MACMILLAN
COMPENDIUM

PHILOSOPHY AND ETHICS

PHILOSOPHY AND ETHICS

SELECTIONS FROM

The Encyclopedia of Philosophy and

Supplement

Donald M. Borchert

Editor-in-Chief

MACMILLAN LIBRARY REFERENCE USA

New York

Copyright © 1999 (Introductory material, updates, index), © 1967, 1996 Macmillan Library Reference

Interior Design by Kevin Hanek
Cover Design by Judy Kahn

Macmillan Library Reference USA
1633 Broadway, 7th Floor
New York, NY 10019

Manufactured in the United States of America

Printing number
1 2 3 4 5 6 7 8 9 10

Library of Congress Cataloging-in-Publication Data

Philosophy and ethics / Donald M. Borchert, editor-in-chief.
    p.   cm. — (Macmillan compendium)
    "Selections from The encyclopedia of philosophy and supplement."
    Includes bibliographical references and index.
    ISBN 0-02-865366-1 (hardcover : alk. paper)
    1. Ethics Encyclopedias.   I. Borchert, Donald M., 1934–
II. Title.   III. Series.
BJ63.E472   1999
170′.3—dc21   99-25219
                                          CIP

Contents

Contents

Preface

Origins

In 1967 Macmillan published the eight-volume *Encyclopedia of Philosophy* under the editorship of Paul Edwards. The *Encyclopedia* soon became not only a standard reference work on the shelves of virtually every college and public library, but also a frequently consulted resource in the personal libraries of countless professors and graduate students. In the three decades following the publication of the *Encyclopedia*, intense and intellectually powerful discussions took place within the discipline of philosophy that resulted in exciting discoveries, fresh insights, and even the emergence of entirely new subfields such as feminist philosophy and applied ethics. Accordingly, early in the 1990s Macmillan decided that the *Encyclopedia* needed updating and asked me to serve as the editor-in-chief to prepare a single-volume Supplement that would survey the past three decades of philosophical development. Fortunately, I had the assistance of a dedicated and competent editorial board: K. Danner Clouser (College of Medicine, Pennsylvania State University), Paul Horwich (University College London), Jaegwon Kim (Brown University), Joseph J. Kockelmans (Pennsylvania State University), Helen E. Longino (University of Minnesota), Vann McGee (Rutgers University), Louis Pojman (U.S. Military Academy, West Point), Ernest Sosa (Brown University), and Michael Tooley (University of Colorado, Boulder). Together we assembled the Supplement to reflect the recent significant developments in every major subfield of philosophy, and Macmillan Library Reference published the volume in 1996. *The Encyclopedia of Philosophy*, now updated with the Supplement, would continue to be a valuable resource for students, library patrons, and professional philosophers.

As the last half of the twentieth century unfolded, one subfield of philosophy—ethics—became increasingly a matter of widespread public interest and concern. In the professions and in business, in politics and in sports, in virtually every field of human endeavor, ethical problems surfaced that needed careful analysis and thoughtful resolution. Many professions and organizations formed ethics committees and instituted codes of ethics. Macmillan Library Reference discerned that the *Encyclopedia of Philosophy* and its Supplement harbored valuable resources that could serve the burgeoning interest in ethics. Accordingly, in 1998 I became the editor-in-chief for the preparation of the single-volume *Macmillan Compendium: Philosophy and Ethics* that would incorporate articles in their entirety, including bibliographies, selected from the *Encyclopedia* and the Supplement. Particular attention was paid to articles dealing with ethics, while not neglecting the other subfields of philosophy and the biographical entries of the major philosophers throughout the centuries. I hope that this single-volume Compendium will increase accessibility of the rich resources in the *Encyclopedia* and the Supplement to a wider audience, to the reading public that wonders about philosophy in general and puzzles over ethical problems in particular.

Features

To add visual appeal and enhance the usefulness of this volume, the page format is designed to include the following helpful features.

- Call-out Quotations: These relevant, often provocative quotations are highlighted in order to promote exploration and add visual appeal to the page.
- Cross-references: Appearing at the end of most articles, cross-references will encourage further reading and research.
- Photographs: Chosen to complement the text, the photo program is designed to further engage the reader.
- Index: An extensive index at the end of the Compendium will provide ample opportunities for further exploration.

Acknowledgments

Macmillan Compendium: Philosophy and Ethics contains more than eighty illustrations. Acknowledgments of sources for the illustrations appear within the captions.

To the entire staff at Macmillan Library Reference

I wish to express our gratitude. Without their hard work and creativity, this work would have been impossible.

Finally, all of us who are enriched by the *Compendium: Philosophy and Ethics* owe a debt of gratitude to the more than 300 scholars who have written the entries and signed their names to the articles appearing in this volume. To them belongs much praise for the benefits we derive from using this resource.

Donald M. Borchert, Editor-in-Chief
Ohio University

ABORTION

The claims to which partisans on both sides of the abortion issue appeal seem, if one is not thinking of the abortion issue, close to self-evident, or they appear to be easily defensible. The case against abortion (Beckwith, 1993) rests on the proposition that there is a very strong presumption that ending another human life is seriously wrong. Almost everyone who is not thinking about the abortion issue would agree. There are good arguments for the view that fetuses are both living and human. ('Fetus' is generally used in the philosophical literature on abortion to refer to a human organism from the time of conception to the time of birth.) Thus, it is easy for those opposed to abortion to think that only the morally depraved or the seriously confused could disagree with them.

The standard antiabortion argument is criticized

on the ground that we do not know

when the soul enters the body.

Standard prochoice views appeal either to the proposition that women have the right to make decisions concerning their own bodies or to the proposition that fetuses are not yet persons. Both of these propositions seem either to be platitudes or to be straightforwardly defensible. Thus, it is easy for prochoicers to believe that only religious fanatics or dogmatic conservatives could disagree. This explains, at least in part, why the abortion issue has created so much controversy. The philosophical debate regarding abortion has been concerned largely with subjecting these apparently obvious claims to the analytical scrutiny philosophers ought to give to them.

Consider first the standard argument against abortion. One frequent objection to the claim that fetuses are both human and alive is that we do not know when life begins. The reply to this objection is that fetuses both grow and metabolize and whatever grows and metabolizes is alive. Some argue that the beginning of life should be defined in terms of the appearance of brain function, because death is now defined in terms of absence of brain function (Brody, 1975). This would

permit abortion within at least eight weeks after conception. However, because death is, strictly speaking, defined in terms of the irreversible loss of brain function, the mere absence of brain function is not a sufficient condition for the absence of life. Accordingly, the claim that the presence of brain function is a necessary condition for the presence of life is left unsupported. Also, the standard antiabortion argument is criticized on the ground that we do not know when the soul enters the body. However, such a criticism is plainly irrelevant to the standard, apparently secular, antiabortion argument we are considering.

The Thomistic premise that it is always wrong intentionally to end an innocent human life is used by the Vatican to generate the prohibition of abortion. This premise is often attacked for presupposing 'absolutism'. This Vatican principle seems to render immoral active euthanasia, even when a patient is in excruciating, unrelievable pain or in persistent coma; it even seems to render immoral ending the life of a human cancer-cell culture. In none of these cases is the individual whose life is ended victimized. Thus, the Vatican principle seems most implausible.

Opponents of abortion are better off appealing to the weaker proposition that there is a very strong presumption against ending a human life (Beckwith, 1993). Because this presumption can be overridden when the victim has no interest in continued life, use of this premise provides a way of dealing with the above counterexamples. However, this tactic provides room for another objection to the antiabortion argument. Some prochoicers have argued that insentient fetuses have no interest in continued life. Because what is insentient does not care about what is done to it and because what does not care about what is done to it cannot have interests, insentient fetuses cannot have an interest in living. Therefore, abortion of insentient fetuses is not wrong (Steinbock, 1992; Sumner, 1981; and Warren, 1987).

If this argument were sound, then it would also show that patients who are in temporary coma, and therefore insentient, do not have an interest in living. M. A. Warren (1987) attempts to avoid this counterexample by making the neurological capacity for sentience a necessary condition for having any interests at all and, therefore, for having an interest in living. This move does not solve the problem, however. Because the argument in favor of permitting the abortion of insentient fetuses generated an untenable conclusion, that argument must be rejected. Because the argument rests on an equivocation between what one takes an interest in and what is in one's interest, there are even better reasons for rejecting it. Accordingly, this objection to the standard antiabortion argument is unsupported.

The classic antiabortion argument is subject to a major theoretical difficulty. Antiabortionists have tried vigorously to avoid the charge that they are trying to force their religious views upon persons who do not share them. However, the moral rule to which the standard antiabortion argument appeals obtains its particular force in the abortion dispute because it singles out members of the species *Homo sapiens* (rather than persons or sentient beings or beings with a future like ours, for example). It is difficult to imagine how the *Homo sapiens* rule could be defended against its competitors without relying upon the standard theological exegesis of the Sixth Commandment and upon the divine-command theory on which its moral standing rests. This leads to two problems. First, arguments against divine-command ethical theory seem compelling. Second, when arguments based on divine-command theory are transported into the Constitutional realm, First Amendment problems arise.

The philosophical literature contains two major kinds of prochoice strategies. The personhood strategy appeals to the proposition that no fetuses are persons. If this is so, then, because a woman plainly has the right to control her own body if she does not directly harm another person, abortion is morally permissible. However, Judith Thomson (1971) has argued that a woman's right to control her own body can justify the right to an abortion in some situations even if fetuses are persons. This second strategy rests on the claim that no one's right to life entails the right to a life-support system provided by another's body even if use of that life-support system is the only way to save one's life. Thus, even if opponents of abortion are successful in establishing that fetuses have the right to life, they have not thereby established that any fetus has the right to anyone else's uterus.

It is widely believed that Thomson's strategy can justify abortion in cases of rape and in cases where the life of a pregnant woman is threatened by pregnancy (Warren, 1973). There is much less unanimity concerning other cases, because it is generally believed that, if we create a predicament for others, we have special obligations to help them in their predicament. Furthermore, let us grant that A's right to life does not entail A's right to B's body even when A needs B's body to sustain life. Presumably, by parity of reasoning, B's right to B's body does not entail B's right to take A's life even if A's continuing to live severely restricts B's choices.

Opponents of abortion claim that fetuses are alive and can thus be killed in defiance of the Sixth Commandment. (Corbis/Owen Franken)

Thus, we have a standoff, and the winner from the moral point of view will be that individual with the strongest right. Although Thomson's strategy has been widely discussed and raises interesting questions about the duty of beneficence, questions both about its philosophical underpinnings and about its scope suggest that philosophically inclined prochoicers would be better off with a personhood strategy.

No doubt, this is why personhood strategies have dominated the prochoice philosophical literature. Such strategies come in many varieties (Engelhardt, 1986; Feinberg, 1986; Tooley, 1972, 1983, and 1994; and Warren, 1973, 1987). Warren's 1973 version is most famous. She argued that reflection on our concept of person suggests that in order to be a person one must possess at least more than one of the following five characteristics: consciousness, rationality, self-motivated activity, the capacity to communicate, and the presence of a concept of self. Since no fetus possesses any of these characteristics, no fetus is a person. If only persons have full moral rights, then fetuses lack the full right to life. Therefore, abortion may never be forbidden for the sake of a fetus.

One might object to such a strategy on the ground that, since fetuses are potential persons, the moral importance of personhood guarantees them a full place in the moral community. The best reply to such an objection is that the claim that X's have a right to Y does not entail that potential X's have a right to Y (think of potential voters and potential presidents; Feinberg, 1986).

Although personhood theorists (like antiabortionists) tend to say little about the moral theories on which their views rest (Engelhardt, 1986, is an interesting exception), presumably most personhood theorists will turn out to be, when driven to the wall, social-contract theorists. Such theories, according to which morality is a self-interested agreement concerning rules of conduct among rational agents, tend to have problems accounting for the moral standing of those who are not rational agents—beings such as animals, young children, the retarded, the psychotic, and the senile. Thus, the personhood defense of the prochoice position tends to have problems that are the inverse of those of the classic antiabortion argument.

Both standard antiabortion and personhood accounts appeal, in the final analysis, to the characteristics fetuses manifest at the time they are fetuses as a basis for their arguments concerning the ethics of abortion. This appeal may be a mistake both defenses share. My premature death would be a great misfortune to me because it would deprive me of a future of value. This is both generalizable and arguably the basis for the presumptive wrongness of ending human life. Such a view seems to imply that abortion is seriously immoral, seems to have a defensible intuitive basis, and seems to avoid the counterexamples that threaten alternative views (Marquis, 1989). However, this view is subject to two major objections. One could argue that the difference between the relation of fetuses to their futures and the relation of adults to their futures would explain why adults are wronged by losing their futures but fetuses are not (McInerney, 1990). One might also argue that because human sperm and ova have valuable futures like ours, the valuable future criterion for the wrongness of killing is too broad (Norcross, 1990). Not everyone believes these objections are conclusive.

[See also Animal Rights and Welfare; Rights.]

BIBLIOGRAPHY

Beckwith, F. J. *Politically Correct Death: Answering Arguments for Abortion Rights.* Grand Rapids, MI, 1993.
Brody, B. *Abortion and the Sanctity of Human Life: A Philosophical View.* Cambridge, MA, 1975.
Dworkin, R. *Life's Dominion: An Argument about Abortion, Euthanasia, and Individual Freedom.* New York, 1993.
Engelhardt, Jr., H. T. *The Foundations of Bioethics.* New York, 1986. An attempt to place the personhood strategy in the context of an ethical theory and other issues in bioethics.
Feinberg, J., ed. *The Problem of Abortion.* Belmont, CA, 1984. An excellent anthology.
———. "Abortion," in Tom Regan, ed., *Matters of Life and Death: New Introductory Essays in Moral Philosophy,* 2d ed. (New York, 1986). The best account of the personhood strategy in a single essay.
Kamm, F. M. *Creation and Abortion: A Study in Moral and Legal Philosophy.* New York, 1992. A defense of Thomson's strategy.
Marquis, D. "Why Abortion Is Immoral," *Journal of Philosophy,* Vol. 86 (1989), 183–202.
McInerney, P. "Does a Fetus Already Have a Future-Like-Ours?" *Journal of Philosophy,* Vol. 87 (1990), 265–68.
Norcross, A. "Killing, Abortion, and Contraception: A Reply to Marquis," *Journal of Philosophy,* Vol. 87 (1990), 268–77.
Pojman, L. J., and F. J. Beckwith, eds. *The Abortion Controversy: A Reader.* Boston, 1994. An excellent anthology.
Steinbock, B. *Life before Birth: The Moral and Legal Status of Embryos and Fetuses.* New York, 1992. A sentience strategy.
Sumner, L. W. *Abortion and Moral Theory.* Princeton, NJ, 1981. A sentience strategy.
Thomson, J. J. "A Defense of Abortion," *Philosophy and Public Affairs,* Vol. 1 (1971), 47–66. A classic paper.
Tooley, M. "Abortion and Infanticide," *Philosophy and Public Affairs,* Vol. 2 (1972), 37–65. A classic paper.
———. *Abortion and Infanticide.* New York, 1983.
———. "In Defense of Abortion and Infanticide," in L. P. Poman and F. J. Beckwith, eds., *The Abortion Controversy: A Reader* (Boston, 1994). Tooley's most recent account of his views.
Warren, M. A. "On the Moral and Legal Status of Abortion," *Monist,* Vol. 57 (1973). 43–61. A classic paper.
Warren, M. A. "The Abortion Issue," in D. VanDeVeer and T. Regan, eds., *Health Care Ethics: An Introduction* (Philadelphia, 1987). A sentience strategy combined with a personhood strategy.

– DON MARQUIS

ACTION THEORY

Action theory's primary concerns are the nature and explanation of human action. The explanatory concern emerged early and prominently in philosophy, in Plato's and Aristotle's ethical writings. In the 1960s action theory came to be seen as a philosophical discipline in its own right, with connections to ethics, metaphysics, and the philosophy of mind. Two questions were central to it then: (1) what is an action? (2) how are actions to be explained? The latter eventually became paramount.

The first question suggests two others: (1a) how do actions differ from nonactions? (1b) how do actions differ from one another (the question of "action individuation")? According to a leading causal position on (1a), actions are like sunburns in an important respect. The burn on Ann's back is a sunburn partly in virtue of its having been caused by direct exposure to the sun's rays; a burn that looks and feels just the same is not a sunburn if it was caused by a heat lamp. Similarly, on the view in question, a certain event is Ann's raising her right hand—an action—partly in virtue of its having been suitably caused by mental items. On an influential version of this view, reasons, constructed as belief/desire complexes, are causes of actions, and an event counts as an action partly in virtue of its having been suitably caused by a reason. Alternative conceptions of action include an "internalist" position, according to which actions differ experientially from other events in a way that is essentially independent of how, or whether, they are caused; a conception of actions as composites of nonactional mental events or states (e.g., intentions) and pertinent nonactional effects (e.g., an arm's rising); and views identifying an action with the causing of a suitable nonactional product by an appropriate nonactional mental event or state—or, instead, by an agent.

Action theorists want to know both what it is

that explanations of actions explain and

how *actions are properly explained.*

By the end of the 1970s a lively debate over (1b) had produced a collection of relatively precise alternatives on action individuation: a fine-grained view, a coarse-grained view, and componential views. The first treats *A* and *B* as different actions if, in performing them, the agent exemplifies different act properties. Thus, if Al illuminates the room by flipping the switch, his flipping the switch and his illuminating the room are two different actions, since the act properties at issue are distinct. The second counts Al's flipping the switch and his illuminating the room as the same action under two different descriptions. Views of the third sort regard Al's illuminating the room as an action having various components, including his moving his arm, his flipping the switch, and the light's going on. Where proponents of the other two theories find, alternatively, a single action under different descriptions or a collection of related actions, advocates of the various component views locate a "larger" action having "smaller" actions among its parts.

Most philosophers agree that actions are explicable at least partly in terms of mental items and that we at least sketch an explanation of an intentional action by identifying the reasons for which the agent performed it. However, whether reasons can provide causal explanations is a contested issue. In 1963 Donald Davidson challenged anticausalists about "reasons-explanations" to provide an account of the reasons for which we act—effective reasons—that does not treat (our having)

those reasons as causes of relevant actions. The challenge is particularly acute when an agent has more than one reason for doing *A* but does it only for some subset of those reasons. For example, Al has a pair of reasons for mowing his lawn this morning. First, he wants to mow it this week and he deems this morning the most convenient time. Second, he has an urge to repay his neighbor for rudely awakening him recently with her early morning mowing, and he believes that mowing his lawn this morning would constitute repayment. As it happens, Al mows his lawn this morning only for one of these reasons. In virtue of what is it true that he mows it for this reason, and not for the other, if not that this reason (or his having it), and not the other, plays a suitable causal role in his mowing his lawn? Although no one has demonstrated that Davidson's challenge cannot be met, the most detailed attempts to meet it are revealingly problematic.

The causal view of action explanation faces problems of its own. It typically is embraced as part of a naturalistic stand on agency, according to which mental items that play causal/explanatory roles in action bear some important relation to physical states and events. Relations that have been explored include identity (both type-type and token-token) and various kinds of supervenience. Each kind of relation faces difficulties, and some philosophers have argued that anything less than type-type identity (which many view as untenable) will fail to avert an unacceptable epiphenomenalism.

Action theorists have fruitfully scrutinized psychological states and events alleged to play crucial causal/explanatory roles in intentional action. At one time belief and desire were assumed to shoulder this burden. By the late 1980s intentions had gained a prominent place in action theory. Some theorists focused on proximal intentions—intentions for the specious present—as the primary link between reasons and action. Others concentrated on the roles of distal intentions—intentions for the nonimmediate future—in guiding practical reasoning and in coordinating one's own behavior over time and interaction with other agents. A lively debate occurred over whether intentions are reducible to belief/desire complexes or, instead, are irreducible states of mind; and the project of constructing a causal analysis of intentional action gained new momentum. Some theorists fruitfully appealed to intentions in attempting to avoid problems that "deviant causal chains" posed for attempted analyses of intentional action featuring reasons (belief/desire complexes) as causes. Briefly, the general alleged problem is this: whatever psychological causes are deemed necessary and sufficient for a resultant action's being intentional, cases can be described in which, owing to an atypical causal connection between the favored psychological antecedents and a pertinent resultant action, that action is not intentional. For example, Ann wants to frighten a prowler away and she believes that she may do so by making a deafening noise. Motivated (causally) by this desire and belief, Ann may search for a suitable object and, in her search, accidentally knock over her aquarium—producing a deafening crash. In so doing, she might frighten the prowler away; but her frightening the prowler is not an intentional action. The task for those who wish to analyze intentional action causally is to specify not only the psychological causes of actions associated with their being intentional but also the pertinent roles played by these causes (e.g., guidance).

Action theorists want to know both what it is that explanations of actions explain and how actions are properly explained. A full-blown theory of action's nature and explanation would not only tell us how actions differ from nonactions and from one another, it would also solve part of the mind–body problem. Further, such a theory would bear directly on the issues of freedom of action and moral responsibility.

[See also Aristotle; Davidson, Donald; Metaphysics; Philosophy of Mind; Plato.]

BIBLIOGRAPHY

Audi, R. *Action, Intention, and Reason*. Ithaca, NY, 1993.
Brand, M. *Intending and Acting*. Cambridge, MA, 1984.
Bratman, M. *Intention, Plans, and Practical Reason*. Cambridge, MA, 1987.
Davidson, D. *Essays on Actions and Events*. Oxford, 1980. Includes his 1963 essay "Actions, Reasons, and Causes."
Ginet, C. *On Action*. Cambridge, 1990.
Goldman, A. *A Theory of Human Action*. Englewood Cliffs, NJ, 1970.
Hornsby, J. *Actions*. London, 1980.
Mele, A. *Springs of Action*. Oxford, 1992.

— ALFRED R. MELE

AESTHETIC ATTITUDE

The aesthetic attitude is the supposed mental state or perspective necessary for aesthetic experience, the mental state in which it is said that human beings are capable of experiencing and enjoying the beauty and symbolic significance of art and natural objects and without which such experiences cannot occur. The aesthetic attitude was therefore understood as the key to the analysis of "aesthetic experience," the central problem of philosophical aesthetics since the early eighteenth century. Although there were isolated discussions by Greek, Roman, and medieval philosophers of topics relating to art and beauty, the idea of an independent science or discipline of aesthetics did not appear until around 1730, when Baumgarten proposed a division of philosophical psychology into "logic" and "aesthetic." Logic dealt with all the cognitive, analytic operations of thinking, while aesthetics would deal with all the intuitive, sensuous areas of human experience, including the experience and enjoyment of natural beauty and art.

The key question was, therefore, What is the nature or essence of aesthetic experience, and how does it differ from other sorts of experiences, especially "logical" experiences? Although various answers were proposed over the next centuries, most aestheticians agreed that there was a peculiar aesthetic point of view or stance that, when directed toward works of art or objects of nature, would yield an aesthetic experience of those objects. A tree, lake, or mountain, for example, could be perceived or considered from other points of view or attitudes—pragmatically, ecologically, and so on, in ways that did not reveal the aesthetic qualities of the object. But by shifting one's attention ("attitude"), looking at an object in a different way, one could become aware of its aesthetic qualities (beauty, charm, and symbolic significance).

What is the nature or essence of aesthetic experience, and how does it differ from other sorts of experiences, especially "logical" experiences?

The major concern, then, was the nature or essence of the "aesthetic attitude." Again, although answers varied considerably, there was general agreement among aestheticians since the early eighteenth century that the aesthetic attitude differed from other mental attitudes in being "disinterested," "detached," and "distanced" from practical and self-interested concerns of real life. This problem of defining the psychological state of mind of the aesthetic observer dominated aesthetics from the early eighteenth century through the early twentieth century. In the twentieth century, however, the interests of aestheticians broadened to include questions of creativity, art history, art institutions, and, generally, the social and political background to art, and interest in the nature of the aesthetic attitude of the perceiver waned. As aestheticians such as Joseph Margolis attempted in the late 1950s and early 1960s to bring aesthetics more firmly within analytic philosophy, problems in clarifying the concept of the aesthetic attitude in terms of "disinterestedness" became increasingly daunting. In the 1960s George Dickie argued against the very existence of an aesthetic attitude. In this same period Arthur Danto argued that it was not adopting the aesthetic attitude that made the appreciation of contemporary art possible but rather art institutions, the "artworld," as he called it, that explained and made possible aesthetic experience. More recently, feminists, "postcolonialists," and others concerned with the marginalization of minority perspectives have wondered if the assumption of a single, monolithic, "normal" aesthetic attitude was not simply the biased, acculturated perspective of a well-educated European male. Despite efforts by Jerome Stolnitz and others to clarify aesthetic-attitude theories, "postmodern" interest in art has tended to reject any monolithic psychological or "intentional" accounts in favor of greater "reader" (observer) participation, diversity, and freedom from supposed norms, emphasizing an institutional, sociological, or political rather than psychological perspective.

[See also Artworld; Beauty; Modernism and Postmodernism.]

BIBLIOGRAPHY

Danto, A. *The Philosophical Disenfranchisement of Art*. New York, 1986.
Dickie, G. *Art and the Aesthetic*. Ithaca, NY, 1974.
Ecker, G. *Feminist Aesthetics*, H. Anderson, trans. Boston, 1985.
Margolis, J., ed. *Philosophy Looks at the Arts*. New York, 1987.
Showalter, E., ed. *The New Feminist Critics: Essays on Women, Literature, and Theory*. New York, 1985.
Silverman, H., ed. *Postmodernism: Philosophy and the Arts*. New York, 1989.
Stolnitz, J. *Aesthetics and Philosophy of Art Criticism*. Boston, 1960.

— H. GENE BLOCKER

AESTHETIC AUTONOMY

That art should be autonomous has its source in the belief that the value of art lies in the aesthetic, a realm disconnected from practical concerns. This eighteenth century idea departs from antiquity's positioning of art as instrumental for cultural and social life.

Kant is the main authority for those who characterize the aesthetic as irreducible to instrumental terms and hence autonomous. For him, each instance of aesthetic gratification is unique and unpredictable because occasioned by the free play of the imagination and understanding. Being not rule governed, aesthetic valuation cannot be equated with cognitive, moral, political, practical, or prudential judgment. In the twentieth century, formalists such as Bell and Adorno further Kant's view by insisting that aesthetic significance consists solely in how the elements of the aesthetic object relate to one another, not in how these elements represent the world external to the aesthetic object.

If aesthetic experience is responsive solely to the perceived aesthetic object and is free of external determinants, its significance must be exclusively aesthetic.

However, the definitive demarcation of the aesthetic from the nonaesthetic has proven elusive, not in the least because contemporary art strives to demonstrate that, given the right context, anything can be an aesthetic object. Fascism and postmodernism even aestheticize political objectives. And scientific and moral experience both contain the intuitive and analogical elements Kant reserved to aesthetic experience. All these considerations challenge the view that the aesthetic is distinct from and undetermined by other realms.

Furthermore, if the aesthetic is autonomous, two implausible conclusions are entailed: first, the aesthetic is thoroughly detached *from* the moral, social, and political environment; second, the aesthetic should be thoroughly detached *about* the moral, social, and political environment. As to the first, recent critical analysis is replete with demonstrations of how aesthetic evaluation is reflective of its environment. As to the second, from antiquity aesthetic significance has been understood to be amplified by rather than detracted from objects' success in celebrating, condemning or otherwise reflecting on the environment from which they emerge.

[See also Kant, Immanuel; Modernism and Postmodernism.]

BIBLIOGRAPHY

Adorno, T. W. *Aesthetische Theorie*. Frankfurt am Main, 1970.
Bell, C. *Art* [London, 1914], 3rd ed. Oxford, 1987.
Kant, I. *The Critique of Judgement*. Oxford, 1928.
Krukowski, L. "Contextualism and Autonomy in Aesthetics," *Journal of Aesthetic Education*, Vol. 24 (1990), 123–34.
Sankowski, E. "Art Museums, Autonomy, and Canons," *Monist*, 75:4 (October 1993), 535–55.

— ANITA SILVERS

AESTHETIC PROPERTIES

Although philosophers in the eighteenth and nineteenth centuries concentrated on beauty and sublimity almost to the exclusion of every other aesthetic property, late-twentieth-century philosophers have done their best to redress the balance and have concentrated on almost every aesthetic property except the two just mentioned. Or at least so it might seem. In truth, their attention has turned from understanding the nature of, or providing criteria of application for, these two admittedly important aesthetic properties to investigating the nature and importance of aesthetic properties as such.

Aesthetic properties include unity, balance, integration, lifelessness, delicacy, dumpiness, loveliness, restlessness, and powerfulness, among many others. Nonaesthetic properties include, again among many others, redness, squareness, noisiness, weighing 50 pounds, being in Philadelphia, and taking up wall space. While lists such as these can be continued almost indefinitely, and there is an intuitive feel to the aesthetic/nonaesthetic property distinction, as well as considerable agreement concerning whether a given property (properly understood) is aesthetic or nonaesthetic, a central philosophical question is what the distinction amounts to or is based on. The problem lies on the aesthetic property side of the distinction.

Late-twentieth-century philosophers have

concentrated on almost every aesthetic property

except *beauty and sublimity—or so it might seem.*

One way to define 'aesthetic property' is epistemologically, in the way such properties are known, or in the manner in which we become acquainted with them. Epistemological definitions can invoke and have invoked special modes of aesthetic perception, but they need not. Frank Sibley, for instance, speaks of the need to see (experience) aesthetic properties, but he does not think that any special perceptual faculty or sensory modality is involved in such perception. What distinguishes aesthetic perception from nonaesthetic perception, he thinks, is that taste is required for the former but not the latter. Given that taste is, according to Sibley, the ability to discern aesthetic qualities, circularity would seem to threaten: aesthetic properties are defined in terms of taste and taste in terms of aesthetic properties.

A different tack is to define 'aesthetic property' semantically or semiotically. Very roughly speaking, the view is that an aesthetic property is one that involves a reference by an object to something else. The object becomes, because it possesses the aesthetic property, a "presentational symbol" of that something else. More precisely, property A of object X is an aesthetic property if and only if X exemplifies A, in the sense that it possesses A and refers to A (inspired by Goodman, 1968). A certain passage of Walter Pater's prose, for example, may be languid and refer to languidness in general. Aesthetic properties, on this view, function in a direct symbolic fashion in a way that nonaesthetic properties do not.

A semiotic or 'symbolic' definition of this sort works well with many literary works and many works of visual art. It does not fare as well, however, with musical compositions (most seem to involve no reference to anything outside themselves), or with natural objects (they do not seem to function symbolically at all), or with many artifacts and human actions (e.g., a perfume may be cloying, or a person's walk graceful). All seem to be about, or refer to, nothing at all, not even themselves.

And there are problems in the other direction. A swatch of cloth—one of Goodman's own examples—may well exemplify kelly green, but kelly greenness is not an aesthetic property.

Another alternative is to define "aesthetic property" in terms of a connection with aesthetic value. An aesthetic property, Monroe Beardsley thinks, is one that contributes, or contributes directly, to the aesthetic value (goodness) or disvalue (badness) of an object (1982). There are two principal problems with this definition, however. One is that some aesthetic properties—austerity or detachedness, for example—seem to be neutral, to count neither for nor against a judgment of aesthetic value, or to be variable, to count positively in one context, negatively in a second, and neither positively nor negatively in a third. The second problem is that unless the notion of aesthetic value, or the aesthetic concept it is defined in terms of, can itself be defined in nonaesthetic terms, circularity would again threaten. Even so, these difficulties may not be insurmountable. Beardsley thinks that the neutrality of certain aesthetic properties is only apparent and evaporates when the vagueness of the corresponding aesthetic term is eliminated; and he has attempted to define (or ground) the aesthetic in nonaesthetic terms.

Another major issue concerning aesthetic properties is their relation to nonaesthetic properties. Speaking in terms of features and terms rather than properties, Sibley has argued that "there are no sufficient conditions, no nonaesthetic features such that the presence of some set or number of them will beyond question logically justify or warrant the application of an aesthetic term" (1979, p. 546). (There are nonaesthetic sufficient conditions for an aesthetic term's not applying, Sibley thinks—for example, a painting that consists solely of two bars of pale blue and one of a very pale gray could not be gaudy.) This is stronger than saying that aesthetic concepts are defeasible, according to Sibley, since defeasible concepts have conditions that are normally sufficient (that apply if they are not 'defeated' because other conditions obtain), and we can be sure they apply if we know that those conditions hold and no 'voiding' conditions do. No such assurance is possible with aesthetic concepts, since the exercise of taste is always required in order to know that they apply. (It should also be noted that Sibley and virtually everyone else hold that there are no nonaesthetic necessary conditions for an aesthetic term's applying. Both a painting and a musical composition may be energetic and yet not share any [interesting] nonaesthetic features.)

As might be expected, Sibley has had his critics. Some have offered counterexamples to his thesis; some have alleged that his arguments are question begging; some have even questioned the existence of a philosophically neutral aesthetic/nonaesthetic property distinction. Putting these issues to the side, there is another matter to consider: aesthetic properties depend on nonaesthetic properties, but not vice versa. A painting may be foreboding (in part) because it has ashen grays that gradually twist into dark browns and deep blacks, but a painting could not be composed of whites and pastel blues because it is joyful; aesthetic properties supervene on nonaesthetic ones. In some cases aesthetic properties may also supervene on other aesthetic properties—a symphony could be triumphant (in part) because it is fiery, for example—but, ultimately, all aesthetic properties are, it is claimed, based on nonaesthetic ones.

What exactly the relation of supervenience is, is not altogether clear. Nor is it clear whether aesthetic supervenience differs from other kinds of supervenience, such as moral supervenience (the moral rightness of an act, for example, supervening on various nonmoral characteristics of it, such as bringing about the most pleasure possible in the circumstances) and mental supervenience (the belief of a person supervening on certain of his/her brain states, for instance). Aestheticians have, however, argued for a number of theses in relation to supervenience. On the skeptical side some have claimed that some aesthetic properties, such as gracefulness, are not supervenient at all, while others have argued that supervenience is not a fruitful notion to use to explain the aesthetic properties of great works of art. More positively, attempts have been made to distinguish between weak and strong supervenience and to argue for (or against) the supervenience relation being causal, logical, or quasi-logical in nature. Efforts have also been made to quell the skeptical doubts just mentioned by arguing that aesthetic properties, including gracefulness, do indeed supervene on nonaesthetic properties, but the determination of such properties also depends on an object's being perceived in the right category, such as fugue or impressionist painting. Supervenience is indeed a useful notion to employ, it is claimed, but its importance may not be fully appreciated if the concept of an artistic category is not brought into play.

[See also Beauty; Goodman, Nelson; Supervenience.]

Today's supermodels are thought by many to embody the aesthetic property of loveliness. (Corbis/Photo B.D.V.)

BIBLIOGRAPHY

Beardsley, M. "What Is an Aesthetic Quality?" in *The Aesthetic Point of View*, edited by M. J. Wreen and D. Callen (Ithaca, NY, 1982).

Bender, J. "Supervenience and the Justification of Aesthetic Judgments," *Journal of Aesthetics and Art Criticism*, Vol. 46 (1987), 31–40.

Casebier, A. "The Alleged Special Logic for Aesthetic Terms," *Journal of Aesthetics and Art Criticism*, Vol. 31 (1973), 357–64.

Cohen, T. "Aesthetic/Non-aesthetic and the Concept of Taste: A Critique of Sibley's Position," *Theoria*, Vol. 39 (1973), 113–52.

Currie, G. "Supervenience, Essentialism, and Aesthetic Properties," *Philosophical Studies*, Vol. 58 (1990), 243–57.

Eaton, M. "The Intrinsic, Non-Supervenient Nature of Aesthetic Properties," *Journal of Aesthetics and Art Criticism*, Vol. 52 (1994), 383–97.

Goldman, A. "Aesthetic Qualities and Aesthetic Value," *Journal of Philosophy*, Vol. 87 (1990), 23–37.

Goodman, N. *Languages of Art*. Indianapolis, 1968. Chap. 2.

Hermeren, G. "Aesthetic Qualities, Value, and Emotive Meaning," *Theoria*, Vol. 39 (1973), 71–100.

Kivy, P. *Speaking of Art*. The Hague, 1973. Esp. chaps. 1–3.

———. "Aesthetic Concepts: Some Fresh Considerations," *Journal of Aesthetics and Art Criticism*, Vol. 37 (1979), 423–32.

Levinson, J. "Aesthetic Supervenience," *The Southern Journal of Philosophy*, Vol. 22 (1983), Supp., 93–110.

Sibley, F. "Aesthetic and Nonaesthetic," *Philosophical Review*, Vol. 74 (1965), 135–59.

———. "Symposium: About Taste, Part II," *British Journal of Aesthetics*, Vol. 6 (1966), 55–69.

———. "Objectivity and Aesthetics," *Proceedings of the Aristotelian Society*, Vol. 42 (1968), Supp., 31–54.

———. "Aesthetic Concepts," in W. E. Kennick, ed., *Art and Philosophy*, 2d ed. (New York, 1979).

Wicks, R. "Supervenience and Aesthetic Judgment," *Journal of Aesthetics and Art Criticism*, Vol. 46 (1988), 509–11.

Zangwill, N. "Long Live Supervenience," *Journal of Aesthetics and Art Criticism*, Vol. 50 (1992), 319–22.

Zemach, E. "The Ontology of Aesthetic Properties," *Iyyun*, Vol. 42 (1993), 49–66.

— MICHAEL WREEN

AESTHETIC RELATIVISM

"There's no disputing about tastes" is a common expression of aesthetic relativism, and indeed, it captures the spirit of relativism, if not the letter. It may be misleading in several respects, however. First, in speaking of "taste," it suggests only a relativism of judgments of aesthetic value (aesthetic goodness or badness). Relativism need not be so confined. Many art critics and philosophers think that all judgments that attribute aesthetic properties to objects behave relativistically and/or that interpretive judgments that say a work of art means or refers to, behave relativistically. Second, the remark suggests individual relativism, the view that judgments are relativized to the individual. Again, relativism need not be so confined. The great majority of relativists hold that judgments are relativized to a group,

usually a culture, or to a set of principles, even if there are many sets of such principles within a single culture. Finally, the expression "no disputing," especially in being coupled with "taste," suggests that mere liking is in question. Few relativists hold that. Sophisticated relativists all leave a great deal of room for reason-giving, and almost all insist that a genuine judgment requires support with reasons.

Still, the maxim captures the important kernel of relativism. To focus only on judgments of aesthetic value: relativism is the view that there are two or more equally true (valid) standards, or sets of standards, of aesthetic value. Just as moral relativism is the view that there is no one true morality, so aesthetic relativism is the view that there is no one true aesthetic. Instead, there is a variety of incompatible aesthetics, no one of which can claim truth to the exclusion of others. So understood, relativism entails that aesthetic goodness and badness are not properties that objects have independent of human beings. In that sense, relativism is a form of subjectivism, the view that aesthetic value is subjective, or mind dependent. Relativism requires more than subjectivism, however, for if aesthetic value is a function of the objective properties of objects as filtered through, or operated on by, subjective but universal features of the human mind (as Kant thought), aesthetic value would be subjective, but there would be only one true aesthetic. If relativism is true, there is no such subjective but universal backing for judgments of aesthetic value.

Actually, relativism, if it is to be interesting, requires even more than that. If there are no such universal features of the human mind involved in judgments of aesthetic value, and if evaluative standards are conventional (and so mind dependent) and variable (meaning that there is more than one set of true or valid standards), relativism would be true. It might still be the case, however, that judgments that attribute aesthetic value to objects are fixed and not variable; it might be that there is only one true answer to the question How much and what kind of aesthetic value (positive or negative) does this object have? Facts about the object, such as what category (e.g., sonata) or categories (e.g., painting, abstract expressionist painting) it is in, could settle which particular set of evaluative principles is the correct one to use in evaluating it. Or, eschewing the notion of categories, other facts about the object might settle the matter. For example, where and when a novel was composed, or what evaluative criteria were operative in the culture or subculture in which it was created, might determine which standards of evaluation are the correct ones to use in evaluating it. What is the right set of principles in one case, for one object, might well be the wrong set of principles in another case, for another object; and yet there is only one correct attribution of aesthetic value in each case. To be interesting, to allow for genuine competing and incompatible judgments of aesthetic value, relativism would have to rule this possibility out as well.

The main argument in favor of relativism has always been the diversity of judgments of aesthetic value. Poetry that one person or culture judges excellent, another thinks mediocre, and a third poor. Moreover, such judgments vary over time, even with a single person or within a culture. A painting judged superior at one time might fall from favor only to regain its place as a superb work of art. In and of itself, such diversity proves nothing, antirelativists are quick to point out, since all it shows is that people disagree. Widespread disagreement is possible about anything, including objective matters, such as the shape of the Earth or the existence of the Loch Ness monster. The best explanation of such disagreement, they think, is that judging aesthetic value is a delicate matter and a difficult business—and also that critics, like everyone else, invest their egos in their pronouncements and thus find it difficult to view matters dispassionately or to change their minds, once made up.

Just as moral relativism holds that there is no one true morality, so aesthetic relativism is the view that there is no one true aesthetic.

The relativist response to this is usually twofold. First, since disagreement over aesthetic matters is not only widespread but has shown and continues to show no sign of abating, it differs markedly from disagreement over objective matters. The best explanation of such continuing, irresolvable disagreement is that, at base, what is in question are differing sets of subjective concerns. Second, regardless of how such disagreement is best explained, the burden of proof is on the antirelativist, who must provide an ontology of aesthetic value that makes it a real, mind-independent property of objects or a real, universally underwritten mind-dependent property of objects; and he or she must provide an epistemology of aesthetic value, one that shows how human beings have access to such a property when it obviously differs radically from objective properties such as shape or size or even 'secondary qualities' such as color or odor.

Antirelativists may see things differently, however. Some, at least, think that the burden of proof is on the relativist. As Monroe Beardsley puts it, relativists hold that what looks like the attribution of a simple, non-

relational property is really an attribution of a two-or-more place relation (Beardsley, 1983). 'This is aesthetically good' is appearance; the reality is 'This is aesthetically good relative to standards A'. Goodness is never simple; it is always goodness in relation to such-and-such standards. Relativists have to complicate matters this way, according to Beardsley, for otherwise they underwrite contradictions: if goodness and badness were simple properties, 'This is aesthetically good' would be logically incompatible with 'this is aesthetically bad'. Thus, since the relational properties the relativist is committed to are more complex than the nonrelational ones we pre-theoretically attribute to objects, the burden of proof is on the relativist; he or she must show that such complex, covertly attributed properties are required. Worse still, Beardsley thinks, that burden can never be met. It is always possible to say, in the face of the widespread disagreement that the relativist cites as evidence (for the need to relativize attributions), that the aesthetic value of an object simply is inaccessible to a person or culture. The critic or culture may not be sufficiently sensitive to the language of a poem, for example, or for other reasons be unable to gauge aesthetic value accurately.

As might be expected, there are a number of relativist responses to this argument. One is to deny that judgments of aesthetic value are covertly relational, but to avoid the contradictions waiting in the wings by also denying that such judgments can be true or false. Rather, they are plausible or implausible, probable or improbable, reasonable or unreasonable, but never true or false. Denying truth to judgments of aesthetic value is a radical move, however, and one that plays havoc with a large number of concepts central to art criticism.

A second response allows such judgments to be true or false but claims that they are not covertly relational in the way alleged. Contradictions are avoided by claiming that the relativizing in question is to an assumed and unstated framework. Just as 'Coughlin Hall is to the left of LaLumiere Hall' is true when one framework (e.g., facing north) is assumed but 'LaLumiere Hall is to the left of Coughlin Hall' is true when another (e.g., facing south) is assumed, so, too, for judgments of aesthetic value. In neither case is the framework, that which is relativized to, part of the predicate of the judgment made. Genuine competing and incompatible judgments of aesthetic value are thus possible, according to this response, because 'aesthetically good' and 'aesthetically bad' are univocal and not telescoped relational terms.

A third response to the antirelativist argument attempts to discharge the burden of proof that (Beardsley and others claim) the relativist bears, and also attempts to show that relativism is required to explain widespread, continuing disagreement. This response notes that, as the antirelativist argument has it, disagreement about aesthetic value can be diminished if people are sensitized to a culture or to the properties of (say) a poem. The problem is that such sensitizing is more like enculturation, or internalizing an ideology, than it is like learning a new science or mastering a new technique of objective inquiry. Relativism is required, then, not just because widespread disagreement is best explained by relativism, but also because the most plausible explanation of how such disagreement is diminished involves an educational process that is itself inherently relativistic.

Another antirelativist argument worth considering is that if widespread disagreement about judgments of aesthetic value shows that such judgments are not objectively true, or true in any universalistic but subjectively underwritten way, so, too, should widespread disagreement about aesthetic relativism show that it is not objectively true, or true in any universalistic but subjectively underwritten way. Indeed, all the arguments and counterarguments the aesthetic relativist marshals in relation to judgments of aesthetic value would seem to apply, mutatis mutandis, in relation to the judgment that aesthetic relativism is true. Aesthetic relativism is, on this argument, hoisted by its own petard.

This, however, is far from the entirety of the debate over relativism. Many of the arguments for or against moral relativism also apply, mutatis mutandis, to aesthetic relativism, although precisely which arguments do apply is itself a matter of dispute.

[See also Aesthetic Properties; Kant, Immanuel; Moral Relativism.]

BIBLIOGRAPHY

Beardsley, M. "Can We Dispute about Tastes?" In M. Singer and R. Ammerman, eds., *Introductory Readings in Philosophy* (New York, 1960).
———. "The Refutation of Relativism," *Journal of Aesthetics and Art Criticism*, Vol. 41 (1983), 265–70.
Crawford, D. "Causes, Reasons, and Aesthetic Objectivity," *American Philosophical Quarterly*, Vol. 8 (1971), 266–74.
Goldman, A. "Aesthetic Qualities and Aesthetic Values," *Journal of Philosophy*, Vol. 87 (1990), 23–27.
Hume, D. "On the Standard of Taste," in G. Dickie and R. Sclafani, eds., *Aesthetic: A Critical Introduction* (New York, 1977).
Kant, I. *Critique of Judgment* [1790], translated by Werner Pluhar. Indianapolis, 1987. Part 1.
Lewis, C. I. *An Analysis of Knowledge and Valuation.* LaSalle, IL, 1946. Book 3, esp. chaps. 12–15.
MacIntyre, A. "Colors, Cultures, and Practices," *Midwest Studies in Philosophy*, Vol. 17 (1992), 1–23.
Mackie, J. L. "Aesthetic Judgments—a Logical Study," in *Selected Papers*, Vol. 2, *Persons and Values* (Oxford, 1985).
McDowell, J. "Aesthetic Value, Objectivity, and the Fabric of the World," in E. Schaper, ed., *Pleasure, Preference, and Value* (Cambridge, 1983).
Olen, J. "Theories, Interpretations, and Aesthetic Qualities," *Journal of Aesthetics and Art Criticism*, Vol. 35 (1977), 425–31.
Pettit, P. "The Possibility of Aesthetic Realism," in E. Schaper, ed., *Pleasure, Preference, and Value* (Cambridge, 1983).
Stolnitz, J. "On Objective Relativism in Aesthetics," *Journal of Philosophy*, Vol. 57 (1960), 261–76.
Walton, K. "Categories of Art," *Philosophical Review*, Vol. 79 (1970), 334–67.

– MICHAEL WREEN

AESTHETICS, HISTORY OF

Despite the problems of such general classifications, contemporary aesthetic theory may be divided into the following major approaches: analytic, pragmatist, Marxist, structuralist and poststructuralist, postmodernist, and feminist. As the first two derive directly from Anglo-American philosophy, the others have been largely inspired by European thought. Though some of the European theories treated here were published before 1960, their influence on Anglo-American aesthetics is more recent and was not previously covered by the Encyclopedia.

Analytic Aesthetics

Analytic aesthetics arose against the tradition of transcendental idealism that dominated early twentieth-century aesthetics through Croce and Collingwood. Assuming that all art shared a common essence, they argued that this essence is intuition-expression and that artworks are therefore all mental or ideal. Croce thus scorned all empirical distinctions between the different arts and their genres. Analytic aesthetics was an attempt to render philosophy of art more empirical and concrete by rejecting metaphysical speculation and adopting the general methods and presumptions of analytic philosophy. Though the different analysts shared a respect for empirical facts and a fervent commitment to conceptual analysis as the proper method of philosophy, they disagreed as to what analysis was. One form of analysis (associated with "ordinary language" philosophy) aims at simply clarifying our actual concepts without trying to revise or reject them. A second form (advocated by Russell, Carnap, and Goodman) sees the goal of clarificational analysis as the replacing of a confused concept by other related concepts that will be more philosophically useful and less problematic—either by breaking down the original concept to more basic ones or by rationally reconstructing the concept to make it more precise and systematic. Both forms are found in analytic aesthetics: most preferred the former, though Goodman was influential in employing the latter in his notational definitions of works of art.

Nonessentialism about art has been a dominant theme in analytic aesthetics and is in part a product of its quest for clarity. The confusions of traditional aesthetics were imputed to its assumption that all art must share a common essence whose discovery could be used as an evaluative standard. This assumption, the analysts argued (relying on Wittgenstein), was mistaken. It led philosophers to ignore, conflate, and homogenize important differences between the arts and propose formulas of putative essence that were distortive, vague, and uninteresting. Thus, Passmore (as also Hampshire, Kennick, Gallie, Weitz [see bibliography]) saw the murky "dreariness" of traditional aesthetics "as arising out of the attempt to impose a spurious unity on things" that are quite different. Rather than generalizations for all art, this analytic current advocated "special study of the separate arts" with real respect for their differences (Passmore, 1954, pp. 44, 55). Nonessentialism also adduced the fact that the subsumption of these various forms under our current general concept of art is only a product of modern history, effected in the eighteenth

century. It is then argued by Wollheim, Margolis, Weitz, and others that art has no essence because it is constituted by its changing history and such history is always open to further change. Viewing art as an open concept whose objects exhibited no common essence but only "strands of similarities," Morris Weitz (1956) argued that aesthetics should eschew impossible attempts to define art (or any of its developing genres) in terms of essence. Theory should instead focus on analyzing the logic of the concept of art (and its genre concepts), in which he distinguished two different logical uses: description (or classification) and honorific evaluation.

Three major analytic aestheticians resisted nonessentialism. Monroe Beardsley (1958) defined all art in terms of its essential use for aesthetic experience. George Dickie (1971) proposed an institutional essence for works of art, defining art (in the nonevaluative sense) as any artifact that is conferred the status of candidate for appreciation by an agent on behalf of the artworld. Art's essence is not in exhibited properties but in genesis, and this allows for openness to any historical development the artworld will allow. Arthur Danto, from

Athens's majestic Parthenon has long been recognized for its aesthetic value. (Corbis/Kevin Shafer)

whom Dickie took the notion of artworld, rejects Dickie's view because it presumes the omnipotence of artworld agents without recognizing the historical constraints that structure their actions. His own form of essentialism identifies art with what art is historically interpreted to be in the artworld. Future history will not upset this definition, since, Danto argues, art's history (though not its actual practice) has reached its end in the recognition that anything can be art if it is so interpreted (Danto, 1981, 1986). These analytic appeals to history and social institutions are, however, rather abstract, "internal," and formal in comparison to Marxist, pragmatist, poststructuralist, and postmodernist theorizing, which emphasize also the wider socioeconomic forces and political struggles that shape the artworld's history.

Central to analytic aesthetics was its self-conception as philosophy of criticism. Rather than offering revisionary manifestos of what art and criticism should be, it sought to elucidate, systematize, and refine the principles of art and criticism as reflected in established practice to make them more logical and scientific. Analytic aesthetics thus got impetus from the growth of scientific art criticism in the academy.

One consequence of this metacriticism was an overwhelming preoccupation with art rather than natural beauty. Another was greater interest in issues of interpretation rather than aesthetic experience. Indeed, despite some early attempts to define the aesthetic (Sibley, Urmson), the dominant recent trend has been to criticize traditional notions of aesthetic experience and aesthetic attitude (Dickie, 1964, 1965). Goodman and Danto even denounce the aesthetic as an oppressive ideology that trivializes art as sensual, emotive pleasure rather than cognition. Another consequence of analytic aesthetic's self-conception as metacriticism was a tendency to avoid evaluative issues, typically by relegating them to the first-order level of criticism itself. Just as academic criticism focused on interpretation rather than evaluation, so did analytic aesthetics. Goodman voiced this attitude in arguing that traditional "concentration on the question of excellence has been responsible . . . for . . . distortion of aesthetic inquiry" (1969, pp. 261–62). It is also expressed in Dickie's attempt to define art in a purely nonevaluative, classificational sense, leaving all normative decisions to the artworld and assuming that the very idea of a candidate for appreciation does not presuppose that art is, in some holistic sense, an evaluative concept, even though not all artworks may be valuable.

Intense preoccupation with the objects (rather than experience) of art was also fostered by the paradigm of metacriticism. Devoted to objective critical truth, it sought to define with great precision the objects of criti-

cism, the exact ontological status and identity of particular works, and the authenticity of their alleged manifestations. Goodman, for example, offers strict notational definitions for works of music and literature, in which, because of the transitivity of identity, one changed letter or note would automatically result in the change of the work's identity.

Pragmatism

After an influential debut Dewey's pragmatist aesthetics of *Art as Experience* (1934) was soon eclipsed by analysis. While analysis emphasized distinctions and objects, Dewey emphasized continuities and transformative aesthetic experience; while analysis privileged clarification of established practice, Dewey advocated progressive reform. If analysts typically followed Moore in thinking of aesthetic qualities as nonnatural and art as disinterested, privileged, and free from practical function, Dewey insisted that the aesthetic is a natural emergence of our animal feelings and practical interests and is designed to serve as well as refine them. Dewey's pragmatist influence is salient in two major analysts. Beardsley's highlighting and account of aesthetic experience (in terms of intensity, harmony, development, and integration) owes much to Dewey. Goodman, like Dewey, insists that art and science are continuous, serving human interests through "their common cognitive function." Despite his own strict definitions of works of art, Goodman insists with Dewey that what matters aesthetically is not what the object is but how it functions in dynamic experience, urging that we replace the question "What is art?" with that of "When is art?" (Goodman, 1978, p. 70; 1984, pp. 142–44). Richard Rorty, Joseph Margolis, and Richard Shusterman continue the Deweyan critique of the reified artwork by showing how interpretation can be transformative of the texts they interpret without thereby depriving us of shared objects to study and discuss. The democratic impulse of pragmatism has been developed in Shusterman's aesthetic defense of popular art. Stanley Cavell, who resists the pragmatist label, connects with pragmatist aesthetics, not only in his sympathetic analyses of popular film, but in the insistence on art's practical functionality as an ethical tool in the perfectionist project of self-improvement.

Marxist and Hermeneutic Theories

Contemporary Marxist aesthetics has its most influential expression in the Frankfurt school tradition of Adorno, Marcuse, and Benjamin that was influenced by Lukacs and in the French blend of structuralist Marxism forged by Althusser. Though Adorno recognizes that art is socially conditioned, he nonetheless insists that its struggle for autonomy and promise of pleasure represents a crucial utopian moment and a critique of the dismal reality from which it seeks to distinguish itself. Criticism must deal with this dialectic between the work's autonomous form and the ideological and historical factors that shape it. Herbert Marcuse probed a related dialectic of art's tendency to affirm our culture even in criticizing it. Adorno (with Horkheimer) influentially condemned popular art as "the culture industry" because it refused the austere autonomy, distance, and demanding formal novelty of high art. Benjamin instead saw popular art as a potentially democratic product of our changing aesthetic sensibilities, which change through material changes in our world. Mechanical reproduction, he argued, has eroded the aura of uniqueness and distance that gave art its sense of monumental autonomy and consequent "cultic" value.

In France Louis Althusser created an original, if problematic, blend of Marxism and structuralism. Though faithful to Marxist insistence on the priority of the material base of production, he argued that the ideological superstructure (including education, art, and culture) must also have an essential role in sustaining that base (e.g., as "ideological state apparatus"), since one is dealing with a structural totality, all of whose parts affect each other. His disciples include Pierre Macherey and the influential Anglophone critics Fredric Jameson and Terry Eagleton. All three provide interesting studies of literature in terms of symbolic production and ideological conflict (which the artwork both embodies and tries to displace or fictionally resolve).

The influential hermeneutics of Heidegger and Gadamer not only provides new holistic accounts of interpretation but, like pragmatism and Marxism, insists that art's experience be fully linked to the historical praxis of life and valued for its truth and not simply for autonomous formal pleasure.

Structuralism and Poststructuralism

Structuralist theory, deriving from Saussure's linguistics, contains three central premises. First, literature is a systematic whole that is more than the sum of its parts, and its underlying rules or structures are more important to study than the particular meanings of individual works, since these basic structures are what are responsible for generating these meanings. Second, linguistic or literary elements are essentially relational or differential, whose meaning is defined in terms of their combination and contrast with each other. Third, these elements are merely conventional, their meaning determined not by inherent qualities but only by the conventional functions they have in the structural system. This holism eventually leads structuralism away from narrow concern with particular artworks toward the larger totality of a culture's codes of social communication (a development we can see in Roman Jakobson, Jan Mukarovsky, Claude Lévi-Strauss, and Roland Barthes). Structuralism thus goes against the traditional attempts at isolating a separate aesthetic domain, just as it resists traditional criticism's concentration on the interpretation and evaluation of particular artworks and their authors. These works are seen more as the rule-governed products of textuality than the expression of an individual creative genius. Even the unconscious was held to be structured like language, according to the influential structuralist psychoanalyst Jacques Lacan.

By the time structuralism gained influence in American aesthetics it was already being eclipsed by poststructuralism.

By the time structuralism gained influence in American aesthetics it was already being eclipsed by poststructuralism, whose leading figures (Barthes, Foucault, Derrida) shared a structuralist background. Poststructuralism (one of whose varieties is deconstruction) agrees that all elements get their meaning from their functional and differential relations to each other, that these relations are conventional rather than natural, and that the systemic meanings are always more than the sum of the individual parts. But by insisting that history and change affect language, it denies the structuralist presumption that the system or structure is ever closed or complete. If language is constantly changing, through new combinations of its elements, so must the meaning of any of its member elements, which raises problems of how any text could have a fixed meaning that would guarantee the possibility of true interpretation. As the work's fixity of meaning is threatened, so is the notion of its organic unity, an explicit target of Foucault, Derrida, and Paul de Man. Deconstructionist flux and relational identity also challenge the firmness of genre distinctions, including the distinction between philosophy and literature; everything is part of the dynamic, generative general text that lacks the closure of a system in the structuralist sense.

Postmodernism and Feminism

Though already used in reference to architecture (in the late 1940s) and literature (by the 1960s), postmodernism emerged as a general trend of aesthetic theory only after the advent of poststructuralism. Like poststructuralism, its heightened sense of flux challenges the stabilities of unity, meaning, and rule-governed structure central to traditional aesthetics. Like postmodern art, postmodern aesthetics challenges the modernist idea of aesthetic autonomy, purity, and distance. Arguing that we cannot compartmentalize art from political and social issues to achieve pure aesthetic experience, it also challenges the strict division between legitimate art and popular culture. Jean-François Lyotard, who made the term famous in philosophy, described the postmodern attitude as an incredulity toward grand metanarratives, toward monolithic unitary views of a topic.

Though independent of postmodernism and not as generally skeptical, feminist aesthetics has most flourished in the climate of postmodern theory, for it represents a challenge to what it sees as the grand metanarrative of "phallogocentric" theory. Like postmodernism, feminism challenges traditional ideas of aesthetic autonomy and distance that support patriarchal culture through the traditional male gaze, which subordinates the female as an object of aesthetic delight. Not surprisingly, embodiment or "writing with the body" is stressed by many feminist theorists, most notably Julia Kristeva, Hélène Cixous, and Luce Irigaray. Feminist and postmodernist perspectives are now making their way into mainstream Anglo-American aesthetics through the work of Elaine Showalter and others (see Korsmeyer & Brand, 1990).

[See also Aesthetic Attitude; Aesthetic Autonomy; Artworld; Beauty; Carnap, Rudolph; Deconstruction; Derrida, Jacques; Foucault, Michel; Gadamer, Hans-Georg; Goodman, Nelson; Heidegger, Martin; Marxism; Poststructuralism; Pragmatism; Russell, Bertrand Arthur William; Wittgenstein, Ludwig Josef Johann.]

BIBLIOGRAPHY

Adorno, T. W. Aesthetic Theory. London, 1984.
Althusser, L. For Marx. London, 1969.
Barthes, R. Image-Meaning-Text. New York, 1977.
Beardsley, M. C. Aesthetics. New York, 1958.
Benjamin, W. Illuminations. New York, 1968.
Cavell, S. Pursuits of Happiness. Cambridge, MA, 1981.
Cixous, H. "Coming to Writing" and Other Essays. New York, 1991.
Danto, A. The Transfiguration of the Commonplace. Cambridge, MA, 1981.
———. The Philosophical Disenfranchisement of Art. New York, 1986.
De Man, P. Blindness and Insight. Minneapolis, 1983.
Derrida, J. Of Grammatology. Baltimore, 1967.
———. Writing and Difference. Chicago, 1977.
Dewey, J. Art as Experience. New York, 1934.
Dickie, G. Aesthetics. New York, 1971.
Eagleton, T. Criticism and Ideology. London, 1976.
Foucault, M. Language, Counter-Memory, Practice. Ithaca, NY, 1977.
Gadamer, H.-G. Truth and Method. New York, 1982.
Gallie, W. B. "The Function of Philosophical Aesthetics," in W. Elton, ed., Aesthetics and Language (Oxford, 1954).
Goodman, N. Languages of Art. Oxford, 1969.
———. Ways of Worldmaking. New York, 1978.
———. Of Mind and Other Matters. Cambridge, MA, 1984.
Heidegger, M. Being and Time. New York, 1962.
———. Poetry, Language, Thought. New York, 1971.
Irigaray, L. This Sex Which Is Not One. Ithaca, NY, 1985.
Jameson, F. Marxism and Form. Princeton, NJ, 1971.
Kennick, W. E. "Does Traditional Aesthetics Rest on a Mistake?" Mind, Vol. 47 (1958).
Korsmeyer, C., and P. Brand. Feminist Aesthetics. Special issue of Journal of Aesthetics and Art Criticism (1990).
Kristeva, J. The Kristeva Reader, edited by T. Moi. New York, 1986.
Lacan, J. Ecrits: A Selection. New York, 1977.
Lukacs, G. History and Class Consciousness. New York, 1971.
Lyotard, J.-F. The Postmodern Condition. Minneapolis, 1984.
Macherey, P. A Theory of Literary Production. London, 1978.
Marcuse, H. Negations. Harmondsworth, Middlesex, 1972.
Margolis, J. Philosophy Looks at the Arts. Philadelphia, 1978.
———. Interpretation: Radical But Not Unruly. Berkeley, 1994.
Moi, T. Sexual/Textual Politics: Feminist Literary Theory. London, 1985.
Rorty, R. Contingency, Irony, and Solidarity. Cambridge, MA, 1989.
Showalter, E. The New Feminist Criticism. New York, 1985.
Shusterman, R. M. Pragmatist Aesthetics. Oxford, 1992.
———. ed. Analytic Aesthetics. Oxford, 1989.
Sibley, F. "Aesthetic Concepts," in J. Margolis, ed., Philosophy Looks at the Arts (Philadelphia, 1978).
Urmson, J. O. "What Makes a Situation Aesthetic?" in F. J. Coleman, ed., Contemporary Studies in Aesthetics (New York, 1968).
Weitz, M. "The Role of Theory in Aesthetics," Journal of Aesthetics and Art Criticism, Vol. 16 (1956), 27–35.
Wollheim, R. Art and Its Objects. New York, 1968.

— RICHARD M. SHUSTERMAN

AESTHETICS, PROBLEMS OF

Aesthetics is the branch of philosophy studying concepts and issues related to art and aesthetic experience. The range of the aesthetic is wider than that of art, since not only works of art but natural objects are objects of aesthetic experience and judgment and display aesthetic qualities. Though different, the concepts of art and the aesthetic have been closely related in modernity, when the specific philosophical discipline of aesthetics was first established, along with the very concept of the aesthetic and the rise of autonomous art. In terms of modernity's tripartite differentiation of cultural spheres (reflected in Kant's three Critiques), art and the aesthetic were linked together in opposition to the domains of pure cognition and practical reason. Much twentieth-century aesthetics is concerned with explaining (or challenging) this differentiation of art and the aesthetic by trying to determine the precise nature of these concepts, often attempting to define art in terms of the aesthetic and vice versa. Besides the issues of art and the aesthetic, this article will treat the problems of art's interpretation and evaluation. Other important issues, not reviewed in this article, include: the ontological status of artworks; the nature of representation in the arts; the nature of fiction, metaphor, and authenticity; the role of emotion in aesthetic appreciation; and the distinction between high and popular art.

The Aesthetic and Aesthetic Experience

Diverse attempts have been made to distinguish the aesthetic from other domains—for example, in terms of a special kind of property (such as beauty), a special kind of attitude, judgment, or experience. Some try to define the property of beauty (Mothersill, Savile), while others try to distinguish aesthetic from nonaesthetic properties in terms of the aesthetic's use of a nonrule-governed logic of application (Sibley). But general skepticism about the robust reality and objectivity of aesthetic properties (Do they exist at all? Are they simply supervenient on more basic physical properties?) has encouraged most recent thinkers to define the aesthetic through the subject-centered notions of attitude and experience. Let us concentrate on aesthetic experience, whose nature has been widely theorized and critiqued in both Anglo-American and Continental philosophy.

Dewey argued that art's essence and value are not in its artifacts but in the dynamic, developing activity through which they are created and perceived.

Aesthetic experience has, through its history, developed the following rough profile. Dynamic, enjoyable, and valuable, it is vividly felt and phenomenologically savored experience, powerfully absorbing us in its immediate presence. Aesthetic experience is also meaningful experience, not mere sensation. In standing out from the ordinary flow of experience by its vividness, pleasure, and greater meaning and unity, it is closely identified with the distinction of autonomous fine art and represents art's prime, autonomous aim. The idea of "art for art's sake" is thus construed as for the sake of art's own experience. Contemporary criticism of aesthetic experience often focuses on its alleged immediacy and its link to the compartmentalizing ideology of art for art's sake.

Dewey's *Art as Experience* concentrates on attacking art's compartmentalization precisely by arguing that art be defined in terms of aesthetic experience and that such experience transcends the institutional boundaries of fine art—for example, in the appreciation of nature and festival. Opposing the fetishization of art's elite objects, Dewey argued that art's essence and value are not in its artifacts but in the dynamic, developing activity through which they are created and perceived. Aesthetic experience, hence art, can be achieved in any domain

of human activity; it is distinguished by its vividness, dynamic development, and integrated satisfying form that makes it stand out from ordinary experience as "*an* experience." It is "directly fulfilling" and, in this sense, immediate, though involving the mediacy of developmental process. Dewey's definition of art as aesthetic experience can be criticized for failing to reflect the actual usage of our established concept of art, even if his real aim was probably instead to transform it radically.

Building on Dewey's theory (but not its critique of differentiation), Monroe Beardsley (1958, 1982) defines art as a function class whose defining function is the production of aesthetic experience. Art's value depends on the basic value and intrinsic pleasure of that experience; better works are those capable of producing aesthetic experiences of "greater magnitude." Aesthetic experience, for Beardsley, is an intrinsically enjoyable, unified, affective, and comparatively intense experience, where the subject's attention is firmly and actively focused on some phenomenal field. Analytic colleagues rejected Beardsley's theory on three grounds: subjective experiences are not the sorts of things that can have unity; aesthetic experience often lacks unity, pleasure, intensity, and affect; and it cannot be defined in positive terms, since some aesthetic experience is bad (e.g., with bad art). The first ground has led some to deny the existence of Beardsley's aesthetic experience (Dickie, 1965) while suggesting that aesthetic experience (conceived as having intrinsic value and positive affect) cannot define art, since such a definition must allow for bad art as well.

To resolve such difficulties, Nelson Goodman (1968, 1978, 1984) offers a definition of aesthetic experience that is nonevaluative and not based on the immediate phenomenological feel of experience. Instead, stressing how aesthetic experience is mediated through symbols, he defines it in purely semiotic terms as "cognitive experience distinguished by the dominance of certain symbolic characteristics": syntactic and semantic density, relative repleteness, exemplification, multiple and complex reference. If an object's "functioning exhibits all these symptoms, then very likely the object is a work of art" (1989, p. 199). However, as Goodman admits, these symptoms do not strictly constitute necessary and sufficient conditions for defining a work of art.

Turning to the Continental critique of aesthetic experience, one may begin with Heidegger's denial that art is for mere "appreciation" divorced from the goal of truth. An artwork is not a gadget for enjoyable experience. "To be a work means to set up a world" and, in setting up a world, to reveal the truth of being. "Art then is the becoming and happening of truth" (1971, pp. 44, 71). Gadamer develops these insights into a critique of aesthetic experience's alleged immediacy and radical differentiation from life. Only by such differentiation can art's appreciation be reduced to an immediate experience, but this does not do justice to art's enduring impact on our lives and world, its roots and effects in our cultural tradition, and its claim to truth. Art's meaning is not immediately given but a developing product of history that reaches beyond compartmentalized aesthetic contexts. True aesthetic experience "becomes an experience changing the person experiencing it" (1982, p. 92); nor is this experience a private subjectivity but the intersubjectively structured play of the work itself. As a game "plays" its players who must follow its rules, so the artwork submits those who want its meaning to the intersubjective structures that guide its experience.

Agreeing that "real aesthetic experience" requires submission "to the objective constitution of the work," Theodor Adorno concludes that it demands a "self-abnegation" inconsistent with immediate, facile pleasure (1984, pp. 474, 476). Art's experience must also go beyond immediate understanding (*Verstehen*), requiring critical "secondary reflection" of its ideological meaning and the sociohistorical conditions that shape it. Though Adorno insists that art's capacity for critical emancipatory truth depends on its distance from the unjust world, he recognizes that art's relative autonomy is only the product of social forces that ultimately condition the nature of aesthetic experience. Since changes in the nonaesthetic world affect our very capacities for experience, aesthetic experience cannot be a fixed natural kind.

This is central to Walter Benjamin's critique of aesthetic experience as immediate *Erlebnis*. Because of the fragmentation and shocks of modern life, immediate experience is no longer capable of any meaningful unity, becoming but a jumble of sensations merely lived through (*erlebt*). Benjamin instead advocates a notion of experience (*Erfahrung*) that requires the mediated, temporally cumulative accretion of coherent transmittable wisdom, though he doubts whether it can still be achieved. Modernization and technology (with its modes of mechanical reproduction) have also eroded aesthetic experience's transcendent "aura" of uniqueness and differentiation from ordinary reality; hence, the aesthetic comes into the world of politics and popular culture. Despite the dangers of the use of aesthetics in fascism, Benjamin, like Dewey, sees the loss of aura and aesthetic compartmentalization as potentially emancipatory.

The Definition of Art

The difficulty of defining art through aesthetic experience and through other familiar criteria (e.g., form, expression, etc.) intensified doubts that art could be adequately defined in any strict sense—that is, in terms of an essence or set of necessary and sufficient conditions. Relying on Wittgenstein, Morris Weitz (1955) and others (e.g., Gallie, Kennick) argue that art's essence could not in principle be defined because it simply had none. If we examine the class of artworks, we find they exhibit no set of properties that is common, peculiar, and essential to all of them. Nor is such essence necessary for the shared meaning of the concept 'art'; the network of similarities and family resemblances among artworks is enough to govern the concept's application. Indeed, art can have no defining essence because it is an intrinsically open, complex, contested, and mutable concept, a field that prides itself on originality and innovation. Thus, any definition that might seem to work would spur art to transcend it. Part of the conceptual complexity of 'art' is having both a mere classificational use and a use that is evaluative, hence contested.

To overcome these problems, a new style of definition was proposed. If evaluative issues make any definition contestable, then definition should be confined to the classificatory sense of art. If artworks exhibit no set of shared properties, then perhaps art's defining essence is not in exhibited properties but in its generative process. Moreover, the notion of family resemblance already implies a common generative core or history. These arguments led to George Dickie's institutional theory of art, which defines an artwork (in a purely classificational sense) as "an artifact . . . upon which some person or persons acting on behalf of a certain social institution (the artworld) has conferred the status of candidate for appreciation" (1971, p. 101).

Though defining art in terms of necessary and sufficient conditions, this influential theory is purely formal or procedural and thus would neither foreclose on innovation nor prejudice with respect to evaluative criteria. Such foreclosures and prejudices are conveniently left to the artworld, as are all other substantive matters. The theory has the merit of highlighting the social context through which art is generated and given properties that are not directly perceived by the senses. Moreover, its flexible formalism can be used to cover whatever the artworld determines to be art. But the theory has problems as well. Though Dickie is right to insist that being an artwork does not entail being valuable, it is wrong to think that art can be defined without reference to value. Indeed, his definition presupposes evaluation in its notion of appreciation, but it provides no substantive insight that would explain *why* art is appreciated and that would enrich our understanding of it. Further, there are problems with seeing the artworld as an institution, since institutions typically involve roles, structures, and practices that are much more clearly codified and strictly administered than in the artworld. To respond that the artworld is a very informal institution is to merge this theory into a far more influential one: that art is a cultural tradition or sociohistorical practice.

Arthur Danto, who propounds this view and whose "discovery" of the artworld inspired Dickie, rejects the institutional theory because of its lack of historical depth. Ignoring Wöllflin's insight that not everything is possible at every time, it gave artworld agents an unlimited power without considering the historical constraints that structure the artworld and thus limit its agents' actions. Even if it could explain how Andy Warhol's Brillo boxes could be art today, it could not explain why such a proposal would not have been accepted in quattrocento Florence. Such acceptance depends on the state of art's history and theory. Nothing, Danto argues, is art unless it is so interpreted, and the artworld "required a certain historical development" to make it possible to interpret the Brillo boxes as art. Since the artworld is but an abstraction from the artistic, critical, curatorial, and theoretical practices that constitute art's history, art is essentially a complex historical practice or tradition best defined historically. Richard Wollheim also asserts that "art is essentially historical," and Adorno concurs that art cannot be defined by any "invariable principle," since it is a historically changing constellation of moments whose constitutive unity is best defined by its concrete development as a distinct practice, at once socially embedded and resistantly autonomous. A new generation of analytic aestheticians (Carroll, Levinson, Wolterstoff) has likewise insisted on defining art by its history as a practice.

Though this strategy has many merits, some pragmatists (such as Shusterman, 1992) find it too quietistic and limited. In defining art as a practice defined by its art-historical narrative, it leaves all decisions as to what counts *as* art or *in* art to the backward-looking practice of art history but does not directly confront such issues. Philosophy of art thus becomes a representation of art history's representation of art, an imitation of an imitation that shirks normative engagement. Moreover, equating art with its historically defined practice involves the shrinking of art's extension, since art as defined by its established historical narrative amounts, in modern times, to the fine art that makes art history, thus essentially limiting art to elite fine art.

Interpretation and Evaluation

The logic of interpretation and evaluation involves two different but related issues: the logical status of interpretive or evaluative statements (i.e., Are they propositions having truth value of some sort, or are they more like performative, creative acts?) and the role of reasons and arguments (i.e., Are they evidence, principles, or merely perceptual or rhetorical devices of persuasion?). Let us concentrate on the first, more basic issue.

In the quest for interpretive truth, authorial intention long served as the aim and criterion, an artwork meaning what its creator intended in creating it. Since correct evaluation should depend on correct understanding, intention thus seemed important for evaluation as well. This standard was successfully challenged in the second half of the twentieth century by analytic philosophers associated with the New Criticism, structuralist and poststructuralist thinkers, and several neopragmatists. Monroe Beardsley opposed what he (with New Critic Wimsatt) called "the intentional fallacy" by arguing that the concept of work-meaning could not be identical with author's meaning, since works can change their meaning without authorial agency (e.g., in the changes of meaning that occur after an author's death). It is the work's meaning that interpretation should seek, since this meaning is available by the norms of language, while access to the author is often not available. Defenders of intentionalism (such as Hirsch) argue that anti-intentionalists fail to distinguish between meaning and significance. Only the latter can change, while meaning must remain fixed to preserve the work's identity. The anti-intentionalists reply that the text itself provides identity enough, while Hirsch says the text itself remains too ambiguous to fix identity without a disambiguating intention.

Nothing, Danto argues, is art unless it is so interpreted, and the artworld "required a certain historical development" to make it possible to interpret Warhol's Brillo boxes as art.

Both Hirsch and Beardsley agree, however, that valid interpretations are true propositions about the meaning of an artwork that preclude the validity of conflicting interpretations. Margolis opposes this with a relativist position, asserting that interpretive statements express cognitive claims having some sort of truth value but that this value is weaker than in standard bivalent logic (involving plausibility, not strict truth). Thus it can allow conflicting interpretations to be valid, as plausible though not as true. For him (as for Ingarden) the ontologically indeterminate status of elements in an artwork provides gaps that can be differently filled in by interpretation. Here, as in critical pluralism, intentionalist interpretation can take its place along with other modes without special privilege.

Like New Critics and pluralists, structuralists and poststructuralists proclaim "the death of the author" as the privileged locus and determiner of work-meaning. Instead, meaning is seen as the product of structural relations among the work's elements and the features of the more general linguistic-cultural sphere. Poststructuralists (including deconstructionists such as Derrida) then argue that meaning is always changing, since these relations of elements are always changing with the changing play of language. Hence, interpretation can never return to recapture the original meaning. Its very use of language to do so involves activity that changes the meaning by changing linguistic relations. Hence, all readings are misreadings. They can nonetheless be productive because of the interesting, insightful meanings they produce.

This theory of interpretation clearly puts its emphasis on productive performativity rather than propositional truth. Harold Bloom, for example, urges that good interpretations are strong, innovative misreadings that help transform the work's meaning into the critic's own. Such a doctrine clearly suits the academy's pressures of constantly producing new interpretations for the professional advancement of its members. Influential pragmatists such as Richard Rorty and Stanley Fish likewise identify the right way of reading with distinctive, novel interpretation, for they argue that, in any case, all reading, like all experience, is always transformative interpretation. But without resorting to foundationalism, Richard Shusterman (1992) argued that we can and often do make a pragmatic distinction between mere acts of reading (or understanding) and interpretations. Such more ordinary (albeit often vague and implicit) understandings remain a necessary background and initial though not apodictic base for innovative interpretation.

Evaluation has received, in recent times, less philosophical attention than interpretation. For Beardsley the standard of artistic value was an artwork's capacity to produce aesthetic experience of some magnitude, but since such experience was subjective he also offered three "objective" canons of critical judgment evaluation: unity, intensity, and complexity. Goodman identifies artistic value with cognitive value achieved through the functioning of aesthetic symbol systems. Anthony Savile has reconstructed Samuel Johnson's theory that an artwork's value is proved by the test of time, while Barbara Smith offers a more complex sociohistorical account of how value is neither intrinsic nor merely subjective but rather the product of social forces and agendas locked in a continuing struggle for greater legitimacy and hegemony.

[See also Aesthetic Attitude; Aesthetic Autonomy; Aesthetic Properties; Aesthetic Relativism; Art, Definition of; Art, Interpretation of; Art, Representation in; Art as Performance; Artworld; Authenticity Regarding the Artist and the Artwork; Beauty; Deconstruction; Derrida, Jacques; Dewey, John; Gadamer, Hans-Georg; Goodman, Nelson; Heidegger, Martin; Kant, Immanuel; Poststructuralism; Wittgenstein, Ludwig Josef Johann.]

BIBLIOGRAPHY

Adorno, T. *Aesthetic Theory*. London, 1984.
Barthes, R. *Image-Meaning-Text*. New York, 1977.
Beardsley, M. C. *Aesthetics*. New York, 1958.
———. *The Possibility of Criticism*. Detroit, 1973.
———. *The Aesthetic Point of View*. Ithaca, NY, 1982.
Benjamin, W. *Illuminations*. New York, 1968.
Bloom, H. *A Map of Misreading*. New York, 1975.
———. *Agon: Towards a Theory of Revisionism*. New York, 1982.
Budd, M. *Music and the Emotions*. London, 1985.
Carroll, N. "Art, Practice, and Narrative," *The Monist*, Vol. 71 (1988), 140–56.
———. *Philosophy of Horror*. New York, 1991.
Cavell, S. *The World Viewed*. Cambridge, MA, 1979.
Danto, A. *The Transfiguration of the Commonplace*. Cambridge, MA, 1981.
———. *The Philosophical Disenfranchisement of Art*. New York, 1986.
Derrida, J. *Of Grammatology*. Baltimore, 1967.
———. *Writing and Difference*. Chicago, 1977.
Dewey, J. *Art as Experience*. New York, 1934.
Dickie, G. "Beardsley's Phantom Aesthetic Experience," *Journal of Philosophy*, Vol. 62 (1965), 129–36.
———. *Aesthetics*. New York, 1971.
Fish, S. *Doing What Comes Naturally*. Durham, NC, 1989.
Gadamer, H.-G. *Truth and Method*. New York, 1982.
Gallie, W. B. "The Function of Philosophical Aesthetics," in W. Elton, ed., *Aesthetics and Language* (Oxford, 1954).
Goodman, N. *Languages of Art*. Oxford, 1968.
———. *Ways of Worldmaking*. Indianapolis, 1978.
———. *Of Mind and Other Matters*. Cambridge, MA, 1984.
Heidegger, M. *Poetry, Language, Thought*. New York, 1971.
Hirsch, E. D. *The Aims of Interpretation*. Chicago, 1978.
Ingarden, R. *The Literary Work of Art*. Evanston, IL, 1973.
Iseminger, G., ed. *Interpretation, Intention, and Truth*. Philadelphia, 1992.
Kennick, W. E. "Does Traditional Aesthetics Rest on a Mistake?" *Mind*, Vol. 47 (1958).
Kivy, P. *The Corded Shell*. Princeton, NJ, 1980.
Levinson, J. *Music, Art, and Metaphysics*. Ithaca, NY, 1990.
Margolis, J. *Art and Philosophy*. Brighton, 1980.
———. *Interpretation: Radical but Not Unruly*. Berkeley, 1994.
Mothersill, M. *Beauty Restored*. New York, 1984.
Novitz, D. *Knowledge, Fiction, and Imagination*. Philadelphia, 1987.
Rorty, R. *Objectivity, Relativism, and Truth*. Cambridge, MA, 1991.
Savile, A. *The Test of Time*. Oxford, 1982.
Shusterman, R. M. *The Object of Literary Criticism*. Amsterdam, 1984.
———. *Pragmatist Aesthetics*. Oxford, 1992.
Sibley, F. "Aesthetic Concepts," in J. Margolis, ed., *Philosophy Looks at the Arts* (Philadelphia, 1978).
Smith, B. *Contingencies of Value*. Cambridge, MA, 1988.

Weitz, M. "The Role of Theory in Aesthetics," *Journal of Aesthetics and Art Criticism,* Vol. 16 (1956), 27–35.

Walton, K. *Mimesis as Make-Believe.* Cambridge, MA, 1990.

Wollheim, R. *Art and Its Objects.* New York, 1968.

Wolterstorff, N. *Works and Worlds of Art.* Oxford, 1980.

———. "Philosophy after Analysis and Romanticism," in R. Shusterman, ed., *Analytic Aesthetics* (Oxford, 1989).

— RICHARD M. SHUSTERMAN

AFFIRMATIVE ACTION

An understanding of affirmative action requires that we distinguish two kinds of discrimination: first, overt discrimination, which always involves prejudice by a perpetrator against a victim; second, institutional discrimination, which occurs when procedures such as selection through personal connections, qualification requirements, and seniority status, although they may be administered by unprejudiced persons, nevertheless have disproportionately adverse impact on minorities and women. While institutional and overt discrimination are distinct concepts, in reality they work together. For example, minorities and women tend to lack seniority protection against layoff because in the past prejudiced supervisors refused to hire them. Also, in large part because of race prejudice, African-Americans are excluded from relations of friendship and intimacy with whites; hence, they lack the personal connections to better jobs where whites predominate.

Affirmative action, a remedy for institutional discrimination, is exemplified, not in passive nondiscrimination, but in efforts to reduce the disparate impact of selection through personal connections, qualification requirements, and seniority status by actively recruiting and promoting significant numbers of minorities and women to positions in employment and as students in universities and professional schools.

Two important affirmative-action measures are, first, ensuring that qualification requirements having disparate impact are relevant to job performance and, second, establishing numerical goals for recruiting and promoting significant numbers of minorities and women. Where underrepresentation is severe, fulfilling a numerical goal may require "preference"—that is, selection of "basically qualified" minorities or women over more qualified white males.

Some critics claim that affirmative action has helped only a few fortunate minorities. But proponents claim that it has brought significant numbers of minority persons from low-status background into professional schools and employment as, for example, police, firefighters, textile workers, and teachers.

Moral critics of affirmative action suggest that preferential treatment is unjust because it undermines our

Allan Bakke took his challenge of a university's affirmative action program all the way to the Supreme Court—and won. (Corbis/Bettmann)

current system of merit selection. Proponents argue that, while being the best candidate is one way to get the job, merit standards are currently ignored in several ways—children of alumni receive preferential admission to elite schools, war veterans are preferred to those without experience in the armed forces, tests that are irrelevant to job performance are used to select employees, and many jobs are filled through personal connections (probably the most widely used recruitment system in American employment).

Moral critics have also argued that preference is unfair to males who are singled out to bear the burden of remedying past discrimination. Some proponents deny that such treatment is unjust, while others, granting that these white males are unfairly singled out, suggest that they be given monetary awards to compensate for their loss.

[See also Racism; Social and Political Philosophy.]

BIBLIOGRAPHY

Boxill, B. *Blacks and Social Justice.* Totowa, NJ, 1984.

Cohen, M., T. Nagel, and T. Scanlon, eds. *Equality and Preferential Treatment.* Princeton, NJ, 1977.

Ezorsky, G. *Racism and Justice: The Case for Affirmative Action.*
  Ithaca, NY, 1991.
Goldman, A. *Justice and Reverse Discrimination.* Princeton, NJ,
  1979.
Wilson, W. J. *The Truly Disadvantaged.* Chicago, 1987.

                                              – GERTRUDE EZORSKY

AFRICAN PHILOSOPHY

As a habit of thought, philosophy is a primeval component of African culture. However, its academic cultivation, although also native to some parts of Africa, has been conducted in Western-style educational institutions in many parts of Africa, on account of the accident of colonization. These two circumstances account, in large measure, for the present character of African philosophy as a discipline.

Flowing directly from the circumstances just alluded to have been two imperatives of philosophical research in postcolonial Africa. They might be called the imperatives of reclamation and of reconstruction. The objective of the first has been to bring out, by means of a firsthand knowledge of African culture and, more especially, of African languages, the true character of the philosophical thought of precolonial Africa, which had suffered neglect or distortion during the colonial period; that of the second to evaluate the results of the first enterprise and, using the insights that might be derived from them in combination with the resources of modern knowledge and reflection, to construct philosophies suitable for present-day existence.

On the first front, available accounts already reveal oral traditions rich in ethical, political, and metaphysical ideas. They reveal, moreover, fundamental contrasts between African and Western conceptions, at least regarding predominant tendencies. Perhaps the most basic of these ideas and also the most illustrative of the contrasts is the idea of human personality. African notions of a human person frequently see human individuality as presupposing the existence of society rather than the other way around. (Good sense, by the way, forbids unqualified universals about the entire continent of Africa.) Two of arguably the most famous quotations in the literature of contemporary African philosophy are about exactly this point. Senghor, the African statesman-philosopher, contrasts the African orientation with the Cartesian one by epitomizing it as "I feel, I dance the other; I am" (1964, p. 73). Mbiti maintains, for his part, that the African individual can only say, "I am because we are, and since we are, therefore I am" (1990, p. 106). The point here is not just that the existence of a person presupposes at least the minimal society of a parental couple. The idea is rather that the notion of a person is intrinsically social; so that

a totally unsocialized being replicating human morphology to perfection would still not be a person. But socialization is only a necessary condition. A person, according to this way of thinking, is a human individual who has matured into a responsible member of the community. Thus, as Menkiti (1984) points out, personhood is not something that one is born with but rather something that one may or may not achieve, and the achievement is susceptible of degree.

Of the various implications of this conception of personhood one of an especial philosophical significance is that the notion has both descriptive and normative components. Normatively, it is indicative of the communalistic ethic of many African societies. In such societies the understanding of the necessity for the adjustment of the interests of the individual to those of the community is developed through bonding to large circles of kinship groups. The multitude of obligations and rights—note the order—that thus emerge go well beyond the province of morality in the strict sense, but this contextualization of the moral sense gives rise, as a rule, to a pragmatic, as opposed to a supernaturalistic, conception of the basis of morality. Contrary to frequent suggestions, in the earlier literature, of the dependency of morality on religion in African thought, recent distinctively philosophical analyses of ethics in various African societies, such as those by Wiredu (1983), Gyekye (1987, chap. 8), and Gbadegesin (1991, chap. 3), converge in the finding that morality is viewed as conceptually grounded on practical and rational considerations about the harmonization of human interests in society rather than on any beliefs of a religious character.

Mbiti maintains that the African individual

can only say, "I am because we are,

and since we are, therefore I am."

In connection with the descriptive dimension of human personhood a very basic fact about much of African ontological thinking becomes apparent—namely, that sharp cleavages are eschewed in the ontological taxonomy of personhood and of reality in general. Thus, a person is commonly conceived to consist of the visible assemblage of flesh, bones, and nerves together with a set of rarefied, not normally visible, constituents of a quasi-material likeness. The number of these subtle components and their exact characterization differ from place to place. But, generally, there are at least two, and they are postulated to account, first, for the fact of animation and, second, for the uniqueness of human individuality.

The Yorubas, for example, attribute life in the human frame to a principle emanating directly from God, which they call 'emi'. (See, e.g., Gbadegesin, 1991, chap. 2.) But they associate the pattern of contingencies of character and circumstance that differentiate one person from another with the 'ori-inu', literally, the inner head, which is supposed to receive the summation of that destiny from God just before earthly incarnation. Two additional constituents are invoked to account for the power of thought. There is the 'okan', literally, the heart, which is regarded as the seat of emotion, and there is the 'opolo', the brain, to which is ascribed the basis of the capacity for ratiocinative thought. It is clear, though easily unnoticed, that if mind is construed, as it so often is in Western thought, as a kind of substance, there is nothing in the Yoruba analysis of personhood that corresponds to it and its associated perplexities. Nor, relatedly, is there any counterpart of the soul of Western dualistic metaphysics. The same is true, mutatis mutandis, of the conceptions of personhood entertained among various African peoples such as the Akans of Ghana and the Banyarwandas of Rwanda.

From the point of view of ontology an even more interesting fact is that, in view of the activities and susceptibilities attributed to the nonbodily constituents of human personality, the difference between them and the physical body is one not of a categorical chasm but only of the degree of materiality. They are only relatively less material than the body in that, although not subject to the grosser limitations of ordinary material bodies, they belong essentially to the general framework of material existence. Ironically, this is more unmistakable from African portrayals of life after death. (See Wiredu, 1992.) The conceptual similarities between African worlds of the dead and the living are so pronounced that they have escaped few students of African thought. This ontological continuity can be seen writ large in the speculative cosmologies of many African peoples. Typically, there is a cosmic order occupied at the apex by a supreme being with, next below him, a variety of extrahuman forces and beings of variable capabilities and virtue. Between this domain and the world of the lesser animals, plants, and inanimate matter is the race of *Homo sapiens*. African ideas of the continual interactions among these orders of being provide little rational incentive for the application to this cosmic picture of metaphysical distinctions familiar in Western philosophy such as those between the natural and the supernatural and the temporal and the nontemporal.

The traditional communal thought of various African peoples owes its origin to the cogitations of individual philosophers, even if usually unnamed. Such indigenous thinkers, practically untouched by Western influences, still exist in Africa. Attention to their views, long overdue, is now being stimulated by works such as Oruka (1991) and, a little indirectly, Hallen and Sodipo (1986). Philosophical thinkers of much longer standing are, of course, known in some parts of Africa. One does not have to go as far as to Pharaonic Egypt for such discoveries. Claude Sumner's five-volume work on Ethiopian philosophy (1974–84), for instance, showcases, among other things, the written philosophy of Za'ra Ya'eqob, who in the seventeenth century propounded an indigenous rationalistic philosophy sterner, perhaps, in its subjection of religious dogma to the canons of reason than Descartes's philosophy. One might mention also earlier leading lights in philosophy in Africa such as Tertullian (160–230) and St. Augustine (354–430).

An urgent question, however, that has arisen for contemporary Africans faced with the challenges of postcolonial reconstruction in philosophy is, How can philosophizing deeply impregnated by foreign ideas or methods, such as the Christ-intoxicated meditations of Tertullian and Augustine or, for that matter, the scientifically oriented analyses of a Western-trained African philosopher of the last half of the twentieth century, lay just claims to African authenticity? The immediate postindependence rulers of Africa, with little spare time for methodological niceties, made their own syntheses of the foreign and the indigenous and in the 1960s produced political philosophies for national reconstruction still worthy of study. (See, for example, Mutiso & Rohio, 1975). Inevitably, African academic philosophers have been especially prone to methodological soul searching, and controversy on the question of the authenticity of African philosophy has absorbed a considerable proportion of their attention, as may be seen in Serequeberham (1991). Still, work in African philosophy sensitive to insights from Western philosophy is being done. Eventually, the imperatives of reclamation and reconstruction will merge.

[See also Augustine, St.; Descartes, René; Philosophy.]

BIBLIOGRAPHY

Appiah, K. A. *In My Father's House: Africa in the Philosophy of Culture.* New York, 1992.

Gbadegesin, S. *African Philosophy: Traditional Yoruba Philosophy and Contemporary African Realities.* New York, 1991.

Gyekye, K. *An Essay on African Philosophical Thought: The Akan Conceptual Scheme.* New York, 1987.

Hallen, B., and J. O. Sodipo. *Knowledge, Belief, and Witchcraft: Analytic Experiments in African Philosophy.* London, 1986.

Hountondji, P. *African Philosophy: Myth and Reality.* Bloomington, IN, 1976. Principal catalyst of the contemporary controversy on the best way of approaching the study of African traditions in relation to the tasks of African philosophy in the world today.

Masolo, D. A. *African Philosophy in Search of Identity.* Bloomington, IN, 1994.

Mbiti, J. *African Religions and Philosophy.* London, 1990.

Menkiti, I. "Person and Community in African Traditional Thought," in R. A. Wright, ed., *African Philosophy: An Introduction* (New York, 1984). Note the bibliography appended to this book.

Mudimbe, V. Y. *The Invention of Africa: Gnosis, Philosophy, and the Order of Knowledge.* Bloomington, IN, 1988. Note the bibliography.

Mutiso, G.-C., and S. W. Rohio. *Readings in African Political Thought.* London, 1975.

Oruka, O. H. *Sage Philosophy: Indigenous Thinkers and the Modern Debate on African Philosophy.* Nairobi, 1991.

Senghor, L. S. *On African Socialism.* New York, 1964.

Serequeberhan, T., ed. *African Philosophy: The Essential Readings.* New York, 1991.

———. *The Hermeneutics of African Philosophy.* New York, 1994.

Sumner, C. *Ethiopian Philosophy,* 5 vols. Addis Ababa, 1974–84. Vol. 2 (1976) is subtitled *The Treatise of Za'ara Ya'eqob and of Walda Heywat, Text and Authorship.*

———. *Classical Ethiopian Philosophy.* Los Angeles, 1994.

Tempels, P. *Bantu Philosophy.* Paris, 1959. Much-discussed philosophical study of an African people by a Belgian missionary. Regarded by some contemporary African philosophers as the paradigm of how not to do African philosophy.

Wiredu, K. *Philosophy and an African Culture.* Cambridge, 1980.

———. "Morality and Religion in Akan Thought," in H. O. Oruka and D. A. Masolo, *Philosophy and Cultures* (Nairobi, 1983).

———. "Death and the Afterlife in African Culture," in K. Wiredu and K. Gyekye, eds., *Person and Community: Ghanaian Philosophical Essays* (Washington, DC, 1992).

– KWASI WIREDU

ANALYTIC FEMINISM

Analytic feminism applies analytic concepts and methods to feminist issues and applies feminist concepts and insights to issues that traditionally have been of interest to analytic philosophers. Analytic feminists, like analytic philosophers more generally, value clarity and precision in argument and use logical and linguistic analysis to help them achieve that clarity and precision. Unlike nonfeminists, they insist on recognizing and contesting sexism and androcentrism (practices that take males or men and their experiences to be the norm or the ideal for human life). Analytic feminism holds that the best way to counter sexism and androcentrism is through forming a clear conception of and pursuing truth, logical consistency, objectivity, rationality, justice, and the good while recognizing that these notions have often been perverted by androcentrism throughout the history of philosophy. Analytic feminists engage the literature traditionally thought of as analytic philosophy but also draw on other traditions in philosophy as well as work by feminists working in other disciplines, especially the social and biological sciences.

Analytic feminists assert the distinction between the biological concept of sex and the socially constructed concept of gender (nonisomorphic to sex), though they may disagree widely on how this distinction is to be

drawn and what moral or political implications it has. Although they share the conviction that the social constructions of gender create a fundamentally unjust imbalance in contemporary social and political arrangements, there is no other political thesis generally held by them. Many analytic feminists are not political philosophers, but those who are defend political views that reflect progressive positions found in contemporary nonfeminist political philosophy, from liberalism (Okin, 1989) to socialism (Jaggar, 1983). They also draw on views of previous generations of feminist political philosophers from John Stuart Mill and Mary Wollstonecraft to Friedrich Engels, Emma Goldman, and Charlotte Perkins Gilman. Analytic feminists, like nonanalytic feminists, have written much about social and political issues such as abortion, pornography, prostitution, rape, sexual harassment, surrogacy, and violence against women. What characterizes analytic feminism here is the use of logical analysis and, sometimes, decision-theoretic analysis (Cudd, 1993).

While postmodern feminism

rejects the universality of truth, justice,

and objectivity and the univocality of "women,"

analytic feminism defends these notions.

Analytic feminists often defend traditional analytic methods and concepts against criticisms from many nonanalytic feminists who charge (in various ways) that the notions of reason, truth, and objectivity or the methods of logical and linguistic analysis are hopelessly masculinist and cannot be reclaimed for feminist purposes. They criticize canonical philosophers, including Aristotle, Descartes, Kant, Rousseau, Frege, Quine, and Rawls, as sexist or at least androcentric, and at times they suggest that these philosophers have nothing useful to say to women. But analytic feminists argue that to reject philosophers on those grounds would indict similarly almost the entire history of philosophy. The question analytic feminists ask is whether those androcentric or sexist writings can be corrected and rescued by an enlightened critical reader. Annette Baier's work on Hume (in Baier, 1994), Marcia Homiak's (1993) work on Aristotle, and Barbara Herman's (1993) work on Kant exemplify such attempts.

Analytic feminism holds that many traditional philosophical notions are not only normatively compelling, but also in some ways empowering and liberating for women. While postmodern feminism rejects the universality of truth, justice, and objectivity and the univocality of "women," analytic feminism defends these notions. It recognizes that to reject a view because it is false or oppressive to women one needs some rational, objective ground from which to argue that it is in fact false or oppressive. An important task for analytic feminism involves investigating the objectivity of science. Helen Longino's *Science as Social Knowledge* (1990) was the first such analytic feminist work. Elizabeth Anderson's "Feminist Epistemology: An Interpretation and a Defense" (1995) shows how a carefully aimed feminist critique can improve the objectivity of science by distinguishing and illustrating four ways that feminist critiques have corrected the distorted lenses of masculinist science: by critiquing gendered structures in the social organization of science, by analyzing gendered symbols in scientific models, by exposing sexism in scientific practices and aims, and by revealing androcentrism in its concepts and theories. In its analysis of traditional philosophical topics such as objectivity and new topics such as sexism in language (Vetterling-Braggin, 1981), analytic feminism reveals the blurriness of the distinction between metaphysics, epistemology, and social/political philosophy.

[See also Abortion; Aristotle; Descartes, René; Feminist Philosophy; Frege, Gottlob; Hume, David; Kant, Immanuel; Liberalism; Mill, John Stuart; Quine, Willard Van Orman; Rawls, John; Rousseau, Jean-Jacques; Wollstonecraft, Mary.]

BIBLIOGRAPHY

Anderson, E. "Feminist Epistemology: An Interpretation and a Defense," *Hypatia,* Vol. 10 (Summer 1995).

Antony, L. M., and C. Witt, eds. *A Mind of One's Own: Feminist Essays on Reason and Objectivity.* Boulder, CO, 1993.

Baier, A. C. *Moral Prejudices.* Cambridge, MA, 1994.

Cudd, A. E. "Oppression by Choice," *Journal of Social Philosophy,* Vol. 25 (1994).

Cudd, A. E., and V. Klenk, eds. *Hypatia,* Vol. 10 (Summer 1995). A special issue devoted to analytic feminism.

Grimshaw, J. *Philosophy and Feminist Thinking.* Minneapolis, 1986.

Herman, B. "Could It Be Worth Thinking about Kant on Sex and Marriage?" in L. M. Antony and C. Witt, eds., *A Mind of One's Own: Feminist Essays on Reason and Objectivity* (Boulder, CO, 1993).

Homiak, M. "Feminism and Aristotle's Rational Ideal," in L. M. Antony and C. Witt, eds., *A Mind of One's Own: Feminist Essays on Reason and Objectivity* (Boulder, CO, 1993).

Jaggar, A. M. *Feminist Politics and Human Nature.* Totowa, NJ, 1983.

Longino, H. *Science as Social Knowledge.* Princeton, NJ, 1990.

Nelson, L. H. *Who Knows: From Quine to a Feminist Empiricism.* Philadelphia, 1990.

Okin, S. M. *Justice, Gender, and the Family.* Boston, 1989.

Vetterling-Braggin, M., ed. *Sexist Language: A Modern Philosophical Analysis.* Lanham, MD, 1981.

— ANN E. CUDD

ANALYTICITY

The idea of analyticity—or truth by virtue of meaning—can be understood in two different ways. On the one hand, it might stand for an epistemic notion, for the idea that mere grasp of the meaning of a sentence suffices for knowledge that it is true. On the other hand, it might stand for a metaphysical notion, for the idea that a statement owes its truth value completely to its meaning, and not at all to "the facts." We may call the first notion "epistemic analyticity" and the second "metaphysical analyticity." On the face of it, these are distinct notions that subserve distinct philosophical programs. Willard Van Orman Quine, whose writings are largely responsible for the contemporary rejection of analyticity, failed to distinguish between them; as a result, many philosophers came to assume that the two notions stand or fall together. However, it is the moral of recent work in this area that this assumption is mistaken: epistemic analyticity can be defended even while its metaphysical cousin is rejected.

What could it possibly mean

to say that the truth of a statement

is fixed exclusively by its meaning

and not by the facts?

The metaphysical concept of analyticity is presupposed by the logical positivist program of reducing all necessity to linguistic necessity. Guided by both the fear that objective, language-independent necessary connections would be metaphysically odd, and that no empiricist epistemology could explain our knowledge of them, philosophers like Rudolf Carnap (1947) and A. J. Ayer (1946) attempted to show that all necessary truths are simply disguised decisions concerning the meanings of words. According to this view, there is no more to the truth of, say, "Either snow is white or it is not" than a decision concerning the meaning of the word "or." On this view, linguistic meaning by itself is supposed to generate necessary truth; a fortiori, linguistic meaning by itself is supposed to generate truth. Hence the play with the metaphysical notion of analyticity.

However, it is doubtful that this makes a lot of sense. What could it possibly mean to say that the truth of a statement is fixed exclusively by its meaning and not by the facts? Is it not in general true that for any statement **S,**

S is true if and only if (iff) for some p, S means that p and p?

How could the mere fact that S means that p make it the case that S is true? Doesn't it also have to be the case that p (see Harman, 1960)?

The proponent of the metaphysical notion does have a comeback, one that has perhaps not been sufficiently addressed. What he will say instead is that, in some appropriate sense, our meaning p by S makes it the case that p.

But this line is itself fraught with difficulty. For how are we to understand how our meaning something by a sentence can make something or other the case? It is easy to understand how the fact that we mean what we do by a sentence determines whether that sentence expresses something true or false. But as Quine (1951) points out, that is just the normal dependence of truth on meaning. What is not clear is how the truth of what the sentence expresses could depend on the fact that it is expressed by that sentence, so that we would be entitled to say that what is expressed would not have been true at all had it not been for the fact that it is expressed by that sentence. But are we really to suppose that, prior to our stipulating a meaning for the sentence

"Either snow is white or it is not"

it was not the case that either snow was white or it was not? Is it not overwhelmingly obvious that this claim was true *before* such an act of meaning, and that it would have been true even if no one had thought about it, or chosen it to be expressed by one of our sentences?

There is, then, very little to recommend the linguistic theory of necessity and, with it, the metaphysical notion of analyticity that is supposed to subserve it. Epistemic analyticity, by contrast, is not involved in that futile reductive enterprise. Its role, rather, is to provide a theory of a priori knowledge.

Intuitively speaking, it does seem that we can know certain statements—the truths of logic, mathematics, and conceptual analysis, most centrally—without recourse to empirical experience. The problem has always been to explain how.

The history of philosophy has known a number of answers to this question, among which the following has been very influential: We are equipped with a special evidence-gathering faculty of intuition, distinct from the standard five senses, that allows us to arrive at justified beliefs about the necessary properties of the world. By exercising this faculty, we are able to know a priori such truths as those of mathematics and logic.

The central impetus behind the analytic explanation of the a priori is to explain the possibility of a priori knowledge without having to postulate any such special

faculty of "intuition," an idea that has never been adequately elaborated.

This is where the concept of epistemic analyticity comes in. If mere grasp of S's meaning by O were to suffice for O's being justified (with a strength sufficient for knowledge—henceforth, we will take this qualification to be understood) in holding S true, then S's apriority would be explainable without appeal to a special faculty of intuition: the very fact that it means what it does for O would by itself explain why O is justified in holding it to be true.

How could mere grasp of a sentence's meaning justify someone in holding it true? Clearly, the answer to this question has to be semantical: something about the sentence's meaning, or about the way that meaning is fixed, must explain how its truth is knowable in this special way. What could this explanation be?

In the history of the subject, two different sorts of explanation have been especially important. Although these, too, have often been conflated, it is crucial to distinguish between them.

One idea was first formulated in full generality by Gottlob Frege (1884). According to this view, a statement's epistemic analyticity is to be explained by the fact that it is transformable into a logical truth by the substitution of synonyms for synonyms. We may call statements that satisfy this semantical condition 'Frege-analytic'.

Quine's enormously influential "Two Dogmas of Empiricism" (1951) complained that there couldn't be any Frege-analytic statements because there couldn't be any synonymies. But, as Herbert P. Grice and Peter F. Strawson showed (1956), the arguments for this claim are highly disputable. And Paul Boghossian (1995) has added to this by arguing that Quine's negative arguments cannot plausibly stop short of his radical thesis of the indeterminacy of meaning, a thesis that most philosophers continue to reject.

The real problem with Frege-analyticity is not that there are not any instances of it, but that it is limited in its ability to explain the full range of a priori statements. Two classes remain problematic: a priori statements that are not transformable into logical truths by the substitution of synonyms for synonyms, and a priori statements that are trivially so transformable.

An example of the first class is the sentence "Whatever is red all over is not blue." Because the ingredient descriptive terms do not decompose in the appropriate way, this sentence is not transformable into a logical truth by substitution of synonyms.

The second class of recalcitrant statements consists precisely of the truths of logic. These truths satisfy, of course, the conditions on Frege-analyticity. But they satisfy them trivially. And it seems obvious that we cannot hope to explain our entitlement to belief in the truths of logic by appealing to their analyticity in this sense: knowledge of Frege-analyticity presupposes knowledge of logical truth and so cannot explain it.

How, then, is the epistemic analyticity of these recalcitrant truths to be explained? The solution proposed by Carnap (1947) and the middle Wittgenstein (1974) turned on the suggestion that such statements are to be thought of as 'implicit definitions' of their ingredient terms. Applied to the case of logic (a similar treatment is possible in the case of the other class of recalcitrant truths), this suggestion generates the semantical thesis we may call:

Implicit definition: It is by arbitrarily stipulating that certain sentences of logic are to be true, or that certain inferences are to be valid, that we attach a meaning to the logical constants. A particular constant means that logical object, if any, which makes valid a specified set of sentences and/or inferences involving it.

The transition from this sort of implicit definition account of grasp to an account of the apriority of logic can then seem immediate, and the following sort of argument would appear to be in place:

1. If logical constant C is to mean what it does, then argument-form A has to be valid, for C means whatever logical object in fact makes A valid.

2. C means what it does.

Therefore,

3. A is valid.

Quine's "Truth by Convention" (1936) and "Carnap and Logical Truth" (1976) raised several important objections against the thesis of implicit definition: first, that it leads to an implausible conventionalism about logical truth; second, that it results in a vicious regress; and third, that it is committed to a notion—that of a meaning-constituting sentence or inference—that cannot be made out.

Even the proponents of implicit definition seem to have agreed that some sort of conventionalism about logical truth follows from implicit definition. However, Nathan Salmon (1994) and Boghossian (1995) have argued that this is a mistake: no version of conventionalism follows from the semantical thesis of implicit definition, provided that a distinction is observed between a sentence and the claim that it expresses.

Quine's second objection is also problematic in relying on a defective conception of what it is for a person to adopt a certain rule with respect to an expression, according to which the adoption of a rule always involves explicitly stating in linguistic terms the rule that is being adopted. On the contrary, it seems far more plausible to construe **x**'s following rule **R** with respect to **e** as consisting in some sort of fact about **x**'s *behavior* with **e**.

In what would such a fact consist? Here there are at least two options of which the most influential is this: **O**'s following rule **R** with respect to **e** consists in **O**'s being disposed, under appropriate circumstances, to conform to rule **R** in his employment of **e**.

According to this view, then, the logical constants mean what they do by virtue of figuring in certain inferences and/or sentences involving them and not in others. If some expressions mean what they do by virtue of figuring in certain inferences and sentences, then some inferences and sentences are constitutive of an expression's meaning what it does, and others are not.

Quine's final objection to implicit definition is that there will be no way to specify systematically the meaning-constituting inferences, because there will be no way to distinguish systematically between a meaning constituting inference and one that is not meaning-constituting but simply obvious. However, although this is a serious challenge, and although it remains unmet, there is every reason for optimism (see, for example, Peacocke, 1994, and Boghossian, 1995).

Quine helped us see the vacuity of the metaphysical concept of analyticity and, with it, the futility of the project it was supposed to underwrite—the linguistic theory of necessity. But those arguments do not affect the epistemic notion of analyticity, the notion that is needed for the purposes of the theory of a priori knowledge. Indeed, the analytic theory of apriority seems to be a promising research program, given reasonable optimism about the prospects both for a conceptual role semantics and for the idea of Frege-analyticity.

[See also Carnap, Rudolf; Frege, Gottlob; Grice, Herbert Paul; Knowledge, A Priori; Quine, Willard Van Orman; Strawson, Peter F.; Wittgenstein, Ludwig Josef Johann.]

BIBLIOGRAPHY

Ayer, A. J. *Language, Truth and Logic.* London, 1946.

Boghossian, P. A. "Analyticity," in C. Wright and B. Hale, eds., *A Companion to the Philosophy of Language* (Cambridge, Eng., 1995).

Carnap, R. *Meaning and Necessity.* Chicago, 1947.

Dummett, M. *Frege: The Philosophy of Mathematics.* Cambridge, MA, 1991.

Frege, G. *Die Grundlagen der Arithmetik: eine logisch-mathematische Untersuchung uber den Begriff der Zahl* [1884], translated by J. L. Austin as *The Foundations of Arithmetic.* Oxford, 1953.

Grice, H. P., and P. Strawson. "In Defense of a Dogma," *Philosophical Review*, Vol. 65 (1956), 141–58.

Harman, G. "Quine on Meaning and Existence I," *Review of Metaphysics,* Vol. 21 (1960), 124–51.

Pap, A. *Semantics and Necessary Truth.* New Haven, 1958.

Peacocke, C. *A Study of Concepts.* Cambridge, MA, 1992.

———. "How Are A Priori Truths Possible?" *European Journal of Philosophy,* Vol. 1 (1993), 175–99.

Putnam, H. *Mind, Language and Reality—Philosophical Papers,* Vol. 2. Cambridge, MA, 1975.

Quine, W. V. O. "Truth by Convention," in O. H. Lee, ed., *Philosophical Essays for A. N. Whitehead* (New York, 1936; reprinted in *The Ways of Paradox,* Cambridge, MA, 1976).

———. "Two Dogmas of Empiricism," *Philosophical Review,* 1951; reprinted in *From a Logical Point of View* (Cambridge, MA, 1953).

———. "Carnap and Logical Truth," [1954]; reprinted in *The Ways of Paradox* (Cambridge, MA, 1976).

———. *Word and Object.* Boston, 1960.

Salmon, N. "Analyticity and Apriority," *Philosophical Perspectives,* 1994.

Wittgenstein, L. J. J. *Philosophical Grammar* [1932–34]. Los Angeles, 1974.

— PAUL ARTIN BOGHOSSIAN

ANAPHORA

The study of *anaphora* (from Greek, "carry back") is the study of the ways in which occurrences of certain expressions, particularly pronouns, depend for their interpretations upon the interpretations of occurrences of other expressions. Problems of anaphora are of interest to philosophy and logic because of their intersection with problems of ontology, quantification, and logical form.

Referential Anaphora

Pronouns understood as anaphoric on referential noun phrases are plausibly viewed as referring to the same things as their antecedents. Sentences (1)–(3) permit such readings (coindexing will be used to indicate an intentional anaphoric connection):

(1) Jim_1 respects students who argue with him_1.
(2) Jim_1 loves his_1 mother.
(3) Jim_1 is here. He_1 arrived yesterday. I think he_1's asleep right now.

We might call these pronouns 'referential anaphors'.

It is sometimes suggested (see, e.g., Soames, 1994) that anaphoric pronouns in such constructions can be understood in a second way. For example, although (2) might be understood as equivalent to 'Jim loves Jim's mother', it might seem to admit of another interpretation that makes it equivalent to 'Jim is a self's-mother-lover', the logical form of which is given by (2′):

(2′) $\lambda x(x$ loves x's mother)Jim.

The contrast between the two readings emerges when (2) is embedded, as in

(4) Mary believes that Jim_1 loves his_1 mother.

Certainly, many of the traditional problems involved in interpreting proper names recur for pronouns anaphoric on names.

Bound-Variable Anaphora

Pronouns anaphoric on quantified noun phrases cannot be treated as straightforwardly referential. Consider the following:

(5) Every man_1 thinks he would be a good $president_1$.
(6) No man_1 respects his_1 brothers' friends.

There is no point inquiring into the referents of the pronouns in examples like these. Following Quine (1960) and Geach (1962), philosophers have tended to treat such pronouns as the natural-language analogs of the variables of quantification theory. Certainly, the logical forms of quantified sentences of the form 'every **F** is **G**' and 'some **F**s and **G**s' can be captured using the standard first-order quantifiers '∀' and '∃'. But a comprehensive semantic theory must treat sentences containing noun phrases formed using 'no', 'the', 'exactly one', 'most', 'few', and so on. This fact highlights two problems. Using the identity sign '=' and the negation sign '¬', it is possible to use '∀' and '∃' to represent sentences containing 'no', 'the', 'exactly one', 'exactly two', and so forth, but the resulting formulae obscure the relationship between the surface syntax of a sentence and its logical form. For example, if Russell is right that 'the F is G' is true if and only if every F is G and there is exactly one F, then the logical form of this sentence is as follows:

(7) $(\exists x)((\forall y)(Fy \equiv y = x) \ \& \ Gx)$.

A more serious problem is that there are sentences that cannot be dealt with in first-order logic—for instance, sentences of the form 'most Fs are Gs'.

Both of these problems are solved if quantification in natural language is viewed as *restricted*. The basic idea here is that determiners combine with their complements (noun complexes) to form restricted quantifiers. So, for example, 'every', 'some', 'most', 'the', and so on combine with simple nouns such as 'pig' (or 'pigs'), 'man' (or 'men'), and so forth (or complex nouns such as 'man who owns a pig', etc.) to form restricted quantifiers such as 'some man', 'most men', 'every man who owns a pig', and so forth. We can represent a restricted quantifier 'every man' as '[every x: man x]'. This quantifier may combine with a predicate phrase such as 'is mortal' (which we can represent as 'x is mortal') to form the sentence 'every man is mortal', which we can represent as

(8) [every x: man x]x is mortal.

Now consider sentences (5) and (6) again. If we treat the anaphoric pronouns in these examples as bound variables, their logical forms will be (abstracting somewhat):

(5') [every x: man x](x thinks x would be a good president).

(6') [no x: man x](x respects x's brothers' friends).

Variable Binding and Scope

Evans (1977) has argued that not all pronouns anaphoric on quantified noun phrases are bound variables. Consider the following examples.

(9) Jim bought some pigs and Harry vaccinated them.

(10) Just one man ate haggis and he was ill afterwards.

A bound-variable treatment of the occurrence of 'them' in (9) yields the wrong result. On such an account, the logical form of the sentence will be

(9') [some x: pigs x](Jim bought x & Harry vaccinated x).

But (9') can be true even if Harry did not vaccinate *all* of the pigs Jim bought, whereas (9) cannot. (If Jim bought ten pigs and Harry vaccinated only two of them, (9') would be true whereas (9) would not.) And if the pronoun 'he' in (10) is treated as a bound variable, the logical form of the sentence will be

(10') [just one x: man x](x ate haggis and x was ill afterwards).

This is also incorrect; if two men ate haggis and only one was ill afterwards, (10') will be true whereas (10) will be false.

There is a plausible syntactic explanation of these facts. In both (9) and (10), the pronoun is located outside the smallest sentence containing the quantifier upon which it is anaphoric and hence lies outside its scope, according to the most promising syntactic characterization of this notion. The scope of an expression α in a sentence of a natural language appears to correspond to the first branching node dominating α at the syntactic level relevant to semantic interpretation. If this is correct, and contemporary syntactic theory suggests

it is, then syntactic theory explains why the pronouns in (9) and (10) are not understood as bound variables. There seem to be, therefore, anaphoric pronouns that are neither bound nor straightforwardly referential.

Unbound Anaphora

A plausible paraphrase of (9) is (9''):

(9'') Jim bought some pigs and Harry vaccinated the pigs Jim bought.

In view of this, Evans (1977) suggests that the pronoun 'them' in (9) is understood in terms of the plural description 'the pigs Jim bought', as what he calls an "E-type" pronoun. An E-type pronoun has its reference fixed by description (in Kripke's sense) and is therefore a rigid designator. On this account, in (9) the pronoun 'them' is taken to refer to those objects satisfying 'pigs Jim bought'.

Problems of anaphora are of interest to philosophy and logic because of their intersection with problems of ontology, quantification, and logical form.

Similarly where the antecedent is singular. A plausible paraphrase of (11) is (11'):

(11) Jim bought a pig and Harry vaccinated it.

(11') Jim bought a pig and Harry vaccinated the pig Jim bought.

According to Evans, the pronoun 'it' in (11) refers to the unique object satisfying 'pig Jim bought'.

This idea forms the basis of Evans's general account of the semantic content of unbound anaphors. The pronoun 'he' in (10) has its reference fixed by 'the man who ate haggis'; and in (12) 'they' has its reference fixed by 'the philosophers who came':

(12) A few philosophers came. They drank far too much.

Evans's proposal can be summarized thus: if P is an unbound pronoun anaphoric on a quantified noun phrase '[DET x: ϕ]' occurring in a sentence '[DET x: ϕ]ψ', then the referent of P is fixed by the description '[the x: ϕ & ψ]'.

Examination of more complex cases reveals weaknesses in Evans's theory (see below). The problems uncovered have tended to steer semanticists in one of two directions. First, there have been attempts to modify or refine Evans's framework (Davies, 1981; Neale, 1990). Second, there have been attempts to replace the entire framework with a uniform, discourse-based approach (Kamp, 1981; Heim, 1982). Both approaches will now be examined.

Descriptive Anaphora

Evans rejected the view that unbound anaphors go proxy for descriptions (in favor of the view that they have their referents fixed by description) on the grounds that such pronouns, unlike overt descriptions, do not give rise to ambiguities of scope. But consider the following:

> (14) A man murdered Smith, but Jim doesn't think he did it.
> (15) A man murdered Smith. The police have reason to think he injured himself in the process.

If 'he' goes proxy for 'the man who murdered Smith', there will be two readings for each of the anaphor clauses in these examples—the so-called *de re* and *de dicto* readings—according as the description for which the pronoun goes proxy is given large or small scope:

> (14a) [the x: man x & x murdered Smith]
>   (Jim doesn't believe that x murdered Smith)
> (14b) Jim doesn't believe that
>   [the x: man x & x murdered Smith](x murdered Smith)

It is natural to interpret (14) as attributing to Jim a noncontradictory belief concerning the murderer to the effect that he is not the murderer. On the proxy view this is captured by the *de re* reading of the second conjunct. The *de dicto* reading is technically available to the proxy theorist but is obviously not the preferred interpretation. But with (15) the *de dicto* reading of the second sentence is actually the more natural; yet Evans's theory explicitly precludes its existence.

Further support for the proxy rather than reference-fixing approach comes from examples containing modal expressions:

> (16) Mary wants to marry a rich man. He must be a banker.

The first sentence in (16) may be read either *de re* or *de dicto*. Moreover, the pronoun 'he' can be anaphoric on 'a rich man' on either reading. But as Karttunen (1976) points out, the modal expression has to be there

for the anaphora to work if the antecedent sentence is to be interpreted *de dicto*. That is, in

> (17) Mary wants to marry a rich man. He is a banker.

it is not possible to get the *de dicto* reading for the antecedent clause if 'he' is anaphoric on 'a rich man'. This contrast between (16) and (17) is explicable on the assumption that the anaphoric pronoun in (16) goes proxy for the description 'the man Mary marries' and may therefore take large or small scope with respect to the modal expression. On the *de dicto* reading of the antecedent clause, the *de re* reading of the anaphor clause is infelicitous because an implication of existence results from giving the description large scope. But the *de dicto* reading of the anaphor clause is fine because on such a reading the description is within the scope of the modal expression. In (17), on the other hand, since there is no modal operator with respect to which the pronoun can be understood with small scope, the sentence has no felicitous reading when the antecedent clause is read *de dicto*.

Donkey Anaphora

Kamp (1981) and Heim (1982) have explored alternative approaches that aim to treat all anaphoric pronouns in a unitary fashion. One motivation is the problem of so called donkey anaphora, typified by sentences like (18) and (19), originally discussed by Geach (1962):

> (18) If a man buys a donkey he vaccinates it.
> (19) Every man who buys a donkey vaccinates it.

Both Evans's theory and the simple proxy theory seem to fail here. For example, if the pronoun 'it' in (19) is analyzed in terms of the singular description 'the donkey he buys' (with 'he' bound by 'every man who buys a donkey') the sentence will be true just in case every man who buys a donkey vaccinates the unique donkey he buys. Consequently, it will be false if any man buys more than one donkey. But this is incorrect; the truth of (19) is quite compatible with some men owning more than one donkey, as long as every man who buys a donkey vaccinates *every* donkey he buys. It would appear, then, that the indefinite description 'a donkey'—which can normally be treated as an existentially quantified phrase—has the force of a *universally* quantified phrase in (19). And in (18) both 'man' and 'a donkey' appear to have universal force.

A common explanation of the "universalization" of the indefinite descriptions in such examples has been proposed by Kamp. The idea (roughly) is that noun phrases introduce variables to which common nouns and predicates supply "conditions" within a "discourse representation" (DR). Typically, the variable is bound by an existential quantifier taking scope over the entire discourse. On this account, an indefinite description is not inherently quantificational; rather, it introduces a variable with conditions on it imposed by, among other things, the predicative material it contains. The DR for (18) might be represented as:

(18′) [man(x) & donkey(y) & buys(x,y)] IFTHEN [vaccinates(x,y)].

Kamp proposes that (18′) is true if and only if every assignment of values to x and y that makes the antecedent true also makes the consequent true. The apparent universalization of the indefinite descriptions 'a man' and 'a donkey' is thus explained as a consequence of a general analysis of conditionals.

In the light of the equivalence of (18) and (19), Kamp suggests that, although (18) is not actually a conditional, because the subject quantifier is universal we get a DR in which the indefinite 'a donkey' has universal force. That is, the DR for (19) is given by

(19′) [man(x) & donkey(y) & buys(x,y)] EVERY [vaccinates(x,y)].

Like (18′), (19′) is true if and only if every assignment of values to x and y that makes '[man(x) & donkey(y) & buys(x,y)]' true, also makes '[vaccinates(x,y)]' true.

One problem with this proposal is that it does not predict that indefinite descriptions "universalize" when they are embedded in *other* quantifiers and thus leads to the so-called proportion problem. Consider

(20) Most men who buy a donkey vaccinate it.

By analogy with (18′) and (19′), the DR for (20) will be

(20′) [man(x) & donkey(y) & buys(x,y)] MOST [vaccinates(x,y)]

which is true just in case *most* assignments of values to x and y that make '[man(x) & donkey(y) & buys(x,y)]' true also make '[vaccinates(x,y)]' true. But on its most natural reading, the truth of (20) requires that most men who buy a donkey vaccinate *every* donkey they buy, whereas (20′) can be true as long as most of the donkeys that are bought by men are vaccinated by their respective buyers. Suppose Alan buys five donkeys, Bill buys one donkey, Clive buys one donkey, and no other man buys any donkeys. Sentence (20′) will come out true if

Alan vaccinates at least four of his donkeys, even if Bill and Clive do not vaccinate their respective donkeys; but in such a situation (20) would be false. (It has been suggested that there is another reading of [20], which requires that most men who buy at least one donkey vaccinate most of the donkeys they buy; but [20′] does not capture this reading either.)

From this brief overview it should be clear that both the simple descriptive theory and the simple DR theory need to be refined if they are to do justice to the full range of antecedent/anaphor relations in natural language. For example, the descriptive approach needs to be modified if it is to handle donkey anaphora, perhaps allowing for the possibility of interpreting some donkey pronouns in terms of 'all of the' rather than 'the' (Davies, 1981; Neale 1990). And the DR approach needs to be modified to avoid the proportion problem and also permit pronouns to be understood with various scopes. At the time of writing, more sophisticated versions of these theories are being developed, as are alternatives to both.

[See also Kripke, Saul Aaron; Logical Form; Ontology; Philosophy of Language; Russell, Bertrand Arthur William.]

BIBLIOGRAPHY

Davies, M. *Meaning, Quantification, Necessity.* London, 1981.
Evans, G. "Pronouns, Quantifiers, and Relative Clauses (I)," *Canadian Journal of Philosophy,* Vol. 7 (1977), 467–536. (Reprinted in Evans [1985], 76–152.)
———. "Pronouns," *Linguistic Inquiry,* Vol. 11 (1980), 337–62. (Reprinted in Evans [1985], 214–48.)
———. *The Collected Papers.* Oxford, 1985.
Geach, P. *Reference and Generality.* Ithaca, NY, 1962.
Heim, I. *The Semantics of Definite and Indefinite Noun Phrases.* Amherst, MA, 1982.
Kamp, H. "A Theory of Truth and Semantic Interpretation," in J. Groenendijk et al., eds., *Formal Methods in the Study of Natural Language* (Amsterdam, 1981).
Karttunen, L. "Discourse Referents," in J. McCawley, ed., *Syntax and Semantics,* Vol. 7, *Notes from the Linguistic Underground* (New York, 1976).
Kripke, S. "Naming and Necessity," in D. Davidson and G. Harman, eds., *Semantics of Natural Language* (Dordrecht, 1972).
Neale, S. *Descriptions.* Cambridge, MA, 1990.
Quine, W. V. O. *Word and Object.* Cambridge, MA, 1960.
Soames, S. "Attitudes and Anaphora," *Philosophical Perspectives,* Vol. 8 (1994), 251–72.

– STEPHEN NEALE

ANIMAL RIGHTS AND WELFARE

Although all the major moral philosophers in the Western tradition have had something to say about the moral status of animals, they have commented infrequently and for the most part only in brief. This tradition of neglect changed dramatically during the last quarter of this century, when dozens of works in ethical theory, hundreds of professional essays, and more than a score of academic conferences were devoted to the moral foundations of our treatment of nonhuman animals.

Two main alternatives—animal welfare and animal rights—have come to be recognized. Animal welfarists accept the permissibility of human use of nonhuman animals as a food source and in biomedical research, for example, provided such use is carried out humanely. Animal rightists, by contrast, deny the permissibility of such use, however humanely it is done.

Differ though they do, both positions have much in common. For example, both reject Descartes's view that nonhuman animals are *automata.* Those animals raised for food and hunted in the wild have a subjective presence in the world; in addition to sharing sensory capacities with human beings, they experience pleasure and pain, satisfaction and frustration, and a variety of other mental states. There is a growing consensus that many nonhuman animals have a mind that, in Charles Darwin's words, differs from the human "in degree and not in kind."

Proponents of animal welfare and animal rights have different views about the moral significance of our psychological kinship with other animals. Animal welfarists have two options. First, they can argue that we ought to treat animals humanely because this will lead us to treat one another with greater kindness and less cruelty. On this view we have no duties to animals, only duties involving them; and all those duties involving them turn out to be, as Kant wrote, "indirect duties to Mankind." Theorists as diverse as Kant, St. Thomas Aquinas, and John Rawls favor an indirect-duty account of the moral status of nonhuman animals.

Second, animal welfarists can maintain that some of our duties are owed directly to animals. This is the alternative favored by utilitarians, beginning with Jeremy Bentham and John Stuart Mill and culminating in the work of Peter Singer. Animal pain and pleasure count morally in their own right, not only indirectly through the filter of the human interest in having humans treated better. The duty not to cause animals to suffer unnecessarily is a duty owed directly to them.

Of the two options the latter seems the more reasonable. It is difficult to understand why the suffering of animals should count morally only if it leads to human suffering in the future. Imagine that a man sadistically tortures a dog and dies of a heart attack as a result of his physical exertion; what he does seems clearly wrong even though he does not live long enough to mistreat a human being. If this is true, then we have at least some direct duties to animals.

Animal welfarists who are utilitarians (Singer is the most notable example) use utilitarian theory to criticize how animals are treated in contemporary industries

Animal rightists deny the permissibility of using animals as a food source and in biomedical research. (Corbis/Raymond Gehman)

(animal agriculture and biomedical research, for example). For in these industries animals are made to suffer and, Singer alleges, to suffer unnecessarily.

Other animal welfarists who are utilitarians disagree. Government and industry leaders agree that some animals sometimes suffer in the course of being raised for food or used in biomedical research; but they deny that they are made to suffer unnecessarily.

Consider organ transplant research. Research on animals in this quarter involves transplanting some internal organ from one healthy animal to another; the "donor" animal, who is under anesthetic, is killed, but the "receiver" animal is permitted to recover and doubtless experiences no small amount of postoperative pain before being humanely killed.

Is the pain unnecessary? In one sense it clearly is. For since the organ was not transplanted for the good of the recipient animal, all the pain that animal experienced was unnecessary. However, this is not the real question, given the utilitarian perspective. The pain caused to this particular animal is only one part of the overall calculation that needs to be carried out. We need also to ask about the possible benefits for humans who are in need of organ transplants, the value of the skills surgeons acquire carrying out animal organ transplants, the value of knowledge for its own sake, and so on. After these questions have been answered and the overall benefits impartially calculated, then an informed judgment can be made about whether organ transplant research involving nonhuman animals does or does not cause unnecessary suffering.

Proponents of animal welfare and animal rights

have different views about the moral significance

of our psychological kinship with other animals.

As this example illustrates, animal welfarists who are utilitarians can disagree about when animals suffer unnecessarily. As such, these animal welfarists can differ in judging whether animals are being treated humanely and, if not, how much reform is called for.

Advocates of animal rights advance a position that avoids the always daunting, frequently divisive challenge of carrying out uncertain utilitarian calculations. Central to their view is the Kantian idea that animals are never to be treated merely as a means to human ends, however good these ends might be. The acquisition of knowledge, including biological knowledge, is surely a good end, as is the promotion of human health. But the goodness of these ends does not justify the utilization of nonhuman animals as means. Thus, even if animal-model organ transplant research can be justified on utilitarian grounds, animal rights advocates would judge it immoral.

Of the two main options—animal welfare and animal rights—it is the latter that attempts to offer a basis for a radical reassessment of how animals are treated. Animal welfare, provided the calculations work out a certain way, enables one to call for reforms in human institutions that routinely utilize nonhuman animals. But animal rights, independent of such calculations, enables one to call for the abolition of all forms of institutional exploitation.

[See also Bentham, Jeremy; Descartes, René; Kant, Immanuel; Mill, John Stuart; Rawls, John; Speciesism; Thomas Aquinas, St.]

BIBLIOGRAPHY

Clark, S. S. L. *The Moral Status of Animals.* Oxford, 1977.
Frey, R. G. *Interests and Rights: The Case against Animals.* Oxford, 1980.
Magel, C. R. *Keyguide to Information Sources in Animal Rights.* Jefferson, NC, 1989.
Midgley, M. *Animals and Why They Matter.* New York, 1983.
Rachels, J. *Created from Animals: The Moral Implications of Darwinism.* Oxford, 1990.
Regan, T. *The Case for Animal Rights.* Berkeley, 1983.
Regan, T., and P. Singer, eds. *Animal Rights and Human Obligations,* 2d ed. Englewood Cliffs, NJ, 1991.
Rollin, B. *Animal Rights and Human Morality.* Buffalo, NY, 1981.
Sapontzis, S. *Morals, Reason, and Animals.* Philadelphia, 1987.
Singer, P. *Animal Liberation,* 2d ed. New York, 1990.

– TOM REGAN

ANOMALOUS MONISM

Originated by Donald Davidson, anomalous monism is a nonreductive, token physicalist position on the relation between the mental and the physical. According to it, each mental event is a physical event, although mental descriptions are neither reducible to nor nomologically correlated with physical ones. In terms that are ontologically more robust than those used by Davidson, the position asserts identities between individual mental and physical events while denying that mental types or properties are either identical with, or nomologically connected with, physical ones. The position specifically concerns intentional mental phenomena such as beliefs and desires, although it is arguable that it can be extended to cover other mental phenomena such as sensations.

Davidson's argument for this position results from an attempt to reconcile three apparently inconsistent principles, two of which he finds independently plausible and the third of which he defends at length. The first is the principle of causal interaction (PCI), which states that mental events cause physical events and vice versa, causality being understood as relating events in extension. The second is the principle of the nomological character of causality (PNCC), which states that events that are causally related have descriptions under which they instantiate strict causal laws. The third is the principle of the anomalism of the mental (PAM), which states that there are no strict laws in which mental terms figure. The principles appear to conflict in that the first two imply what the third seems to deny—namely that there are strict laws governing causal interactions between mental and physical events.

Davidson argues that the principles can be reconciled by adopting the thesis that each mental event has a physical description and so is a physical event. He further suggests that a sound argument can be constructed from these principles to this thesis. Suppose a mental event, m, causes a physical event, p. Then, by the PNCC, m and p have descriptions under which they instantiate a strict causal law. By PAM this cannot be mental in that it cannot contain mental terminology.

Therefore *m* must have a physical description under which it instantiates a strict causal law, which is to say that it is a physical event. Although the argument is formulated in terms of events and their descriptions, it can be formulated equally effectively in the terminology of events and their properties.

Davidson does not take PAM to be obvious. His defense of it involves the idea that laws bring together terms from the same or similar conceptual domains. Using this idea he argues that the constraints that govern the application of mental terms and their associated concepts to things are normative in nature, involving "constitutive" principles of rational coherence, deductive and inductive consistency, and the like. These principles constitute the distinctive rationalistic normativity that is the earmark of the intentional domain; and Davidson argues that they have no place in physical theory.

The argument for anomalous monism appears to work because of the extensionality of the causal relation and the intensionality of nomologicality. Events are causally related no matter how described; but they are governed by laws only as they are described one way rather than another. This opens up a conceptual space between causality and nomologicality that makes it possible to hold both that mental events that interact causally with physical ones are governed by laws and that there are no strict psychological or psychophysical laws.

Events are causally related no matter how described;

but they are governed by laws only as they are

described one way rather than another.

Davidson's argument has had a profound effect on discussions of mental causation and token physicalism. Many have found either the PNCC or the PAM questionable and have taken issue with it. However, the main objection to the argument is that, on a certain conception of the relation between causality and laws, it leads either to inconsistency or to epiphenomenalism. According to this conception, laws link events causally by linking certain, but not all, of their descriptions or properties, the causally relevant ones. The question now arises, In virtue of which of their properties do mental events interact causally with physical ones? If the answer is the mental ones, then anomalous monism is threatened with inconsistency since this implies that there are laws in which mental descriptions/properties figure. If the answer is the physical ones, then anomalous monism is threatened with epiphenomenalism since it is in virtue of their physical properties that mental events are causally efficacious. Since PAM is a crucial premise

in the argument for anomalous monism, it is the epiphenomenalism charge that poses the real threat to the position.

There is a general question of whether nonreductive token physicalist theories count as proper forms of physicalism since they recognize the existence of irreducibly mental properties. Davidson himself favors supplementing his position with some sort of supervenience thesis, according to which, necessarily, if things (events) are the same with regard to their physical descriptions/properties, then they are the same with regard to their mental descriptions/properties. The principal difficulty in formulating such a thesis is in specifying a dependency relation strong enough to ensure that physical properties determine mental ones without leading to reducibility and hence to type physicalism.

[See also Davidson, Donald; Mental Causation; Philosophy of Mind; Physicalism, Materialism; Supervenience.]

BIBLIOGRAPHY

Davidson, D. "Thinking Causes," in J. Heil and A. Mele, eds., *Mental Causation* (Oxford, 1993). Responds to the charge that anomalous monism leads to the causal inefficacy of the mental.

———. "Mental Events," in L. Foster and J. W. Swanson, eds., *Experience and Theory* (Amherst, MA, 1970). Reprinted in D. Davidson, *Essays on Actions and Events* (Oxford, 1980). The classic statement of the argument for anomalous monism.

———. "Psychology as Philosophy," in S. C. Brown, ed., *Philosophy of Psychology* (London, 1974). Reprinted in D. Davidson, *Essays on Actions and Events* (Oxford, 1980). Discusses anomalous monism and the argument against psychophysical laws.

Honderich, T. "The Argument for Anomalous Monism," *Analysis,* Vol. 42 (1982). Classic statement of the inconsistency-or-epiphenomenalism objection to anomalous monism.

Kim, J. "The Myth of Nonreductive Materialism," *Proceedings of the American Philosophical Association,* Vol. 63 (1989), 31–47. Argues that nonreductive materialism leads to epiphenomenalism.

———. "Psychophysical Laws," in E. LePore and B. McLaughlin, eds., *Actions and Events: Perspectives on the Philosophy of Donald Davidson* (Oxford, 1985). Discusses and defends an interpretation of Davidson's argument against psychophysical laws.

LePore, E., and B. Loewer. "Mind Matters," *Journal of Philosophy,* Vol. 84 (1987), 630–41. Discusses the causal efficacy of the mental within the context of physicalism.

LePore, E., and B. McLaughlin, eds. *Actions and Events: Perspectives on the Philosophy of Donald Davidson.* Oxford, 1985. Articles on Davidson's argument for anomalous monism.

Macdonald, C. *Mind–Body Identify Theories.* London, 1989. Surveys various type–type and token identity theories, and defends a version of nonreductive monism.

Macdonald, C., and G. Macdonald. "Mental Causes and Explanation of Action," *Philosophical Quarterly,* Vol. 36 (1986), 145–58. Reprinted in L. Stevenson, R. Squires, and J. Haldane, eds., *Mind, Causation, and Action* (Oxford, 1986). Defends anomalous monism against the charge of epiphenomenalism.

McLaughlin, B. "Type Epiphenomenalism, Type Dualism, and the Causal Priority of the Physical," in *Philosophical Perspectives,* Vol. 3 (1989). Discusses the problem of mental causation for anomalous monism.

— CYNTHIA MACDONALD

ANSCOMBE, GERTRUDE ELIZABETH MARGARET

Gertrude Elizabeth Margaret Anscombe, English philosopher, was born in 1919 and was educated at Sydenham High School and St. Hugh's College, Oxford, where she read *Literae Humaniores* (Greats). She went as a research student to Cambridge, where she became the pupil of Ludwig Wittgenstein. He and Aristotle have been the most important influences on her philosophical thought. Anscombe became a Roman Catholic while in her teens, and her Catholicism has also been a shaping influence. She was a Fellow for many years of Somerville College, Oxford, and held the Chair of Philosophy at Cambridge from 1970 until 1986. A philosopher of great range, she has made important contributions to ethics, philosophy of mind, metaphysics, and philosophy of logic. Much of her most interesting work has been in the history of philosophy; her discussions of ancient, medieval, and modern philosophers combine illuminating accounts of challenging texts with penetrating treatment of the philosophical problems themselves. As one of Wittgenstein's literary executors, as an editor and translator of his writings, and as a writer and lecturer about Wittgenstein, she has done more than anyone else to make his work accessible. Her *Introduction to Wittgenstein's Tractatus* (1959) is a superb introduction to the central themes of that work, making clear the character of the problems (like that of negation) treated in it.

Anscombe's interest in war

and in the concept of murder led her also

to more general philosophical questions

about political authority.

Long before it became fashionable in the 1970s for moral philosophers to concern themselves with practical problems, Anscombe was writing about them. Her first published essay, in 1939, concerned the justice of the European war. She has discussed closely related topics in connection with the honorary degree Oxford University awarded Harry Truman in 1957 and with the policy of nuclear deterrence. She has also written on contraception and euthanasia. All her writings on such questions reflect her belief in the importance for ethics of the concepts of action and intention, in connection especially with questions about our responsibility for the consequences of our actions. She has explained and defended the doctrine of double effect, arguing that its denial "has been the corruption of non-Catholic thought and its abuse the corruption of Catholic thought" (1981, 3:54). Her interest in war and in the concept of murder led her also to more general philosophical questions about political authority. "Modern Moral Philosophy" (1981) has been the most influential of her papers on ethics. In it she defended three theses: that moral philosophy cannot profitably be done until we have an adequate philosophical psychology; that the concepts of moral obligation, moral duty, and the moral "ought" are survivals from a now largely abandoned conception of ethics, are incoherent outside that framework and should therefore if possible be abandoned; and that English moral philosophers from Sidgwick on differ only in superficial ways. In explaining the third thesis Anscombe introduced the term consequentialism for what modern moral philosophers shared, and she argued that consequentialism is a corrupt and shallow philosophy.

In the monograph *Intention* (1957) Anscombe raised and discussed questions about intention, action, and practical thought (practical reasoning and practical knowledge). The prevalent philosophical ideas about intention treat it as some special kind of mental state or event, and Anscombe departed radically from that tradition, beginning with an account of intentional action in terms of the applicability to it of a kind of question asking for the agent's reason. It is thus possible to show the importance of conceptions of good in practical thought. The questions with which she is concerned frequently straddle metaphysics, philosophy of logic, and philosophy of mind, as for example in "The First Person" (1981), in which she explains how we are led into confusion by misunderstandings of "I" on the model of a proper name. In "The Intentionality of Sensation: A Grammatical Feature" (1981) she draws on philosophy of language in explaining grammatical analogies between intention and sensation, and is able to give a very interesting and original account of what is right in sense-impression philosophy and of what is misleading in it.

Anscombe has explored the topic of causation in several papers, questioning in them widely held assumptions. "Causality and Determination" (1981) begins by formulating two such assumptions: that causality is some kind of necessary connection and that it involves a universal generalization connecting events of two kinds. One or other or both of the assumptions is accepted by virtually all writers on causation, but Anscombe questioned both, together with the related idea that, if two courses of events appear similar but have different outcomes, there must be some further relevant difference. She argued that the root idea in all our causal notions is that of derivativeness of one thing from another, and that this need not involve necessitation. In "Times, Beginnings and Causes" (1981) she challenges also two widely accepted views of Hume's, that causal relations never involve logical necessity and that something can, logically, begin to exist without being caused to do so. Questions about time figure centrally in other papers as well, including "The Reality of the Past," which treats a problem raised by Parmenides and shows how attempts to explain the concept of the past by reference to memory must fail; it also contains one of the best short discussions of Wittgenstein's later approach to philosophy.

[See also Aristotle; Causation; Consequentialism; Euthanasia; Hume, David; Metaphysics; Parmenides of Elea; Philosophy of Mind; Sidgwick, Henry; Wittgenstein, Ludwig Josef Johann.]

BIBLIOGRAPHY

Works by Anscombe

Intention. Oxford, 1957.
An Introduction to Wittgenstein's Tractatus. London, 1959.
Three Philosophers (with Peter Geach). Oxford, 1963.
Collected Philosophical Papers. Vol. 1: *From Parmenides to Wittgenstein;* Vol. 2: *Metaphysics and the Philosophy of Mind;* Vol. 3: *Ethics, Religion and Politics.* Oxford, 1981.
"Murder and the Morality of Euthanasia: Some Philosophical Considerations," in L. Gormally, ed., *Euthanasia, Clinical Practice and the Law* (London, 1994).

Works on Anscombe

Diamond, C., and J. Teichman, eds. *Intention and Intentionality: Essays in Honour of G. E. M. Anscombe.* Brighton, 1979. Contains a bibliography, not complete, of writings by Anscombe up to 1979.
Haber, J. G., ed. *Absolutism and Its Consequentialist Critics.* Lanham, MD, 1994.

— CORA DIAMOND

ANSELM, ST.

St. Anselm, of Canterbury (1033–1109), originator of the Ontological Argument for the existence of God and one of the foremost figures of medieval theology. Anselm was born of noble family at Aosta, in Piedmont. After study in the north, he entered the Benedictine order and became prior, later abbot, of Bec. He succeeded his teacher Lanfranc as archbishop of Canterbury in 1093; his primacy was marked by a vigorous defense of the rights of the church against the king.

An Augustinian in theology, Anselm stood firmly against the anti-intellectualism of his day, holding that rational analysis of the Christian faith is not an intrinsic source of doubt and religious skepticism, but, rather, is essential to the understanding of faith and is a religious

St. Anselm is best known among philosophers for Proslogion, *a discourse in which he offers proof for the existence of God. (New York Public Library Picture Collection)*

duty. This claim, and Anselm's application of it in theology, helped to initiate the high Scholasticism of the twelfth and thirteenth centuries. Anselm's own view of the relation of reason to faith is that faith provides conclusions which reason, assured of their truth, can often prove necessary—*credo ut intelligam* ("I believe in order that I may understand") in a very strong sense indeed. Anselm's arguments, therefore, are meant as compelling to any rational mind. To judge them on purely intellectual grounds is to judge them as Anselm would have had them judged.

Anselm's Proofs

Among philosophers, Anselm is chiefly known for his *Monologion* and *Proslogion,* a soliloquy and a discourse, respectively, on the nature and attributes of God. It is on the *Proslogion* that his fame mainly rests, for it contains the Ontological Proof (the term is Kant's) for the existence of God. That proof has often been treated as a gem—or paste—whose worth can be judged apart from its setting; in fact, it must be understood through the *Monologion,* which provides an account of two concepts vital to it, the concepts of existence and of goodness.

The *Monologion* undertakes to prove the existence of "one Nature which is the highest of existing things . . . and which confers upon and effects in all other beings, through its unlimited goodness, the very fact of their existence is good." Two major arguments are offered.

PROOF FROM GOODNESS. The first proof is one from goodness, Anselm's version of an argument of the ancient Academy, that "wherever there is a better, there must be a best." (1) Certain attributes are comparative, that is, admit of degree. Goodness is such an attribute, for one thing may be as good as, better than, or less good than, another. (2) Where an attribute admits of degree, there is some element common throughout its variation; to say that *a* is good and that *b* is good is to use "good" in exactly the same sense, even though *a* may be better than *b*. This argument is restricted: it is not meant to apply to every common term of discourse, but only to comparatives. (3) That through which good things are good is a cause of their goodness; if it did not exist, good things, as good, would not exist. Anselm is offering a theory of universals and a realistic, as opposed to a nominalistic or conceptualistic, theory. (4) That which causes other things to be good must itself be good, and furthermore, supremely good; for since other things are good through it, while it is good only through itself, it can neither be equaled nor excelled by any other good thing. The universal proved to exist, then, is an exemplar: it is the cause of goodness in those things which, in Anselm's phrase, participate in it, and, as cause, itself exemplifies goodness superlatively.

ARGUMENT FROM EXISTENCE. The second main argument of the *Monologion* is from existence. Everything that exists, exists through something. (To exist through *x* is to derive existence from *x*.) Now, it is self-evidently false to suppose that things can exist through each other—Anselm had not heard of Hegel or of "internal relations." Nor can a plurality of things exist independently, through themselves; for then each of them would have the *power* of existing through itself, and therefore all of them would exist in virtue of that power, which is one and the same. Thus there is one and only one thing such that it exists through itself, and all other things must exist through it, for to say of a thing that it exists through nothing is to say that it does not exist.

That through which other things exist is the preeminent existent, and exists through itself. Further, it is identical with the supreme Good. Anselm's argument of this point assumes that a thing is better if it exists through itself than if it exists through something else; since Goodness is supremely good, it must exist through itself; but what exists through itself is Existence. There-

fore, Existence and Goodness are one. Anselm goes on to prove that this Supreme Being must be living, wise, powerful, true, just, blessed, and eternal, since, as the Supreme Good, it must be whatever it is absolutely better to be than not to be.

The Divine Nature, however, does not *have* these characteristics, for that would imply that it has them through something other than, and therefore higher than, itself. The Divine Nature *is* these characteristics. It is the same thing to say of God that he exists and that he is Existence, to say of him that he is good and that he is Goodness. "God is good" and "Socrates is good" are very different statements: in one, the "is" means identity; in the other, roughly, predication. Were this not true, an infinite regress, Plato's Third Man, would arise (*cf. Monologion* VI). And as there is a difference in the meaning of the copula, so there is also a difference in the meaning of the predicate; the difference is indicated by the fact that "God is good" is equivalent in sense to "God is Goodness," whereas no such equivalence holds for "Socrates is good." "Good" has a primary and a derivative use: primarily, it designates Goodness; derivatively, it designates anything that participates in Goodness. Assertions about God, then, are analogical, and the ground of the analogy lies in the fact that God is the source or cause of such absolutely good characteristics as he imparts to things. Anselm's analysis of God's nature adapted Platonic exemplarism to the needs of the Christian church.

Anselm's Theology

Anselm's intellectual interests were essentially theological, and his philosophical speculation was the work of a believer seeking to understand his faith. His view of the theologian's task, however, was anything but narrow. On the one hand, unlike many monastic teachers, he believed that, for all who were capable of it, rigorous reasoning must be an integral part of the quest for closer communion with God. On the other hand, he was a sensitive apologist, concerned to make dissenters and unbelievers appreciate the inherent reasonableness of Catholic Christianity.

Anselm's theology can fairly be described as a rethinking of the Augustinian tradition in the context of the Benedictine life and with a contemporary apologetic aim. While his work was obviously inspired by Augustine's synthesis of Biblical faith and Plotinian philosophy, it bears the stamp of his own original genius and contains few direct references to earlier authorities.

METHOD. Anselm's originality is most apparent in his characteristic use of dialectic—prompted, no doubt, by the philosophical awakening of his time but unparalleled in the theological work of his contemporaries.

Augustine and other Church Fathers had already made use of metaphysical, logical, and ethical notions, borrowed or adapted from Greek philosophy, to defend and expound Christian doctrine. Anselm, however, developed a distinctive systematic method, characterized by a subtle analysis of Christian doctrines and their metaphysical presuppositions (such as truth and rectitude, necessity and liberty, possibility and impossibility), and designed to demonstrate the logical coherence of the Christian faith. An elementary example of his analytic technique, uncomplicated by theological considerations, can be seen in the dialogue *De Grammatico,* in which he introduced the Aristotelian categories in the course of his discussion of a contemporary dialectical question: whether words that occur both as concrete nouns and as adjectives (for instance, the Latin *grammaticus,* which can mean either "grammarian" or "grammatical") signify substances or qualities. Rejecting the initially appealing claim that *grammaticus* sometimes signifies a substance and sometimes a quality, he contrasted the term's direct signification of the quality with its indirect signification of a person. But there is no *thing* signified by the word when the quality is meant; it signifies only being in possession of the quality.

Anselm's intellectual interests were essentially

theological, and his philosophical speculation

was the work of a believer

seeking to understand his faith.

Anselm's analysis of ideas sometimes derived its premises from universal human experience, as in the *Monologion,* which has its starting point in our common awareness of innumerable goods, perceived by the senses or discerned by reason. At other times he drew his conclusion from distinctively Christian premises. Thus the *Cur Deus Homo,* in which faith in Christ is put to a rational test, bases its argument on the dogmatic principles of creation, eternal life, and original sin. Taken as a whole, Anselm's work can be said to move from what we should readily identify as philosophical to more specifically Christian and theological themes. (His *Epistola de Incarnatione Verbi,* in which he defends the dogma of the Trinity against the nominalism of Roscelin, and his *De Processione Spiritus Sancti,* written in response to Greek criticisms of Latin theology, fall to some extent outside the natural line of development of his thought.) It would be misleading,

however, to describe some of Anselm's writings as essentially philosophical and others as theological. From start to finish, his speculative thought is an analysis of the logical structure of Christian faith, rather than an attempt to discover religious truth by philosophical argument.

GOD AS SUPREME GOOD. The central theme of Anselm's theology is the relation of creatures in general, and of mankind in particular, to God. From the *Monologion* and *Proslogion* and the three metaphysical dialogues (*De Veritate, De Libertate Arbitrii, De Casu Diaboli*) to the great Christological works of his later years, the same interest is unmistakable: Anselm wants to explain how the nature of creatures is related to the divine nature and what that relationship involves for human thought and behavior.

The fundamental principle of Anselm's theology is the doctrine of God as the supreme Good and the primordial Truth, self-existent and eternal. The universe is totally dependent on God's creative power, and its nature and purpose are determined by his nature and reason. The essential reality of every creature is measured by its conformity to God, the supreme and creative Truth. Insofar as creatures reflect the divine reason and will, they realize the authentic order of creaturely existence, which Anselm calls truth or rightness (*rectitudo*).

Anselm is most deeply interested in the particular forms that rightness takes in rational creatures—in angels and men. The rational creature is capable of thought, of choice, and of action, and all three capacities are subject to the same ultimate standard. The criterion of the sound mind, the good will, and the right action is its truth, its intelligible rightness, its order grounded in the divine Being itself.

The fundamental form of spiritual order is truth, the rightness of intelligence. Unless the mind is informed by the inherent rational order of God's world, right choice and action are impossible. Furthermore, it is evident that for Anselm a rational understanding of the real order of things is in itself a spiritual good.

The quality of personal life is decisively determined, however, by will and action, rather than by thought. The rational creature, whose mind can apprehend the order of God's truth and whose will can accept that order for its own decisions and actions, is obligated to maintain moral rightness or righteousness (*iustitia*) in the exercise of its freedom, which was bestowed on it for that very purpose. When it freely conforms will, word, and deed to the order of righteousness, the rational creature is right and just.

HIERARCHY OF GOODS. The actual requirements of the moral order are primarily determined by the structure of the Anselmian universe. The fundamental distinction between moral order and disorder presupposes a hierarchy of finite goods ranged beneath the supreme Good. This hierarchy is most clearly depicted in the *Monologion,* in successive affirmations of the supreme Truth and Good which is God, of the complete and adequate expression of that Truth in the divine Word, of the truth of creatures as reflecting the creative Word, and of the possession of the supreme Truth as the end of the rational creature. To live righteously is to subordinate all creaturely loves and relationships to love for God and the quest for communion with him. It is because righteousness is essentially an orientation to the supreme and transcendent Good that Anselm can see in it the supreme value of creaturely life, to be cherished for its own sake, and the gift of God, rather than a human achievement.

Anselm's major Christological works must be read in the light of this doctrine of moral order. In the *De Conceptu Virginali* Anselm presents man's actual state of subjection to sin and death as the result of the Fall, in which Adam lost for all men God's primeval gift of righteousness. In the *Cur Deus Homo* he interprets Christ's satisfaction for sin as God's reversal of the Fall; by Christ's death man is restored to that righteousness which he had lost by his own fault, yet no violence is done to the justice and order of God's treatment of his creatures. It can fairly be claimed that Anselm's analyses of the Christian gospel in the light of his reasoned theory of God and creation constitute his greatest and most influential theological achievement.

BIBLIOGRAPHY

S. Anselmi Opera Omnia, F. S. Schmitt, ed., 6 vols. (Edinburgh, 1946–1961), is the standard edition of the Latin text.

Translations are *St. Anselm,* translated by S. N. Deane (La Salle, Ill., 1903), which includes English translations of the *Proslogion, Monologion,* Gaunilo's reply and Anselm's answer, and *Cur Deus Homo; St. Anselm's 'Proslogion,' With 'A Reply on Behalf of the Fool' by Gaunilo and 'The Author's Reply to Gaunilo,'* translated with an introduction and philosophical commentary by M. J. Charlesworth (Oxford, 1965); *The De Grammatico of Saint Anselm: The Theory of Paronymy,* Latin and English text with discussion by D. P. Henry (Notre Dame, Ind., 1964); and E. R. Fairweather, ed., *A Scholastic Miscellany: Anselm to Ockham* (Philadelphia, 1956), which contains translations of *Proslogion, Cur Deus Homo, De Conceptu Virginali* (in part), some shorter items, and an excerpt from Eadmer's memoir of Anselm.

On Anselm's theology, see J. McIntyre, *St. Anselm and His Critics* (Edinburgh, 1954).

See also R. W. Southern, *St. Anselm and His Biographer* (Cambridge, 1963).

— ANSELM'S LIFE AND THE PROOFS: R. E. ALLEN
ANSELM'S THEOLOGY: EUGENE R. FAIRWEATHER

APPLIED ETHICS

Moral philosophers have traditionally aspired to normative theories of what is right or wrong that are set out in the most general terms. But a practical price is paid for generality in ethical theory: it is often unclear whether and, if so, how theory is to be applied in specific cases and contexts. The terms applied ethics and practical ethics came in vogue in the 1970s, when philosophical ethics began to address issues in professional ethics as well as social problems such as capital punishment, abortion, environmental responsibility, and affirmative action. Philosophers interested in applying their training to such problems share with persons from numerous other fields the conviction that decision making in these areas is fundamentally moral and of the highest social importance.

Philosophers working in applied ethics sometimes do more than teach and publish articles about applications of ethical theory.

Philosophers working in applied ethics sometimes do more than teach and publish articles about applications of ethical theory. Their work involves actual applications. They serve as consultants to government agencies, hospitals, law firms, physician groups, business corporations, and engineering firms. Branching out further, they serve as advisers on ethics to radio and educational television, serve on national and state commissions on ethics and policy, and give testimony to legislative bodies. Occasionally, they draft public policy documents, some with the force of law.

Controversies have arisen about whether philosophers have an ethical expertise suited to such work and also about whether the work is philosophical in any interesting sense. Enthusiasm about applied ethics is mixed in academic philosophy. It has been criticized as lacking in serious scholarship, and many philosophers regard it as reducing ethics to engineering—a mere device of problem solving. Some philosophers are not convinced that philosophical theories have a significant role to play in the analysis of cases or in policy and professional contexts, and others are skeptical that philosophical theories have direct practical implications.

Definitional Problems

'Applied ethics' has proved difficult to define, but the following is a widely accepted account: applied ethics is the application of general ethical theories to moral problems with the objective of solving the problems. However, this definition is so narrow that many will not recognize it as reflecting their understanding of either the appropriate method or content. 'Applied ethics' is also used more broadly to refer to any use of philosophical methods critically to examine practical moral decisions and to treat moral problems, practices, and policies in the professions, technology, government, and the like. This broader usage permits a range of philosophical methods (including conceptual analysis, reflective equilibrium, phenomenology, etc.) and does not insist on problem solving as the objective.

Biomedical ethics, political ethics, journalistic ethics, legal ethics, environmental ethics, and business ethics are fertile areas for such philosophical investigation. However, 'applied ethics' is not synonymous with 'professional ethics' (a category from which business ethics is often excluded). Problems such as the allocation of scarce social resources, just wars, abortion, conflicts of interest in surrogate decision making, whistleblowing, the entrapment of public officials, research on animals, and the confidentiality of tax information extend beyond professional conduct, but all are in the domain of applied ethics. Likewise, professional ethics should not be viewed as a part of the wider domain of applied ethics. The latter is usually understood as the province of philosophy, the former as reaching well beyond philosophy and into the professions themselves.

History

Philosophers from Socrates to the present have been attracted to topics in applied ethics such as civil disobedience, suicide, and free speech; and philosophers have written in detail about practical reasoning. Nonetheless, it is arguably the case that there never has been a genuine practical program of applied philosophy in the history of philosophy (the casuists possibly qualifying as an exception). Philosophers have traditionally tried to account for and justify morality, to clarify concepts, to examine how moral judgments and arguments are made, and to array basic principles—not to use either morality or theories to solve practical problems.

This traditional set of commitments began to undergo modification about the time the *Encyclopedia of Philosophy* was first published in 1967. Many hypotheses can be invoked to explain why. The most plausible explanation is that law, ethics, and many of the professions—including medicine, business, engineering, and scientific research—were profoundly affected by issues and concerns in the wider society regarding individual liberties, social equality, and various forms of abuse and injustice. The issues raised by civil rights, women's rights, the consumer movement, the environmental movement, and the rights of prisoners and the mentally ill often included ethical issues that stimulated the imagination of philosophers and came to be regarded by many as essentially philosophical problems. Teaching in the philosophy classroom was influenced by these and other social concerns, most noticeably about unjust

wars, dramatic ethical lapses in institutions, domestic violence, and international terrorism. Increases in the number of working women, affirmative action programs, escalation in international business competition, and a host of other factors heightened awareness. Classroom successes propelled the new applied ethics in philosophy throughout the 1970s. when few philosophers were working in the area but public interest was increasing.

It is difficult to identify landmark events that stimulated philosophers prior to *Roe* v. *Wade* (the U.S. Supreme Court decision on abortion in 1973), which deeply affected applied philosophical thinking. But at least one other landmark deserves mention. Research ethics had been poorly developed and almost universally ignored in all disciplines prior to the Nuremberg Trials. This apathy was shaken when the Nuremberg Military Tribunals unambiguously condemned the sinister political motivation and moral failures of Nazi physicians. The ten principles constituting the "Nuremberg Code" served as a model for many professional and governmental codes formulated in the 1950s and 1960s and eventually influenced philosophers as well.

In the late 1960s and early 1970s there emerged a rich and complex interplay of scholarly publications, journalism, public outrage, legislation, and case law. The 1970s and 1980s saw the publication of several books devoted to philosophical treatments of various subjects in applied ethics, concentrating first on biomedical ethics and second on business ethics. Virtually every book published in these applied fields prior to 1979 was organized topically; none was developed explicitly in terms of moral principles or ethical theory. Philosophers had by this time been working in areas of applied ethics for several years with an interest in the connection between theory, principles, practical decision making, and policy. However, in retrospect, it appears that these connections and their problems were not well understood prior to the mid-1980s.

Models of Application, Reasoning, and Justification

When applied ethics began to receive acceptance in philosophy, it was widely presumed that the "applied" part involves the application of basic moral principles or theories to particular moral problems or cases. This vision suggests that ethical theory develops general principles, rules, and the like, whereas applied ethics treats particular contexts through less general, derived principles, rules, judgments, and the like. From this perspective applied ethics is old morality or old ethical theory applied to new areas. New, derived precepts emerge, but they receive their moral content from the old precepts. Applied work need not, then, generate novel ethical content. Applied ethics requires only a detailed knowledge of the areas to which the ethical theory is being applied (medicine, engineering, journalism, business, public policy, court cases, etc.).

Many philosophers reject this account because it reduces applied ethics to a form of deductivism in which justified moral judgments must be deduced from a pre-existing theoretical structure of normative precepts that cover the judgment. This model is inspired by justification in disciplines such as mathematics, in which a claim is shown to follow logically (deductively) from credible premises. In ethics the parallel idea is that justification occurs if and only if general principles or rules, together with the relevant facts of a situation (in the fields to which the theory is being applied) support an inference to the correct or justified judgment(s). In short, the method of reasoning at work is the application of a norm to a clear case falling under the norm.

This deductive model is sometimes said to be a top-down "application" of precepts. The deductive form in the application of a rule is the following:

1. Every act of description A is obligatory. (rule)
2. Act b is of description A. (fact)

Therefore,

3. Act b is obligatory. (applied moral conclusion)

This structure directs attention from particular judgments to a covering level of generality (rules and principles that cover and justify particular judgments) and then to the level of ethical theory (which covers and warrants rules and principles).

Ethical theories have rarely been able to raise or answer the social and policy questions commonplace in applied ethics.

This model functions smoothly whenever a fact circumstance can be subsumed directly under a general precept, but it does not adequately capture how moral reasoning and justification proceed in complicated cases. The failure to explain complex moral decision making and innovative moral judgment has led to a widespread rejection of deductivism as an appropriate model for applied ethics. Among the replacements for deductivism as a model of application, two have been widely discussed in the literature: case-based reasoning and reflective equilibrium.

CASE-BASED REASONING (A FORM OF CASUISTRY). This approach focuses on practical decision making about particular cases, where judgments cannot simply be brought under general norms. Proponents are skeptical of principles, rules, rights, and theory divorced from history, circumstances, and experience: one can make successful moral judgments of agents and actions, they say, only when one has an intimate understanding of particular situations and an appreciation of the record of similar situations. They cite the use of narratives, paradigm cases, analogies, models, classification schemes, and even immediate intuition and discerning insight.

An analogy to the authority operative in case law is sometimes noted: when the decision of a majority of judges becomes authoritative in a case, their judgments are positioned to become authoritative for other courts hearing cases with similar facts. This is the doctrine of precedent. Defenders of case-based reasoning see moral authority similarly: social ethics develops from a social consensus formed around cases, which can then be extended to new cases without loss of the accumulated moral wisdom. As a history of similar cases and similar judgments mounts, a society becomes more confident in its moral judgments, and the stable elements crystallize in the form of tentative principles; but these principles are derivative, not foundational.

In addition to having a history dating from medieval casuistry, the case method, as it is often called, has long been used in law schools and business schools. Training in the case method is widely believed to sharpen skills of legal and business reasoning as well as moral reasoning. One can tear a case apart and then construct a better way of treating similar situations. In the thrust-and-parry classroom setting, teacher and student alike reach conclusions about rights, wrongs, and best outcomes in cases. The objective is to develop a capacity to grasp problems and to find novel solutions that work in the context: knowing how to reason and act is more prized then knowing that something is the case on the basis of a foundational rule.

The case method in law has come to be understood as a way of learning to assemble facts and judge the weight of evidence—enabling the transfer of that weight to new cases. This task is accomplished by generalizing and mastering the principles that control the transfer, usually principles at work in the reasoning of judges. Use of the case method in business schools springs from an ideal of education that puts the student in the decision-making role after an initial immersion in the facts of a complex situation. Here the essence of the case method is to present a situation replete with the facts, opinions, and prejudices that one might encounter and to find a way of making appropriate decisions in such an environment.

REFLECTIVE EQUILIBRIUM (A FORM OF COHERENCE THEORY). Many now insist that the relationship between general norms and the particulars of experience is bilateral (not unilateral). Moral beliefs arise both by generalization from the particulars of experience (cases) and by making judgments in particular circumstances by appeal to general precepts. John Rawls's celebrated account of 'reflective equilibrium' has been the most influential model of this sort. In developing and maintaining a system of ethics, he argues, it is appropriate to start with the broadest possible set of considered judgments about a subject and to erect a provisional set of principles that reflects them. Reflective equilibrium views investigation in ethics (and theory construction) as a reflective testing of moral principles, theoretical postulates, and other relevant moral beliefs to make them as coherent as possible. Starting with paradigms of what is morally proper or morally improper, one then searches for principles that are consistent with these paradigms as well as one another. Widely accepted principles of right action and considered judgments are taken, as Rawls puts it, "provisionally as fixed points" but also as "liable to revision."

'Considered judgments' is a technical term referring to judgments in which moral beliefs and capacities are most likely to be presented without a distorting bias. Examples are judgments about the wrongness of racial discrimination, religious intolerance, and political conflict of interest. By contrast, judgments in which one's confidence level is low or in which one is influenced by the possibility of personal gain are excluded from consideration. The goal is to match, prune, and adjust considered judgments so that they coincide and are rendered coherent with the premises of theory. That is, one starts with paradigm judgments of moral rightness and wrongness and then constructs a more general theory that is consistent with these paradigm judgments (rendering them as coherent as possible); any loopholes are closed, as are all forms of incoherence that are detected. The resultant action guides are tested to see if they too yield incoherent results. If so, they are readjusted or given up, and the process is renewed, because one can never assume a completely stable equilibrium. The pruning and adjusting occur by reflection and dialectical adjustment, in view of the perpetual goal of achieving reflective equilibrium.

This model demands the best approximation to full coherence under the assumption of a never-ending search for defects of coherence, for counterexamples to beliefs, and for unanticipated situations. From this perspective moral thinking is analogous to hypotheses in science that are tested, modified, or rejected through experience and experimental thinking. Justification is neither purely deductivist (giving general action guides preeminent status), nor purely inductivist (giving experience and analogy preeminent status). Many different considerations provide reciprocal support in the attempt to fit moral beliefs into a coherent unit. This is how we test, revise, and further specify moral beliefs. This outlook is very different from deductivism, because it holds that ethical theories are never complete, always stand to be informed by practical contexts, and must be tested for adequacy by their practical implications.

Method and Content: Departures from Traditional Ethical Theory

In light of the differences in the models just explored and the enormously diverse literature in applied philosophy it is questionable whether applied ethics has a special philosophical method. Applied philosophers appear to do what philosophers have always done: they analyze concepts, examine the hidden presuppositions of moral opinions and theories, offer criticism and constructive accounts of the moral phenomena in question, and criticize strategies that are used to justify beliefs, policies, and actions. They seek a reasoned defense of a moral viewpoint, and they use proposed moral frameworks to distinguish justified moral claims from unjustified ones. They try to stimulate the moral imagination, promote analytical skills, and weed out prejudice, emotion, misappropriated data, false authority, and the like.

Differences between ethical theory and applied ethics are as apparent over content as over method. Instead of analyzing general terms such as 'good', 'rationality', 'ideals', and 'virtues', philosophers interested in applied ethics attend to the analysis of concepts such as confidentiality, trade secrets, environmental responsibility, euthanasia, authority, undue influence, free press, privacy, and entrapment. If normative guidelines are proposed, they are usually specific and directive. Principles in ethical theory are typically general guides that leave considerable room for judgment in specific cases, but in applied ethics proponents tend either to reject principles and rules altogether or to advance precise action guides that instruct persons how to act in ways that allow for less interpretation and discretion. Examples are found in literature that proposes rules of informed consent, confidentiality, conflict of interest, access to information, and employee drug testing.

However, in philosophy journals that publish both applied and theoretical work no sharp line of demarcation is apparent between the concepts and norms of ethical theory and applied ethics. There is not even a discernible continuum from theoretical to applied concepts or principles. The applied/theoretical distinction therefore needs to be used with great caution.

Competing Theories and Problems of Specificity

One reason theory and application are merged in the literature is that several different types of ethical theories have been employed in attempts to address practical problems. At least the following types of theories have been explicitly invoked: (1) utilitarianism, (2) Kantianism, (3) rights theory, (4) contract theory, (5) virtue theory, (6) communitarianism, (7) casuistry, and (8) pragmatism. Many proponents of these theories would agree that specific policy and practical guidelines cannot be squeezed from appeals to these philosophical ethical theories and that some additional content is always necessary.

Ethical theories have rarely been able to raise or answer the social and policy questions commonplace in applied ethics. General theories are ill suited for this work, because they address philosophical problems and are not by their nature practical or policy oriented. The content of a philosophical theory, as traditionally understood, is not of the right sort. Philosophical theories are about morality, but they are primarily attempts to explain, unify, or justify morality, not attempts to specify the practical commitments of moral principles in public policy or in particular cases. In applied ethics, ethical theory is often far less important than moral insight and the defense and development of appropriate guidelines suited to a complex circumstance.

Every general ethical norm contains an indeterminacy requiring further development and enrichment to make it applicable in a complex circumstance. To have sufficient content, general theories and principles must be made specific for contexts; otherwise, they will be empty and ineffectual. Factors such as efficiency, institutional rules, law, and clientele acceptance must be taken into account to make them more specific. An ethics useful for public and institutional policies needs to prove a practical strategy that incorporates political procedures, legal constraints, uncertainty about risk, and the like. Progressive specification of norms will be required to handle the variety of problems that arise, gradually reducing dilemmas, policy options, and contingent conflicts that abstract theory and principle are unable to handle.

Some philosophers view this strategy of specification as heavily dependent upon preexistent practices. They maintain that major contributions in philosophical ethics have run from "applied" contexts to "general" theory rather than the reverse. In examining case law and institutional practices, they say, philosophers have learned about morality in ways that require rethinking and modifying general norms of truth telling, consenting, confidentiality, justice, and so forth. To the extent that sophisticated philosophical treatments of such notions are now emerging, they move, not from theory application (including specification), but from practice to theory. Traditional ethical theory, from this perspective, has no privileged position and has more to learn from "applied contexts" than the other way around.

Nonetheless, there are problems with attempts to base applied ethics entirely in practice standards. A practice standard often does not exist within the relevant field, group, or profession. If current standards are low, they could not legitimately determine what the appropriate standards should be. Most moral problems present issues that have to be thought through, not issues to which good answers have already been provided, which explains why many in the professions have turned to philosophers for help in developing professional ethics. Applied philosophers are often most useful to those with whom they collaborate in other fields when practice standards are defective or deficient and a vacuum needs filling by reflection on, criticism of, and reformulation of moral viewpoints or standards.

[See also Abortion; Affirmative Action; Biomedical Ethics; Communitarianism; Deontological Ethics; Environmental Ethics; Ethical Theory; Pragmatism; Rawls, John; Rights; Socrates; Virtue Ethics.]

BIBLIOGRAPHY

Beauchamp, T. L. "On Eliminating the Distinction between Applied Ethics and Ethical Theory," *The Monist,* Vol. 67 (1984), 514–31.

Brock, D. W. "Truth or Consequences: The Role of Philosophers in Policy-Making." *Ethics,* Vol. 97 (1987), 786–91.

Caplan, A. L. "Ethical Engineers Need Not Apply: The State of Applied Ethics Today," *Science, Technology, and Human Values,* Vol. 6 (Fall 1980), 24–32.

DeGrazia, D. "Moving Forward in Bioethical Theory: Theories, Cases, and Specified Principlism." *Journal of Medicine and Philosophy,* Vol. 17 (1992), 511–39.

Encyclopedia of Bioethics, 2d ed., edited by Warren Reich. New York, 1995.

Feinberg, J. *The Moral Limits of the Criminal Law,* 4 vols. New York, 1984–87.

Fullinwider, R. K. "Against Theory, or: Applied Philosophy—a Cautionary Tale," *Metaphilosophy,* Vol. 20 (1989), 222–34.

Gert, B. "Licensing Professions," *Business and Professional Ethics Journal,* Vol. 1 (1982), 51–60.

———. "Moral Theory and Applied Ethics," *The Monist,* Vol. 67 (1984), 532–48.

Jonsen, A., and S. Toulmin. *The Abuse of Casuistry: A History of Moral Reasoning.* Berkeley, 1988.

MacIntyre, A. "What Has Ethics to Learn from Medical Ethics?" *Philosophic Exchange,* Vol. 2 (1978), 37–47.

———. "Does Applied Ethics Rest on a Mistake?" *The Monist,* Vol. 67 (1984), 498–513.

Noble, C. "Ethics and Experts," *Hastings Center Report,* Vol. 12 (June 1982), 7–10, with responses by four critics.

Professional Ethics, Vol. 1, nos. 1–2 (Spring–Summer 1992). Special issue on applied ethics.

Rawls, J. *A Theory of Justice.* Cambridge, MA, 1971.

Regan, T., ed. *Matters of Life and Death,* 3d ed. New York, 1992.

Richardson, H. "Specifying Norms as a Way to Resolve Concrete Ethical Problems," *Philosophy and Public Affairs,* Vol. 19 (1990), 279–310.

Singer, P. *Practical Ethics,* 2d ed. New York, 1993.

Winkler, E. R., and J. R. Coombs, eds. *Applied Ethics: A Reader.* Oxford, 1993.

– TOM L. BEAUCHAMP

ARENDT, HANNAH

Hannah Arendt, American philosopher and political scientist, was born in 1906 in Hanover, Germany. In 1928 she completed her Ph.D. under Karl Jaspers at the University of Heidelberg, having previously studied with Martin Heidegger at the University of Marburg. Upon immigrating to the United States in 1941, she became director of several Jewish organizations and served as chief editor of Schocken Books before being appointed to the Committee on Social Thought at the University of Chicago in 1963. She taught at the New School for Social Research in New York from 1967 until her death in 1975. Her most famous disciple and critic is the German social theorist Jürgen Habermas, who traces his own theory of communicative action back to her belief in the existential centrality of communication that she herself had inherited from Jaspers.

Freedom and Action

Arendt's chief concern throughout her life was politics and political action. As the quintessential appearance of human freedom, political action, she argued, must be distinguished from both work and cultural fabrication. Laboring to procure life's necessities is unfree; and the freedom of artistic creation is at best hidden and derivative. As distinct from the solitary application of means in pursuit of ends, true freedom must be communicated publicly, in political deeds and words. For this there must be a public space—exemplified by the Greek *polis* and such modern-day equivalents as the worker council and town-hall meeting—wherein equals representing diverse opinions meet and deliberate together.

Secularization and the Crisis in Culture

Most of Arendt's famous studies—on totalitarianism, evil, revolution, and the Jewish question—document the decline of the public space in the wake of modern secularization. Although she did not blame secularization for this decline (indeed, in her opinion, the glory of the American Revolution resided in its freely enacting a new order without benefit of any traditional precedent), she nonetheless believed that the destruction of the old Roman trinity of religion, tradition, and authority contributed to a crisis of culture that undermined essential differences—between public and private, political and economic, action and work—on which the survival of this space depended. Transcendent authority anchored the autonomy of the public realm as a sacred, if indeed secular, space for manifesting immortal deeds in beautiful words, unsullied by the profane preoccupation with biological self-preservation; the waning of authority diminishes that autonomy, thereby enabling the assimilation of both culture and politics to economics.

> *Most of Arendt's famous studies*
> *—on totalitarianism, evil, revolution,*
> *and the Jewish question—*
> *document the decline of the public space*
> *in the wake of modern secularization.*

Arendt's diagnosis of the crisis in culture bears directly on her political concerns. Like Heidegger, she appealed to the Greek conception of culture as an aesthetic revelation of community that memorializes political actions. In the absence of tradition, art provides perduring standards of judgment so that without it the public space wherein judging and acting complement one another would cease to be meaningful. Political life is thus jeopardized whenever culture becomes the private preserve of elites. Conversely, culture intended for mass consumption loses its enduring authority to memorialize the beauty of deeds and words.

Totalitarianism and Radical Evil

According to Arendt, the culture and politics of mass society reflect the loss of purpose experienced by individuals isolated in their lonely pursuit of self-preservation. Under these conditions it is the state, not the individual, that assumes responsibility for integrating the life of the community. In this connection Arendt banefully observed that the subordination of political life to economic administration substitutes the totali-

Arendt's chief concerns throughout her life were politics and political action. (Corbis/Bettmann)

most persons living in mass society, he confused moral duty of citizenship with doing one's job well, as authority commands. However, Arendt also believed that the "absolute goodness" and violence born of idealism (as personified in Melville's Billy Budd) are as pernicious as the radical evil and destructiveness born of any workmanlike devotion to order.

Moral Judgment and Political Action

Arendt's own idealism clashed with her realism. The "inner dialogue" of moral thought, she noted, is at one remove from the real, *vita activa;* indeed, its critical autonomy depends on maintaining this contemplative distance. Accordingly, she held, following Kant, that the integrity of judgment depends on imaginatively representing things from the standpoint of all others, not as they actually represent them, but as they might represent them, were they to communicate their thoughts and feelings disinterestedly, in abstraction from the real limitations that normally prejudice their sensibilities. Counterbalancing this contemplative idealism, however, is Arendt's conviction that judgment must be cultivated in real political action, where persons are free to communicate their thoughts to one another. But this too accords with Kant's belief that freedom from prejudice—the hallmark of moral autonomy—requires the critical check of engaged interlocutors.

[See also Communicative Action; Evil, Problem of; Habermas, Jürgen; Heidegger, Martin; Kant, Immanuel; Realism; Ricoeur: Evil, Problem of.]

tarian fatalism of work for the spontaneous plurality of action. Ultimately, the administrative organization of masses into a single will and identity must view political dissent as an obstacle to the achievement of social welfare.

However, in Arendt's opinion, what really distinguishes modern totalitarianism from absolute despotism is not suppression of dissent but the total administration of a mass for whom private and political life has ceased to be meaningful. In lieu of constitutionally protected freedom, totalitarianism offers ideological determinism, which conceives history as the necessary realization of some abstract idea. This abandonment of commonsense realism in deference to dogmatic idealism subsequently leads to a permanent revolution hostile to any constitutional stability.

By engendering a system in which human life is made totally superfluous, totalitarianism represents the epitome of "radical evil." Contrary to popular opinion, however, such evil is seldom if ever motivated by diabolical intentions. Eichmann's evil, Arendt observed, simply consisted in his banal "thoughtlessness." Like

BIBLIOGRAPHY

Works by Arendt

The Human Condition. Chicago, 1958.
The Origins of Totalitarianism, enlarged ed. New York, 1958.
On Revolution. New York, 1963.
Eichmann in Jerusalem: A Report on the Banality of Evil. New York, 1965.
Men in Dark Times. New York, 1968.
On Violence. New York, 1970.
Crisis of the Republic. New York, 1972.
Rahel Varnhagen: The Life of a Jewish Woman. New York, 1974.
Between Past and Future: Eight Exercises in Political Thought. New York, 1978.
The Jew as Pariah: Jewish Identity and Politics in the Modern Age. Ron Feldman, ed. New York, 1978.
The Life of the Mind, 2 vols. Mary McCarthy, ed. New York, 1978.
Lectures on Kant's Political Philosophy. R. Beiner, ed. Chicago, 1982.

Works on Arendt

Bernauer, J., ed. *Amor Mundi: Explorations in the Faith and Thought of Hannah Arendt.* Dordrecht, 1987.
Bowen-Moore, P. *Hannah Arendt's Philosophy of Natality.* New York, 1989.
Bradshaw, L. *Acting and Thinking: The Political Thought of Hannah Arendt.* Toronto, 1989.

Carnovan, M. *The Political Thought of Hannah Arendt.* New York, 1974.

———. *Hannah Arendt: A Reinterpretation of Her Thought.* New York, 1992.

Garner, R. ed. *In the Realm of Humanitas: Responses to the Writings of Hannah Arendt.* New York, 1990.

Gottsegen, M. G. *The Political Thought of Hannah Arendt.* Albany, NY, 1994.

Hill, M. A., ed. *Hannah Arendt: Recovery of the Public World.* New York, 1979.

Hinchman, L. P., and K. Sandra, eds. *Hannah Arendt: Critical Essays.* Albany, NY, 1994. Contains essays by Arendt.

Kateb, G. *Hannah Arendt, Politics, Conscience, Evil.* Totowa, NJ, 1984.

Kohn, J., and L. May. *Hannah Arendt: Twenty Years Later.* Cambridge, MA, 1996.

Parekh, B. C. *Hannah Arendt and the Search for a New Political Philosophy.* Atlantic Highlands, NJ, 1981.

Watson, D. *Hannah Arendt.* London, 1992.

Young-Bruehl, E. *Hannah Arendt: For Love of the World.* New Haven, 1982. Contains a bibliography.

— DAVID INGRAM

ARISTOTLE

Aristotle (384–322 B.C.), son of Nicomachus, the court physician to Amyntas II, king of Macedon, was born in the Ionian city of Stagira in Chalcidice. His father died when he was still a boy and he was brought up by a guardian, Proxenus, who sent him to Athens, where he entered Plato's Academy, about 367 B.C. He remained at the Academy until Plato's death in 347 B.C. Plato was succeeded as head of the Academy by his nephew and heir Speusippus, and Aristotle, together with Xenocrates, joined a circle of Platonists living at Assos in the Troad under the protection of the tyrant Hermias of Atarneus. The story that there had earlier been a quarrel and a break in relations between Plato and Aristotle belongs to a later tradition hostile to Aristotle and is contradicted by contemporary evidence.

The story that there had been a quarrel and a break in relations between Plato and Aristotle belongs to a later tradition hostile to Aristotle and is contradicted by contemporary evidence.

But the departure of Aristotle and Xenocrates from Athens did involve the secession of a group of those associated with Plato, and it was probably related to the choice of Speusippus as Plato's successor. After three years in Assos, Aristotle moved in 345 B.C. to Mytilene on the island of Lesbos. A number of details in his biological treatises make it clear that many of his zoological investigations belong to this period. Then in 342 B.C. he accepted an invitation to supervise the education of the thirteen-year-old son of Philip II of Macedon, the future Alexander the Great, at the Macedonian court at Pella. This lasted for some three years. The following five years Aristotle spent at Stagira; and about 335 B.C. he returned to Athens to open a new school in a gymnasium called the Lyceum, a short distance northeast of the city. On the death of Alexander the Great in 323 B.C., the school was in danger of attack from the anti-Macedonian party at Athens, and Aristotle himself took refuge in Chalcis on the island of Euboea, leaving Theophrastus in charge of the school. He died in Chalcis the following year, at the age of 62.

Writings

It is convenient to consider Aristotle's writings under three headings: popular writings, memoranda and collections of material, and scientific and philosophical treatises.

POPULAR WRITINGS. Among Aristotle's popular writings may be included some poems, of which three fragments survive, and also the fragments of certain letters, not all of which are genuine. But far more important are the dialogues and certain other philosophical works constituting what Aristotle refers to in the treatises as "exoteric writings." (The term "exoteric" thus applied is now understood to mean simply "written for those outside the school," and it is opposed to "esoteric," applicable to the treatises and meaning "for those inside the school" without conveying any idea of secrecy or mystery.) Of these exoteric writings the most important are the *Eudemus,* the *Protrepticus, On Philosophy, On the Good,* and *On the Ideas.* None of these survive, but in some cases we have substantial extracts or summaries; and overall there are more than one hundred direct quotations and references in later writers to these works. The dialogues were on the Platonic model, and the high opinion of Aristotle's prose style several times expressed in antiquity clearly refers to them and not to the treatises or memoranda.

MEMORANDA AND COLLECTIONS OF MATERIAL. Over two hundred titles are preserved in the three ancient catalogues of Aristotle's works. Here belong the 158 constitutions of Greek states, of which the *Constitution of the Athenians,* rediscovered in a papyrus in 1890, alone survives; a record of dramatic festivals, called the *Didascaliae,* no longer extant; and perhaps also the surviving *Problems* and *Historia Animalium.* Clearly, Aristotle commissioned others within the school to prepare collections of research materials, and this work continued after his death. Later writers drew extensively on such works as Theophrastus' *Opinions of the Physical Philosophers* and his writings on botany, Eudemus' histories of various branches of mathematics and of theology, and other similar works which may well have been begun during Aristotle's lifetime.

SCIENTIFIC AND PHILOSOPHICAL TREATISES. The scientific and philosophical treatises constitute the surviving corpus of Aristotle's writings and, excluding certain spurious works, they may be listed as follows:

(1) Logical works (the *Organon*)
    Categories
    On Interpretation (De Interpretatione)
    Prior and Posterior Analytics
    Topics
    On Sophistical Refutations (De Sophisticis Elenchis)
(2) Physical works
    Physics
    On the Heavens (De Caelo)
    On Coming-to-be and Passing-away (De Generatione et Corruptione)
    Meteorologics
(3) Psychological works
    On the Soul (De Anima)
    Parva Naturalia: short treatises including *On Memory and Reminiscence, On Dreams, and On Prophesying by Dreams*
(4) Works on natural history
    On the Parts of Animals (De Partibus Animalium)
    On the Movement of Animals (De Motu Animalium)
    On the Progression of Animals (De Incessu Animalium)
    On the Generation of Animals (De Generatione Animalium)
    Minor treatises
(5) Philosophical works
    Metaphysics
    Nicomachean Ethics
    Eudemian Ethics
    Magna Moralia
    Politics
    Rhetoric
    Art of Poetry

The nature of these surviving Aristotelian treatises has been much discussed. Some have supposed that they represent lecture notes, either Aristotle's own or those taken by pupils, while others regard them as essentially textbooks or working notes prepared for the use of students in the Aristotelian School. However they first came to be written down, they seem to have continued in use in the school for a considerable period. Some were edited by members of the School, and it is probable that at least until the death of Theophrastus they remained subject to additions and amplifications. Some of the works now judged spurious may be later revisions of original material going back to Aristotle's own day.

HISTORY OF THE WRITINGS. Before discussing Aristotle's thought in relation to his writings, it is necessary to know something of the external history of them. The treatises passed to Theophrastus on Aristotle's death,

and Theophrastus in turn bequeathed them to Neleus of Scepsis in the Troad. According to the story, they remained in the hands of Neleus' family until they were sold, together with the works of Theophrastus, to Apellicon of Teos, who died about 86 B.C. Apellicon published them, but they had been damaged by damp and vermin, and he filled in the gaps incorrectly. Upon the death of Apellicon, Sulla carried off the books from Athens to Rome. There the elder Tyrannion got possession of them, and together with Andronicus of Rhodes, the eleventh president of the Peripatetic school, he published them sometime between 43 and 20 B.C. The story is told by Strabo, a pupil of Tyrannion, and probably is true in its essentials. There is certainly every reason to believe that all subsequent versions of the treatises stem from this recension by Andronicus of Rhodes.

But the implications of the story have been much discussed. Taken literally, it implies that the Aristotelian treatises were lost to the Peripatetic school during the period from Strato (the successor of Theophrastus) to Andronicus of Rhodes. It is both true and important to

According to Aristotle the basic question in philosophy is "What is being?" (Corbis/Bettmann)

note that the vast majority of references to Aristotle's doctrines in the Hellenistic period before Andronicus are to the dialogues and not to the treatises. This has led to the doctrine of the "lost Aristotle," expounded especially by Ettore Bignone in *L'Aristotele perduto* (2 vols., Florence, 1936). Nonetheless, it is unlikely that the treatises were altogether lost. It is hard to believe that no copies of them were retained in the school at Athens.

The oldest catalogue of Aristotle's writings probably goes back to Ariston of Ceos, head of the school at Athens about 200 B.C. His catalogue lists works known to him at that time, including most but not all of the treatises. The library at Alexandria housed books sought with anxious care from all over the world and is said to have contained forty copies or versions of the *Analytics*—it probably held the rest of the treatises as well as the dialogues. There are some references to the treatises, especially to the biological works, during the earlier Hellenistic period (see Ingmar Düring, "Notes on the Transmission of Aristotle's Writings," in *Göteborgs Högskolas Årsskrift*, Vol. 56, No. 3 (1950), 37–70).

Andronicus' edition undoubtedly gave a fresh stimulus to Aristotelian studies and concentrated attention once again on the treatises. Comparison of the dialogues with the treatises revealed considerable differences in doctrine. In the second century A.D. the successors of Andronicus began the series of great commentaries on the treatises culminating in the work of Alexander of Aphrodisias, who explained that in the treatises Aristotle gave his own opinions and the truth, while in the dialogues he gave the opinions of others, which were false. Other commentators supposed that he preached a doctrine to those inside the school (in the treatises) different from that offered (in the dialogues) to those outside. From Andronicus onward, for over nineteen centuries, it was assumed that Aristotle gave his real doctrines in the treatises. The logical extension of this approach came in 1863, when Valentin Rose concluded that all the dialogues must have been spurious works not written by Aristotle at all (*Aristoteles Pseudepigraphus*, Leipzig, 1863).

Development of Aristotle's Thought

The belief that the Aristotelian corpus gave a systematic statement of Aristotle's thought written mostly in the period after 335 B.C. dominated Aristotelian studies until it was challenged by Werner Jaeger, first in *Studien zur Enstehungsgeschichte der Metaphysik des Aristoteles* (Berlin, 1912), and then in his definitive *Aristoteles, Grundlegung einer Geschichte seiner Entwicklung* (Berlin, 1923), which has had a profound effect on all subsequent discussions. Jaeger maintained that Aristotle's thought went through a gradual development that lasted most of his life. He distinguished three periods. In the first, down to 347 B.C., Aristotle was an emphatic and enthusiastic defender of Platonism. Here belong the dialogues, with the exception of *On Philosophy*, and in them Aristotle holds fast both to the Platonic view of the soul as given in the *Phaedo* and *Republic* and to the doctrine of the Forms. In the second period, from 347 to 335 B.C., Aristotle became increasingly critical of Platonism, above all of the doctrine of Forms. In this period he wrote *On Philosophy*. Finally, in the period after 335 B.C., Aristotle was feeling his way toward a type of thinking based on a wholly new principle, that of empirical science; and by the end of his life he had come to reject all the essential features of Platonic otherworldly metaphysics. In many of the treatises it was, Jaeger held, possible to distinguish quite clearly parts written at different periods and reflecting different and inconsistent stages in Aristotle's thought, ranging all the way from the full-blooded Platonism of the first period, typified by the dialogues, through the period of increasing criticism to the final period, when metaphysics in the old sense was virtually abandoned.

The oldest catalogue of Aristotle's writings probably goes back to Ariston of Ceos, head of the school at Athens about 200 B.C.

Jaeger's radical genetic approach inevitably provoked differing reactions from scholars. Apart from die-hard opposition, the initial tendency was to acknowledge that a new era had dawned in Aristotelian studies. Some adopted Jaeger's scheme wholeheartedly and attempted to apply it in detail to treatises that had not been subject to such analysis in Jaeger's book. But some from the beginning, and an increasing number as time went on, while accepting the genetic approach, were doubtful whether Jaeger had correctly identified the actual stages of Aristotle's development. In particular, Jaeger had argued that Book A of the *Metaphysics* belonged to Aristotle's middle period while admitting that Chapter 8 must have been written toward the end of Aristotle's life. But further study has suggested that Chapter 8 cannot be separated from the rest of the book in this way. It would follow that the whole of Book A must belong to the later period, and this means that Aristotle never abandoned interest in metaphysical problems.

This continued interest in metaphysical problems was suggested also by a fuller investigation into Aristotle's discussion of soul. The biological treatises rest largely on studies made in the Aegean area around Lesbos in Aristotle's second period and may well have been partly written in that period. Aristotle, on this view, began with a Platonist conception of the soul as a separate substance, moved to a view of the body as instrument of the soul in the second or biological period, and in the final period developed the doctrine of the soul as form of the body in the light of his developed theory of substance as expressed in his *Metaphysics* (see F. Nuyens, *L'Evolution de la psychologie d'Aristote*). This comes close to inverting the order of Jaeger's middle and later periods in terms of Aristotle's dominant interests at each stage. This reversal of Jaeger's scheme has been carried a step further, not without an element of deliberate paradox, by Ingmar Düring's apothegm that it would be truer to say that Aristotle began as an empiricist and spent the rest of his life in striving to become a Platonist.

More recently the whole genetic approach has come under fresh attack. It is pointed out that there are many passages in the treatises which imply a systematic order of exposition. In all probability the treatises as we have them represent lecture courses given in the later years of Aristotle's life. The attempt to dissolve them into a series of doctrines classified as earlier or later according to whether they are closer to or more remote from positions adopted by Plato is inherently vicious, in that it assumes at the start what should only be a conclusion, namely, that "nearer to Plato" means "earlier in date." Inconsistencies there certainly are, and no doubt different treatises or parts of treatises were written at different times. But the over-all intention, it is argued, was to produce an organized system of thought. This was no doubt subject to continuous revision, and the process of revision was never completed. Nonetheless, we miss the whole point of Aristotle's undertaking if we reverse his intention in order to dissolve his thought into a series of stages. Even the doctrinal chaos within some of the treatises has been exaggerated, it is claimed, and in the crucial case of the *Metaphysics* it is possible to discern a logical progression from book to book which suggests unitary composition.

So some would say that the break with Platonism was for all practical purposes complete by the time Aristotle went to Assos—all that happened after that was a prolonged and sustained attempt to work out the consequences of the rejection of Plato's metaphysics. Others would attack even the contrast between the treatises and the dialogues, interpreting the dialogues as Aristotelian rather than Platonic in outlook. Above all, it is now quite widely held that there is no evidence anywhere in the dialogues that Aristotle there accepted Plato's theory of the Forms as transcendent, and if this be the case, then Jaeger's thesis is indeed in ruins.

This is a discussion which will long continue. In the present article the view is taken that in most of the dialogues Aristotle accepts a number of Platonic positions which he later abandoned, that a movement away from Platonism occupied most of his life but that he never abandoned or rejected metaphysical interests although he recognized that the rejection of earlier views required modifications in his metaphysical doctrine. On the view assumed here, he was engaged from the start in attempts to present a systematic view of the whole field of knowledge and reality, and he remained throughout a determined and unrepentent systematizer without ever succeeding in producing a fully coordinated system that could satisfy his own high standards of criticism; finally, the right way to present his doctrines, on this account, is not to begin by attempting to distinguish any general stages or layers in his thinking at different periods but to discuss separately the main positions to which he gives expression when discussing different topics, problems, or branches of philosophy, in the expectation that sometimes inconsistencies can be explained along geneticist lines but that at other times Aristotle may have been confronted with difficulties for which he had no solution. Indeed, much of his thinking is what he himself calls aporetic, that is, raising difficulties without solving them; and it may be that the aporetic element is more fundamental than has usually been recognized.

THE PROBLEM OF KNOWLEDGE. In what follows, no account will be offered of Aristotle's important biological studies, and only some of his basic philosophical ideas will be discussed—and then only in the most general terms. But before embarking upon this extremely hazardous undertaking, it may be worth attempting to state some of the guidelines which Aristotle follows in his thinking, above all with reference to the problem of knowledge.

For Plato, knowledge, if it is to be knowledge, must be clear, certain, and not subject to change. It can have these characteristics only if they are found also in the objects known. The objects of knowledge must consequently be definite, real, and unchanging, and so they must be nonsensible and universal—in other words, the Forms. (It may be noted that even if the view is taken that this misrepresents Plato, it is unquestionably what Aristotle attributed to him.) Aristotle came to reject the transcendence of the Platonic Forms, but he retained the Platonic view of knowledge as knowledge of the universal and of the real. His problem, then, was to find a way of giving reality and permanence to the universal without reintroducing the Platonic Forms. Second, Plato had regarded the Forms as the causes of things being or becoming what they are or become. The change in the status of the Forms required of Aristotle a new doctrine of causation and a new source or sources of change and of motion. Third, when Aristotle attempted to systematize the various branches of knowledge on the basis of his changed or changing conceptions of universals and of causes, he was led step by step to make profound changes in the general pictures implied by Plato and by Plato's predecessors, the pre-Socratics. These changes were so vast that we are fully justified in regarding Aristotelianism as a philosophical innovation of the first importance.

Aristotle's problem was to find a way

of giving reality and permanence to the universal

without reintroducing the Platonic Forms,

whose transcendence he had come to reject.

So much has, indeed, been generally recognized. But the interpretation of Aristotle has itself been a part of the subsequent history both of European philosophy and of Christian theology and at many points has provided the terrain for subsequent battles. A sound historical approach to Aristotle must to some extent discard considerations of this kind, and the attempt must be made to see Aristotle against the background of Plato and the pre-Socratics rather than in the light of the subsequent history of philosophy. But not completely. Aristotle was a thinker of great philosophical subtlety and persistence and has much to offer those concerned with the discussion of similar problems today. Ideally, what is wanted is a critical historical approach accompanied by a sympathetic philosophical interest in the many problems which occupied Aristotle's thoughts for a lifetime.

Classification of the Sciences

In *Topics* (I, 14) Aristotle divides propositions into ethical, physical, and logical, thus suggesting the standard Hellenistic division of philosophy into logic, physics, and ethics, a division which Sextus Empiricus tells us (*Against the Logicians* I, 16) originated with Plato but was first made explicit by Xenocrates. However, in *Topics* (VI, 6) Aristotle gives his own famous tripartite division of knowledge into theoretical, practical, and poetic (or, rather, productive). Elsewhere he subdivides theoretical knowledge into first philosophy, physics, and mathematics, and practical knowledge into ethics, politics, and a number of other activities. The bases of these divisions and subdivisions are stated differently on different occasions, but the primary division seems usually to be based on the purpose involved—knowledge pur-

sued for its own sake is theoretical; pursued for the sake of actions, practical; and pursued for the sake of making or producing something, productive. The subdivisions of theoretical knowledge, on the other hand, are usually related to differences in the objects studied. Things that cannot be other than what they are, but can exist separately, are the subject of first philosophy; things that cannot change and cannot exist separately are the subject of mathematics; and things that can change and can exist separately are the subject of physics.

Clearly, this second principle of division leads to an inconsistency with the primary division, since physics, for example, could be pursued either as a part of theoretical or productive or (as in psychology) practical science. A twofold division between theoretical and productive science is found in *Protrepticus* (*Aristotelis Dialogorum Fragmenta*, R. Walzer, ed., Fr. 6), but the primary threefold division may well go back to the dialogue *On Justice*. The problem that results is typical. While all inconsistencies could be removed by positing a series of stages in the development of Aristotle's thought, all stages seem to be combined in *Nicomachean Ethics* (VI, 3–4). It seems probable that Aristotle had not completely systematized his thought on the classification of the sciences, or at the least that he did not intend a single classification to be used for all purposes. His classification was in fact ignored in the Hellenistic period, and its very considerable influence on subsequent thought, down to the present day, probably goes far beyond anything which Aristotle had in mind.

Logic

Whether logic was to be a separate part or merely an instrument of philosophy was a standard subject of debate between the Stoics and the Peripatetics. Aristotle's preferred view did not include logic in his classification of the sciences at all, but treated it as a preliminary to the study of each and every branch of knowledge. Hence, for him it was an instrument (*organon*) of study, and the name *Organon* came later to be applied to the collection of Aristotle's logical treatises. Aristotle's own name for logic was "analytics," and the term "logic" only subsequently came to have its full modern sense. This sense is sometimes said to have occurred first in Alexander of Aphrodisias about A.D. 200. But the term is found in a somewhat restricted sense in Aristotle's own writings (for example, *Topics* I, 14); and there is evidence that it was beginning to be used as the equivalent of dialectic or analytics almost immediately after Aristotle's death, so that it may have been the Stoics who first consciously gave it its modern application.

For Aristotle, the heart of logic was the syllogism. His treatment of syllogistic argument, with some restatements and embroideries, provided the basis of the teaching of traditional formal logic until the beginning of the twentieth century. While it is becoming clear that the traditional formal logic in some ways distorted Aristotle's teaching on particular points, the main lines of his treatment of the syllogism are too well known and also too detailed to justify exposition in this present article. The *Organon* has two preliminary treatises, the *Categories* and *On Interpretation,* dealing respectively with terms and with propositions. Then come the *Prior Analytics,* dealing with the syllogism, and the *Posterior Analytics,* dealing with the conditions of scientific knowledge, including what extra requirements besides consistency are necessary for the attainment of truth. The *Topics,* to which *On Sophistical Refutations* forms an appendix, deals with syllogistically correct kinds of reasoning which fall short of the conditions of scientific accuracy. Genetic studies, without achieving any unanimity, have tended to place the *Topics,* or the greater part of it, earliest in date of composition, on the strong ground that at least part of it was written before the development of the doctrine of the syllogism. An attempt to date the *Posterior Analytics* before the *Prior Analytics* has met with more criticism—while it owes more to Plato than the *Prior Analytics* does, this in itself is not surprising, since the doctrine of the syllogism is not Platonic anyway. The *Categories* and *On Interpretation* are also generally regarded now as early works, but the importance of the *Categories* justifies a fuller discussion.

THE *CATEGORIES.* Since it deals with terms in isolation, it is natural that the *Categories* should be placed first in the *Organon.* It is probable that the second part of the treatise, usually known as the *Post-Predicaments,* is as genuine as the earlier part, although its authenticity was generally doubted until quite recently. According to Aristotle, isolated expressions signify either substance, quantity, quality, relation, place, time, position, condition, action, or passivity. These "categories" were referred to quite frequently elsewhere, but neither the order nor the number was precisely fixed. Most expressions properly signify one category only, but (in *Metaphysics* Δ 10) certain pervasive terms are recognized as able to run through all the categories, terms such as "one," "being," "same," and "other," a fact which is reminiscent of the doctrine of "greatest kinds" in Plato's *Sophist* (254B ff.).

The term "category" properly means "predicate," but it is clear that for Aristotle the expressions with which he is dealing can occur either in the subject or in the predicate position in a sentence. It follows that Aristotle is not simply giving a theory of predication. What is he doing? According to one view, he is classifying terms upon the basis of grammatical distinctions as to their use—noun, adjective, and so on. A second view argues that he is not classifying linguistic symbols but what they symbolize, in other words, things. On this "ontological" interpretation, Aristotle is attempting to classify the main aspects of reality. Others suppose that he is already dealing with strictly "logical" entities. The answer probably is that Aristotle would not have regarded these three views as mutually exclusive—in the words of Porphyry's commentary on the *Categories* (in *Commentaria in Aristotelem Graeca,* A. Busse, ed., Vol. IV, Part I, Berlin, 1887, p. 71, l. 13): "As things are, so are the expressions which primarily indicate them."

It is certainly as part of a theory of reality that Aristotle later uses the categories to criticize Plato's theory of Forms. For Aristotle, Plato was involved in a confusion between the category of substance and the other categories when, for example, he attributed substantiality to predications of quantity, such as "being tall." However, in Chapter 5 of the *Categories* Aristotle distinguishes within the category of substance between "primary substance" and "secondary substance." Primary substances are particular men, horses, and so on, and "secondary substances" are the species and genera to which the individuals belong. It is noteworthy that Aristotle does not, as we tend to do, treat all simple nonrelational predicates as qualities—for him the genus and species to which a thing belongs are substances and not qualities and so belong in the first category. In the *Metaphysics* this treatment of species and genera as involving substantiality seems to have been abandoned, and we have a more simple opposition between substance and the universal. If, then, Aristotle did in fact gradually move farther and farther away from Platonism, this movement would help to support an early date for the *Categories.*

Physics

The Eleatic doctrine of being initiated by Parmenides seemed to make predication impossible by treating identity and being as the same and by arguing that being excludes diversity, so that a thing cannot have any predicate attached to it which is different from itself. To this, Aristotle replied with the doctrine of the *Categories,* distinguishing a number of different senses of being and so making possible a series of different subject–predicate relations. The same Eleatic doctrine of being also seemed to make change and movement impossible by arguing that that which is, always is, and that being cannot come into existence out of nonbeing. The pre-Socratics after Parmenides endeavored to keep change and movement by positing unchanging elements which combine or emerge or separate on varying principles.

Plato in the *Phaedo* struck a death blow at such elements and principles as sources of change by arguing that a thing can never change into its opposite without being itself destroyed. Thereafter there were two predictable courses for physical theory to follow. The first was to seek reality in a substrate behind the elements, a substrate to which varying qualities could attach. This was the course taken by Aristotle. The other alternative was to seek reality in unchanging permanent qualities, the Platonic Forms, with a minimal "location" in which varying temporary projections and combinations of Forms could occur and so constitute the phenomenal world. This second view is the "Platonic" view, and it was the view toward which Plato himself usually tended.

MATTER, PRIVATION, AND FORM. Aristotle's three basic ingredients for the explanation of change are discussed at the beginning of his treatise *Physics* (I, 5–7)—they are the substrate (that which persists through change), the absence of (a particular) form, and the form which appears in the process of change. Change consists in a substrate (matter) acquiring a form which it did not previously possess. Hence we can speak of three principles, matter, privation, and form. Not-being is associated with privation, and the substrate, since it is always in existence, is in itself free of not-being. But since form follows privation, there is a sense in which we do have "genesis out of not-being." The mention of the doctrine of potentiality as an *alternative* explanation of change (191b27 ff.), whether a later insertion or not, is good evidence for the early date of the discussion in the *Physics,* and the first seven books are dated by Jaeger, for example, as belonging originally to the early or Academic period in Aristotle's development. Nonetheless, the doctrine of privation provides a wholly new approach to the problem of change on the part of Aristotle. The doctrine of the substrate clearly has affinities with that of the receptacle in Plato's *Timaeus.* But it inverts Plato's hierarchy of reality between form and substrate, and the doctrine of privation has its roots in the doctrine of the opposites in Plato's *Phaedo.*

SUBSTANCE. In the *Categories* substance is characterized above all by its power to be the recipient of contrary qualifications (4a10), but it alone among the categories has no opposite. In the *Physics* change is from opposite to opposite, and this would seem to exclude the genesis of substances from substances. The logical answer might seem to be to treat only the substrate as a substance, and this is indeed what is implied in the *Physics.* But in *On Coming-to-be and Passing-away* Aristotle has to deal explicitly with the genesis of substance. Once again potential being is considered, but only to be dismissed as a possible source for substance (317b19–33), and an unhappy attempt is made to distinguish certain elements, such as earth, as "not-being" so that another element can come into being out of not-being. In the *Metaphysics* the question is taken up again, and from two points of view. First, the question of substance is much more thoroughly discussed (see below under the heading "Metaphysics"), and second, the doctrine of potential being is used to provide a more nearly adequate solution (*Metaphysics* Z 7–9 and Θ). In the strict sense, substance does not come into existence or pass out of existence either as matter or as form. What comes into existence is a "this-such," or concrete object combining matter and form. Both the matter and the form were already in existence, but in relation to each other their previous existence was only potential. The genesis of a new substance involves the passage from potential to actual existence for both matter and form in a new "this-such" or concrete object.

EFFICIENT AND FINAL CAUSES. The cause of a genesis or of any other change requires for Aristotle a twofold analysis—first, a correct analysis of the process of change itself, and second, the identification of the source or sources of the change. Virtually the same account of the doctrine of "the four causes" is found in the *Physics* and the *Metaphysics* (Δ 2), but there is reason to suppose that the account was first given in the *Physics.* Two "causes" have already been identified in the account of substrate and privation. These are matter and form. Two more must be added, the efficient cause and the final cause. All four can be separately identified in Plato's writings, but they do not form a system as they do for Aristotle. Thus Aristotle can actually criticize Plato for operating only with the formal and material causes, just as he criticized most of the pre-Socratics for employing only the material cause, although he recognized the emergence of efficient causes in Empedocles' Love and Strife.

For Aristotle,

to know is to know by means of causes,

and it is clear that the four Aristotelian causes

are necessary elements in things.

For Aristotle, to know is to know by means of causes, and it is clear that the four Aristotelian causes are necessary elements in things, which must be known or understood if full understanding is to be reached, rather than causes in the modern sense. Viewed in this way, the material cause deals with the substrate, such as the bronze of a statue, while the formal cause is concerned with the shape of the statue. The final cause is the end or purpose for the sake of which the process of making the statue was commenced, and the efficient cause is that which initiates the process of change and so is its primary source. In some cases this might be a person acting as agent. It might seem at first that two of the causes, matter and form, are sited within the object to be explained, and two outside, the efficient and the final causes. This would misrepresent Aristotle's views in two ways. First, it is, strictly speaking, not the object, but the process of change by which it comes into existence, that the doctrine of the four causes is intended to explain. Second, Aristotle tells us (*Physics* 198a24) that in many cases the formal, final, and efficient causes all coincide. In the case of living creatures, the form of an object may also be that at which nature was aiming when the object was produced, and in the case of an artifact the final cause may be the form as known by the artist or manufacturer. In this last case the formal cause may be the efficient cause as well, in that the form as present in the artist's mind and desired by him in the object is the true source of the process of change that results. When applied to objects of different kinds, the doctrine of the four causes is capable of considerable elaboration and subtlety. For example, in the case of a city one might say that the matter is the people, the form is its organization, the final cause is living or living well, and the efficient cause is the realization or acceptance of the final cause as desirable by some or all of the people.

THE ULTIMATE SOURCE OF MOTION. The distinction between external and internal causes raises in an acute way the question of the ultimate source or sources of motion and change in the universe. For the earlier pre-Socratics, *Physics* (Nature) as the object of study by physical philosophers was assumed, rather than consciously concluded, to have its own quasi-living source of motion within itself. Thinkers after Parmenides made increasing use of external agents acting upon the primary elements in order to initiate or maintain change. Plato in the *Laws* (894c ff.) supposed that the primary cause of movement must be that which can move both itself and other things, and this he identified as soul. Soul carries round the sun, moon, and stars, but he leaves it doubtful whether this is because soul is present in the sun as it is in man or because soul pushes the sun from outside or because the sun is moved from outside by soul in some other way. But for Plato the real world itself is not in motion. He supposes that things in the phenomenal world are imitations or reflections of the Forms, and on occasion he can speak of them as endeavoring to reproduce the Forms. When this happens, the Forms and the "love" they inspire are

causes of change in the phenomenal world. Aristotle takes over from the pre-Socratics the concept of nature as possessing a source of motion within itself. In *On Philosophy* three causes of motion are distinguished—nature, force, and free will—and the motion of the stars is attributed to free will. This seems to represent the first stage of Aristotle's thinking, and there seems to be no evidence yet for any single transcendent mover of the heavens.

In *On the Heavens* the doctrine of natural movement is carried a step further. Of the four elements, air and fire naturally move upward and earth and water downward, a doctrine already implied in *On Philosophy*. A fifth element, *aether*, now appears (the later "quintessence"), with a natural circular movement which explains the movements of the stars, since these are composed of aether. We now seem to have only two sources of motion, nature and force, and we are probably justified in concluding that here too Aristotle is not envisaging any transcendent mover, certain passages to the contrary being best explained as later insertions.

Both in *On the Heavens* and in *On Philosophy* it is to be understood that living creatures move themselves and also are moved (on occasion) by forces from without. But what *makes* a living creature move itself? This question is tackled in *Physics* VIII, where it is argued that even a self-moved mover requires a cause outside itself to initiate its movement. If we are to avoid an infinite regress, we must suppose that this leads us to one or more prime movers that are themselves unmoved and that have the power to move by acting as objects of desire. Aristotle actually supposes that the prime mover is one, eternal, and nonmaterial and that there is one first-moved object, namely, the outermost heaven. The introduction of this transcendent mover is sometimes interpreted as the fulfillment rather than the negation of the view found in *On the Heavens* because it is possible to identify what is first moved with the aether. The identification is no doubt correct, but the loss of aether's natural movement is a major change. The unmoved mover is necessarily at rest, and this doctrine clearly is in some danger of introducing a conflict with the doctrine that nature is that which has a source of movement within itself. This would fit in well with an analysis of the *Physics* which would make the first six books represent an earlier stage in Aristotle's thought than Books VII–VIII. But it should be pointed out that if this is correct, the doctrine of the unmoved mover in the later books is nonetheless more Platonic in character than the doctrine of nature in the earlier books.

The final stage comes in *Metaphysics* Λ, the lateness of which is now generally regarded as established by the reference in Chapter 8 to the astronomical theories of

Callippus, which can hardly be earlier than 330 B.C. In this chapter Aristotle puts forward the theory that there are 47 or 55 celestial spheres, each eternal, and for each of them there is a separate unmoved mover. The preceding chapter speaks of an unmoved mover in the singular, and the relation between the two chapters is a considerable problem. But there is a single unmoved mover clearly referred to within Chapter 8, and it is probable that there is no rejection of a single unmoved mover—it should, rather, be regarded as standing on a higher plane than the "departmental" movers assigned to individual planets.

TELEOLOGICAL PHYSICS. Nature for Aristotle makes nothing without a purpose (*On the Heavens* 271a33), and a word must be said about the teleological character of Aristotle's physical theories, which has brought so much censure upon his head. It has tended in modern times to seem a natural but dangerous doctrine in biological studies and wholly wrong in the study of inanimate nature. Its usefulness is clearly a matter for scientists to decide for themselves, but two points seem worth making. Normally Aristotle's teleology is not a doctrine of any over-all pattern of purpose in the universe, nor is it even intended to show how natural objects may serve purposes outside themselves. It is, rather, a doctrine of internal finality, that is, a doctrine that the end of each object is to be itself. Second, his teleology is rooted in his equation of final cause with formal cause. The study of the end or purpose of a thing is the study of its form, and to the extent that a modern scientist is concerned with the formal and universal elements in nature, he is, paradoxically enough, following Aristotle's approach. He would differ in supposing that the achievement of form in inanimate objects cannot profitably be described as their end.

Psychology

For Aristotle, the study of soul and of life is a part of the study of the physical world. In the *Eudemus* he had argued for the pre-existence of the soul, and in refuting the view that the soul was a harmony, he was clearly enough defending the full Platonic doctrine of the soul, even including the doctrine of recollection of knowledge acquired by the soul before birth, and maintaining that the life of the soul in the body is "contrary to nature." In the *Protrepticus,* while the importance of the soul and its superiority to the body are emphatically proclaimed, we have not enough information to say whether there is any change from the view expressed in the *Eudemus.* But in Fragment 60 (*Aristotelis Fragmenta,* Valentin Rose, ed.) the implication that the soul is fitted "part to part" throughout the body clearly involves a view of the soul as a separate substance. In the dialogue

On Philosophy, while apparently disagreeing with Plato on some points, Aristotle puts forward a series of Platonic-type views of the soul, including the attribution of divinity to mind (Fr. 26, Rose).

For Aristotle, the study of soul and of life

is a part of the study of the physical world.

The two-substance view of soul and body is found both in the biological treatises and throughout the *Parva Naturalia,* where the soul is frequently given a physical basis in heat and located or at least concentrated in a central governing place in the body, the heart. This has been called the second stage in the history of Aristotle's view of the soul. If we were dealing with human beings, this conclusion could be accepted with confidence. But since the reference is to animals and plants, we cannot be certain that Aristotle had abandoned his earlier view of the human soul at this stage, and at least one passage suggests that he had not (*On the Generation of Animals* 736b28). In the treatise *On the Soul,* however, we do find a sharply contrasting doctrine, according to which the soul and body constitute a single substance, standing to each other in the relation of form to matter. While it is true that in the *Eudemus* at one point the soul is rather vaguely referred to as a sort of form (Fr. 46, Rose), it is also in the same passage described as "receiving the Forms," implying that it is itself a separate substance. Apart from this there do not seem to be any anticipations of the doctrine presented in *On the Soul.*

ACTIVE AND PASSIVE REASON. The analysis of the functions of the soul in *On the Soul* is elaborate and detailed. After the usual survey of earlier theories, the soul is defined in technical language and its functions treated one by one. In the third and final book we come to the doctrine of Intelligence (*Nous*). The main functions of the soul have earlier been distinguished as the nutritive, the perceptive, the power of initiating movement, and the intelligence. They form a hierarchy, with the intelligence found only in man, so that living creatures can be arranged in a series according to the number of faculties possessed. Thinking is treated by Aristotle as analogous to perceiving. The mind is related to intelligible objects in the same way that sense is related to sensible objects. It is thus impassive and is itself nothing but potentiality (namely, the potentiality of receiving forms), and it has no form of its own.

Generally Aristotle speaks of *Nous* as one, but in the famous fifth chapter of Book III of *On the Soul* he distinguishes two, of which one *Nous* becomes all things like matter and the other makes all things, just as light makes potential colors actual. This latter *Nous* is separable, impassive, and unmixed, and only when it is separated does it have its true nature, immortal and eternal. What Aristotle means by this doctrine of an active and a passive reason is not explained elsewhere and has given rise to a famous controversy lasting over the centuries. Some suppose that we have really only one intellect functioning in two ways. One tradition interprets the active reason as a transcendent entity, identical with the prime mover and in effect God himself, thinking in us. This view began with Alexander of Aphrodisias in the second century A.D. and was developed further by Averroës, who regarded the active reason as a unique separate substance, inferior, however, to God. But Aristotle says that the distinction arises "within the soul," and Themistius cited these words against Alexander in the fourth century A.D. when arguing for a wholly immanent view of the active reason (in this he was followed by Thomas Aquinas).

It could be that we have here a vestige of an earlier Platonic view of the soul (see *Protrepticus* Fr. 61, Rose), but the doctrine seems to arise out of the discussion in earlier chapters in Book III of *On the Soul,* and, obscure though it is, it probably belongs to the latest stage of Aristotle's thought, when he was concerned with the consequences of analyzing the soul–body relationship in terms of form and matter. The question of a divine element in the human soul was possibly related in Aristotle's mind to the doctrine of God as actuality (which will be discussed under the heading "Theology"). His theory of knowledge likewise belongs as much to metaphysics as to psychology. (Another important aspect of Aristotle's psychology, his account of movement and desire, will be discussed under the heading "Ethics.")

Metaphysics

The title *Metaphysics* is of uncertain origin, but it seems clearly to have arisen only after Aristotle's death. The traditional explanation supposes that it refers to the order of the treatises in the Aristotelian corpus as organized by Andronicus of Rhodes, in which the *Metaphysics* comes after the Physics (*meta ta physika*). But there is some evidence that the title may be earlier than Andronicus. However, if its origin was a matter of chance, the meaning of the term was not interpreted as a matter of chance by the Greek commentators. Simplicius, speaking in a Platonizing vein, interpreted *meta* as meaning "beyond" and supposed that the reference was to a hierarchic order in the objects studied—metaphysics was concerned with objects which were beyond or outside the world of nature. The majority supposed that *meta* meant "after" and referred to an order of suc-

cession in knowledge, according to which metaphysical knowledge comes *after* physical knowledge. Aristotle himself uses the term "first philosophy," which he says deals with things that exist separately and are not subject to change or movement (*Metaphysics* 1026a16). Whether for Aristotle first philosophy covered the whole subject matter of the *Metaphysics* or only a part of it depends mainly on what view we take of the ultimate subject of study in the treatise.

The search for substance is for Aristotle

the search for what is,

as distinct from what "is something,"

since if a thing does not exist,

it cannot be anything.

The starting point for Aristotle's thought here, as so often, was his reaction to Plato's two-world doctrine, and in particular to the doctrine of the Forms. On Jaeger's view, Aristotle began by accepting the essentials of Plato's doctrine of the Forms, which Jaeger found clearly implied by *Eudemus* (Fr. 41, Rose). At this stage of Aristotle's thought, metaphysics, it is claimed, was identical with theology. The concept of metaphysics as the science of being-as-such belonged to the second stage, and in the third stage metaphysics either comprised or at least was based on the subject matter of physics. Jaeger's interpretation of the *Eudemus* fragment has since been denied by some, but probably without good reason. A similar controversy, which is currently unresolved, concerns the *Protrepticus* (Fr. 13, Walzer and Ross), which uses highly Platonic language to describe the objects of the theoretical knowledge that is the concern of the true philosopher. There is clearly a reference to the Forms as distinct from phenomena, and while it may be conceded that the fragment does not *say* that the Forms have separate transcendent existence, it does not say they have not; and the conclusion that it is the transcendent Forms to which Aristotle is referring seems the more natural one.

Whether or not Aristotle accepted transcendent Forms in the *Eudemus* and *Protrepticus*, it is clear that he had come to reject them in *On the Ideas*. There (Fr. 187, Rose) he took the view that, while there must be things other than sensible particulars and that these are universals, it does not follow that universals are Ideas or Forms in the Platonic sense; and he brought against the Ideas a number of the objections later elaborated in the *Metaphysics*. In *On Philosophy,* which Jaeger placed in the period after Aristotle left Athens for Assos, we have an attack on the Platonic doctrine of ideal numbers (Fr. 9, Rose). Proclus and Plutarch, apparently independently (Fr. 8, Rose), state that Aristotle rejected the doctrine of Ideas completely in the dialogues as well as elsewhere. But there is no evidence that these statements refer to the *On Philosophy,* so that they cannot be used to argue that that dialogue represents a later stage in Aristotle's thought than, say, *On the Ideas* or any other dialogue. All that we know is that in some of the dialogues Aristotle did criticize the theory of Forms, but this could very well be in the period before he left Athens, when, for all we know, *On Philosophy* itself was composed.

WHAT IS SUBSTANCE? The key to Aristotle's considered rejection of the Platonic Forms lies in his doctrine of substance, which was always for him the basic question in philosophy, as he himself says in the famous sentence in the *Metaphysics* (Z, 1028b2): "The question that was asked long ago, is asked now, and always is a matter of difficulty, 'What is being?' is the question 'What is substance?' " Rightly or wrongly Aristotle interpreted the Platonic Forms as universals and asked from the *Categories* onward how universals stand in relation to substance. He began by distinguishing between primary substance and secondary substance. Primary substance is always the individual concrete thing, and as such it is the subject of attributes in all the categories. The genera and species to which the individual thing belongs are secondary to it and would not exist without some primary substance to which they may apply (*Categories* 2b5). But every genus and species can be the subject of the same attributes as the primary substance of which they are genus and species (apart, of course, from that of coming under the genus and species which they themselves are). Accordingly genus and species, as subjects, can still claim to be substances. In this way the Platonic Forms, as species and genera, retain a kind of secondary existence.

The search for substance is for Aristotle the search for what *is,* as distinct from what "is something," since if a thing does not exist, it cannot be anything. In the *Categories* the Form as genus can still "be something," and so it retains its claim to substance. But Aristotle had already had the basic intuition which was to destroy Platonic transcendence—the substance of the genus or species is not a different substance from the substance of all or any members of the genus or species. In the statement "Socrates is a man," the substantiality of "man" *is* the substantiality of Socrates and not an independent substantiality. So while "man" stands for an entity, this entity *is* the subject of which it is predicated

and not some other entity. In *Metaphysics* Z the priority of substance among the categories rests on three grounds. (1) It can exist alone, while what is signified by the other categories cannot. Of course a substance will have qualities, but it does not depend on them for its existence, while they do depend on it. (2) Substance is prior in definition, since a definition of the substance of a thing must be present in any definition. (3) Substance is prior for knowledge, since we need to know *what* a thing is before we know its quantity, quality, and so on.

There are four objects to which the term "substance" is applied: the essence, the universal, the genus, and the substrate. But substrate in the sense of matter, which in itself is not a particular thing, cannot be substance because both separability and "thisness" are lacking. The same objections are sufficient to show that the universal cannot be a substance, although the opportunity is taken to bring a whole range of other objections against the Platonic Forms; and the objections to the universal as substance apply also to the genus. However, substrate in the sense of subject to which predicates attach may properly be called substance. But we want further information as to what such subjects are. Essence is the traditional rendering of Aristotle's curious coinage of which even the syntax is not altogether clear, but which perhaps should be literally rendered "the what it was to be (something)." (For a discussion of other views, see Joseph Owens, *The Doctrine of Being in the Aristotelian Metaphysics,* 2d ed., pp. 353–354.) But the meaning is clear enough in general—the essence is what a thing is by its very nature, what gives it its identity and makes it what it is. Consequently we may say that the essence of a thing is the thing in its truest sense, and so the essence can be identified with substance.

ESSENCE. A fuller account is needed of the essence of a thing than identifying it with substance. In what does a thing's essence consist? Aristotle's answer is given in terms of the doctrine of causes, which was intended to answer the questions of how and why a thing comes to be what it is. Normally the essence of a thing will be its final cause, which in turn will tend to be the same as its formal cause. We may say, then, that essence consists in form. But here an important distinction must be made. The essence of a thing consists in the form which it has achieved, not in any form which it does not have but might acquire. Achieved form is form actually realized in a concrete thing, and Aristotle uses two virtually interchangeable technical terms for it, "entelechy" and "actuality." (Strictly speaking, "actuality" refers primarily to the process which reaches its termination in the "entelechy.") These are opposed to potentiality. Form without matter exists potentially but not actually, and matter without form would also exist only potentially. Thus the concrete individual object is the essence, which is substance for Aristotle.

THE NATURE OF METAPHYSICS. The discussion of potentiality and actuality provides a bridge to Aristotle's theology. But it also uncovers a major problem as to the nature of metaphysics as Aristotle saw it. Side by side in the *Metaphysics* there appear to be two conceptions. On one view, there is a separate subject of study, the study of being-as-such, distinct from the study of particular kinds of being which form the subject matter of separate sciences. On the other view, the subject matter of metaphysics is separate but unchanging being, in other words, transcendent supersensible being of which God is the outstanding case. The former view is the antecedent of the scholastic general metaphysics, and the latter, which Aristotle tended to call first philosophy or theology, is the later special metaphysics. According to Jaeger, Aristotle's progression was from metaphysics as theology to metaphysics as the science of being-as-such. But Aristotle's fullest discussion of theology comes in *Metaphysics* Λ, which is probably one of the latest parts of the treatise as a whole. The transition to theology begins in the discussion of potentiality and actuality in Book Θ, and the doctrine of actuality, which seems to be a later addition in the *Physics*, looks very like the latest formulation of Aristotle's thinking on the problem of being-as-such. So it could be that Jaeger's order of progression should be inverted—in this case, Aristotle would proceed from being-as-such to theology. A unitarian interpretation of the *Metaphysics* would argue that such a progression is indeed there but that it is a logical progression, a progression in argument, rather than a reflection of any chronological sequence in the stages of Aristotle's thought.

Theology

The relation of the divine world to the physical world was one of the main themes in the dialogue *On Philosophy*. It seems clear that Aristotle had already rejected much of Plato's cosmology as expressed in the *Timaeus*, above all the view (which he thought he found there) that the world had a beginning. But he deployed a whole series of arguments to establish the existence and importance of divine beings. The divinity of the heavenly bodies seems to have been accepted together with the souls in them, which were the sources of their movements. This does not, as has sometimes been claimed, exclude a transcendent mover as well; but there is no positive reference anywhere to such a mover, and Jaeger was not justified in claiming such a mover for this dialogue. The position concerning the unmoved mover is probably the same in the treatise *On the Heavens*, where

there are indeed positive references—but these are probably later additions. The general impression here also is that the outermost heaven is the primary source of movement and that it initiates movement by moving itself.

The highest of the virtues is theoretical wisdom, and this is an activity of which man is capable because of something divine in his nature.

THE UNMOVED MOVER. By the time he wrote the last two books of the *Physics*, Aristotle had come to believe in the necessity of an unmoved mover, and the doctrine is developed fully in the *Metaphysics*. In Book Θ, Chapter 8 he develops the contrast between actuality and potentiality. The potential is actualized only by some actually existing thing acting as cause. Consequently the prime mover must exist actually because it actualizes potential movements throughout the universe, and this is supported by additional arguments. In Book Λ we have a separate treatise on theology which begins with a fresh rehearsal of the doctrines of substance, form, privation, matter, actuality, and potentiality. It is then argued that change must be eternal because the nature of time excludes the possibility of time without change, whether in the past or the future. If change is eternal, then the actuality which causes it must be eternal. Therefore the prime mover must be eternal; and if it is eternal, it must be immaterial, since matter involves potentiality of change and consequently militates against eternal existence. The prime mover, then, as actuality must be pure actuality without matter—a concept of actuality which it is difficult indeed to bring into accord with Aristotle's doctrine of actuality as matter + form. Being immaterial, the prime mover is not extended in space. It moves other objects as the object of their desire and their thought. This is the source of the principle of movement *within* nature which continues to lie at the root of Aristotle's conception of physics. As object of desire it is good, and as actuality it must be substantial because it moves substances. Its freedom from change is explained by identifying it with thought, an identification made the easier for Aristotle because of his normal equation of form without matter and thought. The prime mover turns out to be eternal and thus divine thought or mind, and Aristotle now no longer hesitates to call it God.

But what is this divine thought about? In his famous sentence (*Metaphysics* 1072b19) Aristotle says, "Thought thinks itself as object in virtue of its participation in what is thought." The plain meaning of this is that God is the object of his own thinking. A long tradition going back to Alexander of Aphrodisias and given further currency by Aquinas, maintains that in thinking himself as object, God thinks all the things that are in the world. But this cannot have been Aristotle's meaning. Knowledge of the visible world would involve knowledge of material and so of changeable being, and since the quality of thought depends, for Aristotle as for Plato, on the nature of its objects, to think changeable objects would make the thought itself subject to change, and so God would no longer be immutable. The objects of God's thought must be limited to what is unchangeable and so to himself. This does not mean, however, that Aristotle has produced thought with no object of thought. We should, rather, suppose that God *is* those truths which are free from change and that it is these which he thinks.

This is the theology which there is good reason to suppose represents the latest stage of Aristotle's thinking. While completely un-Platonic in its details, it can not unfairly be characterized as a fresh affirmation of the basic Platonic position that the world of the senses is a derivative world dependent for its continued activity upon a reality outside itself. Metaphysical inquiry understood in this way was clearly something which Aristotle never abandoned. On the other hand, his doctrine of the substantiality of the concrete individual remained with him also, and this marks a decisive break with Platonism.

Ethics and Politics

Of the three major ethical treatises in the Aristotelian corpus—the *Nicomachean Ethics,* the *Eudemian Ethics,* and the *Magna Moralia*—only the first was generally accepted as genuine in the pre-Jaeger period of Aristotelian studies, the *Eudemian Ethics* being attributed to Aristotle's pupil Eudemus of Rhodes and the *Magna Moralia* regarded as a later Peripatetic compilation. Since Jaeger, the *Eudemian Ethics* is usually accepted as also genuine and as representing an earlier stage in Aristotle's ethical thinking. A minority of scholars would regard the *Magna Moralia* as a still earlier work by Aristotle, but most would still regard it as a later Peripatetic compilation based on the *Eudemian Ethics* rather than on the *Nicomachean Ethics.* The relationship between the two works is complicated by the apparent absence of three books in the manuscripts of the *Eudemian Ethics* and the statement made at the end of Book III that the three missing books are identical with Books V, VI, and VII of the *Nicomachean Ethics.* The older view that these three books should be transferred to the *Eudemian Ethics* is now better abandoned in favor

of the view that they represent the latest stage in Aristotle's thinking about the topics dealt with and so are correctly placed in the *Nicomachean Ethics,* the original books of the *Eudemian Ethics* being replaced by them.

The earliest Aristotelian treatment of ethical themes of which we have any knowledge is the *Protrepticus.* There philosophy in a highly Platonic sense is the key to the grasping of the norms of right conduct. No distinction is made between practical and theoretical wisdom, both being called *phronesis,* and ethics is treated as an exact science. *Eudemian Ethics* I, 6 admits an empirical part of ethics but still does not divide *phronesis.* In *Nicomachean Ethics* VI, however, *phronesis* as practical wisdom is contrasted with *sophia* (theoretical wisdom), and both are necessary for achieving "intellectual virtue." All this is most simply explained by the hypothesis that we are witnessing a progressive development of Aristotle's ideas and that the culmination (in the *Nicomachean Ethics*) of this development is the product of his attempt to apply his later metaphysical and psychological doctrines in the sphere of ethics.

It is difficult for a modern philosopher not to either misconstrue or wholly condemn Aristotle's ethical thought. This is because Aristotle begins by implicitly rejecting the basic modern contention that value judgments either are not judgments of fact at all or, if they are, are judgments of a kind of fact altogether different from the facts involved in judgments about the physical world. The good for Aristotle is whatever is in fact aimed at. So the good for man is what man by nature *is* seeking. His seeking is not identical with what he wishes, since his seeking is rooted in his nature in a way in which his wishing need not be. What man is seeking may be given the formal name *eudaimonia,* which we misleadingly translate as "happiness," but if we have to be more explicit as to what *eudaimonia* involves, we will say that the good for man is the fulfillment of his function. This, in terms of Aristotle's metaphysical thought, is expressed as "the actuality of a soul with respect to its function" (1098a16). The soul has a rational part and a nonrational part. The rational part has one aspect which is completely rational and another which is also an aspect of the irrational part, namely, the seat of the appetites and of desire. Insofar as desires conform to reason, the part is rational, and insofar as they do not, it is irrational. The rational control of desires is the province of what Aristotle calls moral virtue. This is confined to cases where a choice is possible. Moral virtue is promoted by regular practice, which induces habits; and it involves following a mean course between extremes, which are vices—as courage is a mean between rashness and cowardice. But action is not virtuous because it follows a mean course—it is virtuous because it is in conformity with reason, and as a result it will in fact involve a mean.

The wholly rational part of the soul is the province of "intellectual virtue," and it is itself twofold inasmuch as one part of it is concerned with the contemplation of unchangeable truths and the other with truths and objects which are subject to change. The virtue of the first part is *sophia,* or theoretical wisdom, and that of the second is *phronesis,* or practical wisdom. It is *phronesis* which discovers what is right in action and so makes it possible for desires to conform to reason by discovering ends and then relating means to ends. But the ultimate end for man, which is living well (*eudaimonia*), is not a matter of deliberation or choice—it is, rather, something given in the nature of man. This is something which could vary, although it is clear that Aristotle does not suppose that in fact it does vary. The highest of the virtues is, however, theoretical wisdom, and this is an activity of which man is capable because of something divine in his nature—in its exercise he approximates to the life of God; and for man, as for God, his highest function is thought. This thought will be about objects which cannot be other than what they are and so never change.

For Aristotle, politics is a branch of practical knowledge, being that part of ethics which deals with men in groups. Some groups have limited purposes, but a polis, or "political" group, is one whose ends are coterminous with the ends of human life. Man is a "political animal," by which Aristotle means that it is his nature to form groups of this kind. These principles are established at the beginning of the *Politics.* Critical and descriptive surveys of various types of constitutions occupy most of Books II–VI, and in Books VII–VIII Aristotle discusses the best form of the polis without actually saying what it is, although earlier he had expressed his approval of rule by the best men, whether a group or an individual. It is possible that the treatise as we have it is unfinished. Attempts to rearrange the books in a more "logical" order must fail, for the present order is that laid down at the end of the *Nicomachean Ethics.* Nor is it plausible any longer to distinguish an empirical trend as representing a later stage in Aristotle's thought than the search for the ideal or best constitution. On this question, as elsewhere, the search for the ideal Form is for Aristotle a search for actuality, and this involves consideration of concrete individual cases.

BIBLIOGRAPHY

The complete works of Aristotle in Greek may be found in *Aristotelis Opera,* I. Bekker and others, eds., 5 vols. (Berlin, 1831–1870); there is a new edition of Vols. I, II, IV, and V, edited by Otto Gigon (Berlin, 1960–1961). The fragments may be found in *Aristotelis Fragmenta,* Valentin Rose, ed. (Leipzig, 1886); *Aristotelis Dialogorum Fragmenta,* R. Walzer, ed. (Florence, 1934); and *Aristotelis Fragmenta Selecta,* W. D. Ross, ed. (Oxford, 1955). There are improved Greek texts for most of the treatises by various editors in the Teubner Series (Leipzig, 1868–1961) and the Oxford Classical Texts (Oxford, 1894–1965); with French translations in the Budé Series (Paris, 1926–1964); and with English translations in the Loeb Series (London, 1926–1965).

The complete works of Aristotle in English may be found in *The Works of Aristotle Translated Into English,* W. D. Ross, ed., 12 vols. (Oxford, 1908–1952).

Medieval Latin translations are *Aristoteles Latinus* (Bruges, 1939—), which is to be in some 34 vols., and *Opera cum Averrois Commentariis,* 12 vols. in 14 (Venice, 1562–1574; reprinted Frankfurt, 1961).

Works of the Greek commentators may be found in *Commentaria in Aristotelem Graeca,* together with *Supplementum Aristotelicum,* 26 vols. (Berlin, 1882–1909).

Major modern editions and commentaries on individual works include the following: *Prior and Posterior Analytics,* W. D. Ross, ed. (Oxford, 1949); *Aristotle's Categories and De Interpretatione Translated With Notes,* translated by J. L. Ackrill (Oxford, 1963); *De Anima,* W. D. Ross, ed. (Oxford, 1961); *De Generatione et Corruptione,* H. H. Joachim, ed. (Oxford, 1922); *L'Éthique à Nicomaque,* R. A. Gauthier and J. Y. Jolif, eds., 3 vols. (Louvain, 1958); *Metaphysics,* W. D. Ross, ed., 2 vols. (Oxford, 1924); *Parva Naturalia,* W. D. Ross, ed. (Oxford, 1955); *Physics,* W. D. Ross, ed. (Oxford, 1936); G. F. Else, *Aristotle's Poetics, the Argument* (Cambridge, Mass., 1957); *Politics,* W. L. Newman, ed., 4 vols. (Oxford, 1887–1902); *Politics,* translated by Ernest Barker (Oxford, 1946); and Ingmar Düring, *Protrepticus, an Attempt at Reconstruction* (Göteborg, Sweden, 1961).

Works on Aristotle's life and writings include Ingmar Düring, *Aristotle in the Ancient Biographical Tradition* (Göteborg, Sweden, 1957), and P. Moraux, *Les Listes anciennes des ouvrages d'Aristote* (Louvain, 1951).

General accounts, including the question of development, are Werner Jaeger, *Aristoteles, Grundlegung einer Geschichte seiner Entwicklung* (Berlin, 1923), translated by Richard Robinson as *Aristotle, Fundamentals of the History of His Development* (Oxford, 1934; 2d ed., 1948); W. D. Ross, *Aristotle* (London, 1923; 6th ed., 1955); P. Wilpert, *Zwei Aristotelische Frühschriften über die Ideenlehre* (Regensburg, 1949); D. J. Allan, *The Philosophy of Aristotle* (London, 1952); J. Moreau, *Aristote et son école* (Paris, 1962); Harold Cherniss, *Aristotle's Criticism of Plato and the Academy* (Baltimore, 1944); and G. E. M. Anscombe, "Aristotle," which is Ch. 1 in G. E. M. Anscombe and P. T. Geach, *Three Philosophers* (Ithaca, N.Y., 1961).

Works on Aristotle's logic are Friedrich Solmsen, *Die Entwicklung der Aristotelischen Logik und Rhetorik* (Berlin, 1929); E. Kapp, *Greek Foundations for Traditional Logic* (New York, 1942); Jan Łukasiewicz, *Aristotle's Syllogistic From the Standpoint of Modern Formal Logic* (Oxford, 1951; 2d ed., 1957); S. McCall, *Aristotle's Modal Syllogisms* (Amsterdam, 1963); G. Patzig, *Die Aristotelische Syllogistik,* 2d ed. (Göttingen, 1963); and J. M. Le Blond, *Logique et méthode chez Aristote* (Paris, 1939).

Aristotle's physics is discussed in A. Mansion, *Introduction à la physique aristotelicienne* (Paris, 1913; 2d ed., Louvain, 1946); Friedrich Solmsen, *Aristotle's System of the Physical World* (Ithaca, N.Y., 1960); and W. Wieland, *Die Aristotelische Physik* (Göttingen, 1962).

For discussions of Aristotle's psychology, see F. Nuyens, *Ontwikkelingsmomenten in de Zielkunde van Aristoteles* (Nijmegen, the Netherlands, 1939), translated by Theo Schillings and others as *L'Évolution de la psychologie d'Aristote* (Louvain, 1948).

For Aristotle's metaphysics, see Joseph Owens, *The Doctrine of Being in the Aristotelian Metaphysics* (Toronto, 1951; 2d ed., 1957), and P. Aubenque, *Le Problème de l'être chez Aristote* (Paris, 1962).

Aristotle's theology is discussed in H. von Arnim, *Die Entstehung der Gotteslehre des Aristoteles* (Vienna, 1931), and W. K. C. Guthrie, "Development of Aristotle's Theology," in *Classical Quarterly*, Vol. 27 (1933), 162–171.

Discussions of Aristotle's ethics may be found in H. von Arnim, *Die drei Aristotelischen Ethiken* (Vienna, 1924); R. Walzer, *Magna Moralia und Aristotelische Ethik* (Vienna, 1929); and J. Léonard, *Le Bonheur chez Aristote* (Brussels, 1948).

Aristotle's mathematics is discussed in T. L. Heath, *Mathematics in Aristotle* (Oxford, 1949).

For Aristotle as a biologist, see M. Manquat, *Aristote naturaliste* (Paris, 1932), and D'Arcy W. Thompson, "Aristotle the Naturalist," in R. W. Livingstone, ed., *The Legacy of Greece* (Oxford, 1922), reprinted in Thompson's *Science and the Classics* (Oxford, 1940).

An invaluable index of Greek words is provided by Hermann Bonitz, *Index Aristotelicus*, which was originally in Vol. V of I. Bekker's edition of *Aristotelis Opera* (Berlin, 1870) and was reprinted separately (Graz, 1955). Of more limited range is Troy Wilson Organ, *An Index to Aristotle in English Translation* (Princeton, N.J., 1949), which is based on the first 11 volumes of W. D. Ross, ed., *The Works of Aristotle Translated Into English*.

– G. B. KERFERD

ARISTOTLE (UPDATE)

Kerferd's 1967 *Encyclopedia* article considers Aristotle in the context of Werner Jaeger's proposal that Aristotle developed gradually from a committed Platonist to an empirically minded anti-Platonist, and that the chronology of his works (and indeed of passages within individual works) may be determined according to the degree of Platonism and empiricism displayed therein. Philosophical discussion of Aristotle is no longer dominated by Jaeger's developmental hypothesis. While questions of chronology and development continue to interest Aristotelian scholars, the dominant goal of post-Jaegerian studies of Aristotle is to elucidate, examine, and criticize the philosophical problems and arguments that Aristotle poses and addresses. The present brief update cannot summarize fully the wide range of questions at issue in Aristotelian studies, but some especially important and interesting areas of consensus and disagreement are described below. For a fuller guide to the issues, the extensive annotated and analytical bibliography in the *Cambridge Companion to Aristotle* (Barnes, 1995) is a valuable resource.

Philosophical Method

Aristotle's *Posterior Analytics* describes scientific knowledge (episteme) as a hierarchical axiomatized system whose characteristic method is demonstration: syllogistic proof from the first principles of a science of all its derivative truths. It is generally recognized that in Aristotle's own scientific and philosophical treatises he employs not this method but one he describes as inductive or dialectical. Aristotle describes his dialectical method as involving three stages: (1) The inquirer begins by collecting the "appearance" (*phainomena*)—a category that includes not only empirical observations but also widely accepted views and the theories of reputable authorities. (2) Next, one generates puzzles (*aporiai*) from the "appearances"—pointing to difficulties and contradictions that result from combining these initially plausible views. (3) In the final, constructive stage of dialectical argument, one resolves the puzzles by revising the "appearances" that give rise to them—maintaining some, rejecting or revising others—with a view to retaining most of the initial appearances, and especially the most important ones (cf. *Nicomachean Ethics* VII, 1145b2–7). It is disputed whether Aristotle thinks the sort of knowledge yielded by dialectical inquiry can be objective, given its tie to "appearances" (M. Nussbaum has argued for the negative answer, T. H. Irwin and others for the affirmative). Such disagreement notwithstanding, it is generally agreed that Aristotle's written works typically do employ, if not always explicitly, the dialectical strategy he describes. One must therefore read Aristotle carefully and consider whether a given passage articulates (1) an appearance he is enumerating but not necessarily endorsing, (2) a puzzle that will dissolve once the appearances have been suitably revised, or (3) an appearance that he is endorsing after resolving the puzzles.

Natural Philosophy

The philosophical innovation of which Aristotle was arguably most proud is his view that there are four different types of cause or explanation. These are generally referred to by scholars as the material, formal, efficient, and final (or teleological) causes. In the case of natural things, Aristotle argues, the formal, final, and efficient causes coincide, so the most basic causal distinction in these cases is between matter and form. Aristotle's use of this distinction to analyze natural and psychological phenomena is sometimes referred to as his *hylomorphism* (from *hyle*, 'matter', and *morphe*, 'form'). The ontological implications of his hylomorphism have been much disputed. Aristotle typically illustrates the distinction between matter and form by citing artifacts. In these examples, the distinction is easy to grasp. The matter of a wall is bricks and mortar, while the form is the shape or arrangement that makes the bricks and mortar into a wall. Artificial examples also make it easy to agree that the form is not an extra element, analogous to the bricks and mortar, that needs to be added to the matter in order to make a wall. Rather, form appears to relate to matter as its shape, arrangement, or proportion. Hylomorphism as applied to natural things is, however, more complicated. Aristotle thinks natural things are significantly different from artifacts in that they have an internal source of growth, development, and activity. He identifies this internal source with form rather than matter. Given the coincidence of formal and final causation in natural things, Aristotle articulates his preference for formal over material explanation via his thesis of natural teleology: natural processes are to be explained with reference to the final rather than the material cause. Some commentators (including J. Cooper, A. Gotthelf, and S. Waterlow) have concluded that the forms of natural things, for Aristotle, involve more than simple arrangements, or proportions, or the like, of the material constituents; forms must be *sui generis* elements whose presence, in addition to matter and its arrangements, is necessary for natural activity to occur. Other scholars (including D. Charles, S. Meyer, and M. Nussbaum) have resisted this conclusion, proposing that Aristotle finds not that the material elements are incapable of constituting natural entities or of causing their natural activities, but rather that the simple invocation of matter, without mention of form or function, does not explain natural processes. On the latter interpretation, the ontological status of form is analogous in the artificial and the natural cases.

Psychology

The interpretation of Aristotle's hylomorphism becomes increasingly difficult and disputed in its application to psychology. Aristotle's *De Anima* gives an account of the soul (*psyche*) or principle of life. While the body of a living thing is its material cause, the soul of a living thing is its formal, final, and efficient cause. The life activities of which the soul is the principle include some that Aristotle also classifies as natural (nutrition and growth), but his list also includes activities (sensation, desire, and thought) that modern philosophers would classify as mental, and to which the application of the hylomorphic model is not straightforward. To David Wiggins, Aristotle's hylomorphism yields a promising account of personal identity over time. Others (e.g., R. Sorabji) have understood it as an alternative both to dualism and to the cruder aspects of some versions of materialism about the mental. Aristotle has been hailed by some (M. Nussbaum, and H. Putnam) as a nonreductive materialist or even a protofunctionalist. Dissenters typically argue that Aristotle's conception of matter (that is, the material cause) has little in common with the post-Cartesian conception assumed by modern forms of materialism (M. F. Burnyeat, W. F. R. Hardie, and H. Robinson).

Metaphysics

The central books of the *Metaphysics* (Zeta, Eta, and Theta) have received much attention. Here Aristotle considers whether sensible individuals, such as particular people or animals, are substances—a question he answers in the affirmative in the *Categories*. The question arises because the hylomorphic analysis of natural substances (which is absent from the *Categories*), together with the *Categories'* criterion that substance is what underlies other things, invites the challenge that not Callias's form but his matter is substance, and so (since Callias is identified with his form rather than with his matter) Callias is not a substance. In Zeta 3 Aristotle addresses this issue by asking whether Callias's form, or his matter, or the compound of the two, is substance. The ensuing discussion ranks among the most intractably difficult of his writings. There is no scholarly consensus about the extent to which Aristotle allows that matter and the compound may be substance, or about whether he retains the criterion that substance is what underlies. While there is agreement that Aristotle's main project in Zeta is to defend the substantial status of forms, it is disputed whether the forms to which he attributes substantial status are individuals (e.g., Callias) or universals (e.g., the species Man). (Proponents of the former view include M. Frede and T. H. Irwin; defenders of the latter include M. Furth and M. Loux.)

Ethics

Aristotle's moral psychology, particularly his conception of reason's role in morality, is generally recognized as an alternative both to Humean and to Kantian views. In contrast to the Kantian picture, Aristotle requires that the proper moral motivation involves having appropriate desires and emotions in addition to the correct judgment. In contrast with Hume, Aristotle allows that reason is not purely instrumental, but may (and should) be exercised to determine one's ultimate ends. Within this consensus, there are still many open questions about the role of reason. For example, it is disputed exactly how reason functions in the decision making (*prohairesis*) of the virtuous agent. One school of thought supposes that the virtuous person has a more or less explicit conception of happiness (*eudaimonia*) to which he or she appeals in making choices and decisions, and that this conception is reflected in the dispositions of desire and emotion that are his or her moral virtues. Others reject this supposition, pointing to Aristotle's remarks that ethical matters belie formulation in general rules, and to his emphasis on the role perception plays in the virtuous person's decision making. The issue comes to a head in the interpretation of Aristotle's account of *akrasia* (weakness of will). One of the most forceful proponents of the latter position (J. McDowell) goes so far as to claim that advocates of the former are thereby committed to a Humean interpretation of practical reason in Aristotle. Yet those sympathetic to the former position (e.g., J. Cooper and T. H. Irwin) typically reject a Humean account of Aristotle.

Another issue of continuing interest concerns Aristotle's apparent indecision (or inconsistency) on the question of whether happiness, properly understood, includes practical activity (this seems to be implied by the attention he devotes, in his ethical writing, to the moral virtues) or whether it involves only pure theoretical reason (this appears to be the import of his remarks on happiness in Book X of the *Nicomachean Ethics*). While the former interpretation has been dominant, the latter is defended anew by Richard Kraut (1989).

BIBLIOGRAPHY

Translations and Commentaries

The old 12-volume Oxford translation has been revised and improved in:
Barnes, J., ed. *The Complete Works of Aristotle: The Revised Oxford Translation*, 2 vols. Princeton, NJ, 1984.

Ancient commentaries:

The enormous extant body of ancient commentary on Aristotle, collected and published in Greek by the Berlin Academy (1882–1909), is being translated into English as the series *The Ancient Commentators on Aristotle,* whose general editor is Richard Sorabji. For a general account of the commentary tradition, see:
Sorabji, R. *Aristotle Transformed: The Ancient Commentators and Their Influence.* London and Ithaca, NY, 1990.

Modern commentaries:

The Clarendon Aristotle Series (1963–) offers generally excellent translations into English, with detailed philosophical notes for the Greekless reader, of many of Aristotle's texts.

Other modern translations and commentaries:

Frede, M., and G. Patzig. *Aristoteles Metaphysik Z.* Munich, 1988.
Furth, M. *Aristotle: Metaphysics Books VII-X.* Indianapolis, 1985.
Irwin, T. H. *Aristotle: Nicomachean Ethics.* Indianapolis, 1985.
Nussbaum, M. C. *Aristotle's De Motu Animalium.* Princeton, NJ, 1978. Includes general essays on Aristotle's teleology.

General books:

Introductory articles on many aspects of Aristotle's philosophy, together with an extensive annotated and analytical bibliography (covering both European and English-language works) are in
Barnes, J., ed. *The Cambridge Companion to Aristotle.* Cambridge, 1995.
A short general account of Aristotle's philosophy is
Ackrill, J. L. *Aristotle the Philosopher.* Oxford, 1981.

Collections of Papers

The proceedings of the triennial *Symposium Aristotelicum* (1957–present) provide excellent examples of post-Jaegerian Aristotelian scholarship by European, British, and North American scholars. The bibliography in Barnes (1995) lists the individual titles.

Other collections include:

Barnes, J., M. Schofield, and R. Sorabji, eds. *Articles on Aristotle,* 4 vols. London, 1975–79.
Frede, M. *Essays on Ancient Philosophy.* Minneapolis, 1987.
Gotthelf, A., and J. Lennox, eds. *Philosophical Issues in Aristotle's Biology,* Cambridge, 1987.
Judson, L., ed. *Aristotle's "Physics."* Oxford, 1991.
Keyt, D., and F. D. Miller, eds. *A Companion to Aristotle's Politics.* Oxford, 1991.
Nussbaum, M. C., and A. O. Rorty, eds. *Essays on Aristotle's de Anima.* Oxford, 1992.
Owen, C. E. L. *Logic, Science, and Dialectic,* edited by M. C. Nussbaum. Cambridge, 1986.
Rorty, A. O., ed. *Essays on Aristotle's Ethics.* Berkeley, 1980.
———, ed. *Essays on Aristotle's "Poetics."* Princeton, NJ, 1992.

Monographs

Broadie, S. *Ethics with Aristotle.* New York, 1991.
Charles D. *Aristotle's Philosophy of Action.* London and Ithaca, NY, 1984.
Cooper, J. M. *Reason and Human Good in Aristotle.* Cambridge, MA, 1975.
Fine, G. *On Ideas: Aristotle's Criticism of Plato's Theory of Forms.* Oxford, 1993.
Halliwell, S. *Aristotle's Poetics.* Chapel Hill, NC, 1986.
Hardie, W. F. R. *Aristotle's Ethical Theory,* 2nd ed. Oxford, 1980.
Hartman, E. *Substance, Body, and Soul.* Princeton, NJ, 1977.
Irwin, T. H. *Aristotle's First Principles.* Oxford, 1988.
Kraut, R. *Aristotle on the Human Good.* Princeton, NJ, 1989.
Loux, M. *Primary Ousia: An Essay on Aristotle's "Metaphysics" Z.* Ithaca, NY, 1991.
Pellegrin, P. *La Classification des animaux chez Aristote.* Paris, 1982. Revised edition translated into English by A. Preus as *Aristotle's Classification of Animals* (Berkeley, 1986).
Sorabji, R. *Necessity, Cause, and Blame: Perspectives on Aristotle's Theory.* London, 1980.
Waterlow, S. *Nature, Change, and Agency in Aristotle's "Physics."* Oxford, 1982.

– SUSAN SAUVÉ MEYER

ARMSTRONG, DAVID M.

David M. Armstrong was born in 1926 in Melbourne, Australia. He was a student of John Anderson's at the University of Sydney and was one of the first of many Australian philosophers to take the B.Phil. degree at Oxford (in 1954). He taught briefly at Birkbeck College, London, before returning to Australia to teach at the University of Melbourne. In 1964 he moved to Sydney, succeeding J. L. Mackie in Anderson's chair.

Armstrong has made influential contributions to a remarkable range of major topics in epistemology and metaphysics, including perception, materialism, bodily sensations, belief and knowledge, laws, universals, and possibility. Recurrent themes have been the need to reconcile what the philosopher says with the teachings of science and a preference for realist over instrumentalist theories.

Armstrong is best known for his *A Materialist Theory of the Mind*. He was originally a behaviorist but was converted to the mind–brain identity theory, the view that mental states are states of the brain, by another Australian philosopher, J. J. C. Smart. In this book he argues that mental states are defined by what they do, in particular by what they do by way of mediating between inputs, outputs, and other mental states. His view was thus an early version of functionalism. Therefore, for him, the question of the identity of a given mental state is simply the (empirical) question of what plays the causally intermediate role distinctive of that state. He observes that it will most likely turn out in each case to be some state or other of the brain that plays the distinctive role. Thus, Armstrong derives the identity theory from a view about what is definitive of a mental state combined with a view about what most likely satisfies the definition.

In the philosophy of perception he argued that we must move away from the tradition that seeks to understand perception as an acquaintance with a special, mental item sometimes called a sense datum and adopt an account that analyzes perception as the acquisition of belief—an account that has the signal advantage of making sense of the role of perception in our traffic with the world.

His treatment of belief follows a suggestion of F. P. Ramsey's that belief is like a map by which we steer. His account of knowledge is a version of reliabilism: *S*'s true belief that *p* is knowledge if it is an empirically reliable sign that *p*. His account of bodily sensations is in terms of the putative perception of goings on in the body and associated attitudes toward those goings on. To give the rough idea: pain is the putative perception of a bodily disturbance combined with a negative attitude toward that perception.

Armstrong is a realist about universals without being a Platonic realist: universals exist, they are not reducible to sets of particulars, they serve as the "truth makers" for predication, but there are no uninstantiated universals.

He draws on his realism about universals in his account of laws of nature and of possibility. He rejects any kind of regularity or neo-Humean account of laws in favor of one in terms of relations of nomic necessitation between universals: roughly, "Every *F* is *G*" is a fundamental law if being *F* necessitates being *G*. Armstrong's account of possibility is a combinatorial one. We can think of how things are as a huge arrangement of particulars and universals. The various possibilities can then be thought of as all the combinations and recombinations of these particulars and universals according to various rules for combining them.

[See also Functionalism; Mackie, John Leslie; Reliabilism; Smart, John Jamieson Carswell.]

BIBLIOGRAPHY

Armstrong, D. M. *Belief, Truth and Knowledge.* Cambridge, 1973.
———. *Berkeley's Theory of Vision.* Melbourne, 1960.
———. *Bodily Sensations.* London, 1962.
———. *A Combinatorial Theory of Possibility.* Cambridge, 1989.
Armstrong, D. M., with N. Malcolm. *Consciousness and Causality: A Debate on the Nature of Mind.* Oxford, 1984.
———. *A Materialist Theory of the Mind.* London, 1968.
———. *Perception and the Physical World.* London, 1961.
———. *Universals: An Opinionated Introduction.* Boulder, CO, 1989.
———. *Universals and Scientific Realism*, 2 vols. Cambridge, 1973.
———. *What Is a Law of Nature?* Cambridge, 1983.

– FRANK JACKSON

ART, DEFINITION OF

Traditionally, the definition of "art" has been the focal point of theorizing about art and has functioned as a kind of summary of a theory of art. Ideally, such a definition is supposed to specify the necessary and sufficient conditions for being a work of art. Traditionally, the conditions given are themselves supposed to be specifiable independently of the notion of art in order to avoid circularity.

What class of objects should be focused on

in trying to define art

in terms of necessary and sufficient conditions?

What class of objects should be focused on in trying to define art in terms of necessary and sufficient conditions? First, the class must include everything that is generally regarded as an artwork. Second, the class's members must be artifacts, because philosophers of art have always theorized about a subset of human artifacts; artifactuality is a built-in necessary feature. Finally, should all the members of the class be valuable? That is, should the definition be evaluational or simply classificatory? This is a controversial issue, but this article will be concerned with classificatory definitions.

In the mid-1950s Paul Ziff, Morris Weitz, and others claimed that defining art is impossible because art is a "family resemblance" concept, one that picks out a class the members of which share no common, essential feature. Instead, they claimed such a class's members merely have overlapping resemblances. They even claimed that a natural object (nonartifact) can be art if it resembles an established artwork. These antiessentialists were so persuasive that for about fifteen years philosophers lost interest in defining art.

The antiessentialists were finally challenged by Arthur Danto (1964) and Maurice Mandelbaum (1965). Danto, ignoring the antiessentialists, claimed that the art theory prevailing at a particular time makes art possible. Danto thus attempted to specify one necessary condition of art. Mandelbaum did not try to specify the conditions of art. He did argue that the antiessentialists focused only on easily noted characteristics and ignored the nonexhibited, relational properties of art that connect it to its producers and appreciators. Mandelbaum claimed that nonexhibited properties are more promising for defining. Danto's visually-indistinguishable-pairs argument (1964, 1973, 1974) also called attention to nonexhibited properties. This argument focuses on indiscernible pairs of objects, one of which is an artwork and one of which is not. One of Danto's examples of such a pair is *The Polish Rider,* which is an artwork, and an accidentally produced canvas and paint object that exactly resembles it, which is not an artwork. Another pair of indiscernibles is Duchamp's artwork *Fountain* and a urinal that looks just like it. *Fountain's* context of (nonexhibited) relations to its producer and appreciators in the artworld makes it art, and the urinal's lack of such a context prevents it from being art.

Once antiessentialism had been challenged, philosophers returned to the task of defining art. But whereas philosophers in the pre-antiessentialist period had used psychological notions such as the expression of emotion and aesthetic emotion, philosophers in the post-antiessentialist period have almost all tried to define art in terms of cultural notions.

Danto's idea of a prevailing art theory is a cultural concept quite unlike the earlier psychological notions. Nelson Goodman (1968) claimed that the arts are symbol systems and defined an artwork as a symbol that functions in an aesthetic way. A symbol system is a cultural notion involving the coordinated interaction of group members. Danto (1973, 1974) changed his view of the kind of cultural context that is necessary for art, claiming that being about something is necessary for being art. In Danto's later view the necessary cultural phenomenon is a linguistic one and resembles to a degree Goodman's notion of art as a symbol.

In 1969 George Dickie began developing a cultural-context theory called the institutional theory of art. His efforts culminated with this definition: "A work of art is an artifact of a kind created to be presented to an artworld public" (1984, p. 80). The definition's circularity is thought by many to be a difficulty, but Dickie has argued that it is a virtue because of the interconnectedness of the elements that make up the artworld and because these related elements are understood from early childhood.

Monroe Beardsley is one of the few post-antiessentialist theorists to attempt to define art in psychological terms, and he did so self-consciously in the face of the prevailing trend. Beardsley wrote, "an artwork can be usefully defined as an intentional arrangement of conditions for affording experiences with marked aesthetic character" (1979, p. 729). The main difficulty of this approach is that it cannot account for nonaesthetic art such as Dadaist works and the like.

As a final example of a cultural account of art, consider the following historical definition offered by Jerrold Levinson (1979, p. 234): "a work of art is a thing intended for regard-as-a-work-of-art: regard in any of the ways works of art existing prior to it have been correctly regarded." As Levinson noted in 1993, the primary problem for such a theory is accounting for the first artwork(s). Cultural theories of art continue to proliferate.

[See also Aesthetics, Problems of; Artworld; Goodman, Nelson; Indiscernibles; Smart, John Jamieson Carswell.]

BIBLIOGRAPHY

Beardsley, M. "In Defense of Aesthetic Value," *Proceedings and Addresses of the American Philosophical Association,* Vol. 52 (1979), 723–49.
———. "Redefining Art," in M. J. Wreen and D. M. Callan, eds. *The Aesthetic Point of View* (Ithaca, NY, 1982).
Binkley, T. "Deciding about Art," in L. Aagaard-Mogensen, ed., *Culture and Art* (Atlantic Highlands, NJ, 1976).
Carroll, N. "Historical Narratives and the Philosophy of Art," *Journal of Aesthetics and Art Criticism,* Vol. 51 (1993), 313–26.
Danto, A. "The Artworld," *Journal of Philosophy,* Vol. 61 (1964), 571–84.
———. "Artworks and Real Things," *Theoria,* Vol. 39 (1973), 1–17.
———. "The Transfiguration of the Commonplace," *Journal of Aesthetics and Art Criticism,* Vol. 33 (1974), 139–48.
———. *The Transfiguration of the Commonplace,* Cambridge, MA, 1981.
Davies, S. *Definitions of Art.* Ithaca, NY, 1991.
Dickie, G. "Defining Art," *American Philosophical Quarterly,* Vol. 6 (1969), 253–56.
———. *Art and the Aesthetic.* Ithaca, NY, 1974.
———. *The Art Circle.* New York, 1984.
Eaton, M. *Art and Nonart.* East Brunswick, NJ, 1983.
Krukowski, L. *Art and Concept.* Amherst, MA, 1987.
Levinson, J. "Defining Art Historically," *British Journal of Aesthetics,* Vol. 19 (1979), 232–50.
———. "Extending Art Historically," *Journal of Aesthetics and Art Criticism,* Vol. 51 (1993), 411–23.

Mandelbaum, M. "Family Resemblances and Generalization Concerning the Arts," *American Philosophical Quarterly*, Vol. 2 (1965), 219–28.

Margolis, J. "Works of Art as Physically Embodied and Culturally Emergent Entities," *British Journal of Aesthetics*, Vol. 14 (1974), 187–96.

Weitz, M. "The Role of Theory in Aesthetics," *Journal of Aesthetics and Art Criticism*, Vol. 15 (1956), 27–35.

Ziff, P. "The Task of Defining a Work of Art," *Philosophical Review*, Vol. 62 (1953), 58–78.

— GEORGE DICKIE

ART, END OF

"End of art" is a concept based on Hegel's claim that art, the first stage in the realization of Absolute Spirit, is now, because of the increasing self-consciousness to which art has itself contributed, a "thing of the past . . . [which] has lost for us genuine truth and life" (Hegel, [1835] 1975, p. 11). On this account art is superseded historically by religion and then philosophy—a progression anticipated in the "symbolic," "classical," and "romantic" stages of art history as the proportions there shift between the sensuous form and the "idea" comprising the individual work. In the last of these stages idea or content "triumphs over" form, and art then loses its efficacy to a more abstract medium. (The phrase "end of art" and its variant, "death of art," are both glosses on Hegel's own words.)

Attempts to reconcile the pronouncement of the end of art with art's apparent persistence have sometimes interpreted the "end" as a recurrent, not a one-time, event, thus as part of an alternating pattern of normalization and obsolescence. On either analysis, however, art is historically contingent and linked to other elements of the social and intellectual context; this contention, together with the related Hegelian claim that the individual stages of art history follow an internal logic, has, although with many variations, greatly influenced modern stylistics and the historiography of art.

The historicist premises of the end of art thesis underlie the recent postmodernist and institutional or "artworld" critiques of essentialist definitions of art, which view the phenomenon of art as humanly or culturally fixed and atemporal. The radical displacement of art is, however, only one possible outcome of art's contingent status; in any event the question of what medium would supersede art depends at least in part on the causal factors identified as bringing about the end.

[See also Aesthetics, History of; Aesthetics, Problems of; Art, Definition of; Artworld; Hegel, Georg W. F.]

BIBLIOGRAPHY

Danto, A. *The Disenfranchisement of Art*. New York, 1986.

Harris, H. S. "The Resurrection of Art," *Owl of Minerva*, Vol. 16 (1984), 5–20.

Hegel, G. W. F. *Aesthetics: Lectures on Fine Art* [1835], 2 vols. T. M. Knox, trans. Oxford, 1975.

Lang, B., ed. *The Death of Art*. New York, 1984.

— BEREL LANG

ART, EXPRESSION IN

The expressive power of art has long drawn the attention of aestheticians no less than it has beguiled artists and appreciators of art alike. In the late nineteenth and early twentieth centuries the so-called expression theory of art was, in one or another of its forms, widely endorsed (by Leo Tolstoy, Eugene Veron, Benedetto Croce, R. G. Collingwood, George Santayana, C. J. Ducasse, and John Dewey) and constituted one of the main tenets of romanticism in aesthetics. This theory defined art in terms of the expressive act of the artist, the embodying or objectifying of the artist's affect or thought in a communicable medium. Gradually, however, it became clear that the expressive properties of art objects are not necessarily the effects of the artist's experiencing the homonymous (i.e., same-named) psychological state: works expressing anguish need not be expressive of an anguished state of the artist. Consequently, philosophical interest largely turned from the creative or expressive act to the puzzles surrounding the idea that art objects are artifacts with expressive properties. The two most important areas of concern became the semantics of expressive predicates and the ontology of expressive properties.

Philosophical interest largely turned

from the creative or expressive act

to the puzzles surrounding the idea that

art objects are artifacts with expressive properties.

In the 1960s and 1970s a variety of philosophical techniques were applied to the semantics of artistic expression. For example, Guy Sircello (1972) employed ordinary-language philosophy and argued that artworks differ in important ways from natural signs and from nonexpressive symbols (expression involving a peculiar "showing" or "standing out" relation) and that their expressive import is not determined conventionally. Sircello claimed that anthropomorphic predicates apply to artworks in virtue of the specific "artistic acts" (such as portraying, presenting, inveighing, etc.) that the artist performs "in" the work.

In contrast, Nelson Goodman, in his influential *Languages of Art* (1968), treated artworks as symbols and defined expression in terms of the semantic relations of reference and denotation. A work expresses φ if and only if the work is a member of the metaphorical denotation of the predicate 'φ' and the work "refers back" to that predicate. Less nominalistically stated, expression is a form of property exemplification for Goodman. A work exemplifies a property if it not only possesses but "highlights" that property, much as a tailor's swatch highlights the texture and design of the material, because of the conventions surrounding its use. Expression is exemplification of properties that a work actually but metaphorically possesses.

Others have wanted to distinguish clearly between, for example, a work's being expressive of anguish and the work's possessing the property of anguish, even metaphorically. Alan Tormey (1971) has proposed that expressive properties are those properties of artworks whose names also designate intentional states of persons. He further suggests that a work's expressive properties are revealed through its perceivable nonexpressive properties, rather as a person's intentional states are revealed through behavior. This area has yet to produce much philosophical consensus, excepting only the conclusion that our language of artistic expression has complex and varied uses.

The ontological problem surrounding expressive properties is to clarify how such properties are related to the more mundane nonaesthetic features of artworks. Most philosophers hold that a work's expressive properties are dependent or supervenient upon, but are not reducible or identical to, its nonexpressive properties.

(Tormey offers a different thesis, viz., that expressive properties are wholly but ambiguously constituted by a work's nonexpressive properties.) The difficulty has been to clarify the nature of this dependency, especially in light of the rather widespread acceptance of an idea of Frank Sibley, that no set of nonexpressive features provides logically necessary and sufficient conditions for the possession of an expressive property. Some—for example, Monroe Beardsley—have suggested that the dependency relation is better construed as a causal and psychological fact about our reactions to artwork rather than a conceptual, quasilogical connection between aesthetic and nonaesthetic descriptions of artworks.

The 1980s and 1990s, in fact, brought renewed discussion of the nature of our reactions to expressive qualities of works of art. It was part of the romanticist theory of expression, or at least certain versions of it, that a work expressive of φ caused its audience to feel φ in the course of their aesthetic appreciation of the work. Peter Kivy, Goodman, and other "cognitivists" have denied that appreciating a work's expressive properties involves arousal of the homonymous emotion. For Kivy (1989) and the case of music such appreciation is a matter of cognitively grasping the way expressive features function "syntactically" in the musical structure. Although it seems clear that artworks expressive of sadness do not necessarily evoke sadness, it is equally obvious that they sometimes do arouse this emotion. The debate between the cognitivist and the emotivist may finally be resolving into the realization that philosophers of art can profitably examine the emotional impact as

The expressive power of art is evident in Picasso's Guernica. *(Corbis/Bettmann)*

well as the cognitive and symbolic functions of the expressive properties of art.

[See also Aesthetics, History of; Aesthetics, Problems of; Dewey, John; Goodman, Nelson.]

BIBLIOGRAPHY

Beardsley, M. "The Descriptivist Account of Aesthetic Attributions," *Revue internationale de philosophie,* Vol. 28 (1974), 336–52.
Goodman, N. *Languages of Art.* Indianapolis, 1968.
Kivy, P. *Sound Sentiment.* Philadelphia, 1989.
Levinson, J. "Aesthetic Supervenience," *Southern Journal of Philosophy,* Vol. 22 (1983), Supplement, 93–110.
Sibley, F. "Aesthetic Concepts," *Philosophical Review,* Vol. 68 (1959), 42–50.
Sircello, G. *Mind and Art.* Princeton, NJ, 1972.
Tormey, A. *The Concept of Expression.* Princeton, NJ, 1971.

– JOHN W. BENDER

ART, INTERPRETATION OF

Traditionally, artworks were thought to be about something, to indirectly refer, symbolize, or mean, and interpreters used ordinary language to open up their meanings. This view is no longer common, in part because of the failure of the dominant critical approaches to give a coherent and workable account of interpretation.

The problem of having to allow as many interpretations as critics, cultures, or historical periods is avoided by postulating some limiting principle (e.g., tradition).

For example, the New Critics suppose understanding literary works to provide the model for all interpretation of artworks. Literary texts are taken to be uniquely and autonomously meaningful, irreducible to extrinsic meanings and ordinary (nonliterary) discourse (cf. Wimsatt & Beardsley, 1954). This position disarms the critic, who must use a language inappropriate to its object—ordinary language and its shared senses. The New Critics, according to their critics, are condemned to silence or to systematic falsification of the sense of the work.

The structuralists suppose that poetic discourse has structural laws of its own analogous to the laws of ordinary discourse. The difference is that poetic meanings are a function of context whereas ordinary meanings are not (cf. Barthes, 1966). According to structuralism's critics, the structuralist then comes to the same end as

does the New Critic, to silence or falsification, because to recast contextual meanings as lexical meanings is grossly to distort them.

The hermeneuticists develop the notion that all meaning, poetic and ordinary, is contextual. Poetic texts provide the model for all meaningful domains; the way they are understood provides the model for every kind of understanding. The problem of having to allow as many interpretations as critics, cultures, or historical periods is avoided by postulating some limiting principle (e.g., tradition). This principle conditions any new interpretation, which is understood as the last remark in a dialogue over time (cf. Gadamer, 1975). Hermeneuticism's critics note that this limits the relativism of understanding by contradicting the basic insight that there is no first, foundational principle limiting the subjectivity of understanding.

Poststructuralists and deconstructionists, in various ways, simply accept the inherent relativity of understanding and license criticism for a variety of pragmatic reasons. They provide a negative but still informative reading of works by unearthing the hidden assumptions, beliefs, cultural fashions, aesthetic influences, and political ideologies that inform and constitute the work. Works can be deconstructed for destructive or playful reasons, or for constructive and even moral purposes (cf. Derrida, 1967). Postcolonial, new historicist, feminist, and Marxist critics may suppose an objective understanding of works is possible; more likely, they understand the force of the idea that meaning is contextual and constituted, and they criticize art to promote the personal, social, or political changes they desire.

It is natural that theory of interpretation has gone from the quest for objectivity to relativism and pragmatism, this being a small chapter in the critique of modernism. Abandoning key concepts of modern philosophy, such as realism, representationalism, and correspondence truth theory, profoundly affects interpretive theory. So does the transformation of art. Nonphysical works, nonart artifacts, natural objects, accidental art, minimal art, and art (including the literary) intended to be minimally meaningful, indefinitely meaningful, meaningless, or merely self-referring, all these bedevil the classical interpreter intent upon meaning and truth. The same is true if one takes the work itself to be an interpretation subject to second-order (i.e., normal) interpretations (cf. Danto, 1981) or to be identifiable as art only in terms of second-order characteristics (cf. Dickie, 1984). Some of these theories contain no implications for interpretive theory (or a theory of evaluation) and suggest none are forthcoming. Not all theorists agree with this general line (e.g., Rosen, 1987), and critics often write as though artworks are intelligible and their remarks helpful to those seeking to understand them.

[See also Aesthetics, Problems of; Deconstruction; Derrida, Jacques; Gadamer, Hans-Georg; Modernism and Postmodernism; Poststructuralism; Realism.]

BIBLIOGRAPHY

Barthes, R. *Critique et vérité.* Paris, 1966.
Berman, A. *From the New Criticism to Deconstruction: The Reception of Structuralism and Post-Structuralism.* Chicago, 1988. A critical overview, typical of a large literature on the evolution of theory of interpretation. Useful bibliography.
Danto, A. C. *The Transfiguration of the Commonplace.* Cambridge, MA, 1981.
Derrida, J. *L'écriture et la différence.* Paris, 1967.
Dickie, G. *The Art Circle.* New York, 1984.
Gadamer, H.-G. *Wahrheit und Methode.* Tübingen, 1975.
Parrinder, P. "Having Your Assumptions Questioned," in R. Bradford, ed., *The State of Theory* (London, 1993). Survey and deconstructive analysis of books on theories of interpretation.
Rosen, S. *Hermeneutics as Politics.* New York, 1987.
The Monist, Vol. 73 (1990), 115–330. Special issue edited by J. Hospers and J. Margolis on "The Theory of Interpretation." Contains eleven articles on the fate of interpretation after the advent of deconstruction.
Wimsatt, W., and M. Beardsley. "The Intentional Fallacy," in W. Wimsatt and M. Beardsley, *The Verbal Icon: Studies in the Meaning of Poetry* (Lexington, KY, 1954).

— MARGARET VAN DE PITTE

ART, REPRESENTATION IN

Both the method (or means) and the values of representations vary across the different artforms and media. Literature represents characters, situations, and events by describing fictional worlds—by generating fictional truths through its descriptions, or prescribing what readers are to imagine is the case. Music sometimes represents sounds in nature or human society by duplicating or imitating those sounds, and it sometimes represents situations or characters through conventional association with its motifs. More often, musical representation shades into expression of emotional states. This is accomplished both by imitating in its pitch, volume, and rhythmic and melodic contours the natural expressions of emotion in voice, demeanor, and behavior and by arousing related emotions in listeners (by harmonic means as well). For example, sad music tends to be slow, low, soft, and in minor keys.

The means by which a painter achieves pictorial representation or depiction, or the criterion for a painting's being a depiction of a particular object or kind of object, is controversial. Of seeming relevance are the artist's intention to depict a certain object, the causal context of the painting's production, conventions for representing certain kinds of objects, and some sort of resemblance relation between the painting and the object represented. Artistic intention is necessary both for depiction in general, since accidental likenesses are not depictions, and for picking out from among the possibilities the actual object represented in a painting. A particular causal relation to its object is not required for a pictorial representation (in this respect paintings differ from photographs), since artists do not necessarily represent the models from which they paint. But the causal context (i.e., marking a surface with paint) is relevant, since photographs and fabric samples do not depict, although they resemble and represent (in a broader sense) their objects.

When music is intensely expressive of emotions

it tends to engage us completely,

and such experience can be its own reward.

Aestheticians differ over the roles of convention and resemblance. In general we do not need to know semantic and syntactic conventions for interpreting parts of paintings and putting those parts together in order to interpret the paintings as depictions. We do so by seeing the objects in the paintings, in virtue of being able to recognize both the objects and the resemblance between our visual experience of the paintings and that of the objects. It is important to emphasize that the relevant resemblance is between visual experiences and not objects themselves; painters must painstakingly learn how to create such resemblances through two-dimensional cues. Convention supplements ordinary recognitional capacities in the depiction of characters or objects that are not (or no longer) recognizable from real life.

We may combine these factors into the following criterion: a painting represents an object when it realizes an artist's intention to mark a surface so as to make the visual experience of it resemble that of the object. This criterion is similar to that first suggested by Plato in the earliest writings in aesthetics, when he held that painters imitate the appearances of objects. This claim raised for him the problem of value in representation: how could a mere imitation possess value approaching the experience of the original?

Kendall Walton has suggested in reply that representations function as props in imaginative games. By imagining ourselves in the fictional worlds of artworks we can try out different roles, learn new responses, and broaden our cognitive and emotional repertoires. If such games of make believe are more common in relation to literature, expression and representation in music and painting serve other aesthetic functions. When music is intensely expressive of emotions it tends to engage us completely, and such experience can be its own reward. Viewing representational paintings can alter the ways we view real objects. Representation in painting can also create higher-order formal structures and intensify the sensuous beauty of pure color and form.

[See also Aesthetics, History of; Aesthetics, Problems of; Art, Resemblance in; Authenticity Regarding the Artist and the Artwork; Plato.]

BIBLIOGRAPHY

Plato. *The Republic,* translated by A. Bloom. New York, 1968. Book 10.
Schier, F. *Deeper into Pictures.* Cambridge, 1986.
Walton, K. *Mimesis as Make-Believe.* Cambridge, MA, 1990.

— ALAN H. GOLDMAN

ART, RESEMBLANCE IN

When a painting depicts a certain object, it seems intuitively that some sort of resemblance enters into that relation of representation. It is easy to show that resemblance is not sufficient for pictorial representation, since, for example, virtually every painting resembles every other painting more than it resembles the objects it represents. But this leaves open the possibility that resemblance is necessary, and it seems so from the fact that an artist's intention and the causal relation between the object and the act of painting do not suffice for depiction. Nor do we need to learn a conventional symbol system before being able to interpret paintings as pictures of objects.

The sort of resemblance that is necessary for depiction is that between visual experience of the object and that of the painting. Painters must learn how to produce such similarity through two-dimensional visual cues. Similarity of shape in the visual field is normally important, but not always crucial (as in the depiction of a leaf by a bright green dot).

If a threshold of such resemblance is necessary for depiction, we may also suppose that the greater its degree, the more true-to-life is the painting.

[See also Aesthetics, History of; Aesthetics, Problems of; Art, Representation in.]

BIBLIOGRAPHY

Neander, K. "Pictorial Representation: A Matter of Resemblance," *British Journal of Aesthetics,* Vol. 27 (1987), 213–26.
Peacocke, C. "Depiction," *Philosophical Review,* Vol. 96 (1987), 383–410.

— ALAN H. GOLDMAN

ART AS PERFORMANCE

Drama, music, and dance are the primary performing arts. In these, executants typically display their skills to an audience. Performances might be freely improvised, but many aim to instance a work, such as a tragedy or symphony, created by an artist.

The artist often supplies a work-specification recorded as instructions (scripts, scores) addressed to performers. The interpretation of the specification presupposes an awareness of the relevant performance tradition, since some things required of the performer may not be indicated and not all aspects of the notation are to be read literally. An accurate rendering of a work-specification results in an instance of the given work; frequently, a work also remains recognizable despite some performance errors or other departures from the artist's specification. The work is completed when its designation is, so a work for performance might have no instances. But such pieces are intended for performance, usually more than once.

Alternatively, the artist might provide a model instance of the work, this being imitated in subsequent

Louis Armstrong's spirited style exemplified art as performance. (Corbis/Bettmann)

presentations. Which features of the model are work properties and which performance properties depends on the relevant genre and conventions. Only the attributes that characterize the work are mandated for its future performances.

Performance is creative because the artist's instructions or model leave much to the performers' discretion. As a result, performances possess finer detail than do the works they exemplify; also, accurate performances of a given piece can differ considerably. A particular manner of realizing a work is an interpretation; this might be repeated in many performances. The audience is as likely to be interested in the interpretation and the talents displayed as in the work itself, especially where the work is well known.

In some arts, such as cinema, performers are employed in the creation of the work. Such works, when finished, are not for performance but for showing.

[See also Aesthetics, History of; Aesthetics, Problems of.]

BIBLIOGRAPHY

Alperson, P. "On Musical Improvisation," *Journal of Aesthetics and Art Criticism,* Vol. 43 (1984), 17–30.

Callen, D. "Making Music Live," *Theoria,* Vol. 48 (1982), 139–68.

Carlson, M. *Theories of the Theatre: A Historical and Critical Survey from the Greeks to the Present.* Ithaca, NY, 1984.

Davies, S. "Authenticity in Musical Performance," *British Journal of Aesthetics,* Vol. 27 (1987), 39–50.

Sparshott, F. *Off the Ground: First Steps to a Philosophical Consideration of the Dance.* Princeton, NJ, 1988.

Thom, P. *For an Audience: A Philosophy of the Performing Arts.* Philadelphia, 1993.

— STEPHEN DAVIES

ARTIFICIAL INTELLIGENCE

Artificial intelligence (AI) tries to enable computers to do the things that minds can do. Although AI research covers cognition, motivation, and emotion, it has focused primarily on cognition.

Some AI researchers seek solutions to technological problems, not caring whether these solutions resemble human psychology. Others want to understand how human (or animal) minds work or even how intelligence in general is possible. The latter approach is more relevant for the philosophy of mind and is central to cognitive science and the computational model of mind. Its practitioners generally accept some form of functionalism (for example, the physical symbol system hypothesis of Newell and Simon).

The things that minds can do include abilities not normally regarded as requiring intelligence, such as seeing pathways, picking things up, and learning categories from experience—all of which many animals can do.

Thus, human intelligence is not the sole focus of AI. Even terrestrial psychology is not since some use AI to explore the range of possible minds.

There are four major AI methodologies: symbolic AI, connectionism, situated robotics, and evolutionary programming. Symbolic AI (also known as classical AI) models thinking on the step-by-step processing of digital computers. Thinking is seen as symbol manipulation, as (formal) computation over (formal) representations. Folk psychological categories are explicitly modeled in the processing. This type of AI is defended by Fodor, who sees connectionism as concerned merely with how symbolic computation can be implemented.

Connectionism, which became widely visible in the mid-1980s, is often said to be opposed to AI. But connectionism has been part of AI from its beginnings in the 1940s and is opposed, rather, to symbolic AI. Connectionism defines associative networks of simple computational units that can tolerate imperfect data and (often) learn patterns from experience. Most philosophical interest is in the type known as PDP (parallel distributed processing), which employs subsymbolic units whose semantic significance cannot be easily expressed in terms of propositional content. (Some classical AI programs employ subsymbolic units too.) PDP representations are embodied as equilibrated activity patterns of the whole network, not as activations of single units or entries in single memory locations.

Although artificial intelligence research covers cognition, motivation, and emotion, it has focused primarily on cognition.

These two AI methodologies have complementary strengths and weaknesses. For instance, symbolic AI is better at modeling hierarchy and "strong" constraints, whereas connectionism copes better with pattern recognition, especially if many conflicting constraints must be considered. But neither can illuminate all of psychology. Both have been criticized by Searle as being concerned only with syntax, not semantics: neither approach, he argues, possesses (or explains) intentionality. He allows, however, that connectionism shows that semantically appropriate inferences can be drawn without the formal symbol manipulations favored by Newell, Simon, and Fodor.

The third AI methodology is situated robotics. Situated robots are described as autonomous systems embedded in their environment (Heidegger is sometimes cited). Instead of planning their actions, as classical robots do, they react directly to environmental cues. Although they contain no objective representations of the world, they may construct temporary, subject-centered (deictic) representations.

In evolutionary programming, a program makes random variations (like biological mutations and crossovers) in its own rules. The most successful rules are automatically selected and (probably) varied again. Eventually, the system is well adapted to its task. This AI method is used within both symbolic and connectionist systems and for both abstract problem solving and evolutionary robotics—wherein the brain and sensorimotor anatomy of robots evolve within a specific task environment.

AI is closely related to artificial life (A-Life). A-Life employs computer simulation to study the emergence of complexity in self-organizing, self-reproducing, adaptive systems. Situated and evolutionary robotics are forms of AI commonly seen as lying within A-Life. However, since psychological properties arise in living things, the whole of AI could be regarded as a subarea of A-Life.

[See also Cognitive Science; Computational Model of Mind, The; Connectionism; Functionalism; Heidegger, Martin; Philosophy of Mind.]

BIBLIOGRAPHY

Boden, M. A., ed. *The Philosophy of Artificial Intelligence*. Oxford, 1990.

———. *Artificial Intelligence and Natural Man*, 2d ed. London, 1987.

Clark, A. J. *Associative Engines: Connectionism, Concepts, and Representational Change*. Cambridge, MA, 1993.

———. *Microcognition: Philosophy, Cognitive Science, and Parallel Distributed Processing*. Cambridge, MA, 1989.

Dreyfus, H. L. *What Computers Can't Do: The Limits of Artificial Intelligence*, 2d ed. New York, 1979.

Fodor, J. A. *Psychosemantics: The Problem of Meaning in the Philosophy of Mind*. Cambridge, MA, 1987.

Holland, J. H., K. J. Holyoak, R. E. Nisbet, and P. R. Thagard. *Induction: Processes of Inference, Learning, and Discovery*. Cambridge, MA, 1986.

Rich. E., and K. Knight. *Artificial Intelligence*, 2d ed. New York, 1991.

Searle, J. R. *The Rediscovery of the Mind*. Cambridge, MA, 1993.

— MARGARET BODEN

Chess champion Gary Kasparov contemplates his next move against Deep Blue, a computer designed to "play" chess. (Agence France Pressel Corbis-Bettmann)

ARTWORLD

"Artworld" designates that complex of individuals and institutions involved in the production and presentation of works of visual art—artists, dealers, collectors, critics, curators, journalists, and the like. The expression achieved philosophical status in Arthur C. Danto's 1964 "The Art World," where it was invoked specifically to explain how certain objects, like Duchamp's ready-mades, get accepted as works of art: "To see something as art requires something the eye cannot descry—an atmosphere of artistic theory, a knowledge of history of art: an artworld." This formulation inspired George Dickie's initial formulations of the institutional theory of art.

[See also Aesthetics, Problems of.]

BIBLIOGRAPHY

Danto, A. C. "The Artworld," *Journal of Philosophy*, Vol. 61 (1964), 571–84.
Dickie, G. *Art and the Aesthetic: An Institutional Analysis*. Ithaca, NY, 1974.

– ARTHUR C. DANTO

AUGUSTINE, ST.

St. Augustine (354–430), also known as Aurelius Augustinus, was one of the key figures in the transition from classical antiquity to the Middle Ages. He was born at Thagaste, in north Africa, and died as the invading Vandals were closing in on his episcopal city, Hippo. He lived through nearly eighty years of the social transformation, political upheavals, and military disasters that are often referred to as the "decline of the Roman Empire." His life also spanned one of the most important phases in the transition from Roman paganism to Christianity. The old Roman pagan tradition was by no means dead, although the Roman emperors had been Christians since Constantine's conversion some forty years before Augustine was born. Augustine's youth saw the brief rule of Julian the Apostate as well as the last great pagan reaction in the empire, which broke out in the 390s. Nevertheless, it was during this period that the Roman state adopted Christianity as the official state religion. Medieval Europe began to take shape within the framework of the Roman Empire.

Augustine belonged to the world of late Roman antiquity, and its cultural and educational system had a decisive and lasting role in shaping his mind. His education, following the standard pattern of the time, was almost entirely literary, with great stress on rhetoric. Its aim was to enable its recipients to imitate the great literary masterpieces of the past. It tended, inevitably, to encourage a conservative literary antiquarianism. The culture it produced rarely rose above the level of the sterile cult of "polite letters" and generally had little contact with the deeper forces at work in contemporary society. There were many creative minds still at work; but even at their best, their thought was largely derivative. This is especially true of the philosophy of the period. Its stock of learning was in large part contained in compendia, though works of Cicero were still widely read, and those of the Neoplatonist thinkers gave inspiration to both pagans and Christians.

Augustine lived through nearly eighty years of the social transformation, political upheavals, and military disasters that are often referred to as the "decline of the Roman Empire."

This culture and its educational system were the two sources that supplied the initial impulse for Augustine's thinking. His search for truth and wisdom began with his reading at the age of 18 of a now lost dialogue by Cicero, the *Hortensius*. The work made an impact that Augustine could not forget and that he often mentions in his later writings. When he recounts the experience in the *Confessions* (III, 4, 7), written in his forties, he tells us that it was this work that changed his interests and gave his life a new direction and purpose: the search for wisdom. The search led him far afield; but looking back on it, Augustine could interpret its start as the beginning of the journey that was finally to bring him back to God.

PHILOSOPHY AND CHRISTIANITY. It was not until 386 that Augustine was converted to Christianity; he was baptized the following year. Meanwhile, his career as a teacher of rhetoric took him from his native Africa to Italy, first to Rome and then to Milan. During this period he was under the spell of the Manichaean religion. Its teachings appeared for a time to offer Augustine the wisdom for which he had been searching, but he became increasingly dissatisfied with it and finally broke with the sect through the influence of his new friends in Milan, Bishop Ambrose and the circle of Christian Neoplatonists around him. In Milan he learned the answers to the questions that had worried him about Manichaean doctrine, and there he encountered a more satisfying interpretation of Christianity than he had previously found in the simple, unintellectual faith of his mother, Monica. There was no deep gulf between the Christianity of these men and the atmosphere of Neoplatonic thought of the time. At this

Augustine's education was almost entirely literary, with great stress on rhetoric. (Gale Research Co.)

stage of his life Augustine saw no need to disentangle exactly what belonged to Christian and what to Neoplatonic teaching: what struck him most forcibly was how much the two bodies of thought had in common. The blend of Neoplatonism and Christian belief won his adherence, and the moral conflict recounted in his *Confessions* (Books VI–VIII) ended with his baptism.

Even in 400, when he wrote his *Confessions,* he spoke of the teachings of the "Platonists" as preparing his way to Christianity. In a famous passage (VIII, 9, 13–14) he describes Neoplatonism as containing the distinctive Christian doctrines about God and his Word, the creation of the world, and the presence of the divine light; all these he had encountered in the books of "the Platonists" before reading of them in the Scriptures. What he had failed to find anticipated in Neoplatonism were the beliefs in the Incarnation and the Gospel account of the life and death of Jesus Christ. Later in life Augustine came gradually to see a deeper cleavage between philosophy and Christian faith; but he never ceased to regard much of philosophy, especially that of the Neoplatonists, as containing a large measure of truth and

hence as capable of serving as a preparation for Christianity.

From Milan he returned to north Africa and retired to live a kind of monastic life with like-minded friends until he was ordained, under popular pressure, to assist the aged bishop of Hippo as a priest. Within four years, in 395, he became bishop of Hippo. From the 390s onward, all of Augustine's work was devoted to the service of his church. Preaching, administration, travel, and an extensive correspondence took much of his time. He continued to lead a quasi-monastic life with his clergy, however, and the doctrinal conflicts with Manichaeans, Donatists, Pelagians, and even with paganism provoked an extensive literary output. Despite this multifarious activity, Augustine never ceased to be a thinker and scholar, but his gifts and accomplishments were turned increasingly to pastoral uses and to the service of his people. The Scriptures took a deeper hold on his mind, eclipsing the strong philosophical interests of the years immediately preceding and following his conversion.

Augustine did not, however, renounce his philosophical interests. He shared with all his contemporaries the belief that it was the business of philosophy to discover the way to wisdom and thereby to show men the way to happiness or blessedness (*beatitudo*). The chief difference between Christianity and the pagan philosophies was that Christianity considered this way as having been provided for men in Jesus Christ. Christianity could still be thought of as a philosophy, however, in that its aim was the same as that of other philosophic schools. The ultimate source of the saving truths taught by Christianity was the Scriptures, which for Augustine had supplanted the teachings of the philosophers as the gateway to truth. Hence, authority rather than reasoning, faith rather than understanding, came to be the emphasis of "Christian philosophy." For although the pagan philosophers had discovered much of the truth proclaimed by the Christian Gospel, what their abstract speculation had not, and could not have, reached was the kernel of the Christian faith: the belief in the contingent historical facts that constitute the history of salvation—the Gospel narrative of the earthly life, death, and resurrection of Jesus.

BELIEF AND UNDERSTANDING. Belief in the above facts was the essential first step along the way to saving truth and blessedness, but it was only a first step. Faith, while required of a Christian, was not in itself sufficient for a full realization of the potential rationality of man. For Augustine, an act of faith, or belief, was an act of rational thinking, but of an imperfect and rudimentary kind. In a late work he defined "to believe" as "to think with assent" (*De Praedest. Sanct.* 2, 5). The act of believing is, therefore, itself an act of thinking and part of a context of thought. What distinguishes it from understanding or knowledge is best brought out by Augustine in passages where he contrasts believing with "seeing." By "seeing" Augustine meant either vision, literally, or, metaphorically, the kind of knowledge to which its object is clear and transparent. This kind of knowledge could be acquired only through direct experience or through logical demonstration, such as is possible in mathematics and other forms of rigorous reasoning. Believing, though a necessary and ubiquitous state of mind without which everyday life would be impossible, is therefore a form of knowledge inferior to understanding. Its object remains distant and obscure to the mind, and it is not intellectually satisfying. Faith demands completion in understanding.

In this emphasis on the priority of belief and its incompleteness without understanding, we may see a reflection of Augustine's own intellectual pilgrimage. His tortuous quest for wisdom, with its false trails, had ultimately led him to consider the Christian faith as the object of his search. But this faith offered no resting place, for Augustine never lost his passion for further intellectual inquiry. His faith was only the first step on the way to understanding. He never ceased to regard mere faith as only a beginning; he often returned to one of his most characteristic exhortations: "Believe in order that you may understand; Unless you shall believe, you shall not understand." The understanding he had in mind could be fully achieved only in the vision of God face to face in the life of blessedness; but even in this life, faith could be—and had to be—intensified in the mind by seeking a deeper insight into it. Progress in understanding, founded on faith and proceeding within its framework, was part of the growth of faith itself. After his conversion, then, reasoning and understanding were for Augustine no longer an independent, alternative route to faith. They still had their work, but now within a new setting and on a new foundation.

Some things, like contingent historical truths, could be the objects only of belief; others could be the objects of either belief or understanding (understanding means having an awareness of grounds and logical necessity). For instance, a mathematical theorem can be believed before it is understood. With understanding, however, belief inevitably follows. God, Augustine thought, belongs among the objects that are first believed and subsequently understood. In the process of gaining this understanding, the ordinary human endowments of rational thought, culture, and philosophy have a part to play. They form the equipment of which a Christian may avail himself in the work of seeking deeper insight into the meaning of his faith.

In his *De Doctrina Christiana* Augustine discusses the ways in which the various intellectual disciplines may serve to assist the Christian in understanding the faith he derives from scriptural sources. Philosophy, along with the other branches of learning, is here seen as subordinated to the service of a purpose outside it, that of nourishing and deepening faith; it is no longer to be pursued for its own sake, as an independent avenue to truth. It is also in *De Doctrina Christiana* that Augustine uses the image of the children of Israel, on their way to the Promised Land, spoiling the Egyptians of their treasures at God's bidding: in the same way, Christians are bidden to take from the pagans whatever is serviceable in understanding and preaching the Gospel. Again, we may see here a reflection of Augustine's narrowing of interests and the growing dominance of pastoral concerns in his mind. The theoretical statement of his subordination of secular learning and culture and their consecration to the service of preaching the Gospel (in its widest sense) is contained in the program laid down in the *De Doctrina Christiana.*

Therefore, Augustine is not interested in philosophy, in the modern sense of the word. Philosophical concepts and arguments play a subordinate role in his work; and where they occur, they are usually employed to help in the elucidation of some aspect of Christian doctrine. Typical examples are his use of Aristotle's *Categories* in an attempt to elucidate the notions of substance and relation in the context of Trinitarian theology, especially in his great work *De Trinitate;* his subtle inquiries into human knowledge and emotions, in the second half of the same work, with a view to discovering in man's mind an image of God's three-in-oneness; and his analysis of the temporal relations "before" and "after," undertaken to elucidate the nature of time in order to solve some of the puzzles presented by the scriptural doctrine of the creation of the world. In all these cases and many more, his purpose would be described today as theological. In Augustine's day the distinction between theology and philosophy did not exist, and "philosophy" could be—and often was—used in a sense so wide as to include what we should call theology.

To study Augustine's thought *as philosophy* is in a sense, to do violence to it: it is to isolate from their purpose and context what he would have regarded as mere techniques and instruments. To focus attention on what Augustine would have regarded as belonging to the sphere of means, however, allows us to see something more than a mere agglomeration of philosophical commonplaces derived, in large measure, from Neoplatonism. Augustine's originality lies not only in his determination to use his inherited philosophical equipment but also in the often slight, but sometimes profound, modification it underwent at his hands. And in the service of Augustine's purpose, many old ideas received new coherence and new power to move. Through his "spoiling of the Egyptians" much of the heritage of late antiquity received a new life in the European Middle Ages.

THE MIND AND KNOWLEDGE. At an early stage of Augustine's intellectual development, the skepticism of the Academic tradition of philosophy appears to have presented him with a serious challenge. His early philosophical dialogues, written in the period immediately after his conversion, are full of attempts to satisfy himself that there are at least some inescapable certainties in human knowledge on which we may absolutely rely. The basic facts of being alive, of thinking, or of simply existing are disclosed in one's immediate awareness of oneself. But Augustine did not limit the range of what was indubitably reliable in one's experience; nor did he seek to build an entire structure of indubitable knowledge on the basis of the absolute certainties of immediate awareness and its strict logical consequences, as Descartes was to do. He tried instead to vindicate the whole range of human knowledge as being capable of arriving at truth, though also liable to err.

It was a basic axiom of Augustine's view of soul and body that while the soul can act on the body, the body cannot act on the soul.

His vindication proceeds on two fronts, according to the fundamental duality of knowledge and of the objects corresponding to it. This duality, like much in his theory of knowledge, is of Platonic origin. Plato is the source of his belief that "there are two worlds, an intelligible world where truth itself dwells, and this sensible world which we perceive by sight and touch" (*C. Acad.* III, 17, 37); and of its corollary, that things can be divided into those "which the mind knows through the bodily senses" and those "which it perceives through itself" (*De Trin.* XV, 12, 21). Although he never departed from this dualistic theory of knowledge, Augustine also always insisted that all knowledge, of either kind, is a function of the mind, or the soul.

He defines the soul as "a substance endowed with reason and fitted to rule a body" (*De Quant. Anim.* 13, 22). Augustine's use of the conceptual framework of the Platonic tradition made it difficult for him to treat man

as a single, substantial whole. He did, nevertheless, attempt to stress the unity of body and soul in man as far as his inherited conceptual framework allowed. In a characteristically Platonic formula he defines man as "a rational soul using a mortal and material body" (*De Mor. Eccles.* I, 27, 52). The soul is one of two elements in the composite, but it is clearly the dominant partner: the relation between it and its body is conceived on the model of ruler and ruled, or of user and tool. This conception gave Augustine considerable trouble in his attempt to work out a theory of sense knowledge.

Sense and Imagination. It was a basic axiom of Augustine's view of soul and body that while the soul can act on the body, the body cannot act on the soul. This is a consequence of the user–tool model in terms of which he understood their relation. The tool cannot wield its user; the inferior in nature has no power to effect or induce any modification in the higher. Augustine could not, therefore, elaborate a theory of sense knowledge in which the bodily affections would in any way cause or give rise to modifications in the soul; nevertheless, he insisted that even sense perception was a function of the soul, one that it carried out through the bodily sense organs. The mere modification of a sense organ is not in itself sense experience, unless it is in some way noticed by the mind. Augustine's problem was to explain this correlation between the mind's awareness and the modification of the organ without allowing the latter to cause or to give rise to the former.

In an early discussion of this problem, Augustine tried to explain the process of seeing as a kind of manipulation by the mind of its sense organs, much like a blind man's manipulation of a stick to explore the surface of an object (*De Quant. Anim.* 23, 41–32, 69). This is very much in line with his general conception of the relation of the body to the mind as that of an instrument to its user, but its inadequacy as an explanation of sense perception may have been apparent to Augustine. At any rate, he later came to prefer an account constructed in quite different terms. This account (elaborated in *De Genesi ad Litteram,* Book XII and generally underlying his later views, for instance, those stated in *De Trinitate*) is based on a distinction between "corporeal" and "spiritual" sight. "Corporeal sight" is the modification undergone by the eyes in the process of seeing and is the result of their encounter with the object seen. "Spiritual sight" is the mental process that accompanies corporeal sight, in the absence of which the physical process cannot be reckoned as sense experience (since all experience is a function of mind). Spiritual seeing is not, however, caused by corporeal seeing, since the body cannot affect the mind. Indeed, spiritual sight is a separate process that may take place in the mind spontaneously, in the absence of its corporeal counterpart—for instance, in dreaming or imagining. The mental processes involved in sight and in dreaming and imagination are identical; what is before the mind is, in all these cases, of the same nature. What the mind sees in each case is not the object outside it, but the image within it. The difference between sensation and imagination is that in sensation a process of corporeal seeing accompanies the mental process; this is absent in imagination.

Augustine never quite answers the question of how we may know the difference between perception and imagination. The part, however, which he attributes to attention in the process of sense perception is important and gives a clue: it is attention that directs the mind's gaze, and it appears that it is attention that checks the free play of imagery in the mind. Thus, perception and imagination can be distinguished in experience by adverting to the presence of attention; its presence immobilizes the creative imagination and insures that the content of the mind has some sort of rapport with the bodily senses and their world. It is difficult to escape the impression that under the guise of "attention" Augustine has introduced what he had begun by excluding—mental process as responsive to bodily change. This is the peculiar difficulty that his two-level theory of man never quite allowed him to escape.

Augustine also speaks of a third kind of sight, one that he calls intellectual. This, the highest kind of sight, is the work of the mind whereby it interprets, judges, or corrects "messages" from the lower kinds of sight. The type of activity Augustine has in mind here is exemplified by any act of judgment on the content of sense perception; for instance, the judgment that an oar partly submerged in water is not actually bent, even though it looks bent. This activity of interpretation and judgment brings us to the second kind of knowledge, that which the mind has independently of sense experience.

Reason and Illumination. In his account of sense knowledge, Augustine's Platonic inheritance was a source of difficulty. In the elaboration of his views on reason and intelligence, the reverse is the case: Augustine's account of these is largely an adaptation of the fundamental tenets of the Platonic tradition. Typical instances of knowledge that the mind has independently of sense experience are the truths of mathematics. Here Augustine discovered the universality, necessity, and immutability that he saw as the hallmarks of truth. Although he did not believe that knowledge obtained through the senses possessed these characteristics, Augustine widened the scope of truth considerably beyond the necessary truths of mathematics and logic. He

thought that our moral judgments and judgments of value, at least of the more fundamental kind, also shared the character of truth. He did not, however, trace this universality and necessity of such propositions to their logical form or to the nature of the definitions and logical operations involved in them. (He wrote 14 centuries before Kant's distinction between analytic and synthetic judgments.)

Like all his predecessors and contemporaries, Augustine thought that this kind of knowledge was just as empirical as sense experience, and that it differed from the latter only in having objects that were themselves superior to the physical objects of sense experience by being immutable and eternal, and therefore capable of being known with superior clarity and certainty. The knowledge open to the mind without the mediation of the senses was conceived as analogous to sight; indeed, Augustine often speaks of it as sight, sometimes qualifying it as "intellectual sight." Its objects are public, "out there," and independent of the mind that knows them, just as are those of physical sight. In its knowing, the mind discovers the objects; it does not create them any more than the eyes create the physical objects seen by them. Together, the truths accessible to this kind of knowledge form a realm that Augustine, following the whole Platonic tradition of thought, often calls the intelligible world. This he identifies with the "Divine Mind" containing the archetypal ideas of all things. He was not, however, the first to take this step; this identification was the key to all forms of Christian Platonism.

Before Augustine, Plato had already used the analogy between sight and understanding. Its details are worked out in the analogy of the sun in the *Republic*. Here the intellectual "light" that belongs to the world of intelligible forms is analogous to the visible light of the material world. Like the latter, it renders "visible" the objects seen by illuminating both them and the organ of perception—in this case, the mind. All understanding is a function of illumination by this light. The intellectual light that illuminates the mind and thus brings about understanding is spoken of in various ways by Augustine. Since it is a part of the intelligible world, it is naturally conceived as a kind of emanation from the divine mind or as an illumination of the human mind by the divine. Augustine also refers to it as the human mind's participation in the Word of God, as God's interior presence to the mind, or even as Christ dwelling in the mind and teaching it from within.

Plato had tried to account for the mind's knowledge of the forms in the theory, expressed in the language of myth, that this knowledge was left behind in the mind as a memory of its life among the forms before it was enclosed in an earthly body. After some early flirtation with this theory of reminiscence, Augustine came to reject it; to hold that the mind's knowledge derived from a premundane existence would have raised serious theological difficulties. Therefore, instead of tracing this knowledge to a residue of a past experience, he accounted for it in terms of present experience; it was the result of continual discovery in the divine light always present to the mind. For this reason, too, his conception of *memoria* became so widened as to lose the reference to past experience that *memory* necessarily implies in English. Augustine's *memoria* included what we should call memory; in it, he thought, were preserved traces of past experience, as in a kind of storehouse or a stomach. But *memoria* included very much more than this. He speaks of our a priori mathematical ideas, numbers and their relations, as being contained in it; and in the course of the tenth book of the *Confessions,* in which he devotes a long discussion to the subject, the scope is so widened as to extend to our knowledge of moral and other values, of all truths of reason, of ourselves, and of God. It is, in effect, identified with all the latent potentialities of the mind for knowledge. *Memoria* and divine illumination are alternative ways of expressing the basis of Augustine's theory of knowledge. The theory is, in its essence, the belief that God is always intimately present to the mind, whether this presence is acknowledged or not. His presence pervades everything and is operative in everything that happens. To this metaphysical principle the human mind is no exception. The only difference between the human mind, in respect to the divine presence within it, and other things is that unlike these other things, the human mind is able to turn freely toward the light and to acknowledge its presence, or to turn away from it and to "forget" it. Whether the mind is present to the divine light or not, however, the light is present to the mind; on this presence is founded all the mind's ability to know.

The manner of operation of this illumination in the mind and what exactly it produces in the mind have been the subject of much debate. This uncertainty is due partly to the enormous variety of expressions used by Augustine to describe the divine light, but it is also partly the result of approaching Augustine's views with questions formulated in terms of concepts between which he would not have made a distinction. It is clear, at any rate, that Augustine did not think that the divine light in the mind gave the mind any kind of direct access to an immediate knowledge of God. This kind of knowledge was, to him, the result of understanding, a goal to be reached only at the end of a long process— and not this side of the grave. If, however, we ask further what exactly he thought illumination did reveal to the mind, the answer is more difficult. In particular, if

we ask whether he conceived illumination primarily as a source of ideas in the mind or, alternatively, as providing the mind with its rules for judgment, the answer is not at all clear. He did not distinguish as sharply as one might wish between the making of judgments and the formation of concepts; he often speaks of both activities in the same breath or in similar contexts, or passes without the least hesitation from one to the other in the course of discussion. Sometimes he speaks of illumination as implanting in the mind an "impressed notion" (*notio impressa*), whether it be of number, unity, wisdom, blessedness, or goodness. Such passages suggest that Augustine thought of illumination primarily as a source of ideas, as providing "impressed notions." It is clear, however, that such "impressed notions" were also to serve as the yardsticks for judging all imperfect participations in individual instances of these notions. And in other passages, again, illumination is spoken of not as supplying any ideas or notions but simply as providing a criterion of the truth or falsity of our judgments.

It was very easy to pass from ideas to judgments in Augustine's way of speaking of illumination. In addition, Augustine's language when he speaks of the mind's judgment made in the light of divine illumination often has further overtones; the judgment he speaks of appears as a kind of foreshadowing of the ultimate divine judgment on all human life and action. The basic reason why Augustine had found Platonic metaphysics so congenial was that it harmonized so easily with the moral bearings of his own views; and its theories, especially in some of their more imaginative and dramatic expressions, allowed themselves to be exploited to serve Augustine's interests as a moralist. In his discussion of knowledge, as in his discussion of the relation of mind and body, ethical considerations very often play the major part. The central theories of Platonic thought buttressed views held by Augustine primarily on account of their moral bearings.

WILL, ACTION, AND VIRTUE. Morality lies at the center of Augustine's thought. There are many reasons for this, the most noteworthy being his conception of philosophy. As we have seen, philosophy was for Augustine far from being an exclusively theoretical study; and morality itself belonged to its substance more intimately than the discussion and analysis of moral concepts and judgments. Philosophy was a quest for wisdom, its aim being to achieve man's happiness; and this depended on right living as much as on true thinking. Hence the practical orientation of Augustine's thought—an orientation that it shared with most contemporary forms of thinking.

On human conduct and human destiny Augustine's thinking was, of course, molded very largely by the New Testament and by the Christian church's tradition in understanding its conceptions of divine law and commandment, of grace, of God's will, of sin, and of love. Much of this, being specifically theological in interest, lies outside the scope of this presentation of Augustine's thought. What is remarkable is the extent to which Augustine was prepared to read back the characteristic teaching of the Christian church into the works of the philosophers, Plato in particular. Thus he held that Plato had asserted that the supreme good, possession of which alone gives man blessedness, is God. "And therefore," Augustine concluded, Plato "thought that to be a philosopher is to be a lover of God" (*De Civ. Dei* VIII, 8). *Rapprochements* of this kind helped to reconcile the Christian and the Platonic teachings to each other; in Augustine's treatment of ethical topics the characteristically Christian themes and distinctively Platonic concepts are so closely interwoven that they are often inseparable.

Augustine's favorite definition of virtue is

"rightly ordered love," which consists in

setting things in their right order of priority,

valuing them according to their true worth,

and in following this right order of value

in one's inclinations and actions.

Augustine is able, therefore, to define blessedness itself in terms that make no reference to any distinctively Christian teaching, for instance, when he says that man is blessed when all his actions are in harmony with reason and truth (*cum omnes motus eius rationi veritatique consentiunt—De Gen. C. Man.* I, 20, 31). Blessedness, according to this view, does not consist simply in the total satisfaction of all desires. In another discussion Augustine makes this more explicit: while blessedness is incompatible with unsatisfied desires, the satisfaction of evil or perverse desires gives no ultimate happiness; hence blessedness cannot be identified simply with total satisfaction. "No one is happy unless he has all he wants and wants nothing that is evil" (*De Trin.* XIII, 5, 8; for the entire discussion, see *ibid.* XIII, 3, 6–9, 12). The only element in all this that is specifically Christian is the insistence that this happiness cannot be attained by man except with the aid of the way revealed by Christ and of God's grace given to men to enable them to follow it.

The dramatic account, given in his *Confessions,* of his own turning to God, though steeped in the language of the Bible and throbbing with the intensity of Augustine's feelings, is, at the same time, an illustration of a central theme in Greek metaphysics. The book opens with a powerful evocation of his coming to rest in God; it ends with a prayer for this rest, peace, and fulfillment. This central theme of longing and satisfaction is a commonplace of Greek thought from Plato's *Symposium* onward. Man, according to the cosmology implicit in this picture, illustrates in his being the forces that are at work in nature in general. Man, like everything else, is conceived as part of a vast nexus of interrelated things within an ordered hierarchy of beings which together form the cosmos. But it is an order in which the components are not stationary but are in dynamic rapport; they are all pursuing their own ends and come to rest only in attaining these ends. Their striving for rest, for completion or satisfaction, is the motive power that drives all things toward their purposes, just as weight, according to this image, causes things to move to the places proper to them in the cosmos—the heavy things downward, the light upward. Augustine thought of the forces that move men as analogous to weight and called them, collectively, love or loves. In a famous passage he wrote, "My weight is my love; by it am I carried wheresoever I am carried" (. . . *eo feror quocumque feror—Conf.* XIII, 9, 10).

Love, Law, and the Moral Order. Man, however, differs from other things in nature in that the forces which move him, his "loves," are very much more complex. Within him there are a great many desires and drives, impulses and inclinations—some of them conscious, others not. The satisfaction of some often involves the frustration of others, and the harmonious satisfaction that forms the goal of human activity appears to be a very distant and scarcely realizable purpose. The reason for this is not only the multiplicity of elements that go into the making of human nature; a further reason is the fact that these elements have been disordered and deprived of their original state of harmony. Augustine interpreted this aspect of the human condition as a consequence of the sin of Adam and the fall of man.

There is, however, a further respect in which man differs from other things in the way his activity is determined. This lies in the fact that even with his disordered impulses, he is not—at least not entirely—at the mercy of the conflicting forces within him. His activity is not, so to speak, a resultant of them: he is, in some degree, capable of selecting among them, deciding which to resist, which to follow. In this capacity for choice Augustine saw the possibility of what he called voluntary action as distinguished from natural or necessary behavior. He called this human capacity "will." It is a source of some confusion that he used the term "love," or its plural, "loves," to designate the sum total of forces that determine a man's actions, whether they are "natural" or "voluntary." As a collective name for natural impulses, "love" is therefore morally neutral; only insofar as the will endorses or approves love of this kind is love morally praiseworthy or blameworthy. Augustine expresses this graphically by distinguishing between loves that ought to be loved and loves that ought not to be loved; and he defines man's moral task in terms of sorting out these commendable and reprehensible loves in himself and putting his loves in their right order.

The physical world concerned Augustine only insofar as it was related either to man or to God.

Augustine's favorite definition of virtue is "rightly ordered love" (as in *De Civ. Dei* XV, 22). This consists in setting things in their right order of priority, valuing them according to their true worth, and in following this right order of value in one's inclinations and actions. The idea of order is central to Augustine's reflections on morals. Before becoming a Christian, he had believed with the Manichaeans that the existence of good and of evil in the world was accounted for by their different origins, respectively from a good and an evil deity. The Neoplatonism of his Christian friends in Milan helped Augustine find an alternative explanation, one that was more in keeping with the Christian doctrine of one world created by one God. According to this theory, evil had no independent, substantial existence in its own right; it existed as a privation, as a distortion or damage within the good. All evil was thus in some sense a breach of the right relation of parts within a whole, a breach of order of some kind. Hence the great emphasis on order in Augustine's thought, from the time of his conversion to the writing of his last works.

Augustine calls the pattern to which human activity must conform "law." Law is, in the first place, the archetypal order according to which men are required to shape their actions and by which their actions are to be judged. Augustine makes it clear that by "law" he means very much more than the actual legal enactments of public authorities. These "human laws" deal only with a part, greater or lesser, of human conduct; they vary from place to place and from time to time; they depend on the vagaries of individual legislators. The true "eternal law" by which all human behavior is judged leaves no aspect of man's life out of its purview; it is the same everywhere and at all times. It is not quite clear how Augustine conceived the relation between divine and human, eternal and temporal, law. His terminology is

variable, and although he thought that human law ought to seek to approach the divine, or at least not to contradict it, he does not appear to have denied its claim to being law even when it failed to reflect the eternal law. Also, as we shall see, he appears to have changed his views on this matter in the course of his life.

The "eternal," or "divine," law is in effect the intelligible world or the divine mind (see discussion of reason and illumination above) insofar as it is considered as the pattern that should regulate activity. The language in which Augustine speaks about the divine law is the same as that which he uses in speaking of the eternal truth, and he believed that the achievement of wisdom consisted in pursuing this truth by understanding and then embodying in oneself the order understood. It is clear that there is no significant difference between "eternal law" and "eternal truth"; the two are identical: eternal law is eternal truth considered under its aspect as a standard of moral judgment. Thus, the problem of how the eternal law is known to men is the same as the problem discussed above of how the eternal truth is known. Here, too, he speaks of the eternal law as being "transcribed" into the human mind or of its "notion" as being impressed on the mind. The deliverance of conscience or reason as manifested in moral judgment is thus no less and no more than the human mind's illumination by the eternal law, or its participation in it; Augustine describes conscience as "an interior law, written in the heart itself" (. . . *lex intima, in ipso . . . corde conscripta*—*En. in Ps.* 57, 1). He refers to this law, inscribed in man's heart or known to him by reason, as "natural." He can thus speak of law (eternal or natural), reason, and order interchangeably when discussing the ordering of human action to bring about its virtuous disposition.

In defining this order of priority in value, the following of which constitutes virtue, Augustine makes a fundamental distinction between "use" and "enjoyment." These two forms of behavior correspond to the twofold classification of things according to whether they are valuable for their own sake or as means, for the sake of something else. Things valued for themselves are to be "enjoyed," things valued as means are to be "used"; the inversion of the relation between use and enjoyment is the fundamental perversion of the order of virtue. To seek to use what is to be enjoyed or to enjoy what is to be used is to confuse means with ends. The only object fit for enjoyment, in this sense, is God; he alone is to be loved for his own sake, and all other things are to be referred to this love. In elaborating this theory, Augustine was expressing the traditional view that it behooves men to journey through their lives on earth as pilgrims and not to regard any earthly goal as a fit resting place. This did not, of course, imply, to Augustine's mind, that nothing but God was a fit object of love; on the contrary, it was a way of stressing the need to put loves in their right order and to love each thing with the kind and degree of love appropriate to it. Although he clearly conceived of love as capable of an endless series of gradations, Augustine is usually content to speak of two kinds of love, which he contrasts: charity (*caritas*) and cupidity (*cupiditas*). The basic distinction is between upright, well-ordered, and God-centered love and perverse, disordered, and self-centered love. A great deal of Augustine's thinking and writing hinges on this distinction.

The individual virtues interested Augustine less than the concept of love. He was content to take over the classical enumeration of the four cardinal virtues. But his own characteristic thoughts on the moral life are always developed in terms of love rather than of any of the virtues. Indeed, as we have seen, he defined virtue in terms of love; similarly, he liked to define the individual cardinal virtues as different aspects of the love of God. This tendency is one of the most important links between what we would distinguish as the theological and philosophical sides of his thought.

THE WORLD AND GOD. Order is a key idea in Augustine's reflections on the morality of human behavior. It also plays a large part in his reflection on the physical universe in its relation to God. The world of nature was not in itself an object of particular interest to Augustine. In cosmological thinking of the kind to be found in Aristotle's *Physics,* for instance, he had little interest. The physical world concerned him only insofar as it was related either to man or to God. Order, then, for Augustine was the expression of rationality. In human action this was something that men should seek to embody in their conduct; in the world of physical and animate nature, which did not share the freedom of human activity, order expressed the divine rationality at work in all natural happenings. To human eyes, however, this order was often glimpsed only in isolated instances, while a great deal of disorder was manifest in the misery, disease, and suffering with which the world is shot through. In part these frustrations of order were held to be due, ultimately, to the initiative of human sin; in part they were held to be merely apparent and capable of being resolved within a perspective larger than that of finite human vision.

Behind the world order stands its author and sovereign ruler, God. All things testify to his presence; the world is full of his "traces" (*vestigia*). God's presence in and behind his creation was, for Augustine, not so much something to be established by argument as it was the premise, taken for granted, of a further argument. This argument, to which Augustine returned on a number of occasions, is particularly well expressed in a chapter

of his *Confessions* (X, 6, 9 and 10). He there speaks of putting things to the question in order to allow them to reveal themselves as dependent on their creator. It is clear that what primarily interested Augustine was the questioner's moral attitude: the point of his argument is not so much that the order and beauty of things imply the existence of God, but rather that since God had created them, we must so discipline ourselves as to see things for what they are—his handiwork—and to value them at their true worth and worship only him, their creator—not his handiwork. Again, the moral concern is uppermost in Augustine's mind.

This is not the case with the discussion of the problem of time, in Book XI of the *Confessions.* The problem was forced on Augustine's attention by the scriptural doctrine of creation, but it is clear that it fascinated him and that he pursued it simply because he was interested in it. Manichaean objectors to the Christian doctrine of creation from nothing had raised difficulties about speaking of an absolute beginning. These critics had pointed out that in our ordinary language there is no room for an absolute beginning of the kind envisaged by adherents of the doctrine; we can always ask what happened before something else, even if this was the first of all happenings. Questions of this kind revealed the arbitrariness and absurdity of the belief that God made the world out of nothing: What was God doing before the creation? Why did he create the world when he did and not sooner, or later?

In answer to these difficulties Augustine in effect undertook a critique of the conception of time that underlay them. Such difficulties arise from the fact that time is thought of as having the same kind of being as the events and happenings going on in time; the question "What happened before time?" was thought to be of the same logical form as questions about what happened before any particular events. Augustine denied this assumed logical similarity behind the grammatical similarity of the questions. He pointed out that whereas it makes sense to ask what happened before any particular event, it does not make sense to ask what happened before all events, because time is the field of the relationships of temporal events, and there could *ex hypothesi* be nothing before the first temporal event. In this argument Augustine in effect rejected the conception of time according to which time has a substantial reality of its own, and he adopted a theory according to which time is the field of temporal relations between temporal events.

He did, however, go further in his reflections on time. Neoplatonic thought had always treated time in close relation to the soul, and Augustine could scarcely avoid discussing this topic. The reality of the past and of the future puzzled him: Can what is not yet but will be, and what is no longer but has been, be said to *be*? If not, then only the present has any reality. But if only the present is real, then reality shrinks to a dimensionless point at which the future is becoming the past. Augustine resolved the whole problem by locating time in the mind and adopting at the end of his discussion, though with hesitation, a definition of time as "extension [*distentio*], I am not sure of what, probably of the mind itself" (*Confessions* XI, 26, 33).

Another question that the doctrine of creation raised for Augustine concerns the natural activity, functioning, and development of creatures. This problem arose from the need to harmonize the story of the creation of the world in seven days or, according to an alternative version, at once, with the fact that some things came into existence only after the creation took place. Augustine's solution of this problem lay essentially in asserting that God created different things in different conditions; some left his hands complete and ready-made, others in a potential or latent state, awaiting the right conditions and environment for their full development. The latter are analogous to seeds, which are thought of as containing in themselves the fully developed plant in potency; and on this analogy, and using the traditional vocabulary, Augustine called these potentialities for later development "seminal reasons" (*rationes seminales,* or *causales*).

Apart from helping him to resolve the apparent contradiction between the belief in a primordial creation and the concept of continued development as a process of natural causality, this theory of "seminal reasons" also prompted Augustine at least to begin to feel his way toward some conception of nature and natural causality. At times, he comes very close to the later medieval distinction between the "First Cause" and the whole range of "second causes," the distinction according to which things depend in different senses both on God (the First Cause) and on their own immediate or distant created causes. Augustine, too, tried to endow the world of created causes with a specific reality of its own, one distinct from the causal activity of God in the world. In this he did not quite succeed. His failure becomes apparent in his treatment of miracles. He did not treat these—as the Scholastics later did as effects of the First Cause (God) produced without the instrumentality of second causes. He allowed the distinction between the two orders of causality (which he had never clearly formulated and which is hinted at, rather than stated, in his writings) to disintegrate during his discussion of miracles. In this context the very idea of "nature" is so widened as to include the miraculous within its scope. Miracles do not contradict the order of nature; they contradict only our idea of this order, an idea based on our re-

stricted view and limited experience. They are not against nature, since nature is God's will; they are only against nature as it is known to us. The distinction between nature and miracle vanishes here, and in his well-known chapter in *The City of God* (X, 12) they become synonymous to the extent that nature itself and man, its crown, become the greatest miracles of all.

MAN IN SOCIETY. Society was not one of the subjects that loomed large in Augustine's earlier thought. Such hints as he gives us of his conception of society in his earlier works (those written before the mid-390s) suggest that he thought that organized human society and the state were part of the worldly dispensation whereby man is assisted to fulfill his destiny. A properly ordered society, like a properly ordered moral life, is a stage on the way to man's ultimate destination in eternity; and as far as Augustine's hints enable us to tell, he expected a properly ordered society to reflect, particularly by means of its legal institutions, the perfection of the eternal, intelligible world.

Although Augustine believed

that man's nature is social,

he did not agree with Aristotle

that it is also political.

In step with his theological development, however, his views on human society underwent profound changes, and by the time that society became an important theme in his reflection, especially in his great work *The City of God* (written 413–427), these views had been radically transformed. An important factor in the course of this transformation was the increasing stress Augustine had come to lay on the power of sin in human life and in all earthly institutions, on man's need for redemption through Christ, and on his need for grace. In the most general terms Augustine came to see man's destiny and his realization of it more in terms of the scriptural pattern of a redemption-history and less in terms of the Neoplatonic theme of the ascent of the soul. Accordingly, human society came to be understood more in terms of its horizontal, historical relationships within the divine plan for men's salvation and less in terms of what we might call its vertical relationship to the intelligible world.

The first event in the course of the Biblical redemption-history, man's fall from grace through Adam's sin, is of decisive importance for Augustine's changed attitude to organized human society. To live in society, according to Augustine, was natural to men; without society they would not be able to realize fully their human potentialities, and the company of their fellow human beings was necessary to them. This, he held, was as true before man's fall as after; even in his state of primal innocence, in full possession of his nature prior to its distortion by sin, man was a social animal by nature; even the life of the blessed in heaven is a social life. But although Augustine believed that man's nature is social, he did not agree with Aristotle that it is also political. Politically organized society—the machinery of authority, government, and coercion—is, in Augustine's view, not natural to man. It was a useful and necessary arrangement for man in his fallen condition, and indeed the purpose of political society was to remedy at least some of the evils attendant upon man's fallen state. Its function was to check the social disorder and disintegration that followed from the general loss of order at the Fall. The institutions of government, the subjection of governed to government, and the coercive power of political authority over its subjects are thus but one instance of the subjection of man to man, and this was something that, Augustine held, did not exist in man's primal state of innocence. No slavery, servitude, or subjection could exist in that state of natural integrity; these things make sense only if understood as God's punishment for the sin that incurred the loss of integrity and, at the same time, as his dispensation for coping with the needs of man's condition in his new, fallen state.

Augustine used the traditional language of Christian theology to state his view of political society. For reasons to be considered below, he never drew out, at least not explicitly, the full implications of this view. In this view of society, however, the legitimate functions of the state are very much more restricted in scope than in theories according to which man is by nature a political animal. In Augustine's view, the state's sphere is confined to the requirements of social order and welfare; the individual's ultimate welfare and eternal destiny lie outside its realm of competence, whereas they are very much a part of the state's interest if the state is thought of as an ordinance of nature, as an indispensable means of man's realizing his ultimate destiny. In Augustine's estimate, the task of the state in the economy of salvation would be rather to establish the conditions in which men may work out their own salvation in relative peace and security than actively to promote their individual salvation through legislation and coercion.

The state was, for Augustine, synonymous with the Roman Empire; and having revised his ideas on the state in terms of the large categories of the scriptural redemption-history, he had inevitably to take the mea-sure of the state he knew in this same perspective. Here his ideas make sense only if seen as a rejection of views of the empire generally current among Christians during the fourth century, after the adoption of Christianity by the emperors. The empire, represented as eternal ever since Vergil's day, was now widely regarded among Christians as an essential instrument of divine purpose in history, bound up with the possibility of salvation and destined to last until the end of time. It had been taken up into the dimension of the Biblical redemption-history. The sack of Rome by the Visigoths in 410 gave a profound shock to this mentality. It led Augustine, whose mind had already moved a long way from the popular picture, to devote his greatest work, *The City of God,* to a reappraisal of the Empire's place in the divine providential plan. The upshot was that the empire was no longer allowed an eternal destiny and was removed from the dimension of the redemption-history; the possibility of salvation was not necessarily bound up with it as a means of God's grace. It was simply one of a series of empirical, historic societies. The eternal categories of sin and holiness, of salvation and reprobation, did not apply to it or, indeed, to any other human assembly; they were embodied only in what Augustine called the earthly city and the heavenly city.

The two "cities" consist, respectively, of those predestined to eternal glory and those predestined to eternal torment or, as Augustine also defined them (clearly intending the various definitions to be equivalent), of those who live according to God and those who live according to man, of the altruistic and the selfish, of those whose love is upright and those whose love is perverse, and so forth. In none of these senses, however, have the two "cities" any discernible reality as communities until their final separation at the Last Judgment. In all discernible human communities they are inextricably intertwined. Here again we may see Augustine's modest estimate of the state's function, for when he discusses it in this context, the realm of the state is identified with the sphere in which the concerns of the two cities overlap. Its task is to secure the temporal peace: the order, security, and material welfare that both the wicked and the righteous cities require during their earthly careers. Its concern is with specifically communal, public matters affecting all its members. Citizens of the heavenly city will not, of course, be content with the welfare and peace thus secured: they will use these things but refer their use to the ultimate enjoyment of a peace beyond the terrestrial.

The general tendency of these views of Augustine's was to undermine the extremely close links that had come to exist between the empire and the Christian church, especially during his own lifetime. He was clearly ill at ease with the current representations of this relationship; but there were considerable pressures working on the minds of his contemporaries to keep them active, and Augustine himself was not exempt from their operation. In the course of the struggle with the Donatist movement in north Africa, a dissenting movement increasingly repressed by the imperial authorities, he came gradually and reluctantly to give his consent to the coercive measures that were being brought into use against the movement. His endorsement of these means of repression ran counter to the most fundamental direction of his thought. Although his endorsement must be regarded as a development in his practical, pastoral, and political attitudes rather than as a reversal of his basic views on the nature of political society, it left deep marks on those views. In later centuries his use of the Gospel phrase "Compel them to come in" (*Coge intrare*—Luke 19.23) and its consecration of repression, persecution, and coercion paved the way to much tragedy. It also helped to obscure the most profound and most original of his contributions to Christian political thinking.

BIBLIOGRAPHY

The most complete and generally reliable Latin edition of Augustine's works is the edition by the Benedictines of Saint-Maur (1679–1700). It supersedes all earlier editions and was reprinted in J. P. Migne's *Patrologia Latina*, Vols. 32–46 (Paris, 1841–1842), with some unfortunate variants and errors. It is also the basis of the texts of the works now being published in *Bibliothèque augustinienne* (with French translation and useful notes). Modern critical editions of many works exist, mainly in *Corpus Scriptorum Ecclesiasticorum Latinorum* (Vienna) and *Corpus Christianorum*. Details are in E. Dekkers, "Clavis Patrum Latinorum," in *Sacris Erudiri*, Vol. 3 (1962).

English translations of many works appear in various series, such as Loeb Classical Library, Library of the Fathers, Select Library of Nicene and Post-Nicene Fathers of the Christian Church, Library of Christian Classics, The Fathers of the Church, Ancient Christian Writers, and the Catholic University of America Patristic Studies. A detailed, convenient, and fairly up-to-date list of translations is included in the bibliography by J. J. O'Meara appended to Marrou's *Saint Augustine.*

Of short introductory works, the best is H. I. Marrou, *Saint Augustine* (London, 1958), translated from the French in the series Men of Wisdom. It contains a brief biography and a discerning characterization of Augustine's thought by a great scholar, as well as a selection of illustrative texts in translation. R. W. Battenhouse and others, *A Companion to the Study of Saint Augustine* (New York, 1955), has now been superseded by G. Bonner, *St. Augustine—Life and Controversies* (London, 1963), as a survey and guide to Augustine's career and literary output. An essential to understanding Augustine in the setting of contemporary education and culture is H. I. Marrou, *Saint Augustine et la fin de la culture antique* (Paris, 1938), completed by his, *Retractatio* (Paris, 1949). On Augustine as a bishop, see F. van der Meer, *Augustine the Bishop* (London, 1962).

Among the many books on Augustine's intellectual development and his conversion, P. Alfaric, *L'Évolution intellectuelle de saint Augus-*tin (Paris, 1918), stands behind much of the subsequent controversy; C. Boyer, *Christianisme et néo-Platonisme dans la formation de saint Augustin* (Paris, 1920), is one of the best-balanced replies provoked by it. P. Courcelle, *Recherches sur les Confessions de Saint Augustin* (Paris, 1950), has put the problem on new footing altogether; it is further pursued, with qualifications, by J. J. O'Meara, *The Young Augustine* (London, 1954).

Of the philosophical aspects of Augustine's thought, the best general account is E. Gilson, *The Christian Philosophy of Saint Augustine,* translated by L. E. M. Lynch (London, 1961). See also the survey by R. A. Markus in *Critical History of Western Philosophy,* D. J. O'Connor, ed. (New York, 1964).

On particular aspects, see C. Boyer, *L'Idée de vérité dans la philosophie de saint Augustin* (Paris, 1941); J. Guitton, *Le Temps et l'éternité chez Plotin et saint Augustin,* 2d ed. (Paris, 1955); and E. Dinkler, *Die Anthropologie Augustins* (Stuttgart, 1934), on the topics named in their titles. M. Schmaus, *Die psychologische Trinitätslehre des heiligen Augustinus* (Münster, 1907), is the classic work on Augustine's theory of mind and the Trinitarian speculations based on it. Also valuable on his theory of knowledge are J. Hessen, *Augustins Metaphysik der Erkenntnis,* 2d. printing (Berlin, 1960), and R. Jolivet, *Dieu soleil des esprits* (Paris, 1934).

On ethical topics, see J. Mausbach, *Die Ethik des heiligen Augustins* (Freiburg, 1909); T. Deman, *Le Traitement scientifique de la morale chrétienne selon saint Augustin* (Paris, 1957); J. Burnaby, *Amor Dei* (London, 1938); and R. Holte, *Béatitude et sagesse: Saint Augustin et le problème de la fin de l'homme dans la philosophie ancienne* (Paris, 1962). On the state and society the least unsatisfactory accounts are R. A. Deane, *The Political and Social Ideas of Saint Augustine* (New York, 1963) and the short treatment by N. H. Baynes, *The Political Ideas of Saint Augustine's De Civitate Dei* (London, 1936).

Many of the most important recent articles on Augustine are to be found in one of the following collections: *Augustinus Magister: Communications et actes du Congrès international augustinien* (Paris, 1954); *Recherches augustiniennes,* Vols. I and II (Paris, 1958–1963); *Studia Patristica,* Vol. VI, F. L. Cross, ed.; *Texte und Untersuchungen zur Geschichte der altchristlichen Literatur,* Vol. 81 (1962); and in the quarterly journal *Revue des études augustiniennes.*

The most up-to-date and best-selected bibliography is *Bibliographia Augustiniana,* appended to C. Andresen, ed., *Zum Augustin-Gespräch der Gegenwart* (Darmstadt, 1962), which is Vol. V in the series *Wege der Forschung.* Gilson's book (see above), in which the classified selection of the original is replaced by an alphabetical list in the English translation; B. Altaner, *Patrologie,* 5th printing (1958); and O. Bardenhewer, *Geschichte der altchristlichen Literatur,* Vol. IV (Freiburg, 1924; reprinted 1962), also have good bibliographies. Current literature is surveyed in the bibliographical supplements to *Revue des études augustiniennes.*

— R. A. MARKUS

AUGUSTINE, ST. (UPDATE)

St. Augustine continues to elicit scholarly discussions of theological issues, but there is an ever-growing number of studies devoted to historical and philosophical issues in their own right. Recent philosophical work has concentrated on deepening our understanding of his arguments, assessing the adequacy of his positions, and contextualizing them in a historically informed way.

P. Brown, *Augustine of Hippo: A Biography* (London, 1967), is a masterful work that situates Augustine in his social and historical surroundings. Accessible overviews of Augustine's life and thought are provided in J. J. O'Donnell, *Augustine* (Boston, 1985), and H. Chadwick, *Augustine* (Oxford, 1986). Our understanding of Augustine's autobiography has been greatly advanced by the fine commentary given in J. J. O'Donnell, *Augustine: Confessions* (3 vols., Oxford, 1992).

Augustine is seen against the background of classical philosophy in J. Rist, *Augustine: Ancient Thought Baptized* (Cambridge, 1994), which provides a guide to Augustine's philosophical views. Another introduction to Augustine as a philosopher is C. Kirwan, *Augustine* (London, 1989), which takes up selected topics in detail. The bibliographies of both these works should be consulted as a guide to the literature. Articles on a variety of topics are usefully collected in R. A. Markus (ed.), *Augustine: A Collection of Critical Essays* (London, 1972); there has been no anthology for philosophers since.

Turning now to particular aspects of Augustine's philosophy, G. J. P. O'Daly, *Augustine's Philosophy of Mind* (London, 1987), and G. Matthews, *Thought's Ego in Augustine and Descartes* (Ithaca, NY, 1992), deal with his philosophical psychology. Epistemology and the theory of illumination are the primary focus of R. H. Nash, *The Light of the Mind: St. Augustine's Theory of Knowledge* (Lexington, KY, 1969); B. Bubacz, *St. Augustine's Theory of Knowledge: A Contemporary Analysis* (New York, 1981); U. Wienbruch, *Erleuchtete Einsicht: Zur Erkenntnislehre Augustins* (Bonn, 1989). Metaphysical problems as well as the issue of Augustine's indebtedness to Plotinus are treated in R. J. O'Connell, *The Origin of the Soul in St. Augustine's Later Works* (New York, 1987). Augustine's account of time is analyzed in R. Sorabji, *Time, Creation, and the Continuum* (Ithaca, NY, 1983), and subjected to a wide-ranging examination in J. Pelikan, *The Mystery of Continuity: Time and History, Memory and Eternity in the Thought of Saint Augustine* (Charlottesville, VA, 1986). Philosophy of language is discussed by M. Burnyeat, "Wittgenstein and Augustine *de Magistro*," in *Proceedings of the Aristotelian Society* (1987, supp. vol.). Augustine's ethical theory is the subject of J. Wetzel, *Augustine and the Limits of Virtue* (Cambridge, 1992), and discussed in G. R. Evans, *Augustine on Evil* (Cambridge, 1982). A recent philosophical study of Augustine's views on freedom, weakness of will, and voluntary action is T. Chappell, *Aristotle and Augustine on Freedom* (New York, 1995). R. Coles, *Self/Power/Other: Political Theory and Dialogical Ethics* (Ithaca, NY, 1992), offers a Foucaultian account of Augustine's political philosophy.

A bibliography of works through 1970 is provided in C. Andresen, *Bibliographia Augustiniana* (Darmstadt, 1973); the next decade of Augustinian studies is covered in T. Miethe, *Augustinian Bibliography, 1970–1980* (Westport, CT, 1982).

[See also Augustine, St.]

– PETER KING

AUTHENTICITY

If there is a single existentialist virtue, it is authenticity (Martin Heidegger's *Eigentlichkeit* and Jean-Paul Sartre's *l'authenticité*). It functions as a kind of ethical gyroscope in a Nietzschean world of moral free-fall. For Heidegger the term denotes my "ownmost" way of being-in-the-world. In *Being and Time* Heidegger advocates resolutely affirming my most authentic possibility, namely, my being-unto-death, and disvalues my prevailing tendency to flee this anguished condition in favor of the average everyday world in which "one dies" (as in Tolstoy's *The Death of Ivan Ilych*). But only I can know how to respond authentically to this fact of my radical finitude because that finitude is most properly my own and not another's. Heidegger introduced the concept to facilitate access to the meaning of being, which was his project in *Being and Time*. Resolutely affirming that I will not be, he argued, reveals what it means to be at all. This use of "authenticity" is ontological and epistemic. Heidegger denied that the term carried moral significance, a claim reinforced by his refusal to write an ethics. But Sartre insisted that it was as moral a concept for Heidegger as it was for him. And so it came to be regarded in the vintage days of existentialism.

Authenticity functions as a kind of ethical gyroscope

in a Nietzschean world of moral free-fall.

Sartre added a footnote to *Being and Nothingness*, promising to write "an ethic of deliverance through authenticity." He wrote hundreds of pages in fulfillment of that promise. But until the posthumous publication of *Notebooks for an Ethics*, his most extended definition of authenticity appeared in *Anti-Semite and Jew*: "Authenticity . . . consists in having a true and lucid consciousness of the situation, in assuming the responsibilities and risks that it involves, in accepting it in pride or humiliation, sometimes in horror and hate" (Sartre, 1948, p. 90). This seemed to yield an ethical style rather than a content.

The publication of *Notebooks* provides the content for this ethics of authenticity by discussions of such concepts as good faith, gift-appeal, generosity, and positive reciprocity. This important text modifies the common conception of Sartre as the prophet of inevitable inauthenticity. It establishes the historical and socioeconomic context in which his more pessimistic assessments are said to apply. To be authentic still includes the acceptance of our human project as simultaneously gratuitous and reflectively appropriated. And it continues to entail a double aspect of unveiling and creation: unveiling of its radical contingency and creation of a reflective relation to this contingency. But authenticity now assumes a social dimension wherein I commit myself to modify others' situations so that they too may act in an authentic manner. Authenticity implies living the tension that arises from appropriating the truth about the human condition: that it is a finite, temporalizing flux, that this fluidity entails profound responsibility for whatever permanence we sustain within that flux, and that mutual recognition among freedoms enhances this concrete freedom even as it increases that lived tension.

Although it is common to read "authenticity" as equivalent to "genuineness," "truthfulness to self," and even "self-realization," these terms are inapplicable to the existentialist use of the term. As the defining maxim of existentialism, "existence precedes essence," implies, there is no pregiven self, essence, or type to realize in one's creative choices. "Truthfulness to one's condition" might better translate "authenticity," provided one respected the contingency, lack of identity, "inner distance," and temporal spread denoted by the term "condition."

Authenticity is often criticized on three grounds: individualism, relativism, and nihilism. Taylor (1991) sketches a nonexistentialist answer to such objections. The existentialist response would note that Heidegger speaks of "authentic being-with" (*Mitsein*) and that Sartre, especially in his later work, emphasizes the concepts of mutual recognition and common action as integral to authentic existence. The charges of relativism and nihilism are answered by the positive value each thinker places on the revelation of Being and the fostering of concrete freedom respectively. "Authenticity" does imply an individuating decision, as does any moral choice. That it is neither the application of a principle nor the following of a rule, but a creative choice, does not leave it arbitrary or random.

[See also Bad Faith; Existentialism; Heidegger, Martin; Sartre, Jean-Paul.]

BIBLIOGRAPHY

Heidegger, M. *Sein und Zeit.* Tübingen, 1927. Translated by J. Macquarrie and J. Robinson as *Being and Time.* New York, 1962.
Martin, M. *Self-Deception and Morality.* Lawrence, KS, 1986.
Santoni, R. E. *Bad Faith, Good Faith and Authenticity in Sartre's Early Philosophy.* Philadelphia, 1995.
Sartre, J.-P. *Cahiers pour une morale.* 1983. Translated by D. Pellauer as *Notebooks for an Ethics.* Chicago, 1992.
———. *L'Etre et le néant.* 1943. Translated by H. E. Barnes as *Being and Nothingness.* New York, 1956.
———. *Réflexions sur la question juive.* 1946. Translated by G. J. Becker as *Anti-Semite and Jew.* New York, 1948.
Taylor, C. *The Ethics of Authenticity.* Cambridge, 1991.
Trilling, L. *Sincerity and Authenticity.* Cambridge, 1972.

– THOMAS R. FLYNN

AUTHENTICITY REGARDING THE ARTIST AND THE ARTWORK

In the main sense of the term an artwork is authentic if it is the artwork it is thought to be—if it has the history of production it is represented as having or gives the impression of having, if it was created where, when, how, and by whom it is supposed or appears to have been created. Thus, a work may be inauthentic in virtue of being a forgery, or a misattribution, or a replica not identified as such. A reproduction (e.g., in an art book) is inauthentic only in a weaker sense: though not the artwork it reproduces, it does not purport to be and runs no danger of being confused with it.

What is wrong with a forgery? or,

What privileges an original artistically?

The chief issue concerning the authenticity of artworks has been the extent to which a work's aesthetic properties, artistic value, and proper appreciation legitimately depend on questions of authenticity in the above sense. The issue is often framed in terms of a challenge: What is wrong with a forgery? or, What privileges an original artistically?

Broadly speaking, there are two opposed views on this issue. On one view an artwork is merely a perceivable structure—for example, a constellation of colors and shapes, a set of notes, a string of words, or the like. Furthermore, this structure is the entire source of its aesthetic and artistic properties and is the only thing relevant to its appreciation and evaluation as art. Thus, anything preserving the artwork's perceivable structure, so as to be perceptually indiscernible from it, is equivalent to it artistically and even ontologically. Such a view underlies the formalism of Clive Bell and Roger Fry, the literary stance of the New Critics, and to some extent the aesthetics of Monroe Beardsley. By these lights there is nothing much wrong with a forgery—provided, of course, that it is a perfect one, not detectably different from the original.

On the other view perceivable structure is not the sole determinant of a work's aesthetic complexion or its artistic character. Rather, a work's context of origination, including the problematic from which it issues, partly determines how the work is rightly apprehended and experienced and thus its aesthetic and artistic properties. Aspects of the context or manner of creation arguably enter even into the identity of the work of art, as essential to its being the particular work it is. By these lights there is quite a lot wrong with a forgery. It differs from the original in numerous respects, both aesthetic and artistic, and as a human product—a making, an achievement, an utterance—it is of an entirely different order, however similar it appears on superficial examination.

If the second view sketched above is sound, then any artwork, *pace* Goodman, can be forged—that is, represented as having a provenance and history other than its own, though how this will be effected differs from artform to artform, especially when one crosses from particular arts (such as painting) to type arts in which structure may be notationally determined (such as music). And this is because, in all artforms, the identity of a work is partly a matter of the historical circumstances of its emergence.

Goodman famously argued, against the aesthetic equivalence of an original painting and an ostensibly perfect forgery, that the possibility of discovering a perceptual difference between the former and the latter constitutes an aesthetic difference between them. Unfortunately, this argument seems to trade on conflating an aesthetic difference and an aesthetically relevant difference between two objects. However, as suggested above, the aesthetic and artistic differences between originals and forgeries, which are ample, rest securely on quite other grounds.

Authenticity of Artwork Instance

In cases of multiple or type arts an instance of a work—a copy, impression, casting, performance, staging, screening, and so forth—may be denominated authentic or inauthentic insofar as it is or is not a correct or faithful instance of the work. And this, according to different accounts, is a matter of its adequately instantiating and representing the structure thought definitive of the work in question, a matter of its having the right sort of causal or intentional relations to the work in question or of being produced in a certain manner, a matter of its conveying the aesthetic or artistic properties believed crucial to the work—or some combination of these.

Authenticity of Artist

Finally, authenticity is sometimes considered a predicate of the artist, describing laudatorily the artist's charac-

teristic mode of creating or the relation between the artist and the content of the works the artist creates. An authentic artist is one thought, variously, to be sincere in expression, pure in motivation, true to self, honest about medium, rooted in a tradition, resistant to ideology yet reflective of society—or all of these. There seems to be only a passing relation between authenticity in this sense and the authenticity of work or instance canvased above.

[See also Aesthetics, History of; Aesthetics, Problems of; Goodman, Nelson.]

BIBLIOGRAPHY

Bailey, G. "Amateurs Imitate, Professionals Steal," *Journal of Aesthetics and Art Criticism,* Vol. 47 (1989), 221–28.

Baugh, B. "Authenticity Revisited," *Journal of Aesthetics and Art Criticism,* Vol. 46 (1988), 477–87.

Currie, G. *An Ontology of Art.* New York, 1989.

Danto, A. *Transfiguration of the Commonplace.* Cambridge, MA, 1981.

Davies, S. "Authenticity in Musical Performance," *British Journal of Aesthetics,* Vol. 27 (1987), 39–50.

———. "The Ontology of Musical Works and the Authenticity of Their Performances," *Noûs,* Vol. 25 (1991), 21–41.

Dutton, D., ed. *The Forger's Art.* Berkeley, CA, 1983.

Godlovitch, S. "Authentic Performance," *The Monist,* Vol. 71 (1988), 258–77.

Goodman, N. *Languages of Art,* 2d ed. Indianapolis, 1976.

———. *Of Mind and Other Matters.* Cambridge, MA, 1984. Chap. 4.

Kennick, W. E. "Art and Inauthenticity," *Journal of Aesthetics and Art Criticism,* Vol. 44 (1985), 3–12.

Levinson, J. *Music, Art, and Metaphysics.* Ithaca, NY, 1990.

———. "Art, Work of," in *The Dictionary of Art* (London, 1995).

Sagoff, M. "Historical Authenticity," *Erkenntnis,* Vol. 12 (1978), 83–93.

———. "On Restoring and Reproducing Art," *Journal of Philosophy,* Vol. 75 (1978), 453–70.

Sartwell, C. "Aesthetics of the Spurious," *British Journal of Aesthetics,* Vol. 28 (1988), 360–67.

Savile, A. "The Rationale of Restoration," *Journal of Aesthetics and Art Criticism,* Vol. 51 (1993), 463–74.

Thom, P. *For an Audience: A Philosophy of the Performing Arts.* Philadelphia, 1992.

Walton, K. "Categories of Art," *Philosophical Review,* Vol. 79 (1970), 334–67.

Wollheim, R. *Art and Its Objects,* 2d ed. Cambridge, 1980.

– JERROLD LEVINSON

AVERROËS

Averroës, or ibn-Rushd (c. 1126–c. 1198), was the foremost figure in Islamic philosophy's period of highest development (700–1200). His pre-eminence is due to his own immense philosophical acuity and power and to his enormous influence in certain phases of Latin thought from 1200 to 1650.

Averroës ("ibn-Rushd" is a more exact transliteration of the Arabic, while "Averroës" is the medieval Latin version) was born in Córdoba into a family of prominent judges and lawyers; his grandfather, bearing the same name, served as the chief *qāḍī* (judge) of Córdoba, and there is a tradition that his father carried out the same duties. (In Muslim society a *qāḍī*'s professional concepts and practical duties were simultaneously civil and religious. Thus, a "lawyer" had expert knowledge of divine law.)

Averroës's preeminence is due to

his immense philosophical acuity and power

and to his enormous influence

in certain phases of Latin thought

from 1200 to 1650.

There are, however, few other specific details about his life and career. Ernest Renan and Salomon Munk mention that he studied under the most learned teachers in theology and law (in the Muslim world the two disciplines are effectively the same). It has been suggested that he studied with such scientists and philosophers as ibn-Tufail (d. 1185) and ibn-Bajja (or Avempace, d. 1138), but the tenuous evidence would indicate that he became acquainted with the former only when he was past forty and that the death of the latter occurred when Averroës was only 11 or 12 years of age. Thus, significant pedagogical influence by these personalities upon Averroës is doubtful.

There remain, nevertheless, scattered pieces of evidence and suggestions of dates delineating his career. Averroës himself mentions that he was in Marrakesh in 1153, on which occasion he observed the star Canope, not visible in Spain at that time. This sighting confirmed for him the truth of Aristotle's claim that the world was round. Some years later he seems to have been associated with the family of the Ibn Zuhr, traditionally physicians and scholars of medicine. He is reported to have been well acquainted with Abū Marwān ibn-Zuhr, perhaps the most outstanding member of the family, and when Averroës composed his medical handbook entitled *Kulliyat* (literally, "generalities," which became latinized to *Colliget*), he encouraged Abū Marwān to write a companion text concerned with the details of specific ailments.

Tradition next reports that Averroës came into the favor of the sultan of Marrakesh, a notable patron of scholarship and research, through the personal recommendation of his friend and presumed mentor, ibn-Tufail. His ready intelligence seems to have pleased the *cālīf,* who, according to a student of Averroës, subsequently encouraged the vast series of commentaries on Aristotle which became known in the West around 1200. It is generally conjectured that the association among ibn-Tufail, the *cālīf,* and Averroës can be dated between 1153 and 1169.

Through the *cālīf*'s offices, Averroës was appointed *qāḍī* of Seville in 1169, and he began his array of commentaries on Aristotle about that time. In 1171 he returned to Córdoba, probably as *qāḍī,* and eventually became chief *qāḍī.* He was, however, continually traveling to Seville and to Marrakesh, as the colophons of various of his writings attest. In 1182 he became physician to the *cālīf* of Marrakesh, continuing as a court favorite until about 1195. At that time he is supposed to have retired, possibly under a cloud as the result of religious controversy, or perhaps to be protected from conservative theologians, to a village outside Seville; details are not available. In any case, he soon returned to Marrakesh, where he died.

His death coincided with the virtual disappearance of the dynamic speculative tradition evidenced in Arabic thinking for the several centuries after 700. Interestingly, it also coincided with the bursting forth of a similarly active tradition in the Latin West, which was greatly stimulated by the translations of Aristotle and Greek science from Arabic and Hebrew manuscripts. All these events—the death of Averroës, the abrupt decline of Arab intellectual dynamism, the translation into Latin of Aristotle (notably the *Metaphysics* and *De Anima* about 1200), and the exponential acceleration of Western philosophizing—occurred virtually within two decades. These are perhaps neither radically causative nor dependent events, but their close association is historically remarkable.

WRITINGS. During the course of his active professional life as *qāḍī,* physician, scientist, and philosopher, Averroës found time to compose an impressive number of scientific, philosophical, and religious writings. It is possible that some of his appointments may have been, in part, preferments for the purpose of sustaining scholarship. Certainly in the medieval Latin West, many a Sorbonne scholar formally designated "canon of Rheims," for example, could rarely be found at Rheims fulfilling his canonic responsibilities.

Most of Averroës's writings that can be dated fall between 1159 and 1195. There is the medical encyclopedia *Kulliyat* (composed before 1162), along with expositions of and commentaries on such medical writers as the Greek Galen and the Eastern Islamic ibn-Sīna (normally latinized as Avicenna). There are writings on astronomy. In religious philosophy there is the famous reply to the philosopher al-Ghazzali's attack on the pretensions of rationalism in matters of divine law *(The Incoherence of the Philosophers);* Averroës's response is titled *The Incoherence of the Incoherence,* in which he strongly affirms the solid adequacy of natural reason in all domains of intellectual investigation. There are many lesser writings, on problems of divine law, on logic, on natural philosophy, and on medicine. Finally, there is the massive set of commentaries on the Aristotelian corpus, which profoundly affected medieval Latin thought—sometimes with official ecclesiastical approbation, sometimes not.

Commentaries on Aristotle. The commentaries on Aristotle are of three kinds: short, often called paraphrases or epitomes; intermediate; and long, usually meticulous and detailed explications. These different versions may well correspond to stages in the educational curriculum.

The commentaries survive in many forms. For some writings of Aristotle, all three commentaries are available, for some two, and for some only one. Since Aristotle's *Politics* was not accessible to him, Averroës wrote a commentary on Plato's *Republic,* under the assumption that Greek thought constituted a coherent philosophical whole. He believed that the *Republic* contributed to this total philosophical construction. In still a further attempt to complete the presumed integrity of all Greek natural philosophy, Averroës supplemented Aristotle's *Physics* and *De Caelo* with a treatise of his own entitled *De Substantia Orbis.*

In supplementing Aristotle in this fashion, Averroës did violence to the original methodology of the Stagirite. For Aristotle the *Physics* and *De Caelo* investigated motions and processes according to two different perspectives—*Physics,* motion as such; *De Caelo,* motion in the particular context of the activities of the heavenly bodies. These investigations were not conceived as standing in any hierarchical order, reflecting any vertical order of being or reality; they were simply different investigations and must not be taken, as did many ancient and medieval commentators, in terms of category and subcategory. Averroës, with methodological dispositions akin to the Platonic, did take them in this way, and thus eventually he found it necessary to provide an all-comprehensive celestial physics—hence, the *De Substantia Orbis.*

Textual Tradition. The actual textual tradition of Averroës's works is extremely complex. Some of the commentaries remain in Arabic versions, some in Hebrew translations from the Arabic, some in Arabic texts recorded in Hebrew script, and many in Latin translations. These categories are not mutually exclusive.

Averroës's commentaries on Aristotle shaped several centuries of Latin philosophy and science. (Corbis/Bettmann)

Beginning in 1472 there appeared numerous printed editions of some, but by no means all, of the commentaries; the format usually consists of a paragraph of Aristotelian text followed immediately by Averroës's comments on and interpretation of that text. This was no doubt an apparatus designed for the practical needs of the teaching of natural philosophy in the Western Latin universities, for it is clear that Averroës's analyses had become influential by the first quarter of the thirteenth century, accompanying as they did the translations of Aristotle, and they remained influential in the traditions of the universities well into the seventeenth century.

Averroës's Philosophy

Averroës's own philosophical position can best be characterized as Aristotle warped onto a Platonic frame. He inherited Greek thought as a literary corpus and, like his Islamic philosophical predecessors, viewed this corpus as an intellectually integrated totality. Aristotle, his commentators (such as Alexander of Aphrodisias and Simplicius) and such thinkers as Plotinus and Proclus were all understood as parts dovetailing into a single coherent philosophical system. Al-Fārābī (died c. 950) is an eminent example of this syncretism: he composed a work entitled *The Harmony between Plato and Aristotle*, and Averroës himself, lacking Aristotle's *Politics*, found little difficulty in incorporating Plato's *Republic* within his compass of speculation.

RELIANCE ON NEOPLATONISM. The doctrinal positions of Greek and Alexandrian thinkers were, in fact, often quite divergent and even incompatible, and to complete the final union of their philosophies into a single intellectual system the Arab philosophers made use of a writing called the *Theology*. Late ancient tradition attributed this treatise to Aristotle, but modern scholarship has established that the *Theology* is fundamentally a compendium based on Plotinus' writings. This work was taken uncritically by Arabic philosophers as the capstone of all Greek speculative thought and, as such, was employed by them to effect the unity of ancient philosophy.

"Mystical" Knowledge. There were at least two reasons for the eager Islamic approval of the *Theology*. First, it strongly reflected the Neoplatonic emphasis especially evident in Plotinus' *Enneads*, on the culminating "mystical" experience at the apex of human knowledge. This experience involved a passing from a condition of ordinary logical ratiocination over into a condition of nondiscursive (although quasi-rational) grasp of ultimate reality. Such an attitude is strongly sympathetic to the Islamic conception of ultimate religious experience, in which there is an analogous passing from individuality into an impersonal fusion with a Whole or Divine Essence.

Hierarchy of Reality. Correlative to its reflection of Neo-platonic "mystical" knowledge, the *Theology* reflected the Neoplatonic methodological conception that is ordered in an organic hierarchy, with interlocking levels indicating superordinate and subordinate dependency. Such relationships involve levels of being and, concomitantly, sources and receivers of being. Such an intellectual structure might be visualized as a series of pyramids successively superimposed, with the preeminent pyramid pointing to an ultimate One which simultaneously comprehends being as such and is the culmination of human reflective experience. This structure is, moreover, dynamic and not static, with a continuing flow of creativity downward and a continuing activity of noetic discovery upward.

ANALYSIS OF THE SOUL. The general methodology described above is evident in many specific places in Averroës's philosophy. In his analysis of the soul, for example, Aristotle's original doctrine undergoes a transformation. Whereas Aristotle's insistence on the physi-

cal principle that every form separate from matter is one in species leads to a presumption against the possibility of individual immortality, Averroës takes the obverse: separate forms or substances can subsist in the general hierarchy of being, and thus immortality, in a purely impersonal sense, is possible.

SCIENTIFIC KNOWLEDGE. The case in natural science is similar to that of the soul. In Aristotle the various sciences are diverse and not necessarily reducible to one another in any formal sense: the *Physics* views natural behavior from one perspective and in accordance with one set of working principles, while the *De Caelo*, in contrast, uses another perspective and another set of principles. Aristotle's natural sciences are irrefragably diversified. In the *Metaphysics* he goes so far as to say that similar terminology is employed in the several sciences; however, this apparent unity of the sciences is qualified by his insistence that the use of the most general metaphysical language is, in disparate domains, only analogous and not semantically equivalent. The particular subject matter that a science encompasses controls the precise significance of the terms and logic used in the analysis and description of that science; the term "being" as it is used in the *Physics* does not possess the same meaning as "being" used in *De Anima*.

Averroës's philosophical position

can best be characterized

as Aristotle warped onto a Platonic frame.

For Averroës, however, such differentiations among the sciences were not the case. "Being" had a univocal significance, not equivocal, as it had for Aristotle; and Averroës viewed nature and reality as exhibiting a single coordinated and coherent structure, proceeding in orderly hierarchical fashion from levels that are lesser (both metaphysically and noetically) to greater and richer levels of being. Aristotle's horizontal and discrete conglomeration of sciences became a harmonious order of vertically structured science with dependent and causative relationships.

ACTIVE AND PASSIVE INTELLECTS. From Aristotle, Averroës understood that the knowing process in man comprised a passive aspect—adumbrant concepts capable of being fully activated—and an active aspect— a power of dynamically activating such concepts. This power, termed during the medieval period the "active intellect," was taken to operate against a "passive intellect" to actualize concepts and thus constituted the thinking activity; and the resulting fusion of function was termed the "acquired intellect." This terminology applicable to the noetic process was based on Aristotle's *De Anima,* and appears, with minor variations, in Greek and Arabic thought down to the time of Averroës. God, as the First Intelligence, provides through the next subordinate level of intelligences—the celestial bodies, upon which he exercises immediate control—activating power for the active intellect controlling man's thought.

However, the active intellect is not personalized because it is Aristotelian form, and each such form is a species and never an individual. Nor is the passive intellect, in its nonnoetic status apart from participation in the acquired intellect—a further pressing of Aristotle impelled by Platonic dispositions. In Averroës' philosophy, consonant with Muslim theology, it is thus a domain of reality which looks upward to God for its sustaining power and with which individual souls strive to fuse impersonally, in knowledge and ultimately in immortality. Thus Averroës, and certainly his medieval interpreters, believed in the unlikelihood of individual immortality—the active intellect with which man hopes to unite at death being a single undifferentiated form—and the soul, as individuated in this life, cannot subsist without the body.

METAPHYSICS, NATURAL PHILOSOPHY, SCIENCE. Averroës's metaphysics, natural philosophy, and science can be classified as a moderate Platonism, tempered with a profound appreciation of Aristotle. Unlike many of his Islamic predecessors, Averroës accepted Aristotle's rigorous rationalism wholeheartedly, although at various crucial points his renderings of Aristotle's laconic texts are governed by his own Platonic methodological predispositions. Against the latter, he held the principle of the univocality of being, flowing downward from a Supreme Principle. God's existence is established from the *Physics,* in that the eternity of motion demands an unmoved mover, which is in itself pure form. In addition to being the source of motion, such pure form is also Intelligence as such, operating not only as the source of the celestial bodies and all subordinate motions but also as the creative originator and sustaining force behind all lesser intelligences.

THEOLOGY AND NATURAL PHILOSOPHY. In the Christian intellectual environment of the thirteenth century, apparent conflicts between argumentation in natural philosophy and argumentation in matters of theological doctrine became exceptionally acute. The newly introduced writings from the ancients—Greek philosophy and science, accompanied by Arabic and Hebrew commentary—rigorously set forth propositions alien to fundamental dicta of Christian faith: for example, the eternity of the world, the impossibility of individual immortality, and the radical noncontingency

of existence as such. Averroës's rendering of the Aristotelian writings contributed heavily to these conflicts. Aristotle was read in the medieval faculties of arts as the staple of natural philosophy and science, and Averroës was read as his primary interpretive adjunct. In fact, in later medieval writings Averroës is merely referred to as "the Commentator." Thus, since he put forward analyses understanding Aristotle to deny the creation of the world in time, personal immortality, and the contingency of existence, such views attained wide currency among masters of arts.

The response from the theological side was early and direct. "Arabic" commentary was forbidden to be read in 1210 and 1215, and permitted only with censoring in 1231, at the University of Paris. Albert the Great published a treatise, *Contra Averroistas,* and Thomas Aquinas wrote about 1269, at a time of great intellectual controversy at Paris, a *Tractatus de Unitate Intellectus Contra Averroistas.*

"Double-Truth" Doctrine. The replies to Averroës were reasoned and moderate, but they seem to have been accompanied by many contemporary declarations that the "Averroists" were actually maintaining a doctrine of "double truth," according to which conclusions in natural philosophy were said to be true, while simultaneously conclusions affirming the contrary in theological argument were held true—presumably an intolerable intellectual situation. Thus there were official condemnations of "unorthodox" doctrines at the University of Paris in 1270 and 1277, including specific injunctions against two standards of truth. It is not, however, clear that any philosophers in the thirteenth century explicitly held such a theory of "double truth"; in the writings that survive, philosophers faced with these conflicts take great pains to concede truth itself to the declarations of faith and say of Aristotelian writings only that they have been properly arrived at according to Aristotle's methods.

Averroës himself composed the short treatise *On the Harmony Between Religion and Philosophy;* his main effort in this work was to establish that there is but one truth to which there are several modes of access—the rhetorical, open to any man through the persuasions of teachers; the dialectical, available for some to explore the probability of truths of divine law; and the philosophical, to be used only by those few capable of exercising pure ratiocination with the fullest competence. Such a variety of methods insures for each man, depending on his individual capability, the possibility of grasping ultimate realities. The fact that in this work Averroës distinguishes between such modes of access to truth has, by many historians, been taken to adumbrate the theory of the "double truth," as attributed to many thinkers in the thirteenth century, but this is not probable. First, this work of Averroës was not available to medieval Latin scholars and thus obviously cannot have been directly influential; second, the doctrine of alternative modes of access to truth is hardly the same as that of maintaining incompatible truths in disparate domains.

Thus, the attribution of a doctrine of "double truth" to medievals cannot be sustained by any writings of Aristotle accompanied by Averroistic commentaries, nor can it be justified explicitly from any Christian medieval master. The oppositions between Aristotelian–Averroist argument and basic Christian doctrine constituted a fundamental intellectual dilemma within Christian speculation—one never resolved by the masters of arts in an explicit proclamation of a logical contradiction between two domains of reflection but always by an absolute accession of truth to faith. Averroës did not contribute specifically to the discussion arising from this dilemma, except insofar as his rigorous analysis of Aristotle made necessary certain conclusions in natural philosophy.

Averroës stands as a philosopher in his own right, but his influence was felt essentially in Western Latin philosophy from 1200 to 1650. His commentaries on Aristotle, an integral part of the educational curriculum in the faculties of arts of western European universities, shaped several centuries of Latin philosophy and science. Despite institutional criticism and even formal condemnation, his powerful statements of Aristotelian doctrine were sustained among Latin scholars and thinkers well into the mid-seventeenth century.

BIBLIOGRAPHY

The most important general references are Ernest Renan, *Averroès et l'averroisme* (Paris, 1852; modern ed., Paris, 1949); Salomon Munk, *Mélanges de philosophie juive et arabe* (Paris, 1859), pp. 418–458; Léon Gauthier, *Ibn Rochd* (Paris, 1948); and G. Quadri, *La Philosophie arabe dans l'Europe médiévale* (Paris, 1947), pp. 198–340. The last two of these studies depend heavily on the first two, which are the unsuperseded (except in occasional detail) classics in the literature on Averroës, although Gauthier properly views some of the indirect traditions with caution. For Averroës's predecessors, mentors, and contemporaries, see George Sarton, *Introduction to the History of Science,* Vol. I (Baltimore, 1927) and Vol. II (Baltimore, 1931), *passim.* Significant recent interpretations, with varying emphases, can be found in Étienne Gilson, *History of Christian Philosophy in the Middle Ages* (New York, 1955); A. A. Maurer, *Medieval Philosophy* (New York, 1962); and D. Knowles, *Evolution of Medieval Thought* (Baltimore, 1962).

For a detailed catalogue of Averroës's writings, see George Sarton, *Introduction to the History of Science,* Vol. II, Part 2, pp. 356–360. Also see Léon Gauthier, *Ibn Rochd,* pp. 12–16, and M. Bouyges, *Notes sur les philosophes arabes connus de Latins au moyen âge,* Vol. IV, *Inventaires des textes arabes d'Averroès* (Beirut, 1922). The latter, a monograph, is in the *Mélanges de l'Université Saint-Joseph* (Beirut, 1922), Vol. VIII, Fascicle 1. H. A. Wolfson has meticulously stated the ambitious program for preparing and publishing modern editions of the Aristotelian commentaries in "Plan for the Publication of a Corpus Commentariorum Averrois in Aristotelem," in *Speculum,* Vol. 6 (1931), 412–427, and "Revised Plan for the Publication of a Corpus Commentariorum Averrois in Aristotelem," in *Speculum,* Vol. 38 (1963), 88–104. The latter article provides the most reliable listing of the surviving writings. There are other modern editions and translations of some works: for instance, E. I. J. Rosenthal, *Averroës's Commentary on Plato's Republic* (Cambridge, 1956); G. F. Hourani, *Averroës on the Harmony of Religion and Philosophy* (London, 1961); and S. Van den Bergh's translation of *The Incoherence of the Incoherence* (Oxford, 1954).

– STUART MACCLINTOCK

B

BAD FAITH

The most common form of inauthenticity in the existentialism of Jean-Paul Sartre, bad faith is paradoxically a lie to oneself. For such self-deception to be possible, the human being must be divided against itself, one level or aspect concealing from the other what it in some sense "knows." The paradox arises from the condition that this operation occurs within the unity of a single consciousness.

The root of Sartrean bad faith is a twofold dividedness of the human being, psychological and ontological. As conscious, humans are prereflectively aware of what they may not reflectively know. Such prereflective awareness or "comprehension," as he will later call it, functions in Sartre's psychology in a manner similar to Freud's unconscious, a concept that Sartre notoriously rejected. The project of bad faith—to keep oneself in the dark about certain matters—is itself in bad faith since prereflective consciousness "chooses" not to acknowledge on reflection what it is concealing from reflective consciousness.

There can be an entire Weltanschauung of bad faith:

the habits, practices, objects, and institutions

that one employs to maintain oneself in a state of

"perpetual distraction."

There can be an entire Weltanschauung of bad faith: the habits, practices, objects, and institutions that one employs to maintain oneself in a state of "perpetual distraction." Sartre's analysis of Second Empire French society in his work on Flaubert is a study in collective bad faith. But the root of the moral responsibility that this term carries lies in the self-translucency of prereflective consciousness: individuals, alone or together, are prereflectively *aware* of more than they reflectively allow themselves to *know.*

The ontological basis of bad faith is the dividedness of the human situation. Every human exists in-situation. Situation is an ambiguous mix of facticity (the given) and transcendence (the surpassing of the given by our projects). Bad faith is our way of fleeing the anguish that this ambiguity causes either by collapsing our transcendence into facticity (as in various forms of determinism) or by volatilizing our facticity into transcendence (like the dreamer who refuses to acknowledge the facts of his or her life). Though the details of bad faith are as singular as our self-defining choices, its moral significance is the same in each instance. Bad faith is basically flight from our freedom-in-situation.

As Sartre's concept of situation expanded to include and even place a premium on socioeconomic conditions, the relation between bad faith and class struggle became more pronounced. He later argued that good faith, which in *Being and Nothingness* he dismissed as a form of bad faith, was fostered by socioeconomic equality and that scarcity of material goods made bad faith almost inevitable. The anti-Semite was in bad faith, but so too was his or her liberal assimilationist defender; likewise the neocolonialist and the industrial capitalist, both of whom fled their responsibility for subscribing to and sustaining a system that made exploitation of others "necessary."

Only in his posthumously published *Notebooks for an Ethics* does Sartre discuss the nature and possibility of good faith at any length. This presumes a "conversion" in which one chooses to live one's anguished dividedness while fostering via generous cooperation a situation that enables others to do likewise.

[See also Authenticity; Determinism and Freedom; Existentialism; Freud, Sigmund; Sartre, Jean-Paul.]

BIBLIOGRAPHY

Beauvoir, S. de. *Pour une morale de l'ambiguité.* Paris, 1947. Translated by B. Frechtman as *The Ethics of Ambiguity.* New York, 1948.

Fingarette, H. *Self-Deception.* London, 1969.

Martin, M. W. *Self-Deception and Morality.* Lawrence, KS, 1986.

Mirvish, A. "Bad Faith, Good Faith, and the Faith of Faith," in R. Aronson and A. van den Hoven, eds., *Sartre Alive* (Detroit, 1991).

Morris, P. "Self-Deception: Sartre's Resolution of the Paradox," in H. J. Silverman and F. A. Elliston, eds., *Jean-Paul Sartre: Contemporary Approaches to His Philosophy* (Pittsburgh, 1980).

Santoni, R. E. *Bad Faith, Good Faith and Authenticity in Sartre's Early Philosophy.* Philadelphia, 1995.

Sartre, J.-P. *Cahiers pour une morale.* Paris, 1983. Translated by D. Pellauer as *Notebooks for an Ethics.* Chicago, 1992.

———. *L'Etre et le néant.* Paris, 1943. Translated by H. E. Barnes as *Being and Nothingness.* New York, 1956.

— THOMAS R. FLYNN

BAYESIANISM

Bayesianism holds that in their cognitive interactions with the world rational agents can be represented as having degrees of belief that are regimented according to the probability calculus. Over time an agent's degrees of belief will change as a result of learning experiences. In the case where such an experience can be characterized as having a propositional content E, it is assumed that the new degrees of belief Pr_{new} are related to the old Pr_{old} by the rule of strict conditionalization: $Pr_{new}(\bullet) = Pr_{old}(\bullet/E)$, where $Pr(X/Y)$ is the conditional probability of X on Y. A more sophisticated rule that allows for uncertain learning has been proposed by Jeffrey (1983).

One justification for regarding the axioms of probability as rationality constraints comes from the demonstration that the failure to conform degrees of belief to the axioms leads to Dutch book: a finite series of bets, each of which the agent regards as fair, with the net result that the agent is guaranteed to lose money. Similarly, diachronic Dutch book arguments have been offered as justifications for the rule of strict conditionalization. Despite their surface appeal, the import of these arguments is controversial (see Maher, 1993).

The subjectivist version of Bayesianism holds that there are no other constraints on rational belief. By such lights the Rev. Thomas Bayes was not himself a pure subjectivist. Bayes's theorem, a result not explicitly stated in Bayes's (1764) original paper, says that $Pr(H/E\&B) = (Pr(H/B)\times Pr(E/H\&B))/Pr(E/B)$. It is helpful to think of H as the hypothesis under investigation, B as the background knowledge, and E as the evidence acquired by observation or experiment. The theorem says that the posterior probability $Pr(H/E\&B)$ of H is equal to the product of the prior probability $Pr(H/B)$ of H and the posterior likelihood $Pr(E/H\&B)$ of E, divided by the prior likelihood $Pr(E/B)$ of E. Bayes thought that the principle of sufficient reason imposes constraints on the prior probability $Pr(H/B)$. This and other attempts to objectify priors run into notorious difficulties. The subjectivists hold that the objectivity of belief is to be gained not by constraints on priors but by the washing out of priors with accumulating evidence. Whether or not mathematical theorems on washing out of priors are applicable to typical cases of scientific inference is a matter of debate (see Earman, 1992).

With conditional probability defined by $Pr(X/Y) = Pr(X\&Y)/Pr(Y)$ (which assumes that $Pr(Y) \neq 0$), Bayes's theorem is a triviality. Alternatively, if conditional probability is taken as primitive, the theorem is an easy consequence of the multiplication axiom $Pr(X\&Y/Z) = Pr(X/Y)\times Pr(Y/X\&Z)$. Although trivial to prove, Bayes's theorem has profound implications for the confirmation of scientific hypotheses. Suppose, for example, that H and B together entail E, as is assumed in the hypotheticodeductive (HD) method. Then an application of Bayes's theorem shows that if $0 < Pr(H/B) < 1$ (one was not certain about H to begin with) and $0 < Pr(E/B) < 1$ (one was not certain that the observation or experiment would yield E or a result incompatible with E), then $Pr(H/E\&B) > Pr(H/B)$. That is, H is incrementally confirmed by E, showing that there is a kernel of truth to the much criticized HD method.

The same machinery can be used to illuminate Hempel's ravens paradox. *Pace* Hempel, it can be shown that, under appropriate background assumptions, the observation of a nonblack nonraven does incrementally confirm the hypothesis that all ravens are black. But it can also be shown that, given plausible assumptions about the relative sizes of the classes of ravens and of nonblack things, the observation of a black raven confirms the ravens hypothesis more than does the discovery of a white shoe.

The Bayesian approach to confirmation must contend with Glymour's (1980) problem of old evidence, the most virulent form of which occurs when the evidence E was known before the hypothesis H was even formulated. Thus, for example, the anomalous advance of the perihelion of Mercury was known to astronomers long before Einstein formulated his general theory of relativity. A naive application of Bayes's theorem would seem to imply that no incremental confirmation takes place, despite the fact that physicists uniformly claim that general relativity receives strong confirmation from its explanation of the perihelion advance.

[See also Probability.]

BIBLIOGRAPHY

Bayes, T. "An Essay Towards Solving a Problem in the Doctrine of Chances," *Philosophical Transaction of the Royal Society (London)*, Vol. 53 (1764), 370–418.

Earman, J. *Bayes or Bust? A Critical Examination of Bayesian Confirmation Theory.* Cambridge, MA, 1992.

Glymour, C. *Theory and Evidence.* Princeton, NJ, 1980.

Howson, C., and P. Urbach. *Scientific Reasoning: The Bayesian Approach,* 2d ed. La Salle, IL, 1993.

Jeffrey, R. C. *The Logic of Decision,* 2d ed. Chicago, 1983.

Maher, P. *Betting on Theories.* Cambridge, 1993.

– JOHN EARMAN

BEAUTY

While it is true that beauty is the central idea of aesthetics from the origins of metaphysics in Plato to the eighteenth century, it is equally true that the attempt

The divorce of artworks from their traditional marriage to beauty is now a commonplace. (Corbis/Francis G. Mayer)

Many of the most innovative efforts in the Continental tradition to reopen the question of beauty in contemporary aesthetics have done so by taking reference to the major text of eighteenth-century aesthetics, Kant's *Critique of Judgment.* Thus, one finds Adorno, Arendt, Gadamer, Derrida, and Lyotard all taking up Kant's text where the question of aesthetics is divided into natural and artistic beauty, and where any claim about beauty is understood as a subjective judgment of taste laying claim to universality. Recent discussions of aesthetic experience frequently follow the Kantian matrix discussing beauty; namely, it is discussed in its difference from the other form of aesthetic experience found in sublimity, in its different significance as natural and artistic beauty, and in the form of subjectivity that is called into play in the judgment of taste.

[*See also Aesthetics, History of; Aesthetics, Problems of; Arendt, Hannah; Derrida, Jacques; Gadamer, Hans-Georg; Hegel, Georg W. F.; Kant, Immanuel; Nietzsche, Friedrich Wilhelm; Plato.*]

BIBLIOGRAPHY

Arendt, H. *Lectures on Kant's Political Philosophy.* Chicago, 1982.
Derrida, J. *Truth in Painting.* Chicago, 1987.
Gadamer, H.-G. *Truth and Method.* New York, 1975. Part 1.
Harries, K. *The Meaning of Modern Art.* Evanston, IL, 1968.

— DENNIS J. SCHMIDT

to understand the significance of the demotion of the idea of beauty from aesthetic theory in most aesthetic treatises written since the time of Baumgarten in both the rationalist and empiricist traditions has been a dominant concern of reflections on art and nature since that time. By the mid-twentieth century art had followed suit: art no longer takes its kinship with the feeling of beauty as its definitive impulse. Moving into the realm of cultural critique, and taking its task to be more concerned with an exploration of the nature and forms of representation in general than the production of beautiful objects, the divorce of artworks from their traditional marriage to beauty is now a commonplace. However, while artworks no longer seem to define themselves by their relation to beauty, it is now the case that aesthetic theories are finding themselves increasingly interested in asking about the prospects of beauty in the contemporary world. Thus, while Hegel can write that beauty is passé from the standpoint of truth, and Nietzsche can write that art should no longer be judged according to the category of beauty, Heidegger, writing in 1935, can suggest that this question of the status of beauty is among the most pressing questions of our age.

BEAUVOIR, SIMONE DE

Simone de Beauvoir, French existentialist feminist, was born in Paris in 1908 and died in 1986, after a prolific career as a philosopher, essayist, novelist, and political activist. Her writings were, by her own accounts, heavily influenced by the philosophy of Jean-Paul Sartre, her intellectual companion for half a century, leading some critics to dismiss her as philosophically unoriginal. Even de Beauvoir, in a 1979 interview, said that she did not consider herself to be a philosopher. In her view, however, "a philosopher is someone like Spinoza, Hegel, or like Sartre, someone who builds a grand system" (quoted in Simons, 1986, p. 168), a definition that would exclude most contemporary professional philosophers. Furthermore, as several recent commentators have argued, de Beauvoir seems to have underestimated her influence on the discipline in general and on Sartre in particular. Although she incorporated Sartrean ideas such as his existentialist conception of freedom in her ethical and political writings, her critiques of Sartre's work-in-progress helped shape his philosophy, which she then extended and transformed in significant ways.

In *The Ethics of Ambiguity,* de Beauvoir attempted to develop an existentialist ethics out of the ontological

De Beauvoir's The Second Sex *explained how women's oppression limits their freedom. (Corbis/Hulton-Deutsch Collection)*

categories in Sartre's *Being and Nothingness.* In Sartre's view, there is no God and therefore no God-given human nature. Nor is human nature determined by biological, psychological, economic, cultural, or any other factors. People are "condemned to be free," and in the course of existing and making choices they construct their own natures (which are continually revisable). Human consciousness is such that, although it is being-for-itself (the being of free and transcendent subjects), it vainly tries to turn itself into being-in-itself (the being of objects, things trapped in their immanence). De Beauvoir called this doomed attempt to synthesize the for-itself and the in-itself the "ambiguity" of the human condition, and she argued that it is because of this inability of human beings to "coincide with" themselves that an ethics is both possible an required. She attempted to ground ethics in individual freedom by asserting that "To will oneself free is also to will others free" (73), but her defense of this claim appears to slip both Kantian and Hegelian presuppositions about human nature into a philosophy that denies that there is such a thing.

In *The Ethics of Ambiguity* de Beauvoir moved beyond Sartrean existentialism in acknowledging certain constraints on freedom, including political oppression and early socialization, that Sartre did not recognize until much later. In her memoirs de Beauvoir recalled conversations she had with Sartre in 1940 about his account of freedom as an active transcendence of one's situation. She had maintained that not every situation offered the same scope for freedom: "What sort of transcendence could a woman shut up in a harem achieve?" Sartre had insisted that even such a limiting situation could be lived in a variety of ways, but de Beauvoir was not persuaded. To defend her view, though, she would "have had to abandon the plane of individual, and therefore idealistic, morality" on which they had set themselves (1962, p. 346).

In *The Second Sex* de Beauvoir continued to move away from a purely metaphysical view of freedom in developing an account of how women's oppression limits their freedom. Although in arguing that "One is not born, but rather becomes, a woman" de Beauvoir applied the existentialist tenet that "existence precedes essence" to the situation of women, she was also influenced by Marxist accounts of the material constraints on our freedom to create ourselves. In addition, she described the ways the socialization of girls and the cultural representations of women perpetuate the view of women as other, thereby limiting their potential for transcendence.

Critics of de Beauvoir's feminism have pointed out tensions between her existentialist premises and her account of the relation between embodiment and oppression. Although, according to existentialism, anatomy is not destiny (nor is anything else), de Beauvoir's discussion of female sexuality at times suggests that women's reproductive capacities are less conducive than men's to the achievement of transcendence. De Beauvoir has also been criticized for advocating (in 1949) that women assume men's place in society, although in interviews (in the 1970s and 1980s) she urged a transformation of both men's and women's roles.

Even de Beauvoir's critics, however, acknowledge her enormous impact on contemporary feminism. Her analysis of what has become known as the sex/gender distinction set the stage for all subsequent discussions. In drawing on philosophy, psychology, sociology, biology, history, and literature in *The Second Sex* and other essays she anticipated the interdisciplinary field of women's studies. Her concern with autobiography, with self-revelation as "illuminating the lives of others" (1962, p. 8), prefigured feminism's preoccupation with the personal as political. It also drew on a philosophical tradition as old as Socrates; her relentless scrutiny of herself and others exemplified, to an extent unmatched by any other twentieth-century philosopher, the maxim that "the unexamined life is not worth living."

In her fiction as well as in her essays and memoirs de Beauvoir discussed numerous philosophical themes— for example, freedom, choice, responsibility, and the

---

De Beauvoir maintained to Sartre that not every situation offered the same scope for freedom: "What sort of transcendence could a woman shut up in a harem achieve?"

---

other—and she also explored the political issues and conflicts of the day, so much so that she has been described as "witness to a century." But she was more than a mere chronicler of events; she was a powerful social critic and an internationally known "public intellectual" whose influence will continue to be felt for a long time.

[See also Existentialism; Hegel, Georg W. F.; Sartre, Jean-Paul; Spinoza, Benedict (Baruch).]

BIBLIOGRAPHY

Selected Works by de Beauvoir

(For a comprehensive bibliography of the publications of de Beauvoir from 1943 to 1977, see Claude Francis and Fernande Gontier, *Les Écrits de Simone de Beauvoir* [Paris, 1979].)

Essays

Pyrrhus et Cinéas. Paris, 1944.
Pour une morale de l'ambiguïté. Paris, 1947. Translated by B. Frechtman as *The Ethics of Ambiguity.* New York, 1948.
Le Deuxième sexe. Paris, 1949. Translated by H. M. Parshley as *The Second Sex.* New York, 1953.
La Vieillesse. Paris, 1970. Translated by P. O'Brien as *The Coming of Age.* New York, 1972.

Fiction

L'Invitée. Paris, 1943. Translated by Y. Moyse and R. Senhouse as *She Came to Stay.* New York, 1954.
Les Mandarins. Paris, 1954. Translated by L. M. Friedman as *The Mandarins.* New York, 1956.

Memoirs

Mémoires d'une jeune fille rangée. Paris, 1958. Translated by James Kirkup as *Memoirs of a Dutiful Daughter.* New York, 1959.
La Force de l'âge. Paris, 1960. Translated by P. Green as *The Prime of Life.* New York, 1962.
La Force des choses. Paris, 1963. Translated by R. Howard as *Force of Circumstance.* New York, 1965.
Tout compte fait. Paris, 1972. Translated by P. O'Brien as *All Said and Done.* New York, 1974.

Selected Works on de Beauvoir

Brosman, C. S. *Simone de Beauvoir Revisited.* Boston, 1991.
Dietz, M. G. "Introduction: Debating Simone de Beauvoir," Signs, Vol. 18 (1992), 74–88.
Gatens, M. "Woman as Other," in *Feminism and Philosophy* (Cambridge, 1991).
Le Doeuff, M. "Simone de Beauvoir and Existentialism," translated from the French by C. Gordon, *Feminist Studies*, Vol. 6 (1980), 277–89.
Mackenzie, C. "Simone de Beauvoir: Philosophy and/or the Female Body," in C. Pateman and E. Gross, eds., *Feminist Challenges: Social and Political Theory* (Boston, 1986).
McCall, D. K. "Simone de Beauvoir, *The Second Sex,* and Jean-Paul Sartre," Signs, Vol. 5 (1979), 209–23.
Simons, M. A. "Beauvoir and Sartre: The Philosophical Relationship," in H. V. Wenzel, ed., *Simone de Beauvoir: Witness to a Century,* special volume of Yale French Studies, No. 72 (1986), 165–79.
Tong, R. "Existentialist Feminism," in *Feminist Thought* (Boulder, CO, 1989).
Whitmarsh, A. *Simone de Beauvoir and the Limits of Commitment.* Cambridge, 1981.

– SUSAN J. BRISON

BELIEF ATTRIBUTIONS

Belief attributions are uses of sentences of the form *N* believes that *s* (where *N* is a noun phrase, *s* a sentence). Their semantic and logical properties have been debated under the assumption that an account of "believes" will carry over to other propositional attitudes such as desire, knowledge, and fear. Most of the debate focuses on two issues: does "believe" pick out a relation, and how do so-called *de re* and *de dicto* attributions differ?

Is "Believes" Relational?

The obvious hypothesis is that in

(1) Maggie believes that Twain lives.

"believes" has the semantic status of a transitive verb, picking out a relation between a believer and something (a proposition) provided by the verb's complement,

(2) that Twain lives.

Grammatical evidence suggests this: "believes" can be followed by names and demonstratives ("I believe Church's thesis," "she believes that") as well as expressions that behave like (nominal) variables ("whenever the Pope says something I believe it").

Gottlob Frege and Bertrand Russell, whose work inspires most subsequent debate about belief attribution, agreed on the obvious hypothesis. Frege held that expressions embedded within "believes that" shift their reference to a way of thinking, or sense, of what they refer to unembedded. Russell held that no such semantic shift occurs; the proposition that *s* is determined by what *s*'s parts pick out when used unembedded.

Since "Twain" and "Clemens" refer to the same author, the Russellian approach seems committed to the identity of the propositions, that Twain lives and that Clemens does, and thus to (1)'s implying

(3) Maggie believes that Clemens lives.

Russell would avoid this by saying that "Twain" and "Clemens" typically function as truncated definite descriptions. This last suggestion is widely thought to have been discredited by Saul Kripke (see Kripke, 1979).

One problem Fregean views face is that sense is idiosyncratic: different people associate with a name different ways of thinking of the referent. It is implausible that when I utter (1) I speak truly only if Maggie thinks of Twain as do I. But if (2) in (1) named Maggie's sense for "Twain lives," the argument "Maggie believes that Twain lives; Seth believes what Maggie does; so Seth believes that Twain lives" would be invalid.

Contemporary Russellians such as Nathan Salmon and Scott Soames hold that to believe a proposition involves grasping or representing it and its constituents; thus, belief is a three-place relation among a believer, a Russellian content, and a representation. Salmon and Soames nonetheless hold that (1) tells us only that Maggie believes ("under some representation") the Russellian proposition that Twain lives; the appearance that (1) and (3) may disagree in truth value results from mistaking a conversational or pragmatic implicature, about the representation under which a belief is held, for part of what a belief attribution, strictly speaking, says.

John Perry and Mark Crimmins have suggested that a belief attribution involves implicit reference to the Russellian's representations or modes of grasping: the complement of "believes" determines a Russellian proposition, but the verb has an "implicit argument place" for representations. A use of (1) makes a claim along the lines of *Maggie believes the Russellian proposition that Twain lives under representation r,* with the representation referred to differing across occasions of use. A problem with this view is that it renders the argument mentioned two paragraphs above invalid.

Some think belief attributions implicitly quotational. The simplest version of such a view sees *that s* as a quotation name of *s,* "believes" naming a relation to sentence types. To this it may be objected that different uses of "Seth thinks I am sad" may have different truth values. Another view sees a "that" clause as picking out a fusion of linguistic items with their interpretations— for example, the result of combining a sentence with the semantic values of its expressions.

Mark Richard's version of this view has *that s* pick out a fusion of the sentence *s* and its Russellian content. In belief attribution, such fusions are offered as "trans-lations" of the believer's thoughts, where a thought is the result of combining a representation that realizes a belief with its Russellian content: (1) is true if the "that" clause provides a translation of a thought of Maggie's. Standards of translation shift from context to context: "Twain" may represent a representation of Maggie's in some but not all contexts. Thus, on this view, the truth of (1) does not demand that of (3).

Donald Davidson denies that (2) is a semantically significant part of (1). "Believes" is a predicate whose second argument is the demonstrative "that"; its referent is the ensuing utterance of "Twain lives." The overall force of (1) is roughly some belief state of Maggie's agrees in content with that utterance. (Davidson made such a proposal for "says" but clearly intended to generalize.) Yet more radical views deny that "believes" is a predicate. Arthur N. Prior took "believes" to combine with a name and sentence to form a more complex sentence; W. V. O. Quine has entertained the idea that "believes that Twain lives" is a predicate without semantically significant structure. A problem for Quine is to explain how infinitely many (semantically unstructured) belief predicates acquire their meanings; Prior thought little useful could be said on such issues.

De Re and De Dicto

There seem to be two ways of interpreting sentences like

(4) Sam believes that Melinda's husband is unmarried.

Sam believes that some Frenchman is not French. One interpretation attributes to Sam necessarily false beliefs; the other, suggested by

(4') Of Melinda's husband, Sam believes he is unmarried.

Of some Frenchman, Sam believes he is not French. does not. Note that (4') ascribes to Sam beliefs in some sense about particular individuals, while this is not true of the interpretation of (4).

The interpretations seem to correspond to different scopes that may be assigned to the quantifier phrases "Melinda's husband" and "some Frenchman." In a *de re* attribution, an expression functioning as a variable within the scope of "believes" is bound by a quantifier outside its scope (and the scopes of other verbs of propositional attitudes). Interpreting the sentences in (4) as in (4') is *de re* attribution: "he" and "she" are bound to "Melinda's husband" and "some women," which are not in the scope of "believes." An attribution that is not *de re* is *de dicto*. If we accept a relational account of "believes," we will say that a *de dicto* interpretation of *N* believes that *s* attributes to *N* a belief in the proposition expressed by *s*. (An attribution might also count as *de re* if it has a term anaphoric on a name outside of the attribution, as in the natural understanding of

(5) Twain was an author, but Seth believes that he was president.)

Not everyone would characterize the *de re–de dicto* distinction as above. Quine held that it is impossible for a quantifier to bind a variable that occurs opaquely—that is, inside a construction, like "believes," which causes failures to substitutivity. If Quine were correct, some other account of the two understandings of (4) is needed. (Quine himself suggested that "believes" is ambiguous.) Quine's view is not widely shared. (See Kaplan, 1986, for discussion.)

The relations between *de re* and *de dicto* attributions are of interest in good part because *de re* attributions are anomalous on some views. A *de re* attribution identifies a belief in terms of the objects it is about, not in terms of how those objects are conceptualized. For a Russellian this is the norm: all there is to belief attribution is identifying the state of affairs believed to obtain. For a Fregean, (4′) is at best an aberration, lacking information about sense, which belief attribution is supposed to convey. *De re* belief attributions provide a focus for the debates among Russellians, Fregeans, and others.

[See also Davidson, Donald; Epistemology; Frege, Gottlob; Kripke, Saul Aaron; Prior, Arthur N.; Quine, Willard Van Orman; Russell, Bertrand Arthur William.]

BIBLIOGRAPHY

Crimmins, M. *Talk about Beliefs*. Cambridge, MA, 1992.

Davidson, D. "On Saying That," in *Essays on Truth and Interpretation* (Oxford, 1984).

Frege, G. "Uber Sinn und Bedeutung," *Zeitschrift fur Philosophie and Philosophische Kritik,* Vol. 100 (1892), 25–50. Translated by P. Geach and M. Black as "On Sense and Reference," in Geach and Black, eds., *Translations from the Philosophical Writings of Gottlob Frege* (Cambridge, 1952).

Higginbotham, J. "Belief and Logical Form," *Mind and Language,* Vol. 6 (1991), 344–69.

Kaplan, D. "Quantifying In," in D. Davidson and G. Harman, eds., *Words and Objections* (Dordrecht, 1969).

———. "Opacity," in L. Hahn and P. Schlipp, eds., *The Philosophy of W. V. Quine* (La Salle, IL, 1986).

Kripke, S. "A Puzzle about Belief," in A. Margalit, ed., *Meaning and Use* (Dordrecht, 1979). Also in Salmon and Soames, 1988.

Perry, J. and M. Crimmins. "The Prince and the Phone Booth," *Journal of Philosophy,* Vol. 86 (1989), 685–711.

Prior, A. N. *Objects of Thought*. Oxford, 1971.

Quine, W. V. "Quantifiers and Propositional Attitudes," *Journal of Philosophy,* Vol. 53 (1956), 177–87.

———. *Word and Object*. Cambridge. MA, 1960.

Richard, M. *Propositional Attitudes*. Cambridge, 1990.

Salmon, N. *Frege's Puzzle*. Cambridge, MA, 1986.

Salmon, N., and S. Soames, eds. *Propositions and Attitudes*. Oxford, 1988.

– MARK RICHARD

BENTHAM, JEREMY

Jeremy Bentham (1748–1832), English Utilitarian and leader of the Philosophical Radicals, was born in Houndsditch, in London. He entered Queen's College, Oxford, at the age of 12, graduated in 1763, and immediately entered Lincoln's Inn to study law, his father's profession. He was called to the bar in 1767 but, although the law was his major preoccupation throughout his long life, he never practiced it. Instead, he set himself to work out a system of jurisprudence and to codify and reform both civil and penal law. His motive was a profound dissatisfaction both with what he witnessed in the courts as a student, and with its theoretical justification by such expositors as Blackstone. The theory did not seem to Bentham either coherent in itself or in accordance with the practice; the practice was brutal, cumbersome, costly, and wrapped in unnecessary obscurity. Bentham's life work was the advocacy of a clear, coherent, humane, and simplified legal system.

Bentham's lifework was the advocacy of a clear, coherent, humane, and simplified legal system.

In pursuit of this aim, Bentham wrote many thousands of pages, but in a curiously desultory way. Before finishing one work, he would start on another; many were left unfinished, and those that he did finish he often did not bother to publish; some were made known to the world only through the French translations of his Swiss follower, Étienne Dumont.

Bentham began his writings on legal reform with a rationale of punishment and an elaborate *Comment* on Blackstone's *Commentaries*. It was about 35 years before the first was published (in Paris by Dumont, in 1811, together with some later material, as *Théorie des peines et des récompenses*); the second escaped publication for nearly 150 years, until 1928. Bentham did, however, publish an extract from it, in which he attacked Blackstone's eulogy of the English constitution, under the title *A Fragment on Government* (London, 1776). The only major theoretical work he published himself was the *Introduction to the Principles of Morals and Legislation* (Oxford, 1789). He did publish a large number of pamphlets on topical issues, attacking the law of libel, the packing of juries, the oath, the extortions of the

Bentham is remembered chiefly as the exponent of utilitarianism. (Corbis)

legal profession, the established church, and much else; or defending the lending of money at interest, reforms in education, and his elaborate scheme for a model prison, on which he spent much time and money. His more theoretical works—such as *The Book of Fallacies* (London, 1824), prepared and edited at Bentham's direction from unfinished manuscripts by Peregrine Bingham; the *Rationale of Judicial Evidence* (London, 1827), similarly edited by J. S. Mill after the publication of a shorter version by Dumont; *Traité des preuves judiciares* (Paris, 1823), edited by Dumont; and the posthumous *Deontology* (London and Edinburgh, 1834), edited by Bowring—were mostly left in an unfinished state by Bentham. The book that did most to make him known was Dumont's *Traités de législation civile et pénale* (Paris, 1802), which was in part an exposition of Bentham's ideas and in part a translation of some of Bentham's published and unpublished works. There are several translations of Dumont's work, the first by John Neal (Boston, 1840).

Bentham tried to interest Catherine of Russia and other European rulers in his *Constitutional Code* (Vol. I first published London, 1830; the complete work first published in the *Works*). He was made a citizen of the infant French republic in 1792, and had some influence there and in other European countries, as well as in that other infant republic, the United States of America. His most abiding influence was, however, in England, where the Benthamites became a powerful political force that attracted men of the caliber of James Mill and his son John Stuart Mill, continued long after Bentham's death, and eventually accomplished at least some of the political and legal reforms Bentham had hoped for. By the time Bentham died, he was already the revered sage of a strong movement. It had a journal, the *Westminster Review,* which Bentham had established in 1824, at his own expense, as an organ of radical opinion to counter the Whig *Edinburgh* and the Tory *Quarterly.* The movement had even succeeded in founding a university—University College, London—in which one of Bentham's most notable disciples, John Austin, became the first professor of jurisprudence. There Bentham's embalmed body, surmounted by a wax model of his head, and dressed in his accustomed clothes, is still to be seen.

MORAL THEORY. It is as the exponent of utilitarianism and as the acknowledged leader of the philosophical radicals, whose program of social reform was firmly based on utilitarian theory, that Bentham is chiefly remembered. He thought of the principle of utility as primarily a guide for legislators. Through it he hoped to impart some order into the chaos and illogic of the law.

Attack on Intuitionism. This chaos was, it seemed to him, partly the result of intuitionism (or the belief in intuitively apprehended absolute principles), which he called "the principle of sympathy and antipathy," or "ipsedixitism." The legislator happened to be revolted by some actions, so he punished them heavily, even though they caused suffering to no one. Bentham cited sexual offenses as one example of this. On the other hand, other types of action that caused great public suffering were either left unpunished or were punished very leniently. This was the inevitable result of basing a penal code on immutable "moral laws" that stigmatized actions as bad in themselves, without regard to their consequences. Nor was it merely penal law that suffered from this error in moral theory. Civil law was traditionally based on contract: the appeal was to an absolute principle, "promises must be kept." But it sometimes happened that the law was unwilling to enforce a contract, perhaps because it was against public policy. Instead of drawing the conclusion that the rule about keeping promises was not absolute, but subordinate to a more binding rule about the public interest, the lawyers said that in this case the contract was null and void, that there never had been a contract. In other words, they saved their moral theory by deliberately falsifying the facts. On the other hand, when the law wished to enforce an obligation that patently did not rest on a contract, since none had been made, it pretended that one had been made, and spoke of a quasi-contract.

Legal Fictions. Bentham put these cases forward as typical examples of the "fictions" by which, he claimed, the law was constantly bedeviled. (Bentham's more general, and more positive, doctrine of "fictions" is discussed below.) These cases also made clear the role that the principle of utility would play in a more rational system. Once legislators were forced to recognize that legal obligations rested, not on arbitrary absolute moral principles but on the single aim of increasing happiness and reducing suffering, it would be possible to lay down much more rational and consistent principles as to which obligations should be waived and which enforced.

Hedonic Calculus. Bentham was, then, the theorist of the philosophical radicals, in that he laid down general principles from which programs of legislative and social reform might follow immediately. But he was much less concerned with the more abstract and metaphysical questions involved. His most characteristic contribution to utilitarian theory was his elaboration of the "hedonic calculus." According to this doctrine, the way to judge between alternative courses of action is to consider the consequences of each, in terms of the pleasure and pain of all the people affected. Let us suppose, for example, that a Benthamite is trying to decide whether to take his small nephew to the circus or to spend his evening at home with a book. He knows that the circus will bore him: he may estimate this boredom at, let us say, 5 units of pain; i.e. −5 units of pleasure. He will, on the other hand, gain some sympathetic pleasure from watching the small boy's pleased excitement, though not enough, certainly, to compensate for his boredom. He may put this at +2 units of pleasure. But the boy may be expected to gain great pleasure from the outing: perhaps 10 units. Taking the child to the circus, then, may be expected to yield (10 + 2) − 5 units of pleasure; i.e., 7 units. Now consider the alternative. A quiet evening at home, though pleasurable, does not transport an adult as much as an evening out does a child: perhaps we may evaluate it at 6 units. His pleasure will be spoiled a little, too, by the sympathetic pain that knowledge of his nephew's disappointment will cause: say −2 units. Then there is that disappointment itself: since both the pains and pleasures of childhood are intense, we may put it at −8 units. To stay at home, then, will cause 6 − 2 − 8 units of pleasure; i.e., 4 units of pain. The choice, then, is between a course of action that will cause, on balance, 7 units of pleasure,

and one that will cause 4 units of pain. The first is clearly the one that will contribute most to the sum of human happiness. It is, then, the right action in these circumstances. Its rightness is not an intrinsic characteristic, but depends entirely on its consequences in any given case: if the uncle found circuses more boring, or the nephew found them less pleasant, staying at home might become the right action.

Utilitarianism presupposes one overriding moral principle: that one ought to aim at the greatest happiness of the greatest number.

This is, of course, a comparatively crude example. Bentham devoted great ingenuity to refining the calculus and working out its implications for legal reform. Punishment, for example, must be just harsh enough to deter, and no harsher. Any more pain than is necessary for this purpose is unjustifiable. On the other hand, too lenient a punishment is a worse evil, since the pain inflicted on the criminal, being insufficient to deter, will not be counterbalanced by the pain spared future victims of similar crimes.

Greatest Happiness Principle. Utilitarianism presupposes one overriding moral principle: that one ought to aim at the greatest happiness of the greatest number. Bentham could not entirely avoid the question of the ontological status of this principle. He did say that it could not be proved, since "it is used to prove everything else," and "a chain of proofs must have their commencement somewhere." This might be taken to mean that it is a self-evident principle known by reason, rather like the principle of the syllogism. But Bentham could hardly insist on this, since he maintained that the appeal to self-evident principles was an appeal to one's own prejudices. He might perhaps have meant that a careful analysis of men's moral judgments would show that the greatest happiness principle always did underlie them, so far as they were consistent: the principle itself could then be accepted just as an aim that men did have, as a matter of fact. In part, this does seem to be Bentham's argument. He could not quite let the matter rest there, however. A prejudice universally held is still a prejudice. He needed an indisputable fact of human nature on which to base his ethics. That men seek their own pleasure would seem to be such a fact. "Why bother about the pleasure and pain of others?" is not a silly question in the sense that "Why bother about one's own pain and pleasure?" is. Bentham's dictum "Nature has placed mankind under the governance of two sovereign masters, pain and pleasure" has all the air of an obvious psychological fact; but only if the pain and pleasure in question are our own.

Psychological Hedonism. The word "pleasure" is notoriously ambiguous. Bentham was not entirely guiltless of using it ambiguously; but J. H. Burton, in his introduction to Bentham's *Works,* took him to mean that "what it pleases a man to do is simply what he wills to do"; and this was perhaps his most consistent meaning. Among his catalogue of pleasures Bentham listed the pleasures of sympathy; and he did not think it necessary, as Hobbes did, to reduce these to self-interest in the narrower sense. If this was his meaning, Bentham's psychological hedonism cannot be dismissed as simply false. But is it, then, just a trivial tautology? What Bentham was saying is that the central fact of human psychology is that men have desires and seek to gratify them. It follows, he thought, that the only rational way to judge between alternative courses of action is to choose the one that gratifies most desires. This is scarcely trivial, since many moralists have held that the gratification of desire is sinful, and that virtue consists in repressing desires. Bentham's central contention was that gratification as such is always good, and that, while it may often be necessary to repress some desires, this is only in order that other desires may be gratified. The opposition between duty and inclination is a false one: the real contest is between conflicting inclinations, and is to be settled by considering which inclinations lead to the greatest pleasure; i.e., the most intense and lasting satisfaction.

There remains a further charge. Is egoism, so interpreted, compatible with utilitarianism? If "pleasure" means "whatever a man wills," he may well take pleasure in the happiness of others. But it certainly does not follow that he must. Moreover, while we can now understand why "Why bother about your own pleasure?" is a silly question (since it means "Why bother about whatever you bother about?"), it is clearer than ever that "Why bother about the desires of others?" is not at all silly. Again, the hedonic calculus implies that men's desires conflict, that the action that will bring pleasure to one man will bring pain to another. Why, then, should either of them worry about the other's pleasure?

Bentham did not give any very explicit answer to this question. He was certainly influenced by the quite elaborate theory of David Hartley, according to which the most satisfying pleasures were those that did not interfere with the cultivation of sympathy. This version of the natural harmony of interests is compatible with the artificial harmony of interests that, according to Bentham, it is the business of the legislator to bring about through an elaborate apparatus of punishments and re-

wards. For, even granted that the course of action that brings most pleasure to the individual in the long run will be the one that also brings most pleasure to others, it may still be necessary for the legislator to intervene. Men are easily seduced by the temptation of the immediate pleasure. The criminal, for example, might eventually find himself, in his old age, looking back on his misspent years with regret; but this prospect is much less likely to deter him in his youth than the threat of imprisonment in the very near future. On the other hand, though Bentham certainly made some use of Hartley's associationism, the presupposition behind the hedonic calculus would seem to be that individual interests may really, and not just apparently, conflict.

The Units of Pleasure. Some of the other stock criticisms of Bentham are easier to answer. One obvious objection to the hedonic calculus is that the units of pleasure and pain of which Bentham spoke are quite fictitious. It is not merely that accurate calculation is difficult, but that the question "how many times greater?" is, in this context, meaningless. There is no homogeneous stuff called "pleasure" that can be weighed and measured; there are many different kinds of pleasurable experience, each yielding its own kind of satisfaction. This is, of course, true, and was quite apparent to Bentham. But it is also true that we cannot avoid, in some quasi-metaphorical sense, weighing pleasures against each other. It is not nonsensical to say that the uncle in our example asks himself whether his nephew's pleasure does or does not outweigh his own boredom, though it is nonsensical to take "outweigh" literally. Yet the notion of quantity is not entirely absent, since it makes a difference if the uncle is very, instead of slightly, bored, and the nephew only slightly, instead of very, pleased.

No doubt Bentham went too far when he tried to specify a unit of pleasure: the minimum state of sensibility that can be distinguished from indifference. But elsewhere he made it clear that there are no real units of pleasure and that reference to them is merely a convenient device for making our calculations as accurate as the nature of the case allows. He did insist that the calculations themselves are indispensable. For example, when fines are imposed in the courts, some alternative punishment must be found for those who cannot, or will not, pay the fine. Clearly we cannot strictly say that the pain of losing five pounds is precisely equivalent to the pain endured during seven days in prison. Yet it is necessary to find some such equivalent, and the job of finding equivalents can be better or worse done. So understood, the weighing of pleasures and pains against each other is not at all absurd. That the process is not mathematically exact can hardly count against it as an analysis of moral evaluation, since moral evaluation is not mathematically exact either.

Quality of Pleasures. It may still be objected, however, that Bentham's hedonic calculus ignores the quality, as distinct from the quantity, of pleasure. This comes out clearly in his famous aphorism that "quantity of pleasure being equal, pushpin is as good as poetry." Quite apart from the difficulty of deciding how many games of pushpin (one million? two million?) are worth one Shakespearean sonnet, it is objected that poetry has a kind of value that is completely absent from pushpin. That is to say, it would be contended that there are "higher" pleasures, such as poetry, that are intrinsically more valuable than "lower" pleasures, such as pushpin. Lower pleasures may sometimes please us more than higher pleasures; but even then the higher pleasures are to be preferred. If this is admitted, the utilitarian contention that pleasure is the sole good would seem to collapse, since the higher pleasures apparently have an element of value, other than the mere quantity of pleasure, that the lower pleasures lack.

Perhaps the crucial question for a utilitarian ethic intended mainly for lawyers and legislators is whether it can account adequately for justice.

Unlike John Stuart Mill, Bentham did not admit this distinction between higher and lower pleasures. But there are two points here that need to be carefully distinguished. As we have seen, Bentham did not deny that pleasures differ in quality as well as in quantity. He gave, indeed, quite an elaborate classification of the different kinds of pleasure. But this is, after all, also true of the lower pleasures. The point about the quality of pleasures, then, is quite distinct from the point about higher and lower pleasures. What Bentham did deny is that the higher pleasure may be better, even though less pleasant, than the lower pleasure. It is true that the lower pleasure may be more intense; but more is involved in quantity of pleasure than just intensity. Bentham distinguished other "dimensions" of pleasure: apart from intensity, these are duration, certainty, propinquity, fecundity, and purity. Now it is arguable that the so-called "higher" pleasures are just those that afford a more lasting satisfaction than the "lower" pleasures (duration), that enlarge our horizons and so open up new possibilities of pleasure (fecundity), and that are less likely to be followed eventually by the pain of satiety and boredom (purity). These are the characteristics that distinguish intellectual activity, for example, from

purely physical pleasure. Once these dimensions are taken into account, it is by no means certain that the difference between higher and lower pleasures is not, after all, a quantitative one. The higher pleasures, it may be argued, are those which men have found, through long experience, to be productive of most pleasure when all these factors are taken into account.

Justice. Perhaps the crucial question for a utilitarian ethic intended mainly for lawyers and legislators is whether it can account adequately for justice. It may be argued that justice requires the equalization as well as the maximization of pleasure. It is not unjust to require me to endure five units of pain on Monday for the sake of ten units of pleasure on Tuesday. But is it just to require Smith to endure five units of pain for the sake of ten units of pleasure for Jones? It is doubtful whether Bentham can meet this objection. He does, however, argue that the maximization of pleasure will itself involve an equalizing tendency. This is because the economist's law of diminishing utility applies to pleasure. The minor amenities of life afford much pleasure to someone whose other pleasures are few, but comparatively little to someone whose pleasures are many. Consequently, while it is true that a utilitarian, forced to choose between a course of action that gives X and Y 10 units of pleasure each and one that gives X 31 units of pleasure and Y 10 units of pain, will prefer the second, it is also true that such choices are most likely to arise when X's life is as a general rule more painful than Y's.

In Bentham's view, our conviction that it is unjust to punish an innocent man is based on nothing but the empirical consideration that punishing the innocent is not likely to deter others from crime. This is, however, not always true: the innocent man may be a hostage, or he may be generally thought to be guilty. Bentham met this kind of criticism by distinguishing between first-order evil, or pain caused to assignable individuals, and second-order evil, or pain caused to the community in general. Insecurity is a very great second-order evil. The point is a general one, of central importance. Utilitarians need to invoke Bentham's distinction between first-order and second-order evil in order to explain the common belief that general rules should be kept even in those cases where some slight increase in the general happiness might seem to result from breaking them. This slight increase in first-order good, it is argued, is outweighed by the second-order evil, which usually consists in the lessening of public confidence. (A *large* increase in first-order good, it is conceded, may justify breaking the rule.)

The argument is plausible, though of course there is no way of proving that the precise point at which we feel justified in breaking the rule is the point at which the first-order good begins to outweigh the second-order evil. It is, however, open to the objection that, while it may be true as a matter of fact that punishing the innocent or breaking a promise will in general cause more pain than pleasure, most of us feel that these actions would be wrong even if this were not the case. The utilitarian can only reply that this is a mistake. Moral rules, he will say, embody human experience about what kinds of action make for the general happiness—human nature and the world in which we live both being what they are. If either were different, morality would be different; it is a mistake, though a natural one, to believe otherwise.

What is the difference, Bentham asked, between

"that luxury which all the world condemns,

and that prosperity which all the world admires"?

POLITICAL AND LEGAL THEORY. If the central question of political philosophy is taken to be: "Why, if at all, should the citizen obey the state?" the utilitarian answer is quite clear. The citizen should obey just so far as obedience will contribute more to the general happiness than disobedience. If the central question is taken to be the nature and ontological status of the state, the answer is equally clear: the state is not a super-entity with purposes and a will of its own, but a human contrivance to enable men to realize as many of their desires as possible. The "general happiness," or "the interest of the community in general," is always, in Bentham, to be understood as the resultant of the hedonic calculus, the sum of the pleasures and pains of individuals.

Accordingly Bentham opposed, on the one hand, those individualist theories of the state that invoke the concepts of "the social contract" and of "natural rights," and, on the other, all "natural law" and "organic" theories of the state.

Criticism of Social Contract Theories. Bentham repeated Hume's arguments against the social contract. His suspicion of it was increased by its being one of those legal fictions in which he saw the root of so much evil. It was not asserted that every citizen had in fact contracted to obey the law, but only that he should be deemed to have so contracted. But this is mischievous unless obeying the laws does in fact make for the general happiness. The principle of utility, then, is the real basis of obedience. To suppose anything else is misleading, since it suggests that the individual need not obey any law to which he has not personally assented—a principle that, if taken seriously, could lead only to anarchy.

Criticism of Natural Rights Doctrines. Bentham attacked natural rights in his *Anarchical Fallacies; being an Examination of the Declaration of Rights issued during the French Revolution* (written about 1791 and first published in French by Dumont as *Sophismes politiques,* Paris, 1816), and declared the whole concept to be "nonsense on stilts." The basic confusion, in Bentham's view, is the failure to distinguish between what is and what ought to be. To say that men have inalienable rights is clearly false, when the assertion is made by way of protest against a government that has in fact alienated rights. There would be no need for revolutions if men were in fact equal, as they are asserted to be: what is meant is that they ought to be treated as equal but are not. On the other hand, if we take the doctrine of natural rights as a statement of what governments ought to do, it will be found untenable. No government could continue to govern if it abstained from ever depriving any of its citizens of life, liberty, or property (still less of happiness), since taxation and punishment would then be impossible. So indeed would law itself, since any law is a restriction on liberty. The only principle that can be justified to the extent that it is backed by coercion, is that the law should not impose restrictions on any individual unless this is necessary to avoid greater pain, on balance, to other individuals: in short, the principle of utility.

Denial of Natural Law. Bentham opposed natural law on much the same grounds. It is a confusion to think of natural law as being literally law, so that an enactment that contravenes it is null and void. This would mean that the "supreme governors," who make the laws, have a *legal* duty not to make certain kinds of law. But "that is my *duty* to do, which I am liable to be *punished,* according to law, if I do not do. . . . Have these supreme governors any such duty? No: for if they are at all liable to punishment, according to law, . . . then they are not, what they are supposed to be, supreme governors" (*A Fragment on Government,* ch. 5, §7). What is meant, doubtless, is that they have either a religious duty or a moral duty. In accordance with Bentham's definition of "duty," a religious duty is one whose neglect renders one liable to punishment by God, and a moral duty is one whose neglect renders one liable, not to punishment in a strict sense, but to various unorganized "mortifications and inconveniences" at the hands of one's fellow men. This is in line with his classification of "sanctions": the "moral sanction" is fear of public opinion. In this sense, moral duties are certainly political realities: Bentham agreed that the ruler is limited by what public opinion will tolerate. But he insisted on distinguishing this from a legal limitation, and both from a nebulous natural law.

It may be objected that Bentham himself was clearly postulating a moral duty in a different sense from the one he allowed. For his main theme is that the legislator ought to make those laws that promote the greatest happiness of the greatest number. He did make some attempt to assimilate this to his "moral sanction," but it is clear that a law that, on balance, causes more suffering than it prevents is not necessarily one so unpopular that it provokes the citizens to active resistance. A similar objection may be made about natural rights: Bentham does seem to have postulated at least one moral right: the right to have one's happiness considered equally with that of other men. This is clearly not the same as the fact that men will seek their own happiness, nor does it follow from the further fact that the legislator, seeking *his* own happiness, will see to it, if he is wise, that he does not provoke his subjects too far. It is here, indeed, that the weakness of Bentham's attempt to base utilitarianism upon egoism shows itself.

Sovereignty. Bentham's theory of sovereignty is the one that he had inherited from Hobbes and that was later to be elaborated by Austin. A man has political authority when other men habitually obey him. The laws are the commands of such men, when enforced by punishment or the threat of punishment. Bentham anticipated some of the objections that were to be made to Austin. It is, he said, quite possible for the same man to be alternately governor and subject: "to-day concurring in the business of issuing a *general* command for the observance of the whole society, amongst the rest of another man in quality of *Judge:* tomorrow, perhaps, punished by a *particular* command of that same Judge for not obeying the general command which he himself (in character of governor) had issued. . . ." His recognition of the moral sanction enabled him to say that the sovereign would find himself compelled to pay attention to those customary ways of behavior that embody the experience of the community about what makes for the general happiness, and so to allow for the part played in law by custom and tradition. He insisted, however, that it is through the command of the sovereign that custom has the force of law.

THEORY OF MEANING. Although his main interest was in moral and political philosophy and jurisprudence, Bentham's numerous if fragmentary writings include an *Essay on Logic* and many passing references to the theory of meaning. An uncompromising nominalist, Bentham drew the conclusion that most of our words refer to fictitious entities and not to real ones. To consider any part or aspect of a real entity in abstraction is to create a fictitious entity. Hence qualities, relations, and classes are all fictions: so are the abstract notions of time, place, motion, and substance. A fiction, Bentham said, is nothing; and a quality of a fiction is equally nothing. Thus most of our talk is strictly nonsense, though it can be given meaning by translating it into terms referring to real entities. The possibility of making such translations gives rise to what he called "definition by paraphrasis." Some words, he said, are best defined by translating the sentences in which they occur into other sentences in which all the words refer to real entities. Examples are "duty," "right," "power," and title," which can be understood only by reference to such concrete situations as one man being punished by another. Legal and political fictions and the mental confusion that results from them are, Bentham thought, largely due to the failure to make such translations; men are caught in what he called "the shackles of ordinary language." "Metaphysical speculations," he said, have as their object "understanding clearly what one is speaking of."

In this Bentham was anticipating both the "definition in use" of the logical atomists and much of their underlying theory. In other ways, too, he anticipated some of the views that became influential early in the twentieth century. Since he regarded mathematics as concerned purely with fictitious entities and as being essentially "a species of short-hand," he was not far from the concept of a postulate set in which the rules of the system itself must be sharply distinguished from the rules governing the application of the system. In a rather different area, he insisted on the distinction between the "eulogistic" and the "dyslogistic" use of words, maintaining that the eulogistic and the corresponding dyslogistic term refer to the same real entity. What is the difference, Bentham asked, between "that *luxury* which all the world condemns, and that *prosperity* which all the world admires"?

To give another example, he claimed that "vanity," "ambition," and "honor" were different names for the same motive. In each case the motive (what moves us) is the love of reputation, which is in itself neither good nor bad. Let us suppose that one father slaves day and night to pay off his son's gambling debts and so clear the family name, while another devotes his energies to marrying his daughter into a titled family. In saying that the former is moved by a sense of honor and the latter by ambition we are expressing a difference in our attitudes to the two men that is, on utilitarian principles, thoroughly justified, since the one course of action is more likely than the other to increase the general happiness. We are not, however, referring to any difference in motive; for both men act from precisely the same motive, the desire that his family shall stand well in the general esteem.

BIBLIOGRAPHY

Bentham's published works and his voluminous unpublished manuscripts were collected by J. Bowring in *The Works of Jeremy Bentham,* 11 vols. (Edinburgh, 1838–1843). This is not complete. Volumes 10 and 11 contain a not very accurate life of Bentham, written by Bowring from Bentham's reminiscences in his old age.

Other biographies include C. M. Atkinson, *Jeremy Bentham* (London, 1905); C. W. Everett, *The Education of Jeremy Bentham* (New York, 1931); Leslie Stephen, *The English Utilitarians,* Vol. 1 (London, 1900).

For critical works, see J. S. Mill, "Bentham," in *London and Westminster Review* (1838), reprinted in Mill's *Dissertations and Discussions* (London, 1859–1875) and in F. R. Leavis, ed., *Mill on Bentham and Coleridge* (London, 1950); Elie Halévy, *La Formation du radicalisme philosophique,* 3 vols. (Paris, 1904), translated by Mary Morris as *The Growth of Philosophical Radicalism* (London, 1928); John Wisdom, *Interpretation and Analysis in Relation to Bentham's Theory of Definition* (London, 1931); C. K. Ogden, *Bentham's Theory of Fictions* (London, 1932), which republishes Bentham's writings on theory of meaning, with a long introductory essay by Ogden; David Baumgardt, *Bentham and the Ethics of Today* (Princeton, 1952); Mary P. Mack, *Jeremy Bentham,* 2 vols. (London, 1962–).

— D. H. MONRO

BERKELEY, GEORGE

George Berkeley (1685–1753), Irish philosopher of English ancestry, and Anglican bishop of Cloyne, was born at Kilkenny, Ireland. He entered Trinity College, Dublin in 1700 and became a fellow in 1707. In 1709 he published his first important book, *An Essay Towards a New Theory of Vision.* This was well received, and a second edition appeared in the same year. The following year *A Treatise Concerning the Principles of Human Knowledge,* Part 1, was published. This is the work in which Berkeley first published his immaterialist philosophy, and although it made him known to some of the foremost writers of the day, its conclusions were not taken very seriously by them. In 1713 Berkeley went to London and there published the *Three Dialogues Between Hylas and Philonous,* a more popular statement of the doctrines of the *Principles.* While in London, Berkeley became acquainted with Addison, Swift, Pope, and Steele and contributed articles to Steele's *Guardian,* attacking the theories of the freethinkers. He traveled on the Continent in 1713–1714 (when he probably met and conversed with Malebranche) and again from 1716 to 1720. During this tour he lost the manuscript of the second part of the *Principles,* which he never rewrote. Toward the end of the tour, he wrote a short essay, in Latin, entitled *De Motu,* published in London in 1721,

criticizing Newton's philosophy of nature and Leibniz's theory of force. In 1724 Berkeley was made dean of Derry.

About this time, Berkeley began to prepare a project for establishing a college in Bermuda, at which not only the sons of American colonists but also Indians and Negroes were to receive a thorough education and be trained for the Christian ministry. Having obtained promises of subscriptions from many prominent people, Berkeley promoted a bill, which was passed by Parliament, providing for considerable financial help from the government. In 1728, before the money was forthcoming, Berkeley, who had just married, left for Rhode Island, where he intended to establish farms for supplying food for the college. He settled in Newport, but the grant never came; and in 1731, when it was clear that the government was diverting the money for other purposes, Berkeley had to return home. While in Newport, however, Berkeley had met and corresponded with the Samuel Johnson who later became the first president of King's College, New York (now Columbia University). Johnson was one of the few philosophers of the time to give close attention to Berkeley's philosophical views, and the correspondence between him and Berkeley is of considerable philosophical interest. While he was in Newport, Berkeley also wrote *Alciphron,* a series of dialogues in part developed from the articles he had written for the *Guardian,* directed against the "minute philosophers," or freethinkers. This was published in 1732.

Berkeley was in London from 1732 to 1734 and there wrote *The Analyst* (1734), a criticism of Newton's doctrine of fluxions and addressed to "an infidel mathematician." This and *A Defence of Free-Thinking in Mathematics* (1735) aimed at showing that the mathematicians so admired by freethinkers worked with concepts that could not withstand close scrutiny, so that the confidence given to them by "the philomathematical infidels of these times" was unjustified. It is not surprising that Berkeley was made bishop of Cloyne, Ireland, in 1734.

Berkeley carried out his episcopal duties with vigor and humanity. His diocese was in a remote and poor part of the country, and the problems he encountered there led him to reflect on economic problems. The result was *The Querist* (1735–1737), in which he made proposals for dealing with the prevailing idleness and poverty by means of public works and education. He also concerned himself with the health of the people and became convinced of the medicinal value of tar water. In 1744 he published *A Chain of Philosophical Reflexions and Inquiries concerning the Virtues of Tar-Water, and divers other Subjects connected together and arising from one another.* When the second edition appeared in the same year, the title *Siris,* by which the book is now known, was added. Much of the book is concerned with the merits of tar water, but Berkeley passed from this subject to the causes of physical phenomena, which, he held, cannot be discovered in the phenomena themselves but must be sought for in the Divine activity. This is in line with his earlier views, but some readers, on the basis of his admiring references to Plato and the Neoplatonists, have considered that by this time he had considerably modified his original system. The *Siris* was Berkeley's last philosophical work. He died suddenly in Oxford nine years later.

An account of Berkeley's life and writings would be inadequate without some reference to his *Philosophical Commentaries.* A. C. Fraser discovered a series of notes by Berkeley on all the main topics of Berkeley's philosophy and published them in 1871 in his edition of Berkeley's works, under the title of *Commonplace Book of Occasional Metaphysical Thoughts.* It was later noticed

that these notes had been bound together in the wrong order, and it has now been shown that they were written by Berkeley, probably in 1707–1708, while he was thinking out his *New Theory of Vision* and *Principles.* This work makes it clear that Berkeley was already convinced of the truth of immaterialism before he published the *New Theory of Vision,* in which that view is not mentioned. The *Philosophical Commentaries* throw valuable light upon Berkeley's sources, bugbears, prejudices, and arguments.

Main Themes of Berkeley's Philosophy

Since the word *idealism* came into use in the eighteenth century, Berkeley has been known as a leading exponent of idealism, and even as its founder. He himself referred to his main view as "the immaterialist hypothesis," meaning by this that he denied the very possibility of inert, mindless, material substance. This description has some advantage over idealism in that it brings out

Berkeley had planned to establish a Christian ministry college in Bermuda, but despite considerable interest among many prominent people, the British government never provided the financial help it had promised. (Corbis/Francis G. Mayer)

Berkeley's radical opposition to materialism; whereas the opposite of idealism is realism, and there are grounds for doubting whether Berkeley intended to deny the realist contention that in perception men become directly aware of objects that persist unchanged when they cease to be perceived. Berkeley's fundamental view was that for something to exist it must either be perceived or else be the active being that does the perceiving. Things that are perceived he called "sensible things" or "sensible qualities," or, in the terminology he had borrowed from Locke, "ideas." Sensible things or ideas, he held, cannot exist except as the passive objects of minds or spirits, active beings that perceive and will. As he put it in the *Philosophical Commentaries,* "Existence is *percipi* or *percipere,*" and he added "or *velle* i.e. *agere*"—existence is to be perceived or to perceive or to will, that is, to be active. Thus there can be nothing except active spirits on the one hand and passive sensible things on the other, and the latter cannot exist except as perceived by the former. This is Berkeley's idealism or immaterialism.

Berkeley has been known as a leading exponent

of idealism, though he himself referred

to his main view as "the immaterialist hypothesis,"

meaning that he denied the very possibility

of inert, mindless, material substance.

CRITICISM OF CONTEMPORARY SCIENCE. The above account of Berkeley's writings emphasizes their apologetic intent, an intent that can be seen in the subtitles of his major writings—that of the *Principles* is typical: *Wherein the chief causes of error and difficulty in the sciences, with the grounds of scepticism, atheism and irreligion, are inquired into.* It will be seen that "the chief causes of difficulty in the sciences" are also prominent. Berkeley considered that in the mathematics and natural sciences of his day insufficient attention was given to what experience reveals to us. Apart from Newton, the mathematicians were, he wrote in the *Philosophical Commentaries,* "mere triflers, mere Nihilarians." For example, they conceived of lines as infinitely divisible, but this is not only absurd, it could be maintained only by men who "despised sense." Thus Berkeley regarded himself as protesting against the excesses of uncontrolled rationalism. Hence he put forward a most antirationalistic view of geometry, although he never developed its implications very far. Similarly he thought

that the natural philosophers deluded themselves with words when they tried to explain the physical world in terms of attractions, forces, and powers. Natural science, as he understood it, was descriptive rather than explanatory and was concerned with correlations rather than with causes. He thus sketched out a view of science that was revived and developed by nineteenth-century and twentieth-century positivists.

SENSIBLE QUALITIES ARE THE SIGNS OF GOD'S PURPOSE. Berkeley's positivism, however, was confined to his account of natural science. The order of phenomena, he held, was willed by God for the good of created spirits. In deciphering the conjunctions and sequences of our sense experience we are learning what God has decreed. Thus sensible qualities are the language in which God speaks to us. In the third and fourth editions (1732) of the *New Theory of Vision* Berkeley said that the objects of sight are a divine visual language by which God teaches us what things are good for us and what things are harmful to us. In the *Alciphron,* published that same year, he argued that "the great Mover and Author of Nature constantly explaineth Himself to the eyes of men by the sensible intervention of arbitrary signs, which have no similitude or connexion with the things signified." We learn that certain visual ideas are signs of certain tactual ones, certain smells signs of certain colors, and so on. There is no necessity about this, any more than things necessarily have the names that convention assigns to them. Just as some sensible qualities are signs of others, so sensible qualities as a whole are signs of the purposes of God who "daily speaks to our senses in a manifest and clear dialect."

Thus, taken as a whole, Berkeley's philosophy is a form of immaterialism combined with an extreme antirationalist theory of science. The regularities between phenomena are regarded as evidence for, and as signs of, God's purposes. Just as a man's words reveal his thoughts and intentions by means of the conventional signs of language, so the sensible order reveals God's will in phenomena that could have been ordered quite differently if he had so decided.

The New Theory of Vision

Although Berkeley did not mention his immaterialism in *An Essay Towards a New Theory of Vision,* this work throws important light upon his quarrel with the mathematicians and his rejection of the rationalist point of view. It contains, too, an interesting statement of what Berkeley then thought about geometry. Furthermore, the *Essay* helps us to see, from what Berkeley said about the objects of vision, how he came to the view that sensible qualities cannot exist "without the mind." Among the main contentions of the book is the claim that distance or "outness" is not immediately perceived by sight; it is "suggested" in part by the sensations we get in moving our eyes but mainly by association with the ideas of touch. According to Berkeley, we see the distance (and size) of things only in the sense in which we see a man's shame and anger. We see his face, and the expression on it suggests to us how he is feeling. In themselves, shame and anger are invisible. Similarly, we see shapes and colors, which are signs of what we would touch if we were to stretch out our hands, but distance itself is no more seen than anger is. In expounding this view, Berkeley developed the thesis that the objects of sight and touch are utterly disparate, so that no feature of the one can have more than a contingent connection with any feature of the other.

DESCARTES'S THEORY OF THE PERCEPTION OF DISTANCE. Consideration should first be given to Berkeley's criticisms of an important geometrical account of how distance is perceived and assessed, the account given by Descartes in his *Dioptrics* (1637). In this work Descartes referred to six "qualities we perceive in the objects of sight," namely, light, color, shape, distance, magnitude, and situation. Descartes argued that one of the ways in which men ascertain the distance of objects is by means of the angles formed by straight lines running from each of their eyes and converging at the object seen. He illustrated this by reference to a blind man with a stick (the length of which he does not know) held in each hand. When he brings the points of the sticks together at the object, he forms a triangle with one hand at each end of the base, and if he knows how far apart his hands are, and what angles the sticks make with his body, he can, "by a kind of geometry innate in all men" know how far away the object is. The same geometry would apply, Descartes argued, if the observer's eyes are regarded as ends of the base of a triangle, and straight lines from them are regarded as converging at the object. The more obtuse the base angles formed by the lines running from this base and converging at the object, the farther away the object must be; the more acute these angles, the nearer the object must be. Berkeley put the matter somewhat differently from Descartes, pointing out that according to the latter's view the more acute the angle formed at the object by the lines converging from the eyes, the farther away it must be; the more obtuse this angle, the nearer the object must be. It is important to notice that this "must" is the "must" of mathematical necessity. From what Descartes said, it is necessarily the case that the more acute this angle is, the farther away the object is; the more obtuse the angle, the nearer the object. "Nearer" and "farther" logically depend upon the obtuseness or acuteness of the angle. In criticizing this

view, therefore, Berkeley was criticizing the view that distance is known a priori by the principles of an innate geometry according to which we know that the distance of the object must vary in accordance with the angle made at the object by straight lines converging there from the eyes of the observer.

BERKELEY'S CRITICISM OF DESCARTES. Against Descartes's view Berkeley brought a complex argument that for purposes of exposition, is here broken up into three parts. The first is that people who know nothing of the geometry of the matter can nevertheless notice the relative distance of things from them. This is not very convincing, for Descartes obviously thought that the geometry he regarded as "innate in all men" might be employed by them without their having reflected on it. The second argument used by Berkeley is that the lines and angles referred to by Descartes "have no real existence in nature, being only an hypothesis framed by the mathematicians. . . ." This argument is of interest in showing how Berkeley thought that mathematicians were inclined to deal in fictitious entities, but it is unlikely that Descartes was deceived by them in this way.

Berkeley's third and main argument was based upon a theory that he expressed in the words, "distance, of itself and immediately, cannot be seen." William Molyneux, from whose *Dioptrics* (1692) Berkeley borrowed this theory, had supported it by the argument that since distance is a line or length directed endwise from the object seen to the eye, it can reach the eye at only one point, which must necessarily remain the same however near or far away the object is. If this argument is accepted, then distance could not possibly be seen, and could only be judged or, as Berkeley believed, "suggested."

DISTANCE IS SUGGESTED BY WHAT IS SEEN. What, then, according to Berkeley, is seen? The answer is not altogether clear, but it would seem that he thought that the immediate object of vision is two-dimensional, containing relations of above and below and of one side and the other, with no necessary connection with a third dimension. Hence the relation between what is immediately seen on the one hand and the distance of objects on the other must be contingent and cannot be necessary. Distance, then, must be ascertained by means of something that has only a contingent relationship with what is seen. Berkeley mentioned the sensations we have when we adjust our eyes, the greater confusedness of objects as they come very close to the eyes, and the sensations of strain as we try to see what is very near. But he mainly relied on the associations between what a man has touched and what he now sees. For example, when a man now sees something faint and dim, he may, from past experience, expect that if he approaches and touches it he will find it bright and hard. When he sees something at a distance, he is really seeing certain shapes and colors, which *suggest* to him what tangible ideas he would have if he were near enough to touch it. Just as one does not hear a man's thoughts, which are suggested by the sounds he makes, so one does not directly see distance, which is suggested by what is seen.

SIGHT AND TOUCH. Berkeley's view that distance is not immediately perceived by sight is rejected by some writers, for instance by H. H. Price, in his *Perception* (1932), on the ground that it is plainly contradicted by experience. We just do see visual depth, it is held, so that it is idle to deny this fact on the basis of an argument purporting to prove that we cannot. Again, some critics, such as T. K. Abbott in *Sight and Touch* (1864) have argued not only that we do get our idea of distance from sight, but also that touch is vague and uninformative by comparison with sight, and hence less effective in giving knowledge of the material world. This discussion need not be developed, however, since, although he said in the *Essay* that by touch we get knowledge of objects that exist "without the mind" (§55), Berkeley's real view was that no sensible thing could so exist. It cannot be denied that on occasion Berkeley's language was imprecise. A crucial example of this occurs in his discussion of the question of whether a man born blind would, on receiving his sight, see things at a distance from him. According to Berkeley, of course, he would not; but to such a man, the most distant objects ". . . would all seem to be in his eye, or rather in his mind" and would appear "(as in truth they are) no other than a new set of thoughts or sensations, each whereof is as near to him as the perceptions of pain or pleasure, or the most inward passions of his soul" (*Essay*, §41). It will be noticed how readily Berkeley passed from "in his eye" to "in his mind," and how he assimilated such very different things as sensations and thoughts. Indeed it is hard not to conclude that he thought that whatever was not seen at a distance must appear to be in the mind. If this is true, then one of the objects of the *Essay* was to show that the immediate objects of vision must be in the mind because they are not seen at a distance.

GEOMETRIES OF SIGHT AND OF TOUCH. As already seen, an extremely important thesis of the *Essay* is that the objects of sight and the objects of touch are radically different from one another. We see visible objects and we touch tangible objects, and it is absurd to suppose that we can touch what we see or see what we touch. According to Berkeley, it follows from this that tangible shape and visible shape have no necessary connection with one another. Geometers certainly supposed themselves to be concerned with shapes in abstraction from their being seen or touched, but Berkeley

did not allow that this is possible. A purely visual geometry would necessarily be confined to two dimensions, so that the three-dimensional geometry that we have must be fundamentally a geometry of touch. He reinforced this strangely pragmatic view with the observation that a sighted but disembodied being that could not touch or manipulate things would be unable to understand even plane geometry, since without a body it would not understand the handling of rulers and compasses and the drawing of lines and the placing of shapes against one another.

Arguments for Immaterialism

The arguments now to be considered are set out in the *Principles* and in the *Three Dialogues*. They are largely concerned with what Berkeley called "ideas," "ideas or sensations," "sensible things," or "sensible qualities." The very use of the word *idea* itself and, even more, its use in apposition with *sensation* had the purpose of indicating something that does not exist apart from the perception of it. Pains and itches are typical sensations, and no one supposes that they could exist apart from a being that experiences them. Rocks do not suffer, and water does not itch. When, therefore, sensible things such as colors, sounds, tangible shapes, tastes, and smells are called ideas, they are assimilated with sensations and hence relate to the perceiving beings that have them. It is now necessary, therefore, to examine the arguments with which Berkeley justified this.

SEVENTEENTH-CENTURY MATERIALISM. Berkeley's arguments for immaterialism can be understood only if we first consider the sort of view it was intended to refute. When Berkeley was forming his views, the natural sciences had been so far advanced by the work of such men as Galileo, Vesalius, Harvey, Boyle, and Newton as to have given rise to a scientific view of the world. Such a view had been elaborated, in its philosophical aspects, by Locke in his *Essay concerning Human Understanding* (1690). Space and time were, so to say, the containers within which material things were situated. The movements and relations of material things could be explored by experiments and characterized in mathematical formulae.

Explanation in Terms of Particles in Motion. The features of the world, thus revealed as fundamental, were those of place, shape, size, movement, weight, and the like; and it was in terms of these that heat and cold and color and sound found their explanation. Heat was thought to be due to the rapid movement of atomic particles, color to the transmission of particles or to the spreading of waves, and sound to the movement of the air between the emitting object and the ear. Whereas solid, shaped, moving objects, and the air and space within which they existed, were regarded as basic features of nature, the colors we see, the heat we feel, and the sounds we hear were held to be the effects that substances possessing only the basic characteristics produced in creatures with sense organs. If all creatures with sense organs and consciousness were removed from the world, there would no longer be any experienced sounds, but only pulsations in the air; particles would increase or decrease their speed of movement, but no one would feel hot or cold; light would be radiated, but there would be no colors as we know them. In such a world colors and sounds, heat and cold, would exist, as Boyle put it, in his *Origins of Forms and Qualities* (Oxford, 1666), only "dispositively," i.e., those primary things would be there that would have given rise to the secondary ones if creatures with the requisite sense organs and minds had been there too.

If all creatures with sense organs and consciousness

were removed from the world,

there would no longer be any experienced sounds,

but only pulsations in the air.

Primary and Secondary Qualities. In this way a distinction was made between the primary qualities of things, which are essential and absolute, and their secondary qualities, which are those among the primary ones that give or would give rise to heard sounds, seen colors, and felt heat. It was an important element of this view that nothing could be perceived unless it acted upon the sense organs of the percipient and produced in his mind an idea. What was immediately perceived was not the external object but an idea representative of it. Locke had made people familiar with this theory, and had maintained that whereas the ideas we have of heat and cold and of color and sound correspond to nothing *like* themselves in the external world; for all that exists in the external world are solid bodies at rest or in movement, the ideas we have of the solid, shaped, moving bodies, i.e., our ideas of primary qualities are like their sources or archetypes outside us. According to the view, then, that Berkeley was considering, material objects are perceived mediately or indirectly by means of ideas, some of which, the ideas of primary qualities, are like their originals; others, the ideas of secondary qualities, are relative to percipients and are unlike anything that exists in the external world.

MATERIALISM LEADS TO SKEPTICISM. Berkeley had two objections to the view that material objects are perceived mediately by means of ideas. One is that since it is held that we never perceive material things directly, but only through the medium of ideas, then we can never know whether any of our ideas are like the qualities of material substances since we can never compare our ideas with them; for to do so we should require direct or immediate acquaintance with them (*Principles,* §18). Indeed, if we accept Locke's position, then the very existence of material substances is in doubt, and we are constantly under the threat of skepticism (*Principles,* §86). Thus Berkeley argued that Locke's theory was in fact, although not by intention, skeptical, and that it could be remedied only by the elimination of material substances that could never be directly apprehended.

DISTINCTION BETWEEN PRIMARY AND SECONDARY QUALITIES UNTENABLE. Berkeley's second objection is that there can be no distinction between ideas of primary qualities and ideas of secondary qualities such as to make secondary qualities relative to the mind in a way in which primary qualities are not. In the *Three Dialogues* Berkeley elaborated the arguments, already used by Locke, to show that the ideas we have of secondary qualities are relative to the percipient and are what they are by reason of his condition and constitution. Things have no color in the dark; the same water can feel hot or cold to different hands, one of which has been in cold water and the other in hot; heat and cold are inseparably bound up with pain and pleasure, which can only exist in perceiving beings; and so on. But Berkeley then went on to argue that just as heat, for example, is inseparably bound up with pleasure and pain, and can therefore, no more than they can, exist "without the mind," so extension is bound up with color, speed of movement with a standard of estimation, solidity with touch, and size and shape with position and point of view (*Principles,* §§10–15). Thus Berkeley's argument is that nothing can have the primary qualities without having the secondary qualities, so that if the latter cannot exist "without the mind," the former cannot so exist either.

ALL SENSIBLE QUALITIES MUST BE EITHER PERCEIVED OR PERCEPTIBLE. The preceding argument, however, is only a hypothetical one to the effect that if secondary qualities cannot exist "without the mind," primary qualities are in like case. What must now be considered are the reasons for holding that secondary qualities and, indeed, all sensible qualities can exist only in the mind so that their being is to be perceived. Berkeley, as already indicated, stated and elaborated well-known arguments to show that heat and cold, tastes, sounds, and the rest are relative to the percipient. Perhaps the most persuasive of these are those that purport to establish an indissoluble connection between heat, taste, and smell on the one hand, and pain or pleasure or displeasure on the other. Since no one denies that pain and pleasure can exist only if felt, then this applies to heat so intense as to be painful and to lesser degrees of heat as well. But in the *Principles,* his systematic treatise on the subject, Berkeley did not make use of these arguments, but said that "an intuitive knowledge may be obtained of this, by any one that shall attend to what is meant by the term *exist* when applied to sensible things" (§3). His view here is that "sensible things" are by their very nature perceived or perceivable. He supported this by asserting that to say there was an odor is to say that it was smelled, to say that there was a sound is to say that it was heard, to say that there was a color or shape is to say that it was seen or touched. According to Berkeley, unsmelled odors, sounds unheard, colors unseen, and shapes unseen or untouched are absurdities or impossibilities; brown leaves could not rustle on a withered tree in a world where life was extinct and God was dead. The very notion is absurd or impossible. Can more light be shed on the matter than is provided by the assertion that we have "intuitive knowledge" of it?

Berkeley held that ideas are passive

and that the only active beings are minds or spirits.

It must be remembered, in the first place, that Berkeley was contrasting the sounds we hear, for example, with the movements in the air, which men of science sometimes call sounds. Sounds in the latter sense, he said, "may possibly be *seen* or *felt,* but never *heard*" (*Three Dialogues,* 1). From this it may be seen that Berkeley looked upon sensible qualities as each the object of its own mode of perception, so that sounds are heard but not seen or touched, colors seen but not heard, heat felt but not seen, and so on. Hence colors require a viewer, sounds a hearer, and heat someone who feels it; and this is one reason why the being of sensible things is held to be their being perceived. The various modalities of sense are distinguished from one another by the mode of perception peculiar to each one, and in making these distinctions it is implied that perception is essential to them all. It is well known, of course, that Berkeley's critics accuse him of failing to distinguish between the object perceived and the perceiving of it. The perceiving of it, they say, can only be an act of a percipient without whom it could not exist, but the perceived object, whether it be a sound or a color or a shape, is distinct from the perceiving and could con-

ceivably exist apart from it. Whatever may be thought of this argument, it should not be used against Berkeley as if he had not thought of it. In fact he put it into the mouth of Hylas in the first of the *Three Dialogues* and rejected it on the ground that in perception we are passive and so are not exerting an act or activity of any kind. It should also be noticed that when Berkeley discussed sensation in detail he stated that sensible things or sensible qualities are perceived *immediately,* i.e., without suggestion, association, or inference. We say that we hear vehicles and that we hear sounds. According to Berkeley, we hear sounds immediately, but vehicles, if they are out of sight, are suggested by or inferred from what we do hear, and so are heard only mediately or by means of the sounds immediately heard. Thus the sound we hear immediately is neither suggested nor inferred, but is heard just as it is. For this to be so, it must be before the mind; for if it were not before the mind, it would have to be inferred or suggested. Thus sensible qualities, as immediately perceived, must be objects of perception; their being is to be perceived.

Inconceivability of a Sensible Object Existing Unperceived. A very famous argument is now to be considered: It is inconceivable that anything should exist apart from, or independent of, mind. This argument was put forward by Berkeley in similar terms both in the *Principles* (§§22, 23) and in the *Three Dialogues* (1) and takes the form of a challenge to the reader to conceive of something—e.g., a book or a tree—existing absolutely unperceived. Berkeley argued that the attempt is impossible of fulfillment, since in order to conceive of a tree existing unperceived we who conceive of it, by the very fact of doing so, bring it into relation to our conception and hence to ourselves. As Hylas admits, in recognizing the failure of his attempt, "It is a pleasant mistake enough. As I was thinking of a tree in a solitary place, where no one was present to see it, methought that was to conceive a tree as existing unperceived or unthought of, not considering that I myself conceived it all the while." This is an argument that was later accepted as fundamental by idealists of such different persuasions as Fichte and Bradley, who held that it shows that mind or experience is essential to the universe.

Sensible Objects Are Complex Ideas. Berkeley's example of a tree makes it necessary to consider how trees and other things in nature are related to ideas, sensible qualities, sounds, colors, shapes, etc. According to Berkeley, such things as trees, books, and mountains are groups of ideas or sensible qualities and are hence as much within the mind as the latter are. Indeed, in his view, books, trees, and mountains *are* ideas, though complex ones. He admitted (*Principles*, §38) that this use of the word *idea* for what is ordinarily called a *thing* is somewhat odd, but held that, the facts being as they are, *idea* is better than *thing*. A tree is a group of ideas touched, seen, and smelled; a cherry, a group of ideas touched, seen, smelled, and tasted. The sensible qualities or ideas, without which we should have no conception of a tree or cherry, do not belong to some unseen, untouched, untasted substance or substratum, for the very conception of such a "something I know not what" (as Locke had called it) is incoherent, and rests upon the false view that we can conceive something in complete abstraction from ideas of sense.

Sensible Objects, as Ideas, Are Perceived Directly. Berkeley therefore concluded that it is his theory that conforms with common sense, not that of the materialists or the dualists. For according to Berkeley we perceive trees and cherries directly by seeing, touching, and tasting them, just as the plain man thinks we do, whereas his opponents regard them as perpetually hidden from us by a screen of intermediaries that may be always deceiving us. Berkeley considered that by this view he had refuted skepticism of the senses, for, according to his theory, the objects of the senses are the things in the world: the trees, houses, and mountains we live among. But trees, houses, and mountains, as compounded of sensible qualities or ideas, cannot exist "without the mind."

SENSIBLE OBJECTS NOT COPIES OF MATERIAL ARCHETYPES. Berkeley's arguments showing that all sensible qualities or ideas exist only as perceived and that, therefore, things in nature, being groups of such ideas, cannot exist "without the mind" have now been expounded. It is now necessary to complete this account of Berkeley's arguments for immaterialism with his argument to show that not only must sensible qualities or ideas exist in the mind, but also that nothing *like* them can exist outside it. For anyone reluctant to accept immaterialism is likely to fall back on the view that our ideas, although in our minds, are copies of material archetypes. Berkeley's objection to this in the *Principles* (§8) is that "an idea can be like nothing but an idea," which he illustrated by saying that a color or shape can only be like another color or shape. In the *Three Dialogues* (1) he expanded the argument in two ways. Ideas, he said, are regarded by some as the perceived representatives of imperceptible originals, but "Can a real thing in itself *invisible* be like a color; or a real thing which is not *audible,* be like a *sound?*" His other reason for holding that ideas cannot be like any supposed external originals is that ideas are "perpetually fleeting and variable," and "continually changing upon every alteration

in the distance, medium or instruments of sensation," while their supposed originals are thought to remain fixed and constant throughout all changes in the percipient's organs and position. But something that is fleeting and relative cannot be like what is stable and absolute, any more than what is incapable of being perceived can be like what is essentially perceptible.

Berkeley carried on a persistent battle against the tendency to suppose that mere abstractions are real things.

SUMMARY. The following are Berkeley's central arguments in favor of immaterialism. They arose out of his exposure of the weaknesses and inconsistencies in the then current scientific view of the world, with its distinction between primary and secondary qualities and its theory of representative perception. According to Berkeley, since primary qualities cannot exist apart from secondary qualities, and since secondary qualities, and indeed all sensible qualities, cannot exist "without the mind," the independent material world of the then current scientific view was a conceptual absurdity. This was supported by the argument that our ideas cannot be likenesses of an external material world, since there is nothing conceivable they could be likenesses of except mind-dependent existences of their own type. The theory of representative perception was held to be essentially skeptical, and Berkeley claimed that his own theory, according to which we directly perceive ideas and groups of ideas that exist only as perceived, eliminates skepticism and accords with common sense.

Metaphysics and Theology

In section 3 of the *Principles,* where Berkeley stated that we have intuitive knowledge of the fact that for sensible qualities to exist they must be perceived, he also stated that when we say that the table is in the room that we have left we mean that if we were to return there we could perceive it "or that some other spirit actually does perceive it." This shows that Berkeley was concerned with the problem of giving an account, within the terms of his immaterialism, of the continued existence of things that are not being perceived by any human being. It also shows that he considered two ways of dealing with this problem. One way was to extend the doctrine that the existence of sensible things is their being perceived into the doctrine that the existence of sensible things is their being *perceptible.* The other way was to argue that when sensible things are not being perceived by human beings they must be perceived by "some other spirit."

BERKELEY NOT A PHENOMENALIST. The first way points in the direction of the modern theory of phenomenalism, the theory according to which, in John Stuart Mill's happily, chosen words, material objects are "permanent possibilities of sensation." But might not anything, even material substances possessing only primary qualities, be perceptible, even if not actually being perceived? Some twentieth-century upholders of phenomenalism have argued that the world was perceptible before there was any life or mind, in the sense that if there had been gods or human beings they would have perceived it. This could not be possible on Berkeley's theory, however, since, as we have seen, he held that only ideas or sensible things can be *like* ideas or sensible things, so that what is perceptible is limited by what is perceived.

PERCEPTIBLE OBJECTS PERCEIVED BY GOD. The perceptible, therefore, is limited to the mind-dependent, and, for Berkeley, the very notion of something that might be perceived, but is not, is unacceptable. Thus it seems that Berkeley was forced to supplement his phenomenalist account of unperceived objects with the view that whatever is not being actually perceived by human beings, but is only perceptible by them, must be an object of perception by "some other spirit." He used this same expression in section 48 of the *Principles,* where he denied that "bodies are annihilated and created every moment, or exist not at all during the intervals between our perception of them." In the *Three Dialogues* (2) he argued that since sensible things do not depend on the thought of human beings and exist independently of them "*there must be some other mind wherein they exist.*" This other mind is God; and thus, according to Berkeley, the existence of sensible things when not being perceived by finite spirits is a proof of the existence of an infinite spirit who perceives them always. Indeed, Berkeley considered it a merit of immaterialism that it enables this brief and, as he thought, conclusive proof to be formulated.

OUR IDEAS COME FROM GOD. In the *Principles* Berkeley put forward another proof of the existence of God, this time a proof based upon God as the cause of our ideas. As has been shown, Berkeley held that ideas are passive and that the only active beings are minds or spirits. Now some of our ideas, namely, ideas of imagination, we ourselves produce, but others, the ideas of sense, come to us without our willing them. "There is therefore some other will or spirit that produces them" (*Principles,* §29). That this is God may be concluded from the regular order in which these ideas come to us.

The knowledge we have of God is analogous to the knowledge we have of other men. Since men are active spirits, we do not have ideas of them, but only of their expressions, words, and bodily movements. Through these we recognize them as possessors of minds and wills like those we know ourselves to have. Similarly, God reveals himself to us in the order of nature: "every thing we see, hear, feel, or in any wise perceive by sense, being a sign or effect of the Power of God."

ACTIVE SPIRITS AND PASSIVE IDEAS. These, then, are the elements of Berkeley's metaphysics. There are active spirits on the one hand and passive ideas on the other. The latter could not exist apart from the former, but the ideas in the minds of human beings are caused in them by God and sustained by him when they are not perceiving them. Regularly recurring groups of ideas are called bodies, and the ideas that form them are arbitrarily connected together and might have been connected quite differently. Thus there is no natural necessity or internal reason about the laws of nature, but the regular sequences of ideas reveal to us a single infinite being who orders things for our benefit. Active spirits and passive ideas are of different natures. The mind is not blue because the idea of blue is in it, nor is the mind extended because it has an idea of extension. Ideas are neither parts nor properties of minds. Berkeley seems to have thought that the relationship is *sui generis,* for he said that sensible qualities are in the mind "only as they are perceived by it, that is, not by way of *mode* or *attribute, but only by way of idea*" (*Principles,* §49).

GOD'S IDEAS AND OUR IDEAS. As already seen, Berkeley held that God was both the cause of the ideas in the minds of embodied finite spirits and also the Mind in which these ideas continued to exist when embodied finite spirits were not perceiving them. Berkeley was thus faced with the problem of how the ideas in finite minds are related to the ideas in God's mind. If we recall Berkeley's claim that he was on the side of common sense against the skeptics, then we should expect the ideas that continue to exist in God's mind to be identical with those that had been in the minds of the embodied finite spirits who had formerly perceived them.

However, he found that there were difficulties in this view. Men perceive ideas of sense by means of sense organs, and their ideas vary in accordance with their position and condition, but God does not have sense organs. Furthermore, some ideas—for example, those of heat and cold, and sensations of smell and taste—are inseparable from sensations of pain and pleasure, but God is impassible, i.e., not subject to feeling or emotion; hence he cannot be supposed to perceive ideas of this nature. In the *Three Dialogues* (3), therefore,

Berkeley concluded that "God knows or hath ideas; but his ideas are not conveyed to Him by sense, as ours are." From this it is natural to conclude that the ideas that God perceives are not identical with the ideas that embodied finite spirits perceive. Berkeley was obviously thinking along these lines when, in the same *Dialogue,* he said that the things that one perceives, "they or their archetypes," must, since one does not cause them, have an existence outside one's mind. Elsewhere in this *Dialogue* he distinguished between what is "ectypal or natural" and what is "archetypal and eternal." Thus Berkeley's arguments and the language he used combine to suggest that the ideas in God's mind are not the same ideas as those in the minds of embodied percipients.

Berkeley's account of arithmetic was even more

revolutionary than his account of geometry.

This point was taken up by the Samuel Johnson referred to earlier, in his correspondence with Berkeley. Johnson suggested that Berkeley's view is that "the real original and permanent existence of things is archetypal, being ideas *in mente Divina,* and that our ideas are copies of them." Johnson was too polite to press the point, but it follows that what we directly perceive are copies or representatives of divine originals, so that Berkeley's claim to have reinstated the direct, unmediated perception of common sense, in place of the representative and skeptical theory of the philosophers and scientists, cannot be substantiated. In his reply, Berkeley hardly met this point when he stated that material substance is an impossibility because it is held to exist apart from mind, whereas the archetypes in the divine mind are obviously inseparable from God's knowledge of them.

Philosophy of Nature

Berkeley carried on a persistent battle against the tendency to suppose that mere abstractions are real things. In the *New Theory of Vision* he denied the possibility of "extension in abstract," saying "A line or surface which is neither black, nor white, nor blue, nor yellow, etc., nor long, nor short, nor rough, nor smooth, nor square, nor round, etc., is perfectly incomprehensible" (§ 123). In the Introduction to the *Principles,* his most explicit discussion of the matter, he quoted Locke's account of the abstract idea of a triangle "which is neither oblique nor rectangle, neither equilateral, equicrural, nor scalenon, but all and none of these at once," and pointed out that any actual triangle must be one of these types and cannot possibly be "all and none" of them. What makes any idea general, he held, is not any abstract

feature that may be alleged to belong to it, but rather its being used to represent all other ideas that are like it in the relevant respects. Thus if something that is true of a triangle of one of these types is not true of it because it is of that one type, then it is true of all triangles whatever. Nothing exists but what is particular, and particular ideas become general by being used as representatives of others like them. Generality, we might say, is a symbolic device, not a metaphysical status. Thus Berkeley's attack on abstractions is based on two principles: (1) that nothing exists but what is particular, and (2) that nothing can exist on its own except what can be sensed or imagined on its own. If we accept the first principle, then abstract objects and Platonic forms are rejected, and if we accept the second, then possibility is limited to the sensible or imaginable.

SPACE, TIME, AND MOTION. We have already seen how Berkeley applied the above two principles to the abstract conception of unperceived existence, and to the abstract conception of bodies with only the primary qualities. It must now be shown how he applied them to some of the other elements in the scientific world view he was so intent on discrediting. Chief among these were the current conceptions of absolute space, absolute time, and absolute motion. According to Berkeley, all these are abstractions, not realities. It is impossible, he held, to form an idea of pure space apart from the bodies in it. We find that we are hindered from moving our bodies in some directions and can move them freely in others. Where there are hindrances to our movement there are other bodies to obstruct us, and where we can move unrestrictedly we say there is space. It follows that our idea of space is inseparable from our ideas of movement and of body (*Principles,* §116).

So too our conception of time is inseparable from the succession of ideas in our minds and from the "particular actions and ideas that diversify the day"; hence Newton's conception of absolute time flowing uniformly must be rejected (*Principles,* §§97, 98).

Newton had also upheld absolute motion, but this too, according to Berkeley, is a hypostatized abstraction. If there were only one body in existence there could be no idea of motion, for motion is the change of position of two bodies relative to one another. Thus sensible qualities, without which there could be no bodies, are essential to the very conception of movement. Furthermore, since sensible qualities are passive existences, and hence bodies are too, movement cannot have its source in body; and as we know what it is to move our own bodies, we know that the source of motion must be found in mind. Created spirits are responsible for only a small part of the movement in the world, and therefore God, the infinite spirit, must be its prime source. "And so natural philosophy either presupposes the knowledge of God or borrows it from some superior science" (*De Motu*, §34).

CAUSATION AND EXPLANATION. The thesis that God is the ultimate source of motion is a special case of the principle that the only real causes are spirits. This principle has the general consequence, of course, that inanimate bodies cannot act causally upon one another. Berkeley concluded from this that what are called natural causes are really signs of what follows them. Fire does not cause heat, but is so regularly followed by it that it is a reliable sign of it as long as "the Author of Nature always operates uniformly" (*Principles*, §107). Thus Berkeley held that natural laws describe but do not explain, for real explanations must be by reference to the aims and purposes of spirits, that is, in terms of final causes. For this reason, he maintained that mechanical explanations of movements in terms of attraction were misleading, unless it was recognized that they merely recorded the rates at which bodies in fact approach one another (*Principles*, §103). Similar arguments apply to gravity or to force when these are regarded as explanations of the movements of bodies (*De Motu*, §6). This is not to deny the importance of Newton's laws, for Newton did not regard gravity "as a true physical quality, but only as a mathematical hypothesis" (*De Motu*, §17). In general, explanations in terms of forces or attractions are mathematical hypotheses having no stable being in the nature of things but depending upon the definitions given to them (*De Motu*, §67). Their acceptability depends upon the extent to which they enable calculations to be made, resulting in conclusions that are borne out by what in fact occurs. According to Berkeley, forces and attractions are not found in nature but are useful constructions in the formulation of theories from which deductions can be made about what is found in nature, that is, sensible qualities or ideas (*De Motu*, §§34–41).

Philosophy of Mathematics

We have already seen that when he wrote the *New Theory of Vision*, Berkeley thought that geometry was primarily concerned with tangible extension, since visual extension does not have three dimensions, and visible shapes must be formed by hands that grasp and instruments that move. He later modified this view, an important feature of which has already been referred to in the account of Berkeley's discussion of Locke's account of the abstract idea of a triangle. A particular triangle, imagined or drawn, is regarded as representative of all other triangles, so that what is proved of it is proved of all others like it in the relevant respects. This, he

pointed out later in the *Principles* (§126), applies particularly to size. If the length of the line is irrelevant to the proof, what is true of a line one inch long is true of a line one mile long. The line we use in our proof is a representative sign of all other lines. But it must have a finite number of parts, for if it is a visible line it must be divisible into visible parts, and these must be finite in length. A line one inch long cannot be divided into 10,000 parts because no such part could possibly be seen. But since a line one mile long can be divided into 10,000 parts, we imagine that the short line could be divided likewise. "After this manner the properties of the lines signified are (by a very usual figure) transferred to the sign, and thence through mistake thought to appertain to it considered in its own nature." Thus it was Berkeley's view that infinitesimals should be "pared off" from mathematics (*Principles*, §131). In the *Analyst* (1734), he brought these and other considerations to bear in refuting Newton's theory of fluxions. In this book Berkeley seemed to suggest that the object of geometry is "to measure finite assignable extension" (§50, Q.2).

If qualities are ideas,

and an idea is identical with its being perceived,

how can different perceivers

perceive the same quality?

Berkeley's account of arithmetic was even more revolutionary than his account of geometry. In geometry, he held, one particular shape is regarded as representative of all those like it, but in arithmetic we are concerned with purely arbitrary signs invented by men to help them in their operations of counting. Number, he said, is "entirely the creature of the mind" (*Principles*, §12). He argued, furthermore, that there are no units and no numbers in nature apart from the devices that men have invented to count and measure. The same length, for example, may be regarded as one yard, if it is measured in that unit, or three feet or thirty-six inches, if it is measured in those units. Arithmetic, he went on, is a language in which the names for the numbers from zero to nine play a part analogous to that of nouns in ordinary speech (*Principles*, §121). Berkeley did not develop this part of his theory. However, later in the eighteenth century, in various works, Condillac argued in detail for the thesis that mathematics is a language, and this view is, of course, widely held today.

Concluding Comments

Berkeley's immaterialism is a strange and unstable combination of theses that most other philosophers have thought do not belong together. Thus he upheld both extreme empiricism and idealism, both immaterialism and common sense, and both subjectivism (as it would seem) and epistemological realism (as it would also seem). Are these mere skillful polemical devices in the war against the freethinkers, or can they be regarded as elements in a distinctive and reasonably coherent metaphysics?

It is odd that Berkeley had so much to say about the relativity of each particular sense and so little to say about our perception of the physical world. He referred to perspectival distortions and the like in the course of defending his view that the existence of sensible qualities is their being perceived, but he did not seem to realize the difficulties they made for his view that perception is direct. Indeed, when, in the *Three Dialogues* (3) he mentioned the case of the oar that looks bent in the water when in fact it is straight, he said that we go wrong only if we mistakenly infer that it will look bent when out of the water. There is something seen to be straight, something else seen to be crooked, and something else again felt to be straight. We go wrong only when we expect that when we see something crooked we shall feel something crooked. But this implies that our perceptions of such things as oars, as distinct from our perceptions of colors and pressures, are not direct as common sense supposes. This reinforces the criticism we have already mentioned, that the ideas perceived by finite spirits with sense organs are different from, and representative of, the ideas in the mind of God. Berkeley was farther from common sense and closer to the views that he was criticizing than he was ready to admit.

It is obvious enough that Berkeley's immaterialism is not in accord with common sense. What place, then, must be given to his empiricism? He certainly rejected the Cartesian conception of a natural world that deceives the senses and is apprehended by the reason. He denied that mathematics reveals the ultimate necessities of things and anticipated to some extent the linguistic theory of mathematics. In arguing that causes are not to be found in nature, and in maintaining that the sciences of nature are primarily concerned with predicting human experiences, he formulated views that Ernst Mach and his twentieth-century followers have advocated. Furthermore, although he did not himself adopt it, he briefly formulated the theory of the physical world known as phenomenalism, the theory that consistent empiricists have adopted in order to avoid postulating objects that transcend sense experience. But, in spite of all this, Berkeley was an idealist rather than an empiricist. He held that sensible qualities or ideas are not independent or substantial existences and that minds or spirits are. On this most important matter, he was in agreement with his great contemporary, Leibniz. Furthermore, Berkeley's antiabstractionism, as we may call it, was constantly leading him towards the conclusion that the universe is a concrete unity in which an infinite mind is manifesting itself. If we look at his writings as a continuing and developing critique of abstraction, then we shall see that the *Siris* is not an aberration or a recantation but, as Bergson said in his lectures on Berkeley, 1908–1909, a natural continuation of Berkeley's earlier views (*Écrits et paroles, 2,* p. 309).

BIBLIOGRAPHY

Life and Principal Editions of Works

Fraser, A. C., *The Works of George Berkeley,* 4 Vols. London, 1871. New (first complete) edition, 1901.

Rand, Benjamin, *Berkeley and Percival.* Cambridge, 1914.

Luce, A. A., and Jessop, T. E., eds., *The Works of George Berkeley, Bishop of Cloyne,* 9 Vols. London and New York, 1948–1957. The Introduction and Notes in this definitive edition are of great value.

Luce, A. A. *The Life of George Berkeley, Bishop of Cloyne.* London, 1949.

Main Themes of Berkeley's Philosophy

Hicks, G. Dawes, *Berkeley.* London, 1932.

Wild, J., *George Berkeley. A Study of His Life and Philosophy.* New York, 1936, 1962.

Warnock, G. J., *Berkeley.* London, 1953.

Leroy, A.-L., *George Berkeley.* Paris, 1959.

The New Theory of Vision

Bailey, S., *A Review; of Berkeley's Theory of Vision,* London, 1842.

Abbot, T. K., *Sight and Touch.* London, 1864.

Turbayne, C. M., "Berkeley and Molyneux on Retinal Images." *Journal of the History of Ideas,* Vol. 16 (1955).

Armstrong, D. M., *Berkeley's Theory of Vision.* Melbourne, 1960.

Vesey, G. N. A., "Berkeley and the Man Born Blind." *PAS,* Vol. 61 (1960–1961).

Arguments for Immaterialism

Laird, J., "Berkeley's Realism." *Mind,* N. S. Vol. 25 (1916), pp. 308 ff.

Moore, G. E., "Refutation of Idealism," in *Philosophical Studies.* London, 1922.

Luce, A. A., "Berkeley's Existence in the Mind." *Mind,* N. S., Vol. 50 (1941), pp. 258 ff.

Luce, A. A., "The Berkeleyan Idea of Sense." *PAS,* Supplementary Vol. 27 (1953).

Broad, C. D., "Berkeley's Denial of Material Substance." *Philosophical Review,* Vol. 43 (1954).

Mates, Benson, "Berkeley Was Right," in *George Berkeley, Lectures Delivered Before the University of California.* Berkeley and Los Angeles, 1957.

Sullivan, Celestine J., "Berkeley's Attack on Matter," *Ibid.*

Bracken, H. M., "Berkeley's Realism." *The Philosophical Quarterly,* Vol. 8 (1958).

Metaphysics and Theology

Luce, A. A., *Berkeley and Malebranche.* London, 1934.

Fritz, Anita D., "Berkeley and the Immaterialism of Male-branche." *Review of Metaphysics,* Vol. 3 (1949–1950).

Gueroult, M., *Berkeley. Quatre études sur la perception et sur Dieu.* Paris, 1956.

Sillem, E. A., *George Berkeley and the Proofs for the Existence of God.* London and New York, 1957.

Bracken, H. M., "Berkeley on the Immortality of the Soul." *The Modern Schoolman,* Vol. 38 (1960–1961).

Myerscough, Angelita, "Berkeley and the Proofs for the Existence of God," in J. K. Ryan, ed., *Philosophy and the History of Philosophy,* Vol 1. Washington, 1961.

Davis, J. W., "Berkeley and Phenomenalism." *Dialogue. Canadian Philosophical Review,* Vol. 1 (1962–1963), 67–80.

Philosophy of Nature and Philosophy of Mathematics

Mach, Ernst, *The Analysis of Sensations.* Chicago, 1914.

Whitrow, G. J., "Berkeley's Critique of the Newtonian Analysis of Motion." Hermathena, Vol. 82 (1953).

Wisdom, J. O., "Berkeley's Criticism of the Infinitesimal." *British Journal for the Philosophy of Science,* Vol. 3 (1953–1954).

Whitrow, G. J., "Berkeley's Philosophy of Motion." *Ibid.*

Popper, K. R., "A Note on Berkeley as Precursor of Mach." *Ibid.*

Myhill, John, "Berkeley's De Motu—An Anticipation of Mach," in *George Berkeley, Lectures Delivered Before the University of California.* Berkeley and Los Angeles, 1957.

Strong, Edward W., "Mathematical Reasoning and Its Object," *Ibid.*

– H. B. ACTON

BERKELEY, GEORGE (UPDATE)

George Berkeley believed that there are only minds and ideas. The existence of minds (or spirits or souls), Berkeley tells us, consists in perceiving, whereas the existence of ideas (including sensations) consists in being perceived. Minds, which are the only substances, are active, and ideas are passive. The existence of physical objects consists in their being perceived: this is so because such objects consist of qualities, and qualities are sensations. Thus, Berkeley endorses the idealist view that the physical world is kept in existence by being perceived and therefore depends upon the mind. Consequently, there is no need for material substance. Indeed, the very concept of material substance is incoherent.

The ideas or sensations that constitute the physical world are given to us by God. Since God is their source, we are in intimate contact with God, and we ought therefore always to be assured of God's existence.

That the foregoing claims are central to Berkeley's philosophy is uncontroversial. However, disagreement persists about Berkeley's views in many areas, including the following.

Abstraction and Immaterialism

Berkeley devotes most of the introduction to *A Treatise concerning the Principles of Human Knowledge,* Part 1, to a refutation of the Lockean belief in abstract ideas. He seems to understand the case against abstraction to be central to his case for thinking that physical objects may not exist apart from perception. But how is the case against abstraction supposed to contribute to the case against mind-independent physical objects?

One strand in his thinking may be that it is wrong to believe things that are incapable of existing apart to exist apart. Physical objects are incapable of existing apart from perception. Hence, it is wrong to believe them to do so. That is, we cannot conceive of, or have an idea of, *a* and *b* as existing apart if *a* and *b* are incapable of existing apart; and since there cannot be existence apart from perception, we are unable to conceive of existence without perception. On this reading the case against abstracting existence from perception requires that it has already been shown that there cannot be existence apart from perception; and the case against abstraction contributes nothing to the defense of Berkeley's philosophy.

Perhaps the idea is that we are incapable of conceiving of sensible things, which are nothing but the sensible ideas we perceive, as existing apart from perception: thus, just as pain is felt pain, so taste is perceived taste, color is perceived color, shape is observed shape, and so forth. Hence, it is impossible for us to believe that physical things exist apart from perception. However, this is not exactly an argument against mind-independent existence. It is closer to being an argument against believing in mind-independent existence; but it really amounts merely to an assertion that we are incapable of believing in this sort of existence.

On this reading the case against abstract ideas is not a premise in an argument against mind-independent existence. At most it is a diagnosis or illumination of the sort of error that is involved in believing that there are unperceived objects, or at least of the sort of error involved in thinking that one is believing in mind-independent existence, since we are told that it is impossible to so believe. Indeed, it seems that the case against abstraction is irrelevant to, and unnecessary for, this line of thought. For if the idea of unperceived existence is contradictory, as Berkeley insists, then even if there were abstract ideas we would still be incapable of conceiving of existence apart from perception, just as we would still be incapable of conceiving of married bachelors or round squares or any other manifestly contradictory concepts even if there were abstract ideas. A further difficulty for this line of thought is that Berkeley actually states that the belief in mind-independent existence is prevalent.

Minds and Bodies

How did Berkeley conceive of the relationship between the mind and the body? A human body, like any other physical object, is—or at least is in part—a set of ideas. Are the ideas that constitute, or partly constitute, physical objects bestowed on finite minds by God? If so, when a human arm is moved, one set of ideas produced by God is followed by another such set. Berkeley says that we move our own limbs and that on this issue he differs from Malebranche. But how can he account for our moving our limbs? (And if he is unable to account for our doing so, on what basis does he think that one finite mind may reasonably conclude that there are other such minds?) Are we able to produce some sensations? Or are we "active beings" who are actually inactive in the world: is the claim that we are able to move our limbs to be reduced to the view that certain sequences of ideas that we produce serve as the occasion for God to grant us certain sensations? Or is it to be reduced to the view that certain sensations (in particular those that constitute, or partially constitute, states of affairs or events that we wish to obtain or occur) can be thought of as being produced by us?

Ideas and the Perception of Ideas

How did Berkeley conceive of the relationship between ideas and their perception? Are there two things, an object and an act, which stand in a certain relationship to each other? (Are there at any rate an object and a process in the mind to be related? For Berkeley says that in sense perception the mind is passive, which incidentally is a view that needs to be reconciled with his idea of the mind as an active, indivisible entity.) Berkeley says that the existence of an idea is identical with its being perceived. His model for the relation between an idea and its perception is the relation between a pain and its perception. That relation is one of numerical identity. If an idea is identical with its being perceived, and if the perception of an idea is a private event in the mental life of an individual, it follows that an idea is something private to the mind in which it occurs.

On the other hand it is natural to think of the qualities of objects, such as the redness of an apple, as something public that different people can perceive. Berkeley would want to preserve this commonsense belief. Yet if qualities are ideas, and an idea is identical with its being perceived, how can different perceivers perceive the same quality?

Perhaps Berkeley should say that different people may perceive numerically the same quality even though they may not perceive numerically the same idea, thereby abandoning his identification of ideas and qualities. Or perhaps he should abandon the view that qualities are public and argue that physical objects are public even though they consist of qualities that are private to the mind that has the ideas with which they are identical.

The Existence of God

Berkeley thought that we can know that God exists because our sensations come to us from an external source. He thought too that since some physical objects continue to exist while unperceived by us, there must be some other mind that perceives them while we do not perceive them; and Berkeley also presents this line of thought as the basis for a case for God's existence. Further, he thought that since the ideas we perceive have an external source, they (or their archetypes) exist apart from us in some other mind that exhibits them to us. Does Berkeley intend to offer three distinct arguments (one that appeals to the source of our ideas, a second that appeals to the continued existence of unperceived objects, and a third that appeals to the independent existence of our ideas or their archetypes), or are these best understood as three strands in a single argument? However Berkeley may have conceived of the connections among these considerations, a case can be made for regarding the appeal to continuity as subsidiary to the appeal to the independent existence of our ideas or their archetypes. For if at all times at which they exist, including times at which we perceive them and times at which we do not perceive them, the objects we perceive by sense exist in another mind, by whom they are exhibited to us, then the fact that they exist when we do not perceive them seems fairly incidental. That is, their existence at times when we are not perceiving them is just a function of the fact that they have an independent existence, an existence that they have both while we perceive them and at times at which we do not perceive them but during which they continue to exist. Yet another argument for God's existence derives from Berkeley's thought that visual sensations are a language in that, for example, they tell us what other sensations we may receive and in that our sensations are often combined in complex patterns. The use of a language requires a mind.

Immediate Perception of Objects

Are physical objects the immediate objects of sense perception, or do we perceive them indirectly by directly perceiving various sensations such as sensations of light, colors, sounds, and odors? Berkeley frequently says that, strictly speaking, nothing is seen but light and colors, nothing is heard but sounds, nothing tasted but tastes, and so on for the other sensory modes. However, if objects consist, or even partly consist, of ideas of sense, perhaps we may perceive them immediately by perceiving some of the ideas that constitute them. It would not be reasonable to object that since, on this view, we immediately perceive them only in part, we do not immediately perceive them: this would be to rule out the direct perception of objects on any conception of an object. Berkeley accepts that there are ideas that are among the constituents of objects that are only suggested to us by the ideas we perceive directly. Thus, the shape and figure of a coach are suggested to us by the sound of the coach. But why think of the object as a whole as being mediately perceived because some of the ideas that are among its components are mediately perceived? Why not think of the object as immediately perceived because ideas that are among its components are immediately perceived?

Ideas and Objects

Berkeley sometimes seems to say that physical objects are just collections of sensations. But he also seems to explain the continued existence of objects that are not currently perceived by us by appealing to God's perceptions and to God's volitions. In addition, as noted above, he says that the ideas we perceive exist apart from our minds at all times at which they exist. But if objects can exist *qua* divine ideas or volitions, or if they have any sort of existence independent of our perception, then they are not just collections of sensations. They are not just families of ideas produced in us by God. Further, God can perceive a great deal more than we can: God can perceive objects from all angles at once and can perceive the interiors of physical objects whose surface alone we can see. It seems that if objects consist of our ideas along with God's ideas, our ideas are in danger of being second-class counterparts of God's. But even if Berkeley were to accept that our ideas are second-class counterparts of God's, he need not also accept that the real objects are in God's mind; and he need not be committed to a representative theory of perception.

[See also Locke, John; Perception.]

BIBLIOGRAPHY

Abstraction and Immaterialism

Bolton, M. B. "Berkeley's Objection to Abstract Ideas and Unconceived Objects," in E. Sosa, ed., *Essays on the Philosophy of George Berkeley* (Dordrecht, 1987).
Pappas, G. S. "Abstract Ideas and the Esse Is Percipi Thesis," in D. Berman, ed., *George Berkeley: Essays and Replies* (Dublin, 1986).

Minds and Bodies

Taylor, C. C. W. "Action and Inaction in Berkeley," in J. Foster and H. Robinson, eds., *Essays on Berkeley: A Tercentennial Celebration* (Oxford, 1985).
Tipton, I. *Berkeley,* London, 1974.

Ideas and the Perception of Ideas

McCracken, C. J. "Berkeley on the Relation of Ideas to the Mind," in P. D. Cummins and G. Zoeller, eds., *Minds, Ideas, and Objects: Essays on the Theory of Representation in Modern Philosophy* (Atascadero, CA, 1992).
Pitcher, G. *Berkeley,* London, 1977.

The Existence of God

Ayers, M. R. "Divine Ideas and Berkeley's Proofs of God's Existence," in E. Sosa, ed., *Essays on the Philosophy of George Berkeley* (Dordrecht, 1987).
Kline, A. D. "Berkeley's Divine Language Argument," in E. Sosa, ed., *Essays on the Philosophy of George Berkeley* (Dordrecht, 1987).

Immediate Perception of Objects

Pappas, G. S. "Berkeley and Immediate Perception," in E. Sosa, ed., *Essays on the Philosophy of George Berkeley* (Dordrecht, 1987).
Pitcher, G. *Berkeley.* London, 1977.

Ideas and Objects

Foster, J. "Berkeley on the Physical World," in J. Foster and H. Robinson, eds., *Essays on Berkeley: A Tercentennial Celebration* (Oxford, 1985).
McKim, R. "Berkeley on Perceiving the Same Thing," in P. D. Cummins and G. Zoeller, eds., *Minds, Ideas, and Objects: Essays on the Theory of Representation in Modern Philosophy* (Atascadero, CA, 1992).

Other Works

Atherton, M. *Berkeley's Revolution in Vision.* Ithaca, NY, 1990.
Berkeley, G. *A Treatise concerning the Principles of Human Knowledge,* edited by C. M. Turbayne. Indianapolis, 1970. With critical essays.
Berman, D. *George Berkeley: Idealism and the Man.* Oxford, 1994.
Dancy, J. *Berkeley: An Introduction.* Oxford, 1987.
Grayling, A. C. *Berkeley: The Central Arguments.* La Salle, IL, 1986.
Jesseph, D. *Berkeley's Philosophy of Mathematics.* Chicago, 1993.
Muehlmann, R. *Berkeley's Ontology.* Indianapolis, 1992.
Winkler, K. *Berkeley: An Interpretation.* Oxford, 1989.

– ROBERT MCKIM

BIOMEDICAL ETHICS

Biomedical ethics, as it is currently known, began in the mid-1960s, around the time of the publication of the *Encyclopedia of Philosophy.* Some date the beginning from the first kidney dialysis unit (1962, in Seattle). Many more people were in need of dialysis than the unit could accommodate; so a committee of community and medical representatives decided who among their kidney-impaired fellow citizens would receive the life-saving procedure. In an important sense this launched the era of biomedical ethics, the thrust of which was to open up moral issues in medicine to public scrutiny. In 1971 the term bioethics was coined, whose connotation was inclusive of but broader than medical ethics (Reich, 1995). "Bioethics" encompassed moral concerns in and about science, scientific research, the treatment of animals, and environmental matters, though it had its beginnings in the concerns of medicine and medical research. Solidifying these moral concerns as a public endeavor were the appointment of national commissions that were constituted to deliberate, analyze, and recommend with respect to selected issues. The terminology gradually shifted from medical ethics to bioethics. As the breadth of bioethics unfolded, "biomedical ethics" was used to distinguish that portion of bioethics devoted to medically related concerns. Eventually, "bioethics" came to be used interchangeably with "biomedical ethics" in denoting this enlarged field of medical ethics. To add to the confusion, "bioethics" and "applied ethics" are often used interchangeably, though applied ethics is the more inclusive term.

When and under what conditions may the doctor,

in order to do "the best" for her patient,

violate that which morality generally requires?

Medical ethics is, of course, a subject probably as old as medicine itself. Nevertheless, the resurgent interest generated in the 1960s was sufficiently strong and different enough to be considered a new era. A confluence of societal forces and events contributed to this rebirth. There was a strong emphasis on individual rights (the civil rights movement), as well as an increasing distrust of authority and institutions. The public no longer showed unquestioning deference to the experts in fields such as medicine, engineering, education, law, and government. Value assumptions were uncovered and questioned. Consumerism was on the rise. Many new medical technologies and therapies were becoming available and more were promised by the "new biology." Inasmuch as there was no clear societal consensus on values, there was considerable need for public discussion of these issues. Though biomedical ethics was the core of this minirevolution, other disciplinary ethics were taking shape—for example, business ethics, engineering ethics, and environmental ethics.

It is hard to overstate the societywide impact of biomedical ethics. Many articles began to appear, especially in medical journals; new journals devoted to such matters were established; courses in biomedical ethics and then in bioethics at the undergraduate level were developed at most colleges and universities (usually within

the religion or the philosophy department); week-long summer workshops in bioethics and professional ethics were attended by persons (totaling thousands) from a wide variety of professional backgrounds. Public discourse of moral issues and scholarly investigation of those issues were well launched by the 1980s.

Many disciplines were involved in the emergence of biomedical ethics. The fields of medicine, religion, journalism, law, social sciences, history, nursing, and others, as well as philosophy, were active in giving shape and substance to this new field. Two important organizations in this development were the Society of Health and Human Values and the Hastings Center. The former, a successor organization to a group called Ministers in Medical Education (mid-1950s), was originally affiliated with the Association of American Medical Colleges, and its members were mostly medical educators. Though continuing to be closely related to the education of health professionals, its membership has become a diverse group from such fields as sociology, nursing, religion, philosophy, law, medicine, literature, and history. The Hastings Center (originally more descriptively named the Institute of Society, Ethics, and the Life Sciences), founded in 1969, similarly had a diverse membership with a core of elected Fellows, most of whom were in the fields of religion, law, medicine, and philosophy. As increasing numbers engaged in clinical ethical consultations, there was a felt need to understand, develop, and assess the emerging phenomenon of bioethical consultation. To meet that need the Society for Bioethics Consultation was created in 1986–87. The American Association of Bioethics, a professional society for bioethics composed primarily of philosophers and lawyers, was organized in 1992–93. The AAB sought to ensure the soundness and continuation of bioethics as an academic discipline, to provide a forum for exchange of ideas and information, and to meet a perceived need for an official organization to engage the issues of bioethics at the national and international level, particularly on matters of policy.

Philosophy and Biomedical Ethics

Many disciplines have contributed to and continue to contribute to the development of biomedical ethics—religion, law, medicine, journalism, social sciences, literature. This entry, however, will focus only on philosophy's involvement. There has been a complicated, reciprocal relationship between philosophy and biomedical ethics. Each has been changed somewhat by the encounter (Clouser, 1989).

Though traditionally ethics has been a major field within philosophy, during roughly the first half of the twentieth century philosophical ethics focused primarily on highly theoretical and metaethical matters. Nevertheless, it may well have been that theoretical orientation that recommended philosophy as a participant in the public moral discourse of biomedical ethical issues, theories, and methods. Neither a professional medical ethic nor a sectarian, religious ethic seemed appropriate as a framework for the public discussion of medically related moral issues. Rather, it was philosophical ethics that appeared to provide the neutrality necessary to nurture the public discussion of practical moral issues in a pluralistic society (Jonsen, 1995).

There is no canonical view of philosophy's involvement. If such a view emerges at all, it will happen only after some histories of this period have been written and debated. Philosophy as a whole did not embrace the new challenge of biomedical ethics, but there were individual philosophers who were drawn to the task. The sheer practicality of the enterprise seemed antithetical

to the tradition of philosophy; on the other hand, there were many intriguing issues and dilemmas that called for philosophy's traditional skills of conceptual analysis. For many philosophers it seemed out of character for philosophers to ponder practical moral decision making in medical clinics and hospitals.

Some Issues

Philosophy's engagement with biomedical ethics took many forms. Primarily it was a matter of individuals trained in philosophy and serving in a variety of different capacities: as teachers of undergraduates; as teachers in medical, nursing, and other healthcare professional schools; as staff members of organizations dealing with bioethics issues, including some appropriate government commissions; as ethics consultants on hospital staffs or in private practice; as providers of educational opportunities in bioethics in venues such as workshops,

Euthanasia crusader Dr. Jack Kevorkian was found guilty of second-degree murder for his role in the assisted suicide of a terminally ill patient. (Corbis/AFP)

continuing education, and conferences; as researchers on special projects involving bioethical issues. There was no formal engagement and no party line coming from philosophy as such. As is typical of philosophy and philosophers, the philosophical input into bioethics was individualistic.

Yet there was a common core of moral issues that, at least in the beginning, were addressed by biomedical ethics and were of particular interest to philosophers. What follows is not a substantive discussion of the issues but a summary revealing those structures of particular interest to philosophers.

From the beginning abortion has been of interest to philosophers. Even after the 1973 *Roe v. Wade* Supreme Court decision, which diminished the urgency of discussion by establishing legal guidelines for practice, the concept of abortion still had many component issues that were natural for philosophy. When does life begin? What constitutes personhood? Does humanity have an essence? Does that essence "enter" at some point in embryonic development? Is there a difference between a potential being and a possible being? Under what circumstances can a right to one's own body justify taking a life? Is one responsible for known but unintended consequences of an action? It was only natural that philosophy would be drawn into this subject matter, which turned more on conceptual analysis than on facts.

Euthanasia is another major concern addressed by biomedical ethics. This bundle of concerns would be better labeled, as it frequently is, "decisions near the end of life." Until the 1990s the focus was seldom on actively killing the patient; rather, the focus was on "allowing the patient to die." The search for moral differences between various methods of "allowing to die" provided many conceptual problems that were ideal for philosophical treatment. For example, is choosing not to save a patient from death (e.g., from a heart attack or a respiratory emergency) the moral equivalent of killing him? Is withdrawing a life-saving therapy (such as a ventilator) from a patient morally the same as not beginning it in the first place? Is there a moral difference between the types of life-saving therapy that are withheld or withdrawn: the patient's regular maintenance medications (e.g., insulin or antihypertensives) versus acute care therapies (e.g., CPR or antibiotics) versus nutrition and hydration? Physicians (and society) had come to recognize that the patient had a right to refuse treatment, and they were equally certain that the physician could not legally acquiesce in the patient's request to kill him directly. But they were unsure whether a patient could refuse the very treatments that, if discontinued, would result in his death, since if withdrawing treatment were morally equivalent to killing the phy-

sician would then be killing at the request of the patient (for contrasting views see Clouser, 1977, and Rachels, 1975). Many of these conceptual problems were circumvented by legislation, state by state, establishing the legality of advance directives (originally called "living wills") whereby an individual, while competent, could give directions for his own care to be followed when he was no longer competent to speak for himself. However, advance directives brought their own ambiguities and conceptual problems, especially with respect to the conditions necessary to activate the advance directive. During the early 1990s several states attempted, by voter referendum, to establish laws allowing physicians to assist patients in committing suicide. Suicide and assisted suicide are matters of long-standing interest to philosophers.

The doctor–patient relationship has generated moral issues for philosophical consideration. It is a given that a physician owes it to her patient always to act in the patient's best interest, but there are varying accounts of why this is so. There are also questions that arise as to the extent of this "fiduciary" obligation. For example, when and under what conditions may the doctor, in order to do "the best" for her patient, violate that which morality generally requires? This is the issue of paternalism, which has been a philosophical topic for many years. Precisely what it is and what would justify it has been a significant concern of biomedical ethics. A closely related issue has been a main thrust of the era of biomedical ethics, namely, establishing the self-determination (or autonomy) of patients. This was provoked by a combination of society's strong insistence on individual rights and the quantum leap of medical progress that entails many more therapeutic options, each with its own inherent advantages and disadvantages. With such a smorgasbord of risk–benefit trade-offs among appropriate therapies, it became prudent for the patient to choose her own therapy.

However, there are ambiguities concerning autonomy, such as determining when a decision is "truly" autonomous. Kant thought a decision to commit suicide could never be an autonomous decision, yet most bioethicists believe that a terminally ill, competent patient's decision to be allowed to die, or even to be killed, is the epitome of an autonomous decision. An inevitable inquiry that emerges from the prominence given autonomy concerns what limits may or must be placed on autonomy. It is argued that the well-being of an individual's family or community have some claim against the autonomous decision. A moral view called communitarianism arose as if in response to unfettered autonomy. Its emphasis is to give voice to the interests and rights of others affected by an individual's decisions.

Among the more interesting philosophical aspects to emerge from the focus on the doctor–patient relationship is the concept of duty. Though duty has often been understood among philosophers simply as a general moral obligation that everyone has toward each other, it is arguable that duties are more helpfully and accurately understood as limited to those moral requirements established by virtue of one's role or relationship to others. Duties thus understood are established through tradition, law, codes, and societal expectations and have important legal and moral implications for how one must, may, and must not act toward the one to whom the duty is owed.

One of the surprises of bioethics

was how little the ethical theories of philosophy

seemed to help in solving the real

and complex moral problems of medicine.

Experimentation on humans for medical and behavioral research constitutes a major area of concern. It was the matter of experimentation with all its attendant moral issues that especially triggered the era of bioethics and brought such matters to public attention. The National Commission for the Protection of Human Subjects of Biomedical and Behavioral Research, established in 1972, was charged with making recommendations for federal regulations to protect the rights and welfare of human subjects of research sponsored by the federal government and to determine the ethical and moral principles governing research with human subjects. This undertaking and the attention it brought to moral concerns in research had far-reaching effects: extensive studies of consent and the conditions necessary for its moral validity (such as the subject's being competent and his decision being informed, free, and voluntary); investigations of the morality of using various populations as research subjects—fetuses, children, prisoners, the senile, the elderly, and the mentally retarded; the establishment of review boards in every institution in the country that uses federal funds for research (a board's function being to assess the moral acceptability of every proposal for research that uses human subjects); and an equally intense parallel concern for the use of animals in research, spawning a new specialty in animal ethics as well as review committees to determine the moral acceptability of research proposals using animals as subjects, known as Institutional Animal Care and Utilization Committees (IACUCs). The major empha-

sis given to the importance of informed consent for research carried over to informed consent for therapy as well. Analyzing what makes a consent (or refusal) valid, and if and when it can be overridden, has been of keen interest to philosophers.

Distributive justice in the world of health care has been a continuing theme in biomedical ethics. In the real world of needy people and limited resources there is pressure to find moral methods or principles for resource distribution. This issue is relevant from the most concrete level (Who should get the next available bed in the intensive care unit? Who should receive the next available organ for transplant?) to the policy level dealing with how goods should be allocated among, for example, hospitals, museums, schools, and road construction. Debated criteria for distribution on the concrete level include equal shares, equal outcome, merit, age, need, health, and personal responsibility for the health deficit (e.g., whether alcoholics should receive liver transplants).

Justice, including distributive justice, has been an issue within philosophy since its inception. During the early years of bioethics the most reflected-upon philosophical work in this context was John Rawls's *Theory of Justice*. Though not originally intended to deal with matters of justice in health care, the book become a paradigm and resource in that area. Rawlsian theory has been ingeniously squeezed for every implication it might have for health-care ethics in general as well as health-care distribution in particular (Daniels, 1985). Another matter dealt with under the rubric of justice is the question of a right to health care: is it a natural human right, or one granted by the government, or one implicit in the U.S. constitution (e.g., following from a guarantee of equal opportunity)?

Reproductive technologies and genetics, though always of concern, rose to prominence in the 1980s, boosted by the increase in related scientific and medical research. The creation of the National Center for Human Genome Research at the National Institutes of Health (1989), dedicated to the mapping and sequencing of the human genome, has especially initiated substantial moral deliberations in and around genetics. Whereas all the other biomedical ethical issues focus especially on weighing harms and benefits and protecting individuals, reproductive technologies and genetics have an additional component. For many the issues are morally challenging because they appear to involve more of an interference with a basic order of nature. Whereas most moral deliberation begins with human nature as a given, genetic engineering raises the possibility of changing that very human nature, either by deleting certain qualities and characteristics or by enhancing them. There are those who regard the creation of human beings as a special and basic order of nature with which no one should tamper. Such metaphysical, religious, or quasi-religious considerations go beyond simply lessening the amount of harm in the world; they entail world views on which it may become very difficult to reach consensus. Meanwhile, practical moral problems must be decided—for example, ownership of preserved sperm or ova or embryos, limits on what may be done with them, and the best policy for handling the various possible combinations of sperm, ova, and hired gestational "mothers." Other issues in genetics pivot around the control and management of knowledge about an individual's genetic makeup, which, in effect, will be significantly predictive of the health status of that individual and thus have important implications concerning privacy, insurability, and life plans.

Philosophical Reflections

Certain questions especially of interest to philosophers are provoked by involvement in the very practical world of biomedical ethics. The following are a few of the matters that, though not necessarily new, have been highlighted for philosophers in the era of bioethics.

"STRETCHING" MORALITY. Inevitably, when confronted with new and unusual circumstances, one questions whether a new ethics is needed in order to deal with such new and different circumstances, or whether somehow the old morality can be "stretched" to cover the new circumstances. Van Rensselaer Potter, who was the first to use the term bioethics (Potter, 1971), believed that what was needed was a more scientifically based ethic, achieved by combining biological knowledge with the knowledge of human value systems. The goal was the survival of the human species. It is not clear that this combination would produce a new ethic, but the scientific aspect, in the service of human values, might sufficiently alert humans to the facts that would both motivate and, by virtue of understanding better the causes and effects in the biological world, give direction to their actions for survival. The idea of inventing new ethics is odd. What would be its justification? Could the new ethics approve of killing a certain group of persons, or causing others pain, or taking away their freedom? It seems that the ethics would have to be fundamentally the same as always, though, given newly discovered facts, capabilities, and causal relationships, the means to a given end may be different. That is, there may be new ways of causing or preventing harm or a new realization that certain actions would result in harms that humans had not realized. Nevertheless, the moral admonition not to cause harm to anyone (unless the moral agent is willing for everyone to know that it

would be acceptable for them also to do the same thing in the same morally relevant circumstances) remains the same as ever. Though much has been made of the new ethics, more likely what has happened is a more intense investigation of the "old ethics" to gain insight and clarity for dealing with situations and problems that had not been encountered.

THEORY AND ITS APPLICATION. One of the surprises of bioethics was how little the ethical theories of philosophy seemed to help in solving the real and complex moral problems of medicine. Philosophy was consulted by those in the medical world seeking help, because philosophy was the traditional academic home for ethics and because philosophy appeared more neutral and nonsectarian, which was an essential feature for an ethic that was becoming a public discussion. But the theories of philosophical ethics were not much help. There was more a chasm between the theory and its use in solving real moral problems than had been suspected. The relentlessness of real circumstances with all their complications seemed more than theory could handle. The early textbooks of biomedical ethics were anthologies, and samples from Mill, Kant, and Rawls constituted the usual fare. Such use of anthologies implicitly suggested either that the reader simply choose whichever she found preferable or that each theory individually was inadequate, but taken all together they might provide enough guidance for making practical moral decisions. One difficulty with the latter interpretation is that there was no overarching theory to resolve conflicts between the individual theories.

The apparent inadequacy of moral theories to deal with practical moral problems produced at least three responses. One was to conclude that moral theories were not helpful because they were too general for the particularity of the circumstances. This led to an antitheory movement (see Clarke & Simpson, 1989). Another response was to conclude that the theories in question were flawed because they were too simple and a more complex theory was needed. Gert (1988), for example, developed a general moral theory showing the integral relationship of applied ethics (biomedical ethics, in particular) to general morality and a procedure for using the theory in dealing with substantive moral problems. A middle position was to limit one's theorizing to the biomedical sphere, wherein the generalities were more immediately related to the particulars of the practice. Among the theoretical frameworks so developed the most popular were "principle based" ethics and "virtue based" ethics. The former was particularly influential and was clearly articulated by Beauchamp and Childress (1994), the latter by Pellegrino and Thomasma (1993). Casuistry also was revisited and renewed in general response to the inadequacy of theory for practical moral problems (Jonsen & Toulmin, 1988).

HOW MANY MORALITIES? While working in bioethics one quickly becomes aware of all the coexisting moral practices and codes of ethics. Not only do we have engineering ethics, business ethics, environmental ethics, dental ethics, nursing ethics, medical ethics, sports ethics, and so forth, but within each of these there are many different groups, each with its own "moral code." Of course it is no surprise to a philosopher that morality may vary from culture to culture, though what constituted a "culture" in this context was never precisely clear. In the practical world of bioethics there are hundreds of moral codes, each designed for the guidance of a particular—usually professional—group. This multiplicity of codes existing side by side in the "same" culture should trouble the cultural relativist. Just as important, this multiplicity of moral practices and codes of ethics raises the question: can a moral code simply be invented by any group or any individual? Certainly that is what has happened through the years. Some of the codes (or aspects thereof) are quite self-serving of the group itself rather than concerned with those with whom they come in professional contact.

The unavoidable awareness of the multiplicity of moralities and moral codes inevitably provokes a basic question: how many moralities are there? Do all the "different moralities" have something in common such that that commonality constitutes "general morality"? If there is just one general morality, what accounts for these various manifestations? These many and various manifestations of morality impel one to search for a system that underlies them and compel one to take the notion of moral system seriously. A traditional, necessary element of morality is impartiality, and that requires a system such that what is moral for one person is moral for anyone else in the same circumstances. Awareness of the multiplicity of "moralities" in the everyday world makes the search for system ever more urgent.

These are important philosophical questions, stimulated by applied ethics inasmuch as applied ethics takes seriously the everyday practical manifestations of morality. Applied ethics has paid more attention to morality as lived and practiced than has traditional philosophical ethics, which tended more to invent ideal moralities.

THE SCOPE OF ETHICS. Scope is a major issue, primarily provoked by applied ethics. The scope of ethics refers to the domain over which ethics has relevance or control. Animals, the environment, fields and streams, fetuses, the senile, and so on, all would fall outside our ordinary scope of morality, whose domain generally is limited to rational agents. But the breadth of bioethics has brought into its circle of concern animals, forests, fields, and streams. This is an enigma to some strands of traditional ethics that have assumed the participants in morality to be rational beings who could reason together and understand what was to their mutual benefit.

Does the physician have a duty to act always

in the best interest of the patient?

All the time? What is duty?

How is one's duty determined?

How the scope of morality is expanded to be more inclusive takes various forms. Some argue that these other entities have rights in and of themselves. Thus, one's actions toward these entities must be guided by considerations of what is for the entities' own good, fulfilling whatever internal goals or purposes that are attributed to them. On the other hand, some argue that the only way such rights can make sense is if the rights are granted by humans in a manner that is ultimately for the benefit of humans. That is, granting such rights may be a heuristic device (e.g., for the protection of aspects of nature, the protecting of which might be seen as ultimately important to humankind).

Many would limit the scope to sentient beings. In general it would be argued that though many sentient beings may not be rational and hence not capable of being held responsible for their own behavior, nevertheless, inasmuch as they are capable of suffering, rational agents have a moral obligation to avoid causing that suffering as well as to prevent it. If the goal of morality is (as many would argue) to reduce the amount of harm incurred in the world, then this extension in scope would seem entirely appropriate.

Scope could even be understood to have an aspect of temporal inclusiveness or exclusiveness. The "problem of future generations" would be an example. In this case it is not the nature of the "beings" or "entities" that is in question, but how far into the future they are owed moral consideration. This was a frequently argued issue in the 1970s and 1980s. Matters of genetic manipulation and the environment would obviously raise these future-oriented reflections. If humans would suffer as a result of actions taken now, then the moral implications of those actions need to be taken seriously. Naturally there is increased uncertainty about the consequences of actions in the distant future; causal chains are difficult enough to estimate even into the much closer future. Furthermore, the seriousness of effects on future generations (for example, of the extinction of a species of plants or animals) often cannot be convincingly argued. Thus, consequences to humans are susceptible to too many "fudge" factors, and, accordingly, other bases for moral judgment are found by those anxious to preserve animals, plants, and the environment in general. It may be that a metaphysical worldview is necessary to set the scope of ethics. That is, it seems that beliefs about the purpose of the world and about the roles and relationships of its inhabitants will inevitably be assumed in arguing for the "proper" behavior of rational agents toward the totality of the planet.

REAL CASES. One of the significant contributions of bioethics is bringing to center stage real moral problems in all their fullness. These are very different from the traditional hypothetical cases offered by philosophers. The former are rich in practical detail and seem relentless in admitting no easy solutions; the latter are usually concocted with a single point in mind to illustrate a theoretical point. The hardness of real cases may be one reason philosophy was slow to acknowledge bioethics. Real cases are often messy; they cannot be dealt with cleanly and decisively; conflicts of claims, rules, and principles abound. It was in the face of these hard cases that many began to suspect that traditional moral philosophies could not help and indeed may even be irrelevant to moral problems in the real world.

The combination of complicated real cases and theories of minimal help led to a focus on facts rather than on theory. Considerable attention had to be given to the facts and their context, because the cases were arising from a variety of complex fields of endeavor such as medicine, engineering, environment, law, and genetics. In order to see the moral issues one had to grasp the nuances, relationships, understandings, and practices within these fields. Thus, the primary work of bioethics was really in gathering and comprehending facts rather than in delving deep into moral theory. Correspondingly, most "moral" disagreements in these areas of bioethics turned out to be disagreements over the facts of the case rather than over morality or moral theory. In clinical settings, for example, once there was a consensus on the facts, there was far more agreement than disagreement on the moral lines of action.

The considerably increased focus on the facts led to two interesting philosophical moves that turned out to be closely related. One was a focused concern for determining which of the infinity of facts were of moral relevance; the other was a realization that there were conceptual clarifications necessary before the moral relevance of some facts could be established.

Though the importance of facts to moral deliberation has never been doubted, perhaps the necessity of establishing criteria for the moral relevance of the facts was not clearly realized until facts became a central focus in bioethics' work with real, concrete cases. The importance of such criteria goes beyond simply trying to sort through the multitude of facts being presented around each case. Such criteria become necessary in making sense of that critical and pivotal phrase "in the same morally relevant circumstances." Without it one situation cannot be compared with another; it is crucial in order to make moral decisions consistent from one time and place to the next. Morality is a system and as such requires uniformity and consistency throughout. If the action of one person is moral (or immoral) in a certain situation, then that action is moral (or immoral) for everyone to do "in the same morally relevant circumstances." Thus, a lot turns on precisely what factors in a situation are morally relevant. One philosopher who has worked explicitly on this matter is Gert (1988), and he continues to do so (Clouser & Gert. 1994; Gert et al., 1996).

The other philosophical move initiated by applied ethics' immersion in facts was the need for conceptual analysis. Of course, conceptual analysis is as old as philosophy, but bioethics was necessarily more focused on conceptual analysis than on ethics. Most of its work was on "preparing" the facts of the case for moral judgment. The ethics was relatively uncomplicated once the facts were properly understood. Is withdrawing life supports the same as killing? Is withholding life supports the same as withdrawing? Is a particular behavior of the physician paternalistic? If it is, must it be morally justified? Does the physician have a duty to act always in the best interest of the patient? All the time? What is duty? How is one's duty determined? Is it a breach of patient confidentiality when a physician gives a patient record to a secretary to type or to a student to study? What is competence to consent and how is it determined? What is the definition of death? When does life begin? What is the moral status of frozen embryos and how is ownership determined? These are simply a sampling of the kinds of conceptual issues that occupy applied ethics (in these instances, biomedical ethics). Notice that traditional moral theories would have little to say about them, yet these are the kinds of issues that bioethics must work through in order to deal with the moral issues at stake.

Contributions of Philosophy to Biomedical Ethics

Philosophy has contributed significantly to biomedical ethics. For all the failure of philosophical theories of ethics to connect with the moral dilemmas of the medical world, the forced dialogue between the theories and the dilemmas has been crucial in helping to systematize, to focus, and to pose the fruitful, organizing questions. Until the late 1960s medical ethics was hardly even an individuated discipline. It was a mixture of religion, tradition, exhortation, legal precedents, miscellaneous rules, epithets, and slogans. It is arguable that philosophy provided the push toward systematization, consistency, and clarity by asking probing and organizing questions, by directing informed attention to assumptions, implications, and foundations, and by locating and analyzing pivotal concepts. Though many disciplines have participated in the recent revival of biomedical ethics, philosophy has provided the framework within which the discussion takes place and within which the contributions of the other disciplines play their part.

[See also Abortion; Animal Rights and Welfare; Applied Ethics; Business Ethics; Communitarianism; Distant Peoples and Future Generations; Engineering Ethics; Environmental Ethics; Euthanasia; Genetics and Reproductive Technologies; Impartiality; Justice; Kant, Immanuel; Mill, John Stuart; Paternalism; Rawls, John; Virtue Ethics.]

BIBLIOGRAPHY

Beauchamp, T. L., and J. F. Childress. *Principles of Biomedical Ethics,* 4th ed. New York, 1994. Earlier editions were more characteristically examples of principlism.
Brody, B. A. *Life and Death Decision Making.* New York. 1988.
Callahan, D. "Bioethics," in *Encyclopedia of Bioethics,* edited by W. Reich. Vol. 1, 2d ed. (New York, 1995).
Clarke, S. G., and E. Simpson. *Anti-Theory in Ethics and Moral Conservatism.* Albany, NY, 1989.
Clouser, K. D. "Allowing or Causing: Another Look," *Annals of Internal Medicine,* Vol. 87 (1977), 622–24.
———. "Bioethics," in *Encyclopedia of Bioethics,* edited by W. Reich, Vol. 1 (New York, 1978).
———. "Ethical Theory and Applied Ethics: Reflections on Connections," in B. Hoffmaster, B. Freedman, and G. Fraser, eds., *Clinical Ethics: Theory and Practice* (Clifton, NJ, 1989).
———, and B. Gert. "Morality vs. Principlism," in R. Gillon, ed., *Principles of Health Care Ethics* (Chichester, England, 1994).
———, and L. Kopelman, eds. "Philosophical Critique of Bioethics," *Journal of Medicine and Philosophy,* Vol. 15 (1990).
Engelhardt, H. T., Jr. *The Foundations of Bioethics.* New York, 1986.
Gert, B. *Morality: A New Justification of the Moral Rules.* New York, 1988.
——— et al. *Morality and the New Genetics.* Boston, 1996.
Jonsen, A. R. "Theological Ethics, Moral Philosophy, and Public Moral Discourse," *Kennedy Institute of Ethics Journal,* Vol. 4 (1994), 1–11.
———, and S. Toulmin. *The Abuse of Casuistry: A History of Moral Reasoning.* Berkeley, 1988.
Mason, C. S., ed. "Theories and Methods in Bioethics: Principlism and Its Critics," *Kennedy Institute of Ethics Journal,* Vol. 5 (1995).

Pellegrino, E. D., and D. C. Thomasma. *The Virtues in Medical Practice.* New York, 1993.
Potter, V. R. *Bioethics: Bridge to the Future.* Englewood Cliffs, NJ, 1971.
Rachels, J. "Active and Passive Euthanasia," *New England Journal of Medicine,* Vol. 292 (1975), 78–80.
Rawls, J. *A Theory of Justice.* Cambridge, MA, 1971.
Reich, W. T., ed. *Encyclopedia of Bioethics.* 5 vols. 2d ed. New York, 1995.
"The Word 'Bioethics': The Struggle over Its Earliest Meanings," *Kennedy Institute of Ethics Journal,* Vol. 5 (1995), 19–34.
Veatch, R. M. *A Theory of Medical Ethics.* New York, 1981.

— K. DANNER CLOUSER

BUSINESS ETHICS

The study of ethics and economics and the analysis of ethical decision making in business are traditions as old as philosophy itself, and the development of reasonable standards for business behavior is part of every culture. Yet the process of integrating and applying ethical standards to management decision making appears to be

Technically defined, business ethics is the study of codes, rules, or principles that govern business conduct; it seeks to understand business practices, institutions, and actions in light of what is right and good.

difficult, because economic goals and exigencies often seem to override other considerations. But ethical issues are part of economics, management, accounting, finance, marketing, and other business disciplines, just as management, marketing, accounting, and so forth are part of business. Not to take into account normative considerations in economic affairs is itself a normative decision that ignores some elementary facts: (1) economic decisions are choices in which the decision makers could have done otherwise; (2) every such decision or action affects people, and an alternative action or inaction would affect them differently; and (3) every economic decision or set of decisions is embedded in a belief system that presupposes some basic values or their abrogation.

Although ethical issues in business are age-old problems, it is an academic discipline that has developed in the latter half of this century, primarily in North America. The discipline of business ethics traces its roots to earlier developments in other areas of applied ethics and to the interest in what was labeled "social issues in management" that developed in the 1950s. During that decade some business schools began to offer courses in "business and society," "corporate social responsibility," or "socio-legal studies" in which emphasis is on the relationship between corporations and society or government. This focus shifted, however, when in 1961, as part of his doctoral work at Harvard, Raymond C. Baumhart did a landmark study of the attitudes of business people toward ethics in their business decision making. The work expanded the study of business ethics to include individual managerial as well as corporate decision making and extended its purview to all normative aspects of business, including issues in management, marketing, finance, accounting, operations, employment, research, technology, multicultural relationships, corporate governance, the environment, and community and government relationships. Although the study of business ethics began in the United States and Canada, the discipline has spread to Europe, Russia, Australia, New Zealand, and Japan and has begun to be taken seriously in other countries as well.

Technically defined, business ethics is the study of codes, rules, or principles that govern business conduct; it seeks to understand business practices, institutions, and actions in light of what is right and good. Business ethics is also descriptive: it engages in behavioral and sociological studies of what in fact managers and companies do. Business ethics analyzes the moral development of managers and how they behave, it studies how corporate culture affects managerial behavior, and it describes the interactions between corporations and government, the environment, and the community. These studies are important descriptions of the causal interrelationships between individuals, corporations, and society and of how those relationships affect individual and corporate choices and actions (Goodpaster, 1992).

Most important, business ethics is normative: it evaluates business and business practices in light of standards elucidating what is right and good, and it offers recommendations and solutions to ethical dilemmas. From this point of view business ethics is defined as a set of normative rules of conduct, a code, a standard, or a set of principles that govern what one ought to do in the practical context of business when the well-being, rights, or integrity of oneself, of other people, of a corporation, or even a nation is at stake.

The subject for business ethics extends beyond individual decision making to include questions about corporate moral responsibility and issues arising from

American financier Ivan Boesky was convicted of illegal insider trading in 1983. (Corbis/Bettmann)

the interrelationships between corporations and society (Goodpaster, 1992). On the individual level questions of managerial character, rights and responsibilities of employees, affirmative action, comparable worth, conflict of interest, and whistleblowing are some of the focal points for analysis and evaluation. Yet most of these issues entail relationships between the individual and the corporation or business.

On the corporate level one central topic is whether and how a corporation or a corporate culture is a moral agent and thus morally responsible. While one must be careful not to anthropomorphize institutions such as corporations, at some level we do hold corporations as well as individuals morally liable. How this is possible is still much in debate, but the literature on collective moral agency is helpful in framing a kind of secondary moral agency for corporations that is unique to collectives (May, 1987; Werhane, 1985). Issues confronting corporations include product safety, marketing and advertising practices, downsizing, mergers, plant relocation, product safety, consumer and company liability, insider trading, pollution, and corporate governance. These issues concern and affect individuals, other corporations, and society. Business ethics also examined social, economic, and political systems that define property arrangements and frame the legal and regulatory environment for commerce.

Milton Friedman (1962) has contended that the primary responsibility of business is its fiduciary responsibility to its shareholders or owners. However, a number of philosophers and management theorists now argue that any good business decision, and thus any ethical decision in business, must weigh the positive and negative consequences to each affected stakeholder, and these consequences are not merely material but involve issues of rights and fairness as well (Evan & Freeman, 1992). So, for example, a decision to downsize a company affects employees, customers, suppliers, shareholders, and the community in which the company is based, and it affects the rights of employees and shareholders as well as their economic interests.

Finally, despite its roots in North America, business ethics is multicultural, and there is a new and growing area of international business ethics in which the emphasis is on multicultural decision making in the context of business. Issues such as exporting unacceptable products, dumping hazardous waste, discriminatory pay of expatriates and nationals, use of indigenous national resources, manufacturing in developing countries, regulatory inconsistencies, demands for sensitive payments to foreign officials, and international trade barriers further complicate decision making. But there is no separate field of "international ethics" that we apply to multinational business. Rather, like business ethics, international business ethics engages in an exploration of the normative dimensions of (cross-cultural) economic activities. These normative dimensions are embedded in these business processes and integral to them.

[See also Applied Ethics.]

BIBLIOGRAPHY

Beauchamp, T., and N. Bowie, eds. *Ethical Theory and Business*, 4th ed. Englewood Cliffs, NJ, 1992.
Boatright, J. R. *Ethics and the Conduct of Business.* Englewood Cliffs, NJ, 1993.
Bowie, N., and R. Duska. *Business Ethics.* Englewood Cliffs, NJ, 1990.
Bowie, N., and R. E. Freeman, eds. *Ethics and Agency Theory.* New York, 1992.
De George, R. *Business Ethics,* 2d ed. New York, 1991.
Donaldson, T. *Corporations and Morality.* Englewood Cliffs, NJ, 1983.
Donaldson, T., *The Ethics of International Business.* New York, 1989.
Donaldson, T., and P. H. Werhane, eds. *Ethical Issues in Business,* 4th ed. Englewood Cliffs, NJ, 1992.
Evan, W., and R. E. Freeman. "A Stakeholder Theory of the Modern Corporation: Kantian Capitalism," in T. Beauchamp and N.

Bowie, eds., *Ethical Theory and Business,* 4th ed. (Englewood Cliffs, NJ, 1992).
Friedman, M. *Capitalism and Freedom.* Chicago, 1962.
Goodpaster, K. "Business Ethics," in *Encyclopedia of Ethics* (New York, 1992).
Hoffman, M., and J. Moore, eds. *Business Ethics,* 3d. ed. New York, 1994.
May, L. *The Morality of Groups.* Notre Dame, IN, 1987.
Sen, A. *On Ethics and Economics.* Oxford, 1987.
Solomon, R. C. *Ethics and Excellence.* Oxford, 1992.
Velasquez, M. *Business Ethics,* 3d ed. Englewood Cliffs, NJ, 1992.
Walton, C. *The Moral Manager.* New York, 1988.
Werhane, P. *Persons, Rights, and Corporations.* Englewood Cliffs, NJ, 1985.
———. *Adam Smith and His Legacy for Modern Capitalism.* New York, 1991.

– PATRICIA WERHANE

BUTLER, JOSEPH

Joseph Butler (1692–1752), moral philosopher and natural theologian, was born at Wantage, Berkshire, to a Presbyterian family. His father, a retired draper, could afford to send Butler to the dissenting academy kept by Mr. Samuel Jones, first at Gloucester and later at Tewkesbury. For reasons now unknown, Butler, when a young man, left Presbyterianism for the Church of England. He entered Oriel College, Oxford, as a commoner. After taking his degree he was ordained a priest in the established church in 1718. Throughout his life Butler held a series of church offices. In 1738 he was made bishop of Bristol, and in 1751 he became bishop of Durham. He also served as clerk of the closet, first to Queen Caroline, and later to George II. When one considers Butler's writings, with their judicious but nonetheless optimistic analysis of human nature, it is well to remember that he was a man of affairs, with ample opportunity to become acquainted with the ways of the world. Butler died at Bath, where he had gone for his health. He was buried in Bristol Cathedral.

MORAL PHILOSOPHY. Since Butler writes as a Christian and a priest, his philosophical interests, moral philosophy, and natural theology are inseparable from his vocation. His moral philosophy must be gleaned from all his writings, the most systematic statement being found in the "Three Sermons on Human Nature."

Butler's writings are a part of the seventeenth- and eighteenth-century effort to find a foundation for morals in something other than appeals to the divine will. Because he believes that nature and revelation are complementary, Butler is willing to eschew appeals to revelation, and search in nature for the basis of morality. But where in nature are the foundations of morality to be discovered? Butler sees two possible ways of proceeding. The first is to inquire into the abstract relations of things; the second is to argue from a matter of fact

Because Butler wrote as a Christian and a priest, his philosophical interests and moral philosophy are inseparable from his vocation. (Corbis/Bettmann)

(the nature of man) to conclusions about the course of life which is fitting for the nature of man. The method of exploring the abstract relations of things had already been used by Butler's older contemporary, Samuel Clarke; and while Butler is not unsympathetic to Clarke's efforts, he finds the method of analyzing the nature of man more appropriate to the limitations of a sermon.

In the task of accounting for morals by appeals to the nature of man, Butler had a set of vigorous and impressive predecessors. On the one hand, he had Thomas Hobbes and his contemporary, Bernard Mandeville, the partisans of self-love; and on the other hand, Shaftesbury, the partisan of an instinct for benevolence. Butler, however, regards his predecessors as having offered only partial analyses of human nature. His method is to show that both self-love and benevolence are part of a larger whole.

Butler claims to have made his observations from the bulk of mankind; and he urges his readers not to be misled about human nature, either by judging only

from their own natures or by giving too much weight to exceptions from the general run of men. Butler finds that men are neither exceptionally self-regarding to the exclusion of benevolence nor exceptionally benevolent to the exclusion of self-interest. What is more, he finds that these affections are not necessarily incompatible and may even reinforce one another. The satisfaction of performing a benevolent action will certainly encourage acts of benevolence in someone who desires the advantages of society.

Butler also argues that self-love and benevolence are but two affections among many; that neither has any priority over the rest; and that neither is such that all other affections can be reduced to it. He points out that self-love is a complex affection, in that its object is not simply the self, but rather the gain of all things pleasing to the self. Butler also claims that there are no affections directly contradictory to self-love and benevolence, namely self-hatred and ill will toward others. Rather, he finds that when self-love or benevolence is opposed, it is by passions for particular things; and it is in the pursuit of these objects that we may harm ourselves or injure others. It must be remembered, here, that Butler means to describe the generality of mankind, and not exceptions.

Thus far, Butler's moral philosophy is a synthesis, with corrections, of the doctrines of his immediate predecessors in the analysis of human nature. But man is something more than a bundle of affections. Butler finds that his predecessors have overlooked the fact that man possesses a faculty superior to affections, which judges both them and the actions which flow from them. This faculty is reflection, or conscience. In his strongest characterization of this "superior principle," he speaks of it as pronouncing "determinately some actions to be in themselves just, right, good; others to be in themselves evil, wrong, unjust." Conscience "without being consulted, without being advised with, magisterially exerts itself, and approves or condemns him the doer of them accordingly . . ." ("Second Sermon Upon Human Nature"). It is conscience (the capacity to reflect on his affections) which distinguishes man from the beasts, by rescuing him from subjection to whatever passion is uppermost at the moment. It is conscience which makes man a moral agent, by enabling him to be a law unto himself—a law which he is obliged to obey, because it is the law of his nature.

Butler might have been clearer about the way conscience works. To characterize it as operating "without being consulted, without being advised with" makes conscience too much of a mechanism in a too mechanical theory of human nature. Here, Butler appears to be caught in the unexamined assumptions of a faulty psychology borrowed from his contemporaries. Nor is Butler as clear as one might wish about the standards in accordance with which conscience makes its judgments. Conscience approves of whatever contributes to the good of the whole man and condemns whatever disproportionately favors some part of the whole. But how does conscience learn to assess these matters? It would seem that this question did not weigh too heavily on Butler, perhaps because of his theology. No questions about how conscience does its job need be asked, since it has been designed by God for its appointed end. As he says, conscience, "if not forcibly stopped, naturally and always of course goes on to anticipate a higher and more effectual sentence, which shall hereafter second and affirm its own" ("Second Sermon Upon Human Nature"). Of course, Butler believes man to be naturally fitted for life in society, and of course, he approves of the social virtues; but in his philosophy society and the social virtues are never reckoned to be inherently valuable.

Something has already been said about Butler's immediate predecessors, but an additional word must be said about the classical springs of his moral philosophy. Oxford tutors think of Butler's sermons as a painless way of conveying Aristotle's *Ethics* to Greekless undergraduates. Canon J. N. D. Kelly, who became the principal of St. Edmund Hall in 1951, has spoken of Butler as "Aristotle, clad in a diaphanous mantle of Christianity." For the distinctive feature of his moral philosophy, the doctrine of conscience, Butler himself cites Arrian's *Discourses of Epictetus*, Book I, Chapter 1, as the source.

NATURAL THEOLOGY. Butler's natural theology is contained in *The Analogy of Religion, Natural and Revealed, to the Constitution and Course of Nature* (London, 1736). The title might lead one to believe that Butler is going to compare religious doctrines with what may be learned by studying nature. But this expectation is not quite right, for Butler does not regard nature as a religiously neutral system. Rather, nature is a product of providential design; by studying nature, one will find confirmation there for the revealed doctrines of Christianity. Appealing to our experience of the conduct of nature with respect to intelligent creatures, Butler states the terms of his analogy in two presumably synonymous ways. He will compare "the known constitution and course of things" with "what is said to be the moral system of nature"; or again, he will compare "the acknowledged dispensations of Providence," that is, "the (natural) government which we find ourselves under," with "what religion teaches us to believe and expect." Through such comparisons we may see whether the terms of these analogies are not "analogous and of a piece."

On an abbreviated scale, the following may be taken as an example of Butler's style of argument. If we begin by assuming that the existence of nature implies an operating agent, then the good and bad consequences of our actions occur by his appointment. Any foresight we have of the consequences of our actions is a warning given by him on how we are to act. The satisfaction we feel at certain consequences, and the pain we suffer at others, are ordained by God and are signs that we are already under his government. Thus, a consideration of nature alone shows that we must acknowledge the place of God in our lives. Hence, if Christian doctrines really are revealed truths (and Butler considers this difficulty with great care), our discoveries in nature have already prepared us to accept the main claims of revelation about God as a creator and judge. Butler does not suppose that his sort of study can do much more than establish the plausibility of the main lines of revelation. We must treat the details with patience and respect, as not being absolutely ruled out by a study of nature.

Butler's writings are a part of the seventeenth- and eighteenth-century effort to find a foundation for morals in something other than appeals to the divine will.

From the assumption that nature implies an operating agent, it seems clear that Butler did not intend his arguments to appeal to the religious skeptic. At best, he may have hoped to convince deists, who already acknowledged the existence of a god, that their convictions might reasonably lead them to accept Christianity. At the very least, he must have expected to make deists acknowledge Christianity's right to be treated as a subject worthy of serious discussion. Followers of Shaftesbury are then his special target.

In the *Analogy*, Butler treated probability (in the Introduction), habit (in Part I, Chapter 5), and body, mind, and death (in Part I, Chapter 1, "Of a Future Life"). He makes a clear distinction between demonstrative reasoning and probable reasoning by pointing out that probability admits of degrees, while demonstration does not. A slight presumption in favor of a thing does not make it probably true. Yet, Butler argues, the slightest possible presumption is, nonetheless, of the nature of probability, for ". . . such low presumption, often repeated, will amount even to moral certainty. Thus a man's having observed the ebb and flow of the tide today, affords some sort of presumption, though the lowest imaginable, that it may happen again tomorrow: but the observation of this even for so many days, and months and ages together, as it has been observed by mankind, gives us a full assurance that it will." While an infinite intelligence must see everything as certainly true or certainly false, for us, with our limited capacities, "probability is the very guide of life."

Habit is examined in Butler's consideration of the acquisition and practice of moral virtues. In the course of the discussion, he includes certain remarks about knowledge and habit which are of the greatest interest. He claims, first, that neither the perception of ideas nor knowledge of any sort is a habit. However, contrary to this, he goes on to observe "that perceptions come into our minds readily and of course, by means of their having been there before"; and this reappearance of perceptions "seems a thing of the same sort as readiness in any particular kind of action, proceeding from being accustomed to it." He then cites, as one of our habits of perception, ". . . our constant and even involuntary readiness in correcting the impressions of our sight concerning magnitude and distances, so as to substitute judgment in the room of sensation imperceptibly to ourselves." And he adds immediately ". . . it seems as if all other associations of ideas not naturally connected might be called *passive habits*." (A natural connection of ideas would be, for example, flame and fire.)

In his discussion of a future life; Butler argues for the probability that the mind may be separable from the body. Hence, death may have no effect on the mind. The programs of Butler and Descartes coincide here, but the statement of Butler's case gains greatly through the force and conciseness of his style.

PERSONAL IDENTITY. The *Analogy* is followed by two short dissertations, Dissertation II, "Of the Nature of Virtue," should be read with the sermons as a supplement to his moral philosophy as stated in them. Dissertation I, "Of Personal Identity," is in part a criticism of Locke. Butler endeavors to clarify the role of consciousness in personal identity. He argues against those whose reason for rejecting consciousness as a source of personal identity is that no two acts of consciousness are identical. Such an argument, Butler says, overlooks what we are really interested in: not an identity of acts of consciousness, but an identity of the object of which we are conscious—ourselves. Of this identity we can be as certain as we are of the identity of any other thing. Anyone who asks for a greater certainty of personal identity than this wishes for something which the subject will not admit.

BIBLIOGRAPHY

Works by Butler

Butler's *Fifteen Sermons,* including the "Three Sermons Upon Human Nature," were first published in London in 1726. *The Works of Joseph Butler,* The Rt. Hon. W. E. Gladstone, ed., 2 vols. (Oxford, 1897) contains the above, along with the *Analogy,* "Six Sermons Preached Upon Public Occasions" and Butler's "Charge to the Clergy of the Diocese of Durham," a moving commentary on the tasks of the clergyman in eighteenth-century England.

Works on Butler

For critical discussions, see A. E. Duncan-Jones, *Butler's Moral Philosophy* (Harmondsworth, Middlesex, 1952); E. C. Mossner, *Bishop Butler and the Age of Reason* (New York, 1936); "Butler," in C. D. Broad, *Five Types of Ethical Theory* (London, 1930), Ch. 3; Leonard G. Miller, "Joseph Butler," in *Encyclopedia of Morals,* V. Ferm, ed. (New York, 1956).

— ELMER SPRAGUE

C

....

CARNAP, RUDOLF

Rudolf Carnap (1891–1970), remained philosophically active throughout his life. Most of his research in his final decade continued to focus on probability, but two other volumes devoted substantially to other issues also came out. The first of these, *The Philosophy of Rudolf Carnap,* appeared in early 1964, though dated 1963. This 1,100-page volume was the result of ten years of work and contains a substantial autobiography, a detailed bibliography (through 1961), as well as twenty-six critical essays (with Carnap's replies) on all aspects of his work. A second nonprobability volume, *Philosophical Foundations of Physics: An Introduction to the Philosophy of Science,* appeared in 1966 (and in very slightly revised form under its less formidable subtitle in 1974). This is essentially a transcript of one of Carnap's seminars edited into very readable form by Martin Gardner.

Carnap concluded that it would be

significantly more convenient to treat probabilities

as applying to propositions rather than,

as he had in earlier work, to sentences.

Carnap's final body of work on probability comprises a very substantial revision (or more accurately the beginnings of such a revision) of the research done twenty years earlier, which had culminated in *Logical Foundations of Probability.* Carnap had agreed in the preface to the second edition of this book that primitive predicates having logical structure were admissible, even though the apparatus therein was unable to cope with them. In various places he had also agreed that, not only was the function c^* too narrow, but so was the whole continuum of inductive methods as well as the first attempts to broaden that continuum. Meanwhile, Carnap concluded that it would be significantly more convenient to treat probabilities as applying to propositions rather than, as he had in earlier work, to sentences. The (revisable) foundation of these changes was to be "A Basic System of Inductive Logic," which Carnap had all but finished at the time of his death on September 14, 1970.

This long (284 pages) article was a progress report in both senses: first, as an announcement of substantial advances on the problems noted and, second, as an interim statement on the way to something better. Perhaps he would have been pleased to have all of his works so viewed: as substantial advances in clarity, power, and generosity to opposing views and as interim statements on the way to something better.

Carnap's Reputation: Decline and Resurgence

Carnap and the other logical empiricists never dominated philosophy to the extent that some have recalled. But beginning perhaps about 1960 their collective reputations began to decline to the point that, twenty years later, discussion of their views was regularly consigned to crude caricatures in the opening paragraphs of works in the philosophy of science. No doubt there are many causes of this decline: continued attacks by Popper, Quine, and Kuhn, Carnap's technical and often inaccessible writing style, his refusal to engage in polemics with his critics, and even the inevitable swings of fashion. In the late 1970s, however, there arose a group of historically minded philosophers who, armed with massive and newly available archival evidence, began reassessing the work of Carnap and other logical empiricists. This work was further spurred by numerous conferences, journal issues, and other activities surrounding the centennial, on May 18, 1991, of Carnap's birth.

Among the emphases of this reappraisal has been a fuller recognition of the important role that Kantianism plays in Carnap's intellectual context, in his own early work, and particularly in such work as the *Aufbau,* which is now seen as focused not on ontology but on the semantics of intersubjective meaning. *The Logical Syntax of Language,* too, has been reappraised and its sophisticated conventionalism and pragmatism more fully understood. Of particular note is the discovery that the program of syntax was broad enough to include a Tarski-type truth theory and that indeed Carnap had himself developed even within that book what we would now call a semantic theory astonishingly close to Tarski's result (*see* Tarski). Similar reexaminations of Carnap's views on observation, analyticity, realism, and probability have shown that many of the standard criticisms were predicated on misunderstandings of these views. Certainly, as the historical reassessment of Carnap and other logical empiricists proceeds, a richer picture of their work emerges, as does a fuller understanding of the extent to which ongoing work both arises out of theirs and can continue to benefit from studying it.

[See also Analyticity; Kuhn, Thomas; Philosophy of Science; Probability; Quine, Willard Van Orman; Realism.]

BIBLIOGRAPHY

Works by Carnap

Philosophical Foundations of Physics: An Introduction to the Philosophy of Science, edited by M. Gardner. New York, 1966.
"A Basic System of Inductive Logic," Part 1, in R. Carnap and R. C. Jeffrey, eds., *Studies in Inductive Logic and Probability*, Vol. 1 (Berkeley, 1971).
"A Basic System of Inductive Logic," Part 2, in R. C. Jeffrey, ed., *Studies in Inductive Logic and Probability*, Vol. 2 (Berkeley, 1980).
"On Protocol Sentences," *Noûs*, Vol. 21 (1987), 457–70.
With W. V. O. Quine, *Dear Carnap, Dear Van: The Quine–Carnap Correspondence and Related Work*, edited by R. Creath. Los Angeles, 1990.

Works on Carnap

Coffa, J. A. *The Semantic Tradition from Kant to Carnap: To the Vienna Station.* Cambridge, 1991. The pioneering study in the area.
Creath, R. "The Unimportance of Semantics," in A. Fine, M. Forbes, and L. Wessels, eds., *PSA 1990*, Vol. 2 (East Lansing, MI, 1990). All these papers by Creath are on analyticity, especially in connection with Quine.
"Every Dogma Has Its Day," *Erkenntnis*, Vol. 35 (1991), 347–89. See this issue for other valuable essays.
———. "Functionalist Theories of Meaning and the Defense of Analyticity," in W. Salmon and G. Wolters, eds., *Logic, Language, and the Structure of Scientific Theories* (Pittsburgh, 1994).
Friedman, M. "Carnap and A Priori Truth," in D. Bell and W. Vossenkuhl, eds., *Science and Subjectivity: The Vienna Circle and Twentieth-Century Philosophy* (Berlin, 1992). This and Goldfarb and Ricketts's paper (see below) are important papers on the a priori and on mathematics.
———. "Epistemology in the *Aufbau*," *Synthese*, Vol. 93 (1992), 15–57. This and Richardson's essay (see below) are valuable essays on Carnap's early Kantianism; other valuable essays appear in this issue.
"Geometry, Convention, and the Relativized A Priori: Reichenbach, Schlick, and Carnap," in W. Salmon and G. Wolters, eds., *Logic, Language, and the Structure of Scientific Theories* (Pittsburgh, 1994).
Goldfarb, W., and T. Ricketts. "Carnap and the Philosophy of Mathematics," in D. Bell and W. Vossenkuhl, eds., *Science and Subjectivity: The Vienna Circle and Twentieth-Century Philosophy* (Berlin, 1992).
Richardson, A. W. "Logical Idealism and Carnap's Construction of the World," *Synthese*, Vol. 93 (1992), 59–92.

– RICHARD CREATH

CAUSAL OR CONDITIONAL OR EXPLANATORY-RELATION ACCOUNTS

Edmund Gettier attacked the traditional analysis of knowledge by showing that inferring a true belief from a false but justified belief produces a justified true belief that does not qualify as knowledge. Subsequent analyses of knowledge were motivated in large part by the wish to avoid examples of the type Gettier used. One way to do so is to insist that a belief must be connected in some proper way to the fact that makes it true in order for it to count as knowledge. In Gettier's examples beliefs are only accidentally true since there are no proper connections between them and the facts that make them true. Analyses that require such connections may either retain or drop the justification condition from the traditional analysis. Without it they are thoroughly externalist analyses since they require only that a belief be externally connected with the fact that makes it true, not that the subject be able to specify this connection.

In Gettier's examples, beliefs are only accidentally true since there are no proper connections between them and the facts that make them true.

One intuitive way to specify the proper connection is to say that it is causal: the fact that makes a belief true must help cause the belief in the subject if the subject is to have knowledge. When this causal relation holds, the truth of the belief is nonaccidental. The causal analysis of knowledge therefore excludes standard Gettier-type cases, but it seems on reflection to be both too weak and too strong: too strong in that knowledge of universal propositions, mathematical truths, and logical connections seems to be ruled out if these cannot enter into causal relations, too weak in allowing knowledge when a subject cannot distinguish a fact that causes her belief from relevant alternatives. Suppose, for example, that a subject S cannot tell red expanses from green ones but believes that there is a red expanse before her whenever either a red or a green expanse is there. Then, on an occasion in which a red expanse is before S the usual sort of perceptual causal connection will hold, but knowledge that the expanse is red will be lacking.

A different way to specify the necessary connection that handles the sort of case just cited is provided by the conditional account. According to this account, S knows that p only if S would not believe that p if p were not true. In close possible worlds in which p is not true, it must be the case that S does not believe it. This rules out the case of the red and green expanses since, in a close world in which the expanse is not red but green, S continues to believe it is red. A further condition required by this account is that in close worlds in which *p* continues to be true but other things change, *S* continues to believe that *p*.

The conditional account handles both Gettier's cases and those that require the distinction of relevant alternatives. But once again there are examples that seem to show it both too weak and too strong. That the first condition is too strong can be shown by a variation on the color expanse example. Suppose that *S* cannot tell red from green but is very good at detecting blue. Then, on the basis of seeing a blue expanse *S* can come to know that there is not a green expanse before her. But if this proposition were false (if there were a green expanse before her), she would still believe it true (she would think she was seeing red). That the second condition is too strong seems clear from the case of a very old person whose mental capacities are still intact but soon will fail him. That there are close worlds in which he does not continue to believe as he does now by exercising those capacities does not mean that he cannot know various facts now through their exercise.

That these conditions are too weak can perhaps be shown by cases in which someone intentionally induces a Gettier-type belief in *S*. In this case, if the belief were not true, it would not have been induced in *S,* and yet *S* does not know. Such a case might or might not be ruled out by the second condition, depending on how it is specified and on how the second condition is interpreted. But there are other cases that seem more certainly to indicate that the conditions are too weak. If *S* steadfastly believes every mathematical proposition that she entertains, then the conditions will be met, but she will not know all the true mathematical propositions that she entertains.

An analysis of knowledge should not only accommodate various intuitions regarding examples; it should also be useful to the normative epistemologist in reconstructing the structure of knowledge and addressing skeptical challenges. The conditional account, as interpreted by its main proponent, Robert Nozick, has interesting implications regarding skepticism. According to it, I can know various ordinary perceptual truths, such as that I am seated before a fire, even though I cannot know that there is no Cartesian demon always deceiving me. This is because in the closest possible worlds in which I am not before the fire, I do not believe that I am (I am somewhere else with different perceptual evidence). But in the closest world in which there is a Cartesian demon, I do not believe there is one (since all my perceptual evidence remains the same). These implications are welcome to Nozick but are troubling to other philosophers. My knowledge of being before the fire depends on the demon world not being among the closest in which I am not before the fire. But, ac-

cording to the conditional account, I cannot know that this last clause is true. Hence, I cannot show that my knowledge that I sit before the fire is actual, as opposed to merely being possible, and it seems that I ultimately lack grounds for being convinced that this is so. Furthermore, implications regarding more specific claims to knowledge and skeptical possibilities are counterintuitive as well. For example, according to this account I cannot know that my son is not a robot brilliantly constructed by aliens, although I can know that I do not have a brilliantly constructed robot son.

A third way of specifying the required connection that makes beliefs true is to describe it as explanatory. If *S* knows that *p*, then the fact that *p* must help to explain *S*'s belief. To see whether this account handles the sorts of cases cited, we would need to define the notion of explanation being used here. One way to do so is in terms of a certain notion of probability: roughly, *p* explains *q* if the probability of *q* given *p* is higher than the probability of *q* in the relevant reference class (reflecting relevant alternatives); put another way, if the ratio of (close) possible worlds in which *q* is true is higher in the worlds in which *p* obtains than in the relevant contrasting set of worlds. Given this interpretation, the analysis handles the perceptual discrimination case. In it *S* does not know there is a red expanse before him because its being red does not raise the probability of his belief that it is relative to those possible worlds in which this belief is based on its being green. The analysis also allows knowledge in the variation that defeats the conditional account. In it *S* knows that there is not a green expanse before her since the fact that the expanse is not green (i.e., it is blue) explains her belief that it is not green. Since the account must allow explanatory chains, it can be interpreted so as to include knowledge of mathematical propositions, which do not enter into causal relations. In the usual case in which *S* has mathematical knowledge that *p* her belief must be explanatorily linked to *p* via some proof. The truth of *p* makes a proof possible, and the ratio of close worlds in which *S* believes *p* must be higher in worlds in which there is a proof than in the overall set of worlds.

The explanatory account needs to be filled out further if it is to accommodate cases involving intentionally produced beliefs resembling Gettier's examples since in such cases the fact that *p* helps to explain why the belief that *p* is induced in *S*. As an externalist account, it would also need to provide defense for the claim that *S* can know that *p* even when, from his point of view, he has no good reasons for believing *p*. The analysis does suggest an approach to answering the skeptic different from that suggested by the conditional account. A proponent of this analysis would answer the skeptic by showing that nonskeptical theses provide better explanations of our ordinary beliefs than do skeptical theses.

[See also Epistemology.]

BIBLIOGRAPHY

Dretske, F. "Conclusive Reason," *Australasian Journal of Philosophy,* Vol. 49 (1971), 1–22.

Gettier, E. "Is Justified True Belief Knowledge?" *Analysis,* Vol. 23 (1963), 121–23.

Goldman, A. H. *Empirical Knowledge.* Berkeley, 1988.

Goldman, A. I. "A Causal Theory of Knowing," *Journal of Philosophy,* Vol. 64 (1967), 357–72.

———. "Discrimination and Perceptual Knowledge," *Journal of Philosophy,* Vol. 73 (1976), 771–91.

Luper-Foy, S., ed. *The Possibility of Knowledge: Nozick and His Critics.* Totowa, NJ, 1987.

Nozick, R. *Philosophical Explanations.* Cambridge, MA, 1981.

— ALAN H. GOLDMAN

CAUSATION

Among the questions that any adequate account of the nature of causation must answer, the following are especially crucial. First, how are causal states of affairs—including both causal laws and causal relations between events—related to noncausal states of affairs? Second, which are more basic—causal laws or causal relations? Third, how should the direction of causation be defined?

Since David Hume's time, reductionist answers have held sway, and philosophers have generally maintained that all causal relations between events are logically supervenient upon causal laws and noncausal states of affairs, that causal laws are supervenient upon non-causal facts, and that the direction of causation is definable in noncausal terms. Since the 1970s, however, these antireductionists have challenged all of these reductionist claims.

Reductionism

Reductionist approaches are of three main types: first, accounts that analyze causation in terms of conditions that in the circumstances are nomologically necessary, sufficient, or both; second, accounts in which subjunctive conditionals play the crucial role; and third, accounts based upon probabilistic relations.

CAUSES AND NOMOLOGICAL CONDITIONS. This first reductionist approach comes in different forms. According to perhaps the most common version, a cause is a condition that is necessary in the circumstances for its effect. To say that event c is necessary in the circumstances for event e is roughly to say that there is some law, l, and some circumstance, s, such that the nonoccurrence of c, in circumstance s, together with law l, logically entails the nonoccurrence of e.

It may be held instead that a cause is a condition that is sufficient in the circumstances for its effect. To say that event c is sufficient in the circumstances for event e is to say that there is some law, l, and some circumstance, s, such that the occurrence of c, in circumstance s, together with law l, logically entails the occurrence of e.

Finally, it has also been suggested that for one event to cause another is for its occurrence to be both necessary and sufficient in the circumstances for the occurrence of the other event.

What problems do such approaches encounter? Perhaps the most serious difficulty concerns the direction of causation. Suppose that our world were a Newtonian one, in which the basic laws are time-symmetric. Then the total state of the universe in 1950 would have been both necessary and sufficient not only for the total state in 2050 but also for the total state in 1850. It would therefore follow that events in 1950 had caused events in 1850.

Less general objections are also important. First, if a cause is necessary in the circumstances for its effect, this precludes cases of causal preemption, in which event d would have caused event e were it not for the presence of event c, which both caused e and prevented d from doing so. In such a case c is not necessary for e since, if c had not occurred, e would have been caused by d. Second, cases of causal overdetermination are also ruled out. For if both c and d are causally sufficient to bring about e, and both do so, then neither c nor d was necessary in the circumstances for the occurrence of e.

These objections can be avoided if one holds instead that a cause is sufficient in the circumstances for its effect. But then other objections emerge. In particular it follows that there can be no causal relations if all the laws of nature are probabilistic. This is a serious difficulty, especially given the indeterministic nature of quantum mechanics.

SUBJUNCTIVE CONDITIONAL APPROACHES. A second important reductionist approach attempts to analyze causation using subjunctive conditionals. One way of arriving at this approach is by analyzing causation in terms of necessary or sufficient conditions (or both) but then interpreting the latter, not as nomological connections, as above, but as subjunctive conditionals. Thus one can say that c is necessary in the circumstances for e if, and only if, had c not occurred e would not have occurred, and that c is sufficient in the circumstances for e if, and only if, had e not occurred c would not have occurred.

John L. Mackie took this tack in developing a more sophisticated analysis of causation in terms of necessary and sufficient conditions. Thus, after defining an INUS condition of an event as an insufficient but necessary part of a condition which is itself unnecessary but exclusively sufficient for the event, and then arguing that *c*'s being a cause of *e* can then be analyzed as *c*'s being at least an INUS condition of *e,* Mackie asked how necessary and sufficient conditions should be understood. For general causal statements, Mackie favored a nomological account, but for singular causal statements he argued for an analysis in terms of subjunctive conditionals.

How are causal states of affairs related to

noncausal states of affairs? Which are more basic:

causal laws, or causal relations? And how

should the direction of causation be defined?

The most fully worked-out subjunctive conditional approach is that of David Lewis. His basic strategy involves analyzing causation using a narrower notion of causal dependence and then analyzing causal dependence counterfactually: (1) an event *c* causes an event *e* if, and only if, there is a chain of causally dependent events linking *e* with *c;* (2) an event *g* is causally dependent upon an event *f* if, and only if, had *f* not occurred *g* would not have occurred.

Causes, so construed, need not be necessary for their effects because counterfactual dependence, and hence causal dependence, are not necessarily transitive. Nevertheless, Lewis's approach is closely related to necessary-condition analyses of causation since the more basic relation of causal dependence is a matter of one event's being counterfactually necessary in the circumstances for another event.

What problems arise for such approaches? One is circularity. Classical analyses of subjunctive conditionals refer to causal laws, and so the question is whether any adequate, alternative analysis can avoid such reference.

Second, Lewis's account falls prey to both overdetermination cases and certain carefully constructed preemption cases, and Mackie's approach, while avoiding the problem of preemption, also rules out overdetermination.

Third, there is once again the problem of explaining the direction of causation. One possibility is to define the direction of causation as the direction of time, but neither Mackie nor Lewis favors that approach: both think that backward causation is logically possible. Mackie's main proposal appeals to the direction of irreversible processes involving the transmission of or-der—such as with outgoing concentric waves produced by a stone hitting a pond—and Lewis advances a somewhat related proposal, in which the direction of counterfactual dependence, and hence causal dependence, is based upon the idea that events in this world have many more effects than they have causes. But the problem with both of these suggestions is that the relevant features are at best contingent ones, and it would seem that, even if the world had neither of these features, it could still contain causally related events.

PROBABILISTIC APPROACHES. Among the more significant developments in the philosophy of causation since the time of Hume is the idea, motivated in part by quantum mechanics, that causation is not restricted to deterministic processes. This has led several philosophers to propose that causation itself should be analyzed in probabilistic terms.

The central idea is that causes must make their effects more likely. This idea can, however, be expressed in two rather different ways. The traditional approach, developed by Hans Reichenbach, I. J. Good, and Patrick Suppes, focuses upon types of events and involves the notion of positive statistical relevance. According to this notion, an event of type C is positively relevant to an event of type E if and only if the conditional probability of an event of type $E,$ given an event of type $C,$ is greater than the unconditional probability of an event of type $E.$ The basic idea, then, is that for events of type C to be direct causes of events of type $E,$ a necessary condition is that the former be positively relevant to the latter.

Other philosophers, including David Lewis, have suggested an alternative approach that focuses instead upon individual events and is formulated in terms of subjunctive conditionals concerning objective chances. The basic idea is that a necessary condition for *c*'s being a direct cause of *e* is that the objective chance of *e*'s occurring was greater, given that *c* occurred, than it would have been had *c* not occurred.

But do causes necessarily make their effects more likely? Consider two diseases, A and $B,$ governed by the following laws. First, disease A causes death with probability 0.1, while disease B causes death with probability 0.8. Second, contracting either disease produces complete immunity to the other. Third, in condition $C,$ an individual must contract either disease A or disease $B.$ (Condition C might be a weakening of the immune system.) Finally, assume that individual *m* is in condition C and contracts disease $A,$ which causes his death. Given these conditions, what if *m,* though in condition $C,$ had not contracted disease A? Then *m* would have contracted disease $B.$ But if so, then *m*'s probability of dying had he not contracted disease A would have been 0.8—higher than his probability of dying given that he had contracted disease *A*. So the claim that lies at the heart of probabilistic approaches—that causes necessarily make their effects more likely—does not appear to be true.

Realism

VARIETIES OF REALISM. Traditional antireductionist approaches have generally held that the concept of causation is primitive and that causal relations are immediately observable. Both these claims, however, seem problematic. Regarding the first, the concept of causation appears to enter into various necessary truths—for example, that causation is irreflexive, asymmetric, and transitive—and if the concept of causation were analytically basic, no explanation of such necessary truths would be forthcoming. As for the second claim, it appears to be incompatible with an empiricist epistemology since the traditional argument from hallucination would seem to show that one cannot have noninferentially justified beliefs about causal states of affairs.

A very different form of causal realism holds, however, that causation is a theoretical relation between events. On this view, all knowledge of causal states of affairs is inferential knowledge, and the concept of causation stands in need of analysis. But unlike reductionist accounts, the relevant analysis does not imply that causal states of affairs are logically supervenient upon noncausal states of affairs.

SINGULARISM AND CAUSAL LAWS. Realist approaches to causation have generally rejected the claim that causal relations between events are reducible to causal laws and to noncausal states of affairs. But in addition, realism frequently has been combined with a singularist concept of causation, according to which events can be causally related even without falling under any causal law. But what reasons are there for accepting this view? The main traditional argument is that causation is directly observable, which would be impossible if causal relations presupposed causal laws—an argument that, as just indicated, involves a dubious premise. But other arguments can be offered, such as the following. Assume that indeterministic laws are logically possible and that, in particular, it is a basic law both that an object's acquiring property *P* causes it to acquire either property *Q* or property *R*, and that an object's acquiring property *S* also causes it to acquire either property *Q* or property *R*. Suppose now that some object simultaneously acquires both property *P* and property *S* and then immediately acquires both property *Q* and property *R*. The problem now is that, given that the relevant laws are basic, there cannot be any noncausal facts that will determine which causal relations obtain. Did the acquisition of *P* cause the acquisition of *Q*, or

did it cause the acquisition of *R*? On a reductionist approach, no answer is possible. So it would seem that causal relations between events cannot be logically supervenient upon causal laws plus noncausal states of affairs.

REDUCTIONISM AND THE DIRECTION OF CAUSATION. What determines the direction of causation? Reductionists have advanced various suggestions, but some arguments seem to show that no reductionist account can work. One such argument appeals to the idea of a very simple world—consisting, say, of a single particle, or of two particles rotating endlessly about one another. Such simple worlds would still involve causation since the identity over time of the particles, for example, requires causal relations between their temporal parts. But since such worlds are time-symmetric, the events in them will not exhibit any noncausal patterns that could provide the basis for a reductionist account of the direction of causation.

A second argument turns upon the idea of possible universes that are temporally inverted twins. Thus, given an instantaneous slice of any Newtonian universe, there could be another universe in which the spatial arrangement of the particles at some instant was the same but with all the velocities reversed. In one universe the direction of causation would agree with the direction of the propagation of order in irreversible processes, the direction of increase in entropy, the direction of open forks, and so on, but in the inverted twin the direction of causation would be opposite. Accordingly, no reductionist account of the direction of causation can generate the correct answer for all possible worlds. It would seem, then, that only a realist account of causation will do.

[See also Hume, David; Mackie, John Leslie; Metaphysics; Philosophy of Science; Reduction, Reductionism.]

BIBLIOGRAPHY

Anscombe, G. E. M. *Causality and Determination.* Cambridge, 1971. A defense of a realist view of causation, arguing that causation is directly observable.

Eells, E. *Probabilistic Causality.* Cambridge, 1991. A detailed exposition of a probabilistic approach, although with sparse discussion of objections.

Fales, E. *Causation and Universals.* London, 1990. A realist approach to causation, defending the view that causation is immediately observable.

Good, I. J. "A Causal Calculus," Parts 1 and 2. *British Journal for the Philosophy of Science,* Vol. 11 (1961), 305–18, and Vol. 12 (1962), 43–51. An early exposition of a probabilistic approach; advocates introducing quantitative causal relations.

Lewis, D. "Counterfactual Dependence and Time's Arrow," *Noûs,* Vol. 13 (1979), 455–76. Reprinted, with postscripts, in *Philosophical Papers,* Vol. 2 (Oxford, 1986). Addresses the problem of the direction of counterfactual dependence.

———. "Causation," *Journal of Philosophy*, Vol. 70 (1973), 556–67. Reprinted, with postscripts, in *Philosophical Papers*, Vol. 2 (Oxford, 1986). An exposition and defense of a counterfactual approach.

Mackie, J. L. *The Cement of the Universe*. Oxford, 1974. A careful exposition of a reductionist approach to causation.

———. "Causes and Conditions," *American Philosophical Quarterly*, Vol. 2 (1965), 245–64. An exposition of the INUS condition account.

Reichenbach, H. *The Direction of Time*. Berkeley, 1956. The earliest exposition of a probabilistic approach to causation.

Salmon, W. C. *Scientific Explanation and the Causal Structure of the World*. Princeton, 1984. A reductionist approach that combines the idea of causal processes with a probabilistic account of causal interaction.

———. "Probabilistic Causality," *Pacific Philosophical Quarterly*, Vol. 61 (1980), 50–74. A critical examination of probabilistic approaches to causation.

Sosa, E., and M. Tooley, eds. *Causation*. Oxford, 1993. An anthology containing contemporary discussions of causation, plus a bibliography.

Strawson, G. *The Secret Connexion: Causation, Realism, and David Hume*. Oxford, 1989. Defends realism and challenges the standard reductionist interpretation of David Hume's approach.

Suppes, P. *A Probabilistic Theory of Causality*. Amsterdam, 1970. An accessible exposition of a probabilistic approach.

Tooley, M. "The Nature of Causation: A Singularist Account," in D. Copp, ed., *Canadian Philosophers, Canadian Journal of Philosophy*, Suppl., Vol. 16 (1990), 271–322. A defense of a singularist approach to causation.

———. *Causation: A Realist Approach*. Oxford, 1987. A defense of a realist view, arguing that causation is a theoretical relation between events.

Von Wright, G. H. *Explanation and Understanding*. Ithaca, NY, 1971. A defense of the view that the concept of causation is to be analyzed in terms of the idea of action.

— MICHAEL TOOLEY

CENSORSHIP

Censorship is the suppression of speech or symbolic expression for reason of its message. Liberal Western

CONDEMNED BOOKS,
From the Painting by Vibert.

In this painting by Vibert, clergymen laugh as they burn books that have been condemned by the church. (Corbis/Bettmann)

constitutionalism has traditionally condemned censorship on both instrumental and intrinsic grounds, classically articulated by John Stuart Mill in *On Liberty*. In this traditional liberal view, freedom of speech instrumentally serves the ends of truth and self-government. Censorship, by entrenching orthodoxy and suppressing dissent, impedes the advancement of truth and the processes of democratic change. Freedom of speech is also intrinsically valuable, in this view, as an aspect of human autonomy. Censorship illegitimately interferes with that autonomy, because speech, unlike action, typically causes others no harm. The proper response to bad speech is more speech, not government regulation.

Censorship, by entrenching orthodoxy

and suppressing dissent,

impedes the advancement of truth

and the processes of democratic change.

Late-twentieth-century critics have challenged both the instrumental and the intrinsic justifications for freeing speech from censorship. First, some suggest that the power to speak is so unequally distributed that free competition in the marketplace of ideas is unlikely to produce either truth or democracy. For example, advocates of regulating campaign advertisements argue that wealthy voices dominate and thus distort political debate, and advocates of hate-speech regulation argue that racial epithets and invective perpetuate a form of cultural white supremacy in which minority voices are effectively silenced. These critics would turn the traditional free-speech principle on its head. In their view freedom of speech helps to entrench the existing status quo while government regulation of the speech of powerful groups can level the playing field. Redistribution of speaking power would advance truth and political equality better than a regime of laissez-faire.

Second, some critics argue that the defense of free speech on autonomy grounds undervalues the harms that speech causes. On this view speech regulation ought to be more widely allowed to protect the countervailing autonomy interests of listeners or bystanders. Liberal constitutional democracies generally permit censorship only to avert a narrow range of material harms. For example, incitement to riot may be forbidden, as may publication of the movements of troops at war. But censorship is rarely permitted on the ground that speech will cause disapproval, anger, alarm, resent-

ment, or offense on the part of the audience. American constitutional law categorically forbids such justifications. Legal systems that permit them do so only in exceptional contexts: for example, British law forbids expressions of racial hatred, and some international human rights laws forbid advocacy of genocide.

Free-speech critics argue that such exceptions should be more the rule. First, some argue, government should be free to prevent injury, not only to bodies, but also to hearts and minds, including the injury caused by expressions of caustic opinion. Second, others argue, speech should be regulable for its social impact, even in the absence of immediate physical harm. On this view speech is not self-regarding but rather helps to structure social life. Thus, for example, pornography, hate speech, and graphic television violence inculcate attitudes that make society more immoral, sexist, racist, lawless, or violent than it would be if a different rhetoric prevailed. Speech helps construct society by socializing behavior, and reconstructing society, in this view, requires regulating speech.

At stake in these debates is whether speech will continue to be understood, like religious and reproductive practices, as presumptively a matter for private resolution, or instead will be subject to greater government regulation in the pursuit of social ends, including that of maximizing the quantity or diversity of speech itself.

[See also Democracy; Liberty; Mill, John Stuart.]

BIBLIOGRAPHY

Bork, R. "Neutral Principles and Some First Amendment Problems," *Indiana Law Journal*, Vol. 49 (1971), 1.

Dworkin, R. "The Coming Battles over Free Speech," *New York Review of Books*, June 11, 1992, 55.

Gates, H. L., Jr. "Let Them Talk," *New Republic*, Sept. 20 & 27, 1993, 37.

MacKinnon, C. A. *Only Words*. Cambridge, MA, 1993.

Matsuda, M. J., et al. *Words That Wound: Critical Race Theory, Assaultive Speech, and the First Amendment*. Boulder, CO, 1993.

Meiklejohn, A. *Free Speech and Its Relation to Self-Government*. New York, 1948.

Mill, J. S. *On Liberty*. 1859.

Scanlon, T. "A Theory of Free Expression," *Philosophy and Public Affairs*, Vol. 1 (1972), 204.

Strossen, N. *Defending Pornography: Free Speech, Sex, and the Fight for Women's Rights*. New York, 1995.

Sunstein, C. R. *Democracy and the Problem of Free Speech*. New York, 1993.

– KATHLEEN M. SULLIVAN

CHISHOLM, RODERICK M.

Roderick M. Chisholm is a twentieth-century American philosopher who has made major contributions in almost every area of philosophy but most notably epistemology and metaphysics. He was an undergraduate at Brown University from 1934 to 1938 and a graduate student at Harvard from 1938 to 1942. He served in the military from 1942 to 1946, and then, after briefly holding a teaching post with the Barnes Foundation and the University of Pennsylvania, he returned in 1947 to Brown University, where he remained until his retirement.

Epistemology

In epistemology Chisholm is a defender of foundationalism. He thinks that any proposition that is justified gets at least part of its justification from basic propositions, which are justified but not by anything else. Contingent propositions are basic insofar as they correspond to self-presenting states, which for Chisholm are states such that whenever one is in the state and believes that one is in it, then one's belief is maximally justified. There are two types of self-presenting states, intentional states (ways of thinking, hoping, fearing, desiring, wondering, intending, etc.) and sensory states (ways of being appeared to by the various senses). A noncontingent proposition is basic if understanding it is sufficient for understanding that it is true and hence also sufficient for making it justified. "2 + 3 = 5" and "If Jones is ill and Smith is away, then Jones is ill" are examples of such propositions, says Chisholm.

Self-presentation and understanding are among the sources of epistemic justification, but according to Chisholm there are other sources as well. The principal of these are perception, memory, belief coupled with a lack of negative coherence (e.g., no inconsistencies among the propositions believed), and belief coupled with positive coherence (i.e., mutual support among the propositions believed). For each of these sources, Chisholm forwards an epistemic principle that describes the precise conditions under which the source produces justified beliefs.

Despite his thinking that there are many sources of epistemic justification, Chisholm is rightly regarded as a foundationalist because all the sources are such that they can produce justified beliefs only because some propositions are justified basically. For example, Chisholm's principles concerning perception and memory make reference to propositions that are justified because they correspond to self-presenting states. In the case of perception the relevant states are sensings, and for memory the relevant states are beliefs (specifically, beliefs to the effect that one remembers something). In a similar spirit, Chisholm says that coherence relations among propositions are not capable of generating justification

for propositions that have nothing else to recommend them; their role instead is to increase the degree of justification that propositions have by virtue of being supported by basic propositions.

Chisholm is also a proponent of internalism in epistemology, in two senses of the term. First, he thinks that epistemic justification supervenes on our conscious states; thus, whether one's beliefs are justified is determined by one's own internal states rather than by conditions obtaining in one's external environment. Second, he thinks that the conditions, if any, that justify one's beliefs are accessible to one; thus, one can determine, if one reflects carefully enough, whether one's beliefs are justified.

Chisholm's epistemology is resolutely antiskeptical. Indeed, he says that the proper way to begin doing epistemology is by presupposing that some of our beliefs are justified and some constitute knowledge. Epistemology, so conceived, becomes primarily a search for the conditions that account for these beliefs being justified. A second task is to define the conditions that turn a true belief into knowledge. Chisholm's approach to this latter task is to defend a nondefeasibility account to knowledge. We know a proposition p, he says, whenever we believe p, p is true, and p is nondefectively evident for us, where p is nondefectively evident for us (some details aside) just in case there is a set of basic propositions that justify p and nothing false for us.

Metaphysics

Chisholm has well-worked-out views on almost every major issue in metaphysics, but his most influential views have been concerned with thought and language, ontology, action, and material bodies.

Chisholm's most influential views

have been concerned with thought and language,

ontology, action, and material bodies.

With respect to thought and language, Chisholm is a defender of the primacy of thought; the intentionality of language is to be understood in terms of the intentionality of thought, he says, rather than conversely. He develops this idea in his direct attribution theory of reference. At the heart of the theory is a proposal that we are able to refer to things other than ourselves by directly attributing properties to them and that we indirectly attribute properties to them by directly attributing properties to ourselves. For example, if you are the only person in a room with me and you are wearing a blue sweater, then by directly attributing to myself the property of being a person X such that the only other person in the room with X is wearing a blue sweater, I indirectly attribute to you the property of wearing a blue sweater and thereby refer to you. Using these notions of direct and indirect attribution, Chisholm provides an account of various semantic notions including sense and reference.

In ontology, Chisholm's view is that there are only two kinds of entities, attributes and the individual things that have these attributes. Everything else, including propositions, states of affairs, possible worlds, and sets, can be understood in terms of two categories. Attributes are possible objects of thought—more specifically, what we are able to attribute, either directly (to ourselves) or indirectly (both to ourselves and other things). Thus, in ontology, Chisholm once again is a defender of the primacy of thought in that he uses the phenomenon of intentionality to identify and understand what kinds of entities there are.

His theory of action is an indeterministic one. The fundamental notions are those of undertaking and causing, and with respect to the latter notion he carefully distinguishes among necessary causal conditions for an event, sufficient causal conditions, and causal contributions. With these notions in hand, he opposes compatibilist attempts to understand what it is for a person to be free to undertake something, insisting that one has undertaken to do something freely only if there was no sufficient causal condition for one to undertake it (although there may have been extensive causal contributions to the undertaking).

Much of Chisholm's work on bodies is concerned with puzzles about the persistence of physical bodies through time, and most of these puzzles, in turn, are concerned with apparent violations of Leibniz's principle of the indiscernibility of identicals. According to this principle, if X and Y are identical, then whatever is true of X is also true of Y. One famous puzzle, for example, is the ship of Theseus. Even if one plank of the ship is replaced at a time t, it is the same ship, namely Theseus's, that exists before t and after t, and yet the ship might appear to have different properties before t and after t. Chisholm attempts to solve this and other puzzles about the identity of physical bodies through time by using his fundamental ontological categories, attributes and individual things, to make precise the seventeenth-century distinction between substances and their modes.

[See also Action Theory; Internalism versus Externalism; Persistence; Reference.]

BIBLIOGRAPHY

Bogdan, R., ed. *Roderick M. Chisholm.* Dordrecht, 1986. Critical essays on Chisholm and a helpful self-profile.

Chisholm, R. *The First Person: An Essay on Reference and Intentionality.* Minneapolis, 1981. A detailed defense of the direct attribution theory of reference.

———. *Theory of Knowledge.* Englewood Cliffs, NJ, 1st ed., 1966; 2d ed., 1977; 3d ed., 1987. His most influential work in epistemology; the later editions contain important modifications of his earlier views.

———. *Person and Object: A Metaphysical Study.* London, 1976. Most of his metaphysical positions are defended in this volume.

———. *Human Freedom and the Self.* Lawrence, KS, 1964. A defense of his indeterministic account of human freedom.

———. *Perceiving: A Philosophical Study.* Ithaca, NY, 1957. His first major work on epistemology.

Lehrer, K., ed. *Analysis and Metaphysics: Essays in Honor of R. M. Chisholm.* Dordrecht, 1975. Critical essays on Chisholm's metaphysics and epistemology.

– RICHARD FOLEY

CHOMSKY, NOAM

Noam Chomsky, born in 1928, is the foremost linguistic theorist of the postwar era, an important contributor to philosophical debates, and a notable radical activist. His influence is felt in many other fields, however, most notably, perhaps, in the area of cognitive studies.

Shifting the linguist's problematic from behavior to the system underlying behavior was probably Chomsky's most important contribution to the development of "scientific" studies of social phenomena.

Chomsky's main achievement was to distinguish linguistic competence from its manifestations in performance and to characterize competence as a system of explicit rules for the construction and interpretation of sentences. Indeed, this achievement provided a model for investigations, in this and other cognitive domains, that replaced then-dominant models based on the notion of analogy and oriented to the causal explanation of behavior.

The competence of individuals to use their language is constituted, on Chomsky's account, by their (tacit) knowledge of a formal grammar (or system of rules); their linguistic performance, involving the deployment of such knowledge, may be influenced by a host of extraneous factors that need not be accounted for by the grammar itself but, instead and if possible, by subsidiary theories (e.g., of perceptual processing, etc.). Furthermore, knowledge of such a system of rules permits a kind of creativity in performance that exhibits itself in the novelty, in relation to speakers' prior linguistic experiences, of (many of) the sentences they actually produce. (Crudely put, they can understand and produce sentences they have never before encountered.)

The competence/performance distinction reflects Chomsky's preference for 'Galiean' theorizing (i.e., for a 'modular' approach), and its introduction was tremendously liberating. A direct attack on performance, under broadly behavioristic auspices, had proved barren, for reasons Chomsky identified with devastating clarity in his review of B. F. Skinner's *Verbal Behavior*. Also pertinent was Chomsky's analysis of linguistic creativity in a second, distinct sense: the appropriateness and yet stimulus-independence (and therefore causal inexplicability) of much of what a speaker says in concrete circumstances. Shifting the linguist's problematic from behavior to the system underlying behavior was probably Chomsky's most important contribution to the development of 'scientific' studies of social phenomena. (Of course, the competence/performance distinction owes much to Ferdinand de Saussure's earlier distinction between *langue* and *parole*. But Saussure did not think of the system underlying behavior as primarily rule-based, and so his distinction proved less fertile than Chomsky's.)

In a series of works beginning with *Cartesian Linguistics*, Chomsky took up what he came to call "Plato's problem"—that of explaining how the gap is bridged between individuals' limited opportunities, as children, for acquiring knowledge of their (native) language(s) and the competence to make many subtle and complex discriminations that, as mature speakers, they do indeed possess. He solved this problem, siding with classical rationalists such as Leibniz, by assuming the existence, as an innate species-wide attribute, of a 'universal grammar'. During the course of language acquisition, limited data fixes the values of free 'parameters' associated with this grammar, thus providing a basis for full-blown knowledge of the language that far exceeds the ordinary 'inductive' implications of these data.

Chomsky has also been a notable advocate, very significantly in a discipline previously marked by instrumentalist assumptions about theorizing, of a realist perspective on theoretical entities and processes. In early work deep structures were postulated as sources, via transformations, of familiar superficial structures of sen-

Chomsky's main achievement was to distinguish linguistic competence from its manifestations in performance. (Gale Research Co.)

tences. So, for instance, a superficially passive sentence was said to be derived from the same deep structure as its active counterpart. And while it might have been more in line with then-contemporary practice to treat these so-called deep structures as pure postulates, useful in simplifying the description and taxonomization of the superficial sentences of our 'experience', Chomsky advocated, instead, that they be treated as having psychological reality and thereby fostered many profound psycholinguistic studies intended to bear out or refute this contention. A topic of continuing importance is whether it is only structures or, instead, derivational processes as well that are to be treated as 'real'.

Less noticed by commentators is Chomsky's profoundly individualistic approach to linguistic phenomena. For him, language itself is a secondary phenomena; primacy is accorded to an individual's competence, a purely psychological phenomenon. Indeed, Chomsky explains the coordination of linguistic interaction, not by reference to any transpersonal system of conventions (as might be thought appropriate in relation to other social phenomena), but, instead, to a harmony—between the competence of the speaker and the marginally different competence of the hearer—that depends largely on the innate constraints on their (typically) quite separate episodes of language acquisition. Even if each learns in isolation from the other, and has quite (though not 'too') different experiential bases for learning, each will acquire an 'idiolect' that is accessible to the other: otherwise rather different data-sets fix the free parameters of the universal grammar in sufficiently similar ways to permit mutual intelligibility.

Other philosophically important themes in Chomsky's work include: (1) his identification of the ideological interests that are served by certain allegedly 'scientific' approaches to the study of human behavior; (2) his argument for treating the capacity for language as species-specific and thus as an aspect of the human 'essence'; (3) his speculations about the possibility that there are innate limitations on the human capacity for knowledge of the world; and (4) his continued defense, in the face of broadly 'postmodernist' opposition, of the role of reason in understanding and improving the human condition and of the viability of the notion of 'progress' in relation to these projects.

[See also Leibniz, Gottfried Wilhelm; Modernism and Postmodernism.]

BIBLIOGRAPHY

Works by Chomsky

Syntactic Structures. The Hague, 1957.
"A Review of B. F. Skinner's *Verbal Behavior*," in J. A. Fodor and J. J. Katz, eds., *The Structure of Language* (Englewood Cliffs, NJ, 1964).
Cartesian Linguistics. New York, 1966.
Language and Mind. New York, 1972.
For Reasons of State. London, 1973.
Language and Problems of Knowledge. Cambridge, MA, 1988.

Works on Chomsky

D'Agostino, F. *Chomsky's System of Ideas.* Oxford, 1986.
Harman, G., ed. *On Noam Chomsky.* Garden City, NY, 1974.
Kasher, A., ed. *The Chomskyan Turn.* Oxford, 1991.
Sampson, G. *Liberty and Language.* Oxford, 1979.

– FRED D'AGOSTINO

CLASSICAL FOUNDATIONALISM

Classical foundationalism maintains that all knowledge and justified belief rest ultimately on a foundation of noninferential knowledge and noninferentially justified belief. Because the classical foundationalist typically assumes an account of knowledge in terms of justified or rational true belief, this entry will focus on the distinction invoked between inferentially and noninferentially justified beliefs.

If we think about most of the beliefs we take to be justified and ask ourselves what justifies them, it seems natural to answer in terms of other justified beliefs. One's justification for believing that it will rain, for example, may consist in part of one's justifiably believing that the barometer is dropping rapidly. But under what conditions can one justifiably infer the truth of one proposition p from another e? The classic foundationalist typically answers this question with what might be called the principle of inferential justification. To be justified in believing p by inferring it from e, one must be (1) justified in believing e and (2) justified in believing that e confirms (makes probable) p.

The principle of inferential justification is a crucial premise in the famous regress argument for foundationalism. If the principle is correct, then to be justified in believing some proposition p on the basis of some other evidence, e_1, one would need to be justified in believing e_1. But if all justification were inferential, then to be justified in believing e_1, one would need to infer it from something else e_2, which one justifiably believes, and so on ad infinitum. This first regress is generated by clause (1) of the principle of inferential justification. If clause (2) is correct, the potential regresses proliferate endlessly. To be justified in inferring p from e_1, one must justifiably believe not only e_1 but also that e_1 makes p likely, and one must infer this from something else, f_1, which one must justifiably infer from some other proposition, f_2, which one justifiably infers. . . . But one must also justifiably believe that f_1 makes likely that e_1 makes likely p, so one must justifiably infer that from some other proposition, g_1, which one justifiably infers. . . . If all justification were inferential, then to justifiably believe any proposition p we would need to complete not one but an infinite number of infinitely long chains of reasoning. The human mind is finite and cannot complete infinitely long chains of reasoning. To avoid the absurd conclusion that we have no reason for believing anything whatsoever, we must suppose that some beliefs are justified without inference and that these noninferentially justified beliefs ground the justification of all other justified beliefs.

Classical foundationalists refer to the foundations of knowledge and justified belief in a variety of ways—non-inferentially justified beliefs, self-evident truths, directly evident truths, incorrigible beliefs, infallible beliefs—but there is no consensus on what confers foundational status on a belief. Some, following René Descartes, seek foundations in beliefs that do not admit the possibility of error. As we shall see, the possibility in question can be interpreted in a number of different ways, but classical foundationalists invoke a very strong concept of possibility—if a belief is foundational, it must be inconceivable that the belief is false. Having the belief must somehow entail its truth.

Many other classical foundationalists sought the source of foundational knowledge in some relation (other than belief) between a believer and the truth conditions of what is believed. One often-invoked metaphor is the concept of acquaintance. When one believes that one is in pain when one is in pain, one is directly acquainted or confronted with the pain itself (the very state that makes true the proposition believed). The knower's direct confrontation with the relevant aspect of reality to which the truth in question corresponds obviates the need for any inference.

There might also be direct acquaintance with logical relations holding between propositions, states of affairs, or properties, direct acquaintance with which yields direct knowledge of necessary truths. On such a view, then, one might locate the source of both a priori and a posteriori foundational knowledge in the same relation of acquaintance. The difference between the two kinds of knowledge might lie more on the side of the relata of the acquaintance relation than on the source of the knowledge.

Classical foundationalists refer to the foundations of knowledge and justified belief in a variety of ways—but there is no consensus on what confers foundational status on a belief.

Classical foundationalism has come under considerable attack from many different directions. Some would argue that the search for infallible beliefs as the foundations of knowledge is both fruitless and misguided, at least if infallibility is understood in terms of a belief's entailing the truth of what is believed. First, it has been pointed out that if one believes a necessary truth, one's belief will trivially entail the truth of what is believed. But surely such a belief would not constitute knowledge if the person held the belief as a matter of pure whimsy. Once one sees that the entailment between belief and the truth of what one believes is not sufficient for any kind of knowledge, one might begin to wonder whether it is ever getting at the heart of any interesting epistemic concept. Still other philosophers have pointed out that beliefs that entail their truth are few and far between and, if knowledge rests on a foundation of these, the foundation is precarious indeed. Consider a favorite example of a foundational belief offered by classical foundationalists—the belief one has that one is in pain. Believing that one is in pain seems to be a state logically distinct from the pain. As such it seems always at least

conceivable that the belief could occur (perhaps produced by some evil demon) without the pain.

Some contemporary philosophers are sympathetic to the idea of direct knowledge, understood in terms of beliefs that cannot be false, but have understood the relevant possibility in causal or nomological terms. Thus, the circumstances that produce my belief that p may be causally sufficient for the truth of p. It is not easy to spell out in an interesting way how one specifies the relevant circumstances causally responsible for a belief, but this approach does succeed in calling into question the classical foundationalists' emphasis on conceivability or logical possibility as the relevant concept to employ in defining epistemically interesting concepts of infallibility.

Reliance on the concept of acquaintance to define the concept of foundational knowledge has not fared much better when it comes to contemporary philosophical fashion. The standard line most often taken is that there is no such relation and, even if there were, it would be of no epistemic interest. Foundational knowledge must be knowledge of propositions if it is to yield the premises from which we can infer the rest of what we justifiably believe. But acquaintance with a fact seems to be a relation that has nothing to do with anything that has a truth value. Facts are not the kinds of things that can be true or false. How does acquaintance with a fact yield access to truth? Indeed, can one even make sense of reference to facts independently of truth? Some philosophers would argue that referring to a fact is just another way of referring to a proposition's being true. If facts are reducible to truths, it would clearly be uninformative to locate the source of noninferential knowledge of truths in terms of acquaintance with facts to which truths correspond.

To attack various versions of foundationalism is not, of course, to respond to the regress argument for foundationalism. It has already been noted that some contemporary foundationalists accept the fundamental idea that there are foundations to knowledge but reject classical accounts of what those foundations consist in. Many externalists, for example, identify justificatory conditions for belief with the circumstances producing the belief. Reliabilists, for example, count a belief as justified if it is reliably produced and allow that a belief might be reliably produced even if the input producing the belief involves no other beliefs. Such reliable belief-independent processes can end a regress of beliefs justified by reference to other beliefs.

The other main alternative to classical foundationalism is the coherence theory of justification. The coherentist rejects the classical foundationalist's assumption that justification is linear in structure. According to the coherentist, there is no escape from the circle of one's beliefs—nothing can justify a belief but other beliefs. But one doesn't justify a belief by reference to other prior justified beliefs. Rather, each belief is justified by reference to its "fit" in an entire system of beliefs.

[See also Coherentism; Descartes, René; Epistemology; Externalism; Reliabilism.]

BIBLIOGRAPHY

Descartes, R. *Discourse on Method and Meditations,* translated by L. Lafleur. Indianapolis, 1960.
Lehrer, K. *Knowledge,* Chap. 4–6. Oxford, 1974.
Price, H. H. *Perception,* Chap. 1, London, 1950.
Russell, B. *The Problems of Philosophy,* Chap. 5. Oxford, 1959.

— RICHARD FUMERTON

COGNITIVE SCIENCE

Cognitive science is the interdisciplinary study of mind in which the concepts and methods of artificial intelligence (AI) are central. The most prominent subdisciplines are AI, psychology, philosophy, and linguistics. Howard Gardner (1985) includes anthropology and sociology, and Mark Turner (1991) adds English studies. Not everyone working in these disciplines is a cognitive scientist; only those taking a computational approach to questions about mind can be given this designation. Relevant subfields include the psychology of human–computer interaction and computational musicology. Nonhuman minds are studied by cognitive and computational ethology and by parts of artificial life (A-Life). Computational neuroscience, which studies computational functions in the brain, also falls within cognitive science.

Cognitive science includes cognitive psychology: the study of language, memory, perception, problem solving, and creativity. Most research has focused on individual human adult cognition, but some research has focused on other aspects of mind: motivation, emotion, development, psychopathology, interpersonal phenomena, motor control, and animal (and artificial) psychology. Cognitive science is not concerned only with cognition.

Cognitive science employs computational models of mind, in two senses. First, the substantive concepts in its theories are computational. The mind is seen as some sort of computational system (just what sort is disputed), and mental processes are described accordingly. Second, computer modeling is often used to clarify and test those theories. If a program produces a given performance, we know that it suffices to do so. Whether real minds use similar processes to produce equivalent performance is another question that must also be addressed.

Many philosophical disputes arise within cognitive science. One concerns the relative merits of two AI approaches: classical (symbolic) AI and connectionism. Some researchers champion only one of these, while others admit both because of their complementary strengths and weaknesses. Another debate concerns the nature and importance of various kinds of internal representation and whether thought requires language. A third asks whether (and if so, how) meaning (intentionality) can be grounded in the real world. And a fourth concerns whether consciousness could be explained in computational (or any other scientific) terms.

Some recent work opposes orthodox (neo-Cartesian) cognitive science, preferring the phenomenological tradition. It rejects both symbolic and connectionist AI, and the concept of representation. It highlights embodied systems (not abstract simulations) that are embedded in their environments and respond directly to them. Examples include situated robotics in AI, dynamical systems theory, ecological psychology, and A-Life studies of evolution and coevolution.

[See also Philosophy of Mind.]

BIBLIOGRAPHY

Boden, M. A., ed. *The Philosophy of Artificial Intelligence.* Oxford, 1990.
———. *Computer Models of Mind: Computational Approaches in Theoretical Psychology.* Cambridge, 1988.
Dennett, D. C. *Consciousness Explained.* Boston, 1991.
Fodor, J. A. *Psychosemantics: The Problem of Meaning in the Philosophy of Mind.* Cambridge, MA, 1987.
Gardner, H. *The Mind's New Science: A History of the Cognitive Revolution.* New York, 1985.
Johnson-Laird, P. N. *The Computer and the Mind: An Introduction to Cognitive Science.* London, 1988.
Turner, M. *Reading Minds: The Study of English in the Age of Cognitive Science.* Princeton, NJ, 1991.
Varela, F. J., E. Thompson, and E. Rosch. *The Embodied Mind: Cognitive Science and Human Experience.* Cambridge, MA, 1991.

— MARGARET BODEN

COHERENTISM

One of the three major views of the nature of epistemic justification, the coherence theory (or coherentism) experienced a revival during the 1970s and 1980s after its near total eclipse earlier in the century. Although its origins can be traced to idealists, including Francis Bradley, Bernard Bosanquet, and Brand Blanshard, the coherence theory has more recently been espoused by empiricist-minded contemporary philosophers such as Wilfrid Sellars, Nicholas Rescher, Keith Lehrer, Gilbert Harman, and Laurence Bonjour. The coherence theory of justification stands as an alternative to both the more traditional foundations theory and the view called reliabilism. It should not be confused with a coherence theory of truth. A coherence theorist about justification can acknowledge a fact that cripples the coherence theory of truth, namely, that there are instances of coherent, hence justified, beliefs in falsehoods.

Although the details of different versions of the coherence theory vary widely, all versions share a positive thesis and a resulting negative claim. The coherence theory's positive thesis is that a belief is justified or warranted for a person to the degree that that belief coheres with the rest of that person's belief system. As a fabric derives its strength from the reciprocal ties and interconnections among its constitutive threads, so, for the coherentist, beliefs derive their justification from their interconnectedness with one's other beliefs. The negative claim endorsed by all coherentists is that foundationalism is in error when it asserts that some of our justified beliefs are privileged or basic—that is, their justification is at least partly independent of their connectedness with other held beliefs.

The coherentist's picture of mutual support or fit among our beliefs departs (to varying degrees) from the strictly linear image of justification that classical foundationalism endorses. For the foundationalist epistemic justification is transmitted to nonbasic beliefs, from those that are basic or foundational, along lines of inference and explanation. Inferred beliefs are justified by those from which they are inferred. For the coherentist the belief's justificatory status has less to do with the grounds on which a belief is based and more to do with the whole cluster of relations (of consistency, implication, probability, explanation, and the like) that more or less strongly fix that belief within the network of other held beliefs.

The exact nature of epistemic coherence, however, is very difficult to clarify, and disagreements occur even among coherentists. Some have argued that coherence is always and ultimately explanatory coherence, a question of whether a belief is a member of the best overall explanatory account accessible to an individual. Others claim that there are justificatory relations of comparative reasonableness of competing beliefs that reflect concerns wider than explanation alone, including measures of subjective probability and the relative informativeness of the proposition believed. Logical consistency seems to be a minimal necessary condition for maximal coherence, but some have argued that at least certain inconsistencies are unavoidable but do not so undermine coherence as to prevent beliefs from being justified. Speaking generally, coherence is a property of a belief system that is determined by the (various) connections of intelligibility among the elements of the system. Most agree that these include deductive, inductive,

and abductive relations, as well as other explanatory and probabilistic connections. Some writers, especially pragmatists, are prepared to add relations such as the relative simplicity or the power of the explanations contained in one's belief system as contributors to overall coherence.

Motivation for the coherence theory comes most directly from finding foundationalism unworkable and believing as a consequence that some version of coherence must be correct. Another motivation comes from the observation that it seems apt and possible to ask about any belief what a person's reasons are for holding it. The theory also appears particularly compatible with the realization that all instances of epistemic justification are defeasible—that is, the justification of a given belief is always liable to undermining by other held beliefs, no matter how strong the initial grounds or evidential basis of the belief might be. Since undermining can come from any element of one's system that might be negatively relevant to a specific belief, it appears that complete epistemic justification, the kind necessary to support claims of knowledge, is sensitive to all of the connections among our beliefs, precisely as the coherence theorist urges. This argument for the coherence theory is not decisive, however, since foundationalists can freely admit that warrant is undermined by a lack of coherence while still rejecting the coherentist's positive claim that coherence is the source of all epistemic justification.

> *Speaking generally, coherence is a property of a belief system that is determined by the (various) connections of intelligibility among the elements of the system—including deductive, inductive, and abductive relations.*

In addition to the unclarities surrounding measuring degrees of coherence, numerous objections have been offered to coherentism. Four have been particularly prominent.

The Circularity Objection

If there are no foundational beliefs that act as the ultimate source of epistemic justification, and if the lines of justification transmission are not infinitely long (which appears absurd given the finitude of our mental capacities), then the coherence theory seems forced to claim that justification can be ultimately but not viciously circular. It is not immediately clear how circularity of this sort is anything but vicious, no matter how wide the circle may be, even though some have argued that wideness of a justificatory circle immunizes against viciousness. But if A is the source of justification for B, how can B be the source of justification for A? The coherentist can reply that the "source" of justification is the entire belief system. The linear model of justification on which the circularity objection is based may not be forceful against a more holistic construal of the relation. Taken as a holistic and higher-order relation constituted by lower-order reciprocal relations (at least some of which are asymmetric, such as "explaining" and "being explained by"), coherence might be able to avoid the problem of vicious circularity.

The Problem of Perceptual Beliefs

Certain simple and apparently immediate perceptual beliefs seem to be justified for us on the basis of the perceptual experience we currently are having rather than on any considerations about how that belief coheres with the rest of our belief system. Experience often seems to warrant beliefs that are anomalous—that is, do not cohere with already-held beliefs. In such cases we do not think that we are justified in rejecting the new belief on grounds of incoherence but often concede that revision of some previously held beliefs is appropriate. Coherentists have replied to this objection by arguing that the justification of even the most immediate perceptual belief requires that that belief cohere with our metabeliefs regarding how reliable or trustworthy we take our perceptual processes to be in the particular conditions. It is such metabeliefs that make it more reasonable to accept the anomalous perceptual experience than it is for us to conclude that we are hallucinating or have been deceived in some fashion. The introduction of metabeliefs into the explanation why immediate perceptual beliefs are often justified for us has struck many, however, as overintellectualizing our epistemic situation, as well as possibly reintroducing foundational principles into the theory of justification.

The Isolation Objection

This objection, closely related to the problem of perceptual beliefs, begins with the observation that coherence is a cognitively internal relation, relating belief to belief. But might not a thoroughly coherent system of beliefs nonetheless fail to be justified because they are not properly linked to the external perceptual circumstances? Would acceptance of a coherent fiction be justified if it were entirely the product of wishful thinking? The continual perceptual input we receive from the world must be assimilated into our belief system or else the justification for those beliefs will often suffer from undermining. The coherence theory seems too internalist to be a complete theory of epistemic justification, the objection concludes. Since coherence does not necessarily serve the epistemic goals of pursuing truth and avoiding error in our belief system, further constraints seem necessary if our notion of justification is to relate appropriately to knowledge. Coherentists respond in a number of ways to the isolation objection.

One alternative is to admit the objection's force and add a requirement that all justified systems include the belief that certain kinds of spontaneously occurring beliefs such as perceptual and memory beliefs are reliable or likely to be true. Demonstrating that this constraint is not an ad hoc amendment to coherentism is a difficult matter. A similar requirement applied to acceptances based on spontaneous wishful thinking would be obviously ad hoc and unacceptable. Some have suggested that metabeliefs about the trustworthiness of our perceptual beliefs in certain circumstances are not ad hoc and are important and legitimate members of our belief system, justified, as all beliefs are, through their coherence with our other beliefs. Whether such beliefs can be noncircularly defended, whether they constitute a sort of foundational belief, and whether they are realistically necessary for epistemic justification are each open matters.

The Inferential-Structure Objection

The foundationalist's traditional view—that whether one is epistemically justified in believing some proposition depends crucially upon the actual course of inference taken in arriving at a belief—is not easily relinquished. Coherence, however, is a relation determined only by the contents of beliefs and not by the order in which they have been inferred. Consequently, it appears possible that a series of beliefs inferred one from the other in a wholly fallacious manner might nevertheless cohere maximally with a background system of beliefs as long as there is another valid (but unused) course of inference that does connect them. This leads to the conclusion that, even if the coherence theory adequately captures the concept of epistemically justifiable beliefs relative to a system, it fails to explicate the notion of being justified in believing a proposition. Coherentists have responded to this challenge by relying once more on metabeliefs, claiming that when we infer A from B and B from C we also accept or believe that A follows from B, and not, for example, that C follows from A. Incorrect metabeliefs will, on some versions of coherentism, cause incoherence and loss of justification, keeping blatantly fallacious reasoning from ending in justified beliefs. This response, however, may generate an infinite regress of metabeliefs. Not all uses of inference schemes contain premises stating that the scheme is valid. One can infer B from A without first having to infer that B follows from A. Some coherentists answer this and other objections by admitting that their proposed conditions for coherence constitute ideals to which human knowers should aspire but seldom in actuality achieve. Debate over the merits of the coherence theory promises to continue unabated.

[See also Classical Foundationalism; Epistemology; Reliabilism; Sellars, Wilfrid.]

BIBLIOGRAPHY

Audi, R. "Foundationalism, Coherentism, and Epistemological Dogmatism," in J. Tomberlin, ed., *Philosophical Perspectives,* Vol. 2, 1988.

Bender, J. W., ed. *The Current State of the Coherence Theory.* Philosophical Studies, Vol. 44. Dordrecht, 1989.

Bonjour, L. *The Structure of Empirical Knowledge.* Cambridge, MA, 1985.

Lehrer, K. *Theory of Knowledge.* Boulder, CO, 1990.

Plantinga, A. *Warrant: The Current Debate.* Oxford, 1993.

Pollock, J. *Contemporary Theories of Knowledge.* Totowa, NJ, 1986.

– JOHN W. BENDER

COLORS

The phenomena of color pose a special puzzle to philosophers characterizing the mind, the world, and the interaction of the two. In various ways, both subjective and objective, both appearance and reality, color has been the subject of wide disagreement. Besides the extreme view that colors are literally sensations—which would imply that they are not in the category of properties and that they last precisely as long as sensations—the main views are these.

Physicalism

D. M. Armstrong, J. J. C. Smart, and others have suggested that red (or being red), for example, is a physical property—perhaps a surface physical characteristic (like Boyle's "textures")—or a propensity to reflect some kinds of light more than others. The threat that physical science might be unable to find a predicate coextensive with "red" seems small; but there are challenges to the idea that any such property can be identified with red. First, will a physical property have the same higher-level properties as red does? Red is a "unique" color—there is a "pure" shade of red with no hint of any other color (unlike orange, every shade of which evidently contains red and yellow); however, it seems nonsense to say that some reflectance characteristic is "unique." The physicalist may perhaps reply: a reflectance characteristic can indeed have the property of "uniqueness"—if that is

understood as the property of *suggesting to a normal observer no hint of any other color.* (That higher-level property will no doubt be the subject of a later reduction.) A second challenge is this: ordinary people surely know, for example, that red is more similar to orange than to blue, but if colors are properties whose true nature is revealed only in science, then (until they know more science) they should be in no position to know this. The physicalist may have a reply: this kind of knowledge is of phenomenal similarity, not physical similarity—and on that ordinary perceivers are authoritative. Both challenges suggest an important point, however—that physicalism can at best be a theory about properties that we think of initially without any thought of physical science.

Dispositional Views

The view that colors are dispositions to produce experiences has long been nearly an orthodoxy in the field. Proposed by Boyle and Locke, it has seemed a perfect way to capture the connections between color concepts and color experience. You cannot, it seems, grasp the idea of red unless things sometimes look red to you. And you cannot have a full grasp of the idea unless you realize that your color judgments will be defeasible if it turns out that either you or the conditions are abnormal. The proposal may be strengthened by adding an actuality operator: to be red, an object needs to look red to such observers and in such conditions as *actually* count as normal. This last phrase shall be abbreviated as "to look red [etc.]."

Galileo, Descartes, and Locke are the first

of many to treat colors as properties of experiences,

which we wrongly "project" onto external objects.

A preliminary worry can perhaps be met. Are there any such things as "normal conditions" and "normal observers"? Normal conditions vary hugely with the nature of the object and with our interests; in some cases (e.g., bioluminescent fish) there may be no clear answer to the question what normal conditions are. "Normal observers" pose a further problem: even when we rule out "color-blind" people, there is surprising disagreement among the remainder (e.g., over which shade of green is "unique"). These problems may not be fatal. If there is indeterminacy in the truth of "x is disposed to look red to normal observers under normal conditions," there may be an exactly corresponding indeterminacy in the truth of "x is red"—the moral may be that some things have no determinate color, not that color is mischaracterized by the dispositional thesis.

Dispositional views vary according to whether they take the experience of a thing's looking red to be a sensation or a representation. The sensationalist version faces the suspicion that the required "sensations of red" (or the "red' regions of the visual field" in Peacocke's language) are mythical creatures of a modern-day sense-datum theory. The view also implies that when an object looks red, it looks disposed to produce red' regions in the visual field. And that seems excessively sophisticated.

The representational version has a related problem: if "red" literally means "disposed to look red [etc.]," then "looks red" will have to mean "looks disposed to look red [etc.]"—which is surely false. This—like related objections about circularity—shows that "red" cannot mean "disposed to look red [etc.]"; but it may not rule out a nonobvious identity of redness and the disposition to look red [etc.], or an a priori necessary coextensiveness.

A final challenge—for both versions of the dispositional view—is more serious. Imagine a yellow object that also emits death rays, so that anyone who looks at it is killed before he can see its color. The object will be yellow but have no disposition to produce experiences as of yellow in normal observers. (The example is due to Kripke.) One can indeed insist that the object would look yellow to normal observers if only we masked the death rays. But we need to mask the death rays without masking or changing the color. And there is no knowledge of what that amounts to, independent of a substantial conception of what color is. We may believe, for example, that the color of a surface is a matter of the way it reflects incident light; so we can change and mask anything that leaves intact the object's *way of changing incident light*. But if we have that belief, it is no thanks to the definition of yellow as simply "the disposition to look yellow [etc.]." Our prime conception of color must have a different source.

Views Available

If the physicalist and dispositional views can at best be true with respect to properties first identified by some other route, then we need a new account of our thought about color and of the object of that thought. If color thinking contains an error, the options are projectivism and eliminativism; more easily overlooked is the possibility that color thinking may contain no error and a nonreductive simple realism be the appropriate view.

Projectivism

Galileo and (at times) Descartes and Locke are the first of many to treat colors as properties of experiences,

which we wrongly 'project' onto external objects. Attractive though the view is, it faces two tasks. It must establish its right to a sensational conception of color vision; and it must clarify what exactly is meant by "projecting" a sensation. The difficulty is to find a precise account of projection that does not make the process so absurd that humans could not commit it or so innocent that it is not actually a mistake.

Representational Error Theory and Eliminativism

Some have suggested that color vision is representational—color vision involves the apparent representation of properties of external objects, but there is in fact no suitable external referent. C. L. Hardin has a related view: colors are properties neither of external objects nor of experiences. Colors are to be "eliminated," though there remain "chromatic perceptual states," which are to be reduced to neural states.

The strengths of these views must lie in the careful analysis of what is involved in naive thought about color. If naive thought makes fundamental assumptions that are false, then error theory must be the right conclusion. But an everyday commitment to the notions of normal observers and normal conditions may (as we have seen) not be disastrous. Incoherence in everyday color thought may have to be sought elsewhere.

Autonomy Views

If color experience apparently represents features of physical objects, what is to prevent us from saying that (in ordinary cases) it correctly represents features of those things, namely colors? These colors would need to be supervenient upon physical properties, though they might or might not be reducible to them. (The model might be Davidson's or Fodor's view of mental properties.) Colors would have their place in a scheme of explanation that was autonomous with respect to physics, in that its legitimacy was not dependent upon ratification by physics. And that explanatory scheme would no doubt make connections between the colors we see and the contingencies of our perceptual system—thus making those colors not only genuine features of external objects but also in a certain way subjective and relative.

The view needs to overcome the suspicions that the only genuine properties are those recognized in physics, or those intelligible from an "absolute" point of view. A defense is needed of the idea that the world (and not just the mind) can contain subjective items, and an account of the mind's thought about such items. Until these tasks are achieved the autonomy view will at best be programmatic. If they cannot be achieved, the option seems to be an error theory. They are large tasks, central in the philosophy of mind and metaphysics, and it is a measure of the difficulty of the topic that they have taken so long to come clearly to light.

[See also Armstrong, David M.; Davidson, Donald; Descartes, René; Kripke, Saul Aaron; Locke, John; Metaphyics; Philosophy of Mind; Qualia; Smart, John Jamieson Carswell.]

BIBLIOGRAPHY

Armstrong, D. M. *A Materialist Theory of the Mind.* London, 1968. Chap. 12.
Boghossian, P., and J. D. Velleman. "Colour as a Secondary Quality," *Mind* (1989), 81–103.
Hardin, C. L., *Color for Philosophers: Unweaving the Rainbow.* Indianapolis, 1988.
Hilbert, D. R. *Color and Color Perception: A Study in Anthropocentric Realism.* Stanford, CA, 1987.
Peacocke, C. *Sense and Content.* Oxford, 1983. Chap. 2.
Westphal, J. *Colour.* Oxford, 1987. 2d ed., 1991.

– JUSTIN BROACKES

COMMUNICATIVE ACTION

"Communicative action" is the central concept in Jürgen Habermas's attempt to displace the subject-centered approaches to reason characteristic of modern Western philosophy with an approach based in a theory of communication. His version of the linguistic turn leads to a 'universal pragmatics' that seeks to reconstruct the 'universal core' of language-in-use or speech. The guiding idea is that not only linguistic competence but 'communicative competence' admits of theoretical rep-

Socially coordinated activities—such as involvement in a fraternity—depend on communicative interaction. (Corbis/Philip Gould)

resentation. Speaker/hearer competence must include, not only an ability to produce and understand grammatical sentences, but also an ability to establish and understand the connections to the world that make situated utterances meaningful. The act of utterance places sentences in relation to the 'external world' of objects and events, the 'internal world' of the speaker's own experiences, and a 'social world' of shared normative expectations. From this pragmatic perspective it becomes clear that mutual understanding in language involves raising and recognizing a variety of 'validity claims'—claims to the truth of assertions in relation to the external world, to the rightness of actions in relation to a shared social world, and to the sincerity of expressions of one's own intentions, feelings, desires, and the like. Naturally, claims of these sorts can be contested and criticized. One way of settling disputed claims, weighing reasons pro and con, appealing to no force but the force of the better argument, has traditionally been regarded as fundamental to the idea of rationality, and is by Habermas as well.

The idea of 'communicative rationality' also serves to develop the categorical framework and normative foundations of Habermas's social theory: "If we assume that the human species maintains itself through the socially coordinated activities of its members and that this coordination is established through communication . . . then the reproduction of the species also requires satisfying the conditions of rationality inherent in communicative action" (Habermas, 1984, p. 397). By stressing that the goal-directed actions of individuals have to be socially coordinated, Habermas directs attention to the broader social contexts of instrumental actions. Thus, the idea of the Lifeworld (*Lebenswelt*)—the taken-for-granted, indeterminate, and inexhaustible background of all our activities—is introduced as a necessary dimension of communicative interaction.

In the course of social and cultural rationalization, the use of reasons or grounds to gain intersubjective recognition for contestable validity claims has taken an increasingly reflective turn in certain domains. Modes of argumentation have been differentiated and discursive institutions established that permit sustained, organized discussions of specific types of validity claims. And this has made learning processes possible in such dimensions as science and technology, law and morality. That means, Habermas argues, that cultural and social changes cannot be understood solely in terms of external, contingent factors; they often evince features that have to be grasped in terms of the differentiation, development, and institutionalization of specific dimensions of communicative reason. It is from this perspective as well that the selectivity of capitalist modernization becomes evident. Habermas argues that many of

the problems and paradoxes of modernity are rooted in a one-sidedly instrumental rationalization of culture and society—that is, in our failure to develop and institutionalize in a balanced way all the different dimensions of communicative reason. In his view the Enlightenment project has not failed but remains unfinished.

[See also Discourse Ethics; Habermas, Jürgen.]

BIBLIOGRAPHY

Works by Habermas

Communication and the Evolution of Society, translated by T. McCarthy. Boston, 1979.
The Theory of Communicative Action, 2 vols., translated by T. McCarthy. Boston, 1984–87.
Postmetaphysical Thinking, translated by W. Hohengarten. Cambridge, MA, 1992.

Works on Habermas

Cooke, M. *Language and Reason: A Study of Habermas's Pragmatics.* Cambridge, MA, 1994.
Honneth, A., and H. Joas, eds. *Communicative Action.* Cambridge, MA, 1991.
White, S. *The Recent Work of Jürgen Habermas.* Cambridge, 1988.

— THOMAS MCCARTHY

COMMUNITARIANISM

In the 1980s communitarians displaced Marxists as the most prominent critics of liberal political theory. Communitarians share a belief that liberalism is excessively "individualistic" or "atomistic," ignoring people's dependence on communal relationships. They differ in

---

Communitarians share a belief that liberalism is excessively "individualistic" or "atomistic," ignoring people's dependence on communal relationships.

---

where they locate this flaw. Some criticize the liberal ideal of freedom of choice, arguing that people's ends in life are defined by their communal ties, not freely chosen (Sandel, 1984). Others accept the ideal of freedom of choice but criticize liberalism for ignoring its social and cultural preconditions (Taylor, 1989). Yet others argue that moral reasoning is dependent on communal traditions, so that liberal claims to universal validity are illegitimate (Walzer, 1983; MacIntyre, 1988).

[See also Liberalism; Marxism.]

BIBLIOGRAPHY

MacIntyre, A. *Whose Justice? Which Rationality?* London, 1988.
Mulhall, S., and A. Swift. *Liberals and Communitarians.* Oxford, 1992.

Sandel, M., ed. *Liberalism and Its Critics.* New York, 1984.

Taylor, C., "Cross-Purposes: The Liberal-Communitarian Debate," in N. Rosenblum, ed., *Liberalism and the Moral Life* (Cambridge, MA, 1989).

Walzer, M. *Spheres of Justice: A Defense of Pluralism and Equality.* New York, 1983.

– WILL KYMLICKA

COMPUTATION

The growth of logic in computer science since the late sixties has been explosive. Several conferences are either devoted to logic or rely heavily on it. Given the enormous body of literature thus produced, a comprehensive survey is out of the question. What follows, therefore, is merely a sampling, with some pointers to other topics and to the literature.

Logic Programming

Let the letters F, M, and A stand respectively for the predicates "father of," "mother of," and "ancestor of." Then the implications $F(x,y) \rightarrow A(x,y)$, $M(x,y) \rightarrow A(x,y)$ and $A(x,z)$ & $A(y,z) \rightarrow A(x,z)$ all hold. These implications, written with a backward arrow ← and ",", replacing "&" become the logic program (1) $A(x,y) \leftarrow F(x,y)$ (2) $A(x,y) \leftarrow M(x,y)$ (3) $A(x,y) \leftarrow A(x,z)$, $A(z,y)$.

It turns out that a proof rule called SLD-resolution allows us to compute all true instances $A(a,b)$ using (1)–(3) if all true instances of F and M are given. This technique, implemented in the programming language Prolog, turns many definitions into programs and is much used in artificial intelligence.

However, we cannot derive true instances $\neg A(a,b)$ this way, even if all true instances of $\neg F$ and $\neg M$ are given. Reiter suggests adding the "closed world assumption" (CWA), which intuitively amounts to adding "and these are all the ancestors" to (1)–(3). However, the CWA cannot be effectively implemented. An effectively implementable alternative is to add the "negation as failure" rule, which says in effect that if the search for a justification of $A(a,b)$ is completed and does not succeed, then we should conclude $\neg A(a,b)$. Unfortunately, infinite but futile searches cannot be handled this way and so this alternative is incomplete.

Logics of Programs

One writes programs to accomplish a task. However, programs do not always accomplish their goals. Hence the need for logics to prove their correctness—that is, that they accomplish the desired goals.

HOARE LOGIC. One strength of Hoare Logic is that it respects modularity. A program is usually made up of simpler parts, and it helps to be able to derive properties of programs from those of their subparts. Another feature of Hoare Logic is that it splits up program correctness into two issues: termination—showing that the program does end, and partial correctness—showing that if the program does end, it yields correct results. The partial correctness statement (PCA) $\{A\}\alpha\{B\}$ says that if the property A holds at the start of the program α then on termination the property B will hold. The properties A and B are usually expressed by first order formulas. One of Hoare's rules is: from $\{A\}\alpha\{B\}$ and $\{B\}\beta\{C\}$ derive $\{A\}\alpha;\beta\{C\}$, where $\alpha;\beta$ is the program: "first do α and then do β." (There are similar rules for the other program constructs such as "if A holds then do α else β" and "while A holds do α"). Now if we want to prove a true assertion $\{A\}\alpha;\beta\{C\}$, we will need to find a B such that $\{A\}\alpha\{B\}$ and $\{B\}\beta\{C\}$ both hold.

One writes programs to accomplish a task,

but programs do not always accomplish their goals.

Hence the need for logics to prove their correctness.

Unfortunately, though the requisite B always exists, it might not be expressible in first order logic even if A and C are, so that the Hoare rule cannot be used.

DYNAMIC LOGIC. Pratt's solution to the Hoare rule problem is to extend the language of first order logic by allowing program modalities $[\alpha]$. $[\alpha]B$ means that B will hold if and when α terminates. Thus $\{A\}\alpha\{B\}$ holds if and only if A implies $[\alpha]B$. Also, to prove $\{A\}\alpha,\beta\{C\}$, the formula $[\beta]C$ will work as the intermediate B whose absence was a problem above. Propositional dynamic logic can be effectively axiomatized, a fact shown independently by Gabbay and Parikh. Dynamic logic also allows us to express dispositions—for example, a substance is fragile if, when thrown, it will break. So we can write *Fragile(x)* ↔ *[thrown]Broken(x)*. Thus dynamic logic may well have a domain of applications even larger than intended. An extension of dynamic logic is game logic, which can be used to show that many-person interactions have certain desired properties—for example, that an algorithm for sharing something among n people is fair.

TEMPORAL LOGIC. An alternative to dynamic logic, followed by Pnueli and others, is to abandon modularity, and reason about one program at a time using temporal reasoning, focusing on the passage of time as a program runs. Thus one will use temporal operators such as "the property A will hold sometime in the future," or "A will hold until B does." The time structure may be linear or it may be branching. The latter case arises if the course of the program is not determined but depends on random events, such as coin tosses, or on external influence.

Non-Monotonic Logics

Tarski's monotonicity condition for the notion of consequence is that if a set of propositions T implies *A* and T ⊂ T′ then T′ also implies *A*. However, there are many situations where this condition fails, especially if *A* is not certain but only very likely given T. A standard example given is that if Tweety is a bird, then Tweety flies, but if we know in addition that Tweety is a penguin, then we conclude that she does not fly. Non-monotonicity occurs in many areas: in default logic, in circumscription, in the logic of knowledge, in the logic of conditionals, and in belief revision. Space limitations prevent us from giving details.

Knowledge and Belief

Formal treatments of knowledge and belief have acquired a great deal of importance in computer science. The TARK (Theoretical Aspects of Reasoning about Knowledge) conferences are devoted to the applications of the logics of knowledge and belief in computer science, economics and artificial intelligence. These logics tend to be multi-modal S4 or S5 logics with several necessity operators, one for each knower, so that interesting questions such as, "does Jill know that Bob does not know that Jill likes tennis?" can be posed and dealt with. Common or mutual knowledge has been a particularly interesting notion. It turns out that if *i* and *j* are individuals and *p* is some fact then the statements "*i* knows *p*," "*j* knows that *i* knows *p*," "*i* knows that *j* knows that *i* knows *p*" are strictly increasing in logical strength. The conjunction of all these infinitely many statements is *mutual knowledge of p* between *i* and *j*. Another important problem is dealing with the lack of logical omniscience, which arises because people fail to know the logical consequences of other facts that they know.

Other Topics

Other issues not touched on here include "denotational semantics," which arises out of the work of Scott, Plotkin, and others on models for the λ-calculus; "non-well-founded sets," a variant of usual set theory, in which a set can contain itself as an element, or where two sets can have each other as elements; and "zero knowledge proofs," whereby I can convince you that I have certain information, perhaps the proof of some theorem, but without actually giving it to you. Computer science has been a rich lode of ideas in logic, and also a user of ideas in logic from philosophy and mathematics. This fruitful interchange promises to continue for quite some time.

[See also Artificial Intelligence; Set Theory.]

BIBLIOGRAPHY

Aezel, P. *Non-well-founded Sets*. Stanford, CA, 1988.
Fagin, R., J. Halpern, Y. Moses, and M. Vardi. *Reasoning About Knowledge*. Cambridge, MA, 1995. (Logic of knowledge)
Goldwasser, S., S. Micali, and C. Rackoff. "The Knowledge Complexity of Interactive Protocols," *Society for Industrial and Applied Mathematics Journal of Computing*, Vol. 18 (1989), 186–208. (Zero-knowledge proofs)
Kozen, D., and R. Parikh. "An Elementary Completeness Proof for PDL," *Theoretical Computer Science*, Vol. 14 (1981), 113–18. (Dynamic logic)
Lloyd, J. W. *Foundations of Logic Programming*, 2d ed. New York, 1987. (Logic programming)
Marek, W., and M. Truszynski. *Non-monotonic Logic*. New York, 1991.
Parikh, R. "The Logic of Games," *Annals of Discrete Mathematics*, Vol. 24 (1985), 111–40. (Game logic)
———. "Logical Omniscience, in D. Leivant, ed., *Logic and Computational Complexity* (New York, 1995).
Plotkin, G. "A Powerdomain Construction," *Society for Industrial and Applied Mathematics Journal of Computing* (1976), 452–87. (Denotational semantics)
Pnueli, A. "The Temporal Logic of Programs," *Proceedings of the 18th Annual IEEE Symposium on Foundations of Computer Science* (1977), 46–57. (Temporal logic)
Pratt, V. "Semantical Considerations on Floyd-Hoare Logic," *Proceedings of the 17th Annual Symposium on Foundations of Computer Science* (1976), 109–21. (Dynamic logic)
Scott, D. "Data Types as Lattices," *Society for Industrial and Applied Mathematics Journal of Computing*, Vol. 5 (1976), 522–87. (Denotational semantics)
van Leeuwen, J., ed. *Handbook for Theoretical Computer Science*, Vol. B. Cambridge, MA, 1980.

– ROHIT PARIKH

COMPUTATIONAL MODEL OF MIND, THE

Computer science has been notably successful in building devices capable of performing sophisticated intellectual tasks. Impressed by these successes, many philosophers of mind have embraced a computational account of the mind. Computationalism, as this view is called, is committed to the literal truth of the claim that the mind is a computer: mental states, processes, and events are computational states, processes, and events.

But what exactly are computational states, processes, and events? Traditionally, computational processes have been understood as rule-governed manipulations of internal symbols or representations (what computer scientists call data structures). Though these representations have meaning (i.e., semantic content), the rules apply to them solely in virtue of their structural properties, in the same way that the truth-preserving rules of formal logic apply to the syntax or formal character of natural-language sentences, irrespective of their semantic content. Developments in computer science in the 1980s, in particular the construction of connectionist machines—devices capable of performing cognitive tasks but without fixed symbols over which their operations are defined—have necessitated a broadening of the notion of computation. Connectionist processes are not naturally interpretable as manipulations of internal symbols. Connectionist devices notwithstanding, philosophers committed to the computational model of mind tend to interpret computation in classical terms, claiming that mental processes are manipulations of symbols in an internal code or language of thought (Fodor, 1974).

Computationalism has been the predominant paradigm in cognitive psychology since the demise of behaviorism in the early 1960s. The failure of behaviorism can be traced in no small part to its refusal to consider the inner causes of behavior, in particular the capacity of intelligent organisms to represent their environment and use their representations in controlling and modulating their interactions with the environment. Computationalism avoids this failing, explaining intelligent behavior as the product of internal computational processes that manipulate (construct, store, retrieve, etc.) symbolic representations of the organism's environment.

Many philosophers of mind find computationalism attractive for two reasons. First, it promises a physicalistic account of mind; specifically, it promises to explain mental phenomena without positing any mysterious nonphysical substances, properties, or events. Computational operations, which apply to the structural properties of objects in their domain (that is, symbols), are physically realized in the computer. Second, it promises a nonreductive account of mind. Although computational processes are physically realized, to describe a device as a computer is not to say anything specific about how the posited computational processes are realized in the device. So too with the mind. If mental processes are computational processes, then these processes are physically realized, but computationalism entails nothing as regards the specific nature of the realization. Indeed, nothing requires that the realization of mental processes be neural. Computationalists take it to be a contingent fact about human mental processes that they are realized in neural matter; these same processes might in other creatures or devices be realized in other ways (e.g., in a silicon-based circuitry). In this respect, computational explanation is a species of functional explanation: it provides an analysis of a cognitive capacity in terms of the organized interaction of distinct components of the system, which are themselves functionally characterized—that is, described in terms of what they do rather than what they are made of.

As a hypothesis about the nature of mind, computationalism is not uncontentious. Important aspects of the mental have so far resisted computational analysis. Computational theorists have had very little to say about the nature of conscious experience. While computers perform many intellectual tasks impressively, no one has succeeded in building a computer that can plausibly be said to feel pain or experience joy. It is quite possible that consciousness requires an explanation in terms of the biochemistry of the brain. In other words, the computationalist strategy of prescinding from the neural details of mental processes may mean that conscious phenomena will escape its explanatory net.

Computationalism is committed to the literal truth

of the claim that the mind is a computer:

mental states, processes, and events

are computational states, processes, and events.

If conscious mental phenomena resist computational analysis, then the computational model of mind cannot be said to provide a general account of the human mind; however, the model might still provide the basis for a theory of those cognitive capacities that do not involve consciousness in any essential way. Cognitive psychologists have applied the computational model to the study of human language processing, memory, vision, and motor control, often with impressive results. Domain-specific processes such as syntactic processing and early vision, about which it might plausibly be argued that the information available to the process is tightly constrained, have proved most amenable to computational analysis. Domain-general or "central" processes such as decision making and rational revision of belief in response to new information have so far resisted computational treatment. Their intractability is due in part to the fact that general constraints on the information that might be relevant to solutions are difficult, if not impossible, to specify. Characterizing how an agent is able to continuously update its knowledge store as the world around it changes is a formidable technical problem known as the "frame problem" in the field of artificial intelligence (AI). Unless it can be solved, or otherwise sidestepped, computationalism has a slim chance of providing a general account of human cognitive capacities, even those not essentially involving consciousness.

Computationalism also requires a psychosemantics—that is, an account of how the internal representations it postulates acquire their meaning. In virtue of what fact does a particular data structure mean Snow is white rather than Snow is red? The meanings of natural-language sentences are fixed by public agreement, but inner symbols must acquire their meaning in some other way. Though there have been several proposals, none enjoys consensus in the field.

A related difficulty for computationalism has been raised by John Searle, who argues that understanding cannot be a computational process. The manipulation of symbols according to rules that operate only on their structural properties is, according to Searle, a fundamentally unintelligent process. The argument, which many have found unconvincing, is formulated explicitly for classical or rule-based computational models, but if Searle is right it would apply to any mechanical model of the mind, hence to connectionist models as well.

[See also Artificial Intelligence; Connectionism; Philosophy of Mind; Physicalism, Materialism.]

BIBLIOGRAPHY

Fodor, J. *The Language of Thought.* New York, 1974.
Haugeland, J. *Artificial Intelligence: The Very Idea.* Cambridge, MA, 1985.
Posner, M., ed. *Foundations of Cognitive Science.* Cambridge, MA, 1989.
Pylyshyn, Z. W. *Computation and Cognition.* Cambridge, MA, 1984.
Searle, J. "Minds, Brains, and Programs," *Behavioral and Brain Sciences,* Vol. 3 (1980), 417–24. Published with critical commentaries.
Sterelny, K. *The Representational Theory of Mind.* Oxford, 1990. A useful introduction to basic issues in computationalism.

— FRANCES EGAN

COMPUTER ETHICS

Computer ethics is a branch of applied ethics that considers ethical issues raised by computing technology. Computing technology, which includes hardware, software, and networks, is both flexible and powerful. Computers can be programmed or trained to perform a wide range of functions, and because of their logical malleability computers have numerous and diverse applications in our society. Computing technology is revolutionizing society, and ethical issues abound.

What rights do people have to use

computer technology and to be protected from it?

Computer ethics is philosophically interesting, not merely because computing technology is widely used, but because computing technology raises intriguing conceptual issues and serious ethical problems for so-

Children may find pornography readily accessible on computer networks, creating an ethical question of responsibility for such material. (Corbis/Hannah Gal)

ciety. What rights do people have to use computer technology and to be protected from it? When computing technology is deployed in a novel way, clear ethical guidelines for its use may not exist. Such policy vacuums are often accompanied by conceptual confusion about how to understand the computerized situation adequately. Hence, computer ethics involves more than simply applying ethical theory to ethical issues in computing. Computer ethics requires a philosophical analysis of the nature and impact of developing computing technology and the corresponding formulation and justification of policies for the ethical use of such technology. Traditionally, computer-ethics research has been trained on at least four broad areas of investigation: privacy, property, power, and professionalism.

Privacy is a central concern of computer ethics because computers rapidly store and search vast amounts of information. Personal information in medical documents, criminal records, and credit histories is easily retrieved and transmitted to others electronically. Individuals are vulnerable to the improper disclosure of sensitive information and to the unwitting introduction of errors into their records. Philosophically, the development of computing technology has necessitated an analysis and expansion of the concept of privacy. Now privacy is routinely understood in terms of protection and control of information as well as the protection against intrusion. Debates about the boundaries of privacy continue, because technological innovations create new informational opportunities and risks.

Property protection is a major issue within computer ethics. To what extent, for example, should computer programs be protected as intellectual property? Computer programs are algorithmic and hence mathematical in nature. Perhaps computer programs, like the Pythagorean theorem, should not be owned at all. However, many computer programs are lengthy, original human expressions and as such are entitled to copyright protection. In their operation on machines computer programs are processes, and, when they are novel, useful, nonobvious processes, they may be properly patentable. How, or even whether, computer programs should be protected depends largely on a philosophical analysis of the nature of computer programs and on a philosophical justification of protecting intellectual property. The issues of protecting computerized property extend well beyond computer programs. Computers process all kinds of data. The information stored on computers, manipulated with computers, displayed by computers, and forwarded on networks to other computers generates complex disputes about what aspects of computerized information can be owned, stolen, and regulated.

Powerful computers and networks allow us to perform tasks more easily and to accomplish some activities that we could never do without them. Those who have access to computers have access to power. One feature of this power is that computer users can act from a distance over networks and thereby accomplish goals without being observed. Like the shepherd with the ring of Gyges, a computer user may act invisibly with an elevated level of protection from harmful consequences. What are the ethical boundaries of actions performed over computer networks and how can they be enforced? And what is the proper distribution of computer power among people? Inequalities in the distribution of computing technology among age groups, sexes, races, and nations raise ethical questions. Unequal distribution of power may require ethical countermeasures to ensure fairness. To what extent, for example, should disabled citizens be assured of equal access to computing technology? Moreover, when computers are introduced into a situation, the balance of power frequently shifts among groups, sometimes quite dramatically. Workers may find themselves no longer needed for their jobs or may become easy targets of surveillance by their own computer tools. Children may find pornography readily accessible on computer networks. To what extent, if any, do rights and responsibilities change with this shifting balance of power?

What are the ethical boundaries

of actions performed over computer networks,

and how can they be enforced?

Many who design and operate computing systems regard themselves as computing professionals. But, given that anyone, regardless of educational background, can be hired to do computing, what does it mean to claim that someone is a computing professional? To what standards, including ethical standards, should computing professionals adhere? Although several debated codes of ethics have been offered to clarify what duties and responsibilities computer professionals have, professional responsibility has been difficult to establish for at least two reasons. First, unlike medicine and law, the field does not have a tradition of professional qualifying examinations and licensing, and therefore enforcement of any code of ethics is difficult. Second, the nature of computing itself makes the assessment of responsibility difficult. Computer programs are often enormously complex, written by dozens of people, and incomprehensible to any one person. Such large computer programs may be brittle in that a tiny, obscure error can shatter the performance of the entire system under certain conditions. To what extent should computing professionals be regarded as liable when such difficult-to-predict errors lead to major failures or even catastrophic results?

Computation and ethics intersect in yet another way. Although most of computer ethics concerns ethical examinations of computing situations, a philosophically rich subfield is computational ethics, which reflects on the impact computing has or theoretically may have on ethics itself. Philosophical issues in this area include questions such as: In what ways can ethical decision making be properly assisted by computational methods? In principle could a computer ever make appropriate ethical decisions? Could a computer, or perhaps a robot, ever have rights or moral responsibilities?

[See also Applied Ethics.]

BIBLIOGRAPHY

Bynum, T. W., ed. *Computers and Ethics.* Special issue of *Metaphilosophy,* Vol. 16 (1985).

Forester, T., and P. Morrison. *Computer Ethics,* 2d ed. Cambridge. MA, 1994.

Gould, C. G., ed. *The Information Web.* Boulder, CO, 1989.

Johnson, D. G. *Computer Ethics,* 2d ed. Englewood Cliffs, NJ, 1994.

Johnson, D. G., and H. Nissenbaum. *Computers, Ethics, and Social Values.* Englewood Cliffs, NJ, 1995.

— JAMES H. MOOR

CONDITIONALS

In the 1960s the problem of conditionals was thought to concern so-called counterfactuals such as "If the match had been struck it would have burned," as contrasted with an indicative conditional such as "If the match was struck it burned," which was thought could be false only if the match was struck but did not burn—that is, was thought to be equivalent to a material conditional (cf. Goodman, 1954). Since then, while the counterfactual has continued to be a subject of controversy, there has been increasing concern with the 'material conditional analysis' of the indicative (MatCond), and no fewer than fifteen books and a hundred scholarly papers on the topic, in fields as disparate as formal logic, artificial intelligence, psychology, and linguistics, appeared between 1967 and 1994. This article will attempt to explain this surge of interest and to outline recent currents of thought, especially on indicatives.

Dissatisfaction with MatCond stems in large part from the fact that it entails 'fallacies' such as that the intuitively absurd inference

I_1 Today is not Tuesday; therefore, if today is Tuesday then tomorrow is Thursday.

is valid because its conclusion must be true if its premise is true. Some of these fallacies have long been known, but more recently other fallacies have been the subject of attention, and new ones have come to light, even apparent counterexamples to the rule of *modus ponens,* one being a variant of counterexamples due to V. McGee (1985):

I_2 If that is a dog, then, if it weighs 500 pounds, it is a 500-pound dog. That is a dog. Therefore, if that weighs 500 pounds it is a 500-pound dog.

While these kinds of examples have been disputed, it is not implausible that a person could assert both premises but deny the conclusion, thinking that whatever 'it' is, if it weighs 500 pounds, it can only look like a dog.

Responses to these challenges to MatCond have tended to be of three kinds: (1) to argue that the theory is right, and seeming fallacies can be explained by ref-

erence to what Grice (1989) called the logic of conversation, as explained below; (2) to advance alternative accounts of the truth conditions of conditional statements; (3) to argue that the concept of truth does not apply to conditionals but that another kind of 'rightness', namely probability, does apply to them, and the premises of inferences such as I_1 have this kind of rightness but their conclusions do not.

The first response distinguishes the truth conditions of ordinary-language statements from what can reasonably be inferred on the assumption that the persons who assert them conform to 'maxims of conversational quality'. Thus, Grice explains the seeming absurdity of inference I_1 by arguing that, while the truth of its premise guarantees the truth of its conclusion, it would violate maxims of conversational quality to assert its conclusion when its premise can be asserted. Others, including Lewis (1974) and Jackson (1987), have followed this general approach while disagreeing with Grice on points of detail. It is noteworthy, incidentally, that many persons who reject this defense of MatCond nevertheless accept the validity and importance of the distinction between truth-conditional logic and 'conversational logic'.

Most of the alternative theories of the truth of "If P then Q" reject the idea that its truth value is determined by the truth values of P and Q, and a more complicated account is required. The best known of these are based on modal concepts, especially that of truth in a world (ModCond). The version due to Stalnaker (1968), variations of which have been proposed by Lewis (1974—for counterfactuals), Nute (1980), and others, holds that "If P then Q" is true in a world w if Q is true in the world 'nearest' to w in which P is true. The notion of nearness of worlds is difficult to explicate, but it can be represented geometrically quite simply. In figure 1 P-worlds and Q-worlds—that is, worlds in which P and

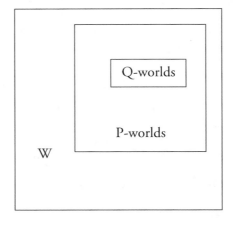

Figure 1

Q are true—are pictured as occupying rectangles in a 'universe of possible worlds', and w is pictured as a point in this universe. Most important, the figure represents "not P" as being true in world w, while "If P then Q" is false, because Q is not true in the world nearest to w in which P is true. It follows that, according to ModCond, inferences of the form of I_1 are invalid, which accords better with intuition than with Mat-Cond.

In application to other patterns of inference, ModCond has the surprising consequence that many inferences that are not usually questioned are invalid. For instance, the reader can easily see that figure 1 pictures contraposition as invalid, because "If P then not Q" is true but "if Q then not P" is false in world w. Moreover, there are ordinary-language examples that confirm this, such as:

I_3 If it rained it didn't rain hard. Therefore, if it rained hard it didn't rain.

In contrast, ModCond does imply the validity of all 'traditionally valid' inferences that do not involve conditionals, as well as such conditional inferences as *modus tollens* and *modus ponens*. Of course, that it implies the validity of the latter means that it cannot account for the seeming invalidity of inference I_2, which is one instance of a general problem that arises in connection with conditionals that are embedded in larger sentences, which will be discussed following comments on the third approach.

This approach, originally proposed independently by Adams (1965), Ellis (1969), and Jeffrey (1964), has many similarities to ModCond, but it considers not the truth-in-worlds of conditionals but their probabilities (ProbCond), and it argues that what is wrong with inferences such as I_1–I_3 is that their premises can be probable while their conclusions are improbable, not that their premises can be true while their conclusions are false. This is intuitively obvious in I_3, since it can be highly probable that if it rained it didn't rain hard, but it would be absurd to claim that if it rained hard it didn't rain. Figure 1 can also be interpreted to picture this, assuming that "It rained" corresponds to region P, "It rained hard" corresponds to region Q, and the probability of "if it rained it rained hard" corresponds to the probability that if a world chosen at random lies inside P then it lies inside Q. This is the same as the proportion of P that lies inside Q, and, similarly, the probability of "if it rained it didn't rain hard" corresponds to the proportion of P that lies outside Q. Assuming this, "If it rained it didn't rain hard" is pictured as probable because most of P lies outside Q, while "If it rained

hard it didn't rain" is pictured as totally improbable since all of Q lies inside P.

Given the foregoing, it will not surprise the reader that there is a kind of 'congruence' between the ModCond and ProbCond theories of the conditional. This has been made precise by Adams (1977) and Gibbard (1981), who proved, assuming a precise definition of 'probabilistic validity', that inferences like I_1 and I_3 that do not involve embedded conditionals are valid according to one theory if and only if they are valid according to the other.

But the above congruence is limited because, while ModCond applies to embedded conditionals, the ProbCond theory does not. This is brought out in application to the controversial principle of the conditional excluded middle, which concerns propositions such as

P_1 Either, if it rained it rained hard, or if it rained it didn't rain hard.

which is true in all possible worlds according to Stalnaker's version of ModCond but not according to Lewis's (1974) version (with the qualification that Lewis applies this only to counterfactuals, which is inessential to the present point). In contrast, ProbCond does not even apply to sentences with embedded conditionals, as in P_1 and, ipso facto, it does not apply to ones such as "If that is a dog, then, if it weighs 500 pounds, it is a 500-pound dog," which enters into I_2. This is explained by some very striking discoveries concerning the ProbCond theory, namely Lewis's (1976) triviality results, which can be pictured intuitively in figure 1.

The probability of a factual proposition such as "It rained" is represented in the figure by the area of the region that corresponds to it, namely rectangle P, and it can be interpreted as the probability of being in a world in which "It rained" is true. On the other hand, the probability of the conditional "If it rained it rained hard" is represented not by an area but by the proportion of rectangle P that lies inside Q. This is a ratio of areas, and it cannot be interpreted as the probability of being in a world in which something is true. Ipso facto, the probability of a disjunction of conditionals as in P_1 cannot be the probability of being in a world in which one of its disjuncts is true. Using the precise mathematical concept of conditional probability, Lewis showed that if ProbCond is right then no 'standard' kind of probability can apply to sentences with embedded conditionals. However, it is noteworthy that a number of writers, including Appiah (1985), Jackson (1987), McGee (1989), and van Fraassen (1976), who accept different versions of the ProbCond theory, have attempted to extend it in 'nonstandard' ways to embeddings of various kinds. Necessarily, all of these extensions are either partial, in the sense that they do not apply to all grammatical sentences with embedded conditionals, or they give up certain basic laws in these applications. Thus, McGee gives up *modus ponens* as applied to I_2, and van Fraassen gives up a basic law of 'probability dynamics'. The latter is important because of its connection with counterfactuals.

Since the 1960s, while the counterfactual has continued to be a subject of controversy, there has been increasing concern with the "material conditional analysis" of the indicative.

The most notable development in the theory of counterfactuals is the application to them of the new 'models' of the indicative, similar to ModCond and ProbCond. For instance, while "If that match had been struck it would have burned" and "If that match was struck it burned" are not equivalent, they can both be diagrammed in the same way as "If it rained it rained hard." Assuming this, Stalnaker argues that if distances between worlds are measured 'counterfactually' the first is right, while if they are measured 'indicatively' the second is right, and Adams (1975, chap. 4) and Skyrms (1981) argue that something very like this holds for probabilities measured counterfactually and indicatively. Thus, probabilities and distances between worlds are 'perspectively-dependent', unlike material truth values, and, in the case of probabilities at least, the counterfactual perspective at one time is often the same as an indicative perspective at another. For instance, the probability that attaches to "If that match had been struck it would have burned" *now* is, plausibly, equal to the probability that *would have* attached to the indicative "If that match is struck it will burn" at some prior time.

But the intertwining of conditionals with 'perspectives' on distance and probability raises complicated issues connected with a still deeper one with which this article will close. Much current controversy centers on the question of whether "If it rained it didn't rain hard" can have the same kind of perspective-independent 'correspondence with the facts' that "It rained" has (cf. Edgington, 1991). ModCond and ProbCond suggest that this is not the case, and, more fundamental, ProbCond's suggestion that perspective-dependent probabilities are logically 'more important' in the evaluation of condi-

tionals than are perspective-independent truth values raises the question of what the values of truth and probability are. That the controversy concerning conditionals raises this question, which goes to the heart of all of logical theory, shows how much is at stake in it.

[See also Artificial Intelligence; Goodman, Nelson; Grice, Herbert Paul; Philosophy of Language; Probability; Truth.]

BIBLIOGRAPHY

Adams, E. W. "On the Logic of Conditionals," *Inquiry*, Vol. 8 (1965), 166–97.
———. *The Logic of Conditionals*. Dordrecht, 1975.
———. "A Note on Comparing Probabilistic and Modal Logics of Conditionals," *Theoria*, Vol. 43, No. 3 (1977), 186–94.
Appiah, A. *Assertion and Conditionals*. Cambridge, 1985.
Edgington, D. "The Mystery of the Missing Matter of Fact," *Aristotelian Society Supplementary Volume*, Vol. 65 (1991), 185–209.
Ellis, B. D. "An Epistemological Concept of Truth," in R. Brown and C. D. Rollins, eds., *Contemporary Philosophy in Australia* (London, 1969).
Gibbard, A. "Two Recent Theories of Conditionals," in W. Harper, G. Pearce, and R. Stalnaker, eds., *Ifs* (Dordrecht, 1980).
Goodman, N. *Fact, Fiction, and Forecast*. London, 1954.
Grice, H. P., "Indicative Conditionals," in *Studies in the Way of Words* (Oxford, 1989).
Jackson, F. *Conditionals*. Oxford, 1987.
Jeffrey, R. C. "If" (abstract), *Journal of Philosophy*, Vol. 61 (1964), 702–3.
Lewis, D. *Counterfactuals*. Cambridge, MA, 1974.
———. "Conditional Probabilities and Probabilities of Conditionals," *Philosophical Review*, Vol. 76 (1976), 297–315.
McGee, V. "A Counterexample to Modus Ponens," *Journal of Philosophy*, Vol. 82 (1985), 462–71.
———. "Conditional Probabilities and Compounds of Conditionals," *Philosophical Review*, Vol. 98 (1989), 484–542.
Nute, D. *Theories of Conditionals*. Dordrecht, 1980.
Pollock, J. L. *Subjunctive Reasoning*. Dordrecht, 1976.
Skyrms, B. "The Prior Propensity Account of Counterfactuals," in W. Harper, G. Pearce, and R. Stalnaker, eds., *Ifs* (Dordrecht, 1981).
Stalnaker, R. C. "A Theory of Conditionals," in N. Rescher, ed., *Studies in Logical Theory*. American Philosophical Quarterly monograph series, no. 2 (Oxford, 1968).
van Fraassen, B. "Probabilities of Conditionals," in W. Harper and C. Hooker, eds., *Foundations of Probability Theory, Statistical Theory, and Statistical Theories of Science*, Vol. 1 (Dordrecht, 1976).

– ERNEST ADAMS

CONFIRMATION THEORY

Confirmation theory seeks to describe normative relations between hypotheses and evidence, relations that measure or indicate whether and how much any body of evidence warrants belief or lends credence to any hypothesis. A related enterprise, decision theory, seeks (among other things) to describe normative methods for deciding whether to reject or to accept hypotheses. Still another related enterprise—variously called estimation theory (in statistics), or learning theory, or reliability analysis (in computer science)—seeks to describe strategies for conjecturing hypotheses from data that under specified assumptions reliably converge to the correct hypothesis. All three methodological strands are represented in philosophy and in statistics.

In statistics, Ronald Fisher developed the most influential confirmation theory in this century. Fisher's work on the testing of statistical hypotheses, on the design and analysis of experiments and their outcomes, and on "fiducial inference" to the probabilities of hypotheses, gave an account of scientific method largely unified by his use of the concept of "information." Biologists, psychologists, medical scientists, and social scientists of every kind continue to be influenced by Fisher's writings, in part because of the wealth of concrete applications he provided and because of the comparative ease with which his calculations can be executed in suitably idealized circumstances. Fisher's views have been debated at length in the statistical literature and examined, defended, or criticized by a number of philosophical writers. Bruno De Finetti proposed a quite different account of confirmation, founded on the idea that probability measures a (rational) individual's degree of belief and that as evidence is acquired, the degree of belief should change by forming the conditional probability on the new evidence. Under the misnomer Bayesian statistics, De Finetti's viewpoint has found an increasing following among economists, social scientists, and others, especially since digital computers have made possible the computation of conditional probability distributions appropriate to many applied issues. Jerzy Neyman and Egon Pearson developed a decision theoretic approach in which a decision is made whether to reject a hypothesis in the light of evidence, and decision rules are justified by the limiting frequency of errors they produce in an infinite sequence of such tests. Corrupted versions of Neyman and Pearson's ideas are widely used in applications. Modern statistical estimation theory also owes a great deal to Fisher, who introduced concepts of likelihood, consistency, bias, sufficiency, and efficiency. Estimation theory seeks rules (functions from data to hypotheses) for conjecturing hypotheses—usually hypotheses about the values of a parameter—such that under appropriate assumptions the rules can be shown to converge to the correct hypothesis as the size of samples increases without bound, and so that the rules have other virtues. Although estimation theory is an investigation of a restricted class of procedures for scientific discovery, the mainstream of the statistical community has adamantly opposed the investigation of rules for discovery in broader contexts, for example rules for conjecturing from data "statistical

models" or parametrized causal hypotheses. Nonetheless, such procedures have been repeatedly proposed in the statistical literature—factor analysis and stepwise multiple regression are examples—but without any rigorous study of their reliability.

A number of philosophical proposals have attempted to analyze confirmation as a logical relation between evidence, represented by a body of propositions, and hypotheses. Carl G. Hempel's well-known proposal held that a body of singular evidence statements confirms a hypothesis statement if the hypothesis statement is true in every domain in which the evidence is true and each member of the domain is named in the evidence. Ludwig Wittgenstein, and later and more successfully, Rudolf Carnap, developed confirmation theories in which hypotheses were given probability measures determined by syntactical relations between hypotheses and evidence. Carnap's theories were restricted to rather simple first order, monadic languages, but later alternatives developed by Richard Jeffrey and Jaakko Hintikka were not so limited. None of these proposals have had much influence on scientific practice, perhaps because they assumed the data to be consistent with the true, nonstatistical, hypothesis, and in most sciences no data are consistent with any interesting hypotheses of that kind. After mid-century, several philosophical writers proposed accounts of confirmation as change of subjective degree of belief measured by probabilities and effected by forming conditional probability distributions given the evidence. Clark Glymour provided a series of puzzles for Bayesian confirmation theory, the most discussed of which, the problem of old evidence, asks how accepted data can confirm a novel theory.

Isaac Levi, Patrick Maher, and others have combined subjective probability with decision theory to represent scientific inference as a series of decision problems involving adjustments of probabilities and utilities for features of hypotheses such as truth, simplicity, and informativeness. The same idea has been pursued by some Bayesian statistical writers. Levi's account includes a carefully developed theory of belief change in which hypotheses may become so accepted that they determine (literally) truth but may nonetheless be abandoned in favor of other, contradictory beliefs that in turn determine a new set of truths.

A standard problem for confirmation theory has been to explain how evidence given under a description bears on hypotheses that are stated in different terms. Hypothetico-deductive accounts of confirmation appear to entail that arbitrary and irrelevant hypotheses are confirmed by data. Herman Weyl, Rudolf Carnap, and Hans Reichenbach suggested that certain hypotheses connecting evidence descriptions and more theoretical language are stipulations that specify (partly) the "meanings" of theoretical terms, and that these stipulations function as tacit premises in relating theory to evidence. Clark Glymour proposed a related "bootstrap" account in which evidence is relevant to a hypothesis only relative to a theory, including possibly a theory that entails the evidence. The latter feature of the proposal was refuted in a series of papers by various authors, principally in issues of the journal *Philosophy of Science*.

The most interesting challenge to the very idea of confirmation theory comes from a literature on reliability analysis that developed from papers in the *Journal of Symbolic Logic* by Hilary Putnam and E. Mark Gold in the 1960s, but which traces a philosophical heritage to Plato's *Meno*. Reliability analysis takes the goal of inquiry to be to settle upon the truth, eventually, and the aim of methodology to study methods by which that may be done reliably. Reliability requires that, no matter which of some collection of hypotheses is true, a method converge to the truth. Methods of inference may be subject to a variety of constraints, for example, constraints on memory, or computability, or number of hypothesis revisions, or amount of data required to succeed, or experimental powers of the inquirer. The sense in which inquiry gets to the truth may also be varied—successful inquiry may be required to reach the truth with certainty at some point; may instead be required only to make at most a finite number of errors; or may be required to assign numerical values (between 0 and 1) to hypotheses in such a way that the sequence of values assigned to true hypotheses, and only true hypotheses, approaches 1 in the limit. Roughly in the spirit of Karl Popper's philosophy of science, or Hans Reichenbach's, an inquirer or scientist is viewed as producing a sequence of hypotheses in response to changing evidence rather than a sequence of confirmations or disconfirmations. Daniel Osherson, Scott Weinstein, and Michael Stob provided the first book-length introduction to the subject, and have also produced a series of methodological results in related papers. The best introduction to the subject now available is Kevin Kelly's *The Logic of Reliable Inquiry* (1995).

The relations between confirmation theory and reliability theory are intricate and interesting. If no limits are imposed on the mathematical powers of a Bayesian inquirer, then for every discovery problem that can be reliably solved in the limit by a Putnam/Gold-style learner, there is a prior probability distribution for which the Bayesian reliably converges to the truth as well. The converse is obviously true. The equivalence fails, however, if both learners must be computable, in the sense that they calculate functions from data to hypotheses (or from data to degrees of belief) that could be computed by some Turing machine. In that case the reliability of Bayesian methods is dominated by that of computable Putnam/Gold-style learners. Other methodological principles championed by philosophers of science are subject to similar criticism; there are discovery problems, for example, that can be solved reliably by computable procedures, but not by any computable procedures that output only hypotheses consistent with the data and background assumptions; Popper's method of generating a hypothesis and testing and holding it until the data conflict can be shown to be suboptimal.

A standard problem for confirmation theory

has been to explain how evidence

given under a description bears on hypotheses

that are stated in different terms.

From a Bayesian or confirmation theoretic perspective, reliable Putnam/Gold learners may be irrational and arbitrary and fail to measure the weight of finite evidence. From the reliabilist point of view, confirmation theories, Bayesian or otherwise, are a codification of prejudices that can interfere with the principal goal of inquiry—finding out something interesting. Reliability analysis challenges the view that confirmation relations and philosophical methodology have any normative force when the aim of inquiry is to discover informative truths. If, further, "ought" implies "can," and humans and their inference devices are all Turing computable, the normative basis for Bayesian and other methodologies is still more dubious. On the other hand, it is easy to show that reliability is impossible to obtain in many contexts without very strong background assumptions, and reliability analysis provides no account of how such assumptions can be justified.

Philosophical confirmation theory has found few applications. One exception is computer science, where machine learning methods as early as the 1960s implemented various confirmation functions as cogs in hypothesis-assessment schemes. Thus Hempel's confirmation theory was used in the Dendral and Meta-Dendral programs designed to infer chemical structure from mass spectroscopy data, and some early programs for medical diagnosis used Bayesian confirmation theory. A Popperian machine learning scheme was developed by Ehud Shapiro. Patrick Langley and his collaborators used bootstrap techniques in some of their programs for reproducing historical scientific discoveries. Reliability analysis has been applied in cognitive psychology to produce constraints on procedures by which children can possibly learn the grammars of natural languages. Most recently, the reliability framework has been applied to study inference strategies in cognitive neuropsychology.

[See also Bayesianism; Carnap, Rudolph; Decision Theory; Plato; Probability; Putnam, Hilary; Wittgenstein, Ludwig Josef Johann.]

BIBLIOGRAPHY

Earman, J., ed. *Testing Scientific Theories.* Minneapolis, 1983.

Glymour, C. *Theory and Evidence.* Princeton, NJ, 1980.

Howson, C., and P. Urbach. *Scientific Reasoning: The Bayesian Approach.* Chicago, 1989.

Kelly, K. *The Logic of Reliable Inquiry.* Oxford, 1995.

Langley, P., et al. *Scientific Discovery.* Cambridge, MA, 1985.

Kotz, S. *Breakthroughs in Statistics.* New York, 1992.

Levi, I. *The Fixation of Belief and Its Undoing: Changing Beliefs Through Inquiry.* Cambridge, 1991.

Maher, P. *Betting on Theories.* Cambridge, 1993.

Osherson, D., M. Stob, and S. Weinstein. *Systems that Learn.* Cambridge, MA, 1985.

Fisher, R. *Statistical Methods for Research Workers.* Oxford, 1990.

Seidenfeld, T. *Philosophical Problems of Statistical Inference: Learning from R. A. Fisher.* Theory & Decision Library, no. 22 (Norwell, MA, 1979).

– CLARK GLYMOUR

CONNECTIONISM

Connectionism is an approach within cognitive science that employs neural networks, rather than computer programs, as the basis for modeling mentality. A connectionist system, or neural network, is a structure of simple neuronlike processors called nodes or units. Each node has directed connections to other nodes, so that the nodes send and receive excitatory and inhibitory signals to and from one another. The total input to a node determines its state of activation. When a node is on, it sends out signals to the nodes to which it has output connections, with the intensity of a signal depending upon both (1) the activation level of the sending node and (2) the strength or "weight" of the connection between it and the receiving node. Typically at each moment during processing, many nodes are simultaneously sending signals to others.

When neural networks are employed for information processing, certain nodes are designated "input" units and others as "output" units, and potential patterns of activation across them are assigned interpretations. (The remaining nodes are called "hidden units.") Typically a "problem" is posed to a network by activating a pattern in the input nodes; then the various nodes in the system simultaneously send and receive signals repeatedly until the system settles into a stable configuration, the semantic interpretation of the resulting pattern in the output nodes is what the system currently represents, hence its "answer" to the problem. Connectionist systems are capable of "learning" from "experience" by having their weights changed systematically in a way that depends upon how well the network has performed in generating solutions to problems posed to it as a training regimen. (Typically the device employed is not an actual neural network but a simulation of one on a standard digital computer.)

The most striking difference between such networks and conventional computers is the lack of an executive component. In a conventional computer the behavior of the whole system is controlled at the central processing unit (CPU) by a stored program. A connectionist system lacks both a CPU and a stored program. Nevertheless, often in a connectionist system certain activation patterns over sets of hidden units can be interpreted as internal representations with interesting content, and often the system also can be interpreted as embodying, in its weighted connections, information that gets automatically accommodated during processing without getting explicitly represented via activation patterns.

Connectionist models have yielded particularly encouraging results for cognitive processes such as learning, pattern recognition, and so-called multiple-soft-constraint satisfaction (i.e., solving a problem governed by several constraints, where an optimal solution may require violating some constraints in order to satisfy others). For example, Terry Sejnowski and Charles Rosenberg trained a network they called NETtalk to convert inputs that represent a sequence of letters, spaces, and punctuation constituting written English into outputs that represent the audible sounds constituting the corresponding spoken English. (The phonetic output code then can be fed into a speech synthesizer, a device that actually produces the sounds.)

Philosophical discussion of connectionism has largely centered on whether connectionism yields or suggests a conception of mentality that is importantly different from the conception of mind-as-computer at the core of classical cognitive science. Several different nonclassical alternatives have been suggested; each has been alleged to fit well with connectionism, and each has been a locus of debate between fans and foes of connectionism. Three proposed interpretations of connectionism deserve specific mention.

On one view, the key difference between classical models of mental processes and connectionist models is that the former assume the existence of languagelike mental representations that constitute a so-called language of thought (LOT), whereas the latter supposedly favor representations that are alleged to be inherently nonlanguagelike in structure: namely, activation patterns distributed over several nodes of a network, so-called activation vectors. On this interpretation connectionism shares with classicism the assumption that cognition is computation over mental representations—that cognitive transitions conform to rules for transforming representations on the basis of their formal structure, rules that could be formulated as an explicit computer program. (In connectionist systems the rules are wired into the weights and connections rather than being explicitly represented. In classical systems some rules must be hard wired; and there may be—but need not be—other rules that are explicitly represented as stored data structures.) The key difference allegedly turns on the languagelike or non-languagelike structure of mental representations.

This construal of connectionism fits naturally with the idea that human cognition involves state transitions that are all essentially associative—in the sense that they reflect statistical correlations among items the system can represent and can be analyzed as the drawing of statistical inferences. Many fans of connectionism, including Patricia Churchland and Paul Churchland, evidently see things this way and tend to regard connectionism as breathing new life into associationism. Prominent foes of connectionism, notably Jerry Fodor and Zenon Pylyshyn, also see things this way; but they regard the link with associationism as grounds for maintaining that connectionism is bound to founder on the same general problem that plagued traditional associationism in psychology: namely, inability to account for the rich semantic coherence of much human thought. To overcome this problem, Fodor and Pylyshyn maintain, cognitive science must continue to posit both (1) mental representations that encode propositional information via languagelike syntactic structure and (2) modes of processing that are suitably sensitive to syntactic structure and are thereby sensitive to propositional content.

A second interpretation of connectionism claims that connectionist models do not really employ internal representations at all in their hidden units (and, a fortiori, do not employ internal representations with languagelike structure). This view has been defended—by Rodney Brooks, for example—on the grounds that putative representations in connectionist systems play no genuine explanatory role. It has also been defended—for instance, by Hubert Dreyfus and Stuart Dreyfus—on the basis of a Heideggerian critique of the notion of mental representation itself. The approach goes contrary to the views of most (but not all) practicing connectionists, who typically posit internal representations in connectionist models and assign them a central explanatory role.

A third interpretation assumes the existence of internal mental representations; and it does not deny—indeed, the version defended by Terence Horgan and John Tienson resolutely affirms—that mental representations often have languagelike structure. It focuses instead on the classical assumption that cognition is computation (see above). This third approach maintains (1) that much of human cognition is too rich and too subtle to conform to programmable rules and (2) that connectionism has theoretical resources for potentially explaining such nonalgorithmic cognitive processing. The approach stresses that there is a powerful branch of mathematics that applies naturally to neural networks: dynamical systems theory. According to this anticomputational construal of connectionism, there can be cognitive systems—subservable mathematically by dynamical systems, which in turn are subservable physically by neural networks—whose cognitive state transitions are not tractably computable. In other words, mental activity in these systems is too refined and too supple to conform to programmable rules. Humans are alleged to be such cognitive systems, and connectionism (so interpreted) is held to yield a more adequate picture of the mind than the classical computational picture.

Connectionist models have yielded particularly encouraging results for cognitive processes such as learning and pattern recognition.

One objection to this third interpretation of connectionism alleges that cognitive state transitions in a connectionist system must inevitably conform to programmable rules, especially since neural networks are simulable on standard computers. Another objection, directed specifically at the version that retains languagelike representations, alleges that the LOT hypothesis is intelligible only on the assumption that cognition is computation.

In much of the early philosophical debate between proponents and opponents of connectionism, the first interpretation was largely taken for granted. But as competing interpretations get articulated, defended, and acknowledged, philosophical discussion of connectionism and its potential implications becomes richer.

[See also Cognitive Science; Language of Thought; Philosophy of Mind.]

BIBLIOGRAPHY

Aizawa, K. "Representations without Rules, Connectionism, and the Syntactic Argument," *Synthese*, Vol. 101 (1994), 465–92.

Bechtel, W., and A. Abrahamsen. *Connectionism and the Mind: An Introduction to Parallel Distributed Processing.* Oxford, 1991.

Brooks, R. "Intelligence without Representation," *Artificial Intelligence*, Vol. 47 (1991), 139–59.

Churchland, P. M. *The Engine of Reason, the Seat of the Soul: A Philosophical Inquiry into the Brain.* Cambridge, MA, 1995.

Churchland, P. S. *Neurophilosophy: Toward a Unified Science of the Mind/Brain.* Cambridge, MA, 1986.

Clark, A., and J. Toribo. "Doing without Representing?" *Synthese*, Vol. 101 (1994), 404–31.

Dreyfus, H., and S. Dreyfus. "Making a Mind versus Modelling the Brain: Artificial Intelligence Back at a Branch-Point," in S. Graubard, ed., *The Artificial Intelligence Debate: False Starts, Real Foundations* (Cambridge, MA, 1988).

Fodor, J., and Z. Pylyshyn. "Connectionism and Cognitive Architecture: A Critical Analysis," *Cognition*, Vol. 28 (1988), 3–71.

Garson, J. "No Representations without Rules," *Mind and Language*, Vol. 9 (1994), 25–37.

Horgan, T., and J. Tienson, "Representations without Rules," *Philosophical Topics*, Vol. 17 (1989), 27–43.

———. "A Nonclassical Framework for Cognitive Science," *Synthese*, Vol. 101 (1994), 305–45.

———, eds., *Connectionism and the Philosophy of Mind.* Dordrecht, 1991.

McLaughlin, B., and T. A. Warfield. "The Allure of Connectionism Reexamined," *Synthese*, Vol. 101 (1994), 365–400.

Ramsey, W., S. Stich, and D. Rumelhart, eds. *Philosophy and Connectionist Theory.* Hillsdale, NJ, 1991.

Sejnowski, T., and C. Rosenberg. "Parallel Networks That Learn to Pronounce English Text," *Complex Systems*, Vol. 1 (1987), 145–68.

Tienson, J. "Introduction to Connectionism," in J. Garfield, ed., *Foundations of Cognitive Science: The Essential Readings* (New York, 1990).

van Gelder, T. J. "What Might Cognition Be if Not Computation?" in R. Port and T. J. van Gelder, eds., *Mind as Motion: Dynamics, Behavior, and Cognition* (Cambridge, MA, 1995).

— TERENCE E. HORGAN

CONSCIOUSNESS IN ANGLO-AMERICAN PHILOSOPHY

Thomas H. Huxley said, "How it is that anything so remarkable as a state of consciousness comes about as a result of irritating nervous tissue, is just as unaccountable as the appearance of Djin when Aladdin rubbed his lamp." We have no conception of our physical or functional nature that allows us to understand how it could explain our subjective experience, or so says one point of view on consciousness. This issue has dominated the discussion of consciousness in recent years.

The Explanatory Gap

Neuroscientists have hypothesized that the neural basis of consciousness is to be found in certain phase-locked 40 Hz neural oscillations. But how does a 40 Hz neural oscillation explain what it is like (in Nagel's memorable phrase) to be us? What is so special about a 40 Hz oscillation as opposed to some other physical state? And why could not there be creatures with brains just like ours in their physical and functional properties, including their 40 Hz oscillation patterns, whose owners' experiences were very unlike ours, or who had no subjective experiences at all? One does not have to suppose that there really could be creatures with brains just like ours who have different experiences or no experiences to demand an account of why not. But no one has a clue about how to answer these questions. This is the heart of the mind–body problem.

Consciousness, in the sense discussed, is phenomenal consciousness. "What's that?," you ask. There is no noncircular definition to be offered; the best that can be done is the offering of synonyms, examples, and one or another type of pointing to the phenomenon. For example, "subjective experience" and "what it is like to be us" were used earlier as synonyms. In explaining phenomenal consciousness, one can also appeal to conscious properties or qualities, e.g., the ways things seem to us, or immediate phenomenological qualities. Or one can appeal to examples: the ways things look or sound, the way pain feels, and more generally the experiential properties of sensations, feelings and perceptual experiences. One could also add that thoughts, wants, and emotions often have characteristic conscious aspects, and that a difference in representational content can make a phenomenal difference. Seeing something as a cloud differs from seeing it as a part of a painted backdrop. What it is like to hear Bulgarian spoken depends on whether one understands the language.

We gain some perspective on the explanatory gap if we contrast the issue of the physical/functional basis of consciousness with the issue of the physical/functional basis of thought. In the case of thought, we do have some theoretical proposals about what thought is, or at least what human thought is, in scientific terms. Cognitive scientists have had some success in explaining some features of our thought processes in terms of the notions of representation and computation. There are many disagreements among cognitive scientists; especially notable is the disagreement between connectionists and classical language of thought theorists. However, the fact is that in the case of thought, we actually have more than one substantive research program, and their proponents are busy fighting it out, comparing which research program handles which phenomena best. But in the case of consciousness, we have nothing worthy of being called a research program, nor are there any substantive proposals about how to go about starting one. Researchers are stumped. There have been many tantalizing discoveries recently about neuropsychological syndromes in which consciousness seems to be in some way missing or defective, but no one has yet come up with a theoretical perspective that uses these data to narrow the explanatory gap, even a little bit.

Perspectives on the Explanatory Gap

There are many different attitudes toward this problem, but five of them stand out. First, we might mention eliminativism, the view that consciousness as understood above simply does not exist (P. S. Churchland, 1983; Dennett, 1988; Rey, 1983). So there is nothing for there to be an explanatory gap about. Second, we have various forms of reductionism, notably functionalsim and physicalism. According to these views, there is such a thing as consciousness, but there is no singular explanatory gap, that is, there are no mysteries concerning the physical basis of consciousness that differ in kind from run-of-the-mill unsolved scientific problems about the physical/functional basis of liquidity, inheritance or computation. On this view, there is an explanatory gap, but it is unremarkable (Dennett, 1991, flirts with both this position and eliminativism). A third view is what Flanagan (1992) calls the new mysterianism. Its most extreme form is transcendentalism, the view that consciousness is simply not a natural phenomenon and is not explainable in terms of science at all. A less extreme form of new mysterianism is that of McGinn (1991), which concedes that consciousness is a natural phenomenon but emphasizes our problem in understanding the physical basis of consciousness. McGinn argues that there are physical properties of our brains that do in fact explain consciousness, but though this explanation might be available to some other type of being, it is cognitively closed off to us. A fourth view, naturalism (Flanagan, 1992; Searle, 1992), holds that though there may be important differences between a naturalistic explanation of consciousness and naturalistic explanations of other phenomena, there is no convincing reason to regard consciousness as non-natural or unexplainable in naturalistic terms. This view is suggested by Nagel's remark that we are like the person ignorant of relativity theory, who is told that matter is a form of energy but who does not have the concepts to appreciate how there could be chains of reference-links leading from a single phenomenon to both "matter" and "energy." The explanatory gap exists—and we cannot conceive of how to close it—because we lack the scientific concepts. But future theory may provide those concepts. A fifth view says the gap is unclosable, but not because we cannot find the right physical concepts. Rather, it is unclosable because reductive expla-

nation requires an a priori functional analysis of the phenomenon to be explained, and no such analysis can be given of our concepts of conscious experience (Levine, 1993). The unavailability of these functional analyses is no accident: if our only concept of consciousness were one that could be analyzed functionally, we would need a different concept of consciousness to capture the features of experience that give rise to the explanatory gap.

Other Concepts of Consciousness

There are other concepts of consciousness—cognitive, or intentional, or functional concepts of consciousness—that are often not distinguished from it, and it is common for deflationists or reductionists about phenomenal consciousness to slide tacitly from phenomenal consciousness to one or another of these cognitive, or intentional, or functional concepts (see Dennett, 1991, and Block, 1995). Three such concepts of consciousness will be mentioned: self-consciousness, monitoring-consciousness, and access-consciousness.

(1) Self-consciousness is the possession of the concept of the self and the ability to use this concept in thinking about oneself. There is reason to think that animals or babies can have phenomenally conscious states without employing any concept of the self. To suppose that phenomenal consciousness requires the concept of the self is to place an implausible intellectual condition on phenomenal consciousness. Perhaps phenomenally conscious states have a nonconceptual content that could be described as "experienced as mine," but there is no reason to think that this representational aspect of the state exhausts its phenomenal properties. After all, if both my experience as of blue and my experience as of red are experienced as mine, we still need to explain the difference between the two experiences; the fact that they are both experienced as mine will not distinguish them. (The "as of" terminology is intended to preclude cases in which red things don't look red.)

(2) Monitoring-consciousness takes many forms. One form is "internal scanning," but it would be a mistake to conflate internal scanning with phenomenal consciousness. As Rey (1983) notes, ordinary laptop computers are capable of internal scanning, but it would be silly to think of one's laptop as conscious. Rey favors supposing that internal scanning is sufficient for consciousness, if there is such a thing, and so he concludes that consciousness is a concept that both includes and precludes laptop computers being conscious, and hence that the concept of consciousness is incoherent. But even if we acknowledge "internal scanning conscious-

ness," we should drop the idea that internal scanning is sufficient for phenomenal consciousness, and so we get no incoherence.

Another form of monitoring consciousness is that of accompaniment by a higher-order thought. That is, a conscious state is one that is accompanied by a thought (grounded noninferentially and nonobservationally) to the effect that one is in that state. If one favors a liberal terminological policy, then there should be no objection to this idea as a concept of consciousness. But one may object to the idea (Rosenthal, 1986) that phenomenal consciousness should be identified with higher-order-thought consciousness. One way to see what is wrong with that view is to note that even if one were to come to know about states of one's liver noninferentially and nonobservationally—as some people just know what time it is—that would not make the states of one's liver phenomenally conscious (see Dretske, 1995). Another objection is that phenomenal consciousness does not require the intellectual apparatus that is required for higher-order thought. Thus, the identification of phenomenal consciousness with higher-order thought shares the over-intellectualism of the identification of phenomenal consciousness with self-consciousness. Dogs and babies may have phenomenally conscious pains without thoughts to the effect that they have those pains.

We gain some perspective on the explanatory gap if we contrast the issue of the physical/functional basis of consciousness with the issue of the physical/functional basis of thought.

A distinction is often made between state consciousness—or intransitive consciousness—and consciousness-of, or transitive consciousness (Rosenthal, 1986). For example, saying "I'm nauseous," ascribes a kind of intransitive consciousness to oneself, and if one says one is now seeing something as a mosquito, one ascribes transitive consciousness. The higher-order thought view purposely collapses these notions. According to the higher-order thought view, a conscious state (intransitive consciousness) is simply a state that one is conscious of (transitive consciousness), and consciousness-of is simply a matter of accompaniment by a thought to the effect that one is in that state. So what it is for a state to be conscious (intransitively) is for it to be accompanied by a thought that one is in that state.

This intentional conflation has an element of plausibility to it, which can be seen by comparing two dogs, one of which has a perceptual state whereas the other has a similar perceptual state plus a representation of it. Surely the latter dog has a conscious state even if the former dog does not! Quite so, because consciousness-of brings consciousness with it. But it is the converse that is problematic. State consciousness makes less in the way of intellectual demands than consciousness-of, and so the first dog could be conscious without being conscious of anything.

(3) Access-consciousness does not make the intellectual demands of self-consciousness or higher-order-thought consciousness, and for that reason, reductionists about phenomenal consciousness would do better to identify phenomenal consciousness with access-consciousness. A state is access-conscious if it is poised for global control. To add more detail, an access-conscious representation is poised for free use in reasoning and for direct control of action and speech. An access-conscious state is one that consists in having an access-conscious representation.

A good way to see the distinction between access-consciousness and phenomenal consciousness is to note cases of one without the other. Consider a robot with a computer brain that is behaviorally and computationally identical to ours. The question arises as to whether what it is like to be that robot is different from what it is like to be us, or indeed, whether there is anything at all that it is like to be that robot. If there is nothing it is like to be that robot, the robot is a zombie. If zombies are conceptually possible, they certainly illustrate access-consciousness without phenomenal consciousness. But there is widespread opposition to the conceptual coherence of zombies (see Shoemaker, 1975, 1981; Dennett, 1991). So for illustrating access-consciousness without phenomenal consciousness, one would rather rely on a very limited sort of partial zombie.

Consider blindsight, a neurological syndrome in which subjects seem to have "blind" areas in their visual fields. If the experimenter flashes a stimulus to one of those blind areas, that patient claims to see nothing at all. But if the experimenter insists that the subject guess, and the experimenter supplies a few alternatives, the blindsight patients are able to "guess" reliably about certain features of the stimulus—features having to do with motion, location, direction—and they are able to discriminate some simple forms. Consider a blindsight patient who "guesses" that there is an 'X' rather than an 'O' in his blind field. The patient has no access-consciousness of the stimulus (because, until he hears his own guess, he cannot use the information freely in reasoning or in rational control of action), and it is plausible that he has no phenomenal consciousness of it either. Now imagine something that does not exist, what we might call super-blindsight. A real blindsight patient can only guess when a given a choice among a small set of alternative ('X'/'O', horizontal/vertical, and so forth). But suppose (apparently contrary to fact) that a blindsight patient could be trained to prompt himself at will, guessing what is in the blind field without being told to guess. Visual information from the blind field simply pops into his thought the way that solutions to problems sometimes pop into ours, or (to use an example given earlier) the way some people just know what time it is without any special perceptual experience. The super-blindsight patient says there is something it is like to see an 'X' in his sighted field, but not in his blind field, and we believe him. This would be a case of access-consciousness without phenomenal consciousness, a sort of partial zombie.

Here is an example of the converse of the zombie cases, namely phenomenal consciousness without access-consciousness. It appears that some areas of the brain specialize in reasoning and rational control of action, whereas other areas subserve sensation. If a person's brain has the former areas destroyed, he is unable to use the deliverances of the senses to control action rationally, to reason or to report sensibly, but he can still have experiences. Such a person has phenomenal consciousness without access consciousness.

Here is a different sort of example. Suppose that you are engaged in intense conversation when suddenly, at midnight, you realize that there is now and has been for some time a deafening pounding noise going on. You had raised your voice in response to the noise, but you had not noticed the noise or that you had raised your voice. You were aware of the noise all along, but only at midnight were you consciously aware of it. That is, you were phenomenally conscious of the noise all along, but only at midnight did you become access-conscious of it. The period before midnight illustrates phenomenal consciousness without access-consciousness. 'Conscious' and 'aware' are roughly synonomous, so it is natural to use one for the period before midnight, and both for the period after midnight, when there are two kinds of consciousness present. The Freudian sense of unconscious means access-unconscious. Suppose a person was tortured in a red room and represses that fact; Freudian theory allows visual images of the red room that lead to desperate flight when the person is in a similarly colored room, but mechanisms of repression can prevent thought, reasoning, and reporting about the torture and the room. The vivid visual image would be phenomenally conscious but access-unconscious.

The cases mentioned earlier of phenomenal consciousness without access-consciousness are also counterexamples to the higher-order-thought theory of phenomenal consciousness. If the subject has no access to the phenomenal state, he cannot think about it either. Before midnight, you have a phenomenally conscious state caused by the noise but no thought to the effect that you are in such a state. The victim of repression has a phenomenally conscious state that he is unable to think about.

Akins (1993) has argued against the distinction between a phenomenal and a representational aspect of experience. She keys her discussion to Nagel's (1974) claim that we cannot know what it is like to be a bat, challenging the reader to imagine that what it is like to be a bat is just what it is like to be us—only all those experiences represent totally different things. Correctly, she says that you cannot imagine that. That is because, as mentioned earlier, representational differences of a certain sort make a phenomenal difference. What it is like to hear a sound as coming from the left is different from what it is like to hear a sound as coming from the right. But from the fact that some representational differences make a phenomenal difference, one should not conclude that the phenomenal character of a conscious state is exhausted by its representational content. Note, for example, that there are phenomenal states that arguably have little or no representational content, orgasm for example (but see Tye, 1995, for the opposite view).

[See also Eliminative Materialism, Eliminativism; Philosophy of Mind; Physicalism, Materialism; Reduction, Reductionism.]

BIBLIOGRAPHY

Akins, K. "A Bat Without Qualities," in M. Davies and G. Humphreys, eds., Consciousness (Oxford, 1993).

Block, N. "On a Confusion about a Function of Consciousness," The Behavioral and Brain Sciences, Vol. 18, No. 2 (1995), 227–47.

Churchland, P. S. "Consciousness: The Transmutation of a Concept," Pacific Philosophical Quarterly, Vol. 64 (1983), 80–93.

Dennett, D. "Quining Qualia," in A. Marcel and E. Bisiach, eds., Consciousness in Contemporary Society (Oxford, 1988).

———. Consciousness Explained. New York, 1991.

Dretske, F. Naturalizing the Mind. Cambridge, MA, 1995.

Flanagan, O. Consciousness Reconsidered. Cambridge, MA, 1992.

Levine, J. "On Leaving Out What It Is Like," in M. Davies and G. Humphreys, eds., Consciousness (Oxford, 1993).

Lycan, W. Consciousness. Cambridge, MA, 1987.

McGinn, C. The Problem of Consciousness. Oxford, 1991.

Nagel, T. "What Is It Like to Be a Bat?" Philosophical Review (1974).

Rey, G. "A Reason for Doubting the Existence of Consciousness," in R. Davidson, G. Schwartz, and D. Shapiro, eds., Consciousness and Self-Regulation, Vol. 3 (New York, 1983).

Rosenthal, D. "Two Concepts of Consciousness," Vol. 3 Philosophical Studies, Vol. 49 (1986), 329–59.

Searle, J. *The Rediscovery of the Mind.* Cambridge, MA, 1992.

Shoemaker, S. "Functionalism and Qualia," *Philosophical Studies,* Vol. 27 (1975), 291–315.

Shoemaker, S. "Absent Qualia Are Impossible—A Reply to Block," *Philosphical Review,* Vol. 90, No. 4 (1981), 581–99.

Tye, M. *Ten Problems of Consciousness: A Representational Theory of the Phenomenal Mind.* Cambridge, MA, 1995.

— NED BLOCK

CONSCIOUSNESS IN PHENOMENOLOGY: HUSSERL

For Husserl, the two basic features of consciousness are intentionality and temporality. Intentionality means that all consciousness is directed to some object. The thesis that consciousness is temporal means, not only that all conscious states have a temporal location, but that each of them has within itself a temporal structure and that the temporal structure of consciousness is the basis for all other determinations of consciousness and its objects.

Husserl's philosophical method proceeds through an analysis of conscious life. However, since all consciousness is intentional, the analysis of the forms and structures of various kinds of consciousness (including volitional, emotional, and evaluative as well as theoretical) is also the appropriate way to analyze the essential forms and structures of various kinds of objects. Since Husserl also believes that consciousness involves at least implicit self-consciousness of one's own mental states, the focus on consciousness shifts the analysis to a sphere that is immediately and directly given in reflection and is therefore the source of apodictic certainty, the transcendental ego. In later works Husserl qualifies this assertion by pointing out that self-givenness even for ideal objects never necessarily involves absolute certainty, so that all purported givenness requires reconfirmation. He also turns his attention to the sphere of passive synthesis, whose results may be directly given to us, while the operations that originally generate them are not, so that a phenomenological reconstruction or intentional analysis is necessary to reveal sedimented or initially hidden and prepredicative elements of consciousness.

[See also Husserl, Edmund; Husserl, Intentionality in.]

BIBLIOGRAPHY

Husserl, E. *Cartesianische Meditationen. Husserliana,* Vol. 1, edited by S. Strasser. The Hague, 1950. Translated by D. Cairns as *Cartesian Meditations.* The Hague, 1960. See especially secs. 6–22 regarding intentionality and reflection. See secs. 30–41 regarding the temporal nature of consciousness and passive genesis.

———. *Formale und transzendentale Logik. Husserliana,* Vol. 17, edited by P. Jannsen. The Hague, 1974. Translated by D. Cairns as *Formal and Transcendental Logic.* The Hague, 1969. Secs. 58ff. distinguish between self-givenness and infallibility.

———. *Ideen zu einer reinen Phänomenologie und phänomenologischen Philosophie, Buch 1. Husserliana,* Vol. 3. The Hague, 1976. Translated by F. Kersten as *Ideas Pertaining to a Pure Phenomenology and Phenomenological Philosophy. First Book.* The Hague, 1982. See especially secs. 34–62 regarding the intentionality of consciousness and its accessibility to pure reflection.

— THOMAS NENON

CONSCIOUSNESS IN PHENOMENOLOGY: SARTRE

Jean-Paul Sartre considered himself a philosopher of consciousness during the first half of his career. He subscribed to the Cartesian ideal of the cogito as the starting point of philosophy and placed a premium on the apodictic evidence it yielded. But he valued consciousness as much for its freedom and spontaneity as for its epistemological translucency. In fact, it was the relevance of translucency to moral responsibility that led

Sartre, here with longtime companion Simone de Beauvoir, valued consciousness as much for its freedom and spontaneity as for its epistemological translucency. (Corbis/Hulton-Deutsch Collection)

169

him to deny both a transcendental ego and the Freudian unconscious and to posit a "prereflective *Cogito*."

In his *The Psychology of Imagination* he describes imaging consciousness as the locus of "negativity, possibility, and lack." Because we are able to "hold the world at bay" and "derealize" perceptual objects imagistically, he argues, we are free. Imaging consciousness becomes paradigmatic of consciousness in general (being-for-itself) in *Being and Nothingness*. Adopting Edmund Husserl's thesis that all consciousness is intentional, he insists that this intentionality is primarily practical, articulating a fundamental project that gives meaning/direction (*sens*) to our existence.

Sartre makes much of the prereflective self-awareness that accompanies our explicit awareness of any object, including our egos as reflective objects. Since we are always implicitly self-aware, it is unnecessary to seek self-consciousness in an endless infinity of reflections on reflections or to chase after a subject that cannot be an object (the transcendental ego). The unblinking eye of prereflective consciousness makes possible both bad faith and its overcoming through what he calls "purifying reflection," the authentic "choice" to live at a creative distance from one's ego.

[*See also Authenticity; Bad Faith; Descartes, René; Sartre, Jean-Paul.*]

BIBLIOGRAPHY

Sartre, J.-P. *L'Etre et le néant*. Paris, 1943. Translated by H. E. Barnes as *Being and Nothingness*. New York, 1956.
———. *L'Imaginaire*. Paris, 1940. Translated by B. Frechtman as *The Psychology of Imagination*. New York, 1966.
———. *La Transcendence de l'ego*. Paris, 1937. Translated by R. Kirkpatrick and F. Williams as *The Transcendence of the Ego*. New York, 1957.

— THOMAS R. FLYNN

CONSEQUENTIALISM

As a name for any ethical theory or for the class of ethical theories that evaluate actions by the value of the consequences of the actions, consequentialism thus refers to classical utilitarianism and other theories that share this characteristic.

Classical utilitarianism, in the philosophies of Jeremy Bentham, John Stuart Mill, and Henry Sidgwick, was consequentialist, judging actions right in proportion as they tended to produce happiness, wrong as they tended to produce pain. In the nineteenth and early twentieth centuries much of the criticism of utilitarianism was directed at the hedonistic value theory on which the ethical theory was founded. Some philosophers, such as G. E. Moore, agreed with the claim of utilitarianism that acts are right insofar as they produce good conse-

quences, wrong as they produce bad consequences, but put forward a richer theory of value, claiming that other things besides pleasure and pain are of intrinsic value and disvalue. Such theories were sometimes labeled ideal utilitarianism. The term consequentialism is now used in a generic sense to include both hedonistic and nonhedonistic theories.

Classical utilitarianism,

in the philosophies of Bentham, Mill,

and Sidgwick, was consequentialist,

judging actions right in proportion

as they tended to produce happiness,

wrong as they tended to produce pain.

The term was probably introduced into usage by Elizabeth Anscombe in "Modern Moral Philosophy" (1958), an essay in which she claims that there is little difference between strictly consequentialist theories and other moral theories from Sidgwick on that permit forbidden acts to be overridden by consequentialist considerations. For example, W. D. Ross, who was an intuitionist in opposition to utilitarianism, even "ideal" utilitarianism, believed that a prima facie wrong action, such as the deliberately unjust punishment of an innocent person, could be outweighed by some consequentialist consideration such as the national interest. One contrast with consequentialism, then, is absolutism, the claim that there are some actions that are never right, whatever the consequences.

In the most usual usage of "consequentialism" as a term for ethical theories, however, it is contrasted, not only to absolutism, but to any theory, such as Kantianism, intuitionism, virtue ethics, rights theories, and so on, that does not in some way make consequences the determinant of right and wrong. The consequences may be considered indirectly. Distinctions have been made between act utilitarianism, which judges acts right or wrong according to the consequences of the particular act, case by case, rule utilitarianism, which judges acts right or wrong according to whether the acts are in accord with or in violation of a useful rule—that is, a rule whose general practice would have good consequences (or better consequences than any feasible alternative rule)—and motive utilitarianism, which judges acts right or wrong if stemming from a motive that, as a motive for action, generally has good consequences.

These distinctions carry over to consequentialism as a generic category of ethical theories, and one can speak of act consequentialism, rule consequentialism, and so on. Consequentialist theories can also have a place for virtues and for rights, if the inculcation of certain virtues or the respect for certain rights has good consequences. But for the consequentialist the virtues or rights are not ultimate. Their value is dependent upon their contribution to good consequences.

Abstracting from the alternative theories of value, there are still important controversies regarding consequentialist theories. Some are problems of measuring consequences or making interpersonal comparisons, whatever the theory of value, but these cannot be addressed in the abstract. Another is the theory of responsibility. One prominent criticism of consequentialism, stated, for example, by Bernard Williams (1973), is that it does not adequately distinguish between positive and negative responsibility. The claim is that consequentialism is indifferent between states of affairs that are produced by what an agent does and those that occur because of what someone else would do that the agent could prevent. It becomes an agent's responsibility to prevent someone else from doing harm as well as not to do harm oneself. Related to this is the claim that consequentialism undermines agent integrity. For example, someone opposed to research in chemical and biological warfare might be required to engage in such research to prevent someone else from doing it more zealously. Another criticism is that if it is formulated as a "maximizing" theory, requiring the maximization of best consequences, consequentialism goes beyond the limits of obligation. For example, one would be morally obligated to spend one's wealth and income on others as long as there is anyone who could benefit more than oneself.

There are four basic kinds of responses that the consequentialist can make to these criticisms. One is to stick to the theory, saying that these things are morally demanded, even if not generally recognized in our selfish and self-centered society, as Peter Singer (1972) argues concerning famine relief. Another is to challenge the implications of the examples, claiming that for moral agents to focus energy and attention on their own lives with integrity to their own principles has better consequences than doing otherwise. A third strategy for a nonhedonist is to attempt to avoid some of these objections by enriching the theory of value, such as to claim that integrity is something that is intrinsically valuable. A fourth strategy is to modify the structure of the theory. Michael Slote (1984) has argued in favor of a "satisficing" rather than a maximizing theory. Samuel Schefeller (1982) has proposed a "hybrid" theory that permits an agent either to maximize best consequences or to pursue the "agent-centered prerogative" of not always doing so.

[See also Anscombe, Elizabeth; Bentham, Jeremy; Deontological Ethics; Ethical Theory; Mill, John Stuart; Rights; Ross, William David; Sidgwick, Henry; Virtue Ethics.]

BIBLIOGRAPHY

Anscombe, G. E. M. "Modern Moral Philosophy," *Philosophy,* Vol. 33 (1958), 1–19.

Bennett, J. "Whatever the Consequences," *Analysis,* Vol. 26 (1965–66), 83–102.

Brandt, R. B. "Utilitarianism and Moral Rights," *Canadian Journal of Philosophy,* Vol. 14 (1984), 1–19.

Kagan, S. "Does Consequentialism Demand Too Much? Recent Work on the Limits of Obligation," *Philosophy and Public Affairs,* Vol. 13 (1983–84), 239–54.

Pettit, P., ed. *Consequentialism.* Brookfield, VT, 1993.

Schefeller, S. *The Rejection of Consequentialism.* Oxford. 1982.

Singer, P. "Famine, Affluence, and Morality," *Philosophy and Public Affairs,* Vol. 1 (1971–72), 229–43.

Slote, M. "Satisficing Consequentialism," *The Aristotelian Society,* Vol. 43 (1984), suppl. vol., 139–63.

Smart, J. J. C. "An Outline of a System of Utilitarian Ethics," in J. J. C. Smart and B. Williams, eds., *Utilitarianism: For and Against* (Cambridge, 1973).

Williams, B. "A Critique of Utilitarianism," in J. J. C. Smart and Bernard Williams, eds., *Utilitarianism: For and Against* (Cambridge, 1973).

— HENRY R. WEST

CONSTRUCTIVISM, CONVENTIONALISM

Conventionalism and constructivism are kindred, often overlapping positions, asserting that the subject matter of some area of inquiry is not fully mind-independent. "Conventionalism" and "constructivism" are not well-defined names of positions but labels adopted—as often by critics as by advocates—to emphasize one positive aspect of positions in a wide range of areas; consequently, these terms group together a variety of positions with varying motivations. In general, the label "conventionalism" is applied to positions that claim the truths in some area are so in virtue of the conventions of a linguistic or conceptual scheme, while "constructivism" emphasizes that a position assigns to the cognitive faculties of humans some role in "making" the objects or facts in the area in question.

Conventionalism

Conventionalists claim either that the truths of some subject matter—such as mathematics or logic, or of a certain sort, such as necessary truths, or some dispute, such as whether Euclid's parallel postulate holds of our physical world—are matters of convention rather than of how the world is independent of mind. Some extreme versions of conventionalism take the fact that it is a matter of convention what our words mean (we could have used *cat* to designate Napoleon) to show that all truth is conventional. However, its being a convention that "Napoleon" names Napoleon hardly makes it conventional that Napoleon was defeated at Waterloo. An interesting conventionalism must assert something more than the conventionality of word meaning and must rest on something more than wild inference from it.

Thomas Kuhn, by virtue of his

The Structure of Scientific Revolutions,

may be considered constructivism's leading protagonist

of the mid-to-late twentieth century.

One area in which conventionalism is familiar, though controversial, is necessary truth. This was one cornerstone of logical positivism; from the seeming a priori nature of necessary truths, the positivists argued (some would say claimed) that since a priori knowledge cannot be of (mind-independent) facts, necessary truths must be analytic, which they understood as true by definition. Given that mathematics is also a priori, their argument was applied there as well. This sort of epistemological argument is typical of conventionalist views: arguing that our methods for ascertaining what is so in some area could not give us knowledge of a mind-independent world, they claim that this knowledge would not be problematic on the assumption that what is fundamentally under investigation are our conventions. Some sorts of conventionalism are also supported by metaphysical considerations such as naturalistic concerns about what, in the mind-independent world, could make for the relevant sort of truth. This sort of argument is common to necessary truths, mathematics, ethics, and other areas with normative import; plainly, such arguments need to be supplemented with an account of how it is that conventions can provide the relevant features.

Saul Kripke's arguments that there are necessary truths that are a posteriori—and, so, not analytic—seemed to some to undermine conventionalism about necessity (Kripke, 1980). It has, however, been argued that conventions could explain the necessity of these truths without the truths themselves being analytic—that is, true by convention (Sidelle, 1989). This may indicate that in general conventionalism, with respect to a subject matter, does not require that all target truths

themselves be analytic but only that conventions be responsible for the features that purportedly cannot be adequately handled within a realistic interpretation.

Aside from the claim that certain truths are so by convention, another common conventionalist position is that some dispute is a conventional rather than factual matter. Poincaré's famous conventionalism about geometry is of this sort. He claims that the choice among systems of geometry, for describing the physical world, is not an issue of which is true but of which is most convenient or useful. By adopting any of them, we could modify our physics so as to have equally full and correct descriptions of the world: indeed, this last claim is the basis for his view that the issue is conventional rather than factual. Carnap offers a similar view about ontological disputes between, for instance, phenomenalists and materialists. Both of these views illustrate that "conventional" does not as such imply 'arbitrary', as pragmatic differences may be quite genuine; we can also see that the plausibility of conventionalism in some area depends largely on how implausible it is to claim that the issue, or truth in question, is a matter of mind-independent fact.

On a more local level, some disputes can appear "purely verbal," as perhaps whether some politician is conservative. When this is plausible, the issue may be said to be a matter of convention or choice rather than fact. The conventionalism of Poincaré, Carnap, and others is akin to this, only in a wider application. In book 3, chapters 7 and 11, of his *Essay*, Locke speculates that many of the "great disputes" are of this sort.

As applied to areas in which the truths are well established (mathematics or logic, for instance), conventionalism is fundamentally a deflationary interpretive position, urging that we not mistake the metaphysical status of these truths. Applied to areas of controversy—ontological or essentialist claims, or whether whales are fish—conventionalism claims that disputes here can only be over what our conventions in fact are, or what they should be, either pragmatically or perhaps morally. In either case, if conventionalism is right, our focus and methods of investigation—and certainly our understanding of what is at stake—for the questions at hand would probably require alteration.

Constructivism

Thomas Kuhn, by virtue of his *The Structure of Scientific Revolutions,* may be considered constructivism's leading protagonist of the mid-to-late twentieth century, despite not adopting the label himself and expressing unease at having it assigned to him. He writes of scientists within different paradigms—roughly, methodological and theoretical traditions or frameworks—as studying different worlds and of their paradigms as in "a sense . . . constitutive of nature" (Kuhn, 1970, p. 110, chaps. 10, 13), at least suggesting a constructivism about the world studied by science. Kuhn's major concerns are epistemological; he argues that scientific procedure is deeply theory laden and encodes ontological and theoretical commitments that it is incapable of testing. How, then, can such a method give us knowledge of the world? Those who see a constructivist in Kuhn have him answer that the world under investigation is itself partly a product of the investigating paradigm. This puts Kuhn in the tradition of Kant, except that the features we "impose" upon the phenomenal world are not (as for Kant) necessary for the possibility of experience, but, rather, contingent features of current science. It is important to note that, even as interpreted, this constructivism does not have scientists making the world out of whole cloth with their paradigms; rather, there is something mind-independent that "filters through" the conceptual apparatus of the paradigm. This is a central difference between constructivism and idealism. The object of scientific study is, however, not this mind-independent world, but rather that which results "through the filter."

Other philosophers, as well as historians and sociologists of science, have taken the supposedly arational or nonobjective features guiding scientific judgment to establish that scientific truth is relative to one's background theory or paradigm. This is sometimes then articulated as the view that these theories or paradigms in part "make" the objects of study—that is, as constructivism. Indeed, many positions that formerly would have simply been called relativist have come, in the late twentieth century, to be called constructivist by their protagonists; arguments in their support tend to be of the familiar relativist sort and thus have the same strengths and problems. It should be noted that neither constructivism nor conventionalism need take a relativistic form.

> *Both conventionalism and constructivism*
>
> *are motivated primarily by negative considerations*
>
> *against a realistic understanding*
>
> *of the subject matter in question.*

Another philosopher associated with constructivism is Nelson Goodman, due largely to his *Ways of Worldmaking*. Goodman argues that no sense can be made of the notion "the (one) way the world is"; rather, there

are lots of ways the world is, depending on the conceptual apparatus one brings. This sort of position is found in many philosophers since Kant, often argued on the trivial ground that one cannot describe or investigate the world without using a system of representation, therefore (*sic*) the world investigated is not mind-independent but partly constructed by our conceptual scheme. This is sometimes added to, or confused with, the relativistic considerations mentioned above. What needs to be explained is how we are supposed to get this substantive conclusion from the banal premise. Why can't the objects represented by the elements of a system of representation—by the name "Tabby," say—be wholly and utterly mind-independent? And even if we add the fact that there can be different schemes of representation, why can it not simply be that they pick out different features of a mind-independent reality? What gives Goodman his special place is that he supplements this argument with the claim that different schemes may be such that their claims conflict with each other, but there can be no grounds for maintaining that one is correct and the other not. Goodman uses as examples the claims that the planets revolve around the sun and that the sun and other planets revolve around the earth. Both, he claims, must be judged as correct (within the appropriately formulated total systems), but they cannot simply be seen as two notationally different descriptions of a single world (thus differing from Poincaré's conventionalism). The success of this argument depends on whether one can simultaneously make out that these claims genuinely do conflict with each other and that, so understood, neither of them can be judged to be true while the other is false.

Prospects

While both Kuhn and Goodman offer relatively global constructivist positions, there are constructivists about essences, moral and aesthetic properties, mathematical objects, and in principle anything. The same is true of conventionalism. Both conventionalism and constructivism are motivated primarily by negative considerations against a realistic understanding of the subject matter in question; this is sometimes supplemented with positive arguments that by understanding the matter as concerning our conventions or choices we can get a better explanation of the phenomena at hand. Often, the negative arguments are very quick and fail to fully consider the range of options available to realists (Scheffler, 1966, presents good discussion), and sometimes they fail to consider whether their positive proposals actually fare any better. Plainly, the plausibility of these positions depends on how well these arguments can be made out, and this may vary drastically across the different subject matters for which conventionalist and constructivist proposals have been offered. Additionally, if these positions are even to be candidates for serious consideration, defenders must be prepared to offer further proof. Conventionalists must specify some sense in which that which is purportedly so by convention would have been otherwise had our conventions been different, and constructivists must describe some sense in which the purportedly constructed objects would not have existed without our input.

[See also Carnap, Rudolph; Goodman, Nelson; Kant, Immanuel; Kripke, Saul Aaron; Kuhn, Thomas; Locke, John.]

BIBLIOGRAPHY

Carnap, R. "Empiricism. Semantics, and Ontology," in *Meaning and Necessity* (Chicago, 1947). A classic exposition of the conventionalist's treatment of apparently ontological questions as fundamentally linguistic.

Dummett, M. *Frege: Philosophy of Language*, 2d ed. Cambridge, 1981. Chap. 16, esp. pp. 560–83. An interesting presentation of what may be seen as a constructivist position on objects or a conventionalist position on identity criteria.

Goodman, N. *Ways of Worldmaking*. Indianapolis, 1978. For useful discussion, see C. G. Hempel, "Comments on Goodman's *Ways of Worldmaking*," and I. Scheffler, "The Wonderful Worlds of Goodman," both in *Synthese*, Vol. 45 (1980),193–209.

Horwich, P. "A Defence of Conventionalism," in G. MacDonald and C. Wright, eds., *Fact, Science and Morality* (Oxford, 1986).

Knorr-Cetina, K. "The Ethnographic Study of Scientific Work: Towards a Constructivist Interpretation of Science," in K. Knorr-Cetina and M. Mulkay, eds., *Science Observed: Perspectives on the Social Study of Science* (London, 1983).

Kripke, S. *Naming and Necessity*. Cambridge, 1980.

Kuhn, T. S. *The Structure of Scientific Revolutions*, 2d ed. Chicago, 1970.

Kyburg, H. E. "A Defense of Conventionalism," *Noûs*, Vol. 11 (1977), 75–95.

Latour, B., and S. Woolger, *Laboratory Life: The Social Construction of Scientific Facts*, 2d ed. Princeton, NJ, 1986.

Lewis, D. *Convention*. Cambridge, 1969. Argues that sense can be made of the idea of nonexplicit conventions, *contra* Quine (1953).

Locke, J. *An Essay Concerning Human Understanding*. 1689. Locke's discussion of substance in book 3, chap. 7, classically expounds his conventionalism about essence and kinds.

Niiniluoto, I. "Realism, Relativism, and Constructivism," *Synthese*, Vol. 89 (1991), 135–62. Critical discussion of constructivism in the social sciences.

Pap, A. *Semantics and Necessary Truth*. New Haven, 1958. An extended argument against conventionalism about necessity.

Poincaré, H. *Science and Hypothesis*. London, 1905.

Putnam, H. "The Refutation of Conventionalism," in *Mind, Language, and Reality* (Cambridge, 1975).

Quine, W. V. O. "Two Dogmas of Empiricism," in *From a Logical Point of View* (Cambridge, 1953). Classical argument against the analytic–synthetic distinction and so against truth by convention.

———. "Truth by Convention," in *The Ways of Paradox and Other Essays* (Cambridge, 1966). A classic argument against the possibility of truth by convention alone.

Reichenbach, H. *Experience and Predication*. Chicago, 1938.

Scheffler, I. *Science and Subjectivity*. Indianapolis, 1966. Responds to arguments based on the history of science against objectivity in science, particularly Kuhn's, which are often used to bolster constructivist positions about the objects of scientific study.

Sidelle, A. *Necessity, Essence, and Individuation: A Defense of Conventionalism*. Ithaca, NY, 1989.

— ALAN SIDELLE

CONSTRUCTIVISM, MORAL

Moral constructivism is a metaethical view about the nature of moral truth and moral facts (and properties), so called because the intuitive idea behind the view is that such truths and facts are human constructs rather than objects of discovery. More precisely, constructivism involves both a semantic thesis about moral sentences and a two-part metaphysical thesis about the existence and nature of moral facts and properties. According to the semantic thesis, ordinary moral sentences purport to be fact-stating sentences and thus purport to be genuinely true or false. And, according to the metaphysical thesis, there are moral facts whose existence and nature are in some sense dependent upon human attitudes, agreements, conventions, and the like. Thus, constructivism represents a metaethical view in partial agreement with versions of moral realism. Like the realist, the constructivist is a so-called cognitivist (descriptivist)—moral sentences have descriptive content and thus purport to be genuinely fact stating. Again, like the realist, the constructivist accepts the view that there are moral facts that serve as the truth makers of true moral sentences. But unlike the realist, the constructivist rejects the idea that there are moral facts (and properties) that are independent of human attitudes, conventions, and the like.

Constructivism, at least in its sophisticated versions,

is supposed to capture what is plausible

about moral realism, leaving behind

what is problematic about realist views.

It is useful to distinguish between simple and sophisticated versions of constructivism as well as between non-relativist and relativist versions. Simple versions of constructivism are represented by certain views that would construe moral truth in terms of the actual attitudes of individuals or actual agreements within cultures about matters of moral concern. More sophisticated versions of constructivism construe moral truths (and associated moral facts and properties) in terms of the hypothetical attitudes of individuals or perhaps hypothetical agreements among members of a group reached under suitably constrained circumstances. Nonrelativist versions of constructivism maintain that all individuals and groups whose attitudes, agreements, and so forth provide the basis for moral truths and facts do or would accept the same set of basic moral norms with the result that there is a single set of moral truths and facts. Usually, such views are wedded to some version or other of sophisticated constructivism. Thus, a version of the ideal-observer view of moral truth—according to which basic moral truths are represented by the moral norms that would be accepted by an ideal observer, where the notion of an ideal observer is so characterized that all ideal observers will agree on the same set of basic moral norms—is a version of sophisticated nonrelativist constructivism. Relativist versions of constructivism allow that there may be more than one individual or group with differing attitudes and agreements that serve as the basis for different (and conflicting) sets of basic moral norms. Versions of moral relativism, according to which moral truths and facts are a matter of what basic moral norms a culture in fact accepts, represent versions of simple, relativistic constructivism; versions of relativism, according to which moral truths and facts are a matter of what would be accepted under conditions that are ideal for choosing such norms, represent sophisticated relativistic versions of constructivism. Versions of the ideal-observer view are relativistic if they allow that there can be ideal observers who would accept different (and conflicting) sets of moral norms. So-called Kantian constructivism of the sort recently elaborated and defended by John Rawls, which appeals to choices made by hypothetical individuals behind a veil of ignorance (a version of contractarianism), is yet another sophisticated and apparently nonrelativistic constructivist view.

Constructivism, at least in its sophisticated versions, is supposed to capture what is plausible about moral realism, leaving behind what is problematic about realist views. Thus, constructivism can accommodate quite well certain 'objective pretensions' of commonsense moral thinking. Some of these pretensions have to do with the form and content of moral discourse. A good many moral sentences are in the declarative mood (e.g., "Abortion, except in cases of rape and incest, is wrong") and are thus naturally interpreted as genuinely fact-stating sentences. Moreover, some such sentences appear to make references to (putative) moral facts and properties (e.g., "The evil of American slavery was partly responsible for its demise as an institution"). Other objective pretensions have to do with such activities as moral deliberation, debate, and argument. These critical practices are seemingly aimed at arriving nonarbitrarily at true or correct moral views, ones that would ideally resolve intrapersonal and interpersonal conflict and uncertainty about moral issues. Like realism, constructivism is attractive in apparently being able to accommodate such objective pretensions of ordinary moral discourse. Moreover, it attempts to accommodate these features without endorsing the sorts of metaphysical commitments to independently existing moral properties and facts countenanced by the realist. In short, at least certain versions of constructivism boast a robust notion of moral objectivity without problematic metaphysical commitments.

One serious challenge to constructivism is represented by the argument from moral error. According to constructivism, moral truths and associated facts are to be understood in terms of the attitudes and agreements of individuals and groups. However, if we take ordinary moral discourse and argument seriously, then since such discourse and argument presuppose that there are right answers to moral questions whose correctness outstrips any actual or even ideal set of attitudes or agreements, the constructivist view cannot be correct. To understand this objection more clearly, it will be useful to distinguish between basic and nonbasic moral truths and facts. Basic moral truths and facts are of a quite general sort, properly expressed by moral principles, and are the direct objects of choice by those under ideal conditions of moral thought and deliberation. Nonbasic moral truths and facts are those truths and facts that, in some sense, follow from the basic ones together with nonmoral information. Now the constructivist can allow for certain sorts of errors in moral judgment. For instance, simple moral relativism can allow that individuals and groups can be mistaken about particular moral judgments owing to misinformation about particular cases or perhaps to faulty reasoning from basic moral principles to concrete cases. However, this kind of moral relativism cannot allow for error at the level of actual agreements, since such agreements constitute basic moral truths. The sophisticated constructivist can allow for error at the level of communal agreement, since it is possible on such views that the actual agreements of actual groups are at odds with those hypothetical choices constitutive of moral truth on this sort of view. However, the sophisticated constructivist cannot allow for error at the level of choice made under ideal conditions—call this 'deep moral error'. After all, the constructivist construes such choice as constitutive and not just evidence of basic moral truths and facts. But, so the objection goes, given our critical practices, we can sensibly raise questions about the truth of those moral principles and norms that are chosen under ideal circumstances. This indicates that moral truth is one thing and the norms and principles chosen even under the most ideal of circumstances is another. Hence, constructivism, in both its simple and sophisticated versions, is not acceptable.

According to constructivism, moral truths and associated facts are to be understood in terms of the attitudes and agreements of individuals and groups.

In response, the constructivist can perhaps block the argument from moral error in the following way. First, the constructivist can note that it is dubious that our critical practices presuppose that deep moral error—error at the level of choice under ideal conditions—is possible. After all, our commonsense critical practices are not finely tuned to subtle differences in metaethical positions, and, in particular, common sense does not (so the constructivist might plead) make any distinction between the sort of realist objectivity that presupposes the possibility of deep moral error and a kind of constructivist objectivity that denies this possibility. Can we, for instance, really make sense of the idea that we might be mistaken about such basic moral principles as one that prohibits torture for fun? Furthermore, the constructivist can question the basic move featured in the argument from moral error—that is, the move from (1) it is quite sensible to raise questions about choices that purport to be made under ideal conditions to (2) an explanation of this phenomenon requires moral realism. Granted, the supposed gap between the truth of moral principles on the one hand and choice of such principles under ideal conditions on the other is one way to explain how we can sensibly raise questions about the truth of moral judgments made under ideal conditions, but this is not the only way to make sense of such critical stances. The constructivist can note that in the context of everyday discussion where we have to judge whether or not to accept the moral judgments of others, one can sensibly raise questions about some judgment by raising questions about the judger herself. After all, whatever is involved according to the constructivist in being ideally well situated for choosing basic moral principles, it is not likely to involve features of the judger and her situation that are easy to detect. For example, part of being ideally well situated would seem to require having all sorts of factual information, being free from certain forms of bias, and properly weighing the interests of parties affected by the choice of principles. But it is difficult to determine that someone has

satisfied these and other relevant desiderata for being well situated. So, even if it is not possible for someone who really is well situated to be mistaken in moral judgment, it is possible for critics who acknowledge that such error is not possible to raise sensible questions about the truth of a person's moral judgment. Hence, although the constructivist cannot allow for the possibility of deep moral error, she can plausibly argue that our commonsense critical practices do not presuppose that deep moral error is possible. Moreover, she can go on to accommodate the idea that it makes sense to criticize those who are ideally situated. The constructivist, it would appear, can plausibly respond to the argument from moral error.

[See also *Ethical Theory*; *Moral Realism*; *Moral Relativism*; *Rawls, John.*]

BIBLIOGRAPHY

Brink, D. O. *Moral Realism and the Foundations of Ethics*. Cambridge, 1989. In chapter 2 Brink uses the argument from moral error against constructivism. Appendix 4 is a critical discussion of Rawlsian constructivism.

Firth, R. "Ethical Absolutism and the Ideal Observer," *Philosophy and Phenomenological Research*, Vol. 12 (1952), 317–45. A classic statement of the ideal-observer version of constructivism.

Milo, R. "Skepticism and Moral Justification," *The Monist*, Vol. 76 (1993), 379–93. Milo defends a contractarian version of constructivism.

O'Neill, O. "Constructivisms in Ethics," in *Constructions of Reason* (Cambridge, 1990). O'Neill criticizes Rawls's version of constructivism and sketches what she takes to be a more plausible version of the view inspired by Kant's writings.

Rawls, J. "Kantian Constructivism in Moral Theory," *Journal of Philosophy*, Vol. 77 (1980), 515–72. An elaboration of a constructivist view that centrally involves a Kantian conception of persons.

Timmons, M. "Irrealism and Error in Ethics," *Philosophia*, Vol. 22 (1993), 373–406. A critical discussion of the argument from moral error.

Wong, D. *Moral Relativity*. Berkeley, 1984. Wong both criticizes various versions of moral relativism and defends his own version.

— MARK TIMMONS

CONTENT, MENTAL

Beliefs, desires, perceptions, and other mental states and events are said to possess content. We attribute such states and events with sentences such as

(1) Arabella believes that the cat is crying.

(1) contains a propositional attitude verb ("believes") and a sentence complement ("the cat is crying"). The verb specifies a type of mental state (belief), and the complement sentence indicates the content of the state. On most accounts this content is the proposition ex-

pressed by that sentence. Propositions have been variously conceived as abstract entities composed of modes of presentation, sets of possible worlds, sets of synonymous sentences, and structured entities containing individuals and properties. All these accounts agree that propositions determine truth conditions. Some mental states and events (e.g., desiring to visit Paris) seem to have contents that are not propositions. However, for most of the current discussion, contents will be identified with propositions and contentful mental states with mental states that possess truth conditions.

Both natural-language sentences and mental states possess contents. The relation between content properties of the two items is controversial. Some philosophers think that natural-language expressions derive their contents from mental states, while others hold that, at least in some cases, the dependency goes the other way. In any case, it is plausible that there are mental states whose contents cannot be expressed or cannot be completely expressed by sentences of English (or other natural languages). For example, the full propositional content of a person watching the sun set is only partially captured by an attribution such as "*A* sees that the sun is setting." Also, some of the states posited by cognitive psychology and the mental states of animals plausibly have contents that fail to correspond to any contents expressible in English.

Content apparently endows mental states with a number of remarkable features. First, they or their constituents refer to extra mental reality. When a person perceives that the sun is setting her perception refers to and thus puts her into contact with the sun. Second, they seem to be essentially normative. For example, a person ought to believe that the sun is setting only if the sun is setting, and if she believes that the sun is setting she ought not believe that the sun is not setting. Third, they apparently cause other mental states and behavior in virtue of their contents. For example, Arabella's belief that the cat is crying causes her to feed it. Fourth, a person can apparently know the contents of her own thought a priori and with an authority available only to her.

It is difficult to see how anything can exemplify all these features. The problem is especially difficult for philosophers who endorse naturalism, the view that all genuine properties are constituted by or realized by properties that are mentioned in true theories of the natural sciences. Content properties are prima facie so different from physical and biological properties as to raise the question of whether they are natural properties.

Hilary Putnam (1975) and Tyler Burge (1979) described thought experiments that have been taken to have important consequences for the nature of mental

contents. Putnam imagined two thinkers, Oscar and twin-Oscar, who are identical with respect to their intrinsic neurophysiological properties but whose environments differ. Specifically, Oscar shares our environment, but twin-Oscar lives on twin-earth where the abundant substance that quenches thirst, fills the twin-earth oceans, and so forth is not H_2O but XYZ. H_2O's and XYZ's superficial properties are identical, and the two substances are indistinguishable without chemical analysis. Putnam claims that, while Oscar's sentence "Water is wet" and the thought he expresses with it are about H_2O, the same sentence in twin-Oscar's language and the thought he expresses with it are about XYZ. The two thoughts differ in their propositional contents, since one is true if and only if (iff) H_2O is wet and the other iff XYZ is wet. Putnam supports these conclusions with the intuition that, were Oscar and twin-Oscar to learn that the substances each refers to with the word water differ in their chemical natures, they would agree that their utterances of "Water is wet" possessed different truth conditions.

Putnam's thought experiment has been taken to establish the truth of content externalism, the thesis that the individuation conditions of mental content are partially external to the thinker. The point generalizes to other mental states whose contents are the same as the contents of sentences containing natural-kind terms such as water. Burge described further thought experiments that he thinks show that practically all thoughts expressible in natural language are externally individuated, and others have argued that all mental states that express extra-mental truth conditions are externally individuated (LePore & Loewer, 1986).

Some philosophers think that natural-language expressions derive their contents from mental states, while others hold that the dependency goes the other way.

Some philosophers (Fodor, 1987; Loar, 1987) react to content externalism by granting that mental states possess externally individuated contents but adding that they also possess narrow contents that are not externally individuated. Oscar's and twin-Oscar's beliefs possess the same narrow content. Philosophers sympathetic to narrow contents raise a number of considerations. One is the Cartesian intuition that thinkers in the same intrinsic state have the same mental lives. It seems essential to our conception of a mental life that it possess content, so there must be some kind of content that such thinkers share. The other consideration is that the causal powers of Oscar's and twin-Oscar's mental states seem to be, in an important way, the same. Fodor (1987) claims that if these causal powers involve the states' contents, then that content must be narrow.

Whether or not these considerations are persuasive, it has proved difficult to formulate a satisfactory notion of narrow content. If natural-language sentences express only externally individuated contents, then we do not attribute narrow content with sentences such as (1). While identity of intrinsic neurophysiological states is sufficient for identity of narrow content, it is not a plausible necessary condition. To adopt it as such would make it enormously unlikely that two people have ever shared the same narrow content state and impossible for a state to maintain its content in the course of reasoning. While some proposals for necessary and sufficient conditions for identity of narrow content have been forthcoming (Fodor, 1987), there is little agreement concerning whether they are correct or, for that matter, whether a notion of narrow content is even needed.

Externalism seems to be in tension with our having a priori knowledge of the contents of our thoughts (Boghossian, 1989). If the content of the thought (e.g., that water is wet) is individuated in part by external factors, then it seems that a person could know that she is thinking this thought only if she knows that those external factors obtain, and thus it is implausible that such knowledge is a priori. One response to this is to grant that we have a priori knowledge only of narrow contents. But a number of philosophers (Burge, 1988; Warfield, 1994) have responded that the tension is only apparent. Burge claims that judgments of the form "I am now thinking that water is wet" are self-verifying, since one cannot make the judgment without thinking the thought that the judgment is about. If this is correct, then externalism and a priori knowledge of content are not always incompatible. But such self-verifying thoughts seem to be a very special case of the thoughts whose contents we seem able to know a priori. It is likely that little progress concerning the epistemology of content can be made without an account of the nature of contentful mental states.

The dominant view in the philosophy of mind is that contentful mental states are functionally individuated internal states. Some philosophers (Dretske, 1981; Fodor 1987) posit that these states are partially constituted by mental representations that are the bearers of propositional content. Mental representations are conceived of as picturelike (mental images), maps, or linguistic expressions. One view (Fodor, 1979) is that mental representations are expressions in a language of thought, Mentalese. On this account thinking that the cat is crying involves tokening a Mentalese sentence with the content that the cat is crying. The thought inherits its content from the semantic properties of its constituent sentence, which in turn obtains its content from the semantic properties of its constituent expressions. Fodor identifies concepts with Mentalese expressions. So, for example, possessing the concept cat is being able to token a Mentalese expression that refers to cats. Some philosophers (Peacocke, 1986) have argued that the contents of perceptual states are nonconceptual. If so, then the contents of these states are not borne by Mentalese expressions.

The nature of the bearers of mental content is best seen as an empirical issue. Fodor (1987) cites the fact that thought is productive and systematic as support for the language-of-thought hypothesis. Productivity is the capacity to produce complicated thoughts by combining simpler thoughts, and systematicity involves being able to think thoughts that are systematically related to each other, as are the thoughts that Bill loves Newt and that Newt loves Bill. Fodor argues that the language-of-thought hypothesis provides the best explanation of these phenomena, since languages are productive and systematic. Further, cognitive scientists have constructed theories of cognitive processes, language comprehension (Pinker, 1994), perception (Marr, 1982), and so forth that involve subpersonal contentful mental representations. For example, on one such theory understanding a natural-language sentence involves tokening a representation of its grammatical structure. These representations are not accessible to consciousness and have contents that are not usually available as the contents of a person's beliefs.

There have been various attempts to specify conditions in virtue of which mental states or mental representations possess their contents. Some of these are attempts to naturalize content properties. Following are brief descriptions of the main proposals.

According to interpretationist theories (ITs; Davidson, 1984; Lewis, 1974) our practices of interpreting one another partially constitute the contents of mental states. On Davidson's approach interpretation is constrained by principles of rationality and charity. These principles say, roughly, that a person's mental states are generally rational and her beliefs are generally true. According to Davidson the evidential base for an assignment of contentful mental states to a person consists of her dispositions to hold true sentences under various conditions. She believes that *p* (desires that *p*, etc.) iff assignments of content to her sentences and to her mental states that systematize these holding true dispositions and that conform to the principles of charity and rationality assign to her the belief that *p* (desire that *p*, etc.).

On ITs, content properties are holistic, since whether or not a person exemplifies a particular contentful mental state depends on what other mental states she exemplifies and on their relations to each other and to environmental conditions. Davidson's IT is externalist, since a state's content is partially determined by relations to environmental conditions. But his account does not provide a naturalistic account of content, since it explains content in terms that presuppose content: holding true, rationality, truth. The primary difficulty with extant ITs is their vagueness. No one has formulated the principles of rationality and charity with sufficient clarity to permit an evaluation of proposed ITs.

It is plausible that there are mental states

whose contents cannot be expressed or cannot be

completely expressed by sentences of English

(or other natural languages).

According to conceptual role semantics (CRS), the content of a mental representation (or mental state) is determined by the inferential relations among representations and causal relations between representations and extramental events (Block, 1986; Loar, 1981; Sellars, 1963). In this respect CRS is similar to IT. The difference is that, whereas ITs employ holistic principles of interpretations (rationality and charity), CRS attempts to spell out inferential patterns associated with particular concepts. CRS seems plausible for the logical connectives. For example, if a thinker is disposed to infer the representation A#B from A and B and vice versa, then # is the thinker's conjunction concept. Some philosophers (Peacocke, 1992) have attempted to formulate conditions that are necessary and/or sufficient for possessing certain predicate concepts. It appears that any such account is committed to a substantial analytic–synthetic distinction, since it will hold that certain inferences involving a concept are necessary to having the concept (Fodor & LePore, 1992). Quine's arguments (1960) that there are no analytic inferences poses an important problem for CRS.

Another approach is informational semantics (Dretske, 1981; Stalnaker, 1984). These theories are supposed to provide naturalizations of content; that is, they specify naturalistic properties that are claimed to be sufficient for possessing content. Informational theories claim that the content of a belief is constituted by the information the belief state carries under certain conditions. A state S carries the information that a property P is instantiated just in case the occurrence of S is caused by and nomically implies the instantiation of P. Informational theories have difficulty accounting for the possibility of error, since if a belief state has the content that *p* it carries the information that *p*. To solve this problem Dretske proposed that the content of a belief is the information that it carries during what he calls "the learning period." A different suggestion (Stalnaker, 1984) is to identify belief content with the information the belief state carries under epistemically optimal conditions. Loewer (1987) has argued that these accounts are not successful as naturalizations, since they appeal to notions—learning, epistemic optimality—that themselves presuppose semantic notions.

Fodor has developed a sophisticated variant of informational theories that applies to the reference of Mentalese predicates. On this account, asymmetric dependency theory (ADT), a Mentalese predicate C refers to, for example, the property of being a cow if it is a law that cows cause Cs, and any other causal relation between something other than cows and Cs depends on this law but not vice versa. That is, if the other causal relations were to fail, it would still be a law that cows cause cows, but if the law were to fail, so would the other causal relation.

ADT is an atomistic account of content in that, contrary to CRS and ITs, it implies that the property of possessing a particular reference is metaphysically independent of inferential connections among thoughts and, indeed, independent of the existence of any other items with content. Whether or not one sees this as an advantage will depend on how one views the analytic–synthetic distinction. Obviously, ADT makes heavy use of metaphysical notions that are less than perspicacious, so one may wonder about its naturalistic credentials. It has also been argued (Boghossian, 1991) that it is equivalent to an optimal-conditions account and is subject to the objections that show that account not to be a naturalization.

Teleological theories of content ground the contents of mental states in biological functions. The biological functions of a system in an organism are those of its features that increased the organism's fitness. Teleological accounts are quite elaborate, but the basic idea (Millikan, 1984; Papineau, 1992) is that there are desire-producing and belief-producing biological systems with certain biological functions. The desire-producing system has the function of producing states that tend to bring about certain effects. The effect associated with a particular desire is its content. The belief-producing systems have the function of producing states that tend to be tokened when certain states of affairs obtain. The state of affairs thus associated with a belief is its content.

Teleological accounts are appealing, since they are naturalistic, assign biological significance to contentful states, and seem to supply them with a kind of normativity. But various serious objections have been raised to teleological theories of content (Fodor, 1992). The most serious is that it is doubtful that teleological considerations are sufficient to assign determinate contents to mental states. A desire state will typically tend to bring about a number of different advantageous effects. Natural selection does not select any one of these effects as the content of the desire. Similarly, natural selection will not single out one of the states of affairs a belief state will typically be associated with as its unique content.

Whether or not content properties can be naturalized is an open question. Some consider it a very important question, since they think that if content properties cannot be naturalized then they are unsuitable to appear in scientific theories or, even worse, that they do not exist or are uninstantiated (Stich, 1983). The unsuitability of content properties for science would be a blow to the emerging cognitive sciences. But the nonexistence of content properties would be devastating to the way we think about ourselves and others, since these ways are permeated with attributions of contentful states. In fact, it has been argued (Boghossian, 1990) that the thesis that there are no content properties is incoherent. Fortunately, no dire consequences strictly follow from the failure of naturalization. It may be that content properties are natural but not naturalizable (McGinn, 1991). It is possible that, while content properties are natural, connections between them and properties that occur in the natural sciences are too unsystematic or too complicated for us to discern. But whether or not this is so is also an open question.

[See also Davidson, Donald; Internalism versus Externalism; Knowledge, A Priori; Language of Thought; Naturalism; Philosophy of Mind; Putnam, Hilary; Quine, Willard Van Orman.]

BIBLIOGRAPHY

Block, N. "Advertisement for a Semantics for Psychology," in *Midwest Studies in Philosophy,* Vol. 10. Minneapolis, 1986.

Boghossian, P. "The Status of Content," *Philosophical Review,* Vol. 99 (1990), 157–84.

———. "Naturalizing Content," in B. Loewer and G. Rey, eds., *Meaning and Mind* (Oxford, 1991).

———. "Content and Self-Knowledge," *Philosophical Topics,* Vol. 17 (1989), 5–26.

Burge, T. "Individualism and the Mental," *Midwest Studies in Philosophy,* Vol. 4. Minneapolis, 1979.

———. "Individualism and Self-knowledge," *Journal of Philosophy,* Vol. 85 (1988), 644–58.

Davidson, D. *Inquiries into Truth and Interpretation.* Oxford, 1984.

Dretske, F. *Knowledge and the Flow of Information.* Cambridge, MA, 1981.

Fodor, J. *The Language of Thought.* Cambridge, MA, 1979.

———. *Psychosemantics.* Cambridge, MA, 1987.

———. *A Theory of Content and Other Essays.* Cambridge, MA. 1990.

———. *Theory of Content and Other Essays.* Cambridge, MA, 1992.

Fodor, J., and E. LePore. *Holism: A Shopper's Guide.* Oxford, 1992.

Grice, P. "Meaning," *Philosophical Review,* Vol. 66 (1957), 377–88.

LePore, E., and B. Loewer. "Solipsistic Semantics," *Midwest Studies in Philosophy* (1986).

Lewis, D. *Convention.* Cambridge, MA, 1969.

———. "Radical Interpretation," *Synthese,* Vol. 23 (1974), 331–44.

Loar, B. *Mind and Meaning.* Cambridge, 1981.

———. "Social Content and Psychological Content," in R. Grimm and D. Merrill, eds., *Contents of Thought* (Tucson, 1986).

Loewer, B. "From Information to Intentionality," *Synthese,* Vol. 70 (1987), 287–317.

Marr, D. *Vision.* San Francisco, 1982.

McGinn, C. *The Limits of Philosophy.* Oxford, 1991.

Millikan, R. *Language, Thought, and Other Biological Categories.* Cambridge, MA, 1984.

Papineau, D. *Naturalism.* Oxford, 1992.

Peacocke, C. *Thoughts: An Essay on Content.* Cambridge, MA, 1986.

———. *A Study of Concepts.* Cambridge, MA, 1992.

Pinker, S. *The Language Instinct.* New York, 1994.

Putnam, H. "The Meaning of Meaning," in *Mind, Language, and Reality* (Cambridge, 1975).

Quine, W. V. O. *Word and Object.* Cambridge, MA, 1960.

Schiffer, S. *Meaning.* Cambridge, MA, 1972.

Sellars, W. *Science, Perception, and Reality.* London, 1963.

Stalnaker, R. *Inquiry.* Cambridge, MA, 1984.

Stich, S. *From Folk Psychology to Cognitive Psychology.* Cambridge, MA, 1983.

Warfield, F. "Externalism and Self-Knowledge," *Analysis* (1994).

— BARRY LOEWER

CONTEXTUALISM

Varying standards seem to govern our practices of attributing knowledge to subjects. In certain contexts we'll say a subject knows provided only that she has a true belief and is in a reasonably strong epistemic position with respect to the proposition in question. In other contexts—when, for instance, a lot rides on whether the subject is right—we may deny that the subject knows unless we think she's in a very strong epistemic position with respect to the proposition in question. Thus, for instance, if over coffee someone asks me merely out of idle curiosity whether I know if my colleague Thelma was in her office on a particular day about a week ago, I'll answer affirmatively if I have a clear recollection of a trustworthy source telling me on the day in question that Thelma was in. But if I were asked the same question in a trial at which Thelma is being charged with committing a murder at the office on the day in question, I'd probably deny that I know that she was in her office, testifying, "I think she was in her office because I remember so-and-so telling me she was in there. But, no, I don't know that she was in." Multiple examples would show that our practices of ascribing knowledge are sensitive to a wide variety of contextual factors that govern the standards a subject must live up to before we'll credit her with having knowledge. Similarly subject to contextually varying standards are our practices of saying that subjects' beliefs are or are not justified.

That such shifting standards govern whether we'll say that a subject knows or doesn't know, or is justified or unjustified in her belief, is not controversial. But invariantists believe that, lying behind the ever-shifting standards that govern whether we'll say that someone knows (is justified in believing), are constant, unchanging standards that govern whether they really know (are justified). Thus, the invariantist will hold that, supposing that Thelma was in fact in her office, since I'm in an equally strong epistemic position with respect to that fact in each of the two situations imagined above, either my claim to know in the first case or my admission in the second case that I don't know must be false, however warranted or conversationally useful this false assertion may be. The contextualist, on the other hand, can hold that both of my assertions are true, for the contextualist believes that the standards that govern whether I can be truthfully credited with knowledge—and not just those that govern whether speakers will in fact credit me with knowledge—vary with context.

Certain skeptical arguments

threaten to show that we know nothing

or very little and are therefore wrong

whenever, or almost whenever,

we claim to know anything.

Contextualism comes in two basic varieties. Contextualists of the first type tend to focus their attention on the context of the putative subject of knowledge, stressing that the epistemic standards to be applied to that subject depend on various features of her context: What form of inquiry is she engaged in? What are the standards of the relevant social group she's a member of? What questions or doubts have been raised in the conversation she's participating in? Contextualists of the second type tend to express their contextualist thesis metalinguistically, saying that the truth conditions, meaning, or content of sentences ascribing knowledge to subjects vary with the context in which those sentences are uttered. These contextualists therefore tend

to focus on the conversational context of the speaker—the person uttering the sentence ascribing knowledge to the subject—rather than on the context of the subject herself, in locating what it is that sets the epistemic standards in force. Of course, in the case of first-person knowledge claims, the speaker and the putative subject of knowledge are one and the same. But the distinction becomes important in treating third-person attributions of knowledge (or in treating first-person claims to have known something in the past: here contextualists of the second type will look to the speaker's context at the time of utterance, and not at the past time being talked about, for what sets the standards).

Suppose you and I are discussing whether Thelma was in her office on the day of the murder, and we're in a context governed by very high standards—so high that I've denied knowing that she was in her office, even though I remember the trustworthy source telling me she was there. You then ask me whether Louise might know if Thelma was in her office. I know that Louise heard the same report I did from the trustworthy source but, like me, has nothing else to go by in the matter. But I also know that Louise is discussing the murder at the local tavern—a place renowned for the low epistemic standards that govern all conversations within its walls. Here it seems clear that I should say that, like me, Louise doesn't know that Thelma was in her office. The standards are set here by features of the speaker's conversational context, and not by the context of the putative subject of knowledge. Of course, for certain purposes, and especially in cases where we're judging whether a subject's belief is justified, we may wish to evaluate her belief relative to standards set by features of her context. But there's nothing in the second version of contextualism to rule this out: among the many standards a speaker's context may select are those relevant to the subject's context.

This case illustrates an important feature of contextualist theories of the second type. On these views, one speaker may truthfully ascribe knowledge of a fact to a subject, while another speaker may truthfully deny that the same subject knows that very fact. Thus, Louise may truthfully say she knows that Thelma was in her office, while at the same time I may truthfully deny that Louise knows that very thing.

Most contextualists hold that, in addition to such factors as the speaker's setting and the importance of being right, epistemic standards are sensitive to what's been said in a given conversation and can change as a conversation progresses. Such sensitivity makes possible one of the most important applications of contextualist theories, which is to the problem of skepticism.

Certain skeptical arguments threaten to show that we know nothing or very little and are therefore wrong whenever, or almost whenever, we claim to know anything. While few are really tempted to accept such skeptical conclusions, many find the arguments for them very powerful. Contextualist theories can sometimes explain the power of these skeptical arguments while at the same time protecting the truth of most of our claims to know. For the contextualist can claim that the skeptic, in presenting his argument, manipulates the standards for knowledge, raising them to such a level as to make his conclusion (that we don't know) true. The skeptic may do this by injecting into the conversation, and thereby making conversationally relevant, certain ordinarily irrelevant alternatives to what we claim to know—alternatives we cannot rule out even if we usually don't have to rule them out to be truthfully credited with knowledge. Or the skeptic's denials that we know may trigger what David Lewis calls a "rule of accommodation"—a rule according to which the "conversational score" tends to adjust to make what's said true—which will raise the standards to the level needed to validate his skeptical denials of knowledge (Lewis, 1979). Whatever conversational mechanism is manipulated, if the skeptical arguments work by raising the standards for knowledge, then, while the skeptic may be able to truthfully state his conclusion, this will not show that we're wrong in other contexts, when, with no pesky skeptics around raising the standards, we claim to know the very things the skeptic truthfully says we don't know. For the fact that we fail to satisfy the skeptic's unusually inflated epistemic standards does not imply that we fall short of meeting the lower standards that govern our other conversations and debates.

[See also Epistemology; Skepticism.]

BIBLIOGRAPHY

Annis, D. "A Contextual Theory of Epistemic Justification," *American Philosophical Quarterly*, Vol. 15 (1978), 213–19.

Cohen, S. "Knowledge, Context, and Social Standards," *Synthese*, Vol. 73 (1987), 3–26.

———. "How to Be a Fallibilist," *Philosophical Perspectives*, Vol. 2 (1988), 91–123.

DeRose, K. "Contextualism and Knowledge Attributions," *Philosophy and Phenomenological Research*, Vol. 52 (1992), 913–29.

———. "Solving the Skeptical Problem," *The Philosophical Review*, Vol. 104 (1995), 1–52.

Dretske, F. "The Pragmatic Dimension of Knowledge," *Philosophical Studies*, Vol. 40 (1981), 363–78.

Hambourger, R. "Justified Assertion and the Relativity of Knowledge," *Philosophical Studies*, Vol. 51 (1987), 241–69.

Lewis, D. "Scorekeeping in a Language Game," *Journal of Philosophical Logic*, Vol. 8 (1979), 339–59.

Unger, P. *Philosophical Relativity*. Minneapolis, 1984.

———. "The Cone Model of Knowledge," *Philosophical Topics*, Vol. 14 (1986), 125–78.

Williams, M. *Unnatural Doubts: Epistemological Realism and the Basis of Scepticism*. Cambridge, MA, 1991.

Wittgenstein, L. *On Certainty*. New York, 1969.

— KEITH DEROSE

CRITERIOLOGY

"Science of criteria" or criteriology is a term, originally neoscholastic, for a theory of knowledge in which judgments are warranted or justified simply by conforming to certain criteria for correct judgment. These criteria are general principles that specify what sorts of considerations ultimately confer warrant on some judgments and that tend (tacitly) to guide self-reflective persons in checking and correcting their judgments. The epistemologist's task is to formulate these principles by reflecting on the considerations present and absent in various judgments we intuitively think of as warranted and unwarranted.

"Criteriology" is a term for a theory of knowledge in which judgments are warranted or justified simply by conforming to certain criteria for correct judgment.

Different criteria may deal with different subject matters, degrees, and sources of warrant (e.g., in perception, memory, inference). Ultimately, there must be warranting considerations other than inferability from other warranted judgments. These must be internally accessible through introspection or reflection without relying on further warranted judgments. They won't be considerations such as whether nature designed us to be reliable judges but ones such as whether we ostensibly see or recall something or intuitively grasp or clearly and distinctly conceive something.

Many epistemologists argue that critical considerations needn't guarantee truth or confer certainty, and whatever warrant they confer may be defeated. For instance, if one ostensibly sees something red, one is prima facie or defeasibly warranted in judging that one actually sees something red. The judgment might not be warranted when, despite ostensibly seeing something red, one has evidence that the illumination makes everything look red. We need additional principles specifying what considerations defeat warrant.

However, if criterial considerations don't guarantee truth, what makes a set of principles genuinely warranting? Putative common contingent features such as their overall reliability rest warrant on something beyond mere conformity to these principles and may allow for alternative principles. Criteriologists (e.g., Pollock, 1974, 1986) often appeal to controversial, nonscholastic, views about concepts and truth influenced by Wittgenstein. Criteria are internalized norms (rules) about when to make and correct judgments ascribing a concept. They characterize what persons must, in order to have a particular concept, tacitly know how to do in their judging and reasoning and be tacitly guided by. Criteria individuate our concepts and thus are necessarily correct. Although warranted judgments needn't be true, we have no idea of their truth completely divorced from what undefeated criterial considerations warrant. Critics often respond: surely this norm conformity must have a purpose beyond itself, like accurately representing the world?

[See also Epistemology; Wittgenstein, Ludwig Josef Johann.]

BIBLIOGRAPHY

Criteriologies

Coffey, P. *Epistemology or the Theory of Knowledge: An Introduction to General Metaphysics,* 2 vols. London, 1917.

Pollock, J. *Knowledge and Justification.* Princeton, 1974.

———. *Contemporary Theories of Knowledge.* Totowa, NJ, 1986.

Critical Discussions

Lycan, W. G. "Non-inductive Evidence: Recent Work on Wittgenstein's 'criteria,' " *American Philosophical Quarterly,* Vol. 8 (1971), 109–25.

Millikan, R. "Truth Rules, Hoverflies, and the Kripke-Wittgenstein Paradox," *Philosophical Review,* Vol. 99 (1990), 323–53.

Plantinga, A. *Warrant: The Current Debate.* Oxford, 1993.

Wright, C. J. G. "Second Thoughts about Criteria," *Synthese,* Vol. 58 (1984), 383–405.

— BRUCE HUNTER

CRITICAL THEORY

"Critical theory" is used to refer to the diverse body of work produced by members and associates of the Frankfurt Institute for Social Research after Max Horkheimer became its director in 1930. The first generation of what came to be called the Frankfurt school included, in addition to Horkheimer, such prominent figures as Theodor Adorno, Herbert Marcuse, Walter Benjamin, Erich Fromm, Leo Löwenthal, Franz Neumann, Otto Kirchheimer, and Frederick Pollock. The most influential members of the second generation are Jürgen Habermas, Karl-Otto Apel, and Albrecht Wellmer. As the variety of backgrounds and interests might suggest, critical social theory was conceived as a multidisciplinary program linking philosophy to history and the human sciences in a kind of "philosophically oriented so-

cial inquiry," as Horkheimer put it. Though very strongly influenced by Kant and neo-Kantianism, Hegel and German idealism, Weber and Freud, it was understood as a renewal of Marxism inspired in part by the earlier work of Georg Lukács and Karl Korsch. This updated Marxism would take account of the altered historical realities of advanced capitalism and integrate areas of inquiry neglected by traditional Marxism, such as philosophy and political theory, cultural studies (including studies of mass culture), and social psychology (appropriating psychoanalysis for social theory). With the rise of National Socialism, the institute moved briefly to Geneva and Paris in 1933 and then in 1934 to Columbia University in New York, where its journal, the *Zeitschrift für Sozialforschung,* continued to be published until 1941, the last volume in English. Early in the 1950s, Horkheimer and Adorno reestablished the institute in Frankfurt. Habermas became an assistant there in 1955.

The insistence on the "truth content" of the

"bourgeois ideals" of freedom, truth, and justice,

the refusal to abandon them as mere ideology,

was severely tested by the horrors of World War II.

The original project of a critical social theory advanced by Horkheimer was a version of Marx's *Aufhebung* of philosophy in social theory and practice. Philosophy was to become a sociohistorical, practically oriented critique of reason and its claimed realizations. While the dominant forms of reason were often distorted in the interests of dominant classes, the aim of critical theory was, not simply to negate them, but, by examining their genesis and functions, to transform them and enlist them in the struggle for a better world. The insistence on the 'truth content' of the 'bourgeois ideals' of freedom, truth, and justice, the refusal to abandon them as mere ideology, was severely tested by the horrors of World War II. Early in the 1940s, in their collaborative reflections on the 'dialectic of enlightenment,' Horkheimer and Adorno offered a much more pessimistic view of the history of reason. Keying on a tendency that Weber had emphasized, the relentless spread of "instrumental" rationality, they revered Marx's positive evaluation of scientific-technological progress. It was now seen as the core of a domination that had spread to all spheres of life and, in the process, had immobilized the potential agents of social change. In this 'totally administered society' with what Marcuse later called its "one-dimensional man," critical theory could at best reveal the unreason at the heart of what passed for reason, without offering any positive account of its own.

Habermas's work since the 1960s might be viewed as an attempt to avoid this impasse by introducing into critical theory a fundamental shift in paradigms from the philosophy of the subject to the theory of communication and from means-ends rationality to communicative rationality. This serves as the basis for an altered diagnosis of the ills of modernity—as rooted, not in rationalization as such, but in a one-sided rationalization driven by economic and administrative forces—and an altered prescription for their cure, the democratization of public opinion and will formation in an effectively functioning public sphere, where issues of general concern are submitted to rational, critical public debate.

[See also Communicative Action; Freud, Sigmund; Habermas, Jürgen; Hegel, Georg Wilhelm Friedrich; Kant, Immanuel; Marx, Karl.]

BIBLIOGRAPHY

Arato, A., and E. Gebhardt, eds. *The Essential Frankfurt School Reader.* New York, 1978.

Bronner, S., and D. Kellner, eds., *Critical Theory and Society: A Reader.* New York, 1989.

Ingram, D., and J. Simon-Ingram, eds. *Critical Theory: The Essential Readings.* New York, 1990.

Jay, M. *The Dialectical Imagination.* Boston, 1973.

Wiggershaus, R. *The Frankfurt School,* translated by M. Robertson. Cambridge, MA, 1994.

— THOMAS MCCARTHY

D

DAVIDSON, DONALD

Donald Davidson, Willis and Marion Slusser Professor of Philosophy at the University of California at Berkeley, was born in 1917 in Springfield, Massachusetts, and graduated from Harvard in 1939. After serving in the United States Navy, Davidson returned to Harvard, writing his doctoral dissertation on Plato's *Philebus*. Receiving his Ph.D. in 1949, Davidson went on to do extensive work in decision theory, in collaboration with Patrick Suppes and others. The methodological challenges of giving empirical application to rational-choice theory have had a lasting influence on Davidson, apparent in his formulation of philosophical questions regarding action, the mental, and linguistic meaning. Davidson's views have come gradually to articulation through series of papers presenting detailed arguments pertaining to specific problems in each of these areas of philosophy, elaborating a set of closely interconnected and highly influential doctrines. This entry looks briefly at each area in turn, emphasizing certain general features characteristic of Davidson's approach, and then concludes with a glance at the key themes of Davidson's more explicitly metaphilosophical work of the 1980s and 1990s.

The Causal Theory of Action

Davidson's view, first set out in print in *Actions, Reasons, and Causes* (1963, see 1980a), is that we must consider the reasons for our actions—combinations of propositional attitudes, paradigmatically belief-desire pairs—to be also their causes (1980a). In this and related papers Davidson grants a main premise of the anti-causalist view prevailing at the time, that the teleological form of action-explanation makes such explanation irreducibly different from the nomological form characteristic of explanation in the natural sciences. What is distinctive about action-explanation is that it identifies the events involved (the action and its explanatory antecedent) in terms that reveal them to be part of a rational pattern. Davidson goes on to challenge anti-causal orthodoxy, however, by arguing that it does not follow from this irreducible difference that action explanation is not a species of causal explanation.

A striking aspect of Davidson's view is the claim that the appeal to reason on which action explanations turn will be genuinely explanatory only insofar as the particular events thus rationally related are also related as cause and effect, and hence, for Davidson, may also be characterized by nomologically related descriptions. But Davidson insists that the explanatory efficacy of the reason-explanation in no way depends on our possessing the explanation that nomologically relates the particular events in question. Indeed, in the typical case we enjoy the full benefits of effective action explanation

> *If a theory of truth is to serve as a theory of meaning for a language, we need to know how an interpreter may arrive at such a theory for a language she does not know.*

without the slightest idea of what the descriptions might be of the relevant events under which they are subsumed by causal law. Davidson thus reconciles the following three fundamental claims. First, when an event is cited in successful explanation of another event, the former is a cause of the latter. Second, causal relations between events entail nomological relations between them. Third, *explanans* and *explanandum* in action explanations are captured in terms that cannot be subsumed under strict law. This reconciliation trades on a particular conception of the relation between cause and law. If two events are causally related, they are so related no matter how described. The nomological relation, however, obtains between kinds of events; laws, as Davidson says, are linguistic, and so while causal relations are extensional, and causally related events necessarily fall under what he terms strict law (that is, law "free from caveats and *ceteris paribus* clauses" [1993, p. 8]), they instantiate such law only under some appropriate description. Hence, the descriptions under which two causally related events appear in successful action explanation may be such that no amount of knowledge of strict causal law would allow us to infer the action from knowledge of the conditions cited in the explanation of it (1980a, 1993).

Anomalous Monism

A crucial element in Davidson's account of action is the distinction between a particular event and the descriptions that sort particular events under kinds. This same distinction is central also to his claims about the nature of the mental and its relation to the physical. In "Mental Events" and subsequent papers (1980a; 1993), Davidson argues that what it is to be a mental event is to be an event that falls under a mental predicate, that is to say, for Davidson, an intentional term. Correspondingly, what it is to be a physical event is to fall under a physical predicate, a predicate suitable for making nomological relations perspicuous. Ultimately, physical predicates are those of developed physics, a vocabulary the constitutive purpose of which is to track the causal structure of the world.

Since Davidson conceives of events as extensionally identified spatio-temporal particulars constituting nodes in the causal network, W. V. O. Quine's basic ontological dictum expresses also for Davidson an important truth; it is the unique business of physics to aim for full coverage. What this means for Davidson is that all events, qua nodes in the causal network, must be describable in the terms of physics. Yet some events are also mental, and Davidson argues that his physicalism supports no reductivist or eliminativist conclusions. For while all particular mental events are also particular physical events, no particular kind of mental event is a particular kind of physical event. The reason for this is that the intentionality, which for Davidson is the mark of the mental, is constituted, in his view, by our efforts to characterize fellow creatures as rational according to an intersubjective standard. We are able to view fellow language users thus because we have at our disposal not only the conceptual resources required to keep track of each other by keeping tabs on objective environmental relations in which we are all embroiled in various and changing ways, but also a set of concepts—of belief, desire, and so on—which allow us to construct accounts of how things seem to someone to be. This system of double bookkeeping allows us to absorb a great deal of variation and irregularity in human behavior by accounting for objective anomalies in terms of subjective variables. But this strategy remains informative and useful only insofar as the essential discrepancies between subjective perspective and objective reality that interpretation exploits are prevented from becoming arbitrary or chaotic—were that to happen, the subjective would lose its explanatory purpose, it would simply mark the place where explanation ends. This is why the interpretive construction of the subjective perspective must be tightly constrained; as Davidson says, making sense of others "we will try for a theory that finds [them] consistent, believer[s] of truths, and lover[s] of the good (all by our own lights, it goes without saying)" (1980a, p. 222). This constraint on the application of inten-

tional terms is often referred to as the "principle of charity." It reflects the fact that only the attitudes (though not only the rational attitudes) of a recognizably rational subject may be invoked in a genuinely explanatory way to account for the subject's behavior. Moreover, as Davidson recently has emphasized, because rationality considerations govern our application of propositional-attitude concepts, these concepts are irreducibly causal, "identified in part by the sorts of action they are prone to cause, given the right conditions" (1991b. p. 162). As he further points out, "the right conditions" are themselves not independently characterizable. The phrase, marking the interdependence of the application conditions of mental predicates, remains an ineliminable qualification of the sort of platitudinous generalizations that express the content of our psychological terms. By contrast, Davidson argues, the application of the predicates of physics—aimed at the formulation of strict causal law—cannot itself depend on causal concepts (1991b). The application conditions of terms related by strict empirical law must be independently specifiable. The real difference, then, between the mental and the physical, and the reason for the irreducibility of one to the other, stems from the fact that the vocabulary of physics and the vocabulary of psychology have evolved under the pressure of distinctively different interests. What we want from the former are modes of description that allow us to interact with each other as persons. What we want from the latter are laws "as complete and precise as we can make them; a different aim" (1991b, p. 163).

Truth and Meaning

In the philosophy of language, Davidson is associated with the view that we may account for linguistic competence by appropriately characterizing the evidence available to and resources required by an idealized interpreter (1984a). There are two fundamental aspects to this position. First, what, Davidson asks, might we know such that by knowing it we would be able to say what a speaker of a given language meant by some arbitrary utterance? His answer is a theory of truth for that language, of the sort which Alfred Tarski showed us how to construct. The condition of adequacy for such a theory is an adaptation of what Tarski called "convention T." We have, Davidson proposes, a theory of meaning for a given language L provided we have a theory that entails for each sentence of L an instance of the schema, 's is true in L if and only if p'. In this schema, 's' would be replaced by an expression that mentions a sentence of L (for example by means of quotation marks), and 'p' is replaced with any sentence of the language in which the theory is stated that is true if and only if the sentence mentioned in 's' is true. Such a theory then provides, based on finite resources, a recursive characterization of the truth conditions for any sentence of L. While all that is demanded by convention T is that the theorems of the theory—known as T-sentences—capture co-extensionality, "the hope," as Davidson says, "is that by putting appropriate formal and empirical restrictions on the theory as a whole, individual T-sentences will in fact serve to yield interpretations" (1984, p. 134). This proposal has spawned a great deal of work in formal semantics, guided by the aim of accounting for natural-language idioms in terms of their deep structure, or logical form, which makes explicit their truth-theoretical composition. For Davidson, the notion of logical form is extremely powerful; constrained on the one hand by our intuitions concerning entailment relations, and on the other by the logical resources of Tarskian truth-theory, the uncovering of logical form functions as a crucible within which crystallize the ontological categories our language commits us to. So for example, support for an ontology of events takes the form of an argument that we cannot account for the entailment relations intuitively characteristic of action sentences within the logical confines of a Tarskian theory of truth for a language unless we are willing to see such sentences as quantifying over events (cf., "The Logical Form of Action Sentences," 1980a).

Davidson's alternative to the representational view of mind is most succinctly expressed in the thesis that there is thought only when there is actual communication.

If a theory of truth is to serve as a theory of meaning for a language, we need to know how an interpreter may arrive at such a theory for a language she does not know. What is required for a recursive truth-theory to have empirical application? This question directs us to the other main aspect of Davidson's position, where Quine's influence is most apparent. Observing the utterances of a speaker but knowing neither what the speaker means nor what she believes, the interpreter can construct a theory of truth for the speaker by proceeding inductively on the assumption that the speaker's responses to her environment are rational, indeed that her mental life constitutes a rational whole (1984a). This assumption of rationality is, of course, defeasible with respect to the attribution of any one particular attitude, within the context of the construction of a

theory of the meaning of someone's words and the contents of her thoughts. Davidson's point is that irrationality is conceptually parasitic, and can be diagnosed only against a background of reason. Thus, in what Davidson dubs radical interpretation, the principle of charity is methodologically indispensable. Even while minimizing irrationality, however, an idealized interpreter will be able to generate for the speaker different theories of belief and meaning that comport equally well with the empirical evidence (i.e., with the speaker's utterances and their contexts). This indeterminacy Davidson regards as innocuous; the salient facts about meaning and mind are what such differing theories have in common (1984a, 1990b, 1991b).

Challenges

With respect to Davidson's view of action, the most serious objection is probably the claim that it fails to illuminate the feature by virtue of which action explanation actually is explanatory. Critics thus doubt the possibility of reconciling the three fundamental claims regarding explanation, cause, and law to which Davidson is committed (see above). One claim—advanced, for example, by Jerry Fodor—is that informative action explanation must somehow draw on the explanatory power of nomic relations, in which case Davidson's irreducibility–claim will be threatened. An alternative view—defended by anti-causalists like George Wilson—is that the explanatory force of reason-explanation is *sui generis,* and does not depend on reasons being causes. This would jeopardize Davidson's conception of event monism.

With regard specifically to anomalous monism, Jaegwon Kim and others have argued that Davidson's view renders the mental causally inert. Partly because of their different views on the individuation of events, this conflict is difficult to assess. However, if we grant Davidson his fundamental claims—that is, that the difference between the mental and the physical is a matter of vocabulary of description, and that events should be extensionally conceived—then his concept of supervenience ensures that a change in the truth value of the relevant kind of mental predicate ascription will entail some difference or other in causal relations. Naturally, alternatives to Davidson's Humean conceptions of causality and of the relations betwen causality and law are frequently at play in criticisms of both anomalous monism as well as Davidson's reconciliation of the irreducibility of action-explanation to nomic explanation with a causal view of action.

As for Davidson's philosophy of language, there have been objections at various levels to the idea that a theory of meaning for a language must take the form of a Tarskian truth-theory. Even while accepting the proposal that a theory of meaning should take the form of a theory of truth, one may ask, for example, why we should restrict ourselves, in producing a formal semantics for a language, to the resources of first-order predicate calculus. And many critics have doubted the prospects of accounting for natural language in purely extensional terms.

Metaphilosophy

It is important to note that Davidson's commitment to the specific contention that theories of truth as Tarski defined them give the structure of theories of meaning is a pragmatic methodological commitment. What supports Davidson's most innovative philosophical conclusions is the more general point that we must understand meaning in terms of truth, in conjunction with his insistence—following Quine—on a third-person perspective to meaning and mind which makes the conditions of interpretation constitutive of content. Together, these commitments yield an account of the concept of truth constrained by the methodological requirements of interpretation (1990b). This account contrasts both with traditional correspondence theories and with epistemic accounts of the sort advanced, for example, by Hilary Putnam, and is distinct from disquotationalist theories such as that of Paul Horwich (1990b).

The significance of these core commitments is readily apparent also in Davidson's argument aimed to discredit the duality of representational scheme and empirical content on the grounds that it presupposes the notion of an untranslatable language ("On the Very Idea of a Conceptual Scheme," 1984a). If truth and meaning are interlocking concepts whose features are illuminated by an account of the methodology of an ideal interpreter, the idea of alternative representations of reality that are mutually semantically impenetrable is not coherent. This argument also marks a dividing line between Davidson and Quine. For the metaphysical opposition between what is given to the mind on the one hand, and the processes brought to bear on that given, on the other, is the very duality in terms of which empiricism faces its defining challenge, namely to articulate a coherent notion of sensory evidence (1982). On this fundamental score, Quine has remained within the bounds of empiricism (1990c). Davidson, on the other hand, has gone on explicitly to reject the basic metaphor of mind as inner space on which empiricism rests. For Davidson the hold of this metaphor reveals itself in the persistence of the interdependent notions of mental states as representational and of truth as correspon-

dence, which, in turn, inextricably entangle us in the problems of relativism and skepticism (1986b, 1987a, 1989a, 1990b).

"A community of minds," Davidson concludes,

"is the basis of all knowledge:

it provides the measure of all things."

Davidson's alternative to the representational view of mind is most succinctly expressed in the thesis that there is thought only when there is actual communication (1989b, 1989c, 1991a, 1991b, 1992a). On this controversial view, knowledge of our own mental states, knowledge of the so-called external world, and knowledge of the mental states of others appear mutually interdependent (1991b). This forecloses the very possibility of a skeptical or relativist challenge, insofar as these are typically constructed around arguments that purport to show the impossibility of deriving any one of the three kinds of knowledge from either or both of the other two. This impossibility is something Davidson accepts—indeed insists on. Against the skeptic or relativist his claim is simply that the three forms of knowledge stand or fall together; denying one is to deny all, and to deny all is just to deprive our intentional concepts of any application. This position rests on two key claims. One is that shared linguistic understanding is a prerequisite for any standard of objectivity (1991b). Such a standard gives content to the very distinction exploited by the propositional attitude verbs between what is and what seems from some perspective to be, and hence, on Davidson's conception, is a prerequisite of thought. The other is the claim that the idea of shared linguistic understanding presupposes actual communication (1986c). The mental is thus what we reveal when we subject a certain vaguely delimited range of causal relations to a particular kind of description, the terms of which presuppose the mutual recognition of subjects interacting in a shared world.

This view carries with it the commitments to event monism, to the constitutive role of rationality for content, and to a view of human agents as an integral part of the natural world, that have always been evident in Davidson's work. The distinction between extensionally conceived particulars and their descriptions remains pivotal. But the upshot is fundamentally at odds with the governing metaphors of modern epistemology-centered philosophy: "A community of minds," Davidson concludes, "is the basis of all knowledge: it provides the measure of all things." And he adds: "It makes no sense to question the adequacy of this measure, or to seek a more ultimate standard" (1991b, p. 164). However we assess the plausibility of the considerations Davidson offers in support of this position, cognizance of the through-going externalism on which it is based should lead us to see it not as a species of antirealism or idealism, but as a fundamental rejection of foundationalist aspirations and as expressing a commitment to a recognizably pragmatist view of the nature of philosophy.

[See also Action Theory; Anomalous Monism; Decision Theory; Logical Form; Meaning; Philosophy of Language; Plato; Putnam, Hilary; Quine, Willard Van Orman; Rationality; Semantics; Skepticism; Supervenience; Truth.]

BIBLIOGRAPHY

Works by Davidson

Essays on Action and Events. Oxford, 1980a.
"Towards a Unified Theory of Meaning and Action," in *Grazer Philosophische Studien*, Vol. 11 (1980b).
"Empirical Content," in *Grazer Philosophische Studien*, Vol. 16/17 (1982), reprinted in LePore, 1986.
Enquiries into Truth and Interpretation. Oxford, 1984a.
Expressing Evaluations (The Lindley Lecture). Lawrence, KS, 1984b.
"First Person Authority," *Dialectica*, Vol. 38 (1984c).
"Judging Interpersonal Interests," in J. Elster and A. Hylland, eds., *Foundations of Social Choice Theory* (Cambridge, 1986a).
"A Coherence Theory of Truth and Knowledge," in E. LePore, ed., *Truth and Interpretation* (Oxford, 1986b). Reprinted, with "Afterthoughts, 1987," in A. Malichowski, ed., *Reading Rorty* (Oxford, 1987).
"A Nice Derangement of Epitaphs," in E. LePore, ed., *Truth and Interpretation* (Oxford, 1986c).
"Knowing One's Own Mind," American Philosophical Association Presidential Address, in *Proceedings and Addresses of the American Philosophical Association*, Vol. 61 (1987a).
"The Myth of the Subjective," in M. Krausz, ed., *Relativism,* (Bloomington, IN, 1989a).
"What is Present to the Mind?" in J. Brandl and W. Gombocz, eds., *The Mind of Donald Davidson* (Amsterdam, 1989b).
"The Conditions of Thought," in J. Brandl and W. Gombocz, eds., *The Mind of Donald Davidson.* (Amsterdam, 1989c).
Plato's "Philebus." New York, 1990a.
"The Structure and Content of Truth," *Journal of Philosophy*, Vol. 87 (1990b).
"Meaning, Truth, and Evidence," in R. Barrett and R. Gibson, eds., *Perspectives on Quine* (Oxford, 1990c).
"Turing's Test," in K. A. Mohyeldin Said, W. H. Newton-Smith, R. Viale, and K. V. Wilkes, eds., *Modelling the Mind* (Oxford, 1990d).
"Representation and Interpretation," in K. A. Mohyeldin Said, W. H. Newton-Smith, R. Viale, and K. V. Wilkes, eds., *Modelling the Mind* (Oxford, 1990e).
"Epistemology Externalized," *Dialectica*, Vol. 45 (1991a).
"Three Varieties of Knowledge," in A. Phillips Griffiths, ed., *A. J. Ayer Memorial Essays*, Vol. 30 (Cambridge, 1991b).

"The Second Person," in P. French, T. Uehling, and H. Wettstein, eds., *Midwest Studies in Philosophy: The Wittgenstein Legacy*, Vol. 17 (Minneapolis, 1992a).
"Thinking Causes," in J. Heil and A. Mele, eds., *Mental Causation* (Oxford, 1993).

Works on Davidson

Brandl, J., and W. Gombocz, eds. *The Mind of Donald Davidson.* Amsterdam, 1989.
Evnine, S. *Donald Davidson.* Palo Alto, CA, 1991.
LePore, E., and B. McLaughlin, eds. *Actions and Events.* Oxford, 1985.
LePore, E., ed. *Truth and Interpretation.* Oxford, 1986.
Malpas, G. *Donald Davidson and the Mirror of Meaning.* Cambridge, 1992.
Preyer, G., F. Siebelt, and A. Ulfig, eds. *Language, Mind and Epistemology: On Donald Davidson's Philosophy.* Dordrecht, 1994.
Ramberg, B. *Donald Davidson's Philosophy of Language: An Introduction.* Oxford, 1989.
Stoecker, R., ed. *Reflecting Davidson.* Berlin, 1993.
Vermazen, B., and M. Hintikka, eds. *Essays on Davidson: Action and Events.* Oxford, 1985.

— BJØRN T. RAMBERG

DECISION THEORY

Along direct and indirect paths contemporary normative decision theory exerts influence on moral theory, political philosophy, epistemology, and the philosophy of science. The subject is a large one with many recent developments, a few of which can be addressed here.

Expected Utility

The expected utility of an action with uncertain outcomes is a weighted average of the utilities of the outcomes, where the weight attached to each is the probability that the act will yield it. $EU(A) = \Sigma_i pr(A$ yields $O_i)\ U(O_i)$. The proposal that A's value is measured by its EU is consequentialist, in that A's utility depends on the utilities of its outcomes. The consequentialism need not be strict, since "outcome" can be construed broadly enough to include A itself. The probability that doing A yields outcome O_i typically depends on unknown states of the world; this is handled by using weights $pr($when S_j, A yields $O_i)$ in a suitable way. Subjective expected utility theory takes pr to reflect the decision maker's beliefs, rather than some objective probability, and takes U to measure value in the eyes of the decision maker rather than some objectively correct value. Such decision theories are meant to explicate subjective practical rationality, the rationality of a decision maker doing the best she can given her information and desires. They leave open the possibility that an account of objective value might be attached to expected utility theory, but normative decision theories as such tend either to embrace subjective utility, or to remain silent on the nature of objectively correct values. The subjective beliefs are often, though not always, taken to be partial beliefs. Bayesians in particular think of beliefs as action-guiding dispositions that come in varying degrees, and they use decision-theoretic arguments to defend this conception of belief. The theories of F. P. Ramsey, Bruno de Finetti, and L. J. Savage are classic examples of that approach.

Decision theorists base their use

of the concept of subjective utility

on axiomatic treatments of preference.

Controversy has long surrounded the concept of utility in philosophy and economics. Decision theorists base their use of the concept of subjective utility on axiomatic treatments of preference. Suppose an agent with a (rich) collection of preferences that meets the standards of rationality. The idea is to show that she can be interpreted as evaluating the objects she prefers in a way that is nonarbitrarily measured by the quantitative utility.

Evidential Decision Theory

The main idea of evidental decision theory (EDT) is that action A's value is measured by the EU that weights each possible outcome O_i by its probability conditional on A, $pr(O_i/A)$. Richard Jeffrey (1965) developed an axiomatic decision theory incorporating this approach. The theory avoids the often questionable objects of preference employed by earlier theories, and it avoids requiring that descriptions of states and acts be so fine-grained that each combination of them deterministically fixes an outcome. The theory takes the objects of an agent's preferences to be (the truth of) propositions; the suggestion is that preferring A to B can be understood as preferring getting the news that A to getting the news that B. For a variety of reasons, including the avoidance of objections to previous theories, the familiarity of the propositional algebra it uses, the generality and elegance of the theory, and the company of Jeffrey's important principle of belief revision for cases of uncertain learning, his theory became well known and influential among philosophers. It is the standard formulation of EDT.

Newcomb's Problem

Statistical correlations often indicate causal connections, but not always. EDT pays attention to the former, but in our deliberations we are most interested in the latter (what will our actions bring about?). EDT was soon confronted with examples where correlations between states and actions on one hand, and outcomes on the other, do not appropriately reflect the causal influence of actions over outcomes. Best known and much debated is Newcomb's problem, introduced by Robert Nozick (1969). A reliable predictor forecasts which of two options the agent will choose: to take the contents of an opaque box (A1), or the contents of both the opaque box and a transparent box that is seen to contain a thousand dollars (A2). On a prior forecast of A1 the predictor places a million dollars in the opaque box; upon forecasting A2 the predictor leaves the opaque box empty. The forecasts are made and the money arranged before the agent makes her choice, and the agent is confident that the problem is as described, with no cheating. EDT straightforwardly applied recommends A1, since the predictor's reliability makes the probability of a filled opaque box conditional on doing A1 high, so A1's evidential EU is also high. This supports the reasoning "most one-boxers get rich and most two-boxers do not, so I will be one of the former." On the other hand, dominance reasoning recommends A2: "The million dollars is there or it is not, and either way it is better also to take the thousand." It is a strange decision problem, but there are other less bizarre examples (e.g., the twin prisoner's dilemma, the smoking gene problem), and the conflict between dominance and evidential reasoning in these cases is real.

Causal Decision Theory

Dominance reasoning is unreliable when acts and states are not independent, and in Newcomb's problem the predictions (and the contents of the opaque box) are correlated with the actions. But there is no causal influence from the action to those states, and that is what really matters. Causal decision theory (CDT) is designed fully to employ the agent's beliefs about relevant causal influences; it has been offered in three versions with much in common by Allan Gibbard and William Harper (1978), Brian Skyrms (1980), and David Lewis (1981). In Gibbard and Harper's theory, the EU worth maximizing employs the weights $pr(A \,\square\!\!\rightarrow O_i)$, where $A \,\square\!\!\rightarrow O_i$ is a causal conditional: $A \,\square\!\!\rightarrow B$ holds when B is a causal consequence of A, or when B is unavoidable whatever the agent does. When M ("the opaque box contains a million") is not under the agent's influence the probabilities of $A1 \,\square\!\!\rightarrow M$ and $A2 \,\square\!\!\rightarrow M$ are equal, dominance reasoning is appropriate, and the theory recommends $A2$. Skyrms's theory avoids causal conditionals by presupposing a partition of states K_j relevant to the problem at hand and outside the influence of the agent. An expanded EU calculation by EDT would employ weights $pr(K_i/A)$. Skyrms's similar calculation uses $pr(K_j)$ instead, since K_j is not under the causal influence of A; this gives results in general agreement with Gibbard and Harper's. Lewis extends the Gibbard and Harper theory by employing causal conditionals with chancy consequents. Notable further developments on CDT are in Ellery Eells (1982), Jeffrey (1983), and Brad Armendt (1988).

Prisoner's Dilemma

Each of two isolated prisoners is invited to confess the guilt of both. The jailers offer these incentives: if both confess (defect from cooperation with the other prisoner), they receive long sentences of nine years; if both refuse to confess (each cooperates), they receive light sentences of one year on trumped-up charges; if just one confesses he goes free and the other is sentenced to ten years. What should they do? Assuming the sentences represent the total relevant payoffs, each prisoner's dominance reasoning recommends confession by each, but that pair of choices yields a much worse outcome for both than would joint cooperation. This two-person game, attributed to A. W. Tucker, has received much attention from game theorists, philosophers, political scientists, and biologists. The symmetry of the problem, and the tension between the individual incentives to defect and the social optimality of joint cooperation, make it a frequently discussed model for many kinds of interaction.

Interactions may be repeated, and, like other games, the PD (with revised payoffs) can be iterated. The iterated PD is one of the games that has most figured in studies of cooperation among rational agents in society, and among populations of biological organisms. When players expect to reencounter their opponents and expect their present play to be remembered on future occasions, the present payoffs and their deliberations become much more complex. Alternatively, organisms with no capacity to deliberate and limited memory of past encounters in iterated PD-like interactions can nevertheless stimulate and be stimulated by the play of others, leading to interesting "strategic play." Influential studies are Robert Axelrod (1981), which includes discussion of his well-known computer tournaments, and John Maynard Smith's work (presented in his 1982 book) on evolutionarily stable strategies. The descendent field of evolutionary game theory is now very active and rapidly growing.

Other Developments

Some of the many significant further topics in current philosophical work on decision theory include: modeling deliberation; the stability of decision; planning and strategic choice; the justification of game-theoretic solution concepts; convention and the coordination of choice; generalized EU and weakened preference principles; and the empirical observations of descriptive decision theory.

[See also Bayesianism.]

BIBLIOGRAPHY

Armendt, B. "Conditional Preference and Causal Expected Utility," in W. Harper and B. Skyrms, eds., *Causation in Decision, Belief Change, and Statistics* (Dordrecht, 1988).

Axelrod, R. "The Emergence of Cooperation among Egoists." *American Political Science Review*, Vol. 75 (1981), 306–18.

Broome, J. *Weighing Goods*. Oxford, 1991.

Eells, E. *Rational Decision and Causality*. Cambridge, 1982.

Gauthier, D. *Morals by Agreement*. Oxford, 1986.

Gibbard, A., and W. Harper. "Counterfactuals and Two Kinds of Expected Utility," in C. Hooker, ed., *Foundations and Applications of Decision Theory* (Dordrecht, 1978).

Jeffrey, R. *The Logic of Decision*. New York, 1965. 2nd ed., Chicago, 1983.

Lewis, D. "Causal Decision Theory," *Australasian Journal of Philosophy*, Vol. 59 (1981), 5–30.

Machina, M. "Decision-Making in the Presence of Risk," *Science*, Vol. 236 (1987), 537–43.

Maynard Smith, J. *Evolution and the Theory of Games*. Cambridge, 1982.

Nozick, R. "Newcomb's Problem and Two Principles of Choice," in N. Rescher, ed., *Essays in Honor of Carl G. Hempel* (Dordrecht, 1969).

Ramsey, F. P. "Truth and Probability" [1926], in D. H. Mellor, ed., *Foundations* (London, 1978).

Skyrms, B. *Causal Necessity*. New Haven, 1980.

———. *The Dynamics of Rational Deliberation*. Cambridge, 1990.

– BRAD ARMENDT

DECONSTRUCTION

To deconstruct a work of philosophy is to give an immanent reading of its conceptual scheme to the point that one begins to locate within the work a certain 'outside' that the scheme excludes but whose traces are nevertheless marked in the text. The term "deconstruction" was introduced by Jacques Derrida in 1967 as a translation of Martin Heidegger's word *Destruktion*, but it became clear almost immediately that with it he intended a major modification of the Heideggerian project. Although deconstruction has spread across the academy, it is with reference to Derrida's relation to Heidegger that the deconstruction of philosophy can be made precise.

Heidegger introduced the term *Destruktion* in *Being and Time* (1927) as part of his attempt to combat the degeneration of tradition into a series of dogmas and categories that had come to be regarded as self-evident by virtue of their longevity. Heidegger's aim was to expand the range of future possibilities by reopening the past and finding what was left unthought, particularly by the Greeks. Derrida's appropriation of the early Heidegger was less favorable to the Greeks because it was mediated by the later Heidegger's project of overcoming metaphysics. However, Derrida also questioned the later Heidegger's account on the grounds that it relied on the idea of the end of philosophy, a notion Derrida dismissed as preeminently metaphysical because it reinscribed classic notions of teleology, unity, and the opposition of inside and outside. In other words, Derridean deconstruction is a response to a fundamental aporia in Heidegger. Heidegger proclaimed the end of metaphysics but was still metaphysical.

Heidegger's aim was to expand the range of future possibilities by reopening the past and finding what was left unthought, particularly by the Greeks.

In his early works Derrida also took over from Heidegger the latter's identification of Western philosophy with the privileging of presence. Derrida found by a close reading of the texts of metaphysics that, although they embodied this privilege within their evaluation of the terms of the binary oppositions that structure metaphysical thought, they were unable to sustain it consistently in this hierarchization. That is why the first deconstructive step of reversing the hierarchy is followed by a second step in which the opposition is displaced in favor of a term that is undecidable between the terms of the opposition.

So, for example, although the overriding value that Western philosophy places on presence leads speech to be privileged over writing, Derrida argued that its articulation has recourse to the model of writing. A text like Plato's *Phaedrus,* which is standardly held to denigrate writing, can also be read as saying the reverse. By interweaving both readings, deconstruction avoids simply deepening the founding concepts of metaphysics, like the early Heidegger, or stepping outside its confines, as the later Heidegger sometimes seems to propose. The principal lesson of deconstruction, that what escapes metaphysics is within the metaphysical text and only accessible through it, has not only negotiated the Heideggerian aporia, it has also led to a more profound reading of Heidegger, in which elements of the early Heidegger are found in the later Heidegger and vice versa.

[See also Derrida, Jacques; Heidegger, Martin.]

BIBLIOGRAPHY

Derrida, J. "La Pharmacie de Platon," *Tel Quel,* No. 32 (1969), 3–48; No. 33 (1969), 18–59. Translated by B. Johnson as "Plato's Pharmacy," in *Dissemination* (Chicago, 1981).

———. "Lettre à un ami japonais," *Psyché* (Paris, 1987), 387–93. Translated by D. Wood and A. Benjamin as "Letter to a Japanese Friend," in D. Wood and R. Bernasconi, eds., *Derrida and Différance* (Evanston, IL, 1988).

Gasché, R. *The Tain of the Mirror.* Cambridge, MA, 1986.

Madison, G. ed. *Working through Derrida.* Evanston, IL, 1993.

— ROBERT BERNASCONI

DEDUCTION

How might one learn a previously unknown proposition q via deduction? A tempting reply: construct a proof of q. But what exactly is the appropriate sense of 'proof' at stake here? A widely accepted answer is that in philosophical discourse any sound and noncircular agrument constitutes a proof of its conclusion. (See, e.g., Cornman, Lehrer, & Pappas, 1982.) And yet it is noteworthy that this orthodox view of proofs seems mistaken. For consider the following pair of arguments:

(1) (a) (Washington, D.C., is the capital of the United States) ⊃ (God exists) [where one must read 'A ⊃ B' as 'It is false that (A is true but B is false)']
    (b) Washington, D.C., is the capital of the United States.
    (c) Thus, God exists.
(2) (d) (God exists) ⊃ (Atlanta, Georgia, is the capital of the United States)
    (e) Atlanta, Georgia, is not the capital of the United States.
    (f) Thus, God does not exist.

By propositional logic, both (1) and (2) are valid and noncircular. Independently, the second premise of each argument is true. Next, observe that the disjunction of premise (1a) with premise (2d) is a tautology in classical propositional logic. It follows, then, that one of (1) and (2) is a sound and noncircular argument. According to the orthodox account of proofs, therefore, one of these two arguments counts as a proof of its conclusion. And the latter result appears just wrong: offered as philosophical proofs of theism and atheism, respectively, both (1) and (2) are decidedly lame. And the reason this is so seems straightforward. Because a material conditional is false if and only if its antecedent is true and the consequent is false, you cannot know which one of (1) and (2) has all true premises unless you already know which argument has the true conclusion. This in turn suggests a crucial agent-and-time-relativized epistemic requirement for the requisite sense of 'proof'—if a sound and noncircular argument a is to constitute a proof of its conclusion for a person S at a time t, then S must be able at t to know the premises of a without already knowing the conclusion.

BIBLIOGRAPHY

Cornman, J. W., K. Lehrer, and G. S. Pappas, *Philosophical Problems and Arguments*, 3d ed. New York, 1982.

— JAMES E. TOMBERLIN

DEMOCRACY

It is generally agreed that people live best in societies regulated by laws. Laws and policies help people cooperate, coordinate their activities, and establish justice in society. 'Democracy' refers to a method in which all minimally competent members of a society can partici-pate in deciding on the laws and policies that regulate the society. The people decide as a single body, and there is some provision for equality in the means to participate. This method contrasts with decentralized methods of decision making such as markets as well as with monarchy, aristocracy, oligarchy, and dictatorship. Theoretical debates about democracy concern its proper range, the nature and strength of the equality that is required, as well as the nature and basis of its worth.

Range

What decisions ought to be made democratically? Some think the people have a right to make decisions on all matters that affect people's lives in society (Walzer, 1981). Others would severely limit it to choices about how to preserve order in society, leaving other matters to private individuals and associations (Hayek, 1960). Most (Christiano, 1996) defend an intermediate position that the people have a right to make decisions on all matters that affect them in common but not to intrude in the lives of individuals. Civil liberties such as freedom of conscience, freedom of association, and freedom from arbitrary treatment by the state ought to be protected against the majority's intrusion. On these grounds some (Arneson, 1993) argue that the people ought to be limited by a constitution that is interpreted by a court with the authority to strike down legislation deemed incompatible with civil liberty. Some (Buchanan & Tullock, 1962) assert that the power of the majority should be tempered by dividing legislative power into two or more branches to make it more difficult to do what it wants. Others (Christiano, 1996) argue that democratic rule can be trusted to limit itself to its appropriate range.

Strength of Equality

Some (Buchanan & Tullock, 1962) argue that each person has a right to an equally weighted vote in elections of representatives to assembly and no more. Others defend a more robust equality requiring public subsidies for political parties and even interest groups to ensure that a broad range of interests and points of views are represented in the political process (Beitz, 1989).

Worth

What, if anything, is worthwhile about democracy? Instrumentalists argue that it is desirable to the extent that it results in more just legislation or efficient policy than other methods. If rule by one person or a small group could produce the same or superior results, they would be just as good or better, but since human beings are naturally inclined to be concerned with themselves first, power must be dispersed so as to avoid abuse (Arneson,

The U.S. Capitol building is a well-known symbol of democracy. (Corbis/Adam Woolfitt)

1993). Others (Nelson, 1980) argue that the people as a whole are likely to be wiser than select, even if individually superior, persons. Instrumentalism has implications regarding the proper range of democracy as well as the nature and proper strength of equality. Those arrangements are best which produce the best results.

Two other approaches attribute intrinsic merits to democracy, in addition to its instrumental virtues. One view is that each has a fundamental right to equal liberty. Individuals are free in a society regulated by law to the extent that they voluntarily make the laws in the democratic process. This approach emphasizes deliberation and consensus, without which many individuals must live under laws to which they are opposed (Cohen, 1989). A different approach makes equality the central ideal of democracy. When people disagree as to how they should order their society, and they must make some decision, the only just way is to give each an equal voice in the decision making. This view emphasizes voting (and access to the relevant information) and majority rule (Christiano, 1996). These two approaches can help us discern the proper range of democratic decision making as well as the appropriate strength of equality among citizens by appeal to the requirements of the underlying ideals of liberty and equality.

[See also Liberty.]

BIBLIOGRAPHY

Arneson, R. "Democratic Rights in National and Workplace Levels," in D. Copp, J. Hampton, and J. Roemer, eds., *The Idea of Democracy* (New York, 1993).

Beitz, C. *Political Equality: An Essay in Democratic Theory.* Princeton, NJ, 1989.

Buchanan, J., and G. Tullock. *The Calculus of Consent: Logical Foundations of Constitutional Democracy.* Ann Arbor, MI, 1962.

Christiano, T. *The Rule of the Many: Fundamental Issues in Democratic Theory.* Boulder, CO, 1996.

Cohen, J. "Deliberation and Democratic Legitimacy," in A. Hamlin and P. Pettit, eds., *The Good Polity: Normative Analysis of the State* (Oxford, 1989).

Hayek, F. A. *The Constitution of Liberty.* Chicago, 1960.

Nelson, W. *On Justifying Democracy.* London, 1980.

Walzer, M. "Philosophy and Democracy," *Political Theory,* Vol. 9 (1981), 379–99.

— THOMAS CHRISTIANO

DEONTOLOGICAL ETHICS

No single idea captures all of the features in virtue of which an ethical theory may deserve the name deontology. In one sense of the term a deontology is simply an account of duty, something most ethical theories have. Yet the term normally conveys more than this when it is used to characterize an ethical theory. Very roughly, a deontological view denies that the good, or

what is of value, takes priority over the right or duty. What this denial means depends on whether the deontology is a normative theory or a metaethical theory. Deontological normative theories argue that at least sometimes it is one's duty to perform an action, or follow a rule, that would not produce the best overall consequences of the available alternatives. Theories holding that there are absolute rights or duties, for instance, are deontological, since they claim that there are some rights or duties that we must not violate even if doing so would bring about the best overall consequences. Sometimes ethicists refer to such prohibitions as agent-relative or deontological constraints, or moral constraints that apply to an agent regardless of whether they bring about the most overall good.

Generally speaking, a deontological view denies that the good, or what is of value, takes priority over the right or duty.

To the extent that a normative theory such as consequentialism holds the view that deontologies deny, it is a teleological theory. But hybrid views are possible. For instance, a rule consequentialist might claim that one should follow those rules of behavior that would produce the best overall consequences if everyone were to follow them. Yet she might also claim that one should follow those rules even when one's individual actions would not bring about the best consequences of the available alternatives. Thus, a normative view could have a teleological theory of the rules we ought to follow but a deontological theory of the actions we ought to perform.

The term deontology may also be used to characterize a metaethical theory. Metaethics includes accounts of moral justification, the nature of moral properties, and the meaning and logic of moral statements. Thus, used in this way, the term may imply several different ideas. A theory may be called a deontology, for instance, because it denies that judgments about what is right are justified only if they are inferred from judgments about what is good, together with judgments about the effects of available actions. Or it may earn the name because it denies that the property of rightness is dependent on the property of causing the most overall good. A deontology in this metaphysical sense insists that rightness is an intrinsic, rather than an extrinsic, property of some actions. A theory may also be viewed as deontological because it denies that statements about what it is right to do can be defined or analyzed in terms of statements about what things are good together with statements about the effects of available actions. Again, at the metaethical level, to the extent that a theory holds a view denied by deontologies, it is teleological.

The positive views deontologists hold are diverse. Some hold that doctrines of the right are fundamental. Thus, to take one metaethical dimension as an example, a deontologist may claim that judgments about what is good are justified only when they are inferred from judgments about what it is right to do (e.g., she may claim that the judgment that a state of affairs is good is justified only when it is inferred from the judgment that it was brought about by a right action). Thus, these sorts of deontologies claim that the good is dependent on (in one of the above metaethical senses) the right. Other deontologists claim that neither the right nor the good are fundamental. For example, deontologists who are also intuitionists may claim that judgments neither about what is good nor about what is right need to be inferred from any other judgments in order to be justified, claiming instead that both are self-justifying or intuited. A deontologist need not be an intuitionist about judgment of right, however. Some argue that, in order to be justified, judgments of right must be inferred from or cohere with some other kinds of judgments. For instance, a divine-command deontologist may hold that judgments about what it is right to do are justified only if inferred from judgments about content of natural law or the will of God. And Kantian deontologists often argue that judgments of right are justified only if derived from a theory of practical reason.

How metaethical and normative theories interrelate is a complex and controversial issue, and so it is with the relationships between deontological theories of both kinds. Some normative deontologists remain quiet on metaethical questions, but others believe that their views have substantial metaethical implications. For instance, they may argue that, if there are any absolute rights or duties, then rightness must be an intrinsic property of actions. On the other hand, some metaethical deontologists remain silent on normative questions, while others argue that their views have normative implications. And some philosophers may pair a normative deontology with a nondeontological metaethics. For instance, an emotivist may claim that judgments of right are mere expressions of noncognitive attitudes and so are not susceptible to rational justification yet also hold the normative view that one must never torture innocents no matter how good the overall consequences of doing so might be.

[See also Consequentialism; Ethical Theory; Ethics, History of; Ethics, Problems of.]

BIBLIOGRAPHY

Donagan, A. *The Theory of Morality.* Chicago, 1977.
Finnis, J. *Natural Law and Natural Rights.* Oxford, 1980.
Fried, C. *Right and Wrong.* Cambridge, MA, 1978.
Gewirth, A. *Human Rights: Essays on Justifications and Applications.* Chicago, 1982.
Herman, B. *The Practice of Moral Judgment.* Cambridge, MA, 1993.
Hill, T. E. *Autonomy and Self-Respect.* Cambridge, 1991.
Nagel, T. *The View from Nowhere.* New York, 1986.
Nozick, R. *Anarchy, State, and Utopia.* Oxford, 1974.
O'Neill, O. *Constructions of Reason.* Cambridge, 1990.
Rawls, J. *A Theory of Justice.* Cambridge, MA, 1971.
Scheffler, S. *The Rejection of Consequentialism.* Oxford, 1982.

– ROBERT NEAL JOHNSON

DERRIDA, JACQUES

Jacques Derrida's name is synonymous with deconstruction. Derrida was born in El-Biar, near Algiers, in 1930. In 1949 he left for Paris and in 1952 began study at the École Normale Supérieure, where he taught from 1964 until 1984. Since 1975 Derrida has spent a few weeks each year teaching in the United States. It was while at Yale University that Derrida collaborated with Paul de Man (1919–1983), leading to the extraordinary impact that deconstruction has had on the study of literature in the United States, an impact that quickly spread to other disciplines and countries.

Most of Derrida's writings operate by close reading, and their impact depends on the capacity of this reading to account for details that more conventional readings either ignore or explain away.

Derrida's record of publications is remarkable. In 1962 he wrote an introduction to a translation of Husserl's *Origin of Geometry* that in many respects anticipates the later works. In 1967 he published a further study of Husserl, *Speech and Phenomena;* a collection of essays, *Writing and Difference;* and a reading of Saussure, Levi-Strauss, and Jean-Jacques Rousseau, *Of Grammatology.* Since then there has been a rapid succession of publications, among the most important of which are *Dissemination* (1972), *Glas* (1974). *The Post Card* (1980), and *Psyché* (1987). He has also published extensively on an increasingly broad range of subjects from literature and politics to art and architecture.

Styles of Deconstruction

Deconstruction is neither a method nor a negative critique. It might be better understood as a strategy for reading texts under the influence of Edmund Husserl, Martin Heidegger, Friedrich Nietzsche, Sigmund Freud, Saussure, and Emmanuel Levinas. In the early years of deconstruction many of the most important readings were devoted to these thinkers, all of whom, except for Husserl, were the focus of Derrida's 1968 lecture "Différance." Derrida justified this cross-fertilization of disparate authors by saying that their names served to define contemporary thought. This practice came to be generalized as intertextuality and is most pronounced in the cumulative layering of Derrida's writing, whereby he draws heavily on his previous readings. Because Derrida's language is both cumulative and parasitic on the texts that he is reading, attempts to formulate Derridean doctrines are often misleading. It is more appropriate to focus on his strategies.

Most of Derrida's writings operate by close reading, and their impact depends on the capacity of this reading to account for details that more conventional readings either ignore or explain away. In clear contrast, not only with most modern trends in philosophy, but also with a widespread image of him, Derrida is immersed in the history of philosophy. For Derrida this is the only way to avoid unwittingly repeating the most classic gestures of philosophy, a danger that threatens every attempt to ignore that history and begin philosophy anew. Deconstruction locates itself within traditional conceptuality in order to find the radical fissures that it believes can be traced in every work of philosophy. Derrida is drawn to the apparent contradictions of the tradition and makes them the starting point of his analysis, whereas a more conventional treatment tends to stop short as soon as a contradiction is identified. Much that is strange, and to some even offensive, about Derrida's analyses arises from the fact that he is attempting to uncover the structures that organize and so transcend conventional reason.

Much that is strange, and to some even offensive,

about Derrida's analyses arises from the fact

that he is attempting to uncover the structures

that organize and so transcend conventional reason.

There is, however, another style of deconstruction that is no less representative of Derrida's thought. It proceeds by the analysis of logico-formal paradoxes. This style is particularly prominent in his treatment of ethics, where he finds a duty to go beyond one's duty. The extent to which this enterprise still reflects the in-terests of the more textual approach to deconstruction is clear. Sometimes, however, Derrida seems to give to the aporias he investigates a universal status, which suggests that in these cases the deconstruction of philosophy no longer depends on the conception of the history of Western metaphysics that is so prominent in his textual readings of philosophy. However, Derrida does not consider these two styles of deconstruction as independent of each other, so that it would be a mistake to suppose that he had compromised the genealogical component of his work.

Equivocity

If deconstruction's initial impact within the United States has been strongest in literature departments, this is in part because Derrida's conviction that absolute univocity is impossible is more readily welcomed by literary critics, who have always celebrated the multiplicity of meaning, than by philosophers, whose discipline has tended to encourage the reduction or controlling of equivocity. Whereas the dominant tendency in philosophy has been to mark different uses of a term in an effort to control the ambiguity, the deconstructive approach is to question the basis of any attempt to limit the associations of language. This approach has sometimes been confused with an invitation to so-called free play, in the sense of arbitrariness in interpretation, although Derrida has often rejected this interpretation of his work. In exploring equivocity, Derrida is recognizing and not ignoring the ambiguity of words. In the literary context the constraints of deconstruction are sometimes neglected for the freedom of literary experimentation. This is less common in Derrida than in some of his followers, but it has given ammunition to the critics of deconstruction.

Criticisms and Responses

The most persistent criticism of Derrida arises from his claim in *Of Grammatology* that "there is nothing outside the text." This has sometimes been understood to mean that all reference to the social and historical context is ruled out, and even that the text has no referent. It is easy to show that Derrida has never practiced such an extreme aestheticization of the text. What he did mean is explained in "Living On," in which he sets out the concept of a text as a differential network that overruns all the limits assigned to it. This, the so-called general text, is not conceived as a totality. It does not have an outside, anymore than it has an inside. As Derrida explained in the 1988 afterword to *Limited Inc,* there is nothing outside context, which is almost the opposite of what he is often accused of saying by many who do not share his philosophical background in phenomenology, psychoanalysis, or structural linguistics and yet fail to make allowance for that fact.

[See also Deconstruction; Freud, Sigmund; Heidegger, Martin; Husserl, Edmund; Levinas, Emmanuel; Nietzsche, Friedrich Wilhelm; Phenomenology; Rousseau, Jean-Jacques.]

BIBLIOGRAPHY

A complete list of works by Derrida in French and English up to 1992, established by Albert Leventure and Thomas Keenan, is available in D. Wood, ed., *Derrida: A Critical Reader* (Oxford, 1992).

Major Philosophical Works

Introduction to *L'Origine de la géométrie* by E. Husserl. Paris, 1962. Translated by J. Leavey, Jr., as *Edmund Husserl's "Origin of Geometry."* Lincoln, NE, 1989.

L'Écriture et la différance. Paris, 1967. Translated by A. Bass as *Writing and Difference.* Chicago, 1978.

De la grammatologie. Paris, 1967. Translated by G. Spivak as *Of Grammatology.* Baltimore, 1976.

La voix et le phénomène. Paris, 1967. Translated by D. Allison as *Speech and Phenomena.* Evanston, IL, 1973.

La Dissémination. Paris, 1972. Translated by B. Johnson as *Dissemination.* Chicago, 1981.

Marges de la philosophie. Paris, 1972. Translated by A. Bass as *Margins of Philosophy.* Chicago, 1982.

Glas. Paris, 1974. Translated by J. Leavey, Jr., and R. Rand as *Glas.* Lincoln, NE, 1986.

La Carte postale. Paris, 1980. Translated by A. Bass as *The Post Card.* Chicago, 1987.

Psyché: Inventions de l'autre. Paris, 1987.

Works on Derrida

Bennington, G., and J. Derrida. *Jacques Derrida.* Paris, 1991. Translated by Geoffrey Bennington as *Jacques Derrida.* Chicago, 1993.

Gasché, R. *The Tain of the Mirror.* Cambridge, MA, 1986.

Lawlor, L. *Imagination and Chance.* Albany, NY, 1992.

Lawlor, L., ed. *Derrida's Interpretation of Husserl.* Southern Journal of Philosophy, Vol. 23 (1993). Supplement.

Llewelyn, J. *Derrida on the Threshold of Sense.* London, 1986.

— ROBERT BERNASCONI

DESCARTES, RENÉ

René Descartes (1596–1650) was one of the founders of modern thought and among the most original philosophers and mathematicians of any age. He was born at La Haye, a small town in Touraine, France. Educated at the Jesuit college of La Flèche, he retained an admiration for his teachers but later claimed that he found little of substance in the course of instruction and that only mathematics had given him any certain knowledge. In 1618 he went to Holland to serve in the army of Maurice of Nassau, and in this capacity he traveled in Germany and perhaps elsewhere; in the following year he was at Ulm, Germany. There, on the night of November 10, after a day of concentrated reflection, he had certain dreams which he interpreted as a divine sign that it was his destiny to found a unified science of

nature based (it would seem) on mathematics. At this time his interest was largely in physics and mathematics, in which he was stimulated by contact with the mathematician Isaac Beeckman. He did not, however, set himself at once to write works of philosophy or science but continued to travel widely. His first substantial work was the never-completed treatise *Regulae ad Directionem Ingenii* ("Rules for the Direction of the Mind"), which was written in 1628 or 1629 but was not printed until 1701. The *Regulae* reveals that Descartes was already preoccupied with method as the clue to scientific advance—a method of basically mathematical inspiration, though it is intended to be the method of rational inquiry into any subject matter whatsoever. This concern with method appears in the *Regulae* in a form that is both more detailed and less metaphysically committed than the form that appears in Descartes's later philosophical works.

On the night of November 10, 1619,

Descartes had certain dreams

which he interpreted as a divine sign

that it was his destiny to found a unified science

of nature based on mathematics.

In November 1628 Descartes was in Paris, where he distinguished himself in a famous confrontation with Chandoux, whose view that science could be founded only on probabilities he eloquently attacked, claiming both that only absolute certainty could serve as a basis of human knowledge and that he himself had a method of establishing this basis. As a result of this incident he was urged to develop his system by Cardinal Bérulle, an Oratorian. (Descartes's close association with the Augustinian and Scotist outlook of the Oratory is significant to his philosophy.) In the same year he retired to Holland, where he remained, with brief interruptions, until 1649.

In Holland, Descartes worked at his system, and by 1634 he had completed a scientific work called *Le Monde.* When he heard, however, of the condemnation of Galileo for teaching the Copernican system, as did *Le Monde,* he immediately had the book suppressed. This incident is important in Descartes's life, for it reveals that spirit of caution and conciliation toward authority which was very marked in him (and which earned the disapproval of some, including Leibniz and Bossuet). The suppression also affected the subsequent course of his publications, which were from then on strategically designed to recommend his less orthodox views in an oblique fashion. In 1637 he published a book containing three treatises on mathematical and physical subjects—the *Geometry,* the *Dioptric,* and the *Meteors*—prefaced by *Discours de la méthode (Discourse on the Method).* This celebrated work is remarkable for a number of things: for its autobiographical tone, for its very compressed exposition of the foundations of the Cartesian system, and for the fact that it was written in French. By writing in French, Descartes intended (as Galileo also did, by writing in Italian) to aim over the heads of the academic community and to reach educated men of *bon sens,* among whom he hoped to get a favorable hearing. The French style that Descartes developed for this purpose has always been regarded as a model for the expression of abstract thought in that language.

Descartes followed this book in 1641 with a more purely metaphysical work, the six *Meditationes de Prima Philosophia (Meditations on First Philosophy),* which were published together with six (later seven) sets of *Objections* from various persons, including Thomas Hobbes, Antoine Arnauld, and Pierre Gassendi, and also with Descartes's *Replies to the Objections;* together these form one of the most important texts of Descartes's philosophy. The exposition of the *Meditations* is heuristic and almost dramatic in tone. A more formal treatise, the *Principia Philosophiae (Principles of Philosophy),* followed in 1644. It contains, besides philosophical matter, a cautious exposition of Descartes's views on cosmology; he expressed the hope that it could "be used in Christian teaching without contradicting the text of Aristotle," an aspiration that, despite his efforts at concealing his real opinions, was optimistic.

In 1649 Descartes yielded, after much hesitation, to the requests of Queen Christina of Sweden that he join the distinguished circle she was assembling in Stockholm and instruct her in philosophy. In this year he also published *Les Passions de l'âme (The Passions of the Soul).* The next year, however, as a result of the Swedish climate and the rigorous schedule demanded by the queen, he caught pneumonia and died.

The Method of Doubt

In Part II of the *Discourse on the Method* Descartes gives an account of four rules that, he says, he had found adequate to express his method:

> The first of these was to accept nothing as true which I did not clearly recognize to be so: that is to say, carefully to avoid precipitation and prejudice in judgements, and to accept in them nothing more than was

Descartes was among the most original philosophers and mathematicians of any age. (Corbis/Bettmann)

> presented to my mind so clearly and distinctly that I could have no occasion to doubt it.
>
> The second was to divide up each of the difficulties which I examined into as many parts as possible, and as seemed requisite for it to be resolved in the best manner possible.
>
> The third was to carry on my reflections in due order, beginning with objects that were the most simple and easy to understand, in order to rise little by little, or by degrees, to knowledge of the most complex, assuming an order, even if a fictitious one, among those which do not follow a natural sequence relative to one another.
>
> The last was in all cases to make enumerations so complete and reviews so general that I should be certain of having omitted nothing. *(The Philosophical Works of Descartes)*

It is immediately obvious that, taken by themselves, these rules are so general, and several of their key terms so vague, that they provide little positive guidance. Thus, there is some justice in a famous sneer of Leibniz' that Descartes's celebrated rules added up to saying

"Take what you need, and do what you should, and you will get what you want." To some extent, at least, Descartes was probably willing to admit that the rules, regarded merely as abstract prescriptions, had no great content, for it is a repeated emphasis of his work that it is only in the actual application of the mind to specific problems that a man will come to recognize what it is to see something "clearly and distinctly," will realize that his ideas have been insufficiently analyzed, and so forth. The problem of the meaning of "clear and distinct perception" is really the central issue of the interpretation of the method, and it will be seen that it recurs at the heart of Descartes's philosophy.

Whatever the difficulties of interpreting the rules, there are two features of Descartes's method that stand out clearly. One is that the method is intended as an analytical or (what Descartes regarded as the same thing) heuristic method; it applies to the situation of one who is confronted with a problem and proceeds to answer it by resolving the situation into a number of constituent elements or ideas. Descartes's model here is in some part that of the resolution of a complex curve or curvilinear motion by use of coordinate geometry, a branch of mathematics whose discovery by Descartes (announced in an obscure and not very general form in the *Geometry* of 1637) is still marked by the use of the expression "Cartesian coordinates." Descartes thought that the great merit of his method, as opposed to the traditional logic, was precisely that it was a method of discovery and not merely a device for the presentation of discoveries already made; in this he represents a characteristic seventeenth-century concern that is also found, for instance, in Bacon and Galileo. Consistent with this concern, he thought that the most illuminating way of expounding his more purely philosophical doctrines was by "the order of discovery," as he expounds them in the *Meditations;* this is indeed the most effective way of understanding Descartes's approach and his problems, and the path of his *Meditations* will, for the most part, be pursued in this article. He opposes to this "analytical" type of exposition a "synthetic" type, a formal deductive exposition on Euclidean lines; in response to a request, he offers such an exposition of his system in the *Second Set of Replies to Objections,* with remarks to the effect that synthetic exposition is inferior to the method he has previously used. Yet in some later developments of rationalism, most notably in Spinoza, the "synthetic" or deductive method of exposition came to be favored as a paradigm of the luminously intelligible.

The second outstanding feature of Descartes's method is that it is intended as a method not only of scientific inquiry, nor only of philosophical inquiry, but

of any rational inquiry whatsoever. In any such inquiry the intellectual power of the mind that the method is supposed to guide is the same; and Descartes indeed had a vision of the unity of all knowledge, philosophical and scientific, that he expressed in an image of the Tree of Knowledge, whose roots were metaphysics, whose trunk was physics, and whose branches were the other sciences (including medicine and morality). Such an image suggests the continuity of metaphysics and science, and much of Descartes's writing implies just such an ideal, with philosophy and the natural sciences unified in one a priori inquiry. However, at other times he seems prepared to admit that one cannot expect the same sorts of arguments to be possible in natural science as in metaphysics.

The method, then, is not a peculiarly philosophical method; it becomes such when it is applied to philosophical issues, in particular to highly general questions about the foundations of knowledge. When it is so applied, the first rule—that nothing should be accepted as true unless it is so clearly and distinctly perceived that there could be no occasion to doubt it—takes on a special character as the chief weapon of Descartes's philosophical inquiry—the famous method of doubt. Descartes proclaims that he intends to doubt as much as possible, in order to see whether anything may then be left which will resist the doubt. If there is, this will constitute an indubitable certainty, from which he may be able to proceed to find other certainties and thus construct his system on solid foundations.

This metaphor of "solid foundations" constantly reappears in Descartes's explanations of his procedure; and it embodies at the very outset a presupposition of Descartes's philosophy (though it was perhaps not consciously seen by him as such) that it is the ideal of knowledge to be systematic, an ordered body of propositions dependent on one another. The same presupposition is present, rather more subtly, in another image that Descartes appeals to in explaining the method of doubt: that he is acting like a man who has a barrel of apples and takes them out one by one to remove any rotten ones, lest they infect the others (*Seventh Set of Replies*). This presupposition, however, does not serve by itself to explain a peculiar feature of Descartes's procedure that has too often gone unquestioned: that while he often states that his aim is merely to discover what is true, he actually sets himself the task of discovering things that are indubitable and, in a strong sense, certain. He apparently regards it as a simple dictate of reason that he should pursue the first by way of the second, but it is not immediately obvious why this should be so. In some part, no doubt, he is influenced by mathematics as a paradigm of knowledge; but this explanation scarcely goes very deep, for Descartes claims that what makes mathematics a paradigm of knowledge is precisely its certainty, and the question remains of why he should think this. Some explanation is to be found in the historical circumstances: a revival of skeptical considerations from ancient sources, notably Sextus Empiricus, was playing a considerable role in contemporary arguments about religious certainty and authority; and some play was made with the idea that all propositions could be rendered equally improbable, so that there was no knowledge at all.

Descartes's basic question is "What do I know?" and he hopes to be able to answer this question by reflection on the beliefs that he finds himself disposed to hold.

Apart from these considerations, however, some motivation for Descartes's preoccupation with the indubitable must be sought; and it can be argued that this preoccupation is already implicit in the egocentric approach which is one of the most characteristic features of his philosophy and which, with its related insistence on epistemology as the starting point of philosophy, serves to distinguish it and much that follows it from most philosophy that preceded it. Descartes's basic question is "What do I know?" and he hopes to be able to answer this question by reflection on the beliefs that he finds himself disposed to hold. One necessary condition of a belief's constituting knowledge is that it is true; but it is difficult to see how any reflection on my beliefs could serve to identify those of them that are true, since the fact that I have these beliefs means that I already suppose them to be true. At this point the only procedure that seems to offer hope of being able to segregate the true beliefs through reflection will be that of selecting just those beliefs whose truth is in some way guaranteed by the fact that they are believed; this is essentially the first rule of the method, the pursuit of the indubitable. Another and slightly different way of putting this is to say that Descartes's task will not have been satisfactorily carried out so long as, for anything I claim to know, it is possible to ask whether I know that I know it; to eliminate this question, genuine knowledge has to be self-guaranteeing—a point emphasized by Spinoza.

Descartes proceeds to apply the method of doubt by suspending his belief in anything in which he can find, or indeed imagine, the slightest ground of doubt. In this way he succeeds (or so he claims) in suspending belief in the entire physical universe, including his own body; in God; in the past; and even in the truth of simple propositions of mathematics (although, as will be seen, some perceptions of logical consequence have to be regarded as immune to the doubt). The arguments by which Descartes so rapidly extends the doubt are sketchy and have given rise to considerable disagreement. In part, he relies on invoking actual occasions of error—for instance, by recalling false judgments based on illusions of the senses; in particular, he refers frequently to the "illusions" of dreams. Yet evidently there can be no very direct route from these considerations to the universal skepticism concerning the physical world that he proceeds to entertain. For, first, if the extension of the doubt involved his claiming to know that he had actually been deceived in the past, it would rest on claims to knowledge of a kind that it itself goes on to disavow; and, second, even if these considerations of past error were allowed to show that *any* occasion of supposed perception might be illusory (because, for instance, I might be dreaming), there would be no valid inference from this to the supposition that *every* supposed occasion of perception might be illusory.

It seems, in fact, doubtful that Descartes did wish to proceed by any direct route from such considerations as illusion and dreaming to the universal skepticism; rather, he is to be taken as invoking those considerations to weaken the reliance on any supposed experience of perception and then going on to entertain the notion of universal illusion. His point is the more immediate one that in this notion he can, at least at this stage of reflection, see no inherent absurdity. Indeed, in the *Meditations* (though not in his earlier writings) he uses a device that seems to make it plain that the universal skepticism has no direct dependence on an appeal to actual types of illusion: he feigns, for the sake of his argument, the existence of a malicious demon, an extremely powerful agency devoted to deceiving him. His question then becomes "If there were such an agency, how many of my normal beliefs could conceivably be the product of his deceit?" To this question Descartes gives the very large-scale answer already indicated, and his reasons for giving this answer seem to come down essentially to the claim that he can see no evident absurdity in supposing that he is so broadly deceived.

Descartes's skepticism has received much attention, but it is fair to say that at no point of his argument is Descartes in any serious sense a skeptic; rather, he is one who uses skeptical arguments as an instrument of analysis. He repeatedly emphasizes—not only in the last of the *Meditations* but also in the *First Meditation,* where the doubt is being invoked—that the extravagant doubts are unreal. He regards the "hyperbolical" doubt, as he sometimes calls it, as running counter to something that is actually the case: that even among our beliefs that are not indubitable, some are, in fact, much more probable than others. The hyperbolical doubt is a device for identifying the indubitable.

"Cogito Ergo Sum"

The doubt comes to a halt, and the first indubitable proposition is identified, when Descartes reflects that one thing, at least, he cannot doubt: his own existence. For if he is to doubt anything, if indeed he is to have any thought at all, then certainly he must exist. In the terms of the *Discourse* (Part IV):

> I noticed that while I was trying to think everything false, it must needs be that I, who was thinking this, was something. And observing that this truth, *I am thinking, therefore I exist* [*Je pense, donc je suis;* Latin version, *cogito ergo sum*] was so solid and secure that the most extravagant suppositions of the sceptics could not overthrow it, I judged that I need not scruple to accept it as the first principle of [the] philosophy that I was seeking. (*Descartes: Philosophical Writings*)

The formulation of the argument in the *Second Meditation* differs from that in the Discourse in three respects: (*a*) there is less suggestion that the particular form of thought that reveals the existence of the thinker is that of doubting—any form of thought will have the same result; (*b*) the famous formula *cogito ergo sum* is not actually employed, Descartes preferring the formulation " 'I am, I exist' is necessarily true whenever I utter it or conceive it in my mind"; (*c*) an additional expression of the basic idea is given in terms of the malicious demon—"there is no doubt that I exist, if he is deceiving me; let him deceive me as much as he likes, he can never bring it about that I am nothing, so long as I think I am something." Although a good deal has been made of the second point, notably by F. Alquié, who inclines to an "existentialist" interpretation of Descartes, these differences from the *Discourse* seem to be of minor importance.

Descartes was, on the whole, content to leave the peculiar certainty or indubitability of the *cogito* unanalyzed, regarding it as a primitive datum that the mind can recognize only when it encounters it. Some modern discussions, however, have sought to give an explanation of the indubitability involved: Ayer, for instance, suggests that the sense of "indubitable" involved here is one by which *p* is indubitable if, and only if, "*p* is true" follows from "I doubt whether *p* is true"; this yields "I exist," "I am doubting," and "I am thinking" (where

this last is taken as following from "I am doubting") as indubitable. A more elaborate logical analysis, involving appeal to a "performatory" element, is offered by Hintikka. Such analyses certainly bring out one logical feature of Descartes's basic propositions: a feature that may also be illustrated, in the spirit of these analyses, by remarking that "I do *not* exist" and "I am *not* thinking" (at least where "thinking" is taken in a sufficiently broad sense, to cover any intelligent and meaningful assertion, as Descartes intended) are necessarily paradoxical assertions that, while not formal contradictions (as, again, Descartes realized), could not possibly be true because their truth would defeat the conditions of their own assertibility.

While these points undoubtedly illuminate certain aspects of the nature of the *cogito,* they are not adequate to bring out all that Descartes intended. For him, *cogitatio* or *pensée* covered more than the modern English term "thought" naturally covers, including not merely ratiocination but also any form of conscious state or process or activity whatsoever; for him, such phenomena as willing and having images are equally forms (in his technical term, *modes*) of *cogitatio*. He makes it clear that the certainty of the *cogito* applies to any mode of *cogitatio;* what can be indubitable is not merely the bare proposition "I am thinking" but also more determinate statements about my states of consciousness—that I am doubting this or that, that I am imagining certain things, that it seems to me (at least) that I am seeing certain physical objects, and so on. All such statements of "immediate experience" are recognized as being, if true, indubitably so. The admission of such statements clearly requires a sense of "indubitable" or "certain" different from that which emerged from the previous analyses of the bare statement "I am thinking"; for the denials of the statements of "immediate experience," unlike the denials of "I am thinking," "I exist" previously considered, are not inherently paradoxical—for instance, they can be used to tell a lie. Here Descartes is disposed to use a model of the mind's states as immediately evident to itself.

A question that has been much discussed is whether Descartes regards *cogito ergo sum* as expressing an inference. His remarks on this issue—as rather often on questions raised by objectors—are not evidently consistent and are quite difficult to interpret. The most probable view of his outlook is that, first, he wishes to deny that the *cogito* presents itself to the mind psychologically as involving an inferential step; and that, second, he wishes to deny that the *cogito* is a *syllogistic* inference resting on the major premise "Everything that thinks, exists" while nevertheless admitting that it does presuppose the rather different principle "In order to think, it is necessary to exist," which he says is merely an "eternal truth" (*vérité éternelle*) that "does not give us knowledge of any existent thing" (see *Principles* I, 10 and a letter to Claude Clerselier, 1646). This last point is one of the clearest indications that Descartes was prepared to admit that there were at least some simple conceptual or a priori truths which must be immune to the doubt and which he must be able to rely on in order to take any step out of the doubt.

The Real Distinction

Many correspondents pointed out to Descartes that the argument of the *cogito* was to be found in several passages of Augustine. To one such correspondent, Andreas Colvius (letter of November 14, 1640), he writes: "I find that it is employed [by Augustine] to prove the certitude of our being, and further to show that there is some image of the Trinity in us . . . in place of the use that I make of it in order to show that this *I*, which thinks, is an immaterial substance which has nothing corporeal about it."

What Descartes here claims to have derived from the *cogito* are in fact two central and closely related doctrines of his: (1) that this "I" whose existence he has proved is a substance whose whole essence is to think and (2) that this substance is "really distinct" from any physical body that he has. It is remarkable that in the passage just quoted Descartes is prepared (in effect) to associate both these doctrines so closely with the *cogito,* for the following year, in replying in the *Third Replies* to some remarks of Hobbes, he is very insistent that in the *Meditations* the "real distinction" is not proved until the *Sixth Meditation* (the last) and not in the *Second Meditation,* where the *cogito* is offered. But while this is literally true, it is difficult to see that much weight can be attached to it or that anything underlies the "real distinction" which is not implicit in the procedure of the *cogito;* and the idea that the essence of the "I" is to be a thinking being or substance is certainly intimately related to both. It will suffice to examine the argument for the "real distinction," together with some comments on Descartes's use of the terms "substance" and "essence."

This "real distinction" between mind and body is regarded by Descartes as one of the two central doctrines of the *Meditations,* as is shown by the full title of the work: "Meditations on First Philosophy, in which the Existence of God and the Real Distinction between Mind and Body are Demonstrated"—a title that Descartes substituted in the second edition for that of the first, which had read ". . . in which the Existence of God and the Immortality of the Soul are Demonstrated." He was moved, most probably, by the consideration that the immortality of the soul is not mentioned in the *Meditations,* let alone demonstrated. The argument for this "real distinction" comes essentially to this: Descartes can be certain of his existence as a thinking thing while still in doubt that he has a body—hence, he and his body (if he has one) must be really distinct one from another. An obvious objection, skillfully pressed by Arnauld in the *Fourth Objections,* is that this argument seems to refer only to a psychological fact about Descartes's understanding, which may depend on Descartes's being confused about the possibilities. In reply, Descartes makes it sufficiently clear that he is here appealing to a clear conception of what is objectively possible, so that his argument is, in effect, that he clearly perceives that it is actually possible that he should exist as a mind or thinking thing without existing as a body—thus, mind and body are really distinct. The weakness of this seems to be that even if the premise is granted, it yields a less strong conclusion than Descartes wanted. The most that this argument could prove is that it is not necessarily the case that, existing as a mind, he must exist also as a body: it does not prove either that mind and body cannot be one and the same, or that they are not, as a matter of fact, one and the same. Yet Descartes quite certainly supposed that in proving mind and body to be "really distinct" in this sense, he had thereby shown them to be actually nonidentical substances.

Even weaker appear to be such independent arguments as Descartes offers for his essence being that of a merely thinking being. Though his treatment is obscure, he is under suspicion of moving directly from the consideration of the *cogito*—that he cannot truly think that he is not thinking, nor that he does not exist—to the stronger claim that thought is his essential property; the latter entails, among other things, that he cannot exist without thinking (see a letter to Guillaume Gibieuf, January 19, 1642).

The considerable difficulties and obscurities involved in Descartes's arguments on these points are most economically explained by recognizing that one is here dealing with a fundamental element of his metaphysical outlook, which is assumed rather than proved. The basic premise, the foundation of his celebrated dualism, is that there are only two essential attributes, thought and extension (though this has not yet been reached at the present stage of Descartes's argument). Thus, all created substances (and Descartes holds that the term "substance" is used univocally of all such substances, both mental and physical, though it is used in a slightly different sense in referring to the uncreated or self-created substance, God) must have their nature explained in terms of one of these essential attributes; indeed, Descartes says that a substance is different from its essential attribute "only by a distinction of reason." Moreover, any other property that a substance possesses must be a *mode* of its essential attribute: all properties of thinking things are (roughly speaking) *ways* of thinking; all properties of physical things, *ways* of being extended. From these premises it immediately follows that if the "I" thinks at all, it cannot also be true of that same thing that it has any physical property—mind and body must be nonidentical. (For this approach to the "real distinction," see particularly the *Third Replies*). What is not shown by any satisfactory (or even clearly identifiable) argument is that thought must be accepted as an essential attribute in this heavily committal sense: the dualism implicit in this conception appears to be the real starting point, as well as the culmination, of Descartes's metaphysics.

The Existence of God

The next step of Descartes's return from the doubt illustrates an essential feature of his thought, very significant to later developments in the history of philosophy. Having established so far only that he exists as a thinking being, he must in order to prove the existence of anything else—and in particular of an "external" physical world—proceed entirely from the contents of his own consciousness. The characteristic feature of Descartes's system is that he proceeds to do this by a transcendental route, by proving next the existence of God, and only from God the existence of other contingent beings. The historical significance of this is that while Descartes's epistemological problem of "working out" from the data of consciousness remained central, his transcendental solution to it rapidly ceased to carry conviction. This is a primary way in which the Cartesian system, which is in itself a religious and dualistic metaphysics containing many scholastic elements, was the true ancestor of many later skeptical, subjectivist, and idealist developments.

Descartes's arguments for the existence of God proceed, as his system demands, only from the contents of his own consciousness and indeed from one item that he claims to find in his consciousness—an idea of God, of a Perfect and Infinite Being. It is essential for Descartes's outlook that an idea (which he defines, *Second Replies* Def. 2, merely as "the form of any thought, that form by the immediate awareness of which I am conscious of that said thought") does not necessarily take the form of an image: he intends, rather, the purely intellectual and rational comprehension of the nature of a thing. Such is his idea of God.

His first and main argument proceeds by applying to this idea a version of a traditional causal principle that he holds to be self-evident, to the effect that the cause of anything must contain at least as much reality or perfection as the effect. This is an entirely general principle, but it has a special application to things, such as ideas, that have a representational character: every idea is an idea of something or has an object (whether that object actually exists or not), and the causal principle just mentioned applies in such cases not merely to the existence of the idea qua idea—on which level all ideas have the same degree of reality or perfection—but also to the idea qua having a certain kind of object: on this level, ideas possess different degrees of reality as their respective objects have different degrees of reality.

Descartes's arguments for the existence of God proceed, as his system demands, only from the contents of his own consciousness.

In the degenerate scholastic terminology that Descartes employs, the cause of any idea must possess at least as much reality as the idea possesses, not only *formally* (intrinsically, qua idea) but also *objectively* (in respect of its having a certain sort of object). If the cause has just as much reality as the effect, the reality of the effect is said to be present in it *formally;* if the cause has a greater degree of reality, it is said to contain the effect *eminently.* The argument then proceeds that alone among the ideas that Descartes has, the idea of God possesses objectively a supreme degree of reality because it is the idea of a Perfect Being; hence its cause must possess formally a similar degree of reality. But this cause is evidently not Descartes himself: among other things, he is in a state of doubt and ignorance, which he clearly recognizes to be imperfections. Hence, there must exist a Being independent of Descartes who is indeed perfect: God.

There are two criticisms of this argument that Descartes himself tries to anticipate. The first is that he might have formed the idea of the infinitely Perfect Being merely by considering his own imperfect state and thinking away its limitations. To this he replies that his idea of God is not that of a being merely negatively infinite—one such that we cannot conceive of limits to his excellence—but of a being actually infinite—such that we know that there are no limits to his excellence. To put the distinction another way, God's excellence is not merely indefinitely, but infinitely, great (*Principles* I, 26 *et seq.;* for a slightly different explanation of these terms, see *First Replies*). The other criticism is that the various perfections of God might actually exist but in different subjects, so that, in fact, there would be no Perfect Being containing them all. To this Descartes replies that "the unity, simplicity or the inseparability of all God's attributes, is itself one of the chief perfections that I conceive him to have" (*Third Meditation;* cf. *Second Objections and Replies*).

What Descartes needs

is something absolutely indubitable,

and if assent can always be withheld,

nothing will be absolutely indubitable.

Two features of the argument are particularly worth remarking in the general context of Descartes's thought. First, there is an obvious tension produced by the fact that on the one hand the argument seems to presuppose an idea of God notably clear and determinate, while on the other hand it turns on the contrast between the infinitude of God and the finite imperfection of Descartes's own mind (an emphasis possibly influenced by Nicholas Cusanus); this can only add force to the traditional view that the human conception of God must necessarily be extremely limited and imperfect. This tension is more generally present in Descartes, and indeed in much seventeenth-century thought, a genuine sense of contingency and limitation being in conflict with a tendency to regard the power of the rational mind as virtually limitless (a peculiar and poignant form of this tension is to be found in Blaise Pascal). Second, the conception of degrees of reality or perfection that Descartes so straightforwardly invokes is not only a very obvious traditional incursion into Descartes's supposedly presuppositionless inquiry but is also more particularly a feature of traditional thought that his own system, it might be supposed, did a great deal to undermine; its ultimately Aristotelian inspiration fits awkwardly into the Cartesian picture of essentially rational minds enjoying equally the "natural light," as against a purely mechanically unified world of matter.

Descartes also uses considerations that introduce God as the cause of Descartes's own existence. He could not have created himself, since it takes greater perfection to create substance than to create any attributes whatsoever. Thus, if he had had the power to create himself as a thinking substance, he would have been able to give himself the perfect attributes which, in the previous argument, he noted that he lacked. (This point depends on a slightly different application of the idea of degrees of perfection, introducing a scale of perfection between

the metaphysical categories of substance, attribute, and mode, not a scale of perfection between substances.) Nor can he suppose that he has existed from all eternity, for it takes as much power to conserve a substance in being from moment to moment as it does to create it in the first place. This argument illustrates how strongly the creative activity of God is involved in the created world, offering as it does (in contrast, for instance, with the outlook of Leibniz) a picture of created things tending constantly to slip out of existence if it were not for God's sustaining activity. Nor, lastly, can he suppose that he has been created merely by his parents or some other contingent being: they also would have to have the idea of God that has been implanted in them, and this, as in the previous argument, must go back to the creative power of God. The use of this last consideration shows that the arguments which refer to the creation of Descartes himself are not, in fact, independent of the first argument, which refers to his idea of God—and Descartes makes it entirely clear that he does not intend them to be independent. In particular, he makes it clear that he does not wish to argue to the existence of God from the mere existence of a contingent being such as himself; for, he says, he can see no evident repugnance in the idea of an infinite series of contingent beings in causal relations—he rejects the traditional Cosmological Argument, which sought to demonstrate the existence of a Necessary Being merely from the existence of contingent beings. It is the presence of the idea of God—"the mark of the workman on his work"—that is the foundation of all of Descartes's reasonings here.

He does, however, have another and independent argument for the existence of God, which he offers in the *Fifth Meditation.* This starts once more from the idea of God, but in this case merely from the content of the idea without reference to the possession of the idea by an imperfect being. The argument relies on the notion that Descartes can discover the attribute of existence to be one of the chief perfections contained in the idea of God. Hence, it is necessary that God exists, just as it is necessary that the angles of a plane triangle add up to two right angles. Thus, this argument is merely an extremely simple version of the Ontological Argument for God's existence, a slightly different version of which was originally propounded by Anselm and had been rejected by Aquinas. Descartes, though he is himself entirely satisfied with the validity of the argument, is aware that it may present an appearance of sophistry; and this is why (he says) he places it second rather than as his leading argument. Later philosophy, particularly after the criticism offered by Kant, has largely agreed in rejecting this argument as based on a false conception of existence.

There are two views that Descartes holds about the nature of God that are worth noting because they have attracted contemporary criticism; the first, in particular, exemplifies the Scotist and Augustinian influences on his outlook. Descartes holds that the omnipotence of God requires that he should be able to do even what we would understand as being logically impossible, and thus that the "eternal truths" are dependent on God's will. God could have brought it about that two and two did not equal four; although, since God has not chosen that this should be so, it must be beyond our finite comprehension how it might have been so (it remains obscure how, on Descartes's view, we can be certain that it is not so, at least in some cases). The second point is of less importance: Descartes, contrary to many theologians, wished to hold that God was the *efficient* cause of himself. Descartes does not wish to press this rather mystifying view too hard, for fear, he says, of "verbal difficulties"; his motive in offering it seems to have been to emphasize that in saying that God was the cause of himself, one was not merely saying something negative—that God had no cause—nor merely that to understand the essence of God is to have a sufficient explanation of his existence (though this indeed follows from Descartes's use of the Ontological Argument). He wishes to stress, in some sense, the dependence of God's existence on God's own activity.

God and the Foundations of Knowledge

There is a property of God that is central to the further construction of Descartes's epistemology: "God . . . is liable to no errors or defect. From this it is manifest that he cannot be a deceiver, since the light of nature teaches us that fraud and deception necessarily proceed from some defect" (*Third Meditation*). This characteristic of God—that he would not deceive us—Descartes is also on occasion disposed to connect with God's benevolence—that he would not wish to lead us, his creatures, into error. It is central to Descartes's system because he founds on it the possibility of knowledge of the external world and of the past. Both of these are matters in which the way of "clear and distinct ideas" does not by itself enable Descartes to reach any certainty from the indubitable contents of consciousness; the mere existence of images and sensations leaves open the possibility, on which the doubt fastened, that there may be neither a past nor an independently existing physical world corresponding to them. At this point, the essence of Descartes's argument is to say that while this possibility remains open, so far as the "natural light" or reason is concerned, we nevertheless have a very strong tendency to believe that there is a reality corresponding to these ideas. This tendency survives the closest scru-

tiny in the light of reason—while the "natural light" reveals no inherent necessity for a corresponding reality, it reveals no inherent impossibility of it either. This being so, Descartes argues that our very strong natural tendency to believe in the reality would be misleading if no such reality existed, and God would then be responsible for our being creatures who, despite the best efforts of their reason, were systematically misled. This would, in effect, make God a deceiver. But God is no deceiver; hence, we may conclude that we are not systematically misled with respect to those things which we have a strong natural tendency to believe and that, accordingly, we are not misled in supposing that there is both a past and an external world.

An essential feature of this argument is that it extends the warrant of God's not being a deceiver only to those beliefs, our strong tendency to hold which survives the scrutiny of reason; the warrant cannot be invoked to support mere "prejudices"—this would obviously frustrate the method of doubt. If one is to avoid error, one must, in effect, do one's own part first by clarifying one's ideas. The result of this activity may well be that the proposition to which one may eventually assent under God's warrant will be different from that to which one was tempted to assent when in the state of prejudice (as in the case of physical objects). Thus, the avoidance of error under God's dispensation involves the correct use of both the understanding and the will; for Descartes, belief is a matter of assent, and assent is something that is given or withheld—it is, in fact, a mode of the will. In this respect there is, of course, a close parallel, consciously sustained by Descartes, between intellectual and moral correctness and error—in both cases God guides the agent toward (respectively) "the true" and "the good," but correct willing on the agent's part is a necessary condition. In both cases, moreover, there exist "temptations" to fall into error—in the pursuit of the good, the tendencies of bodily desire; in the case of the true, the influence of misleading sensations, again a bodily function. Although Descartes seeks to qualify the opposition of rational intellect and misleading bodily sensations implicit in this picture, it plays a prominent part in his philosophy; and the influences of Augustine and, ultimately, of Plato are clearly seen in it.

It appears to be Descartes's doctrine that all belief is a matter of assent and hence depends on the will; and if this doctrine is to have any content, it must imply that, for any proposition, the mind must be able to (though it may not wish to) withhold its assent. However, when the doctrine is applied to the basic propositions of the Cartesian construction, in particular the *cogito* and the proofs of God's existence, two difficulties follow, one inherent in these issues and one systematic.

The inherent difficulty emerges when due weight is given to Descartes's rule, repeatedly appealed to in the construction of the system, that one should give one's assent to all—and only—those ideas which one "clearly and distinctly perceives." Insofar as Descartes expresses himself in these terms, as he sometimes does, it emerges that some of the "ideas" in the mind are of a *propositional* character, besides those ideas that are ideas of various substances, accidents, and modes; this point makes it not altogether easy to apply universally his definitions of clarity and distinctness, by which, he says:

> I term that "clear" which is present and apparent to an attentive mind, in the same way that we see objects clearly when, being present to the regarding eye, they operate upon it with sufficient strength. But the "distinct" is that which is so precise and different from all other objects that it contains within itself nothing but what is clear. . . . Perception may be clear without being distinct, but cannot be distinct without also being clear. (*Principles* I, 45–46)

The difficulty that emerges is this: the sense of "clearly and distinctly perceiving" a proposition in which one ought to give one's assent only to propositions so perceived must also be the sense in which what one clearly and distinctly perceives is that the proposition is *true;* and this indeed emerges from many of Descartes's formulations. But if this is so, there will be no room for a separate function of assent: one who has clearly and distinctly perceived a proposition to be true must thereby already believe it. Thus, the distinction between understanding and will in matters of belief seems to break down at the level of the basic certainties.

This question is connected with the systematic difficulty, which consists in the fact that if assent can always be withheld, even from propositions as compulsive as the *cogito,* it is unclear what could ever suffice to prevent the assent from being withheld. What Descartes needs is something absolutely indubitable, and if assent can always be withheld, nothing will be absolutely indubitable. Here, as his general theory of assent might imply, Descartes finds himself in difficulty and responds to it with considerable ambiguity. On occasion he is disposed to suggest that one might withhold assent from clear and distinct perceptions, but that after God's existence has been proved, we can see an overwhelming reason for not doing so: God's benevolence assures us that our clear and distinct perceptions are really true. But since the proofs of God's existence depend on clear and distinct perceptions, to argue in this way is to argue in a circle, as contemporary critics were quick to point out. (See the *Second Set of Objections, Fourth Set of Objections,* and *Fifth Set of Objections.*)

Descartes's "official answer" (as it might be called) to the charge of circularity is that he applies the justification drawn from God only to those considerations which are not at present clearly and distinctly perceived but are retained in memory. This is consistent with the general structure and ties in with a distinction drawn in the *Regulae* between "intuition" and "deduction," the latter consisting of intuitions held together by memory. However, it cannot be denied that there are many passages, including some of those in which the "official answer" is given, in which the more ambitious and invalid use of God's justification seems to recur (for an example even after the arguments with the critics of the *Meditations,* compare *Principles* I, 13—the "official answer"—with *ibid., 30*). It is doubtful whether any fully consistent view on this issue can be extracted from Descartes's works.

Matter and Physical Science

The conception of physical matter that God ultimately validates is rather different from that which would come to mind before philosophical reflection. Matter, according to Descartes, has the essential attribute of extension, and all genuine properties of matter, must be (quantitative) modes of extension. These modes include duration, which Descartes holds to be necessarily contained in our conception of an existing material thing, since to conceive of it as existing is to conceive of it as continuing to exist. He further holds—none too clearly—that the notion of time adds to that of duration "only a mode of thinking," by which he seems to mean that it introduces a measure of the durations of different things by relating them to some selected reference class of notions (see *Principles* I, 55 and 57).

It is Descartes's final doctrine that no knowledge of the material world is, save in an indirect manner, derived from the senses.

Descartes's conception of matter is a pure idea of reason, which, like the other fundamental Cartesian ideas of mind and God, is innate. He first introduces this idea of matter early in the heuristic order of the *Meditations*—in connection with the famous argument of the piece of wax in the *Second Meditation.* The aim of this argument—which turns on the fact that a piece of wax can be recognized to be present although all its sensible qualities have undergone change—is not to prove at this stage what the essential property of matter must be but to draw attention to an intellectual conception of matter latent in the mind that, reflection shows, is what is being used in forming judgments about matter undergoing sensible change. That this intellectual conception correctly expresses the essence of matter is stated only at a later stage, in the *Fifth Meditation.* It is Descartes's final doctrine that no knowledge of the material world is, save in an indirect manner, derived from the senses. The pure intellectual conception of matter as extension is not derived from the senses, nor (and this for Descartes is a closely related point) can it be adequately represented in images: a favorite argument is that we have a rational comprehension of infinite variations in extension, and this comprehension cannot be adequately expressed in images. Further, not only is the concept of matter intellectual but any perceptual judgment also involves intellectual inference—an inference, ultimately grounded in God's not being a deceiver, from our sensations to the presence of matter that causes them. This representational and causal theory of perception is not only held unquestioningly by Descartes but is also implicit in many of the initial formulations of the doubt and in the approach to the proof of the "external world" as something outside and independent of the mental data certified in the *cogito.*

The conception of matter as extension has a number of important consequences. It implies that the material causes of sensations are not, in fact, as sensation suggests they are to the unreflective mind; in particular, the nature of our sensations may promote the confused—and for Descartes unintelligible—belief that the material world is actually colored, whereas all that is intelligible, and thus can be guaranteed by God's warrant, is that variations in the modes of extension are parallel, but not similar, to variations of perceived color. Thus, Descartes holds the distinction between primary and secondary qualities that is a commonplace of much seventeenth-century scientific thought and is found notably in Galileo and in Locke. There are other consequences of Descartes's views, however, that are more distinctive, following from the fact that his conception of the physical world is totally kinematic and involves no concept that cannot be explained in terms of pure geometry together with time. His physics, in fact, contains no physical (as opposed to mathematical) concept at all; the only departure from a totally abstract geometrical picture is the principle, itself sufficiently abstract, that matter excludes other matter from the place that it occupies.

This excessively geometrical concept of matter has unfortunate results for Descartes's physics. The quantity that is conserved in his system is *motion,* where this is defined as the product of a body's speed and its size, the

"size" being understood as the continuous volume of the body, omitting matter found in its interstices (as water is found in the pores of a sponge). The consequences that Descartes draws from this principle are, not surprisingly, in error, his laws of impact in particular being fundamentally mistaken. But there appear to be striking conceptual difficulties as well, when the question is raised of what is meant in the Cartesian system by the distinction between a body and its environment, or between a body and the contents of its interstices. Descartes does not believe in a void, as will indeed be apparent from his virtual equation of matter and space, an equation that makes plausible for him his basic argument for the impossibility of a void—if there is nothing between two bodies, then they must be contiguous.

Since the material world is a plenum and is continuous, there are no ultimate atoms; Descartes in fact employs atomistic forms of explanation, as in his theories of light, but his conception of the particles involved is merely that of small volumes of matter, each of which, as a matter of fact, moves as a whole. Again, since there is no void for any displaced body to move into, any movement must involve a simultaneous movement of matter in some closed curve; this principle (which was similarly derived by Aristotle from the belief in the plenum) is an important element in the theory of *vortices* that figures in Descartes's physics, notably in his explanations of planetary motion. Thus, the picture of the material world is of one, infinite, three-dimensional, continuous, and homogeneous extended body in the terminology of substance, it seems that while there are indefinitely many thinking substances, there is, strictly speaking, only one extended substance that constitutes the whole material universe. But now it becomes extremely unclear how any body is to be distinguished from its environment. Certainly the Cartesian physics seems to have no room for any concept of *density:* no more matter can ever be put into any volume—the volume must already be full of matter, and matter necessarily excludes other matter from the place it occupies—and thus any quantitative conception of density seems to be ruled out. Related difficulties are to be found with other physical concepts essential for the vortex theory, such as *viscosity.* In fact, the only principle that Descartes can consistently appeal to in distinguishing any body from its environment is differential motion of volumes of the continuous matter with respect to different places; it is not surprising that his explanations do not, in fact, succeed in conforming to this ideal.

It will be evident from Descartes's conception of the physical world that his aims for scientific explanation are that it should be entirely mechanical, with final causation totally excluded, and that mathematical physics should emerge as the fundamental science. However, beyond this point there are certain obscurities about his intentions on two related questions: the connections between physics and metaphysics and the extent to which scientific reasoning was supposed to be pure deduction from evident premises. On the first issue, the model of the Tree of Knowledge suggests that Descartes regards physics as continuous with metaphysics, and the second part of the *Principles* offers supposed derivations of certain fundamental physical laws from the properties of God. Yet elsewhere Descartes writes rather as though metaphysics were to be regarded only as a preliminary to scientific thought, offering foundations in an epistemological rather than an axiomatic sense for the truths of physics. On the question of whether physics can proceed by rigorous deduction from self-evident (or, possibly, metaphysically demonstrated) principles, it is very hard to render Descartes's professions consistent. Two quotations will suffice to illustrate the difficulties:

> ... I only consider [in physics] the divisions, shapes and movements [of quantity, regarded geometrically]; and I do not want to receive as true anything but what can be deduced from these with as much evidence as will allow it to stand as a mathematical demonstration. (*Principles* II, 64)

> To demand of me geometrical demonstrations in a matter which depends on physics is to want me to do the impossible. If one will call "demonstrations" only the proofs of geometers, one will have to say that Archimedes never demonstrated anything in mechanics. ... One is content in such matters if the authors, having presupposed certain things which are not manifestly contrary to experience, go on to speak consistently and without producing any paralogism, even if their suppositions were not entirely true. ... Those who are content to say that they do not believe what I have written because I deduce it from certain suppositions which I have not proved, do not know what they are asking, nor what they should ask. (Letter to Mersenne, May 27, 1638)

Closely connected with this question is that of the role of experiment and observation in Descartes's science. He was always prepared to admit a place for experiment, but his accounts of why it is needed suffer from ambiguities parallel to those just noticed. His favored formulation is to say that there are many different ways in which a phenomenon can be "deduced" from his principles and that experiment is necessary to decide between them; the weakness of this is obviously that if "deduction" is meant strictly, and the principles are

consistent, then there is no decision to be made—all routes of deduction must be equally valid. In this connection, it seems clear that a less strict sense of "deduction" is intended and that Descartes has in mind a method of postulating hypotheses within the general framework of his principles; these hypotheses can then be decided upon by experiment.

In the philosophy of science, it is fair to say that Descartes never arrived at so clear a picture of scientific inquiry, nor as effective scientific results, as Galileo. This may be ascribed to the pervasive effect on his science of some of his metaphysical conceptions (more noticeable in his later work, perhaps, than in his early discussions with Beeckman) and to the drastic assimilation of physics and geometry, which had the paradoxical result that Cartesian physics did not actually admit of the essential type of abstraction performed by Galileo—it cannot isolate a particular force (such as gravity) in terms of how a body would move if free from resistance, for to imagine it moving without any resistance is to imagine it in a void, and this, for Descartes, involves a logical impossibility and is incomprehensible. Nevertheless, it should be added that "ce roman de la physique," as Christian Huygens called it, provided not only certain important results—such as the sine law of refraction and at least an obscure approximation to the law of rectilinear inertia—but also a framework of scientific and cosmological ideas robust enough still to be regarded in the early eighteenth century as a real rival to the Newtonian system; Newton himself considered it worthy of painstaking refutation.

Mind and Body

A human being must be, for Descartes, some kind of union of two distinct things: a soul, or mind, and a body. The body is part of mechanical nature; the mind, a pure thinking substance. Since the body is a mechanical system, the soul is not (as in the opinion of the ancients) the principle of life: live bodies differ from dead ones as stopped watches differ from working ones; the body does not die because the soul leaves it, but the converse (*Passions of the Soul* I, 5 and 6). Moreover, there are many actions that the bodily machine performs on its own, without any intervention of the soul.

Nevertheless, there is a close union between soul and body—what Descartes is sometimes prepared to call, with an utterly misleading use of a traditional scholastic phrase, a "substantial union." He does suggest that this union is in fact a primitive and unanalyzable notion (see letter to Princess Elizabeth, June 28, 1643); but there is a good deal he is prepared to say about it, and in the late work *Passions of the Soul,* he gives a thoroughgoing causal account of the relations involved. Before reaching this account, Descartes has stressed the idea that "my soul is not in my body as a pilot in a ship," meaning by this that the soul is able to move the body "directly" and also that the soul feels pains and other sensations "in" the body; it does not merely appreciate the body's needs and other states intellectually from outside. In the account of the *Passions of the Soul,* this concern is preserved only rather weakly by saying that in a sense the soul is joined to all parts of the body; but, Descartes continues, there is one part in which "it exercises its functions more particularly than elsewhere"—the pineal gland, a structure near the top of the brain. Descartes particularly selected this organ because it appeared unique in the brain in being single and also because he falsely believed that it did not occur in other animals, for which the question of the relations of soul and body did not arise.

For Descartes, a human being must be

some kind of union of two distinct things:

a soul, or mind, and a body.

The picture Descartes offers is that of the soul directly moving the pineal gland and thus affecting the "animal spirits" which he considered the hydraulic transmission system of mechanical changes in the body; consonant with his views on the conservation of motion, it is only the direction, and not the speed, of movement of these spirits that is affected by the soul. This is the direction of action of the *will.* In the opposite direction, changes in the body—such as the effect of external objects on the sense organs—are transmitted to the pineal gland by the spirits and can there affect the soul by causing sensations in it. The further details of this theory need not be pursued here, except to mention that Descartes incorporated into this view a theory that he held before: that in the case of visual sensation, at least, and with visual imagery, a physical picture or representation was formed in the brain, and it was this that the soul was conscious of. There are certain difficulties in understanding exactly how Descartes envisages this consciousness and to what extent a pictorial element recurs at the purely mental level (on this question, see Norman Kemp Smith, *New Studies,* Ch. 6).

The pineal gland theory offered in the earlier parts of the *Passions of the Soul* (a work that also contains other matter, on the emotions and on certain moral issues, which will not be discussed here) was not a part of the Cartesian system that found wide favor; its conception of a local mechanical interaction between two entities, one of which had precisely been defined as having no extended or mechanical properties, seems almost as awkward for the Cartesian system itself as it does to any other point of view. The rejection of Descartes's account led to many important developments in the history of rationalism, notably to the occasionalism of Malebranche and to the theory of pre-established harmony that is particularly associated with Leibniz.

It has already been remarked that in Descartes's view there are certain actions which the body performs "without the intervention of the soul," acting as a purely mechanical system; it is important that these also include certain relations between perception and action or reaction, as when we by reflex throw out our hands to save ourselves from falling or react to certain stimuli by behavior expressive of emotion. In all these cases the body is acting as a reactive machine, the perceptual stimuli producing bodily change merely through the mechanisms of the brain and the nervous system. It is Descartes's view that the behavior of all animals other than man is reactive; and it seems to be his view, further, that while men may have at least some consciousness of the occurrence of these processes—in the form, for instance, of experienced emotions—this is not so with the other animals, which have no soul or mind, and hence no consciousness, at all. This is the famous Cartesian doctrine that animals are machines, a doctrine that aroused particular opposition from two of his English correspondents, Henry More and William Cavendish, the marquess of Newcastle.

Descartes is not always verbally consistent in his accounts of this view, but on the whole it does seem that he held the strong thesis that has usually been ascribed to him; it entails, for instance, that the only sense in which one can hurt an animal is that one can damage it. If this is so, it throws an interesting light on the Cartesian view of the mind or consciousness. Descartes's main grounds for ascribing the possession of mind uniquely to man are grounds concerned with *ratiocination,* particularly that man has a language, which (he supposes) no machine or animal could have; however, free will—again with special reference to conscious intellectual deliberation—is also cited. These distinctions by themselves would seem to have little force in denying that animals possess consciousness of pain or some other kinds of feelings and sensations; and what appears to be Descartes's wholesale rejection of all forms of consciousness in their case is an expression of his concept of the unity of mind under the primary aspect of pure intellect. Totally abandoning any Aristotelian conception of degrees or orders of "soul," he fastens on an intellectual conception that carries all other modes of consciousness with it. This conception emerges also in a certain tendency to regard sensation and feeling, in their purely mental aspects, as confused forms of (intellectual) thought, a tendency that plays some role in his account of perception, for instance, even though it is not consistently carried through either there or in the original descriptions of consciousness given in the *cogito*.

The influence of Descartes has been enormous. The Scottish philosopher Thomas Reid wrote that Malebranche, Locke, Berkeley, and Hume shared "a common system of the human understanding" that "may still be called the Cartesian system," and this very true remark could be extended through the history of philosophy into modern times. As Reid observed, Descartes's influence worked as much on empiricist philosophers as on those of his own rationalist temper; however, different parts of his outlook had these several effects. The influence on empiricism was perhaps the deeper of the two; one can see there, in the particular form of starting with the supposedly indubitable data of the individual consciousness, the effects of Descartes's enterprise of making epistemology the starting point of philosophy. Many postempiricist developments center in the same interest, sometimes (as in the case of Edmund Husserl) with an explicit attempt to recapture the Cartesian approach. The problems posed by Descartes's dualism remain at the heart of much contemporary philosophical inquiry, the work of Gilbert Ryle and Ludwig Wittgenstein, for example, being aimed directly against what are still very powerful Cartesian conceptions.

BIBLIOGRAPHY

The standard edition of Descartes's works is *Oeuvres de Descartes,* Charles Adam and Paul Tannery, eds., 12 vols. (Paris, 1897–1910; Index général, Paris, 1913).

English translations of the philosophical works, or of selections from them, include the following; there are no extensive translations from the correspondence: *The Philosophical Works of Descartes,* translated by E. S. Haldane and G. T. R. Ross, 2 vols. (Cambridge, 1911–1912; corrected ed., 1934; paperback, New York, 1955), is very useful, though the translation is a little heavy and diffuse; selections from the correspondence are included in Vol. II. A vigorous but free translation is found in *Descartes: Philosophical Writings,* selected, translated, and edited by G. E. M. Anscombe and P. T. Geach (Edinburgh, 1954); it also contains brief, useful notes and a good bibliography. Also see *Descartes' Philosophical Writings,* selected and edited by Norman Kemp Smith (London, 1952).

In a special class among the numerous editions of particular works is *Discours de la méthode,* text and commentary by Étienne Gilson, 2d ed. (Paris, 1930), which sheds great light on the *Discourse.*

There are many expository, critical, and historical works on all aspects of Descartes; the following is but a brief selection: Norman Kemp Smith, *Studies in the Cartesian Philosophy* (London and New York, 1902) and *New Studies in the Philosophy of Descartes* (London, 1952); Étienne Gilson, *Études sur le rôle de la pensée médiévale dans la formation du système cartésien* (Paris, 1930); J. Laporte, *Le Rationalisme de Descartes,* 2d ed. (Paris, 1950); G. Milhaud, *Descartes savant* (Paris, 1920); F. Alquié, *La Découverte métaphysique de l'homme chez Descartes* (Paris, 1950); L. J. Beck, *The Method of Descartes. A Study of the Regulae* (Oxford, 1952); and M. Guéroult, *Descartes selon l'ordre des raisons,* Vol. I (Paris, 1953).

Two articles on the *cogito* from an analytical point of view are A. J. Ayer, "Cogito ergo sum," in *Analysis,* Vol. 14 (1953), 27–31, and J. Hintikka, "Cogito, ergo sum: Inference or Performance?" in *Philosophical Review,* Vol. 71 (Jan. 1962), 3–32.

– BERNARD WILLIAMS

DESCARTES, RENÉ (UPDATE)

[*The following bibliographical notes are provided to update the lengthy overview of Descartes's life and thought appearing in the preceding article.*]

The current best original-language text of Descartes's writings is *Oeuvres de Descartes,* edited by Charles Adam and Paul Tannery, 11 vols., originally published in Paris, 1897–1913, and revised, with the addition of a considerable amount of new material (Paris, 1964–74). There is in preparation a new edition for the Bibliothèque de la Pléiade, which will include new and in many cases improved texts of Descartes's French writings, and translations into French of his Latin writings.

The current best English translation of Descartes's writings is *The Philosophical Writings of Descartes,* edited and translated by John Cottingham, Robert Stoothoff, Dugald Murdoch, and Anthony Kenny, 3 vols. (Cambridge, 1984–1991). Vol. 1 contains the *Rules for the Direction of the Mind,* selections from *Le Monde,* the *Discourse on the Method,* selections from the *Principles of Philosophy,* and the *Passions of the Soul.* Volume 2 contains the *Meditations* and the *Objections and Replies,* as well as the dialogue, *The Search after Truth.* Volume 3 contains a generous selection of Descartes's philosophical correspondence, and is an expansion and revision of *Descartes: Philosophical Letters,* edited and translated by Anthony Kenny (Oxford, 1970).

Important recent literature includes Harry Frankfurt, *Demons, Dreamers, and Madmen* (Indianapolis, 1970); Geneviève Rodis-Lewis, *L'oeuvre de Descartes* (Paris, 1971); Jean-Luc Marion, *Sur l'ontologie grise de Descartes* (Paris, 1975); Margaret Wilson, *Descartes* (London, 1978); Jean-Luc Marion, *Sur la théologie blanche de Descartes* (Paris, 1981); Daniel Garber, *Descartes' Metaphysical Physics* (Chicago, 1992); John Cottingham, ed., *The Cambridge Companion to Descartes* (Cambridge, 1992); and Stephen Gaukroger, *Descartes: An Intellectual Biography* (Oxford, 1995).

– DANIEL GARBER

DETERMINISM AND FREEDOM

Determinism is the family of theories that take our choices and the other antecedents of our actions, and our actions themselves, as effects of certain causal sequences. These theories understand effects in the standard way, as necessitated events. An account of choices and actions resting on weaker ideas of causation, perhaps the ideas that effects are merely probable events or events that would not have occurred in the absence of earlier events, would not usually count as a determinism. Indeed, the weaker ideas have sometimes been introduced precisely in order to avoid determinism.

The most discussed theories of determinism are philosophies of mind, which give or assume answers to the questions of how mental events are related to neural events, how mental events come about, and how actions come about.

The most discussed theories of determinism (sometimes spoken of in the past as physical determinism and psychological determinism) are philosophies of mind. That is, they give or assume answers to the questions of how mental events are related to neural events, how mental events come about, and how actions come about. Most other philosophies of mind, worked out as a result of interest in the mind and without concern for the question of determinism and freedom, are in fact also deterministic in nature. It can presumably be assumed, as once it was not, that there do exist conceptually adequate theories of determinism—clear, consistent, and complete.

Is any such theory true? Despite the support of neuroscience, many or most think not, because of interpretations of quantum theory. According to these interpretations there are microlevel things that are not effects. This opposition to determinism is not strengthened by the embarrassing fact, too often glossed over, that no satisfactory interpretation of quantum theory's application to reality has ever been achieved. Are the supposedly undetermined things in fact events? Determinism has no concern with anything other than events, for example, propositions or numbers, that are irrelevant to it. Would a microlevel indeterminism entail macrolevel indeterminism—a denial of theories of the kind with which we are concerned, which take actions and such antecedents as choices and neural events,

all macrolevel, to be effects? It is arguable but not settled that the answer to both questions is no.

Philosophers continue to be more concerned with another matter, that of what follows if determinism is true.

Compatibilists, undaunted by the want of success of their predecessors over centuries, have persisted in arguing that our ordinary idea of freedom, or our only important idea, connected with moral responsibility is that of voluntariness, which evidently is logically compatible with determinism. At bottom a choice or an action is voluntary if it has certain causes rather than others—it is in accordance with the desires and nature of the agent, not compelled or constrained.

Much renewed effort has gone into attempting to prove that our idea of freedom *is* of just voluntariness by elaborating or varying the idea of voluntariness. One elaboration rests on the idea of desires that are themselves desired (Frankfurt, 1988). Another elaboration has to do with the extent and character of the control of our own lives that is consistent with determinism and also with the mistake of thinking that only less is possible because of too-simple models of deterministic behavior (Dennett, 1984).

Incompatibilists, equally undaunted by the fate of their predecessors, have stuck to the redoubtable conviction that our idea of freedom, or our only important idea, connected with moral responsibility is of a choice or action that is both voluntary and originated and hence something incompatible with determinism. A choice or action is originated if it is not the effect of such a causal sequence as supposed by determinists but nevertheless is within some sort of control of the agent.

Perhaps a majority of philosophers are now skeptical about the possibility of making much or sufficient or satisfactory sense of this talk of control. One takes it to involve a hopeless infinite regress (G. Strawson, 1986). Still, a brave attempt has been made to clarify origination in terms of a kind of medley of determined and undetermined events (Kane, 1985). Other incompatibilists, perhaps a majority, have been less ready to try actually to explain origination but have offered arguments designed to show that determinism is *not* compatible with freedom as we ordinarily conceive it. One line of argument is that in order for me to be free in this way today, if determinism were true, I would have to be able to change the past (Ginet, 1990; van Inwagen, 1986).

Other less traditional work on determinism has questioned common assumptions of both the compatibilist and the incompatibilist traditions. One such assumption is that determinism's threat to holding people morally responsible for actions, or crediting them with responsibility for them, is of unique importance. It is said instead that this moral approval and disapproval is one kind of affected attitude among others (P. F. Strawson, 1968). Determinism's consequences for our hopes, our nonmoral feelings about other people, and our confidence in our beliefs are as important, and study of them is less distorted by philosophical habits and investments.

A more fundamental assumption of both compatibilism and incompatibilism has also been disputed. It is that we do have only one conception of freedom, or one important conception, and hence that either compatibilism or incompatibilism must be true. If we have two conceptions of freedom, one as voluntariness and one as voluntariness together with origination, then compatibilism and incompatibilism are both false, and the problem of determinism and freedom must be regarded very differently and, so to speak, less intellectually. It is no longer the problem of analyzing correctly our one conception of freedom. On the assumption that determinism is true it is the problem of giving up attitudes, each of them including desires, that rest on the inconsistent idea of origination (Honderich, 1988, 1993). Against all this, and much else, it has also been maintained that we have no respectable idea of freedom at all but only a kind of mess of inconsistent notions (Double, 1991). Not all have been persuaded.

So much for mainstreams of discussion of freedom and determinism. There have also been side streams, eddies, small whirlpools, and maybe stagnant ponds. They get attention in longer surveys (Clarke, 1995).

[See also Causation; Philosophy of Mind; Strawson, Peter F.]

BIBLIOGRAPHY

Clarke, R. "Freedom and Determinism," *Philosophical Books*, Vol. 36 (1995).

Dennett, D. *Elbow Room: The Varieties of Free Will Worth Wanting.* Cambridge, MA. 1984.

Double, R. *The Non-Reality of Free Will.* New York, 1991.

Frankfurt, H. *The Importance of What We Care About.* Cambridge, 1988.

Ginet, C. *On Action.* Cambridge, 1990.

Honderich, T. *A Theory of Determinism: The Mind, Neuroscience, and Life-hopes.* Oxford, 1988.

———. *How Free Are You?* Oxford, 1993.

Kane, R. *Free Will and Values.* Albany, NY, 1985.

Strawson, G. *Freedom and Belief.* Oxford, 1986.

Strawson, P. F. *Studies in the Philosophy of Thought and Action.* Oxford, 1968.

van Inwagen, P. *An Essay on Free Will.* Oxford, 1986.

– TED HONDERICH

DEWEY, JOHN

John Dewey (1859–1952), American philosopher, educator, and social critic. Dewey was born in Burlington, Vermont. A shy youth, he enjoyed reading books and was a good but not a brilliant student. He entered the University of Vermont in 1875, and although his interest in philosophy and social thought was awakened during his last two years there, he was uncertain about his future career. He taught classics, science, and algebra at a high school in Oil City, Pennsylvania, from 1879 to 1881 and then returned to Burlington, where he continued to teach. He also arranged for private tutorials in philosophy with his former teacher, H. A. P. Torrey. Encouraged by Torrey and W. T. Harris, the editor of the *Journal of Speculative Philosophy* who accepted Dewey's first two philosophical articles, Dewey applied for the graduate program at the newly organized Johns Hopkins University. He was twice refused fellowship aid, but he borrowed $500 from an aunt to begin his professional philosophical career.

> *Shortly after Dewey arrived at Chicago,*
>
> *he helped found the famous laboratory school,*
>
> *commonly known as the Dewey School,*
>
> *which served as a laboratory*
>
> *for testing and developing*
>
> *his psychological and pedagogic hypotheses.*

The external events of Dewey's Vermont years were relatively unexciting, and there is very little to indicate that he would become America's most influential philosopher and educator as well as one of the most outspoken champions of social reform. Yet the New England way of life left a deep imprint on the man and his thought. His modesty, forthrightness, doggedness, deep faith in the workings of the democratic process, and respect for his fellow man are evidenced in almost everything that he did and wrote.

Under the imaginative guidance of Daniel Gilman, the first president of Johns Hopkins, the university had become one of the most exciting centers for intellectual and scholarly activity. Dewey studied with C. S. Peirce, who taught logic, and with G. S. Hall, one of the first experimental psychologists in America. However, the greatest initial influence on Dewey was G. S. Morris, whose philosophical outlook had been shaped by Hegel and the idealism so much in vogue on the Continent and in England.

Dewey was an eager participant in the controversies stirred up by Hegelianism. He dated his earliest interest in philosophy to a course in physiology that he took during his junior year at the University of Vermont, where he read T. H. Huxley's text on physiology. Dewey discovered the concept of the organic and developed a sense of the interdependence and interrelated unity of all things. He tells us that subconsciously he desired a world and a life that would have the same properties as had the human organism that Huxley described. In Hegel and the idealists, Dewey discovered the most profound philosophical expression of this emotional and intellectual craving. From this organic perspective, which emphasized process and change, all distinctions are functional and relative to a developing unified whole. The organic perspective could be used to oppose the static and the fixed and to break down the hard and fast dichotomies and dualisms that had plagued philosophy.

Dewey's writings during his Hegelian period are infused with an evangelical spirit and are as enthusiastic as they are vague. Whatever issue Dewey considered, he was convinced that once viewed from the perspective of the organic, old problems would dissolve and new insights would emerge. Long after Dewey had drifted away from his early Hegelianism, his outlook was shaped by his intellectual bias for a philosophy based on change, process, and dynamic, organic interaction.

After completing his doctoral studies at Johns Hopkins with a dissertation on the psychology of Kant, Dewey joined Morris at the University of Michigan in 1884. He remained there for the next ten years, with the exception of one year (1888) when he was a visiting professor at the University of Minnesota. At Michigan, Dewey worked with G. H. Mead, who later joined Dewey at Chicago. During his years at Michigan, Dewey became dissatisfied with pure speculation and sought ways to make philosophy directly relevant to the practical affairs of men. His political, economic, and social views became increasingly radical. He agreed to edit a new weekly with a socialist orientation, to be called *Thought News,* but it never reached publication. Dewey also became directly involved with public education in Michigan. His scientific interests, especially in the field of psychology, gradually overshadowed his interest in pure speculation. He published several books on theoretical and applied psychology, including *Psychology* (New York, 1887; 3d rev. ed., 1891), *Applied Psychology* (Boston, 1889), and *The Psychology of Number and Its Applications to Methods of Teaching Arithmetic* (New York, 1895). The latter two books were written with J. A. McLellan.

Dewey's appointment in 1894 as chairman of the department of philosophy, psychology, and education at the University of Chicago provided an ideal oppor-

Dewey was one of America's most influential philosophers as well as one of the most outspoken champions of social reform. (Corbis)

tunity for consolidating his diverse interests. In addition to his academic responsibilities, Dewey actively participated in the life of Hull House, founded by Jane Addams, where he had an opportunity to become directly acquainted with the social and economic problems brought about by urbanization, rapid technological advance, and the influx of immigrant populations. Dewey mixed with workers, union organizers, and political radicals of all sorts. At the university, Dewey assembled a group of sympathetic colleagues who worked closely together. Collectively they published the results of their research in a volume of the Decennial Publications of the University of Chicago entitled *Studies in Logical Theory* (Chicago, 1903). William James, to whom the book was dedicated, rightly predicted that the ideas developed in the *Studies* would dominate the American philosophical scene for the next 25 years.

Shortly after Dewey arrived in Chicago, he helped found the famous laboratory school, commonly known as the Dewey School, which served as a laboratory for testing and developing his psychological and pedagogic hypotheses. Some of Dewey's earliest and most important books on education were based on lectures delivered at the school: *The School and Society* (Chicago, 1900) and *The Child and the Curriculum* (Chicago, 1902). When Dewey left Chicago for Columbia in 1904 because of increasing friction with the university administration concerning the laboratory school, he had already acquired a national reputation for his philosophical ideas and educational theories. The move to Columbia, where he remained until his retirement in 1930, provided a further opportunity for development, and Dewey soon gained international prominence. Through the Columbia Teachers College, which was a training center for teachers from many countries, Dewey's educational philosophy spread throughout the world.

There is more to experience, Dewey believed,

than is to be found in the writings of the idealists,

and, indeed, in the writings of most epistemologists.

At the time that Dewey joined the Columbia faculty, *The Journal of Philosophy* was founded by F. J. E. Woodbridge, and it became a forum for the discussion and defense of Dewey's ideas. There is scarcely a volume from the time of its founding until Dewey's death that does not contain an article either by Dewey or about his philosophy. As the journalistic center of the country, New York also provided Dewey with an opportunity to express himself on pressing political and social issues. He became a regular contributor to the *New Republic*. A selection of Dewey's popular essays is collected in *Characters and Events*, 2 vols. (New York, 1929).

Wherever Dewey lectured he had an enormous influence. From 1919 to 1921, he lectured at Tokyo, Peking, and Nanking, and his most popular book, *Reconstruction in Philosophy* (New York, 1920), is based on his lectures at the Imperial University of Japan. He also conducted educational surveys of Turkey, Mexico, and Russia. Although he retired from Columbia in 1930, he remained active and wrote prolifically until his death. In 1937, when Dewey was 78, he traveled to Mexico to head the commission investigating the charges made against Leon Trotsky, during the Moscow trials. After a careful investigation, the commission published its report, *Not Guilty* (New York, 1937). In 1941 Dewey championed the cause of academic freedom when Bertrand Russell—his arch philosophical adversary—had been denied permission to teach at the City College of New York, Dewey collaborated in editing a book of essays protesting the decision.

Although constantly concerned with social and political issues, Dewey continued to work on his more technical philosophical studies. M. H. Thomas's bibliography of his writings comprises more than 150 pages. Dewey's influence extended not only to his colleagues but to leaders in almost every field. The wide effects of his teaching did not depend upon the superficial aspects of its presentation, for Dewey was not a brilliant lecturer or essayist, although he could be extremely eloquent. His writings are frequently turgid, obscure, and lacking in stylistic brilliance. But more than any other American of his time, Dewey expressed the deepest hopes and aspirations of his fellow man. Whether dealing with a technical philosophical issue or with some concrete injustice, he displayed a rare combination of acuteness, good sense, imagination, and wit.

EXPERIENCE AND NATURE. The key concept in Dewey's philosophy is experience. Although there is a development from an idealistic to a naturalistic analysis of experience and different emphases in his many discussions of experience, a nevertheless coherent view of experience does emerge. In his early philosophy Dewey was sympathetic to the theory of experience developed by the Hegelians and the nineteenth-century idealists. He thought of experience as a single, dynamic, unified whole in which every thing is ultimately interrelated. There are no rigid dichotomies or breaks in experience and nature. All distinctions are functional and play a role in a complex organic system. Dewey also shared the idealists' antipathy to the atomist and subjectivist tendencies in the concept of experience elaborated by the British empiricists. But as Dewey drifted away from his early Hegelian orientation he indicated three major respects in which he rejected the idealistic concept of experience.

First, he charged that the idealists, in their preoccupation with knowledge and knowing, distorted the character of experience. Idealists, Dewey claimed, neglected the noncognitive and nonreflective experiences of doing, suffering, and enjoying that set the context for all knowing and inquiry. Philosophy, especially modern philosophy, had been so concerned with epistemological issues that it mistook all experience as a form of knowing. Such bias inevitably distorts the character of both man's experience and his knowing. Man is primarily a being who acts, suffers, and enjoys. Most of his life consists of experiences that are not primarily reflective. If we are to understand the nature of thought, reflection, inquiry, and their role in human life, we must appreciate their emergence from, and conditioning by, the context of nonreflective experience. There is more to experience, Dewey believed, than is to be found in the writings of the idealists and, indeed, in the writings of most epistemologists.

The second major departure from his early idealism is to be found in Dewey's rejection of the idea of a single unified whole in which everything is ultimately interrelated. In this respect, he displayed an increasing sympathy with the pluralism of the British empiricists. He insisted that life consists of a series of overlapping and interpenetrating experiences, situations, or contexts, each of which has its internal qualitative integrity. The individual experience is the primary unit of life.

The third shift is reflected in Dewey's increasingly naturalistic bias. The Hegelians and the nineteenth-century idealists did have important insights into the organic nature of experience, but they had overgeneralized them into a false cosmic projection. Dewey discovered in the new developing human sciences, especially in what he called the anthropological–biological orientation, a more careful, detailed, scientific articulation of the organic character of experience.

Dewey thought of himself as part of a general movement that was developing a new empiricism based on a new concept of experience, one that combined the strong naturalistic bias of the Greek philosophers with a sensitive appreciation for experimental method as practiced by the sciences. He was sympathetic with what he took to be the Greek view of experience, which considers it as consisting of a fund of social knowledge and skills and as being the means by which man comes into direct contact with a qualitatively rich and variegated nature. But Dewey was just as forceful in pointing out that this view of experience had to be reconstructed in light of the experimental method of the sciences. One of his earliest and clearest discussions of the nature of experience as an organic coordination is to be found in "The Reflex Arc Concept in Psychology" (*Psychological Review*, Vol. 3, 1896).

Dewey's interest in developing a new theory of experience led many critics to question the exact status of experience within nature, and some objectors charged him with excessive anthropomorphism. Sensitive to this type of criticism, Dewey, particularly in *Experience and Nature* (Chicago, 1925; 2d ed., New York, 1929), attempted to deal with this criticism and to sketch a metaphysics, "the descriptive study of the generic traits of existence."

Nature, according to Dewey, consists of a variety of transactions that can be grouped into three evolutionary plateaus, or levels. Transaction is the technical term that Dewey used to designate the type of action in which the components and elements involved in the action both condition and are conditioned by the entire coordination. The elements of a transaction play a functional role in the developing coordination. The three plateaus of natural transactions are the physicochemical, the psychophysical, and the level of human experience.

There are no sharp breaks or discontinuities within nature. But there are distinctive characteristics of the different levels of natural transactions that are reflected in their patterns of behavior and in their consequences. From this perspective, human experience consists of one type of natural transaction, a type that has been the latest to evolve. The distinguishing characteristics of this level of natural transaction are to be located in the type of language, communication, and social living that humans have developed. Experience is all-inclusive in the sense that man is involved in continuous transactions with the whole of nature, and through systematic inquiry he can come to understand the essential characteristics of nature. Some of the more specific areas of Dewey's philosophy can be investigated against this panoramic view of experience and nature.

ART AND EXPERIENCE. The ideas contained in Dewey's *Art as Experience* (New York, 1934) provided a surprise for many readers. Popular versions of his philosophy had so exaggerated the role of the practical and the instrumental that art and aesthetic experience seemed to have no place in his philosophical outlook. More perceptive commentators realized that Dewey was making explicit a dimension of his view of experience that had always been implicit and essential to an understanding of his philosophy. The meaning and role of art and aesthetic quality are crucial for understanding Dewey's views on logic, education, democracy, ethics, social philosophy, and even technology.

Dewey had persistently claimed that knowing, or more specifically, inquiry, is an art requiring active experimental manipulation and testing. Knowing does not consist of the contemplation of eternal forms, essences, or universals. Dewey argued that the "spectator theory of knowledge," which had plagued philosophy from its beginnings, is mistaken. He also objected to the sharp division between the theoretical sciences and the practical arts that had its explicit source in Aristotle and had influenced so much later philosophy. Dewey maintained that Aristotle's analysis of the practical disciplines is more fruitful for developing an adequate theory of inquiry than is his description of the theoretical sciences of knowing. Not only is inquiry an art, but all life is, or can be, artistic. The so-called fine arts differ in degree, not in kind, from the rest of life.

Dewey also gave a prominent place to what he called immediacy, pervasive quality, or aesthetic quality. This immediacy is not restricted to a special type of experience but is a distinctive feature of anything that is properly called "*an* experience." The primary unit of life, we have mentioned, is *an* experience, a natural transaction of acting, suffering, enjoying, knowing. It has both temporal development and spatial dimension and can undergo internal change and reconstruction.

But what is it that enables us to speak of an individual experience? Or, by virtue of what does an experience, situation, or context have a unity that enables us to distinguish it from other experiences? Dewey's answer is that everything that is an experience has immediacy or pervasive quality that binds together the complex constituents of the experience. This immediacy or pervasive quality can be directly felt or had. But this qualitative dimension of experience is not to be confused with a subjective feeling that is somehow locked up in the mind of the experiencer. Nor is it to be thought of as something that exists independently of any experiencer. These qualities that pervade natural transactions are properly predicated of the experience or situation as a whole. Within an experiential transaction we can institute distinctions between what is subjective and what is objective. But such distinctions are relative to, and dependent on, the context in which they are made. An experience or a situation is a whole in virtue of its immediate pervasive qualities, and each occurrence of these qualities is unique. As examples of such pervasive qualities, Dewey mentions the qualities of distress or cheer that mark existent situations, qualities that are unique in their occurrence and inexpressible in words but capable of being directly experienced. Thus, when one directly experiences a frightening situation, it is the situation that is frightening and not merely the experience.

Dewey viewed human life as a rhythmic movement from experiences qualified by conflict, doubt, and indeterminateness toward experiences qualified by their integrity, harmony, and funded aesthetic quality.

These pervasive, or "tertiary," qualities are what Dewey calls aesthetic qualities. Aesthetic quality is thus an essential characteristic of all experiences. Within an experience, the pervasive quality can guide the development of the experience, and it can also be transformed and enriched as the experience is reconstructed. Aesthetic quality can be funded with new meaning, ideas, and emotions. A situation that is originally indeterminate, slack, or inchoate can be transformed into one that is determinate, harmonious, and funded with meaning; this type of reconstructed experience Dewey called a consummation. Such experiences are reconstructed by the use of intelligence. For example, when one is confronted with a specific problematic situation that demands resolution, one can reconstruct the situation by locating its problematic features and initiating a course of action that will resolve the situation. Consummations are characteristic of the most mundane practical tasks as well as the most speculative inquiries. The enemies of the aesthetic, Dewey claimed, are not the practical or the intellectual but the diffuse and slack at one extreme and the excessively rigid and fixed at the other. The type of experience that philosophers normally single out as aesthetic is a heightened consummation in which aesthetic qualities dominate.

Dewey viewed human life as a rhythmic movement from experiences qualified by conflict, doubt, and indeterminateness toward experiences qualified by their integrity, harmony, and funded aesthetic quality. We are constantly confronted with problematic and indeterminate situations, and insofar as we use our intelligence to reconstruct these situations successfully we achieve consummations. He was concerned both with delineating the methods by which we could most intelligently resolve the conflicting situations in which we inevitably find ourselves and with advocating the social reforms required so that life for all men would become funded with enriched meaning and increased aesthetic quality.

LOGIC AND INQUIRY. Early in his career, Dewey started developing a new theory of inquiry, which he called instrumental or experimental logic. Dewey claimed that philosophers had lost touch with the actual methods of inquiry practiced by the experimental sciences. The function of instrumental logic is to study the methods by which we most successfully gain and warrant our knowledge. On the basis of this investigation, instrumental logic could specify regulative principles for the conduct of further inquiry.

The central themes of Dewey's conception of logic were outlined in *Studies in Logical Theory* (Chicago, 1903), applied to education in How *We Think* (Boston, 1910), and further refined in *Essays in Experimental Logic* (Chicago, 1916). Dewey also wrote numerous articles on various aspects of logic, but his most systematic and detailed presentation is in *Logic: The Theory of Inquiry* (New York, 1938), in which he defines inquiry as "*the controlled or directed transformation of an indeterminate situation into one that is so determinate in its constituent distinctions and relations as to convert the elements of the original situation into a unified whole*" (p. 104). By itself, this definition is not sufficient to grasp what Dewey intends. But his meaning can be understood when the definition is interpreted against the background of what we have said about the individual experience or situation and the way in which it is pervaded by a unifying quality.

We find ourselves in situations that are qualified by their indeterminateness or internal conflict. From the perspective of the experiencer or inquirer, we can say that he experiences a "felt difficulty." This is the antecedent condition of inquiry. Insofar as the situation demands some resolution, we must attempt to articulate the problem or problems that are to be solved. Formulating the problems may be a process of successive refinement in the course of the inquiry. The next logical stage is that of suggestion or hypothesis, in which we imaginatively formulate various relevant hypotheses for solving the problem. In some complex inquiries we may have to engage in hypothetico-deductive reasoning in order to refine our hypotheses and to ascertain the logical consequences of the hypothesis or set of hypotheses. Finally, there is the stage of experimental testing in which we seek to confirm or disconfirm the suggested hypotheses. If our inquiry is successful, the original indeterminate situation is transformed into a unified whole. Knowledge may be defined as the objective of inquiry. Knowledge is that which is warranted by the careful use of the norms and methods of inquiry. When "knowledge" is taken as an abstract term related to inquiry in the abstract, it means warranted assertibility. Furthermore, the knowledge gained in a specific inquiry is funded in our experience and serves as the background for further inquiry. By reflecting on this general pattern of inquiry, which can be exhibited in commonsense inquiry as well as the most advanced scientific inquiry, we can bring into focus the distinctive features of Dewey's logic.

First, this pattern of inquiry is intended to be a general schema for all inquiry. But the specific procedures, testing methods, type of evidence, etc., will vary with different types of inquiry and different kinds of subject matter. Second, a specific inquiry cannot be completely isolated from the context of other inquiries. The rules, procedures, and evidence required for the conduct of any inquiry are derived from other successful inquiries. By studying the types of inquiry that have been most successful in achieving warranted conclusions, we can abstract norms, rules, and procedures for directing further inquiry. These norms may themselves be modified in the course of further inquiry. Third, all inquiry presupposes a social or public context that is the medium for funding the warranted conclusions and norms for further inquiry. In this respect, Dewey agrees with Peirce's emphasis on the community of inquirers. Inquiry both requires such a community and helps to further the development of this community. Dewey attempted to relate this idea of a community of inquirers to his view of democracy. The essential principle of democracy is that of community; an effective democracy

requires the existence of a community of free, courageous, and open-minded inquirers. Fourth, inquiry is essentially a self-corrective process. To conduct a specific inquiry, some knowledge claims, norms, and rules must be taken as fixed, but no knowledge claim, norm, or rule is absolutely fixed; it may be criticized, revised, or abandoned in light of subsequent inquiry and experience.

Dewey's theory of inquiry as an ongoing self-corrective process and his view of knowledge as that which is warranted through inquiry both differ radically from many traditional theories of inquiry and knowledge.

Dewey's theory of inquiry as an ongoing self-corrective process and his view of knowledge as that which is warranted through inquiry both differ radically from many traditional theories of inquiry and knowledge. Dewey thought of this theory as an alternative to the views of those philosophers who have claimed that there is an epistemological given that is indubitable and known with certainty. According to this epistemological model, some truths are considered to be absolutely certain, indubitable, or incorrigible. They may be considered self-evident, known by rational insight, or directly grasped by the senses. On the basis of this foundation, we then build or construct the rest of our knowledge. From Dewey's perspective, this general model that has informed many classical theories of knowledge is confused and mistaken. There are no absolute first truths that are given or known with certainty. Furthermore, knowledge neither has nor requires such a foundation in order to be rational. Inquiry and its objective, knowledge, are rational because inquiry is a self-corrective process by which we gradually become clearer about the epistemological status of both our starting points and conclusions. We must continually submit our knowledge claims to the public test of a community of inquirers in order to clarify, refine, and justify them.

DEMOCRACY AND EDUCATION. Dewey is probably best known for his philosophy of education. This is not a special branch of his philosophy, however, for he claimed that all philosophy can be conceived of as the philosophy of education. And it is certainly true that all the concepts we have discussed inform his thinking about education. He returned again and again to the subject of education, but the essential elements of his position can be found in *My Pedagogic Creed* (New York, 1897), *The School and Society* (Chicago, 1900), *The Child and the Curriculum* (Chicago, 1902), and especially in his comprehensive statement in *Democracy and Education* (New York, 1916).

It is essential to appreciate the dialectical context in which Dewey developed his educational ideas. He was critical of the excessively rigid and formal approach to education that dominated the practice of most American schools in the latter part of the nineteenth century. He argued that such an approach was based upon a faulty psychology in which the child was thought of as a passive creature upon whom information and knowledge had to be imposed. But Dewey was equally critical of the "new education," which was based on a sentimental idealization of the child. This child-orientated approach advocated that the child himself should pick and choose what he wanted to study. This approach also was based on a mistaken psychology, which neglected the immaturity of the child's experience. Education is, or ought to be, a continuous reconstruction of experience in which there is a development of immature experience toward experience funded with the skills and habits of intelligence. The slogan "Learn by Doing" was not intended as a credo for anti-intellectualism but, on the contrary, was meant to call attention to the fact that the child is naturally an active, curious, and exploring creature. A properly designed education must be sensitive to this active dimension of life and must guide the child, so that through his participation in different types of experience his creativity and autonomy will be cultivated rather than stifled.

Our choices are rational to the extent that

they reflect our developed habits of intelligence;

choices will be perverse or irrational

if they are based on prejudice and ignorance.

The child is not completely malleable, nor is his natural endowment completely fixed and determinate. Like Aristotle, Dewey believed that the function of education is to encourage those habits and dispositions that constitute intelligence. Dewey placed great stress on creating the proper type of environmental conditions for eliciting and nurturing these habits. His conception of the educational process is therefore closely tied to the prominent role that he assigned to habit in human life. (For a detailed statement of the nature and function of habit, see *Human Nature and Conduct*, New York,

1922.) Education as the continuous reconstruction and growth of experience also develops the moral character of the child. Virtue is taught not by imposing values upon the child but by cultivating fair-mindedness, objectivity, imagination, openness to new experiences, and the courage to change one's mind in the light of further experience.

Dewey also thought of the school as a miniature society; it should not simply mirror the larger society but should be representative of the essential institutions of this society. The school as an ideal society is the chief means for social reform. In the controlled social environment of the school it is possible to encourage the development of creative individuals who will be able to work effectively to eliminate existing evils and institute reasonable goods. The school, therefore, is the medium for developing the set of habits required for systematic and open inquiry and for reconstructing experience that is funded with greater harmony and aesthetic quality.

Dewey perceived acutely the threat posed by unplanned technological, economic, and political development to the future of democracy. The natural direction of these forces is to increase human alienation and to undermine the shared experience that is so vital for the democratic community. For this reason, Dewey placed so much importance on the function of the school in the democratic community. The school is the most important medium for strengthening and developing a genuine democratic community, and the task of democracy is forever the creation of a freer and more humane experience in which all share and participate.

ETHICS AND SOCIAL PHILOSOPHY. In order to understand Dewey's moral philosophy, we must again focus on his concept of the situation. Man is a creature who by nature has values. There are things, states of affairs, and activities that he directly enjoys, prizes, or values. Moral choices and decisions arise only in those situations in which there are competing desires or a conflict of values. The problem that a man then confronts is to decide what he really wants and what course of action he ought to pursue. He cannot appeal to his immediate values to resolve the situation; he must evaluate or appraise the situation and the different courses of action open to him. This process of deliberation that culminates in a decision to act is what Dewey calls "valuation." But how do we engage in this process of valuation? We must analyze the situation as carefully as we can, imaginatively project possible courses of action, and scrutinize the consequences of these actions. Those ends or goods that we choose relative to a concrete situation after careful deliberation are reasonable or desirable goods. Our choices are reasonable to the extent that they reflect our developed habits of intelligence.

Choices will be perverse or irrational if they are made on the basis of prejudice and ignorance. Dewey is fully aware that there are always practical limitations to our deliberations, but a person trained to deliberate intelligently will be prepared to act intelligently even in those situations that do not permit extended deliberation. When we confront new situations we must imagine and strive for new goals. As long as there is human life, there will always be situations in which there are internal conflicts that demand judgment, decision, and action. In this sense, the moral life of man is never completed, and the ends achieved become the means for attaining further ends. But lest we think that man is always striving for something that is to be achieved in the remote future, or never, Dewey emphasized that there are consummations—experiences in which the ends that we strive for are concretely realized.

It should be clear that such a view of man's moral life places a great deal of emphasis on intelligence. Dewey readily admitted his "faith in the power of intelligence to imagine a future which is a projection of the desirable in the present, and to invent the instrumentalities of its realization." It should also be clear that ethics conceived of in this manner blends into social philosophy. Valuation, like all inquiry, presupposes a community of shared experience in which there are common norms and procedures, and intelligent valuation is also a means for making such a community a concrete reality. Here, too, ends and norms are clarified, tested, and modified in light of the cumulative experience of the community. Furthermore, it is the objective of social philosophy to point the way to the development of those conditions that will foster the effective exercise of practical intelligence. The spirit that pervades Dewey's entire philosophy and finds its perfect expression in his social philosophy is that of the reformer or reconstructor, not the revolutionary. Dewey was always skeptical of panaceas and grand solutions for eliminating existing evils and injustices. But he firmly believed that with a realistic scientific knowledge of existing conditions and with a cultivated imagination, men could improve and ameliorate the human condition. To allow ourselves to drift in the course of events or to fail to assume our responsibility for continuous reconstruction of experience inevitably leads to the dehumanization of man.

PHILOSOPHY AND CIVILIZATION. Dewey presented a comprehensive and synoptic image of man and the universe. The entire universe consists of a multifarious variety of natural transactions. Man is at once continuous with the rest of nature and exhibits distinctive patterns of behavior that distinguish him from the rest of nature. His experience is also pervaded with qualities that are not reducible to less complex natural transactions. Thus, Dewey attempted to place man within the context of the whole of nature. In addition, Dewey was sensitive to the varieties of human experience. He sought to delineate the distinctive features of different aspects of experience, ranging from mundane practical experience to the religious dimension of experience. Within the tradition of philosophy Dewey may be characterized as a robust naturalist or a humanistic naturalist. His philosophy is both realistic and optimistic. There will always be conflicts, problems, and competing values within our experience, but with the continuous development of "creative intelligence" men can strive for and realize new ends and goals.

"Within the flickering inconsequential acts of separate selves dwells a sense of the whole which claims and dignifies them. In its presence we put off mortality and live in the universal."

This synoptic view of man and the universe is closely related to Dewey's conception of the role of philosophy in civilization. Philosophy is dependent on, but should attempt to transcend, the specific culture from which it emerges. The function of philosophy is to effect a junction of the new and the old, to articulate the basic principles and values of a culture, and to reconstruct these into a more coherent and imaginative vision. Philosophy is therefore essentially critical and, as such, will always have work to do. For as the complex of traditions, values, accomplishments, and aspirations that constitute a culture changes, so must philosophy change. Indeed, in pointing the way to new ideals and in showing how these may be effectively realized, philosophy is one of the means for changing a culture. Philosophy is continually faced with the challenge of understanding the meaning of evolving cultures and civilizations and of articulating new projected ideals. The motif of reconstruction that runs throughout Dewey's investigations dominates his conception of the role of philosophy in civilization. He epitomized the spirit of his entire philosophical endeavor in his "plea for casting off of that intellectual timidity which hampers the wings of imagination, a plea for speculative audacity, for more faith in ideas, sloughing off a cowardly reliance upon those partial ideas to which we are wont to give the name facts." He fully realized that he was giving philosophy a more modest function than had been given by those who claimed that philosophy reveals an eternal reality. But such modesty is not incompatible with boldness in the maintenance of this function. As Dewey declared, "a combination of such modesty and courage affords the only way I know of in which the philosopher can look his fellow man in the face with frankness and humanity" (*Philosophy and Civilization*, p. 12).

BIBLIOGRAPHY

The most exhaustive bibliography of John Dewey's writings is M. H. Thomas' *John Dewey: A Centennial Bibliography* (Chicago, 1962). This excellent guide includes a comprehensive listing of Dewey's writings, translations, and reviews of his works, and a bibliography of books, articles, and dissertations about Dewey.

A less comprehensive bibliography of Dewey's writings can also be found in *The Philosophy of John Dewey*, P. A. Schilpp, ed. (Chicago, 1939).

The following secondary sources are helpful as general introductions to Dewey's life and philosophy. Richard J. Bernstein, *John Dewey* (New York, 1966) focuses on the concept of experience and nature. George R. Geiger, *John Dewey in Perspective* (New York, 1958) stresses the role of aesthetic experience as the key to Dewey's philosophy. Sidney Hook, *John Dewey: An Intellectual Portrait* (New York, 1939) captures both the spirit and letter of Dewey as a man, social reformer, and philosopher. Robert J. Roth, S. J., *John Dewey and Self-Realization* (Englewood Cliffs, N. J., 1962) shows the importance and meaning of religious experience for Dewey.

– RICHARD J. BERNSTEIN

DEWEY, JOHN (UPDATE)

John Dewey has undergone an extraordinary renaissance of scholarly and public concern with his thought. Dewey (1859–1952) was encyclopedic in both his interests and achievements (see original entry). The full and startling range of his written reflections is now apparent with the completed publication of his *Works* in a critical edition of thirty-seven volumes. Commentaries and critical interpretations have followed apace.

In the mediated public mind, prior discussion of Dewey's thought for the most part was devoted to his work on education, both in theory and practice. Unfortunately, these discussions of Dewey's approach to pedagogy and to schooling as an institution in a democratic society were often disconnected from his metaphysics, aesthetics, and social and political philosophy. This interpretive mishap is now being rectified with the appearance of many perceptive studies of Dewey's thought, including his previously neglected thoughts on religion and logic.

Fundamentally, John Dewey is an unregenerate philosophical naturalist, one for whom the human journey is constitutive of its own meaning and is not to be rescued by any transcendent explanations, principles of accountability, or posthumous salvation. Obviously, this position of Dewey is both liberating and baleful, in that it throws us back on our own human resources, for better and for worse. In effect, we are responsible for our actions, for the course of human history, and we are called upon to navigate between the shoals of supine obeisance and arrogant usurpation. In *A Common Faith* (1934), Dewey warns of the danger to human solidarity when we do not accept this responsibility. "Weak natures take to reverie as a refuge as strong ones do to fanaticism. Those who dissent are mourned over by the first class and converted through the use of force by the second."

Leaving no philosophical stone unturned, Dewey addresses the pitfalls and possibilities of the human condition from a wide array of vantage points. His central text is *Experience and Nature*, in which he probes the transactions of the human organism with the affairs of nature. These transactions are to be understood and diagnosed as experiential oscillations between the "precarious" and the "stable." The settings for this trenchant discussion include communication, mind, art, and value. In retrospect, Dewey offered that he should have titled this work *Culture and Nature*, an appropriate reconsideration, for it is helpful to read Dewey as a philosopher of culture, with an eye toward his grasp of human institutions, social, political, and educational.

In the past decade the focus of commentaries on the work of Dewey has been directed to his social and political philosophy, particularly his writings between 1927 and 1935, namely, *The Public and Its Problems, Individualism Old and New*, and *Liberalism and Social Action*. Although Dewey's thought was indigenous to American culture, it is nonetheless remarkable that themes found in Marxist and existentialist traditions are present in these writings, cast differently but equally telling. Of special note is the renewed admiration for Dewey's philosophy of community and his deep grasp of the complex relationships of individuals in communities. For Dewey the irreducible trait of human life is found in the activity of face-to-face communities. Their quality is the sign of how we are faring, humanly. At the end of *Human Nature and Conduct*, he writes a message for his time and for our time as well.

Within the flickering inconsequential acts of separate selves dwells a sense of the whole which claims and dignifies them. In its presence we put off mortality and live in the universal. The life of the community in which we live and have our being is the fit symbol of this relationship. The acts in which we express our perception of the ties which bind us to others are its only rites and ceremonies.

BIBLIOGRAPHY

Works by Dewey

Works of John Dewey, edited by J. A. Boydston. Carbondale, IL, 1969–90. Divided into Early Works (5 vols.), Middle Works (15 vols.), and Later Works (17 vols.). This is a critical edition.
The Philosophy of John Dewey, edited by J. J. McDermott. Chicago, 1981. Complete selections from Dewey's major writings.

Works on Dewey

Campbell, J. *Understanding John Dewey.* Chicago, 1995. The most intelligent and accurate interpretation of Dewey's thought overall.
Hickman, L. A. *John Dewey's Pragmatic Technology.* Bloomington, IN, 1990.
Rockefeller, S. C. *John Dewey: Religious Faith and Democratic Humanism.* New York, 1991.
Ryan, A. *John Dewey and the High Tide of American Liberalism.* New York, 1995.
Schilpp, P. A., and L. E. Hahn, eds. *The Philosophy of John Dewey.* Carbondale, IL, 1989. Contains a bibliography of Dewey's publications with entries and corrections until 1989.
Sleeper, R. S. *The Necessity of Pragmatism: John Dewey's Conception of Philosophy.* New Haven, 1986. An insightful presentation of the relationship between Dewey's thought and major currents in contemporary philosophy.
Welchman, J. *Dewey's Ethical Thought.* Ithaca, NY, 1995.
Westbrook, R. *John Dewey and American Democracy.* Ithaca, NY, 1991. A synoptic and especially perceptive book on Dewey's social thought.

— JOHN J. MCDERMOTT

DISCOURSE ETHICS

"Discourse ethics" refers to an approach to moral theory developed by Jürgen Habermas. It is a reconstruction of Immanuel Kant's idea of practical reason that turns on a reformulation of his categorical imperative: rather than prescribing to others as valid norms which I can will to be universal laws, I must submit norms to others for purposes of discursively testing their putative universality. "Only those norms may claim to be valid that could meet with the approval of all those affected in their capacity as participants in practical discourse" (Habermas, 1990, p. 66). Normative validity, construed as rational acceptability, is thus tied to argumentation processes governed by a principle of universalization: "For a norm to be valid, the consequences and side effects of its general observance for the satisfaction of each person's particular interests must be acceptable to all" (p. 197). Furthermore, by requiring that perspective taking be general and reciprocal, discourse ethics builds a moment of empathy or 'ideal role-taking' into the procedure of practical argumentation.

Like Kant, Habermas distinguishes the types of practical reasoning and the corresponding types of 'ought' connected with questions concerning what is pragmatically expedient, ethically prudent, or morally right. Calculations of rational choice furnish recommendations relevant to the pursuit of contingent purposes in the light of given preference. When serious questions of value arise, deliberation on who one is and wants to be yields insight into the good life. If issues of justice are involved, fair and impartial consideration of conflicting interests is required to judge what is right or just. Again like Kant, Habermas regards questions of the last type, rather than specifically ethical questions, to be the proper domain of theory. (Thus, discourse ethics might properly be called discourse morality.) This is not to deny that ethical discourse is rational or that it exhibits general structures of its own; but the irreducible pluralism of modern life means that questions of self-understanding, self-realization, and the good life do not admit of universal answers. In Habermas's view, that does not preclude a general theory of a narrower sort, namely a theory of justice. Accordingly, the aim of his discourse ethics is solely to reconstruct the moral point of view from which questions of right can be fairly and impartially adjudicated.

By linking discourse ethics to the theory of communicative action, Habermas means to show that our basic moral intuitions are rooted in something deeper and more universal than particularities of our tradition, namely in the intuitive grasp of the normative presuppositions of social interaction possessed by competent social actors in any society. Members of our species become individuals in and through being socialized into networks of reciprocal social relations. The mutual vulnerability that this interdependence brings with it calls for guarantees of mutual consideration to preserve both the integrity of individual persons and the web of their interpersonal relations. In discourse ethics respect for the individual is built into the freedom of each participant in discourse to accept or reject the reasons offered as justifications for norms, and concern for the common good is built into the requirement that each participant take into account the needs, interests, and feelings of all others affected by the norm in question. Hence, the actual practice of moral discourse depends on forms of socialization and social reproduction that foster the requisite capacities and motivation.

[See also Communicative Action; Habermas, Jürgen; Justice; Kant, Immanuel.]

BIBLIOGRAPHY

Habermas, J. *Moral Consciousness and Communicative Action,* translated by C. Lenhardt and S. Nicholsen. Cambridge, MA, 1990.

————. *Justification and Application: Remarks on Discourse Ethics,* translated by C. Cronin. Cambridge, MA, 1993.

Rehg, W. *Insight and Solidarity: The Discourse Ethics of Jürgen Habermas.* Berkeley, 1994.

— THOMAS MCCARTHY

DISTANT PEOPLES AND FUTURE GENERATIONS

Only recently have philosophers begun to discuss the question of whether we can meaningfully speak of distant peoples and future generations as having rights against us or of our having corresponding obligations to them. Answering this question with respect to distant peoples is much easier than answering it with respect to future generations. Few philosophers have thought that the mere fact that people are at a distance from us precludes our having any obligations to them or their having any rights against us. Some philosophers, however, have argued that our ignorance of the specific membership of the class of distant peoples does rule out these moral relationships. Yet this cannot be right, given that in other contexts we recognize obligations to indeterminate classes of people, such as a police officer's obligation to help people in distress or the obligation of food producers not to harm those who consume their products.

Of course, before distant peoples can be said to have rights against us, we must be capable of acting across the distance that separates us. Yet as long as this condition is met—as it typically is for people living in most technologically advanced societies—it would certainly seem possible for distant peoples to have rights against us and us corresponding obligations to them.

By contrast, answering the above question with respect to future generations raises more difficult issues. One concerns whether it is logically coherent to speak of future generations as having rights now. Of course, no one who finds talk about rights to be generally meaningful should question whether we can coherently claim that future generations *will* have rights at some point in the future (specifically, when they come into existence and are no longer future generations). But what is questioned, since it is of considerable practical sig-

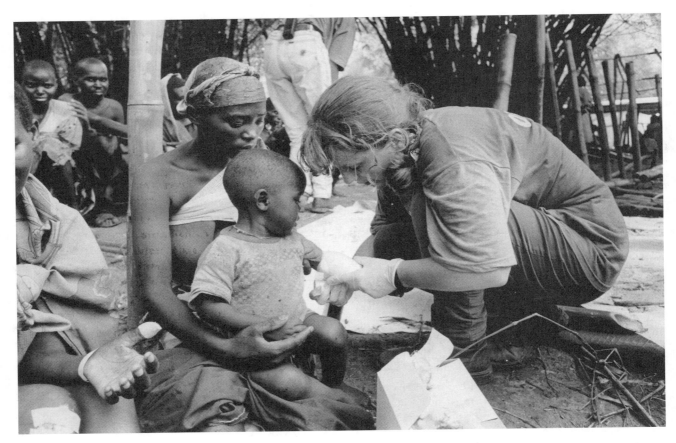

Few philosophers have thought that the mere fact that people are at a distance from us precludes our having any obligations to them. (Corbis/ Howard Davis)

nificance, is whether we can coherently claim that future generations have rights now when they do not yet exist.

Let us suppose, for example, that we continue to use up the earth's resources at present or even greater rates, and as a result, it turns out that future generations will face widespread famine, depleted resources, insufficient new technology to handle the crisis, and a drastic decline in the quality of life for nearly everyone. If this were to happen, could persons living in the twenty-second century legitimately claim that we in the twentieth century violated their rights by not restraining our consumption of the world's resources? Surely it would be odd to say that we violated their rights more than one hundred years before they existed. But what exactly is the oddness?

Is it that future generations generally have no way of claiming their rights against existing generations? While this does make the recognition and enforcement of rights much more difficult (future generations would need strong advocates in the existing generations), it does not make it impossible for such rights to exist. After all, the recognition and enforcement of the rights of distant peoples is also a difficult task, but obviously such rights can exist.

Perhaps what troubles us is that future generations do not exist when their rights are said to demand action. But how else could persons have a right to benefit from the effects our actions will have in the distant future if they did not exist just when those effects would be felt? Our contemporaries cannot legitimately make the same demand, for they will not be around to experience those effects. Only future generations could have a right that the effects our actions will have in the distant future contribute to their well-being. Nor need we assume that, for persons to have rights, they must exist when their rights demand action. Thus, to say that future generations have rights against existing generations, we can simply mean that there are enforceable requirements upon existing generations that would benefit future generations or prevent harm to them.

Most likely what really bothers us is that we cannot know for sure what effects our actions will have on future generations. For example, we may, at some cost to ourselves, conserve resources that will be valueless to future generations who may develop different technologies. Or, because we regard them as useless, we may destroy or deplete resources that future generations will find to be essential to their well-being. Nevertheless, we should not allow such possibilities to blind us to the necessity of a social policy in this regard. After all, whatever we do will have its effect on future generations. The best approach, therefore, is to use the knowledge

we have and assume that future generations will also require those basic resources we now find to be valuable. If it turns out that future generations require different resources to meet their basic needs, at least we will not be to blame for acting on the basis of the knowledge we have.

Most likely what really bothers us

is that we cannot know for sure

what effects our actions will have

on future generations.

Assuming then that we can meaningfully speak of distant peoples and future generations as having rights against us and us corresponding obligations to them, the crucial question that remains is exactly what rights they have against us and what obligations we have to them. While the answer to this question obviously depends on a substantial social and political theory, the expectation is that the rights and obligations that morally bind us to distant peoples and future generations will be quite similar to those that morally bind us to near people and existing generations.

[See also Rights.]

BIBLIOGRAPHY

Elfstrom, G. *Ethics for a Shrinking World.* New York, 1990.
Hardin, G. *Promethean Ethics.* Seattle, 1980.
Partridge, E. *Responsibilities to Future Generations.* Buffalo, NY, 1981.

— JAMES P. STERBA

DUMMETT, MICHAEL ANTHONY EARDLEY

Michael Anthony Eardley Dummett is the most important philosopher of logic of the second half of the twentieth century. Born on 27 June 1925 in London, Dummett completed his formal education at Christ Church, Oxford, and served for many years on the faculty of that university. A fellow of All Soul's College, from 1979 to 1992, Dummett was the Wykeham Professor of Logic. His influential work has made the claim commonplace (though not uncontroversial) that philosophical matters concerning logic and truth are central to metaphysics, understood in roughly the traditional sense. Dummett has profoundly and permanently shifted the ground of debates concerning metaphysical realism.

Much of Dummett's work has taken place in the context of his commentaries on Gottlob Frege, at whose hands, Dummett claims, epistemology was supplanted by the philosophy of language as the fundamental field of philosophical investigation. Frege's reorientation of philosophy, comparable to the Cartesian installation of epistemology as the foundation of philosophical thinking, finally directed philosophers' attention at the proper focus: the relation of language to reality. Dummett is thus a leading advocate of the "linguistic turn." He is heavily influenced by Ludwig Wittgenstein's later work and by intuitionism in the philosophy of mathematics.

Dummett has profoundly and permanently shifted the ground of debates concerning metaphysical realism.

Dummett claims to have articulated a common structure embodied in a number of disputes pitting realists on a given subject matter against opponents of realism on that subject matter. For example, the medieval debate over universals consisted of realists, who held the existence of mind-independent objective properties, against various denials of realism (conceptualism, nominalism). Realism about material objects contrasts with varieties of idealism, all of which share the general view that material objects do not exist mind-independently and objectively (absolute idealism, phenomenalism). In general, these positions antagonistic toward the positing of a given objective, mind-independent realm can be called antirealistic positions. Dummett holds that the proper way to represent the realist/antirealist dispute on a given realm of discourse, a way of understanding the dispute that is deeper than talking about mind independence or objectivity, is to investigate what logical principles that are valid on the realistic view must be abandoned by antirealism. In particular Dummett claims that the law of bivalence, according to which every meaningful statement is determinately either true or false, is the mark of realism.

According to Dummett, the route to antirealism must be a meaning-theoretical one and thus focuses on the role of the notion of truth in explicating meaning. His position on the theory of meaning has been called verificationism but, more properly, should be called neo-verificationism to distinguish him from the logical positivists. Dummett argues that truth cannot be the fundamental notion of a theory of meaning, if truth is conceived realistically—that is, as satisfying the principle of bivalence. He recommends abandoning this classical notion of truth. His positive proposal can be put either of two ways: he sometimes suggests that the classical notion of truth must be replaced by a different concept of truth, one that does not include the bivalence principle. Other times he suggests that truth be replaced by verification as the central meaning-theoretical notion.

The theory of meaning is concerned with the relationships of truth, meaning, and use. Holding to a sophisticated reading of the "meaning is use" idea, Dummett argues that a theory of meaning based on the classical notion of truth cannot successfully analyze the ability of speakers to use their language. That is, the meaning of a sentence cannot be identified (or, more weakly, sufficiently intimately connected) with the sentence's truth conditions if truth is conceived classically, because the resultant theory of meaning will not be able to explain the speaker's linguistic abilities as dependent upon her knowledge of the meaning of her sentences.

Dummett's key arguments to this conclusion have been called the acquisition and manifestation arguments. Because some of the sentences of the language in question are undecidable (their truth or falsity cannot be recognized by means of "decision procedures"), it is inexplicable how a speaker is able to learn their truth-conditional meanings through training. The truth conditions of these sentences transcend the abilities of finite beings to teach them. Similarly, since a grasp of a sentence's meaning must be conclusively manifestable in one's actions, it is inconceivable that a speaker could display competence in the language if this means demonstrating her grasp of a sentence's recognition-transcendent truth conditions. Because of this sensitivity of the theory of meaning to such epistemological concerns, Dummett concludes that the central explanation notion of a theory of meaning cannot be epistemically transcendent. Thus, a notion of truth must be adopted that is responsive to the cognitive limitations of language users. This leads to the intuitionistic concept of truth, whereby bivalence fails and certain sentences cannot be said to possess a truth value despite being meaningful. Examples of such sentences include some past-tense and future-tense sentences, attributions of dispositional properties to no-longer-existent objects that never displayed possession or lack of the dispositions in question, and, crucially, sentences involving unrestricted quantification over infinite domains. Further pursuit of this line leads Dummett into consideration and rejection of meaning-theoretical holism and to an emphasis on the role of logical inference in verification.

Dummett thus rests metaphysical questions upon meaning-theoretical ones and in particular argues that the choice concerning which notion of truth is appropriate, and consequently which logic correctly formalizes the corresponding notion of valid or truth-preserving inference, must depend on a prior investigation in the theory of meaning.

Dummett's importance to philosophy lies in his demonstration of the delicate sensitivity of metaphysics to the philosophy of logic and of both to matters belonging squarely to philosophy of language.

[See also Frege, Gottlob; Intuitionism; Meaning; Philosophy of Language; Realism; Truth; Wittgenstein, Ludwig Josef Johann.]

BIBLIOGRAPHY

"What Is a Theory of Meaning?" in S. Guttenplan, ed., *Mind and Language* (Oxford, 1974).

"What Is a Theory of Meaning? (II)" in G. Evans and J. MacDowell, eds., *Meaning and Truth* (Oxford, 1974).

"The Justification of Deduction," in *Truth and Other Enigmas* (Cambridge, MA, 1978).

"The Philosophical Basis of Intuitionistic Logic," in *Truth and Other Enigmas* (Cambridge, MA, 1978).

"The Significance of Quine's Indeterminacy Thesis," in *Truth and Other Enigmas* (Cambridge, MA, 1978).

Frege: Philosophy of Language, 2d ed. Cambridge, MA, 1981.

The Interpretation of Frege's Philosophy. Cambridge, MA, 1981.

"Frege on the Third Realm," in *Frege and Other Philosophers.* Oxford, 1991.

The Logical Basis of Metaphysics. Cambridge, MA, 1991.

Frege: Philosophy of Mathematics. Cambridge, MA, 1993.

The Seas of Language. Oxford, 1993.

— MICHAEL HAND

ELIMINATIVE MATERIALISM, ELIMINATIVISM

Eliminative materialism espouses the view that our commonsense way of understanding the mind is false, and that, as a result, beliefs, desires, consciousness, and other mental events used in explaining our everyday behavior do not exist. Hence, the language of our "folk" psychology should be expunged, or eliminated, from future scientific discourse.

Our commonsense way of understanding the mind is false; therefore, beliefs, desires, consciousness, and other mental events used in explaining our everyday behavior do not exist.

Two routes have been taken to get to the eliminativist's position. The first and less popular stems from a linguistic analysis of mentalistic language. Paul Feyerabend argues that the commonsense terms for mental states tacitly assume some version of dualism. Insofar as materialism is true, these terms cannot refer to anything in the physical world. Thus they should not be used in discussing ourselves or our psychologies since we are purely physical beings.

The second and better-developed approach comes out of the philosophies of science developed by Feyerabend, David Lewis, Willard Van Orman Quine and Wilfrid Sellars. Two suppositions are important for eliminativism. (1) There is no fundamental distinction between observations (and our observation language) and theory (and our theoretical language), for previously adopted conceptual frameworks shape all observations and all expressions of those observations. All observations are "theory-laden." These include observations we make of ourselves; in particular, observations we make about our internal states. There are no incorrigible phenomenological "givens." (2) The meaning of our theoretical terms (which includes our observational vocabulary) depends upon how the terms are embedded in the conceptual scheme. Meaning holism of this variety entails that if the theory in which the theoretical terms are embedded is false, then the entities that the theory posits do not exist. The terms would not refer.

Two more planks complete the eliminative argument. (3) Our way of describing ourselves in our everyday interactions comprises a rough and ready theory composed of the platitudes of our commonsense understanding. The terms used in this folk theory are defined by the platitudes. (4) Folk psychology is a radically false theory.

In support of this position, Patricia Churchland and Paul Churchland argue that belief-desire psychology wrongly assumes sentential processing; moreover, belief-desire psychology is stagnant, irreducible to neuroscience, and incomplete. Stephen Stich argues that our very notion of belief and, by implication, the other propositional attitudes is unsuitable for cognitive science. Patricia Churchland, Daniel Dennett, Georges Rey, Richard Rorty, and others argue that our notion of consciousness is confused. They all conclude, as do other eliminativists, that folk psychology should be replaced by something entirely different and more accurate, though views differ on what this replacement should be.

Attacks on eliminative materialism generally have come from four fronts, either on premise two, premise three, or premise four of the second approach, or on the eliminativist position itself, without regard to the arguments for it. Premise two asserts meaning holism and a particular theory of reference. If that theory were false, then the eliminativist's second argument would be undermined. There are alternative approaches to reference that do not assume holism; for example, causal-historical accounts do not. If meaning is not holistic, then even if folk psychology were incorrect, the terms used in that theory could still refer, and elimination of folk psychological terms would not be warranted.

Arguments that our folk psychology is not a true theory deny premise three. Here some detractors point out that even if a completed psychology did not rely on the propositional attitudes or consciousness, that fact would not entail that those sorts of mental states do not exist; instead, they just would not be referred to in scientific discourse. Nevertheless, they could still be used as they are now, in our everyday explanations of our behavior.

Others charge that premise four is false; folk psychology might be a rudimentary theory, but it is not radically false. While agreeing that belief-desire explanations or explanations involving conscious events might not be entirely empirically adequate or complete, champions of folk psychology argue that no other theory is either. In addition, our folk psychology has developed over time, is coherent, and its status with respect to neuroscience is immaterial. These arguments are generally coupled with the claim that no other alternative, either real or imagined, could fulfill the explanatory role that the propositional attitudes play in our understanding of ourselves. And until the eliminativist's promise of a better conceptual scheme is fulfilled folk psychology is here to stay. At least some properly revised version of folk psychology would remain.

Lastly, some supporters of folk psychology argue that any eliminativist program would be fatally flawed, regardless of whatever particular arguments are given, for the very statement of eliminative materialism itself is incoherent. In its simplest form, the argument runs as follows: Eliminative materialism claims that beliefs do not exist. Therefore, if eliminative materialism were true, we could not believe it. Therefore, no one can believe eliminative materialism on pain of inconsistency.

Replies to the four sorts of attacks are ubiquitous. However, answering the first three turns on (primarily empirical) issues yet to be settled. Which theory of reference is correct, whether folk psychology is actually a theory, and what revisions are required to make it adequate depend upon facts we do not yet know about ourselves or our linguistic practices.

The last point is more conceptual. In responding to it, eliminative materialists hold that something else will replace "belief," or some instances or aspects of "belief." Call this "schmelief." It is true that eliminative materialists cannot believe that eliminative materialism is true on pain of inconsistency. But, eliminativists maintain, they can "schmelieve it." Defenders of a revised folk psychology answer that, as used in this context, "schmelief" seems to be some other intentional operator or relation, a mere revision of belief. Without better exposition of what the replacement for folk psychology will be (and how it will be radically different), we simply cannot tell what the future holds for our commonsense theory of self: simple revision, peaceful co-existence, or outright replacement.

[See also Folk Psychology; Philosophy of Mind; Quine, Willard Van Orman; Reference; Sellars, Wilfrid.]

BIBLIOGRAPHY

Baker, L. R. *Saving Belief: A Critique of Physicalism.* Princeton, NJ, 1987.

Boghossian, P. "The Status of Content," *Philosophical Review*, Vol. 99 (1990), 157–84.

Churchland, P. "Eliminative Materialism and the Propositional Attitudes," *Journal of Philosophy*, Vol. 78 (1981), 67–90.

Feyerabend, P. "Mental Events and the Brain," *Journal of Philosophy*, Vol. 60 (1963), 295–96.

Horgan, T., and J. Woodward. "Folk Psychology Is Here to Stay," *Philosophical Review*, Vol. 94 (1985), 197–225.

Rey, G. "A Reason for Doubting the Existence of Consciousness," in R. Davidson, S. Schwartz, and D. Shapiro, eds., *Consciousness and Self-Regulation*, Vol. 3. (New York, 1982).

Rorty, R. "Mind-Body Identity, Privacy, and Categories," *Review of Metaphysics*, Vol. 19 (1965), 24–54.

Stich, S. *From Folk Psychology to Cognitive Science: The Case Against Belief.* Cambridge, MA, 1983.

— VALERIE GRAY HARDCASTLE

ENGINEERING ETHICS

Philosophers began to do scholarly work in the area of engineering ethics in the late 1970s; there has been a modest but steady flow of philosophical essays on a variety of issues since that time. Most of the work done by philosophers has been in the United States, although a few philosophers in other countries have begun to contribute to the literature.

As a subfield of applied ethics, the philosophical study of engineering ethics has evolved out of and built on previous philosophical work in areas such as biomedical ethics, business ethics, and the philosophy of technology. More general works on professional ethics (such as Gert, 1992; Hare, 1992) are of direct value to work in engineering ethics.

Engineering ethics has a "gold mine" of resources for doing case studies that is not available for many other professional fields.

A good example of a sustained application to engineering of a topic originally developed in the fields of medical and research ethics appears in a book coauthored by a philosopher. Mike W. Martin and engineer Roland Schinzinger (1983) argue effectively in support of the thesis that most engineering projects involve what can be characterized as social experiments, which for this reason require following informed-consent procedures similar to those used for other experimentation involving human subjects. The most difficult aspect of this approach is the set of complexities associated with identifying the affected parties, providing appropriate information to these parties, and obtaining uncoerced consent from them.

In addition to borrowing from related fields, engineering ethics has contributed to these fields. One of the earliest philosophical essays on engineering ethics,

De George's (1981) analysis of the Pinto gas-tank case in which he proposes necessary and sufficient conditions for justifying whistleblowing, has been widely discussed and reprinted in the literature of business ethics and other fields. Other work on more general topics (e.g., Davis, 1991; Ladd, 1982; Whitbeck, 1992) displays the positive results of interactions between engineering ethics and related fields.

The professional activities of engineers have significant effects—both direct and indirect—on the health of large numbers of persons and other life forms. Bad engineering work (whether at the design, construction/manufacture, or maintenance level) on an automobile, airplane, chemical process, or nuclear power plant could cause serious injury or death to many individuals. Good engineering work can have substantial positive effects in terms of extending the length and improving the quality of the lives of humans and others. The indirect consequences (especially the negative ones) are more difficult to identify but are often more serious in the long run. The general problems of identifying and evaluating the consequences of engineering activities are among the main topics in the philosophy of technology.

Engineering itself evolved as a separate profession during the nineteenth century. National professional societies representing the major fields of engineering (civil, mechanical, electrical, etc.) were well established by 1900. A number of efforts have been made over the past century to establish a single professional organization representing engineers in all fields, but a variety of factors has prevented the lasting success of all such efforts. (Layton, 1986, provides an excellent historical account up to World War II of the political conflicts within and among the major engineering societies and the impact on their ethics activities.)

Most of the engineering societies had formulated and adopted codes of ethics by 1915. As was the case for many professions evolving at the time, the ethics codes of the engineering societies were modeled to a significant degree on the code of medical ethics of the time, with the term "patient" systematically replaced with "employer" or "client."

The ethics codes of the various engineering societies have changed substantially over the years. The most significant change has been in the specification of the "paramount" responsibility of engineers, which was originally identified as the protection of the employer/client's interests. Revisions of the codes in the 1940s required that engineers balance the interests of the employers/clients with the interests of the general public. In the 1970s the paramount responsibility was narrowed to only the public welfare in many (but not all) engineering codes. Although the problematic degree of paternalism in this formulation has been fairly widely discussed in the literature, this element of the codes has not been changed. In fact, the first international model code of engineering, promulgated by the World Federation of Engineering Organizations in 1993, includes the explicit assertion that professional engineers shall "hold paramount the safety, health and welfare of the public."

A feature of the practice of engineering that once set the field apart from many other professions is that most engineers are employees of large organizations and they work as members of teams in which moral responsibility is not clearly assigned to specific individuals. Engineering now provides a model for many other professions, including medicine, law, and accounting, whose members are increasingly employed in large organizations. A related issue that recurs in the literature is that the boundary between professional roles and managerial roles is increasingly blurred (see Werhane, 1991).

Engineers remain different from other professionals such as physicians, nurses, accountants, and lawyers in at least one ethically significant way in that very few engineers (most of them in civil engineering) are required to be licensed. Since only licensed engineers are governed by any legally enforceable code of ethics, the codes of the various engineering societies are essentially statements of ideals.

Engineering ethics has a "gold mine" of resources for doing case studies that is not available for many other professional fields. Because of the public, large-scale nature of many engineering projects, the occurrence of some failures is widely publicized and openly investigated. Congressional hearings (and even presidential commissions, as in the case of the Challenger explosion) have been conducted on a number of important cases, and the published reports are readily accessible. Even when the government has not been the immediate client, regulatory bodies have had sufficient interest to conduct inquiries and publish substantial reports. (In contrast, hearings before state licensing boards for physicians, lawyers, accountants, and other professionals are often held in closed sessions with the transcripts being sealed.) Philosophers have done thoughtful and balanced analyses of a number of cases that provide important insights into the complexities, subtleties, vaguenesses, and ambiguities of situations in which engineers operate and of the ethical issues that arise in those situations (good examples are Fielder, 1988; Fielder & Birsch, 1992; Harris et al., 1995; and Werhane, 1991).

While much of the literature in engineering ethics is concerned with cases involving "disasters" such as the DC-10 case (only a portion of which is included in Fielder & Birsch, 1992), a few important studies have concentrated on the organizational policies and procedures that have been successful in minimizing harm and maximizing benefits of engineering projects (see Flores, 1982).

As with most other professions, engineering ethics still contains much unexplored territory. This is often due (in part, at least) to the fact that certain legal parameters have been created by legislatures and courts; it is then tacitly assumed that the legal principles are also the ethical norms, and no serious examination is made of the issues. For example, until 1976 almost all engineering codes of ethics contained explicit proscriptions against any form of advertising of professional services. After the U.S. Supreme Court ruled in 1976 that such restrictions violate antitrust laws, the proscriptions were dropped from the codes; some codes substituted recommendations that the advertising should not be misleading or in bad taste, but other codes are still completely silent on the matter. There has been no philosophical discussion of the subtle complexities—such as the problem of determining when even accurate quantitative statements may be misleading to potential clients—associated with this aspect of engineering practice. Of an incomplete list of twenty-five issues in engineering ethics in need of philosophical analysis (Baum, 1980, pp. 47–48), most have received little if any attention from philosophers as of the mid-1990s. Some of the topics have received considerable philosophical attention at a more general level (e.g., in Weil & Snapper, 1989), but the specific issues related to engineering have yet to be examined in detail.

[See also Applied Ethics; Biomedical Ethics; Business Ethics; Informed Consent; Paternalism; Philosophy of Technology.]

BIBLIOGRAPHY

Baum, R. J. *Ethics and Engineering Curricula.* Hastings-on-Hudson, NY, 1980.

Baum, R. J., and A. Flores, eds. *Ethical Problems in Engineering,* 2 vols., 2d ed. Troy, NY, 1980.

Davis, M. "Thinking Like an Engineer: The Place of a Code of Ethics in the Practice of a Profession," *Philosophy and Public Affairs,* Vol. 20, No. 2 (1991), 150–67.

De George, R. "Ethical Responsibilities of Engineers in Large Organizations," *Business and Professional Ethics Journal,* Vol. 1, No. 2 (1981), 1–17.

Fielder, J. H. "Give Goodrich a Break," *Business and Professional Ethics Journal,* Vol. 7. No. 1 (1988), 3–25.

Fielder, J. H., and D. Birsch, eds. *The DC-10 Case: A Study in Applied Ethics, Technology, and Society.* Albany, NY, 1992.

Flores, A., ed. *Designing for Safety: Engineering Ethics in Organizational Contexts.* Troy, NY, 1982.

Gert, B. "Morality, Moral Theory, and Applied and Professional Ethics," *Professional Ethics,* Vol. 1, Nos. 1 & 2 (1992), 3–24.

Hare, R. M. "One Philosopher's Approach to Business and Professional Ethics," *Business and Professional Ethics Journal,* Vol. 11, No. 2 (1992), 3–19.

Harris, C. E., Jr., M. S. Pritchard, and M. J. Rabins. *Engineering Ethics: Concepts and Cases.* Belmont, CA, 1995.

Johnson, D., ed. *Ethical Issues in Engineering.* Englewood Cliffs, NJ, 1991.

Ladd, J. "Collective and Moral Responsibility in Engineering: Some Questions," *IEEE Technology and Society Magazine,* Vol. 1, No. 2 (1982), 3–10.

Layton, E. T., Jr. *The Revolt of the Engineers: Social Responsibility and the American Engineering Profession.* Baltimore, 1986.

Martin, M. W., and R. Schinzinger. *Ethics in Engineering.* New York, 1983.

Schaub, J. H., and K. Pavlovic, eds. *Engineering Professionalism and Ethics.* New York, 1983.

Weil, V., and J. Snapper, eds. *Owning Scientific and Technical Information: Value and Ethical Issues.* New Brunswick, NJ, 1989.

Werhane, P. H. "Engineers and Management: The Challenge of the Challenger Incident," *Journal of Business Ethics,* Vol. 10 (1991), 605–16.

Whitbeck, C. "The Trouble with Dilemmas: Rethinking Applied Ethics," *Professional Ethics,* Vol. 1, Nos. 1 & 2 (1992), 119–42.

– ROBERT J. BAUM

ENVIRONMENTAL ETHICS

Spurred by growing environmental concern in the 1960s, philosophers paid increasing attention to environmental ethics in the 1970s and 1980s. The field is dominated by several dichotomies: anthropocentrism versus nonanthropocentrism, individualism versus holism, environmental ethics versus environmental philosophy, organic versus community metaphors, and scientific versus social scientific justifications.

Traditional Western ethics is anthropocentric, as only human beings are considered of moral importance. Because people can help or harm one another indirectly through environmental impact, such as by generating pollution, destroying marshes, and depleting resources, environmental ethics can be pursued as a form of applied ethics in an anthropocentric framework.

Viewed anthropocentrically, environmental ethics is a fertile testing ground for ethical and other theories. Issues of resource depletion, nuclear waste, and population policy, for example, raise questions about the present generation's obligations to future generations. Do future people have rights? Can a meaningful distinction be made between future people and possible people? Why should we care about future people if they can neither harm nor help us? Utilitarian and contractarian theories of ethics are tested in part by their replies to such questions.

In the anthropocentric tradition environmental ethics also includes criticism of cost-benefit analysis (CBA). Translating all values into monetary terms not only jeopardizes future generations (through use of a discount rate that renders impacts 500 years from now insignificant) but also treats present people exclusively as consumers. Ideals of individual excellence and civic virtue are improperly ignored.

Opposed to anthropocentrism are those who consider many nonhuman animals to be worthy of moral consideration in their own right. These views extend some traditional ethical theories, such as utilitarianism and neo-Kantianism, to include nonhuman individuals. Paul Taylor advocates further extension, according equal moral consideration to every living individual, amoeba included.

Many environmental philosophers consider moral extensionism too human-centered and individualistic. It is too human-centered because it justifies valuing nonhumans on the basis of similarities to human beings, such as sentience, consciousness, or merely life itself. Human traits remain the touchstone of all value. Moral extensionism is too individualistic for environmental ethics because some matters, such as species diversity, concern collectives, not individuals. From an individualist perspective, saving ten members of a common species is better than saving one member of an endangered species, other things being equal. Environmentalists concerned to maintain species diversity reject individualism for this reason.

They reject individualism also as ecologically unrealistic. Ecology teaches that ecosystems depend on individuals eating and being eaten, killing and being killed. For example, predators must kill enough deer to avoid deer overpopulation, which would threaten flora on which deer feed. Reduced flora threatens soil stability and the land's ability to support life. So protecting individual deer from untimely death, which valuing deer as individuals may suggest, is environmentally harmful. Such harm threatens natural ecosystems, such as wilderness areas, that foster biological evolution, which is the focus of value for some environmentalists.

Tom Regan calls holistic views "environmental fascism." Sacrificing individuals for evolutionary advance or the collective good resembles Hitler's program, especially when human beings may be among those sacrificed. Human overpopulation threatens species diversity, ecosystemic complexity, and natural evolutionary processes, so consistent environmental holism may be misanthropic.

Holists reply that human individuals, as well as environmental wholes and evolutionary processes, are in-

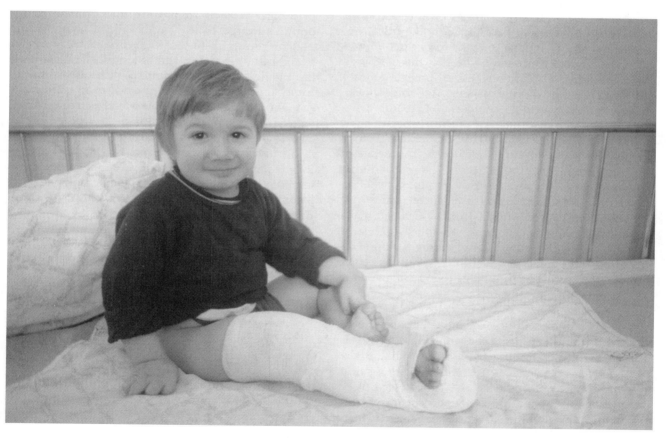

A young victim of the Chernobyl nuclear disaster suffers from bone disease, one of the effects of the catastrophe. (Corbis/Jim McDonald)

trinsically valuable, so individual humans should not be sacrificed to promote the corporate good. However, the casuistry of trade-offs among individuals and corporate entities of various species and kinds is not well developed by the holists. On the other hand, Regan has not shown how all individual nonhuman mammals, for example, could not be accorded the equivalent of human rights without obliterating wilderness areas and causing the extinction of many carnivorous species.

Do future people have rights?

Can a meaningful distinction be made

between future people and possible people?

Why should we care about future people

if they can neither harm nor help us?

Because they value not only nonhumans but holistic entities, many environmental philosophers believe their discipline calls for thorough review of the place of human beings in the cosmos. They reject the title "environmental ethics" in favor of "environmental philosophy" or "ecosophy" to emphasize that their views are not applications of traditional ethics to environmental problems but fundamental metaphysical orientations.

Holistic views tend to compare the environmental wholes they consider valuable in themselves with either communities or organisms. Aldo Leopold's 'land ethic', for example, leans toward the community metaphor. Just as the benefits people derive from their human communities justify loyalty to the group, benefits derived from complex ecological interdependencies justify loyalty to ecosystemic wholes. J. Baird Callicott maintains that community loyalty is emotionally natural to humans, as our ancestors' survival during evolution depended on sentiments of solidarity. Ethics is here based on Humean sentimentalism rather than Kantian rationality or utilitarian calculation.

The Gaia hypothesis and deep ecology stress the similarity of holistic entities to individual organisms, thereby attempting to reconcile individualism with environmentalism. The Gaia hypothesis maintains that life on earth operates as if it were a single organism reacting to altered conditions so as to preserve itself. Deep ecology questions the separateness of any individual from the environmental whole and suggests identifying one's real self with nature. Either way, if life on earth, or nature in general, is an individual, an ethic concentrating on the good of individuals can support

concern for environmental entities that are commonly considered wholes.

Whereas the land ethic and Gaia hypothesis rely primarily on information drawn from science, other environmentalists stress social scientific information. Using the results of anthropological studies, especially of foraging (hunter-gatherer) societies, some environmentalists maintain that human life is better where people do not attempt to master nature in the human interest. Many indigenous societies practice an environmental ethic, similar to the land ethic, of reciprocal exchange with nonhuman environmental constituents such as water, sun, trees, and game animals. This enriches human life and preserves the environment.

Ecofeminists emphasize the relationship between mastering nature in the supposed human interest and the oppression of women. In Western culture men are often associated with heaven, mind, reason, and culture, whereas women are associated with earth, body, emotion, and nature. This explains traditional exclusions of women from high religious offices and from professions emphasizing the use of abstract reason. Because women are associated with nature, the mastery of nature celebrated in modern science and industry involves the oppression of women, from witch trials to the feminization of poverty.

Ecofeminists claim that women tend to think more relationally, organically, and holistically than men, who favor individual rights, commercial success, and mechanistic processes. Whereas typical male patterns of thought and action precipitate ecocrises, typical female patterns ameliorate them. Empowering women can save ecosystems and species diversity.

Because environmental ethics/philosophy questions basic assumptions in economics, technology, metaphysics, ethical theory, moral epistemology, and gender relations, it approaches religion in its attention to the fundamental concerns of human existence.

[See also Animal Rights and Welfare; Applied Ethics; Distant Peoples and Future Generations.]

BIBLIOGRAPHY

Des Jardins, J. R. *Environmental Ethics.* Belmont, CA, 1993. Excellent introduction for the general reader.

Environmental Ethics is the leading journal in this area.

Hargrove, E. C. *The Animal Rights/Environmental Ethics Debate: The Environmental Perspective.* Albany, NY, 1992.

Partridge, E., ed. *Responsibilities to Future Generations.* Buffalo, NY, 1981.

Passmore, J. *Man's Responsibility for Nature.* New York, 1974. Maintains anthropocentrism.

Sagoff, M. *The Economy of the Earth.* New York, 1988. Critiques economics and CBA.

Zimmerman, M. E. *Environmental Philosophy.* Englewood Cliffs, NJ, 1993. Contains seminal articles and essays by P. Singer, T. Regan, P. Taylor, A. Leopold, J. Baird Callicott, A. Naess, C. Merchant, and K. Warren and is an excellent source of information on animal rights, biocentrism, the land ethic, deep ecology, social ecology, and ecofeminism.

— PETER S. WENZ

EPICTETUS

Epictetus (c. 50–c. 130), the enormously influential teacher of Stoicism, was born in Hierapolis, a city in Phrygia, Asia Minor, and died an exile from Rome in Nicopolis, in northwestern Greece. He was born of a slave woman and was for years a slave himself; he was given his freedom sometime after the death of Nero, in 68. His master was Epaphroditus, himself a freedman of Nero who apparently was Nero's administrative secretary. Epaphroditus sent the young Epictetus to perhaps the most powerful Stoic teacher and theoretician since the early Stoa, C. Musonius Rufus, none of whose works survive. Epictetus was banished from Rome by Domitian in 89 or 93. In the Epirus, his place of exile, he drew around him a large thriving school where the logic, physics, and ethics of Stoicism were taught to people from many lands. In his old age he married in order to bring up a child whose parents, friends of his, were going to expose it. In Rome and in Nicopolis he lived in a house with only a rush mat, a simple pallet, and an earthenware lamp (after the iron one was stolen). He was a man of great sweetness, as well as personal simplicity, who was humble, charitable, and especially loving toward children, but he was also possessed of great moral and religious intensity. This disciplined fervor was an excellent example of Stoic tranquillity, which is not simply the absence of feeling but the presence of principled moral and religious tension (*tonos*).

The facts that Epictetus was lame much of his life (some say because of maltreatment when he was a slave) and was for so long a slave have led some commentators to see him as somebody whose only motto was "Anechou kai apechou" ("Bear and forbear"). Indeed, there is in his philosophy a large amount of submissiveness to the inexorable, of seeing all events in a total view and as God's gifts. He was not a political or even a religious activist, as were Zeno and Cleanthes in the early Stoa, and he was not a poised gentleman and a political leader, as was Panaetius in the middle Stoa; he accepted the religion and government of his day without much criticism.

But all of this is only one pole of Epictetus's philosophy, as it is only one pole of the Stoic philosophy throughout its history. Epictetus was a moral activist, insisting on rigorous, continuing moral instruction and effort. Thus, he required daily self-examination, whose ultimate purpose was to learn how to judge one's actions clearly and firmly; he wanted each man to see that he alone was totally responsible for his deeds because he had given his assent to the external circumstances of the deed. The faculty of choice and refusal, the power to use our external impressions, was of immense importance in his philosophy; it was a power even Zeus himself could not interfere with, as Epictetus tells us in the *Discourses*. And when a man finds a fault in his way of using external circumstances, he must root out that fault as ruthlessly and as promptly as a surgeon roots out a dangerous growth. With all his submissiveness Epictetus was one of the great defenders of the *prosopon*, or proper character and personality of a man. He insisted that each man was free to mold it and had an obligation to the rest of the world to display it once it was molded.

The faculty of choice and refusal,

the power to use our external impressions,

was of immense importance

in Epicetetus's philosophy; it was a power

even Zeus himself could not interfere with.

Epictetus was in many respects very close to the Cynics, the proletariat, as E. V. Arnold puts it, of the Greek world, who thought of men as citizens of the universe, not products of local convention, who practiced and preached a simple personal life, and who praised and exemplified *autarkeia*, the independence of the virtuous man from external circumstances. And he shared the Cynics' disdain for theory, though he did not fly in the face of convention and law as they did, nor was he as severe in his ascetism as some of the early Cynics were.

Since Epictetus did not publish anything (in this, as in other things, imitating Socrates), we are confined to the class notes of his pupil Flavius Arrianus, taken in Koine Greek, though Epictetus gave them in Attic. One will not find in these notes the typical Stoic emphasis upon system. The *Discourses* and *Manual* Arrianus recorded did not constitute the texts for formal instruction of the school. The result, however, is felicitous; the *prosopon* of Epictetus himself, with its moral power and personal gentleness, emerges as perhaps the most important lesson he taught.

BIBLIOGRAPHY

Epictetus, translated by W. A. Oldfather, 2 vols. (New York, 1926–1928), is the best edition and one of the best translations into English.

E. V. Arnold, *Roman Stoicism* (London, 1958), is especially informative on Epictetus. See also his article "Epictetus," in James Hastings, ed., *Encyclopedia of Religion and Ethics* (Edinburgh, 1937); this is an excellent article, although it is marred by too heavy an emphasis on Epictetus's doctrine of submissiveness.

A. F. Bonhöffer, *Epiktet und die Stoa* (Stuttgart, 1890), is a crucial work on Epictetus which should be translated into English. It shows how close to the early Stoa Epictetus was in some ways.

— PHILIP P. HALLIE

EPICURUS

Epicurus (341 B.C.–270 B.C.) was born of Athenian parents on the island of Samos. At an early age he began his philosophical studies on the islands of the Aegean and the coast of Asia Minor, where he encountered followers of Plato and Democritus. He first taught at Mytilene, on Lesbos, about 311 B.C.; soon he moved to Lampsacus, a city on the Hellespont, where he recruited a loyal following that included several future leaders of the Epicurean school. In 307–306 B.C. he established at Athens an Epicurean community called the Garden. It was the center of his activity until his death.

The Garden became the prototype of Epicurean groups. Its members included women and at least one slave. The retirement in which the Epicureans lived and their acceptance even of *hetaerae* (courtesans) into their

Epicurus's system undertook to establish something sure and secure in a world of uncertainty. (Corbis/Massimo Listri)

circle exposed them to the ridicule and abuse of their opponents. Yet even their enemies granted a grudging admiration to their cultivation of friendship. Something of Epicurus's affection for his followers and their veneration of him can be gathered from the extant fragments of his extensive correspondence. After his death his school celebrated his memory at a monthly feast, and his teaching spread rapidly through the Greek-speaking world.

Three letters containing summaries of Epicurean doctrine have been preserved in Diogenes Laërtius's *Life of Epicurus* (Book x of the *Lives*): *To Herodotus*, on the atomic theory; *To Pythocles*, on astronomy and meteorology; and *To Menoeceus*, on ethics. Diogenes also preserved a collection of forty *Kuriai Doxai* (*Cardinal Tenets*), presumably formulated by Epicurus for the guidance of his followers. Epicurus's many other writings, now lost, included *Symposium* (a dialogue), *On the Gods, On the Highest Good, Canon* (on the criterion of truth), and, most important of all, *Peri Physeos* (*On Nature*), in 37 books. Fragments of *On Nature* have been recovered from the charred remnants of an Epicurean library at Herculaneum, buried by the eruption of Vesuvius in A.D. 79; they can now be conveniently consulted in Arrighetti's *Epicuro*.

The Philosophy of Epicurus

Epicurus's system, like his Garden, undertook to establish something sure and secure in a world of uncertainty. The social and political changes that followed the death of Alexander had their counterpart in the artistic and intellectual life of Greece; a new skepticism was challenging old ideals and institutions. Epicurus's aim was to build his system on a firm foundation that made no concessions either to skepticism or to idealism. He found his point of departure in the incontestability of immediate experience. Sense data are "true" because they are the ultimate evidence to which all questions must be referred; to question them is to make life itself impossible. The feelings of pleasure and pain that accompany sense experiences are the ultimate good and evil; all statements about good and evil are meaningful only by reference to these feelings.

THEORY OF KNOWLEDGE. The Epicureans gave the name "canonic" to their theory of knowledge. Knowledge arises from sense experience on several levels. First, repeated experiences preserved by memory give rise to "anticipations" (*prolepseis*), which are equivalent to general notions or concepts. These *prolepseis* make possible the use of language; when we hear the word *man* we "anticipate" the kind of object to which the name refers. The *prolepseis* thus classify experiences and fix the limits of variation. The *prolepsis* of man, for instance, is broad enough to include all sorts of men but excludes cattle, trees, gods, etc. And since our *prolepseis* merely register the similarities and differences found in immediate experience, they are themselves "true" and may be used as criteria. Thus Epicurus set up a correspondence among words, notions, and the data of experience without invoking Platonic ideas or Aristotelian essences and accidents. In general, he had little use for logic. We do not need to define words in order to exploit their "natural" meaning, and analysis of the formal aspects of language and thought tells us nothing. No less alien to philosophical inquiry is the language of poetry and myth, which obscures meaning and confuses thought.

Once we are equipped with *prolepseis* we can proceed to form opinions. The truth of opinions is tested in two ways: Where the opinion is about something by nature observable but removed in time or space, the test is verification by actual inspection. Where the opinion is about something by nature unobservable (*physei adelon*), the test is absence of conflict with observable things; if this absence of conflict is such that the denial of a judgment about the unobservable (*adelon*) is incompatible with the data of experience, then the judgment must be true.

PHYSICS. The basic propositions of Epicurean physics are by this means established as necessarily true. Nothing comes from nothing, and nothing returns to nothing; for the denial of these propositions would remove all restraints on what can happen, and the very persistence of uniform patterns in observable similarities and differences is incompatible with the abolition of restraints. Persistence of patterns, in turn, implies some persisting entity, and as the components of experience are all subject to change, there must be something nonexperienceable that is impervious to change. But since changes do occur, the persisting entities must be multiple and capable of interaction. They are, therefore, bodies, for only bodies can act and be acted upon. Bodies interact, moreover, only by blows and rebounds, for they can affect each other only by contact; they have no power of attraction or other means of acting at a distance. How Epicurus defended this last principle we do not know. It created great difficulties for him, for instance, in the explanation of magnets. The physician Asclepiades (first century B.C.), who was influenced by Epicurean atomism, experienced similar difficulty in his physiology, in explaining the function of the kidneys, for example (see Galen, *Natural Faculties,* i.13). Opponents, notably Galen, made much of these difficulties.

Thus Epicurus built his atomic theory, shaping it by reference to the demands of the phenomena it was to explain and overriding theoretical difficulties by appeal to experience. The atoms have parts because they are extended, but they must not be infinitely divisible if they are to provide a secure foundation for the world we know. They lack sensible qualities (colors, tastes, and the like) but produce these qualities by their combinations. Such qualities do not exist per se; they belong either permanently (as properties) or temporarily (as accidents) to atomic compounds. They are, however, no less real than the atoms, for there are no degrees of reality. Life, consciousness, and the flow of experience are as real as the atoms whose movements produce them. Time is an accident of the moving and changing objects that we see around us. Space, however, exists per se, since change requires that the atoms move, and movement requires empty space. The uniformities of experience put limitations on atomic movement, but these limitations must not be so severe that they produce a completely determined system, for experience is not completely determined. The source of indeterminacy is the "swerve" of atoms, a doctrine that accounts also for the crossing of their paths, for by nature they fall downward at a uniform speed. (The atomic swerve is not mentioned in the extant fragments of Epicurus; it is attested to by Lucretius, in *On the Nature of Things,* ii.216–293; and by Philodemus, in *On Methods of Inference,* col. xxxvi.13; cf. Usener, *Epicurea,* pp. 199–201.) Experience sets no limits to space and time; the supply of atoms, then, must also be limitless if they are not to be separated from each other by infinite distances. But the varieties of atoms and their ability to combine must be limited. Most of Epicurus's departures from the atomism of Democritus arose from such considerations as these, inspired in large part by Aristotle's criticisms of Democritus (see, for example, *De Caelo* iii.4 [303a19–20] on the need for limiting the kinds of atoms).

Epicurus's aim was to build his system

on a firm foundation that made no concessions

either to skepticism or to idealism.

The infinite supply of atoms moving in infinite space and time has formed every possible combination, however rare. Everything possible is somewhere actual; indeed, Romano Amerio has suggested, in *L'Epicureismo* (Turin, 1953, pp. 42–44), that the Epicurean doctrine of *isonomia* (equilibrium) rests on the principle that in an infinity of space and time it is not possible to say that any one kind of event occurs more often than any other. The number of coexistent universes is infinite because there is nothing to prevent this (*To Herodotus*, 45). And there is nothing to prevent the existence of innumerable gods, for the gods are compounded of atoms, situated in the intervals between the universes and living forever in a state of supreme bliss because they possess the wisdom and power to protect themselves against all disturbances.

The close tie between the actual and the possible serves also as a principle of method: the actual defines the limits of the possible. The Epicureans recognized that our human experience does not exhaust the range of the actual, and the very variety we observe points to further variety beyond. Other universes need not be exactly like ours. But on another level experience does set limits. It is not possible (to use Lucretian examples) for an animal to be half horse and half man, for a tree to grow in the sky, or for a man to be large enough to wade across the sea.

Changes in the combinations of atoms occur in regular sequences, such as the life cycle of an animal and the disintegration of a universe. These sequences constitute a principle of order: no event occurs apart from the series of events that prepare for it. It is the task of the sciences to discover these sequences, for they provide the causal explanation of all that occurs. The philosopher does not need to know the complete details of a chain of events so long as he knows that it occurs according to fixed principles, that there is no hierarchy of ends or final cause, and that no divine agent guides events or interferes with their course. The existence of evil in the universe is sufficient refutation of the doctrine of an omnipotent and beneficent deity.

When the precise cause of an event cannot be discovered, no possible cause can be rejected. Alternate explanations, therefore, may be entertained, and every possible cause is somewhere operative, if not in our universe then in some other. For the most part the Epicureans used multiple explanations in areas where close observation was not possible, for example, meteorology. Because of their relative indifference to specific details of natural processes, the Epicureans failed to exploit the scientific advances being made in their own times, especially in astronomy and physiology.

MAN. The human organism, for Epicurus, is composed of atoms undergoing characteristic patterns of change. Body and soul are interdependent; neither can survive without the other. The soul's atoms are of four kinds. Three are the same as the atoms that constitute air, wind, and heat; the fourth, the smallest and most mobile, is *sui generis* and nameless. That part of the soul which transmits sensation is spread throughout the body; that which thinks and feels is centered in the region of the heart. There is no nonempirical self. All functions of the human organism are the results of atomic processes. Sight, for example, is caused by atomic films separating from the surfaces of objects and entering the eye. Films of very fine texture, such as those emitted by the gods, are able to impress the mind directly, without the agency of a sense organ. Films that have become scrambled in transit and no longer correspond to stable physical objects account for dreams and fantasies.

The immediate experience of pleasure,

although good in itself,

does not bring with it a guarantee of permanence;

intelligent choice is also needed,

and practical wisdom (phronesis)

is more to be prized than philosophy itself.

Like all other atomic compounds, men come into being when the necessary conditions have been met. They have no creator and no destiny. Their good is pleasure, their highest good a life of secure and lasting pleasure. United by no bond of nature, they form alliances for mutual advantage, and they acquiesce in the restraints of law and government as a protection against injury by their fellows. These measures, however, do not achieve a good life, because of men's false opinions. Men's empty fears of the gods and of death destroy their peace of mind, and in pursuing wealth, power, and fame they seek security where it cannot be found.

ETHICAL DOCTRINES. The good life is attainable only by the philosopher. The immediate experience of pleasure, although good in itself, does not bring with it a guarantee of permanence. Intelligent choice is also needed, and practical wisdom (*phronesis*), Epicurus said, is more to be prized than philosophy itself. Practical wisdom measures pleasures against pains, accepting pains that lead to greater pleasures and rejecting pleasures that lead to greater pains. It counts the traditional virtues (justice, temperance, courage, etc.) among the means for attaining the pleasant life; they have no other justification.

The philosopher distinguishes further between "kinetic" pleasures (for example, eating choice foods), which attend on a motion and cease when the motion ceases, and "catastematic" pleasures (for example, not being hungry), which arise from a state, or stable condition, and are capable of indefinite prolongation. The good life requires catastematic pleasures; kinetic pleasures are mere embroidery. The mind as well as the body has its kinetic and catastematic pleasures. The pleasures of the mind are related more or less directly to physical sensations (a doctrine cited by opposing schools in support of the charge of sensualism); it feels *chara*, delight (a kinetic pleasure), at the well-being of the body, and with the removal of pains and cares it enjoys *ataraxia*, peace of mind (its catastematic pleasure). Peace of mind is achieved when the study of natural philosophy has removed fear of the gods, when death is recognized to be merely the limit of experience and therefore irrelevant to the quality of experience, and when the gratification of desires that go beyond what is necessary and natural is seen to result in greater pains than pleasures.

The mind has also the role of building up a reserve of pleasure to be used as a protection against the onslaughts of fortune. The body lives in the present, but the mind, through memory and expectation, contemplates also the past and the future. Furthermore, the mind is able to select the objects of its attention. The wise man stores up the memory of past pleasures and looks forward to pleasures to come. With such resources he overcomes present distress, as Epicurus overcame the suffering of his final illness with the memory of past conversations with his friends.

WAY OF LIFE. Thus Epicureanism becomes a way of life, with a set of prescriptions for the guidance of the initiates. Epicurus rejected much of traditional education. Geometry does not describe the world as we actually experience it, and rhetoric is an abuse of language. Music and poetry are not fit subjects even for an after-dinner conversation, and happiness does not depend on knowing what side Hector fought on. Epicurus also warned against the assumption of heavy responsibilities and serious involvements, whether public or private, and praised the life that escapes men's notice. These negative features no doubt repelled the intellectual and social elite, but they put the Epicurean life within the reach of the much wider circle of persons who did not enjoy the advantages of wealth, station, and education. To such as these Epicurus recommended the suppression of desires that go beyond natural needs, the cultivation of friendship, the enjoyment of carefree pleasures, and even attendance at religious festivals in order to remind themselves of that complete tranquillity of which the gods are the perfect exemplars.

BIBLIOGRAPHY

Texts and Fragments from Epicurus

Arrighetti, G., ed., *Epicuro, Opere*. Turin, 1960. Contains, along with older material, the first complete collection of the papyrus fragments of Epicurus's *On Nature*. With Italian translation, notes, and a partial *index verborum*.

Bailey, C., ed., *Epicurus, the Extant Remains*. Oxford, 1926. A smaller collection than Usener's (see below), but including the *Vatican Fragments*, discovered soon after Usener's book was published. Bailey supplies an English translation and commentary.

Diano, C., ed., *Epicuri Ethica*. Florence, 1946. An important collection, incorporating material from papyri and from Diogenes of Oenoanda, as well as the *Vatican Fragments*. Contains a useful commentary and a partial *index verborum*.

Usener, H., ed., *Epicurea*. Leipzig, 1887. Still the basic collection of Greek and Latin texts bearing on Epicurus and his school. It contains 607 numbered fragments and much more that is unnumbered.

General Accounts of Epicurean Philosophy

Bailey, C., *The Greek Atomists and Epicurus*. Oxford, 1928. A fundamental work.

Bignone, E., *L'Aristotele perduto e la formazione filosofica di Epicuro*, 2 vols. Florence, 1936. A revolutionary work, portraying Epicureanism as directed primarily against the Platonism of Aristotle's early dialogues, as reconstructed by W. Jaeger.

Cornford, F. M., *Principium Sapientiae*, W. K. C. Guthrie, ed. Cambridge, 1952. The chapter "Epicurus" (pp. 12–30) stresses the deficiencies of Epicureanism viewed as a scientific system.

DeWitt, N. W., *Epicurus and His Philosophy*. Minneapolis, 1954. A sympathetic and at times extravagant account, emphasizing Epicurus' saintly character and his opposition to Platonism.

Festugière, A. J., *Epicurus and His Gods*, translated by C. W. Chilton. Oxford, 1955. A perceptive and rather sympathetic study of Epicurean ethics and religion.

Kleve, K., *Gnosis Theon: Die Lehre von der natürlichen Gotteserkenntnis in der epikureischen Theologie. Symbolae Osloenses* Fasc. Supplet. XIX. Oslo, 1963. A careful examination of a problem much discussed in recent years: how the Epicureans explained, in terms of their theory of knowledge, men's knowledge of the gods.

Schmid, W., "Epikur." *Reallexikon für Antike und Christentum*, Vol. 5 (1961), 681–819. An authoritative article, with extensive bibliography. Especially good on the fortunes of Epicureanism in the early Christian period.

– P. H. DE LACY

EPISTEMOLOGY

There have been numerous exciting developments in epistemology since 1960. The publication of one brief critical article, Edmund Gettier's "Is Justified True Belief Knowledge?," brought about a flurry of activity (Roth & Galis, 1970). Gettier refuted the traditional analysis of knowledge as justified true belief. He showed that a person can have justifying evidence for a belief that happens to be true as a result of a fortunate accident unrelated to that evidence. Such a proposition would not be known. Gettier concluded that justified true belief is not sufficient for knowledge.

With few exceptions, epistemologists responded to Gettier's work by seeking a fourth condition for knowledge. The search for this fourth condition dominated epistemology from the publication of Gettier's paper in

1963 until the mid-1970s. Some philosophers proposed that in any case of knowledge the justification for the belief is "undefeated," meaning roughly that there is no truth that would undermine the believer's evidence for the proposition. Others suggested that in cases of knowledge the justification never involves any falsehood. Others proposed that in cases of knowledge there is an appropriate causal connection between the person's evidence and the truth of the known proposition. Still others claimed that the knower "tracks the truth" of the known proposition, meaning that the person would believe the proposition if it were true and would not believe it if it were false. Counterexamples falsified the original versions of these analyses, increasingly complex analyses replaced the originals, and new sorts of counterexamples cast doubt on the new analyses. Epistemologists learned much about knowledge from these investigations, but they did not reach a consensus on a fourth condition.

Edmund Gettier showed that

a person can have justifying evidence

for a belief that happens to be true

as a result of a fortunate accident

unrelated to that evidence.

In the 1970s epistemology focused on the justifying condition itself. Epistemologists developed and refined coherentism and foundationalism, the two traditional theories of justification. Foundationalists realized that they need not require that foundational beliefs be absolutely certain or infallible. They developed the idea that foundational beliefs need have only some degree of initial justification that is not supplied by other beliefs. Coherentists gave increasing attention to explanatory relations among beliefs as the basis for coherence. A popular coherentist position was that one gets justification by achieving reflective equilibrium—a mutual adjustment of beliefs about particular cases and beliefs about general principles covering these cases that maximizes explanatory relationships among them.

In his seminal paper "What Is Justified Belief?," Alvin Goldman introduced a new approach to justification, reliabilism (Moser, 1986). In its simplest version reliabilism holds that a belief is justified if and only if it is the product of a type of belief-forming process that generally leads to true beliefs. This view has been subject to intense critical scrutiny since its introduction in 1979. Critics identified two main sorts of problems.

The first is that of adequately specifying the types of belief-forming processes to which the theory appeals. The second problem stems from the fact that seemingly unjustified beliefs can result from truth-conducive processes. In response to these and other problems, Goldman and others have revised and transformed reliabilism, sometimes drastically. In some of these theories justification depends upon other epistemic virtues in addition to reliability.

The 1980s also saw extensive discussion of the contrast between internalistic and externalistic accounts of justification. Internalists hold that justification is determined by factors internal to the mind, while externalists impose no such restriction. A typical internalist theory is evidentialism, which holds that the evidence the believer possesses determines the epistemic status of beliefs. Reliability theories exemplify the externalist viewpoint since they maintain that the external and contingent propensity toward truth of the process or mechanism leading to a belief helps to determine the belief's justification. Several philosophers have argued that the central epistemological considerations on both sides of this dispute can be reconciled.

Naturalism was another prominent topic among epistemologists in the 1980s and 1990s. The most frequently cited source of this trend is W. V. O. Quine's 1969 paper, "Epistemology Naturalized" (Kornblith, 1994). A common reading of Quine's position takes him to advocate abandoning traditional epistemology and replacing it with the closest empirical discipline, cognitive psychology. Few philosophers defend this extreme view. However, many urge tying epistemology closely to empirical studies of human cognition. Those who think that epistemology is primarily devoted to recommending ways in which people can improve their reasoning contend that the empirical study of how people actually reason plays a crucial role in developing useful recommendations. Philosophers who believe that the primary role of epistemology is to analyze the concepts of knowledge, justification, and the like usually see less room for empirical input. But some epistemologists in this last group also advocate a form of naturalized epistemology that requires analyzing central epistemic concepts in terms that they deem naturalistically legitimate.

Since 1960 philosophers have continued traditional debates about skepticism. Several new arguments appeared, each having its origin in work in the philosophy of language or the philosophy of mind. One argument, due to Hilary Putnam, is an attempt to refute the much-discussed "brain-in-a-vat" argument. A background assumption of this argument is that a human brain suspended in a vat of nutrients that keep it alive might receive computer-controlled electrical stimulation that duplicates the neural impulses to a brain in an ordinary head in an ordinary world (cf. Descartes's evil demon). The possibility of being such a brain in a vat is a premise in prominent arguments for skepticism. The rest of the argument typically asserts that we cannot know anything about the external world because we cannot rule out the possibility of being a brain in a vat. On one interpretation, Putnam attacks these arguments by a special application of a causal view about reference. He thereby defends the thesis that what envatted brains, lacking all normal environmental interaction, would express by "I am a brain in a vat" would be a falsehood. What people in normal circumstances express by that sentence is also false. The sentence, therefore, does not express a truth, no matter what our actual situation. Thus, the sentence cannot serve as a premise in a successful argument for skepticism. Some critics dispute Putnam's use of the causal theory and deny that this attack refutes any argument for skepticism. Others contend that it refutes only skeptical arguments that are based on certain extreme versions of the brain-in-a-vat hypothesis.

Feminist epistemologists contended

that traditional epistemology would be enhanced,

if not replaced, as a result

of attending to feminist insights.

A second new antiskeptical argument is due to Donald Davidson, who argues that the possibility of interpretation rests on the assumption that most of what the interpreted person believes is true, or at least that the interpreted beliefs must mostly coincide with what the interpreter believes. Since it is possible for there to be an omniscient interpreter, any interpreted beliefs must largely coincide with those of such an interpreter. Thus, any interpreted believer must have mostly true beliefs. Consequently, skepticism cannot be defended on the basis of the possibility of massive error. Again, some critics deny that this argument is sound. Others reply that it refutes only skeptical arguments relying on the possibility of massive error, leaving untouched defenses of skepticism that rely on the possibility, with respect to each individual belief, that it is in error.

A new defense of a skeptical position derives from Saul Kripke's interpretation of Wittgenstein's views concerning rules and private languages. Kripke contends that Wittgenstein in effect, if not by intention, offers a powerful skeptical argument. It threatens our knowledge of the meaning of our own expressions by casting doubt on the existence of the sort of meaning that those expressions otherwise seem to have. The central work of the argument is an attempt to show by an exhaustion of the plausible candidates that there can be no determinate fact as to the extension of any expression beyond its actual application. Critical responses to this argument propose candidates for meanings that do determine the full intuitive extension of our terms. No solution to the problem has been established.

Since 1960 formal work in epistemology has also advanced. Especially notable in this area is the development of and debate over Bayesian epistemology. This approach defends the requirement that rational belief change proceed in accordance with the probability calculus, prominently including the constraint that Bayes's theorem imposes on processing new information.

Several new areas within epistemology emerged in the 1980s and 1990s. Feminist epistemologists contended that traditional epistemology would be enhanced, if not replaced, as a result of attending to feminist insights. Social epistemologists focused on the ways in which social factors affect knowledge and justification. Some philosophers even argued for the "death" of epistemology, contending that its traditional problems or concepts rely on false presuppositions. But the vigor of work, the proliferation of issues, and the liveliness of disputes in a field show its continuing life. A death notice for epistemology therefore seems premature.

[See also Bayesianism; Coherentism; Davidson, Donald; Evidentialism; Internalism versus Externalism; Kripke, Saul Aaron; Moral Epistemology; Naturalism; Naturalized Epistemology; Philosophy of Language; Philosophy of Mind; Pragmatist Epistemology; Putnam, Hilary; Quine, Willard Van Orman; Reliabilism; Skepticism; Subjectivist Epistemology; Virtue Epistemology; Wittgenstein, Ludwig Josef Johann.]

BIBLIOGRAPHY

Alcoff, L., and E. Potter, eds. *Feminist Epistemologies.* London, 1993.

Alston, W. *Epistemic Justification: Essays in the Theory of Knowledge.* Ithaca, NY, 1989.

BonJour, L. *The Structure of Empirical Knowledge.* Cambridge, MA, 1985.

Chisholm, R. *The Theory of Knowledge.* Englewood Cliffs, NJ, 1966; 2d. ed., 1977; 3d ed., 1989.

Davidson, D. "A Coherence Theory of Truth and Knowledge," in D. Henrich, ed., *Kant oder Hegel?* (Stuttgart, 1983).

Dretske, F. *Knowledge and the Flow of Information.* Cambridge, MA, 1981.

French, P., T. Uehling, and H. Wettstein, eds. *Studies in Epistemology,* Midwest Studies in Philosophy, Vol. 5 (Minneapolis, 1980).

Goldman, A. *Epistemology and Cognition.* Cambridge, MA, 1986.

Harman, G. *Change in View: Principles of Reasoned Revision.* Cambridge, MA, 1986.

Kornblith, H., ed. *Naturalizing Epistemology,* 2d ed. Cambridge, MA, 1994. Includes Quine's "Epistemology Naturalized."

Kripke, S. *Wittgenstein on Rules and Private Language.* Cambridge, MA, 1982.

Moser, P., ed. *Empirical Knowledge*. Savage, MD, 1986. Includes Gettier's "Is Justified True Belief Knowledge?" and Goldman's "What Is Justified Belief?"

Nozick, R. "Epistemology," in *Philosophical Explanations* (Cambridge, MA, 1981).

Pappas, G., and M. Swain, eds. *Essays on Knowledge and Justification*, Ithaca, NY, 1978.

Plantinga, A. *Warrant: The Current Debate*. Oxford, 1992.

Putnam, H. "Brains in a Vat," in *Reason, Truth, and History* (Cambridge, 1981).

Rorty, R. *Philosophy and the Mirror of Nature*. Princeton, NJ, 1979.

Roth, M. D., and L. Galis, eds. *Knowing: Essays in the Analysis of Knowledge*. New York, 1970. Includes Gettier's "Is Justified True Belief Knowledge?"

Shope, R. K. *The Analysis of Knowing: A Decade of Research*. Princeton, NJ, 1983.

Sosa, E. *Knowledge in Perspective*. Cambridge, MA, 1991.

Stich, S. *The Fragmentation of Reason*. Cambridge, MA, 1990.

Tomberlin, J. E., ed. *Philosophical Perspectives*, Vol. 2 (1988). Special issue.

– RICHARD FELDMAN
EARL CONEE

EPISTEMOLOGY, RELIGIOUS

The epistemology of religion, as practiced by philosophers, is seldom concerned with the sorts of epistemological questions that emerge on a practical level in ordinary religious life, such as how to determine the correct interpretation of a scriptural text or how to know whether someone's claim to special divine guidance is to be credited. Rather, it tends to focus on the epistemic evaluation of the most basic tenets of the religious worldview in question—the existence of God, the creation of the world and God's relation to it, and the possibility of recognizing divine action in the world and divine revelation. From the 1960s through the early 1990s, religious epistemology has been characterized by a marked decline of fideism, with a renewal of interest in evidentialism and an even more pronounced upsurge of what may be termed experientialism.

The epistemology of religion

tends to focus on the epistemic evaluation

of the most basic tenets

of the religious worldview in question.

Fideism is best characterized as the view that one's basic religious beliefs are not subject to independent rational evaluation. It is defended by urging that religious convictions are the most basic part of a believer's worldview and thus more fundamental than anything else that might be used to evaluate them. It is also said

that to evaluate religious beliefs by standards other than the internal standards of the religious belief system itself is in effect to subject God to judgment and is thus a form of idolatry. In the mid-twentieth century fideism took two main forms, existentialism and Wittgensteinian fideism. In the succeeding decades philosophical existentialism has suffered a massive decline, as has its theological counterpart, neo-orthodoxy. Wittgensteinian fideism, on the other hand, arose largely in response to the positivist contention that God-talk is cognitively meaningless; with the defeat of positivism it has lost much of its relevance. Many religious thinkers, freed from the need to defend religion's cognitive meaningfulness, have felt a renewed impulse to contend for the truth of their faith. And on the other hand, critics of religion have moved readily from the contention that belief in God is meaningless to the logically incompatible assertion that it is false and/or lacking in evidential support.

Evidentialism is the view that religious beliefs, in order to be rationally held, must be supported by other things one knows or reasonably believes to be true. Evidentialist defenses of religion typically rely heavily on theistic arguments, and all of the classical arguments have seen renewed interest in the late twentieth century. Versions of the ontological argument propounded by Charles Hartshorne, Norman Malcolm, and Alvin Plantinga are clearly valid, though their premises remain controversial. William Rowe's work has directed renewed attention to the Clarke-Leibniz version of the cosmological argument, and new versions of the design argument, focusing on God as the source of the basic laws of nature, have been developed by Richard Swinburne and others. Even the moral argument (Robert Adams) and the argument from religious experience (Gary Gutting) have come in for renewed attention. Two new arguments, or versions of arguments, are keyed to developments in cosmology. The "kalam cosmological argument" (William Craig) uses big-bang cosmology to argue that the physical universe as a whole has a temporal beginning and thus is in need of an external cause. And the anthropic cosmological principle is used by John Leslie, among others, to support a new version of the design argument: the apparent fact that the basic laws and initial conditions of the universe are "fine tuned" for life, with no apparent scientific explanation for this fact, is taken as evidence of intelligent design. Both of these arguments benefit from their association with cutting-edge science but also in consequence become vulnerable to future changes in scientific thinking on cosmology.

Evidentialist arguments against religion take a variety of forms. Most basically, evidentialists argue that the theistic arguments are unsuccessful and that theism fails for lack of evidential support. There are various challenges to the coherence and logical possibility of the traditional divine attributes. In most cases, however, these arguments, if successful, lead to a reformulation of the attributes in question rather than to the defeat of theism as such. But by far the most active area of consideration for antireligious evidentialism has been the problem of evil; the volume of writing on its various forms, by both critics and believers, has probably exceeded that on all of the theistic arguments taken together.

Along with the renewed consideration of the various arguments there have been reflections on the requirements for a successful argument. Traditional natural theology claimed to proceed from premises known or knowable to any reasonable person (e.g., "Some things are in motion") by means of arguments any reasonable person could see to be valid. By these standards it is not difficult to show that all of the arguments fail. But the standard is clearly too high; it is difficult to find significant arguments in any area of philosophy that meet it. No doubt a good argument should not be circular or question begging, and its premises must enjoy some kind of support that makes them at least plausible. But what seems plausible, or even evidently true, to one person may not seem so to another, equally rational, person; thus, the recognition emerges that arguments and proofs may be "person-relative" (Mavrodes, 1970). Furthermore, even a good argument is not necessarily decisive by itself, so it is necessary to consider the ways in which a number of arguments, none of them in itself conclusive, can lend their combined weight to establishing a conclusion. One model for this has been developed by Basil Mitchell, who compares arguments for religious beliefs to the kinds of cumulative-case arguments found in fields such as history and critical exegesis as well as in the choice between scientific paradigms. Richard Swinburne, on the other hand, builds a cumulative case for divine existence using the mathematical theory of probability. While it is not possible to assign precise numerical probabilities to the propositions involved in theistic argumentation, Bayes's theorem does provide insight into the way in which evidence contributes in a cumulative fashion to the support or defeat of a hypothesis such as theism. On the other hand, John L. Mackie and Michael Martin have developed what are in effect cumulative-case arguments for atheism.

Experientialism

The most significant development in the epistemology of religion during the 1980s and early 1990s was the rise of a new type of theory distinct from both fideism and evidentialism. This theory, found in the writings of

Richard Swinburne, Alvin Plantinga, and William Alston, lacks a generally recognized label (the term "Reformed epistemology" properly applies only to Plantinga's version) but may be termed *experientialism* in view of its emphasis on the grounding of religious belief in religious experience. Experientialism differs from fideism in that it does not seek to insulate religious belief from critical epistemic evaluation; rather, it affirms that religious experience can provide a sound epistemic basis for such beliefs. Experientialism is also importantly different from the evidentialist "argument from religious

---

The most significant development in the epistemology of religion during the 1980s and early 1990s was the rise of a new type of theory that may be termed experientialism *in view of its emphasis on the grounding of religious belief in religious experience.*

---

experience" in the following respect: the religious experience is not first described in ontologically neutral terms and then made the basis for an inference to the existence of the religious object. On the contrary, the religious belief is grounded directly in the religious experience, without mediation by inference, just as perceptual beliefs are grounded directly in perceptual experience. This difference is important for a couple of reasons. For one thing it is more faithful to the phenomenology of both religious and perceptual belief: in typical cases neither form of belief involves such an inference. But more important, the direct grounding of belief in experience offers better prospects of a favorable epistemic status for the resulting beliefs than does the inferential approach. This is readily apparent in the case of perceptual experience: attempts at a "proof of the external world" have been notably unsuccessful, yet only those in the grip of philosophical theory doubt that we do in fact acquire a great deal of knowledge about the world through our perceptual experience. In the same way it is at least conceivable that believers acquire knowledge of God experientially even if no compelling inferential argument from religious experience is available.

Swinburne, Plantinga, and Alston share what may be termed a weak foundationalist approach to epistemology. That is to say, they accept the distinction between "basic" beliefs, which do not derive their rational acceptability from other beliefs, and "derived" beliefs, which gain their support from the basic beliefs. But they do not accept the traditional foundationalist restriction of basic beliefs to those that are nearly or entirely immune to doubt—beliefs that are self-evident, evident to the senses, or incorrigible. Each of them, furthermore, includes some religious beliefs in the category of basic beliefs. The epistemological task, then, is to show that this inclusion is epistemically proper—to show that such religious beliefs are among our "properly basic beliefs." (The terminology is Plantinga's, but the issue is the same for all three thinkers.) Each of them approaches this issue in a different way, though the approaches are ultimately compatible. Plantinga argues, following Roderick Chisholm, that the proper approach to the question of which beliefs are properly basic is inductive: one first conducts an inventory of the beliefs one takes oneself to hold rationally, then eliminates those that derive their epistemic support from other beliefs, and those that remain will be taken as properly basic. The typical Christian believer, Plantinga thinks, will find that she considers her belief in God to be rational but does not ground it inferentially on other beliefs she holds; thus, she will conclude that this is a properly basic belief. To be sure, atheists or believers in other religions will not concur in this, but Plantinga finds this to be unproblematic: "Followers of Bertrand Russell and Madalyn Murray O'Hair may disagree; but how is that relevant? Must my criteria, or those of the Christian community, conform to their examples? Surely not. The Christian community is responsible to *its* set of examples, not to theirs" (in Plantinga and Wolterstorff, 1983, p. 78).

In contrast with Plantinga's "internal" justification of the rationality of belief, both Swinburne and Alston attempt to show that religious experiences should have some epistemic weight, even for those who do not share the belief system the experiences ostensibly support. Swinburne appeals to the "principle of credulity," which states that "(in the absence of special considerations) if it seems (epistemically) to a subject that x is present, then probably x is present; what one seems to perceive is probably so" (1979, p. 254). He argues that a general denial of this principle lands us in a "sceptical bog" and that there is no justification for excluding religious experience from its scope. Alston, on the other hand, develops a "doxastic practice" approach to epistemology (indebted to both Reid and Wittgenstein), which holds that all socially established doxastic practices are "innocent until proved guilty"; "they all deserve to be regarded as prima facie rationally engaged in . . . pending a consideration of possible reasons for disqualification" (1991, p. 153). Alston's delineation of the "Christian mystical practice" and his defense of its epistemic status

constitute a systematic, detailed, and highly sophisticated presentation of experientialism.

One major difficulty for experientialism is the existence of incompatible experientially grounded beliefs in different religions—in Alston's terms, the existence of a plurality of mutually incompatible mystical practices. Alston concludes that religious experience alone probably cannot resolve this ambiguity and that "the knowledgeable and reflective Christian should be concerned about the situation . . . [and] should do whatever seems feasible to search for common ground on which to adjudicate the crucial differences between the world religions, seeking a way to show in a non-circular way which of the contenders is correct. What success will attend these efforts I do not presume to predict. Perhaps it is only in God's good time that a more thorough insight into the truth behind these divergent perspectives will be revealed to us" (1991, p. 278).

Critics, however, have urged more far-reaching objections to the experientialist program. According to Richard Gale, the analogy between religious experience and sense perception is weak, with the dissimilarities far outweighing the similarities. He also argues that religious experience could not be cognitive—that is, could not provide independent grounds for belief in the existence of its object—and that religious objects such as God or the One are not possible objects of perceptual experience, even if they exist. Alston, on the other hand, has argued in detail that the phenomenological structure of religious experience is perceptual and that "mystical perception" constitutes a genuine species of perception along with sense perception.

[See also Bayesianism; Chisholm, Roderick M.; Evil, Problem of; Existentialism; Mackie, John Leslie; Philosophy of Religion; Probability; Reid, Thomas; Religious Experience; Religious Pluralism; Theism, Arguments for and Against; Wittgenstein, Ludwig Josef Johann.]

BIBLIOGRAPHY

Alston, W. P. *Perceiving God: The Epistemology of Religious Experience.* Ithaca, NY, 1991.

Gale, R. M. *On the Nature and Existence of God.* Cambridge, 1991.

Mackie, J. *The Miracle of Theism: Arguments for and against the Existence of God.* New York, 1982.

Martin, M. *Atheism: A Philosophical Justification.* Philadelphia, 1990.

Mavrodes, G. *Belief in God: A Study in the Epistemology of Religion.* New York, 1970.

Mitchell, B. *The Justification of Religious Belief.* New York, 1981.

Plantinga, A., and N. Wolterstorff, eds. *Faith and Rationality: Reason and Belief in God.* Notre Dame, IN, 1983.

Swinburne, R. *The Existence of God.* Oxford, 1979.

— WILLIAM HASKER

ERROR THEORY

An error theory of ethics is the view that the ordinary user of moral language is typically making claims that involve a mistake. The concepts of ethics introduce a mistaken, erroneous, way of thinking of the world or of conducting practical reasoning. The theory was most influentially proposed by John L. Mackie in his book *Ethics: Inventing Right and Wrong* (1977). Mackie believed that ordinary moral claims presuppose that there are objective moral values, but there are no such things. Hence, the practice of morality is founded upon a metaphysical error.

Mackie's arguments against the existence of objective values are of two main kinds. One is the argument from relativity, which cites the familiar phenomenon of ethical disagreement. Another is the argument from 'queerness'. The moral values whose existence Mackie denies are presented as metaphysically strange facts. They are facts with a peculiar necessity built into them: their essence is that they make demands or exist as laws that 'must' be obeyed. In Kantian terms, the demands made by morality are thought of as categorical, "not contingent upon any desire or preference or policy or choice." The foundation of any such demands or laws in the natural world is entirely obscure. Hence, the right response of a naturalist is to deny that there can be such things. It should be noticed that this is not supposed to be an argument against any particular morality, for instance, one demanding honesty or fidelity, but against the entire scheme of thought of which particular ethical systems are examples.

Another influential theorist whose work bears some resemblance to Mackie's is Bernard Williams, whose *Ethics and the Limits of Philosophy* (1985) equally raises the doubt that ethics cannot possibly be what it purports to be, although Williams's own arguments are more specifically targeted on the morality of duty and obligation.

Responses to the error theory have taken several forms. Both the argument from relativity and that from queerness have been queried, the former on the grounds that, even if ethical opinions differ fundamentally, this does not prevent one from being right and the others wrong, and the latter mainly on the grounds that Mackie suffered from an oversimple, "scientistic" conception of the kind of thing a moral fact would have to be. Perhaps more fundamentally, it is not clear what clean, error-free practice the error theorist would wish to substitute for old, error-prone ethics. That is, assuming that people living together have a need for shared practical norms, then some way of expressing and discussing those norms seems to be needed, and this is all

that ethics requires. Mackie himself saw that ethics was not a wholly illegitimate branch of thought, for he gave a broadly Humean picture of its function in human life. Even projectivists maintain that our need to express attitudes, coordinate policies, and censure transgressions is a sufficient justification for thinking in terms of ethical demands. Ethics does not invoke a strange world of metaphysically dubious facts but serves a natural human need.

[See also Ethical Theory; Mackie, John Leslie.]

BIBLIOGRAPHY

Mackie, J. L. *Ethics: Inventing Right and Wrong*. Middlesex, 1977.

Blackburn, S. "Errors and the Phenomenology of Value," in *Essays in Quasi-Realism* (New York, 1994).

Williams, B. *Ethics and the Limits of Philosophy*. Cambridge. MA, 1985.

— SIMON BLACKBURN

ESP PHENOMENA, PHILOSOPHICAL IMPLICATIONS OF

Since the original *Encyclopedia* article was written, the empirical landscape in parapsychology has changed substantially. For one thing, that article dealt extensively with S. G. Soal's ESP experiments, some of which have since been tainted by evidence of fraud and all of which now must be treated as non-evidential. Since that time, however, parapsychological researchers have introduced some ingenious methodological innovations and research initiatives, and they have amassed a provocative body of new evidence.

Parapsychological researchers have introduced some ingenious methodological innovations and research initiatives, and they have amassed a provocative body of new evidence.

Probably the most impressive recent research into ESP has been the "ganzfeld" experiment, pioneered by the late Charles Honorton. This type of experiment evolved from dream telepathy experiments conducted at Maimonides Hospital in Brooklyn. Unlike the forced-choice experiments that characterized the research of Rhine and Soal, in which the subject's task was to make simple target identifications from a fixed set of presented alternatives (as in card-guessing tests), the ganzfeld experiment is a free-response test. In this type of test the subject does not know what the possible targets are, and instead of mere target identifications the subject's task is to describe the target or reproduce it (say, by drawing).

Subjects in ganzfeld experiments, located in an acoustically isolated room, have Ping-Pong ball halves taped over their eyes, and they listen to white noise through stereo headphones. This state of moderate sensory deprivation presents subjects with a relatively homogeneous visual and auditory field, the purpose of which is to quiet major sources of sensory stimulation or distraction and thereby allow other mental processes (including those produced by psychic functioning) to emerge more clearly. After describing their mental imagery for about thirty minutes, subjects view a set of pictures randomly selected from a larger target pool for the entire experimental series, one of which was viewed during the experiment by a remote "sender." The sub-

ject then tries to identify which picture was the target for that experiment by ranking all of the pictures in the set. In some cases outside judges also rank transcripts of the subject's mentation reports against the possible targets.

Beginning in the 1980s the ganzfeld experiments were subjected to a series of meta-analyses. Although these have not silenced debate about whether the experiments demonstrate the existence of ESP, even some well-known critics of parapsychology have conceded that the meta-analyses demonstrates a rather robust effect across the entire body of experiments. In one analysis Honorton examined twenty-eight studies using only the direct-hit method of scoring (in which the target picture is ranked first out of the set presented to the subject). These twenty-eight experiments included a total of 835 ganzfeld trials conducted in ten different lab-

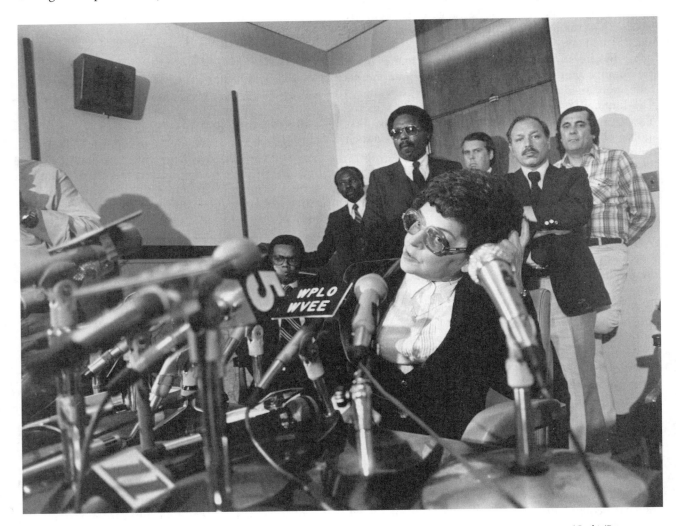

"Psychic detective" Dorothy Allison, who claims to have ESP, has successfully assisted police in solving missing persons cases. (Corbis/Bettmann-UPI)

oratories, and 43 percent produced significant results. The odds against that result occurring by chance are greater than one billion to one. Honorton also addressed what psychologist Robert Rosenthal has called the "file drawer problem," by estimating how many unreported nonsignificant studies there would have to be in order to cancel out this effect. Honorton found that the total number of direct-hit experiments would have to be 451 (rather than twenty-eight), 423 of which were unknown to parapsychologists. Considering that only a small number of scientists work in the field of parapsychology, only some of whom do ganzfeld experiments, and considering also that the ganzfeld experiment is a time-consuming process, it seems likely that there is no file-drawer problem in this case. Honorton and critic Ray Hyman agreed on a set of stringent standards for future ganzfeld work, and the initial results of automated ganzfeld experiments adhering to those standards showed an effect size similar to that found in the original data base of experiments.

Research in psychokinesis (PK) has also charted a new direction during this period. The problem with experiments on tossed dice, coins, and other objects is that it is not clear to what extent those processes are random. For example, the outcome of falling dice depends on many factors that cannot be adequately controlled and are too obscure or complex to permit an accurate assessment of the statistical properties of a series of such falls. These include the physical properties of the tumbler, the initial position of the dice, the material out of which the dice are made, and the number of times the dice are shaken and allowed to tumble. So the "new wave" of PK research looked for effects on simple random processes whose statistical properties were well known. The leading figure in this body of work is physicist Helmut Schmidt, who initially conducted a series of successful experiments using radioactive decay, and then thermal noise, as sources of randomness.

Predictably, Schmidt's work was criticized. Hansel argued that Schmidt's experiments should be dismissed simply because they did not eliminate all possibility of fraud. But even other critics of parapsychology (such as Hyman) have noted that this standard of acceptability would lead to the rejection of virtually every scientific experiment. The more relevant issue is whether there are good reasons for thinking that fraud actually occurred, and no one has supported that charge in connection with Schmidt's work. A more frequent criticism (echoed by Gardner) is that Schmidt's work has not been replicated. But in 1989, Radin and Nelson published a careful meta-analysis of this so-called "micro-PK" work, which covered 597 experimental studies and 235 control studies from sixty-eight different investigators. According to their calculations, the odds of the robust effect they found occurring by chance are approximately 10^{35} to 1.

Perhaps the most philosophically intriguing micro-PK research concerns tests (again pioneered by Schmidt) using prerecorded targets and appearing (at least on the surface) to demonstrate a form of retrocausality. The form for a typical experiment of this sort is as follows. Suppose that on day 1 a binary random generator is automatically activated (in the absence of anyone present) to record sequences of heads and tails onto audio cassettes, heads in the right channel and tails in the left. Suppose twenty such cassettes are recorded, and also that a duplicate record of heads and tails is simultaneously produced on paper punch tape for the purpose of a permanent record. Then on day 2, half of the cassettes are selected by a random process to be test tapes, and the other cassettes are then designated as control tapes. At this point no one knows the contents of any of the tapes. On day 3, the ten test tapes are played back to a subject who thinks he is taking a normal PK test with spontaneously generated targets. The numbers of heads and tails are added up (and a duplicate record again made on punch tape), and it turns out that the test tapes contain a statistically significant excess of heads over tails. Then the control tapes are examined for the first time, and it turns out that they contain only chance levels of heads and tails (and also that they match the punch-tape record for day 1). But the only difference between the test and control tapes is that the test tapes were played for a subject making a PK effort. So it appears that the subject's effort on day 3 biased the random generator on day 1 to produce an excess of heads only for the test tapes (whose selection as test tapes, recall, was not decided until later).

BIBLIOGRAPHY

Braude, S. E. *ESP and Psychokinesis: A Philosophical Examination.* Philadelphia, 1979.
———. *The Limits of Influence: Psychokinesis and the Philosophy of Science.* London, 1991.
Gardner, M. *Science: Good, Bad, and Bogus.* Buffalo, NY, 1981.
Hansel, C. E. M. *ESP and Parapsychology: A Critical Reevaluation.* Buffalo, NY, 1980.
Honorton, C. "Meta-Analysis of Psi Ganzfeld Research: A Response to Hyman," *Journal of Parapsychology,* Vol. 49 (1985), 51–91.
———, et al. "Psi Communication in the Ganzfeld: Experiments with an Automated Testing System and a Comparison with a Meta-Analysis of Earlier Studies," *Journal of Parapsychology,* Vol. 54 (1990), 99–140.
Hyman, R. "Further Comments on Schmidt's PK Experiments," *Skeptical Inquirer,* Vol. 5 (1981), 34–40.
———. "The Ganzfeld Psi Experiment: A Critical Appraisal," *Journal of Parapsychology,* Vol. 49 (1985), 3–49.

———, and C. Honorton. "A Joint Communiqué: The Psi Ganz-feld Controversy." *Journal of Parapsychology*, Vol. 50 (1986), 351–64.

Markwick, B. "The Soal-Goldney Experiments with Basil Shackle-ton: New Evidence of Data Manipulation," *Proceedings of the Society of Psychical Research*, Vol. 56 (1978), 250–77.

Radin, D. I., and R. D. Nelson. "Consciousness-Related Effects in Random Physical Systems," *Foundations of Psychics*, Vol. 19 (1989), 1499–1514.

Rosenthal, R. "Meta-Analytic Procedures and the Nature of Replica-tion: The Ganzfeld Debate," *Journal of Parapsychology*, Vol. 50 (1986), 315–36.

Schmidt, H. "PK Effect on Pre-Recorded Targets," *Journal of the American Society for Psychical Research*, Vol. 70 (1976), 267–91.

Scott, C. "Comment on the Hyman–Honorton Debate," *Journal of Parapsychology*, Vol. 50 (1986), 349–50.

— STEPHEN E. BRAUDE

ETHICAL EGOISM

Generally defined as the view that one ought to do whatever and only whatever is in one's own maximum interest, benefit, advantage, or good, ethical egoism contrasts with (1) psychological egoism, which says that people do in fact, perhaps necessarily, act in that way; and from (2) alternative ethical theories, which claim that we have other fundamental obligations such as to act for the sake of others, even at ultimate cost to our-selves, or in ways having no necessary relation to any-one's benefit.

Is "self-interest" to be understood as one's interest

in certain states unique to one's own self—

as distinct from certain states of other people?

Egoism strikes many as cutting through pretenses and getting down to fundamentals. This appearance soon dissipates when we make essential distinctions. Foremost is that due to the classic work of Bishop Butler (1692–1752). Is "self-interest" in that theory to be un-derstood as one's interest in certain states unique to one's own self—as distinct from certain states of other people? Or is it merely interests of one's own self—the interests one happens to have, whatever they may be? Since action is necessarily motivated by interests of the agent motivated by them, the second interpretation is trivial: whatever we do, we are somehow interested in doing it. But the first interpretation is implausible: peo-ple are notoriously capable of sacrificing themselves—for friends, loved ones, or causes.

Ethical egoism would also be vacuous if it said only that whatever we ought to do, we ought to do it only

if we are motivated to do it. Only when self-interest is construed in the narrow sense, as describing certain of our interests—those focused specifically on oneself—but not others, does it make sense to say that we ought to act self-interestedly. Then the question "Why?" arises, for we have our choice.

This brings up the question of what is the ultimate good or interest of an agent. Alas, we must leave this important issue open in the present discussion. The next question, however, is crucial. What is meant by "ethical"? Here we must distinguish between a wide sense in which "ethical" means something like "ra-tional" and a narrower sense in which specifically moral requirements are intended. I should choose Bordeaux 1989, but that isn't a moral matter; that I should refrain from cheating is.

If ethical egoism is understood in the wider sense, it is a theory about rational behavior; and construing self-interest in Butler's second way, egoism says that a ra-tional agent acts so as to maximize the realization of whatever she or he is interested in attaining. This highly plausible idea is noncommittal about the content of our interests.

Now turn to the moral version. Moral rules call upon us all to do or refrain from certain things, whether we like it or not. Can there be a rational egoistic morality, then?

But the interests of different persons can conflict. This leads to a problem, which becomes clear when we distinguish two possible interpretations of moral ego-ism:

1. "First-person" egoism appraises all actions of all persons on the basis of the interests of the propounder alone. What Jim Jones thinks, if he is this kind of an egoist, is not only that Jim Jones ought to do whatever, and only whatever, conduces to Jim Jones's best interests—but that everyone else should, too. This is consistent, to be sure, but from the point of view of anyone except Jim or his devotees, it is evidently irra-tional, if they too are self-interested.

2. "General" egoism, on the other hand, says that each person ought to do whatever is in that person's interests. If Jim is an egoist of this type, he believes that Jim ought to do whatever is in Jim's interests, but Sheila ought to do whatever is in Sheila's interests, and so on.

Serious conceptual problems arise with general ego-ism. Suppose that Jim's interests conflict with Sheila's: realizing his frustrates hers. Does Jim tell Sheila that it is Sheila's duty to do what's in Sheila's interests? Or what's in Jim's interests? Or both? Every answer is un-acceptable! The first is unacceptable to Jim himself: how can he, as an exclusively self-interested person, support actions of Sheila's that are detrimental to himself? The second is unacceptable to Sheila: If she is exclusively self-interested, why would she take Jim's "advice"? And the third is flatly inconsistent: for their interests to "conflict" means that they cannot both do what is in their own best interest.

A standard reply is to hold that egoism tells each of the differing parties merely to try to do what is in their interests. But this is either just wrong or turns the theory into something else: "Here, all you ought to do is try to bring about your best interests—but it doesn't matter whether you succeed!" But self-interested agents are interested in results.

Or it might be held that the good life consists not in succeeding but in striving. This turns egoism into a game, and in conflict situations, a competitive game. And games are interesting, but also very special, requiring players to abide by certain game-defining rules. True chess-players do not cheat, even if they can—cheating is not really playing the game. They want opponents to do their best, even if they themselves lose. Of course, they prefer to win, but even if they do not, the game is worthwhile. This defense lacks generality. Ethical egoism is not about games, it is about life. Some people may make life into a game, but most people do not. They want results, not just effort; in conflicts, they are not about to cheer for the other side.

So egoism seems to be self-defeating. What to do? The answer requires, first, that we utilize the vital distinction between egoism as (1) a theory of rationality—of what is recommended by reason; and (2) as a theory of morality. The latter is interpersonal, and concerns rules for groups. Such rules require that people sometimes curtail their passions and conform to the rules.

If we view egoism as a theory of rationality, then whether agent A should aim only at bringing about certain states of A is an open question. But that A should aim at bringing about only those states of affairs that A values is not: we can act only on our own values—in acting, we make them our own.

But when we turn to the subject of formulating specifically moral principles, we must attend to the facts of social life. From the point of view of any rational individual, moralities are devices for securing desirable results not attainable without the cooperation of others. To do this, mutual restrictions must be accepted by all concerned. They will be accepted only if they conduce to the agent's interests. Therefore, moral principles, if rational, must be conducive to the interests of all, those to whom they are addressed as well as those of the propounder herself. Thus, egoism leads to contractarianism (qv): moral principles are those acceptable to each person, given that person's own interests, if all comply. Undoubtedly, some will not; but noncompliance, as Hobbes observed, leads to war, which is worse for all.

Rational egoism, then, leads to the abandonment of moral egoism. Sensible people will condemn egotism, and regard selfishness as a vice: we do better if we care about each other, engage in mutually beneficial activity, and thus refrain from one-sided activity that tramples upon others, such as killing, lying, cheating, stealing, or raping. The core of truth in egoism leads to a fairly familiar morality, whose principles must cash out in terms of the good of every agent participating in society.

Ethical egoism would be vacuous if it said only

that whatever we ought to do,

we ought to do it only if we are motivated to do it.

Narrowly egoistic moral principles cannot do this, and thus are the first to be rejected by rational egoists—another of those fascinating paradoxes of which philosophy is full.

[See also Butler, Joseph.]

BIBLIOGRAPHY

Baier, K. *The Moral Point of View.* Ithaca, NY, 1958. Chapter 8, sections 1–4.
Butler, J. *Sermons* [London, 1726], Preface, I, and XI.
Hobbes, T. *Leviathan* [London, 1651]. Chapters VI, XIII–XV.
Fumerton, R. A. *Reason and Morality: A Defense of the Egocentric Perspective.* Ithaca, NY, 1990.
Gauthier, D. *Morals by Agreement.* Oxford, 1986. Chapters I, II, VI, VII.
Kalin, J. "Two Kinds of Moral Reasoning: Ethical Egoism as a Moral Theory," *Canadian Journal of Philosophy* 5 (1975), 323–56.
Medlin, B. "Ultimate Principles and Ethical Egoism," *Australian Journal of Philosophy,* Vol. 35 (1957), 111–18.
Plato. *Republic.* Books 1, 2.

– JAN NARVESON

ETHICAL THEORY

In the decades leading up to the 1960s, the main focus of analytical moral philosophy was not on normative ethical issues of the good and the right but on 'second order', metaethical questions about ethical discourse and thought. Philosophers by and large accepted a distinction between questions concerning ethical concepts, which can be investigated by analyzing the meanings of ethical language, and (normative) ethical issues posed with those concepts and vocabulary. This analytic turn was stimulated, first, by G. E. Moore's influential argument in *Principia Ethica* (1903) that clarity about what ethical questions ask is necessary before attempting to answer them and, second, from the 1930s on, by a Wittgensteinian conception of philosophy as conceptual and linguistic analysis. Reinforcing these was the fact that the ascendant metaethical view during this latter period was noncognitivism, the position that ethical discourse is not fact stating but expressive of states of mind that lack truth values: pro- and con- attitudes, desires, preferences, or feelings. The apparent consequence was that moral philosophy could itself be cognitive only by being restricted to metaethics.

In the 1950s and 1960s various challenges arose to the dominance of noncognitivism as well as to the paradigm of conceptual analysis. On the former front, Elizabeth Anscombe and Philippa Foot argued that ethical language cannot float entirely free of naturalistic criteria. Peter Geach pointed to difficulties noncognitivism faces in accounting for ethical discourse's apparently fact-stating logical structure. W. D. Falk, Kurt Baier, and Stephen Toulmin argued that ethical judgments express convictions about which attitudes are warranted by reasons, not attitudes themselves. Richard Brandt and Roderick Firth maintained along similar lines that ethical discourse is conceptually tied to *idealized* attitudes—those an "ideal observer" would have. Finally, and also to a similar effect, John Rawls argued that consensus about the characteristics of good ethical judges permits treating their considered judgments as evidence for normative ethical propositions and theories.

At the same time the general dominance of conceptual analysis in philosophy was being shaken by forceful arguments of W. V. O. Quine and Nelson Goodman that no principled distinction exists between conceptual, definitional issues and substantive ones. Restricting moral philosophy to metaethics began to look arbitrary at best.

The momentum created by these events increased exponentially (in the United States, especially) with the publication of John Rawls's *A Theory of Justice* in 1971. Although primarily a work in political philosophy, Rawls's book was also read as a general program for normative ethical theory. Following Quine and Goodman, the rejection of a sharp theory/observation distinction in the philosophy of science, and his own earlier work on ethical judgment, Rawls argued that the test of a normative theory should be whether it can be held in "reflective equilibrium" with considered ethical judgments as well as with other relevant beliefs, including empirical theory and other philosophical convictions. The normative theorist's task is thus to articulate principles and ideals that organize and explicate considered convictions.

Rawls's own normative theory, 'justice as fairness', was an impressive example. It had two ordered principles: one mandating a system of equal basic liberties and a second requiring that the social distribution of other 'primary goods' work to the greatest benefit of the least advantaged. Rawls argued that these principles fit better than any traditional theory (specifically, better than utilitarianism) with considered judgments about justice as well as with a compelling underlying philosophical rationale—namely, that they would be rationally chosen over utilitarianism and other rivals from a perspective (the 'original position') in which hypothetical choosers were deprived of information about themselves (the 'veil of ignorance'), except interests they have as 'free and equal moral persons'.

Even if we accept

a particular theory of justice on reflection,

we can nonetheless ask why we should be just.

A Theory of Justice thus represented a major systematic, deontological alternative to utilitarianism, at least so far as questions of justice are concerned. Utilitarianism's critics had usually been content to lodge specific objections, or to defend some set of specific deontological principles, saying little about how these might fit together or be unified by some underlying rationale. By arguing that his principles were rationally choiceworthy from a perspective expressing an ideal of moral persons as free and equal, moreover, Rawls initiated a 'constructivist' interpretation of Kant's ethics that both reinvigorated serious interest in Kant and articulated themes of equal dignity and autonomy that resonated profoundly in normative ethical thought of the period, both in the academy and in the wider culture.

Throughout the next decade, normative ethics flourished in a way unprecedented in this century. But, much as analytical metaethics had driven out normative theory earlier, so during the 1970s was normative theory frequently practiced with little thought of metaethics. No doubt this was due in part to pent-up demand and to reaction against what was increasingly viewed as the sterile and misguided project of conceptual analysis. Encouraged by the method of reflective equilibrium, writers explored specific, 'applied' normative issues no less than general theory by appeal to considered convictions they hoped their readers would share.

Still, even if conceptual analysis remained mostly a dead letter, fundamental questions concerning the metaphysical and epistemological status of ethics could not be wished away. One nagging question, posed pointedly by Philippa Foot, concerned morality's normative force. Even if we accept a particular theory of justice on reflection, we can nonetheless ask why we should be just. Common sense may agree with Kant that morality (justice included) binds categorically, but it can still be asked whether or why this is so. And, Foot replied, the most plausible response is to hold that moral imperatives do *not* bind categorically; their force is only hypothetical, conditional on their furthering the agent's concerns. Philosophers such as Thomas Nagel, David Gauthier, and Kurt Baier argued to the contrary, but more of this below.

By the end of the decade, a number of events transpired to put metaethical concerns back at the center of philosophical discussion, although by no means to the exclusion of normative theory. J. L. Mackie argued startlingly that rejecting noncognitivism—a step with which he agreed—leads ultimately to the 'error theory': the conclusion that all ethical judgments are false. Ethical judgments, he held, attribute properties that are simply too "queer" to exist, since they would have simultaneously to be actual and intrinsically action guiding. How, he asked, could 'to-be-doneness' be part of the "furniture of the universe"? It is we who *project* ethical properties onto the world: we see things *as* having these properties, though they do not in fact. According to Mackie, ethical discourse and practice can proceed despite the massive error it is committed to, but many doubted that this could be so. For them, Mackie's argument from "queerness" stood as a challenge to the viability of ethics itself.

In a not dissimilar vein, Gilbert Harman argued that ethics faces a "problem" that empirical theory does not. Empirical observations can count as evidence of postulated theoretical properties and entities because the relevant theories provide the best explanation of these very observations. A scientist who takes her visual experience before a laboratory monitor as evidence of the existence of a proton, for example, is likely to believe that the proton's existing explains, because it causes, her having the visual experience she does. But it is hard to see how a similar relation could hold between considered ethical convictions and the ethical theories they might be thought to confirm. Which ethical convictions we have appears to have more to do with facts about us than with which ethical propositions, if any, are actually true. But if that is so, what justifies treating considered convictions as evidence?

Worries of these sorts, coupled with the concern, raised by Brandt and R. M. Hare, that ethical 'intuitions' are especially susceptible to infection by prejudice, ideology, and superstition, led to an emerging sense that the viability of normative theory rested ultimately on metaethical issues that could not be indefinitely postponed. The fifteen years that followed saw a reinvigoration of metaethics, although less of conceptual analysis than of more directly metaphysical and epistemological inquiry. Normative theory has thrived also, but especially through the attempt to connect it to issues of fundamental philosophical rationale. This entry's subject, however, is primarily the former phenomenon.

This new life in metaethics has tended to take two different forms dictated by different responses to the problem of placing ethics in relation to the realm of natural fact and empirical method. One trend accepts the challenge in these terms. It holds that ethical methods are continuous with those of science: ethical theories can fit the ethical facts no less than a theory in natural science can fit the facts of nature. Better: ethical facts *are* natural facts, even if ethics is a distinct discipline from, say, psychology. The second insists that the methods and object of ethics are fundamentally different from those of empirical theory but denies that this makes ethics problematic. Prominent among the first trend have been various forms of realist ethical naturalism, both reductionist and nonreductionist. The second trend has collected a wide diversity of approaches: practical reasoning theories, less rationalist forms of constructivism, sensibility theories, and new forms of noncognitivism.

Ethical naturalism had been a prominent casualty early in the century of Moore's arguments in *Principia Ethica*, as well as of the noncognitivist lines of thought these inspired. Naturalism commits the naturalistic fallacy, Moore influentially charged, although it was never clear how any logical error could be involved. More persuasive was what became known as the "open question" argument. Intrinsic value cannot be a natural property. Moore argued, since, for any natural property, it always remains an "open question" whether something having it is good. Later, noncognitivists such as Stevenson and Hare also deployed forms of this thought. The reason that ethical questions remain logically open even when no issue of natural fact remains, Hare argued, is that the former directly engage noncognitive attitudes of commendation and prescription. What is at issue is noncognitive—what to commend or prescribe, not what is the case.

With the undermining of confidence in the analytic/synthetic distinction and in the project of conceptual analysis it underwrote, however, stock in the "open question" argument began to fall. At the same time, important new work in the philosophy of language of Hilary Putnam and Saul Kripke appeared to show that different terms can refer to the same substance or property even if they have different meanings to ordinary speakers. The function of a term such as 'water', for example, is to refer to whatever it is that flows in the rivers and streams. And it can be a later, substantial discovery that 'H$_2$O' refers to the very same stuff. From the fact that, at some point, whether water is H$_2$O is not closed by ordinary meaning it can hardly follow that they are not the same thing. Maybe the same relation could hold between ethical properties and other natural features.

Once these insights were imported into metaethics, ethical naturalism began to find new defenders and new life. There had already been significant movements in this direction. In the late 1950s, for example, Foot had begun to work out a neo-Aristotelian naturalistic alternative to noncognitivism. The new naturalists, however, were characterized by a closer tie to contemporary philosophies of science and language and a desire to use these tools to exhibit a continuity between ethics and the natural sciences.

Thinkers within this broad category include Richard Boyd, Nicholas Sturgeon, David Brink, Gilbert Harman, Richard Brandt, and Peter Railton. They are united by a commitment to metaphysical and methodological naturalism and, with the possible exception of Brandt, to moral realism. In this context, realism differs from cognitivism—the thesis that ethical claims admit of truth value—or even from the additional proposition that some ethical claims are true. Like scientific realism, moral realism holds that ethical facts exist independently of any access we might have to them and that ethical claims and theories are true when they fit the ethical facts. Naturalist moral realism holds, traditionally, that these ethical facts are natural facts.

The new naturalist realists divide on the issue of the reducibility of ethical properties. One group, represented by Boyd, Sturgeon, and Brink, argue from postpositivist theses in the philosophies of science and language to the conclusion that ethical properties can be both natural and irreducible to properties confirmable by any natural science (other than ethics). Only by discreditable positivist criteria, they claim, does ethics itself not qualify as a natural science. The second group holds, by contrast, that ethical properties must earn objectivity and existence "the old-fashioned" (not to say positivist) way—by some form of reducibility to properties confirmable by the (other) natural sciences. Harman, Railton, and Brandt are in this group.

An important area of debate between these two groups concerns the epistemological status of considered ethical convictions or 'intuitions'. While the postpositivist nonreductionists believe that only by discreditable positivist criteria do ethical intuitions not count as genuine observations, the reductive naturalists take Harman's problem seriously. A nonreductionist such as Sturgeon responds to Harman's problem by saying that

ethical facts can indeed explain ethical "observations" in the same way such explanations work in science. For example, that moral opposition to slavery arose only in the eighteenth and nineteenth centuries, despite slavery's long previous history, and then primarily in anglophone and francophone countries, is explainable by the fact that the chattel slavery practiced in English- and French-speaking parts of the New World was worse than earlier and other forms. It is, Sturgeon insists, this ethical fact that best explains the difference in opposition, and, as well, differences in ethical observations or considered judgments people were disposed to make at the time. To this it can be objected that there must have been features of chattel slavery that made it worse than other forms and that it is these, and not the fact of their being worse-making, that explain the differential judgment and opposition. However, the latter explanations may not drive out the former.

This line of thought may help to establish the reality of properties to which ethical vocabulary can refer, but do these exhaust the content of ethical thought and discourse? If, like 'water', ethical terms refer to natural kinds, then the force of Moore's open-question argument is blunted. However, the open question has shown remarkable staying power among philosophers. And the explanation may be that ethical terms have a normative content that is intrinsically regulative of action, feelings, and attitudes. While the function of 'water' is to refer to a natural kind in the causal order, the most general ethical terms, at least, seem less to concern what or how things are in fact than how to respond or act in the face of that.

Reductionist naturalists divide the tasks of securing ethical properties' reality and of establishing their normativity, giving the latter a weight the nonreductionists tend not to. And they generally attempt to do the latter by identifying ethical qualities with natural properties that guarantee an *internalist* connection to motivation or various affective states. In this way they seek to capture the action-, desire-, or emotion-*guiding* character of ethical properties. Taking off from an idea of Brandt's, for example, Peter Railton identifies a person's intrinsic good with what a maximally knowledgeable, experienced, and imaginative extension of that person *would want* for her actual self. Such a claim can be taken either as a synthetic identity thesis or, as Brandt and Railton propose, as a linguistic reform that both satisfies ("old fashioned") naturalist scruples and also secures the normativity of ethical thought and discourse—or, at least, that accomplishes the latter to its closest naturalistic approximation.

A distinctive mark of philosophers who see ethics as fundamentally discontinuous with science is that they deny that ethical properties can be both normative and naturalistic. Recent practical-reasoning theorists, for example, see a discontinuity between the natural and the intrinsically action guiding as arising because of a fundamental difference of perspective—that between the point of view of an observer aiming to describe and understand an independent natural order and the practical perspective of an agent deliberating about what to do. One group, which includes Thomas Nagel, Alan Gewirth, Stephen Darwall, and Christine Korsgaard, have attempted to work out Kantian versions of this approach, arguing that ethical norms are norms of free practical reason. A second, including Kurt Baier and David Gauthier, have pursued a more Hobbesian line. All agree, however, that because it is essentially practical, ethical discourse's truth and objectivity conditions differ fundamentally from those for theoretical disciplines; they must be somehow internal to practical reasoning itself.

Intrinsic value cannot be a natural property,

Moore argued, since, for any natural property,

it always remains an "open question"

whether something having it is good.

For example, Nagel initially argued that any discourse that is not solipsistic must satisfy the constraint that a person be able to make the same judgment of herself from an objective standpoint that she can from her own egocentric point of view. When, however, this is combined with the practical character of deliberative ethical judgments—their intrinsic connection to motivation—Nagel argued that there follows a formal constraint on admissible reasons for acting. Any valid reason must be agent-neutral (e.g., that this will be in someone's interest) rather than agent-relative (that this will be in my—or, indeed, in your—interest); its applicability must not shift with a shift in the agent's point of view. More recently, Nagel has retreated from this strong claim and in a direction that is arguably even more Kantian. Autonomous agency, he now argues, involves an agent's acting on reasons he can reflectively endorse from an objective standpoint, and such a set of reasons can include both agent-relative and agent-neutral ones.

Common to all these Kantian approaches has been the idea that free practical reasoning has a formal structure, with its own internal standards or constraints, and that these provide the truth and objectivity conditions for ethical thought and discourse. Thus, Gewirth maintains that fundamental moral principles are derivable from propositions to which a rational agent is committed from within her deliberative standpoint in acting. And Korsgaard argues that even those who advance "Humean," instrumental theories must believe that practical reasoning requires at least this much form. Once this is admitted, the Kantians hope, debate can take place on a new plane: Is means/end reasoning sufficient for the deliberation of genuine agents? Since, as agents, we regard ourselves as free to adopt and renounce ends, and since what lies behind instrumental reasoning—the hypothetical imperative—is simply a consistency constraint that can be realized as well by renouncing any particular end as by taking means to achieve it, they argue that free practical reasoning requires a formal principle regulating the choice of ends no less than that of means. Agents do things for (and not just because of) reasons and in doing so commit themselves to principles as valid for all. But such a commitment is not, the Kantians claim, a hypothesis about some independently existing order of normative fact to which we might have (theoretical) cognitive access. So the standards to which deliberation is subject must be internal to free practical reasoning itself. But this is possible, they argue, only if practical reasoning is regulated by the categorical imperative: a rule requiring action only on principles that can be willed to regulate the deliberations of all.

Gauthier and Baier reject Kantianism's formalism and apriorism. Both start with the premise that practical rationality must work to the agent's benefit but deny that any purely instrumental or egoistic theory follows from this. Baier argues this is so because a correct theory of rationality cannot be collectively self-defeating, and everyone's acting according to unrestricted self-interest would be mutually disadvantageous. Gauthier rejects this constraint but puts forward another: a theory of rationality cannot be individually self-defeating. The correct theory is one a rational agent would regulate herself by, where a rational agent is one whose rational character—her dispositions to be guided by deliberative principles—is best suited to benefit her. To the extent that our characters are translucent to each other, it will be advantageous to be disposed to constrain self-interest by the requirements of mutually advantageous agreements, since only then will others enter into such agreements with us. This gives Gauthier an opening to argue that at least some aspects of morality are objective, categorical constraints. However, it may be asked of these Hobbesian approaches what the source of their respective self-defeat conditions can be if not some prior account of (free) rational agency?

T. M. Scanlon's constructive contractualism represents another attempt to establish morality's objectivity as a regime of practical reasoning, but without Kantian ambitions. What stands behind morality, Scanlon holds, is "the desire to be able to justify one's actions to others on grounds they could not reasonably reject." An action is wrong if it is contrary to rules no one could reasonably reject to govern their mutual relations. The authority of this moral category, its normative force, derives from the fact that to do what is wrong is to go against the deep desire to be able to justify oneself to others. It follows, however, that although someone having this desire may still apply moral terms to anyone who lacks it, the normative force of this attribution will remain unsecured—there may be no reason why the other person should avoid what one judges to be wrong.

Constructivist and practical-reasoning approaches lay great stress on the role of freely chosen principle, more, it may seem, than ethics can possibly bear. Frequently we discover our ethical convictions, not so much in recognizing principles to which we are or should be committed but through sentiment and response. For sensibility theorists, such as David Wiggins and John McDowell, the epistemology of ethics is modeled more on perception than on anything like working out what rules satisfy various formal or material constraints. Following a broadly Aristotelian outlook, they argue that ethical aspects of situations are there to be seen, at least when these are viewed in the light of the affective responses that virtuous persons have to them.

Perceiving ethical properties is not like detecting aspects of the causal structure of the world. Rather, like color and other so-called secondary qualities, ethical properties are tied to specific human sensibilities, sensibilities we might have lacked without any loss of rationality or capacity to detect causal structure. But, sensibility theorists argue, this does not mean that ethical judgment is noncognitive or that ethical properties are not real, any more than it does in the case of color. Only a "scientistic" view of reality would have these consequences.

Sensibility theory provides a vantage point for arguing simultaneously against noncognitivism and against various forms of intuitionism. Ethical sensibilities and properties come in matched pairs, it holds. As against noncognitivism, it is of the nature of the relevant sentiments that they implicitly involve attribution of the relevant ethical property. We would not understand a sentiment as moral disapproval, for example, unless it involved seeing something *as wrong*. But neither can we understand ethical properties independent of their relation to the relevant sentiments, as part of a freestanding order.

Just as there can be better or worse judgments of color, so can there be better or worse discrimination of ethical properties. And, McDowell argues, we should

not suppose that this is independent of the ethical properties of the perceiver herself. A virtuous person, for example, may be able to see that another person's shyness and sensitivity calls for certain treatment, even if others are oblivious to this. Moreover, because her seeing the situation in this light involves affective response, she must be moved by her perception; she may take it as a reason for acting and, indeed, act for that reason. Tying ethical properties and their detection to sentiment thus gives ethical qualities an internal connection to the will.

Like scientific realism, moral realism holds that ethical facts exist independently of any access we might have to them, and that ethical claims and theories are true when they fit the ethical facts.

Any close analogy between ethical and secondary qualities is bound to break down at some point, however. One disanalogy sensibility theorists themselves admit is that although something counts as having a given color if, and only if, it is such as to elicit the relevant color impression in normal human observers, ethical properties are tied to appropriate or merited response. It is in relation to just such normative notions as these that the most contentious metaethical issues have traditionally arisen, however. Also, to guarantee objectivity to color judgments, it is necessary to "rigidify" the description 'normal human observers' to something like 'normal human observers as they now are'. But although this assures that there are properties to be tracked by our sensibilities, its arbitrariness seems insufficient to support the idea that ethical properties are what should regulate our choices.

These objections recall a fact/value distinction of the sort that fueled earlier versions of noncognitivism. Noncognitivism fell from its dominant position in the 1960s, not least because of the problems Geach had raised concerning the apparently fact-stating logical structure of ethical discourse. Recently, however, Simon Blackburn and Allan Gibbard have breathed new life into noncognitivism, showing how it can take more sophisticated and plausible forms. Blackburn argues that it is because we need terms not only to express emotive attitudes but also to engage in "reflective evaluative practice," and thus "to express concern for improvements, implications, and coherence of attitudes," that we need the objective-looking emotive predicates that are the ethical vocabulary. Within our use of these terms we employ such notions as truth, logical consequence, and so on, as if we were making claims about real properties. Our use is 'quasi-realistic', but not really so. Ethical claims have no cognitive content; their function is not to represent real aspects of the world. Rather, they project our attitudes onto the world, but not in a way that expresses the false belief that the world really has the projected properties.

Gibbard's form of noncognitivism is a norm expressivism rather than an emotivism. The distinctive normative core of ethical notions is the idea of something's being warranted, rational, and supported by reasons; or, in Gibbard's favored phrase, of its "making sense." No real property answers to this idea, Gibbard holds. This can be shown, he argues, by marking what is ultimately at issue between people who disagree about normative questions. For example, theorists may differ over what a person should do in a decision- or game-theoretic situation even when they are completely agreed about the facts of the case, and even when the issue is only what would be most rational in light of the agent's ends. Since there is no disagreement over the facts, Gibbard argues, the remaining disagreement must concern something else. Its source, he suggests, is that the disputants accept conflicting norms of decision or action and that their conflicting judgments express their acceptance of these conflicting norms. Gibbard claims that the mental state of accepting a norm is not a representational state. So to express this state is not to say anything true or false.

Like sensibility theorists, Gibbard agrees that many normative judgments are tied to feelings, but not in the way that either the sensibility theorists or traditional emotivists believed. Gibbard agrees with sensibility theory in rejecting emotivism's view that moral judgments directly *express* feeling; such judgments claim rather that a feeling or sentiment is *warranted*. But, as against sensibility theory, Gibbard maintains that this latter claim is noncognitive; it expresses the acceptance of norms. For example, the judgment that some action is morally wrong expresses the acceptance of norms that warranted feeling impartial anger toward it.

Despite this renewed interest in metaethics, it would be a great mistake to suppose that normative theory has receded into the background in recent years. On the contrary, the area has shown at least as much vitality as metaethics. However, normative theorists have been less than fully satisfied to anchor their theories in a "narrow" reflective equilibrium with considered ethical judgments. More fundamental considerations of rationale and coherence with theory in such areas as moral psychology, theory of action, and the metaphysics of personal identity have come to play a larger role than they did in the "great expansion" of normative theory in the 1970s. In this light the classic debate between consequentialism and deontology has been re-energized. New forms of consequentialism have arisen with more sophisticated theories of the good and accounts of the relation between theories of conduct and theories of moral motivation. The traditional consequentialist complaint that deontology is but a set of "intuitions in search of a foundation" has been given a distinctive form in Samuel Scheffler's charge that no compelling rationale exists for the agent-relative character of deontological constraints—for example, for a requirement not to break one's promise rather than, say, to promote promise keeping in general. After all, if it's bad (in itself) that a promise be broken, it must be worse that several be.

New support for (agent-neutral) consequentialism has also come from Derek Parfit's challenging and influential reductionist theory of personal identity. If no "further fact" of being the same person over time exists beyond a messy set of facts concerning to what degree various relations hold between mental and physical states at various times, then this may tell against deontological theories that apparently require a more robust conception of personal identity and the distinctness of persons.

Thus, if utilitarianism and consequentialism were in retreat after the appearance of Rawls's *A Theory of Justice* in the 1970s, they have managed to gain new ground and go on the offensive more recently. Not that deontology has been on the defensive; far from it. But with a new concern to press fundamental philosophical issues, deontology has been unable to rest on being the theory of moral common sense and has had to seek more deeply satisfying forms.

The deontology/consequentialism debate is rooted in an orthodox tradition of modern moral philosophy that goes back in some form or other to the eighteenth century. One of the more important developments of the 1980s and early 1990s has been a radical critique of this tradition and of the sort of moral theory of which consequentialism and deontology are paradigm examples. Alasdair MacIntyre has argued, for example, that the modern "enlightenment project" of defending universal principles of right without appeal to an essential human aim or *telos* was doomed to failure and that, while we can hardly return to an Aristotelianism that assumes natural final causes, ethics must find foundation in conceptions of virtue and goods that are internal to going traditional practices. It was not necessary to accept MacIntyre's rejection of modern moral theory, however, to agree that, as Philippa Foot put it, "the subject of the virtues and vice" had been "strangely neglected" by analytical moral philosophy. Foot's observation has resonated widely in recent years, and it has combined with the sense of a similar neglect of the moral emotions and sentiments to produce a steadily growing body of work in these areas.

> A distinctive mark of philosophers who see ethics as fundamentally discontinuous with science is that they deny that ethical properties can be both normative and naturalistic.

One particularly important development within this general trend has been an investigation of the ethical dimensions of various forms of human relationships together with a radical, sometimes self-consciously feminist critique of orthodox moral theory as distorting the way ethical issues inevitably arise, not in a general or universal context, but within relationships of concern for *particular* others. Annette Baier's work on trust and a variety of writings on the ethics of care, love, and other forms of particularistic concern, much of it inspired by the psychologist Carol Gilligan, have been especially significant here. Finally, some philosophers have argued that morality itself, and not just moral theory, either has (or should have) a more restricted sphere than orthodox theory supposes or that it is actually worthy of abolition since it embodies an irredeemably defective way of conceiving the ethical life. Susan Wolf is prominent in the first group and Bernard Williams in the second. Partly what worries Williams is, again, that morality's universalism cannot be made fully compatible with the forms of particularistic concern that must take root in a good human life. But equally important is the neo-Nietzschean thought that the 'morality system' involves a form of obligation that requires insupportable metaphysical assumptions about human freedom and that threatens to become a form of bondage, shackling human beings to a profoundly less valuable life.

[See also Action Theory; Anscombe, Elizabeth; Consequentialism; Constructivism, Moral; Decision Theory; Deontological Ethics; Error Theory; Ethical Egoism; Evolutionary Ethics; Goodman, Nelson; Hare, Richard M.; Justice; Kant, Immanuel; Kripke, Saul Aaron; Mackie, John Leslie; Moral Naturalism; Moral Psychology; Moral Realism; Moral Relativism; Moral Skepticism; Nondescriptivism; Personal Identity; Philosophy of Language; Philosophy of Science; Practical Reason Approaches; Projectivism; Putnam, Hilary; Quine, Willard Van Orman; Rationality; Rawls, John; Sensibility Theories; Stevenson, Charles; Virtue Ethics; Wittgenstein, Ludwig Josef Johann.]

BIBLIOGRAPHY

Brandt, R. *A Theory of the Good and the Right.* Oxford, 1979.
Foot, P. "Morality as a System of Hypothetical Imperatives," *Philosophical Review,* Vol. 81 (1972), 305–16. Reprinted in P. Foot, *Virtues and Vices* (Los Angeles, 1978).
Gauthier, D. *Morals by Agreement.* Oxford, 1986.
Gibbard, A. *Wise Choices, Apt Feelings.* Cambridge, 1990.
Harman, G. *The Nature of Morality: An Introduction to Ethics.* New York, 1977.
Mackie, J. L. *Ethics: Inventing Right and Wrong.* Harmondsworth, Eng., 1977.
Nagel, T. *The Possibility of Altruism.* Oxford, 1978.
Rawls, J. *A Theory of Justice.* Cambridge, 1971.
Scanlon, T. M. "Contractualism and Utilitarianism," in A. Sen and B. Williams, *Utilitarianism and Beyond* (Cambridge, 1982).
Wiggins, D. *Needs, Values, Truth: Essays in the Philosophy of Value.* Oxford, 1987.

— STEPHEN DARWALL

ETHICS, HISTORY OF

The term "ethics" is used in three different but related ways, signifying (1) a general pattern or "way of life," (2) a set of rules of conduct or "moral code," and (3) inquiry *about* ways of life and rules of conduct. In the first sense we speak of Buddhist or Christian ethics; in the second, we speak of professional ethics and of unethical behavior. In the third sense, ethics is a branch of philosophy that is frequently given the special name of metaethics. The present discussion will be limited to the history of philosophical or "meta" ethics, for two reasons. First, because it is impossible to cover, with any degree of thoroughness, the history of ethics in either of the first two senses. Practices and the codification of practices are the threads out of which all of human culture is woven, so that the history of ethics in either of these senses would be far too vast a subject for a brief essay. Second, although ethical philosophy is often understood in a broad way as including all significant thought about human conduct, it can well be confined within manageable limits by separating purely philosophical thought from the practical advice, moral preaching, and social engineering which it illuminates and from which it receives sustenance. This distinction, while somewhat artificial, makes sense of the common opinion that philosophy in general, and ethical philosophy in particular, was invented by the Greeks.

The central questions of philosophical ethics are: What do we or should we mean by "good" and "bad"? What are the right standards for judging things to be good or bad? How do judgments of good and bad (value judgments) differ from and depend upon judgments of value-neutral fact? But when these questions are answered, it is important to find out the differences between specific types of value judgments that are characterized by such adjectives as "useful," "right," "moral," and "just." We may therefore divide our subject matter into the search for the meaning and standards of good in general, and of well-being, right conduct, moral character, and justice in particular. Needless to say, these are not watertight compartments. Many philosophers reject sharp distinctions between them. But provisional separation of these topics, subject to reunification in accordance with particular philosophical views, will prove helpful in disentangling the various issues on which philosophers have taken opposing stands, so that the history of ethics can be seen as irregular progress toward complete clarification of each type of ethical judgment.

Greek Ethics

Ethical philosophy began in the fifth century B.C., with the appearance of Socrates, a secular prophet whose self-appointed mission was to awaken his fellow men to the need for rational criticism of their beliefs and practices.

What do we or should we mean

by "good" and "bad"?

What are the right standards

for judging things to be good or bad?

Greek society of the fifth century was in a state of rapid change from agrarian monarchy to commercial and industrial democracy. The religious and social traditions that had been handed down from one generation to the next through the natural processes of social imitation and household training were brought into question by the accession to power of a commercial class, whose members were untrained in and scornful of the ancestral way of life. New rules of conduct were required by a market economy in which money counted more than noble birth and in which men had to be considered equals as buyers and sellers. Men who wished to be elected to public office, but had not been trained at home as rulers of serfs and household servants, needed a more explicit and general code of conduct than was embodied in the sense of honor and *esprit de corps* of the landed aristocracy. Occurring with the

rapid political and social transformation of Greece, and interacting with it as both cause and effect, was the development of basic industrial arts and a scientific technology. These forces both expressed and intensified the developing interest in rational evaluation of beliefs. As Henry Sidgwick put it:

> This emergence of an art of conduct with professional teachers cannot thoroughly be understood, unless it is viewed as a crowning result of a general tendency at this stage of Greek civilization to substitute technical skill for traditional procedure. . . . If bodily vigour was no longer to be left to nature and spontaneous exercise, but was to be attained by the systematic observance of rules laid down by professional trainers, it was natural to think that the same might be the case with excellences of the soul. (*Outlines of the History of Ethics,* p. 21)

Early Greek thinkers drew frequent comparisons between medicine and ethics, describing ethics as the "art of living" and the "care of the soul." Socrates' motto, "A sound mind in a sound body," suggests the medical image of ethics as mental hygiene. Many thinkers took a special interest in medicine, and, recognizing the interdependence of mind and body, they practiced a rudimentary psychiatry. Alcmaeon of Croton, Empedocles, and Democritus were renowned for their psychotherapeutic skills. This biological conception of mind and soul led to a more critical and scientific approach to problems of ethical judgment. Philosophers began to search for reasons for established modes of conduct and, where no reasons were found, to suggest that action could be directed toward individual goals in defiance of tradition. The professional teachers known as Sophists, whose social role was to prepare the uncultivated *nouveaux riches* for positions of power in the rising democracies, employed the new-found weapon of logic with devastating effect against the code of honor of the declining aristocracy. Protagoras, Gorgias, and Thrasymachus taught methods of self-advancement and of attaining virtue. They stressed the difference between subjective values and objective facts, arguing that good and evil are matters of personal decision or social agreement (*nomos*) rather than facts of nature (*phusis*).

SOCRATES. Socrates stood midway between the unexamined, traditional values of the aristocracy and the skeptical practicality of the commercial class. Like the Sophists, he demanded reasons for rules of conduct, rejecting the self-justifying claim of tradition, and for this reason he was denounced as a Sophist by conservative writers like Aristophanes. But unlike the Sophists, he believed that by the use of reason man could arrive at a set of ethical principles that would reconcile self-interest with the common good and would apply to all men at all times.

The central questions of ethical philosophy were raised for the first time by Socrates and the Sophists, but only Socrates realized the difficulty, bordering on impossibility, of finding adequate answers. In this respect, Socrates may be regarded as the first philosopher, in the strictest sense of the term. While the Sophists, after exposing the impracticality of traditional rules of conduct, then offered glib formulas in their place—such as "Justice is the rule of the stronger" (Thrasymachus) and "Man is the measure of all things" (Protagoras)—Socrates applied the same logical criticism with equally devastating results to both aristocratic and market-place morality. He did not find the universal and self-evident code he searched for, but it was his memorable achievement to have revealed to mankind that without such a code its actions will lack justification and that moral perfection is therefore an ideal to which we can only approximate. Perfect clarity about what constitutes moral perfection is no more of this world than is moral perfection itself.

Our knowledge of Socrates is primarily derived from the dialogues of Plato, so it is not possible to draw a sharp line between the ideas of the two men. But since Plato's early dialogues are considerably different in style and content from those which he wrote later in life, one may take the early as fairly representative of Socrates and the late as more expressive of Plato's own thought. The chief differences discernible are the following: the more Socratic dialogues are devoted to the criticism of conventional beliefs and to the demonstration of the need for further inquiry, while the later dialogues argue for positive conclusions; the early dialogues search for definitions of ethical concepts, while the later dialogues are concerned with justifying a contemplative way of life in which pleasures of the senses are spurned in favor of pleasures of the mind; finally, the Socratic style is conversational and argumentative, while that of the later years is more didactic and abstract.

The Socrates of the early dialogues raises questions about the meaning of ethical terms, such as "What is justice?" (*Republic*), "What is piety?" (*Euthyphro*), "What is courage?" (*Laches, Charmides*), "What is virtue?" (*Protagoras*). The answers offered by others to these questions are then subjected to a relentless cross-examination (Socratic dialectic), exposing their vagueness and inconsistency.

Although Socrates did not separate judgments of value from judgments of fact, the negative results of his line of questioning suggest a distinction that was made explicit only in modern times by Hume and Moore. In each of his discussions of ethical concepts like courage or justice, Socrates refutes all efforts to define them in terms of ethically neutral facts. For example, when, in the *Protagoras, Laches,* and *Charmides,* courage is defined as resolute facing of danger, Socrates observes that a man who faces dangers that he would be wise to avoid is a fool rather than a hero. The generalization toward which Socrates points the way, although he does not arrive at it himself, is that ethical concepts can never be adequately defined in terms of observable facts alone. Many philosophers, beginning with the Sophists, have believed that this principle leads to ethical skepticism. Plato attempted to escape such skepticism by means of his theory of Forms, and the modern school of intuitionism proposes a similar way out. Indeed, all the ethical theories developed since Socrates may be considered as alternative explanations of the relation between facts and values, naturalistic theories stressing their interdependence and nonnaturalistic theories stressing their differences. Socrates, in demanding rational grounds for ethical judgments, brought attention to the problem of tracing the logical relationships between values and facts and thereby created ethical philosophy.

The central questions of ethical philosophy

were raised for the first time

by Socrates and the Sophists,

but only Socrates realized the difficulty,

bordering on impossibility,

of finding adequate answers.

PLATO. Plato's thought may be regarded as an endeavor to answer the questions posed by Socrates. From the *Republic* on through the later dialogues and epistles, Plato constructed a systematic view of nature, God, and man from which he derived his ethical principles. The foundation of this metaphysical view was the theory of Forms, whose most succinct formulation may be found in the discussion of the Divided Line, toward the end of Book VI of the *Republic.* Plato divides the objects of knowledge into two main categories and each of these into two subcategories symbolized by unequal sections of the line. The main division is between the realm of changing, sensible objects and that of unchanging, abstract forms. Knowledge of sensible objects acquired by sense perception is inaccurate and uncertain, for the object of sense, like the river of Heraclitus, is in continual flux. In contrast, knowledge of timeless forms is precise and rigorously provable. The realm of sensible objects is subdivided into shadows and images, in the lower section, and natural objects in the upper section. The realm of forms is subdivided into mathematical forms and ethical forms. At the apex of this ascending line is the Form of the Good, in relation to which all other objects of knowledge must be defined if they are to be adequately understood. Thus, ethics is the highest and most rigorous kind of knowledge, surpassing even mathematics, but it is also the most difficult to attain. Mathematics leads us away from reliance on visual images and sense perception, and ethical philosophy demands an even greater effort of abstraction. The objects of ethical knowledge are even less visualizable than geometrical forms and numbers—they are concepts and principles ultimately unified under the all-encompassing concept of the Good.

Although Plato suggests in this and other passages that ethical truths can be rigorously deduced from self-evident axioms, and thus introduces the mathematical model of knowledge that has guided many philosophers ever since, he does not employ a deductive procedure in his discussions of specific ethical problems, perhaps because he did not feel that he had yet attained an adequate vision of the Good that would supply him with the proper axioms from which to deduce rules of conduct. His actual procedure follows what he calls an ascending dialectic, a process of generalization through the give and take of conversation and the consideration of typical cases, a process designed to culminate in an intellectual vision of the structure of reality, from which, by a "descending dialectic" or deduction from general principles, particular judgments of value can be deduced. Plato's main goal in his ethical philosophy is to lead the way toward a vision of the Good.

The Socratic–Platonic ethical theory identifies goodness with reality and reality with intelligible form and thus concludes that the search for value must lead away from sense perception and bodily pleasure. This suggests an ascetic and intellectualistic way of life which is spelled out in full detail in the *Republic*, in the description of the training of the guardians. Some difference in the degree of intensity of the preference for mind over body may perhaps be discerned in the increasing severity of tone from the early dialogues to the later. In the *Protagoras* and *Symposium*, Socrates argues for rational control over the body for the sake of greater pleasure in the long run, but he does not oppose pleasure as such. In the *Symposium* the unity of body and mind is a luminous thread throughout the discussion. Love is regarded as a search for the pleasure that consists in

possession of what is good, and it is shown to exist on many levels, the lowest being that of sexual desire and the highest that of aspiration toward a vision of eternity. While still under the influence of Socrates, Plato distinguishes noble pleasures from base pleasures, rather than condemning pleasure in itself. The image he draws of Socrates is of a man who eats and drinks heartily and enjoys himself on all levels of experience, but in rationally controlled proportions. Socrates enjoys the wine at the symposium as much as anyone else, but unlike the others he remains sober to the end. While the poet Agathon becomes drunk with his own rhetoric, Socrates employs richly sensual language and metaphor in a way sufficiently controlled to make a philosophical point and so remains master of his rhetoric as well as of his body.

In the extraordinarily beautiful dialogue *Phaedo*, which describes the day of Socrates' execution, the theme of superiority of soul to body is dealt with directly, as might be expected of a philosopher who is about to die. Here Socrates commits himself unequivocally to a rejection of the body and its pleasures, maintaining that a wise man looks forward to his own death, when the soul is freed from its corporeal prison. Whether this is an exact expression of Socrates' attitude toward life may, however, be doubted in view of other dialogues, such as the *Protagoras*. In any case, it is natural for a man confronting death to try to set the best possible light on it. But it was this more somber, otherworldly strain in Socrates that Plato in his later works elaborated into a mystical vision of a timeless higher world. Plato has Socrates say, in the *Philebus*, ". . . no degree of pleasure, whether great or small, was thought to be necessary to him who chose the life of thought and wisdom" (translated by B. Jowett, New York, 1933, Para. 33).

In the *Timaeus*, where, significantly, the protagonist is no longer Socrates but the Pythagorean Timaeus, pleasure is described as "the greatest incitement to evil," and Timaeus places the "inferior soul" below the neck, separating it from the intellect. Plato's severe castigations of bodily pleasures, his sharp separation of soul from body and of the eternal from the temporal, and his mystical cosmology entail a more extreme asceticism than that preached or practiced by Socrates.

Plato's mistrust of bodily pleasure and perceptual judgment led him to take an unfavorable view of public opinion and, consequently, of democratic institutions. In the *Republic*, and still more emphatically in the *Laws*, he proposed that society be ruled by an intellectual elite who would be trained to govern in accordance with their vision of eternal forms. He proposed, in the *Laws*, a ruthless system of punishments and the propagation of ideologically useful myths that would preserve social harmony and class distinction. Yet despite his support of severe punishment for social transgressions, Plato followed Socrates in holding, in the *Protagoras, Timaeus,* and *Laws,* that evil is due only to ignorance or madness and that "no man is voluntarily bad," a paradox that Aristotle later tried valiantly to resolve.

ARISTOTLE. One might expect that Aristotle, who studied at Plato's Academy for many years, would take the same view of nature and human conduct as his mentor. But the differences between Plato and Aristotle are more fundamental than the resemblances. Although Aristotle naturally used a similar terminology and shared with Plato certain principles and attitudes expressive of the rationality of Hellenic culture, his method of inquiry and his conception of the role of ethical principles in human affairs were different enough from Plato's to establish a rival philosophical tradition. Plato was the fountainhead of religious and idealistic ethics, while Aristotle engendered the naturalistic tradition. Throughout the subsequent history of Western civilization, ethical views that looked to a supranatural source, such as God or pure reason, for standards of evaluation stemmed from the metaphysics of Plato, while naturalistic philosophers who found standards of value in the basic needs, tendencies, and capacities of man were guided by Aristotle.

Aristotle was born in Stagira, Macedonia, the son of Nicomachus, court physician to Amyntas II. He received early training in biology and physiology and in methods of careful observation and classification, a fact that may account for his later differences with Plato on the role of sense perception in the acquisition of knowledge. While Plato was guided by mathematics as a model of scientific knowledge, Aristotle modeled his system on biology, stressing the importance of observation of recurrent patterns in nature. Thus Plato's goal for philosophical ethics was to make human nature conform to an ideal blueprint, while Aristotle tailored his ethical principles to the demands of human nature.

Aristotle's ethical writings, consisting of the *Eudemian Ethics,* the *Nicomachean Ethics,* and the *Politics,* all edited by his disciples from his lecture notes, constitute the first systematic investigation of the foundations of ethics. Since the *Eudemian Ethics* is superseded by the *Nicomachean Ethics* and the *Politics* is an extension of his ethical principles to social regulation, this discussion will be confined to the ideas contained in the *Nicomachean Ethics.*

In the latter work, Aristotle's main purpose was to define the subject matter and methodology of philosophical ethics. In doing so, he both drew upon and revised the beliefs and values of the Greek society of his time. Aristotle begins his study by searching for the common feature of all things said to be good and, in contrast with Plato, who held that there is a Form of Good in which all good things "participate," Aristotle concludes that there are many different senses of "good," each of which must be defined separately for the limited area in which it applies. Each such "good" is pursued by a specific practical art or science, such as economics, military strategy, medicine, or shipbuilding. But the ends of these particular disciplines can be arranged in order of importance, so that the supreme good can be identified with the goal of the most general practical science to which the others are subordinate. On an individual level, this all-inclusive science is ethics; on a social level, it is politics. The end of ethics is personal happiness and that of politics is the general welfare, and since the good of the whole ranks above that of the part, personal ethics is subordinate to politics. However, this principle does not entail, for Aristotle, that the individual must sacrifice his interests to those of the community, except under unusual conditions such as war, because he assumed that the needs of both normally coincide.

Aristotle identifies the supreme good with "happiness," which he defines as the exercise of natural human faculties in accordance with virtue. His next task is to define virtue as a skill appropriate to a specific faculty, and he distinguishes two classes of virtues—intellectual and moral. There are five intellectual faculties, from which arise art, science, intuition, reasoning, and practical wisdom. He offers a long list of moral virtues, defining each as the mean between the extremes of either emotion or tendencies to action. For instance, courage is the mean between the excess and the deficiency of the emotion of fear, temperance is the mean between the tendencies to eat and drink too much or too little, justice is the mean with respect to the distribution of goods or of punishments. The bulk of the *Nicomachean Ethics* contains detailed analyses of the criteria of specific moral virtues. The final result of Aristotle's investigations is the definition of happiness or the good life as activity in accordance with virtue, and thus as the harmonious fulfillment of man's natural tendencies.

SUMMARY: SOCRATES, PLATO, AND ARISTOTLE. Returning to the central problems of ethical theory, one may hazard an estimation of the contributions of Socrates, Plato, and Aristotle to their clarification. Socrates was the first to recognize the importance of analyzing the meaning of good, right, just, and virtuous, and of articulating the standards for ascribing these properties. Plato charted a spiritualistic direction for finding the answers in a realm of timeless ideals, while Aristotle located the answers in the scientific study of biology, psychology, and politics. Good, for Plato, means resemblance to the pure Form, or universal model of goodness, which serves as the standard for all value judgments. Actions are right, laws are just, and people are virtuous to the degree to which they conform to the ideal model. For Aristotle, good means the achievement of the goals at which human beings naturally aim, the balanced and rational satisfaction of desires to which he gives the name "happiness." Right action, just laws, and virtuous character are the means of achieving individual and social well-being. All three philosophers agree in identifying individual good with social good and in defining moral concepts such as justice and virtue in terms of the achievement of good.

Perfect clarity about what constitutes

moral perfection is no more of this world

than is moral perfection itself.

Moral Responsibility. The concept of moral responsibility that acquired crucial importance in later Christian thought was only obliquely considered by Plato and more fully, although inconclusively, dealt with by Aristotle. Plato, who identified virtue with philosophical understanding, concluded that "no one does evil voluntarily," so that wrong action is always due to intellectual error. Aristotle recognized that intellectual error must be distinguished from moral vice, since the former, unlike the latter, is involuntary. In order to distinguish punishable evil from innocent mistakes, he explained vice as due to wrong desire as well as poor judgment. The will, for Aristotle, is rationally guided desire, formed by moral education and training. But since even voluntary action is determined by natural tendencies and early training, Aristotle searched for an additional factor to account for the freedom of choice necessary for moral responsibility. He thought he found that factor in deliberation, the consideration of reasons for and against a course of action. The further question, as to whether, when an agent deliberates, he has any choice of and consequently any responsibility for the outcome of his deliberation, was not considered by Aristotle and remains an unsettled issue between determinists and libertarians. In general, the concepts of free will and moral responsibility did not become matters of great concern until the rise of Christianity, when people became preoccupied with otherworldly rewards and punishments for moral conduct.

Hellenistic and Roman Ethics

During the two millennia from the death of Aristotle in the fourth century B.C. to the rise of modern philosophy in the seventeenth century A.D., the interests of ethical thinkers shifted from theoretical to practical ethics, so that little advance was made in the clarification of the meanings of ethical concepts, while, on the other hand, new conceptions of the goals of human life and new codes of conduct were fashioned. The philosophical schools of Skepticism, Stoicism, Epicureanism, and Neoplatonism that set the ethical tone of Hellenistic and Roman thought offered a type of intellectual guidance that was more like religious teaching than like scientific inquiry and paved the way for the conquests of Christianity. The popular conception of philosophy as an attitude of indifference to misfortune applies best to this period, in which philosophy and religion were nearly indistinguishable.

The subtlety of Socrates' thought is attested to by the variety of schools that developed out of his teaching. Plato and, through Plato, Aristotle probably represent the Socratic influence most completely. But the Stoics, Epicureans, and Skeptics also owed their guiding principles to Socrates. Aristippus of Cyrene, at first a disciple of Socrates, founded the school of Cyrenaicism, which followed the simple hedonistic principle that pleasure is the only good. Antisthenes, another Socratic disciple, founded the Cynic school on the apparently opposite principle that the good life is one of indifference to both pleasure and pain. The Cynics, of whom Diogenes was the most renowned, rejected the comforts of civilization and lived alone in the forests, like the dogs after whom they named themselves. Cyrenaicism developed into Epicureanism, and Cynicism into Stoicism. Soon after the death of Aristotle, Pyrrho of Elis initiated the philosophy of Skepticism, influenced by both the Sophist and the Socratic criticisms of conventional beliefs. According to Skepticism, no judgments, either of fact or of value, can be adequately proved, so that the proper philosophical attitude to take toward the actions of others is one of tolerant detachment, and toward one's own actions, extreme caution. In the second century B.C., the leaders of Plato's Academy, Arcesilaus and Carneades, adopted Skepticism, and Carneades developed a theory of probability which he applied to ethical judgments. During this period, the Peripatetic school at Aristotle's Lyceum continued the Aristotelian tradition until it merged finally with Stoicism.

EPICUREANISM. Epicurus (c. 341–270 B.C.) founded one of the two dominant philosophical schools of the era between the death of Aristotle and the rise of Christianity. The other dominant school was, of course, Stoicism. These two traditions are often thought of as diametrical opposites, yet it may plausibly be argued that the differences between them were more verbal than substantial. Both views of life were fundamentally pessimistic, directed more toward escape from pain than toward the positive improvement of the human condition. Both encouraged individual withdrawal from the public arena of struggle for economic and political reform, in favor of personal self-mastery and independence of social conditions. The later Roman Stoics modified this extreme individualism and placed more stress on civic duties, but even they preached resignation to the imperfections of social organization rather than efforts at improvement.

Epicurus based his ethics on the atomistic materialism of Democritus, to which he added the important modification of indeterminism by postulating a tendency of the atoms that make up the human body—and particularly its "soul atoms"—to swerve unpredictably from their normal paths, resulting in unpredictable human actions. In this way, Epicurus thought he could account for freedom of the will. He assumed that freedom of choice of action is incompatible with the deterministic principle that all events are necessary results of antecedent causes. But this identification of freedom with pure chance seems to entail that a capricious person is more free than a rational and principled person, and such a conclusion would contradict Epicurus's own vision of moral life. For Epicurus's main difference with his Cyrenaic predecessors lay in his conviction that, by the use of reason, one could plan one's life and sacrifice momentary pleasures for long-run benefit. Like the Cyrenaics, Epicurus held that pleasure is the single standard of good. But he distinguished "natural pleasures," which are moderate and healthful, from "unnatural" satiation of greed and lust. His name for moderate and natural pleasure was *ataraxia,* gentle motions in the body which he regarded as the physiological explanation of pleasure. He proposed, as the ideal way of life, a relaxed, leisurely existence, consisting in moderate indulgence of the appetites, cultivation of the intellect, and conversation with friends, which is how Epicurus himself lived and taught in his famous garden. Two centuries later, Epicureanism was established in Rome by Lucretius (c. 99–55 B.C.), whose influential poem *On the Nature of Things* helped to spread Epicureanism among the Roman aristocracy.

STOICISM. Stoicism was by far the most impressive intellectual achievement of Hellenistic and Roman culture prior to Christianity, providing an ethical framework within which metaphysical speculation, natural science, psychology, and social thought could flourish to such a high degree that Stoicism has not unjustly been identified in the public mind with philosophy itself, that is, with the distinctively "philosophical" attitude toward life. Like every great tradition, Stoicism evolved through many stages and thus comprehends a great variety of specific beliefs. Historians generally distinguish three main stages of its development:

(1) The early Stoa—which derived its name from the portico, or porch, on which the early Stoics lectured—whose important figures were Zeno of Cyprus, Cleanthes, and Chrysippus. Chrysippus made the most substantial contributions to Stoic logic and theory of knowledge. The early Stoics remained close to Cynicism in recommending withdrawal from community life so as to render oneself independent of material comforts, social fashions, and the opinions of one's fellow men. Their ethical goal was the achievement of apathy, the state of indifference to pleasure and pain. They considered reason to be the distinctive nature of man and proposed that one should live "according to nature" and thus according to rational principles of conduct.

Aristotle identifies the supreme good with "happiness," which he defines as the exercise of natural human faculties in accordance with virtue.

With the Stoics, the concept of duty acquired a central place in ethics, as conformity to moral rules which they identified with laws of human nature. The later Roman Stoics developed this doctrine into the theory of natural law on which Roman jurisprudence was largely based. Most of the Stoics were materialists, yet imbued with natural piety, and many identified God with the Logos of Heraclitus, as a universal "fire" or energy of nature embodied in its lawlike processes. Many were fatalists, maintaining that man can control his destiny only by resigning himself to it, a principle that contrasted vividly with their emphasis on rationality and self-control. They sought to reconcile this extreme determinism with freedom and moral responsibility by means of the Aristotelian distinction between external and internal causation, thus suggesting that the free man is one who, in understanding the necessity of what befalls him, accepts it and thus freely chooses it, a solution echoed in modern thought by Hegel's definition of freedom as the recognition of necessity.

(2) The middle Stoics, notably Panaetius and Posidonius, brought Stoicism to Rome, shaping the doctrine to the political-mindedness of the Romans by modifying its extreme individualism and stressing the importance of social duties.

(3) The late Stoics, Seneca, Epictetus, Marcus Aurelius, and, to some extent, Cicero—who accepted only certain parts of Stoic doctrine—developed the ideal of a "cosmopolis," or universal brotherhood of man, in which all men would be recognized as having equal rights and responsibilities, an ideal which Christianity

absorbed into its conception of the "City of God" and which, in the modern age, Kant made the cornerstone of his system of ethics.

NEOPLATONISM. Epicureanism offered a way of life that was open only to the leisure class. Stoicism appealed to highly reflective men of all classes, as evidenced by the fact that the two great figures of late Stoicism were the educated slave Epictetus and the emperor Marcus Aurelius. However, both philosophical views could interest only those of a sufficiently high level of education and thoughtful temperament to place intellectual values above all others. As the Roman Empire declined, and reason seemed powerless to solve the intense economic and social problems of the empire, an atmosphere of pessimism and disaffection with reason began to prevail, a situation which Gilbert Murray has described as "a failure of nerve." Interest increased in finding supernatural routes to salvation of the kind offered by various religious cults, and even in the intellectual schools the study of logic and natural science declined in favor of a search for psychological means of escape from suffering. The philosophy of Neoplatonism fashioned by Plotinus (c. 204–270) offered an intellectual road to salvation, while early Christianity paved an emotional and ritualistic highway toward the same destination. Later, these two roads converged.

Plotinus lectured in Rome and, after his death, his notes were edited by his disciple Porphyry, forming the work entitled *Enneads*—so called because of its division into chapters of nine sections each. Plotinus developed one strain of Plato's thought, the ascetic mysticism of the passages on the Form of the Good in the *Republic* and the *Symposium* and the pantheistic metaphysics of the *Timaeus*. According to Plotinus, the world is a series of emanations or overflowings of the One, the ineffable and ultimate reality of which every determinate thing is a part. The One is so transcendent as to be indescribable, "the One, transcending intellect, transcends knowing." But if the One cannot be described, it can at least be negatively characterized in terms of what it is not, namely, that it is not limited by any finite properties. This negative characterization of the One was the source of Christian "negative theology," the description of God in terms of the denial of all modes of limitation.

The One emanates intelligible Forms or Platonic Ideas, out of which the World Soul produces individual souls which in turn emanate lower beings in a process that approaches, but does not quite reach, pure matter. Matter, as total formlessness, is so far from true being that it does not exist. Identifying evil with matter or formlessness, Plotinus concluded that evil does not exist in an absolute sense, but only as incompleteness or lack of good. This account of evil as having no positive existence was later adopted by Augustine and most subsequent theologians.

Since Plotinus, following Plato, equated goodness with reality and evil with unreality or distance from the One, it followed that virtue consists in purging the soul of reliance on sensual pleasures and imagery, so that it can ascend the ladder of being and return to its source in the One. The culmination of this process of purification through self-denial is the mystical experience of reunion with the One, which Plotinus describes—having experienced it himself at least four times—as "the flight of the Alone to the Alone." Thus virtue, for Plotinus as later for Augustine, is not its own reward but is a means to a metaphysical state of blessedness. In the words of the historian W. T. Jones, "Like other men of his time, Plotinus found this world a sea of troubles and a vale of tears; like them he sought to leave it; and like them he found perfect peace only in otherworldliness." How much of this view was absorbed into Christian, Islamic, and Judaic theology can hardly be overestimated, although the influence of Platonism on Judaism was mainly through Philo Judaeus (fl. 20 B.C.–A.D. 40), an Alexandrian Jew and contemporary of Jesus, who combined elements of Stoicism with a Platonistic interpretation of Judaic theology and ethics.

(The above section on Hellenistic and Roman ethics was prepared in collaboration with Professor Richard O. Haynes of the University of Hawaii.)

Medieval Ethics

The rise of Christian philosophy, out of a fusion of Greco-Roman thought with Judaism and elements of other Middle Eastern religions, produced a new era in the history of ethics, although one that was prepared for by Stoicism and Neoplatonism. The Stoic concern with justice and self-mastery, and the Neoplatonic search for reunion with the source of all being, were combined in early Christian philosophy with the Judaic belief in a personal God, whose commandments are the primal source of moral authority and whose favor is the ultimate goal of human life. Two sources of ethical standards, human reason and divine will, were juxtaposed in one system of ethics, and the tension between them was reflected in conflicting sectarian interpretations of theological principles.

From the second to the fourth century, Christianity spread through the Roman Empire, offering the poor and the oppressed a hope for otherworldly happiness in compensation for their earthly suffering, and thus a way of life with which the more pessimistic and intellectualist schools of philosophy could not compete. By the fourth century, Christianity dominated Western civilization and had absorbed the main ideas and values of the secular schools of thought, as well as rival religions such as Manichaeism, Mithraism, and Judaism. Having converted the masses, it was time to win over the intelligentsia, and doing this required the hammering out of an explicit and plausible system of metaphysical and ethical principles. This task was performed by the Church Fathers, Clement of Alexandria, Origen, Tertullian, Ambrose, and, most completely and authoritatively, by Augustine.

AUGUSTINE. St. Augustine (354–430), born near Carthage, the son of a pagan father and a Christian mother, was first a Manichaean and later became converted to Christianity. He rose in the church to become bishop of Hippo and helped to settle the doctrinal strife among the many Christian sects by constructing a system of theology, ethics, and theory of knowledge that soon became the authoritative framework of Christian thought, modified but not supplanted by subsequent church philosophers. Augustine's major works, *Confessions, The City of God, Enchiridion,* and *On Freedom of the Will,* wove together threads of Stoic ethics, Neoplatonic metaphysics, and the Judaeo-Christian doctrine of revelation and redemption into a many-colored fabric of theology. With Augustine, theology became the bridge between philosophy and revealed religion, the one end anchored in reason and the other in faith, and ethics became a blend of the pursuit of earthly well-being with preparation of the soul for eternal salvation.

Like the Neoplatonists, Augustine rejected almost entirely the claims of bodily pleasures and community life, maintaining, as St. Paul had done, that happiness is impossible in this world, which serves only as a testing ground for reward and punishment in the afterlife. Augustine inherited the Neoplatonic conception of virtue as the purgation of the soul of all dependence on material comforts in preparation for reunion with God. Against the Stoic and Aristotelian reliance on reason as the source of virtue, Augustine maintained that such apparently admirable traits as prudence, justice, wisdom, and fortitude—the four cardinal virtues identified by Plato and stressed by Stoics and Christians—are of no moral worth when not inspired by Christian faith. With the pessimistic view of life characteristic of an era of wars, political collapse, and economic decline—a view already apparent in the Stoic, Epicurean, and Neoplatonic modes of withdrawal from social responsibilities—intensified by his personal sense of guilt and worthlessness, Augustine saw life on earth as a punishment for Adam's original sin. "For what flood of eloquence can suffice to detail the miseries of this life?" he laments in *The City of God.*

Nature. The tension between natural and supernatural values in Augustine's ethical thought shows itself most clearly in his ambivalent attitude toward nature. Nature, as God's creation, must be unqualifiedly good. Natural evils are only apparently evil, and in the long run they contribute to the fulfillment of divine purpose. Natural evil is simply imperfection that makes variety possible and thus, when viewed on a cosmic scale, does not exist at all. On the other hand, since man must be held morally responsible for his sins, human sin cannot be so easily explained away as incompleteness that promotes the cosmic good. Moreover, it is man's bodily desires that tempt him to sin. Without the aid of divine grace, the promptings of human nature, whether impulsive or rational, lead only to vice and damnation. Augustine resolves this paradoxical view of human nature by holding that man, unlike other natural species, was endowed by his Creator with free will and thus with the capacity to choose between good and evil. Through the original sin of Adam he has chosen evil, and it is for this reason, rather than because of any flaw in his original construction, that he is irresistibly inclined to further sin.

Free Will and Divine Foreknowledge. If Augustine's dual conception of nature is explained by his concept of free will, the latter contains new difficulties. The problem of free will is critical in Christian ethics, which emphasizes responsibility and punishment. The Greek ideal of practical reason ensuring physical and mental well-being was supplanted by the ideal of purification of the soul through suffering, renunciation, and humble obedience to divine will.

Where the practice of virtue produces well-being as its natural consequence, as in the Greek view, virtue carries with it its own reward in accordance with the causal processes of nature, so that causal necessity and moral desert are not merely compatible; they normally coincide. But in the Christian view, causal necessity and moral responsibility seem incompatible, for the choice between good and evil is made by the soul, independently of natural processes, and its reward or punishment is independent of the natural effects of human actions. Man is punished or rewarded to the degree to which he voluntarily obeys or disobeys the commands of God. In the Greek view, man suffers from the natural consequences of his mistakes, but in the Christian view, no matter what the natural consequences of his actions, he is held to account for the state of his soul. It is his motives and not his actions that count in assessment of his moral responsibility, and the primary motive is his desire for, or his turning away from, God.

Responsibility is thus transferred from the consequences of a person's actions to the state of his soul. Yet if the soul is created by God, and not subject to its temporary owner's control, then in what sense can man be said to have freedom of choice between good and evil? Augustine describes the soul that chooses evil as "defective," but if so, is not the Creator of the defective soul responsible for its deficiency? In absolution of God, Augustine argues that a defect is not a positive entity, thus not a created thing and not attributable to a creator—a terminological escape that is vulnerable to the objection that, on such grounds, a man who stabs another produces in his victim a deficiency rather than a positive state and therefore is not responsible for his "nonexistent" product.

Augustine's concept of free will is further complicated by his support of the theological principle of divine omniscience, which entails foreknowledge by God of human decisions. The term "predestination," used by later theologians and notably by the Protestant reformers, suggests a determinism that Augustine rejects in his criticism of fatalism. For Augustine, God knows what man will choose to do and makes it possible for man to act on his free choices but does not compel him to any course of action. To the obvious question of how God can know in advance what has not been destined or causally necessitated, Augustine replies by means of his subtle analysis of time. God has knowledge, not of what we are compelled to do but of what we freely choose to do, because his knowledge is not the kind of advance knowledge that is based on causal processes but is due to the fact that, in the mind of God, we have already made our decisions. All of past and future time is spread out in the specious present of the divine mind, so that what, from our limited standpoint, would be prediction of the future is, for God, simply direct awareness of contemporaneous events.

Distinctions Among Ethical Concepts. While Augustine's ethical writings are mainly concerned with the substantive problem of how to achieve redemption, rather than with the clarification of ethical concepts, much of his writing is philosophical in our strict sense, in that it suggests solutions to conceptual or metaethical problems of meaning and method. Augustine opposed the classical tendency to define the moral concepts of rightness and virtue in terms of individual and social well-being and interpreted moral right and virtue as obedience to divine authority. The concept of good is split into a moral and a practical sense. Good as fulfillment of natural tendencies is subordinated to eternal beatitude, the fulfillment of the aspirations of the virtuous soul. Freedom and responsibility are interpreted as internal states of the soul and as excluding, rather than (as for Aristotle) presupposing, causal necessity.

FOURTH TO THIRTEENTH CENTURIES. From Augustine in the fourth century to Abelard in the eleventh century, Christian, Islamic, and Judaic philosophy was dominated by Neoplatonic mysticism and preoccupied with faith and salvation. The outstanding figure of this period was John Scotus Erigena (c. 810–c. 877), whose conception of good was the Platonic one of approximation to timeless being and whose view of life as issuing from and returning to God bordered on heretical pantheism.

With the Stoics, the concept of duty

acquired a central place in ethics,

as conformity to moral rules

which they identified with laws of human nature.

By the eleventh century, interest in rational philosophical speculation had revived, and even those Schoolmen like Bernard of Clairvaux (1091–1153), who continued to defend religious mysticism and denounced reliance upon reason as inimical to faith, nevertheless employed philosophical arguments to refute contrary opinions. Augustine had asserted that one must "believe in order to understand," and St. Anselm (1033–1109) took this to mean that faith is not incompatible with reason but, rather, prepares the soul for rational understanding. The main issues among philosophers of this time were the relation between faith and reason, and the nature of universals.

However, Peter Abelard (1079–1142), an extraordinarily original and independent thinker whose vibrant personality reveals itself in his philosophical writings, rediscovered some of the unsolved problems of ethical philosophy. Abelard brought into clear view the distinctive features of Christian ethics implicit in Augustine's work, in particular, the split between moral and prudential concepts that sharply separates Christian ethics from Greek ethics. Abelard held that morality is an inner quality, a property of motive or intention rather than of the consequences of one's actions, a principle that was later stressed by the Reformation and attained its fullest expression in the ethical system of Immanuel Kant. A somewhat heretical corollary follows from Abelard's principle, namely that, as Étienne Gilson puts it, "Those who do not know the Gospel obviously commit no fault in not believing in Jesus Christ," and it seems clear from all this that Christian faith need not be the foundation for moral rules. Abelard concluded that one can attain to virtue through reason as well as through faith.

THOMAS AQUINAS. The towering figure of medieval philosophy is, of course, Thomas Aquinas (c. 1225–

1274), whose philosophical aim was to reconcile Aristotelian science and philosophy with Augustinian theology. The way to this achievement had already been prepared by the revival in western Europe of interest in Aristotle, whose thought had been preserved and elaborated by Muslim and Jewish scholars such as Avicenna, Averroës, and Maimonides and had been brought to the attention of Christendom by the commentaries of Albert the Great. It remained for Aquinas to prove the compatibility of Aristotelian naturalism with Christian dogma and to construct a unified view of nature, man, and God. This he undertook with remarkable success in his *Summa Theologica* and *Summa Contra Gentiles*.

To a large degree, Aquinas's union of Aristotelianism with Christianity consisted in arguing for the truth of both and in refuting arguments of his predecessors and contemporaries that purported to show their incompatibility. Aristotle's ethics was relativistic, rational, and prudential; Augustinian ethics was absolutist, grounded on faith, and independent of consequences. Now one of these views is totally misguided, or else there must be room for two different systems of ethical concepts and principles. Aquinas adopted the latter alternative and divided the meaning of ethical concepts into two domains, "natural" and "theological." Natural virtues, adequately accounted for by Aristotle, can be attained by proper training and the exercise of practical reason, while theological virtues—faith, hope, and love—require faith and divine grace. Similarly, he distinguished two highest goods, or paramount goals of life, worldly happiness and eternal beatitude (which has precedence); the former is achieved through natural virtue and the latter is achieved through the church and its sacraments. Aquinas thus expressed a considerably more optimistic attitude than did Augustine toward the possibility of improving man's lot on earth through knowledge of nature and intelligent action. This helped to prepare the climate for the rebirth of natural science, whose first stirrings were felt in the thirteenth century.

Natural Law. At the center of Thomistic ethics was the concept of natural law. The medieval doctrine of natural law, stemming from Aristotle's teleological conception of nature and from the Stoic identification of human reason with the Logos, was a fusion of naturalistic Greek ethics with monotheistic theology. On this view, the promptings of informed reason and moral conscience represent an inherent tendency in the nature of man, and conformity to this nature fulfills both the cosmic plan of the Creator and the direct commands of God revealed in the Scriptures. Natural law is the divine law as discovered by reason, and therefore the precepts of the church and the Bible, and scientific knowledge of the universal needs and tendencies of man, provide

complementary rather than competing standards of ethical judgment. Where conflicts between science and religious authority arise, they must be due to inadequate understanding of science, since church authority and dogma are infallible.

The Thomistic unification of scientific and religious ethics in the doctrine of natural law—further elaborated in subtle detail by Francisco Suárez and other legalists—was an effective way of making room, within the religious enterprise of achieving salvation, for the practical business of everyday living in pursuit of personal and social well-being. The ideological supremacy of theology was maintained, but the doctrine of natural law purported to guarantee reliable knowledge of nature, psychology, and political economy. The weakness in this system was that it placed religious barriers in the way of scientific advance, tending to sanctify and render immune from revision whichever scientific principles seemed most congenial to theology, such as instinct theory in psychology, vitalistic biology, and geocentric astronomy.

Augustine describes the soul that chooses evil as "defective," but if so, is not the Creator of the defective soul responsible for its deficiency?

Free Will. Aquinas's account of freedom and moral responsibility was, in general form, similar to that of Augustine, maintaining the compatibility of free will with predestination or divine foreknowledge. Aquinas also maintained the compatibility of free will with causal determinism, thus dealing with the problem on the level of prudential ethics as well on as the theological level of grace and salvation. Aquinas's solution makes effective use of Aristotle's analysis of choice and voluntary action in terms of internal causality and deliberation, and it identifies free will with rational self-determination rather than with the absence of causal influences. On the other hand, Aquinas's concept of freedom is, as a result, more relativistic than Augustine's, and, while it explains the conditions under which an agent may be held responsible for his *actions*—namely, the conditions of desire, knowledge, and deliberation—it does not meet the further issue of whether these faculties that determine action are within the control of the agent, that is, whether a person can freely choose the habits and desires that determine his actions. Later writers, particularly Protestant theologians, tended to interpret Augustine as stressing predestination and Aquinas as stressing free will, but it may be argued to the contrary, that Augustine's conception of free will as an inexplicable and supernatural thrust of the soul allows the agent more independence of his formed character than does Aquinas's, but by that very token, Aquinas's account is more congenial to a scientific view of man.

Subsequent scholastic philosophy, from the fourteenth to the seventeenth centuries, added little to the clarification of metaethical problems, but it probed further into the relation between intellect and will as sources of human and divine action. John Duns Scotus (c. 1266–1308), William of Ockham (c. 1285–1349), and Nicholas of Autrecourt (fl. c. 1335) developed the voluntaristic doctrine that the will is free in a more absolute sense than that accounted for by Aquinas, in that it is independent both of external causality and of determination by the intellect—that is, by the agent's knowledge of what is right and good. Their view in one way strengthened the case for religious faith as against scientific reason, at least in matters of ethical judgment, but, in another way, it helped stimulate an attitude of individualism and independence of authority that prepared the ground for the secular and humanistic ethics of the modern age.

Early Modern Ethics

Philosophy seems to flourish best in periods of rapid social transformation, when the conceptual framework of a culture crumbles, requiring a re-examination of basic concepts, principles, and standards of value. The sixteenth and seventeenth centuries, which saw the demise of medieval feudalism and ushered in the modern age of industrial democracy, were, like the fifth and fourth centuries B.C., a period of intense philosophical ferment. In both cases, the preceding century witnessed the demolition of traditional beliefs, while the succeeding century was one of systematic reconstruction. The development of commerce and industry, the discovery of new regions of the world, the Reformation, the Copernican and Galilean revolutions in science, and the rise of strong secular governments demanded new principles of individual conduct and of social organization.

In the sixteenth century, Francis Bacon demolished the logic and methodology of medieval Scholasticism. Erasmus, Luther, and Calvin, while attempting to strengthen the bond between religion and ethics, undermined the elaborate structure of canon law based on the moral authority of the medieval church, and Machiavelli dynamited the bridge between religious ethics and political science. The task of reconstruction in philosophy was performed in the seventeenth century by Descartes, Hobbes, Leibniz, Spinoza, and Locke.

HOBBES. Modern ethical theory began with Thomas Hobbes (1588–1679). The advent of Galilean natural science had challenged the traditional notions, supported by authority, of purpose, plan, and value in the physical world; it cast into doubt the doctrine of natural law and nullified the anthropomorphic assumptions of theology. New standards of ethical judgment had to be found, not in the cosmic plan of nature or in scriptural revelations of the divine will but in man himself, either in his biological structure, or in his agreements with his fellow men, or in the social and political institutions that he creates. Thus were born, simultaneously and to the same parent, the ethical philosophies of naturalism, cultural relativism, and subjectivism, respectively.

Born in a time of international and domestic strife, Hobbes regarded the preservation of life as the paramount goal of human action and constructed his system of ethics and political science in his major work, *Leviathan,* with the principle of self-preservation as its cornerstone. His enthusiasm for Galileo's physics and his conviction that all fields of knowledge could be modeled on this universal science (following the method of Euclid's geometry) may have suggested to him that the drive to self-preservation is the biological analogue of the Galilean principle of inertia. Hobbes conceived of man as a complex system of particles in motion and attempted to deduce ethical laws from the principle of self-preservation. He offers, however, two formulations of this principle, the first of which is his foundation of ethics, while the second is, in effect, the repudiation of ethics.

The tendency to self-preservation, according to Hobbes, expresses itself in the quest for social harmony through peace-keeping institutions and practices or, alternatively, in the aggressive drive toward power over one's fellow men. Thus he formulates his "first and fundamental" principle in two parts, the "law of nature" to the effect that "Every man ought to endeavor to peace as far as he has hope of obtaining it," and the "right of nature," that "when he cannot obtain it, he may seek and use all the helps and advantages of war." Which of these two forms of the principle of self-preservation should be applied depends, for Hobbes, on whether the agent finds, himself in a well-organized society or in a "state of nature" in which he cannot expect cooperative behavior on the part of his fellow men. Thus, the concept of ethical law applies to social agreements and commitments, while that of rights applies to the exercise of natural powers. In the state of nature one has a right to do whatever one has the power to do.

From his fundamental law of nature, Hobbes derives a number of specific rules that prescribe the means of establishing and maintaining a peaceful society, the primary means being the willingness to make or, if already made, to maintain the social contract in which individual rights or powers are surrendered to a sovereign in return for the guarantee of personal security. The state is thus the artificial creation of reasonable men, a "Leviathan" that maintains peace by means of power relinquished to it by its citizens. Once such a commonwealth has been established by contract or conquest, other general rules of conduct follow in accordance with Hobbes's theory of psychology. To restrain the natural human tendencies to envy, mistrust, self-aggrandizement, and aggression, the virtues of accommodation, gratitude, clemency, obedience to authority, and respect for the equal rights of others are recommended by "laws of nature" as effective means of ensuring social harmony.

Thomas Aquinas's philosophical aim was

to reconcile Aristotelian science and philosophy

with Augustinian theology.

Reason and Ethical Laws. Hobbes's use of the term "laws of nature" in referring to ethical principles is to be distinguished sharply from the medieval concept of natural law that he rejected. There is, for Hobbes, no moral order in the cosmos, nor any natural prompting toward justice and sympathy for others in human nature. Man, like the rest of nature, is a system of particles perpetually moving and colliding in accordance with physical laws whereby direction and intensity of motion are determined solely by preponderance of force. Yet reason plays a role in human action that distinguishes man from the rest of the world machine. Ethical rules are "precepts, found out by reason, by which a man is forbidden to do that which is destructive of his life or taketh away the means of preserving the same."

In his mechanistic physiology, Hobbes explained reason as a mechanical process in the brain consisting in the combining and separating particles that serve as representations of objects and qualities; thus, cognitive processes are a special type of physical process, governed by the same laws. But on this mechanistic view of man, it is difficult for Hobbes to account for the prescriptive character he attributes to ethical laws as distinguished from physical laws. Throughout his discussion, Hobbes vacillates between a conception of ethics as a branch of physical science that describes the behavior of human mechanisms and the quite different conception of ethics as rational advice on how to get along with one's fellow men by consciously restraining one's aggressive impulses. Both sides of the *nomos–phusis* controversy between the Sophists and Plato are represented in Hobbes's thought, and he cites both social authority and prudential reason as sources of ethical obligation. Moral virtue consists in conformity to custom and law, in opposition to the natural aggressiveness that equips a man for survival in the state of nature, yet the "precepts found out by reason" provide a natural basis for the establishment of customs and laws.

Desire and Will. Hobbes's account of desire and will is designed to bridge the gap between rational directives and physical laws. He defines good as "any object of desire" and desire as the motion toward an object that results from physiological processes ("endeavors") within the body. To act rationally does not entail freedom to act contrary to one's physiological impulses, since rationality or deliberation is simply the mediating processes of the central nervous system. The will is not a supernatural power controlling desires but simply the last stage of deliberation that eventuates in overt action, and thus is itself a neurological process governed by laws of physics. Freedom of the will from causal influences is, for Hobbes, a senseless combination of concepts; freedom is the "absence of external impediments" to the will. It is the person who is free or unfree, and not his will, since his freedom consists in the determination of his overt actions by his will rather than by external forces. Yet this mechanistic account of the will seems in paradoxical contrast with his subjectivist account of civil law as deriving its obligatory force from the arbitrary will of the sovereign, an account which comes dangerously close to the Aristotelian and Augustinian notions of the will as a "first cause."

Naturalism and Nonnaturalism. The importance of Hobbes to modern ethical theory is inestimable. In freeing ethics from bondage to revealed theology and its anthropomorphic view of nature, Hobbes brought philosophy back to the problems with which it had begun to wrestle in the time of Socrates and the Sophists, and of which it had lost sight for a millennium. At the same time, he raised the understanding of these problems to a higher level, profiting both from the Christian insight that moral principles have an obligatory force and from the refinements of scientific method introduced by Bacon, Galileo, and Descartes.

If ethics was to become a body of reliable knowledge, it must be grounded on objective laws of psychology and biology, rather than on tradition, sentiment, and church authority. On the other hand, if nature and its scientific description are ethically neutral, then ethics is to be contrasted with science and purged of references to nature, just as natural science must be purged of references to ethical values. In that case, ethical principles must be understood as subjective expressions of emotion and desire, and not as objectively verifiable laws. This dilemma has plagued philosophy ever since, and, if it was not resolved by Hobbes, at least his thought was not completely impaled on either horn but only a bit on both.

EARLY INTUITIONISTS. Reaction to Hobbes's attack on the objectivity of ethical judgment was immediate. The doctrine of natural law and its vision of nature as a moral system were defended in a new form by a group of scholars at Cambridge who became known as the Cambridge Platonists, principally Ralph Cudworth (1617–1688) and Henry More (1614–1687). They maintained that moral principles are self-evident truths, as certain and immutable as the laws of mathematics. Richard Cumberland (1631–1718) attempted to deduce all the principles of ethics from a single "Law of Nature" that later became the cornerstone of utilitarian ethics, namely, the law that all actions should promote the common good. Nicholas Malebranche (1638–1715) developed the Cartesian theory of ethics as a deductive system but gave it an Augustinian slant, attributing to God the sole power to translate knowledge of ethical truth into action. Malebranche realized that the analogy between ethics and mathematics fails to explain the connection between ethics and action, and so he made a virtue of this defect by means of his "Occasionalist" account of causality as divine intervention. Samuel Clarke (1675–1729) developed an intuitionist theory of "natural religion" similar to that of Cudworth and More, holding that the quality of right or "fitness" is an intrinsic property of actions that the mind can perceive as directly as it perceives geometrical relations.

SPINOZA. Born in the Netherlands of Jewish refugees from the Spanish Inquisition, Benedict Spinoza (1632–1677) combined Descartes's faith in the capacity of reason to govern action with Hobbes's mechanistic theory of psychology to express a scientific vision of nature as a unified system of laws. In his *Ethics Demonstrated in the Geometric Manner* Spinoza, like Hobbes but with more formal precision, derived the principles of physics, psychology, and ethics from metaphysical axioms.

The first principle of psychology for Spinoza, as for Hobbes, is the drive to self-preservation and self-aggrandizement, corresponding to the physical principle of inertia. But Spinoza's unique achievement was to derive, as the logical corollary of this egoistic psychology, a rational, humane, and cultivated way of life. A strict determinist in his metaphysics and a thorough naturalist in his ethics, Spinoza held that every event is deducible from antecedent causes and concluded that ethical right is identical with causal necessity. The rules of conduct are therefore laws of human nature, obeyed by all but obeyed blindly by the selfish person enslaved by his passions while understood and accepted by the free man who, in achieving a vision of the necessary order of all things, experiences the "intellectual love of God" that provides both happiness and moral virtue.

While Spinoza tried more consistently than Hobbes to reduce ethics to psychology and thus to make it a branch of natural science, it has often been contended that his program was self-defeating. For if men cannot help acting in accordance with their desires, and if nothing is objectively good or bad but only appears so to those who do not understand the necessity of all events, then what sense can there be to either prudential or moral rules of conduct? Having banished values from nature, Spinoza, like Hobbes, had to relocate them in human consciousness. But then consciousness must be either a supranatural force that interrupts the causal order of nature—as it was for Descartes—or a part of nature and thus ethically neutral, in which case ethics becomes senseless; or, finally, consciousness is an illusory reflection of physical processes in the body, in which case ethics, too, is illusory. Spinoza and Hobbes vacillated between the last two alternatives although, as we have seen, Hobbes's prescriptivist account of moral right as stemming from the will of an authority may be suspected of having slipped an element of supranatural agency back into the picture.

In their social and political theories, both Spinoza and Hobbes argued for the appraisal of institutions and policies in terms of the satisfaction of human needs rather than of conformity to religious tradition. But Hobbes's conception of force as the basis of law led him to support political authoritarianism, while Spinoza's identification of value and right with rational self-interest enabled him to argue, like Locke, for representative government and maximum civil liberty.

LOCKE. John Locke (1632–1704) is generally regarded as the founder of modern utilitarianism, although his applications of utilitarian ethics to social and political theory were more influential than his analysis of standards of individual conduct. He combined the mathematical model of ethical judgment suggested by Descartes and the Cambridge Platonists with a hedonistic theory of psychology according to which pleasure is the goal of all human action and consequently is the fundamental standard of evaluation. In his *Essay Concerning Human Understanding,* Locke criticizes the doctrine of innate ideas of Descartes and Leibniz, in defense of the principle that all knowledge is founded on experience; he then, somewhat paradoxically, offers an account of ethics as a deductive science in which specific rules of conduct are derived "from self-evident propositions, by necessary consequences as incontestable as those in mathematics." The appearance of paradox dissolves, however, on noting that, for Locke, the formation of the ideas of goodness and justice is due to the sensations of pleasure and pain, and thus ethical concepts are derived from experience although their logical relations are then discoverable by reflective analysis.

Locke follows Hobbes in defining good as the object of desire, but then, assuming that the only property of things which provokes desire is their tendency to produce pleasure or reduce pain, he also defines good as "what has an aptness to produce pleasure in us." Again, like Hobbes, Locke defines moral virtue as conformity to custom and law, but he differs from Hobbes in maintaining that custom and law can in turn be evaluated by the more fundamental standards of utility and natural rights. It is in terms of these more basic standards that Locke justifies representative government and civil liberty.

Locke's main contribution to the clarification of the meaning of ethical concepts was in his distinction between "speculative" and "practical" principles. Speculative knowledge is independent of action, while practical principles (including ethical principles) can be said to be believed and known to be true only insofar as they are acted upon. This distinction accounts for the obligatory force of ethical principles and eliminates the need for a supernatural agency, "free will," to translate belief into action, although it makes it difficult to explain why, if practical principles are "self-evident propositions," we do not all behave in a morally impeccable way. Like Hobbes, Locke ridicules the notion of free will as a semantical absurdity similar to the questions "whether sleep be swift or virtue square." Will is the power of the mind to decide on action, and freedom the power to carry out one's decisions, that is, to get what one wants.

MORAL-SENSE THEORIES. The seventeenth-century philosophers found the connection between self-interest and morality in the threat of punishment—divine, natural, or civil—that coerces the individual to be moral for the sake of self-interest. But it was soon noticed that this connection breaks down wherever the expected benefit to the individual of immoral conduct outweighs the likelihood of punishment and that, if morality is grounded in psychology, then human nature cannot be as aggressively self-centered as the apostles of self-preservation and pursuit of pleasure maintained.

The third earl of Shaftesbury (1671–1713) and Francis Hutcheson (1694–1747) proposed that moral obligation has its source in benevolent affections, such as love and pity, that are as natural and universal as the more aggressive tendencies ("self-affections"), such as envy, greed, and the impulse to self-preservation. Moreover, there is a "moral sense" in man that finds unique satisfaction in actions directed toward the common good. This moral sensibility turns us from the pursuit of pleasure toward the performance of duties toward others and explains our admiration of self-sacrifice independently of external reward or punishment.

Bernard Mandeville (c. 1670–1733), in *The Fable of the Bees,* defended egoistic psychology against this attack and ridiculed the concept of moral conscience as a hypocritical device for maintaining social privileges, a view later echoed by Holbach, Marx, and Nietzsche. Bishop Joseph Butler (1692–1752), whose sermons in defense of Christian morality against the cynicism of Hobbes and Mandeville reveal extraordinary analytical power, argued that benevolence and conscience are as deeply rooted in human nature as is self-love. In adding conscience or intuition of duty to benevolence as the psychological source of moral obligation, Butler lessened the stress of earlier moral-sense theorists on emotion and gave more recognition to the role of rational judgment.

Moral-sense theory, refined further by David Hartley (1705–1757) and Adam Smith (1723–1790), who applied utilitarian ethics to economic theory, achieved its most persuasive formulation in the writings of David Hume.

HUME. David Hume (1711–1776), like Hartley and Smith, combined an emotional account of morality with a utilitarian theory of good. Hume's discussions of ethics in the third part of his *A Treatise of Human Nature* and, more fully, in his *An Enquiry Concerning the Principles of Morals* are attempts to answer the metaethical questions of the meaning of good, right, justice, and virtue; by what standards they are attributed to persons and actions; how it is psychologically possible for men to admire and cultivate morality at the expense of self-interest; and by what rules ethical disputes can be decided in favor of one judgment against another. Despite the clarity and good sense that Hume brings to bear on these topics, his discussion shifts inadvertently from one type of question to another, particularly from questions of meaning to questions of motivation, a shift characteristic of moral-sense theories.

Hume begins his studies of ethical judgment with a search for the meanings of ethical terms. Finding no observable facts or logical relations that answer to our concepts of goodness, justice, and moral virtue, Hume concludes that the function of ethical terms is not to denote qualities or relations but to convey a "sentiment of approbation," so that their meaning is to be found in the feelings of the judge rather than in the object judged. We call things good for the same reason that we call them beautiful: because we find them agreeable. An object is good if it is immediately pleasant, or if it is a useful means for attaining something else that is pleasant. Virtues are qualities that render a person agreeable or useful to himself or to others, whether they are "natural virtues" such as talent, wit, and benevolence or "artificial virtues" like honesty and justice. While judgments as to what is useful in producing pleasure, insofar as they rest on knowledge of causal facts, are within the competence of reason, nevertheless they depend, for their distinctively ethical import, on feeling or taste, since rational knowledge alone is "not sufficient" to produce any moral blame or approbation. "Utility is only a tendency to a certain end; and were the end totally indifferent to us, we should feel the same indifference toward the means. It is requisite a certain *sentiment* should here display itself . . ." (*Enquiry Concerning the Principles of Morals*, Appendix I).

Philosophy seems to flourish best

in periods of rapid social transformation, when the

conceptual framework of a culture crumbles,

requiring a reexamination of basic concepts,

principles, and standards of value.

Thus, according to Hume, there are two possible grounds or standards of evaluation, utility and feeling, the one objective and subject to rational confirmation, the other subjective and personal. The objective standard, unfortunately, applies only to instrumental values and not to ultimate ends. However, the subjectivity of feelings is not cause for despair about achieving agreement on ethical judgments, since the sentiment that motivates them, the disinterested pleasure and approval that we feel in contemplating actions directed toward the welfare of others, is, for Hume as for Butler, a universal tendency in human nature.

Moral Reasons and Psychological Motives. In common with Hobbes and Locke, who justified moral conduct by the fear of punishment, and the earlier moral-sense theorists, who explained moral obligation in terms of the benevolent affections, Hume identifies the psychological motives that influence and often prejudice moral judgments with the logical grounds or reasons for moral judgments. From the premise that, were it not for our natural benevolence, we would not care enough about moral issues to make moral judgments, Hume draws the *non sequitur* that the only evidence that supports such judgments lies in the feeling of approval or disapproval that motivates them.

Hume tends to equate moral virtue with the artificial quality of justice, artificial because it is required only for the protection of property rights in a society in which goods are neither too scarce nor sufficiently abundant. The importance for social harmony of strict conformity to laws renders it dangerous and undesirable to make exceptions in the name of expediency. Consequently, the utility of strict justice outweighs the utility of any possible exceptions. But Hume realized that this rather abstract utilitarian consideration can hardly explain our sense of moral obligation and our admiration for those who demonstrate high moral character. He therefore supplements this account with the notion of "disinterested interest" that resembles the rational moral sense appealed to by Butler, Price, and Reid (see below).

However, Hume is not positing any occult faculty, for he explains disinterested moral approbation as a combination of the natural quality of sympathy for others (pain at witnessing another's pain) and the habit of following rules. Since natural sympathy alone would lead us into injustices and considerations of utility alone would seem to justify exceptions to general rules, we come to agree on general principles of conduct and transfer to these principles the sentiment of approbation that we originally felt toward the happiness or release from pain usually produced by following such principles. Thus arises the sense of moral duty and the capacity for disinterested approval. Here again, Hume offers a psychological description of the motivating processes that cause us to approve of moral virtue as an answer to the question of what criteria we use to judge persons and actions to be worthy of moral approval. Once this identity of psychological motive and logical ground is presupposed, it becomes impossible to distinguish between correct and incorrect moral judgments. The question as to whether action that meets with general approbation actually merits such approbation cannot even be raised, since merit has already been identified with the mere fact of approbation.

Freedom. On the issue of free will and its relation to moral responsibility, Hume argued persuasively that responsibility presupposes the causal efficacy of threat of punishment. He developed further the arguments of Hobbes and Locke that freedom is not a quality of the will but a relation between desire, action, and environment, such that a man is free when his actions are caused by his own desires and unimpeded by external restraints, a view that William James later baptized "soft determinism."

COMMON-SENSE INTUITIONISM. Hume's subjective account of moral judgment was countered by the common-sense intuitionism of Thomas Reid (1710–

Voltaire employed acid satire in attacking religious and philosophical obscurantism. (Corbis/Bettmann)

to establish as strong traditions as their British contemporaries. French thought subsequent to the eighteenth century added little to moral philosophy as compared with that of Germany and Great Britain. Due to their intense involvement in political issues, the French writers placed rhetorical effectiveness above clarity and consistency as a standard of philosophical value.

Voltaire (François Marie Arouet, 1694–1778) and Jean-Jacques Rousseau (1712–1778) led the revolt against Cartesian rationalism as well as against political and religious superstition, so transforming philosophy into ideology that *idéologue* became a popular French synonym for *philosophe*. Voltaire employed acid satire in attacking religious and philosophical obscurantism in *Candide, Zadig,* and his *Philosophical Dictionary,* while Rousseau inaugurated the romantic style of soul-stirring emotional intensity, in place of detached analysis and rigorous argument. Denis Diderot (1713–1784) raised philosophical writing to the highest level of literary grace and subtlety since Plato, criticizing conventional morality and religious beliefs in his remarkable essay-novels *Le Neveu de Rameau, Jacques le fataliste,* and *Rêve de d'Alembert.* Yet while appreciating their extraordinary intellectual qualities and the permanence of their place in Western culture, it must be noted that they provided few new concepts and principles on which later ethical philosophers could build.

Rousseau. Rousseau's celebrated exaltation of untutored human nature in his two *Discourses* attributed genial and cooperative tendencies to man's innate disposition and aggressively self-serving tendencies to the harmful influence of civilization. This coincided with the British moral-sense theorists' attacks on Hobbesian egoism. However, unlike Hume (his friend and benefactor prior to their notorious public quarrel), Rousseau considered custom and law to be arbitrary restraints on natural impulses rather than rational methods of channeling self-interest toward the common good. Whatever justification can be given for control of the individual by social institutions lay, for Rousseau, in their claim to represent the "general will," that is, the desires of the majority, independently of whether what is so desired is good. While Rousseau argued forcefully, in *The Social Contract,* for popular sovereignty and the right of revolution, he justified the use by the state of extremely repressive measures, such as the death penalty for atheism. His rather mystical notion of the state as the embodiment of the general will helped to inspire the overthrow in France of absolute monarchy in favor of representative government, yet half a century later it was employed by Fichte, and a century after that by Lenin, in the justification of authoritarianism.

Although Rousseau's religious mysticism and his preference for feeling over rational prudence were con-

1796) and Richard Price (1723–1791), who explained the moral sense, or conscience, that enables man to distinguish right from wrong as a combination of benevolent emotion and rational intuition. Both argued, like Butler, that moral principles are not in need of utilitarian justification but are as natural to man as self-love and desire for pleasure. Reid argued that moral qualities are as directly perceived as physical properties are and thus exist in the object judged rather than in the feelings of the subject who judges. Ethics is as much a matter of objective fact as science is, except that its principles are self-evident and can be discovered by "common sense" alone, uncorrupted by bad philosophy. Reid also defended the belief in freedom of the will as the ground of moral responsibility, arguing that we are introspectively aware of our ability to choose between good and evil independently of our desires.

THE FRENCH ENLIGHTENMENT. Ethical thought in eighteenth-century France paralleled developments in Great Britain, although the French philosophers failed

trary to the general tone of the Enlightenment, his most lasting contribution to ethical philosophy was his insistence that good and evil tendencies are due to social causes, a principle that he shared with Montesquieu, Voltaire, and the Encylopedists. The soundness of this principle is subject to question, but there can be no doubt that it served as a useful guide in the reform of social institutions.

Montesquieu. Charles Louis de Secondat, baron de la Brède et de Montesquieu (1689–1755), in *The Spirit of the Laws* founded the relativistic conception of moral and political principles as grounded in the traditions of particular societies. The "spirit of the laws" is the system of social practices in relation to which new laws are to be evaluated. Western European governments require a division of functions and compensating checks and balances to fulfill the partly republican, partly monarchical values of European society. In treating values as historical and sociological facts, rather than as divine principles or natural laws, Montesquieu developed further the scientific approach to ethics and politics begun by Machiavelli and Hobbes.

The Encyclopedists. Denis Diderot, Claude Helvétius (1715–1771), and Baron Paul Dietrich d'Holbach (1723–1789) derived, from a materialistic theory of nature, an ethical view based on the self-centered pursuit of pleasure as the sole rational motive for action. A well-ordered society, on their view, is one in which the pursuit of personal well-being is unhindered by social authority. Insofar as there are conflicts between morality and self-interest, these are due to defects of social organization and perverse education, rather than to the moral defects of individuals. These Encyclopedists, and kindred spirits in other countries, such as the Italian legal philosopher Beccaria, employed utilitarian moral theory in political campaigns for representative government and humane laws and punishments.

KANT AND THE GERMAN ENLIGHTENMENT. The Enlightenment attack on tradition and authority in favor of individual reason took a nonutilitarian form in the philosophy of Immanuel Kant (1724–1804). The utilitarians identified reason with practical intelligence in the pursuit of happiness. Kant, however, inherited the Cartesian and Leibnizian conception of reason as the intellectual recognition of abstract truths. In fashioning an ethical theory that became the main rival of utilitarianism, Kant combined the Augustinian emphasis, revived by Butler, Price, and Reid, on the internal sense of moral obligation with the rationalistic ideal of knowledge as a deductive system. In his *Critique of Pure Reason,* he attempted to show that the laws of science are imposed by the mind on the objects of its perceptions and can thus be known with certainty through reflection on the a priori structure of knowledge. In his

Critique of Practical Reason he applied the same analysis to ethics, founding morality on the a priori laws with which "practical reason" regulates action. While Kant defended religious faith against the utilitarian freethinkers, he shared their view that ethics is independent of theology, and he followed the deistic tradition of interpreting God as a scientific and ethical ideal, rather than as a supernatural source of revelation and authority.

Hobbes's use of the term "laws of nature"

in referring to ethical principles

is to be distinguished sharply

from the medieval concept of natural law

that he rejected.

In his most influential work on ethics, *The Foundations of the Metaphysics of Morals,* Kant made the most thorough attempt by any philosopher to clarify and explain the difference between ethical principles and laws of nature. The difference lies both in our subjective sense of obligation to obey moral laws, as contrasted with laws of nature, toward which we feel no such obligation, and in the practical—that is, prescriptive—meaning of moral laws, in contrast with the "theoretical"—that is, descriptive—meaning of laws of nature. In virtue of this difference, moral rules are expressed in the imperative mood and laws of nature in the declarative mood. To account for this disparity, Kant distinguished two realms of knowledge dealing with two metaphysically distinct subject matters. Natural science, including scientific psychology, formulates laws of nature that the mind imposes on the objects of perception in accordance with the principle of causal determinism. Ethics articulates the "laws of freedom" that a rational being imposes on his own actions and expects other rational beings to recognize and obey. The justification for these rules lies in the logical fact that to be rational means to act in accordance with general rules and that moral rules are those which can be followed consistently by all rational beings. Thus, insofar as man is moral, he is rational and, in this sense, free; insofar as he is immoral, he is an irrational slave to his natural inclinations. The reward of virtue is not happiness but dignity and freedom.

Moral Virtue: The Supreme Good. Kant's system of ethics is built on three pillars: the examination of the facts of moral experience, the analysis of the logic of ethical judgment, and the formulation of the metaphysical principles presupposed by ethical judgments, as distinct from scientific generalizations. In the first part of the *Foundations* Kant argues, like Reid, that common-sense reflection, uncorrupted by the dialectics of philosophers, informs us with unwavering certainty that duty is distinct from pleasure and utility, that moral virtue or "good will" is the supreme good to which all other values are subordinate, and that moral worth is not measured either by the consequences of a person's actions or by his natural benevolence but by the agent's intention to obey moral laws.

Locke's main contribution

to the clarification of the meaning of ethical concepts

was in his distinction between

"speculative" and "practical" principles.

Categorical Imperatives. In the second section of the *Foundations,* Kant attempts to explain the distinctive character of moral laws by clarifying the logical differences between three types of rules or imperatives: technical "rules of skill," prudential "counsels" as to how to achieve happiness, and moral duties. The first two, he argues, are "hypothetical imperatives" whose directives are contingent on the desires of the agent. Naturalistic ethics mistakes counsels of prudence for moral laws because the desire for happiness is so universal that directives toward this end have the superficial appearance of unconditional laws. But the generalization that all men seek happiness is a law of nature, not a rule commanding action, and the very possibility of a moral code entails that this psychological generalization is subject to exception. For moral duty requires that the agent sacrifice his personal happiness and even the welfare of his community rather than violate a "categorical imperative."

A moral or genuinely categorical imperative is a rule that commands a type of action independently of any desired end, including happiness. Kant accepts the utilitarian account of hypothetical imperatives but argues that the peculiar obligatoriness of moral principles can be explained only by their unrestricted universality and thus by their independence of any facts of human nature or circumstance. It is not in virtue of what satisfies human needs, but in virtue of the demand of reason that action be in accordance with universal law, that we feel obligated to obey moral principles.

Universalizability Criterion. To the question of whether any rule of action can qualify as a moral principle, Kant's answer was in the negative. He maintained

that there is one general or "fundamental" categorical imperative from which all specific moral duties can be derived: "Act only on that maxim which you can will to be a universal law." All maxims or specific rules of conduct can be judged morally right or wrong according to this general criterion. If universal obedience to a proposed rule would contradict the very purpose of the rule, as is the case for rules that under certain circumstances permit lying, stealing, or taking life (somewhat inconsistently, Kant approved of capital punishment), then the rule cannot be part of a true moral code. In contrast, a rule such as "Do not make false promises" can in principle be followed without exception and thus qualifies as a moral duty.

This criterion of universalizability, that is, the logical or psychological possibility of requiring universal obedience to a rule of action (logical for "strict" duties and psychological for "meritorious" duties), was undoubtedly Kant's most original and important contribution to ethical theory. It expresses more precisely and unambiguously the "golden rule" to be found in all the great religions, and it has been incorporated, in one form or another, in most modern systems of ethical theory. Countless writers since Kant have attempted to reformulate the criterion of universalizability in a way sufficiently qualified to avoid reasonable objections, but without complete success.

The obvious objection to Kant's formulation is that no one would want *any* specific rule of action to be followed without exception. No one would want the truth to be told on occasions when unmitigated harm would result—for example, when a murderer demands to know where his intended victim is hiding. Kant's own reply to this objection is that, while one may not be psychologically inclined to tell the truth on such occasions, there is no logical contradiction in willing—that is, commanding—that it be told, come what may.

A second objection is that Kant assumes, for any rule of action, that either it or its negation must be a moral law, and yet there are few rules, if any, which we would care to have followed universally in either positive or negative form. Kant argues that, since it would be self-defeating to will that every person may make false promises when it suits his purposes, we ought to will that false promises never be made. Yet on the same reasoning one could justify all sorts of absurd laws, such as that everyone at all times wear heavy clothing, since we would not and could not will the universal prohibition of heavy clothing.

A third weakness of Kant's theory is that it provides no grounds for deciding what is right in a situation where apparent moral duties collide and one must be sacrificed in favor of another. With respect to this problem, utilitarianism seems clearly superior to Kantian ethics.

Autonomy of the Will. The third part of Kant's ethical theory consists in the metaphysical account of the rational will as a source of action outside the sphere of causal determinism and thus not an object of scientific investigation. The autonomy of the will—that is, the capacity to obey laws of its own conception in defiance of natural causes—is, Kant argues, a necessary presupposition of any moral code. For if all actions were necessary effects of natural causes, then moral evaluation would be pointless. "Ought" implies "can," that is, the obligation to do what is right entails the ability to do it and the ability not to do it. Since science rests on the regulative principle of universal determinism, there can be no scientific proof of freedom of the will. But this only shows the radical difference between science and ethics and the folly of attempting to derive ethics from psychology. Man as an object of scientific inquiry is an organic phenomenon obeying laws of biology and psychology. But man as an object of ethical evaluation is a noumenal being, free to obey or disobey the dictates of practical reason. From this dual conception of man as both inside and outside nature, Kant derives an ideal way of life impressive in its purity and its faith in human perfectibility. Man as a rational agent is a member of a "kingdom of ends" in which he is both subject and sovereign, legislating for himself and for others. The highest goal of human life is to realize this ideal "kingdom" in individual and social practice.

Nineteenth-century Ethics

Nineteenth-century ethical thought became a battleground for two rival traditions. Utilitarianism, stemming from Locke, Hume, and the French Encyclopedists, dominated British and French philosophy, while idealistic ethics was supreme in Germany and Italy. Both traditions took root in the United States, with idealism appealing to the religious vision of Emerson and Royce, while utilitarianism answered to the developing faith in technology that found philosophical expression toward the end of the century in the pragmatic ethics of James and Dewey.

UTILITARIANISM. Christian ethics based on divine authority and natural law was given a utilitarian interpretation by William Paley (1743–1805) in his *Principles of Moral and Political Philosophy.* The source of moral obligation, he agreed with Hobbes, lies in the "violent motive resulting from the command of another," while the ground of goodness is pleasure or utility. But moral duty and self-interest coincide because God, as the paramount authority, commands us through the Scriptures and the promptings of con-

science to seek the general good as well as our own happiness. Moral obligation is supported both by natural pleasure in the welfare of others and by the fear of divine punishment which provides the selfish but rational person with a good reason to sacrifice his pleasure for the common good. Paley's psychological account of morality, like that of earlier moral-sense theories, failed to explain why anyone who lacks natural benevolence ought to have it. His alternative justification of morality in terms of the fear of divine punishment equally fails to explain why such punishment would be just and why a nonbenevolent nonbeliever in Christian theology can nevertheless be expected to behave morally.

Bentham. The mainstream of utilitarian thought was anticlerical. Jeremy Bentham (1748–1832) and James Mill (1773–1836) formed a political movement that helped bring about legislative reforms by criticizing social institutions in terms of their utility in producing "the greatest happiness for the greatest number." In his influential *Introduction to the Principles of Morals and Legislation,* Bentham formulated a theory of ethics and jurisprudence remarkable for its clarity, and consistency. The great appeal of Bentham's theory lay in its apparent simplicity and ease of application, although these virtues may have been more apparent than real. Bentham attempted to make ethics and politics scientifically verifiable disciplines by formulating quantitative standards of evaluation. He began with the psychological generalization that all actions are motivated by the desire for pleasure and the fear of pain: "Nature hath placed mankind under the governance of two sovereign masters, *pain* and *pleasure.* It is for them alone to point out what we ought to do, as well as to determine what we shall do. On the one hand the standard of right and wrong, on the other the chain of causes and effects, are fastened to their throne" (*Principles,* London, 1823, p. 1). From this equation between ethical obligation and psychological necessity, Bentham derived the general principle of utility which "approves or disapproves of every action whatsoever, according to the tendency which it appears to have to augment or diminish the happiness of the party whose interest is in question" (*ibid.*), happiness being understood as the predominance of pleasure over pain.

The most original but also the most dubious part of Bentham's theory is his "hedonic calculus" for measuring pleasures and pains, in computing the over-all value of alternative policies. If such a procedure were feasible, ethical judgments would be as scientific as meteorological forecasts, even though both are subject to considerable error, due to the complexity of the factors involved. But Bentham's ideal of a science of ethics runs afoul of two internal difficulties, the resistance of pleasure to measurement and the impossibility of predicting the long-range consequences of actions. Aside from these internal defects, there remains the general objection that pleasure, unlike pain, is not a bodily sensation but a favorable response to an object grounded on the perception of value in the object, as Thomas Reid had argued. To conclude that an object is good from the fact that it pleases us involves the circular reasoning that it is good because it is judged to be good, a principle too vacuous to provide a guide to ethical judgment. If, on the other hand, pleasure is understood in a more narrow, technical sense as desirable bodily sensations, then Bentham's identification of happiness and welfare with pleasure is unacceptable because it reduces human experience to the level of animal existence. The plausibility of Bentham's theory may be due to the ease with which he shifts inadvertently from one of these senses of "pleasure" to the other.

Despite its theoretical defects, Benthamite utilitarianism, which was more socially oriented than that of Locke and Hume, had a salutary effect on social legislation. His analysis of pleasures into factors of intensity, duration, propinquity, certainty, fecundity, and "extent" (number of persons affected) offered reasonable criteria by which alternative social programs and laws can be evaluated and was a marked improvement over the sanctification of existing laws and customs by which Hobbes, Locke, and Hume had made the transition from self-interest to morality. But there is a missing link in Bentham's chain of reasoning that may not be reparable within the confines of his hedonistic psychology, namely, the link that should connect the desire for one's own pleasure with the willingness to consider "extent" or pleasure of others in deciding on a course of action. Is desire for the pleasure of others also a "sovereign master under which nature hath placed us?" If so, then desire for one's own pleasure cannot be sovereign as well. If not, then on what ground are we required to consider the factor of extent?

Mill. John Stuart Mill (1806–1873) recognized the defects in Bentham's formulation of utilitarianism, and in his essay "Utilitarianism" he offered a more sophisticated version that sought to incorporate the moral insights of rival ethical systems. Realizing that Bentham's emphasis on quantitative aspects of pleasure reduces pleasure to bodily sensation and tends to justify an uncultivated mode of life, Mill proposed a new factor by which pleasures could be compared, the factor of quality. Some pleasurable experiences, notably intellectual, aesthetic, and moral achievements, are qualitatively superior to the satisfaction of bodily needs: "Better to be Socrates unsatisfied than to be a fool satisfied." But like Epicurus's preference for "natural" over "unnatural" pleasures, Mill's criterion of quality introduces a standard of value other than pleasure, by which pleasure itself can be evaluated, and thus contradicts the principle of utility, that pleasure is the single standard of good.

Rousseau's most lasting contribution to ethical philosophy was his insistence that good and evil tendencies are due to social causes, a principle that he shared with Montesquieu, Voltaire, and the Encyclopedists.

Mill also tried to make room in utilitarian theory for the appreciation of the saintly virtues, renunciation and self-sacrifice, by arguing along Humean lines that such virtues are originally valued for their social utility but that we later become attached to them for their own sake, and that this psychological shift from appreciation of virtue as a social instrument to admiration of virtue for itself is a good tendency because it, too, is socially useful. For the appreciation of moral qualities independently of their immediate consequences ensures the social reliability of the agent and, in the long run, produces more good than harm. This utilitarian defense of moral principles rested on an optimistic belief in the generally beneficial tendencies of man. In applying it to political theory, Mill argued for democratic institutions, minimum state interference in social life, and free economic competition. Assuming a general convergence of individual and social benefit, Mill, like Hume and Bentham, left unanswered the question why, in cases of conflict, one *ought* to place public over private interest and confined himself to explaining why we admire the person who does so. Yet if the social utility of moral self-sacrifice is the only rational ground for favorable judgment of it, then it would seem to follow that each of us has reason to approve of self-sacrifice in others but not in himself. If the step from individual happiness to the greatest good for the greatest number is justified only by the long-range coincidence of the two, then whenever we are assured that they will not coincide, we have no reason to prefer public welfare to our own other than the irrational habit of doing so, a habit which, in such case, it would be wise to break. In Kantian terms, utilitarianism, even in Mill's sophisticated version, fails to provide a logical bridge between inclination and obligation, between "is" and "ought."

Later intuitionists, beginning with Henry Sidgwick (1838–1900), attempted to supply this bridge by combining the Kantian theory of rational duty with the utilitarian theory of value, maintaining that we are intuitively aware of the duty to obey moral principles at the expense of self-interest but that moral principles, in turn, are justified by their utility in promoting the common good.

IDEALIST ETHICS. Kant's distinction between man as noumenon, legislating and obeying "laws of freedom," and man as phenomenon, governed by laws of nature, was incorporated into new ethical systems by later German idealists, who assimilated the phenomenal side of the distinction to a part of the noumenal side, making natural science subordinate to ethics. Johann Gottlieb Fichte (1762–1814) extended the noumenal will into a universal force that creates the material world out of its own force and expresses itself partially in the free rational will of the individual conscience but more fully in social institutions and laws. The individual thus achieves self-realization in identifying himself with the universal will and voluntarily accepting his *Beruf* (vocation) as part of the social order.

Fichte. In his early work *Wissenschaftslehre* (*Theory of Science*, 1794) Fichte enlarged Kant's ethical concept of man into a metaphysical picture of the universe. Rejecting Kant's notion of things-in-themselves, Fichte reduced reality to the projections of an absolute mind, and he reduced mind itself to will. The criterion of reality became a practical one: that is real which it is right or good to believe and to act upon (the beginning of pragmatism). Fichte went even further than Kant in stressing moral duty as the goal of life. Kant had sharply separated duty from self-interest in criticizing positions of the kind later referred to as utilitarianism, but Fichte moved full circle by reidentifying moral duty with a higher form of self-interest, the self-realization of an absolute will of which each person is a temporary embodiment. The logical problem created by Fichte's voluntaristic idealism is caused by the fact that it begins with Kant's primacy of moral good over prudential good but concludes with a form of supernatural utilitarianism in which prudential good of a higher self reappears as the ground of morality.

Fichte explained the function of the state as the regulation of conflicts among individuals in protection of their natural rights, and on this basis he supported democratic government. But he advanced the view, later elaborated by Hegel, that governmental restraints on individual action are not limitations of personal freedom but expressions of the higher freedom of the absolute will.

In *The Vocation of Man* (1800) Fichte, who had been accused of atheism, developed a less rationalistic and more religious view of human life. He identified the absolute will with the personal God of Christianity and moral duty with the vocation imposed on man by God. In his later *Addresses to the German Nation* (1808) he applied his notion of divinely ordained vocation to the German nation, which he claimed was destined to raise civilization to a higher level. The evolution of Fichte's thought from austere moralism to religious mysticism and then to chauvinistic nationalism provides an instructive example of the lengths to which thought can go in denying the basic distinctions from which it begins, such as that between self-interest and moral duty or between individual rights and social restraints.

Hegel. G. W. F. Hegel (1770–1831) developed Fichte's social basis of ethics further and in more historical terms. For Hegel value, morality, and law are among the highest forms of self-realization of absolute spirit. The Enlightenment doctrine of abstract rights is only the first stage in the development of ethical consciousness. A higher stage is reached in the Kantian sense of moral duty, which recognizes the conflict between individual rights and social responsibilities, subordinating the former to the latter. But the highest stage of self-realization of "objective mind" involves the incorporation of rights and duties in a rational system of social and political institutions which the individual citizen recognizes as the embodiment of the national will. The perfect freedom that consists in rational self-determination is achieved when individual conscience coincides with custom and law, so that will and reason, subjective motivation and objective necessity, become identical. But this is possible, according to Hegel, only in the modern age of the national state, Christian conscience, and constitutional law. In earlier stages of human history, whatever was necessary for historical progress was, for that age, necessary and therefore right, as, for example, the institution of slavery was necessary and right in ancient Greece. "World history," he declared, "is world justice."

POST-HEGELIAN THEORIES. The impact of Darwin's theory of natural evolution produced naturalistic echoes of Hegelian historical relativism in the utilitarian "survival of the fittest" doctrine of Herbert Spencer (1820–1903), the Marxist philosophy of class conflict, and the cultural elitism of Nietzsche.

Marx. Karl Marx (1818–1883) transformed Hegel's theory of the dialectical self-realization of mind into a doctrine of dialectical development of history through class conflict. In the Marxist theory, moral principles represent the sanctification of the interests of the ruling class at each stage in the development of progressively superior modes of economic organization. Marx criticized both utilitarian and Kantian ethics as variant expressions of bourgeois market-place procedures. Subordinating rules of individual conduct to the historical imperatives of "revolutionary praxis," the *Communist Manifesto* of Marx and Engels called for revolutionary action to achieve a classless society in which "the free development of each is the condition for the free development of all," a society that would require neither the internal repressions of conscience nor the external repressions of laws and punishments. Both morality and the state would "wither away."

Schopenhauer. Arthur Schopenhauer (1788–1860), like Fichte, located the source of both egoistic pursuit of pleasure and moral obligation in the universal will. The morality of equal rights for all represents a higher development of consciousness than that of self-interest, but a still higher stage is reached in the philosophical understanding that the will, in any form, produces illusion and suffering and that the extinction of desire is the only salvation. Schopenhauer gave the Stoic and Buddhist ethic of ascetic renunciation an idealistic metaphysical basis.

Kierkegaard. Søren Kierkegaard (1813–1855) rejected the rationalistic and socially oriented ethic of Hegel in favor of religious individualism. While, like Hegel, he regarded the conflict between self-interest (the "aesthetic attitude") and duty (the "ethical attitude") as reconciled and transcended in a higher stage of consciousness, he denied that this stage could be achieved by reason and described it as a "leap of faith" preceded by tragic anguish. As the contemporary existentialists who have rediscovered Kierkegaard have put it, "The world is absurd" because there are no objective grounds for human decisions. What is right, according to Kierkegaard, is what the individual asserts with the total commitment born of faith, but it is right only for him. Emotional authenticity rather than conformity to rules is the proper guide to action.

Nietzsche. Friedrich Nietzsche (1844–1900) proposed a less mystical but equally individualistic transcendence of moral codes. Like Hobbes and Mandeville, he regarded altruism as contrary to natural impulse and denounced moral restraint as a device created by religion to contravene the natural order of dominance of the strong over the weak. The true source of value lies in the creative self-assertion of the artist and the man of genius who produce new and positive forms of good, while moral prohibitions produce only resentment, envy, and dull conformity.

American Developments. In the United States, the transcendentalists, led by Ralph Waldo Emerson (1803–1882) and the pragmatic idealist Josiah Royce (1855–1916), fashioned still other variations on the idealist theme of self-realization as the goal of human life. The transcendentalists identified the self with the creative force of nature, the "oversoul." Royce, following Hegel, defined the fully realized self as a unity of personal and community interests. All of these post-Hegelian philosophies rejected the Kantian morality of strict adherence to general rules of conduct and proposed ways of transcending the conflict between duty and self-interest through a higher mode of consciousness in which the conflict allegedly disappears.

Toward the end of the nineteenth century, William James and John Dewey developed the philosophy of pragmatism, in which all of human knowledge is regarded as essentially ethical. They rejected both the Kantian separation of ethics from natural science and the traditional conception of scientific knowledge as disinterested contemplation of value-neutral truths. The split between value and fact was bridged by reinterpreting both so that they became indistinguishable. James (1842–1910) combined utilitarianism with a creative individualism similar to that of Nietzsche and the prescriptivism of Hobbes, by identifying the source of value with the human act of making a claim, thus bestowing value on the object claimed. Ethical judgment is a rational process of determining by empirical investigation which policies are likely to satisfy the maximum number of such claims. James defended the indeterminist concept of free will, criticizing what he called the soft determinism of Hume and Mill as a purely verbal escape from the embarrassing consequences of scientific determinism.

BRITISH IDEALISM AND INTUITIONISM. In the last quarter of the nineteenth century the vitality of idealism began to attract even the sober British intellect, and the ethics of self-realization became a powerful rival to utilitarianism through the influence of Green, Bosanquet, and Bradley.

Green. Thomas Hill Green (1836–1882) introduced Oxford students to the lofty vision of idealist metaphysics. In his *Prolegomena to Ethics* (published posthumously) Green derived liberal ethical and political principles from his conception of the individual self as part of a universal and divine self. He criticized both utilitarianism and moral-sense theories for downgrading the role of reason in moral judgment and for reducing human motives to natural causes. A motive, he argued, is a goal previsioned by a rational consciousness, not an event or process in the body. Value is therefore logically prior to desire rather than a product of desire. One can desire or find pleasure only in what one has judged to be good. The source of evil must therefore be found in defects of the understanding, in the failure of the human mind to realize its identity with the universal mind. The highest good is thus as much an object of self-interest as any other, but it is the kind of self-interest that also constitutes morality.

Green was active in social and political controversies, supporting the North in the American Civil War and supporting liberal legislation in England. Green rejected laissez-faire individualism, insisting on the more positive role of government in promoting social welfare.

Green's ethical theory was sharply criticized by Henry Sidgwick in *The Ethics of Green, Spencer and Martineau* (1902). Sidgwick argued that Green's identification of morality with higher self-interest obliterates the all-important distinction between prudence and duty and thus fails to provide a basis for moral responsibility, a defect that, as we have seen, goes all the way back to Plato.

Despite its theoretical defects,

Benthamite utilitarianism,

which was more socially oriented

than that of Locke and Hume,

had a salutary effect on social legislation.

Bosanquet. Bernard Bosanquet (1848–1923), like Green, grounded ethics and politics on idealist metaphysics. Bosanquet stressed somewhat more than Green the uniqueness of individual values while at the same time taking a Hegelian view of the state as the embodiment of objective mind. Like Green, Bosanquet actively supported liberal political causes.

Bradley. Francis H. Bradley (1846–1924), generally considered the most distinguished ethical theorist among the British idealists, criticized both utilitarianism and Kantian formalism and favored a Hegelian conception of the community as an organic unity whose needs, expressed in social institutions, transcend those of individual citizens, a conception which he applied in the defense of conservative social policies. Bradley was probably more consistent than Green and Bosanquet. If law and custom are the expression of a higher self,

then only internal inconsistencies can justify reforms, and individual rights are subordinate to group or national interests. In his *Ethical Studies* (1876) Bradley supported retributive punishment on the ground (which he held to be self-evident to common sense) that punishment is unfair unless it is deserved and that moral desert is independent of social utility. He attempted to reconcile freedom with causal determinism in the notion of an all-encompassing Reality that determines itself in accordance with rational laws. Recognizing that idealism faces the problem of accounting for evil and that its traditional solution—claiming that evil does not exist—is contrary to the judgment of common sense on which Bradley himself always relied, he employed a subtle distinction between existence and reality in holding that evil, though it exists, is unreal. From the standpoint of the totality of knowledge, evil may be seen to contribute to cosmic harmony. This "solution" was later castigated by Bertrand Russell as a morally untenable justification of evil.

Sidgwick. Henry Sidgwick (1838–1900) combined the social utilitarianism of Mill with the intuitionism of Butler and Kant. In *The Methods of Ethics* (1875), a work described by C. D. Broad as "the best treatise on Moral Philosophy that has ever been written," Sidgwick raised ethical analysis to a new level of precision and logical rigor. Setting aside practical moralizing as not the business of objective philosophical analysis, Sidgwick interpreted the task of moral philosophy to be the clarification of the logic of moral judgment, a conception of philosophy that was continued by the contemporary British school of linguistic analysis.

Sidgwick held that there are just three approaches to ethics worth philosophical consideration: egoistic hedonism, utilitarianism, and intuitionism. He pointed out that neither the self-centered ethics of Hobbes and the French Encyclopedists nor the socially oriented ethics of Bentham and Mill can justify the step from psychology to ethics, that is, from the description of human motivation to judgments of moral obligation. Even those who declare that one ought to pursue one's own interests must justify their use of "ought," and this cannot be done on the grounds of psychological facts alone. Sidgwick therefore insisted on distinguishing psychological hedonism from ethical hedonism and grounding the latter on intuition. His argument is reminiscent of Hume's claim that values cannot be deduced from facts, and it anticipates G. E. Moore's later analysis of the "naturalistic fallacy."

All three "methods of ethics" rest, according to Sidgwick, on principles held to be self-evident, and thus intuitionism is, to some extent, inescapable. The egoist must assume the self-evident rightness of pursuing one's own pleasure, and the social utilitarian must assume the rightness of maximizing the common good. Intuitionists differ from utilitarians and egoists only in holding many principles and duties to be self-evident as well, and thus they expose themselves to inevitable counterinstances. The more numerous and specific the rules claimed to be self-evident, the more subject to exception and vulnerable to disproof. Sidgwick concludes that social utilitarianism offers the correct standard of moral judgment but that this standard is in turn grounded on direct awareness of moral obligation. Thus at least one, and probably at most one, moral intuition is essential for moral judgment.

Sidgwick could not finally decide between the conflicting claims of self-interest and social utility. He leaned toward the latter as definitive of moral duty, but he recognized that one's self-interest rightly carries a special weight, other things being equal. Perhaps he would have been able to reconcile these two "intuitions" more easily had he considered utilitarianism in a somewhat weaker form, as the principle that one ought always to refrain from causing unnecessary suffering, rather than the stronger claim that one ought always to aim at maximizing happiness. For while one's own welfare seems naturally to outweigh that of others, it is very close to being self-evident to any morally sensitive person that he ought not to pursue his interests at the cost of substantial suffering to others.

It would appear from our brief glance over the history of ethics through the nineteenth century that philosophers failed to find any conclusive ethical truths and merely argued, more persuasively and with a more impressive display of learning than most, for whatever way of life and standards of conduct they happened to prefer. In some respects this impression would be justified, and it serves to remind us of the differences between scientific knowledge and ethical wisdom. The perennial character of the problems, the lack of general agreement on proposed solutions, and the return of later doctrines to principles advanced by earlier ones all contrast strikingly with the irreversible progress of scientific discovery. It has been suggested by some contemporary philosophers that the endless disputability of ethical issues is rooted in the very nature of ethical language, so that it is not a defect of philosophy to have failed to achieve general agreement on ethics. As W. B. Gallie has put it (*Philosophy and the Historical Understanding*, New York, 1964), ethical concepts are "essentially contestable." It is essential to their meaning that they evoke continual disputes as to the correct standards for their application.

But if we cannot find historical progress in the form of final settlement of issues, we can at least discern some degree of gradual, if irregular, advance toward greater clarity in the formulation of the issues.

On the central issue of the logical relation between facts and values, ethical theories have provided increasingly clear and sophisticated statements of two fundamental positions, naturalism and nonnaturalism (sometimes called teleology and deontology). Naturalistic theories relate values to facts by defining "good" and related concepts in terms of observable criteria, such as fulfillment of natural tendencies (Aristotle), satisfaction of desire (Hobbes and Spinoza), production of pleasure for the greatest number (utilitarianism), conduciveness to historical progress (Spencer and Marx), or efficiency of means to ends (Dewey). Nonnaturalistic theories stress the fact that the meaning of ethical terms goes beyond the observable facts on which ethical judgments are grounded, and they locate the additional component of meaning outside nature. Plato located it in a realm of abstract Forms, Christianity in the will of God, the intuitionists in the direct recognition of the quality of rightness, the moral-sense theorists in the feeling of approbation. Each of these accounts of value and moral right has revealed an additional dimension of the complex logic of ethical judgment. Naturalistic theories have brought to light various ways in which ethical judgment is grounded on the fulfillment of biological and social needs, while nonnaturalistic theories have revealed prescriptive aspects of moral concepts that are independent of prudential considerations. The main effort of twentieth-century ethical philosophy has been to weave together in a consistent pattern all the threads, both naturalistic and nonnaturalistic, that constitute our philosophical heritage.

Contemporary Nonnaturalism

In much of the English-speaking world G. E. Moore's *Principia Ethica* (Cambridge, 1903) is taken to be the starting point of contemporary ethical theory. But it is important to recognize that this primacy is to a considerable degree local and distinctive of the tradition of analytical ethics. On the Continent and in Latin America the work of Max Scheler and Franz Brentano has been a preeminent influence. For much of American thought until fairly recently, the work of John Dewey or Ralph Barton Perry provided the starting point. But, for all that, it is reasonable to begin with G. E. Moore.

MOORE. It is the critical side of Moore's work in ethics that has had the most lasting effect. His delineation of the subject matter of ethics and his very careful effort to show that any form of ethical naturalism involves a fundamental conceptual mistake—the work of the first three chapters of *Principia Ethica*—has been the part of Moore's work that has deeply affected contemporary ethical thought. However, Moore's own positive nonnaturalistic cognitivism, with its reliance on nonnatural characteristics, has found few adherents. Most philosophers—C. L. Stevenson and R. M. Hare are typical—who have been convinced that in essence Moore's case against naturalism is sound have not followed Moore's lead but have adopted some form of noncognitivism.

It was Moore's belief that if moral philosophers simply interest themselves in good conduct, they are not really starting at the beginning, for we cannot know what good conduct is until we know what goodness is. Moore's concern was with a "general enquiry into what is good." Our first question must be "What is good and what is bad?" Such knowledge of good and evil, Moore claims, is the "goal of ethical investigation"; but, he stresses, "it cannot be safely attempted at the beginning of our studies, but only at the end." First we must consider how "good" is to be defined.

Moore clearly is not interested in giving a stipulative definition of "good," and from his disclaimers in *Principia Ethica* about being interested in a merely verbal point, it would seem that he is not interested in a lexical definition either. What he is after, in seeking a definition of "good," is just this: what property, or set of properties is common to and distinctive of anything that could conceivably be properly called intrinsically good, for instance, "answering to interests." Moore thinks "good" stands for a property, and he seeks to determine what it is. Moore's answer, which he is aware will cause discontent, is that "good" is not definable. All we can finally say correctly is that good is good and not anything else. "Good," like "red," is, in the appropriate sense, indefinable. Good is a simple, unanalyzable, nonnatural characteristic. We are either directly aware of it or we are not, but there is no way of defining it or analyzing it so as to make it intelligible to someone who is not directly aware of it.

Such a radical claim on Moore's part would have little force if he could not thoroughly refute naturalistic and metaphysical theories which do purport to give the kind of characterization of intrinsic goodness that he takes to be impossible.

Moore's Case Against Naturalism. Let us consider Moore's case against ethical naturalism. An ethical naturalist holds that moral judgments are true or false empirical statements ascribing an empirical property or set of properties to an action, object, or person. "Good" is defined in terms of this property or set of properties.

But, Moore argues, we will *not* come to know what good is simply by "discovering what are those other properties belonging to all things which are good." Those who commit what Moore calls the naturalistic fallacy think that when they have "named those other properties they were actually defining good; that these properties, in fact, were simply not 'other,' but absolutely and entirely the same with goodness." But to identify good with any other property is to commit the naturalistic fallacy. The naturalists confuse the question of the meaning of the concept of good with the quite different question of what kinds of things are good.

Toward the end of the nineteenth century, William James and John Dewey developed the philosophy of pragmatism, in which all of human knowledge is regarded as essentially ethical.

In a famous argument, which has been dubbed the open-question argument, Moore points out that for whatever naturalistic value we substitute for the variable x in a proposed definition of "good," we can always significantly ask if it is good. If a man says "Happiness is good," or "Self-realization is good," or "The object of any interest is good," we can always significantly ask "Is happiness good?," "Is self-realization good?" "Is the object of any interest good?" Even though we agree, let us say, that happiness is good, it is an evident fact of language that these questions are not without significance. But they would be without significance if "good" did *mean* "happiness," or "self-realization," or "the object of any interest," just as it is pointless to ask if a father is a male parent or a puppy is a young dog. For whatever naturalistic definitions we offer—whatever naturalistic values replace the variable x—it always makes sense to ask if that thing is good. Since this is so, these naturalistic definitions can be seen to be inadequate.

This can be seen in another way as well. If a statement like "The satisfaction of desire is good" were a definition of the sort Moore was searching for, it would be analytic and it would be self-contradictory to assert "This satisfies desire but it is not good." For whatever naturalistic definition one proposes, however, one can assert without self-contradiction "This is x but it is not good," but if x meant the same as "good" this would be impossible, for "*X* is good" would then be analytic. But since this is possible it is clear that the proposed statement is synthetic.

Moore's Influence. The above arguments of Moore's, together with his famous argument in Chapter 3 of *Principia Ethica* against Mill's alleged naturalism, have provided the background for much of the controversy in contemporary ethical theory. While few have accepted all the details of Moore's case against ethical naturalism, it has been felt by many that Moore's essential case is well taken. R. M. Hare in his *The Language of Morals* (Oxford, 1952), P. H. Nowell-Smith in his *Ethics* (Harmondsworth, 1954), and A. C. Ewing in his *Second Thoughts in Moral Philosophy* (London, 1959) try to restate these Moorean insights in such a way as to present a decisive case against ethical naturalism.

It should be noted, however, that the reception of Moore's case against naturalism, even on the part of such eminent nonnaturalists as A. N. Prior and E. W. Hall, has not been that favorable. It is generally thought now that (1) the naturalistic fallacy is not, strictly speaking, a fallacy but is at best a mistake and (2) that it is not really distinctive of naturalism but should be called the definist fallacy, that is, the belief that moral terms are capable of definition in nonmoral terms.

Criticisms of Moore. It is easy to see that someone, though at a certain price, could be a consistent ethical naturalist and that Moore's naturalistic fallacy would not really point to anything necessarily fallacious in such a naturalist's reasoning. An ethical naturalist who is also a hedonist could argue: By "intrinsic good" I am just going to mean "pleasure." This is a stipulative definition on my part and I am making no claim that it squares with ordinary usage, but it will give a clear and consistent definition of "good" that fits well with my preanalytic insight that pleasure and pleasure alone is intrinsically good. It is indeed true that on my theory "Pleasure is good" is a tautology and "Is pleasure intrinsically good?" is a self-answering question. Still, there is a normatively vital question that I can and do ask with perfect conceptual propriety. The vital open question is this: Should an individual seek pleasure and only pleasure as the thing that, morally speaking, he ought always to do? If a man takes this position, Moore's arguments, given above, do not show anything fallacious in his thinking, that is, he has committed no formal or informal fallacy, though it can be shown by some additions to Moore's arguments that he has said something that is mistaken.

There is a further criticism of Moore that can be made with considerable plausibility. Though it is indeed true that "good" taken in isolation cannot be defined, the term "good" is in reality always used in specific contexts, with context-dependent meanings and with such riders as "good at" and "good for." But in such a context "good" can be defined. "A good car," "good teacher," "good at ballet," or even "good man" can be naturalistically defined, even though "good" *sans phrase* cannot. Finally, and perhaps most importantly, it has been pointed out that the open-question and noncontradiction arguments are not conclusive. At best they show why all the naturalistic definitions hitherto proposed do not work. They do not show that naturalistic definitions are impossible.

DEONTOLOGICAL NONNATURALISTS. There are other nonnaturalists who, while holding cognitive metaethical theories, reject Moore's ideal utilitarianism. Moore thought that Bentham and Mill were mistaken in trying to define "good" naturalistically, but that they were not mistaken in regarding good as the fundamental moral concept and were not mistaken in arguing that it is always our duty to seek to bring the greatest total good possible into being. H. A. Prichard, W. D. Ross, E. F. Carritt, and C. D. Broad all agree with Moore that intrinsic good is a unique, nonnatural quality that is indefinable and can only be known directly. But they reject Moore's claim that "right" means "productive of the greatest possible good." "Right," they argue, is also *sui generis;* it is not reducible to "good" or to any teleological concept. To say "This is a right act" means, according to Ross, "This act ought to be done." Furthermore, even what *makes* an act right is not to be completely determined by teleological concepts. An act, even though it may be productive, everything considered, of the best consequences, may still not be the right thing to do. Even Broad, who makes the most concessions to the utilitarians of any of the deontologists (as they are called), argues that in determining what is suitable to the actual situation, we must consider both the total fittingness of the events that are relevant to the act in question and the utilities in question, and then without any precise measure of what is suitable to the situation, we must decide what we are to do. The utilitarians, including Moore, the deontologists agree, oversimplify the situation here.

In 1909 H. A. Prichard, in his celebrated article "Does Moral Philosophy Rest on a Mistake?," set forth in perceptive but uncompromising form the deontological position. But it is W. D. Ross, taking Prichard's position as a starting point, who has been the most influential of these deontological nonnaturalists. Ross's *The Right and the Good* (Oxford, 1930) and his *Foundations of Ethics* (Oxford, 1939) present the classical statement of these views.

Prichard. In "Does Moral Philosophy Rest on a Mistake?" Prichard argued that it was an endemic mistake of moral philosophy to try to give reasons for our obligations. Moral obligation cannot be reduced to acts which ought to be done because by doing them, more good is likely to result than by doing any alternative act. We do not, Prichard contended, come to appreciate an obligation by argument, but in a particular situation we are either directly aware of what it is we ought to do or we are not. Moral philosophy cannot justify these obligations; it can only (1) help us to come to understand the nature of this immediate type of awareness and (2) help us to see through the confused attempts to exhibit the "truly rational foundations" of these obligations by showing how they are grounded in human interests.

Sidgwick held that there are just three approaches

to ethics worth philosophical consideration:

egoistic hedonism, utilitarianism, and intuitionism.

Ross. Ross accepted the Prichardian belief that we have an intuitive insight into our obligations, but he went on from certain hints in Prichard to develop a concept of prima-facie duty. A prima-facie duty is a conditional duty of a very distinctive kind. What is meant by saying that it is "conditional" is that it is something which always would be an actual duty were it not for the fact that in certain circumstances there are more stringent moral considerations that outweigh it. But prima-facie duties are always actual duties unless such conditions obtain. Ross takes it as "self-evident that a promise, simply as such, is something that prima facie ought to be kept, and it does not, on reflection, seem self-evident that production of the maximum good is the only thing that makes an act obligatory." Like Cook, Wilson, and Prichard before him, Ross takes as his data "the moral convictions of thoughtful and well-educated people." They serve as his point of departure and his check on all theorizing concerning morals.

Reasoning from this base, Ross can show that we do not always reason as utilitarian moralists would have us reason. We often have duties of special obligation that conflict with the utilitarian principle that we should always maximize good. If we carefully attend to the data of ethics—our actual moral experiences—we will note that we have prima-facie duties to fidelity, reparation, gratitude, justice, beneficence, nonmaleficence, and self-improvement. Some of these prima-facie duties are more binding than others. *Ceteris paribus,* the duty of nonmaleficence outweighs our obligation to keep a promise. But Ross stresses—as does Broad—that it is not always the case that we have a rule, a general principle, for deciding what to do when there is a conflict in prima-facie duties. Sometimes we simply have to appreciate or come to "see" what is suitable to the situation.

Criticisms of Deontology. Many, though by no means all, philosophers would agree that the deontologists have shown that moral reasoning is not as simple as the classical utilitarians took it to be. But it has been thought by many that consequences play a far larger role in determining what makes an act right than the deontologists have been willing to admit. Their rather antiquated epistemology of intuitions, synthetic a priori judgments, and so forth, and their misleading use of mathematical analogies have stood in the way of an acceptance of deontology. It is, however, quite feasible to argue that such appeals are not essential to a deontological view.

It has also been repeatedly argued that a deontological position, with its list of prima-facie duties and its appeal to the convictions of the thoughtful and the well-educated, is thoroughly ethnocentric. To these objections it is reasonable to reply that most of Ross's prima-facie duties are very similar to the kind of generalities that the anthropologists Ralph Linton and Robert Redfield (among others) have claimed to be cross-culturally sanctioned "universal values." Moreover, the appeal to thoughtful and well-educated people surely need not and should not limit itself to people in one cultural circle.

Rather more important criticisms of deontology have been that it gives us no criteria for deciding what laws, practices, rules, or institutions are worthy of our acceptance. Here the kind of quasi-utilitarian reasoning concerning practices characteristic of the good-reasons approach seems to have decided advantage.

Ewing. It should be mentioned that A. C. Ewing in two closely reasoned books, *The Definition of Good* (New York, 1947) and *Second Thoughts in Moral Philosophy* (London, 1959), works out a theory that in many respects tries to find a middle ground between Moore and Ross. Ewing takes "ought" as his fundamental term, and in the second work he makes far more concessions to the naturalists and noncognitivists than in the first, without abandoning what he takes to be the core of his nonnaturalism.

PHENOMENOLOGICAL VIEWS. Moore, Ross, Broad, and Ewing are not the only nonnaturalists and intuitionists who have exerted a considerable influence on contemporary ethical thought. During a roughly comparable period, Franz Brentano, Nicolai Hartmann, and Max Scheler had a comparable influence on the Continent.

It is necessary to mention that in contemporary philosophical thought there is a fundamental cleavage that divides the English-speaking and Scandinavian countries, on the one hand, from the Continent, Latin America, and the Near East and Far East, on the other. In these latter areas of the world the influence, either direct or indirect, of the philosophers so far discussed has been slight, while the influence in intellectual circles of the philosophers to be discussed in this section and in the section on existentialism has been considerable. Even though Moore, Ross, and Ewing opposed empiricism, their techniques remained analytical, while the work of the philosophers about to be discussed is philosophy in the grand manner; that is, it is comparatively speculative and metaphysical.

Brentano. Franz Brentano's *The Origin of Our Knowledge of Right and Wrong* (Leipzig, 1889) and his later *Grundlegung und Aufbau der Ethik* (F. Mayer-Hillebrand, ed., Bern, 1952) mark the beginning of contemporary Continental ethical theory. In 1903 G. E. Moore remarked that Brentano's work more closely resembled his own than that of any writer with whom he was acquainted. Like Moore, Brentano rejected naturalistic definitions of ethical terms, regarded fundamental moral concepts as *sui generis,* and thought judgments of intrinsic value incapable of being proved.

To gain an adequate understanding of Brentano's ethical theory, it is essential to understand the rudiments of what he called descriptive psychology (the latter, in Husserl's hands, was to become phenomenology). Brentano classified mental phenomena into three fundamental classes: ideas and sensory presentations (images and the like), judgments, and emotions. That is to say, there are three fundamental ways in which one may be intentionally related to something. One may simply think of it, one may take an intellectual stance toward it by either accepting it or rejecting it, or one may take an emotional or attitudinal posture toward it. To do the last is a matter of loving or hating it. (Brentano, of course, uses "love" and "hate" here in a very stretched manner.) Brentano regarded emotions as intentional; he maintained that "certain feelings refer unmistakably to objects and language itself signifies this through expressions which make use of it." Moreover, emotions, like judgments but unlike ideas, can properly be called either correct or incorrect. In this way Brentano differed radically from the emotivists.

How do we decide whether a given emotion is correct or incorrect? Here Brentano, who like Ross was a careful student of Aristotle, was very Aristotelian. We can come to understand what a correct emotion or, for that matter, a correct judgment is only by contrasting actual cases of emotions and judgments taken to be correct by experienced and thoughtful people with cases that are not so regarded.

To say that something is good—where we are talking about "intrinsic good"—is to say that it is impossible to love it incorrectly. To say that something is intrinsically evil is to say that it is impossible correctly to love whatever is in question. "Good" and "evil" are what Brentano called synsemantic terms: they do not refer to concrete particular things, either physical or mental. But such ethical concepts were, on Brentano's view, objective because of the impossibility of loving correctly whatever is hated correctly and of hating correctly whatever is loved correctly. The truth of these fundamental moral judgments is directly evident to the mature moral agent. Any question about the empirical evidence for them is as impossible as it is unnecessary.

In much of the English-speaking world,

G. E. Moore's Principia Ethica *(1903)*

is taken to be the starting point

of contemporary ethical theory.

Scheler. Max Scheler attempted to apply Husserl's phenomenological method to moral concepts. His major works in ethics, *Formalism in Ethics and the Ethics of Intrinsic Value* (Halle, 1916) and *The Nature of Sympathy* (Bonn, 1923), are among his earlier writings (*The Nature of Sympathy* is simply a second and enlarged edition of the early *Zur Phänomenologie und Theorie der Sympathiegefühle,* Halle, 1913); but his later work in philosophical anthropology, *The Forms of Knowledge and Society* (Leipzig, 1926), also has important implications for his ethical theory.

Scheler's ethics is best understood by setting it in relation to that of Kant. Scheler accepted Kant's critique of naturalistic and utilitarian ethical theories. But while he took the categorical imperative as pointing to an essential feature of morality, he thought that such Kantian formalism was incomplete. Like Husserl, Scheler believed that Kant was mistaken in limiting the a priori to the purely formal. The phenomenological method shows that we have a *Wesensschau* (an intuition of essences) in virtue of which we know certain fundamental a priori but nevertheless nonformal moral truths, such as "Spiritual values have a higher place in the scale of values than vital values, and the Holy a higher place than the spiritual."

Given this very extended sense of "a priori," it is correct to say, according to Scheler, that there are objective non-formal moral judgments which are universal, necessary, and synthetic. These moral judgments are said to have an intrinsic content that is given in our intuition of essences.

Scheler argued that there is a hierarchy of objective values, all open to our intuitive inspection. There is, he would argue, nothing subjective about this ordering. In the hierarchy of values phenomenologically given to man, we have at the top religious values, then cultural values (aesthetic, speculative, scientific, and political), and finally, at the bottom, material values (useful things, things that satisfy needs, desires, etc.). All of these values are thought to have an ethical dimension. Questions concerning moral obligation arise when there is a conflict of values. Moral obligation is that which binds us, in such a situation, to take as the order of our incentives the values as they are ordered in the value hierarchy. Scheler was, however, sufficiently Kantian to believe that the ultimate ground of moral obligation lay not in the consequences of moral acts but in the intentions of moral agents. To someone who has studied Mill, Sidgwick, or Ross, this seems like a plain confusion between the moral "grades" we would give a person and an objective consideration of what acts are morally right.

There is another aspect of Scheler's moral theory that should be mentioned, namely, his claim that love and sympathy are the sole means by which we gain an intuitive insight into moral reality. Like Brentano, he thought that these feelings had intentional objects, and like Pascal, he thought that there was a "logic of the heart"—that through the feelings we gain a type of cognition into essential value structures that can be had in no other way.

Hartmann. Nicolai Hartmann's massive work *Ethics* was published in Berlin in 1926. It shows the influence of Scheler and Husserl and is without doubt the most extensive phenomenological discussion of value in the literature. Ethics, for Hartmann, is part of a general theory of value, though, as might be expected, ethical values are the highest values. "Value" for Hartmann, as for Scheler, is a general predicate, and under it there are more specific predicates for determinate values, for instance, "beauty" is to "value" as "red" is to "colored." Values are said to be essences, and we have a direct though emotionally tinged intuition of essences. Being essences, values, like numbers, are thought by Hartmann to have an ideal self-existence (*Ansichsein*). But unlike numbers, values have a "material essence."

Like Scheler, Hartmann believes that if we will but attend patiently to our feelings, we will be able to discern, though vaguely, some hierarchical ordering of those things which are valuable. Putting aside as far as possible our theoretical preconceptions concerning values, we should reflect carefully on our actual experience until we achieve a clear and evident insight into value phenomena. This, of course, is a desideratum that will never be completely achieved, for "morally no age entirely comprehends itself." The real ethical life is "a life deeper than consciousness." But there is a capacity on the part of the human animal to appreciate the valuable, and by ever more carefully attending to this, we can attain both a clearer view and a more purified form of the moral life.

Though values are material essences, they are not, as in Plato, identical with being. Hartmann, no more than Moore or Sartre, will identify what is good or what has worth with what exists. That would destroy the autonomy of ethics and obscure the nature of value. But although values are independent of existence, they are related to existence by a "tendency to reality" which Hartmann calls the ideal Ought-to-Be. We have many different values, but it always remains the case that values ought to be. The criteria for what is good or for what is valuable vary from context to context, but the ought-to-be remains the same: "The ideal Ought-to-Be is the formal condition of value, the value is the material condition of the Ought-to-Be." In contrast with the ideal Ought-to-Be there is the more practical, more directly morally relevant "Ought-to-Do." Here "ought" implies "can," and here practical moral questions arise about making something the case that is not the case.

Recent Developments in Germany. Finally, a brief note is in order about more recent developments in ethics among German philosophers. Heidegger, whose influence is completely overshadowing in Germany, took a dim view not only of the relevance of logic to philosophy but also of philosophical ethics. This has impeded systematic work in ethics in Germany, but nonetheless it is going on. There has been a reaction against the work of Scheler and Hartmann. O. F. Bollnow has argued for a *Situationsethik* and Richard Schattländer has contended that the Scheler-Hartmann approach is too speculative and theoretical and does not adequately handle the moral agent's question: what ought I to do? But the Scheler-Hartmann school is hardly dead, for Hans Reiner, in his *Das Prinzip von Gut und Böse* (Freiburg, 1949), gives us a detailed and vigorous restatement of such a position. Against Heidegger, he defends the philosophical importance of a general theory of value. But in an effort to blunt Heidegger's criticism that such investigations are morally and humanly irrelevant, Reiner concerns himself primarily with moral values. In his concern with moral value, he examines in some detail the problem of ethical relativism, and in this examination he stresses the importance of anthropological investigations to our understanding of morality.

Naturalism in America

While ethical naturalism seemed to have received its quietus in England from Moore and Ross and certainly could not be considered a major force on the Continent, in America in various forms it was, until shortly after World War II, the dominant form of ethical theory.

PERRY. R. B. Perry developed a general theory of value with specific applications to questions of normative ethics, law, politics, economics, and education in his *General Theory of Value* (Cambridge, Mass., 1926) and *Realms of Value* (Cambridge, Mass., 1954). "Value" is used by Perry in a very broad sense as a generic term to group together such terms as "desirable," "good," "worthwhile," "right," "beautiful," "holy," "obligatory," and the like. Perry defines "value" as follows: "a thing—anything—has value, or is valuable, in the original and generic sense when it is the object of an interest—any interest." In an attempt to make his contention overtly verifiable, Perry in turn defined "interest" quasi-behavioristically as "a train of events determined by expectation of its outcome." "Interest" for Perry was an umbrella term for such terms as "like," "desire," "preference," and "need" and their opposites. For something to have positive value, it must be an object of a favorable interest; for something to have negative value, it must be an object of aversion, disapproval, or dislike: in short, it must be an object of negative interest.

It should be understood that this definition of "value" is not taken by Perry to be either a lexical or a purely stipulative definition. It is, rather, a reforming definition. That is to say, it is a deliberate proposal concerning the use of a term in the language, but the proposal is not simply a stipulation, for it has some antecedent basis in the usage in question. It is proposed that this use be adopted as the standard use in order to clear up what are taken to be confusions allegedly resulting from unclear and vacillating usage. By such maneuvers Perry hoped to escape from Moore's arguments concerning the naturalistic fallacy.

Such a theory, initially at least, is extremely attractive, for it holds out a promise for a genuine "normative science" and thus for some objective, if not absolute, knowledge of good and evil. It holds out the promise that we will eventually use the emerging sciences of man to gain some cross-cultural and interpersonally confirmed, and thus objective, knowledge of right and wrong.

The crucial problem for the naturalist is to show how all statements containing ethical terms can be translated into statements that do not contain such terms and are directly or indirectly confirmable or disconfirmable by empirical observation. What must be achieved to develop such a naturalism is to show the tenability of some set of naturalistic definitions of key moral terms.

Working from his initial definition of "value," Perry developed his system from the following definitions:

(1) "*X* has value" equals "*X* is the object of any interest."
(2) "*X* is bad" equals "*X* has negative value."
(3) "*X* is good" equals "*X* has positive value."
(4) "*X* is intrinsically good" equals "*X* is the object of a favorable interest for its own sake."
(5) "*X* is extrinsically good" equals "*X* is the object of a favorable interest because *X*, directly or indirectly, is the most efficient means to something which is intrinsically good."
(6) "*X* is morally good" equals "*X* is the object of interests harmoniously organized by reflective agreement."
(7) "*X* is the highest good" equals "*X* is the object of an all-inclusive and harmonious system of interests."
(8) "*X* is morally right" equals "*X* is conducive to the moral good."
(9) "*X* is morally obligatory" equals "*X* is a social demand that, of any alternative demand, is most clearly called for by the ideal of harmonious happiness."

A theory based on these definitions should, Perry would argue, provide us with a systematic account of our normative concepts and exhibit the rationale of our moral judgments. However, it would be queried by many, including many who are not intuitionists, just how it can be that all moral statements are really a subspecies of empirical statement and how they all could, even in principle, be empirically confirmed or disconfirmed. To take moral statements as empirical statements asserting that so-and-so is the case seems to miss their distinctive, dynamic, and guiding function in the stream of life.

DEWEY. For John Dewey, moral philosophy had a definite normative ethical function. Dewey wanted to criticize normative standards and hoped to indicate more reasonable moral goals. "Philosophy's central problem," he wrote, "is the relation that exists between the beliefs about the nature of things due to natural science and beliefs about values—using that word to designate whatever is taken to have rightful authority in the direction of conduct."

His basic proposal was that we should use what he called experimental intelligence in morals. This means that in moral inquiry we should use the same methodological principles we use in scientific inquiry. We should develop a scientific critique of our institutions and of the patterns of conduct designated "moral." In order to do this we must show the untenability of what

Dewey took to be an unjustified but ancient philosophical preconception that injects a divorce or dichotomy between scientific knowledge, on the one hand, and moral, philosophical, or religious knowledge, on the other. There is but one kind of knowledge, with one reliable method of fixing belief, the experimental method, though this knowledge and method of fixing belief must be applied to different subject matters.

To most people, the use of the experimental method in ethics heralds a drop of any normative ethical standards. In trying to establish that this is a misconception, Dewey tried to establish a severe contextualism. A central mistake of traditional moral philosophies, both naturalist and non-naturalist, was that of looking for one bedrock *summum bonum* or one ultimate moral criterion rather than realizing that there is an irreducible plurality of moral standards and that moral problems are fully intelligible and rationally resolvable only in a definite context. Moral standards are a part of a cultural context in which means and ends are qualitatively continuous and functionally interactive.

This reference to a continuum of means and ends leads to another main element in Dewey's moral philosophy. He argues against the specialist's conception of ethics. To hold this conception, which is traditional with philosophers as different as Plato and Russell, is to stress the distinction between intrinsic good and instrumental good and to contend that intrinsic good is the sole object of philosophical interest. This, according to Dewey, is a mistaken dichotomy rooted in the ancient Greek dichotomy between theory and practice. It is not only intellectually bankrupt but it can, Dewey argues, have vicious social consequences. It even makes for irrationalism in ethics, for given this conception, we are easily led to the assumption that while science can deal with mundane instrumental goods, the highest goods—the basic ends, namely, intrinsic goods—must be grasped by intuition, be vouchsafed by revelation, or be merely a matter of the whims of mortal will. Dewey argued that in concrete moral contexts, answers concerning means actually transform ends. In reasoning morally it is not a matter of discovering the most efficient means to attain a fixed end. If in considering the means it becomes apparent that our ends are utopian, we will, if we are behaving rationally, often give them up or modify them in view of this discovery. Here intelligence has a major role to play in morality. Ends cannot rationally be divorced from means. In fact, they are always functionally interactive. Furthermore, what is an end in one problematic situation is a means in another, and so on. There are never any actual normative goals or ends that are simply intrinsic goods. Ideals are always transformable in the light of what we discover

about our world, and they are always imbedded in a network of other ideals.

Such considerations, it will surely be objected, hardly show that there are no intrinsic goods—but it could be contended that they effectively argue against Aristotelian final ends, or against the belief that in moral appraisal we can justifiably consider intrinsic goods independently of their consequences—and this, after all, is the major point Dewey wanted to establish.

In his celebrated article "Does Moral Philosophy Rest on a Mistake?" (1909), H. A. Prichard argued that it was an endemic mistake of moral philosophy to try to give reasons for our obligations.

Here we hardly have the metaethical concerns that are so distinctive of the work of Moore and Perry. But Dewey—though he didn't call it that—also had a metaethical theory.

Dewey argued that moral judgments are judgments of practice. That is to say, they are made in problematic situations of choice in which a moral agent is trying to decide what to do. This gives them their distinctive normative or *de jure* force. But at the same time they remain *de facto* empirical statements. It is this puzzling amalgam that we must understand if we are to get clear what Dewey was claiming.

Dewey asserted that value judgments are not mere prizings and disprizings. They are predictions about the capacity or incapacity of actions, objects, or events to satisfy desires, needs, and interests. As such they are confirmable and disconfirmable. They predict that certain ends in view will satisfy certain vital impulses under certain conditions. Not everything that is desired is desirable, but those things which are desired "after examination of the relations upon which the object depends" are desirable. In short, to say of something that it is valuable, desirable, or good is to say that it is something which would be desired or approved after reflection upon its relevant causes and consequences.

Criticism of Dewey. Dewey's theory has been subject to some trenchant criticisms by Morton White and Charles Stevenson and has been stanchly defended by Sidney Hook, Gail Kennedy, and Gertrude Ezorsky. The basic considerations here are as follows: even if X is desired after an examination of the causes and consequences of desiring X, it still does not follow that X is desirable or that X ought to be desired. However, to carry out Dewey's program of identifying moral statements as a subspecies of empirical statement, some such identity of meaning must be established.

But the admission that Dewey is wrong in claiming that moral statements are empirical statements or hypotheses is not destructive to his over-all program about the place of reason in ethics. If we ask how we justify our ethical evaluations, it seems that much of Dewey's method of criticism, including much of his use of science, could still be reasonably instituted. Dewey's great failure in talking about morality was in not realizing how very different "values" and "facts" are; his great success was in seeing the extensive relevance of scientific knowledge and scientific method to the making of intelligent moral appraisals.

Contemporary Noncognitivism

Both naturalism and nonnaturalism are cognitive theories. That is to say, they regard moral utterances in the declarative form as statement-making utterances that assert the existence of certain moral facts and are thus either true or false. But first in Sweden, and later in England and America, a quite different kind of metaethical theory developed that has been called a noncognitive theory. According to this theory, moral statements do not assert moral facts; they are neither confirmable nor disconfirmable, and there is nothing to be known by "moral intuition." It is even characteristic of this view to argue that it is either mistaken or at least misleading to characterize moral utterances as true or false.

EMOTIVE THEORY. The noncognitive view, which has subsequently been called the emotive theory, received its first formulation in 1911, when the Swedish philosopher Axel Hägerström drew the outlines of such a theory in his inaugural lecture, "On The Truth of Moral Propositions." In 1917 Hägerström developed his ideas with particular attention to the concept of duty in his *Till Frågan om den Gällande Rättens Begrepp* (Uppsala, 1917). Similar statements of the emotive theory have been developed in Scandinavia by Ingmar Hedenius and Alf Ross. Independently of its Scandinavian formulation, the emotive theory was first stated in the English-speaking world by I. A. Richards and by Bertrand Russell, but it was developed in the Anglo-Saxon world by A. J. Ayer and by Charles Stevenson. There have also been interesting if somewhat atypical statements of it by Richard Robinson, Rudolf Carnap, and Hans Reichenbach.

The emotivists were convinced that moral statements are not a subspecies of factual statement, and they were further convinced that it was impossible to derive a moral statement from a set of purely factual statements. As Hägerström put it, "There is no common genus for

the purely factual and the 'ought.' By using the predicate 'ought to happen' we refer an action to an altogether different category from the factual. That an action 'ought to be done' is regarded as something which holds true altogether without reference to whether it actually is done or not." The whole notion that there is a determinate character of an action that would make a moral statement true or false is, Hägerström argues, an illusion. There is nothing there for an "unmoved spectator of the actual" to observe that would either confirm or disconfirm his moral statements. Moral statements characteristically take a declarative form, but they actually function not to assert that so-and-so is true but to express an attitude toward an action or a state of affairs.

To say that something is good

—where we are talking about "intrinsic good"—

is to say that it is impossible to love it incorrectly.

The emotive theory developed as a *via media* between intuitionism, on the one hand, and ethical naturalism, on the other. Both of these ethical theories displayed crucial difficulties. "Nonnatural qualities" and "nonnatural relations" were obscure, fantastic conceptions, to say the least, and the notion of intuition remained at best nonexplanatory. Furthermore, it was plain that moral judgments are closely linked to one's emotions, attitudes, and conations. But, as Moore in effect showed, neither "A cup of tea before bed is good" nor such general utterances as "Pleasure is good" and "Self-realization is good" are empirical or analytic.

The Function of Ethical Statements. The emotivists maintained that while the grammatical function of a sentence like "A swim before bed is good" is indicative, its actual logical function is much closer to that of an optative or imperative utterance, such as "Would that we could go swimming before bed" or "Swim before bed." Because of this, emotivists have claimed that it is misleading to say that ethical sentences can be used to make statements: they do not function to assert facts.

Similarly, it is a mistake to treat all words as simply functioning to describe or designate some characteristic or thing. Some words so function; but there are other words, like "nasty," "saintly," "graceful," and "wise," that function primarily or in part to express the attitudes of the utterer or to evoke reactions on the part of the hearer. The emotivists claim that "good," "ought," "right," and the like are also emotive words. This gives them their normative function.

Ethical Argument. Hägerström and Ayer contend that the fact that there are no moral facts carries with it the corollary that there can be no genuine moral knowledge. There are no moral facts to be learned; there is no moral information to be gained or forgotten. It makes clear sense to say "I used to know the difference between a pickerel and a pike, but by now I've forgotten it," but what is meant by "I used to know the difference between right and wrong, but by now I've forgotten it"? The word "forgotten" could hardly do its usual job here. The utterance is so deviant that without explanation and a very special context, we do not understand it. Considerations of this sort bring us to the realization that moral utterances are not used to state facts or assert truths; their essential role is a noncognitive one. They typically express emotions, attitudes, and conations and evoke actions, attitudes, and emotional reactions.

Because of this fact about the logical status of moral utterances, it always remains at least logically possible that two or more people might agree about all the relevant facts and disagree in attitude—that is, disagree about what was desirable or worth doing.

We do, however, as Ayer and Stevenson stress, give reasons for moral judgments. If I say "MacDonald did the right thing in killing Janet," it is perfectly in order to ask me to show why this is so. If I say "I don't have any reasons. There aren't any reasons, but all the same I just know that MacDonald did the right thing," I am abusing language. I am saying something unintelligible, for we can't "just know" like that. The person who claims that an action is right *must* always be prepared to give reasons for his moral claim.

Ayer and Stevenson grant all that. This is indeed how we do proceed when we are being reasonable about a moral disagreement. But Ayer says: ". . . the question is: in what way do these reasons support the moral judgments? They do not support them in a logical sense. Ethical argument is not formal demonstration. And they do not support them in a scientific sense either. If they did, the goodness or badness of the situation, the rightness or wrongness of the action, would have to be something apart from the situation, something independently verifiable, for which the facts adduced as the reasons for the moral judgment were the evidence." But this is just what we cannot do. There is *no* procedure for examining the *value* of the facts, as distinct from examining the facts themselves.

If we cannot demonstratively prove or inductively establish fundamental moral claims, then what can it mean to say that a factual statement F is a good reason for a moral judgment E? The emotivist's answer is very simple: if F causes the person(s) to whom E is addressed to adopt E, to share the attitude expressed by E, then F is a good reason for E. It is Ayer's and Stevenson's claim that whatever in fact determines our attitudes is *ipso facto* a good reason for a moral judgment.

Criticisms of Emotive Theory. It has been argued by many moral philosophers (W. D. Falk, Richard Brandt, Errol Bedford, Paul Edwards, and Kai Nielsen, among others) that so to characterize what is meant by "a good reason" in ethics is persuasively to redefine "a good reason" in ethics. As Bedford has well argued against the emotive theory, "we do use logical criteria in moral discussion, however inexplicit, unanalyzed, and relatively vague these criteria of relevance may be." Remarks like "It doesn't follow that you ought to" or "That's beside the point" are just as common and just as much to the point in moral argument as elsewhere. There is no reason to think that these remarks about relevance differ in any essential way from their use in nonevaluative contexts. We don't just seek agreement when there is a moral dispute, but we try to justify one claim over another and we rightly reject persuasion as irrelevant to this task of justification.

Stevenson has replied that to answer in this way is in effect to confuse normative ethical inquiries with metaethical ones. "Good" and "relevant" are normative terms and have their distinctive emotive force. To say that such and such are good reasons is to make a moral statement. Making such a statement involves leaving the normative ethical neutrality of metaethical inquiry. One answer to this is that to say what is *meant* by "good reasons" in ethics is to *mention* "good reasons" and not to *use* them.

EXISTENTIALISM. Noncognitivism is not limited to emotivism. The existentialists do not call themselves noncognitivists, nor do they write metaethical treatises. But reasonably definite metaethical assumptions are implicit in their writings. Their contention that "men create their values," their stress on decision, commitment, and the impossibility of achieving ethical knowledge, strongly suggests a noncognitivist metaethic. We shall limit the examination here to two major figures, Albert Camus and Jean-Paul Sartre.

Camus. Unlike Sartre, Albert Camus wrote no technical philosophy, but in his *Myth of Sisyphus* (Paris, 1942), *The Rebel* (Paris, 1951), and his plays and novels he did articulate an ethical view that has been called the ethics of the absurd. To read Camus is to be immediately thrown into normative ethics via what has been called philosophical anthropology. We are immediately confronted with a picture of man and man's lot. Man is divorced from the world yet is paradoxically thrust into it. The world as we find it—given our hopes, our expectations, our ideals—is intractable. It is incommensurate with our moral and intellectual demands.

Life is fragmented. We seek to discover some rational unity amidst this diversity and chaos. We discover instead that we can only impose an arbitrary unity upon it. *L'homme absurde*, as distinct from *l'homme quotidien*, sees clearly the relativity and flux of human commitment and the ultimate purposelessness of life. Yet man has a blind but overpowering attachment to life as something more powerful than any of the world's ills or any human intellectualization. But the world is ultimately unintelligible and irrational, and man's lot in the world is absurd.

Nicolai Hartmann's massive work Ethics *(1926)*

shows the influence of Scheler and Husserl

and is without doubt the most extensive

phenomenological discussion of value in the literature.

Given this situation, all moral commitments are arbitrary. There is no escaping this: reason will only show us the arbitrariness of human valuations, and a Kierkegaardian leap of faith in the face of the absurd is evasive. It is evasive because it is to consent to absurdity rather than to face up to it, recognizing it for what it is. Man's dignity comes in his refusing to compromise. His very humanity is displayed in his holding on to his intelligence and in recognizing, contra Kierkegaard, that there is no God and, contra Jaspers, that there is no metaphysical unity that can overcome the absurdity of human existence.

Yet paradoxically, and some would claim inconsistently, in his novel *The Plague* (Paris, 1947), and in his essays, collected and published in English under the title *Resistance, Rebellion and Death* (New York, 1961) Camus writes with passion and conviction in defense of human freedom and intelligence. Camus's rationale for this is that we become *engagé* because we see that life has no ultimate meaning and that, finally free from a search for cosmic significance, we can take the diverse experiences of life for what they are in all their richness and variety. Yet beyond that and perhaps because of that, Camus, as a humanist, is espousing the cause of man. By this is meant, as is very evident in *Resistance, Rebellion and Death,* that Camus repeatedly defends human freedom, equality, and the alleviation of human misery and deprivation. We must become involved, but in this involvement Camus urges a reliance on human intelligence in facing the problems of men.

What might be taken to be a conflict between the more theoretical side of Camus's thought and his more directly normative ethical side comes out in his fourth "Letter to a German Friend." Camus agrees with his "German friend" that the world has no ultimate meaning, but he does not and will not conclude from this, as his "German friend" did, "that everything was equivalent and that good and evil could be defined according to one's wishes." Camus then goes on to remark that he can find no valid argument to answer such a nihilism. His only "answer" is "a fierce love of justice, which after all, seemed to me as unreasonable as the most sudden passion." Camus felt he could only resolutely refuse to accept despair and "to fight against eternal injustice, create happiness in order to protest against the universe of unhappiness." Camus concludes with a cry of the heart that while "the world has no ultimate meaning . . . something in it has a meaning, namely man because he is the only creature to insist on having one."

Sartre. Jean-Paul Sartre's views on man's condition are in many important respects like those of Camus, but to a far greater degree than Camus, Sartre in *Being and Nothingness* (Paris, 1943) and *Critique de la raison dialectique* (Paris, 1960) sets his ethical theorizing in the murky atmosphere of metaphysics. The promised systematic work on ethics that was to follow *Being and Nothingness* has not been forthcoming, but in one way or another all of Sartre's works are concerned with ethics. It can be said that there are two Sartres, or at least that the Sartre of *Critique de la raison dialectique* has moved from his earlier existentialism over to a kind of Marxist materialism. Here we shall for the most part (except where specifically noted) be concerned with the earlier Sartre, whose philosophical endeavor centered on his massive *Being and Nothingness.*

Sartre, like Camus, finds man's lot in the world absurd. Since there is no God, life can have no ultimate meaning and there can be no objective knowledge of good and evil. We cannot "decide a priori," or find out by investigation, what we are to do. Man in his forlornness and freedom imposes values. The choices man makes, the projects he forms for himself, and the sum of his acts constitute his values. There is no good and evil to be intuited or in any way discovered by the human animal. Man in anguish creates his values by his deliberate choices, and, to add to his anguish, in making his choices "he involves all mankind." That is to say, Sartre stresses the Kantian claim that moral judgments, in order to be moral judgments, must be universalizable, but, as Sartre adds in his lecture "Existentialism Is a Humanism" (1945), though their "form is universal . . . the content of ethics is variable" and there is no rational way of justifying the acceptance of moral principles with one content rather than another.

Sartre thinks this position is simply a matter of drawing out in a nonevasive manner the implications of a consistent atheism. Only if there were a God could values have an objective justification, but without God "everything is permissible" and "as a result man is forlorn, because neither within him nor without does he find anything to cling to." In this, Sartre is surely mistaken. It does not follow that if there is no God, nothing matters, or that everything is permissible. It is not a contradiction to assert, "Though there is no God, the torturing of children is still vile," and the nonexistence of God does not preclude the possibility of there being an objective standard on which to base such judgments.

Sartre asserts flatly, in good Moorean spirit, "Ontology itself cannot formulate ethical precepts. It is concerned solely with what is, and we cannot possibly derive imperatives from ontology's indicatives." (All the same, his account of morality in *Being and Nothingness* and his account of human action relevant to morality are immersed in "the language of being.") In fact, Sartre goes on to point out that ontology and what he calls existential psychoanalysis can in a given situation constitute "a moral description, for it presents to us the ethical meaning of various human projects." This method of description—though hardly the descriptions themselves—is very like the phenomenological method practiced by Scheler and Hartmann. Yet to proceed in this way hardly constitutes a violation of the is/ought distinction, since Sartre's descriptions of moral evaluations—descriptions of man's ethical life—need not themselves be evaluative, though given the language Sartre uses, they often are.

"Man," he tells us, "pursues being blindly by hiding from himself the free project which is this pursuit." Existential psychoanalysis can reveal to man the real goal of his pursuit. Horrified by the "death of God," man attempts in his anguish to be God. He flees from his freedom—he does not wish to be a creator of values—but in what Sartre ironically calls the spirit of seriousness, he seeks to deny human subjectivity and attributes to value some independent cosmic significance. To the extent that we are caught up in this spirit of seriousness, we will try to fuse "being-for-itself" with the brute facticity of "being-in-itself." (The odd phrase "being-in-itself" is simply the label for the self-contained reality of a thing, while its mate, "being-for-itself," is the label for the realm of consciousness that perpetually strives to transcend itself.) But if we pursue this line, we still condemned to despair, for we "discover at the same time that all human activities are equivalent . . . and that all are on principle doomed to failure." Phenomenological analysis reveals to man that though he perpetually tries to become a thing, a brute existent, the fact that he has

consciousness makes this impossible. Given this ability to think and to feel, man, whether he likes it or not, is slowly led to see that without God he can have no essential nature; that is, though he may form his own projects, there is and can be no purpose to life.

It should be noted that Sartre's view of man's lot is even grimmer than Camus's, for Sartre contends that even in community with others there is no surcease from suffering and alienation, for human relations are essentially relations of conflict and estrangement.

In *Critique de la raison dialectique,* Sartre tries to work out a new kind of Marxism and a new materialist conception of man. But he wishes to integrate his existentialist conceptions into a Marxist materialism in such a way that the latter can come to have a truly "human dimension." Marxism, he argues, must purge itself of its deterministic conceptions of man and acknowledge a rational conception of human freedom. Sartre, in a reversal from *Being and Nothingness,* now argues that there is nothing intrinsic in human nature that makes conflict, war, and a reign of terror inescapable, though, like a good Marxist, he does argue that conflict is a basic factor in human history. It is scarcity, scarcity of goods and materials, that triggers human conflict. Only under these conditions of scarcity is social conflict inescapable and a rational social order impossible. Men make their own history by the choices they make in the face of problems created by history. But man remains the rider, not the horse. Human choices—human projects—are still free choices for which men remain responsible.

Recent Views on Moral Discourse

LINGUISTIC PHILOSOPHY. As has frequently been noted, there are at least superficial resemblances between the existentialists and the otherwise very different, self-consciously metaethical theories of such linguistic philosophers as R. M. Hare, P. H. Nowell-Smith, Bernard Mayo, Alan Montefiore, and John Hartland-Swann.

There is, indeed, this much similarity between these linguistic philosophers and the existentialists. All of the former make the following contentions, all of which would be welcome to the latter:

(1) Moore was essentially right about the naturalistic fallacy. That is to say, moral statements cannot be deduced from any statement of fact, whether biological, historical, psychological, sociological, or religious.

(2) No moral choice or question of value can ever be guaranteed by logical rules.

(3) We are free, as far as language or logic is concerned, to apply evaluative or prescriptive terms to anything we wish to commend or condemn, criticize or approve, prescribe or forbid.

(4) Moral utterances are generalizable decisions, resolutions, or subscriptions.

Given that a man accepts certain moral principles, other moral principles can, together with certain factual statements, be derived from the above principles. But like Ayer and the existentialists, these linguistic philosophers hold that there must be some moral principles which are not derived from any other principles—moral or otherwise—and, being fundamental moral principles, they are not even verifiable in principle. They express moral commitments and can have no rational ground, for what is deemed worthy of acceptance ultimately depends on the very commitments (generalizable decisions, resolutions, or subscriptions) an agent is willing to make.

Many people have thought that such a view of morality is either directly or indirectly nihilistic—that both the linguistic philosophers and the existentialists espouse what is in effect an irrationalism that would undercut the very possibility of a rational normative ethic.

If we consider a reply linguistic philosophers typically make to such criticisms, we will become aware of a crucial dissimilarity between them and the existentialists and a fundamental defect in existentialist ethics.

John Dewey's basic proposal was that we should use what he called experimental intelligence in morals: in moral inquiry we should use the same methodological principles we use in scientific inquiry.

Linguistic philosophers have frequently claimed that the existentialists have merely dramatized a logical point. That moral principles are expressions of commitment or choice, that man cannot simply discover what is good or evil or know a priori that a certain thing must be done but must "create his own values," is not a worrisome fact about the human predicament; it is a conceptual truth concerning the nature of moral discourse. It is not a fact of the human condition that man is born into a world alien and indifferent to human purposes. What is a fact is that the phrases "the universe has a purpose" and "value and being are one" are unintelligible phrases. To say "man creates his own values" is in reality only to say in a dramatic way that a judgment of value is an expression of choice. This statement, it is argued, is not an anguished cry of the human heart but is merely an expression of a linguistic convention.

To say "If *x* is a judgment of value, then *x* is an expression of choice" is not to say "Any choice at all is

justified," "Anything is permissible," or "All human actions are of equal value." These latter statements are themselves value judgments and could not follow from the above-mentioned statement, for it is not itself a statement of value but a nonnormative metaethical statement about the meaning of evaluative expressions, and, as Sartre himself stresses, one cannot derive an "ought" from an "is." In general, Hare and Nowell-Smith, as well as Ayer and Stevenson, stress the normative neutrality of metaethical statements.

Hare. R. M. Hare in two very influential books, *The Language of Morals* (Oxford, 1952) and *Freedom and Reason* (Oxford, 1963), has developed a very closely reasoned metaethical analysis of the type that has been discussed. In *The Language of Morals,* Hare views moral utterances as a species of prescriptive discourse, and he feels that we can most readily come to understand their actual role in the stream of life if we see how very much they are like another form of prescriptive discourse, namely, imperatives. Imperatives tell us to do something, not that something is the case. Moral utterances in their most paradigmatic employments also tell us to do something. Imperative and moral utterances do not, as the emotivists thought, have the logical function of trying to *get* you to do something. Rather, they *tell* you to do something. Furthermore, there are logical relations between prescriptive statements, just as there are logical relations between factual statements.

Moral judgments are viewed as a kind of prescriptive judgment but, unlike singular imperatives, moral judgments (as well as all value judgments) are universalizable. Hare means by this that such a judgment "logically commits the speaker to making a similar judgment about anything which is either exactly like the subject of the original judgment or like it in the relevant respects."

Hare stresses that while almost any word in certain contexts can function evaluatively, "good," "right," and "ought" almost always so function. The evaluative functions of these terms are distinct from their descriptive functions and are an essential part of their meaning. In fact, the distinctive function of all value words is that they in one way or another commend or condemn. But while "good" is a general word of commendation, the criteria for goodness vary from context to context and are dependent on what it is that is said to be "good."

The meaning of "good" or any other value term is never tied to its criteria of application. There is nothing in the logic of our language to limit the content of a moral judgment. As far as logic is concerned, any universalizable prescription that expresses a deep concern or commitment is *ipso facto* a moral prescription, and we can decide without conceptual error to do anything that it is logically or physically possible to do. If we treat the resulting decision as a decision of principle, that is, a universalizable prescription, then it is a value judgment that is in good logical order. As Nowell-Smith has well put it in discussing Hare's theory, "Nothing that we discover about the nature of moral judgments entails that it is wrong to put all Jews in gas-chambers."

Criticism of Hare. Probably the most persistent dissatisfaction with Hare's theory has resulted from the belief that it makes moral reasoning appear to be more arbitrary than it actually is. To say "Nothing that we discover about the nature of moral judgments entails that it is wrong to put all Jews in gas-chambers" is, it will be argued, a *reductio* of such a position. Hare would reply that to argue in such a way is to fail to recognize that he is talking about entailment, and that he is simply making the point that from nonnormative statements one cannot deduce normative ones.

Hare argues that his thesis about the logical status of moral utterances does not commit him to the position that there can be no rational resolution of basic conflicts in moral principle. Returning, in *Freedom and Reason,* to a stress on decisions (though with a new attention to inclinations), Hare contends that to have a morality we must have freedom. Specifically, we must have a situation in which each man must solve his own moral problems. (This is not to moralize about what we should do but to state a logical condition for the very existence of moral claims.)

Philosophers who have criticized Hare, including someone as close to him as Nowell-Smith, have suggested that Hare still has a far too Protestant conception of moral discourse. He fails really to take to heart the Wittgensteinian claim that here, as elsewhere in human discourse, we must have public criteria for what could count as a logically proper moral claim. As F. E. Sparshott—whose book *An Enquiry into Goodness* (Chicago, 1958) deserves more attention than it has received—notes: Hare's individualism leads him to neglect the fact that a morality, any morality, will necessarily incorporate "those rules of conduct that seem necessary for communal living." It is not the case that just any universalizable set of prescriptions can constitute a morality or a set of moral judgments.

THE GOOD-REASONS APPROACH. The last metaethical theory we shall discuss has been dubbed the good-reasons approach. Stephen Toulmin, Kurt Baier, Henry Aiken, Marcus Singer, Kai Nielsen, A. I. Melden, A. E. Murphy, and John Rawls may be taken as representative figures of this point of view. It is an approach which obviously has been deeply affected by the philosophical method that we have come to associate with the work of the later Wittgenstein. These philosophers have centered their attention on the logic of moral reasoning. Their central question has been

"When is a reason a *good* reason for a moral judgment?" Accordingly, the crucial problems center on questions concerning the nature and limits of *justification* in ethics. These philosophers agree with the noncognitivists that moral sentences are used primarily as dynamic expressions to guide conduct and alter behavior. And they would also agree with ethical naturalists that moral utterances usually, at least, also make factual assertions. But they believe that the primary use of moral utterances is not theoretical or just emotive but practical. Hare and Nowell-Smith are right in stressing that they are designed to tell us what to do.

In his novel The Plague *(1947) and in his essays,*

Camus writes with passion and conviction

in defense of human freedom and intelligence.

Yet while moral utterances typically tell us what to do, language with its complex and multifarious uses does not neatly divide into "the descriptive" and "the evaluative," "the constative" and "the performative," "the cognitive" and "the noncognitive." These are philosophers' specialized terms, and they do not help us to understand and clearly characterize moral discourse but actually distort our understanding of it. There can be no translation of moral terms into nonmoral terms, and the ancient problem of bridging "the is–ought gulf" is a muddle, for there is no clear distinction between such uses of language and no single function that makes a bit of discourse normative. Some moral utterances indeed bear interesting analogies to commands or resolutions, but they cannot be identified with them. It is a mistake to think ethical judgments are like scientific ones or like the judgments of any other branch of objective inquiry; yet cognitivist metaethicists were correct, not in pressing this analogy but in maintaining that there is a knowledge of good and evil and that some moral claims have a perfectly respectable objectivity. No matter how emotive or performative moral utterances may be, when we make a moral judgment, it must—logically must—satisfy certain requirements to count as a moral judgment. In making a moral judgment, we must be willing to universalize the judgment in question, and it must be possible to give factual reasons in support of the moral claim.

The advocates of the good-reasons approach in the general tradition of the later Wittgenstein did not take it to be incumbent on the philosopher to translate moral utterances into some clearer idiom. They did not believe that there was some other favored discourse or form of life that moral discourse or morality should be modeled on. What was expected of the philosopher was that he should describe morality so as to perspicuously display the living discourse at work. In particular, philosophers should concern themselves with a conceptual cartography of the nature and limits of justification in ethics. Before we can reasonably claim that moral judgments are at bottom "all subjective" or that no moral claim can be "objectively justified," we must come to understand what can and what cannot count as a good reason in ethics and what the limits of moral reasoning are.

Sartre's view of man's lot is even grimmer than Camus's, for Sartre contends that even in community with others there is no surcease from suffering and alienation, for human relations are essentially relations of conflict and estrangement.

Toulmin. Two books, Stephen Toulmin's *An Examination of the Place of Reason in Ethics* (Cambridge, 1950) and Kurt Baier's *The Moral Point of View* (Ithaca, N.Y., 1958), have most single-mindedly attacked the problem of moral reasoning. They may be taken as paradigms of the good-reasons approach. Toulmin argues that moral rules and moral principles are to be justified by discovering which of these rules or principles, if consistently acted upon, will most likely lead to the least amount of avoidable suffering all around. Those social practices which probably will cause the least amount of suffering for mankind are the social practices which ought to be accepted. Classical utilitarians maintained that a moral rule is justified if it tends to produce greater happiness all around than any alternative rule, but Toulmin favors the negative formulation because (1) though it is very difficult to determine what will make people happy or what they want, it is less difficult to determine what causes suffering, and (2) it is less the function of morality to tell men what the good life is than to tell them what *not* to do so that their interests, including their differing conceptions of the good life, can be realized to the maximum extent.

This theory about moral reasoning, while purporting to be metaethical, is very close to the normative ethical theory sometimes called rule utilitarianism.

Toulmin argues that if we examine closely the way moral reasoning is actually carried on, it will become evident that moral rules and practices are characteristically judged by roughly utilitarian standards, while many individual actions are judged by whether or not

they are in accordance with an accepted moral rule or social practice. Utilitarians point out that it is of the greatest social utility that we characteristically judge moral acts in this seemingly nonutilitarian fashion. However, frequently a decision concerning how to act involves conflicting moral rules with no clear order of subordination, and in some situations there seems to be no moral rule—unless the principle of utility is taken as a moral rule—that is readily applicable. In such a situation, the thing to do is to act on a utilitarian basis when it is at all possible to make some reasonable judgment of the probable beneficial consequences to the people involved of doing one thing rather than another. If that is not possible in a given situation, then we should act as a reasonable man would act. (The concept of a reasonable man, we should not forget, is itself very much a moral concept.)

Criticism of Toulmin. There certainly are a host of objections that spring to mind concerning Toulmin's account. First, it will be said that this is normative ethics, not metaethics: it tells us what we should do, what a good reason is, and how we can justify basic moral rules. Moreover, why should we accept it? Once we see through its modish trappings, it will become apparent that it has all the difficulties attendant on classical utilitarianism.

It could be replied that though the speech is in the material mode and sounds like normative ethics, in reality it is a brief description of how moral reasoning is actually carried on.

Even if this reply is accepted, there are difficulties here too, for viewed this way, Toulmin's account surely looks like an account of a basically sociological sort of how certain people in fact reason. That is to say, it appears to be an impressionistic bit of descriptive ethics and hardly a metaethical account of the *logic* of moral reasoning. It covertly and persuasively redefines as "moral" only a very limited pattern of reasoning—reasoning that expresses the historically and ethnographically limited views of a determinate group of people. The ethnocentric character of this linguistic analysis makes it implicitly, but surreptitiously, normative.

This contention will be rejected by many. It will be argued that moral reasoning, like any other mode of reasoning, is limited. To determine what the moral point of view is and what it is to reason morally, we need first to determine the function (purpose, over-all rationale) of morality.

The function of morality, Toulmin tells us, is to adjudicate conflicting interests and to harmonize desires (that is, moderate our impulses and adjust our demands) so as to reconcile them with our fellows, in such a way that everyone can have as much as possible of whatever it is that, on reflection, he wants.

Given this conception of the function of ethics, something like Toulmin's account of moral reasoning is very plausible, but it has been objected that morality has no *one* such function. Many people have ideals of human excellence that have nothing to do with such a conception of the function of ethics: many Jews and Christians, with their ideals of the love of God, do not conceive the function of moral living in this way, and the Buddhist community with its ideals of *arhat*ship certainly would not accept, either in theory or in practice, such a conception of the function of ethics. Morality is a much more complicated and varied activity. There are diverse and often conflicting functions of morality. Any attempt to claim one function or rationale of morality as *the* function or *the* purpose of morality so circumscribes what can count as moral considerations that its effect is unwittingly to advocate one limited moral outlook as the moral point of view.

Finally, even if Toulmin could make out a case for claiming that the function of morality, or the primary function of morality, is such as he claims it to be, one could still ask, concerning this descriptive account of morality, "Why keep it as the sole or primary function of morality?" If altering the function of morality somewhat alters the meaning of "moral," then why should we be such linguistic conservatives? What is so sacred about that function of morality and its attendant conception of morality?

Probably the most persistent dissatisfaction with

R. M. Hare's theory has resulted from the belief

that it makes moral reasoning appear to be

more arbitrary than it actually is.

Toulmin could claim that now his critic has confused normative issues with metaethical ones. The issues here are complex and lead us into the heart of current discussion about the nature of moral reasoning. Yet a strong case can be made for the contention that there is more to be said for a general approach such as Toulmin's and Baier's than has commonly been thought.

It seems evident that much contemporary thinking about ethics, while devoted to Moore's exacting standards of making perfectly clear precisely what is being claimed, is concerned not with the very general question of the meaning of "good" or, for that matter, "right" or

"ought" but with the rich texture of moral reasoning. This brings once more to the foreground the kind of detailed descriptions of the moral life distinctive of such phenomenologists as Scheler and Hartmann, but given the present care for actual conceptual distinctions, we may develop a kind of linguistic phenomenology which may be of major importance to an understanding of morality. Perhaps the most exciting endeavors from this point of view have been those of John Rawls, Philippa Foot, and Georg von Wright. Rawls, in a series of distinguished essays, has shown the central role of considerations of justice in moral deliberation and the way such considerations modify utilitarian patterns of reasoning; Philippa Foot, also in a series of much-discussed essays, has shown the importance of a discussion of the virtues and the vices and has reinvigorated ethical naturalism. Georg von Wright's recent masterful discussion of the varieties of goodness in his *The Varieties of Goodness* (London, 1963) has contributed immensely to our understanding of morality.

[See also Ethics, Problems of.]

BIBLIOGRAPHY

General Histories of Ethics

Historical and Social Context of Ethical Beliefs

Brinton, C. C., *A History of Western Morals.* London, 1959. A very readable history of ethical beliefs and practices.

Bruce, A. B., *The Moral Order of the World in Ancient and Modern Thought,* 4 vols. London, 1899. A detailed study of the literary and religious background of ethical thought from ancient Greece to the Reformation.

Dittrich, O., *Geschichte der Ethik,* 4 vols. Leipzig, 1926. A scholarly study of the literary and religious origins of Western ethical ideals.

Harkness, G. E., *The Sources of Western Morality.* New York, 1954. An exploration of the ancient origins of modern ethics. Useful comparisons of primitive with Old Testament ethics and of Greek with Christian ethics.

Kropotkin, P. A., *Ethics, Origin and Development,* translated by L. S. Friedland and J. R. Piroshnikoff. New York, 1924. A Marxist account of the development of ethics from primitive to modern Western society.

Lecky, W. E. H., *History of European Morals,* 2 vols. New York, 1919. A justly celebrated study of how moral values reflect, but fail to keep up with, actual practices in the Western world. Vol. I, Ch. 1, discusses modern British ethical philosophy.

Mencken, H. L., *Treatise on Right and Wrong.* New York, 1934. Perceptive and often caustic comments on the evolution of moral ideas in philosophy and religion; a critique of authoritarianism.

Robertson, J. M., *A Short History of Morals.* London, 1920. A relativistic view of the history of ethics, stressing the sociological sources of morality.

Westermarck, E., *The Origin and Development of Moral Ideas,* 2 vols. London, 1908. A monumental work of historical and anthropological scholarship.

Histories of Ethical Philosophy

Broad, C. D., *Five Types of Ethical Theory.* London, 1930. A critical study, by a distinguished intuitionist, of the ethical systems of Spinoza, Butler, Hume, Kant, and Sidgwick.

Kautsky, K., *Ethics and the Materialist Conception of History,* translated by J. B. Agnew. Chicago, 1907. A brief sketch of the evolution of ethical thought by a noted Marxist.

MacIntyre, A., *A Short History of Ethics.* New York, 1966. An important discussion by a contemporary analytic philosopher.

Mackinnon, D. M., *A Study in Ethical Theory.* London, 1957. A comparison of the theories of Kant, Butler, and the utilitarians as alternatives to religious ethics.

Maritain, J., *Moral Philosophy,* translated by M. Suther. New York, 1964. A critical evaluation of secular ethical theories from the standpoint of Catholic theology.

Martineau, J., *Types of Ethical Theory,* 2 vols. Oxford, 1898. Vol. I evaluates the metaphysical and ethical views of Plato, Descartes, Malebranche, Spinoza, and Comte. Vol. II criticizes utilitarian and moral-sense theories.

Rogers, R. A. P., *A Short History of Ethics.* London, 1911. A brief survey of the history of ethical theory. Incomplete but clear and readable.

Sidgwick, H., *Outlines of the History of Ethics.* London, 1886. A brief but illuminating discussion of the most important schools of ethical thought from ancient Greece to nineteenth-century England.

Swabey, W. C., *Ethical Thought From Hobbes to Kant.* New York, 1961. A useful summary of several philosophical systems.

Plato

General Expositions

Dickinson, G. L., *Plato and His Dialogues.* New York, 1932.

Field, G. X., *The Philosophy of Plato.* London, 1951.

Friedländer, P., *Plato,* translated by Hans Meyerhoff. New York, 1958–1964. A multivolume work of tremendous scholarship on the cultural background of Plato's writings.

Shorey, P., *What Plato Said.* Chicago, 1933.

Taylor, A. E., *Plato, the Man and His Work.* London, 1908.

Specialized Studies

Lodge, R. C., *Plato's Theory of Ethics.* New York, 1928. A thorough study limited to Plato's ethical ideas.

Nettleship, R. L., *Lectures on the Republic of Plato.* New York, 1962. An extraordinarily illuminating study of Plato's most important dialogue.

Relation of Plato to Other Greek Thinkers

Burnet, J., *Platonism.* Berkeley, 1928. Distinguishes sharply between Socratic and Platonic views.

Cornford, F. M., *Before and After Socrates.* Cambridge, 1960.

Demos, R., *The Philosophy of Plato.* New York, 1939. Rejects any systematic interpretation of Plato.

Field, G. C., *Plato and His Contemporaries.* London, 1948.

Gould, J., *The Development of Plato's Ethics.* Cambridge, 1955.

Hampden, R. D., *The Fathers of Greek Philosophy.* Edinburgh, 1862.

Merlan, P., *From Plato to Platonism.* The Hague, 1960.

Plato's Ethics and Politics

Crossman, R. H., *Plato Today.* London, 1937. Critical.

Fite, W., *The Platonic Legend.* New York, 1934. Critical.

Koyré, A., *Discovering Plato.* New York, 1945. Favorable.

Levinson, R. B., *In Defense of Plato.* Cambridge, Mass., 1953.

Wild, J. D., *Plato's Modern Enemies.* Chicago, 1959. Favorable.

Aristotle

Aristotle's Ethics

Gauthier, R. A., *La Morale d'Aristote.* Paris, 1958.

Grene, M., *A Portrait of Aristotle.* London, 1963.

Marshall, T., *Aristotle's Theory of Conduct.* London, 1906.

Mure, G. R. G., *Aristotle,* London, 1932.

Oates, W. J., *Aristotle and the Problem of Value.* Princeton, N.J., 1963.

Randall, J. H., *Aristotle.* New York, 1960. Chs. 11–14.

Ross, W. D., *Aristotle.* London, 1930.

Veatch, H. B., *Rational Man.* Bloomington, Ind., 1962.

Walsh, J. J., *Aristotle's Conception of Moral Weakness.* New York, 1963.

Aristotle and Other Ethical Philosophers

Cornford, F. M., *Before and After Socrates.* Cambridge, 1960.

Hampden, R. D., *The Fathers of Greek Philosophy.* Edinburgh, 1862.

Merlan, P., *Studies in Epicurus and Aristotle.* Wiesbaden, 1960.

Taylor, A. E., *Aristotle.* London, 1943.

Hellenistic and Roman Ethics

Epicureanism

DeWitt, N. W., *Epicurus and His Philosophy.* Minneapolis, Minn., 1954.

Hadzsits, G. D., *Lucretius and His Influence.* New York, 1935.

Merlan, P., *Studies in Epicurus and Aristotle.* Wiesbaden, 1960.

Stoicism

Arnold, E. V., *Roman Stoicism.* Cambridge, 1911. Middle and late Stoa.

Bréhier, É., *Chrysippe et l'ancien Stoicisme.* Paris, 1951. Early Stoa.

Brussell, F. W., *Marcus Aurelius and the Later Stoics.* New York, 1910.

Murray, G., *Stoic, Christian and Humanist.* Boston, 1950.

Wenley, R. M., *Stoicism and Its Influence.* Boston, 1924.

Neoplatonism

Elsee, C., *Neoplatonism in Relation to Christianity.* Cambridge, 1908.

Feibleman, J., *Religious Platonism.* London, 1959.

Pistorius, P. V., *Plotinus and Neoplatonism.* Cambridge, 1952.

Switalski, B., *Neoplatonism and the Ethics of St. Augustine.* New York, 1946.

Whittaker, T., *The Neoplatonists.* Cambridge, 1918.

Comparisons

Hicks, R. D., *Stoic and Epicurean.* New York, 1910.

Zeller, E., *Stoics, Epicureans and Sceptics,* translated by O. J. Reichel. London, 1880.

Medieval Ethics

General Histories of Medieval Philosophy

Copleston, F. C., *A History of Philosophy,* Vols. II and III. Westminster, Md., 1950–1953.

Gilson, É., *The Spirit of Medieval Philosophy,* translated by A. Downes. New York, 1936.

Gilson, É., *Reason and Revelation in the Middle Ages.* New York, 1938.

Hawkins, D. J. B., *A Sketch of Medieval Philosophy.* London, 1945.

Husik, I., *A History of Medieval Jewish Philosophy.* New York, 1916.

Augustine

Gilson, É., *Introduction a l'étude de saint Augustin.* Paris, 1943.
Switalski, B., *Neoplatonism and the Ethics of St. Augustine.* New York, 1946.

Aquinas

Copleston, F. C., *Aquinas.* London, 1955. Ch. 5.
D'Arcy, M. C., *St. Thomas Aquinas.* Dublin, 1953. Ch. 9.
Gilson, É., *The Philosophy of St. Thomas Aquinas,* translated by E. Bullough. St. Louis, 1934.
Maritain, J., *St. Thomas and the Problem of Evil.* Milwaukee, Wis., 1942.
Mullane, D. T., *Aristotelianism in St. Thomas.* Washington, 1929.

Erigena and Abelard

Bett, H., *Johannes Scotus Eriugena.* Cambridge, 1925.
Sikes, J. G., *Peter Abailard.* Cambridge, 1932. Chs. 2 and 8.

Seventeenth-century Ethics

Hobbes

Laird, J., *Hobbes.* London, 1934.
Peters, R. S., *Hobbes.* London, 1956.
Stephen, L., *Hobbes.* Ann Arbor, Mich., 1961.
Taylor, A. E., *Hobbes.* New York, 1908.

Spinoza

Bidney, D., *The Psychology and Ethics of Spinoza.* New Haven, 1940.
Broad, C. D., *Five Types of Ethical Theory.* London, 1930. Ch. 2.
Hampshire, S., *Spinoza.* Harmondsworth, England, 1951. Chs. 4 and 5.
Joachim, H. J., *A Study of the Ethics of Spinoza.* London, 1901.
McKeon, R., *The Philosophy of Spinoza.* New York, 1928.

Locke

Aaron, R. I., *John Locke.* Oxford, 1955.
Lamprecht, S. P., *The Moral and Political Philosophy of John Locke.* New York, 1918.

Cambridge Platonists

Cassirer, E., *The Platonic Renaissance in England,* translated by J. P. Pettegrove. Austin, Texas, 1953.
Powicke, F. J., *The Cambridge Platonists.* Cambridge, Mass., 1926.

Eighteenth-century Ethics

Moral-Sense Theories

Bonar, J., *Moral Sense.* New York, 1930.
Raphael, D. D., *The Moral Sense.* London, 1947.

Clarke

Le Rossignol, J. E., *The Ethical Philosophy of Samuel Clarke.* Leipzig, 1892.

Butler

Broad, C. D., *Five Types of Ethical Theory.* London, 1930. Ch. 3.
Duncan-Jones, A. E., *Butler's Moral Philosophy.* Harmondsworth, England, 1952.

Shaftesbury and Hutcheson

Fowler, T., *Shaftesbury and Hutcheson.* London, 1882.

Hume

Basson, A. H., *David Hume.* Harmondsworth, England, 1958. Ch. 5.
Broad, C. D., *Five Types of Ethical Theory.* London, 1930. Ch. 4.
Smith, N. K., *The Philosophy of David Hume.* London, 1941.
Stewart, J. B., *The Moral and Political Philosophy of David Hume.* New York, 1963.

Price and Reid

Raphael, D. D., *The Moral Sense.* London, 1947.

French Enlightenment

Becker, C. L., *The Heavenly City of the Eighteenth Century Philosophers.* New Haven, 1932.
Cassirer, E., *The Philosophy of the Enlightenment,* translated by F. Koelln and J. P. Pettegrove. Princeton, N.J., 1951.
Crocker, L. G., *Nature and Culture.* Baltimore, 1963.
Halévy, É., *The Growth of Philosophic Radicalism,* translated by M. Morris. New York, 1928.
Rouston, M., *The Pioneers of the French Revolution,* translated by F. Whyte. London, 1926. A study of the social and political involvements of the Encyclopedists.

Kant

Broad, C. D., *Five Types of Ethical Theory.* London, 1930. Ch. 5.
Jones, W. T., *Morality and Freedom in the Philosophy of Immanuel Kant.* Oxford, 1940.
Körner, S., *Kant.* Harmondsworth, England, 1955. Chs. 6 and 7.
Lindsay, A. D., *Kant.* London, 1934.
Paton, H. J., *The Moral Law, or Kant's Groundwork of the Metaphysic of Morals.* New York, 1948.
Paton, H. J., *The Categorical Imperative.* Chicago, 1948.
Teale, A. E., *Kantian Ethics.* London, 1951.

Nineteenth-century Ethics

Utilitarianism

Halévy, É., *The Growth of Philosophic Radicalism,* translated by M. Morris. New York, 1928.
Stephen, L., *The English Utilitarians,* 3 vols. New York, 1900.

German Idealism

Dewey, J., *German Philosophy and Politics.* New York, 1942. Highly critical.
Hook, S., *From Hegel to Marx.* New York, 1936.
Löwith, K., *From Hegel to Nietzsche.* translated by D. Green. New York, 1964.
Marcuse, H., *Reason and Revolution.* London, 1941.
Royce, J., *The Spirit of Modern Philosophy.* New York, 1896.

Fichte

Adamson, R., *Fichte.* Edinburgh, 1881.
Royce, J., *The Spirit of Modern Philosophy.* New York, 1896. Part 1, Ch. 5.

Hegel

Findlay, J. N., *Hegel.* London, 1958. Chs. 5 and 11.
Marcuse, H., *Reason and Revolution.* London, 1941.
Stace, W. T., *The Philosophy of Hegel.* New York, 1955.
Royce, J., *The Spirit of Modern Philosophy.* New York, 1896. Part I, Ch. 8.

Schopenhauer

Copleston, F. C., *Arthur Schopenhauer, Philosopher of Pessimism.* London, 1947.

McGill, V. J., *Schopenhauer, Pessimist and Pagan.* New York, 1931.

Mann, T., *Schopenhauer.* Stockholm, 1938.

Nietzsche

Brinton, C. C., *Nietzsche.* Cambridge, 1941.

Copleston, F. C., *Friedrich Nietzsche.* London, 1942.

Lefebvre, H., *Nietzsche.* Paris, 1939.

Marx

Berlin, I., *Karl Marx.* London, 1939.

Hook, S., *From Hegel to Marx.* New York, 1936.

MacIntyre, A. C., *Marxism, an Interpretation.* London, 1953.

Marcuse, H., *Reason and Revolution.* London, 1941.

Tucker, R., *Philosophy and Myth in Karl Marx.* Cambridge, 1961.

American Transcendentalism

Pochmann, H. A., *New England Transcendentalism and St. Louis Hegelianism.* Philadelphia, 1948.

Schneider, H. W., *A History of American Philosophy.* New York, 1946.

Royce and James

Santayana, G., *Character and Opinion in the United States.* New York, 1920.

Smith, J. E., *Royce's Social Infinite.* New York, 1950.

British Idealism

Pfannenstill, B., *Bernard Bosanquet's Philosophy of the State,* translated by Bert Hood. Lund, Sweden, 1936.

Sidgwick, H., *The Ethics of Green, Spencer and Martineau.* London, 1902.

Wollheim, R., *F. H. Bradley.* Harmondsworth, England, 1959. Ch. 6.

Sidgwick

Broad, C. D., *Five Types of Ethical Theory.* London, 1930. Ch. 6.

Twentieth-century Ethics

Assessments of Moore

Adams, E. M., *Ethical Naturalism and the Modern World-view.* Chapel Hill, N.C., 1960. Careful discussion of naturalism–nonnaturalism debate.

Broad, C. D., "G. E. Moore's Latest Published Views on Ethics." *Mind* (1961).

Field, G. C., "The Place of Definition in Ethics." *PAS* (1932). Key discussion of difficulties in Moore's conception of definition.

Frankena, W. K., "The Naturalistic Fallacy." *Mind* (1939). Classical source for discussion of naturalistic fallacy.

Hall, E. W., *Categorial Analysis,* E. M. Adams, ed. Chapel Hill, N.C., 1964. Important defense of Mill against Moore.

Prior, A. N., *Logic and the Basis of Ethics.* Oxford, 1949. Crucial for history of the naturalistic fallacy.

Taylor, P., *Normative Discourse.* Englewood Cliffs, N.J., 1961. Is/ought carefully discussed and a general theory of value developed along linguistic lines.

Warnock, M., *Ethics Since 1900.* Oxford, 1960.

Wellman, C., *The Language of Ethics.* Cambridge, Mass., 1961. Clear statement of difficulties in ethical naturalism.

Deontological Nonnaturalism

Broad, C. D., *Five Types of Ethical Theory.* London, 1930.

Broad, C. D., "Review of Julian S. Huxley's Evolutionary Ethics." *Mind* (1944).

Broad, C. D., "Some Reflections on Moral-sense Theories in Ethics." *PAS* (1944/1945).

Broad, C. D., "Some of the Main Problems of Ethics." *Philosophy* (1946).

Broad, C. D., "Critical Notice of H. A. Prichard, *Moral Obligation.*" *Mind* (1950).

Broad, C. D., "Imperatives, Categorical and Hypothetical." *The Philosopher* (1950).

Broad, C. D., *Ethics and the History of Philosophy.* London, 1952.

Carritt, E. F., *The Theory of Morals.* Oxford, 1928.

Carritt, E. F., "Moral Positivism and Moral Aestheticism." *Philosophy* (1938). Less important than Prichard or Ross but still influential.

Ewing, A. C., *The Definition of Good.* New York, 1947.

Ewing, A. C., *Ethics.* London, 1953.

Ewing, A. C., *Second Thoughts in Moral Philosophy.* London, 1959.

Ewing, A. C., "The Autonomy of Ethics," in I. T. Ramsey, ed., *Prospects for Metaphysics.* London, 1961.

Hall, E. W., *What Is Value? An Essay in Philosophical Analysis.* New York, 1952.

Hall, E. W., *Our Knowledge of Fact and Value.* Chapel Hill, N.C., 1961.

Hall, E. W., *Categorial Analysis,* E. M. Adams, ed. Chapel Hill, N.C., 1964.

Prichard, H. A., *Moral Obligation.* Oxford, 1950. Posthumously collected essays. Primary source for deontology.

Assessments of Deontological Nonnaturalism

Edwards, P., *The Logic of Moral Discourse.* Glencoe, Ill., 1955.

McCloskey, H. J., "Ross and the Concept of a *Prima Facie* Duty." *Australasian Journal of Philosophy* (1963).

Monro, D. H., "Critical Notice of *Second Thoughts in Moral Philosophy.*" *Australasian Journal of Philosophy* (1960).

Schilpp, P. A., ed., *The Philosophy of C. D. Broad.* New York, 1959. Note essays by Frankena, Hare, and Hedenius and Broad's reply. Broad's work, though largely critical of other philosophers, represents a key statement of deontology.

Strawson, P. F., "Ethical Intuitionism." *Philosophy* (1949).

Assessments of Phenomenological Nonnaturalism

Hook, S., "A Critique of Ethical Realism." *International Journal of Ethics* (1929).

Jensen, O. C., "Nicolai Hartmann's Theory of Virtue." *Ethics* (1942).

Schlick, M., "Is There a Factual *A Priori?,*" in Herbert Feigl and Wilfrid Sellars, eds., *Readings in Philosophical Analysis.* New York, 1949.

Walker, M., "Perry and Hartmann, Antithetical or Complementary?" *International Journal of Ethics* (1939).

Ethical Naturalism

Dewey, J., *Essays in Experimental Logic.* Chicago, 1916.

Dewey, J., *Human Nature and Conduct.* New York, 1922.

Dewey, J., *The Quest for Certainty.* New York, 1929.

Dewey, J., *Theory of Valuation.* Chicago, 1939.

Dewey, J., "Ethical Subject Matter and Language." *Journal of Philosophy* (1945).

Dewey, J., *The Problems of Men.* New York, 1946.

Findlay, J. N., *Values and Intentions.* London, 1961.

Findlay, J. N., *Language, Mind and Value.* London, 1963.

Foot, P. R., "Moral Arguments." *Mind* (1958).

Foot, P. R., "Moral Beliefs." *PAS* (1958).

Foot, P. R., "Goodness and Choice." *PAS,* Supp. Vol. (1961).

Pepper, S., *A Digest of Purposive Values.* New York, 1947.

Prall, D. W., *A Study in the Theory of Value.* Berkeley, 1921.

Reid, J. R., *A Theory of Value.* New York, 1938.

Reid, J. R., "The Nature and Status of Values," in R. W. Sellars, V. G. McGill, and Marvin Farber, eds., *Philosophy for the Future.* New York, 1949.

Rice, P. B., *On the Knowledge of Good and Evil.* New York, 1955.

Stace, W. T., *The Concept of Morals.* New York, 1937.

Westermarck, E., *Ethical Relativity.* London, 1932.

Assessments of Ethical Naturalism

Ezorsky, G., "Inquiry as Appraisal: The Singularity of John Dewey's Theory of Valuation." *Journal of Philosophy* (1958).

Frankena, W., "Ethical Naturalism Renovated." *The Review of Metaphysics* (1957).

Frankena, W., "Obligation and Motivation in Recent Moral Philosophy," in A. I. Melden, ed., *Essays in Moral Philosophy.* Seattle, Wash., 1958.

Frankena, W., "Lewis' Imperatives of Right." *Philosophical studies* (1963).

Frankena, W., "C. I. Lewis on the Ground and Nature of the Right." *Journal of Philosophy* (1964).

Frankena, W., "Three Comments on Lewis's Views on the Right and the Good." *Journal of Philosophy* (1964).

Hare, R. M., *The Language of Morals.* Oxford, 1950.

Kennedy, G., "Science and the Transformation of Common Sense: The Basic Problem of Dewey's Philosophy." *Journal of Philosophy* (1954).

Wellman, C., *The Language of Ethics.* Cambridge, 1961.

White, M., *Social Thought in America.* New York. 1949.

White, M., "Value and Obligation in Dewey and Lewis." *Philosophical Review* (1949).

(See also the works by Moore, Ross, Ewing, and Hall previously cited.)

Contemporary Noncognitivism

Ayer, A. J., *Language, Truth and Logic.* London, 1935.

Ayer, A. J., "On the Analysis of Moral Judgments," in his *Philosophical Essays.* New York, 1954.

Carnap, R., *Philosophy and Logical Syntax.* London, 1935.

Cassirer, E., "Axel Hägerström: Eine Studie zur schwedischen Philosophie der Gegenwart." *Goteborgs Hogskolas Arsskrift* (1939).

Edwards, P., *The Logic of Moral Discourse.* Glencoe, Ill., 1955.

Hedenius, I., *Om Rätt och Moral* ("On Law and Morals"); Stockholm, 1941.

Hedenius, I., "Values and Duties." *Theoria* (1949).

Hedenius, I., "Etikens Subjecktivitet," in *Tro och Moral.* Stockholm, 1955.

Reichenbach, H., *The Rise of Scientific Philosophy.* Berkeley and Los Angeles, 1951.

Richards, I. A., *The Meaning of Meaning.* New York, 1933.

Richards, I. A., *Speculative Instruments.* Chicago, 1957.

Robinson, R., "The Emotive Theory of Ethics." *PAS,* Supp. Vol. (1948).

Robinson, R., *An Atheist's Values.* Oxford, 1964.

Ross, A., *Kritik der sogenannten praktischen Erkenntniss.* Copenhagen, 1933.

Ross, A., "On the Logical Nature of Propositions of Value." *Theoria* (1945).

Ross, A., *On Law and Justice.* Berkeley and Los Angeles, 1959.

Ross, A., "On Moral Reasoning." *Danish Yearbook of Philosophy* (1964).

Russell, B., *Religion and Science.* Oxford, 1935.

Schilpp, P. A., ed., *The Philosophy of Rudolf Carnap.* La Salle, Ill., 1964.

Stevenson, C., *Ethics and Language.* New Haven, 1944.

Stevenson, C., "The Scientist's Role and the Aims of Education." *Harvard Educational Review* (1954).

Stevenson, C., *Facts and Values.* New Haven, 1963.

Assessments of the Emotive Theory

Bedford, E., "The Emotive Theory of Ethics," in *Proceedings of the Eleventh International Congress of Philosophy,* Vol. X. Amsterdam, 1953.

Brandt, R., "The Emotive Theory of Ethics." *Philosophical Review* (1950).

Falk, W. D., "Goading and Guiding." *Mind* (1954).

Foot, P. R., "The Philosopher's Defense of Morality." *Philosophy* (1952).

Nielsen, K., "Bertrand Russell's New Ethic." *Methodos* (1958).

Nielsen, K., "On Looking Back at the Emotive Theory." *Methodos* (1962).

Tegen, E., "The Basic Problem in the Theory of Value." *Theoria* (1944).

Assessments of Existentialism

Ayer, A. J., "Albert Camus, Novelist-philosopher." *Horizon* (1946).

Ayer, A. J., "Novelist-philosophers: Jean-Paul Sartre." *Horizon* (1946).

Ayer, A. J., "Philosophy at Absolute Zero." *Encounter* (1955).

Beauvoir, Simone de, *The Ethics of Ambiguity,* translated by Bernard Frechtman. New York, 1948. Important in its own right and in relation to Sartre.

Cranston, M., *Sartre.* Edinburgh and London, 1962. General discussion of the range of Sartre's work. Elementary but clear.

Cruickshank, J., *Camus and the Literature of Revolt.* New York, 1959. Contains a detailed and sympathetic account of Camus's thought.

Cruickshank, J., ed., *The Novelist as Philosopher.* London, 1962.

Hochberg, H., "Albert Camus and the Ethic of Absurdity." *Ethics* (1965). Important analytical criticism.

Jeanson, F., *Le Problème moral et la pensée de Sartre.* Paris, 1947. Sympathetic and informal discussion of Sartre's moral theory.

Murdoch, I., *Sartre: Romantic Rationalist.* New Haven, 1955. Relates Sartre to English thought.

Warnock, M., *Ethics Since 1900.* Oxford, 1960.

Warnock, M., *The Philosophy of Sartre.* London, 1965. Challenging but sympathetic assessment of Sartre.

Wollheim, R., "The Political Philosophy of Existentialism." *Cambridge Journal* (1953).

Wollheim, R., "Modern Philosophy and Unreason." *Political Quarterly* (1955).

Linguistic Noncognitivism

Hare, R. M., "Universalizability." *PAS* (1954).

Hare, R. M., "Descriptivism." *Proceedings of the British Academy* (1963).

Hartland-Swann, J., *An Analysis of Morals.* London, 1960.

Mayo, B., *Ethics and the Moral Life.* London, 1958.

Montefiore, A., *A Modern Introduction to Moral Philosophy.* New York, 1959.

Montefiore, A., "Goodness and Choice." *PAS,* Supp. Vol. (1961).

Nowell-Smith, P. H., *Ethics.* Harmondsworth, England, 1954.

Nowell-Smith, P. H., "Morality: Religious and Secular." *Rationalist Annual* (1961).

Nowell-Smith, P. H., "Contextual Implications and Ethical Theory," *PAS*, Supp. Vol. (1962).

Nowell-Smith, P. H., "Review of *Freedom and Reason*." *Ratio* (1964).

Assessments of Linguistic Noncognitivism

Binkley, L., *Contemporary Ethical Theories*. New York, 1961.

Castañeda, H.-N., "Imperatives, Decisions and 'Oughts. A Logico-metaphysical Investigation," in Héctor-Neri Castañeda and George Nakhnikian, eds., *Morality and the Language of Conduct*. Detroit, 1963.

McCloskey, H. J., "Hare's Ethical Subjectivism." *Australasian Journal of Philosophy* (1959).

McCloskey, H. J., "Nowell-Smith's Ethics." *Australasian Journal of Philosophy* (1961).

Monro, H. D., "Are Moral Problems Genuine?" *Mind* (1956).

Monro, H. D., "Impartiality and Consistency." *Philosophy* (1961).

Monro, H. D., "Critical Notice of *Freedom and Reason*." *Australasian Journal of Philosophy* (1964).

Sparshott, F. E., "Critical Study of *Freedom and Reason*." *Philosophical Quarterly* (1963).

Good-Reasons Approach

Aiken, H. D., *Reason and Conduct*. New York, 1962.

Baier, K., "Decisions and Descriptions." *Mind* (1951).

Baier, K., *The Meaning of Life*. Canberra, 1957.

Falk, W. D., "Morals Without Faith." *Philosophy* (1944).

Falk, W. D., "Obligation and Rightness." *Philosophy* (1945).

Falk, W. D., " 'Ought' and Motivation." *PAS* (1947/1948).

Falk, W. D., "Morality and Nature." *Australasian Journal of Philosophy* (1950).

Falk, W. D., "Goading and Guiding." *Mind* (1953).

Falk, W. D., "Moral Perplexity." *Ethics* (1956).

Falk, W. D., "Action-guiding Reasons." *Journal of Philosophy* (1963).

Falk, W. D., "Morality, Self and Others," in Héctor-Neri Castañeda and George Nakhnikian, eds., *Morality and the Language of Conduct*. Detroit, 1963.

Gauthier, D., *Practical Reasoning*. Oxford, 1963.

Ladd, J., "Reason and Practice," in John Wild, ed., *The Return to Reason*. Chicago, 1953.

Ladd, J., *The Structure of a Moral Code*. Cambridge, Mass., 1957.

Ladd, J., "The Issue of Relativism." *The Monist* (1963).

Melden, A. I., "Two Comments on Utilitarianism." *Philosophical Review* (1951).

Melden, A. I., *Rights and Right Conduct*. Oxford, 1959.

Murphy, A. E., *The Uses of Reason*. New York, 1943.

Murphy, A. E., "Blanshard on Good in General." *Philosophical Review* (1963).

Murphy, A. E., *The Theory of Practical Reason*, A. I. Melden, ed. La Salle, Ill., 1965.

Murphy, A. E.; Hay, William; and Singer, Marcus, eds., *Reason and the Common Good*. Englewood Cliffs, N.J., 1963.

Nielsen, K., "The Functions of Moral Discourse." *Philosophical Quarterly* (1957).

Nielsen, K., "Justification and Moral Reasoning." *Methodos* (1957).

Nielsen, K., "Is 'Why Should I Be Moral?' an Absurdity?" *Australasian Journal of Philosophy* (1958).

Nielsen, K., "The 'Good Reasons Approach' and 'Ontological Justifications of Morality.' " *Philosophical Quarterly* (1959).

Nielsen, K., "Appraising Doing the Thing Done." *Journal of Philosophy* (1960).

Nielsen, K., "Can a Way of Life Be Justified?" *Indian Journal of Philosophy* (1960).

Nielsen, K., "Conventionalism in Morals and the Appeal to Human Nature." *Philosophy and Phenomenological Research* (1962).

Nielsen, K., "Why Should I Be Moral?" *Methodos* (1963).

Nielsen, K., "The Good Reasons Approach Revisited." *Archiv für Rechts- und Sozialphilosophie* (1965).

Rawls, J., "Outline of a Decision Procedure for Ethics." *Philosophical Review* (1951).

Rawls, J., "Two Concepts of Rules." *Philosophical Review* (1955).

Rawls, J., "Justice as Fairness." *Philosophical Review* (1958).

Rawls, J., "Constitutional Liberty and the Concept of Justice," in *Nomos*, Vol. VI, *Justice*, Carl J. Friedrich and John W. Chapman, eds. New York, 1963.

Rawls, J., "The Sense of Justice." *Philosophical Review* (1963).

Rawls, J., "Legal Obligation and the Duty of Fair Play," in Sidney Hook, ed., *Law and Philosophy*. New York, 1964.

Singer, M., *Generalization in Ethics*. New York, 1961.

Singer, M., "The Golden Rule." *Philosophy* (1963).

Singer, M., "Negative and Positive Duties." *Philosophical Quarterly* (1965).

Taylor, P., "Four Types of Ethical Relativism." *Philosophical Review* (1954).

Taylor, P., *Normative Discourse*. Englewood Cliffs, N.J., 1961.

Taylor, P., "On Justifying a Way of Life." *Indian Journal of Philosophy* (1961).

Taylor, P., "The Ethnocentric Fallacy." *The Monist* (1963).

Toulmin, S., "Knowledge of Right and Wrong." *PAS* (1949/1950).

Toulmin, S., *An Examination of the Place of Reason in Ethics*. Cambridge, 1950.

Toulmin, S., "Is There a Fundamental Problem of Ethics?" *Australasian Journal of Philosophy* (1955).

Toulmin, S., "Principles of Morality." *Philosophy* (1956).

Wright, Georg von, "On Promises." *Theoria* (1962).

Wright, Georg von, *The Logic of Preference*. Edinburgh, 1963.

Wright, Georg von, *Norm and Action*. London, 1963.

Wright, Georg von, "Practical Inference." *Philosophical Review* (1963).

Wright, Georg von, *The Varieties of Goodness*. London, 1963.

(Ethics through the nineteenth century)

— RAZIEL ABELSON

(Twentieth-century ethics)

— KAI NIELSEN

ETHICS, PROBLEMS OF

What ethics or moral philosophy is, and at best ought to be, has always been variously conceived by philosophers. There is no uncontroversial Archimedean point from which ethics can be characterized, for the nature and proper office of ethics is itself a hotly disputed philosophical problem. But there are some things which can be said on the subject that will elicit a wide measure of agreement, although in any description of ethics the emphasis and organization will display a particular philosophical orientation.

P. H. Nowell-Smith, in his widely read and influential book *Ethics* (1954), argues that in the past moral philosophers sought to give us general guidance concerning what to do, what to seek, and how to treat others. That is not to say that such philosophers as Plato, Aristotle, Epicurus, Hobbes, Spinoza, and Joseph Butler functioned like parish priests or a citizens' advice bureau; they did not seek to give detailed practical advice as to how we should behave on a particular occasion, but they did believe that they could communicate some general but crucial knowledge of good and evil. It was their belief that there is such a thing as a true moral code or a normative ethical system and that philosophers could show what it is. The philosopher's task, in their view, primarily consists in setting forth systematically the first principles of morality and in showing how it is possible to justify these principles. Such an exposition would include not only the philosopher's theoretical conception of the limits of moral justification but also his conception of the good life for man.

Traditionally, moral philosophy had a practical purpose; moral knowledge was not conceived as purely theoretical knowledge of moral phenomena but as practical knowledge about how we ought to live. The goal was not that we should simply know what goodness is but that we should become good. (Some argued that to know what goodness really is, is to become good.)

Yet this still does not adequately characterize what is distinctive about moral philosophy, for novelists, poets, dramatists, and sometimes even historians, social scientists, and psychologists have functioned, in one way or another, as moral sages and have claimed to give us, in some manner, some knowledge of good and evil. It would be difficult to deny that such men as Tolstoy and Dostoyevsky, Sophocles and Shakespeare, Thucydides and Montaigne have sometimes been very perceptive in what they have said about morality. What distinguishes a specifically philosophical account of morality is its generality, its systematic nature, and its attempt to prove its claims.

Even within this traditional conception of the task of ethics, important disagreements have arisen. Such philosophers as Kant and Henry Sidgwick, unlike Bentham and Nietzsche, stressed the fact that it is not the philosophers' aim to discover *new* truths. Moral philosophy, they thought, should give a systematic account of the knowledge man already possesses; it should try to unify and show the ultimate rationale of the moral knowledge and practices man already has. There should be no wholesale rejection of practical moral claims, but an attempt should be made to unify and show the objective justification of most of these claims. Subjectivists, however, would challenge the latter aim, although in an important way there is less conflict between them and philosophers like Kant and Sidgwick than might at first be supposed. Subjectivists did not so much question specific moral practices as attempt to show, as did

Edward Westermarck in his *Ethical Relativity* (1932), that the alleged objective foundations of these practices are in shambles. They maintained that common expectations notwithstanding, there is, and in reality can be, no such thing as ethics as a body of knowledge demonstrating how we ought to live. Traditional moral philosophers have been concerned to refute such general skeptical conclusions.

There is no uncontroversial Archimedean point from which ethics can be characterized, for the nature and proper office of ethics is itself a hotly disputed philosophical problem.

In attempting to do this, they tried to set forth a true moral code, that is, to determine the objective foundations of ethics and to show the sole grounds on which we can justify our moral beliefs. Skeptical moral philosophers tended to leave commonsense moral beliefs intact but questioned whether it was possible to give an objective underpinning to them.

Nietzsche stands out as stark exception to this in his conception of the task of a moral philosopher. He not only questioned the general methods of moral reasoning; he questioned, criticized, even rejected certain commonsense moral beliefs as well. He would not take morality itself as something given; he stressed the diversity of morals and did not seek to supply a rational foundation for our very common moral convictions but, rather, sought to discover new moral truths.

Yet, in spite of these differences, the writings of nearly all of these philosophers fit Nowell-Smith's over-all characterization of the traditional task of moral philosophy. They did not simply seek to clarify the use of moral discourse or to enable us to gain knowledge of moral phenomena but, skeptics and subjectivists apart, sought to give us objective practical knowledge about how we should live. Even the skeptics and subjectivists lived in the shadow of this goal, for their primary purpose was to show that the moralists could not achieve it.

Normative Ethics and Metaethics

Contemporary analytic philosophers, when they consider moral philosophy, usually construe their task quite differently. In relation to traditional moralists, Nowell-Smith himself is, in the words of R. M. Hare, "their champion, not their imitator." His *Ethics* is an example of the contemporary approach and is described as "a study of the words and concepts that we use for making decisions, advising, warning, and appraising conduct." The direct object of Nowell-Smith's study is not practice but knowledge: knowledge of the distinctive uses or roles of moral language or, to use another idiom, knowledge of the meanings of moral concepts.

Philosophers like Nowell-Smith and Hare do not set forth a moral system and try to show how it is rationally justified; instead, they analyze moral concepts, including moral systems such as hedonism and utilitarianism. They do not, in their philosophical essays, make moral statements themselves (except incidentally); rather, they discuss the meaning and function of such statements—in their works, moral words and statements occur in mention, not in use. Of course, traditional moral philosophers also analyzed moral concepts, but what distinguishes contemporary ethicists is that many regard analysis as their sole philosophical task.

In developing this distinction, we shall call the body of ethical statements, or the actual normative argument, of the moral philosopher his *normative ethics;* discussions of the meanings or uses of moral terms and utterances about the nature of moral concepts will be called *metaethics.* (Other philosophers use different terminologies. Normative ethics is sometimes called substantive ethics or morals. What we shall call metaethics has been referred to as analytical ethics, critical ethics, theoretical ethics, the epistemology of ethics, the logic of ethics, or ethics.)

We should first further distinguish between normative ethical and metaethical statements. Normative ethical statements are actual moral statements: "The treatment of Negroes in Harlem is a glaring evil," "John's leaving her without a word was cruel," "You ought to be more considerate." There are also more abstract and general normative ethical statements that are apt to occur in traditional philosophical treatises. The following are typical examples: "Pleasure and pleasure alone is intrinsically good, and pain and pain alone is intrinsically evil." "One ought not to use one's head but one's feelings in deciding what one ought to do." "Those rules and practices ought to be adopted which harmonize most fully the interests of as many people as possible."

Metaethical statements, by contrast, are about the uses or meanings of normative ethical statements, utterances, or terms, about the logical status of moral claims, about the nature of moral argument, or about what constitutes a morality. The following are typical examples: "Moral utterances are neither autobiographical statements nor statements of nonnatural fact but expressions of emotion." " 'Good' is the name of a simple, unanalyzable, nonnatural quality." "The truth of fundamental moral statements can be known only

through intuition." "The criteria for what can count as 'a good reason' for a moral claim can be determined only by determining the over-all rationale of that discourse."

Not all discussion of normative ethical talk or belief is metaethical, for there are also statements of fact about people's moral opinions, and there are sociological and psychological descriptions of normative ethical beliefs and language, explanations of why people use moral language in the way they do, and accounts of its origin. The following are examples:

Descriptions of moral beliefs: "Most people believe that nuclear warfare under any circumstances is evil."

Descriptions of moral language: "For many children 'cooperative' and 'uncooperative' come to have the same force as 'good' and 'bad'."

Nietzsche not only questioned the general methods of moral reasoning; he questioned, criticized, even rejected certain commonsense moral beliefs as well.

Explanations of moral language: " 'Cooperative' and 'uncooperative' come to have the same force as 'good' and 'bad' because they are used in the same contexts that 'good' and 'bad' are used in and with the same approbative/disapprobative force."

Accounts of the origin of moral language: "Moral discourse arose because people felt the need for some over-all method of control over the native egoism and aggressive impulses of human beings."

Such descriptive talk about moral discourse is not about the meaning or use of moral terms or utterances, the logical status of such utterances, or the method of validation of moral statements—and thus cannot be properly called metaethical. Sociological or psychological questions of fact about moral discourse, or more generally about people's moral beliefs or attitudes, can conveniently be called questions of descriptive ethics. Descriptive ethics can, in various ways, be relevant to metaethics or normative ethics, but it is most certainly distinct from both.

It is sometimes difficult to tell from mere inspection whether a given statement is a part of descriptive ethics, but the following criterion can be utilized: The truth of a statement in descriptive ethics depends on what moral opinions are actually held by the people referred to, or by what beliefs they have about how people actually behave (purely linguistic behavior apart); the truth of a metaethical statement depends on the kind of utterance people would actually be making if they made a certain moral claim, or on the uses or meanings of the terms in the utterance.

For example, the claim that a moral statement is really a statement about the likes and dislikes of the person making the statement is a metaethical assertion. In order to test its truth one might consider whether the utterances "I like to do it" and "I ought to do it" express the same meaning. To show that the claim is false, we need only point out that the sentence "I don't like to do it, but I ought to do it" is not self-contradictory. We do not need to know anything about the actual moral opinions of the people involved; we need only to know what they and we believe counts as an intelligible or possible moral utterance or expression. By contrast, "Most young Catholics do not really believe that birth control is wrong and hope the hierarchy will change its position about this" can be known to be true or false only by knowing something about the actual moral convictions of people.

A normative ethicist tries to set forth a system of true normative ethical statements or at least to show how certain fundamental normative ethical statements are rationally supported. Some ethicists are iconoclasts and moral critics like Nietzsche and Camus, and seek to show that at least some of our actual normative ethical ideals are irrational. Some, like Kant and Sidgwick, are concerned to exhibit the rational foundations of common-sense normative ethics; they seek to state the heterogeneous claims of common-sense morality in some systematic order, to state its fundamental principles, and to show how they can be rationally justified. Some, like Bentham and Dewey, pursue both courses, with emphasis on the latter. (It is important to note that in doing these tasks a very considerable amount of metaethics also is done.)

A metaethicist tries to analyze and perspicuously display normative ethical discourse. He typically starts with everyday first-order moral (normative ethical) talk, but he also concerns himself with the claims and systems of normative ethicists. His object is not to engage directly in moral argument, reasoning, or normative ethical discourse at all but, as a kind of conceptual cartographer, to give a clear description and/or account of that discourse. His effort is not, even in the most general terms, to tell us how to live or to justify living in a certain way but to make clear what morality is all about and, particularly today, to ask whether normative ethics is really possible as a rational inquiry. If it is, how can it be rationally pursued?

Relation of Normative Ethics to Metaethics

Two questions naturally arise: What is the relationship between normative ethics and metaethics? Why should philosophers concern themselves with metaethics at all?

Many philosophers who are antagonistic to analytic philosophy think that contemporary moral philosophy has regressed in so exclusively concerning itself with metaethics. On the other hand, a few purists among analytic philosophers think that since the sole proper concern of philosophy is with the logical analysis of language or the analysis of concepts, philosophers ought *not,* as philosophers, to do normative ethics. Philosophers, they argue, are not seers; they have no special insight into "moral truth," and therefore they have no right at all to preach to their fellow men or tell them how they ought to live. But this, it is argued, is in effect just what they do when they engage in normative ethics.

Many moral philosophers, including this writer, take the less extreme position that to engage in normative ethics properly is not to preach or in a direct, specific, and casuistic way to tell one's fellow man how to order his life. It is, rather, to criticize irrational moral beliefs and to search for certain general, rationally justifiable moral principles. Its aim is finally to discover and articulate a sound normative ethical system. A moral philosopher should do both metaethics and normative ethics; the crucial thing is not to confuse them and to be clear about their intermural relations.

Yet there is a conviction on the part of many philosophers, and perhaps justifiably so, that a philosopher's main task is to do metaethics. This conviction has been engendered by several considerations. There has been the recognition that philosophical attempts to set forth a rational and objective normative ethic have not been notably successful in spite of the fact that philosophers have been engaged in that activity for the last 24 centuries. Furthermore, the arguments for moral skepticism—skepticism about the feasibility of articulating an objective normative ethic—have been very telling. Finally, and most importantly, it is felt by many philosophers that the logical status of moral utterances and the nature of moral reasoning are so unclear that we cannot profitably do normative ethics until we have a far more adequate metaethic than we have at present. Because of such convictions, a central and pervasive question in metaethics is whether normative ethics is possible. If it is, then it is reasonable to argue that the articulation of a rational normative ethical system is, as G. E. Moore believed, the ultimate aim of moral philosophy. If such a system is impossible, then the task of moral philosophy is to show why this is so and to limit itself to metaethical analysis.

Even if we conclude that in some way it is possible to articulate a sound normative ethic, questions still arise about the relevance of metaethics to normative ethics. What is the logical relationship between metaethical statements and normative ethical statements, or between a normative ethic and a metaethic? And what (if anything) is the normative relevance of metaethical analysis? What, in short, is the proper role of a meta-ethic with respect to the moral life?

It is frequently claimed that metaethical theories and metaethical statements are all normatively neutral (the neutrality thesis). This is taken in different ways. To ask if they are normatively neutral is to ask at least one of the following questions: (1) Do metaethical statements or theories entail any normative ethical statements or theories? (2) Do normative ethical statements or theories entail any metaethical statements or theories? (3) Do at least some metaethical theories presuppose certain specific normative ethical doctrines? (4) Do at least some normative ethical theories or doctrines presuppose certain specific metaethical beliefs? (5) Do metaethical theories have a normative ethical role? (6) Do one's metaethical beliefs sometimes alter (causally impinge upon) one's normative ethical beliefs or attitudes?

If in claiming that metaethical contentions are all normatively neutral, one answers (6) in the negative, then one is surely mistaken. Most philosophers no doubt overestimate the extent to which conceptual considerations have causal effects on practical matters—including moral beliefs—but many people, perhaps foolishly, have altered their normative ethical beliefs upon accepting a noncognitive metaethic.

However, most analytic philosophers who have wanted to maintain the neutrality thesis have wanted to contend that (1), (2), (3), and (4) should be answered in the negative. Some, however, have wanted to maintain that only (1) and (2) should be answered in the negative.

The belief that normative ethical statements are about what ought *to be done* or ought *to be* the case, that they are about what is right or good to *do* or good to *make* the case, and that metaethical statements, by contrast, are about what *is* the case strongly inclines one to the neutrality thesis on the ground that a normative statement can never be derived from any nonnormative statement or subset of purely nonnormative statements. Thus there can be no entailment either way.

It might be argued that so to deny an entailment between normative ethical statements and metaethical statements is to presuppose a number of metaethical theses that are themselves quite questionable: that one cannot derive an "ought" from an "is," that there is a clearly demarcated line between factual statements and normative statements or between descriptive discourse and prescriptive and evaluative discourse.

It is, of course, trivially true that if we can make no fundamental or clear demarcation between fact-stating or descriptive discourse and normative discourse, or if

normative discourse is a subspecies of factual discourse, then there will be no general reason to deny an entailment between metaethical statements and normative ones. Whether there is such a demarcation in discourse is one of the central issues of contemporary ethical theory.

Some who would answer (1) and (2) in the negative would answer (3) and/or (4) in the affirmative. There is no entailment between normative ethical claims and metaethical claims, but normative ethical claims presuppose a certain metaethic, or any given normative ethic, is compatible only with a particular metaethic or at least with a certain range of metaethical theories. Where we have an entailment between two statements, p and q, then if p is true, q is true; and if q is false, p is false. But if p is presupposed by q, then if p is false, q as well as not-q is void; but q can be false without p being false. If "Bentley has some students" (p) is presupposed by "Bentley's students are Irish" (q), then "It is false that Bentley's students are Irish" does *not* show that Bentley has no students; but if p is false and Bentley has no students, then neither "Bentley's students are Irish" nor "Bentley's students are not Irish" is false, for both statements are voided when such a condition obtains.

Let our ethical case be "Moral statements can be true or false" (metaethical statement p). Let us try to assert that p is presupposed by normative ethical statement q ("It is patently false to claim that the innocent under certain circumstances ought to be punished"). If p is false, q is not false but in an important sense is meaningless or void, for the falsity of p shows that the very labels "truth" and "falsity" are not applicable to q. In this way the intelligibility, and thus also the truth, of a given normative ethical claim presupposes the truth of a given metaethical statement. If the metaethical statement is false, we cannot assert the normative ethical statement. But it still remains the case that the adoption of that metaethic would not constitute a good reason for accepting the normative ethic or normative ethical statement in question rather than some conflicting normative ethic or normative ethical statement, for if q presupposes p, so does not-q. Since "John's children are bald" presupposes that John has children, so does "John's children are not bald."

The converse does not hold. It is not the case that a given metaethical theory or statement presupposes the correctness of a given normative ethical theory or statement. Consider this case: "Moral utterances are expressions of emotion" does not presuppose "Communism is a glaring evil" or "One ought to experience one's emotional life to the full." These normative statements could be rejected without voiding the metaethical statement. Such a metaethical claim is not voided by any normative ethical statement, no matter how general. Even the falsity of "People ought to do what they are emotionally disposed to do" does not void "Moral utterances are expressions of emotion." The metaethical statement in question only asserts that if an utterance is moral, it expresses the emotions of the speaker; it does not tell one what one ought or ought not to do. It does not say one ought or ought not to do what one is emotionally disposed to do. It only implies that when a speaker asserts "People ought never to do what they are emotionally disposed to do," this utterance, like any moral utterance, expresses the speaker's emotions.

What is the relationship between normative ethics and metaethics? Why should philosophers concern themselves with metaethics at all?

Here we can see in a specific case that a metaethical statement does not presuppose a given normative ethical statement and appears not to presuppose any specific metaethical statement or type of metaethic. It would quite generally appear to be the case that no metaethical statement or metaethic presupposes a normative ethical statement or a given type of normative ethic. If there were no normative ethical claims at all, there could be no metaethics, but that is a different matter.

If correct, the above line of reasoning has important consequences, for it makes it apparent that a given metaethic or metaethical theory does not entail any normative ethical claim, statement, or theory; and the converse relationship also holds. It is also the case that no metaethical theory presupposes any given normative ethics. In these very important respects the defenders of the neutrality thesis seem to be correct. But it would also appear to be the case that we can make certain normative ethical claims only if certain metaethical claims are true. The truth of these metaethical claims does not insure the truth of the normative ethical claims, but the normative ethical claims cannot be true unless the metaethical claims are. In this respect metaethics does not seem normatively neutral.

Finally we consider (5): Do metaethical theories have a normative ethical role? From the above discussion we can see that we are in a position to make one important assertion, namely, that from the truth of any given metaethic or metaethical statement we cannot conclude that a given normative ethic or normative ethical statement is true. But metaethical theories do have normative implications. If "No moral statements can be true

or false" is true, then we cannot assert as a normative ethical statement that it is false to say that communism is evil. Thus there are normative functions of metaethical statements, but it is important to determine just what they are and how they work, for on this turns the pragmatic value of metaethics.

It is sometimes argued that metaethics has normative implications because, without being a normative activity itself, it can still serve as an instrument for greater rationality in our actual moral life. Given the fact that we want to be more rational in our moral thinking, and given the fact that we can be more rational, metaethical analysis can be extremely useful.

There are some important ways in which the above contention is true. Metaethical analysis can undermine certain obscure beliefs about morality and in that way can further the moral life. This is not to say that if a man changes his metaethical beliefs, there is any reason for him to change any given normative ethical belief (such as that the infliction of pain is evil). But metaethical analysis of the meaning of "x is wrong" or "x is right" may enable him to be clearer and more certain in the organization of his moral beliefs and in his efforts to justify them. To take obvious examples, the man who believes that "x is right" means "x is commanded by God" may in certain situations be unsure of how to decide or demonstrate what it is that God has commanded. On the other hand, a man who believes that "x is right" means simply "the speaker feels that x is right" may have difficulty in justifying or finding convincing reasons for doing what he feels is right. However, further metaethical analysis may show that moral judgments do not require special insight into the mind of God or into some nonnatural realm, and moreover that there are rules of valid reasoning appropriate to moral argument. To reason morally may be to reason in accordance with a rule of inference that says "If something causes pain, it is, *ceteris paribus* (all things being equal), not to be done." Thus, moral beliefs may be represented in what is presumably a more coherent and perspicuous way, and one no longer need feel mystified about them and uneasy about their having an objective rationale.

That metaethical beliefs can be helpful in this way assumes that metaethical theory can attain the kind of clarity that would enable us, with some justification, to claim that certain metaethical beliefs are true or at least probable. This is not easy to establish; yet, if it can be shown that some metaethical beliefs are well warranted, then, in the way we have exhibited above, we will have shown how they can clarify normative ethical thought and in this way have an important normative ethical function.

Discourse in Normative Ethics

We must now consider the familiar Kantian question: "Is normative ethics possible?" That is, is it possible to state and rationally defend a normative ethic in such a way that all rational men, after carefully reflecting on the considerations pro and con, would find it acceptable? Is philosophical normative argument possible?

To see, or at least to begin to consider, whether it is or not, let us examine some important normative ethical claims and see if they can be so defended. As this examination proceeds, it will become apparent why so many contemporary philosophers have concerned themselves almost exclusively with metaethics, for when we push normative inquiries to a certain stage, the conclusion often turns to some considerable degree on metaethical issues.

What (if anything) is worthwhile for its own sake

or in itself, quite irrespective of its consequences?

Normative ethics tries systematically to establish the general principles for determining right and wrong or good and evil. In attempting to produce such an answer, many ethical questions are asked, but they can all be subsumed under three general questions: (1) What is right and wrong? (2) What is blameworthy and praiseworthy? (3) What is desirable or worthwhile? Here (2), which presupposes an answer to (1), will be ignored, and we shall concentrate on (1) and (3).

It is important to see that (1) and (3) are distinct questions, for while it may be that everything that is desirable to do is also something that one is obligated to do, it is still not the case that to *say* that something is worthwhile or desirable is the same as saying that one is obligated to do it. Questions about what is desirable to do, what is worthwhile, or what is good in itself may not even strike one as moral questions. If a woman struggles with herself about whether it would be more desirable to be a dentist or a doctor, she is not, at least in typical situations, facing a moral dilemma, although it may be a very crucial personal problem for her; but if a woman struggles over whether to tell her husband that she is going to have a child by another man, she is, in our society at any rate, definitely involved in a moral problem. Yet it is surely not implausible to argue that morality exists for man and not man for morality; that those practices which should be thought of as involving duties and obligations are so labeled because it is believed (perhaps mistakenly) that in the long run they will bring about a better or more desirable life for more people than would the institution of any alternative set of practices. This is not to urge the metaethical thesis that "x is right," "x is obligatory," or "x ought to be done" means "x is the most desirable thing for everybody" or "x is the best possible or most worthwhile act under the circumstances." It is, rather, designed to show the ethical relevance of questions of the third type.

In asking "How should we live?" it is certainly not unreasonable to argue that one ought always to do that act which under the circumstances would have the best or most desirable consequences for everyone involved. After all, what better, more worthwhile thing could we do than to do what is best for everyone? This does not settle the issue in favor of teleologists over deontologists, but it does make the teleological position sufficiently plausible to make it worthwhile to give careful consideration to (3). A teleologist in ethics argues that the only thing we have to know in order to decide whether or not an act is right is whether the act, among all the alternative acts we might perform, would bring about the best total state of affairs. Deontologists, by contrast, assert that there are at least some other considerations, besides the goodness or badness of the consequences of actions or attitudes, that make actions or attitudes right or wrong. Yet even a deontologist can quite consistently consider (3) an ethical question.

Granted that it is crucial in knowing how we ought to live to determine what is worthwhile, desirable, or good in itself, just how would we do it? This issue is a central one in moral philosophy. But before we consider some of the central positions and issues involved in any decision here, it is essential to make an important distinction. In asking our question we are asking what it is that makes something *intrinsically* desirable, good, or worthwhile. That is, what (if anything) is worthwhile for its own sake or in itself, quite irrespective of its consequences?

To say that x is intrinsically desirable (good, worthwhile) is to say that, *ceteris paribus,* the existence or occurrence of x is more desirable (better, more worthwhile) than its nonexistence or nonoccurrence because of its own nature alone, completely apart from any positive or negative desirability possessed by things to which x is conducive. To say that x is extrinsically desirable (good, worthwhile) is to say that x is conducive, directly or indirectly, to something else, y, which is intrinsically desirable (good, worthwhile).

This distinction, like most distinctions made by philosophers, has been vigorously attacked. There are serious questions concerning whether it is a clear distinction; questions concerning its applicability and importance in moral assessment; and, to say the least, it certainly must be questioned whether intrinsic and extrinsic are all the fundamental varieties of goodness. But, historically at least, this distinction has been of considerable moment, for most of the classical normative ethical theories have been theories about what is intrinsically desirable or worthwhile.

Normative ethical theories about what is intrinsically desirable can be conveniently divided into monistic and pluralistic theories. Monistic theories, like hedonism and self-realizationism, claim that one, and only one, kind of experience or reality is intrinsically desirable or good; pluralistic theories maintain that there can be more than one kind of intrinsic desirability or good.

The respective merits of these views will become somewhat more apparent if we examine what could be said for and against ethical hedonism.

ETHICAL HEDONISM. One of the strongest and most persistent theories about what things are intrinsically good is ethical hedonism. An ethical hedonist contends that pleasure, and pleasure alone, is intrinsically good. But hedonism is not just a theory about what is intrinsically good; it also attempts to be a complete normative ethical theory. It aims to tell us which moral principles are justified, what general types of moral rules we should follow, and, in principle at least, it aims to tell us what general types of action are good and what attitudes are desirable. It would, in short, supply us with a complete normative ethical theory, but the whole edifice of such a theory rests on its doctrine about what is intrinsically good. This doctrine is not sufficient to establish hedonism as a complete normative ethic, but it is necessary.

The hedonist's contention is that pleasantness is either identical with or a criterion for intrinsic goodness. To establish either claim involves establishing (1) that pleasure or pleasant (enjoyable) experiences are always intrinsically good and (2) that *only* pleasure or pleasant (enjoyable) experiences are intrinsically good. Neither (1) nor (2) is sufficient by itself.

What can be said for (1)? There is no serious question about whether sometimes a pleasant experience is intrinsically good; the question is whether it is always intrinsically good. There are bad pleasures or evil pleasures, it will be argued. The Klan member who takes pleasure in beating a Negro to death or the sadistic doctor who takes pleasure in hurting his patients does something that is evil. To take pleasure in deliberate acts of cruelty is evil.

To this the hedonist replies that there is nothing wrong with such pleasure per se. Its effects, namely the pain it brings to others, is bad; but if we consider the pleasure in isolation from its effects, it will be seen that there is nothing bad about it taken by itself. It is intrinsically good but extrinsically bad because it is conducive to something that is intrinsically bad, namely pain.

Some will argue that taking pleasure in giving pain to others is both intrinsically and extrinsically evil. Even in the case where an act inspired by sadistic motives has good effects, they will still hold that the act is intrinsically evil. (An example might be a sadistic doctor who enjoys giving shock therapy because he likes to watch his patients suffer but who administers this therapy only in cases where it is the best available treatment to cure the patient.) The nonhedonist may also appeal to majority opinion and maintain that most people will agree that it would be a better world if doctors didn't take pleasure in giving pain. The hedonist will reply that it is not opinion which determines what is intrinsically good or bad. He will point out that the sadistic doctor's pleasure slightly lessens the sum total pain in the world, so in such a situation a world in which he took pleasure in his work would be intrinsically better than a world in which he did not, for the more intrinsic good there is in the world, the better. Those who deny this are either being irrational or are making a miscalculation, for character traits that accompany such sadism usually cause a good deal of unnecessary suffering. But if such behavior has exactly the same effects all around as the behavior of the doctor who does his job with repugnance or just as a matter of routine, then, if one carefully and impartially reflects on it, one will come to appreciate not only that a world with such sadists is not a worse world but is actually a better world, for there will be more pleasure (more intrinsic good) in it than in a world in which this is not so.

The dialectic of this normative ethical argument gives rise, quite naturally, to two metaethical issues. In the first the nonhedonist in effect argues that if x is ordinarily believed to be intrinsically good, then x is intrinsically good—or at least that this ordinary belief is a necessary condition for x's being intrinsically good. The hedonist rejects this and claims instead that only what the clearheaded, impartial, and informed man believes to be intrinsically good is intrinsically good. Both are in reality arguing about what it means to call something "intrinsically good" and about the logic of justification of claims of intrinsic goodness. To do this is to do metaethics.

Suppose the nonhedonist grants that there would be more total pleasure in the sadist's world but still maintains that such pleasure is intrinsically evil and the hedonist, recognizing this, continues to assert it is intrinsically good. How, if at all, could we rationally resolve this issue? Both claims are apparently synthetic, and they are in conflict. To say they are essentially contested or that neither is true or false—for they merely exhibit a disagreement in attitude—is to assume without argument a metaethical position; and exactly the same thing is true if one asserts that one is immediately aware of the truth of the hedonist's or the nonhedonist's claim. Further progress toward resolving this normative issue calls for clarification of the meaning of the terms "good" and "pleasure" and of the logical status of "Pleasure is intrinsically good."

We have noted some, but by no means all, of the difficulties in establishing that pleasure is *always* intrinsically good. But let us assume that we have in some way established its truth. We still have not established the truth of hedonism, for we must also establish what is much harder to establish, that *only* pleasure is intrinsically good. Here most people part company with hedonism and adopt some form of pluralism.

ETHICAL PLURALISM. G. E. Moore argues that the claim of the hedonist is absurd, for it commits him to the belief "that a world in which absolutely nothing but pleasure existed—no knowledge, no love . . . no moral qualities—must yet be intrinsically better worth creating—provided only the total quantity of pleasure in it were *the least bit greater* [italics added], than one in which all these things existed *as well as* pleasure." There are many things of great value. It is, it is argued, absurd to think that only one of them should be classified as worth having for its own sake. Many people who have reflected on the matter regard knowledge, freedom, conscientiousness, a sense of identity, and awareness to be intrinsically good as well.

The hedonist can reply to Moore's argument by agreeing that a world with knowledge and love in it is better than a world without such knowledge, but he will argue that it is not *intrinsically* better. A world with love and knowledge in it will, in the long run, lead to a world with greater happiness in it. We so readily assent to Moore's remarks because we all, on good grounds, believe this; but such a belief is quite compatible with the truth of hedonism.

Part of the difficulty in this argument stems from confusions on both sides about the concept of pleasure. Some critics of hedonism think of pleasure as consisting in delightful sensations. They think that a hedonist is claiming that the only things desirable for themselves alone are things like being rubbed, stroked, or massaged. But this, of course, is an absurd parody of the claims of hedonism. The hedonist does not identify pleasure with such delectable sensations. His use of "pleasure" is identifiable with enjoyable states of consciousness. He claims that something is intrinsically good if, and only if, it is an experience that is enjoyable whenever a person has it. But this is not to treat pleasure, as one treats pain, as a sensation. It is, in a way

that is very hard to characterize correctly, a dimension or quality of experience.

Is it true that the only kind of experiences we want for their own sake are enjoyable experiences? (If true, is it logically true or contingently true?) Are these experiences the only things that are intrinsically desirable? Most philosophers have remained pluralists on these questions. How, for example, does the hedonist know that knowledge always has only extrinsic value? Why not, at least for some kinds of knowledge, both?

How can we tell who is right, or is there in reality no right and wrong—no moral truth—here?

Again metaethics becomes relevant. Suppose a man says: "I don't find self-knowledge or scientific knowledge intrinsically desirable at all. If it leads to happiness, it is worthwhile; if not, not. Similarly, a sense of one's humanity or a sense of identity has no intrinsic merit. To have a sense of identity and an understanding of oneself is valuable only if it leads to happiness; if it does not, it is without intrinsic worth. Pleasure, enjoyment and pleasure, or enjoyment alone is intrinsically good." But, let us further suppose, the ethical pluralist continues to claim that self-identity and some kinds of knowledge are intrinsically good. How, if at all, can we settle this issue? How, if at all, can man either *know* or even have good reason to believe he is right? Here again fundamental metaethical issues lurk behind the scenes.

It is very natural for people to argue here, unwittingly switching to a metaethical argument, that what it *means* to say that something is intrinsically good is that it is enjoyable, pleasant, or productive of pleasure. This is to make a metaethical claim that can be countered by metaethical arguments—that it is an intelligible question to ask if all those things which are enjoyable are intrinsically good; that it is not self-contradictory to assert "It's pleasant but it has no intrinsic worth"; and that it can be pointed out that "Those things which are fecund sources of pleasure are worth seeking for their own sake" is not an analytic statement. We could, by a suitable stipulative redefinition of this last statement, make it true by definition, the one before it self-contradictory, and the question self-answering. But this does not settle the question(s) of why these definitions should be accepted as normative and how a stipulation can reveal "normative truth."

If instead we claim that all men desire or seek pleasure (enjoyment, satisfaction of desire), and only pleasure, for its own sake, this would be, depending on how we took it, either a most questionable psychological claim or a disguised tautology. Whether tautologically true or empirically true, the claim would still not constitute a *normative* claim. That people desire or seek pleasure only for its own sake does not *eo ipso* establish that what they seek is desirable or intrinsically good; and, if the only thing people *can* seek is pleasure or satisfaction of desire, then it makes no sense to say that it is good that they do so, for they cannot do otherwise. But if they do always in fact seek pleasure for its own sake but might seek something else instead, then it is appropriate to ask why they should continue to seek it or why it is good to seek it at all.

If the hedonist, like Sidgwick, claims that on careful reflection he is aware, through immediate or intuitive insight, that only enjoyable states of consciousness are intrinsically good, then he is again engaged in metaethics. He is relying on the possibility and, granted the possibility, the correctness of some intuitions. Sidgwick is not alone in having or claiming to have intuitions, and others, after careful reflection, have intuitions or what they take to be intuitions that conflict with Sidgwick's. Are they all genuine intuitions? How can we know which "intuitions" (if any) are correct? W. D. Ross, for example, has intuitions that are diametrically opposed to Sidgwick's. How can we tell who is right, or is there in reality no right and wrong—no moral truth—here? Are they not both simply expressing their preferences and trying to get others to adopt their attitudes? In trying to assess this normative ethical dispute, we are ineluctably led into fundamental metaethical controversies.

If the hedonist tries to resolve the argument in his favor in another way, he is also led into metaethical controversy and he also, if he so argues, shows how in the interests of his theory he has arbitrarily extended the meaning of "pleasure." Suppose he says that the man who judges some knowledge to be intrinsically good says he *wants* that knowledge for its own sake and not simply because of the pleasure or power it will give him. Similarly, the man who says that, painful or not, he *wants* to keep his self-identity shows that he is, after all, unwittingly reasoning as a hedonist, for in judging knowledge and self-identity to be intrinsically good, he shows that he *wants* them for their own sake; and to say that *x* is pleasant is to say that *x* is a part of experience that all people or most people want to continue on its own account. To be a hedonist is to argue that something is intrinsically desirable if, and only if, it is an experience that the person who has it *wants* to prolong for its own sake.

If this is so, hedonism appears to become true by definition, in which case pluralist theories are unintelligible rather than false. But this may be an arbitrary redefinition of the word "pleasure" in the interests of a normative ethical theory, for ordinarily it would seem that one could understand someone's contention that, even though an experience is painful, he wishes to continue having it because he regards it as having intrinsic value. Such a wish may be irrational, but it certainly does not appear unintelligible. This gives us some reason to believe that such a hedonist is operating with an arbitrarily extended definition of "pleasure."

The hedonist could reply that this is not so, for if we stress, as we should, intrinsic value (that is, an experience worth having "on its own account"), it is not so evident that it makes sense to say that we seek painful experiences on their own account or for themselves, or that we seek nonpleasurable experiences on their own account or for themselves.

Whoever is right here, it is again apparent that to adjudicate this normative ethical issue between the hedonist and the nonhedonist, we must resolve a metaethical dispute about the meaning of "pleasure" and about the relation of "pleasure" to "good."

The hedonist may take yet another tack in his own defense, but again he is led into another metaethical controversy. He may grant, given ordinary moral consciousness and the moral discourse that reflects that consciousness, that it is of course correct to assert that knowledge, self-identity, and many things other than pleasure are intrinsically good. But he still may argue that ordinary moral consciousness is, in many respects, irrational and parochial, and that we cannot rely on it or the discourse it enshrines to give us an understanding of what morality is really about. This raises a cluster of metaethical issues about the nature of justification in ethics.

The point of the discussion about the question of what is intrinsically good or worthwhile has not been to settle this ancient issue in favor of hedonism or in favor of any pluralistic theories, but to show how these normative ethical issues will, when pursued relentlessly, finally turn to a considerable degree, although not entirely, on conceptual controversies. It is these controversies that metaethics is designed to handle.

Normative ethics is actual, so in one plain but trivial sense it is possible; but normative ethical issues lead to metaethical ones, and whether a sound normative ethic is possible turns on the proper answer to certain metaethical questions. (That the relation is not quite that simple will become apparent later. The final constraint on any metaethics is living moral language.)

To settle what is intrinsically good or what is worth seeking for its own sake does not, by any means, exhaust the normative ethical questions that deserve careful treatment. Even the teleologist must go on to determine what is the best thing to do. If he is a pluralist, he must determine which one of various conflicting intrinsic goods is most desirable; and a hedonist must decide what is most pleasurable and *whose* pleasure is to be considered. Other ethical monists have similar problems. But if we are teleologists we will reason in this way, unless we are also egoists: whatever is intrinsically good should be promoted. If the greatest amount of good to everyone involved is realized, then we will have achieved what should be done. Our obligation, as moral agents, is always to promote the greatest possible net good. But, as deontologists and others have been quick to bring out, there are all kinds of questions about this position. Most pressing, perhaps, is the question of whether the rightness of an act depends entirely on its consequences. Is it really the case that an act is right if, and only if, it maximizes intrinsic good?

Suppose act *A* or rule or practice *A* involves breaking a promise or lying, while act *B* or rule or practice *B* does not; but act *A* or rule or practice *A* has *slightly* better consequences. Is it clear that we do the right thing in performing act *A* rather than *B*? It is not so clear. Many moralists would claim that the right thing to do here is *B*. This, they say, is even clearer if the consequences of *A* and *B* both lead to the same amount of total intrinsic good. Where this last situation obtains, teleologists would say that there is no reason for saying one act or one rule is right and the other wrong; but surely an act or rule that involves lying or breaking a promise is, *ceteris paribus,* morally inferior to an act or rule that does not involve lying or breaking a promise. In determining what is right and wrong, it is important to determine what things are intrinsically good and what contributes to a maximum amount of intrinsic good, but such knowledge is not by itself sufficient to give us knowledge of what is the right or wrong thing to do. Moreover, we seem to have a further and independent criterion for justice, for it is not clear that we should always seek the maximum net good; we should be concerned with the equity of its distribution as well. It would seem that we should seek that state of affairs which will, as far as possible, realize the maximum net good for *everyone* involved.

There are a host of questions here about what is the right, just, or fair thing to do that any sound normative ethic must answer. We cannot here examine them in detail, but it should be reasonably apparent that satisfactory answers to them again lead to making a decision about appropriate answers to metaethical questions. Can "right," "ought," "just" be defined or explicated in terms of "good"? Is discovery of the criteria for good also discovery of the criteria for right? Are there independent objective criteria for rightness or justice? What

is the logic of justification in ethics? What is (are) the meaning(s) of "moral"? This discussion would again show that normative ethics, pursued diligently, naturally leads, when pressed to a certain level of abstraction, to the conceptual inquiry called metaethics.

In this section we have sought to establish that many fundamental normative ethical disputes require for their resolution an examination of metaethical issues. Our primary means of achieving this has been through examining some of the conflicts that arise in normative ethics between ethical hedonism and pluralistic theories. In trying to resolve certain fundamental issues in normative ethics, disputes quite naturally arise concerning the intelligibility of the concept of intrinsic goodness, its exact nature, and its centrality in moral reasoning. As we have seen, disputes which arise between ethical hedonists and nonhedonists over whether pleasure and only pleasure is intrinsically good lead to metaethical disputes over the meaning of "pleasure" and over the logical status of such claims as "Pleasure alone is good." Furthermore, even if the normative ethical beliefs of a given normative ethical theory (such as ethical hedonism) conflict with ordinary moral beliefs, it will only follow that this normative ethical theory is in error, if it is true that a normative ethical theory is sound only if it is in accord with ordinary moral beliefs. But this is also a thesis in metaethics and requires metaethical analysis for its rational resolution. Finally, as we have also seen, when normative ethicists consider what is the best thing to do and what ought, everything considered, to be done, metaethical questions concerning the meaning, criteria, and intermural relations of "right," "good," "just," and "ought" come to the fore. To know whether a rational normative ethic is possible, we must have some reasonable answer to such metaethical questions.

Metaethical Relativism and Subjectivism

Given the difficulty in justifying any normative system, we should now examine various forms of the familiar assertion that moral claims, unlike factual claims, are all subjective. There are confusions here and distinctions that must be made before we can profitably pursue some of the metaethical questions that have been central to moral philosophy.

The difficulty in discussing the charge that moral claims are all relative or all subjective is in knowing exactly what the charge is. People who have made such claims have meant many very different things.

To understand clearly what is involved in a conventionalist's challenge concerning morals, a few remarks about metaethical relativism, its cousin ethical skepticism, and subjectivism are in order.

RELATIVISM AND SKEPTICISM. Metaethical relativism claims that there are no objectively sound procedures for justifying one moral code or one set of moral judgments as against another code or set of moral judgments. Ethical skepticism claims that no one can ever say with any justification that something is good or bad, right or wrong. Some actions may be right and others wrong, but there is no way of knowing which is which.

Ethical skepticism claims that no one can ever say with any justification that something is good or bad, right or wrong.

Ethical skepticism at first appears to be a normative ethical doctrine, but it is difficult to understand it as anything other than a claim about the logic of justification in ethics and thus as a part of metaethics. The skeptic leaves open the possibility that some actions or principles are right or wrong, but he claims we can never be in a position to know that this is so. This claim refers to what is logically possible to do and thus is about the nature of moral concepts. This means that if we are to find good arguments for ethical skepticism, they must be found in some metaethical argument about the meaning of ethical terms and/or the nature of moral argument.

SUBJECTIVISM. It is here that subjectivism becomes relevant. Subjectivism, as it is construed by philosophers, is a metaethical contention about the logical status of moral utterances. It is usually taken to mean any one of the following. (1) A moral utterance is merely an autobiographical statement about the attitudes or feelings of the person making the statement. (2) Moral utterances merely express the attitudes or feelings of the utterer and are used by him to evoke or invite similar attitudes in others. (3) Moral judgments *purport* to refer to something outside the speaker's mind, but in reality they only express, although in a disguised way, his approbations and disapprobations. (4) There is no way of rationally resolving *fundamental* moral disputes, for fundamental moral judgments, or *ultimate* moral principles, cannot correctly be said to be true or false independently of the attitudes of at least some people. (A fundamental moral dispute is a dispute that would not be resolved even if there were complete agreement about the nonmoral facts relevant to the dispute. Ultimate moral principles are those which would divide people in such situations of moral dispute, and fundamental moral judgments are the conflicting moral judgments people would make when they disagreed morally,

even when they were in complete agreement about the nonmoral facts relevant to the dispute.)

All four of these metaethical claims are to be contrasted with a fifth sense of "subjectivism" that is not metaethical but probably is closer to what most nonphilosophers would mean by "subjectivism in ethics." This is the contention that the moral judgments people make are all formed or at least very strongly influenced by their emotional biases or prejudices. In short, (5) asserts that all moral judgments are prejudiced judgments.

It is evident that many moral judgments are unwittingly biased and thus are subjective in sense (5), but, unless "bias" and "prejudice" are to be evacuated of all their content, it is clear that this form of subjectivism presupposes the possibility that *some* moral judgments are not subjective in that way. Sometimes people make moral judgments in a calm, impartial way after a due consideration of the facts; and even if this empirical truism would turn out to be false, this would be of a considerably less strictly philosophical consequence than might at first be thought because we would still be able to conceive what it would be like for moral judgments to be objective. The problem would not cause philosophical bewilderment, although it would surely lead to social chaos.

The first characterization of subjectivism given above is a typical way in which analytic critics of subjectivism state the position they are criticizing. Such a subjectivism is plainly untenable. To say (*a*) "One ought never to lie" is not to say (*b*) "the idea of never lying, as a matter of psychological fact, arouses in me a pro-attitude toward never lying." I could surely say, without contradicting myself, that the idea of never lying arouses in me a pro-attitude toward never lying, but all the same I ought to suppress that pro-attitude. But since this is not self-contradictory, (*a*) and (*b*) cannot be identical in meaning; and if they are not identical in meaning, subjectivism in sense (1) is false. What would establish the truth of (*b*) is reasonably evident, but what, if anything, would establish the truth of (*a*) is not at all evident; however, if they have the same meaning, what would establish the truth of one would establish the truth of the other. Nevertheless, we have no reason at all to think they have the same truth-value.

A good case, however, can be made for the claim that this first kind of subjectivism is but the straw man of certain analytic philosophers and that in this form it is seldom maintained by serious philosophers.

Some philosophers, who wish to limit subjectivism to (1) or perhaps to (4), say (2) is not subjectivism at all but a simple and very unsatisfactory variety of emotivism. Others have wished to call emotivism a new subjectivism. It is a moot point whether all forms of emotivism should be called subjectivistic, but (2) would deny any interpersonal validity to moral claims and would deny that they could be true. This would seem enough to warrant calling this form of emotivism a subjective metaethic; later we shall examine whether it is an adequate metaethic. But such a paradoxical claim, if true, would surely give us a negative answer to the Kantian question "Is a normative ethic possible?" It would not entail the impropriety of any normative ethical claim, but if true, there could be no question about justifying a normative ethical claim or a normative ethical system. However, (2) is highly implausible.

Most fundamentally, the question of justification

in ethics is the question of stating, elucidating,

and defending a sound procedure for determining

the truth of conflicting moral claims

and the soundness of moral arguments.

Subjectivism in senses (3) and (4) is a far more serious threat. If (3) were true, no rational normative ethic would be possible; and if (4) were true, it would seem questionable whether we could answer the Kantian question affirmatively. Yet there are powerful considerations favoring (3) and (4). They give substance and greater precision to the frequently voiced and very confused claim that *alles ist relativ.* We could, of course, raise difficulties about (3) and (4), but we would always be faced with the possibility that (3) or (4), more adequately stated or modified, could avoid these difficulties. A more direct approach would be to state an adequate metaethic that was not subjective in any of the above senses and that clarified the nature of the problem about justification in ethics and treated how it could be answered by showing how moral disagreements can be rationally resolved and how they have certain formal and perhaps nonformal conditions of adequacy. Before considering the adequacy of certain traditional nonsubjectivist metaethical theories, we must explain these formal requirements and state the problem of justification somewhat more fully.

Formal Features of Moral Discourse

Most fundamentally, the question of justification in ethics is the question of stating, elucidating, and defending a sound procedure for determining the truth of conflicting moral claims and the soundness of moral arguments. In everyday life we are barraged with a va-

riety of moral claims and counterclaims; the moral arguments in support of them are diverse and conflicting. How are we finally to decide among them? Is it really the case that metaethical relativism or some variety of subjectivism is correct? Moralists have traditionally claimed objectivity for their moral principles, and this claim of objectivity seems to be embedded in our everyday moral discourse. But is this claim actually justified? Can we show that there are objectively true moral judgments or that there are sound moral arguments?

Such a question clearly calls for a characterization of what could be meant by calling a moral judgment objective. A moral judgment is objective if, and only if, it is either true or false and if its truth or falsity does not depend on the peculiarities of the person who makes the judgment or on the culture to which he belongs, but shall be determinable by any rational agent who is apprised of the relevant facts.

It should be noted that there are some metaethicists who claim that there are objective moral judgments and yet deny that moral judgments or statements can properly be called true or false. They recognize that moral judgments do not have the kind of necessary truth characteristic of mathematics, and they argue with considerable plausibility that moral statements are not true or false in the way that empirical statements are true or false—there are no ethical characteristics, rightness and wrongness, goodness and badness, that are either directly or indirectly observable. Since this is so, they conclude that there are no objective moral facts which would make moral judgments true or false; because of this, "truth" and "falsity" are not correctly applicable to moral judgments.

Even if it is true that moral judgments differ from factual judgments in this way, it does not follow that we cannot correctly say that moral judgments are true or false. To assert that a judgment or statement is true is to give a warranted endorsement of that judgment or statement, but what makes the judgment warranted varies according to what we are talking about. To be capable of being true, a statement need not state a fact or assert that certain empirically identifiable characteristics are part of an object or an action. Rather, what is necessary is that the statement in question be publicly warrantable, that is, that it admit of some publicly determinable procedure in virtue of which rational men could come to accept it. If a given statement has a sufficiently powerful warrant to justify our claiming that we are certain of it, then we can properly say it is true. But what and how we warrant what we are talking about depends on *what it is that* we are talking about. We can properly call a statement or judgment in any area objectively true if it would be endorsed without doubt by informed, reasonable, reflective, and careful observers.

Such a publicly determinable judgment, whether true or false, is objective. If, by contrast, its acceptability depends on some cultural or individual idiosyncrasy of the person(s) involved, then the statement is subjective and cannot have the kind of truth required for an objective moral judgment.

There are some features other than the claim to objectivity that are held to be formal requirements of all moral judgments. Moral judgments all make a claim to universality—if I judge that I have a right to disregard a certain regulation or that I ought to do a certain thing, I implicitly judge that relevantly similar persons in relevantly similar situations also have a right to do it or ought to do it. Similarly, if I say that it would be a good thing if x would do y, I give one to understand that it would be a good thing for anyone relevantly like x and similarly situated to do y. And if I say of something, "It's a good one," I must say, on pain of incoherence, that anything exactly like "it" is also a good one. What, exactly, counts as a relevant similarity or a relevant respect cannot be determined apart from the context and nature of what we are discussing, but what constitutes a relevant similarity is often evident enough in a given context. At any rate, this kind of universality or generalizability is built into the very use of moral expressions and helps govern what can count as a moral judgment.

Moral discourse is also a form of practical discourse; its primary use is not that of asserting, questioning, or reaffirming that something is the case but that of making something the case, of criticizing or appraising something that is the case, or of molding attitudes toward certain states of affairs or actions. This is what is meant when we say that moral discourse is essentially action-guiding and attitude-molding.

Beyond the claims to objectivity, universality, and practicality, it is also frequently, but not always, asserted that moral discourse is an autonomous mode of discourse. This means that no moral or normative claim is derivable from, or depends for its validity on, purely nonmoral or nonnormative statements alone. Certain inessential and unimportant qualifications apart, no moral statement is entailed by any set of purely nonnormative statements. Morality, no matter how carefully elaborated, can never become or be reduced to an empirical science. We cannot discover what we ought to do or what is desirable from a knowledge of nonmoral facts *alone,* including the facts about human nature and conduct.

Metaethical Theories

Metaethical theories, where they are not explicitly subjectivistic, attempt to account for four central features of moral discourse: that moral judgments claim universality, autonomy, and objectivity, and that moral discourse is a form of practical discourse—it guides conduct and tends to alter behavior. In handling the problem of justification, these various theories divide on what form the justification of ethical judgments can take, but with one exception about autonomy they agree that a clear characterization of moral discourse must square with the fact that moral discourse in some way satisfies these four conditions.

Not all metaethical theories will be discussed; rather, concentration will be on some of the central aspects of naturalism, intuitionism, and noncognitivism.

NATURALISM. As a distinctively metaethical theory, naturalism contends that moral terms are completely definable in nonmoral terms and that moral judgments are a subspecies of empirical judgments. In reality, moral terms stand for purely natural characteristics.

Naturalism is an attractive theory, for, if correct, ethical theory could become an empirical science. We would have finally uncovered a perfectly objective method for confirming or disconfirming moral judgments, including fundamental moral judgments. There would be no need to appeal to intuition or to regard moral judgments as essentially contested, incapable of rational resolution because ethical naturalism, if true, shows us how we can have a purely empirical knowledge of good and evil.

Whether this desideratum can be realized depends on whether the naturalist can show that all moral terms are actually equivalent in meaning to terms standing for purely empirical characteristics—qualities or relations capable of either direct or indirect observation by empirical methods. It is here that certain objections, first formulated in the twentieth century by G. E. Moore, become relevant. Moore's most central argument has been dubbed the open-question argument.

A naturalist may, for example, try to define "intrinsic good" as "that which satisfies desire," or "moral good" as "that which promotes human survival." But we can intelligibly enough ask, "Is that which satisfies desire intrinsically good?" This is not a senseless question equivalent to asking, "Is that which satisfies desire that which satisfies desire?" We can also with perfect linguistic propriety ask if all those things which promote human survival under any circumstances, cannibalism or incest, for example, are morally permissible. But if the above naturalistic definitions were correct, we could not sensibly ask such questions any more than we can sensibly ask if a father is a male parent. More generally, the argument is this: for any proposed naturalistic definition x we can always, unless x itself contains some normative terms (and thus is not genuinely naturalistic), ask—without making a purely verbal mistake—if x is good, right, or obligatory. This shows that such moral terms are not equivalent to empirical terms. Furthermore, for whatever naturalistic value satisfies the variable *x,* to assert that *x* is good, right, or obligatory is not to assert a statement that cannot be denied without contradiction.

There are many counters to such antinaturalist arguments. One is to claim that moral terms have many contextually dependent meanings and that it is only this, and not the impossibility of naturalism, that the open-question argument shows. It is also argued that there may be a *covert* synonymity between terms, particularly where the correct definition of a term is very complex. Consider this definition of "good": to say "*x* is good" is to say that if there were an omniscient, disinterested, and dispassionate observer, he would approve of *x.* If someone were to inquire whether it made sense to ask if what an omniscient, disinterested, and dispassionate observer would approve is good, we might not know, even after careful reflection, whether such a question is or is not a closed question. In short, a question actually may be closed when it appears to be open. The open-question argument is thus far from decisive.

The critic of naturalism could grant that the open-question argument is not decisive and still argue that nevertheless it counts heavily against naturalism. The criteria for a good woman, a good chisel, and a good horse differ significantly. In this way "good" is a context-dependent word, but as J. O. Urmson has remarked, "good" is not a punning homonym; it has a common use in all these contexts. Furthermore, we can significantly ask, using "good" in a more specific manner, "Is pleasure *intrinsically* good?" or "Is what one's society approves of and regards as having overriding social importance *morally* good?" Thus, even when the kind of normative concept is specified, the moral term in question still is not naturalistically definable. Finally, given the fact that naturalists are trying to define "good" in such a way that their definition, if correct, will show that there are some purely empirical terms that have the same meaning as "good," we must, to have good grounds for asserting such an equivalence, show that an ethical term and its proposed empirical equivalent cannot be used to form an open question. If, after careful reflection, it is possible for someone well acquainted with the language in question to assert that the question is open or even that he is unsure whether it is open or not, we are in no position to assert that the naturalistic definition works. (If the naturalist makes the equivalence a matter of stipulation, he has done something quite arbitrary.) We have very good grounds for believing that all simple naturalistic definitions allow open questions, and the more complex ones also appear to do so.

A more fundamental and perhaps more telling argument for naturalism consists in pointing out that the nonnaturalist assumes something that is quite questionable—that there are two distinct classes of terms; ethical terms and nonethical terms. But the nonnaturalist's distinction has little philosophic value, for no one has given a clear criterion for what counts as an ethical or "evaluative" term, as distinct from a nonethical term. This objection is a two-edged sword, for, if correct, we would have no basic naturalistic or empiricist language made up of terms, logical constants apart, standing for purely empirical realities; and thus we would have no way of knowing whether the naturalist's program could be carried out.

From the above it should be evident that naturalism has not been decisively refuted. If it were a correct metaethic, it would in nonsubjectivist forms show the objectivity and universality of moral discourse. What is, however, very questionable is whether naturalism can adequately account for the practical nature of moral discourse, and naturalism also denies the autonomy of moral claims.

INTUITIONISM. Intuitionists make negative points against naturalism, but they also develop positive contentions of their own. As much as they differ among themselves, they all agree that morality is autonomous: that there must be at least one primitive ethical term that is the vehicle for a nonnatural quality, relation, or concept. This primitive ethical term is indefinable, and the reality it stands for is an objective reality that we must cognize directly. We cannot prove that there is such a reality or confirm or disconfirm its existence by empirical observation. We are either directly aware of it or we are not. It is in this manner that we gain our fundamental knowledge of good and evil.

Moore took "good" as his primitive ethical term. Others have taken "right," "ought," or "fitting" as such a term. Still others have allowed two primitive terms, "right" and "good," but the fundamental point is that there must be at least one such term standing for a unique and unanalyzable object of thought that must simply be apprehended to be known.

There are different types of intuitionism—according to one variety, we intuit the intrinsic goodness of actions; according to another, what we intuit is the obligatory character of an act. Some intuitionists stress that we are directly aware of the rightness, goodness, or obligatoriness of specific actions or attitudes; others argue that we are directly aware only of the self-evidence of certain general, highly abstract principles of conduct. But they all agree that such truths are both necessary and synthetic and that to say we intuit their truth is to say we have a direct, nonsensory, cognitive awareness of the necessary truth of certain moral claims.

If someone reports that he is not aware, on honest reflection, of such a nonnatural characteristic when he judges something to be good or obligatory, but only of a feeling that so and so is good or a feeling that something is obligatory, it will not do for the intuitionist to reply that he must then be morally blind, for, unlike color blindness, there is no agreed-upon criterion for moral blindness. We have physical tests for tone deafness or color blindness, but not for moral blindness. The intuitionist claims to be aware of a nonnatural quality or relation—to see, in a way that is not literal observing, that so and so is good or ought to be done. But what counts as a nonnatural quality? To be told it is not an empirical quality or relation, directly or indirectly given as a sense constituent, is not to be told what it is. The intuitionist has not given us an intelligible description of what it is we must apprehend in order to apprehend a nonnatural quality or relation. His account has all the defects of the *via negativa*. If we are told we just see that it is wrong to kill little children, in the same way that we see that two plus two equals four, the reply must be that we do not see this to be so in a way analogous to our apprehension of logical or mathematical truths; "two plus two equals four," like all logico-mathematical truths, is analytic, while the moral statement, as intuitionists are the first to insist, is synthetic.

The intent of moral language is not simply to describe what is the case but to prescribe that something be done or to evaluate something that is, has been, or may be the case.

There are, it is argued, two even more fundamental errors common to both naturalism and intuitionism. They both operate with a very inadequate conception of how language functions. According to both theories, a word, logical constants apart, is meaningful if, and only if, it stands for something. Naturalists claim that a meaningful word stands for a natural characteristic(s) and intuitionists, noting that it does not seem to stand for a natural characteristic(s), conclude, since moral terms are obviously intelligible, that it *must* stand for a nonnatural characteristic. The mistake is to assume that, to be intelligible, a term must stand for something. Not all terms, not even all adjectives, are property-ascribing words. "Good" and "right" do not stand for properties at all or, more conservatively, do not simply stand for properties, natural or nonnatural; they have a different but distinctive role in that form of social intercourse we call language.

The second error (or alleged error) common to naturalism and intuitionism is that neither can account

properly for the practical functions of moral discourse. To know that one ought to do something involves setting oneself to do it. Moral utterances guide conduct and alter behavior, but naturalism and intuitionism in effect treat moral utterances as property-ascribing theoretical utterances. To regard moral utterances in such a way is to miss their distinctive function. In using moral language we do not, at least typically, tell someone *that* something is the case; we tell someone *to make* something the case. If knowledge of good and evil were simply an apprehending that something is the case, then it would remain inexplicable why to know that one ought to do *x* is to know that one must, if one is a moral agent, *try* to do *x*.

NONCOGNITIVISM. When we consider the common difficulties in naturalism and intuitionism, some form of noncognitivism is likely to become an attractive possibility. ("Noncognitivism," although it has become a fairly standard label, is in a way an unfortunate one, for it suggests what few noncognitivists would affirm, namely that there is no knowledge of good and evil.) Noncognitivists deny that moral utterances are simply, or sometimes even at all, purely property-ascribing utterances, and they likewise deny that moral terms simply or at all stand for characteristics of any sort. We must not, noncognitivists argue, confuse fact-stating and normative discourse. What makes an utterance normative is precisely its dynamism, its trigger function; a normative utterance is an utterance that guides conduct and molds or alters attitudes.

Noncognitivists differ greatly among themselves. Some model moral utterances on imperatives; others model them on decisions of principle, resolutions, or declarations of intention; still others believe that what marks an utterance as moral or normative is that it expresses the attitudes of the speaker and tends to evoke or invite similar attitudes in the hearer. Noncognitivists with greater philosophical sophistication contend that moral utterances are multi-functional. Some function in one way and some in another, but the sophisticated noncognitivists continue to contend that all the various primary functions of moral utterances are always, directly or indirectly, action-guiding.

Some, including A. J. Ayer, maintain that it is misleading to say that statements made by using moral utterances are true or false, for they are not factual statements; others, including C. L. Stevenson, maintain that in virtue of their declarative form and in virtue of the fact that "true" and "false" are typically used to backup or warrant declarative statements of various types, it is perfectly proper to follow everyday usage and say of such moral statements that they are true or false. But all noncognitivists agree that fundamental moral judgments cannot be verified (confirmed or disconfirmed) and that we can never have an a priori or purely conceptual warrant for claiming that fundamental moral conflicts can be resolved by empirical methods alone. It will always remain at least a logical possibility that we might agree about all the facts and still disagree about what we ought to do or about what is good or worth having for its own sake. On these issues the noncognitivists side with the intuitionists against the naturalists. But like the naturalists they deny that we have any intuitive knowledge of good and evil. Fundamental moral claims are not matters of knowledge but expressions of attitude, decisions of principle, or declarations of intention. Hence the label noncognitivist. The intent of moral language is not simply to describe what is the case but to prescribe that something be done or to evaluate something that is, has been, or may be the case.

Since not all noncognitivist views are the same, different difficulties will apply to different views. If the noncognitivist is an emotivist and contends that to be a moral utterance, an utterance must be attitude-expressing and attitude-evoking, a question immediately arises about the logical status of this claim. Presumably it must be analytic. (If it were empirical, it would not show what makes an utterance a moral utterance.) The statement "His attitudes and emotional reactions are those of a segregationist, but he knows segregation to be wrong" does not appear to be self-contradictory, and as children we are not taught any rule of language to the effect that an utterance must be attitude-expressing to be moral. We know that there is a close link between attitudes ("the passions") and morality, but this is perfectly compatible with a cognitivist metaethic. How, then, do we know that moral utterances must be attitude-expressing? We are tempted to say that moral dispute is at an end when, and only when, we attain agreement in attitude; but this does not appear always to be so. Two people may have the same attitudes concerning the white power structure vis-à-vis Harlem; they both, let us say, disapprove of the behavior of the city officials, yet they still disagree morally about the issue because they have different reasons for their disapproval of the city officials. And it is not the case that any consideration that leads the hearer to share the expressed attitude of the speaker will *ipso facto* count, as the emotivists claim it will, as a morally relevant reason for adopting that attitude. Emotional appeals and nonrational persuasion are irrelevant in moral reasoning. What motivates one to act in a certain way or to adopt a certain attitude may or may not justify one in so acting, and what justifies one in doing it may or may not so motivate one to do it.

Other noncognitivists, such as Hare, argue that moral utterances are much more like imperatives than expressions of attitude. It is their primary logical function to tell us to do something, to guide our actions; whether or not they actually succeed in persuading us or goading us into so acting, they still remain perfectly intelligible moral utterances. But there are also difficulties in such an imperativist view. Imperativists claim that all moral utterances entail imperatives, but while "You ought to vote Socialist" functions very like an imperative and entails "Vote Socialist," no imperative is entailed by "He ought to have voted Socialist" or "He will come to appreciate that he ought to vote Socialist." Furthermore, the contradictories of moral utterances entailing imperatives do not themselves entail imperatives, although surely the moral terms in both utterances have the same meaning.

Besides, whether we liken moral utterances to imperatives, resolutions, declarations of intention, or decisions of principle, it remains the case that the "ought" in the antecedent clause of conditional sentences does not have any of the above noncognitive functions. The "ought" in "If he ought to be told, he should be told now" has the same meaning as the "ought" in "He ought to be told," but the "conditional ought" clearly does not entail an imperative, declare an intention, or express a resolution. Thus, the "ought" in the latter sentence cannot have as an essential part of its meaning any such function.

Lastly, any form of noncognitivism would in effect undermine the objectivity of moral judgments. (This should not be taken to mean that noncognitivists do not have moral principles they are willing to stand by or that they advocate that everything be permitted. To take the remark in this way is to confuse metaethical claims with normative ethical ones.) We have seen that the minimal requirement for the objectivity of a judgment is that it can be interpersonally validated; in the case of moral judgments, this means that an objective moral judgment is a judgment that every rational agent will accept if he reasons disinterestedly, is apprised of the nonmoral facts, and takes the matter to heart. But if moral utterances are essentially resolutions to act in a certain way, declarations of intention, expressions of attitude, or decisions of principle, it follows that moral utterances do not, given such a logical form, require such interpersonal agreement. A man may resolve or decide, even as a matter of principle, to do what no one else does or would resolve or decide to do after careful reflection, and yet there would be nothing logically inappropriate about his decision or resolution.

Moral Reasoning

Those philosophers who tried to bridge the "is/ought gap" were trying, although perhaps in a mistaken way, to do something that is very important. It is a fact of moral reasoning that certain facts are good reasons for moral judgments. Without at all committing oneself to ethical naturalism, and without denying the insight of the noncognitivists that one cannot demonstratively prove or inductively establish fundamental moral claims, it remains the case that we do conclude from "He is my father" that "He has a right to special consideration from me" or from "He promised to return" that "He is under an obligation to return." It is an obvious fact of moral discourse that we give reasons for moral claims, that these reasons are typically statements of fact, and that sometimes we can conclude that if a given factual statement, F, is true, then a certain moral conclusion, E, follows.

It does not, however, follow from this that there is no logical gap between facts and norms. Such ethical conclusions hold only in virtue of certain canons of relevance; when these canons of relevance are explicitly stated, they will be found to invoke normative principles. Moreover, there must be some normative principles used in our judgments of relevance that will not be derived from, or even made in accordance with, other higher-order normative principles.

Such neonaturalists as Philippa Foot and A. I. Melden are perfectly right in claiming that certain matters of fact constitute good and sometimes even conclusive reasons for acting in a certain way, *given* the assumption of the conceptual structures constitutive of our ordinary moral reasoning. But in accepting these we accept a structure that has as constitutive elements certain normative principles, such as "Similar cases are to be treated similarly," "In deciding what is to be done, every person concerned has a right to equal consideration," and "There can be no arbitrary inequalities." It is in virtue of certain very general but still normative principles that we can derive certain moral conclusions from certain factual premises and that certain factual statements become good reasons for certain moral conclusions.

It is also crucial to see, as such philosophers as Stephen Toulmin, Kurt Baier, and Marcus Singer have stressed, that in morality, as in science, we have a limited but distinctive mode of reasoning with its own pragmatic point. If we are ever to understand the nature of moral reasoning, we must not simply fix our attention on the meaning of moral terms or expressions taken in isolation; we must seek to grasp the over-all point or rationale of the discourse in question. Subservient to the over-all purposes for which we have the discourse, each mode of discourse has its distinctive procedures, and in accordance with these procedures we judge whether something is or is not good evidence for or a good reason for a certain claim. Without such ground

rules we cannot correctly speak of the evidence or reasons for or against any contention.

If we examine actual moral discourse when it is being conducted, we will come to see that there is a complicated network of procedural rules connected with morality that limit and partially specify what can count as good reasons for a moral claim. Furthermore, if we reflect on why we have a morality, any morality at all, moral discourse and moral action will be seen to have a point; and the procedural rules that help define morality will be found to be instrumental to the continuance of this activity.

Moral discourse is a form of practical discourse.

Moral questions are fundamentally questions

about what we are to do.

Moral discourse is a form of practical discourse. Moral questions are fundamentally questions about what we are to do. The primary intent of moral utterances is not to assert that so and so is the case, but to advise, admonish, suggest, proclaim, or protest that so and so be done. Moral knowledge is knowledge about what to do or about what attitude to take toward what has been done, is being done, or is intended. In pointing out that moral judgments do not assert something to be the case and thus are not confirmable, Ayer and the emotivists in effect are showing that moral utterances are not theoretical statements about what is the case but are bits of practical discourse about what to *make* the case. As we want and need to know what is the case, so we want and need to know what to do. Indeed, we could not know what to do if we did not know something about what is the case—something about how the world goes—but we also need to know what to do. There are no grounds for assuming that questions about what we should do are more subjective than factual questions or that moral language is more untrustworthy than theoretical discourse. It is just different. In life we need both these activities and the diverse uses of language embedded in them.

Many might concede that morality has its distinctive procedural rules and still object that this does not give it the required objectivity. It has been argued that while the procedural rules connected with the making of factual judgments are cross-culturally valid, the procedural rules connected with moral discourse are purely conventional.

Moral rules, such a conventionalist or metaethical relativist will argue, are rationalizations of custom. Morality is constituted by certain social rules and the actions and attitudes appropriate to those rules. Any attempt to appraise these rules as sound or unsound will at best be question-begging.

In challenging metaethical relativism, we must show how it is possible to assert correctly and objectively that certain social practices either are or are not morally justifiable; and in a like manner we must show how it is possible to assert correctly that the whole moral order either does or does not have a rational claim to our assent.

The metaethical relativist is indeed on solid ground when he points out that morality is a rule-governed activity that guides conduct and molds and alters actions and attitudes. In determining the content and structure of a strange tribe's morality, we would have to discover the social practices to which that tribe was most deeply committed and elicit the rules defining these social practices. We would have to know much more as well, but we would have to know at least that.

Morality necessarily involves a cluster of practices. "Practices" here refers to social activities that contain a set of rules which specify rights and duties, permissible and impermissible steps. The rules that so define a practice we may call procedural rules. Games and ceremonies are good examples of practices. If in playing baseball I hit into center field, I cannot wonder if I really must go to first before I go to second, but I can deliberate about whether to hold up at first or try for second. That a runner must go to first before going to second is a rule of procedure which helps define the practice of baseball. Although not so strictly codified, moral behavior is also a rule-governed activity, a complex cluster of practices with procedural rules that define those practices.

Promising is one such practice. It involves public rules of procedure, rules that are readily taught. We can say that a person has made a promise only when he acts in accordance with certain procedural rules. If I have promised to meet a friend, it is not open to me to excuse my failure to meet him simply on the ground that I had subsequently thought it through and decided that slightly more good would be served by not meeting him. I cannot offer that excuse and still act in accordance with the practice of promise-keeping, any more than I can have three strikes and still be at bat. We could, of course, deliberately change the practice, but given the practice and given the fact that I accept the practice, there are some things I must do. My failure to do these things would, exceptional circumstances apart, show that I either did not really accept the practice or did not properly understand it. There are, of course, legitimate excuses, but the very rules of the practice

itself specify what is to count as a legitimate excuse for not acting in accordance with the practice. There are, for example, conditions that excuse fulfilling a promise, but they are built into the very practice of promise-keeping.

If my action falls under an existing practice that I accept, and if my action does not also fall under a conflicting practice that I also accept, then I have no moral alternative, while accepting the practice, but to try to act in accordance with it. In a contrasting situation where conflicting practices are involved, I must see if there are any principles which I accept that give some moral priority to one or another of the conflicting practices. Where there is such priority, I must acknowledge it and try to act in accordance with it. There are indeed moral questions that cannot without strain and ambiguity be answered by subsumption under any procedural rule, but this does not disconfirm the claim that there are practices which specify and limit how we are to act while acting as moral agents.

What has been said so far might be taken as giving aid and comfort to metaethical relativism, but so far only a very partial account of moral reasoning has been given. The justification of moral beliefs does not terminate in the statement of rules that partially codify our social practices; we can reason about and ask for a justification of the practices themselves. There is a whole battery of objective tests for evaluating social practices, and they are clearly recognizable as a part of our first-order moral discourse. Understanding what morality is involves knowing how to use these procedures for appraising social practices.

Morality has developed in such a way that it is now correct to say that in morality we are concerned with the reasoned pursuit of the interests of all rational agents. That is to say, from the moral point of view, we are concerned with the most extensive welfare of all concerned. When, as with the Nazis or the segregationists, there is both an overriding of some individuals' rights and a pretension to moral rectitude, this oppression is accompanied by rationalization. The victims are thought of in such a way that they are not regarded as fully human, that is, they are not regarded as rational agents capable of the sensibilities of moral agents. That even Nazis and segregationists are committed to act in accordance with such a conception of morality is evidenced by the fact that they must depersonalize their victims in order to justify to themselves their treatment of them. From the moral point of view, we are concerned with the most extensive welfare of all persons concerned. In theory, such racists do not reject such a principle but through rationalization convince themselves that Jews or Negroes are not fully human.

Terms such as "human welfare" and "well-being" are not so vague that certain states of affairs could not be said to be incompatible with them. Social practices that drastically frustrate our need for sleep, food, sex, drink, or elimination; or practices that pointlessly diminish self-esteem, the appreciation of and concern for others, creative employment and diversion; or practices that seek to destroy our tendencies to prize integrity, conscientiousness, knowledge, and the contemplation of beautiful things are practices which must be said to be morally inferior to social practices which do not so frustrate us. This is not to deny the obvious, namely that there are sharp disagreements over the value of some things and that there is even considerable disagreement about the moral priority of those very things we universally prize, approve of, or admire. But even with our less than exact conception of human welfare, we can still show that there are many sets of social practices both imaginable and actual that intelligent and correctly informed people judge without equivocation to be morally inferior to comparable sets of practices. As our knowledge of man develops and as our superstitions—particularly our religious superstitions—diminish, it is reasonable to expect that moral deliberation will enable us to achieve a greater understanding of and agreement about those attitudes and styles of behavior that are taken to be desirable or admirable.

There is a further procedural rule to be considered. In a moral situation we cannot be concerned only with the maximum welfare; we must also be concerned with the welfare of everyone involved. Quite independently of what we judge human welfare to be, these distinctively human values must, from a moral point of view, be distributed as equitably as possible to all the people involved. If I decide I have a right to do x, I must, if I am reasoning morally, be prepared to grant that others relevantly like me and similarly situated have a right to do x as well. As Marcus Singer has shown in his *Generalization in Ethics* (1961), what count as "relevantly like me" and as "similarly situated" cannot be specified apart from a determinate context. Too much depends on who I am and what I am doing, but in determinate contexts there frequently are criteria for an objective determination of these matters.

It is also a procedural rule of morality that the moral agent (as well as the moral critic) must, in making moral judgments, try to assume the viewpoint of an impartial but sympathetic observer. *Ideally,* moral judgments are made in the light of full knowledge and appreciation of the relevant facts; and they *must* be made in the light of the facts that the moral agent can be reasonably expected to have in his possession when he makes the judgment. In making moral judgments we must at-

tempt to make impartial judgments in the light of the relevant facts, using the relevant consideration-making beliefs; but to gain the moral insight that mature morality requires, we should also, before rendering judgment, vividly imagine and emphatically rehearse and review what we know. We should strive to enter unreservedly into the feelings and attitudes of the persons involved in the action; we should seek to see the situation as they see it. After this exercise in imagination, we should then make our moral appraisals as impartial but understanding observers. The attempt to view the situation impartially is a minimum requirement for correct moral appraisal, but mature moral thinking requires sympathy and imagination as well. In utilizing these methods, we have additional checks on our moral beliefs. Any man who will take the trouble to attend carefully to moral discourse will find procedures for its critical appraisal and correction built into its very use.

We have tried to show that while morality involves reasoning in accordance with certain practices, there remain generally acknowledged ways of appraising these practices. This being so, metaethical relativism or subjectivism cannot be true.

The metaethical relativist or subjectivist may well claim by way of rebuttal that all these tests are conventional and that the rationality of the whole moral enterprise is spurious. Only our conditioned virtue—our psychological involvement with morality—blinds us to the fact that it is merely a matter of convention or arbitrary decision whether we accept the requirements of the moral order or become nonmoral rational egoists.

Against the conventionalist claim one can point out that there are good Hobbesian reasons for rational and self-interested people to accept the moral point of view. A rational egoist will naturally desire the most extensive liberty compatible with his own self-interest, but he will also see that this is most fully achievable in a context of community life where the moral point of view prevails. Thus, in a quite nonmoralistic sense of "reasonable," it is reasonable for men, even self-interested men, to acknowledge that it is better for people to behave morally than amorally or immorally.

It is not the case that there is no logical limit to what could count as a valid moral judgment. If what we have claimed is correct, there are unequivocal material procedural rules that help define morality. They limit the scope of what counts as a moral judgment, and they have a rational point. Thus, under certain conditions certain moral judgments are objectively true and others are false. That is to say, there are certain moral truths that do not at all depend on the personal idiosyncrasies or cultural perspective of anyone but would be affirmed by any rational agent apprised of the relevant facts. If this is so, neither metaethical relativism nor any form of subjectivism can be an adequate account of moral reasoning. Although moral utterances express attitudes and have a moving appeal, moral reasoning remains a rule-governed activity with an objective rationale.

[See also Ethics, History of.]

BIBLIOGRAPHY

Classic Sources

Plato, *The Republic,* translated and edited by F. M. Cornford. Oxford, 1941; New York, 1945.

Aristotle, *The Nichomachean Ethics,* in *The Basic Works of Aristotle,* R. M. McKeon, ed. New York, 1941.

Epicurus, *Letter to Menoeceus,* in *Epicurus, the Extant Remains,* translated and edited by Cyril Bailey. Oxford, 1926.

Thomas Aquinas, *Summa Theologica,* translated by the Fathers of the English Dominican Province. London, 1920–1924; New York, 1947. Part II.

Butler, Joseph, *Sermons.* London, 1726.

Hume, David, *An Inquiry Concerning the Principles of Morals,* C. W. Hendel, ed. New York, 1957.

Spinoza, Baruch, *Ethics,* in *The Chief Works of Spinoza,* translated and edited by R. H. M. Elwes. New York, 1955. Especially Parts III-V.

Selby-Bigge, L. A., ed., *British Moralists,* 2 vols. Oxford, 1897; New York, 1965. An important collection of the principal writings of the classical British moralists of the eighteenth century.

Bentham, Jeremy, *The Principles of Morals and Legislation.* London, 1789. Reprinted in Hafner Library of Classics and edited by L. J. Lafleur. New York, 1948.

Mill, J. S., *Utilitarianism.* London, 1861.

Kant, Immanuel, *The Moral Law, or Kant's Groundwork of the Metaphysic of Morals,* translated with analysis and notes by H. J. Paton. London, 1948; 3d ed., 1956.

Kant, Immanuel, *Critique of Practical Reason,* translated and edited by L. W. Beck. Chicago, 1949.

Hegel, G. W. F., *The Philosophy of Right,* translated by T. M. Knox. Oxford, 1942.

Kierkegaard, Søren, *The Concept of Dread,* translated by Walter Lowrie. London, 1944.

Schopenhauer, Arthur, *The Basis of Morality,* translated by A. B. Bullock. London, 1903.

Marx, Karl, *Capital,* translated by Samuel Moore and Edward Aveling. Chicago, 1912.

Kamenka, Eugene, *The Ethical Foundations of Marxism.* London, 1962. Classical examination of Marx's scattered writings on the problems of ethics.

Sidgwick, Henry, *The Methods of Ethics.* London, 1874–1878; 7th rev. ed. by Constance Jones, Chicago, 1962.

Nietzsche, Friedrich, *The Genealogy of Morals,* in *The Complete Works,* Oscar Levy, ed. Edinburgh and London, 1909–1913.

Bradley, F. H., *Ethical Studies.* Oxford, 1876; New York, 1954.

Modern Writings

Baier, Kurt, *The Moral Point of View. Ithaca,* N. Y., 1958. A much-discussed account of the logic of moral reasoning.

Blanshard, Brand, *Reason and Goodness.* New York, 1961.

Brentano, Franz, *The Origin of the Knowledge of Right and Wrong,* translated by Cecil Hague. London, 1902.

Broad, C. D., *Five Types of Ethical Theory.* London, 1930.

Dewey, John, *Human Nature and Conduct.* New York, 1922.

Dewey, John, *The Quest for Certainty.* New York, 1929.

Edwards, Paul, *The Logic of Moral Discourse.* Glencoe, Ill., 1955. An attempt to square crucial features of the emotive theory and a modified ethical naturalism. Important discussion of previous contemporary metaethical theories.

Ewing, A. C., *The Definition of Good.* London, 1947.

Ewing, A. C., *Second Thoughts in Moral Philosophy.* London, 1959. A cognitivist, nonnaturalist analysis that tries to develop a *via media* between Moore and the deontologists.

Gauthier, David, *Practical Reasoning.* Oxford, 1963. An analysis of the logic of moral reasoning from the point of view of linguistic analysis.

Ginsberg, Morris, *On the Diversity of Morals.* New York, 1957.

Ginsberg, Morris, *On Justice in Society.* Ithaca, N.Y., 1965. An account by a distinguished British sociologist of the problem of relativism and some of the central problems of justice.

Hägerström, Axel, *Inquiries Into the Nature of Law and Morals,* translated by C. D. Broad. Stockholm, 1953.

Hägerström, Axel, *Philosophy and Religion,* translated by Robert T. Sandin. London, 1964.

Hare, R. M., *The Language of Morals.* Oxford, 1952.

Hare, R. M., *Freedom and Reason.* Oxford, 1963. A much-discussed and closely reasoned statement of nondescriptivist metaethic.

Hartmann, Nicolai, *Ethics,* translated by Stanton Coit. London, 1932.

Lewis, C. I., *An Analysis of Knowledge and Valuation.* La Salle, Ill., 1947.

Lewis, C. I., *The Ground and Nature of the Right.* New York, 1955. An important statement of a general theory of value and a discussion of the unique role of the concept of right.

Mayo, Bernard, *Ethics and the Moral Life.* New York, 1958. An important examination of the logic of moral reasoning from the point of view of linguistic analysis.

Moore, G. E., *Principia Ethica.* Cambridge, 1903.

Moore, G. E., *Ethics.* London, 1912.

Nowell-Smith, P. H., *Ethics.* London, 1954. A book, covering a wide range of metaethical topics, that is characteristic of contemporary linguistic philosophy.

Perry, R. B., *General Theory of Value.* Cambridge, Mass., 1926.

Perry, R. B., *Realms of Value.* Cambridge, Mass., 1954. A classical statement of ethical naturalism.

Prichard, H. A., *Moral Obligation.* Oxford, 1949. A collection of crucial essays from a deontological point of view.

Prior, A. N., *Logic and the Basis of Ethics.* Oxford, 1949. A careful statement of the central issues between naturalism and nonnaturalism. The history of the dispute is displayed.

Raphael, D. D., *Moral Judgment.* London, 1955. An analysis of the meanings of certain central moral concepts and a discussion of the ground of obligation and the problem of free will.

Rice, Philip B., *On the Knowledge of Good and Evil.* New York, 1955. A restatement, in the light of the criticisms of it by noncognitivism, of a variety of ethical naturalism. Important discussions of contemporary metaethical theories.

Robinson, Richard, *An Atheist's Values.* Oxford, 1964. A lucid discussion of important normative ethical problems by a distinguished British philosopher.

Ross, W. D., *The Right and the Good.* Oxford, 1930.

Ross, W. D., *The Foundations of Ethics.* Oxford, 1939. The major statement in contemporary philosophy of the deontological position.

Russell, Bertrand, *Human Society in Ethics and Politics.* New York, 1955. An attempt to combine a utilitarian account of moral reasoning with an emotive metaethic. Interesting discussion of specific normative ethical issues.

Scheler, Max, *The Nature of Sympathy,* translated by Peter Heath. New Haven, 1954.

Singer, Marcus, *Generalization in Ethics.* New York, 1961. A careful study of the force of the generalization argument in moral reasoning. Important discussions on Kant and the utilitarians.

Sparshott, F. E., *An Enquiry Into Goodness.* Chicago, 1958. An attempt to develop a theory of moral reasoning and an explication of the concept of goodness. A useful discussion of the nature of moral philosophy.

Stevenson, Charles, *Ethics and Language.* New Haven, 1944.

Stevenson, Charles, *Facts and Values.* New Haven, 1963. A much-discussed and complex statement of an emotive metaethic.

Toulmin, Stephen, *The Place of Reason in Ethics.* Cambridge, 1950. A pioneer account, from the point of view of linguistic analysis, of the nature of moral reasoning.

Wellman, Carl, *The Language of Ethics.* Cambridge, Mass., 1961. A discussion of contemporary ethical theories and a careful cataloguing of the meanings of ethical sentences.

Westermarck, Edward, *Ethical Relativity.* London, 1932; Paterson, N.J., 1960.

Wright, G. H. von, *The Varieties of Goodness.* New York, 1963. A very careful account of the varieties of goodness, together with important remarks about justice and duty.

Anthologies

The following books are excellent selections of recent and original work in analytical ethics.

Brandt, Richard, ed., *Social Justice.* Englewood Cliffs, N.J., 1962.

Castañeda, Héctor-Neri, and Nakhnikian, George, eds., *Morality and the Language of Conduct.* Detroit, 1963.

Melden, A. I., ed., *Essays in Moral Philosophy.* Seattle, 1958.

Olafson, Frederick, ed., *Justice and Social Policy.* Englewood Cliffs, N.J., 1961.

Ramsey, I. T., ed., *Christian Ethics and Contemporary Philosophy.* London, 1965.

Sellars, Wilfrid, and Hospers, John, *Readings in Ethical Theory.* New York, 1952.

The following anthologies contain good selections from classical and contemporary sources.

Brandt, Richard, ed., *Value and Obligation.* New York, 1961.

Dewey, Robert E.; Gramlich, F. W.; and Loftsgordon, Donald, eds., *Problems of Ethics.* New York, 1961.

Katz, Joseph; Nochlin, Philip; and Stover, Robert, eds., *Writers on Ethics: Classic and Contemporary.* Princeton, N.J., 1962.

Melden, A. I., ed., *Ethical Theories,* 2d ed. Englewood Cliffs, N.J., 1955.

Mothersill, Mary, ed., *Ethics.* New York, 1965.

Munitz, Milton K., ed., *A Modern Introduction to Ethics.* Glencoe, Ill., 1958.

Taylor, Paul, ed., *The Moral Judgment.* Englewood Cliffs, N.J., 1963. Contemporary sources only.

Texts

Baylis, Charles, *Ethics: The Principles of Wise Choice.* New York, 1958. Elementary.

Brandt, Richard, *Ethical Theory.* Englewood Cliffs, N.J., 1959, Advanced. A detailed and careful text that examines the central metaethical and normative ethical theories.

Dewey, John, *Theory of the Moral Life.* New York, 1960. A description of classical ethical theories, together with a complex evaluation of them by a famous pragmatist.

Ekman, Rosalind, ed., *Readings in the Problems of Ethics.* New York, 1965. Important collection of contemporary writings on ethics.

Ewing, A. C., *Ethics.* London, 1953. Elementary.

Frankena, William, *Ethics.* Englewood Cliffs, N.J., 1963. Elementary.

Hospers, John, *Human Conduct.* New York, 1962. A full discussion of classical and contemporary ethical theories. Readable and full of examples.

Montefiore, Alan, *A Modern Introduction to Moral Philosophy.* New York, 1959. An analytical introduction to ethics by a linguistic philosopher.

Wilson, John, *Reason and Morals.* Cambridge, 1961. An attempt to state contemporary metaethical analysis in a popular form and show its moral relevance.

Wilson, John, *Logic and Sexual Morality.* Harmondsworth, England, 1965. Attempts to use the techniques of modern analysis to say something about the problems of sexual morality.

— KAI NIELSEN

EUTHANASIA

Euthanasia used to refer to an easy and gentle death, but it now refers to methods of inducing that kind of death or, more precisely, methods of bringing about death sooner and usually with less pain and suffering than would have occurred otherwise. Euthanasia used to be limited to patients in the terminal stage of an illness, but it is now thought to be appropriate in some cases of nonterminal patients—for example, those in a persistent vegetative state and those suffering from an incurable and very painful chronic disease.

If a patient requests the physician to do something, the physician is not morally required to do it if in his judgment it is inappropriate for him to do so, regardless of the kind of treatment.

Voluntary active euthanasia (VAE) is when a physician accedes to a rational request of an adequately informed competent patient for the physician to kill him, with a lethal intravenous injection of pentothal, for example.

Physician-assisted suicide (PAS) is when a physician, at a rational request of an adequately informed competent patient who plans to commit suicide, knowingly provides that patient with the medical means to commit suicide and the patient uses those means to commit suicide.

Voluntary passive euthanasia (VPE) is when a physician abides by a valid rational refusal of treatment by an adequately informed competent patient knowing that doing so will result in the patient's dying—for ex-

Despite her parents' decision to remove her from life support, Karen Quinlan lived for years in a vegetative state. (Corbis/Bettmann-UPI)

ample, complying with the refusal of a ventilator-dependent patient with motor neuron disease to receive further mechanical ventilatory support. Abiding by patient refusal of hydration and nutrition (PRHN) is another example of VPE, as is abiding by such refusals given in advance directives, either living wills or durable powers of attorney for health care, even though the patient is incompetent at the time the treatment is withheld or withdrawn.

Patients are competent to make a decision about their health care if they have the capacity to understand and appreciate all the information necessary to make a rational decision. They are adequately informed when they have been given all the information necessary to make a rational decision. Patient competence, the receipt of adequate information from the physician, and no coercion by the health care team are the elements of valid (informed) consent or refusal of treatment.

A decision by a patient is irrational if he knows it will result in harm—for example, death, pain, or disability—to him and he does not have an adequate reason, such as avoiding suffering an equal or greater harm, for that decision. Only those decisions count as irrational that result in the person's suffering harm and for which almost no one in the person's culture would rank

the benefit gained or harm avoided as providing an adequate reason. Often, however, rational people rank harms in different ways. It is rational to rank immediate death as worse than several months of suffering from a terminal disease, and it is also rational to rank that suffering as worse than death.

Involuntary active euthanasia (IAE) is when, out of concern for the patient, a physician kills a permanently incompetent patient—for example, one in a permanent vegetative state. Involuntary passive euthanasia (IPE) is when, in the absence of an advance directive, but out of concern for the patient, a physician ceases treatment of a permanently incompetent patient, knowing that doing so will result in the patient's dying.

At the present time PAS, VAE, and IAE are illegal in the United States, but some people have begun to argue for their legalization, especially PAS, in carefully controlled circumstances. IPE is also illegal, except when continuing treatment is considered futile, but some have recommended that the definition of futility be broadened so that all treatment of permanently unconscious patients be classified as futile.

VPE has been declared acceptable by the U.S. Supreme Court and is approved by the American Medical Association and all other medical and legal organizations. Thus, there have been many attempts by philosophers to provide an account of VPE that explains its almost universal acceptance. All of these attempts have identified VAE with killing and VPE with allowing to die. Two of the most common ways of distinguishing between VAE (killing) and VPE (allowing to die) are (1) acts versus omissions and (2) withholding versus withdrawing.

The philosophical distinction between acts and omissions seems a natural way to distinguish between killing and allowing to die. If a physician does something, performs an action—for example, injects an overdose of morphine or turns off the respirator—that action counts as VAE, is considered killing, and is prohibited. If the physician does nothing, but rather simply fails to do something—for example, does not turn on the respirator or does not provide essential antibiotics—that omission counts as VPE, is considered allowing to die, and is permitted. However, it seems pointless to distinguish between an authorized physician who turns a knob that stops the flow of life-sustaining antibiotics and one who omits filling the bag when it runs out of those antibiotics. Those who have used the distinction between acts and omissions to distinguish between VAE (killing) and VPE (allowing to die) have usually concluded that the distinction has no moral significance.

The distinction between withholding and withdrawing treatment seems to have great appeal for some doctors as a way of distinguishing VAE and VPE. Some doctors maintain that if a patient validly refuses to start life-saving treatment, they do not have a duty to force it on him and so are only allowing him to die. However, once treatment is started, if discontinuing would lead to the patient's death, they have a duty to continue, and it is killing not to. Doctors are not required to force a patient to go on the ventilator if the patient refuses, but once the patient has accepted going on the ventilator, they have a duty to keep him on if taking him off would result in his death, even if he has changed his mind.

Like the previous distinction between acts and omissions, there seems to be no morally significant difference between withholding and withdrawing treatment. Physicians do not have a duty to continue treatment if an adequately informed competent patient rationally refuses to have it continued. Imagine two unconscious patients who are going to be put on a respirator: one becomes conscious before she is put on and the other after she is put on, but both are competent, adequately informed, and rationally refuse treatment. This accident of timing is morally irrelevant. Further, this way of distinguishing between active and passive euthanasia may create serious practical problems. Patients who had not been adequately evaluated (often at the scene of an accident) were sometimes judged inappropriate for rescue efforts because the doctors believed that once the patient was on a ventilator they could not legitimately withdraw him from it.

The inadequacy of these two attempts to distinguish between VAE and VPE has led many to doubt that there is a morally relevant distinction between them. However, closer attention to the way the distinction is actually made, both in law and medicine, shows that what was overlooked is the crucial role played by the patient. When a patient rationally and validly refuses what is offered, the physician is legally and morally required not to overrule that refusal. Abiding by a valid rational refusal, knowing that death will result, counts as VPE, whether this involves (1) an act or an omission or (2) withholding or withdrawing. That everyone acknowledges that a physician must abide by a valid refusal of treatment, whether this involves an action or is a case of withdrawing, explains why VPE is almost universally considered to be morally acceptable.

If a patient requests the physician to do something, however, the physician is not morally required to do it if in his judgment it is inappropriate for him to do so, regardless of the kind of treatment. Physicians may accede to patient requests if they regard them as appropriate, but rarely are they required to do so. If a patient requests that they do something illegal or that they consider immoral, they are never required to do so. Killing patients at their rational request is VAE. It is illegal, and even if it were to be legalized many physicians would

still consider it to be immoral. Even if it is sometimes morally acceptable for physicians to kill patients at their request, it should never be legally or morally required for them to do so. This is sufficient to distinguish VAE from VPE, for it is legally and morally required for physicians not to overrule the rational valid refusals of their patients.

Confusion sometimes arises when a patient's refusal is framed in terms resembling a request. For example, a patient's "request" that no cardiopulmonary resuscitation (CPR) be attempted on him is actually a refusal of permission for CPR. Similarly, written advance directives "requesting" the cessation of other therapies or of hydration and nutrition are really refusals of treatment.

Using valid refusal versus requests as the way of distinguishing VPE from VAE, while it explains the moral acceptability of VPE, does not make VAE morally unacceptable. Given present knowledge and technology, one can kill a patient absolutely painlessly within a matter of minutes. If patients have a rational desire to die, why wait several months for them to die, why not kill them quickly and painlessly in a matter of minutes? If there were no way for patients to shorten the time of their dying, or for their pain to be controlled, VAE would seem to be clearly morally acceptable. However, PRHN, which contrary to common belief does not cause suffering, allows patients to become unconscious within a week and to die within another week, and medication is available to control their other pain during that time. Further, all proposals to employ VAE involve at least a two-week waiting period. Thus, it seems pointless to employ VAE, which is controversial, rather than VPE, which is already universally accepted.

Abiding by the refusal in an advance directive of a competent patient, when that patient becomes incompetent, is usually regarded as similar in all moral respects to abiding by the refusal of a currently competent patient. If competent patients explicitly state in an advance directive that, should they become permanently incompetent, they want life-prolonging treatments to be discontinued, then the physician is morally required to abide by that refusal. However, this view is challenged by those claiming that the views of the competent person who filled out the advance directive are not always the same as the views of the incompetent person to whom they are being applied.

Some hold that advance directives need not be followed if the physician believes that the incompetent person would not choose to have life-prolonging treatment withdrawn. One must judge a public policy, however, in terms of the effects that this policy would have on everyone involved if all knew of the policy. Competent persons who fill out advance directives refusing life-prolonging treatment if they become permanently incompetent consider it distasteful and devoid of dignity to live as a permanently incompetent person. The now-incompetent person, however, having no sense of dignity, does not view her life with distaste.

If everyone knew that advance directives would not be honored in these cases, some permanently incompetent persons would live longer than they would if such advance directives were honored. This might be a positive result, but it is not clear whether the incompetent person views it in that way. However, it is clear that another result of having everyone know that their advance directives would not be honored would be anxiety, anger, and other unpleasant feelings. This could result in an increase in deaths of such competent persons in order to avoid the unwanted prolongation of their lives as incompetent persons. The consequences of a public policy of not honoring such advance directives seem to be worse than those of the present policy of honoring them.

[See also Biomedical Ethics; Informed Consent; Paternalism.]

BIBLIOGRAPHY

Bernat, J. L., B. Gert, and R. P. Mogielnicki. "Patient Refusal of Hydration and Nutrition: An Alternative to Physician Assisted Suicide or Voluntary Euthanasia." *Archives of Internal Medicine,* Vol. 153 (Dec. 27, 1993), 2723–28.

Brock, D. W. *Life and Death.* Cambridge, 1993. Esp. pp. 95–232.

Clouser, K. D. "Allowing or Causing: Another Look," *Annals of Internal Medicine,* Vol. 87 (1977), 622–24.

Dresser, R. S., and J. A. Robertson. "Quality of Life and Nontreatment Decisions for Incompetent Patients," *Law, Medicine, and Health Care,* Vol. 17. no. 3 (Fall 1989), 234–44.

Gert, B. *Morality: A New Morality of the Moral Rules.* New York, 1988.

The Hastings Center. *Guidelines on the Termination of Life-Sustaining Treatments and Care of the Dying.* Bloomington. IN, 1987.

Lynn, J., ed. *By No Extraordinary Means.* Bloomington, IN, 1986.

President's Commission for the Study of Ethical Problems in Medicine and Biomedical and Behavioral Research. *Deciding to Forgo Life-Sustaining Treatment.* Washington, DC, 1983.

Rachels, J. *The End of Life: Euthanasia and Morality.* New York, 1986.

Van er Maas, P. J., et al. *Euthanasia and Other Medical Decisions concerning the End of Life.* Lancet, 1991.

Wanzer, S. J., et al. "The Physician's Responsibility toward Hopelessly Ill Patients: A Second Look," *New England Journal of Medicine,* Vol. 320 (1989), 844–49.

Weir, R. F. *Abating Treatment with Critically Ill Patients.* New York. 1989.

— BERNARD GERT

EVENT THEORY

An event is anything that happens, an occurrence. The idea of an event began to take on a philosophical life of its own in the twentieth century, due to a reawakening of interest in the concept of change, to which the concept of an event seems inextricably tied, and to the growing use of the concept of an event in scientific and metascientific writing (see Broad, 1933, 1938; McTaggart, 1927; and Whitehead, 1929). Interest in events has also been sparked by versions of the mind–body identity thesis formulated in terms of events and by the idea that a clearer picture of events will facilitate discussion of other philosophical issues.

The idea of an event began to take on a philosophical life of its own in the twentieth century, due to a reawakening of interest in the concept of change.

Discussions of events have focused on whether there are events and, if so, what the nature of events is. Since whether there are events depends in part on what they would be like if there were any, the two issues have usually been treated together.

Some philosophers (e.g., J. J. Thomson) simply assume that there are events; others argue for that assumption. Donald Davidson has asserted that there are events (and actions) by arguing that, to explain the meanings of claims involving adverbial modifiers (e.g., "Jones killed Smith in the kitchen") and singular causal claims (e.g., "the short circuit caused the fire"), we should suppose that such claims implicitly quantify over, or posit, actions and events (e.g., killings, short circuits, and fires). Opponents of Davidson's analyses (e.g., Terence Horgan) have argued that alternative semantic theories, which do not posit events, are able to explain the semantic features of Davidson's target sentences.

While some singular terms purporting to refer to events are proper names (e.g., "World War I"), many are definite descriptions (e.g., "the killing of Caesar by Brutus"). The semantics of singular descriptions for events has been studied by Zeno Vendler and Jonathan Bennett. Of particular interest is the distinction between perfect nominals, like "Quisling's betraying of Norway," which refer to events (or actions or states), and imperfect nominals, like "Quisling's betraying Norway," which refer to fact-like entities. Bennett has argued that much of what is wrong in Jaegwon Kim's theory of events can be traced to confusions involving these two sorts of nominals and to expressions (e.g., "the betrayal") that are ambiguous and can refer either to events or to facts.

Most philosophers take events to be abstract particulars; particulars in that they are nonrepeatable and spatially locatable, abstract in that more than one event can occur simultaneously in the same place. Some philosophers who think this way (e.g., Lombard) take events to be the changes that objects undergo when they alter. (Others, such as Bennett, have doubts about this; others, like Kim and David Lewis, deny it outright.) Thus, the time at which an event occurs is the (shortest) time at which the subject of that event changes from the having of one to the having of another, contrary property. Since no object can have both a property and one of its contraries simultaneously, there can be no instantaneous events.

Events inherit their spatial locations from the spatial locations, if any, of the things in which those events are changes. Events do not get their spatial locations by occupying them; if they did, then distinct events, like distinct physical objects, could not occur in the same place simultaneously. But more than one event apparently can occur at the same time and place. However, some philosophers (e.g., Quine) hold that events are concrete and that events and physical objects do not belong to distinct metaphysical kinds.

Though it seems clear that some events are composed of others, it is not clear what the principles are that determine when events compose more complex events.

Some views of events (perhaps Whitehead's) seem compatible with there being subjectless events, events that are not changes in anything whatsoever. However, subjectless events could not be changes, for it seems absurd to suppose that there could be a change that was not a change in or of anything.

Theories about the nature of entities belonging to some metaphysically interesting kind must address the issue of what properties such entities essentially have. In the case of events, the issue is made pressing by the fact that certain theories concerning causation (e.g., David Lewis's) require that judgments be made about whether certain events would occur under certain, counterfactual circumstances.

In the literature on events, attention has been given to four essentialist issues. The first is whether the causes (or effects) of events are essential to the events that have them; Peter van Inwagen has suggested that an event's causes are essential to the events that have them, while Lombard has argued that neither the causes nor the effects of events are essential to them. The second concerns the subjects of events; Bennett and Lewis suggest that the subjects of events are not essential, while Lombard and Kim argue that they are. The third is whether

an event's time of occurrence is essential to it. Lombard has argued in favor of this essentialist claim, while Bennett and Lewis have argued against it. And the fourth is whether it is essential that each event be a change with respect to the properties to which it is in fact a change. Though the first three issues have received some attention, the fourth has attracted the most, due to the prominence given to debates between the defenders and opponents of Kim's and Davidson's views on the identity of events.

Theories about events typically contain, as a chief component, a "criterion of identity," a principle giving necessary and sufficient conditions for an event e and an event e' to be identical. Though there is no general agreement on this, such a principle is sought because, when it satisfies certain constraints, it becomes a vehicle for articulating a view about what it is to be an event and how events are related to objects belonging to other kinds.

Quine holds that events are the temporal parts of physical objects and thus that events and physical objects share the same condition of identity: sameness of spatiotemporal location.

Kim's interest in events centers in part on the idea that they are the objects of empirical explanations. Since what is typically explained is an object's having a property at a certain time, Kim takes an event to be the exemplification of a property (or relation) by an object (or objects) at a time. This idea, combined with some others, led him to hold that an event e is the same as an event e' if and only if e and e' are the exemplifications of the same property by the same object(s) at the same time. Kim's view has been criticized, principally by Lombard and Bennett, on the grounds that what it says about events is more plausibly seen as truths about facts. Kim's view has also been criticized by those whose intuitions concerning the identity of events more closely match Davidson's.

Davidson once proposed that events, being essentially the links in causal chains, are identical just in case they have the same causes and effects. He has since abandoned this position in favor of Quine's.

Another view that places causation at the heart of the idea of an event is due to David Lewis, who has tried to construct a theory in which events have just those features that would allow them to fit neatly into his counterfactual analysis of causation. In some respects, Lewis's view is like Myles Brand's in that both are moved in part by the idea that more than one event can occur simultaneously in the same place. Lewis takes an event to be a property-in-intension of a spatio-temporal region, so that events that in fact occur simultaneously in the same place but could have had different spatio-temporal locations are distinct.

Bennett thinks that the concept of an event is not precise enough to withstand much critical examination on its own and that events should be thought to be (only) whatever they need to be in order to make constructive use of them in the discussion of other philosophical issues. Like Lewis, Bennett takes an event to be a property; but, for Bennett, the property seems to be a property-in-extension and is a particular. That is, Bennett thinks that events are tropes.

Lombard's view is, like Kim's, a variation on a property exemplification account. Lombard's version is derived from the idea of events as the changes that objects undergo when they alter, and it takes events to be the exemplifyings of "dynamic" properties at intervals of time. Such alterations are the "movements" by objects from the having of one to the having of another property through densely populated quality spaces, where each quality space is a class of contrary properties, the mere having of any member of which by an object does not imply change.

[See also Davidson, Donald; Metaphysics; Quine, Willard Van Orman.]

BIBLIOGRAPHY

Bennett, J. *Events and Their Names.* Indianapolis, 1988.
Brand, M. "Particulars, Events, and Actions," in M. Brand and D. Walton, eds., *Action Theory* (Dordrecht, 1976).
Broad, C. D. *An Examination of McTaggart's Philosophy.* Cambridge, 1933.
Davidson, D. *Essays on Actions and Events.* New York. 1980.
———. "Reply to Quine on Events," in E. LePore and B. P. McLaughlin, eds., *Actions and Events: Perspectives on the Philosophy of Donald Davidson* (Oxford, 1985).
Horgan, T. "The Case Against Events," *Philosophical Review,* Vol. 87 (1978), 28–47.
Kim, J. "Events and Their Descriptions: Some Considerations." in N. Rescher et al., eds., *Essays in Honor of Carl G. Hempel* (Dordrecht, 1969).
———. *Supervenience and Mind,* Chaps. 1, 3. New York, 1993.
Lewis, D. "Events," in *Philosophical Papers,* Vol. 2 (New York, 1986).
Lombard, L. B. *Events: A Metaphysical Study.* London, 1986.
McTaggart, J. M. E. *The Nature of Existence,* Vol. 2. Cambridge, 1927.
Quine, W. V. O. "Things and Their Place in Theories," in *Theories and Things* (Cambridge, MA, 1981).
———. "Events and Reification," in E. LePore and B. P. McLaughlin, eds., *Actions and Events: Perspectives on the Philosophy of Donald Davidson* (Oxford, 1985).
Thomson, J. J. *Acts and Other Events.* Ithaca, NY, 1977.
van Inwagen, P. "Ability and Responsibility," *Philosophical Review,* Vol. 87 (1978), 201–24, esp. 207–9.
Vendler, Z. "Facts and Events," in *Linguistics and Philosophy* (Ithaca, NY, 1967).
Whitehead, A. N. *The Principles of Natural Knowledge.* Cambridge, 1919.
———. *Process and Reality.* Cambridge, 1929.

— LAWRENCE BRIAN LOMBARD

EVIDENTIALISM

Evidentialism is the view about epistemic justification that identifies the extent to which a person is justified in believing a proposition with the extent to which the evidence the person has supports the truth of the proposition. Other doxastic attitudes such as withholding judgment and denying are also justified by the character of the person's evidence.

A full-scale evidentialist theory would explain what constitutes evidence, what it means to have a certain body of evidence, and what it means for a body of evidence to support a proposition to any given extent. Ordinarily, people count as evidence external things such as fingerprints and bank records. However, according to evidentialists, our fundamental evidence is constituted by our perceptual experiences, our apparent memories, and other mental states. A full-scale theory requires an account of what we have as this ultimate sort of evidence: it is unclear, for example, whether someone's unactivated memories are part of the person's current evidence. The evidential support relation to which evidentialists appeal is not a familiar logical relation. Perceptual states can support beliefs about the external world, yet there is no familiar logical relation between those states and the beliefs they support. Furthermore, one's evidence on its own does not support its distant and unnoticed logical consequences. A complete evidentialist theory would clarify the justifying connection between a body of evidence and a proposition.

Leading skeptical controversies are usefully understood to concern what sort of evidence is required for knowledge. For example, if knowledge requires complete epistemic justification, and this requires having entailing evidence, then skeptics can cogently argue that we have no such evidence for any empirical proposition and that therefore we have no empirical knowledge. On the other hand, standard skeptical arguments fail if nonentailing evidence can completely justify belief. An evidentialist theory can resolve this dispute either way.

Diverse theories of justification can be understood as evidentialist views that differ on the nature of evidence, its possession, and how it supports belief. For instance, a typical coherentist theory in effect holds that a person has her beliefs as evidence and that support by evidence consists in coherence with it. A typical foundationalist theory in effect holds that justified beliefs must include some that are defended by a foundational sort of evidence—for example, by perceptual states—and that this evidence is had by the person by being consciously accessible.

Evidentialism entirely discounts factors that figure centrally in some theories of justified belief. These factors include the intellectual pedigree of the belief, the believer's capacity or intention to fulfill intellectual duties or to exemplify cognitive virtues, and the normal functioning of the operative belief-forming mechanism. Justifying evidence for a belief might happen to arise in an irresponsibly haphazard inquiry with no attempt to fulfill any epistemic duty, as a fluke result of some abnormal cognitive activity lacking in intellectual virtue. The evidentialist view is that regardless of all this, belief is justified because the evidence possessed supports the proposition.

[See also Coherentism; Epistemology; Skepticism.]

BIBLIOGRAPHY

Chisholm, R. "A Version of Foundationalism," in *The Foundations of Knowing* (Minneapolis, 1982).
Feldman, R., and Earl Conee. "Evidentialism," *Philosophical Studies,* Vol. 48 (1985), 15–34.
Goldman, A. *Epistemology and Cognition.* Cambridge, MA, 1986. Pp. 87–93.
Haack, S. *Evidence and Inquiry.* Oxford, 1993.
Moser, P. *Knowledge and Evidence.* Cambridge, 1989.
Plantinga, A. *Warrant and Proper Function.* Oxford, 1993. Pp. 185–93.

— EARL CONEE
RICHARD FELDMAN

EVIL, PROBLEM OF

Many people feel that the evils that occur in our world, particularly the amount and severity of human and animal suffering, make it difficult to believe in the existence of God, where God is understood to be the perfectly good, infinitely powerful, all-knowing creator of the world. This difficulty for belief in God is held by some to be logical, by others to be evidential, depending on whether one believes that such evils logically preclude the existence of God or that such evils, although perhaps logically consistent with the existence of God, nevertheless constitute evidence against his existence.

Logical Problem of Evil

The proponent of the logical problem of evil asserts that it is logically impossible both that God (the infinitely powerful, perfectly good, all-knowing creator of the world) exists and that the world contains the evils we observe. But how can this be proved? If it were necessarily true that God would prevent some of the evils we

observe in our world, and we knew that this was so, we could then prove that it is logically impossible both that God exists and that the world contains the evils we observe. But is it necessarily true that God would prevent some of the evils in our world? Presumably God would prevent evils only if he could do so without losing goods that outweigh those evils. So if it is necessarily true that God would prevent some of the evils that occur in the world, it is necessarily true that he could

---

The proponent of the logical problem of evil asserts that it is logically impossible both that God exists and that the world contains the evils we observe. But how can this be proved?

---

prevent those evils without losing any outweighing goods. Since God is omnipotent, one might think that he must be able to prevent those evils without losing any outweighing goods. But what if God's permitting those evils is itself logically required for outweighing goods? If this were so, then, since most philosophers think power extends only to what is logically possible, few would think that God's omnipotence implies that he could prevent those evils without losing any outweighing goods. Furthermore, even if it is necessarily true that God could prevent some evils we observe in the world without losing any outweighing goods, how could we come to know that this is so? For unless we know that it is so, we cannot prove that God's existence is logically inconsistent with the evils we observe. Consideration of these difficulties has led many philosophers to conclude that the efforts to prove that God's existence is logically inconsistent with the existence of the evils we observe have not been successful. In addition, on the assumptions that our world is a good world and that an act is free only if it is undetermined, a formidable argument (the free-will defense) has been developed by Alvin Plantinga to show that it is logically possible that God could not create a world better than ours that contains less evil. If it is logically possible that God could not create a world better than ours that contains less evil, God's existence is not logically inconsistent with the evils we observe in the world.

Evidential Problem of Evil

The proponent of the evidential problem of evil holds that, although the evils we observe may be logically consistent with the existence of God, they (or what we know about them) provide us with evidence against the existence of God. If we think of a pointless evil as an evil that God would not be justified in permitting, it is clear that if God exists no pointless evils exist. One popular evidential argument from evil claims that we have good reasons to believe that our world contains pointless evils. Proponents of this argument point to particular cases of horrendous evils—a fawn's being severely burned in a forest fire and undergoing several days of terrible agony before death relieves its suffering, a five-year-old girl being savagely beaten, raped, and strangled—as examples of evils they believe to be pointless. They argue that, when we consider particular instances of horrendous, apparently pointless evil, or reflect on the magnitude of severe human and animal suffering, it is simply staggering to suppose that an omnipotent, omniscient, and perfectly good being is in charge. What could possibly justify his permitting such monstrous evils? When we try to envisage goods whose realization might justify God (if he exists) in permitting these evils, we encounter one or the other of the following difficulties. First, it is clear that many of the goods we can envisage are not good enough to justify God in permitting such horrendous evils. Second, when we envisage goods that do seem to outweigh these horrendous evils, it is reasonable to believe that these goods are realizable by an omnipotent being without his having to permit these horrendous evils. Of course, it is logically possible that there are some outweighing goods beyond our comprehension whose realization by God requires him to permit these horrendous evils. But in the absence of any special reason to think that God would not make himself and his realization of such goods known to us, it is claimed that what we know of the magnitude of horrendous evils we observe in our world gives us reason to think that some of these evils are pointless and that, therefore, the God of traditional theism does not exist.

Theistic responses to this line of argument take various forms. Some theists tend to agree that we cannot envisage goods whose realization by God would justify him in permitting many of the evils we observe, but they argue that this is just what we should expect if the theistic hypothesis is true. Since God's knowledge is infinite and his power unlimited, they believe that the goods that justify God in permitting many of the evils we observe would be goods we cannot comprehend. Just as an infant or very young child cannot grasp the good purposes for which the loving parent may allow the child to suffer, so we with our limited minds cannot possibly be aware of the goods that justify God (if he exists) in permitting the multitude of horrendous evils we observe. Other theists reject the view that we are unable to envisage goods whose realization would justify God in permitting so many horrendous evils. They advance theodicies that purport to single out various kinds of goods whose realization by God may justify him in permitting these evils. They suggest that horrendous evils need to occur if human beings are to acquire knowledge of how to do great harm. They also think that the knowledge of how to do great harm is essential if humans are to be free to choose between good and evil and to develop into morally praiseworthy beings. Still other theists argue that, given the human cognitive situation, we are in no position to conclude that no good we know of justifies God in permitting horrendous evils. As opposed to those theists who claim that we can see that some goods we know of could be God's justification for permitting the evils we observe, these theists argue that we are in no position to make an affirmative or negative judgment about whether these goods could be God's justification for permitting the evils we observe. We must remain agnostics about this matter. Finally, it should be noted that a theist may grant that the evidential argument from evil makes God's existence significantly less likely than it would otherwise be, but the theist would argue that the reasons, whether propositional or nonpropositional, in support of the existence of such a being outweigh the evidence against provided by the argument from evil.

These objections and various responses to them are indicative of an ongoing debate between theists and nontheists over one form of the evidential problem of evil. Another form of the evidential argument seeks to undermine the theistic hypothesis by showing that there are naturalistic hypotheses that far more adequately explain certain facts about good and evil. For example, it is known that much pleasure and pain serves a biological function in that it is useful for survival and reproduction. It is argued that this known fact is a good deal more likely on the hypothesis that sentient creatures did not come to be as the result of the good or bad intentions of a supernatural person than it is on the theistic hypothesis. For on the theistic hypothesis one would expect that pain and pleasure would serve distinctly moral purposes. Thus, since the competing hypothesis to theism better explains the known facts about pleasure and pain, it is more likely than the theistic hypothesis relative to the evidence we have concerning the function of pleasure and pain in sentient life. Against this argument, theists have urged that it is a mistake to view theism as an explanatory hypothesis whose justification rests on evidence. Moreover, even if theism is treated as an explanatory hypothesis, theists may argue that certain data often confirm one hypothesis over its competitor, while other data do just the opposite. The question then would be whether the total data is better explained by theism than by its competitors.

[See also Philosophy of Religion.]

BIBLIOGRAPHY

Adams, R. M. "Middle Knowledge and the Problem of Evil." *American Philosophical Quarterly,* Vol. 14 (1977), 109–17.

Alston, W. P. "The Inductive Problem of Evil and the Human Cognitive Condition," in J. E. Tomberlin, ed., *Philosophical Perspectives,* Vol. 5, *Philosophy of Religion* (Atascadero, CA, 1991).

Draper, P. "Pain and Pleasure: An Evidential Problem for Theists," *Noûs,* Vol. 23 (1989). 331–50.

Mackie, J. L. "Evil and Omnipotence," *Mind,* Vol. 64 (1955), 200–12.

Pike, N. "Hume on Evil," *Philosophical Review,* Vol. 72 (1963), 180–97.

Plantinga, A. "God, Evil, and the Metaphysics of Freedom," in *The Nature of Necessity* (Oxford, 1974).

———. "The Probabilistic Argument from Evil," *Philosophical Studies,* Vol. 35 (1979), 1–53.

Rowe, W. L. "The Problem of Evil and Some Varieties of Atheism." *American Philosophical Quarterly,* Vol. 16 (1979), 335–41.

———. "Evil and the Theistic Hypothesis: A Response to Wykstra," *International Journal for Philosophy of Religion,* Vol. 16 (1984), 95–100.

———. "William Alston on the Problem of Evil," in T. Senor, ed., *The Rationality of Belief and the Plurality of Faith* (Ithaca, NY, 1995).

Russell, B. "The Persistent Problem of Evil," *Faith and Philosophy,* Vol. 6 (1989), 121–39.

Swinburne, R. "The Problem of Evil," in *The Existence of God* (Oxford, 1979).

Tooley, M. "The Argument from Evil," in J. E. Tomberlin, ed., *Philosophical Perspectives,* Vol. 5, *Philosophy of Religion* (Atascadero, CA, 1991).

van Inwagen, P. "The Problem of Evil, the Problem of Air, and the Problem of Silence," in J. E. Tomberlin, ed., *Philosophical Perspectives,* Vol. 5. *Philosophy of Religion* (Atascadero, CA, 1991).

Wykstra, S. J. "The Humean Obstacle to Evidential Arguments from Suffering." *International Journal for Philosophy of Religion,* Vol. 16 (1984), 73–93.

– WILLIAM L. ROWE

EVOLUTIONARY ETHICS

Evolutionary theory came of age with the publication of Charles Darwin's *Origin of Species* in 1859, where he argued that all organisms, living and dead, including humans, are the end result of a long, slow, natural process of development from one or a few simple forms. Believing this new world history to be the death knell of traditional ways of thinking, many were inspired to extrapolate from the science a deeper meaning for life. Attempts were made to find within the process of evolution appropriate guides for proper human conduct ("substantive ethics"), as well as the justificatory foundations for all such social behavior ("metaethics").

At the substantive level the evolutionary ethicist's usual move was from Darwin's own suggested mechanism of change—the "natural selection" of the "fittest" organisms in life's struggle for existence—to some analogous process supposedly operating in the world of humans. Although this philosophy became known as social Darwinism, its widespread popularity, especially in America, owed less to Darwin himself and more to the voluminous writings of his fellow countryman Herbert Spencer. Notoriously, Spencer was an enthusiast for an extreme libertarian *laissez-faire,* although today scholars realize that Spencer's beliefs owe at least as much to the self-help philosophy of his nonconformist Christian childhood as to anything to be found in biology.

The evolutionary ethicist's usual move was from Darwin's own suggested mechanism of change (natural selection) to some analogous process supposedly operating in the world of humans.

In later writings Spencer tempered the harshness of his philosophy, seeing a definite role for cooperation in society, and (since he was not much given to retraction) this ambiguity about what was his real position led to his followers, claiming quite contradictory things, all in the name of the same philosophy. At one end of the spectrum there were conservative businessmen like John D. Rockefeller and supporters like the sociologist J. B. Sumner, who saw a place only for the success of the successful, and at the other end were the American Marxists (not to mention all of the would-be reformers in prerevolutionary China), who likewise saw in biology, as mediated by Spencer, the true rules of moral conduct. Softer and more subtle forms of social Darwinism tried to combine social responsibility with enlightened capitalism. Most influential was the iron and steel magnate Andrew Carnegie, who devoted much of his fortune to the founding of public libraries, where the poor but "fit" children might raise themselves in life's struggles.

In this century the debt to Spencer is ignored and unknown, and the term social Darwinism, burdened by history, is avoided. Nevertheless, particularly among biologists and politicians, the tradition has continued of seeking the rules of conduct in what are believed to be the sound principles of the evolutionary process. At the beginning of the century there was the exiled Russian anarchist. Prince Peter Kropotkin, arguing that all animals are subject to a cooperating tendency toward "mutual aid" and that this can and will function once we dismantle the apparatus of the modern state. Later, the

MR. BERGH TO THE RESCUE.

THE DEFRAUDED GORILLA. "That *Man* wants to claim my Pedigree. He says he is one of my Descendants."

MR. BERGH. "Now, Mr. DARWIN, how could you insult him so?"

An 1871 cartoon depicts Henry Bergh admonishing Charles Darwin for slighting a gorilla by claiming that man may be descended from apes. (Corbis)

English biologist Julian Huxley operated as the first director general of UNESCO according to a biologically based religion of humanity directed toward the survival of the species. And today we have the Harvard entomologist and sociobiologist Edward O. Wilson, who urges the preservation of the rain forests else humans, who live in symbiotic relation with the rest of nature, fade and die. It is less than obvious, from a historical or conceptual point of view, that some of the more vile racist ideologies of this century owe much to evolutionary biology. The Nazis, for instance, shrank from the implication that all humans have a common origin, ultimately simian.

Evolutionary ethics has long fallen from favor in philosophical circles, chiefly because of its supposed metaethical inadequacy. In his *Principia Ethica* (1903), G. E. Moore penned the classic critique, complaining that systems like that of Spencer commit the "naturalistic fallacy" trying to define the nonnatural property of goodness in terms of natural properties, in Spencer's case the happiness supposedly produced by the evolutionary process. Psychologically, however, enthusiasts for evolutionary ethics find this critique most unconvincing. It is therefore more effective to point to the earlier attack of Thomas Henry Huxley (Julian's grandfather), who argued that systems deriving morality from evolution invariably rely on the hidden—and dubious—premise that evolution is in some sense progressive and that value is thus increased as one goes up the scale. As Huxley noted, in a post-Darwinian world, where fitness is a relative concept, the old picture of evolution "from monad to man" owes more to the Christianized Chain of Being than to the history of the organic world. It may be true that humans value humans and their well-being more than we do that of other organisms, but this is something we read into evolution.

Recently, with the increased biological interest in the evolution of animal social behavior ("sociobiology"), there has been renewed interest by philosophers in the possibility of fruitful connections between biology and morality. In his influential *A Theory of Justice*, John Rawls suggested that social contract theorists might explore fruitfully the possibility that in real life morality is the end result of the evolutionary process rather than the construct of a hypothesized group of rational beings. In support Rawls drew attention to the similarities between his own beliefs in "justice as fairness" and the results of such sociobiological mechanisms as "reciprocal altruism."

At the metaethical level also there has been renewed thought. Since the search for foundations seems so misguided, could it not be that the evolutionist is directed toward some noncognitivist "ethical skepticism," where there simply are no foundations at all? This is the approach taken by Wilson collaborating with the philosopher Michael Ruse. Following up on the thinking of the late John L. Mackie, they suggest that ethics (at the substantive level) might be simply a collective illusion of our genes, put in place by natural selection to make humans into good cooperators. To this they add the related suggestion that the reason ethics works is that our biology makes us "objectify" our moral sentiments; thus, we are psychologically convinced that morality, despite its lack of real foundation, is more than mere subjective sentiment. Whether these and related suggestions will bear fruit will probably owe as much to developments in human biology as to refined philosophical analysis.

[*See also* Ethical Theory; Mackie, John Leslie; Rawls, John.]

BIBLIOGRAPHY

Huxley, T. H. *Evolution and Ethics* [1894]. Princeton, NJ, 1989.
Mackie, J. L. "The Law of the Jungle," *Philosophy,* Vol. 53 (1978), 553–73.
Moore, G. E. *Principia Ethica.* Cambridge, 1903.
Richards, R. J. *Darwin and the Emergence of Evolutionary Theories of Mind and Behavior.* Chicago, 1987.
Ruse, M. *Taking Darwin Seriously.* Oxford, 1986.
Ruse, M., and E. O. Wilson. "Moral Philosophy as Applied Science." *Philosophy,* Vol. 61 (1986), 173–92.
Spencer, H. *The Principles of Ethics.* 2 vols. London, 1892.
Wilson, E. O. *On Human Nature.* Cambridge, MA, 1978.

— MICHAEL RUSE

EXISTENTIALISM

The development of existentialism in the last years of its leading French proponents, Jean-Paul Sartre and Maurice Merleau-Ponty, occurred in the areas of social philosophy and existential psychoanalysis in the case of Sartre and the philosophy of language and fundamental ontology for Merleau-Ponty. Partly in response to the latter's critiques, but chiefly as a result of his own political commitment, Sartre constructed a social ontology and a theory of history in his *Critique of Dialectical Reason.* Faithful to his existentialist emphasis on the primacy of the individual, but replacing his earlier philosophy of consciousness with one of *praxis* (roughly, purposive human activity in its historical and socioeconomic context), Sartre formulated a set of concepts, especially praxis, seriality, and the practico-inert, that respected the power of social forces to countermand, deviate, and reverse our undertakings without totally robbing the organic individual of existentialist freedom and responsibility. He allowed far greater play to the force of circumstance in assessing human action and underscored the determining power of family and early childhood experience in his massive existential biography of Flaubert, *The Family Idiot*. This last, combining the discourse of *Being and Nothingness* with that of the *Critique,* forms a kind of synthesis of Sartre's work.

Sartre's massive existential biography of Flaubert,

The Family Idiot, *combines the discourse of*

Being and Nothingness *with that of the*

Critique of Dialectical Reason *to form*

a kind of synthesis of Sartre's work.

At the time of his death in 1961 Merleau-Ponty was at work on a manuscript that has come to be known as *The Visible and the Invisible,* a work that some consider his version of Heidegger's "What Is Metaphysics?" It reveals a growing interest in an ontology that avoids the pitfalls of "philosophies of consciousness," with their subject–object relation, which has defined and limited philosophy in the West for centuries. Inspired by the painter's articulation of the world and building on the concepts of chiasm and flesh, introduced in his earlier *The Phenomenology of Perception,* Merleau-Ponty was moving beyond the boundaries of phenomenology to elaborate an "indirect ontology" in which language questioning being questions itself.

[See also Authenticity; Merleau-Ponty, M.; Phenomenology; Sartre, Jean-Paul.]

– THOMAS R. FLYNN

EXPLANATION, THEORIES OF

Although explanations of many sorts occur in daily life, philosophical theories of explanation have dealt mainly with scientific explanation. Explanation in science in the *Encyclopedia of Philosophy* focused on Carl G. Hempel's covering law theory of explanation, which included the deductive-nomological (D-N) model as expounded in Hempel and Oppenheim, (1948) and the inductive-statistical (I-S) model as presented in Hempel (1962). It qualified as "the orthodox view" during most of the 1960s and 1970s.

This approach received a definitive statement in Hempel's essay, "Aspects of Scientific Explanation" (1965), published too late for mention in the *Encyclopedia of Philosophy.* Here Hempel discussed many of the objections that had been brought against the D-N model, offered a much-improved version of the I-S

model, and articulated for the first time the deductive-statistical (D-S) model. This article was the major point of departure for discussions of scientific explanation for about three decades.

The Orthodox View

According to the orthodox view, all legitimate scientific explanations fall into one of four categories, depending on the type of phenomenon to be explained (a particular fact or a general law) and on the type of law used in the explanation (universal or statistical), as shown in Table 1. Every explanation is a logically correct deductive or inductive argument, and every explanation requires a general law in its premises; thus, every explanation represented in this table qualifies as a covering-law explanation. Statistical laws, it should be noted, are just as general as universal laws. "All tritium atoms have a probability of one-half of decaying within 12.32 years" applies to all tritium atoms just as "All green plants contain chlorophyll" applies to all green plants.

The D-S model of explanation differs little from the D-N model as applied to explanations of general laws. Both types explain general laws by deduction from other general laws; the only difference is whether the law to be explained is statistical or universal. Since no statistical law can be deduced from universal laws alone, every D-S explanation contains at least one statistical law among its premises.

Hempel and Oppenheim attempted to offer a precise explication of D-N explanation but had to admit failure regarding explanations of general laws. As they point out (Hempel & Oppenheim, 1948, n. 33), a derivation of Kepler's laws of planetary motion from Newton's laws of gravitation and motion has genuine explanatory value, but a derivation of Kepler's laws from the conjunction of Kepler's laws and Boyle's law (obviously a valid deduction) has no explanatory merit. They can offer no explicit criterion for distinguishing worthy

		Type of phenomenon to be explained	
		Particular fact	General law
Type of	Universal law	Deductive-Nomological	Deductive-Nomological
Law	Statistical law	Inductive-Statistical	Deductive-Statistical

Table 1. Types of scientific explanation.

from worthless explanations of generalizations. The same problem plagues the D-S model. It has received little attention in the philosophical literature and has not been solved (in Hempel, 1965, it is not addressed). Therefore, both types of explanation in the second column stand under a cloud.

The explanations in the first column are explanations of particular facts or events. In each case, deductive or statistical, the explanation is an argument to the effect that the event to be explained was to be expected by virtue of the explanatory facts. This means that, had we possessed the explanatory facts early enough, we could have predicted the explanandum event. In the D-N case, given the explanans, we could have predicted the event with deductive certainty; in the I-S case, given the explanans, we could have predicted the event with high inductive probability.

Probabilistic/Statistical Explanation

Richard Jeffrey (Salmon et al., 1971) and Wesley Salmon (ibid.) severely criticized the I-S model of explanation. According to this model, an event can be explained only if it has a high probability relative to a suitable body of background knowledge. Jeffrey argued that events having low probabilities can sometimes be explained in terms of the stochastic mechanisms that give rise to them. The magnitude of the probability has no bearing on the value of the explanation. A run of ten heads with a fair coin is improbable (1/1024) but is fully comprehensible as an outcome of that chance process. Thus, statistical explanations of individual events need not be inductive arguments that render their conclusions highly probable.

Arguing that statistical relevance rather than high probability is the key to statistical explanation, Salmon rejected the I-S model and offered the statistical-relevance (S-R) model instead. Suppose that Mary Smith suffers from a psychological problem; she undergoes extensive psychiatric treatment and recovers. Suppose, further, that the probability of recovery from that problem with such treatment is 90 percent. Does the psychotherapy explain her recovery? If the spontaneous remission rate is also 90 percent, the answer is no, because the treatment has no bearing on the chance of recovery. This example fits the I-S model, but it does not constitute a genuine explanation. If, however, she had been afflicted with a different problem, for which the rate of recovery under psychotherapy is 40 percent but the spontaneous remission rate is 1 percent, the psychotherapy would explain her recovery even though the probability is not high. In this case the psychotherapy is statistically relevant; it makes a significant difference to the chance of recovery. These examples show

that high probability is neither necessary nor sufficient for sound statistical explanation. According to the S-R model, a statistical explanation is not an argument, but rather an assemblage of factors relevant to the occurrence of the event to be explained.

Every explanation is a logically correct deductive or inductive argument, and every explanation requires a general law in its premises.

When Salmon pointed out the problem of irrelevance in connection with I-S explanation, Henry E. Kyburg, Jr., observed that the same problem arises regarding D-N explanation. The following patently misguided explanation satisfies the D-N pattern: John Jones (a male) avoided becoming pregnant last year because he regularly consumed his wife's birth control pills, and any man who regularly takes oral contraceptives will avoid pregnancy. Thus, because of problems of relevancy, both patterns in the first column of Table 1 are undermined. Although the orthodox view retained its popularity for some time, it had been seriously shaken by the early 1970s. Three major approaches emerged as successors: the causal/mechanical view, the unification view, and the pragmatic view.

EXPLANATION AND CAUSATION. Michael Scriven has maintained that to give an explanation of an occurrence is simply to cite its cause, and this squares well with our intuitions. Hempel's orthodox theory, while not denying the existence of causal relations, deliberately avoids allowing them any role in explanation. One suspects that the main reason many philosophers adopt this view lies in David Hume's critique of causality. Those philosophers who claim that at least a major subset of explanations are causal take two different lines. One group, including Michael Scriven and Larry Wright, maintains that causal relations are among the givens of experience, and that causality needs no analysis. The other group, including James Fetzer, Paul Humphreys, and Salmon, among many others, have tried to furnish satisfactory analyses. These proffered explications differ markedly from one another.

Reflection on the S-R model also indicates the need for causality in explanation. For example, white spots on the inside of the cheek (known as Koplik spots) invariably accompany measles and appear before the other symptoms of the disease. The appearance of Koplik spots does not explain the occurrence of measles because they do not cause it; they are only a symptom. They are, however, strongly correlated with the occurrence of measles. This example shows that statistical relevance is insufficient for scientific explanation; causal relevance is what matters.

In discussing the role of causality in explanation

we must remember that statistical explanation

and causal explanation are not mutually exclusive.

In discussing the role of causality in explanation we must remember that statistical explanation and causal explanation are not mutually exclusive; indeed, a number of authors have promulgated theories of probabilistic causality (see Patrick Suppes, 1970; Fetzer, 1981; Salmon, 1984; Humphreys, 1989; Ellery Eells, 1991). No consensus has developed regarding which analysis is correct.

EXPLANATION AND UNIFICATION. The Newtonian synthesis is a stunning achievement in the history of science. Three simple laws of motion and one law of gravitation suffice to unify, and thereby explain, a tremendous variety of phenomena—e.g., planetary motions, falling bodies, tides, and comets. According to Michael Friedman (1974) this case exemplifies a general principle—our understanding is increased when we can subsume diverse phenomena under a small number of basic assumptions. Friedman's technical account proved defective (see Salmon, 1989). Philip Kitcher (1989), though critical of Friedman's theory, subsequently developed a different version of the unification approach in which types of argument forms, rather than scientific laws, are the instruments of unification.

PRAGMATICS AND EXPLANATION. Pragmatics is the study of contextual factors associated with the uses of language. Although advocates of the orthodox theory, the causal/mechanical approach, and the unification view all recognize that explanations have contextual features, they focus on such objective factors as laws of nature, causal relations, and logical entailments. Philosophers who deal with the pragmatics of explanation emphasize aspects like the interests and background knowledge of people who seek and who give explanations. Sylvain Bromberger did pathbreaking work in this area in the 1960s (see Salmon, 1989), but much greater attention has been drawn to this topic by Bas van Fraassen (1980).

According to van Fraassen, explanations are answers to why-questions. Questions arise in contexts and have presuppositions; if the presuppositions are not fulfilled the question cannot be answered but must be rejected. A why-question has three aspects, a topic, a contrast class, and a relevance relation. When Willie Sutton, the notorious bank robber, was asked by a reporter, "Why do you rob banks?" he replied. "Because that's where the money is." The topic of this question is the fact to be explained, "You rob banks." The question, as stated, is ambiguous because two different contrast classes are available. The journalist presumably had in mind the class {being a bank robber, being a doctor, being a plumber, . . .}. Sutton's answer involved a different class {robbing banks, robbing liquor stores, robbing private homes, . . .}. The humor in his answer plays on his ambiguity. The relevance relation on either interpretation is motivational.

Van Fraassen claims that attention to pragmatic features enables us to avoid the traditional problems surrounding the concept of explanation. His critics hold that he has failed to specify adequately what constitutes an explanatory relevance relation, and that to do so would involve precisely the problems faced by those who focused on the noncontextual aspects of explanation. No doubt investigation of the pragmatics of explanation is illuminated, but objective factors seem indispensable to an adequate theory of explanation.

[See also Causation; Explanation, Types of; Hume, David; Philosophy of Science; Pragmatics; Probability.]

BIBLIOGRAPHY

Eells, E. *Probabilistic Causality.* Cambridge, 1991.

Feigl, H., and G. Maxwell, eds. *Scientific Explanation, Space, and Time,* Vol. 3, *Minnesota Studies in the Philosophy of Science.* Minneapolis, 1962. Contains Hempel's first article on statistical explanation (superseded by his "Aspects of Scientific Explanation") and articles on explanation by M. Brodbeck, P. Feyerabend, and M. Scriven.

Fetzer, J. H. *Scientific Knowledge.* Dordrecht, 1981.

Friedman, M. "Explanation and Scientific Understanding," *Journal of Philosophy,* Vol. 71 (1974), 5–19.

Hempel, C. G. *Aspects of Scientific Explanation and Other Essays in the Philosophy of Science.* New York, 1965. Contains Hempel's "Aspects of Scientific Explanation," and a reprint of Hempel and Oppenheim, "Studies in the Logic of Explanation" (1948).

Humphreys, P. *The Chances of Explanation.* Princeton, NJ, 1989.

Kitcher, P., and W. C. Salmon. *Scientific Explanation,* Vol. 13, *Minnesota Studies in the Philosophy of Science.* Minneapolis, 1989. Contains nine articles by well-known experts, including Kitcher's "Explanatory Unification and the Causal Structure of the World," and Salmon's "Four Decades of Scientific Explanation." A rich source of bibliographical information, especially Salmon's contribution.

Salmon, W. C. *Scientific Explanation and the Causal Structure of the World.* Princeton, NJ, 1984.

———, et al. *Statistical Explanation and Statistical Relevance.* Pittsburgh, 1971. Contains Jeffrey. "Statistical Explanation vs. Statistical Inference," and Salmon, "Statistical Explanation."

Suppes, P. *A Probabilistic Theory of Causality.* Amsterdam, 1970. The classic work on probabilistic causality.

van Fraassen, B. C. *The Scientific Image.* Oxford, 1980.

— WESLEY C. SALMON

EXPLANATION, TYPES OF

Various types of explanation appear in the natural and social sciences. How these are understood depends considerably on one's overall theory of scientific explanation. Deductive and statistical theories such as those of Hempel and Salmon attempt to reduce scientific explanation to one or two basic forms. Aristotle's theory, which postulates different kinds of explanatory factors in nature, is nonreductionistic. So are pragmatic theories of the sort proposed by Achinstein and van Fraassen, which recognize many nonreducible types of questions that scientific explainers can answer. In what follows three important categories of explanation will be considered.

Causal Explanation

WHAT IS A CAUSAL EXPLANATION? For Aristotle, who held a broad view, a causal explanation is one that cites one or more of the four causes or determining factors that exist in nature and correspond to the meanings of the question Why?: the material cause (the matter or constituents of which something is composed); the formal cause (the form or structure); the efficient cause (an external source of motion or change); and the final cause (the end, purpose, or function of something).

For Aristotle all explanations are causal, since by an explanation he means something that gives one or more of his four causes.

Many contemporary philosophers focus on a concept of cause corresponding roughly to Aristotle's efficient cause, with the idea that this is central in science, other types of causes being reducible to it. Since the 1940s the most influential of these accounts is the deductive-nomological model due to Hempel. To explain a particular event, on this account, one cites universal laws and facts about specific conditions that obtain, from which a statement describing the event is derivable. Such an explanation is causal if all the specific conditions cited occurred prior to the event being explained. This accords with Hume's definition of causation, which requires the cause to precede the effect. Salmon has provided a more complex Humean account of

causal explanation that involves distinguishing three aspects of causation: causal processes (e.g., the motion of a missile through space), causal interaction (e.g., the projection of the missile by a firing device), and conjunctive forks (the projection of several missiles together by a common firing device). Achinstein's pragmatic theory analyzes causal explanation by offering a semantical account of the kinds of questions causal explanations answer.

ARE ALL EXPLANATIONS CAUSAL? For Aristotle all explanations are causal, since by an explanation he means something that gives one or more of his four causes. Some contemporary philosophers who do not champion such a broad notion of cause nevertheless answer the question affirmatively. David Lewis holds that to explain an event is to provide some information about its causal history. Depending on the context, this might include just one prior event or maximally and ideally a complete causal chain starting from the big bang.

Other writers deny that explanations, including scientific ones, are always causal. For Hempel, noncausal deductive-nomological explanations are possible in which the events cited in the explanans (the explaining sentences) occur contemporaneously with, or even after, the event being explained. Achinstein characterizes several types of noncausal scientific explanations, including those that explain a regularity (e.g., a projectile continuing in motion) by bringing it under a more general noncausal law (e.g., the law of inertia) and those that explain why something has a given property (e.g., why this gas has the temperature it does) by citing an identical theoretical property (e.g., its mean molecular kinetic energy). Cases of the latter sort are also explored by Ruben.

Statistical Explanation

Some events are explained by citing conditions statistically but not universally associated with the event to be explained. We may say that Jim recovered from strep throat because he took penicillin, even though not all people recover under such conditions. For Hempel these explanations are inductive, not deductive, arguments (by contrast to the deductive-nomological cases). They contain premises describing conditions that obtained (e.g., "Jim had strep throat and took penicillin") together with probabilistic laws (e.g., "the probability of recovery from strep, given a penicillin injection, is such and such"); and they make the conclusion describing the event to be explained ("Jim recovered") probable.

Hempel's statistical model requires laws with high probabilities for the events being explained. Salmon and

Railton develop contrasting statistical models that permit laws assigning any probabilities—high or low—to the event in question. On Salmon's statistical relevance model, for example, one can explain why a certain atom decayed when it did by citing the fact that the atom is an atom of radioactive element E and the statistical law that the probability of an atom of element E decaying at a given time is p, where the latter may be low but not zero. For Salmon, unlike Hempel, a statistical explanation cites facts and probability laws that do not necessarily make the event to be explained probable but show with what probability such an event can be expected. Railton defends what he calls a deductive-nomological-probabilistic (d-n-p) model of statistical explanation. First, from a theory supplying some causal mechanism, a law of the following form is derived deductively: at any time anything that has property F has a probability p to have property G. Second, a fact is cited concerning the event e to be explained—namely, that e has property F at time t. From this and the previous law we deduce: e has a probability p to have property G at time t. Finally, we add, parenthetically, according to what transpired: e did (not) have G at time t. This will constitute a d-n-p explanation of why e did (not) have G at t.

Functional Explanation

A functional explanation is one that explains the existence of some item (e.g., the heart, the rain dance in some society) by citing its function (e.g., to pump the blood, to promote group solidarity). Such explanations frequently occur in biology as well as the social sciences.

WHAT ARE FUNCTIONS? Most philosophical accounts fall into four categories. First is a "good consequence" doctrine, according to which doing y is x's function if and only if doing y confers some good. For biological functions the good is "survival and reproduction" (Ruse; Woodfield). Second, there is a "goal" doctrine, which states that y is x's function if and only if doing y contributes to some goal-state associated with x, the latter usually being defined causally (Nagel). Third, there is an "explanation" doctrine, according to which y is x's function if and only if x exists because it does y and y is a consequence of x's existing (Wright; Cummins and Millikan offer other versions). Fourth is a "means" doctrine that distinguishes various types of functions—including design, use, and service—all of which involve a means-end relationship; for example, "the function that x was designed to serve is to do y" is true if x was designed to serve as a means of doing y (Achinstein).

ARE FUNCTIONAL EXPLANATIONS LEGITIMATE IN SCIENCE? For Hempel a functional explanation to be scientifically legitimate would have to conform either to the deductive-nomological or the inductive-statistical model of explanation. But this is usually impossible, Hempel claims. Suppose we seek to give a functional explanation of the existence of the heart in mammals. To do so we must cite universal or statistical laws that either entail or make probable the heart's existence. So we might say: (1) mammals exist; (2) mammals exist only if their blood is circulated; (3) their blood is circulated only if they have hearts. But, says Hempel, (3), understood as a law, is false, since it is possible for devices other than (natural) hearts to circulate the blood. We could transform (3) into a truth by changing "only if" to "if." But with this change (1), (2), and the revised (3) would not entail or make probable that hearts exist in mammals. According to Hempel, the problem with functional explanations, whether in biology or the social sciences, is that they usually offer no basis for inferring the existence of the item with the function rather than any other item that could also have served that function.

Hempel's claims are rejected by Wright, who maintains that one can give a functional explanation of the existence of an item without also showing that only that item could serve the function. According to Wright, a functional explanation is a certain type of causal explanation: it explains the existence of an item x with a function y by saying that doing y in the past has been a cause or an important part of the cause of x's existence. Part of the cause of the heart's existing in mammals is that hearts have circulated the blood and continue to do so, even if in principle other blood circulators could have existed.

Both Hempel's attack on functional explanations and Wright's defense of them are based on the idea that teleological claims involving functions, to be legitimate in science, must be reducible to causal or lawlike assertions. This is in fundamental opposition to Aristotle's position that teleological claims are *sui generis* (final causes are not reducible to efficient ones). Achinstein's "means" doctrine of functions is a contemporary representative of the latter tradition. One can explain why hearts exist in mammals not only by answering (1) what caused them to exist (what evolutionary, chemical, or other processes were involved) but also by answering (2) what ends are served by means of hearts for which they exist? Answers to (1) and (2) may be independent.

Explanatory Reductionism

Philosophers such as Hempel, Salmon, and Railton, who provide "models" of explanation, attempt to show that various types of explanations in the sciences conform to one of these models. But their models have counterexamples. One, to which the models of Hempel and Railton are subject, involves an intervening cause. Suppose that Jones eats a pound of arsenic and that it is a law that anyone who does so dies within twenty-four hours. For Hempel and Railton a correct explanation of Jones's death is his arsenic feast, even if there was an unrelated intervening cause such as a truck accident that killed poor Jones. Modelists generally build two features into their models: first, the presumption that, except for the truth of the explanans, whether or not the conditions required by the model are in fact met can be decided a priori; and second, a requirement that the description of the particular events invoked in the explanans does not by itself, without invoking laws, entail the event to be explained. Achinstein argues that models having both these features are always subject to counterexamples and hence that explanations in science cannot be reduced to the basic types demanded by modelists. For example, in the arsenic case, to avoid the problem noted and satisfy the a prior condition, one could add to the explanans the sentence "Jones's eating a pound of arsenic caused his death"; but this violates the second condition, since, without explicitly invoking laws, it entails the event to be explained.

[See also Aristotle; Causation; Explanation, Theories of; Hume, David; Philosophy of Science; Probability.]

BIBLIOGRAPHY

Achinstein, P. *The Nature of Explanation*. New York, 1983.
———. "A Type of Non-Causal Explanation," in P. A. French, T. E. Uehling, and H. K. Wettstein, eds., *Causation and Causal Theories*, Midwest Studies in Philosophy, Vol. 9 (Minneapolis, 1984).
Aristotle. *Physica*, Book 2.
Cummins, R. "Functional Analysis," *Journal of Philosophy*, Vol. 72 (1975), 741–65.
Hempel, C. G. *Aspects of Scientific Explanation*. New York, 1965.
Lewis, D. "Causal Explanation," in D.-H. Ruben, ed., *Explanation* (Oxford, 1993).
Milliken, R. *Language, Thought, and Other Biological Categories*. Cambridge, MA, 1984.
Nagel, E. *Teleology Revisited and Other Essays in the Philosophy and History of Science*. New York, 1979.
Pitt, J. C., ed. *Theories of Explanation*. New York, 1988.
Railton, P. "A Deductive-Nomological Model of Probabilistic Explanation," *Philosophy of Science*, Vol. 45 (1978), 206–26.
Ruben, D.-H., ed. *Explanation*. Oxford, 1993.
Ruse, M. *The Philosophy of Biology*. London, 1973.
Salmon, W. C. *Scientific Explanation and the Causal Structure of the World*. Princeton, NJ, 1984.
———. *Four Decades of Scientific Explanation*. Minneapolis, 1989.
———, et al. *Statistical Explanation and Statistical Relevance*. Pittsburgh, 1971.
van Fraassen, B. *The Scientific Image*. Oxford, 1980.
Woodfield, A. *Teleology*. Cambridge, 1976.
Wright, L. *Teleological Explanations*. Berkeley, 1976.

— PETER ACHINSTEIN

EXTRINSIC AND INTRINSIC PROPERTIES

An intrinsic property is one whose possession by an object at a time involves nothing other than the object (and its parts) at that time; an extrinsic property is one whose possession at a time involves something else. We might say, therefore, that the properties of being red and round are intrinsic to this ball, but the properties of being in Rhode Island, being less than five feet away from a tree, and having once been owned by my sister are extrinsic to it.

Two extreme views are that

all properties are really intrinsic and that

all properties are really extrinsic.

Geach has made a corresponding distinction among changes. There is change whenever 'F(x) at time t' is true and 'F(x) at time t'' is false. Socrates will change when he puts on weight; he will also change when he comes to be shorter than Theaetetus merely in virtue of Theaetetus' growth. Changes of the second kind—intuitively less genuine—Geach calls "mere Cambridge changes," without proposing a rigorous criterion. We might define a mere Cambridge property as a property, change in an object's possession of which is a mere Cambridge change. Mere Cambridge properties are plausibly taken to be the same as extrinsic properties.

The matter is important, among other things, for the clear statement of a Humean view of the world. For a Humean there is in principle a description in intrinsic terms of the state of the world at any one time that is both complete and free of implications for the state of the world at any other time. "Solidity, extension, motion; these qualities are all complete in themselves, and never point out any other event which may result from them" (Hume, *Enquiry*, sec. 8, 1) It is not clear, however, that what Hume says can be true: the motion of an object is hardly free of implications about the state of the world at other times. (If an object at place *p* is said to be moving at time *t*, this is standardly in the sense that, at other times more or less near to *t*, the object is in other places more or less near to *p*.) We may have to decide between complete description and a purely intrinsic one.

Two extreme views are that all properties are really intrinsic and that all properties are really extrinsic. Leibniz holds the first: "There are no purely extrinsic denominations." His insistence resulted in the drastic denial of the reality of relations and, most notably, of space and time; it has not been widely accepted. A moderate version of the opposite view, that all properties are really extrinsic, might be held by someone, like Popper, who believes that physical properties are essentially dispositional. Both extremes, in different ways, represent a sense that the nature of one thing cannot be divorced from the nature of others. Confidence in a firm distinction between the intrinsic and the extrinsic, on the other hand, is more characteristic of an optimistic Humean.

It is not easy to give a precise characterization of intrinsic properties, and there may not even be a unique idea, so to speak, waiting to be characterized. We might try saying that extrinsic properties are relational properties and intrinsic properties nonrelational. But many intuitively intrinsic properties still in some way involve a relation—squareness involves a relation among the sides of an object. Can we say that intrinsic properties are those that do not involve a relation to anything that is not a part of the object? This is perhaps the clearest criterion, but it may still be incapable of capturing all our intuitions at once. The power to open locks of kind k, for example, apparently involves a relation to external things of a certain kind—which would seem to make it extrinsic. Yet it is a property that a key can have if it is, so to speak, alone in the world—which would seem to make it intrinsic.

It may be helpful to invoke a distinction between relational descriptions of a property and descriptions of a relational property. But that distinction is itself perplexing. Is 'possessing what is actually Jane's favorite intrinsic property' a relational description of a first-order property or a description of second-level relational property?

Philosophers have argued in many cases that apparently intrinsic properties are in fact extrinsic. Terms such as *old, great,* and *imperfect,* Locke says, "are not looked on to be either relative or so much as external denominations," but they conceal a tacit relation (*Essay*). More worrying are challenges even to the idea that primary qualities, like size and shape, are intrinsic. The size of the ball is, we may think, intrinsic to it. We can describe a scenario where everything else in the universe is twice its actual size while the ball remains the same.

But can we properly distinguish this from a scenario where the rest of the world is the same but the ball is half its actual size? Some will argue that length is relational, and the two scenarios make a distinction without a difference: size, after all, is extrinsic. Others will argue instead that even if our descriptions of size are relative, for example, to standard measures, what is described is still an absolute and intrinsic property.

Are any or all of a person's mental properties intrinsic to her? The question is in part about the limitations of methodological solipsism. If Jane could not possess the property of thinking of Bertrand Russell if Russell did not exist, then that property must be extrinsic to her. Some will try to segment referential thought into an internal and an external component; but if that proposal fails, referential thought will typically be extrinsic to the thinker. (Another option is that the thinker, or her mind, extends more widely than her body—and actually includes Russell.) One might argue a similar point with respect to thought about properties as well as about individuals. (A brain that has never been out of a vat does not know what a meter is.) Maybe there are very few mental properties intrinsic to a person; or maybe we should think again about what the notion of the intrinsic is, and what exactly it is supposed to do for us.

[See also Hume, David; Internalism versus Externalism; Leibniz, Gottfried Wilhelm; Locke, John; Metaphysics.]

BIBLIOGRAPHY

Geach, P. T. *God and the Soul.* London, 1969.
Leibniz, G. W. "Primary Truths" and "Letters to Des Bosses," in *Philosophical Essays,* translated by R. Ariew and D. Garber. Indianapolis, 1989. See esp. pp. 32, 203.
Lewis, D. K. *On the Plurality of Worlds.* Oxford, 1986. Chaps. 1.5, 4.2.
Lewis, D. K. "Extrinsic Properties," *Philosophical Studies,* Vol. 44 (1983), 197–200.
Locke, J. *Essay concerning Human Understanding.* Bk. 2, Chaps. 25, 28.
Popper, K. *The Logic of Scientific Discovery.* London, 1959. Pp. 424–25.

— JUSTIN BROACKES

F

FEMINIST ETHICS

The umbrella of feminist ethics covers many approaches to ethics arising from overlapping motivations and histories. The motivations are feminist (many varieties); the histories are of women's oppression in what Iris Young calls its five faces: socially sanctioned exploitation, marginalization, powerlessness, cultural imperialism, and violence against women and girls. Despite the popularity of certain themes—opposition to hierarchies and dualisms, favoring circles and centers, deep suspicion of competition—feminist ethics is not a set of doctrines or positions, nor is it a single theory or world view, but it is a cluster of theorizings manifesting feminist perspectives on women's lives and motivated by commitments to resist further oppression, undo the damage of past oppression, and inspire better future alternatives. It has moved from an early approach emphasizing issues such as abortion and affirmative action to wide-ranging, pluralistic, and multileveled theorizing. Although inspired by women's lives, it is not only about women but about living well in the world. Its concerns range from domestic to environmental.

In its efforts to command a respect for women largely absent from centuries of philosophical writing, feminist ethics aims also to avoid either glorifying women's experience or presenting women merely as victims.

In 1957 African-American playwright Lorraine Hansberry (1930–65) wrote to *The Ladder,* a lesbian magazine, calling for women to analyze ethical questions produced by a male-dominated culture (Card, 1991). French philosopher Simone de Beauvoir (1908–86) was already doing it long before it had a label. The Second Wave of feminist politics of the late 1960s and early 1970s became a major influence on the feminist ethics that followed. In 1978 Sarah Hoagland used the term "lesbian ethics" in a workshop at a Women's Learning Institute in Maidenrock, Wisconsin, and in Boston Mary Daly subtitled her treatise *Gyn/Ecology*

"The Metaethics of Radical Feminism." The term "feminist ethics" was soon heard in feminist responses to Carol Gilligan's study of patterns in women's moral development.

From such beginnings feminist ethics has struggled with tensions between rebellion against damaging, patriarchally constructed femininities and insistence upon respect for women's voices wherever they are heard, between emphasis on what women have suffered and emphasis on what women have done. In its efforts to command a respect for women largely absent from centuries of philosophical writing, it aims also to avoid either glorifying women's experience or presenting women merely as victims.

Feminist ethics is theorized at many levels of abstraction and has many traditions. Many theorists define and critique issues in particular areas such as reproduction, education, work, government, sexuality, self-defense, friendship, spirituality, or food. Some, in the tradition of applied ethics, draw upon classical texts and principles, extending their applications; others, such as Janice Raymond, take their findings as bases for new theorizing. Historically oriented traditions critically reexamine classical texts, as Elizabeth V. Spelman (1988) does with Plato and Aristotle, exposing misogyny and stereotypes but also searching out unexamined assumptions or even explicitly defended ideals that support oppressive social structures, or as Annette Baier (1985) does with René Descartes in arguing that we are, first of all, "second persons," addressed as "you" by caretakers who socialize us. Some reclaim past defenses of women, such as those of Mary Wollstonecraft and John Stuart Mill, against sexist attitudes and practices or seek out positions and values supporting feminist ideals, as Annette Baier does with the ethics of David Hume (Kittay & Meyers, 1987).

Yet others, wishing to begin anew, articulate new theories, explore new principles, reexamine everyday moral concepts, and analyze such concepts as bitterness and attentive love, that have not been central to influential theories of the past. A major tradition in this vein is feminist care ethics, the revaluing, analysis, and development of caring as a fundamental moral value, taking as paradigmatic relationships central to many women's lives—female friendships, mother–child relationships, nursing, lesbian bonding. Care ethics focuses on relationships with particular others, encounters with real individuals. It values emotional responses and respects material needs. Its focus on agency allies it with character ethics, in contrast with act-oriented duty and consequentialist theories of the modern era. Responsibility in care ethics suggests responsiveness to needs rather than a duty or obligation correlated with the rights of others.

Yet care ethics is not always feminist. Patriarchally constructed femininity has included care ethics that requires service and emotional bonding of wives to husbands and children, as well as philanthropic community service where possible, and requires unmarried women to devote themselves to a masculine God or to their nearest earthly kin. Women's voices speaking out of such contexts without a feminist perspective may simply endorse these requirements. Because of the possibility that a care ethic may be traditionally feminine rather than critically feminist, major questions for any proposed feminist care ethic are whether it valorizes women's subordination as servants and whether it glorifies female martyrdom (or whether it can readily be used to do either). Care ethics based on women's past experiences as mothers or nurses is vulnerable to these pitfalls.

Nevertheless, mothering is a significant part of many women's histories, and, accordingly, feminists have mined that experience for the wisdom it can yield. Sensitive to the dangers of endorsing servitude or glorifying martyrdom, Sara Ruddick articulates a theory of "maternal thinking," arguing for its extension into the sphere of international relations, and Virginia Held proposes a feminist morality that would take as paradigmatic relationships that would characterize ideal post-patriarchal families. Sara Ruddick's maternal thinking embodies ideals, such as "attentive love" (following Simone Weil and Iris Murdoch), that she finds implicit in three tasks that together define mothering as an activity. They are the tasks of preserving the child's life, fostering its growth, and making it acceptable to a society wider than its family of origin. Her goal is a nonviolent world where peace is the enduring outcome of the virtues of maternal thinking rather than the precarious outcome of adversarially oriented conflict resolution through mutual concessions.

Virginia Held's feminist morality for a noncontractual society includes postpatriarchal mothering as one among many paradigms that she would have displace from dominance the contract paradigms of human relationship pervasive in modern European moral philosophy. Aspects of mothering and family living that she finds important for ethics are the affectional nature of family bonding, the intrinsic character of the value of

these relationships in contrast with the instrumental character of contractual ones, and the degree to which such relationships are not voluntary, all of which are aspects of social relationships not well captured by contract models.

Some theorists,

such as Iris Young and Patricia Williams,

call for a feminist, antiracist theory of justice,

articulated from the perspectives

of those with legacies of oppression

rather than from perspectives of privilege.

An alternative to the mother model is Sarah Hoagland's lesbian ethics, a feminist care ethic that takes as paradigmatic relationships between lesbians primarily bonded with each other and not with men. She rejects mother–child paradigms for the ethics of adult interaction, because such relationships exemplify nonreciprocal caring, a problem for women's relationships with other adults in sexist societies (Card, 1991). Although she addresses lesbians living in community with lesbians and her work is inspired by the need for conflict resolution that would strengthen lesbian bonds and preserve lesbian community, the sense of community she intends is not geographical, and she leaves for others to answer whether such an ethic might also be valuable for them. Like Sara Ruddick, she explores "attending" as a form of ethical caring, citing midwifery as an example, and offers it as an alternative to the social-control orientation predominant in modern moral philosophy. Like Virginia Held, she is concerned about contexts we have not chosen but within which we can still make choices that make a difference.

Proponents of feminist care ethics disagree over the value of justice, rights, impartiality, and institutions, concepts that evoke what Seyla Benhabib has called the "generalized other" rather than the "concrete other" of particular caring relationships (Kittay & Meyers, 1987). Sarah Hoagland does not find justice and rights useful concepts for lesbian community. Nel Noddings finds justice a poor substitute for caring in any community. Virginia Held finds justice indispensable but needing supplementation by care. Janice Raymond, reflecting on histories of female friendships ("gyn/affection"), finds that supportive institutions facilitate female bonding.

And Marilyn Friedman acknowledges as a limit of the social conception of the self its inability to ground an unmediated global concern (Card, 1991).

Justice is defined as being at least partly independent of agents' motivations. A common assumption of those who reject justice is that caring is a remedy or a prophylactic against violence, hostility, and neglect. Some of the data of mothering, nursing, and friendship encourage this view; many data of heterosexual interactions, and even of women's interactions with women as lovers or primary caretakers, raise questions about it. If violence, hostility, and neglect are also partly definable as independent of motives, some such concept as justice may be required to address them adequately. Thus, some theorists, such as Iris Young and Patricia Williams, call for a feminist, antiracist theory of justice, articulated from the perspectives of those with legacies of oppression rather than from perspectives of privilege. Reflecting on a bill of sale for her great-great-grandmother, impregnated at age eleven by her white owner, Patricia Williams (1991) finds the sound of rights "deliciously empowering." Iris Young (1990) calls for a theory of justice centered, not on distributive issues, as modern theories have been, but on issues of decision making, division of labor, and culture, taking domination and oppression as paradigmatic injustices rather than as unfairness in the economies of power and rights.

María Lugones makes cultural pluralism the center of her theorizing, introducing a concept, " 'world'-traveling," that helps mediate the concerns of care and justice. World-traveling, willful exercise of a flexibility acquired spontaneously by members of a minority in an oppressive society, is shifting perceptually and emotionally from a construction of life where one is at home although many others are outsiders to other constructions of life in which some former outsiders are now at home and in which one may figure as an outsider oneself. Finding it an antidote to arrogance, which blocks both love and justice, María Lugones advocates animating world travel with nonagonistic playfulness. She illustrates with a tale of traveling to her mother's world, explaining that she could not love her mother well until she could enter that world.

Feminist perspectives on justice permeate feminist bioethics (or biomedical ethics), as feminist conceptions of care permeate ecofeminism (ecological feminism). Susan Sherwin notes that prefeminist bioethics posed questions of justice regarding rights of access to traditional health-care systems but ignored the ill design of such systems for responding to health needs created for many groups of women by an oppressive social system, needs such as those of women battered by partners or at risk for developing addictions or lacking adequately nutritious food supplies. Jan Raymond challenges reproductive liberalism's focus on choice, arguing that supporters and promoters of technological and contractual reproduction undermine women's reproductive rights. Both critique so-called surrogacy (contractual pregnancy) and new reproductive technologies (NRTs), especially in vitro fertilization (IVF; "test tube babies"), and between them cover further issues ranging from premenstrual syndrome and medical constructions of homosexuality to the international traffic in fetal tissue and in women and children for organ transplants.

Ecofeminism joins to holistic environmental ethics a feminist sensitivity to parallels between oppressions of women and of other animals and the natural environment. Vegetarianism, defended vigorously by Carol Adams, is the most concrete issue widely discussed. Otherwise, ecofeminism has been more abstract than feminist bioethics, exploring issues ranging from who (or what) counts as "morally considerable" to the viability of such traditional philosophical dualisms as reason and feeling (or emotion), mind and matter, culture and nature. Karen Warren exposes a "logic of domination" common to oppressions of women and nature. Val Plumwood critiques dominant forms of rationality, arguing that philosophical dualisms have protected against acknowledging human dependency on nature and men's dependency on women.

[See also Abortion; Affirmative Action; Applied Ethics; Aristotle; Beauvoir, Simone de; Biomedical Ethics; Consequentialism; Descartes, René; Environmental Ethics; Feminist Philosophy; Genetics and Reproductive Technologies; Hume, David; Impartiality; Justice; Mill, John Stuart; Pluralism; Rationality; Rights; Speciesism; Violence; Wollstonecraft, Mary.]

BIBLIOGRAPHY

Adams, C. J. The Sexual Politics of Meat. New York, 1990.
Baier, A. "Cartesian Persons," in Postures of the Mind (Minneapolis, 1985).
Beauvoir, S. de. Le Deuxième sexe, 2 vols. Paris, 1949. Translated by H. M. Parshley as The Second Sex. New York, 1952.
Card, C., ed. Feminist Ethics. Lawrence, KS, 1991.
Gilligan, C. In a Different Voice: Psychological Theory and Women's Development. Cambridge, MA, 1982.
Held, V. Feminist Morality. Chicago, 1993.
Hoagland, S. Lesbian Ethics. Palo Alto, CA, 1988.
Kittay, E. F., and D. T. Meyers, eds. Women and Moral Theory. Totowa, NJ, 1987.
Lugones, M. "Playfulness, 'World'-Traveling, and Loving Perception," Hypatia, Vol. 2 (1987), 3–19.
Murdoch, I. The Sovereignty of Good. London, 1970.
Noddings, N. Caring. A Feminine Approach to Ethics and Moral Education. Berkeley, 1984.
Plumwood, V. Feminism and the Mastery of Nature. London, 1993.

Raymond, J. G. *A Passion for Friends*. Boston, 1986.
———. *Women as Wombs*. San Francisco, 1993.
Ruddick, S. *Maternal Thinking*. Boston, 1989.
Sherwin, S. *No Longer Patient: Feminist Ethics and Health Care*. Philadelphia, 1992.
Spelman, E. V. *Inessential Woman: Problems of Exclusion in Feminist Thought*. Boston, 1988.
Warren, K. "The Power and Promise of Ecological Feminism," *Environmental Ethics*, Vol. 12 (1990), 125–46.
Weil, S. *La Pesanteur et la grace*. Paris 1974. Translated by E. Craufurd as *Gravity and Grace*. London, 1952.
Williams, P. *The Alchemy of Race and Rights*. Cambridge, MA, 1991.
Young, I. *Justice and the Politics of Difference*. Princeton, NJ, 1990.

— CLAUDIA CARD

FEMINIST PHILOSOPHY

Feminist uses and adaptations of Western philosophies can be found in almost all historical periods. In the early modern period theorists such as Mary Wollstonecraft and Harriet Taylor adapted the democratic philosophies of Rousseau and the utilitarians to argue for the equality of women. Socialists such as Flora Tristan and Clara Zetkin used the theories of utopian socialists, socialist anarchists, and Marxists to argue for women's rights as workers. African abolitionists such as Sojourner Truth drew on black liberationist theology and Africanist social theory to argue against slavery. In the revolutions of the 1960s and 1970s racial feminists found inspiration in the philosophy of black power and black separatism. Much feminist theory developed along lines of nonfeminist social theory, moving from liberal democratic rights and equality, to socialist or Marxist claims to economic freedom and parity, to radical demands for reform in sexual, family, and social life.

Prominent in feminist philosophy

is the use of gender as an analytic category,

a change not easily accommodated

within the scope of the philosophical

as it has been understood since ancient Greece.

Inherent in early modern classics of feminist democratic and socialist theory such as Harriet Taylor and John Stuart Mill's *The Subjection of Women* (1869), Wollstonecraft's *Vindication of the Rights of Women* (1792), and Alexandra Kollantai's Marxist *The Social Basis of the Woman Question* (1909) were distinct approaches and problematics. In the last three decades of the twentieth century these approaches generated distinct lines of feminist philosophizing that have introduced sexuality and family life as questions of philosophical interest and also changed how the method, purpose, and origin of philosophy are conceived (Nye, 1995).

Prominent in feminist philosophy is the use of gender as an analytic category, a change not easily accommodated within the scope of the philosophical as it has been understood since ancient Greece. For Greek philosophers and subsequent philosophers man's essence, nature, rights, and proper life is the proper subject of philosophy, "man" understood as a general term for what is human with no specific reference to gender. Even as some philosophers overcame prejudice and admitted that women or non-white races and peoples were human and capable of philosophical thought, they typically continued to philosophize about morality, knowledge, and truth without reference to race or sex.

Feminist insistence on gender as a crucial determinant of meaning and reference has interjected the specificity and physicality of bodies and sexuality into philosophical inquiries traditionally framed in general and abstract terms. Attention to gender has also introduced questions elided in the public affairs of politics, the state, religious establishments, and centers of learning which were the matrix for establishment philosophizing. Because ideas of gender change from one culture and historical era to another, insistence on gender as an analytic category has introduced a controversial historical element. The distinction of philosophy had been taken to be its timelessness, its concern with the eternal, the universal, the nature of man beyond history, culture, ethnicity. Feminists focused on gender as a category with reference to a diversity of private lives as well as to generalized procedures of public life, turned away from essentialist accounts of man to the examination of complex and diverse interactions between social structures and individual subjects.

The antiphilosopher Karl Marx compromised philosophical truth by claiming its dependence on "class consciousness" and inspired an independent line of social feminist philosophizing. But in much Marxist philosophy "class" and "production" were universals in their own right, ultimate determinants of social experience and reality. Feminist theorists, concerned with large areas of family life left out of Marxist theory and communist agendas for social reform, were critical of material as well as conceptual forms of philosophical foundationalism. Instead, they tended to find in the experiences, lives, and needs of diverse women interlocking determinants of class, race, gender, and culture that admitted of no abstracted or essentialist treatment.

Feminist theories in the 1970s and 1980s held out hope that "postmodern" nonfoundationalist and non-essentialist paradigms could be used to feminist advantage. In Britain and North America after World War II, a dominant positivist/analytic style of philosophy had mutated to less ambitious and more professionalized ordinary-language philosophy, naturalized epistemology, or cognitive psychology. English-speaking philosophers no longer saw themselves as dictating standards of truth and knowledge but as describing and clarifying in relatively minor ways the evolving logic of successful sciences. Analytic feminists such as Janet Radcliffe Richards and Jean Grimshaw promoted these humbler forms of linguistic and logical analysis as useful ways to clarify issues of interest to women. Others such as Louise Antony and Lynn Nelson found in the postpositivist logicist philosophy such as that of W. V. O. Quine an alternative to foundationalism that might further feminist attempts to change systems of beliefs. Jane Duran championed a new cognitivism in academic philosophy of mind, arguing that the empirical study of thinking processes leaves open the possibility of diverse feminine thinking styles.

In France, Husserl's phenomenology and the structuralism of the 1950s had given way to Michel Foucault's post-Nietzschean studies of the generation of forms of knowledge as modes of power and Jacques Derrida's deconstruction of any attempt to ground linguistic or logical structure in human presence, mind, or voice. Many feminists welcomed in these poststructuralist theories a radicalism missing from the increasingly solipsistic and academic turnings of English-speaking philosophy. In Germany the Frankfurt school of critical theorists attempted a less dogmatic version of Marxism to repair the practical and theoretical failures of orthodox Marxist theory, grafting onto materialism theories of consciousness and subjectivity. Feminist social theorists such as Nancy Fraser, Seyla Benhabib, and Iris Young found critical theory in general, and Habermas's theory of human needs and communicative truth in particular, useful in understanding and addressing the ideological and cultural roots of women's oppression.

A Feminist History of Philosophy

One major feminist innovation was in the history of philosophy. In the 1970s and 1980s came revisionary feminist philosophical readings of virtually the entire established canon of major philosophers. A number of these rereadings were published in a groundbreaking 1983 collection of articles (*Discovering Reality*) edited by Merrill Hintikka and Sandra Harding.

In that volume and elsewhere Aristotle, like Plato one of the canonical founders of philosophy, was a frequent

The cultural and ethnic variety of African-American sexual and family experience, as described by social theorists like Angela Davis, inspired new social models. (Corbis/Bettmann)

subject of feminist critique. Feminists found misogyny and an oppressive gender and racial subtext in Aristotle's metaphysics, ethics, biology, and politics. Also given special attention was the entire body of liberal democratic theory: Locke, Rousseau, Hobbes, as well as John Rawls. Susan Okin, Carole Pateman, Lorenne Clark, Lynda Lange, and Jean Elshtain all uncovered in supposedly gender-neutral philosophical theories of democratic rights and freedoms—theories that had established much of the agenda for modern social theory—assumptions and implications concerning family life, reproduction, and male/female relations that were prejudicial to women.

There were accompanying attempts to find women philosophers to supplement a canon almost uniformly male. Work in this area has been conservative as well as revisionary. Radical critiques of the philosophical tradition, including standards of rationality and logic generated in philosophy, have been rejected by some women philosophers as extremist and even dangerous, playing into the hands of those who proclaim philosophy off limits to women. The hope was that, just as some male philosophers were relatively free of bias, so women philosophers could be found who had contributed to the mainstream history of philosophy. Margaret Atherton and others have researched historical figures such as Mary Astell and Damaris Masham, who took Descartes's rationalism as support for a gender-neutral mental capacity. Attention was paid to contemporary analytic philosophers such as Iris Murdoch and Elizabeth Anscombe, well known in university circles, as well as to important but marginalized twentieth-century thinkers such as Rosa Luxemburg, Simone Weil, and Susanne Langer. Milestones were Mary Ellen Waithe's three-volume collection of women philosophers (*A History of Women Philosophers*) and the establishment of a Society for the Study of Women Philosophers affiliated with the American Philosophical Association.

More radical rereadings came from feminist philosophers interested in contemporary Continental styles of philosophy open to psychoanalytic and other interpretive perspectives in psychology. Susan Bordo (1987) used the structural psychology of Jean Piaget to argue that Cartesianism, usually taken as establishing the agenda for modern philosophy of knowledge, was in fact a "flight" from a "mother-world" of the Middle Ages to a masculine world of science. Using the post-Freudian object-relations theory of Nancy Chodorow, psychoanalyst Jane Flax argued that Descartes's rationalism was a form of pathology generated in masculine upbringing. Eva Kittay analyzed Plato's symptomatic use of the metaphor of philosophy as midwife. Perhaps most dazzling of all, the French analyst Luce Irigaray adapted Lacanian post-Freudian psychoanalysis to expose in philosophical texts a "phallomorphic" masculine imaginary.

Other radical critiques have drawn on the experiences of women of color. The Hispanic philosopher Maria Lugones used considerations of gender, class, and race in her interpretation of the uses and abuses of philosophical theory. The Indian-American critical theorist Gayatri Spivak called deconstruction to account for its own ethnocentricity. Gloria Anzaldua promoted a conceptual bilinguality that puts concepts into motion rather than establishes monolingual and rigid philosophical definitions.

Feminist philosophical readings of the history of philosophy have introduced new philosophical problematics. If the philosophical mind could not rise above its bodily, historical, social, or racial situation by way of reason or logic, then in what sense can there be a subject that has a sense of herself and can act free of social constraints and established meanings? To act effectively, knowledge is needed. The establishment of standards of rational justification and inference that define knowledge had been a mainstay of philosophical thought, but if standards of rationality are gender or class specific, then how is any justification possible?

As the French philosopher Michele LeDoeuff put it in her 1991 Hipparchia's Choice, *feminist philosophy was modeled, not after Kant's "island of truth," but rather after a great seaport, trading ground for foreign goods and practices.*

The question for feminists was not only academic but directly related to concerns about viable feminist practice. The energy with which it was discussed reflects feminist philosophy's characteristic mix of passionate practical concerns and abstract theory, of fact and normative judgment. Questions of the nature of mind, knowledge, or truth had been at the heart of philosophy since its inception, but much work of the canonical philosophers had been systematic, a striving for metaphysical grasps of ultimate determinants, ultimate structures of reality. Feminist philosophers, even as they looked for causes, conditions, or remedies, constantly returned to the concrete facts of women's lives and experience.

Feminist Philosophies of Subjectivity

A quiet explosion of feminist philosophy appeared in the 1980s and 1990s, scattered here and there in establishment journals and published in *Hypatia*, the flourishing journal of the new Society for Women in Philosophy. The self-identity and autonomy of those not in positions of power to form concepts and ideas was a frequent concern. On this question feminist philosophies of subjectivity tended to oscillate between two poles: promotion of an ideal of rational mental autonomy supposedly accessible to both men and women and the postmodern realization that our identities, beliefs, and desires are constructed in systems of thought and language beyond individual control. Much of feminist philosophy of mind and subjectivity between 1970 and 1990 was an attempt to negotiate a path between these two extreme positions. The first ruled out radical reforms in philosophical style, method, and content championed by many feminists; the second seemed to rule out autonomous understanding and action.

In her paper for *Discovering Reality,* Naomi Scheman expanded Wittgensteinian arguments against the possibility of a private language. Scheman gave a feminist interpretation of the tendency in modern philosophy to reify mental objects, citing men's interests in the privilege of science and the competitive capitalist free market, as well as child-rearing practices that leave parenting to women.

Drawing on phenomenological and existentialist approaches to the study of consciousness, Marilyn Frye in *The Politics of Reality* focused not on the private lives of subjects but on oppressive relations between subjects. Given that selves are always relationally defined, women and other inferiorized groups will have maimed identities. Frye brought the discussion of self and other, often highly abstract and illustrated with examples from a very limited range of experience, back to a fuller consideration of human identities and the reality of the actuality of unequal relations.

Similarly broadened were feminist treatments of the constitution of subjects in language and discourse popularized by French theorists such as Derrida and Foucault. Students of postmodernism such as Linda Alcoff and Rosemary Hennessey problematized the apparent political stasis inherent in the view that subjects have no individual autonomy or capability of self-definition, making of the very position of being oppressively defined by others a possible progressive stance. Sandra Bartky and Judith Butler expanded Foucault's genealogical methods to describe the discipline exercised on the female body by the beauty industry as well as the construction of sexual identity in scientific discourse and literature.

These lines of thought led feminist philosophers to wider consideration of personal identity, especially the identity of those stigmatized by sex or sexual preference or because of race, class, or ethnicity. Major catalysts were lesbian philosophers and women of color. In the discursive structures of elitist and mass culture, in the very grammar of spoken language, sex is a primary positioning factor. Philosophers such as Judith Butler, Sarah Hoagland, Claudia Card, and Monique Wittig problematized sexual identity and the assumption of heterosexuality that holds it in place, going past questions of surface logical grammar to meanings that lay behind uses of words.

Persons of color had been virtually nonexistent in professional philosophy in North America and Europe and remained a small minority throughout the 1980s and 1990s. A few, such as Maria Lugones, taught phi-

losophy and were active in the Society for Women in Philosophy; other women of color, not trained as professional philosophers—social theorist Bell Hooks, sociologist Patricia Hill Collins, critical theorist Gayatri Spivak—participated in feminist philosophical discussions that were increasingly interdisciplinary, introducing new ways of understanding the self and relations between selves and others not authorized in mainstream philosophy of exclusively European origin.

Mainstream philosophy in North America and Britain, as well as an important core of philosophy in France and Germany, tended to draw disciplinary boundaries around a specialty seen as threatened in an age of science. Feminist philosophers, concerned with existential problems of identity and human relation, forced those boundaries to draw back into philosophy insights from psychology, social theory, literary criticism, and other fields. As the French philosopher Michele LeDoeuff put it in her 1991 *Hipparchia's Choice,* feminist philosophy was modeled, not after Kant's "island of truth," but rather after a great seaport, trading ground for foreign goods and practices.

Feminist Epistemology

Women's exclusion from the production of knowledge in all fields had long been of concern to feminists. The limited success of equal-opportunity and fair-employment politics to enlist women in science, technology, economics, and other fields noted for the rigor and rationality of their methodologies posed for feminist philosophers a deeper question about the nature of, and access to, knowledge. Again, the masculinity of rationality was in question. Is knowledge as designed by men—currently exemplified by empirical physicalist science—unsuited to the feminine mind? More important, is knowledge as it has been designed by men knowledge at all?

The question of distinguishing what is knowledge from mere opinion was posed by Plato as a founding question of philosophy. Again, considerations of gender and interlocking considerations of economic and racial privilege has led to distinctive and destabilizing lines of feminist epistemological thought. Of foremost interest, as it was for most philosophers in the modern period, is the status of science. A number of nonfeminist studies of changing paradigms in the history of science, such as Thomas Kuhn's *The Structure of Scientific Revolutions* (1970), had opened the door to "sociological" studies of the origins and genesis of science, which seemed to relativize science's claim to truth. Feminist studies in the history of science—for example, those by Carolyn Merchant (1980) and the theoretical biologist Evelyn Fox Keller (1985)—further noted the important role gender metaphors played in the seventeenth century's reconceptualization of nature and science.

Although the logic of empiricist models for the decisive verifiability or falsifiability of empirical theories was already undergoing revision by establishment philosophers such as Quine who questioned the possibility of reference to scientific objects independent of theory, feminist studies constituted a more radical undermining of the positivistic attempt to establish scientific truth as objective and value free. If the constitutive methods of science could be linked to race or gender, then no adherence to a logic that reflected only those methods could ensure objectivity. Instead, there was, as Susan Bordo put it, a "flight to objectivity" motivated by subjective drives and intentions and specific personal and political interests.

This radical questioning of the possibility of objectivity in science was treated with skepticism by some feminist philosophers who defended "feminist empiricism" as a rigorous attempt to apply the standards of "good science" to eliminate bias and unwarranted conclusions in science. Feminist standpoint epistemology, as developed by Hilary Rose, Nancy Hartsock, and Sandra Harding, was another alternative, especially in the social sciences. Originally modeled on the Marxist claim that philosophy reflects the interest of a particular class, feminist standpoint theories claimed that a different view of reality is possible when science is done from the perspective of women's lives and not from the perspective of male generals and captains of industry. In the social sciences, Sandra Harding (1991) suggested the cognitive value of a "strong" objectivity and a "strong" reflexivity in feminist science that takes its own starting position and interests into consideration. Lorraine Code (1991) accepted a degree of relativism, emphasizing the moral choice that needs to be made between different forms of knowledge. Helen Longino (1990) mapped out ways in which scientific objects are constituted in research projects as social knowledge that underlies what is considered supporting evidence for theories. In all of these cases the distinction commonly made by philosophers between "a context of justification" and "a context of discovery," a distinction that validates the possibility of an "internal" logicist history of science without reference to social context or gender, was called into question.

Equally in question was the possibility of a purely logical and ahistorical philosophical knowledge. A central concern of twentieth-century philosophers, both in the United States and Europe, had been to define the specific nature of philosophical knowledge. On the Continent Husserl argued that the historical lifeworld could be bracketed, allowing a generalized study of phenomenological essences constitutive of objectivity; in England analytic philosophers defended the possibility of a study of logical or grammatical structures that would produce a nonempirical knowledge different from that of the scientist. Feminist epistemologists, many of them cognizant of new postmodern and poststructuralist questioning of essence and form, blurred boundaries between philosophy and linguistics, philosophy and psychology, philosophy and sociology. Perhaps most challenging was their questioning of the objectivity of philosophers' pretension to a "God's eye" view of the truth.

Feminist Social Philosophy

Twentieth-century mainstream philosophy tended to focus on questions of knowledge and meaning, sidelining considerations of politics and social justice as conceivable applications of first principles but peripheral to the core of philosophy. Feminist studies of the social nature of scientific knowledge reintroduced social theory as philosophically central. Instead of establishing self-evident truth and deducing a politics from it, a procedure that feminists argued may only constitute blindness to background assumptions that frame first principles, feminist epistemologists such as Sandra Harding and Helen Longino understood the social as epistemologically prior.

One of the most significant innovations of feminist social philosophy was attention to the family. In the mainstream philosophical tradition the political had been defined in opposition to private life. The family for many male philosophers was a "state of nature" assumed in political theory but subject to biological law rather than to normative political judgment. Feminist philosophers such as Susan Okin (1989) have argued that a necessary condition for justice in public life is justice in the family. Again, feminist concerns for shared parenting, equal responsibility for housework, support for working mothers, and childcare introduced a new concreteness into philosophical discussions of social justice.

If the liberal tradition had neglected the family, so had Marxists. Although many feminists approved Marxism's extension of philosophical scrutiny to the economic sphere, in which women were disadvantaged even more than men, they also noted the continued restricted scope of the social as understood by Marxist philosophers. Much of the essential work done by women—housework, service work, clerical work—was not considered productive and so outside the engine of transformative materialist dialectics; in addition, Marx and Engels assumed a substratum of biological reproduction—birth, child rearing, sexuality—not subject to change or critical scrutiny. Feminist philosophers have been drawn to Marxism's critique of idealist ideology and to a materialist philosophy that takes the concrete facts of daily life as the primary reality, but they have done much conceptual work in adapting Marxist concepts and positions to feminist aims. Michelle Barrett, Anne Ferguson, Alison Jaggar, and Christine Delphy all developed versions of Marxism that reworked central Marxist concepts of production, alienation, and exploitation to accommodate the oppression of women.

An independent line of feminist philosophy of law developed with critical attention to prejudice to women in legal theory and practice.

Mainstream philosophers had also neglected sex. With a few exceptional treatments of love, since Plato sex had been the distraction from which the philosopher liberated his mind if not his body. One source for feminist critical work on sexuality was Foucault's historical studies of sexuality as a form of bodily discipline more intimately oppressive than laws or economic arrangements. With Foucault the very concept of the sexual as a natural fact of human life gave way to sexuality as constructed in variable discourses of power. In Foucault's account ultimate categories such as nature/society, public/private, body/mind shift in meaning with changes in institutional power. Jana Sawicki, Judith Butler, and others used Foucault as authority for a denaturalized sexuality subject to critical social judgment as well as to possible transformation.

Again, feminist philosophy was influenced by ideas and approaches outside philosophy. The poet Adrienne Rich's much-cited essay "Compulsory Heterosexuality and Lesbian Existence" introduced a socially enforced rather than "natural" heterosexuality. Nancy Chodorow's object-relations psychology laid out a social origin for differing masculine and feminine approaches to intimacy. The cultural and ethnic variety of African-American sexual and family experience, as described by social theorists such as Angela Davis, Patricia Hill Collins, and Bell Hooks, inspired new social models.

Lines of thought developed within philosophy were used in original ways, as in Judith Butler's (1993) innovative use of speech-act theory to show the "performative" rather than biological nature of sexual identity or in Carole Pateman's (1988) re-formation of the social

contract, backbone of much liberal philosophy, as a "sexual contract"—a contract prior to more superficial political agreements theorized by democratic philosophers. Unnoticed by male philosophers, the sexual contract, Pateman argued, is enforced in practices such as prostitution, forced marriage, dating and courting customs, rape, and pornography.

An independent line of feminist philosophy of law developed with critical attention to prejudice to women in legal theory and practice. Susan Brownmiller examined concepts underlying rape laws. Catharine MacKinnon, the feminist legal scholar, critiqued the legal language devised by men and called attention to painful experiences of women for which there was no legal language. In a direct application of feminist philosophy, MacKinnon and other feminists were successful in winning legal recognition of sexual harassment as a legal offense and launched a movement to have pornography, described alternatively as free speech or as obscenity, redescribed in feminine terms as a systematic depiction of the degradation of women.

Inherent in MacKinnon's and other feminists' work was a philosophy of language. For MacKinnon language was not a structure to be mapped or the grammar of a form of life to be described but a shifting and changing instrument of understanding and response. Such a philosophy of language exemplifies visionary hope for a common language and a society that responds to men and women.

A further extension of that possibility came in the philosophies of women such as Gloria Anzaldua and Maria Lugones. Hispanic, Asian, and African-American feminist philosophers emphasized the importance of travel between social worlds, of a culturally literate philosophy that did not insist on one method, conceptual scheme, logic, or language but that negotiated incommensurate social forms and idioms. Here the vision was less of a common language than it was of a multilingual internationalist philosophy in constant motion as concepts and perceptions clash and mix.

Feminist Values

Plato identified philosophy as concern about what is of value rather than what exists as fact. Feminist studies in philosophical epistemology and psychology indicate that no knowledge is free of considerations of value. Intermingled even in the factual sciences are considerations of what is desirable in appearance, conduct, character, and social and economic arrangements. Feminist philosophers, however, showed little interest in developing an axiology or general theory of value that would underlie judgments in morals, aesthetics, and politics.

Instead, what emerged were networks of interlocking, broadly based concerns about the quality of human life in ethics, art, relations with nature, and life-styles.

In moral philosophy the social psychologist Carol Gilligan's researches into an alternative feminine voice in ethics cleared the way for new paradigms such as Nel Nodding's ethics of care and Sara Ruddick's maternal ethics. Problems of living within as well as separated from discriminatory society were addressed in Sara Hoagland's *Lesbian Ethics*. Annette Baier reunited moral passion and critical judgment in a nonfoundational feminist Humean ethics. Applied ethics was of particular interest to feminist philosophers, especially in medical practice, reproductive technologies, pedagogy, and animal rights. Feminist work in these areas did not simply apply established theories such as deontology or utilitarianism to new issues, as did much mainstream work in applied ethics, but, consistent with its mingling of the practical and theoretical, feminist philosophy tended to draw out from ethical situations new ways of conceiving value.

Feminists were also critical of mainstream aesthetics, with its historical beginnings in eighteenth-century elitist and Eurocentric definitions of fine art. Aestheticians such as Hilde Hein, Patricia Mills, Estella Lauter, and Heide Gottner-Abendroth blurred the line between craft or folk art and fine art, critiqued the objectification of women's bodies in art, took popular culture seriously as a determinant of taste, and developed original concepts of creativity, beauty, and artistic intention.

Many feminist philosophical concerns—the historical constitution of knowledge, the justice of social arrangements, the ethics of conduct, the critique of patriarchal religions, and the experience of beauty in nature—were linked to work identified as ecofeminist. Susan Griffin's (1978) critical examination of concepts of femininity, science, nature, the body, and God in the context of a poetic descriptive account of women's and men's experience opened lines of questioning that both converged with and diverged from developing theoretical perspectives in environmental, animal rights, and peace movements. Collections of papers followed (Diamond, 1990) that integrated work in feminist philosophy of knowledge, ethics, aesthetics, and society.

Twentieth-century philosophy in both the United States and Europe had tended to become increasingly academic, professionalized, and concerned with defending its own identity. Feminist philosophy, in contrast, has defined itself as interdisciplinary, has insisted on historical understanding, and has mingled theory with the personal and political, reconceiving philosophy as a humane inquiry into issues of human concern common to all sexes, races, and cultures.

[See also *African Philosophy; Anscombe, Elizabeth; Applied Ethics; Aristotle; Critical Theory; Deconstruction; Deontological Ethics; Derrida, Jacques; Descartes, René; Feminist Ethics; Feminist Social and Political Philosophy; Foucault, Michel; Habermas, Jürgen; Hobbes, Thomas; Husserl, Edmund; Kuhn, Thomas; Liberation Theology; Locke, John; Marx, Karl; Marxism; Meaning; Mill, John Stuart; Naturalized Epistemology; Personal Identity; Philosophy; Philosophy of Language; Philosophy of Mind; Plato; Postmodernism; Quine, Willard Van Orman; Rationality; Rawls, John; Rousseau, Jean-Jacques; Truth; Wollstonecraft, Mary.*]

BIBLIOGRAPHY

Overviews of Feminist Philosophy

Nye, A. *Feminist Theory and the Philosophies of Man.* New York, 1989.

———. *Philosophy and Feminism: At the Border.* New York, 1995.

Tong, R. *Feminist Thought.* Boulder, CO, 1989.

Representative Collections of Papers in Feminist Philosophy

Antony, L., and L. Nelson, eds. *A Mind of One's Own: Feminist Essays on Reason and Objectivity.* Boulder, CO, 1993.

Garry, A., and M. Pearsall, eds. *Women, Knowledge, and Reality.* Boston, 1989.

Harding, S., and M. Hintikka. *Discovering Reality.* Dordrecht, 1983.

Nicholson, L., ed. *Feminism/Postmodernism.* New York, 1990.

Feminist Philosophy of Subjectivity

Anzaldua, G. *Making Face Making Soul-Hacienda: Creative and Critical Perspectives by Women of Color.* San Francisco, 1990.

Bartky, S. *Femininity and Domination: Studies in the Phenomenology of Oppression.* New York, 1990.

Butler, J. *Bodies that Matter.* New York, 1993.

Fry, M. *The Politics of Reality.* Trumansburg, NY, 1983.

Feminist Epistemology

Bordo, S. *The Flight to Objectivity.* Albany, NY, 1987.

Code, L. *What Can She Know: Feminist Theory and the Construction of Knowledge.* Ithaca, NY, 1991.

Harding, S. *Whose Science? Whose Knowledge? Thinking from Women's Lives.* Ithaca, NY, 1991.

Keller, E. F. *Reflections on Gender and Science.* New Haven, 1985.

Longino, H. *Science as Social Knowledge: Values and Objectivity in Scientific Inquiry.* Princeton, NJ, 1990.

Merchant, C. *The Death of Nature: Women, Ecology, and the Scientific Revolution.* San Francisco, 1980.

Social Philosophy

Fraser, N. *Unruly Practices: Power, Discourse, and Gender in Contemporary Social Theory.* Minneapolis, 1989.

Jaggar, A. *Feminist Politics and Human Nature.* Totowa, NJ, 1983.

LeDoeuff, M. *Hipparchia's Choice.* Oxford, 1989.

Okin, S. *Justice, Gender, and the Family.* Princeton, NJ, 1989.

Pateman, C. *The Sexual Contract.* Stanford, 1988.

MacKinnon, C. *Feminism Unmodified.* Cambridge, 1987.

Feminist Values

Card, C., ed. *Feminist Ethics.* Lawrence, KS, 1991.

Diamond, I., and G. Orenstein, eds. *Reweaving the World.* San Francisco, 1990.

Ecker, G., ed. *Feminist Aesthetics.* Boston, 1986.

Griffin, S. *Women and Nature.* New York, 1978.

Held, V. *Feminist Morality: Transforming Culture, Society, and Politics.* Chicago, 1993.

Hoagland, S. *Lesbian Ethics. Towards a New Value.* Palo, 1988.

Noddings, N. *Caring: A Feminist Approach to Ethics and Education.* Berkeley, 1984.

Ruddick, S. *Maternal Thinking.* Boston, 1989.

— ANDREA NYE

FEMINIST SOCIAL AND POLITICAL PHILOSOPHY

Feminism recognizes gender structures as fundamental to virtually all societies; it is committed to the normative equality of women and rejects the view that the inferior position of women is inevitable. Feminism does not seek to replace domination by men with domination by women, but to overcome domination. Some feminists argue that gender is the most fundamental form of domination, underlying such other forms as racial, class, and ethnic domination.

The work of feminists

dealing with society and politics

is often described in terms of such categories

as liberal feminism, socialist feminism,

and radical feminism.

To restructure something as fundamental and pervasive as the gender structure of society is usually seen by feminists as revolutionary. It is a revolution thought to be taking place in consciousness and culture as well as in the arenas of political power, legal decision, and economic activity. Most feminists hold that this revolution is well underway but is subject to much resistance and many reverses. Feminist social and political philosophy has developed feminist critiques of traditional social and political philosophy and is rethinking social and political theory and practice from a feminist point of view.

Categories of Feminist Social and Political Philosophy

The work of feminists dealing with society and politics is often described in terms of such categories as liberal feminism, socialist feminism, and radical feminism. The views expressed within these categories often overlap, but arguments for them tend to have developed out of different traditions and to address different problems.

All three approaches have recognized the need to concern themselves with racial and class diversity and with global and environmental problems.

In the United States liberal feminism developed in the late 1960s with the awareness that the liberal principles of freedom and equality proclaimed by democratic political theory and such foundational documents as the U.S. Declaration of Independence and the French Declaration of the Rights of Man were not being applied to women. Liberal feminists pressed for increased representation of women in government and elsewhere and an end to legal and other gender inequalities. They called for equal opportunities for women in occupations previously closed to or prejudiced against women. Liberal feminists demanded an end to sexual double standards and demanded that women have rights to control their own reproduction, hence that legal prohibitions against abortion be ended. The implications of equality for family structures were thought to require that men share responsibility for childcare and housework, and women for obtaining income; some thought this would require a fundamental restructuring of capitalism.

Socialist feminism developed out of the Marxist tradition and saw the need for women to overcome the oppressions of both class and gender. Socialist feminists saw capitalism as deeply implicated in the oppression of women. Equal opportunities alone would not liberate women unable to make use of such opportunities, and the disempowerment women suffered was often of a kind not addressed by the liberal agenda. Socialist feminists went far beyond Marxism in seeing women as oppressed, not only by economic dependence, but also by such factors as the division of labor within the household and in characteristic relations in which women provide more emotional support for men than men provide for women. Concepts such as alienation were adapted to analyze the ways in which women are alienated as women—for instance, from their bodies, constantly under male sexual scrutiny—not only as workers or nonworkers under capitalism. In general, whereas liberal feminism tends to take capitalism as a given economic system in need of reform, socialist feminism tends to think capitalism must be replaced.

Radical feminism has fewer roots in established traditions of political and social philosophy. Some radical feminists have been influenced by anarchist thought; others have asserted that feminism must build only on feminism itself, not on any of the male-dominated social or political theories of the past or present. Radical feminism has often seen sexuality, rather than political inequality or the economic system, as central to the oppression of women. Many radical feminists argue that male sexuality has been constructed in conjunction with the domination of women, and often with violence against women. They see pornography and domestic violence as highly important contributors to male domination and female disempowerment. Some radical feminists argue for separatism for women, advocating that women form cultural and other communities of their own. Many feminists argue that women should evaluate their work by the standards of other women rather than seek the approval of male elites. Lesbian separatism is a strand of radical feminism. Lesbian feminism has developed critiques of mainstream feminism on sexuality, family structure, ethics, strategies for liberation, and the concept of woman.

All branches of feminist social and political philosophy deplore discrimination against women of color, but work by black and Latina feminists has gone beyond countering discrimination. It offers distinctive perspectives and insights on such issues as domination, race and gender identity, and social knowledge.

Feminists in the non-Western world have argued for the construction of their own theories and interpretations of what feminism implies for their often very different cultures and circumstances. Western formulations of demands for equality are not always helpful. Non-Western feminists face the task of empowering women within their own cultures without accepting cultural nationalisms that see preserving non-Western cultures as requiring the maintenance of norms and practices that disempower women. Non-Western feminists often urge Western feminists to consider how Western economic and military policies and colonialist attitudes harm non-Western women.

Feminist Reconceptualizations

Attention has been paid by feminist theorists to many specific social and political issues such as affirmative action remedies for discrimination; strategies to achieve equal pay and advancement for women; reproductive choice, including abortion; contracted motherhood and its risks for the further exploitation of women; the double burdens of women of color; rape and domestic violence; pornography, prostitution, and the formation of male sexuality; compulsory heterosexuality and injustices toward lesbians; and sexual harassment, especially in the workplace.

In addition, feminists have recognized the need for thoroughgoing reconceptualizations of many of the fundamental concepts of social and political thought. These reconceptualizations have in turn deeply affected the development of feminist social and political philosophy. Among such reconceptualizations are the following.

THE DISTINCTION BETWEEN PUBLIC AND PRIVATE. Feminists from all approaches and fields have questioned traditional distinctions between public and private, noting that personal relations between women and men are deeply affected by the greater social, economic, and political power of men in the public sphere. Public law and policy on everything from marriage regulations, to restrictions on abortion, to policies that fail to provide social support for childcare and fail to protect women from domestic violence and rape all structure women's private lives. From a feminist perspective what had been thought to belong to a private sphere beyond politics is seen instead to be deeply embedded in the power relationships of the political. The early feminist slogan "the personal is political" reflects this insight. But the implications are even deeper than at first realized. Not only should such considerations as equality and self-determination be applied to the personal realm and to women, but when the concerns of women are taken as seriously as the concerns of men, society and politics themselves may require almost total restructuring. For instance, concern for the upbringing and education of children, and protection of children and women from violence and abuse, would have to be accorded central rather than peripheral importance in how society would be structured.

THE CONCEPT OF PERSON. In a wide range of areas from psychology and moral development to law and sociology feminists have recognized the need for a more satisfactory concept of the person than those previously dominant. Many feminists criticize the liberal political concept of the autonomous, atomic, individual as a construct reflective of a male point of view that artificially ignores human relatedness and interdependence. But many feminists are also critical of communitarian views of persons in which women are defined by their roles in the practices and traditions of their communities. Feminist views recognize that a person is partly constituted by her relations with others—for instance with her parents, her friends and lovers or spouse, her children; at the same time such a person has the capacity to restructure radically her relations with others and to her community. When persons are seen in this light, the social and political structures thought appropriate for such persons will be different from traditional ones. Instead of government and law being built to serve the self-interest of individuals, as advocated by liberal political theory, government may be evaluated in terms of the human relationships it reflects or affects. Relationships of trust and caring will be seen as relevant to political life as well as to personal life. But persons will not be the communal members of much communitarian and some conservative thought; they will be continually changing persons shaping their own development in relationships with others.

REQUIREMENTS FOR EQUALITY. An unresolved debate among feminists has centered on how to interpret what equality requires. It is recognized that gender-blind categories that ignore the ways women differ from men—for instance, that only women get pregnant—can put women at a serious disadvantage in provisions such as those for health care and family leave. On the other hand feminists often argue that traditional distinctions between women and men used in law and social norms to uphold the subordination of women must be ended. Thus, when the law specifies, as it has, that the husband has a right to decide where a couple will live, gender becomes, to feminists, a "suspect category," and a commitment to equality requires that it not be used. Some feminists see a solution in seeking equally advantageous outcomes for women and men. Then, recognizing gender when it contributes to such an outcome is appropriate, but when gender distinctions lead to disadvantages for women, they should not be made.

Traditional social and political theory has been criticized as inadequate for dealing with issues of race and culture. Feminists have attended to inequalities among women and to differences of history, experience, and outlook among women of different racial or ethnic groups and different nations and regions of the world. Feminists have argued that differences between women and men and between members of different racial or cultural groups can be noted and appreciated without supposing that to see persons as different is to see some as superior to others. Difference need not imply hierarchy; equality need not require sameness. At the same time many feminists have argued that to reject the concept of "woman" entirely, on the grounds that there is no "essential" woman, only many different women, can undermine the feminist project itself. Arguments for the equality of women—whatever the differences between them—continually need to be reaffirmed.

FREEDOM AND OPPRESSION. Liberal political theory has seen freedom in negative terms, as freedom from hindrance or interference. It has recommended a scheme of rights in which individuals are as free as possible from interference by others and by government, consistent with similar freedom for all others. Marxists have criticized this conception of freedom as failing to consider the material resources needed for a human being to be a free agent: being free to starve or freeze is not really being free to act. Feminists usually share with Marxists a recognition that to be free one must have

the capacity to act freely, as well as to be free from interference, but feminists are aware of a wide range of interferences and incapacitations to which neither liberals nor Marxists have attended.

Socialist feminism developed out of the Marxist tradition and saw the need for women to overcome the oppressions of both class and gender.

The liberation of women requires an end to oppressive state interferences with women's reproductive choices and to oppressive domestic situations where women are subject to abuse; and it requires economic independence for women through employment or some equivalent such as family allowances. It also requires the psychological empowerment of women to overcome traditional practices of disregarding and trivializing women and their views and of seeing women as sexual objects and exploitable caregivers.

THE VALUE OF CARE IN POLITICAL LIFE. Much feminist work has been done in ethics and moral theory. Care and nurturing, empathy and compassion, and the cultivation of human relatedness have been recognized as important moral values and concerns. The emphasis on justice and abstract rules in dominant moral theories such as Kantian ethics and utilitarianism have been thought by many feminists to provide a distorted view of morality as a whole. Though justice and rules may be necessary for political and legal theory and organization, many feminists have found such rationalistic and individualistic approaches deficient for much of morality. As feminists have developed alternative, more satisfactory views, the term 'ethics of care' has often been used to indicate what many take to be a central concern.

Some feminists think an adequate feminist ethic can be based on care rather than on justice. Others think these and other values must be integrated into a feminist ethic. With the questioning of the distinction between public and private has come a realization that traditional efforts to associate care with the household and the supposedly "natural" mothering done by women, and to associate justice with men and public life, are misguided. Women need justice and fairness in the household and in how the tasks of caring labor are divided; women and children need justice and protection against violence in the private sphere. At the same time public policies, law, and international affairs need to be much more influenced than they have been by feminist values of care and concern. For instance, the way children and old people are cared for should be a social concern, not something for which government takes no responsibility. The ways bureaucracies might deal with persons in caring ways that foster self-determination, rather than with insensitive disregard, is an important public issue. And how nations can come to trust one another so that more resources can be devoted to meeting people's needs and fewer wasted on armaments should be an important concern of international affairs.

Feminists often believe that feminist perspectives and values should influence how we deal with global and environmental problems: we should recognize the responsibilities of persons and nations to care about and for the victims of famine, genocide, armed conflict, and exploitation, to take needed measures to prevent these, and to take proper care of the environment to be inhabited by future generations.

[See also Abortion; Affirmative Action; Deontological Ethics; Feminist Ethics; Feminist Philosophy; Justice; Liberalism; Marxism; Nationalism and International Relations; Racism; Violence.]

BIBLIOGRAPHY

Bartky, S. L. Femininity and Domination: Studies in the Phenomenology of Oppression. New York, 1990.

Bartlett, K. T., and R. Kennedy, eds. Feminist Legal Theory: Readings in Law and Gender. Boulder, CO, 1991.

Benhabib, S. Situating the Self: Gender, Community, and Postmodernism in Contemporary Ethics. New York, 1992.

Collins, P. H. Black Feminist Thought: Knowledge, Consciousness, and the Politics of Empowerment. Boston, 1990.

Eisenstein, Z. The Radical Future of Liberal Feminism. New York, 1981.

Ferguson, A. Blood at the Root: Motherhood, Sexuality, and Male Domination. London, 1989.

Fraser, N. Unruly Practices: Power, Discourse, and Gender in Contemporary Social Theory. Minneapolis, 1989.

Friedman, M. What Are Friends For?: Feminist Perspectives on Personal Relations and Moral Theory. Ithaca, NY, 1993.

Gould, C. C., ed. Beyond Domination: New Perspectives on Women and Philosophy. Totowa, NJ, 1984.

Hartsock, N. C. M. Money, Sex, and Power: Toward a Feminist Historical Materialism. New York, 1983.

Held, V. Feminist Morality: Transforming Culture, Society, and Politics. Chicago, 1993.

Jaggar, A. M. Feminist Politics and Human Nature. Totowa, NJ, 1983.

Lugones, M. C., and E. V. Spelman. "Have We Got a Theory for You! Feminist Theory, Cultural Imperialism, and the Demand for 'The Woman's Voice,' " Women's Studies International Forum (Hypatia), Vol. 6 (1983), 573–81.

MacKinnon, C. A. Toward a Feminist Theory of the State. Cambridge, MA, 1987.

Okin, S. M. Justice, Gender, and the Family. New York, 1989.

Ruddick, S. Maternal Thinking: Toward a Politics of Peace. Boston, 1989.

Shanley, M. L., and C. Pateman, eds. Feminist Interpretation and Political Theory. University Park, PA, 1991.

Tong, R. Feminine and Feminist Ethics. Belmont, CA, 1993.

Tronto, J. C. Moral Boundaries: A Political Argument for an Ethic of Care. New York, 1993.

Young, I. M. Justice and the Politics of Difference. Princeton, 1990.

— VIRGINIA HELD

FICTIONALISM, MATHEMATICAL

Mathematical fictionalism is the view that mathematical theories are strictly speaking false but that it is often useful to pretend they are true. It thus combines a skeptical rejection of mathematical theories with the recommendation that we should embrace them as useful fictions.

Mathematical fictionalism combines a skeptical rejection of mathematical theories with the recommendation that we should embrace them as useful fictions.

Fictionalists argue that their view is preferable to both realist and reductionist philosophies of mathematics. Mathematical realists hold that mathematical objects such as numbers and sets really exist, though not in the world of space and time. The central problem facing mathematical realism is to explain how we can have knowledge of these mathematical objects, given that our normal senses give us no access to them. Fictionalists, however, simply sidestep this difficulty by denying that we have any knowledge of mathematical objects to start with.

Mathematical reductionists offer a different solution to the problem of mathematical knowledge. They argue that it is wrong to read mathematics as making claims about objects outside space and time in the first place. Versions of reductionism are that mathematics is about marks on paper, or that it consists of hypothetical claims about what follows from axions, or that it simply abbreviates logical truths. Fictionalists make the same objection to all these versions of reductionism. They argue that they misrepresent the real meaning of mathematical claims. Reductionist views may make mathematical claims knowable, but only by changing what mathematicians say. Fictionalists admit that they too recommend a change in normal mathematical practice, namely that we should stop believing mathematical claims. But they point out that it is far easier to change our attitude to mathematics than to change its content.

One obvious objection to fictionalism is that natural science as well as mathematics seem to commit us to mathematical objects. Does this mean that fictionalists have to disbelieve natural science, along with mathematics? Hartry Field addresses this and other objections to fictionalism in his influential *Science without Numbers* (1980). In Field's view natural science's commitment to mathematical objects is relatively superficial. He argues that most familiar scientific theories can be given "nominalistic" reformulations that are free of reference to mathematical objects and, moreover, yield superior explanations of the empirical data.

Field allows that it is convenient for scientific reasoning to be able to appeal to mathematical objects and associated mathematical theories. This is why he thinks mathematics is a useful fiction. But he insists that this usefulness is no reason to believe mathematics is true. This leaves him with a problem, however. If mathematics is not true, why should we trust the inferences it underpins? Field's answer is that it is nevertheless "conservative," in the sense that any inferential moves it allows between nominalist claims could in principle, though not in practice, be made by logic alone.

There are a number of technical objections to Field's views. Critics have complained that his nominalized science in effect still requires a continuum of space-time points and elements of higher-order logic. How far this reduces the attraction of fictionalism is a matter for debate. But in any case fictionalism poses a serious challenge to more traditional positions in the philosophy of mathematics.

[See also Mathematical Logic.]

BIBLIOGRAPHY

Field, H. *Science without Numbers.* Oxford, 1980. The original statement of the fictionalist point of view.
———. *Realism, Mathematics, and Modality.* Oxford, 1989. Field develops his position and responds to criticisms.
Irvine, A., ed. *Physicalism in Mathematics.* Dordrecht, 1990. Contains a number of articles on fictionalism.
Papineau, D. "Mathematics and Other Non-natural Subjects," in *Philosophical Naturalism* (Oxford, 1993). Defends fictionalism against competing views.

— DAVID PAPINEAU

FOLK PSYCHOLOGY

In everyday commerce with our fellows all of us attribute propositional attitudes—beliefs, desires, intentions, and the like—to aid in explaining and predicting behavior. These attitudes possess intentional mental content; we attribute the belief that *p* and the desire that *q*. When, for example, Achilles returns to battle, we may explain his action so: Achilles wants to avenge the death of Patroklos, and he believes that killing Hektor, and so reentering the fray, is the best way to accomplish this. This commonsense framework of intentional description, explanation, and prediction has come to be termed *folk psychology.* (Strictly speaking, *folk psychology* applies both to nonintentional qualitative as well as to intentional psychological phenomena. Philosophers have concentrated their attention upon folk intentional psychology.) The chief philosophical issues are engaged when we turn to various efforts to characterize the nature and status of folk psychological explanation.

The most influential view (in part, at least, the result of the dominance of functionalist accounts of the mental) is that folk psychology constitutes an empirical theory of mind and behavior (Churchland, 1981; Sellars, 1963). According to this "theory-theory" (Morton, 1980), we make use of an implicit theory when offering folk psychological explanations. *Belief, desire, intention,* and the like are theoretical terms whose meaning and reference are secured by their place in a network of implicit folk psychological laws. One such law might be stated as follows: If *A* desires or intends that *v* and believes that *k* is necessary for *v*, then, *ceteris paribus, A* tries to bring it about that *k*. The point is, however, quite general. Our ability to offer folk psychological explanations is a matter of our drawing upon a store of commonsense laws that connect behavior, internal states, and stimuli.

Much of the discussion of folk psychology has focused upon the consequences of the theory-theory. One immediate consequence is that folk psychology might be false in the way that any empirical theory might be false. Vindicationists argue that folk psychology is very likely a correct theory of mind and behavior. Eliminativists argue that folk psychology is very plausibly a false theory. In its role as a causal explanatory theory, folk psychology awaits replacement by a neurological—or, at least, a non-intentional—account of behavior (Stich, 1983).

The eliminativist-vindicationist debate hinges upon the anticipated relationship between folk psychological explanation and scientific psychological explanation. Since both folk psychology and a scientific psychology offer causal explanations of what is intuitively the same class of explananda, if we are to regard folk psychology as, by and large, a correct theory, we are presumably committed to thinking that the cognitive sciences will, in some way, serve to vindicate the explanations of folk psychology (Kim, 1989).

A notable advocate of this brand of vindicationism. Jerry Fodor, has argued that a scientific psychology will count as vindicating folk psychology just in case it postulates states that (1) are semantically evaluable; (2) have causal powers; and (3) are found to conform to the tacit laws of folk psychology (Fodor, 1987). Each of these has given rise to eliminativist complaint.

Insofar as intentional content figures essentially in folk psychological explanation, it may seem quick to demonstrate that such explanations are not respectable:

1. The causes of behavior supervene upon the current, internal, physical states of the organism.
2. Intentional mental content does not supervene upon such states.
3. The science of psychology is concerned to discover the causes of behavior.
4. Therefore, psychology will not trade in the intentional idiom.

If the argument is correct, folk psychological explanation would be deeply suspect because intentional mental content would be irrelevant to the causal explanation of behavior. The argument is, however, suspect on many fronts. First, one might dispute the sense of behavior in (1) and with it the notion that respectable explanation must be "individualistic" (Burge, 1986). Second, one might grant that while truth-evaluable content is "wide" and so fails to supervene upon states of the individual, there is a kind of content—"narrow" content—that respects individualist scruples.

Content-based objections such as the above focus upon the puzzling status of intentional properties in a physical universe; and many theorists point to the allegedly irreducible nature of intentional mental content as a way of undermining the integrity of folk psychology (Churchland, 1986). Another family of eliminativist worries focuses upon matters structural. It is claimed that if certain connectionist models of our cognitive architecture are correct, then there will literally be no states or events that play the causal role that intentional mental states play in folk psychology. Folk psychology appears committed to the view that intentional mental states are "functionally discrete" internal states possessed of a specific causal syndrome (Ramsey, Stich, & Garon, 1991). Yet on connectionist models there are no such discrete internal states with the causal roles that belief, desire, and so forth are presumed to play.

If these objections give some taste of the eliminativist assault, they serve as well to highlight an assumption held by many vindicationists and eliminativists alike: folk psychology possesses (in Fodor's terminology) theoretical "depth" (1987, p. 6). It posits unobservable states and events in aid of the explanation of observed phenomena. The explanations of folk psychology are, then, structurally informative insofar as they offer information about the structure of causal relations that hold between behavior, stimuli, and unobservable internal states. Only on such a supposition is it plausible

to suggest that folk psychology will go the way of caloric and phlogiston. And this is why the vindicationist holds that the survival of folk psychology demands that there be a scientific level of description of our cognitive architecture that mirrors the folk psychological one.

Much hinges upon the resolution of this dispute. If the eliminativist is correct, there are no beliefs and desires and no actions. It is, for example, just false that human beings very often intend to do what they most desire. Nothing will remain of our conception of ourselves as deliberators and actors. This seems incredible, but of course the eliminativist will answer that this is but another case in which what has appeared patently obvious to folk turns out to be radically false.

Even so, it is argued that, more than incredible, eliminativism is self-refuting or pragmatically incoherent (Baker, 1987). The charge here is not that eliminativism is self-contradictory or internally inconsistent. Rather, the claim is that there is no perspective from which the doctrine can be coherently put forth. For if eliminativism is true, there are no actions. Yet the eliminativist asserts the truth of eliminativism, and assertion is certainly an action. Moreover, the eliminativist presumably asserts eliminativism because he takes it to be true, because he takes it to be well-supported by the available evidence. But what sense can be made of justification or even truth without the intentional framework of folk psychology? This argument is sometimes developed in concert with the suggestion that folk psychological principles are, not contingent regularities, but normative principles that are true a priori.

Whatever the merits of the foregoing line of argument, the prima facie oddity that attaches to radical eliminativism suggests that while it is one thing to assert that intentional mental states will not figure in the ontology of some ideal cognitive science, it is quite another to assert that there are, really, no intentional mental states. In hopes of saving the folk psychological phenomena, an alternative conception of the nature of folk psychology rejects the assumption that folk psychology does offer such informative causal explanations. Rather, folk psychological explanations are silent about the internal mechanisms and processes of cognition and behavior. Since its explanations are not informative enough to be in competition with the cognitive sciences, folk psychology can be understood to be insulated from scientific advances.

In an influential series of papers, Daniel Dennett (1987) advocates such a view. According to him, folk psychological explanation and prediction proceed on the assumption of rationality. When we predict what an agent will do, we ask what it would be rational to do given the subject's beliefs and desires. And, to be an intentional system, to have beliefs truly attributable to one, is just to be a system whose behavior is so predictable. Folk psychological description, then, does not aim at the description of internal mental processes. And, while an empirically informative psychology will reject the intentional idiom, folk psychological explanation is adequate in its own preserve. Even so, it is not easy to see how this brand of instrumentalism about the intentional makes folk psychology anything more than a *façon de parler*.

The most influential view

is that folk psychology constitutes

an empirical theory of mind and behavior.

Other philosophers who offer versions of this suggestion emphasize that many of the folk explanations we regard as true bear no easy relation to science (Chastain, 1988; Horgan & Graham, 1991; Horgan & Woodward, 1985). We may, for example, explain why Ajax slipped by pointing out that the ground was slimy. In such a case we are in command of a folk law to the effect that slimy surfaces are apt to produce slippings. But sliminess and slipperiness are certainly not scientific kinds—nothing like them will figure in the explanations of science. Still, it would be mad to suggest the explanation is false or that there are no slippery or slimy things; nor need we be instrumentalist about such things.

Such explanations can survive most any developments in the sciences. Moreover, we are likely to regard a more fundamental scientific account as a way of spelling out, and so vindicating, the folk slimy/slippery account. With such folk explanations all we demand is that there be some more basic scientific account of the processes we describe in terms of "slimy" and "slippery." The source of the robustness of such explanations is precisely their relative uninformativeness. Indeed, we folk recognize the fact that sliminess and slipperiness don't play any deep or informative role in the causal explanations in which they figure. Rather, their role would appear to be of the following nature: there is something about the substance picked out as "slimy" that causes events picked out as "slippings." And so, just by virtue of the fact that they offer scant information about the relevant causal processes, they are insulated from any threat of elimination posed by developments in the sciences.

Finally, it is urged that we adopt a similar view of the status of folk psychology. Thus, just as there are slimy things, there are beliefs and desires; and just as it is true that Ajax slipped because the ground was slimy, so it is true that Achilles behaved so because he believed and desired as he did. It should nonetheless be emphasized that this appealing conclusion has been secured at some considerable price: folk psychological explanations, though serviceable for everyday purposes, are about as uninformative and superficial as causal explanations can be. It is not at all clear that, for example, our conception of ourselves as reasoners—a conception that appears to demand a certain view of the nature of mental processes—can withstand so deflationary a reading. One might well conclude that this gives to the eliminativist everything but what she wants.

In broad terms, then, the theory-theory has one of two results. First, folk psychology is an informative account of mind and behavior but one that is gravely at risk of elimination; second, folk psychology is extraordinarily unlikely to be displaced, but this because it is an exceedingly uninformative theory.

Perhaps what demands reevaluation is the theory-theory itself. According to that view our mastery of the psychological vocabulary as well as our capacity to explain and to predict are grounded in a command of psychological laws. But, it is argued that no one has succeeded in stating such laws in an adequate fashion and that, in any case, the information necessary for the construction of such laws is far beyond the ken of folk (Goldman, 1993; Schiffer, 1991). After all, even very young children have an impressive grip upon the folk psychological framework. Moreover, the theory-theory seems to result in a particularly strange account of the self-attribution of the propositional attitudes. Indeed, it has been alleged that the theory-theory results in troubling asymmetries between first and third personal folk psychologizing (Blackburn, 1992; Moran, 1994).

If we wish to deny that folk psychological explanation is founded upon theorizing, we will need another account. Robert Gordon (1986) and Alvin Goldman (1989) have resuscitated the view that our comprehension of others proceeds via simulation. In the effort to understand others we make adjustments for their cognitive and affective conditions and then, using these as inputs, allow our own psychological processes to run "offline." In prediction, the resulting simulated belief or intention is attributed to the subject.

Advocates of this account claim that simulation is a far simpler and more psychologically plausible account of our folk psychologizing. The verdict of developmental psychologists is, however, mixed (Harris, 1993;

Wellman, 1990). One benefit of simulation theoretic accounts is, nonetheless, clear: if folk psychology is not a theory it cannot be a false theory. On such a conception, the eliminativist worry cannot so much as be raised.

[See also Cognitive Science; Eliminativism; Rationality; Philosophy of Mind.]

BIBLIOGRAPHY

Baker, L. R. *Saving Belief.* Princeton, NJ, 1987.

Blackburn, S. "Theory, Observation, and Drama," *Mind and Language,* Vol. 7 (1992), 187–203.

Burge, T. "Individualism and Psychology," *Philosophical Review,* Vol. 45 (1986), 3–45.

Chastain, C. "Comments on Baker," in R. Grimm and D. Merrill, eds., *Contents of Thought* (Tucson, AZ, 1988).

Churchland, P. S. *Neurophilosophy.* Cambridge, MA, 1986.

Churchland, P. "Eliminative Materialism and the Propositional Attitudes," *Journal of Philosophy,* Vol. 78 (1981), 67–90.

Dennett, D. *The Intentional Stance.* Cambridge, MA, 1987.

Fodor, J. *Psychosemantics.* Cambridge, MA, 1987.

Goldman, A. "Interpretation Psychologized," *Mind and Language,* Vol. 4 (1989), 161–85.

———. "The Psychology of Folk Psychology," *Behavioral and Brain Sciences,* Vol. 16 (1993), 15–28.

Gordon, R. "Folk Psychology as Simulation," *Mind and Language,* Vol. 1 (1986), 158–71.

Harris, P. "From Simulation to Folk Psychology: The Case for Development," *Mind and Language,* Vol. 7 (1992), 120–44.

Horgan, T., and G. Graham. "In Defense of Southern Fundamentalism," *Philosophical Studies,* Vol. 62 (1991), 107–34.

Horgan, T., and J. Woodward. "Folk Psychology Is Here to Stay," *Philosophical Review,* Vol. 44 (1985), 197–226.

Kim, J. "Mechanism, Purpose, and Explanatory Exclusion," *Philosophical Perspectives,* Vol. 3 (1989), 77–108.

Morton, A. *Frames of Mind.* Oxford, 1980.

Ramsey, W., S. Stich, and J. Garon. "Connectionism, Eliminativism, and the Future of Folk Psychology," in J. Greenwood, ed., *The Future of Folk Psychology* (Cambridge, 1991).

Schiffer, S. "*Ceteris Paribus* Laws," *Mind,* Vol. 100 (1991), 1–17.

Sellars, W. "Empiricism and the Philosophy of Mind," in *Science, Perception, and Reality* (New York, 1963).

Stich, S. *From Folk Psychology to Cognitive Science.* Cambridge, MA, 1983.

Wellman, H. M. *The Child's Theory of Mind.* Cambridge, MA, 1990.

— DION SCOTT-KAKURES

FOUCAULT, MICHEL

Michel Foucault, French philosopher, historian, and social critic, was born in Poitiers in 1926. He studied at the Sorbonne, earning his licence de psychologie in 1950 and the diplôme de psycho-pathologie from the Université de Paris in 1952. He directed the Institut Français in Hamburg as well as the Institut de Philosophie at the Faculté des Lettres in the Université de Clermont-Ferrand. Foucault lectured widely at universities throughout the world, and he was awarded a chair at the Collège de France. He died in 1984.

Foucault's scholarly career is commonly divided into three fairly distinct periods. In his "early," archaeological writings Foucault investigated the internal relations that obtain between language and knowledge and the discursive practices within which both are produced. In the genealogical writings of his "middle" period he focused on the historical transformations and manifestations of power. In the ethical writings from his "late" period he turned his attention to the historical conditions that have collectively presided over the formation of the modern subject. By Foucault's own reckoning this periodization charts a shift, not in the guiding interest of his scholarly activity, but in his critical orientation to it. Throughout his career he sought to account for the emergence within modernity of the self-constituting subject, a being contingently endowed with a historically circumscribed complement of powers and potentialities.

The most significant development

in Foucault's thinking occurred in the late 1960s,

when he diverted his primary focus

from discursive practices to the power relations

that inform and sustain them.

The most significant development in Foucault's thinking occurred in the late 1960s, when he diverted his primary focus from discursive practices to the power relations that inform and sustain them. The defining characteristic of power is its capacity for "infinite displacement" within a complex network of discursive practices. All discourse is ultimately concerned with power, albeit in complicated, disguised ways. Because power can be effective only when it remains partially hidden, it always shelters itself within a discourse about something else. Power is both ubiquitous and capillary in its manifestations, and it announces its presence only as a diversion from its more central concerns.

In order to investigate hidden power relations, and to deliver a critique of concrete social practices, Foucault developed the method known as genealogy. By tracing the historical descent of authoritative discursive practices the genealogist is able to chart the shifting relationships between power and knowledge within the historical transformation of these practices. The genealogist can glimpse power only as it adjusts and reconfigures itself within the social and political relations it strategically inhabits, as it silently transforms institutions and discursive practices. Foucault was especially concerned to investigate the exclusionary power of discursive practices, including those responsible for the institutionalized definitions of madness, criminality, and sexual deviancy.

Foucault's turn to ethics comprised an extension of the development of his genealogical method. His contribution to ethics involved neither the articulation of a new moral theory nor the advocacy of an alternative to the signature techniques of bio-power. He was concerned rather to investigate the conditions under which particular subjects are formed and to expose the hidden power interests that are served by each type of subject. He consequently centered his ethical investigations on the process he called subjectivation, whereby human beings are gradually transformed into subjects invested with unique powers and limitations. Of specific concern to him, especially in his final writings, were the techniques of subjectivation deployed by bio-power, which organizes the resources of modern societies under the pretense of attending to the care of the species and the health of individual human beings.

Foucault's ethical period is marked by his rejection of the "repressive hypothesis," which maintains that power, in all of its manifestations, is strictly juridical and coercive. Foucault opposed this hypothesis with his own genealogy of the various transformations responsible for the emergence in the modern period of bio-power, which displaces its self-aggrandizing designs behind a numbing reverence for health and well-being. The success of the regimes devoted to the expansion of bio-power demonstrates that truth is, not the enemy of power, but its silent partner in a complex network of totalizing strategies.

Foucault's ethical investigations revealed that regimes of power can realize their ends only if human beings are transformed into productive subjects, invested with a limited capacity for self-legislation. Although he located in the dominant regimes of bio-power a masked impulse toward domination, he also acknowledged their productive, empowering roles in the formation of the modern subject. The subjects depicted in his later genealogies are not simply the unwitting products of clandestine discursive practices, for they are able to resist the totalization of power within its most ambitious and monolithic regimes. To expose the mobilization of power within mechanisms of transformation is to render it temporarily less effective and less dangerous. Power can neither be eradicated nor contained, but its inexorable tendency toward domination can often be neutralized within local regimes.

Foucault developed the method known as genealogy in order to investigate hidden power relations and critique concrete social practices. (Vanity Fair/Condé Nast Publications, Inc.)

Foucault never completed the ambitious genealogical agenda he set for himself. The guarded optimism conveyed by his final writings has been taken up by successor genealogists, and the articulation of a Foucaultian political position remains, for some, an ongoing project.

BIBLIOGRAPHY

Major Works by Foucault in English Translation

The Archaeology of Knowledge. Translated by Alan M. Sheridan Smith. New York, 1972.

The Order of Things: An Archaeology of the Human Sciences. Unidentified translation. New York, 1973.

Madness and Civilization: A History of Insanity in the Age of Reason. Translated by R. Howard. New York, 1973.

The Birth of the Clinic: An Archaeology of Medical Perception. Translated by A. M. Sheridan Smith. New York, 1975.

Language, Counter-Memory, Practice: Selected Essays and Interviews. Edited by D. Bouchard. Translated by D. Bouchard and S. Simon. Ithaca, NY, 1977.

Discipline and Punish: The Birth of the Prison. Translated by A. Sheridan. New York, 1979.

The History of Sexuality, Vol. 1, *An Introduction.* Translated by R. Hurley. New York, 1980.

Power/Knowledge: Selected Interviews and Other Writings 1972–1977. Edited by C. Gordon. Translated by C. Gordon, L. Marshall, J. Mepham, and K. Soper. New York, 1980.

The Foucault Reader. Edited by P. Rabinow. New York, 1984.

The History of Sexuality, Vol. 2, *The Use of Pleasure.* Translated by R. Hurley. New York, 1985.

The History of Sexuality, Vol. 3, *The Care of the Self.* Translated by R. Hurley. New York, 1986.

Politics, Philosophy, Culture: Interviews and Other Writings 1977–1984. Edited by L. D. Kritzman. Translated by A. Sheridan, et al. New York, 1988.

The Final Foucault. Edited by J. Bernauer and D. Rasmussen. Cambridge, MA, 1988.

Works on Foucault

Dreyfus, H. L., and P. Rabinow. *Michel Foucault: Beyond Structuralism and Hermeneutics,* 2d ed. Chicago, 1983.

Miller, J. *The Passion of Michel Foucault.* New York, 1993.

— DANIEL CONWAY

FREGE, GOTTLOB

By far the most important event for Frege scholarship that took place after 1967 was the publication of a volume containing all those of Frege's unpublished writings that had not been destroyed in the wartime bombing of Münster: the *Nachgelassene Schriften* (1969). This allowed a far clearer view of Frege's philosophical development than had been obtainable from his published writings alone. It was translated into English as *Posthumous Writings* (1979) and was followed by the publication of Frege's surviving correspondence in *Wissenschaftlicher Briefwechsel* (1976). The main items of this were translated in *Philosophical and Mathematical Correspondence* (1980).

In the Encyclopedia of 1967, the division of Frege's career into five periods was misjudged. It is better to recognize only three: from his earliest writings up to 1886 (the early period); from 1891 to July 1906 (the middle or mature period); and from August 1906 until his death in 1925. He published nothing in the years 1887–90, during which, by his own account, he was rethinking his logical doctrines. The early period, which includes the two masterpieces *Begriffsschrift* and *Grundlagen,* was one of rapid development. The middle period was introduced by the lecture "Function und Begriff," in which he expounded his new views in concise form, and includes the famous essays "Über Sinn und Bedeutung" and "Über Begriff und Gegenstand" of 1892 and both volumes of *Grundgesetze* (1893 and 1903). Its termination was marked by Frege's realization that his attempted solution of the Russell contradiction would not work; thanks to the *Nachgelassene Schriften,* this can be precisely dated. During the middle period, no changes of mind can be detected, so that the writings of that period may be treated as presenting a single body of ideas. The acknowledgment that his attempt to solve the Russell contradiction was a failure affected Frege profoundly: it meant that his life's work had failed. Although it had led him into many side-turnings, he had, almost from the beginning, devoted himself to accomplishing a single large task: the construction of a definitive foundation for number theory and analysis; virtually everything he had written had been directed toward that end. Now it appeared that his attempt had been vitiated by a single huge error, which he had came to see as the admission of classes, which he had characterized as the extensions of concepts. (In *Grundgesetze,* the notion of a class is generalized to that of a value-range, the extension of a function; both the more and the less general notions Frege now saw as chimerical.) At first he sought to isolate and expound systematically what remained intact, his logical doctrines purged of the extensions of concepts; but he fell for many years into a condition of discouragement and abandoned the project. He took it up again, with some vigor, in the years after World War I and, toward the very end of his life, began an attempt at constructing a geometrical foundation for arithmetic.

The sense of a sentence—the thought it expresses— is what is grasped *by one who understands it: it comprises what, in knowing the language, he knows about it that is relevant to its truth or falsity.*

In the 1967 Encyclopedia article the change from the early to the middle period was presented as consisting principally in the addition of some important new doctrines, notably that of the distinction between sense (*Sinn*) and reference (*Bedeutung*). It was much more than that. The distinction was not a mere systematization of what had been left unsystematic; it was the first acknowledgment of *any* distinction between the significance of a term and that which it signified. In the writings of the early period no such distinction is anywhere to be found. The attempt has been made, in particular by Baker and Hacker (1984), to present Frege's ideas of that period as together forming a coherent theory as systematic and as tenable as that of the middle period; but such an attempt must fail, because no coherent theory that altogether ignores that distinction can be devised. This is why Frege's dual use of "concept" (*Begriff*) is so puzzling to those who read *Grundlagen* for the first time: sometimes he speaks of attaining a concept, at others he says that a statement of number serves to say something about a concept. We cannot coherently run together what we talk about with the meaning of the term we use to talk about it.

The sense of a sentence—the thought it expresses— is what is *grasped* by one who understands it: it comprises what, in knowing the language, he knows about it that is relevant to its truth or falsity. It does not comprise anything that one need not know in order to know the language (extraneous information); nor does it comprise any aspect of the sentence's meaning that does not bear on its being true or otherwise (such aspects Frege classifies as its 'coloring'). The sense of a component expression is its contribution to the sense of the whole: what, in virtue of knowing the language, one must grasp concerning that expression in order to understand the sentence. The notion of *Bedeutung* is always presented by Frege as stemming from the relation of a name to its bearer; but its function in the philosophy of his middle period is essentially that of the semantic value of an expression. The theory concerns the mechanism whereby the truth-value of a sentence is determined: the *Bedeutungen* of its component expressions are what have to be determined in the process of determining the truth-value of the whole. This is why, if the truth-value of a sentence in which it occurs can be affected by the presence of an expression, the possession of a *Bedeutung* by that expression cannot be called in question; it is also why sentences must be accorded a *Bedeutung,* since they can be components of more complex sentences.

Sluga (1980) has shown that Georg W. F. Hegel's influence had waned in Germany when Frege was writing; it was therefore wrong to credit him with helping to overcome that influence. He was nevertheless unquestionably a realist. Jean van Heijenoort, followed by Hintikka, attributed to Frege a rejection of semantics as an impossible attempt to survey language as if from outside language. This is probably a correct account of his view in his early period. The context principle, as stated in *Grundlagen,* denies that the connection between a term and its content in reality can be apprehended by a mental association between them: all legitimate questions, in the formal mode, concerning the content of expressions, are equivalent to questions in the material mode, that is, framed *within* the language. This yields a view of content or reference analogous to the minimalist view of truth propounded by Frank Plumpton Ramsey: the principle exemplified by "The content of the name 'Chicago'" enshrines the *whole* explanation of the notion of content. But van Heijenoort's interpretation does not apply to the views of Frege's middle period. The theory of *Bedeutung* is, precisely, a semantic theory. It is not possible to view language, as such, from outside; but it is possible to speak in one language about another, as Frege stated in German the semantics of the formal language of *Grundgesetze.* The distinction between object-language and metalanguage is made explicitly in the late unpublished fragment "Logical Generality."

In *Grundlagen* the context principle serves, in practice. as a guide to finding a correct definition of number. So viewed, it requires one to find a means of specifying, without circularity, the truth-conditions of those sentences in which we normally employ the term to be defined: it is then a requirement on a correct definition of it that it yield those truth-conditions for such sentences. It will confer truth-conditions on other sentences, which we do not ordinarily use and are not interested in; their possible unnaturalness is no objection to the definition, which has done all that is required of it.

This left an unanswered question: how can we come to understand the primitive expressions of a formal theory and, in particular, the domain over which its variables range? Frege attempted to answer this question in *Grundgesetze,* as it applied to terms for value-ranges: it there took the form. "How can we secure *Bedeutungen* for such terms?" His answer was an appeal to the context principle. Admittedly, though he still allowed a salient role for sentences in the theory of sense, he no longer recognized them as categorically different from singular terms in the theory of *Bedeutung;* but in practice this made no difference. Without a distinction between significance and thing signified, it has some plausibility to maintain that, if all sentences containing certain terms have been assigned truth-conditions, all that is needed to give those terms a content has been done. But Frege continued to maintain this about *Bedeutung:* he supposed that the *Bedeutung* of a term could be fixed by laying down the *Bedeutungen* of more complex terms (and the truth-conditions of sentences) containing it. He thus attempted simultaneously to specify the *Bedeutungen* of value-range terms and the domain of the individual variables. The result was a grossly ill-founded set of inductive specifications, which, partially incorporated into the axioms, led to contradiction. The problem of how we attain a grasp of the intended range of the variables of a fundamental mathematical theory remains unsolved. Frege's attempt to solve it was indeed a failure; he deserves credit for formulating and for facing it.

[See also Hegel, Georg W. F.; Reference; Russell, Bertrand Arthur William; Sense.]

BIBLIOGRAPHY

Works by Frege

Collected Papers. Edited by B. McGuinness. Oxford, 1984.
Nachgelassene Schriften. Hamburg, 1969.
Philosophical and Mathematical Correspondence. Edited by B. McGuinness. Oxford, 1980.
Posthumous Writings [translation of *Nachgelassene Schriften*]. Translated by P. Long and R. White. Oxford, 1979.

Wissenschaftlicher Briefwechsel. Hamburg, 1976.

Works on Frege

Baker, G. P., and P. M. S. Hacker. *Frege: Logical Excavations.* Oxford, 1984.

Dummett, M. *Frege: Philosophy of Language,* 2d ed. London, 1981.

———. *Frege: Philosophy of Mathematics.* London, 1991.

———. *Frege and Other Philosophers.* Oxford, 1991.

———. *The Interpretation of Frege's Philosophy.* London, 1991.

Haaparanta, L., and J. Hintikka, eds. *Frege Synthesized.* Dordrecht, 1986.

Klemke, E. D., ed. *Essays on Frege.* Urbana, IL, 1968.

Resnick, M. *Frege and the Philosophy of Mathematics.* Ithaca, NY, 1986.

Schirn, M., ed. *Studien zu Frege.* Bad Canstatt, 1976.

Sluga, H. *Gottlob Frege.* London, 1980.

———, ed. *The Philosophy of Frege,* 4 vols. New York, 1993.

van Heijenoort, J. "Logic as Calculus and Logic as Language," *Synthese,* Vol. 17 (1967), 324–30.

von Kutschera, F. *Gottlob Frege.* Berlin, 1989.

Wright, C. *Frege's Conception of Numbers as Objects.* Aberdeen, 1983.

———, ed. *Frege: Tradition and Influence.* Oxford, 1984.

— MICHAEL DUMMETT

FREUD, SIGMUND

Sigmund Freud has seen an explosion in historical scholarship, accelerated by the publication of Freud's correspondence with Wilhelm Fleiss and by the appearance of other original source materials. As a result, the sources of Freud's psychoanalytic work are now firmly placed in late-nineteenth-century biology, physiology, medicine, and neurology. Freud's philosophy of science and methodological views are understood as adaptations of standard opinions in those subjects at the time; much more is known about the outcomes of Freud's treatments and the backgrounds of his patients; and his changes of opinion have been thoroughly and repeatedly documented. Minor questions of interpretation and major questions of the motives for changes in Freud's doctrines remain. The picture of Freud that has emerged shows him to have been largely unsuccessful in the early years of psychoanalytic practice in

---

Minor questions of interpretation

and major questions of the motives

for changes in Freud's doctrines remain.

---

curing patients, justifiably dubious in the late 1890s about the reliability of his methods of diagnosis and inference, and subsequently disingenuous, or at least very inaccurate, about the development of his views.

Freud's doctrine, his evidence, his arguments, and ahistorical reinterpretations of his work by Paul Ricoeur and by Jürgen Habermas have been scathingly criticized by Adolf Grunbaum in a sustained series of essays and in two books. Grunbaum emphasized that Freud offered a "tally argument" for the correctness of psychoanalytic interpretation, based on the assumption that only correct interpretations of the source of a disorder will cause permanent removal of symptoms. Grunbaum argues that data on placebo effects and spontaneous remission provide overwhelming empirical evidence against this "necessary condition thesis." A substantial portion of the literature written on Freud by philosophers in the 1980s and 1990s consists of responses to Grunbaum, none disputing his empirical claims (see the contribution by Edward Erwin in Earman et al., 1993).

Perhaps because of these historical and critical developments, and almost certainly because the rise of cognitive psychology has offered better prospects, there are few positive projects in recent philosophy that are framed around Freud, Freudian theory, or Freudian themes. One such is accounts offered by Donald Davidson, Herbert Fingarette, and others of paradoxes of rationality—weakness of will, self-deception, and others—in terms of a self divided into parts with competing beliefs, desires, and resources. Weakness of will is then explained as a compromise result, or as the temporary dominance of one part over another; self-deception is explained by the existence of separate memory structures, each accessible only to one of two or more inner agents, and so forth.

Influenced by neo-Wittgensteinian literature, Marcia Cavell has propounded a view in which the truth or falsity of claims of meaning, as in dream interpretation, are determined socially, not by any history of private thoughts. The maneuver may be aimed at saving Freudian theory from charges of falsehood or at least unreliability, but if so whether it succeeds or fails depends largely on the community selected. The general scientific society has decided that Freud was wrong about a great deal and that Cavell is wrong about what makes for truth and falsehood. Cavell also raises interesting questions about what neonates and babies experience and how they subsequently come to be able to describe their own experiences. Similar questions that have recently been the subject of a large body of research in developmental psychology (see Alison Gopnik, 1996) seem remote from any Freudian theory.

Patricia Kitcher has offered a historical/philosophical reconstruction of Freud's enterprise as an attempt to construct a multidisciplinary science of the mind, drawing on psychology, anthropology, biology, physiology, and, of course, clinical phenomena. So read, Freud's effort is almost unique in the human sciences, which have more typically been formed by emulating developments in some particular influential science, most recently cognitive psychology.

The similarities between Freud's general theoretical views before the turn of the century and those of contemporary cognitive psychology, especially "connectionist" models of mental processing, has been noticed by several writers. The scientific ambition Freud embraced—to identify the structure and processes of mind chiefly from observational evidence—is not unlike the similar task contemporary cognitive psychologists undertake on the basis of experimental behavior. The methodological issues on which Freud took a stand confront contemporary cognitive psychologists almost exactly as they did Freud: the appropriate role for statistical reasoning as against reasoning from example and counterexample; the value of evidence from abnormal subjects in reasoning about normal mental structure; the proper reconstruction of causal hypotheses and the

nature of sound inference to causal relations; how to separate universal features from individual idiosyncrasies; how to obtain any evidence about the mentation of the very young; the relation between theoretical descriptions of mental processes and those of everyday belief-desire psychology; the relation, if any, between behavioral evidence and physiological evidence; and, most generally, whether theoretical claims about normal mental processing are radically underdetermined by behavioral evidence, no matter whether clinical or experimental. These parallelisms suggest that many of those methodological criticisms of the Freudian enterprise that do not turn on Freud's idiosyncrasies might usefully be addressed to pieces of contemporary cognitive science. Thus far few philosophers have been inclined to turn the tables.

[See also Connectionism; Davidson, Donald; Habermas, Jürgen; Ricoeur, Paul; Self; Truth.]

The sources of Freud's psychoanalytic work are now firmly placed in late-nineteenth-century biology, physiology, medicine, and neurology. (Corbis/Bettmann)

BIBLIOGRAPHY

Cavell, M. *The Psychoanalytic Mind.* Cambridge, MA, 1993.

Cohen, R., and L. Laudan, eds. *Physics, Philosophy, and Psychoanalysis.* Reidel, 1983.

Earman, J., et al., eds. *Philosophical Problems of the Internal and External Worlds: Essays on the Philosophy of Adolf Grunbaum.* Philadelphia, 1993.

Erwin, E. *A Final Accounting: Philosophical and Empirical Issues in Freudian Psychology.* Cambridge, MA, 1996.

Gopnik, A. *Words, Thoughts, and Things.* Cambridge, MA, 1996.

Grunbaum, A. *The Foundations of Psychoanalysis.* Berkeley, 1984.

———. *Validation in the Clinical Theory of Psychoanalysis.* Rome, 1993.

Kitcher, P. *Freud's Dream: A Complete Interdisciplinary Science of Mind.* Cambridge, MA, 1992.

Macmillan, M. *Freud Evaluated.* Cambridge, MA, 1996.

Masson, J. *The Complete Letters of Sigmund Freud to Wilhelm Fleiss.* Cambridge, MA, 1985.

Neu, J., ed. *The Cambridge Companion to Freud.* Cambridge, 1991.

Pribram, K., and M. Gill. *Freud's Project Reassessed.* New York, 1976.

Sulloway, F. *Freud: Biologist of the Mind.* New York, 1979.

Wollheim, R., ed. *Freud: A Collection of Critical Essays.* Garden City, NY, 1974.

– CLARK GLYMOUR

FUNCTIONALISM

Functionalism is one of the major proposals that have been offered as solutions to the mind–body problem. Solutions to the mind–body problem usually try to answer questions such as: What is the ultimate nature of the mental? At the most general level, what makes a mental state mental? Or more specifically, what do thoughts have in common in virtue of which they are thoughts? That is, what makes a thought a thought? What makes a pain a pain? Cartesian dualism said the ultimate nature of the mental was to be found in a special mental substance. Behaviorism identified mental states with behavioral dispositions; physicalism, in its most influential version, identifies mental states with brain states. Functionalism says that mental states are constituted by their causal relations to one another and to sensory inputs and behavioral outputs. Functionalism is one of the major theoretical developments of twentieth-century analytic philosophy, and provides the conceptual underpinnings of much work in cognitive science.

Functionalism has three distinct sources. First, Putnam and Fodor saw mental states in terms of an empirical computational theory of the mind. Second, Smart's "topic neutral" analyses led Armstrong and Lewis to a functionalist analysis of mental concepts. Third, Wittgenstein's idea of meaning as use led to a version of functionalism as a theory of meaning, further developed by Sellars and later Harman.

One motivation behind functionalism can be appreciated by attention to artifact concepts such as *carbu-*

retor, and biological concepts such as *kidney.* What it is for something to be a carburetor is for it to mix fuel and air in an internal combustion engine—*carburetor* is a functional concept. In the case of the kidney, the *scientific* concept is functional—defined in terms of a role in filtering the blood and maintaining certain chemical balances.

The kind of function relevant to the mind can be introduced via the parity-detecting automaton illustrated in the figure below, which tells us whether it has seen an odd or even number of '1's. This automaton has two states, S_1 and S_2; one input, '1' (though its input can be nothing) and two outputs, it utters either the word "Odd" or "Even." The table describes two functions, one from input and state to output, and another from input and state to next state. Each square encodes two conditionals specifying the output and next state given both the current state and input. The left box says that if the machine is in S_1 and sees a '1', it says "odd" (indicating that it has seen an odd number of '1's) and goes to S_2. The right box says, similarly, that if the machine is in S_2 and sees a '1', it says "even" and goes back to S_1.

Now suppose we ask the question: "What is S_1?" The answer is that the nature of S_1 is entirely relational, and entirely captured by the table. We could give an explicit characterization of 'S_1' as follows:

Being in S_1 = being in the first of two states that are related to one another and to inputs and outputs as follows: being in one of the states and getting a '1' input results in going into the second state and emitting "Odd"; and being in the second of the two states and getting a '1' input results in going into the first and emitting "Even."

Making the quantification over states more explicit:

Being in S_1 = Being an x such that $\exists P \exists Q$[If x is in P and gets a '1' input, then it goes into Q and emits "Odd"; if x is in Q and gets a '1' input it gets into P and emits "Even" & x is in P] (Note: read '$\exists P$' as 'There is a property P'.)

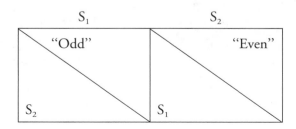

This illustration can be used to make a number of points. (1) According to functionalism, the nature of a mental state is just like the nature of an automaton state: constituted by its relations to other states and to inputs and outputs. All there is to S_1 is that being in it and getting a '1' input results in such and such, and so forth. According to functionalism, all there is to being in pain is that it disposes you to say 'ouch', wonder whether you are ill, it distracts you, and so forth. (2) Because mental states are like automaton states in this regard, the illustrated method for defining automaton states is supposed to work for mental states as well. Mental states can be totally characterized in terms that involve only logico-mathematical language and terms for input signals and behavioral outputs. Thus functionalism satisfies one of the desiderata of behaviorism, characterizing the mental in entirely nonmental language. (3) S_1 is a second order state in that it consists in having *other* properties, say mechanical or hydraulic or electronic properties, that have certain relations to one another. These other properties, the ones quantified over in the definitions just given, are said to be the *realizations* of the functional properties. So, although functionalism characterizes the mental in nonmental terms, it does so only by quantifying over realizations of mental states, which would not have delighted behaviorists. (4) One functional state can be realized in different ways. For example, an actual metal and plastic machine satisfying the machine table might be made of gears, wheels, pulleys and the like, in which case the realization of S_1 would be a mechanical state; or the realization of S_1 might be an electronic state, and so forth. (5) Just as one functional state can be realized in different ways, one physical state can realize different functional states in different machines. This could happen, for example, if a single type of transistor were used to do different things in different machines. (6) Since S_1 can be realized in many ways, a claim that S_1 *is* a mechanical state would be false (at least arguably), as would a claim that S_1 is an electronic state. For this reason, there is a strong case that functionalism shows physicalism is false: if a creature without a brain can think, thinking cannot be a brain state. (But see the section on functionalism and physicalism below.)

The notion of a realization deserves further discussion. In the early days of functionalism, a first-order property was often said to realize a functional property in virtue of a 1-1 correspondence between the two realms of properties. But such a definition of realization produces far too many realizations. Suppose, for example, that at t_1 we shout 'one' at a bucket of water, and then at t_2 we shout 'one' again. We can regard the bucket as a parity-detecting automaton by pairing the physical configuration of the bucket at t_1 with S_1 and

the heat emitted or absorbed by the bucket at t_1 with "odd"; by pairing the physical configuration of the bucket at t_2 with S_2 and the heat exchanged with the environment at t_2 with "even"; and so on. What is left out by the post hoc correlation way of thinking of realization is that a true realization must satisfy the *counterfactuals* implicit in the table. To be a realization of S_1 it is not enough to lead to a certain output and state given that the input is a '1'; it is also required that had the input been a '0', the S_1 realization would have led to the other output and *state*. Satisfaction of the relevant counterfactuals is built into the notion of realization mentioned in (3) above (see Lycan, 1987).

Functionalism is one of the major theoretical developments of twentieth-century analytic philosophy, and provides the conceptual underpinnings of much work in cognitive science.

Suppose we have a theory of mental states that specifies all the causal relations among the states, sensory inputs, and behavioral outputs. Focusing on pain as a sample mental state, it might say, among other things, that sitting on a tack causes pain, and that pain causes anxiety and saying 'ouch'. Agreeing for the sake of the example to go along with this moronic theory, functionalism would then say that we could define 'pain' as follows: being in pain = being in the first of two states, the first of which is caused by sitting on tacks, which in turn causes the other state and emitting 'ouch'. More symbolically

Being in pain = Being an x such that $\exists P \exists Q$[sitting on a tack causes P & P causes both Q and emitting 'ouch' & x is in P]

More generally, if T is a psychological theory with n mental terms of which the 17th is 'pain', we can define 'pain' relative to T as follows (the 'F_1' ... 'F_n' are variables that replace the n mental terms, and i_1, etc. And o_1, etc. indicates):

Being in pain = Being an x such that $\exists F_1$ ... $\exists F_n$ [$T(F_1$ ... F_n, i_1, etc., o_1, etc.) & x is in F_{17}]

In this way, functionalism characterizes the mental in nonmental terms, in terms that involve quantification over realizations of mental states but no explicit mention of them; thus functionalism characterizes the mental in terms of structures that are tacked down to reality only at the inputs and outputs.

The psychological theory T just mentioned can be either an empirical psychological theory or else a commonsense "folk" theory, and the resulting functionalisms are very different. In the latter case, conceptual functionalism, the functional definitions are aimed at capturing our ordinary mental concepts. In the former case, "psychofunctionalism," "the functional definitions are not supposed to capture ordinary concepts but are only supposed to fix the extensions of mental terms. The idea of psychofunctionalism is that the scientific nature of the mental consists not in anything biological, but in something "organizational," analogous to computational structure. Conceptual functionalism, by contrast, can be thought of as a development of logical behaviorism. Logical behaviorists thought that pain was a disposition to pain *behavior*. But as Geach and Chisholm pointed out, what counts as pain behavior depends on the agent's beliefs and desires. Conceptual functionalists avoid this problem by defining each mental state in terms of its contribution to dispositions to behave—and have other mental states.

Functionalism and Physicalism

Theories of the mind prior to functionalism have been concerned both with (1) what there *is,* and (2) what gives each type of mental state its own identity, for example what pains have in common in virtue of which they are pains. Stretching these terms a bit, we might say that (1) is a matter of ontology and (2) of metaphysics. Here are the ontological claims: dualism told us that there are both mental and physical substances, whereas behaviorism and physicalism are monistic, claiming that there are only physical substances. Here are the metaphysical claims: behaviorism tells us that what pains (for example) have in common in virtue of which they are pains is something behavioral; dualism gave a nonphysical answer to this question, and physicalism gives a physical answer to this question. Turning now to functionalism, it answers the metaphysical question without answering the ontological question. Functionalism tells us that what pains have in common— what makes them pains—is their function; but functionalism does not tell us whether the beings that have pains have any nonphysical parts. This point can be seen in terms of the automaton described above. In order to be an automaton of the type described, an actual concrete machine need only have states related to one another and to inputs and outputs in the way described. The machine description does not tell us how the machine works or what it is made of, and in particular it does not rule out a machine which is operated by an immaterial soul, so long as the soul is willing to operate in the deterministic manner specified in the table (see Putnam, 1988 and the paper by Fodor in Block, 1980).

> *The idea of psychofunctionalism*
>
> *is that the scientific nature of the mental*
>
> *consists not in anything biological,*
>
> *but in something "organizational,"*
>
> *analogous to computational structure.*

In thinking about the relation between functionalism and physicalism, it is useful to distinguish two categories of physicalist theses: one version of physicalism competes with functionalism, making a metaphysical claim about the physical nature of mental state properties or types (and is thus often called "type" physicalism). As mentioned above, on one point of view, functionalism shows that type of physicalism is false.

However, there are more modest physicalisms whose thrusts are ontological rather than metaphysical. Such physicalistic claims are not at all incompatible with functionalism. Consider, for example, a physicalism that says that every actual thing is made up entirely of particles of the sort that compose inorganic matter. In this sense of physicalism, most functionalists have been physicalists. Further, functionalism can be modified in a physicalistic direction, for example, by requiring that all properties quantified over in a functional definition by physical properties. Type physicalism is often contrasted with *token* physicalism. (The word 'teeth' in this sentence has five letter tokens of three letter types.) Token physicalism says that each pain (for example) is a physical state, but token physicalism allows that there may be nothing physical that all pains share, nothing physical that makes a pain a pain.

It is a peculiarity of the literature on functionalism and physicalism that while some functionalists say functionalism shows physicalism is false (see the papers by Putnam, Fodor, and Block and Fodor in Block [1980], some of which are also in the other anthologies), others say functionalism shows physicalism is true. (See the papers by Lewis and Armstrong in Block [1980], and Rosenthal [1991].) In Lewis's case, the issue is partly terminological. Lewis is a conceptual functionalist about "having pain." Having pain on Lewis's regimentation could be said to be a rigid designator of a functional property. (A rigid designator names the same thing in each possible world. 'The color of the sky' is nonrigid, since it names red in worlds in which the sky is red. 'Blue' is rigid, since it names blue even in worlds in which the sky is red.) 'Pain', by contrast, is a nonrigid designator conceptually equivalent to a definite description of the form 'the state with such and such a causal role'. The referent of this phrase in us, Lewis holds, is a certain brain state, though the referent of this phrase in a robot might be a circuit state, and the referent in an angel would be a nonphysical state. Similarly, 'the winning number' picks out '17' in one lottery and '596' in another. So Lewis is a functionalist (indeed a conceptual functionalist) about having pain. In terms of the metaphysical issue described above—what do pains have in common in virtue of which they are pains— Lewis is a functionalist, not a physicalist. What a person's pains and the robot's pains share is a causal role, not anything physical. Just as there is no numerical similarity between 17 and 596 relevant to their being winning numbers, there is no physical similarity between human and Martian pain that makes them pains. And there is no physical similarity of any kind between human pains and angel pains. However, on the issue of the scientific nature of pain, Lewis is a physicalist. What is in common to human and Martian pain in his view is something conceptual, not something scientific.

Functionalism and Propositional Attitudes

The discussion of functional characterization given above assumes a psychological theory with a finite number of mental state terms. In the case of monadic states like pain, the sensation of red, and so forth, it does seem a theoretical option simply to list the states and their relations to other states, inputs and outputs. But for a number of reasons, this is not a sensible theoretical option for belief-states, desire-states, and other propositional attitude states. For one thing, the list would be too long to be represented without combinatorial methods. Indeed, there is arguably no upper bound on the number of propositions, any one of which could in principle be an object of thought. For another thing, there are systematic relations among beliefs: for example, the belief that John loves Mary and the belief that Mary loves John. These belief states represent the same objects as related to each other in converse ways. But a theory of the nature of beliefs can hardly just leave out such an important feature of them. We cannot treat 'believes-that-grass-is-green', 'believes-that-grass-is-blue', and so forth, as unrelated primitive predicates. So we will need a more sophisticated theory, one that involves some sort of combinatorial apparatus. The most promising candidates are those that treat belief as a relation. But a relation to what? There are two distinct issues

here. One issue is how to state the functional theory in a detailed way. (See Loar [1981] and Schiffer [1987] for a suggestion in terms of a correspondence between the logical relations among sentences and the inferential relations among mental states.) A second issue is what types of states could possibly realize the relational propositional attitude states. Field (1978) and Fodor (in Block, 1980) argue that to explain the productivity of propositional attitude states, there is no alternative to postulating a language of thought, a system of syntactically structured objects in the brain that express the propositions in propositional attitudes. (See Stalnaker, 1994, chapters 1–3, for a critique of Field's approach.) In later work, Fodor (1987) has stressed the systematicity of propositional attitudes mentioned above. Fodor points out that the beliefs whose contents are systematically related exhibit the following sort of empirical relation: if one is capable of believing that Mary loves John, one is also capable of believing that John loves Mary. Fodor argues that only a language of thought in the brain could explain this fact.

Externalism

The upshot of the famous "twin earth" arguments has been that meaning and content are in part in the world and in the language community. Functionalists have responded in a variety of ways. One reaction is to think of the inputs and outputs of a functional theory as *long-arm* as including the objects that one sees and manipulates. Another reaction is to stick with *short-arm* inputs and outputs that stop at the surfaces of the body, thinking of the intentional contents thereby characterized as *narrow*—supervening on the nonrelational physical properties of the body. There has been no widely recognized account of what narrow content is, nor is there any agreement as to whether there is any burden of proof on the advocates of narrow content to characterize it. (See the papers by Burge, Loar, and Stalnaker in Rosenthal, 1991; see also Goldman, 1993.)

Meaning

Functionalism says that understanding the meaning of the word 'momentum' is a functional state. On one version of the view, the functional state can be seen in terms of the role of the word 'momentum' itself in thinking, problem solving, planning, and so forth. But if understanding the meaning of 'momentum' is this word's having a certain function, then there is a very close relation between the meaning of a word and its function, and a natural proposal is to regard the close relation as simply identity, that is, the meaning of the word just *is* that function. (See Peacocke, 1992.) Thus functionalism about content leads to functionalism about meaning, a theory that purports to tell us the metaphysical nature of meaning. This theory is popular in cognitive science, where in one version it is often known as procedural semantics, as well as in philosophy where it is often known as conceptual role semantics. The theory has been criticized (along with other versions of functionalism) in Putnam (1988) and Fodor and LePore (1992).

Holism

Block and Fodor (in Block, 1980) noted the "damn/darn" problem. Functional theories must make reference to any difference in stimuli or responses that can be mentally significant. The difference between saying 'damn' and 'darn' when you stub your toe can, in some circumstances, be mentally significant. So the different functionalized theories appropriate to the two responses will affect the individuation of every state connected to those utterances, and for the same reason, every state connected to those states, and so on. His pains lead to 'darn', hers to 'damn', so their pains are functionally different, and likewise their desires to avoid pain, their beliefs that interact with those desires, and so on. Plausible assumptions lead to the conclusion that two individuals who differ in this way share almost nothing in the way of mental states. The upshot is that the functionalist needs a way of individuating mental states that is less fine-grained than appeal to the whole theory, a molecularist characterization. Even if one is optimistic about solving this problem in the case of pain by finding something functional in common to all pains, one cannot assume that success will transfer to beliefs or meanings, for success in the case of meaning and belief may involve an analytic/synthetic distinction (Fodor and LePore, 1992).

Qualia

Recall the parity-detecting automaton described at the beginning of this article. It could be instantiated by two people, each of whom is in charge of the function specified by a single box. Similarly, the much more complex functional organization of a human mind could "in principle" be instantiated by a vast army of people. We would have to think of the army as connected to a robot body, acting as the brain of that body, and the body would be like a person in its reactions to inputs. But would such an army really instantiate a mind? More pointedly, could such an army have pain, or the experience of red? If functionalism ascribes minds to things that do not have them, it is too liberal. Lycan (1987) suggests that we include much of human physiology in our theory to be functionalized to avoid liberalism; that is, the theory T in the definition described earlier would

be a psychological theory plus a physiological theory. But that makes the opposite problem, chauvinism, worse. The resulting functional description will not apply to intelligent Martians whose physiologies are different from ours. Further, it seems easy to imagine a simple pain-feeling organism that shares little in the way of functional organization with us. The functionalized physiological theory of this organism will be hopelessly different from the corresponding theory of us. Indeed, even if one does not adopt Lycan's tactic, it is not clear how pain could be characterized functionally so as to be common to us and the simple organism. (See Block, "Troubles with Functionalism," which appears in all the anthologies in the bibliography.)

It is a peculiarity of the literature

on functionalism and physicalism

that while some functionalists say

functionalism shows physicalism is false,

others say functionalism shows physicalism is true.

Much of the force of the problems just mentioned derives from attention to phenomenal states like the look of red. Phenomenal properties would seem to be intrinsic to (nonrelational properties of) the states that have them, and thus phenomenal properties seem independent of the relations among states, inputs and outputs that define functional states. Consider, for example, the fact that lobotomy patients often say that they continue to have pains that feel the same as before, but that the pains do not bother them. If the concept of pain is a functional concept, what these patients say is contradictory or incoherent—but it seems to many of us that it is intelligible. All the anthologies have papers on this topic: see also Lycan (1987), chapters 8, 9, 14, and 15 of Shoemaker (1984), and Hill (1991).

The chauvinism/liberalism problem affects the characterization of inputs and outputs. If we characterize inputs and outputs in a way appropriate to our bodies, we chauvinistically exclude creatures whose interface with the world is very different from ours—for example, creatures whose limbs end in wheels or, turning to a bigger difference, gaseous creatures who can manipulate and sense gases but for whom all solids and liquids are alike. The obvious alternative of characterizing inputs and outputs themselves functionally would appear to yield an abstract structure that might be satisfied by, for example, the economy of Bolivia under manipulation by a wealthy eccentric, and would thus fall to the opposite problem of liberalism.

It is tempting to respond to the chauvinism problem by supposing that the same functional theory that applies to a person also applies to the creatures with wheels. If they thought they had feet, they would try to act like us, and if we thought we had wheels, we would try to act like them. But notice that the functional definitions have to have some specifications of output organs in them. To be neutral among all the types of bodies that sentient beings could have would just be to adopt the liberal alternative of specifying the inputs and outputs themselves functionally.

Teleology

Many philosophers (see the papers by Lycan and Sober in Lycan, 1990, and Lycan, 1987) propose that we avoid liberalism by characterizing functional roles teleologically. We exclude the armies and economies mentioned because their states are not for the right things. A major problem for this point of view is the lack of an acceptable teleological account. Accounts based on evolution smack up against the swamp-grandparents problem. Suppose you find out that your grandparents were formed from particles from the swamp that came together by chance. So, as it happens, you do not have any evolutionary history to speak of. If evolutionary accounts of the teleology underpinnings of content are right, your states do not have any content. A theory with such a consequence should be rejected.

Causation

Functionalism dictates that mental properties are second-order properties, properties that consist in having other properties that have certain relations to one another. But there is at least a prima facie problem about how such second-order properties could be causal and explanatory in a way appropriate to the mental. Consider, for example, provocativeness, the second-order property that consists in having some first-order property (say redness) that causes bulls to be angry. The cape's redness provokes the bull, but does the cape's provocativeness provoke the bull? The cape's provocativeness might provoke an animal protection society, but is not the bull too stupid to be provoked by it? (See Block, 1990.)

Functionalism continues to be a lively and fluid point of view. Positive developments in recent years include enhanced prospects for conceptual functionalism and the articulation of the teleological point of view. Critical developments include problems with causality and holism, and continuing controversy over chauvinism and liberalism.

[See also Armstrong, David M.; Causation; Chisholm, Roderick M.; Cognitive Science; Computational Model of Mind, The; Language of Thought; Meaning; Metaphysics; Ontology; Physicalism, Materialism; Philosophy of Mind; Putnam, Hilary; Qualia; Sellars, Wilfrid; Smart, John Jamieson Carswell; Wittgenstein, Ludwig Josef Johann.]

BIBLIOGRAPHY

Beakley, B., and P. Ludlow, eds. *Philosophy of Mind: Classical Problems, Contemporary Issues.* Cambridge, MA, 1992.
Block, N., ed. *Readings in Philosophy of Psychology,* 2 vols. Vol. 1. Cambridge, MA, 1980.
————. "Can the Mind Change the World?" in G. Boolos, ed., *Meaning and Method: Essays in Honor of Hilary Putnam,* (Cambridge, 1990).
Field, H. "Mental representation." *Erkenntniss,* Vol. 13 (1978), 9–61.
Fodor, J. *Psychosemantics.* Cambridge, MA, 1987.
———— and E. LePore. *Holism.* New York, 1992.
Goldman, A. *Readings in Philosophy and Cognitive Science.* Cambridge, MA, 1993.
Hill, C. S. *Sensations.* Cambridge, 1991.
Loar, B. *Mind and Meaning.* Cambridge, 1981.
Lewis, D. "Reduction of Mind," in S. Guttenplan, ed., *A Companion to Philosophy of Mind* (Oxford, 1995).
Lycan, W. G. *Consciousness.* Cambridge, MA, 1987.
————, ed. *Mind and Cognition.* New York, 1990.
Peacocke, C. *A Study of Concepts.* Cambridge, MA, 1992.
Putnam, H. *Representation and Reality.* Cambridge, MA, 1988.
Rosenthal, D., ed. *The Nature of Mind.* Oxford, 1991.
Schiffer, S. *Remnants of Meaning.* Cambridge, MA, 1987.
Shoemaker, S. *Identity, Cause and Mind.* Cambridge, MA, 1984.
Stalnaker, R. C. *Inquiry.* Cambridge, MA, 1984.

– NED BLOCK

FUZZY LOGIC

Fuzzy logics are multivalued logics intended to model human reasoning with certain types of imprecision. The field of fuzzy logic originated with a 1965 paper by Lotfi Zadeh, a professor of engineering at the University of California, Berkeley. It is significant that the inventor of fuzzy logic was neither a philosopher nor a linguist. Since 1965 research in fuzzy logic has always had an engineering and mathematical bent, while the philosophical foundations of fuzzy logic have always been under attack.

Many different formal systems have been proposed under the general name of fuzzy logic, but there is wide acceptance that the fundamental principles of fuzzy logic are

(1) $t(A \wedge B) = \min\{t(A), t(B)\}$
(2) $t(A \vee B) = \max\{t(A), t(B)\}$
(3) $t(\neg A) = 1 - t(A)$.

In these axioms A and B represent arbitrary propositions. The truth value of A, a real number between 0 and 1, is denoted $t(A)$. The first axiom above says that the truth value of $A \wedge B$ is the lesser of the truth value of A and the truth value of B. The second and third axioms concerning disjunction and negation are to be understood similarly.

At the same time that Zadeh introduced fuzzy logic, he also introduced fuzzy set theory, a variant of naive set theory (i.e., everyday set theory as opposed to a foundational set theory such as the Zermelo-Fraenkel axioms) with the basic axioms

(1) $\mu(x \in P \cap Q) = \min\{\mu(x \in P), \mu(x \in Q)\}$
(2) $\mu(x \in P \cup Q) = \max\{\mu(x \in P), \mu(x \in Q)\}$
(3) $\mu(x \in P^c) = 1 - \mu(x \in P)$.

Here $\mu(x \in P)$ denotes the degree to which x is a member of the set P. Since 1965 many branches of mathematics have been generalized along fuzzy set theory lines.

There are two fundamental differences between fuzzy logics and conventional logics such as classical predicate calculus or modal logics. Although these differences are technical, they are of considerable philosophical significance. First, conventional logics (except intuitionistic logics) require for every proposition that either it or its negation be true, that is, that $t(A \vee \neg A) = 1$ in fuzzy logic notation. In fuzzy logics this "law of the excluded middle" does not hold. Second, there is no consensus about a semantics for fuzzy logic that is well-defined independently of its proof theory, that is, the inferential axioms given above. In contrast, conventional logics have well-accepted semantics, for example Tarskian model theory for predicate calculus, and Kripkean possible worlds semantics for modal logics.

Fuzzy logics are claimed to be capable of representing the meanings of intrinsically imprecise natural language sentences, such as "Many Texans are rich," for which the law of excluded middle fails. There is disagreement as to whether fuzzy methods successfully represent the complexities of concepts such as "many" and "rich." What is clear is that the rules of fuzzy logic cannot be used for reasoning about frequentist or subjective types of uncertainty, whose properties are captured by standard probability theory. The central issue here is that the probability of a compound proposition such as $A \wedge B$ is not a function just of the probabilities of the propositions A and B: the probability of $A \wedge B$ also depends on the relationship between the propositions A and B, in particular on their independence or correlation.

The tolerance for ambiguity found in fuzzy logic, and specifically the rejection of the law of the excluded middle, is a revolutionary idea in mathematical logic. Some advocates of fuzzy logic claim that tolerance for ambiguity is also revolutionary philosophically, since Western philosophy, from Plato through Descartes, has supposedly been an intrinsically dualistic tradition. According to this argument, fuzzy logic has been better received in Japan and other Asian countries than in the West because of the holistic, subtle nature of the Eastern intellectual tradition. Apart from the dualistic oversimplification of the distinction between "Western" and "Eastern" thought, this claim also ignores the continuous holistic tradition in European philosophical thought, from Zeno through Pascal to Heidegger and Wittgenstein.

Research in fuzzy logic has always had

an engineering and mathematical bent,

while the philosophical foundations of fuzzy logic

have always been under attack.

There has been much artificial intelligence research on using fuzzy logic for representing real-world knowledge, and there has been some recent convergence between this work and parallel work by a distinct research community on knowledge representation using classical logics, nonmonotonic logics, and probability theory. So far this research has remained almost exclusively theoretical. In contrast, engineering work on using fuzzy logic for controlling complex machines heuristically has been highly successful in practice.

A fuzzy controller is a device, usually implemented as software for an embedded microprocessor, that continually monitors readings from sensors, and makes decisions about actuator settings. For example, a controller for the automatic transmission of a car monitors road speed, the position of the accelerator pedal, and other factors, and decides whether to shift gears down or up, or not to shift. The knowledge possessed by a fuzzy controller is typically represented as rules such as

$$\mu(speed, \text{MODERATE}) \wedge \mu(pedal, \text{FULL-DOWN}) \rightarrow \mu(shift, \text{DOWN})$$

Here *speed* and *pedal* are sensory readings, *shift* is a possible actuator setting, and MODERATE, FULL-DOWN, and DOWN are fuzzy sets. Through inference rules for the fuzzy connectives $\wedge$ and $\rightarrow$, the degree of membership of *speed* in MODERATE and of *pedal* in FULL-DOWN determines the desired degree of membership of *shift* in DOWN. Given a set of rules, a *fuzzy* controller continually computes the degree to which the antecedents of each rule are satisfied, and selects a conclusion that is the weighted average of the conclusion of each rule, where rules are weighted using these degrees.

Fuzzy controllers are widely used for two basic reasons. First, since the action chosen at each instant is typically the result of interpolating several rules, their behavior is smooth. Second, fuzzy controller rule sets are easy for humans to read and understand intuitively, hence easy to construct by trial and error.

[See also *Artificial Intelligence; Descartes, René; Heidegger, Martin; Kripke, Saul Aaron; Mathematical Logic; Modal Logic; Model Theory; Philosophical Logic; Plato; Probability; Proof Theory; Set Theory; Wittgenstein, Ludwig Josef Johann.*]

BIBLIOGRAPHY

Elkan, C. "The Paradoxical Success of Fuzzy Logic," *IEEE Expert,* Vol. 6 (August 1994), 3–8.
Mamdani, E. H. "Application of Fuzzy Algorithms for Control of Simple Dynamic Plant." *Proceedings of the Institution of Electrical Engineers,* Vol. 121 (1974), 1585–88.
Zadeh, L. A. "Fuzzy Sets," *Information and Control,* Vol. 8 (1965), 338–53.
Zimmermann, H.-J. *Fuzzy Set Theory—And Its Applications.* Holland, 1991.

– CHARLES ELKAN

G

GADAMER, HANS-GEORG

Hans-Georg Gadamer, a Heidelberg philosopher and student of Martin Heidegger, is best known for his hermeneutic philosophy put forward in his *Wahrheit und Methode* (*Truth and Method*, 1960). Widely regarded as the most significant German philosopher after Heidegger, Gadamer wrote on Plato, Georg Wilhelm Friedrich Hegel, Heidegger, Aristotle's practical philosophy, reason in an age of science, aesthetics, poetics, Paul Celan, and other topics.

Biography

Gadamer was born in Marburg in 1900 and grew up in Breslau. His mother died when he was four. His father was a well-known university research scientist in pharmacological chemistry. In 1919 Gadamer's father was called from the University of Breslau to a research chair at the University of Marburg. Gadamer entered Marburg as a second-year student with interests in literature, art history, and classical philology. But he was soon drawn to the great neo-Kantian philosopher and Platonist, Paul Natorp, under whom he completed his doctoral dissertation in 1922 on pleasure in the Platonic dialogues. In 1923 Gadamer journeyed for the summer semester to Freiburg to hear Martin Heidegger, who was offering bold new interpretations of Aristotle and other philosophers. When Heidegger moved to Marburg in the fall of that year, Gadamer became his assistant and he remained so until 1928. During this time Gadamer also studied with Nicolai Hartmann, took seminars in classical philology under Paul Friedländer and others, and in 1927 was certified in classical philology. In 1928 he completed his habilitation under Heidegger on "Plato's dialectical ethics," based on the *Philebus*.

Gadamer remained another ten years in Marburg waiting for a call to a full-time teaching appointment. After 1933 his chances for a call were practically blotted out by his not being in good standing with the Nazis. But he remained active in the academic life at Marburg, which boasted some of Germany's leading intellectuals—Rudolf Bultmann in theology; Nicolai Hartmann; Stefan George, the charismatic poet; Richard Hamann, the iconoclastic art historian; and finally, Friedländer and others, who represented the great philological tradition of Ulrich von Wilamowitz-Moellendorff.

In 1938 Gadamer was finally called to a chair in philosophy at Leipzig, where he was able to survive through the war years as a politically unthreatening classical humanist. Because of his political integrity he was elected rector at Leipzig after the war. In 1947 he managed to escape the stultifying atmosphere of the new communist regime by being called to a position at Frankfurt University. He was at Frankfurt but two years when in 1949 he was called to fill Karl Jaspers's chair at the University of Heidelberg.

> *Widely regarded as the most significant German philosopher after Heidegger, Gadamer wrote on Plato, Hegel, Aristotle's practical philosophy, aesthetics, poetics, and many other topics.*

Gadamer remained in Heidelberg as chair in philosophy until his retirement in 1968. A gifted lecturer, he concentrated in the 1950s on topics that later became part of *Truth and Method*. At the same time, he worked to revive Hegel studies in Germany, and rebuilt a war-shattered department into one of the strongest in Germany. In 1952, along with Helmut Kuhn, he founded the *Philosophische Rundschau*, a journal dedicated to reviewing current books and discussing major issues in philosophy.

After 1968 Gadamer continued to lecture and offer seminars in Heidelberg as an honored emeritus professor, but now he allowed himself to accept invitations to speak in other countries and to serve as a guest professor at various universities, especially in the United States and Canada. This fed a growing interest in hermeneutics in the United States, an interest manifested in the number of dissertations and books being written on the subject. English translations of Gadamer's works began to appear: *Truth and Method* (1975), *Philosophical Hermeneutics* (1976), and *Hegel's Dialectic* (1976) being among the first.

In *Truth and Method* Gadamer's concepts can be logically divided into those within *Truth and Method* and those in the shorter writings after it. The latter category includes further writings defending and defining hermeneutics, writings in modern and ancient philosophy, and in aesthetics and poetics.

In *Truth and Method* Gadamer articulated the most detailed and nuanced account of the "event of understanding" in the history of philosophy. He based much of his thinking on Heidegger, Hegel, and Plato. From Heidegger's *Origin of a Work of Art* he drew strength for a powerful reassertion of the "truth" of art, and from Heidegger's *Being and Time* and later writings he drew concepts that called into question the goal of objectivity in interpretation. From Hegel and Plato he drew emphases on tradition, history, and dialogue. From Wilhelm Dilthey and Heidegger he drew an emphasis on the horizonal character of consciousness and the operativeness of history in all understanding. Understanding, he argues, takes place in a consciousness in which history—that is, tradition—is always already at work, shaping, predisposing, predefining what the process of understanding involves. His term for this is *wirkungsgeschichtliches Bewußtsein*, "effective historical consciousness," and the encounter with the other, as person or as text, is a matter of *Horizontverschmelzung* (fusion of horizons).

In Truth and Method *Gadamer articulated*

the most detailed and nuanced account

of the "event of understanding"

in the history of philosophy.

In *Truth and Method* Gadamer shows the development after Kant of fateful conceptual turns in the course of eighteenth- and nineteenth-century philosophy, philology, and hermeneutics that have led to present presuppositions about understanding and the conditions for its possibility. He traces the dream of scientific objectivity in humanistic and social scientific knowledge in the nineteenth century, especially in Friedrich Daniel Ernst Schleiermacher and Dilthey, and the promising philosophical transformation of this "problematic" of understanding through Heidegger's phenomenological analysis of existential temporality and the historical situatedness of and the participation of history in understanding. He accepts Heidegger's description of the "forestructure" of understanding, adding to it his concept of an "anticipation of completeness" in all understanding. He argues that the process of understanding has the structure of a dialogue and can be likened to a game in that it follows rules and operates in a language

that transcends it; thus, he emphasizes the "linguisticality" (*Sprachlichkeit*) of understanding and even ultimately its ontological character: "Being that can be understood is language," he asserted (*Truth and Method*, p. 432). Finally, one of the most distinctive and important of the contributions of *Truth and Method* is its insistence on a moment of "application" in all understanding.

The book's overarching goal, however, was to cause the artwork to be seen in a new way. While the title might lead one to expect it to be concerned with methods in the *Geisteswissenschaften*, Gadamer's professed aim is to defend the claim of artworks to be "true." In Gadamer's view the experience of encountering truth in great works of art demonstrates the limits of a science-oriented concept of understanding; the meaning and power of such artworks elude scientific modes of understanding. Gadamer wrote a good deal in explanation and defense of *Truth and Method*. These writings are now collected in volume 2 of his collected works.

Gadamer's writings on modern philosophy range through the Continental tradition since Kant and are influenced principally by Plato, who casts a shadow even over his modern writings; by Heidegger, about whom he has written more than about any other modern philosopher; by Hegel, whose importance in modern philosophy Gadamer repeatedly defended; and by Edmund Husserl whose phenomenology Gadamer used and treated as a major element in his thought. Most of his essays on ancient philosophy are directly or indirectly connected with Plato. From Plato he draws his model of dialogue, in which partners participate in quest of a truth that transcends the individual seeker. Gadamer's ethical thinking as well as his dialectical hermeneutics go back to Plato's "dialectical ethics" of respect for the other person, of openness, of seeking to strengthen the partner's case in order not merely to win a debate to one's own satisfaction but to move together toward truth, a result that benefits both sides and that both sides affirm.

Art and poetry are a major theme in Gadamer's writings throughout his career. In 1934 Gadamer wrote on "Plato and the Poets," and in the 1940s he was writing essays on Hölderlin, Goethe, Immerman, and Rilke. His articles after *Truth and Method* tend to select more sober and difficult poets like Stefan George, Gottfried Benn, and Paul Celan. His essays on aesthetics and poetics continue to emphasize the truth of art, the need for dialogical openness, and the priority of the artwork's character of play. At the same time, another issue arises: What about basically nonrepresentational poetry? What about the "no longer beautiful" poetry of the modern (or postmodern) dark lyric? After a number of writings that struggle successfully with the dark lyric, such as

Wer bin ich und wer bist du? ("Who Am I and Who Are You?", 1973), on poet Paul Celan, Gadamer poses the problem in somewhat different terms. For Gadamer it is a "task of philosophy" to develop a context within which one can still recognize and deal with—or "understand"—modern and postmodern art.

Gadamer's essay "The Relevance of the Beautiful" presents a twentieth-century defense of such art. In this essay experience becomes the reference point, even group experiences as one finds them in the historical record. Gadamer includes, not just experiences recorded in artworks or great poetry, which would create a circular argument, but in anthropological records of such things as (1) the role of play in human life, (2) the high experiences of festiveness in our own and other cultures, and (3) the power of participation in symbolic religious rites. In groping for an explanation of the power of art and a defense of its legitimacy, Gadamer offers an analysis of three categories—play, symbol, and festival.

In his essay "The Truth of the Artwork" (1960), Gadamer pointed to a threefold insufficiency of scientific thinking: (1) the insufficiency of scientific thinking, by itself and without recourse to standards outside itself, to grapple with ethical problems such as human rights, abortion, ecology, or planning the future; (2) its incapacity to account for the experience of beauty in art and poetry or to lay down principles for its creation; and (3) its insufficiency to meet, or even account for, the spiritual needs of human beings. All these suggest that a recourse to the absolute priority of scientific presuppositions cannot serve us well in dealing with the encounter with ethical problems, artworks, or the divine. Art, like ethics and the divine, seems to move beyond the competence of the categories of scientific thinking. And they can claim to be "true." This is a major theme both in *Truth and Method* and in later writings.

In "Wort und Bild" ("Word and Image," 1992) Gadamer takes the final step and attempts to articulate aesthetic categories that apply both to plastic/pictorial arts and arts of the word. Among the several concepts to which he turns are the Greek concept of the fine (*kalon*) and to our experience of the rightness and absoluteness of art.

[See also Aristotle; Hegel, Georg W. F.; Heidegger, Martin; Hermeneutic Philosophy; Husserl, Edmund; Plato.]

BIBLIOGRAPHY

Major Works by Gadamer

Platos dialektische Ethik: Phänomenologische Interpretationen zum "Philebos," 3d ed. Leipzig, 1931. Translated by R. M. Wallace as *Plato's Dialectical Ethics: Phenomenological Interpretations Relating to the "Philebus."* New Haven, 1991.

Wahrheit und Methode: Grundzüge einer philosophischen Hermeneutik. Tübingen, 1960. Translated as *Truth and Method,* edited by G. Barden and J. Cumming. New York, 1975; rev. ed., 1989.
Hegels Dialektik: Fünf hermeneutische Studien. Tübingen, 1971. Translated by P. C. Smith as *Hegel's Dialectic: Five Hermeneutical Studies.* New Haven, 1976.
Wer bin ich und wer bist du?: Ein Kommentar zu Paul Celans Gedichtfolge "Atemkristall." Frankfurt, 1973.
Vernunft im Zeitalter der Wissenschaft: Aufsätze, Frankfurt, 1976. Translated as *Reason in the Age of Science.* Cambridge, MA, 1981.
Die Aktualität des Schönen: Kunst als Spiel, Symbol, und Fest. Stuttgart, 1977. Translated by N. Walker as "The Relevance of the Beautiful." In R. Bernasconi, ed., *The Relevance of the Beautiful and Other Essays* (Cambridge, 1986).
Die Idee des Guten zwischen Plato und Aristoteles. Heidelberg, 1978. Translated as *The Idea of the Good in Platonic-Aristotelian Philosophy.* New Haven, 1986.
Heideggers Wege. Tübingen, 1983. Translated as *Heidegger's Ways.* Albany, NY, 1994.
Gessamelte Werke. 10 vols. Tübingen, 1985–. Contains all of the above works.

Collections of Gadamer's Works in English

Philosophical Hermeneutics, edited and translated by D. E. Linge. Berkeley, 1976.
Dialogue and Dialectic: Eight Hermeneutical Studies on Plato, translated by P. C. Smith. New Haven, 1980.
The Relevance of the Beautiful and Other Essays, edited by R. Bernasconi. Cambridge, 1986.
Dialogue and Deconstruction: The Gadamer–Derrida Encounter, edited by D. Michelfelder and R. E. Palmer. Albany, NY, 1989. Includes five essays by Gadamer.
Hans-Georg Gadamer on Education, Poetry, and History, edited by Dieter Misgeld and G. Nicholson. Albany, NY, 1992.
Literature and Philosophy in Dialogue: Essays in German Literary Theory, translated by R. H. Paslick. Albany, NY, 1992.

Works on Gadamer

Hoy, D. C. *The Critical Circle: Literature, History, and Philosophical Hermeneutics.* Berkeley, 1978.
Schmidt, L. K. *The Epistemology of Hans-Georg Gadamer.* New York, 1985.
Warnke, G. *Gadamer: Hermeneutics, Tradition, and Reason.* Stanford, CA, 1987.
Weinsheimer, J. C. *Gadamer's Hermeneutics: A Reading of "Truth and Method."* New Haven, 1985.
Wright, K., ed. *Festivals of Interpretation: Essays on Hans-Georg Gadamer's Work.* Albany, NY, 1990.

– RICHARD E. PALMER

GENETICS AND REPRODUCTIVE TECHNOLOGIES

Modern genetics and technological aids to human reproduction, like other advances in science and technology, have created ethical problems heretofore unencountered. Biomedical developments have also posed new conceptual, epistemological, and metaphysical problems. This article addresses these philosophical concerns as well as the more widely discussed ethical implications of contemporary genetics and reproductive technologies. One conceptual and ethical link between these two fields is the prospect of "designing our descendents." This prospect has been viewed by some as a boon to humankind (Fletcher, 1974) and by others as a fearsome possibility to be avoided at all costs (Ramsey, 1970).

The Human Genome Initiative, a "big science" project launched by the U.S. government to map and sequence the entire human genome, has heightened concerns about the privacy and confidentiality of genetic information, the uses to which such information might be put, and the possibility of stigmatizing individuals or groups because of their genetic constitution. The knowledge the human genome project can yield is massive in contrast to previous efforts to acquire information about human genetics.

The contemporary science of genetics provides, not only an understanding of heritable traits, but also the

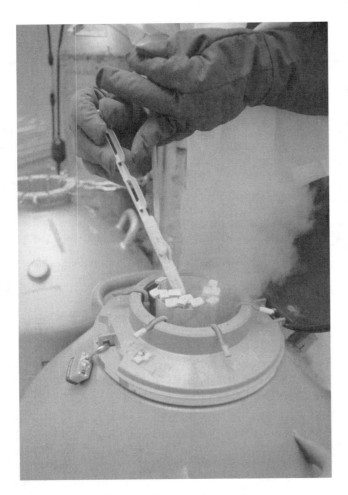

Sperm banks foster eugenic practices by allowing their patrons to choose sperm from a donor whose traits they hope to replicate in the child. (Corbis/Stephanie Maze)

capability to diagnose the probability or certainty of transmitting to offspring genetic conditions such as sickle-cell disease, Tay Sachs disease, or cystic fibrosis. The ability to identify and locate specific genes that render a person likely to manifest heritable conditions, such as Huntington's disease and certain forms of cancer, raises profound questions about the wisdom and desirability of learning about future contingencies when no cure exists and preventive measures are of uncertain efficacy.

A conceptual question is prompted by the rapid advances in genetics: What constitutes genetic disease? The traditional concept of disease relies on the ability of medical scientists to identify deviations from the normal physiological functioning of an organism. Asymptomatic diseases, such as hypertension, can be detected by diagnostic instruments even though the individual feels no symptoms of illness. With the discovery of genes that render an individual with a family history highly likely to develop a particular disease later in life, how should the individual who carries the gene be characterized? Does the person in whom the gene is found have a genetic disease or not? The individual has no symptoms and the disease may never express itself. Yet merely being susceptible opens the possibility of harm to the interests of such individuals, making them vulnerable to actions by others such as insurance companies who seek to deny insurance on grounds of a pre-existing condition or employers who refuse to hire workers with a known propensity for illness.

Beyond the problems posed by diagnosis and prediction in genetics are those of intervention: Is gene therapy intrinsically different from traditional medical therapy? Even if gene therapy by means of manipulating somatic cells poses no special problem, what about altering germ-line cells, a procedure that would affect future generations? If genetic manipulation to correct defects is ethically permissible, what, if anything, would be wrong with alterations intended to provide genetic enhancement? Are efforts to improve human intelligence, appearance, or other attributes by genetic means essentially different from the traditional methods of education, physical or mental training, or behavior modification (President's Commission for the Study of Ethical Problems, 1982)?

Attempts to improve the quality of the human gene pool, or "positive eugenics," have generally been viewed with disfavor, especially after the policies in Nazi Germany promoting racial hygiene (Proctor, 1988). Yet eugenic practices remain at the level of individual choice. The recipients of donated sperm are typically given information about physical and other personal characteristics of donors, allowing them to choose sperm from a donor whose traits they hope to replicate in the child. The prospect of genetic enhancement using the techniques of recombinant DNA manipulation can allow for more precision and wider applications than older approaches such as selective sperm banking.

Knowledge that one carries a gene for a heritable disease can pose a profound dilemma for the individual. An early form of this dilemma arose when carrier screening was the only way to determine whether a couple would pass on a genetic disease to their offspring. A couple then had to decide whether to take the chance that a child would be born with the heritable condition. With the advent of various forms of prenatal diagnosis (amniocentesis, chorionic villus sampling, blood tests), the presence of some genetic diseases in a fetus can be detected. The ethical question in such cases is whether to abort an afflicted fetus. In the case of both carrier screening and prenatal diagnosis, trained genetics counselors have uniformly taken a nondirective approach. The norm in genetics counseling has generally been to provide unbiased information to enable individuals or couples to make an informed decision whether to initiate a pregnancy or to abort a fetus found to have a genetic disease (Lappe, 1971; President's Commission for the Study of Ethical Problems, 1983).

As the science of genetics yields an increasing amount of information, individuals are faced with making decisions about prophylactic medical interventions. For example, a woman who learns that she carries a gene for an inherited form of breast cancer may contemplate bilateral mastectomy before any clinical signs appear. The epistemological problem posed by such scenarios is a familiar philosophical one: decision making under risk and uncertainty. If the woman decides to undergo a major, disfiguring operation, she does so with the knowledge that she might escape the disease entirely. But if she forgoes the preventive step, she runs the risk of developing a dread disease that may be curable if detected early but that also has a high mortality rate.

The knowledge by individuals or couples that they are at risk for transmitting a genetic disease to offspring is one indication for embarking on the use of reproductive technologies. The couple may elect to use donated sperm or ova. A far more common indication for the use of reproductive technologies, however, is infertility or sub-fertility on the part of one or both members of a couple. Methods include in vitro fertilization (IVF)—fertilizing a human ovum outside the womb; the use of sperm of ova contributed by third parties or the womb of a woman not intended to be the rearing parent (surrogacy); cryo-preservation (freezing) of fertilized ova, which are termed 'preembryos'; and embryo splitting.

Frequently discussed ethical issues include concerns about destruction of the traditional family when third parties are used as gamete donors or surrogates (Macklin, 1991); worries about the effect on children who learn that they were born as a result of these techniques; and the opposite worry about harmful effects of struggling to maintain family secrets. Prior to the first IVF birth in 1978, fears were expressed that IVF would produce a higher than normal incidence of birth defects, but scientific evidence gathered over the years has shown this concern to be unwarranted. The objection that being created with the aid of gametes from a third party can harm the interests of children is countered by the metaphysical observation that these are children who would never have existed but for the use of these techniques.

Frequently discussed ethical issues

include concerns about destruction

of the traditional family when third parties

are used as gamete donors or surrogates.

Different religions are opposed to the use of some or all of these reproductive technologies. The Roman Catholic Church has urged prohibition of virtually all forms of assisted reproduction (Congregation for the Doctrine of the Faith, 1987). The church's opposition is based on the fact that these techniques separate the procreative and unitive functions of marriage. Some authorities in Orthodox Judaism allow insemination from non-Jewish sperm donors but prohibit donation from Jews, in order to prevent consanguinity; others oppose all third-party donations out of fear of consanguinity and also by analogy with adultery. Islamic law prohibits the use of sperm or eggs from anyone other than the married couple on grounds that the results are similar to adultery (Serour, 1992). Since the identity of gamete donors is normally kept confidential, a secular concern is that a brother and sister may unwittingly mate or marry, unaware that they have a genetic parent in common.

Possibly the most intriguing philosophical issues posed by reproductive technologies are those that arise from the newfound ability to separate the genetic from the gestational procreative functions. IVF permits an ovum from one woman to be fertilized and the resulting embryo implanted in a different woman. This creates the entirely novel situation of two different "mothers": the genetic mother, who supplies the egg; and the gestational mother, who undergoes pregnancy and child-birth. Apart from the emotional or other psychological consequences that may result from such arrangements, the separation of the woman's procreative role into two distinct biological functions requires a conceptual decision of whether the individual who performs each function properly deserves the appellation 'mother' (Macklin, 1991).

A variation on this conceptual theme stems from research that demonstrates the capability of transplanting ovaries from an aborted fetus into an adult woman who lacks ovaries of her own. The woman into whom the ovaries are transplanted is a mother in the traditional sense of one who is pregnant and gives birth to the child. Is it appropriate to construe the aborted fetus as the "genetic mother"? The conceptual oddity of this construal suggests that "mother" is a concept laden with connotations that do not permit its expansion to include aborted fetuses. Although the aborted fetus is without question the source of the genetic material from which the new life was created, it is semantically odd to conclude that the aborted fetus is the genetic mother.

A persistent quandary relates to the status of extra-corporeal embryos. The product of IVF is termed a 'preembryo,' partly because of its early developmental stage but also because it is unimplanted. The ability to freeze embryos indefinitely and thaw them for use later poses both conceptual and ethical questions. When disputes arise concerning the ownership of embryos, should the embryos be construed as "people" or as "property" (Annas, 1989; Robertson, 1990)? Should anyone other than the couple who contributed the gametes have the authority to destroy frozen embryos? If it is permissible to destroy embryos that are not intended for implantation, is it permissible to do experiments on the embryos? Controversy exists over the splitting of embryos, a technique sometimes called cloning (Robertson, 1994). One objection holds that such deliberate duplication destroys genetic individuality and thus devalues the uniqueness of each individual.

Genetics and reproductive technologies pose new philosophical questions about the scope and limits of such familiar concepts as disease, individuality, parent, mother, and the family. The importance accorded to human reproduction and lineage throughout history is a reminder that such questions are not merely abstract concerns of philosophers but deeply rooted in the lives of individuals and communities.

[See also Abortion; Biomedical Ethics; Distant Peoples and Future Generations; Informed Consent.]

BIBLIOGRAPHY

Annas, G. J. "A French Homunculus in a Tennessee Court," *Hastings Center Report*, Vol. 19 (1989), 20–22.

Congregation for the Doctrine of the Faith. *Instruction on Respect for Human Life in Its Origin and on the Dignity of Procreation.* Vatican City, 1987.

Fletcher, J. *The Ethics of Genetic Control: Ending Reproductive Roulette.* Garden City, NY, 1974.

Lappe, M. "The Genetic Counselor: Responsible to Whom?" *Hastings Center Report*, Vol. 2 (1971), 6–8.

Macklin, R. "Artificial Means of Reproduction and Our Understanding of the Family," *Hastings Center Report*, Vol. 21 (1991), 5–11.

Milunsky, A., and G. J. Annas, eds. *Genetics and the Law III.* New York, 1985.

President's Commission for the Study of Ethical Problems in Medicine and Biomedical and Behavioral Research. *Splicing Life.* Washington, DC, 1982.

President's Commission for the Study of Ethical Problems in Medicine and Biomedical and Behavioral Research. *Screening and Counseling for Genetic Conditions.* Washington, DC, 1983.

Proctor, R. N. *Racial Hygiene: Medicine under the Nazis.* Cambridge, MA, 1988.

Ramsey, P. *Fabricated Man: The Ethics of Genetic Control.* New Haven, 1970.

Robertson, J. A. "In the Beginning: The Legal Status of Early Embryos," *Virginia Law Review*, Vol. 76 (1990), 437–517.

Robertson, J. A. "The Question of Human Cloning." *Hasting Center Report*, Vol. 24 (1994), 6–14.

Serour, G. I. "Medically Assisted Conception: Islamic Views," in G. I. Serour, ed., *Proceedings of the First International Conference on Bioethics in Human Reproduction Research in the Muslim World* (Cairo, 1992).

– RUTH MACKLIN

GÖDEL, KURT

Kurt Gödel (1906–78), logician, was born in Brno, Czech Republic, and educated at the University of Vienna, where he became Privatdozent in 1933. In 1940 he joined the Institute for Advanced Study in Princeton, New Jersey, where he remained for the rest of his career. Following Hilbert, Gödel was instrumental in establishing mathematical logic as a fundamental branch of mathematics, achieving results such as the incompleteness theorems that have had a profound impact on twentieth-century thought. In philosophy, by contrast, he represents the path not taken. His few publications in this area tend to focus on the more immediate ramifications of his own (and closely related) mathematical work. A fair amount of synthesis and reconstruction is needed if one is to consider him as a philosopher.

A close student of the history of philosophy, Gödel follows Plato, Leibniz, and Husserl as opposed to the more fashionable Aristotle, Kant, and Wittgenstein. (On Kant, however, see Gödel, 1946–49 and 1961.) Methodologically, two patterns in his thinking stand out. First, a tendency to move from the possible to the actual is revealed, via the notion of necessity, in his Leibnizian ontological argument for the existence of God (Gödel, 1970). He relies here on the S5 modal principle, (possibly necessarily P ⊃ necessarily P). It can also, arguably, be discerned in his mathematical Platonism— since the distinction of the possible from the actual, relevant to material being, collapses in the formal realm of mathematics. (See Yourgrau, 1991.) Finally, in relativistic cosmology (Gödel, 1949, 1950) he concludes from the possible existence of rotating universes, where time is merely 'ideal', to its ideality in the actual world. Second, he is preoccupied with probing mathematically the limits of 'formal' methods in systematizing 'intuitive' concepts. In his first incompleteness theorem, for example, by applying an ingenious arithmetization of metamathematics to a formal system of arithmetic, he is able to construct a formula expressing its own unprovability and thus to prove (as he made explicit later) the indefinability within the system of the 'intuitive' concept of arithmetic truth. (See Feferman, 1983.) Along the same lines one might view his results in cosmology as demonstrating the limits of relativistic space-

time in representing the 'intuitive' concept of time, although here, interestingly, Gödel's response is to abandon the 'intuitive' concept. (See Yourgrau, 1991, 1995.)

From a broader perspective Gödel isolates two basic philosophical worldviews: one with a "leftward" direction, toward skepticism, materialism, and positivism, the other inclined toward "the right," toward spiritualism, idealism, and theology (or metaphysics; Gödel, 1961). He puts empiricism on the left and a priorism on the right and points out that although mathematics, qua a priori science, belongs "by its nature" on the right, it too has followed the spirit of the times in moving toward the left—as witnessed by the rise of Hilbert's formalism. With Frege Gödel resists this trend, pointing to his incompleteness theorems as evidence that "the Hilbertian combination of materialism and aspects of classical mathematics . . . proves to be impossible"

Kurt Gödel (second from right), seen here with Albert Einstein (far left), was a student of mathematics. In philosophy, by contrast, he represents the path not taken. (Corbis/Bettmann-UPI)

(1961, p. 381). But Frege's mathematical philosophy is held together by two strands that may appear to be in tension with one another: on one side his Platonism and conceptual realism, on the other his conception of arithmetic as analytic (that is, as resting on our definitions and on the laws of logic) and his "context principle" (which seems to put our sentences—hence language—at the center of his philosophy). (See Dummett, 1991.) This second aspect of Frege's thought, via Russell and Wittgenstein, helped persuade the positivists of the Vienna Circle (whose meetings Gödel attended) that mathematics is "without content," a mere matter of (more or less arbitrary) linguistic conventions concerning the syntax of (formal) language. This conclusion was, however, rejected by both Frege and Gödel (1944; 1951; 1953–59), Frege hoping, contra Kant, "to put an end to the widespread contempt for analytic judgments and to the legend of the sterility of pure logic" (1884, p. 24; see also 1879, p. 55). Gödel, for his part, insists that " 'analytic' does not mean 'true owing to our definitions', but rather 'true owing to the nature of the concepts occurring therein' " (1951, p. 321). (See Parsons, 1994.)

Gödel was instrumental

in establishing mathematical logic

as a fundamental branch of mathematics,

achieving results such as the

incompleteness theorems that have had

a profound impact on twentieth-century thought.

Frege and Gödel are in further agreement, "against the spirit of the times," that the fundamental axioms of mathematics should be not simply mutually consistent but (nonhypothetically) true. They also reject Hilbert's conception of axiom systems as 'implicit definitions', Gödel insisting that a formal axiomatic system only partially characterizes the concepts expressed therein. Indeed, his incompleteness theorem makes the point dramatically: "Continued appeals to mathematical intuition are necessary . . . for the solution of the problems of finitary number theory. . . . This follows from the fact that for every axiomatic system there are infinitely many undecidable propositions of this type" (1947 [1964], p. 269). And it is in our ability—if indeed we possess it—to 'intuit' new axioms in an open-ended way that Gödel sees a possible argument to the

effect that minds are not (Turing) machines (Gödel, 1951; Wang, 1974). What kind of intuitions, however, are these? Gödel does, it is true, employ a Kantian term here, but he does not mean concrete immediate individual representations, and on just this point he faults Hilbert: "What Hilbert means by 'Anschauung' is substantially Kant's space-time intuition. . . . Note that it is Hilbert's insistence on *concrete* knowledge that makes finitary mathematics so surprisingly weak and excludes many things that are just as incontrovertibly evident to everybody as finitary number theory" (1958 [1972], p. 272, n. b). (See also 1947 [1964], p. 258.) Note, further, that mathematical intuition, though a form of a priori knowledge, does not ensure absolute certainty, which Gödel rejects (Wang, 1991); rather, as with its humbler cousin, sense perception, it too may attain various degrees of clarity and reliability. (See Gödel, 1951, his remarks on Husserl in 1961, and Parsons, 1995, 1995a.)

Frege and Hilbert, then, serve as useful coordinates in mapping Gödel's philosophy, in its tendency to "the right." What, then, if one chooses Einstein as a third coordinate? Note first that "idealistic" in the title of Gödel (1949) is not a gesture toward a mind-centered philosophy like that of Berkeley. Rather, Gödel is pointing to the classic Platonic distinction between appearance and reality. Though the world may appear (to the senses) as if temporal, this is in fact an illusion. Only 'reason'—here, mathematical physics—can provide a more adequate cognition of reality (i.e., of Einstein-Minkowski space-time). Gödel makes a sharp distinction between intuitive time, which 'lapses', and the 'temporal' component of space-time. By his lights, already in the special theory of relativity (STR) intuitive time has disappeared, since "the existence of an objective lapse of time means . . . that reality consists of an infinity of layers of 'now' which come into existence successively" (Gödel, 1949, pp. 202–3), whereas the relativity of simultaneity in the STR implies that "each observer has his own set of 'nows', and none of these various systems of layers can claim the prerogative of representing the objective lapse of time" (p. 203).

These observations, however, rely on the equivalence of all 'observers' or reference frames in the STR, whereas in the general theory of relativity (GTR), of which the STR is an idealized special case, the presence of matter and the consequent curvature of space-time permit the introduction of 'privileged observers', in relation to which one can define a 'world time' (which, one might say, objectively lapses). Gödel's discovery is that there exist models of the GTR—the rotating universes—where, probably, no such definition of a world time is possible. In particular, these worlds permit 'time travel', in the sense that, "for *every* possible definition of a world time one could travel into regions of the universe which are past according to that definition," and "this again shows that to assume an objective lapse of time would lose every justification in these worlds" (1949, p. 205). The idea, here, is clearly that if a time has 'objectively lapsed' it no longer exists and so is not *there* to be revisited (in the future). Hence, by contraposition, if it can be revisited, it never did 'objectively lapse' in the first place. To describe the Gödel universe as 'static', however, as opposed to our own, would be misleading. The time traveler's rocket ship, for example, would move at a speed of at least $1/\sqrt{2}$ of the velocity of light! It would seem to observers, just as in our world, to be moving at great speed, and in general the denizens of Gödel's universe would experience time much as we do. And, indeed, that is why Gödel moves from the mere possible existence of the Gödel universe to the ideality of time in the actual world, since "the experience of the lapse of time can exist without an objective lapse of time, no reason can be given why an objective lapse of time should be assumed at all" (p. 206; see Saritt, 1994; Stein, 1970, 1994; Wang, 1995; and Yourgrau, 1991, 1994.)

Here, then, is another example of the Janus-faced quality of Gödel's thinking (presaged already in his arithmetization of metamathematics)—contributing, mathematically, to "the left" while at the same time, as he sees it, pointing to "the right."

[*See also* Aristotle; Berkeley, George; Frege, Gottlob; Husserl, Edmund; Kant, Immanuel; Leibniz, Gottfried Wilhelm; Materialism; Mathematical Logic; Plato; Platonism, Mathematical; Russell, Bertrand Arthur William; Skepticism; Wittgenstein, Ludwig Josef Johann.]

BIBLIOGRAPHY

Works by Gödel

The Foundations of Arithmetic [1884], translated by J. L. Austin. Evanston, IL, 1980.
"Russell's Mathematical Logic" [1944], in *Collected Works,* Vol. 2. New York, 1990.
"What Is Cantor's Continuum Problem?" [1947; 1964], in *Collected Works,* Vol. 2. New York, 1990.
"A Remark about the Relationship between Relativity Theory and Idealistic Philosophy" [1949], in *Collected Works,* Vol. 2. New York, 1990.
"Some Observations about the Relationship between Theory of Relativity and Kantian Philosophy" [1950], in *Collected Works,* Vol. 3. New York, 1994.
"Some Basic Theorems on the Foundations of Mathematics and Their Implications" [1951], in *Collected Works,* Vol. 3. New York, 1994.
"Is Mathematics Syntax of Language?" [1953–59], *Collected Works,* Vol. 3. New York, 1994.

"On an Extension of Finitary Mathematics Which Has Not Yet Been Used" [1958; 1972], translated by L. F. Boron, rev. K. Gödel, in *Collected Works,* Vol. 2. New York, 1990.
"The Modern Development of the Foundations of Mathematics in the Light of Philosophy" [1961], translated by E. Köhler and H. Wang, in *Collected Works,* Vol. 3. New York, 1994.
"Ontological Proof" [1970], in *Collected Works,* Vol. 3. New York, 1994.

Works on Gödel and Related Topics

Buldt, B., et al., eds. *Wahrheit und Beweisbarkeit: Leben und Werk Kurt Gödels.* Vienna, 1995.
Dawson, J. *Logical Dilemmas: The Life and Work of Kurt Gödel.* Wellesley, 1995.
Dummett, M. *Frege: Philosophy of Mathematics.* Cambridge, MA, 1991.
Feferman, S. "Kurt Gödel: Conviction and Caution," in S. G. Shanker, ed., *Gödel's Theorem in Focus* (London, 1988).
Frege, G. "Begriffsschrift: A Formula Language, Modeled upon That of Arithmetic, for Pure Thought" [1879], translated by S. Bauer-Mengelberg, in J. van Heijenoort, ed. *From Frege to Gödel: A Source Book in Mathematical Logic, 1879–1931* (Cambridge, MA, 1967).
Kreisel, G. "Kurt Gödel," *Biographical Memoirs of Fellows of the Royal Society,* Vol. 26 (1980), 149–224.
Parsons, C. "Quine and Gödel on Analyticity," in P. Leonardi, ed., *On Quine: New Essays* (San Marino, 1995).
———. "Platonism and Mathematical Intuition in Kurt Gödel's Thought," *The Bulletin of Symbolic Logic,* Vol. 1, No. 1 (1995a), 44–74.
Savitt, S. "The Replacement of Time," *Australian Journal of Philosophy,* Vol. 72, no 4 (1994), 463–74.
Shanker, S. G., ed. *Gödel's Theorem in Focus.* London, 1988.
Stein, H. "On the Paradoxical Time-Structures of Kurt Gödel," *Philosophy of Science,* Vol. 37 (1970), 589–601.
———. "Introductory Note to Gödel, 1946/9," in K. Gödel, *Collected Works,* Vol. 3 (New York, 1994).
Wang, H. *From Mathematics to Philosophy.* New York, 1974.
———. *Reflections on Kurt Gödel.* Cambridge, MA, 1987.
———. "Philosophy through Mathematics and Logic," in R. Haller and J. Brandl, eds., *Wittgenstein—towards a Re-Evaluation: Proceedings of the Fourteenth International Wittgenstein-Symposium* (Vienna, 1990).
———. "To and From Philosophy: Discussions with Gödel and Wittgenstein," *Synthese,* Vol. 88 (1991), 229–77.
———. "Time in Philosophy and in Physics: From Kant and Einstein to Gödel," *Synthese,* Vol. 102 (1995), 215–34.
Yourgrau, P. "Review Essay: Hao Wang, *Reflections on Kurt Gödel,*" *Philosophy and Phenomenological Research,* Vol. 1 (1989), 391–408.
———. *The Disappearance of Time: Kurt Gödel and the Idealistic Tradition in Philosophy.* Cambridge, 1991.
———. "Philosophical Reflections on Gödel's Cosmology," in B. Buldt et al., eds., *Wahrheit und Beweisbarkeit: Leben und Werk Kurt Gödels* (Vienna, 1995).

– PALLE YOURGRAU

GOODMAN, NELSON

Nelson Goodman, one of the foremost philosophers of the twentieth century, has produced works that have transformed epistemology, metaphysics, and the philosophy of art. *The Structure of Appearance,* which grew out of his Ph.D. dissertation, shows how to develop interpreted formal systems that solve or dissolve perennial epistemological problems. *Fact, Fiction, and Forecast* poses and solves the new riddle of induction, demonstrating that to block the inference to 'All emeralds are grue', we must consider the ways our terms have actually been used inductively in the past. *Languages of Art* reconceives aesthetics, arguing that the arts function cognitively, so aesthetics is a branch of epistemology.

Despite Goodman's recognition

of multiple ways of worldmaking

and multiple worlds made, he does not contend

that every version makes a world.

Only right versions do.

Goodman attended Harvard, both as an undergraduate and as a graduate student. During graduate school, he supported himself by running an art gallery. He spent most of his academic career as professor of philosophy at the University of Pennsylvania. During the final decade of his teaching career he was professor of philosophy at Harvard. He founded Project Zero, an ongoing research program in arts education at the Harvard Graduate School of Education, and the Harvard Summer Dance program. He is an avid, eclectic collector of art.

Art

Nelson Goodman's trailblazing *Languages of Art* reorients aesthetics. Active engagement, not passive contemplation, marks the aesthetic attitude. Understanding rather than appreciation is its goal. Aesthetics, as Goodman construes it, belongs to epistemology.

Works of art are symbols that require interpretation. *Languages of Art* provides a taxonomy of syntactic and semantic systems deployed in the arts and elsewhere, detailing their strengths and limitations. Two modes of reference are basic. Denotation links names to bearers, predicates to instances, representations to the things they represent. 'George Washington', 'the first U. S. president', and the Gilbert Stuart portrait all denote Washington. In exemplification, a symbol points up, hence refers to properties it serves as a sample of. A fabric swatch exemplifies its pattern; a Mondrian painting, squareness. Ubiquitous in art, exemplification is also widespread in science, advertising, indeed anywhere we adduce samples and examples (Goodman, 1976).

Reference need not be literal. Metaphorical reference, Goodman maintains, is real reference; metaphorical truth, real truth. 'Bulldog' genuinely, albeit metaphorically, denotes Churchill. 'Churchill is a bulldog' is genuinely, although not literally, true. Michelangelo's *Moses* genuinely, albeit metaphorically, exemplifies rage. Expression is metaphorical exemplification by a work of art functioning as such. The *Moses* thus expresses the rage it exemplifies (Goodman, 1976; 1984).

Some reference is complex. In allusion, a referential chain composed of denotational and exemplificational links connects a symbol to its referent (Goodman, 1984). Two chains figure in variation, one exemplifying features that a variation shares with its theme, the other exemplifying features that contrast with the theme (Goodman and Elgin, 1988).

Scientific symbols, Goodman maintains, are relatively attenuated, aesthetic symbols relatively replete. A scientific symbol is normally univocal, its full import readily apparent. An aesthetic symbol may bear multiple correct interpretations and symbolize along several dimensions simultaneously. Exactly what it symbolizes may never be settled. The same item may qualify as a symbol of either kind, depending on how it functions. So 'When is art?' not 'What is art?' is the crucial question. When, how, and to what effect does a symbol function aesthetically (Goodman, 1978)?

Art advances understanding, not only because interpretation is a cognitive process. Encounters with art afford insights that extend beyond the aesthetic realm. Discoveries made, orientations adopted, and patterns discerned in aesthetic contexts transfer and make sense of other aspects of experience.

Worldmaking

In *Ways of Worldmaking* Goodman returns to constructionalist themes first explored in *The Structure of Appearance.* Worlds, he contends, are made, not found. Since the elements of any group are alike in some respects and different in others, mere examination will not reveal whether two manifestations are of the same thing or two things of the same kind. To settle such matters requires criteria of individuation and classification. Category schemes supply them. But category schemes are human constructs. In devising them we demarcate the individuals and kinds that make up a world. Different demarcations yield divergent but equally tenable world versions. One might characterize light as a stream of particles; another, as a sequence of waves. Each may be right relative to its own world version, wrong relative to its rival's. Neither is right or wrong absolutely.

If overlapping world versions all supervened on a single base, such differences would be ontologically innocuous. They do not. A physicalist version, for example, neither supervenes on nor underlies a phenomenalist version. Nor does any neutral version underlie them both. Since we can and do construct multiple, individually adequate, but irreconcilable world versions, there are, Goodman concludes, many worlds if any.

Worldmaking is not always deliberate. Also in *Ways of Worldmaking,* Goodman analyzes a series of psychological experiments and shows how, with only sparse cues, the visual system constructs the apparent motion it detects. Nor is worldmaking always discursive. Nonverbal schemes structure things in ways no description precisely captures. The arts as well as the sciences construct viable world versions.

Despite Goodman's recognition of multiple ways of worldmaking and multiple worlds made, he does not contend that every version makes a world. Only right versions do. Rightness does not reduce to truth, for some truths are wrong, some falsehoods right, and some symbols right though neither true nor false. Rightness involves fitting and working—fitting with past cognitive practice and working to promote cognitive ends. Consistency, cogency, projectibility, and fairness of sample figure in the rightness of tenable world versions (Goodman, 1978; Goodman and Elgin, 1988).

[See also Aesthetic Attitude; Aesthetics, History of; Aesthetics, Problems in; Art, Interpretation of; Epistemology; Metaphysics; Reference.]

BIBLIOGRAPHY

Works by Goodman

Problems and Projects. Indianapolis, 1972.
Languages of Art, 2d ed. Indianapolis, 1976.
The Structure of Appearance, 3d ed. Dordrecht, 1977.
Ways of Worldmaking. Indianapolis, 1978.
Fact, Fiction, and Forecast, 4th ed. Cambridge, MA, 1983.
Of Mind and Other Matters. Cambridge, MA, 1984.
Reconceptions in Philosophy and Other Arts and Sciences, with C. Z. Elgin. Indianapolis, 1988.
Esthétique et connaissance: Pour changer de sujet, with C. Z. Elgin. Combas, 1990.
A Study of Qualities. New York, 1990. Goodman's Ph.D. dissertation.

Works on Goodman

Elgin, C. Z. *With Reference to Reference.* Indianapolis, 1983.
Scheffler, I. "The Wonderful Worlds of Goodman," in *Inquiries* (Indianapolis, 1986).
Schwartz, R. "The Power of Pictures," *Journal of Philosophy,* Vol. 82 (1985), 711–20.

Stalker, D., ed. *Grue: The New Riddle of Induction.* La Salle, IL, 1994.

— CATHERINE Z. ELGIN

GRICE, HERBERT PAUL

Herbert Paul Grice (1913–1988), was born and educated in England. He taught at St. John's College, Oxford, until 1967, when he moved to the University of California at Berkeley. He taught there until his death. He published little until near the end of his life but had a great influence through students and the wide circulation of unpublished manuscripts. His earliest work dealt with perception, but he subsequently moved to problems in language, ethics, and metaphysics. Concern about reason and rationality unites these investigations. His historical idols were Aristotle and Kant.

A conversational implicature of an assertion

is something that is conveyed to

a thoughtful listener by the mode of expression

rather than by the words themselves.

One early concern was a defense of the causal theory of perception. This defense required separating the scientific part of the task of analyzing perception from that of the philosopher. This distinction relies on an underlying notion of analysis closely related to the analytic/synthetic distinction for which Grice and Strawson provided a brief spirited defense. Three subsequent papers represent intricate attempts to define meaning using only commonsense psychological concepts such as intention, belief, and desire. If this program had succeeded it would have provided a more elaborate defense of the analytic/synthetic distinction.

Grice's best-known contribution is that of a conversational implicature. A conversational implicature of an assertion is something that is conveyed to a thoughtful listener by the mode of expression rather than by the words themselves. Implicatures arise from the fact that conversation is normally governed by principles including cooperation, truthfulness, and informativeness and that both parties are aware of these. The two best-known applications of this concept are to perception and logic. Grice was concerned to provide an account of sense-data discourse in terms of how things seemed to the perceiver. An objection to this is that it is odd to say in a normal case of the perception of a table that it seems to the subject that a table is present. Grice's concept of conversational implicature can explain the oddity as a result of the fact that a stronger statement can be made, thus leaving room for the seems statement to be true.

Grice also scouts the possibility of defending the claim that the logician's material conditional is an adequate representation of the indicative conditional of English by explaining the apparent divergence as a matter of conversational implicatures. If one knows the truth values of P and Q, then one can make a more informative statement than P ⊃ Q, so the only conversationally appropriate use of P ⊃ Q is when the speaker does not know the truth of either component but only that they are so connected that the truth of P guarantees the truth of Q. The conversational use of P ⊃ Q requires a connection that is not part of the truth condition of the compound. Part of the definition of a conversational implicature requires that the hearer should be able to reason out the intentions of the speaker and, in conjunction with the conversational principles, discern the implicit message. This places an important role on reasoning, especially inasmuch as in typical cases the reasoning is not conscious in the hearer.

Grice devotes considerable energy to investigating rationality, reasoning, and reasons. He emphasizes that reasoning is typically directed to the goal of producing reasons relevant to some end in view. This intentional activity involves the ability to make reason-preserving transitions. Grice defines "reason preserving" as analogous to "truth preserving" in deductive logic. A transition is reason preserving just in case; if one has reasons for the initial set of thoughts, beliefs, actions, or intentions, then one does for the subsequent set as well.

Grice uses this general account of reasoning to investigate moral reasoning and moral reasons. He emphasizes the connections between reasons, actions, and freedom. Strong rational evaluation—which Grice sees as essential to freedom—involves the rational evaluation and selection of ends, including ultimate ends.

How are we to choose ultimate ends? Grice answers that we should choose ends that have unrelativized value. Grice grants that the concept of unrelativized value requires defense. Typically, things have value only relative to ends and beneficiaries. My concern for the focus of relativization gives the value concept a "bite" on me, it ensures that the value concept carries weight for me. So how are we to understand unrelativized value?

Grice turns to final causation for a special kind of value. A tiger is a good tiger to the degree it realizes the final end of tigers. Grice defines a good person as one who has as part of his or her essential nature an autonomous finality consisting in the exercise of rationality. Grice's philosophical psychology supports this conception of persons as end-setters. Freedom intimately involves the ability to adopt and eliminate ends. One does not (ideally) arbitrarily select and conform to ends; one does so for reasons. This makes being an end-setter an instance of unrelativized value; for to take a consideration as an ultimate justification of action is to see it as having value. Grice defines unrelativized value in Aristotelian style as whatever would seem to possess such value in the eyes of a duly accredited judge; and a duly accredited judge might be identifiable as a good person operating in conditions of freedom. Of course, we are still talking about what is of value for and to persons. But the point was not to avoid this "relativization"; the point was to avoid relativization to this or that kind of person.

[See also Aristotle; Kant, Immanuel; Perception; Rationality; Strawson, Peter F.]

BIBLIOGRAPHY

Works by Grice

Studies in the Way of Words. Cambridge, MA, 1989. A collection including most of the important works published during his lifetime.

The Conception of Value. New York, 1991. A posthumous publication of the John Locke Lectures, delivered 1979.

"In Defence of a Dogma," with P. F. Strawson, *Philosophical Review,* Vol. 65 (1957), 141–58. A defense of the analytic/synthetic distinction, widely reprinted and discussed.

Work on Grice

Grandy, R. E., and R. Warner. *Philosophical Grounds of Rationality: Intentions, Categories, Ends.* Oxford, 1986. A festschrift celebrating Grice's work, with an introduction and a response by Grice.

– RICHARD E. GRANDY
RICHARD WARNER

H

HABERMAS, JÜRGEN

Jürgen Habermas, German philosopher and leading representative of the Frankfurt school of critical theory, was born in 1929 in Düsseldorf. After World War II he studied in Göttingen, Zürich, and Bonn, where he submitted a dissertation on Schelling in 1954. From 1955 to 1959 he was Theodor Adorno's assistant at the Institute for Social Research in Frankfurt. After habilitating at Marburg University in 1961, he taught philosophy and sociology at the universities of Heidelberg and Frankfurt before becoming co-director of the Max Planck Institute in Starnberg. In 1983 he returned to the University of Frankfurt, where he was professor of philosophy until his retirement in 1994.

Habermas's scholarly work,

which aspires to a comprehensive critical theory

of contemporary society, ranges across many

of the humanities and social sciences.

Habermas's life and work have remained deeply influenced by the traumatic events of his youth under National Socialism. From the time of his involvement with the German student movement in the 1960s he has been one of Germany's most prominent public intellectuals, speaking out on a wide array of issues, from violations of civil liberties and the attempted "historicizing" of the Holocaust to immigration policy and the manner of German reunification.

Habermas's scholarly work, which aspires to a comprehensive critical theory of contemporary society, ranges across many of the humanities and social sciences. His early and influential *Strukturwandel der Öffentlichkeit* (1962) was a historical, sociological, and philosophical account of the emergence and transformation of the liberal public sphere as a forum for critical public discussion of matters of general concern. While the historical structures of that sphere reflected the particular constellations of interests that gave rise to it, the idea it claimed to embody, the idea of legitimating political authority through rational discussion and reasoned agreement, remains central to democratic theory.

Habermas returned to these themes three decades later in *Faktizität und Geltung* (1992), where he applied the idea of justification by appeal to generally acceptable reasons to the deliberations of free and equal citizens in a constitutional democracy. The primary function of the system of basic rights, he argued, is to secure personal and political autonomy; and the key to the latter is the institutionalization of the public use of reason in the legal-political domain.

One might read Habermas's extensive writings in the intervening decades as a protracted examination of the cultural, psychological, and social preconditions of and barriers to accomplishing this. The essays of the early 1960s, a number of which were collected in *Theorie und Praxis* (1963), introduced the idea of studying society as a historically developing whole for purposes of enlightening political consciousness and guiding political practice. The methodology and epistemology behind this approach were elaborated in the later 1960s in *Zur Logik des Sozialwissenschaften* (1967) and *Erkenntnis und Interesse* (1968). A principal target in both books was the neopositivist thesis of the unity of scientific method, particularly the claim that the logic of inquiry in the human sciences is basically the same as in the natural sciences. The former work started from an examination of the nature and role of *Verstehen* in social inquiry and argued that access to symbolically prestructured object domains calls for interpretive procedures designed to grasp the meanings on which social interactions turn. Intersubjective meanings constitutive of sociocultural lifeworlds can neither be wholly objectified, as positivism supposes, nor simply reappropriated, as hermeneutics proposes. Psychoanalysis suggests an alternative approach, in which explanatory and interpretive procedures are combined with a critique of ideology in a historically oriented theory with practical intent.

In *Erkenntnis und Interesse* Habermas undertook a historical and systematic study of "the prehistory of modern positivism" in an attempt to free the ideas of reason and rationality from what he regarded as a "scientistic misunderstanding." Tracing the development of the critique of knowledge from Kant through German idealism to Marx, and its transformation into the methodology of science in early positivism, he elaborated his own position in critical encounters with three classic but flawed attempts to overcome positivism from within methodology: Peirce's reflections on natural science, Dilthey's on cultural inquiry, and Freud's on self-reflection. In each case he examined the roots of cognition in life and argued for an internal connection of knowledge with 'anthropologically deep-seated' human interests. A key feature of this 'quasi-transcendental' theory of cognitive interests was the basic distinction between the interest in prediction and control of objectified processes and the interests in mutual understanding and distortion-free communication with speaking and acting subjects.

There followed a series of studies of basic structures of communication, organized as a three-tiered research program. The ground level consisted of a general theory of communication in natural languages, a 'universal pragmatics', as Habermas called it. This served as the foundation for a general theory of socialization in the form of a developmental account of the acquisition of communicative competence. Building on both of these, Habermas sketched a theory of sociocultural evolution as the historical development of forms of communicative interaction and mutual understanding. These accounts of communication, socialization, and social evolution enabled him to anchor moral theory in the theory of social action. Arguing that our basic moral intuitions spring from something deeper and more universal than contingent features of particular traditions, his discourse ethics sought to reconstruct the intuitive grasp of the normative presuppositions of social interaction possessed by competent social actors generally.

The work of the 1960s and 1970s culminated in the monumental *Theorie des kommunikativen Handelns* (1981), in which Habermas developed a concept of communicative rationality freed from the subjectivistic and individualistic premises of modern social and political theory, together with a two-level concept of society that integrated the competing paradigms of 'lifeworld' and 'system'. On this basis he then sketched a critical theory of modern society that focused on 'the colonization of the lifeworld' by forces arising from the economy and the state: systemic mechanisms such as money and power drive processes of social integration and symbolic reproduction out of domains in which they cannot be replaced. The phenomena that Max Weber pointed to in his vision of an 'iron cage' and that Marxists have dealt with in terms of 'reification' arises from an ever-increasing 'monetarization' and 'bureaucratization' of lifeworld relations. This relentless attack on the communicative infrastructures of society can be contained, he argued, only by a countervailing expansion of the areas of life coordinated via communication, and in particular by the subordination of economic and administrative subsystems to decisions arrived at in open and critical public debate. Thus, the antidote to colonization is democratization, and the key to the latter is an effectively functioning cultural and political public sphere. What distinguishes this critique of modernity from the welter of counterenlightenment critiques during the last two centuries is Habermas's unflinching defense of enlightenment rationality—a defense, to be sure, that is itself informed by the critique of rationalism and that emphasizes the ongoing, unfinished character of the project of enlightenment.

[See also Communicative Action; Critical Theory; Democracy; Discourse Ethics; Freud, Sigmund; Kant, Immanuel; Marx, Karl; Peirce, Charles Sanders; Rights.]

BIBLIOGRAPHY

Works by Habermas

Knowledge and Human Interests, translated by J. Shapiro. Boston, 1971.
Theory and Practice, translated by J. Viertel. Boston, 1973.
Communication and the Evolution of Society, translated by T. McCarthy. Boston, 1979.
Autonomy and Solidarity: Interviews with Jürgen Habermas, edited by Peter Dews. London, 1986.
The Theory of Communicative Action, 2 vols., translated by T. McCarthy. Boston, 1984, 1987.
The Structural Transformation of the Public Sphere, translated by T. Burger and F. Lawrence. Cambridge, MA, 1989.
Moral Consciousness and Communicative Action, translated by C. Lenhardt and S. Nicholsen. Cambridge, MA, 1990.
Between Facts and Norms: Contributions to a Discourse Theory of Law and Democracy, translated by W. Rehg. Cambridge, MA, 1995.

Works on Habermas

Bernstein, R., ed. *Habermas and Modernity.* Cambridge, MA, 1985.
McCarthy, T. *The Critical Theory of Jürgen Habermas.* Cambridge, MA, 1978.
Rehg, W. *Insight and Solidarity: The Discourse Ethics of Jürgen Habermas.* Berkeley, 1994.
White, S., ed. *The Cambridge Companion to Habermas.* Cambridge, 1995.

— THOMAS MCCARTHY

HARE, R. M.

R. M. (Richard M.) Hare, sometime White's Professor of Moral Philosophy at Oxford University, is famous as the inventor of universal prescriptivism. This is a metaethical doctrine, a thesis about what moral words mean. But Hare uses his metaethic to generate an ethic. Anyone who employs the moral concepts consistently in full awareness of the facts must wind up a utilitarian. Hare claims that his utilitarianism is the product of conceptual analysis rather than of moral intuition. To rely on intuitions is a philosophical sin, since it leads to relativism (Hare, 1991). His theory is developed in three books, *The Language of Morals* (1952), *Freedom and Reason* (1963), and *Moral Thinking* (1981).

Prescriptivism is a variant of noncognitivism. Moral judgments are action guiding, and the explanation of this is that they are prescriptive: they are not primarily

---

In Hare's view moral judgments are universalizable.

Thus, if Bligh asserts that Burkitt ought to be

flogged, he is committed to the view

that anyone in relevantly similar circumstances

ought to be flogged likewise.

---

designed to state facts but to prescribe actions. They are more akin to orders than statements or propositions. Nevertheless, moral judgments do have descriptive content, though this will depend upon the moral opinions of the speaker (Hare, 1963). Thus, if Captain Bligh says that Burkitt is a scoundrel, we can assume he is disobedient. Indeed, even words such as ought have descriptive content, though this too will vary with the moral opinions of the speaker. Typically, the descriptive content of an ought judgment will consist in the factual considerations—the reasons—that can be advanced in its support. Thus, if Bligh asserts that Burkitt ought to be flogged, this will be because it would be an act of punishing disobedience. That the flogging would be such an act is the descriptive content of "Burkitt ought to be flogged." (Whence it follows that, if Burkitt has not been disobedient, the ought judgment will be factually false.) In Hare's view moral judgments are universalizable. Thus, if Bligh thinks that Burkitt ought to be flogged, he is committed to the view that anyone in relevantly similar circumstances—anyone who has been similarly disobedient to a king's officer—ought to be flogged likewise. He must assent to the imperative "Let me be flogged in the hypothetical case in which I am in Burkitt's position!"—which includes having committed Burkitt's heinous acts of disobedience (Hare, 1963). Finally, moral judgments are overriding. They take precedence over any other imperatives the subject may accept. Thus, if Bligh thinks himself morally obliged to have Burkitt flogged, this takes precedence over his aesthetic obligation not to sully the pure air of the Pacific with Burkitt's distasteful groans. Sincere moral commitment entails action. Weakness of the will as traditionally conceived is not a genuine possibility. Thus, Hare reinstates the Socratic paradox that we cannot willingly do wrong (Hare, 1952; 1963).

What about utilitarianism? Hare first points out that the metaethic generates a method for refuting moral "conjectures." Bligh considers the maxim "I ought to have Burkitt flogged." He universalizes this to derive the principle that anyone in relevantly similar circumstances ought to be flogged likewise. This in turn entails the imperative "Let me be flogged if I am in Burkitt's position!" But Bligh cannot assent to this unless he is a fanatic—someone who prefers flogging the disobedient to remaining unflogged himself. Thus, Bligh must rescind his original "ought" (Hare, 1963). But this is only a method for vetoing moral maxims and a method, moreover, that leads to moral paralysis. As Hare himself points out, a guilty prisoner could challenge the judge to universalize the maxim that the accused ought to be put away and derive the imperative "Let me be imprisoned if I am in the accused shoes!"—an imperative she could accept only if she had a fanatical preference for imprisoning the guilty rather than staying out of jail herself (Hare, 1963). Nonfanatical judges would have to give up sentencing and justice would founder! But Hare offers a utilitarian solution. The correct course is to go the rounds of the affected parties and opt for the action that is subject to the weakest veto[es]. Thus, the judge must take into account the likely depredations of the prisoner and ask herself whether she can accept such imperatives as "Let me be robbed if the prisoner is released and allowed to carry on with his course of crime and I am one of his victims!" If not, and if the vetoes of the prisoner's potential victims outweigh his preference not to go to jail, then to jail he must go. The criminal-justice system can survive without fanaticism, and Hare's method becomes utilitarian. But does Hare derive utilitarianism from his conceptual analysis or assume utilitarianism to rescue that analysis from disaster (Roxbee Cox, 1986)?

The fanatic remains a problem. She can consistently subscribe to a persecuting principle if she assents to the imperatives in which she is on the sharp end. In *Moral Thinking* Hare deprives her of this possibility. He claims it is a conceptual truth that if I fully represent to myself what an unpleasant experience is like for someone—an experience that they would prefer to stop—I now acquire an equally strong preference not to have that experience were I in their shoes. Hence, a fanatic who fully represents to herself the sufferings of her potential victims cannot assent to the imperative that she should suffer were she in their position. For she has a preference as strong as theirs that she should not. If, however, Hare's conceptual truth is neither conceptual nor a truth, then fanaticism remains an option (Seanor & Fotion, 1991).

[See also Ethical Theory; Nondescriptivism.]

BIBLIOGRAPHY

Works by Hare

The Language of Morals. Oxford, 1952. Hare sets forth his metaethic.

Freedom and Reason. Oxford, 1963. Hare develops his metaethic and devises an engine of moral argument to enforce utilitarian conclusions. But he admits the fanatic is immune.

Moral Thinking: Its Levels, Methods, and Point. Oxford, 1981. Hare draws a distinction between intuitive and critical thinking and invents a conceptual truth to dispose of the fanatic. Only amoralists can avoid utilitarianism.

Essays in Ethical Theory. Oxford, 1989a. Hare develops and defends his ideas and attacks his philosophical rivals. Contains a memorably savage critique of John Rawls for relying on intuition, a reply to J. L. Mackie, his chief Oxford opponent, and a bibliography of his extensive writings.

Essays on Political Morality. Oxford, 1989b. A collection on applied ethics.

Works on Hare

Roxbee Cox, J. W. "From Universal Prescriptivism to Utilitarianism," *Philosophical Quarterly,* Vol. 36 (1986), 1–15. Challenges Hare's derivation of utilitarianism.

Seanor, D., and N. Fotion, eds. *Hare and Critics: Essays on Moral Thinking with Comments by R. M. Hare.* Oxford, 1991. The best essays are by Brandt, Singer, Gibbard, and Vendler. Hudson's essay lists some of the important criticisms Hare has faced. Extensive bibliography.

Singer, P. *Practical Ethics,* 2d. ed. Oxford, 1993. Hare's method is applied to practical affairs by his most gifted disciple.

Taylor, C. C. W. "Critical Notice of R. M. Hare's *Freedom and Reason,*" *Mind,* Vol. 74 (1965), 280–90. Still perhaps the best critique of Hare.

— CHARLES R. PIGDEN

HEGEL, GEORG WILHELM FRIEDRICH

Hegel became famous and influential at the University of Berlin. (Corbis/Bettmann)

Georg Wilhelm Friedrich Hegel (1770–1831), German idealist philosopher, was born at Stuttgart and entered the theological seminary at the University of Tübingen in 1788. Among his fellow students were Schelling and the poet Friedrich Hölderlin. After graduating he became, in 1793, a resident tutor in the home of an aristocratic family at Bern, and in 1796 he took a similar post in Frankfurt. In 1800 he went to Jena, where Schelling had succeeded Fichte as professor of philosophy and was developing an idealist philosophy of nature and metaphysics. Having been accepted as a teacher at Jena on the strength of his dissertation, *De Orbitis Planetarum* (1801), Hegel collaborated with Schelling in editing the philosophical journal *Kritisches Journal der Philosophie* and published his first book, *Differenz des Fichte'schen und Schelling'schen Systems der Philosophie* (1801). Notable articles by Hegel in the *Kritisches Journal* were "Glauben und Wissen" (1802) and "Über die wissenschaftlichen Behandlungsarten des Naturrechts" (1802–1803). At Jena, Hegel wrote his first major work, *Phänomenologie des Geistes* (*Phenomenology of Mind,* Würzburg and Bamberg, 1807). Completed about the time of Napoleon's victory over the Prussians at Jena in 1806, it was not published until 1807, after Hegel had left Jena to become editor of a daily paper at Bamberg in Bavaria.

In 1808, Hegel was appointed headmaster of a school in Nuremberg, a post he held until 1816. While at Nuremberg, Hegel published his *Wissenschaft der Logik* (*Science of Logic*)—Vol. I, *Die objective Logik* (2 vols.), Nuremberg, 1812–1813, and Vol. II, *Die subjective Logik oder Lehre vom Begriff* (Nuremberg, 1816). From 1816 to 1818, Hegel was professor of philosophy at Heidelberg. There he published *Encyklopädie der philosophischen Wissenschaften im Grundrisse* (*Encyclopedia of the Philosophical Sciences in Outline*) in 1817. In 1818, Hegel was appointed professor at the University of Berlin, where he became famous and influential. *Na-*

turrecht und Staatswissenschaft im Grundrisse (*Philosophy of Right*) appeared there in 1821; a second edition, edited by E. Gans as *Grundlinien der Philosophie des Rechts,* was published in Berlin in 1833. In 1827 a second, much enlarged edition of the *Encyclopedia* appeared.

Hegel died during a cholera epidemic in 1831. After his death a group of his friends compiled an edition of his works in 18 volumes (Berlin, 1832–1840). Several of Hegel's works were published for the first time in this edition: *Vorlesungen über die Aesthetik* ("Lectures on Aesthetics," translated as *The Philosophy of Fine Art,* H. G. Hotho, ed., 2 vols., 1835–1838); *Vorlesungen über die Philosophie der Geschichte* (*Lectures on the Philosophy of History,* E. Gans, ed., 1837); *Vorlesungen über die Philosophie der Religion* (*Lectures on the Philosophy of Religion,* Philipp Marheineke, ed., 2 vols., 1832); and *Vorlesungen über die Geschichte der Philosophie* (*Lectures on the History of Philosophy,* K. L. Michelet, ed., 2 vols., 1833–1836). This edition also contains notes taken by students of Hegel's comments on the *Encyclopedia* and on *Philosophy of Right,* which he was in the habit of using as textbooks.

In his biography, *Georg Wilhelm Friedrich Hegels Leben* (Berlin, 1844), Karl Rosenkranz referred to and quoted from the manuscripts of works written by Hegel prior to the publication of the *Phenomenology of Mind.* Not all the manuscripts known to Rosenkranz have survived, but toward the end of the nineteenth century Wilhelm Dilthey made a study of those that have and published an account and discussion of them in the *Proceedings of the Berlin Academy* in 1905. This has since received the title *Die Jugendgeschichte Hegels* and is reprinted in the fourth volume of Dilthey's collected works. Dilthey's pupil and editor, Herman Nohl, then published, under the title *Hegels theologische Jugendschriften,* the text of a great part of what Hegel had written while he was at Bern and Frankfurt. The chief of the writings unpublished during Hegel's lifetime are the essay "Das Leben Jesu" ("Life of Jesus," 1795), *Die Positivität der christlichen Religion* (*The Positivity of the Christian Religion,* 1796), and *Der Geist des Christentums und sein Schicksal* (*Spirit of Christianity and Its Destiny,* 1799). In 1915, Hans Ehrenberg and Herbert Link published, under the title *Hegels erstes System* (Heidelberg, 1915), an early version, written at Jena but never published by Hegel, of what later became the system sketched in the *Encyclopedia.* Since then Georg Lasson (*Hegels Jenenser Logik,* Leipzig, 1923) and Johannes Hoffmeister (*Hegels Jenenser Realphilosophie,* 2 vols., Leipzig, 1932) have published still other writings that Hegel had left unpublished. Thus, much more is

now known about Hegel's writings and philosophical development than was generally known in the nineteenth century.

Main Themes of Hegel's Philosophy

MIND. In the Preface to the *Phenomenology,* Hegel wrote that only mind (*Geist*) is real, and he constantly reiterated this view. (I have translated Hegel's *Geist* as "mind," in agreement with Wallace's view that "to average English ears the word Spiritual would carry us over the medium line into the proper land of religiosity"—*Hegel's Philosophy of Mind,* Oxford, 1894, p. 1.) Thus, he must be regarded as a philosophical idealist. He wrote rather slightingly of Berkeley, however, whose works he does not seem to have studied closely, and is sometimes described as an objective idealist in order to absolve him from suspicion of the subjective idealism that has often been attributed to Berkeley. Hegel's idealism presupposed the work of Kant and was influenced by Fichte and Schelling, but his early unpublished writings show that he had preoccupations of his own, independent of his famous German predecessors.

When Hegel said that only mind is real, he did not mean that material things do not exist and that only minds do. Mind was not, in Hegel's view, a plurality of immaterial substances but a system of individuals actively developing their potentialities by embodying them in increasingly complex forms. A fundamental feature of mind, according to Hegel, is freedom, and nothing that is partial or finite can be wholly free. The mind that is the only reality is therefore infinite. Furthermore, no one is free unless he is conscious of what he is doing, and infinite mind is therefore self-conscious mind. Artists and statesmen, merchants and saints, all busy themselves with their more or less partial tasks without necessarily concerning themselves with what it is that they are doing. According to Hegel, it is the function of the philosopher to make men conscious of what art and politics, commerce and religion, are, so that mind can exert itself to its utmost range and thus become absolute. Like Pythagoras, Plotinus, and Spinoza, Hegel was a philosopher who held that philosophy is an activity which purifies and frees the mind.

DIALECTIC. Hegel is, of course, famous for his dialectical method, but it is enormously difficult to explain this in a brief compass. It should first be noted that Hegel set out his systematic writings in dialectical triads comprising a thesis, antithesis, and synthesis. Thus, he divided his *Encyclopedia,* in which he expounded his system as a whole, into three fundamental division sections—"Logic," "Philosophy of Nature," and "Philosophy of Mind." In the first he expounded the categories as developing forms of thought; in the second, he said "the Idea" is considered in its "otherness" (*Anderssein*) or externality; and in the third, mind is considered as existing "for itself," as conscious of itself and of the institutions it has given rise to. Within these main divisions there are further triadic subdivisions, although a very large number of subdivisions are not of this nature. It is therefore clear that Hegel himself regarded his whole work as a dialectical construction, with thought and nature as opposites united in mind and society, in the artistic and religious products of man, and, ultimately, in the activity of philosophical self-consciousness.

When Hegel said that only mind is real,

he did not mean that material things do not exist

and that only minds do.

Hegel's system, then, has a dialectical structure, but what is his dialectical method? Hegel, like Spinoza, held that error resides in incompleteness and abstraction, but, unlike Spinoza, he held that the incompleteness and abstraction can be recognized by the contradictions they generate. It is the business of the philosopher, he held, to bring out the contradictions latent in partial or abstract views and to emphasize and elaborate them in such a way that less partial and less abstract views can be constructed that nevertheless retain in themselves what there was of truth in the original views. The same method is to be brought to bear on the less partial and less abstract views in their turn and to be pressed as thoroughly as it can be. This method of pressing and accentuating contradictions is not to be used merely to discard error but also to preserve truth. Because of the happy circumstance that in German *aufheben* means both "to cancel" and "to preserve"—its literal meaning is "to lift up"—Hegel was able to express this aspect of his view with brevity and acuity. The concept or view that is *aufgehoben* is transcended without being wholly discarded. Hegel's *Phenomenology of Mind* was an account of how various human attitudes—reliance on sense experience, the belief in substance, otherworldliness, strenuous moralism, and so on—all have some point and are yet contradictory, leading to the conclusion that "truth is a bacchanalian revel where not a member is sober," as Hegel put it in the Preface. His *Logic* gave an account of how the categories are related in this way. In his *Lectures on the History of Philosophy* he sought to show that the major philosophical outlooks from that of the Ionians on are, on the one hand, posi-

tive contributions that we could not do without and, on the other hand, contradictions that we have to overcome.

HISTORY. Another feature of Hegel's philosophy is its concern with history. Much as Hegel admired Plato's philosophy, he held that it was impossible to be a Platonist in the nineteenth century, when the philosophical context differed so greatly from that of Plato's day. In his *Lectures on the Philosophy of History*, Hegel argued that the history of man in the concrete was as much a progression as the history of his thought. This he deduced from the thesis that mind is of its very nature free. Thus, each historical epoch, according to Hegel, embodied some aspect of or stage in the development of man's free mind, and it would be absurd for an individual to go counter to his time except insofar as he was preparing the way for future epochs. Hegel borrowed this "progressivism," as it may be called, from the philosophers of the Enlightenment. It has greatly influenced Marxism.

CHRISTIANITY. Hegel thought his system provided a defense of Christianity, and both supporters and opponents of his system have taken this view of it. Those known as right Hegelians considered Hegel's apologetic successful, whereas the left Hegelians argued that his Christianity had been only superficial and his Christian terminology a disguise for something very different. In his system Hegel placed philosophy above religion in the dialectical scale, and this may give some support for the interpretations of the left. Yet there is ambiguity in Hegel's view on this, as on other important matters. On one hand, he held that only infinite mind is real; on the other hand, he held that infinite mind cannot be distinct from or beyond the finite and partial. He thought that these views were not incompatible, but it has been argued that the second is a denial of the first and, hence, a denial of any form of theism.

This article will briefly describe Hegel's early works that were posthumously published in *Hegels theologische Jugendschriften*. It will continue with an account of the *Phenomenology of Mind*, Hegel's first important book, and conclude with a brief discussion of the Hegelian system based chiefly on the *Encyclopedia*.

Early Unpublished Writings

"LIFE OF JESUS." Even before he wrote his "Life of Jesus," Hegel had written some comments on Christianity in which he criticized it for its belief in the efficacy of prayer and had contrasted it, to its detriment, with the this-worldly, social religion of the Greeks. Jesus, he held, was obscurantist and narrow-minded in comparison with Socrates. In the "Life of Jesus" it almost seems as if Hegel had decided to rewrite the Gospels in the form of a Kantian manifesto. He began by claiming that God is pure reason. He described Jesus as the son of Joseph and Mary. The only miracles Hegel mentioned he interpreted naturalistically, bringing the work to an end with the death and burial of Jesus. The central theme is the conflict between the virtuous Jesus acting dutifully for the sake of the moral law and the Jewish priesthood calling for the meticulous observance of a set of irrational rules said to be commanded by God. Jesus is depicted as saying to the Pharisees, "When you regard your ecclesiastical statutes and positive commands as the supreme law given to mankind, you fail to understand the dignity of man and the power he has of creating out of himself the idea of the divinity and knowledge of his will." This improbable allocution is typical of the way in which this work denudes the Gospel narrative of what is individual and poetical.

THE POSITIVITY OF THE CHRISTIAN RELIGION.

The theme of *The Positivity of the Christian Religion*—the place in the Christian religion of the rational, on the one hand, and of the merely factual and historical, on the other—was already raised in the "Life of Jesus." Developing the implications of the then current distinctions between natural law and positive law and between natural religion and positive religion, Hegel argued that the positive element rested on authority and was not wholly based on the dignity of man. In Christianity, according to Hegel, the main positive element was provided by Judaism, a highly authoritarian religion. But Jesus himself brought elements of positivity into the rational morality that it was his prime aim to teach; he could not have obtained a hearing from the Jews of his day if he had not claimed God's authority for his teachings. "Jesus therefore demands attention for his teachings, not because they are adapted to the moral needs of our spirit, but because they are God's will" (*Early Theological Writings*, p. 76). In claiming to be the Messiah, Jesus was using the language his listeners would understand. His followers, from a natural interest in the details of his life, developed these positive elements into Christianity. They appealed to miracles as proofs of Jesus's divinity and virtue, and instead of revering him for his teaching about virtue, they revered his teaching about virtue because of the miracles he was supposed to have performed.

Hegel asked how it happened that the pagan religion of the Greeks and Romans was overcome by Christianity. His answer was that at the periods of their greatness the Greeks and Romans were free peoples each individual of which regarded his own good as inseparable from the good of his community. When they lost their freedom, they lost the motives that bound them to their fellows; government and authority were now imposed from without, weighing down upon isolated individuals who came to regard their lives as individual possessions to be preserved irrespective of the social whole that alone gave them meaning.

> Thus the despotism of the Roman emperors had chased the human spirit from the earth and spread a misery which compelled men to seek and expect happiness in heaven; robbed of freedom, their spirit, their eternal and absolute element, was forced to take flight to the deity. [The doctrine of] God's objectivity is a counterpart to the corruption and slavery of man. (*Ibid.*, pp. 162–163)

THE SPIRIT OF CHRISTIANITY. In *The Spirit of Christianity* Hegel continued and sharpened his attack on Judaism, which he regarded as a religion of domination. He now criticized Kantian ethics as well, however, finding in it elements of the same positivity he had criticized in the Jewish religion and had seen as a contamination in the teachings of Jesus. Kant had contrasted his rational religion with the religion of the Siberian shamans on the ground that these primitive men, as well as some civilized prelates and puritans, irrationally worshiped alien forces that they regarded as exerting domination over men. But according to Hegel, the difference between the believers in these positive creeds and the follower of the religion approved by Kant is "not that the former make themselves slaves, while the latter is free, but that the former have their lord outside themselves, while the latter carries his lord in himself, yet at the same time is his own slave" (*ibid.*, p. 211). Hegel here first used the word "morality" (*Moralität*) as a pejorative description of the Kantian morality, which he now considered to be a submission of man's inclinations, including his impulses and his feelings of love, to a universal reason held to be free from and above all passion. He held that virtue demands more than this and that in the Sermon on the Mount Jesus made higher demands. "The Sermon does not teach reverance for the laws; on the contrary, it exhibits that which fulfils the law but annuls it as law and so is something higher than obedience to law and makes law superfluous" (*ibid.*, p. 212). Thus, duty takes a lower place than love. ". . . Jesus makes a general demand on his hearers to surrender their rights, to lift themselves above the whole sphere of justice or injustice by love, for in love there vanish not only rights but also the feeling of inequality and the hatred of enemies which this feeling's imperative demand for equality implies" (*ibid.*, p. 218). Hegel here saw in the ethics of the Sermon on the Mount and in the conduct of Jesus something of the "beautiful soul" described by Goethe in *Wilhelm Meis-*

ter. Jesus retained his dignity by refusing to defend himself or to uphold his rights.

Hegel went on to discuss with subtlety the possible consequences for the individual and for other men of resistance to evil, on the one hand, and of withdrawal from conflict, on the other. In this part of the work the beginnings of dialectical method as it was used a few years later in *Phenomenology of Mind* may already be discerned.

Phenomenology of Mind

The *Phenomenology* is the most obscure and the most interesting of Hegel's works. On the title page it is described as a "System of Science, Part I. The Phenomenology of Mind," but this arrangement of Hegel's system was not continued in the *Encyclopedia,* where the section headed "Phenomenology of Mind" is contained in the third part and deals with only some of the topics of the original *Phenomenology.* Hegel put the *Phenomenology* together rather hastily and was uncertain what to call it. Different copies of the first edition have slightly differing titles, and what seems like a new title, "Science of the Experience of Consciousness," is placed after the Preface and before the Introduction. Insofar as there is a central theme, it consists of an account of the various stages of human consciousness from mere sense awareness to absolute knowledge, but there are many digressions into topics of current interest, such as Goethe's description of the "beautiful soul," the Reign of Terror, and F. J. Gall's phrenology. The difference between the dialectical progression of the *Phenomenology* and of the *Encyclopedia* was cited soon after Hegel's death as evidence of the inadequacy of the dialectical method (C. F. Bachmann, *Über Hegels System und die Nothwendigkeit einer nochmaligen Umgestaltung der Philosophie,* Leipzig, 1833). In the twentieth century Marxists have preferred the *Phenomenology* to Hegel's other writings because Marx himself admired it and because of its account of how man develops by transforming the natural world through his labor. Existentialists have preferred it to the later system because of its account of man as maker of himself; no doubt they are also impressed by Hegel's references to death and the fear of death.

The *Phenomenology* begins with a dialectical discussion of sense perception in which it is argued that knowledge of physical things presupposes the view that the physical world consists of forces interacting according to laws. Hegel maintained that knowledge of such a world is really a type of self-knowledge, since in penetrating to the forces behind phenomena we become aware of what we ourselves have devised and put there. "Behind the so-called curtain which is to hide the internal constitution of things, there is nothing to be seen unless *we ourselves* go behind." The physical world of scientific theory presupposes self-conscious beings. When he analyzed self-consciousness, Hegel argued that it presupposed a plurality of living and desiring beings each of whom seeks to subdue the world to his own wishes, to make it part of himself.

MASTER AND SLAVE. No individual will rest satisfied with a conquest that fails to secure the conscious acknowledgment of other men. Hence, there is a struggle for both power and recognition. In this struggle some will take greater risks than their competitors; those who risk the least will become the slaves or bondsmen of those who face death by risking their lives. In order to preserve his life, the slave submits to the master, who regards the slave as nothing but a means to his own designs. The slave is forced to work, whereas the master can enjoy leisure in the knowledge that the slave is reshaping the natural world to provide the products of his labor for the master to consume. Thus, the master's leisure protects him from experience of the negativity of nature, whereas the slave, in struggling with nature's recalcitrance, learns its secrets and puts mind into it. The master, in consuming, destroys; the slave, in working, creates. But the master's consumption depends upon the slave's work and is thus impermanent, whereas the slave's labor passes into things that have a permanent existence. Hegel argued, too, that the slave's work in transforming the natural world is a consequence of his fear of the master, who can kill him. Death is overcome by the works of civilization. The man who risks his life and becomes the first master breaks the bonds of nature and starts the process that will incorporate mind into it.

Phenomenology of Mind *is the most obscure*

and the most interesting of Hegel's works.

It is not surprising that this section in the *Phenomenology* has greatly interested Marxists. Both Georg Lukács, in *Der junge Hegel,* and Herbert Marcuse, in *Reason and Revolution* (2d ed., London and New York, 1955), contrived to discuss it without mentioning Hegel's emphasis on the fear of death. In *Introduction à la lecture de Hegel,* Alexandre Kojève brought out the importance of the fear of death and showed, too, that Hegel was here concerned with the transition from nature to history, from mere life to thought, from animality to freedom.

THE UNHAPPY CONSCIOUSNESS. The next dialectical transition is from mind that is attempting to master nature to mind that seeks freedom and independence in itself, that says, "It is in thinking that I am free because I am not in another but remain completely with myself alone," an attitude exemplified in stoicism. But stoicism passes over into skepticism, for the stoic finds freedom in himself as a rational, thinking being, whereas the skeptic, pushing freedom still further, uses thought to dissipate its own categories. This, according to Hegel, was the state of mind that prevailed when the Roman Empire was dissolving. Christianity was an attempt on the part of men in intellectual despair to find stability in an eternal and infinite God.

Hegel called this frame of mind the unhappy consciousness. The individual is divided within himself, conscious of his own isolation, attributing all that is good to the activity of God. What Hegel said here was elaborated from a passage in *The Positivity of the Christian Religion* describing how the eternal and absolute in man had been "forced to take flight to the Deity." The unhappy consciousness was regarded by Hegel as a characteristic of both Judaism and Christianity and as the condition of all men at all times who believe in a transcendent God before whom they are as nothing. It is a stage on the way to higher forms of self-mastery.

It will be noted that in this part of the *Phenomenology* Hegel passed from epistemology through a sort of speculative sociology to an account of historical stages in human consciousness. According to Rosenkranz, Hegel, in his last years, used to refer to the *Phenomenology* as his philosophical "voyage of discovery," and it does seem that the course of the argument, although arresting, was not altogether foreseen. Royce was right when he said that in this book Hegel described "in serial order, some varieties of experience which . . . are at once characteristic of the general evolution of the higher intellectual life, and are examples of the transition from common sense naiveté to philosophical reflection and to the threshold of an idealistic system" (*Lectures on Modern Idealism*, J. Loewenberg, ed., New Haven, 1919, p. 139).

REASON AS "OBJECTIVITY." After discussing certain scientific theories of his time under the heading "Reason as Observer," Hegel went on to consider some of the ways in which reason becomes practical. He depicted the man who, like Faust, tries to make the passing moment stay. When this attempt fails, as inevitably it must, ideals are sought in a spirit of sentimental disillusionment, but such romantic crusades are never really serious. In reaction to this frivolity there develops a taste for the hard intellectual pursuits of disinterested scholarship, the concern for "objectivity," for facts, for "the thing itself." But these allegedly disinterested researchers actually go into a sort of intellectual jungle (*das geistige Thierreich*) where, deceiving one another and themselves, they tear one another to pieces in the service of truth. It soon emerges that it is not the facts that matter

but a certain proprietorship that scholars working in their special fields claim over the facts.

THE DIALECTIC OF MORALITY. In the next part of the *Phenomenology*, entitled "Mind," Hegel considered how the mind of man is embodied in his rules and institutions. This part constitutes both an account of the main types of moral attitude and a philosophy of history. These two lines of thought come together insofar as Hegel regarded the historical development from the Greek and Roman civilizations through early and medieval Christianity to Protestantism and the French Revolution as an unfolding of the main aspects and stages of freedom and, hence, as a dialectical actualization of what was merely latent and implicit in the morality of the ancient world. This unfolding is dialectical because it proceeds by oscillations and because it is made possible by conflict, in the ancient world by the conflict between the gods of the family and the laws of the city and in the modern world by the conflict between the claims of the individual and the demands of society.

In this part Hegel gave indications of the doctrine of alienation that attracted Marx in the 1840s. In building his civilization, man creates institutions and rules that are simultaneously his own products and alien constraints upon him. He may not even understand them, so that they appear strange to him. It was Hegel's view, of course, that without these institutions and rules and without the restrictions upon willfulness that they impose, mind could not reach its higher levels.

RELIGION AND ABSOLUTE KNOWLEDGE. In the last two parts of the *Phenomenology*, Hegel presented the dialectic of religion and the passage to absolute knowledge. In the earlier developments of mind the individual has to find his place in the natural world and in society, but in religion he gains consciousness of the Absolute Being. This is first approached in the primitive religions of nature, in which men worship trees, streams, or animals. Next come those forms of religion in which the Absolute Being is approached through such works of art as temples and statues. This type of religion reached a high level in ancient Greece, but when God was represented in human form, he came to be regarded as merely human and hence was lost sight of in the tragic heroes of Greek drama. As the religious element was discarded from tragedy, it gave way to comedy, in which the contingencies of human life were paraded and criticized, and God was completely ignored in favor of human self-knowledge. "The individual self is the negative force through and in which the gods . . . disappear."

This skeptical and sophisticated humanism is succeeded by Christianity, in which God is revealed to man in Christ. Here the human and the divine are no longer sundered, and God is seen to be present in the world. But it is easy to overemphasize the historical features of Christianity and, as Hegel put it, to neglect the spiritual revelation in the attempt to uncover the often commonplace ideas of the early Christians and to gain knowledge of the mere externality and particularity of Jesus. Thus, no religious experience, not even that of Christianity, can bring absolute knowledge. The historical element in Christianity, although necessary in order to avoid regarding the Absolute Being as apart from the world, is nevertheless inseparable from perception and imagination. The events of the Gospels are, so to speak, pictured or represented. Religion therefore leads on but is subordinate to the supreme form of knowledge, the philosophical, in which human history is "conceived history, the recollection of the Absolute Mind and its graveyard, the actuality, truth and certainty of its throne, without which it would be for ever alone and devoid of life." In these last words of the *Phenomenology*, Hegel made it clear that the course of history, philosophically conceived, was in his view the incarnation of the Absolute Mind. Apart from the history of man God would be alone and lifeless (*das leblose Einsame*). It would seem, indeed, that without the historical development of man and his freedom there would be no God.

The Hegelian System

It has already been mentioned that before writing the *Phenomenology*, Hegel had written but had left unpublished some attempts at a complete system of philosophy and that the *Phenomenology* was described on its title page as the first part of a system of science. It turned out that the *Science of Logic* (1812–1816) became the first part of Hegel's final system. A shortened and revised version of the *Science of Logic* appeared in 1817 as the first part of the *Encyclopedia,* a book intended for use at his lectures. A second, very much elaborated edition of the *Encyclopedia* appeared in 1827, and a third in 1830. This last edition was reprinted in the edition of Hegel's collected works published soon after his death, with inserted "additions" taken from the notebooks of students who had attended Hegel's lectures. These additions, which are most frequent in the first and second parts of the *Encyclopedia,* help greatly in the understanding of Hegel's argument but do not have quite the authority of the main text. Such additions are less frequent at the end, since the editors considered that the *Philosophy of Right,* first published in 1821, and some of the sets of lectures, provide commentary of this sort.

THE *ENCYCLOPEDIA.* The *Encyclopedia* starts with a discussion of "Logic"—a revision of *Science of Logic*—and proceeds to the sections "Philosophy of Nature" and "Philosophy of Mind." The transition from the "Logic" to the "Philosophy of Nature" is not easy to understand. There are statements which say that the idea decides to allow nature to go forth freely from itself (Sec. 244), that "Nature has come to pass as the Idea in the form of otherness" (Sec. 247), and that nature is "the unresolved contradiction" (Sec. 248). The last main heading in the "Philosophy of Nature" is "The Animal Organism." Toward the end of this section there is an account of the individual animal as having "an original sickness" and "an innate germ of death" (Sec. 375), which leads to the assertion that with the subjectivity of living organisms the "outside-itself-ness" (*Aussersichsein*) of nature is transcended by the "interiority" (*Insichsein*) of actuality (Sec. 376). Hegel later claimed (Sec. 381) that mind presupposes nature but is "the truth [of nature] and its absolute ground [*deren absolut Erstes*]." He also stated that the essence of mind is freedom (Sec. 382). A fundamental comment on the dominating triadic division must be made before going further into the details of the system. The revised "Science of Logic" that appeared in the *Encyclopedia* was concerned with the categories of thought, proceeding from the most inadequate and abstract to the most concrete and adequate, from being to the Absolute Idea. The inadequacies of the abstract categories show themselves through the contradictions they give rise to. Being is more abstract than becoming; becoming, more abstract than being-for-self; these early categories, more abstract than the latter categories of life, and so on. But Hegel was always concerned with the categories of thought and their relations to one another. When he wrote that the idea decided to allow nature to go forth freely from itself, was he saying that thought is the Divine Being that created nature? The religious overtones that accompany Hegel's major transitions cannot be ignored, but those who wish to interpret him naturalistically—an interpretation his early writings and the *Phenomenology* may well justify—can take the view that the decision and the free going forth are meant to indicate that nature is not deducible from the categories of thought, that there is a contingency about it that no system of logic and no elaboration of concepts can eliminate. In *Subjekt-Objekt* (Berlin, 1951) Ernst Bloch suggested that the free decision of the Absolute Idea is reminiscent of the arbitrary act of an absolute monarch, and he quoted a passage from Schelling's *Philosophie und Religion* (Tübingen, 1804) which held that "the descent of finite things from the Absolute" is a "primal accident [*Urzufall*]." In the third part of the *Encyclopedia,* Hegel described mind as it develops in the natural world, mind as it transforms the natural world in creating the works of civilization, and mind fully aware of itself in the complete self-consciousness of philosophical thought. The "Logic" culminates in the Absolute Idea, the most adequate category but still a category. In the "Philosophy of Nature," where there is no Absolute, the culminating point consists of mortal individuals belonging to persisting animal species. The "Philosophy of Mind" culminates in Absolute Mind, the consciousness man gains of himself through understanding his own history in a civilization that he has imposed upon the contingencies of nature.

A prominent feature in the

"Doctrine of the Concept"

is Hegel's critical treatment and reorganization

of the traditional formal logic.

"LOGIC." Like the Hegelian system as a whole, each of its three main sections—"Logic," "Philosophy of Nature," and "Philosophy of Mind"—is again divided into three. The "Logic" is divided into the "Doctrine of Being," the "Doctrine of Essence," and the "Doctrine of the Concept [*Begriff*]." The difficulties in presenting a comprehensible summary of Hegel's views are at their greatest in relation to the "Logic," and all that will be attempted is an indication of a few of Hegel's most characteristic views.

"Doctrine of Being." In the "Doctrine of Being" Hegel was concerned with the most abstract categories. Being itself, the most abstract of all, amounts to the same as nothing. Like Russell in his theory of descriptions, Hegel held that nothing can be said to be unless some characteristic is attributed to it; hence, in Hegel's terminology being leads on to determinate being, which involves the notion of quality. On the ground that a quality is something distinct from other qualities, Hegel argued that quality implies the category of a unit (*das Eins*) and that this in turn leads on to quantity. This part of the "Logic" was completed by transitions to degree and measure.

Hegel's object in the "Doctrine of Being" was to show that these categories are not independent of one another but develop from one to the other in an ascending order of adequacy. We know more about something when we know the proportions of its parts than when we know only how many parts it has, that it is, or that it is something or other. An important element in this part of the "Logic" is Hegel's criticism of infinite numerical series as the false infinite and his contrast

between the false and the true infinite, which is not an incompletable progression of similar items but a completed, complex whole of supplementary parts. The true infinite is not to be reached by attempting the impossible task of moving from one finite to the next but must comprise the finite.

"Doctrine of Essence." The "Doctrine of Essence" is concerned with such distinctions as that between a thing's nature and its appearances, forces and their manifestations, form and matter. Hegel exploited the difficulties ("contradictions") that arise when these oppositions are so accentuated that we are left with featureless essences, on the one hand, and unattached appearances, on the other. Typical of his treatment of these topics is his claim that "the explanation of an appearance in terms of a force is an empty tautology" (Sec. 136) and his assertion that as a man's outward actions are, so his inner aims and intentions must be (Sec. 140).

"Doctrine of the Concept." A prominent feature in the "Doctrine of the Concept" is Hegel's critical treatment and reorganization of the traditional formal logic. Thus, he classified judgments in terms of his own division of "Logic" into being, essence, and concept. The classification progresses from the mere factual attribution of a quality, through disjunctive and necessary judgments in which the predicate belongs essentially to the subject, to judgments of value which assert that a thing is good or bad just because it is that individual thing. Judgments gain in adequacy as they advance from mere factual attribution to attribution for reasons contained in the subject. Hence, the more developed forms of judgment are indistinguishable from inferences. In his account of the syllogism Hegel placed inferences in which the terms are only contingently connected at the bottom of a scale leading up to the disjunctive syllogism, in which a genus is exhaustively specified.

Although Hegel retained the terms and distinctions of the traditional formal logic, the use he made of them was highly original. Instead of setting out the types of judgment and the figures and moods of the syllogism as equally valid forms, he regarded judgment as implicit inference and inference as ordered in a scale of ascending rationality. This conception of logic influenced such later writers as Christoff Sigwart and R. H. Lotze and was developed in both F. H. Bradley's *Principles of Logic* (London, 1883) and Bernard Bosanquet's *Logic: The Morphology of Knowledge* (2 vols., Oxford, 1888).

The argument of Hegel's "Logic" can be very briefly summarized. The least that can be said about anything is that it is. More is said about it when it is qualified, numbered, or measured; still more is said about it when it is explained in terms of essences, grounds, or causes.

Most is said about it when it is placed in the context of life, purpose, will, and value.

"PHILOSOPHY OF NATURE." At the end of the eighteenth and the beginning of the nineteenth century there was a great deal of philosophizing about nature. Electricity was held to have cosmic significance, and Schelling made much of the opposition between positive and negative poles. Poets as dissimilar as Blake and Goethe rejected what they regarded as the unduly quantitative physics of Newton. Spinoza was revived, and among German poets and philosophers much was said about the ἐν καὶ πᾶν, the one and the all. It is not surprising, therefore, that Hegel's dissertation of 1801, *De Orbitis Planetarum,* was critical of Newton and sought to provide an a priori justification of Kepler's laws. At the end of the dissertation Hegel mentioned some numerological accounts of the distances and number of the planets and expressed the opinion that if Plato was right in the *Timaeus,* there could be no planet between Mars and Jupiter. Hegel did not then know that Ceres, an asteroid between these two planets, had been discovered at the beginning of the year. However, even after he had heard of this discovery and of the discovery of several other asteroids soon after, he continued to hope that philosophical reasons could be given for the positions of the heavenly bodies. In an addition to Section 270 of the *Encyclopedia,* Hegel tried to show that these asteroids filled a gap that would otherwise have been unreasonable. The addition ends with the words: "Specialists do not think about such matters. But a time will come when in this science there will be a demand for concepts of the Reason."

It should be mentioned here that Hegel accepted and developed Kant's distinction between the reason and the understanding. According to Hegel, the understanding, although a necessary stage of thought, is less philosophical than the reason. To think in terms of the understanding, as is done in mathematics, the natural sciences, and traditional metaphysics, is to think in terms of fixed and uncriticized categories, to think undialectically or in prephilosophical terms. The reason moves dialectically toward completeness in terms of fluid categories that constantly amend themselves. Thus, when Hegel wanted astronomers to pay attention to "concepts of Reason," he wanted astronomy to take its place within a system of philosophy. This place must be a subordinate one, for Hegel wrote in the Introduction to the "Philosophy of Nature" (Sec. 248): "Even if arbitrary will, the contingency of mind, leads on to wickedness, this is nevertheless something infinitely higher than the regular movements of the planets or than the innocence of the plants: for what goes wrong in that way is nevertheless mind." Here Hegel was emphasizing

the gulf between mind and nature, even though he held that the understanding does not give a complete knowledge of nature.

Mechanics. The three main divisions of the "Philosophy of Nature" are concerned with mechanics, physics, and organic nature. The astronomical theories expounded in the first part have already been touched upon. This part also contains a brief discussion of space and time. Following Kant, Hegel regarded them both as "forms of sensibility," or, more strikingly, as "the non-sensible sensible." Although he regarded arithmetic and geometry as sciences of the understanding, he considered the possibility of a philosophical mathematics at the level of measure or proportion (mass).

Physics. The second part of the "Philosophy of Nature" moves through various triads from light, the elements, sound, heat, to electricity and chemical combination. Hegel commented upon the philosophical significance of each form of matter. The comment on heat is characteristic:

> Heat is the re-establishment of matter in its formlessness, its fluidity, the triumph of its abstract homogeneity over its specific determinations. . . . Formally, that is in relation to spatial determinations in general, heat therefore appears expansive, as cancelling the limitations which the specification of the indifferent occupation of space is. (Sec. 303)

That is, when heat spreads out from a heated thing, that thing is not confined to one place, as it would be if it were not heated. Or as Hegel put it in the next section, heat is the "real negation of what is specific and exclusive in body."

Organic Nature. In the last main triad of the "Philosophy of Nature," Hegel passed from geological nature through vegetable nature to the animal organism. The most interesting part of this triad is the last, in which Hegel discussed animal species and their relationships. He seems to have thought that violent death is, in the animal world, "the natural fate of the individual" and that because of the contingency of nature animal life is "uncertain, anxious, and unhappy" (Sec. 369). But other members of the same species are not only hostile to the individual; they are also, like him, continuations of the species, and, hence, the individual feels a need to unite himself to the species (*Gattung*) and to continue it by copulation (*Begattung*)—the play on words is, of course, deliberate. Thus, Hegel seems to have held that animal sexual union is not merely a contingent affair. On the other hand, since the new individuals produced in this way only repeat the features of their parents and other ancestors, their constant reproduction is an instance of the false infinite, not of the true infinite in which completeness and perfection are achieved.

"PHILOSOPHY OF MIND." The major triad in the "Philosophy of Mind" consists of "Subjective Mind," "Objective Mind," and "Absolute Mind."

Subjective Mind." Under the heading "Subjective Mind" and the subheading "Anthropology," Hegel dealt with the soul as a natural entity in the physical world; the soul as a sensitive, feeling being; and the soul as a being that can express itself and act upon the world through its body. The upright body, the hand "as the absolute tool" (Sec. 411), the mouth, and the power of weeping and laughing all enable man to express in nature—to externalize—his thoughts and feelings. Furthermore, the world has effects upon man's body that are internalized by him—Hegel here made a play on the word *Erinnerung,* which means "recollection" but, if taken in the literal sense of its German etymology, can be taken to mean "internalization." When the organism reacts to immediate stimuli in the light of its own experience, mind has evolved beyond the mere animal level and has reached the stage of consciousness.

Hegel discussed the next moment of subjective mind under the heading of the "Phenomenology of Mind," going through the main phases distinguished in the earlier chapters of his book with that title—namely, sense experience, perception, understanding, desire, the self-consciousness that recognizes others (containing the discussion of master and slave), reason.

The third triad of subjective mind, which is headed "Psychology," contains descriptions of such intellectual functions as intention, representation, recollection, imagination, memory, and thought and descriptions of the practical drives, impulses, and seekings after satisfaction.

This part ends with a brief section headed "Free Mind." Here it is asserted that the unity of theoretical and practical mind is free will. Hegel meant that human freedom is possible only on the dual basis of thought and impulse and consists of the rationalizing and systematizing of the impulses and passions. "This will to freedom," he said, "is no longer an impulse that demands satisfaction, but the character—the mind's consciousness grown into something non-impulsive" (Sec. 482).

Objective Mind." At the very end of his discussion of subjective mind Hegel wrote that the freedom which is the culmination of subjective mind is only a concept, "a principle of mind and heart destined to develop into the objective phase, into legal, moral, religious and scientific actuality" (Sec. 482). The rest of the system is therefore concerned with the ways in which the human will, in which thought and impulse ("mind and heart") are combined in freedom, becomes effective (this is the idea behind the word "actuality," which translates *Wirklichkeit*) in the public world, the world in which men act and in which their thoughts and deeds give rise to rules, institutions, and organizations. These rules, institutions, and organizations are independent of each man and thus may be regarded as kinds of objects, though not as physical objects. Men build up in the natural world a world other than the natural world by working on nature and transforming it and by creating systems of property, economic organizations, class differentiations, and the like. The triad that makes up objective mind comprises law (*Recht*), subjective morality (as Wallace translated *Moralität*), and social morality (as Wallace translated *Sittlichkeit;* Knox translated it as "ethical life"). The first part covers legal rights and duties as exemplified in property, contract, and punishment. The second is concerned largely with the morality of intention and conscience—the term *Moralität* was used by Hegel somewhat pejoratively to mean a sort of ethics (of which Kant was, in his view, the chief exponent) in which the agent is unduly governed by the subjective and internal aspects of decision and action.

According to Hegel, the understanding, although a necessary stage of thought, is less philosophical than the reason.

The third part is itself a triad. The first stage of social morality is the family, "the natural or immediate phase" of objective mind (*Philosophy of Right,* Sec. 152). When members of the family have matured, they detach themselves from it and enter the world of independent men who compete in an economic arena free from tribal allegiances. This phase of social life Hegel called "civil society." It is the world of intelligent, responsible individuals in their business relationships, free from irrational tribal loyalties, allowing their connections with one another to be formed by the coincidence of wants in a market of wide extent. Indeed, it is the aspect of human society that the classical economists, whom Hegel admired, had analyzed and justified. But civil society cannot exist as a mere market, for markets need to be policed, whereas trades and industries themselves find common concerns that unite the individuals in corporations of various kinds.

There is thus a double necessity for the state—as the upholder of fair dealing and as the ultimate curb on the selfishness of corporations within civil society. In the

Encyclopedia, Hegel wrote of "the unification of the family principle with that of Civil Society" and described it as a unification of the love that is essential to the family with the conscious universality that is the mark of civil society (Sec. 535). In the *Philosophy of Right* (Sec. 257) the state was described as "the actuality [*Wirklichkeit*] of the ethical Idea"—that is, as its effective embodiment. In the same section of the *Philosophy of Right,* Hegel wrote that "the mind of a nation (Athene for instance) is the divine, knowing and willing itself," and in an addition to Section 258 is the famous phrase "The march of God in the world, that is what the State is." But this section has been misunderstood. In the sentence before that in which he had written that the state is divine, Hegel had said, with the family in mind, "The *Penates* are inward gods, gods of the underworld," so that it is not only to the state that he attributed divinity. Furthermore, in the same addition as that in which he claimed that the state is "the march of God in the world," he said that the state "stands on earth and so in the sphere of caprice, chance and error, and bad behaviour may disfigure it in many respects." Hegel's main concern was, as he stated, to analyze the state at its best. Although, like Aristotle, he regarded the state as the highest social achievement of man, he also held, again like Aristotle, that within the state there should be guarantees against arbitrariness and despotism. He did not take a favorable view of "popular suffrage" on the grounds that "in large states it leads inevitably to electoral indifference" and that "election falls into the power of a few, of a caucus" (*Philosophy of Right,* Sec. 311). He strongly believed that all important interests should be represented and thought that there should be a constitutional monarchy with considerable powers advised by an upper and a lower house.

This brings us to the most controversial part of Hegel's account of objective mind, his philosophy of history. Whatever else is involved in his view that the state is man's highest social achievement, it undoubtedly implies that there is no superior body or group by which its claims may be assessed. States are necessarily independent beings. Their relations are regulated to some degree by custom, and there is an international law that regulates dealings between subjects of different states and requires adherence to treaties, as if they were a sort of contract. When the vital interests of states clash, however, there is no alternative except war. War between states, Hegel had said in his "Die Verfassung Deutschlands" ("Constitution of Germany," 1802; first published in Georg Lasson, ed., *Schriften zur Politik und Rechtsphilosophie,* 2d ed., Leipzig, 1923), does not decide which of the rights of the conflicting states is the true right—for both are—"but which right has to give way to the other." Hegel believed that war performs the function of keeping before the minds of men the realities of death and destruction. He held that states are individuals and that all individuals persist in their existence by ensuring that other individuals recognize them as they recognize the others. The very concept of a state therefore requires that there be a plurality of them, and this makes war a part of the system of states even though war is not their natural condition but an interruption of the normal state of peace. Hegel argued that since war is a relation between states and not a relation of individual men to one another, the rights and interests of noncombatants should be maintained to the utmost. For the same reason he was in favor of professional armies and against conscription or any form of levy en masse.

Whatever else is involved in Hegel's view that the state is man's highest social achievement, it undoubtedly implies that there is no superior body or group by which its claims may be assessed.

Each nation is limited by geographical and other accidental features and hence can build up only a particular culture and can have only a particular, not a universal, history. Thus, nations, when they reach the level of statehood, make their contribution to the whole in the part they play in world history (*Encyclopedia,* Sec. 548). World history is not wholly an affair of chance or contingency; as the work of mind it could not be. Therefore, the history of the world has a rational structure, and any historical writing that ignored this "would be only an imbecile mental divagation, not as good as a fairy-tale" (Sec. 549). This rational structure, according to Hegel, is the development of freedom.

"Absolute Mind." The triad which completes the Hegelian system is composed of art, revealed religion, and philosophy. It will be remembered that at the end of the *Phenomenology* Hegel proceeded from the religion of nature to the religion of art and then to the philosophical knowledge of the history of the world. In the *Encyclopedia* art is given what seems to be a more independent status, but the details of the argument hardly bear out the general scheme, since the transitional sections describe a transition from objective mind to religion, as in the *Phenomenology.* Thus, in the concluding sections of the *Encyclopedia* art is regarded as an inadequate form of religion, religion as a more adequate form of art, philosophy as religion freed from picture think-

ing and wholly rationalized, and all three as manifestations of Absolute Mind. Art is the embodiment of Absolute Mind in material things fashioned by the artist, who, in a sense, is thus "the master of the God" (*Encyclopedia,* Sec. 560). In classical art the embodiment takes place without any antithesis between the embodiment and the mind that is embodied. In the art of the sublime, which preceded classical art, the Absolute Mind is regarded as something that defies embodiment and remains forever beyond and behind the sensible forms that succeed only in symbolizing it. The defect of artistic representation is that the sensible symbols may be taken to refer to another world beyond, which is as limited as this world is falsely taken to be. Thus, men worship idols or even bones, "which point to the unspiritual objectivity of that other world" (*ibid.,* Sec. 562).

God is therefore not something grander and more powerful than the natural world yet fundamentally like it, nor is he something beyond the world that must remain forever inaccessible to man. God is manifested in the world, and this is the truth that revealed religion has expressed most adequately in the Christian doctrine of the Incarnation. Without this doctrine God would still be regarded as beyond the world and, thus, as incomplete and finite. Even with this doctrine he is conceived of through the medium of particular historical events that introduce an element of contingency and irrelevance into our conception of him. In philosophy the artist's external vision and the mystic's internal vision are united in a mode of thought in which there is no further conflict. The philosopher who achieves ultimate self-knowledge is freed from the conflicts that inevitably disturb the inferior levels of knowledge. By philosophizing to the end, he has made himself free (*ibid.,* Sec. 576).

The Dialectical Method

CONTRADICTION. It is now necessary to give more detailed attention to Hegel's dialectical method. There are interpreters of Hegel who say that Hegel denied the principle of contradiction in that he held that contradictories can both exist and that contradictory propositions can therefore both be true. Others deny this interpretation, maintaining, instead, that, according to Hegel, since contradiction is a mark of inadequacy and falsehood, contradictions are to be found in the lower categories but are absent from or resolved in the Absolute Idea. This view is summed up in Michael Oakeshott's reference to "the element of self-contradiction inherent in all abstraction" (*Experience and Its Modes,* Cambridge, 1933, p. 328). Those who take the first view can quote some convincing passages from Hegel's

Science of Logic. For example, there he wrote that "all things are in themselves contradictory," that "movement is existing contradiction itself," and that "only insofar as something has contradiction in itself does it move, have impulse or activity."

If Hegel had rejected the principle of contradiction in the sense that that principle is understood by formal logicians, his case would indeed be serious, for it follows from the rejection of this principle that any proposition can be true and false and that there is thus no means of distinguishing truth from falsehood. It is important, therefore, to see whether Hegel did reject the principle of contradiction in this sense and whether its rejection is part of his dialectical method. That these questions are not easy to answer becomes apparent if we consult some of the commentators on the passages I have just quoted. J. M. E. McTaggart, in his *Commentary on Hegel's Logic,* was dissatisfied with the whole section and claimed that in it Hegel had allowed himself to be too much influenced by Schelling's view on polarity and opposition. "The whole point of the dialectic," McTaggart protested, "is that the perception of a contradiction is a reason for abandoning the category which we find contradictory." Indeed, he found this part of the *Logic* so unsatisfactory that he proposed to amend the sequence of categories by leaving out contradiction altogether.

McTaggart said nothing, however, about Hegel's statement that there are existing contradictions. G. R. G. Mure, in his *A Study of Hegel's Logic,* did not evade this difficulty. Examining Hegel's text more closely than McTaggart had done, he pointed out that on the ground that "the contradictory cannot be imagined or thought" Hegel rejected the common-sense view that things cannot be self-contradictory but that thought can be. Mure called attention, too, to Hegel's statement that self-contradiction is not a mere disease of thought but something which it must pass through on its way to truth. Furthermore, according to Hegel, it is finite things that are self-contradictory, and they are contradictory not in relation to one another but by virtue of their relation to what is infinite; Hegel "is not suggesting that Big Ben can now read both 9 P.M. and not 9 P.M." (p. 105). Although this is an improvement on McTaggart, it left out of account Hegel's statement that for something to move, it must be both here and not here at the same time. What Hegel said about movement is not altogether unlike Mure's example of Big Ben. So the difficulty remains.

In the "Logic" sections of the *Encyclopedia* which was written later than the *Science of Logic* contradiction is not a separate category at all. Perhaps the reason for this difference is that Hegel had second thoughts and gave up the idea of contradiction in the nature of things. But although contradiction is no longer a category in the *Encyclopedia,* Hegel still sometimes wrote as if there were contradictions in the nature of things. For example, he stated that although such concepts as "square circle," "many-sided circle," and "straight curve" are self-contradictory, geometers nevertheless regard circles as polygons composed of very short sides and "the center and circumference of a circle as opposite and contradictory to one another" (*Encyclopedia,* Sec. 119). Hegel also suggested that polarity in physics goes against the ordinary logic—but he used the word "opposition" (*Entgegensetzung*) rather than "contradiction" (*Widerspruch*).

In *Geschichte der neueren Philosophie* (Heidelberg, 1901, Vol. VIII, Part 2) Kuno Fischer tried to overcome the difficulty by distinguishing between two sorts of contradiction, "necessary contradiction" and "impossible contradiction." The example of a square circle illustrates the notion of an impossible contradiction, a *contradictio in adjecto,* for it is impossible for the same thing to be both circular and square. When a circle is regarded as a many-sided polygon, however, the contradiction is not *in adjecto* but in *subjecto,* for the circle is then being regarded as in the process of being formed or generated from these many sides. This, Fischer held, is the contradiction involved in all becoming (the first concrete category of the "Logic," the synthesis of being and nothing). Fischer's suggestion is therefore that there is not a vicious or stultifying contradiction involved in becoming or in movement, contradictory though they must in some sense be. But although this may be a correct exposition of Hegel's view, it is hardly a defense of it, since it merely repeats without explaining his claim that there are contradictions in the objective world.

By drawing this distinction, Fischer has nevertheless raised the question of whether Hegel intended the word "contradiction" to be used in the way it is used in formal logic. The answer is clear enough. Hegel did not regard formal logic as a philosophical science, and he therefore rejected any idea that its categories should dominate philosophical thought. Thus, the fact that the word "contradiction" is used in a certain way by formal logicians was not for him a reason for confining himself to that meaning. When Hegel was advocating the dialectical method, he had in mind a method in which oppositions, conflicts, tensions, and refutations were courted rather than avoided or evaded. Hegel was a student of the classical, laissez-faire economists who held that wealth would be maximized by the free play of competition. In this view if traders and producers ceased to compete with one another, the whole level of economic life would be lowered. General prosperity

could be reached only at the expense of labor and anxiety. So it is, Hegel believed, with the categories of our thought, the systems of philosophers, and the forms of life and society. There is no tranquillity to be had by withdrawal and isolation. Our categories compete with one another, and out of their competition emerges something better than either of them could have accomplished alone. But it is not possible for the superior category to go into retirement, for without the spur of competition it would fall into decay. Furthermore, just as competition requires the competitors to continue in business—for if one destroys the others, there is monopoly and stagnation—so the competing categories cannot be swallowed up and lost in the Absolute Idea but must all play their part in maintaining its life and stability. There is nothing fanciful in this comparison. Indeed, it gains support from Hegel's "System der Sittlichkeit" of 1802 ("System of Morality"; in *Schriften zur Politik und Rechtsphilosophie,* Georg Lasson, ed., 2d ed., Leipzig, 1923), in which it is quite clear that Hegel's systematic thinking was influenced by his understanding of economic theory. For example, in this essay he developed the triad need–labor–enjoyment and described labor as "the destruction of the object . . . but in such a way that another is put in its place." Here Hegel compared labor with knowledge and undoubtedly had in mind (in accord with his tendency to take German words in the sense of their roots) the element of negation (*nicht*) in the word for destruction (*Vernichtung*). The destruction of the natural object is the creation of an artificial one.

NEGATION. Negation, indeed, is the vital notion in Hegel's account of the dialectic. In the Preface to the *Phenomenology* Hegel wrote, "The life of God and divine knowledge may, if we wish, be described as love disporting with itself; but this idea is degraded into mere edification and insipidity if it lacks the seriousness, the pain, the patience and the labour of the negative." "Seriousness," "pain," "patience," and "labor" would be strange words to use of the negative symbol of formal logic. Expressed in theological–economic terms Hegel's view is that God cannot be a mere consumer, for there is no consumption without labor, and labor has to face a recalcitrant nature that has to be understood and humored. Thus, there is no God apart from nature. In moral terms there is no good without evil, and in logical terms there is no truth without error. These, according to Hegel, are central truths of dialectics.

But surely, it will be said, this conflicts with such obvious facts as that there are some who consume without working, that in mathematics there are sequences of necessarily true propositions with no admixture of falsity, and that some things—for example, conscientious action—are good without qualification. As to the first point, Hegel argued in the *Phenomenology* that the master who consumes what his slave produces for him destroys what he consumes, whereas the slave shapes the external world in such a way that mind is embodied in it. Hence, the slave is on the road to freedom, whereas the master, who does not work, destroys without creating. As to mathematics, Hegel was inclined to hold it in contempt. There is no space here to consider the strange things he said about it, and it need only be remarked that he held that philosophical truth is utterly different from mathematical truth in that false philosophical views are taken up into true philosophy whereas false mathematics is not taken up into true mathematics. As to the alleged unmixed goodness of conscientious action (the Kantian "good will"), Hegel held that the morality of conscience contained in itself the seeds of willfulness and arbitrariness, for the most atrocious deeds can be defended on the ground that the man who committed them genuinely thought them right. Obedience to one's own conscience, Hegel thought, is an advance over obedience to the commands of an external lord but is nevertheless an unstable basis for morality.

Hegel did not regard formal logic

as a philosophical science,

and he therefore rejected any idea that its categories

should dominate philosophical thought.

Several ways in which the negative element is important in Hegel's method have been discussed. There is the conceptual competition without which thought must decay. Then, there is the polar character of certain fundamental notions which makes the one unthinkable without its opposite. At the prephilosophical level Hegel gave above and below, right and left, father and son, as examples. At the philosophical level his examples, were good and bad, master and slave, thought and nature. But not only do these opposites require each other; they also pass into each other. Good will can pass over into atrocity; philosophical truth is the result of errors that supplement each other; the master satisfies his desires but becomes dependent upon the labor of the slave in order to do so; and the slave, by work, controls his desires and develops a rational will. The life of thought in conceptual conflict, the mutual dependence of polar opposites, and the instability or oscillations of philosophical and moral attitudes are different sorts of dia-

lectic which Hegel emphasized on different occasions. If they have anything in common, it is the activity of negation.

There are two other aspects of the dialectic to discuss, the role of reason and understanding and the role of skepticism.

REASON AND UNDERSTANDING. First, Hegel, following Kant, contrasted the reason, the source of dialectical thinking, with the understanding, the predialectical mode of thought. The understanding, as Hegel saw it, is the type of thinking that prevails in common sense, in the natural sciences, and in mathematics and those types of philosophy that are argued in quasi-scientific or quasi-mathematical ways. Fixed categories are uncritically adhered to, demonstrations are produced (only to be demolished), analyses are made, and distinctions are drawn. Analyzing and distinguishing are necessary foundations of philosophical activity but only to prepare the way for the more sinuous and subtle method of the dialectic. Once an analysis has been made, the elements of it are seen to conflict and collide as well as to cohere. First, the understanding isolates, then comes the Reason's negative moment of criticism or conflict, and after that its speculative moment of synthesis. It should be mentioned that distinctions somewhat similar to the distinction between the understanding and the reason had already been made by Plato when he distinguished between the highest knowledge and knowledge in the various sciences, by Spinoza in his second and third kinds of knowledge, by Pascal with his *esprit de géometrie* and *esprit de finesse*, by Hume with his reason and imagination, and by Burke when he contrasted the abstract rationalism of the Enlightenment with the organic, evolutionary view of society that he preferred. These distinctions are not all quite like that drawn by Hegel, but in his theory there is something corresponding to each of them.

SKEPTICISM. Second, Hegel thought that skepticism was an important forerunner and essential ingredient of the dialectical method. In a review of a book by G. E. Schulze that appeared in 1802, Hegel wrote appreciatively of the skepticism of Sextus Empiricus and of the skeptical features in the philosophy of Parmenides, of whom he wrote, "This skepticism, which in its pure *explicit* form comes forward in Parmenides, is to be found *implicit* in every genuinely philosophical system, for it is the free aspect [*die freie Seite*] of every philosophy" ("Verhältnis des Skeptizismus zur Philosophie," in *Kritisches Journal der Philosophie*, Vol. 2 (1802), 1–74; quoted from *Sämtliche Werke*, Georg Lasson, ed., Vol. I, pp. 174–175). In the same essay Hegel wrote that when Spinoza held that God is the immanent but not the transcendent cause of the world, he was equating the cause with the effect, even though the very notion of an effect implies that it is distinct from the cause. Hegel agreed with Spinoza's equation but concluded that it shows that the reason can accept the principle of contradiction only as a formal principle. In "genuine" philosophy cause and effect are seen as both distinct and identical.

Freedom, according to Hegel,

is something that has to be achieved,

and it therefore would be impossible

in the absence of opposition and negation.

Hegel illustrated his comment that skepticism is "the free aspect" of philosophy in the following way. Dogmatists, he said, regard individual men as objects in the power of rules, laws, and customs. The more the dogmatists study man, the more they show him in subjection to these forces. When, however, the skeptics attack dogmatism, "they raise the freedom of Reason above this necessity of nature." An example of this is the way in which Europeans came to question their own concepts of law and morals when they were brought face to face with cultures very different from their own. When such skeptics as Montaigne mockingly insisted on these differences, men became more conscious of their own institutions and recognized the possibility of changing them. In theoretically breaking down men's traditional views and institutions, the skeptic frees men from the unconscious power of these views and institutions. Hegel repeated his general assessment of skepticism in the *Encyclopedia* (Sec. 81, addition 2) and in his *Lectures on the History of Philosophy*. In these lectures Hegel said that skepticism is "the demonstration that all that is determinate and finite is unstable." Hegel went on to say that "positive philosophy," by which he meant philosophy that is not content to remain in total skepticism, "has the negative to Scepticism in itself; thus it does not oppose, nor is it outside of it, for Scepticism is a moment in it" (Haldane and Simpson, 1955, Vol. II, p. 330).

Freedom

From what has just been said, it is clear that Hegel's account of dialectic and of reason is closely linked with his view of freedom. The exercise of thought in its most developed forms involves the negation of what had seemed firm and certain and the opening up of new possibilities. That mind is freedom applies both to the understanding and the reason, since both are spontaneous activities that interpret and arrange. But because the understanding is confined to a fixed system of categories, it is less free than the reason that criticizes, stretches, and transforms the categories of the understanding.

Freedom is, of course, logically connected with will, and according to Hegel, will is as essential to mind as intellect is. Reference has already been made to Section 482 of the *Encyclopedia*, in which Hegel asserted that the unity of theoretical and practical mind is free will. In the preceding sections he had argued that thought presupposes mind as practical, since classifying and explaining are activities through which the world is, so to speak, appropriated by the mind. In the sections of the *Encyclopedia* in which he expounded the categories of cognition and of will, Hegel endeavored to show that mere cognition is at a lower stage than will and that will is thus the actuality of what is only potential in knowledge. He also argued that the freedom and necessity that are opposed to each other are abstractions and that what is concrete must combine both. The very nature of necessity, he continued, presupposes a will on which it is a constraint.

At the logical–metaphysical level, therefore, Hegel held a view which implied that freedom is essential to mind, both the presupposition and outcome of intelligence, and in its concrete form inseparable from constraint and necessity. This view of the matter pervaded his account of freedom in the social and political sphere. Freedom is not something merely opposed to constraint; on the contrary, it presupposes and requires restraint. This is true of concrete freedom. However, abstract or negative freedom, when it is more than a moment in actual or positive freedom, is a purely destructive force. Hegel considered that this negative freedom played a large part in the French Revolution. The old corporations and institutions were destroyed in such a frenzy of annihilation that it took several years for new institutions to be created and recognized as authoritative. Furthermore, when the conflicting interests in society are overcome, individuals come to be treated as equal, undifferentiated, replaceable, and expendable units. The events of the Reign of Terror thus led Hegel to hold that purely negative freedom was associated with force and death. The logical connections are not altogether clear, but it may well be that the links between egalitarianism, antinomianism, violence, and contempt for human life are not wholly accidental.

Freedom, according to Hegel, is something that has to be achieved, and it therefore would be impossible in the absence of opposition and negation. Hence, although negative freedom in its abstract form is a "fury of destruction," it is a necessary element in concrete freedom. Free will is not the liberty of indifference but the rational organization of the feelings and impulses.

Rationality is not a power that could reside in an isolated individual, however. To be rational, the individual must draw upon the resources of an organized and differentiated society and must be "formed" and educated to do this. His will is then in harmony with the ends of the various social groups by which he has been influenced and, in civilized societies, with the more complex ends of the state. In conforming to these pressures and in obeying the laws of the state, the individual is achieving his own rational ends and in so doing is free.

Hegel, like Rousseau, also held that an individual might be free even when he was being coerced, for although he might dislike the force applied against him, this dislike would be an expression of his particular whims, not of his rational insight, as can be seen when he approves of the imposition of a like force upon other people in like circumstances. Insofar as the criminal who is being punished would wish others to be punished who committed a like crime against him, he wills his own punishment.

FREEDOM IN HISTORY. Hegel considered that the history of the human race is a development from less to greater freedom and from less adequate forms of freedom to freedom in its perfection. Thus, his philosophy of history can be understood only in terms of his conception of freedom. In the Oriental world there was no freedom for the subjects and only an arbitrary, irrational freedom for the despot who ruled over them. In the classical world of Greece and Rome there was a more adequate conception of freedom, and more men achieved freedom than in the Oriental despotisms. In the Greek city-state the citizens often regarded themselves as finding their fulfillment in the achievements of their city, apart from which they conceived of no life for themselves. Indeed, they might accept personal defeat and misfortune and submit to what they called destiny and still regard themselves as free in so doing. Of course, there were slaves who had no part in this activity and had no freedom.

Christianity offered the prospect of freedom to all men, a freedom, furthermore, that transcended the given social order. In what Hegel called the Germanic world—that is, the Christian civilization that grew out of Protestantism—this latest form of freedom was being realized in the manifold institutions of Europe and America and in the states in which these institutions flourished and by which they were regulated and protected. In Christianity the individual is regarded as of infinite value, as a candidate for eternal salvation, and

although the emphasis on subjective freedom can lead, as it did in the French Revolution, to contempt for social institutions, it comprises the form and aspect of freedom that gives its special quality to modern civilization, with its romantic art, romantic love, and support for the rights of conscience (*Philosophy of Right,* Sec. 124).

It is apparent from the foregoing that Hegel rejected the liberal view that man is free to the extent that he is guaranteed a sphere within which he can do what he wishes without interference from others who are guaranteed a like position. Such freedom he stigmatized as negative, abstract, or merely willful. Men enjoy concrete freedom when the various orders and groups of civilized life are maintained in and by the state. In this passage of the *Lectures on the Philosophy of History* (Hoffmeister, Vol. XVIIIA, p. 111) Hegel also emphasized that in submitting their private wills to the laws of the state and to the rules of its subordinate but free institutions, men were submitting their passions to the control of reason. Thus, the argument comes full circle. The theoretical reason is inseparable from will and from freedom; necessity and negative freedom are only abstractions; in concrete freedom the negative, destructive element is held in check and rendered fruitful by being realized in institutions; the individual enjoys concrete freedom when he is educated to live in a civilized state and to be guided by the reason that permeates it.

There is no space here to criticize this view in any detail, for in a way it is a cross section of the whole Hegelian metaphysic. It should be noted, however, that when a critic maintains that real freedom is what Hegel called negative or abstract freedom and when he goes on to maintain that "concrete freedom" is not freedom but indoctrinated submission, then he is criticizing Hegel's terminology rather than the substance of his view. To say that freedom consists of a willing acceptance of the tasks imposed by a civilized state is certainly to extend and perhaps to distort the ordinary senses of the term and to capture a word from the liberal vocabulary for use in a far from liberal scheme of concepts. It was Hegel's view, however, that the thoughts that the liberal phraseology expressed necessarily move in the directions he described and that societies themselves, the embodiments of men's thoughts and aims, move in these directions, too.

Aesthetic Theory

We have already seen that Hegel discussed the nature of art and of beauty toward the end of both the *Phenomenology* and the *Encyclopedia.* Art, according to Hegel, is one of the manifestations of Absolute Mind, of which religion and philosophy are the other two. Thus, although art presupposes the civilized life of the state, it also transcends it. In his lengthy *Vorlesungen über die Aesthetik* ("Lectures on Aesthetics") Hegel developed his theories of art and beauty in great detail. The lectures possess great power and attraction, and so much of their value resides in the details that a summary treatment is bound to be difficult.

THREE STYLES OF ART. Hegel's account of beauty is a modification of Schiller's view, in his *Letters on the Aesthetic Education of Mankind* (1795), that beauty is the mediation between the sensible and the rational. According to Hegel, beauty is the rational rendered sensible, the sensible appearance being the form in which the rational content is made manifest. This sensible embodiment of the rational, he held, can take place in three principal ways, symbolic art, classical art, and romantic art.

Symbolic Art. In the first and least adequate form, symbolic art, the sensible shape merely symbolizes the rational content without penetrating and transforming it. A lion may symbolize courage; a bird, the soul; or a temple, the presence of a god who nevertheless remains a mystery. Thus, in symbolic art the sensible object refers away from itself to a rationality that is enigmatically and mysteriously beyond it. In thus referring away from the sensible symbol to something vast and merely adumbrated, symbolic art sometimes achieves the sublime.

Classical Art. In classical art, the second form of sensible embodiment, the sensible expression is adequate to the idea that it gives expression to and does not point vaguely beyond itself. This is typified in sculptures of the human body so formed that the divine ideal is realized in the stone, not merely hinted at. A temple makes us think of the god but is not the god. In a statue of Apollo the god is visible and tangible in the stone. Hegel pointed out that works of classical art have independence and completeness, so that when they have been created, it seems that there is nothing more left to do done. "Nothing more beautiful," he wrote, "can be or become."

Romantic Art. Christianity, however, with its emphasis on the infinite value of the individual and upon subjective freedom, made classical art seem somewhat unsatisfactory. More is required than works of art in which reason, as Hegel put it, "stands in quiet and blessedness in bodily form." When the self and its inner life are regarded as of infinite value, the forms of art must move on from balance and harmony to the storm and turmoil of the subjective. According to Hegel, it is in romantic art that this progress to subjectivity and self-consciousness is achieved. Romantic art turns its back on the quiet and balanced beauty of the classical and "weaves the inner life of beauty into the contingency of

the external form, and allows full scope to the emphatic features of the unbeautiful." In romantic art, as in symbolic art, there is much that is bizarre and even grotesque, but romantic art is on a higher level than symbolic art because the mind expressed in it is more complex and sophisticated. And in romantic art the mind has achieved a greater measure of freedom than in classical art because romantic art is less involved in and hampered by the sensible embodiment.

PRODUCTS OF ART. Hegel's view of the three main types of beauty is closely linked with his view of the main types of artistic product. Hegel divided the arts into architecture, sculpture, painting, music, and poetry. Works in any of these mediums may be produced in the symbolic, classical, or romantic styles, but, according to Hegel, architecture is particularly appropriate to symbolic art, sculpture to classical art, and painting, music, and poetry to romantic art.

Architecture. Architecture, Hegel held, is the basic art, the art that men first practice, for its material is mindless and its forms depend upon the weight and physical properties of this mindless medium. The architecture of early men, by bringing them together to worship the gods in temples, served to bring unity into their societies. Hegel imagined the men who built the first temples as they cleared the ground on which to build them, and he described this as "clearing the undergrowth of finitude."

Sculpture. In architecture a house is provided for the god, and the god is prepared for and expected. He is not, however, embodied or manifested in the stones of a mere building. In classical sculpture the god is embodied in the stone in such a way that all the parts of the statue combine in expressing and proclaiming him. Hence, it is not a mindless symbol of the mind beyond but a unified expression of it. Hegel contrasted the stiff regularity of Egyptian sculpture with the harmonious independence of the Greek, the acme of classical art. In Christian sculpture this Greek ideal does not predominate, and even when, as with Michelangelo, it is fully understood and mastered, it is associated with "the kind of inspiration that is found in romantic art."

Painting, Music, and Poetry. The three romantic arts of painting, music, and poetry differ from the arts of sculpture and architecture, according to Hegel, by being more "ideal." One thing he seems to have meant was that the productions of these arts are not three-dimensional like the productions of architecture and sculpture. Painting, of course, is two-dimensional, and Hegel thought it is more ideal than sculpture because it is further removed from the solid substance of material things. He appears to have argued that the painter transforms to an extent that the sculptor has no need to do. In reducing the three dimensions to two, space is somehow rendered more "inward" and "subjective," and the first step has been taken on the road to poetry.

The next step toward subjectivity is taken by music, which abandons all the dimensions of space as well as the senses of sight and touch. Hearing, according to Hegel, is a "more subjective" sense than sight because it is less practical and more contemplative.

In romantic art, as in symbolic art,

there is much that is bizarre and even grotesque,

but romantic art is on a higher level

than symbolic art because the mind expressed in it

is more complex and sophisticated.

In poetry the sensible elements of music, the notes or tones, are replaced by words that stand for thoughts. "The art of poetry," Hegel wrote, "is the universal art of mind that has become free and is no longer dependent upon external sensible material for its realization." Within poetry as a whole he distinguished epic, lyric, and dramatic poetry. Hegel's account of dramatic poetry is particularly interesting. "In tragedy," he wrote, "individuals destroy themselves through the onesidedness of their upright will and character, or they are forced to resign themselves and identify themselves with a course of action to which they are fundamentally opposed." In comedy, on the other hand, there is no such reconciliation, the characters pursue courses of action that have only subjective significance. Indeed, in comedy, according to Hegel, the subjectivity characteristic of romantic art is taken to such an extreme that all unity is dissolved; with it goes beauty, too. In comedy there is merely a series of subjective interests playing against one another, as opposed to the aim of all art, which is the revelation of the eternal and divine in sensible form.

NATURAL BEAUTY. The discussion has thus far been confined to the beauty of works of art (*das Kunstschöne*). It is with this that by far the greater part of the "Lectures on Aesthetics" is concerned. In the second chapter, however, Hegel did say something about natural beauty (*das Naturschöne*). He discussed the notions of regularity, symmetry, harmony, and conformity to law and also the beauty claimed for plants, animals, and human beings. He concluded his discussion of the subject with some comments on how natural beauty falls short of artistic beauty. Plants and animals, he granted, are more beautiful than inanimate natural objects, but what we see of them is their outward coverings, not the soul that works within, for that is concealed by the visible feath-

ers, hair, scales, fur, and the like that cover them. Hegel referred to natural beauty as the "prose of the world." Although Hegel did not altogether deny the beauty of nature, it is clear that he ranked it very low. Indeed, the structure of his system made this inevitable, for it is the self-conscious achievements of man that form its culmination.

It would seem that the triadic divisions of the "Lectures on Aesthetics" constrained and even corrupted Hegel's argument. An example of this occurs in his account of dramatic poetry, into which he introduced a species called "drama," the function of which was to add one species to tragedy and comedy and thus make three species of dramatic poetry.

Hegel also tended to confuse conceptual and historical relationships. For example, the distinction between symbolic, classical, and romantic art was intended to be made on conceptual grounds, but, on the other hand, Hegel had in mind historical progression. Here, as elsewhere, Hegel confused historical types, such as romanticism, with conceptual types, such as tragedy, which have no necessary temporal sequence. Perhaps the most interesting case of this is Hegel's suggestion that art comes to an end with the highest flights of romanticism. We have already seen that Hegel brought his account of dramatic poetry to an end with comedy, the most subjective of all art forms. At the very end of the "Lectures on Aesthetics" he said that "in this culmination comedy is leading straight to the dissolution of art in general." It is unlikely that Hegel believed that art was coming to an end, any more than he believed that with the Prussian state, history was coming to an end. Yet in each case he argued in such a way as to suggest that the culmination of a conceptual sequence must also be the conclusion of a historical progress. Insofar as he held that history was the movement of the Divine in the world, it was natural to make this identification, extravagant as it is. Bosanquet, who denied that Hegel believed that art was on the point of final dissolution, held that he did foresee that it was about to suffer an eclipse in the new form of society. "But we must claim extraordinary insight for him, who, still under the spell of Schiller and Goethe, described the present exhaustion of the art-impulse and the conditions hostile to it in language approaching that of Ruskin and William Morris" (*A History of Aesthetic*, 4th ed., London, 1917, p. 361).

Philosophy of Religion

A few commentators have regarded Hegel's philosophy as atheistic, but most have considered it to be either theistic or pantheistic. Certainly religious expressions abound in his writings, even in the *Logic*. It has been shown how closely he associated art with religion and how he applied religious epithets to the state. It was also pointed out that the *Phenomenology* might with some justification be interpreted in atheistic terms. It would be obviously overstraining the evidence, however, to interpret Hegel's mature system in this way, for in the system religion is a form of Absolute Mind, along with art and philosophy, which is the supreme expression of the Absolute Mind. According to Hegel, religion represents or pictures the Absolute, whereas philosophy conceives or thinks it. The same truth, that is, expressed in quasi-imaginative form in one and in conceptual form in the other.

CHRISTIANITY. Since the concept is supreme and ultimate, philosophy surpasses religion to this extent, but in doing this, it finally and fully justifies Christianity, which is the absolute religion. The doctrine that elevates Christianity above all other religions is the doctrine of the Incarnation, which, according to Hegel, is the religious expression of the philosophical truth that the Infinite Being is not distinct from what is finite but is necessarily manifested in it. Hegel also interpreted the doctrine of the Trinity in philosophical terms. In the "Science of Logic" God is revealed as he is before the creation of the world; in the "Philosophy of Nature," in his material embodiment; and in the "Philosophy of Mind," as reconciling the finite and the Infinite. In this way the Father, the Son, and the Holy Spirit are explained in terms of the main themes of the Hegelian system. Again, Hegel interpreted the doctrine that God is love to mean that although the Infinite Being cannot exist without negation and opposition, the negation and opposition are finally reconciled. Finally, it should be mentioned that Hegel gave a series of lectures on the traditional proofs for the existence of God. He admitted the force of Kant's criticisms of these proofs but claimed to have reformulated the arguments so as to meet the criticisms. In particular, he held that the Ontological Argument, which Kant had regarded as vital but unsound, was valid when properly understood.

Undoubtedly, Hegel's later writings are much closer to orthodox Christianity than his earlier ones. The early "Life of Jesus" had nothing to say about the Resurrection, whereas in the *Lectures on the Philosophy of Religion* this doctrine was stated and defended. Hegel here wrote of "the death of death," of "the triumph over the negative," of mind as "the negative of this negative which thus contains the negative in itself," and of "the division of the divine idea and its reunion" that is "the whole of history." Although Hegel said that God appeared in the flesh at a particular time and in a particular individual, his account of the matter seems to be extremely general. In the Christian doctrine of the Incarnation, God became man in Jesus Christ at a particular time and place, whereas Hegel's God is incorporated in the finite world.

It would seem that a highly specific historical view is replaced by a highly general metaphysical one. Hegel himself did not take this view of his own work, nor did a younger contemporary of his, Karl Friedrich Göschel, in his *Aphorismen über Nichtwissen und absolutes Wissen im Verhälnisse zur christlichen Glaubenserkenntnis* (Berlin, 1829). In the *Encyclopedia* (Sec. 564) Hegel recommended this book, which is generally regarded as giving a theistic account of the Absolute. Just before referring to Göschel's book, Hegel had written, "God is only God in so far as he knows himself; his self-knowledge is moreover his consciousness of himself in man and man's knowledge *of* God, a knowledge that extends itself into the self-knowledge of man *in* God."

What cannot be doubted is that Hegel's philosophy of religion contained elements that could easily be developed in ways that go counter to orthodox Christianity. Thus, when D. F. Strauss argued, in his *Life of Jesus* (1835), that the Gospel story was a set of myths, he was consciously working out what he thought was the consequence of Hegel's view that in religion the truth about God is understood in representative or pictorial terms. Again, Ludwig Feuerbach, in his *The Essence of Christianity* (1841), endeavored to interpret the Christian doctrines in human and psychological terms as the imaginary fulfillment of wishes that cannot be satisfied here on earth. We have already referred to the passage in Hegel's *The Positivity of the Christian Religion,* in which he said that in the days of imperial Rome men who had been robbed of their freedom in this world sought for it in a heaven beyond. Feuerbach, who, of course, had not seen this work, could have read something similar in the *Phenomenology*. It is a very short step from Hegel's view that the infinite is manifested in the finite to the view that it is a projection of it. Perhaps the truth of the matter is that the Christian religion, according to Hegel, is adequate in its own sphere and that the philosophy of religion is required to counteract false religious views and false views about religion but is not a substitute for it. This is the interpretation given by Lasson in the Introduction to Hegel's philosophy of religion printed at the end of his edition of Hegel's *Lectures on the Philosophy of Religion.*

BIBLIOGRAPHY

Works by Hegel

The edition of Hegel's collected works, *Werke. Vollständige Ausgabe,* published soon after his death has already been mentioned. This was republished in 26 volumes under the editorship of Hermann Glockner (Stuttgart, 1927–1940) as the jubilee edition. Volumes 23–26 of this edition are an invaluable *Hegel-Lexikon* (1st ed., 1935; rev. ed., 2 vols., 1957). Mention must be made of Georg Lasson's edition, *Georg Wilhelm Friedrich Hegels Sämtliche Werke* (Leipzig, 1905–); this was to have been revised and re-edited by Lasson and

Johannes Hoffmeister, and some volumes were published (Hamburg, 1949—). As a result of the death of Lasson and of Hoffmeister, the plan was altered. The *Sämtliche Werke, neue kritische Ausgabe,* which Hoffmeister started to edit, will continue under the editorship of various scholars. This edition contains Hegel's letters in *Briefe von und an Hegel,* 4 vols. (1952–1960). The unpublished writings prior to 1800 will appear in this new critical edition under the editorship of Gisela Schüler. Another collection with still earlier documents is *Dokumente zu Hegels Entwicklung,* edited by Hoffmeister (Stuttgart, 1936).

Some of Hegel's early writings were translated from Herman Nohl, ed., *Hegels theologische Jugendschriften* (Tübingen, 1907) by T. M. Knox as *Early Theological Writings* (Chicago, 1948). There is a translation of the *Phenomenology of Mind* by J. B. Baillie (London, 1910; 2d ed., 1931). William Wallace translated the Encyclopedia "Logic," with excellent Prolegomena in *The Logic of Hegel* (Oxford, 1873); there are subsequent editions. He also translated the last part of the *Encyclopedia* (in *Hegel's Philosophy of Mind,* Oxford, 1894). See also *The Science of Logic,* translated by W. H. Johnston and L. G. Struthers, 2 vols. (London, 1929); *The Philosophy of Right,* translated and edited by T. M. Knox (Oxford, 1942), a very fine work of scholarship; *The Philosophy of Fine Art,* translated by F. P. B. Osmaston, 4 vols. (London, 1920); *Lectures on the Philosophy of Religion,* translated by E. B. Speirs and J. B. Sanderson, 3 vols. (London, 1895); and *Lectures on the History of Philosophy,* translated by E. S. Haldane and F. H. Simson, 3 vols. (London 1892–1896; reprint, 1955). J. Sibree's translation of the *Lectures on the Philosophy of History* (London, 1857) has been reprinted several times. See also *Hegel's Political Writings,* translated by T. M. Knox with an introductory essay by Z. A. Pelczynski (Oxford, 1964). There is a translation of the *Encyclopedia* with notes by Gustav E. Mueller (New York, 1959). There are two useful books of selections, *Hegel: Selections,* edited by Jacob Loewenberg (London and New York, 1929), and *The Philosophy of Hegel,* edited by C. J. Friedrich (New York, 1953).

Works on Hegel

The System

Caird, Edward, *Hegel.* London and Edinburgh, 1883.

Copleston, Frederick, *A History of Philosophy,* Vol. VII, *From Fichte to Nietzsche.* London, 1963. Chs. 9–11.

Croce, Benedetto, *Ciò che è vivo e ciò che è morto della filosofia di Hegel.* Bari, Italy, 1907. Translated by Douglas Ainslie as *What Is Living and What Is Dead in the Philosophy of Hegel.* London, 1915.

Findlay, J. N., *Hegel: A Re-examination.* London, 1958. Emphasizes the *Logic* and interprets Hegel in somewhat nonmetaphysical terms.

Glockner, Hermann, *Hegel,* 2 vols. Stuttgart, 1929. These are Vols. XXI–XXII of the jubilee edition of Hegel mentioned above.

Grégoire, Franz, *Études hégéliennes.* Louvain, Belgium, and Paris, 1958. Contains detailed and fruitful discussions of the central issues.

Haering, T. L., *Hegel: Sein Wollen und Sein Werk,* 2 vols. Leipzig, 1929. A leading authority.

Hartmann, Nicolai, *Die Philosophie des deutschen Idealismus,* Vol. II, Hegel. Berlin and Leipzig, 1929.

Kaufmann, Walter, *Hegel: Reinterpretation, Texts and Commentaries.* New York, 1965.

Kline, George L., "Some Recent Re-interpretations of Hegel's Philosophy." *The Monist,* Vol. 48 (1964), 34–73.

McTaggart, J. M. E., *Studies in Hegelian Cosmology.* Cambridge, 1901. Stimulating and idiosyncratic.

Mure, G. R. G., *An Introduction to Hegel.* Oxford, 1940. Emphasizes Hegel's debt to Greek philosophy, Aristotle in particular.

Pringle-Pattison, A. S., *Hegelianism and Personality,* 2d ed. London and Edinburgh, 1887. The first edition was published under the name Andrew Seth. See the article "The Absolute."

Seeberger, Wilhelm, *Hegel: Oder die Entwicklung des Geistes zur Freiheit.* Stuttgart, 1961. A new statement of the "orthodox" interpretation.

Stace, W. T., *The Philosophy of Hegel.* London, 1924; New York, 1955. A detailed account based on the *Encyclopedia.*

Serreau, René, *Hegel et l'hégélianism.* Paris, 1962. Brief but informative book with good introductory account of the various Hegelian schools.

Early Writings

Asveld, P., *La Pensée religieuse du jeune Hegel.* Louvain, Belgium, 1953.

Dilthey, Wilhelm, *Die Jugendgeschichte Hegels.* Berlin, 1906. It is included as Vol. IV of Dilthey's *Gesammelte Schriften* (Berlin and Leipzig, 1921).

Hyppolite, Jean, *Introduction à la philosophie de l'histoire de Hegel.* Paris, 1948. A valuable account of Hegel's early views on history and politics.

Kaufmann, Walter, "The Young Hegel and Religion," in his *From Shakespeare to Existentialism.* Boston, 1959. Ch. 8.

Lukács, Georg, *Der junge Hegel.* Berlin, 1948. An interesting Marxist interpretation.

Peperzak, A. T. P., *Le Jeune Hegel et la vision morale du monde.* The Hague, 1960.

Walsh, W. H., "The Origins of Hegelianism," in his *Metaphysics.* London, 1963. Ch. 9.

Phenomenology of Mind

Hyppolite, Jean, *Genèse et structure de la Phénomenologie de l'Esprit de Hegel.* Paris, 1946.

Kojève, Alexandre, *Introduction à la lecture de Hegel.* Paris, 1947. Gives the "atheistic" interpretation.

Loewenberg, Jacob, "The Exoteric Approach to Hegel's Phenomenology. I." *Mind,* N.S. Vol. 43 (1934), 424 ff.

Loewenberg, Jacob, "The Comedy of Immediacy in Hegel's Phenomenology. II." *Mind,* N.S. Vol. 44 (1935), 21 ff.

Wahl, Jean, *Le Malheur de la conscience dans la philosophie de Hegel.* Paris, 1929; 2d ed., 1951.

Logic

Hyppolite, Jean, *Logique et existence.* Paris, 1953.

McTaggart, J. M. E., *Commentary on Hegel's Logic.* Cambridge, 1910.

Mure, G. R. G., *A Study of Hegel's Logic.* Oxford, 1950.

Dialectic

Coreth, E., *Das dialektische Sein in Hegels Logik.* Vienna, 1952.

Grégoire, Franz, *Études hégéliennes.* Louvain, Belgium, and Paris, 1958. See Study II.

McTaggart, J. M. E., *Studies in the Hegelian Dialectic.* Cambridge, 1896; 2d ed., 1922.

Mueller, Gustav E., "The Hegel Legend of Thesis, Antithesis and Synthesis." *Journal of the History of Ideas,* Vol. 19 (1958), 411–14.

Popper, Karl, "What Is Dialectic?" *Mind,* N.S. Vol. 49 (1940), 403–26, Revised and reprinted in his *Conjectures and Refutations* (London, 1963), Ch. 15.

Social and Political Philosophy

Foster, M. B., *The Political Philosophies of Plato and Hegel.* Oxford, 1935. An original and valuable discussion.

Grégoire, Franz, *Études hégéliennes.* Louvain, Belgium, and Paris, 1958. See Study IV.

Haym, Rudolf, *Hegel und seine Zeit*. Berlin, 1857; reprinted, Hildesheim, 1962.

Kaufmann, Walter, "The Hegel Myth and Its Methods," in his *From Shakespeare to Existentialism*. Boston, 1959. Ch. 7 is a criticism of Ch. 12 of Popper's *The Open Society and Its Enemies*.

Knox, T. M., "Hegel and Prussianism." *Philosophy*, Vol. 15 (1940), 51–63.

Plamenatz, John, *Man and Society*, 2 vols. London and New York, 1963. Vol. II. Chs. 3–4. "The Social and Political Philosophy of Hegel."

Popper, Karl, *The Open Society and Its Enemies*, 2 vols. London, 1945. See Vol. II, Ch. 12.

Rosenzweig, Franz, *Hegel und der Staat*, 2 vols. Oldenburg, Germany, 1920.

Weil, Eric, *Hegel et l'état*. Paris, 1950.

Aesthetics

Bosanquet, B. *History of Aesthetic*. London, 1892. Chs. 2, 12.

Teyssèdre, B., *L'Esthétique de Hegel*. Paris, 1958.

Philosophy of Religion

Chapelle, A., *Hegel et la religion*, Vol. I, *La Problématique*. Paris, 1964—. The first of four projected volumes on the subject.

Grégoire, Franz, *Études hégéliennes*. Louvain, Belgium, and Paris, 1958. Study III.

Iljin, I., *Die Philosophie Hegels als kontemplative Gotteslehre*. Bern, 1946.

McTaggart, J. M. E., *Studies in Hegelian Cosmology*. Cambridge, 1901. Especially Chs. 2, 3, 6 ("Sin"), and 8 ("Hegelianism and Christianity").

Mueller, Gustav E., "Hegel's Absolute and the Crisis of Christianity," in D. C. Travis, ed., *A Hegel Symposium*. Austin, Tex., 1962.

For further discussion see *Hegel-Studien*, Vol. I (Bonn, 1961), Vol. II (Bonn, 1963), and Supp. Vol. I (Bonn, 1964). This is edited by F. Nicolin and O. Pöggeler and contains articles, reviews, and bibliography. See also *Études hégéliennes*, (Neuchâtel, 1955), containing articles by Alexandre Kojève, Georges Bataille, R. Queneau, Jean Wahl, and Eric Weil, and *A Hegel Symposium* (Austin, Texas, 1962), with articles by C. J. Friedrich, Sidney Hook, Helmut Motekat, Gustav E. Mueller, and Helmut Rehder.

– H. B. ACTON

HEGEL, GEORG W. F. (UPDATE)

Georg W. F. Hegel changed his major philosophical views very little from the publication of his first major work, the *Phenomenology of Spirit*, in 1807 until his death in 1831. This stability and continuity have not made it any easier for commentators to agree on what those views were. Disagreement about Hegel's basic position and its implications is still widespread, even more so after a great resurgence of Hegel studies after World War II.

In the Anglophone philosophical world, Hegel's position is still often summarized as an objective idealism, thanks largely to his influence on early twentieth-century British objective idealists such as Bradley. He is said to have believed that only "mind" (the preferred translation of *Geist* until the A. V. Miller translation of *Phenomenology of Spirit* was first published in 1977) was "real"; or that no determinate individual object could be said to be real. Such an object was really a "moment" of the interrelated and temporally developing structure of the one true substance, the absolute, or absolute mind. Such a substance was said to develop over time; the nature of that development was a process of greater self-consciousness, and this development was reflected in, or the underlying basis of, the great social and political changes of world history, as well as intellectual changes in philosophy, art, and religion. Since Hegel appeared to have claimed a full and final "absolute knowledge," an "encyclopedic" account of such a structure, or the relation between "logic," philosophy of nature, and philosophy of spirit could be given. (A compelling demonstration that such an objective-idealist or "internal relations" view could *not* have been Hegel's position was published by the German Hegel scholar Rolf-Peter Horstmann in 1984, *Ontologie und Relationen*.)

Some aspects of such views of what Hegel really meant persist in many postwar interpretations but have not provoked much serious discussion or the interpretive variants that once characterized the work of McTaggart. Mure, Caird, and Stace. Other interpretations and emphases have predominated. Many commentators have become interested in Hegel less as an object of purely historical research and more as a possible contributor to perennial and current philosophical controversies.

Charles Taylor's 1975 study *Hegel*, while offering a comprehensive commentary on all aspects of Hegel's work, emphasized Hegel's insights into the emerging problems of the modern social and political world—problems such as social fragmentation, alienation, and the proper understanding of the modern goals of freedom and some sort of harmony with self. Taylor showed that many of Hegel's theoretical intentions could also best be understood against the backdrop of such concerns, and his approach became influential.

Hegel's understanding of the intellectual and social dimensions of modernization was also important in the work of many critical theory or Frankfurt school neo-Marxist philosophers (a group sometimes even designated as "neo-Hegelian" Marxists because of their attention to the social function of ideas and culture without a reliance on traditional Marxist versions of economic materialism). In the work of the most important "second generation" critical theorist, Jürgen Habermas, Hegel also plays a large role in what Habermas calls, in a book title, *The Philosophical Discourse of Modernity*. Hegel is called "the first philosopher who made modernity a problem" (p. 4)—this by raising many questions about the sufficiency of the modern notions of subjectivity and rationality.

In other developments, Klaus Hartmann in several influential articles proposed what he called a "non-metaphysical" reading of Hegel, one that emphasized Hegel's category theory and the unusual "logic" of categorial relations, all as more or less autonomous

---

Hegel's understanding of the intellectual

and social dimensions of modernization

was important in the work

of many critical theory or Frankfurt school

neo-Marxist philosophers.

---

philosophical problems, not necessarily wedded to any metaphysics of absolute mind. A group of German philosophers who came to be known as the Heidelberg school began to work in a more contemporary way on the single greatest problem that preoccupied the German idealists as a whole, and Hegel especially: the problem of self-consciousness, or "reflection," how the mind could be said to be both the subject of its own consciousness and object to itself at the same time. (The most important and influential work on this aspect of the idealists and Hegel in particular has been Dieter Henrich's.) Since, for many post-Kantian idealists, any possible cognitive or practical relation to the world was an active comporting of oneself toward the world, or a "self-relation in relation to an other," the problem of self-relation was argued to be fundamental in any epistemology or account of human agency. These elements have also been emphasized by those who argue that Hegel should be read much more as a post-Kantian idealist, as much more decisively influenced by Kant's founding arguments about the possibility of any self-conscious experience than by, say, Spinoza or Schelling.

Hegel's contributions to all such problems—the nature and implications of modern social life, the possibility of self-consciousness and self-knowledge, the nature of the mind-world, and agency problems—reappear with great urgency in his ethical and social theory and in many interpretations. Debates about whether Hegel's 1821 *Elements of the Philosophy of Right* encouraged an accommodation of the conservative rulers of the Prussian state, or whether he was guilty of a kind of "organicist" antiindividualism, have been replaced by an emerging consensus that Hegel belongs within, if idiosyncratically, the modern liberal political

tradition. This recognition has been somewhat complicated by "communitarian" writers and "traditionalist" writers suspicious of the modern reliance on claims of rationality as decisive in ethical life. Many such writers have occasionally enlisted arguments in a case against the classical liberal tradition. Hegel's position on the importance and "priority" of the ethical community in ethical life (*Sittlichkeit*) has sometimes been understood such that anyone who believes in the priority of prevolitional attachments or commitments in ethical deliberation (e.g., such attachments are necessary for deliberation to get started or have direction but cannot themselves be products of such deliberation) is labeled a neo-Hegelian. But Hegel believes that modern ethical life (the institutions and practices of modern social existence, the modern family, civil society, and the legal, constitutional state) are not just "ours" and "prior." He believes they are rational, raising the still much-debated question of how he distinguishes rational from nonrational ethical communities.

A great deal of scholarly work has been done in the postwar period on Hegel's texts, especially on the dating and organization of his Jena-period lecture materials. Karl-Heinz Ilting has compiled, edited, and published an extensive collection of Hegel's lecture notes on political philosophy, and a new critical edition of Hegel's works has begun to appear. New English translations of the *Phenomenology*, the *Logic*, the *Philosophy of Right*, the *Aesthetics* lectures, Hegel's letters, and many other works have also appeared.

[See also Communitarianism; Critical Theory; Habermas, Jürgen; Kant, Immanuel; Liberalism; Marxism; Rationality; Spinoza, Benedict (Baruch); Subjectivity.]

BIBLIOGRAPHY

Works by Hegel

German

Gesammelte Werke, edited by Rheinisch-Westfälischen Akademie der Wissenschaften. Hamburg, 1968– . Of great value to serious students of Hegel in the original.

Philosophie des Rechts: Die Vorlesung von 1819/20, edited by D. Henrich. Frankfurt, 1983.

Vorlesungen über Rechtsphilosophie 1818–31, edited by K.-H. Ilting. Stuttgart, 1974. Contains an invaluable collection of student notes and additions.

Werke in zwanzig Bänden. Frankfurt, 1971. Useful paperback version of the 1832–45 Moldenhauer and Michel edition.

English

The Difference between Fichte's and Schelling's System of Philosophy, translated by H. S. Harris and W. Cerf. Albany, NY, 1977.

Elements of the Philosophy of Right, edited by A. Wood, translated by H. B. Nisbet. Cambridge, 1991.

Faith and Knowledge, translated by W. Cerf and H. S. Harris. Albany, NY, 1977.

Hegel: The Letters, translated by C. Butler and C. Seiler. Bloomington, IN, 1984.

Hegel's Aesthetics: Lectures on Fine Art, translated by T. M. Knox. Oxford, 1965.

Lectures on the Philosophy of Religion: The Lectures of 1827, edited by P. Hodgson, translated by R. F. Brown, P. C. Hodgson, J. M. Stewart, and H. S. Harris. Berkeley, 1983.

Phenomenology of Spirit, translated by A. V. Miller. Oxford, 1977.

Science of Logic, translated by A. V. Miller. London, 1969.

Works on Hegel

Hegel's Intellectual Development

Dickey, L. *Hegel: Religion, Economics, and the Politics of the Spirit.* Cambridge, 1977.

Görland, I. *Die Kantkritik des jungen Hegel.* Frankfurt, 1966.

Harris, H. S. *Hegel's Development.* 2 vols. Oxford, 1972–83.

Henrich, D., and K. Düsing, eds. *Hegel in Jena.* Bonn, 1980.

Kimmerle, H. *Das Problem der Abgeschlossenheit des Denkens: Hegels System der Philosophie in den Jahren 1800–1804.* Bonn, 1970.

Peperzak, A. *La jeune Hegel et la vision morale du monde.* The Hague, 1960.

Hegel's Basic Position and His System

Adorno, T. *Hegel: Three Studies,* translated by S. W. Nicholsen. Cambridge, MA, 1993.

Beiser, F., ed. *The Cambridge Companion to Hegel.* Cambridge, 1993. Contains a comprehensive bibliography of recent work on Hegel.

Brockard, H. *Subjekt: Versuch zur Ontologie bei Hegel.* Munich, 1970.

DeVries, W. *Hegel's Theory of Mental Activity.* Ithaca, NY, 1988.

Fackenheim, E. *The Religious Dimension in Hegel's Thought.* Chicago, 1967.

Harlander, K. *Absolute Subjektivität und kategoriale Anschauung.* Meisenheim, 1969.

Hartmann, K. *Die ontologische Option.* Berlin, 1976.

Henrich, D. *Hegel im Kontext.* Frankfurt, 1971.

Hösle, V. *Hegels System.* 2 vols. Hamburg, 1987. Includes a comprehensive bibliography of recent work on Hegel.

Houlgate, S. *Freedom, Truth, and History: An Introduction to Hegel's Philosophy.* London, 1991.

Inwood, M. J. *Hegel.* London, 1983.

———, ed. *Hegel.* Oxford, 1985. Contains a comprehensive bibliography of recent work on Hegel.

MacIntrye, A., ed. *Hegel: A Collection of Critical Essays.* Notre Dame, IN, 1972.

McCumber, J. *The Company of Words: Hegel, Language, and Systematic Philosophy.* Evanston, IL, 1993.

O'Brien, G. D. *Hegel on Reason and History.* Chicago, 1975.

Peperzak, A. *Selbsterkenntnis des Absoluten: Grundlinien der Hegelsche Philosophie des Geistes.* Stuttgart, 1987.

Pinkard, T. *Hegel's Dialectic: The Explanation of Possibility.* Philadelphia, 1988.

Pippin, R. B. *Hegel's Idealism: The Satisfactions of Self-Consciousness.* Cambridge, 1989. Includes a comprehensive bibliography of recent works on Hegel.

Plant, R. *Hegel.* Bloomington, IN, 1973.

Rockmore, T. *Hegel's Circular Epistemology.* Bloomington, IN, 1986.

Rose, G. *Hegel Contra Sociology.* Atlantic Highlands, NJ, 1981.

Rosen, S. *G. W. F. Hegel: An Introduction to the Science of Wisdom.* New Haven, 1974.

Soll, I. *An Introduction to Hegel's Metaphysics.* Chicago, 1969.

Taylor, C. *Hegel.* Cambridge, 1977.

White, A. *Absolute Knowledge: Hegel and the Problem of Metaphysics.* Athens, OH, 1983.

Wohlfahrt, G. *Der spekulative Satz: Bemerkungen zum Begriff der Spekulation bei Hegel.* Berlin, 1981.

Hegel's Phenomenology and Logic

Baum, M. *Die Entstehung der Hegelschen Dialektik.* Bonn, 1986.

Bubner, R. *Dialektik und Wissenschaft.* Frankfurt, 1962.

Düsing, K. *Das Problem der Subjektivität in Hegels Logik.* Bonn, 1976.

Flay, J. *Hegel's Quest for Certainty.* Albany, NY, 1984. Includes a comprehensive bibliography of recent work on Hegel.

Forster, M. *Hegel and Scepticism.* Cambridge, MA, 1989.

Fulda, H. *Das Problem einer Einleitung in Hegels Wissenschaft der Logik.* Frankfurt, 1965.

———, ed. *Materialen zu Hegels Phänomenologie des Geistes.* Frankfurt, 1973.

———. *Hegels Wissenschaft der Logik: Formation und Rekonstruktion.* Stuttgart, 1986.

Henrich, D. *Die Wissenschaft der Logik und die Logik der Reflexion.* Bonn, 1987.

Horstmann, R.-P. *Ontologie und Relationen: Hegel, Bradley, Russell, und die Kontroverse über interne und externe Relationen.* Königstein, 1984.

Labarriere, P. *La Phénoménologie de l'esprit de Hegel.* Paris, 1979.

Marx, W. *Hegel's Phenomenology of Spirit: Its Point and Purpose—A Commentary on the Preface and Introduction.* New York, 1975.

Pinkard, T. *Hegel's Phenomenology: The Sociality of Reason.* Cambridge, 1994.

Pöggeler, O. *Hegels Idee einer Phänomenologie des Geistes.* Freiburg, 1973.

Puntel, B. *Darstellung, Methode, und Struktur: Untersuchungen zur Einheit der systematischen Philosophie G. W. F. Hegels.* Bonn, 1973.

Robinson, J. *Duty and Hypocrisy in Hegel's Phenomenology of Mind.* Toronto, 1977.

Rohs, P. *Form und Grund: Interpretation eines Kapital der Hegelschen Wissenschaft der Logik.* Bonn, 1969.

Rosen, M. *Hegel's Dialectic and Its Criticism.* Cambridge, 1982.

Shklar, J. *Freedom and Independence: A Study of the Political Ideas in Hegel's Phenomenology of Mind.* Cambridge, 1976.

Solomon, R. *In the Spirit of Hegel.* Oxford, 1983.

Theunissen, M. *Sein und Schein: Die kritische Funktion der Hegelschen Logik.* Frankfurt, 1978.

Westphal, M. *History and Truth in Hegel's Phenomenology.* Atlantic Highlands, NJ, 1978.

Hegel's Practical Philosophy

Avineri, S. *Hegel's Theory of the Modern State.* Cambridge, 1972.

Brod, H. *Hegel's Philosophy of Politics: Idealism, Identity, and Modernity.* Boulder, CO, 1992.

Cullen, B. *Hegel's Social and Political Thought: An Introduction.* Dublin, 1979.

D'Hondt, J. *Hegel in His Time: Berlin 1818–1831,* translated by J. Burbidge. Peterborough, NH, 1988.

Fessard, G. *Hegel, le Christianisme, et l'histoire.* Paris, 1990.

Fleischman, E. *La Philosophie politique de Hegel.* Paris, 1964.

Hardimon, M. *The Project of Reconciliation: Hegel's Social Philosophy.* Cambridge, 1993.

Henrich, D., and R.-P. Horstmann. *Hegels Philosophie des Rechts: Die Theorie der Rechstformen und ihre Logik.* Stuttgart, 1982.

Marcuse, H. *Reason and Revolution.* Boston, 1960.

Pelczynski, Z. A., ed. *Hegel's Political Philosophy: Problems and Perspectives.* Cambridge, 1971.

———. *Hegel and Civil Society.* Cambridge, 1984.

Peperzak, A. *Philosophy and Politics: A Commentary on the Preface to Hegel's Philosophy of Right.* The Hague, 1987.

———. *Hegel's praktische Philosophie: Ein Kommentar zur enzyklopädischen Darstellung der menschlichen Freiheit und ihre objektive Verwirklichung.* Stuttgart, 1991.

Pinkard, T. *Democratic Liberalism and Social Union.* Philadelphia, 1987.

Riedel, M. *Theorie und Praxis im Denken Hegels.* Frankfurt, 1965.

———. *Materialen zu Hegels Rechtsphilosophie.* 2 vols. Frankfurt, 1975.

Ritter, J. *Hegel and the French Revolution,* translated by R. D. Winfield. Cambridge, MA, 1982.

Siep, L. *Hegels Fichtekritik und die Wissenschaftslehre von 1804.* Freiburg, 1970.

———. *Praktische Philosophie im Deutschen Idealismus.* Frankfurt, 1992.

Smith, S. *Hegel's Critique of Liberalism.* Chicago, 1989.

Stepelevich, L. S., and D. Lamb. *Hegel's Philosophy of Action.* Atlantic Highlands, NJ, 1983.

Taylor, C. *Hegel and Modern Society.* Cambridge, 1979.

Theunissen, M. *Hegels Lehre vom absoluten Geist als theologisch-politischer Traktat.* Berlin, 1970.

Tunick, M. *Hegel's Political Philosophy: Interpreting the Practice of Legal Punishment.* Princeton, NJ, 1992.

Walsh, W. H. *Hegelian Ethics.* London, 1969.

Wasczek, N. *The Scottish Enlightenment and Hegel's Account of Civil Society.* Dordrecht, 1988.

Wildt, A. *Autonomie und Anerkennung: Hegels Moralitätskritik in Lichte seiner Fichte Rezeption.* Stuttgart, 1982.

Wood, A. *Hegel's Ethical Thought.* Cambridge, 1990.

Aesthetics

Bungay, S. *Beauty and Truth: A Study of Hegel's Aesthetics.* Oxford, 1986.

Desmond, W. *Art and the Absolute: A Study of Hegel's Aesthetics.* Albany, NY, 1986.

Fulda, H., ed. *Hegel und die Kritik der Urteilskraft.* Stuttgart, 1990.

— ROBERT B. PIPPIN

HEIDEGGER, MARTIN

Martin Heidegger (1889–1976), German philosopher, counts as one of the major forces of twentieth-century European thought. Once considered to be principally an "existentialist" thinker, Heidegger insisted to the end that his only concern was the question about the meaning of 'Being', and his later work justified the claim.

Beginning of the Way

Asked in 1962 to describe the origins of his experience, Heidegger explained that his question was given to him by reading Franz Brentano's doctoral dissertation, "On the Manifold Meaning of Being [*Seiendes*] in Aristotle" (1862). If a being (*Seiendes,* Aristotle's *on*) is understood as what-is, then "is" obviously has manifold meanings. "How can they be brought into comprehensible accord? This accord can not be grasped without first raising and settling the question: whence does Being as such (*Sein*) (not merely beings as beings) receive its determination?" (Preface to Richardson, 1974). Accordingly, Being (*Sein*), as different from beings (*Seiende*), would be the Is of what-is, the process of letting everything that is

show itself as what it is. What is the meaning of such a being-process as different from the beings it lets be manifest (the "ontological difference"), even if these be taken in their ensemble?

In private conversation Heidegger would expand this to say that his initial reading of ancient authors offered no answer to his question. Hence, equally original with the experience of the question was the experience of its inherent negativity, or finitude—that is, its forgottenness. Yet the word "is" was everywhere, and those who used it (especially the philosophers) had to have some understanding of what it meant, even if they remained oblivious of that meaning. The only way to get an answer to the question would be to interrogate this obscured understanding in the being (human) that was gifted with it.

Once considered principally

an "existentialist" thinker,

Heidegger insisted to the end that his only concern

was the question about the meaning of "Being."

Given the question, Heidegger relates that three factors were especially significant in his pursuit of an answer: (1) the discovery (through Husserl) of phenomenology as a method, the term being derived from the Greek *logos* (to make manifest) and *phainesthai* (to show oneself)—a process eventually identified as the Greek sense of *hermeneuein,* hence a hermeneutic phenomenology of its very nature; (2) the experience of truth as essentially revelation (in Aristotle's *Metaphysics,* book 9, and *Nicomachean Ethics,* book 6); (3) the experience of being (*ousia*) as a noun born of a participle suggesting presence (*Anwesenheit*) or the present (*Gegenwart*)—in any case something of a temporal nature. The being that says "is"—the "There" (or "Here": *Da*) among beings through which the Is (Being: *Sein*) becomes articulated—will be referred to as *Dasein,* a term that later became anglicized. But already a temporal structure in it could be discerned, at least in retrospect: its openness to the Being-process, its coming-to-be-itself, by reason of this openness, is a coming that may be called its future (*Zukunft*); but such a future comes to a Dasein that already is, with an alreadiness that may be called its past (*Gewesenheit*); finally, by reason of what it is already coming-to-be, Dasein can let every being (including itself) be present as showing itself as what it is, a structure that may be called its present (*Gegenwart*). Future, past, and present—these are the components (eventually "ecstases") of time. They would have to be

German philosopher Martin Heidegger counts as one of the major forces of twentieth-century European thought. (Corbis/Bettmann)

justified by phenomenological analysis, of course, but with the advantage of hindsight one can appreciate the import of Heidegger's subtitle for part 1 of *Being and Time,* indisputably his major work (1927): "The Interpretation of Dasein in Terms of Temporality, and the Explication of Time as the Transcendental Horizon for the Question of Being."

Given this conception of what makes Dasein to be what it is (its "essence": *Wesen*), which Heidegger named "existence" (later elaborated as self and care), it is understandable how the phenomenological/hermeneutic analysis, beginning with the everyday facticity of Dasein as simply being-in-the-world, could be taken to be an "existentialism." But Heidegger's own project was never lost sight of: to understand Dasein's temporality and consequent historicity as propaedeutic to questioning the meaning of Being itself in its relation to time.

The Turn (*die Kehre*)

The philosophical public first heard Heidegger speak of a "turn" in his way with the publication of the *Letter*

on Humanism (1947), but those close to his unpublished work (courses, lectures, etc.) could hardly be unaware of a shift of emphasis in his approach to the Being-question that could be dated from at least 1930. Precisely what the shift consists in and how it came about are issues of debate among specialists, but the simplest way to understand it may be within the context of the essay "On the Essence of Truth," a lecture first delivered in 1930 but not published until 1943.

After reviewing classical conceptions of truth as some kind of correspondence between knower and known, Heidegger analyzes the knowing process as involving an openness of Dasein to the Open that permits a being to come to presence as to-be-known. This Open he calls *Aletheia,* which he will henceforth understand in the radical Greek sense of non- (alpha privative) concealment (-*lethe*). But in part 6 of the essay, Aletheia is experienced as more than the horizon within which beings are encountered and reveal themselves as true. Rather, it is experienced as an active force, a process that assumes an initiative of its own by revealing itself to Dasein—but concealing itself as well. The concealing takes a double form: (1) concealing its own concealment so that its self-concealment is forgotten ("mystery": *das Geheimnis*); (2) compounding the forgottenness by seducing Dasein into wandering about in ever deeper forgetfulness of the mystery ("errancy": *die Irre*). This shift of focus from Dasein as disclosing Being to Being as revealing itself to, and concealing itself from. Dasein characterizes the entire later period of Heidegger's address to the Being-question. Whatever else is said about the celebrated "turn," it must take account of this fact.

One immediate consequence of this shift of focus was a new way of conceiving history, no longer in terms of Dasein, but now in terms of Being-as-Aletheia sending/withdrawing itself, always in finite fashion. This self-sending (*sich-schicken*) is received by Dasein, and the correlation of the two Heidegger calls "destiny" (*Geschick*), which, in turn, constitutes an "epoch" of history. Sometimes the self-sending of Being is taken in a limited sense as bestowed upon an individual thinker (e.g., Parmenides); sometimes it is taken in a very broad sense as determining the entire history of metaphysics. In any case, the combination of these epochs constitutes the history of Being—that is, Being-as-history (*Seinsgeschichte*)—and, to think the Being-question, one must do so in terms of its history, through retrieval (*Wiederholung*) of its past.

The "Later" Heidegger

This is a general term that refers to no identifiable date but designates Heidegger's effort to think the Being-question after the turn in his way. It is marked by certain differences of style and terminology (e.g., Dasein comes to be called the "clearing" [*Lichtung*] of Being) as well as by the shift of focus just mentioned, but Heidegger's basic preoccupation remains the same. The period is represented by no dominant published work comparable in stature to *Being and Time* but rather by published versions of lecture courses, interpretations of poetry, and sundry collections of essays. For heuristic purposes one may survey the drift of Heidegger's thought after the turn by polarizing remarks around three separate moments that may be considered as "early," "middle," and "late" with regard to this period itself: *Introduction to Metaphysics* (1935); *Letter on Humanism* (1947); *Time and Being* (1960).

Heidegger's conception of human being is not

at all a humanism in the metaphysical sense but,

if the term must be retained,

offers a humanism of a higher sort.

Introduction to Metaphysics was not published until 1953 and, in retrospect, made unmistakably clear the import of the turn, though echoes of *Being and Time* remained. (After reformulating the Being-question, Heidegger examines the Greek grammar and syntax of Being and then reflects on the limitation of its meaning through its differentiation from modalities with which it is often associated—Being "and" Becoming/Seeming/Thinking/the Ought.) The spine of the course is the meditation on Being and thinking in terms of Parmenides' gnome: *to gar auto noein estin te kai einai* ("for thinking and Being are one"). Here Being (*einai*) is interpreted as emerging-abiding-presence (*physis*), or (by analogy with Heraclitus's *logos*) as a primordial gathering into presence, or (always by implication) Aletheia. Thinking (*noein*), the function of Dasein, is the effort to bring to containment the overpowering advance of Being or (less dramatically) to respond to (correspond with) its self-sending. To say that Being and thinking are *auto* does not mean that they are the same in the sense of identical but that they are "one" because they are necessarily correlative. If Dasein's only function is to be the There of Being, Being reciprocally has need of its There as the clearing through which it can reveal itself. It is this correlation that constitutes the destiny (*Geschick*) of Being in any given epoch.

Letter on Humanism is the published response to several questions posed by the French student of Jean-Paul Sartre, Jean Beaufret, the first of which was: "How can we restore meaning to the word 'humanism'?" Heidegger, in substance, replies that humanism is a metaphysical notion: "Every humanism is either grounded in a metaphysics or is itself made to be the ground of one," with its standard conception of human being as a "rational animal." But this conception sells human being short, measures it by a zoological standard of sheer animality rather than in terms of its unique prerogative of access to Being. Accordingly, Heidegger's conception of human being is not at all a humanism in the metaphysical sense but, if the term must be retained, offers a humanism of a higher sort.

With this much said, the import of the letter derives in large degree from the fluid epistolary style that permits the author to discourse freely on a wide range of significant issues that receive more thorough treatment elsewhere. By way of summary, several of these are worth noting:

THE POLEMIC AGAINST METAPHYSICS. Heidegger's complaint about metaphysics is that it is oblivious of the very Being that makes its enterprise possible. In the early years he spoke about laying the groundwork for metaphysics through fundamental ontology. Later the project was called the overcoming of metaphysics. Defined by Aristotle as the interrogation of *on hei on*, of beings as beings, metaphysics became either the study of beings in their commonality (ontology) or of beings in their ultimate ground in a supreme being (theology)—hence, it is onto-theo-logical in its very structure. Dealing exclusively with beings, metaphysics is utterly forgetful of Being (i.e., Aletheia-as-history), their ground.

THE CRITIQUE OF TECHNOLOGY. When Nietzsche, in the final paroxysm of the epoch of metaphysics (see "Nietzsche's Word 'God is dead' "), speaks of "mastery over the earth" (*Erdherrschaft*) as the proper task for human being under the sway of will-to-power, this for Heidegger is harbinger of another, more ominous, epoch, one marked by the destiny (*Geschick*) of Being in his own time whose effect he describes as *die Technik*, ambiguously translated as "technology" (see "The Question Concerning Technology"). The menace in this, as he sees it, is not scientific progress as such but the way an instrument is used in achieving this progress (e.g., a hydroelectric dam on the Rhine)—as no more than a "standby reserve" (*Bestand*) of power to be subjected increasingly to human control. To give a name to the self-disclosure of Being whose effect is this steady submission of beings to human manipulation, Heidegger invents the word *Gestell:* the collective prefix *Ge-* combining the various forms of *stellen* (*vor-/nach-/gegen-/zurück-*, etc.) that suggest such control. So far,

English has had to settle for a more or less literal translation of the banal meaning of *Gestell* in German: "enframing." In any case, failure to recognize this destiny for what it is—this is the true "danger" (*Gefahr*) of the epoch. Is there any "salvation" (*Rettung*) from such a danger? Only by recognizing both danger and destiny as signs of Being's bestowal—and withdrawal—in/as an epoch of history.

Heidegger's complaint about metaphysics

is that it is oblivious of the very Being

that makes its enterprise possible.

LANGUAGE: HOUSE OF BEING. This celebrated metaphor, introduced to the public in the letter to Beaufret, signals the importance that language had assumed for Heidegger in his pursuit of the Being-question by the mid-1940s. In *Being and Time* the problem of language found a place in the phenomenological analysis only as one of the existential components of Dasein under the name of *Rede* ("discourse"), which translated the Greek *logos*. After the turn, logos in *Introduction to Metaphysics* is thought of homologously with physis, einai (and Aletheia) in Heraclitean terms. Thus interpreted, logos is understood as a gathering process that collects all beings unto themselves and lets them be manifest as what they are. It is precisely in this guise that logos comes to be thought of as aboriginal language—language in its origins. Heidegger elaborates this theme in a lecture course of 1944, entitled " 'Logos' (Heraclitus Fg. 50)" (see *Vorträge und Aufsätze*), adding that the task of humans is to respond to—rather, to correspond with (*homologein*)—Being as it reveals itself as logos, bringing it into words. To attend in this fashion to the address of Being is to "poetize" (*Dichten*), and in this respect thinker and poet share a common task. The problem is to understand how the two tasks differ.

Heidegger does not claim that Heraclitus thought the relation between Being and language in this fashion explicitly but rather that the relation is accessible to subsequent thinking through a retrieve of Heraclitus's experience. This conception of the origin of language, suggestive though it be, is limited, at best, to a specifically Greek phenomenon and, as such, takes no account of the Judaic experience of language (also a part of the Western tradition), still less of non-Western experiences of language and thought, with all of their untold wealth.

Time and Being brings Heidegger's endeavor full circle. The title of this lecture was especially provocative, for it was the same formula that announced the third section (which never appeared) of part 1 of *Being and Time*. For many readers, much of the work published after the turn performed the task that had been projected there. The themes discussed had been wide-ranging. Besides those already mentioned, there had been essays on various issues, for example, on the origin of a work of art, on building, on dwelling, and on "things" in their relation to the world—that is, to the fourfold of earth and sky, the gods and mortals. Finally, the task of thought that Heidegger sought to pursue and to urge, whether under the rubric of "thinking-as-thanking" (*Danken*) (see *What Is Called Thinking*, part 2) or "releasement" (*Gelassenheit*) (see *Conversation on a Country Path*), parallelled, after the turn, what *Being and Time* called "resoluteness," the gesture of acquiescence by which Dasein achieves authenticity.

What readers at the time were not aware of was a major manuscript, entitled *Beiträge zur Philosophie: Vom Ereignis,* that Heidegger drafted but did not edit (1936–38) and was published only posthumously (1989). The most decisive word in the essay, *Ereignis,* normally translated as "event," is here given the sense of an event that "gives" or "appropriates." Though this term occurs with increasing frequency and shifting significance after 1936, its sense as "appropriating event" did not receive full development for the reading public until *Time and Being*. In *Being and Time* the author declares that "there is" (*es gibt,* literally "it gives") Being only insofar as Dasein is. In *Letter on Humanism* he interprets the earlier formula to mean that the giver is Being itself. In *Time and Being,* Being does not do the giving; it is, itself, given.

In this essay Heidegger returns to the earliest form of the question that first set him on his way: what is the meaning of Being in terms of time? Clearly, Being is not a being but rather is given (*es gibt Sein*). Nor is time a being; it, too, is given (*es gibt Zeit*). Neither is prior to the other, yet each reciprocally determines the other, and in this reciprocity each is given unto its own (*Eigene*). Being is understood as coming-to-presence (*Anwesen*) but includes a nonpresencing (*Abwesen*), a withdrawal, too. For the present (*Gegenwart*) that emerges out of the presencing process implies a nonpresent of a twofold kind: that of the past (*Gewesen*), which is no longer present; that of the future (*Sukunft*), which is still withheld from the present. Pres-absencing (*An-/Abwesen*), then, comes to this:

Approaching (*Ankommen*), being not yet present, at the same time gives and brings about what is no longer present, the past, and, conversely, what has been offers future to itself. The reciprocal relation of both at the same time gives and brings about the present (*Time and Being,* 13).

The two modes of the nonpresent in the pres-absencing process constitute, then, the withdrawal that is ingredient to Being's self-donation. Where, for whom, does this take place? For human being!

If man were not the constant receiver of the gift given by the "It gives presence," if that which is extended in the gift did not reach man, then not only would Being remain concealed in the absence of the gift, not only closed off, but man would remain excluded from the scope of: It gives Being. Man would not be man. (*Time and Being,* 12)

But what is "It" (*Es*) that does the giving of Being and time, each unto its own and to the other? The appropriating event (*Ereignis*)!

What remains to be said? Only this: Appropriation appropriates. Saying this, we say the Same, in terms of the Same about the Same. . . . But what if we take what was said and adopt it unceasingly as the guide for our thinking, and consider that this Same is not even anything new, but the oldest of the old in Western thought: that ancient something which conceals itself in *A-letheia?* (*Time and Being,* 24)

The appropriating event, then, anticipated in the *Beiträge* (1936), here (1960) comes into its own as the final name for Aletheia, which is, for Heidegger, the first name of all.

Conclusion

No one (beginning with Heidegger himself) denies the density of *Time and Being,* with which his effort at thought comes, in effect, full circle. Here at last was one way to answer the question. Whence does Being as such (not merely beings as beings) receive its determination? Any attempt to assess Heidegger's contribution to the history of twentieth-century philosophical thought must begin with the single-mindedness of his enterprise. Everything turns on how one assesses his experience of Aletheia: on the one hand this term surely characterizes the uniqueness of Heidegger's own extraordinary philosophical gift; on the other, as in Greek tragedy, it may help to account for the singularity of the failure for which history will hold him responsible. Confronted by mystery and errancy, he, too, was subject to the finitude of Aletheia as it revealed itself in him. It is in this context that the question of Heidegger's political involvement must be raised: did the very nature of the enterprise lead to his transient tryst with Nazism (and if so, how?) or simply fail to prevent it? This leaves to Heidegger's readers the delicate task of trying to make for themselves a judicious assessment of the relationship between the content of his thought and the conduct of his life.

[See also Authenticity; Heraclitus; Hermeneutic Phenomenology; Husserl, Edmund; Nietzsche, Friedrich Wilhelm; Parmenides; Sartre, Jean-Paul; Self; Truth.]

BIBLIOGRAPHY

Works by Heidegger

Gesamtausgabe (1973–93, Frankfurt)

PUBLISHED WORKS, 1910–76
Frühe Schriften [1912–16], ed. F.-W. von Herrmann. 1978.
Sein und Zeit [1927], ed. F.-W. von Herrmann. 1977.
Sein und Zeit, 17th ed., reprint of 15th rev. ed. Tübingen, 1993.
Kant und das Problem der Metaphysik [1929], ed. F.-W. von Herrmann. 1991.
Erläuterungen zu Hölderlins Dichtung [1936–68], ed. F.-W. von Herrmann. 1978.
Holzwege [1935–46], ed. F.-W. von Herrmann. 1978.
Wegmarken [1919–58], ed. F.-W. von Herrmann. 1976.
Unterwegs zur Sprache [1950–59], ed. F.-W. von Herrmann. 1985.
Aus der Erfahrung des Denkens [1910–76], ed. H. Heidegger. 1983.
Seminare [1951–73], ed. C. Ochwadt. 1986. (Heraklit: Freiburg 1966/1967, with E. Fink; Vier Seminare: Le Thor 1966, 1968, 1969; Zähringen 1973; Züricher Seminar: Aussprache mit Martin Heidegger am 6. 11. 1951.

Lecture Courses, 1919–44

MARBURG LECTURE COURSES, 1923–28
Einführung in die phänomenologische Forschung [Winter], ed. F.-W. von Hermann. 1994.
Platon: Sophistes [Winter 1924–25], ed. I. Schüssler. 1992.
Prolegomena zur Geschichte des Zeitbegriffs [Summer 1925], ed. P. Jaeger. 1979.
Logik: Die Frage nach der Wahrheit [Winter 1925–26], ed. W. Biemel. 1976.
Grundbegriffe der antiken Philosophie [Summer 1926], ed. F.-K. Blust. 1993.
Die Grundprobleme der Phänomenologie [Summer 1927], ed. F.-W. von Herrmann. 1975, 1989.
Phänomenologische Interpretation von Kants Kritik der reinen Vernunft [Winter 1927–28], ed. I. Görland. 1977, 1990.
Metaphysische Anfangsgründe der Logik im Ausgang von Leibniz [Summer 1928], ed. K. Held. 1978, 1990.

FREIBURG LECTURE COURSES, 1928–44
Die Grundbegriffe der Metaphysik: Welt-Endlichkeit-Einsamkeit [Winter 1929–30]. ed. F.-W. von Herrmann. 1983, 1992.
See also: "Unbenutzte Vorarbeiten zur Vorlesung vom Wintersemester 1929/30: *Die Grundbegriffe der Metaphysik: Welt-Endlichkeit-Einsamkeit,*" Heidegger Studies, Vol. 7 (1991), 5–14.
Vom Wesen der menschlichen Freiheit: Einleitung in die Philosophie [Summer 1930], ed. H. Tietjen. 1982.
Hegels Phänomenologie des Geistes [Winter 1930–31]. ed. I. Görland. 1980, 1988.

Aristoteles: Metaphysik θ 1–3 [Summer 1931], ed. H. Hüni. 1981, 1990.

Vom Wesen der Wahrheit: Zu Platons Höhlengleichnis und Theätet [Winter 1931–32], ed. H. Mörchen. 1988.

Hölderlins Hymnen "Germanien" und "Der Rhein" [Winter 1934–35], ed. S. Zeigler. 1980, 1989.

Einführung in die Metaphysik [Summer 1935], ed. P. Jaeger. 1983.

Die Frage nach dem Ding: Zu Kants Lehre von den transzendentalen Grundsätzen [Winter 1935–36], ed. P. Jaeger. 1984.

Schelling: Über das Wesen der menschlichen Freiheit [Summer 1936], ed. I. Schüssler. 1988.

Nietzsche: Der Wille zur Macht als Kunst [Winter 1936–37], ed. B. Heimbüchel. 1985.

Nietzsches metaphysische Grundstellung im abendländischen Denken: Die Lehre von der ewigen Wiederkehr des Gleichen [Summer 1937], ed. M. Heinz. 1986.

Grundfragen der Philosophie: Ausgewählte "Probleme" der "Logik" [Winter 1937–38], ed. F.-W. von Herrmann. 1984, 1992.

Nietzsches Lehre vom Willen zur Macht als Erkenntnis [Summer 1939], ed. E. Hanser. 1989.

Nietzsche: Der europäische Nihilismus [2d trimester 1940], ed. P. Jaeger. 1986.

Die Metaphysik des deutschen Idealismus: Zur erneuten Auslegung von Schelling "Philosophische Untersuchungen über das Wesen der menschlichen Freiheit und die damit zusammenhängenden Gegenstände" (1809) [1st trimester 1941], ed. G. Seubold. 1991.

Nietzsches Metaphysik [for Winter 1941–42, not delivered] and *Einleitung in die Philosophie: Denken und Dichten* [Winter 1944–45], ed. P. Jaeger. 1990.

Grundbegriffe [Summer 1941], ed. P. Jaeger. 1981, 1991.

Hölderlins Hymne "Andenken" [Winter 1941–42], ed. C. Ochwadt. 1982, 1992.

Hölderlins Hymne "Der Ister" [Summer 1942], ed. W. Biemel. 1984.

Parmenides [Winter 1942–43], ed. M. Frings. 1982.

Heraklit 1: Der Anfang des abendländischen Denkens (Heraklit) [Summer 1943]; and *Heraklit 2: Logik—Heraklits Lehre vom Logos* [Summer 1944], ed. M. Frings. 1979, 1987.

EARLY FREIBURG LECTURE COURSES, 1919–23

Zur Bestimmung der Philosophie: 1. Die Idee der Philosophie und das Weltanschauungsproblem [War Emergency Semester 1919]; *2. Phänomenologie und transzendentale Wertphilosophie* [Summer 1919], ed. B. Heimbüchel. 1987.

Grundprobleme der Phänomenologie [Winter 1919–20], ed. H.-H. Gander. 1992.

Phänomenologie der Anschauung und des Ausdrucks: Theorie der philosophischen Begriffsbildung [Summer 1920], ed. C. Strube. 1993.

Phänomenologie des religiosen Lebens: 1. Einleitung in die Phänomenologie der Religion; 2. Augustinus und der Neuplatonismus; 3. Die philosophischen Grundlagen der mittelalterlichen Mystik, edited by M. Jung and T. Regehly. 1995.

Phänomenologische Interpretationen zu Aristoteles: Einführung in die phänomenologische Forschung [Winter 1921–22], ed. W. Bröcker and K. Bröcker-Oltmanns. 1985.

Ontologie: Hermeneutik der Faktizität [Summer 1923], ed. K. Bröcker-Oltmanns. 1988.

Unpublished Manuscripts

Beiträge zur Philosophie (Vom Ereignis), ed. F.-W. von Herrmann. 1989.

Hegel: 1. Die Negativität. Eine Auseinandersetzung mit Hegel aus dem Ansatz in der Negativität 1938–39, 1941; 2. Erläuterung der "Einleitung" zu Hegels Phänomenologie des Geistes 1942, ed. I. Schüssler. 1993.

Feldweg—Gespräche [1944–45], ed. I. Schüssler, 1995.

Bremer und Freiburger Vorträge: 1. Einblick in das Was ist [Bremen, 1949]; *2. Grundsätze des Denkens* [Freiburg, 1957], ed. P. Jaeger, 1994.

Works not in Gesamtausgabe

Antwort: Martin Heidegger im Gespräch, ed. G. Neske and E. Kettering. Pfullingen, 1988. (Contains "Die Selbstbehauptung der deutschen Universität" [the rectoral address], "Das Rektorat, 1933/34: Tatsachen und Gedanken," "Nur noch ein Gott kann uns retten" [the *Spiegel* interview], and "Martin Heidegger im Gespräch: Mit Richard Wisser.")

"Aus einer Erörterung der Wahrheitsfrage," in *Zehn Jahre Neske Verlag* (Pfullingen, 1962).

Der Begriff der Zeit: Vortrag vor der Marburger Theologenschaft Juli 1924. Tübingen, 1989.

"Brief an Jean Beaufret," *Heidegger Studies*, Vol. 3/4 (1987/1988), 3–4.

"Brief an William J. Richardson" (April 1962), in W. J. Richardson, *Heidegger: Through Phenomenology to Thought*, 3d ed. (The Hague, 1974).

Der Feldweg [1949], 3d ed. Frankfurt, 1962.

Gelassenheit [1959], 9th ed. Pfullingen, 1988.

Hebel—der Hausfreund [1957], 5th ed. Pfullingen, 1985.

"Hegel und die Griechen" [1958]. in *Die Gegenwart der Griechen im neueren Denken*. Festschrift für Hans-Georg Gadamer zum 60. Geburtstag (Tübingen, 1960).

"Hölderlins Himmel und Erde" [1959], in *Hölderlin Jahrbuch* (Tübingen, 1960).

"Die Idee der Phänomenologie und der Rückgang auf das Bewußtsein," Versuch einer zweiten Bearbeitung eines Artikels von E. Husserl. *Husserliana*, Vol. 9 (The Hague, 1962).

Identität und Differenz [1957], 8th ed. Pfullingen, 1986.

Die Kunst und er Raum. St. Gallen, 1969.

Martin Heidegger, zum 80. Geburtstag von seiner Heimstadt Messkirch. Frankfurt, 1969.

Nietzsche, Vols. 1 and 2 [1961], 4th ed. Pfullingen, 1982.

"Phänomenologische Interpretationen zu Aristoteles: Anzeige der Hermeneutische Situation." ed. H.-U. Lessing, in *Dilthey Jahrbuch für Philosophie und Geschichte der Gewissenschaften*, Vol. 6. Göttingen, 1989.

Phänomenologie und Theologie. Frankfurt, 1970. (Includes "Phänomenologie und Theologie" [1927]; "Einige Hinweise auf Hauptgesichtspunkte für das theologische Gespräch über 'Das Problem eines nichtobjektivierenden Denkens und Sprechens in der heutigen Theologie' " [1964].)

Der Satz vom Grund [1957], 6th ed. Pfullingen, 1986.

"Sprache und Heimat," in *Dauer und Wandel*. Festschrift zum 70. Geburtstag von Carl J. Burckhardt (München, 1961).

Die Technik und die Kehre [1962], 7th ed. Pfullingen, 1988.

Überlieferte Sprache und technische Sprache [1962], ed. H. Heidegger. St. Gallen, 1989.

"Die Unumgänglichkeit des Da-seins ('Die Not') und Die Kunst in ihrer Notwendigkeit (Die bewirkende Besinnung)," *Heidegger Studies*, Vol. 8 (1992), 6–13.

Vorträge und Aufsätze [1954], 5th ed. Pfullingen, 1985.

Vom Wesen des Grundes [1929?], 7th ed. Frankfurt, 1983.

"Vom Ursprung des Kunstwerkes: Erste Ausarbeitung," *Heidegger Studies*, Vol. 5 (1989), 5–22.

"Vorbemerkung des Herausgebers, zu: Edmund Husserls Vorlesungen zur Phänomenologie des inneren Zeitbewußtseins," *Jahrbuch für Philosophie und phänomenologische Forschung* [Halle], Vol. 9, 367–68.

Was heißt Denken? Tübingen, 1954.

Was ist das—die Philosophie? [1955], 9th ed. Pfulligen, 1988.

Zur Frage nach der Bestimmung der Sache des Denkens, ed. H. Heidegger. St. Gallen, 1984.

Zur Sache des Denkens [1963–66], 2d ed. Tübingen, 1976.

Zur Seinsfrage [1955], 4th ed. Frankfurt, 1977.

"Zu Überwindung der Aesthetik: Zu 'Ursprung des Kunstwerks,' " *Heidegger Studies,* Vol. 6 (1990), 5–10.

Letters

Martin Heidegger, Elizabeth Blochman: Briefwechsel, 1918–1969, ed. J. Storck. Marbach am Neckar, 1989.

Martin Heidegger, Karl Jaspers: Briefwechsel, 1920–1963, ed. W. Biemel and H. Saner. Frankfurt, 1990.

Martin Heidegger, Erhart Kastner: Briefwechsel, 1953–1974, ed. Heinrich Petzet. Frankfurt, 1986.

English Translations

GESAMTAUSGABE

Sein und Zeit
Being and Time, trans. J. Macquarrie and E. Robinson. New York, 1962.

Kant und das Problem der Metaphysik
Kant and the Problem of Metaphysics, trans. R. Taft. Bloomington, IN, 1990.

Erläuterung zu Hölderlins Dichtung
"Remembrance of the Poet," trans. D. Scott, in Werner Brock, ed., *Existence and Being* (Chicago, 1949).
"Hölderlin and the Essence of Poetry," trans. D. Scott, in *Existence and Being.*

Holzwege
"The Origin of the Work of Art," trans. A. Hofstadter, in *Poetry, Language, Thought* (New York, 1971).
"The Age of the World Picture," trans. W. Lovitt, in *The Question Concerning Technology* (New York, 1977).
"The Word of Nietzsche: 'God Is Dead,' " in *The Question Concerning Technology.*
"What Are Poets For?" in *Poetry, Language, Thought.*
"The Anaxamander Fragment." trans. D. F. Krell and F. Capuzzi, in *Early Greek Thinking* (New York, 1975).
"Hegel's Concept of Experience," trans. K. R. Dove, in *Hegel's Concept of Experience* (New York, 1970).

Wegmarken
"What Is Metaphysics?" trans. D. F. Krell, in *Basic Writings* (New York, 1977).
"On the Essence of Truth," trans. J. Sallis, in *Basic Writings.*
"Postscript to 'What Is Metaphysics?' " trans. R. F. C. Hull and A. Crick, in *Existence and Being.*
"Plato's Doctrine of Truth." trans. J. Barlow, in *Philosophy in the Twentieth Century,* Vol. 3, *Contemporary European Thought,* ed. W. Barrett and H. D. Aiken (New York, 1971).
"Letter on Humanism," trans. F. A. Capuzzi, with J. G. Gray and D. F. Krell, in *Basic Writings.*
"The Way Back into the Ground of Metaphysics," trans. W. Kaufmann, in *Existentialism from Dostoevsky to Sartre* (Cleveland, 1956).
"Kant's Thesis about the Thing," trans. T. E. Klein and W. E. Pohl, *Southwestern Journal of Philosophy,* Vol. 4, No. 3 (Fall 1973), 7–33.
"On the Being and Conception of Physis in Aristotle's Physics, B,1," trans. T. J. Sheehan, *Man and World,* Vol. 9 (1976), 219–270.

Unterwegs zur Sprache
On the Way to Language, trans. P. D. Hertz. New York, 1971.
"Language," in *Poetry, Language, Thought.*

Aus der Erfahrung des Denkens
"Why Do I Stay in the Provinces?" trans. T. J. Sheehan, in T. J. Sheehan, ed., Heidegger: *The Man and the Thinker* (Chicago, 1981).

Seminare (1951–73) [Heraklit]
Heraclitus Seminar, 1966/1967, with Eugen Fink, trans. C. H. Seibert. University, AL, 1982.

Prolegomena zur Geschichte des Zeitbegriffs
History of the Concept of Time: Prolegomena, trans. T. Kisiel. Bloomington, IN, 1985.

Die Grundprobleme der Phänomenologie
The Basic Problems of Phenomenology, trans. A. Hofstadter. Bloomington, Ind. 1982.

Metaphysische Anfangsgründe der Logik im Ausgang von Leibniz
The Metaphysical Foundations of Logic, trans. M. Heim. Bloomington, IN, 1984.
Fundamental Concepts of Metaphysics: World, Finitude, Solitude, trans. W. McNeill and N. Walker. Bloomington, IN, 1995.

Hegels Phänomenologie des Geistes
Hegel's Phenomenology of Spirit, trans. P. Emad and K. Maly, 1988.
Aristotle's Metaphysics Theta, 1–3: On the Essence and Actuality of Force, trans. W. Brogan and P. Warnek. Bloomington, IN, 1995.

Einführung in die Metaphysik
Introduction to Metaphysics, trans. R. Manheim. New Haven, 1959.

Die Frage nach dem Ding
What Is a Thing?, trans. W. B. Barton and V. Deutsch. Chicago, 1967.

Grundfragen der Philosophie: Ausgewählte "Probleme" der "Logik"
Basic Questions of Philosophy: Selected "Problems" of "Logic," trans. R. Rojcewicz and A. Schuwer. Bloomington, IN, 1994.

Grundbegriffe
Basic Concepts, trans. G. E. Aylesworth. Bloomington, IN, 1993.

Parmenides
Parmenides, trans. A. Schuwer and R. Rojcewicz. Bloomington, IN, 1993.

WORKS NOT IN GESAMTAUSGABE

Antwort: Martin Heidegger im Gespräch
Martin Heidegger and National Socialism: Questions and Answers, trans. L. Harries. New York, 1990. (Contains "The Self-Assertion of the German University" [the rectoral address], "The Rectorate 1933/34: Facts and Thoughts," "Only a God Can Save Us" [the *Spiegel* Interview], and "Martin Heidegger in Conversation, with Richard Wisser.")

Der Begriff der Zeit
The Concept of Time, trans. W. McNeill. Oxford, 1992.

Brief an William J. Richardson
"Letter to Father Richardson," in *Heidegger: Through Phenomenology to Thought,* 3d. ed. (The Hague, 1974).

Der Feldweg
The Pathway, trans. T. R. O'Meara, O. P. (Revisions: Thomas J. Sheehan), *Listening,* Vol. 8 (1973).

Gelassenheit
Discourse on Thinking, trans. J. M. Anderson and E. H. Freund. New York, 1966.

Identität und Differenz
Identity and Difference, trans. J. Stambaugh. New York, 1969. German text included in appendix.

Die Kunst and der Raum
"Art and Space," trans. C. H. Siebert, *Man and World*, Vol. 6, (1973).

Martin Heidegger, zum 80. Geburtstag von seiner Heimstadt Messkirch
"Homeland," trans. T. F. O'Meara, *Listening*, Vol. 6 (1971), 231–38.

Nietzsche, Volume One
Nietzsche, Vol. 1, *The Will to Power as Art*, ed. and trans. D. F. Krell. New York, 1979.
Nietzsche, Vol. 2, *The Eternal Recurrence of the Same*, ed. and trans. D. F. Krell. New York, 1984.
Nietzsche, Vol. 3, *The Will to Power as Knowledge and as Metaphysics*, ed. D. F. Krell, trans. J. Stambaugh, D. F. Krell, and F. A. Capuzzi. New York, 1987.

Nietszche, Volume Two
Nietzsche, Vol. 3, *The Will to Power as Knowledge and as Metaphysics*, "The Eternal Recurrence of the Same and the Will to Power."
Nietzsche, Vol. 4, *Nihilism*, "European Nihilism," ed. D. F. Krell, trans. F. A. Capuzzi. New York, 1982.
Nietzsche, Vol. 3, *The Will to Power as Knowledge and as Metaphysics*, "Nietzsche's Metaphysics."
Nietzsche, Vol. 4, *Nihilism*, "Nihilism as Determined by the History of Being."
"Metaphysics as the History of Being," trans. J. Stambaugh, in *The End of Philosophy* (New York, 1973).
"Sketches for a History of Being as Metaphysics," in *The End of Philosophy*.
"Recollection in Metaphysics," in *The End of Philosophy*.

Phänomenologische Interpretationen zu Aristotles
"Phenomenological Interpretations with respect to Aristotle: Indications of the Hermeneutic Situation," trans. M. Baur, *Man and World*, Vol. 25 (1992), 355–93.

Phänomenologie und Theologie
"The Problem of Non-Objectifying Thing and Speaking," in J. Gill, ed., *Philosophy and Religion* (Minneapolis, 1968).

Der Satz vom Grund
The Principle of Reason, trans. R. Lilly. Bloomington, IN, 1991.

Die Technik und die Kehre
"The Question Concerning Technology," trans. W. Lovitt, in *The Question Concerning Technology*.
"The Turning," trans. W. Lovitt, in *The Question Concerning Technology*.

Vorträge und Aufsätze, Volume One
"The Question Concerning Technology," in *The Question Concerning Technology*.
"Science and Reflection," in *The Question Concerning Technology*.
"Overcoming Metaphysics," in *The End of Philosophy*.
"Who Is Nietzsche's Zarathustra?" trans. B. Magnus, *Review of Metaphysics*, Vol. 20 (1967), 411–31.

Vorträge und Aufsätze, Volume Two
"Building, Dwelling, Thinking," in *Poetry, Language, Thought*.
"The Thing," in *Poetry, Language, Thought*.
". . . Poetically Man Dwells . . .," in *Poetry, Language, Thought*.

Vorträge und Aufsätze, Volume Three
"Logos (Heraclitus, Fragment B 50)," in *Early Greek Thinking*.
"Moira (Parmenides VIII, 34–41)," in *Early Greek Thinking*.
"Aletheia (Heraclitus, Fragment B 16)," in *Early Greek Thinking*.

Vom Wesen des Grundes
The Essence of Reasons, trans. T. Malick. Evanston, IL, 1969.

Was heißt Denken?
What Is Called Thinking? trans. F. D. Wieck and J. G. Gray. New York, 1972.

Zur Sache des Denkens
On Time and Being, trans. J. Stambaugh. New York, 1972.

Zur Seinsfrage
The Question of Being, trans. J. T. Wilde and W. Kluback. New Haven, 1958.

Other Translations

Basic Writings, ed. D. F. Krell. New York, 1977.
Early Greek Thinking, trans. D. F. Krell and F. Capuzzi. New York, 1975.
The End of Philosophy, trans. J. Stambaugh. New York, 1973.
Existence and Being, ed. W. Brock. Chicago, 1949.
Hegel's Concept of Experience, trans. K. R. Dove. New York, 1970.
Identity and Difference, trans. J. Stambaugh. New York, 1969.
Kant and the Problem of Metaphysics, trans. R. Taft. Bloomington, IN, 1990.
The Piety of Thinking, trans. J. Hart and J. Maraldo. Bloomington, IN, 1976.

Works on Heidegger

Bibliographies and Indexes

Franzen, W. *Martin Heidegger*. Stuttgart, 1976.
Index zu Heideggers "Sein und Zeit," ed. H. Feick, 4th ed., updated by S. Zeigler, Tübingen, 1991.
Martin Heidegger: A Bibliography, ed. J. Nordquist. Santa Cruz, CA, 1990.
Sass, H.-M. *Martin Heidegger: Bibliography and Glossary*. Bowling Green, OH, 1982.
The Cambridge Companion to Heidegger, ed. C. Guignon. Cambridge, 1993.

General

Antwort: Martin Heidegger im Gespräch. Hrsg. E. Kettering. Pfullingen, 1988.
Barash, J. *Martin Heidegger and the Problem of Historical Meaning*. The Hague, 1988.
Beaufret, J. *Dialogue avec Heidegger*. 4 vols. Paris, 1973–85.
Bernasconi, R. *The Question of Language in Heidegger's History of Being*. Atlantic Highlands, NJ, 1985.
Birault, H. *Heidegger et l'expérience de la pensée*. Paris, 1978.
Bourdieu, P. *The Political Ontology of Martin Heidegger*, trans. P. Collier. Stanford, CA, 1991.
Caputo, J. *Demythologizing Heidegger*. Bloomington, IN, 1993.
Dallmayer, F. *The Other Heidegger*. Ithaca, NY, 1993.
Derrida, J. *Of Spirit: Heidegger and the Question*, trans. G. Bennington and R. Bowlby. Chicago, 1989.
Dreyfus, H. *Being-in-the-World: A Commentary on Heidegger's "Being and Time," Division I*. Cambridge, MA, 1990.
Foti, V. *Heidegger and the Poets*. Atlantic Highlands, NJ, 1992.
Grondin, J. *Le Tournant dans la pensée de Martin Heidegger*. Paris, 1987.
Haar, M. *Heidegger and the Essence of Man*, trans. W. McNeill. Albany, NY, 1993.
Janicaud, D. *L'Ombre de cette pensée: Heidegger et la question politique*. Grenoble, 1990.
Kisiel, T. *The Genesis of Heidegger's "Being and Time."* Berkeley, 1993.
Kockelmans, J. *On the Truth of Being: Reflections on Heidegger's Later Philosophy*. Bloomington, IN, 1984.
Kolb, D. "Heidegger at 100, in America," *Journal of the History of Ideas*, Vol. 52 (1991), 140–51.
Krell, D. *Intimations of Mortality: Time, Truth, and Finitude in Heidegger's Thinking of Being*. University Park, PA, 1986.

Lacoue-Labarthe, P. *Heidegger, Art, and Politics: The Fiction of the Political,* trans. C. Turner. Oxford, 1990.

Marx, W. *Heidegger and the Tradition,* trans. T. Kisiel and M. Greene. Evanston, IL, 1971.

Mehta, J. *Martin Heidegger: The Way and the Vision.* Honolulu, 1976.

Okrent, M. *Heidegger's Pragmatism.* Ithaca, NY, 1988.

Ott, H. *Martin Heidegger: A Political Life,* trans. A. Blunden. New York, 1993.

Pöggeler, O. *Martin Heidegger's Path of Thinking,* trans. D. Magurshak and S. Barber. Atlantic Highlands, NJ, 1987.

Richardson, W. *Heidegger: Through Phenomenology to Thought.* Preface by M. Heidegger. 3d. ed. The Hague, 1974.

Petzet, H. *Encounters and Dialogues with Martin Heidegger, 1929–1976,* trans. P. Emad and K. Maly. Chicago, 1993.

Rosen, S. *The Question of Being: A Reversal of Heidegger.* New Haven, 1993.

Schürmann, R. *Heidegger on Being and Acting: From Principles to Anarchy,* trans. C.-M. Gros. Bloomington, IN, 1987.

Taminiaux, J. *Heidegger and the Project of Fundamental Ontology,* trans. M. Gendre. Albany, NY, 1991.

The Heidegger Case: On Philosophy and Politics, ed. T. Rockmore and J. Margolis. Philadelphia, 1992.

Von Herrmann, F.-W. *Subjekt und Dasein: Interpretationen zu "Sein und Zeit."* Frankfurt, 1974; 2d. ed., 1985.

Zarader, M. *Heidegger et les paroles de l'origine.* Préface de E. Levinas. Paris, 1990.

Zimmerman, M. *Heidegger's Confrontation with Modernity.* Bloomington, IN, 1990.

Collections

Heidegger: A Critical Reader, ed. H. Dreyfus and H. Hall. Oxford, 1992.

Heidegger and Modern Philosophy: Critical Essays, ed. M. Murray. New Haven, 1978.

Heidegger et la question de Dieu, ed. R. Kearney and J. O'Leary. Paris, 1980.

Heidegger: Perspektiven zur Deutung seines Werkes, ed. O. Pöggeler. Köln, 1969.

Heidegger: The Man and the Thinker, ed. T. Sheehan. Chicago, 1981.

Martin Heidegger, ed. M. Haar. Paris, 1983.

Reading Heidegger: Commemorations, ed. J. Sallis. Bloomington, IN, 1993.

The Cambridge Companion to Heidegger, ed. C. Guignon. Cambridge, 1993.

— WILLIAM J. RICHARDSON

HERACLITUS OF EPHESUS

Heraclitus of Ephesus, pre-Socratic philosopher. Exact dating of Heraclitus's life is impossible, since the two different ancient chronologies are probably worthless; the more plausible of the two connects him with Darius of Persia (d. 486 B.C.). References by Heraclitus to other writers make it impossible to date his work much before 500 B.C.; references to him (not by name) in Parmenides and the Sicilian poet Epicharmus are uncertain. Since Heraclitus ignores Parmenides, one can scarcely date his work after 460 B.C. Little is certain, about his life, except for his domicile in Ephesus, an Ionian city of Asia Minor. Hellenistic biographers invented biographical facts, either to fill the void or to take the only

revenge open to them for Heraclitus's insults to mankind. The story most often believed—that he gave up his (not necessarily exclusive) kingship to his younger brother—could be based on the traditional motif of philosophers' unworldliness coupled with his own statement from another context, "The kingdom is a child's." The legend of the "weeping philosopher" is late and based on a combination of a Platonic joke, Heraclitus's theory of flux, and a misunderstanding of Theophrastus' word "melancholia," which originally meant "impulsiveness."

Ancient opinion, generally unfavorable,

nicknamed Heraclitus "the obscure,"

mentioning ambiguities of word order and division.

WORK. The nine "Letters of Heraclitus" are spurious, having been produced by Cynic or Stoic rhetoricians of the first century A.D. Heraclitus wrote one book, title (if any) unknown. The fact that it was a connected exposition and not merely a collection of sayings is suggested by the elaborate introductory sentence still extant. The book itself is now lost, and how long it survived is uncertain. Several ancient commentaries and metrical "versions," mostly Stoic, are also lost. Fortunately, many ancient authors from Plato on quoted Heraclitus; but citations may often come from anthologies or metrical versions, are often torn from context, and are seldom verbally reliable. Heraclitus must be pieced together, a process hindered by ancient misunderstandings.

STYLE. Ancient opinion, generally unfavorable, nicknamed Heraclitus "the obscure," mentioning ambiguities of word order and division. The problems of interpreting fragments are deepened by frequent metaphors and pregnant utterances; Heraclitus probably compared his own style to that of the Sibylline oracles. The fragments offer more instances of illustration than of argument, almost confirming Aristotle's imputation that Heraclitus was guilty of not reasoning. Connection between topics was probably more verbal (in the Archaic manner) than logical. Accustomed to poetic vocabulary, Heraclitus used few technical terms or verbal abstracts, and those he did use were for cognitive rather than external processes. Personal knowledge of his homely illustrations adds force to his statements. But he polished his sentences, anticipating such devices of rhetoric as alliteration, homoeoteleuton, and rhythmic balance. His doctrine of the unity of opposites invited antithesis and juxtaposition of contrasting descriptions at the expense of normal word order. His style was thus appropriate to his matter, as in his numerous puns, which were not intended to amuse but reflected the untutored assumption that a word's form resembles the thing it signifies. Heraclitus' style is biting, earnest, and prophetic.

PHYSICAL VIEWS. Heraclitus abandoned genetic explanations of the world, believing it uncreated. In his view, all events take place according to a "Logos," a term he left undefined. Since the Logos can be heard, it must be expressible in words; but it would appear that "Logos" signifies far more than Heraclitus's book, since the philosopher reproaches men for not understanding the Logos before they hear it and advises listening to the Logos, not to himself. Logos is both discourse and contents, both the truth about things and the principle on which they function. Being common to all things, the Logos would be accessible to men if it were not for their folly. In this objective sense, there is also a Logos of the soul, although deeply hidden. The Greek word *logos* can mean "proportion," and for Heraclitus one change takes place in the same proportion as the reverse change. The English word that best covers Heraclitus' philosophical uses of "Logos" is "formula." But this Logos has a material aspect in the form of Fire. We find it difficult to conceive of a "formula" as being material, but the concept of incorporeal existence was not available to Heraclitus. His idea that an abstract "formula" was the world's ruling stuff was a significant step toward the availability of such a concept, not its attainment. Symbolized by "thunderbolt" in its function of "steering all things," Fire is also associated with human wisdom and doubtless governed the world intelligently. The truth expressed in the Logos is principally the unity of opposites. These opposites, however, are engaged in perpetual strife, and Strife is not only right and normal, but is also, like the Logos, "common," and everything happens according to it. It is tempting simply to identify Fire, Logos, and Strife, but that is an oversimplification; we have not so much a formally coherent system as several lines of thought closely associated but not fully integrated. The unity of the opposites struck Heraclitus so forcibly that he leaped to the conclusion that all things are one.

Unity of Opposites. Pairs of opposites exemplify the unity of all things by standing in several different relationships to each other. First, they may be logically indistinguishable, as in "Beginning and end are 'common' on the circle." Second, they may be in unvarying mutual succession: thus, day and night are one, because, in modern terms, they are "temporally continuous"—a possible sense for "one" Greek. Other examples of this type, harder to interpret, are living–dead, awake–asleep, and young–old. Hot–cold and wet–dry should

perhaps be included here: of each pair, one member changes invariably and solely into the other, without significant temporal discontinuity. The remaining types are liable to give the impression of relativism; but it should be stressed that Heraclitus was insufficiently aware of epistemological problems to ask himself the relevant questions, and also that strife (and therefore opposition) was fundamental to his natural philosophy. When Heraclitus says "the road up and down is one and the same," he does not mean that "up" and "down" are relative terms, but that their unity in opposition results from their predicability of the same object. The same holds for another saying, "In writing, the course taken, straight and crooked, is one and the same"; one is tempted to say that curvature and straightness "inhere" in the movement, but the word "inhere" and the distinction between qualities and objects are anachronistic. Also, only superficially relativistic is the following type of assertion: "The sea is both purest and foulest; drinkable and salutary for fish, to men undrinkable and poisonous." Here Heraclitus deduces the unity of opposites from the opposite effects of one thing on different creatures; but he does not deduce the absence of opposition. Lastly, one opposite may be a necessary condition for the perception of another: "Disease makes health pleasant and good, hunger satiety, weariness rest." Opposition remains, but the impossibility of experiencing one fully without the other connects the opposites. The tempting word "connection" is justified by Heraclitus's use of a similar word: "Men do not understand how what is being borne apart is being brought together with itself; a backward-stretching *harmonia* as of bow and lyre." "Harmonia" here cannot be purely musical, nor does it mean "concord"; "connection" seems the best proposed rendering, referring to the strings connecting the arms of bow and lyre. For Heraclitus, such a connection proved opposites the same. Those who find difficulty in understanding this mode of thought may recall that to distinguish between different senses of one word was (except for obvious homonyms) an unknown logical venture. If opposites were one in the sense (in our terms) of "connected" or "continuous," they were also one in the sense of being "identical"; Heraclitus could not make the Aristotelian distinction between unity as continuity and as identity. Furthermore, beginning and end *are* indistinguishable on the circle, and the road up and down *is* physically the same; Heraclitus can hardly have made the distinctions offered here between types of opposition. Heraclitus believed both connection and difference between opposites to be valid, but considered the unity more important and valuable, because less obvious. This valuation reappears in the combined statements: "The human character does not have insights, but the divine does," and "To the god all things are beautiful and good and just, but men opine that some are just and some unjust." The same valuation, taken together with the status of Logos and Fire, probably evoked the remark, "God is day, night; winter, summer; war, peace; satiety, hunger," adding "He changes as fire (?) does when mixed with things sacrificed and called by the name appropriate to the taste of each." Here Heraclitus apparently implies that each pair of opposites is united in the deity, that each is of equal standing, and that all are somehow divine. The relation of this deity to the Logos must be close, but is undefined.

When Heraclitus says

"the road up and down is one and the same,"

he does not mean

that "up" and "down" are relative terms,

but that their unity in opposition

results from their predicability of the same object.

Change and Measure. For Heraclitus change takes place between opposites, but like his predecessors and successors he also talked of change between cosmic masses (a better term than "elements," since Heraclitus hardly analyzed the composition of particulars). He thought these masses to be three in number; fragments that name four are suspected to be Stoic perversions. The three are fire (associated particularly with the bright sky), sea, and earth, and they correspond to our gaseous, liquid, and solid states of matter; but other philosophers ignored Heraclitus's hint, and four became the canonical number. Heraclitus wrote, "The turnings of fire are: first sea, of sea half earth and half 'prester,'" and "Earth is fused as sea and is measured in the same proportion as before (? before it became earth)." "Prester" is a meteorological phenomenon, possibly lightning, representing fire or a way of changing into fire. Either the sea *is* half fire, half earth, or it *is turning* half to fire and half to earth. Heraclitus' statement, which is not cosmogonical, describes the course of changes in the existing world. Theophrastus applied the saying about the "way up and down" to this course—an application of doubtful correctness. Details of the proportions are obscure, and so is the integration of opposites with cosmic masses. This fact is not surprising, for the assignment of opposites to "elements" remained a standing problem

of Greek thought. The importance of proportion in change is clear, however; without its maintenance, the balance of the opposites would be destroyed, and Strife would cease. The world's stability depends on balanced strife between opposites, and compensation of local or temporary imbalance. Nevertheless, Fire has some preeminence: "All things are an equal exchange for fire, and fire for all things, as goods for gold and gold for goods." In this instance, Fire is set against all things, as in the statement about "turnings." Again, "No god or man created this world order, but it always was and is and will be: an ever-living fire, being kindled in measures and extinguished in measures." These fragments do not justify the Stoic interpretation of Heraclitus's Fire as an ultimate universal conflagration; the emphasis on balance and measure is strong enough to refute that interpretation. The probably Heraclitean notion of a Great Year need not imply the conflagration either. This period of 10,800 years (360 thirty-year generations) may represent either an eschatological cycle for souls or a physical cycle in which a given piece of matter returns to its original position. The "exchange" of all things for fire is the part extinction and part rekindling of the fire which is the world order; perhaps each thing has an exchange value in terms of fire. This extinction and rekindling show that changes really take place from and into fire and that individual nonfiery objects are not fire; fire is not a substratum. The reasons for Fire's primacy in Heraclitus's thought were, doubtless, complex. In the first place, the ebb and flow of flame afforded an apt symbol for constant balanced change; second, Anaximander had written of one stuff "holding the helm" of all things; and furthermore, heat was associated with life, and early Greek thinkers often transferred animate states and processes to inanimate Nature.

In details also measure was important; Heraclitus wrote of the sun's measures, which were not to be overstepped without punishment. But little is known of his detailed astronomical and meteorological views. He cannot have meant that the sun is literally "only a foot wide." Doxographical tradition records his interpretation of the heavenly bodies as bowls containing fire; he explained the moon's phases by the gradual turning of its bowl and apparently asked no further questions. He thought the sun new every day, probably as being extinguished each sunset and rekindled when fire gathered in the bowl each morning. The sun's fire was nourished by a bright exhalation from earth or sea. Theoretically, absence of sunlight should suffice to cause darkness, and Heraclitus even said, "If there were no sun it would be night." Doxographical evidence suggests, however, that he postulated a second, dark exhalation to quench the sun's fire. The stars, more distant, were beyond reach of this exhalation. Doxographers allege this exhalation in explanation of seasons, months, years, rains, winds, and so forth; the extent and manner of its operation are uncertain, and in this report some have suspected Peripatetic "interpretation." To integrate the exhalations with opposites and cosmic masses is difficult. Theophrastus's reproach of "incompleteness" perhaps indicates the absence of a systematic astronomy or meteorology. Heraclitus' naïveté in such matters may reasonably be attributed to his being less interested in them than in his logical discovery about opposites and its physical implications.

Flux. One elaboration of that discovery, was of immediate physical importance, namely, the theory of flux. Although this theory has often been exaggerated, it did not signify that everything, without physical or logical exception, was continually changing and therefore inaccessible to knowledge, for such was the theory of Cratylus, sharply distinguished by good evidence from Heraclitus' theory. One explanation of the latter's theory is that Heraclitus, comparing all things to a river, meant that they all changed all the time; applied to natural objects, this means that even apparently stable things are changing, although total balance is always maintained. This view is sometimes rejected as being precluded by common sense and Heraclitus's acceptance of sense evidence. It is then maintained that the river illustrates not perpetual, but measured, change. But in the various "river statements" extant, there is nothing explicit about measures; the concept of the river's remaining the same amid the flow of different waters is consistent with either interpretation. Heraclitus valued the senses highly, but emphasized their need of an understanding mind as interpreter, and the probably Heraclitean remark that one cannot step twice into the same river sounds more like an emphatic parable of continuous change.

For Heraclitus change takes place between opposites,

but like his predecessors he also talked

of change between cosmic masses.

PSYCHOLOGY. Although skeptical of final knowledge of the soul, Heraclitus arrived, partly by introspection, at a psychology that neatly dovetailed into his cosmology. Souls fit into the cosmic flux, apparently occupying the same place as Fire: "It is death for souls to become water." Total wateriness means death, but in life the fiery soul is wisest and best when kept dry. A drunkard, having a wet soul, does not know where he

is going, but is led by a child. This implies that a dry soul guides the body just as Fire steers all things. Partial extinction and rekindling obtains in man as in Nature, for sleep extinguishes certain senses. The afterlife in Heraclitus is obscure; we know that "there await mankind after death things they do not expect," and that at least "souls smell in Hades"—whatever Heraclitus meant by "Hades." Perhaps some special fate awaited the dead in battle, whom "gods and men honor," for "Greater deaths are allotted greater portions"; but if everything joins the cosmic flux anyway, this statement is difficult to understand; these fragments, out of context, constitute an uncertain foundation for theory. Life and death, as alternate states, are the same. This concept need not imply metempsychosis and more probably reflects either the tradition of a grandfather's rebirth in his grandson or the alternate dissolution of the body and formation of another from similar materials; either view would also explain the mutual succession of young and old. The living and dead are also somehow continuous: in an epistemological context, "The living touches the dead in sleep, the waking touches the sleeping." In sleep, the Greek Skeptic Sextus Empiricus records, the soul is cut off from the outside world by the blocking of passages used by the senses. Thus, the soul loses memory, but recovers it on awakening. The soul in sleep maintains residual contact with externals by breathing; to this contact (obviously lost in death) the soul owes some of its intelligence.

The Senses. Heraclitus was perhaps the first Greek speculative philosopher to raise the question of the validity of sense perception. So far as the senses go, he did not believe that they actually deceive: "I prefer things of which there is sight, hearing, learning." He called the eyes more accurate witnesses than the ears—perhaps intending a warning against hearsay. An injunction to independent inquiry, "Lovers of wisdom must be good inquirers into many things," is not contradicted by "Learning of many things does not teach insight"; Heraclitus distinguishes true philosophical insight from indiscriminate gathering of facts, believing facts to be necessary but not sufficient for insight. The soul is both agent and interpreter of sensations; its relation to the body is that of spider to web. The soul, being firmly and "proportionally" joined to the body, rushes to any injured part of it. If the soul interpreter is barbarous—that is, if it does not understand the language—insight will not result. Heraclitus frequently abuses men for their lack of understanding; he compares their opinions to children's playthings, denounces them as deaf to what they hear and as asleep even when awake, and rebukes them for relying on individual, rather than on "common," thought, which he associates with insight. The object of insight is the way in which the world functions—"how all things are steered through all things." Thus, the intelligent Fire and Logos are objects of knowledge by the fiery human soul at its most intelligent.

Theology. The comparison with children is developed theologically: man is to god as child to man; similarly, compared with a god, man resembles an ape. Divine insight contrasts with human lack of it. Heraclitus disapproved of many popular cults: he compares purification of blood guilt by blood sacrifice to washing off mud with mud and compares praying to statues with talking to walls. He condemns the mystery cults, perhaps for a similar lack of spirituality, as "conducted in an unholy manner." The best that can be said for oracles is that their style, by which they "neither speak nor conceal but give a sign," deserves approving imitation. All that can be said for the procession and the hymn to Dionysus (otherwise a shameful phallic rite) is that they imply the identification of Dionysus with Hades, here possibly representing life and death, respectively. But there is a wide gulf between disapproval of polytheist cults and espousal of monotheism, and there is insufficient evidence that Heraclitus crossed it. The question of monotheism versus polytheism was not raised in Archaic Greece. In referring to "the one wise thing" which "is willing and unwilling to be called Zeus," he doubtlessly means that Fire or Logos is supreme but lacks the personal attributes attached to Zeus in cult and myth. But even though a tendency toward monotheism is observable, we cannot credit Heraclitus with solving a problem he probably never considered. He attacked myth when it conflicted with his theories; he criticized Hesiod for distinguishing Day and Night, and Homer for recounting a prayer for an end to strife.

Ethics. In the statement "Character is *daemon* to man," theology merges with ethics. According to traditional belief, a divine being, or *daemon,* accompanied man through life, bringing him good fortune or bad: Heraclitus ascribed men's fortunes to internal forces. Although he implies the possibility of action in accordance with the Logos, he gives little detail. One should not get drunk or reveal ignorance; what men want is not good for them; punishment awaits liars—there is little system here. From contemptuous words about "the many" it appears that Heraclitus considered glory more permanent and valuable than sensual gratification. It is unlikely that he abolished ethics by completely identifying good and evil. Theology merges with politics in the doctrine of the one divine law that nourishes and gives strength to all human laws. Anaximander had projected justice into the world, but Heraclitus introduced the first extant connection of divine (unwritten) law with the laws of states, which was the origination of the theory of "natural law." Other political views of Heraclitus, expressing mainly typical antidemocratic sentiments, are less significant.

Heraclitus was perhaps the first Greek speculative philosopher to raise the question of the validity of sense perception.

INFLUENCE. Heraclitus's doctrine of simultaneously converging and diverging opposites generated only faint echoes. It supplied some minor Hippocratic writers with an excuse for thoughtless paradox and may be said to reappear in Anaxagoras's refusal to separate the opposites in "the one cosmos," and again in Diogenes of Apollonia's argument that action of one thing on another implies their constitution from one substance. Possibly Empedocles' theory of alternate states of unity (under Love, or *Harmonia*) and diversity (under Strife) owes something to Heraclitus's theory of opposition, as well as to Eleaticism. Later, more emphasis was laid on flux. Plato's "Heracliteans . . . around Ephesus" may be jocular, but the Athenian Cratylus adopted the concept of flux and also made explicit the "natural" resemblance between name and object. In Plato's *Cratylus,* Socrates demonstrates the difficulties in this combination, and Cratylus was later driven to abandoning language and communicating by gesture. Exaggerating Heraclitus's river statement, Cratylus said that you could not step into the same river once. His importance derives from Aristotle's statement that he introduced Heraclitean flux to the young Plato, who was (partly) thereby persuaded to deny knowability and reality to particulars. Aristotle not only depreciated Heraclitus, but vitiated later understanding of him by assimilation to his Milesian predecessors and by propagation of the world conflagration interpretation appropriated by the Stoics. Many aspects of genuinely Heraclitean doctrine appealed to the Stoics: Heraclitus's psychology gave them the image of spider and web; Cleanthes drew on the concept of the primacy of fire as well as the Heraclitean ideas of unity, harmony, war, and insight, but gave them a deeper religious import. For Stoics too the soul was material and the Logos common to mind and external world; for both the Heracliteans and the Stoics, the Logos was divine, eternal, all-pervading. The Stoics added a creative power whereby the Logos informed objects, creatures, and thoughts. Philo's connection of this Logos with the Divine Wisdom prepared for the transcendent yet incarnate Logos of Christianity. Later Christian writers either, like Clement of Alexandria, found in Heraclitus one middle way between pagan rationalism and Christian anti-intellectualism or, like Hippolytus, rebutted heresies by assimilation to Heraclitean paganism.

BIBLIOGRAPHY

Texts

Volume I of H. Diels and W. Kranz, *Die Fragmente der Vorsokratiker,* 10th ed. (Berlin, 1961) contains the standard critical text with a competent German translation, but is over-optimistic in attribution to Heraclitus. R. Walzer, *Eraclito* (Florence, 1939) prints contexts of ancient citations more fully.

Introductions

W. K. C. Guthrie, *History of Greek Philosophy,* Vol. I (Cambridge, 1962) has a sober, impartial survey. G. S. Kirk and J. E. Raven, *The Presocratic Philosophers,* 2d ed. (Cambridge, 1960) contains a critical account and selected texts and translations. H. Fränkel, *Dichtung und Philosophie des frühen Griechentums,* 2d ed. (Munich, 1962) sets Heraclitus in both literary and philosophical context.

Bibliography

E. Zeller and R. Mondolfo, *La filosofia dei Greci,* Part I, Vol. IV (Florence, 1961) is a monumental survey, with copious ancient and modern references.

Additional Background

K. Reinhardt, *Parmenides und die Geschichte der griechischen Philosophie* (Bonn, 1916) is fundamental, but unsound on chronology and Orphic influence. O. Gigon, *Untersuchungen zu Heraklit* (Leipzig, 1936) is a stimulating work, more incisive on psychology than cosmology. G. S. Kirk, *Heraclitus, the Cosmic Fragments* (Cambridge, 1954) is exemplary in its field for thoroughness in study of text and interpretation. It is well criticized by G. Vlastos, "On Heraclitus," in *American Journal of Philology,* Vol. 76 (1955), 337–68.

— MICHAEL C. STOKES

HERMENEUTIC PHENOMENOLOGY

Dilthey scholars such as Georg Misch and Eduard Spranger already regarded Edmund Husserl's phenomenology as hermeneutical, as a process of exposing hidden meaning and as a method of explicating the implicit structures of experience. But it was Martin Heidegger who expressly brought the two traditions together in what he in 1919 first called a phenomenological hermeneutics. More than a superficial grafting, the addition of "hermeneutic" to phenomenology is meant to explicate its essence more originally. Instead of a spontaneous self-showing readily accessible to intuition, the primal phenomena are regarded as concealed and so in need of the labor of exposure. Heidegger therefore displaces Husserl's experiential structure of intentionality as intuitive fulfillment of initially empty signification with a more basic structural process of explication of implicit but already understood meaning. Interpretive exposition and not intuition becomes the basic mode of knowing, understanding and not signifying intending is the basic mode of human being.

More than a superficial grafting,

the addition of "hermeneutic" to phenomenology

is meant to explicate its essence more originally.

The early Heidegger's "hermeneutics of facticity" of the contextually situated "historical I" (later *Dasein*) in fact draws its proximate inspiration, not only from the philosophical hermeneutics of Schleiermacher and Dilthey, but also from the neo-Kantian tradition from Fichte (he coined the term facticity) to Emil Lask, which sought to found historical science in the factic categories of "value individuality" and "motivation." But Heidegger undermines this twofold tradition's hermeneutic distinction between the "understanding" historical-cultural sciences and the "explanatory" natural sciences by posing the more rudimentary phenomenological problem of the "genesis of the theoretical" as such from the background of protopractical understanding and interpretation, from that human experience that spontaneously articulates itself in "getting around" the world by "getting by" with things, "getting along" with others, and "getting with" oneself. Thus, the "hermeneutic 'as' " is first exemplified from human commerce with tools in a contextured world that already implicates us in a tradition of "usage," to which we comply in this interpretive instance of explicative appliance by "letting the implication apply." A life rooted in care already implicitly interprets itself, from circumspective concern to inspective or solicitous regard to the lucid perspicuity of distressed self-caring. Historically situated existence in its facticity is thoroughly hermeneutical, so that an overtly phenomenological hermeneutics *of* facticity, in its expository interpretation of care in its temporal and discursive structures, is but a repetition of an implicit panhermeneutic process already indigenous to life.

A radically hermeneutic ontology accordingly assumes the focal task of explicating the central interpretive tendency operative in the various basic movements of the life that "in its being goes about [*geht um* = is concerned with] this very being." This formula of the self-referential movement of Being itself in *Being and Time* (1927) becomes the formal indication of the understanding-of-Being that defines the very being of factic Dasein. This self-referential movement preceding any subject–object reflectivity, accordingly a temporal-historical circular movement of being to being circumscribing the understanding *of* Being that Dasein is, is the temporalized translation of the seemingly static reflective "*self*-directedness toward" of the phenomenological structure called intentionality, the source of the giving of meaning in human experience. Inescapably situated in the hermeneutic-ontological magnitudes of tradition and language, temporally driven by the erotic question of the sense of Being, the understanding-of-Being is the all-pervasive central core of all of Heidegger's thought. Thus, the later Heidegger (1959) still identifies the accustomed "usage" of the human being by Being itself, through the "hidden pull" of its tradition of language, as the "hermeneutic relation."

The dislocating circular dynamics of situated meaning-formation is first made manifest in the historically precedented structure indigenous to the "hermeneutic situation" of understanding. This prestructure of the understanding is tensed temporally by a prepossession, preview, and preconception that circularly structure meaning into a "toward-which-according-to-which" something becomes understandable as something. Meaning thus indicates the articulative direction for cultivating the prestructure of understanding into the as-structure of interpretation. Already inescapably finding itself in a hermeneutic situation, following the temporal promptings of dispositioning understanding in a discursive medium of self-mediating meaning, Dasein appropriates and explicates its most immediate conditions of access to itself and to its world. Through historical self-explication, by working out the presuppositional constellation already at work in interpreting anything whatsoever, self-referential understanding-*of*-Being becomes fully itself, comes full circle again and again "to its matter itself." Being itself is accordingly the "event" of situated *hermeneia,* of unconcealing concealing, of the original "clearing" of sense in human experience.

Repeated review and deepening re-vision of his hermeneutic situation is the strategy that Heidegger himself applies to his own ever more radical philosophical discourse, as it develops from the fundamental-ontological hermeneutics of human being to the destructive retrieve of the fundamental historicity of the thinking of Being itself. The merit of Hans-Georg Gadamer's less radical "philosophical hermeneutics" is the reapplication of the situational dynamics of Heidegger's "hermeneutics of facticity" to its more customary loci in the humanities. Gadamer's masterwork, *Truth and Method,* based in the hermeneutic intentionality of our "thrown" belonging to the project of tradition, proposes no method but seeks simply to understand phenomenologically how the understanding (contextualized "truth") that is bound by tradition naturally "happens" by way of that tradition in our humanistic experiences of art, history, and language. Unique features of Gadamer's account of "hermeneutic experience" are the dialectical encounter between interpreter and transmitted text itself taken as interrogating dialogue partner, the productivity of the temporal distance between them that exposes precedented possibilities mediating present and past into a fusion of horizons, the resulting translation of that tradition to a new (thus unprecedented) whole, how history itself is at work in restoring our understanding of an initially alien past, how the "speculative" play of language itself is the ultimate source of this healing productivity ("the medium mediates"), and insistence on the completion of the process of understanding interpretation in the moment of application (to our time, to our language, the two transcendental magnitudes of hermeneutics).

[See also Gadamer, Hans-Georg; Heidegger, Martin; Hermeneutic Philosophy; Husserl, Edmund; Husserl, Intentionality in.]

BIBLIOGRAPHY

Gadamer, H.-G. *Gesammelte Werke.* Tübingen, 1986–.
Gadamer, H.-G. *Wahrheit und Methode: Grundzüge einer philosophischen Hermeneutik.* Tübingen, 1960. Published as Vols. 1–2 of *Gesammelte Werke.* Translated and newly revised by J. Weinsheimer and D. G. Marshall as *Truth and Method.* New York, 1989.
Heidegger, M. "A Dialogue on/from Language between a Japanese and an Inquirer," in *Unterwegs zur Sprache* (Pfullingen, 1959). Translated by P. D. Hertz as *On the Way to Language.* New York, 1971.
———. *Gesamtausgabe.* Frankfurt, 1975–.
———. *Sein und Zeit.* Halle, 1927. 16th ed., Tübingen, 1986. Translated by J. Macquarrie and E. S. Robinson as *Being and Time.* New York, 1962.
Kisiel, T. *The Genesis of Heidegger's "Being and Time."* Berkeley, 1993.

– THEODORE KISIEL

HERMENEUTIC PHILOSOPHY

While hermeneutics, per se, is generally identified with the "art of understanding"—that is, with the methods and principles for understanding texts—in the twentieth century it was transformed into a philosophical position closely associated with Hans-Georg Gadamer and Paul Ricoeur. Two forerunners to Gadamer and Ricoeur are Wilhelm Dilthey, who in 1990 saw hermeneutics as a methodological foundation for the human sciences, and Martin Heidegger, who, as early as 1919 and later in *Being and Time* (1927), used the word *Hermeneutik* to indicate an alternative kind of interpretation embedded in existential understanding.

After the publication of *Truth and Method,* Gadamer encountered opposition from Emilio Betti and E. D. Hirsch, Jr., who objected that Gadamer offered no means of achieving objectively valid interpretations, and from the neo-Marxist Jürgen Habermas, who found in Gadamer's affirmation of tradition no room for the "moment of critique."

Paul Ricoeur spent World War II in a concentration camp writing a translation of Husserl's *Ideas* between the lines. In early work on phenomenology of the will and the fallibility of man he turned to the interpretation of symbols and devoted a volume to the symbolism of stain and evil (1960). He then wrote on Freud's view of interpretation (1965), and in *The Conflict of Interpretations* (1968) he tried to mediate the conflict between Anglo-American and Continental philosophy. His book on the living metaphor (1974) and a three-volume work on time and narrative also contributed to hermeneutics.

Beginning in 1967 Jacques Derrida offered a continuation of Heideggerian thought that contrasts with that of both Gadamer and Ricoeur, yet since it deals heavily with the question of interpretation one may include it within the category of hermeneutic philosophy. In 1979 Richard Rorty's *Philosophy and the Mirror of Nature* made hermeneutics a new paradigm for philosophizing, a contrast with the philosophizing that invents systems and seeks to lay foundations for future thought.

[See also Derrida, Jacques; Freud, Sigmund; Gadamer, Hans-Georg; Habermas, Jürgen; Heidegger, Martin; Husserl, Edmund; Ricoeur, Paul; Ricoeur, Metaphor.]

BIBLIOGRAPHY

Betti, E. "Hermeneutics as the General Methodology of the *Geisteswissenschaften,*" in J. Bleicher, ed., *Contemporary Hermeneutics* (London, 1980).

Bruns, G. *Hermeneutics Ancient and Modern.* New Haven, 1993.

Dilthey, W. "The Rise of Hermeneutics," *English Literary History,* Vol. 3 (1972), 230–44.

Gadamer, H.-G. *Wahrheit and Methode.* Tübingen, 1960. Translated as *Truth and Method,* edited by G. Barden and J. Cumming. New York, 1975; rev. trans., 1989.

Grondin, J. *An Introduction to Philosophical Hermeneutics.* New Haven, 1994.

Habermas, J., "The Hermeneutic Claim to Universality," in J. Bleicher, ed., *Contemporary Hermeneutics* (London, 1980).

Heidegger, M. *Sein und Zeit.* Tübingen, 1927. Translated by J. Macquarrie and E. Robinson as *Being and Time.* New York, 1962.

Hirsch, E. D., Jr. "Gadamer's Theory of Interpretation," Appendix 2 in *Validity in Interpretation* (New Haven, 1967).

Palmer, R. E. *Interpretation Theory: Schleiermacher, Dilthey, Heidegger, Gadamer.* Evanston, IL, 1969. An introduction to hermeneutic philosophy.

Ricoeur, P. *La symbolique du mal.* Paris, 1960. Translated by E. Buchanan as *Symbolism of Evil.* Boston, 1969.

———. *De l'interprétation. Essais sur Freud.* Paris, 1965. Translated by Denis Savage as *Freud and Philosophy: An Essay on Interpretation.* New Haven, 1970.

———. *Le conflit des interprétations.* Paris, 1969. English title: *Conflict of Interpretations,* edited by D. Ihde. Evanston, IL, 1974.

———. *Métaphore vive.* Paris, 1975. Translated by R. Czerny as *The Rule of Metaphor.* Toronto, 1977.

———. *Temps et récit.* Paris, 1983–85. Translated by K. McLaughlin and D. Pellauer as *Time and Narrative.* 3 Vols. Chicago, 1984–88.

Rorty, R., "From Epistemology to Hermeneutics," and "Philosophy without Mirrors," in *Philosophy and the Mirror of Nature* (Princeton, NJ, 1979).

– RICHARD E. PALMER

HIPPOCRATES OF COS

Hippocrates of Cos (c. 460–c. 380 B.C.), the patron saint of scientific medicine, taught, according to Plato, that it is impossible to treat any part of the body without taking account of the whole body (*Phaedrus* 270A); according to the history of medicine written by Aristotle's pupil Meno, he explained illness as being brought about by air secreted by undigested food. This is all that is known about Hippocrates from testimonies of the

---

The Hippocratic Oath,

probably of Pythagorean origin,

was the document that for the Middle Ages

and later centuries embodied

the highest aspirations of the doctor,

who is here "not to harm but to help."

---

classical age. It is, however, a method of treatment and a theory of disease that are not basic to any of the so-called Hippocratic writings. In the Hellenistic age, Hippocrates was most often hailed as an empiricist, and various books of the *Corpus Hippocraticum* are quoted as his, whether they are books on prognosis, on surgery, or on the etiology and cure of diseases along the lines of both empirical and rational medicine. In the second century Galen, a Platonist by persuasion, saw in Hippocrates the philosophical doctor who, before Plato, had taught much of what Plato was to teach. His interpretation of the Hippocratic doctrine and the Hippocratic work became canonical by the end of antiquity, although Galen himself was quite aware that he was merely interpreting the evidence available and that the genuineness of any Hippocratic treatise had to be demonstrated. From then on, through the Middle Ages and the Renaissance, and until the beginning of the nineteenth century, Hippocrates' name stood as the symbol of a medical wisdom that understands the nature of the human body as dependent on the nature of the universe, and the Hippocratic treatises were studied as the incunabula as well as the perfection of medical insight.

In the course of the nineteenth century, Hippocrates was dethroned as the scientific authority. For historical scholarship only the earliest evidence was acceptable as a basis on which to judge the achievement of Hippocrates, and one tried to account for the change in the ancients' evaluation of his teaching, especially for the attribution of the so-called Hippocratic treatises to him. The most likely hypothesis is that the medical writings of the fifth and fourth centuries B.C. circulated without the names of their authors and that from early Alexandrian times on, literary critics and medical scholars had attempted to find among them works of Hippocrates, in whom they were interested. This interest stemmed from the fact that Plato and Aristotle spoke of Hippocrates and quoted him. He may also have been remembered as an unusually successful physician, for a doctor gains renown not only as a writer and theoretician but also, if not above all, as a practitioner. One of the great Hellenistic schools of medicine traced its origins to the Coan medical tradition. In the eyes of Galen and his contemporaries, it was in Hippocrates' favor that he lived in the classical era, in which the archaism of the second century discovered the beginnings of all things.

Whether or not this is the right explanation for the ascendancy of Hippocrates, it is certain that no more can be said about his achievement than what is told by Plato, and by Aristotle and his school. For the historian, his "writings," with the exception of a few books that are probably of a later date, represent medicine as it was practiced at the turn of the fifth to the fourth century B.C. and are, for that reason, of great interest. They show, first of all, that by that time Greek medicine had learned not only to describe the details of a disease, as had Oriental medicine, but also to grasp its whole course, to give a picture of disease entities. Etiologies varied from a one-humor theory to a four-humor theory; explanations of the causes of illness ranged from the air inhaled to the food and drink taken in. Treatment consisted predominantly in changes in regimen; the use of drugs was relatively restricted and of secondary importance. Outstanding surgery was performed on fractures, dislocations, and wounds of the head but was

The Hippocratic Oath *infused morality into medical craft. (Corbis)*

almost never undertaken in cases of an affliction of the internal organs. (Anatomy was animal anatomy, not human anatomy.) Prognosis was as highly developed as diagnosis and included, in addition to a prediction of the outcome of an illness, a "foretelling" of the present condition of the patient—without gathering information from him—and even of previous stages of his sickness. As early as the classical age, Greek medicine concerned itself with the healthy as well as with the sick, prescribing for the rich a very rigorous regimen that hardly left the individual free to do as he pleased at any given moment, and for the poor, at least a set of precautionary measures meant to avert the worst dangers of haphazard living.

Since the *Corpus Hippocraticum* is a collection of treatises by diverse authors, one can find in it support for a variety of principles. Bacon and Galileo quoted "Hippocrates" as the protagonist of experiment and observation; Voltaire admired his renunciation of an empty metaphysics. (The *facies Hippocratica* was famous as the embodiment of cool and detached observation; the first aphorism—life is short; art, long—was the proverbial slogan of skepticism.) Leibniz invoked Hippocrates' endorsement of the harmony and interconnection of all things; Berkeley compared Newton's physics to his teaching. The multiplication of disease entities was defended by reference to his authority, as was the insistence on including the various forms of an illness under one name. Treatment based on the dogma of *contraria contrariis* (cure opposites with opposites)—no less than that based on the dogma of *similia similibus* (cure like with like)—was called Hippocratic.

Two features can perhaps be called characteristic of all the medical treatises of the classical age. Whatever the explanation of diseases, whatever their cure, the individuality of the patient was never lost sight of. The art of the physician lay in his ability to strike a balance between knowledge that abstracts from particular conditions and that is, of necessity, general, and the specific requirements of the situation at hand. Moreover, medical treatment was not divorced from ethical considerations. In most of the Hippocratic writings, medical ethics is, to be sure, an ethics of performance. Since he is a craftsman, by ancient social standards, the physician wants to do his job well, that is, as a competent and responsible craftsman should. But some of the treatises infuse philosophical morality into medical craft. The *Hippocratic Oath,* probably of Pythagorean origin, was the document that for the Middle Ages and later centuries embodied the highest aspirations of the doctor, who is here "not to harm but to help." It has kept the name of Hippocrates alive even in a world in which the knowledge of the Greece of old has become obsolete and the past of medicine mere history.

BIBLIOGRAPHY

The complete works of "Hippocrates" must still be read in E. Littré, ed., *Oeuvres complètes d'Hippocrate,* 10 vols. (Paris, 1839–1861).

In the four-volume Loeb edition of Hippocrates (Cambridge, Mass., 1948–1953), Vol. III, W. H. S. Jones and E. T. Withington, eds., is a selection of the most important treatises and is valuable for the introduction to the various essays.

The interpretation of Hippocrates given here is set forth in detail in Ludwig Edelstein, ΠΕΡΙ ΑΕΡΩΝ *und die Sammlung der Hippokratischen Schriften* (Berlin, 1931), and in A. Pauly and G. Wissowa, eds., *Realencyclopädie der classischen Altertumswissenschaft,* Supp. VI (Stuttgart, 1935), Cols. 1290 ff. For survival in the Middle Ages and later centuries, see Pauly and Wissowa, Cols. 1335 ff.

Concerning later literature, see Ludwig Edelstein's "The Genuine Works of Hippocrates," in *Bulletin of the History of Medicine,* Vol. 7 (1939), 236 ff. Also see his paper "The Hippocratic Oath," which is *Supplement to the Bulletin of the History of Medicine,* Vol. 1 (1943).

— LUDWIG EDELSTEIN

HOBBES, THOMAS

Thomas Hobbes (1588–1679), often called the father of modern analytic philosophy, was born in Malmes-

Thomas Hobbes is often called the father of modern philosophy. (Macmillan)

bury, Wiltshire, England. Hobbes later enjoyed jesting about the significance of his manner of entry into the world. (He was born prematurely when his mother heard of the approach of the Spanish Armada.) "Fear and I were born twins," he would say, adding color to his conviction that the fear of death and the need for security are the psychological foundations both of worldly prudence and of civilization itself. He died at the age of 91 in Hardwick, Derbyshire, after a life of travel, study, polemical controversy, and philosophical and literary activity that in his later years had virtually established him as an English institution.

EARLY YEARS. Hobbes's father, Thomas Hobbes, was vicar of Westport, an adjunct of Malmesbury, but his conduct reflected little credit on his cloth. After being involved in a brawl outside his own church, he had to flee to London, leaving Thomas to be brought up by a wealthy uncle, who took the matter of his education very seriously. When he was only 14, Hobbes was sent to Magdalen Hall, Oxford, where he remained for five years before taking his bachelor's degree. He seems to have been bored by his Aristotelian tutors, although he acquired considerable proficiency in logic. The strong

Puritan tradition of his college impressed Hobbes, but the drunkenness, gaming, and other vices that were prevalent equally impressed him. On leaving Oxford in 1608, Hobbes had the good fortune to become tutor to the young son of William Cavendish, earl of Devonshire. This circumstance introduced him to influential people, to a first-class library, and to foreign travel.

In 1610, on the first of Hobbes's visits to the Continent, he discovered the disrepute into which the Aristotelian system of thought was beginning to fall. Kepler had recently published his *Astronomia Nova,* and Galileo had just discovered the satellites of Jupiter through his telescope. Hobbes returned to England determined to devote himself to the pursuit of learning, a resolve that was probably strengthened by his meetings with Francis Bacon. Hobbes, however, thought little of Bacon's so-called method of induction, with its stress on observation and experiment, which was later to become the inspiration of the Royal Society. Nevertheless, he agreed with Bacon in his contempt for Aristotelianism, in his conviction that knowledge means power to be used for the improvement of man's estate, and in his advocacy of clear and concrete speech instead of the vague abstractions of the schools.

At this period of his life Hobbes had turned to the classics to gain an understanding of life and of philosophy, which, he thought, could not be found in the schools. After a period of reading and reflection, he decided to translate Thucydides into English, a significant choice. Like Thucydides, Hobbes believed that history was written for instruction, and he wished to instruct his countrymen on the dangers of democracy. In 1628, when Hobbes published his translation, Charles I had been on the throne for three years and was already at loggerheads with Sir John Eliot and John Pym. Hobbes's translation was the first of his many attempts to bring his countrymen to their senses and to make them aware of the tragedy that they courted: that of civil war, from which proceed "slaughter, solitude, and the want of all things."

PHILOSOPHICAL AWAKENING. It was not until the time of his second journey to the Continent that Hobbes's career as a philosopher began. His patron had died, and as a temporary economy, Catherine, the countess of Devonshire, had dispensed with Hobbes's services. Hobbes took similar employment with Sir Gervase Clinton and, in 1629, accompanied Clinton's son on a journey to the Continent. There Hobbes developed a passionate interest in geometry, which impressed him as a method for reaching indubitable conclusions. Could not his convictions about the dangers of democracy be demonstrated? Could not his opinions about man, gleaned from his observation of the con-

temporary scene, from his insight into his own nature, and from his perusal of the pages of Thucydides and Machiavelli, be postulated as axioms from which theorems about the conditions of a commonwealth might be generated?

Like Thucydides, Hobbes believed that history was written for instruction, and he wished to instruct his countrymen on the dangers of democracy.

Hobbes's discovery of geometry gave him a method of analysis and a conception of scientific method, but he still lacked a conceptual scheme to give content to his demonstrations about man and society. In Paris, during his third journey to the Continent (1634–1637), again in the service of the Devonshires as tutor to William, the succeeding earl, he became a member of the intellectual circle of the Abbé Mersenne, who patronized Descartes and Gassendi. (Gassendi later became one of Hobbes's firmest friends.) Hobbes also made a pilgrimage to Italy in 1636 to visit Galileo, the leading exponent of the new natural philosophy. By the time of his return to England in 1637, he had conceived, perhaps at Galileo's suggestion, the main outlines of his philosophical system, in which the method of geometry and the concepts of the new science of motion were to be applied to man in society.

It is a mistake to think of Hobbes's interests as purely political. Hobbes claimed originality for his optics as well as for his civil philosophy, and at some point between his discovery of geometry and his return from his third journey to the Continent, he wrote his first philosophical work, the *Little Treatise,* in geometrical form, in which he sketched an explanation of sensation in terms of the new science of motion. His interest in sensation, according to his prose autobiography, arose from an encounter with some learned men who were discussing the cause of sensation. One of them asked derisively what sensation was, and Hobbes was astonished to find that none of them could say. From then on, he was haunted by the problem of the nature and cause of sense. He began to think he was near an explanation after it struck him that if bodies were always at rest or always moved at a constant rate, the ability to make discriminations would vanish, and with it all sensation. He concluded that the cause of everything, including that of sensation itself, must be in variations of motion.

In his verse autobiography, Hobbes graphically related how, on his third journey, he was obsessed by the omnipresence of motion. He was acclimating himself to Galileo's audacious suggestion that motion is the natural state of bodies and that they continue in motion to infinity unless they are impeded. This went against the crude evidence of the senses as well as against the established Aristotelian world view, in which rest was regarded as the natural state. But if Galileo's supposition could be entertained, Hobbes thought, even apparition itself could be explained as a meeting place of motions, and from Galileo's law of inertia the phenomena of sense and imagination could be deduced.

The state of turmoil in England on his return drove Hobbes to make his first systematic attempt to employ his geometrical approach and mechanistic psychology to present the realities beneath the appearances of the contemporary issues. His *Elements of Law,* circulated in 1640 in manuscript form during the session of Parliament, was the result. This work, which demonstrated the need for undivided sovereignty, was published in 1650 in two parts, *Human Nature* and *De Corpore Politico.* However, its arguments were taken from general principles of psychology and ethics, rather than from appeals to divine right. Many regard Hobbes's *Human Nature* as one of his best works. It consists largely of traditional psychology coordinated and underpinned by the conceptual scheme he had learned from Galileo.

EXILE IN FRANCE. Hobbes claimed later that his life would have been in danger because of the views expressed in *Elements of Law,* had not the king dissolved Parliament in May 1640. Six months later, when the Long Parliament impeached Thomas Wentworth, earl of Strafford, Hobbes fled to the Continent in fear for his life, later priding himself on being "the first of all that fled." A warm welcome awaited him in Mersenne's circle, and he settled down in Paris to his most productive philosophical period.

His first work was the composition of some 16 objections to Descartes's *Meditations,* which Mersenne submitted to Descartes in advance of its publication. This led to a rather acrimonious exchange between Descartes and Hobbes. In 1642 Hobbes published his *De Cive,* an expanded version in Latin of Part 2 of his *Elements of Law* (later to appear as *De Corpore Politico*). The additional sections dealt largely with a more detailed treatment of the relationship between the church and the civil power. During the period from 1642 to 1646, Hobbes published his *Minute or First Draught of the Optiques,* which he considered one of his most important and original works. He also started work on his most ambitious scheme—the construction of a trilogy on body, man, and citizen, in which everything in the world of nature and man was to be included in a conceptual scheme provided by the new science of mechanics. Hobbes made a beginning with *De Corpore,* which was to be the first work in the trilogy.

In 1646, however, political events again interfered with Hobbes's more abstract speculations. He was on the verge of accepting an invitation to retire in peace to a friend's house in Languedoc, in the south of France, when he was requested to act as tutor in mathematics to the future Charles II, who had just fled to Paris. Hobbes's tutorship, however, was interrupted, if not terminated, by a severe illness in 1647. He recovered after having consented to receive the sacrament on what he took to be his deathbed, and he was drawn again into political controversy by the presence of so many Royalist *émigrés.* A second edition of *De Cive* was published in 1647, but this was in Latin and had only a limited circulation. Hobbes therefore decided to blazon abroad his views on man and citizen for all to read, in English, with the arresting title of *Leviathan.* With Mersenne's unfortunate death in 1648, Hobbes began to feel increasingly isolated, for he was suspected of atheism and was an outspoken enemy of the Catholic church.

Political events in England provided a fitting prelude to the publication of *Leviathan.* Charles I was executed in 1649 and, until 1653, when Cromwell was made Protector, there was constant discussion and experimentation to find an appropriate form of government. *Leviathan,* published in 1651, was therefore very topical. It came out strongly in favor of absolute and undivided sovereignty, without the usual arguments from divine right. Indeed, Hobbes conceded popular representation but, by an ingenious twisting of the social contract theory, showed that it logically implied the acceptance of undivided sovereignty.

RETURN TO ENGLAND. Hobbes returned to England in 1651 after a severe illness and soon became embroiled in a heated debate with John Bramhall, bishop of Derry, Ulster, on the subject of free will. In 1645, in Paris, Hobbes had discussed the problem of free will with the bishop, and they both wrote their views on the matter soon afterward. A young disciple of Hobbes published his contribution in 1654, without Hobbes's consent, under the title *Of Liberty and Necessity.* Bramhall was understandably indignant and, in 1655, he published the whole controversy under the title *A Defence of True Liberty from Antecedent and Extrinsical Necessity.* In 1656 Hobbes replied by printing Bramhall's book, together with his own observations on it, which he called *The Questions Concerning Liberty, Necessity, and Chance.* Bramhall replied in 1658 with *Castigations of Hobbes his Last Animadversions,* which carried an appendix called "The Catching of Leviathan the Great Whale." Bramhall died in 1663, and Hobbes had the last word a few years later.

There was another controversy in which Hobbes was caught up for the major part of the twenty years that were left to him. This one involved John Wallis, professor of geometry at Oxford, who mercilessly exposed Hobbes's attempt in *De Corpore* (1665) to square the circle—not then such a ridiculous enterprise as it now seems—and Seth Ward, professor of astronomy, who launched a polemic against Hobbes's general philosophy. These two men were members of the "invisible college" that the king had recognized as the Royal Society in 1663. They were Puritans in religion and Baconians in their approach to science. Hobbes had annoyed them not simply by his attack on their religion and his contempt for the method of induction, but also by his diatribes on the universities as hotbeds of vice and sedition. Hobbes replied to their published criticisms with an emended English version of *De Corpore* with "Six Lessons" appended for Wallis. This was in turn attacked by Wallis, and the controversy dragged on for many years, often descending into personal vituperation on both sides.

Hobbes's first work was the composition of some 16 objections to Descartes's Meditations, *which led to a rather acrimonious exchange between the two philosophers.*

Not all of Hobbes's remaining years, however, were spent on this abortive controversy. *De Homine,* the second part of his trilogy, was published in 1657. This dealt with optics and human nature, matters on which Hobbes's opinions were already well known; accordingly, it attracted little attention and was not translated.

After the Restoration, Hobbes was granted a pension and "free access to his Majesty, who was always much delighted in his witt and smart repartees" (John Aubrey, *Brief Lives,* pp. 152–153). Only once again did he fear for his life. After the Great Plague (1665) and the Great Fire of London (1666), some reason was sought for God's displeasure, and a spasm of witch-hunting shook Parliament. A bill was passed by Parliament for the suppression of atheism, and a committee was set up to investigate *Leviathan.* The matter was eventually dropped, probably through the king's intervention, but Hobbes was forbidden to publish his opinions thereafter.

In 1668 Hobbes finished his *Behemoth*—a history of the period from 1640 to 1660, interpreted in the light of his beliefs about man and society. He submitted it

to King Charles, who advised against its publication (it was published posthumously in 1682).

Even at this advanced age Hobbes was still capable of exerting himself both physically (he played tennis until he was 75) and philosophically. John Aubrey, later his biographer, sent him Bacon's *Elements of Common Law* for his comments; and Hobbes, after protesting his age, managed to produce his unfinished *Dialogue between a Philosopher and a Student of the Common Laws of England* (published posthumously in 1681). This minor work was interesting in that Hobbes anticipated in it the analytical school of jurisprudence of the nineteenth century and came out unequivocally in favor of what has been called the command theory of law. At the age of 84 Hobbes wrote his autobiography in Latin verse after completing one in prose. At 86, for want of something better to do, he published a verse translation of the *Iliad* and the *Odyssey.*

Logic and Methodology

Hobbes lived during the emergence of men who challenged not only traditional tenets about political and religious authority but also the wisdom of the past, especially that of Aristotle. Men were exhorted to find out things for themselves, to consult their own consciences, and to communicate with God directly, instead of through the established religious hierarchy. It was widely believed that all men have the gift of reason but that they make poor use of it through lack of a proper method. Books such as Bacon's *Novum Organum,* Descartes's *Regulae* and *Discourse on Method,* and Spinoza's *Ethics* were written to remedy this defect. Thus, Hobbes was not exceptional in believing that knowledge, which meant power, could be obtained only by adopting a certain kind of method.

According to Hobbes, the knowledge whereby most men live is the knowledge gleaned from experience, culminating in prudence and history—"the register of knowledge of fact." Hobbes described experience as "nothing but remembrance of what antecedents have been followed by what consequents." Bacon had tried to set out this sort of knowledge explicitly in his *Novum Organum,* and it was taken by the Royal Society to be the paradigm of science.

DOCTRINE OF NAMES. Hobbes, however, was very contemptuous of such grubbing around and peering at nature, not only in natural philosophy but also in civil philosophy. Had Galileo or Harvey, the pioneers of the new philosophy, made a laborious summary of their experience? And in civil philosophy, what store is to be placed on the dreary saws of practical politicians or the ossified ignorance and superstitions of the common lawyers? Mere prudence, which is the product of experience, should not be mistaken for wisdom. Wisdom is the product of reason, which alone gives knowledge of "general, eternal, and immutable truths," as in geometry.

Hobbes described experience as

"nothing but remembrance of what antecedents

have been followed by what consequents."

In geometry, definitions are of paramount importance. Therefore, claimed Hobbes: "The only way to know is by definition." Thus, science is "knowledge of all the consequences of names appertaining to the subject in hand." It gives knowledge not of the nature of things but of the names of things. We start with certain terms or names about whose definition we agree. We connect these into such statements as "A man is a rational, animated body," just as we add items in an account. We then find that if we follow certain methods of combining the statements so created, conclusions can be drawn that are contained in the premises but of which we were ignorant before we started reckoning. "For reason, in this sense, is nothing but reckoning, that is adding and subtracting, of the consequences of general names agreed upon for the marking and signifying of our thoughts."

Obvious objections to such an account of scientific knowledge immediately come to mind. How, for instance, can we be sure that such a train of reasoning applies to anything? How are the meanings of Hobbes's names fixed, and how are the rules for their combinations determined?

Hobbes supposed that "names are signs not of things, but of our cogitations." Words are not the only things that can be signs; for instance, a heavy cloud can be a sign of rain. This means that from the cloud we can infer rain. This is an example of a natural sign; other examples are animal warnings of danger and summonses to food. These natural signs are to be distinguished from language proper, which consists of sounds, marks, and other such significations determined—as are the ruler of civil society—by decision. Animal noises come about by necessity, not by decision, as human speech does. That is why, on Hobbes's view, animals, though capable of imagery, cannot reason; for reasoning presupposes words with meanings fixed by decision.

Hobbes thought that every man has his own private world of phantasms or conceptions, for which words are signs that function for him like a private system of

mnemonics. These words act as signs to others of what a man thinks and feels. Although some words signify conceptions, they are not names of conceptions; for Hobbes seemed to use the word "name" for the relation of reference between names and things, and words like "signify" for the relationship between particular occurrences of a name and the idea in a person's mind. Some names are names of things themselves, such as "a man," "a tree," or "a stone," whereas others, such as "future," do not stand for or name things that as yet have any being. Such words signify the knitting together of things past and things present. In a similar way there are names, such as "impossible" and "nothing," that are not names of anything. Such names are signs of our conceptions, but they name or stand for "things" that do not exist.

Hobbes's doctrine was not altogether clear. He seemed to mean that all names serve as mnemonics to us of our conceptions and as signs to others of what we have in mind, but that only some names actually denote things in a strict sense. This leads to the distinctions that Hobbes introduced in relation to the logical function of names. Names can be either concrete or abstract. Concrete names can denote bodies, their accidents, or their names. Abstract names come into being only with propositions and denote "the cause of concrete names."

UNIVERSALS. There are two classes of concrete names: proper names and universal names. A proper name, such as "Peter," is singular to one thing only; a universal name, such as "man," denotes each member of a class of things. A universal name, "though but one name, is nevertheless the name of diverse particular things; in respect of which together, it is called a universal; there being nothing in the world universal but names; for the things named are every one of them individual and singular."

Hobbes's doctrine of universal names was crucial to his attack on the scholastic belief in essences. The world, Hobbes maintained, contains no such essences for universal names to designate. "Universal" is the name of a class of names, not of a diaphanous type of entity designated by a name. The error of those who believe in essences derives from their tendency to treat a universal name as if it were a peculiar kind of proper name. It is the *use* of a name that makes it universal, not the status of the thing that the name designates.

Hobbes's doctrine of abstract names was more obscure but of cardinal importance in his account of scientific knowledge. Abstract names come into being when names are joined in propositions. A proposition is "a speech consisting of two names copulated, by which he that speaketh signifieth the latter name to be the name of the same thing whereof the former is the name." For instance, in saying "man is a living creature," the speaker conceives "living creature" and "man" to be names of the same thing, the name "man" being comprehended by the name "living creature." This relation of "comprehension" can be brought out in some languages by the order of words without employing the verb "to be." The copulation of the two names "makes us think of the cause for which these names were imposed on that thing," and this search for the causes of names gives rise to such abstract names as "corporeity," "motion," "figure," "quantity," and "likeness." But these denote only the *causes* of concrete names and not the things themselves. For instance, we see something that is extended and fills space, and we call it by the concrete name "body." The cause of the concrete name is that the thing is extended, "or the extension or corporeity of it." These causes are the same as the causes of our conceptions, "namely, some power of action, or affection of the thing conceived, which some call the manner by which anything works upon our senses, but by most men they are called accidents." Accidents are neither the things themselves nor parts of them, but "do nevertheless accompany the things in such manner, that (saving extension) they may all perish, and be destroyed, but can never be abstracted." Among such accidents some are of particular importance for science, those which Hobbes sometimes referred to as "universal things" or "such accidents as are common to all bodies." These are the abstract concepts by means of which a theory is developed about the underlying structure of nature. The endeavor of the scientist is to understand, by means of the resoluto-compositive method of Galilean mechanics, the universal cause—motion—without knowledge of which such fundamental theories could not be developed.

MISUSES OF WORDS. Hobbes has often been called the precursor of modern analytical philosophy because he was particularly sensitive to the manner in which ridiculous (and dangerous) doctrines can be generated through confusion about how words have meaning. One class of absurdities is generated by failure to understand the different ways in which the copula "is" can function. Such terms as essence, reality, and quiddity, beloved by the schools, "could never have been heard among such nations as do not copulate their names by the verb 'is,' but by adjective verbs as runneth, readeth. . . ." The word "is" in a proposition such as "Man is a living body" has the function of "comprehension" or class inclusion. Something of the form "If *x* is a man, then *x* is a living body" is being stated. There is no commitment to the existence of men that is implied when "is" occurs in such statements as "Here is Thomas Hobbes."

Absurdities also arise if names of accidents are assimilated to names of bodies. For instance, those who say that faith is "infused" or "inspired" into a person treat faith as if it were the name of a body, for only bodies can be poured or breathed into anything. An accident is not in a body in the same sort of way that a body can be in a body—"as if, for example, redness were in blood, in the same manner, as blood is in a bloody cloth." Hobbes was also eloquent on the subject of names that name nothing.

SCIENTIFIC TRUTH. Hobbes's theory of scientific truth was not altogether consistent. He started with the important insight that "true" and "false" are attributes of speech, not of things. Truth, then, "consisteth in the right ordering of names in our affirmations." It characterizes propositions in which names of limited generality are "comprehended" by those of wider generality: for example, "Charity is a virtue." Hobbes held, it therefore seems, that all true propositions are analytically true, which is a plausible enough view if only geometrical truths are at issue. But Hobbes often spoke as if all truth must conform to this model. He saw that this raises the question of how the initial definitions are to be fixed, and about these definitions he often seemed to take a conventionist view by suggesting that "truth therefore depends upon the compacts and consents of men." He often linked the contract theory of the origin of civil society with a theory about agreement on definitions. When he was speaking about natural science, however, his position was not so clearly conventionist. The difference was caused by his assumption that men construct states just as they construct circles or triangles. But since they do not construct natural bodies in the same way, the problem therefore arises as to how Hobbes thought that propositions of natural science, which did not come into being through decisions of men, say what is true about the natural world.

Hobbes thought that all the propositions of natural science are deductions from the basic theory of motion, in which there are primary propositions containing such simple unanalyzable concepts as motion, extension, and straightness. These are "well enough defined, when, by speech as short as may be, we raise in the mind of the hearer perfect and clear ideas of the thing named" (*De Corpore*). Such conceptions are featured in Hobbes's account of evidence, which is "the concomitance of a man's *conception* with the *words* that signify such conception in the act of ratiocination" (*Human Nature*). A parrot could speak truth but could not know it, for it would lack the conceptions that accompany the speaking of truth by a man who knows truth. "Evidence is to truth, as the sap to the tree . . . for this evidence, which is meaning with our words, is the life of truth.

Knowledge thereof, which we call *science,* I define to be *evidence of truth,* from some beginning or principle of *sense. . . ."*

Conceptions, in Hobbes's view, are explained causally in terms of motions that arise in the head and persist after the stimulation of sense organs by external bodies. Names, which are joined together in true propositions, are signs of these conceptions in that they mark them for the individual and enable other people to make inferences about what he thinks. Thus, Hobbes must have thought that when a man knows (as distinct from when he merely speaks) what is true, his conceptions, as it were, keep pace with what he is saying. Some of these conceptions, those involved in understanding primary propositions, are clear and distinct ideas of things named. Thus, scientific systems are somehow anchored to the world of nature by means of names that refer to attributes of bodies of which we have a clear and distinct idea.

This theory resembles, in certain respects, the self-evidence theory of the Cartesians. However, it seems inconsistent with the conventionalism of Hobbes's other remarks about basic definitions and is a very confused account in itself, not very helpful in elucidating what makes scientific propositions true. In the empirical sciences the clarity of the ideas in the initial postulates is neither here nor there. What matters is whether statements deduced from them can be observationally confirmed.

SCIENTIFIC INQUIRY. The ambiguity in Hobbes's account of truth is paralleled by the ambiguity in his account of scientific method, which he equated with the search for causes. One of his most famous definitions of philosophy or scientific knowledge (he did not distinguish between the two) occurs at the start of *De Corpore* (Molesworth ed.): "philosophy is such knowledge of effects or appearances, as we acquire by true ratiocination from the knowledge we have first of their causes or generation: And again, of such causes or generations as may be from knowing first their effects." By "cause" Hobbes meant, of course, antecedent motion, and he was unusual in thinking that even geometrical figures are to be explained in terms of motion because of the movements involved in constructing them.

Hobbes's distinction between these two forms of philosophical knowledge is important. In the case of acquiring knowledge of effects from knowledge of causes or generation, his conventionist account of truth holds good. For instance, in the case of deciding that a figure must be a circle from our knowledge of the motions from which it was produced, "the truth of the first principles of our ratiocination, namely definitions, is made and constituted by ourselves, whilst we consent and agree upon the appellation of things." He used this method in *De Corpore* to explain parallel lines, refraction and reflection, circular and other forms of motion, angles, and similar concepts. It also seems that he had this model in mind when he thought about the generation of the artificial machine of the commonwealth.

When dealing with knowledge of causes from effects, however, Hobbes's account is far less clear-cut and conventionist. At the beginning of Part 4 of *De Corpore,* for instance, he said: "The principles, therefore, upon which the following discourse depends, are not such as we ourselves make and pronounce in general terms, as definitions: but such, as being placed in the things themselves by the Author of Nature, are by us observed in them. . . ." The explanations that we give in the natural sciences may be true, but it is impossible to demonstrate that they are necessarily true, for the phenomena are not generated by human contrivance, as are the phenomena of geometry and politics.

The method on which Hobbes was relying in both these types of scientific inquiry was, of course, the resoluto-compositive method of Galilean mechanics. In this method a typical phenomenon, such as the rolling of a stone down a slope, was taken. Such properties as color and smell, which were regarded as scientifically irrelevant, were disregarded, and the situation was resolved into simple elements that could be quantified—the length and angle of the slope, the weight of the stone, the time the stone takes to fall. The mathematical relations disclosed were then manipulated until functional relations between the variables were established. The situation was then synthesized or "composed" in a rational structure of mathematical relations. This is what Hobbes called analysis—the search for causes, given the effects. "Synthesis" consisted in starting from the known causes and deducing effects from them. In Galileo's hands this method was highly successful because he tested such deductions by observation. In Hobbes's hands the method was not so fruitful because it always remained an imaginary experiment.

Similar ambiguities in Hobbes's methodology complicate our effort to understand his conception of his trilogy on body, man, and citizen. He thought of geometry as the science of simple motions that could demonstrate how figures are generated by varieties of motion. Second came the philosophy of motion, as usually understood in the Galilean system, in which the effects of the palpable motions of one body on another were considered. Third came physics, the investigation of the internal and invisible motions that explain why "things when they are the same, yet seem not to be the same, but changed." Sensible qualities, such as light, color, heat, and sound, were to be explained, together with the nature of sensation itself. After physics came moral philosophy, the study of the motions of the mind—appetites and aversions. Such motions of the mind had their causes in sense and imagination. Finally, there was civil philosophy, the study of how states are generated from the qualities of human nature.

Hobbes has often been called the precursor of modern analytical philosophy because he was particularly sensitive to the manner in which ridiculous (and dangerous) doctrines can be generated through confusion about how words have meaning.

It is probable that Hobbes did not view the hierarchy of sciences as a rigorous deductive system. To start with, he never worked out the deductions in any detail—for instance, in the transition from what he called physics to moral philosophy, or psychology. Furthermore, what he said about the possibility of a self-contained science of politics contradicts his suggestion that it must be deduced from the fundamental theory of motion and that it supports the conventionist account of truth in politics. Hobbes said that even those who are ignorant of the principles of physics and geometry might attain knowledge of the principles of politics by the analytical method. They could start, for instance, with the question of whether an action is just or unjust; "unjust" could be resolved into "fact against law," and "law" into "command of him or them that have coercive power"; "power" could in its turn be derived from the wills of men who established such power so that they might live in peace.

This line of argument, developed in *De Corpore* after admitting the possibility of using the synthetic method to start from the first principles of philosophy and deduce from them the causes and necessity of constituting commonwealths, is confirmed by Hobbes's injunction in the Introduction to *Leviathan* that a man who is to govern a whole nation must "read in himself, not this or that particular man; but mankind: which though it be hard to do, harder than to learn any language of science; yet when I shall have set down my own reading, orderly and perspicuously, the pains left another, will be only to consider, if he find not the same in himself. For this kind of doctrine admitteth no other demonstration." It appears that Hobbes envisaged a relatively self-contained doctrine of politics based on introspection. His trilogy was, therefore, probably not conceived as forming a strictly deductive system. Its various elements were to be more loosely bound together by the fact that all three were sciences of motion.

Philosophy of Nature

Hobbes's natural philosophy seems to have been stimulated largely by the problem of the nature and cause of sensation that had so long haunted him. His theory was that the cause of everything, including sensation itself, lies in the varieties of motion. His first sketches of such a theory were in his *Little Treatise* and his early optical treatises, and his *De Corpore* was an ambitious development of this fundamental idea. Geometry, physics, physiology, and animal psychology were all incorporated within the theory of motion. Sensation occupied a shadowy middle position between the gross motions of the external world and the minute motions of the bodily organs.

The strange thing about Hobbes's preoccupation with sensation is that he seems to have been little troubled by the problems that are almost the stock in trade of philosophers—the problems of epistemology. He assumed that things exist independently of our perceptions of them and was convinced that "conceptions and apparitions are nothing really but motions in some internal substance of the head." The "nothing but" is very hard to accept, for obviously when we speak of "thoughts" and "conceptions," we do not *mean* the same as when we talk of motions in the brain.

MOTION AND QUALITIES. On the status of the various sense qualities, Hobbes held, as did such natural philosophers as Kepler and Galileo, that secondary qualities—such as smells, colors, and sounds—are only appearances of bodies, whose real properties are those of extension, figure, and motion. Such secondary qualities are phantasms in the head, caused by the primary properties of external objects interacting with the sense organs, but the secondary qualities represent nothing outside. Hobbes argued that images and colors are "inherent in the sentient" because of illusions and because of images produced in other ways—for example, by blows on the optic nerve. But this proved too much, for representations of primary qualities are equally liable to deceive. Hobbes also proved too little, for he argued that secondary qualities represent no qualities of external objects because tastes, smells, and sounds seem different to different sentients. But there are standard tests for establishing the fact, for example, that a man is color-blind; and, as Berkeley later showed, the perception of primary qualities is infected with a similar relativity owing to the point of view and peculiarities of the percipient. Hobbes, in fact, gave but a halting philosophical patter to justify a distinction deeply embedded in the thought and practice of the new natural philosophers, for the basic tenet of these thinkers was that bodies in motion exist independently of our perception of them and that mathematical thinking about them discloses their real properties.

Hobbes regarded sensation and apparition as a meeting place of motions. Sense organs, he thought, are agitated by external movements without which there would be no discrimination and, hence, no sensation. Therefore, to give the entire cause of sense, an analysis is required of all movements in external bodies, which are transmitted to the sense through a medium. But sensation is not simply the end product of external motions; it also functions as an efficient cause of actions of sentient beings. Actions, in Hobbes's view, are really reactions to stimuli that are passed on by means of the sense organs. Sensation acts as a bridge between movements in the external world and the behavior of animals and men.

Hobbes's mechanical theory was distinctive in that he extended the Galilean system in two directions: into geometry at one end, and into psychology and politics at the other. He thought that no one could understand the definitions of geometry without grasping how motion is involved in the construction of lines, superficies, and circles. Geometry is the science of simple motions. It paves the way for mechanics, which explains the effects of the motions of one body on another, and for physics, which deals with the generation of sensible qualities from the insensible parts of a body in contact with other moving bodies.

CAUSATION. All causation, in Hobbes's view, consists in motion. "There can be no cause of motion except in a body contiguous and moved," If bodies are not contiguous and yet influence one another, this influence has to be conveyed either by a medium or by emanations of minute bodies that impinge on others (the theory of effluxes), There can be no action at a distance. Hobbes combined this principle with his rendering of Galileo's law of inertia.

Hobbes extended this conception of causation to human actions: "A final cause has no place but in such things as have sense and will; and this also I shall prove hereafter to be an efficient cause." To bring about this transition from mechanics to physiology and psychology, Hobbes introduced the concept of "endeavour," which he defined as "motion made in less space and time than can be given ... that is, motion made through the length of a point, and in an instant or point of time." In other words, he used the term to postulate infinitely, small motions, and by means of this notion

he tried to bridge the gap between mechanics and psychology. He thought that external objects, working on the sense organs, produce not only phantasms but also minute motions that proceed to the heart and make some alteration in the vital motions of the circulation of the blood. When these vital motions are thereby helped, we experience pleasure; when they are hindered, we experience pain. The body will be regulated in such a way that it will preserve the motions that help the vital motions and get rid of or shun those that hinder. This brings about animal motion. Even habits are nothing but motions made more easy by repeated endeavors; they are comparable to the bend of a crossbow.

Hobbes has often been called a materialist, but it is more appropriate to regard him as a great metaphysician of motion. He took concepts that have an obvious application to one realm of phenomena (mechanics) and developed a conceptual scheme that, he thought, could be applied to all phenomena. The plausibility of such a scheme derives from stressing tenuous similarities and ignoring palpable differences. There is a sense in which social life is a matter of bodies moving toward and away from other bodies, just as there is a sense in which work is moving lumps of matter about. But such descriptions are either unilluminating truisms, or, if they carry the "nothing but" implication, they are misleading. Habits, for example, may be formed in part by a variety of movements, but to suggest that by "habit" we mean nothing but a build-up of movements is ridiculous. This either confuses a question of meaning with a question of genetic explanation or it demonstrates the length to which Hobbes was prepared to go in rigging appearances to suit his metaphysical redescription.

SUBSTANCE AND ACCIDENT. In his *De Corpore* Hobbes defined "body" as "that which having no dependence upon our thought, is coincident and coextended with some part of space." Bodies need not be visible. Indeed, "endeavours," which featured so widely in his system, are movements of minute unobservable bodies. Hobbes held that there is nothing else in the world but bodies, and he therefore did not flinch from the conclusion that "substance incorporeal" is a contradiction in terms. He argued that God cannot be such a substance. To Bishop Bramhall's question of what he took God to be, Hobbes replied, "I answer, I leave him to be a most pure, simple, invisible, spirit corporeal."

By "accident" Hobbes meant a property or characteristic that is not a part of a thing but "the manner by which any body is conceived." Most accidents, with the exception of figure and extension, can be absent without destruction of the body. But Hobbes was not altogether clear about the grounds for such an exception. If the grounds are the inconceivability of a body without figure and extension, why should not color be in the same category as figure? Hobbes regarded color as a subjective appearance brought about by the interaction of sense organs with the primary qualities of external objects; but if the criterion is one of conceivability, as Berkeley pointed out, it is as difficult to conceive of a body without color as it is to conceive of one without figure. Hobbes in fact defined "body" in terms of accidents that are mathematically tractable in mechanics and geometry. He tried to provide some kind of rationale for this basic assumption of the new natural philosophy by introducing the criterion of conceivability, which will not really do the work required of it.

The strange thing about Hobbes's preoccupation with sensation is that he seems to have been little troubled by the problems that are almost the stock in trade of philosophers— the problems of epistemology.

Hobbes defined space as "the phantasm of a thing existing without the mind simply." By this he meant that what is called space is the appearance of externality. If the world were to be destroyed, and a man were left alone with his imagination and memories, some of these would appear external to him, or located in space, for the system of coordinates used to describe the relative position of bodies is a subjective framework. "Place is nothing out of the mind nor magnitude anything within it." A body always keeps the same magnitude, whether in motion or at rest, but it does not keep the same place when it moves. Place cannot, therefore, be an accident of bodies; place is feigned extension—an order of position constructed from experience of real extended things to provide a framework for their externality. Similarly, time is "the phantasm of before and after in motion." Time systems are constructed from the experience of succession.

Hobbes never made clear the relationship between any particular temporal or spatial system that an individual may devise and the system of coordinates adopted by the natural philosophers. Here again, Hobbes typically took for granted the system used by the scientists and tacked on a very brief philosophical story about its relation to the "phantasms" of the individual.

Psychology

Hobbes's psychology was not behavioristic, as it has sometimes been said to be, except insofar as behaviorism has often been associated with a materialistic metaphysical theory or with mechanical modes of explanation. Hobbes stressed the indispensability of introspection in the analysis and explanation of human behavior.

When Hobbes looked into himself he found, of course, motions that were in conformity with Galilean principles. He boldly proclaimed in *De Corpore* that "we have discovered the nature of sense, namely, that it is some internal motion in the sentient." The external body, either directly or via a medium, presses on the organ of sense, "which pressure, by the mediation of the nerves, and other strings and membranes of the body, continues inwards to the brain and heart, causeth there a resistance, or counterpressure, or endeavour of the heart to deliver itself, which endeavour, because outward, seemeth to be some matter without." Sensations are thus nothing but motions. They have the character of externality because of the "outward endeavor" of the heart.

PERCEPTION. Having provided a mechanical starting point for his psychology, Hobbes then tried to describe what was known about psychological phenomena in terms compatible with a mechanical theory. One of the most obvious features of perception is that it involves seeing something as something, some sort of discrimination or recognition. Hobbes's way of saying this was that sense always has "some memory adhering to it." This was to be explained by the sense organs' property of acting as retainers of the movements of external bodies impinging on them. Without this retention of motions, what we call sense would be impossible, for "by sense we commonly understand the judgment we make of objects by their phantasms; namely, by comparing and distinguishing those phantasms; which we could never do, if that motion in the organ, by which the phantasm is made, did not remain there for some time, and make the same phantasm return."

The selectivity of perception raised a further problem. Why is it that men do not see many things at once? Hobbes again suggested a mechanical explanation: "For seeing the nature of sense consists in motion; as long as the organs are employed about one object, they cannot be so moved by another at the same time, as to make by both their motions one sincere phantasm of each of them at once." But this does nothing to explain why one object rather than another is selected. Hobbes's ideomotor theory made it hard to give a plausible account of the influence of interests, attitudes, and sets on what is selected in perception.

Hobbes also attempted a mechanical explanation of the phenomena of attention and concentration. When a strong motion impinges on the sense organ, the motion from the root of the sense organ's nerves to the heart persists contumaciously and makes the sense organ "stupid" to the registering of other motions.

IMAGINATION AND MEMORY. Hobbes's account of imagination was explicitly a deduction from the law of inertia. "When a body is once in motion, it moveth, unless something else hinder it, eternally . . . so also it happeneth in that motion, which is made in the internal parts of a man when he sees, dreams, etc. For after the object is removed, or the eye shut, we still retain an image of the thing seen, though more obscure than when we see it . . ." Imagination, therefore, is "nothing but decaying sense." This decay is not a decay in motion, for that would be contrary to the law of inertia. Rather, it comes about because the sense organs are moved by other objects, and subsequent movements obscure previous ones "in such manner as the light of the sun obscureth the light of the stars."

Memory, Hobbes claimed, differs from imagination only in that the fading image is accompanied by a feeling of familiarity. "For he that perceives that he hath perceived remembers," and memory "supposeth the time past." Hobbes thus seems to have more or less equated what is past with what is familiar, which is most implausible even if familiarity is often a hallmark of what is past. It is also difficult to see how, in his view, remembering something could be distinguished from seeing it for a second time, if the second impression of the thing is not very vivid.

Hobbes's fundamental mistake in all such descriptions and explanations was to attempt to distinguish performances, such as perceiving and remembering, by reference to subjective hallmarks vaguely consistent with his mechanical theory, rather than by reference to the epistemological criteria written into them. The fundamental difference between perception and imagination, for instance, is not one of vividness or any other such accidental property; it is an epistemological difference. To say that a person imagines a tree rather than perceives it is to say something about the status of what is claimed. To perceive is to see something that really is before one's eyes; to imagine is to think one sees something that is not there. Similarly, to remember is to be right in a claim one makes about something in the past that one was in a position to witness, whereas to imagine is to be mistaken in what one claims. There are, of course, further questions about the mechanisms by means of which people perceive, imagine, and remember; and it could be that some such mechanical story as told by Hobbes might be true about such mechanisms.

But in the language of such a story the basic epistemological differences between these mental performances could never be made, and although the mechanical story might give an account of some of the necessary conditions of such performances, it is difficult to see how it could ever serve as a sufficient explanation of them.

THOUGHT. The same general critique concerning neglect of epistemological criteria must be made of Hobbes's treatment of thought, which he equated with movements of some substance in the head. There may be movements in the brain that are necessary conditions of thought, but no description of such conditions should be confused with what is meant by "thought." We do speak of "the movement of thought," but this is a description of transitions, as from premises to conclusions or from problems to solutions, not of movements explicable in terms of mechanical laws.

Hobbes's mechanical theory was distinctive in that

he extended the Galilean system in two directions:

into geometry at one end,

and into psychology and politics at the other.

Even though Hobbes's general account of thought was rather hamstrung by his obsession with mechanics, he nevertheless had some quite illuminating things to say about trains of thought, an account that owed more to Aristotle than to Galileo. Hobbes distinguished "unguided" thought from that directed by a passionate thought or plan. Unguided thought followed principles that later came to be called principles of association—for example, spatiotemporal contiguity and similarity. Hobbes, however, made no attempt to formulate principles of this kind. He was much more interested in, and attached much more importance to, guided thought, in which desire for an end holds the train of thought together and determines the relevance of its content.

Hobbes distinguished two main types of regulated thinking. The first was the classic Aristotelian case of deliberation, where desire provides the end, and the means to this end are traced back until something is reached that is in a person's power to do. This faculty of invention is shared by the animals, but they do not share the other sort of guided thinking that Hobbes called prudence. In prudence the starting place is an action that is in a person's power to perform, and the store of past experience is used to speculate on its probable effects. In this case, deliberation leads forward to an end that is either desired or feared. Hobbes seemed to think that people's prudence is in proportion to the amount of past experience on which they can draw. This sounds improbable, for although children cannot be prudent, many old people miss the relevance of their past experience.

DREAMS. Dreams fascinated Hobbes. He attempted to determine what distinguishes them from waking thoughts and to develop a mechanical theory to explain them. He claimed that they lack coherence because they lack the thought of an end to guide them. Dreams consist of compounded phantasms of past sensations, for "in the silence of sense there is no new motion from the objects, and therefore no new phantasm." Dreams are clearer than the imaginations of waking men because of the predominance of internal motion in the absence of external stimulation. There is no sense of time in dreams, and nothing appears surprising or absurd.

There is an intimate connection between dreams and bodily states. Lying cold, for instance, produces dreams of fear and raises the image of a fearful object. The motions pass both from the brain to the inner parts and from the inner parts to the brain. So, just as anger causes overheating in some parts of the body, overheating of the same parts can cause anger and, with it, the picture of an enemy. Dreams are thus the reverse of waking imaginations. Motion begins at one end during waking life and at the other end during sleep. This tendency to project images produced by bodily states gives rise to belief in apparitions and visions. Hobbes's treatment of dreams typified his approach to such matters. He seemed uninterested in the epistemological questions to which they give rise, as, for instance, in the thought of his contemporary, Descartes.

PASSIONS. Hobbes's mechanical theory of human action hinged on his concept of "endeavour," by means of which he tried to show how the gross movements of the body in desire and aversion could be explained in terms of minute unobservable motions in the body. He postulated two sorts of motion in the body. The first is its vital motion, manifest in such functions as circulation of the blood, breathing, and nutrition, which proceeds without external stimulation or the help of the imagination. The second is animal motion, which is equivalent to such voluntary movements as walking and speaking. This is always "first fancied in our minds" and is produced by the impact of external stimuli on the sense organs, an impact that gives rise both to phantasms in the brain and to internal motions that impinge on the vital motions of the heart. If the motion of the blood is helped, this is felt as pleasure; if it is impeded, as pain. Pleasure, Hobbes said, is "nothing really but

motion about the heart, as conception is nothing but motion in the head." In the case of pleasure, the spirits—which were thought of as vaporous substances flowing through the tubes of the nerves—are guided, by the help of the nerves, to preserve and augment the motion. When this endeavor tends toward things known by experience to be pleasant, it is called appetite; when it shuns what is painful, it is called aversion. Appetite and aversion are thus the first endeavors of animal motion. We talk about "will" when there is deliberation before acting, for will is "the last appetite in deliberating."

Hobbes's theory of the passions was an attempt to graft the traditional Aristotelian account of them onto his crude mechanical base. Love and hate are more or less the same as appetite and aversion, the only difference being that they require the actual presence of the object, whereas appetite and aversion presuppose its absence. These, together with joy and grief, which both involve foresight of an end rather than just an immediately perceived object, are the simple passions out of which others are compounded. Social life is a race for precedence that has no final termination save death. "So that in the first place, I put for a general inclination of all mankind, a perpetual and restless striving of power after power, that ceaseth only in death." To endure in the race requires foresight and scheming; to fail to compete is to die. A man who is convinced that his own power is greater than that of others is subject to what Hobbes called glory; its opposite is humility or dejection. Pity is grief for the calamity of another, arising from imagination that a like calamity may befall ourselves. Laughter is the expression of sudden glory caused by something new and unexpected in which we discover some superiority to others in ourselves.

Hobbes also introduced motion into his theory of individual differences. He thought that such differences are derivative from differences in passions and in the ends to which men are led by appetite, as well as to the sluggishness or agility of the animal spirits involved in the vital motions of their respective bodies.

The basic difficulty in understanding Hobbes's theory of motivation arises from his attempt to underpin a psychology derived from introspection, from the shrewd observation of others, and from the tradition going back to Aristotle with a mechanical theory whose outline was only very briefly sketched. Perhaps the essential criticism of any such theory is that actions cannot be analyzed into mere movements because, in any action proper—as distinct from a nervous tic or a reflex—the movements take place because of an end that the person has in mind. This end is what makes the action one of a certain sort, and, provided that the movements are directed toward this end, an almost indefinite range of movements can form part of the same action. Similarly, the movements involved in raising one's hand can form part of quite different actions, depending on the purpose for which the hand is raised—for example, to signal, to test the direction of the wind, to stretch the muscles, and so on.

Having something in mind—which is part of the concept of "action"—is not a movement, still less a movement of some internal substance of the head, if this is what Hobbes really believed. But Hobbes was not at all clear on the relationship between movements, whether observable or unobservable, and the cognitive components of appetites, aversions, and the various passions. Indeed, he seems to have held an extremely paradoxical and overintellectualistic view about the cognitive component of the passions. For he saw that passions are to be distinguished by their objects and by the judgment of the possibility of attaining such objects, yet he injected into his account a bizarre kind of egocentricity. For Hobbes, in all cases of passions the notion of "self" was part of the content of cognition. He seemed to think that all such "phantasms" of objects, by reference to which the passions are to be distinguished, involve the thought of ourselves doing something or of our power to do something. Pity is thus seen as grief arising from our imagining ourselves in the same predicament as that of the one pitied. Hobbes's analysis of laughter palpably suffered from the same injection of egocentricity. Furthermore, how the highly sophisticated and narcissistic type of appraisal involved in the passions is to be reconciled with any attempt to represent them all as movements of the body and of some internal substance in the head is very difficult to determine.

For all its ambiguities, oversights, and obvious defects, Hobbes's psychology was remarkable, for he attempted to establish it as an objective study untrammeled by theological assumptions. To suggest that man is a machine was a great step forward in thought. Even though the hypothesis is probably untenable, it marked the beginning of the effort to use scientific methods and objective concepts in the sphere of human behavior. In the seventeenth century this was a novel undertaking, as well as a dangerous one.

Ethics

Hobbes thought that, by employing the resolutive method, he could demonstrate the absolute necessity of leagues and covenants and the rudiments of moral and civil prudence from his two principles of human nature—"the one arising from the concupiscible part, which desires to appropriate to itself the use of those things in which all others have a joint interest; the other proceeding from the rational which teaches every man to fly a contranatural dissolution, as the greatest mischief that can arrive to nature." These two principles underlie Hobbes's account of the personal good, as well as his account of civil duty.

Hobbes was scornful of the notion that "good" and "evil" name any metaphysical essence. These words are "ever used with relation to the person that useth them: there being nothing simply and absolutely so; nor any common rule of good and evil, to be taken from the nature of the objects themselves." They name objects of our desires and aversions. We call a horse "good," for instance, because it is "gentle, strong, and carrieth a man easily." The desires of the individual determine what qualities are selected to furnish the ground for saying that an object is good.

Hobbes introduced a further refinement of this theory when he contrasted short-term goods with long-term goods. "Reason," he said, "declaring peace to be good, it follows by the same reason, that all the necessary means to peace be good also." This he contrasted with the sway of irrational appetite, whereby men "greedily prefer the present good." He thought that a man might not desire peace at a particular moment when influenced by some insistent desire; but when he sat down soberly in a cool hour, he would see that peace is a necessary condition of satisfying most of his desires in the long run. Thus, peace is something that he must desire both because of his fear of death and because of the other things he desires to do that a state of war would make impossible.

Hobbes was a nominalist, and he thought that all words have meaning, as if they were some kind of name. He did not see, as Berkeley seems to have seen a little later, that words like "good" have a prescriptive function and cannot be treated merely as if they were names. To say that something is good is to say that it is what it ought to be; it is to commend it. But also it implies that there are grounds for such commendation. It is to guide a person by suggesting grounds for his choice; it is not to order him or goad him. Hobbes saw that "good" is always thus connected with reasons, but he gave a very circumscribed account of what such reasons must be like, that is, characteristics of things desired. This was modified somewhat by what he said a man desires insofar as he uses his reason, that is, insofar as his "rational" as well as his "concupiscible" nature is involved. Hobbes's account of what a man desires would not be implausible if his account of human nature were acceptable, for then what men *must* desire could be predicted. But, if his account of human nature is rejected as oversimple, there cannot be quite such a tight connection as Hobbes suggested between "good" and what is, or will be, desired.

The connection is probably looser; given that words such as "good" have the practical function of guiding people's choices, it would be impossible to explain their effectiveness in this function if it were not generally the case that what was held up as good was something that people in general wanted. But it does not follow from this that any particular individual desires, or must desire, what is held up to him as good. Indeed, half the business of moral education consists in drawing people's attention to characteristics of things that they ought to desire but do not in fact desire.

Dreams fascinated Hobbes.

He attempted to determine what distinguishes them

from waking thoughts and to

develop a mechanical theory to explain them.

STATE OF NATURE AND LAWS OF NATURE. Morality is not concerned simply with the pursuit of personal good; it is also concerned with the acceptance of rules that limit the pursuit of good when it affects that of others. A tradition going back to the Stoics held that there was a small corpus of such rules, called the law of nature; these rules, which were universal preconditions of social life, did not depend, as do custom and law, on local circumstances. The Dutch jurist Grotius regarded this law of nature as a self-evident set of principles binding on all men (on kings as well as on their subjects) that would provide a rational basis for a system of international law; it was, he claimed, fundamental in the sphere of social rules in the same sort of way that Galileo's postulates were fundamental in the realm of nature. Morals could be brought within the expanding empire of the mathematical sciences.

Hobbes, therefore, was not original in his claim that "the true doctrine of the laws of nature is the true moral philosophy," nor was he original in likening its precepts to axioms. What was original was his claim that its precepts were axioms of prudence, insofar as "prudence" implies considerations limited to those that affect only the agent. For Grotius, the maintenance of society was a major need of man as a *social* animal, irrespective of purely private benefits. Hobbes, however, maintained that more or less the same set of rules that Grotius regarded as binding (such as keeping faith and fair dealing) could be shown to be axioms that must be accepted by any man who is both rational and afraid of death.

"All society, therefore, is either for gain or for glory; that is, not so much for love of our fellows as for love of ourselves."

Man, Hobbes argued, shuns death "by a certain impulsion of nature, no less than that whereby a stone moves downward." This is what saves man from anarchy and civilizes him, for if man were driven merely by his "concupiscible" part, there would be no society, and the life of man would be "solitary, poor, nasty, brutish, and short." Men are equal enough in body and mind to render negligible any palpable claims to superior benefits, and even the weakest is able to kill the strongest. But man's fear of death brings him up short in his pursuit of power and leads him to reflect upon the predicament of a state of nature. His reason tells him that peace is necessary for survival and also "suggesteth certain articles of peace, upon which men may be drawn to agreement. These articles are they, which otherwise are called the Laws of Nature." One of these laws is that "men perform their covenants made." In this way Hobbes claimed to demonstrate "the absolute necessity of leagues and covenants, and thence the rudiments both of moral and of civil prudence."

Hobbes's demonstration gave only the semblance of validity because he isolated the concupiscible and rational aspects of man's nature from each other and, as in a Galilean imaginary experiment, explored the consequences of each independently. Given only man's self-assertion, then there must be a state of nature; given only his overwhelming aversion to death, then he must accept the conditions necessary for avoiding death. These axioms of prudence are hypothetical in relation to man's assumed fear of death. They are rules that a rational man must accept insofar as he wants to avoid death. But men are only partly rational and, although they have an overwhelming fear of death, they also want other things, such as power and glory. Presumably Hobbes, like Machiavelli, could also have laid down rules for obtaining power and glory that would have borne no resemblance to the laws of nature. Thus, Hobbes could not have been trying to show that virtue, as defined by adherence to the laws of nature, is natural to man or a deduction from his nature, as have many thinkers who have adopted a psychological starting point. Indeed, the general relationship between Hobbes's psychology and his ethics is too obscure for us to know quite what he was doing.

The key to Hobbes's "demonstration" really lies in what he did with it, for he went on to point out that the laws of nature are only theorems that any rational man would accept. Since these laws need the backing of the sword to insure peace, men have need of a "common power to keep them in awe, and to direct their actions to the common benefit." The rationale of Hobbes's demonstration can now be seen, for at the time that Hobbes was writing, England was precariously poised between anarchy and civil disorder. Hobbes's analysis was a Galilean "resolution" of such a situation into the simple components of human nature that formed its basis. He pointed out that, insofar as men want peace and security (and all men do want this, although they want other things as well), then they must see that, human nature being what it is, there are certain means that they must accept if they are to have what they want. It is irrational to want something and yet to refuse to take the only means that will ensure that what is wanted is obtained. Since the acceptance of social rules is based only on the fear of death, it is only the fear of death that will ensure that these rules are obeyed. Men therefore cannot have the peace they all desire unless they accept the sword of the sovereign that will make death the consequence of breaking the rules that are a necessary condition of peace.

DETERMINISM AND FREE WILL. The indeterminate position of Hobbes's psychology in relation to his ethics was encouraged by his belief in determinism—or "necessitation," as he usually called it—which he outlined in his controversy with Bishop Bramhall. Hobbes denied that there is any power in men to which the term "will" refers; what is commonly called will is but the last desire in deliberating. Furthermore, he argued, only a man is properly called free, not his desires, will, or inclinations. The liberty of a man "consisteth in this, that he finds no stop, in doing what he has the will, desire, or inclination to do." Liberty is "the absence of all the impediments to action that are not contained in the nature and intrinsical quality of the agent." To speak of liberty is not to make any suggestions about the determinants or absence of determinants of man's deliberations or decisions; it is to suggest that man is not externally constrained in his actions. There is, therefore, no contradiction in saying that a man acts freely and that his actions are also determined. Since all actions have causes and thus are necessitated, it is pointless to use "free" in the sense of "free from necessitation," as distinct from "free from compulsion." There are no such actions, although we may think that there are because we are ignorant of the causes of actions.

There is much to be said for Hobbes's recommendation on the use of the word "free"; many others, such as Locke and Hume, have followed him in confining it to the absence of constraint on a man's actions. But Hobbes's claim that all actions are necessitated is not so straightforward. Certainly he was right in suggesting that all actions are explicable—if that is what is meant by saying that they have causes—but so many different things can count as causes, ranging from deliberation

and understanding to a stab of pain or a crack on the skull. Since Hobbes thought of man as a natural machine, he therefore viewed all causes as mechanical pushes. His doctrine carried the suggestion that the behavior of men is not only explicable but also somehow unavoidable because men's decisions and choices are simply manifestations of internal pushes.

Significantly enough, Bramhall did not object to Hobbes's doctrine insofar as it related to actions shared with animals or to spontaneous actions. What he could not allow was that voluntary actions, which follow on election and deliberation, should also be "necessitated." Bramhall pointed out the difficulties of likening actions and the grasp of objects and of means of obtaining them, which are inseparable from the concept of "action," to processes in nature explicable in terms of antecedent motions. In this contention Bramhall was substantially right, for although actions may involve movements, they are not reducible to movements.

Hobbes also disagreed with Bramhall on the implications of his doctrine of "necessitation" for moral judgments and for the operation of the law. Bramhall argued that if human actions are necessitated, then praise and blame, reward and punishment, are both unjust and vain. To the charge that they are vain, Hobbes replied that they are to be viewed as further determinants of choice. Praise and blame, reward and punishment "do by example make and conform the will to good and evil." To the charge of injustice, Hobbes argued that "the law regardeth the will and no other precedent causes of action"; also that punishments annexed to breaches of the law function as deterrents and necessitate justice. He went out of his way to distinguish punishment from acts of revenge or hostility and to stress its deterrent purpose, which is a sound position. Hobbes saw clearly that retribution is part of the meaning of punishment, but that it is the connection with authority that distinguishes it from other sorts of retributive acts. He also saw that, although retribution may be written into the meaning of punishment, its justification is not therefore necessarily retributive. Rather, it is to be justified for its preventive and deterrent function.

Political Philosophy

In his political philosophy Hobbes tried to conceptualize the relationship between the new nation-state, which had been emerging under the Tudors, and the individual citizen, who could no longer be regarded simply as having a set place in a divinely instituted order. In the old medieval society a man was bound by ties attaching to his status and by duties prescribed for him by the church. Tradition was the main form of social control, and traditions stretching back into the distant past assigned to a man his relatively fixed place in society. Aristotle's doctrine of natural kinds and natural places and his account of man as a social animal provided a fitting naturalistic foundation for the theological world view that was accepted by rulers and ruled alike. But with the rise of individualism and the social mobility that accompanied the rise of commerce and capitalism, this old conception of man in society no longer applied. Men had shaken off the ties of their guilds and local communities, and the new natural philosophy was beginning to render the naturalistic foundations of the former world view untenable.

Hobbes's picture of life as a race, in which we

"must suppose to have no other good,

nor other garland, but being foremost,"

was a gruesome caricature of an age

of individualism, restless competition,

and social mobility.

Hobbes's picture of life as a race, in which we "must suppose to have no other good, nor other garland, but being foremost," was a gruesome caricature of an age of individualism, restless competition, and social mobility. But if the fetters of tradition were being cast away, what other form of social control could take its place to prevent the anarchy of a state of nature? The answer was to be found, of course, in the increasing executive power of the state and in the growth of statute law, together with the development of the individual conscience, whereby regulation from within replaced the external authority of the Catholic church. Hobbes distrusted the anarchic tendencies of the individual conscience as much as he loathed the extramundane authority of the Church of Rome. Both were to be banished, along with traditional ties; civil society could be reconstructed as a simple mechanical system.

SOCIAL CONTRACT. Hobbes had a model ready at hand by means of which he might present his Galilean analysis of the rationale of civil society—the social contract theory. The social contract theory, despite its obvious flaws, was an attempt to rationalize political obligation, to substitute an intelligible bargain for mystifying appeals to tradition and divine right.

The contract theory was resorted to mainly by those who wanted to challenge the absolutist claims of monarchs, to uphold the claims of the common law, or to lay down some sort of moral limits on control and in-

terference by the central executive. Hobbes's feat was to employ this model to demonstrate that absolutism is the only possible logical outcome of consistent concern for individual interests. Indeed, he prided himself on grounding the authority of sovereigns, as well as the liberty and duty of subjects, upon axioms of human nature rather than on tradition and supernatural authority. In his attitude toward tradition and divine right, he was at one with the defenders of government by consent. But because of his overriding concern for security, and because of his rather depressing estimate of human nature, he came to the somewhat gleeful conclusion—highly displeasing to those who believed in government by consent—that absolutism could be the only rationally defensible form of government.

Hobbes did not seriously consider the social contract, as some did, as a quasi-historical hypothesis on how civil society might have come into existence. In his account the contract was featured as a framework for a Galilean resolution of civil society into its simple elements. Hobbes imagined the individual in a state of nature as having an unlimited right to "protect his life and members" and "to use all the means, and do all the actions, without which he cannot preserve himself." But he also has a right to all things "to do what he would, and against whom he thought fit, and to possess, use, and enjoy all that he would, or could get." Hobbes here was employing a very strange concept of right, for usually, when we talk about a right, we are indicating a rule that protects or should protect a person from interference in the doing of something that he might want to do. Hobbes, however, used the term in this way to talk about both what a person is entitled to do (when it is correlative with duties of noninterference on the part of others) and what a person cannot be obliged to renounce. When Hobbes declared that men have a "right of self-preservation," he meant not that an individual is entitled by some rule (of law, tradition, or morals) to life but that he cannot be obliged to renounce it because it is psychologically impossible for him to do so. "Natural rights" therefore have a quite different meaning in Hobbes's writing than in the works of Locke, Pufendorf, and other such defenders of natural rights. In these classical theories, natural rights are interests protected by natural law against the interference of others. Hobbes's natural-law theory is not connected in this way with his rather bizarre concept of natural rights.

Hobbes's "rights" of nature are derivative from man's tendency to assert himself and to seek power. But, as already shown, Hobbes held that man would also be driven by his fear of death to accept certain laws of nature, the second of which prescribed that every man should lay down his right to all things and "be contented with so much liberty against other men, as he would allow other men against himself." This could be done either by not interfering with others' enjoyment of their rights or by transferring one's right to another, in which case the transferrer is obliged not to hinder the recipient. Injustice consists in hindering a person whom it is a duty not to hinder. The mutual transferring of such rights is called a contract, and the third law of nature is "that men perform their covenants made."

COMMONWEALTH. Hobbes deduced a mutual transfer of rights from his postulate of rational action under the impetus of fear. But men are not yet safe, for there may be danger in keeping covenants and it may be, on occasion, in people's interest to break them. "And covenants, without the sword, are but words, and of no strength to secure a man at all." Matters must be arranged so that it will never be in anyone's interest to break covenants, which cannot exist where there is no "common power" to enforce them. Thus, a social contract must be presumed in which it is *as if* every man should say to every other man, "I authorize and give up my right of governing myself, to this man, or to this assembly of men, on this condition, that thou give up thy right to him, and authorize all his actions in like manner." This contract unites the multitude into one people and marks the generation of "that great Leviathan, or rather, to speak more reverently, of that mortal God, to which we owe under the immortal God, our peace and defence." The definition of commonwealth is, therefore, "one person, of whose acts a great multitude, by mutual covenants one with another, have made themselves every one the author, to the end he may use the strength and means of them all, as he shall think expedient, for their peace and common defence." The person that results is called sovereign, and everyone else is his subject. The sovereign is created by the contract but is not party to it. Thus, the people rule even in monarchies; a multitude becomes a people by having some device, such as that of representation, by means of which decisions binding on all are made on behalf of all. Some such "covenant" is implicit in speaking of a commonwealth as a people, as distinct from a multitude of men.

Up to this point there is much to be said for the sort of analysis that Hobbes gave, although some of its details are peculiar. He had considerable insight into the sort of thing we mean when we speak of a civil society, as distinct from a mere multitude of men. He saw clearly that societies are not natural wholes like toads, turnips, or colonies of termites. They exist because individuals act in accordance with rules that can be rejected, broken, or altered; they are artificial wholes. Therefore, if we are to speak of the "will" or "decision" of such an entity, there must be some higher-order rules of procedure, such as that of representation, by reference to which what is to count as a corporate decision is constituted. Individuals or groups of individuals are put in authority for such a purpose.

Hobbes saw clearly that societies are not natural wholes like toads, turnips, or colonies of termites. They exist because individuals act in accordance with rules that can be rejected, broken, or altered; they are artificial wholes.

When Hobbes proceeded to the more concrete details of what must constitute the duties of rulers and subjects, however, he was not equally convincing, for this next step depended on his questionable account of human nature. The basic principle of human nature revealed by his Galilean resolution was "that the dispositions of men are naturally such that, except they be restrained through fear of some coercive power, every man will dread and distrust each other." No motive in human nature, except the fear of death, is strong enough to counteract the disruptive force of man's self-assertion. The fear of death must, therefore, be the explanation of the existence of civil society (insofar as there is a social order and not anarchy), and security must be the sole reason for the institution of the social order; there is simply no other reason for which men could be induced to give up their natural right to self-assertion. Since this is the sole reason for having a commonwealth, it follows logically that a commonwealth must be devised that will accomplish the end for which it exists. Sovereignty must be perpetual, undivided, and absolute, for to divide or limit sovereignty would be to risk anarchy; and such limitation would be illogical because it would be inconsistent with the *raison d'être* of sovereignty. *Salus populi suprema lex* ("The safety of the people is the supreme law"). Moreover, complete safety entails complete submission to an absolute sovereign. Thus, absolutism is the logical consequence of government by consent, once the real interest of individuals, which is the presupposition of the institution of commonwealth, has been clearly understood.

There are two obvious flaws in this stage of Hobbes's argument. The first is the assumption that the desire for security, deriving from the fear of death, is the sole reason for the institution of commonwealth, a reason that Hobbes more or less wrote into the meaning of "commonwealth." It is obviously a very important reason, but that it should be the only reason is plausible only if Hobbes's psychology were to be accepted. Even so, Hobbes should not have written the reason for instituting a commonwealth into what is *meant* by "commonwealth." The second flaw was well brought out by Locke, who argued that, even if security were the sole reason for the institution of commonwealth, absolute authority is a dangerous expedient from the point of view of individual interest. For the hypothesis is that the timid individual would exchange the possible threat to life presented by 100,000 men, all of whom individually might attack him, for the threat to his life made possible by the arbitrary authority of one man who has 100,000 men under his command. "Are men so foolish that they take care to avoid what mischiefs may be done them by polecats or foxes, but are content, nay think it safety, to be devoured by lions?"

Hobbes was led to his advocacy of undivided sovereignty by his interest in constitutional and legal matters. When Hobbes was writing, there was a clash between the higher-order principles of common law and of statute law. The common-law principle that custom, as interpreted by the judges, is to be consulted in declaring what the law is, existed alongside the principle of statute law, that rules laid down by a determinate body or person (for example, Parliament or the king) determine what the courts must recognize as valid law. Statute law was on the increase during this period, and it was intolerable to any clearheaded man that these two principles should operate side by side. Hobbes advocated the unambiguous supremacy of the principle of statute law and the abolition of common law. The need to introduce clarity and coherence into the confused constitutional situation that prevailed in Hobbes's time was obvious enough. But for Hobbes to suggest that it was a logical truth that there must be an absolute sovereign in any commonwealth was to introduce dubious logical deductions into a field where a solution was more likely to be found by practical adjustments and compromises that reflected the strength of competing interests and were consonant with deep-seated traditions.

One of the traditions that Hobbes's geometric solution ignored was that of the liberty of the subject. In Hobbes's view, civil liberty lay "only in those things, which in regulating their actions, the sovereign hath praetermitted." It is unlikely, Hobbes suggested, that laws would be necessary to regulate buying and selling, and choice of abode, diet, a wife, a trade, and education. But whether such laws are necessary is entirely up to the sovereign. The liberty of the subject also consists in the lack of proscription of such acts that it would be vain to forbid because they are psychologically impossible for the subject to refrain from committing. These

acts involve the right of the subject to preserve himself and to resist imprisonment. Hobbes also suggested that "in the act of submission consisteth both our obligation, and our liberty." Both the obligation and the liberty are to derive from the words "I authorize all his actions," which the subject is imagined to have expressed in instituting a commonwealth. The subject is released from his obligation only if the sovereign fails to do what he is there to do, namely, to guarantee security. This marks the extent of the subject's much-lauded "right to resist." Presumably Hobbes meant to stress that subjects submit voluntarily to authority. This is true enough, but what it has to do with the liberty of the subject, in any straightforward sense of "liberty," is difficult to grasp.

LAW. Hobbes's concept of the role of natural law, once the law of the state had been established, was not altogether clear. He maintained that the laws of nature were "but conclusions, or theorems concerning what conduceth to the conservation and defence of themselves; whereas law, properly, is the word of him that by right hath command over others. But yet, if we consider the same theorems, as delivered in the word of God, that by right commandeth all things; then they are properly called laws." These "laws" always obligate *in foro interno*—that is, in matters of private conscience—in prescribing a general readiness of mind; but *in foro externo,* that is, in actions, the laws may not be obligatory if certain conditions, such as peace and security, are absent. Such conditions, when present, will in fact render it to the interest of the subject that he follow the laws of nature. A law properly so called always obligates *in foro externo* because of its source in the command of the sovereign, as well as because civil society, by definition, provides the conditions of security and the sanction that will make it always against a man's interest to disobey it. But do the laws of nature oblige *in foro externo,* if not incorporated in the civil law, when the security of civil society prevails? This depends on how seriously Hobbes meant his reference to theorems as authoritative edicts from God, for such derivation would give them a determinate source, as in the case of laws properly so called. Some take Hobbes seriously and claim that he really thought that the laws of nature oblige *in foro externo* as well as *in foro interno* whenever conditions of security prevail. Others hold that Hobbes never really thought that laws of nature oblige in a full sense *in foro externo* because his reference to their authoritative source is but a tactful concession to piety. He really thought of them merely as axioms of reason that oblige in a full sense only when they are issued by a temporal sovereign as commands and when conditions of security, together with sanctions, prevail in civil society.

Hobbes took this somewhat ambiguous view about the status of natural laws (or moral precepts) because of his extreme hardheadedness about laws properly so called. Law, he held, is the *command* of the sovereign, "the word of him that by right hath command over others." It is authority, not conformity with custom or reason, that makes a law. In this forthright view he was attacking the fiction of the common law that the law was there to be discovered, immanent in the customs of the people.

Whatever the merits of Hobbes's view—later adopted by the analytic school of John Austin—that laws are commands, Hobbes made a valuable contribution in helping to distinguish questions about law that are often confused. The question "What is a law?" should be distinguished from such other questions as "Is the law equitable or reasonable?" and "What makes a law valid?" Hobbes argued that a law is simply a rule issued by someone in authority. Whether it is reasonable or equitable is a further question, as are the questions of its validity, of its conformity with custom, and of the grounds on which a man could be obliged to obey it.

To claim that laws are *commands* was an oversimple and misleading way to bring out the prescriptive force of laws. But it was useful insofar as it connected law with authority, for laws, like commands, are utterances issuing from people in authority. In stressing the necessary connection between law and authority, Hobbes made an important contribution to political philosophy, for there is no necessary connection between authority and moral precepts or "laws of nature."

On the question of the person or body of men by whose authority laws should be made, Hobbes was more open-minded than is often realized. He thought that this was not a matter that could be demonstrated; it was a matter of factual argument. He believed that the relative advantages of each form of government had to be considered in the light of the sole end of security. It was a factual matter which type of government was most likely to promote such an end. On the whole, he argued, monarchy is preferable because it is more likely to be undivided, strong, and wise.

Religion

At the time Hobbes wrote, ethics and politics were inseparable from religion. Even the Royal Society was founded by men who believed that science would reveal more of the details of God's creation and thus enhance his worship. Hobbes was one of the pioneers in the process of distinguishing religious questions from other sorts. He rigorously excluded theology from philosophy and tried to map the proper domains of faith and knowledge. He outlined a theory of the causes of religion and superstition and discussed the grounds of religious belief, and he conducted an elaborate inquiry into the use of various terms in the Scriptures. But all this analysis and theorizing was subordinate to his main interest in religion as a possible source of civil discord. It is seldom realized that more than half of *Leviathan* is concerned with religious matters, with Hobbes trying to defend the "true religion" from both Catholicism and the priesthood of all believers. He saw clearly that these doctrines were two of the main obstacles in the way of the absolutism that he advocated.

Hobbes made some interesting speculations about the natural causes of religion, which he said were "these four things, opinion of ghosts, ignorance of second causes, devotion toward what men fear, and taking of things casual for prognostics. . . ." These seeds of religion could be cultivated according to natural invention, which leads to superstition and nature worship, or according to God's commandments. "Fear of power invisible, feigned by the mind, or imagined from tales publicly allowed, religion; not allowed, superstition. And when the power imagined is truly such as we imagine, true religion."

NOTION OF GOD. What, then, constituted true religion for Hobbes? To reasonable men, God's commands amounted to the laws of nature. God's nature, however, was a much more baffling matter, even for a rational man. Certainly God must have "existence," which Hobbes took to be an attribute of God, in spite of his remarks elsewhere about the ambiguities of the verb "to be." In *Leviathan* Hobbes held that God is the cause of the world, "that is, a first and an eternal cause of all things; which is that which men mean by the name of God." In his later *De Corpore,* however, he indicated the difficulties in the notion of an unmoved mover. This was a difficult question for philosophers to determine and had better be handed over for decision to the lawful authorities. Hobbes also stressed God's irresistible power and maintained that the only solution to the problem of evil was to be found in this power. Did not God reply to Job: "Where wast thou, when I laid the foundations of the earth?" Job had not sinned; his suffering was an unfortunate consequence of God's manifestation of power.

The main function of reason, however, is to show what God cannot be—at ease, finite, figured, having parts, occupying a place, moved or at rest, plural, and having passions, rational appetite, sight, knowledge, and understanding. If we rely on natural reason, we must either qualify God in a negative way by adjectives, such as "infinite" and "incomprehensible," or by a superlative, such as "most high," and an indefinite, such as "holy," which are not really descriptions of his nature but expressions of our admiration. Thus, rational disputations about the nature of God are pointless and a dishonor to him, "for in the attributes which we give to God, we are not to consider the signification of philosophical truth; but the signification of pious intention, to do him the greatest honour we are able." The sovereign, therefore, must decide on God's attributes; and public, uniform worship must be instituted.

REASON AND REVELATION. Reason, however, should not be "folded up in the napkin of an implicit faith, but employed in the purchase of justice, peace, and true religion." There is nothing in God's word contrary to reason. We must, however, be prepared in this world "to captivate our understanding to the words; and not to labour in sifting out a philosophical truth by logic, of such mysteries as are not comprehensible, nor fall under any rule of natural science." Reason should be kept very much to the fore when one is confronted with those who claim revelation, for if a man says that God spoke to him in a dream, this "is no more than to say he dreamed that God spoke to him." There are psychological explanations of such phenomena that cast doubt on their reliability as valid communications with God.

Dreams, visions, and inspiration, however, should not be dismissed altogether, for it is by such means that prophets have been informed of the will of God. What is needed are criteria for detecting true prophets. Hobbes suggested two necessary criteria: the working of miracles and the teaching of doctrines not at variance with those already established. Since miracles had by then ceased, there was no sign left to single out true prophets. And, in any case, the Scriptures, since the time of Jesus, had taken the place of prophecy.

Reliance on the Scriptures, Hobbes realized, is not altogether straightforward. Even supposing that it could be decided which books are authentic, and that the sovereign, by his authority, could make their teaching law, there is still the problem of what many of the terms used in the Scriptures mean. Hobbes went through most of the key terms in the Scriptures, giving meaning to them in a way consistent with his mechanical theory. He argued, for instance, that God must have a body and that the proper signification of "spirit" in common speech is either a subtle, fluid, and invisible body or a ghost or other idol or phantasm of the imagination; it may also have a figurative use in such a phrase as "spirit of wisdom." "Angels" signify images raised in the mind to indicate the presence of God. Hobbes made acute remarks about the nature of miracles that mingled rad-

ical probing with subtle irony (indeed, one often wonders whether his whole treatment of "the true religion" is not a colossal piece of irony).

Hobbes concluded Leviathan *with his famous section on the Kingdom of Darkness, in which he castigated superstition and Catholicism as enemies of the true religion.*

On the relationship between church and state, Hobbes of course adopted an uncompromising Erastian position. A church he defined as "a company of men professing Christian religion, united in the person of one sovereign, at whose command they ought to assemble, and without whose authority they ought not to assemble." There is, therefore, no universal church to which all Christians owe allegiance, for there is no supreme sovereign over all nations.

Hobbes concluded *Leviathan* with his famous section on the Kingdom of Darkness, in which he castigated superstition and Catholicism as enemies of the true religion. The papacy, he remarked "is no other than the ghost of the deceased Roman empire, sitting crowned upon the grave thereof." The papacy ruthlessly exploits the fears of ignorant men to perpetuate the power of unscrupulous priests as a rival to the secular power.

Hobbes held that there is only one article of faith necessary for salvation: that Jesus is the Christ. On what authority did such a belief rest? Hobbes had some interesting things to say about the difference between knowledge and faith. The object of both is propositions, but in the case of knowledge we consider the proposition and call to mind what its terms signify. Truth here is a matter largely of following the consequences of our definitions. But when reasons for assent derive "not from the proposition itself but from the person propounding, whom we esteem so learned that he is not deceived, and we see no reason why he should deceive us; our assent, because it grows not from any confidence of our own, but from another man's knowledge, is called faith." Faith, therefore, depends on our trust in a man rather than on our grasp of truth. The faith that Jesus is the Christ must therefore come from the Scriptures and our trust in those who wrote them. But who is to interpret them? "Christian men do not know, but only believe the Scripture to be the word of God." St. Paul said, "Faith cometh by hearing," and that, according to Hobbes, means listening to our lawful pastors, who are appointed by the sovereign to interpret the Scriptures for us. Charles II and Cromwell must have been flattered by the magnitude of the problems on which they were required to issue authoritative edicts: the creation of the world, God's attributes, the authenticity of miracles, and the proper interpretation of the Scriptures. Hobbes regarded religion more as a matter of law than of truth.

Hobbes's treatment of religion leaves obscure exactly what he himself thought about such matters. His technique was always to push radical probing to the limit, and when the basis for the traditional doctrines seemed about to be cut away, the sovereign was summoned as a sort of *deus ex machina* to put everything in its orthodox place. Hobbes was obviously extremely skeptical about what could be demonstrated in the sphere of religion, but it is difficult to say whether his suggestion that the sovereign should pronounce on such matters as the creation of the world and the attributes of God was a subtle piece of irony, a pious protestation to protect himself against the charge of atheism, or yet another manifestation of his overwhelming conviction that there must be nothing touching the peace of the realm that the sovereign should not decide.

BIBLIOGRAPHY

Works by Hobbes

English Works of Thomas Hobbes, 11 vols., and *Opera Philosophica* (Latin works), 5 vols., Sir William Molesworth, ed. London, 1839–1845; reprinted Oxford, 1961. All quotations in the text of this article are from this edition of the English works.

The Elements of Law, Natural and Political, Ferdinand Tönnies, ed. London, 1928. This also includes extracts from the *Little Treatise, or A Short Tract on First Principles and Excerpta de Tractatu Optico.*

Leviathan, Michael Oakeshott, ed. Oxford, 1947; New York, 1962. Latter is paperback with introduction by Richard S. Peters.

Body, Mind, and Citizen, Richard S. Peters, ed. New York, 1962. Paperback, with introduction by Peters, that contains selections from the Molesworth and Tönnies editions.

Works on Hobbes

Aubrey, John, *Brief Lives,* E. O. Dick, ed. London, 1950. Contains biography of Hobbes.

Brandt, Frithiof, *Thomas Hobbes' Mechanical Conception of Nature,* translated by Vaughan Maxwell and Annie I. Fausbøll. London, 1928.

Laird, John, *Hobbes.* New York and London, 1934.

Peters, Richard S., *Hobbes.* Harmondsworth, England, 1956. Paperback.

Robertson, G. C., *Hobbes.* London and Edinburgh, 1886.

Stephen, Leslie, *Hobbes.* London, 1904.

Strauss, Leo, *The Political Philosophy of Thomas Hobbes.* New York and London, 1936; Chicago, 1963. The 1963 edition is paperback.

Warrender, J. H., *The Political Philosophy of Thomas Hobbes.* New York and London, 1957.

Watkins, John W. N., *Hobbes's System of Ideas.* London, 1965.

— R. S. PETERS

HOBBES, THOMAS (UPDATE)

Thomas Hobbes became the subject of a great increase in the rate of publications after 1967, an increase that is largely attributable to the three hundredth anniversary of his death, marked in 1979, and the four hundredth anniversary of his birth, marked in 1988. The second of these saw the establishment of *Hobbes Studies,* a journal devoted to Hobbes, though the International Hobbes Association and its newsletter were established some years earlier. Interest in Hobbes's work—though more low-key—had existed beforehand.

Of the work done on Hobbes since 1967,

most has been concerned with

his moral and political philosophy.

The interest in Hobbes expressed itself not only in new writings about him but also in new editions of his work and the publication of some of his previously unpublished work. The major project of producing the Clarendon edition of Hobbes's works, begun by Howard Warrender, received a setback with his death in 1985 after only two volumes were completed, but an editorial board was set up to carry on the work. The first English translation of part of *De Homine* appeared in 1972, and Jones's translation of *Thomas White's De Mundo Examined* appeared in 1976.

Little has been added to our detailed knowledge of the events of Hobbes's life. Miriam M. Reik published *The Golden Lands of Thomas Hobbes,* an intellectual biography, and Arnold Rogow published *Thomas Hobbes: Radical in the Service of Reaction.* But the most interesting source to read on the subject remains Aubrey (1898).

Of the work done on Hobbes since 1967, most has been concerned with his moral and political philosophy. Other aspects of his work have not been completely ignored: Maurice Goldsmith's *Hobbes's Science of Politics* (1966) encouraged concern with Hobbes's ideas of science and scientific method, and J. W. N. Watkins's *Hobbes's System of Ideas* argued that Hobbes's argument was intended to move smoothly all the way from his philosophical ideas to his political theory. Thomas Spragens's *The Politics of Motion* concerned itself with the relationship between Hobbes's ideas about cosmology and his ideas about politics. Similar issues have been of interest to Richard Tuck in some of his papers. Very few publications dealt with Hobbes's views on scientific matters just for their own sake, though a notable exception was Shapin and Schaffer's *Leviathan and the Air Pump*, an account of the dispute between Hobbes and Boyle about the value of the experimental method.

The most influential book on Hobbes since 1967 has probably been David Gauthier's *The Logic of Leviathan* (1969). This book led the reaction to Warrender's interpretation of Hobbes, which was until then the most generally accepted interpretation. Gauthier introduced into discussion of Hobbes's moral theory the use of game theory, starting from the idea that "Hobbes takes seriously . . . the supposition that . . . all men are naturally selfish" (p. 90); then, working from the further claim that, on Hobbes's account, "both rights and obligations must have a prudential foundation" (p. 93), Gauthier constructed a Hobbesian argument that rational people must set up a sovereign if they are to achieve their own advantage and concludes that the Hobbesian "moral" system is nothing more than universal prudence (p. 98). Despite the work of Bernard Gert (in, for example, "Hobbes and Psychological Egosim," 1967) designed to show that Hobbes did not, in fact, regard people as naturally selfish, this general approach to Hobbes achieved great popularity and for some time was the received approach. Jean Hampton employed the games-theoretical approach to interpreting Hobbes in its finest detail in *Hobbes and the Social Contract Tradition* (1986). She did purport to be interpreting Hobbes, making the undefended claim that there is nothing anachronistic in using modern games theory to elucidate Hobbes and going on to say that "Euclid would feel himself vindicated rather than violated if his faulty proofs were corrected so that his conclusions could be derived from his axioms, and Hobbes would feel the same" (p. 137). But better arguments are not the same as the arguments they are better than; in fact, the games-theoretic versions of Hobbes's arguments cannot be what Hobbes actually intended.

Many people writing of Hobbes in the games-theoretic school do not claim to be arguing for an interpretation of Hobbes's text but simply use Hobbes as a starting point. This is true, for example, of Gregory Kavka's *Hobbesian Moral and Political Theory*, a very popular member of the games-theoretic set that makes the point explicit at the start. This is also true of many of the attempts to sort out a Hobbesian model for the study of international affairs, a move that has shared with the games-theoretic approach the assumption that the strong form of Hobbes's condition of mere nature is at least a coherent notion and can therefore constitute part of such a model.

Arguments against the prevailing games-theoretic interpretations of Hobbes came from Deborah Baumgold in *Hobbes's Political Theory* and R. E. Ewin in *Virtues and Rights* (1991), the latter arguing that the condition of mere nature is not a coherent notion and was intended by Hobbes as part of a *reductio* argument. Gert's work began a trend away from reading Hobbes as a psychological egoist (1967).

Work has been done, by Richard Tuck and others, on the historical Hobbes, most of it started off by Keith Thomas's "The Social Origins of Hobbes's Political Thought" and such writings of Quentin Skinner as "The Context of Hobbes's Theory of Political Obligation" (1966). More such work would be welcome. It has become common to distinguish between the "philosophers' Hobbes"—the Hobbes who saw himself as setting up a science of morality and of politics and as making a large part of his contribution to the debates by doing so—and "the historians' Hobbes"—the Hobbes who quite clearly saw himself as making a contribution to the debates about practical affairs of his time. Debates in the field of Hobbes scholarship will move further forward as these two strands come closer together again.

BIBLIOGRAPHY

Aubrey, J. *Brief Lives,* edited by E. O. Dick. London, 1950.
Chappell, V., ed. *Essays on Early Modern Philosophers: Thomas Hobbes.* New York, 1992.
Curley, E. "Reflections on Hobbes: Recent Work on His Moral and Political Philosophy," *Journal of Philosophical Research,* Vol. 15 (1990), 169–250.
Ewin, R. E. *Virtues and Rights: The Moral Philosophy of Thomas Hobbes.* Boulder, CO, 1991.
Gauthier, D. *The Logic of Leviathan.* Oxford, 1969.
Gert, B. "Hobbes and Psychological Egoism," *Journal of the History of Ideas,* Vol. 27 (1967), 503–20.
Goldsmith, M. M. *Hobbes's Science of Politics.* London, 1966.
Hampton, J. *Hobbes and the Social Contract Tradition.* Cambridge, 1986.
Skinner, Q. "The Context of Hobbes's Theory of Political Obligation," *Historical Journal,* Vol. 9 (1966), 286–317.
Zagorin, P. "Hobbes on Our Mind," *Journal of the History of Ideas,* Vol. 51, No. 2 (1990), 317–35.

– ROBERT E. EWIN

HUME, DAVID

David Hume (1711–1776), Scottish philosopher and historian, was born in Edinburgh. His father owned a

In the 1700s there existed a lack of contemporary minds capable of understanding Hume. (Corbis)

small estate called "Ninewells" near Berwick and was a distant cousin of the earl of Home. His mother, Katherine Falconer, came from a family of lawyers, and young Hume was steered toward this profession. But soon after leaving Edinburgh University at the age of 15, he conceived a dislike for the law and embarked on a course of intense study of his own devising, which eventually led to the formulation of a complete philosophical system, published anonymously in 1739 as *A Treatise of Human Nature.*

Hume was deeply disappointed at the reception of his revolutionary book. He expected fury and learned controversy; he received neglect, mockery, and incomprehension. Indeed, Immanuel Kant and Thomas Reid were probably the only contemporary philosophers capable of understanding Hume. Blaming his own literary inexperience, Hume published anonymously in 1740 *An Abstract of a Treatise of Human Nature* and in 1748 and 1751 respectively *Philosophical Essays concerning the Human Understanding* and *An Enquiry concerning the Principles of Morals. Philosophical Essays* was retitled *An Enquiry concerning the Human Understanding* in a 1758 edition. From 1748 on, Hume acknowledged author-

ship of all major works except the *Treatise* and the *Abstract.* In his advertisement to a later edition of the two *Enquiries,* Hume expressly desired that they and not the *Treatise* should be "regarded as containing his philosophical sentiments and principles."

The *Enquiries* differ from the *Treatise* in style, in the omission of a number of elaborate psychological speculations, particularly concerning space, time, and sense perception, and in the inclusion of chapters on miracles, providence, and the theological implications of the free-will problem, all of which Hume had omitted from the *Treatise* because of their openly antireligious tendency.

Hume made no further important contributions to philosophical literature, except the *Dialogues concerning Natural Religion,* published posthumously and probably written in the 1750s. The reasons for this were, first, the lack of contemporary minds capable of understanding Hume and stimulating him to further researches and, second, the fact that Hume's dominant passion was not scientific curiosity but, in his own words, "love of literary fame."

Having restated his philosophy to his own satisfaction, Hume sought literary fame in other fields, principally in history and secondarily in moral and political thought, including economics, in which he won a reputation during his lifetime comparable to that of his great friend Adam Smith.

Hume was never an academic, though he made two unsuccessful applications for chairs of philosophy, at Edinburgh and at Glasgow. He was a man of letters and to a lesser extent a man of affairs. His principal appointments were as secretary to General St. Clair from 1746 to 1749 on a military expedition to Brittany and a diplomatic mission to Turin; as keeper of the Advocates Library, Edinburgh, where he wrote his *History of Great Britain,* from 1752 to 1757; as private secretary to Lord Hertford, British ambassador in Paris, from 1763 to 1766, where for a time Hume was *chargé d'affaires;* and as undersecretary of state, Northern Department, from 1767 to 1768.

Hume was a deservedly popular figure in the literary world of the period. Sociable, witty, kind, ingenuous in his friendships, innocently vain, and devoid of envy, he was known to French friends as "le bon David," and in Scotland as "Saint David." He never married, though he had many women friends, and the manner in which he faced his death from cancer was a paradigm of cheerful philosophic acceptance of annihilation, in the ancient Epicurean tradition.

The Origins of the *Treatise*

Though one may, as Hume desired, judge his philosophy by the *Enquiries,* it is to the *Treatise* that one must look first in order to understand him. This work seems to have been conceived in a moment of inspiration when Hume was about eighteen. In a letter to a physician, dated 1734, Hume related that after long and unsatisfactory study of the various systems of philosophy, he felt a growing boldness of temper and sought for himself a "new medium by which truth might be established." At last "there seemed to be opened up to me a new scene of thought, which transported me beyond measure and made me, with an ardor natural to young men, throw up every other pleasure or business to apply entirely to it." After five years of this exertion, Hume was a sick young man—hence the letter to the physician. A change of occupation in a Bristol merchant's office helped him; and in a quiet retreat at La Flèche, in Anjou, where Hume stayed for three years, the book was finally completed, a long book, a young man's book, the outcome of eight years' intense intellectual labor.

We shall never know what the "new scene of thought" was. But we can identify the main currents in contemporary thought with which Hume was concerned and describe his response to them as presented in his completed work.

First, there was the influence of the great seventeenth-century rationalistic metaphysical systems of Hobbes, Descartes, Leibniz, Spinoza, and Malebranche. These thinkers all argued deductively, most of them professedly in the manner of Euclid, to prove the truth of sweeping propositions about the nature of the universe, God, and the human soul.

Second, there was the influence of Sir Isaac Newton, who by confining himself to hypotheses capable of being tested experimentally had shed immense light on the phenomena of nature. Newton's doctrines were taught in Edinburgh, around the time when Hume was a student, by two successive professors of mathematics, James Gregory and Colin Maclaurin.

Third, there was the influence of the British empiricist school of philosophy of Locke, Shaftesbury, Mandeville, Hutcheson, and Joseph Butler, in whose footsteps Hume professed to be following. These thinkers viewed with suspicion the grandiose systems of the Continental rationalists and sought by an unprejudiced examination of the faculties and principles of the human mind to establish the limits of our knowledge and the foundations of our duties.

Fourth, there was the influence of rationalistic systems of ethics, of which Samuel Clarke's provides the best example. Clarke combined an admiration for Newton with a completely a priori system of ethics, in which the principles of right and wrong that oblige not only men but God were held to be as self-evident or demonstrable as the propositions of Euclid.

Fifth, there were the great religious controversies of the preceding centuries, between Catholics and Protestants and, later, between theists and deists.

Finally, and closely connected with the religious controversies, there was the intense preoccupation of French thinkers with skepticism. This ancient discipline, rediscovered during the Renaissance in the text of Sextus Empiricus, aimed at the complete suspension of judgment, to be achieved by posing a counterargument to any argument that might be produced. Since the time of Montaigne, skepticism had been employed by Catholics and Reformers against one another, and since Descartes's unsuccessful attempt to silence it once and for all, its chief protagonist had been Pierre Bayle, one of Hume's favorite authors. Berkeley, generally regarded as a British empiricist, was not classed as such by Hume, but as a skeptic and a very powerful one.

Hume was deeply disappointed

at the reception of his revolutionary book,

A Treatise of Human Nature (1739).

He expected fury and learned controversy;

he received neglect, mockery, and incomprehension.

Hume's policy, both in the *Treatise* and in the *Enquiries*, was to apply the Newtonian experimental method to the British empiricists' investigations into the powers and principles of the human mind. The intended result was to be a truly experimental science of human nature. The findings of this science were to provide a touchstone by which the arbitrary hypotheses of the rationalist metaphysicians could be tested. In the youthful ardor of his introduction to the *Treatise*, Hume even promised "a complete system of the sciences, built on a foundation almost entirely new." But in Part IV of Book I of the *Treatise*, a new force appeared—skepticism. Hume first used skepticism to discomfort his enemies and then drew its fangs in order to live with it himself. But in the *Treatise* this approach was only hinted at; and in the final chapter of Book I Hume seemed distinctly frightened of his new tool. In the first *Enquiry* and the *Dialogues concerning Natural Religion* the policy is clearer. The main enemy in the *Enquiry* is not metaphysics but religion. The metaphysical jungle must be cleared, because it is a dangerous lurking place for superstition. Skeptical arguments are logically unanswerable but powerless against the natural sentiments and convictions that govern our judgment in daily life. They can, therefore, safely be used to tease the theologians and set them quarreling with one another ("Natural History of Religion") and to serve as an antidote to dogmatism and overcertainty of every kind. They offer no threat to common sense, to mathematics, to morals, or to the experimental sciences, all of which, unlike metaphysics, are protected by the force of the natural sentiments and convictions. Naturalism deprives the skeptic of his sting, and reconciles him with the experimental scientist.

Hume's Logic

PLAN OF THE *TREATISE*. According to Hume, the four main divisions of the science of man are "logic, morals, criticism, and politics." Logic, whose end is said to be to "explain the principles and operations of our reasoning faculty and the nature of our ideas," occupies Book I of the *Treatise* and the whole of the first *Enquiry*. Morals and politics occupy Book III of the *Treatise* and the second *Enquiry*. Criticism, by which Hume meant roughly what we should call aesthetics, is supposed to be covered in Book II of the *Treatise* ("Of the Passions") and in the dissertation "*On the Passions.*"

According to Hume,

the four main divisions of the science of man are

"logic, morals, criticism, and politics."

The main purpose of Book I of the *Treatise* is to establish empiricism as an empirical fact and thereafter to examine several metaphysical systems and philosophical problems. Hume's empiricism may be summed up in two propositions.

(1) All our ideas are derived from impressions of sense or inner feeling. That is, we cannot even conceive of things different in kind from everything in our experience.

(2) A matter of fact can never be proved by reasoning a priori. It must be discovered in, or inferred from, experience.

From these two propositions it follows that metaphysical systems telling us of the existence of God, the origin of the world, and other matters transcending human experience, have no meaning, and even if they had, could not be shown to be true.

There were two principal groups of concepts by means of which metaphysicians had claimed to transcend the limits of experience: space, time, number, geometry, and arithmetic, on the one hand; and cause and effect, force, energy, and necessity, on the other. Plato had argued from the unalterable exactitude of geometrical and arithmetical truths to the existence of intelligible forms more perfect than their approximations in the shifting world of sense. Leibniz argued from the infinite divisibility of space, and therefore of matter, to the unreality of both; for if infinitely divisible, they have no constituent parts, and the whole cannot exist without its parts. Only if the universe consists of an infinite number of indivisible souls, distinguished from one another solely by the differences in their ideas, and each mirroring the whole from a different point of view, can infinite divisibility and individuality be reconciled. The arguments based on causality were many and varied. Material things are plainly inert and inactive and therefore cannot cause anything, said Malebranche and Berkeley; therefore, the only true causes are spirits, finite and infinite. The cause, said Descartes, must possess at least as much reality as the effect. The cause of my idea of a Perfect Being is therefore a Perfect Being.

For this reason we find that Book I, Part II of the *Treatise* is devoted to our ideas of space, time, and number, and much of Part III to cause and effect.

The plan of Book I is as follows: Part I, evidence for the general proposition that ideas are derived from impressions; Part II, evidence for the empirical origin and application of our ideas of space, time, number, and existence; Part III, evidence for the purely conceptual character of questions decidable by reason a priori, for the empirical character of all questions of fact, and for the part played by the cause–effect relation in deciding such questions; Part IV, various metaphysical systems and problems considered.

THE ORIGIN OF IDEAS. For the professed founder of a new experimental science, Hume began in a distressingly dogmatic and a priori manner. "All the perceptions of the human mind resolve themselves into two distinct kinds, which I shall call impressions and ideas." Exhaustive dichotomies always merit suspicion, and this one is no exception. Hume did not in fact succeed in maintaining it. Impressions are supposed to be either sensations, passions, or emotions, but he soon introduced a number of familiar experiences which are none of these, for instance: the order in time of the five notes of a tune is not a *sixth* impression, but a *manner* in which the five impressions occur; an "idea of an idea" is distinguished, not by the impressions which it represents, but by the representation of a certain indefinable "je-ne-sais-quoi"; belief is said to be neither part of the idea believed nor a distinct impression produced by that idea, but a special *manner* in which the idea is conceived.

Hume came to accept this cramping dichotomy because he was unable entirely to throw off a picture of the mind that, with slight variations, had dominated philosophical thinking for over a century. The mind was pictured as an immaterial thing with the powers of receiving representations of things in the world which it inhabits, of reasoning about these representations, and of making decisions that are somehow translated into physical action by the body to which the mind is temporarily attached. These representations were usually called "ideas." This word, now so familiar, but not to be found in the Authorized Version of the Bible or in Shakespeare, was a technical term of the Platonic philosophy, originally signifying those perfect intelligible archetypes which were the only objects of true knowledge, which the soul had seen before incarnation, and of which the soul is now sometimes reminded by sensible things, such memories appearing as a priori knowledge. The Christian Platonists, disbelieving in the prenatal existence of the soul, substituted for the inborn memories of the archetypes, inborn representations of them, which they called "innate ideas." It was from the possession of and by reflection on these innate ideas that we came by the knowledge of such necessary truths of metaphysics, mathematics, and morals as our Maker had thought it necessary for us to have and which could not be discovered from experience.

Empiricists—for instance, Locke—denied the existence of these innate ideas; but in doing so, they accepted the accompanying general picture of mind informed about the world around it by means of the ideas it possesses. Not being innate, these ideas must come from experience, which Locke defined as "sensation and reflection." Ideas of sensation come from our sense organs, ideas of reflection from our consciousness of our mental processes. The former are representations of things outside us and entirely sensuous in character; the latter, entirely subjective, representing in some mysterious way such processes as perceiving, combining, comparing, and abstracting. Memory somehow stores these representations, or copies of them, and has them handy when required for thinking. From this it was an obvious and inevitable step to treat the "ideas," which were supposed to provide the means of thinking, as mental images. Locke sometimes seems to have done so; Hume did so openly and consistently.

Hume's first departure from Locke's position was purely terminological. He called Locke's ideas of sense and reflection "impressions" and reserved the term "idea" for representations of imagination and memory. But Hume saw very clearly that if our primary information consists of nothing but representations and our thoughts of nothing but copies of those representations,

then we can never find out how accurate the representations of sense may be, nor can we form any ideas of the real world, as distinct from our impressions of it. Hume also rejected the immaterial substance that supposedly possesses the ideas, professing to be unable to discover any such thing. These moves are not made until Book I, Part IV of the *Treatise,* but their logical effect is to vitiate Book I, Part I altogether. For with no mind to have the ideas and no hope of the ideas representing the world to us, the notion of ideas should have been abandoned altogether. But so persuasive was the prevailing picture of the mind and its ideas that Hume kept them in his scheme even when they had nothing to represent or belong to, and he still endeavored to construct his world picture entirely out of them. So, for that matter, did several great philosophers who succeeded him.

For the professed founder

of a new experimental science,

Hume began in a distressingly dogmatic

and a priori manner.

In Book I, Part I, Hume was content to remain silent about the material world, from which our impressions are thought to come and which they are supposed to represent, and also about the mind, which has the impressions. Impressions of sense "arise in the soul from unknown causes," and impressions of reflection stem from ideas of impressions of sense; fear, for instance, is an impression of reflection resulting from an idea of pain, and pain in turn is an impression of sense. Hume's concern was with the relation between impressions and ideas, in terms of which he found a deceptively simple way of stating the first of the two basic propositions of empiricism: "Every simple idea is derived from a corresponding impression." Thinking is a matter of mental imagery, and the constituents of all our mental pictures, however varied and fanciful, are representations of impressions of sense. This doctrine effectively restrained the human mind within the limits of experience and provided Hume with the first two of his three principal tools of philosophical inquiry—his microscope, his razor, and his fork.

The "microscope" is described in the *Treatise,* Book I, Part III, Section II, and more fully in the first *Enquiry,* Section VII, Part I, where it is actually called a microscope. Its use is as follows. To examine and understand an idea, first reduce it to its simple constituent ideas.

Then, if any one of these is still obscure, produce the impression from which it is derived. By "producing" the impression, as opposed to the idea, Hume should have meant arranging for the actual occurrence of the impression. Anything short of this can only be considering the idea in a different way. The use of the microscope, therefore, ought to be a genuine psychological experiment. It is doubtful whether Hume fully realized this implication, and how often he made genuine experiments is not known. The only clear case is the experiment with a spot of ink on paper (*Treatise,* Bk. I, Pt. II, Secs. I, IV). Probably Hume did not distinguish between the literal "production of the impression" and a quite different procedure, the illustration of a general idea, whether simple or complex, by concrete particular cases, imaginary or recorded. This confusion was assisted by the fact that certain impressions of reflection in which Hume was greatly interested, such as moral approval, can be actually produced in the mind by considering imaginary cases. (For an example of the use of imaginary cases under the title of "experiments," see the *Treatise,* Bk. II, Pt. II, Sec. II.)

The use of concrete cases to clarify conceptual problems in general and philosophical problems in particular is a method by which Hume and many others have achieved valuable results. But giving oneself impressions is likely to be of interest only to the physiologist, if to anyone.

Hume's "razor" is closely associated with his "microscope." If a term cannot be shown to evoke an idea that can be analyzed into simple constituents for which impressions can be produced, then it has no meaning. There is an affinity between Hume's "razor" and the verification principle of the logical positivists. Both attempt to formulate precisely the general principle that to understand a word or expression one must know how one would use it in relation to concrete cases one has met or might meet in experience. Assuming that this was the principle Hume in fact often employed, one can understand how he came to make so many important contributions to philosophy, in spite of his mistaken doctrine of impressions and ideas. Hume's "fork" will be considered later, when his skepticism is treated.

ABSTRACT IDEAS. Empiricists who maintained that all our ideas are derived from experience had found difficulty in accounting for general ideas, for which general terms such as "man," "triangle," "red," or "motion" were supposed to stand. For we see only particular men, triangles, shades of red, and bodies moving. Locke had supposed that we have a power of abstraction, by which from the particular ideas of sense we manufacture general ideas, which represent only the features common to all individuals of the same sort and omit what is peculiar to each. But Berkeley had pointed out that if you eliminate from your idea, or image, of a particular man all the features peculiar to him and not shared by all other men, you have no image left. This was particularly clear in the case of an idea like "red." There is no imaginable feature common to all shades of red. My general idea of red must either be no shade of red at all, which is absurd; or all shades at once, which is impossible because they are mutually exclusive; or none and all at once, which is self-contradictory. Berkeley maintained that the idea in the mind answering to a general term is always particular and specific but that the use made of it is general. It is used to stand for all other particular ideas of the same sort or similar to it in some respect. Hume followed Berkeley, acclaiming this view as a great discovery, but went further in attempting to explain what is meant by the particular idea "standing for" all others of the same sort. To do so he invoked the doctrine of association of ideas. Ideas whose impressions are alike or contiguous in space or time become associated in the mind; that is to say the mind has a tendency to pass from one to another. A general term is associated by contiguity—that is, by the times and places of its use—with the several particular things to which it is applied; the ideas of these are associated by resemblance with one another and with any others like them in the same way. So the term "stands for" the general idea, in that it tends to evoke by association particular members of a family of ideas associated by resemblance and unlimited in number.

The merit of this theory is that it explains how I, for instance, can understand a general term without either forming "a general abstract idea" or conceiving an infinite number of particular ones. My understanding consists in nothing that I actually do, but in what I am prone to do if necessary, that is, to go on visualizing other instances. This was the first of many uses Hume made of the principle of association of ideas. This principle was not his own discovery, but he did claim in the *Abstract* that the use he made of the principle was the most original part of his work, and in the *Treatise* he compared its importance in the mental world with that of attraction in the physical world. There is an element of truth in Hume's theory of abstract ideas. One way in which understanding of a general term can show itself is in the ability to visualize particular instances. But he failed to see, first, that there are many other abilities in which understanding of a general term can be shown, such as the abilities to recognize, depict, and make instances, to carry out instructions, and to construct significant sentences in which the term occurs; second, what is required for understanding of a general term is not merely a tendency to continue in a certain direction, such as association might account for, but an ability to avoid and correct mistakes in its use.

SPACE, TIME, AND EXISTENCE. In the *Treatise*, Book I, Part II, Hume tried to explain the nature of those ideas which provide the framework and outline of our world. He wanted to show that they are such as to provide no basis for metaphysical arguments about the nature of the universe.

Hume explained how we can talk intelligently about a vacuum, even though our idea of space is derived entirely from the order of sensible points and we consequently have no idea of empty space.

Space and Time. Space and time are nothing but the manners in which our impressions occur—alongside one another if they are impressions of sight and touch, and one after the other in all cases. Following Berkeley, though without acknowledgment, Hume maintained that neither our impressions nor our ideas are infinitely divisible, but rather reach a minimum beyond which we can neither see, feel, nor imagine anything smaller in size or shorter in duration. These minima Hume called visible and tangible points. Their existence was said to be an empirical fact, and the experiment with the spot of ink was adduced to support it. Hume then, by a dubious application of the doctrine of impressions and ideas, argued that since none of our ideas are infinitely divisible, we have no idea of infinite divisibility, and the expression is therefore meaningless.

Considering the objections of mathematicians to such a view, Hume maintained first that his perceptible points were proof against the objections which mathematicians bring against the traditional conception of an indivisible point; second, that the geometers' definitions of surface, line, and point were unintelligible unless we suppose indivisibles, so that they cannot without self-contradiction base arguments against indivisibles on these concepts; and finally, that no geometrical arguments can be decisive with regard to minute quantities, because the ideas of geometry are derived from the imprecise appearances of sense, and the "maxims" concerning them are therefore "not precisely true." He illustrated this lack of precision by asking whether geometers have any more exact standard of equality or of flatness or of straightness than the sensible propor-

tions of bodies and by what right they maintain that two straight lines have no common segment when they meet at a very small angle or that a tangent only touches the circle at a single point when the circle is very large.

Finally, Hume explained how we can talk intelligently about a vacuum, even though our idea of space is derived entirely from the order of sensible points and we consequently have no idea of empty space. The idea of a vacuum is derived from such impressions as those of two points of light in complete darkness, which, though nothing lies between them, are visibly related to one another in the same way as pairs of impressions which have others between them.

Hume apparently gave considerable further thought to the philosophy of mathematics. In the first *Enquiry* (Sec. XII, Pt. II) the equally convincing arguments for and against indivisible minima are represented as the main source of skepticism with regard to reason. Hume held, however, that we cannot be content with skepticism on this point. For he held that mathematics is one of the two kinds of valid reasoning. In a footnote he suggested that it might be possible to resolve the contradictions concerning infinite divisibility by recourse to Berkeley's theory of abstract ideas. He wrote, "It is sufficient to have dropped this hint at present, without prosecuting it any further." It is clear, therefore, that Hume either had not read or did not accept Berkeley's own resolution of this problem in his *Principles of Human Knowledge,* sections CXVIII–CXXXIV. Hume's letters reveal that he later wrote a dissertation on geometry to be included with the *Four Dissertations* published in 1757 but suppressed it after receiving decisive criticisms from the second earl of Stanhope.

Existence. Hume's account of the idea of existence is of greater philosophical interest. In the *Treatise* (Bk. I, Pt. II, Sec. VI) Hume argued that every idea is the idea of a being. Existence must therefore be either a separate idea that accompanies every other idea or the very same with the idea of the object we think of. The former suggestion being plainly false, Hume chose the latter. Therefore, he concluded, "Any idea we please to form is the idea of a being; and the idea of a being is any idea we please to form." Several important consequences follow. First, we cannot form an idea of anything specifically different from ideas and impressions. The representative theory of perception is therefore nonsensical, for it maintains that the ideas in the mind represent material substances specifically different from them. Second, since to conceive of God or any other being and to conceive of the existence of that being are the same thing, it is nonsense to say that the idea of God has the peculiar characteristic of also entailing the idea of existence. Though Hume did not explicitly draw this conclusion or mention the Ontological Argument, he probably had the argument in mind and certainly anticipated Kant's reason for rejecting it, i.e., that existence is not a predicate. Third, the traditional account of judgment as the uniting of ideas is false, for in the judgment "God exists," there is only one idea present.

Farhang Zabech, in his *Hume: Precursor of Modern Empiricism,* and John Passmore, in *Hume's Intentions,* have maintained that Hume was unable on this basis to explain the idea of nonexistence. Hume did in fact offer an account of this idea (*Treatise,* Bk. I, Pt. I, Sec. V). The idea of nonexistence, he claimed, is the idea of the object together with the exclusion of the object from all times and places in which it is supposed not to exist. If I think of mermaids as nonexistent, I think of mermaids and the seas of this planet and "exclude" the former from the latter. It will be considered later whether there is any intelligible interpretation of "exclusion," as used in this context.

A PRIORI AND EMPIRICAL KNOWLEDGE. Both the *Treatise* (Bk. I, Pt. III) and the first *Enquiry* (Sec. IV, Pt. I) begin by drawing a distinction of the greatest importance. In the *Treatise* it is between "knowledge" and "probability"; in the *Enquiry,* between "relations of ideas" and "matters of fact." Hume claimed that these two classes exhaust the field of discoverable truth. The distinction, often referred to as "Hume's fork," corresponds roughly to the traditional one between necessary and contingent truths but not as closely as some have thought to the later distinction between analytic and synthetic propositions.

The essence of the distinction is the same in both works. Some truths depend on our ideas. They state relations between our ideas that cannot be altered without altering the ideas, because any attempt to do so results in a "contradiction." These are relations of ideas, the subject matter of knowledge and science. Other truths do not depend on the ideas concerned. They can be conceived to be false without any contradiction. Relations of ideas can be discovered in two ways, by intuition and by demonstration. I may consider two ideas and perceive a relation between them, for example, that two is half four; or I may discover a relation by the interposition of other ideas, as in Euclid's demonstration that the internal angles of a triangle are equal to two right angles. Matters of fact can also be discovered in two ways, by observation and by inference. The validity of observation was, for the purposes of this argument, taken for granted, as Hume elsewhere said it always must be.

The question Hume considered here was the nature of nondemonstrative inference. He stated that such inferences always rest on the relation of cause and effect. If I observe *A* and infer *B*, it can only be because I believe *A* and *B* to be causally connected. This is true in the rather odd sense that Hume chose to give to the word "cause." The man who sees the feet of the passersby from a basement window and infers the presence of their bodies and heads, would not ordinarily be said to argue from effects to causes or vice versa. But Hume would say that such an inference was based on knowledge of causes and effects, simply because it is based on knowledge of what usually does and does not happen.

The importance of Hume's doctrine lies not in his definition of an effect as an unvaried and expected sequel, but in his insistence that there is no other way of anticipating or supplementing our observations than by inferences based on our experience of what always or usually happens. It does not matter whether we use the term "cause" to refer to any kind of regular conjunction or keep it for some special sort. Hume's point is that there are no cause and effect relationships that provide a way of bypassing the appeal to experience on questions of fact. For the question whether *A* causes *B* depends on, even if it is not identical with, the question whether *A* in fact happens without *B*, which only experience can decide.

There is a second important contention that Hume based on the distinction between relations of ideas and matters of fact. In the *Treatise* it remains unstated, though often implied. In the first *Enquiry* (Sec. XII, Pt. III) it is stated explicitly, "Whatever *is* may *not be.* . . . The non-existence of any being, without exception, is as clear and distinct an idea as its existence." Every existential proposition states a matter of fact. Its truth must be determined empirically. So God's existence cannot be proved a priori.

What exactly is the nature of the distinction between relations of ideas and matters of fact? One solution Hume would not accept was the view that a proposition expressing a relation of ideas is true by definition. Following Locke, who called propositions true by definition "trifling propositions," Hume poured scorn on such a truth as "that where there is no property there can be no injustice," which is supposed to rest on the definition of injustice as the violation of property. He contrasted this proposition with the Pythagorean theorem, which, he said, cannot be known without thinking it out, "let the terms be ever so exactly defined" (first *Enquiry,* Sec. XII, Pt. III). The ensuing denunciation of all "syllogistic reasoning" must be taken to apply to deductions from premises which are "trifling." Hume himself did plenty of syllogistic reasoning, but his premises, he would have said, were matters of empirical fact or, occasionally, relations of ideas.

If one remembers that Hume thought of ideas as images, and primarily as visual images, it is easier to understand what he meant by "relations of ideas." He said in the *Treatise* (Bk. I, Pt. III, Sec. I) that the relations which depend on ideas are "resemblance, contrariety, degrees in quality, and proportions in quality and number." Causation, identity, and spatiotemporal relations are not relations of ideas.

As an analogue to "ideas," consider a typically graphic representation, a map of the world. Cornwall and Italy resemble each other in shape. How would you remove this resemblance from the map except by altering the shape of one or both countries? Consider another map, representing the international date line as passing to the east of a certain island, whereas the first map makes it pass to the west of the island. This contrariety cannot be removed except by altering one of the maps (although it can, of course, be explained in other ways). The central Atlantic is bluer than the North Sea; Iceland is bigger than the Isle of Wight; there are more islands in the Swedish archipelago than in the Hebrides. None of these relations can be altered without changing the graphic representation of the terms.

Hume found that all inferences

from the existence of one object to that of another

are nondemonstrative and based on

the relation of cause and effect.

By contrast, consider causation, identity, and position. The whole map might be produced by a different process and look the same. The representation of any island could be moved toward or away from any other, without altering the appearance of either. Is this Pacific island that is on the right-hand edge of the map the same as that Pacific island on the left-hand edge, or is it another island of the same shape? The appearance on the map would be the same in either case.

Hume used three other formulas, with variants, to express the nature of a necessary truth. The first is that "whatever objects are different are distinguishable, and whatever objects are distinguishable are separable by the thought and imagination" and conversely that "whatever objects are separable are also distinguishable and whatever objects are distinguishable are also different" (*Treatise,* Bk. I, Pt I, Sec. VII). The second is that it is impossible "for the imagination to conceive anything contrary to a demonstration" (*Treatise,* Bk I, Pt. III, Sec. VII). The third is that if a proposition were demon-

strably false, it would imply a contradiction (*Enquiry,* Sec. IV, Pt. I).

All three principles apply to the examples considered above: the first draws our attention to the objects (the impressions corresponding to the ideas), the second to the ideas, and the third to the "proposition" (the sentence) expressing the relation of ideas or its denial.

The resemblance between Cornwall and Italy is nothing different or distinguishable or separable from the shapes of the two peninsulas. The contrariety between the two maps is nothing distinct from what is represented in each. Nor are the differences in degree of blueness, in size, or in number different and distinct from either the degrees of blueness of the two seas, or the sizes of the two islands, or the numbers of the two archipelagoes.

We cannot imagine a change in resemblance without a change in the resembling objects, a removal of contrariety without a change of the contrary representations, a change of relation in degree, size, or number without imagining a change in the qualities, sizes, or numbers of the related terms.

Finally, if we try to understand a sentence that denies an actual relation of ideas, that is, if we try to "conceive the ideas according to the proposition," we find the ideas display a contradiction. If it is said that the shape of Cornwall is not like the shape of Italy, one must first visualize the shapes of the two peninsulas as they are, then alter them so that they are no longer alike, but at the same time keep them as they are. Thus the denial of a relation of ideas is a self-canceling cue for visualization. This is clearest in the case of numerical proportion: "Jones has six children, two sons and three daughters"; visualize this family according to the meaning (the customary associations) of the words, and you will find yourself alternately including and excluding a sixth child.

The above is only a suggested interpretation of Hume. What light it throws on the problem of necessary truths is another matter.

An interpretation of Hume's theory of nonexistence can now be given. "There are no mermaids" is a proposition instructing us to visualize seas and mermaids, but forbidding us to visualize the latter in the former. In this view, a negative existential statement presupposes a field or spatiotemporal region, suggests the idea of an object, and by the use of the negated verb, activates a disposition to inhibit or cancel the visualization of the object in the field.

CAUSE AND EFFECT. Hume found that all inferences from the existence of one object to that of another are nondemonstrative and based on the relation of cause and effect. He then showed that they are not even indirectly demonstrative, for neither any specific causal relation, nor the proposition that every event has a cause, nor even the claim that the unobserved resembles the observed can be known either by intuition or demonstration. An exception to any causal connection is clearly imaginable; so is a pure fluke or a sudden change in the course of nature. Only by experience can we know whether any of these occur.

Hume therefore had to answer two questions: What is our idea of cause and effect? How does experience enable us to discover causes and make inferences?

Hume maintained that the terms "cause" and "effect" do not stand for any features, observed or inferred, in the objects to which they are applied; aside from their contiguity in space, succession in time, and the constant conjunction of like objects in past experience. There are no other features to observe; and if there were concealed "powers" that we infer from the conjunction, we should not be able to explain or predict the phenomena any better than we can without them. For we should not know why, but only that, certain objects have certain powers, and the persistence of the powers and the nature of their effects would be predictable only from the same empirical data and with the same degree of accuracy as they are at present. A similar criticism is leveled at the power of providence, as it is supposed to be inferred from its effects.

But over and above contiguity, succession, and constant conjunction, there is, Hume said, another element in our idea of cause, the idea of necessary connection, although as we have seen, Hume's microscope can find no impression corresponding to it. Therefore, Hume examined the way in which we actually discover causal relations and base inferences on them. It is, he said, a simple matter of association of ideas. Experience shows *A* to have been frequently followed by *B* and never to have occurred without *B*. The idea of *B* is therefore associated with *A* in a way in which no other idea is. As a result, when the idea of *A* occurs, the mind is determined to pass to the idea of *B*, and when the impression of *A* occurs, it is determined not only to form the idea of *B* but to transfer to that idea a share of the "vivacity" of the impression of *A*.

In terms of this account Hume could explain four things. The inference is the transition from the impression of *A* to the lively idea of *B*. The lively idea of *B*, associated with the present impression of *A*, is belief in *B*; and the feeling we have of being determined to pass from the idea of *A* to that of *B*, or from the impression of *A* to the belief in *B*, is the origin of our idea of necessary connection. Finally, since this "determination" of the mind depends solely on repetition (of past conjunctions) and not on any reasoning, it is due to custom or habit. By a customary association Hume

meant an association reinforced by repetition. This identification of the impression of necessary connection was supported by the following argument: "The necessary connection betwixt causes and effects is the foundation of our inference from one to the other. The foundation of our inference is the transition arising from the accustomed union. These are, therefore, the same" (*Treatise*, Bk. I, Pt. III, Sec. XIV).

Consequently, any talk of power, efficacy, energy, force, or necessity which implies that it is something existing in the cause, whether material or spiritual, natural or supernatural, is pronounced meaningless.

Finally Hume offered two definitions of cause: (1) "an object precedent and contiguous to another, and where all objects resembling the former are placed in like relations of precedency and contiguity to those objects that resemble the latter"; and (2) "an object precedent and contiguous to another and so united with it that the idea of the one determines the mind to form the idea of the other, and the impression of the one to form a more lively idea of the latter."

In the first *Enquiry* (Sec. VII, Pt. II) Hume added to the former of the two definitions the following alleged equivalent: "Or in other words where, if the first object had not been, the second had never existed." In fact this proposition is neither entailed by nor equivalent to the first definition.

BELIEF. Could Hume reconcile his definition of belief as a "lively idea associated with a present impression" with his thesis that all beliefs about matters of fact rest on causal inference? If other associations, for instance, resemblance or contiguity, do not enliven ideas, why does constant conjunction? If they do, why do they not produce belief?

Hume first replied that the other relations do enliven ideas already believed in as realities. But if an idea is only "feigned," such as the idea of someone resembling an illustration in a fairy story, the other relations make little difference to its liveliness. But Hume did not feel satisfied with this reply and went on to describe a difference between a "feigned" idea resembling a present impression and an idea customarily associated with one. The former is arbitrary, variable at will, capricious, inconstant. The latter is involuntary, fixed by the unalterable past, and a member of a whole system of ideas similarly enlivened, which together with our impressions and our memories form a stable and coherent world picture, which we please to call "reality." But the essence of belief was no longer the vivacity of the picture; it was also its coherence with a general picture, its constancy, its involuntariness.

The same criteria were invoked to deal with the problem of beliefs resulting from education. Education, by repeated conjunction of ideas, sets up habits of association. Most of our beliefs result from education and endure in the face of experience to the contrary, so firmly does repetition infix ideas in our minds. But when we reflect on such beliefs and remember that educators can say what they please and when we find that they contradict both one another and our experience, we form a general distrust of such beliefs.

Ideas are merely copies of impressions.

Therefore, we cannot conceive of, know of, or

believe in anything of which we have no impression.

By the time Hume came to write the "Appendix" to the *Treatise* he saw the need to give a revised account of belief, which would connect it with the features characteristic of inferences from experience and differentiate it from those characteristic of the fancies of superstition, propaganda, and poetical imagination. Accordingly, he added to "vivacity" a range of other terms, "force," "solidity," "firmness," and "steadiness." Belief was "something felt by the mind, which distinguishes the ideas of the judgment from the fictions of the imagination. It gives them more force and influence; it makes them appear of greater importance; infixes them in the mind; and renders them the governing principles of all our actions." In the final clause of the above quotation Hume at last grasped the central characteristic of belief, that it manifests itself in conduct. Compared with this, its effects on our mental imagery are of secondary importance.

DETERMINATION OF THE MIND. The feeling of "determination," to which Hume traced the idea of necessary connection, is not the same as the feeling of belief. For determination carries the mind from the idea of the cause to that of the effect, as well as from the impression of the cause to a lively idea of—that is, to a belief in—the effect. The term "determination" expresses the relation of precise dependence, with none of the metaphysical overtones of "force," "energy" "agency," or "power." A modern psychologist might say, "What we expect is determined by our past experience and our present percepts," and mean exactly what Hume meant.

The feeling of determination was postulated to distinguish between a transition of thought that is determined by imposed factors and one that is arbitrary and alterable at will. There are some things that I cannot help thinking and others that I only choose to suppose; but the presence or absence of a feeling of determination surely cannot be a decisive mark of the distinction between the two classes.

Many critics have thought that Hume's use of the determiniation of the mind in his account of causality and necessary connection made that account circular, and in his second definition of a cause there is a kind of circularity. He did not define cause in general in terms of itself under the same or another name. The circularity is not like that of defining pain as the anticipation of an increase in suffering. But he did define the causal relation between *A* and *B* as their regular conjunction, plus their effect on the mind. So *A* is the cause of *B* partly in virtue of the fact that their regular conjunction is the cause of something else. The worst kind of circular definition leaves the problem untouched. This kind shifts the problem but does not solve it.

Hume should have eschewed the method of formal definition. Instead of offering a paraphrase of "*A* caused *B*," he should have told us what a man is doing who says that *A* is the cause of *B*. Such a man is not, as Hume's definition suggests, conjoining two assertions, one about the objects, the other about his mind; he is making one assertion, that *A* without *B* would be unprecedented, and also, by the (causal) terms which he uses, expressing the "determination of his mind," or whatever we choose to call it. This feeling of determination is caused; but then so is everything.

Some have felt that Hume's account is circular in an even simpler way, that he was saying, "The necessity of natural processes is only the necessity of our thoughts projected onto things." This is clearly not what Hume meant and he was at pains to say so (*Treatise*, Bk. I, Pt. III, Sec. XIV). He opened the door to such misunderstandings when he said that "upon the whole, necessity is something that exists in the mind, not in the objects." But this idiom is similar to "beauty is in the eye of the beholder." And no one would take this to mean that pictures and sunsets are not really beautiful but that the eyes of the people who look at them are so.

A final difficulty concerning the feeling of determination is the question whether we have an impression of causation when we have this feeling, that is, whether the customarily associated ideas, as they succeed one another in the mind, seem connected and not merely conjoined? If they do not, it is not clear how the feeling can be the source of the idea of necessary connection. If they do, then Hume's unrestricted statement that events seem conjoined but not connected (first *Enquiry*, Sec. VII, Pt. II) must be qualified: We have a wide variety of feelings—feeling sick, hungry, sleepy, inclined to do this, unable to do that, obliged to do the other—feelings which seem connected with the states of which they are symptoms. Nor does it seem plausible to say that we have to learn by experience what to expect when we have one of these feelings. It seems clear that

Hume should have spoken only of external events as never seeming to be connected.

Albert Edouard Michotte in *The Perception of Causality* claimed to have shown experimentally that even some external events seem causally connected; he held that under certain precisely specifiable stimulus conditions we experience definite impressions of mechanical causality of two main types, which he called "the launching effect" and "the entraining effect." The former would apply precisely to Hume's favorite case of the impact of the billiard balls. Michotte differed from Hume on another point, the role of experience in the discovery of causes. He denied that we need a build-up of repeated conjunctions to give belief in causality. A single case often suffices, even without a background of scientific knowledge. A child needs to be scratched only once by a cat to connect the cat, the injury, and the pain. The function of experience, Michotte claimed, is to show which of the seemingly necessary conjunctions are not really so. A somewhat similar view was elaborated by Karl Popper in *The Logic of Scientific Discovery*. According to him, the function of experiments in science is only to disprove the hypotheses that seem to be worth testing. Induction plays no part in scientific method.

Hume would undoubtedly answer that, nevertheless, the man of sense trusts and employs a theory, a machine, or an institution with a confidence proportionate to the number and variety of the tests it has survived. The more it has survived, the more it is likely to survive. There would seem to be room, in science and in ordinary life, for both methods: confirmation and disproof.

PROBABILITY. The teaching of experience is not always unequivocal. A die always falls flat on one of its sides, but there are six of them, and experience does not tell us on which of them it will settle on a given occasion. Four out of every five men recover from a certain disease, but we do not know if a given patient will be one of the unlucky ones.

Hume would have called the first example a case of the probability of chances, the second a case of the probability of causes (*Treatise*, Bk. I, Pt. III, Secs. XI and XII). Reason, said Hume, is powerless in either case. Although four of the six sides of the die are marked with a cross and only two with a circle, there is no reason why the event should fall on that side where there is a superior number of chances. Similarly, four out of the next five patients will recover, but reason cannot tell us which.

Hume's criticism of the logic of chance is admirable. His psychological solution is dubious. He said that in both types of case the force of custom, which determines us to expect what we have experienced before, is

split up into as many parts as there are chances; so we have six lively ideas of the fall of the die, four representing it with a cross uppermost, two with a circle; four lively pictures of the patient recovering, one of his dying. The similar images reunite, forming two ideas in each case, one of which is stronger and livelier than the other in proportion to the greater number of constituent images that concur in it. A probability is a stronger belief opposed by a weaker and incompatible one.

Mind and Matter

In the *Treatise*, Book I, Part IV, and in the first *Enquiry*, Section XII, Hume considered two perennial problems of philosophy, our knowledge of the external world and the relations of mind and matter. His semantic and epistemological principles made his solution almost inevitable.

To conceive, to know, or to believe are nothing but to have ideas, to have ideas unalterably related, or to have vivid and steady ideas. Ideas are merely copies of impressions. Therefore, we cannot conceive of, know of, or believe in, anything of which we have no impression. We have no impression of the mind, save as an assemblage or "bundle" of impressions and ideas. We have no impression of a physical thing distinct from our impressions of it. "Spiritual substances" and "corporeal substances" are therefore meaningless metaphysical jargon.

But Hume saw that we do talk quite significantly about and believe in both ourselves and the things around us. The problem was to describe the nature of these two beliefs and discover their causes. Hume admitted breakdowns in his answers to both problems but affected to welcome his failures as additional support for his skepticism.

Hume's theory of moral judgments is that

to consider a character trait or

an act which springs from it as virtuous or vicious

is to have a special sort of feeling of pleasure

or displeasure toward it.

Both accounts start from the initial assumption, mistaken by Hume for an empirical fact, that our primary data are nothing but sensations, feelings, and images. So Hume had to conclude that the mind is nothing but a bundle of perceptions related by resemblance, succession, and causation, to which we ascribe an identity by a kind of fiction. A succession of related perceptions feels to the mind very like an identical, that is, an uninterrupted and unvaried, perception. We are apt to confuse things that feel alike, so we mistake the series of related but different perceptions that make up the mind for a single unvarying perception; hence the illusion of a permanent self. But this account, Hume recognized, in his "Appendix" to the *Treatise*, failed to explain how the successive perceptions are united in consciousness. Hume pleaded the privilege of a skeptic" and left the question unresolved.

The bundle theory of the self helped Hume explain the external world. Perceptions are distinct, independent, self-sufficient entities; they occur in bundles, so far as we know. But the idea of a perception that is not a member of any bundle is not self-contradictory, as Berkeley had supposed. So if I think of a set of impressions that are related to one another (as are those which I call a shoe) but are not part of any bundle or person, I am thinking of a shoe which nobody is seeing. And if such a set of ideas were enlivened, I should be believing in the existence of an unseen shoe.

It remained for Hume to explain what suggests and enlivens such ideas to our minds. Two features of our impressions, he said, suggest to us the idea of unperceived perceptions—"constancy" and "coherence."

My impressions of a mountain are like one another. It looks much the same each time. The impressions form a constant series. Since they are very similar but interrupted, they feel to the mind like an uninterrupted and unvarying series and are mistaken for one. So I come to think of the mountain as a continuous object. When I notice the interruptions in my impressions of it, I resolve the contradiction by supposing unperceived perceptions to fill up the gaps in the series. These ideas are enlivened by their association with the impressions I have. So I have a vivid picture of, a belief in, a mountain existing continuously and therefore independently of my interrupted perceptions.

Changing objects are believed to exist independently if the impressions of them display *coherence*. If I sit and watch my fire die slowly down, I get an uninterrupted series of varying impressions. If I leave the room and then return, I get an interrupted series; but it matches the uninterrupted series, allowing for the gaps. Moreover, the effects of the two series are the same. In both cases the room gets colder; the effects seem to be independent of the gaps. The supposition of unperceived perceptions to fill the gaps restores to me a regular picture of the behavior of fires and their effects on room temperature. The ideas of the unseen dying coals are enlivened by association with all my experiences of watched fires.

But again Hume's thought takes a skeptical turn. This everyday world-picture provides the field in which we investigate causes and effects, including the causes of our impressions. We find our impressions to be wholly dependent on our sense organs and nervous system. It is therefore empirically impossible that perceptions should exist in the absence of a percipient, that there should be perceptions that are unperceived. Common sense presupposes unperceived perceptions; science is founded on common sense, but science disproves the existence of unperceived perceptions.

The scientist has an answer. He distinguishes between objects and our perceptions of them. The former are independent and continuous, the latter fleeting and subjective. But the sensible qualities of objects, their color, temperature, sound, smell, taste, depend on our nerves and sense organs; they must be merely apparent. The objects, the scientist says, have only the "primary" qualities of extension, that is, size and figure, motion, and solidity. Hume followed Berkeley in denying that we can form any idea of a thing having only these qualities. Hume argued that motion presupposes a body moved; a body presupposes something extended and solid. The idea of extension is that of juxtaposed colored and/or solid minimal parts. Color being merely apparent, all depends on solidity. But solidity means impenetrability; impenetrability involves two bodies which will not unite. And we have no qualities left in terms of which to conceive these bodies. "Our modern philosophy leaves us no just or satisfactory idea of matter." "There is a direct and total opposition betwixt our reason and our senses" (*Treatise*, Bk. I, Pt. IV, Sec. IV).

Hume next examined the traditional arguments about the conjunction and interaction of mind and body (*Treatise*, Bk. I, Pt. IV, Sec. V). Spiritual substance and material substance are equally inconceivable. The distinction between unextended and extended lies elsewhere, between the impressions of sight and touch, which alone provide us with an idea of extension, and those of smell, taste, sound, feeling, and passion, which do not. The idea of local conjunction is simply inapplicable to the latter variety of impressions. They exist, but exist nowhere. There is no mystery about motion causing thought, for no causal relation is intelligible. Anything may cause anything, and cause and effect are always distinct. Motion and thought are in no way peculiar: reflection shows them to be distinct; experience shows them to be constantly conjoined.

Skepticism

Hume outlined his general position with regard to skepticism in the *Treatise*, Book I, Parts IV and VII, and in the first *Enquiry*, Section XII. Apart from differences in emphasis and tone, the position is the same in both works. He distinguished two main forms of skepticism, "antecedent" and "consequent." Each may take either an extreme, "Pyrrhonian" form or a mitigated and moderate form.

By "antecedent" skepticism Hume meant a procedure like that of Descartes's method of doubt, by which, before any sort of examination of our faculties or methods of reasoning, we doubt them all and demand some antecedent, infallible criterion for deciding which faculties, if any, to trust. Such a skepticism, Hume held, is in fact unattainable and would be quite incurable if it were attained. But in a mitigated form, as a general counsel of diffidence and caution, it has its use.

Consequent skepticism is the method Hume himself practiced. That is, he based his doubts as to the certainty and extent of our knowledge on an examination of our faculties. That is why, in the *Treatise,* skepticism was not introduced until Book I, Part IV, *after* the discussion of knowledge and probability, and in the *Enquiry* the discussion of those same topics in Section IV, is headed "Skeptical Doubts concerning the Operations of the Understanding." Consequent skepticism, again, may take a Pyrrhonian form, appearing in the *Treatise* as the first attack of utter despair. Belief has been shown to be nothing but a feeling, its causes to lie in the imagination. Moreover, the processes which give rise to belief, if allowed to continue, eventually destroy it. Belief in our reason, senses, and memory is nothing but a natural instinct, safeguarded by natural defense mechanisms, which alone save it from self-destruction.

Even the most extreme ancient skeptics admitted that we must live; and since reason cannot tell us how to live, they recommended that we follow nature, under which they included natural appetites and instincts, the sensible appearances of things, and the traditions of one's city. Hume, who regarded both mathematical and empirical reasoning as natural, since each follows a natural "determination" of the mind, found that he could maintain his skepticism and still perceive, remember, calculate, and infer, provided he confined himself to "common life," whose problems natural reasoning is adapted to meet. Since "nature by an absolute and uncontrollable necessity has determined us to judge as well as to breathe and feel," Hume would be as unorthodox a skeptic if he stopped judging as an ancient skeptic would have been had he stopped breathing.

Hume thus reached his final stage of mitigated consequent skepticism. Its two main characteristics are an undogmatic moderation and a refusal to go beyond common life. Nevertheless, it permitted rich intellectual life. The science of man, on which it was founded, was

also permitted by it, for its conclusions are only "those of common life, methodized and corrected." Metaphysics, if it consists in the empirical study of our "sublimer" ideas, is also natural—for curiosity is as natural a motive as any and its gratification a natural pleasure. Further, if we do not prosecute such studies, the theologians will, and will take advantage of our ignorance to give metaphysical coverage to their dangerous dogmas.

Mathematics, though at first sight a source of unanswerable skeptical arguments, had been restored to the fold of natural activities by Hume's demolishment of the dogma of infinite divisibility. And all the experimental sciences, as well as history and geography, are merely extensions of the natural ways of thinking, which we cannot help using in common life. Hume's "fork," his third implement, was now completed, and he could use it to stoke the bonfire of unprofitable books described in the famous peroration to the first *Enquiry:* of every piece of pretended reasoning he demanded, "Is it abstract reasoning concerning quantity and number?" or "Is it experimental reasoning concerning matters of fact?" If the answer was "neither," he consigned it to the flames.

If right and wrong are discoverable

by intuition or demonstration,

they must depend on some relation of ideas.

The attitude of mitigated skepticism was supposed to follow from a proper understanding of "the force of the Pyrrhonian doubt, and of the impossibility that anything but the strong power of natural instinct, could free us from it." No doubt nature would save us from Pyrrhonism; but is it not possible that there are some holes in the skeptics' arguments, quite apart from the fact that in undermining all arguments they undermine themselves?

The Pyrrhonian arguments that Hume presented are as follows: (1) his own argument about the nature of causal inference; (2) the mathematical arguments about infinite divisibility, which he thought could be met; (3) the argument from the unavoidability and incoherence of the representative theory of sense perception; and (4) a peculiar argument, apparently of Hume's own invention, used in the *Treatise,* Book I, Part IV, Section I, and not repeated in the *Enquiry.* The first and third of these correspond to perennial problems in the theory of knowledge that have seemed to most philosophers to demand and to defy solution, the problem of induction and the problem of perception. The former problem was given its classical statement by Hume in the *Treatise,* Book I, Part III; the latter he stated very well in Book I, Part IV, Section II.

The skeptic tries in both these contexts to make it appear that when he asks "How do you know?" or "What right have you to be sure?" the only possible sort of answer is to produce direct observations and inferences from them. The only alternative is supposed to be a blind reliance on instinct. Intelligent anticipation must, therefore, be composed of past observations plus an inference—but what sort of inference? Sense perceptions must be awareness of sensations (or impressions or sense data) plus an inference—but what sort of inference? Hume showed quite clearly that no sort of inference known to logicians would fill the bill in either case.

The answer is that between the formal procedures of observation and deduction and the mechanical operation of instinct lies the whole field of acquired abilities, of which observation and deduction are themselves rather advanced instances. Knowledge comes from having learned to use our eyes and our memories, as well as from having learned how to talk, to record, to tabulate, and to deduce.

The skeptic makes it appear that induction (commonly known as intelligent anticipation) is peculiar in that it will only work if things behave regularly. In fact, every sort of ability is in the same position. In an irregular world there could be neither learned nor unlearned abilities of any kind whatever. The verb "can" would have no application. In fact, all language would be impossible.

The mathematical arguments need no further discussion. There are still unsolved problems in mathematical philosophy, but they are not the same as Hume's.

The last argument, peculiar to Hume, is introduced by a harmless truth: however "certain and infallible" the rules of a demonstrative science may be, I may always make a mistake in applying them. Whether I have done so is a question of fact, that is, of probability. So all demonstrations degenerate into probability, the probability of there having been no mistake. But in any probable judgment I may have misassessed the evidence; so I must review my past form to determine the likelihood of error; in this review too I may have made mistakes, and so the argument may be repeated to infinity. Each judgment, "however favorable to the preceding one," raises a new doubt; each doubt detracts a little from the probability of the original judgment, which, unless the process is arbitrarily stopped, must eventually wither away altogether.

Thus, Hume concluded, the natural and proper procedures of probable reasoning, as employed by every prudent man, would totally destroy our belief in everything if allowed to proceed unchecked. Nature usually saves us by forcing us to make up our mind and stop bothering. If we do continue the process, she prevents it having any considerable effect on our beliefs. Hume clearly regarded this argument as unanswerable, but unconvincing. He said that his intention in producing it was to show that "belief is more properly an act of the sensitive, than of the cogitative part of our nature." If belief were a voluntary act, owing allegiance to logic alone, it would on every occasion destroy itself.

The argument is plainly sophistical but phrased in such vague terms that it would be a lengthy task to set out all the various possible cases covered and explain the fallacy in each. Take one case. I judge (1) that Bucephalus will probably win the 2:30. But then I reflect (2) that I am not a good judge of form. Then I reflect (3) that I am not a very good critic of my own performances in these matters. The force of (3) is to counteract (2) and leave (1) unchanged but subject—as it always should have been—to the proviso "unless I am mistaken." And how am I supposed to proceed further in this regress? Where shall I find evidence of my powers of criticizing my own criticisms of my judgments, distinct from the evidence of my powers of criticizing my own judgments? I have reached an assessment of my powers of picking up my own mistakes, and beyond this it is not possible to go. Every further step is the same step repeated.

To conclude, Hume was right to remind us that in no species of reasoning whatever are we immune from error; in the end, after the most careful possible use of analytical and experimental techniques, we must pronounce what *seems* to us the probable or inevitable conclusion and await the judgment of others. But to appreciate the merits of this procedure it is not necessary, as Hume supposed, to be baffled by Pyrrhonian sophistries.

Moral Philosophy

Hume's theory of moral judgments is that to consider a character trait or an act which springs from it as virtuous or vicious is to have a special sort of feeling of pleasure or displeasure toward it. The distinctive character of this feeling is that it is aroused only by human characters and actions, that it is aroused only when the type of the character or action is considered in general, neglecting any individuating features of a particular case, and that the feeling is affected by no features of the character or action other than its pleasantness or unpleasantness, its usefulness or harmfulness, either to its possessor or to others affected by it.

This theory of moral judgments bears a very close analogy to Hume's theory of beliefs about questions of fact. In neither case is the judgment a voluntary act in accordance with a priori principles of logic or of natural law. In both cases it is a kind of feeling that arises irresistibly, given the appropriate conditions of past experience and present perception. Both can be "regulated," or indirectly controlled, in accordance with general rules, by reflecting on certain aspects of our experience and neglecting others. Such regulation is itself a propensity natural to the more intelligent mind, motivated by a desire for consistency with oneself and agreement and cooperation with others.

So close is this analogy that Norman Kemp Smith, in *The Philosophy of David Hume,* argued that Hume's theory of belief was modeled on his theory of moral approval, which was substantially derived from Francis Hutcheson. According to Kemp Smith the discovery that this account of judgment could be extended from value judgments to judgments of fact was the "new scene of thought" which so transported Hume at the age of 18.

Though Hume's theory of morals is derived from Hutcheson, Hume would surely have been more explicit about it had he been consciously extending his theory of moral judgment to other judgments. Probably no one, not even Hume himself, quite realized that this is what he had in fact done until Kemp Smith pointed it out.

In spite of this close analogy, there are important differences, according to Hume, between judgments of fact and judgments of value. Judgments of fact, like judgments concerning relations of ideas, can be true or false. Judgments of taste and of morals cannot. On the strength of this distinction, Hume introduced a definition of "reason" as "the discovery of truth or falsehood," a definition according to which moral distinctions cannot be "the offspring of reason." Judgments of fact, like judgments concerning relations of ideas, are "inactive." They can never by themselves produce or prevent any action. Judgments of value can do so. Judgments of value form a class that is logically isolated from relations of ideas and matters of fact, as the latter two classes are logically isolated from one another. No probable or demonstrative inference can be made from a relation of ideas to a matter of fact, from either to a judgment of value, from a value judgment to a relation of ideas or to a matter of fact, or from a matter of fact to a relation of ideas.

Hume's theory of morals may be considered under three heads: his contention that reason alone cannot decide moral questions, his contention that a "moral sentiment" decides such questions, and his contention that the moral sentiment is actuated only by what is either pleasant or useful. In the first two contentions can be seen the beginnings of modern subjectivism and a strong resemblance to the views of C. L. Stevenson in his *Ethics and Language.* In the third can be seen one of the origins of the utilitarianism of Bentham and Mill.

Hume devoted much space

both in the Treatise *and in the second* Enquiry

to proving that principles of justice depend

entirely on the inventions and traditions of men

and that the obligation to observe and enforce them

arises solely from their utility.

ANTIRATIONALIST ARGUMENTS. Moral decisions sometimes produce and prevent actions; decisions of reason have no such power. Therefore moral decisions are not decisions of reason. The second premise is the conclusion of arguments offered in the *Treatise* (Bk. II, Pt. III, Sec. III). These run as follows: abstract reasoning concerning relations of ideas can never affect action, which is concerned with "realities," not ideas. The only practical employment of mathematics is to "direct," or quantify, our judgments concerning causes and effects, as in engineering and accountancy. Knowledge of causes and effects, whether purely qualitative or refined by measurement and calculation, only affects our actions if the objects so connected are of some interest to us. Nothing can make them of interest to us but the pleasure or pain we expect from them. It is not the reasoning concerning causes and effects which moves us to action, but the desire of the pleasures and fear of the pains which we foresee by this reasoning.

Nor can a rationalist escape by admitting that actions are always due to passion and then distinguishing between reasonable and unreasonable passions. Passions, since they neither represent nor assert anything, cannot be untrue to facts or incompatible with propositions. They may be excited by false or unreasonable judgments concerning the existence of desirable or undesirable objects or concerning the means of achieving or avoiding them. It is the judgments which are reasonable or unreasonable, and not the passions. It is in this context that Hume produced that notoriously provocative overstatement, "Reason is, and ought only to be, the slave of the passions." An error of reasoning is a mistake. If the rationalists are correct, wrongdoing must be some kind of mistake. But mistakes of fact and miscalculations are not blameworthy; and if wrongdoing were defined as a mistake about right and wrong, the definition would be circular.

If right and wrong are discoverable by intuition or demonstration, they must depend on some relation of ideas. The relations concerned in other abstract reasoning are resemblance, contrariety, degrees in quality, and proportions in quantity and number. Morality cannot consist in any of these, since they apply equally to irrational and inanimate objects, whereas morality does not. If morality consists in some other relation, it must satisfy two requirements. First, it must hold only between an action of the mind and an external object. If it can hold between states of mind, we may be guilty of crimes without doing anything to, or even thinking about, any object in the world. If it can hold between external objects, then they, as well as persons, can be guilty or praiseworthy. Second, the relation must be such as to be intuitively or demonstrably obligatory on the will of every rational being. Hume, oddly regarding obligation as a causal relationship, concluded from his account of causation that this requirement cannot be met.

Morality does not consist in any matter of fact inferable from experience. Consider willful murder. "Examine it in all lights, and see if you can find that matter of fact . . . which you call *vice*. The vice entirely escapes you as long as you consider the object." All you can find is a sentiment of disapprobation in your own breast. This sentiment in you is the vice of the action, just as a certain sensation in you is, "according to modern philosophy," the color of an object.

Hume's two main arguments against rationalism appear to be valid against views of the type he had in mind, which assimilated moral reasoning either to mathematical or to empirical reasoning. Hume's paradigm of practical unreason, the man who prefers the destruction of the entire world to the scratching of his finger, is guilty of no miscalculation or faulty inference from the available evidence. Nevertheless, most readers feel dissatisfied with Hume's arguments: first, because many types of wrong conduct, like the preference above cited, do seem to be, in an ordinary sense of the word, unreasonable; and second, because Hume depicted an unreal separation between the "idle judgments" of "inactive" understanding and the busy "passions" which push us into or hold us back from action.

The reasons by which I justify doing or approving something must resemble the reasons by which I justify believing something, in the sense that if they are good reasons, they must be equally good for anyone else in a similar situation doing or approving the same action, just as what is good reason for my believing any proposition is good reason for anyone else's believing it. But no such reasons can be given for the preference above cited. No one else would accept any reason for this preference or this preference as a reason for the corresponding action, nor would the man himself approve of similar preferences and actions in others. To select one's own fingers, out of all the fingers in the world, to be preserved at any cost is arbitrary, and the arbitrary is commonly opposed to the rational.

Both Hume and Kant were aware that this principle of justification by general and universally applicable criteria is central to the moral judgment. Hume imputed our observance of it to a "calm passion," dislike of muddle and controversy; this dislike makes use of another calm passion, "sympathy," in order to provide itself with a common and impartial standard for judging human character. Calm passions are often confused with reason, because their tranquil (but often efficacious) working feels very similar. Therefore, he said, this sense of "reason" and "reasonable" is an improper one.

But if Hume downgraded the universalization principle to the level of a mere matter of minor convenience, Kant upgraded it to too high a level, making it not only the sole source of moral distinctions but also the essence of that rationality which is the essential nature of man's "noumenal self." Kant's most valuable countermove to Hume was to regard moral judgments as imperatives, not expressions of feeling; and imperatives (instructions, advice, and commands, for example), unlike feelings, can be logically related to one another and, thus, are subject to appraisal as self-contradictory or coherent, as arbitrary or capable of being subsumed under a principle—that is, as rational or irrational.

Hume exaggerated the gulf between the "idle" judgments of understanding and the motivating passions. Acting, believing, and wanting are not distinct processes causally related; the concepts are logically dependent on one another. The character of an action, as distinct from a mere bodily response like vomiting, is determined by its intention, that is, by what the agent wants and how he thinks his voluntary movements will bring it about. The reality of a belief is determined by the agent's readiness to do what will satisfy his wants if the proposition believed is true. The reality of his want is determined by his readiness to do what he thinks will realize its object. Hume represented believing and wanting as "distinct objects" inexplicably causally related; they are really two logically interdependent aspects of intelligent behavior. This mistake gives many of his arguments an air of unreality.

Hume concluded the *Treatise,* Book III, Part I, Section I, with an "observation" which he could not "forbear adding, . . . which may be found of some importance." It has in fact enjoyed endless discussion and been canonized as the principle, "No *ought* from an *is.*" Hume said that in all "systems of morality" he had met, the author would start in "the ordinary way of reasoning," proving, for example, the existence of God or describing human society, then suddenly would switch from "is" and "is not" to "ought" and "ought not," for example, from "God *is* our creator" to "We *ought* to obey him." No explanation was ever given of this "new relation" or of how it could be a deduction from others which were entirely different from it; let the reader try to give this explanation, and all "the vulgar systems of morality" would be overthrown, for he would see that moral distinctions are not "founded merely on the relation of objects, nor perceived by reason."

Hume was probably wrong in thinking justice

an artificial virtue esteemed for its utility alone.

It has been claimed by Geoffrey Hunter in "Hume on 'Is' and 'Ought' " (*Philosophy,* Vol. 37, 1962, and Vol. 38, 1963) that Hume did not say that "ought" is deducible from "is," but that if we try to explain how "ought" is deducible from "is," we shall see that the rationalists' explanations were wrong. Hunter suggested that Hume meant that his system and no other could explain the inference from "is" to "ought"; it is an inference from a cause, the agreeable or useful character, to its effect, the sentiment of approbation.

This cannot have been what Hume meant. The whole of Section I of the *Treatise,* Book III, Part I, is directed to prove that moral decisions, which must include an "ought" judgment, are not discoverable by any kind of inference. Is Hunter's suggestion what Hume ought to have meant? If virtue is approval and approval is an effect, why can virtue not be inferred from its cause, like any other effect? Hume's probable answer can be extracted from the following passage of the same section. "You can never find it [the viciousness of willful murder] until you turn your reflection into your own breast, and find a sentiment of disapprobation, which arises in you, towards this action. Here is a matter of fact; but it is the object of feeling, not of reason. It lies in yourself, not in the object." You must look into your *own* breast; the vice lies in *yourself.* What all or most other people feel is irrelevant except insofar as the

thought of it affects *your* feelings. Your sentiment is "the object of feeling, not of reason." I think Hume would have said that there is no such thing as inferring one's own present feelings. If there were, they would be subconscious ones, and nobody decides between right and wrong by what he infers his subconscious approvals and disapprovals to be. Other people's feelings are no doubt a matter of inference; but what would we think of someone who said, "It looks as if most people disapprove of corporal punishment, so it must be wrong, though I personally feel no disapproval at all?" Several critics (for example, C. D. Broad in *Five Types of Ethical Theory*) have thought Hume maintained virtue to be what all or most men approve of. Their mistake may arise from confusing the procedure Hume recommended for the moral philosopher (in Appendix I of the *Enquiry concerning the Principles of Morals*) with that which he claimed underlies the making of moral judgments in ordinary life.

In the second *Enquiry* Hume postponed discussion of the rationalist versus sentimentalist controversy until he had shown that utility and nothing but utility is the determinant of our approval and disapproval. He then dealt more sympathetically with reason, emphasizing the richness and diversity of the preparatory work it has to do before a moral judgment can be made. But from these concessions he derived a new antirationalist argument. The moral judgment cannot be finally made until reason has done all that it can do in analyzing the facts and implications of the case. If anything relevant still remains to be discovered by reason, it is too soon to pass a moral judgment; if nothing relevant still remains to be discovered, "the understanding has no further room to operate," and the moral judgment must be executed by some other faculty (*Enquiry concerning the Principles of Morals,* Appendix I).

THE MORAL SENTIMENT. Hume ascribed moral decisions to sentiment for several reasons: because that seemed the only alternative to reason, which he had rejected; because sentiment was the only impression he could find for the idea of vice; and because moral decisions influence action, something which only feelings and passions can do. The view was thus partly dictated to him by his philosophy of mind.

The moral sentiment is pleasant if it is a feeling of approval, unpleasant if one of disapproval. Its object is always a human character or quality; actions are only concerned insofar as they indicate character. The sentiment therefore contains an element of love or hatred if its object is another's character and of pride or humility (or shame) if it is one's own. This differentiates it from our favorable or unfavorable feelings toward inanimate objects. The moral sentiment arises only when a character or quality is considered generally. This differentiates the feeling of moral sentiment from all partial and interested feelings and frees it from fluctuations due to variations in temporal or spatial distance from the observer. Finally, no feature of a character, when so considered, influences this sentiment except the tendency of that character to be pleasant and useful, or unpleasant and harmful, either to its possessor or to others.

This is a very plausible account of moral approval and disapproval in regard to their objects, the associated feelings (such as shame), and the conditions under which they are properly felt. It should be noted that Hume was not talking about deciding whether actions are right or wrong, that is, forbidden or permitted by existing rules. He was talking about goodness and badness, virtue and vice, which are qualities from which actions spring. He often called disapprobation a "sentiment of blame." Blaming someone is imputing his error to a fault in his character.

What is doubtful is the categorization of moral approval as a "sentiment" or "feeling." If disapprobation is blame, presumably approval is praise; blame and praise are not "feelings." Is the degree of disapprobation really commensurate with the strength of feeling? How "calm" can a passion be and still be a passion? If it is calm, what is the measure of its strength? What common quality do the pleasure of moral approval, the pleasure of sweet music, and the pleasure of struggling to the summit of a mountain share? Do they *feel* at all alike?

These considerations have led modern philosophers to class approval and similar states as dispositions, tendencies to act in certain ways, dispositions which may intimate their existence to their possessor by a feeling (as tiredness does) but are not themselves feelings. But several who take this view, C. L. Stevenson (*Ethics and Language*), P. H. Nowell Smith (*Ethics*), and the present writer (*David Hume, His Theory of Knowledge and Morality*), have made a miscategorization as bad as Hume's in calling these dispositions "attitudes." Attitudes are assumed, taken up, or adopted voluntarily and usually disingenuously; approval and disapproval are not assumed at will, any more than beliefs are. We experience them involuntarily (if we are honest men). That was Hume's reason for calling them both feelings.

Finally, Hume considered how the general tendency of a character to promote happiness arouses this sentiment of approbation, either through a psychological mechanism of sympathy or through an original instinct of benevolence or humanity. The former explanation prevailed in the *Treatise* and the second *Enquiry* (Sec. V). The latter replaced it in Appendix II to the second *Enquiry*. Sympathy is a general psychological process whereby a lively idea of any passion tends to become

that passion itself in a mild form. In this way the supposed pleasures of others become my pleasures. Humanity is a special original instinct prompting me, *ceteris paribus,* to prefer pleasure to pain, no matter whose.

JUSTICE AND UTILITY. Justice is commonly opposed both to expedience and to sentiment; it seems, therefore, a stumbling block to Hume's theory and a potential stronghold for the rationalist. Hume therefore devoted much space both in the *Treatise* and the second *Enquiry* to proving that principles of justice depend entirely on the inventions and traditions of men and that the obligation to observe and enforce them arises solely from their utility.

In the *Treatise* Hume first proved the artificiality of justice, then proceeded to show that such artifices are devised only for their usefulness. In the second *Enquiry,* he first proved their usefulness, then showed their artificial character, though he tactfully avoided labeling justice an "artificial virtue," as he had in the *Treatise.*

The argument for the artificiality of justice in the *Treatise* is that justice is a virtue; a virtue is a praiseworthy motive to action; and the praiseworthy motive to just acts cannot be merely the desire to be just, on pain of vicious circularity. There is no natural motive which always points to the just act. Justice does not necessarily conform to either the agent's private interest, his personal friendships, or the public interest. It must therefore arise from some artifice whose merits we learn. In the *Enquiry* Hume stressed the complicated procedures by which jurists work out a vast variety of different criteria for the determination of rights in varying circumstances; he pointed out that what is just depends, in particular contexts, on such various and plainly artificial conventions as the prohibited degrees of marriage, the rules of courtly love, the rules of war, of games, of the road.

Hume's arguments for the utilitarian foundation of justice consist, in both works, in inviting us to consider real or imaginary situations in which justice would be useless and admit that in these cases it either ceases or would cease to be a virtue. These situations are unlimited abundance of transferable goods, unlimited benevolence in the hearts of men, extreme dearth of necessities in famines and sieges, transactions with animals and savages, who are incapable of or ignorant of the rules. Hume added that perfect equality is not considered a requirement of justice, simply because the attempt to preserve it would be impracticable and pernicious.

On what kind of artifice does justice depend? Not, as many philosophers have supposed, on a contract, for contracts are themselves artifices of the kind in question. It depends on conventions. By a convention or agreement, Hume meant the manifestation to one another by two or more persons of the intention each has to behave, so long as others do likewise, in a certain way that is beneficial to all if followed by all. The longer such intentions are normally fulfilled, the more trustworthy and useful are such agreements. Hume's paradigm case is that of two men pulling the oars of a boat. It is, he maintained, simply because the use of such words as "I promise" or "I give" are governed by conventions that we are able by their use to undertake contractual obligations and transfer proprietary rights. Contracts and promises are not the foundation of human cooperation, but a special case of it. A footnote on this subject (second *Enquiry*, Sec. III, Pt. II) is a remarkable anticipation of J. L. Austin's discoveries concerning the performatory use of language.

In the *Treatise* Hume pointed out that the use of such agreements to regulate the conjunction of forces, partition of tasks, and distribution of products is a lesson men learn in the natural society of the family and is a biological necessity for the survival and prevalence of the human species. Hume's views on politics follow from his theory of justice. Governments, laws, and institutions are useful to human society. Their justification is in their utility, which depends largely on the habitual trust men have in one another's allegiance to them. Consequently, an established trusted government should never be overthrown on grounds of religion or hereditary claims to thrones or in order to experiment with utopian theories. Nor does the authority of governments rest on a contract. Rather the authority of both governments and contracts rests on their utility ("of the Original Contract"). Hume was a conservative. Unlike later utilitarians, he hoped to overthrow nothing and would have liked to overthrow nothing except the Church.

Hume was probably wrong in thinking justice an artificial virtue esteemed for its utility alone. His arguments only prove that property, promises, governments, laws, rules of games, and the like are useful devices, which no man is obliged to respect unless others do likewise. These, or the respect for them, he equated with justice. But there is another, more usual sense of "justice," in which laws and the systems of property can themselves be unjust, in which a mother even in the golden age could be unjust to one child in favor of another. The idea of justice seems, as both Hume and Plato saw, to be somehow connected with the fact that mankind lives by cooperation, by sharing tasks and exchanging products. The man who, or system which, allocates to one man fewer of the tasks or more of the products than it does to another—unless for some reason equally valid for and acceptable to all—is unjust, or as we more usually say, "unfair." The willingness to be fair, the lack of which makes a man unfit to participate in any form of cooperation and distribution, whether instinctive or devised, is no more an "artificial" virtue than courage. And being essentially concerned with distribution, not with aggregation, it cannot be justified by its utility, unless equality, as well as "happiness," be admitted as an ultimate end.

God, Freedom, and Miracles

A believer in God might justify his belief, if asked to, in several ways. He might offer an a priori argument—for instance, the Ontological Argument; he might offer a posteriori arguments, from the marvels of creation to a designing Mind; he might appeal to revelation and cite the miracles recorded in Scripture; he might say that, without an all-powerful Providence, human choices and endeavors are pointless; he might appeal to anthropology to show that it was unnatural for man to live without a religion and attempt to find some converging direction in the developments of particular faiths.

Hume had an answer to each such move. The first two are considered in the *Dialogues concerning Natural Religion*. The existence of God is a matter of fact. Therefore, as already shown in the *Treatise* and first *Enquiry* it cannot be proved a priori, but only from experience by an argument from effect to cause. But we have no experience of the origins of worlds. We must therefore rely on analogy, comparing the world to things of whose origin we have experience. But the world is as like an animal or a vegetable as it is like a machine. So it arose as likely from insemination as from design. Moreover, if God is known only as the cause of the world, we can know nothing of him except that he is such as to create the world we find. We can draw no inferences from his existence except such as are already warranted by our knowledge of the world. He is an empty hypothesis (first *Enquiry*, Sec. XI).

The third move is dealt with in the essay "On Miracles" (first *Enquiry*, Sec. X). Since a miracle is by definition a breach of a law of nature, a known miracle must be a breach of a known law. But a known law of nature by definition carries the highest possible degree of probability, derived from extensive and uniform experience. A miracle can therefore only be accepted if the falsity of the testimony for it would be an even greater miracle, that is, a more glaring improbability than the miracle first alleged. Hume did not deny that this could ever happen. Laws of nature do have to be amended in the light of startling new experiments. He did deny that a miracle can ever be proved as a justifiable foundation for a system of religion. His reason is that the record of known fabrications of marvels of this sort is so black that it is always more probable that a story of a miracle imputed to the action of a god has been made up than that it happened. Moreover, if not all religions are true and if all religions produce miracles, most miracles must be deceptions. All religions do produce miracles. There is, therefore, always a high probability that any one of them is a deception.

The idea of justice seems,

as both Hume and Plato saw,

to be somehow connected with the fact

that mankind lives by cooperation,

by sharing tasks and exchanging products.

The fourth move is met by Hume's section "On Liberty and Necessity" (first *Enquiry*, Sec. VIII; *Treatise*, Bk. II, Pt. III, Secs. I, II). An event, Hume said, is either caused or it is not; in the former case it is causally determined, or necessary. In the latter case it is a pure fluke, or happens by chance. Nobody believes that human actions are of the latter kind, least of all moralists and theologians. How then can they scruple to admit that they are of the former kind? Because, Hume said, they confuse the liberty of indifference with the liberty of spontaneity. It is one thing to perform an uncaused action (if one can conceive such a thing), another to do what you want. Conversely, it is one thing to act from intelligible and natural motives, quite another thing to be compelled to do what you do not want or prevented from doing what you want. Everyone really agrees that, except for prisoners, men enjoy the liberty of spontaneity but not that of indifference, that they are subject to the necessity of causes but not that of constraint.

Three factors assist this confusion: Imagining that we find an objective necessity in physical causation and not finding it in the will, we conclude that there is no causality in the will. Finding that I can first raise and then lower my hand without any alteration of the conditions, I suppose there must be a total indifference between these movements—failing to notice that the cause of the difference on the second occasion was my desire to demonstrate my liberty. Theology confuses the question of freedom with its own problem of the origin of evil. In the *Treatise* Hume said that "religion has been very unnecessarily interested in the question"; he insisted that a causal connection between actions and motives is essential to the concepts of praise and blame, reward and punishment, whether human or divine. In the *En-quiry* Hume proceeded more archly. His argument was quite intricate; the following interpretation of the logical structure behind Hume's camouflage of irony was made by Antony Flew (*Hume's Philosophy of Belief*, Ch. 7).

Hume's causal determinism combined with theism entails that God is the originator of our actions. (All events with causes trace their causal ancestry to him, and our actions have causes.) Hence it follows that either no actions are evil, being due to God, or that God is responsible for our sins. Hume pretended to regard this as an objection to causal determinism; he really meant it as an objection to theism, for he had already shown that there is no alternative to causal necessity except chance, which is unacceptable to all parties.

Hume then examined the objection. The first alternative, that no actions are evil, can be avoided; even if our actions are precontrived by God, and the "bad" ones are as necessary as the good to the goodness of the whole, their badness consists in the sentiments they naturally arouse in the human breast, which are unaffected by such remote considerations. We are left with the second alternative, real moral evil for which God is responsible. Hume saw no way to meet this difficulty. With tongue in cheek, he concluded that such "sublime mysteries" are beyond the reach of unassisted reason and, therefore, of philosophy.

Finally, he argued that no one should suppose that a belief in theism is natural to mankind. In "The Natural History of Religion," an entertaining exercise in armchair anthropology from secondary sources, Hume maintained that there is no evidence of any specific instinct for religious belief. Some races have no religion. In all known cases the earliest religions were polytheistic and idolatrous, with no notion whatever of an intelligent cause of the whole frame of nature. They were as truly atheistic as would be the beliefs of a contemporary person who acknowledged elves and fairies but denied the existence of God. The polytheistic systems were not, according to Hume, primitive systems of science. Primitive man was not interested in accounting for the regular phenomena of nature; he took the familiar for granted, however marvelous. It was the bewildering successions of floods and droughts, sickness and health, calm and tempest, victory and defeat, birth and death, that alternately terrified and comforted, nourished and destroyed him; it was these contrary and diverse events which, by a natural tendency to see external things in his own likeness, he ascribed to diverse and warring invisible persons, amenable to flattery and bribes and even to threats and force of arms.

In short, it was not God as the author of nature but God as a particular providence for which primitive religions were an origin and prototype. The only original instincts involved were the fear of death and pain and the desire for security and pleasure, together with a tendency to personify inanimate things.

Hume constantly pretended, how sincerely it is difficult to say, to distinguish "true" or "philosophical" religion from superstition as above described. But the concession is in the end an empty one, for all that Hume's philosophical theism amounted to was that probably, and not in any scientifically respectable sense of "probably," the universe was due to something remotely analogous to a designing mind (*Dialogues concerning Natural Religion,* Pt. XII). But the moral attributes of God, providence, immortality, and the whole Christian story from the Fall to the Day of Judgment he regarded as superstition.

BIBLIOGRAPHY

Works by Hume

A Treatise of Human Nature, Bks. I and II, 2 vols. London, 1739. Bk. III, London, 1740. Modern editions are by L. A. Selby Bigge (Oxford, 1888 and 1896) and by A. D. Lindsay (London and New York, 1911, 2 vols.). A recent edition of Book I only, by D. G. C. Macnabb (New York, 1962), also includes the *Abstract.*

An Abstract of a Treatise of Human Nature. London, 1740. Modern edition by J. M. Keynes and Piero Sraffa, eds. Cambridge, 1938.

Essays, Moral and Political, 2 vols. Edinburgh, 1741–1742.

Three Essays ("Of Natural Character," "Of the Original Contract," and "Of Passive Obedience"). London, 1748.

Enquiry concerning Human Understanding. London, 1748. Published as *Philosophical Essays concerning Human Understanding* as were all the early editions prior to that of 1758. Modern edition by C. W. Hendel. New York, 1955.

Enquiry concerning the Principles of Morals. London, 1751. Modern edition by C. W. Hendel. New York, 1957.

Hume's Enquiries, L. A. Selby Bigge, ed. Oxford, 1894. Contains both *Enquiries.*

Political Discourses. London, 1752.

Four Dissertations ("The Natural History of Religion," "Of the Passions," "Of Tragedy," and "Of the Standard of Taste"). London, 1757.

Two Essays ("Of Suicide" and "Of the Immortality of the Soul"). London, 1777.

The Life of David Hume, Esq., Written by Himself, Adam Smith, ed. London, 1777. Reprinted in Mossner, E. C., *The Life of David Hume* and in Greig, J. Y. T., *The Letters of David Hume.* Often found under its original manuscript title, *My Own Life.*

Dialogues concerning Natural Religion. London, 1779. Recent edition by Norman Kemp Smith. Oxford, 1935; Edinburgh, 1947; New York, 1962.

History of Great Britain from the Invasion of Julius Caesar to the Revolution of 1688, 6 vols. London, 1754–1762. More recent edition by R. Worthington. New York, 1880.

Hume's Philosophical Works, T. H. Green and T. H. Grose, eds. 4 vols. London, 1874–1875. Includes all works listed above except the *Abstract* and the *History.*

Works on Hume

Life and Letters

Greig, J. Y. T., *David Hume.* London, 1931.

Greig, J. Y. T., ed., *The Letters of David Hume,* 2 vols. Oxford, 1932.

Klibansky, Raymond, and Mossner, E. C., eds. *New Letters of David Hume.* Oxford, 1954.

Mossner, E. C., *The Life of David Hume.* Austin, Texas, London, and Edinburgh, 1954.

Critical Works

Church, R. W., *Hume's Theory of the Understanding.* Ithaca, N.Y., 1935. The author contends that the constructive side of Hume's philosophy, particularly his theory of belief, is independent of his doctrine of impressions and ideas.

Flew, Antony, *Hume's Philosophy of Belief.* London and New York, 1961. A serious attempt to meet Hume's request to be judged by his *Enquiries* and not the *Treatise,* with special emphasis on his philosophy of religion.

Green, T. H., *General Introduction to Hume's Treatise.* London, 1874. A classical exposition from the idealist point of view of the traditional account of Hume's philosophy as a negative and untenable subjectivism.

Hendel, C. W., *Studies in the Philosophy of David Hume.* Princeton, N.J., 1925. Revised edition, New York, 1963. A sympathetic and scholarly interpretation of Hume's contribution to philosophy.

Kemp Smith, Norman, *The Philosophy of David Hume.* London, 1941. An authoritative assessment of Hume, stressing the parallelism between his ethics and his epistemology and the priority of the former.

Laing, B. M., *David Hume.* London, 1932. An attack on the traditional view of Hume's philosophy as a bankrupt atomistic sensationalism.

Laird, John, *Hume's Philosophy of Human Nature.* London, 1932. An acute and learned analysis of Hume's arguments and their relations to earlier and contemporary philosophers.

Leroy, André-Louis, *David Hume.* Paris, 1953. A lively discussion of Hume as seen through the eyes of a modern Continental.

Macnabb, D. G. C., *David Hume, His Theory of Knowledge and Morality.* London, 1951. An attempt to clarify Hume's arguments to the modern reader.

Michotte, Albert Edouard, *La Perception de la causalité.* Louvain, Belgium, 1954. Translated by T. R. Miles and E. Miles as *The Perception of Causality.* London, 1962. An account and discussion of experiments at the University of Louvain, claimed to prove the existence of an unlearned visual impression of mechanical causality.

Passmore, J. A., *Hume's Intentions.* Cambridge, 1952. A brief but acute analysis of the distinct but related trends in Hume's thought.

Price, H. H., *Hume's Theory of the External World.* Oxford, 1940. An original attempt to extract the elements of truth in Hume's account of sense perception.

Stewart, J. B., *The Moral and Political Philosophy of David Hume.* New York, 1963.

Taylor, A. E., "David Hume and the Miraculous," in his *Philosophical Studies.* London, 1934.

Zabech, Farhang, *Hume: Precursor of Modern Empiricism.* The Hague, 1960. An analysis of Hume's opinions on meaning, metaphysics, logic, and mathematics in relation to later philosophy.

— D. G. C. MACNABB

HUME, DAVID (UPDATE)

David Hume (1711–1776), has traditionally been viewed, in epistemology and ethics alike, as the exponent of a radical, destructive skepticism that results when the empiricist premises of Locke and Berkeley are pursued to their remotest consequences. Though this remains the view of the generality of philosophers, there is a growing consensus among specialists in Hume's thought that, far from being an innovator in the subjectivist theory of ideas, he merely exploited the skeptical arguments of his predecessors to clear the ground for a moderate, realist naturalism.

Hume's general account of identity in terms of fictions of imagination is generally regarded as the weakest point in his epistemology.

The subordination of skepticism to naturalism stems from the work of Norman Kemp Smith in the early twentieth century, and he remains the outstanding proponent of this view. He distinguished two components in Hume's naturalism: (1) the thesis that our beliefs and actions are founded not on reason but on sentiments rooted in human nature; and (2) the attempt to explain these beliefs and actions causally by means of quasi-mechanical associative propensities. Some commentators give pride of place to the second component, principally because it was in the course of elaborating and defending his explanations that Hume begat the notions that have influenced subsequent philosophy (Beauchamp & Rosenberg; Fogelin; Stroud; Wright). However, most historically focused naturalist interpretation emphasizes the first component, particularly in the guise of a "philosophy of common life" (Baier; Capaldi; Livingston). The central idea is that Hume's entire corpus, from the *Treatise* to the *Essays* and *History of England,* is set within the framework of historically grounded, continuously evolving social institutions and public language. Even Hume's talk of 'perceptions' and 'association of ideas' should be referred not to a solipsistically isolated, individual consciousness—a bundle of perceptions that is neither mind nor body—but to our ordinary, everyday selves. The theme of common life thus bestows a unity, a grand design, on the whole of Hume's intellectual achievement.

Epistemology

PSYCHOLOGY. Though the rise of the naturalist view has discouraged interpreters from examining in detail Hume's claims to be an innovator in the subjectivist theory of ideas, there are some exceptions. First, Hume's relation to Husserlian phenomenology has been the object of considerable attention (Murphy), as has his relation to intentionality theory (Livingston). Second, the increasing tendency to regard Hume as a metaphysical realist (see examples below) has focused attention on relative ideas (relations with an imperceptible term) and inconceivable suppositions (realities posited in the absence of any impression or idea). Third, since Kemp Smith's case for naturalism is predicated on peculiar construals of such key notions of Hume's philosophy as vivacity, relation, and association, antinaturalist interpreters have offered alternatives and, in the process, illuminated Hume's accounts of sense certainty, memory, time consciousness, and aspect seeing (Waxman).

INDUCTION, CAUSATION, AND PHILOSOPHY OF SCIENCE. Hume's skepticism about induction is a subject of considerable controversy, with some interpreters treating it as a restricted critique of a narrowly philosophical, Cartesian view of empirical rationality, while others relate it to a broader, more ordinary notion of probable reasoning. Either way, naturalist interpreters treat Hume's skepticism as epistemic rather than ontological or conceptual and tend to combine it with ontological realism about both causation and bodies (Beauchamp & Rosenberg; Stroud); some contend that he was a realist about necessary connections as well as regularities and so classify him among Cartesian rationalists (Strawson; Wright). Methodologically, much attention has been paid to how the normative principles of science Hume derived from his naturalist account of causation (in *Treatise,* bk. 1, pt. 3. sec. 15) are self-consciously exemplified in his own philosophizing (Baier; Wilson).

BODY AND MIND. Hume's general account of identity in terms of fictions of imagination is generally regarded as the weakest point in his epistemology, though an exception tends to be made for his way of framing the problem of personal identity and his critique of alternative accounts. The main focus of interpreters is whether Hume's subjectivist approach is compatible with belief in the ontological reality of bodies, minds, and substances and, if so, whether he adopted a commonsense ("vulgar") realism or a scientific ("double existence") realism. Hume's assertion that "we may well ask, *What causes induce us to believe in the existence of body?* but 'tis in vain to ask, *Whether there be body or not?*" (*Treatise,* bk. 1, pt. 4, sec. 2) is widely taken to confirm that he accepted the mind-independent reality of the external world. Those belonging to the common-life school emphasize the continuum between vulgar and scientific belief, while dissenters attribute to Hume one or another form of indirect realism (skeptical in the case of Wright, scientific in that of Wilson). In general, naturalist interpreters suppose that Hume's account of personal identity, wittingly or not, premises the reality of the external world (Bricke, Pears) and perhaps human society and language as well (Baier; Livingston). The reverse, however, has also been maintained (Waxman) on the ground that there can be no standard for the externality and independence of objects other than relation to the mind (a corollary of Hume's espousal of Locke's account of temporal succession).

Moral Philosophy

Hume's theory of the passions was long denigrated as evincing the worst features of the associationalist. "Newtonian" strand of his thought: blind mechanism substituted for contextualized understanding, theory riding roughshod over data, psychology smothering philosophy. Thanks to several fine historical and textual studies (Àrdal; Baier; Norton), a new appreciation of the subtlety and explanatory power of the theory has emerged and, with it, of how for Hume human nature is inherently a moral nature. For example, if we accept that Hume viewed moral reason as inherently social (Baier) and practical—a "we-do," not an "I-think," reason (Capaldi)—the traditional picture of him, as moral subjectivist and skeptic, becomes untenable (holdouts include Fogelin and, to a lesser extent, J. L. Mackie). Nor can it be taken for granted any longer that Hume's antirationalist sentimentalism is incompatible with moral realism or moral cognitivism (Norton).

Scholarship

Under the ægis of the Hume Society and its journal, *Hume Studies* (1975–), Hume scholarship has burgeoned. Long-neglected aspects of his thought—religion, aesthetics, politics, philosophy of history—have begun to receive the scholarly attention they require and deserve. A new critical edition of Hume's philosophical, political, and literary writings under the editorship of Tom L. Beauchamp, David Fate Norton, and M. A. Stewart is planned by Oxford Clarendon Press and should further promote this process.

[See also Berkeley, George; Causation; Epistemology; Locke, John; Mackie, John Leslie; Naturalism; Personal Identity; Phenomenology; Realism; Skepticism.]

BIBLIOGRAPHY

Àrdal, P. S. *Passion and Value in Hume's "Treatise."* Edinburgh, 1966. A detailed textual analysis of Hume's theory of the passions.

Baier, A. *A Progress of Sentiments.* Cambridge, MA, 1991. An authoritative, highly persuasive vision of the *Treatise* as reason's onerous progress toward self-comprehension, which it finds in society.

Beauchamp, T. L., and A. Rosenberg. *Hume and the Problem of Causation.* New York, 1981. An attempt to defend Hume's views on induction and causation against contemporary views.

Bricke, J. *Hume's Philosophy of Mind.* Edinburgh, 1980.

Capaldi, N. *Hume's Place in Moral Philosophy.* New York, 1989. Maintains that Hume wrought a Copernican revolution in philosophy by substituting a "we-do" orientation for the "I-think" of his predecessors. Contains an extended, if jaundiced, survey of Hume scholarship.

Chuo University. *David Hume and the Eighteenth Century British Thought: An Annotated Catalogue,* edited by S. Ikeda. Tokyo, 1986, 1988.

Fogelin, R. *Hume's Skepticism in the "Treatise of Human Nature."* London, 1985. Aspires to restore Hume's skepticism to a status equal, and complementary, to his naturalism, both in epistemology and in morals.

Gaskin, J. C. *Hume's Philosophy of Religion,* 2d ed. New York, 1988.

Hall, R. *50 Years of Hume Scholarship.* Edinburgh, 1978.

Harrison, J. *Hume's Moral Epistemology.* Oxford, 1976.

Levine, M. *Hume and the Problem of Miracles: A Solution.* Dordrecht, 1989.

Livingston, D. W. *Hume's Philosophy of Common Life.* Chicago, 1984. Maintains that Hume adopted the approach of the social historian even in epistemology.

Mackie, J. L. *Hume's Moral Theory.* London, 1980. A projectivist reading of Hume's sentimentalism, with a keen analysis of his account of virtue.

Murphy, R. *Hume and Husserl: Towards Radical Subjectivism.* Boston, 1980.

Norton, D. *David Hume: Common-Sense Moralist, Sceptical Metaphysician.* Princeton, 1984. Contains an excellent account of Hutcheson and examines other influences on Hume.

———, ed. *The Cambridge Companion to Hume.* Cambridge, 1993. Contains an excellent bibliography.

Pears, D. *Hume's System.* Oxford, 1990. Attempts to balance Hume's empiricism and naturalism by correlating the first to a theory of meaning and the second to a theory of truth.

Snare, F. *Morals Motivation and Convention: Hume's Influential Doctrines.* Cambridge, 1991.

Stove, D. C. *Probability and Hume's Inductive Scepticism.* Oxford, 1973.

Strawson, G. *The Secret Connexion: Causation, Realism, and David Hume.* Oxford, 1989.

Stroud, B. *Hume.* London, 1977. Presents Hume as advancing a theory of human nature in which the traditional conception of man as rational animal is overturned.

Waxman, W. *Hume's Theory of Consciousness.* Cambridge, 1994. A critique of the premises of the naturalist interpretation and a defense of the traditional view of Hume as a more extreme subjectivist, skeptical successor to Locke and Berkeley.

Whelan, F. G. *Order and Artifice in Hume's Political Philosophy.* Princeton, 1985.

Wilson, F. *Laws and Other Worlds.* Dordrecht, 1986.

Wright, J. *The Skeptical Realism of David Hume.* Manchester, 1983. Presents Hume as an epistemological skeptic but ontological realist about bodies and causes.

— WAYNE WAXMAN

HUSSERL, EDMUND

Edmund Husserl (1859–1938), German philosopher and the central figure in the phenomenological movement, began his career in mathematics, receiving his Ph.D. in 1881. After a brief assistantship to the noted mathematician Karl Theodor Weierstrass, he moved to Vienna, where he attended the lectures of the philosopher Franz Brentano from 1884 to 1886, and decided to devote himself to philosophy. He taught in Halle (1887–1901), Göttingen (1901–1916), and Freiburg (1916–1929), where he spent the remainder of his life, during the last few years exposed to various social and political pressures because of his Jewish ancestry.

Philosophy, for Husserl, was not just his occupation; it was of the utmost seriousness to him. He spoke of it as some men speak of their call to the priesthood or others of their most sacred moral duties. Were he to waver in his devotion, he would be untrue to himself; were he to lose faith in philosophy, he would lose faith in himself.

Philosophy, as he committed himself to it, was first and foremost a science. His conception of this philosophical science changed more than once, but he never wavered in his conviction that only a body of indubitable and objective truths deserves to be called "science." The truths he sought do not concern this or that particular subject matter. He sought the truths on which all other human knowledge rests.

Devoted to his pursuit with a moral fervor, he worked steadily throughout most of his long life, publishing eight books or long articles and writing 45,000 manuscript pages in shorthand, some of it practically ready for publication, the rest in less finished form. His search was for the unshakable foundation of human knowledge, which he often referred to as the "Archimedean point." More than once he was led to abandon earlier views, for it was all-important that the beginning should be made correctly. He spoke of himself with pride, mixed with sadness, as "a perpetual beginner." His writings, both the published and unpublished ones, are best regarded as more or less polished working papers. There is no Husserlian "system"; there are no incontestable phenomenological truths; there is no unambiguous and incontrovertible description of the phenomenological method.

The requirement that philosophy be scientific is specified in several imperatives for philosophers. The philosopher must seek complete clarity. He must seek apodictic certainty, at least for the starting points of his inquiry. He must be "radical" in the sense that he must take nothing for granted. Ideally, at least, philosophy is presuppositionless; no statement is to be admitted as true without scrutiny, no conception to be used without examination.

The search for clarity and understanding prompted Husserl's first philosophical inquiries. He was not sat-

Philosophy, as Husserl committed himself to it, was first and foremost a science. (Austrian National Library, Vienna)

isfied with doing mathematics without complete clarity about the meaning of basic mathematical concepts. Encouraged by Brentano, he turned to the philosophy of mathematics, and in 1891 he published the first volume of his *Philosophie der Arithmetik*. In this book he attempted a psychological analysis of certain basic logical and mathematical notions. The concept of number, for instance, was to be elucidated by talking about the activity of counting. In his review of this book, the mathematician Gottlob Frege argued that logical and mathematical concepts differ from the psychological acts in which they may occur and that, therefore, the discussion of the latter does not serve to explicate the former. He accused Husserl of confusing psychology and logic.

CRITIQUE OF PSYCHOLOGISM. Husserl was impressed by Frege's objections. The promised second volume of the *Philosophie der Arithmetik* never appeared. Instead, he brought out his *Logische Untersuchungen*, in two volumes (1900–1901). The first of these volumes contains a thorough critique of the assumption underlying the earlier book, the assimilation of logic and psychology, a view which he called "psychologism." Psychologism is now rejected; the foundations of logic and mathematics are not to be found in psychology, for psychology is an empirical science. Logic and mathematics are a priori sciences. Philosophy, too, is a priori, dealing with rational concepts and necessary truths. Later, in an essay called "Philosophie als strenge Wissenschaft" (1910), Husserl generalized this new conception of philosophy by attacking "naturalism"—the claim that statements in the existing sciences are premises in philosophic argument—and "historicism"—the view that philosophic truths are not eternal truths but are relative to historical epochs. The second view had been defended by Dilthey and his followers.

Husserl's search was for the unshakable foundation of human knowledge, which he often referred to as the "Archimedean point."

The concept of philosophy as a science thus changes from philosophy as a part of empirical natural science to philosophy as an a priori, autonomous science. This science Husserl called "phenomenology" without knowing very clearly, at first, what that term meant to him. In the first edition of the *Logische Untersuchungen*, Husserl identified it with "descriptive psychology" in spite of his earlier polemic against psychologism. He soon realized that it was a mistake to use the word "psychology" to describe what he was doing and argued at length in "Philosophie als strenge Wissenschaft" that phenomenology and psychology must be distinguished. But he continued to insist that phenomenology is descriptive. This distinguishes the method of phenomenology, he thought, from the established practice of philosophy, which deduces what must be true of the world from prior assumptions instead of looking at the world and discovering what it is like. It is not altogether clear which other philosophers are genuinely open to this criticism; Husserl may well have been unfair to his predecessors. But his insistence that phenomenology is descriptive is another expression of the imperative that we must philosophize without presuppositions.

The second volume of the *Logische Untersuchungen* contained six separate essays concerned with concepts important in logic, such as "meaning" and "judgment." In these essays Husserl first discussed the concept of intentionality in detail. Following Brentano, he held that all mental acts are intentional. This means that a true description of a mental act—for example, "Husserl thought that all mental acts are intentional"—does not entail the existence or the truth of the intentional object, in this example, "mental acts are intentional." The doctrine of intentionality recognizes that all mental acts are, in principle, fallible.

TRANSCENDENTAL PHENOMENOLOGY. In the fifth essay of the *Logische Untersuchungen,* Husserl provided a description of the several elements of intentional acts. But what sort of descriptions are these? How are we to distinguish these phenomenological descriptions from ordinary psychological ones? In answer to this question, he introduced the "transcendental–phenomenological reduction" in a series of lectures entitled *Die Idee der Phänomenologie* (1907). These lectures were not published, however, until after his death. The "reduction" first appeared in print in his lifetime in his *Ideen zu einer reinen Phänomenologie und phänomenologischen Philosophie* (1913). The transcendental-phenomenological reduction is a methodological device, required before one can begin to do phenomenology. Roughly, it is the transition from an ordinary, straightforward attitude toward the world and the objects in it to a reflective attitude. However, the precise nature of this device always remained an acute problem for Husserl.

Once we perform the reduction, Husserl claimed, we discover what he called the "transcendental ego," or "pure consciousness," for which everything that exists is an object. We discover that whatever is in the world is only as object for our pure consciousness. The task of describing the workings of this pure consciousness falls to the phenomenologist. Phenomenology is now characterized as the exploration and description of a realm of being, previously unsuspected, which is the absolute foundation of the experienced world, a realm of being, moreover, which is not accessible to empirical observation but only to phenomenological description and to something Husserl called "eidetic intuition."

Because the existence of the transcendental ego is indubitable, its discovery serves both to distinguish phenomenology from the empirical sciences and to provide the Archimedean point at which to begin our studies. These doctrines caused considerable stir, particularly among the members of the phenomenological movement, many of whom regarded them as regrettable lapses into metaphysics, a straying away from the primrose path of descriptive phenomenology.

For the next 10 or 15 years, Husserl held some rather extreme views on the transcendental ego. He said more than once that this ego would remain in existence even if the entire world were destroyed and that this ego is an individual entity, distinct from the self which is the object of my empirical self-observations or the observations of the psychologist. It sounds very much as if I had two selves, one of them the familiar empirical one, the other a transcendental and generally unknown one which would remain in existence even if my empirical self were destroyed together with the destruction of the world. One may well doubt that such a claim is supported by the description of phenomena.

True to his methodological maxims, Husserl refused to be discouraged by this sort of doubt. He was perfectly well aware of them; he continued to raise them himself, both in his later publications and in his unpublished notes. But true to the maxim that phenomenology describes and does not argue, he saw in these objections only a sign that the descriptions given of the transcendental ego so far were not adequate, and he tried to give better ones.

In the *Formale und transcendentale Logik* (1929) he still held that the transcendental ego exists "absolutely" and that all other things exist "relative" to it. But in his lectures given in 1935 and published under the title *Die Krisis der europäischen Wissenschaften und die transcendentale Phänomenologie* (Belgrade, 1936), the transcendental ego was said to be "correlative" to the world; it had lost its absolute status. Equally important is another change. The world is no longer said to be what it is for any transcendental individual but for an intersubjective community of individuals. The problem of the intersubjectivity of transcendental egos was first discussed in the *Cartesianische Meditationen*, which originated in a series of lectures given in Paris in 1929.

Husserl's insistence that phenomenology is descriptive is another expression of the imperative that we must philosophize with presuppositions.

The concept of phenomenology now changed once again. Phenomenology was no longer the description of a separate realm of being but, rather, the reflection on and description of the ways in which our communal experience comes to be, what are the criteria for the coherence of different sorts of experiences and for their adequacy, Phenomenology no longer differed from the empirical sciences because it had a different subject from them but because it dealt with the world in a different way, the reflective, and reflected not on matters of fact but on the necessary conditions for coherence and adequacy of experience.

One other major change in the conception of phenomenology had occurred. Earlier, phenomenological reflection was to have provided the foundations of scientific knowledge (in a large sense of "scientific") by reflecting about scientific knowledge. Now Husserl distinguished sharply between the world as known to science and the world in which we live, the *Lebenswelt*.

Scientific knowledge, he now believed, can be understood only if we first understand the *Lebenswelt*. The study of that lived world and of our experience of it becomes the first task of phenomenology.

[See also Phenomenology.]

BIBLIOGRAPHY

Works by Husserl

Husserliana, Edmund Husserl, Gesammelte Werke. The Hague, 1950– . Nine volumes have been published thus far, and other volumes are in preparation. Vols. I–IX primarily contain unpublished writings and relevant working notes.

Philosophie der Arithmetik. Halle, Germany, 1891.

Logische Untersuchungen, 2 vols. Halle, Germany, 1900–1901. Translated by Hubert Elie as *Recherches logiques.* Paris, 1959–1963.

"Philosophie als strenge Wissenschaft." *Logos,* Vol. I (1910), 289–314. Translated by Quentin Lauer as "Philosophy as Rigorous Science," in Edmund Husserl, *Phenomenology and the Crisis of Philosophy.* New York, 1965.

Ideen zu einer reinen Phänomenologie und phänomenologischen Philosophie, Vol. I. Halle, Germany, 1913. Translated by W. R. Boyce Gibson as *Ideas—General Introduction to Pure Phenomenology.* London, 1931. The second and third volumes were published posthumously in *Husserliana, op. cit.,* Vols. IV–V (1952).

"Phenomenology," translated by C. V. Salmon in *Encyclopaedia Britannica,* 14th ed. Chicago, 1929. Vol. XVII, pp. 700–702.

Formale und transcendentale Logik. Halle, 1929. Translated by Suzanne Bachelard as *Logique formelle et logique transcendantale.* Paris, 1957.

Cartesianische Meditationen, in *Husserliana, op. cit.,* Vol. I (1950). Translated by Dorion Cairns as *Cartesian Meditations.* The Hague, 1960.

Die Krisis der europäischen Wissenschaften und die transcendentale Phänomenologie, in *Husserliana, op. cit.,* Vol. VI (1954).

Works on Husserl

Bachelard, Suzanne, *La Logique de Husserl.* Paris, 1957. An insightful and instructive commentary on Husserl's *Formale und transcendentale Logik* that contains some of the most intelligible statements about transcendental phenomenology.

Diemer, Alwin, *Edmund Husserl, Versuch einer systematischen Zusammenstellung seiner Phänomenologie.* Meisenheim am Glan, Germany, 1956.

Fink, Eugen, "Die phänomenologische Philosophie Edmund Husserls in der gegenwärtigen Kritik." *Kantstudien,* Vol. 38 (1933), 319–83. A defense of Husserl against Neo-Kantian critics by Husserl's assistant. The article has Husserl's official approval.

Spiegelberg, Herbert, *The Phenomenological Movement,* 2 vols. The Hague, 1960. Discusses Husserl in Vol. I, pp. 73–167. Bibliography.

Szilasi, Wilhelm, *Einführung in die Phänomenologie Edmund Husserls.* Tübingen, Germany, 1959.

– RICHARD SCHMITT

HUSSERL, EDMUND (UPDATE)

Between 1970 and 1995 several of Husserl's major works (including, most prominently, *Logische Untersuchungen, Krisis der europäischen Wissenschaften und die transzendentale Phänomenologie, Formale und transzendentale Logik, Phänomenologische Psychologie,* and *Ideen II*) were translated into English. Twenty additional volumes in the *Husserliana* series appeared, some making important works easily available again (such as Husserl's early writings on mathematics and formal logic), others making available for the first time Husserl's lectures and research manuscripts on intersubjectivity, ethics, the constitution of spatiality, and imagination and memory. Moreover, the scholarly reception of two volumes published shortly before 1970, one on passive synthesis and the other a critical edition of Husserl's lectures on time-consciousness, have strongly influenced the way that scholars view Husserl's work. These developments have not led to a whole-scale revision of the general view of Husserl's phenomenology that had been based primarily upon the *Cartesianische Meditationen* and the *Ideen I.* Scholars continue to agree that for Husserl intentionality is the fundamental structure of consciousness, that the objects of human cognition are intentional objects, and hence that the analysis of consciousness and its correlative objects is the proper starting point for philosophy. The method of phenomenological reduction retains its central position in discussions of Husserlian phenomenology. The publications and translations between 1970 and 1995 have nonetheless influenced the discussion significantly.

First of all, they have allowed readers to come to a better understanding of the internal motives for the development of Husserl's thinking. Previously, it was common to attribute many of the changes in Husserl's positions between major works to outside influences. Shifts in Husserl's thinking between the *Philosophie der Arithmetik* and the *Logische Untersuchungen* were attributed to a critical review of the former work by Frege, and the emphasis upon the lifeworld in the *Krisis* was widely viewed as a response to Heidegger's *Sein und Zeit.* The edition of Husserl's early essays on logic and the foundation of mathematics in *Aufsätze und Rezensionen (1890–1910),* however, establishes that Husserl himself had become dissatisfied with many of his earlier formulations and adopted positions similar to those of the *Logische Untersuchungen* before Frege's review was composed. Similarly, closer attention to Husserl's analyses of the personalistic world in *Ideen II* and to other manuscripts such as the lectures on passive synthesis and those published in *Erfahrung und Urteil* show that his analyses of the lifeworld emanate from phenomenological research conducted prior to the appearance of Heidegger's major work. At the same time, however, the publication of a critical edition of the *Sechste cartesianische Meditation* and of the intersubjectivity lectures demonstrate the collaborative aspects of Husserl's relationship to his assistants Eugen Fink and Edith Stein

and their influence on his work. The publication of Husserl's correspondence also makes it possible to situate Husserl much better against the backdrop of his age and his intellectual and cultural milieu.

> *Phenomenology turns out to be more than just a method. It also involves the project of exploring the structures of an extremely wide range of regions and the foundational relationships that govern them.*

Second, these publications demonstrate that Husserl's painstaking phenomenological analyses extended to a much wider range of areas than logic and the theory of perception and thereby shifted much of the discussion from questions of methodology to specific topics. The focus of *Ideen I* and *Cartesianische Meditationen* is the proper methodology for phenomenology. For many years *Ideas I* was the only major work by Husserl available in English. It was joined by *Meditations* and two shorter works, *The Idea of Phenomenology* and "Philosophy as a Rigorous Science," both programmatic pieces, during the early 1960s. Thus, it was natural for questions of phenomenological method to dominate the discussion, especially since much of what Husserl himself published during his lifetime dealt more with the general outlines of the program of phenomenology than with concrete phenomenological analyses of specific domains. (Of course, in works that were long available in German, one finds concrete phenomenological analyses, but these are limited primarily to the foundations of logic, mathematics, and the natural sciences.) The *Husserliana* volumes completed since 1966 have not only provided much more detailed discussions of Husserl's analyses of perception and his work on the foundations of mathematics and logic, but have also made accessible for the first time extended discussions of intersubjectivity, the foundations of the human sciences, ethics, and religion. Phenomenology turns out to be more than just a method. It also involves the project of exploring the structures of an extremely wide range of regions and the foundational relationships that govern them. It also becomes apparent that the ultimate object of analysis is concrete human life as a culturally situated, practically involved, historical interaction with cultural objects, persons, and institutions—along with unique abstractive cultural formations such as modern natural science, logic, and mathematics. Husserl shows how such complex formations are constituted first on the basis of simpler operations beginning with the simplest acts of sense perceptions on the part of individuals, up through the formation of theoretical judgments, and how these are conjoined with acts of willing and valuing, to form practical and evaluative judgments. Moreover, after tracing out the simple elements involved in the constitution of intersubjectivity, all of this takes place within an intersubjective, cultural, and historical environment. Finally, Husserl tries to show how all of these developments are guided by the norm of rationality, of intentions and anticipations that each in its own way claims to have some basis in experience and may be justified or refuted through recourse to the simple or complex experiences that they implicitly aim at. Husserl tries to show how the guiding concept of evidence is not limited to the scientific or philosophical realm but is rather the expression of a fundamental structure of conscious life that ultimately issues in the norms of autonomy and self-responsibility that are exemplified explicitly in truly philosophical existence but also serve as the implicit norm for all human existence.

Finally, the new publications have made scholars careful about identifying Husserl's phenomenology with the Cartesian project of finding an absolute foundation for knowledge in truths that are eternal, completely certain, and irrefutable through reflection of a conscious ego that is completely and immediately self-transparent. The very confident and final tone of Husserl's early pronouncements concerning the possibility of constructing transcendental phenomenology as a science that can achieve results once and for all with absolute certainty has been called into question. Already in *Formale und transzendentale Logik*, Husserl points out that evidence with regard to ideal objects (which includes meanings or senses, the primary objects of phenomenological analysis) is not apodictic in the sense of being beyond doubt. Scholars have come to see that Husserl also recognized the important role of passive, prepredicative elements in valuing and knowing that are not easily and directly accessible to subjective reflection. Analysis of kinaesthesis in *Phänomenologische Psychologie, Ideen II*, and *Analysen zur passiven Synthese* make clear that the subject of knowledge is not just a pure consciousness but an embodied agent. Much of the impetus for the reevaluation of Husserl has also come as a response to challenges from Emanuel Levinas, Maurice Merleau-Ponty, and Jacques Derrida, who have joined the previously well-known Martin Heidegger in claiming to be followers of Husserl in phenomenology while rejecting what each identifies as inappropriate Cartesian elements in Husserl's phenomenology. These figures have exhibited new directions in which Husserl's phenomenological project may be taken and have also prompted Husserl's defenders to emphasize those in-

sights that anticipate many of his successors' positions and to reinterpret Husserl's work as a whole in a way that makes him less open to the charges of Cartesianism.

[*See also Consciousness in Phenomenology: Husserl; Derrida, Jacques; Heidegger, Martin; Husserl, Intentionality in; Levinas, Emmanuel; Merleau-Ponty, M.; Phenomenology.*]

BIBLIOGRAPHY

Works by Husserl

Logische Untersuchungen. Husserliana, Vols. 18–19. The Hague, 1984. Translated by J. N. Findlay as *Logical Investigations*. New York, 1970.

Cartesianische Meditationen. Husserliana, Vol. 1. The Hague, 1950. Translated by D. Cairns as *Cartesian Meditations*. The Hague, 1960.

Ideen zu einer reinen Phänomenologie und phänomenologischen Philosophie: Erstes Buch (Ideen I). Husserliana, Vol. 3. The Hague, 1950. Translated by F. Kersten as *Ideas Pertaining to a Pure Phenomenology and to a Phenomenological Philosophy*. The Hague, 1982. The first translation by R. Gibson was available after 1931 and had a decisive influence on the understanding of Husserl.

Die Krisis der europäischen Wissenschaften und die transzendentale Phänomenologie. Husserliana, Vol. 6. The Hague, 1954. Translated by D. Carr as *The Crisis of European Sciences and Transcendental Phenomenology*. Evanston, IL, 1970. Husserl's extensive discussion of the lifeworld makes clear that the concrete world of pretheoretical experience is the basis for the abstract spheres that had often been taken as fundamental for Husserl.

Ideen zu einer reinen Phänomenologie und phänomenologischen Philosophie: Zweites Buch (Ideen II). Husserliana, Vol. 4. The Hague, 1952. Translated by A. Schuwer and R. Rojcewicz as *Ideas Pertaining to a Pure Phenomenology and Phenomenological Philosophy: Book Two*. Dordrecht, 1989.

Phänomenologischen Psychologie. Husserliana, Vol. 9. The Hague, 1962. Translated by J. Scanlon as *Phenomenological Psychology*. The Hague, 1977.

Zur Phänomenologie des inneren Zeitbewußtseins (1893/1917). Husserliana, Vol. 10. The Hague, 1966. Translated by J. Brough as *Concerning the Phenomenology of Inner Time Consciousness*. Dordrecht, 1991. Previous translation by J. Churchill in 1964. The new translation makes available supplementary texts from the critical edition in German that illuminate the history of the development of Husserl's thinking on the issue.

Analysen zur Passiven Synthesis. Husserliana, Vol. 11. The Hague, 1966. The most extended treatments (along with *Erfahrung und Urteil*) of the genesis of predicative thinking out of the realm of prepredicative experience.

Philosophie der Arithmetik: Mit ergänzenden Texten (1890–1901). Husserliana, Vol. 12. The Hague. 1970.

Zur Phänomenologie der Intersubjektivität. Husserliana, Vols. 13–15. Extensive excerpts from lectures and research manuscripts make available for the first time detailed analyses of Husserl's thinking on intersubjectivity. Prefaces by the editor, I. Kern, are especially helpful.

Formale und transzendentale Logik. Husserliana, Vol. 17. The Hague, 1974. Translated by D. Cairns as *Formal and Transcendental Logic*. Evanston, IL, 1969.

Aufsätze und Renzensionen (1890–1910). Husserliana, Vol. 22. The Hague, 1979. Husserl essays and reviews during this period concerned primarily logic and the foundation of mathematics.

Makes available once again several important documents that make clear how Husserl's views in these areas evolved.

Phantasie, Bildbewußtsein, Erinnerung: Zur Phänomenologie der anschaulichen Vergegenwärtigungen. Husserliana, Vol. 23.

Vorlesungen über Ethik und Wertlehre, 1908–1914, Husserliana, Vol. 18. First publication of lectures on the theory of values and the principles of rational practical choice.

Aufsätze und Vortrage (1922–37). Husserliana. Vol. 27. Dordrecht, 1989. The "Kaizo articles" locate Husserl's phenomenological philosophy within a broader project of cultural and ethical renewal and bring out clearly the ethical dimension of the notion of evidence.

Erfahrung und Urteil. Meiner, 1985. Translated by J. Churchill and K. Ameriks as *Experience and Judgment*. Evanston, IL, 1973.

"Philosophie als strenge Wissenschaft," in *Husserliana*, Vol. 25 (Dordrecht, 1987). Translated by Q. Lauer as "Philosophy as a Rigorous Science," in E. Husserl, *Phenomenology and the Crisis of Philosophy* (New York, 1965).

Works on Husserl

Bernet, R., I. Kern, and E. Marbach. *An Introduction to Edmund Husserl's Phenomenology.* Evanston, IL, 1993. A good overview of the development of Husserl's thinking in terms of his attempts to come to grips with central issues that emerge in his early work.

Derrida, J. *Introduction à "L'Origine de la géométrie" de Husserl*. Paris, 1962. Translated by J. Leavey as *Edmund Husserl's Origin of Geometry. An Introduction*. Stony Brook, NY, 1978.

———. *La Voix et le phénomène.* Paris, 1967. Translated by D. Allison as *Speech and Phenomena*. Bloomington, IN, 1973.

Elliston, F., and P. McCormick, eds. *Husserl: Expositions and Appraisals*. Notre Dame, IN, 1977. Assembles classic essays on controversial questions concerning Husserl's phenomenology.

Heidegger, M. *Sein und Zeit.* Tübingen, 1972. Translated by J. Macquarrie and E. Robinson as *Being and Time*. San Francisco, 1972.

Levinas, E. *Totalité et infini*. The Hague, 1961. Translated by A. Lingis as *Totality and Infinity*. Pittsburgh, 1969.

Merleau-Ponty, M. *Phénoménologie de la perception*. Paris, 1946. Translated by C. Smith as *Phenomenology of Perception*. London, 1962.

Mohanty, J. N., and W. McKenna, eds. *Husserl's Phenomenology: A Textbook*. Lanham, MD, 1989. Helpful introductory essays.

Sepp, H. R. *Edmund Husserl und die phänomenologische Bewegung*. Freiburg, 1988. Documents in texts and photographs Husserl's life, intellectual development, and influences.

— THOMAS NENON

HUSSERL, INTENTIONALITY IN

For Husserl the doctrines of his teacher Franz Brentano form the point of departure for his analyses of intentionality. Like Brentano, he thinks that intentionality is the distinguishing mark of mental states, that intentionality concerns the directedness of these states to objects, and that the object to which the intention is directed may or may not exist apart from its "mental inexistence." In Husserl's first extended discussion of intentionality in the fifth logical investigation, he analyzes intentionality in terms of subjective acts of meaning. Here he distinguishes between the material and the quality of an act. The material or content pertains to the object of the act, for instance, a person or a state of affairs; it is not to be confused with the "sense experiences" upon which the perception or representation of the object is based, since these are not intentions or even the object of an intention but exist only as nonindependent moments of the intention as a whole. The quality refers to the way in which the act is related to that material or content—for instance, perceiving, imagining, desiring, hating, or esteeming it. Together the matter and the quality make up the "intentional essence" of the act.

In Husserl's first extended discussion of intentionality in the fifth logical investigation, he analyzes intentionality in terms of subjective acts of meaning.

Husserl also follows Brentano in his thesis that complex forms of intentions, such as desiring or valuing, are based on simple representational acts that found them: one cannot desire or have an aversion to ice cream without some idea of ice cream. Particularly important for Husserl are the objectifying acts, those that establish a relationship to their object in such a way that they may be fulfilled or disappointed through intuitions. In the case of a complete fulfillment the identity of intention and object would be established, so that the object would be both intentional and being. In the case of disappointment the object turns out to be otherwise than intended or nonexistent except as intended. The object of the intention in the case of an object like a tree or a house is accordingly not a psychic but a transcendent physical object that may or may not exist and be as it is intended. The analyses of the sixth logical investigation turn on the intimate relationship between intention and fulfillment in the relationship to the intended object. "Meaning" then emerges as the particular way of being directed to the object or some aspect of it, which may or may not be fulfilled. The object itself is simply that which is given in an adequately fulfilled intention.

In *Ideen I* Husserl continues to place intentionality at the center of his analyses of consciousness, but he introduces a new terminology to explain the relationship between intention and object. The term "noesis" is employed to describe the subjective side of intending an object; "noema" is the name for the object as intended. Again, as in *Logische Untersuchungen*, experience in the form of intuition may or may not show that there is an actual object corresponding to the noema. However, there is necessarily a parallel between noesis and noema, so that an analysis of the essential noetic structures of consciousness can also reveal essential noematic or ontological structures as well. In this work Husserl not only differentiates between the quality of an intention and its matter (which he now calls its "noematic core"). He also introduces into the full notion of the noema the mode of attentiveness—that is, whether it is presented as background or foreground, as the focal point of consciousness or as part of the horizon for the current focal point. Furthermore, he introduces into the notion of the noema the doxic modality, the degree or kind of belief attached to the core that corresponds to the noetic believing. He asserts that the *Urdoxa,* of which all other modalities are modifications, is a sure belief in the actuality of the posited entity. Here he also introduces the controversial notion of "hyletic data." Husserl classifies together the strictly sensual components of an intention, using the Greek term *hyle,* "matter" or "stuff." He contrasts this with the intentional *morphé* or form that makes up the specifically intentional character of the intention, which is most closely associated with the noesis. In fact he even states: "The stream of phenomenological being has a material and a noetic stratum" (*Ideen I,* sec. 85). Most commentators agree that this presents a problem for the noetic-noematic parallel, since the noematic core clearly includes those elements of the object that correspond to our sense impressions. One's evaluation of Husserl's position here depends upon how strongly one reads the opposition between matter and form, passively received sense impressions, and the active operations of consciousness that organize the sensual elements in such a way as to establish an intentional relationship to a perceived object. In any case intentionality is associated more closely with the active, conscious, synthetic side of consciousness than with the passive, receptive elements. At the same time Husserl believes that the telos of intentionality, its rationality, is directed to evidence—that is, the confirmation of the intention through the appropriate intuition, which in the case of physical objects includes sense impressions but may take on other forms for other kinds of nonphysical objects that correspond to other kinds of intentions.

In much of his later work Husserl tried to correct an overemphasis upon the propositional, focused, clearly active elements of consciousness involved in intentionality and strike a balance between them and the passive, pre-predicative syntheses that underlie them. Here the implicit intentionalities involved in habitualities of thinking. feeling, and acting become recognized as important elements in concrete intentionality. The emphasis upon the background horizon for theory and practice counterbalances the continued interest in questions of formal logic, mathematics, and science. In those analyses in which Husserl analyzes the intentionality involved in concrete human existence he also sets the stage for later phenomenologists such as Merleau-Ponty to conceive of intentionality, not only as an activity of consciousness, but as bodily intentionality, as the fundamental characteristic of an organism as a whole. For Husserl, however, his emphasis upon phenomenology as a pure science pursued in a reflective attitude led him to continue to think of intentionality above all as a feature of consciousness and as an activity that at least ideally should be evaluated in terms of its suitability for an autonomous, self-responsible, and self-aware agent.

[*See also* Husserl, Edmund; Merleau-Ponty, M.; *Phenomenology.*]

BIBLIOGRAPHY

Dreyfus, H., ed. *Husserl, Intentionality, and Cognitive Science.* Cambridge, MA, 1982. An anthology that includes several classic articles on the concept of intentionality in Husserl and discussions of its contemporary relevance.

Husserl, E. *Cartesianische Meditationen. Husserliana,* Vol. 1, edited by S. Strasser. The Hague, 1950. Translated by D. Cairns as *Cartesian Meditations.* The Hague, 1960. The fourth meditation indicates how intentionality is related to temporality and how intentionality involves passive as well as active genesis.

———. *Logische Untersuchungen.* Tübingen, 1968. Translated by J. N. Findlay as *Logical Investigations.* New York, 1970. Esp. the first investigation regarding meaning-bestowing acts, the fifth investigation regarding the structure of intentionality, and the sixth investigation regarding fulfillment and the relation to objects.

———. *Ideen zu einer reinen Phänomenologie und phänomenologischen Philosophie, Buch 1. Husserliana,* Vol. 3. The Hague, 1976. Translated by F. Kersten as *Ideas Pertaining to a Pure Phenomenology and Phenomenological Philosophy. First Book.* The Hague, 1982. Secs. 84ff. describe intentionality as the main theme of phenomenology and introduce the concepts of hyletic data, noesis, and noema. Sec. 128 deals with the relationship between noema and object and defines the concept of a "noematic core."

— THOMAS NENON

HYPATIA

Hypatia, A.D. 370/75–415, was a philosopher, mathematician, and astronomer who, though female and pagan, achieved the honor of being named by the Christian Roman government to the position of philosopher at the museum of Alexandria. Students reading philosophy at the Alexandrian school would also study mathematics and astronomy as technical, applied disciplines of the more traditional studies of metaphysics and cosmology. Hypatia's father, Theon of Alexandria, was the museum's most famous mathematician-astronomer, and it is largely through Theon that we have a reliable source of Ptolemy's *Syntaxis Mathematica (Almagest)*. Hypatia likely assumed the directorship of the school of philosophy circa 400. The recently converted Christian, Synesius of Cyrene, later the Bishop of Ptolemais, became her student in 393. From Synesius's works we

---

Hypatia was an eclectic philosopher

with a cynic's literary and personal style

that may have had as much to do

with her risky status as both woman and pagan

as with her philosophical affiliation.

---

surmise that Hypatia's early philosophical teachings concentrated on Plato's metaphysical works, especially the *Timeaus*. Her later mathematical and astronomical writings can be understood primarily as applications of Neoplatonist metaphysical and cosmological theories. Hypatia was an eclectic philosopher with a Cynic's literary and personal style that may have had as much to do with her risky status as both woman and pagan as with her philosophical affiliation. Accounts of outrageous tactics to counter sexist male student behavior may be apocryphal (Lewis, 1921; Toland, 1720). Nevertheless they provide insight into the personality of a defensive female professor in a brutally misogynist environment. A traditional middle platonist, Hypatia was sympathetic to Porphyryian metaphysics and to stoicism. In 415, she was savagely dismembered by a gang of monks. She appears to have been succeeded by Hierocles.

[See also Metaphysics.]

BIBLIOGRAPHY

Bregman, J. *Synesius of Cyrene: Philosopher-Bishop*. Berkeley, 1982.

Evrard, E. "A Quel titre Hypatie enseigna-t-elle la philosophie?" *Revue des études grecques*, Vol. 90 (1977), 69–74.

Halma, N. B. *Theon et Hypatie, Commentaires de Theon d'Alexandrie sur le troisième livre de l'almageste de Ptolemee*. Paris, 1820.

———. *Almageste de Ptolémée, Commentaires de Théon D'Alexandrie sur le premier livre de la composition mathématique de Ptolémée*. Paris, 1821.

Heath, T. *A History of Greek Mathematics*. Oxford, 1921.

———. *Greek Astronomy*. Oxford, 1932.

———. *Diophantus of Alexandria*. New York, 1960.

Index Bibliothecae Medicae. Florence, 1882.

Knorr, W. *Textual Studies in Ancient and Medieval Geometry*. Boston, 1989.

Lampropoulou, S. "Hypatia philosophe Alexandrine," *Athenai, Bibliopholeion*. Athens, 1977.

Lewis, T. *The History of Hypatia, a Most Impudent School-mistress of Alexandria. . . .* London, 1921.

Ligier, H. *De Hypatia philosopha et eclectismi alexandrini fine*. 1879.

Meyer, W. A. *Hypatia von Alexandria*. Heidelberg, 1886.

Montulca, J. F. *Histoire des mathématiques*. Paris, 1960.

Rome, A. "Le Troisième livre des commentaires sur l'almageste par Théon et Hypatie," *Annales de la société scientifique de Bruxelles*, Vol. 46 (1926), 1–14.

———. "Observations d'équinoxes et de solstices dans le chapitre 1 du livre 3 du commentaire sur l'almageste par Théon d'Alexandrie," *Annales de la société scientifique de Bruxelles*, Vol. 57 (1937), 213–36 (première partie); Vol. 58 (1938), 6–26 (second partie).

———. *Commentaires de Pappus et de Théon d'Alexandrie sur l'almageste, tome III, Théon d'Alexandrie commentaire sur les livres 3 et 4 de l'almageste*. Studi e testi 106. Vatican City, 1943.

Suidae [sic] S. *Lexicon*. Stuttgart, 1967–71.

Tannery, P. *Diophanti Alexandrini Opera Omnia*. 2 vols. Lipsiae, 1893–95.

———. "L'Article de Suidas sur Hypatia," *Annales de la faculté des lettres de Bordeaux*. Bordeaux, 1880.

———. *Mémoires scientifiques*. Toulouse, 1912.

Toland, J. *Hypatia, or the History . . .* in *Tetradymus*. London, 1720.

Usener, H. "Fasti Theonis Alexandrini," in T. Mommsen, ed., *Chronica Minora Sasc. IV, V, VI, VII*. (Berlin, 1898).

Waithe, M. E. "Hypatia of Alexandria," in *A History of Women Philosophers*, Vol. 1, *Ancient Women Philosophers 60 BC-500 AD* (Dordrecht, 1987).

— MARY ELLEN WAITHE

I

IDENTITY

The word 'is' is multiply ambiguous. When it can be expanded to read 'is the same thing as', or 'is identical with', or (in numerical contexts) 'is equal to', it expresses the relation of identity. The simplest identity statements contain the 'is' of identity flanked by singular terms, either names or definite descriptions: 'Samuel Clemens is Mark Twain'; 'The U.S. president in 1996 is Bill Clinton'; 'Four is the sum of two and two'. A more complex identity statement might, for example, combine the 'is' of identity with quantifiers: 'Every even number is the sum of two primes'.

Identity, on its face, is simple and unproblematic: it is that relation that everything bears to itself and to nothing else. Yet discussions of identity in contemporary philosophical logic and metaphysics are brimming with controversy. From where does this controversy arise? Some of it is not genuine, being based on confusion; and some of it, though genuine, is not genuinely about identity. However, a residue of controversy survives, owing to the view, perpetrated by Peter Geach, that identity statements are meaningless unless relativized, that there is no absolute relation of identity.

Sources of Confusion

One source of confusion is the ambiguity of 'identical' in English. We do sometimes say that two things are identical, as when we speak of identical twins, or say that some coat is identical with some other. This is qualitative identity: things are qualitatively identical if they resemble one another sufficiently in relevant qualitative respects. Numerical identity is different: two things, no matter how closely they resemble one another, are never numerically identical. Numerical identity is the topic of this article.

A second source of confusion is English grammar, which allows, for example, 'Clemens is identical with Twain' to be rewritten equivalently as 'Clemens and Twain are identical' or as 'they are identical'. But then it seems that two persons (or two *somethings*) are being said to be identical, which is absurd. A general response is familiar from other cases: surface grammar often misrepresents the underlying logic: one must beware inferring logical from grammatical form. More specifically, it can be verified that plural noun phrases in English do not, in all contexts, entail or presuppose reference to a plurality.

A third source of confusion is Frege's puzzle of informative identity statements, sometimes introduced by the following argument. To say of something that it is identical with itself is trivial, to say of something that it is identical with something else is false; therefore, identity statements are all either trivial or false, and there can be no point in asserting them. This conclusion is manifestly incorrect: identity statements are often both true and informative, as witness, 'the capital of Honduras is Tegucigalpa'. The puzzle is to say where the argument goes wrong.

Discussions of identity in

contemporary philosophical logic and metaphysics

are brimming with controversy.

From where does this controversy arise?

One response rejects the second premise by taking identity to be a relation between names or descriptions rather than between the objects named or described: identity is then the relation of co-designation, the relation that holds between singular terms whenever those terms designate the same object. That would indeed allow identity statements to be both true and informative. But the response is not viable, for many reasons. For one, it fails to account for uses of identity that do not involve singular terms, such as: 'Everything is identical with itself'. For another, it fails to allow identity statements between different singular terms to be uninformative, as they are when the singular terms are synonymous. For another, it fails to provide a unified solution to analogous puzzles of informativeness, such as how 'the capital of Honduras is in Honduras' and 'Tegucigalpa is in Honduras' can differ in informativeness, even though both ascribe the same property to the same thing.

A better response is due to Frege. Identity is a relation between objects; a simple identity statement is true just in case the objects referred to by the singular terms stand in that relation. But singular terms have sense in addition to reference; a true identity statement is informative just in case its singular terms differ in sense. (Just what is included in the sense of a singular term varies from theory to theory; but note that senses must be rich enough to allow co-designative proper names—such as 'Mark Twain' and 'Samuel Clemens'—to differ in sense.) Now the puzzle may be solved by rejecting the argument's first premise: one can say informatively of an object that it is identical with itself by referring to the object twice over. using singular terms that differ in sense. That is how 'The capital of Honduras is Tegucigalpa' manages to be both true and informative. Identity statements are useful in ordinary language because we often refer to the same object from different points of view, using terms with different senses. (Frege's statement of the puzzle, and his solution, is in Frege, 1892; see also Kripke, 1980; Salmon, 1986.)

The Logic of Identity: Leibniz's Law

Relations may be classified according to their general, logical characteristics. The logical characteristics of the identity relation are easily enumerated. First, as already noted, identity is reflexive: every object is identical with itself. Second, identity is symmetric: if an object x is identical with an object y, then y is identical with x. Third, identity is transitive: if an object x is identical with an object y, and y is identical with an object z, then x is identical with z. A relation that is reflexive, symmetric, and transitive is called an equivalence relation. Finally, identity is the strongest equivalence relation, entailing all other equivalence relations: if an object x is identical with an object y, then x bears R to y, for every equivalence relation R. Since being the strongest equivalence relation (or, equivalently, being the strongest reflexive relation) uniquely characterizes identity in purely logical terms. identity may properly be classified as a logical relation and the theory of identity as a branch of logic.

All of the logical characteristics of identity can be derived from a single principle, sometimes called Leibniz's law: An object x is identical with an object y if and only if every property of x is a property of y and vice versa. Leibniz's law is a biconditional and thus the conjunction of two conditionals, one giving a necessary, the other a sufficient, condition for identity to hold. Say that an object x is indiscernible from an object y just in case every property of x is a property of y and vice versa. The half of Leibniz's law that gives a necessary condition proclaims the indiscernibility of identicals: if x is identical with y, then x is indiscernible from y. This principle is useful for establishing nonidentity: to show that x is not identical with y, it suffices to find a property had by x but not by y or vice versa. Most famously, perhaps, the principle has been used to argue that persons are

not identical with their bodies. The half of Leibniz's law that gives a sufficient condition proclaims the identity of indiscernibles: if x is indiscernible from y, then x is identical with y (more on this below).

(Note that Leibniz's law is stated within second-order logic: it involves quantification over properties. The first-order theory of identity substitutes for Leibniz's law an axiom schema containing, for each [monadic] predicate of the language, an axiom stating: if x is identical with y, then x satisfies the predicate if and only if y satisfies the predicate. This schema, together with an axiom of reflexivity, entails the entire first-order theory of identity. The first-order theory is weaker than the full second-order theory; in particular, no logically sufficient condition for identity is expressible within first-order logic.)

The indiscernibility of identicals is beyond dispute: if x and y are identical, then there is only one thing; how can that one thing both have and not have some property? Nonetheless, the principle has been disputed. Consider the following attempt at a counterexample (discussed in Quine, 1953). It is true that Giorgione was so called because of his size, let us suppose, and that Giorgione is identical with Barbarelli; yet, apparently contrary to the principle, it is not true that Barbarelli was so called because of his size. But to see this as a violation of the indiscernibility of identicals, one would have to hold that the predicate 'is so called because of his size' expresses some genuine property of objects and expresses the same property when applied to 'Giorgione' as when applied to 'Barbarelli'. On the contrary, when considered in isolation the predicate expresses no property at all but rather a relation between objects and names. When applied to 'Giorgione' it expresses the property was-called-Giorgione-because-of-his-size; and that property is true of Barbarelli, in accord with the indiscernibility of identicals. Other attempts at counterexamples are more subtle than this; but all seem to involve naively reading subject-predicate sentences as simple property-to-object attributions. (For examples involving modality see Cartwright, 1971: Quine, 1953).

Identity of Indiscernibles

The other half of Leibniz's law proclaims the identity of indiscernibles; but now one must be careful just what 'indiscernible' means. If indiscernibles have *all* of their properties in common, where properties are conceived abundantly, then the identity of indiscernibles is trivially true. For, on an abundant conception of property, for any object y there is the property is-identical-with-y. Now suppose that x is indiscernible from y. Then, since y has the property is-identical-with-y, x must have this property too; that is, x is identical with y, as was to be shown.

If we interpret 'indiscernible' instead in terms of properties more sparsely conceived, for example, as 'indiscernible in all qualitative respects', then we arrive at a substantial metaphysical principle, the identity of qualitative indiscernibles; the trivial "proof" above is blocked because properties such as is-identical-with-a (where 'a' names some object) are not (or, at any rate, are not trivially) qualitative. There are different versions of the principle, however, corresponding to different interpretations of 'qualitatively indiscernible'; and for each version one might ask whether the principle is logically necessary, is contingently true, or neither. Let us consider three versions.

Can identity be understood in terms not involving identity?

According to the strongest (and least plausible) version, objects that share all of their intrinsic qualitative properties—intrinsic duplicates—are identical. This principle seems to be false even at the actual world: according to current physics, distinct elementary particles of the same kind—for example, distinct electrons—have all of their intrinsic properties (charge, mass, etc.) in common.

According to the second (and most familiar) version, objects that share all of their intrinsic and extrinsic qualitative properties—absolute indiscernibles—are identical. Absolute indiscernibles must not only be intrinsic duplicates, they must be exactly similarly situated with respect to all of their surroundings. But, surely it is at least possible that there be distinct yet absolutely indiscernible objects; that is, the principle is not necessarily true. For, to take the standard counterexample (from Black, 1952), it is logically possible that the world contains nothing but two perfectly round globes, exactly similar down to their smallest parts and separated, say, by one meter. The globes share all of their intrinsic qualitative properties, having the same mass, shape, and so on. And the globes share all of their extrinsic qualitative properties—for example, each is one meter from a globe of a certain mass, shape, and so on. (Note that properties that would only be expressible using names for the globes, such as is-one-meter-from-globe$_1$, are not qualitative.) In short, the globes are absolutely indiscernible; yet they are two, not one.

A defender of the identity of absolute indiscernibles might simply deny that there is any such possibility; but there is a substantial cost. The claim that it is logically possible that there be nothing but two absolutely indiscernible globes can be backed up by a subsidiary argument (Adams, 1979). Surely, there could be nothing but two almost indiscernible globes, differing, say, only in the placement of a single atom. To hold that that atom could not have been shifted in a certain way (because, if it had, there would have been two absolutely indiscernible globes), but that any other atom could have been shifted in that way, would amount to an implausibly inegalitarian approach to what is and is not possible.

Perhaps an even weaker version of the principle should be considered: objects that share all of their qualitative properties, and stand in the same qualitative relations to any given object—relative indiscernibles—are identical. (On absolute vs. relative indiscernibility, see Quine, 1960.) The possibility just considered of the two globes is not a counterexample to the necessity of this version: the globes are discerned by spatial relations; each globe is one meter from the other globe but not one meter from itself. A counterexample, however, is not far to seek. Consider the possibility that there be nothing but two absolutely indiscernible globes standing in no spatial relation (or other qualitative external relation) to one another, two absolutely indiscernible 'island universes'. (This possibility can be motivated, too, by first considering 'almost' island universes, connected, say, by a single 'wormhole'.) Such globes would be relatively, as well as absolutely, indiscernible; they stand in no relations that could serve to discern them. So even this weakest version of the identity of qualitative indiscernibles seems not to be a necessary truth. (Indeed, it may not be contingently true: so-called 'identical particles' in quantum mechanics are arguably distinct but absolutely and relatively indiscernible.)

Is Identity Definable?

Identity has been characterized many times over. Do any of these characterizations provide a (noncircular) definition of the identity relation? Can identity be understood in terms not involving identity? Our initial characterization—that everything is identical with itself and with nothing else—clearly will not do as a definition: to be 'else' is to be other, that is, nonidentical. Moreover, the characterization of identity as the strongest equivalence relation fares no better: identity characterized by quantifying over all relations, identity included.

Leibniz's law gives a necessary and sufficient condition for identity by quantifying instead over properties. But among the quantified properties are haecceities, properties of being identical with some given object. The question whether an object x shares with an object

y the property of being identical with y is just the question whether x is identical with y; the purported definition takes one around in a circle. Similarly defective is the oft-heard definition 'x is identical with y if and only if x and y belong to the same classes'. The question whether x, like y, belongs to the class whose only member is y is just the question whether x is identical with y.

If one bathes in the river on Monday,

and returns to bathe at the same place on Tuesday,

one has not bathed in the same river twice.

What if some version of the identity of qualitative indiscernibles were necessarily true (contrary to what was argued above)? That would indeed provide a noncircular criterion for the identity of *objects*. But the identity or distinctness of qualitative properties (and relations) would remain undefined. Indeed, any purported definition of identity would have to quantify over some sort of entity; the definition could not be understood without a prior understanding of the identity and distinctness of the entities quantified over. We must conclude, then, that identity, at least as applied to the most basic entities, must be taken as primitive and unanalyzable; there is no fully general (noncircular) definition of identity.

Questions remain, some of which might seem to pose problems for the classical conception of identity. We shall see, however, that in each case replies exist that leave classical identity unscathed. (Each of the issues raised below is discussed in Lewis, 1993.)

Partial Identity

Classical identity is all or nothing; it never comes in degrees. Yet, when objects overlap, we may say they are 'partially identical, partially distinct'; and when objects extensively overlap, we may say they are 'almost identical'. Do we have here a challenge to classical identity? No, we have an ambiguity: identity, in the sense that admits of degrees, is simply overlap; identity, in the classical sense, is equivalent to the extreme case of total overlap. The two notions of identity are not in conflict; they fit together as well as you please.

Vague Identity

Classical identity is determinate and admits of no borderline cases. That is not to say that identity statements cannot be vague or indeterminate in truth value. If I say 'that cloud in the sky is identical with A', where 'A'

names some precisely specified aggregate of water molecules, what I say may be neither determinately true nor false. But such vagueness resides in the reference of singular terms—in this case, 'that cloud in the sky'—not in the identity relation itself.

Some philosophers, however, hold that there is vagueness, not only in our reference to objects, but in the objects themselves; not only in our language and thought, but in the world. Let us suppose, charitably, that such a view makes sense. Might not these vague objects be vaguely identical? That depends. If vague identity is understood so that vaguely identical objects are neither determinately identical nor determinately not identical, then the answer is no, as the following argument shows. (Versions are in Evans, 1978; Salmon, 1981.) Suppose a and b are vaguely identical; then they differ in some property, namely, being vaguely identical with b. For although a has the property, b does not: nothing is vaguely identical with itself. By the indiscernibility of identicals, then, a is (determinately) not identical with b. So, vaguely identical objects are (determinately) not identical! That sounds odd; but there is no contradiction if vague identity is understood in some way that detaches it from indeterminacy of truth value. So understood, vague identity poses no challenge to classical identity.

Temporary Identity

The Greek philosopher Heraclitus argued that one cannot bathe in the same river twice, something as follows. Rivers flow. The stretch of water that comprises the river on Monday is not the same as the stretch of water that comprises the river on Tuesday. But a river is not something separate and distinct from the stretch of water that comprises it; be it on Monday or on Tuesday, the river and the stretch of water are one and the same. It follows, by a double application of the indiscernibility of identicals, that the river on Monday is not the same as the river on Tuesday. If one bathes in the river on Monday, and returns to bathe at the same place on Tuesday, one has not bathed in the same river twice.

One wants to say: on Monday, the river is identical with a certain stretch of water; on Tuesday, the same river is identical with a different stretch of water. More generally, identity can be temporary, holding at some times but not at others. Temporary identity, however, is disallowed by the above argument, not just for rivers, but for all entities whatsoever. Should we abandon the classical notion of identity that the argument presupposes?

There are at least two responses to Heraclitus's problem compatible with classical identity. According to the first response (inspired by Aristotle), when we say that a river *is* just a certain stretch of water, we are using not the 'is' of identity but the 'is' of constitution; and constitution is never identity (see Lowe, 1989). On this view there are two fundamentally different kinds of entities that occupy space and persist through time. There are ordinary material objects, such as rivers, trees, statues, and tables; and there are portions of matter that may temporarily constitute the ordinary objects. At any time an ordinary object is constituted by some portion of matter or other; but at no time is it identical with that portion of matter, either wholly or in part. In particular, the very same river is constituted by one stretch of water on Monday and by a different stretch of water on Tuesday. No conflict arises with the laws of classical identity, and Heraclitus's problem is solved.

This response, however, is not without problems. A dualism of ordinary objects and the portions of matter that constitute them is neither necessary nor sufficient to solve the general problem of temporary identity. It is not sufficient, because some cases of temporary identity have nothing to do with constitution. Consider a tree that, at some bleak stage of its career, consists of nothing but a trunk. Later, however, the tree sprouts new branches and leaves. Then we have another prima facie case of temporary identity: the tree is identical with the trunk at the bleak time but not identical with the trunk at the happier time. In this case, however, invoking constitution is of no avail: neither the trunk nor the tree constitutes the other, in the relevant sense. (This example is from Hirsch, 1982.)

Nor is such a dualism necessary to solve the problem of temporary identity, because another response is available, one (arguably) more economical in its ontological commitments (see Hirsch, 1982; Quine, 1950). On this second response objects that persist through time are composed of (more-or-less) momentary stages, of temporal parts. A persisting river is a sum of stages unified in a way appropriate for rivers; a persisting aggregate of water molecules is a sum of stages unified in a way appropriate for portions of matter. A persisting river and a persisting aggregate of water molecules may overlap by having a stage in common; in that case a stage of the river and a contemporaneous stage of the aggregate of water molecules are identical. But the persisting river is not identical with the persisting aggregate of water molecules: later stages of the river are in about the same place as earlier stages and are no less spatially continuous; later stages of the aggregate of water molecules are downstream of earlier stages and are spatially scattered. When we say that, at any time, a river is nothing separate and distinct from the water that comprises it, this must be understood as asserting not an identity between persisting objects but an identity between stages. Identity between stages, however, is all one needs to avoid the uneconomical dualism of the constitution view. All objects that occupy space and persist through time are composed of a single kind of entity: stages of portions of matter. (The stage view of persistence is argued for in Lewis, 1986.)

Heraclitus's problem is now easily solved. One cannot bathe in the same river stage twice; but one can bathe in the same river twice by bathing successively in two river stages belonging to a single persisting river. That these two stages are not stages of a single persisting aggregate of water molecules is irrelevant. There is no conflict with classical identity.

Contingent Identity

A change in example, however, makes trouble for the stage view of persistence. Consider a statue called *Goliath* that consists entirely of a lump of clay called *Lumpl*; and suppose that the statue and the lump came into being, and ceased to exist, at exactly the same times. Then, on the stage view, every stage of *Goliath* is identical with a stage of *Lumpl* and vice versa; *Goliath* and *Lumpl* are the same sum of stages and so are identical. But, surely, they are not necessarily identical. *Goliath* could have been destroyed without destroying *Lumpl*— say, by being squashed—in which case *Goliath* would have lacked *Lumpl*'s final stages and would have been a distinct sum from *Lumpl*. So, *Goliath* and *Lumpl* are identical, but only contingently identical. (The example is from Gibbard, 1975.)

Trouble arises because contingent identity, no less than temporary identity, is incompatible with identity, classically conceived—or so the following argument seems to show. Consider the property is-necessarily-identical-with-*y*, for some object *y*. Surely *y* has it: everything is necessarily identical with itself. Now suppose an object *x* is identical with *y*. Then, by the indiscernibility of identicals, *x* has the property as well; that is, *x* is necessarily identical with *y*. Thus, objects are necessarily identical if identical at all; objects are never contingently identical.

Whether this argument is unassailable will depend upon one's interpretation of modal properties, of modality *de re*. If objects have their modal properties absolutely, in and of themselves, then the argument is sound. Since *Goliath* and *Lumpl* are not necessarily identical, they are not identical at all. *Goliath* and *Lumpl* are numerically distinct objects that occupy the same place at all times that they exist. *Goliath* is not identical with any sum of matter-stages, contradicting the stage view of persistence.

The stage view can be preserved, however, if one takes the view that modal predicates do not apply to objects absolutely, in and of themselves; their application is relative to how the objects are conceived, classified, or referred to. For example, could the lump of clay—that is, the statue—have survived a squashing? *Qua* lump of clay, it could; *qua* statue, it could not. There is no violation of the indiscernibility of identicals because the modal predicate 'could survive a squashing' expresses no property when considered out of context and expresses different properties when attached to 'the lump of clay' (or 'Lumpl') and to 'the statue' (or *Goliath*). In this way the stage view can accept the contingent identity of Lumpl and *Goliath*, without forfeiting classical identity. (For versions of this strategy, see Gibbard, 1975; Lewis, 1971.)

Relative Identity

Classical identity is absolute: whether identity holds between objects does not depend upon how those objects are conceived, classified, or referred to. In ordinary language we often say '*a* is the same *F* as *b*', for some general term '*F*'; but this is naturally analyzed as a restriction of absolute identity: *a* is *F*, and *b* is *F*, and *a* is (absolutely) identical with *b*.

Geach has argued, on the contrary, that all identity statements are relative: '*a* is the same *F* as *b*' cannot be analyzed as restricted absolute identity, because there is no absolute identity; when we say simply '*a* is the same as *b*', some general term '*F*' must be supplied by context, or what we say is meaningless (Geach, 1970). To support his claim, Geach has presented examples in which we would say: *a* and *b* are the same *F*, and *a* and *b* are *G*'s, but *a* and *b* are not the same *G*. Consider the word 'tot'. It contains three letter tokens, two letter types. The first letter token and the last letter token are not the same letter token, but they are the same letter type. That contradicts the claim that 'the same *F*' is to be analyzed as restricted absolute identity.

The defender of classical identity has a simple and natural reply: sometimes the relation is-the-same-*F*-as is not restricted identity but rather some weaker equivalence relation; that is, sometimes it is a species of qualitative, rather than numerical, identity (see Perry, 1970). For example: if I say that you are wearing the same coat as I am, I (probably) do not mean the numerically same coat. Similarly, letter tokens of the same type are qualitatively similar—equiform—not numerically identical. To the extent that Geach's point is just that 'the same *F*' cannot always be analyzed as restricted identity, it is a point no one should deny.

Any rejection of absolute identity, it seems, must be based upon arguments of a more abstract sort. Indeed, Geach explicitly rejects the standard characterization of

identity through Leibniz's law on the grounds that second-order quantification over properties leads to paradox. And he rightly points out that, within first-order logic, characterizations of identity are inevitably relative to the predicates of the language. But how does this impugn the meaningfulness of absolute identity? Does Geach's argument simply amount to the demand, Define absolute identity, or count it as meaningless? That demand, certainly, is too strong. No fundamental notion of logic or metaphysics could meet it.

[See also Aristotle; Frege, Gottlob; Heraclitus; Kripke, Saul Aaron; Leibniz, Gottfried Wilhelm; Properties; Quine, Willard Van Orman; Vagueness.]

BIBLIOGRAPHY

Adams, R. M. "Primitive Thisness and Primitive Identity," *Journal of Philosophy*, Vol. 76 (1979), 5–26.

Black, M. "The Identity of Indiscernibles," in *Problems of Analysis* (Ithaca, NY, 1954).

Cartwright, R. "Identity and Substitutivity," in M. Munitz, ed., *Identity and Individuation* (New York, 1971).

Evans, G. "Can There Be Vague Objects?" *Analysis*, Vol. 38 (1978), 208.

Frege, G. "Uber Sinn und Bedeutung." *Zeitschrift fur Philosophie und philosophische Kritik*, Vol. 100 (1892), 25–50. Translated by P. Geach and M. Black as "On Sense and Reference," in *Philosophical Writings of Gottlob Frege* (Oxford, 1952).

Geach, P. T. "Identity." *Review of Metaphysics*, Vol. 21 (1967), 3–12.

Gibbard, A. "Contingent Identity," *Journal of Philosophical Logic*, Vol. 4 (1975), 187–221.

Hirsch, E. *The Concept of Identity*. Oxford, 1982.

Kripke, S. *Naming and Necessity*. Cambridge, MA, 1980.

Lewis, D. "Counterparts of Persons and Their Bodies," *Journal of Philosophy*, Vol. 68 (1971), 203–11.

———. *On the Plurality of Worlds*. Oxford, 1986.

———. "Many, But Almost One," in K. Campbell, J. Bacon, and L. Reinhardt, eds., *Ontology, Causality, and Mind: Essays in Honour of D. M. Armstrong* (Cambridge, 1993).

Lowe, E. J. *Kinds of Being*. Oxford, 1989.

Perry, J. "The Same *F*," *Philosophical Review* (1970), 181–200.

Quine, W. V. O. "Identity, Ostension, and Hypostasis," *Journal of Philosophy*, (1950).

———. "Reference and Modality," in *From a Logical Point of View* (New York, 1953).

———. *Word and Object*. Cambridge, MA. 1960.

Salmon, N. *Reference and Essence*. Princeton, NJ, 1981.

———. *Frege's Puzzle*. Cambridge, MA, 1986.

– PHILLIP BRICKER

IMPARTIALITY

A more complex concept than is generally recognized, impartiality does not require giving equal weight to the interests of all, as many philosophers assume, but at most involves giving equal weight to the interests of all those whose interests are being appropriately considered. Often, impartiality does not even involve considering the interests of people in any straightforward sense of interests. An impartial baseball umpire should call balls and strikes without being influenced by how his calls will affect any of the players on the competing teams.

The most common characterization of impartiality is that it requires that like cases be treated alike. This characterization is taken as trivially true by almost all philosophers, but it is mistaken. Consider an umpire who changes the strike zone every three innings, starting with a wide zone, going to a narrow one, and then returning to a wide one, because he is upset and believes that umpires are not appreciated. If he changes it without regard to which team benefits or is harmed by this change, then he is impartial with regard to the two teams in calling balls and strikes. Although his not treating like cases alike (i.e., calling balls and strikes differently in the first and fifth innings) makes him a bad umpire, it does not affect his impartiality.

Even if he changes the strike zone whenever he feels like it but is not influenced by which pitcher, batter, or team is benefited or harmed by this erratic change in the strike zone, he remains impartial with regard to the two teams. He is not consistent, but impartiality should not be confused with consistency. A good umpire is supposed to be consistent as well as impartial. An inconsistent umpire will be suspected of not being impartial, but if he is not influenced by who is benefited or harmed, he remains impartial with respect to calling balls and strikes with regard to the two teams.

Jurors are required to be impartial in hearing and deciding cases. Impartiality requires that like cases be treated alike. (Reuters/Bettmann)

Thus, understanding what it means to say that a person is impartial requires specifying the group with regard to which she is impartial and the respect in which she is impartial with regard to that group. A person is impartial in the most fundamental sense insofar as she acts impartially. The following is an analysis of the basic concept of impartiality: *A is impartial in respect R with regard to group G if and only if A's actions in respect R are not influenced at all by which member(s) of G are benefited or harmed by these actions.*

Impartiality at most involves giving equal weight to the interests of all those whose interests are being appropriately considered.

Acting impartially is not sufficient for acting morally, for one may be impartial in an unacceptable respect (e.g., a burglar who does not discriminate on the basis of race, sex, or any other irrelevant characteristic in choosing his victims) or with regard to an unacceptable group (e.g., a racist who hires impartially with regard to all members of the favored race when he should be impartial with regard to qualified people of all races who apply for the job). Making explicit the respect in which a person is impartial and the group with regard to which she is impartial enables one to examine whether or not the respect and group are acceptable. Impartiality is taken to be praiseworthy only because it is usually presupposed that a person is impartial with regard to an acceptable group in an acceptable respect. The person herself need not be included in the group with regard to which she is impartial. A mother can be impartial with regard to all of her children with respect to providing them with spending money; that she keeps more money for herself does not affect her impartiality with regard to her children.

One must include oneself in the group toward whom one acts impartially when the concern is with the impartiality required by morality, but that one is included in the group is not an adequate specification of that group. All agree that this group must include, at least, all currently existing actual moral agents, but people disagree about who else is included. Disputes about abortion and the treatment of animals are disputes about whether or not fetuses or nonhuman animals are included in the group toward which morality requires impartiality.

The respect in which morality requires one to be impartial is only with regard to those moral rules prohibiting killing, causing pain, deceiving, breaking prom-

ises, and so on. For it is only with regard to these kinds of moral rules, those that can be formulated as prohibitions, that it is humanly possible to act impartially with regard to a group that contains all other moral agents. No one can act impartially with regard to all in this group with respect to relieving or preventing pain or acting on any other positive moral ideal. Thus, morality cannot require such impartiality.

[See also Abortion; Animal Rights and Welfare; Ethical Theory.]

BIBLIOGRAPHY

Baier, K. *The Moral Point of View.* Ithaca, NY, 1958.
Firth, R. "Ethical Absolutism and the Ideal Observer," *Philosophy and Phenomenological Research,* Vol. 12 (1952), 317–45.
Gert, B. *Morality.* New York, 1988. See especially chapter 5, "Impartiality."
Hare, R. M. *Moral Thinking.* Oxford, 1981.
Kant, I. *Grounding for the Metaphysics of Morals.* 1785.
Singer, M. G. *Generalization in Ethics.* New York, 1961.

— BERNARD GERT

INDEXICALS

Suppose that Natasha says "I am right and you are wrong" to Joey. Natasha's utterance of "I" designates Natasha and her utterance of "you" designates Joey. The truth-conditions of her statement are that Natasha is right and Joey is wrong.

Now suppose that Joey responds by uttering the exact same words back to Natasha: "I am right and you are wrong." He has said the same words, with the same meaning, but he has not said the same thing. Joey's utterance of "I" designates Joey and his utterance of "you" designates Natasha. The truth-conditions of his statement are that Joey is right and Natasha is wrong. Joey has directly disagreed with Natasha.

In this article, "meaning" refers to the rules or conventions that are associated by a language with the expressions in it, the rules that one learns when one learns the language. Given this, the meanings of Natasha's words and of Joey's are the same. What differs is the objects the particular expressions designate and the truth conditions of the statements. This aspect of utterances will be called "content."

The crucial differences between the first and second utterances were the speakers and the addressees. Such facts about an utterance can be called its "context." Differences in the contexts of the utterances account for the differences in their contents.

(The role of context in this case differs from that in a case of homonymity or ambiguity. With homonymity the context helps us determine which word is being used; with ambiguity, which meaning of a word or phrase is being used. But in this case context still has a role to play after questions of words and meanings have been settled. The meanings of "I" and "you" direct us to features of the context, to determine who is designated.)

The content of an utterance using "I" or "you" is determined by contextual facts about the utterance in accord with their meaning. Such expressions we call indexicals.

In addition to "I" and "you," the standard list of indexicals includes the personal pronouns "my," "he," "his," "she," "it," the demonstrative pronouns "that" and "this," the adverbs "here," "now," "today," "yesterday," and "tomorrow," and the adjectives "actual" and "present" (Kaplan, 1989). The words and aspects of words that indicate tense are also indexicals. And many other words—for instance, "local"—seem to have an indexical element.

According to David Kaplan's account, each indexical, and each sentence containing an indexical, has a meaning or character that is a function from contexts to content. The character of "I" is a function whose value, for each context, is the speaker or agent of that context. The character of "now" is a function whose value, for each context, is the time of that context. The character of "you" is a function whose value, for each context, is the person addressed by the speaker in that context. The character of the sentence spoken by Natasha and Joey is a function whose value, for a context with a speaker *x* and an addressee *y*, is the proposition that *x* is right and *y* is wrong. Natasha and Joey's words have the same characters, but their utterances have different contents.

According to David Kaplan's account,

each indexical, and each sentence containing

an indexical, has a meaning or character

that is a function from contexts to content.

In the formal development of his theory, Kaplan equates content with the intensions of intensional semantics. He criticizes earlier attempts to provide a formal theory within this framework for treating contexts on a par with "circumstances of evaluation" (Kaplan, 1989, pp. 507ff.). The context determines which proposition is expressed by Joey's utterance of "I am right and you are wrong"; the circumstance of evaluation determines whether or not the proposition is true. The necessity for such a distinction was seen by Hans Kamp (1971).

(Kaplan notes that at the level of character it makes sense to talk about the logic of indexicals. "I am here now" is a truth in the logic of indexicals, because, given its character, this sentence will have a true content at each context. The content will be contingent and can be expressed by a sentence that is not a logical truth.)

Kaplan's concept of content corresponds to "what is said" by an utterance (let us call this "official" content). This is what someone who knows the meaning and the context grasps. Other philosophers have thought it important also to bring in the concept of token-reflexive or diagonal content. This is what someone who knows the meaning but does not know the context grasps (Burks, 1949; Perry, 1993; Stalnaker, 1981).

Consider an utterance **u** of "Je ne comprends pas l'anglais" made by Erin during a cocktail party. Suppose that Natasha hears the words and understands French but does not see who said them. Joey hears the words, understands French, and also sees that Erin said them. Based on her knowledge of French, Natasha can assign utterance-reflexive truth conditions to **u**: Natasha knows that **u** is true iff (if and only if) (1) the speaker of **u** does not understand English. Joey, since he knows who is talking, can assign nonreflexive truth conditions to **u**: Joey knows that **u** is true iff (2) Erin does not understand English. Natasha knows what the world has to be like for **u** to be true, given the meaning of the words in **u**. Joey knows what the world has to be like, given the meaning of the words in **u** *and* the relevant facts about context. What Joey knows, (2), is the official content of Erin's remark. It is what we would ordinarily say Erin *said*. Erin did not *say* (1); she did not make a remark about her own utterance. Nevertheless, (1) corresponds to an important level of understanding that we must take account of to explain the cognitive significance of sentences containing indexicals. (When Erin said what she did, she probably wanted her listeners to grasp that the person in front of them, at whom they were looking and with whom perhaps trying to converse in English, did not understand that language. This would be an easy inference from the proposition expressed by (1)—that the person who was producing the utterance they were hearing did not understand English. To understand Erin's plan, we seem to need the reflexive content of Erin's remark, and not only its official content.)

[See also Philosophy of Language.]

BIBLIOGRAPHY

Burks, A. "Icon, Index, and Symbol," *Philosophical and Phenomenological Research*, Vol. 9 (1949), 673–89.

Castañeda, H.-N. " 'He': A Study in the Logic of Self-Consciousness," *Ratio*, Vol. 8 (1966), 130–57.

Evans, G. "Understanding Demonstratives." in H. Parret and J. Bouveresse, eds., *Meaning and Understanding* (Berlin, 1981).

Kamp, H. "Formal Properties of 'Now,'" *Theoria,* Vol. 37 (1971), 237–73.

Kaplan, D. "Demonstratives," in J. Almog, J. Perry, and H. Wettstein, eds., *Themes from Kaplan* (New York, 1989).

Nunberg, G. "Indexicality and Deixis," *Linguistics and Philosophy,* Vol. 16 (1993), 1–43.

Perry, J. *The Problem of the Essential Indexical and Other Essays.* New York, 1993.

Recanati, F. *Direct Reference: From Language to Thought.* Oxford, 1993.

Stalnaker, R. "Indexical Belief," *Synthese,* Vol. 49 (1981), 129–51.

Yourgrau, P., ed. *Demonstratives.* Oxford, 1990.

– JOHN PERRY

INDISCERNIBLES

When artworks indiscernible from real counterparts became a historical possibility, accounting for the difference became philosophically urgent. These included Marcel Duchamp's 1917 "ready-made" *Fountain,* in fact an ordinary urinal; Constantin Brancusi's 1927 *Bird in Space,* which looked to customs officials more like a kitchen utensil than a sculpture; and Andy Warhol's 1964 *Brillo Box,* which looked like a soap-pad carton. The possibility of such works makes it plain that the art–reality difference cannot be regarded as perceptual, for though there are minor observable differences in all these cases, they are hardly of a kind to ground the distinction between art and reality. And since for any artwork an ordinary object can be imagined indiscernible from it, the meaning of "artwork" cannot be taught by means of examples. These works raise questions of whether aesthetic considerations belong to the definition of art. Moreover, since the possibility of artworks indiscernible from real counterparts was not an artistic option before the twentieth century, these works raise the further question of how historical considerations relate to artistic understanding, for not even the artist's intention that they be regarded as artworks could have been formed in earlier historical periods.

[See also Art, Definition of.]

BIBLIOGRAPHY

Danto, A. C. *The Transfiguration of the Commonplace.* Cambridge. MA, 1981. Chapter 1.

———. *Connections to the World: The Basic Concepts of Philosophy.* New York, 1985. Chapter 2.

– ARTHUR C. DANTO

INFERENCE TO THE BEST EXPLANATION

In an inductive inference, we acquire a belief on the basis of evidence that is less than conclusive. The new belief is compatible with the evidence, but so are many competing hypotheses we are unwilling to infer. This raises a question of description and a question of justification. What are the principles that lead us to infer one hypothesis rather than another? Do we have any reason to believe that these principles are good ones, leading us to accept hypotheses that are true and to reject those that are false? Inference to the best explanation offers partial answers to both questions.

According to this model, explanatory considerations are a fundamental guide to inductive inference. We decide which of the competing hypotheses the evidence best supports by determining how well each of the competitors would explain that evidence. Seeing the ball next to the broken vase, I infer that my children have been playing catch in the house, because this is the best explanation of what I see. Having measured the red shift of a star's characteristic spectrum, the astronomer infers that the star is receding from the earth with a specified velocity because no other hypothesis would explain the evidence so well.

Although inference to the best explanation gives a natural account of many inferences in both science and ordinary life, the model needs further development before it can be properly assessed. What, for example, should be meant by *best?* It is sometimes taken to mean likeliest, but inference to the likeliest explanation is a disappointingly uninformative model since the main point of an account of inference is to say what leads one hypothesis to be judged likelier than another. A more promising approach construes *best* as loveliest. On this view, we infer the hypothesis that would, if correct, provide the greatest understanding.

This is a promising approach, but it raises questions that the literature has only begun to answer. An account is needed of the explanatory virtues, specifying what makes one explanation lovelier than another. Then it needs to be shown that loveliness is in fact our guide to judgments of likeliness. If this can be done, then the model may give an illuminating description of inductive practice.

Inference to the best explanation has also been used in attempts to justify our inductive practices, to show that those hypotheses we judge likely to be correct really are so. For example, it has been argued that we have good reason to believe that our best scientific theories are true since the truth of those theories is the best explanation of their wide-ranging predictive success. This argument has considerable plausibility, but it faces serious objections. If scientific theories are themselves accepted on the basis of inferences to the best explanation, then to argue in the same way that those inferences lead to the truth seems to beg the question. Moreover, it is not clear that the truth of a theory really is the best explanation of its predictive success since this seems no better an explanation than would be the truth of a competing theory that happens to share those particular predictions.

[See also Epistemology.]

BIBLIOGRAPHY

Harman, G. "The Inference to the Best Explanation," *Philosophical Review*, Vol. 74 (1965), 88–95.

Lipton, P. *Inference to the Best Explanation*. London, 1991.

Thagard, P. "The Best Explanation: Criteria for Theory Choice," *Journal of Philosophy*, Vol. 75 (1978), 76–92.

— PETER LIPTON

INFINITESIMALS

The ubiquitous use of infinitely small quantities in mathematics dates back at least to the seventeenth century. Despite continuing qualms as to their legitimacy and their supposed elimination as a result of the thoroughgoing reform movement of the nineteenth century, infinitesimals have continued to be used, especially in applied mathematics. The logician Adolf Fraenkel gave what was no doubt the widely accepted view when he stated, "The infinitely small is only to be understood as a manner of speaking based on the limit concept, hence a *potential* infinite; it is a matter of variable . . . [positive] numbers or quantities that can ultimately decrease below any arbitrarily small positive value. A fixed [positive] number different from zero that can serve as a lower bound to all finite positive values is not possible" (1928, p. 114, my translation, emphasis in original). In 1960 Fraenkel's one-time student Abraham Robinson showed how to obtain just such a "fixed number" and thereby vindicated the discredited infinitesimal methods.

The benefits of the free use of infinitesimal methods were amply demonstrated by the success of Leibniz's version of the differential and integral calculus and the continued use of these methods by the Bernoulis and especially by Leonhard Euler. Working mathematicians had no difficulty in knowing just which properties of ordinary numbers infinitesimals could be assumed to possess and just when it was legitimate to equate such quantities to zero. But the lack of any clear justification for these methods provided an opening for scathing attacks such as that of George Berkeley. The need for rigorous methods was felt by mathematicians themselves and eventually supplied (Edwards, 1979; Robinson, 1974).

Robinson's key insight was that the methods of model theory could be used to construct a powerful

rigorous theory of infinitesimals. Thus, for example, we may consider a first-order language in which a constant symbol is provided as a "name" for each real number, a function symbol is provided as a "name" for each real-valued function defined on the real numbers, and the only relation symbols are $=$ and $<$. Let T be the set of all true sentences of this language when each symbol is understood to have its intended interpretation. Let δ be a new constant symbol, and let W consist of the sentences of T together with the infinite set of sentences:

$$\delta > 0$$
$$\delta < 1, \, \delta < \frac{1}{2}, \, \delta < \frac{1}{3}, \, \delta < \frac{1}{4}, \ldots$$

Since any finite subset of W can be satisfied in the ordinary real numbers by interpreting δ as a sufficiently small positive number, the compactness theorem for first-order logic guarantees that W has a model. But in that model, the element serving to interpret δ must be positive and less than every positive real number (i.e., infinitesimal). The structure with which we began of real numbers and real-valued functions can readily be embedded in the new model. Thus if r is a real number and c_r is the constant of the language that names r, we may regard the element of the new model that serves to interpret c_r as simply r itself. Functions can be embedded in the same way. One speaks of the new model as an enlargement.

Abraham Robinson's key insight was that the methods of model theory could be used to construct a powerful rigorous theory of infinitesimals.

Moreover, because $T \subseteq W$, all true statements about the real numbers that can be expressed in our language are also true in this enlargement. A false statement about the real numbers is likewise false in the enlargement: if the statement S is false, then $\neg S$ is a true statement about the reals and hence is also true in the enlargement. It is this transfer principle, the fact that statements are true about the real numbers if and only if they are true in the new enlarged structure, that makes precise just when an assertion about ordinary numbers can be extended to apply to infinitesimals as well.

The enlargement will contain infinitely large as well as infinitesimal elements. This is readily seen by applying the transfer principle to the statement that every nonzero real number has a reciprocal. One may even speak of infinite integers; their existence follows on applying the transfer principle to the statement that for any given real number there is a positive integer that exceeds it.

The basic facts of real analysis can be established on this basis using modes of argument that would earlier have been quite correctly regarded as illegitimate. For example, the basic theorem that a continuous function on a closed interval assumes a maximum value can be proved by dividing the interval into infinitely many sub-intervals, each of infinitesimal length, and selecting an endpoint of such a subinterval at which the function's value is greatest (Davis, 1977; Robinson, 1974). By beginning with a more extensive language, it is possible to apply infinitesimal methods to branches of mathematics requiring a more substantial set-theoretic basis (e.g., topology, functional analysis, probability theory). It has even proved possible to use these "nonstandard" methods to settle certain open questions in mathematics.

For those with qualms concerning nonconstructive methods in mathematics, these infinitesimal methods are bound to seem unsatisfactory. Because the underlying language is built on an uncountable "alphabet," the use of the compactness theorem hides an application of some form of the axiom of choice. This in turn is reflected in a basic indeterminacy; we can establish the existence of enlargements but cannot specify any particular enlargement. Robinson himself has emphasized that although nonstandard analysis "appears to affirm the existence of all sorts of infinitary entities," one always has the option of taking the "formalist point of view" from which "we may consider that what we have done is to introduce *new deductive procedures* rather than new mathematical entities" (1974, p. 282, emphasis in original).

[See also Berkeley, George; Leibniz, Gottfried Wilhelm; Mathematical Logic; Model Theory.]

BIBLIOGRAPHY

Davis, M. *Applied Nonstandard Analysis*. New York, 1977.
Edwards, C. H., Jr. *The Historical Development of the Calculus*. New York, 1979.
Fraenkel, A. *Einleitung in die Mengenlehre*, 3d ed. Berlin, 1928: reprint, New York, 1946.
Robinson, A. *Nonstandard Analysis*, 2d ed. Amsterdam, 1974.

– MARTIN DAVIS

INFORMED CONSENT

A fundamental requirement of both ethics and the law is that medical treatment cannot be given to competent patients without their informed consent. This represents a rejection of more traditional authoritarian or paternalistic accounts of the physician/patient relationship in which the physician had decision-making authority in favor of a process of shared decision making between physicians and patients. In this respect informed consent helps shape the nature of nearly all health-care treatment decision making. Informed consent also has special importance in a narrower class of cases in which patients and their physicians are unable to agree on a course of treatment. In these cases a competent patient is given the right to refuse any recommended treatment, even including life-sustaining treatment, no matter how strongly the physician or others believe that the treatment should be undertaken.

There are two principal moral values that are served by and justify the informed-consent requirement in health care. The first is patient well-being—arguably the fundamental goal of all health care. The concept of patient well-being, as opposed to the apparently more objective goals of protecting and promoting patients' health and lives, signals the important respect in which what will best serve a particular patient's well-being is often to a significant degree a subjective determination that depends on the particular aims and values of the patient in question. Increasingly, there are medically acceptable alternative treatments (including the alternative of no treatment), no one of which is best for all patients with a particular medical condition. The patient's participation in decision making is therefore necessary in order to select the treatment that best fits his or her aims and values. The other fundamental moral value that under-girds the informed-consent requirement is individual self-determination or autonomy. Self-determination in this context is the moral right of ordinary persons to make significant decisions about their lives for themselves and according to their own aims and values. Requiring that health care not be rendered without a competent patient's informed consent respects this right of self-determination. The informed-consent requirement reflects the fundamental moral point that it is the patient and the patient's body that undergo the treatment, and so it should be the patient who is morally entitled to authorize or refuse the treatment.

Three conditions are necessary for ethically valid informed consent—that the patient's decision be informed, voluntary, and competent. The requirement that the decision be informed places a responsibility on the patient's physician to provide the patient with information, in an understandable form, about the patient's condition or diagnosis and the prognosis if no treatment is provided, together with the alternative treatments that would improve that prognosis, along with their risks and benefits. This typically does not require that the physician provide, or that the patient understand, complex medical and scientific information, but rather information about how the various alternatives would likely affect the patient's pursuit of his or her plan of life. Legal requirements regarding how much and which information must be provided vary, but the ethical ideal is to provide the information that the particular patient would reasonably want to know in order to make his or her decision.

The requirement that the consent be voluntary means that treatment must not be rendered against the patient's will, either by force or by coercing the patient's choice. More important, it also forbids physicians from manipulating the patient's choice through selective provision of information, playing on the patient's fears, and other means. Ethically objectionable manipulation, as opposed to appropriate informing and persuasion, aims to produce a different choice from what a competent patient would have made if fully informed and freely choosing.

The third requirement of competence is the most complex. Usually, patients are either clearly competent, with their normal decision-making capacities intact, or clearly incompetent, unable to make any decision. In

The Tuskegee Study consisted of experiments on syphilis-infected African-American men without informing them of their condition or treating them for it. (Corbis/Bettmann)

borderline cases in which there is significant, but not total, impairment of the patient's decision-making capacities, the competence determination is often controversial. The competence evaluation should address the process of the patient's decision making in order to determine whether there are significant impairments, limitations, or mistakes in that process that have resulted in a choice different from what the patient would have wanted in the absence of those impairments, limitations, or mistakes. The proper standard of competence in borderline cases is controversial but increasingly understood to be a variable standard, requiring a higher level of understanding and reasoning when the patient's well-being would be seriously affected by the decision in question and a lower level when there would be only limited impact on the patient's well-being. While treatment refusal may reasonably trigger an evaluation of the patient's competence, it should not serve as any evidence of the patient's incompetence—that evidence must come from impairments or limitations that cannot be remedied in the process of the patient's reasoning. When the requirements for ethically valid informed consent (that is, informed, voluntary, and competent) are met, the patient's choice should be reasonably in accord with his or her well-being, and his or her self-determination will have been respected.

Three conditions are necessary for ethically valid

informed consent: that the patient's decision

be informed, voluntary, and competent.

When the patient has been determined to be incompetent to make his or her own treatment choices, a surrogate or proxy, typically a close family member, should substitute for the patient in the decision-making and consent process. The patient's informed consent is also not required in emergency conditions, when taking time to obtain consent would involve serious risks to the patient's well-being, or when the patient has waived his or her right to give consent and has authorized another to make the treatment decision.

[See also Applied Ethics; Biomedical Ethics; Paternalism.]

BIBLIOGRAPHY

Appelbaum, P. S., C. W. Lidz, and A. Meisel. *Informed Consent: Legal Theory and Clinical Practice.* New York, 1987.
Faden, R., and T. L. Beauchamp. *A History and Theory of Informed Consent.* New York, 1986.

– DAN W. BROCK

INTENSIONAL LOGIC

There are two central uses of the term 'intensional': (1) one semantic, and (2) one ontological.

1. A language (or its logic) is said to be extensional if, within it, equivalent formulas can be substituted for one another salva veritate: $(A \leftrightarrow B) \rightarrow (\ldots A \ldots) \leftrightarrow (\ldots B \ldots)$. A language is said to be intensional if it is not extensional, that is, if it violates this substitutivity principle. For example, "x is a creature with a heart" and "x is a creature with a kidney" are equivalent (they apply to the same things). But when we substitute the former for the latter in the true sentence "It is necessary that, if x is a creature with a kidney, x has a kidney," we get a false sentence, "It is necessary that, if x is a creature with a heart, x has a kidney." Intensional language is used for such matters as modality, propositional attitudes, probability, explanation, and counterfactuality.

2. An entity x is said to be extensional if it satisfies the following principle of extensionality: for every entity y in the same ontological category as x, if x and y are equivalent, they are identical. An entity x is said to be intensional if it is not extensional, that is, if this principle of extensionality does not hold for it (i.e., there is some equivalent entity y in the same ontological category that is not identical to x). Sets are paradigmatic extensional entities; properties, relations, concepts, and propositions are paradigmatic intensional entities. For example, even though being a creature with a kidney and being a creature with a heart are equivalent properties (the same things have them), they are not identical.

The leading view is that the underlying source of intensionality in natural language is a certain sort of complex abstract singular term known as an "intensional abstract." Examples are 'that' clauses, gerundive phrases. infinitive phrases, and so on. The connection between the two uses of 'intensional' is that intensional abstracts are terms for intensional entities. For example, 'that 5 + 7 = 12' denotes the proposition that 5 + 7 = 12; 'being red' denotes the property of being red; and so on.

There are two main projects in intensional logic, one for each of the two uses of the term. The first project is to formulate logical laws governing substitutivity conditions for intensional abstracts. The main challenge is to find techniques for representing systematically the subtle distinctions arising in intensional language. The second project is to formulate logical laws governing the fundamental logical relations relative to which the intensionality of an entity is characterized. In the case of properties, for example, this fundamental logical relation is the relation of having a property. In the case of a concept, it is the relation of falling under a concept. The main challenge in this area is to find systems of laws for such relations which are faithful to our intuitions and which, at the same time, avoid logical paradoxes (e.g., the intensional version of Russell's paradox—the property of being a property which does not have itself).

Russell and Whitehead's *Principia Mathematica* (1910) undertook both projects at once, as did Church's Frege-style "A Formulation of the Logic of Sense and Denotation" (1952). In connection with the second project mentioned above, these logicians avoided the logical paradoxes by imposing a rigid type theory. From about 1960 there has been a burst of activity in intensional logic. Throughout this period, until his death in 1995, Church continued to work on his own Frege-style approach. In the 1960s and early 1970s, however, most of the new work on intensional logic was inspired by Carnap's *Meaning and Necessity* (1947), in which Carnap attempted to explicate the informed notion of a possible world. Montague, Kaplan, Bressan, Cocchiarella, T. Parsons, D. Lewis, Gallin, Partee, and a host of others applied Carnapian possible-worlds semantics—and enrichments of it (following Bayart, Kanger, Kripke, and Hintikka)—to various intensional languages. Most of the efforts were carried out in the setting of some form of type theory. In the case of Montague, this took the form of a categorial grammar, which led to a flurry of work on natural language syntax.

Two main difficulties, one for each use of 'intensional', confront all these approaches to intensional logic. The first has to do with the use of rigid type theories to resolve the paradoxes. There is overwhelming linguistic evidence that natural languages do not have the sort of rigid type structure posited by Russell and Church. Indeed, there are various ways in which natural language is type-free. For example, everything (regardless of category) is self-identical, even self-identity. Moreover, the sentence just used is not infinitely ambiguous along type lines, as Russell thought. Appreciation of such facts has led a number of logicians to develop type-free resolutions of the paradoxes. Contributions along these lines have been made by Fitch, Gilmore, Feferman, Aezel, Turner, and many others.

The second difficulty, associated with the logic for intensional abstracts, is the problem of fine-grained content. On the standard *possible-worlds* approach, intensional abstracts (e.g., 'that 5 + 7 = 12' and 'that

1 + 1 = 2') denote the same thing as long as they are necessarily equivalent. But this is clearly mistaken: for example, it is possible to be thinking that $1 + 1 = 2$ and not to be thinking that $5 + 7 = 12$.

A fine-grained intensional logic must accommodate not only intensional distinctions but also those associated with the paradox of analysis.

Certain possible-worlds theorists working within a type-theoretic framework (e.g., Cresswell) have attempted a reductionist approach to fine-grained content; on this approach "complex" intensional entities (e.g., propositions) are identified with sequences or abstract trees whose elements are possible-worlds constructs. A reductionist approach (adopted by, e.g., Perry & Barwise, 1983) which is not wedded to type theory takes certain intensions as primitive and then reduces all remaining "complex" intensions to set-theoretical constructions out of these primitive intensions. There is also a nonreductionist algebraic approach (e.g., Bealer, Menzel, Parsons) which is type-free and which takes all intensional entities, "complex" and "noncomplex," at face value as *sui generis* entities.

A fine-grained intensional logic must accommodate, not only intensional distinctions of the above sort, but also those associated with the paradox of analysis (Langford & Moore, 1942), Mates's puzzle (1950), and Frege's original 1892 puzzle (how can 'that Hesperus = Phosphorous' and 'that Hesperus = Hesperus' denote different propositions?). Around 1970 Donnellan and Kripke mounted persuasive arguments undermining Frege's own solution to the latter puzzle (a solution upon which Church's approach to fine-grained content is based), according to which proper names express descriptive intensions (e.g., 'Aristotle' expresses the descriptive concept of being the most famous philosopher of antiquity). Evidently, the nonreductionist theory is the most promising approach to these further problems of fine-grained intensional logic.

[See also Carnap, Rudolph; Explanation, Theories of; Explanation, Types of; Frege, Gottlob; Modality, Philosophy and Metaphysics of Probability; Russell, Bertrand Arthur William.]

BIBLIOGRAPHY

Barwise, J., and J. Perry. *Situations and Attitudes.* Cambridge, MA, 1983.

Bealer, G. *Quality and Concept.* Oxford, 1982.

———. "A Solution to Frege's Puzzle," in J. Tomberlin, ed., *Philosophical Perspectives* 7 (Atascadero, CA, 1993), pp. 17–61.

Church, A. "Outline of a Revised Formulation of the Logic of Sense and Denotation," *Noûs*, Vol. 7 (1973), 23–33, and *Notûs* Vol. 8, (1974), 135–56.

Chierchia, G., B. Partee, R. Turner, eds. *Property Theories, Type Theories, and Semantics*. Dordrecht, 1988.

Cresswell, M. J. *Structured Meanings*. Cambridge, MA, 1985.

Feferman, S. "Toward Useful Type-free Theories," *The Journal of Symbolic Logic*, Vol. 49 (1984), 75–111.

Gallin, D. *Intensional and Higher-Order Modal Logic*. Amsterdam, 1975.

Gilmore, P. C. "The Consistency of Partial Set Theory Without Extensionality," *Proceedings of Symposia in Pure Mathematics* 8, Part II (1974), 147–53.

Kaplan, D. *Foundations of Intensional Logic*, doctoral dissertation, University of California in Los Angeles, 1964.

Kripke, S. *Naming and Necessity*. Cambridge, MA, 1980.

Thomason, R. *Formal Philosophy: Selected Papers of Richard Montague*. Hew Haven, 1974.

— GEORGE BEALER

INTERNALISM VERSUS EXTERNALISM

Internalism and externalism are positions regarding the nature of positive epistemic status. The central claim of internalism is that the epistemic status of a belief depends importantly on factors internal to the believer's perspective or point of view, as opposed to factors such as the causal genesis of the belief or the reliability of the believer's cognitive faculties. Different versions of internalism spell out the internalist constraint in different ways, but all focus on the importance of S's perspective where epistemic evaluation is concerned. Externalism is simply the denial that epistemic status so depends on the believer's perspective. An example of internalism is the position that the epistemic status of a belief depends only on what S knows to be the case. An externalist opposing such a view might think that the status of S's belief depends on how the belief was caused, even if S does not know how the belief was caused.

Two important kinds of internalism are perspectival internalism and access internalism. Perspectival internalism claims that epistemic status depends entirely on what is internal to the actual perspective of the believer. Different versions of perspectival internalism define actual perspective in different ways, but usually it is in terms of what the believer believes, justifiably believes, or knows. Access internalism claims that epistemic status depends only on what is easily accessible to the believer's perspective. Access internalism also has many versions, depending on how one defines the believer's perspective and on what kind of accessibility is required.

The internalist constraints posited by access and perspectival internalism are very general. More restricted kinds of internalism place constraints only upon specific factors contributing to epistemic status. Thus grounds internalism is the position that the grounds or evidence for S's belief must be appropriately internal to S's perspective. Norm internalism is the position that the rules or norms governing S's beliefs must be appropriately internal. For each of the versions of internalism specified we may define a version of externalism as the denial of that position.

Why would someone be an internalist? Historically, internalists have accepted a deontological conception of positive epistemic status, or a conception that closely associates epistemic status with the concepts of responsibility, praise, and blame. But since whether one's believings are responsible seems to depend more on one's perspective than on factors outside that perspective, internalists have argued for analogous constraints on epistemic status.

[See also Epistemology.]

BIBLIOGRAPHY

Alston, W. "Concepts of Epistemic Justification." *Monist*, Vol. 68 (1985), 57–89.

———. "Internalism and Externalism in Epistemology," *Philosophical Topics*, Vol. 14 (1986), 179–221.

BonJour, L. "Externalist Theories of Empirical Knowledge," in P. A. French, T. E. Uehling, and H. K. Wettstein, eds., *Studies in Epistemology*, Midwest Studies in Philosophy, Vol. 5 (Minneapolis, 1980).

Goldman, A. "The Internalist Conception of Justification," in P. A. French, T. E. Uehling, and H. K. Wettstein, eds., *Studies in Epistemology*, Midwest Studies in Philosophy, Vol. 5 (Minneapolis, 1980).

Greco, J. "Internalism and Epistemically Responsible Belief," *Synthese*, Vol. 85 (1990), 245–77.

Plantinga, A. *Warrant: The Current Debate*. Oxford, 1993.

Pollock, J. *Contemporary Theories of Knowledge*. Totowa, NJ, 1986.

— JOHN GRECO

INTROSPECTION

The term 'introspection' might be defined as the direct, conscious examination or observation by a subject of his or her own mental processes. The term is derived from two Latin words, *spicere* ("to look") and *intra* ("within").

From at least the time of René Descartes up to the early twentieth century, it would have been considered unproblematic that the mind can reflect (or bend its attention back) upon itself. In the eighteenth and nineteenth centuries, if not earlier, self-reflection began to be interpreted, in the main, as introspection. In turn, to introspect one's own mental processes was explained in terms of the capacities (1) to focus the full glare of one's conscious attention upon the task of observing some particular, first-level, conscious process (or mental act), which was an item in one's stream of consciousness, and (2) to report in a privileged and incorrigible way upon the results of such observation. This introspective act was considered to be a form of inner, though nonsensuous, perception, and deliberate parallels were frequently drawn between it and ordinary outer perception by means of our senses, such as those of vision or hearing.

In the nineteenth century, Franz Brentano and other philosophical psychologists were at pains to distinguish introspection (sometimes called inner observation) from its close relative self-consciousness (sometimes called inner perception). Introspection was a deliberate act of focusing a subject's attention on some inhabitant in his stream of consciousness. Self-consciousness was an indeliberate but inescapable, though partial, concomitant awareness on the part of a subject of at least some features of some of his first-level conscious mental acts. To put it metaphorically, introspection was a deliberate ogling with the inner mental eye; self-consciousness was unavoidably catching sight of something out of the corner of one's mental eye.

However, even as this canonical version of introspection was being formulated, doubts were being voiced about the possibility of splitting consciousness into two processes that operated at two different levels at the same time. Pushing aside these doubts, the early psychological introspectionists—such as Wilhelm Wundt, Edward B. Titchener, Narziss Ach, Karl Bühler, and William James—believed that either introspection proper or some version of self-consciousness was nevertheless the only possible method for inaugurating a truly empirical, that is, scientific, psychology. For only the subject of mental acts or processes can have "eye witness," knowledge by acquaintance of the denizens of his or her stream of consciousness. So, the very first psychological laboratories were devoted to introspection (for this term came to be used for both introspection proper and for scientific versions of self-consciousness). In carefully designed laboratories bristling with chronograph and tachistocope, subjects were asked to produce detailed introspective reports on various aspects of the inner conscious effects of carefully controlled stimuli applied to their senses.

These experiments resulted in some of the most tedious literature that psychology has ever produced. Also, there could be found little or no agreement about results across schools or from one laboratory to the next. Yet another consequence, which Wundt, for example, readily admitted, was that introspection experiments seemed confined to a study of comparatively trivial mental episodes.

Surprisingly, the failure of introspectionism did not lead many people to question the inherent model of introspection. As psychology and philosophy wound their way through behaviorism and versions of the mind–brain identity theory to contemporary forms of physicalism, such as functionalism, both were faithful to the original, classical model of introspection. They abandoned the Cartesianism of the psychological introspectionists and questioned the privileged status of introspection reports, but they did not question the basic two-level picture—that introspection was a second-level monitoring, observing, registering, or tracking of some first-level process or processes.

In the nineteenth century, Franz Brentano and other philosophical psychologists were at pains to distinguish introspection from its close relative self-consciousness.

Thus, classical psychological behaviorists such as John Broadus Watson or B. F. Skinner gave, as at least one account of one employment of introspection, that it was a literal monitoring by the subject of his thinking (which for a classical behaviorist was to be analyzed as inner truncated movements in the muscles of speech, or "stopped short" speech). Only the repeated failure of experiments seeking to verify this theory led to the abandonment of that particular, and now notorious, explanation.

The philosophers, or most of them, also championed some version of the two-level account of introspection, and still do. Even the most tough-minded of the physicalists, such as David M. Armstrong or Daniel Dennett, stick resolutely to a two-level monitoring account of introspection. Thus, in *A Materialist Theory of the Mind* Armstrong describes introspection as one part of the brain scanning another part of the brain such that the subject, whose brain it is, generates (in entirely causal fashion) a belief about the nature of the first-level, scanned, brain process. In *Content and Consciousness* and again in *Brainstorms* and *Consciousness Explained,* in an uncompromising functionalist account of mind, Dennett describes introspection in terms of one part of the brain "accessing" another (like one part of a computer accessing another) and then, via the speech center, "printing out" the results.

In philosophy and psychology since the 1950s, there has been a minority view that this two-level account of introspection is simply mistaken. Humans have no such second-level inspecting or scanning or monitoring capacity. Earlier, Gilbert Ryle (1949) argued convincingly that this two-level account did not make theoretical sense. Unfortunately, he substituted for it an unconvincing behaviorist account (in terms of the ordinary perceptual "retrospection" of ordinary behavior). More recently, psychologists and philosophers (such as Wilson and Nisbett, 1977, and Lyons, 1986) have suggested that, besides those theoretical grounds for rejecting the two-level account of introspection, there are also empirical grounds for rejection drawn from contemporary experimental psychology, anthropology, and the brain sciences. In contemporary introspective experiments subjects produced reports that were more like stereotyped and predictable "folk" interpretations than detailed eyewitness accounts of inner events. Besides, it seems that in cultures more or less uninfluenced by European culture people do not claim to have powers of introspection. More important, there does not seem to be any part of the brain that functions as a monitor of those neurophysiological states that maintain and control conscious states. Finally, it seems both possible and more plausible to give an account of what humans are doing, when they claim to be introspecting, in terms of the exercise of the internal but quite ordinary capacities of memory and imagination. This opposition of views has not yet been resolved, and, because of this, introspection (like consciousness itself) is likely to receive more direct and sustained treatment in the closing years of the century.

[See also Armstrong, David M.; Descartes, René; Functionalism; James, William; Philosophy of Mind; Physicalism.]

BIBLIOGRAPHY

In Philosophy

Armstrong, D. M. *A Materialist Theory of the Mind.* London, 1968.
Brentano, F. *Psychology from an Empirical Standpoint* (1874). Edited by O. Kraus and L. McAlister. Translated by A. C. Rancurello, D. B. Terrell, and L. McAlister. 1973.
Churchland, P. M. *Matter and Consciousness: A Contemporary Introduction to the Philosophy of Mind.* Cambridge, MA, 1984.
Dennett, D. *Content and Consciousness.* London, 1969.
———. *Brainstorms: Philosophical Essays on Mind and Psychology.* Brighton, 1979.
———. *Consciousness Explained.* Boston, 1991.
Dretske, F. "Introspection," *Proceedings of the Aristotelian Society,* Vol. 94 (1994), 263–78.
Hamlyn, D. W. "Self-Knowledge," in *Perception, Learning, and the Self: Essays on the Philosophy of Psychology* (London, 1983).
Lyons, W. *The Disappearance of Introspection.* Cambridge, MA, 1986.
Ryle, G. *The Concept of Mind.* London, 1949.

In Psychology

Boring, E. G. "A History of Introspection," *Psychological Bulletin,* Vol. 50 (1953), 169–89.
Danziger, K. "The History of Introspection Reconsidered," *Journal of the History of the Behavioral Sciences,* Vol. 16 (1980), 241–62.
Hebb, D. O. "The Mind's Eye." *Psychology Today,* Vol. 2 (1969), 55–68.
Humphrey, N. *Consciousness Regained: Chapters in the Development of Mind.* Cambridge, 1983.
James, W. *The Principles of Psychology* (1890), 2 vols. 1950.
Miller, G. *Psychology: The Science of Mental Life.* Middlesex, 1966.
Titchener, E. B. *A Primer of Psychology.* London, 1899.
Nisbett, R. E., and T. D. Wilson. "Telling More than We Can Know: Verbal Reports on Mental Processes," *Psychological Review,* Vol. 84 (1977), 231–59.
Wundt, W. *An Introduction to Psychology.* Translated by R. Pintner. London, 1912.

– WILLIAM LYONS

INTUITION

In the history of philosophy intuition has been used primarily as a term for an intellectual, or rational, episode intimately tied to a priori knowledge. The term has sometimes been used in a broader way to include certain sensory episodes (appearances) and certain introspective episodes (e.g., inner awareness of the passage of time). In contemporary philosophy this broader use has fallen out of fashion (except among Kantians), and the narrower use prevails.

An intuition in this sense is simply a certain kind of seeming: for one to have an intuition that P is just for it to seem to one that P. This kind of seeming is intellectual, not sensory or introspective, in the following sense: typically, if it is possible for someone to have the intuition that P, then it is possible for someone to have the intuition that P in the absence of any particular sensory or introspective experiences relevant to the truth or falsity of the proposition that P. For this reason, intuitions are counted as "data of reason" not "data of experience." In this connection, intuitions are sometimes called "a priori intuitions" or "rational intuitions."

Intuition must be distinguished from belief: belief is not a seeming; intuition is. For example, I have an intuition—it still seems to me—that the naive set-abstraction axiom from set theory is true despite the fact that I do not believe that it is true (because I know of the set-theoretical paradoxes). There is a rather similar phenomenon in sense perception. In the Müller-Lyer illusion, it still seems to me that one of the two arrows is longer than the other, despite the fact that I do not believe that one of the two arrows is longer (because I have measured them). In each case, the seeming persists in spite of the countervailing belief. Similar considerations show that intuitions must likewise be distinguished from guesses, hunches, and common sense.

Many philosophers identify intuitions with linguistic intuitions. But this is mistaken if by "linguistic intuition" they mean intuitions about words, for most of our intuitions simply do not have any linguistic content. Other philosophers think of intuitions as conceptual intuitions. Nothing is wrong with this if "conceptual intuition" is understood broadly enough. But there is a common construal—originating in Hume's notion of relations of ideas and popular with logical positivists—according to which conceptual intuitions are all analytic. The problem is that countless intuitions are not analytic on the traditional construal of that term (convertibility into a logical truth by substitution of synonyms). For example, the intuition that, if region r_1 is part of region r_2 and r_2 is part of region r_3, then r_1 is part of r_3. Possibility intuitions are also not analytic (e.g., in epistemology the intuition that the Gettier situations are possible). In response, some philosophers have countered that possibility intuitions are just intuitions of consistency, but this view is mistaken on several counts. For example, it is consistent to hold that region r_1 is part of r_2, r_2 is part of r_3, but that r_1 is not part of r_3, despite the fact that such a thing is not possible.

Intuition must be distinguished from belief:

belief is not a seeing; intuition is.

Standard practice in logic, mathematics, linguistics, and philosophy is to use intuitions as evidence. (For example, in epistemology Roderick Chisholm uses intuitions to show that traditional phenomenalism is mistaken, and Edmund Gettier uses intuitions to show that the traditional identification of knowledge with justified true belief is mistaken. In metaphysics Saul Kripke uses intuitions to show that, if water is H_2O, then it is necessary that water is H_2O. In philosophy of mind, Hilary Putnam uses intuitions to show that logical behaviorism is mistaken, and so forth.) A great many philosophers believe that use of intuitions is essential to the indicated disciplines.

Radical empiricists, who doubt that intuitions have evidential weight, usually defend their view by pointing to the fact that intuitions can be unreliable. They cite, for example, the fact that our intuitions about naive set theory are in conflict with our intuitions about classical logic. But this shows only that traditional infallibilism is mistaken, not that intuitions lack evidential weight. After all, sense perceptions have evidential weight even though they can be unreliable. (Incidentally, although various cognitive psychologists—Wason, Johnson-Laird, Rosh, Nisbett, Kahneman, Tversky, and oth-

ers—have examined human rationality with a critical eye, their studies have not attempted to test empirically the reliability of intuitions, and it will be quite difficult to do so.)

Why should intuitions have evidential weight? A plausible answer is that intuitions have an appropriate tie to the truth: as a noncontingent fact, if a subject's cognitive conditions (intelligence, attentiveness, and so forth) were suitably close to ideal, the subject's intuitions would be sufficiently reliable to permit the subject to arrive at a mostly true theory regarding the subject matter of those intuitions. This is a consequence of an analysis of what it is to possess concepts determinately: a necessary and sufficient condition for determinately possessing one's concepts is that one's intuitions have this kind of tie to the truth; if the subject's intuitions lacked this sort of tie to the truth, that would only show that the subject did not determinately possess those concepts (or that the subject's cognitive conditions were not sufficiently good). In contemporary philosophy, many have come to accept (some form of) this moderate rationalist theory of intuitions and concept possession.

[See also Chisholm, Roderick M.; Hume, David; Kripke, Saul Aaron; Philosophy of Mind; Putnam, Hilary; Truth.]

BIBLIOGRAPHY

Bealer, G. "A Priori Knowledge and the Scope of Philosophy," *Philosophical Studies* (1966), with replies by E. Sosa and W. Lycan in the same volume.
BonJour, L. "Against Naturalized Epistemology," *Midwest Studies in Philosophy*, Vol. 19 (1994).
Kahneman, D., and A. Tversky. "On the Study of Statistical Intuitions," in D. Kahneman, P. Slovic, and A. Tversky, eds., *Judgment Under Uncertainty* (Cambridge, 1982).

– GEORGE BEALER

INTUITIONISM

Intuitionism is a form of constructivism about mathematics and logic that has its origins in the work of L. E. J. Brouwer and A. Heyting. It should be distinguished both from other forms of constructivism (e.g., finitism, Bishop's constructive mathematics, recursive mathematics, predicativism) and from classical or platonistic viewpoints.

Philosophical research on intuitionism has been greatly stimulated by the work of Michael Dummett (1976, 1977, 1978). Dummett has offered a meaning-theoretic argument in favor of intuitionism and against classical or platonistic viewpoints. On the classical truth-conditional view of meaning, truth is understood in such a way that the principle of bivalence ($A \lor \neg A$) holds, and truth is divorced from the ability to recognize truth. This view is supported by a platonistic or realistic metaphysics, according to which all statements have definite truth values by virtue of some mind-independent reality. Dummett, however, wishes to proceed from general conditions about language use and the ability to learn and communicate meaning, rather than from metaphysical views about whether or not there is a mind-independent mathematical reality. He argues that we cannot justify a notion of truth on which the principle of bivalence holds.

The core of the argument is that the meaning of a statement must be construed in terms of what it is for a person to know the meaning. Knowledge of meaning must ultimately be implicit. That is, if we define the meaning of an expression by using other expressions then there must be knowledge of the meaning of these other expressions. To avoid an infinite regress, we must finally arrive at expressions for which meaning is implicit. Implicit knowledge can be ascribed to a person only if it is fully manifestable in our behavior or practice. This is Dummett's version of Wittgenstein's idea that meaning is determined by use. Intuitionism satisfies the condition that the user of a language must be able fully to manifest his or her knowledge of meaning because it explains meaning in terms of constructions (= proofs). The knowledge of truth-conditions of undecidable statements (e.g., involving quantification over infinite domains), however, cannot be fully manifestable if truth is understood platonistically or according to the classical view of logic and mathematics.

Dummett has claimed that the conclusion of his argument depends upon the rejection of meaning holism, and he has provided a deep investigation into its other conditions. By linking knowledge of meaning with the full manifestability of that knowledge in linguistic practice, Dummett's view of intuitionism is quite different from Brouwer's solipsistic view. Brouwer held that not only could mental constructions not be adequately captured in formal systems, but they were fundamentally languageless.

The core of the argument is that the meaning of a statement must be construed in terms of what it is for a person to know the meaning.

Dummett's work has thus shown how intuitionism is related to many broader philosophical issues about semantics and the realism/antirealism debate. An extensive literature has developed on this basis, and various aspects of Dummett's views, on intuitionism have been widely discussed and criticized. Some critics have claimed that the requirement of 'full' manifestability is too strong and should be weakened (see Prawitz, 1977). Another response is that a finitist could apply Dummett's argument to intuitionism itself to show that its idealizations, like those of the platonist, are unfounded (see Wright, 1993). Some critics think that manifestability is actually compatible with the existence of classical mathematics. It has been argued that mathematics does not seem to involve a molecular meaning theory, and that Dummett's approach is focused too narrowly on logic and arithmetic (see Troelstra & van Dalen, 1988). There has also been some concern about how intuition has disappeared from intuitionism as a consequence of the focus on meaning-theoretic issues. It has been argued that intuitionism needs a (nonsolipsistic) notion of intuition (see Parsons, 1986). Moreover, this concern about intuition does not have to preclude a theory of meaning (see Tieszen, 1994).

Many other significant conceptual advances in intuitionism are related to work that is more technical in nature (see Troelstra & van Dalen, 1988). There has been much interest in the metamathematics of intuitionism, and a good deal of research has been carried out on the proof theory of intuitionistic formal systems. Beth and Kripke models for intuitionistic logic have been developed and used extensively. These models are now seen as special cases of categorical semantics, which also includes topos semantics and sheaf models. The intuitionistic type theories of Per Martin-Löf (1984) constitute an important new development and have been studied extensively. There has been further research on intuitionistic set theory. Theories of choice and lawless sequences have been greatly expanded, leading to further results in intuitionistic real analysis. This work will, it is hoped, lead to a deeper understanding of the nature of the continuum. There has also been some interesting work on the theory of the creative subject.

Continuing efforts to reconstruct other areas of mathematics in an intuitionistically acceptable fashion have met with some success, and there have been some especially interesting efforts to forge connections between intuitionism and computer science.

[See also Dummett, Michael; Kripke, Saul Aaron; Meaning; Truth; Wittgenstein, Ludwig Josef Johann.]

BIBLIOGRAPHY

Brouwer, L. E. J. *Collected Works I*, edited by A. Heyting. Amsterdam, 1975.

Dummett, M. *Elements of Intuitionism*. Oxford, 1977.

———. "The Philosophical Basis of Intuitionistic Logic," in *Truth and Other Enigmas* (Cambridge, MA, 1978).

George, A. "How Not to Refute Realism." *Journal of Philosophy,* Vol. 40 (1993), 53–72.

Martin-Löf, P. *Intuitionistic Type Theory.* Naples, 1984.

McDowell, J. "Anti-Realism and the Epistemology of Understanding," in H. Parrett and J. Bouveresse, eds., *Meaning and Understanding* (Berlin, 1981).

McGinn, C. "Truth and Use," in M. Platts, ed., *Reference, Truth and Reality* (London, 1980).

Parsons, C. "Intuition in Constructive Mathematics," in J. Butterfield, ed., *Language, Mind and Logic* (Cambridge, 1986).

Prawitz, D. "Meaning and Proofs: On the Conflict Between Classical and Intuitionistic Logic," *Theoria,* Vol. 43 (1977), 1–40.

Sundholm, G. "Proof Theory and Meaning," in D. Gabbay and F. Guenther, eds., *Handbook of Philosophical Logic II* (Dordrecht, 1986).

Tieszen, R. "What Is the Philosophical Basis of Intuitionistic Mathematics?" in D. Prawitz, B. Skyrms, and D. Westerståhl, eds., *Logic, Methodology and Philosophy of Science IX* (Amsterdam, 1994).

Troelstra, A., and van Dalen, D. *Constructivism in Mathematics,* Vols. I and II. Amsterdam, 1988.

Wright, C. *Realism, Meaning and Truth,* 2d ed. Oxford, 1993.

– RICHARD TIESZEN

J

JAMES, WILLIAM

William James (1842–1910), American philosopher and psychologist, was born in New York City to Mary Robertson Walsh James and Henry James, Sr., the eccentric Swedenborgian theologian. James's paternal grandfather and namesake was an Irishman of Calvinist persuasion who immigrated to the United States in 1798 and became very rich through felicitous investment in the Erie Canal. James had three brothers and a sister; one of them, the novelist Henry James, achieved equal fame.

James's early environment was propitious; his father's enthusiastic and unconventional scholarship, his personal and unorthodox religion, his literary association with men like Oliver Wendell Holmes, Sr., and Ralph Waldo Emerson all stimulated free intellectual growth. Even more important was the rather extraordinary respect that the elder James lavished upon the youthful spontaneities of his children; each, he thought, must go his own way and become that most valuable of creatures, himself. There was no strait-laced dogmatism in the James household, and William James was free to accept or reject the ideas of his father and his father's friends. The thought and sympathies of these transcendentalists and romantic humanitarians of the New England tradition never seemed to James the ultimate answers to his own philosophical and personal problems, but they dealt with genuine issues which he did not evade in his later work.

James's primary education took place at his father's table; its main constituents were the spirited discourse that the family held on every topic and the example of the parents, loving and unworldly. Formal education took place irregularly in various private establishments. From 1855 to 1860 James (often in the company of his younger brother Henry) attended schools in England, France, Switzerland, and Germany. There, as his father said, he and his brother were able "to absorb French and German and get a better sensuous education than they are likely to get here" (Ralph Barton Perry, *The Thought and Character of William James,* p. 59). During this European sojourn James's interest was divided between natural science and art, especially painting.

In spite of his continuing enthusiasm and talent for scientific inquiry, James's interest in painting became so strong by 1860 that he resolved to spend a trial period learning to paint. The elder James was not anxious for his son to become a painter, thereby prematurely cutting himself off from the rest of life's possibilities; any definite vocation, according to the father, was sadly "narrowing" (*ibid.,* p. 171). It was nevertheless arranged that James should begin study with William M. Hunt in Newport. This experiment convinced James that he lacked the ability to be anything more than a mediocre artist, than which there was, he thought, nothing worse. The lesson at Newport permanently discouraged James's pursuit of an artistic vocation, but throughout his scientific and philosophical career he retained the artist's eye, his predilection for concrete sensuous detail, and his concern for style.

James was essentially an original thinker,

and he borrowed only what fitted his own design.

In 1861, James entered the Lawrence Scientific School, Harvard, studying first in the chemistry department under Charles W. Eliot, later in the department of comparative anatomy and physiology under Jeffries Wyman and Louis Agassiz. From Wyman he learned the importance of evolution; from Agassiz, an appreciation of "the world's concrete fulness" (William James, *Memories and Studies,* p. 14) and of acquaintance with empirical facts as against abstraction. In 1864, James transferred to the medical school, though without the intention of ever practicing medicine. His medical studies, although fruitful, were attenuated and sporadic.

While at medical school James joined Agassiz as an assistant on the Thayer expedition to Brazil during 1865/1866. In Brazil he contracted smallpox and suffered from sensitivity of the eyes. This was the first serious manifestation of that constitutional failure which was to recur throughout James's life, imposing upon it a pattern of interrupted work and of periodic flights to Europe which were always, at least in part, searches for health.

In 1867 ill health and the desire to study experimental physiology led James to Europe, to Germany in particular. While little formal study of physiology proved to be possible, James read widely and thoughtfully. His first professional literary effort, a revision of Herman

Grimm's *Unüberwindliche Mächte,* published in the *Nation* (Vol. 5, 1867), dates from this period.

James returned to Cambridge in November 1868 and received his medical degree in June 1869. After a period of illness and retirement, he began teaching anatomy and physiology at Harvard in 1873, psychology in 1875, and philosophy in 1879. This order is very nearly accidental and gives no adequate indication of James's development. Philosophy was an early interest which grew with his scientific studies; for James the more narrowly scientific questions could never be separated, even theoretically, from the more general questions which philosophy considers.

It was indeed a specifically philosophical concern which precipitated James's profound emotional crisis of 1870. He had been suffering from a sense of moral impotence which only a philosophical justification of the belief in the freedom of the will could cure. In the *Essais de critique générale* of Charles Renouvier, James found the basis of the justification he sought. And throughout his life the problem of maintaining free will and the moral attitude in the face of either religious monism or scientific determinism, as well as the problem of legitimating belief despite various intellectual skepticisms, continued to engage James's attention and to influence his mature philosophy. That philosophy, growing out of personal need and agitation, has a strong eschatological flavor. It cannot, however, be reduced either to a scheme of personal salvation or to an apology for some special way of life. James offered a philosophical, not an emotional, defense of free will, moralism, and belief. These topics became important test cases for a general metaphysics which James sought to elaborate not for its own sake but to satisfy interests which were distinctly rational and theoretical.

Having settled into the career of philosopher and teacher, if one may speak of James's settling into anything, he maintained close but not constant association with Harvard until his final resignation in 1907. He married Alice Howe Gibbens in 1878; the marriage seems to have increased his sense of purpose and coincided with a noticeable improvement in James's health. Thenceforth, he led an intensely active life, teaching at Harvard, lecturing widely, and publishing a series of books which became undeniable classics of American philosophy. Three series of James's lectures deserve special mention. He gave the Gifford lectures at Edinburgh in 1901/1902, published as *The Varieties of Religious Experience* (1902); lectures on pragmatism at the Lowell Institute and Columbia in 1906 and 1907, published as *Pragmatism* (1907); and the Hibbert lectures at Oxford in 1908/1909, published as *A Pluralistic Universe* (1909).

James offered a philosophical, not an emotional, defense of free will, moralism, and belief. (Corbis)

CHARACTER OF JAMES'S PHILOSOPHY. This brief biography gives no indication of that range and richness of James's experience which so struck those who knew him and which entered into everything he wrote. James was a highly social man whose friends formed an intellectual community of great distinction. Chauncey Wright, C. S. Peirce, Shadworth Hodgson, Charles Renouvier, Josiah Royce, George Santayana, John Dewey, Henri Bergson, and F. H. Bradley were a few of those whom James knew as friends and fellow laborers.

From all of these men and others James drew philosophical nourishment, and the very number of sources and influences renders the search for antecedents otiose. James was essentially an original thinker, and he borrowed only what fitted his own design. This must be maintained in spite of James's habitual humility and his characteristic generosity of acknowledgment.

James impressed his friends with his vitality and strength of character, with his open-mindedness and sympathy. His spirit and attitude were admired even by those whose philosophical conclusions differed radically from his own. Santayana, for example, in his witty and condescending memoir *Character and Opinion in the United States* is forced to praise James, at least as an enthusiastic and explosive force. Because James wrote as he talked, much of his vividness and personal style is retained in his works. The majority of James's books are simply transcriptions of lectures; they have all the virtues and vices of spoken discourse, and the circumstances of their presentation must help to determine the kind of analysis to which they can be fruitfully subjected.

James addressed himself to the people, not especially to other philosophers, and he listened to the people to find out what life meant to them. He respected not so much their common sense as their common feelings and hopes and would not allow his philosophy to dismiss cavalierly that which figured largely in the experiences of men. The people listened to James, and his books sold well. By the end of his life he was nearly a legendary figure, and he was generally regarded as the chief representative of American philosophy. Nevertheless, professional philosophers, when they have discussed James at all, have tended to concentrate on those of his ideas which, separated from the body of his work and often distorted, have achieved currency. To this general picture there are important exceptions, such as Ralph Barton Perry, who has done more for James scholarship than anyone else.

To provide a proper perspective for the study of James, three corrective measures must be taken. First, attention must be diverted from his life, however interesting, to his published philosophy. For all its validity the biographical motive can be, and has been, pressed to the point where it precludes philosophical clarity. Second, James must be seen within the general philosophical tradition, in relation to the fundamental philosophical problems that he attempted to solve and not in relation to his position as a distinctly American thinker. To attempt to evaluate James's philosophy in terms of his American background is neither more nor less rewarding than to attempt to evaluate Kant, say, in terms of his German background. Third, the objective aspect of James's philosophy must be stressed. James himself thought that philosophy involved the subjective factors of temperament and personal vision. In the first chapter of *Pragmatism,* he drew a very plausible correlation between tough-minded and tender-minded temperaments and empirical and rationalist philosophical positions. Again, in the essay "The Sentiment of Rationality" James argued that there can be no adequate definition of reason which ignores the feeling of rationality, the ultimate sense of logical fit. James believed that the subjective (or what might better be called the aes-

thetic) dimension was a feature of philosophy as such. James's philosophy is subjective, therefore, because it is philosophy, not because it is James's philosophy. Objectivity, like truth and reality, was redefined, not abandoned, by James.

The remainder of this article is divided into sections on James's psychology, philosophy of religion, pragmatism, and metaphysics. This arrangement is simply an expository device. If pragmatism is a theory of all belief, then religious philosophy is a subdivision of pragmatism. If pragmatism is a description of what actually happens when men seek truth, then it is part of psychology. If the dualism between human and natural processes is finally inadmissible, then psychology is a chapter of general metaphysics. The interdependence of the various parts of James's philosophy, suggested here, will be exhibited below.

Psychology

The *Principles of Psychology* (1890) is, according to James himself, "mainly a mass of descriptive details"; certainly, this work more than any other justifies Whitehead's remark that James's primary task was philosophical assemblage. The *Principles* "assembles" in two senses. First, there is a brilliant gathering, through extensive quotation and reference as well as careful documentation, of relevant material from the Scottish, English, French, and German schools. Second, there is the exhibition of facts which may never have appeared prominently in any system, either of psychology or of philosophy.

It has become customary,

and it is certainly legitimate,

to praise James's Principles of Psychology *for its*

sensitive evocation of the evanescent inner life.

It has become customary, and it is certainly legitimate, to praise the *Principles* for its sensitive evocation of the evanescent inner life. It is indeed a kind of generalized psychic autobiography by a master of introspection, but it is much more than a document of literary psychology. The concrete rendering of experience is an essential element in the development of James's mature philosophy, for when he spoke of the world as "a world of pure experience," he referred to experience as it is described in the *Principles*. If experience had not the ramifications and possibilities so lovingly and exuberantly detailed by James in his "psychological" writings, it could never have become, as it did for James, the central image of complete reality. Moreover, James was not in his early days merely "collecting" facts whose subsequent careers happened to include the incident of being generalized into a total world view. James, as he said himself, "hated collecting" (Perry, *op. cit.,* p. 225). The material of the *Principles* is already thrown into philosophical form, is already illuminated or stained (however one decides the matter) by the foundational metaphysical categories which recur, with greater generality, in the later works.

DESCRIPTION. If the *Principles* is to be regarded as primarily a descriptive work, one must be clear about what is involved in description as James understood it. He was convinced that pure description in the manner of phenomenology is impossible. Description cannot be other than conceptual; concepts, in turn, are tools of classification that have inexpugnable conventional and theoretical elements. Concepts do not passively mirror; they select according to human interests and purposes. Assumptions, James maintained, have a way of establishing themselves "in our very descriptions of the phenomenal facts" (*Principles,* Vol. I, p. 145). Naive phenomenology attempts to eliminate assumptions from descriptive statements. This is an impossible task if for no other reason than that every allegedly assumption-free phenomenology must itself make doubtful assumptions, including the assumption that there can be description without classification. James's own approach was to examine the assumptions involved in all descriptions, making those assumptions "give an articulate account of themselves before letting them pass" (*loc. cit.*). Pragmatism as it appears in the *Principles* consists simply in spelling out what claims our theories and assumptions make for us and in eliminating elements which are superfluous, elements, that is, which can be eliminated without changing the tenor of what we really want to say. Pragmatism here can be fruitfully regarded as a general theory of theory criticism, as an attempt to make clear what we are actually committed to by the theories we entertain. The chapters which criticize the conscious automaton theory (Vol. I, Ch. 5) and the mind-stuff theory (*ibid.,* Ch. 6), respectively, are indeed the first extended exercises in pragmatic criticism.

SCIENCE AND METAPHYSICS. Purely phenomenological description being considered impossible by James, the question arises as to what is scientific about the *Principles.* The standard interpretation—the interpretation upon which the judgment of its great historical importance is based—finds the work very nearly the first attempt to treat psychology from the standpoint of a natural science—that is, descriptively and apart from metaphysical theories. The sharp distinction which we

are likely to draw between scientific theories and metaphysical theories is difficult to sustain from James's own point of view and therefore cannot be used to differentiate the *Principles* from metaphysical treatments of the same subject matter.

A much more pregnant distinction is that between a priori and a posteriori metaphysics. A priori metaphysics was, for James, a totally illegitimate enterprise consisting of vacuous abstractions excogitated apart from any experience of the world. Throughout his work James often referred to a priori metaphysics simply as "metaphysics," and his frequent criticisms of metaphysics must therefore be carefully interpreted in their contexts. The *Principles* is antimetaphysical where metaphysics means "scholastic rational psychology" or "philosophical pyschology."

The more interesting problem is defining the relation between the *Principles* and the kind of metaphysics of which James did approve, a posteriori metaphysics, which is continuous with science and, like science, is both descriptive and theoretical. Here the differentiation must be emphatic rather than absolute. The *Principles* may be regarded as a deliberate (and artificial) restriction of general metaphysical scope. Science, as James saw it, must grow into metaphysics. Explanation must become more complete and more comprehensive even if, as James certainly believed, it cannot become total and absolute. But science must *be* science before it can become metaphysics. In the *Principles* metaphysics is, necessarily, postponed; its positivism is provisional rather than dogmatic and final.

The relative autonomy which science is given in the *Principles* is "for the sake of practical effectiveness exclusively," as James said in his essay "A Plea for Psychology as a 'Natural Science' " (*Collected Essays and Reviews,* p. 317). Science left to itself, with its "convenient assumptions" unquestioned, is best able to accumulate a mass of factual details which lead to the subsequent enrichment and "thickening" of the content of metaphysics. The danger of premature metaphysical reconstruction is thinness, impoverishment of content, and abstraction.

MENTAL STATES. The basic assumption of the *Principles* and its "convenient" point of departure is the existence of mental states. The first task of psychology is to describe the conditions of these mental states with as much detail and completeness as possible. Chapter 2 of the *Principles* is an extended examination of the ways in which various brain states condition various mental states. The search for conditions among bodily experiences generally and brain experiences particularly is the only alternative to treating mental states as frankly miraculous. James, the evolutionary naturalist, had to maintain that mental states grow out of physical states, in spite of whatever difficulties this view entails. Since mental states, in addition to arising from physical antecedents, themselves give rise in all cases to changes in the physical world, it seems utterly impossible to create any kind of dualistic ontological chasm between the two types of process, mental and physical. There is indeed a discriminable subject matter of psychology, which James referred to both as "mental states" and as "mental life." This subject matter must be treated autonomously, which means, in practice, guarding against the reduction of mental phenomena to nothing but physical phenomena in the interest of some schematic monism. In this context James at times spoke of "irreducible dualisms," but what he meant to emphasize might perhaps better be called "irreducible dualities," discriminations which remain what they are no matter what supervenient integrations may also be pointed out.

The whole question of the dualism between the physical and the mental is complicated by the fact that James was, even in the *Principles,* developing a view of physical nature at large which departed radically from the familiar deterministic, mechanical model. It is often maintained, for example, that James's treatment of the will as irreducible to antecedent mechanical factors creates a dualistic chasm between natural processes and characteristically human processes. This would be true only if James had retained the customary deterministic model of nature. However, James did not retain this model; he would sooner have conceived of all nature as willful than of man's will as an exception to nature.

James himself came to believe

that all of reality must be describable in terms

like those used for human experience.

James believed that the border line of the mental is vague. Mentality, as James defined it, exists wherever we find the choice of means for the attainment of future ends. Mental life is purposive in a way which involves the overcoming, through suitable invention and appropriation, of any obstacles lying in the way of its purpose. The mind is a tactical power which reveals itself in the struggle with its environment. The only kind of world in which minds can conceivably develop and be found is one in which success is neither automatic nor impossible. An interesting consequence of James's view is that an omnipotent God could not have a mind; neither could a purely contemplative deity. The notion of mind as an instrument within the general economy of pur-

pose and resistance to purpose, a notion which has justly been called "biological" and "Darwinian," is simply an ungeneralized expression of pragmatism.

Although it is necessary to consider mental states as "temporal events arising in the ordinary course of nature" (*ibid.,* p. 319), with emphasis on their natural antecedents and results, it is also necessary to consider mental states in themselves as realities to be described as they are found with their generic particularity and variety intact. Here again, it must be emphasized that James was not attempting a phenomenology of mental life or consciousness. What he was attempting was the provision of adequate description that would not be guilty of gross oversimplification or distortion.

INTROSPECTION. Adequate description must, of course, be based somehow upon observation, and, James maintained, the principal method of psychology is introspective observation. Introspection, as an observational process, is similar to other kinds of observation. James could find in introspection no peculiar epistemological characteristic; it is neither more nor less fallible than other kinds of observation. Its frequently alleged infallibility, based on some notion of the immediate relation obtaining between a mind and its contents, is simply contradicted by experience. Even if feeling is unmistakably what it is, our "naming, classing, and knowing" (*Principles,* pp. 189–190) of every feeling share in the notorious general human fallibility. The truth of any observation, introspective or otherwise, is not to be found in the character of the source of observation but in the consequent service, especially theoretical service, which the observation and its correlative preservation in description can be made to render. There is therefore no simple and immediate verification of observations, no once and for all validation of descriptions. For James "the only safeguard [of truth] is the final *consensus* of our farther knowledge about the thing in question, later views correcting earlier ones until at last the harmony of a consistent system is reached" (*ibid.,* p. 192). James's own descriptions in the *Principles* must lend themselves to this kind of pragmatic corroboration.

THOUGHT. The famous "descriptive" chapter, "The Stream of Thought" (perhaps the heart of the *Principles*), cannot be evaluated from a simply empirical point of view. What is described and how it is described are determined by markedly theoretical affinities and avoidances. James singled out five traits of thought in that chapter: (1) Thought tends to be part of personal consciousness—that is, thought is not experienced as simply *a* thought but as *my* thought; (2) thought is always changing; (3) within each personal consciousness thought is sensibly continuous; (4) thought deals with objects independent of itself; and (5) thought is selective and has interests. The metaphysical model which James had in mind here is of a process that is partially determined and partially self-determining—that is, centered or focused and essentially temporal. Although the analysis in the *Principles* is limited to one kind of process, consciousness, the structure of the analysis is similar to that Whitehead offers of all actual occasions. James himself came to believe that all of reality must be describable in terms like those used for human experience. This belief is elaborated in *Essays in Radical Empiricism* as the notion of a world of "pure experience."

Each of the five traits of thought which James distinguishes repudiates some important philosophical position. One dimension of James's work clearly apparent in the *Principles* is a sustained criticism of the "classic-academic" version of mind. No easy summary of what this meant to James is available, but its main features would seem to be the marshaling of instances of mental phenomena according to a priori canons of clarity and rationality, the overwhelming influence of the assertive paradigm (as opposed to the judgments implicit in making and doing) in construing the problems of belief and judgment, and allegiance to the spectator theory of knowledge with whatever passivity is therein involved. These attitudes James attacked in the name of a richer experience, encompassing all the concrete information we possess about the functions of mind. This is the information, so carefully assembled and considered in the *Principles,* which James urged the epistemologist to work into his official model and the philosopher generally to consider in making his pronouncements.

EXPERIENCE. The appeal to experience is not new in philosophy; James was solidly in the venerable tradition of empiricism. But empiricism in its classic British form is essentially an epistemological position which regards experience as an exclusive witness before a cognitive tribunal in which other sources of evidence are ruled out of court as uncertain or unreliable. The genius of James's empiricism lies precisely in ruling nothing out of court. His theory of experience, the object of so much of James's later labor, is perhaps the first such theory which is cosmological, rather than strictly epistemological, in intention and logical form. This shift of the total frame of reference within which experience is considered has, for better or worse, influenced a subsequent movement in philosophy typified by Whitehead and his disciples. It is this influence which points to the main philosophical significance of the *Principles.*

Philosophy of Religion

Even in the Introduction to *The Literary Remains of the Late Henry James* (1885), a relatively early work which

might be thought no more than an act of filial devotion, James's own ideas about religion were quite clear. There is, of course, a sympathetic exposition of his father's superpersonal theological monism, for William James could honestly admire his father's "instinct and attitude" even if he could not condone the "cold accounts" and abstract formulations of the elder James's system. It is religious experience, rather than religious doctrine, that matters. Unless it is a part of vital experience, religion becomes "fossil conventionalism." Here James shared his father's attitude; his father wrote so much, according to James, because he was dissatisfied with every verbal encapsulation. Writing was a necessary evil and, like the labor of Sisyphus, self-stultifying.

The doctrine of the will to believe,

with all its genial encouragement of risking belief,

is balanced, in James, by an unremitting fallibilism.

That James could not accept in any unqualified way the religious vision of his father is evident. The difficulty is simply this: "Any absolute moralism is a pluralism; any absolute religion is a monism" (*The Literary Remains,* p. 118). The recognition of the essential opposition of morality and religion was clearly made by the elder James. The logic of his system required him to reject the finite moral agent with his frantic moral efforts. It is certain that James benefited from his father's insight even though he aligned himself with morality and pluralism. The working attitude of the healthy mind must always be, for James, a moral one which takes seriously the difference between good and evil and which commits itself to struggle for the first and against the second. To adopt the religious attitude is to step out of life's fight and to justify that withdrawal by some belief about the character of the world and either the ineffectiveness or superfluity of action within it. For James the character of the world, the nature of reality, does not justify, as a general attitude, the quietism that religion counsels. On the contrary, the world is the kind of place in which moral endeavor is, as a rule, supremely worthy. James neither denied the satisfaction that religion gives to many nor declared that satisfaction illusory. The very fact of pluralism allowed him to suppose at least some aspect, however fragmentary, of reality which justifies the religious option. Religious belief gives us, in James's famous phrase, a "moral holiday." Like any holiday it may be enjoyed for its own sake; more important to James, however, holidays indirectly affect the work week.

EVOLUTIONARY THEORY. James was strongly influenced by the Darwinian theory of evolution and was therefore predisposed to find in all feelings, including religious feelings, clues about what the world is like. Feelings that evolved in the world must somehow reflect the world. The most eccentric fancy, for example, tells us that we have the kind of world in which such a fancy is possible.

Evolutionary theory, as James saw it, begins with the presupposition that each part of reality has a function, that each part is in some way or other good for something or other. The strictly useless, according to such a theory, cannot endure, and all flourishing realities command a certain minimal respect. Religious experience is not especially justified by evolution because nothing is *especially* justified. Religion and irreligion, insofar as they both exist, are exactly equal before the evolutionary tribunal. Belief in evolution, at least as James interpreted that belief, makes simple dismissal impossible; even that which is evil cannot be negligible. The questions must be asked of religion as it must be asked of everything. How is it that it came to be what it is? What is it for?

ANTECEDENTS AND VALUE OF RELIGION. In his major work on religion, *The Varieties of Religious Experience,* James attempted to account for the antecedents and value of religion. The question of how it came to be what it is, is a matter of classifying religious feelings and religious propensities with other kinds of human experience which are found to be similar to them. The initial task, therefore, of *The Varieties* is the provision of a "descriptive survey" beginning with as many and as varied examples of typically religious experience as possible. The emphasis, here as elsewhere, is on spontaneous religious emotions rather than theological interpretations or institutional prolongation and regularization.

James was scrupulously careful to explain religious phenomena by ordinary scientific laws and principles, if at all possible. Accordingly, religious visitations of all kinds are classed as sudden influxions from the subject's own subconsciousness. Conversion is seen as the radical rearrangement of psychic energy around some new center of interest. Examples of this kind of felicitous theorizing could be multiplied.

James, however, was equally concerned with promoting the thesis that nothing said about the history or genesis of religious phenomena can shed the slightest light on the spiritual worth and significance of those phenomena. The older dogmatists attempted to justify religion once and for all by pointing to its privileged origin in some kind of revelation; newer dogmatists—the "medical materialists"—attempted to discredit religion once and for all by pointing to its disreputable origin in some curious bodily state. Neither approach is acceptable. Religion must be judged in the same way that everything else is judged, by proving itself useful (in specifiable ways) in some possible future. Religion must "run the gauntlet of confrontation with the total context of experience" (*The Varieties,* p. 426). This context includes the collection of all our established truths as well as all the exigencies of our affective and intellectual natures. Therefore, the defense of religion that can be found in James is not based on appeals to either mere social utility or subjective feeling. The question of the truth of religion arises only when religion makes some concrete, specific prediction about the world's future. Religion having framed its hypotheses, these hypotheses are supported or refuted in terms set out by James's general theory of belief, known as pragmatism.

BELIEF. James's notorious defense of the right to believe in the widely read essay "The Will to Believe" and elsewhere, though generally given a limited religious interpretation, is, in fact, not primarily a defense of religious belief but of moral belief, belief in the efficacy of action, including, as an important instance, the active experimentalism of modern science. The point of James's doctrine is its repudiation of the methodological caution epitomized by the Baconian injunction not to "suffer the understanding to jump and fly from particulars to remote and most general axioms" or by the Cartesian rule "that the understanding should always know before the will makes a decision." James was making a general statement in support of the method of empirical science, with special emphasis upon the initially unwarranted character of every scientific hypothesis. We must at least believe our hypotheses sufficiently to bestir ourselves to test them; without our active interest in and partisanship of belief the enterprise of science would come to a silent, ghostly end. It is the theoretical daring of science which inspired James. His doctrine on the will to believe is no fuzzy *ad hoc* concession to self-indulgent piety but an integral part of his general theory of belief.

The doctrine of the will to believe, with all its genial encouragement of risking belief, is balanced, in James, by an unremitting fallibilism. Belief, however justified originally, is always conditional. Belief must continue to justify itself; there is no possibility of a definitive, once and for all certification. Both the options of practical life and the tenets of religion may be justified as peculiar kinds of scientific hypotheses, the first sort peculiar because of their limitation to some particular matter or situation, the second because of their elusive generality. There seems to be no difficulty in interpreting the practical decisions of life, with their inherent predictions about relevant future events, as closely analogous to the predictive, if not to the explanatory, activity of science. Religious belief, on the contrary, may seem intrinsically isolated from the arena of confirmation and disconfirmation and, therefore, alien to the scientific pattern. For James all genuine belief, including religious belief, must address itself to the tribunal of experiment. If all possible procedures of verification are irrelevant to some religious doctrine, then that doctrine cannot rightly be the object of any belief; such a doctrine, having no positive content, would be meaningless.

James did, in fact, think that at least a few religious hypotheses were truly empirical, that they made a difference which somewhere could be noticed. James was careful not to prejudice the case against religion by adopting some single restrictive paradigm of verification. If religious belief makes a difference, it is not altogether surprising that we should have to look for that difference with greater sympathy, imagination, and patience than we are used to exercising in more straightforward cases.

JAMES'S RELIGIOUS BELIEF. James's own religious belief, expressed without dogmatism in the last chapter and the Postscript of *The Varieties* and again in the last chapter of *Pragmatism,* consists essentially in the affirmation that the world is richer in realities than conventional science is willing to recognize. Religious experience at least suggests that there is what James called a "higher part of the universe" (*ibid.,* p. 516) which, though beyond the immediate deliverance of the senses, is nevertheless effective in the world in a way that makes a noticeable difference. This assertion that the higher part makes concrete and local differences constitutes James's famous "piecemeal supernaturalism" (*ibid.,* p. 520), really only a name for an enlarged and tolerant naturalism. The higher part is perhaps impossible to define given the present state of our knowledge. Certainly, for James it cannot be the infinite and omnipotent God of traditional theism who guarantees the successful outcome of the universe. The higher part is better conceived as a finite power (or perhaps even a polytheistic medley of powers) which, like men, works toward the good and helps achieve it. This is a theological notion compatible with the significance of moral choice in a way that the conventional notion is not.

The vagueness of much of James's treatment, a vagueness he frequently admitted to, has been amply noted by his critics. What must also be noted, however, is the forceful way in which a fundamental idea of our tradition, the idea of God, has been radically reconstructed by James in a manner that makes the idea more consonant with religious experience and that frees it from the congeries of paradoxes associated with the problems, among others, of free will and of evil.

Pragmatism

The chief locus for James's pragmatism is, of course, his immensely popular and influential work *Pragmatism: A New Name for Some Old Ways of Thinking.* The origin of pragmatism, however, as James always acknowledged, is found in C. S. Peirce's essay "How To Make Our Ideas Clear," published in 1878. This essay remained generally unnoticed until James's 1898 lecture on pragmatism, "Philosophical Conceptions and Practical Results," at the University of California (in *Collected Essays and Reviews*). This lecture may be taken as the beginning of pragmatism as an explicit, although never a unified, movement, but the essentials of the doctrine as developed by James are found earlier in the *Principles of Psychology* and even in the Introduction to *The Literary Remains of the Late Henry James.* Indeed, James rarely wrote anything, early or late, which did not at least imply pragmatism.

Pragmatism may be approached as a mere method, an eristic device which vouchsafes hints as to either the meaning or truth of propositions or to both together; it may be taken as a theory of meaning or a theory of truth or, once again, as a theory of both meaning and truth. A. O. Lovejoy in "The Thirteen Pragmatisms" insisted upon distinctions such as these and chided James for neglecting them. In fact, though James erred in emphasizing the autonomy of the various aspects of pragmatism, he wished to persuade his readers of the truth of whichever part he was recommending at the moment, and he therefore tended to stress the self-contained plausibility of elements which, if plausible at all, are so only when taken together in the total view.

It is the contention of James's sympathetic commentators that his pragmatism is plausible as nothing less than a theory of reality. It is the descriptive naturalism central to James which saves pragmatism from being merely a convenient device for settling philosophical disputes. The fundamental assumption which generates pragmatism is the assumption that "knowledge," "truth," and "meaning," as well as any other possible object of discourse or any other possible subject matter for philosophical discussion, must be explicable as a natural process or as a functional medley or competition of natural processes. The world, for James, is a plurality of temporal processes related in so many specifiable and concrete ways that it cannot be accounted for by abstract speculation alone.

James believed that a man's personal, peculiar vision counts most in philosophy; not surprisingly, it is vision, not method, which is primary in James. Reality dictates the method by which it may be known. The gross encounter with the world is primary in the determination of what character the world will have for us. Theories of knowledge and of method, existing at a high level of abstraction, are second to the ineluctable fact of experience breaking in upon us.

TRUTH AND MEANING. James's pragmatism is an attempt to formulate a metaphysics of truth and of meaning. Logically, such an attempt is exactly on a par with the metaphysical treatment of any discriminable subject matter. By metaphysics James meant the quest for adequate general descriptions either of reality as a whole or of some distinguishable part of it. The descriptions offered by metaphysics are, in principle, continuous with those offered by science, although their range and focus may differ. The distinction between science and metaphysics was not crucial for James; he saw the possibility of unrestricted intercourse and cooperation exactly where later thinkers are likely to see division and competition for cognitive respectability. It is therefore helpful from James's own point of view to regard pragmatism's description of truth in the same light, say, as geology's description of continental drift. Both are characterizations of natural processes, and both attempt to portray what actually happens.

The metaphysical perspective of *Pragmatism* itself (even apart from the context of James's total work) is so unmistakable that the prevailing interpretation of pragmatism as a set of newly devised rules that serve a certain practical purpose seems totally unjustified. If James was right, men have always unwittingly followed the "pragmatic method." A purely theoretical illumination like pragmatism will indeed clarify practice and improve it; for James no process—least of all, a process where human influence intervenes—is so canalized that modifications are utterly beyond hope. Metaphysics must recognize the plasticity of its subject matter as well as the limits of plasticity.

Pragmatism discusses truth without falling into the epistemological frame of mind habitually assumed by professional philosophers. James's description of actual processes rejects the usual question of what we ought to believe. If there is something we "ought" to believe, the authority of the "ought" itself must be explained concretely. There is no authority which is merely formal. Pragmatism therefore becomes the justification of truth's prestige in terms of the world's exigencies.

One factor discernible in the complex process called "believing truly" is the compulsion of fact or the unavoidability of a residual nonplastic pole in determination of what is true. It is here that we find truth's authority and importance.

Truth, for James, is what we must somehow take account of if we are not to perish. Men cannot in the long run believe what is false not because truth extracts from them a categorical imperative in its own behalf but because reality compels men in spite of themselves, and it is from this that the authority of truth is derived. "Agreement with reality" as a criterion of truth cannot be taken to indicate any fixed structural relation (such as the "copying" relation). The truth relation is characterized not by stasis but by the fluid resourcefulness of functional harmony. The character of the harmony itself may be anything that is compatible with survival. Even in the Darwinian world that James pictured, there is more than one way to survive as truth.

The origin of pragmatism,

as James always acknowledged,

is found in C. S. Peirce's essay

"How to Make Our Ideas Clear" (1878).

Raw compulsion may account for the authority of truth, but truth is hardly a mute registry of bruises received from the world. Indeed, men create truth, and truth is so exclusively the result of human activity that James's own view has been called "humanism." Central to this humanism is the distinction (so often insisted on by James, so often neglected by his critics) between ideas and objects, between what takes account and what is taken account of. The objects constitute what James referred to as the "unhumanized fringe," the yet to be conceptualized. What must be taken account of is presumably just what it is. Truth and falsity, however, apply not to objects but only to our ideas of objects. Our ideas of objects are mutable in the sense that we can modify ideas or replace one idea by another. In such a situation ideas are to be judged better or worse; such judgments fall between the ideal limits of complete good and complete bad. These are the same limits usually called "truth" and "falsity." Truth is viewed by James as one species of the good. The good is itself interpreted as a plurality of "good fors." In this view ideas are instruments for taking account theoretically, practically, aesthetically, and so on, of reality.

The point of James's view of truth, as Bergson suggests in *The Creative Mind* (p. 256), is that truth is to be described as an invention rather than a discovery. Truth, or propositions which are true, might be compared to cleverly made maps or apt predictions. If they serve us as we expect them to serve us, we have no legitimate complaint. There are, of course, ontological relations between inventions like maps, predictions, and propositions (as well as inventions like light bulbs and cotton gins) and what, in summary fashion, is referred to as reality. Inventions are conventional but not arbitrary. They are not arbitrary because they must somehow take account of reality; they are conventional because they embody one way (among alternatives) for that taking account.

In the seminal essay "Does Consciousness Exist?" (1904), James asks us to assume that there is just one "primal stuff" of which everything in the world is made.

The relationship between two processes within experience constitutes truth—(1) the inventive process or activity of proposing, of framing propositions, and (2) the particular chain of natural processes with which the proposition in question is concerned. The emphasis on the truth relation as a relation within experience and totally construable in terms of "positive experienceable operation" (*Meaning of Truth*, p. x) is one instance of James's general metaphysical position that all relations are within experience. Experience, as it were, forms a cohesive, self-explanatory whole; it hangs together, as James liked to say, and needs no transcendental connectives or supports.

Since the truth relation was taken by James's contemporaries as transcending experience, the strategic function of pragmatism is apparent. It is an extension of radical empiricism, an attempt to place the particularly troublesome truth relation within the total perspective of metaphysical naturalism.

James spoke of true ideas as those which "work," which "lead" propitiously, which give various kinds of satisfaction, and which bring about various kinds of success. He also spoke approvingly of the "cash value" of ideas and thought that meaningful ideas are those which make "practical differences." These highly (and obviously) metaphorical expressions have confused many commentators.

There are those who have found James vague. He intended, however, that all these metaphors should be functionally specific and indeterminate only in respect to instances. "Working," "leading," "satisfying," and "succeeding" are generic terms as respectable and as precise as terms like "copying" and "agreeing." They are,

however, functional rather than static. For those who see functions as inherently insubstantial, shadowy, and vague, any functional definition of truth will be unacceptable, but this hardly seems to be an insurmountable objection.

Other commentators have seized upon the prominence of the "practical" in James's account of meaning and truth. Surely, this is a difficult term in James, if for no other reason than that he used it as it is used in ordinary language—that is, variously. His prevailing usage, however, cannot be equated with some narrow notion of commercial efficiency. Pragmatism is not a philosophical vindication of the businessman's common sense or acumen. It was James, after all, who saw the tendency to worship "the bitch goddess, success," as the principal weakness in the American character. It is especially in our theoretical and moral practice that meaningful ideas, according to James, are to make a difference. Belief divorced from action may well be morally effete, and James set forth this point, though not in its crudely athletic form; his main thesis, however, was that belief divorced from action is *theoretically* inexplicable. James's quest was not for a formula which would rouse his fellows to civic virtue or efficiency of some peculiarly American sort but for criteria which would be descriptively adequate to belief. His philosophical purpose was to find out what it means to believe, what it means to entertain ideas which may be meaningful and true.

Metaphysics

Although frequently attempted, it is not possible to isolate a final "metaphysical" period in James. The theory of the various kinds of belief, which formed his philosophy of religion and of pragmatism, has as a conspicuous feature the assumption that anything which can be meaningfully said about belief must take into account the grounding of belief in natural processes, particularly human processes. It is possible to formulate a theory of belief apart from a general metaphysics only by adopting an assumption which James explicitly rejected. This is the epistemological assumption that an existentially neutral *logic* of belief can be constructed. In fact, on this assumption existential reference is regarded as the indication of a certain categorial confusion frequently labeled "psychologism." James insisted, even in his least metaphysical passages, that "knowledge," "belief," "truth," and "meaning" indicate discriminable natural existences in the same way that all terms do, or at least all terms that figure as possible subjects of philosophical discussion. This is simply the corrective application of the basic postulate of metaphysical naturalism to the recalcitrant subject matter of epistemology.

James regarded the prominence accorded this subject matter since the time of Kant as a distortion of perspective which his own philosophy was intended to correct.

But for the development of James's metaphysics, the psychology—or the treatment of characteristically human processes—was even more important than the theory of belief. His metaphysics was simply the attempt to apply to all reality categories originally framed for human experience. The radical generalization of the concept of experience, so central in James, is necessitated by two ideas. First, James believed that metaphysical dualism is always unacceptable. Whatever dualities or pluralities are distinguished for certain purposes, ultimately the philosopher cannot operate with irreducible categories. Second, if one categorial set or one metaphysical model must be adopted, James believed that this categorial set or metaphysical model must arise from the consideration of our own experience. It is only of human experience that we have anything like "complete concrete data." Anthropocentrism is therefore thought to be a consequence of any genuine empiricism. For James even panpsychism is at least a possible and interesting empirical hypothesis.

In the seminal essay "Does Consciousness Exist?" (1904), James asks us to assume that there is just one "primal stuff" of which everything in the world is made. This stuff, called "pure experience," is not a single entity, like Thales' water; "pure experience" is a collective name for all sensible natures, for all the "that's" which anywhere appear. The monism implied in this concept of the *one* primal stuff is therefore merely formal. Explanatory monism must be accepted before specific metaphysical descriptions may be attempted. In the same essay James provided a sample of metaphysical description. Consciousness is there described as a certain relation of parts of experience to one another. Consciousness is not an unanalyzable substance but simply the name which is given to a certain discriminable function within experience, the knowing function. All other functions are to be explained in the same way as consciousness. Functional explanations in terms of related strands of experience allow the abrogation of traditional dualisms because the same isolable part of experience may enter into many and various relations. What is subject may also be object; what is object may be subject. The knower may also be the known and vice versa, depending on the "context of associates" within which the part of experience so labeled is considered.

James's frequent use of the expression "part of experience" was not meant to suggest that experience has an atomistic constitution. Indeed, James constantly argued against the "pulverization" of experience in British empiricism. We experience not isolated parts but continuities of indeterminate extension. Parts and the relations between parts, both directly experienced, form new functional wholes. The use of the word "part" indicates nothing more than the theoretical and practical need for emphatic focus.

James regarded the "concrete" data appealed to by British empiricism as abstract, intellectual products; he accused that empiricism of committing what Whitehead later called "the fallacy of misplaced concreteness." If James's philosophy is to be classified historically as a criticism of British empiricism, it must also be emphasized that it is self-consciously offered as an alternative to the criticism of empiricism by idealists from Kant to Royce.

If the facts pointed to by the usual empiricism are abstract in the sense of being incomplete, inadequate, or partial, it still cannot be said, as it is said by absolute idealism, that there are no facts at all or that there is just one fact, the immovable "block-universe," as James referred to this notion that he always found slightly ridiculous. There are no general grounds, according to James, for the rejection of the obvious particularity and individuality which characterize the plural parts of experience. James certainly held that any allegedly self-sufficient fact may turn out from some point of view or for some purpose, intellectual or practical, to be partial or abstract. But there are many points of view and many purposes with equal titles to rationality. There are therefore many levels of fact, and words like "part," "whole," "unity," "concrete," "abstract," "particular," and "individual" do not qualify any reality simply or always. These words are definable only within purposive contexts. Absolute idealism, in contrast, sets up a single standard of rationality and develops a characteristic vocabulary which it applies *simpliciter.* This procedure yields a certain clarity and neatness but suffers from "vicious intellectualism" or *"the treating of a name as excluding from the fact named what the name's definition fails positively to include"* (A Pluralistic Universe, p. 60).

James constantly argued against the

"pulverization" of experience in British empiricism.

The notion of self-sufficient centers within experience emphasized by James as particulars or individuals is a generalization of that first trait of the stream of thought referred to in *Principles of Psychology.* Although made familiar by Whitehead, it was James who first used the concept of personal order to replace the traditional concept of some fundamental and thinglike substance.

Other traits of existence which impressed themselves on James are first annunciated in the *Principles* as traits of the stream of thought or of the central human process. So, for example, the doctrine that thought is always changing becomes the doctrine that reality is always changing. Again, human freedom is eventually interpreted as a special case of universal indeterminism. My future, though continuous with my past, is not determined by it. Just so the future of the world; although it grows out of the total past, it is not a mere result of that past. If I am creative—that is, if human freedom is effectual—then the world is creative, if for no other reason than that I am part of the world. What is constant in my behavior is the result of habits which never entirely lose their flexibility. In the same way the constancies charted by the laws of science are only more inveterate habits.

Objections can be raised against all these contentions, especially in the enthusiastic, unguarded form in which James made them. They do, however, add up to a serious philosophical position which has, in fact, borne fruit in the subsequent history of philosophy and is worthy of continuing serious study.

[See also Pragmatism.]

BIBLIOGRAPHY

Works by James

Only James's chief works are listed here. For a complete list see Perry's bibliography, below. Secondary literature is copious, and only the most important works are listed here. Those who wish to sample the periodical literature are advised to consult the fifty-year (1904–1953) index of the *Journal of Philosophy* (New York, 1962), under the heading "James."

The Literary Remains of the Late Henry James, with an introduction by William James, ed. Boston, 1885.

Principles of Psychology, 2 vols. New York, 1890. Regarded by many as James's major work, it is a prime source not only for his psychology but also for his metaphysics.

The Will To Believe and Other Essays in Popular Philosophy. New York, 1897. In addition to the title essay, the essay "The Sentiment of Rationality" is, if interpreted in the context of James's total thought, an important source of his basic convictions. The book also contains the famous essay "The Dilemma of Determinism," James's fullest statement of his views on free will.

The Varieties of Religious Experience: A Study in Human Nature. New York, 1902.

Pragmatism: A New Name for Some Old Ways of Thinking. New York, 1907.

The Meaning of Truth: A Sequel to "Pragmatism." New York, 1909. A collection of polemical essays; the Preface is especially important, for it answers certain criticisms of pragmatism and states James's conception of the relation between pragmatism and radical empiricism.

A Pluralistic Universe. New York, 1909. A sustained criticism of absolute idealism and intellectualism; contains chapters on Hegel, Fechner, and Bergson.

Some Problems of Philosophy: A Beginning of an Introduction to Philosophy. New York, 1911. James's last project; it is incomplete. Valuable for its many very clear formulations; three chapters outline his theory of perception.

Essays in Radical Empiricism. New York, 1912. A related series of essays expounding James's mature philosophy; the essays "Does Consciousness Exist?" and "A World of Pure Experience" are especially important.

Memories and Studies. New York, 1912. Fifteen popular essays and addresses selected by James's son Henry James; includes commemorative addresses on Agassiz and Emerson, an essay on Spencer, and several essays on psychical research and academic life.

Collected Essays and Reviews. New York, 1920. Thirty-nine articles, selected by Ralph Barton Perry, extending from 1869 to 1910; many historically important works, including the California lecture "Philosophical Conceptions and Practical Results."

Letters, Henry James, ed., Boston, 1920. Charming letters, primarily of biographical and historical significance, edited by James's son.

Works on James

Aiken, H. D., "American Pragmatism Reconsidered: William James." *Commentary,* September 1962, pp. 238–266.

Bergson, Henri, "On the Pragmatism of William James: Truth and Reality," in his *The Creative Mind,* translated by Mabelle L. Andison. New York, 1946. Brief but provocative development of the thesis that to understand James's pragmatism, we must modify our general conception of reality.

Dewey, John, *Characters and Events,* Vol. I. New York, 1929. Book I, Ch. 12. "William James" consists of three occasional pieces which together provide an informal but penetrating analysis of James's contribution to and place in American philosophy.

Lovejoy, Arthur O., *The Thirteen Pragmatisms and Other Essays.* Baltimore, Md., 1963. In addition to the very influential title essay, there are eight other essays on James or pragmatism.

Moore, G. E., *Philosophical Studies.* London, 1922. "William James' 'Pragmatism' " attempts to refute James from the commonsense point of view.

Perry, Ralph Barton, *Annotated Bibliography of the Writings of William James.* New York, 1920. A listing of 312 items from 1867 to 1920, with helpful indications of each item's content and value.

Perry, Ralph Barton, *The Thought and Character of William James,* 2 vols. Boston, 1935. A massive, richly documented study; the single most important work on James.

Perry, Ralph Barton, *In the Spirit of William James.* New Haven, 1938. A solid and sympathetic philosophical interpretation of James. The chapters "An Empirical Theory of Knowledge" (Ch. 2) and "The Metaphysics of Experience" (Ch. 3) are especially noteworthy.

Royce, Josiah, *William James and Other Essays on the Philosophy of Life.* New York, 1911. An attempt to show James's place in American social history.

Russell, Bertrand, *Philosophical Essays.* London and New York, 1910. See "William James' Conception of Truth" and "Pragmatism."

Santayana, George, *Character and Opinion in the United States, With Reminiscences of William James and Josiah Royce and Academic Life in America.* New York, 1920. Unsympathetic but extremely interesting in its own right.

— WILLIAM JAMES EARLE

JAMES, WILLIAM (UPDATE)

William James is to classical American philosophy as Plato was to Greek and Roman philosophy, an originating and inspirational fountainhead. Thinkers as diverse as C. S. Peirce, Josiah Royce, John Dewey and the late work of A. N. Whitehead took their point of departure from William James, especially his monumental *Principles of Psychology*. Influential philosophers elsewhere were also deeply influenced by James, for instance Henri Bergson, Edmund Husserl, Miguel de Unamuno, and Ludwig Wittgenstein.

In reading James the first response

is one of elation at the apparent simplicity

and obvious elegance of the literary style.

With the completed publication of all of James's writings, including his manuscripts and notebooks, the full range and philosophical virtuosity of his work comes into focus. For too long the thought of William James was taken to be novel and intriguing but lacking in technical sophistication. In reading James the first response is one of elation at the apparent simplicity and obvious elegance of the literary style. After several careful and close readings, however, the philosophical depth and complexity emerge. The consequence of these more mature readings of James's thought are now found in many areas of contemporary philosophy, for example, the philosophy of mind, ethics, and the philosophy of religion. More significant still is that James represents a very helpful philosophical stance, one that is chary of narrowness and rigid conceptual schematisms and affirms the messages of human experience no matter the source. William James believes that philosophy itself is "the habit of always seeing an alternative." He was convinced as well that no matter how recondite the issue in question—for example, the meaning of consciousness or his innovative doctrine of radically empirical relations—the kernel of the position taken could be articulated in prose accessible to the intelligent reader as well as to the philosopher.

The most salutary result of recent commentaries on the philosophy of William James has been the rescue of two of his most beleaguered positions, that of the pragmatic theory of truth and his doctrine of "The Will to Believe." In both areas James's thought was often subject to mocking dismissal and shallow interpretations. With the completion of James's *Works*, the girth and sophistication of his philosophy is now apparent. Witness, for example, the sterling introductory essays by H. Standish Thayer on James's theory of truth as found in "Pragmatism" (*Works*, 1975) and "The Meaning of Truth" (*Works*, 1975). Similarly, one finds an equivalently clarifying essay by Edward H. Madden in his introductory essay to "The Will to Believe" (*Works*, 1979).

The divide that has existed between mainstream analytic philosophy and pragmatism is no longer purposeful. Transformations of this conflict are now at hand. Hilary Putnam, for decades a major figure in contemporary philosophical thought, writes in his *Pragmatism* (1995) as follows:

> I believe that James was a powerful thinker, as powerful as any in the last century, and that his way of philosophizing contains possibilities which have been too long neglected, that it points to ways out of old philosophical "binds" that continue to afflict us. In short, I believe that it is high time we paid attention to Pragmatism, the movement of which James was arguably the greatest exponent.

Although in no way gainsaying the importance of specific philosophical contentions held by James, nonetheless it can be said that the most signal reason for paying serious attention to this work is found in his philosophical attitude, his approach to philosophical inquiry. William James was no stranger to philosophical debate or argument, as one finds in his brilliant and jousting correspondence with F. H. Bradley. Yet James was uneasy about closure, answers, and finality of any kind. In a "Notebook" entry of 1903 James writes of "bad taste," by which he means

> All neat schematisms with permanent and absolute distinctions, classifications with absolute pretensions, systems with pigeon-holes, etc., have this character. All 'classic,' clean, cut and dried, 'noble,' fixed, 'eternal,' *Weltanschauungen* seem to me to violate the character with which life concretely comes and the expression which it bears of being, or at least of involving, a muddle and a struggle, with an 'ever not quite' to all our formulas, and novelty and possibility forever leaking in.

For the thought and person of William James, the novel call of experience inevitably trumps categories of explanation. Consequently, possibility rather than solution becomes the philosophical watchword, especially in matters of profound human importance.

[See also Dewey, John; Husserl, Edmund; Peirce, Charles Sanders; Philosophy of Mind; Philosophy of Religion; Plato; Pragmatism; Pragmatist Epistemology; Putnam, Hilary; Wittgenstein, Ludwig Josef Johann.]

BIBLIOGRAPHY

Since the original publication of *The Encyclopedia of Philosophy*, virtually all of William James's writings have been published in a critical edition. Under the general editorship of Frederick Burkhardt, see *The Works of William James*, 19 volumes (Cambridge, MA, 1975–88). Williams James is widely admired for his brilliant style of writing, and nowhere is that more apparent than in his letters. To that end, with John J. McDermott as general editor, publication has begun on a critical edition of *The Correspondence of William James*, edited by Ignas Skrupskelis and Elizabeth Berkeley (Charlottesville, 1992–). Four of the twelve volumes have been published. Of recent commentaries the finest and most thorough is that of Gerald Myers, *William James: His Life and Thought* (New Haven, 1986). Other recent studies of note include: Charlene Haddock Seigfried, *William James's Radical Reconstruction of Philosophy* (Albany, NY, 1990); Eugene Fontinell, *Self, God, and Immortality: A Jamesian Investigation* (Philadelphia, 1986); George Cotkin, *William James: Public Philosopher* (Baltimore, 1990); Samuel Henry Levinson, *The Religious Investigations of William James* (Chapel Hill, 1981); and T. L. S. Sprigge, *James and Bradley: American Truth and British Reality* (Chicago, 1993). For an "Annotated Bibliography of the Writings of William James" and complete selections from his major works, see John J. McDermott, ed., *The Writings of William James* (Chicago, 1977). The entire family is chronicled by R. W. B. Lewis in *The Jameses: A Family Narrative* (New York, 1991).

— JOHN J. MCDERMOTT

JUSTICE

The subject of justice—and in particular distributive or social justice as distinguished from criminal or corrective justice—has received more philosophical attention during the last third of the twentieth century than during the entire rest of the century, and arguably the topic has been more central to recent ethical theory than to the ethical thought of any other historical period. The cause of these developments has in large measure been the work of John Rawls who, in a series of articles culminating in his book *A Theory of Justice*, reintroduced political philosophy in "the grand manner" after decades of less ambitious and more semantically oriented work in that area.

Rawls explicitly introduced his own theory of justice as a way of countering utilitarian ideas about social ethics that had never, even in the heyday of analysis and metaethics, entirely lacked for influence. His view is an idealized version of traditional social-contract theory, understood through the lens of Kantian views about autonomous choice. According to Rawls, justice is best understood in terms of those principles that free and equal beings would agree to as defining the terms of their future social cooperation, given fair conditions for the making of such a choice. Rawls imagines the choice thus characterized as being made in an "original position" by rationally self-interested but nonenvious contractors who are behind a "veil of ignorance" that prevents them from tailoring principles to their own advantage because they are ignorant of what in fact would be to their advantage. Perhaps most notable in the conditions Rawls sets for social justice are his insistence that in contemporary societies civil liberties trump considerations of individual well-being or social welfare (rights of association and free speech cannot be abridged simply in order to promote the prosperity of any group) and his claim, known as "the difference principle," that inequalities in social benefits and burdens are justified only if they make the least advantaged group better off than they otherwise could be.

> *The subject of justice*
>
> *—especially distributive or social justice*
>
> *as distinct from criminal or corrective justice—*
>
> *has received more philosophical attention*
>
> *during the last third of the twentieth century*
>
> *than during the entire rest of the century.*

From the moment of its appearance, *A Theory of Justice* called forth a great number and variety of criticisms, as well as further developments, of Rawls's views. Early on, Robert Nozick, in *Anarchy, State, and Utopia*, argued that the whole idea of "distributive justice" mistakenly treats social rewards and goods as if they were part of a pie waiting to be distributed by some central social mechanism. On Nozick's libertarian view, social justice is not some sort of ideal social pattern that must be maintained by whatever mechanisms are required, as Rawls and others have thought, but consists, rather, in letting economic and social choices be made freely over time, even if considerable inequalities in welfare eventually result.

Others have criticized Rawls for the emphasis he places on individual liberties at the expense of community or communitarian values, and in a related criticism it has been argued by William Galston and Michael Sandel, among others, that, by keeping ideas about human and social flourishing out of sight in discussing the principles of justice, Rawls unnecessarily impoverishes and undermines the plausibility of his theory.

Others, like Norman Daniels, have discussed the difficulties for Rawls's difference principle of considerations about the just distribution of medical services and technology. If those needing the most medical attention are the worst off in society, then making them as well off as possible will likely cause an enormous drain on all other social resources and thus on the well-being of others in society, and it is far from clear what justice really requires in this familiar kind of situation. Recently, too, philosophers and others inspired by Carol Gilligan's *In a Different Voice* have held that interrelatedness is more basic to human social reality than atomistic contractarian views like Rawls's can allow for, and Susan Okin, in *Justice, Gender, and the Family*, has questioned Rawls's assumption that issues of justice do not arise within families.

Over the years, however, many philosophers influenced by Rawls have in a variety of ways departed from Rawls's specific views while seeking to retain some of the Kantian, social-contractarian, and/or egalitarian tendencies of the original. This has been true of Okin's work but also, for example, of the writings of Ronald Dworkin, Thomas Nagel, and Thomas Scanlon.

In *Taking Rights Seriously*, Dworkin argues that Rawls's theory of justice is based in the idea of rights, rather than being goal based or duty based, and goes on to offer a rights-based account of social justice (which he takes to be implicit in Rawls's views) centered on the idea that all men and women have a right to equality of concern and respect. Nagel, in *Equality and Partiality*, explores Rawls's view that just social arrangements must be acceptable to *all* parties (the unanimity condition) and delves into the practical and moral difficulties that result from the insistence on unanimity. Scanlon in various papers accepts Rawls's unanimity condition but has attempted to apply it more widely as a basis for morality in general, not just political or social justice, relying, to that end, on the idea of *reasonableness* in accepting or rejecting rules (in contrast with Rawls's idea of nonenvious self-interested rational contractors).

In the meantime, reawakened by Rawls's challenge, utilitarians and sympathizers of utilitarianism have sought to revitalize their approach to social morality and demonstrate its superiority to Rawls's proposal. Still others have been inspired in large measure by the way Rawls mines the history of philosophy for the means of large-scale political theorizing. Some of Rawls's own students have taken the cue more from Kant himself than from Rawls's modified Kantian approach and have used that as the basis for ideas about social justice. In *Constructions of Reason*, for example, Onora O'Neill, using Kant's ethics of the individual as a basis for social criticism, criticizes certain capitalistic social arrangements as unjust because they involve treating workers or women or children as mere means.

Even virtue ethics, which has long been thought to be hopelessly mired in antidemocratic political values (of the sort one finds in Plato and Aristotle), has found new sustenance in the rather more enlightened and democracy-friendly notions of human brotherhood [*sic*] and human dignity that are to be found in ancient stoicism. (Kant is thought to have gotten the idea that humans have a dignity beyond price from Seneca's *Epistles*.) Thus, as Martha Nussbaum points out, Aristotle defends a rather democratic and egalitarian notion of social cooperation except for the conditions he attaches to citizenship; so that, if, in the way suggested by Stoic ideals, one extends the rights of citizens to women and manual laborers and, indeed, to all adults, we get a conception of social justice that is rather "social democratic" and modern.

In a slightly different vein. Michael Slote has argued that egalitarian democratic values can be justified by reference to the Stoic ideal of *autarkeia* (self-sufficiency), expanded so that it includes, not only a certain independence from "worldly goods," but also a refusal to be parasitical upon others. On such a virtue-ethical conception, social justice depends on the extent to which a society's members possess and its institutions reflect motivations that accord with this ideal.

Although all these theories owe some sort of debt to Rawls, they differ in important ways, and the debate among them is likely to remain a central focus of ethical and political thought for the foreseeable future.

[See also Aristotle; Ethical Theory; Kant, Immanuel; Plato; Rawls, John; Rights; Social and Political Philosophy; Virtue Ethics.]

BIBLIOGRAPHY

Daniels, N. *Just Health Care.* New York, 1985.
——. *Reading Rawls: Critical Studies on Rawls's "A Theory of Justice."* Standford, CA, 1989.
Dworkin, R. *Taking Rights Seriously.* Cambridge, MA, 1978.
Galston, W. *Justice and the Human Good.* Chicago, 1980.
Gilligan, C. *In a Different Voice.* Cambridge, MA, 1982.
Nagel, T. *Equality and Partiality.* New York, 1991.
Nozick, R. *Anarchy, State, and Utopia.* New York, 1974.
Nussbaum, M. "Aristotelian Social Democracy," in R. B. Douglass, G. Mara, and H. Richardson, eds., *Liberalism and the Good* (London, 1990).
Okin, S. *Justice, Gender, and the Family.* New York, 1989.
O'Neill, O. *Constructions of Reason: Explorations of Kant's Practical Philosophy.* New York, 1990.
Parfit, D. *Reasons and Persons.* New York, 1984.
Rawls, J. *A Theory of Justice.* Cambridge, MA, 1971.
Sandel, M. *Liberalism and the Limits of Justice.* New York, 1982.
Scanlon, T. "Contractualism and Utilitarianism," in A. Sen and B. Williams, eds., *Utilitarianism and Beyond* (New York, 1982).
Slote, M. "Virtue Ethics and Democratic Values," *Journal of Social Philosophy,* Vol. 24 (1993), 5–37.

— MICHAEL SLOTE

K

KANT, IMMANUEL

Immanuel Kant (1724–1804), propounder of the critical philosophy. Kant was born at Königsberg in East Prussia; he was the son of a saddler and, according to his own account, the grandson of an emigrant from Scotland. He was educated at the local high school, the Collegium Fridericianum, and then at the University of Königsberg, where he had the good fortune to encounter a first-class teacher in the philosopher Martin Knutzen. After leaving the university, about 1746, Kant was employed for a few years as a tutor in a number of families in different parts of East Prussia. He kept up his studies during this period and in 1755 was able to take his master's degree at Königsberg and to begin teaching in the university as a *Privatdozent*. He taught a wide variety of subjects, including physics, mathematics, and physical geography as well as philosophy, but nevertheless remained poor for many years. It was not until 1770, when he was appointed to the chair of logic and metaphysics at Königsberg, that his financial stringencies were eased.

Kant's first book, *Gedanken von der wahren Schätzung der lebendigen Kräfte* ("Thoughts on the True Estimation of Living Forces"), was published as early as 1747 (Königsberg), and between 1754 and 1770 he produced an impressive stream of essays and treatises. His earlier works are primarily contributions to natural science or natural philosophy, the most notable being his *General History of Nature and Theory of the Heavens* of 1755; it was not until after 1760 that philosophical interests in the modern sense became dominant in his mind. Kant's publications had already won him a considerable reputation in German learned circles by the time he obtained his professorship. The ten years following his appointment form a period of literary silence during which Kant was engaged in preparing his magnum opus, the *Critique of Pure Reason*. The appearance of the *Critique* was eagerly awaited by Kant's friends and philosophical colleagues, but when it at last came out in 1781 the general reaction was more bewilderment than admiration. Kant tried to remove misunderstandings by restating the main argument in the *Prolegomena to Every Future Metaphysics* of 1783 and by rewriting some of the central sections of the *Critique* for a second edition in 1787. At the same time he continued, with most remarkable energy for a man of his years, the elaboration of the rest of his system. By 1790 the *Critique of Practical Reason* and the *Critique of Judgment* were in print, and of the major treatises only *Religion Within the Bounds of Mere Reason* (1793) and *Metaphysic of Morals* (1797) had still to appear. Kant then enjoyed a tremendous reputation throughout Germany and was beginning to be known, though scarcely to be understood, in other European countries. In his declining years, however, he suffered the mortification of seeing some of the ablest young philosophers in his own country, among them Fichte, Schelling, and J. S. Beck, proclaim that he had not really understood his own philosophy and propose to remedy the deficiency by producing "transcendental" systems of their own. There is reason to believe that the work on which Kant was engaged in the last years of his life was intended as a counterblast to such critics. But Kant was not able to complete it before his death, and all that remains of it are the fragments gathered together under the title *Opus Postumum*.

Kant was the first of the major philosophers

of modern times to spend his life

as a professional teacher of the subject.

Kant's outer life was almost entirely uneventful. He never married. The one occasion on which he might have become politically prominent was in 1794 when, after the appearance of his book on religion, the Prussian king asked him not to publish further on a topic on which his views were causing alarm to the orthodox. But Kant duly promised, and no scandal ensued. For the rest, he fulfilled the duties of his professorship and took his turn as rector of the university; dined regularly with his friends; admired Rousseau and the French Revolution from afar; conversed eagerly with travelers who brought him news of a wider world he never saw himself. Never very robust in body, he carefully conserved his physical resources and was in good health until a relatively short time before his death. He was nearly eighty when he died.

Character of Kant's Philosophical Work

Kant was the first of the major philosophers of modern times to spend his life as a professional teacher of the

Kant is the only eighteenth-century philosopher who at once appreciated the greatness of Newton and was fully aware of the challenges for ethics Newton's work presented. (Corbis)

subject. He was required by university regulation to base his philosophy lectures on particular texts, and he used for this purpose not the works of major thinkers like Descartes and Locke, but the handbooks of his professorial predecessors, notably Christian von Wolff, Alexander Baumgarten, and G. F. Meier. Wolff and Baumgarten had dressed out the philosophy of Leibniz in what they took to be decent academic garb, presenting Leibniz' thoughts in the form of a system and with an air of finality foreign to the original; Meier did the same for the doctrines of formal logic. Their example had a near-fatal effect on Kant, for he too thought that philosophy must be thorough if it is to be academically respectable—meaning, among other things, technical and schematic. In the *Critique of Pure Reason* he set out his theories in what he later called progressive order, starting from what was logically first and working forward to familiar facts; in that work he also employed an elaborate terminology of his own and an apparatus of "parts," "divisions," and "books" whose titles are alarming and whose appropriateness to the subject mat-

ter is not immediately obvious. It is not surprising that his first readers were unable to discover what the work as a whole was about. The *Critique of Practical Reason* and the *Critique of Judgment* were still more pedantic in form, since in them Kant persisted with much of the formal framework already used in the *Critique of Pure Reason,* in each case proceeding from a part labeled "Analytic" to another labeled "Dialectic," uncovering one or more "antinomies" in dealing with the dialectic, and ending with an untidy appendix irrelevantly entitled "Doctrine of Method." The fact that Kant was already an old man when he composed these works doubtless explains his attachment to what some commentators have called his architectonic; it is a major obstacle to the proper grasp and unprejudiced evaluation of his ideas. Yet, as passages in his ethical writings in particular show, Kant was capable of expounding his thoughts with clarity, even with eloquence. He was not by nature a bad writer, but he accepted uncritically the scholastic manner cultivated by his fellow professors.

The first task in reading Kant is thus to cut through the formal academic dress in which he clothes his opinions. When this is done, what emerges is not a provincial pedant like Wolff or Baumgarten, but a person of remarkable intellectual and moral stature. Kant's knowledge of the major European philosophers was often no more than superficial, and his estimate of the work of some of his own contemporaries was certainly overgenerous. But he had, for all that, a sure sense of what was intellectually important at the time; he alone among the eighteenth-century philosophers at once appreciated the greatness of Newton and was fully aware of the challenge for ethics Newton's work presented once its seemingly deterministic implications were understood. To sum up Kant's mature philosophy in a single formula: He wished to insist on the authority of science and yet preserve the autonomy of morals. To achieve this result was a gigantic task, involving consideration of the whole question of the possibility of metaphysics as well as the construction of a theory of scientific knowledge and the elaboration of an ethical system. Nor was Kant one to be content with mere generalities; he sought to work out his position in detail, with many specific arguments, as well as to state a general case. But the obscurities of his language combine with the extent of his intellectual ambitions to prevent the average reader from grasping precisely what Kant was after; individual points are picked up, but the shape of the whole is not discerned. Yet to be fair to Kant the reader must see the individual views in the wide setting in which Kant saw them himself. To estimate their philosophical value without taking account of their position in the Kantian system, as many critics have tried to do, is quite indefensible.

Precritical Writings

Kant's philosophical career is commonly divided into two periods, that before 1770, usually referred to as "precritical," and that after 1770, usually referred to as "critical." The word "critical" comes from Kant's own description of his mature philosophy as a form of "critical idealism," an idealism, that is to say, built on the basis of a critique of the powers of reason. The precritical period of Kant's thought is interesting primarily, though not exclusively, for its anticipations of his later ideas. Kant was educated by Knutzen in the Wolff–Baumgarten version of Leibniz, and he was, like his master, an independent Leibnizian from the first, although it was many years before he made a decisive break with the Leibnizian way of thinking. The main influence operating against Leibniz in Kant's early thought was Newton, to whose work he had also been introduced by Knutzen. In the more narrowly philosophical field another independent Leibnizian, Christian August Crusius, proved an important subsidiary influence. Just when Hume awakened Kant from his "dogmatic slumber" is uncertain, but it seems likely that Kant had moved some way in the direction of empiricism before that event took place.

CAUSATION. How little the early Kant had learned from Hume can be seen from some of his first metaphysical essays. In the *Principium Primorum Cognitionis Metaphysicae Nova Dilucidatio* (Königsberg, 1755) he discoursed in effect on the subject of causality, discussing at length the relationship of the Leibnizian principle of sufficient reason to the logical principles of identity and contradiction. Kant knew at this stage, as Crusius did, that Wolff's attempt to subordinate the real to the logical was a mistake, but he had only a hazy idea of what he was later to call the synthetic nature of propositions asserting real connections. He moved a step nearer his mature view in the 1763 essay on negative quantities (*Versuch, den Begriff der negativen Grössen in die Weltweisheit einzuführen,* Königsberg) when he pointed out that opposition in nature is quite different from opposition in logic: Two forces acting against one another are quite unlike a proposition in which the same predicate is simultaneously affirmed and denied. But in none of his writings of the time did Kant explicitly raise the question of the sphere of application of the causal principle, as Hume did.

EXISTENCE. Kant's failure to press home his questions on causation is paralleled in his otherwise striking treatment of existence in another work published in 1763, "The Only Possible Ground of Proof of God's Existence." He began this work by declaring that even if the proposition that existence is no predicate or determination of anything seems "strange and contradictory," it is nevertheless indubitable and certain. "It is not a fully correct expression to say: 'A sea unicorn is an existent animal'; we should put it the other way round and say: 'To a certain existing sea animal there belong the predicates that I think of as collectively constituting a sea unicorn.'" On these grounds Kant rejected the Cartesian version of the Ontological Argument. But he held, even so, that an alternative conceptual proof of God's existence could be found: Nothing could be conceived as possible unless (as the point had already been put in the *Nova Dilucidatio*) "whatever of reality there is in every possible notion do exist, and indeed, absolutely necessarily. . . . Further, this complete reality must be united in a single being." There must, in other words, be a perfect being if there are to be any possibilities. Kant was to recall this proof in his derivation of the idea of the *ens realissimum* in the *Critique of Pure Reason,* but he then no longer believed that it had constitutive force. His treatment of attempts to produce causal proofs of God's existence in the *Critique* was also altogether more trenchant than in the precritical works, for though he saw there that the ordinary First Cause Argument was unsatisfactory, he regarded the Argument from Design as generally acceptable, even if not logically compulsive.

METAPHYSICAL PROPOSITIONS. Kant was more successful in another treatise written at the same period, "Untersuchungen über die Deutlichkeit der Grundsätze der natürlichen Theologie und der Moral" ("On the Distinctness of the Principles of Natural Theology and Morals," 1764). The Berlin Academy had proposed the question, Are metaphysical truths generally, and the fundamental principles of natural theology and morals in particular, capable of proofs as distinct as those of geometry? if not, what is the true nature of their certainty? Kant answered by drawing a series of radical distinctions between argument in philosophy and argument in mathematics. The mathematician starts from definitions that are in effect arbitrary combinations of concepts; the philosopher must work toward definitions, not argue from them, since his business is to "analyze concepts which are given as confused." Mathematics contains few unanalyzable concepts and indemonstrable propositions; philosophy is full of them. Then too, the relationship between mathematical ideas can always be observed *in concreto,* whereas the philosopher, having nothing to correspond to mathematical diagrams or symbolism, necessarily works on a more abstract level. The lesson of all this might seem to be that philosophical truths are incapable of strict demonstration, but Kant did not draw this conclusion in the case of natural theology, where he held to his attempted conceptual proof, though he inclined toward it in respect to "the primary grounds of morals." In general, Kant's tendency was to say that metaphysics must be an analytic activity that should follow a method that is fundamentally Newtonian: "It is far from the time for proceeding synthetically in metaphysics; only when analysis will have helped us to distinct concepts understood in their details will synthesis be able to subsume compounded cognitions under the simplest cognitions, as in mathematics" (*Critique of Practical Reason and Other Writings,* Beck translation, 1949, p. 275).

The first task in reading Kant

is to cut through the formal academic dress

in which he clothes his opinions.

Kant viewed the prospects of attaining genuine metaphysical knowledge with increasing skepticism as the 1760s went on. In the enigmatic *Dreams of a Spirit-Seer* of 1766 he compared the thought constructions of metaphysics to the fantasies of Swedenborg, in a manner that is scarcely flattering to either. Metaphysical contentions are groundless, since metaphysical concepts such as spirit cannot be characterized in positive terms. To survive, metaphysics must change its nature and become a science of the limits of human knowledge. Kant's skepticism about metaphysics was increased by his discovery of the antinomies, which is often dated 1769 although something like the third antinomy is to be found in the *Nova Dilucidatio.* Astonishingly, however, in his inaugural dissertation in 1770 he reverted in some degree to the old dogmatic conception of the subject and argued for the possibility of genuine knowledge of an intelligible world. But the main interest of the dissertation lies in its account of sensory knowledge, which prepared the way for the fundamental criticisms of metaphysical pretensions in the *Critique of Pure Reason.*

The Inaugural Dissertation

Kant's Latin dissertation, "On the Form and Principles of the Sensible and Intelligible Worlds," publicly defended on August 21, 1770, was his inaugural lecture as professor of logic and metaphysics at Königsberg. At least one of the themes of the dissertation, the status of the concept of space, represented a long-standing inter-

est. As early as 1747 Kant had argued that the proposition that space has three dimensions is contingent; given a different law of the effects of different substances on one another, "an extension with other properties and dimensions would have arisen. A science of all these possible kinds of space would undoubtedly be the highest enterprise which a finite understanding could undertake in the field of geometry" ("Living Forces," Handyside translation, in *Kant's Inaugural Dissertation and Early Writings on Space,* p. 12). Later, however, he regarded three-dimensionality as a necessary property of space, and used its necessity as a ground for rejecting Leibniz' account of the concept. In a short essay on space published in 1768 Kant had seemed to suggest that Newton's view of space as an absolute reality was the only alternative to Leibniz, but in the dissertation he rejected both theories and widened his treatment of the question so that it covered time as well as space. Despite this extension the dissertation is best viewed as directed mainly against Leibniz.

SPACE AND TIME. In general, Leibniz had followed the other great rationalists in interpreting perception as a confused form of thinking. Like Descartes, he had treated the deliverances of the senses as sometimes clear but never distinct. In the dissertation Kant developed two main arguments against this position. He maintained in the first place that it could not do justice to the special character of space and time, which are not, as Leibniz supposed, systems of relations abstracted from particular situations and confusedly apprehended, but rather unique individuals of which clear knowledge is presupposed in all perceptual description. The ideas of space and time are intuitive rather than conceptual in character; moreover, they are "pure" intuitions insofar as the essential nature of their referents is known in advance of experience and not as a result of it.

SPACE AND GEOMETRY. To reinforce this point Kant brought forward his second argument, that Leibniz' theory could not account for the apodictic character of geometry. There was, Kant supposed, an essential relation between geometry and space, for geometry "contemplates the relations of space" and "does not demonstrate its universal propositions by apprehending the object through a universal concept, as is done in matters of reason, but by submitting it to the eyes as a singular intuition, as is done in matters of sense" ("Dissertation," *ibid.,* Sec. 15 C). But if space is what Leibniz said it was and if, as Kant added, "all properties of space are borrowed only from external relations through experience," then:

geometrical axioms do not possess universality, but only that comparative universality which is acquired through induction and holds only so widely as it is observed; nor do they possess necessity, except such as depends on fixed laws of nature; nor have they any precision save such as is matter of arbitrary convention; and we might hope, as in empirical matters, some day to discover a space endowed with other primary affections, and perhaps even a rectilinear figure enclosed by two straight lines. (*Ibid., Sec. 15 D*)

Kant's own account of space at this stage was that it "*is not something objective and real,* neither substance, nor accident; nor relation, but [something] *subjective and ideal;* it is, as it were, a schema, issuing by a constant law from the nature of the mind, for the co-ordinating of all outer sensa whatever" (*ibid.*). One major advantage of this subjectivist view, in Kant's eyes, was that it explains the possibility of applying geometry to the physical world. Space being a universal form of sensibility, "nothing whatsoever . . . can be given to the senses save in conformity with the primary axioms of space and the other consequences of its nature, as expounded by geometry" (*ibid., Sec. 15 E*).

APPEARANCE AND REALITY. Kant's view had another, more startling implication, namely that we cannot know things as they really are through sense perception. If space and time are contributed by the knowing mind, spatial and temporal objects will be altered in the very act of being apprehended. It follows that the world known through the senses—the world investigated by the physical sciences and familiar in everyday experience—can be no more than a phenomenal world. Kant was prepared to accept this conclusion in the dissertation, but he balanced it by saying that over and above this phenomenal world is another world of real objects, knowable not by the senses but by reason. Reason lacks intuitive powers—we cannot be acquainted with things as they are. But (and in this the contrast with the *Dreams* is at its strongest) reason possesses certain concepts of its own, among them "possibility, existence, necessity, substance, cause," by means of which it can arrive at a "symbolic cognition" of such things; that is, know some true propositions about them. The intellect, in its real as opposed to its logical use, can form the concept of a perfect being and use this both to measure the reality of other things and for moral purposes.

ACHIEVEMENTS. The doctrine of pure intellectual concepts in the dissertation is at best impressionistic and had to be completely rethought in the ten years that followed. But against this may be set Kant's positive achievements in the dissertation, seen from the point of view of his future work. First, Kant had convinced himself that there is an absolute difference between sensing

and thinking, and that sense experience need not be in any way confused. Second, he had worked out the main lines, though by no means all the details, of what was to be his mature theory of space and time. Third, he had revived the old antithesis of things real and things apparent, objects of the intellect and objects of the senses, to cope with the consequences of his views about space and time; in this way he was able to show (or so he thought) that physics gives us genuine knowledge, though only of appearances, and that the task of telling us about things as they really are is reserved for metaphysics. Fourth and last, he had recognized the existence of a special class of concepts, "given through the very nature of the intellect," and had seen that these have an important bearing on the question of the possibility of metaphysics.

If space and time are contributed

by the knowing mind, spatial and temporal objects

will be altered in the very act of being apprehended.

What Kant had not done was to pose the problem of metaphysics with all its wider implications. As in the *Dreams,* he treated the question whether we have any knowledge of a world of pure spirit as one that is asked primarily for its theoretical interest. It was intellectual curiosity, that is to say, which at this stage prompted Kant to inquire whether physics and metaphysics could coexist, and, if they could, what should be said of their respective objects. He retained this curiosity when he wrote the *Critique of Pure Reason,* but it was not by then his only motive. For he had seen by 1781 that the question of the possibility of metaphysics was important not only to the academic philosopher, but because of its bearing on the universally interesting topics of God, freedom, and immortality, to the plain man as well; that it was a matter not just of intellectual, but also of moral, concern.

Critique of Pure Reason: Theme and Preliminaries

Kant's principal task in the *Critique of Pure Reason* was to determine the cognitive powers of reason, to find out what it could and could not achieve in the way of knowledge. The term "reason" in the title was intended in its generic sense, to cover the intellect as a whole; Kant was not exclusively interested in the reason that he himself distinguished from and opposed to understanding. He was, however, particularly concerned with the capacities of "pure" reason, that is, with what reason could know when operating by itself and not in association with another faculty. Kant believed it important to answer this question for two reasons. He saw that there are spheres (mathematics, for instance) in which it is plausible to claim that pure reason is a source of important truths. He also saw that in another field, that of metaphysics, remarkable claims were advanced on reason's behalf: It was alleged that, by simply thinking, we could arrive at ultimate truth about the world, establishing thus a series of propositions whose certainty was unassailable and whose subject matter was of supreme importance. Kant, who had himself made this sort of claim in the dissertation, never doubted that what the metaphysician wants to say matters, but he did question his competence to say it. The fact that reason "precipitates itself into darkness and contradictions" once it enters this field struck him as deeply significant; the "intestine wars," the interminable disputes, of metaphysicians could only mean that their claims were pitched too high. Nor was the scandal of metaphysics—the fact that nothing in metaphysics could be regarded as settled—of concern only to metaphysicians. By failing to make good his proofs, the metaphysician brought doubt on the acceptability of his conclusions, including such fundamental articles of belief as that God exists and that the will is free. In proposing a radical reexamination of the capacities of pure reason, Kant's ultimate motive was to safeguard such convictions by making clear that although they cannot be matters of knowledge, they can all the same be held to as matters of what he called pure rational faith.

TYPES OF JUDGMENT. In the preface to the *Critique,* Kant formulates his main question as "how much can understanding and reason know apart from all experience?" (A xvii). (The first edition is customarily referred to as A, the second edition as B.) In the introduction, he takes his first step toward an answer by substituting the formula "How are synthetic a *priori* judgments possible?" Two closely connected sets of distinctions lie behind these celebrated words. First, Kant distinguishes propositions that are a priori from all others; an a priori judgment "in being thought is thought as *necessary*" and is also thought "with strict universality, that is, in such a manner that no exception is allowed as possible" (B 3–4). A priori judgments have the twin characteristics of necessity and universality, neither of which can be found in conclusions from experience.

In holding that experience can present us with no more than contingent truths Kant echoes the views of many of his predecessors. But in his other distinction, between synthetic and analytic judgments, he shows greater originality. A judgment is analytic, he explains, if what is thought in the predicate-concept has already been thought in the subject-concept; a judgment is syn-

thetic if this condition does not obtain. Thus, "All bodies are extended" is analytic because our idea of a body is of something that is extended or occupies space; "All bodies have weight" is synthetic because the notion of weight is not comprised in the notion of body (we learn by experience that bodies have weight). In analytic judgments, again, the connection of subject and predicate is "thought through identity"; or, as Kant puts it elsewhere in the *Critique,* the highest principle of all analytic judgments is the principle of contradiction. It follows from this that every analytic judgment is a priori in that it is true or false without regard to experience; every analytic judgment is either necessarily true or necessarily false, and we establish its truth or falsity by reference only to definitions of the terms it contains and to the principle of contradiction. Synthetic judgments, by contrast, require for their authentication a different sort of reference, since in their case the connection of subject and predicate terms is "thought without identity." In the case of everyday judgments of fact, for example, we need to consult experience to see whether the connection asserted actually holds.

So far Kant's distinction is simply a more elaborate version of Hume's division of propositions into those that assert relations of ideas and those that express matters of fact and existence, a version inferior to Hume's in that it is formally tied to statements of the subject—predicate form. But at this point Kant gives the distinction a fresh twist by asserting that there are judgments that are both synthetic and a priori, thus cutting across the usual classifications. Nearly all the propositions of mathematics answer this description, according to Kant; he also thinks it obvious that *"natural science (physics) contains* a priori *synthetic judgments as principles."* He gives two examples: "in all changes of the material world the quantity of matter remains unchanged; and . . . in all communication of motion action and reaction must always be equal" (B 17). The very existence of these judgments shows that reason has special cognitive powers of its own, and so lends plausibility to the claims of metaphysicians. But before accepting the claims of metaphysicians, Kant suggests, we need to ask ourselves how (under what conditions) it is possible to assert judgments of this type in the two fields concerned. Only when this question is answered can we decide whether metaphysicians can draw support from the example of mathematics and "pure" physics. This inquiry is what Kant is concerned with in the first half of the *Critique.*

ANALYTIC AND SYNTHETIC. The terms in which Kant states his problem seem at first sight clear, but the clarity diminishes on closer inspection. There is the criticism that he offers a dual account of the analytic—

synthetic distinction, once in psychological and once in logical terms, and the criticism that reference to the principle of contradiction alone is inadequate for the logical formulation of the distinction (he should have referred to logical laws generally). Apart from these two matters, Kant's treatment is marred by a failure to offer any discussion of his key idea, "what is thought in a concept." This omission is the more remarkable because Kant in fact had views on the subject of definition, views that are hard to reconcile with his apparent assumption that every judgment is unequivocally analytic or synthetic. Elsewhere in the *Critique* he states that, according to the real meaning of "definition," an empirical concept "cannot be defined at all, but only made explicit" (B 755). He means that we cannot give the "real essence" (in Locke's terminology) of such a concept, but only its "nominal essence," or conventional signification, which is liable to change as knowledge increases or interests shift. If this is correct, it seems to be only by convention, or provisionally, that the judgment "All bodies are extended" is analytic and the judgment "All bodies have weight" synthetic.

Some critics speak as if Kant's failure

to produce a satisfactory philosophy of mathematics

invalidated the whole "Aesthetic."

Nor is Kant's other distinction, between a priori and a posteriori, as simple as he pretends. He tries to clarify it by explaining that the first class of judgments have the characteristics of necessity and universality, which serve as criteria that are "inseparable from one another." He fails to notice, however, that the necessity that belongs to synthetic a priori judgments must on his own account differ from that which characterizes analytic judgments. Analytic judgments are, or rather claim to be, logically necessary—to deny a true analytic judgment would be, if Kant is correct, to dispute the validity of the law of contradiction. But though no synthetic judgment can contravene the laws of logic, none can be true in virtue of these laws and of meanings alone. Accordingly, if any synthetic judgment is to be described as necessary, it must be necessary in some further sense.

Kant recognizes in practice that the synthetic a priori judgments he takes to be valid have their own special kind of necessity. In his own terminology, they are "transcendentally" necessary; necessary, that is to say, if we are to have the knowledge and experience we actually have. But he would have done better to acknowledge the ambiguity in his term "a priori" from the outset. It

would also have been helpful had he given some elucidation of his statement that, when a judgment is thought with strict universality, "no exception is allowed as possible." He cannot mean that no exception is logically possible, or every a priori judgment would be analytic. But he does not, at least at this early stage, make clear what other sort of possibility he has in mind.

Transcendental Aesthetic

Kant's next step in the solution of the problem of how synthetic a priori judgments are possible is to examine the two types of case in which, in his view, we undoubtedly can make synthetic a priori judgments, and then to exhibit the bearing of his results on the possibility of metaphysical knowledge. In his short but important *Prolegomena to Every Future Metaphysics* he approaches these tasks directly. In the *Critique* itself his method is more roundabout, since he proposes there to delineate the entire cognitive powers of the mind and so to clarify the background against which synthetic a priori judgments are made. This leads him to undertake an inquiry first into the a priori elements involved in sensory knowledge (the "Transcendental Aesthetic") and then into the corresponding elements involved in thought (the "Transcendental Logic"). The sharp distinction between the senses and the intellect argued for in the dissertation is the obvious basis of this division.

A PRIORI INTUITIONS. It seems at first sight contradictory to say that there might be a priori elements involved in sensory knowledge. According to an old philosophical and psychological tradition, sensation is an essentially passive affair; the senses present us with data and we have no choice but to accept. Kant was quite ready to agree to this as a general account of sensation. But he was persuaded that there are some features of sensory experience that cannot be accepted as empirically given.

Kant identifies these features by a process similar to that in the dissertation: an examination of our ideas of space and time. These ideas, he argues, represent the form of experience rather than its matter; through them we structure the sensory given in the very act of sensing it. To establish this position Kant appeals to a variety of considerations.

First, he insists on the fundamental and ubiquitous character of space and time, as opposed to features like color and sound. Spatial predicates apply to whatever we know through the five senses, temporal predicates both to these and to the immediately experienced flow of our inner lives. Second, he argues that we cannot acquire the ideas of space and time by reflecting on what is empirically given. Some philosophers had said that we come by the idea of space by noticing such things as that one object is adjacent to another, and that we come by the idea of time by observing the way in which events succeed, are simultaneous with, or precede one another. Kant points out that the very description of such situations presupposes familiarity with space and time as such. For to know what is meant by saying that one thing is "next to" or "on top of" another we need to appreciate how the things in question are situated in a wider spatial framework, which in turn falls within a yet wider spatial system, until we come to the thought of space as a whole. Particular spaces are not instances of space, but limitations of it, and space is accordingly a special sort of particular. The same argument applies to time. Adding to these two points the fact that we know certain things to be necessarily true of space and time (space has only three dimensions, different times are not simultaneous but successive), Kant infers that the ideas of space and time are not only "intuitions," but "*a priori* intuitions."

MATHEMATICS. Kant finds confirmation for his view of space and time exactly as he had in the dissertation: in the thought that this view alone can explain the possibility of pure and applied mathematics. Pure geometry is possible because we are able to "construct," or show the real possibility of, its concepts in pure intuition. An experiment conducted in imagination shows at once that a triangle is a real spatial possibility, whereas a figure bounded by two straight lines is not. Applied geometry is possible because whatever is apprehended by the senses must necessarily accord with the forms of sensibility. Kant attempts at various points in his writings to extend his doctrine of the importance of pure intuition for mathematical thinking from geometry to the other parts of mathematics, but it cannot be said that he is ever convincing on this point. His reasons for saying that "seven and five are twelve" is a synthetic proposition were sharply and properly criticized by Gottlob Frege. His account of algebra (B 745, 762) is so sketchy as to be virtually unintelligible. Kant tries to say that in algebra there is a "symbolic construction" corresponding to the "ostensive construction" of the concepts of geometry, but it is not in the least clear what this has to do with the pure intuition of either space or time.

Some critics speak as if Kant's failure to produce a satisfactory philosophy of mathematics invalidated the whole "Aesthetic," and it is true that the central point of this part of his work is destroyed if his main contentions about mathematics are rejected. Kant's explanations fall to the ground if it turns out that there is no intrinsic connection between mathematics and space and time, or if it is held that mathematical propositions are analytic, not synthetic a priori. But it does not im-

mediately follow that the whole Kantian doctrine of space and time must be rejected, for many of his arguments on this matter are independent of his philosophy of mathematics. Nor is it decisive against him that the treatment of space and time in modern physics is very different from his; he claims to be dealing with the space and time of immediate perception.

In the first part of the "Analytic"

Kant has much to say not only about

concepts, judgments, and the understanding

but also about the imagination.

SIGNIFICANCE. Apart from the questions about truth, however, it is vital to appreciate the importance of the conclusions of the "Aesthetic" in the economy of the *Critique of Pure Reason* as a whole. The "transcendental ideality" of space and time carries with it, for Kant, the proposition that whatever we know through the senses (including "inner sense") is phenomenal; Kant's celebrated distinction between appearances and things-in-themselves has its origin, if not its justification, at this point. And the view that space and time are a priori forms of intuition is not only the model on which Kant constructed his theory of categories as concepts embodying the pure thought of an object in general; the view is carried over intact into the "Transcendental Analytic," and plays a crucial part there. To treat the theories of the "Aesthetic" as if they merely embodied a series of views that Kant had outgrown by the time he completed the *Critique*, as some commentators have proposed to do, is not in accord with Kant's own intentions. It is also to ignore a series of arguments that are of independent philosophical interest, and that demand careful notice from anyone writing on the philosophy of perception.

Pure Concepts of the Understanding

The main contentions of the aesthetic are to be found in the dissertation. Of the doctrine of pure intellectual concepts put forward in that inaugural lecture, on the other hand, almost nothing survives in the *Critique of Pure Reason*.

OBJECTIVE REFERENCE. In the dissertation Kant argues along two lines: First, that pure intellectual concepts are not derived from sense experience (they could not be described as "pure" if they were); and second, that they serve to give us information about things as they really are. Soon after writing this work, however,

Kant realized that there was a fundamental difficulty in this position, a difficulty he stated at length in a letter to his friend Marcus Herz dated February 21, 1772. It was that of knowing how "pure" concepts could be said to determine an object of any kind. To elucidate the difficulty, Kant isolated two contrasting types of intelligence, *intellectus ectypus,* "which derives the data of its logical procedure from the sensuous intuition of things," and *intellectus archetypus,* "on whose intuition the things themselves are grounded." The concepts of the first type of intelligence, deriving as they do from objects, have a guaranteed relationship to objects. The concepts of the second type determine objects, because, in this sort of case, thinking itself brings objects into existence in the same way in which "the ideas in the Divine Mind are the archetypes of things." But the human intelligence, as described in the dissertation, answers to neither description, for some of its concepts are not empirically derived and yet none of its thinking is creative in the sense specified. The problem then arises, How can these concepts be said to have objective reference; how can we know that in using them we are thinking about anything actual? It is this problem that Kant professes to have solved in the *Critique of Pure Reason.* Roughly speaking, his solution is that pure concepts can be shown to determine an object if the object is phenomenal. By contrast, when an attempt is made to use them to specify characteristics of "things in general," there is no guarantee that anything significant is being said.

ANALYTIC AND DIALECTIC. The details of Kant's explanation of how pure concepts can be said to have objective reference is to be found in the lengthy section of the *Critique* labeled "Transcendental Logic" and divided into two main parts, "Transcendental Analytic" and "Transcendental Dialectic."

The first part contains an inventory of what at this point Kant calls pure concepts of the understanding, or categories, with an account of the function they perform in human knowledge and a series of arguments purporting to show that, in the absence of such pure concepts, objective knowledge would be impossible for human beings. In addition, the "Analytic" lists the principles that rest on these pure concepts and offers independent proofs of these principles. Transcendental analytic is said by Kant to be a "logic of truth," insofar as "no knowledge can contradict it without at once losing all content, that is, all relation to an object, and therefore all truth" (B 87). It deals, in short, with the proper use of a priori concepts, which is the use they have when they provide a framework for empirical inquiries.

Transcendental dialectic is introduced as if it were merely the negative counterpart of analytic—as if its sole purpose were to expose the illusions generated when dogmatic philosophers, unaware of the sensuous conditions under which alone we can make successful use of a priori concepts, attempt to apply them outside the sphere of possible experience. In fact a large part of the section entitled "Dialectic" is devoted to the exposure of metaphysical sophistries. But insofar as Kant recognizes in this part of his work the existence of a further set of intellectual operations involved in scientific inquiry, he seeks to show that the faculty of theoretical reason as well as that of the understanding has its appropriate pure employment.

JUDGMENT OR BELIEF. A good way to approach the central doctrines of the analytic is to see them as an intended answer to Hume. Kant's knowledge of Hume was limited—he had no firsthand acquaintance with the *Treatise of Human Nature*—but he grasped the importance of many of Hume's most challenging points. For instance, Hume had argued that *"belief is more properly an act of the sensitive, than of the cogitative part of our natures"* (*Treatise,* L. A. Selby-Bigge, ed., 1888, Book I, Part IV, Sec. 1, p. 183); in the last resort it is a matter of subjective conviction. It is one of Kant's main objects in the analytic to demonstrate that such a view cannot do justice to an all-important feature of what Hume calls belief and he calls judgment, namely, its claim to be true. When I judge that something is the case I do not merely commit myself to a certain assertion; there is a sense in which I commit all rational persons too, for I purport to state what holds objectively, that is to say for everyone. To make judgment primarily a matter of feeling, something private to an individual person, is to leave out what is most characteristic of it. Similarly, to explain thinking about matters of fact and existence in terms of the association of ideas, as Hume did, is to confuse the objective with the subjective, to put science on the level of idle reverie. Empirical thinking, to deserve its name, must proceed according to rules, and there is all the difference in the world between a rule, which cannot of its nature be private, and association, which is the connecting of ideas on a purely personal plane.

THE UNITY OF EXPERIENCE. There are many philosophers who would accept this criticism of Hume but would deny that empirical thinking involves not only rules, but rules that are a priori or necessary rules. To understand why Kant asserts that thinking must proceed according to necessary rules, we must explain his attitude to another of Hume's doctrines, the famous contention that "all our experimental conclusions proceed upon the supposition that the future will be conformable to the past" (*Enquiry Concerning Human Understanding,* Sec. IV, Part II). Kant agrees with Hume that empirical knowledge involves connecting one part or element of experience with another; he agrees too that connection of this sort ("synthesis") proceeds on a principle that is neither analytically true nor empirically probable. But he refuses to follow Hume in deriving the principle from "Custom or Habit," for he sees more clearly than Hume the consequences of adopting this "sceptical solution." If it were really the case that events were as "loose and separate" as Hume supposed, not only should we be deprived of any insight into the connections of things, but we should have no unitary consciousness of any sort. For it is a necessary condition of having a unitary consciousness that we be able to relate what is happening here and now to things and events that lie outside our immediate purview; if the ability to relate is not a real possibility, then neither is unitary consciousness. What Kant calls in one place (A 113) "the thoroughgoing affinity of appearances" (the fact that appearances are capable of being connected in a single experience) thus relates closely to the ability of the observer to recognize himself as a single person with diverse experiences. In fact the relation is one of mutual implication.

It may be useful to cite Kant's explanation as he gave it in the first edition of the *Critique,* in a passage in which all the most characteristic ideas of the "Analytic" appear and which also illustrates Kant's persistent but nonetheless questionable tendency to move from saying that unity of consciousness means that appearances must be capable of connection to the conclusion that they must be capable of connection according to universal and necessary laws.

> There can be in us no items of knowledge, no connection or unity of one item of knowledge with another, without that unity of consciousness which precedes all data of intuitions, and by relation to which representation of objects is alone possible. This pure original unchangeable consciousness I shall name *transcendental apperception.* . . . This transcendental unity of apperception forms out of all possible appearances, which can stand alongside one another in one experience, a connection of all these representations according to laws. For this unity of consciousness would be impossible if the mind in knowledge of the manifold could not become conscious of the identity of function whereby it synthetically combines it in one knowledge. The original and necessary consciousness of the identity of the self is thus at the same time a consciousness of an equally necessary unity of the synthesis of all appearances according to concepts, that is, according to rules, which not only make them necessarily reproducible but also in so doing determine an object for

their intuition, that is, the concept of something wherein they are necessarily interconnected. (A 107–108)

ROLE OF CATEGORIES. If the synthesis of appearances is to proceed in accordance with necessary laws, we must clearly operate not just with empirical but also with a priori concepts. But this must not be taken to mean that some items or features of fact can be known apart from all experience. For the role of an a priori concept is fundamentally different from that of its empirical counterpart. Categories are concepts of a higher order than empirical concepts; like the ideas of space and time, they have to do with the form of experience rather than its matter. Our possession of categories accordingly supplies no knowledge of particular things; categories are fertile only when brought to bear on empirical data. Thus, because we hold to the a priori concept of cause, we interrogate nature in a certain way; thanks to it, we refuse to believe that there could be an uncaused event. But the answers we get to our interrogation depend primarily not on the form of our questions, but on what turns up in experience. Those who accuse Kant of having believed in the material a priori have failed to understand his theory.

To summarize this part of Kant's argument: If we are to have knowledge (and it is Kant's assumption that we do), various conditions must be fulfilled. The different items that fall within our experience must be capable of being connected in a single consciousness; there can be no happenings that are genuinely loose and separate. But the connections thus demanded must be objective connections—they must hold not just for my consciousness, but for "consciousness in general," for everyone's. An objective connection for Kant is a connection determined by a rule, and a rule is of its nature something that claims intersubjective validity. Finally, if we are to establish the operation of empirical rules we must proceed in accordance with nonempirical rules of a higher order, rules that insure that our different experiences are capable of connection within a single experience.

JUDGMENTS. In view of the close relation Kant sees between the making of judgments and the use of a priori concepts, it is perhaps not surprising that he tries to arrive at a full list of such concepts by scrutinizing the formal properties of judgments. In this connection he invokes the doctrines of general or formal logic, a science he believed had been brought to completion at a single stroke by Aristotle. Few scholars have been convinced by this section of his argument, for it seems clear that Kant adapted the list of judgment forms to suit his list of categories, rather than deriving the categories from the judgment forms. In any case, it is not obvious how formal logic, which is a logic of consistency, can supply a clue to the content of what professes to be a logic of truth.

IMAGINATION AND UNDERSTANDING. In the first part of the "Analytic" Kant has much to say not only about concepts, judgments, and the understanding but also about the imagination. For example, he remarks in a cryptic passage:

> Synthesis in general is the mere result of the power of imagination, a blind but indispensable function in the soul, without which we should have no knowledge whatsoever, but of which we are scarcely ever conscious. To bring this synthesis to concepts is a function which belongs to understanding, and it is through this function of the understanding that we first obtain knowledge properly so called. (B 103)

The contrasting and, in places, overlapping roles of understanding and imagination are among the most puzzling features of Kant's exposition. The reason why they are both introduced is related to the fact that, in the second edition of the *Critique of Pure Reason* in particular, Kant was concerned with two quite distinct questions. He first asked himself what conditions have to be fulfilled if any sort of discursive consciousness is to have objective knowledge; he then went on to put the question as it relates to the human discursive consciousness, which not only intuits data passively, but does so under the particular forms of space and time. When the first question is uppermost Kant tends to speak of the understanding; when the second is to the fore, he brings in the imagination as well. The passage quoted above, typical of many, suggests that it is the business of the imagination to connect, whereas that of the understanding is to make explicit the principles on which the connecting proceeds. But in one chapter, "Schematism of the Pure Concepts of Understanding," a more satisfying account of the relationship is offered.

SCHEMATA. The problem of the chapter on what Kant called "schematism" is the central problem of the analytic: How can concepts that do not originate in experience find application in experience? At first Kant speaks as if there were no comparable difficulty in the case of concepts originating in experience, although he later makes clear that there are schemata corresponding both to empirical and to mathematical concepts. To possess the concept triangle is to know its formal definition, to be able to frame intelligible sentences containing the word "triangle," and so on; to possess the schema corresponding to the concept triangle is to be able to envisage the variety of things to which the word

"triangle" applies. Thus for Kant a schema is not an image, but a capacity to form images or (perhaps) to construct models. Pure concepts of the understanding are such that they "can never be brought into any image whatsoever" (B 181); the thought they embody, springing from the pure intellect, cannot be pictured or imagined. Yet there must be some connection between the abstract idea and the experienced world to which that idea is expected to apply; it must be possible to specify the empirical circumstances in which pure concepts of the understanding can find application. Kant thinks that for the categories this requirement is met by the fact that we can find for each of them a "transcendental schema," which is, he explains, a "transcendental determination of time." Without such a schema the categories would be devoid of "sense and significance," except in a logical (verbal) way. With it, use of the categories is clearly restricted to the range of things that fall within time—meaning, for Kant, restricted to phenomena.

Causality for Kant as for Hume

is a relation between successive events;

a cause is an event that regularly precedes its effect.

The meaning of this baffling doctrine can perhaps best be grasped through Kant's examples of schemata:

> The schema of substance is permanence of the real in time, that is, the representation of the real as a substrate of empirical determination of time in general. . . . The schema of cause . . . is the real upon which, whenever posited, something else always follows. It consists, therefore, in the succession of the manifold, in so far as that succession is subject to a rule. . . . The schema of necessity is existence of an object at all times. (B 183–184)

It emerges from these cryptic sentences that the transcendental schema is something like an empirical counterpart of the pure category. It is what the latter means when translated into phenomenal terms. In Kant's own words, the schema is "properly, only the phenomenon, or sensible concept, of an object in agreement with the category" (B 186). A category without its corresponding "sensible concept" would be a bare abstraction, virtually without significance. Insofar as he argues that schematization is the work of the imagination, Kant has found a genuine function for the imagination to perform.

ANALYTIC OF PRINCIPLES: PURE PHYSICS. In the first half of the "Analytic" Kant undertook to produce a "transcendental deduction," that is, a general proof of validity, of the categories. In the second half of the "Analytic" he gives a series of demonstrations of the synthetic a priori principles that rest on individual categories.

The categories are divided, for this and other purposes, into four groups: quantity, quality, relation, and modality. The four sets of corresponding principles are labeled axioms of intuition, anticipations of perception, analogies of experience, and postulates of empirical thought in general. Only one principle falls under each of the first two classes; the third contains a general principle and three more specific principles; the fourth contains three separate though closely connected principles. The first two classes are grouped together as "mathematical" principles; the third and fourth are described as "dynamical." Mathematical principles are said to be "immediately evident" and again to be "constitutive of their objects"; they apply directly to appearances. Dynamical principles are concerned with "the existence of such appearances and their relation to one another in respect of their existence." They are no less necessary than mathematical principles, but must be distinguished from them "in the nature of their evidence" and in that they are not "constitutive" but "regulative."

Behind this formidable façade some interesting ideas are hidden. In the first place, Kant makes stimulating though not altogether convincing remarks on the subject of proving principles of the understanding. The statement that every event has a cause carries strict necessity with it and therefore cannot be grounded on an inductive survey of empirical evidence. But equally it is not analytic, and so not open to straightforward conceptual proof. To be assured of its authenticity we consequently require a different type of argument altogether, which Kant calls a "transcendental" argument "from the possibility of experience." His idea is that only if the principles of the understanding are taken to be operative and in order can we have the type of experience we in fact have. Kant perhaps supposes that this type of proof is logically compulsive, but if so he overlooks the difficulty of setting up the original premise, of being sure that only if such-and-such were true should we have the experiences we have. But even with this defect his procedure has an immediate appeal, and is not without modern imitators.

AXIOMS OF INTUITION. The details of the particular arguments for the principles corresponding to the categories also deserve careful attention. The principle of axioms of intuition, that "all intuitions are extended magnitudes," is perhaps the most difficult to take seriously, since what it purports to prove has apparently already been dealt with in the "Aesthetic." Kant is once more asking questions about the application of mathematics to the world; in this section of the *Critique* the problem that apparently troubles him is how we know that inquiries about sizes or areas are always appropriate when we are dealing with things that occupy space. His solution is that they must be appropriate, since every such thing can be regarded as an aggregate of parts produced by the observer as he synthesizes his experiences. "I cannot represent to myself a line, however short, without drawing it in thought, that is, generating from a point all its parts one after another" (B 203).

Kant's acceptance of the distinction between

phenomena and things-in-themselves

has met with much criticism.

ANTICIPATIONS OF PERCEPTION. Under the term "anticipations of perception" Kant is concerned with the question of the applicability of mathematics to sensations. What guarantee have we, he asks, that every sensation will turn out to have a determinate degree, in principle quantifiable? Might we not find, for instance, that an object is colored but with no precise depth of saturation, or a smell present in a room but with no specific magnitude? Kant attempts to rule out such possibilities by attention to the formal properties of sensations. We cannot anticipate the matter of sensation, but we can say in advance of experience that every sensation will have intensive magnitude, that is, a determinate degree, because it is possible to think of any given sensation as fading away until it is imperceptible, and conversely as being built up by continuous transitions on a scale from zero to the magnitude it has. Whatever may be the merits of this solution, there can be no doubt of the importance, and for that matter the novelty, of the question Kant asks here.

ANALOGIES OF EXPERIENCE. The section on the analogies of experience contains ideas as significant as any in Kant's writings.

The Permanence of Substance. The principle of the first analogy is that of the permanence of substance: "in all change of appearances substance is permanent; its quantum in nature is neither increased nor diminished." To believe in the permanence of substance is to believe that, whatever happens, nothing goes completely out of existence and nothing totally new is created: all change is transformation. Kant justifies the acceptance of this presupposition (which in his view, it should be remembered, applies only to things phenomenal) by arguing that without it we could not have a unitary temporal system. Coexistence and succession make sense only against a background that abides, and since time itself cannot be perceived, that background has got to be one of permanent things. This does not mean that we can determine a priori what form the permanent will take; empirical scientists are to pronounce on that question, and their answers may obviously change from time to time. All that Kant seeks to rule out is the possibility that there might be no permanent at all. His argument is defective at a vital point here, but presumably he is saying that if things could go completely out of existence, so that it would make no sense to ask what became of them, the establishment of connections between one part of experience and another would be impossible. Experience would be (or at least might be) full of unbridgeable gaps, with the result that no one set of happenings could be integrated with another, and the unity of time would be totally destroyed.

Causation. Kant carries his argument further in his discussion of the second and third analogies, in which he argues for the necessary operation of the concepts of cause and reciprocity (causal interaction). But just as the notion of substance he justifies is very different from that held by metaphysicians, so is the Kantian concept of cause different from that of, say, Leibniz; it seems at first sight much closer to Hume's idea of a cause as an invariable antecedent. Causality for Kant as for Hume is a relation between successive events; a cause is an event that regularly precedes its effect. But whereas Hume is content to treat the occurrence of regular sequences as an ultimate and entirely contingent fact, Kant believes that without the presumption of sequences that are regular (determined by a rule) there could be no knowledge of objective succession. His reason is that we have to distinguish successions that happen only in ourselves, successions merely in our apprehension, from those that occur in the objective world and are independent of us. We can do this only if an objective sequence is defined as a sequence happening according to a rule. The objective world is a world of events the occurrence of each of which determines the precise place in time of some other event. But though events are necessarily connected in this way, we must not conclude that causal connections can be established a priori; for Kant as for Hume causal propositions are one and all synthetic and empirical. All we can know a priori is that there are such connections to be found, provided we have the skill or good fortune to discover them.

POSTULATES OF EMPIRICAL THOUGHT. One way of expressing Kant's attitude to substance and causality is to say that he thinks the principle of substance licenses us to ask the question, What became of that?

whenever something happens, and that the principle of causality licenses the parallel question, What brought that about? If someone tried to say that things might go out of existence altogether, or happen for no reason at all, Kant would say that these were logical but not real possibilities. The contrast between real and logical possibility is explored by Kant in the section "The Postulates of Empirical Thought." This section contains an explanation of the notions of possibility, actuality, and necessity from the critical point of view. By "really possible" Kant means "that which agrees with the formal conditions of experience, that is, with the conditions of intuition and of concepts" (B 265). A two-sided figure enclosing a space is not really possible, though its concept is not self-contradictory, because such a figure does not accord with the formal conditions of intuition. Telepathy and precognition are not real possibilities; they "cannot be based on experience and its known laws" (B 270), presumably because their actuality would violate some principle of the understanding, although Kant fails to make the point clear. The notion of real possibility is for Kant intermediate between logical and empirical possibility. We need it and can use it only because the world we have to deal with is a world that is not independently existent, but has its being in essential relation to consciousness.

PHENOMENA AND THINGS-IN-THEMSELVES. The distinction between phenomena and things-in-themselves, insisted on in the "Aesthetic" to explain our having a priori knowledge of the properties of space and time, is invoked again in the "Analytic" to account for "pure physics." If the world we confronted were one of things-in-themselves, a priori knowledge of it, even of the very restricted sort for which Kant argues, would be quite impossible. The fact that we have such knowledge—that we possess the principles discussed above—is taken by Kant as proof that the objects of our knowledge are phenomena or appearances. He does not mean by this, however, that they are private objects, at least insofar as they are spatial. The world we know in everyday and scientific experience is common to many observers; if not independent of consciousness as such, it is independent of particular consciousnesses. Parts of it are known only to particular experiencers—my inner life, for example, is accessible only to me—but that does not affect the general point.

Kant's acceptance of the distinction between phenomena and things-in-themselves has met with much criticism. Without the idea of the thing-in-itself, said his contemporary F. H. Jacobi, we cannot enter the world of the *Critique of Pure Reason;* with it we cannot remain inside. At the end of the "Analytic" Kant tries to defend himself against criticism of this sort by arguing that though he says that the objects of experience are phenomena and is prepared to admit that the obverse of a phenomenon is a noumenon or intelligible object, he is committed to noumena only in a negative sense. Having said that the categories, one of which is existence, apply only to phenomena, he cannot with consistency hold any other view. Nor is his position at this stage as devoid of logic as some have tried to make out. After all, to describe things as phenomena he does not need to assert that there actually are things of a different kind; he needs only the idea of such things. To talk about things as they might be in themselves is no more objectionable than to speak of an *intellectus archetypus,* as Kant did in the letter to Herz, or of an intuitive understanding, as he constantly does in both the *Critique of Pure Reason* and the *Critique of Judgment.*

The Elimination of Dogmatic Metaphysics

At the end of the section of the *Critique of Pure Reason* devoted to the transcendental analytic, there is a passage that can be taken as summarizing the second stage in Kant's emancipation from Leibnizian rationalism:

> The Transcendental Analytic leads to this important conclusion, that the most the understanding can achieve *a priori* is to anticipate the form of a possible experience in general. And since that which is not appearance cannot be an object of experience, the understanding can never transcend those limits of sensibility within which alone objects can be given to us. Its principles are merely rules for the exposition of appearances; and the proud name of an Ontology that presumptuously claims to supply, in systematic doctrinal form, synthetic *a priori* knowledge of things in general . . . must, therefore, give place to the modest title of a mere Analytic of pure understanding. (B 303)

Kant thus repudiates the possibility of knowledge through pure concepts of things as they really are; in 1770 he had still clung to it. Having disposed of ontology, Kant needed to consider, to complete the negative side of his work, the tenability of the remaining parts of metaphysics (rational psychology, rational cosmology, and natural theology in Baumgarten's classification), and this he did in the section entitled "Transcendental Dialectic." To complete his own alternative to rationalism he needed to clarify the status of the propositions involved in "pure practical faith." His attempt to meet this requirement is made at the very end of the *Critique,* especially in the chapter "The Canon of Pure Reason" (B 823 ff.).

REASON. Most of the conclusions of the "Dialectic" follow directly from those of the "Analytic," though there are new points of interest. As in the "Analytic,"

Kant's views are expressed inside a framework that is heavily scholastic. Kant claimed that human beings have an intellectual faculty in addition to the understanding. This additional faculty is reason, and it is equipped with a set of a priori concepts of its own, technically known as ideas of reason. An idea of reason can have no object corresponding to it in sense experience, for the ambition of reason is to arrive at absolute totality in the series of conditions for the empirically given, and in this way to grasp the unconditioned that falls outside experience altogether. However, this ambition can never be realized, and the only proper function for reason in its theoretical capacity is to regulate the operations of the understanding by encouraging it to pursue the search for conditions to the maximum extent that is empirically possible.

THE KNOWING SUBJECT. Kant's handling of the "psychological idea" at the beginning of the main part of the "Dialectic" is exceptionally brilliant. He maintains in the "Analytic" that what he there calls the "I think," or the unity of apperception, is the ultimate condition of experience, in the sense of being the logical subject of experience or the point to which all experience relates. All experience is experience for a subject; whatever thoughts or feelings I have I must be capable of recognizing as *my* thoughts or feelings. But the subject here referred to is not something substantial; it is merely a logical requirement, in that nothing follows about the nature of my soul or self from the fact that I say "I think." So far from being "an abiding and continuing intuition" (the sort of thing Hume vainly sought in the flow of his inner consciousness), for Kant the "representation 'I' . . . [is] simple, and in itself completely empty . . . we cannot even say that this is a concept, but only that it is a bare consciousness which accompanies all concepts. Through this I or he or it (the thing) which thinks, nothing further is represented than a transcendental subject of thoughts = X" (B 404). The same view is expressed in an earlier passage in the *Critique,* where Kant says that "in the synthetic original unity of apperception, I am conscious of myself, not as I appear to myself, nor as I am in myself, but [I am conscious] only that I am. This *representation* is a *thought,* not an *intuition*" (B 157).

REFUTATION OF RATIONAL PSYCHOLOGY. These subtleties are unknown to the exponents of rational psychology, who develop the whole of their teaching around a "single text," which is "I think." From the fact that I am the subject of all my thoughts they infer that I am a thinking substance; from the fact that the "I" of apperception is logically simple they conclude that I am, in substance, simple and not composite. The proposition that "in all the manifold of which I am conscious

I am identical with myself" is taken by them as implying that I am possessed of continuing personal identity. Finally, my distinguishing my own existence as a thinking being from that of other things, including my own body, is put forward as proof that I am really distinct from such things and so could in principle exist in complete independence of them. None of these inferences is justified, for in each case a move is attempted from an analytically true premise to a synthetic conclusion. As Kant remarks, "it would, indeed, be surprising if what in other cases requires so much labour to determine—namely, what, of all that is presented in intuition, is substance, and further, whether this substance can be simple . . .—should be thus given me directly, as if by revelation, in the poorest of all representations" (B 408).

Kant perhaps intended originally to make

the Critique of Pure Reason *the vehicle*

of his entire philosophy, but it was clear

before he completed it that some of his views,

especially those on ethics,

could be only touched on there.

MIND AND BODY. Kant presents the doctrines of rational psychology in his own idiosyncratic way, but anyone who reflects on the theories of Descartes will see that Kant was by no means attacking men of straw. Kant's treatment of the fourth paralogism, "of Ideality," is of special interest in this connection. Descartes inferred from his *cogito* argument that mind and body were separate in substance, which meant that the first could exist apart from the second. Bound up with this was the view that I am immediately aware of myself as a mind, but need to infer the existence of material things, which is in principle open to doubt. A great many philosophers have subscribed to this opinion, but Kant thought he could show it to be definitively false. In order to say that my inner experiences come one before another I need to observe them against a permanent background, and this can only be a background of external objects, for there is nothing permanent in the flow of inner experience. As Kant put it in the second edition, in which he transposed the argument to the discussion of existence in connection with the postulates of empirical thought, "*The mere, but empirically determined, consciousness of my own existence proves the*

existence of objects in space outside me" (B 275). Kant is in no sense a behaviorist; he thinks that empirical self-knowledge is to be achieved through inner sense and declares in one passage that, for empirical purposes, dualism of soul and body must be taken as correct. Yet his commitment to "empirical realism" is quite unambiguous.

THE ANTINOMIES. Of the remaining parts of the "Dialectic," only the sections on the antinomies and on the existence of God can be discussed here. In the "Antinomy of Pure Reason," Kant first sets out a series of pairs of metaphysical doctrines (which he says have to do with cosmology but which are in fact of wider interest). The two doctrines in each pair seem to contradict one another directly. He then produces for each pair what he regards as watertight proofs of both sides of the case, maintaining that if we adopt the dogmatic standpoint assumed without question by the parties to the dispute, we can prove, for example, both that the world has a beginning in time and that it has no beginning in time, both that "causality in accordance with laws of nature is not the only causality" and that "everything in the world takes place solely in accordance with laws of nature." Thus Kant exhibits in systematic form the famous contradictions into which, as he notes, reason precipitates itself when it asks metaphysical questions. Kant is enormously impressed by the discovery of these contradictions, and it is regrettable only that he does not sufficiently discuss their formal character or illustrate them with genuine examples.

The only way to avoid these antinomies, in Kant's opinion, is to adopt his own (critical) point of view and recognize that the world that is the object of our knowledge is a world of appearances, existing only insofar as it is constructed; this solution enables us to dismiss both parties to the dispute in the case of the first two antinomies, and to accept the contentions of both parties in the case of the other two. If the world exists only insofar as it is constructed, it is neither finite nor infinite but indefinitely extensible and so neither has nor lacks a limit in space and time. Equally, if the world is phenomenal we have at least the idea of a world that is not phenomenal; and natural causality can apply without restriction to the first without precluding the application of a different type of causality to the second. This is admittedly only an empty hypothesis so far as theoretical reason is concerned, but Kant argues that it can be converted into something more satisfactory if we take account of the activities of practical (moral) reason.

THE EXISTENCE OF GOD. The fourth antinomy is concerned with God's existence. Kant's full treatment of the subject is not in the section on the antinomies but in that headed "The Ideal of Pure Reason," the *locus classicus* for Kant's criticisms of speculative theology. These criticisms have proved as devastating as those he brought against rational psychology.

Speculative Proofs. There are, Kant argues, only three ways of proving God's existence on the speculative plane. First, we can proceed entirely a priori and maintain that the very idea of God is such that God could not *not* exist; this is the method of the Ontological Argument. Second, we can move from the bare fact that the world exists to the position that God is its ultimate cause, as in the First Cause, or Cosmological, Argument. Finally, we can base our contention on the particular constitution of the world, as in the "physicotheological proof" (the Argument from Design).

If he had published nothing else but the

Groundwork of the Metaphysic on Morals

Kant would be assured a place

in the history of philosophy.

Kant argues that all three types of proof are fallacious. The Ontological Argument fails because it treats existence as if it were a "real predicate," whereas "it is not a concept of something which could be added to the concept of a thing. It is merely the positing of a thing, or of certain determinations, as existing in themselves" (B 626). The First Cause Argument fails on several counts: because it uses the category of cause without realizing that only in the schematized form is the category significant; because it assumes that the only way to avoid an actually infinite causal series in the world is to posit a first cause; finally and most important, because it presupposes the validity of the Ontological Proof, in the step which identifies the "necessary being" or First Cause with God. The Argument from Design makes all these mistakes and some of its own, for even on its own terms it proves only the existence of an architect of the universe, not of a creator, and such an architect would possess remarkable but not infinite powers.

The Moral Proof. In spite of Kant's criticisms of the classical arguments for God's existence, he is neither an atheist nor even a believer in the principle of *credo quia impossibile.* He both believes in God and holds that the belief can be rationally justified. For although speculative theology is, broadly, a tissue of errors, moral theology is perfectly possible. But the moral proof of God's existence differs from the attempted speculative proofs in at least two significant respects. First, it begins neither from a concept nor from a fact about the world, but from an immediately experienced moral situation. The moral agent feels called upon to achieve certain results, in particular to bring about a state of affairs in which happiness is proportioned to virtue, and knows that he cannot do it by his own unaided efforts; insofar as he commits himself to action he shows his belief in a moral author of the universe. Affirmation of God's existence is intimately linked with practice; it is most definitely not the result of mere speculation. Again, a proof like the First Cause Argument claims universal validity; standing as it does on purely intellectual grounds it ought, if cogent, to persuade saint and sinner alike. But the moral proof as Kant states it would not even have meaning to a man who is unconscious of moral obligations; the very word "God," removed from the moral context that gives it life, is almost or quite without significance. Accordingly Kant states that the result of this proof is not objective knowledge but a species of personal conviction, embodying not logical but moral certainty. He adds that "I must not even say '*It is* morally certain that there is a God . . .,' but '*I am* morally certain' " (B 857). In other words, the belief or faith Kant proposes as a replacement for discredited metaphysical knowledge can be neither strictly communicated nor learned from another. It is something that has to be achieved by every man for himself.

Ethics

Kant perhaps intended originally to make the *Critique of Pure Reason* the vehicle of his entire philosophy, but it was clear before he completed it that some of his views, especially those on ethics, could be only touched on there. In the years immediately following its publication he displayed exceptional energy in defending and restating the theories he had already put forth and in extending his philosophy to cover topics he had hitherto not treated, or not treated in detail. By 1788 he had not only published the second, substantially revised edition of the *Critique of Pure Reason,* but had laid the foundations for his ethics in his short but influential *Groundwork of the Metaphysic of Morals* (1785) and had undertaken a more elaborate survey of moral concepts and assumptions in the *Critique of Practical Reason* (1788). He had also, in passing, written his essay *Metaphysical Foundations of Natural Science* (1786), intended as a first step toward a projected but never completed metaphysics of nature. Two years after the *Critique of Practical Reason* he produced yet another substantial work, the *Critique of Judgment,* in which he expressed his views on, among other topics, aesthetics and teleology.

MORAL ACTIONS. If he had published nothing else but the *Groundwork of the Metaphysic of Morals* Kant would be assured a place in the history of philosophy.

Difficult as it is to interpret in some of its details, this work is written with an eloquence, depth of insight, and strength of feeling that make an immediate impact on the reader and put it among the classics of the subject. Kant says that his "sole aim" in the book is "to seek out and establish *the supreme principle of morality*." He wishes to delineate the basic features of the situation in which moral decisions are made, and so to clarify the special character of such decisions.

The situation as he sees it is roughly as follows. Man is a creature who is half sensual, half rational. Sensuous impulses are the determining factor in many of his actions, and the role of reason in these cases is that assigned to it by Hume; it is the slave or servant of the passions. But there is an identifiable class of actions in which reason plays a different part, leading rather than following. This is the class of moral actions. Such actions have the distinguishing feature that they are undertaken not for some ulterior end, but simply because of the principle they embody.

INTENTIONS AND MORAL JUDGMENTS. The moral worth of an action, as Kant puts it (*Grundlegung*, 2d ed., p. 13), lies "not in the purpose to be attained by it, but in the maxim in accordance with which it is decided upon." Whether or not I attain my ends does not depend on me alone, and my actions cannot be pronounced good or bad according to the effects they actually bring about. But I can be praised or blamed for my intentions, and I can, if I choose, make sure that the maxim or subjective principle of my action accords with the requirements of morality. To do this I have only to ask myself the simple question whether I could will that the maxim should become a universal law, governing not merely this particular action of mine, but the actions of all agents similarly circumstanced. For it is a formal property of moral as of scientific judgments, recognized in practice even by the unsophisticated, that they hold without distinction of persons; the result is that an action can be permissible for me only if it is permissible for anyone in my situation.

PRACTICAL REASON. There are difficulties in this position of which Kant seems to have been unaware. In particular, he never asks how I am to decide what is the correct description, and hence the maxim, of my act or proposed act. Nor is it obvious how the theory shows the falsity of Hume's view that "reason alone can never be a motive to any action of the will"—how it can be shown, in Kant's language, that pure reason really is practical. The practical effectiveness of reason is manifested not in the capacity to reflect, which both Kant and Hume allow, but in the power to originate or inhibit action. Kant obviously thinks that the facts of temptation and resistance to temptation, which he sees as ubiquitous in the moral life, have a clear bearing on

the question whether reason really has such a power. Recognition that I ought to follow a certain course of action, whether I want to or not, and that anything that is morally obligatory must also be practically possible, is enough in his view to show that I am not necessarily at the mercy of my desires. In favorable cases, at any rate (Kant pays too little attention to the factors that diminish and sometimes demolish responsibility), I am free to resist my sensuous impulses and to determine my actions by rational considerations alone.

CONSEQUENCES OF THE MORAL LAW. Some commentators have seen Kant as an ethical intuitionist, but this view is clearly mistaken. His "practical reason" is not the faculty of insight into the content of the moral law; it is rather the capacity to act. In determining what the moral law commands, I have initially no other resources at my disposal than the reflection that it must be applied impartially. But in practice this criterion carries others with it. If the moral law applies without distinction of persons, Kant believes it follows that I must treat all human beings as equally entitled to rights under it, and that therefore I must regard them as ends in themselves and never as merely means to my own ends. Further, once I recognize that other people are morally in the same position as I am myself, and that we belong to the same moral community, I recognize both that I can legitimately pursue those of my purposes that do not conflict with the moral law and that I also have a duty to facilitate the like pursuit on the part of my fellows. So though Kant is a formalist in his view of moral reason (as in his view of the theoretical intellect), he sees his ethics as having practical consequences of the first importance. He sets these consequences out in his lectures on ethics and develops them in detail later in his 1797 *Metaphysic of Morals*. To judge him by the *Groundwork* alone, or even by the *Groundwork* and the *Critique of Practical Reason* taken together, is to do less than justice to the scope of his ethical reflection.

MORAL IMPERATIVES. Previous moral philosophies, Kant writes, whether they put their stress on moral sense or on moral reason, have all been vitiated by a failure to recognize the principle of the autonomy of the will. Utilitarianism, for instance, is a heteronomous ethical theory because, according to its supporters, the point of a moral action is to promote an end or purpose beyond the action, the greatest happiness of the greatest number. Kant is not unaware of the importance of ends and purposes in actions: in the *Critique of Practical Reason* he corrects the one-sidedness of the *Groundwork* by discoursing at length on the concept of "good" as well as on that of "duty." But he holds, even so, that consideration of ends cannot be of primary importance for the moral agent, since a moral action is one that is commanded for its own sake, not with a view to some purpose it is expected to bring about. The imperatives of morality command categorically, unlike those of skill or prudence, which have only hypothetical force (*ibid.,* pp. 39–44). A rule of skill or a counsel of prudence bids us take certain steps *if* we wish to attain a certain end—good health or over-all happiness, for example. There is no "if" about a command of morality; it bids me act in a certain way whether I want to or not, and without regard to any result the action may bring about. It represents a course of conduct as unconditionally necessary, not just necessary because it conduces to a certain end.

FREEDOM AND NECESSITY. The concepts of duty, the categorical imperative, the moral law, and the realm of ends (in which we are all at once subjects and lawgivers) are intended by Kant to illuminate the moral situation. But even when we know what that situation is, there are many features of it that remain mysterious. Morality as Kant expounds it involves autonomy of the will, and such autonomy clearly makes no sense except on the supposition of freedom. But how we can think of the will as free and at the same time regard ourselves as subject to the moral law, that is, as under obligation, has still to be explained. To throw light on this question, Kant invokes the concept of the two worlds, the sensible and the intelligible, to which he made appeal in the *Critique of Pure Reason.* Insofar as I exercise the faculty of reason I have to regard myself as belonging to the intelligible world; insofar as I exercise my "lower" faculties I am part of the world of nature, which is known through the senses. Were I a purely rational being, possessed of what Kant sometimes calls a "holy will," all my actions would be in perfect conformity with the principle of autonomy, and the notions of obligation and the moral law would have no meaning for me. They would similarly have no meaning if I were a purely sensuous being, for then everything I did would occur according to natural necessity, and there would be no sense in thinking that things ought to be otherwise. The peculiarities of the human moral situation arise from the fact that men are, or rather must think of themselves as being, at once intelligible and sensible. Because I regard myself as belonging to the intelligible order, I see myself as "under laws which, being independent of nature, are not empirical but have their ground in reason alone" (*ibid.,* p. 109). But I am also a natural being, and those laws therefore present themselves to me in the form of commands that I acknowledge as absolute because I recognize that the intelligible world is the ground of the sensible. We can thus see "how a categorical imperative is possible."

What we cannot see, if Kant is to be believed, is how freedom is possible. "All men think of themselves as having a free will. . . . Moreover, for *purposes of action* the footpath of freedom is the only one on which we can make use of reason in our conduct. Hence to argue freedom away is as impossible for the most abstruse philosophy as it is for the most ordinary human reason" (*ibid.,* pp. 113–115). Yet freedom remains what it is in the *Critique of Pure Reason,* "only an idea whose objective reality is in itself questionable," and there is a prima facie clash between the claim to freedom and the knowledge that everything in nature is determined by natural necessity. Kant seeks to dissolve the antinomy of freedom and necessity by means of two expedients. First, he insists that the idea of freedom required for morals is not a theoretical but a practical idea. Freedom does not need to be established as a metaphysical fact; it is enough that we find it necessary to act on the assumption that freedom is real, since "every being who cannot act except under the idea of freedom is by this alone—from the practical point of view—really free" (*ibid.,* p. 100). The status of the proposition that the will is free is identical with that of the proposition that there is a God. Both are postulates of practical reason—beliefs that we "inevitably" accept; but they are emphatically not items of knowledge in the strict sense of that term. Second, Kant sees no difficulty in our accepting the postulate of freedom, because there is no contradiction in thinking of the will as free. As an object of theoretical scrutiny I must regard myself as a phenomenon; as a moral agent possessed of a will I transfer myself to the intelligible world of noumena. I can be at once under necessity qua phenomenon and free qua noumenon. But the question of how I can be free leads to the extreme limits of practical philosophy. Freedom cannot be explained, for we lack all insight into the intelligible world; the most we can do is make clear why it cannot be explained. The critical philosophy purports to have performed this task.

EPISTEMOLOGY AND ETHICS. Kant advocates a form of nonnaturalist theory in ethics. But neither his ethics nor his theory of knowledge can be fully understood in isolation one from the other. The two together constitute an over-all theory that is not so much a metaphysics as a substitute for a metaphysics: a theory that argues that human insight is strictly limited, but urges that, so far from being regrettable, this testifies to "the wise adaptation of man's cognitive faculties to his practical vocation" (*Critique of Practical Reason and Other Writings,* Beck translation, 1949, p. 247). If we knew more, we might indeed do as we ought, for "God and eternity in their awful majesty would stand unceasingly before our eyes," but we should not then do things as a matter of duty, but rather out of fear or hope. And thus the world would be poorer, for we should lose the opportunity to manifest "good will," the only thing in the world, "or even out of it, which can be taken as good without qualification."

The Critique of Judgment

None of Kant's other writings is as forceful or original as the first two *Critiques* and the *Groundwork*. The *Critique of Judgment* contains some fresh ideas of remarkable power, but it constitutes a series of appendixes or addenda to Kant's earlier work rather than something wholly new. It should really be seen as three or four separate essays whose connecting link is the concept of purpose.

SYSTEM OF SCIENCE. The first essay, the introduction, begins with a pedantic discussion of the status of the power of judgment. It then takes up a problem aired in the appendix to the "Dialectic" in the *Critique of Pure Reason*—the problem of the special assumptions involved in the belief that we can construct a system of scientific laws. If we are to have such a system, Kant argues, we must proceed on the principle that nature is "formally purposive" in respect of empirical laws; that nature is such that we can make sense of it not merely in general, but also in detail. Kant's object is to show that this principle is not a constitutive principle of things, but simply a subjective maxim of judgment.

Judgments of taste, as Kant calls them,

are peculiar in that they not only rest on feeling

but also claim universal validity.

In the *Critique of Pure Reason* (B 670 ff.) Kant argues for what he calls the regulative employment of the ideas of reason: the use of ideas to order empirical inquiries in such a way that we try at once to find greater and greater diversity of form in the material before us and to group different species and subspecies together under ever higher genera. In actual practice we assume that nature will display the unity-in-diversity required for this program to be carried out, but we cannot prove that it will do so as we can prove that whatever falls within experience will conform to the categories. Hence we are concerned not with objective rules, but only with maxims, defined in this connection as "subjective principles which are derived, not from the constitution of an object but from the interest of reason in respect of a certain possible perfection of the knowledge of the object" (B 694).

In the *Critique of Pure Reason* Kant ascribes these maxims to reason. In the *Critique of Judgment,* he assigns them to judgment, in effect the identical doctrine. The difference is accounted for by two facts. First, by the time Kant wrote the *Critique of Judgment,* the term "reason" suggested to him nothing but practical reason.

Second, he had come to think that if the power of judgment is genuinely separate from understanding on the one hand and reason on the other it must have a priori principles of its own. A division within the power of judgment itself, into determinant and reflective activities, had helped to make this last point plausible, at least in the eyes of its author.

AESTHETICS. The "Critique of Aesthetic Judgment," the first major division of the *Critique of Judgment,* uses the term "aesthetic" in what has become its modern sense. The discussion is Kant's contribution to the controversies initiated by Lord Shaftesbury and Francis Hutcheson when they made both moral and aesthetic judgments matters of feeling; Kant rejects this view and also explains why he yet cannot approve of Alexander Gottlieb Baumgarten's attempt to "bring the critical treatment of the beautiful under rational principles, and so to raise its rules to the rank of a science" (B 35, note *a*). Kant needs to show, for the purposes of his general philosophy, that aesthetic judgments are essentially different from moral judgments on the one hand and scientific judgments on the other. This need apart, he had a long-standing independent interest in the subject; in 1764, thirty years before the *Critique of Judgment,* he published an essay on the beautiful and the sublime (*Beobachtung über das Gefühl des Schönen und Erhabenen,* Königsberg). Such an interest may seem surprising in view of the obvious limitations of Kant's own aesthetic experience; he had some feeling for literature, especially for satire, but little or no real knowledge of either painting or music. But what he has in mind in discussing the beautiful is the beauty of nature as much as anything, and his main interest is not in making aesthetic judgments, but in deciding on their logical status.

Judgments of taste, as Kant calls them, are peculiar in that they not only rest on feeling but also claim universal validity. That they rest on feeling seems to him obvious: when I ascribe beauty to an object or scene I do so not because I have observed some special character in it, but because contemplation of its form gives me immediate delight. But it is an entirely disinterested form of delight, quite different from that we feel concerning things that are agreeable, or even things that are good. When we take pleasure in something beautiful we are not desiring to possess it, or indeed taking up any attitude toward its existence. The fact that aesthetic delight is disinterested allows us to think of it as universally shared:

Since the delight is not based on any inclination of the subject (or any other deliberate interest), but the Subject feels himself completely *free* in respect to the liking which he accords to the object, he can find as reason for his delight no personal conditions to which his own subjective self might alone be party. Hence he must regard it as resting on what he may also presuppose in every other person; and therefore he must believe that he has reason for demanding a similar delight from every one. (*Critique of Judgment*, Meredith translation, Sec. 6)

Because they claim universal validity, judgments of taste appear to rest on concepts, but to think that they do is a mistake. The universality attaching to judgments of taste is not objective but subjective; to explain it we must refer to "nothing else than the mental state present in the free play of imagination and understanding (so far as these are in mutual accord, as is requisite for *cognition in general*)" (*ibid.*, Sec. 9). As in the *Critique of Pure Reason*, Kant argues that both imagination and understanding are involved in the apprehension of any spatiotemporal object but that when we simply contemplate any such object aesthetically, no definite concept is adduced; and so the two faculties are in free play. It is the harmony between the faculties in any act of aesthetic contemplation that Kant takes to be universally communicable, and believes to be the basis for the pleasure we feel.

In addition to analyzing judgments about the beautiful, Kant devoted considerable attention in the *Critique of Judgment* to another concept which figured prominently in the aesthetics of his day, that of the sublime. Burke and others had given what was in effect a psychological description of the conditions in which we judge, say, the sight of a mountain range or a storm at sea to be sublime. Kant was all the more anxious to specify more exactly the meaning of such judgments and to establish their transcendental conditions because he was convinced that we here also have to do with a feeling that is held to be universally communicable. The feeling for the sublime, as he explained it, is connected not with the understanding, as is that for the beautiful, but with reason. To put his view somewhat crudely, we are at first abashed by the formlessness of some parts of nature, only to be elevated when we reflect on the utter inadequacy of these objects to measure up to our own ideas, and in particular to our moral ideas. Thus the sublime is not, as might at first sight be supposed, a quality which inheres in natural objects, but a feeling which the contemplation of natural objects provokes in us. It could have no existence for a being totally lacking in culture (a savage might feel fear on observing "thunderclouds piled up the vault of heaven," to use one of Kant's own examples, but could not recognize their sublimity), yet it is not a mere product of culture or social convention. "Rather is it in human nature that its foundations are laid, and, in fact, in that which, at once with common understanding, we may expect everyone to possess and may require of him, namely, a native capacity for the feeling for (practical) ideas, that is, for moral feeling" (*ibid.*, Sec. 29).

In addition to analyzing judgments about the beautiful, Kant devoted considerable attention in the Critique of Judgment *to another concept which figured prominently in the aesthetics of his day, that of the sublime.*

TELEOLOGY. One of Kant's motives for wanting to avoid making beauty an objective characteristic was that he thought such a view would lend force to the Argument from Design, and so encourage the revival of speculative theology. If things could be said to possess beauty in the same sort of way in which they possess weight, it would be a short step to talking about the Great Artificer who made them to delight us. Arguments of the same general kind were still more vividly present to his mind when he came to write the second main section of the *Critique of Judgment*, the "Critique of Teleological Judgment." Indeed, he ended the book with a lengthy section that underlines yet again the shortcomings of "physicotheology" and points up the merits of "ethicotheology."

Before confronting theology directly, Kant embarked on a detailed and penetrating discussion of the nature and use of teleological concepts. The existence of organic bodies, he argues, is something for which we cannot account satisfactorily by the mechanical principles sanctioned by the physical sciences; to deal with organic bodies we must employ a distinct principle, the principle of teleology, which can do justice to the fact that "*an organized natural product is one in which every part is reciprocally both means and end*" (*ibid.*, Sec. 66). Such a principle cannot be used for cognitive purposes in the strict sense; it can be employed only by reflective judgment to guide "our investigation of . . . [organic bodies] by a remote analogy with our own causality according to ends generally, and as a basis for reflection upon their supreme source" (*ibid.*, Sec. 65). Teleology is a concept that occupies an uneasy intermediate position between natural science and theology. We cannot help using it to describe the world about us, yet we cannot assign to it full scientific status. Kant mitigates the austerities of this position by suggesting in his section "The Antinomy of Judgment" that in the end the mechanical and teleological principles stand on the same level, both belonging to reflective judgment. But it is hard to see how this can be made consistent with the doctrines of the *Critique of Pure Reason,* which ascribes constitutive force to the concepts of "pure physics," or even with the distinction in the *Critique of Judgment* itself between explaining something and merely "making an estimate" of it. We use the categories to explain, but can employ teleological concepts only for the purpose of making an estimate. Kant's underlying attitude to the whole question is revealed most clearly in the passage at the end of Sec. 68 of the *Critique of Judgment,* where he asks why teleology "does not . . . form a special part of theoretical natural science, but is relegated to theology by way of a propaedeutic or transition." He answers:

This is done in order to keep the study of the mechanical aspect of nature in close adherence to what we are able so to subject to our observation or experiment that we could ourselves produce it like nature, or at least produce it according to similar laws. For we have complete insight only into what we can make and accomplish according to our conceptions. But to effect by means of art a presentation similar to organization, as an intrinsic end of nature, infinitely surpasses all our powers. (Meredith translation)

It would be interesting to know if Kant would say the same were he alive today.

Other Philosophical Writings

After publishing the three *Critiques*—Kant was 66 when the *Critique of Judgment* appeared—he continued to publish essays and treatises on a wide variety of philosophical subjects. Most of these are in fact contributions to applied philosophy, for he took the view that scientific inquiries and practical activities alike stand in need of philosophical foundations. In many cases he attempts to supply these foundations by means of the principles established in his main works—hence the general shape of his philosophies of science and religion, and of his political philosophy. It would, however, be wrong to see these as no more than mechanical applications of general Kantian conclusions. For although Kant was deeply and indeed unduly devoted to system, he also had a wide and in some cases penetrating knowledge of many different branches of learning and human activity, and there are few philosophical topics that he touchs without illuminating; in fact, Kant gave the names still in use to most of the branches of applied philosophy he took up.

PHILOSOPHY OF NATURE. In the preface to his *Metaphysical Foundations of Natural Science,* Kant argues that the very concept of scientific knowledge is such that we can use the term properly only when dealing with truths that are both apodictically certain and systematically connected. A discipline that is thoroughly and entirely empirical cannot comply with these requirements; hence Kant pronounces chemistry to be no better than "systematic art or experimental doctrine." But the situation is different in physics. Although Kant was as firmly persuaded as any empiricist that detailed knowledge of the physical world could be arrived at only by observation and experiment, he was also sure that physics has an unshakable a priori basis that makes it worthy of the name of science. It owes this, in Kant's judgment, to the fact that its fundamental concepts are capable of mathematical expression, as those of chemistry are not, and to the close connection of these concepts with the categories, the basic concepts of rational thought. The main object of the *Metaphysical Foundations* is to demonstrate the second of these points by means of an examination of the idea of matter. Starting from what professes to be an empirically derived definition of matter, "that which is capable of movement in space," Kant proceeds to a deduction of its main properties in the light of the table of categories. The result is, in effect, a rereading or reinterpretation of then-current physical theory in which all the main doctrines of Newton find their place, but which is distinctive in that the atomism professed by many physicists of the day is rejected in favor of a dynamical theory of matter resembling that of Leibniz. Kant argues in the *Critique of Pure Reason* that only mistaken metaphysics leads scientists to think they must accept the notions of absolutely homogeneous matter and absolutely empty space. In the *Metaphysical Foundations* he works out an alternative conception of matter in terms of moving forces, omnipresent but varying in degree, and puts it forward as both theoretically satisfactory and consistent with the empirical findings.

It is difficult not to see in these views the beginnings of *Naturphilosophie* as it was to be practiced by Schelling and Hegel, the more so if we read the *Metaphysical Foundations* in the light of Kant's further treatment of the subject in the notes published as *Opus Postumum.* But in 1786 at any rate Kant was still far from committing the extravagances of the speculative philosophers of nature. For one thing, he was both more knowledgeable about and more respectful of the actual achievements of physical scientists than were his romantic successors, doubtless because, unlike them, he was something of a physical scientist himself. For another, the lesson he drew from his 1786 inquiries was not how much physical knowledge we can arrive at by the use of pure reason, but how little. To establish the metaphysical foundations of natural science was a useful task, but it was in no sense a substitute for empirical investigation. Despite these differences from *Naturphilosophie*, it must be allowed that *Metaphysical Foundations* testifies, in name as well as in content, to the extent of Kant's commitment to rationalism (his theory of science could scarcely be further from Hume's) and to the way in which he was at least tempted by the constructivism favored by some of his younger contemporaries.

Kant treats religion as essentially,

if not quite exclusively,

a matter of purity of heart—

thus dispensing with speculative theology altogether

and assigning a meager importance

to the institutional side of religion.

PHILOSOPHY OF HISTORY. Although Kant was quite unaware of the problems about historical knowledge and explanation with which philosophers since Wilhelm Dilthey have dealt, he made an important and characteristic contribution to speculative philosophy of history in his essay "Idee zu einer allgemeinen Geschichte in Weltbürgerlicher Absicht" ("Idea of a Universal History from a Cosmopolitan Point of View," *Berliner Monatsschrift*, November 1784, 386–410). Observing that the actions of men, when looked at individually, add up to nothing significant, he suggests that nature or providence may be pursuing through these actions a long-term plan of which the agents are unaware. To see what the plan may be we have to reflect on two points: first, that nature would scarcely have implanted capacities in human beings if she had not meant them to be developed, and second, that many human intellectual capacities (for example, the talent for invention) are such that they cannot be satisfactorily developed in the lifetime of a single individual. The development of such capacities belongs to the history of the species as a whole. Kant suggests that the hidden plan of nature in history may well be to provide conditions in which such capacities are more and more developed, so that men move from barbarism to culture and thus convert "a social union originating in pathological needs into a moral whole." The mechanism of the process lies in what Kant calls the "unsocial socia-

bility" of human beings—the fact that they need each other's society and help and are nevertheless by nature individualists and egotists—which insures that men develop their talents to the maximum extent, if only to get the better of their fellows, and at the same time necessitates man's eventually arriving at a form of civil society that allows for peaceful rivalry under a strict rule of law. But such a "republican" constitution would be of no value unless it had its counterpart in the international sphere, for the struggles of individuals against one another are paralleled by the struggles of states. We must accordingly conclude that the final purpose of nature in history is to produce an international society consisting of a league of nations, in which war is outlawed and the way is finally clear for peaceful competition between individuals and nations.

The difficulty with this as with other lines of Kant's thought is to understand its relation to empirical inquiries. From what Kant says it seems clear that he intended "philosophical" history to be an alternative to history of the everyday kind, not a substitute for it. Nor did he pretend to be writing philosophical history himself; his essay merely puts forward the idea of or offers a "clue" to, such a history, leaving it to nature to produce someone really capable of making sense of the historical facts as Kepler and Newton made sense of physical facts. It is difficult to see, even so, how Kant could have possessed the idea of history as meaningful without knowing the facts, or alternatively how he could know that the idea throws light on the facts when it was discovered without any reference to them.

PHILOSOPHY OF LAW AND POLITICS. Kant's views about law and politics, like his philosophy of history, are obviously tied up with his ethics. Kant holds that legal obligations are a subspecies of moral obligation; thus the rational will, and neither force nor the commands of God, is the basis of the law. His standpoint in philosophy of law is thus broadly liberal, though his attitude on many particular legal issues is far from liberal as the term is now understood. He holds, for instance, that if one of the partners to a marriage runs away or takes another partner, "the other is entitled, at any time, and incontestably, to bring such a one back to the former relation, as if that person were a thing" (*Metaphysic of Morals*, Sec. 25). He is notorious as a strong supporter of the retributive theory of punishment and an uncompromising advocate of the death penalty for murder. The explanation of his harshness in these matters is to be found in his legalistic approach to ethics, which leaves little room for sympathy or forgiveness.

In politics also Kant combines a fundamentally liberal attitude with specific views that are conservative, if not reactionary. Following Rousseau, he attempts to explain political authority partly in terms of the general will and partly in terms of the original contract. Insofar as he insists on the contract, which he interprets not as a historical fact but as a regulative idea, he is advocating a version of political liberalism which lays particular emphasis on the rule of law; insofar as he grounds supreme political authority in the will of the people as a whole, he is obviously flirting with more radical doctrines—from whose consequences he is quick to draw back. An admirer of the French Revolution, he nevertheless denies that the subjects of the most ill-governed states have any right of rebellion against their rulers. And though the mixed constitution he favors is one in which citizens can make their voices heard through their representatives, he is for confining the franchise to persons who possess "independence or self-sufficiency," thus excluding from "active" citizenship (according to Sec. 46 of the *Metaphysic of Morals*) apprentices, servants, woodcutters, plowmen, and, surprisingly, resident tutors, as well as "all women." The truth is, however, that Kant's political theorizing was done in a vacuum; in his day there was no real chance for a Prussian professor of philosophy to influence political events.

PHILOSOPHY OF RELIGION. In the sphere of religion the views of a professor of philosophy could be influential, and Kant's views on this subject were certainly provocative. He treats religion as essentially, if not quite exclusively, a matter of purity of heart—thus dispensing with speculative theology altogether and assigning a meager importance to the institutional side of religion. To adopt the religious attitude, as Kant sees it, is to look on duties as if they were divine commands. But this, he explains, is only to insist on the unconditioned character, the ineluctability, of moral obligation; it is a way of representing morality, not a way of going beyond it. Knowledge of the supersensible, as Kant thought he had shown in the *Critique of Pure Reason,* is impossible; and although moral practice carries with it belief in God and a future life, the whole meaning and force of that belief is to be found in a persistence in moral endeavor and a determination to repair moral shortcomings. The pure religion of morality needs no dogma apart from these two fundamental articles of belief, which are accessible immediately to the simplest intelligence. Still less has it any need of the external trappings of religion—priests, ceremonies, and the like—although the body of believers must think of themselves as belonging to a church, universal but invisible, and the practices of visible churches sometimes serve to stimulate or strengthen moral effort, in a way which is useful but not indispensable.

The religion of morality is on this account a religion of all good men. Despite this, Kant took a particular interest in Christianity, which he saw as at least approximating true religion though corrupted by the presence of extraneous elements derived from Judaism. His book *Religion Within the Bounds of Mere Reason* (1793) is in effect a commentary on and a reinterpretation of Christian doctrine and practice, written with the object of making this conclusion clear. In this reinterpretation the doctrine of original sin is transformed into a doctrine of the radical evil in human nature, which is the positive source of moral failing; and that of the Incarnation is replaced by an account of the triumph of the good principle over the bad, the part of the historical Jesus being taken by an idea of reason, that of man in his moral perfection. Kant sets aside the historical elements in Christianity as having no importance in themselves: Whatever is true in the religion must be derivable from moral reason. To think of the uttering of religious formulas or the performance of formal services to God as having a value of their own is to fall into the grossest superstition. It is perhaps scarcely surprising that these sentiments, whose attraction for youth can be seen in Hegel's *Jugendschriften,* should have struck the Prussian authorities as subversive and led the orthodox King Frederick William II to demand that Kant refrain from further pronouncements on religion. Though Kant, in his letter acceding to this demand, protested that he had no thought of criticizing Christianity in writing his book, it is hard to take his protest quite seriously, for he had certainly meant to suggest that many of the beliefs and actions of practicing Christians were without value, if not positively immoral. Indeed, the originality and continuing interest of his work on religion connect directly with that fact.

THE *OPUS POSTUMUM.* In the last years of his life—from about 1795 on—Kant was engaged in the composition of what would have been a substantial philosophical work; the preparatory notes for it have been published as *Opus Postumum.* Its original title was "Transition from Metaphysical Foundations of Natural Science to Physics," and in its original form its object was to carry further the process, begun in 1786 in the *Metaphysical Foundations of Natural Science,* of finding an a priori basis for physics. No longer content with the formal structure for which he had argued earlier, Kant thought he had to show that some of the particular laws of nature could be known in advance of experience. The broadest types of physical possibility were determined by the constitution of the human mind; it was this, for example, which explained the presence in nature of just so many fundamental forces, and even of an omnipresent ether. These speculations about the foundations of physics led Kant to epistemological considerations of a wider kind. The whole subject of the relation of the form of experience to its matter, with the question how far the form shapes the matter, arose in his mind anew, doubtless because of the criticisms directed against the formalist position of the *Critique of Pure Reason* by self-professed disciples like Fichte. In 1799 Kant dissociated himself publicly from the views expressed in Fichte's *Wissenschaftslehre,* according to which the subject of knowledge "posits" the objective world and so, in a way, creates nature. Yet the evidence of the *Opus Postumum* is that at this time, or shortly thereafter, Kant was toying with similar ideas and was even using some of the same vocabulary. It is perhaps fortunate for Kant's reputation that he was not able to get his final philosophical thoughts into publishable form.

BIBLIOGRAPHY

Works by Kant

Collected Works

Gesammelte Schriften, 23 vols., edited under the supervision of the Berlin Academy of Sciences. Berlin, 1902–1955. The standard collected edition of Kant's writings; contains his correspondence and hitherto unpublished notes (including those for the *Opus Postumum*) as well as everything he published. Further volumes covering Kant's lectures are in preparation.

Kants Werke, 10 vols., Ernst Cassirer, ed. Berlin, 1912–1922. Contains the published works, with full indications of the contents of the original editions.

Philosophische Bibliothek series. Leipzig and Hamburg, 1904—. Separately bound editions of all the treatises listed below under the head "Main Treatises," with useful introductions; also includes *Kleinere Schriften zur Geschichtsphilosophie, Ethik, und Politik.*

Main Treatises

Allgemeine Naturgeschichte und Theorie des Himmels. Königsberg and Leipzig, 1755. English translation by W. Hastie in *Kant's Cosmogony* (Glasgow, 1900).

Der einzig mögliche Beweisgrund zu einer Demonstration des Daseins Gottes. Königsberg, 1763. No serviceable translation.

Träume eines Geistersehers, erläutert durch Träume der Metaphysik. Königsberg, 1766. Translated into English as *Dreams of Spirit-Seer* by E. F. Goerwitz (New York, 1900).

De Mundi Sensibilis atque Intelligibilis Forma et Principiis Dissertatio. Königsberg, 1770. Translated into English in Handyside's *Kant's Inaugural Dissertation and Early Writings on Space* (Chicago, 1929).

Kritik der reinen Vernunft. Riga, 1781; 2d ed., Riga, 1787. The first edition is customarily referred to as A, the second edition as B. The most useful modern edition is by Raymond Schmidt (Leipzig, 1926). There are English translations by Francis Heywood (London, 1838); J. M. D. Meiklejohn (London, 1854), F. Max Müller (2 vols., London, 1881), and N. Kemp Smith (London, 1929). Kemp Smith's version is the fullest and most reliable.

Prolegomena zu einer jeden künftigen Metaphysik die als Wissenschaft auftreten können. Riga, 1783. English translations are available by John Richardson (*Prolegomena to Future Metaphysics,* in *Metaphys-*

ical Works of the Celebrated Immanual Kant, London, 1836), J. P. Mahaffy and J. H. Bernard (*The Prolegomena,* London, 1872), E. B. Bax (*Kant's Prolegomena and Metaphysical Foundations of Natural Science,* London, 1883), Paul Carus (*Prolegomena to Any Future Metaphysics,* Chicago, 1902), L. W. Beck (same title as Carus', New York, 1951), and P. G. Lucas (same title as Carus', Manchester, 1953). The Beck and Lucas translations are much the best.

Grundlegung zur Metaphysik der Sitten. Riga, 1785; 2d ed., Riga, 1786. Translated into English by T. K. Abbott as *Fundamental Principles of the Metaphysic of Morals* (in *Kant's Critique of Practical Reason and Other Works on the Theory of Ethics,* London, 1873), by L. W. Beck as *Foundations of the Metaphysics of Morals* (in *Critique of Practical Reason and Other Writings in Moral Philosophy,* Chicago, 1949), by H. J. Paton (from the 2d edition) as *The Moral Law, or Kant's Groundwork of the Metaphysic of Morals* (London, 1948). All three versions are good; Paton's is the most elegant. Quotations in the text of this article are from Paton's translation; the citations to page numbers in the 2d edition are taken from Paton's marginal notation.

Metaphysische Anfangsgründe der Naturwissenschaft. Riga, 1786. Translated into English by E. B. Bax (in *Kant's Prolegomena and Metaphysical Foundations of Natural Science,* London, 1883).

Kritik der praktischen Vernunft. Riga, 1788. Translated into English by T. K. Abbott, and also by L. W. Beck, as *Critique of Practical Reason* in the books cited for the *Grundlegung zur Metaphysik der Sitten.* The Beck translation is accurate but somewhat clumsy; it has been published separately (New York, 1956).

Kritik der Urteilskraft. Berlin and Liebau, 1790. Translated into English by J. H. Bernard as *Kritik of Judgement* (London, 1892; later reprinted as *Critique of Judgement*). Also translated by J. C. Meredith in two parts, *Critique of Aesthetic Judgement* (Oxford, 1911) and *Critique of Teleological Judgement* (Oxford, 1928), which were reissued together as *The Critique of Judgement* (Oxford, 1952). Both the Bernard and the Meredith versions are of poor quality; Meredith's is slightly the better. Kant wrote an introduction to the *Kritik* which he discarded; it is available as *Erste Einleitung in die Kritik der Urteilskraft,* Vol. V, *Kants Werke* (Berlin, 1922), and in English translation by H. Kabir as *Immanuel Kant on Philosophy in General* (Calcutta, 1935).

Die Religion innerhalb der Grenzen der blossen Vernunft. First part published separately, Berlin, 1792; published complete at Königsberg, 1793. Translated into English by John Richardson as *Religion Within the Sphere of Naked Reason* (in *Essays and Treatises,* London, 1798), by J. W. Semple as *Religion Within the Boundary of Pure Reason* (Edinburgh, 1838), T. M. Greene and H. H. Hudson as *Religion Within the Limits of Reason Alone* (Chicago, 1934; 2d ed., with new matter by J. R. Silber, New York, 1960). The 1960 edition (Greene-Hudson-Silber), is the best.

Zum ewigen Frieden: ein philosophischer Entwurf. Königsberg, 1795. The two best English translations are L. W. Beck's *Perpetual Peace* (in *Critique of Practical Reason and Other Writings in Moral Philosophy,* Chicago, 1949; separately bound, New York, 1957) and C. J. Friedrich's *Inevitable Peace* (New Haven, 1948).

Metaphysik der Sitten, Part I, *Metaphysische Anfangsgründe der Rechtslehre;* Part II, *Metaphysische Anfangsgründe der Tugendlehre.* Separately bound, Königsberg, 1797. Part I translated into English by W. Hastie as *Kant's Philosophy of Law* (Edinburgh, 1887). Part II translated into English by James Ellington as *Metaphysical Principles of Virtue* (Indianapolis, 1964) and by Mary Gregor as *The Doctrine of Virtue* (New York, 1964).

Anthropologie in pragmatischer Hinsicht. Königsberg, 1798. No English translation.

Kant on History. Indianapolis, 1963. Translations by L. W. Beck, R. E. Anchor, and E. L. Fackenheim; contains Kant's minor essays on philosophy of history.

Eine Vorlesung über Ethik, edited from student's notes by P. Menzer. Berlin, 1924. Translated into English by Louis Infield as *Lectures on Ethics* (London, 1930).

Works on Kant

Life

The main sources for Kant's life, apart from his letters, are three memoirs published in Königsberg in 1804: L. E. Borowski's *Darstellung des Lebens und Characters Immanuel Kants;* R. B. Jachmann's *Immanuel Kant, geschildert in Briefen an einen Freund;* and E. A. C. Wasianski's *Immanuel Kant in seinen letzten Lebensjahren.* Wasianski's memoir is extensively used in Thomas De Quincey's "The Last Days of Kant" (*Works,* Vol. XII). See also Ernst Cassirer's *Kants Leben und Lehre* (Berlin, 1921), and for a useful short life Karl Vorländer's *Immanuel Kants Leben* (Leipzig, 1911).

Commentaries

Rudolf Eisler's *Kantlexicon* (Berlin, 1930) and Heinrich Ratke's *Systematisches Handlexicon zu Kants Kritik der reinen Vernunft* (Leipzig, 1929) are valuable aids to the Kantian student. The periodical *Kantstudien* has published many important contributions to Kantian scholarship and discussion.

For commentaries on the *Critique of Pure Reason,* see Hans Vaihinger, *Kommentar zur Kritik der reinen Vernunft,* 2 vols. (Stuttgart, 1881–1892), which covers the opening sections only; N. Kemp Smith, *A Commentary to Kant's Critique of Pure Reason* (London, 1918; rev. ed., 1923), which is strongly influenced by Vaihinger's "patchwork" theory; H. J. Paton, *Kant's Metaphysic of Experience,* 2 vols. (London, 1936), which covers the first half only and is sharply critical of Kemp Smith; A. C. Ewing, *A Short Commentary on Kant's Critique of Pure Reason* (London, 1938); T. D. Weldon, *Kant's Critique of Pure Reason* (Oxford, 1945; 2d ed., 1958).

On the theory of knowledge see also H. A. Prichard, *Kant's Theory of Knowledge* (Oxford, 1909); A. C. Ewing, *Kant's Treatment of Causality* (London, 1924); W. H. Walsh, *Reason and Experience* (Oxford, 1947); Graham Bird, *Kant's Theory of Knowledge* (London, 1962); R. P. Wolff, *Kant's Theory of Mental Activity* (Cambridge, 1963).

For commentaries on the *Critique of Practical Reason* and other works on ethics, see L. W. Beck, *A Commentary on Kant's Critique of Practical Reason* (Chicago, 1960), a good source; H. J. Paton, *The Categorical Imperative* (London, 1947), a detailed commentary on the *Grundlegung;* W. D. Ross, *Kant's Ethical Theory* (Oxford, 1954); A. R. C. Duncan, *Practical Reason and Morality* (Edinburgh, 1957); M. J. Gregor, *Laws of Freedom* (Oxford, 1963), which expounds the *Metaphysic of Morals;* P. A. Schilpp, *Kant's Pre-Critical Ethics* (Evanston, Ill., 1938); A. E. Teale, *Kantian Ethics* (London, 1951).

For commentaries on the *Critique of Judgment,* see Konrad Marc-Wogau, *Vier Studien zu Kants Kritik der Urteilskraft* (Uppsala, Sweden, 1938); H. W. Cassirer, *A Commentary on Kant's Critique of Judgment* (London, 1938).

Commentaries on other aspects of Kant's thought are also available. On the precritical writings, see Giorgio Tonelli, *Elementi metafisici e metodologici in Kant precritico* (Turin, 1959). On Kant's philosophy of religion, see C. C. J. Webb, *Kant's Philosophy of Religion* (Oxford, 1926) and F. E. England, *Kant's Conception of God* (London, 1929). On Kant's philosophy of history, see Klaus Weyand, *Kants Geschichtsphilosophie* (Cologne, 1964). On Kant as a scientist, see Erich Adickes, *Kant als Naturforscher,* 2 vols. (Berlin, 1924–

1925). On the *Opus Postumum,* see Erich Adickes, *Kants Opus Postumum dargestelt und beurteilt* (Berlin, 1920).

General Studies

S. Körner, *Kant* (Harmondsworth, 1955) is the best general introduction; see also G. J. Warnock's chapter in D. J. O'Connor, ed., *A Critical History of Western Philosophy* (New York, 1964).

Edward Caird, *The Critical Philosophy of Kant,* 2 vols. (Glasgow, 1889), criticizes Kant from the Hegelian position. Martin Heidegger, *Kant und das Problem der Metaphysik* (Bonn, 1929) examines Kant as an "ontologist." H. J. de Vleeschauwer, *La Déduction transcendentale dans l'oeuvre de Kant,* 3 vols. (Antwerp, 1934–1937), presents an exhaustive survey of Kant's writings on the problem; de Vleeschauwer offers a one-volume summary in *L'Évolution de la pensée kantienne* (Paris, 1939), which has been translated into English by A. R. C. Duncan as *The Development of Kantian Thought* (London, 1962). Gottfried Martin, *Immanuel Kant, Ontologie und Wissenschaftstheorie* (Cologne, 1951), translated into English by P. G. Lucas as *Kant's Metaphysics and Theory of Science* (Manchester, 1955), is influenced but not dominated by Heidegger. Richard Kroner, *Kants Weltanschauung* (Tübingen, 1914), translated into English by J. E. Smith as *Kant's Weltanschauung* (Chicago, 1956), stresses Kant's emphasis on the practical. R. Daval, *La Métaphysique de Kant* (Paris, 1951), presents "schematism" as the key idea in Kant's thought.

— W. H. WALSH

KANT, IMMANUEL (UPDATE)

Immanuel Kant continues to exercise significant influence on philosophical developments, and his philosophy continues to generate an ever-growing body of

---

Special areas of interest are the essential role of imagination in perception and experience, the distinction between inner sense and apperception, and the relation between subjective or psychological and objective or logical grounds of knowledge.

---

scholarly literature. Work on Kant has progressed in two main directions. Central doctrines of the *Critique of Pure Reason* have been reconstructed, examined, and revised in the light of current philosophical concerns and standards; and the focus of scholarship has widened to include aspects and parts of Kant's work hitherto neglected, especially in his practical philosophy and aesthetics. Both in style and substance there has been a considerable convergence between the Anglo-American ("analytic") and the German ("Continental") interpretation of Kant.

Critique of Pure Reason

Further advances in interpreting the first *Critique* have occurred in three related areas: the nature and validity of Kant's overall argumentative procedure, with special emphasis on the deduction of the categories; the meaning and function of transcendental idealism and the associated distinction between things in themselves and appearances; and the role of mental activity in Kant's theory of experience.

The deduction of the categories, in which Kant sought to identify and justify the basic concepts underlying all our experience and its objects, has become the center of major interpretive efforts. Stimulated by the neo-Kantian analytic metaphysics of Peter F. Strawson, philosophers have attempted to distill a type of argument from Kant's text that refutes skeptical doubts about the reality of the external world and other minds by showing how the skeptical challenge tacitly and unavoidably assumes the truth of the very assumptions it sets out to deny—the reality of external objects and other minds.

While the force of such "transcendental arguments" remains controversial, the analytic-reconstructive approach to the deduction of the categories has also resulted in more text-based interpretations that reflect the whole spectrum of Kant scholarship. Readings of the deduction start either from the assumption of experience and proceed from there analytically to the necessary conditions of experiences (the categories and the principles based on them) or take as their starting point some conception of self-consciousness or self-knowledge, either understood in Cartesian purity (a priori unity of apperception) or in phenomenological embeddedness (empirical self-consciousness), and argue from there to the synthetic conditions for the very possibility of such self-awareness. A key insight shared by many interpreters is the mutual requirement of object knowledge and self-knowledge in Kant.

In interpretations of Kant's transcendental idealism a major alternative has opened up between those scholars that see things in themselves and appearances as different aspects of one and the same things ("two-aspect view") and those that regard the two as so many different sets of objects ("two-object view"). On the former view appearances are genuine objects. On the latter view they are representations. While the textual evidence is not conclusive for either view, the two-aspect theory has found many adherents because of its ontological economy and its avoidance of a phenomenalist reduction of things to representations.

The central role of human subjectivity in the deduction of the categories and in the defense of transcendental idealism has led to a renewed interest in Kant's philosophy of mind. Kant's philosophical psychology is more and more seen as an integral part of his theoretical philosophy. Special areas of interest are the essential role of imagination in perception and experience, the distinction between inner sense and apperception, and the relation between subjective or psychological and objective or logical grounds of knowledge. While no one advocates the derivation of the logical from the psychological in the manner of a reductive psychologism, the exact function of specifically psychological considerations in transcendental philosophy remains controversial. There is a minimal consensus that the self involved in the grounding of experience is distinct from the transcendent, noumenal self of the metaphysics of the soul, so forcefully rejected by Kant in the transcendental dialectic of the first *Critique,* and equally to be distinguished from the empirical self known through inner experience. Interpreters typically stress the formal and functional rather than material and substantial sense of this "third," transcendental self in Kant.

Other Works

Important new work on other parts of Kant's philosophy has occurred in three main areas: practical philosophy, especially ethics; the *Critique of Judgment,* especially its aesthetics; and philosophy of science.

Scholarship on Kant's ethics has widened beyond the limited concern with the principle of morality (categorical imperative) to include other aspects of Kant's ethics as well as the position of Kant's moral theory within his practical philosophy as a whole and within the wider architectonic of the critical philosophy. A main inspiration of the work on Kant's ethics has been the neo-Kantian political philosophy of John Rawls, who seeks to extract from Kant's formal approach to morality procedural guidelines for the ideal construction of the principles of social conduct. Increased attention has been paid to Kant's account of agency, the possible grounding of the categorical imperative in a generic conception of practical rationality, and the key features of Kant's moral psychology—including the theory of motivation, the role of moral judgment, and the function of subjective principles of action (maxims). The move beyond the traditional confines of Kant's foundational ethical writings extends to his philosophy of law and doctrine of virtues as contained in the *Metaphysics of Morals,* his philosophy of religion, and his political philosophy and philosophy of history contained in a number of smaller pieces written in a more popular vein. The picture of Kant's practical philosophy that emerges from these reconstructions, revisions, and rediscoveries is that of a highly complex theory that is well able to respond to the charges and challenges posed by utilitarianism and communitarianism.

In work on the *Critique of Judgment* the standard emphasis on Kant's theory of aesthetic judgments has been widened considerably in recognition of the role of the third *Critique* as a synthesis of theoretical and practical philosophy in a comprehensive philosophy of human cultural development. Much of the scholarship on Kant's philosophy of the natural sciences has focused on the *Opus Postumum* and its attempts to specify the transition from an a priori theory of material nature to physics proper.

[See also *Communitarianism; Descartes, René; Rawls, John; Skepticism; Strawson, Peter F.*]

BIBLIOGRAPHY

Works by Kant

The Cambridge Edition of the Works of Immanuel Kant, 14 vols., edited by P. Guyer and A. Wood. Cambridge, 1992–. Once completed, this edition will contain all of Kant's published works, plus substantial selections from his lectures on logic and metaphysics, his handwritten literary remains, and his correspondence—all in English translation. The following volumes have been published so far: *Theoretical Philosophy, 1755–1770*, edited by M. Walford with R. Meerbote; *Lectures on Logic*, edited by M. Young; *Opus Postumum*, edited by E. Förster.

Works on Kant

Allison, H. E. *Kant's Transcendental Idealism*. New Haven, 1983.
——. *Kant's Theory of Freedom*. Cambridge, 1990. Allison's books are sympathetic accounts of the main doctrines of the first *Critique* and Kant's ethics, respectively.
Ameriks, K. *Kant's Theory of Mind*. Oxford, 1982. Emphasizes the metaphysical dimension of Kant's philosophical psychology.
Aquila, R. E. *Representational Mind*. Indianapolis, 1983.
——. *Matter in Mind*. Indianapolis, 1989. Aquila's books are phenomenological readings of the transcendental aesthetics and the deduction, respectively.
Friedman, M. *Kant and the Exact Sciences*. Cambridge, MA, 1992. Special emphasis on the *Opus Postumum*.
Guyer, P. *Kant and the Claims of Taste*. Cambridge, MA, 1979.
——. *Kant and the Claims of Knowledge*. Cambridge, MA, 1987.
——. *Kant and the Experience of Freedom*. Cambridge, MA, 1993. Guyer's three books are critical accounts of Kant's aesthetics, his epistemology, and his theory of culture, respectively.
——, ed. *The Cambridge Companion to Kant*. Cambridge, MA, 1992. Fourteen essays on the major aspects of Kant's work by the leading scholars in the field; includes extensive bibliography.
Henrich, D. *The Unity of Reason*. Cambridge, MA, 1994. Essays on Kant's theoretical and practical philosophy, including the influential study "Identity and Objectivity" (1976).
Herman, B. *The Practice of Moral Judgment*. Cambridge, MA, 1993. Argues for a complex conception of moral judgment and moral personality in Kant.
Kersting, W. *Wohlgeordnete Freiheit: Immanuel Kants Rechts- und Staatsphilosophie*. Frankfurt, 1993. A comprehensive account of Kant's legal and political philosophy.
Kitcher, P. *Kant's Transcendental Psychology*. Oxford, 1990. Reads Kant as a precursor to contemporary functionalist philosophy of mind.
Makkreel, R. A. *Imagination and Interpretation in Kant*. Chicago, 1990. Stresses the hermeneutical dimension of Kant's critical philosophy.
O'Neill, O. *Constructions of Reason*. Cambridge, 1989. Places Kant's ethics in the context of his theories of reason, agency, and freedom.
Prauss, G. *Erscheinung bei Kant*. Berlin, 1971.
——. *Kant und das Problem der Dinge an sich*. Bonn, 1974.
——. *Kant über Freiheit als Autonomie*. Frankfurt, 1983. Prauss's three books are critical studies on things in themselves, the constitution of experience, and the relation between moral autonomy and the spontaneity of the mind in Kant, respectively.
Strawson, P. F. *The Bounds of Sense: An Essay on Kant's Critique of Pure Reason*. London, 1966. The classic analytic commentary on the core doctrines of the first *Critique*.
Sullivan, R. *Immanuel Kant's Moral Theory*. Cambridge, 1989. A sympathetic account of Kant's ethics and other practical philosophy.
Walker, R., ed. *Kant on Pure Reason*. Oxford, 1982. Includes the two classic pieces: B. Stroud, "Transcendental Arguments" (1968), and D. Henrich, "The Proof-Structure of Kant's Transcendental Deduction" (1969).
Yovel, Y. *Kant and the Philosophy of History*. Princeton, NJ, 1980. Examines the relation among morality, history, and religion.

— GÜNTER ZÖLLER

KIERKEGAARD, SØREN AABYE

Søren Aabye Kierkegaard (1813–1855), Danish philosopher and religious thinker, frequently considered the first important existentialist, was the youngest son of Mikaël Pederson Kierkegaard and Anne Sørensdatter Lund, born when his father was 56 years old and his mother was 44. His early childhood was spent in the close company of his father, who insisted on high standards of performance in Latin and Greek, inculcated an anxiety-ridden pietist devotion of a deeply emotional kind, and awakened his son's imagination by continually acting out stories and scenes. Kierkegaard thus felt early the demand that life should be at once intellectually satisfying, dramatic, and an arena for devotion. Confronted with the Hegelian system at the University of Copenhagen, he reacted strongly against it. It could not supply what he needed—"a truth which is true *for me*, to find *the idea for which I can live and die*" (*Journal*, Aug. 1, 1835). Nor could contemporary Danish Lutheranism provide this. He ceased to practice his religion and embarked on a life of pleasure, spending heavily on food, drink, and clothes. The melancholy which originated in his childhood continued to haunt him, however, and was increased by his father's confiding in him his own sense of guilt for having somehow sinned deeply against God. For Kierkegaard, the question of how a man can be rescued from despair was consequently intensified. He resolved to return to his studies and become a pastor. He finished his thesis *On the Concept of Irony* (1841) and preached his first sermon. He became engaged to the 17-year-old Regine Olsen. But as he became aware of the uniqueness of the vocation which he felt within himself, he found himself

The epitaph that Kierkegaard composed for himself was simply "That individual." (Corbis/Bettmann)

conformism and the inward and personal character of Christian faith. He died shortly after refusing to receive the sacrament from a pastor. "Pastors are royal officials; royal officials have nothing to do with Christianity."

Kierkegaard's biography is necessarily more relevant to his thought than is the case with most philosophers, for he himself saw philosophical enquiry neither as the construction of systems nor as the analysis of concepts, but as the expression of an individual existence. The epitaph which he composed for himself was simply, "That individual." From his own point of view, any verdict on his thought can only be the expression of the critic's own existence, not a critical assessment which could stand or fall according to some objective, impersonal standard. Hence all attempts at an objective evaluation of his thought were condemned by him in advance. He predicted and feared that he would fall into the hands of the professors. Moreover, the initial difficulty created by Kierkegaard's subjectivism is compounded by his style and manner of composition. Although he attacked Hegel, he inherited a large part of Hegel's vocabulary. Passages of great and glittering brilliance tend to alternate with paragraphs of turgid jargon. Both types of writing often prove inimical to clarity of expression. A great many of his books were written for highly specific purposes, and there is no clear thread of development in them. One device of Kierkegaard's must be given special mention: he issued several of his books under pseudonyms and used different pseudonyms so that he could, under one name, ostensibly attack his own work already published under some other name. His reason for doing this was precisely to avoid giving the appearance of attempting to construct a single, consistent, systematic edifice of thought. Systematic thought, especially the Hegelian system, was one of his principal targets.

THE SYSTEM, THE INDIVIDUAL, AND CHOICE. In Hegel's philosophical system, or rather in his successive construction of systems, the linked development of freedom and of reason is a logical one. Out of the most basic and abstract of concepts, Being and Nothing, there is developed first the concept of Becoming and the various phases of Becoming in which the Absolute Idea realizes itself during the course of human history. Each phase of history is the expression of a conceptual scheme, in which the gradual articulation of the concepts leads to a realization of their inadequacies and contradictions, so that the scheme is replaced by another higher and more adequate one, until finally Absolute Knowledge emerges and the whole historical process is comprehended as a single logical unfolding. It is this comprehension itself that is the culmination of the process, and this point was effectively reached for Hegel

unable either to share his life with anyone else or to live out the conventional role of a Lutheran pastor. For him, breaking off his engagement was a decisive step in implementing his vocation. (This cosmic view of the breach does not appear to have been shared by his young fiancée, whose natural hurt pride and rejected affection led to her marriage to Fritz Schlegel, afterwards governor of the Danish West Indies.) From then on Kierkegaard lived a withdrawn life as an author, although he did involve himself in two major public controversies. The first followed his denunciation of the low standards of the popular Copenhagen satirical paper *The Corsair. The Corsair* in turn caricatured Kierkegaard unmercifully. The second sprang from his contempt for the established Danish Lutheran church, and especially for its primate, Bishop Mynster, who died in early 1854. When Mynster's about-to-be-appointed successor, Professor Hans Martensen, declared that Mynster had been "a witness to the truth," Kierkegaard delivered a series of bitter attacks on the church in the name of the incompatibility he saw between established ecclesiastical in his own philosophy. Thus, in *The Science of Logic* he was able to write that he was setting out not merely his own thoughts, but the thoughts of God—the idea of God being simply an anticipation of the Hegelian conception of the Absolute.

Kierkegaard issued several of his books

under pseudonyms and used different pseudonyms

so that he could, under one name,

ostensibly attack his own work

already published under some other name.

In the Hegelian view, both moral and religious development are simply phases in this total process. In *The Phenomenology of Mind*, Hegel described the moral individualism of the eighteenth century, for example, in terms of a logical progress from the hedonistic project of a universal pursuit of private pleasure, through the romantic idealization of "the noble soul," to the Kantian scheme of duty and the categorical imperative, trying to show how each was brought into being by the contradiction developed by its predecessor. In terms of the Hegelian view, an individual is essentially a representative of his age. His personal and religious views must give expression to his role in the total moral and religious development of mankind—a role which is imposed upon him by his place in the historical scheme. He can at best express, but not transcend, his age.

For Kierkegaard, Hegel dissolved the concreteness of individual existence into abstractions characteristic of the realm of concepts. Any particular conceptual scheme represents not an actuality but a possibility. Whether a given individual realizes this possibility, and so endows it with existence, depends upon the individual and not upon the concepts. What the individual does depends not upon what he understands, but upon what he wills. Kierkegaard invokes both Aristotle and Kant in support of his contention that Hegel illegitimately assimilated concepts to individual existence; he praises in particular the manner of Kant's refutation of the Ontological Argument. But Kierkegaard, in his doctrine of the primacy of the will is, in fact, more reminiscent of Tertullian or Pascal.

Kierkegaard buttressed his doctrine of the will with his view of the ultimacy of undetermined choice. He maintained that the individual constitutes himself as the individual he is through his choice of one mode of existence rather than another. Christianity is not a phase in the total development of man's religious and moral ideas; it is a matter of choosing to accept or to reject God's Word. But choice is not restricted to this supreme decision; it is the core of all human existence. The Hegelian view that human existence develops logically within and through conceptual schemes is not merely an intellectual error. It is an attempt to disguise the true facts, to cast off the responsibility for choice, and to find an alibi for one's choices. Moreover, speculative system building falsifies human existence in another way, for it suggests that although those who lived prior to the construction of the system may have had to make do with a partial and inadequate view of reality, the arrival of the final system provides an absolute viewpoint. But according to Kierkegaard, such a viewpoint must be an illusion. Human existence is irremediably finite; its standpoint is incorrigibly partial and limited. To suppose otherwise is to yield to a temptation to pride; it is to attempt to put oneself in the place of God.

This conclusion is only a special case of Kierkegaard's general doctrine that his intellectual opponents are guilty fundamentally not of fallacies and mistakes, but of moral inadequacy. That Kierkegaard should have thought this not only reflects his unfortunate personality; it was a necessary consequence of his doctrine of choice. Another necessary consequence was his mode of authorship. On his own grounds, he cannot hope to produce pure intellectual conviction in his readers; all that he can do is to confront them with choices. Hence he should not try to present a single position. This explains Kierkegaard's method of expounding incompatible points of view in different books and using different pseudonyms for works with different standpoints. The author must conceal himself; his approach must be indirect. As an individual, he must testify to his chosen truth. Yet, as an author he cannot conceal the act of choice. From these views, it is apparent that Kierkegaard utilized a special concept of choice.

The essence of the Kierkegaardian concept of choice is that it is criterionless. On Kierkegaard's view, if criteria determine what I choose, it is not I who make the choice; hence the choice must be undetermined. Suppose, however, that I do invoke criteria in order to make my choice. Then all that has happened is that I have chosen the criteria. And if in turn I try to justify my selection of criteria by an appeal to logically cogent considerations, then I have in turn chosen the criteria in the light of which these considerations appear logically cogent. First principles at least must be chosen without the aid of criteria, simply in virtue of the fact that they are first. Thus, logical principles, or relationships between concepts, can in no sense determine a person's intellectual positions; for it is his choices that determine the authority such principles have for him. Is man then not even limited by such principles as those which enjoin consistency and prohibit contradiction? Apparently not. For even paradox challenges the intellect in such a way as to be a possible object of choice. The paradoxes which Kierkegaard has in mind at this point in his argument are those posed by the demands of ethics and religion. He is prepared to concede that in fields such as mathematics the ordinary procedures of reason are legitimate. But there are no objective standards where human existence is involved.

THE AESTHETIC AND THE ETHICAL. In *Either/Or: A Fragment of Life* (1843), the doctrine of choice is put to work in relation to a distinction between two ways of life, the ethical and the aesthetic. The aesthetic point of view is that of a sophisticated and romantic hedonism. The enemies of the aesthetic standpoint are not only pain but also, and above all, boredom. As Kierkegaard wrote of the protagonist of aestheticism in *Purify Your Hearts!*, "See him in his season of pleasure: did he not crave for one pleasure after another, variety his watchword?" The protagonist tried to realize every possibility, and no possibility furnishes him with more than a momentary actuality. "Every mood, every thought, good or bad, cheerful or sad, you pursue to its utmost limit, yet in such a way that this comes to pass *in abstracto* rather than *in concreto*; in such a way that the pursuit itself is little more than a mood. . . ." But just because boredom is always to be guarded against, so its threat is perpetual. In the end, the search for novelty leads to the threshold of despair.

By contrast, the ethical constitutes the sphere of duty, of universal rules, of unconditional demands and tasks. For the man in the ethical stage "the chief thing is, not whether one can count on one's fingers how many duties one has, but that a man has once felt the intensity of duty in such a way that the consciousness of it is for him the assurance of the eternal validity of his being" (*Either/Or*, II, p. 223). It is important to note how intensity of feeling enters into Kierkegaard's definition of the ethical stage. He thought that what his own age most notably lacked was passion; hence one must not be deceived by the Kantian overtones of his discussions of duty. Kierkegaard's categorical imperative is felt rather than reasoned. He is an heir of such romantics as the Schlegel brothers in his attitude toward feeling, just as he is the heir of Hegel in his mode of argument. Kierkegaard is a constant reminder of the fact that those who most loudly proclaim their own uniqueness are most likely to have derived their ideas from authors whom they consciously reject.

In *Either/Or* the argument between the ethical and the aesthetic is presented by two rival characters: an older man puts the case for the ethical, a younger for the aesthetic. The reader, as we should expect, is allegedly left to make his own choice. But is he? The description of the two alternatives seems heavily weighted in favor of the ethical. The difficulty is that Kierkegaard wished *both* to maintain that there could be no objective criterion for the decision between the two alternatives, *and* to show that the ethical was superior to the aesthetic. Indeed, one difference between the ethical and the aesthetic is that in the ethical stage the role of choice is acknowledged. Kierkegaard frames this criticism of the man who adheres to the aesthetic: "He has not chosen himself; like Narcissus he has fallen in love with himself. Such a situation has certainly ended not infrequently in suicide." Remarks like this suggest that in fact Kierkegaard thinks that the aesthetic fails on its own terms; but if he were to admit this, his concept of interested choice would no longer apply at this critical point. In one passage Kierkegaard asserts that if one chooses with sufficient passion, the passion will correct whatever was wrong with the choice. Here his inconsistency is explicit. According to his doctrine of choice, there can be no criterion of "correct" or "incorrect," but according to the values of his submerged romanticism, the criterion of both choice and truth is intensity of feeling.

> *Kierkegaard is a constant reminder*
>
> *of the fact that those who most loudly proclaim*
>
> *their own uniqueness are most likely*
>
> *to have derived their ideas*
>
> *from authors whom they consciously reject.*

This inconsistency is not resolved; rather it is canonized in the thesis that truth is subjectivity. On the one hand Kierkegaard wants to define truth in terms of the way in which it is apprehended; on the other he wants to define it in terms of what it is that is apprehended. When inconsistency results, he is all too apt to christen this inconsistency "paradox" and treat its appearance as the crowning glory of his argument.

Kierkegaard is not consistent, however, even in his treatment of inconsistency. For he sometimes seems to imply that if the ethical is forced to its limits, contradiction results, and one is therefore forced to pass from the ethical to the religious. "As soon as sin enters the discussion, ethics fails . . . for repentance is the supreme expression of ethics, but as such contains the most profound ethical contradiction" (*Fear and Trembling*, p. 147, footnote). What is this but Hegelianism of the purest kind?

Kierkegaard describes the transition from the ethical to the religious differently at different periods. In *Either/Or* the ethical sometimes seems to include the religious. By the time the *Concluding Unscientific Postscript* (1846) was written, the religious seems to have absorbed the ethical. In *Fear and Trembling* (1843), the passage from the ethical to the religious is even more striking than that from the aesthetic to the ethical. One of the heroes of this transition is Abraham. In demanding from Abraham the sacrifice of Isaac, God demands something that, from the standpoint of the ethical, is absolutely forbidden, a transgression of duty. Abraham must make the leap to faith, accept the absurd. He must concur in a "suspension of the ethical." At such a point the individual has to make a criterionless choice. General and universal rules cannot aid him here; it is as an individual that he has to choose. However, according to Kierkegaard, there are certain key experiences on the margins of the ethical and the religious through which one may come to censure oneself as an individual. One such experience is the despair that Kierkegaard describes in *The Sickness Unto Death;* another is the generalized fear and anxiety that is characterized in *The Concept of Dread* (1844). Despair and dread point in the same direction. The experience of each forces the individual to realize that he confronts a void and that he is, in fact, responsible for his own sick and sinful condition. In the state of despair he is brought to recognize that what he despairs of are not the contingent facts (such as the loss of a loved one) that he claims to be the objects of his despair; the individual despairs of himself, and to despair of oneself is to see oneself confronting an emptiness that cannot be filled by aesthetic pleasure or ethical rule-following. Moreover, it is in order to become conscious that one has brought oneself to this point. In analyzing despair, we recognize guilt; so too with dread. Kierkegaard contrasts the fear that has a specific and identifiable object with the dread that is objectless; or rather he identifies the fear which is a fear of nothing in particular as a fear of Nothing. (The reification of negatives into noun phrases is typically Hegelian.) In the experience of dread I become conscious of my bad will as something for which I am responsible, and yet which I did not originate. Original sin is seen as a doctrine deduced from the analysis of experience.

In these works of Kierkegaard it is plain that the existentialist philosophy of choice is in some danger of being submerged in the romantic philosophy of feeling. But the testimony of feeling serves as a propaedeutic to the encounter with Christianity.

CHRISTIANITY. Kierkegaard regarded his own central task as the explanation of what is involved in being a Christian. Apart from Christianity, the only religions he discusses are those of the Greeks and the Jews, and those only as a foil to Christianity. At first sight, Kierkegaard's doctrines of choice and of truth stand in an uneasy relationship to his allegiance to Christianity. For surely Christianity has always claimed to be objectively true, independently of anyone's subjective commitment, and Kierkegaard recognized this. "Not only does it [Christian revelation] express something which man has not given to himself, but something which would never have entered any man's mind even as a wisp or an idea, or under any other name one likes to give to it" (*Journal*, 1839).

If what we believe depends on the believer's own ultimate choice of rational criteria, then surely all beliefs have an equal moment, or rather equal lack of moment, for claiming objective truth. Kierkegaard, however, tried to evade this conclusion and continued to argue both that ultimate choice is criterionless and that one choice can be more correct than another.

Unfortunately, Kierkegaard never considered the issues raised by religions other than Christianity; for it would clarify our view of his position considerably if we could know what he would have said about an account of Islam or Buddhism that was logically parallel to his account of Christianity, in that it made their claims rest on a doctrine of ultimate choice. But the choices that Kierkegaard discusses are always those that might arise for an educated Dane of the nineteenth century. The foil to Christianity is not another religion, but secular philosophy.

This particular contrast is most fully elucidated in the *Philosophical Fragments* (1844), in which Kierkegaard begins from the paradox posed by Socrates in Plato's *Meno*. How can one come to know anything? For either one already knows what one is to come to know, or one does not. But in the former case, since one already knows, one cannot come to know; and in the latter case, how can one possibly recognize what one discovers as being the object of one's quest for knowledge? Plato's answer to this paradox is that in coming to know, we do not discover truths of which we had hitherto been totally ignorant, but truths of which we were once aware (when the soul pre-existed the body), but which we had forgotten. These truths lie dormant within us, and to teach is to elicit such truths. So Socrates makes the slave boy in the *Meno* aware that he knows geometrical truths which he did not know that he knew.

Suppose, however, Kierkegaard asks, that the truth is not within us already. It will then be the case that we are strangers to the truth, to whom the truth must be brought from outside. It will follow that the moment at which we learn the truth and the teacher from whom we learn the truth will not stand in a merely accidental relationship to us. On the Socratic view, one may learn geometry from this teacher or that, but the question of the truth of a geometric theorem is independent of the question from whom we learned it. Not so, on Kierkegaard's view. There are two possible conceptions of the truth that we must choose between, and the Socratic view represents only one alternative. It is important to note that in the *Philosophical Fragments* (1844) Kierkegaard does not say, as he says elsewhere, that one view of the truth is appropriate in matters of geometrical truth, but another is appropriate in matters concerning moral and religious truth. He speaks of two alternative views of the truth, which apparently cover every kind of subject matter, although for the rest of the book he discusses only religion.

Kierkegaard's doctrine of choice

raises at least two fundamental questions:

Are there criterionless choices?

And is it by such choices that we either

can or do arrive at our criteria of true belief?

Following Kierkegaard's preferred view of the truth, if the truth is not within us, it must be brought to us by a teacher. The teacher must transform us from beings who do not know the truth to beings who are acquainted with it. It is impossible to conceive any greater transformation, and only God could bring it about. But how could God become the teacher of man? If He appeared as He is, the effect on man would be to overawe him so that he could not possibly learn what God has to teach. (Kierkegaard cites the story of the prince in the fairy tale who could not appear to the swine girl as a prince because she would not have come to love him for himself.) Thus, Kierkegaard argues that if God is to be the teacher of man, He must appear in the form of a man, and more specifically, in the form of a servant. From the standpoint of human reason, the idea that God should come as a teacher in human form is an impossible paradox which reason cannot hope to comprehend within its own categories. But according to Kierkegaard, it is in encountering this paradox that reason becomes aware of the objective character of what it encounters.

To be a Christian is thus to subordinate one's reason to the authority of a revelation that is given in paradoxical form. The Christian lives before God by faith alone. His awareness of God is always an awareness of his own infinite distance from God. Christianity initially manifests itself in outward forms, and Kierkegaard reproaches Luther for having tried to reduce Christianity to a pure inwardness—a project that has ended in its opposite, the replacement of inwardness by an ecclesiastical worldliness. Nonetheless, an inward suffering before God is the heart of Christianity.

As previously mentioned, Kierkegaard saw his own age as lacking in passion. The Greeks and the medieval monastics had true passion. The modern age lacks it, and because of this, it lacks a capacity for paradox, which is the passion of thought.

CRITICISMS OF KIERKEGAARD. Kierkegaard used Friedrich Trendelenburg's exposition of Aristotle's logic to criticize Hegel. But he never took the question of the nature of contradiction seriously, and hence he never explained the difference, if any, between paradox (in his sense of the word) and mere inconsistency. But without such a clarification, the notion is fatally unclear. The lack of clarity is increased by Kierkegaard's failure at times to distinguish between philosophy, as such, and Hegelianism. Kierkegaard sometimes seems to have thought that any philosophy that claims objectivity must consist solely of tautologies (*Papirer* III, B, 177).

His doctrine of choice raises at least two fundamental questions: Are there criterionless choices? And is it by such choices that we either can or do arrive at our criteria of true belief? Actual cases of criterionless choice usually seem in some way to be special cases. Either they are trivial, random selections (as of a ticket in a lottery) or they arise from conflicts of duties in which each alternative seems equally weighted. But none of these are choices of criteria. Such choices arise precisely at the point at which we are not presented with objective criteria. How do we arrive at such criteria? They appear to be internally connected with the subject matter of the relevant beliefs and judgment. Therefore we cannot choose our ultimate criteria in mathematics or physics. But what about morals and religion? Can one choose to consider the gratuitous infliction of pain a morally neutral activity? We are strongly inclined to say that an affirmative answer would indicate that the word "morally" had not been understood. But what is certain is that Kierkegaard's fundamental positions must remain doubtful until some series of questions such as this has been systematically considered. Kierkegaard himself never tried to ask them.

BIBLIOGRAPHY

Works by Kierkegaard

Texts

Samlede Vaerker, 2d ed., A. B. Drachmann, J. L. Heiberg, and H. O. Lange, eds., 14 vols. Copenhagen, 1920–1931.
Papirer, P. A. Heiberg, V. Kuhr, and E. Torsting, eds., 20 vols. Copenhagen, 1909–1948.

Texts in English Translation

The following listing is in order of original date of publication.
Either/Or, 2 vols. Vol. 1, translated by D. F. Swenson and L. M. Swenson. Princeton, 1941. Vol. II, translated by W. Lowrie. Princeton, 1944.
Fear and Trembling, translated by R. Payne. London, 1939. Also translated by W. Lowrie. Princeton, 1941.
Repetition: An Essay in Experimental Psychology, translated by W. Lowrie. Princeton, 1941.
Philosophical Fragments: Or, A Fragment of Philosophy, translated by D. F. Swenson. Princeton, 1936.
The Concept of Dread, translated by W. Lowrie. London, 1944.
Stages on Life's Way, translated by W. Lowrie. Princeton, 1940.
Concluding Unscientific Postscript, translated by D. F. Swenson and W. Lowrie. Princeton, 1941.
The Sickness Unto Death, translated by W. Lowrie. Princeton, 1941.
The Point of View, translated by W. Lowrie. Princeton, 1941.
Training in Christianity, translated by W. Lowrie. Princeton, 1944.
Purify Your Hearts!, translated by A. S. Aldworth and W. S. Fine. London, 1937.
For Self-examination, translated by W. Lowrie. Princeton, 1941.
The Present Age, translated by A. Dru and W. Lowrie. London, 1940.
Christian Discourses, translated by W. Lowrie. London, 1939.
Works of Love, translated by D. F. Swenson. Princeton, 1946.
The Attack Upon "Christendom," translated by W. Lowrie. Princeton, 1944.
The Journals of Søren Kierkegaard: A Selection, edited and translated by A. Dru. Oxford, 1938.

Works on Kierkegaard

Anthologies, Biography, and Critical Studies

Bretall, R., *A Kierkegaard Anthology.* Princeton, 1946.
Geismar, E. O., *Lectures on the Religious Thought of S. Kierkegaard.* Minneapolis, 1937.
Hohlenberg, J. E., *Søren Kierkegaard.* London, 1954.
Jolivet, R., *Introduction to Kierkegaard.* London, 1950.
Lowrie, W., *Kierkegaard.* New York, 1938.
Lowrie, W., *A Short Life of Kierkegaard.* Princeton, 1942.
Swenson, D. F., *Something About Kierkegaard.* Minneapolis, 1941.
Wahl, J. *Études Kierkegaardiennes.* Paris, 1938.

Additional Background

Barrett, W., *Irrational Man.* New York, 1958.
Blackham, H. J., *Six Existentialist Thinkers.* New York, 1952.
Collins, J., *The Existentialists. A Critical Study.* Chicago, 1952.
Grene, M., *Introduction to Existentialism.* Chicago, 1959.
Shestov, L., *Athènes et Jérusalem.* Paris, 1938.

— ALASDAIR MACINTYRE

KIERKEGAARD, SØREN A. (UPDATE)

Søren A. Kierkegaard has been the subject of sharply rising scholarly interest in recent years. In addition to several important works devoted to reexamining Kierkegaard's relation to Hegel, and numerous specialized treatments of key themes and problems in the authorship, newer studies have explored the significance of Kierkegaard's thought from literary, political, and historical viewpoints.

M. Jamie Ferreira offers a compelling refutation of the popular but mistaken assumption that Kierkegaard viewed ethical and religious choice as criterionless and hence immune to critical appraisal.

Niels Thulstrup (1967) traces the development of Kierkegaard's critical engagement with Hegel from 1835 to the conclusion of the pseudonymous authorship in 1846. Thulstrup carefully delineates the main sources of Kierkegaard's knowledge of Hegelian philosophy. This is an invaluable service, considering that much of what Kierkegaard knew about the German philosopher was actually gleaned from secondary sources. Of special interest are the Danish Hegelians, Heiberg and Martensen, and the anti-Hegelians, Sibbern and Møller. Thulstrup also examines the influence of important German writers such as Erdmann, Fichte, Schelling, Trendelenburg, Marheinecke, and Werder. The notable tendency in this work to read Hegel through a Kierkegaardian lens leads the author to conclude that the two "have nothing in common as thinkers." However, this conclusion has been challenged by other commentators who claim to find deeper parallels in their thought.

Several such parallels are noted by Mark C. Taylor (1980). Taylor points out, for instance, that both thinkers see the spiritlessness of modernity as the chief obstacle to selfhood and that both attempt to recover spirit through a process of "aesthetic education." For Hegel, however, spiritlessness represents a form of self-alienation that can be overcome only by a reconciliation of self and other, a mediation of the individual's personal and social life, while for Kierkegaard, the threat to spirit lies in the modern tendency to objectify and systematize, to dissolve the distinction between the individual and "the crowd." Taylor argues that Kierkegaard's exclusive emphasis on the individual is ultimately self-negating, since the self is never merely the self but bears a necessary and internal relation to the other. Hegel's relational conception of selfhood is thus shown to be more adequate and more comprehensive than Kierkegaard's, which "necessarily passes over into its opposite—Hegelian spirit" (p. 272). There remains a genuine question, however, about whether Kierkegaard's critique of "the crowd" precludes the possibility of a genuine human community in which individual responsibility is preserved.

Stephen N. Dunning (1985) goes even further than Taylor, suggesting that a relational conception of selfhood is implicit in the dialectical structure of Kierkegaard's writings. Dunning argues that the solitude of the self is "always a moment in a development that embraces interpersonal relations that can be contradictory (the aesthetic stage), reciprocal (the ethical stage), or paradoxically both incommunicable and reciprocal (the religious stage)" (pp. 248–49). According to this reading the *Postscript* describes a religious dialectic that culminates in a paradoxical unity of the self as both "other to itself (in sin) and restored to itself by God" (p. 249), and at the same time related to the entire community of Christians by a deep bond of sympathy. In this way, the theory of stages confirms the Hegelian insight that the solitary self is incomprehensible apart from the relational structures that give it meaning. It has been noted, however, that the formal similarities between Kierkegaardian and Hegelian dialectic may mask important conceptual differences noted by Thulstrup and Taylor.

Three studies of Kierkegaard's moral and religious philosophy deserve special mention. The first is Gregor Malantschuk's excellent study (1968). Working mainly from the journals, Malantschuk shows that the authorship is governed by a qualitative dialectic, which is aimed at illuminating the subjective dimensions of human existence, while the later polemical writings make use of a quantitative dialectic, which invokes the visible degradation of Christ as a judgment on Christendom. The dialectical method is thus seen to be the golden thread that runs through all of Kierkegaard's writings and places the individual works in the larger context of his avowed purpose as a religious author.

C. Stephen Evans's study of the *Fragments* and *Postscript* (1983) is widely recognized as one of the best general introductions to the Climacus writings available in any language. Though the book is written for the "ordinary" reader rather than the specialist—there is no critical engagement with the secondary literature—students and scholars alike have found it immensely useful for its coherent presentation of the main themes in Kierkegaard's religious philosophy, including his complex

use of irony and humor in connection with the theory of indirect communication. The clarity of Evans's exposition is unsurpassed, even by his 1992 book, which returns to many of the issues addressed in the earlier work.

M. Jamie Ferreira (1991) explores one of the most difficult conceptual problems in the authorship: the nature of religious conversion. Challenging volitionalist and antivolitionalist accounts of the Kierkegaardian leap, Ferreira reconceptualizes the transition to faith as a "reorienting, transforming, shift in perspective" (p. 57). Central to this account is the concept of surrender, which is explicated in terms of the imaginative activities of suspension and engagement. Based on this analysis, Ferreira offers a compelling refutation of the popular but mistaken assumption that Kierkegaard viewed ethical and religious choice as criterionless and hence immune to critical appraisal. Her analysis suggests rather that the more wholeheartedly one chooses, the more likely one is to discover whether one has made the wrong choice. On this reading passionate engagement is not meant to guarantee that one will continue in a choice no matter what, but it does ensure that one will experience more fully what is implied by a choice. In this way passionate engagement is seen to facilitate the possibility of critical appraisal.

Louis Mackey (1971) uses the tools of literary criticism to explore the complex relation between the literary and philosophical dimensions of Kierkegaard's authorship. Mackey argues that even the most philosophical of Kierkegaard's books, the *Fragments* and *Postscript,* call into question the very nature of the philosophical enterprise. His use of literary devices, intended to create a poetic indirection, always leave the reader somewhere between assertion and irony. Mackey goes on to make a more general point about the relation between philosophy and poetry, observing that "all humane philosophy is a poetic and for that reason an indirect communication" (p. 295). Indeed, the philosophers of Western tradition have in this sense, he claims, "always been poetic philosophers" (p. 295). This theme is developed further in Mackey (1986), which attempts to situate Kierkegaard in relation to current trends in deconstructionist thought and literary practice.

Bruce Kirmmse (1990) traces the political, economic, and social history of Denmark from 1780 to 1850, giving us a detailed picture of the cultural milieu in which Kierkegaard lived and wrote. Focusing on the boundaries between the public and the private, between politics and religion, Kirmmse lays a foundation for understanding the connection between Kierkegaard's critique of society and his attack on the established church. The exposition is facilitated by a discussion of Kierkegaard's important religious writings, which are frequently overlooked in major surveys of his thought. Until recently Kierkegaard's social and political views had received scant attention in the secondary literature. Other notable discussions can be found in chapters 8 and 9 of Alastair Hannay (1982) and in Merold Westphal (1987).

[See also Hegel, Georg Wilhelm Friedrich.]

BIBLIOGRAPHY

Dunning, S. N. *Kierkegaard's Dialectic of Inwardness: A Structural Analysis of the Theory of Stages.* Princeton, NJ, 1985.

Evans, C. S. *Kierkegaard's "Fragments" and "Postscript": The Religious Philosophy of Johannes Climacus.* Atlantic Highlands, NJ, 1983.

———. *Passionate Reason: Making Sense of Kierkegaard's "Philosophical Fragments."* Bloomington. IN, 1992.

Ferreira, M. J. *Transforming Vision: Imagination and Will in Kierkegaardian Faith.* Oxford, 1991.

Hannay, A. *Kierkegaard.* London, 1982.

Kirmmse, B. H. *Kierkegaard in Golden Age Denmark.* Bloomington, IN, 1990. Contains an extensive scholarly bibliography.

Mackey, L. *Kierkegaard: A Kind of Poet.* Philadelphia, 1971.

———. *Points of View: Readings of Kierkegaard.* Tallahassee, FL, 1986.

Malantschuk, G. *Dialektik og Eksistens hos Søren Kierkegaard* [1968]. Translated by H. V. Hong and E. H. Hong as *Kierkegaard's Thought.* Princeton, NJ, 1971.

Taylor, M. C. *Journeys to Selfhood: Hegel and Kierkegaard.* Berkeley, 1980.

Thulstrup, N. *Kierkegaards forhold til Hegel.* Copenhagen, 1967. Translated by G. L. Stengren as *Kierkegaard's Relation to Hegel.* Princeton, NJ, 1980.

Westphal, M. *Kierkegaard's Critique of Reason and Society.* Macon, GA, 1987.

— STEVEN M. EMMANUEL

KNOWLEDGE AND MODALITY

The modalities have played a central role in discussions of a priori knowledge largely through the influence of Immanuel Kant ([1781] 1965), who maintained that

(1)   all knowledge of necessary truths is a priori; and

(2)   all a priori knowledge is of necessary truths.

Saul Kripke (1971, 1980) has challenged the Kantian account by arguing that some necessary truths are known a posteriori and some contingent truths are known a priori. A cogent assessment of the controversy requires some preliminary clarification.

The distinction between a priori and a posteriori knowledge is epistemic. S knows a priori that p just in case S knows that p and S's justification for believing that p is independent of experience. The distinction between necessary and contingent propositions is metaphysical. A necessarily true (false) proposition is one that is true (false) but cannot be false (true). Anthony

Quinton (1963–64), R. G. Swinburne (1975), and others have defended the Kantian account by defining the a priori in terms of the necessary. Such definitions beg the substantive philosophical issue in question.

When discussing knowledge of modality, one must take into account the following distinctions: (A) S knows the general modal status of p just in case S knows that p is necessary (necessarily true or necessarily false) or that p is contingent; (B) S knows the specific modal status of p just in case S knows that p is necessarily true or S knows that p is contingently true or S knows that p is necessarily false or S knows that p is contingently false; and (C) S knows the truth value of p just in case S knows that p is true or S knows that p is false.

Utilizing these distinctions, three different readings of (1) can be discerned:

(1A)   If p is a necessary truth and S knows that p is necessary, then S knows a priori that p is necessary.

(1B)   If p is a necessary truth and S knows that p is necessarily true, then S knows a priori that p is necessarily true.

(1C)   If p is a necessary truth and S knows that p is true, then S knows a priori that p is true.

Kant's defense of (1) is based on the premise that experience teaches us what is the case but not what must be the case. This premise supports (1A) but not (1B) or (IC). For it does not rule out a posteriori knowledge of the truth value of necessary propositions. Yet Kant goes on to argue that knowledge of the truth value of mathematical propositions is a priori since such propositions are necessary. This argument presupposes (1C). But from the fact that S knows a priori that p is necessary, it does not follow that S knows a priori that p is true. Hence, Kant's argument overlooks the distinction between knowledge of general modal status and knowledge of truth value.

The distinction between a priori and

a posteriori knowledge is epistemic.

Kripke's argument against (1) involves a related oversight. He maintains that (a) if P is an identity statement involving rigid designators or a statement asserting that an object has an essential property, then one knows a priori that if P then necessarily P. Since (b) one knows that P by empirical investigation, Kripke concludes (c) one knows a posteriori that necessarily P. Kripke's argument, if sound, establishes that knowledge of the specific modal status of some necessary propositions is a posteriori. This result does not contravene (1A), which is the principle Kant defends. Kripke's claim to the contrary overlooks the distinction between knowledge of general modal status and knowledge of specific modal status. From the fact that S knows a posteriori that p is necessarily true, it does not follow that S knows a posteriori that p is necessary. Kripke's (b), however, does contravene (1C), which Kant does not defend but presupposes.

Reading (1A) has not gone unchallenged. Philip Kitcher (1980) argues that even if knowledge of the general modal status of propositions is not based on experiential evidence, it does not follow that such knowledge is a priori, since it might still depend on experience. Albert Casullo (1988) argues that the Kantian claim that a posteriori knowledge is limited to the actual world overlooks the fact that much of our practical and scientific knowledge goes beyond the actual world.

Kripke also argues that some contingent truths are known a priori. His examples are based on the observation that a definite description can be employed to fix the reference, as opposed to give the meaning, of a term. Consider someone who employs the definition description 'the length of S at t_0' to fix the reference of the expression 'one meter'. Kripke maintains that this person knows, without further empirical investigation, that S is one meter long at t_0. Yet the statement is contingent, since 'one meter' rigidly designates the length that is in fact the length of S at t_0 but, under certain conditions, S would have had a different length at t_0. In reply, Alvin Plantinga (1974) and Keith Donnellan (1979) contend that, without empirical investigation, the reference fixer knows that the sentence 'S is one meter long at t_0' expresses a truth but not the truth that it expresses.

[See also Epistemology; Knowledge, A Priori; Kripke, Saul Aaron; Meaning; Reference.]

BIBLIOGRAPHY

Casullo, A. "Kripke on the A Priori and the Necessary," Analysis, Vol. 37 (1977), 152–59.

———. "Necessity, Certainty, and the A Priori," Canadian Journal of Philosophy, Vol. 18 (1988), 43–66.

Donnellan, K. "The Contingent A Priori and Rigid Designators," in P. French, T. Uehling, and H. Wettstein, eds., Contemporary Perspectives in the Philosophy of Language (Minneapolis, 1979), 45–60.

Kant, I. Critique of Pure Reason [1781]. Translated by N. K. Smith. New York, 1965.

Kitcher, P. "Apriority and Necessity," Australasian Journal of Philosophy, Vol. 58 (1980), 89–101.

Kripke, S. "Identity and Necessity," in M. K. Munitz, ed., Identity and Individuation (New York, 1971), 135–64.

———. Naming and Necessity. Cambridge, 1980.

Plantinga, A. "The Nature of Necessity." Oxford, 1974.

Quinton, A. "The A Priori and the Analytic," Proceedings of the Aristotelian Society, Vol. 64 (1963–64), 31–54.

Swinburne, R. G. "Analyticity, Necessity, and Apriority," Mind, Vol. 84 (1975), 225–43.

– ALBERT CASULLO

KNOWLEDGE, A PRIORI

For as long as the concept of knowledge has been the subject of systematic theorizing, it has seemed obvious to most philosophers that there are at least two kinds: knowledge whose justification depends on outer, empirical experience, and knowledge whose justification does not. The former is referred to as "a posteriori" knowledge and the latter as "a priori."

Historically, the truths of logic (Not both p and not p), mathematics ($7 + 5 = 12$), and conceptual analysis (All bachelors are unmarried) have been regarded as the paradigm examples of a priori knowledge. One important feature that all these examples have in common is that they involve necessary truths. Saul Kripke (1980) has suggested that we may have a priori knowledge even of some contingent propositions; however, this claim remains controversial (see Donellan, 1977).

The central question is: What does it mean for knowledge "not to depend on outer, empirical experience"? It is generally agreed that what is at issue here is the independence of the warrant or the justification for the belief, rather than any of its other features. In particular, it is consistent with a belief's constituting a priori knowledge that experience is required for the thinker to acquire the concepts ingredient in it.

So our central question becomes: What does it mean for the warrant for a belief not to depend on empirical experience? This being a philosophical term of art, it would be pointless to seek that single meaning which ordinary users of the phrase might be said to express by it. Rather, the correct procedure is to define various possible notions that could reasonably be said to fall under the concept of an "experience-independent warrant," and then investigate which of them, if any, best fits the paradigm examples.

The weakest relevant notion is this: S knows that p a priori if and only if (1) S possesses a justification for believing that p that's of a strength sufficient for knowledge; (2) this justification does not appeal to outer empirical experience; and (3) the other conditions on knowledge are satisfied. We may call this "weak a priori knowledge."

Weak a priori knowledge is by no means uninteresting. That there are propositions that can be justified with a strength sufficient for knowledge without recourse to empirical experience is a very significant claim in the theory of knowledge. Moreover, it does seem that, prima facie anyway, the three classes of proposition outlined above satisfy this definition. Hence, this concept can legitimately lay claim to constituting the minimal core of the notion of a priori knowledge.

Is there a conception of apriority that is stronger than weak and that equally well fits the paradigm examples? Historically, philosophers have insisted that the correct conception of apriority goes beyond that of weak apriority in incorporating the idea of immunity to rational revision.

The central question is:

What does it mean for knowledge

"not to depend on outer, empirical experience"?

What does it mean to say that a belief is "immune to rational revision"? And is it plausible to claim that the concept of apriority demands it?

Beginning with the first question, there are a number of different ways to understand immunity to rational revision between which philosophers have perhaps not always sufficiently distinguished. There are at least two independent dimensions along which disambiguation must be sought. First, does "rationally unrevisable" mean unrevisable in light of *any* future evidence, or only: unrevisable in light of any future *empirical* evidence? Second, does "rationally unrevisable" mean *known* not to be rationally revisable in light of the right sort of future evidence, or only: not in fact rationally revisable in light of that sort of evidence, whether or not that fact is known?

It is hard to see what motivation there could be for incorporating a notion of unrestricted unrevisability into the concept of a priori knowledge, as opposed merely to that of unrevisability in light of future empirical evidence. In general we do not insist that a source of justification be infallible as a condition of its being a source of justification: why should we insist on such a stringent condition in the case where the justification is a priori (see Albert Casullo, 1988)? Certainly, the paradigm examples do not support such a condition: it is easy to describe intuitively compelling cases of mathematical belief that are warranted a priori though false. We may, therefore, safely put to one side the idea of unrestricted unrevisability.

What about the more restricted idea of unrevisability in light of future empirical evidence? This idea is more compelling—not in the sense that the concept of weak a priori knowledge entails it, but in the sense that at least some of the paradigm examples support it.

Thus, it not only seems true of the logical principle of noncontradiction that it is justifiable without recourse to empirical evidence; it also seems true of it that it cannot be disconfirmed by any future empirical evidence. If this is right, then the theory of knowledge has reason to take seriously not merely the concept of weak a priori knowledge, but also a conception of such knowledge that incorporates a condition of rational unrevisability in light of future empirical evidence. We may call such a conception one of "strong" a priori knowledge.

Now, strictly speaking, to say that a proposition is not defeasible in light of future empirical evidence and to say that it is known not to be defeasible by such evidence, are two different things. It is one thing to say of a given proposition that no further empirical evidence could bear on it, and another to say of that proposition that it is known to have that property. Nevertheless, there has been a persistent tendency in the literature to run these two thoughts together.

This tendency has been most clearly manifest in writings that have wanted to promote a skepticism about the a priori. Willard Van Orman Quine (1951), and following him Hilary Putnam (1983), have pointed out that we have often been wrong in the past about which propositions are rationally immune to empirical disconfirmation. For example, Euclid's parallel postulate used to be regarded as strongly a priori, even when interpreted as a claim about physical space. However, later developments in mathematical and physical theory showed how such a claim could be false after all. From the existence of such cases of mistaken classification, these philosophers have wanted to conclude that there is no such thing as a priori knowledge in the first place.

But this sort of skepticism overshoots the arguments adduced in its favor by quite a margin. At most what those arguments show is that we do not always know when a proposition is strongly a priori. And that is very different from saying that there are not any strongly a priori propositions.

One will be tempted to suppose that any proposition that is strongly a priori must also be known to be strongly a priori only if one conflates the idea of the a priori with that of the certain. A certain belief is precisely a belief of which one can correctly claim that it will not be disconfirmed by any possible future evidence. Nothing, however, in the paradigm examples of the a priori suggests that we have certain beliefs in this sense.

Much recent writing has tended to be skeptical about the existence of a priori knowledge. As just mentioned, some of these skeptical arguments depend upon assuming an implausibly demanding conception of a priori knowledge. However, the best skeptical arguments proceed by pointing out that no one has satisfactorily explained how any proposition might be known a priori, even when this is construed as involving only weak apriority. There is a genuine puzzle here: How can we be warranted in believing a factual proposition without recourse to empirical evidence?

Historically, philosophers attempted to answer this question by appealing to a faculty of intuition. However, no one has succeeded in giving a satisfactory account of this faculty and of how it is able to deliver warranted judgments.

More promising has been the project of attempting to explain a proposition's apriority by appeal to its epistemic analyticity. An epistemically analytic proposition is such that a thinker's grasp of it by itself suffices for his being justified in believing it to be true. If a significant range of a priori propositions were analytic in this sense, then their apriority would be explainable without recourse to a peculiar evidence-gathering faculty of intuition.

Quine (1951, 1976), and following him Gilbert Harman (1960), have attempted to establish that there are no analytic propositions in this sense. However, Paul Boghossian (1995) has argued that those arguments are far from conclusive. And both Boghossian (1995) and Peacocke (1993) have tried to provide a model for how the mere grasp of a proposition by a thinker could suffice for the thinker's being justified in believing that proposition to be true.

[See also Epistemology; Intuition; Kripke, Saul Aaron; Putnam, Hilary; Quine, Willard Van Orman.]

BIBLIOGRAPHY

Boghossian, P. "Analyticity," in C. Wright and B. Hale, eds., *A Companion to the Philosophy of Language* (Cambridge, 1995).

Casullo, A. "Revisability, Reliabilism, and A priori Knowledge," *Philosophy and Phenomenological Research*, Vol. 49 (1988), 187–213.

Donellan, K. "The Contingent A priori and Rigid Designators," *Midwest Studies in Philosophy*, Vol. 2 (1977), 12–27.

Harman, G. "Quine on Meaning and Existence I," *Review of Metaphysics*, Vol. 21 (1960), 124–51.

Kripke, S. *Naming and Necessity.* Cambridge, MA, 1980.

Peacocke, C. "How are A Priori Truths Possible?" *European Journal of Philosophy*, Vol. 1 (1993), 175–99.

Putnam, H. " 'Two Dogmas' Revisited," in *Realism and Reason* (Cambridge, 1983).

Quine, W. V. O. "Two Dogmas of Empiricism," *Philosophical Review* (1951), reprinted in *From a Logical Point of View* (Cambridge, MA, 1953).

———. "Carnap and Logical Truth" [1954], reprinted in *The Ways of Paradox* (Cambridge, MA, 1976).

— PAUL ARTIN BOCHOSSIAN

KRIPKE, SAUL AARON

Saul Aaron Kripke, American philosopher and logician, was born in Bay Shore, New York, in 1940. He received his B. A. from Harvard in 1962, and subsequently held positions at Harvard, Rockefeller, and elsewhere. Since 1977 he has been McCosh Professor of Philosophy at Princeton.

Philosophy

Only a rough, brief treatment of the philosophy of language and analytic metaphysics in Kripke's two books is possible here. Applications to philosophy of mind, and puzzles about belief and other issues in lesser works, have also generated much discussion.

Names, unlike descriptions, designate "rigidly," continuing to designate the same thing even when discussing counterfactual hypotheses.

In *Naming and Necessity* Kripke supports, using intuitive counterexamples and other arguments, the following doctrines among others about naming. Proper names do not denote or refer through mediation of descriptive connotation or sense (as maintained by G. Frege) but "directly" (as maintained by J. S. Mill); proper names (e.g., "Phosphorus") are not synonymous with definite descriptions (e.g., "brightest object in the eastern sky before sunrise"). Names, unlike descriptions, designate "rigidly," continuing to designate the same thing even when discussing counterfactual hypotheses (e.g., "If there had been a brighter object, Phosphorus would have been only second brightest"). It is usually contingent that the bearer of the name also satisfies the description but always necessary that the bearer of the name is itself (e.g., Phosphorus could have failed to be brightest but not to be Phosphorus).

Also defended are the following doctrines about necessity. Something may be necessary (e.g., Hesperus, alias Phosphorus, could not have failed to be identical to itself, Phosphorus, alias Hesperus), though it is neither linguistically analytic nor epistemologically a priori (e.g., it is synthetic a posteriori that planets seen morning and evening and named "Phosphorus" and "Hesperus" are the same). A thing has nontrivial "essential" properties, ones it could not have existed without, including being what it is (e.g., identical with Phosphorus) and being the sort of thing it is made of or from what it is (e.g., made of rock).

A mechanism for direct reference is suggested: the first user of the proper name or "initial baptist" may fix its reference by some description ("the bright object over there by the eastern horizon"), the second user may use the name with the intention of referring to whatever the first user was referring to, while perhaps being ignorant of the original description, and so on in a "historical" chain. (Some commentators say "causal" chain, but there need not be any causal connection between initial baptist and thing named, which may be a mathematical object.)

Kripke adapts his doctrines to other designating expressions, especially natural-kind terms. Kripke's work and the partly complementary, partly overlapping work of K. Donnellan (descriptions), D. Kaplan (demonstratives), and H. Putnam (natural-kind terms) together constitute what in the 1970s was the "new," and has become the received, theory of reference.

In *Wittgenstein: On Rules and Private Language*, Kripke advances as noteworthy, though not as sound, an argument inspired by his reading of the *Philosophical Investigations*, though these are not unqualifiedly attributed to their author, the later Wittgenstein. On Kripke's reading the target of the argument is any theory (like the "picture theory" of the early Wittgenstein in the *Tractatus Logico-Philosphicus*) that conceives of meaning as given by conditions for truth, conceived as correspondence with facts. Kripke compares his reading of Wittgenstein to the reading of Hume that takes seriously Hume's protestations that he is only a mitigated, not an extreme, skeptic. So read, Wittgenstein's attack on correspondence theories of meaning consists, like Hume's attack on rationalist theories of inference, of two phases.

First, a "skeptical paradox." Consider an ascription of meaning, say that according to which by "plus" I mean *plus,* so that 125 is the right answer to the question "what is 68 plus 57?" as I mean it. To what fact does this correspond? Not the record of how I have worked sums in the past. (Perhaps I have never worked this one before, and many rules are compatible with all the ones I have worked so far.) Not my ability to state general rules for doing sums, since this only raises the question what fact corresponds to my meaning what I do by the words in these rules. Not my behavioral dispositions (nor anything in my brain causally underlying them), since what answer I am disposed to give is one question and what answer would be the right one another question; and I am disposed to give wrong answers fairly often. Further considerations suggest it cannot be introspectable feelings accompanying calculation either. No candidates seem to remain, so if meaning consists in conditions for truth and truth of correspondence with facts, then ascriptions of meaning like "What I mean by 'plus' is *plus,*" are neither true nor meaningful, and no one ever means anything by anything.

Second, a "skeptical solution." This suggests an alternative to the corresponding theory of meaning. The suggested alternative involves community usage but

otherwise defies concise summary, as does the critical literature on Kripke on Wittgenstein, almost coextensive with Wittgenstein studies from the 1980s on.

One objection (actually anticipated by Kripke) is that Wittgenstein does, following F. P. Ramsey, accept talk of "truth" and "facts" in a deflated sense, in which sense to say "It is true or a fact that by 'plus' I mean *plus*" amounts to no more than saying "By 'plus' I mean *plus,*" which Wittgenstein would on Kripke's reading want to say, being no extreme skeptic. So a straightforward statement of Wittgenstein's view as the thesis that there are no "facts" corresponding to meaning ascriptions will not do. But as Kripke notes, one of the tasks of a reading of Wittgenstein is precisely to explain why he does not state his view in straightforward philosophical theses. One rival reading explains this by interpreting Wittgenstein as a "therapist" who aims not to answer philosophical questions but to dissuade us from asking them, and criticizes Kripke for overlooking this "therapeutic" aspect. But such a reading may be less utterly irreconcilable with the reading of Wittgenstein as skeptic than its proponents recognize, since historical skepticism was itself a form of psychotherapy, aiming to achieve philosophic *ataraxia.*

Logic

Kripke has worked on recursion theory on ordinals, intuitionistic analysis, relevance logics, and other branches of logic. Perhaps best known to philosophers, and cited also in the literature on linguistics semantics, theoretical computer science, category theory, and other disciplines, is his work on relational models for modal logics, consisting of a set X (of "states of the world"), a binary relation R (of "relative possibility") thereon, plus an assignment to each atomic formula p of the set of those x in X at which p is true. The assignment extends to all formulas, taking $\square A$ to be true at x if A is true at every y with xRy. Truth at all x in all models with R reflexive (and transitive) (and symmetric) coincides with provability in the modal system **T** (respectively **S4**) (respectively **S5**). For sentential modal logic, such results follow on combining work from the 1940s on algebraic modelings by A. Lindenbaum and J. C. C. McKinsey with representations of algebraic by relational structures due to B. Jónsson and A. Tarski (circa 1950), but this was noted only after Kripke's independent discovery (late 1950s). Despite this anticipation and others he cites, it was Kripke's papers of the early 1960s, presenting with full proofs modelings for predicate as well as sentential logic, and intuitionistic as well as modal logic, with applications to decision and other problems, that transformed the field—in recognition whereof relational models are customarily called Kripke models. While Kripke *qua* philosopher defends the thesis that things that are identical are necessarily so (as in the Hesperus example), Kripke *qua* logician provides a modeling method for modal predicate logic that is equally applicable to systems with and without this thesis and similarly for other controversial theses.

Also well known is Kripke's work on truth. A truth predicate in a language *L* permitting quotation (or other self-reference) would be a predicate *T* such that the following holds with any sentence of *L* in the blanks:

(1) 'T("_____")' is true if and only if "_____" is true.

The liar paradox shows there cannot be a truth predicate in *L* if *L* has no truth-value gaps. There are several treatments of such gaps, including S. C. Kleene's trivalent and B. van Fraasen's supervaluational schemes. Each, given a partial interpretation *I* of a predicate *U* (under which *U* is declared true of some items, declared false of others, not declared either of the rest), dictates which sentences containing *U* are to be declared true, declared false, or not declared either. If *U* is being thought of as "is true," this amounts to dictating a new partial interpretation *I** of *U*. For a partial interpretation with *I* = *I**, or fixed point, (1) holds. Assuming a rather special treatment of gaps, R. M. Martin and P. Woodruff established the existence of a fixed point. Kripke's work, in addition to more purely philosophical contributions, shows how theorems on inductive definitions yield a minimal fixed point (contained in any other, and explicating an intuitive notion of "groundedness"), a maximal intrinsic fixed point (not declaring true anything declared false by any other fixed point), and many others, for any reasonable treatment of gaps.

[*See also Frege, Gottlob; Hume, David; Liar Paradox; Mill, John Stuart; Modal Logic; Philosophy of Language; Philosophy of Mind; Putnam, Hilary; Recursion Theory; Wittgenstein, Ludwig Josef Johann.*]

BIBLIOGRAPHY

"Semantic Considerations on Modal Logic," *Acta Philosophica Fennica*, Vol. 16 (1963), 83–94. A less technical member of the series of papers presenting Kripke models.

"Outline of a Theory of Truth," *Journal of Philosophy*, Vol. 72 (1975), 690–715.

Naming and Necessity. Cambridge, MA, 1980. Transcript of lectures given in 1970; this book version supersedes earlier publication in an anthology.

Wittgenstein: On Rules and Private Language. Cambridge, MA, 1982. This book version supersedes earlier partial publication in an anthology.

— JOHN P. BURGESS

KUHN, THOMAS S.

In the 1960s the philosophy of science saw some upheaval in its general orientation. In the earlier decades more or less steady progress seemed to have been achieved within the framework of logical positivism, at least in some of the key questions. But now some of these results were challenged—for instance, about explanation and reduction, together with some of their underlying presuppositions. As it turned out, the most important figure in this new movement was Thomas S. Kuhn, who was trained as a theoretical physicist, then turned to the history of science, and finally moved on to the philosophy of science. He became world famous with his 1962 book, *The Structure of Scientific Revolutions (SSR)*, which is the most widely distributed book ever written in the history and philosophy of science. Why was the impact of this book so strong?

Kuhn became world famous with his 1962 book,

The Structure of Scientific Revolutions,

the most widely distributed book ever written

in the history and philosophy of science.

First, *SSR* challenged the existing tradition in the philosophy of science by exposing its discrepancies with the history of science. This was a controversial move, since in the decades before *SSR*, philosophy of science was mostly understood as normative, and criticizing it by the results of a descriptive discipline apparently meant to commit the naturalistic fallacy. But the discrepancies had to be understood anyway, and from the 1960s on this brought the history of science in closer contact with the philosophy of science.

Second, some of *SSR*'s central terms have had a tremendous career, not only in philosophy of science, but also in many other fields, especially the term 'paradigm', which meant "scientific achievements that some particular scientific community acknowledges for a time as supplying the foundation for its further practice" (*SSR*, p. 10). This specific practice of science in which there is a consensus about foundations was not seen in standard philosophy of science before Kuhn; he called it 'normal science', another of Kuhn's key terms. Furthermore, at this point a sociological element of Kuhn's philosophy became apparent, namely an explicit reference to scientific communities. Along with other factors this sort of reference made Kuhn very influential in many branches of the social sciences.

Third, Kuhn directed attention to what he called 'scientific revolutions'. These episodes of scientific development were seen to terminate one phase of normal science and commence a new one. Because of scientific revolutions, the development of science is not, as was often thought, a cumulative accretion of knowledge. Rather, revolutionary breaks bring about change in concepts, problems, legitimate solutions, and, in a sense, the world in which the community works. The relation between the two phases of normal science is thus of a special (and controversial) nature; Kuhn termed this relation 'incommensurability'. Incommensurability makes the comparison of competing theories more difficult and subtle than simply balancing the number of correct and incorrect predictions of the two theories, though comparison is not entirely impossible. Neither does it necessitate a conception of scientific change that is devoid of any progress. Rather, science is progressive, but not in the sense of approaching the truth. The sciences' progress is purely instrumental in the sense that the accuracy of predictions indeed becomes better and better, but not in the sense that we know more and more about the nature of things.

Finally, as a consequence of incommensurability, the commonly held view about reduction was seriously called into question. Whereas, under the image of cumulative scientific development, earlier theories seemed reducible to their successors, the meaning change usually accompanying revolutions prohibited such clear-cut reductions.

[See also Philosophy of Science.]

BIBLIOGRAPHY

Works by Kuhn

The Copernican Revolution: Planetary Astronomy in the Development of Western Thought. Cambridge, 1957.
The Structure of Scientific Revolutions. Chicago, 1962. 2d ed., 1970.
The Essential Tension: Selected Studies in Scientific Tradition and Change. Chicago, 1977.
Black Body Theory and the Quantum Discontinuity, 1894–1912. Oxford, 1978.
With J. L. Heilbron, P. Forman, and L. Allen. Sources for the History of Quantum Physics: An Inventory and Report. Philadelphia, 1967.

Works on Kuhn

Barnes, B. T. S. Kuhn and Social Science. London, 1982.
Gutting, G., ed. Paradigms and Revolutions: Applications and Appraisals of Thomas Kuhn's Philosophy of Science. Notre Dame, IN, 1980.
Horwich, P., ed. World Changes: Thomas Kuhn and the Nature of Science. Cambridge, 1993.
Hoyningen-Huene, P. Reconstructing Scientific Revolutions: Thomas S. Kuhn's Philosophy of Science, translated by A. T. Levine. Chicago, 1993. Includes bibliographies of Kuhn's works and of the secondary literature.
Lakatos, I., and A. Musgrave, eds. Criticism and the Growth of Knowledge. London, 1970.

— PAUL HOYNINGEN-HUENE

L

LANGUAGE

What is a language? Is it an internal component of a speaker's mind, or is it wholly dependent on our external behavior? Is it a matter of social practice, or are languages to be viewed as independently existing abstract objects? Arguments have been offered in favor of each of these conceptions.

Adherents to these different positions can agree that linguistic theories provide the most precise way of characterizing particular languages. A theory, or grammar, supplies a set of rules describing the semantic properties of the basic expressions and their permissible syntactic combinations into meaningful wholes. The disagreements that arise concern the interpretation of linguistic theories and the nature of the linguistic objects and properties they describe.

Platonists, for instance, argue that languages are purely formal, or abstract entities, whose natures are fully specified by formal theories. For the platonist, linguistics is a branch of mathematics. In contrast, mentalists see linguistics as a branch of cognitive psychology and take linguistic theories to be about the psychological states or processes of linguistically competent speakers. For others, linguistic theories can be seen as systematizing a vast range of facts about the behavior of an individual or community of speakers, with the rules describing regularities in individual or social practice.

For platonists, such as Katz and Soames, languages with their properties of meaning and structure exist independently of speakers. A firm distinction is drawn between languages and linguistic competence: theories of the former are not to be confused with theories of the latter. The formal properties of a language, on which its identity depends, owes nothing to its users. Speakers of those languages may be blind to some of its properties of meaning or structure, although these may be deduced from the theory. Moreover, languages with just these formal properties exist whether anyone speaks them or not. They may be defined, according to Lewis, as sets of expression meaning-pairs, with the set of human (or natural) languages making up a very small portion of the set of all possible languages. The task for platonists is to explain what makes one rather than another of these abstract entities the language of a given individual or population. To explain this the platonist must define an *actual-language relation* between speakers, or populations, and particular abstract objects (see Schiffer for discussion). This may depend, as Lewis thinks, on facts about the conventions that exist among a population of speakers. Or it may be based upon psychological facts about speakers' competence such as the claim that speakers have internalized a grammar that somehow generates either the set, or a subset, of the sentences described by the formal theory.

Is a language a matter of social practice,

or are languages to be viewed

as independently existing abstract objects?

Mentalists, such as Chomsky and Fodor, insist to the contrary that the best account of speakers' actual languages should fit the facts about the meanings and structures individuals actually give to expressions: theories of language should be tailored to the contours of linguistic competence. Thus for Chomsky, a theory of language is a theory of a speaker's knowledge of language. The formal entities described by platonists are just projections of the linguistic properties that speakers give to the expressions they produce and respond to. For mentalists, language is not in the world. The world contains only marks and sounds. Language is in the mind of speakers and consists in the assignments of meaning and structure given to particular marks and sounds.

For Chomsky, a grammar is a theory of the speaker's linguistic competence: an internalized system of rules or principles a person uses to map sounds to meanings. This is a body of tacit knowledge that the speaker puts to use in the production and comprehension of speech. It contains a largely innate, and species-specific, component common to all human language users. The workings of this component are described by universal grammar. Linguistic competence is just one of the factors affecting linguistic performance. Memory, attention, and other cognitive factors contribute to the actual production of speech. For Fodor, by contrast, the rules of grammar describe the actual psycholinguistic mechanisms at work in our production and comprehension of language. Language is just one of the perceptual modules, or sensory input systems, that serve our central cognitive processing.

In contrast to the platonist and mentalist construals of language, behaviorists insist that grammars are merely theoretical representations of a speaker's practical abilities: the ability to use expressions in particular ways.

For Chomsky, a grammar is a theory

of the speaker's linguistic competence:

an internalized system of rules or principles

a person uses to map sounds to meanings.

For Quine, a language is a set of dispositions to verbal behavior. Quine argues that the only evidence for linguistic theory is linguistic behavior, and that many grammars will serve equally well to generate the set of sentences a speaker is disposed to produce and respond to. Thus grammars and the sentence structures they describe are construed as artifacts of theory. Chomsky denies that behavior provides the only evidence for testing theories of grammar. Psycholinguistic evidence and language acquisition are also relevant. He also argues that we could not have learned to produce and respond to so many novel sentences just on the basis of observed behavior. The data are too impoverished to support such inductive inferences: sentences alike in surface structure differ in underlying levels of structure, and speakers respond to them differently. Chomsky concludes that speakers must bring their own internally generated representations of structure to bear on the evidence. Predictions of the sentences they find acceptable and unacceptable, and the interpretations they can and cannot allow, will be based on the fewest linguistic generalizations that fit the pattern of elicited data, and explain any gaps in the data. Claims about a speaker's grammar are thus based on inference to the best explanation about the principles by which she generates structural descriptions (SDs) for the utterances she hears. A speaker's language is an internally generated set of structures.

Davidson, like Quine, accepts that all facts about meaning must be exhibited in behavior. But unlike Quine, he holds that the assignments of meaning depend on facts about what the speaker believes and intends. Thus linguistic meaning cannot be reduced to behavior. The notions of belief and meaning are settled together by a total theory for interpreting what a speaker says and does.

Finally, is language an essentially social phenomenon? Dummett argues that a language is a shared social practice upon which the possibility for communication among speakers depends. Lewis, although a platonist, also argues that facts about the conventional regularities maintained by populations relate them to particular languages. Chomsky and Davidson, on the other hand, conclude that the fundamental notion of language is that of an individual's language, or idiolect. Differences in grammar and vocabulary between speakers ensure that no two speakers have exactly the same language: they can still communicate because there is often overlap in idiolects, and they can work out what others are saying. Chomsky distinguishes between E-languages, which are ill-assorted, externally described, and extensionally characterized social practices, and I-languages, which are the intensionally characterized, internalized grammars of individuals that assign SDs to expressions. For Chomsky, the former notion is ill-defined, so only the latter is of use in the scientific study of language. He argues that a language L cannot be identified apart from its structure, and the structure of L is the structure assigned to it by its speaker(s). He thus casts doubt on behaviorism. Many languages will share the same sounds: whether a string of sounds is a sentence depends on how different speakers perceive those sounds. Relative to one structural assignment, the sound string may be grammatical, relative to another it may not. Quine's and Lewis's idea of a set of well-formed strings, which can be generated by different grammars, becomes problematic; instead we have a set of structures that speakers assign to sounds and signs. We might reconstruct the notion as follows: an E-language is a set of grammatical strings, where a 'string' is grammatical if it has at least one structural description (SD), which is permitted by the I-language of some set of speakers in the sense that it conflicts with no principles of universal grammar (UG).

In the case of meaning, Tyler Burge has argued that word meaning depends on the social norms operating in the speaker's community; while Putnam stresses that the meaning and reference of natural terms are settled by a group of experts to whom ordinary speakers defer in their use of these terms. These social factors are compatible with the claim that the primary notion of language is that of an idiolect, as they concern vocabulary items only. Each of these different conceptions of language may coexist, all of them serving a different philosophical or scientific interest.

[See also Chomsky, Noam; Davidson, Donald; Dummett, Michael; Inference to the Best Explanation; Meaning; Philosophy of Language; Putnam, Hilary; Quine, Willard Van Orman; Reference.]

BIBLIOGRAPHY

Burge, T. "Wherein Is Language Social," in A. George, ed., *Reflections on Chomsky* (Cambridge, MA, 1989).

Chomsky, N. *Knowledge of Language: Its Nature, Origin, and Use.* Westport, CT, 1986.

Davidson, D. "Radical Interpretation," in his *Inquiries into Truth and Interpretation* (Saffron Walden, Essex, Eng., 1984).

Dummett, M. "Language and Communication," in A. George, ed., *Reflections on Chomsky* (Cambridge, MA, 1989).

Fodor, J. "Some Notes on What Linguistics Is About," in J. Katz, ed., *The Philosophy of Linguistics* (Saffron Walden, Essex, Eng., 1983).

Katz, J., ed. *The Philosophy of Linguistics.* Saffron Walden, Essex, Eng., 1983.

Lewis, D. "Languages and Language," in his *Philosophical Papers,* Vol. 1 (Saffron Walden, Essex, Eng., 1983).

Putnam, H. "The Meaning of Meaning," in his *Philosophical Papers,* Vol. 2 (Saffron Walden, Essex, Eng., 1975).

Quine, W. V. O. "Methodological Reflections on Current Linguistic Theory." in D. Davidson and G. Harman, eds., *Semantics of Natural Language* (Norwell, MA, 1972).

Schiffer, S. "Actual-Language Relations," in J. Tomberlin, ed., *Philosophical Perspectives* (Atascadero, CA, 1973).

Soames, S. "Semantics and Psychology," in J. Katz, ed., *The Philosophy of Linguistics* (Saffron Walden, Essex, Eng., 1985).

— BARRY C. SMITH

LANGUAGE AND THOUGHT

Should questions about thought—about intentionality, beliefs, and concept possession, for example—be approached directly or, instead, indirectly via the philosophy of language? There are two slightly different ways in which questions about language and meaning might seem to offer illumination of issues concerning thought. One way relates to language that is explicitly about thoughts, as when someone says, "Bruce believes that boomerangs seldom come back." The idea that a philosophical investigation of thought should proceed via a study of the logical properties of language that is about thoughts is a particular case of a more general view that philosophy of language enjoys a certain priority over metaphysics.

The other way relates to the use of language to *express* thoughts, and this provides the topic for the present entry. Suppose that Bruce believes that boomerangs seldom come back, and expresses this thought in the English sentence: "Boomerangs seldom come back." Which takes priority, the meaning of the English sentence or the content of Bruce's thought?

A claim of priority is the converse of a claim of one-way dependence: X enjoys priority over Y if Y depends on X but X does not depend on Y. Thus, a question of the relative priority of X and Y has four possible answers: X has priority; Y has priority; X and Y are mutually dependent; X and Y are independent. But the question of the relative priority of thought and language

is still unclear, until the relevant kind of priority has been specified. It is useful to distinguish three kinds of priority question: ontological, epistemological, and analytical (see Avramides, 1989, for a similar distinction).

To say that thought enjoys *ontological priority* over language is to say that language is ontologically dependent on thought, while thought is not so dependent on language. That is, there can be thought without language, but there cannot be language without thought. To say that thought enjoys *epistemological priority* over language is to say that the route to knowledge about language (specifically, about linguistic meaning) goes via knowledge about thought (specifically, about the contents of thought), while knowledge about thought can be had without going via knowledge about language.

> *To say that thought enjoys* ontological priority over language is to say that language is ontologically dependent on thought, while thought is not so dependent on language.

Donald Davidson denies both these priority claims. As for ontological priority, he argues (1975) that there cannot be thought without language: in order to have thoughts (specifically, beliefs), a creature must be a member of a language community, and an interpreter of the speech of others. As for epistemological priority, Davidson argues (1974) that it is not possible to find out in detail what a person believes without interpreting the person's speech.

Analytical priority is priority in the order of philosophical analysis or elucidation. To say that X is analytically prior to Y is to say that key notions in the study of Y can be analyzed or elucidated in terms of key notions in the study of X, while the analysis or elucidation of the X notions does not have to advert to the Y notions. On the question of the relative analytical priority of thought and language, there are, then, four positions to consider: two priority views, and two no-priority views.

Priority for Thought

A philosophical account of the content of thoughts—of intentionality—can be given without essential appeal to language, and the notion of linguistic meaning can then be analyzed or elucidated in terms of the thoughts that language is used to express. The analytical program of Paul Grice was aimed at an analysis of linguistic meaning in terms of the beliefs and intentions of language users, though Grice did not offer any account of the intentionality of mental states themselves (Grice, 1989; see also Schiffer, 1972). There are many proposals for explaining the intentionality of mental states without appeal to linguistic meaning, and these might be coupled with an elucidation of linguistic meaning in terms of mental notions. It is widely reckoned, however, that the Gricean analytical program cannot be carried through (Schiffer, 1987).

Priority for Language

An account of linguistic meaning can be given without bringing in the intentionality of thoughts, and what a person's thoughts are about can then be analyzed in terms of the use of language. This view can be found in Michael Dummett's work (1973, 1991, 1993). If a theorist attempts to give a substantive account of linguistic meaning in accordance with this view, then the resources that can be invoked are seriously limited, since the account cannot presume upon everyday psychological notions such as belief and intention. Because of this, it would not be surprising to find hints of behaviorism in work that is influenced by this view.

No Priority—Interdependence

There is no way of giving an account of either intentionality or linguistic meaning without bringing in the other member of the pair. The two notions have to be explained together. This is Davidson's view (Davidson, 1984). He thus maintains an ontological, epistemological, and analytical no-priority position. While the three no-priority claims go together quite naturally, it is important to note that they are separable claims and that the analytical no-priority claim is not entailed by the ontological and epistemological no-priority claims.

No Priority—Independence

The notions of intentionality for mental states and of linguistic meaning are unrelated. This view might be defended if a language is considered as an abstract entity, composed of a set of expressions together with a function that assigns a value to each expression (a proposition to each sentence, for example). On such a conception, meaning is a purely formal notion. But for the notion of linguistic meaning as it applies to a public language in use, this fourth view is implausible.

[See also Davidson, Donald; Dummett, Michael; Grice, Herbert Paul; Language; Meaning; Philosophy of Language.]

BIBLIOGRAPHY

Avramides, A. *Meaning and Mind: An Examination of a Gricean Account of Language*. Cambridge, MA, 1989.

Davidson, D. "Belief and the Basis of Meaning," *Synthese*, Vol. 27 (1974), 309–23.
———. "Thought and Talk," in S. Guttenplan, ed., *Mind and Language*. (Oxford, 1975).
Dummett, M. *Frege: Philosophy of Language*. London, 1973.
———. *Truth and Other Enigmas*. London, 1978.
———. *Inquiries into Truth and Interpretation*. Oxford, 1984.
———. *The Logical Basis of Metaphysics*. Cambridge, MA, 1991.
———. *The Seas of Language*. Oxford, 1993.
Grice, H. P. *Studies in the Way of Words*. Cambridge, MA, 1989.
Schiffer, S. *Meaning* [1972]. Oxford, 1988.
———. *The Remnants of Meaning*. Cambridge, MA, 1987.
Sellars, W. S., and R. M. Chisholm. "Intentionality and the Mental," in H. Feigl, M. Scriven, and G. Maxwell, eds., *Minnesota Studies in the Philosophy of Science, Volume 2: Concepts, Theories, and the Mind-Body Problem* (Minneapolis, 1958).

— MARTIN DAVIES

LANGUAGE OF THOUGHT

Simply stated, the language-of-thought thesis (LOT) holds that thinking (i.e., cognition) is carried out in a languagelike medium, where the thoughts that constitute thinking are themselves sentencelike states of the thinker. Since the demise of philosophical behaviorism in the early 1960s the LOT thesis has enjoyed considerable support as a central tenet of a more encompassing representationalist theory of mind (RTM). Proponents of RTM, led by Jerry Fodor, have mounted a sustained defense of LOT.

RTM offers an account of propositional attitudes—beliefs, desires, doubts, and so on—according to which propositional attitudes relate the possessor of the attitude to a mental representation (cf. Fodor, 1981). Mental representations have both semantic and physically realized formal properties: they are semantically evaluable (e.g., as being true or false, as being about or referring to certain entities or properties); they stand in inferential relations to other mental representations; and, like words, pictures, and other representations, they also have certain formal properties (e.g., shape, size, etc.) in virtue of being physical, presumably neural, entities. Mental representations, and hence propositional attitudes, have their causal roles in thinking and behavior in virtue of their formal properties. Propositional attitudes inherit semantic properties from the mental representations that are one of their relata. RTM is silent as to what kind or sort of representation these mental representations are (cf. Fodor, 1987, pp. 136–38).

LOT supplements RTM with a specific proposal or hypothesis about the character of mental representations: like sentences of a language, they are structured entities, and their structures provide the basis for the particular semantic and causal properties that propositional attitudes exhibit. More specifically, they are syntactically structured entities, composed of atomic constituents (concepts) that refer to or denote things and properties in the world. The semantic properties of a mental representation, including both truth conditions and inferential relations, are determined by the representation's syntactic structure together with the semantic properties of its atomic constituents. Mental representations, in other words, have a combinatorial semantics. The causal properties of a representation are similarly determined by the representation's syntactic structure together with the formal properties of its atomic constituents.

Mental representations,

and hence propositional attitudes,

have their causal roles in thinking and behavior

in virtue of their formal properties.

Three sorts of arguments have been advanced in support of LOT. The first makes much of the apparent semantic parallels between thoughts and sentences. Both beliefs and declarative sentences, for example, are typically meaningful, truth valued, and intentional (in the sense of being about something). Both stand in various inferential relations to other beliefs and assertions. One obvious explanation of these parallels is that thought has a languagelike character, individual thoughts a sentencelike structure. A second sort of argument focuses on the productivity and systematicity of thought. Thought, like language, is productive in the sense that there are indefinitely many, indefinitely complex thoughts. Whatever can be said can also be thought. Thought, like language, is also systematic in the sense that you can think one thought (e.g., that the child bit the monkey) if and only if one can also think certain other systematically related thoughts (that the monkey bit the child). Again, one obvious explanation is that thought has a languagelike character, individual thoughts a sentencelike structure. A third sort of argument claims that much cognitive scientific theorizing seems committed to LOT. Specifically, our best theories of rational choice, perception, and learning seem committed to the claim, not simply that cognition is a matter of the creation and manipulation of mental representations, but also that these representations are sentential in character. It is claimed, for example, that our best theories of learning are a species of hypothesis

testing. But such a procedure, it is argued, presupposes the existence of a language, that is, a language of thought in which the hypothesis being tested is formulated.

Proponents of LOT readily concede that these arguments are not decisive. Each is an instance of inference to the best explanation, and as such each is vulnerable to refutation by some alternative explanation that does not appeal to a language of thought.

Critics of LOT find the foregoing sorts of arguments unpersuasive for any of a number of reasons. Either they believe that there are equally good explanations that don't appeal to a language of thought, or they deny the phenomena that LOT is said to explain, or they hold that the proposed explanations either rest on false presuppositions or are so sketchy and incomplete as not to merit the name, or they believe that these explanations have entailments so implausible as to impugn the explanatory premise that there exists a language of thought. Thus, for example, the argument from learning discussed above apparently entails that to learn a language one must already know a language. Many critics find in this entailment a reductio of LOT. Proponents such as Fodor, by contrast, have courageously embraced this entailment, arguing that all concepts, including, for example, our concept of a Boeing 747, are innate. Whatever the specific merits and defects of the arguments and counterarguments, it seems fair to say that the existence of a language of thought remains an open empirical question.

[See also Inference to the Best Explanation; Mental Representation; Philosophy of Mind.]

BIBLIOGRAPHY

Defending LOT

Field, H. *The Language of Thought.* New York, 1975.
———. "Mental Representations," *Erkenntnis,* Vol. 13 (1978), 9–61.
———. *Representations.* Cambridge, MA, 1981.
———. "Why There Still Has to Be a Language of Thought," in *Psychosemantics* (Cambridge, MA, 1987).

Criticizing LOT

Churchland, P. M., and P. S. Churchland. "Stalking the Wild Epistemic Engine," *Noûs,* Vol. 17 (1983), 5–18.
Dennett, D. C. "Brain Writing and Mind Reading," in *Brainstorms* (Cambridge, MA, 1978).
———. "A Cure for the Common Code," in *Brainstorms* (Cambridge, MA, 1978).
Loar, B. "Must Beliefs Be Sentences?" in P. Asquith and T. Nickles, eds., *Proceedings of the PSA, 1982* (East Lansing, MI, 1983).
Schiffer, S. *Remnants of Meaning.* Cambridge, MA, 1987.

– ROBERT J. MATTHEWS

LAWS OF NATURE

The laws of nature are the general ways of working of the physical and mental world. Many natural scientists have as one of their great aims the uncovering of these laws. The topic of laws of nature has been the subject of vigorous discussion in contemporary philosophy. Three broad tendencies have emerged, with a number of important variations within these tendencies.

The Regularity or Humean View

Since the work of David Hume, at least, there have been many philosophers, particularly those in the empiricist tradition, who have tried to analyze both causes and laws (which they tend not to distinguish very clearly) in terms of mere regular successions or other regularities in the behavior of things. Laws tell us that, given a phenomenon of a certain sort, then a further phenomenon of a certain sort must occur in a certain relation to the first phenomenon. Particularly since the rise of quantum physics, this may be modified by saying that there must be a certain probability that the further phenomenon will occur. Regularity theorists see this "must" as mere universality: this is what always happens.

The topic of laws of nature has been the subject

of vigorous discussion in contemporary philosophy.

A great many difficulties have been raised against this position (for a fairly full listing see Armstrong, 1983, pt. 1). The most important of these are as follows.

1. The intuitive difference between merely accidental uniformities and nomic (lawlike) uniformities. The traditional example is the contrast between the accidental uniformity that every sphere of gold has a diameter of less than one mile and the nomic uniformity that every sphere of uranium 235 has a diameter of less than one mile, because that diameter would ensure "critical mass" and the explosion of the sphere.

2. Laws of nature "sustain counterfactuals." If it is a law that arsenic is poisonous, then if, contrary to the facts, you had drunk arsenic, then you would have been very sick. But from the fact that no human being of Neanderthal race ever spoke English, it by no means follows that if, contrary to fact, some of them had lived in an English-speaking society, they would not have spoken English. The uniformity that Neanderthals spoke no English does not sustain counterfactuals.

3. A regularity theorist cannot give a satisfactory solution to the problem of induction. If laws are mere regularities, what rational grounds have we for believing that observed uniformities will continue to hold in the future and for the unobserved generally?

4. A regularity theorist is likely to identify merely probabilistic laws with actually occurring frequencies. This identification is difficult, because such laws do not actually rule out distributions with the "wrong" frequencies. All that probabilistic laws do is to make such frequencies improbable; they do not make them nomically impossible.

5. Science admits certain laws that may well have no positive instances falling under them. The most famous example is Newton's first law of motion. An uninstantiated law would have to be a vacuous uniformity, but there are far too many such uniformities all to be laws.

Those who continue to work in the regularity tradition try to meet these and other difficulties largely by distinguishing "good" uniformities that deserve to be called laws and "bad" ones that do not. There are two main approaches, the epistemic and the systematic.

Epistemic theorists emphasize the nature of the evidence that we have for claiming that certain uniformities obtain. References and criticism may be found in Suchting (1974), Molnar (1974), Dretske (1977), and Armstrong (1983). Brian Skyrms's (1980) resiliency account is a sophisticated epistemic approach. His basic idea is that we give assent to a generalization, and count it lawlike, only if we find it to hold under a wide variety of circumstances and conditions. For criticism of Skyrms, see Tooley (1987) and Carroll (1990).

The systematic approach has been championed by David Lewis, explicitly basing himself on a suggestion made by F. P. Ramsey. Lewis says that "contingent generalization is a *law of nature* if and only if it appears as a theorem (or axiom) in each of the true deductive systems that achieves the best combination of simplicity and strength" (1973, p. 73). Further discussion may be found in Lewis (1986). He himself finds that his greatest difficulties are associated with probabilistic laws. For criticism of Lewis see Armstrong (1983), Tooley (1987), Carroll (1990).

Strong Laws

One who judges that no regularity theory of laws can succeed may wish to argue that laws are something stronger than mere uniformities or statistical distributions. Laws may be called strong if their existence entails the existence of the corresponding uniformities and so on but the reverse entailment fails to hold.

Traditional theories of strong laws tended to see these laws as holding necessarily. Given all the antecedent conditions, the consequent is entailed. In the days when

Euclidean geometry was unchallenged, geometrical models were attractive (see, among many, Descartes, Hobbes, Locke). As with geometrical theorems, this necessity was thought to be discoverable, at least potentially, a priori. Granted that laws might in practice be discovered by experience, just as the Pythagorean theorem might be discovered by measuring and adding areas, it was still thought that a sufficiently powerful intellect might spell out the necessity involved without the aid of experience. This approach seems to have been abandoned by contemporary philosophers (though there are hints in Martin, 1993). It now seems agreed, in general, and in agreement with regularity theorists, that the laws of nature can be discovered only a posteriori.

Upholders of strong laws do, however, differ among themselves whether these laws are contingent or necessary. The contingency view (also held by regularity theorists) is represented by Fred Dretske (1977), Michael Tooley (1977, 1987) and D. M. Armstrong (1983). These three evolved their rather similar views independently and almost simultaneously. Laws are argued to be dyadic relations of necessitation holding contingently between universals, schematically N(F,G). Such a relation entails the regularity that all Fs are Gs, but the regularity does not entail N(F,G). Dretske presents the central idea with particular clarity; Tooley and Armstrong develop the theory more fully. Tooley argues that the possibility of certain sorts of uninstantiated laws demands uninstantiated universals, leading him to what he calls a factual Platonism about universals. Armstrong, however, tries to get along with instantiated universals only.

The theory appears to be able to handle probabilistic laws (see Armstrong, 1983, chap. 9; Tooley, 1987, chap. 4). The connection between universals envisaged by the theory may be thought of as involving connections of differing strength holding between antecedent and consequent universals. The greatest strength, one (exactly one, not one minus an infinitesimal), represents the probability involved in an old-style deterministic law. The consequent universal must be instantiated if the antecedent universal is. Numbers between nought and one give the lesser probability of the consequent being instantiated under these conditions. This probability is an objective one. The antecedent universal, if instantiated, bestows an objective propensity, as some say, for the instantiation of the consequent.

An obvious cost of this sort of theory is that it must postulate universals. This is a stumbling block to many. But by far the most important criticism of this account has been developed by Bas van Fraassen (1989, chap. 5; see also the discussion-review of this book by him,

Earman, Cartwright, and Armstrong, 1993). He poses two difficulties: the identification problem and the inference problem. The first is the problem of identifying in a noncircular way the nature of the necessitation relation supposed to hold between the universals involved in the law. The second is the problem, given a concrete account of this relation, of understanding why it is legitimate to infer from the fact that the universals are so related to the existence of corresponding uniformities or frequencies in the world. Van Fraassen argues that solving the one problem makes it impossible to solve the other. A clear account of the relation makes the inference problematic; a clearly valid inference makes the relation no more than something that validates the inference.

One response to the difficulties

of the regularity theory of laws—

a response rather typical of our age—

is not to propose a strengthened theory of laws

but to take the deflation further and argue

that there are no such things as laws.

The view that laws of nature are necessities discovered a posteriori is developed by Sydney Shoemaker (1980) and Chris Swoyer (1982). They build on Saul Kripke's (1980) arguments for a posteriori knowledge of necessity, and Kripke hints that laws of nature may have this status. Their view depends upon taking a different view of properties from that found in Dretske, Tooley, and Armstrong. For the latter, properties are conceived of as 'categorical' or self-contained entities. But for Shoemaker and Swoyer, properties, either singly or in combination, are nothing apart from the laws they enter into. They might be described as pure powers or dispositions to produce law-governed consequences.

On this view, therefore, if it is a law that property F ensures possession of property G, then it is the very essence of F so to ensure G, and so the law is necessary. That there are things having property F is contingent, but that F ensures G is necessary. It seems, then, that the dispute between contingent strong laws and necessary ones depends on the true theory of properties. See Richard Swinburne's (1983) critical comments on Shoemaker.

The view of properties just discussed might be called dispositionalism as opposed to categoricalism. There are theorists who favor a view of properties that gives them both a categorical and a dispositional (or power) side; see Evan Fales (1990) and C. B. Martin (1993). It is to be noted that both in pure dispositionalism and this mixed theory there is a strong tendency to regard laws as not fundamental but rather analyzable in terms of causal relations holding between individual events and particulars (singular causation). These causal relations, and so their laws, are determined by the nature of the dispositions or powers that particulars have.

Eliminativism About Laws

The regularity theory of laws is a deflationary theory. It holds that there is less to being a law than one might naturally think. It also faces a number of serious difficulties. One response, rather typical of our age, is to meet the difficulties, not by proposing a strengthened theory of laws, but by taking the deflation further and arguing that there are no such things as laws. This is the position taken by van Fraassen in *Laws and Symmetry* (1989). A natural comparison is with eliminative materialism, which denies the existence of the mind in favor of the brain.

Van Fraassen begins with a systematic criticism, first of Lewis's version of the regularity theory, and then of various strong views. The rejection of laws he links to his "constructive empiricism," according to which the aim of science is not truth in general but only empirical adequacy, defined as truth with respect to what is observed. Beyond the observable, all that can usefully be done is the constructing of models that are in a deep way adequate to the phenomena and that may be true but about which we can have no special reason to think them true. In these constructions considerations of symmetry play an energizing role.

A certain skepticism about laws is also to be found in Nancy Cartwright's *How the Laws of Physics Lie* (1983). Her skepticism concerns the fundamental as opposed to more messy phenomenological laws. The former may explain better, but the latter are truer to the facts! The distinction she is concerned with is one made by physicists, and the "phenomenological" laws go far beyond van Fraassen's observables. Cartwright accepts these laws because the entities they deal with, though perhaps unobserved, appear to exist and to act as causes. In *Nature's Capacities and Their Measurement* (1989), she argues that the world is a world of singular causes, individual entities interacting with each other. The nature of these interactions is determined by the capacities of these entities. Her capacities seem close to the dispositions and powers that contemporary necessitarians identify with properties.

[See also Armstrong, David M.; Descartes, René; Eliminative Materialism, Eliminativism; Hobbes, Thomas; Hume, David; Kripke, Saul Aaron; Locke, John; Probability.]

BIBLIOGRAPHY

Armstrong, D. M. *What Is a Law of Nature?* Cambridge, 1983.
Carroll, J. "The Humean Tradition," *Philosophical Review*, Vol. 99 (1990), 261–76.
———. *Laws of Nature.* Cambridge, 1994. Contains a useful set of references.
Cartwright, N. *How the Laws of Physics Lie.* Oxford, 1983.
———. *Nature's Capacities and Their Measurement.* Oxford, 1989.
Dretske, F. "Laws of Nature," *Philosophy of Science*, Vol. 44 (1977), 248–68.
Fales, E. *Causation and Universals.* London, 1990.
Kripke, S. *Naming and Necessity.* Oxford, 1980.
Lewis, D. *Counterfactuals.* Cambridge, MA, 1973.
———. *Philosophical Papers*, Vol. 2. New York, 1986.
Martin, C. B. "Power for Realists," in J. Bacon, K. Campbell, and L. Reinhardt, eds., *Ontology, Causality, and Mind* (Cambridge, 1993).
Molnar, G. "Kneale's Argument Revisited," in T. Beauchamp, ed., *Philosophical Problems of Causation* (Belmont, CA, 1974).
Shoemaker, S. "Causality and Properties," in *Identity, Cause, and Mind* (Cambridge, 1984).
Skyrms, B. *Causal Necessity.* New Haven, 1980.
Suchting, W. A. "Regularity and Law," in R. S. Cohen and M. W. Wartofsky, eds., *Boston Studies in the Philosophy of Science* (Dordrecht, 1974).
Swinburne, R. "Reply to Shoemaker," in L. J. Cohen and M. Hesse, eds., *Aspects of Inductive Logic* (Oxford, 1983). See also Shoemaker's paper in the same volume.
Swoyer, C. "The Nature of Natural Laws," *Australasian Journal of Philosophy*, Vol. 60 (1982), 203–23.
Tooley, M. "The Nature of Laws," *Canadian Journal of Philosophy*, Vol. 7 (1977), 667–98.
———. *Causation: A Realist Approach.* Oxford, 1987.
van Fraassen, B. *Laws and Symmetry.* Oxford, 1989.
———, J. Earman, D. M. Armstrong, and N. Cartwright. "A Book Symposium on Laws and Symmetry." *Philosophy and Phenomenological Research*, Vol. 53 (1993), 411–44.

– DAVID M. ARMSTRONG

LEIBNIZ, GOTTFRIED WILHELM

Gottfried Wilhelm Leibniz (1646–1716), German philosopher, scientist, mathematician, historian, and diplomat. Leibniz was born in Leipzig; his father was a professor, and his mother was the daughter of a professor at the University of Leipzig. A precocious child, he read widely in the library of his father, who died when Leibniz was six. Although Leibniz studied philosophy and law at the university, he was not permitted to present himself for the doctorate of laws in 1666, on the ground that he was too young. Thereupon he left Leipzig and graduated at Altdorf, where he was offered a professorship. He declined this, and went to Nurem-

German philosopher Gottfried Leibniz developed the early foundations of calculus. (Corbis)

berg, where he became secretary of the Rosicrucian Society. In Nuremberg he met Johann Christian von Boyneburg, a statesman and diplomat who had formerly been first minister at the court of Mainz but was now in retirement although still active. Through Boyneburg, Leibniz was introduced to Johann Philipp von Schönborn, elector of Mainz, who took him into his service. During this period Leibniz wrote a number of papers furthering Boyneburg's schemes and cooperated with Dr. Lasser, one of Schönborn's lawyers, in revising Roman law. However, his position as a Protestant in a Catholic court was never very secure, and in 1672 he went to Paris, partly on Boyneburg's private affairs and partly for personal reasons. After four years in Paris he went to Hanover (October 1676) in the service of Johann Friedrich, the reigning duke. He remained in Hanover until his death, serving under Ernst August after the death of Johann Friedrich in 1679, and then under Georg Ludwig, who in 1714 became king of Great Britain. In 1685 Ernst August set Leibniz the task of writing the history of the house of Brunswick, and to gather material for this history in 1687 he began a

journey that lasted nearly three years, going through Munich and Vienna to Italy and returning to Hanover in June 1690. He succeeded in showing the connection between the houses of Brunswick and Este.

Sophie, the wife of Ernst August, and her daughter Sophie Charlotte, who became queen of Prussia, were very close to Leibniz, and much of his writing, including the *Théodicée,* was occasioned by his discussions with them. While Sophie Charlotte was alive, he frequently visited Berlin, where in 1700 the Berlin Society of Sciences (later the Prussian Royal Academy) was founded, with Leibniz as president for life. However, after Sophie Charlotte's death in 1705, Leibniz' presence in Berlin was more and more unwelcome, and by 1711 he had altogether ceased to go there.

Throughout his life Leibniz sought to promote cooperative activity in scientific and medical research and in the systematic collection and arrangement of facts already known, whether about things or about technical processes. He also sought to bring together Christians of all sects by presenting a body of doctrine containing everything essential for Christian faith, on which all could agree. He wrote innumerable letters to advance these projects and drafted innumerable prefaces. His later years were marred, however, by the controversy with the Newtonians over priority in the discovery of the calculus, a strong blow to his own ideal of scientific cooperation. And, although during a stay in Vienna from 1712 to 1714 Leibniz was made an imperial privy councilor and given the title of Freiherr, he was generally neglected. His death passed almost unnoticed by both his royal patrons and the intellectual world.

Early Views

A few general points may be noted in regard to Leibniz' views before he went to Paris.

He knew of Descartes's work mainly through the writings of some of Descartes's followers; but he was more familiar with Bacon, Gassendi, and Hobbes. He read very widely and rapidly, generally assimilating what stimulated his own thinking; and, although his university studies had made him thoroughly familiar with the Aristotelian tradition and his own early reading had given him a wide range of ideas from the Scholastics, he decided strongly in favor of the modern outlook, with its stress on explanation through efficient causes, its atomism, and its experimental approach to the study of nature.

FINAL CAUSES. Leibniz did not completely abandon the traditional views, but he thought it possible to harmonize them with the new. In particular, he thought that for ultimate explanations of the nature of things,

God's existence and the consideration of final causes could not be neglected. The world was a harmonious whole produced by God to serve the divine ends, and although the fundamental workings of things in the world were in accordance with laws of efficient causes, these laws brought about the divine ends. Efficient causes did not rule out final causes.

MIND, BODY, AND FREE WILL. During this early period Leibniz did not think of mind and body as being sharply separated, any more than the Scholastics or atomists, such as Gassendi and Bacon, did, or than Hobbes did. His inclination to consider body in terms of mind rather than to read mind in terms of body is epitomized in his statement, "A body is a momentary mind, but without memory." In various letters to Johann Friedrich and others, he outlined the view that the human mind is implanted in an imperishable bodily kernel that remains as the seat of the mind even when the rest of the body is dissipated. Later, in some of his Parisian writings, he linked minds with vortices, suggesting that the unity of body comes from minds. All these speculations were crude, but they formed a natural basis for his more mature views.

Throughout his life Leibniz

sought to promote cooperative activity

in scientific and medical research

and in the systematic collection and arrangement

of facts already known.

Leibniz was greatly interested in what he called the two most important labyrinths that perplex and imprison the human mind—that of fate and free will and that of the continuum.

LOGIC AND THE UNIVERSAL LANGUAGE. Leibniz's earliest philosophical interest, almost before he was in his teens, was in logic. Here his main emphasis (as was Bacon's) was on classification; deduction was a natural consequence of combining classified items into new classes. In an early academic exercise on the principle of individuation ("De Principio Individui," 1663) he listed as one of the corollaries on which he was ready to dispute, the principle "Things are like numbers." By this Leibniz meant that statements about complex things can be derived from statements about their simpler constituents by a process of combination analogous to multiplication of numbers. This was a kind of con-

ceptual atomism that resulted in a fundamental schema for an alphabet of human thought, haunting him throughout his whole life and becoming more and more unrealizable the more he worked on it. Leibniz thought that if man could discover the fundamental concepts involved in all possible existence, the derivation of all possible truths would be within his reach. On the lowest level there would be combinations of fundamental concepts; on the next level (as Leibniz put it) "conternations" or "con3nations"—that is, combinations of concepts taken three at a time, with corresponding combinations at higher levels. It can be seen that the classification is the basis for deduction within this schema.

UNIVERSAL ENCYCLOPEDIA. Related to Leibniz's notion of a conceptual alphabet was his conception of an encyclopedia of human knowledge. Leibniz held that there already exist vast stores of experience held by groups of skilled workers, or by individuals, that are not fully utilized. These must be collected and systematically arranged, if their full fruits are to be obtained for understanding and practical application. Leibniz thought that the fuller knowledge of the world made available by such an encyclopedia would be conducive to piety by bringing out the richness and variety in the world, and thus testifying to God's wisdom and power. Leibniz desired a fuller knowledge of the nature of things because he believed it would increase piety and devotion to God.

JURISPRUDENCE. During his university years one of Leibniz' fundamental interests was to see how philosophical disciplines could help in the clarification of other studies, especially legal studies, and his academic theses in his legal course were devoted to this. His *Nova Methodus Docendae Discendaeque Jurisprudentiae* ("New Method of Teaching and Learning Jurisprudence," 1667), dedicated and presented to von Schönborn, led to his appointment to assist Dr. Lasser in the work of reforming the corpus juris.

New Physical Hypothesis

Most important to the next step in Leibniz's career was his 1671 work, *Hypothesis Physica Nova* ("New Physical Hypothesis," Gerhardt 1875–1890, Vol. IV, pp. 177 f.), which was divided into two parts: a theory of concrete motion, dedicated to the Royal Society in London, and a theory of abstract motion, presented to the Academy of Sciences in Paris.

CONCRETE THEORY. The concrete theory, a hypothesis designed to explain the most important complex phenomena in terms of simpler phenomena, was based on the relative circulation of the ether through and around the materials that made up the earth in its earliest state. In his abstract theory Leibniz showed how all cohesion of bodies depends on the motion of their constituent particles. This motion is due to the impact of the ether upon the particles and is the ultimate explanatory cause of all the physical characteristics of bodies.

ABSTRACT THEORY. The abstract theory turns on two main lines of thought: Leibniz's study of the labyrinth of the continuum and his reaction to the laws of motion given by Wren and by Huygens in the *Proceedings of the Royal Society,* laws that Leibniz thought could not be fundamental. He also based his idea of continuity in space and time on Hobbes's concept of "endeavor" (conatus), defined by Hobbes as movement over a space less than any given space in a time less than any given time. Leibniz conceived the conatus as unextended but insisted that both points and instants, although unextended, have parts. His account of the laws of motion depended on the view that particles of matter completely at rest offer no resistance to a moving body; it is only because of the inner movements of their parts that bodies have either resistance or cohesion. A moving body, however small, will sweep along with it those parts of a body completely at rest, however large, that stand in its way.

The "New Physical Hypothesis" must be looked upon as a stage, soon to be superseded, in Leibniz's thought about the problems of motion. It was during his stay in Paris that Leibniz first learned to handle competently the problems of the continuum and of motion. He was indebted for his new skill to the encouragement of Christian Huygens, whom he met there and who showed him what he must study in mathematics. Huygens' methods of handling problems of motion gave Leibniz his fundamental principle that in all physical transactions (which he regarded as resulting from impacts) the total effect is equal to the entire cause.

Paris Years

Leibniz's sojourn in Paris (1672–1676) was one of the most profitable periods of his life. He made many important contacts with mathematicians, physicists, philosophers, and men of affairs. The most important of these contacts, after Huygens, were the philosophers Antoine Arnauld, Nicolas Malebranche, and Simon Foucher, canon of Dijon; the physicist Edmond Mariotte; and Walther von Tschirnhaus, who came to Leibniz with an introduction from Henry Oldenburg, secretary of the Royal Society. During these same years Leibniz studied the works of Pascal, Descartes, and Huygens; made discoveries in the calculus that brought

him into contact with Sir Isaac Newton and other British mathematicians; and constructed a calculating machine capable of multiplying large numbers.

PHILOSOPHICAL NOTES. In Paris, Leibniz composed a series of philosophical notes, dating from the end of 1675 to April 1676 (edited by Iwan Jagodinski and published in 1913 as *Leibnitiana Elementa Philosophiae Arcanae de Summa Rerum*). Of the wide range of topics covered, only a few that throw light on his later development can be mentioned here. Leibniz took for granted the notions of the harmony of all things and the perfection of the world as created by God, and utilized them in the discussion of other topics. The greatest possible amount of essence exists and, since thought and perception mirror things, this mirroring increases the variety of the world—and hence increases its perfection. That is why particular minds exist.

SENSATION. The harmony of all things is also increased by there being an infinite number of creatures in the smallest particle, and they also have their own perceptions that mirror their world (Jagodinski 1913, pp. 28–40). This later led Leibniz, in the course of a discussion of Descartes, to raise the question as to what our perception assures us of. He concluded, as Descartes had, that all we can be certain of is that we sense and that we sense things congruous to each other. The difference between dreams and waking life lies in the regularities that are observed in our sensings in ordinary life, so that reasons can be given for them and predictions about further sensings can be made. There is no need to suppose that what different people sense is the same, so long as (as is the case) what each person senses is congruent to himself. Each person's sensings have the same cause and therefore are in conformity. There is no need to posit interaction.

The External World. Leibniz went on to suggest that there is likewise no need to ask whether space and body exist outside our minds. Space, as he put it, is what makes many perceptions cohere among themselves—the perception of space relations among one's perceptions enables one to make predictions about the space relations of new perceptions to the old ones. However, he seemed to imply that there is such a thing as "our" world—that "we" all perceive the same space; and he went on to conclude that other creatures can have other spaces (that is, they can have perceptions that are linked among themselves by spatial laws other than ours), in which case there would be no conformity between them and us. Indeed, to ask whether there can be another world and other spaces is only to ask whether there are other minds that have no communication with ours. It will be seen that Leibniz was assuming that, although two persons need not have qualitatively the same sense experiences, they can and do communicate, and that this communication somehow depends on the nature of the space relations underlying the congruity of each person's perceptions.

Causation. The philosophical notes contain another point very significant in relation to Leibniz's later doctrine. In a paper dated April 1, 1676, and headed "Meditatio de Principio Individui" (Jagodinski 1913, p. 44), Leibniz started from the common notion that an effect involves its cause, so that anyone who understands some effect perfectly would also be able to come to a perfect understanding of the cause. This involves the idea that it is impossible for a particular effect to be produced in two alternative ways by two different causes (as, for instance, a square might be produced either by joining two rectangles or by joining two right-angled isosceles triangles). Leibniz decided that no two things can be alike, but in a material thing there is always something that bears the traces of its earlier state, so that its cause can be discovered in it. This element, he said, is mind, since matter itself is incapable of containing such traces.

Leibniz uses an interesting argument (*ibid.,* p. 46) to show that effect involves cause: "It is true of the effect that it was produced by such a cause. Therefore there is at present in it a quality of such a kind as carries this fact, which even though relative, has something objective"; that is, in the effect itself. The implication of this—that whatever is true of anything is expressed in some way in the thing—is also found in another passage: "When another thing becomes greater than me by increasing, there also occurs some change in me, since a denomination of me is changed . . . and in this way all things are contained in all things" (*ibid.,* p. 122).

These two passages are consistent with the more general view, which Leibniz enunciated later, that if man had a perfect knowledge of the present state of an individual thing, he should be able to deduce its whole past and future states, and even the past and future states of the whole universe. The notion of the individual mirroring the universe was thus given enormous significance. The principle (discussed below) enunciated in the *Discourse on Metaphysics* of 1686—that in the complete notion of an individual is to be found whatever can be said about the individual, past, present, and future—gave a rather special twist to the general thesis, based on the further proposition that all true statements consist in attributing diverse predicates to a complex subject that "in some way" contains them all.

Identity of Indiscernibles. The argument showing that effect involves cause also contains one of the main reasons for Leibniz's later principle of the identity of indiscernibles, the principle that there cannot be two things

in the universe that are exactly alike. A characteristic expression of this principle is to be found in a paper printed by Couturat (*Opuscules et fragments,* p. 9). The point is that a thing *A* cannot have a spatiotemporal position different from another thing *B* without this difference being intimately linked with differences within the natures of the things themselves. The identity of indiscernibles is significantly connected with the principle that in every true proposition the predicate is contained in the subject. Elsewhere (*ibid.,* p. 519) the principle is found connected with the principle of sufficient reason; if there are two different things, some reason for this difference must be present in the natures of the things themselves. The whole complex of ideas is very close to the argumentation in the papers of 1676.

Simple and Complex Ideas. There are also in the philosophical notes many discussions of simple ideas and of their combination to form complex ideas. Leibniz noted (Jagodinski 1913, p. 124) that there are some complex ideas that represent things that are impossible, such as the swiftest motion or the greatest number. He therefore sought examples of maxima and minima that are possible, and also noted that the ontological proof of God's existence from the concept of the greatest possible being or the most perfect being is incomplete until it is shown that such a being is possible (*ibid.,* p. 112; cf. letter to Oldenburg of December 28, 1675, in Gerhardt 1849–1863, p. 85).

One would expect Leibniz to argue that since (1) all complex concepts are derived from simple concepts, (2) all simple concepts are both purely positive and completely independent of one another, and (3) God is the being to whom all positive attributes belong (if this is possible), it therefore follows that the concept of God is possible and hence that God exists (cf. Jagodinski 1913, p. 122).

Origin of Created Beings and the Creation. However, if Leibniz's account of simple and complex concepts is correct, it is not easy to see how any complex concept could represent an impossible being, or how any negation or incompatibility could arise at all. Yet if some particular things are to exist rather than others, there must be negation and incompatibility. Leibniz never satisfactorily solved this problem. In the Parisian notes he took refuge in the thought that particular things result from forms (simple concepts) combined with a subject. This, he said, involved some kind of modification of the forms, although in what manner this occurred was not made clear. "How things result from forms I cannot explain otherwise than by analogy with numbers arising from unities, with this distinction that all unities are homogeneous whereas forms are different" (*ibid.*). This explanation did not help in the least.

At a later period he referred the distinction between God and created beings to the concept of difference, or negation, which must be a constituent of every thing created; and his analogy then was not with numbers arising from unities but with the fact that in the dyadic notation all numbers are expressible in terms of the two characters 1 and 0. Thus, Pure Being (God) and nonbeing are the two ultimate constituents of all created things, and nonbeing brings about profound modifications in the constituent concepts of things. Leibniz associated nonbeing with imperfection and evil; nonbeing makes it impossible for God to create a completely perfect world, and allows him to create only the best of all possible worlds. It is not clear that Leibniz ever asked himself how nearly the best possible world approaches the perfection of God himself; he would probably have regarded the question as unanswerable by finite beings. In one passage (Bodemann 1895, p. 120) he suggested that the world improves with the passage of time, although it never arrives at fullest maturity. He never even seems to have raised the question of whether the concept of a best possible world is possible, although presumably he would have said that it must be, since that is what God creates. However this may be, it seems clear that there must be an infinite difference between the Creator and any created world.

Pacidius Philalethi

The notes published by Jagodinski are our main evidence for Leibniz's philosophical explorations in Paris. In the early part of 1676 he made an abbreviated translation of Plato's *Theaetetus* and *Phaedo,* and he had a discussion with Malebranche on the question of whether matter is to be equated with extension.

In that October Leibniz left Paris to take up his new position at Hanover, traveling by way of London and Holland, where he visited Spinoza, among others. While delayed on board his boat in the Thames, Leibniz composed a long dialogue, *Pacidius Philalethi* (Couturat, pp. 594 ff.), in the form of a letter from Pacidius to Philalethes, in which Pacidius relates a conversation between himself and some friends. (The title may be translated "Godfrey [or Gottfried], to the lover of truth.") The dialogue shows familiarity with the stock arguments associated with the labyrinth of the continuum.

The fundamental problem of the continuum arises through regarding any motion as analyzable into successive states, in each of which a body occupies a position different from that in the next state. In this analysis there is no way of avoiding the problem of how the body gets from one position to the other, or of avoiding the problem of how the two positions are spatially re-lated. The solution adopted by Leibniz used a form of the principle that the continued existence of material things is their continual re-creation by God. Leibniz used the word *transcreation* in the early part of the dialogue to express the idea that when a body moves, it goes out of existence in the earlier position and is re-created in the later position, there being a gap between the two positions. Motion was thus resolved into a series of rests, without any leaps by any actually existing thing. Leibniz showed that this notion was open to a variety of objections, and he finally arrived at a different conception of transcreation, in which the successive positions are contiguous, without any gaps. However, he still resolved motion into a series of rests, God letting the body go out of existence at one point and re-creating it at the next.

Leibniz took for granted

the notions of the harmony of all things

and the perfection of the world as created by God,

and utilized them in the discussion of other topics.

This solution did not satisfy Leibniz, but he could see no way out so long as space and motion were regarded as objectively real (substantial), and he was forced to the conclusion that there is something phenomenal in both. The difficulties of the continuum were thus instrumental in leading Leibniz to the view that motion itself cannot be a real entity, because it never exists; only what can exist in a moment of time can be real. This view was important for his dynamical conception of substance.

New Formulation of Laws of Motion

Leibniz appears to have gradually come to accept Huygens's view of the fundamental principles governing the laws of the impact of bodies, and soon after his arrival in Hanover he began to enunciate these principles, although the evidence (as so far published) is scanty and gives only the barest facts. Thus, in December 1676 Leibniz wrote that any effect taken in its totality is equal (quantitatively) to its entire cause (Grua 1948, p. 263). In March 1677 he enunciated two rules of impact: that the motive power of two impinging bodies (taken together) is the same before and after impact, and that the center of gravity of the two bodies proceeds with equal velocity before and after their impact, so that the direction of the aggregate of bodies is the same before and after the impact. "From these we derive the rest"

(Bodemann, *op. cit.,* p. 328, Bl. 144). These are Huygens's rules. In January 1678 a paper headed "De Concursu Corporum" began: "Force is the quantity of effect. Hence the force of a body in motion should be measured by the height to which it can ascend" (*ibid.,* p. 328, Bl. 86–91). This rule, which was inspired by Huygens (although not used by him in precisely this form), is based on Galileo's discussion of falling bodies. Huygens, and Leibniz after him, assumed that however a body was moving, it could always—in theory—be supposed to have all its force directed upward, so that the height to which it could ascend against gravity could be measured. Thus, a body moving with velocity v could rise against gravity to a height proportional to v^2 before its active force was used up. Hence, Leibniz took this height as the measure of the force of the moving body in terms of the square of its velocity.

There were two further points for which Leibniz was indebted to Huygens. One was that the center of gravity of a set of mutually interacting bodies cannot be raised through their interactions. If it could, there would be a system making perpetual mechanical motion possible. Leibniz used this principle (for instance, in the *Discourse on Metaphysics*) in his criticism of Descartes's measure of force in terms of mass multiplied by velocity, which he claimed would make perpetual motion possible.

Leibniz associated nonbeing with imperfection

and evil; nonbeing makes it impossible

for God to create a completely perfect world,

and allows him to create only the best

of all possible worlds.

The second point was the use Huygens made of relative motion in what he called his "method of a boat." Leibniz generalized this method, arguing that there was no way of determining, by a mere consideration of the motions of a set of bodies moving relative to one another, which of the motions were the real ones. This point was an additional reason for concluding that there is something not completely real—something phenomemal—in motion, and for deciding that the nature of substance must be found in something other than body (since body gets all its positive attributes through motion).

NEW CONCEPTION OF SUBSTANCE. Stress has been laid on Huygens's work because it was Leibniz's studies of motion and of the laws of motion that were responsible for what can only be described as a complete about-face on the question of fundamentals of dynamics.

Leibniz had essentially agreed with the outlook of the most modern of his contemporaries, for whom extension, figure, and motion were the outstanding examples of what is clear and distinct, not only making rational investigation possible in science but also justifying the claim that what science was investigating was the nature of reality itself. He had held to this outlook even though in his view the world of nature interpreted in this way was not metaphysically self-sufficient but needed God as creator and sustainer, and even though he sometimes treated bodies in terms of minds, through his notion of the conatus.

DYNAMICAL LAWS NOT BASIC. Toward the end of the 1670s Leibniz began to think of extension, figure, and motion as containing something imaginary, and held that the basic laws of motion cannot be derived from a study of their nature. Nevertheless, he continued to hold that, given basic laws derived from other sources, extension, figure, and motion could provide a means for explaining and predicting the course of phenomena. This is a noteworthy point. For Descartes and for Malebranche extension was real only because one can reason on it. Leibniz was now insisting that one can reason on it even though, like sound or color, there is something imaginary about it.

ACTIVITY ESSENTIAL TO MATTER. Metaphysical considerations were now necessary for the basic laws. The question arises, however, of what Leibniz meant by this. In two letters, one to Johann Friedrich, probably written in the autumn of 1679 (Preussische Akademie, Series II, Vol. I, p. 490), and one to the Jesuit Father de La Chaise, Louis XIV's confessor, probably from May 1680 (*ibid.,* p. 512), he spoke of re-establishing substantial forms, and stated that the nature of body does not consist in extension, but in "an action which relates itself to extension" (a remarkable anticipation of the view he expressed in the 1690s). The then current view of matter treated it as inert substance; Leibniz insisted that activity (effort) is essential to substance.

However, there was still much that was obscure in this work, and not until the dynamical discussions after 1690 was there any major clarification.

Doctrine of Propositions

A further development of Leibniz's views must be referred to at this point—his generalization in the *Discourse on Metaphysics* that in every true affirmative proposition, whether necessary or contingent, the predicate is contained in the notion of the subject. All the other basic ideas contained in the *Discourse* can be found in

Leibniz's writings up to and including 1680, but this doctrine concerning true propositions, and the ideas immediately dependent on it, appear to have been formulated just prior to the writing of the *Discourse.* It emerged from a long series of investigations into logic (Couturat, *op. cit.*). Perhaps it is a natural outcome of Leibniz' early view of knowledge as resulting from combinations of simple concepts, taken with his speculations—already alluded to—about modifications of pure concepts arising through their application to subjects. If *a, b, c,* and *d* are completely simple concepts having no common content (although Leibniz found some difficulty in this), then the proposition *abc is a* is true and the proposition *abc is d* is false. The first is an identical (necessary) proposition, and the second is self-contradictory (impossible).

CONTINGENT PROPOSITIONS. However, there are many propositions that are not of either type—for instance, "Caesar crossed the Rubicon." All such propositions, concerning existing individuals, are contingent. Leibniz constantly asserted that they are ultimately reducible to identities, but he had to admit that such truths of fact are not capable of being reduced to identities by human beings or even, in a straightforward sense, by God. He was also compelled to distinguish these truths from necessary propositions of the type *abc is a,* because he was unwilling to admit that everything that happens, happens necessarily. His studies of the endless discussions of free will had left him insistent on the contingency of what actually exists, and this was combined with stress on the freedom of God as creator of the best possible world and on the freedom of human beings in that world. However, Leibniz was unable to find any ultimate principle of demonstration other than that of the ultimate reducibility of true propositions to identities. He therefore tried to give this principle a form that would not jeopardize contingency.

It is clear that this attempt is not consistent with any account of the ultimate concepts as positive, separate, and containing nothing in common. The formula *abc is a* obviously will not apply to contingent propositions. On the basis of this formula, the predicate must be in the subject literally. In the *Generales Inquisitiones* of 1686 (Couturat, Secs. 132–136, p. 388), he said that contingent propositions are proved by "continued resolution" that is never completed, and in a paper on liberty (Foucher de Careil 1857, p. 182), he stated that this resolution is never completed, even by God, since it has no end. This means that more and more reasons can be given that make it likely that the predicate does belong to the subject. Thus, for God, who sees the infinite, the result is certain, although not necessary. Leibniz compared this continual progress toward identities

with the continued approach of a curve to its asymptote. Elsewhere he compared contingent propositions with incommensurable numbers. While all this shows how much he stressed the views that contingent propositions are not necessary, it is incompatible with any formal account that could be given of basic concepts and of complex concepts as simply results of combinations of basic ones.

POSSIBILITY. As has been shown, Leibniz had long held the view that every individual, whether person or thing, in some way reflects everything that is happening in the universe. He also asserted that there is an infinity of possible individuals that has never existed and never will, each possible individual being part of a possible universe and mirroring that universe. The Adam in our world was tempted and sinned; there are other possible worlds containing Adams who were tempted and did not sin. From this point of view, one can say that it would not be self-contradictory for the Adam in our world not to sin, although, given all his characteristics up to the time of his temptation, it was certain that he would sin. This makes Adam's sin contingent and not necessary; he could, Leibniz insisted, have refrained.

On the other hand, if the Adam in our world had refrained, our world—and, consequently, all the substances other than Adam in it—would have been different. An Adam without sin would have been possible, but would not have been compossible with the rest of the things in our world. From this point of view, God must be conceived as surveying all the different compossible worlds and decreeing the existence of the one containing the greatest perfection.

Perhaps a remote parallel is to be found in the activity of a dramatist working out alternative developments of his plot, always endeavoring to make characters act freely in accordance with their own natures but not admitting them into his drama if their behavior does not suit his purposes.

The point to be stressed is that the concept of a possible individual is always relative to the concept of a possible world, and cannot be considered independently. The notion of a possible individual in a possible world is a summary of God's complete knowledge of this and all the other individuals in that world, showing the individual's complete behavior but in no way constraining his action.

Denial of Interaction

The most important immediate consequence Leibniz derived from his conception of individual substance was the denial of any interaction between substances. In this he was doing no more than the occasionalists had already done, the difference between his view and theirs being that they made God the only immediate agent in the world, while Leibniz made every individual substance evolve in accordance with its own determinate nature, which was admitted into existence by God when he created the world.

ATTACK ON OCCASIONALISM. In contrast to Malebranche, whose *Méditations chrétiennes* he had studied in 1679 with great interest, Leibniz emphasized the view that individual substances are responsible for their own activity. He told de L'Hôpital in a letter of September 30, 1695 (Gerhardt 1849–1863, Vol. II, p. 299), that his view was a development from Malebranche's doctrine of occasional causes "and it is to him that I owe my foundations on this subject." He also wrote to Wolf on December 8, 1705 (Gerhardt 1860, p. 51), that he would not have discovered his harmonic system if he had not found laws of motion that overturn occasional causes. Thus, it seems that for Leibniz both logic and laws of motion lead to metaphysics.

APPEARANCE OF INTERACTION EXPLAINED. The denial of interaction led Leibniz to an account of the appearance of interaction in terms of the correspondence between all creatures established by God. He held that one could still speak of action and passion; changes in a substance as it evolves are changes in the degree of perfection with which it expresses the universe. A substance can be said to act when it passes to a lower degree of expression. In addition, one substance can be said to act on another when (*a*) it contains a clearer expression than any other substance of the changes that are about to occur in the substance that is said to be acted upon, and (*b*) the latter substance passes to a less perfect expression.

EACH SOUL EXPRESSES THE UNIVERSE. The relation between the human mind and the body is explained in terms of the view that the soul, evolving spontaneously, always expresses the entire state of the universe. It does this "according to the relation of other bodies to its own." This expression is contained in its "perception"—Leibniz's word for the most rudimentary awareness, sensuous in nature, of an object. It follows that the perceptions of the soul must correspond most directly to what is happening in its body, and this is what makes it appropriate to call one's body one's own. Monads, as Leibniz said later, have no windows (*Monadology,* Sec. 7) and need none. They know what is going on outside through the effect of the outside world on their own bodies; and, as we have seen, such effects mirror their causes.

OTHER POINTS. It also follows that our sense perceptions must contain much that is confused, which we are not able to perceive clearly. Leibniz had already noted this in 1676 (Jagodinski 1913, p. 96), and it is the basis of his later doctrine of *petites perceptions.*

There are many points in the *Discourse* that have not been explicitly referred to. Mention must be made of two: the account of the rules governing God's action in the world, which are regular—aside from occasional suspensions for miracles—but are such as to produce the maximum richness of effects; and the discussion of the sense in which man can be said to have ideas of all things. The first point was touched upon very early, but was reinforced and given definition by Leibniz' study of Malebranche's writings in 1679, and the second can be compared with the study "Ideas" ("Quid Sit Idea," Gerhardt 1875–1890, Vol. VII, p. 263).

There is a strong note of piety struck in the *Discourse* in the account of the City of God, of which all rational creatures are members. As has been shown, Leibniz held that the accumulation of knowledge of the universe naturally increases the devotion of men to its creator.

Substantial Unity of the Human Body

Leibniz sent a paragraph-by-paragraph summary of the *Discourse* to Count Ernst von Hessen-Rheinfels for transmission to Antoine Arnauld. This led to a long correspondence (first published with the *Discourse,* 1846) in which the main points raised by Arnauld arose from Leibniz's account of the concept of an individual substance and of the individual's complete lack of interaction with other substances. Five specific issues may be noted: (1) Arnauld's fear that the derivation of whatever will happen to an individual from his complete notion renders all events necessary and deprives not only the individual but also God of all freedom; (2) the difficulty of understanding how the events in the body can fit in completely with the events in the mind, if both interaction and occasionalism are denied; (3) in what way the human body, which is extended and divisible, can be a substance, which is, on Leibniz's view, unextended and indivisible; (4) the manner in which mind can express what is in the body; (5) of what things there are substantial forms.

SUBSTANTIAL FORMS. Here only the third issue, that of the substantial unity of the human body, will be treated. Leibniz had no really satisfactory answer to this question. He made it clear that he did regard the human body as forming a true unity with the mind, which is the substantial form of the body; but he was unable to say how mind unifies body. The body is, of course, an organism, but it is body; and everything happens in it according to the laws of motion. In this correspondence Leibniz did not, as he later did, stress the notion of an organism as fundamental to a substance. Assuming that the human being, consisting of mind and body, is a true unity, he extended the notion of organism to cover all beings endowed with substantial forms. A substantial form, for Leibniz, was something analogous to a mind and capable of "perception" (the lowest degree of mental activity, not involving either self-consciousness or thought). It is through its perceptions that any individual "expresses" what goes on in the universe.

BODIES AS BODIES ARE MERE PHENOMENA. Leibniz insisted that unless bodies are made up of constituents that have substantial forms, they have no reality but are mere phenomena. If there are such substantial forms, then bodies have such reality as belongs to their constituents; but even so, when they are considered only as bodies (the substantial forms not taken into account), they are mere aggregates, phenomenal and not real. This is important because it indicates one of the things Leibniz often had in view when he spoke of something as phenomenal. Take something real, consider some aspect of it that does not directly involve the substantial forms that make it real, and that aspect is phenomenal. Or take a number of real things, aggregate them, and consider the aggregate as a single thing; as a single thing it is phenomenal and not real. The phrase "well founded phenomena" (*phenomena bene fundata*) was used by Leibniz of things that, although phenomenal in the above sense, are based on something real; an example is the rainbow, which is based on light refracted from water drops, which in turn are based on monads.

Leibniz had long held the view

that every individual, whether person or thing,

in some way reflects everything

that is happening in the universe.

SUBSTANCES HAVE ORGANIC BODIES. The letter to Arnauld dated October 6, 1687, was the last in the series, for Leibniz went traveling. On March 23, 1690, he wrote to Arnauld once more, this time from Venice, sending a résumé of his metaphysics (much shorter than his previous résumé and, apart from one point, of interest chiefly for its omissions). Bodies are not substances but aggregations of substances—these substances are indivisible, incorruptible, and not capable of being generated, and possess something analogous to souls. This view stresses that these substances have been and will always be united to *organic* bodies capable of diverse transformations. The view that substances are united to bodies was not new to Leibniz, but his stress on the organic nature of these bodies seems to be new. Nothing was said about substantial forms, about the notion of individual substance, or about bodies apart from forms being phenomena. Substances were still spontaneously active and self-contained, but the new

formula was less provocative. "Each substance contains in its nature the law of continuation of the series of its own operations and all that has happened to it and all that will happen to it." The notions of expression of the union of soul and body and of action of one thing on another are explained as in the *Discourse*. The remainder of the final letter corresponds briefly to the sections in the *Discourse* dealing with God as the head of the republic of spirits, with a brief note about physics.

In Leibniz' later writings the stress on every substance's having an organic body, and on the substance's having in it the law of continuation of the series of its operations, predominated. The *notion* of an individual substance was rarely mentioned.

Pre-Established Harmony

While in Italy, Leibniz saw a review of Newton's *Principia* in the *Acta Eruditorum* of June 1688, and was stimulated by it to develop his own views in a manuscript on dynamics (Gerhardt 1849–1863, Vol. VI, pp. 281–514). He left the manuscript in Florence, to be criticized by friends before publication, but it was not published in his lifetime.

From the time Leibniz returned home, he published aspects of his new views in the various journals. In March 1694 his "First Philosophy and the Notion of Substance: An Emendation" (Gerhardt 1875–1890, Vol. IV, p. 468) appeared in the *Acta Eruditorum*. In this article Leibniz stressed the concept of force as essential to substance, contrasted it with the scholastic notion of power, and called substance by the Aristotelian word *entelechy*. In April 1695 he published his "Specimen Dynamicum" in the same journal (Gerhardt 1849–1863, Vol. VI, pp. 234 f.), giving a more technical and systematic account of his conception of force; and on June 27, 1695, he published his "Système nouveau de la nature et de la communication des substances" (*ibid.*, Vol. IV, pp. 477 f.), containing a discussion of the problem of the relation between mind and body, in the *Journal des sçavans*. In this latter paper, Leibniz expounded his view that every substance is completely self-contained, but did so in consequence of his inability to see how one could solve the problem otherwise, rather than in relation to the doctrine of propositions. Interaction is inconceivable because of the disparity between matter and mind; occasional causes show the power of God but not his wisdom; therefore, Leibniz said, he was led gradually to a view that surprised him: that God created each substance in such a way that everything that happens to it arises from its own nature, in complete spontaneity and without any influence from anything outside, apart from God, and yet in complete harmony with what happens to every other substance. In January 1696 (Gerhardt 1875–

1890, Vol. IV, p. 499), he publicly described his hypothesis as "the way of pre-established harmony," a phrase that has provided the most popular description of Leibniz' system (first used in a 1695 paper; see Gerhardt 1849–1863, Vol. II, p. 298).

Monads

The common term "monad" was first used by Leibniz in 1695 (not in 1696, as popularly held) in a letter (*ibid.*, p. 295) to de L'Hôpital (who in 1696 wrote the first treatise on the integral calculus, using Leibniz's symbols and methods). There were so many examples of the use of the word *monas* in the seventeenth century to signify the unit that it is impossible to say which of them stimulated Leibniz to use it. However, Euclid's word for the unit (*Elements*, Bk. VIII, Def. I) is *monas* and, since Leibniz had recently, in the *Acta Eruditorum*, quoted the *Elements* (Bk. V, Def. V) in his reply to Nieuwentijt's criticisms of the calculus, this may have been an important influence on Leibniz's choice of the term in a letter to a mathematician and thereafter.

MONADS AND THE PHYSICAL WORLD. Leibniz's fundamental stress was on the unity and spontaneous activity of monads, but he insisted that monads are in the real world and mirror the world only because of their association with their organic body. A monad without a body would be "a deserter from the general order" ("On Principles of Life," written 1705; Gerhardt 1875–1890, Vol. VI, p. 546). Since everything that happens anywhere in the physical world has some effect everywhere else, the body belonging to a monad is receiving such effects at every moment and is in correspondence with these effects—although not as a causal consequence of them—in such a way that the monad is able to mirror what is happening everywhere.

The Adam in our world was tempted and sinned;

there are other possible worlds containing Adams

who were tempted and did not sin.

As has been shown, the fundamental physical process is impact, and in order to preserve the law of continuity—which Leibniz claimed to have introduced—all bodies must have some degree of elasticity and some degree of hardness. When two bodies impinge, each gradually changes shape through its elasticity and then rebounds; thus, speeds change gradually. Each body derives the whole of its force of rebound from its own inner structure; it depends on the force of the other body only for the amount of force it itself displays (thus echoing the independence of the monads). Elasticity is

possible only because an elastic fluid circulates between the parts of the body, but this fluid in turn can be elastic only by means of an elastic fluid circulating between its parts, and so on ad infinitum, so that we must admit bodies within bodies without end. (Leibniz welcomed such infinite regresses.)

All bodies are moving diversely, and all have effects on the organism of any monad and are thus mirrored by the monad. Although monads are not extended, they nevertheless have a certain kind of situation in extension: ". . . a certain ordered relation of coexistence with all others, through the machine over which they are, though this situation cannot be designated by precise points" (letter to de Volder, March–June 1703, *ibid.*, Vol. II, p. 253). There is no particle of matter, however small, that is not composed of organisms, each with its dominant monad. When Leibniz was asked the use of this elaboration of organisms—why God could not have been satisfied with monads and their perceptions—he replied that a part of the function of the monad is to express its body, and that without bodies nature would lack the "bond of order" between all things (letters to Foucher, September 1695, *ibid.*, Vol. IV, pp. 492–493; to Jaquelot after September 1704, *ibid.*, Vol. VI, p. 570).

OBJECTIVITY OF THE PHYSICAL WORLD. Leibniz' view of monads and the physical world is quite in accordance with his account of phenomena, by which matter is phenomenal because the monads that give it reality are omitted from consideration, but it is difficult to reconcile this with any account that makes phenomena entirely subjective. Leibniz quite often spoke as if all that is necessary in the universe is God and individual monads with their inner states, so that the whole appearance of spatiotemporal material objects is entirely within each monad (letters to de Volder, June 30, 1704, *ibid.*, Vol. II, p. 270, and after November 14, 1704, *ibid.*, p. 275).

But what then becomes of Leibniz's stress on organisms as essential to the "bond of order"? The wisdom of God in harmonizing efficient and final causes requires that there should really be efficient causes, and efficient causes require that extended bodies in time have at least some degree of reality. Although space and time considered in themselves are abstractions, extended and enduring things are concrete. Even if they are "phenomenal" (in some sense) when reference to their underlying monads is left out of account, they nevertheless make up the real world, taken along with their monads. In abstracts the wholes are prior to the parts, so that parts are mere limitations of the wholes; but abstracts are derived from concretes, and in concretes the parts are prior to the wholes. Space and time, being abstract, are derived from enduring things; and enduring things, being concrete, are dependent on the monads composing them. Therefore, unless there are unitary monads that themselves have no parts, there are no concretes from which space and time can be abstracted.

This was one of Leibniz's main arguments, many times repeated, in favor of monads other than rational spirits. However, this whole elaborate structure vanishes if material things are merely contents of the perceptions of monads in a modern subjective sense. The student of Leibniz's conflicting writings must make what he can of this topic.

Space and time *considered by themselves* are not real; that is, they are not substances: they are ideal and abstract. Leibniz certainly regarded ideal space as having the structure given to it by Euclidean geometry, and he thought of this structure as being imposed on whatever is spatially extended. Space in this sense is also the form of possible coexistences, as time is the form of possible successive existents.

ORGANISMS AND "VIS VIVA." At this point one of the most obscure parts of Leibniz' doctrine is involved. To get organisms into his world even as aggregates, Leibniz somehow had to derive them from his monads. To do this, he stated that (1) every monad is an entelechy (primitive active force) combined indissolubly with primary matter (primitive passive force); (2) derived forces, both active and passive, are modifications of primitive forces; (3) impenetrability of extended bodies is derived from the prime matter (*materia prima*) of monads, as is their inertia, although this in some way involves active force as well; (4) extension presupposes something diffused or spread out—something capable of resistance and which Leibniz further seems to have identified with the prime matters in a multitude of monads, although every such monad is involved as a whole; (5) in this way secondary matter (*materia secunda*) results; this is not just an extended mass of matter, but an aggregate of monads spatially related through their matters.

Derived active force, *vis viva*, belongs to *materia secunda*. Since primary active forces in the monads display themselves as derived active forces to the degree made possible by the interlinking of matter in space, a body can get the amount and kind of movement allowed it only through the moving bodies that environ it (May 1702, *ibid.*, Vol. IV, pp. 393 f., printed also in Gerhardt 1849–1863, Vol. VI, pp. 98 f.; *ibid.*, pp. 235, 247; Gerhardt 1875–1890, Vol. IV, pp. 364, 467; *ibid.*, pp. 510–511; and many other places).

It does not seem that there is any way of making out Leibniz's views in detail. An infinity of monads would have to contribute primary active force toward the *vis viva* of the smallest particle of *materia secunda*. Again,

Leibniz always rejected the idea that there is any active power inside a monad that can actually produce a movement, so the link between primary active force and the force said to be derived from it is difficult to understand. Even if the derivation were successful, it would do nothing to justify the existence of organisms (as distinct from mere unorganized bodies); and Leibniz stated that while organisms are not essential to matter, they are essential to matter organized by a supreme wisdom (letter to Lady Masham, June 30, 1704, *ibid.*, Vol. III, pp. 356–357).

There is also the general difficulty of reconciling the dynamical account of monads as active centers of force impeded by primary matter with the psychological account of them as active–passive producers of confused and clear perceptions through appetition; it is hard to see how the monad could be both things, although Leibniz thought that it could (letter to des Bosses, March 11, 1706, *ibid.*, Vol. II, p. 307). Certainly overstress on the psychological account was liable to endanger the entire development based on the dynamical account.

General Principles

Leibniz claimed that his philosophy was based on certain general principles concerning necessary truths and concerning truths of fact, which are contingent.

PRINCIPLE OF IDENTITY. The fundamental principle of necessary truths is the principle of identity, which Leibniz always associated with noncontradiction: *A* is *A* and cannot be non-*A*. The opposites of necessary truths are self-contradictory.

PRINCIPLE OF THE BEST. A contingent truth is one whose opposite is not self-contradictory. The fundamental principle of contingent truths is the principle of the best, which arises from the free choice of God in creating the world. God, being perfectly wise, powerful, and good, is obliged to choose the best among possibles if he decides to admit any possibles to existence. However, this is a moral, not a metaphysical, necessity; he could refrain from creating any world, and it would not be self-contradictory (since he chose freely) if he chose to create a world less good than the best, although it is certain he would not do so.

The main difficulty here is that if God's wisdom, power, and goodness are necessary characteristics (and they seem to be if the standard proof of his existence from his essence, as amended by Leibniz, is sound), it is hard to see how there could be even the possibility of his doing something not in accordance with these characteristics.

PRINCIPLE OF SUFFICIENT REASON. The principle of sufficient reason holds for all truths, but its main application was to contingent truths, since identity is the sufficient reason for necessary truths. It was used by Leibniz to show the impossibility of identical atoms: there would be no possible reason why any one such atom should be where it is rather than elsewhere. He similarly rejected the idea of the world's being created at a particular moment of time, on the ground that there could be no reason why it should not have been created earlier or later than that particular moment. Sometimes he used sufficient reason as the basis of the principle of the identity of indiscernibles. It is not impossible, he told Clarke, that there should be two things exactly alike, but God would not admit two such things into existence because he would have no reason for treating them differently (Alexander 1956, 5th letter, Sec. 25).

METAPHYSICALLY NECESSARY PRINCIPLES. There are a number of principles that Leibniz considered metaphysically necessary, although he did not actually reduce them to identities; for instance, that everything possible demands (*exigit*) to exist, and will exist unless hindered. Here it must be remembered that what exists depends on God's will, and that unless possibles demanded existence, God would have no reason for admitting any of them into existence. However, once this reason is given God, he can and does impose conditions of perfection.

Other examples are the principle that activity is essential to substance, which Leibniz thought would hold in any world (Gerhardt 1875–1890, Vol. II, p. 169), and the axiom that a thing remains in its own state unless there is reason for change (*ibid.*, p. 170).

PRINCIPLES OF ORDER. Very important for the understanding of Leibniz's philosophy of science are the laws that he called systematic, or laws of order ("Specimen Dynamicum," Gerhardt 1849–1863, Vol. VI, p. 241). These are the principle of continuity, the principle that every action involves a reaction, and the principle of the equality of cause and effect.

The principle of continuity has a wide range of application, since it covers changes in perception and all changes in degrees of perfection in monads. It also requires that there be no sudden qualitative alterations as an observer goes from one point of space to another. This principle, however, must be linked with an equally general one, that of maximum variety. There are no two locations, however close together, where there is not some divergence in every aspect of every feature. Leibniz also stressed two principles together: *tout comme ici*, and *che per variar la natura e bella:* nature is everywhere the same, everywhere varied (letter to Queen Sophie Charlotte, May 8, 1704, Gerhardt 1875–1890, Vol. III, pp. 343–348). To all these must be added the principle of maximum determination. Nature does not always seek

the shortest paths, but always acts in the most determinate way.

CORRESPONDENCE OF EFFICIENT AND FINAL CAUSES. One other important general point is the correspondence between efficient and final causes. The higher monads act in accordance with what appears their greatest good; final causes apply to them. In matter everything occurs through efficient causation, including the increase and diminution of organisms, although neither the origination nor the destruction of an organism is possible through mechanical means. The two realms of efficient and final causation correspond perfectly and in complete independence, the lower realm being so contrived as to "serve" the higher. The laws of efficient causation cannot be derived from matter, although they are "natural" to it.

In abstracts the wholes are prior to the parts,

so that parts are mere limitations of the wholes;

but abstracts are derived from concretes,

and in concretes the parts are prior to the wholes.

CONCEPT OF THE "NATURAL." The conception of what is "natural" to a thing plays a significant part in Leibniz' system. The natural is intermediate between the essential and the accidental. It is, he held, capable of being derived from the nature of the thing as an explicable modification (Preface to *New Essays, ibid.,* Vol. V, p. 59). What God allows to exist, what he chooses as best, is chosen from natural characteristics, since to give things what is not natural to them would involve a constant miracle. Leibniz came to believe that the natural tendency of a body moving in a curved path is to move along the tangent to the curve; that bodies cannot naturally attract one another; that matter is not naturally capable of thinking; that there is a natural and not a merely arbitrary connection between our perceptions of secondary qualities and the bodily movements giving rise to these perceptions (for instance, *New Essays,* Book IV, Ch. 6, Sec. 7).

There is no clear justification for these views, but they show how anxious Leibniz was to avoid anything purely arbitrary in the construction of the universe. He was sure that God would not do anything merely because he willed it: if there were no objective reason to determine God's will, he would not act at all.

Discussions of Contemporary Philosophy

Leibniz was moved by the publication in 1704 of Coste's French translation of Locke's *Essay on Human*

Understanding to lay his thoughts in detail alongside those of Locke. Leibniz' *New Essays* (*Nouveaux Essais sur l'entendement humain*) was not a systematic criticism of Locke's philosophy. It contains occasional discussions of Locke's views, but in general Leibniz expounded his own views, without giving reasons, on the points raised by Locke. The book is thus more valuable as a collection of passages relating to aspects of Leibniz' system than as a thoroughgoing criticism of Locke. Leibniz had intended to publish the *New Essays* and get Locke's views on them, but Locke died in 1704, the year in which Leibniz wrote them, and he gave up the idea. They were first published at Amsterdam and Leipzig in 1765.

CRITICISMS OF DESCARTES. Leibniz had also thought of publishing his papers on Descartes, but never succeeded in getting them ready. By comparison with his criticisms of Locke, Leibniz's criticisms of Descartes were much more searching. This was natural, in view of the strength of Cartesianism in France.

LEIBNIZ AND SPINOZA. Leibniz was never a Spinozist. He thought highly of Spinoza, but held that his view that only what is actual is possible involved a denial of God's providence and of all freedom. His statement to Bourguet (Gerhardt 1875–1890, Vol. III, p. 576)— "Spinoza would be right if there were no monads"— emphasized a further point, the need for a "substantial foundation in things" other than God.

THE *THEODICY*. Leibniz's only large book on philosophy that was published during his lifetime, *Essais de Théodicée sur la bonté de Dieu, la liberté de l'homme et l'origine du mal* (the *Theodicy*), was the outcome of discussions with Sophie Charlotte on matters concerning free will, evil, and the justification of God's creation, many of which had been raised by Bayle. The *Theodicy,* written in French, was published at Amsterdam in 1710; a Latin translation by des Bosses, at Frankfurt in 1719. In this work Leibniz was at his ease, pouring out his vast learning with an avoidance of technicality and finding no difficulty in replying to objections in such a way as to appeal to Sophie Charlotte, who, while interested and intelligent, was not a professional philosopher. One of the interesting things about the *Theodicy* is the way in which Leibniz' memory unearthed ideas and views from his early years; a lifetime's ideas are in it. It is not to be put aside as mere recreation for a queen; unsystematic though it is, it contains many passages that give clear and explicit expression to many of Leibniz's views.

Later Correspondence

Of Leibniz' philosophic correspondence in his later years three sets may be singled out: that with Simon de Volder, a physicist and philosopher of Leiden and the literary executor of Huygens (*ibid.*, Vol. II, pp. 148 ff.); that with des Bosses, a Jesuit priest of Hildesheim (*ibid.*, pp. 291 ff.); and that with Samuel Clarke. In this correspondence Leibniz showed his mettle, not merely expressing his views but also defending them. De Volder, who forced Leibniz to discuss the notion of substance when Leibniz wanted to discuss the measurement of forces, remained unconvinced by Leibniz's accounts, although he compelled Leibniz to bring out explicitly many points in his view of substance.

The letters between Leibniz and Clarke, which concern Newton's views on space, time, and matter and Leibniz's views on these topics and the principle of sufficient reason, grew in length, and Leibniz died before he could receive Clarke's reply to his fifth letter. These letters went via the princess of Wales, whom Leibniz had known in Hanover, and national pride was at stake on both sides. The situation for Leibniz was embittered by the attack on his integrity that had been begun 15 years earlier by Fatio de Duillier, who charged that Leibniz had used—without acknowledgment—Newton's discoveries on the calculus, an attack that had been fully endorsed by the large-scale inquiry made by the Royal Society. The whole dispute was caused by misconceptions on both sides, and would have been unnecessary had Newton been less secretive and more ready to publish his work.

Des Bosses, in his correspondence with Leibniz, began by expounding certain difficulties he felt with regard to Leibniz' system, but gradually the discussion began to turn on the doctrine of transubstantiation. To explain how the blood and body of Christ could be literally present in the sacramental bread and wine, Leibniz suggested the notion of a substantial bond (*vinculum substantiale*) conferring substantiality on material bodies (such as bread and wine) so as to make them more than mere entities by aggregation (mere phenomena), as they were in Leibniz's system. What Leibniz himself wanted was not to confer substantiality on ordinary material bodies as such, but to show how an organism has unity through the presence in it of its dominant monad. While he never succeeded in showing this, he constantly asserted it (although sometimes he did deny it). However, a substantial bond of the sort discussed in these letters would be somewhat of an excrescence, since it would be affected by the monads but they would not be affected by it. The supplementary note at the end of the letter to des Bosses of August 19, 1715 (*ibid.*, p. 506), containing Leibniz's classification of entities, shows no trace of a need for any such bond.

The Papers of 1714

Mention must be made of two important papers of 1714, "Principes de la nature et de la grâce, fondés en raison" ("The Principles of Nature and of Grace," first published in *L'Europe savant,* 1718), written for Prince Eugene of Savoy, and the "Monadologie" ("Monadology," which first appeared in Erdmann, *Opera Philosophica*), begun for Remond. These two papers have much in common, although the "Monadology" is more complete and gives references throughout to the relevant sections of the *Theodicy.* Together they give a synoptic view of Leibniz's philosophy. It must be remembered, however, that for the working out of his views in detail, one must go to Leibniz's letters and papers; the synoptic views are insufficient.

Leibniz's general philosophical views could be made out pretty well from the papers published in his lifetime, along with the *Theodicy* and the correspondence with Samuel Clarke, published by Clarke in 1717. These do not, however, enable one to understand the grounds for his views, and without this, misunderstanding is only too easy. Publication of his writings came only slowly. Among the important works are the *New Essays,* published by R. E. Raspe in 1765, the *Discourse on Metaphysics* and correspondence with Arnauld, published by C. L. Grotefend in 1846, and the logical essays, published by Louis Couturat in 1903.

Leibniz thought highly of Spinoza, but held that his view that only what is actual is possible involved a denial of God's providence and of all freedom.

One personal characteristic of Leibniz helps to explain much in his work. He said he had a weak memory but strong gifts of invention and judgment (Guhrauer, *Life,* Vol. II, Appendix, p. 60). Much of his original work was done over and over: "When I have done something, I forget it almost completely in a few months, and rather than hunt for it among a chaos of sheets that I never had time to sort out and index, I have to do the work all over again" (Gerhardt 1849–1863, Vol. II, p. 228). His papers show how true this is. They were never reduced to order in the past, and it is only during the twentieth century, under the auspices of the Berlin and Paris academies, that a systematic attempt has been made to classify and catalogue them.

BIBLIOGRAPHY

Bibliographical Sources

Bodemann, Eduard, *Der Briefwechsel des G. W. Leibniz in der Königlichen Öffentlichen Bibliothek zu Hannover.* Hanover, 1889; reprinted Hildesheim, after September 1965.

———, *Die Leibniz-Handschriften zu Hannover.* Hanover, 1895; reprinted Hildesheim, after September 1965.

Ravier, Émile, *Bibliographie des oeuvres de Leibniz.* Paris, 1937. Corrections and additions by Paul Schrecker in *Revue philosophique de la France et de l'étranger,* Vol. 126 (1938), 324 ff.

Works

Opera Omnia, Louis Dutens, ed., 6 vols. Geneva, 1768. Still the most complete collection.

Leibniz's deutsche Schriften, G. E. Guhrauer, ed., 2 vols. Berlin, 1838–1840; reprinted Hildesheim, after September 1965.

Opera Philosophica, J. E. Erdmann, ed., 2 vols. Berlin, 1840; reprinted Aalen, 1958. Still the most useful compact edition.

Oeuvres, Amédée Jacques, ed., 2 vols. Vol. I, Paris, 1845; Vol. II, Paris, 1842.

Briefwechsel zwischen Leibniz, Arnauld und dem Grafen Ernst von Hessen-Rheinfels, C. L. Grotefend, ed. Hanover, 1846. First publication of the *Discourse on Metaphysics* (1685–1686).

Mathematische Schriften, C. I. Gerhardt, ed., 7 vols. Berlin and Halle, 1849–1863; reprinted Hildesheim, 1962. Much valuable philosophical matter.

Nouvelles Lettres et opuscules inédits, L. A. Foucher de Careil, ed. Paris, 1857. Still very useful.

Oeuvres, L. A. Foucher de Careil, ed., 7 vols. Paris, 1859–1875.

Briefwechsel zwischen Leibniz und Wolf, C. I. Gerhardt, ed. Halle, 1860; reprinted Hildesheim, 1963.

Philosophische Schriften, C. I. Gerhardt, ed., 7 vols. Berlin, 1875–1890; facsimile reprint Hildesheim, 1960–1961. Indispensable.

Mittheilungen aus Leibnizens ungedruckten Schriften, G. Mollat, ed. Leipzig, 1893.

Briefwechsel von G. W. Leibniz mit Mathematikern, C. I. Gerhardt, ed. Berlin, 1899; reprinted Hildesheim, 1962.

Opuscules et fragments inédits de Leibniz, Louis Couturat, ed. Paris, 1903; reprinted Hildesheim, 1961. A model of what such an edition should be. Exceedingly valuable for logic and theory of knowledge.

Nachgelassene Schriften physikalischen, mechanischen, und technischen Inhalts, Ernst Gerland, ed. Leipzig, 1906.

Leibniz. Avec de nombreux textes inédits, Jean Baruzi, ed. Paris, 1909.

Leibnitiana Elementa Philosophiae Arcanae de Summa Rerum, Iwan Jagodinski, ed. Kazan, Russia, 1913. Text with Russian translation. In spite of errors, this is a precious record. Review with many corrections by A. Rivaud, in *Revue de métaphysique et de morale,* Vol. 22 (1914); 94–120.

Leibnitiana Inedita. Confessio Philosophi, Iwan Jagodinski, ed. Kazan, Russia, 1915. Text with Russian translation. *Confessio* edited and translated into French by Yvon Belaval. Paris, 1961.

Ausgewählte philosophische Schriften im Originaltext, Herman Schmalenbach, ed., 2 vols. Leipzig, 1915.

Sämtliche Schriften und Briefe, edited under the supervision of the Preussische Akademie der Wissenschaft. Darmstadt and Leipzig, 1923—. Only one volume of the philosophical letters and two of the philosophical writings have appeared so far. The remaining volumes are historical and political.

Lettres et fragments inédits, Paul Schrecker, ed. Paris, 1934.

Textes inédits, Gaston Grua, ed., 2 vols. Paris, 1948. A most useful addition to the published material.

Revisions of Texts

Discours de métaphysique, Henri Lestienne, ed. Paris, 1907; 2d ed., 1929; reprinted 1952. This diplomatic edition contains all the variants of Leibniz' drafts.

Lettres de Leibniz à Arnauld, Geneviève Lewis, ed. Paris, 1952. Gives text as received by Arnauld, but Arnauld's replies are not given.

Malebranche et Leibniz, André Robinet, ed. Paris, 1953. Large collection of texts from original sources.

Principes de la nature et de la grâce fondés en raison; Principes de la philosophie ou monadologie, André Robinet, ed. Paris, 1954. Gives all variants.

Correspondance Leibniz-Clarke, André Robinet, ed. Paris, 1957.

Commentaries

Boutroux, Émile, *La Monadologie.* Paris, 1881; reprinted Paris, 1956.

Burgelin, Pierre, *Commentaire du Discours de métaphysique.* Paris, 1959.

Costabelle, Pierre, *Leibniz et le dynamique. Les textes de 1692.* Paris, 1960.

Le Roy, Georges, *Discours de métaphysique et Correspondance avec Arnauld.* Paris, 1957.

English Translations

Philosophical Works, translated by G. M. Duncan. New Haven, 1890.

The Monadology and Other Philosophical Writings, translated by Robert Latta. Oxford, 1898.

Discourse on Metaphysics, Correspondence With Arnauld, Monadology, translated by G. R. Montgomery. Chicago, 1902. Contains many mistranslations. Edited with corrections by A. R. Chandler. Chicago, 1924.

New Essays Concerning Human Understanding, translated by A. G. Langley. Chicago, 1916; reprinted 1949. Many errors in translation.

Monadology, translated by H. W. Carr. London and Los Angeles, 1930.

Philosophical Writings, translated by Mary Morris. London, 1934.

Theodicy, translated by E. M. Huggard, Austin Farrer, ed. London, 1951.

Selections, translated by Philip Wiener. New York, 1951. A wide and very representative collection.

Monadology, translated by P. G. Lucas and Leslie Grint. Manchester, 1953; reprinted with minor corrections, 1961. Based on Lestienne's edition.

Leibniz-Clarke Correspondence, H. G. Alexander, ed. Manchester, 1956. Gives Clarke's translation of Leibniz' letters.

Philosophical Papers and Letters, translated by L. E. Loemker, 2 vols. Chicago, 1956. The widest and most useful collection in English, with an admirable selected, annotated bibliography.

German Translations

Hauptschriften, translated by Ernst Cassirer and Artur Buchenau, 5 vols. Leipzig, 1904–1906; 2d ed., 2 vols., Leipzig, 1924.

Schöpferische Vernunft, translated by Wolf von Engelhardt. Marburg, 1952. A very useful collection, containing much not translated elsewhere; for instance, *Pacidius Philalethi.*

Fragmente zur Logik, translated by Franz Schmidt. Berlin, 1960.

A microfilm negative of unpublished manuscripts in Hanover, selected by Paul Schrecker, is deposited in the University of Pennsylvania Library. Permission for a positive copy to be made must be obtained from the Niedersachsische Landesbibliothek in Hanover.

Biographies

Fischer, Kuno, *Gottfried Wilhelm Leibniz. Leben, Werke und Lehre,* 5th ed., Willy Kabitz, ed. Heidelberg, 1920. Of great value, with appendix containing many new details and corrections.

Guhrauer, G. E., *Gottfried Wilhelm, Freiherr von Leibniz,* 2 vols. Breslau, 1842; 2d ed., 1846; reprinted Hildesheim, after September 1965. The only full-scale life.

Huber, Kurt, *Leibniz.* Munich, 1951.

Merz, J. T., *Leibniz.* Edinburgh and London, 1884; reprinted New York, 1948. Still useful.

Wiedeburg, Paul, *Der junge Leibniz, das Reich und Europa,* Part I, *Mainz,* 2 vols. Wiesbaden, 1962.

Interpretations

Belaval, Yvon, *Leibniz, critique de Descartes.* Paris, 1960.

——, *Leibniz. Initiation à sa philosophie.* Paris, 1962. Replaces *La Pensée de Leibniz* (1952).

Blondel, Maurice, *Une Énigme historique: Le Vinculum substantiale d'après Leibniz.* Paris, 1930.

Boehm, A., *Le "Vinculum substantiale" chez Leibniz.* Paris, 1934.

Brunner, Fernand, *Études sur la signification historique de la philosophie de Leibniz.* Paris, 1950.

Cassirer, Ernst, *Leibniz' System in seinen wissenschaftlichen Grundlagen.* Marburg, 1902; reprinted 1962. Classical study.

Couturat, Louis, *La Logique de Leibniz.* Paris, 1901; reprinted Hildesheim, 1961. Classical study.

Friedmann, Georges, *Leibniz et Spinoza.* 2d ed., Paris, 1946; 3d ed., 1963. Useful correction of wrong ideas.

Galli, Gallo, *Studi sulla filosofia de Leibniz.* Padua, 1948.

Grua, Gaston, *Jurisprudence universelle et théodicée selon Leibniz.* Paris, 1953.

——, *La Justice humaine selon Leibniz.* Paris, 1956.

Gueroult, M., *Dynamique et métaphysique leibniziennes.* Paris, 1934. An admirable full-scale study of Leibniz' dynamics.

Hildebrandt, Kurt, *Leibniz und das Reich der Gnade.* The Hague, 1953.

Iwanicki, Joseph, *Leibniz et les démonstrations mathématiques de l'existence de Dieu.* Strasbourg, 1933.

Jalabert, Jacques, *La Théorie leibnizienne de la substance.* Paris, 1947.

——, *Le Dieu de Leibniz.* Paris, 1960.

Joseph, H. W. B., *Lectures on the Philosophy of Leibniz.* Oxford, 1949.

Kabitz, Willy, *Die Philosophie des jungen Leibniz.* Heidelberg, 1909. A very good account.

Le Chevalier, L., *La Morale de Leibniz.* Paris, 1933.

Mahnke, Dietrich, *Leibnizens Synthese von Universalmathematik und Individualmetaphysik.* Halle, 1925. Still one of the best discussions of Leibniz; contains full-scale criticisms of Cassirer, Couturat, and Russell works.

Martin, Gottfried, *Leibniz: Logik und Metaphysik.* Cologne, 1960. Translated by P. G. Lucas as *Leibniz: Logic and Metaphysics.* Manchester, 1963.

Moreau, Joseph, *L'Universe leibnizien.* Paris, 1956.

Naert, Émilienne, *Leibniz et la querelle du pur amour.* Paris, 1959.

——, *Mémoire et conscience de soi selon Leibniz.* Paris, 1961.

Piat, Clodius, *Leibniz.* Paris, 1915.

Pichler, Hans, *Leibniz.* Graz, 1919.

Russell, Bertrand, *A Critical Exposition of the Philosophy of Leibniz.* Cambridge, 1900; 2d ed., 1937.

Schmalenbach, Herman, *Leibniz.* Munich, 1921.

Stieler, Georg, *Leibniz und Malebranche und das Theodicee Problem.* Darmstadt, 1930.

Wundt, Wilhelm, *Leibniz.* Leipzig, 1917.

Christian Unification

Baruzi, Jean, *Leibniz et l'organisation religieuse de la terre.* Paris, 1907. The best book on the subject.

Leibniz as Historian

Davillé, L., *Leibniz historien.* Paris, 1909.

Schischkoff, Goerge, ed., *Beiträge zur Leibniz-Forschung.* Reutlingen, 1946.

— L. J. RUSSELL

LEIBNIZ, GOTTFRIED WILHELM (UPDATE)

Gottfried Wilhelm Leibniz and the entire range of current scholarship concerning him have, since 1969, been the subjects of a single bibliographic source created by the Leibniz Archiv of the Niedersachsische Landesbibliothek in Hanover, namely, the periodical *Studia Leibnitiana*. Two other volumes should be noted in this regard: Albert Heinekamp's edition of *Leibniz Bibliographie: Die Literatur über Leibniz* (Frankfurt, 1984), which covers the secondary literature on Leibniz up to 1980; and Wilhelm Totok's *Leibniz Bibliographie,* vol. 14 of his *Handbuch der Geschichte der Philosophie* (Frankfurt. 1981).

The following aims to supplement L. J. Russell's 1967 bibliography in the original *Encyclopedia,* using the categories he employed, with some of the significant items that have appeared since then.

BIBLIOGRAPHY

Works by Leibniz

Sämtliche Schriften und Briefe. Four volumes of Leibniz's philosophical works and one volume of his philosophical correspondence have appeared to date. The philosophical work is covered through 1676 and the correspondence through 1685. In addition, another volume contains the *Nouveaux essais sur l'entendement humain.* Volumes completing coverage of the philosophical work to 1690 are scheduled to appear.

Various relatively short pieces of Leibniz's philosophical work and correspondence have appeared; for details, consult the bibliographies published in *Studia Leibnitiana.* There have also been numerous revisions of texts, for which the same source is recommended.

Commentaries and Interpretations

Adams, R. *Leibniz: Determinist, Theist, Idealist.* New York, 1994.
Becco, A. *Du simple selon G. W. Leibniz.* Paris, 1975.
Belaval, Y. *Études leibniziennes.* Paris, 1976.
Broad, C. D. *Leibniz: An Introduction.* Cambridge, 1975.
Brown, S. *Leibniz.* Minneapolis, 1984.
Burkhardt, H. *Logik und Semiotic in der Philosophie von Leibniz.* Munich, 1980.
Costabel, P. *Leibniz and Dynamics.* Ithaca, NY. 1973.
Dascal, M. *La Sémiologie de Leibniz.* Paris, 1978.
———. *Leibniz: Language, Signs, and Thought.* Amsterdam. 1987.
———, and E. Yakira, eds. *Leibniz and Adam.* Tel Aviv. 1993.
Duchesneau, F. *Leibniz et la méthode de la science.* Paris, 1993.
———. *La dynamique de Leibniz.* Paris, 1994.
Fichant, M., ed. *Gottfried Wilhelm Leibniz, la réforme de la dynamique.* Paris, 1994.
Frankfurt, H., ed. *Leibniz: A Collection of Critical Essays.* Garden City, 1972.
Heinekamp, A. *Das Problem des Guten bei Leibniz.* Bonn. 1969.
———, W. Lenzen, and M. Schneider, eds. *Mathesis rationis: Festschrift für Heinrich Schepers.* Munster, 1990.
Hooker, M., ed. *Leibniz: Critical and Interpretive Essays.* Minneapolis, 1982.
Ishiguro, H. *Leibniz's Philosophy of Logic and Language,* 2d ed. Cambridge, 1990.

Jolley, N. *Leibniz and Locke: A Study of the "New Essays Concerning Human Understanding."* Oxford, 1984.
———, ed. *The Cambridge Companion to Leibniz.* Cambridge, 1995.
Kauppi, R. *Uber die leibnizsche Logik.* New York, 1985.
Kulstad, M., ed. *Essays on the Philosophy of Leibniz.* Houston, 1977.
Kulstad, M., ed. *Leibniz on Apperception, Consciousness, and Reflection.* Munich, 1991.
Lamarra, A., ed. *L'infinito in Leibniz problemi e terminologia.* Rome, 1990.
Leclerc, I., ed. *The Philosophy of Leibniz and the Modern World.* Nashville, 1973.
Mates, B. *The Philosophy of Leibniz: Metaphysics and Language.* New York, 1986.
McRae, R. *Leibniz: Perception, Apperception, and Thought.* Toronto, 1976.
Mugnai, M. *Leibniz's Theory of Relations.* Stuttgart, 1992.
Okruhlik, K., and J. R. Brown, eds. *The Natural Philosophy of Leibniz.* Dordrecht, 1985.
Parkinson, G. H. R. *Logic and Reality in Leibniz's Metaphysics.* Oxford, 1965.
Rescher, N. *Leibniz: An Introduction to His Philosophy.* Totowa, NJ, 1979.
———. *Leibniz's Metaphysics of Nature.* Dordrecht, 1981.
———. *G. W. Leibniz's "Monadology." An Edition for Students.* Pittsburgh, 1991.
Robinet, A. *Architectonique disjonctive, automates systémiques et idéalité dans l'oeuvre de G. W. Leibniz.* Paris, 1986.
MacDonald Ross, G. *Leibniz.* Oxford, 1984.
Rutherford, D. *Leibniz and the Rational Order of Nature.* Cambridge, 1995.
Sleigh, C. R., Jr. *Leibniz and Arnauld: A Commentary on Their Correspondence.* New Haven, 1990.
Wilson, C. *Leibniz's Metaphysics.* Princeton, NJ, 1989.
Wilson, M. *Leibniz' Doctrine of Necessary Truth.* New York, 1990.
Yost, R. M., Jr. *Leibniz and Philosophical Analysis.* New York, 1985.
Woolhouse, R. S., ed. *Leibniz: Metaphysics and Philosophy of Science.* New York, 1981.

English Translations

De Summa Rerum: Metaphysical Papers, 1675–1676, trans. G. H. R. Parkinson. New Haven, 1992.
Discourse on Metaphysics, trans. P. Lucas and L. Grint. Manchester, 1953.
"Discourse on Metaphysics" and Related Writings, trans. R. Niall, D. Martin, and S. Brown. Manchester, 1988.
General Investigations Concerning the Analysis of Concepts and Truths, trans. W. H. O'Briant. Athens. GA, 1968.
The Leibniz-Arnauld Correspondence, trans. H. T. Mason. Manchester, 1967.
Logical Papers, trans. G. H. R. Parkinson. Oxford, 1966.
"Monadology" and Other Philosophical Essays, trans. P. Schrecker and A. M. Schrecker. New York, Macmillan, 1965.
New Essays on Human Understanding, trans. P. Remnant and J. Bennett. Cambridge, 1981.
Philosophical Essays, trans. R. Ariew and D. Garber. Indianapolis, 1989.
Philosophical Papers and Letters, trans. L. E. Loemker, 2d ed. Dordrecht, 1969.
Philosophical Writings, trans. M. Morris and G. H. R. Parkinson. London, 1973.
The Political Writings of Leibniz, trans. P. Riley. Cambridge, 1972.

Biographical

Aiton, E. J. *Leibniz: A Biography.* Bristol, 1985.

Müller, K., and G. Krönert. *Leben und Werk von Gottfried Wilhelm Leibniz.* Frankfurt, 1969.

— ROBERT SLEIGH

LEVINAS, EMMANUEL

Emmanuel Levinas was born in 1906 in Kaunas, Lithuania, of Jewish parents. His education familiarized him with the Hebrew Bible and the Russian novelists. After having studied at the gymnasiums in Kaunas and Charkow, Ukraine, he traveled to Strasbourg, where he studied philosophy from 1924 to 1929. He spent the academic year of 1928–29 in Freiburg, where he attended the last seminars given by Edmund Husserl and the lectures and seminars of Martin Heidegger. His dissertation, *La théorie de l'intuition dans la phénoménologie de Husserl,* was published in 1930. In 1930 Levinas settled in Paris, where he worked for the Alliance Israélite Universelle and its schools located throughout the Mediterranean. In 1947 he became the director of the École Normale Israélite Orientale, the training facility for teachers of those schools. In 1961 he was appointed professor of philosophy at the University of Poitiers and in 1967 at the University of Nanterre. In 1973 he moved to the Sorbonne, where he became an honorary professor in 1976. Levinas died on December 25, 1995, a few days before his 90th birthday.

Works

Until World War II most of Levinas's writing focused on introducing the phenomenology of Husserl and Heidegger into France. His early commentaries on their work were collected in *En découvrant l'existence avec Husserl et Heidegger* (1949). His first personal essay was the article "De l'évasion" (1935), whose central question was whether it is possible to evade the totalizing tendency of being. The search for an answer coincided with the beginning of his criticism of Heidegger's ontology. Levinas's first personal book, with the anti-Heideggerian title *De l'existence à l'existant* (*From Existence to Existents* or *From Being to Beings*), was published in 1947. In the same year he gave a lecture series under the title *Le temps et l'autre* (*Time and the Other*),in which some central thoughts of his later work are anticipated. A part of *De l'existence à l'existant* to which Levinas later refers with approval is its phenomenology of *il y a* ('there is'), that is, being in its most general and indeterminate or empty sense, preceding all determination, order, and structure. Levinas describes it as a formless and obscure night and a silent murmur, an anonymous and chaotic atmosphere or field of forces from which

no being can escape. It threatens the existing entities by engulfing and suffocating them. As such, being is horrible, not because it would kill—death is not an evasion from it—but because of its depersonalizing character. All beings are caught in the anonymity of this primordial materiality—much different from the giving essence of *es gibt* as described by Heidegger.

The work that made Levinas famous,

Totalité et infini. Essai sur l'extériorité *(1961),*

was an attack on the entirety of Western philosophy,

including Heidegger's ontology.

The work that made Levinas famous is *Totalité et infini. Essai sur l'extériorité* (1961). As an attack on the entirety of Western philosophy, including Heidegger's ontology, this work tries to show why philosophy has not been faithful to the most important facts of human existence and how its basic perspective should be replaced by another one. The "totality" of the title stands for the absolutization of a panoramic perspective from which reality is understood as an all-encompassing universe. All kinds of relation, separation, exteriority, and alterity are then reduced to internal moments of one totality. Borrowing from Plato's *Sophist,* Levinas affirms that Western philosophy reduces the other (*to heteron*) to 'the Same' (*tauton*). The resulting tautology is an egology because the totalization is operated by the consciousness of an ego that does not recognize any irreducible heteronomy.

The relative truth of the ego's autonomy is shown in a phenomenology of the way in which human beings inhabit the world. Levinas characterizes this "economy" (from *oikos* = house, and *nomos* = law) as vitality and enjoyment of the elements. Implicitly polemicizing against Heidegger's description of *Dasein's* being-in-the-world, he focuses on the dimension of human eating, drinking, walking, swimming, dwelling, and laboring, a dimension more primordial than the handling of tools and much closer to the natural elements than scientific or technological objectification.

The infinite (*l'infini*), which Levinas contrasts with the totality, is another name for "the Other" insofar as this does not fit into the totality. In order to determine the relation between consciousness, the totality, and the infinite, Levinas refers to René Descartes's *Meditations on the First Philosophy,* in which Descartes insists on the fact that the idea of the infinite is original and cannot be deduced from any other idea. It surpasses the capacity of consciousness, which in it "thinks more than it can think" (see Levinas's *Collected Philosophical Papers,* p. 56). The relation between the ego and the infinite is one of transcendence: the infinite remains exterior to consciousness, although this is essentially related to its "height."

The concrete sense of the formal structure thus indicated is shown through a phenomenology of the human other, whose "epiphany" reveals an absolute command: as soon as I am confronted, I discover myself to be under an absolute obligation. The fact of the other's existence immediately reveals to me the basic ought of all ethics. On this level is and ought are inseparable. Instead of the other (*l'autre* or *autrui*), Levinas often uses the expressions "the face" (*le visage*) or "the speech" (*la parole,* also *le langage*) because the other's looking at me and speaking to me are the two most striking expressions of the other's infinity or "height." As the relation between an economically established ego and the infinite other, the intersubjective relation is asymmetrical: the other appears primarily not as equal to me but rather as "higher" and commanding me. I am responsible for the other's life, a responsibility that puts infinite demands on me, but I cannot order another to give his or her life for me.

In his second major work, *Autrement qu'être ou au-delà de l'essence* (1974), Levinas continues his analyses of the relationship between the ego and the other but now emphasizes the basic structure of the ego, or rather of the "me" in the accusative, as put into question, accused, and unseated by the other. The relationship is described as nonchosen responsibility, substitution, obsession, being hostage, persecution. Subjectivity (the "me" of *me voici*) is determined as a nonchosen being-for-the-other and, thus, as basically nonidentical with itself, a passivity more or otherwise passive than the passivity that is opposed to activity. Subjectivity is primarily sensibility, being touched and affected by the other, vulnerability.

In the course of his analyses Levinas discovered that the other, me, and the transcendence that relates and separates them do not fit into the framework of phenomenology: neither the other nor I (me) is phenomenon; transcendence does not have the structure of intentionality. Through phenomenology Levinas thus arrived at another level of thinking. He did not join Heidegger's call for a new ontology, however.

In *Autrement qu'être* Levinas gives a new description of the way being "is": *esse* is *interesse;* being is an active and transitive "interestingness" (*intéressement),* which permeates all beings and weaves them together in a network of mutual interest. If ontology is the study of (this) being, it is not able to express the other, transcendence,

and subjectivity. Transcendence surpasses being. Appealing to Plato, who characterized the good as *epekeina tès ousias,* Levinas points at transcendence, infinity, and otherness as "otherwise" and "beyond" the realm of being (or essence).

The other, subjectivity, and transcendence—but then also morality, affectivity, death, suffering, freedom, love, history, and many other (quasi-)phenomena—resist, not only phenomenology and ontology, but all kinds of objectification and thematization. As soon as they are treated in a reflective discourse, they are converted into a said (*dit).* The saying (*dire),* in which the "otherwise than being" (that which is not a phenomenon, a being, or a theme) addresses itself to an addressee, is lost in the text of the said. However, thematization and objectification are inevitable, especially in philosophy and science, but also in the practical dimensions of law, economy, and politics. The organization of justice cannot do without generalization and grouping of individuals into totalities. The transition from the asymmetrical relation between the other and me to the generalities of justice is founded in the fact that the other human who, here and now, obligates me infinitely somehow represents all other humans.

How does the intersubjective and asymmetric transcendence differ from the relationship to God? "Otherness," "infinity," and "beyond" do not apply to God in the same way as to the human other. God is neither an object nor a you; no human being can meet with God directly, but God has left a trace. The infinite responsibility of the one for the other refers to an election that precedes freedom. In coming from an immemorial, anachronical "past," responsibility indicates the "preoriginary" "illeity" of God. The *il* or *ille* of "the most high" is sharply distinguished from the chaotic anonymity of *il y a;* the dimensions of economy, morality, and justice separate the indeterminacy of being from the beyond-all-determinacy of God. However, as the practical and theoretical recognition of the relationship between God and humans, religion cannot be separated from ethics: the only way to venerate God is through devotion to human others.

Besides the two books summarized here, Levinas wrote many articles. Most of these were collected in *Humanisme de l'autre homme* (1972), *De Dieu qui vient à l'idée* (1982), *Hors sujet* (1987), and *Entre nous* (1991).

Like all other philosophers, Levinas has convictions that cannot be reduced to universally shared experiences, common sense, or purely rational principles. In addition to his philosophical work he wrote extensively on Jewish questions from an orthodox Jewish, and especially Talmudic, point of view. In his philosophical writings he quotes the Bible perhaps as often as Shakespeare or Dostoyevsky, but these quotations are not meant to replace philosophical justification of his assertions. Phenomenological rigor and emphasis are typical of his method, even where he points beyond the dimensions of phenomena and conceptuality.

[See also Descartes, René; Heidegger, Martin; Husserl, Edmund; Plato.]

BIBLIOGRAPHY

A complete bibliography of primary and secondary texts published between 1929 and 1989 is given in Roger Burgraeve, *Emmanuel Levinas; une bibliographie primaire et secondaire (1929–1985) avec complément 1985–1989*. Leuven, 1990.

The most important philosophical books of Levinas are:

La théorie de l'intuition dans la phénoménologie de Husserl. Paris, 1930; 2d. ed. 1963. Translated by A. Orianne as *The Theory of Intuition in Husserl's Phenomenology.* Evanston, IL, 1973.

De l'existence à l'existant. Paris, 1947; 2d. ed., 1978. Translated by A. Lingis as *Existence and Existents.* The Hague, 1978.

En découvrant l'existence avec Husserl et Heidegger. Paris, 1949; 2d. ed., 1967. Partially translated by A. Lingis in *Collected Philosophical Papers (v. infra).*

Totalité et Infini. Essai sur l'extériorité. The Hague, 1961. Translated by A. Lingis as *Totality and Infinity: An Essay on Exteriority.* Pittsburgh, 1969.

Humanisme de l'autre homme. Montpellier, 1972.

Autrement qu'être ou au-delà de l'essence. The Hague, 1974. Translated by A. Lingis as *Otherwise than Being or Beyond Essence.* The Hague, 1981.

Le temps et l'autre. Montpellier, 1979 (2d. ed. of Levinas's contribution to *Le choix, le monde, l'existence* [Paris, 1948]). Translated by R. Cohen as *Time and the Other.* Pittsburgh, 1987.

De Dieu qui vient à l'idée. Paris, 1982.

Collected Philosophical Papers, trans. A. Lingis. Boston, 1987. Contains the English translation of twelve thematic essays from several volumes and journals.

Hors sujet. Montpellier, 1987.

Entre nous: Essais sur le penser-à-l'autre. Paris, 1991.

Secondary Literature

Bernasconi, R., and S. Critchley, eds. *Re-reading Levinas.* Bloomington, IN, 1991.

Bernasconi, R., and D. Wood, eds. *The Provocation of Levinas: Rethinking the Other.* London, 1988.

Chalier, C., and M. Abensour, eds. *Emmanuel Levinas.* Paris, 1991.

Cohen, R., ed. *Face to Face with Levinas.* Albany, NY, 1986.

Peperzak, A. *To the Other. An Introduction to the Philosophy of Emmanuel Levinas.* West Lafayette, IN, 1993.

———, ed. *Ethics as First Philosophy. The Significance of Emmanuel Levinas for Religion, Literature and Philosophy.* New York, 1995.

Greisch, J., and J. Rolland, eds. *Emmanuel Levinas. L'éthique comme philosophie première.* Paris, 1993.

Wyschogrod, E. *Emmanuel Levinas: The Problem of Ethical Metaphysics.* The Hague, 1974.

— ADRIAAN PEPERZAK

LIAR PARADOX, THE

Attributions of truth and falsehood under certain conditions generate the liar paradox. The most famous illustration of this comes from the Epistle to Titus, in which St. Paul quotes approvingly a remark attributed to Epimenides: "One of themselves, even a prophet of their own, said, The Cretans are always liars, evil beasts, slow bellies. This witness is true" (King James version). Let us suppose that Epimenides, the Cretan prophet, did say that the Cretans are always liars, and let us consider the status of his utterance—call it *E*—under the following two conditions. (1) A Cretan utterance counts as a lie if and only if it is untrue. (2) All Cretan utterances, except perhaps *E*, are untrue. Now, if *E* is true, then, since *E* is a Cretan utterance, not all Cretan utterances are untrue. Hence, Cretans are not always liars (by (1)), and so *E* must be untrue. On the other hand, if *E* is untrue, then indeed all Cretan utterances are untrue (by (2)). Hence, Cretans are always liars (by (1)), and so *E* is true after all. Both the hypotheses, that *E* is true and that *E* is not true, yield, therefore, a contradiction. Yet the steps in the argument are all apparently valid, and the initial setup is not impossible. This is the liar paradox.

The liar and related paradoxes

raise a number of difficult conceptual problems,

among them the normative problem

of designing paradox-free notions

of truth and reference.

The paradox was discovered by Eubulides of Miletus (fourth century B.C.E.) and has exercised logicians down the ages to the present time. (See Bocheński, 1961; Spade, 1988.) For principally two reasons, interest in the paradox has been especially great in this century. First, arguments similar to that found in the liar wreaked havoc in several prominent logical systems (e.g., those of Gottlob Frege and Alonzo Church). This prompted a search for systems that were immune from paradox. Second, the rise of semantical studies created a need for a better understanding of the notions of truth, reference, and the like. The notions are fundamental to semantical investigations, but the paradoxes reveal a profound gap in our understanding of them. (The notion of reference, like other semantical notions, exhibits, under certain conditions, paradoxical behavior.)

The liar and related paradoxes raise a number of difficult conceptual problems. One is the normative problem of designing paradox-free notions of truth, reference, and the like. Another is the descriptive problem of understanding the workings of our ordinary, paradox-laden notions. The work on the paradoxes in the first half of this century is, perhaps, best viewed as addressing the normative problem. The work in the second half is best viewed as addressing the descriptive problem. Some of this work is outlined below.

Let us sharpen the descriptive problem a little. For simplicity, let us restrict our attention to a fragment, *L*, of our language that contains no problematic terms other than 'true'. All other terms in *L* have, let us suppose, a classical interpretation. How should 'true' be interpreted? A natural demand is that the interpretation must validate the T-biconditionals, that is, all sentences of the form.

(T) '*B*' is true if and only if (iff) *B*,

where *B* is a sentence of *L*. The argument of the liar paradox shows, however, that every possible classical interpretation of 'true' is bound to make some T-biconditionals false. (This is a version of Alfred Tarski's indefinability theorem.) How, then, should we interpret 'true'? Should we abandon the natural demand? Or the classical framework? Or the naïve reading of the T-biconditionals? Essentially, the first course is followed in the contextual approach, the second in the fixed-point approach, and the third in the revision approach.

The Contextual Approach

This approach takes 'true' to be a context-sensitive term. Just as the interpretation of 'fish this long' varies with contextually supplied information about length, similarly, on the contextual approach, with 'true': its interpretation also depends upon contextual information. There is no consensus, however, on the specific information needed for interpretation. In the levels theory due to Tyler Burge and Charles Parsons, the context supplies the level at which 'true' is interpreted in a Tarskian hierarchy of truth predicates. In the Austinian theory of truth developed by Jon Barwise and John Etchemendy, the relevant contextual parameter is the "portion" of the world that a proposition is about. In the singularity theory of Keith Simmons, the relevant information includes certain of the speaker's intentions.

Contextual theories assign to each occurrence of 'true' a classical interpretation, though not the same one to all occurrences. This has several characteristic consequences: (1) Occurrences of 'true' do not express global truth for the entire language (by Tarski's indefinability theorem). They express instead restricted or "quasi" notions of truth; the former possibility is realized in the levels theory, the latter in the singularity

theory. (2) Truth attributions, even paradoxical ones, have a classical truth value. Paradox is explained as arising from a subtle, unnoticed, shift in some contextual parameter. (3) Classical forms of reasoning are preserved. But caution is in order here: Whether an argument exemplifies a classically valid form turns out to be nontrivial. For example, the argument "*a* is true, *a* = *b*; therefore, *b* is true" exemplifies a classically valid form only if 'true' is interpreted uniformly, but this is nontrivial on the contextual approach.

The Fixed-Point Approach

This approach interprets 'true' nonclassically. It rests on an important observation of Saul Kripke. Robert Martin, and Peter Woodruff. Consider again the language *L*, and assign to 'true' an arbitrary partial interpretation $\langle U, V \rangle$, where *U* is the extension and *V* the anti-extension (i.e., the objects of which the predicate is false). We can use one of the partial-valued schemes (say, Strong Kleene) to determine the sentences of *L* that are true (U'), false (V'), and neither-true-nor-false. This semantical reflection defines a function, κ, on partial interpretations; $\kappa(\langle U, V \rangle) = \langle U', V' \rangle$. The important observation is that κ has a fixed point: There exist $\langle U, V \rangle$ such that $\kappa(\langle U, V \rangle) = \langle U, V \rangle$.

Certain partial-valued schemes have a least fixed point, which is a particularly attractive interpretation for 'true'. It is also the product of an appealing iterative construction: we begin by supposing that we are entirely ignorant of the extension and the anti-extension of 'true': we set them both to be $\varnothing$ (the null set). Despite the ignorance, we can assert some sentences and deny others. The rule "Assert '*B* is true' for all assertible *B*; assert '*B* is not true' for all deniable *B*" entitles us to a new, richer, interpretation, $\kappa(\langle \varnothing, \varnothing \rangle)$, for 'true'. But now we can assert (deny) more sentences. The rule entitles us to a yet richer interpretation $\kappa(\kappa(\langle \varnothing, \varnothing \rangle))$. The process, if repeated sufficiently many times, saturates at the least fixed point.

Under fixed-point interpretations, the extension of 'true' consists precisely of the truths and the anti-extension of falsehoods. The T-biconditionals are, therefore, validated. They are not, however, expressible in *L* itself: fixed points exist only when certain three-valued functions, including the relevant 'iff', are inexpressible in *L*.

The Revision Approach

This approach holds truth to be a circular concept. It is motivated by the observation that truth behaves in a strikingly parallel way to concepts with circular definitions. Suppose we define *G* thus:

$$x \text{ is } G =_{Df} x \text{ is a philosopher distinct from Plato } or$$
$$x \text{ is Plato but not } G.$$

The definition is circular, but it does impart some meaning to G. G has, like truth, unproblematic application on a large range of objects. It applies to all philosophers distinct from Plato and fails to apply to non-philosophers. On one object, Plato, G behaves paradoxically. If we declare Plato is G, then the definition rules that he is not G; if we declare he is not G, the definition rules that he is G. This parallels exactly the behavior of truth in the liar paradox.

The revision account of truth rests on general theories of definitions, theories that make semantic sense of circular (and mutually interdependent) definitions. Central to these theories are the following ideas. (1) A circular definition does not, in general, determine a classical extension for the definiendum (the term defined). (2) It determines instead a rule of revision. Given a hypothesis about the extension of the definiendum G, the definition yields a revised extension for G, one consisting of objects that satisfy the definiens (the right side of the definition). (3) Repeated applications of the revision rule to arbitrary hypotheses reveal both the unproblematic and the pathological behavior of the definiendum. On the unproblematic the revision rule yields a definite and stable verdict, irrespective of the initial hypothesis. On the pathological this ideal state does not obtain.

The ingredient needed to construct a theory of truth once we have a general theory of definitions is minimal: it is just the T-biconditionals, with 'iff' read as '$=_{Df}$'. This reading was suggested by Tarski, but, as it results in a circular definition, it can be implemented only within a general theory of definitions. Under the reading, the T-biconditionals yield a rule of revision. Repeated applications of this rule generate patterns that explain the ordinary and the pathological behavior of truth. The revision approach thus sees the liar paradox as arising from a circularity in truth. The approach has been developed by, among others, Anil Gupta, Hans Herzberger, and Nuel Belnap.

The three approaches, it should be stressed, do not exhaust the rich array of responses to the paradoxes in this century.

[*See also Frege, Gottlob; Kripke, Saul Aaron; Russell, Bertrand Arthur William.*]

BIBLIOGRAPHY

Antonelli, A. "Non-Well-Founded Sets via Revision Rules," *Journal of Philosophical Logic,* Vol. 23 (1994), 633–79.

Barwise, J., and J. Etchemendy. *The Liar: An Essay on Truth and Circularity.* New York, 1987.

Bocheński, I. M. *A History of Formal Logic.* Notre Dame, IN, 1961.

Chapuis, A. "Alternative Revision Theories of Truth," *Journal of Philosophical Logic,* Vol. 24 (1996).

Epstein, R. L. "A Theory of Truth Based on a Medieval Solution to the Liar Paradox," *History and Philosophy of Logic,* Vol. 13 (1992), 149–77.

Gaifman, H. "Pointers to Truth," *Journal of Philosophy,* Vol. 89 (1992), 223–61.

Gupta, A., and N. Belnap. *The Revision Theory of Truth.* Cambridge, MA, 1993.

Koons, R. C. *Paradoxes of Belief and Strategic Rationality.* Cambridge, 1992.

McGee, V. *Truth, Vagueness, and Paradox.* Indianapolis, 1991.

Martin, R. L., ed. *The Paradox of the Liar,* 2d ed. Reseda, CA, 1978. Contains a useful bibliography of material up to about 1975; for later material consult the bibliography in Gupta and Belnap, 1993.

———, ed. *Recent Essays on Truth and the Liar Paradox.* New York, 1984. Contains the classic papers of Parsons, Kripke, Herzberger, and others; a good place to begin the study of the three approaches.

Priest, G. *In Contradiction.* Dordrecht, 1987.

Russell, B. "Mathematical Logic as Based on the Theory of Types," in *Logic and Knowledge* (London, 1956).

Sainsbury, R. M. *Paradoxes.* Cambridge, 1988.

Simmons, K. *Universality and the Liar.* New York, 1993.

Spade, P. V. *Lies, Language, and the Logic in the Late Middle Ages.* London, 1988.

Tarski, A. "The Semantic Conception of Truth," *Philosophy and Phenomenological Research,* Vol. 4 (1944), 341–76.

Visser, A. "Semantics and the Liar Paradox," in D. Gabbay and F. Guenthner, eds., *Handbook of Philosophical Logic,* Vol. 4 (Dordrecht, 1989).

Yablo, S. "Hop, Skip, and Jump: The Agonistic Conception of Truth," in J. Tomberlin, ed., *Philosophical Perspectives,* Vol. 7 (Atascadero, CA, 1993).

Yaqūb, A. M. *The Liar Speaks the Truth.* New York, 1993.

— ANIL GUPTA

LIBERALISM

Liberalism is commonly defined as a political philosophy that places a primary value on liberty, especially the liberty of individuals from interference by the state.

Since the 1950s liberals

have increasingly defined liberty

as the neutrality of the state with regard to

differing conceptions of the good life.

Since the 1950s liberals have increasingly defined liberty as the neutrality of the state with regard to differing conceptions of the good life. Liberal thinkers have combined this commitment to "value neutrality" with a belief in the necessity of economic growth for providing the prosperity required for a just society.

The most important philosopher to reformulate liberalism in these terms is John Rawls. In his book *A Theory of Justice,* Rawls justifies a liberal welfare state that could provide a basis for the equal enjoyment of individual liberties. Rawls combined advocacy of a principle of "an equal right to the most extensive basic liberty" with his "difference principle," which justified only those inequalities that were "to the greatest benefit of the least advantaged" in society. Rawls hypothesized that individuals would derive these two principles through rational deliberation in an "original position" in which "knowledge of the circumstances of one's own case" was excluded. Rawls's theory revitalized social contract theory in Anglo-American philosophy, after its virtual eclipse by utilitarianism.

The first major criticism of Rawls's work, by Robert Nozick, emphasized the distance that Rawls's welfare-state liberalism had gone from the classical liberal (now "libertarian") view that espoused the value of a minimal state. Nozick argued that redistributive schemes such as Rawls's were inherently unjust, since they imposed an "end-state" in violation of previous consensual exchanges between individuals.

Isaiah Berlin's distinction between negative and positive freedom—between a freedom from interference and a freedom to achieve certain ends—lay at the root of this divergence between libertarians and liberals. In response, Gerald MacCallum argued that all conceptions of freedom combined negative and positive elements; one implication of this argument was that there could not be a coherent liberalism that did not include a positive conception of the role of the state in furthering particular social goals.

Subsequently, Ronald Dworkin asserted that liberalism is primarily a philosophy of equality, not of liberty per se, since liberties were best secured through the achievement of an equal society in which all could pursue their own ends. Dworkin argued that a consequence of this egalitarianism was that liberalism should be based on a strong conception of human rights. In his work *Taking Rights Seriously,* he argues that human rights generally were based not on a right to liberty as such but on a right to "treatment as an equal."

In the 1980s philosophers criticized the Rawls-Dworkin view of an egalitarian liberalism in two ways. First, Joseph Raz criticized Dworkin's emphasis on rights-based theories of morality and law. In particular, Raz maintained that the idea of liberty was best understood not as a right to treatment as an equal but as a

collective good. Raz attacked both the concept of a "rights-based morality" and the notion of a liberal theory of equality as unable to account for moral reasons for action such as might be found in concepts of virtues, goods, or consequences.

Second, Michael Sandel and Charles Taylor criticized the Rawlsian conception of justice on the basis of a philosophy of communitarianism derived from rereadings of Aristotle and Hegel. The communitarian critique of liberalism was based on the idea that individuals come to have desires and ends only through socialization within a particular society; liberalism cannot therefore account for how individuals come to have an interest in liberty at all. Sandel and Taylor, as well as Michael Walzer, argued that Rawls simply assumed the existence of autonomous individuals without acknowledging the constitutive role of an already existing community in forming these individuals.

Rawls responded to this criticism by reformulating his theory as a "political liberalism" rather than as a general theory of justice. Rawls's "justice as fairness" was therefore a theory of the best distribution of goods within a particular political culture—that of the Anglo-American liberal democracies. As Walzer subsequently maintained, communitarianism could then be seen as a corrective to an overemphasis in liberal theory on the presumed autonomy of individuals in modern capitalist societies.

The devolution of most communist societies in the early 1990s encouraged a brief triumphalist mood within liberalism. In the most notable expression of this mood, Francis Fukuyama argued that modern liberal democracy should be universally acknowledged as the only legitimate form of government at the end of the twentieth century. The most important question about liberalism was therefore whether it could withstand assaults from antiliberal societies—now more frequently based on ethnic nationalism or religious fundamentalism than on Marxism-Leninism.

Two themes of liberalism in the 1990s were to some extent responses to this view. On the one hand, some liberal thinkers such as Rawls turned to a consideration of how liberal principles might be applied to relations between states and peoples on the global level. On the other hand, thinkers such as Benjamin Barber criticized liberalism for its advocacy of representative democracy to the exclusion of participatory institutions.

In response to these new problems, liberals increasingly reconceptualized liberal society as one that protects diverse ways of life through a political procedure guaranteeing agreement of all concerned. Both Rawls's political liberalism and the discourse ethics of the German philosopher Jürgen Habermas are examples of this procedural approach. The dialogue between these two figures in the mid-1990s suggests that liberalism at the millennium may well be understood as a procedural theory of democracy that can serve to protect diverse cultures within which individuals can claim autonomy. Whether such a theory can withstand the developing criticisms by ecologists and feminists of the other assumption of liberalism—that of the value of a growth-oriented society—remains to be seen.

[See also Aristotle; Communitarianism; Habermas, Jürgen; Hegel, Georg Wilhelm Friedrich; Justice; Rawls, John; Rights.]

BIBLIOGRAPHY

Barber, B. *Strong Democracy.* Berkeley, 1984.

Berlin, I. *Four Essays on Liberty.* Oxford, 1969.

Dworkin, R. *Taking Rights Seriously.* Cambridge, MA, 1977.

———."Liberalism." in S. Hampshire, ed., *Public and Private Morality* (Cambridge, 1978).

Fukuyama, F. "The End of History?" *National Interest,* no. 16 (1989), 3–18.

Habermas, J. *Theorie des Kommunikativen Handelns.* Frankfurt, 1981.

———. "Reconciliation Through the Public Use of Reason: Remarks on John Rawls' *Political Liberalism,*" *Journal of Philosophy,* Vol. 92 (1995), 109–31.

MacCallum, Jr., G. C. "Negative and Positive Freedom," *Philosophical Review,* Vol. 76 (1967), 312–34.

Nozick, R. *Anarchy, State, and Utopia.* New York, 1974.

Rawls, J. *A Theory of Justice.* Cambridge, MA, 1971.

———. "The Law of Peoples." in S. Shute and S. Hurley, eds., *On Human Rights: The Oxford Amnesty Lectures 1993* (New York, 1993).

———. *Political Liberalism.* New York, 1993.

———. "Reply to Habermas." *Journal of Philosophy,* Vol. 92 (1995), 132–80.

Raz, J. *The Morality of Freedom.* Oxford, 1986.

Sandel, M. J. *Liberalism and the Limits of Justice.* Cambridge, 1982.

Taylor, C. *Philosophical Papers,* Vol. 2: *Philosophy and the Human Sciences.* Cambridge, 1985.

Walzer, M. *Spheres of Justice.* New York, 1983.

———. "The Communitarian Critique of Liberalism," *Political Theory,* Vol. 18 (1990), 6–23.

— OMAR DAHBOUR

LIBERATION THEOLOGY

Theology of liberation is the name of a movement that arose in the churches, both Catholic and Protestant, of Latin America during the last third of the twentieth century. It also describes a theological trend that is found, sometimes under different names and with somewhat different emphases, across the world.

The earliest and still definitive statement of the movement is *A Theology of Liberation* by Gustavo Gutierrez (1988). The basic principles he sets forth are as follows.

First, theology is critical reflection on Christian praxis. Faith, charity, and commitment to God and others in the struggle for humanity and justice are primary. Theology relates this praxis to the sources of revelation and the history of the church.

Second, biblical revelation commits the church to God's "preferential option for the poor." The poor are, by their condition, involved in a struggle to realize their humanity, to become "subjects of their own history," against the political, economic, and social powers that marginalize and oppress them. This struggle is revolutionary, not reformist. The church belongs with the poor in the midst of it, doing theology in a revolutionary situation.

How is the truth claim

of liberation theology validated?

How are the poor defined?

What does liberation theology owe to Marxism,

and is that debt theologically legitimate?

Third, the struggle of the poor for social justice is a work of human self-creation that finds its source, meaning, and hope in God's work. Salvation history is at the heart of human history, in creation, covenant, Christ's incarnation, and the coming kingdom of God. Political liberation is a partial salvific event, a historical realization of the kingdom that looks forward to its ultimate fulfillment by divine grace operating in the human struggle, informing its character and directing it toward ever larger goals of human community.

Three developments of this theology, in response to both defenders and critics, are especially important.

First, How is the truth claim of liberation theology validated? Juan Luis Segundo (1976) describes it as a hermeneutical circle. Experience of reality from the perspective of the poor leads to ideological suspicion toward received structures of authority, morals, and dogma. This leads to a new awareness of God, which in turn creates a new hermeneutic for interpreting the biblical story. One does not escape ideology through this circle. But biblical revelation at one pole and the human condition of the poor on the other direct and correct it toward political and spiritual liberation. Paulo Freire develops the same line of thought as a teaching method in *The Pedagogy of the Oppressed,* with its emphasis on learning to be human in Christian base communities through defining and struggling against oppressive powers while being transformed by God's saving love in the struggle.

Second, How are the poor defined? The Latin American theologians have clearly a universal dependent economic class in mind, created by exploiting landlords, industrialists, and bankers with their political and military agents. Black theologians in the United States and South Africa, however, have maintained that the defining category is race. Dalit Christians in India find it in the religion-based caste system. A chorus of ethnic minorities throughout the world define it in terms of their own culture, language, or nation, seeking liberation from a dominant, oppressive majority. All these agree on God's preference for the poor and on divine promise in the human struggle. They differ in defining the poor and therefore on the universality versus the particularity of that promise.

Third, What does liberation theology owe to Marxism, and is that debt theologically legitimate? The question arises on two levels. First, the hermeneutic of suspicion, which probes the roots of all truth claims in social experience and interest and defines theology as reflection on social praxis, owes much to Marx. It contradicts the teaching of St. Thomas Aquinas about the universality of reason and natural law as perfected by revelation. It reflects, however, the reformation's understanding of reason distorted by human sin and is rooted, liberation theologians would claim, in the way God is known in the biblical history of calling, covenant, and promise. The question remains how divine revelation corrects and redeems the self-understanding also of the poor.

Defining the social condition of the poor in terms of dehumanizing economic exploitation and class struggle clearly borrows from Marx. Miguez Bonino (1976) acknowledges this explicitly, as do many others. They claim, however, that this analysis is the secular expression in modern industrial society of a theme in Christian history that finds its source in the Hebrew prophets and the incarnation of Christ: the saving work of God liberating the people from the economic and political power of organized human sin. Regardless of the future of Marxism as an analytical tool, this struggle and this promise will continue. The question is how the power analysis it requires can become a more subtle and insightful guide to Christian understanding and action than Marxism was.

[See also Justice; Marx, Karl; Marxism; Thomas Aquinas, St.]

BIBLIOGRAPHY

Freire, P. *Pedagogy of the Oppressed.* New York, 1971.
Gutierrez, G. *The Power of the Poor in History.* Maryknoll, NY, 1983.
————. *A Theology of Liberation,* rev. ed. Maryknoll, NY, 1988.
Miguez Bonino, J. *Doing Theology in a Revolutionary Situation.* Philadelphia, 1975.
————. *Christians and Marxists: The Mutual Challenge to Revolution.* Grand Rapids, MI, 1976.
Segundo, J. L. *The Liberation of Theology.* Maryknoll, NY, 1976.

— CHARLES C. WEST

LIBERTY

One of the central concerns of social and political philosophy has been the issue of what limits, if any, there are to the right of the state to restrict the liberty of its citizens. Unless one is convinced of the truth of anarchism, there are some actions with which the state may legitimately interfere, and unless one accords no value to personal liberty, there are some actions the state must leave to the discretion of the individual. One of the tasks of political philosophy is to develop and elaborate a theory to determine where these boundaries lie.

A nineteenth-century cartoon depicts anarchism, socialism, communism, and others trying to bring down America's Statue of Liberty. (Corbis)

In his classical defense of liberalism—*On Liberty*—John Stuart Mill gave one influential answer to this question. The only reason that could justify the use of coercion against a person is to prevent harm to other people. Such a reason might not be decisive—it might be that the use of coercion would be ineffective or too costly or would violate the rights of privacy—but it brings the action in question within the scope of legitimate state power.

What limits, if any, are there

to the right of the state

to restrict the liberty of its citizens?

Other reasons, according to Mill, do not justify legal coercion. One cannot restrict someone's actions because they are harmful to that person; paternalism is not legitimate. One cannot restrict someone's actions because they are wrong or immoral (but not harmful to others); legal moralism is not legitimate. One cannot restrict someone's actions because their character would be improved by doing so; moral paternalism is not legitimate.

Obviously, a theory that puts such heavy weight on the notion of harm gives rise to disputes about the nature and limits of that notion. If conduct is offensive to others, does that count as harming them? If not, do we need a separate principle to justify prohibiting offensive conduct such as public nudity or racist graffiti? If we are competing for a job and you get it, am I harmed by this? Does only physical damage count as harm or emotional damage as well? Am I harmed by simply knowing that behind the walls of your house you are engaged in activities that I would find repulsive or wicked? If someone defaces the flag, is anyone harmed by this? If I consent to some action that is otherwise damaging to me, am I still harmed? Can I be harmed after my death—for example, by attacks on my reputation?

One of the most fully developed views that seeks to provide answers to these and similar questions is that of Joel Feinberg. He argues that any notion of harm that is going to play a role in answering normative questions will itself be normative in character. He accordingly defines the notion of harm in terms of a wrongful setback to a person's interests. To some extent, naturally, this shifts philosophical attention to the concept of interests.

Paternalism

The normative issue raised by paternalism is when, if ever, the state or an individual is entitled to interfere with a person for that person's good. Examples of laws that have been justified in paternalistic terms include requiring motorcyclists to wear helmets, forcing patients to receive blood transfusions against their wishes, or requiring individuals to save for their retirement (Social Security).

The reasons that support paternalism are those that support any benevolent action—promoting the welfare of a person. The reasons against are those that militate against any interference with the autonomy of individuals—respect for their desire to lead their own lives. Normative debates about the legitimacy of paternalism involve disputes about many issues including the nature of welfare (can we produce good for a person against that individual's preferences and evaluations?), the correctness of various normative theories (consequentialism vs. autonomy or rights-based theories), and the relevance of hypothetical consent (in Mill's famous example of the man walking across a bridge that, unknown to him, is about to collapse, we may stop him, since he would not want to cross the bridge if he knew its condition).

Legal Moralism

The issue of whether the state may enforce morality—the subject that was brought to philosophical prominence by the debate between Lord Devlin and H. L. A. Hart—is present in discussions of the legalization of homosexuality, pornography, surrogate motherhood, and active euthanasia. The focus of such discussion is not the harm of such activities but their immorality and whether if they are immoral that is sufficient reason for the state to proscribe them. Since it is clearly the case that one of the grounds for proscribing murder is its immorality, the question arises as to what it might mean to deny that the state should take morality into account in limiting liberty. The best answer is that we may distinguish within the immoral different realms—for example, matters having to do with rights as opposed to matters having to do with ideals of conduct. Those who are opposed to the enforcement of morality are really opposed to enforcing certain areas of morality. Much of the discussion goes on under the heading of the "neutrality" of the liberal state.

[See also Consequentialism; Euthanasia; Liberalism; Mill, John Stuart; Paternalism; Rights; Social and Political Philosophy.]

BIBLIOGRAPHY

Devlin, P. *The Enforcement of Morals.* London, 1965.
Dworkin, G. "Paternalism," *The Monist,* Vol. 56 (1972), 64–84.
Feinberg, J. *The Moral Limits of the Criminal Law,* 4 vols. New York, 1984–88.

Mill, J. S. *On Liberty.* London, 1959.

Hart, H. L. A. *Law, Liberty, and Morality.* Stanford, CA, 1963.

— GERALD DWORKIN

LOCKE, JOHN

John Locke (1632–1704), English empiricist and moral and political philosopher. He was born in Wrington, Somerset. Locke's father, an attorney and for a time a clerk to the justices of the peace in Somerset, fought on the parliamentary side in the first rebellion against Charles I. Locke was reared in a liberal Puritan family and early learned the virtues of temperance, simplicity, and aversion to display. Though his father was severe and remote from him in early youth, as Locke matured they became close friends.

When his lifelong friend James Tyrrell

voiced his suspicion that Locke had written

the Two Treatises of Government *(1690),*

Locke was evasive and would not admit the fact.

In 1646 Locke entered Westminster School, where he studied the classics, Hebrew, and Arabic. Little time was given at Westminster to science and other studies, and its harsh discipline, rote learning, and excessive emphasis on grammar and languages were later condemned by Locke.

In 1652 Locke was elected to a studentship at Christ's Church, Oxford. He received his B.A. in 1656 and remained in residence for the master's degree. He was not happy with the study of Scholastic philosophy and managed to inform himself of many new areas of thought. As a master, Locke lectured in Latin and Greek and in 1664 was appointed censor of moral philosophy.

His father's death in 1661 left Locke with a small inheritance and some independence. During these years he became acquainted with many men who were to have a profound influence upon his life. From Robert Boyle Locke learned about the new sciences and the corpuscular theory, as well as the experimental and empirical methods. Confronted with the choice of taking holy orders, continuing as a don, or entering another faculty, Locke chose medicine. Though well trained, he never practiced medicine, nor was he permitted to take the medical degree, which would have permitted him to teach the profession, until 1674, although in 1667 he began to collaborate with the great physician Thomas Sydenham, who deeply influenced him.

In 1665 Locke was sent on a diplomatic mission accompanying Sir Walter Vane to the elector of Brandenburg at Cleves. He subsequently rejected a secretaryship under the earl of Sandwich, ambassador to Spain, and returned to Oxford. It was at this time that his interests began to turn seriously to philosophy. Descartes was the first philosopher whom Locke enjoyed reading and the first to show him the possibility of viable alternatives to the Schoolmen.

Locke had met Lord Ashley, earl of Shaftesbury, in 1662 at Oxford. They found much pleasure in each other's company, and the astute Shaftesbury quickly recognized Locke's talents. In 1667 he invited Locke to live with him in London as his personal physician. Later Locke served him well in many other capacities. Under Shaftesbury Locke found himself in the center of the political and practical affairs of the day. He assisted Shaftesbury in the framing of a constitution for the colony of Carolina. For a time he was secretary for the presentation of benefices and then secretary to the Council of Trade and Plantations. Locke was always at home in the world of practical affairs, and many of his philosophical attitudes reflect this interest. At the same time he became a fellow in the Royal Society, where he continued to be in touch with learning.

Locke, never robust in health, in 1675 went on a prolonged visit to France, where he made many friends and came into contact with the foremost minds of his day. His studies and criticisms of Descartes were deepened under the influence of various Gassendists.

In 1679 Locke returned to an England torn by intense political conflicts. Shaftesbury, who had become the leader of the parliamentary opposition to the Stuarts, alternated between political power and impotence. The close association with Shaftesbury brought Locke under suspicion; he was kept under surveillance. Shaftesbury was tried for treason in 1681, but acquitted. He subsequently fled England for Holland, where he died in 1683. Locke, at Oxford, uncertain of his position and fearing persecution, also fled England, arriving in Holland in September 1683. The king had demanded that Locke be deprived of his studentship at Oxford, and news of this demand caused Locke to prolong his stay. After the death of Charles II and the ascension of James II to the throne, the duke of Monmouth attempted a rebellion, which failed. Locke was denounced as a traitor, and the crown demanded of the Dutch that he be returned to England. No great effort was made to comply with the demand, and Locke remained in Holland.

During his stay in Holland, Locke again acquired a wide circle of distinguished friends and wrote extensively. He contributed an article as well as reviews to the *Bibliothèque universelle* of Jean Leclerc; these were his first published works. He wrote in Latin the *Epistola de Tolerantia,* which was published anonymously in 1689 and translated as the *First Letter Concerning Toleration.* He also worked assiduously on the *Essay Concerning Human Understanding,* which he had been writing off and on since 1671. In 1688 the *Bibliothèque universelle* published an abstract of the *Essay.*

These activities did not prevent him from being deeply engaged in politics. The plot to set William of Orange on the throne of England was well advanced in 1687, and Locke was, at the very least, advising William in some capacity. The revolution was accomplished in the fall of 1688, and in February 1689 Locke returned to England, escorting the princess of Orange, who later became Queen Mary.

In 1689 and 1690 Locke's two most important works, the *Essay Concerning Human Understanding* and the *Two Treatises of Government,* were published. From 1689 to 1691 Locke shuttled between London and Oates, the home of Sir Francis and Lady Masham, the daughter of Ralph Cudworth. He had declined an ambassadorial post only to accept a position as commissioner on the Board of Trade and Plantations. Apparently his practical wisdom was invaluable, for when he wished in 1697 to resign because of ill health, he was not permitted to do so. He remained until 1700, serving when he could, although his health was extremely poor.

In 1691 Locke made Oates his permanent residence at the invitation of Lady Masham. It was, for the aging Locke, a place of refuge and joy; there he received visits from Newton, Samuel Clarke, and others. These were productive years for Locke. *Some Thoughts Concerning Education* appeared in 1693. The second edition of the *Essay* was published in 1694. In the following year the *Reasonableness of Christianity* was published anonymously. He answered criticism of it in *A Vindication of the Reasonableness of Christianity* (London, 1695) and in a second *Vindication* in 1697. From 1697 to 1699 Locke engaged in an epistolary controversy with Edward Stillingfleet, bishop of Worcester.

However, Locke's health steadily failed him. After 1700, when the fourth edition of the *Essay* appeared, he remained almost constantly at Oates. He was engaged in editing the *Two Treatises of Government,* for no edition which pleased him had yet appeared. In his last years he wrote extensive commentaries on the epistles of St. Paul, which were published posthumously. On October 28, 1704, while Lady Masham was reading the Psalms to him, Locke died. Lady Masham wrote of him, "His death was like his life, truly pious, yet natural, easy and unaffected."

The great affection and respect that so many had for Locke are testimony to his charm and wisdom. (Corbis/Bettmann)

CHARACTER. The Lovelace Collection of Locke's personal papers in the Bodleian Library, Oxford, shows that Locke's character and personality were more complex than had been suspected. The great affection and respect that so many men and women had for him are testimony to his charm and wisdom. That he was modest, prudent, pious, witty, and eminently practical was long known. But he was also extremely secretive and apparently given to excessive suspicion and fears. When his lifelong friend, James Tyrrell, voiced his suspicion that Locke had written the *Two Treatises,* Locke was evasive and would not admit the fact. When he suspected that Tyrrell was spreading the report that Locke was the author, Locke angrily demanded an explanation. At the same time, Locke showed great affection for many friends and a real fondness for children. In maturity he could not abide religious intolerance or suffer tyranny. He was passionately devoted to truth and strove constantly to state the truth as he saw it, but always with a caution that distrusted all dialectic, even his own, when it appeared to go beyond common sense.

INFLUENCES ON LOCKE. Locke's philosophy is grounded in medieval thought, though he, like Descartes, turned away from it as far as possible. The Cambridge Platonists, notably Ralph Cudworth and Benjamin Whichcote, influenced him greatly with respect to religious tolerance, empirical inquiry, and the theory of knowledge. Locke was indebted to Richard Hooker in his political thought. Hobbes probably influenced him somewhat, though Locke was concerned not to be classed as a Hobbist. The two most important philosophical influences upon him were Descartes and Pierre Gassendi. From Descartes he learned much that is incorporated in the *Essay,* and in Gassendi and the Gassendists he found support to challenge the doctrine of innate ideas and the radical rationalistic realism of Descartes. Gassendi helped to convince Locke both that knowledge begins in sensation and that intellect, or reason, is essential to the attainment of truth and knowledge.

Essay Concerning Human Understanding

Locke's position in the history of Western thought rests upon *The Essay Concerning Human Understanding* and *Two Treatises of Government.* He spent long years working out the thought of each, and he carefully and lovingly revised and corrected them for subsequent editions. Locke wrote two drafts of his *Essay* in 1671, and in 1685 he wrote a third. The first edition, though dated 1690, appeared in late 1689. During the years between 1671 and 1689 Locke revised and reorganized many of his original concepts. In response to criticisms of the first edition of the *Essay,* he introduced a number of changes in subsequent editions. This long period of gestation and Locke's subsequent modifications of his initial public statement disclose primarily the refinement and clarification of his philosophy by way of certain important additions, but never by a radical or fundamental departure from his basic position.

From the outset Locke was persuaded

that our understanding and knowledge

fall far short of all that exists;

yet he was equally certain that men have a capacity

for knowledge sufficient for their purposes

and matters enough to inquire into.

From the first appearance of the *Essay* Locke was criticized for being inconsistent in his theory of knowledge, vague in the presentation and development of many of his ideas, and wanting in thoroughness in developing

other ideas. But these criticisms have in no way diminished either the importance or the influence of the *Essay* on subsequent thinkers. By no means the first of the British empiricists, Locke nonetheless gave empiricism its firmest roots in British soil, where it still proudly flourishes. It must be remembered that Locke was also a rationalist, though one of quite different orientation from such Continental thinkers as Descartes, Spinoza, and Malebranche. In Locke many strands of traditional thought are rewoven into a new fabric. Subsequent thinkers, notably Berkeley, Hume, and Kant, perhaps fashioned more coherent and consistent systems, but it is doubtful whether they were more adequate to what Locke might have called the plain facts. Locke's tendency toward inconsistency can be seen in his definition of knowledge as "the perception of the connection and agreement, or disagreement and repugnancy, of any of our ideas" (*Essay,* IV.i.2). This is plainly incompatible with his later contention that we have intuitive knowledge of our own existence, demonstrative knowledge of God's existence, and sensitive knowledge of the existence of particular things. Nonetheless, Locke would not abandon his position for the sake of consistency alone. He was persuaded that common sense and the facts justified his conviction and that whatever faults there were in his position lay in the difficulty of stating a coherent theory of knowledge, not in the reality of things. If this made him an easy prey to a skillful dialectician, like Berkeley, it also left him closer to the common conviction of most of us when we think about anything other than epistemology. It is this viewpoint, almost unique in philosophy, that accounts for the abiding interest in Locke's thought and the great extent of his influence despite the shortcomings of his work.

PURPOSE OF THE *ESSAY.* In the "Epistle to the Reader" Locke related that some friends meeting in his chamber became perplexed about certain difficulties that arose in their discourse about a subject (left unnamed). He proposed that before they could inquire further, "it was necessary to examine our own abilities and see what objects our understandings were, or were not, fitted to deal with." This discussion in 1670 or 1671 first started Locke on the inquiries that were to continue intermittently for twenty years. What Locke first set down for the next meeting is not known, unless it was Draft A (1671) of the *Essay.* That the initial suggestion became the abiding purpose of the *Essay* is clear from Locke's assertion that his purpose was "to inquire into the original, certainty, and extent of human knowledge, together with the grounds and degrees of belief, opinion, and assent" (I.i.2). At the same time he disavowed any intention to examine "the physical consideration of the mind, . . . wherein its essence consists, or by what motions of our spirits or alterations of our bodies we come to have any sensation by our organs or any ideas in our understandings, and whether those ideas do in their formation any or all of them depend on matter or no" (I.i.2).

Locke did not, in fact, offer any detailed or explicit accounts of these matters. He would have considered that a subject for natural philosophy. Nonetheless, he did, as indeed he had to, deal with the physical considerations of the mind, as well as all the other matters mentioned.

From the outset Locke was persuaded that our understanding and knowledge fall far short of all that exists; yet he was equally certain that men have a capacity for knowledge sufficient for their purposes and matters enough to inquire into. These convictions, pragmatic and utilitarian, set Locke apart from most of the other major philosophers of the seventeenth century, who, impressed by the new developments in mathematics and the new physical sciences, boldly plunged ahead with a rationalistic realism in the belief that their new methods would enable them in large measure to grasp reality. Locke saw that the very advances made in the new sciences put reality farther from the reach of the human mind. This did not make Locke a nominalist or an idealist in any modern sense; rather, he persistently affirmed the real objective existence of things or substances. What he denied was that the human understanding could know with certainty the real essences of substances. If "ideas" stand between reality and the understanding, it is to link them, even if only under the form of appearances. It is not to obliterate any connection between them or to justify a negation of substance—God, mind, or matter.

IDEAS. The key term in Locke's *Essay* is "idea," which he defined as ". . . whatsoever is the object of the understanding when a man thinks, . . . whatever is meant by phantasm, notion, species, or whatever it is which the mind can be employed about in thinking" (I.i.8). Any object of awareness or of consciousness must be an idea. But then how can we have any knowledge of anything other than ideas and their relationships? It is true that Locke spoke of ideas as the "materials of knowledge." Yet knowledge itself, when possessed and made the object of the mind, must be an idea. For example, to perceive that *A* is equal to *B* is to perceive the agreement between *A* and *B*. This agreement as perceived must be an idea, or it cannot be an object of the mind when it thinks. Despite this difficulty Locke clung tenaciously to his term "idea" in his disputes with Stillingfleet. He actually intended something other than he stated, namely, that knowledge is an operation, an activity of the mind, not initially one of its objects. It would have served his purpose better had he spoken of "knowing" rather than of "knowledge," even though

this would not have entirely removed the difficulty, since to set the mind at a distance where we may look at it, in order to know what knowledge is, is still to have an idea.

Locke argued that we have no innate

moral or practical principles,

for there is no universal agreement

about such principles; great varieties

of human vice have been at one time or place

considered virtues.

Locke, however, went beyond ideas to assume the real existence of things, substances, actions, processes, and operations. Ideas, except when they are the free constructs of the mind itself, signify and represent, however imperfectly, real existences and events. So deep was Locke's conviction on this point that no argument could shake him, although he constantly tried to remove the difficulties implicit in his definitions of "ideas" and "knowledge." This conviction is evident in the first two books of the *Essay,* in which Locke inquired into the origin of our ideas.

NO INNATE IDEAS. It was Locke's central thesis, developed extensively in Book II of the *Essay,* that we get all our ideas from experience. The whole of the first book is given to an overlong criticism, at times not germane to the subject, of the doctrine that we have innate ideas and innate knowledge.

Locke contended that there are no innate principles stamped upon the mind of man and brought into the world by the soul. In the first place, the argument that people have generally agreed that there are innate ideas, even if true, would not demonstrate the innateness of ideas. Moreover, there are no principles to which all give assent, since principles such as "Whatever is, is" and "It is impossible for the same thing to be and not to be" are not known to children, idiots, and a great part of mankind, who never heard or thought of them. Locke here assumed that innateness was equivalent to conscious perceiving and argued that to be in the mind is to be perceived or to be readily recalled to perception. Locke allowed that there is a capacity in us to know several truths but contended that this lent no support to the argument that they are innate.

To argue that all men know and assent to certain truths when they come to the use of reason proves nothing, since they will also come to know many truths that are not innate. It would appear, then, that all truth is either innate or adventitious. Again, why should the use of reason be necessary to discover truths already innately in the mind? Locke allowed that the knowledge of some truths is in the mind very early, but observation shows such truths are about particular ideas furnished by the senses; for example, a child knows the difference between the ideas of sweet and bitter before it can speak and before it knows abstract ideas. Even assent at first hearing is no proof of innateness, for many truths not innate will be assented to as soon as understood.

The ideas that are furnished by experience

are the materials of reason and knowledge.

On the contrary, the senses first furnish us with particular ideas, which the mind by degrees becomes familiar with, remembers, and names. The mind subsequently abstracts from these particular ideas and gives names to general ideas. Thus, general ideas, general words, and the use of reason grow together, and assent to the truth of propositions depends on having clear and distinct ideas of the meaning of terms. Locke held it to be evident that particular propositions are known before the more universal and with as much certainty.

We have natural faculties or capacities to think and to reason. This is not, however, the same thing as having innate ideas, for if anyone means by innate ideas nothing but this natural capacity, he uses terms, according to Locke, in a manner plainly contrary to common usage.

In a similar fashion, Locke argued that we have no innate moral or practical principles, for there is no universal agreement about such principles; great varieties of human vice have been at one time or place considered virtues. We all have a desire for happiness and an aversion to misery, but these inclinations give us no knowledge or truth. Locke was persuaded that there are eternal principles of morality, which men may come to know through the use of reason about experience. This, however, is far from proving them innate.

In the third chapter of Book I Locke argued that no principles can be innate unless the ideas contained in them are innate, that is, unless men can be conscious of them. Impossibility and identity are hardly innate, yet without them we cannot understand the supposedly innate principle of identity, that it is impossible for the same thing both to be and not be. Similarly, the proposition that God is to be worshipped cannot be innate, for the notion of God is so diverse that men have great difficulty agreeing on it, while some men have no conception of God whatsoever.

Locke's Target. Who was Locke criticizing in his long and repetitious attack on the doctrine of innate ideas? Was the position he denounced held by anyone in the form in which he presented the theory? Why did he examine the question at such length?

Since the *Essay* was first published tradition has held that Locke's target was Descartes and the Cartesians. Certainly Leibniz thought so, as did others after him. In the late nineteenth century, critics pointed to Locke's own rationalism and noted that his recognition of men's natural faculties and innate powers to think and reason is not far from the position of Descartes, who wrote, "Innate ideas proceed from the capacity of thought itself," and "I never wrote or concluded that the mind required innate ideas which were in some sort different from its faculty of thinking." Various other possible objects of Locke's attacks were suggested, the Cambridge Platonists, certain groups in the universities, and various clergymen. Recently R. I. Aaron has argued persuasively that the older tradition, that Descartes, the Cartesians, and certain English thinkers were the targets of Locke's attack, is the correct one and that Locke was not simply striking at a straw man of his own making.

Reasons for Attacking Innate Ideas. Locke suggested that the doctrine of innate ideas lends itself to a certain authoritarianism and encourages laziness of thought, so that the foundations of knowledge are not likely to be examined. The expression "innate ideas" is an unfortunate one and admittedly extremely vague. It carries with it the suggestion that certain ideas and knowledge are, in Locke's sense, imprinted on the mind and are in no way dependent on experience. Certainly there are passages in Descartes which strongly suggest that certain ideas are innately in the mind, and more than a few thinkers took this to be Descartes's meaning. Furthermore, Locke wished to prepare the ground for his own thesis that all ideas and all knowledge are acquired. If he overemphasized the crude sense of the theory of innate ideas, he also showed that even the refined doctrine is unnecessary in accounting for knowledge.

There is another point that Locke discussed later in the *Essay.* Descartes asserted that the essence of the mind is to think. To Locke this meant that the mind could not both be and not think. He argued that the mind does not think always and that its real essence cannot be thinking. If the mind thinks always, either some ideas must be innate or the mind comes into being only after it has been furnished with ideas by experience. Neither alternative was acceptable to Locke.

SOURCE OF IDEAS. Locke, in his positive thesis in Book II, valiantly and sometimes awkwardly endeavored to show that every idea we have is ultimately derived from experience, either from sensation or reflection. Locke began by asserting that a man is conscious of two things, the fact "that he thinks" and "the ideas" in the mind about which he thinks. Locke's initial concern was with the question of how a man comes by his ideas; and he made an assumption in terms of several similes. "Let us then suppose the mind to be, as we say, white paper, void of all characters, without any ideas. How comes it to be furnished? . . . Whence has it all the materials of reason and knowledge?" (II.i.2). Locke replied to his own questions that we get all our ideas from experience, the two fountainheads of which are sensation and reflection. Our senses are affected by external objects (bodies) and afford us ideas, such as yellow, white, heat, cold, soft, hard, bitter, and sweet. Perceiving the operations of our own minds when we reflect, we are furnished with ideas of perception, thinking, doubting, believing, reasoning, knowing, and willing.

The ideas that are furnished by experience are the materials of reason and knowledge. These materials are either the immediate objects of sense, such as color, or the unexamined but direct awareness of such acts as doubting or knowing. Locke's meaning becomes explicitly clear in his account of solidity. He held that we get the idea of solidity by touch. "That which . . . hinders the approach of two bodies, when they are moving one towards another, I call solidity" (II.iv.1). He sharply distinguished this sense from the purely mathematical use of the term. Impenetrability is an acceptable alternative name for solidity. It is clearly distinct from space and hardness. After an extensive discussion Locke stated, "If anyone asks me what this solidity is, I send him to his senses to inform him. Let him put a flint or a football between his hands and then endeavour to join them, and he will know" (II.iv.6). All philosophical and scientific discourse about solidity, however complex and sophisticated it may be, must ultimately refer back to that from which it began, namely the experience or sensation we have when we put something such as a flint or a football between our hands. Similarly, we cannot by discourse give a blind man the idea of color or make known what pain is to one who never felt it. All knowledge about the physics of light and color or sound refers back to what we perceive when we see and hear. It is in this sense, then, that we get all our ideas from sensation and reflection. Locke nowhere, however, suggested that we can or should stop there. Once the mind is furnished with ideas, it may perform various operations with them.

IDEAS AND THE REAL WORLD. Throughout the first book of the *Essay* Locke assumed the real existence of an external physical world and the substantial unity of a man in body and mind. He undoubtedly accepted the thesis that the external physical world is corpuscular and acts by bodies in motion that possess only those qualities which Locke called primary. Locke spoke of sec-

ondary qualities as powers in bodies to produce in our minds ideas that are signs of these powers but that in no way resemble the powers which produce them. Often he suggested that if we had the means of observing the minute motions of the particles making up gross bodies, we might have a clearer notion of what we mean when we call secondary qualities powers. Locke's position here is physical realism. It is not simply a manner of speaking. The ideas we have do represent real things outside of us and do constitute the links by which we know something of the external physical world.

IDENTITY. Among the bodies that exist are those of plants, animals, and men. Existence itself constitutes the principle of individuation. Identity is not applied in the same way to a mass of matter and a living body. The identity of an oak lies in the organization of its parts, which partake of one common life. So it is with animals. Again, "the identity of the same man consists: viz. in nothing but a participation of the same continued life, by constantly fleeting particles of matter, in succession vitally united to the same organized body" (II.xxvii.6).

Origin of Sensation. With these controlling hypotheses in the *Essay* in view, we may return to Locke's invitation to consider the mind as a blank sheet of paper without any ideas. Is a mind without ideas anything but a bare capacity to receive ideas? If we ask what a man is without ideas, we can say he is an organized body existing in a world of other bodies and interacting with them. Experience is a matter of contact of the organized human body with other bodies before it is a matter of sensation or perception. Not every body impinging on our body gives rise to sensation; if it does not, we take no notice of it. However, if some external bodies strike our senses and produce the appropriate motions therein, then our senses convey into the mind several distinct perceptions. How this takes place Locke avoided considering, but that it takes place he was certain; a man, he asserted, first begins to think "when he first has any sensation" (II.i.23).

SIMPLE AND COMPLEX IDEAS. Locke proceeded to distinguish between simple and complex ideas. A simple idea is "nothing but one uniform appearance or conception in the mind, and is not distinguishable into different ideas" (II.ii.1). A color seen, a sound heard, warmth felt, an odor smelled, are all simple ideas of sense. Once it is furnished with a number of simple ideas, the mind has the power to repeat, compare, and unite them into an almost infinite variety of combinations; but it is utterly incapable of inventing or framing a new simple idea. Thus, with respect to simple ideas the mind is mostly passive; they are simply given in experience. The ideas are given not in isolation from each other but in combinations, as when we simultaneously feel the warmth and softness of wax or the cold-ness and hardness of ice; nevertheless, simple ideas are distinct from each other in that the mind may mark off each from the other, however united the qualities may be in the things that cause the simple ideas in the mind. Moreover, only those qualities in things that produce ideas in us can ever be imagined at all. Thus, our knowl-edge of existence is limited by the ideas furnished by experience. Had we one sense less or more than we now do, our experience and knowledge would be respectively decreased or increased.

We have certain ideas, such as color or odor, from one sense only; others, like figure and number, from more than one sense. Reflection alone provides us with experience of thinking and willing. Other ideas, such as pleasure, pain, power, existence, and unity, we have from both sensation and reflection.

PRIMARY AND SECONDARY QUALITIES. Locke made a second basic distinction—between primary and secondary qualities. In doing so he clearly went beyond ideas. He wrote, "Whatsoever the mind perceives in itself, or is the immediate object of perception, thought, or understanding, that I call idea; and the power to produce any idea in our mind, I call quality of the sub-ject wherein that power is" (II.viii.8). Primary qualities, he argued, are utterly inseparable from body. They are known to be primary because sense constantly finds them there if body can be perceived at all, and the mind by critical reflection finds them inseparable from every particle of matter. Solidity, extension, figure, and mo-bility are all primary qualities. Our ideas of these qual-ities resemble the qualities themselves, and these qual-ities really exist in body, whether or not they are perceived. Berkeley was to show that to speak of resem-blance supposes that a comparison, an observation, can be made. Locke was aware of the difficulty, as is shown in his *Examination of Malebranche*. Apparently he be-lieved it was the only explanation plausible in spite of its difficulties.

Secondary qualities, in Locke's terms, were nothing but powers to produce various sensations. Bodies do so by the action of their bulk, figure, and texture, and by the motion of their insensible parts on our senses. Somehow they produce in us such ideas as color, odor, sound, warmth, and smell. These ideas in no way re-semble the qualities of bodies themselves. They are but signs of events in real bodies. Locke also frequently called these ideas secondary qualities. He would have been clearer had he called them sensory ideas of sec-ondary qualities, preserving the distinction between qualities as attributes of a subject and ideas as objects in the mind. A third class of qualities (sometimes called tertiary) is the power of a body to produce a change in another body, for example, the power of the sun to melt wax.

Nowhere is Locke's physical realism more evident than in his distinction between primary and secondary qualities. Whatever epistemological difficulties the dis-tinction might entail, Locke was persuaded that the new physics required it. Indeed, the distinction was made by Boyle, Descartes, Galileo, and others before him and was thoroughly familiar in his day. Admittedly there is a problem in the assertion that a certain motion in body produces in us the idea of a particular color. Neverthe-less, Locke was persuaded that it was so. In such difficult cases Locke fell back upon the omnipotence and wis-dom of God and the fact that our knowledge is suited to our purpose.

IDEAS OF REFLECTION. Locke observed that per-ception is the first faculty of the mind and without it we know nothing else. Hence, the idea of perception is the first and simplest idea we have from reflection. What perception is, is best discovered by observing what we do when we see, hear, or think. Locke added that judgment may alter the interpretation we make of the ideas we receive from sensation. Thus, if a man born blind gains his sight, he must learn to distinguish be-tween a sphere and a cube visually, though he can do so readily by touch. By habit the ideas of sensation are gradually integrated into the unified experience of com-plex ideas, and by judgment we come to expect things that look a certain way to also feel or smell a certain way. It is worth noting that Locke was persuaded that animals have perception and are not, as Descartes held, mere automatons.

Memory and Contemplation. The second faculty of the mind that Locke held indispensable to knowledge is the retention manifested in both contemplation and memory. Contemplation consists in holding an idea be-fore the mind for some time. Memory, however, gave Locke some difficulties. He asserted that "our ideas be-ing nothing but actual perceptions in the mind—this laying up of our ideas in the repository of the memory signifies no more but this: that the mind has a power in many cases to revive perceptions which it has once had, with this additional perception annexed to them, that it has had them before" (II.x.2). The inadequacy of this statement is at once evident. It proposes no more than a kind of subjective conviction that may often be in error. Locke's analysis of memory was more psycho-logical than philosophical. He passed over the consid-eration of how memory is possible at all and the criteria by which a true memory may be distinguished from a false memory. He did say, however, that attention, repe-tition, pleasure, and pain aid memory and are the conditions under which memory is strengthened or weakened. Again he asserted that animals have memory.

Other Ideas of Reflection. Other faculties of the mind are discerning and distinguishing one idea from another, comparing and compounding, naming, and abstracting. Locke considered each point also in respect to animals, holding, for example, that animals compare and compound ideas only to a slight extent and do not abstract ideas at all. At the conclusion of this chapter (II.xi.15) Locke asserted that he thought he had given a "true history of the first beginnings of human knowledge."

Just as the mind observes that several combinations

of simple ideas are found together, so too,

it can by its own action voluntarily join

several simple ideas together into one complex idea.

COMPLEX IDEAS. Locke next considered complex ideas. Just as the mind observes that several combinations of simple ideas are found together, so too, it can by its own action voluntarily join several simple ideas together into one complex idea. There are three categories of complex ideas—modes, substances, and relations. Modes are dependencies or affections of substances. Simple modes are variations or different combinations of one simple idea, whereas in mixed modes several distinct ideas are joined to make a complex idea. Ideas of substances represent distinct particular things subsisting in themselves. Complex ideas of relation consist in comparing one idea with another.

This classification is not entirely satisfactory because ideas of modes invariably entail relations in the broadest sense. Locke seems to have been closer to Aristotle than to modern usage in his employment of the term "relation." Under modes Locke included space, duration and time, number, infinity, motion, sense qualities, thinking, pleasure and pain, power, and certain mixed modes. Under substance he placed the idea of substance in general, the ideas of particular substances, and collective ideas of substances. In the category of relation, he considered a number of ideas, including cause and effect, relations of place and time, identity and diversity, and others that he classified as proportional, natural, instituted, and moral.

The greater number of these concepts have in other philosophies been credited with some a priori and extraempirical character. They are not direct objects of sensory experience; and they appear to have a certainty

not found in the mere coexistence of sensory ideas. They are more abstract and universal than the simple ideas of sensation and reflection. Locke's broad use of the term "ideas" tends to confuse and obscure the distinction between sensory percept and concept. Nevertheless, Locke undertook to show how the mind actively constructs these complex ideas, abstract and conceptual though they may be, out of the materials of knowledge, the simple ideas of sensation and reflection. In this undertaking Locke's rationalism was most evident, for he held that while the mind constructs complex ideas, it cannot do so arbitrarily. In this sense, Locke could claim for them an objective reality.

The Mode of Space. Examination here will be limited to only those complex ideas that are most important and difficult. Among modes, only space, duration, number, thinking, and power will be considered. Locke contended that the modifications of a simple idea are as much distinct ideas as any two ideas can be. Space in its first manifestation is a simple idea, since in seeing and touching we immediately perceive a distance between bodies and the parts of bodies. Though the idea of space constantly accompanies other sensory ideas, it is distinguishable from them. All our modes of the idea of space derive from the initial sensory experience. Thus space considered as length is called distance, considered three-dimensionally is capacity, considered in any manner is termed extension. Each different distance, especially when measured by stated lengths, is a distinct idea, including the idea of immensity, which consists in adding distance to distance without ever reaching a terminus. So too, figure allows an endless variety of modifications of the simple idea of space. Place is distance considered relative to some particular bodies or frame of reference.

Locke disagreed with Descartes's assertion that extension is the essence of matter, although he agreed that we cannot conceive of a body that is not extended. But a body has solidity, and solidity is distinct from the notion of space; for the parts of space are inseparable in thought and in actuality and are immovable, whereas a solid body may move and its parts are separable. Descartes's argument that the physical universe is a plenum was dismissed by Locke as unsound, for there is no contradiction in the conception of a vacuum. If body is not infinite, we can conceive of reaching out beyond the physical limits of the universe to a place unoccupied by matter. The idea of pure space is necessarily infinite, for we can conceive of no limit or terminus to it. Locke professed not to know whether space was a substance or an accident and offered to answer the question when the ideas of substance and accident were clarified. He was more confident of the idea of pure space than he was of the traditional philosophical categories. Locke placed a great load on the simple idea of space, and by the activity of his reason he went beyond the bounds of possible experience.

Duration and Time. The idea of duration is broader than that of time. If we consider the train of ideas that passes through our minds, we observe that one idea constantly succeeds another, and so we come by the idea of succession. By reflection we acquire the idea of duration, which we may then apply to motion and sensory ideas. Where there is no perception of the succession of ideas in our minds, there is no sense of time. Locke insisted that motion does not furnish us with the idea of duration, and he directly opposed Aristotle's definition that "time is the measure of motion with respect to before and after."

Once we have the idea of duration, we need a measure of common duration. Time is the consideration of duration marked by certain measures such as minutes, hours, days. The most convenient measures of time must be capable of division into equal portions of constantly repeated periods. We cannot be certain of the constancy of motions or of the time spans they measure. Locke was concerned with liberating time from motion. Consequently, he argued that we must consider duration itself as "going on in one constant, equal, uniform course; but none of the measures of it which we make use of can be known to do so" (II.xiv.21). Once time is liberated from motion, Locke held, we can conceive of infinite duration even beyond creation. Thus we can expand by endless addition the idea of duration to come to the notion of eternity.

Were it not for the implicit realism of Locke's arguments, it would be possible to agree with those scholars who have seen in his arguments about duration and expansion a vague groping for a position somewhat similar to Kant's a priori aesthetic. For both men, space becomes the framework of body, and duration or time the structure of the mind, or the inner sense.

Number. The idea of unity is everywhere suggested to the mind, and no idea is more simple. By repeating it we come to the complex modes of number. Once we have learned to perform this operation, we cannot stop short of the idea of infinity. Locke regarded both finite and infinite as modes of quantity. Because we are able to apply the idea of number to space and time, we are capable of conceiving of them as infinite. The idea of infinity is essentially negative, since we come to it by enlarging our ideas of number as much as we please and discover that there is no reason ever to stop. We may know that number, space, and duration are infinite, but we cannot positively know infinity itself. Locke insisted that however remote from the simple ideas of sensation

and reflection these ideas may be, they have their origin in those simple ideas.

The Modes of Thinking. Locke gave only casual and formal attention to the modes of thinking, such as sensation, remembrance, recollection, contemplation, attention, dreaming, reasoning, judging, willing, and knowing. Equally superficial was his consideration of modes of pleasure and pain, which consisted of little more than definitions of various emotions.

Power. The chapter on power is the longest in the *Essay,* and Locke felt obliged to rewrite portions of it time and again, for each new edition.

Where there is no perception

of the succession of ideas in our minds,

there is no sense of time.

It is evident that power is not perceived as such. Locke observed that the mind, taking note of the changes and sequences of our ideas and "concluding from what it has so constantly observed to have been, that the like changes will for the future be made in the same things, by like agents, and by the like ways . . . comes by that idea which we call power" (II.xxi.1). From this it hardly seems that the idea of power is a simple idea, unless Locke meant no more than that the idea of power is only the observation of the regular order and connection of our ideas. But Locke wrote that "since whatever change is observed, the mind must collect a power somewhere able to make that change, as well as a possibility in the thing itself to receive it" (II.xxi.4). Here the idea of power is a necessary idea of reason, grounded in certain other experiences. Locke never made clear this distinction. He admitted that the idea of power included some kind of relation but insisted that it was a simple idea.

Power is both passive and active. Whether or not matter has any active power, Locke pointed out, we have our idea of active power from the operations of the mind itself. We find by direct observation that we have the power to begin, continue, or stop certain actions of our minds and motions of our bodies. This power we call will, and the actual exercise of this power, volition, or willing. Action is voluntary or involuntary insofar as it is or is not consequent upon the order or command of the mind.

Locke proceeded to explore the ideas of will, desire, and freedom in terms of the idea of power. "The idea of liberty is the idea of a power in any agent to do or forbear any particular action, according to the determination or thought of the mind, whereby either of them is preferred to the other" (II.xxi.8). Where this power is absent, a man is under necessity. Locke consequently dismissed as unintelligible the question of whether or not the will is free. The only intelligible question is whether or not a man is free. Freedom is one power of an agent and will is another; one power cannot be the power of another. "As far as this power reaches, of acting or not acting, by the determination of his own thought preferring either, so far is a man free" (II.xxi.21). Freedom then, for Locke, was the absence of constraint. If we distinguish will from desire, we cannot make the mistake of thinking the will is free.

What then determines the will with respect to action is some uneasiness in a man that may be called the uneasiness of desire. Good and evil work on the mind but do not determine the will to particular actions. The only thing that can overcome the uneasiness of one desire is the greater uneasiness of another. The removal of uneasiness is the first and necessary step to happiness. Since it is present desire that moves the will to action, good and evil contemplated and known in the mind can move us to action only when that knowledge is accompanied by a greater uneasiness than any other. Since we have many desires and can have knowledge of desired good in the future as well as feared evil, we can suspend the pursuit of any desire until we have judged it. Thus, government of our passions is possible whenever there is a greater uneasiness in not doing so. This power is the ground on which we hold men responsible for their actions. Good and bad are nothing but pleasure or pain, present or future. Error in choice is usually due to the greater strength of present pleasure or pain in comparison with future pleasure and pain. A true knowledge of what contributes to our happiness can influence a choice only when to deviate from that choice would give greater uneasiness than would any other action. Thus it is possible to change the pleasantness and unpleasantness of various actions by consideration, practice, application, and custom.

Locke's conception of power, like his ideas of cause and effect, was inadequate and vague. It was both a simple idea and a complex one; it was the notion of regular sequence and that of efficacious cause; and it was at once given and a priori. The rational and empirical elements in Locke were at war here. Locke was at his best in showing how the word "power" is commonly used. His analysis of the will and freedom was likewise involved in difficulties. The will is not free and thus man's actions are determined; but at the same time we can suspend the execution of any desire by our judgment. Locke was aware of these difficulties, but he saw no satisfactory alternative.

Mixed Modes. Mixed modes are made by the mind and are exemplified by drunkenness, a lie, obligation, sacrilege, or murder. To a great degree we get these ideas by the explanation of the words that stand for them.

SUBSTANCE. Of all the ideas considered by Locke none gave him more difficulty than that of substance, and nowhere was his empiricism more in conflict with his rationalism. The diverse trends of Locke's thought concerning substance and the problems he raised prepared the ground for Berkeley, Hume, Kant, and many others who struggled with the same questions. At every opportunity throughout the *Essay* he returned to consider particular substances and the general idea of substance. Locke held that we are conversant only with particular substances through experience; yet his rationalism and realism would not permit him to abandon the general idea of substance.

The mind is furnished with many simple ideas by the senses, and it observes by reflection that certain of them are constantly together. It then presumes that these belong to one thing and for convenience gives them one name. In this way the mind arrives at the complex idea of particular substances, such as gold, which we observe to be yellow and malleable, to dissolve in aqua regia, to melt, and not to be used up in fire. A substance so defined gives us only a nominal definition.

Locke added that "not imagining how these simple ideas can subsist by themselves, we accustom ourselves to suppose some substratum wherein they do subsist, and from which they do result; which therefore we call substance" (II.xxiii.1). This idea of a substratum is extremely vague, and Locke called it a "something we know not what." Our ideas do not reach, and we cannot have, a knowledge of the real essence of substances. Nonetheless, Locke continued to believe that real essences do exist, although our knowledge comes short of them.

Our knowledge of corporeal substances consists of ideas of the primary and secondary qualities perceived by the senses and of the powers we observe in them to affect or be affected by other things. We have as clear an idea of spirit as of body, but we are not capable of knowing the real essence of either. Locke observed that we know as little of how the parts of a body cohere as of how our spirits perceive ideas or move our bodies, since we know nothing of either except our simple ideas of them. Locke even suggested that God could if he wished, as far as we know, add to matter the power to think, just as easily as he could add to matter a separate substance with the power to think.

Even our idea of God is based on simple ideas that are enlarged with the idea of infinity. God's infinite essence is unknown to us. We can only know that he exists.

RELATIONS. The mind can consider any idea as it stands in relation to any other; and thus we come by ideas of relation, such as father, whiter, older. Frequently, the lack of a correlative term leads us to mistake a relative term for an absolute one. Locke distinguished the relation from the things related and appears to have made all relations external. Indeed, he held that many ideas of relation are clearer than ideas of substances; for example, the idea of brothers is clearer than the perfect idea of man.

Though there are many ideas and words signifying relations, they all terminate in simple ideas. There is a difficulty here. If the idea of relation is not a simple idea or a combination of simple ideas, then it is distinct from them. Like the general idea of substance, it is a concept derived from reason. No doubt the mind is capable of comparing the relation of one idea with another, but our perception of this operation must have for its object either a simple idea or the operation itself. On this point Locke was obscure and evasive and avoided the difficulties by the vague assertion that all relations terminate in simple ideas.

Causation. The relation to which Locke first turned was cause and effect. His discussion was inadequate and marked by the duality found in his consideration of other ideas. We observe the order and connection of our ideas and the coming into existence of things and qualities. In pointing this out Locke was on strictly empirical grounds. When, however, he defined cause as "that which produces any simple or complex idea," and "that which is produced, effect" (II.xxvi.1), he went beyond experience and rested his argument on reason. Locke undoubtedly saw the difficulties of his position. He was concerned, on the one hand, to show how we have the ideas of cause and effect from experience. On the other hand, he was not satisfied with a mere sequence theory. The difficulty arose, as it did with power and substance, because he was persuaded that there is a reality beyond the ideas manifest to us. It is a reality, however, about which he could say little in terms of his representationalism.

Identity and Diversity. Under relation Locke also examined identity and diversity, by which he meant the relation of a thing to itself, particularly with respect to different times and places. As was stated above, the identity of a plant, an animal, or a man consists in a participation in the same continued life. To this Locke added an examination of personal identity. He argued that personal identity is consciousness of being the same thinking self at different times and places.

Locke also discussed other relations, such as proportional, natural, instituted, and moral, which are not es-

sential to the main argument of the *Essay* and which will, therefore, not be discussed here.

The remaining chapters of Book II of the *Essay* are devoted to "Clear and Obscure, Distinct and Confused Ideas," "Real and Fantastical Ideas," "Adequate and Inadequate Ideas," "True and False Ideas," and "The Association of Ideas." All of them have merit in clarifying other parts of the *Essay* but add little that is new and not discussed elsewhere. Consequently, they will be passed over.

LANGUAGE. At the end of Book II of the *Essay* Locke related that he had originally intended to pass on to a consideration of knowledge. He found, however, such a close connection between words and ideas, particularly between abstract ideas and general words, that he had first to examine the "nature, use, and signification" of language, since all knowledge consists of propositions. Book III, therefore, was incorporated into the *Essay.*

Of all the ideas considered by Locke

none gave him more difficulty

than that of substance,

and nowhere was his empiricism

more in conflict with his rationalism.

The merits of Book III are the subject of some controversy. Most scholars have dismissed it as unimportant and confused. Some, such as Aaron, see many merits in it despite its manifest inadequacies.

The primary functions of language are to communicate with our fellow men, to make signs for ourselves of internal conceptions, and to stand as marks for ideas. Language is most useful when general names stand for general ideas and operations of the mind. Since all except proper names are general, a consideration of what kinds of things words stand for is in order. "Words, in their primary or immediate signification, stand for nothing but the ideas in the mind of him that uses them" (III.ii.2). We suppose they stand for the same ideas in the minds of others. Words stand for things only indirectly. General words stand for general ideas, which become general by separation from other ideas and from particular circumstances. This process Locke called abstraction.

Definition. Definition by genus and differentia is merely a convenience by which we avoid enumerating various simple ideas for which the genus stands. (In this, Locke prepared the way for descriptive definition, which makes no pretense of defining the real essence of things.) It follows that general or universal ideas are made by the understanding for its own use. Thus the essences of so-called species are nothing but abstract ideas. Locke asserted that every distinct abstract idea is a distinct essence. This must not be taken in a Platonic sense, for it is the mind itself that makes these abstract ideas. If essences are distinguished into nominal and real, then with respect to simple ideas and modes there is no difference between nominal and real essence. In substances, they are decidedly different, in that the real essence of substance is unknowable to us.

Names. Locke asserted that the names of simple ideas are not definable. One wonders, Is blue a general idea? If so, what is this blue as against that blue? What is separated out? What retained? Locke never examined these questions, with the result that his conception of abstraction is vague and vacillating. Locke gave several distinct meanings to such terms as "general ideas" and "universal ideas," shifting from one meaning to another and never clarifying them.

Complex ideas consisting of several simple ideas are definable and intelligible provided one has experience of the simple ideas that compose them. Without experience how can a blind man understand the definition of a rainbow?

Simple ideas are "perfectly taken from the existence of things and are not arbitrary at all" (III.iv.17). Ideas of substances refer to a pattern with some latitude, whereas ideas of mixed modes are absolutely arbitrary and refer to no real existence. They are not, however, made at random or without reason. It is the name that ties these ideas together, and each such idea is its own prototype.

Since names for substances stand for complex ideas perceived regularly to go together and supposed to belong to one thing, we necessarily come short of the real essences, if there are any. One may use the word "gold" to signify the coexistence of several ideas. One man may use the term to signify the complex idea of *A* and *B* and *C*. Another man of more experience may add *D,* or add *D* and leave out *A*. Thus, these essences are of our own making without being entirely arbitrary. In any case, the boundaries of the species of substances are drawn by men.

Connective Words. In a brief chapter, "Of Particles," Locke pointed out that we need words signifying the connections that the mind makes between ideas or propositions. These show what connection, restriction, distinction, opposition, or emphasis is given to the parts of discourse. These words signify, not ideas, but an action of the mind. Again a difficulty arises. If "is" and "is not" stand for the mind's act of affirming or denying, then either the mind directly apprehends its own ac-

tions in some way or we do have ideas of affirmation or denial. If we do have ideas of the mind's acts, then these words ought to signify the ideas of these acts; if we do not have ideas which these words signify, then either we do not apprehend them or something besides ideas is the object of the mind when it thinks.

The remainder of Book III concerns Locke's thoughts on the imperfection of words, the abuse of words, and his suggested remedies for these imperfections and abuses.

KNOWLEDGE. The first three books of the *Essay* are largely a preparation for the fourth. Many scholars see a fundamental cleavage between Book II and Book IV. Yet Locke saw no conflict between the two books, and whatever split existed in Locke's thought runs throughout the *Essay,* as J. W. Yolton and others have pointed out. An effort can be made to reconcile Locke's empiricism and his rationalism, his grounding of all ideas and knowledge in experience and his going beyond experience to the existence of things.

Many of Locke's difficulties stem from his definition of "idea." It is so broad that anything perceived or known must be an idea. But Locke showed, in Books I and II, that we get all our ideas from experience, not in order to claim that nothing exists except ideas, but to show that there is an alternative to the theory of innate ideas. For Locke, experience is initially a contact of bodies and subsequently a reflection of the mind. He never doubted the existence of an external physical world, the inner workings of which are unknown to us.

Sources of Knowledge. There are two sources of knowledge—sensation and reflection. The ideas we have from reflection are in some important ways quite different from those we have from sensation. In Book II Locke asserted that the mind "turns its view inward upon itself and observes its own actions about those ideas it has (and) takes from thence other ideas" (II.vi.1). The important point here is that in reflection the mind observes its own action. It is true that Locke spoke of modes of the simple ideas of reflection, such as remembering, discerning, reasoning, and judging. Nonetheless, if the mind does observe its own action, then something more than ideas are the object of the mind in reflection, or else ideas of reflection are somehow importantly different from the ideas of sensation. This point will show up in a consideration of Locke's theory of knowledge.

Propositions. Locke defined knowledge as "the perception of the connection and agreement, or disagreement and repugnancy, of any of our ideas" (IV.i.2). This agreement or disagreement is in respect to four types: identity and diversity, relation, coexistence or necessary connection, and real existence. Perceiving agreement or disagreement is quite different from just barely perceiving the ideas that are said to agree or disagree. Strictly speaking, this perception must be a distinct idea of either agreement or disagreement. Yet this was not Locke's meaning. Where there is knowledge, there is judgment, since there can be no knowledge without a proposition, mental or verbal. Locke defined truth as "the joining or separating of signs, as the things signified by them do agree or disagree one with another" (IV.v.2). There are two sorts of propositions: mental, "wherein the ideas in our understandings are, without the use of words, put together or separated by the mind perceiving or judging of their agreement or disagreement" (IV.v.5); and verbal, which stand for mental propositions.

Judgments. In this view, ideas are the materials of knowledge, the terms of mental propositions. They are, insofar as they are given in sensation and reflection, the subject matter of reflection. If perception of agreement or disagreement in identity and diversity is the first act of the mind, then that act is a judgment. If we infallibly know, as soon as we have it in our minds, that the idea of white is identical with itself and different from that of red, and that the idea of round is identical with itself and different from that of square, we must distinguish between the bare having of these ideas and the knowledge of their identity and diversity. The knowledge of their identity and diversity is a judgment. It is reflective, and in it the mind perceives its own action or operation. There can be no distinction between the judgment and the idea of it. This is perhaps Locke's meaning, which is unfortunately obscured by his broad use of the term "idea." This perception of its own action is quite distinct from the abstract idea of the power of judgment. We may be uncertain as to how the mind makes judgments, what determines it to judge, or in what kind of a substance this power inheres, but we may be sure that in the actual making of a true judgment the mind perceives its own act. This position may be beset with difficulties, but it makes some sense out of Locke's definition of knowledge.

Degrees of Knowledge. Locke recognized two degrees of knowledge, in the strict sense of the term—intuition and demonstration. Of the two, intuition is more fundamental and certain. "The mind perceives the agreement or disagreement of two ideas immediately by themselves, without the intervention of any other" (IV.ii.1). Such knowledge is irresistible and leaves no room for hesitation, doubt, or examination. Upon it depends all the certainty and evidence of all our knowledge. Here, clearly, what the mind perceives is not any third idea, but its own act. In demonstration the mind perceives agreement or disagreement, not immediately, but through other mediating ideas. Each step in demonstration rests upon an intuition. This kind of knowledge is most evident in, but is not limited to, mathematics.

A third degree of knowledge is "employed about the particular existence of finite beings without us, which going beyond bare probability and yet not reaching perfectly to either of the foregoing degrees of certainty, passes under the name of knowledge" (IV.ii.14). Locke called this sensitive knowledge. Fully aware of the dialectical difficulty entailed in this position, he grounded his reply to critics on common sense. The differences between dreaming and waking, imagining and sensing, are strong enough to justify this conviction. Hunger and thirst should bring a skeptic to his senses. For Locke, it was enough that common sense supported him, for he always took sensory ideas to be signs or representations of something beyond themselves.

Limits of Knowledge. Locke asserted that knowledge extends no farther than our ideas and, specifically, no further than the perception of the agreement or disagreement of our ideas. We cannot have knowledge of all the relations of our ideas or rational knowledge of the necessary relations between many of our ideas. Sensitive knowledge goes only as far as the existence of things, not to their real essence, or reality. Two examples were given. In the first, Locke argued that though we have the ideas of circle, square, and equality, we may never find a circle equal to a square and know them to be equal. In the second, he observed that we have ideas of matter and thinking but may never know whether mere material being thinks. This has been discussed earlier.

In his controversy with Stillingfleet, Locke never abandoned this latter thesis. And throughout this section (IV.iii) Locke showed that many relations of coexistence give us no certainty that they will or must continue to be so. He seemed persuaded that the continued discovery of new knowledge suggests that there are vast horizons of reality that we may advance upon but can never reach. With respect to the relations between abstract ideas we may hope to advance very far, as in mathematics. To this he added the belief that a demonstrable science of morality is possible. On the other hand, he held that we can have no certain knowledge of bodies or of unembodied spirits.

Knowledge of Existents. Locke argued that though our knowledge terminates in our ideas, our knowledge is real. "Simple ideas are not fictions of our fancies, but the natural and regular productions of things without us, really operating upon us; and so carry with them all the conformity which is intended; or which our state requires" (IV.iv.4). On the other hand, he argued: "All our complex ideas, except those of substances, being archetypes of the mind's own making, not intended to be copies of anything, nor referred to the existence of anything, as to their originals, cannot want any conformity necessary to real knowledge" (IV.iv.5).

Universal propositions, the truth of which may be known with certainty, are not concerned directly with existence. Nonetheless, Locke argued that we have intuitive knowledge of our own existence. Here the argument is much the same as Descartes's, and it is valid only if we accept the view that the mind in reflection perceives its own acts. This knowledge of our own existence has the highest degree of certainty, according to Locke.

Many of Locke's difficulties

stem from his definition of "idea."

It is so broad that anything perceived or known

must be an idea.

We have a demonstrable knowledge of God's existence, Locke held. He used a form of the Cosmological Argument: starting with the certainty of his own existence, he argued to the necessary existence of a being adequate to produce all the effects manifest in experience. The argument assumed the reality of cause, the necessity of order, and the intelligibility of existence.

Of the existence of other things, as has been shown, we have sensitive knowledge. Locke felt the inconsistency of his position on this matter, yet accepted what he believed common sense required. We know of the coexistence of certain qualities and powers, and reason and sense require that they proceed from something outside themselves. Throughout these arguments about existence Locke went beyond his own first definition of knowledge.

PROBABILITY. The remaining portions of the *Essay* are concerned with probability, degrees of assent, reason and faith, enthusiasm, error, and the division of the sciences. Though Locke's treatment of probability is inadequate, he recognized its importance. The grounds of probability lie in the apparent conformity of propositions with our experience and the testimony of others. Practical experience shows us that our knowledge is slight, and action requires that we proceed in our affairs with something less than certainty.

Faith was, for Locke, the acceptance of revelation. It must be sharply distinguished from reason, which is "the discovery of the certainty or probability of such propositions or truths, which the mind arrives at by deduction made from such ideas which it has got by

the use of its natural faculties, viz. by sensation or reflection" (IV.xviii.2). Though reason is not able to discover the truth of revelation, nevertheless, something claimed to be revelation cannot be accepted against the clear evidence of the understanding. Thus, enthusiasm sets reason aside and substitutes for it bare fancies born of conceit and blind impulse.

Error. Error cannot lie in intuition. Locke found four sources of error: the want of proofs, inability to use them, unwillingness to use them, and wrong measures of probability. Locke concluded the *Essay* with a brief division of science, or human knowledge, into three classes—natural philosophy, or φυσική, practical action and ethics, or πρακτική, and σημειωτική, or the doctrine of signs.

INFLUENCE OF THE *ESSAY*. Many minds of the seventeenth century contributed to the overthrow of the School philosophies and the development of the new sciences and philosophies. Descartes and Locke between them, however, set the tone and direction for what was to follow. Certainly Locke was the most prominent figure in the early eighteenth century, the indispensable precursor of Berkeley and Hume as well as a fountainhead for the French Encyclopedists. If it is said that the two strains of Cartesian rationalism and Lockian empiricism met in Kant, it can be added that Hume built on Locke's foundation and Kant formalized much that was first a vague groping in Locke. Though Locke was not a wholly satisfactory thinker, his influence on thought in England and America has never completely abated, and even now there appears to be a revived interest in the *Essay*.

Political Thought

Locke's earliest known political writings were the *Essays on the Law of Nature,* written in Latin between 1660 and 1664 but not known until the Lovelace Collection was examined in 1946. They were first published in 1954 with a translation by W. von Leyden. Though much in these essays appears in the *Essay Concerning Human Understanding* and the *Two Treatises,* there remain many points at which the early essays are in conflict with parts of both later works. This fact and the bother of translating them may have deterred Locke from publishing them, despite the urging of Tyrrell. Since von Leyden can find no evidence of direct influence of these essays on anyone other than Tyrrell and Gabriel Towerson, the student of Locke is referred to von Leyden's publication for additional information.

THE "TWO TREATISES." The *Two Treatises of Government* appeared anonymously in 1690, written, it is said, to justify the revolution of 1688, or, according to the preface, "to establish the Throne of Our Great Restorer, our present King William; to make good his Title, in the Consent of the People." Locke acknowledged his authorship only in a codicil in his will listing his anonymous works and giving to the Bodleian Library a corrected copy of the *Two Treatises*. He never felt that any of the editions printed during his lifetime had satisfactorily rendered his work. Only in 1960 did Peter Laslett publish a critical edition based on the Coste master copy of the *Two Treatises*.

THE FIRST TREATISE. It has long been suspected that the first treatise was written in 1683 and that the second treatise was written in 1689. Laslett has presented much evidence to show that the second treatise was the earlier work, written between 1679 and 1681. If his thesis is correct, it was a revolutionary document, whose purpose was not primarily to philosophize but to furnish a theoretical foundation for the political aims and maneuvers of Shaftesbury and his followers in their struggle with Charles II. Only further scholarly probing will resolve this question.

Certainly Locke was the most prominent figure

in the early eighteenth century,

the indispensable precursor of Berkeley and Hume

as well as a fountainhead

for the French Encyclopedists.

In his preface, Locke stated that the greater part of the original work had been lost. He was satisfied that what remained was sufficient, since he had neither the time nor the inclination to rewrite the missing sections. The evidence is clear that it was portions of the first treatise that were lost.

The first treatise is a sarcastic and harsh criticism of Sir Robert Filmer's *Patriarcha*, which argued for the divine right of kings. Locke's treatise is more of historical than philosophical importance. It argued that Adam was not, as Filmer claimed, divinely appointed monarch of the world and all his descendants. Neither was the power of absolute monarchy inherited from Adam. Adam had no absolute rights over Eve or over his children. Parents have authority over children who are dependent upon them and who must learn obedience as well as many other things for life. The function of the parent is to protect the child and to help him mature. When the child comes to maturity, parental authority ends. In any case, the relation of parent and child is not the same as that of sovereign and subject. Were Filmer

right, one would have to conclude that every man is born a slave, a notion that was utterly repugnant to Locke. Even if Filmer were correct, it would be impossible to show that existing rulers, especially the English kings, possess legitimate claims to their sovereignty by tracing it back to lawful descent from Adam.

THE SECOND TREATISE. Locke began the second treatise with the proposition that all men are originally in a state of nature, "a state of perfect freedom to order their actions, and dispose of their possessions, and persons as they think fit, within the bounds of the Law of Nature, without asking leave, or depending upon the Will of any other man" (II.ii.4). Although Locke sometimes wrote as if the state of nature were some period in history, it must be taken largely as a philosophical fiction, an assumption made to show the nature and foundation of political power, a fiction at least as old as Plato's treatment of the Prometheus myth in the *Protagoras*. It is a state of equality but not of unbounded license. Being rational and being a creature bound by God, man must be governed by the law of nature.

Natural Law. Though the concept of the law of nature is as old as antiquity, it flourished in the seventeenth century in the minds of a considerable number of ethical and political thinkers. In general it supposed that man by the use of reason could know in the main the fundamental principles of morality, which he otherwise knew through Christian revelation. Locke was extremely vague about the law of nature, but in his *Essays on the Law of Nature* he held that that law rests ultimately on God's will. Reason discovers it. It is not innate. When, however, Locke spoke of it as "writ in the hearts of all mankind," he suggested some kind of innateness. There are obvious difficulties here, for sense and reason may fail men, even though the law of nature is binding on all. Moreover, the various exponents of the law of nature differ on what it consists of, except that it presupposes the brotherhood of man and human benevolence.

State of Nature. In a state of nature, according to Locke, all men are bound to preserve peace, preserve mankind, and refrain from hurt to one another. The execution of the law of nature is the responsibility of each individual. If any man violates this law, he thereby puts himself in a state of war with the others, who may then punish the offender. The power that one man may hold over another is neither absolute nor arbitrary and must be restrained by proportion. The state of nature was for Locke a society of men, as distinct from a state of government, or a political society.

Social Contract. There are certain inconveniences in a state of nature, such as men's partiality and the inclination on the part of some men to violate the rights of others. The remedy for this is civil government, wherein men by common consent form a social contract and create a single body politic. This contract is not between ruler and ruled, but between equally free men. The aim of the contract is to preserve the lives, freedom, and property of all, as they belong to each under natural law. Whoever, therefore, attempts to gain absolute power over another puts himself at war with the other. This holds in the political state as well as the state of nature. When a ruler becomes a tyrant, he puts himself in a state of war with the people, who then, if no redress be found, may make an appeal to heaven, that is, may revolt. This power is but an extension of the right of each to punish an aggressor in the state of nature. Unlike Hobbes, Locke was persuaded that men are capable of judging whether they are cruelly subjected and unjustly treated. Since one reason for men entering into the social contract is to avoid a state of war, the contract is broken when the sovereign puts himself into a state of war with the people by becoming a tyrant.

Slavery. Curiously, Locke justified slavery on the grounds that those who became slaves were originally in a state of wrongful war with those who conquered them and, being captive, forfeited their freedom. Apart from being bad history, this argument ignores the rights of the children of slaves. Locke's inconsistency here may mercifully be passed over.

Property. Property was an idea which Locke used in both a broad and a narrow sense. Men have a right to self-preservation and therefore to such things as they need for their subsistence. Each man possesses himself absolutely, and therefore that with which he mixes his labor becomes his property. "God has given the earth to mankind in common." No man has original, exclusive rights to the fruits and beasts of the earth. Nevertheless, man must have some means with which to appropriate them. This consists of the labor of his body and the work of his hand. By labor, man removes things from a state of nature and makes them his property. Without labor, the earth and things in general have but little value. However, only so much as a man improves and can use belongs to him, nor may a man deprive another of the means of self-preservation by overextending his reach for property.

Though the right to property is grounded in nature, it is not secured therein. It is one of the primary ends of the state to preserve the rights of property, as well as to make laws governing the use, distribution, and transference of property. In communities or countries under government, there are fixed boundaries to the common territory, and there is land and property held in common which no one may appropriate to himself and to which those not members of the community have no

right at all. Money, being something which does not spoil, came into use by mutual consent, serving as a useful means of exchange. At the same time it made possible the accumulation of wealth greater than warranted by need or use.

Political Society. Having established several rights and duties belonging to men by nature and having shown certain inconveniences and disadvantages of the state of nature, Locke turned to political society. The first society consists of the family, whose aims are not initially or primarily those of political society, but which may be included under political society.

In political society "any number of men are so united into one Society, as to quit everyone his Executive power of the law of nature, and to resign it to the public" (II.vii.89). The legislative and executive powers are "a right of making laws with penalties of Death, and consequently all less Penalties, for the regulating and preserving of property, and of employing the force of the community, in the execution of such laws, and in the defense of the commonwealth from foreign injury, and all this only for the public good" (II.i.3). By the social contract men give up, not all their rights, but only the legislative and executive right they originally had under the law of nature. This transference of power is always subordinate to the proper and true ends of the commonwealth, which are "the mutual preservation of their lives, liberties and estates."

Each man must voluntarily consent to the compact either explicitly or implicitly. An individual who at age of discretion remains a member of the community tacitly consents to the compact.

Since the compact is made between the members of the community, sovereignty ultimately remains with the people. The sovereign, in the form of a legislative body, and executive, or both, is the agent and executor of the sovereignty of the people. The community can act only by the rule of the majority, and everyone is bound by it, because an agreement of unanimity is virtually impossible. It is the people who establish the legislative, executive, and judiciary powers. Thus, an absolute monarch is incompatible with civil society.

Locke's theories so far are compatible with either monarchy, oligarchy, or democracy so long as it is recognized that ultimate sovereignty lies with the people. He believed that a constitutional monarchy with executive power, including the judiciary, in the hands of the monarch, and legislative powers in a parliamentary assembly elected by the people was the most satisfactory form of government. The supreme power he held to be the legislative, for it makes the laws that the executive must carry out and enforce. Whenever the executive violates the trust that he holds, no obligation is owed him and he may be deposed. The legislature may also violate its trust, though Locke believed it less likely to do so. Whenever this occurs, the people have a right to dissolve it and establish a new government. For this reason a regularly elected legislative body is desirable.

Rebellion. Locke explicitly recognized, as the events during his lifetime had shown, that men may become tyrants to those whom they were bound to serve. It may be a king, an assembly, or a usurper that claims absolute power. In such cases the people have a right to rebellion if no other redress is possible. Locke was not unmindful of the fact that the executive needs latitude and prerogative so that he may govern, and that the legislative body must deliberate and make laws which they believe to be in the public good. The right to rebellion is warranted only in the most extreme conditions, where all other means fail. Locke did not believe that men would lightly avail themselves of this power, for men will suffer and endure much before they resort to rebellion.

In transferring to the government the right to make and execute law and make war and peace, men do not give up the natural light of reason, by which they judge good and evil, right and wrong, justice and injustice. In specific laws or executive decisions judgment must be allowed to the legislature and the executive. If, however, a long train of acts shows a tyrannical course, then men, judging that the sovereign has put himself into a state of war with them, may justly dethrone the tyrant. On the other hand, the legislative and executive power can never revert to the people unless there is a breach of trust.

The dissolution of government is not the dissolution of society. The aim of revolution is the establishment of a new government, not a return to a state of nature. The dissolution of a government may occur under many circumstances, but foremost among them are when the arbitrary will of a single person or prince is set in place of the law; when the prince hinders the legislature from due and lawful assembly; when there is arbitrary change in elections; when the people are delivered into subjection by a foreign power; and when the executive neglects and abandons his charge. In all such cases sovereignty reverts to the society, and the people have a right to act as the supreme power and continue the legislature in themselves, or erect a new form, or under the old form place sovereignty in new hands, whichever they think best. On the other hand, "the power that every individual gave the society, . . . can never revert to the individuals again, as long as the society lasts" (II.xix.243).

As theory, Locke's second treatise is full of inadequacies, but its magnificent sweep of ideas prepared the ground for popular and democratic government.

Education and Religion

Locke's thought on education and religion was not presented in strictly philosophical terms. It was, however, deeply rooted in the fundamental concepts of the *Essay* and the *Two Treatises.* His works in these areas display clearly the liberal bent of his mind as well as his love of freedom, tolerance, and truth. His attitude was pragmatic and based on considerable psychological insight into the motives, needs, passions, and follies of men. *Some Thoughts Concerning Education,* several letters on toleration, and *The Reasonableness of Christianity* profoundly affected educational and religious thought in the eighteenth century and after. Two of these works, *Some Thoughts Concerning Education* and the first *Letter on Toleration,* continue to be fresh and relevant.

EDUCATION. When Locke was in Holland, he wrote a number of letters to Edward Clark advising him on the education of his son, a young man of no particular distinction. Locke had in mind the education of a gentleman who would one day be a squire. In 1693 Locke modified these letters somewhat and published the contents as *Some Thoughts Concerning Education* in response to "so many, who profess themselves at a loss how to breed their children." His thought was marked by a ready understanding of, and warm sympathy with, children. Three main thoughts dominate the work. First, the individual aptitudes, capacities, and idiosyncrasies of the child should govern learning, not arbitrary curricular or rote learning taught by the rod. Second, Locke placed the health of the body and the development of a sound character ahead of intellectual learning. In the third place, he saw that play, high spirits, and the "gamesome humor" natural to children should govern the business of learning wherever possible. Compulsory learning is irksome; where there is play in learning, there will be joy in it. Throughout he placed emphasis on good example, practice, and use rather than on precepts, rules, and punishment. The work was an implicit criticism of his own education at Westminster and Oxford, which he found unpleasant and largely useless.

Writing almost as a physician, Locke advised "plenty of open air, exercise, and sleep; plain diet, no wine or strong drink, and very little or no physic; not too warm and strait clothing; especially the head and feet kept cold, and the feet often used to cold water and exposed to wet." The aim in all was to keep the body in strength and vigor, able to endure hardships.

Locke urged that early training must establish the authority of the parents so that good habits may be established. The prime purpose is the development of virtue, the principle of which is the power of denying ourselves the satisfaction of our desires. The child should be taught to submit to reason when young. Parents teach by their own example. They should avoid severe punishments and beatings as well as artificial rewards. Rules should be few when a child is young, but those few should be obeyed. Mild, firm, and rational approval or disapproval are most effective in curbing bad behavior. Children should be frequently in the company of their parents, who should in turn study the disposition of the child and endeavor to use the child's natural desire for freedom and play to make learning as much like recreation as possible. High spirits should not be curbed, but turned to creative use. Curiosity too should be encouraged, and questions should be heard and fairly answered. Cruelty must always be discouraged and courageousness approved.

Locke's works on education and religion

display clearly the liberal bent of his mind

as well as his love of freedom,

tolerance, and truth.

As the child grows, familiarity should be increased so that the parent has a friend in the mature child. Virtue, breeding, and a free liberal spirit as well as wisdom and truthfulness were the goals set by Locke in all his advice. Affection and friendship were for him both means and ends of good education.

Learning, though important, Locke put last. First, he would have the child learn to speak and read his own language well by example and practice, not by grammar. In the study of all languages, he would put off the study of grammar until they can be spoken well. He would begin the learning of a second modern language early. Reluctantly he would allow a gentleman's son to learn Latin, but he did not recommend much time on Greek, Hebrew, Arabic, rhetoric, or logic, which constituted the curricula of the universities of his day. Rather, time should be given to the study of geography, arithmetic, astronomy, geometry, history, ethics, and civil law. Dancing he encouraged, and music as well, in moderation. He was less sympathetic to poetry. Remarkably, he urged that everyone learn at least one manual trade and make some study of accounting. Finally, travel was valuable if not done before one could profit by it.

If much of this is familiar and even trite, it must be remembered that Locke was among the first to formulate these ideas. His influence on educational thought and practice was enormous and is still very much with us in its fundamental outlook and method.

RELIGION. Locke saw some merits in all the competing claims of various religious groups. He also saw the destructive force that was released when these claims sought exclusive public dominion at the expense of individual conscience. He looked in several directions at once. This tendency has earned for him the reputation of being timorous and compromising. Nonetheless, it is on this trait of mind that much of his great influence and reputation rests. For Locke, fidelity to the evidence at hand always outweighed cleverness, consistency, and dialectic. It is the chief testimony to his claim that truth was always his aim, even when he might have won an easy victory by dogmatic consistency.

Locke's writings on religion are voluminous. When he died he was working on extensive commentaries on the *Epistles of St. Paul,* as well as a draft of a fourth *Letter on Toleration.* Earlier he had written and published three letters on toleration, *The Reasonableness of Christianity* (1695), and two *Vindications* (1695 and 1697) of the latter work. Moreover, Locke's three letters to Stillingfleet, the bishop of Worcester, are concerned with religious questions as well as epistemological ones.

Religious Tolerance. Locke's first *Letter Concerning Toleration* stated his position clearly, and he never deviated from it substantially. It was originally written in Latin as a letter to his Dutch friend Philip van Limborch. In 1689 it was published on the Continent in Latin, and in the same year a translation of it by William Popple appeared in English.

Locke was not the first to write in advocacy of religious toleration. His was, however, a powerful, direct, and passionate plea. It was linked with the *Essay* by its recognition of the limits of human knowledge and human fallibility, and with the *Two Treatises* by his deep commitment to individual rights and freedom.

Locke took toleration to be the chief characteristic mark of the true church, for religious belief is primarily a relation between each man and God. True religion regulates men's lives according to virtue and piety, and without charity and love religion is false to itself. Those who persecute others in the name of Christ abjure his teachings, seeking only outward conformity, not peace and holiness. Who can believe that in torture and execution the fanatic truly seeks the salvation of the soul of his victim? Moreover, the mind cannot be forced or belief compelled. All efforts to force or compel belief breed only hypocrisy and contempt of God. Persuasion is the only lever that can truly move the mind.

A church is "a voluntary society of men, joining themselves together of their own accord in order to the public worshipping of God in such manner as they judge acceptable to Him, and effectual to the salvation of their souls." It is sharply distinct from a state, or commonwealth. The state is concerned with the public good, protecting life, liberty, and property. It has no authority in matters of the spirit. "Whatever is lawful in the commonwealth cannot be prohibited by the magistrate in the church."

Locke's influence was wide and deep.

In political, religious, educational, and

philosophical thought he inspired

the leading minds of England, France, America,

and, to some extent, Germany.

It is to be doubted that any man or group of men possess the truth about the one true way to salvation. In the Scriptures we have all that may reasonably be claimed by Christians to be the word of God. The rest are the speculations and beliefs of men concerning articles of faith and forms of worship. Sincere and honest men differ in these matters, and only tolerance of these differences can bring about public peace and Christian charity. Jews, pagans, and Muslims are all equally confident in their religious faith. Mutual tolerance is essential where such diversity exists. This is most evident when we observe that it is the most powerful party that persecutes others in the name of religion. Yet in different countries and at different times power has lain in the hands of different religious groups. It is physical power, not true faith, which decides who is persecuted and who persecutes.

Throughout Locke's argument the liberty of person and the liberty of conscience are decisive. He limited this liberty only by denying to religion the right to harm directly another person or group or to practice clearly immoral rites. By a curious and probably prudential exception, he denied tolerance to atheists, because promises, covenants, and oaths would not bind them, and to any church so constituted "that all those who enter into it do thereby *ipso facto* deliver themselves up to the protection and service of another prince."

Despite these limitations, Locke's letter moved subsequent generations to a greater spirit of tolerance in religious matters. It is still part of the liberal democratic ideal and transcends the time of its composition.

Faith and Reason. The Reasonableness of Christianity and the *Vindications* are works more bound to Locke's own time. Locke was probably neither a Socinian nor a deist, even though certain deists and Unitarians found comfort and inspiration in his work. He was a sincere Christian, who tried to diminish the flourishing schisms and sects by proposing a return to the Scriptures and an abandonment of the interminable theological disputes of his day. He accepted the divine inspiration of the Bible. Nevertheless, he held that even revelation must be tested by reason. In the New Testament, Christianity is rational and simple. The core of Christian faith lies in the belief in the fatherhood of God, the divinity of Christ the Messiah, the morality of charity, love, and divine mercy. Justification by faith means faith in Christ, whose essential revelation is that God is merciful and forgives the sinner who truly repents and strives to live a life of Christian morality. The Mosaic law, God's mercy, and Christian morality are all consonant with human reason. Revelation discloses to man what unaided reason could not discover—the mysteries, the Virgin Birth, the Resurrection, the divinity of Christ. But when disclosed, these do not violate the canons of reason. Here as elsewhere, Locke's emphasis on reason was circumscribed, reason must be followed where possible, but it does not carry us far enough by itself.

Locke's influence was wide and deep. In political, religious, educational, and philosophical thought he inspired the leading minds of England, France, America, and, to some extent, Germany. He disposed of the exaggerated rationalism of Descartes and Spinoza; he laid the groundwork for a new empiricism and advanced the claims for experimentalism. Voltaire, Montesquieu, and the French Encyclopedists found in Locke the philosophical, political, educational, and moral basis that enabled them to prepare and advance the ideas which eventuated in the French Revolution. In America, his influence on Jonathan Edwards, Hamilton, and Jefferson was decisive. Locke's zeal for truth as he saw it was stronger than his passion for dialectical and logical niceness, and this may account for the fact that his works prepared the ground for action as well as thought.

[See also Personal Identity.]

BIBLIOGRAPHY

Works by Locke

The Correspondence of John Locke and Edward Clarke, B. Rand, ed. Oxford, 1927.

An Early Draft of Locke's Essay (Draft A), R. I. Aaron and J. Gibb, eds. Oxford, 1936. Valuable as a study of the development of the *Essay.*

Epistola de Tolerantia. Gouda, 1689. Translated by William Popple as *A Letter Concerning Toleration.* London, 1689. Several defenses appeared in the 1690s and fragments of a fourth in 1706.

An Essay Concerning Human Understanding. London, 1690; 2d ed. with large additions, London, 1694; 3d ed., London, 1695; 4th ed., with large additions, London, 1700; 5th ed., with many large additions, London, 1706. Best modern edition, from which all quotes in this article are taken, is a reprint of the fifth edition, J. W. Yolton, ed., 2 vols. New York and London, 1961.

An Essay Concerning the Understanding, Knowledge, Opinion and Assent (Draft B), B. Rand, ed. Cambridge, Mass., 1931. Valuable, but superseded by manuscript in Bodleian Library.

Essays on the Law of Nature. Translated from the Latin and edited by W. von Leyden. Oxford, 1954. Also gives an account of the Lovelace Collection.

A Letter to the Right Rev. Edward Ld. Bishop of Worcester, concerning Some Passages relating to Mr. Locke's Essay of Human Understanding. London, 1697. Two further letters appeared, in 1697 and 1699.

A Paraphrase and Notes on the Epistles of St. Paul to the Galatians [etc.]. London, 1705.

Posthumous Works of Mr. John Locke, 6 vols. London, 1706.

The Remains of John Locke, E. Curl, ed. London, 1714.

Works of John Locke, 3 vols. London, 1714; 10th ed., 10 vols., London, 1801.

The Reasonableness of Christianity. London, 1695. Defenses of this work were published in 1695 and 1697.

Some Considerations of the Consequences of the Lowering of Interest and the Raising of the Value of Money. London, 1692. Two additional papers on money appeared in 1695.

Some Thoughts Concerning Education. London, 1693.

Two Treatises of Government. London, 1690. The critical and collated edition of Locke's corrected copy by Peter Laslett (Cambridge, 1960) surpasses all previous editions.

For the remainder of Locke's published and unpublished papers, consult the works listed below by Aaron, Christopherson, von Leyden, Long, Ollion, and Yolton. See von Leyden and Long particularly for the Lovelace Collection.

Works on Locke

Biographies

Bourne, H. R. Fox, *Life of John Locke*, 2 vols. London, 1876. Excellent, but inadequate since Lovelace Collection became available.

Cranston, Maurice, *John Locke, a Biography*. London, 1957. A thorough study of the life of Locke, using all materials available at present.

King, Lord Peter, *The Life and Letters of John Locke*. London, 1829. Not good, but contains original material.

Critical Commentaries

Aaron, R. I., "Locke's Theory of Universals." *PAS*, Vol. 33 (1932/1933). Useful and enlightening.

———, *John Locke*. Oxford, 1937; rev. ed., Oxford, 1955. Best general commentary.

Adamson, S. W., *The Educational Writings of John Locke*. Cambridge, 1922.

Bastide, C., *John Locke, ses théories politiques et leur influence en Angleterre*. Paris, 1906. Still valuable work on Locke's political philosophy.

Christopherson, H. O., *A Bibliographical Introduction to the Study of John Locke*. Oslo, 1930. Incomplete.

Clapp, J. G., *Locke's Conception of the Mind*. New York, 1937.

Cranston, Maurice, "Men and Ideas; John Locke." *Encounter*, Vol. 7 (1956), 46–54.

Czajkowski, C. J., *The Theory of Private Property in Locke's Political Philosophy*. Notre Dame, Ind., 1941. Useful on the labor theory of value.

DeMarchi, E., "Locke's Atlantis." *Political Studies*, Vol. 3 (1955), 164–65.

Gibson, James, *Locke's Theory of Knowledge*, Cambridge, 1917. Emphasizes Locke's rationalism.

———, *John Locke*. British Academy, Henriette Hertz Lecture, 1933.

Gierke, Otto von, *Naturrecht und deutsches Recht*. Translated and edited by Ernest Barker as *Natural Law and the Theory of Society*, 2 vols. Cambridge, 1934. A major study.

Gough, J. W., *John Locke's Political Philosophy. Eight Studies*. Oxford, 1950. Important.

Jackson, Reginald, "Locke's Distinction Between Primary and Secondary Qualities." *Mind*, Vol. 38 (1929), 56–76.

———, "Locke's Version of the Doctrine of Representative Perception." *Mind*, Vol. 39 (1930), 1–25.

James, D. G., *The Life of Reason. Hobbes, Locke, Bolingbroke*. London, 1949.

Krakowski, E., *Les Sources médiévales de la philosophie de Locke*. Paris, 1915. One of the few studies of influences on Locke.

Lamprecht, S. P., *The Moral and Political Philosophy of John Locke*. New York, 1918.

Laslett, Peter, "The English Revolution and Locke's Two Treatises of Government." *Cambridge Historical Journal*, Vol. 12 (1956). Interesting and controversial.

Leibniz, G. W., *Nouveaux Essais sur l'entendement humain*. Leipzig and Amsterdam, 1765. Translated by A. G. Langley as *New Essays concerning Human Understanding*. New York and London, 1896. An important critique of Locke by a contemporary.

Leyden, W. von, "John Locke and Natural Law." *Philosophy*, Vol. 31 (1956). A useful examination.

Long, P., *A Summary Catalogue of the Lovelace Collection of Papers of John Locke in the Bodleian Library*. Oxford, 1959.

O'Connor, D. J., *John Locke*. Harmondsworth, England, 1952.

Ollion, H., *Notes sur la correspondance de John Locke*. Paris, 1908.

Polin, R., *La Politique de John Locke*. Paris, 1960. Interesting contrast to Laslett.

Pollock, Sir Frederick, "Locke's Theory of the State," in his *Essays in the Law*. London, 1922. Ch. 3.

Ryle, Gilbert, *Locke on the Human Understanding*. Oxford, 1933.

Smith, N. K., *John Locke*. Manchester, England, 1933.

Ware, C. S., "The Influence of Descartes on John Locke." *Revue internationale de philosophie* (1950), 210–30.

Webb, T. E., *The Intellectualism of Locke. An Essay*. Dublin, 1857. Presents Locke as a precursor to Kant.

Yolton, J. W., "Locke's Unpublished Marginal Replies to John Sergeant." *Journal of the History of Ideas*, Vol. 12 (1951), 528–59.

———, "Locke and the Seventeenth-Century Logic of Ideas." *Journal of the History of Ideas*, Vol. 16 (1955), 431–52.

———, *Locke and the Way of Ideas*. Oxford, 1956. A careful study.

———, "Locke on the Law of Nature." *Philosophical Review*, Vol. 67 (1958), 477–98.

– JAMES GORDON CLAPP

LOCKE, JOHN (UPDATE)

John Locke (1632–1704), has been, for the last three decades, the subject of a rapid expansion of interest, stimulated by Oxford University Press's Clarendon edition of his works. The eight-volume edition of Locke's correspondence has opened new areas of information and exploration. So far in that series, we have definitive editions of the *Essay* (including editions of the drafts and other relevant writings), the work on education, his paraphrases of St. Paul's epistles, and the papers on money. The *Reasonableness of Christianity* is in press, the journals will soon appear (again, opening a vast and important insight into Locke's reading, book buying, travels, opinions), and other works will follow. These editions, and the research that went into their production, have provided new resources for work on almost all aspects of Locke's life and writings, as well as material relating to his intellectual environment.

Oxford University Press's Clarendon edition

of Locke's works has stimulated

a rapid expansion of interest in the philosopher.

Antedating the Clarendon series was another medium for interest in Locke: *The Locke Newsletter,* founded and edited by Roland Hall. Beginning in 1970, published once a year (more or less), the newsletter has published articles on all aspects of Locke's thought. Included in each number is a list of recent books and articles on Locke, in many languages. This is a valuable source for keeping up to date on the publications about Locke. Another source of information on publications about Locke is the *Reference Guide* by Yolton and Yolton. Two other bibliographic resources are Attig's listings of Locke editions, and the much fuller descriptive bibliography of all editions of Locke's publications by Jean S. Yolton. The latter, a work long overdue, describes many different copies of Locke editions, which were located and examined in many different libraries and countries.

Among the topics in Locke's *Essay,* three have received special attention: the representative theory of perception, personal identity, and matter theory. The first of these in recent discussions has involved a debate over the nature of ideas: are they special entities (e.g., images) standing between perceivers and objects, or are they simply the means for our access to the physical world? On the second topic it is becoming increasingly recognized that memory is not the crux of Locke's concept of person; it is consciousness, a wider and richer process (one with clear moral overtones) that focuses our awareness of self. A person for Locke is a moral being composed of the thoughts, feelings, and actions performed throughout a life. Consciousness is not a property of some immaterial substance, at least not so far as we can discover. The third topic has been given detailed attention via Locke's use of the corpuscular the-

ory (see Alexander, 1985). Some recognition has been given to Locke's movement toward the Newtonian concept of matter as force and power. Locke anticipated this development in his talk of the qualities of body being primarily powers. The substantiality of matter begins to fade under Locke's analysis of primary and secondary qualities. The chapter on power in the *Essay,* the power of persons and the power of matter, is the longest and most complex chapter in that work (see J. W. Yolton, 1993).

Locke's social and political thought has received even more attention throughout the decades, especially over the last dozen or so years. Laslett's early dating of *Two Treatises,* and his locating that work in its historical context, have been developed by writers such as Dunn, Harris, and Marshall (and many others). The central role of property and the relation of that concept to the person is generally recognized (see Tully, 1980). His *Two Treatises* elaborates a concept of property that starts with each person's having property in his person. Acquisition of other possessions is a function of that original self-property. The tension between the interests and rights of the individual and those of society (or the community of mankind) is much discussed (see especially Gobetti, 1992). The focus on consciousness as defining the person in his *Essay* indicated the central place of the individual in Locke's civil society. At the same time majority decisions were allowed to restrain individual actions. The power of the people is sanctioned by a social contract that obliges the ruler or legislative body to act for the good of the citizens, in conformity with the laws of nature. The interconnections between Locke's moral views and his social and political thought have been discussed by Marshall (1984). The issue of religious toleration has focused some of the recent treatments of Locke's political and religious writings, but all of the toleration writings by Locke await their inclusion in the Clarendon editions.

Locke's religious interests in the Bible and in what is required of a Christian have been clarified by recent studies (e.g., Wainwright's edition of the *Paraphrases,* 1987), but this area will be further illuminated when the Clarendon edition of *Reasonableness* appears. Locke's relation to the Latitudinarians and the role of original sin in his thinking have been explored by Spellman (1988). Coleman's (1983) systematic study of Locke's moral theory set the stage for some of the recent attention to this aspect of Locke's thought.

Another newly developing area of Locke studies concerns the reception of his doctrines in Europe, especially in France. The difficulties the French had with the term 'consciousness' when translating this English term have been interestingly analyzed by Davies (1990). Reactions to Locke's books in French-language journals and the impact of his doctrines (especially thinking matter) on Enlightenment thinkers have been presented by several writers (Hutchison, 1991; Schøsler, 1985, 1994; J. W. Yolton, 1991). The full story of the reception of Locke's doctrines in Europe (especially in Germany, Portugal, and Holland) in the eighteenth century has yet to be written. Fruitful research programs are waiting for scholars.

A number of collections of articles can be consulted to fill out this brief sketch of newer developments in Locke studies (Chappell, 1994; Harpham, 1992; Thompson, 1991).

[See also Consciousness in Anglo-American Philosophy; Perception; Personal Identity.]

BIBLIOGRAPHY

Recent Editions of Locke's Works

De Beer, E. S., ed. *The Correspondence of John Locke.* 8 vols. Oxford, 1976–89.

Kelly, P., ed. *Several Papers relating to Money, Interest, and Trade.* Oxford, 1991.

Laslett, P., ed. *Two Treatises of Government,* 3d ed. Cambridge, 1989.

Nidditch, P. H., ed. *Essay concerning Human Understanding.* Oxford, 1975.

———, and G. A. J. Rogers, eds. *Drafts for the Essay concerning Human Understanding and other Philosophical Writings,* Vol. 1. Oxford, 1990. Includes drafts A and B: other volumes planned.

Wainwright, A. P., ed. *Paraphrases and Notes on the Epistles of St. Paul.* 2 vols. Oxford, 1987.

Yolton, J. W., and J. S. Yolton. eds. *Some Thoughts concerning Education.* Oxford, 1989.

Works on Locke

Alexander, P. *Ideas, Qualities, and Corpuscles: Locke and Boyle on the External World.* Cambridge, 1985.

Ashcraft, R. *Revolutionary Politics and Locke's "Two Treatises of Government."* Princeton, 1986.

Attig, J. C., ed. *The Works of John Locke: A Comprehensive Bibliography from the Seventeenth Century to the Present.* Westport, CT, 1985.

Ayers, M. *Locke.* 2 vols. London, 1991.

Chappell, V., ed. *The Cambridge Companion to Locke.* Cambridge, 1994.

Colman, J. *John Locke's Moral Philosophy.* Edinburgh, 1983.

Davies, C. *"Conscience" as Consciousness: The Self of Self-Awareness in French Philosophical Writing from Descartes to Diderot.* Studies on Voltaire and the Eighteenth Century, 272. Oxford, 1990.

Dunn, J. *The Political Thought of John Locke: An Historical Account of the Argument of the "Two Treatises of Government."* Cambridge, 1969.

Franklin, J. H. *John Locke and the Theory of Sovereignty: Mixed Monarchy and the Right of Resistance in the Political Thought of the English Revolution.* Cambridge, 1978.

Gobetti, D. *Public and Private: Individuals, Households, and Body Politic in Locke and Hutcheson.* London, 1992.

Goyard-Fabre, S. *John Locke et la raison raisonnable.* Paris, 1986.

Harpham, E. J., ed. *John Locke's "Two Treatises of Government": New Interpretations.* Lawrence, KS, 1992.

Harris, I. *The Mind of John Locke: A Study of Political Theory in Its Intellectual Setting.* Cambridge, 1994.

Hutchison, R. *Locke in France, 1688–1734.* Studies on Voltaire and the Eighteenth Century, 290. Oxford, 1991.

Mackie, J. L. *Problems from Locke.* Oxford, 1976.

Marshall, J. *John Locke: Resistance, Religion, and Responsibility.* Cambridge Studies in Early Modern British History. Cambridge, 1994.

Passmore, J. "Locke and the Ethics of Belief," *Proceedings of the British Academy,* Vol. 64 (1978), 185–208.

Rogers, G. A. J. "Locke, Anthropology, and Models of the Mind," *History of the Human Sciences,* Vol. 6 (1993), 73–87.

———, ed. *Locke's Philosophy: Content and Context.* Oxford, 1994.

Schochet, G. J. "Toleration, Revolution, and Judgment in the Development of Locke's Political Thought," *Political Science,* Vol. 40 (1988), 84–96.

Schøsler, J. *La Bibliothèque raisonnée (1728–1753): Les Réactions d'un périodique français à la philosophie de Locke au XVIIIᵉ siècle.* Odense, 1985.

———. "Le Christianisme raisonnable et le débat sur le 'Socianisme' de John Locke dans la presse française de la première moitié du XVIIIᵉ siècle," *Lias,* Vol. 21, no. 2 (1994), 295–319.

Schouls, P. A. *Reasoned Freedom: John Locke and Enlightenment.* Ithaca, NY, 1992.

Spellman, W. M. *John Locke and the Problem of Depravity.* Oxford, 1988.

Thiel, U. *Locke's Theorie der personalen Identität.* Bonn. 1983.

Thompson, M. P., ed. *John Locke und Immanuel Kant.* Berlin, 1991.

Tomida, Y. "Idea and Thing: The Deep Structure of Locke's Theory of Knowledge," *Analecta Husserliana,* Vol. 66 (1995), 3–143.

Tuck, R. *Natural Rights Theories: Their Origin and Development.* Cambridge, 1979.

Tully, J. *A Discourse on Property: John Locke and His Adversaries.* Cambridge, 1980.

Vaughn, K. I. *John Locke, Economist and Social Scientist.* Chicago, 1980.

Vienne, J.-M. *Expérience et raison: Les fondements de la morale selon Locke.* Paris, 1991.

Walmsley, P. "Locke's Cassowary and the Ethos of the Essay," *Studies in Eighteenth-Century Culture,* Vol. 22 (1992), 253–67.

———. "Dispute and Conversation: Probability and the Rhetoric of Natural Philosophy in Locke's *Essay,*" *Journal of the History of Ideas,* Vol. 54 (1993), 381–94.

Winkler, K. P. "Locke on Personal Identity," *Journal of the History of Philosophy,* Vol. 29 (1991), 201–26.

Wood, N. *The Politics of Locke's Philosophy: A Social Study of "An Essay concerning Human Understanding."* Berkeley, 1983.

Yolton, J. S. *John Locke: A Descriptive Bibliography.* Bristol, England, 1996.

———, and J. W. Yolton. *John Locke: A Reference Guide.* Boston, 1985.

Yolton, J. W. *Locke and the Compass of Human Understanding: A Selective Commentary on the Essay.* Cambridge, 1970.

———. *Locke and French Materialism.* Oxford, 1991.

———. *A Locke Dictionary.* Oxford, 1993.

– JOHN W. YOLTON

LOGIC, NONSTANDARD

Logic is that discipline that aims to give an account of what inferences are valid and why. Although it is common to distinguish between two sets of criteria for validity—inductive and deductive—most work in the history of logic has focused on deductive validity. Since the mathematization of logic around the turn of this century, accounts of deductive validity have been given for inferences couched in formal languages. A common practice is to specify validity in terms of some set of axioms or rules and justify it by way of some semantics. To obtain applications of the account, an understanding of the relationship between the formal language and the vernacular (often in the form of some imprecisely specified translation manual) has also to be provided.

The 1960s and 1970s saw not only

the development of many older nonstandard logics

but the production of many new kinds.

The correct characterization of and justification for validity have historically been matters of philosophical contention. There is, however, an orthodoxy (if not unanimity) on the issue that dates back to around the 1920s. The account is essentially that of Frege's *Begriffschrift* and Russell and Whitehead's *Principia Mathematica*, as cleaned up and articulated by subsequent logicians such as Hilbert and Gentzen. It is often known (rather inappropriately) as classical logic and is to be found in virtually any modern logic textbook.

Despite the relative orthodoxy, classical logic faces a number of problems. These have bred dissatisfaction and attempts to articulate rival accounts of deductive validity. Such accounts are commonly referred to as nonstandard logics.

Modal and Intuitionist Logics

Criticisms of classical logic go back to the 1920s. One was given by C. I. Lewis, who objected to paradoxes of "material implication" such as $\alpha \rightarrow (\neg\alpha \rightarrow \beta)$. He constructed systems of logic that contained a notion of strict implication that avoided these paradoxes. This led to an investigation of the logic of modalities, such as necessity and possibility, and modal logic developed. Lewis's original critique of classical logic is now generally thought to be based on a confusion of the connective 'if' and the relation of entailment. Consequently, modal logic is now usually thought of as an augmentation of classical logic by modal functors rather than as a rival. This development was accentuated by the discovery of world semantics for modal logics in the 1960s by Kripke and others. World semantics have, however, provided the basis for the semantics of many new logics. One of these, another augmentation of clas-

sical logic, tense logic, was invented by Prior. In this, temporal operators—for example, F (it will be the case) and P (it was the case)—are added to the language and given suitable semantic conditions.

A second early critique was provided by Brouwer and other intuitionists. Arguing on the basis of a critique of a Platonist philosophy of mathematics, they rejected a number of principles of classical logic, such as $\neg\neg\alpha \rightarrow \alpha$, $\neg\forall x\alpha \rightarrow \exists x\neg\alpha$. For example, the second of these fails because the mere fact that you can show, for instance, that not all numbers have a certain property does not show how to construct a number that does not have it, which is what is required to ground an existence claim. In the light of these criticisms Heyting formulated an axiom system for intuitionist logic with an informal semantics in terms of provability. After a fairly quiet period the study of intuitionist logic took off again in the 1960s and 1970s. Kripke demonstrated that the logic has a world semantics; Dummett introduced new arguments for intuitionism (not just in mathematics) based on the philosophy of language: and applications of the logic in computer science were discovered.

Many-Valued and Quantum Logics

A third critique dating back to the 1920s was provided by Lukasiewicz. Arguing on the basis of the indeterminacy of future events, he introduced a system of logic where sentences can be neither true nor false, and so classical principles such as a $\alpha \lor \neg\alpha$ fail. The system was quickly generalized to ones where sentences can have arbitrarily many semantic values, many-valued logics. The study of many-valued logics accelerated in the 1960s and 1970s. Many logicians suggested that certain kinds of sentences might have no truth value: for example, they are "meaningless" ('It's 3 P.M. at the North Pole'); they are paradoxical ('This sentence is false'); they are vague ('Dry grass is green'). Consequently, we have seen the articulation of various three-valued logics (sometimes called partial logics). Consideration of vagueness also makes it tempting to suppose that truth comes by degrees. A natural way of handling this insight is by using a different sort of many-valued logic, where sentences can have as truth value any real number between 0 (wholly false) and 1 (wholly true). Under the influence of writers such as Zadeh, such logics, now usually called fuzzy logics, have found applications in artificial intelligence.

In the 1930s Reichenbach and Destouches-Février suggested that various problems in quantum mechanics made it appropriate to use a three-valued logic there. These ideas were not very successful, but similar problems led Birkhoff and von Neumann to suggest a more sophisticated approach around the same time. This is now usually called quantum logic (and has, again, received much further attention by logicians such as Putnam since the 1960s). They argued that the classical principle of distribution, $\alpha \wedge (\beta \vee \gamma) \vdash (\alpha \wedge \beta) \vee (\alpha \wedge \gamma)$, fails in the microworld. For example, it may be true (verifiable) of a particle that it has a position and one of a range of momenta, but each disjunct attributing to it that position and a particular momentum is false (unverifiable). To construct a logic in which distribution fails, they proceeded essentially as follows. In standard world semantics, sentences can be thought of as taking subsets of the set of worlds as semantic values, and the logical constants can be interpreted as Boolean operations. In quantum mechanics the possible states of the system form a mathematical structure known as a Hilbert space, and it is natural to take the semantic values to be subspaces of this space. Logical constants are then interpreted as appropriate operations on subspaces. For example, disjunction is interpreted as the span of (the smallest space containing) two subspaces.

Relevant and Paraconsistent Logics

The 1960s and 1970s saw not only the development of many older nonstandard logics but the production of many new kinds. One of these was relevant logic. This grew, like modal logic, from dissatisfaction with the paradoxes of material implication (and those of strict implication, such as $\alpha \wedge \neg\alpha \vdash \beta$). Building on early work of Church and Ackermann, Anderson, Belnap, and co-workers constructed axiom systems for three propositional (and later predicate) logics *E*, *R*, and *T*, which satisfied the criterion that if $\alpha \rightarrow \beta$ is provable, α and β share a propositional parameter. Semantics for the systems came a little later. In particular, world semantics were provided by Routley and Meyer. In the light of these it became clear that there are many more, and possibly more important, systems in the family. One of these is closely related to linear logic, proposed independently in the 1980s by Girard for its applications in computer science.

There are two features of world semantics for relevant logics that distinguish them from those of modal logic. The first is that a ternary relation (instead of a binary one) is used to give the truth conditions of the conditional: $\alpha \rightarrow \beta$ is true at world *w* if and only if (iff) for all worlds *x*, *y* such that *Rwxy*, if α is true at *x*, β is true at *y*. The second is that some technique is required to produce worlds that are inconsistent or incomplete. This can be done in two ways. The first is to have an operator on worlds, *, such that α is true at world *w* iff α is not true at world *w**, (For the worlds of ordinary modal logic, * can be thought of as just the identity function.) The second is to allow sentences to take one

of four truth values: true only, false only, both, neither ($\{1\}$, $\{0\}$, $\{1, 0\}$, ϕ). These semantics therefore combine the techniques of both modal and many-valued logic. Standard relevant logics invalidate not only the paradoxes of material implication but also the disjunctive syllogism: $\neg\alpha \wedge (\alpha \vee \beta) \vdash \beta$. Much of the critique of relevant logic has focused on this fact.

A related contemporary nonstandard logic is paraconsistent logic. A logic is paraconsistent iff the inference $\alpha, \neg\alpha \vdash \beta$ fails. (A paraconsistent logic may or may not be relevant.) Paraconsistent logics were developed independently by Jaśkowski, da Costa, and others. Their principle concern was the use of such a logic to make inferences in a sensible way in situations where the information from which conclusions are drawn may be inconsistent—for example, from scientific theories whose principles conflict, or where the information is that in some computational data base, Semantics for paraconsistent logics use techniques such as those used in relevant logic to allow contradictions to be true in an interpretation. Some (though not all) paraconsistent logicians, such as Priest, have endorsed the view that some contradictions may actually be true (*simpliciter*): dialetheism. A major argument for this view is provided by the paradoxes of self-reference. Consistent solutions to these are notoriously problematic.

Conditional and Free Logics

Dissatisfaction with the material conditional (at least as an account of English subjunctive conditionals) triggered another nonstandard logic around the 1970s: conditional logics. A number of counterexamples were provided by Stalnaker and others to classical principles such as transitivity ($\alpha \rightarrow \beta$, $\beta \rightarrow \gamma \vdash \alpha \rightarrow \gamma$) and antecedent strengthening ($\alpha \rightarrow \beta \vdash (\alpha \wedge \gamma) \rightarrow \beta$). For example, if you strike this match it will light; hence, if you strike this match and it is under water it will light. In conditional logics these inferences are invalid. The major technique used to achieve this end is a selection function, *s*, which, given a world, *w*, and a sentence, α, picks out a set of worlds $s(w, \alpha)$. Intuitively, this can be thought of as the set of worlds relevantly similar to *w* where α is true. The truth conditions are then as follows: $\alpha \rightarrow \beta$ is true at *w* iff β is true at every world in $s(w, \alpha)$. Standard conditional logics validate the paradoxes of strict implication, but relevant conditional logics may be obtained by combining the appropriate semantic techniques.

Another kind of nonstandard logic takes issue with the principle built into classical semantics that every name denotes (an existent object). (Consider, e.g., 'Sherlock Holmes'.) Logics that reject this are called free logics. One approach to free logics is to take all sentences containing nondenoting terms to be truth valueless. This idea gives rise to various three-valued logics, proposed in the 1960s by Smiley and others. A sophistication of this idea was proposed by van Fraassen. Given any evaluation of this kind, a supervaluation is any two-valued evaluation that agrees with it except where it makes a sentence neither true nor false. Logical validity is now defined in terms of supervaluations rather than evaluations. This construction allows all classical validities to be preserved.

Logic is not a set of received truths

but a discipline

where competing theories concerning validity

vie with each other.

A rather different approach was suggested by Leonard, Lambert, and others around the same time. This approach modifies the classical rule of existential generalization, $\exists x\alpha(x) \rightarrow \alpha(c)$ (and its dual, universal instantiation), by adding a conjunct to the antecedent to the effect that c exists. An appropriate semantics can be obtained by allowing constants to denote objects outside the domain of quantification. This is a form of Meinongianism, since it allows nonexistent objects to be named (but not quantified over). Some neo-Meinongians (e.g., Routley) allow them to be quantified over as well. This requires no change to the formal machinery of classical logic. All that has to be changed is the canonical interpretation of the quantifiers in English. Thus '$\exists x\alpha$' is now read, not as 'There exists an x such that α', but as 'For some x, α', where this expression is devoid of any existential commitment.

Whether or not any of the nonstandard logics discussed here are correct, their presence serves to remind that logic is not a set of received truths but a discipline where competing theories concerning validity vie with each other. The case for each theory—including a received theory—has to be investigated on its merits. This requires detailed philosophical investigations concerning existence, truth and contradiction, truth in quantum mechanics, or whatever is appropriate. Detailed discussions can hardly be attempted here. Some can be found in the items cited in the bibliography, which should also be consulted for further historical and technical details.

[*See also Artificial Intelligence; Dummett, Michael; Frege, Gottlob; Fuzzy Logic; Intuitionism; Kripke, Saul Aaron; Mathematical Logic; Modal Logic; Philosophical Logic; Philosophy of Language; Prior, Arthur N.; Putnam, Hilary; Russell, Bertrand Arthur William; Vagueness.*]

BIBLIOGRAPHY

Anderson, A., N. Belnap and J. M. Dunn. *Entailment: The Logic of Relevance and Necessity*, 2 vols. Princeton, NJ, 1975–92. A reference book for the original systems of relevance logic.

Dummett, M. *Elements of Intuitionism*. Oxford, 1977. A discussion of the foundations of intuitionist logic.

Gabbay, D., and F. Guenthner. *Handbook of Philosophical Logic*, 4 vols. Dordrecht, 1983–89. For discussions of temporal logic, conditional logic, partial logic, many-valued logic, relevance logic, intuitionist logic, free logic, and quantum logic, see, respectively, Vol. 2, chaps. 2, 8; Vol. 3, chaps. 1, 2, 3, 4, 6, and 7.

Haack, S. *Deviant Logic*. Cambridge, 1974. An introduction to the general philosophical issues surrounding nonstandard logics and to some of the logics.

Harper, W. L., R. Stalnaker, and G. Pearce, eds. *Ifs*. Dordrecht, 1981. A collection of papers on aspects of conditional logic.

Lambert, J. K. *Philosophical Applications of Free Logic*. Oxford, 1991. A collection of essays on various aspect of free logic.

Mittelstaedt, P. *Quantum Logic*. Dordrecht, 1978. An exposition of quantum logic.

Priest, G. *In Contradiction: A Study of the Transconsistent*. The Hague, 1987. A defense of dialetheism and dialetheic logic.

Priest, G., R. Routley, and J. Norman. *Paraconsistent Logic: Essays on the Inconsistent*. Munich, 1989. A reference book for paraconsistent logic.

Prior, A. *Past, Present, and Future*. Oxford, 1967. A classic exposition of tense logic and its philosophical aspects.

Rescher, N. *Many-valued Logic*. New York, 1969. A modern survey of many-valued logics.

Routley, R., V. Plumwood, R. K. Meyer, and R. T. Brady. *Relevant Logics and Their Rivals*. Atascadero, CA, 1982. A reference for the newer systems of relevant logic.

Yager, R. R., and L. A. Zadeh. *An Introduction to Fuzzy Logic Applications in Intelligent Systems*. Dordrecht, 1992. An introduction to the applications of fuzzy logic in AI.

— GRAHAM PRIEST

LOGICAL CONSEQUENCE

Logical consequence is a relation between a set of sentences and a sentence said to follow logically from it. Closely related notions are logical validity and logical truth: an argument is logically valid iff (if and only if) its conclusion is a logical consequence of the set of its premises; a sentence is logically true iff it is a logical consequence of any set of sentences. Other notions definable in terms of logical consequence are logical consistency, logical equivalence, theory, and so forth.

Modern logic offers two distinct concepts of logical consequence: a proof-theoretical concept, "derivability" or "provability," symbolized by $\vdash$, and a semantic concept, "logical consequence (proper)," "logical implication," or "logical entailment," symbolized by $\vDash$. Given a formal system $\mathscr{L}$ (a formal language together with a proof system and a system of models), the two concepts are defined as follows: if σ is a sentence and Σ is a set of sentences, then $\Sigma \vdash \sigma$ iff there is a proof of σ from Σ, and $\Sigma \vDash \sigma$ iff every model of Σ is a model of σ, i.e., iff there is no model in which all the sentences of Σ are true and σ is false. Gödel's 1930 completeness theorem establishes the coextensionality of ⊢ and ⊨ in standard first-order logic, but in general the two notions are not coextensional. The term "logical consequence" is usually reserved for the semantic notion, a tradition followed in this article.

The semantic definition of logical consequence is due to Alfred Tarski (1936). An informal version of this definition was implicit in earlier works by Gödel, Hilbert, and others, but it was Tarski's treatment of logical consequence and related semantic notions that allowed a rigorous mathematical study of these notions and led to the modern conception of logic as constituted by two equally fundamental disciplines: proof theory (the theory of ⊢) and model theory (the theory of ⊨).

Tarski claimed his definition captured the intuitive, everyday notion of logical consequence. He characterized this notion by the following two traits: (i) if σ is a logical consequence of Σ, then "it can never happen" (1936, p. 414) that all the sentences of Σ are true and σ is false; (ii) logical consequences are formal, and as such they are dependent on the form of the sentences involved, not on the particular objects referred to in these sentences. Neither the proof-theoretical definition nor the substitutional definition of logical consequence, Tarski contended, accurately captures the intuitive notion. The proof-theoretical definition leaves some genuinely logical consequences unaccounted for, and it follows from Gödel's incompleteness theorem that no matter how many new (finite, structural), rules we add to the proof-theoretical apparatus, any reasonably rich (higher-order) deductive theory would have consequences which follow logically from it in the intuitive sense yet are not provable from its theorems. The substitutional definition fails in languages with an insufficient stock of nonlogical (substitutional) terms. This definition says that σ is a logical consequence of Σ iff there is no substitution under which all the sentences of Σ are true and σ is false (where substitutions preserve grammatical categories, are uniform, and are restricted to nonlogical constants), but if the language lacks in expressive resources, a failure to satisfy (i) may not be witnessed by an appropriate substitution. Tarski's own definition uses semantic tools (1933). Semantics, according to Tarski, deals with concepts relating language to the "world" (objects in a broad sense), the basic notion being satisfaction—a relation between a formula and a sequence of objects (in the universe of discourse). Model of σ (Σ) is defined in terms of satisfaction: Let σ (Σ) be a sentence (a set of sentences) of a formalized language L. By replacing all the nonlogical constants of σ (Σ) by variables in a proper manner, i.e., preserving syntactic categories as well as identities and differences, we obtain an open formula (a set of open formulas), σ*

(Σ*). A sequence of objects is a model of σ (Σ) iff it satisfies σ* (all the sentential functions in Σ*).

Tarski ended his discussion of logical consequence with a qualifying note: the semantic definition of logical consequence is adequate given the standard division of terms to logical and nonlogical, but while this division is not arbitrary, an adequate criterion for logical terms might never be found. Tarski's semantic definition of logical consequence was likened (by Berg, 1962, and others) to an earlier substitutional definition due to Bolzano (1837). It is important, however, to keep in mind the differences between the semantic and the substitutional methods, in particular, the objectual nature of Tarskian semantics as opposed to the purely linguistic or conceptual nature of substitutional semantics. Another debated historical issue is the relation between Tarski's 1936 notion of model and the modern notion (see Etchemendy, 1988; Hodges, 1986; Sher, 1991).

The notion of logical consequence is sensitive to choice of logical terms, order of variables, and compositional structure.

The intuitive adequacy of the semantic definition was questioned by several authors. Boolos (1985), Kreisel (1967), and McGee (1992) examined the limitations incurred by restricting logical models to structures whose universes are proper sets: the semantic definition reduces logical consequence to preservation of truth, or validity, in all set structures, but intuitively logical consequence is validity in all structures whatsoever, including structures whose constituents are proper classes. Kreisel concluded, based on Gödel's completeness theorem, that at least in the case of standard first-order languages, preservation of truth in all set models ensures preservation of truth in all class models. Boolos and McGee found the restriction of models to set-theoretical structures problematic in second-order languages.

Etchemendy (1990) investigated the semantic definition from a broader perspective, distinguishing between two basic types of semantic theories, so-called representational and interpretational theories. In representational semantics models represent possible worlds, and preservation of truth in all models is preservation of truth under all possible changes in the actual world relative to a fixed language. In interpretational semantics, models represent variations in language, and preservation of truth in all models is preservation of truth under all reinterpretations of the nonfixed (nonlogical) vocabulary relative to a fixed world (the actual world). Interpretational semantics is an upgraded, objectual version of substitutional semantics (the range of reinterpretation of terms is not restricted by the lexical resources of the given language), and Etchemendy regarded modern semantics as exemplifying this type of theory. The semantic definition of logical consequence, however, fails in interpretational semantics. The conceptual resources of interpretational semantics are rather restricted, and as a result: (i) interpretational semantics cannot establish an adequate distinction between logical and nonlogical terms; and (ii) interpretational semantics cannot distinguish between accidental and necessary generality (truth in all models is no more than accidental generality). It follows that the interpretational notion of logical consequence collapses to that of material consequence. Etchemendy's interpretational construal of Tarskian semantics and the underlying dichotomy of interpretational vs. representational semantics were criticized by García-Carpintero (1993) and Sher (1996). Alternative conceptions designed to vindicate the semantic definition were developed by the above two authors, and a more restricted defense was proposed by McGee (1992).

The notion of logical consequence is sensitive to choice of logical terms, order of variables, and compositional structure (e.g., linear vs. branching quantifier-prefixes). This means that a theory of the scope of logic (logical form) must take into account considerations pertaining to the resulting notion of logical consequence. Quine (1970) regarded the "remarkable concurrence" of diverse definitions of logical consequence in standard first-order logic—in particular, the coextensionality of the semantic and proof-theoretical definitions (completeness)—as a reason for drawing the line there, ruling out second-order logic as well as branching quantification as part of logic proper, but other philosophers (e.g., Boolos, 1975) contested Quine's restrictions. Following Mostowski (1957), Lindström (1966) and Tarski (1966) proposed invariance under isomorphic structures or, more restrictedly, invariance under permutations of the universe, as a criterion for logical terms, leading to a generalized (abstract, model-theoretic) conception of first-order logic. McCarthy (1981), Peacocke (1976), Sher (1991), and Tharp (1975) examined this and other criteria for logical terms in light of the adequacy of the resulting notion of logical consequence, arriving at a wide array of views on the scope of logical terms and logic.

[See also Gödel, Kurt; Logical Terms; Mathematical Logic; Model Theory; Philosophical Logic; Proof Theory; Quine, Willard Van Orman.]

BIBLIOGRAPHY

Berg, J. *Balzano's Logic.* Stockholm, 1962.

Bolzano, B. *Wissenschaftslehre.* Sulzbach, 1837. Translated by B. Terrell as *Theory of Science.* Dordrecht, 1973.

Boolos, G. "On Second-Order Logic," *Journal of Philosophy* 72 (1975), 509–27.

———. "Nominalist Platonism," *Philosophical Review,* Vol. 94 (1985), 327–44.

Etchemendy, J. "Tarski on Truth and Logical Consequence," *Journal of Symbolic Logic,* Vol. 53, (1988), 91–106.

———. *The Concept of Logical Consequence.* Cambridge, MA, 1990.

García-Carpintero, M. "The Grounds for the Model-theortic Account of the Logical Properties," *Notre Dame Journal of Formal Logic,* Vol. 34 (1993), 107–31.

Hodges, W. "Truth in a Structure," *Proceedings of the Aristotelian Society,* 1986, 135–51.

Kreisel, G. "Informal Rigour and Completeness Proofs," in I. Lakatos, ed., *Problems in the Philosophy of Mathematics* (Amsterdam, 1967), 138–71.

Lindström, P. "First Order Predicate Logic with Generalized Quantifiers," *Theoria,* Vol. 32 (1966), 186–95.

McCarthy, T. "The Idea of a Logical Constant," *Journal of Philosophy,* Vol. 78 (1981), 499–523.

McGee, V. "Two Problems with Tarski's Theory of Consequence," *Proceedings of the Aristotelian Society,* Vol. 92 (1992), 273–92.

Mostowski, A. "On a Generalization of Quantifiers," *Fundamenta Mathematicae,* Vol. 42 (1957), 12–36.

Peacocke, C. "What Is a Logical Constant?" *Journal of Philosophy,* Vol. 73 (1976), 221–40.

Quine, W. V. O. *Philosophy of Logic.* Englewood Cliffs, NJ, 1970.

Sher, G. *The Bounds of Logic: A Generalized Viewpoint.* Cambridge, MA, 1991.

———. "Did Tarski Commit 'Tarski's Fallacy'?", *Journal of Symbolic Logic,* Vol. 61 (1996).

Tarski, A. "Pojecie Prawdy w jezykach nauk dedukcyjnych," monograph. *Prace Towarzystwa Naukowego Warszawskiego, Wydzial III Nauk Matematyczno-fizycznych,* 34, Warsaw, 1933. Translated by J. H. Woodger as "The Concept of Truth in Formalized Languages." English translation and a postscript by the author appear in Tarski (1983), 152–278.

———. "O Pojciu Wynikania Logicznego," *Przeglad Filozoficzny,* Vol. 39 (1936), 55–68. Translated by J. H. Woodger as "On the Concept of Logical Consequence," English translation by J. H. Woodger appears in Tarski (1983), 409–20.

———. *Logic, Semantics, Metamathematics,* 2d. ed. Indianapolis, 1983.

———. "What Are Logical Notions?" (1966), *History and Philosophy of Logic,* Vol. 7 (1986), 143–54.

Tharp, L. H. "Which Logic Is the Right Logic?" *Synthese,* Vol. 31 (1975), 1–21.

– GILA SHER

LOGICAL FORM

Consider the argument

All amanitas are mycorrhizas;
all mycorrhizas are symbionts;
therefore all amanitas are symbionts.

You can discern its validity without fully grasping its content. How? One answer is that you recognize its form as one that guarantees that if its premises are true, so is its conclusion. Now consider

> Aaron was a father;
> Esau was a father;
> therefore Aaron and Esau were fathers.

This too is patently valid. But replace "father(s)" by "brother(s)" throughout and one gets an argument of the same apparent form, with true premises and a false conclusion. Such examples abound. So if logical validity depends on form, it cannot be apparent grammatical form. (Parallel considerations apply with consistency in place of validity—the two are interdefinable.) Usually, when one tries to spell out the logically relevant difference between corresponding arguments, it does seem to be a difference in form. Hence the hypothesis of logical form: statements (derivatively arguments) have a special kind of form responsible for their logical properties.

Formalization

More support for the hypothesis comes from the success of formalization, the translation of arguments from natural language into an interpreted formal language for which there are formal analogues of logical properties. For a formal language there must be a specification of sentences, of admissible interpretations, and of truth/falsehood of a sentence under an admissible interpretation. An argument in a formal language is formally valid just when there is no admissible interpretation in which the premises are true and the conclusion false. Any formal language is so designed that sentences with the same syntactic form have the same logical properties; hence, syntactically matching arguments are all formally valid if one of them is. Formalization of a part of one's natural language is validity preserving when all clearly logically (in)valid arguments in that part are translated into formally (in)valid arguments. Formalization is successful only if it is validity preserving, the more successful the more it translates.

A significant part of English is successfully formalizable in the language of first-order predicate calculus with identity (PC), and formalization of ever larger parts supports the idea of logical form as syntactic form in some validity-preserving comprehensive formalization.

Doubts

One source of doubt about the hypothesis of logical form is that certain practices of formalization are quite counterintuitive yet seem optimal. Consider

> Bill ran for office in 1993;
> so Bill ran for office.

To get a validity-preserving translation of such arguments in an interpreted version of PC, we construe the original sentences as existential:

> There is a running for office and it was by Bill and it was in 1993;
> so there is a running for office and it was by Bill.

If the original sentences were really existential, it would be self-contradictory to claim that, though Bill ran for office, there are no such things as runnings for office. But this is ontological thrift, not self-contradiction.

Perhaps two statements have the same logical form when they have the same semantic structure and the same logical constants in the same positions.

Such counterintuitive construals do not threaten the hypothesis of logical form, since they can be dispensed with by enriching the syntax of the language of PC with a category of predicate modifiers. Members of this category combine with a predicate to form another predicate, satisfied only by satisfiers of the first. Treating "in 1993" as a predicate modifier, satisfiers of "ran for office in 1993" are guaranteed to be satisfiers of "ran for office"; thus a validity-preserving formalization is available consonant with logical intuition.

A second source of doubt is the availability of seemingly acceptable nonequivalent formalizations of a statement. For example, "red is the color of blood" may be formalized in at least four nonequivalent ways, using "R" and "B" for predicates "is red" and "is blood," "r" and "b" as constants (names) for the color red and the substance blood, and "c" for the function expression "the color of": Rb; $(\forall x)(Bx \to Rx)$; $r = c(b)$; $(\forall x)(Bx \to r = c(x))$. Adding categories to PC only exacerbates the problem, but restriction to PC is not a complete escape, and some types of expression force us beyond PC—for example, binary quantifiers (Barwise & Cooper, 1981).

Considerations of uniformity will narrow down the class of validity-preserving comprehensive formalizations of a natural language; but there may remain more than one. If so, arguments may have more than one logical form (Sainsbury, 1991). However, if only one of these formalizations presents forms we actually respond to in making judgments of validity, the hypothesis of logical form would still be part of the explanation of our logical intuitions.

Semantic Structure and Logical Form

As logical form so often diverges from apparent syntactical form, yet seems to be a structural aspect of the way we understand statements, a natural speculation is that logical form is semantic structure.

The basic units of semantic structure are semantic categories of semantically simple expressions, two expressions belonging to the same category if they have the same type of value (e.g., individual, function from individuals to truth values, truth value). Assuming that an unambiguous statement is composed in a unique way from semantically simple constituents, its semantic structure is representable by its compositional tree, with constituents replaced by their categories. On this account, semantic structure is too gross to be logical form: statements of the form "P and Q" and "P or Q," though not logically equivalent, have the same semantic structure, since "and" and "or" both serve as functions from pairs of truth values to truth values, hence belong to the same semantic category (Evans, 1976).

Perhaps two statements have the same logical form when they have the same semantic structure and the same logical constants in the same positions. If so, choices of formalization may be guided by intuitions of semantic structure as well as by logical intuitions. This would favor, for example, the binary formalization of universal quantifiers, instead of the hidden-"if" version (Davies, 1981); and the number of acceptable formalizations may be reduced.

Against the view of logical form as semantic structure with positioned logical constants stands the difficulty of defining the class of logical constants. On one view there is no such class (Etchemendy, 1983). When defining admissible interpretations, we can choose to hold constant the interpretations of any expressions we like. In addition to the usual list we could also hold constant the interpretations of "knows that" and "believes that"; then the argument

> George knows that Bill has won;
> hence, George believes that Bill has won.

would be valid, since there would be no admissible interpretation under which the formalized premise is true and the formalized conclusion untrue. Such examples are sometimes treated as evidence that there is nothing intrinsic to an expression that makes it a logical constant. But this is a mistake. The semantic value of a logical constant must be a function from the semantic values of the expressions it combines with. "Knows that" fails this test: in the case above "knows that" takes the individual George and the proposition that Bill has won to a truth value, but which truth value depends on a contingent, hence variable, relation between George and that proposition; the same goes for "believes that." Although the hidden-"if" universal quantifier also fails this test, the binary universal quantifier does not. For example, in "all men are sinners" the binary "all" takes the extension of "men" and the extension of "sinners" (in that order) to truth if the first is included in the second, to falsehood if not.

Though passing this test is necessary for logical constanthood, it is not sufficient, as "and 7 is prime and" passes. Perhaps an expression is a logical constant just when it is semantically simple and passes the test, or is composed of such expressions. Until we have grounds for confidence in a definition of logical constanthood, the view of logical form as semantic structure with positioned logical constants remains uncertain.

Syntactic Structure and Logical Form

The divergence between logical form and apparent grammatical form does not entail that logical form is nonsyntactical. In some theories of syntax a sentence has more than one syntactical level; apparent grammatical form is only surface-level phrase structure, so logical form may be closely linked with (or even coincide with) syntax at another level. If some level of syntax is appropriate for semantic interpretation, the prospect of a unified account of syntax, semantics, and logical form emerges (Neale, 1944).

One of the major approaches to syntax, Government and Binding theory, associates three levels with each sentence. Structure at one of these levels, s-structure, represents apparent grammatical form; by a series of syntactically constrained moves (especially of quantifier noun phrases) from s-structure one reaches the level known as LF, at which quantifier scope is made explicit (May, 1985). LF appears to present structural representations to which a formal truth definition is applicable and would therefore be the level of syntax appropriate for semantic interpretation (Larson & Ludlow, 1993; Neale, 1994). Thus, logical form may be LF with positioned constants.

This approach brings two other benefits. First, by providing a systematic account of the derivation of LF from s-structure, it helps solve the problem of finding a comprehensive system of translation into an appropriate formal language. Second, the approach is formulated so as to distinguish those aspects of syntax common to all natural languages, thus promising to illuminate what in logical form the human mind is generally sensitive to.

Logical and Linguistic Knowledge

If logical form has a linguistic explication, knowledge of validity based on form would be partly linguistic knowledge. But this seems wrong, because the situation described by the conclusion of a valid argument must accompany the situation described by the premises, however those situations are described. Taking the comparative suffix "er" followed by "than" as a logical constant guaranteeing transitivity, the following is valid:

Jack is older than Bob and Bob is older than Ted; therefore, Jack is older than Ted.

The premise of this argument describes exactly the same situation as "Jack was born before Bob and Ted was born after Bob." Had we used this sentence as the premise instead, the resulting argument would still have been recognizably valid, but not on the basis of logico-linguistic form.

This does not warrant skepticism about linguistic accounts of logical form. We must distinguish between what constitutes validity and ways of recognizing validity. An argument is logically valid when it is recognizably valid from its logical form. Validity is more comprehensive than logical validity, and the aim of explicating it in information-based terms (Barwise, 1989) is not in conflict with the aim of clarifying logical validity in terms of linguistic forms.

[See also Mathematical Logic; Philosophy of Language; Semantics; Syntax.]

BIBLIOGRAPHY

Barwise, J. *The Situation in Logic.* Stanford, 1989.
Barwise, J., and R. Cooper. "Generalized Quantifiers and Natural Language," *Linguistics and Philosophy,* Vol. 4 (1981), 159–219.
Davies, M. *Meaning, Quantification, Necessity.* London, 1981.
Etchemendy, J. "The Doctrine of Logic as Form," *Linguistics and Philosophy,* Vol. 6 (1983), 319–34. The case against.
———. *The Concept of Logical Consequence.* Cambridge, MA, 1990. Argues against the Tarskian view.
Evans, G. "Semantic Structure and Logical Form," in G. Evans and J. McDowell, eds., *Truth and Meaning* (Oxford, 1976).
Kamp, H., and U. Reyle. *From Discourse to Logic.* Dordrecht, 1993. Formal semantics with representations of discourse rather than sentences as the units for interpretation.
Larson, R., and P. Ludlow. "Interpreted Logical Forms," *Synthese,* Vol. 95 (1993), 305–55.
May, R. *Logical Form: Its Structure and Derivation.* Cambridge, MA, 1985. A study of the syntactical level LF.
Neale, S. "Logical Form and LF," in C. Otero, ed., *Noam Chomsky: Critical Assessments* (London, 1994).
Sainsbury, M. *Logical Forms.* Oxford, 1991. The best starting point. See especially chap. 6.

− MARCUS GIAQUINTO

LOGICAL KNOWLEDGE

Logical knowledge can be understood in two ways: as knowledge of the laws of logic and as knowledge derived by means of deductive reasoning. Most of the following is concerned with the first of these interpretations; the second will be treated briefly at the end. Furthermore, only deductive logic will be treated: as yet, there is no set of laws of inductive logic enjoying the kind of consensus acceptance accorded to deductive logic.

To begin with, we must specify what is a law of logic—not an entirely straightforward task. There are three, not all mutually exclusive, conceptions of logic laws. First, one could take them to be valid schemata (of statements), such as the familiar law of excluded middle, ⌜p or not p⌝. A second conception is that they are valid rules of inference, such as the familiar *modus ponens*—that is, from ⌜p → q⌝ and p infer q. The third conception of logic law, due to Gottlob Frege and Bertrand Russell, takes them to be maximally general, true (not valid) second-order quantified statements (see Goldfarb, 1979). The following discussion is confined, by and large, to the second conception; but the philosophical problems canvased arise with respect to the other conceptions as well.

To appreciate the problems involved

in the analysis of knowledge of logical laws,

note that, however these laws are conceived,

knowledge of them appears to be propositional.

In order to appreciate the problems involved in the analysis of knowledge of logical laws, note first that, however these laws are conceived, knowledge of them appears to be propositional. That is, to know a law of logic is to know that a rule of inference (or a schema) is valid (or a statement true). But, given the classical analysis of knowledge as justified true belief, it follows that knowledge of the validity of a rule of inference requires justification. There are two uncontroversially entrenched forms of justification: inductive and deductive justification. By the nature of inductive reasoning an inductive justification of validity shows, at best, that a rule of inference usually leads from true premises to a true conclusion (or that it is sufficiently highly likely to do so). This is too weak; a valid rule of inference, as noted above, necessarily leads from true premises to true conclusions. So it appears that the justification of validity must be deductive.

On the basis of this conclusion it can be shown that the justification of the validity of any rule of inference either is circular or involves an infinite regress. The argument has two parts. To begin with, there certainly are deductive justifications of rules of inference that raise no serious philosophical questions. Take the justification of the rule "existential specification" in Benson Mates's widely used *Elementary Logic:* "To justify this rule, . . . we observe that . . . we may . . . obtain the inference it permits [using certain basic rules] . . . Assuming . . . that the basic rules . . . are [valid], . . . the above description of how any [existential specification] inference can be made using only [those] rules . . . shows that [existential specification] is [valid], too" (Mates, 1972, p. 123). The rule is justified by explicitly assuming the validity of other rules, so the justification here is only relative. If all logical laws are justified in this way, then, plausibly, the justification of any given rule will be either circular, by explicitly assuming its own validity, or will involve an infinite regress.

One might conclude from this that there must be some set of rules that are not justified on the basis of the assumed validity of other rules. Let us call these rules fundamental. Unfortunately, there is a simple argument that the justification of fundamental rules will involve a similar circularity or infinite regress.

What counts as a deductive justification of a proposition depends on what forms of inference are taken to be valid. For, if any rule of inference used in an argument is invalid, then the argument could not constitute a deductive justification of anything. Let us formulate this point as: a deductive argument presupposes the validity of the rules of inference it employs. Given this formulation, we can state an intuitive principle: if an argument for the validity of a rule of inference presupposes the validity of that very rule, then the argument is circular. To distinguish this notion of circularity from the one used above, let us call this pragmatic circularity, and the former, direct circularity.

Suppose a fundamental rule of ρ is justified by an argument π. Now either π employs nonfundamental rules, or it does not. Suppose π employs a nonfundamental rule σ. By the first part of the argument, σ is justified by assuming the validity of fundamental rules. Again, either the justification of σ assumes the validity of ρ or it does not. Now assume further that if an argument employs a rule whose justification assumes the validity of another, then it presupposes the validity of the second. Thus, in the first case, the justification of ρ is pragmatically circular. In the second case, the justification of ρ presupposes the validity of a set of other fundamental rules.

Now suppose that π does not employ nonfundamental rules. Then, either it employs ρ or it does not. In the first case the justification is pragmatically circular. In the second, again, the justification of ρ presupposes the validity of a set of other fundamental rules. Hence, the justification of any fundamental rule either is pragmatically circular or involves an infinite regress. (See Goodman, 1983, pp. 63–64; see also Bickenbach, 1978; Dummett, 1973; and Haack, 1976.)

One might object to the notion of circularity of argument used in the second part of the argument. Unlike the more familiar variant of circularity, the conclusion in this case is not actually assumed as a premise but is presupposed by the inferential transitions. Thus, it is unclear that this sort of circular argument suffers from the principal difficulty afflicting the more familiar sort of circular argument, namely, that every conclusion is justifiable by its means.

This, however, is not a very strong objection. One might reply, to begin with, that pragmatically circular arguments are just as objectionable as directly circular ones in that both assume that the conclusion is not in question, by assuming its truth in the one case and by acting as if it were true in the other. Moreover, while it is unclear that every rule of inference is justifiable by a pragmatically circular argument, it is clear that such an argument can justify both rules that we take to be valid and rules that we take to be fallacies of reasoning. For example, the following is an argument demonstrating the validity of the fallacy of affirming the consequent (see Haack, 1976):

1. Suppose $\ulcorner p \rightarrow q \urcorner$ is true.
2. Suppose q is true.
3. By the truth table for "$\rightarrow$," if p is true and $\ulcorner p \rightarrow q \urcorner$ is true, then q is true.
4. By (2) and (3), p is true and $\ulcorner p \rightarrow q \urcorner$ is true.
5. Hence, p is true.

Second, one might accept that deductive justification is not appropriate for fundamental logical laws but conclude that there is another kind of justification, neither deductive nor inductive, for these laws. There have been two proposals about a third kind of justification.

One proposal, due to Herbert Feigl (1963), claims that fundamental logical laws require pragmatic, instrumental justification. An immediate difficulty is, What counts as a pragmatic justification of a logical law? Surely, if there is anything that a rule of inference is supposed to do for us, it is to enable us to derive true conclusions from true premises. So, it looks as if to justify a logical law pragmatically is to show that it is suited for this purpose. And that seems to require showing that it is valid. Feigl is aware of this problem and argues that, in the context of a pragmatic justification, circularity is not a problem, since all that such a justification is required to do is provide a recommendation in favor of doing things in some particular way, not a proof that this way necessarily works. It is not clear, however, that this constitutes a compelling response to the philosophical problem of justifying deduction, since, far from needing a letter of reference before employing deductive reasoning, its use is inescapable.

How do we identify the fundamental laws of logic?

Is there such a thing as criticism or justification,

as opposed to mere acceptance of a deductive practice?

Another proposal for a third kind of justification is due to J. E. Bickenbach (1978), who argues that rules of inference are justified because they "fit with" specific instances of arguments that we accept as valid; for this reason he calls this kind of justification "instantial." The problem with this approach is that, in the case of rules of inference having some claim to being fundamental, such as *modus ponens,* it is plausible that we take the validity of the rule to be conceptually prior to the validity of any instance of it. For example, in the case of *modus ponens,* where there appear to be counterinstances to the rule, such as the sorites paradox, we take the problem to lie not in *modus ponens* but in vague concepts. Hence, whatever force "instantial" justification has, it seems incapable of conferring on fundamental rules of inference the kind of conceptual status we take them to have.

One might simply accept the conclusion of the argument, that fundamental logical laws cannot be justified, as indicating the philosophical status of these laws: they are simply constitutive rules of our practice of deductive justification. That is, there is no such thing as deductive justification that fails to conform to these rules, just as there is no such thing as the game of chess in which the queen is allowed to move in the same way as the knight. This third response leads to at least two philosophical questions: (1) How do we identify the fundamental laws of logic? (2) Is there such a thing as criticism or justification, as opposed to mere acceptance of a deductive practice?

A natural way to answer the first question is to take the fundamental rules to be determined by the meanings of the logical constants. This answer has been developed in some detail by Dag Prawitz (1977) and Michael Dummett (1991). Following Gerhard Gentzen (1969), they take the natural deduction introduction and elimination rules for a logical constant to be determined by the meaning of that constant. (More detail on the answer is provided in the final paragraph of this article.) Part of an answer to the second question has been provided by A. N. Prior (1967) and Nuel Belnap (1961), who showed that there exist sets of rules of inference that we can recognize as internally incoherent.

This third response has the consequence that our relation to the fundamental laws of logic is not one of knowledge classically construed and, hence, is different from our relation to other laws, such as the laws of physics, or of a country.

We turn now to the notion of knowledge derived from deductive reasoning. The question this notion raises, first studied by J. S. Mill (1950, bk. 2, chap. 3), is to explain how deductive reasoning could be simultaneously necessary and informative. It is undeniable that we can understand the premises and the conclusion of an argument without knowing that the former implies that latter; this is what makes it possible for us to gain information by means of deductive reasoning. This fact does not by itself conflict with the necessity of deductive implication, since there is no conflict between the existence of something and our lack of knowledge thereof. But, a problem can arise if the explanation of the necessity of deductive implication entails constraints on the notion of understanding. The following are two ways in which the problem of deduction arises.

First, consider Robert Stalnaker's (1987) analysis of the notions of proposition and of understanding. The proposition expressed by a statement is a set of the possible worlds, the set of those worlds in which the proposition is true. To understand a statement is to know the proposition it expresses; hence, to understand a statement is to know which possible worlds are those in which the proposition it expresses is true. These claims have two consequences: first, that all necessary statements, and hence all deductive valid statements, express the same proposition, namely, the set of all possible worlds; second, to understand any necessary statement is to know that the proposition it expresses is the set of all possible worlds. From these consequences it would seem to follow that in virtue of understanding any valid statement, one would know that it is necessarily true. It seems plausible that if one understands the premises and the conclusion of a valid argument, then one must also understand the conditional whose antecedent is the conjunction of the premises and whose consequent is the conclusion. But if the argument is valid, so is this conditional. Hence, if an argument is valid, then anyone who understood its premises and conclusion would know that this conditional expressed a necessary truth. It is now plausible to conclude that one can know whether an argument is valid merely on the basis of understanding its premises and conclusion by knowing whether the corresponding conditional expressed a necessary truth.

Next, consider Dummett's (1973, 1991) analysis of deductive implication. According to this analysis, deductive implication is based on the meanings of the logical constants. Thus, for example, the fact that p and q imply $\ulcorner p$ and $q\urcorner$ is explained by the fact that the meaning of "and" is such that the truth condition of $\ulcorner p$ and $q\urcorner$ is satisfied just in case those of p and of q are. Similarly, the meaning of the existential quantifier is such that if the truth condition of $\ulcorner a$ is $F\urcorner$ is satisfied, then so must the truth condition of $\ulcorner$There is an $F\urcorner$. Thus, corresponding to each logical constant, there is an account of the truth conditions of logically complex statements in which that constant occurs as the principal connective, in terms of the truth conditions of its substatements. This account explains the validity of rules of inference to those statements from their substatements and hence determines the set of fundamental rules, rules whose validity must be acknowledged by anyone who understands the meanings of the logical constants. But there are, as we have seen, cases in which we can understand the premises and the conclusion of an argument without knowing that the former implies the latter. So, how is deductive implication to be explained in those cases? This question is easy to answer if all the inferential transitions in these arguments are instances of fundamental rules determined by the senses of the constants. But the fact is otherwise; we acknowledge a number of rules of inference that are not reducible to fundamental rules. The problem is thus not an epistemological one; it arises because our conception of deductive implication includes rules whose necessity is not explainable on the basis of our understanding of the logical constants.

[See also Dummett, Michael; Frege, Gottlob; Knowledge, A Priori; Mill, John Stuart; Prior, Arthur N.; Russell, Bertrand Arthur William.]

BIBLIOGRAPHY

Belnap, N. "Tonk, Plonk, and Plink," in P. F. Strawson, ed., *Philosophical Logic* (Oxford, 1967).

Bickenbach, J. E. "Justifying Deduction," *Dialogue,* Vol. 17 (1979), 500–516.

Dummett, M. A. E. "The Justification of Deduction," in *Truth and Other Enigmas* (Cambridge, MA, 1973).

———. *The Logical Basis of Metaphysics.* Cambridge, MA, 1991.

Feigl, H. "De Principiis Non Disputandum . . . ?" in M. Black, ed., *Philosophical Analysis* (Englewood Cliffs, NJ, 1963).

Gentzen, G. "Investigations into Logical Deduction," in *Collected Papers,* edited by M. E. Szabo (Amsterdam, 1969).

Goldfarb, W. D. "Logic in the Twenties," *Journal of Symbolic Logic,* Vol. 79 (1979), 1237–52.

Goodman, N. *Fact, Fiction, and Forecast.* Cambridge, MA, 1983.

Haack, S. "The Justification of Deduction," *Mind,* Vol. 85 (1976), 112–19.

Mates, B. *Elementary Logic.* Oxford, 1972.

Mill, J. S. *A System of Logic,* in *Philosophy of Scientific Method,* edited by E. Nagel (New York, 1950).

Prawitz, D. "Meaning and Proof: On the Conflict between Classical and Intuitionistic Logic," *Theoria,* Vol. 48 (1977), 2–4.

Prior, A. N. "The Runabout Inference Ticket," in P. F. Strawson, ed., *Philosophical Logic* (Oxford, 1967).

Stalnaker, R. *Inquiry.* Cambridge, MA, 1987.

Strawson, P. F., ed. *Philosophical Logic.* Oxford, 1967.

– SANFORD SHIEH

LOGICAL TERMS

The two central problems concerning logical terms are demarcation and interpretation. The search for a demarcation of logical terms goes back to the founders of modern logic, and within the classical tradition a partial solution, restricted to logical connectives, was established early on. The characteristic feature of logical connectives, according to this solution, is truth-functionality, and the totality of truth functions (Boolean functions from n-tuples of truth values to a truth value) determines the totality of logical connectives. In his seminal 1936 paper, "On the Concept of Logical Consequence," Tarski demonstrated the need for a more comprehensive criterion by showing that his semantic definition of logical consequence—the sentence σ is a logical consequence of the set of sentences Σ iff (if and only if) every model of Σ is a model of σ—is dependent on such a demarcation. (Thus suppose the existential quantifier is not a logical term, then its interpretation will vary from model to model, and the intuitively logically valid consequence, "Rembrandt is a painter; therefore there is at least one painter," will fail to satisfy Tarski's definition. Suppose "Rembrandt" and "is a painter" are both logical terms, then the intuitively logically invalid consequence, "Frege is a logician; therefore Rembrandt is a painter," will satisfy Tarski's definition.) Tarski, however, left the general demarcation of logical terms an open question, and it was not until the late 1950s that the first steps toward developing a systematic criterion for logical predicates and quantifiers were taken.

In his 1957 paper, "On a Generalization of Quantifiers." A. Mostowski proposed a semantic criterion for first-order logical quantifiers that generalizes Frege's analysis of the standard quantifiers as second-level cardinality predicates. Technically, Mostowski interpreted a quantifier, Q, as a function from universes (sets of objects), A, to A-quantifiers, Q_A, where Q_A is a function assigning a truth value to each subset B of A. Thus, given a set A, the existential and universal quantifiers are defined by: for any $B \subseteq A$, $\exists_A(B) = T$ iff $B \neq \phi$ and $\forall_A(B) = T$ iff $A - B = \phi$. Intuitively, a quantifier is logical if it does "not allow us to distinguish between different elements" of the underlying universe. Formally, Q is logical iff it is invariant under isomorphic structures of the type $<A,B>$, where $B \subseteq A$; that is, Q is a logical quantifier iff for every structure $<A,B>$ and $<A',B'>$:if$<A,B> \cong <A',B'>$, then $Q_A(B) = Q_{A'}(B')$. Quantifiers satisfying Mostowski's criterion are commonly called *cardinality quantifiers,* and some examples of these are "!δx" ("There are exactly δ individuals in the universe such that . . ."), where δ is any cardinal, "Most x" ("There are more x's such that . . . than x's such that not . . ."), "There are finitely many x," "There are uncountably many x," and so forth. In 1966, P. Lindström extended Mostowski's criterion to terms in general: A term (of type n) is logical iff it is invariant under isomorphic structures (of type n). Thus, the well-ordering predicate, W, is logical since for any A,A', $R \subseteq A^2$ and $R' \subseteq A'^2$: if $<A,R> \cong <A',R'>$, then $W_A(R) = W_{A'}(R')$. Intuitively, we can say that a term is logical iff it does not distinguish between isomorphic arguments. The terms satisfying Lindström's criterion include identity, n-place cardinality quantifiers (e.g., the 2-place "Most," as in "Most A's are B's"), relational or polyadic quantifiers like the well-ordering predicate above and "is an equivalence relation," and so forth. Among the terms not satisfying Lindström's criterion are individual constants, the first-level predicate "is red," the first-level membership relation, the second-level predicate "is a property of Napoleon," and so forth. Tarski (1966) proposed essentially the same division.

The search for a demarcation of logical terms

goes back to the founders of modern logic.

The Mostowski-Lindström-Tarski (MLT) approach to logical terms has had a considerable impact on the development of contemporary model theory. Among the central results are Lindström's characterizations of elementary logic, various completeness and incompleteness theorems for generalized (model-theoretic, abstract) logics, and so forth. (See Barwise & Feferman, 1985). But whereas the mathematical yield of MLT has been prodigious, philosophers, by and large, have continued to hold on to the traditional view according to which the collection of (primitive) logical terms is restricted to truth-functional connectives, the existential and/or universal quantifier and, possibly, identity. One of the main strongholds of the traditional approach has been Quine, who (in his 1970 book) justified his approach on the grounds that (1) standard first-order logic (without identity) allows a remarkable concurrence of diverse definitions of logical consequence, and (2) standard first-order logic (with or without identity) is complete. Quine did not consider the logicality of nonstandard quantifiers such as "there are uncountably many," which allow a "complete" axiomatization. Tharp (1975), who did take into account the existence of complete first-order logics with nonstandard generalized quantifiers, nevertheless arrived at the same conclusion as Quine's.

During the 1960s and 1970s many philosophers were concerned with the interpretation rather than the identity of logical terms. Thus, Marcus (1962, 1972) and others developed a substitutional interpretation of the standard quantifiers; Dummett (1973) advocated an intuitionistic interpretation of the standard logical terms based on considerations pertaining to the theory of meaning; many philosophers (e.g., van Fraassen) pursued "free" and "many-valued" interpretations of the logical connectives; Hintikka (1973, 1976) constructed a game theoretic semantics for logical terms. In a later development, Boolos (1984) proposed a primitive (non-set-theoretic) interpretation of "nonfirstorderizable" operators, which has the potential of overcoming ontological objections to higher-order logical operators (e.g., by Quine).

In the mid-1970s philosophers began to search for an explicit, general philosophical criterion for logical terms. The attempts vary considerably, but in all cases the criterion is motivated by an underlying notion of logical consequence. Inspired by Gentzen's proof-theoretic work, Hacking (1979) suggests that a logical constant is introduced by (operational) rules of inference that preserve the basic features of the traditional deducibility relation: the subformula property (compositionality), reflexivity, dilution (stability under additional premises and conclusions), transitivity (cut), cut elimination, and so forth. Hacking's criterion renders all and only the logical terms of the ramified theory of types genuinely logical. Koslow's (1992) also utilizes a Gentzen-like characterization of the deducibility relation. Abstracting from the syntactic nature of Gentzen's rules, he arrives at a "structural" characterization of the standard logical and modal constants. Both Koslow and Hacking incorporate lessons from an earlier exchange between Prior (1960, 1964) and Belnap (1962) concerning the possibility of importing an inconsistency into a hitherto consistent system by using arbitrary rules of inference to introduce new logical operators.

Peacocke (1976) approaches the task of delineating the logical terms from a semantic perspective. The basic property of logical consequence is, according to Peacocke, a priori. α is a logical operator iff α is a noncomplex n-place operator such that given knowledge of which objects (sequences of objects) satisfy an n-tuple or arguments of α, $<\beta_1, \ldots, \beta_n>$, one can know a priori which objects satisfy $\alpha(\beta_1, \ldots, \beta_n)$. Based on this criterion Peacocke counts the truth-functional connectives, the standard quantifiers, and certain temporal operators ("In the past . . .") as logical, while identity (taken as a primitive term), the first-order membership relation, and "necessarily" are nonlogical. Peacocke's criterion is designed for classical logic, but it is possible to produce analogous criteria for nonclassical logics (e.g., intuitionistic logic). McCarthy (1981) regards the basic property of logical constants as topic neutrality. He considers Peacocke's condition as necessary but not sufficient, and his own criterion conjoins Peacocke's condition with Lindström's invariance condition (MLT). The standard first-order logical vocabulary as well as various nonstandard generalized quantifiers satisfy McCarthy's criterion, but cardinality quantifiers do not (intuitively, cardinality quantifiers are not topic-neutral). Sher (1991) considers necessity and formality as the two characteristic features of logical consequence. Treating formality as a semantic notion, Sher suggests that any formal operator incorporated into a Tarskian system according to certain rules yields consequences possessing the desired characteristics. Viewing Lindström's invariance criterion as capturing the intended notion of formal operator, Sher endorses the full-fledged MLT as delineating the scope of logical terms in classical logic.

The theory of logical terms satisfying Lindström's criterion has led, with various adjustments, to important developments in linguistic theory: a systematic account of determiners as generalized quantifiers (Barwise & Cooper, Higginbotham & May); numerous applications of "polyadic" quantifiers (van Benthem, Keenan); and an extension of Henkin's 1961 theory of standard branching quantifiers, applied to English by Hintikka (1973), to branching generalized quantifiers (Barwise and others).

[See also Dummett, Michael; Frege, Gottlob; Marcus, Ruth Barcan; Mathematical Logic; Model Theory; Philosophical Logic; Prior, Arthur N.; Quine, Willard Van Orman.]

BIBLIOGRAPHY

Barwise, J. "On Branching Quantifiers in English," *Journal of Philosophical Logic,* Vol. 8 (1979), 47–80.
———, and R. Cooper. "Generalized Quantifiers and Natural Language," *Linguistics and Philosophy,* Vol. 4 (1981), 159–219.
———, and S. Feferman, eds. *Model-Theoretic Logics.* New York, 1985.
Belnap, N. "Tonk, Plonk, and Plink," *Analysis,* Vol. 22 (1962), 130–34.
Boolos, G. "To Be Is to Be a Value of a Variable (or to Be Some Values of Some Variables)," *Journal of Philosophy,* Vol. 81 (1984), 430–49.
Dummett, M. "The Philosophical Basis of Intuitionistic Logic," in *Truth and Other Enigmas.* Cambridge, MA, 1978.
Hacking, I. "What Is Logic?" *Journal of Philosophy,* Vol. 76 (1979), 285–319.
Henkin, L. "Some Remarks on Infinitely Long Formulas," in *Infinitistic Methods.* Warsaw, 1961.
Higginbotham, J., and R. May. "Questions, Quantifiers and Crossing," *Linguistic Review,* Vol. 1 (1981), 41–79.
Hintikka, J. "Quantifiers vs. Quantification Theory," *Dialectica,* Vol. 27 (1973), 329–58.
———. "Quantifiers in Logic and Quantifiers in Natural Languages," in S. Körner, ed., *Philosophy of Logic* (Oxford, 1976), 208–32.
Keenan, E. L. "Unreducible n-ary Quantifiers in Natural Language," in P. Gärdenfors, ed., *Generalized Quantifiers* (Dordrecht, 1987).
Koslow, A. *A Structuralist Theory of Logic.* Cambridge, 1992.
Lindström, P. "First Order Predicate Logic with Generalized Quantifiers," *Theoria,* Vol. 32 (1966), 186–95.
McCarthy, T. "The Idea of a Logical Constant," *Journal of Philosophy,* Vol. 78 (1981), 499–523.
Marcus, R. Barcan. "Interpreting Quantification," *Inquiry,* Vol. 5 (1962), 252–59.
———. "Quantification and Ontology," *Noûs,* Vol. 6 (1972), 240–50.
Mostowski, A. "On a Generalization of Quantifiers." *Fundamenta Mathematicae,* Vol. 42 (1957), 12–36.
Peacocke, C. "What Is a Logical Constant?" *Journal of Philosophy,* Vol. 73 (1976), 221–40.
Prior, A. N. "The Runabout Inference-Ticket," *Analysis,* Vol. 21 (1960), 38–9.
———. "Conjunction and Contonktion Revisited," *Analysis,* Vol. 24 (1964), 191–95.
Quine, W. V. O. *Philosophy of Logic.* Englewood Cliffs, NJ, 1970.
Sher, G. *The Bounds of Logic: A Generalized Viewpoint.* Cambridge, MA, 1991.
Tarski, A. "On the Concept of Logical Consequence" [1936], in *Logic, Semantics, Metamathematics,* 2d ed. (Indianapolis, 1983), 409–20.
———. *Logic, Semantics, Metamathematics,* 2d. ed. Indianapolis, 1983.
———. "What Are Logical Notions?" [1966], *History and Philosophy of Logic,* Vol. 7 (1986), 143–54.
Tharp, L. H. "Which Logic Is the Right Logic?" *Synthese,* Vol. 31 (1975), 1–21.
van Benthem, J. "Polyadic Quantifiers," *Linguistics and Philosophy,* Vol. 12 (1989), 437–64.
van Fraassen, B. C. "Singular Terms, Truth-Value Gaps, and Free Logic," *Journal of Philosophy,* Vol. 63 (1966), 481–95.

– GILA SHER

M

MACHIAVELLI, NICCOLÒ

Niccolò Machiavelli (1469–1527), Italian politician and political thinker, is famous for his treatise on princeship entitled *The Prince* (*Il principe*) and for a discussion of how to establish a good republican government, *The Discourses* (*Discorsi sopra la prima deca di Tito Livio*). Machiavelli also wrote poems and comedies (including the *Mandragola*), a *History of Florence,* and a book entitled *Art of War.* They contain many original ideas and were widely read, but today these writings arouse interest mainly because their author was the man who, with *The Prince* and *The Discourses,* inaugurated a new stage in the development of political thought.

When Machiavelli wrote *The Prince* and *The Discourses,* he was aware that he was saying things about politics that had not been expressed before; in the introduction to *The Discourses* he stated that he was resolved "to open a new route which has not yet been followed by anyone." Nevertheless, Machiavelli would not have claimed to be a systematic political philosopher. *The Prince* was written in 1512/1513; the date of *The Discourses* is less certain, but it was certainly completed by 1517. Machiavelli was then in his forties and, in the preceding years of his life, he had been a practical politician who had never shown interest in becoming a political writer or in embarking on a literary career.

In 1498, after the expulsion of the Medici from Florence and the fall of Savonarola, Machiavelli had entered the Florentine chancellery, where his special function was to serve as the secretary of The Ten, a group of magistrates charged with the conduct of diplomatic negotiations and the supervision of military operations in wartime. In this position Machiavelli carried out a number of diplomatic missions in Italy, France, and Germany. His ability attracted the attention of Gonfalonier Piero Soderini, the official head of the Florentine government, and Machiavelli became Soderini's confidant—his "lackey," according to Soderini's enemies. Machiavelli's close relationship with Soderini became a serious handicap when, in 1512, the republican regime was overthrown and the Medici returned to Florence. Other members of the chancellery were permitted to continue in office, but Machiavelli was dismissed and forced to withdraw to a small estate near Florence, where he lived in straitened economic circumstances.

It was at this time that Machiavelli turned to literary work in the hope that through his writings he would gain the favor of influential men who might help him to regain a position in the Florentine government. *The Prince* was dedicated to Lorenzo de' Medici, a nephew of Pope Leo X, who was the actual ruler of Florence. *The Discourses* was dedicated to members of the Florentine ruling group, and his *History of Florence* was written at the suggestion of Cardinal Giulio de' Medici, who in 1523 became Pope Clement VII. In the 1520s Machiavelli's efforts began to bear fruit. Clement VII entrusted him with a number of minor political commissions, and Machiavelli devoted himself to this kind of work, relegating the completion of his literary projects to the background. However, in 1527, before Machiavelli had been firmly re-established in a political position—actually, at a moment when his future had again become uncertain because the Medici had once more been driven from Florence—he died.

When Machiavelli wrote

The Prince *and* The Discourses,

he was aware that he was saying things

about politics that had not been expressed before.

Thus, Machiavelli's attitude in composing *The Prince* and *The Discourses* was not that of a disinterested scholar; his aims were practical and personal. He wanted to give advice which would prove his political usefulness, and he wanted to impress those who read his treatises. Therefore, Machiavelli was inclined to make numerous startling statements and extreme formulations. A characteristic example is his saying that the prince "must abstain from taking the property of others, for men forget more easily the death of their father than the loss of their patrimony" (*The Prince,* Ch. 17).

ARTS OF WAR. Machiavelli's statements were startling not only because of their form of presentation but also because of their content. One aspect of political affairs with which Machiavelli had been particularly concerned and in which he was especially interested was the conduct of military affairs. He thought deeply about the reasons why the French had so easily triumphed over the Italians in 1494 and had marched from the north

Machiavelli's views have frequently been misinterpreted to mean that wickedness is more effective than goodness. (Corbis/Bettmann)

to the south of Italy without meeting serious resistance. Machiavelli's explanation was that the governments of the various Italian states, whether they were republican regimes or principalities, had used mercenary soldiers led by hired *condottieri*. He therefore recommended that in case of war the prince should lead his troops himself and that his army should be composed of his own men; that is, the Italian governments should introduce conscription. Moreover, Machiavelli polemicized against other favorite notions of his time on military affairs; for instance, he denied that artillery was decisive in battle or that fortresses could offer a strong defense against an invading army.

MORALS AND POLITICS. Machiavelli's rejection of traditional political ideas emerged most clearly in his discussions of the relation between morals and politics. The most revolutionary statements on these issues are found in chapters 15–19 of *The Prince,* which deal with the qualities a prince ought to possess. In the Mirror of Princes literature of the ancient world and of the Middle Ages, a prince was supposed to be the embodiment of human virtues; he was expected to be just, magnanimous, merciful, and faithful to his obligations, and to do everything which might make him loved by his subjects. Machiavelli objected to such demands. According to him, a prince "must not mind incurring the scandal of those vices without which it would be difficult to save the state, and if one considers well, it will be found that some things which seem virtues would, if followed, lead to one's ruin and that some others which appear vices result in one's greater security and well-being." This sentence and chapters 15–19 have frequently been understood as meaning that instead of being mild a prince ought to be cruel; instead of being loyal, treacherous; instead of aiming to be loved, he should aim to be feared. But this is a misunderstanding. A closer reading shows that Machiavelli admonishes a prince to disregard the question of whether his actions would be called virtuous or vicious. A ruler ought to do whatever is appropriate to the situation in which he finds himself and may lead most quickly and efficiently to success. Sometimes cruelty, sometimes leniency, sometimes loyalty, sometimes villainy might be the right course. The choice depends on circumstances. To illustrate his point of view Machiavelli used as an example the career of Cesare Borgia, which he outlined in Chapter 7 of *The Prince.*

Machiavelli's views have frequently been interpreted as meaning that wickedness is more effective than goodness. This distortion of his views has been regarded as the essence of Machiavelli's teaching, as identical with what later centuries called Machiavellism. It should be stated that Machiavelli was not concerned with good or evil; he was concerned only with political efficiency. His rejection of the *communis opinio*—whether in the special area of military affairs or in the general field of ethics—was a reflection of a new and comprehensive vision of politics. Before Machiavelli, the prevailing view had been that the task of government was distribution and maintenance of justice. Machiavelli believed that the law of life under which every political organization existed was growth and expansion. Thus, force was an integral, and a most essential, element in politics.

Machiavelli's interest in military affairs had its basis in his conviction that possession of a powerful and disciplined military force was a requisite for the preservation of political independence. Moreover, because political life was a struggle, the conduct of life according to Christian virtues could endanger political effectiveness; Christianity, by preaching meekness and selflessness, might soften men and weaken a political society. Machiavelli directed some very strong passages against the effeminacy to which Christianity had led. Political man needed not virtues but *virtù,* "vitality." The possession of *virtù* was the quality most necessary for a political leader, but according to Machiavelli both individuals and entire social bodies could and should possess *virtù.* That is why, in *The Prince,* Machiavelli could write a "handbook for tyrants," while in *The Discourses* he could advocate a free republican regime. Every well organized, effective political organization must be permeated by one and the same spirit and must form an organic unit. There are few if any passages in Machiavelli in which he uses the word state (*stato*) in the modern sense of an organic unit embracing individuals and institutions. However, there can be no doubt that his concept of an organized society producing *virtù* among its members comes very close to the modern concept of state.

METHOD OF ARGUMENT. The new vision of the character of politics required a new method of political argumentation. Rules for the conduct of politics could not be formulated on the basis of theoretical or philosophical assumptions about the nature of a good society; successful political behavior could be learned only through experience. Machiavelli stated in his dedication of *The Prince* that he wanted to tell others what he had "acquired through a long experience of modern events and a constant study of the past." Thus, experience was not limited to those events in which a person participated but embraced the entire field of history. To Machiavelli the most instructive period of the past was that of republican Rome. Machiavelli thought that, because the Romans succeeded in extending their power over the entire world, no better guide for the conduct of policy could be imagined than that of Roman history. It is indeed true that previous writers on politics, particularly the humanists, had used historical examples, but to rely exclusively on historical experience in establishing political laws was an innovation; Machiavelli's writings implied that every true political science ought to be based on history.

It has been said that, in rejecting the validity of the doctrines of theology and moral philosophy for the conduct of politics, Machiavelli established politics as an autonomous field. He could do so because he regarded political bodies not as creations of human reason but as natural phenomena. In Machiavelli's opinion all political organizations, like animals, plants, and human beings, are subject to the laws of nature. They are born, they grow to maturity, they become old, and they die. Well organized political bodies might live longer than others, but even the best-constructed political society, even Rome, could not escape decline and death. This view of the instability and impermanence of all things gives Machiavelli's recommendations their particular tenor. Men or political bodies are entitled to use all possible means and weapons because the moments when they can flourish and triumph are brief and fleeting. Despite Machiavelli's claim that political success depended on acting according to the political laws he established in his writings, he was always conscious of the role of accident and fortune in human affairs.

INFLUENCE. It is of some importance to distinguish between the shocking novelty of Machiavelli's particular recommendations and his general concepts of politics from which his practical counsels arose. Such a distinction helps to explain the contradictory reception his ideas found in the following centuries. Machiavelli's writings soon became known in Italy and then in other European countries, particularly France and England, although in 1559 his works were placed on the Index. Generally he was considered an adviser of cruel tyrants, an advocate of evil; Cardinal Reginald Pole said that Machiavelli wrote "with the finger of the Devil." Although nobody in the sixteenth century dared publicly to express anything but abhorrence, a school of political writers arose in Italy who explained that the criteria of a statesman's or ruler's actions were the interests of the state. These advocates of the doctrine of "reason of state"—even if they did not acknowledge their obligations to Machiavelli—followed the course Machiavelli had charted. The Enlightenment, with its belief in the harmony of morality and progress, could only condemn Machiavelli's view that political necessity permitted the neglect of ethical norms. An example is the *Anti-Machiavel* which Frederick II of Prussia composed as a young man. However, some eighteenth-century thinkers recognized truth in Machiavelli's approach to politics. For instance, Mably and Rousseau admired Machiavelli because he had realized that the strength of a political organization depends on the existence of a collective spirit which is more than a summation of individual wills.

Machiavelli's rejection of traditional political ideas

emerged most clearly in his discussions

of the relation between morals and politics.

In the nineteenth century, students of Machiavelli, following the interpretation which the German historian Leopold von Ranke had given, did not believe that Machiavelli had wanted to separate ethics and politics. Because the last chapter of *The Prince* contains an appeal for the liberation of Italy from the barbarians, they assumed that Machiavelli had permitted the violation of moral rules only for the purpose of a higher ethical goal; that his purpose had been to point the way toward the foundation of a unified Italy. Thus, in the nineteenth century Machiavelli became respectable as the prophet of the idea of the national state. In the later part of the century Machiavelli was also referred to by those who wanted to free man from the oppressive shackles of traditional morality and believed that man's faculties could be fully developed only if he placed himself "beyond good and evil." Nietzsche's superman was supposed to have "virtue in the style of the Renaissance, *virtù*, virtue free from morality."

BIBLIOGRAPHY

The literature on Machiavelli is very extensive. The most recent critical edition of Machiavelli's works is that edited by Sergio Bertelli and Franco Gaeta and published by Feltrinelli in its Biblioteca di classici italiani. So far four volumes containing Machiavelli's literary works and three volumes containing his *Legazioni e commissarie* have appeared (1960–1964). This edition provides a critical discussion of the Machiavelli literature. The best recent translation is Allan Gilbert, *Machiavelli: the Chief Works and Others,* 3 vols. (Durham, N.C., 1965).

Older biographies have become obsolete since the appearance of Roberto Ridolfi's *Vita di Niccolò Machiavelli* (Rome, 1954), translated by Cecil Grayson as *The Life of Niccolò Machiavelli* (New York, 1963). Machiavelli's intellectual development is well analyzed by Gennaro Sasso in his *Niccolò Machiavelli: Storia del suo pensiero politico* (Naples, 1958). For the relation of Machiavelli's thought to that of his contemporaries, see Felix Gilbert, *Machiavelli and Guicciardini* (Princeton, 1965). The main lines of the influence of Machiavelli's ideas on the political thought of later centuries are traced in Friedrich Meinecke, *Die Idee der Staatsräson in der neueren Geschichte* (Berlin, 1924), translated by Douglas Scott as *Machiavellism* (New Haven, 1957). For Machiavelli's impact on English political thought, see Felix Raab, *The English Face of Machiavelli: A Changing Interpretation 1500–1700* (London and Toronto, 1964).

— FELIX GILBERT

MACKIE, JOHN LESLIE

John Leslie Mackie was born in Sydney, Australia, in 1917, and educated under John Anderson at the University of Sydney and at Oxford, where he graduated with a first in literae humaniores in 1940. After the war he returned to an academic position at the University of Sydney. In 1955 he took up the Chair in Philosophy at the University of Otago, then in 1959 he returned to the University of Sydney to replace Anderson in the Challis Chair. He left for Great Britain in 1964, going first to fill the foundation Chair of Philosophy at the new university in York. In 1967 he became Fellow of University College, Oxford, where he remained, becoming University Reader in 1978, until his death in 1981.

His work is characterized by an acute, unwearied, dispassionate analysis of alternative solutions to problems, striving for full and plain clarity, and by careful exploration and appraisal of alternative arguments in support of proposed solutions. Mackie applied this analytic reason across a very broad field. He made contributions to, among other topics, logic (particularly the understanding of paradoxes; conditionals and the theory of causality; the interpretation of counterfactual conditionals; the theory of space and time; the theological problem of evil; the theory of ethics; the relations between reason, morality, and law; the philosophy of mind; the philosophy of biology; and the interpretation of Locke's epistemology and metaphysics and of Hume's ethics.

Mackie's work is characterized by an acute, unwearied, dispassionate analysis of alternative solutions to problems, and by striving for full and plain clarity.

For many years he published a succession of important articles but no books. This pattern changed in 1973, with the appearance of *Truth, Probability, and Paradox,* a collection of essays on logical themes. It was followed in rapid succession by *The Cement of the Universe,* which presents his views on causation; *Problems from Locke,* which concerns characteristically Lockean themes, including primary and secondary qualities, perception, substance, universals, identity, and innate ideas; *Ethics: Inventing Right and Wrong,* a sustained argument for an error-projection account of human moral thinking; and *Hume's Moral Theory.* In 1982 appeared the posthumous *The Miracle of Theism,* whose subtitle—*For and Against the Existence of God*—sufficiently indicates its contents. This burst of productivity propelled Mackie to the forefront among British philosophers of his generation.

The distinctive theses for which he is principally celebrated are four: in philosophical theology the patiently argued insistence on the failure of all attempts to reconcile the existence of evil with the classical Christian conception of God as omnipotent, omniscient, and completely benevolent; in philosophical logic the theory that counterfactual conditionals, despite appearances, are not really propositions but, rather, condensed and elliptically expressed arguments from their antecedent as premise to their consequent as conclusion; in metaphysics the account of causal factors as INUS conditions—that is, Insufficient but Necessary parts of Unnecessary but Sufficient conditions for the occurrence of the effect; in ethics his thesis that there are no moral facts of the sort required by the semantics of moral discourse, which must therefore be expounded as arising from a widespread error.

The denial of objective moral facts is the aspect of his thought that most clearly shows the influence of his Andersonian education. When considering our behavior and its effects, our attitudes and feelings are what lead us to assume, falsely, the existence in human situations of objective features of right or wrong, good or bad, corresponding to and validating those attitudes and feelings. As there are no such validating properties, we must take on ourselves the responsibility for the judgments we make.

[See also Causation; Conditionals; Evil, Problem of; Hume, David; Locke, John; Nondescriptivism; Philosophy of Biology; Philosophy of Mind; Time.]

BIBLIOGRAPHY

Works by Mackie

Truth, Probability, and Paradox: Studies in Philosophical Logic. Oxford, 1973.
The Cement of the Universe: A Study of Causation. Oxford, 1974.
Problems from Locke. Oxford, 1976.
Ethics: Inventing Right and Wrong. Harmondsworth, Middlesex, 1977.
Hume's Moral Theory. London, 1980.
The Miracle of Theism: Arguments for and against the Existence of God. Oxford, 1982.
Mackie, J., and P. Mackie, eds. *Selected Papers,* 2 vols. Oxford, 1985.

Works on Mackie

Honderich, T., ed., *Morality and Objectivity: A Tribute to J. L. Mackie.* London, 1985. Contains comprehensive Mackie bibliography.

— KEITH CAMPBELL

MARCUS, RUTH BARCAN

Ruth Barcan Marcus, though she has published in a number of areas, is best known for her groundbreaking papers in modal and philosophical logic. In 1946 she initiated the first systematic treatment of quantified modal logic (see Barcan, 1946), therein provoking W. V. O. Quine's decades-long attack upon the meaningfulness of quantification into alethic modal contexts. The ensuing dispute focused attention on the phenomenon of referential opacity and led to important developments in logic, metaphysics, and philosophy of language. In subsequent papers Marcus extended the first-order formalization to second order with identity (Barcan, 1947) and to modalized set theory (Marcus, 1963, 1974). Particularly significant theses presented in these works were the axiom $\blacklozenge(\exists x)Fx \rightarrow (\exists x)\blacklozenge Fx$, known as the Barcan formula (Barcan, 1946), and the proof of the necessity of identity (Barcan, 1947; Marcus, 1961). It is of some historical interest that Marcus introduced the now standard "box" operator for necessity.

Marcus's response to criticisms of quantified modal logic took many forms and was a theme to which she returned repeatedly throughout her career. In her 1961 paper (and elsewhere) she sought to dispel certain puzzles about substitutivity of identity in modal contexts; she was an early advocate of a substitutional interpretation of the quantifiers for certain purposes (Marcus, 1961, 1962, 1972), as for example in modal and fictional discourse; she maintained that quantification into modal contexts involves no commitment to an objectionable essentialism (Marcus, 1961), and she later developed and defended a version of Aristotelian essentialism within a modal framework (Marcus, 1967, 1976). Finally, in the mid-1980s she offered an explicit defense of the metaphysical actualism that had informed her early papers in modal logic (Marcus, 1985/86). Here once again Marcus employed an objectual interpretation of the quantifiers, construing our core modal discourse as counterfactual discourse about actual objects.

Allied doctrines of enduring significance either originated or evolved in other writings by Marcus. For example, she introduced a flexible notion of extensionality whereby languages and theories are extensional to the extent that they identify relatively stronger equivalence relations with relatively weaker ones (Marcus, 1960, 1961). She also proposed that ordinary proper names are contentless directly referential tags (Marcus, 1961). In so doing, Marcus rejected earlier "descriptivist" accounts, often associated with Gottlob Frege and Bertrand Russell, and laid the cornerstone of the so-called new theory of direct reference later elaborated by Saul Kripke, Keith Donnellan, David Kaplan, and others.

Writing in moral theory, Marcus exposed defects in the structure of standard deontic logic (Marcus, 1966). She also argued that moral dilemmas are real and, moreover, that their reality is compatible with the consistency of the moral principles from which they derive (Marcus, 1980). Reasoning from a straightforward analogue of semantic consistency, she called into question familiar arguments from the existence of moral dilemmas to ethical antirealism. The resulting account also yielded some second-order principles of conflict avoidance.

Marcus argued that moral dilemmas are real and that their reality is compatible with the consistency of the moral principles from which they derive.

Finally, in a series of papers on the nature of belief (Marcus, 1981, 1983, 1990), Marcus rejected language-centered theories according to which beliefs are attitudes to linguistic or quasi-linguistic entities (sentences of English or "Mentalese," for instance). Her proposal was that an agent *X* believes that *S* if and only if *X* is disposed to respond as if *S* obtains, where *S* is a possible state of affairs and what is to count as such a response is a function of environmental factors and internal states such as *X*'s needs and desires. This object-centered theory, as opposed to the language-centered views of Donald Davidson and Jerry Fodor, for example, more naturally accommodates unconscious beliefs and beliefs of infralinguals and nonlinguals. It also accommodates a more robust notion of rationality and explains, as its rivals cannot, why a fully rational agent would not believe a contradiction. In the wide sense of the term, a rational agent is one who, among other things, strives to maintain the global coherence of the behavioral—that is, verbal as well as nonverbal—indicators of his beliefs. Thus, although a rational agent might assent to a contradiction, his assent would not "go over" into a belief. Indeed, upon discovering the contradiction, he would retract his earlier (contradictory) belief claim. On Marcus's view, just as one cannot know what is false, one cannot believe what is impossible.

Ruth Barcan Marcus was professor of philosophy and chair of the department at the University of Illinois at Chicago from 1964 to 1970, professor of philosophy at Northwestern University from 1970 to 1973, and the Reuben Post Halleck Professor of Philosophy at Yale, where she succeeded her mentor Frederick B. Fitch, from 1973 to the time of her retirement in 1992. In addition to her scholarly achievements Marcus changed the face of the philosophical profession by her efforts on behalf of women. Perhaps most noteworthy in this connection was the reform of hiring practices instituted by the American Philosophical Association during her tenure as an officer and subsequently as chairman of its National Board of Officers.

[See also Davidson, Donald; Ethical Theory; Frege, Gottlob; Kripke, Saul Aaron; Logic; Metaphysics; Modal Logic; Philosophy of Language; Quine, Willard Van Orman; Rationality; Russell, Bertrand Arthur William.]

BIBLIOGRAPHY

Barcan, R. C. "A Functional Calculus of First Order Based on Strict Implication," *Journal of Symbolic Logic,* Vol. 11 (1946), 1–16.

———. "The Identity of Individuals in a Strict Functional Calculus of First Order," *Journal of Symbolic Logic,* Vol. 12 (1947), 12–15.

Marcus, R. B. "Extensionality," *Mind,* Vol. 69, No. 273 (1960), 55–62.

———. "Modalities and Intensional Languages," *Synthese,* Vol. 13 (1961), 303–22.

———. "Interpreting Quantification," *Inquiry,* Vol. 5 (1962), 252–59.

———. "Classes and Attributes in Extended Modal Systems," *Proceedings of the Colloquium in Modal and Many Valued Logic, Acta philosophica fennica,* Vol. 16 (1963), 123–36.

———. "Iterated Deontic Modalities," *Mind,* Vol. 75, No. 300 (1966), 580–82.

———. "Essentialism in Modal Logic," *Noûs,* Vol. 1 (1967), 91–96.

———. "Essential Attribution," *Journal of Philosophy,* Vol. 67 (1971), 187–202.

———. "Quantification and Ontology," *Noûs,* Vol. 6 (1972), 240–50.

———. "Classes, Collections, and Individuals." *American Philosophical Quarterly,* Vol. 11 (1974), 227–32.

———. "Dispensing with Possibilia," Presidential Address, *Proceedings of the American Philosophical Association,* Vol. 49 (1976), 39–51.

———. "Moral Dilemmas and Consistency," *Journal of Philosophy,* Vol. 77, No. 3 (1980), 121–35.

———. "A Proposed Solution to a Puzzle about Belief," in P. French, T. Uehling, H. K. Wettstein, eds., *Foundations of Analytical Philosophy,* Midwest Studies in Philosophy, Vol. 6 (Minneapolis, 1981).

———. "Rationality and Believing the Impossible," *Journal of Philosophy,* Vol. 75 (1983), 321–37.

———. "Possibilia and Possible Worlds," in R. Haller, ed., *Grazer philosophische Studien,* Vols. 25 & 26 (1985/86), 107–32.

———. "Some Revisionary Proposals about Belief and Believing," *Philosophy and Phenomenological Research* (Supplement 1990), 133–54.

———. *Modalities.* Oxford, 1994.

— DIANA RAFFMAN
G. SCHUMM

MARX, KARL

Karl Marx (1818–1883), German revolutionary socialist, social and economic theorist, and source of most of the important currents in modern socialism. Marx was born in Treves (Trier) in the Rhineland. His family was Jewish but converted to Lutheranism when he was six. Marx studied law in Bonn and philosophy and history in Berlin, where the intellectual legacy of Hegel, dead five years earlier, "weighed heavily on the living," as Marx later said. He received a doctorate from the University of Jena in 1841 for a thesis on Epicurus and Democritus. As an undergraduate Marx had identified himself with the left wing of the young Hegelians and was known as a militant atheist whose creed was (and remained): "Criticism of religion is the foundation of all criticism." This reputation made an academic career impossible under the Prussian government. Instead he became editor of a liberal businessmen's newspaper in Cologne, the *Rheinische Zeitung.* This paper was suppressed in 1843, and Marx decided to continue the struggle against Prussian autocracy from Paris, thus beginning a lifelong exile. In Paris he became friendly with Friedrich Engels, and they began what was probably the most momentous literary partnership in history. In his *Economic and Philosophic Manuscripts of 1844,* written in Paris, Marx roughed out, in a more metaphysical form than his later work, a brilliantly original view of human society, whose three components were French socialism, English economics, and German philosophy (the Hegelianism of his student days corrected by Feuerbach's materialism).

Expelled from France in 1845, Marx went to Brussels, where he continued his economic studies and made his first contact with the workingmen's movement. Asked to draft a statement of principles for one of their leagues, he and Engels produced the immensely influential *Communist Manifesto* (1848). The *Manifesto* is an analysis of capitalism, a criticism of "false" socialism, an interpretation of history as the preparation for the coming of true socialism, and a call to revolutionary action. During the 1848 revolutions, Marx was expelled from Brussels; he went first to Paris and then to Cologne, where he edited the *Neue Rheinische Zeitung* during an abortive experiment in parliamentary democracy. Upon the defeat of the democracy, Marx was arrested, tried for sedition, acquitted, and expelled in 1849.

He lived the rest of his life in London, supported financially by Engels, who had returned to his prosperous textile business. Apart from some journalism for Horace Greeley's New York *Tribune,* Marx never had regular work. He lived a life of poverty that was complicated by his own notions of respectability, worsened by chronic illness, and saddened by the death of three children. His only notable political activity was domination of the International Working Men's Association (the "First International"), formed in 1864 and scuttled by Marx himself in 1872 after prolonged factional strife, notably between Marx and Michael Bakunin. Most of those years Marx spent in the British Museum, gathering material for his great historical analysis of capitalism, *Das Kapital,* of which he was able to publish only one volume (Hamburg, 1867); Engels had to construct the other two volumes from posthumous papers. Marx's other writings were mostly exercises in political pamphleteering, in which his keen but often overhasty analysis was backed by unusual gifts for rhetoric and invective. At his death Marx was, in his own words, "the best hated and most calumniated man of his time." His life had been dedicated to political fanaticism and to a passionate quest for a vast synthetic view of all history and culture.

That synthesis was only partially achieved, yet it succeeded well enough to provide an ideology and a fairly coherent world view for attempts to produce a new civilization, supposedly better and more advanced than the one produced by democracy and industrialism in western Europe and North America. Philosophy played little part in the Marxian synthesis, which was intended to be positive, historical, and sociological—"scientific," as Engels called it. It has been argued that any such generalizing world view is by definition philosophical or even religious and that therefore Marx must be classed with such great metaphysical synthesizers as Aristotle,

A statue of Karl Marx in Moscow bears testament to his influence on modern socialism. (Corbis/Bettmann)

Aquinas, and Hegel. But that begs the very question Marx posed; whether the study of history and economics, free of all philosophical speculation, religious prejudice, and overt ethical promotion, cannot show us the course that humanity will follow on this earth.

Marx's system began with an economic theory. Goods were exchanged at rates decided by the amount of labor that went into them (the labor theory of value). The price of labor itself was no exception to this law; labor was paid subsistence wages, just what was needed to "make" workers, i.e., to keep them alive and reproducing themselves. Yet labor produced goods worth more than its wages, and the difference belonged to the capitalists. Thus the misery of the masses was not due to wickedness that might respond to preaching, but to the operation of economic laws. However, a critical study of political economy showed that these laws were peculiar to capitalism, which was merely one stage of historical development, one soon to be destroyed by its internal contradictions. As the masses became poorer and more numerous, the capitalists became fewer and controlled greater concentrations of productive equipment, whose full productiveness they throttled back for their own gain. The capitalists would soon be swept aside as a restraint on production, and the masses would take over the already socialized industrial economy, which had been carried to the edge of perfection by self-liquidating capitalism. There would succeed a progressive, rational society with no wages, no money, no social classes, and, eventually, no state—"a free association of producers under their [own] conscious and purposive control."

The Communist Manifesto *(1848)*

is an analysis of capitalism,

a criticism of "false" socialism,

an interpretation of history as the preparation

for the coming of true socialism,

and a call to revolutionary action.

Marx was the author of the doctrine of historical materialism, the theory that the "material conditions of life" and specifically "the mode of production of the material means of existence" determine much else in human consciousness and society. Neither Marx nor any of his followers, in a century-long debate, ever succeeded in stating this theory both rigorously and plausibly at the same time. Yet, because it stressed economic and technological factors in human affairs that previously had been overlooked or veiled by hypocrisy, the theory has had an extensive and generally fruitful influence over much thinking and writing about society. Marx "flirted with" Hegel's triadic dialectic to express some parts of his economic and historical theories, but it was Engels who developed dialectical materialism as a metaphysics or a theory of reality. Marx remained, like many Germans in his day, marked by the influence of Hegel, which revealed itself in a taste for metaphysical bombast but also in certain specific doctrines, such as that history progresses by struggle and opposition and that change occurs in revolutionary leaps rather than in gradual, quantitative stages. Not surprisingly, the Hegelian imprint is clearest in the earliest work: Marx's Paris manuscripts are a fusion of political economy and Hegelianism, each interpreted in terms of the other. But as Marx extended his knowledge of history and eco-

nomics, he abandoned the metaphysical-moral critique of capitalism for an approach that sought to be factual and scientific.

BIBLIOGRAPHY

Works by Marx

The nearest approach to a complete edition of Marx's work is in Russian, Karl Marx and Friedrich Engels, *Sochineniya,* 32 vols. (Moscow, 1955–), of which the parallel German version is *Werke,* 30 vols. (Berlin, 1957–). Previously scholars used *Marx–Engels Gesamtausgabe,* 12 vols. (Berlin and Moscow, 1927–1935). Neither contains all of Marx's output, which is catalogued in Maximilien Rubel, *Bibliographie des oeuvres de Karl Marx* (Paris, 1956).

In English there are several selected editions: Marx and Engels, *Selected Works,* 2 vols. (London, 1942; and, slightly different, 1951); and Marx and Engels, *Selected Correspondence 1846–1895* (London, 1934). Selections dealing with philosophical subjects include Marx and Engels, *Selected Writings in Sociology and Social Philosophy,* Maximilien Rubel and T. B. Bottomore, eds. (London, 1956); and Marx and Engels, *Basic Writings on Politics and Philosophy,* L. S. Feuer, ed. (New York, 1959).

Separate works in English by Marx alone are: *Capital,* translated by S. Moore, E. Aveling, and E. Untermann, 3 vols. (Chicago, 1906–1909); *A Contribution to the Critique of Political Economy,* translated by N. I. Stone (Chicago, 1904); *Economic and Philosophic Manuscripts of 1844,* translated by M. Milligan (London, 1959); *Letters to Dr. Kugelmann* (New York, 1934); *The Poverty of Philosophy,* translated by H. Quelch (Chicago, 1910); *Theories of Surplus Value* (London, 1951).

Separate works in English by both Marx and Engels are *The Holy Family* (Moscow, 1956) and *The German Ideology,* R. Pascal, ed. (New York, 1933); *The Communist Manifesto* has had numerous editions, whose history is told in Bert Andreas, *Le Manifeste communiste de Marx et Engels* (Milan, 1963); the most useful in English are those of Max Eastman (New York, 1932) and Harold Laski (London, 1948).

Works on Marx

Biographies include *Karl Marx: Chronik seines Lebens in Einzeldaten* (Moscow, 1934); Isaiah Berlin, *Karl Marx* (London, 1939); E. H. Carr, *Karl Marx, A Study in Fanaticism* (London, 1934); Franz Mehring, *Karl Marx,* 4th ed. (Leipzig, 1923), translated by E. Fitzgerald (London, 1936); Maximilien Rubel, *Karl Marx. Essai de biographie intellectuelle* (Paris, 1957); Otto Rühle, *Karl Marx,* translated by Eden Paul and Cedar Paul (New York, 1929); D. Ryazanov, *Marks i Engels* (Moscow, 1923), translated by J. Kunitz as *Karl Marx and Friedrich Engels* (London, 1927).

The literature on Marxism is enormous. See the section "Bibliographie marxologique" by Maximilien Rubel in the journal *Études de marxologie,* published in Paris since 1959. Notable theoretical studies include H. P. Adams, *Karl Marx in His Earlier Writings* (London, 1940); Jean-Yves Calvez, *La Pensée de Karl Marx* (Paris, 1956); Max Eastman, *Marxism: Is It Science?* (New York, 1940); Sidney Hook, *Toward the Understanding of Karl Marx* (New York, 1933), Sidney Hook, *From Hegel to Marx* (New York, 1936); Karl Korsch, *Karl Marx* (New York, 1938); Antonio Labriola, *Marx nell'economia e come teorico del socialismo* (Lugano, 1908); George Lichtheim, *Marxism* (London, 1961).

— NEIL MCINNES

MARXISM

Post–World War II Marxist theory has been decisively shaped by social changes: the growing irrelevance of orthodox Marxist political movements and the moral and economic decline (and eventual collapse) of the Soviet empire; the emergence of politically radical social movements based in nationalism, gender, and race rather than economic class; changes in the world capitalist economy; and increasing environmental degradation. These developments are reflected in divergent formulations of historical materialism; the adaptation and transformation of Marxism by the new social movements; neo-Marxist theories of contemporary capitalism; and "eco-Marxism."

Western Marxists such as Herbert Marcuse, the early Jürgen Habermas, and Jean-Paul Sartre resisted the dogmatic and positivist versions of historical materialism found in Marx and in the Second and Third Internationals. These writers denied that a theoretical analysis of capitalist society could provide laws of historical development. Rather, they believed that at best economic theory could describe certain continuing contradictions in the social order, the resolutions of which necessarily depended on the self-awareness and political organization of contending social groups. Given the rise of fascism out of the depression and the triumph of capitalist hegemony over the industrial working classes after World War II, political revolution could no longer be thought of as a direct consequence of predictable economic collapse. It was necessary to investigate social forces that seemed to make the working class not only politically passive but also psychically attached to bourgeois authority. These forces included, not just conscious beliefs, but unconscious personality structures; not just the experience of work, but those of sexuality and family life as well. Consequently, Marxist theory had to encompass psychology and cultural theory as well as economics and politics. It was further claimed that any assimilation of Marxism into a natural-science model was itself an element in political totalitarianism. Habermas (1970) developed this position into a critique of "science and technology as ideology." When we identify social theory with natural science, he argued, we fail to distinguish between science's goal of controlling nature and social theory's goal of understanding and liberating human beings. As a result we end up treating people like things.

French Marxist Louis Althusser posed an influential counterview (1970), arguing that, while different aspects of society did possess a "relative autonomy" from the economy, it was class structure that always determined historical outcomes "in the last instance." Claim-ing to present the scientific view of Marxism, and in a move that anticipated later developments of postmodern thought, Althusser asserted that subjectivity was an effect of social structures and not a primary constituent of them.

Anglo-American philosophy has seen a sophisticated reformulation of some of Marx's original claims about the social primacy of technological development. Analytical Marxist G. A. Cohen developed a "functional" analysis in which a universal human drive to develop forces of production conditioned social relations to change to support such development. Other analytic Marxist philosophers attempted to articulate a distinct moral perspective in Marx to ground claims about the immorality of capitalist exploitation and to critique the individualism of the dominant liberal paradigms of writers such as John Rawls.

With the rise of radical social movements of racial minorities and women, Marxist theory was challenged to integrate accounts of patriarchy and racism with its traditional focus on class exploitation and technological development. Theorists argued that racism and sexism were not reducible to or simple consequences of class power. They were embedded in Western culture and conferred certain limited privileges on the white and/or male working class itself. Rather than depending solely on the concept of economic exploitation, or the traditional Marxist notion that the liberation of the working class would liberate all other subject groups, socialist or Marxist-feminist theorists and black liberationists analyzed the mutually supportive, conflicting, and at times disparate elements of class, racial, and gender domination.

From the 1960s to the 1990s the structural evolution of capitalism led to new versions of Marxist economic and sociological theory. Baran and Sweezy's analysis (1966) revealed how dominant sectors of the economy had become controlled by a small number of firms and that consequently the classic price competition and overproduction oscillations of the nineteenth and early twentieth centuries had given way to stagnation as a result of an unutilizable surplus. Other theorists (e.g., Wallerstein, 1974–80) redefined capitalism as a capitalist "world-system" constituted by exploitative trade relations between a developed Western core and an underdeveloped periphery. Both the monopoly capital and the world-system models were challenged by the "global capitalism" perspective (Ross & Trachte, 1990), which sees an international economy dominated by multinational firms, intranational competition rather than a dominant Western core, and increased power for capitalists as international mobility allows them to evade local labor movements, governments, and environmental regulations.

Many writers claimed that the increased role of the state in the national economy mitigated the business cycle and redirected class struggles to competition over state resources. James O'Connor (1973) foresaw that contradictions between state support of capitalist accumulation and democratic legitimation would eventually cause a "fiscal crisis of the state." Habermas (1975), writing under the shadow of the political uprisings of the 1960s and 1970s, described conflict between ideals of democracy and equality and state support of capitalist accumulation as causing a "legitimation crisis."

It was necessary to investigate social forces

that seemed to make the working class

not only politically passive

but also psychically attached to bourgeois authority.

Responding to the continued dominance of capitalism and the failure of almost all state-controlled communism, theorists of socialism have also raised the possibility of alternative forms of a socialist economy, especially a socialism in which consumer demand is allocated by markets but is not at the same time controlled by private ownership of the forces of production.

Marxist theoreticians have responded to the worsening environmental crisis, not only by using familiar Marxist concepts to explain it, but by positing (O'Connor, 1988) an "eco-Marxist" analysis in which capitalist destruction of the environment becomes the "Second Contradiction of Capital." On this view capitalism's tendency to destroy its own physical basis of production (through ecological devastation) now coexists with the resistance it generates from the labor force as a major source of its own undoing.

In sum, Marxism continues to evolve and mutate, with many of its basic concepts (the critique of ideology, the analysis of capitalism) still essential to socially critical perspectives such as postmodernism and feminism. If it is now virtually impossible to delineate any simple Marxist orthodoxy, or to say where Marxism ends and other left perspectives begin, one can (as in other intellectual traditions) trace the historical roots of philosophical perspective and revolutionary social intent from Marx, through enormous historical change, to the Marxisms of the present.

[See also Feminist Social and Political Philosophy; Habermas, Jürgen; Liberation Theology; Marx, Karl; Modernism and Postmodernism; Racism; Rawls, John; Sartre, Jean-Paul.]

BIBLIOGRAPHY

Althusser, L. *For Marx.* New York, 1970.
Baran, P., and P. Sweezy. *Monopoly Capital.* New York, 1966.
Buchanan, A. E. *Marx and Justice: The Radical Critique of Liberalism.* Totowa, NJ, 1982.
Cohen, G. A. *Karl Marx's Theory of History: A Defence.* Princeton, NJ, 1978.
Eisenstein, Z., ed. *Capitalist Patriarchy and the Case for Socialist Feminism.* New York, 1979.
Gottlieb, R. S. *History and Subjectivity: The Transformation of Marxist Theory.* Atlantic Highlands, NJ, 1993.
Habermas, J. *Towards a Rational Society.* Boston, 1970.
——. *Legitimation Crisis.* Boston, 1975.
Kuhn, A., and A. Wolpe, eds. *Feminism and Materialism.* London, 1978.
Le Grand, J., and S. Estrin, eds. *Market Socialism.* Oxford, 1989.
Marcuse, H. *Eros and Civilization.* New York, 1962.
——. *One-Dimensional Man.* Boston, 1964.
O'Connor, J. *The Fiscal Crisis of the State.* New York, 1973.
——. "Capitalism, Nature, Socialism: A Theoretical Introduction," *Capitalism, Nature, Socialism,* Vol. 1 (1988).
Reich, M. *Racial Inequality: A Political-Economic Analysis.* Princeton, NJ, 1980.
Ross, R., and K. Trachte. *Global Capitalism: The New Leviathan.* Albany, NY, 1990.
Sargent, L., ed. *Women and Revolution.* Boston, 1981.
Sartre, J.-P. *Search for a Method.* New York, 1963.
Wallerstein, I. *The Modern World-System,* 2 vols. New York, 1974–80.

— ROGER S. GOTTLIEB

MATHEMATICAL LOGIC

Mathematical logic is the study of logic by mathematical methods. The field has developed since the mid-twentieth century, like others in mathematics, dividing into branches whose mutual connections are often looser than the connections each has with outside fields. The volume of philosophically oriented work has decreased in relative terms but has still increased in absolute terms, owing to the overall growth of the field. The many subdivisions of mathematical logic are grouped into four main divisions: model theory, proof theory, recursion theory, and set theory.

Set Theory

Axiomatic set theory provides the framework within which mainstream mathematics is developed, and so it is a major object of logical investigation. The mainstream axiom system for set theory (ZFC) consists of the Zermelo-Fraenkel axioms (ZF) plus the axiom of choice (AC). By the incompleteness theorem of K. Gödel, for this or any similar system (assuming it consistent), there is a hypothesis that is both consistent with the system (irrefutable) and independent of the system (unprovable). Gödel conjectured that for the system ZFC the old conjecture about sets of real numbers known as the continuum hypothesis (CH) is such a hypothesis. Besides thus conjecturing that CH is consistent with but independent of ZFC, he also conjectured that AC is consistent with but independent of ZF, and he proved consistency in both cases.

The most important development in set theory and arguably in all mathematical logic since the mid-twentieth century has been the proof in the early 1960s of independence for both cases by P. J. Cohen. His method of "forcing" has since been applied by R. M. Solovay and others to establish the consistency and independence of many hypotheses. Anticipating such developments, Gödel had urged that new axioms should be sought, axioms that might be justifiable intrinsically as further expressions of an intuitive conception of set only partially expressed by the axioms of ZFC, or extrinsically as having attractive or useful consequences in areas nearer mainstream practice in pure or applied mathematics. Two directions have especially been pursued in seeking new axioms.

So-called large cardinal axioms, for which some claim an intrinsic justification, assert the existence of sets far larger than any that can be proved to exist in ZFC, which already include sets far larger than any encountered in mainstream mathematical practice. The so-called determinacy axiom for a class of sets of real numbers pertains to infinite games in which a set from the class is dealt to two players, who then generate a real number by alternately choosing the digits of its decimal expansion, with the first or second player winning accordingly as the number thus generated does or does not belong to the set; the axiom states that, given any set from the class, for one or the other player there will be a winning strategy, a rule telling that player what to choose as a function of the opponent's previous choices, which if followed will result in a win for the player in question. An extrinsic justification has been claimed for such axioms, since they imply that simply definable sets of real numbers are also well behaved in various respects; for instance, there is no counterexample to CH among them.

Work of the self-styled "cabal" of A. Kechris, D. A. Martin, Y. N. Moschovakis, J. Steel, and H. Woodin culminated in the 1980s in a proof of a close connection between the two kinds of axioms: suitable large cardinal axioms imply enough determinacy axioms to settle most outstanding questions of interest about simply definable

sets of real numbers. There is also a partial converse. But the question whether or not there is a counterexample to CH among arbitrary, as opposed to simply definable, sets of real numbers is not decided by large cardinal or any other widely accepted axioms: the status of CH (if regarded as having a definite truth value) remains open.

Recursion Theory

Recursion theory begins with a rigorous definition of decidability for sets of natural numbers (or of objects like logical formulas that can be indexed by natural numbers), in terms of the existence of an algorithm of a certain specified kind that will for any given number in finite time determine whether or not it is in the set. The core area of pure recursion theory as a subject in its own right is degree theory, the classification of undecidable sets of natural numbers (or in a subsequent generalization called α-recursion theory, of certain ordinal numbers) by their degree of undecidability. Work in this area displays immense technical sophistication but claims little philosophical relevance and so will be slighted here, as will be the many positive and negative results about the decidability or undecidability of various particular mathematically significant sets of formulas. But to mention at least the most famous of these, work of Y. Matijacevič in the early 1970s showed the undecidability of the set of polynomial equations in several variables for which there is a solution in integers. This implies that no reasonable axiom system will be able to settle the status of all such simple-seeming equations.

Recursion theory includes a general theory of definability applicable to undecidable sets of natural numbers and to sets of real numbers, which has played a large role in work in set theory. It also includes complexity theory, concerned with the subclassification of decidable sets by considering how fast the number of steps of computation needed to determine whether a given n belongs to the set grows as a function of n. For instance, if there is a polynomial function of n that bounds this number of steps for all n, then the set is said to be polynomial-time decidable. The distinction between sets that are and that are not polynomial-time decidable is an idealization of the philosophically interesting distinction between sets for which it is feasible in practice and sets for which it is only possible in principle to decide whether a given number belongs.

Complexity theory is an example of an area on the border between mathematical logic and theoretical computer science, which was historically an offshoot of recursion theory but has long since far outgrown its parent discipline. Today, computer science is the locus of many of the most important applications of all branches of mathematical logic. Areas of application range from the design of circuits to questions of more direct philosophical interest connected with artificial intelligence.

Model Theory

Model theory begins with a rigorous definition of logical consequence, in terms of the nonexistence of countermodels or interpretations of a certain specified kind in which the premise is true and the conclusion false. Model-theoretic methods have played a large role in set theory. The core area of pure model theory is stability theory, the classification of theories by the number of their models of any given uncountable size (pursued especially by S. Shelah). This work is more technically sophisticated than philosophically relevant and will be passed over here, along with the many applications of model theory to abstract algebra and related areas of mathematics. One such application has, however, captured the imagination of philosophers, namely A. Robinson's nonstandard analysis.

Another area of model theory that has generated philosophical interest is the study of extensions of classical or first-order logic. These are of two kinds. In logics with infinitary connectives of conjunction and disjunction, or generalized quantifiers such as "there exist uncountably many," the classical notion of model due to A. Tarski (essentially, a set with some distinguished relations on it) is retained. Closely related to the study of such logics is abstract or comparative model theory, inaugurated by a result of P. Lindström, according to which classical logic is in a sense that can be made precise the only logic for which both the compactness theorem of Tarski and the transfer theorem of L. Löwenheim and T. Skolem hold.

In logics with operators for necessity and possibility, or related notions of special philosophical interest, a different notion of model, elaborated by S. Kripke and others in the years around 1960 (essentially an indexed family of Tarski models, the indices being called possible worlds), is used. For this, among other reasons, the study of such logics is sometimes considered to fall outside mathematical logic; but however classified, it is a philosophically significant area of applications of model-theoretic and other methods of mathematical logic. Several such logics have applications in theoretical computer science (though such applications often involve abandoning any literal adherence to their original philosophical interpretations and motivations).

Proof Theory

Proof theory begins with a rigorous definition of logical deducibility, in terms of the existence of proofs or sequences of steps leading by rules of a certain specified kind from premise to conclusion. The traditional core of proof theory has been the comparative study of classical mathematics on the one hand and nonclassical, restricted forms of mathematics on the other hand. Three of these latter, in order from most to least restrictive, are finitism, constructivism, and predicativism. It had been the original goal of D. Hilbert to prove (finitistically) that any finitistically meaningful and classically provable mathematical statement is finitistically provable: in jargon the goal was to prove that orthodox mathematics is conservative over finitist mathematics, with respect to the class of finitistically meaningful statements. Such a conservativeness result would have provided, from a finitist standpoint, an indirect justification of classical mathematical practice. However, it follows from Gödel's incompleteness theorem that classical mathematics as a whole is not thus conservative over finitist, constructive, or predicative mathematics.

Mathematical logic has developed

since the mid-twentieth century,

like others in mathematics,

dividing into branches whose mutual connections

are often looser than the connections

each has with outside fields.

A modified program has had the goal of proving the conservativeness of one or another significant fragment of classical mathematics with respect to one or another significant class of statements over one or another significantly restricted form of mathematics. An indispensable preliminary to this program was to find formal theories codifying finitist or constructive or predicative mathematics at least as well as ZFC codifies classical mathematics. This preliminary task was largely accomplished by the end of the 1950s, since which time there has been considerable progress on the program proper.

Noteworthy has been the work of the schools of S. Feferman (an important contributor to codifying predicativism) and H. Friedman. The former has steadily produced more and more flexible systems more and more comfortably accommodating more and more substantial fragments of classical mathematics, while remaining conservative (for an appropriate class of statements) over restrictive forms of mathematics. The latter, with its program of *reverse mathematics,* has produced increasingly stronger fragments WKL_0, ACA_0, ATR_0, $\Pi^1_1\text{-}CA_0$ of classical mathematics that are conservative over finitist, constructive, predicative, and a liberalized predicative mathematics respectively, and that are claimed to constitute natural stopping points within classical mathematics, in the sense that most often when a major classical theorem is not provable in one system in the series, it actually implies the characteristic axioms of the next stronger system. The same school has also continued the project, which began with the work of J. Paris and L. Harrington, of identifying simple and natural results of finite combinatorics that, in a sense that can be made precise, lie just beyond the power of finitist or constructive or predicative mathematics to prove.

In a sense proof-theoretic study of proposed restrictions of classical mathematics and set-theoretic study of proposed extensions (in both of which recursion-theoretic and model-theoretic methods are indispensable) are complementary activities, working at opposite ends of the same continuum. Between them they supply a picture that is steadily growing clearer of just how far ordinary practice in pure and applied mathematics does or does not exploit the irreducibly infinistic and nonconstructive and impredicative methods that classical axioms in principle supply.

[*See also Artificial Intelligence; Computation; Gödel, Kurt; Infinitesimals; Intuitionism; Kripke, Saul Aaron; Logic, Nonstandard; Logical Consequence; Logical Terms; Modal Logic; Model Theory; Proof Theory; Provability; Recursion Theory; Set Theory.*]

BIBLIOGRAPHY

Barwise, J., ed. *Handbook of Mathematical Logic.* Amsterdam, 1977. A comprehensive survey of all branches of the field.

Bulletin of Symbolic Logic. Established in 1995 as an official organ of the Association for Symbolic Logic. Contains in each issue survey/expository articles intended for a nonspecialist readership, which chronicle the progress of the field.

Gabbay, D., and F. Guenthner, eds. *Handbook of Philosophical Logic,* 4 vols. Dordrecht, 1983–89. A comprehensive survey of its field, covering classical logic as well as philosophically motivated non-classical logics.

Mueller, G. H. et al., eds. Ω-*Bibliography of Mathematical Logic,* 6 vols. Berlin, 1987.

See also the bibliographies of the articles on the separate branches of mathematical logic.

– JOHN P. BURGESS

MEANING

What is it for a sentence—or a substantial expression, such as a word or phrase—to have a particular meaning in a given language? While it is widely agreed that the meaning of a sentence, phrase, or word must have something to do with the way that the expression is used by speakers of the language, it is not at all obvious how to move from that vague idea to a precise answer to our question. One problem is that utterances of a given sentence might be used to convey all manner of messages, many of which would be far removed from what we intuitively regard as the literal linguistic meaning of the sentence. Any account of meaning in terms of use must find a way to avoid having every innovative or idiosyncratic feature of use registered as an aspect of meaning. There are two ideas about linguistic meaning that might help with this problem. One is the idea that linguistic meaning is a matter of convention. The other is the idea that linguistic meaning is compositional; that is, the linguistic meaning of a sentence depends in a systematic way on the meanings of the words and phrases from which the sentence is constructed.

LINGUISTIC MEANING IS CONVENTIONAL. To define the meaning of a sentence as the message or messages that the sentence is, or can be, used to convey is inadequate, because too inclusive. In order to exclude the innovative or idiosyncratic features of language use, we might reach for the notion of a rule of language: what it is for a sentence to mean that p is for there to be a rule saying that the sentence is to be used (or may be used) to convey the message that p. However, if a rule is something that is formulated explicitly (in language), then the proposal may just reintroduce the notion of linguistic meaning; and that would be unsatisfactory if the project is to define or analyze the notion of linguistic meaning in other terms. So, instead of the notion of an explicitly formulated rule we can make use of the notion of a convention, defined as a rationally self-perpetuating regularity (Lewis, 1969). The resulting proposal is that what it is for a sentence S to mean that p in the language of a given population is for there to be a convention in that population to use utterances of S to convey the message that p.

LINGUISTIC MEANING IS COMPOSITIONAL. The term 'theory of meaning' can be applied to two very different kinds of theory. On the one hand, there are semantic theories that specify the meanings of the expressions of some particular language; on the other hand, there are metasemantic theories that analyze or explain the notion of meaning. We should expect the idea that meaning is compositional to be reflected in semantic theories. The way in which the meanings of sentences depend on the meanings of words and phrases should be revealed in a semantic theory by having the meaning specifications for whole sentences derived logically from more basic principles that specify the meanings of words and phrases.

Any account of meaning in terms of use

must find a way to avoid having

every innovative or idiosyncratic feature of use

registered as an aspect of meaning.

Many features of the messages conveyed by the use of a sentence will not be seen simply as the results of contributions to meaning made by the words in the sentence—contributions that would be repeated in other sentences—but rather as the products of interaction between the meaning of the sentence and other background assumptions. (The study of this interaction is called pragmatics. See Davis, 1991.) It is true, for example, that a letter of reference that says only. "Mr. X's command of English is excellent, and his attendance at tutorials has been regular," is likely to convey the message that Mr. X is not a talented philosopher (Grice, 1975). But this message is not the logical product of the meanings of the words and phrases used. Rather, the letter writer is able to convey that message by relying on shared assumptions about what information would be relevant in the circumstances. (See Grice's early [1961] proposals about pragmatics.)

TWO APPROACHES TO THE STUDY OF MEANING. These ideas, that meaning is conventional and compositional, can be seen at work in two important approaches to the study of linguistic meaning, on which this article focuses. One is Paul Grice's program for analyzing the concept of literal linguistic meaning in terms of psychological notions such as belief and intention (Grice, 1989). The other is Donald Davidson's project of illuminating the notion of meaning by considering how to construct compositional semantic theories for natural languages (Davidson, 1984).

Grice's Analytical Program

The Gricean analytical program can be regarded as having two stages (for overviews, see Avramides, 1989; Neale, 1992). The first stage aims to characterize a concept of speaker's meaning that corresponds, roughly, to the idea of conveying, or attempting to convey, a particular message (Grice, 1957, and other papers, 1989).

The second stage then aims to use the concept of speaker's meaning, along with the notion of a convention, to build an analysis of literal linguistic meaning. (In fact, Grice himself did not introduce the notion of convention, but used a slightly different idea. See Grice, 1989; Lewis, 1969, 1975; Schiffer, 1972.)

The basic idea of the first stage of the program is that an agent who is attempting to convey a message—perhaps the message that it is time for tea—makes an utterance (which might or might not be linguistic in nature) with the intention that the hearer should come to believe that it is time for tea and should believe it, at least in part, in virtue of recognizing that this is what the utterer intends him or her to believe. The analysis of speaker's meaning was refined and complicated in the face of counterexamples (Grice, 1989; Strawson, 1964; Schiffer, 1972), but it retained the crucial feature of not itself importing the notion of literal meaning. This feature is shared by the analysis of convention as a rationally self-perpetuating regularity, and so the prospects are good that the analysis of meaning resulting from Grice's program can meet the requirement of noncircularity.

PROBLEMS WITH GRICE'S PROGRAM. Grice's program does, however, face a number of serious objections. One problem concerns the application of the program to sentences that are never used at all—perhaps because they are too long or too implausible. Clearly, the Gricean analysis of literal meaning cannot be applied directly to these sentences. If we want to say that there is, nevertheless, a fact of the matter as to what unused sentences mean, then we seem bound to appeal to the meanings of the words and phrases from which unused sentences are built. But now we come to the most serious problem for the program, namely, how to analyze the notion of meaning as it applies to subsentential expressions.

Parties to a convention know what the relevant regularity is, and their belief that they and others have conformed to the regularity in the past gives them a reason to continue conforming to it. Thus, the Gricean program involves crediting speakers of a language with knowledge about regularities of use. While this is plausible in the case of the use of complete sentences, it is problematic when we move to subsentential expressions. Words and phrases are used in complete sentences, and they make a systematic contribution to the meanings of the sentences in which they occur. Regularities of use for words and phrases are regularities of contribution to the messages that sentences are used to convey. But spelling out in detail how words and phrases (and ways of putting them together) contribute to the meanings of complete sentences is a highly nontrivial project. So, it is not plausible that every speaker of a language knows what these regularities of contribution are.

The problem for the Gricean program is that it seems bound to attribute to ordinary language users knowledge that they do not really have. It may be that we can deal with this problem by invoking some notion of *tacit* (Chomsky, 1986) or *implicit* (Dummett, 1991, 1993) knowledge (Loar, 1981). But the dominant consensus—and the view of one of the most authoritative exponents of Grice's program (Schiffer, 1987)—is that the project of analyzing literal meaning in terms of intentions and beliefs cannot be completed.

Davidson and Truth-Conditional Semantics

Any metasemantic theory can be used to provide conditions of adequacy on semantic theories. Thus, consider the Gricean metasemantic proposal:

Sentence S means that *p* in the language of population G if and only if (iff) there is a convention in G to use utterances of S to convey the message that *p*.

And suppose that a semantic theory for a particular language L delivers as one of its meaning specifications:

Sentence S1 means (in L) that wombats seldom sneeze.

Then, according to the metasemantic proposal, one necessary condition for the correctness of the semantic theory is that there should be a convention in the population of L-speakers to use utterances of S1 to convey the message that wombats seldom sneeze.

This kind of transposition can be carried out in the opposite direction too. Any condition of adequacy on semantic theories can be reconfigured as a partial elucidation of the concept of meaning—or of whatever other concept plays a key role in the semantic theory—and a great deal of philosophical work on the concept of meaning proceeds by considering constraints on semantic theories. Davidson's work (1984) provides an important example of this approach.

THE TRUTH-CONDITIONAL FORMAT. As we introduced the notion, a semantic theory is a theory that tells us what expressions mean. It is natural to suppose, then, that the key concept used in a semantic theory will be the concept of meaning, and that the format of the meaning specifications for sentences will be either:

The meaning of sentence S = *m*

or else:

Sentence S means that *p*

according as meanings are or are not regarded as entities. But Davidson (1967) rejects both these formats, and argues instead for the truth-conditional format:

Sentence S is true if and only if *p*.

His argument comes in two steps.

The first step is intended to rule out the idea that, to each word, each phrase, and each sentence, there should be assigned some entity as its meaning. This step proceeds by showing that, under certain assumptions about the assignment of entities, all true sentences would be assigned the same entity. (The argument that is used here is sometimes called the Frege argument.) Clearly, no such assignment of entities could be an assignment of meanings, since not all true sentences have the same meaning. However, it is possible to resist this first step by arguing that an assignment of meanings would not conform to the assumptions that are needed to make the Frege argument work.

Even though the first step is controversial, the second step in Davidson's argument remains important for anyone who begins by favoring the format:

Sentence S <u>means that</u> *p*.

We said that, given the compositionality of meaning, we should expect that, in a semantic theory, the meaning specifications for whole sentences will be derived from more basic principles that specify the meanings of words and phrases. But Davidson points out that the logical properties of the 'means that *p*' construction raise problems for the formal derivation of meaning specifications for sentences. In contrast, the truth-conditional format is logically well understood. And from the work of Alfred Tarski on certain formal languages (1944, 1956) we can carry over methods for deriving truth-condition specifications for sentences from axioms that assign semantic properties to words and phrases.

CONDITIONS OF ADEQUACY. If what a semantic theory tells us about each sentence of a language is to be cast in the truth conditional format:

Sentence S is true if and only if *p*

then what are the conditions of adequacy on semantic theories? We have already seen an adequacy condition on the internal structure of a semantic theory; namely, that it should reveal how the truth conditions of complete sentences depend on the semantic properties of words and phrases. But what conditions must the truth condition specifications themselves meet, in order to be correct?

Tarski imposed, in effect, the condition that the sentence that fills the 'p' place should translate (or else be the very same sentence as) the sentence S. (This is Tarski's Convention T [1956].) This condition of adequacy can be transposed into a partial elucidation of the concept of truth in terms of the concept of translation. The concept of translation is sufficiently closely related to the concept of meaning that we can move from here to a partial elucidation of truth in terms of meaning:

If a sentence S means that p then S is true iff p.

But we cannot shed any light on the concept of meaning itself without bringing in extra resources.

The key notion that Davidson introduces is that of 'interpretation'. We imagine using the deliverances of a semantic theory to help interpret the linguistic behavior of speakers. For these purposes, we can abstract away from the details of the format, and use deliverances in the schematic form:

Sentence S ——————— p

to license the redescription of utterances of a sentence S as linguistic acts of saying or asserting that p. Now, by providing a way of understanding speakers' specifically linguistic behavior, a semantic theory can play a part in the project of interpreting, or making sense of, them. So, any constraints on the project of overall interpretation of people can be reconfigured as partial elucidations of the key concepts used in semantic theories.

One problem faced by Grice's program

concerns the application of the program

to sentences that are never used at all—

perhaps because they are too long or too implausible.

Two suggestions for overarching constraints on interpretation emerge from Davidson's work. One possible constraint is that speakers should be so interpreted that what they say and believe about the world turns out to be by and large correct. This is the "principle of charity" (Davidson, 1967, 1973). The other possible constraint—widely reckoned to be more plausible—is that speakers should be so interpreted that what they say and believe about the world turns out to be by and

large reasonable or intelligible. This is sometimes called the "principle of humanity" (see Wiggins, 1980).

In the imagined project of interpretation, the deliverances of a semantic theory are used in schematic form. For these purposes, at least, it does not matter whether the semantic theory uses the 'means that p' format or the 'is true if and only if p' format. So we can, if we wish, say that the constraints on interpretation shed light on the concept of meaning and thence—by way of the connection between meaning and truth—on the concept of truth.

Meaning and Use

We began from the vague idea that meaning has something to do with use, and have focused on two approaches to the study of meaning, both of which lay stress upon such notions as conveying the message that p, saying that p, and asserting that p. Both approaches take the basic way of specifying the meaning of a sentence to involve a 'that p' clause, and both permit the straightforward connection between meaning and truth. However, there are other ways to develop the idea of a link between meaning and use. For example, we might regard knowing the meaning of a sentence as knowing how to use it appropriately. Or we might say that knowing the meaning of a sentence is knowing under what circumstances a speaker would be warranted in using the sentence to make an assertion. Many of these ways of linking meaning with use do not lead to specifications of meaning by way of a 'that p' clause, and so do not support the direct transfer of elucidation from the concept of meaning to the concept of truth. It is to metasemantic theories of this kind that the term 'use theory of meaning' is usually applied. Use theories of meaning are often coupled with the claim that there is nothing substantive to be said about the concept of truth (see Field, 1994; Horwich, 1990, 1995).

[See also Chomsky, Noam; Davidson, Donald; Dummett, Michael; Frege, Gottlob; Grice, Herbert Paul; Philosophy of Language; Pragmatics; Reference; Strawson, Peter F.; Truth.]

BIBLIOGRAPHY

Avramides, A. *Meaning and Mind: An Examination of a Gricean Account of Language.* Cambridge, MA, 1989.

Chomsky, N. *Knowledge of Language: Its Nature, Origin, and Use.* New York, 1986.

Davidson, D. *Inquiries into Truth and Interpretation.* Oxford, 1984.

Davis, S. *Pragmatics: A Reader.* Oxford, 1991.

Dummett, M. *The Logical Basis of Metaphysics.* Cambridge, MA, 1991.

————. *The Seas of Language.* Oxford, 1993.

Field, H. "Deflationist Views of Meaning and Content," *Mind,* Vol. 103 (1994), 249–85.

Grice, H. P. "Meaning," *Philosophical Review,* Vol. 66 (1957), 377–88. Reprinted in Grice, 1989.

———. "The Causal Theory of Perception," *Proceedings of the Aristotelian Society*, supplementary vol. 35 (1961), 121–52. Reprinted in Grice, 1989.

———. "Logic and Conversation," in P. Cole and J. Morgan, eds., *Syntax and Semantics, Volume 3: Speech Acts* (London, 1975). Pp. 41–58. Reprinted in Grice, 1989.

———. *Studies in the Way of Words*. Cambridge, MA, 1989.

Horwich, P. *Truth*. Oxford, 1990.

———. "Meaning, Use and Truth," *Mind*, Vol. 104 (1995), 355–68.

Lewis, D. *Convention*. Cambridge, MA, 1969.

———. "Languages and Language," in K. Gunderson, ed., *Language, Mind and Knowledge* (Minneapolis, 1975).

Loar, B. *Mind and Meaning*. Cambridge, 1981.

Neale, S. "Paul Grice and the Philosophy of Language," *Linguistics and Philosophy*, Vol. 15 (1992), 509–59.

Schiffer, S. *Meaning* [1972]. Oxford, 1988.

———. *The Remnants of Meaning*. Cambridge, MA, 1987.

Strawson, P. F. "Intention and Convention in Speech Acts," *Philosophical Review*, Vol. 73 (1964), 439–60.

Tarski, A. "The Concept of Truth in Formalized Languages," in A. Tarski, *Logic, Semantics, Metamathematics* (Oxford, 1956). Pp. 152–278.

Wiggins, D. "What Would Be a Substantial Theory of Truth?" in Z. van Straaten, ed., *Philosophical Subjects* (Oxford, 1980). Pp. 189–221.

— MARTIN DAVIES

MEMORY

Philosophical work on memory continues to focus on the factive and epistemological notion of remembering that *p* for a given proposition *p*. It is widely agreed that if a subject *S* now remembers that *p* from some prior time *t*, then it is a fact that *p*, *S* knew at *t* that *p*, and *S* now knows that *p*.

Since 1960, discussions of memory knowledge have moved from the question of whether memory involves representations to the question of what memory involves over and above representations. One issue is the extent to which remembering that *p* entails a causal relation between the subject's current and past knowledge that *p*. Participants in this debate agree that remembering is not the mere retention of knowledge over time since one can remember that *p* after having for a time forgotten that *p*. Rather, remembering is the retaining or reacquiring of knowledge from internal sources (Locke, 1971). As Norman Malcolm puts it, *S* now remembers that *p* from a time *t* when *S* now knows that *p* because *S* knew that *p* at *t* (Malcolm, 1963). A key question is whether the "because" relation is a causal relation (Zemach, 1983) and, if so, what kind of causal relation *S* might know that *p* as a result of reading that *p* in his or her diary without thereby remembering that *p*. Remembering is accordingly taken by some to require a certain kind of causal chain between *S*'s current knowledge that *p* and *S*'s past knowledge that *p*—a chain that is psychologically internal to *S* in a way that a diary entry is not (Martin & Deutscher, 1966).

A second issue on which discussions of memory knowledge have focused is whether memory knowledge is justified at a temporal distance, so that memory knowledge is indebted to our past justification and thus susceptible to epistemic luck. Remembering that *p* is

---

Since 1960, discussions of memory knowledge have moved from the question of whether memory involves representations to the question of what memory involves over and above representations.

---

commonly taken to entail currently being justified in believing that *p*. On a traditional account of memory justification, one is currently justified in believing that *p* by memory in virtue of (or on the basis of) a current mental event (e.g., one's memory impression that *p* or one's beliefs that one remembers that *p*; Ginet, 1975; Pollock, 1974). On a nontraditional account, one is now justified by memory from a prior time *t* on the basis of one's original grounds for believing *p* at *t* (Naylor, 1983). The nontraditional account differs from the traditional one in entailing that there is memory justification at a temporal distance: one can be currently justified in believing that *p* by memory even if one has forgotten one's original grounds for believing that *p* and even if one lacks any other grounds deriving from a current mental event; indeed, one can remember without there being any memory impression and without its seeming to one that one remembers.

[See also Epistemology; Locke, John.]

BIBLIOGRAPHY

Ginet, C. *Knowledge, Perception, and Memory*. Dordrecht, 1975.

Locke, D. B. *Memory*. London, 1971.

Malcolm, N. "A Definition of Factual Memory," in *Knowledge and Certainty: Essays and Lectures* (Englewood Cliffs, NJ, 1963).

Martin, C. B., and M. Deutscher. "Remembering," *Philosophical Review*, Vol. 75 (1966), 161–96.

Naylor, A. "Justification in Memory Knowledge," *Synthese*, Vol. 55 (1983), 269–86.

Pollock, J. *Knowledge and Justification*. Princeton, NJ, 1974.

Zemach, E. M. "Memory: What It Is, and What It Cannot Possibly Be," *Philosophy and Phenomenological Research*, Vol. 44 (1983), 31–44.

— FREDERICK F. SCHMITT

MENTAL CAUSATION

By 'mental causation' is meant cause and effect relationships in which mental phenomena act as causes.

Mental phenomena—beliefs, desires, intentions, emotions, memories, experiences, bodily sensations, and the like—seem to have causal effects, both mental and physical. The very activity of conscious thinking seems to be a causal process involving thoughts and experiences; moreover, our sensory experiences work in conjunction with our prior beliefs to produce beliefs about our environment; and our bodily sensations can make us aware of bodily damage or irritation, and lead to our wincing, or moaning, or moving our bodies; when we act intentionally, our behavior is caused, in part, by our mental states; further, we can make decisions based on what we think, want, and value, and act on them so as to causally effect the course of events for better or worse through our behavior. Minds, it seems, have causal efficacy: they can change the world.

Philosophical issues arise when one begins

to reflect on how mental causation is possible.

Philosophical issues arise when one begins to reflect on how mental causation is possible. Suppose that a mental state M (e.g., a desire) has a causal effect E. The question arises: how did M cause E? This question is intended here to ask not what other states M caused en route to bringing about E, but rather to ask what the underlying mechanism is by which M caused E. One possible answer is that there is no underlying mechanism: the causal transaction between M and E is basic, unmediated by any underlying mechanism. While this answer has not been conclusively refuted, it has seemed to many just too incredible to believe. Indeed, one reason many philosophers reject Cartesian interactionism—the doctrine that mental states are states of an immaterial, nonspatial substance that causally interact in the first instance with physical states of the brain and then, via such interactions, with other physical states—is that it appears to imply that there is basic mental causation. The assumption that mental causation is basic does not require the assumption of dualism, however. It could be claimed that while all substances are physical, certain mental properties are fundamental force-generating properties. On the evidence, however, this claim is false. Mechanics has no need of the hypothesis that individuals have mental properties (McLaughlin, 1992).

There is compelling evidence for the following physical determination thesis: for any physical occurrence P, there is (on any cross-section of the backward light-cone of P) some physical state that determines P (or, if causal determinism is false, that determines the objective chance of P). The claim that mental state M caused a physical effect P in a way unmediated by any underlying physical mechanism is logically compatible with physical determination. However, M would then cause P in a way that is independent of any physical causal chains leading to P. While this sort of causal overdetermination seems logically possible, many philosophers have found it too incredible to believe. Mental causes of physical effects, it is widely held, could not act independently of every physical cause of those effects. For a mental state M to have a physical effect P, the causal transaction between M and P would have to be implemented by some physical mechanism (Kim, 1993; McLaughlin, 1994).

Causal interactions between mental states themselves also seem to require implementation by a physical mechanism. On the evidence, every actual state (or event) that occurs in time, occurs in space-time. Given that, causal transactions between mental states are transactions between states occurring within space-time. The following principle of causation via physical effects seems plausible: if a state has an effect that occurs within a certain region of space-time, then it is has a physical effect that occurs within that region of space-time. (Notice that if two distinct states can occur within exactly the same region of space-time, then this principle does not imply that all causal effects are physical effects.) Since mental states occur within space-time, if this principle is correct, then every mental state that has any causal effects whatsoever, has physical effects. Given that a mental cause of a physical effect does not act independently of every physical cause of the effect, it is plausible that when a mental state M acts as a cause of an effect E, there is some physical state occurring within the same space-time region as M that acts as a cause of E. The physical state will be a stage of a physical causal process leading to E that implements the causal relationship between M and E. It should be apparent that essentially the same line of argument can be employed to argue that macrocausation—cause and effect relationships in which macrostates act as causes—is nonbasic causation: whenever a macrostate has an effect, there is always some underlying microphysical causal mechanism (of the sort postulated by microphysics) by which it has that effect (Kim, 1993; McLaughlin, 1994).

It is a received view today that to have a mind is not to possess an immaterial substance, or, for that matter, to possess any sort of substance at all. Rather, to have a mind is just to possess certain sorts of capacities, such as the capacity to think and the capacity to feel. On the evidence, properly functioning brains serve as the material seat of such capacities, though whether artifacts can serve as the seat of mental capacities is regarded as an open empirical question—this is the question of whether artificial intelligence is possible. In any case, we come to be in mental states at least partly through the exercise of mental capacities, and, on the evidence, the exercise of such capacities is somehow implemented by neurophysiological processes that are, in turn, implemented by chemical processes that are, themselves, implemented by quantum mechanical processes involving subatomic states and events.

On these assumptions, one natural suggestion, then, is that mental states are high-level macrostates of the brain, and that mental causation is thus a kind of macrocausation (Searle, 1991). This suggestion is, however, controversial: it is controversial whether mental states bear a macro/micro relationship to physical states. It is not understood how physical states could combine to constitute mental states. Indeed, we lack a well-supported theory of the nature of mental states.

It might be thought that if nonreductive materialism is true, the issue of the nature of mental states need not be addressed to explain how mental causation is possible. Nonreductive materialism combines the materialist thesis that every mental-state token is some physical-state token or other, and the nonreductive thesis that types of mental states do not reduce to types of physical states. The *relata* of causal relations are state tokens, not state types. Mental causation is just physical causation in which the physical cause happens to be a mental state as well (Davidson, 1980).

While nonreductive materialism avoids token epiphenomenalism—the doctrine that no mental state has any causal effects—it faces the threat of another sort of epiphenomenalism. While the relata of causal relations are indeed state tokens, it is, nevertheless, fairly widely held that when two state tokens are causally related, they are so in virtue of something about them. The following principle of physical causal comprehensiveness seems true: whenever two physical states causally interact, they do so in virtue of falling under physical types. If every state is a physical state, then whenever any two states causally interact, they do so in virtue of falling under physical types. Since the nonreductive materialists deny that mental state types are physical state types, they face the problem of whether type epiphenomenalism is true: the thesis that no state has any causal effects in virtue of falling under a mental type (Kim, 1993; McLaughlin, 1989, 1994).

It has been widely argued that states can be causes in virtue of falling under macrostate types, even though such state types often fail to be identical to physical state types of the sort postulated by microphysics. Macrostate types seem to figure in counterfactual supporting causal

patterns that can ground causal relations between particular state tokens. When macrocausation occurs, often the microphysical stages of the underlying mechanism will involve many elements that are irrelevant to the bringing about of an effect of the sort in question. Often a state's falling under a macrostate type will "screen-off" a state's falling under a microphysical state type for causal relevance vis-a-vis a certain sort of effect: that is, often, so long as an instance of the macrostate type occurred, the effect would have occurred even if the microphysical state type in question had not been instanced (albeit, then, some other microphysical state type would have been—see LePore & Loewer, 1987; Putnam, 1975; and Yablo, 1992). Everyday examples of this are in ample supply: the turning of a key with such-and-such macrofeatures may cause a lock with such-and-such macrofeatures to open; most of the microphysical details underlying this key turning will be irrelevant to whether the sort of lock in question will open when the sort of key in question is turned. If that sort of key turning had occurred, that sort of lock would have opened, even if the underlying microphysical states had been different. It has thus been argued that there are genuine causal patterns to be found at each level of organization of reality. These causal patterns are the business of the special sciences. Underlying mechanisms are nevertheless relevant: they are relevant to how the macrostates bring about their effects.

It is a received view today that to have a mind

is not to possess an immaterial substance,

or, for that matter,

to possess any sort of substance at all.

Macrostate types are typically not identical with any microphysical state types. Rather, it is claimed, macrostate types are realized by microphysical state types; and a given macrostate type may be multiply realizable, realizable by many distinct microstate types. It might be argued that mental state types are macrostate types that are realizable, perhaps multiply realizable, by microphysical state types. But for the causal relevance of mental types to be vindicated in this way, it must be the case that mental state types bear macro/micro relationships to physical state types. However, whether they do is, as we noted, a controversial issue.

It has been widely argued that state types can be realized by microphysical states without being related to them as macrostates to microstates, and realized in a way that renders the state types causally relevant. Functional states, for example, can be realized by physical states, even though they do not bear micro/macro relationships to them. According to the leading version of functionalism, functional states are second-order states: to be in a functional state is to be in some state that has a certain causal role. Dispositional states are arguably functional states. For something to be soluble, for instance, is (arguably) for it to be in some state such that, under appropriate conditions, it would begin to dissolve when immersed in a liquid. The states that have the causal roles in question are first-order states relative to the functional states, and are said to realize the functional states. Functional states, in worlds such as ours, the functionalist claims, are realized (perhaps multiply realized) by microphysical states.

The functionalist approach to the nature of mental states is today the leading approach. Mental states, it is fairly widely claimed, are functional states that, like all functional states in worlds such as ours, are realized by microphysical states. However, a prima facie problem arises for mental causation on this functionalist view. It has been argued that such second states are not causally relevant; that, rather, it is their first-order realizations that are relevant to bringing about effects. Thus, it has been argued that it is not the solubility of an object that has causal effects, but rather the first-order structural state that realizes solubility that has effects. The view that functional states are causally irrelevant (though their first-order realizations are not) is, however, controversial; some philosophers argue that functional states do indeed have causal effects (for discussion see Jackson & Pettit, 1988; Block, 1990).

However this issue is resolved, problems of mental causation remain. Even if intentional mental states—propositional attitude states—are functional states, and such states have contents. The contents of intentional states play an essential role in explanations in which the states figure. For example, that the content of the belief that 'there is a snake in the room' figures essentially both in the rationalizing explanation, 'He decided not to enter the room because he believed there was a snake in the room', and in the nonrationalizing explanation, 'He began to quiver in fear because he believed there was a snake in the room'. According to externalist theories of content, however, the contents of intentional states are individuated, in part, by environmental factors. For this reason, it has been argued that an intentional state's having a certain content is a causally irrelevant feature of it. This issue is, however, also highly controversial. There are various theories that purport to explain how contents can be causally relevant, despite being individuated in part by environmental factors (Dretske, 1988).

A final problem should be noted. Even if intentional states such as beliefs, desires, and intentions are functional states, there is reason to think that certain mental states, phenomenal mental states, are not. Phenomenal mental states such as, for instance, states of pain seem to be essentially intrinsic states, not second-order states of being in states with certain causal roles. If this is right, then we lack an account of the nature of phenomenal states since functionalism is false for them. Yet phenomenal states seem paradigmatically causal: pains can make us wince, nagging headaches can put us in a bad mood, visual experiences can lead to beliefs about the scene before our eyes. That phenomenal states are epiphenomena seems quite implausible. Even if we could somehow know in our own case, without causal mediation, that we occupy them, how could we know that others are in phenomenal states if such states lack causal effects? However, philosophers who maintain that phenomenal states act as causes and that such causal action is implemented by physical mechanisms must either show how, despite appearances to the contrary, phenomenal states are functional states, or else explain in some other way how phenomenal states can be realized by physical states in such a way as to be causally efficacious.

The issues raised above are subjects of intensive philosophical investigation. Suffice it to note that philosophical problems concerning mental causation cannot be addressed independently of addressing the nature of mental states, and that the nature of mental states remains a topic of controversy.

[See also Artificial Intelligence; Davidson, Donald; Functionalism; Philosophy of Mind; Putnam, Hilary.]

BIBLIOGRAPHY

Block, N. "Can the Mind Change the World?" in G. Boolos, ed., *Meaning and Method: Essays in Honor of Hilary Putnam* (Cambridge, 1990).

Davidson, D. *Actions and Events.* Oxford, 1980.

Dretske, F. *Explaining Behavior: Reasons in a World of Causes.* Cambridge, MA, 1988.

Heil, J., and A. Mele, eds. *Mental Causation.* Oxford, 1993.

Jackson, F., and P. Pettit. "Broad Contents and Functionalism," *Mind*, Vol. 47 (1988), 381–400.

Kim, J., ed. *Supervenience and Mind.* Cambridge, 1993.

LePore, E., and B. Loewer. "Mind Matters," *Journal of Philosophy*, Vol. 4 (1982), 630–42.

McLaughlin, B. P. "Type Dualism, Type Epiphenomenalism, and the Causal Priority of the Physical," *Philosophical Perspectives*, Vol. 3 (1989), 109–35.

———. "The Rise and Fall of British Emergentism," in A. Berckermann, H. Flohr, and J. Kim, eds., *Emergence or Reduction?* (Berlin, 1992).

———. "Epiphenomenalism," in S. Guttenplan, ed., *A Companion to the Philosophy of Mind* (Oxford, 1994).

Putnam, H. "Philosophy and Our Mental Life," in H. Putnam, ed., *Philosophical Papers*, Vol. 2 (Cambridge, 1975). Cambridge University Press.

Searle, J. *Rediscovering the Mind*. Cambridge, 1992.

Yablo, S. "Mental Causation," *Philosophical Review*, Vol. 101 (1992), 245–80.

— BRIAN P. MCLAUGHLIN

MENTAL IMAGERY

Does Lincoln's nose point right or left on American pennies? If you drilled a hole through the floor of your upstairs bathroom, which room would the drill tip end up in? Does the tip of a racehorse's tail extend below its rear knees? Questions like these typically prompt people to form mental images. But just what are mental images?

Mental images are not seen with real eyes;

they cannot be hung on real walls;

they have no objective weight or color.

According to the pictorial view, held by Aristotle, Descartes, and the British Empiricists, for example, mental images—specifically visual images—are significantly like pictures in the way that they represent things in the world. Notwithstanding its widespread acceptance in the history of philosophy, the pictorial view is deeply puzzling. Mental images are not seen with real eyes; they cannot be hung on real walls; they have no objective weight or color. What, then, can it mean to say that images are pictorial? Mental images are also frequently indeterminate. For example, a mental image of a striped tiger need not represent any definite number of stripes. But, according to some philosophers, a picture of a striped tiger must be determinate with respect to the number of stripes. So, again, how can images be pictures? And what evidence is there for accepting a pictorial view of images?

Historically, the philosophical claim that images are picturelike rested primarily on an appeal to introspection. But it seems plausible to suppose that what introspection really shows about visual images is not that they are pictorial but only that what goes on in imagery is experientially much like what goes on in seeing (Block, 1983).

Perhaps the most influential alternative to the pictorial view has been what is now standardly labeled 'descriptionalism'. This approach has some similarity with the claim made by some behaviorists—that imaging is a matter of talking to oneself beneath one's breath—

for the basic thesis of descriptionalism is that mental images represent in the manner of linguistic descriptions. This thesis, however, should not be taken to mean that during imagery there must be present inner tokens of the imager's spoken language in movements of the larynx. Rather, the hypothesis is that there is some languagelike neural code within which mental images are constructed.

Descriptionalism has its advocates in philosophy (e.g., Dennett, 1981) and has significant support in contemporary psychology. Nevertheless, since the early 1980s the pictorial view has made a comeback after having fallen out of favor. What has been responsible for this change more than anything else is the work of some cognitive psychologists, notably Stephen Kosslyn, who has developed an empirical version of the pictorial view that seems much more promising than any of its philosophical predecessors.

Kosslyn's view is complex, and only the barest sketch of its central idea can be provided in this entry. According to Kosslyn, mental images are to be conceived of on the model of displays on a cathode ray tube screen connected to a computer. Such displays are generated on the screen from information stored in the computer's memory. Now the screen may be thought of as the medium in which the picture is presented. This medium is spatial and is made up of a large number of basic cells, some of which are illuminated to form a picture. Analogously, according to Kosslyn, there is a functional spatial medium for mental imagery. In Kosslyn's view mental images are functional pictures in this medium.

It is not easy to see exactly what Kosslyn means by calling images functional pictures in a functional spatial medium. One important part of the position is that mental images function with respect to the representation of relative distance relations as if they were screen displays (even though, in reality, they need not be laid out in the brain with just the same spatial characteristics as real displays). Kosslyn hypothesizes that the imagery medium, which he calls the "visual buffer," is shared with visual perception. Each cell in the medium represents a tiny, just perceptible patch of object surface. The cells representing adjacent object parts need not themselves be physically adjacent (as in a real picture). Rather, like the cells in an array in a computer, they may be widely scattered.

This view is motivated by many intriguing experiments (see Tye, 1991, for a summary). Not all cognitive scientists agree with Kosslyn, however. Zenon Pylyshyn, for example, maintains that mental images are structural descriptions no different in kind from the representations involved in other areas of cognition. According to Pylyshyn, Kosslyn's experiments on imagery can be accounted for by reference to the task demands placed on subjects by the experimenter's instructions together with facts the subjects already tacitly know. No inner picturelike entity is needed.

It is far from clear that the appeal to tacit knowledge can explain all the imagery data (Kosslyn, 1980). But there are other descriptional theories of imagery that have no need of the doctrine of tacit knowledge (e.g., Hinton, 1979). The controversy between pictorialists and descriptionalists in psychology about imagistic representation has not been settled yet.

Another topic of interest to philosophers that also remains a source of considerable puzzlement is the phenomenal or subjective character of images. What is responsible for the technicolor phenomenology of a mental image of a striped tiger? Some philosophers maintain that the phenomenal aspects of imagery derive from images having special, intrinsic, introspectively accessible, nonintentional properties (or qualia). But there is no general agreement.

[See also Aristotle; Descartes, René; Introspection; Philosophy of Mind; Qualia.]

BIBLIOGRAPHY

Block, N. "Mental Pictures and Cognitive Science," *Philosophical Review*, Vol. 92 (1983), 499–542.
Dennett, D. "The Nature of Images and the Introspective Trap," in *Content and Consciousness* (London, 1969).
Hinton, G. "Some Demonstrations of the Effects of Structural Descriptions in Mental Imagery," *Behavioral and Brain Sciences*, Vol. 3, (1979), 231–50.
Kosslyn, S. *Image and Mind*. Cambridge, MA, 1980.
———. *Image and Brain: The Resolution of the Imagery Debate*. Cambridge, MA, 1994.
Pylyshyn, Z. "The Imagery Debate: Analog Media versus Tacit Knowledge," *Psychological Review*, Vol. 88 (1981), 16–45.
Tye, M. *The Imagery Debate*. Cambridge, MA, 1991.

— MICHAEL TYE

MENTAL REPRESENTATION

Mental representations are the coin of contemporary cognitive psychology, which proposes to explain the etiology of subjects' behavior in terms of the possession and use of such representations. "How does a subject manage to move through her darkened bedroom without stumbling over the furniture? She has an accurate mental representation of the room's layout, knows her initial position in the room, and is able to use this representation, in roughly the way a mariner uses a chart, to navigate through the room." "How does a sighted subject manage to recover information, available in the retinal image, about 'what's where' in her environment? She computes a series of representations, using information present in the retinal image, that eventuates in

a three-dimensional representation of the distal objects present in the subject's visual field." "Why do native speakers of English have difficulty recognizing the grammaticality of so-called garden-path sentences such as 'The horse raced past the barn fell'? In recovering the meaning of a sentence, a speaker first constructs a representation of the syntactic structure of the sentence. In the case of garden-path sentences, the parsing processes that construct this representation mistakenly take the sentence's subject noun phrase to be a complete sentence, thus concluding that the entire sentence is ungrammatical." Cognitive ethologists offer similar explanations of many animal behaviors: foraging red ants are said to practice a form of dead reckoning to maintain a representation of their current location relative to their nest, which they use to find their way back; migratory birds are said to navigate using representations of various sorts (celestial, magnetometric, topographic, etc.) that are either innate or learned as juveniles.

The point of describing the representations as mental is simply to emphasize the particular explanatory role that these representations play in these explanations.

If, as these explanations apparently assume, mental representations are real entities that play a causal role in the production of a subject's behavior, then presumably it makes sense to ask about the form in which the information contained in these representations is encoded. This question has been the focus of considerable debate, especially with respect to mental imagery. Descriptionalists argue that, subjective impressions to the contrary notwithstanding, all mental representation, including mental imagery, is descriptional in form; mental representations are said to represent in a way similar to the ways linguistic descriptions represent. Descriptionalists subscribe to a language of thought hypothesis, according to which all human cognition is conducted in a quasi-linguistic medium. Pictorialists, by contrast, argue at least some mental representation, notably those involved in mental imagery, represent in ways similar to the ways pictures represent. The issues in dispute here are not straightforwardly empirical. Neither party believes that we literally have descriptions or pictures in our heads; rather, their claims are about similarities to the respective ways that pictures and descriptions represent. But it is precisely these similarity claims that render this debate obscure. What are the respective ways that pictures and descriptions represent, and what are the salient similarities such that if they hold they would justify characterizing mental representations as being of one form rather than the other? It is not obvious that there are definitive answers to either of these questions.

To describe the representations to which psychological and ethological explanations appeal as mental is not to imply that their possessors are conscious of them; typically the representations are nonconscious or subconscious. Nor is it to imply that these representations are nonphysical; there is no commitment here to dualism. Psychologists and ethologists presume that the representations to which their explanations appeal are neurologically realized, physical structures. The point of describing the representations as mental is simply to emphasize the particular explanatory role that these representations play in these explanations. The explanations undertake to explain a kind of purposive behavior on the part of a subject, in which the particular behavior exhibited by the subject is typically modulated in a characteristic fashion, not only by the goal or purpose of the behavior, but also by the environment in which the behavior is exhibited. Thus, for example, our subject's movement through her darkened bedroom is modulated by her knowledge of the current layout of the room. The mental representations that figure in these explanations serve two distinct explanatory roles: (1) they explain why a subject behaves in one way rather than another—she behaves as she does because she currently has this particular representation rather than another, and this representation is causally efficacious in the etiology of her behavior—and (2) they explain how the subject's behavior manages to be modulated (in characteristic ways) by her environment. Mental representations are able to play this dual explanatory role by virtue of possessing both physico-formal and semantic (intentional) properties that are linked in such a way as to ensure that a subject's environment can modulate her behavior. Basically, the cognitive processes that make use of mental representations are causally sensitive to the physico-formal properties of these representations that encode their semantic properties in much the way that sound-reproduction processes are sensitive to the physico-formal properties of records, tapes, and CDs.

Commonsense psychological explanations of behavior standardly appeal to beliefs, desires, intentions, and other so-called propositional attitudes (e.g., "Jones went to the refrigerator because he wanted a beer and believed there to be one there"). Behaviorists and eliminativists have challenged the legitimacy of these explanations, arguing that propositional attitudes either do not exist or do not figure in the etiology of behavior. Impressed with the prominent explanatory role of mental representations in cognitive psychological and ethological explanations, many philosophers of mind, notably Jerry Fodor, have proposed establishing the materialistic respectability of these explanations by appeal to the notion of mental representation. Their strategy is to explicate propositional attitudes in terms of mental representations. They defend a doctrine called the "Representational Theory of Mind" (RTM, for short), which holds that possessing a propositional attitude (e.g., believing that it is sunny today) is a matter of having a mental representation that (1) expresses the propositional content of that attitude (viz., that it is sunny today) and (2) plays a causal-functional role in the subject's mental life and behavior characteristic of the attitude in question (viz., the characteristic role of beliefs in modulating goal-satisfying behavior). More formally, for any organism O, any attitude A toward the proposition P, there is a mental representation MR such that MR means that (expresses the proposition that) P and a relation R (which specifies the characteristic causal-functional role of the MRs that are associated with a given A); and O bears attitude A to P if and only if O stands in relation R to MR. So formulated, RTM is silent as to the form of the mental representations that express the propositional contents of attitudes; however, proponents of RTM invariably assume that these representations are syntactically structured entities, composed of atomic constituents (concepts) that refer to or denote things and properties in the world. More colorfully, these representations are sentences in the language of thought. The structure and meaning of these sentential representations purportedly explain the particular semantic and causal properties that propositional attitudes exhibit.

RTM is clearly realist in its construal of propositional attitudes: it purports to explain, not only what they are, but also how they could have both the causal and semantic properties that common sense attributes to them (viz., of being causally efficacious in the production of other thoughts and of behavior, and of being semantically evaluable, as, e.g., true or false). RTM is equally realist in its construal of mental processes, which, it holds, are causal sequences of the tokenings of mental representation. These sequences are said to be proof-theoretic in character, with the sequential states in a thought process functioning like premises in an argument. Thought processes are, like arguments, generally truth preserving.

Proponents of RTM claim to find strong empirical support for the doctrine in the apparent explanatory (and predictive) successes of cognitive science, whose theories are heavily committed to the existence of mental representations. Critics tend to dismiss this claimed support, arguing that what is at issue is not whether there are mental representations but whether there are mental representations with the particular properties demanded by RTM. Critics argue that propositional-attitude contents cannot always be paired with mental representations in the way that RTM requires: a subject may bear a certain attitude to a proposition but lack, among the many mental representations that cognitive scientific theories attribute to her, any mental representation of that particular proposition. Thus, for example, more than one critic has pointed out that, while David Marr's computational theory of early vision (see his *Vision* [1982]) attributes to the visual system the assumption that objects in the visual field are rigid in translation, the theory does not attribute to the visual system an explicit representation of that assumption; rather, the assumption is implicit in the operation of visual processes. Proponents, for their part, have tended to dismiss such counterexamples as "derivative" cases, arguing that RTM nonetheless holds for what they term the "core" cases of propositional attitudes. Such a response presumes that there is a non-question-begging characterization of the class of core cases. It also presumes that the class so characterized includes those propositional attitudes that figure in the commonsense psychological explanations that RTM is intended to vindicate. It remains an open question whether either of these presumptions can be met.

Commonsense psychological explanations of behavior standardly appeal to beliefs, desires, intentions, and other so-called propositional attitudes.

Other critics of RTM have challenged the doctrine's apparent commitment to "classical" cognitive architectures that presume a principled distinction between mental representations, on the one hand, and the computational processes that are defined over these representations, on the other. These critics point out that connectionist computational models of cognition do not preserve such a distinction, so that, if, as these critics presume, cognitive architecture is connectionist rather than classical, then RTM is untenable. Not surprisingly, proponents of RTM have been in the forefront of efforts to demonstrate that cognitive architecture is not connectionist.

Still other critics of RTM have focused on the semantics of the postulated mental representations, arguing that, if RTM is to provide a materialistic vindication of explanations that appeal to propositional attitudes, it must be possible to provide a "naturalistic" semantics, a theory of content, for these representations. By such a semantics these critics understand a materialistic account, invoking no intentional or semantic notions, of how it is possible for mental representations to have the semantic properties that they do (of being about things in the world, of being truth valued, etc.). There is general agreement among critics and proponents alike that none of the proposed naturalistic semantics is adequate, but, where critics see in these failures the symptoms of RTM's untenability, proponents see the beginnings of a difficult but eventually successful research project. There is disagreement among critics as to the import for cognitive science itself of there possibly being no naturalistic semantics for mental representations. Some argue that it would impugn the claimed explanatory role of mental representations; others argue that it would not. Whatever the upshot of these arguments, the untenability of RTM would not in and of itself impugn the explanatory role of mental representations in cognitive science, since that commitment to mental representations does not entail RTM. One can perfectly well be a representationalist in the way that most cognitive scientists are without also being a proponent of RTM.

[See also Cognitive Science; Connectionism; Eliminative Materialism, Eliminativism; Language of Thought; Mental Causation; Mental Imagery; Philosophy of Mind.]

BIBLIOGRAPHY

Block, N., ed. *Imagery.* Cambridge, MA, 1981. A collection focusing on debate between descriptionalists and pictorialists regarding mental imagery.

Field, H. "Mental Representation," *Erkenntnis,* Vol. 13 (1978), 9–61.

Fodor, J. A. "Fodor's Guide to Mental Representation," *Mind,* Vol. 94 (1985), 55–97.

———. "The Persistence of the Attitudes," in *Psychosemantics* (Cambridge, MA, 1987).

Marr, D. *Vision.* Cambridge, MA, 1982.

Matthews, R. "Troubles with Representationalism," *Social Research,* Vol. 51 (1984), 1065–97.

———. "Is There Vindication through Representationalism?" in B. Loewer and G. Rey, eds., *Meaning in Mind: Fodor and His Critics* (Oxford, 1991).

Pylyshyn, Z. "The Explanatory Role of Representations," in *Computation and Cognition* (Cambridge, MA, 1984).

Sterelny, K. *The Representational Theory of Mind: An Introduction.* Oxford, 1990.

Stich, S., and T. Warfield, eds. *Mental Representation: A Reader.* Oxford, 1994. An excellent collection of papers on theories of content for mental representation; includes Field (1978) and Fodor (1985).

— ROBERT J. MATTHEWS

MEREOLOGY

Mereology (from Greek *meros,* "part") is the theory (often formalized) of part, whole, and cognate concepts. The notion of part is almost ubiquitous in domain of application, and for this reason Husserl assigned its investigation to formal ontology. Aristotle observed that the term part was used in various ways such as for a subquantity, a physical part (leg of an animal), a part in definition (animal is part of man), a part in extension (man is part of animal). Part concepts had obvious applications in geometry and were among Euclid's undefined terms. Several senses of "part" are expressible using the preposition "in," but not all uses of "in" express parthood.

Until the twentieth century it was generally assumed that the concept of part was sufficiently clear not to require elucidation, but gradually the need for a formal treatment became apparent. Euclid's maxim that the whole is greater than the part appeared to be contradicted by infinite classes, for example. In 1901 Husserl proposed a general theory of part and whole and distinguished several kinds of parts, notably dependent and independent parts. Explicit formal theories of part and whole were developed around 1914 to 1916 by Whitehead and Leśniewski, who worked independently of each other. They had different motivations: Whitehead wanted an empirical basis for geometry, whereas Leśniewski wished to offer a paradox-free class theory. Mereology was later formulated within first-order predicate logic by Leonard and Goodman, who called it "the calculus of individuals." Mereology has often been employed by nominalists as a partial substitute for set theory, but it is not intrinsically a nominalistic theory: part relations are definable via endomorphisms in many mathematical domains.

The most natural basic concept of mereology is that of a (proper) part to its (larger) whole. A coincident of an object is the object itself or something that shares all parts with it. An ingredient of an object is a part or coincident of it. Two objects overlap if and only if they share an ingredient, and they are disjoint if and only if they do not. The relation of part to whole has some minimal formal properties: it is (1) existence entailing; (2) asymmetrical; (3) transitive; and (4) supplementative. That means (1) that if one thing is part of another, if either the part or the whole exists, so does the other; (2) that if one thing is part of another, the second is not part of the first; (3) that a part of a part of a whole is itself a part of the whole; and (4) that if an object has a part, it has another part disjoint from the first. Principles (3) and (4) have occasionally been doubted, (4) unconvincingly. Some meanings of "part" are not tran-sitive; for example, a hand is said to be part of the body, but an arbitrary chunk of flesh is not, and for such concepts counterexamples to (3) may sound plausible, but only because they restrict the general (and transitive) concept, to mean, for example, organ, functional part, immediate part, assembly component.

The most natural basic concept of mereology

is that of a (proper) part to its (larger) whole.

Beyond such minimal properties mereologists often make further assumptions. Very often it is assumed that objects with the same ingredients are identical: such a mereology is extensional. Extensionality makes good sense for homogeneous domains such as regions of space or masses of matter, but some objects of distinct sorts seem to be able to coincide, at least temporarily, without identity. Another assumption often made is that any two objects make up a third, indeed that any nonempty collection of objects constitutes a single object, their mereological sum. The minimal properties together with extensionality and this general-sum principle constitute the classical mereology of Leśniewski and Leonard/Goodman: it is as rich in parts as an extensional theory can be, differing algebraically from Boolean algebra only in lacking a null element. It does, however, have an ontologically maximal object or universe, the sum of all there is, which by extensionality is unique. Whitehead denied that there was a universe: for him every object is part of something greater, so he rejected the sum principle. Whitehead also denied there are atoms, that is, objects without parts: for him, every object has a part. This antiatomism, together with supplementarity, ensures that every object has nondenumerably many parts. Whitehead thus denies geometrical points, and his method of extensive abstraction is directed to logically constructing substitutes for points out of classes of extended objects, an idea also carried through by Tarski. As the examples indicate, the issue whether atomism or antiatomism holds is independent of general mereology. Formally, the best worked-out forms of mereology are those of Leśniewski and his followers; they have shown that any of a wide range of mereological concepts may be taken as sole primitive of the classical theory.

Beyond extensional mereology attention has focused on the combination of mereological notions with those of space, time, and modality. Thus, Whitehead and a number of more recent authors combine mereological with topological concepts to define such notions as two regions' being connected, or their abutting (externally or internally), using mereology as its modern authors intended, as an alternative framework to set theory. When time is considered, matters become more complex. Some objects have temporal parts, including phases, and perhaps momentary temporal sections. States, processes, and events (occurrents) are uncontroversial cases of objects that are temporally extended, but many modern metaphysicians apply the same analysis to ordinary things such as bodies and organisms, giving them a fourth, temporal dimension, though this view is not uncontested. Whether or not continuants (spatially extended objects with a history but not themselves temporally extended) are thus reduced to occurrents, a number of chronomereological concepts may be defined and applied, such as temporary part, initial part, final part, permanent part, temporary overlapping, growth, diminution, and others, though their formulation will vary as applying to occurrents or continuants.

Embedding mereological notions within a modal framework likewise opens up a wider range of concepts such as essential part, accidental part, dependent part, accidental overlapping. Combining these in their turn with temporal notions allows the definition of concepts such as accidental permanent part, essential initial part, and so on. In general, where mereological notions are enriched with others, their interactions become multifarious and lose the algebraic elegance of the classical theory while gaining in applicability and usefulness.

In modal mereology much attention has been paid to R. M. Chisholm's thesis of mereological essentialism, which states that every part of a continuant is both essential and permanent to that continuant (though, conversely, a part may outlast the whole and need not have it as whole). Chisholm's position is presaged in Leibniz and Brentano. Since it appears to be contradicted by everyday experience of such things as rivers, mountains, organisms, and artifacts, it is natural for Chisholm to regard such mereologically fluctuating things as not "real" continuants but as *entia successiva,* supervenient upon successions of continuants for which mereological essentialism holds.

The ubiquity and importance of mereological concepts ensure them a growing place within cognitive science and formal representations of commonsense knowledge, and there is no doubt that mereology is firmly established as a part of formal ontology.

[See also Aristotle; Chisholm, Roderick M.; Cognitive Science; Goodman, Nelson; Husserl, Edmund; Leibniz, Gottfried Wilhelm; Metaphysics.]

BIBLIOGRAPHY

Chisholm, R. M. *Person and Object: A Metaphysical Study.* London, 1976.

Husserl, E. "On the Theory of Wholes and Parts." in *Logical Investigations,* 2 vols. (London, 1970).

Leonard, H. S., and N. Goodman. "The Calculus of Individuals and Its Uses," *Journal of Symbolic Logic,* Vol. 5 (1940), 45–55.

Leśniewski, S. "On the Foundations of Mathematics," in *Collected Works* (Dordrecht, 1992).

Simons, P. M. *Parts: A Study in Ontology.* Oxford, 1987.

Whitehead, A. N. "Principles of the Method of Extensive Abstraction," in *An Enquiry Concerning the Principles of Natural Knowledge* (Cambridge, 1919).

– PETER SIMONS

MERLEAU-PONTY, MAURICE

[*This entry consists of three articles. In his first essay, Martin C. Dillon presents an overview of the French philosopher's contributions to the field. In his second piece, Dillon discusses Merleau-Ponty's philosophy of psychology. The third article, contributed by Sonia Kruks, presents Merleau-Ponty's views on political theory.*]

MERLEAU-PONTY, MAURICE

Maurice Merleau-Ponty (1908–61), French philosopher associated with existential phenomenology, was the youngest philosopher ever to be appointed to the chair once occupied by Henri Bergson at the Collège de France. He is known primarily for developing an ontology that recognizes the philosophical significance of the human body. His early interest in the resonance between the emergent school of gestalt psychology and the phenomenology of Edmund Husserl and Martin Heidegger, coupled with lively participation in contemporary debates in politics, human sciences, and the arts, led to a radical reassessment of transcendental philosophy. He died abruptly at the age of fifty-three, leaving his last major work, *Le Visible et l'invisible,* unfinished. Claude Lefort has edited the extant text, four chapters and an appendix, and published it together with extensive working notes dated from January 1959 to March 1961.

The Lived Body

Merleau-Ponty revolutionized Western thinking about the body, which since ancient Greece had taken it to be either insignificant or a detriment to knowledge, by demonstrating its constitutive role in the process of human understanding. He showed, for example, that it is through bodily motility that the various adumbrations or perspectival views of an object can be synthesized into a unitary whole. Our understanding of objective space, the three-dimensional Cartesian grid of length, breadth, and height, is an abstraction from lived space, space articulated by the body's capacity to move purposively, to grasp things, to maintain the equilibrium that allows for stable visual coordinates, to interrogate its environment. Furthermore, the body's ability to perceive the world is grounded in the body's double role as sensor and sensed, subject and object of experience: I could not touch an object were I not myself, as body, an object capable of being touched, nor could I see were my eyes not themselves objects located within the surroundings to which they are sensitive. The classical dualism, which views the body and otherworldly objects as disjunct from the mind as the subject or agency of disembodied thought, is replaced with Merleau-Ponty's model of corporeal intentionality, in which the body is revealed as having an intelligence of its own, manifest in reflex as in habitual activities, which allows it to interact with the world at a level prior to the reflexivity of deliberate conceptualization.

Merleau-Ponty is known primarily

for developing an ontology that recognizes

the philosophical significance of the human body.

Reversibility Thesis

The transcendental role of the body, its ability to project its organizational schemas into the world, is inseparable from the body's own status as physical object subject to the worldly forces impinging upon it. These roles are inseparable, but not coincident. There is a divergence of the body as sensing from the body as sensed: the finger that touches the thumb or is touched by it does not form an identity with the thumb; rather, the two bodily parts co-exist in an ambiguous relationship of reversibility within the encompassing matrix of bodily being-in-the-world. Finger and thumb can reverse roles, the erstwhile sensor becoming the sensed, just as the hand that feels the table can sense itself being touched by the table, yet neither of these roles would be possible were it not for the other.

The Flesh of the World

Merleau-Ponty takes the reversibility of subject and object roles in the case of human flesh as emblematic of a global manner of being, which he designates as chiasm or intertwining. The term 'flesh' is generalized to encompass worldly being as such. The world is taken as an arena of interaction in which every entity is what it is in relation to every other. This is not a pananimism, but rather an attempt to rectify the post-Socratic reduction of nature to inert materiality in a movement of thought which is as consonant with the ancient concept of *physis* as it is with the contemporary notion of world as ecosystem. The figure of the chiasm, the intersection or intertwining marking the point at which things touch each other as they cross, refers to the dynamics of worldly unfolding or global temporality in which the interaction of things brings about change. The brute or savage being of the world, the factuality of its transcendence, is counterbalanced with the relatedness of its denizens apparent in the relatively abiding structures human intelligence organizes under the heading of science. We are that aspect of the flesh of the world that is capable of the reflective relationship of conceptualization or understanding, but other aspects of the world betray other forms of corporeal reflexivity in the complex of interaction that encompasses organic cycles, weather systems, geological formation, and so forth as each of these contributes and responds to all the others.

Visible and Invisible

Merleau-Ponty's thesis of the primacy of perception evolves from the middle phase of his thinking, when he published *Phénoménologie de la perception* and set forth the view that "the perceived world is the always presupposed foundation of all rationality, all value and all existence," to later phases in which this thesis had to be expanded to accommodate the findings of extensive analyses of language based on his unique interpretation of the philosophical significance of Saussurean semiotics. There is controversy regarding his later thinking on the relative primacy of language and perception, but general agreement that the relationship between the two is that of intertwining: language, conceived as sign system, might be conceived as an invisible nexus of relations that is apparent in the visible world and is itself perceptible in speech and writing. The controversy centers on two questions regarding origins or foundations. Does the invisible structure of language reflect organization perceived in the world or does it constitute that nexus of relations? The second question challenges the legitimacy of asking the first: is it possible to separate perception from language in such a way that one could even ask about the primacy of one with respect to the other? Merleau-Ponty regards language as flesh, akin to the flesh of the body in its reflexivity, its relatedness to itself and world, but "less heavy, more transparent." In general, the structure of the visible-invisible relation can be defined as asymmetrical reversibility: just as the object I touch can be seen (although its tactile aspect remains invisible as such), so can the hidden or horizonal aspects of a given theme be brought into focal vision, but only through the loss of their horizonality.

[See also Heidegger, Martin; Husserl, Edmund; Perception; Phenomenology; Rationality.]

BIBLIOGRAPHY

Works by Merleau-Ponty

Les Aventures de la dialectique. Paris, 1955. Translated by J. Bien as *Adventures of the Dialectic.* Evanston, IL, 1973.

Les Philosophes célèbres. Paris, 1956.

Le Visible et l'invisible. Edited by C. Lefort. Paris, 1964. Translated by A. Lingis as *The Visible and the Invisible.* Evanston, IL, 1968.

Résumés de cours, Collège de France, 1952–1960. Paris, 1968. Translated by J. O'Neill as *Themes from the Lectures at the Collège de France, 1952–1960.* Evanston, IL, 1970.

La Prose du monde. Paris, 1969. Translated by J. O'Neill as *The Prose of the World.* Evanston, IL, 1973.

Existence et dialectique. Paris, 1971.

Consciousness and the Acquisition of Language. Translated by H. J. Silverman. Evanston, IL, 1973.

Texts and Dialogues. Edited by H. J. Silverman and J. Barry, Jr. Atlantic Highlands, NJ, 1991.

Works on Merleau-Ponty

Burke, P., and J. Van der Vecken, eds. *Merleau-Ponty in Contemporary Perspective.* Dordrecht, 1993.

Busch, T., and S. Gallagher, eds. *Merleau-Ponty, Hermeneutics, and Postmodernism.* Albany, NY, 1992.

Casey, E. S. "Habitual Body and Memory in Merleau-Ponty." *Man and World,* Vol. 1 (1984), 279–98.

Dillon, M. C. *Merleau-Ponty's Ontology.* Bloomington, IN, 1988.

———, ed. *Merleau-Ponty Vivant.* Albany, NY, 1991.

Johnson, G. *The Merleau-Ponty Aesthetics Reader.* Evanston, IL, 1993.

Johnson, G., and M. Smith, eds. *Ontology and Alterity in Merleau-Ponty.* Evanston, IL, 1990.

Langer, M. M. *Merleau-Ponty's Phenomenology of Perception: A Guide and Commentary.* Tallahassee, 1989.

Madison, G. B. *The Phenomenology of Merleau-Ponty.* Athens, OH, 1981.

Pietersma, H., ed. *Merleau-Ponty: Critical Essays.* Lanham, MD, 1989.

Silverman, H. J. *Inscriptions: Between Phenomenology and Structuralism.* New York, 1987.

Watson, S. "Language, Perception, and the Cogito in Merleau-Ponty's Thought," in John Sallis, ed., *Merleau-Ponty: Perception, Structure, Language* (Atlantic Highlands, NJ, 1981).

— MARTIN C. DILLON

MERLEAU-PONTY, MAURICE: PHILOSOPHY OF PSYCHOLOGY

From the earliest of his writing until the last, Merleau-Ponty maintained the thesis of the irreducibility of the figure-ground or theme-horizon structure articulated by gestalt theory. This thesis holds that perception and cognition are fundamentally relational, hence stand in opposition to such standpoints as that of sense-data theory based on the notions of perceptual atoms, elemental simples, or discrete qualia.

In his *Phénoménologie de la perception,* Merleau-Ponty offers an extended case study of Schneider, a World War I soldier debilitated by a shrapnel wound in the occipital region of his brain. The point of the study is to demonstrate the inadequacy of the standpoints of empiricism or physicalism, on the one hand, and intellectualism or transcendentalism, on the other, to provide an accurate description of Schneider's afflictions, which are neither purely physiological nor purely intentional but involve a degeneration of the lived body resulting in aberrant forms of substitution behavior in such domains as sexual responsiveness, existential spatiality, motility, expression, and memory.

Merleau-Ponty is unique among phenomenologists in reinterpreting Freudian notions regarding the unconscious in a positive way and reintegrating them within his own body of theory.

Merleau-Ponty is unique among phenomenologists in reinterpreting Freudian notions regarding the unconscious in a positive way and integrating them within his own body of theory. This appropriation involved some modification, to be sure, specifically that of asserting a continuity between conscious and unconscious aspects of human experience at the level of prereflective horizonality. Merleau-Ponty steers a middle course between Freud's relatively mechanistic account of such phenomena as repression, which attributes it to an autonomous function of censorship and dissemblance, and Jean-Paul Sartre's relatively voluntaristic account, which attributes repression to an act of self-deception on the part of a consciousness recoiling from the implications of its own freedom. Merleau-Ponty interprets behavior traditionally subsumed under the heading of repression in terms of a process of habituation operating at prepersonal or unreflective levels in which the body's response to worldly events becomes sedimented as a style of contending with a domain of existence permeated with negative significance. Thus, the aphonia and anorexia of a girl whose family has forbidden her to see her lover is understood, neither as a reversion to an infantile phase of oral sexuality, as Freud would have it, nor as a recoil from responsibility in the mode of magical transformation, as Sartre would have it, but as a refusal of coexistence, a withdrawal from the communal world of eating and talking, which acquires the autonomy of a habit exacerbated by former habitualities favoring oral modes of responding to the world.

In addition to his interests in gestalt psychology and Freudian psychoanalysis, Merleau-Ponty was also well acquainted with the work done by his sometime colleague Jean Piaget in developmental psychology and the work of Jacques Lacan, a contemporary known for his reinterpretation of Freudian themes along semiological lines. There are frequent references to Piaget in *La Structure du comportement* and *Phénoménologie de la perception*, and an extended response to Lacan's seminal thinking on the mirror stage in a late essay entitled "Les Relations avec autrui chez l'enfant." Perhaps Merleau-Ponty's greatest contribution to psychological theory lies in his articulation of an ontological framework capable of consolidating the findings of thinkers across the full spectrum of ideologies from eidetic analysis to experimental and behavioral research: he unremittingly refused to endorse the radical distinctions between the a priori and the a posteriori, between transcendental and empirical approaches, which have functioned to isolate the various schools through polarized opposition.

[See also Freud, Sigmund; Perception; Physicalism; Qualia; Sartre, Jean-Paul.]

BIBLIOGRAPHY

Works by Merleau-Ponty

"Les Relations avec autrui chez l'enfant," in *Les Cours de Sorbonne* (Paris, 1960). Translated by W. Cobb as "The Child's Relations with Others," in J. M. Edie, ed., *The Primacy of Perception* (Evanston, IL, 1964).

"Phenomenology and Psychoanalysis: Preface to Hesnard's *L'Oeuvre de Freud*," trans. A. L. Fisher, *Review of Existential Psychology and Psychiatry*, Vol. 18 (1982–83), 67–72.

Works on Merleau-Ponty

Dillon, M. C. "Merleau-Ponty and the Psychogenesis of the Self," *Journal of Phenomenological Psychology*, Vol. 9 (1978), 84–98.

———. "The Implications of Merleau-Ponty's Thought for the Practice of Psychotherapy," in Kah Kyung Cho, ed., *Philosophy and Science in Phenomenological Perspective* (The Hague, 1984).

Giorgi, A. *Psychology as a Human Science*. New York, 1970.

Kockelmans, J. J. "Merleau-Ponty on Sexuality," *Journal of Existentialism*, Vol. 6 (1965), 9–30.

———. "The Function of Psychology in Merleau-Ponty's Early Works," *Review of Existential Psychology and Psychiatry*, Vol. 18 (1982–83), 119–42.

Krell, D. F. "M. Merleau-Ponty on 'Eros' and 'Logos,'" *Man and World*, Vol. 7 (1974), 37–51.

Levin, D. M. "Eros and Psyche: A Reading of Merleau-Ponty," *Review of Existential Psychology and Psychiatry*, Vol. 18 (1982–83), 219–39.

Lingis, A. *Libido: The French Existentialist Theories*. Bloomington, IN, 1985.

O'Connor, T. "Behaviour and Perception: A Discussion of Merleau-Ponty's Problem of Operative Intentionality," *Human Context*, Vol. 7 (1975), 32–48.

Olkowski, D. "Merleau-Ponty's Freudianism: From the Body of Consciousness to the Body of Flesh," *Review of Existential Psychology and Psychiatry*, Vol. 18 (1982–83), 97–116.

O'Neill, J. "The Specular Body: Merleau-Ponty and Lacan on Infant Self and Other," *Synthese*, Vol. 66 (1986), 201–17.

Pontalis, J. B. "The Problem of the Unconscious in Merleau-Ponty's Thought," trans. W. Ver Eecke and M. Greer, *Review of Existential Psychology and Psychiatry*, Vol. 18 (1982–83), 83–96.

– MARTIN C. DILLON

MERLEAU-PONTY, MAURICE: POLITICAL THEORY

Merleau-Ponty engaged with both liberalism and Marxism as he sought a political theory that could support concrete human freedom. Because human beings are embodied and situated subjects, he argued that freedom can arise only in engagement with an already given world. This world includes residues of prior human action "sedimented" in such social institutions as language, class, and political organizations. Freedom is an ambiguous venture. For although rooted in the given world, it always outstrips our ability to know opening onto an unpredictable and contingent future. Particularly in the world of politics, where power is at issue and multiple projects always intersect, good intentions may thus give rise to unintended, often violent, consequences. However, Merleau-Ponty insisted, political actors must always bear responsibility for such unintended consequences, otherwise all checks on violence would cease.

Immediately after World War II, Merleau-Ponty was particularly critical of liberalism, which, he argued, used abstract principles of freedom to justify capitalist exploitation and the violence of colonial rule.

Such views led Merleau-Ponty to be critical of traditional normative political theory, which attempts to develop universal principles and erroneously posits the theorist as standing "nowhere," a surveying, disembodied consciousness. Worse, pursuing normative principles without regard for their actual consequences can function ideologically to legitimize violence. Immediately after World War II Merleau-Ponty was particularly critical of liberalism, which, he argued, used abstract principles of freedom to justify capitalist exploitation and the violence of colonial rule. Instead, Merleau-Ponty turned to Marx for a theory of human "existence and coexistence" that resonated with his own commitment to a concrete humanism.

In the late 1940s Merleau-Ponty offered "critical support" to communist movements. But at the same time he also argued that twentieth-century "orthodox" forms of Marxism (i.e., Soviet and Communist Party Marxism) were dangerously abstract. Their claims about the universal and indubitable logic of history, much like liberalism's abstract universal principles, served to justify a disregard for actual consequences and a willingness to sacrifice human lives and well-being for abstract truths—as evidenced in Stalinist terror.

By the mid-1950s Merleau-Ponty ceased privileging Marxism, arguing that the objective and subjective aspects of the Marxian dialectic had come asunder, with crude objectivism dominating in Soviet-style Communism and subjectivism in a theory such as Sartre's. Instead, he argued for a "heroic liberalism," one that would realize that its own principles were relative and that would permit their contestation by opposing forces.

Some commentators have suggested that Merleau-Ponty's critique of universal principles and historical logic anticipated the work of later poststructuralist critics of Western thought. However, unlike such later thinkers, Merleau-Ponty eschewed extreme relativism, arguing that certain general values do continuously emerge from human existence. Since we all share the experience of embodiment and since our subjectivities and freedom are intrinsically interconnected, our own freedom demands a politics of mutual respect for the freedom of others. Thus, in both his existential Marxism of the 1940s and his heroic liberalism of the 1950s, Merleau-Ponty called for a politics that would allow space for otherness and ambiguity and would facilitate plurality rather than oneness.

[See also Liberalism; Marx, Karl; Marxism; Moral Relativism; Violence.]

BIBLIOGRAPHY

Works by Merleau-Ponty

Les Aventures de la dialectique. Paris, 1955. Translated by J. Bien as Adventures of the Dialectic. Evanston, IL, 1973.

Humanisme et terreur. Paris, 1947. Translated by J. O'Neill as Humanism and Terror. Boston, 1969.

Sens et non-sens. Paris, 1948. Translated by H. L. Dreyfus and P. A. Dreyfus as Sense and Non-Sense. Evanston, IL, 1964.

Signes. Paris, 1960. Translated by R. McCleary as Signs. Evanston, IL, 1964.

Works on Merleau-Ponty

Cooper, B. Merleau-Ponty and Marxism: From Terror to Reform. Toronto, 1979.

Kruks, S. The Political Philosophy of Merleau-Ponty. Atlantic Highlands, NJ, 1980.

Whiteside, K. H. Merleau-Ponty and the Foundation of an Existential Politics. Princeton, NJ, 1988.

    — SONIA KRUKS

METAPHOR

Metaphors have an emotive force and aesthetic dimension that have long been recognized. What has made metaphor so compelling to contemporary philosophers, however, has been its importance to cognition. Aesthetics and philosophy of religion are no longer the sole province of the study of metaphor. Instead, most of the research is located in philosophy of language, philosophy of science, and cognitive science. The ubiquity of metaphor and its contribution to all forms of discourse, the apparent anomaly of metaphor in light of standard accounts of language, and the increased interest by philosophers to provide theories for natural (rather than formal or artificial) languages have made an account of metaphor an important criterion of adequacy for theories of language. The limits of literality have similarly been felt in accounts of science and cognition. Max Black's (1962) seminal work connecting the use of scientific models to metaphors opened an area of inquiry now pursued by psychologists and cognitive scientists as well as philosophers of science. Some philosophers join questions of the role of metaphor in science to debates concerning scientific realism (Boyd, 1979; Hesse, 1970). The work emanating from theories of language and theories of science and cognition converge in concerns about meaning change, computer modeling of discovery processes, linguistic competencies, creativity, and religious discourse (Soskice, 1985).

While many questions remain, a few issues have been settled. The view of metaphor as an isolated word or phrase that is an occasional, unsystematic, and deviant phenomenon in language valued for its rhetorical force but disdained for its ability to mislead or be used in place of proper argument has been challenged. Metaphors have come to be understood as syntactically complex (Black, 1962; Tirrell, 1991) attributions that may or may not be grammatically deviant (Stern, 1985). In the tradition of I. A. Richards (1936) and Black, metaphors are generally taken to implicate entire conceptual domains or semantic fields (Kittay, 1987) through which a metaphor is interpreted, extended, and even systematically integrated into the language (Lakoff & Johnson, 1980). They either exploit some similarity between the metaphorically used term (the vehicle or source) and the concept spoken of (the topic or target) or create or intimate a similarity. While the similarity appealed to in earlier discussions pertained to intrinsic properties or properties associated with vehicle and topic, similarity has increasingly come to mean a relational or structural similarity—akin to models and analogies—between the contexts or domains (Black, 1962; Goodman, 1968) implicated in the metaphor.

While earlier debates concerned metaphor's cognitive value, current debates accept its cognitive function and ask if this function is properly assigned to metaphoric meaning and whether it is a distinctive form of cognition not reducible to other forms such as the capacity to recognize similarity and make comparisons. The outcome of the debate is important to the nature of language, of thought, and of epistemic enterprises such as science. If metaphors have meaning, then a theory of language must explain how such meaning is determined, and any account of mind in which linguistic capacity plays a central role for cognition must similarly explain how cognitive faculties make use of, and make possible, metaphorical thought. Similarly, if the use of metaphorical language in knowledge domains such as science is not reducible to literal language, then we need metaphor in order to understand and explain what is knowable. Furthermore, if we need metaphor to access scientific knowledge, as well as for aesthetic or evocative purposes, then the domains such as art and religion may be more akin to science—or related in more interesting ways—than we have presumed (Fleischacker, 1994). But if metaphors perform their cognitive function without generating a distinctive meaning, then theories of language that are based on literal language suffice; metaphoric contributions to cognition are assimilable to other, already understood or accepted cognitive abilities; the cognitive role of metaphor would be valuable only as heuristic (although, in the case of combinatorially complex problems, the heuristic contribution of metaphor itself may be irreplaceable), and we maintain a clear delineation between the scientific and the poetic.

What has made metaphor

so compelling to contemporary philosophers

has been its importance to cognition.

The position propounding metaphoric meaning and the cognitive irreducibility of metaphor was staked out by Black and has been buttressed by arguments and evidence gathered by philosophers of science, cognitive psychologists, philosophers of language, and linguists. However, the parsimony of the opposing position, and its elegant articulation by Donald Davidson (1978), continues to make it attractive, despite the counterintuitive claim that metaphors have no meaning and the weighty evidence of metaphor's importance in all cognitive endeavors.

Philosophers claiming that metaphors have meaning generally begin by accepting some version of the inter-

action theory of metaphor but have utilized the resources of many different semantic theories (e.g., possible-world semantics [Bergman, 1982; Hintikka & Sandu, 1994], semantic-field theory [Kittay, 1987], cognitive semantics [Gibbs, 1994; Lakoff & Johnson, 1980; Sweetser, 1990], a componential semantics [Levin, 1977], a Wittgensteinian semantic, and David Kaplan's semantics for demonstratives [Stern, 1985]). Some use speech-act theory, claiming that metaphors are a feature of speaker meaning rather than sentence meaning (Searle, 1981) or that metaphors are, in the end, elliptical similes after all (Fogelin, 1988).

Newer comparison theories, versions of the theory that metaphors are elliptic similes or implicit comparisons and so do not have a distinctive meaning, explore the notion of figurative rather than literal similarity (Glucks & Keysar, 1990; Ortony, 1979). Some of these theories offer a causal theory, opposing it to a semantic theory, claiming that metaphors cause us to make comparison by "intimating similarities" and have a causal effect of creating intimacy among speaker and listener (Cohen, 1978; Cooper, 1986). Questions remain concerning the relation between metaphor and literal language (e.g., Can the distinction be drawn in a clear fashion? Is the interpretative process the same or different? Is language originally metaphorical or literal?) and other nonliteral languages (see Hintikka & Sandu, 1994; Jakobson, 1960).

The importance of metaphor in science was stressed by Mary Hesse (1970), who developed the understandings of metaphors as systematic analogies in which the "neutral"—that is, unexplored analogical relations—provide a distinctive source for predictive claims. Dedre Gentner (1982), a cognitive psychologist, along with her associates has identified features, such as systematicity and higher-order relations, that make some metaphors more productive for cognitive purposes than others.

Noting the affinity between metaphor and analogy has permitted a number of researchers in philosophy and psychology to make headway with computational approaches to metaphor—a promising tool for testing theories of metaphor and for understanding the extent to which accounts of metaphor are amenable to formal and precise accounts (Holyoak & Thagard, 1989; Steinhart & Kittay, 1994). Making use of advances in our understanding of metaphor, theorists have explored the role of metaphor in creativity, in language acquisition and concept formation, and in both the consolidation and the breakdown of habituated patterns of thought such as cultural prejudice. These latter developments (which have especially been taken up by feminist philosophers and other social critics) bring the question of the cognitive role of metaphor full circle, reconnecting it to its rhetorical force.

[See also Aesthetics; Cognitive Science; Davidson, Donald; Goodman, Nelson; Philosophy of Language; Philosophy of Religion; Philosophy of Science.]

BIBLIOGRAPHY

Bergman, M. "Metaphorical Assertions," *Philosophical Review,* Vol. 91 (1982), 229–45.

Black, M., ed. *Models and Metaphors.* Ithaca, NY, 1962.

Boyd, R. "Metaphor and Theory Change: What Is 'Metaphor' a Metaphor For?" in A. Ortomy, ed., *Metaphor and Thought* (Cambridge, 1979).

Cohen, T. "Metaphor and the Cultivation of Intimacy," *Critical Inquiry,* Vol. 5 (1978), 3–12.

Cooper, D. *Metaphor.* Oxford, 1986.

Davidson, D. "What Metaphors Mean," in S. Sacks, ed., *On Metaphor* (Chicago, 1978).

Fleischacker, S. "Frustrated Contracts, Poetry, and Truth," *Raritan,* Vol. 13, No. 4 (Spring 1994), 47–70.

Fogelin, R. *Figuratively Speaking.* New Haven, 1988.

Gentner, D. "Are Scientific Analogies Metaphors?" in D. S. Maill, ed., *Metaphor: Problems and Perspectives* (New York, 1982).

Gibbs, R. *The Poetics of Mind: Figurative Thought, Language, and Understanding.* Cambridge, 1994.

Goodman, N. *Languages of Art.* Indianapolis, 1968.

Glucksberg, S., and B. Keysar. "Understanding Metaphorical Comparisons: Beyond Similarity," *Psychological Review,* Vol. 97 (1990), 3–18.

Hesse, M. *Models and Analogies in Science.* Notre Dame, IN, 1970.

Hintikka, J., and G. Sandu. "Metaphor and Other Kinds of Nonliteral Language," in J. Hintikka, ed., *Aspects of Metaphor* (Dordrecht, 1994).

Holyoak, K. J., and P. Thagard. "Analogical Mapping by Constraint Satisfaction," *Cognitive Science,* Vol. 13 (1989), 295–355.

Jakobson, R. "Closing Statement: Linguistics and Poetry," in T. A. Sebeok, ed., *Style in Language* (Cambridge, MA, 1960).

Kittay, E. F. *Metaphor: Its Cognitive Force and Linguistic Structure.* Oxford, 1987.

Lakoff, G., and M. Johnson. *Metaphors We Live By.* Chicago, 1980.

Levin, S. R. *The Semantics of Metaphor.* Baltimore, 1977.

Ortony, A. "The Role of Similarity in Similes and Metaphors," in A. Ortony, ed., *Metaphor and Thought* (Cambridge, 1979).

Richards, I. A. *The Philosophy of Rhetoric.* Oxford, 1936.

Searle, J. "Metaphor," in M. Johnson, ed., *Philosophical Perspectives on Metaphor* (Minneapolis, 1981).

Soskice, J. M. *Metaphor and Religious Language.* Oxford, 1985.

Steinhart, E., and E. F. Kittay. "Generating Metaphors from Networks: A Formal Interpretation of the Semantic Field Theory of Metaphor," in J. Hintikka, ed., *Aspects of Metaphor* (Dordrecht, 1994).

Stern, J. "Metaphor as Demonstrative," *Journal of Philosophy,* Vol. 82 (1985), 677–710.

Sweetser, E. *From Etymology to Pragmatics: The Body-Mind Metaphor in Semantic Structure and Semantic.* Cambridge, 1990.

Tirrell, L. "Reductive and Nonreductive Simile Theories of Metaphor," *Journal of Philosophy,* Vol. 88 (1991), 337–58.

— EVA F. KITTAY

METAPHYSICS

The period since 1960 has featured a great deal of work on issues in metaphysics. Much of this work is best considered under more specific headings such as philosophy of mind, action theory, philosophy of language, philosophy of mathematics, philosophy of science, and metaethics. Hence, such vital topics as the mind–body problem, personal identity, personal freedom, the theory of truth, the nature of mathematical truth and existence, determinism, causation, the nature of theoretical entities, and the existence and nature of moral facts will be set aside. Furthermore, limitations of space exclude consideration of several other important topics such as the debate between realists and antirealists.

The period under review has included a number of surprising developments in metaphysics. The most general and important is the restoration of metaphysics itself to its historically central position in philosophy. It is no exaggeration to say that 'metaphysics' was a term of derision for most of the first half of the century and that even in 1960 metaphysics was often either regarded as nonsense or viewed with great suspicion. By 1990 this legacy of positivism had largely disappeared. One reason is that a number of philosophers produced work that undeniably was metaphysics but, just as undeniably, was meaningful, lucid, rigorous, and important. Three closely related and central topics arguably constitute the most significant development in metaphysics since 1960.

Perhaps the most striking of the three is the rehabilitation of Aristotelian essentialism, initiated prominently by Ruth Barcan Marcus and Saul Kripke. The doctrine of essentialism holds that some things have nontrivial essential (or necessary) properties—that they could not exist without having those properties. For example, an essentialist might hold that any specific dog is necessarily a mammal. It is important to distinguish this from the claim that it is necessary that all dogs are mammals. For that claim could still be true even if all the actual dogs had been ducks and hence not mammals. Since in that circumstance they would not be dogs, their nonmammality would not threaten the necessity of all dogs' being mammals. The existence of such nontrivial essential properties would apparently undercut the common assumption that knowledge of necessity cannot be empirical. The effort to rehabilitate essentialism was resisted by many, notably and influentially by Willard Van Orman Quine.

The discussion of essentialism was part of a surge of interest in all aspects of modality, including purely logical and semantic topics as well as philosophical. Quine's suspicions about essentialism partly reflected a more general worry that the very concept of necessity was hopelessly obscure, and much effort was expended in trying to provide the concept with clear philosophical foundations. Many hoped to achieve this by appealing to the Leibnizian notion of possible worlds. Some sought to analyze necessity (roughly, as truth in all possible worlds). Others attempted no analysis but hoped nevertheless to illuminate the notion by appealing to worlds. Several ontologically different conceptions of possible worlds emerged. These included: worlds as (at least partly) concrete entities, like our own universe: worlds as idealized linguistic or quasi-linguistic entities; worlds as special states of affairs or propositions; and worlds as mere metaphor. Key contributors to the foundational discussion included Robert Merrihew Adams, Roderick Chisholm, Kit Fine, David Kaplan, David Lewis, Alvin Plantinga, Arthur N. Prior, and Peter van Inwagen (in addition to Kripke, Marcus, and Quine).

Many philosophers, notably Jaakko Hintikka and Robert Stalnaker, used possible worlds in treating a variety of other topics. Examples include the semantics of counterfactual conditionals and the analysis of dispositionality, theories of propositional attitudes, especially belief, and even the analysis of such notions as rationality and obligation. Although possible worlds became widely accepted, partly as a result of their seeming success in these sorts of projects, a fair amount of skepticism has persisted, even among those who do not find the notion of necessity obscure.

The surge of interest in modality may be seen as reflecting the decline of a certain metaphysical and methodological dogma that was another legacy of positivism. In its metaphysical aspect the dogma asserts the obscurity of intensional notions as compared with extensional. Methodologically, it counsels us to work as much as possible in strictly extensional terms. Modality was a prime target of the dogma because it did not seem clearly amenable to a fully extensional treatment. (For example, it has been claimed that the substitution of coreferential expressions in modal contexts does not always preserve truth value.)

Significant developments in metaphysics include revivals of Aristotle's essentialism and Plato's theories of properties. (Corbis/Ted Spiegel)

But another main target of the dogma is intensional entities—for example, properties. They are intensional in the sense that distinct properties may have the same 'extension', that is, exactly the same instances. This is in sharp contrast with sets, no two of which may have just the same members. So, champions of the dogma of extensionalism, in particular Quine, urged that if abstract entities are to be tolerated at all, sets should be preferred over properties. The period witnessed a good deal of ingenious work in which various notions were held to be reducible to set-theoretic constructions. But the growing respectability of modality loosened the grip of extensionalism. This made the philosophical world safe for a revival of Platonism, especially concerning properties, relations, and propositions. Of course, Platonism was never really dead. Many leading philosophers—for example, Chisholm—did not embrace nominalism or even extensionalism. The revival consisted in a new willingness of many nominalists to take a fresh look at Platonistic positions, and in the emergence of defenses of properties (Putnam, 1970) and theories of properties (Bealer, 1982). Property theories quickly found promising applications in such areas as natural-language semantics.

> *The most important development concerning metaphysics since 1960 has been its restoration to its historically central position in philosophy.*

The decline of extensionalism has also had significant effects in other areas of metaphysics. (For example, it seems indirectly implicated in a revived interest in mind–body dualism.) But extensionalism still has able defenders—an obituary is premature.

[See also Action Theory; Causation; Chisholm, Roderick M.; Colors; Conditionals; Constructivism, Conventionalism; Determinism and Freedom; Event Theory; Extrinsic and Intrinsic Properties; Identity; Kripke, Saul Aaron; Marcus, Ruth Barcan; Mereology; Modality; Nonexistent Object, Nonbeing; Persistence; Personal Identity; Philosophy of Language; Philosophy of Mind; Philosophy of Science; Plato; Platonism, Mathematical; Prior, Arthur N.; Projectivism; Properties; Putnam, Hilary; Quine, Willard Van Orman; Time, Being, and Becoming; Truth.]

BIBLIOGRAPHY

Bealer, G. *Quality and Concept.* Oxford, 1982.

French, P. A., T. E. Uehling, Jr., and H. K. Wettstein, eds. *Studies in Essentialism,* Midwest Studies in Philosophy, Vol. 11. Minneapolis, 1986.

Kripke, S. A. *Naming and Necessity.* Cambridge, MA, 1972.

Lewis, D. *On the Plurality of Worlds.* Oxford, 1986.

Marcus, R. B. *Modalities.* Oxford, 1993.

Putnam, H. "On Properties," in N. Rescher, ed., *Essays in Honor of Carl G. Hempel* (Dordrecht, 1970).

Quine, W. V. O. *Word and Object.* Cambridge, MA, 1960.

— MICHAEL JUBIEN

MILL, JOHN STUART

John Stuart Mill (1806–1873), English philosopher, economist, and administrator, was the most influential philosopher in the English-speaking world during the nineteenth century and is generally held to be one of the most profound and effective spokesmen for the liberal view of man and society. In the belief that men's opinions are the dominant influence on social and historical change, Mill tried to construct and to propagate a philosophical position which would be of positive assistance to the progress of scientific knowledge, individual freedom, and human happiness. Despite numerous flaws in his theories, he succeeded in providing an alternative to existing views on morals and politics and their foundations which was both specific and cohesive enough to give a markedly liberal tendency to social and political opinion, and also sufficiently tolerant and inclusive to gain it access to an extraordinarily large and diverse public. Mill cannot be ranked among the greatest of pure philosophers, either for his originality or for his synthesizing power. His work in logic, however, broke new ground and gave a badly needed impetus to the study of the subject, while his reformulations of classical British empiricism and Benthamite utilitarianism gave these positions a relevance and continuing vitality which they would not otherwise have had.

Although Mill's views on economics will not be discussed in the present article, an excellent summary of them is contained in the article on Mill by F. Y. Edgeworth in Palgrave's *Dictionary of Political Economy.*

LIFE. John Stuart Mill was born in London, the son of James and Harriet Burrow Mill. Outwardly his life was not eventful. He was educated by his father and never attended school, although for a short time he read law with John Austin. In 1823 he became a clerk in the East India Company, where his father was a high official, and worked there until 1858. Eventually he became chief of his department, a post involving considerable administrative responsibility. In 1831 he was introduced to Harriet Taylor, the wife of a successful merchant and mother of several children. Friendship between Mill and Mrs. Taylor rapidly developed into deep though Platonic love, and for the next twenty years they saw each other constantly, despite the increasing social isolation this involved. Mill was convinced that

Mrs. Taylor was a great genius: he discussed all of his work with her and attributed to her an enormous influence on his thought. Her husband died in 1849, and three years later she married Mill. In 1858, while the Mills were on a tour of France, Harriet died in Avignon. Mill bought a house nearby so that he could always be near her grave.

In 1857 Mill had written a brilliant defense of the East India Company for the parliamentary debate on renewal of the company's charter. When renewal was not granted, Mill retired, refusing an offer of a position in the government as an official for Indian affairs. In 1865 he was invited to stand for election to Parliament as an independent member for Westminster. He accepted, and although he refused to campaign, contribute to expenses, or defend his views, he won, and served until the next election, in 1868, when he was defeated. Thereafter he spent his time alternately in London and in Avignon, admired and sought after by many, accessible to few. He died after a very brief illness, attended by his wife's daughter Helen, who had looked after him since her mother's death.

Education and Philosophical Radicalism. Until 1826 Mill's thought was completely controlled by his father. James Mill gave him one of the most formidable educations on record, starting him on Greek at the age of three and Latin at eight. By the age of fourteen he had read most of the major Greek and Latin classics, had made a wide survey of history, and had done intensive work in logic and mathematics. He had also been prepared for acceptance of the central tenets of philosophical radicalism, a set of economic, political, and philosophical views shared by the group of reformers who regarded Jeremy Bentham and James Mill as their intellectual leaders. When at the age of fifteen Mill read Bentham's *Traité de législation,* it had the effect on him of a religious revelation. It crystallized his thoughts and fixed his aim in life—to be a reformer of the world. Guided by his father, he threw himself into the work of the radicals; he edited Bentham's manuscripts, conducted a discussion group, wrote letters to the press and articles critical of laws, judicial decisions, and parliamentary debates and actions.

Depression and Change of Views. Late in 1826, Mill suffered a sudden attack of intense depression, which lasted for many months. The attack led him to reconsider the doctrines in which he had been raised and to seek other than Benthamite sources of thought. He believed that his capacity for emotion had been unduly weakened by strenuous training in analytic thought, with the result that he could no longer care for anything at all. In the poetry of Wordsworth he found something of a cure—an education of the feelings that helped to

Although Mill cannot be ranked among the greatest of pure philosophers, his work in logic broke new ground and provided badly needed impetus to the study of the subject. (Corbis)

balance the education of intellect given to him by his father. In 1828 he met Gustave d'Eichthal, a French follower of Saint-Simon, who sent him an early essay by Auguste Comte and a great deal of Saint-Simonian literature. He also met John Sterling, a disciple of Coleridge. Mill came to admire both the Saint-Simonians and the Coleridgeans, and he attempted to incorporate into his own thinking what he took to be sound in their doctrines. In 1829 he published nothing at all, but by the following year he had reached a philosophical position that seemed to him far more adequate than the older Benthamism. He never again changed his philosophical views so radically.

Comte and Saint-Simon. The historical standpoint of the Saint-Simonians, as well as the appreciation of the value of old institutions emphasized by Coleridge, impressed Mill as important additions to Benthamism, which, he thought, simply neglected such factors. He accepted the outlines of the Saint-Simonian–Comtian philosophy of history, and particularly its theory that in social change there is an alternation between "critical" periods, in which society destroys outmoded forms of life and tends toward disintegration, and "organic" periods, in which new forms of common life are evolved and social cohesion is re-established. He agreed also with the French view that in his own times society had come to the end of a critical period. From Coleridge he learned to think of the cultured class as the leader of opinion in a nation. He also came to believe that the problem he had in common with other intellectuals was that of assisting the world, and especially England, to emerge from the critical period and progress toward a new organic period. Unless this was done, he thought, the tendency toward disintegration might possibly grow too strong to be controlled.

The most influential philosopher

in the English-speaking world during

the nineteenth century, Mill is generally held

to be one of the most profound

and effective spokesmen for the liberal view

of man and society.

Three important consequences followed from this. First, merely negative remarks upon institutions, laws, and political arrangements were no longer sufficient. Although much remained that needed to be changed, it was necessary now to replace what had been destroyed with something better. Second, the views of those who defended the old and outmoded could no longer be dismissed, in Benthamite fashion, as mere lies used in defense of vested interests. What is now outmoded must, at one stage of historical development, have served a valuable purpose; otherwise it could not have survived. Those who defend it are those who see the good still in it; hence we must seek for the truth in their views, and not merely reject the falsity. The particular vice plaguing social thought is not the tendency to make mistakes of fact or faulty inferences from facts, but the great ease with which data can be overlooked: in a word, one-sidedness. Hence, if we are to obtain sound social views, our greatest need is for a complete survey of data, and this is possible to achieve only if we can appreciate the truth that our opponents have learned. For each man is naturally one-sided and can overcome this only by education and effort. Third, the tactics of a reformer must be adapted to the period in which he lives. In particular, during a critical period there is no point in promulgating an entire system: no one will listen, and the ideas will not serve to improve social cohesion. One must proceed cautiously, piecemeal, educating one's public as one goes. One must—especially in England, Mill held, where any appearance of system is abhorrent—confine oneself to particular issues, only slowly insinuating more general principles; or else work only from points on which there is general agreement, so as to avoid any shocking appearance of novelty.

This set of views dictated the program that Mill followed for the next twenty or more years. He did not abandon his early epistemology or ethical beliefs, but in developing them he always tried to emphasize their inclusiveness and their constructive power, rather than their critical and destructive powers. He refrained (with one major exception) from publishing a systematic account of his ideas, but wrote instead occasional essays dealing with fairly specific issues, in which he always tried to bring out the value of the books he was criticizing. (These tactics are largely responsible for the common view of Mill as a wavering, halfhearted, muddled thinker, appreciative of what others had to say but holding no clear opinions of his own.) He defended what he held to be sound views on philosophy, but he did not explicitly link these views together, except in his *System of Logic*, which was an entirely different case. Methods of investigation, Mill held, could be relatively neutral as regards political and moral opinion. Since these methods could be discovered from analysis of subjects like physical science, in which there was widespread agreement on results, there was a good chance of obtaining general agreement on the methods. The methods could thus serve as a cohesive, rather than a disruptive, social force.

THE *SYSTEM OF LOGIC*. Mill's *Logic* is in fact by no means neutral with regard to substantive issues. It is the first major installment of his comprehensive restatement of an empiricist and utilitarian position. It presents (sometimes, to be sure, only as "illustration") a fairly complete outline of what would now be called an "empiricist" epistemology, although Mill himself used "empiricist" in a deprecatory sense to mean "miscellaneous information," as contrasted with "scientific knowledge." It begins the attack on "intuitionism" which Mill carried on throughout his life, and it makes plain his belief that social planning and political action should rely primarily on scientific knowledge, not on authority, custom, revelation, or prescription. The *Logic* had a rapid and wide success. Adopted as a text first at Oxford and eventually at Cambridge, it was also read by many outside the universities, including workmen.

Its success can be explained in part by its enormous superiority to any book then existing in the field, but credit must also be given to its clear and unmistakable relevance to social problems (and to religious questions: it was attacked as atheistic by some of its earliest reviewers).

With the publication of the *Logic,* Mill took a major step toward showing that the philosophy of experience, which had hitherto been identified primarily as a skeptical position, could offer at least as much in the way of constructive thinking as any other kind of view. His treatment of deductive inference was far more sympathetic to formal logic than that of previous empiricists; and by arguing that, with care, certainty could be attained even in inductive reasoning, he made it plain that empiricism was not committed to a Humean standpoint. Mill held that the philosophy of experience was more likely than any other to encourage the development of society along liberal lines. He therefore held that it was a matter of considerable importance to show that empiricism was a viable alternative to the less progressive views—notably, Scottish common-sense philosophy and German idealism—which were then dominant. The *Logic* succeeded in doing this.

The *Logic* is primarily a discussion of inferential knowledge and of the rules of inference. (The discussion of noninferential, or as Mill also called it, immediate or intuitive, knowledge belongs, in Mill's view, to metaphysics.) It contains six books. In the first two, Mill presented an empiricist theory of deductive inference, and, since mathematics is the chief deductive science, a discussion of the nature of the truth of mathematics, especially of its axioms. In Book III, Mill discussed induction, its grounds, its methods, and its results. Book IV, entitled "Of Operations Subsidiary to Induction," contains chapters on observation and description, abstraction, naming, and classification. Book V is a discussion of fallacies. Book VI contains Mill's attempt to extend the methods of the physical sciences, as derived in Book III, to what were then called "moral sciences," that is, psychology and sociology. He argued for the possibility of a science of human nature and action, and assessed the value of the various methods for attaining it. He concluded with a chapter on the logic of morality, discussing primarily the relation between rules for actions and the factual statements which serve as their foundations.

No adequate summary of the contents of the *Logic* can be given here, but some of Mill's leading views may be indicated.

Deductive Reasoning. Mill's argument in Book I of the *Logic* is intended to show the mistake of those who say that deductive inference (as found, for example, in

the syllogism) is entirely useless because it involves a *petitio principii,* but at the same time to make it clear that deduction in general is never the source of new knowledge. Mill agreed that the conclusion of a syllogism may not contain more than is contained in the premises and that "no reasoning from generals to particulars can, as such, prove anything, since from a general principle we cannot infer any particulars, but those which the principle itself assumes as known."

With the publication of his System of Logic, *Mill took a major step toward showing that the philosophy of experience could offer at least as much in the way of constructive thinking as any other kind of view.*

It is useless to defend deduction by saying that it shows us what was "implicit" in our premises, unless we can go on to explain how something can be implicitly contained in what we already know. Mill's solution to this problem and his explanation of the value of rules of deduction rest on his view that "all inference is from particulars to particulars." When we reason "All men are mortal; Jones (not yet dead) is a man; so Jones is mortal," our real evidence for the assertion that Jones will die is our knowledge that Smith, Peters, Wilkins, and many other individuals who resemble Jones in many respects did die. We infer from their deaths to his. The general premise that all men are mortal is not itself our evidence. It is rather a note, or register, of the particular evidence on which the conclusion really depends, together with the prediction that what we have found in cases which we have already observed will also hold in similar cases not yet observed. The real inference, Mill thought, comes in constructing the general proposition on the basis of observation of particular cases. Deduction is to be understood as a way of interpreting the note that has been made of our previous inference. It is valuable because misinterpretation is very easy; but it no more gives us new information than do propositions that are true by definition. Such propositions, which Mill called "verbal," only pull out of a word what was previously put into it; and in the same way, a syllogism simply retrieves from a general proposition a particular one that was previously assumed to be in it. Since there is no real progress of thought in deduction, deductive inference is merely *apparent* inference. Induction is the only procedure that gives us nonverbal general propositions that go beyond what has actually been observed. Hence, only in induction do we make *real* inferences.

According to Mill, there are four inductive methods:

the method of agreement, the method of difference,

the method of residues, and

the method of concomitant variations.

Mathematical knowledge is no exception to this. Taking geometry first, as the deductive science par excellence, Mill argued that its conclusions are necessary only in the sense that they necessarily follow from the premises from which they are deduced. But the premises themselves—ultimately, the axioms—are grounded on observation and are generalizations from what we have always experienced. (The definitions are in a somewhat different position, although an experiential element is involved in the belief that the entities they define, such as a geometric point or line, really exist.) That two straight lines do not enclose a surface is evident to us every time we look at two straight lines which intersect. The laws of psychology, operating on such experiential data, are sufficient to explain the production in us of the belief that such lines cannot possibly enclose a surface: hence we need not appeal to intuition or to some other nonexperiential source to explain the belief. Even the inconceivability of the denial of the axioms of geometry does not show, Mill argued, that they are not based on experience. For inconceivability is psychological, and the fact that we cannot think of something does not show that that thing cannot exist. Mill went on to offer an account of the way in which arithmetic and algebra are founded on experience. Here the essential point is that groups of four items, for example, may be rearranged into, or formed from, two groups of two items each, or a group of three items together with a group of one item. Seeing that this is always so, we come, through the operation of psychological laws, to believe that $2 + 2$, or $3 + 1$, *must* be the same as 4. Algebra is simply a more abstract extension of this sort of belief.

With these explanations Mill hoped to show how mathematics can yield propositions which are not merely verbal and which are certainly true of the world of experience, but which do not depend on any nonexperiential sources of knowledge. His account has never been accepted by philosophers as it stands, but there have been some attempts, among thinkers influenced by pragmatism, to work out a philosophy of mathematics along lines analogous to Mill's.

Inductive Reasoning and Scientific Explanation. In Mill's view, induction is clearly of central importance, since it is the only possible source of substantive general propositions. While the details of his theory are complicated, its main lines may be concisely indicated. All methodical and critical induction rests on the fundamental principle of the uniformity of nature; namely, that what has happened once will happen again, if circumstances are sufficiently similar. Mill thought that this is a factual proposition which is itself derived by a primitive and natural process of induction: we first note a few limited regularities and predict that they will hold in the future. After our predictions come true, we spontaneously generalize, saying that since some events have been found to occur in repeating patterns, all events will be found to occur in repeating patterns. Belief in the uniformity of nature is thus derived from, and resolvable into, belief in the existence of less sweeping patterns of occurrences, or into particular causal laws. Mill defined "cause of a phenomenon" as "the antecedent, or concurrence of antecedents, on which it is invariably and unconditionally consequent." Like the "axiom" of the uniformity of nature, the principle that every occurrence has a cause is confirmed by all our experience. It is, in fact, simply a more precise way of stating the principle of the uniformity of nature. The hope of science is to formulate propositions about specific sequences of phenomena that can be relied on to the same degree as the law of causation. And the problem of methodical induction—which is the core of the problem of scientific reasoning—arises when it is discovered that the simplest method of induction (that of assembling positive instances of a sequence of phenomena and generalizing directly from them) often leads to general propositions which turn out to be false. We then seek ways of obtaining better results. The fundamental technique is to obtain evidence which will allow us to argue as follows: either *A* is the cause of *a*, or else there are some events which have no cause; and since we are certain that every event has a cause, we may be certain that *A* causes *a*.

According to Mill, there are four inductive methods: the method of agreement, the method of difference, the method of residues, and the method of concomitant variations. He also discussed a combination of the first two, calling it the joint method of agreement and difference. We use the first two methods in this way. If we find that *A* under circumstances *BC* is followed by *abc*, while under circumstances *DE* it is followed by *ade*, then *A* cannot be the cause either of *bc* or of *de*, since they sometimes do not occur when *A* occurs (and hence by the definition of "cause," cannot be caused by it). But *a* occurs under both sets of conditions; hence it could be the effect of *A*: this illustrates the method of agreement. To ascertain if something other than *A* might be the cause of *a* we use the method of difference. Will *BC* without *A* be followed by *a*? If not, we have so far confirmed our view that *A* causes *a*, for, in the cases we have examined, *A* is always followed by *a* and *a* never occurs without being preceded by *A*. Hence, by the definition of "cause," *A* is, so far as our evidence goes, the cause, or part of the cause, of *a*—or else there are events without any regular cause.

Science does not rely upon induction and experiment alone. It is only infrequently, Mill thought, that we will find genuine causal laws, that is, absolutely invariable sequences. More frequently we will find regularities which hold as far as a limited experience shows but which, we have reason to believe, might well not hold under quite different circumstances. These "empirical laws" are not to be considered basic laws of nature. Much of the practical application of science depends on them, but we cannot claim to have truly scientific knowledge until we can deduce empirical laws from basic laws of nature, showing why the combination of circumstances and laws renders inevitable the limitations within which the empirical laws hold. This makes clear the aim of science: to discover laws of nature and empirical laws, and to connect them, in a deductive system, in such a way as to show how the unrestricted laws would give rise to the regularities reported by the empirical laws. The various sciences are differentiated by the ways in which these two types of laws must be discovered and connected. In some sciences it is possible to discover laws of nature directly, deduce what the empirical laws must be, and then proceed to verify the deductions by checking against experimental data. In others, empirical laws are discovered first, and laws of nature are presented as hypotheses to explain them. These alleged laws of nature are then tested by deducing further empirical laws from them and testing these deductions. In any science, however, explanation comes to an end when laws of nature are reached: these are simply ultimate facts which are to be accepted.

The Moral Sciences. In the last book of the *Logic*, Mill argued that the phenomena of individual or social human life are no exception to the law of causation, and that consequently it must be possible to determine what are the natural laws of human behavior. He investigated the various modes of inquiry used in the different physical sciences to determine which are most suited to this sort of investigation, and he sketched an outline of what a completed science of man will be. Here as elsewhere, Mill thought that "however complex the phenomena,

all their sequences and co-existences result from the laws of the separate elements." Since the separate elements in this instance are men, it is the basic laws of psychology from which, when the science is completed, all the laws and regularities concerning social phenomena must be deduced. Because of the enormous number of interacting elements, however, the complexity of social action is so great that no direct deduction of its regularities from basic psychological laws will be possible. In order to make this deduction it will be necessary first to construct a science of human character that will cover both the development of human character and the tendencies to action of different types of persons. From the laws of this science, which Mill called "ethology," we may hope eventually to get sociological laws. Even then, however, we will at best obtain statements of tendencies toward action, for the enormous number of factors involved in determining social action will not allow any more accurate predictions. Still, Mill held, "knowledge insufficient for prediction may be most valuable for guidance" in practical affairs. His chief interest lay in the possibility of obtaining scientific guidance for the direction of political decisions.

Mill held that we must know some things intuitively, without inference, if we know anything at all, and he rejected skepticism as failing to make a relevant distinction between knowledge and doubt.

How far, then, had social science actually progressed? Mill thought that the basic laws of psychology were by then well established: they were the laws put forward by psychologists of the associationist school, among whom James Mill was pre-eminent. But the science of ethology, which John Stuart Mill had hoped to found himself, eluded him, and he gave up work on it shortly after he published the *System of Logic*. Although the absence of the intermediate laws that this science was designed to contribute made impossible the completion of sociology, Mill thought that at least one basic law of social change had been discovered and substantially proven: Auguste Comte's Law of Three Stages. One element, Mill argued, is more important than any other single factor in causing change in society: "This is the state of the speculative faculties of mankind, including the nature of the beliefs which . . . they have arrived at concerning themselves and the world by which they are surrounded. . . . the order of human progression in all respects will mainly depend on the order of progression in the intellectual convictions of mankind." Comte had shown that opinion always passes through the same three phases. Men first try to understand their universe in theological terms, then in metaphysical terms, and finally in scientific or, as he called them, positive terms. He had also shown that correlated with these three stages of opinion are types of social organization, which change as opinions change. This generalization, for Mill, was enormously important to our understanding of history and to our practical decisions, and up to that time it was the sole example of a well-founded sociological law. But Mill had high hopes that, with work, much progress could be made in constructing a social science; and he looked forward to a time when "no important branch of human affairs will be any longer abandoned to empiricism and unscientific surmise."

EPISTEMOLOGY AND METAPHYSICS. With respect to metaphysics in the contemporary sense of systematic knowledge transcending experience, Mill claimed to have none; and his epistemology consists largely of an account of experiential knowledge in which he intended to show why nothing beyond such knowledge is either possible or necessary. Mill presented an empiricist theory of our knowledge of the external world and of persons which is equally free of the skepticism of Hume and the theology of Berkeley. He consequently covered quite thoroughly a good deal of the ground that was gone over again in the discussions among empiricists and logical positivists in the second and third decades of the twentieth century.

Aim and Method. Mill held that we must know some things intuitively, without inference, if we know anything at all, and he rejected skepticism as failing to make a relevant distinction between knowledge and doubt ("In denying all knowledge it denies none"). For if all knowledge were inferential, there would be no firm starting point for inference, and we should be led into a vicious infinite regress of premises. But because whatever can be known only by intuition is beyond the realm of rational discussion and experimental test, such intuitive knowledge is not easily distinguished from dogmatic opinion. Hence, it was Mill's aim to reduce to an absolute minimum the number of points at which intuitions are required. In the *Logic* he argued that no intuitions are necessary for mathematics, logic, or the procedures of natural science. In the *Examination of Sir William Hamilton's Philosophy* (1865), he pursued these questions further and explicitly took up the questions he had claimed to avoid in the earlier work—especially

those concerning the foundations and nature of our knowledge of bodies and of minds.

Mill argued that we cannot tell by intuition or by introspection what we know intuitively. In order to distinguish what is directly given to consciousness from what is there as a result of inference, we must try to investigate the *origins* of the present contents of our minds. And again, this cannot be done directly, because the minds of infants are not accessible to us. Hence, Mill concluded, "the original elements can only come to light as a residual phenomena, by a previous study of the modes of generation of the mental facts which are confessedly not original." This is the psychological method that was originated by Locke. In using it, Mill attempted always to show how experience, acting in accordance with known laws of psychology, can explain all of our knowledge. If successful, such accounts make unnecessary (and therefore unwarranted, according to sound scientific methodology) any appeal to extraordinary faculties or to nonexperiential sources of knowledge.

Matter and Mind. Mill attempted to explain our belief in the existence of matter and in the existence of our own and other minds by using a psychological method. The "Psychological Theory of the Belief in an External World," as he called it, postulates first, a mind capable of expectation (that is, of forming the conception of possible sensations which would be felt if certain conditions were realized), and second, the psychological laws of association. The claim is that these two factors, operating on experienced sensations and reminiscences of them, would generate not only a belief in an external world but, in addition, a belief that this belief was immediate or intuitive. Mill argued first that by an external object we mean only something that exists whether it is thought of or not, that stays the same even if the sensations we get from it change, and that is common to many observers in a way that sensations are not. One's concept of the external world, Mill said, is made up only to a slight degree, at any moment, of actual sensations, but to a large degree of possible sensations— not of what I am sensing, but of what I would sense *if* I moved, or turned my head, and so forth. These possible sensations, moreover, are thought of as being in groups: numbers of them would be present if I did this, numbers of others if I did that. Contrasted with any particular actual sensation, these groups of possible sensations seem stable and permanent. Moreover, there is not very much regularity in the sequences of our actual sensations, but there is considerable regularity associated in our minds with the groups of possible sensations: we will regularly get this sensation following that one if we do this following that. Hence ideas of cause and power, which (as had been argued in the *Logic*) depend on regularity and succession, are associated with the groups of possible sensations, and not with the actual sensations. At this stage we begin to refer any actual sensation to some group of possible sensations, and even to think of the possibilities as the cause or root of the actual sensation. The groups of possibilities, having permanence and causal power, are so different from fleeting actual sensations that they come to be thought of as being altogether different from them. When it finally becomes clear that the permanent possibilities are publicly observable, we have a concept answering in all respects to our definition of externality. Hence, Mill said, matter "may be defined, a Permanent Possibility of Sensation"; this is all, he held, that the plain man believes matter to be, and indeed, Mill shared this belief. Mill's aim, however, was not so much to defend the belief, as to account for it. And his account, which appeals only to psychological laws known to operate in many other kinds of cases, is simpler than accounts that would make the belief in matter an original part of our mind or an intuitive belief: consequently, he held, it is a better account.

Agreement on moral beliefs

is the most important single factor

making for cohesion in society,

and where it is lacking,

society cannot be unified.

Mill went on to ask how far a similar theory is adequate to account for mind. The theory will work, he thought, to a large extent, since we know nothing of our mind but its conscious manifestations, and since we know other minds only through inference from the similarities of other bodies and their actions to ours. But memory and expectation pose a fatal difficulty. They involve a belief in something beyond their own existence, and also the idea that I myself have had, or will have, the experience remembered or expected. Hence, if the mind is really a series of feelings, it is an extraordinary series, for it is one that is "aware of itself as a past and future." And if it is not this paradoxical series, it is something more than a series—but what that can be we have no idea. Mill concluded that at this point we are "face to face with that final inexplicability at which . . . we inevitably arrive when we reach ultimate facts," and all we can do is accept the facts as inexplicable. Hence, mind is not simply a permanent possibility of sensation.

Sensations and feelings—the data of experience—are, then, intuitively known; the fact of memory (a consequence of which Mill thought to be expectation) is also known directly; and the kind of link between past and present involved in memory (which Mill took to be the central inexplicable reality about the self) is known directly. Aside from these, there is only one additional inexplicable fact, and that is belief—the fact that there is a difference between contemplating, or imagining, or supposing, and actually believing. Mill rejected his father's analysis of belief, but could develop no adequate account of his own.

ETHICS. According to Mill, agreement on moral beliefs is the most important single factor making for cohesion in society, and where it is lacking society cannot be unified. In his own times he saw and recognized the significance of the first serious widespread breakdown of belief in the Christian moral scheme. He thought it a task of first importance to provide an alternative view of morality which would be both acceptable to those who still clung, in part, to their older views, and capable of redirecting these older moral attitudes into newer paths. He was a utilitarian in ethics: that is, he held that an action is right if, and only if, it brings about a greater balance of good over bad consequences than any other act open to the agent, and he also believed that only pleasure is intrinsically good and only pain intrinsically bad. Bentham and James Mill had held a similar position, but John Stuart Mill modified their view in a number of ways, attempting always to show that utilitarianism need not be a narrow or selfish view and that it did not force one to rely, for social progress, purely on impersonal institutional arrangements and thereby compel one to leave human personality out of account. By arguing that the utilitarian could appreciate the wisdom embodied in traditional morality as well as offer rational criticism of it, and that he could also accept and account for the high value of self-sacrifice and could make the development and perfection of individual character the key obligation of morality, Mill sought to rebut the most frequent criticisms of the Benthamite morality and thereby make it more generally acceptable. Although his ethical writings (especially *Utilitarianism*) have been much criticized, they contain the most influential philosophical articulation of a liberal humanistic morality that was produced in the nineteenth century.

In his ethical writings, Mill pursued the attack on intuitionism which was so constant a feature of his other work. This issue is especially important with regard to moral problems. Intuitionism, he said in the *Autobiography,* is "the great intellectual support of false doctrines and bad institutions" because it enables "every inveterate belief and every intense feeling . . . to dispense with the obligation of justifying itself by reason. . . . There never was such an instrument devised for consecrating all deep-seated prejudices." The intuitionists supposed, Mill believed, that only their view could account for (1) the uniqueness of moral judgments, (2) the rapidity with which the plain man passes moral judgments, and (3) the authority to be given to common-sense moral judgments. To the first point, Mill answered with the theory that moral feelings may have unique properties, just as water has, and yet may still be derived, by a chemical compounding process, from simpler elements which do not have those properties. Hence, so far there is no need to say that these feelings are caused by unique intuitions. To the second point he replied that rapidity of judgment may be due to habit and training as well as to a faculty of intuition. And with regard to the third point, which is the crucial one, he argued that the utilitarian can give at least as good an account as the intuitionist of the authority of common sense in moral matters. Rules such as those that enjoin the telling of truth, the paying of debts, the keeping of promises, and so forth (Mill called these "secondary rules") were taken by him to indicate, not widespread intuitions, but the results of hundreds of years of experience of the consequences of actions. These rules, based on so much factual knowledge, are of considerable value in helping men to make correct decisions when time or data for a full calculation of the results in a particular case are lacking. The wisdom of the ages, thus embodied in the rules and precepts of common-sense morality, is an indispensable supplement to the limited knowledge and almost inevitable one-sidedness of any single person. It is for these reasons, utilitarians claim, that these rules and precepts have a certain cognitive authority. There is no need to appeal to a faculty of intuition to explain the authority, and therefore such an explanation is, from a scientific point of view, unwarranted.

Mill thus gave a prominent place to moral directives other than the utilitarian principle. But he was basically an act-utilitarian, believing that each particular obligation depends on the balance of pleasure and pain that would be produced by the act in question. The utilitarian principle is so abstract, Mill thought, that it is unlikely to be actually used, except in cases where two secondary rules come into conflict with each other. But it serves the invaluable function of providing a rational basis for the criticism of secondary rules (this is brought out especially well in the essay on justice, Ch. 5 of *Utilitarianism*), and there was no doubt in Mill's mind that there can never be a right act which contravenes the principle. This is true even with regard to the rule (to

which Mill gave so much emphasis) dictating the development and perfection of individual character. It often seems that Mill placed more stress on individuality, or self-realization, than on general welfare, and critics frequently claim that he contradicted himself by saying that both of these constitute the sole highest good. But there is no contradiction in his views, for he held that self-development is the best way for an individual to work for the common good.

Mill was profoundly worried

about the tendency of democracies

to suppress individuality and override minorities.

Mill's concern with the problem of free will sprang from his view of the importance of self-development. (He presented this view both in the *Logic* and in the *Examination of Hamilton*.) The doctrine of necessity, which he had been taught to believe, seemed to him to make a man a creature of his environment, and this doctrine depressed and disturbed him for many years. When he realized that the desire to improve oneself could be a powerful motive and that actions dictated by this desire, although not contravening the law of causation, are properly said to be due to oneself rather than to one's environment, he felt "as if an incubus had been raised off him." He thought that this view enabled him to make determinism compatible with his emphasis on the individual's responsibility for his own character.

Two aspects of Mill's *Utilitarianism* have been attacked more frequently than any others. The first is his attempt to broaden utilitarianism by making a distinction between *kinds* of pleasure, so that an act producing a smaller amount of a more valuable kind of pleasure might be obligatory, rather than an act producing a larger amount of a less valuable kind of pleasure. This line of reasoning has been said to involve him in flagrant contradictions, or else to be sheer nonsense.

The second aspect is his attempt to give some sort of reasoned support to the utilitarian principle itself, which led G. E. Moore to accuse him of committing the "naturalistic fallacy." Moore thought Mill was trying to give a conclusive proof of a first moral principle, but he was mistaken. Throughout his life, Mill consistently held that no such proof of the principle was possible, either deductively or inductively. There is, however, no agreement as to the manner in which Mill attempted, in the fourth chapter of *Utilitarianism*, to support his first principle so that he would not be open to the same reproach of dogmatism that he had made against the intuitionists. Mill's remarks here are extremely unclear. His problem arises because, while he insisted that there must be a factual basis for moral judgments, he held that moral judgments are different in kind from factual propositions and therefore cannot be strictly derived from them. Although he failed to solve this problem, he at least propounded it in precisely the form in which it has perplexed (not to say obsessed) recent moral philosophers.

SOCIAL AND POLITICAL PHILOSOPHY. Mill was more aware than were the older Benthamites of the importance of nonrational and noninstitutional factors to an understanding of society and was consequently less disposed to rely on legal and governmental reforms for the improvement of it. He believed in democratic government, but he was convinced that it could not work well unless the citizens who lived under it were reasonably well educated, tolerant of opposing views, and willing to sacrifice some of their immediate interests for the good of society. He was profoundly worried about the tendency of democracies to suppress individuality and override minorities: indeed, this, and not the problem of forcing those who control government to work for the interests of the people, seemed to him the crucial problem of his times. Hence, in his writings on social and political philosophy, his central concern was to show the importance of personal freedom and the development of strong individual character and to devise ways of encouraging their growth.

Economic Theory. With regard to economic theory Mill at first supported a general policy of laissez-faire, but increasing awareness of the uselessness to the individual of political freedom without economic security and opportunity led him to re-examine his objections to socialism. By the end of his life he had come to think that as far as economic theory was concerned, socialism was acceptable. His reservations about it sprang from his fear that it would give overwhelming strength to the tendencies of the age toward suppression of individuality.

On Liberty. Mill thought that his essay *On Liberty* was the most likely of all his works to be of enduring value. In it he maintained the view, which he had expressed as early as 1834, that "the sole end for which mankind are warranted, individually or collectively, in interfering with the liberty of action of any of their number, is self-protection." Mill argued for this view especially in regard to freedom of thought and discussion. "We can never be sure," he wrote, "that the opinion we are endeavoring to stifle is a false opinion; and if we were sure, stifling it would be an evil still": these are the lines of his defense, which rests ultimately on his assessment of the importance of sociological knowledge to the direction of social action and on his view of the peculiar difficulties in obtaining it. In the third

chapter, Mill argued at length for the importance of "individuality," which, he held, comes from, or indeed is identical with, continued effort at self-development. Even eccentricity is better, he held, than massive uniformity of personality and the stagnation of society that would result from it. Mill's strong emphasis on this point stems from his conviction, here strongly influenced by de Tocqueville, that the chief danger of democracy is that of suppressing individual differences and of allowing no genuine development of minority opinion. Democratic tyranny would be far worse, he held, than aristocratic or despotic tyranny, since it would be far more effective in utilizing the most efficient of means of social control, the pressure of public opinion. Against this the only reliable safeguard would be the development of personalities strong enough to resist such pressures.

Representative Government. In more specifically political matters the same concerns are evident. Mill defended representative democracy, but not solely on the grounds used by the older Benthamites. Representative government, he held, is ideally the best form of government because it does more to encourage the growth and development of individuality than any other form of government. By leading people to participate in the processes of governing, representative government makes them more active, intelligent, and well rounded than even the best-intentioned of despotisms could. It thereby gives them vitally important moral training, by cultivating their public sympathies, strengthening their habit of looking at social questions from an impersonal point of view, and aiding their identification of personal interests with the interests of society. Care must be taken, however, to get a true democracy, one in which minorities as well as majorities are represented. For this reason Mill enthusiastically endorsed Thomas Hare's scheme of proportional representation. He also favored plural voting, which would allow educated and responsible persons to have more influence than the uneducated, by giving the former several votes. Mill's view of the function of the representative also shows his concern to get as much intelligence as possible into government. A properly educated constituency, he held, would be able and willing to select the best men available; and since those elected would be better informed and wiser on particular issues than the electorate, it would be absurd to bind the representatives to anything but a very general agreement with the beliefs and aims of the electors.

Individuals and Society. Mill is frequently criticized for overlooking the organic elements in society and for thinking of society as a mere aggregate of units in which each unit is what it is regardless of its membership in the whole. Mill certainly held this view as far as the most fundamental laws of psychology are concerned. But his view of individual character involves new considerations. Individuals, he held, are radically affected by their membership in society and inevitably formed by the customs, habits, morality, and beliefs of those who raise them. There is, however, no impersonal assurance, metaphysical or otherwise, that the individual will feel himself an organic member of any group. He will do so, Mill thought, only if he is educated to do so. Mill cannot be accused of underestimating the importance of ensuring that men are so educated, and it is not clear that an organic theory has anything better to offer on a practical level.

In "The Utility of Religion,"

Mill argued that much of the social usefulness

attributed to religion is actually due

to the influence of a widely accepted

and instilled moral code, and to

the force of public opinion guided by that code.

RELIGIOUS VIEWS. Mill maintained for the most part a determined silence on religious questions. Although he had written "On Nature" and "The Utility of Religion" by 1858, and although he lived during a period of increasingly free discussion of all possible religious subjects, he thought that the British public would not listen patiently to what he had to say on these questions and that he could not publish his views without alienating readers and losing public influence. And this, as he made quite clear in his correspondence with Auguste Comte, he was determined not to do. Despite his precautions, however, he was generally taken to be atheistic, and he was sometimes criticized for not openly stating the views which, so it seemed, he insinuated but did not defend. The consternation of his followers and the delight of his opponents was therefore considerable when it became apparent from the posthumously published *Three Essays on Religion* (1874) that Mill did not entirely condemn religious aspirations and hopes and even thought that there might be some faint possibility of the existence of rational support for a religious view of the world. Admirers felt betrayed, and religious critics proclaimed that Mill's secular education and materialistic position here issued in collapse and evident moral and intellectual bankruptcy.

Goodness of God. Mill's most famous pronouncement on religion occurs not, however, in the *Three Essays,* but

in the *Examination of Hamilton.* Discussing the use made by one of Hamilton's philosophical followers, Mansel, of Hamilton's view that we cannot know the Absolute, Mill particularly criticized Mansel's theory that even the moral terms we apply to God do not mean what they mean when we apply them to men. Mill objected to this theory in the name of logic: if terms are not to be used in their usual sense, they ought not to be used at all. But, more strongly, he went on to say that a being, no matter how powerful, whose acts are not sanctioned by the highest human morality conceivable, is not deserving of worship. If Mill were convinced of the existence of such a being he would not worship him. "I will call no being good," Mill proclaimed, "who is not what I mean when I apply that epithet to my fellow creatures, and if such a being can sentence me to hell for not so calling him, to hell I will go."

Nature. Of the *Three Essays,* the first two, at least, show no reversal or collapse of Mill's views. In "On Nature" Mill argued that the maxim "Follow Nature" is of no use as a guide to action. For "Nature" either means "everything that happens, good as well as bad," in which case it offers no guidance whatsoever; or it means "what happens without any human interference," and in that case the maxim is self-contradictory. Nature in the second sense, Mill went on to argue, offers at least as much evil to our observation as good; it is rather a challenge to amendment than an ideal for imitation. From this, two conclusions follow. First, it is our job to improve nature, especially human nature; for it is only insofar as men have intervened to change things that the world has become civilized, safe, and happy, even to the limited extent that it has. Human virtues are not natural: they are pre-eminently the results of cultivation. Even justice is an artificial virtue, Mill said, and the idea of natural justice does not precede, but follows, it. Second, in view of the suffering and ugliness presented by much of the natural world, the only religious view that is at all tenable is one which holds that the deity is not omnipotent, that "the Principle of Good *cannot* at once and altogether subdue the powers of evil," and that, consequently, men should think of themselves as the far from useless helpers of a limited but benevolent God.

Utility of Religion. In "The Utility of Religion," Mill argued that much of the social usefulness attributed to religion is actually due to the influence of a widely accepted and instilled moral code, and to the force of public opinion guided by that code. The belief in the supernatural origin of morality may once have helped it to gain acceptance, but is no longer needed, or indeed, even effectual, in maintaining this acceptance. The effect of religion on individuals springs largely from our need to have ideal conceptions that move us to action.

"The essence of religion is the strong and earnest direction of the emotions and desires towards an ideal object, recognized as of the highest excellence, and as rightfully paramount over all selfish objects of desire." But a religion of humanity, Mill argued, can have this effect to an even greater extent than a supernatural religion. The religion of humanity would cultivate our unselfish feelings and would free us from any need for intellectual juggling or willful blindness with regard to its tenets, since it would rather point out than deny the evil in the world and urge us to work to remove it.

God. Thus, the first two essays of the *Three Essays* together suggest that the alternative to a supernatural religion is not simple acceptance of Nature, but the construction of an alternative way of living based on education and convention; and these themes are to be found throughout Mill's thought. The third essay, "Theism," drafted from 1868 to 1870, which assesses arguments in support of a supernatural religious view, seems to make more concessions to traditional religiosity than the other essays; but even these are slight. In this essay, Mill discussed the possibilities of rational support for supernatural beliefs. Dismissing all a priori reasoning, he found only the Argument from Design at all convincing, and this argument gives us at best "no more than a probability" that some intelligent creator of the world exists. For the same evidences that thus support the existence of a creator also go to show that he was not omnipotent and do not prove that he was omniscient. Mill suggested that we think of a limited deity faced with the independent existence of matter and force. To this picture of a Platonic demiurge, Mill thought we are entitled to add that benevolence may have been one (although surely not the only) moral attribute of the creator. But Mill emphasized strongly the importance of the work of man in improving the world. "If man had not the power," he said, "by the exercise of his own energies for the improvement both of himself and of his outward circumstances, to do for himself and other creatures vastly more than God had in the first instance done, the Being who called him into existence would deserve something very different from thanks at his hands."

Immortality and Miracles. Mill argued that there is no evidence for the immortality of the soul and none against it. After a lengthy discussion of Hume's arguments on this point he found that roughly the same is true of miracles. But in each case he pointed out that there is room for *hope:* one may, if it is comforting and encouraging, hope that the soul is immortal and that the revelations attested by miracles are true. And it is this point more than any other in the essay that upset Mill's admirers. For while he concluded that the proper rational attitude to supernatural religion is skepticism rather than belief or positive disbelief and that "the whole domain of the supernatural is thus removed from the region of Belief into that of simple Hope," he also held that it may be valuable and justifiable to encourage religious hopes. This, he said, can be done without impairing the power of reason; and indulgence in such hopes may help some men to feel that life is more important and may strengthen their feelings for others. Furthermore, to construct a picture of a person of high moral excellence, such as Christ, and form the habit of seeking the approval of this person for one's acts, may aid that "real, though purely human, religion, which sometimes calls itself the Religion of Humanity, and sometimes that of Duty." Critics may wish to call these views objectionable, but in Mill at least they are not inconsistent. They hark back to his early discovery of the importance of cultivating the feelings and develop the further implications of his idea of the moral importance of educating the emotions. His assessment of the degree to which scientific support can be given to a supernaturalist theory by evidences of design, low though it is, may seem far too high; but his interest in the theory of a limited deity with whom we must cooperate to bring about improvement in the world is hardly great enough or personal enough to lend credence to the accusations that he had undergone an emotional collapse.

BIBLIOGRAPHY

Works by Mill

Mill's works have not yet been collected. Even the projected University of Toronto Press edition of his *Works* will probably not contain all of them. Mill's own *Bibliography*, edited by M. MacMinn, J. R. Hainds, and J. M. McCrimmon (Evanston, Ill., 1945), is not quite complete.

Mill's books (all of which were published in London, unless otherwise noted) are as follows: *System of Logic*, 2 vols. (1843; 8th ed., 1872); *Essays on Some Unsettled Questions of Political Economy* (1844; written 1830–1831); *Principles of Political Economy*, 2 vols. (1848; 7th ed., 1871; variorum ed., W. J. Ashley, ed., 1909); *On Liberty* (1859); *Dissertations and Discussions*, periodical essays, 2 vols. (1859), 4 vols. (1875); *Considerations on Representative Government* (1861); *Utilitarianism*, reprinted from *Frasers Magazine*, 1861 (1863); *An Examination of Sir William Hamilton's Philosophy* (1865; 6th ed., 1889); *Auguste Comte and Positivism* (1865); *Subjection of Women* (1869; written in 1861); *Autobiography* (1873; more complete edition, J. J. Coss, ed., New York, 1924).

Among Mill's shorter writings of philosophical interest (most reprinted in *Dissertations and Discussions*) are the following: "Whately's Elements of Logic," *Westminster Review* (1828); "The Spirit of the Age," in the *Examiner* (1831), included in F. Hayek, ed., *The Spirit of the Age* (Chicago, 1942); "Prof. Sedgwick's Discourse" (1835); "Civilization" (1836); "Bentham" (1838); "Coleridge" (1840); "M. de Tocqueville on Democracy in America" (1840); "Bailey on Berkeley's Theory of Vision" (1842); "Michelet's History of France" (1844); "Dr. Whewell on Moral Philosophy" (1851); "Bain's Psychology" (1859); "Austin on Jurisprudence" (1863); "Plato" (1866);

"Inaugural Address to the University of St. Andrews" (1867); "Berkeley's Life and Writings," *Fortnightly Review* (1871); "Grote's Aristotle" (1873); "Chapters on Socialism," *Fortnightly Review* (1879), reprinted as *Socialism*, W. O. P. Bliss, ed. (Linden, Mass., 1891).

Of Mill's literary essays, the best known are "What Is Poetry?" and "The Two Kinds of Poetry," in *Monthly Repository* (1833), reprinted in part in *Dissertations and Discourses* as "Thoughts on Poetry and Its Varieties."

Works on Mill

Life

For Mill's life, see his *Autobiography;* F. E. Mineka, ed., *Earlier Letters,* 2 vols. (Toronto, 1963); H. S. R. Elliott, ed., *Letters,* 2 vols. (1910); J. Stillinger, ed., *Early Draft of Mill's Autobiography* (Urbana, Ill., 1961). See F. Hayek, ed., *John Stuart Mill and Harriet Taylor* (1951), for their correspondence. See also the standard M. St. John Packe, *The Life of John Stuart Mill* (1954); A. Bain, *John Stuart Mill* (1882); and W. L. Courtney, *Life of John Stuart Mill* (1886); H. O. Pappe, *John Stuart Mill and the Harriet Taylor Myth* (Melbourne, 1960); A. W. Levi, "The Writing of Mill's Autobiography," in *Ethics*, Vol. 61 (1951).

Among many estimates of Mill's life and character are those by R. H. Hutton, reprinted in *Criticism on Contemporary Thought and Thinkers*, Vol. 1 (1894); J. Martineau, in *Essays*, Vol. 3 (1891); J. Morley, in *Critical Miscellanies*, Vol. 2 (1877); B. Russell, in *Proceedings of the British Academy* (1955); W. Ward, in *Men and Matters* (1914).

General Works

For general commentary on the thought of Mill see Sir Leslie Stephen, *English Utilitarians*, Vol. 3 (1900); R. P. Anschutz, *Philosophy of John Stuart Mill* (Oxford, 1953); Karl Britton, *John Stuart Mill* (1953).

Logic

See O. A. Kubitz, *Development of John Stuart Mill's System of Logic*, Illinois Studies in the Social Sciences, VIII (Urbana, Ill., 1932); R. Jackson, *Deductive Logic of John Stuart Mill* (Oxford, 1941); W. Whewell, *Of Induction, with especial reference to Mr. J. Stuart Mill's System of Logic* (1849), and see E. A. Strong, "W. Whewell and John Stuart Mill," *Journal of the History of Ideas* (1955). Classic criticisms include: T. H. Green, "The Logic of John Stuart Mill," *Works*, Vol. II (1886); F. H. Bradley, *Principles of Logic* (Oxford, 1883), Bk. II, Part II, Chs. 1–3; W. S. Jevons, "John Stuart Mill's Philosophy Tested," reprinted in *Pure Logic* (1890).

Metaphysics

Among older studies of interest are: W. L. Courtney, *The Metaphysics of John Stuart Mill* (1879); C. M. Douglas, *John Stuart Mill, A Study of His Philosophy* (Edinburgh and London, 1895); J. McCosh, *An Examination of Mr. John Stuart Mill's Philosophy* (London and New York, 1866); and John Grote, *Exploratio Philosophica* (Cambridge, 1865; 2 vols., 1900). Few recent discussions center explicitly on Mill.

Ethics and Utilitarianism

E. Halévy, *La Formation du radicalisme philosophique*, 3 vols. (Paris, 1901–1904), translated into English by Mary Morris as *Growth of Philosophic Radicalism* (London, 1928), is the basic study of the development of Benthamite doctrine; see also E. Albee, *History of English Utilitarianism* (1900) and J. Plamenatz, *The English Utilitarians* (Oxford, 1949). Especially valuable older critical works are John Grote, *Examination of the Utilitarian Philosophy* (Cambridge, 1870) and F. H. Bradley, *Ethical Studies* (Oxford, 1876), Ch. 3. Recent dis-

cussions start from the criticisms of G. E. Moore, *Principia Ethica* (Cambridge, 1903), Chs. 1 and 3. Compare J. Seth, "Alleged Fallacies in Mill's Utilitarianism," in *Philosophical Review*, Vol. 17 (1908); E. W. Hall, "The 'Proof' of Utility in Bentham and Mill," in *Ethics*, Vol. 9 (1949); J. O. Urmson, "Interpretation of the Moral Philosophy of John Stuart Mill," in *Philosophical Quarterly*, Vol. 3 (1953). I. Berlin's lecture, "John Stuart Mill and the Ends of Life" (London, 1962), is more general.

Political Philosophy

See G. H. Sabine, *History of Political Theory*, 3d ed. (New York, 1961); M. Cowling, *Mill and Liberalism* (Cambridge, 1963). J. F. Stephen, *Liberty, Equality, Fraternity* (1873) is an interesting early attack; others are summarized in J. C. Rees, *Mill and His Early Critics* (Leicester, 1956). B. Bosanquet, *Philosophical Theory of the State* (1899) and D. G. Ritchie, *Principles of State Interference* (1891) present representative criticism. J. H. Burns, "John Stuart Mill and Democracy," in *Political Studies*, Vol. 5 (1957), traces the development of Mill's views. For criticisms of Mill's views on sociological method, see K. Popper, *Open Society and Its Enemies*, 2 vols. (1945), Ch. 14, and P. Winch, *Idea of a Social Science* (1958), especially Ch. 3.

— J. B. SCHNEEWIND

MILL, JOHN STUART (UPDATE)

The publication of the *Collected Works* of John Stuart Mill, in thirty-three volumes (1963–91), has provided a mine of information about Mill's life and thought and will do so for years to come. The six volumes of letters and many volumes of essays, speeches, and journals show that most of his writing was not on narrowly philosophical topics. Much of it was on concrete political issues of his day.

The Mill Newsletter began publication in 1965 under the editorship of John M. Robson. It carried long and short articles, news of new and forthcoming books and articles, and a continuing bibliography of works on Mill. In 1989 it merged with *The Bentham Newsletter* to become *Utilitas: A Journal of Utilitarian Studies*. It has provided a vehicle for Mill scholarship including but not limited to his philosophy.

The most widely read philosophical works of John Stuart Mill continue to be his essays *Utilitarianism* and *On Liberty*. Debates concerning utilitarianism in the second half of the twentieth century, such as the distinction between act utilitarianism and rule utilitarianism and the plausibility of each, have included controversies on the interpretation and plausibility of Mill's position on these issues. Also, those attacking or defending liberalism have inevitably included references to Mill's essay as one of the most representative statements of the liberal position. With the development of feminist philosophy his essay *The Subjection of Women* has also received renewed attention as an early feminist statement, sometimes dismissed as the "liberal feminist" position but sometimes defended against its critics.

Two controversial topics in Mill's utilitarianism continue to receive attention: his distinction between pleasures on grounds of superiority or inferiority of quality as well as quantity and his alleged "proof" of the principle of utility. In the early part of the twentieth century, the first of these was generally regarded as either inconsistent with his hedonism or as nonsense, and the second was regarded as a classic case of fallacious reasoning. In the second half of the twentieth century, these have been defended, although not always in the same ways. Some "friends" of Mill have tried to reduce the distinction of qualities to a quantitative distinction; others have insisted that Mill is correct in recognizing the phenomenal diversity of pleasurable experiences; but even among the latter there is disagreement about whether Mill is correct in correlating the distinction to the distinctively human (as opposed to nonhuman animal) faculties and whether qualitatively distinct pleasures are consistently preferred by those who are qualified by experiences of both.

Mill's "proof" has been the subject of numerous interpretations and controversy. It is no longer dismissed as a collection of fallacies, but whether it is a sound argument with plausible assumptions is still a matter of great debate.

The consistency between Mill's apparently hedonistic utilitarianism and his essay *On Liberty* has been another topic of extensive discussion. Here again the discussion has been more friendly to Mill, but with differences in interpretation. Some commentators have claimed consistency for him by a reinterpretation of his utilitarianism to make it nonhedonistic, with a conception of happiness that essentially involves the free exercise of rational capacities. Others have seen in Mill's psychological assumptions, with a complex phenomenal account of pleasure including "higher" and "lower" and the necessity for self-development as a necessary condition for the higher pleasures, a basis for consistency which remains hedonistic.

Whether Mill was a rule utilitarian was one of the questions that generated the distinction between act utilitarianism and rule utilitarianism. The essay by J. O. Urmson (1953) interpreting Mill as a rule utilitarian has been challenged and supported by citations both pro and con from Mill texts. A middle position, argued by Fred R. Berger (1984) and others, is that Mill endorsed a "strategy" for achieving the greatest happiness that was ostensibly rule utilitarian but that he seemed to think that if all hidden utilities were taken into consideration there would be no conflict between the two positions. Acts that violate useful rules weaken the rules and undermine the rule-abiding character of the agent. Acts that form part of a collection of acts that have bad consequences can theoretically be assigned a fraction of those bad consequences. Whether these moves are adequate to remove the conflict is suspect.

In chapter 5 of *Utilitarianism* Mill has a theory of rights correlative to some but not all morally significant actions, and he restricts the morally obligatory to those actions for which punishment has utility; in *August Comte and Positivism* (in *Collected Works,* Vol. 10:337–39) he clearly states a theory of morally meritorious action that goes beyond what is morally required. These would indicate that Mill's moral theory has a structure that is more complicated than any simple act- or rule-formulation.

The consistency between Mill's apparently hedonistic utilitarianism and his essay On Liberty *has been a topic of extensive discussion.*

Mill's *On Liberty* attempts to distinguish between conduct that concerns others and conduct that concerns only oneself. Strictly construed, very little conduct concerns only oneself. Studies of *On Liberty* by C. L. Ten (1980), John Gray (1983), and J. C. Rees (1985) have reinterpreted the distinction in terms of concerning the "interests" of self or others. Mill is seen to be holding the view that there is a right to liberty that is a right to autonomy. There is controversy, however, over the substance of this right and also over the "harm principle" that limits it.

Mill's contribution to the development of psychological theory and the applications of his theory in classical economics and in moral philosophy is the subject of an important study by Fred Wilson (1990).

[*See also Feminist Philosophy; Liberalism; Liberty.*]

BIBLIOGRAPHY

Berger, F. R. *Happiness, Justice, and Freedom: The Moral and Political Philosophy of John Stuart Mill.* Toronto, 1982.

Donner, W. *The Liberal Self: John Stuart Mill's Moral and Political Philosophy.* Ithaca, NY, 1991.

Edwards, R. B. *Pleasures and Pains: A Theory of Qualitative Hedonism.* Ithaca, NY, 1979.

Gray, J. *Mill on Liberty: A Defence.* London, 1983.

Laine, M. *Bibliography of Works on John Stuart Mill.* Toronto, 1982.

Lyons, D. "Mill's Theory of Morality," *Noûs,* Vol. 10 (1976), 101–20.

———. "Liberty and Harm to Others," in W. E. Cooper, K. Nielsen, and S. C. Patten, eds., *New Essays on John Stuart Mill and Utilitarianism* (Guelph, Ont., 1979).

McCloskey, H. J. *John Stuart Mill: A Critical Study.* London, 1971.

Mill, J. S. *Collected Works of John Stuart Mill,* 33 vols. Toronto, 1933–91.

The Mill Newsletter, Vols. 1–23 (1965–89).

Rees, J. C. *John Stuart Mill's "On Liberty."* Oxford, 1985.

Ryan, A. *John Stuart Mill.* New York, 1970.

———. *J. S. Mill.* London, 1974.

Skorupski, J. *John Stuart Mill.* London, 1989.

Ten, C. L. *Mill on Liberty.* Oxford, 1980.

Urmson, J. O. "The Interpretation of the Moral Philosophy of J. S. Mill," *Philosophical Quarterly,* Vol. 3 (1953), 33–39.

Utilitas, Vol. 1– (1989–).

West, H. R. "Mill's "Proof" of the Principle of Utility," in H. B. Miller and W. Williams, eds., *The Limits of Utilitarianism* (Minneapolis, 1982).

Wilson, F. *Psychological Analysis and the Philosophy of John Stuart Mill.* Toronto, 1990.

– HENRY R. WEST

MODAL LOGIC

The main developments since 1960 fall mainly under four headings: (1) formal analysis of modal logic, (2) epistemic logic, (3) conditional logic, (4) dynamic logic, and (5) the provability interpretation of modal logic.

Formal Developments

By 1960 a great many modal logics had been proposed. Thanks to the advent of possible worlds semantics a unified, systematic treatment became possible. The central concept was the normal modal logic, a logic in which all truth-functional tautologies and all instances of the so-called Kripke schema $\Box(A \supset B) \supset (\Box A \supset \Box B)$ are valid and which respects the rules of modus ponens (if $A \supset B$ and A are valid, then so is B) and of necessitation (if A is valid, then so is $\Box A$). The 1970s saw a great number of formal results of an increasingly mathematical character. Particularly interesting from a philosophical point of view was the discovery, by Kit Fine and S. K. Thomason, independently, that the relational Kripke semantics has a certain limitation—there are normal modal logics incomplete with respect to that semantics.

Epistemic Logic

In his book *Knowledge and Belief* (1962), Jaakko Hintikka proposed to give indexed modal operators epistemic or doxastic interpretations; that is, a box operator $\Box_i$ would be read as "the agent i knows that" or "the agent i believes that." One contentious topic was the status of this kind of logic: is it normative or descriptive or neither? Moreover, knowledge in Hintikka's sense implies various forms of omniscience. For example, is it reasonable that, as in Hintikka's system, agents should know all logically valid propositions or that they should know all logical consequences of their knowledge? Yet another topic was the so-called KK-thesis. Discussing the schemata $\Box_i A \supset \Box_i \Box_i A$ and $\neg \Box_i A \supset \Box_i \neg \Box_i A$, Hintikka felt the former ("positive introspection") should be regarded as valid, the latter ("negative introspection") not. In the theoretical computer science community, which became interested in epistemic logic

in the 1980s, the general consensus, reached without much debate, is that both are valid.

The main developments in modal logic since 1960 have been in formal analysis of modal logic; epistemic logic; conditional logic; and the provability interpretation of modal logic.

In 1969 David Lewis introduced the concept of common knowledge, which has since become important not only in philosophical analysis but also in theoretical computer science and economics. A proposition A is common knowledge within a group of agents if and only if, for every number n and every choice $i_1, \ldots, i_n$ of agents in the group, $\Box_{i_1} \ldots \Box_{i_n} A$ obtains (that is, i_1 knows that $\ldots i_n$ knows that A). It has been shown that common knowledge can make a crucial difference to problems concerning communication or other forms of rational action.

Conditional Logic

Toward the end of the 1960s, Robert C. Stalnaker and David Lewis, independently, presented logical analyses of conditional propositions, including counterfactuals ("if it were the case that A, then it would be the case that B" and "if it were the case that A, then it might be the case that B"). Both give a possible-worlds account according to which the truth of a conditional (of the kind in question) relative to a world depends on the truth of the consequent in one or several worlds selected from among those in which the antecedent is true (worlds in which the antecedent is true "under ideal circumstances," to use a phrase of Lennart Åqvist). Thus to determine, in a certain situation, the truth of the counterfactual proposition "If I had struck this match five seconds ago, it would have lighted" one has to consider, perhaps as a thought experiment, those situations which differ from the given situation *as little as possible except that* the match is struck; if it lights in those situations the counterfactual is true, otherwise it is not. The difficulty is to elucidate the expression "as little as possible except that."

Brian F. Chellas has shown that there is a close connection between Stalnaker's and Lewis's semantics and ordinary possible worlds semantics for modal logic; on Chellas's account "if it were the case that A, then it would be the case that B" can be read as "it is A-necessary that B"; and "if it were the case that A then it might be the case that B" can be read as "it is A-possible that B" (in symbols, $\square_A B$ and $\diamond_A B$, respectively). Chellas's reduction has the methodological advantage that it allows techniques of formal modal logic to bear on the formal problems of analyzing conditionals.

Dynamic Logic

In modal logic the only nonclassical operators are the box $\square$ (the necessity operator), and the diamond $\diamond$ (the possibility operator). Dynamic logic, created by Vaughan Pratt in the late 1970s, may be seen as a generalization over modal logic inasmuch as it postulates a set of terms such that for each term α there is one box operator and one diamond operator, for typographical reasons written as $[\alpha]$ and $<\alpha>$, respectively. Originally the intended interpretation of terms was as computer programs, but other interpretations are also possible, for example, as actions or events. If A is a formula then $[\alpha]A$ may be read as "after α it is always the case that A" and $<\alpha>A$ as "after α it is sometimes the case that A."

The interest of dynamic logic depends on the many operations on terms and formulas that are possible. For example, interpreting terms as actions, if α and β are actions, then $\alpha + \beta$ is the disjunctive action consisting in doing either α or β, and $\alpha;\beta$ is the composite action consisting in doing first α and then, without interruption, β. If α is an action, then α^* is the action consisting of doing α any finite number of times. If A is a proposition, then ?A is the action consisting in testing the truth of A; if A obtains, the answer is affirmative, if A is false there is no answer. It is worth noting that in Pratt's semantics $[\alpha + \beta]C \equiv ([\alpha]C \wedge [\beta]C)$ is generally valid but $[\alpha][\beta]C \equiv [\beta][\alpha]C$ is not.

The operations $+$, ; and $*$ (sum, composition, and the Kleene star) are called the three regular operations. Much of the early interest in dynamic logic was due to the fact that important aspects of reasoning about actions could be formalized within the new language. For example, there is a sense in which commands like "if it is true that A then do α else do β" and "while it is true that A do α" can be rendered. From a philosophical point of view the importance lies in the fact that in dynamic logic and extensions of dynamic logic one is able to refer to and talk about actions directly.

Other Developments

In a series of papers in the late 1960s and the early 1970s, Richard Montague undertook to apply the techniques achieved in the study of intensional logic to natural languages. Although this grandiose development falls outside this entry, it is worth noting that the Montague program may be seen as taking to an extreme but logical conclusion ideas originating at least in part in the analysis of modal logic.

[See also Conditionals; Kripke, Saul Aaron; Mathematical Logic; Philosophical Logic; Provability.]

BIBLIOGRAPHY

Guenthner, F., and D. M. Gabbay. *Handbook in Philosophical Logic*, Vol. 2. Dordrecht, 1984.

Fagin, R., J. Y. Halpern, Y. Moses, and M. Y. Vardi. *Reasoning about Knowledge*. Cambridge, MA, 1995.

Lenzen, W. *Recent Work in Epistemic Logic*. Amsterdam, 1978.

Lewis, D. *Counterfactuals*. Oxford, 1973.

Montague, R. *Formal Philosophy*. Edited by R. H. Thomason. New Haven, 1974.

– KRISTER SEGERBERG

MODALITY, PHILOSOPHY AND METAPHYSICS OF

This has received considerable attention in metaphysics and other areas of philosophy since the 1950s. During this period the notion has flourished, despite some determined resistance. This entry will first treat the foundations of modality, including modal skepticism, and then two specific issues important to those who accept modal notions. The discussion will be confined to logical modality—that is, to necessity and possibility as (supposed) modes of truth and predication. There will be no specific discussion of modal logic or its semantics.

Consider the sentence

(1) Necessarily, nine is odd.

What does it mean? Clarence Irving Lewis, a pioneer of modal logic, would likely have taken its meaning as captured by

(2) "Nine is odd" is analytically true.

where "analytically true" means true in virtue of the meanings of the terms it contains. Willard Van Orman Quine, a persistent and important critic of modal notions, has at least two objections (Quine, 1960). First, (2), unlike (1), does not refer to the number nine but rather to the sentence "Nine is odd." So, it is an unlikely candidate for making clear sense of (1). Second, although Quine would not automatically object to necessity taken as a predicate of sentences (provided it expressed a coherent concept), he is famous for having questioned the coherence of the notion of analyticity.

In (1) "necessarily" apparently attaches to a complete sentence to form a new sentence. If so, it functions as what logicians call an operator, like the negation operator of first-order logic. But such operators may also attach to open formulas. So, a modal logic built on this model will contain analogues of sentences like

(3) Something is necessarily odd.

We will see below that Quine would find any such account obscure and unacceptable. But the modern development of quantified modal logic, initiated in the work of Ruth Barcan Marcus, has favored precisely this approach. And the development of formal semantics for such systems, notably in the (independent) work of Stig Kanger, Saul Kripke, and Jaakko Hintikka, convincingly vitiates any charge of formal obscurity or incoherence. If modality is obscure or incoherent, it is so for philosophical reasons, perhaps of the sort Quine offered in attacking analyticity. But recent discussion of necessity, following Kripke, has sharply distinguished necessity from analyticity.

To say that a sentence expresses a necessary truth is to say that what it expresses could not have failed to be true. To say that a sentence is analytically true is to say that it is true solely in virtue of the meanings of the words it contains. These are clearly different notions. A common tendency to confuse them undoubtedly stemmed from the conviction that, even if they were different, they were still coextensive. But, having called attention to the confusion, Kripke (1972) argued that various sentences that are not analytically true nevertheless express necessary truths.

Saying that necessary truths are those that could not have failed to be true gives, not so much a helpful characterization of necessity, as a mere paraphrase of 'necessary'. We still want to know what the necessity of a truth consists in—that is, what insulates it from possible falsity. The need for a clear characterization intensified as more philosophers came to believe that some nontrivial truths really are necessary and as modal skeptics continued to press charges of obscurity or incoherence.

One approach to this foundational problem would be to provide an explicit analysis of the modal notions using more basic concepts that may independently be held to be clear and coherent. Another would be to claim that the notions of necessity and possibility are primitive—that there are no more fundamental concepts with which to analyze them. Certainly this approach would not convert many skeptics unless accompanied by some new and convincing illumination of the modal notions.

An important foundational first step is to distinguish logical, or what is sometimes called metaphysical, modality from that reflected in other modal idioms, especially epistemic and physical. Such modal concepts often concern what is necessary (or possible) given that certain conditions hold. In contrast, metaphysical necessity is the notion of what is necessary, period. If, say, physical necessity is conceived as what is necessary given the actual laws of physics, then physical necessity has been characterized in terms of metaphysical necessity, for questions of physical necessity are reduced to questions of the metaphysical necessity of conditional statements.

Discussion of modal foundations has almost always involved the notion of possible world(s). (In fact, a fascination with worlds has sometimes obscured the foundational problem, leaving it addressed only indirectly or not at all.) A proposition is held to be necessary if it is true at all (relevant) worlds; a proposition is possible if it is true at some world or other. These formulations may be taken variously: as genuine analyses of the modal notions; as important characterizations of the modal notions; or merely as providing a picturesque metaphor, helpful in thinking about modality. The recent interest in possible worlds is, of course, partly inspired by Leibniz but also by formal developments in the semantics of quantified modal systems.

Proponents of worlds have offered several different conceptions falling into two major kinds that may (somewhat misleadingly) be called concrete and abstract. Concrete worlds are entities like the actual physical world around us but causally isolated from the actual world and from each other. (There is room here for partly or entirely nonphysical worlds and perhaps also for an entirely empty world.) Concrete worlds are existing entities, and each is held to be actual with respect to itself. Because these worlds do not overlap, no entity existing in any world also exists in any other world. Hence, questions about what is possible or necessary for a given individual are answered by appeal to a counterpart relation that may hold between pairs of individuals in different worlds. Something is possible for a given individual if it is true at some world of a counterpart of that individual. Theories of modality along these lines are called counterpart theories. Such theories conform to possibilism—the view that there truly are merely possible objects. (Actualism is the denial of possibilism.) The originator and leading proponent of this conception of modality is David Lewis (1986). For Lewis modal operators are quantifiers over possible worlds. So, a noniterated assertion of necessity is simply an assertion that a certain nonmodal state of affairs holds at all possible worlds. Thus, it is natural to see counterpart theories as offering an analysis of modality. But it has been argued that, even if there are other isolated concrete worlds, it is difficult to see how goings on there can be relevant to modal questions here (Jubien, 1988).

There are several treatments of worlds as abstract entities. For example, they have been taken to be entities of their own special kind (Davies, 1981); certain propositions (Prior & Fine, 1976); certain states of affairs (Plantinga, 1974); and certain sets of propositions (Adams, 1974). Such treatments are often similar in structure and spirit and share certain virtues and (alleged) vices.

A proposition is held to be necessary

if it is true at all (relevant) worlds;

a proposition is possible

if it is true at some world or other.

Robert Adams (1974) takes worlds to be maximal consistent sets of propositions. But consistency is explicitly understood in terms of the possible (joint) truth of propositions. So the treatment cannot support an analysis of possibility in terms of worlds. Its virtue lies in providing a precise concept for the often vaguely conceived notion of possible world and thereby enhancing whatever illumination worlds can provide for modality in general. It has. however, been argued that this and other maximality-driven accounts produce paradox (Jubien, 1988).

A crucial issue for those who accept modal notions is whether contingent entities like people or physical objects have nontrivial essential properties, properties that they could not have failed to have. The leading proponent of an affirmative answer has been Kripke, and many have been converted to his position.

Essentialism is often characterized as the acceptance of (nontrivial) *de re* necessities, in which a property is held to be necessarily instantiated by a thing (or a necessary property is held to be instantiated). In ordinary English,

(4) Necessarily, Cicero is human.

and

(5) Cicero is necessarily human.

are perhaps not normally taken as making distinct assertions. But if (5) is taken to entail

(6) Something is necessarily human.

then the modality is genuinely *de re* and goes beyond the merely *de dicto* sense in which (4) may be taken to entail "Necessarily, something is human" but not to entail (6).

Quine (1960) found the very notion of necessary properties nonsensical, arguing that any necessity or contingency in an attribution of a property to a thing must depend on how that thing is described, not on how the thing is, independent of any particular description. But Kripke (1972) insisted that this cannot be right. He urged, with respect to a variety of examples, that one simply cannot imagine the thing in question not having the property in question. Thus, one might ask whether we could imagine Cicero himself but without his being human. Whereas we find no difficulty imagining Cicero to fail of being an orator or being Roman, it seems much more difficult, if not impossible, to imagine him not being human.

It is vital that we assume for the sake of such thought experiments that the thing in question actually does have the property in question. The reason is that we are asking whether any of a thing's (actual) properties are essential. So, epistemic cases, in which we have been incorrect all along about the actual properties, are ruled out. (It is irrelevant that Cicero might prove to have been a robot or an extraterrestrial.) It is also vital that we take our inability to imagine something as good evidence of its impossibility.

Many who initially thought they could, for example, imagine Cicero not being human became persuaded that there is a better way to describe what they imagined, one that does not entail that Cicero is not necessarily human. It has been argued that, while such thought experiments do support nontrivial essentialism, they do not support necessity *de re,* and thus that there are really two doctrines where there is commonly thought to be one (Jubien, 1993).

A central question for essentialists is whether the essential properties of a thing include its 'haecceity' (or 'thisness'). Cicero's haecceity is the supposed property of being Cicero, a property that is normally taken to be primitive and nonqualitative. Such a property would also be an essence of Cicero. In possible-worlds terminology, an essence of a thing is an essential property that no other thing has in any world. But one may accept essences without accepting haecceities.

Defenders of haecceities, like Adams (1979), often make their case using an example borrowed from Max Black. Here is one version. Imagine that the world consisted simply of two qualitatively indistinguishable globes. Then it seems that there must be another world that is qualitatively indistinguishable from the first but in which the positions of the globes are interchanged. It is hard to make sense of this intuitive possibility (or perhaps even of the initial idea that there are two globes rather than one) without thinking that there is some nonqualitative way in which the globes differ. So it has been held that they differ by having different haecceities, and haecceities have been held to provide the conceptual underpinning for all of the alternative possibilities for things.

One version of this view is that haecceities are needed to account for transworld identity and hence that any illuminating treatment of possibility in terms of possible worlds rests on the acceptance of haecceities. But Kripke (1972) emphatically denied that there is a problem of transworld identity in the first place. To think that there is would be to imagine that worlds are presented to us purely qualitatively and that we must somehow figure out whether a given individual exists in another world from the qualitative features displayed by individuals in that world. But Kripke would insist that we do not normally think of worlds in this way at all. We normally describe worlds partly in terms of specific individuals that they contain. Thus, we say, for example, "Consider a world in which Cicero is not an orator." Assuming we are right that there are such worlds, it is automatic that Cicero inhabits them, and there is no problem of checking the features of various individuals to determine which one is Cicero. For Kripke it is a matter of stipulation that Cicero inhabits these worlds, and this is quite independent of the matter of haecceities. Those who see a problem of transworld identification and invoke haecceities in order to solve it are very likely assuming that the role of worlds is to provide an analysis of the modal notions, an assumption that Kripke rejects.

Others have argued for different reasons that haecceities are not needed to make sense of genuine possibilities for things (Chisholm, 1986). It has also been argued that things have qualitative essences that, for example, support a distinction between the two-globe worlds but that no such property could serve as an essence of, say, Cicero (Jubien, 1993).

Obviously, there can be no problem of transworld identification in counterpart theories since it is impossible for an individual to inhabit different worlds. So the question of haecceitism must take a different form. For Lewis (1986) the key question is whether what an individual's otherwordly counterparts represent as possible for that individual depends strictly on qualitative features of those counterparts. He claims it does and considers himself an antihaecceitist on this basis.

Important contributors to the contemporary philosophical discussion of modality not mentioned above include David M. Armstrong, Graeme Forbes, David Kaplan, Richard Montague, Hilary Putnam, Nathan Salmon, Brian Skyrms, Robert Stalnaker, and Peter van Inwagen.

[See also Analyticity; Armstrong, David M.; Chisholm, Roderick M.; Kripke, Saul Aaron; Leibniz, Gottfried Wilhelm; Marcus, Ruth Barcan; Metaphysics; Modal Logic; Putnam, Hilary; Quine, Willard Van Orman.]

BIBLIOGRAPHY

Adams, R. M. "Theories of Actuality," *Noûs*, Vol. 8 (1974), 211–31.
———. "Primitive Thisness and Primitive Identity," *Journal of Philosophy*, Vol. 76 (1979), 5–26.
Chisholm, R. M. "Possibility without Haecceity," in P. A. French, T. E. Uehling, Jr., and H. K. Wettstein, eds., *Studies in Essentialism*, Midwest Studies in Philosophy, Vol. 11 (Minneapolis, 1986).
Davies, M. K. *Meaning, Quantification, Necessity: Themes in Philosophical Logic.* London, 1981.
Forbes, G. *The Metaphysics of Modality.* Oxford, 1985.
French, P. A., T. E. Uehling, Jr., and H. K. Wettstein, eds. *Studies in Essentialism*, Midwest Studies in Philosophy, Vol. 11. Minneapolis, 1986. A valuable collection.
Jubien, M. "Problems with Possible Worlds," in D. F. Austin, ed., *Philosophical Analysis* (Dordrecht, 1988).
———. *Ontology, Modality, and the Fallacy of Reference.* Cambridge, 1993.
Kripke, S. A. *Naming and Necessity.* Cambridge, MA, 1972.
Lewis, D. *On the Plurality of Worlds.* Oxford, 1986.
Marcus, R. B. *Modalities.* Oxford, 1993.
Plantinga, A. *The Nature of Necessity.* Oxford, 1974.
Prior, A. N., and K. Fine. *Worlds, Times, and Selves.* London, 1976.
Quine, W. V. O. *Word and Object.* Cambridge, MA, 1960.

— MICHAEL JUBIEN

MODEL THEORY

Model theory began as a branch of mathematics, and its main advances between 1960 and 1995 lay in mathematics. But some aspects of model theory interested philosophers and linguists during this period, and by the 1990s it was also becoming an important tool in computer science.

Nonstandard analysis—invented by Abraham Robinson in 1960—is an application of model theory that uses the compactness theorem to add infinitesimals to the field of real numbers. One can then use these infinitesimals roughly as Leibniz intended; for example, one calculates a derivative as (almost) a ratio dy/dx of two infinitesimals dy and dx. In 1976 Jerome Keisler published an undergraduate textbook of calculus using nonstandard methods.

Though nonstandard analysis soon lost contact with the mainstream of model theory, it set a paradigm.

Thus, one could apply model theory to branches of mathematics by identifying the first-order relations (i.e., those relations defined by first-order formulas) in certain structures, and then using the compactness theorem or other general theorems of model theory. Two remarkable successes along these lines were the proof by James Ax, Simon Kochen, and Yuri Ershov in 1965 of a number-theoretic conjecture of Emil Artin (so far as it is true), and Ehud Hrushovski's proof in 1993 of a diophantine conjecture of Serge Lang.

The 1960s saw an invasion of model theory by techniques from combinatorial and descriptive set theory. Set theorists realized that certain model-theoretic methods (ultraproducts and indiscernibles) yielded information about the set-theoretic universe and especially about the effects of large cardinals. In 1965 Michael Morley used indiscernibles to prove an old conjecture describing those first-order theories, which in some uncountable cardinality have only one model up to isomorphism.

Morley's work formed a new paradigm, in which model theorists classified first-order theories according to whether their models are chaotic or form a well-structured family. In 1982 Saharon Shelah proved that the class of all models of a complete theory in a countable first-order language is either highly structured, in the sense that one can catalogue the models by intuitively meaningful invariants, or hopelessly unstructured. This took Shelah some twelve years' work, during which he created stability theory. In the mid-1980s model theorists realized that stability theory is a model-theoretic analogue of algebraic geometry, and many links with algebraic geometry (particularly the theory of algebraic groups) came to light.

The period 1982–92 saw axiomatic descriptions of important classes of definable sets in algebraic geometry. One consequence was the creation (by Lou van den Dries, Anand Pillay, and Charles Steinhorn) of a new branch of function theory dealing with O-minimal fields, whose first-order relations resemble those of the field of real numbers.

Here we turn from mathematics to applications in philosophy and elsewhere.

Around 1990 several philosophers attacked what they took to be a consensus that logical truth means truth in all models, thinking of models as possible worlds. In fact there never was such a consensus. For first-order logic (though not in general) one can show by the completeness theorem that the logical truths are exactly the sentences true in all models; but as Georg Kreisel in 1969 and Willard Van Orman Quine in 1970 made clear, this argument does not involve possible worlds.

However, there are ways to represent possibility and other modalities in terms of models. During the 1950s several writers explored how one might axiomatize the notion that one structure is possible relative to another. Saul Kripke gave in 1959 the formulation that came to be accepted: one considers a set of structures and a binary relation of possibility between them. In the model theory of modal logic, a sentence 'Necessarily A' is true in a structure M if and only if A is true in all structures possible relative to M.

The 1960s saw an invasion of model theory by techniques from combinatorial and descriptive set theory.

One can apply these notions to various kinds of possibility. An important example is time, where the structures possible relative to a structure M are those representing times later than M. During the 1970s Vaughan Pratt and others used similar ideas to represent the execution of computer programs through time. By the mid-1980s model-theoretic techniques appeared in the theory of processes in computer science. For example, the model-theoretic technique of back-and-forth, a device for comparing two structures by choosing elements alternately from the first and second structure, yielded the bisimulation test for comparing two processes.

In 1970 Richard Montague adapted the model theory of modal logic to formalize the semantics of a fragment of English containing problematic expressions such as 'necessarily', 'believe that', 'wish to', and 'change'. This heroic effort created Montague semantics, a sophisticated application of models to the semantics of natural languages. In 1985 the generalized phrase structure grammar (GPSG) of Gerald Gazdar et al. used a modified form of Montague semantics as its semantic component. Nevertheless it became clear that language devices such as cross-reference between sentences need ideas that depart further from classical model theory. For example, the discourse representation theory of Irene Heim and Hans Kamp uses the notion of an element in a structure being accessible to an expression.

Another development was to stay with models in the classical sense, but to study properties definable in non-first-order languages. This work began within mathematics, but by 1990 it had moved completely to computer science. For example, one can represent a data base as a finite structure; then a query to the data base asks whether a certain formal sentence is true in the structure. Data-base queries often ask questions that have no first-order formalization, such as whether one element can be reached from another in a finite number of steps. The model-theoretic technique of back-and-forth has proved invaluable for measuring the expressive power of database query languages.

[See also Infinitesimals; Kripke, Saul Aaron; Leibniz, Gottfried Wilhelm; Mathematical Logic; Modal Logic; Quine, Willard Van Orman; Semantics; Set Theory.]

BIBLIOGRAPHY

Hodges, W. A. *Model Theory.* Cambridge, 1993.
van Benthem, J. *A Manual of Intensional Logic.* 2d ed. Stanford, CA, 1988.

— WILFRID A. HODGES

MODERNISM AND POSTMODERNISM

Modern philosophy is construed as beginning sometime in the Renaissance. A philosophy that seeks new foundations for knowledge was offered as an alternative to that provided by the ancient philosophers. Modern philosophy was presented as starting afresh from new beginnings—turning to nature directly (Bacon), turning to the mind directly (Descartes), turning to experience directly (Hobbes). The "quarrel between the ancients and the moderns" resulted from this basic disagreement as to the sources of philosophical knowledge.

Modern philosophy was presented

as starting afresh from new beginnings—

turning to nature directly (Bacon),

to the mind directly (Descartes),

or to experience directly (Hobbes).

Modern philosophy turned away from the past and toward the future, toward the advancement of knowledge, toward human understanding, and toward progress through method or through experience. With the break between the continental rationalists (Descartes, Malebranche, Leibniz, and Spinoza) and the British empiricists (Hobbes, Locke, and Hume) at the end of the eighteenth-century Enlightenment, a new formulation in modern philosophy was called for. Kant brought together in his "critical" philosophy the commitments to the analytic exercise of the mind, on the one hand, and the empirical reception through the senses on the other. With Kant, modern philosophy combined the "tran-

scendental unity of apperception" with the "manifold of experience." Modern philosophy was no longer based on a theory of representation—representation to the mind through reason or representation to the mind through experience—but on the linking of transcendental subjectivity and empirical objectivity. This "doublet," as Foucault came to name it, accounted for a whole new way of philosophizing.

Modernism is distinguished from modern philosophy in that it is linked to certain movements in art and literature that began sometime around the end of the nineteenth century. While drawing upon some similar characteristics of "modern philosophy," modernism in art, literature, and philosophy involved novelty, break with tradition, progress, continuous development, knowledge derived either from the position of the subject or from claims to objectivity, and concomitantly the crisis in knowledge produced by this very dichotomy. Hence in modernism, at the same time that certain theories based knowledge on a centered, transcendental, interpreting subjectivity, and others based knowledge on certain, atomistic, analytic, empirical objectivity, the crisis in knowledge created a sense of uncertainty, paradox, incompleteness, inadequacy, emptiness, and void. Modernism in art and literature involved a shift away from the dichotomies of romanticism and realism to the stream of consciousness, lived and internal time-consciousness, transcendental subjectivity, narrated remembrance and awareness, portrayed speed, mechanisms, objects, and abstractions. Latent content was allowed to penetrate through the surfaces of manifest content. Understanding would have to delve more deeply than surfaces and mere appearances. A phenomenology would be needed in order to inventory the contents of consciousness (Husserl) or a psychoanalysis to delve the depths of what the mind was really thinking (Freud); or a logical positivism would take the alternative tack by excluding all knowledge that cannot be verified logically and empirically (Russell, early Wittgenstein, Ayer). Modernism in philosophy involved at each stage the Kantian combination of the empirical and the transcendental, the objective and the subjective, the material and the intellectual—but each time measuring the doublet with weight on one side or the other.

The disintegration of modernism in philosophy was internal. The radical claims of logical positivism excluded all that was of value: metaphysics, aesthetics, axiology, and so forth. The rigorous science of transcendental phenomenology excluded the very existence of what it was investigating. The dualism of creative evolutionism left an irreparable dichotomy between lived experience and objective knowledge. The pragmatism of radical empiricism failed to provide a way to interpret the meanings of experience. The center of modernism in philosophy could not hold because its very foundations were in question. But attempts to retrieve it from itself by the turn to language—ordinary language, analytic philosophies of language, hermeneutics of language, semiologies of language—could not resolve the dilemmas of human existence. Modernism in philosophy faced the absurd, the ambiguous, and the dialectical. And it worked these theories to their limits.

In the mid-1960s philosophy came to look at its epistemological formations and to ask whether the humanisms and anthropologisms of modern philosophy had not circumscribed themselves. Merleau-Ponty's interrogations were reformulated in Foucault's archeology of knowledge. The human sciences placed the optimisms and pessimisms of modern philosophy in question by circumventing the theory of "man." Knowledge formations were articulated in terms of multiple spaces of knowledge production and no longer according to a central source or position, or ego, or self, or subject, nor according to a multiplicity of sense-data, objective criteria, material evidence, or behaviors. Knowledge formations crossed disciplines and operated in multiple spaces where questions of structure, frame, margin, boundary, edge, limit, and so on, would mark any discursive practice. In other words, knowledge was no longer produced from a center, foundation, ground, basis, identity, authority, or transcendental competency. Knowledge was dispersed, multiple, fragmented, and theoretically varied. Knowledge was no longer based on continuity, unity, totality, comprehensiveness, and consistency. Knowledge began to be understood in terms of discontinuity, difference, dissemination, and differends.

By the early 1970s postmodernism—a term that Daniel Bell used in connection with postindustrial society in the 1950s, that architects appealed to in the 1960s, and that art and literary historians invoked in the 1970s—had still not been invoked in connection with philosophy. Derrida's grammatology and theory of "difference" in 1967 (building upon Heidegger's account of "the end of philosophy and the task of thinking") turned into a full-fledged deconstruction in the 1970s. Deleuze and Guattari's notion of the rhizomal thinking (as opposed to hierarchical, authorizing arborescent thinking) marked a move against psychoanalytic theories based on Oedipal authority and paternal insistence. Their idea of nomadism placed emphasis on knowledge, experience, and relations that were not organized around a central concept. Kristeva's account of the revolution in poetic language marked the distinction between the semiotic and the symbolic. Where symbolic—scientific, theoretical, phallic, paternal—

thinking had pervaded philosophy and science, Kristeva invoked the semiotic as the poetic, fluid, receptacle-like, maternal thinking that has been hidden in modern thought. Yet postmodern was hardly the term that was invoked to describe this kind of philosophizing. Correspondingly, the more restricted study of phenomenology and existentialism in philosophy gave way to the more multiple and diverse theories implicit in continental philosophy: deconstruction, archeology of knowledge, semanalysis, schizoanalysis, feminist theory, and so forth. Yet, while poststructuralism (in connection with Foucault, Derrida, Deleuze, Kristeva, et al.) was hailed as the successor to structuralism (Lévi-Strauss, Barthes, Lacan, Althusser), and existential phenomenology (Heidegger, Sartre, Merleau-Ponty, de Beauvoir), postmodernism was still not a relevant category in philosophy until well into the 1980s. As time passed, postmodernism and postmodern thought came to take precedence over poststructuralism as the prevalent theoretical formulation.

Modernism is distinguished from modern philosophy in that it is linked to certain movements in art and literature that began sometime around the end of the nineteenth century.

Postmodern thought means the appeal to differences—differences in theories, differences in formulations, differences in identities. Postmodern thought rejects hierarchies and genealogies, continuities and progress, resolutions and overcomings (*Überwindungen*). Postmodern thought, in fact, cannot operate outside of the modern, for it is itself what can be called an "indecidable." The postmodern signals the end of modernity, but it operates at the same time necessarily within the modern. To claim that the postmodern is outside the modern is to identify it as other than the modern, but that which is outside or other reinscribes the identity of the modern and therefore the postmodern inscription within it. Hence the postmodern both marks places of difference within the modern and calls for an alternative to the modern. The postmodern in any case does not call for the destruction of the modern, not does it seek to deny the modern, since it is necessarily part of the modern.

The postmodern involves the question of the end or limit or margin of what is in question. History, man, knowledge, painting, writing, the modern—each is posed in terms of its end. The end is not as much a matter of termination or conclusion any more than a matter of goal and aspiration. The postmodern involves, as Vattimo notes, a *Verwindung* of modernity—a getting over, a convalescence, a recovering from modernity. This means that modernity is itself placed in question and no longer taken as an unquestioned given. The cracks and fissures in modernity, the places where modernity cannot be fully aware of itself, the moments of unpresentability in the modern—these are the concerns of postmodern thought. As Lyotard has noted in his famous *The Postmodern Condition* (1984), the postmodern involves the presentation of the unpresentable in presentation itself—that is, in modernity, the concern was to present something new, something unheard of, something unique, something shocking, something unpresentable. The postmodern involves the presentation of the unpresentable in presentation itself—the

---

By the 1970s postmodernism

—a term that Daniel Bell used in connection with

postindustrial society in the 1950s—

had still not been invoked

in connection with philosophy.

---

formulation of the moments of unpresentability as they mark what is presented. Lyotard calls attention to the role of the "differend" as the place of conflict between two alternative positions. The differend does not belong to either side. It belongs only to the place between, to the gap between the two presentations on either side. This is the postmodern moment—such moments or events with which the modern is distinctively scarred and animated.

[See also Beauvoir, Simone de; Deconstruction; Derrida, Jacques; Descartes, René; Existentialism; Foucault, Michel; Freud, Sigmund; Heidegger, Martin; Hobbes, Thomas; Hume, David; Husserl, Edmund; Kant, Immanuel; Language; Leibniz, Gottfried Wilhelm; Locke, John; Merleau-Ponty, M.; Phenomenology; Poststructuralism; Realism; Russell, Bertrand Arthur William; Sartre, Jean-Paul; Self; Spinoza, Benedict (Baruch); Wittgenstein, Ludwig Josef Johann.]

BIBLIOGRAPHY

Derrida, J. *Margins of Philosophy.* Translated by A. Bass. Chicago, 1982.
Foucault, M. *The Order of Things.* Translator anon. New York, 1970.
Kristeva, J. *Revolution in Poetic Language.* Translated by M. Waller. New York, 1984.
Lyotard, J.-F. *The Postmodern Condition.* Translated by G. Bennington and B. Massumi. Minneapolis, 1984.
———. *Toward the Postmodern.* Translated by R. Harvey and M. Roberts. Atlantic Highlands, NJ, 1993.
Natoli, J., and L. Hutcheon, eds. *A Postmodern Reader.* Albany, NY, 1993.
Silverman, H. J., ed. *Postmodernism—Philosophy and the Arts.* New York, 1990.
———. *Textualities: Between Hermeneutics and Deconstruction.* New York, 1994.
Vattimo, G. *The End of Modernity.* Translated by J. R. Snyder. Baltimore, 1988.

— HUGH J. SILVERMAN

MORAL EPISTEMOLOGY

Moral epistemology is concerned with the epistemic evaluation of moral judgments and theories. It does not seek to determine whether specific moral judgments or theories are known, justified, warranted, rational, reasonable, or what have you. It is the business of moral theorists and the ordinary people who make and act upon moral judgments to make such determinations. The moral epistemologist's interest in the evaluation of moral judgments and theories is more general: her aim is to determine how, if at all, moral judgments or theories might be justified, rational, and so forth. Other areas of epistemology are similar: for example, epistemologists studying perception seek a general understanding of how visual perception justifies beliefs, not to determine whether specific perceptual beliefs are justified.

Questions about moral epistemology are fundamental, and attempts to answer them go back at least to Plato and Socrates. Nonetheless, it can seem the field developed only in the last quarter of the twentieth century. Though moral epistemology has always been included in metaethics, which is defined as the study of the meaning and justification of moral statements, the inclusion of epistemological questions under this definition is misleading since twentieth-century metaethics has focused almost exclusively on questions of meaning. Moreover, after flirting with intuitionism (which either left moral knowledge mysterious or subsumed it under our knowledge of our concepts or language—see, e.g., Moore, 1903, and Ross, 1930), metaethics settled in for a long infatuation with nondescriptivism (see, e.g., Gibbard, 1990, Hare, 1952, and Stevenson, 1937). Because nondescriptivism holds that the point of moral language is not to state facts, and that moral claims are therefore neither true nor false, questions about the justification of moral statements drop out of nondescriptivist metaethics, at least if these questions are understood as epistemological. Intelligible questions about the justification, reasonableness, or rationality of moral statements remain. But such questions are practical, not epistemological: they seek, for example, a reason for believing that it is in one's own interest to abide by the dictates of morality.

Normative ethics has emphasized questions of meaning as well, and this has also dampened the development of moral epistemology. If substantive moral questions are answered by analysis of moral language or concepts, there is nothing distinctive about moral knowledge. The epistemology of conceptual analysis should apply equally well whether the analysis produces ethical theories or theories in another area of philosophy.

Two developments in the 1970s focused attention on moral epistemology. One was the widespread self-conscious adoption of reflective equilibrium as a method of moral injury. (The method was [arguably] employed by philosophers long before it was explicitly described and self-consciously employed.) Goodman (1965) first described reflective equilibrium and advocated it for justifying principles of induction. Rawls (1971) further developed the method and applied it to moral inquiry. Reflective equilibrium is a coherence method. One must begin the process of theory construction with one's considered moral judgments, which can be of any level of generality, and formulate a system of principles that yield these judgments. But then one must proceed via a process of mutual adjustment. When the emerging theory is found to conflict with central, very confidently made considered judgments, the inquirer must revise the theory. But if a well-confirmed element of the theory that is independently plausible is found to conflict with less firmly held considered judgments, then these judgments are revised. The decision regarding what to revise is made for each case on the basis of what seems most likely to be correct to the inquirer, all things considered. (This description fits Goodman's original approach, known as narrow reflective equilibrium. Rawls advocated a method of wide reflective equilibrium, which directs the inquirer to bring her moral judgments and theory into coherence with any background beliefs or theories that might be relevant, again via a process of mutual adjustment. [On wide versus narrow reflective equilibrium, see Daniels, 1979, or DePaul, 1993.].)

Since reflective equilibrium seems to grant first the inquirer's considered moral judgments and later her judgments of what is more likely to be correct crucial roles in inquiry, it has been widely criticized as a sophisticated version of intuitionism, which makes for an unreliable and extremely conservative method. (Brandt, 1979, is a representative critic of the use of reflective equilibrium in ethics. Stich, 1990, criticizes reflective equilibrium as a general philosophical method.) One

response admits that an argument for the reliability of considered moral judgments is needed while stressing that the required argument cannot be produced prior to employing the equilibrium method. The fact that we cannot now produce the required argument therefore is no decisive objection since the argument can only emerge as part of the coherent system that reflective equilibrium will eventually produce. (See Daniels, 1979.) Although no one has done so in this context, one might also respond by appealing to a general coherentist epistemology and rejecting the critic's apparent demand to have the foundations of moral knowledge established. (Brink develops this natural line of argument while defending moral realism. See below.) Finally, one can respond by recognizing that there are a number of significant dimensions of epistemic evaluation. One might then grant that because reflective equilibrium relies on human intuition, it is likely unreliable and hence, if reliability is required for justification, unlikely to yield justified beliefs. One then defends the method by showing either that it, or that only it, yields other significant epistemic goods—for example, rational belief. (Using different terminology, and focusing on reflective equilibrium as a method for ethics or as a general philosophical method respectively, De Paul, 1993, and Sosa, 1991, have pursued this approach.)

The moral epistemologist's interest in the evaluation of moral judgments and theories is, generally, to determine how moral judgments or theories might be justified, rational, and so forth.

The second development that prompted work in moral epistemology concerned metaphysical rather than methodological issues. The nondescriptivism of traditional analytic philosophy, which dominated metaethics through the middle of the twentieth century, left little room for substantive moral inquiry. But moral philosophers could not resist the lively debates about the pressing moral and political issues of the 1960s. They became involved in these debates, bringing argumentative strategies familiar in other areas of philosophy to bear upon substantive moral questions. These debates proceeded as though a question of truth were at stake, as though there were a fact of the matter to be determined, and as a consequence moral philosophy seemed tacitly to assume moral realism. It is, therefore, perhaps true to say that analytic nondescriptivism was abandoned more because philosophers simply became bored with the limits it imposed than because it was refuted. It is no surprise, then, that this tacitly accepted realism and descriptivism regarding moral language was challenged.

The new debate tended to focus more on the metaphysical issue regarding realism rather than on descriptivism. One reason for this was that Mackie (1977), one of the most important critics of realism, was willing to grant that our ordinary moral language is in fact descriptive. But he went on to argue that the kind of realism about ethics to which our moral language commits us is metaphysically and epistemologically untenable. Moral facts are metaphysically "queer"; they cannot happily be fit into the natural world (a point also forcibly made by Harman, 1977), and our epistemic access to moral facts is at best problematic. On the metaphysical front, efforts to defend moral facts have for the most part attempted to assimilate them either to natural facts of the sort discovered by science (Boyd, 1988, and Brink, 1989) or to secondary qualities such as colors (McDowell, 1985, and Wiggins, 1987). (See also Goldman, 1988, who assimilates moral facts and inquiry to legal facts.)

Efforts to respond to the epistemological challenge to realism have followed suit. Those who see moral facts as akin to natural facts argue that something very much like reflective equilibrium is the method of scientific inquiry, that this is also the method of moral inquiry, and that in both cases the method is supported by a coherence account of epistemic justification. (Boyd, 1988, and Brink, 1989.) Those who assimilate moral properties to secondary qualities naturally take some sort of perceptual knowledge as a model for their moral epistemology. (McNaughton, 1988.) The model need not be something simple such as color perception. Moral epistemology is more plausibly modeled on more complicated types of perception—for example, perception of the tonal qualities of a complex musical composition, which requires special sensitivity acquired through extensive experience and perhaps a course of training.

Some philosophers are interested in modeling moral epistemology upon perception because of concerns about the way philosophical inquiry into morality is conducted rather than because of metaphysical worries about realism. They are dissatisfied with the rather dry, artificial nature of the traditional type of moral theorizing that is based on a scientific model and is so far removed from our ordinary experience of making moral judgments and decisions. One problem with such theorizing is that it tends to focus exclusively on abstract principles and thinly described, highly stylized examples. As a result, moral theorists tend to miss the very

particular elements of real cases that can be morally crucial and have failed to notice what is involved in the kind of sensitivity required to notice and respond to such particulars (Nussbaum, 1990).

Although work in moral epistemology has flourished after the passing of traditional analytic nondescriptivism, such work tends to be done in the service of other interests and not because of the kind of pure interest that motivated, for example, much work on the epistemology of perception. In such circumstances there is more than the usual danger of distorting the object of inquiry to fit the theory.

[See also Coherentism; Epistemology; Goodman, Nelson; Hare, Richard M.; Mackie, John Leslie; Meaning; Moral Realism; Nondescriptivism; Perception; Plato; Rationality; Rawls, John; Realism; Ross, William David; Socrates; Stevenson, Charles.]

BIBLIOGRAPHY

Boyd, R. "How to Be a Moral Realist," in G. Sayre-McCord, ed., *Moral Realism* (Ithaca, NY, 1988).

Brandt, R. B. *A Theory of the Right and Good.* New York, 1979.

Brink, D. O. *Moral Realism and the Foundations of Ethics.* Cambridge, 1989.

Daniels, N. "Wide Reflective Equilibrium and Theory Acceptance in Ethics," *Journal of Philosophy,* Vol. 76 (1979), 256–82.

DePaul, M. R. *Balance and Refinement: Beyond Coherence Methods in Ethics.* London, 1993.

Gibbard, A. *Wise Choices, Apt Feelings.* Cambridge, MA, 1990.

Goldman, A. *Moral Knowledge.* London, 1988.

Goodman, N. *Fact, Fiction, and Forecast.* Indianapolis, 1965.

Hare, R. M. *The Language of Morals.* Oxford, 1952.

Harman, G. *The Nature of Morality.* New York, 1977.

Mackie, J. L. *Ethics: Inventing Right and Wrong.* New York, 1977.

McDowell, J. "Values and Secondary Properties," in T. Honderich, ed., *Morality and Objectivity* (London, 1985).

McNaughton, D. A. *Moral Vision.* Oxford, 1988.

Moore, G. E. *Principia Ethica.* Cambridge, 1903.

Nussbaum, M. *Love's Knowledge.* Oxford, 1990.

Rawls, J. *A Theory of Justice.* Cambridge, MA, 1971.

Ross, W. D. *The Right and the Good.* Oxford, 1930.

Sosa, E. "Equilibrium in Coherence?" in *Knowledge in Perspective: Selected Essays in Epistemology* (Cambridge, 1991).

Stevenson, C. L. "The Emotive Meaning of Ethical Terms," *Mind,* Vol. 46 (1937), 14–31.

Stich, S. *The Fragmentation of Reason.* Cambridge, MA, 1990.

Wiggins, D. *Needs, Values, and Truth: Essays in the Philosophy of Value.* Oxford, 1987.

— MICHAEL R. DEPAUL

MORAL NATURALISM

Philosophical naturalism, considered in general, is not a unified doctrine but a broad label applied both to methodological stances (e.g., "The methods of philosophy are continuous with those of empirical science") and to substantive positions (e.g., "For a belief to be epistemically warranted is for it to be the product of a certain kind of causal process"). The two are often combined, as when a naturalistic interpretation of a given domain of discourse is justified as "the best explanation" of associated practices. However, the two are in principle independent. In the moral case, for example, it has been argued that a projectivist or noncognitivist interpretation gives a better explanation of moral practice than any substantive naturalism (Blackburn, 1984; Gibbard, 1990).

Kant frankly accepted that he could see no way of reconciling the deliberative standpoint of morality with the causal perspective of science.

But what makes a method or interpretation naturalistic? Attempts to give an explicit definition have largely been abandoned in favor of pointing. Roughly, naturalistic methods are those followed in actual scientific research (including—according to some but not all naturalists—mathematics and social sciences as well as natural sciences). And a naturalistic interpretation of a discourse is one based upon predicates or terms that play a role in the explanatory theories that research has generated.

This characterization of naturalism is informative but incomplete. There are vigorous debates within the philosophy of science over just what the methods, concepts, or posits of contemporary science are. Moreover, interpretation based upon naturalistic terms encompasses some quite different tasks. Some examples follow, but first we should ask, Why stay within naturalistic terms at all? Science is a theoretical, descriptive/explanatory enterprise while morality is held to be essentially practical and normative. One might think, no sooner did morality emerge from the shadow of religion than philosophers began trying to push it into the shadow of science. Is it never to be allowed to stand in its own right as a distinctive domain of inquiry?

An answer of sorts is possible. Morality by its nature cannot stand entirely on its own. Moral discourse is supervenient upon the nonmoral and, specifically, the natural—two actions or agents cannot differ in their moral qualities unless there is some underlying difference in their natural qualities. This and other truisms about morality, such as 'Ought' implies 'can', tie moral evaluation to the natural world in ways that no ethical theory can altogether ignore. Moreover, morality presents us with various epistemic and metaphysical puzzles. We believe that we have come to possess at least some moral knowledge—but how? (See Harman, 1977.) We

treat moral statements as if they stated genuine propositions—but can this idea be sustained in light of the normative role of moral judgment? We freely make moral judgments, but do they have presuppositions or make claims that are incompatible with our understanding of the natural world?

Hard determinists, for example, have challenged intuitive attributions of moral responsibility by arguing that the notion of free agency they presuppose is incompatible with the world revealed by physics. And J. L. Mackie is led to an "error theory" of morality by his diagnosis that moral evaluation attributes to states of the world an objective "to-be-pursuedness" that cannot be fit with any plausible empirical theory (Mackie, 1977).

Kant, for one, frankly accepted that he could see no way of reconciling the deliberative standpoint of morality with the causal perspective of science. Rational agents must, he held, postulate the compatibility of moral agency with the natural order, even though this remains inexplicable to them. But few philosophers have been willing to stop there. Empirical science affords the best-developed picture we have of ourselves and our world. Without the special authority of religion to back it up, morality inevitably becomes a focus of practical and theoretical concern.

Substantive moral naturalists in effect propose to overcome some of the mystery and potential conflict surrounding the relation of morality to our empirical self-understanding by showing just how much of morality might be found within the domain of the natural. This could be done by providing a naturalistic account of moral discourse that affords an analysis of moral terms (Lewis, 1989), or permits a worthwhile revision of moral language that nonetheless can serve virtually all the same functions (Brandt, 1979), or enables us to reduce moral properties to natural properties (Railton, 1993), or shows moral properties to be natural properties in their own right (e.g., thanks to their contribution to empirical explanation; see Boyd, 1988; Miller, 1985; Sturgeon, 1985). Substantive moral naturalism promises to explain such important features of moral discourse and practice as the applicability of notions of truth and falsity to moral claims, the supervenience of the moral upon the natural, the role of natural properties in justifying moral claims, and the possibility of semantic and epistemic access to moral notions through ordinary experience.

The first half of the twentieth century had not been kind to substantive moral naturalism (for a brief history, see Darwall et al., 1992). Condemned by G. E. Moore (1903) for committing the "fallacy" of trying to close an "open question" by analytic means and rejected by nonfactualists (emotivists, prescriptivists, etc.) for failing to capture the special relation of moral evaluation to motivation and action, naturalism fell into disuse. But by mid-century naturalism had begun to win its way back. The initial steps were taken, independently, by Philippa Foot (1958–59) and Geoffrey Warnock (1967), who argued that one could not be competent in moral discourse unless one possessed some substantive, contentful moral concepts. Moral evaluation is distinguished from aesthetic or prudential, for example, in part because it has a certain descriptive, arguably natural content—namely, a concern with the effects of our actions on the well-being of others. If we came upon a society in whose behavioral code the key notion was *guleb*, a term applied in the paradigm case to warriors who have killed an enemy bare-handed, we would certainly mislead if we translated *guleb* as 'morally good' or 'just' rather than 'valiant' or 'courageous'.

Meanwhile, Peter Geach (1965) showed convincingly that existing nonfactualist views could not account for the full grammar of moral discourse, in particular, the logical behavior of unasserted moral claims in conditionals.

Foot (1972) took the next step as well, challenging the 'internalist' conception of the relation of moral evaluation to motivation that served as the basis for nonfactualism. She argued that ordinary moral agents are able to see themselves as motivated by a rationally optional concern for others. Those who lack such a concern might lack moral character, but they do not make a linguistic mistake in using the moral vocabulary.

This sort of moral 'externalism' offers an alternative explanation of why moral evaluation and motivation are so intimately related, at least in paradigm cases. Concern for others is a very basic part of normal human life. An Aristotelian would say that human nature itself is social; a Darwinian would emphasize the contribution of concern for others to inclusive fitness and to the possibility of benefiting from reciprocal altruism. Speculative biology apart, it is possible to see how social norms involving concern for others, keeping promises, and so forth might emerge and be sustained in virtue of their contribution to solving various serious coordination and collective-action problems. Such norms will function best only if well internalized by a major part of the population. It should therefore be unsurprising that moral judgment is usually accompanied by a positive attitude. Moreover, it should not be forgotten that moral judgment is a species of assertion and that assertion itself involves, not only signaling a cognitive attitude of belief, but also various forms of active endorsement or encouragement, as well as associated claims of authority. Moral externalism, by drawing upon these ingredients (and others) for an alternative explanation of the evidence—such as it is—offered on behalf of internalism, has attracted a number of defenders (see, for example, Boyd, 1988; Brink, 1989; Railton, 1986).

Another sort of naturalism, however, takes the opposite tack. It treats the purported relation to motivation as fundamental but interprets it in a subjectivist rather than nonfactualist manner. Subjectivist interpretations of moral discourse have historically faced difficulties in accommodating all the elements of an interconnected set of features of morality: the critical use of moral assessment, the nonrelativistic character of moral judgment and the possibility of genuine moral disagreement across social or cultural differences, the limits on empirical methods in resolving moral disputes, and the seemingly normative character of the relation between moral judgment and motivation. Can new forms of subjectivism succeed where others have failed?

No moral naturalism has emerged

that meets all the desiderata

of an account of moral discourse and practice.

Consider the simple subjectivist formula:

(1) Act A is morally good $=$ A is such that one would approve of the performance of A.

Since approval is a positive attitude, (1) establishes a relationship with a source of motivational force. But is it the right relationship?

We do not typically regard our current tendencies to approve or disapprove as morally authoritative—they might, for example, be based upon hasty thinking or false beliefs. This has led naturalists to modify (1) to require that the approval be well informed and reflectively stable. (See, for example, Brandt, 1979, and Firth, 1952. For criticism, see Velleman, 1988.)

Moreover, not all species of approval have a moral flavor. I can approve of an act because of its aesthetic or pious qualities, for example. Some naturalists therefore amend (1) to restrict the object of approval (e.g., to the set of rules one would—reflectively, informedly, etc.—approve for a society in which one is going to live [cf. Brandt. 1979]). Others attempt to identify in naturalistic terms a specifically moral sort of attitude of approval or disapproval (e.g., an attitude of impartial praise or anger). Critics have argued that no noncircular characterization of this kind is possible (for a subjectivism without reductive ambitions, see Wiggins, 1987).

Formulas like (1) also threaten to yield relativism. Since they introduce a necessary link to facts about motivation, moral attribution becomes tied to contingencies of individual psychology. That seems wrong, since moral evaluation purports to abstract from individual interest and motive and to prescribe universality. If one is not correspondingly motivated, that is a deficiency in oneself rather than an excusing condition or a limit on the reach of moral judgment. Each of us recognizes that he or she can in this sense be motivationally defective from a moral point of view. (But see Harman, 1975, for a defense of a naturalistic moral relativism.) This has led naturalists to modify the formula away from the individualistic language of 'one' or 'I' and in the direction of a more inclusive 'we' or 'everyone' or even 'normal humans' (see, respectively, Lewis, 1989; Smith, 1994; and Firth, 1952). New problems arise. The notion of 'normal human' threatens to introduce a term that itself requires naturalization—since we believe that statistically "normal" humans might be motivationally defective from a moral point of view—for example, in lacking sympathy with those from other groups. (Of course, one could at this point also embrace circularity.) If we insist that everyone approve, there is again a risk that contingencies of motivational idiosyncrasies will receive authority—this time, in preventing us from attributing moral value to states of affairs virtually all (but still not quite all) of us approve heartily on reflection. A less ambitious alternative is to replace 'one' with 'us' and seek moral consensus where we may. This would help explain the "outreach" function of moral discourse without altogether removing the account's relativism.

An alternative approach avoids relativism by "rigidifying" the subjectivist formula (cf. Wiggins, 1987). One fixes the truth conditions of moral judgments by reference to the motivations *actually* prevalent in one's moral community (e.g., '*A* is such that we, with our actual motives and with full and informed reflection, would approve of it'). This secures the desirable result that changes in our motives will not in themselves change what is morally good. But it undermines some of the critical role of moral assessment in our own society (since, again, we can imagine that our actual motives are morally defective) and will have the result that those brought up in different social environments with different acquired motivations will lack a common subject matter even though they believe they are having a genuine moral disagreement (for discussion, see Johnston, 1989).

No moral naturalism has emerged that meets all the desiderata of an account of moral discourse and practice. Nonnaturalists and nonfactualists attribute this to a mistaken starting point. But no alternative account has met all the desiderata, either. Moral naturalists have often been accused of "changing the subject"—shifting the locus of attention from the position of the agent involved in practical deliberation to that of the scientist engaged in theoretical description. But this criticism begs the question. Naturalists seek to explain, not ignore, moral experience; if they are right, the phenomena they study are the very stuff of moral thought and action.

[See also Conditionals; Determinism and Freedom; Ethical Theory; Kant, Immanuel; Mackie, John Leslie; Moral Relativism; Naturalism; Philosophy of Science; Projectivism; Supervenience.]

BIBLIOGRAPHY

Blackburn, S. *Spreading the Word.* Oxford, 1984.
Boyd, R. "How to Be a Moral Realist," in G. Sayre-McCord, ed., *Essays on Moral Realism* (Ithaca, NY, 1988).
Brandt, R. *A Theory of the Good and the Right.* New York, 1979.
Brink, D. O. *Moral Realism and the Foundations of Ethics.* Cambridge, 1989.
Darwell, S., et al. "Toward *Fin de siècle* Ethics," *Philosophical Review,* Vol. 101 (1992), 317–45.
Firth, R. "Ethical Absolutism and the Ideal Observer," *Philosophy and Phenomenological Research,* Vol. 12 (1952), 317–45.
Foot, P. "Moral Beliefs," *Proceedings of the Aristotelian Society,* Vol. 59 (1958–59), 83–104.
———. "Morality as a System of Hypothetical Imperatives," *Philosophical Review,* Vol. 81 (1972), 305–16.
Geach, P. "Assertion," *Philosophical Review,* Vol. 74 (1965), 445–65.
Gibbard, A. *Wise Choices, Apt Feelings.* Cambridge, 1990.
Harman, G. "Moral Relativism Defended," *Philosophical Review,* Vol. 84 (1975), 3–22.
———. *The Nature of Morality.* New York, 1977.
Johnston, M. "Dispositional Theories of Value," *Proceedings of the Aristotelian Society,* Vol. 63 (1989), suppl., 139–74.
Lewis, D. "Dispositional Theories of Value," *Proceedings of the Aristotelian Society,* Vol. 63 (1989), suppl. 113–37.
Mackie, J. L. *Ethics: Inventing Right and Wrong.* New York, 1977.
Miller, R. "Ways of Moral Learning," *Philosophical Review,* Vol. 94 (1985), 507–56.
Moore, G. E. *Principia Ethica.* Cambridge, 1903.
Railton, P. "Moral Realism," *Philosophical Review,* Vol. 95 (1986), 163–207.
———. "Reply to David Wiggins," in J. Haldane and C. Wright, eds., *Reality, Representation, and Projection* (Oxford, 1993).
Smith, M. *The Moral Problem.* Oxford, 1994.
Sturgeon, N. "Moral Explanations," in D. Copp and D. Zimmerman, eds., *Morality, Reason, and Truth* (Totowa, NJ, 1985).
Velleman, D. "Brandt's Definition of 'Good,'" *Philosophical Review,* Vol. 97 (1988), 353–71.
Warnock, G. *Contemporary Moral Philosophy.* London, 1967.
Wiggins, D. "A Sensible Subjectivism?" In *Needs, Values, and Truth: Essays in the Philosophy of Value* (Oxford, 1987).

— PETER RAILTON

MORAL PSYCHOLOGY

The intellectual division of labor makes a sharp distinction between moral philosophy and moral psychology. Moral philosophy is in the business of saying what ought to be, what is really right and wrong, good and evil: what the proper moral principles and rules are, what counts as genuine moral motivation, and what types of persons count as genuinely good. Most important, the job of moral philosophy is to provide philosophical justification for its shoulds, and oughts, for its principles and its rules.

Moral psychology—what Kant called

the "empirical side of morals"—

might tell us what people think ought to be done,

what they believe is right or wrong,

what they think makes a good person.

Moral psychology, what Kant called the "empirical side of morals," might tell us what people think ought to be done, what they believe is right or wrong, what they think makes a good person, and so on. But all the psychological facts taken together, including that they are widely and strongly believed, could never justify any of these views. Mottoes abound to express the basic idea: one cannot make inferences from 'is' to 'ought'; one cannot derive values from facts; the empirical tells us what is the case, the normative tells us what ought to be the case.

In the *Groundwork* (1785), Kant writes that a "worse service cannot be rendered morality than that an attempt be made to derive it from examples." Trying to derive ethical principles "from the disgusting mishmash" of psychological, sociological, or anthropological observation, from the insights about human nature that abound "in the chit-chat of daily life" and that delight "the multitude" and upon which "the empty headed regale themselves" is not the right way to do moral philosophy.

What is the right way to do moral philosophy? We need "a completely isolated metaphysics of morals, a pure ethics unmixed with the empirical study" of human nature (1785, pp. 408–10). Once moral philosophy has derived the principles that ought to govern the wills of all rational beings, then and only then should we seek "the extremely rare merit of a truly philosophical popularity" (p. 409). This is "Kant's dogma."

The sharp separation was not always the rule. Kant's target in the passages about the "disgusting mish mash" of observations that pervade "the chit-chat of ordinary life" includes not just ordinary people but the entire philosophical tradition, from Plato to Hume. Indeed,

until the eighteenth century moral philosophy was thought to involve close attention to human nature, character, motivation, the passions and emotions, the social bases of moral life, the virtues and vices of everyday life, moral education, the relation between being a decent person and living in a decent community, and individual and cultural difference.

Moral psychology has had a revival in the second half of the twentieth century. It involves work done both by empirical psychologists and philosophers and is devoted to reflection on how morals are acquired or developed, the role of emotions in moral life, how resistance to evil is inculcated, and so on. Of the many reasons for this revival, these are three of the most prominent: (1) How was the Holocaust possible? That is, how could seemingly decent people go off the moral deep end in the way they did during the Nazi era? (2) How can schools, especially schools in a secular society, teach moral values and encourage the development of decent character, moral sensitivity, and so on, without teaching a specific religious morality? (3) How does moral philosophy, especially the moral philosophical project of trying to find the right way to live, respond to the facts of pluralism and individual and cultural difference?

Immediately after the Second World War, a spate of literature appeared— *The Authoritarian Personality* (Adorno et al., 1993) being the most famous—which traced the roots of compliance to moral evil and moral conventionalism. Work by Stanley Milgram and Hannah Arendt and more recent work on the character of rescuers during the Holocaust reinforce the idea that in times of moral crisis individuals who believe in abiding conventional norms will do great moral harm.

With regard to issues of moral education and moral development, Lawrence Kohlberg's moral stage theory attempted to fill a vacuum. According to Kohlberg, there are universal stages of moral development (six in total). Most people reach only the middle conventional stages, but development to the postconventional stages (five and six), where one will resist evil such as the Holocaust, can be promoted by engaging children, adolescents, and adults in discussion of complex moral issues; this can be done without bringing religion into the discussions.

Carol Gilligan (1982), a colleague and collaborator of Kohlberg's, challenged the comprehensiveness of his stage theory. Distilled to its essence, the claim was that the theory was sexist. Gilligan describes a moral universe in which men, more often than women, conceive of morality as substantively constituted by obligations and rights and as procedurally constituted by the demands of fairness and impartiality, while women, more often than men, see moral requirements as emerging from the particular needs of others in the context of particular relationships. Gilligan dubs this latter orientation the "ethic of care," and insists that the former, the "ethic of justice," with its exclusive focus on justice reasoning, obscures both the care ethic's psychological reality and its normative significance.

Gilligan characterizes the two ethics as "different ways of viewing the world" that "organize both thinking and feeling," and that involve seeing things in different and competing ways. The justice orientation organizes moral perception by highlighting issues of fairness, right, and obligation. Whereas the ethic of justice involves seeing others thinly, as worthy of respect purely by virtue of common humanity, morally good caring requires seeing others thickly, as constituted by their particular human face, their particular psychological and social self. Caring also involves taking seriously, or at least being moved by, one's particular connection to the other. Gilligan claims that once the dispositions that underlie such caring are acknowledged, the dominant conception of moral maturity among moral psychologists and moral philosophers will need to be reconceived.

At the same time the Kohlberg-Gilligan debate was getting hot, many philosophers were questioning impartial conceptions of moral life. The debate about impartiality, led by philosophers such as Lawrence Blum, quickly brought to the fore questions about the nature of love and friendship (are we supposed to be impartial to our friends and loved ones?), the role of emotions in moral life, questions about the legitimacy of different moral conceptions in a multicultural society, as well as general questions about how realistic our moral theories ought to be.

[See also Arendt, Hannah; Hume, David; Impartiality; Justice; Kant, Immanuel; Plato.]

BIBLIOGRAPHY

Adorno, T. W., et al. *The Authoritarian Personality.* New York, 1993.

Blum, L. *Impartiality and Particularity.* New York, 1994.

Flanagan, O. *Varieties of Moral Personality: Ethics and Psychological Realism.* Cambridge, MA, 1991.

Gilligan, C. *In a Different Voice: Psychological Theory and Women's Development.* Cambridge, MA, 1982.

Kohlberg, L. *Essays on Moral Development.* Vol. I., *The Philosophy of Moral Development: Moral Stages and the Idea of Justice.* San Francisco, 1981.

———. *Essays on Moral Development.* Vol. II., *The Psychology of Moral Development: The Nature and Validity of Moral Stages.* San Francisco, 1984.

— OWEN FLANAGAN

MORAL REALISM

Moral realism holds that there exist moral facts and therefore properties (such as goodness, evil, rightness, wrongness, virtue, vice) that are not reducible to nonmoral facts or properties; these facts and properties, the theory holds, are independent of our awareness, the manner in which we think or speak, our beliefs and attitudes, and our feelings and desires. Moral properties may be exemplified by persons, actions, institutions, and so forth; their exemplifications are moral facts, correspondence to which constitutes the truth of moral judgments. Sophisticated moral antirealism need not reject all of these theses; it may accept some or all of them, but only after reinterpreting them, especially the conception of truth as correspondence to facts (Blackburn, 1984, 1993; Wright 1992). Such reinterpretations are motivated by the plausibility of moral realism and would be needed only if it were found seriously deficient.

Moral realism is often called cognitivism,

but properly speaking the latter

is the view that moral beliefs and statements do

or at least can express knowledge.

Moral realism is often called cognitivism, but properly speaking the latter is the view that moral beliefs and statements do or at least can express knowledge. And there may be moral facts of which we cannot have knowledge—for example, whether a certain action would ultimately produce more goodness than any of its alternatives would (Butchvarov, 1989; Fumerton, 1990). Cognitivism is opposed to moral skepticism, not to moral realism. On the other hand, if by cognitivism we mean merely that moral statements have truth value, then it might coincide with moral realism, but only if it also holds that some moral statements are true.

The issues moral realism raises are essentially metaphysical. First, what is it for something to be real? To be a part of the causal spatiotemporal network that science investigates? But we must add that we mean a real, not an imaginary, network, and then we would be guilty of circularity. Inattention to this metaphysical issue would vitiate any realism or antirealism, regardless of its subject matter. A second issue is whether there are such entities as properties at all and, if there are, what they are, especially whether they are universals (i.e., capable of being exemplified by many particulars at the same time), as was held by Plato and George Edward Moore (1903). A third issue concerns the relationship between moral properties and the nonmoral (whether natural or nonnatural) properties in virtue of which they can be attributed to particulars. Moral goodness can be attributed to a person only if the person has certain nonmoral properties such as kindness (Brink, 1989; Butchvarov, 1989; Moore, 1922; Ross, 1930). How is this relationship between moral and nonmoral properties to be understood? If the moral properties are defined in terms of the nonmoral properties, then we have abandoned moral realism. If we claim that there is a law like connection between them (Brink, 1989), then we must ask what the nature of such "laws" might be; they are hardly scientific laws, and anyhow the nature of scientific laws is too obscure and controversial to support a helpful analogy. If we appeal to the formal supervenience of moral on nonmoral properties (Post, 1987)—meaning by this that in particular cases the former could not be different unless the latter were different—but deny that the presupposed substantive relation of dependence of the moral on the nonmoral is causal, semantical, or logical, then we may be moral realists but we appeal to a relation at least as mysterious as Moore's nonnatural property of goodness (Moore, 1903, chap. 1), especially if we add that the nonmoral properties must be physical. Another view (Butchvarov, 1989, chap. 4) is that nonmoral properties exemplify moral properties in the distinctive way specific properties (e.g., red) exemplify their generic properties (e.g., color) and that particulars (such as persons and actions) exemplify moral properties only indirectly, by exemplifying nonmoral properties that exemplify moral properties directly. A person's kindness is a species, a kind, of goodness, not goodness itself, and the person exemplifies goodness indirectly, which is exemplified by kindness directly. But a genus such as goodness is not definable in terms of its species except as their disjunction, which is seldom possible and also violates the notion of definition. Even then it is the genus that guides us in the selection of the disjuncts. (Color cannot be defined as the disjunction of the specific shades of color, which are perhaps infinite in number. And while the species of goodness are probably not infinite in number, their disjunction can be arrived at only through a prior grasp of their genus.) But, although familiar, the genus-species relation requires extensive metaphysical elucidation. All three metaphysical issues can be properly resolved only by metaphysics, not by ethics.

The chief argument for moral realism is that it is the view implicit in common sense. We sometimes just "see" that something, say, an action or a person, is morally good, or bad, or right, or wrong. We regard moral judgments as true or false, disagree and argue about them, and sometimes attempt to live in accordance with them. We do not think that their meaning or use is to express attitudes or prescriptions of behavior or that they are about certain thoughts and feelings. Even a

moral antirealist such as Mackie (1977) admits this but draws the conclusion that common sense is in error in its moral judgments, since there is nothing in reality to make them true. Could common sense be that wrong? There are philosophical arguments against moral realism. In ethics, as in all disciplines, one must begin with common sense, but one need not end with it.

One argument is phenomenological. Hume ([1739] 1888) claimed that when we perceive a case of murder we do not perceive the vice in it, nor can we infer it from what we do perceive by any legitimate principles of inference. A counterargument is that such a view rests on a rather primitive phenomenology, as contrasted, say, with that of Max Scheler ([1913–16] 1973), probably also on the failure to recognize that moral properties are strictly speaking properties of properties and thus not discernible in the way properties directly exemplified by particulars are discernible. (You do not see color in the way you see a specific shade of red, but obviously you are, or on reflection can become, aware of it, in a quite nonmysterious way; nor are you tempted to identify color with red, since then you would also have to identify it with green, with blue, etc., thus implying that these are not different colors.) It has been argued that our awareness of moral properties is a mere "projection" of our attitudes (Blackburn, 1984; 1993, part 2; Hume, [1752] 1957). But this cinematographic metaphor requires detailed metaphysical unpacking, which is not provided.

A second argument is that moral properties have no place in the "scientific image" of the world, in particular that their existence is incompatible with physicalism, the view that everything is physical. They are not part of the subject matter of physics, they can enter in no causal relations, and appeal to them has no explanatory value, even with respect to our having the moral opinions we do have (Harman, 1977, chap. 1). But numbers and God are also not physical things, and it would be presumptuous and unphilosophical to deny their existence for just that reason. Nor has anyone shown that the reality of something requires it to have a causal or explanatory role. At any rate, it is not at all clear that moral properties do not have such a role. Much depends on what we understand by causality and explanation, topics so obscure and controversial (as evident in the philosophy of science, where they really belong) that a major position in ethics should not depend on opinions about them. (Scientific realism itself has been rejected by some on the grounds that it is insufficiently explanatory of our scientific observations and beliefs.) Why exactly may we not explain the Holocaust, as well as our belief that it was evil, in part by the evil of Hitler's character? And was not the evil of his character in part a cause of the Holocaust, as well as of our belief that it was evil? (See Sturgeon, 1984.)

A third argument draws attention to the existence of moral disagreement, especially among cultures (Mackie, 1977). There are three common responses. First, the extent and depth of the disagreement can be competently judged only outside ethics—by anthropologists. Second, disagreement may be due to ignorance of the moral facts, not to their nonexistence. Disagreement seems to be chiefly about the details of morality, for example those concerning sexual behavior. We know too little about these details, especially about their nonmoral properties. Disagreements about economic policies and effective child raising are also widespread, but is this a reason for rejecting realism in economics and child psychology? Third, moral disagreement is often due to misunderstanding (the concepts used, whether moral or nonmoral, are often too vague and unclear), to moral immaturity, and to clashes of self-interest (the rich and the poor may disagree on distributive justice).

The issues moral realism raises

are essentially metaphysical.

First, what is it for something to be real?

A fourth argument is that the relevance of moral facts to motivation and thus behavior is obscure, perhaps nonexistent (Mackie, 1977). A common response is that this too can be competently judged only outside ethics—this time, by psychology, since it concerns motivation (unless the issue is whether the recognition of moral facts logically entails the appropriate motivation, something moral realism need not and should not assert). But psychology is hardly advanced enough to provide an answer, and if we think that someday neuroscience will, we are just speculating.

[See also Causation; Ethical Theory; Explanation, Theories of; Hume, David; Justice; Mackie, John Leslie; Moral Skepticism; Philosophy of Science; Physicalism; Plato; Realism; Ross, William David; Supervenience.]

BIBLIOGRAPHY

Blackburn, S. *Spreading the Word.* Oxford, 1984.
———. *Essays in Quasi-Realism.* Oxford, 1993.
Brink, D. O. *Moral Realism and the Foundations of Ethics.* Cambridge, 1989.
Butchvarov, P. *Skepticism in Ethics.* Bloomington, IN, 1989.
Copp, D., and D. Zimmerman, eds. *Morality, Reason, and Truth.* Totowa, NJ, 1984.
Fumerton, R. A. *Reason and Morality.* Ithaca, NY, 1990.
Harman, G. *The Nature of Morality.* New York, 1977.
Hume, D. *A Treatise of Human Nature* [1739]. London, 1888.
———. *An Inquiry Concerning the Principles of Morals* [1752]. Indianapolis, 1957.
Mackie, J. L. *Ethics: Inventing Right and Wrong.* New York, 1977.
Moore, G. E. *Principia Ethica.* Cambridge, 1903.
———. "The Conception of Intrinsic Value," in *Philosophical Studies* (London, 1922).
Post, J. F. *The Faces of Existence: An Essay in Nonreductive Metaphysics.* Ithaca, NY, 1987.
Ross, W. D. *The Right and the Good.* Oxford, 1930.
Scheler, M. *Formalism in Ethics and Non-Formal Ethics of Values,* trans. M. S. Frings and R. L. Funk. Evanston, IL, 1973.
Sturgeon, N. "Moral Explanations," in D. Copp and D. Zimmerman, eds., *Morality, Reason, and Truth* (Totowa, NJ, 1984).
Wright, C. *Truth and Objectivity.* Cambridge, MA, 1992.

– PANAYOT BUTCHVAROV

MORAL RELATIVISM

Moral relativism (e.g., Wong, 1984) involves two claims: (1) a moral judgment can be assigned objective truth conditions only relative to some moral framework; (2) there is no single objectively true morality; instead, there is a variety of moral frameworks, none of which can be objectively distinguished as the correct moral framework.

Moral relativism is opposed by moral absolutism on one side and moral nihilism on the other side. Moral absolutism insists that there is a single objectively true morality. Moral nihilism agrees with moral relativism in rejecting a single true morality but goes on to abandon morality and moral judgments, including relative moral judgments.

In arguing against moral absolutism, moral relativists point to the apparent impossibility of objectively resolving moral disagreements over abortion, vegetarianism, egoism, and many other issues. Moral relativists argue (a) that we cannot settle by objective inquiry which moral framework is correct and (b) that this provides a strong reason to believe that there is no single correct moral framework. (Moral relativists take the latter reason to be analogous to the strong reason we have to believe there is no privileged spatiotemporal framework.)

Moral absolutists (e.g., Brink, 1989) reject either (a) or (b) or both. They observe that the mere existence of different opinions does not establish relativism and note that, even if there is no way objectively to demonstrate the correctness of any one moral framework, that may be more a limitation on our powers of demonstration than an argument that there is no single true morality.

On the other hand, nihilists, who agree with the conclusion that there is no single true morality, take this conclusion to provide a reason to reject morality altogether, just as those who believe that there is no single true religion tend to reject religion altogether rather than accepting "religious relativism." Moral relativists prefer an analogy with Einstein's theory of relativity: talk of right and wrong, like talk of before and after, does make sense even though such talk has objective truth conditions only in relation to a choice of framework.

Conflict Between Frameworks

People who accept different moral frameworks typically have conflicting affective attitudes. One person may wish to end abortions, another may be indifferent to most abortions. In some sense they disagree with each other, but moral relativism does not appear to provide them with any way to express their disagreement. Each agrees that abortion is wrong relative to the first moral framework and that abortion is not wrong relative to the second.

Emotivists (Stevenson, 1944; 1963) argue against restricting moral terminology in the relativistic way and in favor of using moral terminology to express affective attitudes. In its crudest form emotivism offers a "Boo! Hurrah! Who cares!" account of the meaning of moral discourse. "Abortion is morally wrong" means something like "Boo to abortion!" and "Abortion is not wrong" means something like "Abortion, who cares?"

Somewhat more sophisticated versions of emotivism (Hare, 1952) treat moral judgments as imperatives: "Don't ever have an abortion!" versus "Have an abortion if you want to!" All these views differ from moral relativism in denying that moral judgments have a truth value. "Boo to abortion!" and "Don't have an abortion!" are neither true nor false.

Emotivism, unlike pure moral relativism, allows people with different moral frameworks to express moral disagreements. On the other hand the crudest forms of emotivism allow only the simplest forms of moral judgment and do not address more complex judgments such as (3) "Either contraception is morally wrong or abortion is not always morally wrong."

There is a variety of moral frameworks,

none of which can be objectively distinguished

as the correct moral framework.

The most sophisticated form of emotivism, sometimes called projectivism (Blackburn, 1993), attempts to handle these more complex judgments as objective projections of subjective values. For example, a moral relativist might in this sense project his or her moral framework onto the world and then use moral termi-

nology as if the projected morality was the single true morality, while at the same time admitting that this way of talking is only "as if." The supposed advantage of this projectivist usage is that it allows people with different moral frameworks to disagree with each other. Critics of the proposal might claim that it only allows such people to appear to disagree with each other!

Truth

If projectivism is intelligible, it may appear to threaten the relativist's principle (1). Stevenson (1963) and Stoljar (1993) observe that projectivist moral judgments can be treated as having truth conditions, given a redundancy or disquotation theory of truth. Let us use all capital letters to indicate the projectivist usage, as in "MORALLY WRONG." Then, in this view of truth, the truth conditions of the nonrelative emotivist or projectivist judgment, "Abortion is MORALLY WRONG," are given disquotationally as follows: (4) "Abortion is MORALLY WRONG" is true if and only if abortion is MORALLY WRONG. Such a condition is not relative to a moral framework, which may appear to conflict with (1). However, the truth condition is also not an objective truth condition, since (in this view) it is not an objective matter whether abortion is MORALLY WRONG, so (4) does not in the end actually conflict with (1).

Is There a Need for Relative Moral Judgments?

Let us return to the issue between moral relativism and nihilism. Moral relativism denies that we should simply give up on morality in the way that a religious skeptic might give up on religion. There are practical reasons to want to retain morality and relative moral judgments.

Now projectivism claims to provide a nonrelativistic usage that may be more useful than a purely relativistic usage in allowing a way to express moral disagreements between people with different moral frameworks. If so, does that mean we can simply forget about relative moral judgments? Not necessarily, since projectivist moral judgments may be projections of relative moral judgments and unintelligible apart from an understanding of such relative judgments.

[See also Abortion; Ethical Theory; Hare, Richard M.; Projectivism; Stevenson, Charles.]

BIBLIOGRAPHY

Blackburn, S. *Essays in Quasi-Realism.* Oxford, 1993.
Brink, D. *Moral Realism and the Foundations of Ethics.* Cambridge, 1989.
Hare, R. M. *The Language of Morals.* Oxford, 1952.
Harman, G. "Moral Diversity as an Argument for Moral Relativism," in D. Odegard and C. Stewart, eds., *Perspectives on Moral Relativism* (Millikan, Ont., 1991).

Mackie, J. *Ethics: Inventing Right and Wrong.* Harmondsworth, Middlesex, 1977.

Odegard, D., and C. Stewart. *Perspectives on Moral Relativism.* Millikan, Ont., 1991.

Stevenson, C. L. *Ethics and Language.* New Haven, 1944.

———. *Facts and Values.* New Haven, 1963.

Stoljar, D. "Emotivism and Truth Conditions," *Philosophical Studies,* Vol. 70 (1993), 81–102.

Wong, D. *Moral Relativity.* Berkeley, 1984.

— GILBERT HARMAN

MORAL SKEPTICISM

The two main forms of skepticism about morality are skepticism about moral truths and skepticism about reasons to comply with moral considerations. These doctrines challenge the cognitive significance or rational authority of morality.

Skepticism about moral truths denies that there are—or that we can know that there are—true moral propositions (or facts) that entail that something has a moral attribute. This form of skepticism seems to imply that rational and informed agents would give moral claims no credence. It has been supported by a variety of arguments, including arguments about moral disagreement. One deep motivation for it is the difficulty of explaining the normativity or action-guiding nature of moral claims.

Noncognitivists attempt to explain the normativity of moral judgments by supposing that their function is to express states of the speaker and to affect behavior rather than to express propositions. Noncognitivists would agree that there are no true moral propositions, since they hold that moral claims do not express propositions. Yet they do not view moral claims as defective. According to noncognitivists, one who makes a claim, such as "Truthfulness is morally required," expresses a moral attitude or acceptance of a moral norm (Ayer, [1936] 1946; Gibbard, 1990; cf. Hume, [1739–40] 1978).

Cognitivists object that our moral thinking cannot be understood except on the assumption that moral claims express propositions. To avoid skepticism, cognitivists must believe that there are moral properties that are sometimes exemplified. For if no moral property exists, or if none is exemplified, it follows that there are no moral requirements, no moral goods or bads, no moral virtues or vices. It may follow that there are no *honest* persons, for example, although there may be truthful persons.

A skeptic might hold that moral properties exist but that none is exemplified. This position seems implausible, however, for if there is the property of wrongness, it would be astonishing if nothing were ever wrong. Alternatively, a skeptic might argue that there are no

moral properties. According to widely accepted views about propositions, however, the proposition that lying is wrong, for example, would attribute the property wrongness to acts of lying. The property would be a constituent of the proposition. Hence, if there are no moral properties, these views about propositions may lead to the conclusion that no proposition is expressed by sentences such as "Lying is wrong."

Skepticism about moral truths denies that there are

—or that we can know that there are—

true moral propositions (or facts)

that entail that something has a moral attribute.

J. L. Mackie argued that there are no moral properties (1977). We conceive of moral properties as intrinsic; if an action is wrong, it is wrong "as it is in itself." But we also conceive of moral properties as intrinsically action guiding; we can be motivated to act in an appropriate way simply by coming to know that an action would be wrong, regardless of any antecedent motivations. Yet, Mackie thought, it is not intelligible that it be intrinsic to an action's having an intrinsic property that the mere recognition that the action has the property could motivate a person. The idea of a moral property is not intelligible; moral properties would be metaphysically "queer."

Gilbert Harman (1977) argued for an epistemic version of skepticism about moral truths. He argued that there seems to be no good reason to affirm any moral proposition, for moral hypotheses are never part of the best explanation of any observation. There is always a better nonmoral explanation. The belief that there are true moral propositions is therefore unwarranted.

Skepticism about moral truth appears to have a life of its own in secular cultures, independent of skeptical arguments. Some people believe that moral truths are grounded in God's commands. A secular culture would tend to think, however, that all substantive facts are empirical and "natural." And natural facts do not seem to be normative in the way moral facts are normative. It is therefore difficult to see how a natural fact could be a moral fact.

The second skeptical doctrine is the thesis that there need be no reason to comply with moral considerations. According to this thesis, rational agents would not give attention to moral considerations, as such, in deciding how to live their lives. To be sure, we may desire to live morally, and this desire may give us a reason to live morally. Or we may find ourselves in a context in which living morally is in our interest. Yet these possibilities do not show that there is necessarily a reason to comply with moral considerations (Nielsen, 1974); they do not distinguish moral considerations from considerations of etiquette, for example.

Skepticism about compliance is typically motivated by the idea that morality can require actions that are not to the agent's advantage. Assuming that there are reasons for one to do something just in case it would be to one's advantage, this idea implies that there may be no reason to comply with morality.

The two main skeptical doctrines are closely linked, on certain ways of thinking. First, it may seem, we cannot be guaranteed to have reasons to comply with moral considerations unless there are moral truths of which we have knowledge. Second, a kind of "internalist" theory holds that moral facts are "constituted" by reasons. On this view there are no moral facts unless there are reasons of a relevant kind.

Internalist antiskeptical theories attempt to defeat both skeptical doctrines at once. Immanuel Kant held, in effect, that if a moral imperative corresponds to a truth, it does so in virtue of the fact that it would be complied with by any fully rational agent (Kant, [1785] 1981). "Externalist" theories attempt to deal with skepticism about moral truths independently from skepticism about compliance (Sturgeon, 1985). Those who believe that moral truths are grounded in God's commands may suppose, for example, that God necessarily gives us reasons to comply.

Philosophers who accept one of the skeptical doctrines typically try to defuse it. Skeptics about rational compliance may argue that people with normal psychologies invariably have reasons to comply with morality. Skeptics about moral truth may argue that there nevertheless are reasons to engage in the practice of judging things morally.

[See also Ethical Theory; Hume, David; Kant, Immanuel; Mackie, John Leslie; Moral Realism; Moral Skepticism; Skepticism.]

BIBLIOGRAPHY

Ayer, A. J. Language, Truth, and Logic [1936]. London, 1946.
Copp, D. "Moral Skepticism," Philosophical Studies, Vol. 62 (1991), 203–33.
Gibbard, A. Wise Choices, Apt Feelings: A Theory of Normative Judgment. Cambridge, MA, 1990.
Harman, G. The Nature of Morality: An Introduction to Ethics. Oxford, 1977.
Hume, D. A Treatise of Human Nature [1739–40]. Edited by P. H. Nidditch. Oxford, 1978.
Kant, I. Grounding of the Metaphysics of Morals [1785]. Translated by James W. Ellington. Indianapolis, IN, 1981.
Mackie, J. L. Ethics: Inventing Right and Wrong. Harmondsworth, Middlesex, 1977.
Nielsen, K. "Why Should I Be Moral?" in W. K. Frankena and J. T. Granrose, eds., Introductory Readings in Ethics (Englewood Cliffs, NJ, 1974).
Nietzsche, F. Basic Writings of Nietzsche. Edited and translated by Walter Kaufmann. New York, 1968. See The Genealogy of Morals and Beyond Good and Evil.
Sturgeon, N. "Moral Explanations," in D. Copp and D. Zimmerman, eds., Morality, Reason, and Truth (Totowa, NJ, 1985).

— DAVID COPP

MULTIPLE REALIZABILITY

Multiple realizability (MR) marks the pivotal point upon which a number of debates have turned. Most notably, Hilary Putnam and Jerry Fodor reject the doctrine of reductive materialism on grounds that mental properties are "multiply realized" by the physical (Fodor, 1974; Putnam, 1967). At stake is the identity of types or properties, the values of the abstract singular terms and predicates that factor crucially in the formulation of scientific laws. Briefly, property identity requires necessary coextension, with the aforementioned items always occurring together (cf. "water = H_2O").

The degree of variability exhibited

by psychofunctional types might preclude a theory

that is at once an image of psychology

and roughly isomorphic to physical theory.

Reductive materialism thus holds that all properties are necessarily coextensive with physical properties. Yet, by employing a functional analysis, Putnam and Fodor argue that mental properties fail to correlate with the physical in the requisite way, since the same function can be instantiated in (or subserved by) radically different physical structures. Hence, any attempt at reducing psychology on the basis of such correlations must ultimately fail.

This suggests a general definition, where A and B are sets of properties, with A representing the realized properties and B serving as their realization base:

A property F in A is subject to multiple realization in a set B if and only if there are distinct properties G and H in B such that (1) it is possible that an object realizes F by virtue of G but not H; (2) it is possible that an object realizes F by virtue of H but not G; and (3) there is no property K in the set B such that, necessarily, every object realizes F by virtue of K.

Clauses (1) and (2) jointly express the desired "variability," meaning that the base properties G and H are individually sufficient but not necessary to bring about F; while clause (3) expresses a form of "irreducibility," meaning that no other property in the set B is both necessary and sufficient for F, nothing coextensive in the way that would license identifying F with a property in the designated set B.

So defined, MR appears satisfied in a number of cases: the properties implicated in the classification of Aristotelian form to matter, various construals of function to substance, folk classifications of mental to physical, and their scientific progeny, a functionalist psychology vis-à-vis neuroscience. There is the much-heralded plasticity of psychological functions within the primate cerebral cortex (Johnson, 1993), and more so if these functions are distributed over physically diverse mechanical devices, as computer engineering will attest. For example, (1) an object can add by virtue of having a human cell assembly rather than, say, the Intel 80386 microprocessor, and (2) vice versa, with (3) no property in that set underlying every possible occurrence while serving to realize the adding function. This is the initial data to which Putnam and Fodor appeal, and this much goes virtually uncontested (but cf. Kim, 1972; Zangwill, 1992). Whether one may wield these facts against the doctrine of reductive materialism, however, depends upon the resolution of substantive philosophical issues. The debate is waged on three fronts.

First, there is a concern about reduction. For applying MR to a suitable range of psychofunctional and neuroscientific properties delivers nonreductivism in the proprietary sense that no identities exist between the specified types. Yet this is compatible with a different understanding of reduction that entails no identities or lawful coextensions. Alternative accounts are legion. One of the more interesting is Paul Churchland's (1979) suggestion that an explanatorily equipotent image of psychology might be derived from physical theory on the basis of a structural isomorphism (also Bickle, 1992). On the other hand, it remains a point of some consequence that MR forbids strict property identities, seeing that they underwrite claims about the ontology of reduction (Causey, 1977; Enc, 1983) and serve to distinguish reductive materialism from its eliminativist rival. Moreover, the degree of variability exhibited by psychofunctional types might preclude the possibility envisaged, namely, a theory that is at once an image of psychology and roughly isomorphic to physical theory. For if psychology is radically incommensurate with physical theory, then so too is any approximate image (Endicott, 1993).

Second, there is a concern about the significance of MR. Specifically, many claim that the Putnam-Fodor-style argument is vitiated by the fact that mental and physical properties both enjoy this variability in their instances. Jaegwon Kim (1972) mentions the case of temperature (also Enc, 1983; Wilson, 1985). Others draw a parallel with Mendelian genetics (Richardson, 1979). The point is that a property can be undeniably physical and a paradigm of reduction in spite of its multiple realizability. So why, on account of that selfsame phenomenon, should one believe that psychological properties are nonphysical and irreducible? Still, critics of reductionism see important differences on this score. Some argue that only mental properties are initially excluded from the class of physical properties by any criterion of "physical" at play in the debate, and mental properties are consequently irreducible to the entire range of physical properties, given their realization base with respect to this class (Endicott, 1989). Others describe how mental types are conspicuously more diverse in their instances (Horgan, 1993; Pereboom & Kornblith, 1991).

Third, and finally, there is a concern about the correct interpretation of the properties. For one may reconstruct either the multiply realized types or their realization base so that MR no longer applies. Thus, the base properties might be extended by means of logico-mathematical operations, generating physical coextensions (e.g., Kim, 1978; cf. Owens, 1989; Teller, 1983). Or, a strategy more closely tied to scientific practice, Kim (1972, 1992) appeals to domain-specific properties and species-relative laws that promise local reductions of psychological phenomena (also Enc, 1983). So, whereas pain per se is realized in various ways across sentient creatures, the more restricted human pain is not. On the contrary, only human neurophysiology subserves human pain, and any physical diversity that underlies pain in other species is simply irrelevant. Nevertheless, critics respond that this reductive strategy misses important generalizations across domains (Block, 1978); ignores physical differences within the same species (Pereboom & Kornblith, 1991); and cannot overcome plasticity within the same individual over time without collapsing the distinction between type and token identities (Endicott, 1993). Such concerns illustrate the metaphysics and philosophy of science behind the debate over multiple realizability.

[See also Eliminative Materialism; Functionalism; Identity; Philosophy of Mind; Philosophy of Science; Properties; Putnam, Hilary; Reduction, Reductionism.]

BIBLIOGRAPHY

Bickle, J. "Multiple Realizability and Psychophysical Reduction," *Behavior and Philosophy*, Vol. 20 (1992), 47–58.

Block, N. "Troubles with Functionalism." *Minnesota Studies in the Philosophy of Science*, Vol. 9 (1978), 261–325.

Causey, R. *Unity of Science*. Dordrecht, 1977.

Churchland, P. *Scientific Realism and the Plasticity of Mind.* Cambridge, MA, 1979.

Enc, B. "In Defense of the Identity Theory," *Journal of Philosophy,* Vol. 80 (1983), 279–98.

Endicott, R. "On Physical Multiple Realization," *Pacific Philosophical Quarterly,* Vol. 70 (1989), 212–24.

———. "Species-Specific Properties and More Narrow Reductive Strategies," *Erkenntnis,* Vol. 38 (1993), 303–21.

Fodor, J. "Special Sciences, or the Disunity of Science as a Working Hypothesis," *Synthese,* Vol. 28 (1974), 77–115.

Horgan, T. "Nonreductive Materialism and the Explanatory Autonomy of Psychology," in S. Wagner and R. Warner, eds., *Naturalism: A Critical Appraisal* (Notre Dame, 1993).

Johnson, M. *Brain Development and Cognition: A Reader.* Oxford, 1993.

Kim, J. "Phenomenal Properties, Psychophysical Laws, and the Identity Theory," *Monist,* Vol. 56 (1972), 177–92.

———. "Supervenience and Normological Incommensurables," *American Philosophical Quarterly,* Vol. 15 (1978), 149–56.

———. "Multiple Realization and the Metaphysics of Reduction," *Philosophy and Phenomenological Research,* Vol. 52 (1992), 1–26.

Owens, D. "Disjunctive Laws," *Analysis,* Vol. 49 (1989), 197–202.

Pereboom, D., and H. Kornblith. "The Metaphysics of Irreducibility," *Philosophical Studies,* Vol. 63 (1991), 125–45.

Putnam, H. "Psychological Predicates," in W. Capitan and D. Merrill, eds., *Art, Mind, and Religion* (Pittsburgh, 1967).

Richardson, R. "Functionalism and Reductionism," *Philosophy of Science,* Vol. 46 (1979), 533–58.

Teller, P. "Comments on Kim's Paper," *Southern Journal of Philosophy,* Vol. 22 (1983), suppl. 57–61.

Wilson, M. "What Is This Thing Called 'Pain'?: The Philosophy of Science behind the Contemporary Debate," *Pacific Philosophical Quarterly,* Vol. 66 (1985), 227–67.

Zangwill, N. "Variable Realization: Not Proved," *Philosophical Quarterly,* Vol. 42 (1992), 214–19.

– RONALD ENDICOTT

N

NATIONALISM AND INTERNATIONAL RELATIONS

The publication of Elie Kedourie's *Nationalism* in 1960 marked the beginning of a renaissance of scholarship about nationalism and national identity. Kedourie saw nationalism as an unsuccessful attempt to solve the problem of political legitimacy in modern society by regarding the state as an expression of the will of a people. For Kedourie, who traced the ideology of nationalism to Enlightenment philosophies of the will (particularly those of Kant and Fichte), the very idea of a self-determining political community was flawed; legitimacy should be solely a result of the ability of governments to manage conflicts.

In contrast to Kedourie, Ernest Gellner saw nationalism as an ideology of modern industrial society—promulgated by the educational institutions that train elites to manage modern bureaucracies. Both Kedourie and Gellner regarded nations as essentially modern phenomena. Anthony Smith, among others, held what has sometimes been characterized as a primordialist view of national identity. On this account nationalism constitutes the political response of traditional ethnic communities to the effects of modern market and state institutions. The modernist view of Walker Connor is more in accord with Kedourie and Gellner in regarding nations as groups who come to believe that they are ancestrally related. Thus, on this account, nations are a creation of nationalist ideology rather than a product of the interaction of already existent ethnic nationalities with modernization.

Discussions within international law concerning the consequences of decolonization in the 1960s paralleled the debate about the nature of national identity. For instance, Rupert Emerson argued that the concept of self-determination used by anticolonial movements did not necessarily apply to noncolonial settings. In earlier international law peoples who claimed a right to political independence were presumably non-self-governing. But once the concept of a people is given an ethnic or national meaning, there is no definite way to determine which nations ought to have rights to states. As Emerson pointed out, the definition of a nation as a culturally homogeneous people (or ethnic group) can be used to disrupt internationally recognized borders and self-governing political communities.

There has been much subsequent discussion about whether ethnically defined nations in the postcolonial world have distinct rights. A number of philosophers have argued recently that culturally homogeneous groups have rights to their own states, either as a result of the good of collective membership (Avishai Margalit & Joseph Raz), the desirability of consent to membership in a political community (Harry Beran), or the necessary presumption of communal membership for any theory of distributive justice (Michael Walzer). Critics of the principle of national self-determination have argued that group identity cannot justify rights to territorial takings (Lea Brilmayer) and that granting self-determination to nations undermines agreements that can safeguard environmental preservation and international peace (Jeremy Brecher).

Discussions within international law

concerning the consequences

of decolonization in the 1960s

paralleled the debate about

the nature of national identity.

Walzer, in his book *Just and Unjust Wars,* connected the issue of the rights of nations to theories of a just war. In his view nations could claim rights if they were able to conduct legitimate and successful secessions, even if these resulted in civil wars. However, Allen Buchanan argues that, while secessions may be justified as a means of avoiding systematic discrimination by a central government, they cannot be so justified simply as a result of the political assertion of a will to form a new state. With regard to international terrorism, Virginia Held has written that it is no different in principle from other forms of political violence and is therefore subject to the same considerations of justification as wars. Charles Beitz has similarly challenged the presumption against foreign interventions found not only in Walzer, but in international law generally, by arguing that its assumption of the autonomy of states is unwarranted. Finally, in response to Walzer, Robert Holmes has renovated a pacifist position regarding modern war in particular, since, he argues, modern war is so inherently destructive of innocent life that it can never be justified as a legitimate exercise in self-defense.

The renovation of concepts of national identity and just war put into question the idea that there were ever any universal entitlements or rights that could bridge the divisions between peoples and states. Two possible applications of universal ideas to international relations are the concepts of international distributive justice and human rights. Charles Beitz and Thomas Pogge have both written in defense of extending a conception of distributive justice based on John Rawls's theory to the global level, thus mandating a redistribution of wealth on a world scale. At the same time Jack Donnelly has attempted to give international human rights a philosophical foundation that avoids problems with both will- and interest-based notions of rights.

The attempts to justify national rights, along with arguments for universal human entitlements, raise the problem of which persons are entitled to membership in which states. Walzer has argued that citizenship cannot be determined in relation to prior considerations of justice, since it is only within a community in which some are members and others are not that a conception of justice has meaning. In response, Joseph Carens has presented the case for "open borders," arguing that there are no clear reasons in any contemporary theory of justice for restricting the freedom of movement of immigrants.

While the idea of the nation-state, which some regard as an unrealizable ideal at the end of the twentieth century, has been the most prevalent conception of a political community for some time, other ideas are being reconsidered. On the one hand Charles Taylor and Will Kymlicka advocate a multicultural community in which different cultural groups are explicitly recognized. On the other hand Jürgen Habermas, in discussing the viability of the European Community, has maintained the

The United States, which allows aliens to become naturalized citizens, is a creation of nationalistic ideology. (Corbis/Bettmann)

importance of keeping ascribed cultural identities separate from discursive political ones in the construction of political communities. It remains to be seen, however, whether concepts of cultural diversity or political discourse are sufficient for a new understanding of community.

[See also Habermas, Jürgen; Justice; Kant, Immanuel; Rawls, John; Rights; Social and Political Philosophy.]

BIBLIOGRAPHY

Beitz, C. R. *Political Theory and International Relations.* Princeton, NJ, 1979.

Beran, H. *The Consent Theory of Political Obligation.* London, 1987.

Brecher, J. " 'The National Question' Reconsidered from an Ecological Perspective," *New Politics,* Vol. 1 (1987), 95–112.

Brilmayer, L. "Secession and Self-Determination," *Yale Journal of International Law,* Vol. 16 (1991), 177–201.

Buchanan, A. E. *Secession.* Boulder, CO, 1991.

Carens, J. H. "Aliens and Citizens," *Review of Politics,* Vol. 49 (1987), 251–73.

Connor, W. *Ethnonationalism.* Princelon, NJ, 1994.

Donnelly, J. *The Concept of Human Rights.* New York, 1985.

Emerson, R. "Self-Determination," *American Journal of International Law,* Vol. 65 (1971), 459–75.

Gellner, E. *Nations and Nationalism.* Ithaca, NY, 1983.

Habermas, J. "Citizenship and National Identity." *Praxis International,* Vol. 12 (1992), 1–19.

Held, V. "Violence, Terrorism, and Moral Inquiry," *The Monist,* Vol. 67 (1984), 605–26.

Holmes, R. *On War and Morality.* Princeton, NJ, 1989.

Kedourie, E. *Nationalism.* London, 1960.

Kymlicka, W. *Liberalism, Community, and Culture.* Oxford, 1989.

Margalit, A., and J. Raz. "National Self-Determination," *Journal of Philosophy,* Vol. 87 (1990), 439–61.

Pogge, T. *Realizing Rawls.* Ithaca, NY, 1989.

Smith, A. D. *The Ethnic Origins of Nations.* Oxford, 1986.

Taylor, C. "The Politics of Recognition," in A. Gutmann, ed., *Multiculturalism and "The Politics of Recognition"* (Princeton, NJ, 1992).

Walzer, M. *Just and Unjust Wars.* New York, 1977.

– OMAR DAHBOUR

NATIVISM, INNATISM

Although the thought that some human knowledge is innate (that is, not the product of learning) is an ancient one, it was revived with the 1957 publication of *Syntactic Structures,* Noam Chomsky's short but groundbreaking treatise in linguistics. In that and much subsequent work, Chomsky argued for the intelligibility and desirability of an empirical study of language that would take as its central goal the explicit and precise characterization of the linguistic knowledge of competent speakers. Not only must this characterization satisfy the obvious criterion of descriptive adequacy—namely, it must be faithful to the intricate range of facts regarding the nature of, and relations between, sound, structure, and meaning in human languages—but it must also make possible an account of language acquisition.

For Chomsky and many linguists, the most prominent features of first-language learning are that it proceeds without the benefit of explicit training; that all normal children display approximately the same patterns of acquisition; and that, relative to the wealth of knowledge the child acquires in just five or so years, language learning takes place rapidly and on the basis of little information. These features of language acquisition, Chomsky has contended, lead immediately to what he calls "Plato's Problem": how do humans manage to acquire such extensive linguistic knowledge so quickly and on the basis of such impoverished data?

A brief example from Chomsky (1980, pp. 160–61) may serve as an illustration. Consider the following four sentences of English:

(1) John betrayed the woman he loved.
(2) The woman he loved betrayed John.
(3) Everyone betrayed the woman he loved.
(4) The woman he loved betrayed everyone.

Any competent speaker of English will recognize certain facts about the interpretations of these sentences. In (1), "he" may refer to John. The same applies for (2), which can thus mean that the woman who he, John, loved betrayed John. Both (1) and (2) differ in this respect from a sentence such as "He betrayed the woman John loved," in which the pronoun cannot refer to John. If we replace the name "John" in (1) and (2) by the quantificational expression "everyone," we get (3) and (4), respectively. One might expect interpretations corresponding to those of (1) and (2). This is borne out for (3), which may indeed be understood to mean that every person x is such that x betrayed the woman whom x loved. But (4), surprisingly, cannot mean that every person x is such that the woman who x loved betrayed x; instead, we must take "he" to refer to some independently identified individual.

These as well as countless other subtle and superficially anomalous facts about their language are known to speakers without their having been taught them, and without their ever having observed any use of the relevant sentences. Indeed, it seems hard to see how such linguistic phenomena could have been explicitly conveyed to speakers, for the principles that organize them and reveal the deeper regularities they instance involve abstract concepts only recently articulated and of which speakers have no conscious grasp at all.

The only plausible hypothesis, according to Chomsky and others, is that the child is born already knowing much about his or her future language. But since children are not genetically predisposed to acquire a particular language (children of Hungarian parents would not find it any easier to learn Hungarian than they would Greek), it must be that they are born with considerable knowledge about any human language they might encounter. This could be, however, only if all possible natural languages share many underlying characteristics, that is, only if there are linguistic universals true for all languages despite their variegated surface appearance. In the face of the poverty of the stimulus to which the learning child is exposed and the richness of the linguistic knowledge that develops, it is natural to infer that the child is genetically endowed with innate knowledge of many universals that characterize fundamental properties of all learnable languages. (Some of these universals will, for instance, be involved in a deep explanation of such phenomena as the admissible interpretations of (1)–(4).) The process of language acquisition, on this view, consists in the child's determining which of all possible human languages—each one of which he innately knows a great deal about—is actually his own, that is, is the one spoken around him.

Linguistic knowledge

seems not to require justification,

as do many familiar cases of knowledge.

There is an interdependence between this conclusion about innate knowledge and the goal of descriptive adequacy mentioned above. The second informs the first, for as the characterization of human languages—what the child eventually comes to acquire, quickly, and on the basis of little evidence—reveals greater complexity, so the argument to innateness becomes the more plausible. And the first informs the second, for the assumption that there is innate knowledge of linguistic universals encourages the search for a level of linguistic description that is deep enough to reveal the hidden kinship between superficially very different languages.

Linguistics, on this conception, becomes the branch of psychology that studies both the intricate knowledge speakers possess that enables their use of language, and the information available to them at birth that makes acquisition of this knowledge possible. In what came to be known as the cognitive revolution, other areas in psychology patterned themselves on linguistics: they sought to characterize the knowledge that underlay a particular range of abilities and they also strove to account for its acquisition, sometimes by appeal to knowledge or concepts innately given.

Chomsky and others have argued that the successes of this approach to linguistics, and to other areas in psychology, constitute a vindication of seventeenth-century rationalist thought over its empiricist opponents. Empirical research into language shows, it is claimed, that those who treat the human newborn as an empty vessel waiting to be filled by Nature are mistaken.

These claims have come in for considerable attack by philosophers, as have some of the methods and concepts of modern linguistics. It has been argued, for example, that it is unintelligible to attribute to the learning child propositional knowledge of the relevant kind (e.g., knowledge that a particular regularity holds for all human languages) on the grounds that such knowledge involves thoughts, and thoughts can be attributed only to creatures who already possess a language. We make no headway, this argument runs, in explaining how humans acquire language by attributing to them knowledge that they could intelligibly possess only if they had a language.

Even the contention that knowledge must be attributed to competent speakers in an explanation of their linguistic abilities (whether or not this knowledge is partly innate) has generated opposition. Worries have been expressed about a concept of knowledge that to some appears quite different from the standard one. Thus linguistic knowledge seems not to require justification, as do many familiar cases of knowledge. Furthermore, we are not conscious of our linguistic knowledge as we are of much other knowledge: we could not articulate the principles that constitute our knowledge of language—indeed, we very likely would not even be able to recognize them were they presented to us, involving as they do concepts of which we have no conscious understanding.

Such criticisms have led linguists and sympathetic philosophers to defend vigorously the coherence and importance of Chomsky's conception of linguistic knowledge. One of the most sustained and interesting debates has been between Chomsky and the philosopher W. V. O. Quine. Their fundamental disagreement is sometimes assumed to revolve around the issue of innateness, with Quine, the empiricist, portrayed as unwilling to countenance the appeal to innate knowledge. This way of putting the matter is only half right, however. It is correct that Quine finds Chomsky's notion of innate linguistic knowledge problematic, but that is not because Quine has objections to innateness; Quine himself believes that no learning is possible without something being given innately. Rather, what Quine finds troublesome is the notion of linguistic knowledge. For as conceived by Chomsky, it cannot be understood as a place holder for a collection of behavioral dispositions: someone may lack the ability to use language but still possess linguistic knowledge (this is what we might say, according to Chomsky, of one who, for whatever reason, temporarily loses her capacity to speak). This construal of knowledge of language, according to which it can be present but unmanifestable, is in tension with Quine's emphasis on the public nature of meaning.

What this and other debates may ultimately indicate is less that there is disagreement about whether innate structures exist pertaining to the cognitive functioning of humans than that there is confusion and controversy over the precise nature of these structures.

[See also Chomsky, Noam; Epistemology; Language; Meaning; Quine, Willard Van Orman.]

BIBLIOGRAPHY

Chomsky, N. *Syntactic Structures.* The Hague, 1957.
———. *Aspects of the Theory of Syntax.* Cambridge, 1965.
———. *Cartesian Linguistics.* New York, 1966.
———. *Reflections on Language.* New York, 1975.
———. *Rules and Representations.* New York, 1980.
Otero, C., ed. *Noam Chomsky: Critical Assessments.* Vol. 2. New York, 1994.
Quine, W. V. O. "Methodological Reflections on Current Linguistic Theory," in D. Davidson and J. Hintikka, eds., *Semantics of Natural Language* (Boston, 1972).
———. "Linguistics and Philosophy," in *The Ways of Paradox and Other Essays* (Cambridge, 1976).

– ALEXANDER GEORGE

NATURALISM

Philosophical naturalism might be characterized in rough terms as the view that nature is all there is and all basic truths are truths of nature. But even those who can accept this description differ widely on three questions: (1) What is nature? (2) What kind of "is" expresses its identity with what there is? (3) What sorts of truths are basic, and in what way? Naturalism is more often presupposed than stated, and naturalists differ in their conceptions of the position. Thus, (1) may be answered ontologically, in terms of what kinds of entities count as natural, or methodologically, in terms of the methods of investigation that determine what counts as natural, or in other ways.

Naturalisms may be global, applying to everything, or domain specific, targeting one category of phenomenon, such as the mental. Any naturalism may be reductive or nonreductive. Reductive naturalisms may attempt either conceptual or nonconceptual reduction. Thus, in the philosophy of mind logical behaviorism seeks to reduce mental phenomena to behavioral (hence natural) phenomena by philosophical analysis; a mind–brain identity theory could claim that it is only an empirical fact that mental phenomena are physical (and thereby natural).

Nonreductive naturalism requires special comment. Its main division is perhaps between substantive and methodological versions. The former maintain that everything they apply to—e.g., mental phenomena, properties, numbers—is some specified kind of natural entity; the latter specify only a methodology, characteristically one deemed scientific, such that everything it applies to is thereby properly called natural. Thus, a substantive, nonreductive naturalism in the philosophy of mind might hold that mental properties are natural though not reducible to physical properties—the paradigmatically basic kind of natural properties. This claim might be defended by arguing that mental properties supervene on physical ones, where "supervene" implies that our mental properties, and thereby all psychological truths about us, are determined by physical properties and physical truths. It might also be held that any moral properties and truths there are depend similarly on physical properties and truths. By contrast, a methodological naturalist might hold that what counts as a natural property is determined, not by any specific ontological base of, say, physical properties, but rather by the success of scientific investigations, and scientific legitimation even of psychic properties not supervening on physical properties is not ruled out.

What is nature?

What kind of "is" expresses its identity

with what there is?

What sorts of truths are basic,

and in what way?

One way to avoid reduction of putative nonnatural entities is to eliminate them. Eliminative materialism, which claims that there are no mental phenomena, can be driven by naturalism. Elimination, even when motivated by naturalism, should be distinguished from *naturalization*: the latter brings the target phenomena into the natural domain; the former discountenances them. Thus, although eliminativism motivated by naturalism is not reductive regarding mental phenomena, it contrasts sharply with what is called nonreductive naturalism.

Naturalization can be attempted in any domain. Let us consider just three in which there has been much theorizing.

In metaphysics, although a naturalist need not be a physicalist—holding that only physical phenomena are real, not even excepting such comparatively well-behaved abstract entities as sets—naturalism may be in some way derived from, or at least be motivated by, physicalism. But how well do we understand the physical? It need not be, for example, the corporeal: consider the physical forces in action at a distance. If, however, we do not characterize the physical intrinsically in terms of some kind of property, we appear forced to define it by appeal to what physical scientists discover, or perhaps would ultimately discover. Then we cannot know a priori that, for example, irreducibly mentalistic explanations will not ultimately be part of what the people we call physicists consider their best overall account of reality. It could turn out, moreover, to be impossible to account adequately for science, not to mention philosophy, without positing some abstract entities such as numbers, propositions, and possible worlds.

A further question concerns causation, which appears central for either substantive or methodological naturalisms. Suppose that mental properties in some sense must depend on physical properties, as nonreductive supervenience requires. Robust naturalists tend to want more. Many naturalists seem committed to the causal closure of the physical world, roughly the view that all causes are, or depend exclusively on, physical causes, as opposed to the causal sufficiency of the physical: the existence of physical nomically sufficient conditions for every event. Causal sufficiency implies the possibility of a *comprehensive* physical science, but is not exclusive in the way closure is.

In epistemology consider just reliabilism—roughly, the view that knowledge and justified beliefs are constituted by beliefs that are reliably produced (i.e., produced or sustained in a way that makes them likely to be true). Reliabilists may try to naturalize epistemology in at least two contrasting ways. They may hold that epistemology, properly practiced, is a branch of psychology or that epistemology is committed to no irreducibly normative, and thereby nonnatural, properties. We might call the view that the truths of epistemology are empirical substantive epistemological naturalism, and the view that its only irreducible concepts are natural—with its apparent implication that all its truths are naturalistically expressible—conceptual epistemological naturalism. The latter view does not entail the former: an epistemologist could use only (naturalized) concepts and still countenance nonempirical epistemic principles.

In ethics reductive naturalism—the view that moral properties (e.g., obligatoriness) are natural properties remains controversial. We could, however, have conceptual naturalism here without substantive naturalism: even if moral concepts are reducible to natural ones, some moral truths could be a priori. A weaker view is

normative naturalism, the nonreductive position that there are naturalistic, contingently necessary and sufficient conditions for applying moral terms. A position that leaves reductive naturalism open is explanationist naturalism—the view that moral properties are explanatory and ethical truths are confirmable by natural facts about individuals and society. As elsewhere, naturalists may proceed by elimination. An analogue of eliminativism in philosophy of mind is ethical noncognitivism: just as there are no mental properties, there are no moral ones. But whereas the former eliminativists commonly hold that we can have better ways to explain behavior than the mentalistic modes now employed, noncognitivists generally embrace moral discourse as invaluable—they simply decognitivize it: moral predicates are expressive or prescriptive, not descriptive or explanatory. Again we may have conceptual naturalism without substantive naturalism: even if moral concepts are reducible to natural ones, some moral truths could be a priori.

In any attempt to understand naturalism there is a danger of speaking as if it is clear when a view is reductive; but 'reduction' may be no clearer than when two predicates express the same property. Do they express the same property provided they are (1) synonymous, (2) analytically equivalent, (3) conceptually equivalent, (4) logically equivalent, (5) metaphysically equivalent, (6) synthetically a priori equivalent, (7) explanatorally equivalent, (8) nomically equivalent, (9) causally equivalent, or (10) something else again? The weaker the criteria for reduction, the more readily reductive naturalization can be achieved; the stronger these criteria, the more significant a nonreductive, substantive naturalization can be. As to methodological naturalism, if it takes scientific method as the only route to knowledge—and some such conviction also largely motivates substantive naturalisms—this leaves unclear just what is ruled out by a commitment to scientific method. And if we cannot characterize scientific method in quite definite terms and instead must conceive it as the investigative procedure the scientific community uses, where that community is understood—in the spirit of naturalism—historically and sociologically, then naturalism is functionally defined, in terms of how well the thesis or project in question fits whatever worldview has suitable scientific sanction. How clear, then, is our conception of naturalism if scientific method is essential to it? It may seem as clear—or contested—as our present understanding of scientific method. The question remains whether this understanding is firm enough to anchor a philosophical worldview.

[See also Causation; Eliminative Materialism, Eliminativism; Epistemology; Metaphysics; Naturalized Epistemology; Philosophy of Mind; Physicalism, Materialism; Reduction, Reductionism; Reliabilism; Supervenience.]

BIBLIOGRAPHY

Armstrong, D. M. *The Nature of Mind and Other Essays.* Ithaca, NY, 1981.

Kim, J. "The Myth of Nonreductive Materialism," *Proceedings of the American Philosophical Association* 63 (1989), 31–47.

Kitcher, P. "The Naturalists Return," *Philosophical Review,* Vol. 101 (1992), 53–114.

Kornblith, H., ed. *Naturalized Epistemology.* Cambridge, MA, 1985.

Nagel, E. *The Structure of Science.* New York, 1961.

Sellars, R. W. "Why Naturalism and Not Materialism," *Philosophical Review* 36 (1927), 216–25.

Post, J. *The Faces of Existence.* Ithaca, NY, 1987.

Quine, W. V. O. "Epistemology Naturalized," in *Ontological Relativity and Other Essays* (New York, 1969).

Wagner, S. J., and R. Warner, eds. *Naturalism: A Critical Appraisal.* Notre Dame, 1993.

— ROBERT AUDI

NATURALIZED EPISTEMOLOGY

Movements to naturalize are influential in almost every area of philosophy, from philosophy of mind to philosophy of language to moral philosophy. The aim of these movements is to ensure that our philosophical theories are compatible with science—that is, make reference only to those properties and entities that science can countenance. Naturalized epistemologists share this aim, but they also argue that the practices and findings of science should play a more positive, active role in epistemological theorizing.

W. V. O. Quine coined the expression "naturalized epistemology" and is the movement's most influential proponent. He rejects the analytic-synthetic distinction, and this in turn leads him to emphasize the holistic nature of our belief systems. Our beliefs cannot be neatly divided into those that purport to capture analytic truths, which are known a priori and as such are not subject to empirical disconfirmation, and those that capture synthetic truths, which are known a posteriori and are subject to empirical disconfirmation. Rather, our beliefs face the test of experience as a whole. When experiences fail to turn out as expected, we know that something in our belief system has gone wrong and is in need of revision, but no part of the system is in principle immune from revision. It is a short step from this conclusion to the view that there is no sharp separation between epistemology and science. Epistemology cannot be done without empirical input. It has to be naturalized.

Quine's most famous characterization of naturalized epistemology is that it turns epistemology into a chapter of psychology. This is accomplished by reformulating the traditional questions of epistemology to make them proper subjects of empirical studies. For example, the question, Do our sensory experiences justify our beliefs about the external world? is replaced with, How do sensory experiences cause us to believe what we do about the external world? The strategy is to make epistemology into a part of natural science and hence, in Quine's view, respectable.

W. V. O. Quine coined the expression "naturalized epistemology" and is the movement's most influential proponent.

Some other epistemologists who see themselves as doing naturalized epistemology reject many of Quine's positions, but they share his distaste for a priori theorizing in epistemology. Cartesian epistemology, in particular, is the common enemy. Descartes thought of epistemology as first philosophy; the epistemologist's task is to tell us what intellectual methods and procedures we are justified in employing. Science can be of no help in this project, since a part of the project's motivation is to lay down rules for science itself.

In the eyes of naturalized epistemologists, this conception of epistemology forced Descartes and epistemologists influenced by him to resort to armchair speculation about what intellectual procedures, methods, and practices are to be trusted. Not surprisingly, they came to different conclusions. Descartes recommends the method of doubt; Locke recommends the way of ideas; Russell insists that all knowledge ultimately depends on direct acquaintance with facts; and Chisholm says that it is prima facie reasonable for us to trust introspection, memory, and perception. The problem common to all these recommendations, say naturalized epistemologists, is that they are the result of a priori reflections about what methods are to be trusted. The alternative is to abandon the Cartesian project and instead to make full use of science in thinking about epistemological questions.

Naturalized epistemologists appeal to science in a variety of ways. Some engage in detailed studies of the methods and practices of science. The assumption is that, insofar as we are interested in which intellectual procedures are trustworthy, we need to look carefully at how science works, since it is the most successful of all human intellectual enterprises.

Others have attempted to use the theory of evolution to address some of the central questions of epistemology, including, for example, the question of what reasons we have for trusting our cognitive faculties. For example, some evolutionary epistemologists argue that natural selection favors reliable cognitive faculties, since they are survival enhancing. So, it is to be expected that our cognitive faculties are reliable.

Still others apply the findings of cognitive science to epistemology, citing studies that show recurrent patterns of errors in the way we reason. The errors arise, for example, from an insensitivity to sample size, an underutilization of known prior probabilities in making predictions, a tendency in certain kinds of situations to assign a higher probability to a conjunction than to one of its conjuncts, and so on. The assumption behind these projects is that epistemology has traditionally been interested in fashioning advice for the improvement of our intellectual lives, but for this we need to look at empirical studies that document the kinds of mistakes we have a tendency to make. We will then be in a position to guard against them.

Yet others follow Quine's advice more literally, focusing their attention on how our sense experiences lead to our beliefs, hypotheses, and theories. The emphasis is on how cognition actually functions, and the relevant sciences are psychology and neurobiology.

A recurrent objection to naturalized epistemology is that it is not normative and thus constitutes an abandonment of epistemology. If we turn epistemology into a chapter of psychology, in which its principal task is to describe how a relatively restricted sensory input produces a rich array of beliefs, then we are no longer interested in assessing which procedures, methods, and practices we are justified in believing. We are simply describing how we come to believe what we do.

In general, naturalized epistemologists have been eager to respond that they have no intention of abandoning the normative element within epistemology. Quine's view is that the normative is not jettisoned; it merely becomes a part of what he calls the "engineering" of truth seeking. If we assume that one of our goals is to believe truths and assume also that this goal is valuable, then the various sciences, from physics to psychology to mathematics, are in a position to give us advice about how to achieve this goal—advice that has normative implications. For example, physics advises us not to take soothsayers seriously, since their claims to reliability are incompatible with what physics tells us; psychology provides us with information about the conditions in which we are subject to perceptual illusions, wishful thinking, and other such cognitive problems; mathematics warns us against various kinds of statistical mistakes; and so on.

Alvin Goldman has a different response to the objection that naturalized epistemology is not normative. Unlike Quine, he does not altogether reject the analytic-synthetic distinction, and as a result he is more comfortable than Quine in proposing a conceptual analysis of epistemic justification. The analysis he defends is a reliabilist one; epistemic justification is essentially a matter of having one's beliefs generated by reliable cognitive processes. Goldman points out that a naturalized approach to epistemology fits comfortably with this reliabilist account of epistemic justification, and it is this that allows epistemology to be both naturalized and normative. Reliabilism tells us that we are justified in employing an intellectual procedure, method, or practice insofar as the practice is reliable, and then science tells us which procedures, methods, and practices are in fact reliable.

Hilary Kornblith has yet another way of arguing that naturalized epistemology is normative. He claims that questions about how people ought to reason cannot be sharply separated from questions about how they actually reason, since any attempt to understand how people ought to reason has no choice but to begin with facts about how they do reason. This constraint, according to Kornblith, suggests that the two cannot radically come apart. But if so, studies of how we actually reason will always have important lessons for how we should reason.

A related problem for naturalized epistemology can be expressed in the form of a dilemma: the less closely a naturalized epistemology aligns itself with the methods and findings of science, the less distinct it will be from traditional approaches of epistemology; on the other hand, the more closely it aligns itself with the methods and findings of science, the less room there will be for radical challenges of those methods and findings.

Most naturalized epistemologists grasp the second horn of this dilemma, since they are not disposed to engage in radical critiques of science in any event. So, if it turns out to be impossible on their view to engage in such critiques, this is a small price to pay for an alternative to a priori epistemology. However, their opponents think that none of our intellectual endeavors, not even science, should be protected from radical challenges. They also point out that the tendency of naturalized epistemologists not to take seriously radical critiques of science is part of a larger refusal to take seriously any kind of radical skeptical worry.

Most naturalized epistemologists are more than willing to admit that they are unconcerned with refuting radical skeptical hypotheses such as Descartes's evil-demon hypothesis. In helping themselves to the conclusions of science at the beginning of their theorizing, they are presupposing the falsity of the radical skeptical hypotheses, and they see nothing wrong with this. On the contrary, they regard attempts to disprove radical skeptical hypotheses as examples of a failed epistemological tradition that sees it as the task of the epistemologist to vindicate simultaneously all of our intellectual capacities and methods. The alternative is to recognize that epistemological questions arise only at a relatively late stage of inquiry and that we have no choice but to use the results of previous inquiries to investigate these questions.

[See also Chisholm, Roderick M.; Cognitive Science; Descartes, René; Epistemology; Introspection; Locke, John; Memory; Perception; Philosophy of Language; Philosophy of Mind; Quine, Willard Van Orman; Reliabilism; Russell, Bertrand Arthur William.]

BIBLIOGRAPHY

Goldman, A. *Epistemology and Cognition.* Cambridge, MA, 1986. A defense of a reliabilist theory of knowledge and epistemic justification.

Kornblith, H., ed. *Naturalizing Epistemology.* Cambridge, MA, 1994. The volume contains many of the most important articles on naturalized epistemology and a useful introduction.

Quine, W. V. O. "Epistemology Naturalized," in *Ontological Relativity and Other Essays* (New York, 1969). This is the article that has had the greatest influence on the naturalized epistemology movement.

———. *Pursuit of Truth.* Cambridge, MA, 1990. The first chapter contains a clear summary of Quine's epistemology as well as a discussion of why his naturalized epistemology is normative.

Stich, S. *The Fragmentation of Reason.* Cambridge, MA, 1990. The book explains the relevance of cognitive science to epistemology, criticizes the idea that the processes of natural selection ensure that our cognitive faculties are reliable, and defends a pragmatic account of cognitive evaluation.

– RICHARD FOLEY

NIETZSCHE, FRIEDRICH

Friedrich Nietzsche (1844–1900), German philosopher and poet, is one of the most original and influential figures in modern philosophy. His life has attracted more attention from interpreters of his thought, major novelists, psychiatrists, and others than the life of other major philosophers. Misrepresentations of almost every facet of his life have been crucial, for they bear on an understanding of his significance. It is also difficult to obtain reliable information on the authenticity and relative importance of his works and his posthumously published notes, on his madness, and on his relation to Wagner. These problems will therefore be stressed in the following discussion.

Life and Pathology

Nietzsche was born in Röcken, Prussia. His father, Ludwig Nietzsche, a Lutheran minister and the son of a minister, was 31, and his mother, the daughter of a Lutheran minister, was 18. His paternal grandfather had written several books, including *Gamaliel, or the Everlasting Duration of Christianity: For Instruction and Sedation . . .* (1796). Many of Nietzsche's ancestors were butchers; none of them seem to have been, as he believed, Polish noblemen. His father christened him Friedrich Wilhelm after King Friedrich Wilhelm IV of Prussia, on whose birthday he was born. The king became mad a few years later; so did Nietzsche's father. Nietzsche later shed his middle name, along with his family's patriotism and religion, but in January 1889 he, too, became insane.

As a student at Leipzig, Nietzsche discovered

Schopenhauer and Richard Wagner,

the two greatest influences on his early thought.

In an early autobiographical sketch Nietzsche wrote, "In September 1848 my beloved father suddenly became mentally ill." When Elisabeth Förster-Nietzsche (born 1846) published this sketch in her biography of her brother (1895), she changed the wording to read, ". . . suddenly became seriously ill in consequence of a fall." (She also published, as addressed to her, letters actually addressed to her mother and drafts of letters to others, but there is no evidence of any forgery that affects Nietzsche's philosophy.) In fact, the diagnosis of Ludwig Nietzsche's doctor was softening of the brain (*Gehirnerweichung*), and after the elder Nietzsche's death in 1849, his skull was opened, and the diagnosis was confirmed. Nevertheless, most experts agree that the philosopher's later insanity was not inherited.

In January 1850, Nietzsche's widowed mother lost her youngest son (who was born in 1848) and moved her family to Naumburg. The household there consisted of Friedrich, his mother (who died in 1897) and sister, his father's mother, and two maiden aunts. This, as well as his sister's character, helps to account for some of Nietzsche's snide remarks about women.

In 1858 Nietzsche accepted free admission to Pforta, a famous boarding school a few miles from Naumburg. He was often at the head of his class and acquired an excellent classical education. In 1861 he wrote an enthusiastic essay on his "favorite poet," Hölderlin, "of whom the majority of his people scarcely even know the name." Hölderlin had spent the last decades of his life in hopeless insanity, but sixty years after Nietzsche wrote his essay, Hölderlin was widely recognized as Germany's greatest poet after Goethe. The teacher wrote on the paper, "I must offer the author the kind advice to stick to a healthier, clearer, *more German* poet."

The medical records of the school contain an entry, recorded in 1862: ". . . shortsighted and often plagued by migraine headaches. His father died early of softening of the brain and was begotten in old age [actually, when his father was 57, his mother 35]; the son at a time when the father was already sick [most experts deny this]. As yet no grave signs are visible, but the antecedents require consideration."

In 1864 Nietzsche graduated with a thesis on Theognis. He studied theology and classical philology at the University of Bonn, but in 1865 he gave up theology and went to Leipzig. There is no evidence that he contracted syphilis in Cologne while he was a student at Bonn, although this story has gained currency; there is, however, inconclusive evidence that two physicians in Leipzig treated Nietzsche for syphilis without telling him their diagnosis. Wilhelm Lange-Eichbaum, a psychiatrist, writes that a Berlin psychiatrist told him this and added that the names of the two doctors were known. Another psychiatrist, P. J. Möbius, is said to have possessed letters which were written by these two men but which no longer exist. Be that as it may, Nietzsche evidently never thought he had syphilis, and most of his life he was sexually a complete ascetic. The most that has been claimed is that as a student he may have visited a brothel once or twice. The matter has been much debated because his madness was probably tertiary syphilis, and Thomas Mann's novel *Doktor Faustus,* which draws on Nietzsche's life, has given these questions additional prominence.

Throughout his life Nietzsche's health was poor. His doctors kept warning him to preserve his very bad eyesight by reading and writing less. He disregarded this advice, fought severe migraine and gastric pains with long walks and much writing, and took pills and potions to purchase a little sleep. His books became his life. As they found no response, his style became shrill, and losing his inhibitions, he said in his later books what he had said earlier only in some of his letters. Out of context some phrases sound mad. Many of Nietzsche's dicta are redeemed by his wit, which has escaped many translators and interpreters.

In January 1889, Nietzsche collapsed in a street in Turin while embracing a horse that had been flogged by a coachman. His last letters, mailed on the first days of 1889, are mad but meaningful and moving. After the first week of 1889 nothing of even this pathetic bril-

Misrepresentations of almost every facet of Nietzsche's life have been crucial, because they bear on an understanding of his significance. (Corbis/Hulton-Deutsch Collection)

liance relieved the utter darkness of his mind. He vegetated until his death. But none of his books can be discounted as a product of madness; all repay close study.

The various accounts of Nietzsche's pathology disagree on many points, but none of them illuminates Nietzsche's philosophy. When the novelist Arnold Zweig wanted to write a book on Nietzsche, Freud wrote him that Nietzsche's psychological development could not be reconstructed, and according to Ernest Jones, Freud's biographer, Freud "several times said of Nietzsche that he had a more penetrating knowledge of himself than any other man who ever lived or was ever likely to live." Lesser psychologists and would-be psychologists have been more condescending.

As a student at Leipzig, Nietzsche discovered Schopenhauer and Richard Wagner, the two greatest influences on his early thought, as well as F. A. Lange's *History of Materialism.* In a letter dated November 1866, Nietzsche wrote, "Kant, Schopenhauer, and this book of Lange's—more I don't need." But he also worked on Aeschylus and published papers on Theognis (1867) and a prizewinning essay on Diogenes Laërtius (1868–1869). Although the appearance of these articles in Professor Friedrich Ritschl's journals was a triumph, Nietzsche wrote his friend Erwin Rohde (later a famous classical philologist) that he found his prize paper "repulsive" and utterly inadequate. "What is Diogenes Laërtius? Nobody would lose a word over the philistine physiognomy of this scribbler if he were not by accident the clumsy watchman guarding treasures whose value he does not know. He is the night watchman of the history of Greek philosophy: one cannot enter it without obtaining the key from him."

In October 1867, Nietzsche commenced his military service. In March 1868, while jumping on his horse, he hit the pommel of the saddle with his chest and was badly hurt, but he rode on as if nothing had happened. In August 1868, after prolonged suffering from the injury, he returned home and was formally discharged from the army in October.

Back in Leipzig, he complained, in a letter to Rohde of November 20, "I must again see the swarming philologists' breed of our day from nearby, and daily have to observe the whole molish business, the full cheek pouches and blind eyes, the delight at having caught a worm, and indifference toward the true and urgent problems of life." He published scholarly book reviews but at one point considered writing a doctoral thesis on Kant. Early in 1869 he even thought of taking up chemistry, "throwing philology where it belongs, with the household rubble of our ancient ancestors."

During the following winter the chair of classical philology at the University of Basel fell vacant, and Ritschl recommended him for the post: he had never published contributions from another student nor seen a student like Nietzsche in 39 years of teaching. Nietzsche had not yet written a doctoral thesis, let alone the dissertation generally required before a doctor of philosophy becomes a *Privatdozent,* or the additional book required for an associate professorship, yet he was appointed an associate professor at Basel at the age of 24. Ritschl wrote that "in *Germany* that sort of thing happens absolutely never" but reassured the authorities at Basel that although Nietzsche had concentrated on Greek literature and philosophy, "with his great gifts he will work in other fields with the best of success. He will simply be able to do anything he wants to do." Leipzig conferred the doctorate without thesis or examination, and in April 1869, Nietzsche went to Basel and became a Swiss subject. In 1870 he became a full professor.

In August 1870 he received leave to volunteer as a medical orderly in the Franco-Prussian War. Early in

September he returned to Germany with dysentery and diphtheria; he may also have infected himself with syphilis while ministering to sick soldiers. Without waiting to regain his strength, he returned to Basel in October to teach at both the Gymnasium and the university. During the following months he also audited the lectures of Jakob Burckhardt, the art historian, visited Richard Wagner in Tribschen near Lucerne whenever possible, and finished his first book.

What requires explanation is not so much why Nietzsche became mad, but how he could ever have written over ten books that stamp him as one of Germany's greatest masters of prose as well as the most influential and inexhaustible German philosopher since Kant and Hegel.

In summing up this account of Nietzsche's first 28 years, three points merit emphasis. First, although the historical-critical edition of Nietzsche's *Werke* (discontinued after five volumes) only includes material published before 1869 and the literature on the young Nietzsche keeps growing, this period commands attention only as the background of his later work. However, legions of errors about Nietzsche's early period have been used in support of false claims about his philosophy. Second, Nietzsche's eventual insanity seems overdetermined; no explanation of it has been proved, but so many explanations are available that what requires explanation is not so much why he became mad but how he could ever have written over ten books that stamp him as one of Germany's greatest masters of prose as well as the most influential and inexhaustible German philosopher since Kant and Hegel. Third, he might never have subjected himself to all the requirements for a professorship had it not been offered to him practically gratis.

Writings

THE BIRTH OF TRAGEDY. Nietzsche's first book, *Die Geburt der Tragödie aus dem Geiste der Musik* (1872), advances theories about the birth and death of Greek tragedy that are unsupported by footnotes or Greek quotations; in 1874 a version with slight textual changes appeared. In 1886 both versions were reissued with a new introduction and a title page that read *The Birth of Tragedy, or Hellenism and Pessimism: A New*

Edition with an Attempt at a Self-Criticism. This self-criticism is the best critique ever written of the book, which for all its faults has the touch of genius. Only the later introduction shows human greatness.

In 1872, immediately after *The Birth of Tragedy* was published, Ulrich von Wilamowitz-Moellendorff, who had just received his doctorate and much later was to achieve great fame as a Greek philologist, published a pamphlet *Philology of the future! A reply to Friedrich Nietzsche's birth of tragedy* (*Zukunftsphilologie!*). Rohde replied with a polemic called *Afterphilologie,* which means "pseudophilology"; but *After,* a word Luther liked to use abusively in various combinations, also means posterior, and the title suggests a perversion of philology. Nietzsche wrote Rohde that his friend Franz Overbeck, church historian at Basel had suggested this title. He did not mention that Schopenhauer, in his diatribe against *Die Universitätsphilosophie* had spoken of Hegel's *Afterphilosophie.* In 1873 Wilamowitz published another reply. All three pamphlets were unworthy of their authors; they were never reprinted and have since become rarities.

Wilamowitz was utterly blind to the merits of *The Birth of Tragedy,* of which F. M. Cornford was to write in *From Religion to Philosophy* (1912) that it was "a work of profound imaginative insight, which left the scholarship of generation toiling in the rear." Wilamowitz tried to establish his own erudition by cataloguing faults, and Rohde then tried to show that they were not faults. But Rohde who had just received the title of professor, constantly called Wilamowitz "our Dr. phil." or "the pasquinader" and quite failed to see that Wilamowitz had a point in being worried about the future of philology if purple prose were to become a fashionable substitute for exact scholarship. (By now the Nietzsche literature offers many horrible examples.)

More than any other single work, *The Birth* changed the prevalent conception of the spirit of Greece, which owed much to Winckelmann and Goethe, and replaced "sweetness and light" (to use Matthew Arnold's phrase) with a more complex analysis, since further developed by Cornford, Jane Harrison, and E. R. Dodds (see Dodds's *The Greeks and the Irrational,* Berkeley, Calif., 1951, for recent literature).

Nietzsche distinguishes two tendencies: the "Apollinian," stressed hitherto—the genius of restraint, harmony, and measure that found expression in Greek sculpture and architecture—and the "Dionysian," a cruel longing to exceed all norms that found an outlet in the drunken frenzy of the Dionysian festivals and the music associated with them. Nietzsche argues that the Apollinian achievements cannot be fully appreciated until one realizes what powers had to be harnessed to make them possible. This point was missed by many interpreters because, in his later works, Nietzsche identified himself with Dionysus. In the late works, however, Dionysus is no longer opposed to Apollo; he stands for a synthesis of both gods and is played off against the crucified Christ. In Nietzsche's *Twilight of the Idols,* written in 1888, the old Goethe, who was certainly not anti-Apollinian, could therefore be celebrated as superbly Dionysian.

In *The Birth* the contrast between the Dionysian and Apollinian is indebted to Schopenhauer's contrast between will and representation. Even so, the book is a declaration of independence from Schopenhauer. Nietzsche explains the birth of Greek tragedy out of the music and dances of the Dionysian cult as a triumph of Apollinian form. He envisages "the sublime as the artistic conquest of the horrible," and he celebrates the Greeks who, facing up to the terrors of nature and history, did not seek refuge in "a Buddhistic negation of the will," as Schopenhauer did, but instead created tragedies in which life is affirmed as beautiful in spite of everything.

Ideally, the book should end, as a draft did, with Section 15; the remaining sections are a rhapsody on the rebirth of tragedy in Wagner's operas and obscure the conclusions of the original analysis. In *Ecce Homo,* written in 1888, Nietzsche said of *The Birth,* "It smells offensively Hegelian, and it is only in a few formulas affected by the cadaverous perfume of Schopenhauer." As Nietzsche pointed out, Dionysus and Apollo are "*aufgehoben* into a unity" in tragedy (*aufgehoben* is a characteristic Hegelian term meaning "canceled," "preserved," "lifted up"); this synthesis is then confronted by another idea, rationalism, symbolized by Socrates. Euripides was "a mask only: the deity who spoke out of him was . . . Socrates."

Rationalism antedated Socrates but "gained in him an indescribably magnificent expression." Even as the Greeks had needed tragedy to survive, they needed Socratism a little later. "If one were to think of this whole incalculable sum of energy . . . as *not* employed in the service of knowledge," Greek culture might have perished in "wars of annihilation," in "suicide," and in "pessimism." Rationalism brought about the demise of Greek tragedy, yet "the influence of Socrates necessitates ever again the regeneration of art." The two sections (14–15) that contain these conclusions suggest the need for a further synthesis—an "artistic Socrates."

Here one might think of Plato, but the *Republic* and *Laws* illustrate Nietzsche's claim that Socrates' rationalist-moralist heritage was opposed to the spirit of Aeschylus and Sophocles. The "artistic Socrates" is Nietzsche himself. Far from denouncing the development he described, he found his own task suggested by its projected culmination. What is wanted is a philosophy that faces what the Greek tragedians knew without sacrificing sharp rational analysis; a philosophy that does not share Socrates' optimistic assurance that knowledge, virtue, and happiness are inseparable; a philosophy that avails itself of the visions and resources of art.

THE FOUR MEDITATIONS. From 1873 to 1876, Nietzsche published his four meditations.

First Meditation. In 1873 Nietzsche published the first of his four "untimely meditations" (*Unzeitgemässe Betrachtungen,* translation published as *Thoughts out of Season*), a polemic entitled *David Strauss, The Confessor and Writer.* Strauss is best remembered for his influential *Life of Jesus* (1835). What enraged Nietzsche, however, was the immense success of Strauss's *The Old Faith and the New* (1872; 6th ed., 1873). It was the *Zeitgeist* that Neitzsche meant to attack, not Strauss, whom he was soon sorry to have hurt.

Nietzsche was roused from his dogmatic slumber by Darwin, as Kant had been roused by Hume a century earlier, and he sought to serve humanity and humaneness by resurrecting "the image of man."

In his attack on the *Kulturphilister* ("cultural philistine"), Nietzsche abandoned the patriotism of his childhood, foresaw "the extirpation of the German spirit in favor of the 'German *Reich,*' " and denounced all "deification of success." Strauss "proclaims with admirable frankness that he is no longer a Christian, but he does not want to disturb any comfortableness of any kind." He praises Darwin, but his "ethics is quite untouched," as we see when Strauss exhorts us never to forget "that you are a human being and not merely something natural." Strauss fails to recognize that "preaching morals is as easy as giving reasons for morals is difficult."

Second Meditation. In *Of the Use and Disadvantage of History for Life* (1874), Nietzsche distinguished three types of historiography. "Antiquarian history," cultivated at the universities, aims reverently to consolidate our knowledge of the past; "critical history" passes sentence; and "monumentalistic history" concentrates on past heroes in order to confront contemporary mediocrity with the possibility of greatness. While each type has its uses and disadvantages, Nietzsche dwelled particularly on the life-inhibiting consequences of the hypertrophy of the historical sense and on the usefulness

of monumentalistic history, which was later cultivated under his influence by the Stefan George Circle in Germany. Their best studies include Friedrich Gundolf's monographs; their worst, Ernst Bertram's influential *Nietzsche: versuch einer Mythologie* ("Nietzsche: Attempt at a Mythology").

Nietzsche then introduced the suprahistorical (*über-historisch*) man "who does not envisage salvation in the process but for whom the world is finished in every single moment. . . . What could ten new years teach that the past could not teach?" Nietzsche denounced "admiration for success" and "idolatry of the factual" as leading to a "yes" to "every power, be it a government, public opinion, or a majority of numbers." He rejected the optimism of nineteenth-century Hegelians and Darwinists. "The *goal of humanity* cannot lie in the end [*Ende*] but only *in its highest specimens.*"

Like the Greeks, confronted with a chaotic flood of older cultures, some of us might yet "*organize the chaos*" and appropriate the Greek "conception of culture as another and improved *physis* . . . culture as a harmony of living, thinking, appearing, and willing." In a later note Nietzsche complained that "the Germans alternate between complete devotion to the foreign and a vengeful craving for originality," as if originality consisted "in the complete and over-obvious *difference;* but the Greeks did not think that way about the Orient . . . and they *became* original (for one *is* not original to begin with, but one is raw!)" (*Werke,* Musarion edition, Vol. XI, p. 110).

Third Meditation. Schopenhauer as Educator (1874) picks up the motif of self-perfection. "The man who would not belong in the mass needs only to cease being comfortable with himself; he should follow his conscience which shouts at him: 'Be yourself! You are not really all you do, think, and desire now.' " As Nietzsche put it later, one must become what one is. To find what one is in this sense, it helps to ask oneself what one has loved until now. The answer reveals your "true self," which is not within "but immeasurably high above you, or at least above what you usually take for your ego." Nietzsche then introduces Schopenhauer as the educator whom he has loved, in order to reveal his own true self.

State and church intimidate us into conformity; a new conception of humanity is needed. In the second meditation Nietzsche had already said of the Darwinian doctrine "of the fluidity of all . . . species, of the lack of any cardinal distinction between man and animal," that it was "true but deadly" and that in another generation, when the full implications would become apparent, a widespread practical nihilism would probably result (he did not use the word "nihilism" until later). Nietzsche was roused from his dogmatic slumber by Darwin, as Kant had been roused by Hume a century earlier, and he sought to serve humanity and humaneness by resurrecting "*the image of man.*"

He criticized Rousseau's image of man as representative of a Dionysian return to nature and the unleashing of savage and destructive forces. Schopenhauer's man—the kind Nietzsche decided then and there to become—"destroys his earthly happiness through his courage; he must be hostile even to the human beings he loves and the institutions from whose womb he issued; he may spare neither human beings nor things, though he himself suffers with them in hurting them; he will be mistaken for what he is not and long be considered an ally of powers he abominates."

Later, Nietzsche asked to be read with consideration for context in order to avoid misunderstanding—*rück- und vorsichtig* (Preface to *The Dawn*). He warned that his meaning was "plain enough, assuming—as I do assume—that one has first read my earlier writings and not spared some trouble in doing this" (Preface to *Genealogy of Morals*). He pleaded, "*Above all, do not mistake me for someone else!*" (Preface to *Ecce Homo*). This is the reason for giving so much space to Nietzsche's earlier writings, which are less familiar and accessible in English. A brief essay cannot adequately summarize Nietzsche's thought; it can serve only as an introduction.

Philosophically, the third meditation is not sophisticated. Its ethic is based on the intuition of conscience, which commands us to realize our true self, and a complementary intuition of the purpose of nature, which "wants to make the life of man significant and meaningful by generating the philosopher and the artist." We are asked to help nature, which will not succeed without our assistance. This is similar to the challenge of Zarathustra, the founder of Zoroastrianism, according to which we should help Ormuzd, the god of light, whose eventual triumph over Ahriman, the force of darkness, depends on us. In his earlier works Nietzsche does not mention the Persian prophet, but nine years later he used him as his mouthpiece in his best-known book.

Fourth Meditation and Break with Wagner. Nietzsche had now come up against philosophic problems he could not solve. During the next three years he published only one short book, his meditation on *Richard Wagner in Bayreuth* (1876). From 1878 to 1889 he published one book a year. But in 1875 he approached a crisis that was not only philosophical but also personal.

The first three meditations had appeared about six months apart; the fourth, on Wagner, was postponed several times and finally was published after a two-year

interval. Meanwhile, Nietzsche anticipated in his notes some of the basic points of his later attack on Wagner, *The Case of Wagner* (1888). In 1878 their friendship came to an end.

Three reasons suffice to account for the break, although others may have contributed. First, according to Nietzsche, "one cannot serve two masters, when one is called Wagner" (*The Case of Wagner*). Wagner appreciated Nietzsche as an apostle of Wagnerism, as a professor who brought prestige to the cause, and as a young friend who could be asked to do one's Christmas shopping and other chores. Wagner had asked for changes in the endings of *The Birth* and the third meditation and had frowned on the second meditation, which made no special reference to him. In order to come into his own, Nietzsche had to break with Wagner.

In The Dawn, *Nietzsche tried to determine,*

among other things,

to what extent behavior might be explained

in terms of power and fear.

Second, Nietzsche had had growing misgivings about many of Wagner's pet ideas, such as his nationalism and his hatred of the French and the Jews. As long as the composer lived at Tribschen, Switzerland, such idiosyncrasies could be discounted. After all, it meant a great deal to have a close relationship with the greatest German artist of the time. But when Wagner moved to Bayreuth, made his peace with the new German Empire, and became a cultural influence of the first order, Nietzsche had to take a stand.

His objection to Wagner's *Parsifal*, which is widely held to have precipitated the break between them, was that coming from Wagner, it was a betrayal of integrity. How could the self-styled modern Aeschylus celebrate the anti-Greek ideal of "pure foolishness"? How could Schopenhauer's foremost disciple, hitherto an avowed atheist, use Christianity for theatrical effects? Yet the break was not sealed in January 1878, when Wagner sent Nietzsche his *Parsifal*; it was sealed in May when Nietzsche sent Wagner *Human, All-too-human*, with a motto from Descartes and a dedication to Voltaire. In August, Wagner attacked Nietzsche in the *Bayreuther Blätter*. The third reason for the break, then, is that Nietzsche's development from Schopenhauer to Voltaire and from essays with romantic overtones to aphorisms after French models, as well as his abandonment of nationalism for the ideal of the "good European," were at least as unforgivable from Wagner's point of view as *Parsifal* was from Nietzsche's.

Nietzsche "never forgave Wagner . . . that he became *reichsdeutsch*" (*Ecce Homo*). In fact, Wagner's anti-Semitic essays profoundly influenced his son-in-law H. S. Chamberlain, author of *The Bases of the Nineteenth Century* (*Die Grundlagen des neunzehnten Jahrhunderts*); the Nazis' official philosopher, Alfred Rosenberg, author of *Der Mythus des 20. Jahrhunderts* ("The Myth of the Twentieth Century"); and, above all, Hitler. Nietzsche's cleanliness vis-à-vis Wagner's influence and vis-à-vis Bernhard Förster, the Wagnerian anti-Semitic leader whom the philosopher's sister married in 1885, merits emphasis.

THE FIVE APHORISTIC BOOKS. *Human, All-too-human* (*Menschliches, Allzumenschliches*, 1878) was subtitled "A Book for Free Spirits." During the winter of 1877/1878, Nietzsche's ill health had forced him to obtain leave from the Pädagogium. His eyes, head, and stomach continued to make him so miserable that in May 1879 he resigned from the university. In June he was granted a modest pension. Henceforth, he was entirely free and alone and devoted all his remaining strength to his writing.

Two sequels appeared in 1879 and 1880—"Mixed Opinions and Aphorisms" (*Vermischte Meinungen und Sprüche*) and "The Wanderer and His Shadow" (*Der Wanderer und sein Schatten*). In later editions all three books were subsumed under the general title, *Human, All-too-human*. All three consist of aphorisms, mostly a page or less in length, with little continuity between them. Also aphoristic are *The Dawn: Reflections on Moral Prejudices* (*Morgenröthe: Gedanken über die moralischen Vorurteile*, 1881, translated as *The Dawn of Day*) and *The Gay Science* (*Die fröhliche Wissenschaft*, 1882, translated as *The Joyful Wisdom*), surely Nietzsche's best books up to that time. Readers who are put off by the shrillness of his later style may find them more likable; the prose is superb, and they abound in penetrating observations.

Having reached a philosophical impasse in his meditations, Nietzsche tried a new tack, which some have called positivistic. In an exceptionally open-minded and experimental spirit, he assembled observations on which his later suggestions were built—for example, the psychology of the will to power and the contrast of master and slave moralities.

In *The Dawn*, Nietzsche tried to determine, among other things, to what extent behavior might be explained in terms of power and fear. In one long aphorism (number 113) he argued in some detail that "the

striving for excellence is the striving to overwhelm one's neighbor, even if only very indirectly or only in one's own feelings," and also that "there is a long line of degrees of this secretly desired overwhelming, and a complete list of these would almost amount to a history of culture." At the top of the ladder stands "the ascetic and martyr." In other aphorisms Nietzsche stresses his contempt for the German Empire and those who worship strength; "Only the degree of reason in strength" can establish "worthiness of being honored." Corresponding to the early dualism of Dionysus and Apollo, of empirical and true self, we now have strength and reason, but there are many suggestions that self-integration evinces greater power than either asceticism or undisciplined strength.

In *The Gay Science* (290) "giving style to one's character" is shown to be a sign of power, while "it is the weak characters without power over themselves who hate the constraint of style," who "become slaves as soon as they serve," and who "hate to serve." The one thing needed is "that a human being attain his satisfaction with himself"; those who do not will make others pay for it. In the same book we find the dictum "The secret of the greatest fruitfulness and the greatest enjoyment of existence is: *to live dangerously*" (250). Rilke's later poetry rings beautiful variations on this theme.

THUS SPOKE ZARATHUSTRA. Thus Spoke Zarathustra (*Also sprach Zarathustra*) contains the first comprehensive statement of Nietzsche's mature philosophy. Nietzsche called it "the most profound book" of world literature, and an apologist has asked which books, excepting the Bible, are more profound. It is widely considered Nietzsche's magnum opus. The Victorian style of the early English translations misrepresents the original, which in itself does not sustain the stylistic perfection of *The Gay Science* or *Nietzsche Contra Wagner*. Magnificence alternates with parodies, epigrams with dithyrambs, wit with bathos. Part IV derides the holy mass, as well as various types of men who were attracted to Nietzsche's philosophy. Unlike the first three parts, it relates a continuous story. It is full of laughter, some at Zarathustra's expense. Philosophically, there is an utter lack of sustained argument, but Nietzsche's later works support and develop the same ideas with attention to detail and ramifications.

THE LAST SEVEN BOOKS. Most British and American philosophers find *Beyond Good and Evil* (*Jenseits von Gut und Böse*, 1886) and *Toward a Genealogy of Morals* (*Zur Genealogie der Moral*, 1887) Nietzsche's most philosophic works. *Beyond Good and Evil* offers about 200 pages of 296 consecutively numbered aphorisms, framed by a preface and a poem. This book covers the whole range of Nietzsche's interests in nine chapters, each of which deals consecutively with one group of topics, such as religion and "the natural history of morals."

The *Genealogy* comprises three essays. The first contrasts good and evil as characteristic of slave morality with good and bad as characteristic of master morality. Nietzsche argues that slave morality is born of resentment and that evil is its primary concept, with good as an afterthought. In master morality, which is basically affirmative, "good" is primary and "bad" is an afterthought, a term of contempt for what is undistinguished and not noble. Nietzsche plainly prefers master morality to slave morality, without accepting or preaching either; these are merely two types of morality. Contemporary Western morality, according to Nietzsche, is an inconsistent mixture. The second essay deals with guilt, bad conscience, and related matters, and the third with the meaning of "ascetic ideals."

In 1888 Nietzsche published *The Case of Wagner* (*Der Fall Wagner*) and completed four other short books. *The Twilight of the Idols* (*Die Götzen-Dämmerung,* 1889), a 100-page summary of Nietzsche's philosophy, originally was to be entitled "A Psychologist's Leisure." Peter Gast, a disciple, pleaded for a more flamboyant title, and the master obliged with a dig at Wagner's *Götterdämmerung,* adding the subtitle "How One Philosophizes With a Hammer." This alludes to an image in the Preface, which was written before the title was changed: idols "are here touched with a hammer as with a tuning fork" to determine whether they are hollow.

The Antichrist (*Der Antichrist,* 1895) was subtitled *Attempt at a Critique of Christianity,* but shortly before his collapse Nietzsche struck out this subtitle, substituting "Curse on Christianity." It seems reasonable to retain the earlier subtitle.

Ecce Homo, Nietzsche's incomparably sarcastic review of his work, was withheld by his sister until 1908. Its four chapter headings are "Why I Am So Wise," "Why I Am So Clever," "Why I Write Such Excellent Books" (which comprises reviews of all his books through *The Twilight of the Idols*), and "Why I Am a Destiny." The similarity to George Bernard Shaw is striking, but many critics have discounted the book and failed to profit from its exceedingly interesting self-interpretation. Indeed, most interpreters have lacked an appreciation of Nietzsche's sense of humor and irony, and without that, *Ecce Homo*—and Nietzsche in general—cannot be understood.

The Preface to *Nietzsche Contra Wagner,* which is the last book Nietzsche completed, is dated Christmas 1888. Nietzsche's intent in the 25-page work was to

show that *The Case of Wagner* involved no betrayal of his previous thought and that he had not waited for Wagner's death to publish his criticisms of him. So, according to the Preface, he assembled relevant passages from his earlier books, "perhaps clarified here and there, above all shortened. Read one after another, they will leave no doubt either about Richard Wagner or about myself: we are antipodes." If it had been better known, the book, whose prose is superb, might have obviated many misunderstandings.

In sum, the books of 1888, which are very short, are among Nietzsche's best, and they afford a good approach to his thought.

POETRY AND FORGERY. Nietzsche was also a highly influential poet. *The Gay Science* begins with a section of verse, and in the second edition another chapter, as well as another section of poetry, was appended. *Zarathustra* contains several long poems, and Nietzsche's *Dionysus-Dithyramben* were appended with separate pagination to Part IV of *Zarathustra* (1891). These dithyrambs have been often reissued, with slight textual changes. The poems are all by Nietzsche, but he did not prepare any final version for the printer, and he considered using some of them to conclude his books of 1888. Although the poems are very uneven, they influenced Rilke's *Duino Elegies.*

My Sister and I (New York, 1951) was published over Nietzsche's name. Allegedly, the original was lost, and only a vermin-eaten carbon copy of a translation survived. The book is a clumsy forgery with no literary or philosophic value whatsoever.

"THE WILL TO POWER." The book published under the title *Der Wille zur Macht* (*The Will to Power*) consists of some of the notes Nietzsche accumulated from 1884 to 1888, systematically arranged by his sister. Her first version (Vol. XV of the "collected works," 1901) contained some 400 "aphorisms." In 1904, 200 pages of further notes were included in the last volume of her biography of her brother. Finally, a second edition in two volumes (1906) offered 1,067 notes, the new material being mixed with the old. In the best edition, *Gesammelte Werke* (Musarion edition), the approximate date of every note is given in an appendix. The systematic arrangement makes it easy to see what Nietzsche had to say about religion, morality, epistemology, art, and so forth, although many notes might equally well be placed in another section. But those who regard *The Will to Power* as Nietzsche's magnum opus overlook that he utilized many of these notes in his later books, often giving them an unexpected twist, and that many of the notes not used by him presumably did not satisfy him.

For a time Nietzsche planned to write a book to be called "The Will to Power," but he never finished a single chapter. He later decided to call his main work "Revaluation of All Values" (*Umwertung aller Werte*), and he referred to *The Antichrist*, which draws heavily on notes included in *The Will to Power*, as Book I of the "Revaluation."

Friedrich Würzbach's rearrangement of the notes according to a scheme of his own has met with no acclaim. Karl Schlechta's arrangement, offered as part of a three-volume edition of the *Werke*, has been widely accepted and also widely criticized. By printing the material as found in the notebooks, in which Nietzsche sometimes wrote on right-hand pages first, then on left-hand pages, and sometimes started from the back, Schlechta eliminates all order, along with any pretense that this is a major work, and makes these notes almost unreadable. His claim that they contain "nothing new" and merely duplicate the books is exaggerated; for example, much of the material on nihilism, with which Nietzsche's sister's arrangement begins, is not found elsewhere. In sum, *The Will to Power* is of very great interest, but it must be used cautiously and compared with Nietzsche's later books and with the notes the sister did not include—notes that are to be found, for instance, in the Musarion edition of the *Werke* but not in Schlechta's edition.

Philosophy

THE WILL TO POWER. The conception of the will to power is central in Nietzsche's philosophy. In his aphoristic books he had found the will to power at work in all sorts of human behavior and valuations; in *Zarathustra* he proclaimed it man's basic motive and suggested that it is to be found in all living things (in his later works, he even ascribed it to inorganic nature). This is frankly presented as a "hypothesis," one which Nietzsche does not claim to have proved even in the realm of psychology—the only field in which he assembled a great deal of evidence. As a metaphysical theory about the universe or ultimate reality, the doctrine need not be taken seriously, not even in an effort to understand Nietzsche. Heidegger's interpretation of Nietzsche, which makes this metaphysic the center of his thought and significance, depends on a complete disregard for the context of the passages he cites and the *Gestalt* of Nietzsche's thought generally. He assigns to Nietzsche a totally uncongenial role in the history of Western thought, disregards the bulk of his writings, and stresses a few formulations in which Nietzsche opposes the will to power to Schopenhauer's blind will. Like all serious interpreters, however, Heidegger rejects the notion that the will to power is protofascist.

Nietzsche's psychological theory depends on his concept of sublimation (a word Nietzsche himself used),

and he found more power in self-control, art, and philosophy than in the subjugation of others. Nietzsche's notion of resentment (*Ressentiment*) is another facet of the psychology of the will to power; so is the discussion of slave morality, created by "the resentment of those who are denied the real reaction, that of the deed, and who compensate with an imaginary revenge" (*Genealogy*). The noble man, being powerful, "shakes off with one shrug much vermin that would have buried itself deep in others"; free of resentment, he can respect and even love his enemies.

Nietzsche's psychological theory depends on his concept of sublimation (a word he himself used), and he found more power in self-control, art, and philosophy than in the subjugation of others.

Nietzsche's doctrine developed out of his early reflections on the contest (agon) among the Greeks. The tragic poets sought triumphs over one another and also power over their audience, the language, and themselves. Socrates before his judges, Socrates in prison, Socrates meeting death is a paragon of power. But the weak also seek power; Nero, unsuccessful as an artist, became a tyrant, burned Rome, and fiddled on the roof.

Nietzsche's belief that Socrates is more powerful than Nero—the example is that of the present writer—is far clearer than his right to translate cultural power into *more* power. It seems that he reasoned more or less as follows. The only thing that all men want is power, and whatever is wanted is wanted for the sake of power. If something is wanted more than something else, it must represent more power. Men would rather be Socrates in prison than Nero on the roof; hence, Socrates must be more powerful. No argument of this form is found in Nietzsche's writings, and he may have found it evident, at least at times, that the acme of power is embodied in the perfectly self-possessed man who has no fear of other men, of himself, or of death and whose simple personality, unaided by any props, changes the lives of those who meet him and even imposes itself on the minds of those who encounter him only at second hand, in literature. Some of Nietzsche's objections to Socrates fit this account perfectly. We must surpass even Socrates insofar as he "suffered life"; "to *have* to fight the instincts—that is the formula for decadence." In Nietzsche's view Goethe was superior even to Socrates.

Nietzsche's admiration for Julius Caesar bears out our account: it is Caesar's personality and his rarely equalled self-mastery that he found exemplary. Nietzsche had reservations about Napoleon, calling him "this synthesis of the inhuman and superhuman." Cesare Borgia was not one of Nietzsche's heroes; he merely suggested that there was more hope "even" for the Borgia than for Parsifal because a man of passion might come to master his passions, while a pure fool, destitute of passion, is hopeless. When Nietzsche expressed the wish that Cesare Borgia might have become pope (*Antichrist*), his point was that this might have finished the church. Among his heroes there was not one he admired for conquests; all were men of surpassing intelligence, passionate men who mastered their passions and employed them creatively.

The overman (Übermensch) *is the type approximated by Goethe—the human being* (Mensch *includes women as well as men) who has organized the chaos of his passions, given style to his character, and become creative.*

What is open to criticism is Nietzsche's assumption that the only thing wanted for its own sake is power. To be sure, it is not true that by finding the will to power at work everywhere, he necessarily empties "power" of all meaning. On the contrary, it is surprising how much of human behavior Nietzsche illuminates by calling attention to the will to power and its hidden workings; in this respect he invites comparison with Freud. What he overlooks is the point Freud made in *The Interpretation of Dreams* (1900), in the footnote about *Hamlet*. Neurotic symptoms, dreams, works of literature, and, one might add, human behavior generally "are capable of overinterpretation, and indeed demand nothing less than this before they can be fully understood." Even if almost all behavior can be illuminated by finding the will to power at work in it, it does not follow that this is the only ultimate motive and the only way of illuminating such behavior. Moreover, in some cases an appeal to the will to power is farfetched and not very illuminating. Nietzsche never gave systematic attention either to apparently negative instances or to possible alternative hypotheses.

Another objection could be met, at least partially, by Nietzsche. Would all men really rather be Socrates in prison than Nero on the roof or be Goethe rather than Hitler? Nietzsche's psychology would stress that Hitler, like Nero, was an artist *manqué* and that his behavior

was, again and again, typical of frustration. No poll could settle the question of what all men would prefer. What matters is not what they might say they prefer but what they really prefer, and we could say that something is really wanted if, and only if, failure to get it results in frustration that disappears with attainment.

THE OVERMAN. The overman (*Übermensch*) is the type approximated by Goethe—the human being (*Mensch* includes women as well as men) who has organized the chaos of his passions, given style to his character, and become creative. Aware of life's terrors, he affirms life without resentment. Except for an ironic, self-critical passage in the chapter "On Poets" in *Zarathustra,* the word "overman" is used in the singular; it is always intended as a this-worldly antithesis to God. Instead of conceiving perfection as a given, man should conceive it as a task (not as *gegeben,* Kant might have said, but as *aufgegeben*). The term is never applied to an individual, and Nietzsche plainly considered neither himself nor Zarathustra, whom he often ridiculed, an overman.

The concept of the overman involves no bifurcation of humanity; neither does the contrast between master and slave moralities, which is a sociological distinction and refers to the origin of moral valuations either in a ruling group or among the oppressed. Indeed, no sooner has Nietzsche introduced these terms (in *Beyond Good and Evil,* 260) than he feels compelled to "add immediately" that mixed types are common and occur "even in the same human being, within a single soul."

In *Ecce Homo* Nietzsche says that only "scholarly oxen" could have construed the overman Darwinistically. But some of the metaphors in the Prologue to *Zarathustra* invite this misunderstanding if one has not read Nietzsche's other books.

Still, Darwin did influence Nietzsche's conception of the overman, and at times Nietzsche did approximate a bifurcation of humanity, albeit not in the manner usually supposed. Unlike David Strauss and legions of other moralists, Nietzsche concluded that if we renounce supernatural religions and accept a scientific approach to man, we lose the right to attribute to man as such a unique supranatural dignity. Such dignity is not *gegeben* but *aufgegeben,* not a fact but a goal that few approach. There is no meaning in life except the meaning man gives his life, and the aims of most men have no surpassing dignity. To raise ourselves above the senseless flux, we must cease being merely human, all-too-human. We must be hard against ourselves and overcome ourselves; we must become creators instead of remaining mere creatures. Therefore, Nietzsche wishes to those whom he wishes well "suffering, being forsaken, . . . profound self-contempt, the torture of mistrust of oneself, and the misery of him who is overcome" (*Will to Power*, 910). He has no pity for his "disciples" when they endure all this, for there is no other way in which one can attain or prove one's worth.

The bifurcation implicit in this position was formulated by Ortega y Gasset:

> The select man is not the petulant person who thinks himself superior to the rest, but the man who demands more of himself than the rest. . . . The most radical division that it is possible to make of humanity is that which splits it into two classes of creatures: those who make great demands of themselves, piling up difficulties and duties; and those who demand nothing special of themselves, but for whom to live is to be every moment what they already are, without imposing on themselves any effort towards perfection; mere buoys that float on the waves. (*The Revolt of the Masses,* Madrid, 1930; English translation, New York, 1932, Ch. 1)

Nietzsche acknowledged that a man's contemporaries may be poor judges of his nobility.

ETERNAL RECURRENCE. The Nietzschean doctrine of the eternal recurrence of the same events may be summarized as follows. After our planet has been destroyed, it will eventually be reconstituted as the power quanta that make up the universe once again reach a previous configuration and thenceforward repeat all the following patterns, to the point where Nietzsche is born again in 1844 and so forth. What is, has been and will be innumerable times at immense intervals. As a young scholar Nietzsche had encountered essentially the same doctrine among the Greeks. In 1882, while taking a walk, it suddenly struck him with the force of a revelation that this was the most scientific of all hypotheses and that the prospect of eternal recurrence is gruesome unless one has succeeded in giving style to one's character and meaning to one's life to such an extent that one can joyously affirm one's existence and say, unlike Goethe's Faust: Abide, moment—but if you cannot abide, at least return eternally!

The Will to Power contains attempts to show why eternal recurrence is the most scientific hypothesis. If we assume a finite number of power quanta in a finite space and an infinite time, only a finite number of configurations are possible. But no end state has been reached yet; hence, unless we follow Christianity in positing a beginning of time, the same configurations must recur eternally. Georg Simmel has pointed out in his *Schopenhauer und Nietzsche* (Leipzig, 1907, pp. 250 f.) that even if there were only a very few things in a finite space in an infinite time, they need never repeat the same configuration. Imagine three wheels of equal size, rotating on a single axis, one point marked on the circumference of each and the three points lined up in one straight line. If the second wheel rotated twice as fast as the first and if the speed of the third was $1/\pi$ of the speed of the first, the initial line-up could never recur. In his books Nietzsche attempted no scientific proof of this doctrine but stressed its potential ethical impact and, even more, the experience of believing it—the horror that will be felt as long as one's life is all-too-human and the joy that can be felt by the exceptional person. The claim that this doctrine is incompatible with Nietzsche's conception of the overman arises from a misunderstanding of both doctrines, according to which the doctrine of eternal return held that history is punctuated by constant repetitions and the doctrine of the overman proclaimed that there is progress in history.

RELIGION. *The Antichrist* is Nietzsche's most sustained attempt at a critique of Christianity, but most of his books contain related material. Nietzsche thought that Jesus was like Prince Myshkin in Dostoyevsky's *The Idiot* (he alludes to the novel without citing it)—wonderfully pure and free of resentment but profoundly pathological. Jesus' disciples misunderstood him, and Christianity was, from the start, opposed to Jesus' spirit; it stressed faith and was deeply resentful toward unbelievers and, indeed, toward "the world." Nietzsche criticizes the Christian faith both as an illicit alternative to Jesus' way of life and as opposed to reason. These two criticisms are also important for an understanding of Nietzsche's attitude toward reason, which he esteemed highly. His most original criticism of Christianity is his attempt to show how from the very start resentment has been central in the so-called religion of love. (This point is made most succinctly in *The Antichrist*, Sec. 45, where Nietzsche quotes, *inter alia*, Mark 6.11, 9.42, and 9.47, and I Corinthians 1.20 ff.)

As for Judaism, he sometimes speaks of the Old Testament with the utmost enthusiasm as being infinitely superior to the New Testament, and even to the literature of the ancient Greeks, but elsewhere he tries to show how Christianity is the culmination of all that was worst in Judaism and traces back resentment and dishonesty to what he considers the priestly editing of the Old Testament. He rarely speaks of Jews and Judaism without using them, one way or another, to attack Christians and Christianity. Anti-Semitism, however, he derided consistently.

Nietzsche occasionally refers to Buddhism and Hinduism, usually to suggest that for all their faults they were also preferable to Christianity in some ways. Personally, he rejected all religions. He considered supernaturalism opposed to reason, sought the roots of otherworldiness in a resentment against this world, found Buddhism a religion of weariness, and objected to the Hindus' treatment of the untouchables as an outrage against humanity.

METAPHYSICS AND EPISTEMOLOGY. Nietzsche did not see himself as a metaphysician and opposed all two-world doctrines (for example, in the chapter "On the Afterworldly"—"afterworldly" was probably intended as a translation of "metaphysicians"—in *Zarathustra;* and in the chapters " 'Reason' in Philosophy" and "How the 'True World' Finally became a Fable" in *The Twilight of the Idols*). His own concept of the will to power is primarily a psychological notion, but in a few passages, directed at Schopenhauer, it becomes a theory about ultimate reality. The doctrine of eternal recurrence is also a metaphysical theory, although this is not the aspect that most concerned Nietzsche. Nietzsche might therefore be called a metaphysician in spite of himself. But he insisted that we must turn to the sciences for knowledge of reality, and he had high hopes for the future development of psychology and physiology and their relevance to issues previously considered philosophical.

If metaphysics is understood as reflection about categories rather than about ultimate reality, then the chapter "The Four Great Errors" in *The Twilight of the Idols* is metaphysics because it deals with the error of confusing cause and effect, the error of a false causality, the error of imaginary causes, and the error of free will. But even here Nietzsche's concern is primarily with morality and religion, and his intent is antimetaphysical. Morality and religion teach, for example, that if you are good, you will be happy. Nietzsche argues that virtue is the effect of happiness or that vice is bred by unhappiness—a commonplace in the twentieth century but not in the nineteenth. Against the "error of a false causality" Nietzsche argues that "there are no mental causes at all," no spirits as entities or agents. "Imaginary causes" include events in dreams that "explain" ex post facto such events as noises outside, but they also include "sin" as a supposed cause of suffering. Here Nietzsche includes Schopenhauer in his critique. There is more material about metaphysical questions in *Beyond Good and Evil* and in the notes, especially in *The Will to Power.*

There is also more about epistemology in the notes than in the books, for Nietzsche was never sufficiently satisfied with his thoughts on these topics to put them into print. Two of his more interesting suggestions might be summed up as a not very thoroughly worked out perspectivism and a theory of fictions comparable to that of Hans Vaihinger, who conceived his independently and published it nine years after his book on Nietzsche.

ON CLASSIFYING NIETZSCHE. Nietzsche's philosophy is not readily separable into metaphysics, epistemology, ethics, aesthetics, and other fields (frequently, the same passage is relevant to many such areas), and most attempts to classify his philosophy are untenable. His ethics, for example, is definitely not evolutionist; neither was he an irrationalist. Positivistic elements appear side by side with existentialist concerns.

The poet Gottfried Benn (1886–1956) wrote in an essay on Nietzsche, "Really everything my generation discussed, thought through—one could say, spun out [*breittrat*]—all that had already been expressed and exhausted by Nietzsche; he had given the definitive formulations, all the rest was exegesis."

Nietzsche thought that Jesus was like Prince Myshkin in Dostoyevsky's The Idiot—*wonderfully pure and free of resentment but profoundly pathological.*

Nietzsche's 1886 Preface to the second edition of *Human, All-too-human* begins, "One should speak only where one may not remain silent, and speak only of that which one has overcome—everything else is chatter." Wittgenstein had probably read this years before he concluded his *Tractatus* with the statement "Of what one cannot speak, one must remain silent" (his ladder metaphor is also reminiscent of Nietzsche's "has overcome"). Still, Nietzsche was perhaps replying to an ancient author quoted by Wittgenstein. In any case, Nietzsche was not content to remain silent about subjects that cannot be discussed with scientific precision. His myriad suggestions have an existential unity, but this unity includes the determination to bring to bear science, especially psychology, on traditional philosophic concerns and not to let religion and morality escape unscathed.

Nietzsche was also an influential poet and offered many interesting remarks about language—for example, "epistemologists who have got stuck in the snares of grammar (the metaphysics of the people)" (*Gay Science*, 354); "language . . . talks of opposites where there are only degrees and many refinements of gradation" (*Beyond Good and Evil*, 24); "the misleading errors of language (and the fundamental fallacies of reason which have become petrified in it), which understands, and misunderstands, all activity as due to an agent, a 'subject' " (*Genealogy*, I, 13; the parentheses show where Nietzsche differs from many analytic philosophers). Other remarks may be found in *The Will to Power*, 484; *Beyond Good and Evil*, 16 f.; and the chapter " 'Reason' in Philosophy" in *The Twilight of the Idols*, especially Section 5, which ends, "We are not rid of God because we still have faith in grammar."

INFLUENCE. Under the Nazis an expurgated edition of *The Antichrist*, a few anthologies of Nietzsche's works, and some unconscionable books about him gained currency, but Plato and quotations about "the Jews" from the Gospel of John were used far more. Hitler, who was steeped in Wagner, probably never read one of Nietzsche's books, nor could any of them have been used by the Nazis in an unexpurgated form. Some of Nietzsche's coinages and even whole sentences torn out of context could have been made serviceable, but his ideas and spirit were clearly opposed to those of the National Socialist German Labor Party. In fact, few writers have been so hard on nationalism, socialism, the Germans, labor movements, and "party men" (see, for example, *The Twilight of the Idols* and, on the last point, *Antichrist*, 55: "Of necessity, the party man becomes a liar").

Nietzsche's influence on literature has been incalculable. It is especially marked in the poetry of Rainer Maria Rilke, Stefan George, Christian Morgenstern, and Gottfried Benn; in the novels of Thomas Mann, Hermann Hesse, André Gide, and André Malraux; in Shaw and Yeats; and in psychoanalysis and existentialism. Besides the many philosophers who have written books on him, Albert Camus, Jean-Paul Sartre, Max Scheler, Oswald Spengler, and Paul Tillich, are especially indebted to him.

At the age of 83, Martin Buber published *Begegnung; Autobiographische Fragmente* (Stuttgart, 1961) and included "encounters" with two philosophers, Kant and Nietzsche. In a footnote he revealed that at 17 he was so impressed by *Zarathustra* that he began to render it into Polish "and actually did translate the First Part." It is to be expected that in years to come it will be shown how many major writers were much more deeply influenced by Nietzsche than had been suspected.

After Freud's death Ernest Jones published a letter in which his master, at 78, said of Nietzsche, "In my youth he signified a nobility which I could not attain."

Nietzsche's appeal was confined neither to men of only one type nor to those who have published essays on him. To use the weighty word he applied to himself in *Ecce Homo*, he really became a "destiny" for many, including some of the leading spirits of the twentieth century.

BIBLIOGRAPHY

Works by Nietzsche

Collected Works

Gesammelte Werke, Musarionausgabe, 23 vols. (Munich, 1920–1929), features a chronological arrangement of Nietzsche's works and notes with indexes. Only the 20-volume *Grossoktavausgabe*, 2d ed. (Leipzig, 1901–1913), is nearly as good. Karl Schlechta's edition, *Werke in drei Bänden* (Munich, 1954–1956), contains all of the books, but far fewer of Nietzsche's notes than several previous editions. It also contains 278 letters, a 50-page philological postscript in which Elisabeth Förster-Nietzsche's petty forgeries (none of which affect his philosophy) are detailed, and a 24-page chronological table covering Nietzsche's life. Schlechta finds small faults in previous editions, but his own editing has been sharply criticized by E. F. Podach in his edition, *Nietzsches Werke des Zusammenbruchs* (Heidelberg, 1961). None of the disputed points, however, affects our understanding of Nietzsche's philosophy.

Letters

Gesammelte Briefe, Elisabeth Förster-Nietzsche, Peter Gast, et al., eds., 5 vols. in 6 (Leipzig, 1900–1909), was later supplemented by separate editions of *Nietzsches Briefwechsel mit Franz Overbeck*, C. A. Bernoulli and Richard Oehler, eds. (Leipzig, 1916); E. Förster-Nietzsche, *Wagner und Nietzsche zur Zeit ihrer Freundschaft* (Munich, 1915), translated by C. V. Kerr as *The Nietzsche-Wagner Correspondence* (London, 1922); and Karl Strecker, *Nietzsche und Strindberg, mit ihren Briefwechsel* (Munich, 1921). There are additional letters in various places. *Historisch-Kritische Gesamtausgabe der Werke und Briefe*, Wilhelm Hoppe, Karl Schlechta, Hans Joachim Mette, and Carl Koch, eds. (Munich, 1933–1942), includes five volumes of works up to 1869 and four volumes of letters to 1877. This edition was discontinued during World War II.

Translations

The Complete Works, Oscar Levy, ed., 18 vols. (Edinburgh and London, 1909–1913, reissued 1964), is marred by poor and unreliable translations. *The Portable Nietzsche* (New York, 1954), translated and edited by Walter Kaufmann, contains *Thus Spoke Zarathustra, Twilight of the Idols, The Antichrist*, and *Nietzsche Contra Wagner* (all complete) and selections from the other books, the notes, and the letters, with 60 pages of editorial material. *Basic Writings of Nietzsche* (New York, 1966), edited and in part newly translated, with notes, by Walter Kaufmann, contains *The Birth of Tragedy, Beyond Good and Evil, The Genealogy of Morals, The Case of Wagner, Ecce Homo* (all complete) and additional selections. *The Will to Power* (New York, 1966), translated by Walter Kaufmann and R. G. Hollingdale, and edited, with notes, by Walter Kaufmann, furnishes the approximate date of every note and cross references to parallel passages in the books Nietzsche finished.

Works on Nietzsche

Biography

C. A. Bernoulli, *Franz Overbeck und Friedrich Nietzsche*, 2 vols. (Jena, 1908), important for its biographical material, takes issue with the version of Nietzsche's life presented by his sister. Elisabeth Förster-Nietzsche, *Das Leben Friedrich Nietzsches*, 3 vols. (Leipzig,

1895–1904), contains much important material, but, like all her publications, is quite unreliable. By far the best biography in English is R. G. Hollingdale, *Nietzsche: The Man and His Philosophy* (Baton Rouge, La., 1965), in which Nietzsche's ideas are discussed in the context of his life. E. F. Podach, *Nietzsches Zusammenbruch* (Heidelberg, 1930), translated by F. A. Voigt as *Nietzsche's Madness* (London and New York, 1931); *Gestalten um Nietzsche* (Weimar, 1931); and *Friedrich Nietzsche und Lou Salomé* (Zurich, 1938), are three books containing important biographical documents and information.

Commentaries

Martin Heidegger, *Nietzsche*, 2 vols. (Pfullingen, 1961), and "Nietzsches Wort 'Gott ist tot,'" in *Holzwege* (Frankfurt, 1952), are interesting for students of Heidegger who know Nietzsche well enough to appreciate Heidegger's approach. Karl Jaspers, *Nietzsche* (Berlin and Leipzig, 1936), translated by C. F. Walraff and F. J. Schmitz as *Nietzsche* (Tucson, Ariz., 1965), exposes oversimplifications about Nietzsche in a stunning array of quotations, but Jaspers discounts all of Nietzsche's conclusions. Without regard for chronology or context, apparently contradictory statements from books and notes are methodically contrasted to persuade us of the inadequacy of all positions and of the need for Jaspers' existentialism. In the English version all page references are omitted, so the Nietzsche quotations cannot be located. Karl Jaspers, *Nietzsche und das Christentum* (Hameln, 1938), translated by E. B. Ashton (Chicago, 1961), is similar in approach to the preceding, but is less than one tenth its length. Walter Kaufmann, *Nietzsche* (Princeton, N.J., 1950; rev. ed., New York, 1956), is the book on which the present article is based; the original edition contains a long bibliography. Walter Kaufmann, *From Shakespeare to Existentialism* (Boston, 1959; rev. ed., New York, 1960), British edition entitled *The Owl and the Nightingale* (London, 1960), contains five chapters on Nietzsche, including three chapters on his relation to Rilke and to Jaspers. Walter Kaufmann, *Twenty German Poets: A Bilingual Collection* (New York, 1962), contains 11 of Nietzsche's poems and assigns him a place in the development of German poetry from Goethe to Benn. Walter Kaufmann, "Nietzsche Between Homer and Sartre: Five Treatments on the Orestes Story," in *Revue internationale de philosophie*, No. 67 (1964), 50–73, demonstrates Nietzsche's immense influence on Sartre's play *The Flies*. Walter Kaufmann, "Nietzsche in the Light of His Suppressed Manuscripts," in *Journal of the History of Philosophy*, Vol. 2 (1964), 205–225, includes discussions of *The Antichrist* and *Ecce Homo* and of the way Nietzsche's works have been edited. Ludwig Klages, *Die psychologischen Errungenschaften Nietzsches* (Leipzig, 1926), is an extremely interesting work in which Nietzsche is criticized for his Socratism and rationalism. George Allen Morgan, *What Nietzsche Means* (Cambridge, Mass., 1941), is a systematic epitome that deliberately ignores how Nietzsche came to think as he did; informed, avoids criticism of Nietzsche, useful for reference. A valuable commentary is Hans Vaihinger, *Nietzsche als Philosoph* (Berlin, 1902). Vaihinger's "Nietzsche und seine Lehre vom bewusst gewollten Schein," in *Die Philosophie des Als-Ob* (Berlin, 1911), translated by C. Ogden as *The Philosophy of As-If* (New York, 1924), is a chapter containing interesting material on Nietzsche's epistemology.

Bibliography

H. W. Reichert and Karl Schlechta, *International Nietzsche Bibliography* (Chapel Hill, N.C., 1960), lists 3,973 items about Nietzsche in over 24 languages, arranged in alphabetical order by author within each language. It is selective, with some unfortunate oversights, and includes some very brief summaries and evaluations.

— WALTER KAUFMANN

NIETZSCHE, FRIEDRICH (UPDATE)

Friedrich Nietzsche exerted much influence upon modern philosophy and literature, as Walter Kaufmann noted in his article on Nietzsche in the 1967 edition of the *Encyclopedia of Philosophy*. Yet Kaufmann could scarcely have imagined the explosion of interest in Nietzsche's works, particularly in philosophical circles, that began in the mid-1960s and still continues unabated. Kaufmann's bibliography lists only two secondary works on Nietzsche written in English—his own *Nietzsche* and George A. Morgan's *What Nietzsche Means*. But since 1967 there have appeared almost two thousand volumes focused primarily on Nietzsche—more than half of them in English, the rest in French and German—and perhaps ten times that number of essays, articles, or book chapters have been published.

Charting the expanding horizons of Nietzsche's influence quickly becomes a sociological study of the dominant motifs of late twentieth-century culture, and charting the influence within philosophical inquiry is equally complex. There may in fact be no philosopher whose works admit less happily to a canonical or consensual interpretation, a claim supported by the staggering diversity of interpretations of Nietzsche's philosophy that have appeared since 1967. Nevertheless, some general observations can be made concerning the range of these new interpretations.

One can locate at least three primary factors in the increased philosophical attention to Nietzsche since 1967. First is the tremendous influence of Martin Heidegger's reading of Nietzsche. Published in Germany in 1960, translated into French in 1962 and into English between 1979 and 1987, Heidegger's overarching interpretation of Nietzsche as the culminating figure in the history of metaphysics inspired an enormous range of exegetical and critical response while leading several generations of philosophers and philosophy students back to Nietzsche's texts.

A second reason can be located in the discovery of a "new Nietzsche" that emerged in conjunction with the rise of recent French philosophy. While perhaps most widely associated with Jacques Derrida and the deconstructionist attention to questions of textuality and the styles of philosophical discourse, Nietzsche's inclusion, along with Marx and Freud, as one of the three "masters of suspicion," and his importance in the philosophical works of Michel Foucault and Gilles Deleuze have shown him to be an intellectual influence on much of what is called poststructuralist thought. And, as in the case of Heidegger, the popularity of poststructuralist French thought brought with it a renewed interest—among literary critics and theorists, historians, political theorists, and philosophers—in Nietzsche's thinking.

The third reason for the increased attention to Nietzsche concerns the transformation of philosophy within the Anglo-American tradition. In the 1960s Kaufmann's and Arthur Danto's texts had first to justify Nietzsche as a philosopher whose ideas warranted serious philosophical consideration. As the scope of English-language philosophy has broadened there has appeared a distinctly Anglo-American tradition of Nietzsche interpretation informed by the ethical, metaphysical, and epistemological questions that occupy analytically trained philosophers.

To be sure, there is still much work offering interpretations of the "classical" Nietzschean themes: will to power, eternal recurrence, Übermensch, nihilism, perspectivism, and so forth. But other issues have appeared as well. For example, an attention to questions of texts and textuality has played a role in much of the recent literature. It has become increasingly common to distinguish between his published texts and his unpublished notes, especially as concerns themes whose primary expression is to be found in the "book" constructed by his literary executors after his death and titled *The Will to Power*. One also finds an increasing tendency to read Nietzsche's texts *as* texts, following their internal development as opposed to simply viewing them as collections of remarks from which one can pick and choose the comments relevant to one's own argument. A third theme emerging from the recent interest in textuality is an attention to the various styles of Nietzsche's philosophical prose—in other words, an attention to his use of metaphor, to the "literary" character of much of his writing (in particular, *Thus Spake Zarathustra*), to the different genres of writing (aphorism, essay, polemic, poem, etc.), and to other issues characterized collectively as the question of style.

A second range of topics within the recent literature addresses some of the classical philosophical questions. Does Nietzsche have a "theory of truth"? Does he have a "theory of knowledge"? An "ontology"? Is Nietzsche a metaphysician in the way that Heidegger defines metaphysics? Is Nietzsche an ethical naturalist? Within these questions a topic that continues to draw attention is the issue of self-reference: when Nietzsche makes claims (about truth, reality, being, subjectivity, etc.), do these claims refer or apply to or hold true for his own philosophical conclusions? The most obvious case where the question of self-reference arises concerns the question of truth and interpretation: if Nietzsche claims that "there is no Truth," or that "everything is an interpretation," are these claims put forward as "true"? If they are, then they appear to contradict themselves; but if they are not true, then why should we be interested in them? The issue has been extended beyond the confines of epistemology, however, and one finds discussions of the eternal recurrence or the *Übermensch* or the ascetic ideal in terms of the question of self-reference.

Charting the expanding horizons

of Nietzsche's influence quickly becomes

a sociological study of the dominant motifs

of late twentieth-century culture,

and charting the influence

within philosophical inquiry is equally complex.

A third and final set of issues that warrants noting is the extension of Nietzschean themes into new areas not discussed, or only hinted at, in Kaufmann's initial entry. Among the most important topics producing much recent scholarship are Nietzsche's influence on postmodernism, his position on "woman" and his relevance for feminism, and his political philosophy and impact on twentieth-century political and social movements.

"Some are born posthumously," Nietzsche wrote in 1888. "One day my name will be associated with the memory of something tremendous," he claimed in *Ecce Homo*, at the beginning of a chapter entitled "Why I Am a Destiny." One hundred years later, these remarks appear prophetic, and at the end of the twentieth century it would be difficult to find a philosopher whose influence on matters philosophical and cultural exceeds that of Nietzsche.

[See also Deconstruction; Derrida, Jacques; Foucault, Michel; Freud, Sigmund; Heidegger, Martin; Marx, Karl; Poststructuralism.]

BIBLIOGRAPHY

Works by Nietzsche

Nietzsche Briefwechsel: Kritische Gesamtausgabe, edited by G. Colli and M. Montinari. Berlin, 1975–. A complete edition of Nietzsche's correspondence.

Nietzsche Werke: Kritische Gesamtausgabe, edited by G. Colli and M. Montinari. Berlin, 1967–. Without question the most important publication since 1967.

Works on Nietzsche

Abel, G. *Nietzsche: Die Dynamik der Willen zur Macht und die ewige Wiederkehr.* Berlin, 1984.

Allison, D. B., ed. *The New Nietzsche: Contemporary Styles of Interpretation.* New York, 1977.

Aschheim, S. E. *The Nietzsche Legacy in Germany, 1890–1990.* Berkeley, 1992.

Clark, M. *Nietzsche on Truth and Philosophy.* Cambridge, 1990.

Deleuze, G. *Nietzsche et la philosophie.* Paris, 1962. Translated by H. Tomlinson as *Nietzsche and Philosophy.* New York, 1983.

Derrida, J. *Spurs: Nietzsche's Styles,* translated by B. Harlow. Chicago, 1979.

Granier, J. *Le Problème de la vérité dans la philosophie de Nietzsche.* Paris, 1966.

Heidegger, M. *Nietzsche.* 2 vols. Pfullingen, 1961. Edited and translated by D. F. Krell et al. as *Nietzsche.* 4 vols. New York, 1979–87.

Janz, C. P. *Friedrich Nietzsche: Biographie.* 3 vols. Munich, 1978–79. The most definitive biography.

Klossowski, P. *Nietzsche et le cercle vicieux.* Paris, 1969.

Kofman, S. *Nietzsche et la métaphore.* Paris, 1972. Translated by D. Large as *Nietzsche and Metaphor.* Stanford, CA, 1994.

Krell, D. F., and D. Wood, eds. *Exceedingly Nietzsche: Aspects of Contemporary Nietzsche Interpretation.* London, 1988.

Lampert, L. *Nietzsche's Teaching: An Interpretation of "Thus Spake Zarathustra."* New Haven, 1987.

Magnus, B. *Nietzsche's Existential Imperative.* Bloomington, IN, 1978.

Müller-Lauter, W. *Nietzsche: Seine Philosophie der Gegensätze und die Gegensätze seiner Philosophie.* Berlin, 1971.

Nehemas, A. *Nietzsche: Life as Literature.* Cambridge, 1985.

Nietzsche-Studien: Internationales Jahrbuch für die Nietzsche-Forschung, Vols. 1– (1972–).

Schacht, R. *Nietzsche.* London, 1983.

Solomon, R. C., and K. Higgins, eds. *Reading Nietzsche.* New York, 1988.

Strong, T. B. *Friedrich Nietzsche and the Politics of Transfiguration.* Berkeley, 1975.

Warren, M. *Nietzsche and Political Thought.* Cambridge, MA, 1988.

— ALAN D. SCHRIFT

NONDESCRIPTIVISM

Nondescriptivists (or noncognitivists) hold that the function of normative judgments is not, or not primarily, to describe or state facts and that because of this, these judgments lack a truth value. A strong form of ethical nondescriptivism says that moral judgments have no descriptive function, but weaker forms say only that their nondescriptive function is primary or dominant.

Differing accounts of the nondescriptive function of moral language generate a variety of nondescriptivisms. Moral judgments have been said to express emotions, feelings, attitudes, or stances; and they have been characterized as tools for performing other nondescriptive tasks such as commanding, requesting, endorsing, or commending. A. J. Ayer, whose position is called emotivism, said that "ethical terms" express emotions or feelings and that they "are calculated also to arouse feelings, and so to stimulate action" (1952, p. 108). C. L. Stevenson, whose metaethical theory is called noncognitivism, argued that the major use of "ethical statements" is dynamic rather than fact stating. They are not, he said, primarily used to describe interests or attitudes but rather to change or intensify attitudes and to influence behavior. What Stevenson called the emotive meaning of ethical terms makes this dynamic use possible and also explains why ethical judgments, unlike factual ones, are capable of moving us to action.

From the thought that moral judgments are exclamations and disguised commands Ayer concluded that they "have no objective validity whatever" and that "it is impossible to dispute about questions of value" (1952, p. 110). Stevenson tried to show that there is a place for ethical arguments, but he did not go beyond the claim that a reason is "relevant" when it is likely to influence some attitude. This means, at least to the critics of Stevenson, that the relation between the premises and the conclusion of an ethical argument is psychological rather than logical and that there is no clear distinction between ethical argument and propaganda.

Both Ayer and Stevenson were in the positivist tradition, but by the 1950s an interest in ordinary language also led increasing numbers of analytic philosophers to nondescriptivism. These thinkers acknowledged that moral language can be used descriptively, but they insisted that its "primary" (basic, fundamental) use is to perform any of a number of nondescriptive speech acts. R. M. Hare argued that the primary function of the word 'good' is to commend and that when we commend anything "it is always in order, at least indirectly, to guide choices, our own or other people's, now or in the future" (1952, p. 127). Words such as 'right' and 'ought' are used for giving advice or, as he said, for prescribing. According to Hare, the claim that something is good has both descriptive and prescriptive meaning. The descriptive meaning of the word 'good' changes as it is applied to different things, but the prescriptive meaning remains constant because 'good' is invariably used to commend. This is why the prescriptive meaning is primary.

Hare described his own position as nondescriptivism, but he was more positive than Ayer and Stevenson about the role and value of logic in ethical arguments. Moral judgments, he said, are a subclass of "prescriptive" rather than "descriptive" language—they are "universalizable prescriptions." Unlike attempts to persuade or to influence attitudes, a judgment that something is good or right is a prescription that is complete in itself, even if no change is brought about in the hearer's attitudes or behavior. Hare believed that there could be logical relations among prescriptive judgments, even commands; and he developed a logic of prescriptive discourse to account for those relations. In the end he concluded that while we can argue logically about what to do, a complete justification of a moral decision will always require the adoption, without justification, of some basic principle or principles as a part of a freely chosen "way of life."

P. H. Nowell-Smith offered a form of nondescriptivism he called multifunctionalism. He said that evaluative language is used "to express tastes and preferences, to express decisions and choices, to criticize, grade, and evaluate, to advise, admonish, warn, persuade and dissuade, to praise, encourage, and reprove, to promulgate and draw attention to rules; and doubtless for other purposes also" (1954, p. 98). Though his position is more complex than Hare's, he does agree that "the central activities for which moral language is used are choosing and advising others to choose" (p. 11).

A strong form of ethical nondescriptivism says that moral judgments have no descriptive function, but weaker forms say only that their nondescriptive function is primary or dominant.

After the contributions of Ayer, Stevenson, Hare, Nowell-Smith, and others, nondescriptivism was neglected as interest in applied ethics flourished and as those who did think about metaethics developed naturalistic forms of descriptivism. The new naturalists conceded that normative language has nondescriptive functions, but they then pointed out how those functions are compatible with simultaneous descriptive intent and therefore with the possibility of evaluating normative pronouncements in terms of truth and falsity. In the 1980s interest in metaethics was stimulated by new forms of nondescriptivism developed by Simon Blackburn and Allan Gibbard. The dominant issue at that time, however, was the dispute between moral (or ethical) realists and antirealists. Nondescriptivists are more likely to be antirealists, and descriptivists are more likely to be realists, but there are complications.

Formerly, both intuitionists and naturalists were descriptivists. Intuitionists identified moral facts with nonnatural facts, and naturalists identified moral facts with natural facts. If one who believes that moral facts are natural facts can be said to be a moral realist, then both naturalists and intuitionists were moral realists and were in a position to say that moral judgments are true when they correctly describe some natural or nonnatural reality. But there is a way to combine descriptivism with antirealism and another way to combine nondescriptivism with at least the practices of the realist. J. L. Mackie develops a descriptivist account of much normative language, but he argues that judgments of moral obligation, which are thought to be both objective and prescriptive, and judgments of "intrinsic" value are always false. One who says that something is "good in itself" is always speaking falsely because nothing is good in itself.

Both Blackburn and Mackie begin with a Humean projectivism according to which the normativity we think we discover in nature is projected onto a value-free world by us. When we see and are moved by cruelty to the bull, we objectify our negative attitude, and promote it too, by saying that bullfighting is wrong. Projectivists are antirealists. Mackie combines his antirealism with descriptivism and takes this to result in an error theory. Blackburn begins with antirealism, adds his version of nondescriptivism or "expressivism," and emerges with what he calls quasi-realism, the idea that the linguistic practices of the realist—saying that bullfighting is really wrong, for example—are perfectly in order and that no error is made. One of his main concerns is to defend this quasi-realism by showing how we "earn the right" to "practice, think, worry, assert, and argue" as though moral commitments are true in some straightforward way (1984, p. 257).

Blackburn's view is that we do not describe reality correctly or incorrectly when we make moral claims—we express "stances." He characterizes a stance as a "conative state or pressure on choice and action" but admits that we could also call this an attitude. But whatever we call it, "its function is to mediate the move from features of a situation to a reaction, which in the appropriate circumstances will mean choice" (1993, p. 168).

Allan Gibbard also defends a nondescriptivist or "expressivist" account of normative judgments. Normative judgments, he says, take the form of saying that some act, belief, or feeling is "rational," or "makes sense." The point of making such a judgment is not to describe something, not to attribute a property to it, but "to express one's acceptance of norms that permit it" (1990, p. 7). A norm, according to Gibbard, is "a linguistically encoded precept," and the capacity to be motivated by norms "evolved because of the advantages of coordination and planning through language" (p. 57). There are norms of many kinds, but when we say that what someone did was morally wrong, we are expressing and endorsing norms that govern feelings of guilt by the agent and of anger by others.

Three arguments are traditionally deployed against nondescriptivists. According to the grammatical argument, since moral judgments are phrased in ordinary indicative sentences, there is a prima facie reason to treat them as statements and to treat those who make them as attempting to make statements. Nondescriptivists will reply that here the grammar is misleading, but they can then be asked to explain why this should be so. There is also a logical argument against nondescriptivism. If moral judgments lack a truth value, then it is impossible for them to play a role in truth-functional constructions (implication, conjunction, and negation, for example) and in arguments. It is also difficult to know how they are to be interpreted when they occur embedded in complex constructions such as statements of belief and doubt. According to what has been called the phenomenological argument, not only do moral claims look and behave like descriptive utterances, they "feel" like them too. When we claim that something is good or right, we do not seem, even to ourselves, to be merely expressing ourselves or ordering others to do things. Nondescriptivists will try to explain why these judgments have this distinctive feel, but descriptivists will insist that the feeling is important data that cannot easily be explained away.

Nondescriptivism is alive and well,

but its prospects are uncertain

because it is truly difficult to develop

convincing and definitive answers to the objections

from grammar, logic, and phenomenology.

Starting with Ayer, each nondescriptivist has been forced to develop some reply to these, as well as to other, difficulties. Blackburn, for example, responds to the logical argument by developing an expressivist account of truth. He wants to show how it makes sense to claim moral truth even if there are no moral facts and even if our moral claims are no more than expressions of stances or attitudes. Gibbard sketches a solution to the embedding problem that exploits the idea that when we make a normative statement we are expressing a state of mind that consists in "ruling out various combinations of normative systems with factual possibilities." He develops a formalism that allows him to use this idea to account for "the logical relations that hold among normative statements" (1990, p. 99).

Owing to the work of Blackburn and Gibbard, nondescriptivism is alive and well, but its prospects are uncertain because it is truly difficult to develop convincing and definitive answers to the objections from grammar, logic, and phenomenology. Furthermore, nondescriptivism needs a fact/value distinction, and this is something about which philosophers have become increas-

ingly nervous. The early descriptivists tried to reduce values to facts, or they accepted the fact/value distinction and then relegated values to a philosophically insignificant pragmatic limbo. Since then there has been a tendency to argue that many statements that appear to be safely descriptive must be understood to have nondescriptive elements. Nondescriptivists now point out that even if the line between facts and values is blurred or moved, we can still draw an important distinction between assertions and expressions. This claim, however, will continue to be challenged by those who are impressed by the descriptive nature of norms or the normative nature of descriptions.

[See also Applied Ethics; Ethical Theory; Hare, Richard M.; Mackie, John Leslie; Moral Realism; Projectivism; Stevenson, Charles.]

BIBLIOGRAPHY

Ayer, A. J. *Language, Truth, and Logic.* New York, 1952.
Blackburn, S. *Spreading the Word: Groundings in the Philosophy of Language.* Oxford, 1984.
———. "Wise Feelings, Apt Reading," *Ethics,* Vol. 102 (1992), 342–56.
———. "How to Be an Ethical Anti-realist," in *Essays in Quasi-Realism* (New York, 1993).
Darwall, S., A. Gibbard, and P. Railton. "Toward *Fin de Siècle* Ethics: Some Trends," *Philosophical Review,* Vol. 101 (1992), 115–89.
Gibbard, A. *Wise Choices, Apt Feelings: A Theory of Normative Judgment.* Cambridge, MA, 1990.
Hare, R. M. *The Language of Morals.* Oxford, 1952.
———. *Freedom and Reason.* Oxford, 1963.
Mackie, J. L. *Ethics: Inventing Right and Wrong.* Harmondsworth, Middlesex, 1977.
Nowell-Smith, P. *Ethics.* Harmondsworth, Middlesex, 1954.
Stevenson, C. L. *Ethics and Language.* New Haven, 1944.
———. "The Emotive Meaning of Ethical Terms," in *Facts and Values* (New Haven, 1963).
Urmson, J. O. *The Emotive Theory of Ethics.* New York, 1969.

– RICHARD GARNER

NONEXISTENT OBJECT, NONBEING

We think and talk about things that do not exist—or so it seems. We say that Santa Claus lives at the North Pole and that unicorns are white. We admire Sherlock Holmes or judge him to be less or more clever than J. Edgar Hoover. People look for the Fountain of Youth. A childless couple may hope for a daughter. So, according to Alexius Meinong and others, there are things that do not exist. In order even to deny that Santa Claus or the Fountain of Youth exists, it seems, we must be able to identify what it is whose existence we are denying.

Bertrand Russell's rejection of this line of thought is well known. Expressions that appear to denote nonexistents are among those which, according to his theory of descriptions, lack denotation. (Russell shifted the emphasis from thoughts and other intentional attitudes, which appear to have nonexistents as objects, to the language in which they are expressed.) Many later analytic philosophers shared with Russell a distaste for what they saw as Meinong's bloated universe. Even those who rejected the theory of descriptions often assumed that apparent references to nonexistents can somehow be paraphrased away. But there have been few serious attempts since Russell's to show how this is to be done, and the task has proven to be much more difficult than it once seemed. Several sophisticated realist theories were developed after 1970 (Castañeda, 1979; Parsons, 1980; Routley, 1980; Van Inwagen, 1977; Wolterstorff, 1980; Woods, 1974). These have been countered by antirealist theories based on notions of pretense or make-believe (Evans, 1982; Walton, 1990; see also Currie, 1990).

Many recent discussions focus primarily or exclusively on fictional characters and other objects introduced by works of fiction. The issues concerning fictions may or may not differ significantly from those concerning other nonexistent objects of thought, but they are in some ways more compelling.

We speak easily and elaborately about fictional characters as though they are ordinary people, describing Sherlock Holmes as a detective who lives on Baker Street, and so on. Some take such descriptions at face value, understanding characters to possess the same kinds of ordinary properties that real people do and to differ only in being fictional rather than actual. Such literalists, as Fine (1982) calls them, usually accept that, unlike existing objects, most nonexistents are incomplete (Holmes neither has a mole on his back nor lacks one), and some are impossible (e.g., the round square).

Literalism threatens to get out of hand. We readily describe Holmes as a person and a detective, but we are also prepared to say, in much the same spirit (i.e., speaking "within the story"), that he and other characters exist. (Macbeth's dagger is a mere figment of his imagination, but Macbeth himself exists.) If Holmes and Macbeth are people, it is awkward to deny that they exist. How, in general, are we to treat propositions that are true-in-(the-world-of)-a-story, or fictional (Walton, 1990)? It is fictional both that Holmes is a person and that he exists. Other fictional propositions do not involve fictional particulars at all. It may be fictional in a story that Napoleon has magical powers or that there are such things as ghosts. "Napoleon has magical powers" and "There are such things as ghosts." "Napoleon has magical powers" and "There are such things as ghosts," understood literally and straightforwardly, are false. Why should "Holmes is a person and a detective" be treated differently?

The most obvious alternative to literalism is to treat fictional propositions as elliptical, to understand "Holmes is a detective," for instance, as short for "It is fictional (true-in-the-story) that Holmes is a detective." So Holmes is not, literally, a person or a detective; he is such that it is fictional that he possess these attributes. And although he exists-in-the-story, this does not mean that he exists. Some allow that Holmes actually (not fictionally) possesses other properties: he was created by Conan Doyle, he is a fictional character, he is admired by millions of readers.

In order even to deny

that Santa Claus or the Fountain of Youth exists,

it seems, we must be able to identify

what it is whose existence we are denying.

Literalists about nonexistents generally take the golden mountain to be, literally, golden and a mountain, and a wished-for child to be, literally, a child. Those who reject literalism while allowing that nonexistents possess properties may understand the golden mountain merely to be thought to be golden and a mountain and regard the nonexistent child to be such that the couple wishes it to be a child.

Some take properties such as being a person and a detective to constitute (rather than characterize) fictions, identifying Holmes with the class of properties attributed to him in the stories or with an abstract particular corresponding to it (e.g., a "theoretical entity" or a "kind"). Variations on this strategy give different answers to questions about the identity and individuation of nonexistents. Are they platonic entities which are (some even say exist) necessarily and eternally, or are they created when, for example, the relevant story is written? If characters in different unrelated stories happen to have exactly the same characteristics attributed to them, are they identical? Can the same character appear in different stories if the characteristics attributed to it in them are not exactly the same?

Pretense or make-believe theories return to a more intuitive understanding of statements such as "Holmes is a detective" without embracing literalism. The speaker pretends to refer to an ordinary person and to attribute to him, in the ordinary way, the property of being a detective. Nothing is actually referred to, and what is said is not literally true. But this is pretense with a serious purpose. The speaker does actually assert something by engaging in the pretense, and the theory must explain what it is. Some statements are less easily construed as uttered in pretense than others. There are statements of propositions that are not fictional in a work of fiction (e.g., "Holmes is a fictional character"), ones that do not concern fiction at all (statements about wished-for children, Vulcan, etc.), and claims of existence and nonexistence. Pretense may figure in the explication of such statements even if they are not uttered in pretense.

[See also Metaphysics; Realism; Russell, Bertrand Arthur William.]

BIBLIOGRAPHY

Castañeda, H.-N. "Fiction and Reality—Their Fundamental Connections: An Essay on the Ontology of Total Experience," Poetics, Vol. 8 (1979), 31–62.

Chisholm, R. "Beyond Being and Nonbeing," Philosophical Studies, Vol. 24 (1973), 245–57.

Crittenden, C. Unreality: The Metaphysics of Fictional Objects. Ithaca, NY, 1991.

Currie, G. The Nature of Fiction. Cambridge, 1990.

Donnellan, K. "Speaking of Nothing," Philosophical Review, Vol. 83 (1974), 3–31.

Evans, G. The Varieties of Reference, edited by J. McDowell. Oxford, 1982.

Fine, K. "The Problem of Non-Existence: I. Internalism," Topoi, Vol. 1 (1982), 97–140.

Geach, P. "Intentional Identity," Journal of Philosophy, Vol. 20 (1967), 627–32.

Hintikka, J. "Are There Nonexistent Objects? Why Not? But Where Are They?" Synthese, Vol. 60 (1984), 451–58.

Howell, R. "Fictional Objects: How They Are and How They Aren't," Poetics, Vol. 8 (1979), 129–77.

Ingarden, R. The Literary Work of Art: An Investigation on the Borderlines of Ontology, Logic, and Theory of Literature. Translated by G. G. Grabowicz. Evanston, IL, 1973.

Katz, J. J., "Names without Bearers," Philosophical Review, Vol. 103, No. 1 (1994), 1–39.

Lewis, D. "Truth in Fiction," in Philosophical Papers, Volume I (New York, 1983). Pp. 261–80.

Meinong, A. "The Theory of Objects." in R. Chisholm, ed., Realism and the Background of Phenomenology (New York, 1960).

Parsons, T. Non-Existent Objects. New Haven, 1980.

Quine, W. V. O. "On What There Is," in From a Logical Point of View (New York, 1953).

Routley, R. Exploring Meinong's Jungle and Beyond: An Investigation of Noneism and the Theory of Items. Canberra, 1980.

Russell, B. "On Denoting," Mind, n.s. 14 (1905), 479–93.

Ryle, G. "Symposium: Imaginary Objects," Proceedings of the Aristotelian Society, Supp. Vol. 12 (1933).

Van Inwagen, P. "Creatures of Fiction," American Philosophical Quarterly, Vol. 14 (1977), 299–308.

Walton, K. L. Mimesis as Make-Believe: On the Foundations of the Representational Arts. Cambridge, MA, 1990.

Wolterstorff, N. Works and Worlds of Art. Oxford, 1980.

Woods, J. The Logic of Fiction: A Philosophical Sounding of Deviant Logic. The Hague, 1974.

— KENDALL L. WALTON

ONTOLOGY

For much of this century the discussion of ontology has been shaped by philosophical naturalism, according to which whatever exists is part of the natural world. Natural ontology is understood to exclude supernatural entities, Cartesian mental entities, and Platonic universals. From the naturalist perspective, any ontological question is, ultimately, a scientific question. The period since about 1960 has included significant work in ontology that, like typical earlier work in the century, falls under the aegis of naturalism. A prominent example is the development, within 'physicalism', of an array of different reductive, 'functional', and even 'eliminative' accounts of the mind and mental phenomena. But the period is perhaps more notable for the appearance of a variety of nonnatural ontological theories (even including versions of Cartesian dualism). This entry focuses on recent nonnatural ontology, along with naturalistic counterpoints.

Since 1960 much work in ontology has been influenced—in one way or another—by the prominent naturalist philosopher, Willard Van Orman Quine. Quine is well known for three contributions to the discussion. One is his 'criterion of ontic commitment' (Quine, 1960, section 49), often captured in the slogan, 'to be is to be a value of a bound variable'. Another is his doctrine of 'ontological relativity' (Quine, 1969, essay 2). The third is his influential insistence that the postulation of entities of any kind be accompanied by a statement of their identity conditions' (Quine, 1960, sections 42–3). It is ironic that Quine conceded the existence of sets—hardly occupants of the natural world—on the grounds that they are indispensable for physics and linguistics. Not only did this constitute a departure from strict naturalism, it also opened the floodgates for further 'indispensability' claims, often in favor of entities he would find much less acceptable than sets.

For Quine, the need for postulating nonnatural entities came most urgently from the effort to understand how human language works. But when we try to find specific linguistic pressure for sets, we fail. Instead, we find a need for 'intensional' entities like propositions (for example, to serve as 'meanings' of sentential utterances and as objects of 'attitudes' like belief), and properties and relations (to serve as meanings of predicates).

Quine was fully aware of this (as were earlier contributors, notably Frege, Russell, Carnap, and Church). But he thought the roles of these entities could be adequately played by (impure) sets, and that sets were more acceptable ontologically. Quine held that the principle of extensionality provided adequate identity conditions for sets, but that since no such conditions were available for intensional entities, they were (comparatively) obscure and therefore dubious.

Natural ontology is understood to exclude supernatural entities, Cartesian mental entities, and Platonic universals.

But the strength of the direct pressure for intensional entities—from a variety of sources—became much more widely appreciated. Even naturalistically inclined philosophers found it hard to resist (Putnam, 1970). One important source was a growing interest in overtly intensional notions, especially alethic modality (Marcus, 1993) and 'essentialism' (Kripke, 1972), which gave rise to the postulation of possible worlds. The acceptance of intensional entities was often accompanied by an effort to provide identity conditions (Putnam, 1970), but the demand for such conditions has also been questioned (Plantinga, 1974), and even rejected (Jubien, 1996).

The 1980s and 1990s not only witnessed an increased acceptance of intensional entities, it also featured them as objects of study in their own right. Notable here are theories of properties and theories of possible worlds, which sometimes draw heavily on mathematical logic, especially set theory and modal logic. A contemporary theory of properties that aspires to naturalism is D. M. Armstrong's (1978), which takes properties and relations to be constituents of 'states of affairs' in the spatiotemporal world. An important nonnaturalist theory is George Bealer's (1982), in which properties and relations are seen as independently existing entities of their own special kinds, and constituting part of the proper subject matter of logic.

The discussion of modality resulted in a variety of different theories of possible worlds. Several of these may be thought of as 'proposition-style' theories because their treatment of worlds crucially involves propositions (or other proposition-like entities). (See Alvin Plantinga, 1974.) For example, one may take worlds to be 'maximal consistent' propositions. (A proposition is consistent if it is possibly true, and maximal if, for any proposition P, it either entails P or the negation of P.) Proposition-style theories are far from naturalistic since they take propositions to be irreducible, Platonic entities. But these theories are seen by their proponents as 'actualistic' in virtue of relying only on entities that actually exist.

A sharply contrasting view of worlds (and properties) is the 'counterpart' theory of David Lewis (1982). This theory is naturalistic, at least in spirit, but far from actualistic. According to Lewis, there exists a plenitude of 'possible worlds' in addition to the world we inhabit. These other worlds, however, are not abstract entities like propositions. They are concrete, spatiotemporal realms, more or less like our own world, but physically inaccessible from our world (and from each other). Each possible world is 'actual' from its own perspective and nonactual from the perspective of every other world. Because other worlds exist, but do not actually exist, they count (for us) as 'merely possible objects', and Lewis's theory is hence a version of ontological 'possibilism'. This strikingly lavish (though entirely naturalistic) ontology enables Lewis to give analyses of the modal notions, and reductive treatments of intensional entities like properties, relations, and propositions.

The period since 1960 has included a number of developments in ontology that we have not considered here. (One example is a renewed interest in mereology as it bears on the topic of physical objects; another is the discussion of the nature of events.) Important contributors to ontological discussions so far unmentioned include Robert M. Adams, Paul Benacerraf, Jonathan Bennett, John Bigelow, Hector-Neri Castañeda, Richard Cartwright, Roderick Chisholm, Donald Davidson, Michael Dummett, Hartry Field, Graeme Forbes, Jerrold Katz, Jaegwon Kim, J. L. Mackie, Terence Parsons, Richard Routley, Brian Skyrms, Robert Stalnaker, and Peter van Inwagen.

[See also Armstrong, David M.; Carnap, Rudolph; Chisholm, Roderick M.; Davidson, Donald; Dummett, Michael; Eliminative Materialism, Eliminativism; Frege, Gottlob; Kripke, Saul Aaron; Mackie, John Leslie; Marcus, Ruth Barcan; Mathematical Logic; Mereology; Modal Logic; Modality, Philosophy and Metaphysics of; Naturalism; Properties; Propositions; Putnam, Hilary; Quine, Willard Van Orman; Russell, Bertrand Arthur William; Set Theory.]

BIBLIOGRAPHY

Armstrong, D. M. *Universals and Scientific Realism,* 2 vols. Cambridge, 1978.

Bealer, G. *Quality and Concept.* Oxford, 1982.

Jubien, M. "The Myth of Identity Conditions," *Philosophical Perspectives,* Vol. 10 (1996).

Kripke, S. A. *Naming and Necessity.* Cambridge, MA, 1972.

Lewis, D. *On the Plurality of Worlds.* Oxford, 1986.

Marcus, R. B. *Modalities.* Oxford, 1993.

Plantinga, A. *The Nature of Necessity.* Oxford, 1974.

Putnam, H. "On Properties," in N. Rescher, ed., *Essays in Honor of Carl G. Hempel* (Dordrecht, 1970).

Quine, W. V. O. *Word and Object.* Cambridge, MA, 1960.

———. *Ontological Relativity and Other Essays.* New York, 1969.

— MICHAEL JUBIEN

P

PACIFISM

Pacifism is moral opposition to war. The concept embraces a wide range of positions from an absolute prohibition of all use of force against persons to a selective and pragmatic rejection of particular forms of such force under varying circumstances. Pacifists vary on their moral grounds for rejecting war and on their commitments to varieties of nonviolence.

Pacifism's opposition to war is much more frequently

reflected in philosophical literature

than is its active creation of peace.

Etymologically, pacifism comes from the Latin *pax, pacis,* "peace" (originally "compact") + *facere,* "to make," and literally means "peacemaking." Often, pacifism is incorrectly identified as passivism, which derives from the Latin *passivus,* "suffering," and means being inert or inactive, suffering acceptance. Pacifists may be passivists but often are activists, choosing nonviolent means to resolve conflict and achieve personal and social goals.

Pacifism consists of two parts: the moral opposition to war and the commitment to cooperative social and national conduct based on agreement. Beyond the mere absence of war, peace is a condition of group order arising from within by cooperation among participants rather than order imposed from outside by domination by others. Pacifism's opposition to war is much more frequently reflected in philosophic literature than is its active creation of peace.

Moral opposition to war is discussed across the history of Western philosophy. While early considerations of the morality of war can be found in ancient Greek texts (e.g., Plato, *Republic,* Book IV, 469c–471c), more thorough treatments are much later—notably from Erasmus in the sixteenth century and Kant in the late eighteenth. Adin Ballou articulated pragmatic pacifism in the mid-nineteenth century, and William James explored pacifist philosophy in the early twentieth. Arguments for pacifism tend to focus on the evils of war, including human suffering—especially of innocents—

and moral degradation of participants as well as the uncontrollability of modern warfare.

The case for pacifism varies with the form of pacifism being put forth. Absolute pacifism, the view that it is wrong under all circumstances to use force against persons, may rest on one interpretation of Kant's categorical imperative, on Gandhi's Satyagraha (truth force), on King's notion of Christian love, or on other moral bases. Weaker forms of pacifism may rest on interpretations of these same principles or on other grounds. Epistemological pacifists stress the impossibility of knowing sufficiently to warrant taking lives, while pragmatic pacifists trace the empirical history of war to em-

Pacifists often are activists, choosing nonviolent means to resolve conflict and achieve personal and social goals. (Corbis/Bettmann)

phasize failures in achieving the ends that were to justify carnage. Nuclear pacifists focus on the projected effects of thermonuclear exchange, and ecological pacifists consider the effects of modern war on ecosystems.

[See also James, William; Kant, Immanuel; Plato; Social and Political Philosophy; Violence.]

BIBLIOGRAPHY

Ballou, A. "Christian Non-Resistance," in S. Lynd, ed., *Nonviolence in America: A Documentary History* (Indianapolis, 1966).

Cady, D. L. *From Warism to Pacifism: A Moral Continuum.* Philadelphia, 1989.

Erasmus, D. *Complaint of Peace.* 1517.

———. *Praise of Folly.* 1512.

Gandhi, M. K. *Nonviolent Resistance,* ed. B. Kumarappa. New York, 1951.

Holmes, R. L. *On War and Morality.* Princeton, NJ, 1989.

James, W. "The Moral Equivalent of War" [1910], in R. Wasserstrom, ed., *War and Morality* (Belmont, CA, 1970).

Kant, I. *Perpetual Peace* [1795], ed. and trans. L. W. Beck. New York, 1957.

King, M. L., Jr. *A Testament of Hope: The Essential Writings of Martin Luther King, Jr.,* ed. J. M. Washington. New York, 1986.

Ruddick, S. *Maternal Thinking: Toward a Feminist Peace Politics.* Boston, 1989.

Sharp, G. *Power and Struggle,* part 1 of *The Power of Nonviolent Action.* Boston, 1973.

Teichman, J. *Pacifism and the Just War.* Oxford, 1986.

Tolstoy, L. *The Kingdom of God and Peace Essays* [1909], 2d ed. Oxford, 1951.

— DUANE L. CADY

PARMENIDES OF ELEA

Parmenides of Elea, the most original and important philosopher before Socrates, was born c. 515 B.C. He changed the course of Greek cosmology and had an even more important effect upon metaphysics and epistemology. He was the first to focus attention on the central problem of Greek metaphysics—What is the nature of real being?—and he established a frame of reference within which the discussion was to be conducted. The closely related problem of knowledge, which to a great extent dominated philosophy in the fifth and fourth centuries, was raised at once by his contrast between the Way of Truth and the Way of Seeming. His influence can be found in Empedocles, Anaxagoras, and the atomists; it is strong in most of Plato's work, particularly in the vitally important dialogues *Parmenides, Theaetetus,* and *Sophist.*

Plato in his dialogue *Parmenides* describes a meeting in Athens of Parmenides, Zeno, and Socrates. Parmenides was then about 65, Zeno about 40, and Socrates "very young." Though the meeting is probably fictitious, there is no reason why the ages should be unrealistic. Since Socrates died in 399, when he was about 70, and since he was old enough in Plato's dialogue to talk philosophy with Parmenides, the meeting would have to be dated about 450, making Parmenides' birth about 515. An alternative dating (Diogenes Laërtius, *Lives* IX, 23, probably from Apollodorus' *Chronica*) puts his birth about 25 years earlier, but this can be explained away.

Plato's remark (*Sophist* 242D) that the Eleatic school stems from Xenophanes is not to be taken seriously. Parmenides founded the school in the Phocaean colony of Elea in southern Italy, and its only other noteworthy members were his pupils Zeno and Melissus (the tradition that the atomist Leucippus was from Elea is probably false).

Parmenides changed the course of Greek cosmology and had an even more important effect on metaphysics and epistemology.

WRITINGS. The work of Parmenides is not extant as a whole. Plato and Aristotle quote a line or two; from later writers, particularly Sextus Empiricus and Simplicius, about 150 lines can be recovered. Parmenides wrote in hexameter verse. All the fragments seem to come from a single work, which may have been called *On Nature;* it is unlikely to have been very long, and the fragments may amount to as much as a third of the whole. The survival of a long consecutive passage of more than sixty lines (Fr. 8) is of the greatest importance; it is the earliest example of an extended philosophical argument.

The poem begins with a description of the poet's journey to the home of a goddess, who welcomes him kindly and tells him that he is to learn "both the unshakeable heart of well-rounded Truth, and the beliefs of mortals, in which there is no true reliability" (Fr. 1). The rest of the poem consists of the speech of the goddess in which she fulfills these two promises.

The interpretation of Parmenides is thoroughly controversial, and a short article cannot do more than offer one possible account, with a brief mention of the more important and plausible variants. In the interests of brevity many expressions of doubt have been omitted.

THE PROEM. Sextus Empiricus (*Adversus Mathematicos,* VII, 111 ff.) quotes 32 lines which he asserts to be the beginning of Parmenides' *On Nature* (Fr. 1). The poet describes his journey in a chariot, drawn by mares that know the way and escorted by the Daughters of the Sun. The Sun Maidens come from the Halls of Night and unveil themselves when they come into daylight. There is a gateway on the paths of Night and Day, with great doors of which the goddess Justice holds the key. The Sun Maidens persuade Justice to open the gates for themselves and Parmenides, and they pass through. "The goddess" welcomes him kindly as a mortal man in divine company, shakes his hand, and sets his mind at rest by telling him that it is right and just that he should have taken this road. He must now learn both the truth and the unreliable beliefs of mortals.

Although few examples of contemporary poetry have survived for comparison, it is safe to say that this proem is a mixture of tradition and innovation. The "journey" of the poet is a literary figure closely paralleled in an ode by Pindar (*Olympian* 6). There, as for Parmenides, the journey is an image of the course of the song; the poet rides in a chariot, a gate has to be opened, the team knows the way, and the road is notably direct. The route followed by Parmenides' chariot, although straight and swift, is impossible to chart. The details are vague. What is clear is that the whole journey is nowhere on earth, but in the heavens, and that it begins in the realm of darkness and ends in the realm of light. This imagery is confirmed by other indications—the escort of Sun Maidens and their unveiling.

It can hardly be doubted that the journey symbolizes progress from ignorance to knowledge on a heroic or even cosmic scale. The epic verse form signifies a deliberately heroic context, for earlier philosophers probably wrote in prose (though Parmenides may also have chosen verse as being more memorable). Parmenides' journey in search of knowledge must recall Odysseus's journey to Hades (*Odyssey* XI) to get directions from Teiresias to guide him on his way home. The location of Parmenides' journey recalls the magic regions of this part of the *Odyssey*, where in one place dawn follows immediately upon nightfall because "the ways of night and day are close together" (X, 86) and where in another place there is no daylight at all, since Night envelops everything (XI, 19). There may also be reminiscences of the journey of Phaethon in the chariot of the Sun.

Sextus, after quoting Fragment 1, gives a detailed allegorical interpretation of it, and in this he has been followed by some modern scholars. But this is wrong; it is impossible to trace a consistent allegory, and in any case detailed allegory was a later invention.

The identity of the goddess is puzzling. The wording of the proem itself suggests that she is the same as the goddess Justice who holds the keys of the gates; in a later fragment, however, she speaks of Justice in the third person (possibly even in Fr. 1.28; certainly in Fr. 8.14). It may be that Parmenides left the identification intentionally vague. Simplicius does not mention the goddess at all but introduces his quotations as if the first

person referred to Parmenides himself. The Neoplatonists appear to have called her "the nymph Hypsipyle" (that is, High Gate; Proclus, "Commentary on the *Parmenides*" Book IV, Ch. 34).

It is probably wrong to say that in his proem Parmenides is setting himself up as a mystic or that he is claiming to have received a divine revelation. If mysticism entails some privileged access to truth through nonrational means, then Parmenides was no mystic. The fragments show that he argued for his conclusions; his goddess tells him to use his reason to assess her words (Fr. 7.5). A single visionary experience is ruled out by the opening of the proem, in which the tenses show that the journey is a repeated one—perhaps repeated every time the poem is recited. Unless the claim of every poet to be inspired by the Muses is itself a claim to a divine revelation, this seems to be an inappropriate description of Parmenides' experience.

At the time of its composition, the proem was probably understood as a claim that the poet had something of great importance to say. The course of his divinely inspired song was a path that led to the light of knowledge. By making Justice responsible for opening the gate for him, he claimed that this was a right and proper path for him to follow and, therefore, a path that led to truth. By putting the whole of his doctrine into the mouth of a goddess, he claimed objectivity for it; it was not beyond criticism, since the goddess instructed him to judge it by reason, but it was not to be regarded as a merely personal statement by Parmenides.

THE THREE WAYS. The goddess begins by telling Parmenides what are the only possible ways of inquiry. She describes three ways, produces reasons for ruling out two of them, and insists on the remaining one as the only correct one.

First two ways are stated, each being defined by a conjunctive proposition. The first is "that it *is*, and cannot not be; this is the way of Persuasion, for she is the attendant of Truth." The second is "that it *is not*, and must necessarily not be, this I tell you is a way of total ignorance" (Fr. 2).

The literal meaning of Parmenides' Greek in these propositions is hard to see. The verb "to be" is used in the existential sense. He uses it in the third person present indicative without any subject expressed. Some interpreters say that there is no subject to be understood; however, without any subject the sentence is incomplete, and no doubt the impersonal subject "it" is to be regarded as contained in the verb, as it often is. What this "it" refers to has to be derived from the rest of the argument and will be discussed shortly.

Immediately after the statement of the first two ways, the second way is ruled out on the ground that it is impossible to know or to utter what does not exist: "Whatever is for thinking and saying *must* exist; for it can exist [literally, 'is for being'], whereas nothing cannot" (Fr. 6). The line of thought seems to be that the object of thought *can* exist, and since "nothing" cannot exist, the object of thought cannot be nothing. But it must either exist or be nothing; hence, it *must* exist. The basic premises then are that "nothing" is nonexistent (presumably regarded as tautological) and that the object of thought *can* exist (that is, it is possible to think of something).

Parmenides makes it quite plain, by the use of inferential particles, that there *is* an argument in this passage (though this has been denied) along the lines described. It is therefore legitimate to fill in the basic proposition of the Way of Truth ("it is") from the grounds on which it is based. The unexpressed subject of this proposition must be "the object of thought or knowledge" (this is convincingly shown by G. E. L. Owen, "Eleatic Questions"). The Way of Truth will therefore show what can be said of a thing if it is to be a proper object of thought; the first step is to assert that it must *be,* that it should not *be* is unthinkable. Subsequently, the subject is referred to as τὸ ἐόν ("that which is," "what is real," "what exists").

After ruling out the second way, the goddess continues with a warning against a third way, the way followed by mortal men, who wander about senselessly, knowing nothing and getting nowhere. Their characteristic error is that they have made up their minds that "to be and not to be is the same and not the same" (Fr. 6). The third way can be identified with "the beliefs of mortals" mentioned at the end of the proem and discussed in detail in the main body of Parmenides' work, after the Way of Truth (this identification is often denied). Mortals treat existence and nonexistence as the same in that they attach them both to the same objects by supposing that things sometimes exist and sometimes do not (that is, that there is change) and by supposing that some things exist which contain less of being than others and therefore contain some nonexistence (that is, that there is difference). They treat them as not the same in that they suppose they have different meanings. The language in which the censured doctrine is expressed is reminiscent of Heraclitus, but Heraclitus is certainly not the only mortal who suffers from Parmenides' lash here.

The third way is ruled out by pointing to an alleged contradiction in it. It asserts that "things that are not, are" (Fr. 7). From the arguments of the recommended way, described later, it would appear that what is objectionable in the third way is its assumption of intermediate degrees of existence, of things that exist at one

time but not another, at one place but not another, or in one way but not another. Ordinary habits of speech and the data of sense perception would lead a man along this path; the goddess gives a warning to "judge by *reason* the hard-hitting refutation that I have uttered."

THE WAY OF TRUTH. The Way of Truth has now been shown by elimination to be the right way. The long Fragment 8 proceeds to make deductions from the basic proposition that "it" (the object of thought and knowledge if the analysis given above is correct) "exists and must exist."

The goddess begins by telling Parmenides what

are the only possible ways of inquiry.

Its first property is that it is ungenerated and indestructible. It cannot have come into being out of what does not exist since what does not exist is absolutely unthinkable and since there would, moreover, be no explanation of why it grew out of nothing at one time rather than another. There is no growth of what exists (and no decay either, but Parmenides offers no separate argument for that); hence, "either it is or it is not" (Fr. 8.16)—and that decision has already been made. It *is,* as a whole, entirely.

Since there is no growth or decay of what exists Parmenides argues that no distinctions can be made within it. There are no degrees of being—differences of density, for instance; the whole is full of continuous being. What exists is single, indivisible, and homogeneous. Here Parmenides apparently moves from the temporal continuity of being to its spatial uniformity; in the same way Melissus, his pupil, argues for the absence of a beginning or end in time and then assumes the absence of a beginning or end in space (Melissus, Frs. 3–4).

Next follows an assertion that since there is no generation or destruction, there is no motion or change in what exists. This argument is expanded by Melissus (Fr. 7). Any form of change or rearrangement implies the destruction of a state of affairs that exists and the generation of one that does not exist. Thus, Parmenides concludes that what exists "remains the same, in the same . . . held fast in the bonds of limit by the power of Necessity" (Fr. 8.29). It already is whatever it can be. Motion, as a species of change, is apparently denied by the same argument.

The last section of the Way of Truth is particularly difficult. Parmenides repeats his assertion that there is no not-being and there are no different degrees of being; what exists is equal to itself everywhere and reaches its limits everywhere. From this he concludes that it is "perfect from every angle, equally matched from the middle in every way, like the mass of a well-rounded ball" (Fr. 8.42–44). There is no agreement among modern scholars as to whether this is a literal assertion that what exists is a sphere (a view held by Burnet and Cornford) or only a simile indicating that it is like a ball in some respect other than shape (a view held by Fränkel and Owen). The latter view seems more probable. Parmenides' stress lies on the qualitative completeness, or perfection, of what exists, not on its spatial extension. The point of the simile might be put like this: As a ball is equally poised about its center so that it would make no difference which direction you took if you examined it from the center outward, so what exists is all the same from any center.

THE WAY OF SEEING. Having completed her account "about truth," Parmenides' goddess fulfills her promise to describe mortal beliefs. Only about forty lines survive from this part of the poem. The fundamental difference from the Way of Truth is made clear at the outset: Mortals give names to two forms, and that is where they are wrong, for what exists is single. They assume the existence of two opposites, Fire and Night, probably characterized in terms of sensible opposites such as hot-cold, light-dark, light-heavy, soft-hard. Using these two forms as elements, the Way of Seeing apparently offered a detailed account of the origin of the stars, sun, moon, earth and all the things on the earth "as far as the parts of animals" (Simplicius, *In de Caelo* 559.25), some embryology, sense perception, and doubtless other things. The details are unimportant (though Parmenides is credited with the first assertion that the morning star is identical with the evening star, according to Diogenes Laërtius, *Lives* IX, 23); the interesting and puzzling thing is that he should have added a cosmogony to the Way of Truth at all. Modern scholars differ about his intention.

Zeller took the cosmogony to be an account of the beliefs of Parmenides' contemporaries; Burnet called it "a sketch of contemporary Pythagorean cosmology." However, there is no evidence for this. Such a review would seem to be pointless, and in antiquity the cosmogony was recognized as Parmenides' own. One can ignore the suggestion that it represents those of his early beliefs which were later superseded. The discussion now turns on this point: Is the Way of Seeing granted relative validity as a sort of second best, or is it wholly rejected? If it is wholly rejected, why did Parmenides write it?

Recently, the first view has been defended as follows by, for example, Verdenius, Vlastos, Schwabl, and Chalmers. The goddess in the prologue promised that Parmenides would learn about mortal beliefs as well as

truth and would hardly have done so if they had no validity at all. Unless the phenomenal world is granted some degree of reality, the philosopher himself, the learner of truth, appears to be condemned to nonexistence; however, the mind, described in physical terms in the Way of Seeing (Fr. 16), is the faculty which grasps what is real in the Way of Truth. Moreover, some of the language of the way of Seeing deliberately echoes that of the Way of Truth. The two opposites, Fire and Night, transgress the canons of truth by being distinguished from each other, but they are each described as self-identical and as containing no nonexistence, like the real being of the Way of Truth (Frs. 8.57–59, 9.4). Later writers in antiquity, notably Aristotle (*Metaphysics* A5, 986b27–34), took Parmenides to be yielding to the necessity of providing his own account of the phenomenal world. For reason, Aristotle said, there was just one being, but for sense perception more than one. Others have argued that the Way of Truth is the way an immortal looks at the world *sub specie aeternitatis*, whereas the Way of Seeing is the way mortals see the same world in time. Many variations on these themes have been suggested.

The contrary view, defended recently in differing forms by Owen, Long, and Taran, has more justification in the text of Parmenides. The goddess makes it clear enough that the Way of Seeing is wholly unreliable (Frs. 1.30, 8.52) and that the Way of Truth leaves no room whatsoever for intermediate degrees of reality. The text itself contains a statement of the intention: "Thus no judgment of mortals can ever overtake you" (Fr. 8.61; the metaphor is from chariot racing). Although this is ambiguous, the likeliest sense is that Parmenides is equipped by the Way of Seeing to defeat any mortal opinion about the phenomenal world. All descriptions of the phenomenal world presuppose that difference is real, but the Way of Truth has shown that what exists is single and undifferentiated. The transition to the Way of Seeing is made by pointing to the fundamental mistake in assuming even the minimum of differentiation in reality—that is, in assuming that two forms of what exists can be distinguished (Fr. 8.53–54). Once this assumption is made, a plausible description of the phenomenal world can be offered, but anyone who has followed Parmenides thus far will recognize the fundamental fallacy in even the most plausible description. This explanation is more consistent with the later history of Eleaticism, for Zeno and Melissus showed no interest in positive cosmology.

PARMENIDES AND GREEK PHILOSOPHY. There is general agreement that Parmenides followed the Milesians, Heraclitus, and Pythagoras and preceded Empedocles, Anaxagoras, and the atomists (the thesis of Reinhardt that Heraclitus answered Parmenides has been generally rejected). Ancient tradition credits him with a Pythagorean teacher, Ameinias (Diogenes Laërtius, *Lives* IX, 21). It is often said that the rigorous deductive method of the Way of Truth was learned from the mathematicians, who at that time in Italy were likely to be Pythagoreans, but the truth is that too little is known of the mathematics of the time to allow this to be more than a guess.

Plato inherited from Parmenides the belief

that the object of knowledge must exist

and must be found by the mind

and not by the senses.

In general, the relevance of Parmenides to earlier philosophy is fairly clear, though there is room for doubt about his attitude toward individual men. (Various scholars have found in the text attacks on Anaximander, Anaximenes, Heraclitus, and the Pythagorean school.) All previous systems had assumed the reality of change in the physical world and attempted to explain it. Thales, Anaximander, and Anaximenes held that the world evolved from a simpler state into a more complex one. Anaximander's view was that different substances ("the opposites") grew out of a primitive undifferentiated "indefinite"; Anaximenes gave a more precise description of the manner of differentiation and said that the original substance, air, turned into other substances by rarefaction and condensation. Heraclitus apparently abandoned the idea of an original simple state, asserting that everything in the world is always changing—"an ever-living fire." In somewhat less materialistic language the Pythagoreans produced a cosmogony based on the imposition of limit upon the unlimited. Parmenides' critique was equally damaging to all of these theories, since his argument, if accepted, condemned all difference as illusory.

It is often said that Parmenides' attack on the reality of the physical world depends on his confusion of two senses of the verb "to be"—the existential and copulative. It cannot logically be true that a subject *is* and at the same time *is not* (existentially); from this Parmenides is supposed to have concluded that it cannot be true that a subject *is* black and at the same time *is not* white and hence that all differentiation is impossible. The surviving text does not bear this out. Parmenides' premise (and his fundamental fallacy) was, rather, that "what is not" is absolutely unthinkable and unknowable. Every change would involve the passage of

what is into what is not, and hence every attempt to describe a change would involve the use of an unintelligible expression, "what is not."

The argument of the Way of Truth is metaphysical and would apply to any subject matter whatsoever; it is false to suppose that it applied only to Pythagorean cosmogony or only to the materialist cosmogonies of the Ionians. But that Parmenides' primary intention was to criticize the earlier cosmogonists seems clear from the addition of the Way of Seeming to the Way of Truth. His own Real Being was certainly not a ball of matter, as Burnet and others thought. On the other hand, it was not something to which spatial terms were wholly inapplicable. It filled the whole of space and thus was in some sense a competitor of other accounts of the cosmos. The main effects of his work, too, were on cosmology.

The error of Parmenides' ways was not seen immediately, perhaps not until Plato's *Sophist*. Their immediate effect was to produce theories which attempted to save the natural world from unreality without transgressing Parmenides' logical canons. In brief, they produced theories of elements. Empedocles envisaged a cosmos made of the four elements which were later made standard by Aristotle—earth, water, air, and fire. He satisfied some of Parmenides' criteria by making his elements unchangeable and homogeneous. What he refused to accept from Parmenides was that difference was impossible without diminution of reality; his four elements were asserted to be different from one another yet equally real. He explained apparent change as the rearrangement in space of the unchanging elements. Anaxagoras went further to meet Parmenides by asserting that all natural substances, not just a privileged four, were elementary and unchangeable. The atomists responded in a different way; they accepted that no qualitative difference is possible but rescued the phenomenal world by asserting that "what is not" exists in the form of void—that is, as empty space separating pieces of real being from each other. (The equation of void with "what is not" is sometimes attributed to Parmenides himself, but it was probably first made by his follower Melissus, who explicitly denied its existence in his Fragment 7.)

Plato inherited from Parmenides the belief that the object of knowledge must exist and must be found by the mind and not by the senses. He agreed that the object of knowledge is not something abstracted from the data of sense perception but a being of a different and superior order. He differed, however, in that he allowed the sensible world to have an intermediate status, as the object of "belief," rather than no status at all (*Republic* 477B and elsewhere). He differed more significantly, too, in that be reimported plurality into the real and knowable by distinguishing different senses of "not-being" (*Sophist* 237B ff. and 257B ff.).

BIBLIOGRAPHY

Fragments and ancient testimonia are in H. Diels and W. Kranz, eds., *Fragmente der Vorsokratiker,* 10th ed. (Berlin, 1961), the standard collection. Fragments with English translation and commentary are in G. S. Kirk and J. E. Raven, *The Presocratic Philosophers* (Cambridge, 1957), but the commentary is rather inadequate. They are also found in Leonardo Taran, *Parmenides* (Princeton, N.J., 1965), and in Italian, with a long bibliography, in Mario Untersteiner, *Parmenide* (Florence, 1958).

The most important recent studies are H. Fränkel, "Parmenidesstudien," in his *Wege und Formen frühgriechischen Denkens* (Munich, 1955), and G. E. L. Owen, "Eleatic Questions," in *Classical Quarterly,* N.S. Vol. 10 (1960), 84–102.

Other studies are H. Diels, *Parmenides, Lehrgedicht* (Berlin, 1897); John Burnet, *Early Greek Philosophy* (London, 1892); K. Reinhardt, *Parmenides und die Geschichte der griechischen Philosophie* (Bonn, 1916); W. Kranz, "Über Aufbau und Bedeutung des Parmenideischen Gedichtes," in *Sitzungsberichte der Deutschen Akademie der Wissenschaften zu Berlin,* Vol. 47 (1916), 1158–1176; Eduard Zeller, *Die Philosophie der Griechen,* 6th ed., Vol. I (Leipzig, 1919), Ch. 1; F. M. Cornford, "Parmenides' Two Ways," in *Classical Quarterly,* Vol. 27 (1933), 97–111, and *Plato and Parmenides* (London, 1939); G. Calogero, *Studi sul eleatismo* (Rome, 1932); and Harold Cherniss, *Aristotle's Criticism of Presocratic Philosophy* (Baltimore, 1935).

Some more recent studies are W. J. Verdenius, *Parmenides: Some Comments* (Groningen, the Netherlands, 1942); Olof Gigon, *Der Ursprung der griechischen Philosophie von Hesiod bis Parmenides* (Basel, 1945); Gregory Vlastos, "Parmenides' Theory of Knowledge," in *Transactions of the American Philological Association,* Vol. 77 (1946), 66–77; Hans Schwabl, "Sein und Doxa bei Parmenides," in *Wiener Studien,* Vol. 66 (1953), 50–75; C. M. Bowra, *Problems in Greek Poetry* (Oxford, 1953); Eric A. Havelock, "Parmenides and Odysseus," and Leonard Woodbury, "Parmenides on Names," in *Harvard Studies in Classical Philology,* Vol. 63 (Cambridge, Mass., 1958); W. R. Chalmers, "Parmenides and the Beliefs of Mortals," in *Phronesis,* Vol. 5 (1960), 5–22; A. A. Long, "The Principles of Parmenides' Cosmogony," in *Phronesis,* Vol. 8 (1963), 90–107; J. Mansfeld, *Die Offenbarung des Parmenides und die menschliche Welt* (Assen, 1964); and W. K. C. Guthrie, *A History of Greek Philosophy,* Vol. II (Cambridge, 1965).

– DAVID J. FURLEY

PATERNALISM

This term has long been in currency among moral and political philosophers, but its circulation became much wider, and its definitions much more precise, following the widely read debate over "the legal enforcement of morality" between Patrick Devlin (*The Enforcement of Morals,* 1965) and H. L. A. Hart (*Law, Liberty, and Morality,* 1963). Hart had endorsed the liberal doctrine of J. S. Mill, that the only legitimate reason for state interference with the liberty of one person is to prevent him from harming other persons. Mill was especially emphatic in denying that the actor's "own good, either physical or moral," is ever an adequate reason for in-terference or criminal prohibition ([1859], 1985, p. 9). What Mill denied in this passage is precisely what came to be called "legal paternalism" in the writings of his followers, including Hart nearly a century later. Thus, paternalism was regarded as a thoroughly unacceptable view by nineteenth-century liberals.

Physical and Moral

In his exchange with Devlin, however, Hart conceded that a certain amount of physical paternalism could be accepted by twentieth-century liberals, here departing from Mill who, he wrote, "carried his protests against paternalism to lengths that may now appear to us as fantastic" (Hart, 1963, p. 32). He cited, for example, Mill's criticism of restrictions on the sale of drugs. Devlin then responded by drawing a distinction between "physical paternalism," which protects people from physical harm that could be caused by their own voluntary conduct, and "moral paternalism," which offers similar protection against "moral harm" of the actor's own causing. Devlin could see no consistent way in which the physical paternalist like Hart could avoid commitment to moral paternalism, for if it is the prevention of harm that justifies prohibition in the one case, why not use state power to prevent an equal amount of harm, though of a different kind, in the other case? Similarly, Devlin concluded, there is no relevant difference between criminalization meant to prevent moral harm and criminal prohibitions meant to "enforce the moral law as such." The view that "enforcement of morality," quite apart from harm prevention, is a valid reason for criminal prohibitions is widely called "legal moralism." It is anathema to liberals.

Paternalism was regarded as a thoroughly

unacceptable view by nineteenth-century liberals.

One way in which liberals sometimes defend themselves from Devlin's argument is by maintaining that Devlin's moves from physical to moral harm and from preventing moral harm to "enforcing the moral law" do not follow logically. One liberal critic, Joel Feinberg (1986), even goes so far as to deny, in the teeth of the immense combined authority of Plato and Aristotle to the contrary, that "moral harm" is a coherent concept.

Hard and Soft

A distinction is commonly made between hard (or strong) paternalism and soft (or weak) paternalism. Hard paternalism justifies the forcible prevention of some dangerous but self-regarding activities even when those activities are done in a fully voluntary (i.e., free and informed) way. Soft paternalism, on the other hand, permits individuals or the state to prevent self-regarding dangerous behavior only when it is substantially nonvoluntary or when temporary intervention is necessary to establish whether it is voluntary or not.

Most soft paternalists are liberals strongly opposed to paternalism. Most of them, when they think of the paternalism they oppose, think of what is here called hard paternalism. Therefore they would prefer to go by the name of soft antipaternalists. The term hard antipaternalism could be reserved for the totally uncompromising liberal who would oppose interference even with some choices known to be involuntary, and with temporary compulsory intervention that is only for the purpose of determining whether the intended conduct truly is voluntary, and even with the imposition of compulsory education about risks or state-administered tests to assess the dangerous actor's understanding of the risks, with licenses required for self-regarding dangerous behavior, like mountain climbing. Clarity would be improved if philosophers would speak of paternalism only when what is meant is hard paternalism, justifying prohibition even of wholly voluntary self-regarding conduct, when dangerous. Then soft and hard antipaternalism would be the names of a moderate and extreme liberalism, respectively.

The controversy over paternalism in the criminal law is genuine and difficult. Those who are strongly opposed to paternalism find it not only mistaken but arrogant and demeaning. It is very difficult to reconcile it with even a minimal conception of personal autonomy (rightful self-government) when it proclaims that state officials may rightfully intervene even against my protests to "correct" my choices, and this on the ground that they know what is good for me better than I do myself. But if we reject paternalism altogether, we seem to fly in the face both of common sense and of long-established customs and laws. The state, for example, does not accept "consent" as a justification for mayhem or homicide. Similarly, the law of contracts will not validate certain agreements even though they are voluntary on both sides—when, for example, they are usurious or bigamous. One would be hard put to accept these traditional state-created disabilities without abandoning one's opposition to paternalism. But if we continue our adherence to paternalism, we may discover that in other areas paternalism justifies too much, the flat-out prohibition, for example, of whiskey, cigarettes, and fried foods, which tend to be bad for people too, whether they know it or not.

Medical Contexts

Writers on medical ethics confront paternalism at every turn, often in human contexts that are less familiar to those whose interest is primarily focused on criminal law. Those characteristic social situations have led to some forms of ethical analysis supplementary to those that prevail among the critics and defenders of "legal paternalism." For example, not all of the moral problems raised by paternalism in medical settings are problems for legislators drafting mandatory rules or other governmental officials such as judges or police officers. Moreover, paternalism is not exclusively a criterion for the legitimacy of coercion. Sometimes what is at issue is some other practice that normally has high moral costs, most notably deception rather than coercion, as in false but comforting statements to frightened patients or the unacknowledged or mendacious use of placebos. Sometimes a medical provider may have to decide whether to tell a "white lie" to his patient, not for the sake of her health, but rather as a way of preventing her from experiencing intense despair in her final hours about a matter having no direct connection with medical treatment. In a hypothetical case invented by Culver and Gert (1976, p. 46), a woman on her deathbed asks her physician how her son is doing, and the doctor replies that he is doing well even though he knows that "the son has just been killed trying to escape from jail after having been indicted [a fact unknown to his mother] for multiple rape and murder." An opponent of (hard) paternalism would probably consider the doctor's mendacity to be a violation of the patient's autonomy. A medical paternalist would probably argue that the truthful alternative in this case would be cruel to the point of indecency. They might both be right.

Pros and Cons

Problems involving paternalism in medical contexts are quite diverse. They include not only truth-telling cases but also suicide attempts, requests for euthanasia, and the use of human volunteers in dangerous experiments. The paternalist position in these conflicts is that protecting volunteers or patients from harm and promoting their benefit should take precedence over respecting their autonomy by permitting them to act freely on their well-informed choices in matters that are almost exclusively self-regarding.

Beauchamp (1977) and Beauchamp and Childress (1979) in their influential works rejected hard paternalism nearly categorically, emphasizing that to overturn the deliberate choices of adult human beings that affect only them, or only them clearly and directly, is to deny that their lives really belong to them. The apparent exceptions—cases in which commonsense morality would seem to justify interference with the patient's voluntary choice—invariably turn out to be cases in which that choice is not fully voluntary after all; that is, the patient or volunteer subject had not been adequately informed about the risks he would be accepting, or he was not perfectly free of coercive influences, or some other condition, such as infancy, drug intoxication, high fever, rage, or depression, had diminished his capacity to act rationally. To restrict his liberties in such circumstances, or to motivate him by telling him a lie, would be to interfere with actions that are not fully voluntary in the first place. To interfere with dangerous self-regarding but less-than-voluntary behavior can be justified by soft paternalism (that is by soft *and* hard antipaternalism). Another example illustrates the point.

Problems involving paternalism in medical contexts

include not only truth-telling cases

but also suicide attempts, requests for euthanasia,

and the use of human volunteers

in dangerous experiments.

"If we see a normally calm person who we know has been experimenting with hard drugs, go into a sudden frenzy, and seize a butcher knife with the clear intention of cutting his own throat, then [of course!] we have the right to interfere. In so doing we will not be interfering with his real self or blocking his real will. . . . His drug-deluded self is not his 'real self,' and his frenzied desire is not his 'real choice,' so we may defend him against these internal threats to his autonomous self, which is quite another thing than throttling that autonomous self with external coercion" (Feinberg, 1986, p. 14). Interference on this ground is no more paternalistic than interference designed to protect an individual from an attack by some berserk assailant. Paternalists have been quick to point out, however, that this example, and others like it, hardly fit the more usual examples of risky choice making.

Writing from the practical point of view, and a philosophical position more friendly to paternalism, Culver and Gert (1982), in response to Beauchamp, point out that many crucial questions remain for the soft antipaternalist analysis. Most of these stem from the vagueness of the distinction between voluntary and nonvoluntary. Culver and Gert remind us that voluntariness is usually a matter of degree with no conveniently placed bright lines to guide us. In this respect it resembles the concept of harm (which is also crucially involved in hard paternalists' calculations) and the degree of violation of a moral rule, like that forbidding telling

lies, or that condemning coercion, and even the degree to which the overruled choices of, say, a patient, are purely self-regarding—another essential variable.

Culver and Gert, however, do not endorse the hard paternalistic position without limit. Rather, they hold that some (hard) paternalistic interventions are justified, and some are not, but reject the unqualified antipaternalism of Beauchamp and Childress, which denies that (hard) paternalistic prohibitions and interferences are ever justified, and the unqualified paternalism of many utilitarian writers, which holds that *all* paternalistic behavior is justified, except that which will be counterproductive in the long run.

[See also Aristotle; Biomedical Ethics; Liberty; Mill, John Stuart; Plato.]

BIBLIOGRAPHY

Beauchamp, T. L. "Paternalism and Bio-behavioral Control," *The Monist*, Vol. 60 (1977), 62–80.

———, and J. F. Childress. *Principles of Biomedical Ethics*. New York, 1979.

Brock, D. "Paternalism and Promoting the Good," in R. Sartorius, ed., *Paternalism* (Minneapolis, 1983). This is one of the leading statements of a qualified utilitarian theory of paternalism.

Culver, C. M., and B. Gert. "Paternalistic Behavior," *Philosophy and Public Affairs*, Vol. 6 (1976), 45–7.

———. *Philosophy in Medicine*. New York, 1982.

Devlin, P. *The Enforcement of Ethics*. London, 1965.

Dworkin, G. "Paternalism," *The Monist*, Vol. 56 (1972), 64–84. An influential early article that helped shape twenty years of discussion.

———. "Paternalism: Some Second Thoughts," in R. Sartorius, ed., *Paternalism* (Minneapolis, 1983), 105–13.

Faden, R. R., and T. L. Beauchamp. *A History and Theory of Informed Consent*. New York, 1986. The definitive work on its subject.

Feinberg, J. *Harm to Self*. New York, 1986.

Hart, H. L. A. *Law, Liberty, and Morality*. Stanford, CA, 1963.

Kleinig, J. *Paternalism*. Totowa, NJ, 1983.

Mill, J. S. *On Liberty* [1859]. Indianapolis, 1985.

Sartorius, R., ed. *Paternalism*. Minneapolis, 1983. This excellent collection includes, in addition to the selections by Brock and Dworkin already cited, fifteen useful articles and a superb bibliography.

VanDeVeer, D. *Paternalistic Intervention: The Moral Bounds of Intervention*. Princeton, NJ, 1986.

— JOEL FEINBERG

PEIRCE, CHARLES SANDERS

Charles Sanders Peirce (1839–1914), American philosopher, physicist, and mathematician and the founder of pragmatism, was born in Cambridge, Massachusetts. His father, Benjamin Peirce, was the leading American mathematician of the time and Perkins professor of mathematics and astronomy at Harvard. Young Charles was born and bred a scientist, and from his earliest years

Peirce came to philosophy as a student of Kant, from whom he had acquired the architectonic theory of philosophy. (Corbis/Bettmann)

he showed great promise in mathematics and the physical sciences. He attended Harvard, graduated in 1859, and subsequently studied at the Lawrence Scientific School, from which he received his degree in chemistry *summa cum laude* in 1863. During the next 15 years, Peirce simultaneously pursued several distinct careers. He worked as an astronomer at the Harvard Observatory, where he did pioneer work in photometric research. He also worked as a physicist for the United States Coast and Geodetic Survey, of which his father was superintendent, and achieved some distinction for his discovery of hitherto undetected errors in pendulum experiments used to determine the force of gravity. And he worked, more or less privately, at philosophy and logic, steadily publishing works on these subjects from 1866 on. By 1879 he had achieved sufficient stature in these last two fields to be appointed lecturer in logic at the newly organized Johns Hopkins University in Baltimore, Maryland. He remained at Johns Hopkins from 1879 until 1884, meanwhile continuing to work for the Coast and Geodetic Survey—a connection which he sustained until 1891. In 1887, after having inherited

some money, he retired to Milford, Pennsylvania, where he lived in relative isolation until his death. Peirce was twice married—in 1862 to Harriet Melusina Fay, whom he divorced in 1883, and in 1883 to Juliette Froissy, who survived him. He had no children.

PHILOSOPHICAL ORIENTATION. Peirce was a systematic philosopher of great breadth, and his writings cover almost all fields of philosophy. His greatest contributions were in the field of logic, but he wrote extensively on epistemology, scientific method, semiotics, metaphysics, cosmology, ontology, and mathematics, and less extensively on ethics, aesthetics, history, phenomenology, and religion. Since Peirce's views underwent considerable change as he grew older, it is not possible to speak of his philosophy as a single system: rather, he formulated several systems, each of which represents a different phase in his development. These different systems, however, deal with the same problems and embody the same fundamental concept of philosophy.

Peirce came to philosophy as a student of Kant, from whom he had acquired the architectonic theory of philosophy. In brief, this theory holds that the domain of knowledge can be so characterized that general assertions can be proven true of all possible knowledge; the theory also holds that it is the dependence of all knowledge upon logic that makes such a characterization possible. Accordingly, the doctrine holds that it is possible to derive from logic the fundamental categories and principles which form the basis of all that can ever be known. In formulating this theory, Kant assumed that logic was a completed, unchanging science. But Peirce was one of that group of men, including George Boole, Augustus De Morgan, Gottlob Frege, and others, who revolutionized logic and prepared the way for Whitehead and Russell's *Principia Mathematica*. Hence, for Peirce, logic was a growing, changing subject, and as it changed, so, according to the architectonic theory, Peirce's philosophy had to change with it. Thus the major shifts in Peirce's system are correlated with his major discoveries in logic and reflect the modifications that he thought those discoveries entailed. In the following exposition, Peirce's work will therefore be dealt with chronologically, and each system will be treated in order.

The First System, 1859–1861

Pierce's first system is a form of extreme post-Kantian idealism. The sources of this idealism are not known: whether he evolved it himself or derived it from some other source, such as Emersonian transcendentalism, cannot now be determined. What is clear is that by

1857 he was seeking to combine the Transcendental Analytic with Platonic idealism.

CATEGORIES. From Kant's doctrine of the Transcendental Sciences, Peirce derived a threefold ontological classification of all there is into matter (the object of cosmology), mind (the object of psychology), and God (the object of theology). Peirce referred to these three categories as the It (the sense world), the Thou (the mental world), and the I (the abstract world), respectively; and it was from these pronouns that he subsequently derived the names Firstness, Secondness, and Thirdness, by which he usually called his categories.

Peirce was a systematic philosopher of great breadth, and his writings cover almost all fields of philosophy.

Having divided all there is into these three categories, Peirce's problem was then to define the relations among them. Specifically, the problem of knowledge as it appears in the first system is how the ideas in the mind of God can be known by human minds. Peirce thought he had found the solution to this problem in the Kantian principle that all phenomena and all concepts—all that can be before the mind—are representations, for he understood this to imply that the ideas in the mind of God, which Peirce conceived as Platonic archetypes, are first given a material embodiment in the form of the objects of our experience and are then derived by us from those objects by abstraction. So Peirce took the Transcendental Analytic to be a description of this process: the synthesis in intuition is the synthesis of the divine idea (already present in an unconscious form within the soul) with "the matter of sensation" to form the empirical object which is also, by virtue of the divine idea, the transcendental object; and the concept is derived by abstraction from the object given in intuition. But when it came to explaining just how the Kantian categories served to effect so un-Kantian a synthesis as that demanded by his own semiotic idealism, Peirce found himself in grave difficulties, and after struggling with the problem for some time he was forced to conclude that the Kantian table of categories was simply inadequate.

Transitional Period: Study of Logic

According to the architectonic principle, the inadequacy of the table of categories implies the inadequacy of Kant's logical classification of propositions. In 1862, therefore, Peirce began the serious study of logic, and he naturally turned to the Scholastics for instruction. Although he began his study in the belief that the fun-

damental problem was the classification of propositions, he soon learned from Duns Scotus that the classification of arguments, or forms of inference, was more fundamental, since the significance of propositions depends upon the role they play in inference. He was therefore led to investigate the irreducible forms of inference, and so to study Kant's famous paper "The Mistaken Subtlety of the Four Syllogistic Figures," in which Kant argued that all inference is reducible to Barbara or to a combination of Barbara and immediate inference. In the "Memoranda Concerning the Aristotelian Syllogism," which he published in 1866, Peirce showed that Kant's argument is invalid, for the syllogism by which the reduction of the second and third figures is made is itself in the figure from which the reduction is being made. Peirce therefore concluded that the first three figures are irreducible. Moreover, Peirce noted that if the first figure is defined as the deduction of a conclusion from a major and a minor premise, then the second figure can be described as the inference of the major from the minor and conclusion and the third figure as the inference of the minor from the major and conclusion. Accordingly, Peirce held that the first figure is purely deductive, the second figure inductive, and the third figure hypothetical.

For Peirce this discovery had great importance. His previous belief in the existence of synthetic a priori propositions had rested on the two doctrines, derived from Kant, that all thought involves inference and that all inference is in Barbara. Granting these doctrines, it is clear that the major premises must be innate in the mind. But with the discovery of the role of hypothesis and induction, all synthetic propositions can be regarded as inferred, and so the problem shifts to the process of synthetic inference and to scientific inquiry.

At about the same time that he discovered the irreducibility of the three figures, Peirce made another important discovery in logic—namely, that the copula can be interpreted as the sign relation. This view, which was probably derived from the scholastic theory of supposition, enabled him to regard all propositions as instances of a single fundamental relation, and the analysis was quickly extended to inferences also by treating the conclusion as a sign that is determined by the premises to represent the same state of affairs which they themselves represented. Such a result was thoroughly in line with Peirce's early semiotic idealism, and it meant that the fundamental logical relation from which the categories must be derived is signhood.

The Second System, 1866–1870

In 1867 Peirce published a paper entitled "On a New List of Categories," in which he attempted to solve the problem of relating his three ontological categories of mind, matter, and God.

THE SIGN RELATION. Starting from Kant's position that knowledge occurs only when the manifold is reduced to the unity of a proposition, Peirce asked what that unity consisted in. Since he conceived the proposition in subject-predicate form, this is equivalent to asking how the predicate is applied to the subject. On the basis of the reduction of the copula to signhood, Peirce argued that the predicate is applied to the subject by being made to stand for the same object for which the subject stands. Thus a proposition would be impossible without reference to some object. But how does the predicate come to stand for this object? Only, Peirce held, by being interpreted as standing for it by some interpreting representation, or mind, so that no proposition is possible unless such an interpretant also exists. And how does the mind make this interpretation? Only, Peirce held, by the sign's representing its object in some respect, that is, by referring to some attribute of the object. Hence, propositions would be impossible if there were no pure abstract attributes embodied in the object to form the basis of comparison among them. So his argument, in essence, was that all synthesis involves the sign relation, that the sign relation consists in a sign standing for something to someone in some respect, and therefore that unless there are things, minds, and abstractions, there is no knowledge. But since the pure abstract attribute is the Platonic Form in the mind of God, what Peirce was really arguing is that without his three ontological categories signhood would be impossible.

Aspects of Reference. In the "New List," Peirce did not present his categories directly as ontological classes; rather, he began with the problem of unifying the manifold by joining the predicate to the subject through the sign relation and then analyzed signhood into the three aspects of reference: reference to abstraction, reference to an object, and reference to an interpretant. These three aspects are then made the basis for a systematic classification of signs according to the prominence given to each reference, and this mode of classification is applied to terms, propositions, and arguments. In the case of arguments, Peirce rederived the division into hypothesis, induction, and deduction, thus presenting the three forms of syllogistic as consequences of his analysis of signs.

Logic, however, is not the only science of signs; indeed, it is but one of three, each of which studies a particular aspect of the subject. The first is speculative grammar, which studies the relation of signs to the abstraction; the second is logic, which investigates the relation of signs to their objects; and the third is speculative rhetoric, which investigates the reference of signs to their interpretants. Peirce could therefore derive his three ontological categories by abstraction from the three references of signs, but he had to show further how we can know the objects referred to and whether or not they are real. For these purposes he needed a theory of cognition and a theory of reality.

Many empiricists would agree with Peirce

that if the object is real,

then if inquiry does go on forever,

our hypotheses will converge

to a final true description.

COGNITION. Peirce stated his new theories of cognition and reality in three articles published in 1868 in the *Journal of Speculative Philosophy.* These papers simply develop the implications of the "New List." Since the reference of a sign to its object is established by its being predicated of another sign which already refers to that object, and since the predication exists only because there is an interpreting sign which so interprets it, it is clear that the series of signs is doubly infinite. Peirce accepted this conclusion and asserted that there is neither a first nor a last cognition. While this doctrine appears bizarre, it has a clear purpose. What Peirce was trying to avoid was the classic dilemma of the empiricist who, having tracked cognition back to an original impression of sense, finds himself completely unable to prove the accuracy of that first impression.

Peirce held that if we examine what actually occurs in cognition, we find the process to be something like the following. In the flood of sensory stimuli that pours in upon us, we detect certain relations which lead us to segregate some stimuli and to interpret these as having a common referent. We do not know what the first such stimulus having that referent may have been, and the question is meaningless, since it is only after many stimuli have occurred that we note their relations. As experience progresses and we acquire more relevant stimuli, we further conceptualize this referent, and in time we acquire a progressively more and more complete and precise idea of it. But our knowledge is never fully complete, so that this process of learning and inquiry is endless. It is true that once we have a relatively detailed concept of the referent, we assume that the object antedated our experience of it and in fact caused that experience; epistemologically, however, it is the experience which comes first and the notion of the object which comes later. The object, then, is a hypothesis designed to give coherence to our experience, and this hypothesis is derived by hypothetical and inductive reasoning; hence, the process of cognition can be fully described by the three forms of inference. Moreover, it follows that the object must be as we conceive it, since it is only as we conceive it that it is postulated at all, and therefore there can be no such thing as an incognizable cause of cognition, for the postulate that an object exists is warranted only by the coherence it gives to experience. Accordingly, whatever is, is cognizable.

REALITY. The above theory of cognition leads at once to a theory of reality. The object is real, Peirce held, only if as the number of cognitions goes to infinity, the concept of the object tends to a limiting form. It follows, therefore, that although the object is not independent of being thought (since it is only as it is thought that it exists at all), it is nevertheless independent of the thought of any particular man and represents what would be agreed upon by an ideal community of investigators if inquiry were to go on forever.

Many empiricists would agree with Peirce that if the object is real, then if inquiry does go on forever, our hypotheses will converge to a final true description. But few would follow him in holding that the object is real because inquiry converges. What Peirce was attempting to do in this instance was to propound a doctrine which was at once phenomenalistic and realistic. To do this, he had to give a phenomenal definition of reality which would compromise neither the inexhaustibility of the real nor the particularity of the phenomenal, and the infinite series of cognitions seemed to do just that. But could Peirce prove that the infinite series is convergent? In 1868 he thought he could do this by means of an argument which purported to show that the concept of a universe in which induction and hypothesis would not lead to agreement was self-contradictory. When he subsequently discovered that this argument was fallacious, his theory of reality had to be substantially revised.

Universals. Peirce's theory that reality consists in the convergence of inquiry led to a further consequence. For it follows that the real object must be as we conceive it to be, and since, as the "New List" showed, the predicate of a judgment is always general, it further follows that universals are real. On this basis Peirce declared himself a scholastic realist of the moderate, or Scotist, school. The claim is misleading, for whereas the scholastic doctrine rests on the assertion that the universal in the mind and the individual out of the mind have a common nature, Peirce's argument rests on the fact that no cognition is wholly determinate—that is, that there is no true individual, and that therefore everything is to

some degree general. Peirce's "realism" was thoroughly idealistic throughout.

The Third System, 1870–1884

By 1870 Peirce had propounded, in outline at least, an architectonic philosophy based upon the principles that all cognition involves the sign relation; that the sign relation involves three classes of referents; and that these referents are real and can be adequately known by scientific inquiry. But this theory depended upon logical doctrines that Peirce was forced to abandon when he discovered the logic of relations.

The Logic of Relations. The first work on the new logic had been done by Augustus De Morgan, but little progress was made with the subject until Peirce entered the field in 1870. It was in this area that Peirce made his greatest contributions to logic, and it is no exaggeration to say that it was he who created the modern logic of relations. Philosophically these new discoveries in logic had important consequences, for the logic of relations forced Peirce to abandon the subject–predicate theory of the proposition which underlies the "New List," and so required that he overhaul his basic position. Probably the most notable revisions directly attributable to the new logic are the doctrines of pragmatism and the doubt–belief theory of inquiry.

Pragmatism is Peirce's most famous philosophical doctrine, although it was made famous by William James rather than by Peirce.

THE DOUBT–BELIEF THEORY OF INQUIRY. Peirce formulated the doubt–belief theory in 1873, but it was first published in a series of six papers in *Popular Science Monthly* in 1877 and 1878. These papers do not constitute a rejection of the earlier theory of cognition; rather, they elaborate the earlier theory and set it in the context of biological evolution.

Any organism that is to survive, Peirce held, must develop habits of behavior that are adequate to satisfy its needs. Such habits are rules of behavior that prescribe how we should act under given conditions in order to achieve a particular experiential result. Now such habits, when thoroughly adopted, Peirce called beliefs. Since to possess beliefs is to know how to satisfy one's wants, belief is a pleasant state: doubt, or the absence of belief, is an unpleasant state, since one is then uncertain how to act and is unable to attain the desired goals. The organism will therefore seek to escape from doubt and to find belief. The process by which the organism goes from doubt to belief Peirce defined as inquiry. Clearly, there are various methods of inquiry, and the most satisfactory method will be that which leads most surely to the establishment of stable belief—that is, to beliefs that will stand in the long run.

PRAGMATISM. From the standpoint of the inquiring organism, a belief concerning a particular object is significant because it permits the organism to predict what experiences it will have if it acts toward the object in a given way. Recalling Kant's use of the term "pragmatic," namely, ". . . contingent belief, which yet forms the ground for the actual employment of means to certain actions, I entitle *pragmatic belief*" (*Critique of Pure Reason*, A 824, B 852), Peirce propounded what he called the pragmatic theory of meaning, which asserts that what the concept of an object means is simply the set of all habits involving that object. This doctrine involves a major change in Peirce's thinking, and one which is directly due to the logic of relations.

Prior to 1870, Peirce conceived the meaning of a term as the embodied abstraction that it connotes. The meaning of the concept of an object is therefore the same abstraction that is the essence of the object. But once relations were admitted as propositional constituents coordinate with quality, it became possible to conceive the object not only in terms of indwelling qualities but also in terms of relations among its states and with other objects—that is, in terms of its behavior. Accordingly, instead of regarding the behavior of the object as determined by its qualitative essence, the behavior itself may now be regarded as the essence. The meaning of the concept of an object may therefore be given by the set of laws completely specifying the behavior of the object under all conditions. These laws are conditional statements relating test conditions to phenomenal results, and such laws, considered as governing behavior, are habits relating action to experiential effects. Hence, the principle of pragmatism asserts that the concept of the object is synonymous with the set of all such conditionals. Since actual synonymy is asserted, it follows that the concept of a real object can be completely translated into phenomenal terms, but only, it should be noted, into dispositionally phenomenal terms—a point which was to cause Peirce considerable trouble.

Pragmatism: A Theory of Meaning. Pragmatism is Peirce's most famous philosophical doctrine, although it was made famous by William James rather than by Peirce. As Peirce defined it, pragmatism is purely a theory of meaning—not of truth. Moreover, it is a theory of meaning which combines two rather distinct emphases. First, Peirce intended pragmatism to be a principle of scientific definition. By permitting the translation of a concept into phenomenal results that are observable under stated test conditions, the principle legitimizes the use of theoretical constructs in science and thus does much to clarify the nature and status of scientific theory and proof. But when Peirce chose to call the doctrine pragmatism and insisted that the concept must be translatable into "practical effects," the choice of Kantian terminology was not accidental. Peirce was also stressing the utilitarian aspect of science and of all knowledge—that is, the fact that significance lies in the relation to ends desired. Peirce drew no distinction between these two aspects of pragmatism: for him they formed a single doctrine.

Scientific Method. Taken together, pragmatism and the doubt–belief theory imply that the stable beliefs sought by inquiry are in fact the laws of science. The problem of finding the best method of inquiry therefore becomes that of the justification of scientific method, which in Peirce's terms means the justification of induction and hypothesis. Although Peirce formally presented this justification in terms of the operating characteristics of the procedures, he admitted that the relative frequency with which inductive and hypothetical inferences lead to the truth cannot be calculated; hence, our assurance that synthetic inference does ultimately lead to truth comes from the fact that inquiry will converge to a limiting result which is true by definition. Thus, in this instance Peirce admitted that the convergence of inquiry to a final opinion cannot be proven but must be assumed, and since his definition of reality rests upon the convergence of inquiry, this is equivalent to saying that the existence of the real is unprovable and must be assumed. But even as an assumption the doctrine presents problems, for it amounts to saying that if inquiry were to go on forever it would converge, and thus involves fundamental questions concerning counterfactuals.

Counterfactuals. The problem of counterfactuals is central to Peirce's philosophy, and his failure to solve it was one of the chief reasons that his system of the 1870s had to be rejected. Pragmatism requires that the concept of a real object be wholly translatable into a set of conditionals relating test conditions to observations. But then it would seem that the concept of the real object is devoid of content: that is, if the concept of the real object is synonymous with the set of conditionals, each of which is purely phenomenal, then the assertion of reality adds nothing to which a nominalist might object. Peirce, however, did not regard the concept of reality as vacuous; he argued that the conditionals are asserted to be true always, whether actually under test or not. The real, therefore, is a permanent possibility of sensation—not merely a series of sensations. But this leads directly to the counterfactual problem, or the equivalent problem of real possibility. Peirce's theory requires that there be real possible sensations—an assertion that is not only unprovable but pragmatically meaningless, since possible sensations are pragmatically equivalent to actual sensations. Thus, far from proving phenomenalism realistic, Peirce found his position reduced to a subjectivism which was the exact antithesis of the scholastic realism he had hoped to establish.

The Fourth System, 1885–1914

During the years he spent at Johns Hopkins, Peirce was extremely productive in the field of logic. He further developed and extended the calculus of relations and applied it to problems in mathematics. He also clarified and revised his theory of synthetic inference, began the study of the Cantor set theory, and in 1885, with the help of his student, O. H. Mitchell, discovered quantification—a discovery in which Frege had anticipated him by six years. These new developments in logic, together with the rather serious difficulties in his own philosophical position which had become apparent by the end of the 1870s, led Peirce to attempt a radical reformulation of his position in 1885. This reformulation involved a complete revision of the categories, the theory of cognition, and the theory of reality.

THE CATEGORIES. In the 1885 version of the categories, Peirce distinguished sharply between their formal and material aspects. Formally considered, the categories (Firstness, Secondness, and Thirdness) are simply three classes of relations—monadic, dyadic, and triadic. Moreover, Peirce held that these classes are irreducible and that all higher relations (quartic, quintic, etc.) are reducible to some combination of these three. The irreducibility of monadic and dyadic relations is generally admitted. The irreducibility of triadic relations is argued on the ground that all combinatorial relations are triadic, since they involve a relation between two elements and a resulting whole. Granting this, it follows that triadic relations are irreducible, because analysis could only resolve them into components and a combinatorial relation, and that combinatorial relation would itself be triadic. But once the notions of element and combination are given, relations of more than three correlates are easily generated, and so all higher relations may be regarded as being constructed from the three basic types.

Among triadic relations Peirce distinguished pure and degenerate species. A pure triadic relation is one in which no two of the correlates would be related without the third. His example of such a relation is signhood, for the sign relates object and interpretant, the interpretant relates sign and object, and the object, by establishing the identity of the extensional domain, relates

sign and interpretant. Since Peirce held that all thought is in the form of signs, it follows that all thought is irreducibly triadic, which is another way of stating the Kantian doctrine that all thought is synthetic.

Throughout the 1890s Peirce labored at the problem of reconstructing the architectonic theory.

Since a monadic relation is a one-place predicate, the material aspect of Firstness must be qualitative, and Peirce therefore called it quality; what he meant by this term in 1885, however, was not the embodied abstraction that he had described in 1867. Quality now refers not to a concept but to a phenomenal suchness which is the immediate, nonconceptual given of sensation. In the 1885 version, not the concept red, but that suchness of an object which leads us to classify it as red, is a quality.

Peirce called the material aspect of Secondness haecceity, a term derived from Scotus' *haecceitas,* meaning "thisness." As experienced, haecceity is known as shock or brute resistance: Peirce described it as an immediately given, nonconceptual experience of dyadic opposition or "upagainstness." The fact that the experience implies the dynamic interaction of two things, and is therefore dyadic in structure, permits it to qualify as the material aspect of Secondness. For Scotus, haecceity was the principle of individuation, and Peirce accepted this meaning: only individual things have haecceity. It was apparently the discovery of quantification theory which led Peirce to this formulation, for in the variable of quantification theory he found a sign capable of referring directly to an object without describing it, and "thisness" was intended as that property of the object by virtue of which such a reference can be made.

The material aspect of Thirdness is less clearly defined than that of the other two categories. Peirce described it as combination, or mediation, where the latter term signifies either connection or means–ends relations among things. Signhood may also be regarded as part of the material aspect of Thirdness, and so too may generality, since the general constitutes a connection among particulars. Clearly, what Peirce was describing in this instance has much less the character of the immediately given than is the case for the other two categories. The reason is that Peirce not only regarded all thought as triadic—he also regarded all pure triads as conceptual. The material aspect of Thirdness is therefore the experience of thought or rationality. One of Peirce's problems was to explain just how so immaterial a thing can be perceived.

COGNITION. The revision of the categories raised some important problems in regard to cognition. Not only did Peirce have the problem of demonstrating how Thirdness can be perceived, but he also had the problem of explaining how quality and haecceity could be perceived. For in his earlier writings on cognition, Peirce had explicitly denied the existence of first impressions of sense of precisely the sort that he now introduced as the material aspects of his first two categories. Moreover, a further set of problems relating to cognition arose from the doubt–belief theory itself. For in that theory, logic, both deductive and synthetic, is treated as a method whereby an inquiring organism seeks belief. The status of logic, therefore, is that of a useful but contingent means to a sought end—contingent both upon our seeking this particular end, which is a characteristic of the present evolutionary state, and upon our choosing the most efficient of the several available means. Thus, in the doubt–belief theory, logic loses that necessary relation to all possible knowledge which is asserted by the architectonic theory and required to prove the universality of the categories.

Classification of Knowledge. Throughout the 1890s Peirce labored at the problem of reconstructing the architectonic theory. Since the architectonic theory presupposes a classification of knowledge into two classes—logic, and all other knowledge—Peirce's problem was to develop this classification so as to ensure the universality of the categories, while at the same time not contradicting his theory of inquiry. The final system of classification was not attained until 1902. In that system, Peirce divided knowledge into practical (or applied) and theoretical sciences, and then further subdivided the theoretical sciences into sciences of discovery and sciences of review (the latter merely summarizing the findings of the sciences of discovery). The major portion of the classification thus deals with the sciences of discovery. The classification is by presupposition.

The first science is mathematics, which Peirce regarded as presupposed by all others. Mathematics is divided into three branches: mathematics of logic, mathematics of discrete series, and mathematics of continua. It is to the mathematics of logic that Peirce assigned the threefold classification of relations which constitutes the formal aspect of the categories. Next after (and presupposing) mathematics comes philosophy, which Peirce divided into phenomenology, normative science, and metaphysics. Phenomenology, which here appeared in Peirce's writing for the first time, is defined as the study of all that can be before the mind, but in practice, it is devoted to proving that all phenomenal experience is resolvable into three factors, which are the material aspects of the three categories. Thus Peirce sought to show

that his categories, in both their formal and material aspects, are presupposed by all other knowledge.

Normative science has three divisions: aesthetics, ethics, and logic. In this classification logic appears explicitly as the science of how we ought to reason in order to obtain our objectives—whatever they may be. Thus the contingent and utilitarian aspect of logic, first brought out by the doubt–belief theory, is here made central. But reasoning as we ought is only one aspect of acting as we ought, which is the proper subject of ethics: hence, logic presupposes the science of ethics, or the science of how conduct should be regulated to attain our ends. But what our conduct ought to be depends on our aims, and these Peirce held to be the subject of aesthetics, which is the science of what is desirable in and of itself. Hence Peirce subscribed to an aesthetic theory of goodness and made the good and the beautiful coincide.

Following and presupposing philosophy is idioscopy, which Peirce subdivided into the physical and psychical sciences. Each division is further subdivided to yield what we would ordinarily regard as the physical, biological, and social sciences. All domains of science thus fall within the classification, and so depend upon the categories. The classification thus serves the purpose of preserving the architectonic while ensuring the normative role of logic.

Perception. Peirce's determination to preserve both the universality and phenomenal observability of the categories as well as the normative character of logic is evident in the theory of percepts and perceptual judgments which he propounded at this time. According to Peirce, physiology and psychology tell us that our percepts are synthesized from the myriad neural stimuli which assail us from without. Of these neural stimuli themselves and of the process of synthesis we are entirely unaware; the earliest step in cognition of which we are at all conscious is the percept. But we cannot really be said to know the percept; what we know is a perceptual judgment, which is a proposition telling us what the nonlinguistic percept was. The perceptual judgment, such as "red patch here now," is a hypothesis that explains the percept, but it is a peculiar hypothesis, since it is immediate and indubitable. Even if the perceptual judgment is immediately followed by a contradictory perceptual judgment, still that second perceptual judgment relates to a later percept, and it remains indubitable that my first and now forever vanished percept was truly red. Perceptual judgments, therefore, form the real starting point in knowledge and must be taken as the ultimate evidence statements.

Peirce described the processes of synthesis which precede and lead to the perceptual judgment as unconscious inference. Their inferential character is defended, here as in his earlier writings, by an argument that identifies the psychological processes of association with the forms of inferences. But since these processes are unconscious, they are beyond our control and thus are not subject to logical criticism—for logical criticism, being normative, is applicable only to voluntary and controllable behavior. On the other hand, conscious inferences, such as the processes whereby we derive knowledge from the perceptual judgments, are thoroughly subject to logical criticism. Accordingly, Peirce could hold both that there is no first impression of sense and that the object (percept) is given to us by a synthesis in intuition. He could further hold that our knowledge has a definite starting point in propositions which give direct reports of phenomenal observation and that whatever is asserted in those judgments of perception must be accepted as given. Thus, in the theory of percepts and perceptual judgments, Peirce tried to reconcile his denial of first impressions with his doctrine of direct phenomenal contact with the world.

Like all students of scientific method,

Peirce was perplexed by the problem

of how we discover true hypotheses.

On the basis of this theory, Peirce held that the material aspects of all three categories are empirically observable. Quality and *haecceity* are argued to be directly observable aspects of the percept. But so, too, according to Peirce, is Thirdness, for what is asserted in the perceptual judgment is necessarily true, and the perceptual judgment, being a proposition, has a predicate which is general. Since the generality is given in the perceptual judgment, and since criticism cannot go behind the perceptual judgment, this generality must be regarded as given in perception, and hence as being observable. Thus, by phenomenological analysis, all the categories can be shown to be present in experience.

REALITY. In the course of his study of the logic of relations, Peirce noted that the analysis of certain relations leads to an infinite regress. Thus the relation "in the relation R to" must itself be related to its subjects by the same relation, for example, "in the relation 'in the relation R to' to," and so on. Such relations, which can be analyzed only into relations of the same sort, Peirce called continuous relations, since they fit the definition of the continuum as that of which every part is of the same nature as the whole. They are, according to Peirce's theory, pure triadic relations; therefore their irreducibility follows from the irreducibility of Thirdness. Moreover, since every relation must be related to its

subjects by some such relation, Peirce drew the conclusion that all relations involve a continuous relation.

Continua. During the 1880s, Peirce had become acquainted with Georg Cantor's work on set theory, which bears directly on the problem of continuity. Recognizing at once the great importance of Cantor's work for both logic and mathematics, Peirce undertook the study of the foundations of mathematics and attempted to construct his own theory of cardinal and ordinal numbers. Peirce's papers on this subject are highly technical, and only the briefest summary of them can be given here. In developing his theory of cardinal numbers, Peirce discovered a form of the paradox of the greatest cardinal. His efforts to solve this paradox led him to the erroneous conclusion that the series of transfinite cardinals is only countably infinite and has an upper limit which is the power of the linear continuum. It follows that if the continuum consisted of discrete elements, then there would exist a greatest cardinal, and to avoid this conclusion he held the continuum to be a "potential" set consisting of possible points. Accordingly, although subsets of any multitude may be actualized from the continuum, nevertheless, not all of the possible points are actualizable, since if they were, we should have a greatest cardinal and hence a contradiction. Peirce believed that by such arguments he had established that whatever is truly continuous involves unactualized possibility; hence the problem of the existence of real possibility, which he had found insoluble in the 1870s, was now reduced to that of the reality of continuity. Peirce used the arguments of Zeno in an attempt to prove that space and time must be truly continuous in his (Peirce's) sense, and he went on to argue that continuous relations are truly continuous both intensively and extensively. In defining the continuum as that of which every part is the same sort as the whole, Peirce was brought to the conclusion that real relations, and so real laws, are in some sense continua.

Synechism. The doctrine that the world contains real continua Peirce called synechism. He regarded this as his most important philosophical doctrine and preferred to have his whole philosophy called by this name. He also asserted that it was a modern form of scholastic realism. Scholastic or not, it is certainly realistic, for it holds that the external referents of true laws are real continua which, since they involve unactualized possibilities, contain real generality. To support this doctrine, Peirce had to define an ontology which would explain what those referents might be. Peirce was no stranger to such an enterprise. He began his work in philosophy in the 1850s, with the doctrine of the three ontological categories, and although he subsequently redefined the categories several times in less ontological fashion, he never forgot the question of what realities lay behind his categories. It is therefore not surprising that following the 1885 revision of the categories, Peirce returned to the problem of ontology, and this soon led him to propound an evolutionary cosmology.

EVOLUTIONARY COSMOLOGY. Peirce had several reasons for formulating an evolutionary cosmology in the 1890s. Not only did synechism require a clarification of his ontological commitments, but he was also impelled toward such a formulation by problems arising within the theory of cognition. First, the doubt–belief theory, by imbedding inquiry within an evolutionary context, made the utility of scientific method relative to a particular evolutionary adaptation, the permanence of which is by no means guaranteed and must therefore be investigated.

A second reason for Peirce's formulating an evolutionary cosmology in the 1890s springs from his doctrine of critical common sense. Like all students of scientific method, Peirce was perplexed by the problem of how we discover true hypotheses. Considering the infinity of possible false hypotheses, it is evident that not even Peirce's theory of synthetic inference could account for the remarkable frequency with which we do, in fact, find a true explanatory hypothesis. Utilizing the evolutionary doctrines current at the time (including the inheritance of acquired characteristics), Peirce argued that the human mind must possess some innate adaptation which enables us to guess the correct laws of nature more readily than pure chance would allow. Such an adaptation would mean that true hypotheses appear to us peculiarly simple and natural. According to Peirce, it follows, then, that judgments of common sense, conceived through the mechanism of the inheritance of acquired characteristics as quasi-instinctual beliefs that have been built up through centuries of experience, should have a greater probability of being true than have parvenu doctrines. But this probability is at best low, so that common-sense judgments cannot be accepted without critical analysis and careful test. Thus Peirce's doctrine of common sense is thoroughly critical: common sense is to be regarded as a likely source of true hypotheses, but no hypothesis is to be accepted without empirical validation. But in terms of the doubt–belief theory, this doctrine leads to a serious problem. Should the course of evolution alter significantly, our innate adaptation, which has proven so useful in the past, would become positively harmful, since it would direct us to seek explanations in terms of an adaptation that no longer obtains. Accordingly, it becomes a question of considerable moment to inquire what the future course of evolution will be.

The Continuous External Referent. In the doubt–belief theory, Peirce had formulated the principle that a law, which he conceived as governing the behavior of an organism, is a habit. Now a habit, considered as a psychological entity, is a connection among feeling states and actions, and this connection, Peirce held, must consist in an actual substantive continuity among them. Peirce based this assertion on a variety of arguments, including the felt continuity of mental phenomena (the impossibility of memory without continuous connection between past and present) and certain arguments drawn from the behavior of protoplasm under stimulation. It was therefore Peirce's doctrine that habit, considered as a psychological entity, is a continuum corresponding to a law that is conceived as governing behavior. To find continuous external referents for all laws, Peirce asserted that the universe is itself a living organism possessed of feelings and habits and that our laws of nature describe the habits of the universe. Thus, after 1885, the subjective idealism of Peirce's early writings became an extreme form of objective idealism.

When the doubt–belief theory

is applied to the organic universe itself,

the result is an evolutionary cosmology.

Knowledge, Feeling, Volition. From the position that the universe is an organism, it follows that all our experience of the external world must be describable as experience of some state or behavior of this organism. But the possible forms of experience are defined by the material aspects of the categories, while Peirce took the possible components of mind to be defined by the traditional division into knowledge, volition, and feeling. He had already identified knowledge with belief-habit and made it the correspondent of law, or Thirdness. He now identified feeling as the correspondent of Firstness and volition as the correspondent of Secondness. But the doctrine asserts more than mere correspondence, for Peirce seeks to account for the fact that all our experience can be classified by the categories, and his explanation for this fact is that what is for the cosmic organism feeling, volition, and belief is experienced by the individual as Firstness, Secondness, and Thirdness.

Chaos and Order. The habits created through inquiry are, objectively viewed, laws of behavior. What then, according to Peirce, is doubt, or the absence of belief? In the state of doubt, there will be feeling, but no habit and no order—hence, objectively viewed, the state of doubt will appear as purely random or chance behavior. Thus, objective orderliness or randomness corresponds to states of the universe in which habit is either strong or weak. The irritation of doubt is redefined as an intense consciousness associated with states of unordered feeling; as order or habit increases, the intensity of consciousness declines until, in the case in which virtually complete regularity has been established, it is so low as to be all but undetectable. Mind that is so hidebound with habit we regard as dead matter.

When the doubt–belief theory is applied to the organic universe itself, the result is an evolutionary cosmology. In the beginning, Peirce held, there is nothing but an undifferentiated continuum of pure feeling wholly without order—a primal chaos. From this starting point, the universe evolves by means of the development of habits. We have here the typical Spencerian passage from homogeneity to heterogeneity, but without benefit of Spencer's mechanical model. In the course of time, the universe becomes ever more orderly, but at any given time its habits remain less than perfectly regular and there are still areas requiring the further fixation of belief.

This cosmology is the basis for Peirce's doctrine of tychism—that there is absolute chance in the universe. For as law is the objective manifestation of habit, so chance is the objective manifestation of lack of habit; hence the primal undifferentiated continuum of feeling is literally a world of pure chance. Evolution constantly diminishes the amount of objective chance in the universe, but only in the limit does it wholly disappear. At any given time, some chance remains, and the laws of nature are not yet wholly exact.

Pragmatism and Universal Evolution. The doubt–belief theory describes inquiry as an attempt to escape the irritation of doubt. But it is hardly proper to say that the universe seeks to escape from doubt, and some better motive is required. The state toward which the universe is evolving is, according to Peirce's theory, one of complete order. Since such a state involves the complete subjection of feeling and action to belief, Peirce regarded it as the realization of rationality in the concrete, or, in his terms, of "concrete reasonableness." But it is also a state of maximum beauty, for Peirce's aesthetic is a coherence theory of beauty. Accordingly, the normative theory of inquiry may be brought to bear in explaining the evolutionary process. The end sought is concrete reasonableness; the means, supplied by ethics, is the regulation of conduct by this aim. In the area of inquiry, this implies the discovery of those laws necessary to regulate behavior. Thus pragmatism, or pragmaticism, as Peirce renamed his doctrine after 1905 in order to distinguish it from James's, also serves the cause of evolution, for in translating the concept into a set of habits we discover the practical effects of the object— that is, how our conduct is affected. It remains for scientific inquiry, then, to discover the truth or falsity of potential habits and hence to fix belief. Thus the course of universal evolution and our modes of inquiry must remain ever in harmony, for the objective logic of evolution is identical with the logic of discovery. All nature works by a common process to a common end, and the duty of the individual man is to aid that process by devoting himself to scientific inquiry.

BIBLIOGRAPHY

Works by Peirce

The Collected Papers of Charles Sanders Peirce, Vols. I–VI, Charles Hartshorne and Paul Weiss, eds., Cambridge, Mass., 1931– 1935; Vols. VII–VIII, Arthur Burks, ed., Cambridge, Mass., 1958. This is the basic published collection of Peirce's writings. (The usual method of citation to these volumes is by volume number, followed by a decimal point and the paragraph number—for example, 3.456.)

Charles S. Peirce's Letters to Lady Welby, Irwin Leib, ed. New Haven, 1953. These letters, written between 1903 and 1911, are largely devoted to the theory of signs and contain some of Peirce's best writings on that subject.

Works on Peirce

Buchler, Justus, *Charles Peirce's Empiricism.* New York, 1939. An incisive study of Peirce's more empirical doctrines, with particular emphasis on pragmatism and common-sensism.

Feibleman, James, *An Introduction to Peirce's Philosophy, Interpreted as a System.* New York, 1946. A broad but superficial survey.

Gallie, W. B., *Peirce and Pragmatism.* Harmondsworth, England, 1952. A thoughtful book devoted chiefly to Peirce's pragmatism.

Goudge, Thomas A., *The Thought of C. S. Peirce.* Toronto, 1950. Goudge holds that Peirce's work contains two contradictory positions, which he calls naturalism and transcendentalism. The book is an exposition of this thesis and of its implications.

Lewis, Clarence I., *A Survey of Symbolic Logic.* Berkeley, 1918. Ch. 1, Sec. 7. This is still the best essay on Peirce's work in logic.

Moore, Edward C., and Robin, Richard S., eds., *Studies in the Philosophy of Charles Sanders Peirce, Second Series.* Amherst, Mass., 1964.

Murphey, Murray G., *The Development of Peirce's Philosophy.* Cambridge, Mass., 1961. An attempt to interpret Peirce's work chronologically and systematically through the architectonic principle.

Thompson, Manley, *The Pragmatic Philosophy of C. S. Peirce.* Chicago, 1953. A thoughtful and systematic study of Peirce's pragmatism and related problems.

Wiener, Philip and Young, Harold, eds., *Studies in the Philosophy of Charles Sanders Peirce.* Cambridge, Mass., 1952. This collection of essays on Peirce's philosophy is extremely uneven: it contains some excellent articles and some very poor ones. The papers by Savan, Thompson, Fisch and Cope, and Weiss are particularly good.

Weiss, Paul, "Charles Sanders Peirce," in *Dictionary of American Biography.* New York, 1934. Vol. XIV. A very fine biographical article on Peirce.

– MURRAY G. MURPHEY

PEIRCE, CHARLES SANDERS (UPDATE)

Charles Sanders Peirce (1839–1914), one of America's most original philosophers, produced a body of work remarkable for its scope and enduring relevance. For many years Peirce's principal contributions to mainstream philosophy were in logic and philosophy of science, but changes in the philosophic terrain since 1967 have brought new areas of his thought to prominence. The resurgence of interest in pragmatism, due in large measure to its promotion by Richard Rorty, and the adoption of Peirce by the Frankfurt School as the philosopher who may hold the key to the problem of modernity, have brought attention to Peirce's unique brand of pragmatism and to his philosophy of signs. Outside of philosophy, the active interdisciplinary field of semiotics that began in Chicago with Charles Morris acknowledges Peirce as the founder of modern sign theory.

> *Peirce was a late child of the Enlightenment,*
>
> *a staunch believer in the universal applicability*
>
> *of mathematics and in the continuous growth*
>
> *of knowledge through sustained inquiry.*

Peirce was a late child of the enlightenment, a staunch believer in the universal applicability of mathematics and in the continuous growth of knowledge through sustained inquiry. He was a diligent student of the history of science and understood that the advancement of knowledge is crucially linked to nondeductive (inductive and abductive) reasoning and shared experimental methods. He was convinced that a prerequisite for successful experimentation is an external world resistant to actions arising from misconceptions of it. These views led Peirce to an anti-Cartesian epistemology rooted in perceptual experience and committed to fallibilism and the repudiation of deductive foundationalism. Peirce generalized his view of the advancement of science to all forms of learning from experience, and he concluded that all meaningful conceptions are necessarily related to experiential expectations (conceived consequences). This is the epistemological motivation for his meaning-focused pragmatism (pragmaticism).

Sometimes Peirce is said to have equated truth with settled belief, but that applies only when belief is settled as the result of a steadfast application of scientific method. Other methods for overcoming doubt and settling belief, such as the a priori method or the methods of tenacity and authority, while not without some advantages, do not provide grounds for confidence that truth will be reached. Even the sustained application of scientific method can never issue in a guarantee that inquiry has "stormed the citadel of truth." Truth is always relative to propositions and is, therefore, grounded in the conventionality of symbolism (for propositions can only be expressed symbolically). The true represents the real precisely insofar as inquiry forces beliefs to yield to the dictates of an independent reality, but the "correspondence" of truth and reality that is hoped for at the end of inquiry is at best an ideal limit; we can never be certain that we have reached the truth. This is Peirce's fallibilism. It is typical of Peirce's philosophy that truth and reality are correlates in a triadic relation, where the mediating relate involves a community of inquirers (interpreters).

Peirce believed that the key to intelligence of any kind is sign action (which is always goal directed), and he formulated an elaborate semiotic theory to facilitate the analysis and classification of signs. Peirce's division of signs into icons, indexes, and symbols is his best-known semiotic bequest—although his distinction between tones, tokens, and types is also widely used—but these are only two of many triads that permeate his philosophy. Peirce held that minds are sign systems and thoughts are sign actions, and it is not too far-fetched to say that the mission of his semiotic is similar to that of modern-day cognitive science. Peirce's epistemological shift from a focus on ideas to signs marks him as a forerunner, if not a founder, of philosophy's so-called linguistic turn and, also, of the modern—and postmodern—emphasis on textualism. Peirce's triadic theory of signs distinguishes semiotics from semiology, a generally dyadic theory of signs stemming from the work of Ferdinand de Saussure. Recently there have been attempts to reconcile these two approaches.

Current interest in Peirce's thought extends over most of philosophy. Peirce's graphical logic (his existential graphs) is used as a basis for computational linguistics. The recent move away from logicism has led to renewed interest in Peirce's philosophy of logic, according to which logic is not the epistemic foundation for mathematics. The rehabilitation of systematic and speculative thought has attracted attention to Peirce's evolutionary cosmology, which holds that the principal constituents of the universe are chance, law, and habit formation. Peirce insisted that change is really operative in nature (his tychism), that continuity, in general, prevails (his synechism), and that love or sympathy has a real influence on the course of events (his agapism). He contributed America's most original and thoroughgoing phenomenology (his phaneroscopy), and he advanced unique views on religion and on the significance of sentiment and instinct. He stressed the importance of the existent and the individual while, at the same time, admiring the ideal and insisting that rationality is rooted in the social. Peirce's intellectual legacy is a rich system of thought that helps organize and unify a broad array of issues in modern philosophy.

[See also Cognitive Science; Philosophy of Science; Pragmatism; Truth.]

BIBLIOGRAPHY

Works by Peirce

Complete Published Works Including Selected Secondary Material (microfiche edition), edited by K. L. Ketner et al. Greenwich, CT, 1977. A companion bibliography is also available: *A Comprehensive Bibliography of the Published Works of Charles Sanders Peirce with a Bibliography of Secondary Studies,* edited by K. L. Ketner. Greenwich, CT, 1977. Rev. ed., Bowling Green, OH, 1986.

The Essential Peirce: Selected Philosophical Writings, 2 vols., edited by N. Houser and C. Kloesel. Bloomington, IN, 1992–97.

A History of Science: Historical Perspectives on Peirce's Logic of Science, 2 vols., edited by C. Eisele. The Hague, 1985.

The New Elements of Mathematics by Charles S. Peirce, 4 vols., edited by C. Eisele. The Hague, 1976.

Reasoning and the Logic of Things: The Cambridge Conferences Lectures of 1898, edited by K. L. Ketner. Cambridge, MA, 1992.

Writings of Charles S. Peirce: A Chronological Edition, edited by the Peirce Edition Project. Bloomington, IN, 1982–.

Works on Peirce

Apel, K.-O. *Charles S. Peirce: From Pragmatism to Pragmaticism,* trans. J. M. Krois. Amherst, MA, 1981.

Brent, J. *Charles Sanders Peirce: A Life.* Bloomington, IN, 1993.

Burch, R. W. *A Peircean Reduction Thesis.* Lubbock, TX, 1991.

Delaney, C. F. *Science, Knowledge, and Mind: A Study in the Philosophy of C. S. Peirce.* Notre Dame, IN, 1993.

Eisele, C. *Studies in the Scientific and Mathematical Philosophy of Charles S. Peirce,* edited by R. M. Martin. The Hague, 1979.

Esposito, J. L. *Evolutionary Metaphysics: The Development of Peirce's Theory of Categories.* Athens, OH, 1980.

Fisch, M. H. *Peirce, Semeiotic, and Pragmatism,* edited by K. L. Ketner and C. J. W. Kloesel. Bloomington, IN, 1986.

Freeman, E., ed. *The Relevance of Charles Peirce.* La Salle, IL, 1983.

Hausman, C. R. *Charles S. Peirce's Evolutionary Philosophy.* Cambridge, 1993.

Hookway, C. *Peirce.* London, 1985.

Houser, N., D. D. Roberts, and J. Van Evra, eds. *Studies in the Logic of Charles S. Peirce.* Bloomington, IN, 1996.

Ketner, K. L., ed. *Peirce and Contemporary Thought: Philosophical Inquiries.* New York, 1995.

Murphey, M. G. *The Development of Peirce's Philosophy.* Cambridge, MA, 1961.

Raposa, M. L. *Peirce's Philosophy of Religion.* Bloomington, IN, 1989.

Roberts, D. D. *The Existential Graphs of Charles S. Peirce.* The Hague, 1973.

— NATHAN HOUSER

PERCEPTION

Broadly speaking, the Kantian tradition on the topic of perception is the view that perception is essentially a conceptual event or act. That is, each event or act of perception either is, or essentially includes, a conceptual component, usually regarded as a judging or the making of a judgment. And since judgments, when made, have propositional form, we can speak by extension of perception being or essentially including some propositional component. Of course, it is granted that there is more to perception than the conceptual element; there is also a sensory constituent, related in an important but variously specified way to the conceptual.

One familiar account of this relation is provided in causal theories of perception. On such a theory, as a result of a causal relation to the world a person experiences a sensation, which experience in turn occasions a judging or a taking something to be the case. On many versions of this theory, it is this latter element— the judging or taking—that, strictly speaking, is the perception. The experience of the sensation is causally necessary for, and so is a constant accompaniment of, a perception; but the sensory element is not strictly a constituent element in the event of perception.

The Kantian tradition is somewhat different from the causal theory, inasmuch as the conceptual factor and the sensory factor are both reckoned constituent elements in the perception. A perceptual event is an organic whole, a single event that has conceptual and sensory events as parts in something like the way that a complex event has simpler events as parts. An event of perception, then, is not to be identified with just the judging element, nor with the sensory element taken alone. Instead, perception is construed as the combined entity—sensing-and-judging.

The Kantian tradition has been well represented in philosophical work on perception over the past few decades. A case in point is the work of Wilfrid Sellars. On Sellars's view, sensations are theoretical entities we must postulate as occurring in perceptual experiences if we are adequately to explain perceptual propositional attitudes. These posits, what Sellars terms sense impressions, are not themselves objects of perceptual awareness, such as sensa. Instead, he construes sense impressions as events of sensing, along the lines of the adverbial account of sensations, so that a sense impression of red is the event of sensing red-ly. These sensing events, moreover, are wholly nonconceptual, not to be thought of as cognitive events.

The conceptual component included in every perception is a judging. Sellars typically represents a perception of an object as perceiving there to be something present before one. So, seeing a teacup on the table he takes as seeing there to be a teacup on the table. Sellars rejects the suggestion that the judging ingredient in this simple perception is to be expressed by "This is a teacup which is on a table" because he holds that the pure demonstrative "this" does not do justice to the complexity of the situation. Instead, he would express the judgment made as "This-teacup-before-me-now is on the table." This complex demonstrative is a fused expression, mental tokening of which Sellars treats as a taking *as* or a believing *in*. And, though the tokening is directed at the teacup on the table, in fact he tells us that the demonstrative refers to the sense impression. This is *mis-taking as,* which occurs even in veridical perception.

The judging proper Sellars takes to be a believing-*that*. It is believing, of what is in fact a sense impression, that it is on a table. The judging alone, however, is not itself the perception of the teacup. That event is the complex event consisting of the event of sensing, which is a cause of the events of tokening the relevant demonstrative and the judging.

Sellars's theory, here given just for what he terms the "manifest image," is a species of direct realism. It does not countenance phenomenal entities as perceived intermediaries, as in the causal theory; and the mental tokening of the complex demonstrative is "directed at" the external physical object.

Another species of direct realism which stresses the importance of judgments is the theory of Romane Clark. Clark holds that the occurrence of a sense impression in a simple context of object perception literally is or contains demonstrative reference, typically to the cause of that occurrence. Sense impressions are not phenomenal individuals, and thus do not function as perceptual intermediaries, just as in Sellars's account. Their demonstrative reference will vary with context, just as the reference of linguistic demonstratives varies with change in context. However, unlike either Sellars or Kant, Clark takes the sense impressions themselves also to be conceptual entities: ". . . sense impressions are fully constitutive of sensuous judgments. They are not the contexts in which such judgments occur. They make up such judgments. They are, then, after all, conceptual entities" (Clark, 1973, p. 53).

Marginally related to the Kantian tradition are epistemic theories of perception. These theories, developed by David M. Armstrong and George Pitcher, may be characterized negatively as dispensing with sensations, at least for purposes of explicating perception; and positively as the thesis that perception is essentially an observer's acquisition of specific beliefs in certain ways, such as by the use of the sense organs. In the simplest case of veridical perception of a teacup, for example, the perception is just the acquisition of sundry teacup beliefs on that occasion and in that causal context. In cases where the perceived object appears differently from the way it is, as when a round pond appears elliptical, it is held that one acquires an inclination to believe that the pond is elliptical, where an inclination to believe is ac-

tually a belief (that the pond is elliptical) which is held in check or overridden by some stronger beliefs, perhaps by the background belief that this pond is actually round. And in a small number of cases, where it seems neither beliefs nor inclinations thereto are acquired, perception is identified with coming to be in a potential belief state (Armstrong), or with acquisition of a suppressed inclination to believe (Pitcher). Their ideas are similar: in these cases one comes to be in a state which would have been a belief state had certain inhibiting factors, most commonly other beliefs, not been present.

Husserl takes perception to be

a paradigm case of an intentional act,

and so it is an act directed at an object.

The beliefs or inclinations to belief one acquires will naturally be causally prompted by some object, in typical cases; and the beliefs or inclinations are held to be about this object, though of course they need not be in all cases correct. But in the normal case of veridical perception, this event just is the acquisition of true beliefs about the object.

Epistemic theories are marginally related to the Kantian tradition. They stress belief acquisition, and so require possession and utilization of various concepts as a constituent element in each perception. But these theories include no provision for demonstrative reference, do not reckon perception as having a judgmental ingredient, and dispense with the role of sensations, however construed, in perception.

Another theory, which has but a slight connection to the Kantian tradition, is Husserl's. Husserl distinguishes between perception of objects and perception of facts. The latter he would take as including a judgment, but then so would everyone. There is no judging in the account Husserl gives of perception of objects, however, even though there is a role for concepts.

Husserl held that in every case of perception of objects there is some sensory input, what he calls "hyle" or "hyletic data." These are experiences that are not themselves conceptual events, and neither are they objects of perception. In these respects, Husserl's view of hyle is similar to Sellars's account of sense impressions.

Husserl takes perception to be a paradigm case of an intentional act, and so it is an act directed at an object—in the typical, veridical case, an external physical object or a quality of one. The directed nature of the act is not achieved by the fact that the hyle is caused by the external object, but rather by means of the hyle being "informed" or "filled." This filling or informing, any instance of which Husserl calls a *noesis,* is a bestowal of meaning to the hyle. The complex act, hyle-plus-meaning bestowal, constitutes perception of an object.

The example of the teacup can again be used. One looks at the teacup and, in the normal case, one is caused to have certain sensory experiences (hyle), which are interpreted as of a teacup. The latter interpreting is the meaning-bestowing phase or noesis; it supplies the directedness ingredient in the act. Semantically, the result of hyle thus informed by a noesis is best expressed by a complex demonstrative, perhaps, "This teacup now before me . . ." For this meaning-bestowal to occur, the agent must possess the relevant concept, and indeed this concept is used since it informs the hyle. But it is not used to make a judgment, or to predicate anything of the referent of the demonstrative. Instead, it is what gives sense to the demonstrative.

As a result of the meaning-bestowal phase acting on the hyle, one sees the teacup as a teacup. This event is strictly analogous, I believe, to Sellars's notion of "believing-in," and is connected in the same way to a complex demonstrative. But for neither of these philosophers is the seeing-as to be construed as a judging or as a predication, despite the fact that concepts are necessary if meaning-bestowing or interpretation is to occur.

Theories that seem to lie completely outside the Kantian framework have also been developed since the late 1960s. A nonepistemic account of seeing was proposed by Fred Dretske, where a nonepistemic theory is one in which a person's seeing an object does not logically require that the person thereby acquire any beliefs (nor, presumably, any knowledge) about that object. It requires, at most, that the agent visually discriminate the object from its background and from neighboring objects. Nor, for a nonepistemic theory, is perception to be explicated so as to include the making of a judgment.

A more general version of Dretske's view, applying to all of perception, has been worked out by James Cornman. For him, the sensory element of perception is explicated along adverbial lines; seeing something red, e.g., is taken to include sensing red-ly. More generally, perception of an object E is taken to include an event of E-sensing. What distinguishes Cornman's version of direct realism is that the event of E-sensing is held to be all there is to perception of an object or a quality of an object. He says that "Each event of a person having an experience of something, E, is identical with some event of the person E-sensing" (Cornman, 1975, p. 340). What is interesting is the manner in which Cornman construes E-sensing. Where Q is a minimal sensible quality of an object E (roughly, observable occurrent properties), then E-sensing is thought of as E-as-Q-sensing. In this way, Cornman's view is akin to

Husserl's, though Cornman makes no mention of the concepts necessary to perceive an object E as Q.

[See also Armstrong, David M.; Epistemology; Husserl, Edmund; Kant, Immanuel; Realism; Sellars, Wilfrid.]

BIBLIOGRAPHY

Armstrong, D. M. *A Materialist Theory of the Mind.* New York, 1968.
Clark, R. "Sensuous Judgments," *Noûs,* Vol. 7 (1973).
———. "Considerations for a Logic for Naive Realism," in P. Machamer and R. Turnbull, eds., *Studies in Perception* (Columbus, OH, 1978).
———. "Seeing and Inferring," *Philosophical Papers,* Vol. 22, 1993.
Cornman, J. *Perception, Common Sense and Science.* New Haven, 1975.
Dretske, F. *Seeing and Knowing.* New York, 1969.
Husserl, E. *Logical Investigations* [1901]. Translated by J. J. Findlay. New York, 1970.
———. *Ideas: General Introduction to Pure Phenomenology* [1913]. Translated by W. Boyce Gibson. London, 1931.
Pitcher, G. *A Theory of Perception.* Princeton. NJ, 1971.
Sellars, W. *Science, Perception and Reality.* New York, 1963.
———. "Givenness and Explanatory Coherence," a typescript widely circulated in 1973. A much shorter version of this paper, with no material on perception, was published in *Journal of Philosophy,* 1973.
———. "Reflections on Perceptual Consciousness," a typescript widely circulated in 1975 and presented as a lecture at Marquette University.
———. "Berkeley and Descartes: Reflections on the Theory of Ideas," in P. Machamer and R. Turnbull, eds., *Studies in Perception* (Columbus, OH, 1978).
———. "Sensa or Sensings: Reflections on the Ontology of Perception," *Philosophical Studies,* Vol. 41 (1982).
Soltis, J. *Seeing, Knowing and Believing.* London, 1966.

Commentary

Follesdal, D. "Brentano and Husserl on Intentional Objects and Perception," and "Husserl's Theory of Perception," in H. Dreyfus, ed., *Husserl, Intentionality and Cognitive Science* (Cambridge, MA, 1982).
Maund, J. B. "The Non-Sensuous Epistemic Account of Perception," *American Philosophical Quarterly,* Vol. 13 (1976).
Mulligan, K. "Husserl on Perception," in D. Smith and B. Smith, eds., *The Cambridge Companion to Husserl* (New York, 1995).
Pappas, G. "Perception Without Belief," *Ratio,* Vol. 19 (1977).
Smith, D., and R. McIntyre. *Husserl and Intentionality.* Dordrecht, 1984.

– GEORGE S. PAPPAS

PERSISTENCE

The data of theories of persistence—that is, of identity across time—are cross-temporal identity sentences. For example:

The huge elm in the garden is the sapling Grandfather planted on his tenth birthday.

Cross-temporal identity sentences (CTISs) seem to be equivalent to regimented cross-temporal identity sentences, sentences consisting of two time-involving definite descriptions (or terms) flanking the identity sign. Thus, the above CTIS seems to be equivalent to:

> The x such that x is now a huge elm in the garden = the x such that Grandfather planted x on his tenth birthday and x was then a sapling.

Theories of identity across time may be usefully categorized by reference to CTISs and regimented CTISs.

According to temporal-slice theories, the terms of a regimented CTIS refer—if they refer to anything—to instantaneous slices of temporally extended four-dimensional objects. For example. 'The x such that x is now a huge elm in the garden' refers to a huge, elm-shaped thing that exists only at the present moment.

There are two temporal-slice theories. According to revisionist temporal-slice theory, a CTIS is equivalent to the regimented CTIS it seems to be equivalent to. Since no regimented CTIS is true (its terms refer to objects that do not simultaneously exist and are therefore not identical), our everyday utterances of CTISs express falsehoods. According to reconciliationist temporal-slice theory, a CTIS is not equivalent to the regimented CTIS it seems to be equivalent to. The words, phrases, or grammatical constructions in CTISs that seem to express numerical identity instead express 'gen-identity', the relation that holds between two temporal slices just in the case that there is some extended four-dimensional whole of which they are both slices. (The question, In what cases is a certain region of space-time occupied by a "whole"? will not be addressed in this article.) A CTIS—a misnomer, because the class of sentences so designated are not identity sentences—can very well be true. It might be, for example, that 'the huge elm in the garden' and 'the sapling Grandfather planted on his tenth birthday' designate two instantaneous slices of one temporally extended four-dimensional object.

There are two theories of identity across time that are not temporal-slice theories. According to temporal-whole theory, the terms of a regimented CTIS denote four-dimensional wholes and could well denote the same whole. Regimented CTISs can therefore easily be true. CTISs are equivalent to the regimented CTISs they seem to be equivalent to and can easily be true. According to continuant theory the terms of regimented CTISs denote 'continuants', things that exist at more than one time and are capable of having different—in fact, logically incompatible—properties at different times. Continuants are not extended in time in any way that is analogous to spatial extension. Continuants have no proper temporal parts; there is no such thing as 'the temporal part of the elm that occupied the

year 1952', for such a thing would have been spatially coextensive with the elm throughout 1952, and no other thing has ever been spatially coextensive with the elm. Regimented CTISs can well be true. It might well be that one could write the two phrases 'the x such that x is now a huge elm in the garden' and 'the x such that Grandfather planted x on his tenth birthday and x was then a sapling' on two slips of paper, paste both slips on a certain tree, and thus twice correctly label it. (And doing that would not be twice labeling either a four-dimensional tree or one of its slices but rather a thing that is in the garden now and was in the garden when it was younger and smaller.) CTISs are equivalent to the regimented CTISs they seem to be equivalent to and can easily be true.

There are several well-known arguments

for and against temporal-whole theory

and continuant theory, and there are

well-known "standard" replies to these arguments.

Temporal-whole theory seems to be superior to both versions of temporal-slice theory. The three theories require more or less the same ontology, but temporal-whole theory seems to provide a more satisfying account of the way in which the objects contained in that ontology are related semantically to CTISs.

There are several well-known arguments for and against temporal-whole theory and continuant theory, and there are well-known "standard" replies to these arguments. (Only arguments directly related to the problem of identity across time will be considered here.)

First, it could be said that continuant theory implies that a persisting object must have incompatible properties. The sapling is not a full-grown elm; if, therefore, the sapling and the elm are numerically identical, there is an object that both is and is not a full-grown elm. To this objection continuant theory replies that there is one object that *is now* a full-grown elm and *was once* a sapling. Continuant theory, therefore, does not ascribe incompatible properties to this object. The "temporally relativized" properties being-a-full-grown-elm-now and being-a-sapling-on-Grandfather's-tenth-birthday do indeed belong ("timelessly") to the same continuant, but these two properties are compatible. (David Lewis, 1986, has posed a problem for continuant theory—"the problem of temporary intrinsics"—that is based on a more sophisticated version of this argument.)

Second, temporal-whole theory faces "counting" problems. Suppose there is now one elm in the garden.

Temporal-whole theory implies that there are now in the garden (in the only sense in which any extended four-dimensional object can be 'now in the garden') a vast number of things—temporal parts of the 'whole tree'—that now have just the properties that the referent of 'the elm in the garden' is supposed to have. But only *one* thing now in the garden has those properties. To this, temporal-whole theory replies that there is nothing paradoxical about this, as a simple spatial analogy shows: the river that flows past this point has a vast number of parts that have *here* the same properties as the "whole river."

Third, temporal-whole theory implies that change is an illusion. A four-dimensional tree would be static; it could "grow" only in the sense of having a temporal part that comprised successively larger spatial "cross-sections." The reply to this is that a river may grow wider as it proceeds along its course; temporal change is precisely analogous to such "spatial change."

[See also Identity; Metaphysics.]

BIBLIOGRAPHY

Chisholm, R. M. *Person and Object: A Metaphysical Study.* La Salle, IL, 1976.

Heller, M. *The Ontology of Physical Objects.* Cambridge, 1990.

Jubien, M. *Ontology, Modality, and the Fallacy of Reference.* Cambridge, 1993.

Lewis, D. *On the Plurality of Worlds.* Oxford, 1986.

———. "Survival and Identity," in A. O. Rorty, ed., *The Identities of Persons* (Berkeley, 1976). Reprinted in D. Lewis, *Philosophical Papers,* Vol. 1 (New York, 1983), with postscripts. See particularly postscript B, "In Defense of Stages."

Thomson, J. J. "Parthood and Identity across Time," *Journal of Philosophy,* Vol. 80 (1983), 201–20.

van Inwagen, P. "Four-Dimensional Objects," *Noûs,* Vol. 24 (1990), 245–55.

— PETER VAN INWAGEN

PERSONAL IDENTITY

At the center of the debate about personal identity since the 1970s has been the work of Derek Parfit, whose ideas, first published in his article "Personal Identity" (1971) and then extended and elaborated in his monumental *Reasons and Persons* (1984, part 3) revitalized and to some extent transformed the topic. The following discussion explains how this has come about and relates Parfit's ideas to those of other influential writers on personal identity from the 1960s on, in particular Bernard Williams, Sydney Shoemaker, Robert Nozick, Roderick M. Chisholm, David Wiggins, and Richard Swinburne.

The starting point for the development of Parfit's ideas was provided by Bernard Williams in his article "Personal Identity and Individuation" (1956–57), in which he puts forward his famous reduplication argu-ment, intended as an objection to any account of personal identity that entailed the possibility of reincarnation. No such account, he claimed, could rule out the possibility of a situation in which there were two equally good "candidates" for identity with an earlier person, and hence no such account could provide a sufficient condition of personal identity.

A consensus quickly emerged, however, among other writers on personal identity that the significance of Williams's argument was greater than he had seen. Though Williams himself remained recalcitrant, others saw that his argument consequently challenged, not just any account of personal identity that allowed for such possibilities as reincarnation, which involves a radical separation of personal identity from bodily identity, but any account of personal identity that proposed as a sufficient condition of personal identity a conceivably duplicable relation—that is, a relation that could conceivably take a one–many form. The result of this was to focus attention on the principle underlying Williams's argument, called "the only x and y rule" by David Wiggins in his discussion of the reduplication problem (1967, extensively revised and republished 1980), which emphasized the generality of the argument. The correct formulation of this principle is difficult, but roughly speaking it asserts that the question whether later x is the same person as earlier y can depend only on facts about x and y and the relationship between them, and no facts about any other individuals can be relevant to whether x is y.

One response to Williams, then, is simply to reject the only x and y rule and to elaborate an account of personal identity that explicitly packs into its sufficient condition the constraint that x is identical with y only if there is no third individual z who can be considered a better or equally good candidate for identity with y. Such an account of personal identity, in terms of psychological continuity, is elaborated by Sydney Shoemaker in his article "Persons and Their Pasts" (1970), in which he also fashions the important concept of quasi-memory as a way of responding to the objection that a vicious circle must necessarily be involved in explaining personal identity in terms of, possibly among other things, memory. Another sophisticated development of the best candidate approach is contained in Robert Nozick's book *Philosophical Explanations* (1981).

But the straightforward rejection of the only x and y rule is implausible, unless some account of its attractiveness is given. It is at this point that Parfit's ideas become relevant. In response to Williams's argument he proposes (1971, 1984) that identity does not matter in survival. What does matter is a relation of psychological connectedness-cum-continuity that does conform to the only x and y rule, but it seems plausible that identity obeys the only *x* and *y* rule only because we mistakenly identify this relation with identity.

The contention that identity does not matter in survival, which is Parfit's most discussed claim, is one component of the reductionist view of personal identity he recommends. Another component is that there need be no answer to a question of personal identity: personal identity may in some cases be indeterminate. In addition, Parfit holds that there are no facts about personal identity other than facts about mental states, their relations to one another, and their relations to physical bodies and the happenings therein. Persons are not "separately existing" entities, and a complete description of reality could be wholly impersonal.

The starting point for the development

of Derek Parfit's ideas on personal identity

was provided by Bernard Williams in his article

"Personal Identity and Individuation" (1956–57).

Of these three components of the reductionist view the first is the most obscure. What Parfit means by it, however, is that we do not have among our basic concerns a desire for our own continued existence and well-being. Insofar as we are concerned about these our concern is derivative from a concern for those future people (in the actual world, contingently, ourselves) linked by certain relations of psychological continuity and connectedness to ourselves as we are now. The contention that personal identity may be indeterminate is a more straightforward claim. What Parfit has in mind is that in at least some of the puzzle cases described in the literature on personal identity our concepts, suited as they are in the first place to our actual circumstances, have no determinate application. Whether such indeterminacy is to be regarded as due merely to vagueness in language or to vagueness in the world is, however, a debatable point (see Evans, 1978, for the argument that it must be regarded as due merely to vagueness in language). Parfit's third contention, that facts about personal identity are nothing over and above facts about the relations of mental states, indicates the Humean influence on his views.

Opponents of the reductionist view are described by Parfit as nonreductionists, or as proponents of the simple view. One such nonreductionist is Roderick Chisholm, whose work (see Chisholm, 1976) is perhaps the most careful working out of such a view in the literature. Chisholm defends the simple view as the development of the views on personal identity of Bishop Butler and Thomas Reid (Butler, 1897; Reid, 1941). Another philosopher who has defended the simple view, and has done so in conscious opposition to Parfit, is Richard Swinburne (see Swinburne, 1973–74). Swinburne emphasizes in particular the difficulty of making sense of the idea that one's own personal identity may be indeterminate and in doing so draws on arguments from Bernard Williams (1970).

These philosophers reject the whole Parfitian reductionist package. But the elements of the package are, arguably, separable. Or at least, so some philosophers have thought. Thus Sydney Shoemaker (1985) rejects the Parfitian claim that persons are reducible to their experiences in any sort of Humean way but accepts both that identity does not matter in survival and that personal identity can be indeterminate. Again David Lewis (1976) rejects Parfit's claim that identity does not matter in survival while accepting that personal identity can be indeterminate.

Parfit's reductionist thesis about personal identity is not easy to assess or respond to. But, just as no philosopher writing on personal identity can afford to ignore the work of Locke or Hume, so, from now on, Parfit's work must be regarded similarly. Certainly, no other philosopher in this century has had such an impact on the debate about personal identity.

[See also Butler, Joseph; Chisholm, Roderick M.; Hume, David; Locke, John; Philosophy of Mind; Reid, Thomas.]

BIBLIOGRAPHY

Chisholm, R. M. *Person and Object.* La Salle, IL, 1976.

Evans, G. "Vague Objects." *Analysis,* Vol. 38 (1978), 208.

Lewis, D. "Survival and Identity," in A. Rorty, ed., *The Identities of Persons* (Berkeley, 1976).

Nozick, R. *Philosophical Explanations.* Oxford, 1981.

Parfit, D. *Reasons and Persons.* Oxford, 1984.

———. "Personal Identity," *Philosophical Review,* Vol. 80 (1971), 3–27.

Reid, T. *Essays on the Intellectual Powers of Man,* ed. A. D. Woozley. London, 1941.

Shoemaker, S. "Critical Notice: Parfit's *Reasons and Persons,*" *Mind,* Vol. 44 (1985), 443–53.

———. "Persons and Their Pasts," *American Philosophical Quarterly,* Vol. 7 (1970), 269–85.

Swinburne, R. G. "Personal Identity," *Proceedings of the Aristotelian Society,* Vol. 74 (1973–74), 231–47.

Wiggins, D. *Sameness and Substance.* Oxford, 1980.

———. *Identity and Spatiotemporal Continuity.* Oxford, 1967.

Williams, B. A. O. "Personal Identity and Individuation," *Proceedings of the Aristotelian Society,* Vol. 57 (1956–57), 229–52. Reprinted in Williams, B. A. O., *Problems of the Self* (Cambridge, 1973).

– HAROLD W. NOONAN

PHENOMENOLOGY

The development of phenomenology is a consequence of the interpretation of the texts of the major figures, especially Husserl, and of independent phenomenological research. Quite often, the two projects have gone hand in hand. One major factor in the development of phenomenology during the period under review has been the ongoing publication of the Nachlass of the major figures (*Husserliana*, Heidegger's *Gesamtausgabe*, as well as Merleau-Ponty's lectures). Another is the continuing conversation with analytic philosophy in the English-speaking countries, with structuralism and deconstructionism in France, and with hermeneutics, critical theory, and the tradition of German idealism in Germany.

One major starting point in the conversation with analytic philosophy has been Dagfinn Føllesdal's (1969) paper, which argues that Husserl's concept of Noema is a generalization of the Fregean notion of *Sinn*. Both the Sinn and the Noema are abstract entities, to be distinguished from the object toward which an intentional act may be directed. While the historical claim underlying this thesis—namely, that Frege's was a major influence on the development of Husserl's thinking around the turn of the century—has been challenged (e.g., by Mohanty), the systematic thesis of Føllesdal (as opposed to Gurwitsch's thesis, that the Noema is the perceived object qua perceived and the object intended is but a system of noemata), has been influential. Jaakko Hintikka developed another aspect of Husserl's theory of intentionality by construing the Noema as a function from possible worlds to individuals in those worlds. The resources of the semantics of Frege and of possible worlds have been pulled together to interpret Husserl in the work of David Smith and Ronald McIntyre. Mohanty and Seebohm have cautioned against reducing the intentional thesis of Husserl to an extensional thesis of possible worlds and have emphasized the need for a theory of constitution of possible worlds, if the latter are not to be posited in a naively ontological thesis. Still others, notably Sokolowski and Bell, have questioned the validity of ascribing to Husserl a Fregean-type theory. Sokolowski takes the Husserlian Noema to be identical with the object (with the proviso "as intended"), and Bell reads Husserlian Gegenstand to be a component of the intentional act and so quite unlike the Fregean reference. From another perspective, Searle has found the Husserlian intentionality thesis useful for his own work but goes beyond Husserl by appropriating, from Heidegger via Dreyfus, the idea of Background of skills and practices, and more recently by developing a theory of we-intentionality that is irreducible to I-intentionalities (reminiscent of the Hegelian *Geist* as well as of a thesis advanced by David Carr). This last discussion connects with the way phenomenology has related itself to cognitive science. Fodor's methodological solipsism has been related by Dreyfus to Husserl's,

while Searle's emphasis on Background clearly falls on the Heideggerean side of the divide.

The tension between Husserlian phenomenology and hermeneutics lies in that the former is concerned with consciousness, its contents and structures, the latter with the individual's ontological relatedness to his world and to others. This issue becomes, Is interpretation to be construed as the gift of a transcendental ego, or is it to be construed as an ontological feature of the mode of being of *Dasein?* Hans-Georg Gadamer's theory of interpretation develops the latter alternative, while Paul Ricoeur comes closest to mediating between Husserlian thinking, especially of the *Logical Investigations,* and an ontologically construed hermeneutics. We must also recall Ricoeur's work on metaphor, in which, going beyond the traditional rhetorical and semantic theories of analytic philosophy, Ricoeur integrates them in such a manner as permits the poetic and disclosive dimension of language to emerge. Ricoeur's researches have also sought to mediate between time (the most radical subjectivity) and narrative (by which reality is redescribed, as by metaphors) and reestablish a certain reciprocity between them.

The most influential critique of classical phenomenology is offered by Jacques Derrida. While it is more common to look upon Derrida's work as refuting Husserl's transcendental phenomenology, it is also possible to maintain that Derrida's work is a further radicalization of Husserl's genetic phenomenology, an alleged result of which is the demonstration that constitution involves a perpetual deferral and difference, also that a radicalization of Husserl's concept of horizonal character of intentionality would call into question all fixity and univocity of meanings, and that possibilities of non-fulfillment of intention are necessarily inherent in all intentionality. But those who ascribe to Husserl a metaphysics of presence fall into the opposite trap of reifying 'absence'. As Sokolowski has shown, Husserl's thinking rather exhibits a mutual involvement of presence and absence.

Of those from analytic philosophy who have pursued some kind of phenomenology, mention must be made of Castañeda's rich phenomenology of indexical reference and of 'I' thought. In the latter context, he distinguishes between the ground floor of empirical I-guise and successive phases of transcendental I-guises, among all of which there is a sameness that is yet not strict identity.

In the United States there is a continuing tendency, inaugurated by Dreyfus and Rorty, to see in Heidegger a pragmatist philosopher, whereby clearly Heidegger's ontological concern with the meaning of being and the historical concern with the historicity of understanding of Being are either underplayed or sought to be altogether set aside. While it was at first usual to look upon Heidegger as an anti-science thinker, now—largely owing to the work of von Weizsäcker, Kockelmans, and Heelan—one has come to realize that Heidegger's thinking could form the basis for an understanding and appreciation of science and technology. In general, phenomenological thinking about science has exhibited three distinct features: First, following Husserl in the *Crisis,* some have attempted to reestablish the proper connection between science and lifeworld. The most important work on this front is due to Mittelstrass. Second, following also Husserl's work in the *Crisis,* but more inspired by Heideggerean thought about historicity of *Dasein* as also by Kuhn's work on history of science, some have looked upon science as a historical accomplishment marked by epochal changes, epistemological breaks, shifts of paradigm—thereby rejecting the prevailing obsession with the logical structure of scientific theories and also the reigning prejudice in favor of a naively realistic and positivist theory of science. But within phenomenology itself, this time following Husserl's original concern, there is also a continuing concern with the nature and structure of logic and mathematics as theories and with the origin of such theories, their relation to practice and also to the lifeworld, on the one hand, and the transcendental, thinking ego on the other.

The most influential critique of classical phenomenology is offered by Jacques Derrida.

Patrick Heelan has developed the view, using the conceptual resources of Husserl, Heidegger, and Merleau-Ponty, that scientific observation, like all perception, is hermeneutical. Hermeneutical phenomenology of science focuses, in his view, not so much on theory as on experimental phenomena. Heelan defends a sort of realism called by him hermeneutic or horizonal realism as opposed to the instrumentalism of some phenomenologists. Thus, according to Heelan, in particle physics many phenomena have actual existence only within the context of the measurement processes. Kockelmans emphasizes what he regards as the ontological aspect of science: he draws attention to the role of "objectifying thematization," which lies at the root of every scientific activity. In this latter concept he brings together Husserl's idea of "thematization" and Heidegger's idea that a certain fundamental understanding of being makes possible science, philosophy, and technology. Although Kockelmans accepts the Kuhnian thesis of epochs in the history of science, he nevertheless holds that history of science is guided by an ideal of reason and that each new paradigm is necessarily a historical synthesis.

From its inception phenomenology had a special relation of love and hate toward psychology; at a later phase, it developed a special interest in history. With regard to psychology, there has been a long tradition of original work in what is known as phenomenological psychology. To the period under review belong some works of Medard Boss, Aron Gurwitsch, Minkowski, and Ricoeur. Boss has applied his Heideggerean conception of *Daseinsanalytik* to such contexts as sexual perversion, dream, and psychosomatic illness. Drawing upon his work on lived space and lived time, Minkowski studies how these can undergo modifications in psychoses, schizophrenia, manic-depression and hallucinations. Gurwitsch's *Marginal Consciousness,* posthumously published, continues the work done in *The Field of Consciousness.* However, for research in descriptive psychology, possibly the most important results are to be found in Edward Casey's two books on imagining and remembering. This research has opened out new fields of investigation. For example, in his work on remembering, Casey explores a number of neglected, nonrepresentational forms of remembering, including body memory and place memory, reminiscing and commemorating.

In the phenomenology of history, a brief reference may be made to the important work done by Ricoeur, who seeks to mediate between lived time and cosmic time. The past is irrevocably gone, and our access to it across the historical distance is made possible by creative imagination. Here fiction, by its quasi-historical character, comes to our help. History is not a totality, an absolute mediation. Nevertheless, there is a search for meaning, which is open-ended without a Hegelian *Aufhebung.* The idea of one history is a Kantian-type regulative idea.

[See also *Cognitive Science; Critical Theory; Deconstruction; Derrida, Jacques; Frege, Gottlob; Gadamer, Hans-Georg; Heidegger, Martin; Hermeneutic Phenomenology; Hermeneutic Philosophy; Husserl, Edmund; Indexicals; Intentionality; Kuhn, Thomas; Merleau-Ponty, M.; Ricoeur, Paul; Ricoeur, Paul: Metaphor.*]

BIBLIOGRAPHY

Bell, D. *Husserl.* London, 1990.

Castañeda, H.-N. *Thinking, Language, and Experience.* Minneapolis, MN, 1989.

Casey, E. S. *Imagining: A Phenomenological Study.* Bloomington, IN, 1976.

———. *Remembering: A Phenomenological Study.* Bloomington, IN, 1987.

Derrida, J. *Speech and Phenomena,* trans. D. Allison. Evanston, IL, 1973.

Dreyfus, H., ed. *Husserl, Intentionality, and Cognitive Science.* Cambridge, MA, 1982.

Føllesdal, D. "Husserl's Notion of Noema," *Journal of Philosophy,* Vol. 66 (1969), 680–87.

Gurwitsch, A. *Studies in Phenomenology and Psychology.* Evanston, IL, 1966.

———. *Marginal Consciousness,* ed. L. Embree. Athens, OH, 1985.

Heelan, P. *Space Perception and the Philosophy of Science.* Berkeley, CA, 1983.

Hintikka, J. *The Intentions of Intentionality and Other New Models for Modalities.* Dordrecht, 1975.

Kockelmans, J. *Ideas for a Hermeneutic Phenomenology of the Natural Sciences.* Dordrecht, 1993.

———, ed. *Phenomenological Psychology: The Dutch School.* Dordrecht, 1987.

Mittelstrasse, J. *Die Möglichkeit von Wissenschaft.* Frankfurt am Main, 1974.

Mohanty, J. N. *Husserl and Frege.* Bloomington, IN, 1982.

———. *The Possibility of Transcendental Philosophy.* Dordrecht, 1985.

Ricoeur, P. *Time and Narrative,* trans. K. Blamey and D. Pellauer. Chicago, 1988.

Searle, J. *Intentionality.* New York, 1983.

Smith, D., and R. McIntyre. *Husserl and Intentionality.* Dordrecht, 1982.

Sokolowski, R. "Husserl and Frege," *Journal of Philosophy,* Vol. 84 (1987), 523–28.

von Weizsäcker, C. F. *Zeit und Wissen.* Munich, 1992.

– JITENDRA N. MOHANTY

PHENOMENOLOGY AND SCIENCE

In his later work, *Crisis of European Sciences,* Edmund Husserl thematized the prescientific lifeworld as the foundation of the sense of the positive sciences. However, since the emergence of modern mathematical physics this prescientific world could be approached only from the fact that a stock of unquestionably obvious scientific knowledge was added to it. Hence, for any particular scientific theory (of any epoch) a reawakening of the formerly activated constitution of its sense is needed. To show, then, how entirely specific constitutions of scientific formations come about, all sedimentations must be reactivated down to the ultimate procedures that constitute science; these procedures were originally encountered in the world of plain intuitive givenness and everyday practical activity. Husserl himself attempted to articulate such a description for the paradigmatic case of geometry. The contemporary crisis of reason results from the shifts in the sense of what is given in the lifeworld, shifts that science itself does not question and cannot detect because they have become increasingly unintelligible.

Martin Heidegger's reflections on science are concerned with the function of modern science within the totality of meaning and being. He finds an unbridgeable gap between the mode of scientific explanation and philosophical radicality because science cannot even account for the essence of its own field of study: it aims at technical domination (the capacity to control and predict results), but technique is not yet understanding. Therefore, any genuine reflection on the part of science must be extrascientific, in the sense that it must clarify the ontological status of its claims. Science is a mode of theoretical knowledge, which is itself a mode of being-in-the-world. The classical example for the ontological genesis of science is the rise of mathematical physics. What is decisive for its development consists neither in the emphasis on "facts" nor in its application of mathematics; it consists in the manner in which nature is mathematically projected. That is, modern science gives credit to the mathematical as that evident aspect of material things within which we are always moving (as original praxis) and according to which we experience them as things at all. Between us and the things the dialogue does not know of any limitation as long as we retain of nature what is calculable. The resulting harmony between the discovery of beings and the prior projection of their ontological structure is exemplified in the process of experimentation, which in modern science is always concomitant with mathematization. Elaboration precedes contemplation, whereas for the Greeks the passivity in the contemplative gaze was the decisive element of theory. To the rootlessness that has been a fruit of technical success, Heidegger ultimately opposes a return to the sources of our earthly lives.

Extending Husserl's reflections on the crisis of contemporary reason, Maurice Merleau-Ponty points out that phenomenology has disavowed scientism, not science. The problem is that contemporary science has generated a cult of superstition and idolization, since it defies common science, and yet is capable of changing the world. In particular, physics abounds in paradoxes that contradict the classical representation of a world of things in themselves, and yet it has abandoned the search for ultimate foundations. Against this situation Merleau-Ponty argues that a rational basis of science actually lies in the prescientific reason implicated in our existence in a common world of perception. A broadened conception of reason should emerge from the investigation of the ambiguities of the perceptual field itself. Science and its paradoxes contribute to this investigation, even though the brute facticity of the world cannot be exhausted in terms of science's intelligible essences.

[See also Explanation, Theories of; Heidegger, Martin; Husserl, Edmund; Merleau-Ponty, M.]

BIBLIOGRAPHY

Bachelard, S. *La Conscience de Rationalité.* Paris, 1958.

Becker, O. "Beiträge zur phänomenologischen Begründung der Geometrie und ihrer physikalischen Anwendungen," *Jahrbuch für*

Philosophie und phänomenologische Forschung, 6 (1923), 385–560.

Grieder, A. "Husserl on the Origin of Geometry," *Journal of the British Society for Phenomenology*, 20 (1983), 277–289.

Heelan, P. *Space Perception and the Philosophy of Science*. Berkeley, 1983.

Husserl, E. *The Crisis of European Sciences and Transcendental Phenomenology*, trans. D. Carr. Evanston, IL, 1970.

Kockelmans, J. *Phenomenology and the Physical Sciences*. Pittsburgh, 1966.

————. *Heidegger and Science*. Washington, DC, 1985.

Kockelmans, J., and T. Kisiel, eds. *Phenomenology and the Natural Sciences*. Evanston, IL, 1970.

Margenau, H. "Phenomenology and Physics," *Philosophy and Phenomenological Research*, 5 (1944), 269–80.

Ströker, E. *Philosophical Investigations of Space*, trans. A. Mickunas. Athens, OH, 1986.

— PIERRE KERSZBERG

PHILOSOPHICAL LOGIC

While the years since 1960 have seen a number of significant developments in philosophical logic, it seems safe to say that the farthest reaching of these has been the advent of possible-world semantics. Taking at face value a slogan loosely attributed to Leibniz—"To be necessary is to be true in all possible worlds"—Saul Kripke developed semantics for modal logic, according to which '$\square P$' (read, 'Necessarily P') means that 'P' is true in all possible worlds, while '$\lozenge P$' (read, 'Possibly P') means that 'P' is true in at least one possible world; or, more precisely, since, on some conceptions of modality, what is possible may depend on what is actual, for '$\square P$' to be true in the actual world, 'P' must be true in all worlds accessible from the actual world. (This development had a number of antecedents, going back to the work of J. C. C. McKinsey in the 1940s, but Kripke's contributions were unmistakably paramount.)

The metaphysical status of possible worlds is much disputed. David Lewis contends that other possible worlds are no less real than the actual world, though spatiotemporally disconnected from it. Others regard possible worlds as merely a mathematically useful fiction, with a wide variety of positions in between. Whatever their metaphysical inclinations, philosophers have found possible-world talk useful in understanding necessity and in a surprisingly wide variety of other applications.

The most striking effect of the new semantics on our understanding of necessity has been to facilitate a revival of essentialism, which had fallen into disrepute since the downfall of Aristotelian physics. Before the revival, philosophers had principally been interested in logical necessity, the sort of necessity that attaches to sentences whose truth is ensured by conventions of language. The new notion—not new to metaphysics, surely, but new to formal modal logic—is metaphysical necessity, according to which, even though 'Socrates was an alien from outer space' is conceptually possible, it is metaphysically necessary that Socrates, if he existed, was a human being, because humanity is part of Socrates' essence.

The farthest-reaching of recent developments in philosophical logic has been the advent of possible-world semantics.

One impediment to the development of modal predicate calculus, stressed by W. V. O. Quine, was this: the true premises '$\square 9 = 9$' and '$9 =$ the number of planets' would appear logically to entail the absurd conclusion '$\square 9 =$ the number of planets'. To understand why this inference fails required a deep analysis of the role of proper names, which, in turn, led to extensive and insightful investigations of the various ways we refer to things; notable here is David Kaplan's work on indexicals and demonstratives. A further consequence has been the general abandonment of the thesis that there are contingently true identity statements, in particular, of the thesis that the mind is contingently identical to the brain.

The formal logic is susceptible to many other interpretations, notably epistemic logic, developed by Jaakko Hintikka, which takes '$\square P$' to mean 'It is known that P'. This has been extended to a general theory of propositions that identifies a proposition with the set of possible worlds in which it is true. There are difficulties with the program—for example, according to it, all necessary truths express the same proposition, so that, in some sense, if we believe any necessary truth, we believe all of them—but it has nonetheless won many adherents.

Taking '$\square P$' to mean that 'P' is provable in, say, Peano arithmetic, we can use modal logic to investigate issues surrounding Gödel's second incompleteness theorem. Robert Solovay has given a complete set of axioms; its surprising axiom is the formal version of Löb's theorem: '$(\square(\square P \to P) \to \square P)$'.

Combining the possible world semantics for S4 (one of several modal deductive calculi invented by C. I. Lewis) with Gödel's 1931 result that questions about deducibility in intuitionistic logic could be reduced to questions about S4, Kripke got a semantics for intuitionistic logic, in which we can think of the "possible worlds" as representing the mathematician's epistemic state at various stages of inquiry. The importance of this result was increased by the revived interest in intuitionism inspired by the work of Michael Dummett, who advocated intuitionist logic on the basis of considerations from the philosophy of language separate from the mathematical concerns that motivated Brouwer and his followers.

Redeploying the machinery by identifying a possible world with an instant of time and letting the instants accessible from the present instant be those prior to it, we can read "$\diamond$ Spot runs" as "Spot ran" and "$\square$Spot runs" as "Spot has always run." Adopting analogous operators for future times, one gets an elegant theory of tense.

There are other applications of possible-world semantics besides the many applications we get by varying the interpretation of '$\square$'. The most important of these is Robert Stalnaker's theory of conditionals, according to which, to say that if Sonia had struck the match, it would have ignited, is to say that, among the worlds in which Sonia struck the match, the world most similar to the actual world is a world in which the match ignited. The notion of similarity of worlds requires a great deal of clarification, of course, and attempts to clarify it have contributed a great deal to our understanding of conditionals. (While the acceptance of Stalnaker's account has been widespread, a rival theory deserves mention here. Ernest Adams developed a probabilistic account, according to which the probability of a simple conditional is the conditional probability of the consequent given the antecedent. David Lewis showed that this thesis cannot be directly extended to compound conditionals.)

As a final application of possible worlds, mention should be made of supervenience. To say that the mental supervenes upon the physical will be to say that, for any worlds W and V, if there is a one-one correspondence between the individuals existing in the two worlds such that individuals in W have the same physical properties and stand in the same physical relations as the corresponding individuals in V, then individuals in W have the same mental properties and stand in the same mental relations as the corresponding individuals in V. Numerous variations in detail are possible. For many purposes, supervenience provides an attractively priced substitute for reducibility, since it enables us to express the idea that the physical facts determine the mental facts without being embarrassed by the fact that no one has any idea how to reduce the mental to the physical.

The development of modal, epistemic, and conditional logics was part of a broader pattern of going beyond the confines of the first-order predicate calculus in trying to give formal models of natural languages. Second-order logic has figured prominently, for example, in Boolos's result that plural quantification, as found in such locutions as 'There are some critics who

only admire one another', is intertranslatable with second-order quantification. There are many other forms of quantification in English, a number of which have been investigated by Jon Barwise and Robin Cooper. Another departure from classical logic is 'free logic' (short for 'presupposition-free logic'), which eschews the classical presumption that proper names always denote.

Apart from the many applications of possible worlds, the busiest area of research has been the logic of truth, looking for ways to circumvent the liar paradox. All contemporary work on the liar paradox takes as its starting point Tarski's 1935 paper, "The Concept of Truth in Formalized Languages," and nearly all of it accepts Tarski's fundamental conclusion: in formulating a theory of truth, the language we talk about (the object language) must be essentially poorer in expressive power than the language we speak (the metalanguage). In particular, having no essentially richer metalanguage, we cannot hope to formulate an account of what it is for a sentence of English to be true. All we can hope for is to describe various useful fragments of English.

Again Kripke has been at the forefront, developing an account of truth-value gaps, according to which the paradoxical sentences fall into the gap between truth and falsity. We know from Tarski's formalization of the liar paradox that, in a language with classical logic that can describe its own syntax, it is not possible to assign an extension to the word 'true' in such a way that " 'P' is true" comes out true or false according as 'P' is true or false. Yet Kripke has shown that, in a language with truth-value gaps, it is possible to arrange things so that " 'P' is true" is true, false, or undecided according as 'P' is true, false, or undecided.

An alternative treatment is the 'revision theory' of Hans Herzberger, Anil Gupta, and Nuel Belnap, which provides a strategy, within classical, two-valued logic, for devising better and better candidates for the extension of 'true'. One starts out by making a blind guess what the extension of 'true' might be. Having a candidate for the extension of 'true' and assuming we already know the meanings of all the other terms, we get a model for the language, and we can say what sentences are true in the model. Our second candidate for the extension of 'true' will be the set of sentences true in the model in which the extension of 'true' is taken to be the first candidate. The process continues into the transfinite, giving us candidates for the extension of 'true' which better and better accord with our intuitions. This story has been extended by Gupta and Belnap to a general theory of circular definitions.

The third prominent approach, developed by Charles Parsons, Tyler Burge, and others, starts with Tarski's suggestions that we can construct a metalanguage for a given object language merely by adding a new predicate 'true in the object language', and that this process can be iterated, getting a metalanguage, a metametalanguage, and so on. To apply this construction to English, treat the English world 'true' as ambiguous, taking a given use of 'true' to mean 'true in the nth level metalanguage', for some contextually determined number n.

Apart from the many applications of possible worlds,

the busiest area of research has been

the logic of truth, looking for ways to circumvent

the liar paradox.

A rather different discussion about truth has contrasted disquotational theories of truth—which take sentences that follow the paradigm " 'Snow is white' is true if and only if snow is white" as true by definition, being constitutive of the meaning of 'true'—with correspondence theories—which take it that the thoughts and practices of speakers fix a connection between expressions and the objects those expressions are about, and this connection, together with the nonlinguistic facts, makes true sentences true and false ones false. This discussion originates out of work by W. V. O. Quine and others that has seemed to show that the connections between words and their referents are much less direct than we would have hoped.

The 'sorites' paradox starts with the seemingly harmless observation that giving a single penny to a poor man still leaves him poor and leads, by a billion iterations, to the seemingly preposterous conclusion that giving ten million dollars to a poor man still leaves him poor. An especially prominent response has been Kit Fine's, which employs a technique of Bas van Fraassen's called 'super-valuations': say an ordinary, classical model of the language is acceptable if the extension it assigns to 'poor' includes all people who are definitely poor, excludes all the people who are definitely not poor, and, in adjudicating borderline cases, respects the principle that, if x is better off financially than y and x is poor, then y is poor. A sentence containing the word 'poor' is true if and only if it is assigned the truth value 'true' in all acceptable models. Under this proposal, we get to say that, if Nell is a borderline case of 'poor', then the sentence 'Nell is poor' is neither true nor false, and yet we get to maintain classical logic. (An analogous application of supervaluations enabled Kripke to get a version of his theory of truth that upholds classical logic in spite of truth-value gaps.) Other approaches require

giving up classical logic in favor of either 3-valued, intuitionist, or fuzzy logic. Fuzzy logic, invented by Lofti Zadeh, assigns sentences numerical values between 0 (falsity) and 1 (truth). Yet other approaches involve denying that there are borderline cases, either by denying that anyone is either genuinely rich or genuinely poor (Peter Unger and Samuel Wheeler), or by insisting that the border between poor and nonpoor is, in fact, sharp, appearances to the contrary arising from our epistemic inability to determine who the richest poor person is (Timothy Williamson and Roy Sorensen).

A great deal must be left out of such a survey as this. Two more items need mention: (1) logical consequence, which contrasts Tarski's model-theoretic approach—taking a sentence to be a logical consequence of a set of premises just in case it is true in every model of the premises—with Gentzen's proof-theoretic approach, according to which the meaning of the logical operators is given by the rules of inference. (2) Relevant logic, which, taking offense at the classical doctrine that everything follows from a contradiction, insists that one's conclusions be connected to one's premises.

In all the sciences, contemporary research has been characterized by the increasing use of mathematical methods; for philosophy, this has principally meant the use of logical methods. We may expect this trend to continue.

[See also Conditionals; Dummett, Michael; Fuzzy Logic; Gödel, Kurt; Indexicals; Intuitionism; Kripke, Saul Aaron; Leibniz, Gottfried Wilhelm; Liar Paradox; Logical Consequence; Mathematical Logic; Modal Logic; Philosophy of Language; Propositions; Quine, Willard Van Orman; Semantics; Supervenience; Truth.]

BIBLIOGRAPHY

Adams, E. W. *The Logic of Conditionals.* Dordrecht, 1975.

Barwise, J., and R. Cooper. "Generalized Quantifiers and Natural Language," *Linguistics and Philosophy*, Vol. 4 (1981), 159–219.

———, and J. Etchemendy. *The Liar.* New York, 1987. Uses non-well-founded set theory to give a highly sophisticated contextualist solution to the liar paradox.

Belnap, N., and A. Anderson. *Entailment.* Princeton, NJ, 1975. Relevant logic.

Boolos, G. "To Be Is to Be the Value of a Variable (or to Be Some Values of Some Variables)," *Journal of Philosophy*, Vol. 81 (1984), 430–49. Connects second-order and plural quantification.

———. *The Logic of Provability.* New York, 1993. Includes Solovay's results.

Cresswell, M. J. *Logic and Languages.* London, 1973. Propositions as sets of possible worlds.

David, M. *Correspondence and Disquotation.* New York, 1994.

Dummett, M. *Elements of Intuitionism.* Oxford, 1971.

Etchemendy, J. *The Concept of Logical Consequence.* Cambridge, MA, 1990. A relentless attack on Tarski's theory.

Field, H. "The Deflationary Conception of Truth," in G. MacDonald and C. Wright, eds., *Fact, Science, and Morality* (Oxford, 1986). Disquotational vs. correspondence theories of truth.

Fine, K. "Vagueness, Truth, and Logic," *Synthese,* Vol. 30 (1975), 265–300. Uses supervaluations to solve the 'sorites' paradox.

Gabbay, D., ed. *Handbook of Philosophical Logic.* 3 vols. Boston, 1983. A useful guide to all areas of philosophical logic.

Gentzen, G. *Collected Papers.* Amsterdam, 1969. Classics of proof theory.

Gupta, A., and N. Belnap, Jr. *The Revision Theory of Truth.* Cambridge, MA, 1993. Embeds the revision theory of truth into a general account of circular definitions.

Harper, W., R. Stalnaker, and G. Pearce, eds. *Ifs.* Dordrecht, 1981. Fundamental papers on conditionals, including those of Stalnaker and Lewis.

Hintikka, J. *Models for Modalities.* Dordrecht, 1969. Important papers on modal and epistemic logic.

Horwich, P. *Truth.* Oxford, 1990. Defends a disquotational theory.

Hughes, R. I. G. *Philosophical Companion to First-Order Logic.* Indianapolis, 1993. A useful anthology.

Kaplan, D. "Demonstratives," in J. Almog, J. Perry, and H. Wettstein, eds., *Themes on Kaplan* (New York, 1976).

Kim, J. *Supervenience and Mind.* New York, 1993. Seminal papers on supervenience.

Kripke, S. "Semantical Analysis of Intuitionistic Logic I," in J. N. Crossley and M. A. E. Dummett, eds., *Formal Systems and Recursive Functions* (Amsterdam, 1965).

———. *Naming and Necessity.* Oxford, 1980. Fundamentally changed philosophical thinking about reference and modality.

Lambert, K. *Philosophical Applications of Free Logic.* New York, 1991.

Lewis, D. *On the Plurality of Worlds.* New York, 1986. Defends possible-world realism: other worlds are every bit as real as this one.

Linsky, L., ed. *Reference and Modality.* London, 1971. Fundamental papers by Kripke, Quine, and others. Arthur Smullyan's response to Quine's '□ 9 = the number of planets' argument is noteworthy.

Loux, M., ed. *The Possible and the Actual.* Ithaca, NY, 1979. Papers explore the status of possible worlds.

Martin, R., ed. *Recent Essays on Truth and the Liar Paradox.* New York, 1984. Includes the papers by Belnap, Burge, Gupta, Herzberger, Kripke, and Parsons.

McGee, V. *Truth, Vagueness, and Paradox.* Indianapolis, 1991. Attempts a self-contained theory of truth, without recourse to a richer metalanguage.

Montague, R. *Formal Philosophy.* New Haven, 1974. Important papers on modal logic and on the semantics of English.

Prior, A., and K. Fine. *Worlds, Times, and Selves.* Amherst, MA, 1977. Modal logic and tense logic.

Quine, W. V. O. *Philosophy of Logic,* 2d ed. Cambridge, MA, 1986.

———. *Ontological Relativity.* New York, 1990. Inscrutability of reference, among other topics.

Sorensen, R. *Blindspots.* Oxford, 1988. Vagueness as ignorance.

Tarski, A. *Logic, Semantics, Metamathematics,* 2d ed. Indianapolis, 1983. Includes the papers on truth and consequence.

Unger, P. "There Are No Ordinary Things." *Synthese,* Vol. 41 (1979), 117–54. Denies that vague terms refer.

Wheeler, S. "On That Which Is Not," *Synthese,* Vol. 41 (1979), 155–74. Denies that vague terms refer.

van Benthem, J. *A Manual of Intensional Logic,* 2d ed. Stanford, CA, 1988. Applications of possible world semantics.

van Fraassen, B. "Singular Terms, Truth Value Gaps, and Free Logic," *Journal of Philosophy,* Vol. 63 (1966), 464–95. Introduces supervaluations as a technique for free logic.

Williamson, T. *Vagueness.* London, 1994. Vagueness as ignorance.

Zadeh, L. "Fuzzy Logic and Approximate Reasoning," *Synthese,* Vol. 30 (1975), 407–28.

– VANN MCGEE

PHILOSOPHY

Conceptions of philosophy have varied dramatically throughout its history. Western philosophy originated in ancient Greece, mainly in the writings of Plato and Aristotle. Such questions as the following occupied Plato and Aristotle: What is being? What is knowledge? What is justice? These questions take the form "What is *X*?", a form common to philosophical inquiry. What exactly do such questions seek? In particular, what, if anything, constitutes the correctness or incorrectness of an answer to a philosophical question of the form "What is *X*?" The latter two questions have attracted various answers from philosophers engaged in metaphysics, epistemology, and ethics. Still, those questions lead naturally to inquiry about the objectivity or subjectivity of answers to philosophical questions having the form "What is *X*?"

A fifteenth-century work depicts "philosophy personified." (Corbis/ Leonard de Selva)

Plato and Aristotle regarded philosophical "What is X?" questions as inquiring about the essences of things. Plato's question "What is knowledge?" in the *Theaetetus,* for example, seeks to identify what knowledge itself is, what is essential to (or definitive of) all instances of knowledge. In general, Plato's "What is X?" questioning aims for a statement of the essence of X (*Meno* 72b; cf. *Euthyphro* 11a). Such a statement, according to Plato, would provide a definition (*logos*) of the essence of X (*Republic* 534b). Similarly, Aristotle regards philosophy as knowledge of essences, which on his view amounts to knowledge of definitions (*Metaphysics* 983a27f). The relevant definitions are neither stipulative nor conventional but real—that is, essence specifying in virtue of their signifying the properties that locate something in its proper genus or species. Aristotle was explicit about this approach to real definitions (*Categories* 2b28–3a5).

Plato and Aristotle were essence realists; they denied that essences depend on someone's conceiving of them as essential. They held, accordingly, that the correctness of answers to philosophical "What is X?" questions is conceiving independent and, in that respect, objective. Philosophical truths, according to Plato and Aristotle, are correspondingly objective. In addition, Plato and Aristotle distinguished philosophical truths from the empirical sciences. Aristotle regarded the subject of metaphysics, for instance, as "first philosophy": that is, the science that investigates things apart from the classifications peculiar to the special sciences. Metaphysics, according to Aristotle, is the science of being as such: being qua being. The views of Plato and Aristotle gave rise to a tradition holding that philosophy is autonomous—in both its methods and its truths—with respect to the empirical sciences. This tradition holds that philosophical truths are (1) necessary rather than contingent, (2) knowable a priori, and (3) substantive rather than merely prescriptive, stipulative, or conventional.

Another long-standing tradition, inspired by Hume and various other empiricists, endorses the methodological and doctrinal autonomy of philosophy but denies that philosophical truths are substantive. This tradition regards philosophical truths as analytic, resulting from stipulative or conventional definitions, and as knowable a priori. In contrast, substantive truths, according to this tradition, are contingent and knowable a posteriori. Such twentieth-century positivists as A. J. Ayer and Rudolf Carnap represented this tradition; they opposed the rationalist view that philosophical truths are synthetic a priori. As philosophical truths are logically necessary, according to such philosophers, they are a priori, but they are not substantive or synthetic. In general, this empiricist tradition characterizes philosophy as offering conceptual truths that define general categories fundamental to the empirical sciences.

A more recent tradition, stemming from the views of W. V. O. Quine, proposes that philosophy be "naturalized," that it be regarded as continuous with the natural sciences. Quine himself rejects the analytic–synthetic distinction as philosophically irrelevant and contends that there is no first philosophy, no philosophy prior to the natural sciences. Philosophy, Quine holds, is methodologically and doctrinally continuous with the natural sciences. Epistemology, for instance, is a branch of psychology; it is not a discipline that offers independent standards of assessment for the natural sciences. Quine denies, then, that philosophy is autonomous with respect to the natural sciences. He denies, accordingly, that philosophical truths are necessary or knowable a priori. Some other philosophers have offered less austere ways to naturalize philosophy, but Quine's approach attracts the most attention in contemporary philosophy.

A pressing issue for Quine's approach is, In the absence of any first philosophy, how are we to discern which of the various so-called sciences are genuinely reliable and thus regulative for purposes of theory formation? Our list of genuine sciences will perhaps include the dominant physics and chemistry but exclude astrology and parapsychology. Such a list, regardless of its exact components, seemingly depends on some first philosophy, some philosophical commitments prior to the natural sciences in question. It is an open question, however, whether such philosophical commitments are analytic or synthetic.

A very recent approach to philosophy emerges from the writings of Richard Rorty, who has acknowledged the influence of Thomas Kuhn's social-political approach to the sciences. If Quine's approach exalts the natural sciences, Rorty's elevates the social sciences. Rorty proposes, in particular, that we replace first philosophy with philosophy as the comparing and contrasting of cultural traditions. He offers a kind of pragmatism that aims to change the subject from Platonic and positivistic questions about the nature of truth and goodness to intellectual history of a certain sort. Rorty endorses the Hegelian view that philosophy is "its own time apprehended in thoughts," and he understands talk of "our own time" as including the notion of "our view of previous times." Rorty's pragmatism apparently merges philosophy with intellectual history and literary criticism, leaving no special subject matter for the discipline of philosophy.

Even if pragmatists wish to change the subject, we can still ask whether one approach to our intellectual history is more reliable—closer to the truth—than another. Indeed, we shall naturally raise such an issue when faced with incompatible lessons from alternative approaches to intellectual history. In raising such an issue, however, we shall also open questions about the nature of truth, questions that appear to be philosophical and not merely historical or literary. Rorty's pragmatism owes us, at the least, an explanation of how philosophical issues about the nature of truth can actually be set aside. Such issues, contrary to Rorty's pragmatism, may be unavoidable in the end.

The characterization of philosophy

is a philosophical problem in its own right,

and as such it resists any quick and simple treatment.

The original *Encyclopedia of Philosophy* article on philosophy identified the distinctive feature of philosophy as its being a critical discussion of critical discussion. It proposed that philosophy is distinctively metaphilosophy, or metainquiry: an inquiry about the character of inquiry. "The philosopher," according to the original article, "interests himself in such topics as the good, the beautiful, and the public interest, just because the mechanism for discussing differences of opinion about them strikes him as being inadequate" (p. 223). This is, it seems, an empirical claim to be assessed on the basis of evidence concerning what actually motivates philosophers. If this is so, the claim seems doubtful, at least given the ordinary significance of the term philosopher. Many philosophers investigate the nature of the good, the beautiful, the public interest, and so on without any particular interest in the adequacy of the mechanism for discussing difference of opinion. Special interest in the latter mechanism typically characterizes epistemologists, decision theorists, and students of methodology, but not philosophers in general. Perhaps philosophers should always be interested in the mechanism for discussing difference of opinion, but this normative proposal may fail to characterize all actual philosophers. It would be useful to have a characterization of philosophy that captures all those thinkers commonly called philosophers.

The later Wittgenstein is famous for characterizing philosophy as a kind of therapeutic metaphilosophy: philosophy dissolves philosophical problems by removing conceptual muddles. Even if philosophy can serve such a therapeutic purpose on occasion, it is debatable whether philosophy serves only that purpose. One controversial issue is whether every long-standing philosophical problem can be dissolved by the removal of conceptual confusion. Another relevant issue is whether

philosophy might offer conceptual clarification for explanatory problem-solving purposes without thereby dissolving problems. Perhaps philosophy has a constructive explanatory role apart from the therapeutic dissolution of problems. In any case we must be especially careful not to identify one feature of philosophy as the distinctive trait of philosophy. Philosophy as commonly characterized is, for better or worse, a multifaceted discipline that resists simple characterization. Philosophy now includes, for instance, applied philosophy of various sorts, such as applied ethics involving business and health care.

One might say that philosophy is what philosophers characteristically do. Given this theme, the discipline of philosophy will be as diverse as the works of its practitioners. This theme may capture what philosophy is, at least as commonly characterized. The explanatory burden would then fall to the notion of a philosopher, and the latter notion may be as contested as the notion of philosophy itself. Still, some inquirers may make progress by beginning with their notion of a philosopher, a notion that is perhaps less abstract for them than is the notion of philosophy itself. The concluding lesson is that the characterization of philosophy is, in its own right, a philosophical problem, and as such it resists any quick and simple treatment. The wages of philosophy are, more often than not, difficulty and complexity, even when philosophical progress ensues.

[See also Applied Ethics; Aristotle; Biomedical Ethics; Business Ethics; Carnap, Rudolph; Hume, David; Kuhn, Thomas; Plato; Pragmatism; Quine, Willard Van Orman; Truth; Wittgenstein, Ludwig Josef Johann.]

BIBLIOGRAPHY

Baynes, K., J. Bohman, and T. McCarthy, eds. *After Philosophy: End or Transformation?* Cambridge, MA, 1987.

Cohen, A., and M. Dascal, eds. *The Institution of Philosophy: A Discipline in Crisis?* LaSalle, IL, 1989.

Mays, W., and S. C. Brown, eds. *Linguistic Analysis and Phenomenology.* London, 1972.

Moser, P. *Philosophy after Objectivity.* New York, 1993.

Moser, P., and D. H. Mulder, eds. *Contemporary Approaches to Philosophy.* New York, 1994.

Rajchman, J., and C. West, eds. *Post-Analytic Philosophy.* New York, 1985.

Rescher, N. *The Strife of Systems: An Essay on the Grounds and Implications of Philosophical Diversity.* Pittsburgh, 1985.

Rorty, R., ed. *The Linguistic Turn: Recent Essays on Philosophical Method.* Chicago, 1967.

Russell, B. *The Problems of Philosophy.* New York, 1912.

Unger, P. *Philosophical Relativity.* Minneapolis, 1984.

— PAUL K. MOSER

PHILOSOPHY OF BIOLOGY

Revolutionary changes in molecular and evolutionary biology over the last half of the twentieth century have brought biology to the center of attention in the philosophy of science. The result has been significant advance in the traditional problems of teleology and functional analysis, reductionism and physicalism, the nature of biological laws, theories and explanations, as well as new philosophical interest in biological questions about taxonomy and sociobiology.

Evolutionary Theory

After a period of midcentury eclipse, Charles Darwin's account of the appearance of design as the result of natural selection over blind but heritable variation regained its philosophical influence in the 1980s. It has been exploited to analyze intentionality, function, moral goodness, reliable belief production, and science's progress as the results of purely mechanical, purposeless processes. But this application required a vindication of the theory's status as cognitively significant. A traditional objection charges the theory of natural selection with being an empty tautology on the ground that its key explanatory term, fitness, is defined in the theory by appeal to what it explains—reproductive success. The result is that fitness differences simply redescribe reproductive-rate differences and cannot explain them. No evidence about differential rates of reproduction could falsify the claim that they reflect fitness differences. Even after the eclipse of strict falsification as a criterion for a theory's being scientific, opponents of Darwinism, creationists, and other antiphysicalists laid the charge of vacuousness against the theory.

That the theory of natural selection is not an empty tautology is a matter of agreement among philosophers of biology, in spite of the fact that many biology textbooks inadvertently trivialize the theory by defining fitness as reproductive rate. It is widely held that the source of this mistake in the textbooks is a failure to make a simple distinction. The theory is saved from vacuity because fitness is not to be defined in terms of reproductive rates. Rather fitness must be defined as the probabilistically expected rate of reproduction, which is distinct from the actual rate of reproduction, and provides a probabilistic explanation for the actual rate. Thus, the theory of natural selection asserts a causal chain between environmental forces of selection, a probabilistic propensity to reproduce in that environment, and an actual level of reproduction, which leads to differential perpetuation of traits. Biologists inadvertently trivialize the theory when they fail to distinguish the probabilistic propensity to reproduce from the actual level of reproduction.

One difficulty with the probabilistic propensity definition of fitness is that it identifies fitness with the units in which it is measured, rather like defining heat in terms of degrees on a thermometer. But heat is mean kinetic energy, not the units in which it is measured. Mutatis mutandis, one is tempted to ask, what is fitness, over and above the units in which it may be measured? Answers to this question reveal one of the most important features of biological phenomena and biological theory.

Supervenience

Fitness is a relational term: an organism or trait has a level of fitness only in relation to an environment. A white coat in the Arctic is fitter than the same color in a rain forest. Two different traits in the same environment, say camouflage and running speed, may accord the same level of fitness. Similarly, different traits in different environments may accord the same level of fitness, as measured by the level of reproductive success they cause. If a large number of different packages of traits-in-environments can give rise to the same level of fitness, then fitness differences cannot be exhaustively defined in terms of their causes; the full definition will be an indefinitely long disjunction of different combinations of traits and environments. Fitness is supervenient on these packages: for any organism with a given fitness level, any other organism with the same traits in the same environment will have the same level of fitness. An organism's fitness is completely fixed by the relation between its traits and the environment, even though the reverse does not hold. Supervenience allows us to express the claim that fitness is nothing over and above the relation between traits and environments even though it is not reducible to this relation. Accordingly, we cannot define fitness in terms of its causes. When fitness is defined in terms of its effects—reproduction—the theory of natural selection is trivialized. When philosophers define it in terms of an intermediate probabilistic disposition, the result is foreign to the biologist's conception of fitness.

However, the relationship of supervenience turns out to characterize intertheoretical relations throughout biology and to enable the philosophy of science to explain the autonomy of biology from physical science consistent with physicalism. For when properties such as fitness are supervenient, but not reducible, then the regularities, generalizations, and laws expressed in these terms will not be reducible either. (See the discussion of the reduction of genetics below.)

Biological Theories, Laws, and Models

Many philosophers have long denied the existence of biological laws, either because they argue for the distinctiveness of biology as a historical discipline or because they deny its status as a separate science. Beyond evolutionary theory's laws, generalizations in biology do not have features traditionally required of scientific laws: they are never exceptionless, their *ceteris paribus*—other things equal—clauses cannot be made precise, they advert to species and environments restricted to the Earth. For example, Mendel's "laws" of the segregation and assortment of genes have been disconfirmed by crossover, linkage, meiotic drive, and other genetic effects. But the result has not been replacement of Mendel's principles by more precise ones. Instead, biological theorizing has resorted to the development of models with local applicability. This has led philosophers to hold that biological theory does not proceed by the identification of explanatory laws of increasing generality. Instead, biological theory is a sequence of models that vary in the domains of phenomena to which they apply and are similar only in mathematical formalization, or underlying mechanism, or domain of application. Thus, the structure of biological theory differs significantly from theory structure elsewhere in natural science.

That the theory of natural selection is not

an empty tautology is a matter of agreement

among philosophers of biology, in spite of the fact

that many biology textbooks inadvertently

trivialize the theory by defining fitness

as reproductive rate.

The puzzle remains why there are few strict laws in biology. One answer brings together supervenience and biological teleology.

Functional Analysis and Explanation

Branches of biology, and especially anatomy, have always been organized around the search for the functions of organelles, cells, tissues, and organs. Before Darwin the best explanation for functions, (co-)adaptations, and biological purposiveness was the existence of a designer. Darwin recognized that by substituting for global design a succession of local environmental filters through which pass only the fitter among heritable variations he could explain apparent purposiveness as the result of long-term adaptation. Since Darwin biologists have employed the hypothesis that most traits and capacities have resulted from selection among randomly produced variants to provide powerful explanations for the ad-

aptations biologists uncover. But it took philosophers over a century after the publication of *On the Origin of Species* to reach something approaching consensus on the role of Darwin's theory in the analysis of biological function.

"The function of the heart beat is to pump the blood." This truth discovered in the seventeenth century by William Harvey explains why hearts beat. But the explanation is problematical in two ways: first, the explainer—pumping the blood—is an effect of what it explains. This reverses the causal order that scientific explanation elsewhere honors. Second, the function of a heart is to pump the blood even when through deformity, injury, or disease it does not do so. Under these circumstances the explanatory power of a functional claim is mysterious. Philosophers long sought an analysis of functional systems that cashed them in for sets of causal claims about these systems as complexes of subsystems causally connected by feedback and feedforward loops. Functional claims thus understood are abbreviations for complex causal claims (Nagel, 1977). Feedback/feed-forward analyses of function were, however, prone to counterexamples, and they made unwarranted distinctions between natural and artifact function. Such analyses also failed to exploit the biological foundation of functions in natural selection. It was Larry Wright (1976) who provided such an account: an event has many effects. The heart's beating has the effect of displacing a certain volume of air in the chest, of pushing the stomach down, stretching the tissue of the aorta, changing the color of the blood in the extremities, moving plaques of cholesterol along blood vessels, of making sounds a stethoscope detects. None of these effects are its functions. Another one of the heart beat's effects is pumping the blood, and this indeed is a function. Functions are effects, but not just any effects. They are effects that have been historically selected for their contributions to evolutionary fitness. In vertebrates the function of the heart's beating is to circulate blood, because the beating of every vertebrate heart has a certain *etiology*: over the course of evolutionary history vertebrate hearts and their predecessors were selected for their properties of efficient blood circulation; or the genes that code for hearts were selected for their phenotypic effects in efficient blood circulation. Wright's "etiological" analysis of function enables us to see how Darwinian theory underwrites functional claims in biology while preserving their continuity with artifact functions: for example, a bust functions as a door stop because of its etiology in literal, not natural, selection.

Above the level of the macromolecule, almost all biological concepts are functional ones, because they describe traits, dispositions, behaviors, and systems in terms of the effects that make them adaptations. But different structures can all have the same type of effect and thus fulfill the same function. Consider all the different mechanisms that keep time and therefore function as clocks. For this reason functional classifications that reflect selection for effects are blind to structural differences. Together with supervenience, the blindness to structure of selection or function explains much about biological theorizing. To see this consider the concept of 'gene'.

Reduction, Emergentism, and Autonomy

Until Francis Crick and James D. Watson uncovered the molecular mechanism of the Mendelian gene in the nucleic acids, the claim that biological processes were nothing but physical processes lacked concrete detailed evidence. Since their work biologists and philosophers have wrestled with the problem of how molecular biology and the rest of the sciences are related to one another. The problem is to reconcile the claim that the biological processes are nothing but physical ones, as Watson and Crick seemed to show for heredity, with the difficulty of actually effecting the reduction of Mendelian genetics or biological processes to purely physical ones.

Classical criteria for successful reduction require that the terms of the reduced theory be linked in definitions or general laws to the terms of the reducing theory and that the laws of the former be explained by the laws of the latter through deductive derivation. Meeting the first test requires a characterization of gene in terms of nucleic acids molecules. However, no satisfactory molecular characterization of the Mendelian gene is possible. "Mendelian gene" is a functional term; like most biological entities, genes are individuated by their functions: the phenotypes they help produce. Any number of physically quite different stretches of nucleic acid can in principle produce the same phenotypic effect, thus share a function, and so be classified as realizing the same Mendelian gene. In short, the Mendelian gene is supervenient on an indefinitely long disjunction of packages of molecular material, each of which will have the same phenotypic effect. Accordingly, no Mendelian gene is reducible to any single or small number of nucleic acid sequences, even though each Mendelian gene is nothing but a complex macromolecule. Without a connection between Mendelian genes and molecular ones, no Mendelian laws can be reductively explained by derivation from molecular ones.

But there are no strict Mendelian laws to be derived in any case. On the etiological analysis of function it is easy to see why. A biological generalization would link a functionally characterized kind either to another functional kind or to a structural kind: since the generalization's antecedent names a functional kind, its instances will differ from one another in physical properties because of the supervenience of functional kinds on a motley of structural properties. Thus, there will be no general structural kind common to this motley to figure in the consequent of the law we seek. If instead we seek a generalization linking the functional antecedent to a functional consequent, the diversity of physical structures on which the antecedent supervenes will almost certainly have no other common property that selection can turn into a function and so make the consequent of a law about functions linked to functions.

Controversy over reductionism

has spread from the molecular/Mendelian interface

to sociobiology and behavioral biology.

The supervenience of biological properties on physical ones, together with the absence of laws of the sort to be expected in physical sciences, leaves biology's relation to these disciplines problematical. The argument that biological explanations are somehow basic and autonomous from lower-level explanations that advert only to the physical constituents of biological systems is greatly strengthened by the impossibility of reduction. By the same token modern biology's physicalist commitments seem to be undermined by this conclusion.

Consider a concrete case: a Mendelian gene is nothing but a nucleic acid molecule. Thus, its causal properties are identical to those of the molecule. Consequently, if a Mendelian explanation of inheritance is autonomous from a molecular one, the autonomy cannot be grounded in differences between the causal processes they report. One alternative is that the autonomy is explanatory. Biological theories meet our explanatory needs and interests even when the processes they report are physical. An alternative strategy bases biology's autonomy on a denial of supervenience, asserting that biology discovers emergent nonphysical properties—ones that cannot be fully explained in terms of more basic underlying physical properties and relations. This approach has become unattractive in the light of advances in molecular biology.

Levels and Units of Selection

Controversy over reductionism has spread from the molecular/Mendelian interface to sociobiology and behavioral biology. Because of its attempts to explain human and infrahuman social and cultural traits genetically, sociobiology is often accused of reductionism in a different sense: of unwarranted reduction of the number of causal determinants of a trait or behavior by excluding environmental causes. This is a mistake sociobiologists rarely make, for the theory of natural selection clearly teaches that the environment works with the gene to create phenotypes and selects for those that confer heritable fitness. Conflicts among biologists and philosophers about the bearers of these traits have become a new arena of debate about reductionism.

Individual organisms are presumably the bearers of heritable traits selected for environmental fitness. However, some biologists long held that there can be selection for traits of groups of individuals, in particular social groups. Such group selection was held to best explain the emergence of cooperation among otherwise self-interested fitness maximizers. Groups of organisms might be selected for adaptive traits that were not adaptive for their members taken individually. Groups would thus constitute units of selection with traits not reducible to individuals' traits. A number of biologists, including G. C. Williams (1966) and Richard Dawkins (1976), rejected this argument for a mixture of biological and philosophical arguments. They held the reductionist view that the unit of selection is neither the group, nor the individual, but the gene. All evolution of species, populations, families, and individuals was to be understood as selection for traits of individual genes. Their arguments included appeals to parsimony in theory construction, the unlikelihood that the specialized conditions required for group selection would ever materialize, and the claim that the apparent adaptation of a group or individual trait could be explained by the actual adaptation of one or more traits of genes. The debate surrounding this thesis of 'genic' selection has focused on the question of whether there are significant generalizations about selection at higher levels of organization—the genotype, the individual, or a group of individuals—that genic selection cannot explain. Or can selection of "selfish" fitness-maximizing genes explain the cooperative fitness-reducing behavior and individual organisms that contain the "selfish" genes? Solving this problem requires clarity on a number of broad issues in the philosophy of science: what counts as a significant generalization and a reductive explanation, what counts as a group, as a reproducing individual, and as a trait to be acted on by selection?

Issues in Taxonomy

Since Aristotle species names have been held to characterize "natural kinds." But the absence of any set of conditions necessary and sufficient—essential—for membership in any species makes taxonomy problem-atical. This absence of "essentialism" in classification distinguishes biology from the physical sciences, which seek the essence of kinds on the model of the atomic structure of the chemical elements. Some biologists and philosophers have sought to account for "nonessentialism" about species by arguing that species, such as *cygnis olor,* the swan, or *Didus ineptus,* the dodo, are not kinds with instances but (spatiotemporally distributed) historical individuals—the lineage—with parts—the individual swans or dodos. This thesis may explain why no unique biological taxonomy seems forthcoming, why species concepts constitute more fundamental categories than higher taxa such as genus, order, or phylum. If species are individuals, it will be no surprise that there are no laws about them, nor a single mechanism of speciation.

Beyond these questions in the philosophy of science biology is widely held to have direct relevance to philosophers' concerns about the nature of life, thought, action, meaning, and value. Thus, its recent revolutionary developments have been applied to illuminate areas of biomedical ethics, animal rights and welfare, ecological protection, as well as traditional topics in moral philosophy. Whether descriptive biology can have normative or prescriptive implications for individual and social policy hinges on questions that have vexed moral philosophers since David Hume first objected to inferences from what happens to be the case to what ought to be the case.

[See also Animal Rights and Welfare; Aristotle; Biomedical Ethics; Hume, David; Philosophy of Science; Physicalism, Materialism; Reduction, Reductionism; Supervenience.]

BIBLIOGRAPHY

Brandon, R., and R. Burian. *Genes, Organisms, and Populations.* Cambridge, 1984.
Darwin, C. *On the Origin of Species.* London, 1859.
Dawkins, R. *The Selfish Gene,* 2d ed. Oxford, 1989.
Ereshefsky, M. *The Units of Evolution: Essays on the Nature of Species.* Cambridge, MA, 1992.
Hull, D. *Science as a Process.* Chicago, 1989.
Kitcher, P. *Vaulting Ambition: Sociobiology and the Quest for Human Nature.* Cambridge, MA, 1985.
Maynard Smith, J. *Evolution and the Theory of Games.* Cambridge, 1982.
Mayr, E. *Towards a New Philosophy of Biology.* Cambridge, MA, 1988.
Nagel, E. *Teleology Revisited.* New York, 1977.
Rosenberg, A. *The Structure of Biological Science.* Cambridge, 1985.
Ruse, M. *The Philosophy of Biology Today.* Albany, NY, 1988.
Sober, E. *Conceptual Issues in Evolutionary Biology,* 2d ed. Cambridge, 1994.
———. *The Nature of Selection,* 2d ed. Chicago, 1994.
Wilson, E. O. *On Human Nature.* Cambridge, MA, 1978.
Wright, L. *Teleological Explanation.* Berkeley, 1976.

— ALEXANDER ROSENBERG

PHILOSOPHY OF LANGUAGE

A number of influences contrived to keep the philosophy of language at the center of analytical philosophy in the years following 1960. One was the continued influence of the *Philosophical Investigations* of Wittgenstein. A second fertile source of interest was the theory of speech acts, as it was developed in the work of J. L. Austin, whose untimely death in 1960 was closely followed by influential collections of his lectures and papers. A further influence was the emergence of linguistics as a full-fledged theoretical discipline, in the work of Noam Chomsky and his followers. Paul Grice's seminal paper "Meaning" (1957) was becoming the primary focus of discussion of the relationship between a speaker's intentions in making an utterance and the meaning of the words occurring in it. Finally, W. V. O. Quine's *Word and Object* appeared in 1960; perhaps more than any other single work it dictated the subsequent directions in which the philosophy of language traveled.

Although Wittgenstein's work had alerted philosophers to a certain flexibility in our concept of what is meant by any human utterance, particularly by emphasizing concepts such as that of a family resemblance, or that of the open texture of terms, it was Quine who defended the wholesale skepticism about determinate meaning known as the thesis of the 'indeterminacy of radical translation'. In chapter 2 of *Word and Object* he presented the scenario of the radical translator, confined to the use of observation and scientific method in attempting to form hypotheses about the meanings of the sentences and words of a foreign people. Quine's thesis was that such hypotheses are underdetermined by the data: there will always be an indefinite number of ways of translating the foreign speech, no one of which can claim to be the single correct way. Quine was not merely pointing out the kind of choices that translators in practice make. His thesis was the more radical one that the rival translations need stand to each other in "no kind of equivalence, however loose," yet still nothing in the peoples' reactions or dispositions would determine one to be right and the others wrong. Nor is his point intended to be only one about learning a second language or a foreign language, for he immediately applied it to the "home" case, arguing that even in familiar interactions expressed in our first native language, the same massive indeterminacies arise. Finally, his point is not simply an instance of the familiar underdetermination of scientific theory by data, for in the general case of theoretical science we may believe that further facts exist to make true one theory or another, even if our empirical evidence leaves those further facts undetermined,

whereas in the case of meaning there exists nothing—no mysterious mental fact—except the peoples' perceptions, actions, and behavior. There is here no further determining fact making it true that they mean one thing rather than another.

It might well be noticed that Quine and Wittgenstein are here surprisingly representative of cultural movements and philosophical traditions that at first blush seem quite alien to them. It was not only in the philosophical academies but in the wider culture that confidence in determinate meanings began to slip at this time. The loss of confidence, the fragmentations of authority, and the denial of uniquely correct "voices" or "versions" of history, experience, or even science were not only skeptical fantasies from the philosophical study, but also becoming matters of urgent concern in the humanities and in the culture in general. So, although Quine's thesis seemed incredible and even self-refuting to many philosophers (for we appear to have to understand, determinately, the rival interpretations suggested by different translation schemes), it focused attention in ways that were immediately recognized on the actual practices of translation, interpretation, and understanding that determine social relationships outside the study. In this way what might seem to be a domestic problem for abstract philosophical study became also an emblem of the 'postmodernist' climate, with many authors celebrating in different ways the denial of the 'given' or of any authoritative pivot on which practices of understanding would hinge.

In the following years Quine's austere conception of scientific method was enriched with other suggestions for the epistemology of interpretation. In particular Davidson influentially emphasized two aspects that had perhaps been underplayed by Quine. One was the importance of systematic semantic structure: to understand a language involves knowing how words and other subsentential elements contribute to the indefinite number of sentences in which they can occur. This knowledge, Davidson argued, can best be described by a fully formalized semantic theory of the kind that Tarski had developed for the rather different project of defining truth in a formal language. It would take as axioms whatever can properly be regarded as semantically primitive in the language studied (the object language) and deliver as theorems T-sentences, which are sentences saying of each sentence S of the language that S is true if and only if *p*. Such a theory therefore associates a truth condition with each sentence of the object language. Formally, Davidson's suggestion inaugurated the project of actually developing such a description of actual languages (a project about which Tarski had always been skeptical) and led to work on recalcitrant elements such as intensional contexts and descriptions of actions and events. Philosophically, it sparked a prolonged debate over the relationship between such a formal description of a language and the competence actually possessed by native speakers. Obviously, normal speakers do not explicitly know such theories, for even inadequate and simplified ones are extremely complex. The suggestion must be that they implicitly or tacitly know such theories, or at least that they have a competence that is modeled by such a theory even if there is no sense at all in which they know it. Problems of indeterminacy arise here also, since there will typically be an indefinite variety of formal theories capable of delivering the same theorems, so the question of which, if any, represents any truth about the speakers' actual psychologies is not easy to solve. Michael Dummett's work dominated this discussion and allied troubles about whether the notion of a truth condition is one that should be regarded as foundational.

What might seem a domestic problem for

abstract philosophical study became also

an emblem of the "postmodernist" climate,

with many authors celebrating the denial of the

"given" or of any authoritative pivot

on which practices of understanding would hinge.

The second feature of Davidson's position has been the emphasis on a principle of charity as a key element in the interpretation of others. We learn what people mean by their sayings, it seems, only by supposing them to be rational. We must suppose them to be, by and large, believers in what is true (and, perhaps, lovers of what is good). If their motives and delusions were sufficiently bizarre and widespread, practices of translation would grind to a halt. Again, there is a question of the status of this imputation of rationality and what it teaches us about our own propensities to truth. And there is the urgent question of what else, apart from system and charity, is involved in interpretation. For if these were all that is involved, once more indeterminacy would threaten, since a speaker may be interpreted as speaking truly but about subject matter that may on other grounds seem foreign to their interests and concerns. The problem becomes one of deciding which perceptual and causal links to the world also constrain interpretation.

This is, in effect, the problem of reference, and the same period saw a resurgence of concern with the particular links to the world afforded by our practices of naming and using demonstratives to refer to things in our immediate environment. Since Frege it has been customary to think of reference as mediated by sense: we refer to things by words that present their references in a certain way, as, for example; "Homer" presents the man only indirectly, as the apparently blind ninth-century B.C.E. Greek poet who wrote the *Iliad* and the *Odyssey*, and this way—the sense of the referring expression—mediates between it and the thing referred to. This model, essentially similar to that of Russell's theory of definite descriptions, was attacked by Ruth Marcus, David Kaplan, and Saul Kripke, and their work gave rise to a new paradigm of 'direct reference' in which names are thought to function very much as Russell believed logically proper names to behave but in which the restriction of their references to Russell's items of immediate experience is dropped.

This approach to semantics coincided with a new interest in theories of the mind that see it in computational terms, making transformations on elements thought of as elements in basic programming languages. This kind of functionalist model of the mind threatens the notion of reference, since to the computer the reference of elements is immaterial (it does not affect the software or hardware that '$' refers to a certain amount of money, for example). The principal lifeline for a genuine semantic notion of reference in the face of this challenge has usually been thought to be a causal theory, capable of selecting the "right" causal linkage to the external world to connect signs to objects. It is widely agreed that something must be added to causation to give a genuinely cognitive element, the relation that exists when we fix attention on a thing and form belief about that thing, but there exists no consensus on the right way to enrich the account. Many suggestions involve what Quine would call switching muses, already attributing cognitive grasp of a determinate kind to the subject whose reference to objects is being analyzed. Apart from these problems in the philosophy of mind, the main purely semantic problems faced by the direct theory of reference have been Russell and Frege's old reasons for avoiding it: the possibility of understanding differently two names for the same thing and of understanding a name that in fact has no bearer. Direct theories try in various ways to avoid or deny these phenomena.

The indeterminacy Quine explored includes indeterminacy of reference, or the possibility of multiple interpretations of the objects about which a speaker is concerned. Further indeterminacy emerged in Kripke's interpretation of Wittgenstein's "rule-following considerations." In *Wittgenstein on Rules and Private Language* Kripke interpreted the central texts of the *Philosophical Investigations* as a response to a skeptical paradox similar to Quine's. The paradox suggests that no fact either in a subject's behavior or in occurrences in their mind can be sufficient to identify a single rule governing the application of functions and predicates that they use. Wittgenstein held that this would be true of the private language he describes, which is the reason why the hypothesis of such a language is a delusion, but Kripke's discussion suggests that the threat encompasses any language. Kripke offers a solution that involves both social elements, whereby persons manage to deem one another to be following specific rules, and an "anti-realist" element, whereby rule following is seen not as a real fact but rather as a kind of fiction or compliment we pay each other. Both elements of this position have excited fierce controversy, particularly among rival commentators wishing to show that they are untrue to Wittgenstein.

We have very little access to mind,

apart from language.

But we have very little access to language

apart from mind.

We have very little access to mind, apart from language. But we have very little access to language apart from mind. That is, the philosophies of mind and language are inextricably intertwined. Probably in 1960 it was easier to believe that authority flowed one way only, from the study of language to that of mind. By the late twentieth century this was no longer so. It was by then widely recognized that computational approaches to mind are unlikely to welcome sharp division between the mental lives of language-using creatures (or computers) and those who live their lives or conduct their programs nonlinguistically. The lowly creature that perceives and responds, focuses attention on aspects of the environment, or is adapted for fleeing or feeding on some of its elements, may be a better starting point for a philosophy of reference or even predication and truth than the full-fledged competent user of a language. Not only did this change in the flow of authority affect writings of the late twentieth century, but it was abetted by developments within the philosophy of language itself. Certainly since Carnap, but prominently in Wittgenstein, there have surfaced doubts about the very possibility of a substantive philosophy of language, a 'semantics' that would represent in some scientific way the function of parts of language and the epistemological status of the whole. Pursuing such a project might seem to be attempting to step outside our own skins, attempting to occupy a standpoint available only to some fantasized being that could theorize about language and the world without itself standing inside a particular linguistic clothing. A characteristic reaction to this problem became the adoption of varieties of "minimalisms," or philosophies counseling that in the end there is little substantive that we can say about the centrally contested concepts of semantics: truth, reference, and meaning.

[See also Analyticity; Anaphora; Carnap, Rudolph; Chomsky, Noam; Computational Model of Mind, The; Conditionals; Davidson, Donald; Dummett, Michael; Frege, Gottlob; Grice, Herbert Paul; Indexicals; Kripke, Saul Aaron; Language; Logical Form; Marcus, Ruth Barcan; Meaning; Metaphor; Modernism and Postmodernism; Philosophy of Mind; Phonology; Pragmatics; Propositions; Quine, Willard Van Orman; Reference; Rule Following; Russell, Bertrand Arthur William; Semantics; Sense; Syntax; Truth; Vagueness; Wittgenstein, Ludwig Josef Johann.]

BIBLIOGRAPHY

Austin, J. L. *How to Do Things with Words.* Oxford, 1962.
Barrett, R., and R. Gibson. *Perspectives on Quine.* Oxford, 1990. A good entry to the debates that have centered on Quine's work.
Blackburn, S. *Spreading the Word.* Oxford, 1984. An introductory overview of the field.
Dummett, M. *The Seas of Language.* Oxford, 1993.
Evans, G., and J. McDowell, eds. *Truth and Meaning.* Oxford, 1976. A useful collection of essays largely representing a Davidsonian outlook.
Grice, P. *Studies in the Way of Words.* Cambridge, MA, 1989.
Horwich, P. *Truth.* Oxford, 1992. The best statement of modern minimalism, especially about the concept of truth.
Kripke, S. *Naming and Necessity.* Oxford, 1980.
———. *Wittgenstein on Rules and Private Language.* Oxford, 1982.
Martinich, A. P., ed. *The Philosophy of Language.* New York, 1985. The standard collection of important papers on the subject.
Quine, W. V. O. *Word and Object.* Cambridge, MA, 1960.

— SIMON BLACKBURN

PHILOSOPHY OF LAW, PROBLEMS OF

The philosophy of law has come a long way since 1967. At that time, the field was dominated by the legal positivism of H. L. A. Hart, who wrote the original essay on philosophy of law, problems of, in *The Encyclopedia of Philosophy.* There were critics, of course, including Lon Fuller, a natural law theorist; but a much wider variety of approaches sprang up in the 1970s and 1980s.

Probably the most prominent individual has been Ronald Dworkin (1978, 1986), who began by distinguishing rules, such as "Don't drive over 65 MPH," from principles that specify requirements of morality, such as "People should not profit from their own wrongs," and from policies that set out goals, such as "Automobile accidents are to be decreased." According to Dworkin, Hart's legal positivism captured rules but not principles or policies, so it failed to include all parts of law. As a result, Hart ascribed discretion to judges whenever they are not bound by rules, but Dworkin argued that judges do not have discretion if they are still bound by principles. Dworkin also denied that the distinction between morality and law is as clear as Hart assumed.

Dworkin's alternative approach invoked an ideal judge named Hercules who develops a theory of political morality to justify all of the substantive and procedural precedents and statutes in the jurisdiction. Hercules' "soundest theory of law" then determined which rules and principles are valid and which legal obligations exist. Dworkin argued that Hercules would and judges should base their decision only on rules or principles rather than on policies (the rights thesis), but there are enough principles to determine one right answer in every legal case, at least in the United States and Britain.

In his later work Dworkin has emphasized interpretation and analogized strings of judicial decisions to a chain novel game in which each successive player writes a new chapter and tries to make the whole novel as good as it can be. Just as previous chapters constrain chain novelists, so previous decisions constrain judges: and just as chain novelists rely on their views about what makes a novel good, so judges cannot make decisions without appealing to some moral values. More specifically, Dworkin argued that judges should ultimately base their decisions on a substantive moral theory whose fundamental principle requires the government to show equal concern and respect for all citizens but not necessarily to treat them all equally.

Although Dworkin's views attracted many followers, he was also criticized from many sides. Some conservative critics (e.g., Bork, 1990) objected that Dworkin's theory gives too much power to judges. These critics claimed instead that the original intentions of lawmakers and the original meanings of the words in laws determine what the law is and what judges should decide, so judges should not use their own moral beliefs to make legal decisions. Such judicial restraint was supposed to be the only way to maintain a legitimate separation of powers.

At the opposite extreme, pragmatists (e.g., Posner, 1990) have argued that Dworkin is too restrictive in his claim that judges should base their legal decisions only on rules and principles rather than on policies. According to pragmatists, court decisions are and should be based on the practical consequences of those decisions. One version of this claim has been espoused by members of the law and economics movement, who use the methods of economics to understand the content and evolution of law and claim that laws and judicial decisions do and should seek to maximize society's wealth. This focus on consequences would force judges to look at particular situations and thereby would take judges far from the traditional view of legal reasoning in terms of rules and rights.

According to critical legal studies,

there are usually or always

enough precedents on both sides and

enough vagueness in statutes

for a judge to support any decision

that she or he wants to make.

Pragmatists' skepticism about rules has been shared by members of the critical legal studies movement (e.g., Unger, 1986). This group is diverse, but it is often associated with leftist political views and with strong claims about the indeterminacy of law. According to critical legal studies, there are usually or always enough precedents on both sides and enough vagueness in statutes for a judge to support any decision that she or he wants to make. In this respect, critical legal studies is often seen as a descendant of American legal realism.

Another movement that gained prominence during the 1970s and 1980s is feminist jurisprudence. Many feminists have espoused a new methodology that pays more attention to the particular context of acts, laws, and judicial decisions. For example, the common construct of a genderless legal subject has been criticized as a myth, both because it overlooks important aspects of the context in which a person acts (namely, that person's gender and social stereotypes about that gender) and because of the context in which this construct itself arose. In their more substantive work feminist jurisprudes exposed the ways in which laws favor males or represent male perspectives in many areas including abortion, reproductive technology, sexual harassment, rape, battering, pornography, sex discrimination, and pregnancy leaves. Of course, feminists have disagreed in their approaches to these issues. Some have emphasized similarities between men and women, such as in mental capacity; others have emphasized differences between men and women, such as regarding pregnancy (Minow, 1990); and still others have emphasized the subtle ways in which law supports the dominance of men over women, such as by making it difficult to convict rapists and batterers (MacKinnon, 1987). Despite these and other disagreements, all feminists share the goal of improving the legal and social status of women.

Critical race theory has also questioned both the method and the substance of traditional jurisprudence (Bell, 1987, 1992). Its advocates have often employed fiction and first-person narratives (also used by some feminists) to show what law looks like from the perspective of a member of an underprivileged minority. Critical race theorists have focused on the law of discrimination and affirmative action and have shown how and why racial problems persist. An important debate within critical race theory has concerned whether the rhetoric of rights aids or impedes the progress of racial minorities.

These movements mainly concern the nature of law and how judges ought to reason. There have also been developments regarding the substance of law and its evaluation. Some of these substantive developments were stimulated by new kinds of government programs and laws. For example, since the 1970s affirmative action programs have created great controversy. Some philosophers of law argued that affirmative action was justified as retribution or compensation for past injustices or that it served important social goals without violating any rights. Critics saw affirmative action as a form of discrimination, because it treated individuals according to their race, gender, or ethnic group. Then, in the 1980s new kinds of laws against pornography and against hate speech were proposed by some as necessary to achieve sexual and racial equality and criticized by others as vague and thus dangerous to speech that should be protected against censorship. Such substantive debates have occupied many philosophers of law, who have used their general theories of law to illuminate these particular issues and to argue for or against proposed laws.

Philosophers of law have also developed new theories for evaluating laws in several particular areas. One prominent example is punishment, where several philosophers have defended new versions of retributivism, some of which proportion punishment, not only to the harm done by the criminal, but also to the degree of responsibility of the criminal or instead to the unfair advantages gained by the criminal. There have also been advances in the theory of justice. John Rawls (1971) raised liberalism to new levels of sophistication, Robert Nozick (1974) countered with a forceful argument for libertarianism, and communitarians criticized both the-

ories for oversimplifying the nature of persons (e.g., Sandel, 1982). Such theories of justice might belong to political theory rather than to the philosophy of law itself, but they are discussed by philosophers of law, because these theories have very different implications about what kinds of laws should be passed or overturned. This interest in theories of justice is one instance of a general tendency of philosophers of law to use theories from related fields—a tendency that grew during the decades after 1967.

[See also Abortion; Affirmative Action; Communitarianism; Genetics and Reproductive Technologies; Justice; Liberalism; Racism; Rawls, John; Rights.]

BIBLIOGRAPHY

Bell, D. *And We Are Not Saved*. New York, 1987.
———. *Faces at the Bottom of the Well*. New York, 1992.
Bork, R. *The Tempting of America*. New York, 1990.
Dworkin, R. *Taking Rights Seriously*. Cambridge, 1978.
———. *Law's Empire*. Cambridge, 1986.
MacKinnon, C. *Feminism Unmodified*. Cambridge, 1987.
Minow, M. *Making All the Difference*. Ithaca, NY, 1990.
Nozick, R. *Anarchy, State, and Utopia*. New York, 1974.
Posner, R. *Problems of Jurisprudence*. Cambridge, 1990.
Rawls, J. *A Theory of Justice*. Cambridge, 1971.
Sandel, M. *Liberalism and the Limits of Justice*. Cambridge, 1982.

— WALTER SINNOTT-ARMSTRONG

PHILOSOPHY OF MEDICINE

The subject matter unique to philosophy of medicine—as opposed to those issues that are best seen under the heading of philosophy of biology—is clinical medicine and its underlying methodology and assumptions. Crucial to philosophy of medicine is the family of terms disease, malady, health, normal, abnormal, condition, syndrome, all of which have evaluative aspects to their definitions. For all its scientific base, medicine must be a value-laden practice guided by the values of its practitioners and its public. It is in this regard, but not only in this regard, that the claim "Medicine is an art and a science" should be understood.

Disease, Health, and Normality

A stable departure from physiological normality that causes death, disability, pain, loss of pleasure, or inability to achieve pleasure is the sort of entity that is called disease (Clouser, Culver, & Gert, 1981). The departure has to be stable enough so that it causes similar problems in similar people and so that it is recognizable by different medical practitioners as the same disease entity. When the departure is less clearly individuatable than a disease, the entity is referred to as a syndrome.

Normality and health are relative terms. They are relative to species, age, gender, (perhaps) social status, race, and ultimately to one's own physiology. A healthy (normal) eighty-five-year-old is quite different from a healthy (normal) twenty-year-old; and a healthy (normal) professional athlete is quite different from a healthy (normal) philosophy professor. Normal health is also relative to one's values. Unless a person feels comfortable doing what she wants to do, she can claim to be unhealthy by saying things like: "I just don't feel up to par." In this sense health is a theoretical state of a person.

The concept of biological variability derives its useful sense from the relativity of "normal." Biological variability makes generalization problematic in a way that generalizing from one billiard ball to any such object is not. Biological variability, meaning that no two organisms are exactly alike, is trivially true. It is unhelpful, except as a reminder that generalization is problematic.

Diseases are real to the extent that they are stable departures from normality (sometimes called "baseline") as defined above. Obviously, diseases are not like traditional physical objects. They can overlap and be in two places at the same time. (Mental diseases present their sorts of problems, which parallel issues in philosophy of mind and philosophy of psychology.) Diseases are real in that they cause real pain, disability, or both. Diseases are real in the sense that they can be reduced to physiological occurrences. Diseases are theoretical in the sense that they are not traditional physical objects, *and* they are identified only relative to a value structure that then becomes part of the medical theory. For example, given the current medical theory of Western scientific medicine, chronic fatigue syndrome is a disease. But against the backdrop of eighteenth-century medicine, it would have been seen primarily as a characteristic of some women and lazy men. Chiropractic medicine sees disease only in terms of misalignment of vertebrae. The reality of disease, a sense for reduction, and the theory-ladenness of disease exemplify traditional questions in philosophy of science.

What is classifiable as a disease is also a function of what physicians are willing to do, what they are interested in, and what will be reimbursed. Thus, infertility

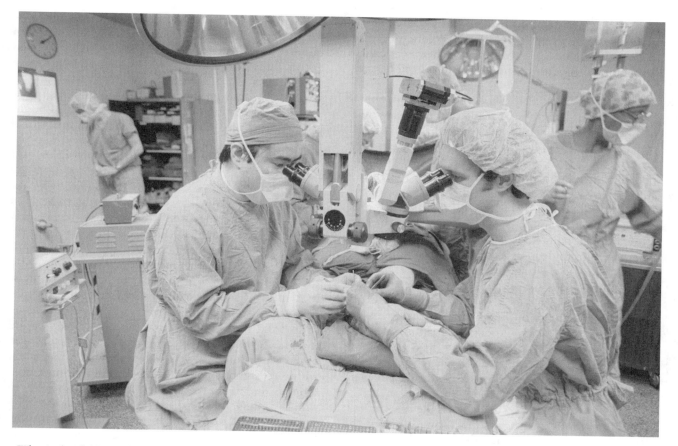

What is classifiable as a disease is also a function of what physicians are willing to do, in what they are interested, and what will be reimbursed. (Corbis/Bettmann)

is treated as a disease in large part because it is a terrible burden to some, it is interesting to deal with medically, and people are willing to pay for treatment. Being short is also treated as a condition worth reversing (in children) for the same sorts of reasons. This makes disease relative to culture and economic conditions.

Crucial to philosophy of medicine

is the family of terms disease,

malady, health, normal, abnormal, condition,

syndrome—all of which have evaluative aspects

to their definitions.

Treating a condition as if it were a disease makes it a disease in a stipulative sense but not in the physiological sense. Baldness and bad breath would be conditions that might be very troublesome, most effectively treated medically, and yet still not classified as diseases. However, if they are caused by a disease, they may be considered signs of an underlying medical condition. Psychiatry periodically redecides whether certain psychological conditions should be considered diseases.

The Logic of Diagnosis

Diagnosis and scientific explanation present similar philosophical problems, especially with respect to explanation, causality, and laws. Diagnosis begins with history taking and moves on to the physical examination. The standard history questions assume that disease entities have a typical natural history to them.

Signs are objective characteristics such as blood pressure and broken bones. Symptoms are the subjective characteristics reported by the patient—for example, pain and lightheadedness. The signs and symptoms of disease vary with the stage of the disease. Thus, an early stage of any disease may be confused for the later stage of another. Physicians look for the best overall explanation for the condition, given the patient's individuating factors such as age, gender, occupation, stress factors, and so forth. The best explanation is assumed to be the most probable explanation, where the disease is considered to be the cause of the condition being investigated.

A standard procedure in diagnosis is the rule-out test. A physician limits the diagnosis to a few conditions and then does a test, which, if negative, will rule out one of the possible causes. This procedure is repeated until only one likely answer is left. This is in keeping with a simplistic version of falsification.

Doctors also use a simple confirmation strategy in diagnosis. Usually, more than one confirmatory test result is required before the diagnosis is accepted. Other predictions will have to be borne out by test results as well as physical findings and consistent history. Laboratory tests are crucial to modern-day diagnoses, although they present problems. Results are subject to false positives (disease reported when absent) and false negatives (disease not reported when present). The best test has a high true positive ratio and a low false positive ratio. Bayes's theorem can be used to calculate the probability that a person with a positive test actually does have the disease in question.

Since test results are continuous, cutoff points must be chosen. The cutoff points are chosen based on how serious an error would be. If a disease is fatal and can be treated safely, then a high false positive rate would be acceptable. For less worrisome conditions, compromise between the two figures is possible. Again, values are part of what looks like a very objective aspect of medicine. In this sense, medical diagnosis may be different from the usual picture of the scientific method. There are other differences as well.

Some of the crucial aspects of physical diagnosis—for example, interpreting heart sounds and kinds of rashes—are subjective and cannot be taught so much as they must be learned by practice. The apprenticeship of medical students and physicians (residents) is, in this sense, different from the time graduate students in science spend learning bench laboratory skills. Also, anecdotes play a role in diagnosis in a way that they would not in physics or most other sciences. Related to the reliance on anecdotes is that the best physicians just seem to "sense" that, no matter where the facts are pointing, something else is going on. Subjectivity, anecdotes, and intuition seem not, in general, to be good scientific methodology, and yet it seems to be precisely what separates the great clinicians from the ordinary ones. The key to understanding these great diagnosticians is probably pattern recognition.

Physicians often wait in order to let a disease show itself more clearly, sometimes confirming their diagnoses by followup: did the condition follow its predicted course; did the treatment have the expected effect and in the expected manner? If not, the diagnosis may well have been incorrect. Even if the followup is consistent with the diagnosis, the actual condition may have been different and may have remitted on its own or have been similar enough to the disease suspected so that it responded to the treatment. In these sorts of cases, physicians do not know that they were wrong. They will count these cases as successes and so use them to support a similar diagnosis the next time. There is no practical defense against this failing.

Holism and Reductionism

Holistic medicine assumes that diseases are primarily a function of lifestyle and life events of the patient. A holistic approach to diagnosis will focus as much on psychosocial history as it will on traditional signs and symptoms. Stress as a factor in disease is very important in holistic accounts. Reductionistic medicine focuses more on physiology as the key to diagnosis, treatment, and taxonomy of disease. The reductionistic approach is the legacy of scientific medicine begun in the mid-nineteenth century.

[See also Bayesianism; Causation; Explanation; Laws of Nature; Philosophy of Biology; Philosophy of Mind; Philosophy of Science; Reduction, Reductionism.]

BIBLIOGRAPHY

Bursztajn, H., R. Feinbloom, R. Hamm, and A. Brodsky. *Medical Choices, Medical Chances.* New York, 1990. Parts 1 and 2.

Clouser, K. D., C. M. Culver, and B. Gert. "Malady: A New Treatment of Disease," *Hastings Center Report* (June 1981), 11, 29–37.

Kelley, W., ed. *Textbook of Internal Medicine.* Philadelphia, 1992. Chaps. 6–8.

Margolis, J. "Thoughts on Definitions of Disease," *Journal of Medicine and Philosophy,* Vol. 11, No. 3 (Aug. 1986), 233–36.

Maull, N. "The Practical Science of Medicine," *Journal of Medicine and Philosophy,* Vol. 6, No. 2 (May 1981), 165–82.

McNeil, B., et al. "Primer on Certain Elements of Medical Decision Making," *New England Journal of Medicine,* Vol. 293, No. 5 (July 31, 1975), 211–15.

Merskey, H. "Variable Meanings for the Definition of Disease," *Journal of Medicine and Philosophy,* Vol. 11, No. 3 (Aug. 1986), 215–32.

Munson, R. "Why Medicine Cannot Be a Science," *Journal of Medicine and Philosophy,* Vol. 6, No. 2 (May 1981), 183–208.

Murphy, A. E. *The Logic of Medicine.* Baltimore, 1976.

Passmore, R., ed. *A Companion to Medical Studies,* vol. 3. Oxford, 1974.

Schaffner, K. "Philosophy of Medicine," in M. Salmon et al., eds. *Philosophy of Science* (Englewood Cliffs, NJ, 1992).

Wulff, H. *Rational Diagnosis and Treatment.* Oxford, 1976.

— ARTHUR ZUCKER

PHILOSOPHY OF MIND

During the 1960s the philosophy of mind was shaking off its Cartesian and behaviorist past and entering a hopeful new phase. In Australia, J. J. C. Smart and U. T. Place, prodded by C. B. Martin, had advanced an identity theory, according to which mental kinds (visual experiences of red, for instance) were held to be identical with physical (neurological) kinds (Smart, 1959). Identities of this sort, like the identification of water with H_2O, do not imply interdefinability: water is H_2O, even though the terms *water* and *H_2O* are not interdefinable.

The identity theory afforded a way of seeing how dualism could be avoided and the traditional mind–body problem solved without a commitment to behaviorism. Even so, the theory came under attack from a variety of sources. Donald Davidson (1970) pointed out that it was one thing to suppose that every mental token or particular is identical with some physical token or particular and quite another matter to imagine a one–one pairing of mental and physical types. My thinking of Vienna is identical, perhaps, with some neural event of type N_1; your thinking of Vienna could be identical with some neural event of type N_2. Mental particulars might be physical particulars, then, even though the relation between mental and physical kinds is not principled or reductive.

The identity theory purported to demystify the mind by showing how it might be possible to understand mental episodes as nothing more than physical occurrences.

Why then should we suppose that every mental particular, every instance of a mental property or kind, is identical with some physical particular? How could such identities be anything more than fortuitous? To answer this question, Davidson appealed to supervenience, long a staple of ethical theorists. If the mental supervenes on the physical, two agents could not differ mentally without differing in some physical respect. Davidson regarded supervenience as nonreductive: if mental properties supervene on physical properties, this implies neither that mental properties are physical properties nor that there are strict laws relating the mental and the physical. Davidson dubbed the resulting view anomalous monism: mental events are physical events, though there are no strict psychophysical laws.

Subsequent refinements of the notion of supervenience, notably those proposed by Jaegwon Kim (1984), have cast doubt on its anomalousness. One way of characterizing mental–physical supervenience is as follows: necessarily, if anything, x, has a mental property, M, there is some physical property, P, such that x has P, and necessarily, if anything, y, has P, y has M. Such a characterization allows for principled relations between mental properties and physical properties, or at any rate between mental properties and disjunctions of physical properties.

Functionalism represents another line of response to the identity theory: mental properties are identified with second-order, functional properties (Fodor, 1968). My thinking of Vienna is a matter of my being in a state with particular sorts of causal or dispositional relations to other states. If I am thinking of Vienna, then I am disposed to act in certain ways (to respond, perhaps, to your query, "A penny for your thoughts," with "Vienna") and to entertain other, related thoughts. What I actually do or think will depend on my other states of mind. I will not say that I am thinking of Vienna if I believe that I might be punished for having such a thought or if I want to deceive you. In this respect functionalism differs from old-fashioned behaviorism, which identified the having of particular kinds of thoughts with tendencies to behave in specific ways. Still, functionalism can be seen as a refinement rather than a rejection of behaviorism.

One sort of functionalism, computationalism, depicts states of mind as relations between agents and syntactically defined internal symbols (Fodor, 1975). These symbols—sentences in a language of thought—owe their meaning to relations they bear to one another and to inputs and outputs. Mental operations, however, are fully characterizable syntactically—that is, without reference to the semantic features of mental items.

This picture, which underlies research in cognitive psychology and artificial intelligence (AI), has been challenged by connectionist (or neural network) models of mind. Connectionists regard minds, not as syntactic engines serially manipulating well-defined symbols, but as interconnected arrays of nodes whose relations yield outputs resembling the "fuzzy" categories of ordinary human cognition.

The computationalist model has been attacked as well by John Searle in a much-discussed thought experiment. Imagine that Wanda is placed in a room and Chinese characters are passed to her through a slot. When she receives these characters Wanda consults a code book that instructs her to pass other characters out through the slot. Wanda may be computationally equivalent to a Chinese speaker, yet she does not understand Chinese. So, Searle contends, computationalism (and functionalism generally) cannot account for a central component of our mental lives.

The identity theory purported to demystify the mind by showing how it might be possible to understand mental episodes as nothing more than physical occurrences. Inspired by W. V. O. Quine and Wilfrid Sellars, Richard Rorty (1965) argued that we might see ascriptions of states of mind on the model of a scientific theory: mental terms resemble theoretical terms deployed in the sciences. Mental items are "posited" to explain behavior just as electrons are introduced to explain chemical phenomena. We "eliminate" entities postulated by a theory when we abandon the theory, however. We once explained the transfer of heat by positing a fluid, caloric, that flowed between material bodies. With the emergence of thermodynamics we eliminated

caloric from our ontology. A similar, fate might await beliefs, desires, and pains if neurobiology has its way (Churchland, 1981).

Externalism and the Reemergence of the Mind-Body Problem

Consider the so-called propositional attitudes: belief, desire, intention, and the like. In believing (or desiring, or intending) we take up an attitude toward some proposition. I can believe, or hope, or fear, or (if I am a rainmaker) intend that it will rain. Could such states of mind supervene on our physical features? The question is pressing owing to the widely held supposition that the propositional content of agents' states of mind depends, not merely on agents' intrinsic physical features, but on relations that agents bear to their circumstances.

Contextual accounts of mental content are motivated by appeals to "Twin Earth" cases of a sort pioneered by Hilary Putnam and extended by Tyler Burge (Burge, 1979; Putnam, 1975). What makes my thoughts about water concern water? Imagine a twin me existing on a planet indiscernible from Earth in all but one respect: on Twin Earth oceans and rivers contain, not water, not H_2O, but XYZ. When my Twin Earth counterpart has thoughts he would express by saying "there's water," his thoughts concern, not water, but XYZ, twin water. Mental differences between my twin and me are due, not to our intrinsic physical makeup, but to our circumstances. My thoughts concern water, and my twin's concern twin water, because my environment includes water, and his contains XYZ.

Such externalist or anti-individualist conceptions of mind might be thought to be incompatible with supervenience. We can, however, suppose that contextually fixed mental features of agents supervene on their physical features, provided we include among those physical features relations agents bear to their surroundings. Impressed by such considerations, Putnam, Jerry Fodor, and others have promoted a distinction between broad and narrow mental content: broad content is exhibited by states of mind whose supervenience base includes agents' contexts; narrow content supervenes on agents' intrinsic features. Agents, identical with respect to their intrinsic physical features but distinct with respect to their circumstances, have the same narrow states of mind even if they differ with respect to their broad mental states.

Fodor has argued that a properly scientific psychology can appeal only to agents' narrow features in explaining behavior: how I behave, including how I respond to incoming stimuli, depends on my intrinsic features (Fodor, 1981). To the extent that some states of mind are determined by relations I bear to my surroundings, these cannot be relevant to what I do. Fodor has cited such considerations as evidence for narrow content; others, skeptical of the notion, have concluded either that the explanation of behavior in terms of content is a nonstarter (Stich, 1983) or that psychological explanation is inherently anti-individualistic (Burge, 1979).

The rise of externalism has reinvigorated the mind–body problem. In identifying mental and physical properties, classical identity theories showed how mental and physical events could be causally related. Token identity and supervenience, however, reintroduce the problem. Suppose every mental particular is a physical particular. Suppose further that my thinking of Vienna is identical with some neurological event in my brain and that this event leads me to utter the sentence "Vienna is congested." The neurological event is a thinking of Vienna, and this event causes my utterance, but in what sense does the event's being a thinking of Vienna make any difference at all to what it causes? If we assume that the physical world is causally closed, it would apparently be possible in principle to offer a complete explanation of my behavior without reference to any mental properties I might happen to instantiate. Mental properties appear in this light to be epiphenomenal.

Since the 1960s philosophers of mind

have tended to repress the question

of how consciousness fits into the physical world.

The problem is not merely that my thinking of Vienna might depend on my circumstances, although this makes the difficulty particularly acute. Assuming closure, two agents, indistinguishable with respect to their intrinsic physical characteristics, must behave identically given identical stimuli. If such agents differ mentally, these differences apparently lack causal relevance. Even if we reject externalism, however, so long as we suppose that the mental supervenes on the physical, it is hard to see how agents' mental properties could matter causally. Supervenience establishes property correlations. But the presence of a correlation, even a principled correlation, between the mental and the physical does not support the conclusion that the mental makes a causal difference if the physical does.

Other Developments

Since the 1960s philosophers of mind have tended to repress the question of how consciousness fits into the physical world, focusing instead on intentionality, the "ofness" or "aboutness" of thought. As a result, it remains unclear how best to understand the place of conscious phenomena. A functionalist account would seem

unpromising (though see Dennett, 1991, and Shoemaker, 1975). Some philosophers, following Thomas Nagel (1974), have elected to home in on the "what-it's-likeness" of ordinary conscious experiences, arguing that attempts to accommodate consciousness to the physical world as we now understand it are bound to fail.

Since Smart's defense of materialism in 1959 the philosophy of mind has grown and diversified. At times solutions to long-standing philosophical problems seemed imminent. At other times the prospects have appeared less hopeful. Progress in philosophy is measured, not by the discovery of settled solutions to such problems, however, but by an improved and deepened understanding of the domain. So measured, progress in the philosophy of mind has been remarkable.

[See also *Action Theory; Anomalous Monism; Artificial Intelligence; Computational Model of Mind, The; Connectionism; Consciousness in Anglo-American Philosophy; Consciousness in Phenomenology; Davidson, Donald; Eliminative Materialism, Eliminativism; Folk Psychology; Functionalism; Language of Thought; Mental Causation; Mental Imagery; Mental Representation; Multiple Realizability; Personal Identity; Physicalism, Materialism; Putnam, Hilary; Qualia; Quine, Willard Van Orman; Reduction, Reductionism; Self; Sellars, Wilfrid; Smart, John Jamieson Carswell; Subjectivity; Supervenience.*]

BIBLIOGRAPHY

Burge, T. "Individualism and the Mental," *Midwest Studies in Philosophy,* Vol. 4 (1979), 73–121.

Churchland, P. M. "Eliminative Materialism and the Propositional Attitudes," *Journal of Philosophy,* Vol. 78 (1981), 67–90.

Davidson, D. "Mental Events," in L. Foster and J. Swanson, eds., *Experience and Theory* (Amherst, MA, 1970). Reprinted in *Essays on Actions and Events* (Oxford, 1980).

Dennett, D. C. *Consciousness Explained.* Boston, 1991.

Fodor, J. "Methodological Solipsism Considered as a Research Strategy in Cognitive Psychology," *Behavioral and Brain Sciences,* Vol. 3 (1981), 63–73.

———. *The Language of Thought.* New York, 1975.

———. *Psychological Explanation.* New York, 1968.

Kim, J. "Concepts of Supervenience." *Philosophical and Phenomenological Research,* Vol. 45 (1984), 153–76.

Nagel, T. "What Is It Like to Be a Bat?" *Philosophical Review,* Vol. 83 (1974), 435–50.

Putnam, H. "The Meaning of 'Meaning,' " in *Mind, Language, and Reality* (Cambridge, 1975).

Rorty, R. "Mind-Body Identity, Privacy, and Categories," *Review of Metaphysics,* Vol. 19 (1965), 24–54.

Searle, J. "Minds, Brains, and Programs," *Behavioral and Brain Sciences,* Vol. 3 (1980), 417–24.

Shoemaker, S. "Functionalism and Qualia," *Synthese,* Vol. 27 (1975), 291–315.

Smart, J. J. C. "Sensations and Brain Processes," *Philosophical Review,* Vol. 68 (1959), 141–56.

Stich, S. P. *From Folk Psychology to Cognitive Science.* Cambridge, MA, 1983.

– JOHN HEIL

PHILOSOPHY OF PHYSICS

Of all the special sciences to which philosophy has given birth, physics is perhaps the oldest and most successful, as its archaic name, natural philosophy, attests. But despite its venerable status as an independent discipline, the more recent history of physics has highlighted its intimate interconnections—both epistemological and metaphysical—with philosophy. Radical developments in twentieth-century physics have prompted reflection on the character and reliability of scientific knowledge while at the same time challenging some of our most basic assumptions concerning the nature of the world and our relation to it. Moreover, physicists have sometimes appealed to characteristically philosophical arguments in the course of developing or defending their views. Most important to philosophy, perhaps, are the conceptual issues raised by fundamental physics itself.

Relativity

Einstein created two theories of relativity, known as the special and the general theory. Each in turn involved radically new conceptions of space and time. Einstein (1905) based the special theory on two principles. The principle of relativity states that all states of uniform motion are physically equivalent. The principle of the constancy of the speed of light states that light travels at a definite speed in a vacuum, independent of the motion of its source. For Einstein the principle of relativity derived support from both experiment and symmetry considerations. The constancy of the speed of light was a consequence of the then accepted wave theory of light, for which there was much experimental support. Einstein was able to construct a theory from these principles only by modifying certain intuitive assumptions about time incorporated into physics since Newton. He took these modifications to follow from a definition of simultaneity for events at different places, in accordance with which light travels at the same speed (in a vacuum) in both directions between these places.

Most important to philosophy, perhaps, are the conceptual issues raised by fundamental physics itself.

Einstein's teacher Minkowski (1908) presented this special theory of relativity as explicitly postulating a radically new four-dimensional structure incorporating time as well as space. Minkowski spacetime is a generalization of Euclidean geometry. The analogues of points of Euclidean space are points of Minkowski spacetime, at each of which an instantaneous, spatially

unextended, event may occur. A point in Euclidean space can be labeled by three numbers (x,y,z), which specify how far away it is from a fixed point o, as measured along each of three fixed, mutually perpendicular, directions. These numbers are called the point's coordinates, and o and the three directions define the corresponding Cartesian coordinate system with o as origin. Pythagoras's theorem implies that the square of the distance Δs between the points p and q is equal to the sum of the squares of the differences between p's coordinates and q's coordinates, as follows.

$$(1) \qquad \Delta s^2(p,q) = (x_p - x_q)^2 + (y_p - y_q)^2 + (z_p - z_q)^2$$

The distance between two points does not depend on the choice of the Cartesian coordinate system. This invariance of distance characterizes the intrinsic geometric structure of Euclidean space. Analogously, each point in Minkowski spacetime may be labeled by four numbers (x,y,z,t): the first three numbers are Cartesian coordinates of the point's spatial location, and the fourth specifies the time an event may have occurred at the point. The fundamental invariant quantity defining the structure of Minkowski spacetime is the spacetime interval $\Delta I(p,q)$ defined by

$$(2) \qquad \Delta I(p,q) = c^2\,\Delta t^2(p,q) - \Delta s^2(p,q)$$

(where $\Delta t(p,q)$ is the elapsed time, and $\Delta s(p,q)$ is the spatial distance, between the points p,q of Minkowski spacetime, and c is a number equal to the speed of light in a vacuum). Now let K,K' be two states of uniform, unaccelerated motion: suppose that (x,y,z,t) is a system of coordinates for Minkowski spacetime such that the (spatial) origin o of the Cartesian coordinate system (x,y,z) remains at rest in K, and (x',y',z',t') is a similar system whose spatial origin o' remains at rest in K'. Then the invariance of the Minkowski spacetime interval means that

$$(3) \qquad c^2\Delta t'^2(p,q) - \Delta s'^2(p,q) = c^2\Delta t^2(p,q) - \Delta s^2(p,q)$$

Newton maintained that both the spatial distance and the temporal interval between every pair of spatiotemporally localized events constituted intrinsic relations between them. In such a Newtonian spacetime the interval given by equation (2) is consequently also invariant, provided that $\Delta t(p,q)$ represents the intrinsic temporal interval and $\Delta s(p,q)$ represents the intrinsic spatial distance between p and q. But if $\Delta s(p,q)$ is calculated according to equation (1) in the (x,y,z,t) system, and $\Delta s'(p,q)$ is given by an analogous equation in the (x',y',z',t') system, then equation (3) cannot hold in

Newtonian spacetime if K,K' represent different states of motion. For in that case $\Delta t(p,q) = \Delta t'(p,q)$, but $\Delta s(p,q) \neq \Delta s'(p,q)$.

Equation (3) can hold in Minkowski spacetime because neither the spatial distance nor the temporal interval between any pair of noncoincident spatiotemporally localized events is an intrinsic quantity. In Minkowski spacetime not only the spatial distance but also the temporal interval between a pair of nonincident spatiotemporally localized events depends on the state of motion to which one chooses to relativize these quantities: it is only the Minkowski spacetime interval that remains an absolute quantity, independent of state of motion. Note that, relative to a state of motion, there is still an absolute distinction between spatial and temporal intervals, as the minus sign in equation (2) indicates.

Points p,q are said to be respectively timelike, spacelike, or null separated, depending on whether the spacetime interval $\Delta I(p,q)$ is positive, negative, or zero. Events at p,q are spacelike (timelike) separated just in case they occur at different places (times) with respect to all states of uniform motion. $\Delta I(p,q)$ may be zero even if $p \neq q$. Fixing any point o as the origin of a system of spatiotemporal coordinates (x,y,z,t), the locus of points q that are null separated from o forms the three-dimensional "surface" of a four-dimensional generalization of a cone in Minkowski spacetime with vertex at o—an important part of the intrinsic structure of Minkowski spacetime that is not relative to any state of motion. A light pulse emitted from o in a vacuum would form a spherical shell expanding about the place it was emitted. This expanding shell traces out what is called the forward null cone or light cone at o, consisting of all points of Minkowski spacetime at null separation from and invariantly later than o: points at null separation from and invariantly earlier than o are said to form the backward null cone at o.

The null-cone structure of Minkowski spacetime allows for processes (including light traveling in a vacuum) that propagate with invariant speed c. Requiring all other physical processes also to conform to the principle of relativity ensures that the laws of physics do not single out any privileged state of absolute rest.

Einstein's teacher Minkowski presented a special theory of relativity that explicitly postulated a radically new four-dimensional structure incorporating time as well as space. (Corbis/Dennis di Cicco)

This is one way in which the special theory of relativity goes beyond the claim that spacetime is Minkowski.

The natural modifications required to make Newton's laws of motion conform to the principle of relativity imply that no massive body can be accelerated to or beyond the speed of light in a vacuum. But tachyons—hypothetical particles that always travel faster than light—are not thereby excluded. The special theory of relativity alone does not imply that the (invariant) speed of light in a vacuum forms an upper limit to the speed of signaling and information transmission. Nor does the theory itself imply that an event may be influenced only by events in or on its past null cone and may influence only events in or on its future null cone. But these conclusions do indeed follow, given plausible but not unquestioned substantive assumptions about causation and information transmission.

The special theory of relativity abandons previously unquestioned assumptions about time. The temporal interval between a pair of events is no longer an absolute quantity but a relation between these events and a state of motion. If the events are timelike separated, then any spacetime path joining them that represents a possible history of a point mass defines such a state of motion, and the length of this path corresponds to the elapsed time according to an ideal clock whose history coincides with that path. If the events are spacelike separated, then it is not only their temporal separation but also their temporal order that is relative to an arbitrarily chosen state of uniform motion. Hence, there is no absolute simultaneity: any pair of spacelike separated events are simultaneous relative to one state of uniform motion but occur at different times relative to other states of uniform motion. While this relativity of simultaneity is a basic consequence of relativity theory, Reichenbach's (1928) further claim, that it is conventional which pairs of spacelike separated events we take to be simultaneous relative to a given state of uniform motion, sparked extensive philosophical debate. Against Reichenbach's claim one may note that the null-cone structure of Minkowski spacetime singles out a unique notion of simultaneity for distant events that implies the constancy of the one-way speed of light in a vacuum. Insofar as special relativity postulates Minkowski spacetime, it seems inappropriate to regard either Einstein's "definition" of distant simultaneity, or the constancy of the one-way speed of light, as true by convention. The revised assumptions about space and time imply a number of surprising, but well-confirmed, empirical predictions, while a number of alleged paradoxes are readily resolved by their consistent application.

Einstein realized that, despite its unprecedented empirical success, Newton's law of universal gravitation was incompatible with his special theory of relativity. He developed a radically new theory that came to be called the general theory of relativity, largely because Einstein (1916) took it to incorporate a generalization of his earlier principle of relativity to cover all states of motion, accelerated as well as uniform. According to the general theory of relativity, while spacetime approximates to the structure of Minkowski spacetime in any sufficiently small region, its large-scale structure may be quite different. For both the global four-dimensional structure of spacetime and the three-dimensional spatial geometry that derives from it depend on how matter and energy are distributed. When an apple falls to the earth, rather than being forced by gravity to execute a nonuniform motion in a fixed, background Minkowski spacetime, its trajectory is actually a spacetime geodesic, or "straightest path," in a spacetime whose structure deviates systematically from that of Minkowski spacetime, largely because of the nearby presence of the massive Earth. There is no force of gravity: there are just matter-induced deviations from Minkowski spacetime.

Since the structure of spacetime depends on the distribution of matter, many different spacetime structures are equally compatible with the general theory of relativity.

Since the structure of spacetime depends on the distribution of matter, many different spacetime structures are equally compatible with the general theory of relativity. An empty spacetime may (but need not!) have the global structure of Minkowski spacetime. Observations indicate that our universe is expanding. While the global structure of the observable universe conforms closely to one of a class of expanding, isotropic general relativistic spacetimes, it remains an open question which member of that class best represents it.

Other general relativistic spacetimes represent very different states of matter. According to the general theory, a sufficiently massive star will collapse irreversibly, and the spacetime structure around this collapse will be so distorted that not even light can escape from a spatial region surrounding the star, which is consequently called a black hole. Black holes contain spacetime singularities. A singularity is not a region of spacetime but rather constitutes an edge or boundary of spacetime. According to the theory, an object falling into a black hole will reach the singularity in a finite time, as recorded by an ideal clock carried with it: it will then no longer exist. But according to an ideal clock located far from the black hole, the object will never enter the black hole, and its clock will slow down indefinitely as it nears the black hole.

Spacetimes describing black holes have been widely applied as descriptions of distant objects in the observable universe. Other general relativistic spacetimes that do not appear to describe anything in our universe nevertheless pose intriguing philosophical problems. The famous logician Kurt Gödel (1949) discovered one such general relativistic spacetime that appears to allow for the possibility of time travel into one's own past, even though its structure in fact rules out any global distinction between past and future. This discovery has prompted philosophical debate concerning whether this is indeed a possibility, and if so in what sense.

Other philosophical debates have been transformed by the development of relativity theory. Leibniz denied the substantial reality of space and time, arguing that spatial and temporal facts were reducible to relations between material objects and events: he further claimed that temporal relations were themselves reducible to causal relations. While Reichenbach took Leibniz's relationism to be vindicated by relativity, this verdict proved to be premature. Although spatial and temporal relations are relativized to states of motion, Minkowski spacetime itself is no more and no less substantial than Newtonian space and time. The dynamic nature of spacetime in general relativity appears to render it even more substantial, but on further analysis general relativity so transforms the substantivalist/relationist debate that it is difficult to award victory to any traditional view.

Robb (1914) developed Minkowski spacetime on the basis of a primitive relation of absolute (temporal/causal) precedence. Some interpret this as supporting a causal theory of time. But all general relativistic spacetimes are not so readily developed, and the epistemic and/or metaphysical credentials of the allegedly causal primitive have been questioned.

Following seminal work of Poincaré (1902), Reichenbach (1928), and Grünbaum (1973) argued that equality of spatial distance and temporal interval, or in relativity the spacetime interval, is conventional. But realists such as Friedman (1983) have countered their arguments.

Quantum Mechanics

Serious difficulties arose when physicists attempted to apply the physics of Newton and Maxwell to atomic-sized objects. By the 1920s a theory called quantum mechanics emerged that seemed capable of replacing classical physics here and, in principle, in all other domains. Quantum mechanics quickly proved its empirical success. But this was purchased at a high conceptual cost: there is still no consensus on how to understand the theory.

In Newton's mechanics the state of a system at a time is fixed by the precise position and momentum of each of its constituent particles. Their values determine the precise values of its energy and all other dynamical quantities. The state typically changes under the influence of forces, in accordance with Newton's laws of motion. At least in the case of simple isolated systems these laws imply that the initial state of a system determines its state at all later times, given the forces acting on it. In this sense the theory is deterministic.

While any particular method of observing a system may disturb its state, there is no theoretical reason why such disturbances cannot be made arbitrarily small. An ideal observation of a system's state would then not only reveal the precise position and momentum of each of its constituent particles at one time but also permit prediction of its exact future state, given the forces that will act on it and setting aside computational difficulties. (Though in certain so-called chaotic systems the future state may depend so sensitively on the exact initial state that practical limitations on measurement accuracy effectively preclude such predictions.)

Although it uses almost the same dynamical quantities, quantum mechanics does not describe a system to which it applies (such as an electron) by a state in which these all have precise values. Instead, the state of an isolated system is represented by an abstract mathematical object (i.e., a wave function or, more generally, a state vector). If it is left alone, a system's state vector evolves in such a way that the vector representing the system's state at later times is uniquely determined by its initial value. But this vector specifies only the probability that a measurement of any given dynamical quantity on the system would yield a particular result; and not all such probabilities can equal zero or one. Moreover, no attempt to establish a system's initial state by measuring dynamical quantities can provide more information than can be represented by a state vector. It follows that no measurement, or even theoretical specification, of the present state of a system suffices within the theory to fix the value that would be revealed in a later measurement of an arbitrary dynamical quantity. This is the sense in which the theory is indeterministic.

The famous two-slit experiment illustrates these features of quantum mechanics. If a suitable source of electrons is separated from a detection screen by a barrier in which two closely spaced parallel slits have been cut, then impacts of individual electrons on different regions of the screen may be detected. Quantum mechanics is able to predict the probability that an electron will be observed in a given region of the screen. The resulting probability distribution is experimentally verified by noting the relative frequency of detection in different regions, among a large collection of electrons. The resulting statistical pattern of hits is characteristic of phenomena involving interference between different parts of a wave, one part passing through the top slit and the other part through the bottom slit.

Now, according to quantum mechanics, the electrons have a wave function at all times between emission and detection. But the theory does not predict, and experiment does not allow, that any electron itself splits up, with part passing through each slit. The electrons' wave function specifies no path by which any particular electron travels from source to screen: it specifies only the probability that an electron will be detected in a given region of the screen. The theory neither predicts just where any electron will be detected on the screen nor has anything to say about how individual electrons get through the slits.

After heated discussions at Bohr's institute in Copenhagen in the 1920s, there emerged among many physicists a consensus that became known as the Copenhagen interpretation. A central tenet of this interpretation is that the quantum-mechanical description provided by the state vector is both predictably and descriptively complete. The most complete description of a system at a given time permits only probabilistic predictions of its future behavior. Moreover, this description, though complete, fails to assign a precise value to each dynamical quantity.

As an example, if a system's wave function makes it practically certain to be located within a tiny region of space, then the system's momentum must be very imprecise. A quantitative measure of the reciprocal precision with which quantities such as position and momentum are simultaneously defined is provided by the Heisenberg indeterminacy relations. According to the Copenhagen interpretation, rather than restricting our knowledge of an electron's precise simultaneous position and momentum, these relations specify how precise their simultaneous values can be.

Some, including Einstein, have objected to the Copenhagen interpretation of quantum mechanics because of its rejection of determinism in physics. But Einstein's main objections to the Copenhagen interpretation sprang from his conviction that it was incompatible with realism. In its most general form realism is the thesis that there is an objective, observer-independent reality that science attempts (with considerable success)

to describe and understand. To see how the Copenhagen interpretation seems to conflict with this thesis, consider once more the two-slit experiment.

If one performs an observation capable of telling through which slit each individual electron passes, then one will indeed observe each electron passing through one slit or the other. But performing this observation will alter the nature of the experiment itself, so that the pattern of detections on the screen will now look quite different. The characteristic interference pattern will no longer be observed: in its place will be a pattern that, ideally, corresponds to a simple sum of the patterns resulting from closing first one slit, then opening it and closing the other.

Observation of the electrons passing through the slits therefore affects their subsequent behavior. The Copenhagen interpretation further implies that it is only when this observation is made that each electron passes through one slit or the other! The observed phenomenon then so depends on its being observed that its objective reality is threatened. Moreover, the quantum-mechanical probabilities explicitly concern results of just such observations. Quantum mechanics, on the Copenhagen interpretation, then appears to be a theory not of an objective world but merely of our observations. If there is an objective world somehow lying behind these observations, then quantum mechanics seems notably unsuccessful in describing and understanding it!

A proponent of instrumentalism could rest easy with this conclusion: according to instrumentalism, the task of a scientific theory is simply to order previous observations and predict new ones, and quantum mechanics succeeds admirably at this task. But if the Copenhagen interpretation is correct, then the theory does so without even permitting a description of what lies behind these observations. Realists such as Einstein and Popper have therefore rejected the Copenhagen interpretation while attempting to accommodate the great success of quantum mechanics itself by offering an alternative interpretation of that theory.

According to the simplest realist alternative, a quantum system always has a precise value of every dynamical quantity such as position and momentum. The state vector incompletely describes a large number of similarly prepared systems by specifying the fraction that may be expected to have each value of any given quantity. On this view each electron follows its own definite path through one slit or the other in the two-slit experiment, and the wave function simply specifies the relative fractions that may be expected to take paths ending in each particular region of the screen.

Unfortunately, there are strong objections to this simple variety of realistic interpretation of quantum mechanics (see, e.g., Redhead, 1987). A technical objection is that this interpretation is inconsistent with features of the mathematical representation of quantities in the theory. More fundamentally, it turns out to conflict with Einstein's own assumption that the state of a system cannot be immediately affected by anything that is done far away from where it is located.

If quantum mechanics is a universal theory,

then it must apply not only to atoms

and subatomic particles but also to ordinary objects

like beds, cats, and laboratory apparatus.

Einstein had two main arguments against the Copenhagen thesis that quantum mechanics is complete. He developed a version of the first argument in consultation with his colleagues Podolsky and Rosen, and their joint paper (Einstein, Podolsky, & Rosen, 1935; hereafter EPR) became a classic. The paper described a thought experiment in which quantum mechanics implies the possibility of establishing, with arbitrary accuracy, either the position or the momentum of one particle solely by means of a measurement of the corresponding quantity performed on a second particle. They argued that such a measurement would not affect the state of the first particle, given that the two particles are physically separated. They concluded that the first particle has both a precise position and a precise momentum, despite the fact that no quantum-mechanical wave function describes these quantities as having such simultaneous precise values.

Bohr (1935) rejected the conclusion of the EPR argument. His reply may be interpreted as maintaining the completeness of quantum mechanics by rejecting some of the argument's assumptions. Later work by Bell (1964) showed how one crucial assumption could be experimentally tested. This locality assumption is that the total state of two physically separated systems is given by the states of those two systems, in such a way that the state of one cannot be immediately affected by anything that is done to the other. In an experimental setup very similar to the one EPR had themselves described this assumption turns out to imply predictions that conflict with those of quantum mechanics itself! Subsequent verification of the quantum-mechanical predictions has provided strong evidence against this locality assumption (see, e.g., Redhead, 1987).

The failure of such unorthodox alternatives does not imply that the Copenhagen interpretation is correct, and several rival interpretations have been proposed by physicists, philosophers, and mathematicians. An examination of Einstein's second main argument against the Copenhagen interpretation may help explain why people have made such proposals.

If quantum mechanics is a universal theory, then it must apply not only to atoms and subatomic particles but also to ordinary objects like beds, cats, and laboratory apparatus. Now, while it may seem unobjectionable for an electron to have no definite position, it is surely ridiculous to suppose that my bed is nowhere in particular in my bedroom. The Copenhagen interpretation seems committed to just such ridiculous suppositions. For it is possible to transfer the alleged indeterminateness of a microscopic object's state to that of a macroscopic object by means of an appropriate interaction between them. Indeed, this is exactly what happens when a macroscopic object is used to observe some property of a microscopic object.

In Schrödinger's (1935) famous example, a cat is used as an unconventional apparatus to observe whether or not an atom of a radioactive substance has decayed. The cat is sealed in a box containing a sample of radioactive material. A Geiger counter is connected to a lethal device in such a way that if it detects a radioactive decay product, then the device is triggered and the cat dies. Otherwise, the cat lives. The size of the sample is chosen so that there is a 50 percent chance of detecting a decay within an hour. After one hour the box is opened.

The quantum-mechanical description couples the wave function describing the radioactive atoms to the wave function describing the cat. The coupled wave function after one hour implies neither that an atom has decayed nor that no atom has decayed: but it also implies neither that the cat is alive nor that it is dead. If this wave function completely describes the state of the cat, it follows that the cat is then neither alive nor dead! This is hard to accept, since cats are never observed in such bizarre states. Indeed, when an observer opens the box she will observe either a dead cat or a live cat. But if she finds a corpse, she is no mere innocent witness: rather her curiosity killed the cat.

Most proponents of the Copenhagen interpretation would reject this conclusion. They would claim that an observation had already taken place as soon as the decay of a radioactive atom produced an irreversible change in a macroscopic object (such as the Geiger counter), thus removing any further indeterminateness and causing the death of the cat. But this response is satisfactory only if it can be backed up by a precise account of the circumstances in which an observation occurs, thereby leading to a determinate result.

The problem of explaining just why and when a measurement of a quantum-mechanical quantity yields some one determinate result has come to be known as the measurement problem. The problem arises because if quantum mechanics is a universal theory, it must apply also to the physical interactions involved in performing quantum measurements. But if the Copenhagen interpretation is correct, then a quantum-mechanical treatment of the measurement interaction is either excluded in principle or else leads to absurd or at least ambiguous results.

One radical response to the measurement problem is due originally to Everett (1957). It is to deny that a quantum measurement has a single result: rather, every possible result occurs in some actual world! This implies that every quantum measurement produces a splitting, or branching, of worlds. A measurement is just a physical interaction between the measured system and another quantum system (the observer apparatus) that, in each world, correlates the result with the observer apparatus's record of it. One can show that the records built up by an observer apparatus in a world will display just that pattern that would have been expected if each measurement had actually had a single result.

In 1929 Hubble concluded from observations

that distant galaxies are receding from one another,

with velocities proportional to their distances apart.

Since every possible result actually occurs in every quantum measurement, the evolution of the physical universe is deterministic on this interpretation. Not only indeterminism but also nonlocality turns out to be a kind of illusion resulting from the inevitably restricted perspective presented by the world of each observer apparatus.

Though embraced by a number of prominent physicists, Everett's interpretation faces severe conceptual difficulties. It must distinguish between the physical universe and the "worlds" corresponding to each observer apparatus. But the status of these "worlds" is quite problematic. Moreover, it is unclear what can be meant by probability when every measurement outcome is certain to occur in some "world."

After writing a classic textbook exposition of the Copenhagen interpretation, Bohm (1952) rejected its claims of completeness and proposed an influential alternative that sought to restore determinism. On this alternative the state of a particle is always completely specified by its position. Changes in this position are produced by a physical force generated by a field described by the wave function of the entire system of which the particle is a component. Measurements of

quantities such as energy and momentum are analyzed into observations of some system's position. Quantum mechanics is understood as offering probabilities for the results of these observations. Since each result is actually determined, in part by the initial positions of measured system and apparatus (which are not described by the wave function), quantum indeterminism is just a consequence of the incompleteness of the quantum description.

Bohm's interpretation clearly involves interactions that violate the locality assumption. A measurement on one particle can immediately affect the state of a distant particle by altering the force acting on it—a theoretical violation of the principle of relativity. But if the interpretation is correct, it turns out that this instantaneous action as a distance cannot be exploited to transmit signals instantaneously. The violation of locality and the principle of relativity is unobservable.

Cosmology

In 1929 Hubble concluded from observations that distant galaxies are receding from one another, with velocities proportional to their distances apart. Subsequent observations confirmed and refined this picture of an expanding universe, which is well modeled by a symmetric general relativistic spacetime with an initial singularity, on the order of ten billion years ago. Theoretical investigations showed that this singularity is not merely an artifact of the symmetry of these models. If classical general relativity is true, then the initial singularity corresponds to an origin of the universe. This would imply that the universe did not come into existence at some moment in time—rather, time is coeval with the universe.

But there are grounds for doubting the applicability of general relativity to the extreme conditions of the hot, dense early universe: in these conditions qauntum effects are expected to be of crucial importance. Now despite its empirical success in less extreme conditions, the general theory of relativity does not mesh well with quantum theory: a fully satisfactory quantum theory of gravity has proven elusive. However, this has not prevented theoretical astrophysicists from speculating on how such a theory might prompt revisions in our understanding of the origin of the universe.

Linde has speculated that the vast observable universe originated as a tiny random quantum fluctuation within a "mother" universe, then briefly "inflated" at an enormous rate before settling down to its present stately rate of expansion. Such "baby universes" have continually formed in this random fashion from within preexisting universes in a potentially infinite sequence.

Hawking has suggested that the approximately classical general relativistic spacetime of our present universe may have emerged from a quantum spacetime whose temporal aspect cannot be distinguished from its spatial aspect. It would follow that as we trace the universe back in time we find no singularity: rather, what we call time merges gradually into a structure that does not possess a recognizably temporal aspect.

Statistical Mechanics

Philosophical debates on the atomic theory began with the pre-Socratics. In the nineteenth century these debates were continued within physical science as the atomic hypothesis came to play an increasingly important role in physics as well as chemistry. At issue was not merely the ontological status of unobservables, but also difficulties that arose in reconciling the putative microscopic constitution of matter with its irreversible macroscopic behavior, given the reversibility of the underlying mechanical laws. Boltzmann's struggles to understand the thermodynamic behavior of gases introduced probability into physical theory and thereby gave rise to statistical mechanics, a theory whose conceptual foundations remain controversial. Boltzmann's thesis—that the basis of our distinction between past and future is ultimately just those statistical asymmetries that underlie thermodynamic irreversibility—was taken up and defended by Reichenbach and others against objections of some philosophers and physicists.

Replacement of classical mechanics by quantum mechanics as a fundamental microtheory has changed the context of such debates without resolving them. Indeed, quantum statistical mechanics raises fascinating philosophical issues of its own concerning the identity and individuality of different kinds of fundamental particles—issues that also arise in attempts to understand the empirically successful relativistic quantum field theories that, by formulating quantum mechanics in a relativistic spacetime, yielded physicists' deepest level of understanding of the world at the turn of the twenty-first century.

[See also Gödel, Kurt; Leibniz, Gottfried Wilhelm; Realism.]

BIBLIOGRAPHY

Bell, J. S. "On the Einstein-Podolsky-Rosen Paradox," *Physics,* Vol. 1 (1964), 195–200.

Bohm, D. "A Suggested Interpretation of the Quantum Theory in Terms of 'Hidden Variables,' " Parts 1–2. *Physical Review,* Vol. 85 (1952), 166–93.

Bohr, N. "Can Quantum-Mechanical Description of Physical Reality Be Considered Complete?," *Physical Review,* Vol. 48 (1935), 696–702.

———. *The Physical Writings of Niels Bohr,* Vols. 1–3. Woodbridge, CT, 1987. These essays develop Bohr's distinctive and influential philosophy of physics.

Cartwright, N. *How the Laws of Physics Lie.* Oxford, 1983. Argues that while physics reveals true causes, its fundamental laws explain only by distorting the truth.

Earman, J. *World Enough and Space-Time.* Cambridge, MA, 1989. A thorough treatment of the absolutist/relationist debate in historical context.

Earman, J., C. Glymour, and J. Stachel. *Foundations of Space-Time Theories.* Minneapolis, 1977. Contains a number of papers on the causal theory of time.

Einstein, A. "Zur Elektrodynamik bewegter Körper," *Annalen der Physik,* Vol. 17 (1905). Translated as "On the Electrodynamics of Moving Bodies" in H. A. Lorentz, A. Einstein, H. Minkowski, and H. Weyl, eds., *The Principle of Relativity* (London, 1923).

———. "Die Grundlage der allgemeinen Relativitäts-theorie," *Annalen der Physik,* Vol. 49 (1916). Translated as "The Foundation of the General Theory of Relativity" in H. A. Lorentz, A. Einstein, H. Minkowski, and H. Weyl, *The Principle of Relativity* (London, 1923).

———, B. Podolsky, and N. Rosen. "Can Quantum-Mechanical Description of Physical Reality Be Considered Complete?" *Physical Review,* Vol. 47 (1935), 777–80.

Everett, H., III. " 'Relative State' Formulation of Quantum Mechanics," *Reviews of Modern Physics,* Vol. 29 (1957), 454–62.

Friedman, M. *Foundations of Spacetime Theories.* Princeton, NJ, 1983.

Gödel, K. "A Remark about the Relationship between Relativity Theory and Idealistic Philosophy," in P. Schilpp, ed., *Albert Einstein: Philosopher-Scientist* (Evanston, IL, 1949).

Grünbaum, A. *Philosophical Problems of Space and Time,* 2d ed. Dordrecht, 1973.

Hawking, S. *A Brief History of Time.* New York, 1988. A provocative and superficially nontechnical book in which an influential mathematical physicist attempts to bring contemporary physics to bear on basic cosmological questions.

Horwich, P. *Asymmetries in Time.* Cambridge, MA, 1987. Contains a provocative defense of Gödel's analysis of the sense in which his model of general relativity would permit time travel to one's past.

Linde, A. *Inflation and Quantum Cosmology.* Boston, 1990.

Lorentz, H. A., A. Einstein, H. Minkowski, and H. Weyl, eds., *The Principle of Relativity.* London, 1923. Reprinted, New York, 1952.

Minkowski, H. "Space and Time," address delivered in Cologne, Germany (1908), in H. A. Lorentz, A. Einstein, H. Minkowski, and H. Weyl, *The Principle of Relativity* (London, 1923).

Poincaré, H. *La Science et l'hypothèse.* Paris, 1902. Translated by W. J. Greenstreet as *Science and Hypothesis.* New York, 1952.

Popper, K. R. *Quantum Theory and the Schism in Physics.* London, 1982.

Redhead, M. L. G. *Incompleteness, Nonlocality, and Realism: A Prolegomenon to the Philosophy of Quantum Mechanics.* Oxford, 1987.

Reichenbach, H. *Philosophie der Raum-Zeit-Lehre.* Berlin, 1928. Translated by M. Reichenbach and J. Freund as *The Philosophy of Space and Time.* New York, 1958.

Robb, A. A. *A Theory of Time and Space.* Cambridge, 1914.

Schilpp, P. *Albert Einstein: Philosopher-Scientist.* Evanston, IL, 1949. Contains Einstein's thoughtful intellectual autobiography as well as a number of philosophically rich exchanges between Einstein and his commentators.

Schrödinger, E. "Die gegenwärtige Situation in der Quantenmechanik," *Naturwissenschaften*, Vol. 23 (1935), 807–12; 823–28; 844–49. Translated by J. D. Trimmer as "The Present Situation in Quantum Mechanics: A Translation of Schrödinger's 'Cat Paradox' paper," in J. A. Wheeler and W. H. Zurek, eds., *Quantum Theory and Measurement* (Princeton, NJ, 1983).

Sklar, L., *Space, Time, and Spacetime*. Berkeley, 1974. An introduction to some main topics of philosophical reflection on the nature of space and time stimulated by developments in physics.

———. *Philosophy of Physics*. Boulder, CO, 1992. A useful nontechnical introduction to the field.

———. *Physics and Chance*. Cambridge, 1993. A wide-ranging introduction to philosophical issues raised by statistical mechanics.

Teller, P. *An Interpretive Introduction to Quantum Field Theory*. Princeton, NJ, 1995. A ground-breaking attempt by a philosopher to come to grips with the concepts of quantum field theory.

van Fraassen, B. *The Scientific Image*. Oxford, 1980. Develops an influential but controversial account of the structure and role of scientific theories focused especially on examples from physics.

Wheeler, J. A., and W. H. Zurek, eds. *Quantum Theory and Measurement*. Princeton, NJ, 1983. Contains reprints of Bell (1964), Bohm (1952), Bohr (1935), EPR (1935), and Everett (1957).

— RICHARD HEALEY

PHILOSOPHY OF RELIGION

Analytical philosophy of religion, still in its infancy in 1967, has developed markedly since then. Other approaches have certainly continued to play a part in philosophy of religion written in English, even more so in other languages. Process philosophy, for example, inspired by the thought of Alfred North Whitehead and exemplified in the ongoing work of Charles Hartshorne and others, has retained influence in philosophy of religion and in theology, probably more than in other areas of philosophy. Phenomenology, postmodernism, and other approaches characteristic of the European continent inspire important contributions to the subject. Indeed, there is often not a sharp line between different approaches. Continental writers such as Kierkegaard figure extensively in undoubtedly analytical writing about religion, and analytical philosophy of religion makes such extensive use of medieval material as to be more or less continuous with neoscholastic treatments of the subject.

Although there had been a few earlier analytical essays about various religious issues, the main development of analytical philosophy of religion may be said to have begun in the 1950s with discussion of the "logical positivist" challenge to the cognitive significance of religious language. Most analytical philosophers then held, or were strongly tempted to hold, as an empiricist principle, that every (logically contingent) assertion, in order to have any cognitive meaning, must be verifiable or, more broadly, testable, in principle, by experience. It was charged, by Alfred Jules Ayer, Antony Flew, and others, that the affirmations of religious belief typically

do not satisfy this criterion of meaning (A. Flew, R. M. Hare, and B. Mitchell in Brody, 1974).

How, then, were the apparent truth claims of religions to be understood? Some were prepared, with Ayer, to treat major religious assertions as mere expressions of emotion, without any cognitive significance. Others sought ways of understanding such assertions as empirically verifiable in principle. John Hick (in Brody, 1974) argued, for instance, that "eschatological verifiability," in a life after death, provides at least a partial solution to the problem. Still others, while granting that empirical testability is decisive for the meaning of typical factual assertions, sought to establish a different, and not merely emotive, type of meaning that could be ascribed to religious assertions. The most influential attempts of this type were inspired by the later writings of Ludwig Wittgenstein, particularly by his account of "language games" and their relation to forms of life.

The Wittgensteinian approach, as developed, for example, by Norman Malcolm (in Brody, 1992) and D. Z. Phillips (1970), has generated very interesting studies of the relation of religious language to religious life. It is widely criticized, by some as giving inadequate weight to the apparent straightforwardly realistic intent of typical religious assertions, and by some as improperly shielding religious claims from rational criticism by relativizing them to religious language games. It remains, nevertheless, an important strand in contemporary discussion. Of all that has been done in analytical philosophy of religion, it is probably the discussion of religious language in general, and Wittgensteinian themes in particular, that have most interested professional theologians, perhaps because these themes have seemed more relevant than more metaphysical discussions to the work of interpretation and reinterpretation of traditions in which theologians are so much engaged.

Within analytical philosophy during the 1950s the verifiability criterion of meaning was already undergoing severe criticism and has since been virtually abandoned in anything like its original form. Many analytical philosophers continue to consider themselves empiricists and seek alternative ways of excluding claims that they regard as objectionably metaphysical. Many others, however, see the permanent contribution of analytical philosophy, not in a form of empiricism, or in any set of doctrines, but in a method, style, or discipline that can be applied to virtually all the historic issues of metaphysics and ethics and can be used in developing and espousing almost any of the classic philosophical doctrines.

The majority of work done in analytical philosophy of religion since 1967 has been inspired by the later conception of analytical philosophy and has not focused on issues about religious language. It is characterized by metaphysical realism, taking the religious claims under discussion to be straightforwardly true or false. (For defense of this stance, see, e.g., Swinburne, 1977, chaps. 2–6.) Some have suggested calling it philosophical theology rather than philosophy of religion, because the principal subject of most of it is God rather than human religious phenomena, though atheists as well as theists have certainly been important participants in the discussion. On this basis, mainly since 1960, a very substantial body of literature, dealing with most of the traditional issues of philosophical theology and some new ones too, has been created.

Among the traditional topics the attributes of God received rather early analytical attention. (For general treatments see Swinburne, 1977, chaps. 7–15; Kenny, 1979; Wierenga, 1989.) Analysis of the concept of God was easily seen as an appropriate subject for analytical philosophy, and issues about the attributes had been connected, since the Middle Ages, with problems about predication, an appealing point of entry into philosophical theology for those interested in the philosophy of language. According to some of the most influential medieval theologians, God is so different from creatures that positive attributes of creatures cannot in general be predicated of God univocally, that is, in the same sense in which they are predicated of creatures. How then can we predicate anything of God? Various Scholastic theologians developed various solutions, the best known being the theory of analogical predication of Thomas Aquinas. Analytical philosophers of religion have taken up the problem and some of the medieval views, along with more contemporary concerns—for instance, about the ascription of psychological predicates to a being who is supposed not to have a body. (Cf. Maimonides, Aquinas, and Alston in Brody, 1992).

The two divine attributes that have received the most extensive analytical discussion are omniscience and eternity. The central issue about eternity is whether to understand it (as medieval and early modern theology generally did) as involving existence outside of time or rather as involving existence without beginning or end in time, as many contemporary thinkers have proposed. Critics of divine timelessness, such as Nelson Pike

Some philosophers have treated major religious assertions as mere expressions of emotion, without any cognitive significance. (Corbis/Owen Franken)

(1970) and Nicholas Wolterstorff (in Brody, 1992), have questioned the compatibility of timelessness with God's consciousness or action or interaction with creatures. Eleanor Stump and Norman Kretzmann, however, have presented an influential defense of the traditional timeless conception (in Brody, 1992), and the issue remains vigorously debated.

The main development of analytical philosophy of religion may be said to have begun in the 1950s with discussion of the "logical positivist" challenge to the cognitive significance of religious language.

Omniscience and eternity are related topics, for one of the most discussed issues about God's knowledge concerns God's relation to time: does God have complete knowledge of the future? In particular, does God know, infallibly and in every detail, how free creatures will use their freedom? Traditional theologies generally gave an emphatically affirmative answer to this question; but some modern philosophers and theologians have disagreed, arguing that the doctrine of total, infallible foreknowledge compromises the freedom of the creatures. The extensive analytical literature on this issue (e.g., in Fischer, 1989) is continuous with older discussions, and opinion remains divided.

A related old debate, recently revived, concerns what has been called "middle knowledge": does God know, completely and infallibly, what every actual and even merely possible free creature would freely do (or would have freely done) in every possible situation in which that creature could act freely? In the late sixteenth century, Luis de Molina, a Jesuit, proposed an ingenious theory of divine providence according to which God uses such subjunctive (and largely counterfactual) conditional knowledge to control the course of history without having to interfere metaphysically with the freedom of creatures. This theory of middle knowledge was widely embraced by Jesuits, but opposed by Dominicans, who argued that there cannot be such determinate conditional facts about everything that would be freely done by particular creatures in all possible circumstances. This historic controversy was introduced into current analytical discussion by Anthony Kenny (1979) and Robert Adams (1987), who have both defended the Dominican objection to middle knowledge; but the opposite position has been argued by a vigorous school of contemporary Molinists, including Alvin Plantinga (1974) and Alfred Freddoso (1988).

Regarding the relation of God to ethics, it was almost universally held in the 1960s that fundamental ethical principles must be independent of theology and that an acceptable theological account of the nature of ethical facts is impossible. Since then, however, it has come to be widely held by theists, and granted by many nontheists, that facts about God, if God exists, could play a central role in explaining the nature of ethics and that theistic philosophers should be expected to avail themselves of this possibility. The most discussed type of theological theory in this area is the divine-command theory of the nature of ethical obligation, or of right and wrong (Helm, 1981). Several thinkers, such as Philip Quinn (1978), have tried to reformulate and explain the theory in such a way as to defend it against the traditional objections to it. Robert Adams (1987) has proposed a form of the theory that rests on semantical assumptions very similar to those of some of the most influential contemporary exponents of metaethical naturalism but employs different (theistic) metaphysical assumptions.

The grounds proposed for belief or disbelief in the existence of God have naturally claimed at least as much analytical attention as the attributes of God. This is a subject so intensively discussed for centuries that one might have expected little novelty in the treatment of it. But in fact investigations have been rather innovative, and the state of debate has changed significantly since 1960. One striking change is that the traditional arguments for the existence of God, then widely dismissed, even by theologians, as hopelessly discredited, have many defenders now.

This is connected with a more general phenomenon, which is that analytical philosophers, especially those inclined to construct and defend constructive metaphysical theories, demand less of arguments than has commonly been demanded in the past. Virtually no one thinks any one "theistic proof" conclusive; but if arguments must be either conclusive or worthless, there would be little useful reasoning about any of the most important philosophical issues. Theistic apologists are accordingly less apt to seek a single "knockdown" proof than to try to show that several traditional (and perhaps also novel) arguments have something of value to contribute to a "cumulative case" for theism, an approach exemplified by Richard Swinburne (1979). Extensive work has been done interpreting, developing, and criticizing all the main types of theistic arguments. Those that have probably received the most attention and development are the "ontological" and the "teleological" (to give them their Kantian names).

The fallaciousness of any ontological argument and the contingency of all real existence had become such commonplaces, especially among empiricists, that it had a certain "shock value" when Norman Malcolm in 1960 published a defense of an ontological argument (reprinted in Brody, 1992). Malcolm claimed to find in Anselm's *Proslogion,* besides the famous argument of its second chapter, a second ontological argument in which it is not existence but necessary existence that figures as a perfection. Malcolm also held that necessary existence cannot be excluded from theology on general philosophical grounds. Whether a statement expresses a necessary truth, he argued, depends on the language game in which it figures; and a religious language can treat the existence of God as a necessary truth. These two features of Malcolm's article foreshadow the main tendencies in the development of ontological arguments since then: (1) attention to more modal versions of the argument and (2) the attempt to rehabilitate the idea of necessary existence.

Ontological argument studies have been greatly influenced by the dramatic development of modal logic, which was gathering momentum in the 1960s and burst into the center of American philosophical consciousness in the 1970s. In 1962 Charles Hartshorne published a modal proof of the existence of God relying only on the premises that God's existence must be necessary if it is actual and that God's existence is at least possible. Subsequent discussion has established that this proof, and related proofs from slightly slenderer assumptions, are valid in the system of modal logic most widely thought to be appropriate for the context. David Lewis (in Brody, 1974) and Alvin Plantinga (1974) have given the argument a form that takes account of developments in modal predicate logic as well as modal propositional logic (or in *de re* as well as *de dicto* modality). The argument is still of limited value for proving the existence of God, because those who would otherwise doubt the conclusion are likely to doubt the possibility premise, given the rest of the argument. But the modal development of the argument is helpful in structuring discussion of questions about necessary existence.

In the 1950s it was the opinion of almost all analytical philosophers that the existence of a real being, such as God (as distinct from merely abstract objects, such as numbers), cannot be necessary in the strongest, "logical" sense. This opinion has come to be widely doubted, however, and the traditional view that God should be conceived as an absolutely necessary being has regained a following. (For contrasting views see Adams, 1987, chaps. 13–14, and Swinburne, 1977, chaps. 13–14.) Several factors have contributed to this change. The identification of necessity with analyticity, on which the rejection of necessary existence was commonly based, is under attack. W. V. O. Quine's influ-

ential doubts about the adequacy of the notion of analyticity led Quine himself to skepticism about necessity. But others, influenced in some cases by an interest in necessity *de re,* have been inspired to seek a more robustly metaphysical conception of necessity. Since a conception of the latter sort was generally held by the great philosophers of the Middle Ages and the seventeenth century, a growing and more sympathetic understanding of those periods of the history of philosophy has also tended to undermine the most dismissive attitudes toward the idea of necessary existence.

The two divine attributes that have received

the most extensive analytical discussion

are omniscience and eternity.

The most popular argument for the existence of God in the eighteenth century was the teleological or design argument, usually in a pre-Darwinian form drawing its evidence largely from biological adaptations. This type of argument was discredited both by the devastating critique it received in David Hume's *Dialogues Concerning Natural Religion* and by the development of an alternative explanation of the biological phenomena in terms of natural selection. A major rehabilitation of the design argument has been undertaken by Richard Swinburne (1979). Instead of the biological evidence, he takes as his principal evidence the most pervasive, highest-level regularities in the universe. Since they constitute the most fundamental laws of nature, to which all scientific explanations appeal, he argues, there cannot be any scientific explanation of them. There may therefore be no viable alternative to a theological explanation for them, if they are to be explained at all. Deploying the apparatus of Bayesian probability theory, and responding to Hume's objections, Swinburne tries to establish that a theological explanation is indeed more plausible than no explanation at all. Swinburne's argument depends at some points on controversial metaphysical theses and has inspired an extended atheistic response by J. L. Mackie (1982); but the teleological argument has at least been shown to have much more philosophical life in it than had been thought.

The leading argument for atheism, aside from the various critiques of theistic arguments, has long been the argument from evil. The evils that occur in the world are incompatible, it is argued, with the existence of an omnipotent, omniscient, perfectly good God. In the earlier years of analytical philosophy of religion this was usually a charge of demonstrable, logical incompatibility; and attempts to provide theists with a "solution" to the "problem of evil" concentrated accordingly on trying to show the possibility of a perfect deity having permitted the evils. Borrowing a Leibnizian idea, for instance, Nelson Pike argued that for all we know, this might be the best of all possible worlds (in Adams & Adams, 1990). Alvin Plantinga (1974) developed a much-discussed version of the traditional "free will defense," arguing that even if there are possible worlds containing less evil, and as much moral good, as the actual world, an omnipotent God may have been unable to create them because it may be that creatures (whether humans or angels) would not have freely done what they would have to do freely in order for one of those worlds to be actual. The adequacy of such theistic responses to the "logical" form of the argument from evil has been keenly debated, but it has probably become the predominant view that the argument does not afford much hope of a tight, demonstrative proof of atheism.

There has therefore been increasing interest in probabilistic arguments from evil, as presented, for example, by William Rowe (in Adams & Adams, 1990), whose thesis is that evils show theism to be implausible, or at least constitute evidence against theism, which might contribute to a cumulative case for atheism. Theistic responses to this type of argument must address issues of plausibility and not merely of possibility. Some have been methodological, attempting to show that the relevant probabilities cannot be determined, or that the explanatory structure of the situation keeps the evils from being even relevant evidence (e.g., Stephen Wykstra in Adams & Adams, 1990). Others have tried to give plausible accounts of why evils might have been necessary for greater goods. One widely debated hypothesis, developed in different ways by John Hick (in Adams & Adams, 1990) and Richard Swinburne (1979), for instance, is that evils, and possibilities of evil, play an essential part in making the world a context for the moral and spiritual development of free creatures.

All such explanations of why God would permit great evils have seemed to some morally or religiously objectionable. Among theists who take this view, Marilyn Adams has argued that we should accept that we simply do not know why God has permitted horrendous evils but that within a religion that affirms, as Christianity does, God's love for individuals who suffer them, it is important to have a coherent account of how God may be seen as redeeming them (Adams & Adams, 1990). She points to traditional religious ideas of suffering shared with God or with Christ as suggesting how horrendous evils might be "defeated" by forming an or-

ganic whole with incommensurably great religious goods.

One of the more dramatic developments of the period under review is the development of a defense of the rationality of theism that professes not to be based on arguments or evidence. Alvin Plantinga maintains that belief in the existence of God can be "properly basic," a basic belief being one that is not inferentially based on any other belief (in Plantinga & Wolterstorff, 1983). It has been held by many that some beliefs (formed, perhaps, in sensation or memory) do not need inferential support from other beliefs for their justification. Plantinga argues that more beliefs than some have supposed are reasonably held without being based on the evidence of other beliefs and that there is no compelling reason to deny that some religious beliefs have this basic status. He suggests that religious beliefs not based on "evidence" constituted by other beliefs may nonetheless be based on other sorts of "grounds," which might be found, for example, in religious experience. Plantinga's view (which he has dubbed "Reformed epistemology") has been keenly debated. One of the most discussed issues is whether it allows an adequate basis for distinguishing between rational and irrational religious beliefs. (For a moderately critical view see R. Audi in Audi & Wainwright, 1986).

For philosophy of religion

as for contemporary theology,

the problem of conflicting-truth claims

of different religions

is coming into increasing prominence.

A related but importantly different view has been developed by William Alston (1991). Religious experience has been a major subject of discussion in philosophy of religion (e.g., W. James, W. T. Stace, and C. B. Martin in Brody, 1974; Wainwright, 1981), as it has been in modern theology. Not all of the discussion has been epistemological or focused on the justification of belief. Nelson Pike (1992), for instance, has written about the phenomenology of mysticism, arguing, against the older theory of Walter Stace, that there are mystical experiences of theistic as well as nontheistic content. Alston's approach is thoroughly epistemological, however, and he focuses on the experience of more ordinary religious believers rather than of those adepts typically singled out as "mystics."

Relying on carefully discussed analogies with sense perception, Alston argues that in some circumstances experiences as of God addressing, or being present to, a person can reasonably be regarded as perceptions of God. His argument is placed in the context of a "doxastic practice" conception of the justification of beliefs. He argues that we are able to form and justify beliefs only in socially established practices in which we have learned to be responsive to such factors as experiential cues and communal traditions as well as to beliefs that we hold. In Alston's view we have no choice but to rely on socially established doxastic practices, and it is presumptively rational to do so, even though we typically have little or no independent evidence of the reliability of the practice. He argues that this presumption of rationality applies also to religious doxastic practices that are socially established, and in particular to practices in which participants have learned to form beliefs of having perceived God in various ways. Alston offers vigorous rebuttals of several major objections to basing religious beliefs on religious experience. In his opinion the most serious problem for his view, which he treats at some length, is that posed by the existence of diverse religious traditions whose well-established doxastic practices lead them to form apparently conflicting beliefs on the basis of their religious experience.

For philosophy of religion as for contemporary theology, the problem of conflicting truth claims of different religions is, if not a new issue, one that is coming into increasing prominence. John Hick (1989) has done much to draw attention to it. He argues that it is not plausible to suppose that one traditional form of religious experience is veridical while others are not, and he tries to articulate a way in which many apparently conflicting forms could all be at bottom veridical, proposing to regard them as apprehending different "phenomenal" manifestations of a single "noumenal" transcendent "reality." Not that Hick thinks all religious beliefs equally acceptable; the main criterion he proposes for the value of religious traditions and belief systems is their fruitfulness in producing morally and spiritually recognizable saints, people notably advanced in a transformation from self-centeredness to Reality-centeredness. Among the issues in the vigorous debate about Hick's view are the adequacy of the conceptual apparatus he borrows from Kant and whether it is compatible (as he means it to be) with a fundamentally realist and cognitivist conception of religious belief.

[See also Bayesianism; Epistemology, Religious; Evil, Problem of; Hare, Richard M.; Hume, David; James, William; Kant, Immanuel; Kierkegaard, Søren Aabye; Mackie, John Leslie; Modal Logic; Phenomenology; Postmodernism; Quine, Willard Van Orman; Religious Experience; Religious Pluralism; Theism, Arguments for and Against; Thomas Aquinas, St.; Wittgenstein, Ludwig Josef Johann.]

BIBLIOGRAPHY

Adams, M. M., and R. M. Adams, eds. *The Problem of Evil*. Oxford, 1990.

Adams, R. M. *The Virtue of Faith and Other Essays in Philosophical Theology*. New York, 1987.

Alston, W. P. *Perceiving God*. Ithaca, NY, 1991.

Audi, R., and W. J. Wainwright, eds. *Rationality, Religious Belief, and Moral Commitment: New Essays in the Philosophy of Religion*. Ithaca, NY, 1986.

Brody, B. A., ed. *Readings in the Philosophy of Religion: An Analytic Approach*. Englewood Cliffs, NJ, 1974; 2d ed., 1992. Somewhat different selections, both comprehensive and both excellent, in the two editions.

Freddoso, A. J., intro. and trans., L. de Molina. *On Divine Foreknowledge* (Part IV of the *Concordia*). Ithaca, NY, 1988.

Fischer, J. M., ed. *God, Foreknowledge, and Freedom*. Stanford, 1989.

Hartshorne, C. *The Logic of Perfection and Other Essays in Neoclassical Metaphysics*. Lasalle, IL, 1962.

Helm, P., ed. *Divine Commands and Morality*. Oxford, 1981.

Hick, J. *An Interpretation of Religion*. London, 1989.

Kenny, A. *The God of the Philosophers*. Oxford, 1979.

Mackie, J. L. *The Miracle of Theism*. Oxford, 1982.

Phillips, D. Z. *Faith and Philosophical Enquiry*. New York, 1970.

Pike, N. *God and Timelessness*. New York, 1970.

———. *Mystic Union*. Ithaca, NY, 1992.

Plantinga, A. *The Nature of Necessity*. Oxford, 1974.

———, and N. Wolterstorff, eds. *Faith and Rationality*. Notre Dame, IN, 1983.

Quinn, P. L. *Divine Commands and Moral Requirements*. Oxford, 1978.

Swinburne, R. *The Coherence of Theism*. Oxford, 1977.

———. *The Existence of God*. Oxford, 1979; 2d ed. 1991.

Wainwright, W. J. *Mysticism*. Madison, WI, 1981.

Wierenga, E. R. *The Nature of God*. Ithaca, NY, 1989.

— ROBERT M. ADAMS

PHILOSOPHY OF SCIENCE

From 1960 to 1995 the philosophy of science experienced explosive growth, despite the often alleged death of logical positivism, which had served as the dominant school of thought for the preceding twenty-five years. Quantitative measures of this explosion can be provided through an examination of the number of new journals (at least ten such as *Economics and Philosophy, Biology and Philosophy*, and *Perspectives on Science*) that appeared in that time period, the number of Ph.D. programs specializing in or offering a specialty area in philosophy of science, the appearance of research centers dedicated to the philosophy of science (such as the University of Pittsburgh's Center for Philosophy of Science and Boston University's Center), and new departments or programs concentrating in this general area. More impressive than these numbers is the change in focus, best seen against the background of logical positivism.

At its core logical positivism can best be understood as metascience. Its subject matter was science, as the subject matter of science is the world. It was concerned with articulating the logic of concepts constitutive of science. Partially in response to what they considered the excesses of nineteenth-century German metaphysics, the early positivists viewed philosophical problems as problems of language. Their solution was to take the linguistic turn and focus on the construction and/or analysis of formal languages, using highly controlled mechanisms for introducing definitions and a clear logical structure. Since positivism held science to be the premier knowledge-producing activity, such an analysis guaranteed value both for understanding what knowledge is and for the reform of nonscientific knowledge. As a consequence, this attention to the logic of such general concepts as explanation, confirmation, and evidence, approached as linguistic phenomena, kept work in the philosophy of science at some remove from the worries of particular sciences. The argument in defense of this approach resembled an abstract solution to the problem of demarcating science from nonscience. Before biology, geology, or psychology could qualify as sciences the abstract conditions for being a science had to be established through the explication of these central concepts, understood as necessary and sufficient conditions of scientific status. A number of other assumptions were at work as well. For example, the positivist program was heavily reductionist, with physics understood as both foundational and the best justified of sciences. While not appreciated as such, for most of the years from the beginning of the positivist movement until deep into the 1970s, positivist philosophy of science was philosophy of physics, concentrating on specific problems within physics often under the guise of clarifying the more general conceptual problems of science at large.

It is fashionable to speak of the death of positivism and to associate its decline with the appearance of Thomas Kuhn's *The Structure of Scientific Revolutions* in 1962). But positivism is not dead, and most of the severest blows were dealt to its viability as a successful philosophy of science before the publication of Kuhn's book. To recognize that positivism is not dead but flourishing is not to deny that it has undergone significant transformations. Some of its older characteristics, such as the attempt to display the structure of concepts using first-order predicate calculus, are no longer universally employed. Nor is it fashionable to attempt explications of universal concepts that apply across the sciences without modification. But a great deal of important work in philosophy of science still aims to uncover the strong logical relations between theory and evidence, with the

primary goal of understanding the logical structure of science and scientific knowledge. In this context the development of the semantic view of theories (see the work of Bas van Fraassen and Fred Suppe) can easily be seen as an extension of the positivist agenda in the light of the knowledge gained concerning the limits of a strictly linguistic framework exploited using only basic logical techniques.

While it would be historically inaccurate to deny the importance of Kuhn's contribution to the transformation of the philosophy of science from a positivistic philosophy of physics to its current state, it is also important to note that positivism was under serious fire before his work appeared. Attacks on the justifiability of central assumptions, such as W. V. O. Quine's rejection of the analytic-synthetic distinction and Wilfrid Sellars's attack on epistemological foundationalism, appeared in the 1950s. Likewise, what has come to be called the historical turn, incorrectly credited to Kuhn, was well under way at the same time in the work of Norwood Russell Hanson (1961). Further, positivistically trained philosophers such as Carl Hempel were highly sensitive to the limits of the approaches they employed and were undertaking continual modifications of key assumptions in attempts to meet the most severe objections, some of which were of their own making.

To be fair to positivism, despite the unjustifiable claims of hegemony, it was a vibrant and exciting research program that insisted on intellectual rigor and logical consistency, which is one reason why it continues to exercise a profound influence on the contemporary scene. Positivism gave us a standard for the philosophy of science that philosophers are largely unwilling to relinquish. This explains in part why contemporary critics of the philosophy of science refer to it as being in a state of crisis. But such criticism is misguided: in contrast, the philosophy of science is far more exciting than ever before, precisely because of its positivistic heritage, in two distinct ways. First, that heritage anchors philosophers of science either as they respond to current challenges to the role of philosophy in the analysis and understanding of science or as they work their way toward a new and better understanding of science. Second, because of positivism's goal of universal criteria there now exists a healthy dynamic tension between efforts to remain true to that objective and the need to deal with the particulars that form the focus of newer developments, such as those discussed below.

As noted above, during the heyday of positivism, there was an illusion of hegemony in the philosophy of science. Today there is no such illusion. Further, with the loss of hegemony comes the problem of explaining what is going on in the field. It is complicated, but four central features stand out on the contemporary landscape: (1) increasing attention to the problems of the individual sciences; (2) the historical turn; (3) new challenges to standard methodologies from feminists and from sociologists; and (4) the rise of the new experimentalism.

Positivism is not dead,

and most of the severest blows

were dealt to its viability

as a successful philosophy of science

before the publication of Kuhn's

The Structure of Scientific Revolutions *(1962).*

First, increasing amounts of work are now devoted to philosophical problems of individual sciences. This is not to say that the attempt to provide a characterization of science *tout court* has been abandoned. That ideal remains. But directing attention to the problems of the individual sciences—for example, explanation in biology—forces us to deal with the actual practice of science. In so doing we necessarily fall short of achieving an account—of explanation, for example—that meets a general ideal. This new focus on the particular drives a kind of dialectic between the general ideals for science and the needs generated by remaining true to the practices of actual scientists. As we focus on the practices of scientists we see a proliferation of philosophies of. . . . For example, the philosophy of biology is now a firmly established field of its own with a substantial cadre of researchers and its own journal. Philosophical problems of biology are sufficiently distinct from the old standard problems in the philosophy of physics that entrée into its discussion requires substantial background. The same is true for the philosophy of economics and the philosophy of psychology. Further, as philosophical work concerning science moves closer into specific sciences it becomes increasingly necessary to know something about the science and, perhaps more important, something about the literature on the philosophical topic at hand. Thus, when considering the problem of what constitutes a species in biology, it would be easy to consider this as merely an instance of a type-token problem and as a simple instance of the perennial philosophical problem of universals. But the interesting part of the problem comes from the biology itself, considering not only the functional role of species in biological

theory but the peculiarities of the many-one problem in the context of an intrinsically changing "one." In addition, as we move toward the specific sciences, philosophical problems become increasingly tied to methodological problems within those sciences. For example, referring again to the problem of species, the difficulty of devising an adequate definition is exacerbated by the real-world difficulty of delimiting the individuals who are members of a species, not just in space, but also in time.

A second notable feature of contemporary philosophy of science is, of course, the turn to history. But in the context of contemporary developments, it is not too strong to claim that the turn to history alone is passé. On the one hand, like species, scientific methods and our understanding of evidential relations and the like have been shown to be evolving. Hence, analyses that go into any detail of the alleged timeless and universal concepts of evidence and explanation will fail. Yet, the still viable positivist ideal calls for just such universal accounts of the logic of the concepts involved in order to understand the sense of "science" at work. Further, from a methodological point of view, much recent philosophy of science has been enhanced and challenged by work in both history and sociology of science, not to mention critical theory, economics, and political science. To appreciate fully the force of the dynamic tension between the pull of general ideals and the push for detail, interdisciplinarity is increasingly demanded.

In *Structure*, Kuhn alerted the positivists to the fact that a detailed look at the history of science rendered a number of positivistic methodological and substantive assumptions nonoperative. Thus, Kuhn argued that a single instance of falsification was rarely, if ever, sufficient to justify rejection of a theory. Likewise, given the structure of the development of science that Kuhn proposed and defended, the very question of the rationality of scientific change was brought into doubt. Although subsequent historical work left many of Kuhn's own claims in question, this challenge motivated philosophers to test their ideas against history. What remained unclear was the methodology appropriate to meeting this challenge. Philosophers first began to use history to substantiate and illuminate philosophical theses without much awareness or acknowledgment of the canons of historiography. More often than not it appeared that one simply went out and found a historical case study that substantiated the philosophical assumptions being asserted. Philosophers of science became well versed in their individual favorite historical episode or two, but rarely was the history taken on its own ground. Historians of science naturally objected to this usurpation of history. And despite the turn to history, a genuine rift was developing in the 1970s between historians and philosophers of science.

In addition to the attacks of historians of science, the late 1970s saw the rise of the ironically named Strong Programme in the sociology of science. Advocates of the Strong Programme defended an extreme position regarding the claims of scientific knowledge—that they are merely the results of negotiations among the practitioners of science and that the world, as such, has nothing to do with scientific claims. Science, on this view, is social all the way down. This particular form of severe relativism arose at the same time as the newest version of the battle over scientific realism developed.

In addition to the attacks of historians of science, the late 1970s saw the rise of the ironically named Strong Programme in the sociology of science.

The old debate was between scientific realism and instrumentalism, and it concentrated on what can be called theory realism because of the positivistic turn to language and the characterization of theories as languages. Defenders of the new scientific realism—for example, Richard Burian and Ian Hacking—endorse the view that entities named in scientific theories and discovered through experimentation are real and that knowledge of them and their behavior is possible and in some cases actual. Philosophers in this camp found that, under this attack from the sociologists, they needed secure knowledge of the science and of its history to mount a reasonable counterattack. The problem was to find a way to reinsert the world into our account of science. On this point historians and philosophers of science kept common ground: science is about the world, and the activities of scientists are worth studying because they reveal important things about how we come to know what the world is like. For some philosophers it looked as if the philosophical arguments over the reality of nonobservable scientific entities paled in the face of the dogmatic assertions of the Strong Programme regarding the irrelevance of the nonsocial factors (i.e., the world) in understanding both the activities of scientists and the epistemic authority of scientific claims.

Another problem arose out of the turn to history and the reaction to the relativism of the sociology of science: as philosophers of science became more and more embroiled in arguments over the accuracy of historical details or immersed in the sophistication of their understanding of the subtleties of the science in question, the traditional normative role of philosophy appeared to disappear. That is, the strategy philosophers undertook was to become more like historians or scientists. In doing so the philosophical issues seemed to slip between the cracks. Here again we can see the effect of the dynamic tension between the goals of normative universal account and the need for accurate description.

Further, for some on the contemporary scene, the normative role of philosophy should be usurped and transformed into a political role. This attack comes on two fronts. The first is the result of the move to interdisciplinarity. The second comes from a different direction and leads us to the third major aspect of the contemporary landscape. First, the attack from interdisciplinarity.

Philosophy of science has always been under attack. The positivists were often misunderstood and withstood such charges as aiming to tell scientists how to do science—this despite the fact that they saw their normative role in the construction of criteria for adequate explanations, laws, theories, and evidence, satisfaction of which would guarantee that the claims under analysis were in fact scientific. They were concerned with showing that a science, reconstructed after the fact, met these criteria. But they were often charged with trying to reform the practice of science. Now the new interdisciplinarity has a name: science studies. It is not yet clear whether the mix of disciplines will produce a new discipline with its own methodology and domain of inquiry or whether it will result in an uneasy alliance of interests, methods, and criteria of adequacy. Nevertheless, there are subgroups within science studies with their own explicit normative agendas that range over a continuum. At one end, unlike the positivists, is a group that does want to tell scientists what to do. This goal is announced under the rubric of the democratization of science and represents an interesting blend of ideologies—primarily Marxists looking for a last venue but also extreme democrats who believe that if the people are going to pay for scientific research, they ought to have a significant say in where it goes. At the other end there are the scientists who reject any normative intrusions from outside.

Political agendas are not the exclusive property of sociologists of science, Marxists, and scientists. A new and refreshing voice has entered the discussion, sometimes with a political agenda, sometimes not. This is the voice of feminist philosophers of science. Their challenges to more standard philosophy of science, which sometimes amount to recirculated positivism, usually incorporate a healthy appreciation of the social domain of scientific inquiry. In some cases this amounts to a significant challenge to key epistemological assumptions ranging over yet another continuum. At one end of this continuum, seen in the work of Sandra Harding, is a set of issues concerning the impact of what is perceived to be a patriarchal social structure within the scientific community on both the role of women within science and, subsequently, on the range of acceptable points of view in the formulation and evaluation of scientific claims. At the other of the spectrum, found most prominently in the work of Helen Longino, is the acknowledgment of the problems created by the social environment but a strong defense of nongender-rendered epistemological criteria and standards.

The introduction of political and feminist agendas, however, has not answered the question concerning the normative dimensions of the philosophy of science, even within interdisciplinary science studies. This question requires an answer that focuses on the criteria for being scientific. One attempt to deal with this demand has been to take yet another turn, one that relies on history and sociology in part but that takes science to be the foremost player. This is the turn to naturalize the philosophy of science. Naturalized philosophy of science, the most recent incarnation of Quine's naturalized epistemology, is defended by Ronald Giere, Philip Kitcher, Larry Laudan, and a number of philosophers who took the turn to an examination of the problems of individual sciences. The move here is simple: biology, for example, is what biologists do. Who is a biologist is determined by appeal to historical and sociological criteria. The answer to the question of what constitutes good biology must come from the biologist or the practices of biology. It is then the philosopher's role to subject the criteria proposed by the scientist to rigorous analysis to see if they meet the standards of consistency and logical rigor common to all discourse. And there is one further job for the philosopher of science—that is, to see whether the criteria meet the goals and objects of the scientists working in the area under discussion.

There are at least two problems stemming from this approach that need solutions. First, what is the normative philosophical role here? Second, can whatever results philosophical analysis produces be taken beyond the boundaries of the particular scientific domain under discussion? The first problem resembles a similar problem confronting Quine's attempt to naturalize epistemology. Simply put, if we give up epistemology for, say, psychology, we are still left with questions such as, How does this account of how the human brain works explain what knowledge is? That is, a fully descriptive account of what, from a sociohistorical point of view, scientists do still leaves us with the question of whether or not it is good science. This question remains even if we answer positively the questions concerning logical

rigor and whether or not the results of philosophical analyses show that the scientific results meet the scientists' objectives. The second problem speaks directly to the role and objectives of philosophy itself. If, as Sellars proposed, philosophy aims at a full-blown understanding of how the world in all its peculiarities hangs together, thus enabling us to make our way around in it successfully, the fragmentation represented by the historical and naturalistic turns, as well as the rise of philosophies of various sciences, seems to render this goal unobtainable. Philosophy as a synthesizing activity would appear to be increasingly out of fashion and difficult, if not impossible, to do.

Paradoxically, to accept this perspective would be to take an unphilosophical and at the same time characteristically philosophical point of view. This view is unphilosophical in the sense that it assumes that the current state of philosophical work is in some sense a final state. But there is no reason to assume that the current state of affairs will dominate in the future, and a few reasons why are suggested below when we turn to the fourth and final major feature of the contemporary landscape. This pessimistic point of view is, however, characteristically philosophical in the sense that announcements of the death of philosophy are a persistent feature of its history. One of its most vocal advocates in the period under discussion is Richard Rorty. But saying so does not make it so.

Challenges by feminist philosophers of science

usually incorporate a healthy appreciation

of the social domain of scientific inquiry.

One way to revitalize some of the more praiseworthy aspects of the philosophy of science in the face of the apparent fragmentation occurring as a result of challenges from the history of science, the sociology of science, feminist critiques, and the naturalistic turn is to look at yet one more new feature of the landscape, the New Experimentalism. It is both possible and reasonable to understand these various challenges to the traditional philosophy of science as a reaction to the philosophy of science as history of ideas (i.e., ideas about science). Each of the new dimensions discussed above can be seen as an attempt to put some content into the philosophy of science, to give the philosophy of science some point of contact with the world of science as it actually works. This feature is characteristic of the New Experimentalism as well. Further, the analysis and appreciation of the role of experiments and the problems they both solve and present can be legitimate aspects of each of the other new features of the philosophy of science landscape. In short, philosophical issues surround experimentation, and experiments are or can be a common thread in discussions of science, irrespective of whether the main approach is historical, sociological, feminist, or naturalistic. And, obviously enough, this is because experiments are a common feature of science. There is also traditional philosophical content in the turn to experiments, overlooked by many positivists, since experiment is the heart of science's means of obtaining and evaluating evidence. There are many levels on which the role of experiments can be addressed. There are epistemological problems presented by the creation and use of experimental devices. After constructing a device for measuring certain features of a field, the first problem is to calibrate the device (see Hacking, 1983; Hanson, 1961). This involves a variety of aspects, certain assumptions about standard conditions, questions about the reliability of calibration devices and readouts, and a theory of calibration itself. Then there is the question of accurately reporting what is revealed. Here we have the basic question of working out how the results bear on the hypothesis under investigation and the theory being tested or developed. It is a problem of framing the results in the proper terms to make their precise relevance perspicuous. In addition, we have problems of separating the signal from the noise and detecting the object presented as an object and not a creation of the experimental device. And while work on experiments is fairly recent, incorporating sociological perspectives (Andy Pickering), historical/sociological perspectives (Steven Shapin and Simon Schaffer), historical perspectives (Jed Buchwald, Peter Galison), and philosophical perspectives (Robert Ackermann, Nancy Cartwright, Allan Franklin, Ian Hacking), the importance of experiments and experimental apparatuses for the epistemological authority of science already was well appreciated by Gaston Bachelard in the 1930s.

The recent emergence of the importance of understanding experiments for understanding science, and for an appreciation of the philosophical problems experiments present, has also made it possible to see how the philosophy of science, enriched by its new developments, can work through its recent fragmentation to a new and deeper holistic appreciation of the scientific enterprise. As work on experiments progresses, two things are increasingly evident: (1) experiments do not occur in a vacuum and (2) the broader context in which we need to see experiments provides the platform for the reemergence of a more traditional, normative, and

synthetic role for the philosophy of science. To take these points in order, first consider the fact that experiments are not merely theory dependent. That is, we do not start with a theory and then construct an experiment to document some aspect of that theory. There is an important and overlooked interactive symbiosis between theories and instruments that generates highly creative and inventive experimental environments that are constantly being readjusted in the light of changes in any and all of its components (see the work of Hans-Joerg Rheinberger). There is a certain sense in which the instruments and techniques of experimentation, on the one hand, and theories, on the other hand, come to the experimental environment as equal partners. If we identify the science exclusively with the theories, we do an injustice to history. Nevertheless, we cannot discuss the design and significance of experiments without appreciating the theories. And yet, it is the experimental platform that increasingly seems to mold the theories as the science matures, and that platform increases in complexity (e.g., as instruments are embedded in computer arrays and stacked programs).

The shift from the universal criteria of positivism to the pervasive technological infrastructure is not perfectly smooth.

The New Experimentalism therefore provides us with the basis for reconceptualizing the development and character of science in the context of its technological infrastructure. The infrastructure also provides the vehicle for the incorporation of all of the various new facets of the philosophical landscape in the philosophy of science and also provides the philosophy of science with a new framework. Instead of seeing science as merely a collection of theories that meet certain logical criteria of adequacy, these recent developments give us science as a thoroughly human activity generating knowledge about the world through a technologically interactive framework.

If the New Experimentalism, fleshed out with detailed historical, social studies of the sciences, offers a promising new framework for the new philosophy of science, where does that leave the positivistic foundation, which, it was argued above, is still functioning? To begin with, that positivism is the foundation for contemporary work is a historical fact. From that fact it does not follow that for positivism to be an influence on the contemporary scene its original program must still be intact. We have noted throughout the dynamic tension between the universalistic goals of positivism and the fragmentation brought about by the increased attention to the details of the sciences. The proposal here is that the still-functioning search for universal criteria is the motivation to turn to the technological infrastructure of science. Mature sciences are increasingly characterized, if not captured, by their technological bases. This is yet another fact on the contemporary scientific landscape. The universal features and, perhaps, problems of contemporary science are increasingly a direct function of the supporting and interacting technological systems in which the science is embedded. It can be argued that the technological side provides the more encompassing framework in which to consider the scientific.

The shift from the universal criteria of positivism to the pervasive technological infrastructure is not perfectly smooth. The positivists' linguistic framework is not being exchanged for the technological. The manner in which we phrase our theories, our hypotheses, and our evidential claims remains crucial to the scientific process. Nor does the appeal to the technological deal well with the emergence of new sciences, since the claim is that the technological infrastructure is most evident in mature sciences. Nevertheless, the search for some universal feature(s) remains a deeply rooted feature of contemporary philosophy of science.

[See also Critical Theory; Explanation, Theories of; Explanation, Types of; Kuhn, Thomas; Laws of Nature; Naturalized Epistemology; Philosophy of Biology; Philosophy of Physics; Philosophy of Social Sciences; Quine, Willard Van Orman; Realism; Reduction, Reductionism; Scientific Theories; Sellars, Wilfrid.]

BIBLIOGRAPHY

Ackermann, R. J. *Data, Instruments, and Theory: A Dialectic Approach to Understanding Science.* Princeton, NJ, 1985.

Buchwald, J. Z. *The Creation of Scientific Effects: Heinrich Hertz and Electric Waves.* Chicago, 1994.

Burian, R. M. "Realist Methodology in Contemporary Genetics," in N. Nersessian, ed., *The Process of Science,* Vol. 3 of *Science and Philosophy* (Dordrecht, 1987).

Cartwright, N. *How the Laws of Physics Lie.* Oxford, 1983.

Franklin, A. *The Neglect of Experiment.* Cambridge, 1986.

Galison, P. L. *How Experiments End.* Chicago, 1987.

Giere, R. N. *Exploring Science: A Cognitive Approach.* Chicago, 1988.

Hacking, I. *Representing and Intervening: Introductory Topics in the Philosophy of Natural Science.* Cambridge, 1983.

Hanson, N. R. *Patterns of Discovery: An Inquiry into the Conceptual Foundations of Science.* Cambridge, 1961.

Harding, S. G. *Whose Science? Whose Knowledge? Thinking from Women's Lives.* Ithaca, NY, 1991.

Hempel, C. G. *Aspects of Scientific Explanation and Other Essays in the Philosophy of Science.* New York, 1965.

Kitcher, P. *The Advancement of Science: Science without Legend, Objectivity without Illusions.* New York, 1993.

Kuhn, T. S. *The Structure of Scientific Revolutions.* Chicago, 1962.

Laudan, L. *Progress and Its Problems: Towards a Theory of Scientific Growth.* Berkeley, 1977.

Longino, H. E. *Science as Social Knowledge: Values and Objectivity in Scientific Inquiry.* Princeton, NJ, 1990.

Pickering, A. *Constructing Quarks: A Sociological History of Particle Physics.* Chicago, 1984.

Quine, W. V. O. "Two Dogmas of Empiricism," *Philosophical Review,* Vol. 60 (1951), reprinted in *From a Logical Point of View.* Cambridge, MA, 1953.

Rheinberger, H. J. "Experiment, Difference, and Writing I: Tracing Protein Synthesis." *Studies in History and Philosophy of Science,* Vol. 23 (1994), 305–31.

———. "Experiment, Difference, and Writing II: The Laboratory Production of Transfer RNA," *Studies in History and Philosophy of Science,* Vol. 23 (1994), 389–422.

Rorty, R. *Philosophy and the Mirror of Nature.* Princeton, NJ, 1979.

Sellars, W. "Empiricism and the Philosophy of Mind," *Minnesota Studies in the Philosophy of Science,* Vol. 1 (1956), 253–329.

Shapin, S., and S. Schaffer. *Leviathan and the Air Pump: Hobbes, Boyle, and the Experimental Life.* Princeton, NJ, 1985.

Suppe, F. *The Semantic Conception of Theories and Scientific Realism.* Urbana, IL, 1988.

van Fraassen, B. C. *The Scientific Image.* Oxford, 1980.

– JOSEPH C. PITT

PHILOSOPHY OF SOCIAL SCIENCES

The philosophy of social sciences comes in three varieties, as the metaideology, the metaphysics, and the methodology of the disciplines involved. The metaideology looks at how far different, traditional legitimations of social sciences succeed. The metaphysics looks at questions having to do with what social science posits—what things it says there are—and at how far those posits are consistent with more or less commonplace beliefs. And the methodology looks at questions regarding the nature of observations, laws, and theories in social science, the logic of induction and confirmation, the requirements of understanding and explanation, and so on.

Metaideology

The social sciences were conceived and pursued, from the very beginning, under the influence of ideals (particularly of scientific objectivity and progress) deriving from the eighteenth-century enlightenment (Hawthorn, 1976). The first social scientists were economists and sociologists, as we would call them today, and they were self-consciously concerned about producing something that would count, not as philosophy, not as literature, not as common sense, but as science: as a project faithful to the image forged by natural science.

The scientific intention—the intention to make science—has remained characteristic of work in the social sciences. It puts social scientists, paradoxically, under an obligation of an ideological kind: the obligation to show that the sort of analysis they pursue is of a properly scientific kind. The metaideology of social science interrogates and assesses the ideologies whereby the social sciences try to legitimate what they do, to show that what they do is genuinely scientific in character.

Broadly speaking, there are three main ideologies that have been invoked—individually or in various combinations—by social scientists in the scientific legitimation of their enterprise. Each of these marks a feature that putatively distinguishes social science from mere common sense, mere social lore. The first ideology hails social science as an explanatory enterprise of culturally universal validity; the second as an enterprise that is interpretatively neutral, not being warped by people's self-understanding; and the third as an enterprise that enjoys evaluative independence: value-freedom. The universality, neutrality, and independence claimed are each meant to establish social science as objective, and therefore scientifically respectable, in a way in which common sense is not; each notion offers an explication of what scientific objectivity involves. Some approaches in the metaideology of social science, particularly those of a postmodern cast (Rosenau, 1992), reject all three ideologies out of hand: they reject any notion of objectivity in the area; others consider them one by one, under the assumption that they may come apart.

The first social scientists were economists

and sociologists, as we would call them today,

and they were self-consciously concerned

about producing something that would count,

not as philosophy, not as literature,

but as science.

Social lore is always lore about a particular social milieu and culture, and an aspiration to cultural universality, if it can be vindicated, would certainly give social science a distinctive status. Such an aspiration is supported in a variety of traditions: among anthropologists and sociologists of a Durkheimian cast, among many Marxist scholars, and among those economists who think that all human behavior, and the patterns to which it gives rise, can be explained by reference to *homo economicus.*

But the metaideologists of social science have claimed many reasons to question the possibility of any universalist, or at least any straightforwardly universalist, theory. Hermeneutic philosophy, which has long been dominant in Germany, and the analytical tradition sponsored by the work of the later Wittgenstein both suggest that any explanation of human behavior has to start with the culturally specific concepts in which people understand their environment and cannot aspire, therefore, to a substantive universality (McCarthy, 1978; Winch, 1958). The debate on these questions ranges widely, encompassing issues of cultural and other forms of relativism (Hollis & Lukes, 1982).

Social lore is not only particularistic, it is also designed to represent people as subjectively understandable or interpretable. We, the local consumers of such lore, know what it is like to be creatures of the kind represented and know how we would go about communicating with them. The second, and perhaps least persuasive, ideology of social science suggests that this disposition to represent people as subjectively understandable comes of a limited perspective that social science transcends. It suggests that social science can aspire to an objective explanation of people's behavior without worrying about whether the explanation fits with their self-understanding: without being anxious to ensure that it makes native sense of them and facilitates interpersonal communication. The ideology suggests that social science, in the received phrases, can aspire to a form of *Erklären,* or explanation, that need not service the needs of interpersonal *Verstehen,* or understanding.

Metaideologists of social science have claimed many reasons to question this aspiration to *Verstehen*-free explanation. Hermeneutic and Wittgensteinian thinkers both reject the idea that people can be properly understood without facilitating communication (Winch, 1958). And the many philosophers who follow the lead of Donald Davidson on interpretation argue that there is no interpreting human subjects without representing them as more or less rational and more or less interpersonally scrutable (Macdonald & Pettit, 1981).

Social lore is often evaluatively committed as well as particularistic and oriented to subjective understanding. It takes a form premised on an evaluative characterization of the status quo. Thus, it may characterize the beliefs and explain the behavior of rulers on the assumption that the regime they sustain is unjust. The third and most common legitimating ideology of social science, one associated in particular with the German sociologist Max Weber, holds that in this respect—and perhaps in this respect only—social science can do scientifically better than social lore. It can acknowledge that the agents in the society have evaluative beliefs, and it can take account of these in its explanation of what they do, without itself endorsing any such beliefs; it can be objective, in the familiar sense of remaining uncommitted on evaluative questions.

Metaideologists of social science have also sought reasons to doubt this claim, but the debate has been confused by differences over what sorts of evaluative commitments would really be damaging to the pretensions of social science. The critique of social science on the grounds of not escaping a commitment to value has been nurtured by the appearance, in the later part of the century, of a variety of realist positions on the nature of value. If values are taken to be objective features of the world, then a social scientist's beliefs as to what those features are may well affect their interpretation of how certain subjects think and act; interpretation, after all, is bound to be influenced by the interpreter's view of the subject's environment (Hurley, 1989, chap. 5; Macdonald & Pettit, 1981, chap. 4; Taylor, 1981).

The metaideology of social science may concern itself with other issues: for example, whether the models used in social science, in particular within economics, are really empirical, scientific models and not just pieces of mathematics or exercises in a conversational rhetoric (Hausman, 1991: McCloskey, 1985; Rosenberg, 1992). These issues are not discussed here.

Metaphysics

The metaphysics of social science usually takes it as granted that there is no society without individual intentional agents: without subjects who apparently act, other things being equal, on the basis of their beliefs and desires (Pettit, 1993, pt. 1). The question that metaphysics raises bears on what more we should include in our metaphysical stock-taking of society; and on how the more we should include, if there is any, relates to individual intentional subjects.

There are two aspects of social life that are particularly relevant to this question. There is the social interaction between individuals in virtue of which various relationships get formed: relationships involving communication, affection, collaboration, exchange, recognition, esteem, or whatever. And there is the social aggregation of individual attitudes and actions in virtue of which various institutions get established: these institutions will include common instrumentalities such as languages, cultures, and markets; groups such as the club, union, or party, whose essence it is to have a mode of collective behavior; groups that may have only a non-behavioral collective identity such as genders, races, and classes; and shared resources of the kind illustrated by museums, libraries, and states.

The metaphysics of social science concerns itself both with issues raised by interaction and with questions associated with aggregation, specifically with social interaction and aggregation. (On the definition of "social," see Ruben, 1985).

On the side of interaction the main issue in social philosophy is that which divides so-called atomists from non-atomists (Taylor, 1985). The atomist holds that individual human beings do not depend—that is, noncausally or constitutively depend—on social relationships for the appearance of any distinctive, human capacities. The non-atomist holds that they do. The atomist defends an image of human beings under which they come to society with all the characteristic properties that they will ever display; social life does not transform them in any essential manner. The nonatomist denies this, believing that it is only in the experience of social relationships that human beings come properly into their own.

The debate between atomists and nonatomists has centered on the connection between thought and language. Atomists have taken their lead from Hobbes, who argues that, however useful language is for mnemonic, taxonomic, and communicative purposes, thinking is possible without speech, even without any inchoate form of speech. Nonatomists have tended to follow Rousseau and the Romantic tradition with which he is associated—a tradition also encompassing Herder and Hegel—in arguing, first, that language is social and, second, that thought requires language.

The atomist tradition has been dominant in English-speaking philosophy, while the nonatomist has had a considerable presence in France and Germany. One source of nonatomism in the English-speaking world has been the work of the later Wittgenstein, in which it is suggested that following a rule—and, therefore, thinking—is possible only in the context of social practices and relationships (Wittgenstein, 1968). This very strong nonatomist thesis may also be weakened, so that the claim is that following a rule of a characteristic kind—say, a suitably scrutable kind—requires such a social context (Pettit, 1993, chap. 4). Another source of nonatomism in recent English-speaking philosophy has been the argument that the content of a person's thoughts is fixed, not just by what goes on in his head, but by the linguistic community to which he belongs and to which he aspires to remain faithful (Burge, 1979; Hurley, 1989).

What now of the issues generated by the aggregative aspect of society? There are a number of interesting questions raised by the aggregative structure of society, some having to do with the reducibility of aggregative theory to theory of a more psychological cast, others having to do with the status of aggregative individuals and the standing of the causal relevance we ascribe to such entities (Gilbert, 1992; James, 1984; Ruben, 1985; Tuomela, 1996). Perhaps the most pressing question, however, is whether the entities that appear with the social aggregation of individual attitudes and actions give the lie to our ordinary sense of intentional agency: whether it means that, contrary to appearances, we are in some way the dupes of higher-level patterns or forces (Pettit, 1993, chap. 3). The individualist, to use a name that also bears further connotations—see under "Methodology"—denies that aggregate entities have this effect; the nonindividualist insists that they do.

The metaphysics of social science usually takes it as granted that there is no society without individuals who act on the basis of their beliefs and desires.

One extreme sort of individualism would say that intentional agency is not compromised by any aggregate, social entities, because in strict truth no such entities exist. A more plausible form of the doctrine would say that while there are indeed a variety of aggregate entities, there is nothing about those entities that suggests that our received, commonplace psychology is mistaken. No doubt, there are aggregate regularities associated with such entities: for example, a rise in unemployment tends to be followed by a rise in crime; the fact that something is in an organization's interest generally means that agents of the organization will pursue it; and so on. But the individualist will argue that those regularities do not signal the presence of forces unrecognized in commonplace psychology or the operation of any mechanism—say, any selection mechanism—that belies the assumptions of that psychology. That the regularities obtain can be explained within that psychology, given the context in which the relevant agents find themselves and given their understanding—perhaps involving relevant aggregate-level concepts—of that context.

Methodology

There are two sorts of methodological questions raised in the philosophy of social science: first, questions imported from the methodology of natural science having to do with such matters as observations and laws and theories, realism and nonrealism in theory interpretation, statistical inference, confirmation, and explanation; second, questions that arise only, or arise distinctively, within the social sciences. Perhaps the two major

questions of the latter kind bear on whether it is good explanatory practice to follow the individualistic and economistic assumptions, respectively, that characterize much social science. Here the emphasis will be on the issues of individualism and economism.

The methodological individualist, as characterized in the literature, is associated with a number of more or less outlandish doctrines: for example, that individuals each play indispensable roles, so that things would always have been significantly different if the actual individuals had not been around or if they had not done the things they actually did; that individuals are unaffected by their circumstances, or their relationships with one another, in the things they come to think and want; or that all social facts can be expressed in terms of a nonsocial psychology and that all social laws can be derived from the laws of such a psychology.

Methodological individualism is better understood, however, as a doctrine that has more clearly had respectable defenders as well as opponents: specifically, as the doctrine that it is always good explanatory practice to try to explain social events in terms of finer-grain, individualistic factors rather than by reference to aggregative antecedents. Such an explanatory individualism has been defended by Jon Elster (1985). He argues that aggregative antecedents are causally relevant in virtue of the causal relevance of individual factors and that staying at the aggregative level means leaving the productive mechanism in a black box; it amounts to a willful neglect of relevant facts.

Suppose that we have found a good aggregative explanation of some social phenomenon: say we find that secularization is explained adequately by urbanization or a rise in crime by a rise in unemployment. We gain further information about the causal history of such a phenomenon as we are informed about the individual-level factors at work in producing secularization or crime. But it may still be that the aggregative story gives us equally important causal information. It may be, for example, that while we learn more about the detail of the actual causal process in going individualistic we learn more about what would be enough to ensure an increase in secularization or crime—that there should be urbanization or unemployment—in spotting the aggregative connections. After all, we might have known the individual-level explanations without having come to recognize the aggregative connections. Perhaps the right line is neither explanatory individualism nor explanatory nonindividualism but explanatory ecumenism (Jackson & Pettit, 1992).

The second question bears on whether it is a good explanatory strategy in social science to make economistic assumptions about individual agents: to assume, as economists tend to do, that agents are rational in the way they form and reform their preferences and that their preferences are generally egoistic in character. There are lots of persuasive arguments for following an economistic strategy: arguments that point to the precision in model building and prediction that economistic assumptions allow (Becker, 1976). But it seems manifest, on the other hand, that the economistic story is not the whole truth about human beings (Hollis, 1977). For example, it is surely obvious that most of us do not make our decisions on the self-concerned, calculative basis that that story would seem to suggest.

But this consideration may not be decisive against economism. For what is possible is that while agents often do not calculate economistically, they tend sooner or later to give up on patterns of behavior that are not at least comparatively satisfactory in economistic terms (Pettit, 1993, chap. 5). Perhaps the fact that a pattern of behavior satisfies such economistic constraints is necessary to explain the resilience, if not the actual production and reproduction, of the behavior.

[See also Confirmation Theory; Davidson, Donald; Explanation, Theories of; Explanation, Types of; Hegel, Georg Wilhelm Friedrich; Hermeneutic Philosophy; Hobbes, Thomas; Philosophy of Science; Postmodernism; Realism; Rousseau, Jean-Jacques; Scientific Theories; Wittgenstein, Ludwig Josef Johann.]

BIBLIOGRAPHY

Becker, G. *The Economic Approach to Human Behavior.* Chicago, 1976.

Burge, T. "Individualism and the Mental," *Midwest Studies in Philosophy,* Vol. 4 (1979), 73–121.

Elster, J. *Making Sense of Marx.* Cambridge, 1985.

Gilbert, M. *On Social Facts.* Princeton, NJ, 1992.

Hausman, D. *The Separate and Inexact Science of Economics.* Cambridge, 1991.

Hawthorn, G. *Enlightenment and Despair: A History of Sociology.* Cambridge, 1976.

Hollis, M. *Models of Man: Philosophical Thoughts on Social Action.* Cambridge, 1977.

———, and S. Lukes, eds. *Rationality and Relativism.* Oxford, 1982.

Hurley, S. *Natural Reasons: Personality and Polity.* New York, 1989.

Jackson, F., and P. Pettit. "In Defence of Explanatory Ecumenism," *Economics and Philosophy,* Vol. 8 (1992), 1–21.

James, S. *The Content of Social Explanation.* Cambridge, 1984.

Macdonald, G., and P. Pettit. *Semantics and Social Science.* London, 1981.

McCarthy, T. *The Critical Theory of Jürgen Habermas.* Cambridge, MA, 1978.

McCloskey, D. *The Rhetoric of Economics.* Madison, WI, 1985.

Papineau, D. *For Science in Social Science.* London, 1978.

Pettit, P. *The Common Mind: An Essay on Psychology, Society, and Politics.* New York, 1993.

Rosenau, P. M. *Post-Modernism and the Social Sciences: Insights, Inroads, and Intrusions.* Princeton, NJ, 1992.

Rosenberg, A. *Economics: Mathematical Politics or Science of Diminishing Returns?* Chicago, 1992.

Ruben, D.-H. *The Metaphysics of the Social World.* London, 1985.

Ryan, A. *The Philosophy of the Social Sciences.* London, 1970.

Taylor, C. "Understanding and Explanation in the *Geisteswissenschaften,*" in S. H. Holtzman and C. M. Leich, eds., *Wittgenstein: To Follow a Rule* (London, 1981).

——— *Philosophy and the Human Sciences.* Cambridge, 1985.

Tuomela, R. *The Importance of Us.* Stanford, CA, 1996.

Winch, P. *The Idea of a Social Science and Its Relation to Philosophy.* London, 1958.

Wittgenstein, L. *Philosophical Investigations,* 2d ed., trans. G. E. M. Anscombe. Oxford, 1968.

– PHILIP PETTIT

PHILOSOPHY OF TECHNOLOGY

To the three traditional sets of philosophical questions concerning being (metaphysics), knowledge (epistemology), and human action (ethics) modern philosophy added a fourth concerning history: What is the structure of history? What is the character of the mod-

The twentieth century saw the characterization of human history in terms of technology. (Corbis/Bettmann)

ern (or any other) historical epoch? From the beginning, response to the fourth kind of question has involved reference to technology. For Francis Bacon, for instance, the modern period is defined by the inventions of printing, gunpowder, and the compass (*Novum organum,* book 1, aphorism 129). Historical anthropologies commonly periodized human history on the basis of material artifacts: the stone age, the bronze age, the iron age, and so forth. And the substructure of "postmodernity" is constituted by advances in electronic communication from TV to computers.

Two Traditions in the Philosophy of Technology

In the late nineteenth and early twentieth centuries the characterization of human history in terms of technology gave way to the first explicit theories about technology itself. For example, Franz Reuleaux's *Theoretische Kinematik* (1875) was the founding text in mechanical engineering. From a more general perspective Ernst Kapp's *Grundlinien einer Philosophie der Technik* (1877) outlined a theory of culture grounded in technics understood as the extension and differentiation of human anatomy, physiology, and behavior. The hammer, for instance, can function as an extension of the fist, the train as an extension of legs and feet, the camera as an extension of the eye; and vice versa the fist is a kind of hammer, the train a kind of foot, the eye a kind of camera. Elaborations of this view of technology as "organ projection" are at the foundation of a tradition of what Carl Mitcham (1994) has termed "engineering philosophy of technology" and can be seen reflected in the work of philosophers such as the Russian Peter Englemeier, the German Friedrich Dessauer, the Frenchman Gilbert Simondon, and the Spaniard Juan David García Bacca (all of whom have been largely ignored by Anglo-American philosophy).

The recognition of technology

as a philosophical issue

is based upon its parallel emergence

as a social problem.

Research engineer Dessauer, for instance, developed a neo-Kantian critique of the transcendental possibility of technological invention that sees technology as bringing noumenal power into the world. Simondon explores relations between parts, artifacts, and technical systems and the evolutionary manifestation of what he terms "technicity." Englemeier and García Bacca both see

technological change as engendering world-historical transformations that are at once humanizing and transcending of the merely organically human. Additional contributions to this perspective can be found in the work of cybernetics and artificial intelligence theorists from Norbert Wiener (1948) to Kevin Kelly (1994). (The collections edited by Alan Ross Anderson [1964] and John Haugeland [1981] constitute good overviews of philosophical debates in this particular field.) Philosophical anthropologist Arnold Gehlen, media theorist Marshall McLuhan, as well as contemporary engineers Samuel Florman and Henry Petroski provide other takes on engineering philosophy of technology. But for two of the most sophisticated alternative presentations of aspects of this philosophy see scientific philosopher Mario Bunge's (1985) metaphysics, epistemology, and ethics of technology, and David Rothenberg's (1993) comprehensive reduction of nature and the nontechnical to technology.

Philosophy of technology is more commonly identified, however, with what could be termed a counterphilosophy of technology that interprets technology, not as extending, but as encroaching on or narrowing the categories of human experience. Following Kant's attempt "to deny [scientific] *knowledge,* in order to make room for *faith*" (*Critique of Pure Reason,* B), this "humanities philosophy of technology" seeks to limit technological action in order to make room for human culture in all its diversity. This tradition has been elaborated especially by the Continental philosophical tradition in the work of José Ortega y Gasset, Martin Heidegger, and Jacques Ellul.

Until quite recently, however, the problematic character of the phenomenon of technology remained in the background of philosophy. Technology constitutes what can be called a new philosophical issue, one that entered mainstream philosophical discourse only in the latter half of the twentieth century.

Technology as a Social Problem

The recognition of technology as a philosophical issue is based upon its parallel emergence as a social problem. A general name for this problem is that of technocracy—that is, the control of society by technical experts or by technical ways of thinking and acting. However, the precise understanding of the challenge of technocracy has varied from engineer apologists who see technocracy as a necessary good to humanities critics who reject it as an unnecessary evil. Indeed, one of the first requirements in the philosophy of technology is to clarify the problematic of technocracy.

Speaking generally, one can identify at least five competing and overlapping interpretations of technology as a social problem. First, there is a problem of the just distribution of technological products and powers—that is, technology as a political issue. Since the Industrial Revolution the social-justice question has found a variety of expressions in authoritarian and democratic regimes, in developed and developing countries. Second is the problem of the alienation of workers from their labor under conditions constituted by the industrial means of production, which has been presented especially by Marxists as an economic and by some non-Marxist social scientists as a psychological issue. Third is the problem of the destruction or transformation of culture by modern science and the technological development of new means of transportation and communication. Fourth is the problem of democratic participation. How are those who are not scientists or engineers to participate in technoscientific decision making or even decision making about science and technology? Indeed, the apparent need to rely on technical experts in many of the social institutions of high-tech democracies constitutes the challenge of technocracy in its restricted form. Fifth is the industrial pollution of the natural environment, which is often seen as an ecological issue. Competing proposals for "sustainable development" highlight this issue. Contemporary discussions of a range of applied ethics issues—from biomedical ethics to nuclear, environmental, and computer ethics—prolong these interpretations of technology as a social problem and are often taken to constitute the substance of the philosophy of technology.

Again, speaking generally, one can note two broad approaches to such problems. One attempts to explain modern technology as rooted in human nature and culture (engineering philosophy of technology), the other interprets modern technical methods and effects as unwarranted constraints on action (humanities philosophy of technology). The engineering philosophical approach calls in one way or another for more technology, the humanities philosophical approach for some delimitation of technology.

In its most extreme form, then, the foreground of philosophical reflection on technology centers on questions of whether technology is good or bad—on arguments between utopian and dystopian views of technology (Ihde, 1986). This pro/con, positive/negative approach is inadequate for two reasons. It treats technology as a unified whole when in truth it is a complex amalgam of artifacts, knowledge, activities, and volition, each with diverse structural features scattered across historical epochs and social contexts. Second, it assumes clarifications of the meaning of good and bad, right and wrong, just and unjust as these have developed

in the traditions of philosophy largely independent of any sustained reflection on technology. Reflection on ethics in technology or technologies may, however, demand a reevaluation of traditional ethical concepts and principles.

Underlying competing interpretations of technology as a social problem are variations of the three traditional philosophical questions. One concerns the epistemological question of the structure of technological (as related to or contrasted with scientific and aesthetic) knowing. Another is the metaphysical question of the relation between nature and artifice. Still a third is the ethical question of the proper creation and utilization of technoscientific powers, both within technoscientific institutions and in society at large. Philosophy of technology constitutes a progressive deepening and clarification of these questions by both engineering and humanities philosophers of technology.

Technology, Technicity, Technicism: European Philosophy of Technology

The attempt to speak of "technology" rather than "technologies" rests on an ability to clarify some inner or essential feature of all technologies. Call this hypothetical essential feature "technicity." We can then immediately note that, prior to the modern period, technicity was at a minimum scattered throughout and heavily embedded within a diversity of human engagements, and indeed that philosophy took a stand against any separating of technicity from its embedding in particulars. Plato's argument in the *Gorgias,* for example, is precisely an argument against disembedding *techne* from social or cultural contexts and traditions, not to mention ideas of the good. What is distinctive about modern philosophy, by contrast, is the attempt, beginning with Galileo Galilei and René Descartes, to disembed technics from particular human activities, to study them in systematic ways, and thus to create technology.

John Stuart Mill in his *Logic* (1843) already assumes the success of this disembedding project when he explains the practical value of science. For Mill the rationality of any art is grounded in a corresponding science.

> The art proposes to itself an end to be attained, defines the end, and hands it over to the science. The science receives it, considers it as a phenomenon or effect to be studied, and having investigated its causes and conditions, sends it back to art with a theorem of the combinations of circumstances by which it could be produced. Art then examines these combinations or circumstances, and according as any of them are or are not in human power, pronounces the end attainable or not. (*Logic,* book 6, chapter 12, section 2)

The pattern of technicity thus outlined is of the form $C \to E$, where E is an end or effect to be attained and C is the cause or condition of E. The remarkable thing about Mill's analysis is that art (or traditional technics) is not thought of as including any knowledge of means. Art is concerned only with determining the end and then putting into operation a means derived from science. It is the scientific study of means that constitutes what even during Mill's lifetime is coming to be called technology. Modern technicity can thus be defined as a systematic or scientific study of means that suspends examination of ends.

Among the first philosophers to analyze such a disembedding of means from ends was Ortega y Gasset. In the English translation of his *La rebelión de las masas* (1929), Ortega writes that "Three principles have made possible [the] new world: liberal democracy, scientific experiment, and industrialism. The two latter may be summed up in one word: technicism" (1932, p. 56). Ortega himself uses the more straightforward "técnica," but the term technicism is significant, and this in fact constitutes one of its first English occurrences with this sense. Prior to the 1930s "technicism" simply meant excessive reliance on technical terminology, whereas now it designates a unification of science and technics.

As part of a further "Meditación de la técnica" (1939) Ortega outlines a historical movement from the chance inventions that characterize archaic societies, through the trial-and-error techniques of the artisan, to the scientific technologies of the engineer. According to Ortega, the difference between these three forms of making lies in the way one creates the means to realize a human project—that is, in the kind of technicity involved in each case. In the first epoch technical discoveries are accidental; in the second, techniques emerge from intuitive skill. In both instances they are preserved and elaborated within the confines of myth and tradition. In the third, however, the engineer has undertaken scientific studies of technics and, as a result, "prior to the possession of any [particular] technics, already possesses technics [itself]" (*Obras completas*, 5:369). It is this third type of technicity that constitutes "modern technicism" (and here Ortega himself uses the term "tecnicismo").

But technicism, understood here as the science of how to generate all possible technical means, disembedded from any lived making and using, creates a unique historical problem. Prior to the modern period human beings were commonly limited by circumstances within which they at once were given a way of life and the technical means to realize it. Now, however, they are given in advance many possible ways to live and a plethora of technical means but no well-defined life. "To be an engineer and only an engineer is to be

everything possibly and nothing actually," all form and no content (*Obras completas*, 5:366). There is in the midst of modern technicism what Ortega calls a crisis of imagination and choice. Insofar as people can be anything, why should they be any one thing at all?

According to Heidegger, as well, technicism covers over its own foundations. For Heidegger (1954) scientific technics or technology constitutes a new kind of truth: truth not as correspondence, not as coherence, and not as functional knowledge, but as revelation. Technology reveals Being in a way that it has never previously been revealed in history: as *Bestand*, or resource. A castle constructed with traditional technics on a cliff overlooking the Rhine River makes more fully present than before the stone that invests the landscape with its particular contours while it sets off the curve of the river against the backdrop of its walls and towers. A poured-concrete, hydroelectric power station, by contrast, compels the river to become an energy resource and converts the landscape into, not a place of human habitation, but a machine for the generation of electricity. The modern technicity that manifests itself in the disclosure of nature as resource Heidegger names *Gestell* or enframing.

Gestell at first sight appears to be a human work, something human beings in the course of history have chosen to do for their own benefit. It gives them power over nature. But as it digitalizes nature physically (dimensioned vectors), geographically (longitude and latitude), chemically (molecules, atoms, subatomic particles), and biologically (genetic mapping), it also transforms language (computer signal processing) and art (pixel imaging) so that impact outstrips original intentions. Hidden in the midst of *Gestell* is Being as event, that which lets this dominating transformation come to pass. *Gestell* is at once destiny and, precisely because it appears so clearly to be the result of a human activity, an obscuring of the transhuman destining that is its ground.

In the same year that Heidegger's *Die Frage nach der Technik* appeared Ellul published *La Technique*, later translated into English as *The Technological Society* (1964). For Ellul too what is happening is something transhuman, or at least transindividual, the emergence of a new social order in which people give themselves up to the systematic analysis of actions into constituent $C \to E$ elements, which are then evaluated in terms of output/input metrics. The scientific analysis of techniques extends technoscientific methods into economics, politics, education, leisure, and elsewhere and creates what he calls the technical milieu.

But in contrast to Heidegger Ellul's phenomenological characterization of this new reality—its rationality, artificiality, self-directedness, self-augmentation, indivisibility, universality, and autonomy—reveals the technical milieu as something opposed to the human. The human experience of the technical milieu is not as something human—although, insofar as one is able to look through it, all one is able to see is either the human of certain inexorable laws of artifice (such as those of supply and demand). Just as the natural milieu once provided a framework for human life, a differentiated but overriding order to which human beings adapted in a variety of ways, so now a much more homogeneous technical milieu presents itself, not as a realm of freedom that human beings have constructed, but as that which constructs them. In the words of social psychologist Kenneth Keniston, the problem is that "in our highly developed technological society we have adopted, usually without knowing it, the implicit ideology called 'technism,' which places central value on what can be measured with numbers, assigns numbers to what cannot be measured, and redefines everything else as self-expression or entertainment" ("The Eleven-Year-Olds of Today Are the Computer Terminals of Tomorrow," *New York Times,* Feb. 19, 1976, p. 35). Manfred Stanley (1978), in the single, most extended critique of technicism, likewise sees it as an ethos of collective mentality in which "the entire world is symbolically reconstituted as one interlocking problem-solving system according to the . . . technological language of control" (p. 10).

Toward a New Philosophy of Technology

The humanities philosophies of technology of Ortega, Heidegger, and Ellul constitute nodal points in Continental philosophy of technology, although the extent to which what such critiques define as modern technicity sufficiently reflects engineering and technological practice remains problematic. At least some philosophers (such as Friedrich Rapp, 1981) and engineers (such as David Billington, 1983, and Walter Vincenti, 1990) argue that the engineer is as much concerned with socially determined priorities and aesthetics as with efficiency, thus going beyond the $C \rightarrow E$ relationship. Nevertheless, by analogy with scientism, which refers to the unwarranted extension of science or the scientific method beyond its legitimate boundaries (which Kant attempted to determine), technicism can be described as the overextension of technicity. And it is unclear whether engineering philosophy of technology, imbued with the achievements of modern technicity whatever its form, ever adequately addresses the challenge of technicism. Against this background there has emerged a new philosophy of technology that, while continuing attempts to define the theoretical and practical limits of

technology, has promoted more socially, technically, and historically detailed epistemological, metaphysical, and ethical studies.

One inspiration for a more technoscientifically sensitive approach is the work of John Dewey. In his *Theory of Valuation* (1939), for example, when Dewey turns from analysis of the valuation of ends to the valuation of means, he begins by citing Charles Lamb's satiric essay "A Dissertation upon Roast Pig" (1822). According to the story, which Lamb in typically modern fashion uses to poke fun at the nonscientific determination of means, roast pork was first accidentally discovered when a building burned down with some piglets in it. The owner, after singeing his fingers on the carcass and putting them to his lips for relief of the pain, then set about building houses, confining pigs in them, and burning them down in order to enjoy such a delicious taste again and again.

Now, in the modern period,

people are given many possible ways to live

and a plethora of technical means,

but no well-defined life.

For Dewey, this is to pursue the $C \rightarrow E$ rational vengeance that artificially isolates E (the taste of roast pork) from other experiences and relates it only to a narrowly defined C (burning houses). It fails to appreciate the ways in which C itself is embedded in a network of human experiences that include other ends (shelter), which it destroys at the same time that it produces roast pork. The problem with the $C \rightarrow E$ model lifted from its social context is at least twofold: it fails to note how C is itself the E_P of a prior C_P and how the original C produces not only E but also supplementary or side effects $E_{S1}, E_{S2}, \ldots E_{Sn}$ as well as secondary and tertiary effects $E_2, E_3, \ldots E_n$ that can in fact be negative and undermine or counter the original value of E. Traditional technics, because of its limited rational analysis, kept means embedded in networks of custom and culture; modern technology, because of its more extensive rationality, transcends tradition. But according to Dewey, rational disembedding from traditional culture must be complemented by the conscious re-embedding in a rationally reconstructed social life and aesthetic experience.

Lewis Mumford's well-known criticism of what he calls monotechnics, the technics of power, which he contrasts to poly- or biotechnics, can be interpreted in similar terms. The problem with monotechnics is that it disembeds the $C \rightarrow E$ relation from the larger contexts of life and the biological world. For Mumford the "myth of the machine" is that the $C \rightarrow E$ relation is the source of all human benefit. In fact, it constitutes an unrealistic narrowing of technical action itself in a way that inevitably leads to the production of negative side effects and second-order consequences. Indeed, once these negative side effects became widely recognized during the late 1960s, a number of attempts at the rational re-embedding of technology emerged in the development of social institutions such as the Environmental Protection Agency (established 1970) and the U.S. Congress Office of Technology Assessment (1972).

Parallel to the public philosophical discussions from which these institutions emerged, Hans Jonas undertook fundamental inquiries into the phenomenon of life and the inherently practical character of modern science, an expression of life that can appear to deny its relationships to the organic. Further grounded in his studies of the metaphysics and epistemology of the scientific and technological revolutions of the seventeenth century and after, studies which in their own way re-embedded techno-science in modern history, Jonas (1979) undertook an extended philosophical scrutiny of the technicist projects of nuclear weapons and biomedical health care. In the presence of technical powers to end or alter human life Jonas reformulates the Kantian categorical imperative as "Act so that the effects of your action are compatible with the permanence of genuine human life" (1984, p. 11). Such a reformulation of the fundamental deontological principle again constitutes an attempt at the re-embedding of technology in moral philosophy.

Langdon Winner's (1986) conception of "technologies as forms of life" and call for the abandonment of "technological somnambulism" in favor of the comprehensive public design of technological projects constitute another attempt to re-embed technology in human practice. Winner's call is not unrelated to Ihde's (1990) phenomenology of the techno-lifeworld, which discloses two fundamental human-technology-world relations: instrumental relations, in which the technology is integrated into the human sensorium as its extension (the blindman's cane), and hermeneutic relations, in which the technology becomes part of the world to be interpreted (a thermometer). Both relations manifest an invariant structure that amplifies some aspect of the world (exact metric of temperature) while simultaneously reducing others (general sense of climate). Such an analysis reveals the strengths and weaknesses of both engineering and humanities philosophies of technology: the one stresses amplification, the other reduction. But amplification-reduction is in invariant pattern that,

once appreciated, can serve as a foundational recognition for the reintegration of technology into human experience transformed into what Ihde calls techno-pluriculture. Paradoxically enough, Michel Foucault's (1988) idea of "technologies of the self" may constitute an *extendo ad transformandum* of the idea of technicism.

There is in the midst of modern technicism

what Ortega y Gasset calls a

crisis of imagination and choice.

Insofar as people can be anything,

why should they be any one thing at all?

Two related contributions to the re-embedding of technology can be found in the work of Albert Borgmann and Kristin Shrader-Frechette. Borgmann (1984) explains technicism as a political economy of the manufacture and consumption of products partaking of what he terms the device paradigm (the ideal of an artifact disengaged from bodily engagements). Against such patterns of techno-economic behavior he appeals to the ideal of a way of life lived with what he calls focal things and practices. Shrader-Frechette (1991), by contrast, explains technicism as a restricted conception of risk analysis that must be broadened in ways pointed to by Dewey. What unites both Borgmann and Shrader-Frechette is an attempt to throw bridges between philosophy of technology, economics, and public policy.

Among all these approaches to a new philosophy of technology is an attempt to recognize technology as a social construction that nevertheless exhibits tendencies to escape conscious human direction. The dangers and challenges of such a technicism are to be met, however, by the disciplined pursuit of philosophical reflection that merges with practical and public citizen participation in the transformation no longer simply of nature but of technology itself.

[See also Applied Ethics; Artificial Intelligence; Biomedical Ethics; Computer Ethics; Democracy; Descartes, René; Dewey, John; Environmental Ethics; Epistemology; Ethical Theory; Foucault, Michel; Heidegger, Martin; Justice; Kant, Immanuel; Marxism; Metaphysics; Mill, John Stuart; Plato; Postmodernism.]

BIBLIOGRAPHY

Anderson, A. R., ed. *Minds and Machines*. Englewood Cliffs, NJ, 1964.
Billington, D. P. *The Toward and the Bridge: The New Art of Structural Engineering*. New York, 1983.

Borgmann, A. *Technology of the Character of Contemporary Life: A Philosophical Inquiry.* Chicago, 1984.

Bunge, M. "Technology: From Engineering to Decision Theory," in *Treatise on Basic Philosophy,* vol. 7, *Philosophy of Science and Technology,* part 2, *Life Science, Social Science, and Technology* (Boston, 1985).

Ellul, J. *La Technique ou l'enjeu du siècle.* Paris, 1954. Rev. ed., Paris, 1990. Translated as *The Technological Society.* New York, 1964. See also two supplements: *Le Système technicien.* Paris, 1977. Translated as *The Technological System.* New York, 1980. *Le Bluff technologique.* Paris, 1988. Translated as *The Technological Bluff.* Grand Rapids, MI, 1990.

Foucault, M. *Technologies of the Self: A Seminar with Michel Foucault.* Edited by L. H. Martin, H. Gutman, and P. H. Hutton. Amherst, MA, 1988.

Haugeland, J., ed. *Mind Design: Philosophy, Psychology, Artificial Intelligence.* Cambridge, MA, 1981.

Heidegger, M. "Die Frage nach der Technik," in *Vorträge und Aufsätze* (Pfullingen, 1954). Translated as "The Question concerning Technology," in *The Question concerning Technology and Other Essays* (San Francisco, 1954).

Ihde, D. *Philosophy of Technology: An Introduction.* New York, 1986.

———. *Technology and the Lifeworld: From Garden to Earth.* Bloomington, IN, 1990.

Jonas, H. *Das Prinzip Verantwortung: Versuch einer Ethik für die technologische Zivilisation.* Frankfurt, 1979. Translated as *The Imperative of Responsibility: In Search of an Ethics for the Technological Age.* Chicago, 1984.

Kelley, K. *Out of Control: The Rise of Neo-Biological Civilization.* Reading, MA, 1994.

Mitcham, C. *Thinking through Technology: The Path between Engineering and Philosophy.* Chicago, 1994.

Mitcham, C., and R. Mackey. *Bibliography of the Philosophy of Technology.* Chicago, 1973.

———, eds. *Philosophy and Technology: Readings in the Philosophical Problems of Technology.* New York, 1972.

Mumford, L. *The Myth of the Machine,* Vol. 1: *Technics and Human Development.* New York, 1967.

Ortega y Gasset, J. *La rebelión de las masas.* Madrid, 1929. Translated as *The Revolt of the Masses.* New York, 1932.

———. "Meditación de la técnica," in *Ensimismamiento y alteración* (Buenos Aires, 1939).

Rapp, F. *Analytische Technikphilosophie.* Freiburg, 1978. Translated by R. Carpenter and T. Langenbruch as *Analytical Philosophy of Technology.* Boston, 1981.

Rothenberg, D. *Hand's End: Technology and the Limits of Nature.* Berkeley, 1993.

Shrader-Frechette, K. S. *Risk and Rationality: Philosophical Foundations for Populist Reforms.* Berkeley, 1991.

Stanley, M. *The Technological Conscience: Survival and Dignity in an Age of Expertise.* New York, 1978.

Vincenti, W. G. *What Engineers Know and How They Know It: Analytical Studies from Aeronautical History.* Baltimore, 1990.

Wiener, N. *Cybernetics of Control and Communication in the Animal and the Machine.* Cambridge, MA, 1948.

Winner, L. *The Whale and the Reactor: A Search for Limits in an Age of High Technology.* Chicago, 1986.

— CARL MITCHAM

LEONARD WAKS

PHONOLOGY

Phonology is the branch of linguistics concerned with the articulatory and auditory domain of grammar— that is, with the theory of what Austin (1962) called phonetic acts. Its subject matter links with but is distinct from that of syntax, semantics, and pragmatics. It covers the forms in which the sounds of words are kept in memory and the manner in which the motions of speech organs are shaped by grammar.

Unlike syntax, semantics, and pragmatics (but like closely related morphology), phonology has been largely ignored by philosophers. On the whole, philosophers consider the fact that natural languages are primarily spoken rather than written as of little interest for what Dummett (1986) calls a "philosophical explanation" of language. This attitude stems largely from the mistaken but widely held view that spoken signs are arbitrary sounds whose individuating traits are those of noises. On that view, utterances contemplated apart from their semantic and syntactic features are merely tokens of acoustical types, bereft of grammatical properties, fully described by the physics of noises, and available for human communication simply because humans can perceive and produce them; there is nothing intrinsically linguistic about them. Nor is this attitude an accident. Historically, philosophers have had little incentive to reflect on the sound of language. Most belong to traditions that admit no crucial differences (except perhaps those that pertain to pragmatics) between natural languages and notational systems developed by scientists, mathematicians, or philosophers for the elaboration of their theories. Such notational systems have a syntax and a semantics of sorts, but they have no phonology. Their constituent elements are typically spatial ideographs that share little with the phonological structures of natural languages. Studying language with such a bias offers few reasons, if any, to focus on what is spoken rather than written. It can, however, entrap one in a false conception of linguistic signs, so false, in fact, as seriously to weaken philosophic doctrines built on it.

Phonology rests on a series of presumptions—each supported by a vast body of observations—that together entail that the sounds of natural languages are not arbitrary human noises, on a par with grunts or snorts, whose individuating attributes lie entirely outside the domain of grammar.

The first such presumption is that when people acquire a word they memorize the underlying phonological representation of that word, a representation that defines—but often only partially—how the word is pronounced. These representations have the structure of linearly arrayed discrete timing positions that are assigned pointers to articulatory organs (lips, blade of tongue, dorsum of tongue, root of tongue, velum, vocal cords) implicated in the pronunciation of the word, and pointers to actions these organs execute during speech. The first timing position for the English 'pin', for instance, points to the lips, the vocal cords, the velum, full closure of the first, stiffening of the second, and nonlowering of the third.

Phonology rests on a series of presumptions that together entail that the sounds of natural languages are not arbitrary human noises.

A second presumption is that these pointers (called phonological features) on timing positions are drawn from a finite repertoire, common to all languages, and that they are combined within and across timing positions in rule-governed ways. Some rules are common to all languages and reflect innate linguistic endowments, others are language specific and reflect the influence of linguistic exposure. No language, for instance, avails itself of nasal snorts. French admits rounding of the lips in combinations of features that English excludes (thus the sound *ü* in French but not in English). Korean, unlike English (except for *h*), admits aspiration in underlying phonological representations. German, unlike English, admits initial sequences corresponding to sounded *k* followed by sounded *n*. All languages assemble features in similar (three-dimensional-like) structures.

A third presumption is that underlying phonological representations, in isolation or when compounded in complex words, are subject to rule-governed processes that add, subtract, or modify phonological features, which group them into syllables, feet, and prosodic words, which assign stresses and (in some languages) tones, and which ultimately yield final articulatory instructions, so-called surface phonological representations related to, but often very different from, the underlying representations in memory. Processes of this sort account for the fact that, for example, 'leaf' occurs as 'leavz' (with *v* instead of *f*) in the plural, or that 'serene' is pronounced differently when alone than when a constituent of 'serenity', or that 'p' gets aspirated in 'pin' though not in 'spin'. The details of these rules, the manner of their application, the universality of their formats, and the options fixed by different languages are all objects of intense research and controversies. But the evidence in behalf of their reality seems irrefutable.

Phonology is of philosophic interest, not only because it brings into question analogies between contrived notational systems and natural languages, but also because it raises conceptual issues of its own. Two can be mentioned here.

First, individual spoken utterances are analyzable in both acoustical and phonological terms. No generalizable exact correspondences between these two analyses are known. None may be forthcoming. For instance, nothing acoustical corresponds to word division. How can this dualism be reconciled? Is there a cogent sense in which the objects of speech production are the same (or belong to the same types) as those of speech perception? Offhand, the problem resembles that raised by other events amenable to multiple descriptions. But in this case solutions must be attuned to much that is already understood about both phonology and acoustics. It is not a simple task.

Second, phonological theory associates multiple representations with each utterance—including an underlying representation and a surface one—and it describes them all in the same notation. Surface representations can be conceptualized as instructions (or intentions) to move articulators in certain ways; their ontological status, though unclear, is at least comparable to that of other familiar cases. Not so the other phonological representations. They do not have familiar analogues. The semantic domain of phonological notation therefore cannot be ontologically homogeneous. Furthermore, part of that domain is deeply perplexing.

[See also Dummett, Michael; Philosophy of Language; Pragmatics; Semantics; Syntax.]

BIBLIOGRAPHY

Anderson, S. R. *Phonology in the Twentieth Century.* Chicago, 1985.
Austin, J. L. *How to Do Things with Words.* Cambridge, MA, 1962.
Bromberger, S., and M. Halle. "The Ontology of Phonology," in S. Bromberger, ed., *On What We Know We Don't Know* (Chicago, 1992).
Dummett, M. In E. LePore, ed., *Truth and Interpretation: Perspectives on the Philosophy of Donald Davidson* (Oxford and New York, 1986).
Kenstowicz, M. *Phonology in Generative Grammar.* Cambridge, MA, 1994. An introduction to the field and a complete bibliography.
Quine, W. V. O. *Word and Object,* chap. 3. Cambridge, MA, and New York, 1960.

– SYLVAIN BROMBERGER
MORRIS HALLE

PHYSICALISM, MATERIALISM

Physicalism, of which materialism is a historical antecedent, is primarily an ontological doctrine concerning the nature of reality and, specifically, mental reality. It is the view that reality is ultimately constituted or determined by entities—objects, events, properties, and so on—that are physical. This thesis is often combined with a claim about the explanatory supremacy of physical theory (physics).

Any formulation of physicalism raises the question, What is meant by 'physical'? It is difficult to formulate a conception of the physical that is neither too strong, making physicalism obviously false, nor too weak, making physicalism trivially true. For example, what is physical may be simply identified through the language of physics. However, a problem arises over the conception of physics appealed to. Current physics seems too narrow since future extensions of physics would not count as physical; but the idea of a completed physics is too indeterminate since we have no clear idea of what that physics might include. One could attempt to characterize the physical in more general terms such as having spatial location or being spatiotemporal. However, this threatens to make physicalism trivially true since mental phenomena seem clearly to have spatial location in virtue of having subjects—persons—who have bodies. It may be preferable to appeal to the idea of a completed physics. Although at any particular time we may not know exactly what is physical and what is not (since we may not know whether we have completed physics), nevertheless what is physical is all and only what a completed physics countenances.

There are two main types of physicalist theses. First, there is eliminative materialism, or physicalism. According to this there are not, and never have been, any mental entities, events, properties, and so forth. Strictly speaking, this is not a view about the nature of mental reality. Second, there is a group of doctrines that fall under the general heading of identity theories, some of which are stronger than others. These can be divided into two main categories. The stronger doctrines may be called type–type identity theories, or type physicalist theories, and the weaker doctrines may be called token identity theories, or token physicalist theories.

Type Physicalism

Consider any mental phenomenon, such as my being in pain now. We can talk about this phenomenon as an individual occurrence of a certain kind in the mental life of a person and discuss its properties. We can also talk about the kind of phenomenon—pain—of which this event is an individual instance. Physical phenomena can be discussed in both of these ways. Type physicalism is the view that the mental types, properties, or kinds under which mental phenomena fall are identical with physical types, properties, or kinds. Pain—that type of phenomenon, occurrences of which are individual pains—is identical with some single type of physical phenomenon such as C-fiber stimulation.

Type physicalism has its origins in the doctrines espoused by the logical positivists and central-state materialists. It is a strong form of physicalism because it is reductionist. Many who endorse it believe that nothing short of it counts as a proper physicalism. They argue that even if it is in practice impossible for sentences containing mental terminology to be translated into or replaced by sentences containing physical and topic-neutral terminology, any view that holds that all mental phenomena are physical phenomena, but mental properties or kinds are not physical properties or kinds, is not worthy of the name 'physicalism'.

However, type physicalism suffers from two serious objections. The first, from phenomenal properties, specifically concerns sensations such as pain, afterimages, and the like. It is that phenomena of these kinds or types have "felt" properties, such as being dull, or stabbing, whereas phenomena of physical types do not. Given this, and given Leibniz's principle of the indiscernibility of identicals, it follows that sensation types are not identical with physical types since the phenomena that fall under them do not share all the same properties. A variant of this objection focuses on the distinctive point of view a subject has on its own experiences: a subject knows what it is like to have experiences in a way that others do not, and this subjective mode of access reveals the phenomenal aspect of the experience, whereas an "other" oriented point of view does not.

Physicalism is the view that reality

is ultimately constituted or determined by entities

—objects, events, properties—

that are physical.

The second objection to type physicalism is that from multiple realizability. This claims that mental kinds or properties may be realized in physically diverse types of ways, hence that there is no single physical type with which a given mental type may be identified. The point is that even if each mental type were in fact to be realized by a single physical type, it is possible for pain to be realized by physically diverse types of states. The reason is that the introspective and behavioral basis upon which attributions of mental properties are typically made is silent on the potential internal physical realizers of mental properties. Given the claim that identical things are necessarily identical, the mere possibility that a given mental type should be realized by a physical type of state other than that which in fact realizes it is sufficient to refute the claim that that mental type is identical with any physical type that may realize it. This objection is not independent of a modal argument that trades on the thesis that identical things are necessarily identical. This argument concludes that, since it is possible that pain should exist in the absence of any type of physical phenomenon, pain is not identical with any type of physical phenomenon.

One response is to argue that mental types are identical with disjunctions of physical types. For example, pain may not be identical with C-fibre stimulation, but it may be identical with the disjunctive property, C-fibre stimulation, or A-fibre stimulation, or . . . , and so on. However, it is unclear whether these are bona fide properties. They do not have a unity of their own, viewed from a physical perspective: and it is arguable that we need a reason, apart from the fact that they all realize a given mental property, to think that they are properties in their own right.

Token Physicalism

Many consider one or the other of the above objections to be decisive against type physicalism and have opted instead for a weaker view, token physicalism. According to this, each individual mental event or phenomenon is identical with some physical event. One influential version of this is the view known as anomalous monism. Token physicalism is compatible with the multiple realizability of mental properties by physical ones since it is not committed to the view that each individual occurrence of a given mental kind is identical with an occurrence of the same type of physical phenomenon. It also appears to avoid the objection from phenomenal properties in its original form since it can concede that mental kinds have associated with them felt aspects with which no physical kinds are associated. To the objection that mental events are not identical with physical events because it is no part of the nature of any physical event that it have a felt aspect, the following reply can be made. If token physicalism is true, no physical event is essentially of a mental type; but given that it is of a given mental type, it has what is essential to being of that type. Thus, if this pain is identical with this C-fibre stimulation, then it is not essentially a pain. However, given that it is, as it happens, a pain, it has (though not essentially) what is essential to being of that type, namely being felt.

Without an explanation of how mental types relate to physical ones, token physicalism threatens to succumb to the charge that it is dualist because it countenances the existence of nonphysical properties or types. A common strategy is to advance a supervenience doctrine concerning the relation between mental and physical properties, according to which physical properties, although distinct from mental ones, in some

sense determine them. There are many varieties of supervenience theses. The main difficulty is in finding one strong enough to do justice to the claim that physical properties determine mental ones without being so strong as to entail identities between mental and physical properties or types, and with these, reducibility.

[See also Anomalous Monism; Eliminative Materialism, Eliminativism; Leibniz, Gottfried Wilhelm; Multiple Realizability; Philosophy of Mind; Reduction, Reductionism; Supervenience.]

BIBLIOGRAPHY

Armstrong, D. M. *A Materialist Theory of Mind.* London, 1968. Defense of a type–type identity theory of the mental and physical.

Block, N., ed. *Readings in the Philosophy of Psychology,* Vol. 1. Cambridge, MA, 1980. Articles on type–type identity theories, token identity theories, reductionism, and functionalism.

Davidson, D. "Mental Events," in Lawrence Foster and J. W. Swanson, eds., *Experience and Theory* (Amherst, MA, 1970). Highly influential argument for a token identity of the mental and physical.

Hellman, G., and F. W. Thompson. "Physicalism: Ontology, Determination, Reduction," *Journal of Philosophy,* Vol. 72 (1975), 551–64. Defense of a supervenience doctrine.

Jackson, F., R. Pargetter, and E. Prior. "Functionalism and Type–Type Identity Theories." *Philosophical Studies,* Vol. 42 (1982), 209–25. Discussion of the relation between functionalism and type–type identity theories.

Kim, J. "Supervenience as a Philosophical Concept," *Metaphilosophy,* Vol. 12 (1990), 1–27. Discusses supervenience as a covariance relation and its relation to reduction.

Kripke, S. *Naming and Necessity.* Cambridge, MA, 1980. A modal argument against type–type and token identity theories.

Lewis, D. "An Argument for the Identity Theory," *Journal of Philosophy,* Vol. 63 (1966), 17–25. An argument for a type–type identity theory.

Macdonald, C. *Mind-Body Identity Theories.* London, 1989. A survey of type–type and token identity theories, and a defense of a token identity theory.

Nagel, T. "What Is It Like to Be a Bat?," *Philosophical Review,* Vol. 83 (1974), 435–50. Argues against identity theories of the mental and the physical.

Place, U. T. "Is Consciousness a Brain Process?," *British Journal of Psychology,* Vol. 47 (1956), 44–50. A defense of central-state materialism for sensations.

Smart, J. J. C. "Sensations and Brain Processes," *Philosophical Review,* Vol. 68 (1959), 141–56. A defense of central state materialism for sensations.

– CYNTHIA MACDONALD

PLATO

Plato's life began some thirty years before the end of the fifth century B.C. and ended soon after the middle of the fourth century. Yet this rich literary epoch yields little direct information about Plato's life or personality. Partly, this lack of information is due to the code of the prose writers of that period against making explicit mention of living contemporaries. The orator Isocrates, who was Plato's contemporary, does not mention Plato by name in any of his numerous orations that have come down to us or even in his letters. Aristotle, who was 37 when Plato died, alludes anonymously to Plato, Speusippus, Xenocrates, Isocrates and other contemporaries far more often than he names them, and many of the passages in which he does name them were most likely written after their deaths. In some places Aristotle oddly refers to Plato under the name "Socrates," as when he speaks of Socrates composing the *Republic.*

Plato's own dialogues nearly always have Socrates for hero or at least as a minor character. As Socrates was executed in 399, these dialogues could not, without anachronism, have mentioned any incident belonging to the last 52 years of Plato's own life. In fact, Plato is mentioned by name only in the *Apology,* where he is listed with other adherents of Socrates as attending his trial. However, Plato does not altogether avoid anachronism in his dialogues. There are some clear allusions to historical events which took place many years after Socrates' death. In the *Republic* Socrates is made to approve a major development in geometry which was the work of Theaetetus, though Theaetetus was only in his teens when Socrates died; and in several dialogues Socrates is made the spokesman of the Theory of Forms, which, as Aristotle explicitly says, was not a Socratic, but a Platonic theory. Where some anachronisms are certain, others are likely. So it is justifiable to expect to find in the dialogues clues to Platonic, as distinct from Socratic history. But the strengths and weaknesses of these clues must always be debatable.

Diogenes Laërtius, in his *Life of Plato,* cites Plato's will verbatim. The will is interesting for two things. It indicates that when Plato drew it up, he was not wealthy, though also not in great poverty. Its total silence about the buildings, grounds, and contents of his school, the Academy, pretty well proves that by this time Plato had ceased to be the owner of the Academy. It must already have acquired the semi-religious, "college" status that the will of Theophrastus shows to have been the status of Theophrastus's school. This status was that of a dedicated and endowed foundation, legally under the control of a board of trustees. Plato did not bequeath the Academy to Speusippus, nor did Speusippus bequeath it to Xenocrates. These two were elected to its headship, and Speusippus seems to have resigned from its headship.

There have come down to us thirteen letters reputedly written by Plato. Most of these letters are unanimously rejected by scholars as forgeries or imitations. There remain Letters III, VII, VIII, and XIII, some or all of which are accepted as authentic by most, though not by all scholars. Of these four, Letter VII is by far

Plato almost certainly trained pupils of his own in the Socratic Method. (Corbis/Bettmann)

the most important. It is or purports to be a piece of Plato's autobiography, giving a fairly general account of his career as a young man and a very detailed account of his last two visits to Sicily in 367–366 and 361–360 and of his relations with the tyrant of Syracuse, Dionysius the Younger, and with the tyrant's opponent, Dion. As it also contains an excursus on the Theory of Forms, this letter, if authentic, shows that Plato adhered to this theory at least until his mid-seventies. There exists, however, the skeptical minority view that this letter is also a forgery. It is unmentioned by Aristotle, even in any of the many passages in which he criticizes the Theory of Forms. Nor do all latter-day philosophers find the letter's exposition of the Theory of Forms genuinely Platonic either in doctrine or in argumentation. According to one variant of the skeptical view, this letter is, with Letters III, VIII, and XIII, a contemporary political forgery intended to misrepresent, for Sicilian political purposes, Plato's relations with Dion and Dionysius. It needs to represent Plato as the confidant and supporter of Dion and the critic and opponent of Dionysius just in order to put Dion's political actions and policies in a good light and those of Dionysius in a bad light. The letter concludes by stating that conflicting stories are already rife, as if, half a dozen years before Plato died, many people did not yet think of Plato as the supporter of Dion or the opponent of Dionysius.

It is often assumed that Plato began to compose

his Socratic dialogues when he was in his thirties

or even in his late twenties,

before the death of Socrates,

though there is no evidence to support this idea.

Even if the skeptical view of the Seventh Letter and the other three letters were accepted, they would, if contemporary forgeries, continue to be useful sources of information. A forger, to remain undetected, must not deny or garble things already well known to the readers of his forgeries. So there are some things, including some biographically important things, said in these four letters which must be true, in substance if not in coloration, even if these letters are forgeries; *a fortiori* they will be true if the letters are authentic.

Aristotle, who was 37 when Plato died, had belonged to the Academy for the last twenty years of Plato's life. Yet in his voluminous writings that have come down to us there is next to no personal information about Plato. Aristotle constantly draws examples from Plato's dialogues and frequently criticizes Plato's doctrines, especially his Theory of Forms. But about Plato's character or about the course of his life we learn next to nothing from Aristotle.

Even our natural supposition that the young Aristotle and his fellow students had been taught philosophy by Plato has been attacked. Nowhere does Aristotle indisputably mention anything taught by Plato that could not have been learned from Plato's writings or else from the lecture (or lectures) on the Good that Plato on one occasion gave but did not transmit in writing to posterity. In his *Politics* Aristotle more than once criticizes Plato's *Republic* for being inexplicit about fairly cardinal arrangements in the Ideal State. None of Plato's students or colleagues seems to have asked Plato in person to fill these gaps.

Certainly Aristotle's lectures would not have been thought the proper places for casual anecdote or personal gossip; but we search them equally vainly for reports of Plato's replies to objections or of his developments or revisions of his earlier ideas. Hardly one

whisper of the tutorial voice of Plato is relayed to us by Aristotle, even on philosophical matters.

The orator Isocrates lived in Athens for nearly a hundred years. Though he was born before Plato and outlived him, in his orations he never mentions by name Plato or the Academy or Speusippus, Xenocrates, Eudoxus or Aristotle or, for that matter, any contemporary politician or rhetorician. His speeches and letters do contain, however, a number of indubitable anonymous references, as well as many other likely or merely possible references to Plato and the Academy and even one or two to Aristotle. These references tend to be acidulated. A careful sifting, especially of his *Helen, Busiris, Antidosis,* and *Panathenaicus,* might give us more information about Plato than all that we can cull from Plato's other contemporaries.

Xenophon, who wrote three pieces about Socrates, mentions Plato only once, though he was alive until Plato was in his seventies. Demosthenes mentions Plato twice, but quite uninformatively.

For the rest we have to draw almost entirely on philosophers, historians, scholars and anecdote collectors who wrote three, four or more centuries after Plato's death. These writers had access to earlier sources that are lost to us, and some of these sources were good authorities. But Diogenes Laërtius, say, and Plutarch were not very critical. They transmit some gold but much dross. In particular, they and others of these late writers assumed the authenticity of Letter VII.

PLATO'S LIFE. Plato died in 347 B.C. at the age of about 81. He never married. He came from an aristocratic and wealthy family, several members of which had been politically prominent on the anti-democratic side. The victory of the democratic cause left Plato and his surviving relatives without political influence or prospects. Plato's attitude toward the leaders of the democracy—that is, the demagogues—is what could be expected. The account in Letter VII of the frustration of Plato's political ideals and ambitions is likely to be true in substance. Plato certainly saw military service in the war against Sparta. It is probable that he belonged to the cavalry. He was a close associate of Socrates, anyhow during the last few years of Socrates' life, which ended when Plato was about 31. The story is quite likely true that after the execution of Socrates Plato and others of Socrates' circle found it politically expedient to take refuge in Megara, where Euclides seems to have had some sort of school.

Later, probably in the earliest 380s, Plato traveled to Egypt, among other places. During these travels he paid the first of his three visits to Syracuse in Sicily, where Dionysius the Elder was military governor, or tyrant.

The often repeated stories of a quarrel between Plato and this tyrant deserve no credence; they are standard anti-tyrant stories. They are not even faintly echoed in Letter VII, though this letter is unsparing of invective against Dionysius's son, Dionysius the Younger.

At some time after Plato's first visit to Syracuse and before his second visit in 367 he founded the Academy. The still prevalent idea that he founded the Academy in the early 380s rests entirely on one vague phrase in Diogenes Laërtius's *Life of Plato*, suggesting that after his travels Plato lived at the Academy. "Academy" was the name of Plato's house, and we have nothing to indicate that Plato started his school in this house at the moment he began to reside there or even that he began to reside there immediately or soon after his return from his travels. There is some evidence that Plato was teaching young men at the Academy before the inauguration of the school that we think of as "the Academy," with the curriculum described in Book VII of the *Republic*.

It is often assumed that Plato began to compose his Socratic dialogues when he was in his thirties or even in his late twenties, before the death of Socrates. There is no evidence to support this idea. On the other hand there is some fairly strong internal evidence that Plato's *Euthydemus* and *Crito* were written at least some way on in the 370s, that the *Symposium* was written after 371, and that the *Phaedo* was written just before Plato left for Sicily in 367; so it may be that Plato's career as a writer of dialogues began fifteen or twenty years after the execution of their hero, Socrates, that is, when Plato was well past middle age.

In 367 Plato sailed again to Syracuse, where he stayed as the guest of Dionysius the Younger for over a year. Letter XIII is or purports to be, *inter alia*, Plato's thank-you letter. Its tone of voice toward Dionysius is quite incongruous with the story in Letter VII of a wide and deep breach between Plato and Dionysius over the young tyrant's maltreatment of Dion, whom, a few months after Plato's arrival, Dionysius had banished for treasonable correspondence with Carthage.

The story given in Letters III, VII and XIII is that Plato came to Sicily on the joint invitation of Dion and Dionysius the Younger after the latter's accession to the tyranny. As the death of Dionysius the Elder cannot have occurred more than a couple of months before Plato left Athens and may have occurred only a few days before Plato reached Syracuse, this story cannot be true. Plato's invitation to Syracuse must have come, not from Dionysius the Younger, but from his father, during 368 or 369. If so, these three letters must be forgeries, since Plato himself could not have got wrong the identity of his inviter. It happens that we possess a letter from Isoc-rates to Dionysius the Elder, written in 368, regretting that he cannot risk the long journey to Sicily. As two other philosophers or sophists from Athens, Aristippus and Aeschines, were in Syracuse with Plato, it looks as if Dionysius the Elder had in 368 or 369 invited several Athenian luminaries, including Plato, to visit his court in 367. If so, then the so-called Platonic letters are in error not only about the source of Plato's invitation but also about the reasons for it, since these reasons would presumably be the reasons also for the invitations to Isocrates, Aristippus and Aeschines.

In 361 Plato visited Syracuse for the third and last time and was again, for part of his sojourn, the personal guest of Dionysius the Younger. This time he came with Aristippus, Aeschines, Speusippus, Xenocrates and probably Eudoxus, the last three being teachers in the Academy. No mention is made in the so-called Platonic Letters of their presence, the reasons for which could not have been the reasons alleged by these letters for Plato's visit. On these grounds too, the letters must be forgeries, and they are likely to be pro-Dion propaganda forgeries, since the motives that they allege for Plato's visit are pro-Dion motives. Plato returned from Syracuse via Olympia, where he attended the Games of July 360.

Some time not long after his return to Athens, when he was nearly seventy, Plato suffered, according to Seneca, a serious illness caused by the hardships of his long voyages. He survived this illness and was able to go on working for quite a long time. He died, aged about 81, in 347. He was succeeded as Head of the Academy by his nephew Speusippus. At about the same moment Aristotle left Athens and did not return for several years.

Many years before the death of Socrates there had been introduced into Athens a special debating exercise, sometimes called "eristic," though called "dialectic" by Plato and Aristotle.

There must have been other biographically important events in Plato's life, but most of these must either remain hidden from us or be inferred or conjectured from clues provided by his dialogues, with, at best, snippets of corroboration from outside sources. One such event is this: Diogenes Laërtius says that Dionysius the Younger gave Plato the enormous sum of 80 talents. The amount is doubtless exaggerated, but the story that Dionysius treated Plato very handsomely is borne out by a number of mostly malicious yarns from other sources, according to which Plato was the beneficiary of Dionysius. The so-called Platonic Letters, in their hostility to Dionysius, have to deny that Plato benefited from the tyrant's monetary lavishness, as if there were stories already current to the opposite effect, which needed to be denied. This story of Diogenes Laërtius and the account in Letter VII of Plato's relations with Dionysius the Younger cannot easily be reconciled, and Diogenes Laërtius makes no attempt to reconcile them.

Socrates and Plato

It is certain that during some of Socrates' last years before his execution in 399 Plato was closely associated with him. There was some sort of circle of adherents who loved Socrates as a person and both admired and studied his practice of the Socratic Method. Whether they or some of them were in any formal sense his pupils is debatable. In the *Apology* Socrates is made to deny that he had ever been a teacher of students, as well as to deny, somewhat inconsistently, that he had ever charged fees for his teaching. On the other hand Aristophanes in his *Clouds* certainly represents Socrates as conducting a school for young men, some of whom lived in Socrates' house. A writer of comedies can, of course, play fast and loose with fact, and we know that Aristophanes credits Socrates with theories really held by Diogenes of Apollonia; he also attributes to Socrates things for which Protagoras seems to deserve the credit or discredit. Nonetheless, the Athenian public would have found less fun in a comic account of Socrates' school if he had been known not to have had one than in a caricature of a school which he was known to have.

Isocrates in his *Busiris* denies that Alcibiades had ever been a pupil of Socrates, not apparently on the score that Socrates had no pupils but only on the score that Alcibiades was not one of them. In his *Life of Socrates* Diogenes Laërtius says that Socrates taught, not philosophy or disputation, but rhetoric, though we hear nothing of this from Plato or Xenophon. We should therefore treat with some skepticism the *Apology*'s denial that Socrates was a teacher of students. Even if he did teach students, it would not follow that Plato's association with Socrates had been that of a pupil with his teacher.

Although our picture of Socrates derives chiefly from Plato's dialogues, especially his early dialogues, with some reinforcement from Xenophon's *Symposium, Apology* and *Memorabilia*, these sources give us very little factual information about Socrates. Only in his *Apology, Crito* and *Phaedo* does Plato mention Socrates' sons; only in his *Phaedo* does Plato mention Socrates' wife. He tells us nothing about Socrates' house and nothing about the profession or craft from which he made his

modest living. The story that Socrates was a sculptor does not come from either Plato or Xenophon.

We know that Socrates was tried in the King Archon's Court for "impiety" or "irreligion" and that he was executed for this. He could hardly have been so prosecuted and convicted just for privately harboring heretical opinions. He must have made his opinions known to Athens and even have been thought to have indoctrinated his pupils with them. The second charge against Socrates was that of corrupting the young men. Plato's *Apology* purports to be the speeches made by Socrates in his own defense. Yet of its two dozen pages only two or three are concerned with the charge of "impiety." The bulk of Plato's *Apology* is given up to Socrates' defense of his practice of the Socratic Method—that is, his practice of cross-examining politicians, orators, poets and artisans and driving them by his chains of questions into logical *impasses*. Near the end of the *Apology* Socrates is made to say, by implication, that he is being executed for his practice of the Socratic Method. The King Archon's Court was empowered to try only for the two capital crimes of murder and impiety. Socratic questioning was not even illegal, but if it had been illegal, it could not have been a capital offense or, therefore, one tried in this particular court. So Plato's *Apology* must, in bulk, be totally unhistorical. Plato must have had special reasons for publishing a defense of dialectic, and he did this by putting into his dramatic hero's mouth only a perfunctory answer to the charge of impiety but a protracted defense of the practice of elenctic questioning.

In the *Gorgias* and *Meno* there are apparent references, dramatically in the future tense, to the trial and condemnation of Socrates. Not a word is said here or in a partly analogous reference in the *Politicus* about the accusation of impiety. There is much more fiction than is sometimes supposed in the dialogues' pictures of Socrates.

We have no good reason to doubt that the real Socrates did in fact practice the Socratic Method, save that Diogenes Laërtius in his *Life of Socrates* says nothing about it and that Isocrates in his *Against the Sophists* and *Helen* reprobates Protagoras and other practitioners of what he calls "eristic" without any mention of Socrates by name or any clear allusion to him.

THE SOCRATIC METHOD. Many years before the death of Socrates there had been introduced into Athens and probably into other Greek cities a special debating exercise, sometimes called "eristic," though called "dialectic" by Plato and Aristotle. There are fairly good reasons for thinking that it was the sophist Protagoras who introduced it into Athens and taught its procedures and techniques to students. Possibly he was its inventor.

The exercise took the following form. Two debaters or disputants, a questioner and an answerer, are put up. The answerer undertakes to defend a thesis or proposition; the questioner has to try to demolish it. The questioner may, with certain reservations, only ask questions and questions so constructed that the answerer can answer Yes or No to them. The answerer in his turn is, with certain reservations, allowed to give only Yes or No answers. The questioner tries to pose such chains of questions that some of the answerer's Yes or No answers will turn out to conflict with the thesis that he had undertaken to defend. If the questioner is successful, he has confuted his opponent. If the answerer remains unconfuted until the time is up, he is the victor. The tournament, or logic duel, is fought out before an audience, which may act as a sort of jury to decide who has won or whether one of the duelists has been guilty of a foul.

The fact that we neither possess nor hear

of any students' notes of lectures by Plato,

other than his public lecture on the Good,

suggests that Plato himself did not often,

if ever, give lectures.

These set combats may sometimes have been controlled by an umpire. We may borrow the title "moot" for these organized disputations. In moots the same thesis is commonly debated time after time. Today's questioner may, but need not be tomorrow's answerer, or a new questioner and a new answerer may be brought in. The thesis need not be something of which the answerer is himself convinced. He is only its advocate for today, charged with the task of making the strongest possible case for it. Similarly, the questioner is charged with, so to speak, the prosecution of the thesis. He may have no doubts of its truth. His business is the barrister-like one of making the strongest possible case against it. Today's disputation will partly follow the course taken in yesterday's debate of the same thesis. If a line of argumentation has proved efficacious, it can be re-employed, perhaps with some condensations. But if it has proved inefficacious or frail, it is either dropped or strengthened. Sometimes, if not usually, some kind of written record is kept of the course of the argumentation, so that tomorrow's questioner and answerer can take over, with or without their own modifications, the arguments of yesterday and last week. There is no personal property in arguments, any more than there is in chess

moves. When a thesis has thus been debated many times, the final *pro* and *contra* arguments are crystallizations of the accumulated contributions of many different debaters.

If the questioner succeeds in confuting the answerer's thesis, the result of the duel is necessarily negative, in the sense that what has been proved is either that the thesis is false or that the answerer's case for it contains one or more logical flaws. When, for example, Socrates defeats Protagoras in Plato's *Protagoras,* he has proved either that virtue is *not* teachable or that there is a fallacy in Protagoras' arguments in support of the thesis that virtue is teachable. An *elenchus,* or confutation, has to be a demolition. No constructive doctrines can be established in discussions of this pattern. In such discussions the questioners are in search of illogicalities in the answerers' cases for their theses. The debate is concluded when such illogicalities are found.

Protagoras taught the art of elenctic disputation to young men and did so for a fee; the teaching of this art subsequently became widespread. Often, if not usually, it was taught to students who were also studying rhetoric. Eloquence and clarity of presentation were reinforced by cogency in destructive argumentation. Probably Protagoras thought of this new exercise only as a good training for future politicians and "lawyers"; and, to start with, young men paid to be coached in the exercise partly because it was an amusing and exciting contest but chiefly because of its career value. What is of importance to us is that it proved to be the beginning of methodical philosophical reasoning.

In the early dialogues of Plato we find, presented in the form of mimes or dramas, discussions between Socrates and interlocutors, conducted not under formal moot conditions but in unplanned and even casual conversations. Socrates is usually the questioner and is usually victorious, though in the *Euthydemus* he is, for part of the time, a hapless answerer. We need to see Plato's Socratic dialogue against this background of the rule-governed dialectical moot. If, as some clues suggest, Plato himself did for some time coach young men in elenctic disputation, his early dialogues are likely to reflect, in their argument sequences, the recorded proceedings of moots steered, arbitered and perhaps minuted by himself.

The idea, deriving entirely from the *Apology,* that the real Socrates had practiced his method by cross-examining in the market place people whom he happened to come across there is not credible. In no Platonic dialogue nor in the Socratic writings of Xenophon do Socrates' questioner-answerer tussles take place in such unsuitable surroundings. Instead, the other Platonic dialogues represent the discussions as taking place in a private house, a lecture hall or a gymnasium, and very often the disputants and their listeners are described as sitting down. Like the other teachers of dialectic, probably including Plato himself and certainly including Aristotle, the real Socrates would usually have conducted dialectical disputations under formal moot conditions. It is for dramatic ends that these discussions are, in the dialogues, informalized and enlivened with interactions between interesting persons.

Plato's Academy

When Plato was young there existed in Athens no organized higher education for lads who were finished with school, save for the few who were individually apprenticed, for example, to doctors or architects. This gap was partly filled by the sophists. A sophist was usually an itinerant lecturer who charged fees for the classes that he conducted. The main subject taught by sophists was rhetoric, the art of making forensic, political and panegyric speeches. Since most of the young men for whom the sophists catered came from the upper class, what they required was training for public life. The rhetoric taught by the sophists might include more than eloquence and clarity of presentation. Some sophists also taught embryonic linguistic subjects; some of them certainly taught eristic disputation; some of them seem to have taught literary criticism; and some, maybe, political history of a superficial sort. A few sophists taught scientific subjects. Hippias of Elis certainly taught astronomy and mathematics; others seem to have taught elementary medicine.

It seems that as a rule a sophist would flit from one city to another, giving the same lectures in each. The young Athenian might sit at the feet of Hippias or Prodicus of Ceos for a few days or weeks and then never hear him again, unless he attached himself as a fellow migrant to the sophist's retinue. A few sophists, like Gorgias, ultimately settled down in Athens and thus inaugurated the stationary "school" or "college." Aristophanes' *Clouds* makes it appear that Socrates conducted a static school. Antisthenes certainly did so. These were single-teacher schools. As far as is known, Socrates and Antisthenes employed no assistants. The static school of which most is known is that of Plato's contemporary, Isocrates, who taught rhetoric in Athens. His pupils may have remained under his tutelage for three or four years. Though apparently no fees were charged to the sons of Athenians, they were charged to the sons of non-Athenians, and Isocrates prospered from these fees. As Isocrates was far on in his nineties when he died, it is a plausible guess that the teaching in his school was, in his later years, partly done by subordinates.

Plato's Academy certainly resembled the school of Isocrates, presumably that of Antisthenes, and quite likely that of Socrates in providing a continuous education. Aristotle came to the Academy at the age of 17 and remained there for some years as a student and then for many years as a teacher. Nearly all of the Academy's students of whom anything is known came, like Aristotle, from cities other than Athens.

In two extremely important respects the Academy was unlike the school of Isocrates. First, the Academy was from its start a school with a many-sided curriculum and, correspondingly, with more than one teacher. The mathematician Theaetetus taught in the Academy and is said to have been there from its start. Probably the astronomer and mathematician Eudoxus was in the same position. He had previously had a school of his own at Cyzicus and seems to have migrated to Athens with several of his students, who then became members of the Academy. In Book VII of the *Republic* the higher education prescribed for the young men is an education that Theaetetus and Eudoxus alone could at that time have provided.

Second, where Isocrates' school trained young men in things necessary or helpful for subsequent careers in public life, the subjects taught in the Academy were, for a long time, quite unvocational—that is, "academic." It could and did produce scientists and mathematicians, but it was not at the start a seminary for future politicians, orators or "lawyers," It was left to Aristotle, in his middle twenties, to add rhetoric to the Academy's curriculum and so to bring the Academy into competition with the school of Isocrates.

It is often taken for granted that the young students in the early Academy were taught not only mathematics and astronomy but also, and above all, philosophy; Aristotle is accordingly often described as having been taught philosophy by Plato. But in Book VII of the *Republic* Socrates quite violently forbids the teaching of dialectic to young men. We have some external evidence that this was the policy of the early Academy. For whatever reasons the young Aristotles were not trained to thrash out conceptual questions according to the Socratic Method. It was Aristotle who in the fairly early or middle 350s first gave this training to the Academy's students. Xenocrates may have cooperated. Though Plato was the Head of the Academy, he did not teach his own forte, dialectic, in it.

It is not clear that Plato taught there at all. Certainly Aristotle knew the scientific content of Plato's *Timaeus*. He draws on and criticizes this dialogue far more often than he does any other Platonic dialogue. But not one of his numerous comments indicates that the *Timaeus* had been more than a basic textbook. He nowhere unmistakably suggests that Plato ever developed or modified anything in the book; or that Plato conducted *Timaeus* classes in which he told the students anything in addition to, or in correction of what is in the text of the *Timaeus*. Aristotle also shows good or moderate knowledge of many, though not all of Plato's philosophical and political writings. But of things said in class by Plato, whether in response to questions or in reply to objections, whether in jest or in annoyance, not one certain echo is transmitted by Aristotle. Our very natural and congenial idea that the Academy was a seminary in which the main teacher was Plato and the main subject taught and discussed was philosophy seems to be a long way wide of the truth.

Plato nearly always puts the questioner's words

into the mouth of his dramatic Socrates, but

no Athenian would have expected of these dialogues

much biographical fidelity to the real Socrates.

When was the Academy founded? That is, when did Plato, Theaetetus and probably Eudoxus start, at Plato's residence, which was named "Academy," the school the curriculum of which is described and justified in Book VII of the *Republic*? The traditional story that it was started in the early 380s cannot be true. Theaetetus had conducted a school of his own at Heraclea on the Black Sea before coming to the Academy, and we know from Plato's *Theaetetus* that Theaetetus was only a lad in 399. If Eudoxus was a fellow founder of the Academy, which is not certain, then the Academy could not have been started until late in the 370s. Isocrates' *Helen,* which should probably be dated late, perhaps very late, in the 370s, seems to castigate Plato, though without mentioning him by name, for teaching eristic to young men, and eristic, or dialectic, is precisely what the Academy debars young men from learning. So the founding of the Academy must have been later than the *Helen.* It is arguable that the Academy began not twenty years, but only three, four or five years before Aristotle joined it in 367.

We have no information about the number of students studying in the Academy at any one time. The temptation to liken the size of the Academy to that of a modern university or even of a college needs to be resisted. The Academy's students in a given year could probably have been counted in two figures, and very likely in the not very high two figures. Nor should it be supposed that the Academy resembled modern or even medieval universities in their most characteristic features. Nothing like their degrees, examinations, halls of residence or professorial and sub-professorial ranks can be supposed to have existed in Plato's or in Aristotle's days. Continuing lecture courses were certainly given; Aristotle's surviving books largely consist of such lecture courses. He made use of the Greek counterpart of our blackboard, and references are made here and there to anatomical diagrams, maps and the astronomers' orreries. It is not certain that the Academy even had a library in its early years.

The students took down notes of the lectures that they heard, and therefore they listened sitting down. The fact that we neither possess nor hear of any students' notes of lectures by Plato, other than his public lecture on the Good, suggests that Plato himself did not often, if ever, give lectures.

Whether, like Isocrates' school, the Academy charged fees to the sons of non-Athenians cannot be decided. We know that neither Theaetetus nor Eudoxus had inherited any private wealth, and they are likely to have had to make their livings from their own earlier schools at Heraclea and Cyzicus. There is evidence of debatable strength that Plato had become a relatively poor man shortly before the Academy was founded. If so, then it would seem inevitable that the Academy would have charged enough fees to support its Head and its two other teachers. On the other hand in a letter of questioned authenticity Dionysius the Younger reproaches Plato's successor, Speusippus, for charging fees where Plato had not done so. Plato's will seems to show that the Academy became, some time before Plato's death, an endowed foundation, controlled by trustees. So perhaps the Academy had charged fees to start with and ceased to charge them when it got the endowment that enabled it to acquire "college" status. It is tempting to identify this postulated endowment with the bounty of 80 talents that Dionysius the Younger is alleged to have given to Plato. No such wealth is bequeathed in Plato's will.

Plato's Dialogues

Plato wrote some two dozen compositions, which are known as his dialogues. A few of these are not really dialogues but addresses in monologue with a bit of conversational preamble. The *Laws,* on which Plato was still working when he died, seems originally to have been a sequence of addresses. This, after its original composition, was, during Plato's last years, in process of being reconstructed into conversational shape, but this reconstruction was never completed.

The *Menexenus* seems to be an orthodox funeral oration, to which an incongruous conversational preamble and close were subsequently added. The *Apology* is Plato's version of Socrates' speeches at his trial. The *Symposium* is, save for some brief stretches of conversation and debate, a sequence of short orations given by seven different speakers. The unfinished *Critias* and the *Timaeus* are both addresses in monologue prefaced by a little conversation. There is no philosophy in the *Menexenus*, the *Apology* or the *Critias;* almost no philosophy in the *Laws,* except for Book X, or in the first six speeches in the *Symposium;* and almost none in the *Phaedrus.* The *Republic* is a mixed bag, of which some of the contents, like its educational requirements and its political diagnoses and prescriptions, exhibit Plato as the designer of utopian policies of political reform. The program of the *Laws* is relatively unutopian, and probably Plato hoped that this program would be realized.

No contemporary testimony tells us how Plato and the many other writers of dialogues published their compositions. Nor have scholars given much consideration to the matter. What follows is a hypothesis, based on a lot of little individually tenuous clues. There was, of course, no printing in ancient Greece. Compositions published in book form were individually handwritten by scribes. There is the evidence of silence from Plato, Isocrates and others that in Plato's day there were no libraries. Very likely there were no bookshops displaying stocks of ready-made handwritten books. We do not hear of anyone browsing in such a bookshop until half a century after Plato's death. The number of individual collectors of books must have been very small. Reading books was a fairly rare thing. Inside the Academy itself the young Aristotle seems to have acquired the nickname "Reader" because he was exceptional in being a voracious reader.

The normal mode of publishing a composition, whether in verse or prose, was oral delivery to an audience. Conjecturally, the compositions of dialogue writers, including Plato, Antisthenes, Xenophon and Aristotle, were no exception. The public got to know a new dialogue by hearing the author recite it. Normally, Plato orally delivered the words of his dramatic Socrates. The dialogues were dramatic in form because they were composed for semi-dramatic recitation to lay and drama-loving audiences, consisting largely of young men. A dialogue had therefore to be short enough not to tax the endurance of its audience. The only two mammoth dialogues, the *Republic* and the incompletely conversationalized *Laws,* must have been intended for special audiences that would reassemble time after time to hear the successive installments. There are special reasons for thinking that of Plato's dialogues only the *Timaeus* and the second part of the *Parmenides* were composed just for Academic listeners.

It is customary, and not seriously misleading, to divide Plato's writing career into three periods.

THE FIRST PERIOD. The dialogues of Plato's earliest period are the *Lysis, Laches, Euthyphro, Charmides, Hippias Major* and *Hippias Minor, Ion, Protagoras, Euthydemus, Gorgias* and *Meno.* The *Alcibiades,* I and II, if Plato wrote them, are in this group also, as is the bulk of the first book of the *Republic,* which would seem to have been originally intended for an independent dialogue, the name of which would have been *Thrasymachus.* All these are dialectical or elenctic dialogues, in the sense that in all of them the debating exemplifies the Socratic Method.

Often in these early dialogues the answerer's thesis is a suggested definition of some general notion, like Piety or Valor or Beauty, but often it is a general proposition, such as "Virtue can be taught" or "It is worse to suffer than to do wrong." In either case the disputants are in search of knockdown arguments against these positions or of rebuttals of such arguments.

It may be that Plato was considerably influenced

by a special need to establish dialectic

as an autonomous and paramount science.

To us, as to some contemporary critics of Socrates and Plato, such dialectical checkmates are disappointing. We think of philosophers as trying to resolve *impasses,* not create them. But when Plato was composing these early dialectical dialogues, the word "philosophy" had not yet acquired the constructive connotations that it has for us and that it had for Aristotle and the terminal Plato.

Socrates must have trained his associates, including Plato, Antisthenes and Aeschines, in disputing according to the Socratic Method. Plato almost certainly and Antisthenes certainly subsequently trained pupils of their own in this method, as, later on, Aristotle did too. It is likely, therefore, that these early dialogues of Plato reflect, in dramatized form, moots conducted by Plato himself before the foundation of his Academy, in which dialectical disputation was forbidden to its young students. Plato nearly always puts the questioner's words into the mouth of his dramatic Socrates, but no Athenian would have expected of these dialogues much biographical fidelity to the real Socrates. The art of biography did not yet exist. The young men for whom these dialogues were chiefly written had not known Socrates, nor could they read any Socratic writings, since Socrates had published nothing.

THE MIDDLE PERIOD. In his *Gorgias* and what probably was to have been his *Thrasymachus*, now Book I of the *Republic*, Plato reaches the peak of his genius in the combination of lively dramatization with powerful elenctic argumentation. Then quite suddenly this genre of argumentation almost vanishes from Plato's dialogues, until the very undramatic second part of his late dialogue, the *Parmenides*. Only here and there and only for short stretches is the Socratic Method now practiced; and the conversations between the discussion leader and his interlocutors are no longer duels and often not even debates. In the last eight and a half books of the *Republic* Glaucon and Adeimantus merely acquiesce most of the time, without any theses of their own to champion or to surrender.

It seems plausible to connect Plato's near-abandonment of the Socratic Method with Socrates' startling veto on the participation in dialectic of the young guardians-to-be (*Republic* VI, 537–539). As the description of the higher education of these guardians is the description of the initial curriculum of the Academy, we have to conclude that in the early Academy itself young men in their teens or twenties were not allowed to take part in dialectical moots. The young Aristotle was not taught philosophy during his student years. Plato's teaching of dialectical disputation stopped with the foundation of his Academy. His composition of dialectical dialogues seems to have stopped at the same time, presumably for the same unrecorded reason.

It is in dialogues immediately succeeding the last of the dialectical dialogues that we first hear of the famous Theory of Forms. Here for the first time we find Plato putting forward a positive philosophical doctrine.

If Plato's middle period can be demarcated by the virtual disappearance of the *elenchus* and by the presence of the Theory of Forms, then the *Timaeus* has to be dated fairly close to the *Phaedo* and the *Republic*. Most commentators, however, hold that the *Timaeus,* and with it the *Philebus,* are among Plato's latest compositions and consequently that the Theory of Forms remained Plato's doctrine from the beginning of his middle period to the end of his third period. They have, in consequence, to construe Plato's criticisms of the theory in his *Sophist* and *Parmenides* as either unserious or merely peripheral. According to the other view, the minority view that is adopted here, the *Timaeus* was composed in close proximity to the *Symposium, Phaedo* and *Republic,* with the *Philebus* succeeding the *Timaeus* fairly closely, so that the middle period dialogues are these five plus the unphilosophical *Critias* and the unphilosophical *Phaedrus*. The original unconversational version of Books III–VII of our *Laws* seems likely to belong to this period also. This is also unphilosophical.

THE THIRD PERIOD. The dialogues of the third period are the *Theaetetus, Sophist, Politicus* and *Parmenides*. The *Cratylus* should probably be included, but this is a matter of controversy. The later books of the *Laws* would seem to have been composed during this period.

It is a new feature of these dialogues that they deal with sophisticated and semi-professional issues. For whatever recipients Plato ostensibly wrote them, he clearly had in mind Academic colleagues and students who were already discussing methodological and embryonically logical or semantic matters. The atmosphere of these dialogues is the atmosphere in which Aristotle was preparing his *Rhetoric, Categories, De Interpretatione, Topics* and *Peri Ideon*. The Academy's initial veto on the teaching of dialectic to young men has clearly been rescinded. Aristotle's *Topics* is a course of instruction in the techniques and rationale of elenctic disputation; in his *Parmenides* Plato makes old Parmenides advise the youthful Socrates to practice argumentation of the Zenonian pattern if he is to develop into a philosopher. In the *Sophist* and *Politicus* Plato exhibits at tedious length the division of generic concepts into their species and sub-species, and whole books of divisions were correspondingly composed by Aristotle, Xenocrates, Speusippus and Theophrastus.

In the *Cratylus, Theaetetus* and *Sophist* Plato, like Aristotle in, for example, his *De Interpretatione* and *Categories,* is beginning to consider grammatical and semantic questions about the elements and the compositions of truths and falsehoods and of the sentences that convey them. We know from Isocrates' *Antidosis* that dialectic, or eristic, was a part of the Academy's curriculum for young men by or before the middle of the 350s. It is to the 350s that Plato's third period dialogues seem to belong.

The Theory of Forms

It has been shown that the series of Plato's elenctic dialogues is abruptly terminated with the *Gorgias* or the unfinished *Thrasymachus*, which is now the substance of Book I of the *Republic*. No matter what sort of crisis this drastic change of direction was due to, Plato's succeeding dialogues are markedly different from their predecessors. Negatively, they differ in being devoid or almost devoid of argumentative checkmating; positively, they differ in presenting constructive philosophical doctrines. Of these by far the most famous is Plato's Theory of Forms.

This theory is first adumbrated in the *Symposium*. It is fairly fully stated, argued and exploited in the *Phaedo*. It is expounded and made use of in the *Republic*. It is rather briefly defended in the *Timaeus,* as if it had been already subjected to criticism; here not much positive use is made of the theory. It is mentioned with respect in the *Philebus,* but as a theory which is up against radical objections; the main arguments of this dialogue do not depend on it.

In the *Sophist* the Theory of Forms is treated quite unparentally, and a modification is required of it which, if accepted, would make it a very different doctrine. In the first part of the *Parmenides* old Parmenides not only marshals a battery of powerful, almost Aristotelian, objections to the theory but also adjures its youthful inventor, Socrates, to take serious training in dialectic if he wishes to become a philosopher. In the *Cratylus* and *Theaetetus* the theory is unmentioned and unused, save that one important strand of it is reaffirmed, though without reference to the theory as a whole.

Plato's own schooling can have contained no

natural science, though he later read for himself

books of Ionian cosmologists

and he knew something of the contents

of past and contemporary medical handbooks.

Historians of thought and commentators are apt to speak as if the Theory of Forms was the whole of Plato's thinking. It was indeed of great importance, but it has to be remembered not only that the theory is unthought of in the elenctic dialogues and is either ignored or criticized in the late dialogues; but also that during the very heyday of the theory, from the *Symposium* to the *Timaeus,* the page space given to the theory is only a small fraction of all that Plato uses. In the *Phaedo,* which seems to have been the source of most of Aristotle's ideas of the theory, the theory is employed as providing only one or two among several disparate reasons for believing in the immortality of the soul. In six of the ten books of the *Republic* nothing is said or needs to be said about the Forms. "Platonism" was never the whole of Plato's thought and for much of his life was not even a part of it.

What was this Theory of Forms?

It originated out of several different and partly independent features of the general ideas or notions that constituted the recurrent themes of dialectical disputations.

DEFINITIONS. Every discussion of a general issue turns ultimately upon one or more general notions or ideas. Even to debate whether, say, fearlessness is a good quality is to work with the two general notions of fear and goodness. Two disputants may disagree whether fearlessness is a good or a bad quality, but they are not even disagreeing unless they know what fear and goodness are. Their debate is likely, at some stage, to require the explicit definition of one or more of the general terms on which the discussion hinges. They may accept a proffered definition, but even if a proffered definition is justly riddled by criticism, this criticism teaches what the misdefined notion is not. If "fearlessness" were misdefined as "unawareness of danger," the exposure of the wrongnesses of this definition would by recoil bring out something definite in the notion of fearlessness. The Socratic demolition of a proffered definition may be disheartening, but it is also instructive.

STANDARDS OF MEASUREMENT AND APPRAISAL. Some general notions, including many moral notions and geometrical notions, are ideal limits or standards. A penciled line is, perhaps, as straight as the draftsman can make it; it deviates relatively slightly, sometimes imperceptibly, from the Euclidean straight line. The notion of absolute straightness is the standard against which we assess penciled lines as crooked or even as nearly quite straight. Rather similarly, to describe a person as improving in honesty or loyalty is to describe him as getting nearer to perfect honesty or loyalty.

IMMUTABLE THINGS. Ordinary things and creatures in the everyday world are mutable. A leaf which was green yesterday may be brown today, and a boy may be five feet tall now who was two inches shorter some months ago. But the color brown itself cannot become the color green, and the height of four feet, ten inches, cannot become the height of five feet. It is always five feet minus two inches. A change is always a change from something A to something else B, and A and B cannot themselves be things that change.

TIMELESS TRUTHS. What we know about particular things, creatures, persons and happenings in the everyday world are tensed truths, and what we believe or conjecture about them are tensed truths or tensed falsehoods. The shower is still continuing; it began some minutes ago; it will stop soon. Socrates was born in such-and-such a year; the pyramids still exist today; and so forth. But truths or falsehoods about general notions such as those embodied in correct or incorrect definitions are timelessly true or timelessly false. Just as we cannot say that 49 used to be a square number or that equilateral triangles will shortly be equiangular, so we cannot say, truly or falsely, that fearlessness is now on the point of becoming, or used to be, indifference to recognized dangers. If this statement is true, it is eternally or, better, timelessly true. We can ask questions about fearlessness or the number 49 but not questions beginning "When?" or "How long?"

ONE OVER MANY. It is often the case that we can find or think of many so-and-so's or the so-and-so's, for example, of the numerous chimney pots over there or of the prime numbers between 10 and 100. Things, happenings, qualities, numbers, figures, can be ranged in sorts or characterized as sharing properties. Hence, where we speak of the so-and-so's—say, the storms that raged last week—we are talking of storms in the plural, and we are thereby showing that there is something, some *one* thing, that each of them was—namely, a *storm.* Or if there are twenty idle pupils, there is *one* thing that all twenty of them are—namely, *idle.* Sometimes we do not and even cannot know how many leaves, say, there are in a forest, and we may ask in vain, How many leaves are there? But however many or few there are, there must still be *one* thing—namely, *leaf*— which each of them is. It is one or singular; they are many or plural. We have not seen and may never see all or most of them. But *it,* that which each of them is, is in some way known to us before we could even begin to wonder how many leaves there are.

INTELLECTUAL KNOWLEDGE. For our knowledge of, and our beliefs and opinions about the things, creatures and happenings of the everyday world, we depend upon our eyes, ears, noses and so on, and what our senses tell us is sometimes wrong and is never perfectly precise. There is nobody whose vision or hearing might not be even slightly better than it is. On the other hand, our apprehension of general notions is intellectual and not sensitive.

CONCEPTUAL CERTAINTIES. Last, but not least in importance, dialectical debates are concerned only with general ideas, like those of fearlessness, goodness, danger and awareness. The answerer's thesis is a general proposition, such as "Virtue is (or is not) teachable" or "Justice is (or is not) what is to the advantage of the powerful." When such a thesis has been conclusively demolished, something, if only something negative, has been conclusively established about virtue or justice. In the domain of general ideas or concepts certainties, if seemingly negative certainties, are attainable by argument. About things or happenings in the everyday world no such purely ratiocinative knowledge is possible.

ONTOLOGY OF FORMS. Most of the above ways of characterizing general ideas or concepts had been brought out severally or together in Plato's elenctic dialogues. Yet his Socrates did not in these dialogues put forward the Theory of Forms. The Theory of Forms, as first fully developed in the *Phaedo,* is a unified formulation of these several points, but it is also more than this. For Plato now proffers an ontology of concepts. A general idea or concept, according to this new doctrine, is immutable, timeless, one over many, intellectually apprehensible and capable of precise definition at the end of a piece of pure ratiocination *because it is an independently existing real thing or entity.* As our everyday world contains people, trees, stones, planets, storms and harvests, so a second and superior, or transcendent world contains concept-objects. As "Socrates" and "Peloponnesus" name perceptible objects here, so "justice," "equality," "unity," and "similarity" name intellectually apprehensible objects there. Furthermore, as the human mind or soul gets into contact, though only perfunctory and imperfect contact, with ordinary things and happenings in this world by sight, hearing, touch and so on, so the human mind or soul can get into nonsensible contact with the ideal and eternal objects of the transcendent world. We are ephemerally at home here, but we are also lastingly at home there. The immortality of the soul is proved by our ability to apprehend the everlasting concept-objects that Plato often calls the Forms. For what reasons and from what intellectual motives did Plato take this big stride beyond anything that his Socrates of the elenctic dialogues had established about general notions or concepts?

It is often suggested that Plato derived his ontology of Forms from the following seductive, though erroneous, semantic considerations. All statements of truths and falsehoods, or at least the basic ones, can be analyzed into a subject of which something else is truly or falsely predicated and a predicate, or that which is truly or falsely predicated of that subject. As both the subject word of such a sentence and the predicate word or predicate phrase must be significant for the whole subject-predicate sentence to be significant, both this subject word ("Socrates," say) and the predicate word ("wise," say) must name, stand for or denote something. Now the name "Socrates" names or stands for the particular snub-nosed philosopher who died in 399 B.C. But the word "wise" names or stands for a spiritual quality which can be possessed or lacked by anyone at all of any date whatsoever. Wisdom, or what the word "wise" names or stands for, is an eternal or timeless entity and one in which the fifth-century man Socrates was just one temporary participant. He exemplified it for a time, but it was and is there to be exemplified, whether by Socrates or by anyone else, at all possible times.

It may be that Plato did unwittingly take for granted such a view of the anatomy of truths and falsehoods into subjects and predicates. But there is certainly a big anachronism in the idea that Plato came to his Theory of Forms as a result of considering this semantic analysis. It is only in his late dialogues, the *Cratylus, Theaetetus* and especially the *Sophist,* that we find Plato inaugurating the analytical study of the structures of truths and falsehoods and the study of the grammatical parsing of Greek sentences. Here even the, to us, elementary distinction between nouns and verbs is, for the first time, being established by fairly complex arguments. The technical terminology of "subject and predicate" was the creation not of Plato but of Aristotle.

Toward the end of the Meno, *Socrates,*

despairing of proving that virtue is teachable

and is, consequently, a piece of knowledge,

reminds Meno that in many daily affairs

correct opinion, doxa, *serves us*

just as well as knowledge.

Rather, far from the Theory of Forms issuing out of the recognition of the subject–predicate structure of truths and falsehoods, this recognition seems to have been achieved only after the Theory of Forms had already been subjected to radical criticism. The task of distinguishing the subjects from the predicates of truths and falsehoods and the nouns from the verbs in sentences was undertaken partly in order to diagnose the ills from which the Theory of Forms had proved to be suffering. The theory that Socrates is one entity in this world and wisdom a second and separate entity in another world and that the former for a time "participates" in or "takes after" the latter came to grief partly because of the ambivalent nature of this bridge notion of "participating" or "taking after." It was because Plato did not and could not yet distinguish predicate expressions, like "is wise," from subject expressions, like "Socrates," that wisdom, say, seemed to be required to be an entity counterpart to, and existing separately from Socrates or anyone else who can be asserted to be or not to be wise. Plato did not deduce the Theory of Forms from the false premise that verbs and verb phrases function like extra nouns. Rather, it was because he had not and could not have thought about such semantic and grammatical matters that he was for a time unsuspicious of his independently based treatment of wisdom, say, and equality as transcendent things.

One consideration which certainly did move Plato in developing his ontology of Forms was that geometry and arithmetic were certainly sciences and sciences the certainties of which were higher than, or rather of an order different from the limited convincingness of the speculations of the natural scientists, such as the astronomers and the doctors. The lines, angles and areas, the numbers, equalities and ratios that we discover in our geometrical and arithmetical thinking are not particular penciled lines, sketched areas or assembled couples. When we prove that the two base angles of an isosceles triangle are equal, we are not finding out by more or less rough measurements that these two penciled angles are so nearly the same as to make no difference. Nor in calculating $7 \times 7 = 49$ are we finding out by more or less careful counting that the number of nuts or drops of water in this container matches the total number of nuts or drops of water that had previously been in those seven containers.

Geometry and arithmetic are sciences of the line, the angle, the area, number, the ratio and so on in abstraction from their more or less rough and unstable approximations in our penciled diagrams and manipulatable objects. A geometrical truth is true of, say, the base angles of all possible isosceles triangles. The objects of which geometry is the science are, in an essential way, general objects, or to put it in a later idiom, geometrical truths are unrestrictedly general truths embodying ideal limit concepts. Geometry and arithmetic are sciences, and what they are sciences of are realities exempt from the imprecisions and the instabilities that belong to the things and happenings of the everyday world.

Another consideration that influenced Plato was that in a dialectical disputation the questioner and answerer are concerned with such general notions or concepts as justice, friendship, beauty, unity, plurality, identity, pleasure and so on. Their debating about these notions requires extracting the implications and incompatibilities of truths or falsehoods embodying these concepts; and often, also, the testing and re-testing of various suggested definitions of such concepts. When a conclusive argument has been found, then something, even if only a negative something, has been established about one or more of the concepts operated on. Here too, as in a different way in mathematics, abstract truths are established with certainty by pure ratiocination. The conclusions of a dialectical argument seem consequently to be scientific conclusions; like theorems of mathematics, the conceptual points established by Socratic demolitions are of an unrestricted generality and of a precision unattainable by the most plausible findings of the observational sciences.

But if dialectic is, in this way, also a science, then, it seems, what it is the science of must also be realities or real things. As the would-be science of astronomy has the visible stars and planets for its objects, so the objects dealt with by the dialectician—namely, abstract concepts—must also be things in the real world, though in this case their real world is a transcendent world of timeless and purely intelligible entities.

THE CREDENTIALS OF DIALECTIC. It may be that Plato was considerably influenced by a special need to establish dialectic as an autonomous and paramount science. For the Theory of Forms appears in his dialogues so swiftly after his sudden divorce from the practice of elenctic disputation and the composition of elenctic dialogues that we may conjecture that this divorce was forced upon Plato against his will, and that he needed to justify the now ostracized practice of dialectic. He had to satisfy some of his fellow Athenians, but also to satisfy himself, that the Socratic Method was something much better than the youth-demoralizing game that its enemies took it to be. It was, rather, a science, with such a supremacy over the other sciences or would-be sciences that without it as their foundation they were without foundation. This hypothesis is partly borne out by the fact that the examples of Forms given in the middle period dialogues are nearly always concepts constantly operated on in actual dialectical debates. At this stage we hear little of the concepts of natural kinds, of kinds of artifacts, or of sensible qualities; that is, we hear little or nothing of the Forms of Dog, Tree, Silver or Water or, with one or two exceptions, of the Forms of Spade, Knife or Table or of the Forms of Green, Sour, Shrill or Rough. Only later did Plato see that the arguments for taking Justice, say, and Unity as Forms would establish Tree, Silver, Knife and Sour as Forms too. To start with, he was thinking, above all, of those concepts that must and do get dialectical examination, as these other concepts do not. Socratic probings into the nature of Copper, say, or Elephant could get nowhere. It is for the metalworker and the zoologist to find out by experiment and observation what can be found out about such subjects. But Socratic probings do fix the boundaries between such concepts as virtue and knowledge or justice and skill.

It may be, therefore, that Plato's Theory of Forms was, in part, a defense of dialectic, which woefully needed defense. The partial parallels of geometry and arithmetic, which needed no such defense, were cited as providing collateral reinforcements for the defense of dialectic. As they were recognized sciences, so it was an unrecognized science. When dialectic was described in the *Republic* as "the coping-stone of the sciences," Plato was not just gratuitously complimenting his darling ratiocinative exercise; he was contrasting the intellectual homage which it deserved with the contempt and hostility with which his Athens actually treated it—and him. When Plato made Socrates sternly refuse parti-

cipation in dialectic to his young guardians-to-be on the ground that early participation demoralizes its participants, we must suppose that Plato was being politic. His Academy would indeed forbid dialectic to its young students, but because Athens demanded this, not because Plato's heart endorsed this demand.

The Timaeus *seems to have been used in the Academy as a basic textbook of natural science and to have been written for this end.*

In his *Parmenides,* of perhaps a decade or more later, he makes Parmenides urge the youthful Socrates to take training in the dialectical exercise if he wishes to become a philosopher. The supposed risk of the young man's being demoralized goes unmentioned, just as in the early dialogues Socrates encourages lads to join in elenctic debates without any warnings of dangers to their morals.

APPLICATIONS OF THE THEORY. The Theory of Forms is put to an ancillary use in the *Republic,* Book VI, where Socrates is challenged to explain why he requires philosophers to rule the Ideal State, when in real life philosophers are notoriously devoid of worldly sagacity. Socrates concedes the depressing fact but claims that the true philosopher's apprehension of the Forms and especially of the Form of the Good is analogous to our vision of sunlit objects and of the sun itself. Cave dwellers, when first let out into the sunlight, are dazzled by the bright light, though they soon see more than ever before. Conversely, on their first return to their cave they are worse at discerning its dimly illuminated objects than are those who have never looked at anything lit by the rays of the sun. The intellect is subject to its counterparts of dazzlement and night blindness.

In Book X of the *Republic* the Theory of Forms is employed for another subsidiary task. Painters, actors, sculptors and dramatists are all producers of representations or "imitations." The picture of a tree is not itself a tree; the stage hero does not perform real acts of heroism. To this distinction between realities and representations of them there corresponds the distinction between the man who apprehends the realities and the man who attends only to the imitations—that is, between the philosopher and, say, the theatergoer. Truths about realities are not to be looked for in Homer or Euripides. This contrast of representation with reality is then given a further application. A painter may produce a likeness of the real bed that the carpenter manufactures. But the carpenter, in manufacturing beds, is in a supposedly analogous way "imitating" the concept of Bed. What he produces in wood is a good or a bad specimen of Bed. Socrates pretends that it stands to what it is a specimen of somewhat as the picture of a wooden bed stands to the actual bed. As the painter has to know things about the real bed if he is ever to try to produce a good likeness of it, so the carpenter has to know what a bed is if he is ever to try to make a good specimen of a bed. In the *Timaeus* God, the cosmic artificer, is similarly described as modeling the things in his new world after eternal or timeless thing-patterns.

For us, as for Aristotle, the cardinal task of the Theory of Forms is to answer the question How are Forms related to the particular things in our everyday world which partially or completely exemplify these Forms? But this question had not been the cardinal question for Plato at the start. Then, apparently, he had needed his separate world of concept-objects to give objectivity and autonomy to conceptual inquiries—that is, to dialectic. Only later did he come under pressure to reunite the conceptual with the factual, the other world with this world. Later still, in his *Sophist* and in *Parmenides*, Part I, he argues as forcibly as Aristotle against that very separateness of his concept-objects, which had, at the start, seemed requisite for the scientific primacy of conceptual inquiries.

Plato and Natural Science

Plato's own schooling can have contained no natural science, though he later read for himself books of Ionian cosmologists and he knew something of the contents of past and contemporary medical handbooks. He also picked up a little astronomy. He was better grounded in geometry and arithmetic, although we have no reasons for thinking that he was ever an original mathematician. His Academy became the main seedbed of original mathematicians, and Plato gave his support and blessing to their researches. But Theaetetus and Eudoxus were the teachers who instructed the new generation of mathematicians.

In the *Phaedo* Socrates is made to declare his personal renunciation of natural science and his resultant recourse to conceptual inquiries. With surprising inconsistency he almost concludes his conversation with an exposition of "someone's" geophysical theories about the spherical shape and internal structure of the earth, about its hydraulics and about the causes of volcanoes and earthquakes. Parts of this geophysics belong to a period well after the death of the real Socrates, so the passage is likely to record things that Plato himself had newly learned at about the time he completed the *Phaedo*. Socrates is careful to avoid saying that these geophysical ideas are his own. In the *Republic* the astronomy and harmonics prescribed for the education of the young guardians are to have no touch with stellar observation or with acoustic experiments. In a different context, also in the *Republic,* medical science is likewise treated very scathingly.

It is therefore a remarkable fact that by the time, whenever it was, that Plato wrote his *Timaeus,* his attitude toward natural science had been completely revolutionized. For the *Timaeus* is in large part a synoptic digest of contemporary Italian and Sicilian natural science. After an introductory story of creation, the allocution given by Timaeus, whose description is the description of Archytas of Tarentum, is devoted almost entirely to astronomy, theoretical chemistry, anatomy, physiology, pathology and the mechanism of sense perception. It is true that Timaeus does not claim for his doctrines anything higher than probability and that he professes that the study of nature is only a pastime. But Plato certainly intended his *Timaeus* to be used in the Academy for the instruction of students, and we know that Aristotle was in fact steeped in its scientific content. Aristotle does not treat very seriously its theology or cosmogony, but he takes very seriously and treats very critically such things as its geometrical atomism, anatomy, physiology and theory of visual perception.

Scholars disagree whether it was in the middle or at the end of his writing life that Plato composed the *Timaeus.* The view adopted here is that Plato composed the *Timaeus* during his second visit to Syracuse, in 367–366, that this was very shortly after he had composed the *Phaedo* and the political core of his *Republic;* and that Plato's *Philebus* and *Theaetetus* were written later than the *Timaeus* and contain echoes from it. But this is a minority view. The matter is of great importance. If the view here adopted is correct, Plato's later thinking differs drastically from his earlier thinking. In the *Phaedo* and the *Republic* knowledge or science is possible only of what belongs to the transcendent world of Forms, including the objects of pure mathematics. Of the mutable things and the dated happenings that constitute nature nothing better than opinion and conjecture is possible. Our world is one of mere semblances. But after Plato had learned what Archytas and Philistion had to teach, he no longer thought that knowledge of nature was unattainable and no longer thought that the temporariness of things and processes in our world was incompatible with our discovering truths about them. An important part of what is commonly meant by "Platonism" was not what Plato thought after the *Timaeus.* In the *Sophist* he argues explicitly against the "friends of the Forms" that temporal things and events are genuine realities—that is, that nothing prevents tensed truths from being perfectly true or certainly true. Plato may well have continued for some time to think that Forms are eternally or timelessly existing objects, but he no longer thinks of them as the only objects of which scientific knowledge is possible.

In the *Timaeus* itself Plato had defended the Theory of Forms, apparently against some of its critics, by the antithesis between what is known and what merely appears to be so-and-so, taking it that Forms and only Forms are accessible to knowledge and only to knowledge, while whatever exists or happens in our everyday world is a matter of mere belief or opinion. In the *Theaetetus* Plato argues conclusively that we can make mistakes about timeless objects like numbers and that we can know for certain truths about things and events in our everyday world. For example, the eyewitness to a crime, unlike the jurors, is not persuaded of what took place; he knows what took place.

Plato's Theaetetus *is a head-on inquiry*

into the notion of knowledge.

In the *Philebus* Socrates is made to allow that as long as knowledge of conceptual matters retains its primacy, subordinate inquiries can be admitted as authentic sciences. The reputed otherworldliness or epistemological utopianism of Plato really did belong to him when he wrote the *Phaedo* and the *Republic*. He is somewhat on the defensive about it in the earlier part of the *Timaeus*. If the *Timaeus* belongs to Plato's middle period, then after the *Timaeus,* and possibly because of its detailed, elaborate and copious exposition of Italian and Sicilian natural science, Plato ceases to think of this world as a place of unreliable semblances, in which the intellect of man is an exile, forever sick for its other home.

In the *Parmenides,* Part I, Plato deploys the young Socrates' arguments for, and the old Parmenides' arguments against the Theory of Forms. No student of the quality of the argumentation can doubt that Parmenides' arguments are Plato's arguments or that what Parmenides rejects is what Plato now rejects. Since the second part of the *Parmenides* is a protracted and highly scholastic exercise in two-way question-answer dialectic, we can take it that the veto on dialectic for the young men in the Academy has by now been lifted or forgotten. Plato no longer needs the Theory of Forms to vindicate dialectic against contempt and suppression; he no longer needs the Theory of Forms to represent genuine science against the unstable pretensions of the natural scientists. His own Academy, without Athenian hostility, now teaches dialectic, mathematics, astron-

omy, zoology and, most likely, anatomy and physiology. Utopia evaporates into a dream. The Academy of the late Plato is the Academy of the young Aristotle. The same air is breathed by both.

Theory of Knowledge and Logic

In the early dialogues prior to the *Meno* problems in the theory of knowledge are hardly touched on, save for the recurrent question *Is virtue teachable?* and the ancillary question about the relation between possessing knowledge and possessing virtue. Here the puzzles canvassed are puzzles about the nature of virtue rather than about the natures of knowledge, learning and teaching.

In the *Meno* the situation changes. At one point, when Socrates wishes to investigate the nature of virtue, Meno puts forward a debater's teaser about investigations of any sort. If a man does not know something, how can his inquiry succeed? For he will not recognize whether what he arrives at is what he had been looking for. Alternatively, if he had known what he was looking for, he would not have needed to look for it. For example, if I do not know what 7×8 makes, then whatever number I get, I shall not recognize it for the required number; I cannot recognize 56 as the object of my search, since I searched in ignorance of this product. The conclusion of this obviously sophistical argument, if accepted, would show that it is never any use trying to find out anything. Neither thinking nor any other kind of investigation could possibly achieve its aim.

DOCTRINE OF RECOLLECTION. Socrates rejects this conclusion and argues for a positive doctrine about inquiry, thought and knowledge, the doctrine known as his doctrine of reminiscence or recollection. A slave boy who had been taught no geometry is cross-examined about a geometrical problem. To start with, the boy jumps to tempting but false answers. He is quickly satisfied that the answers are false and in the end comes out with the correct answer. Yet Socrates has told him nothing, but only asked him questions. In short, the boy thinks out a geometric truth that is new to him from considerations stimulated in him by Socrates' interrogations.

Socrates now argues that in some way this truth must already have been in the boy, since it was elicited from him by questions and not introduced into him by telling it to him. But if this geometrical truth was already in the boy and had not got into him by any new instruction in geometry, then he must have acquired it in a previous existence. It must have been latently in him when he was born—that is, innate. Socrates' questions served as reminders of things that the boy had known before but had forgotten in the passage from an earlier life to this life. Thus, an immortality of the soul is apparently proved, though not yet an eternal life after death or an endless series of lives after death, for it is only an eternal life or an endless series of lives preceding this life. This argument reappears in the *Phaedo,* now in association with the Theory of Forms, which had had no place in the *Meno.* The doctrine of recollection seems also to be alluded to in the *Phaedrus.*

How much does Socrates' argument prove? It certainly proves that if a slave boy, say, thinks out for himself a truth that no one has taught him, then this discovery was in some sense already "in" him. But in this sense a poet's compositions, a humorist's new jokes or an inventor's inventions were antecedently "in" their producers, for they possessed the intelligence and the equipment to compose new poems, make new jokes or invent new inventions. Today's poem was not previously lodged away, ready-made, inside the poet, like the seed inside a berry. What the poet possessed was the talent or ability, plus the vocabulary and the prosody, to compose new poems. In this sense of "in," the exploit of climbing this tree was "in" the strong and adventurous boy—namely, that he had it in him to climb it, that is, he possessed the requisite strength, dexterity and courage. So the slave boy had it in him to think out the solution to his geometrical problem because he possessed the intelligence, application and interest. That the solution was "in" him in any other way is not proved by Socrates' argument, which, in effect, reduces thinking something out to having one's memory refreshed, without any answer to the resultant question, How did it ever get into him, even in some previous life? But it cost Plato and especially Aristotle much intellectual effort to separate out the notions of ability, capacity and skill from the notions of performance, application and exercise. Only then was it possible to distinguish the qualities that must have been possessed by the slave boy for him to think out the solution from his being already in actual, though latent, possession of that solution.

KNOWLEDGE AND OPINION. Toward the end of the *Meno* Socrates, despairing of proving that virtue is teachable and is, consequently, a piece of knowledge, reminds Meno that in many daily affairs correct opinion, *doxa,* serves us just as well as knowledge. The guide who only thinks that this is the road to Larissa but is quite right gets us to Larissa as effectively as if he actually does know it. The defect of opinion, even when correct, is that, unlike knowledge, it can be shaken by criticism, conflicting evidence, authority, etc. This opposition of knowledge to opinion, even to correct opinion, is of great importance. Much of Plato's *Theaetetus* is given up to the discussion of the antithesis. For the moment it is necessary to point out that *doxa* covers a good deal more than our "opinion." It includes any case of something seeming or appearing. The seeming convergence of the receding railway lines would be a case of *doxa,* as well as its seeming that the earth is flat, that $7 \times 8 = 54$, or that this is the road to Larissa.

It is in the *Phaedo* that we first find Plato systematically contrasting intellectual apprehension with sense perception, knowledge of what is exact and timeless with the temporary and imprecise deliverances of our senses, the true and permanent home of the philosopher with the temporary habitat of sense-tethered men. Here we get the opposition between the equalities established in, say, geometry and the more or less rough approximations toward equality that are exhibited by our wooden sticks or our tape measures. In assessing this quantity as approximately the same as that one we are applying the ideal limit of absolute sameness of quantity. This absolute standard is prior to its rough approximations. It is what these approximate toward or diverge from. Soul and body, reason and sense, ideal limit and approximation, eternal and ephemeral, sunshine and twilight, heaven and earth, knowledge and opinion, reality and semblance, invisible and visible, imperishable and perishable, divine and earthy—all these dualities are one duality. The philosopher who dies in an Athenian prison this morning lives in the other world not only forever after but already. The true objects of his pure thought had never been on this earth.

To think is to have an answer,

correct or incorrect, to a question;

the verbal expression of a thought

must be a complete sentence.

There is no great difference on these matters between the *Phaedo* and the *Republic,* especially Book VI. At this stage Plato's need is to distinguish or separate the ideal from the actual, the intelligible from the sensible, thought from sense perception, the measure from the things measured. He needs to establish that there is a separate world, of the realities of which philosophy and mathematics are the sciences. Only later does he feel the need to reunite the other world to this world by, among other things, considering how thought and sense perception can and sometimes must cooperate if our mundane inquiries are to result in new knowledge. The very crevasse between Forms and particulars, between the one and the many, between the objects of knowledge and those of *doxa*, which had been opened in order to ensure the autonomy of reason and the separateness of its proper objects, later had to be bridged in order to make communications possible; for example, to make nature amenable to science.

TELEOLOGY. At one stage in the *Phaedo* Socrates recounts how, after having for a time been fascinated by the speculations of the cosmologists, he had come to renounce, for his purposes, their causal or mechanical explanations. The explanations that he required were teleological explanations, answers to the question, What for? and not to the questions, Owing to what? and By means of what? It is not clear that he thinks that mechanical explanations fail to explain anything. In the *Timaeus* they are allowed to be genuine explanations, but only auxiliaries to the ultimate explanation. There is no sign that Plato rejects such auxiliary explanations merely on the grounds that they are still purely speculative and unproved. Least of all is Socrates in the *Phaedo* forswearing explanations of what is temporal or this-worldly on the grounds that such things are not worthy or susceptible of explanation; for he contrasts a mechanical with a teleological explanation of his own recent decision to stay in prison and die. Rather, it seems that Socrates is telling why he himself had preferred to concentrate on conceptual or perhaps dialectical problems, above all, those hinging on concepts of value. Ultimate explanations must be answers to the question, What is the good of it?

THEORY OF THE SCIENCES. The *Republic,* Book VII, moves beyond the *Phaedo* in developing not so much a theory of knowledge as a theory of the sciences. The education prescribed for the young guardians-to-be, which reflects the initial curriculum of Plato's own Academy, is a training in mathematics, harmonics and astronomy. Harmonics and astronomy, however, are to be studied as branches of pure theory, without recourse to acoustic experiments or to stellar observations. Although, before they reach the age of 30, the students are forbidden to take part in dialectic, still dialectic is the "coping-stone of the sciences." Even the purely theoretical sciences of arithmetic and geometry remain merely provisional or hypothetical until dialectic gives its guarantee to their postulates or so-called axioms. These sciences, at present, rest only on "hypotheses" or "sub-theses," and their conclusions are necessarily insecure as long as their starting points are insecure. Only dialectic can make these secure, by trying to test them to destruction.

In the *Timaeus* the Theory of Forms is briefly stated and championed, apparently against some skeptics. The case for the theory here rests wholly on the antithesis between knowledge or reason and true opinion. This distinction is made to derive from the differences between the timeless and immutable objects of knowledge and the short-lived objects of sense-given opinion.

The *Timaeus* seems to have been used in the Academy as a basic textbook of natural science and to have been written for this end. As one part of it gives the results of observational astronomy and other parts the results of anatomical dissections, both probably learned by Plato from the scientists of Italy and Sicily, his strictures on the senses as incapable of yielding teachable knowledge must by now have been attended by some mental qualifications. He could not consistently have believed both that no teachable truths about nature existed and that, among other subjects, human anatomy could and should be taught out of his own *Timaeus* to the young Aristotles in his Academy.

KNOWLEDGE IN THE *THEAETETUS*. Plato's *Theaetetus* is a head-on inquiry into the notion of knowledge. It begins with a destructive examination of the theory that knowledge is sense perception, that is, that to know something is to be in receipt of a deliverance from the eyes, the ears, the nose, etc. It is not being debated whether human knowledge requires or depends on the receipt of these deliverances but whether knowing just amounts to such receipt. Socrates is not out to establish that we could know some things, or all knowable things, even though deprived of sight, hearing, touch and the rest, but only that knowing things is more than getting sensations. Among several powerful arguments, Socrates produces a conclusive refutation of the theory that knowing something is simply equivalent to having a sensation. What I have found out, he argues, I continue to know until I forget. I can know that there was a noise when my hearing of the noise is over. So I now know this truth, though I can no longer hear the noise. Knowing the truth about the noise is therefore not equivalent to hearing it, since the former continues to exist when the latter has ceased to exist. To know something is to retain what has been got, and this retaining cannot be equated with this getting, though it presupposes it. Correspondingly, an expert may know how something is going to taste, feel or sound. He knows this future-tense truth before he sees or hears the thing foretold. If the knowing exists already when the seeing or hearing has not yet occurred, then the knowing cannot be identified with the seeing or hearing, or else the date of the one would be the date of the other.

Socrates now establishes a positive or constructive point. When I find out something by using my eyes, ears or tongue, and even when, on using my eyes, ears or tongue, it just seems to me that something is the case, what I have come to know, or even merely surmise, always embodies some element or feature other than the colors, noises and tastes that my senses present to me. For example, I know or surmise that one thing is similar in color to another; or that one noise is shriller than, and therefore not identical with another; or I know or surmise that there are two or several specks of red or only one speck; or I know or surmise that something exists now, has existed or will still exist; or that something else is not occurring, has not occurred yet, but will shortly occur. But these elements or features conveyed by "similar," "identical," "single," "several," "two," "exist," "not occur," "was," "will" and others are not, like colors, sight-given as opposed to taste-given or, like noises, heard as opposed to smelled. They are not proprietary to any one particular sense. They are neutral as between the different senses. There is not one of them of which a man blind or deaf from birth is therefore uncognizant. Though unable to see or hear, he is, unless also a moron, cognizant of these non-proprietary, or "common," elements because he can think. They are thought-given, not sense-given. Value notions, like good, beautiful, and just seem to be, in the same way, "common" or sense-neutral. It follows that our knowledge even about what is visible, tangible or audible demands intelligence as well as eyesight, hearing, etc. Thus knowledge or opinion is the product of thought in cooperation with sense perception. So on this score too, bare sensing does not amount to knowledge. Our knowings, supposings, surmisings, our recognizings and even our misrecognizings must contain the element of the thinking of thoughts.

In the Gorgias *the young interlocutor, Polus,*

champions the sub-thesis that it is better

to do wrong than to suffer it,

and Socrates duly confutes this sub-thesis.

Thought. What then is thinking? This question is now explicitly posed. The young Theaetetus, abandoning the equation of knowing with sensing, suggests instead that knowing should be equated with thinking—or rather, since thinking can be mistaken, that knowing should be equated with unmistaken thinking or correct thinking. Patently, a person who knows that something is the case is not mistaken, or else he could not be said to know.

Socrates postpones discussing this new equation in its own right. He first discusses very exhaustively the interim question. How is mistaken thinking possible? The difficulty is this. The things that we see, touch, hear, eat, hold, meet and carry are there to be seen, carried, etc. But if, perhaps in a fog, I misidentify Theaetetus as Theodorus, this identity of Theaetetus with Theodorus is *not* there, since they are really two different people. So what I mistakenly think is not there for me to think it. Yet I cannot be thinking nothing. Indeed, if you, in the same fog, misidentify Theaetetus as Socrates, your mistake is a different mistake from mine. You think something different from what I think, yet neither the something that you think nor the something different that I think is there to be thought, since the identity of Theaetetus with Socrates is no more really there than is his identity with Theodorus. Similarly, if my memory is at fault, the event I misremember did not happen. So, it seems, this event, which is what I misremember, did not occur—and how can an event be without occurrence?

A person who knows neither Theodorus nor Theaetetus, or who knows one but not the other, cannot misidentify either as the other. If he does know both, he knows that they are different people and so are not one and the same person. He cannot then think the thought "Theaetetus and Theodorus are one and the same person." Yet, in a fog, he may very well think "That man yonder [who is actually Theaetetus] is Theodorus." The relative clause in the square brackets is not his rider, but ours.

Similarly, the child may very well think that $7 \times 8 = 54$ [though it actually is 56]; so he thinks that the product of 7 and 8 [which in fact is 56] is 54, without thinking, what he could not think, that the number 54 is the number 56. Again, I may not know who it is that is yonder in the fog, although I do know the man Theodorus [who is actually over there]. Thus I can mistakenly think that the man over there is Theaetetus, whom I know, when it is really Theodorus, whom I also know. In making this mistake, I am not thinking that Theodorus is Theaetetus, but that the man yonder [who is really Theodorus] is Theaetetus. In retrospect I shall never say, "I thought that Theaetetus was Theodorus," but only, "I mistakenly thought that the man looming out of the fog was Theaetetus, but to my surprise it now turns out that he was Theodorus." This sort of misidentification is possible and common, but it is quite a different sort of misidentification from the impossible one, easily confused with the first, namely, thinking that Theaetetus, whom I know, and Theodorus, whom I know, are the same person or that the number 54 is the number 56.

Socrates sees that underlying his question What is it to think falsely? or How can a person mistake something for what it is not? there is this perfectly general feature of thinking, whether correct or mistaken thinking: to think is to have an answer, correct or incorrect, to a question; the verbal expression of a thought must be a complete sentence. What I think is that this is the road to Larissa or that the product of 7 and 8 is 54. This already weakens the early argument that as what I see, hear, eat or carry must be there for me to see it, etc., then what I think must be there for me to think it. For what I see or eat is a thing, and what I hear or remember may be a happening. But what I think is not a thing or a happening; it is a truth or a falsehood about one or more things or happenings. I can meet or hear Theodorus, but I cannot think *him,* but only *that* he is approaching through the fog or *that* he is not a mathematician, etc.

Suppose that you and I both see a man in a fog, and you say and think correctly that it is Theaetetus while I say and think incorrectly that it is Theodorus. Then, in some way, Theodorus seems to have got into my words and my thought instead of Theaetetus. I have made some sort of inadvertent swap or substitution of Theodorus, who ought not to be there, for Theaetetus, who ought, though necessarily I know that they are different persons. I have jumbled them in my thought but not, of course, thought them to be identical with one another. Socrates deploys in great detail impossibilities and difficulties in this initially tempting theory of mistakes, namely, that in saying or thinking something false we somehow substitute one person or one thing for another person or thing. Socrates seems here to be testing to destruction a view about what was later to be labeled the subject-predicate structure of true and false statements, and therewith of correct and incorrect thoughts, the view, namely, that just as the subject expression in an elementary statement stands for or names a person or an animal or a thing, etc., so its predicate expression stands for or names a second person or thing or animal, etc. He does not even mention here what he had mentioned in the *Cratylus* and analyzes in the *Sophist,* that is, statements of which the predicates are verbs, like "runs" and "flew," which no one could take to be the names of particular persons, animals or things. In the *Theaetetus* he operates almost wholly with false or true statements of the pattern "That man yonder is Theodorus," "The sum of 7 and 5 is the number 11." In his so-called "dream" he expounds the theory that a statement, true or false, is a combination of the names of the basic elements of which reality consists, though in the preceding and succeeding dialogues an elementary statement is a combination, not of two names, but of a name with a verb or a verb phrase. Such a verb or

verb phrase is, in the *Sophist,* rightly denied to function as the name of anything.

In the *Theaetetus,* therefore, Plato rightly argues that knowledge requires thinking; that thoughts, with the statements of them, can be false as well as true; that false thoughts are *not* thoughts of two different things, or persons, etc., treated as the same thing or person, etc.; that in a false thought about a real thing or person what is wrong is not any sort of a substitution of one thing or person for another different thing or person, that is, by implication, predicate expressions, unlike subject expressions, are not also names of things or persons, etc.

True Belief Plus a "Logos." When the discussion at last reverts to the original question What is knowledge? it is quickly shown that knowledge is not to be equated, as Theaetetus had suggested, with correct opinion. The jurors may be persuaded of truths about an event that they have not witnessed. The eyewitness knows what happened, but they do not know it, but only believe correctly that what he reports to them did happen. So knowing is not the same as correctly believing. It is now suggested that knowledge must be not just true belief, but true belief *plus* something else, namely, a *logos.* It is soon shown that "*logos*" has many different senses and that in three of its senses, which are not its only senses, possession of a *logos* is not enough to entitle a person who believes something and is right, to claim that he knows it. The original question What is knowledge? does not get its final answer—and, incidentally, it has not got it yet.

THEORY OF MEANING IN THE *SOPHIST*. In the succeeding dialogue, the *Sophist,* the central question discussed belongs not to the theory of knowledge but to logic, or rather, to a part of the theory of meaning that is prefatory to logical inquiries proper. For Plato is now explicitly considering, side by side, questions about the grammatical structures of sentences conveying elementary truths or falsehoods, and the structures of those truths and falsehoods themselves. In an elementary statement, like "Theaetetus is flying," the nominative expression names or denotes a particular person or thing, but the predicate expression, in this case the verb, cannot possibly be doing this, since a sequence of two names, like "Theaetetus-Theodorus," says nothing, true or false. It merely lists two persons. For a sentence to say something true or false about Theaetetus, its predicate expression, say, the verb, must convey something that Theaetetus is or is doing or is undergoing. Moreover, the verb is tensed. It conveys what Theaetetus was doing or will be undergoing or is now looking like, etc. Finally, a sentence like "Theaetetus is (or was) flying" says something true or else, as in this instance, something false which can be negated. "Not" can be attached to the predicate expression, as it cannot be attached to the subject expression. If a falsehood is negated, as in "Theaetetus was not flying," a truth results and *vice versa*.

As the Ideal State is a coordination or integration

of three different classes, each with its own

economic and political role, so the soul is

an integration of three different parts or elements,

each with a role proper to it

in the conduct of personal life.

The central problem of the philosophical core of this dialogue is the problem, How can a statement to the effect that something is *not* the case be a true statement and, therefore, one which says what *is* the case? How can it really *be* the case that Theaetetus is not flying, when his *not flying* seems to be an example of something *not* being done by Theaetetus? Yet even to word the issue in this way is to take part of the heart out of the puzzle as it existed at Plato's time. Its natural formulation then was, How can we tell or think what *is not?* or How can we tell or think something that *is not?* For surely there cannot be, that is, exist, non-existent somethings. We cannot eat or see or carry an apple that is not there, so how can we tell or think what is not? This question can be taken as asking how we can significantly assert or believe something *false;* or it can be taken as asking how we can significantly assert or believe a *negative* proposition, true or false. Plato moves from a discussion of the former issue to a discussion of the latter one, which underlies the former. The Eleatic thinker, Parmenides, had set the problem to which Plato's *Sophist* gives at least a big part of the correct answer. For Parmenides the problem was this: Since what is not, is not anything, it is not to be thought about or mentioned; so there can be no thought or statement that not so-and-so. No truth or falsehood can be negative. What is not cannot be what I think or declare, since it cannot be anything at all. Obviously even these statements of Parmenides' doctrine, being themselves negative, come under their own proscription.

Plato shows that this proscription is self-destroying by this shrewd argument. To say anything at all about that which *is* not, or about things that *are* not, is to speak either in the singular or in the plural. But then

there must *be* one or more than one of what are spoken of in the singular or the plural. Yet we cannot *not* use the singular or the plural; so we cannot even say, with Parmenides, that that which is not is unthinkable or that things which are not cannot be spoken of. Parmenides' problem has therefore to be reformulated. How can we think or say about something or some things that it is or they are not so-and-so? The problem is not the unstatable problem, How can there be negative things? It is rather, How can things be truly or falsely denied to be so-and-so? In Aristotelian parlance, "not" cannot be attached to the subject of a truth or falsehood; but it can be attached to what is predicated of that subject. We can say truly of Theaetetus that he is not flying or falsely of him that he is not sitting. What we cannot do is say anything at all about not-Theaetetus or un-Theaetetus. Statements can be negative, though their subject names cannot. So the authentic problem is, What is it to deny or to affirm something, truly or falsely, of, say, Theaetetus? It is at once clear that the part of the sentence by which something is affirmed or denied or even asked of a named subject cannot itself be a second subject name. To affirm or deny something of Theaetetus is not to affirm or deny some *thing,* but that he is or is not so-and-so. A proposition is not a conjoining of two named subjects. This is made very clear by examples of elementary propositions of which the predicate is a tensed verb, as in "Theaetetus was (or is) sitting." It is just because the contribution of the verb to the proposition is entirely different from the contribution of its subject name that we can, for example, say that Theaetetus is *not* flying, without entrapping ourselves in the Parmenidean idea that we are thereby mentioning an un-thing or a not-person.

In his very abstract and intricate discussion of the "highest kinds" Plato seems to be developing a positive answer to the ensuing question, What is it to attach a negated verb or predicate to a subject? The somethings that verbs convey belong to one or other of a set of "families," so that to deny something of Theaetetus is thereby positively to ascribe to him some other member of the family to which the negated something belongs. If Theaetetus is *not* a fish, then there is something else in the family of fish-or-bird-or-man, etc., that he *is.* The denial of one predicate entails the affirmation of some other "brother" predicate and *vice versa.* Negative truths are the obverses of affirmative truths and *vice versa.* Negativeness, far from being the death of thought and statement, is an essential part of their daily lives.

Here then we find Plato investigating the bi-polar structures of integral truths and falsehoods. He is no longer spellbound by the idea of special entities, such as the concept-objects, or Forms, of his earlier days.

Indeed in one passage in the dialogue he seems to hold himself aloof from the "friends of the Forms," whom he criticizes for their reluctance to concede the reality of any objects other than their timeless concept-objects. Doubtless one thing that moved Plato in this new direction was the impotence of the Theory of Forms to cope with Parmenides' difficulties with negation. For if there cannot be negative things, there cannot be negative concept-objects either. But then there would be no place in the reality constituted by these concept-objects for not being so-and-so; and consequently no negative truths, and therewith no affirmative truths, could be known or thought or stated about even these concept-objects themselves. Only if verbs or predicates are *not* names, even of concept-objects, can truth and falsehood, affirmation and negation, knowledge and opinion be accounted for. The road is now opened for Aristotle's inquiries into the implications and non-implications of truths by other truths.

Moral and Political Theory

The dialogues of Plato's first period often have ethical subjects for their disputation themes. Sometimes, as in the *Laches* and *Charmides,* Socrates demolishes a succession of attempted definitions of moral virtues, for example, of courage and self-control. Sometimes, as in the *Protagoras* and *Meno,* Socrates discusses the thesis that virtue can be taught. But the subject of the *Lysis* is friendship, that of the *Hippias Major* is beauty, while the *Gorgias* is concerned with the nature and worth of rhetoric. These themes are not ethical.

As the finale of an elenctic debate is a confutation, a dialogue exhibiting the Socratic Method in action cannot yield a positive theory. It is often said that in these dialogues Socrates is made to teach the doctrine that virtue is knowledge. But in the *Protagoras* and *Meno* Socrates argues against this equation. For knowledge is what can be taught; so if virtue cannot be taught, it is not knowledge. Elsewhere, as in the *Euthydemus,* Socrates does argue in the other direction.

In the *Gorgias* the young interlocutor, Polus, champions the sub-thesis that it is better to do wrong than to suffer it, and Socrates duly confutes this sub-thesis. In the *Protagoras* Socrates had, to our surprise, argued for a hedonistic calculus, like that of Bentham, but in the *Gorgias* and the much later *Philebus* his arguments are anti-hedonistic. It is in the *Republic* that Plato first puts forward a constructive ethical theory. A dominant theme of the *Republic* is the nature and worth of justice. In Book I, which is of the familiar elenctic pattern, some cynical views are defended by the sophist Thrasymachus and are duly confuted, though some of Socrates' argumentative tactics leave us uneasy. In the remainder of the *Republic* there is almost no questioner-answerer disputation; instead Plato makes Socrates give a positive definition of justice. He defines it, as self-control had been defined in the *Charmides,* as "the performance of one's proper function"—almost as "minding one's own business."

In the Republic,

and especially in the political core of Books II–V,

Plato delineates his famous Ideal State,

or "Callipolis."

STRUCTURE OF THE SOUL. Socrates builds up a description of the constitution of the human soul paralleling his description of the constitution of the Ideal State. As the Ideal State is a coordination or integration of three different classes, each with its own economic and political role, so the soul is an integration of three different parts or elements, each with a role proper to it in the conduct of personal life. All people have in them the appetitive or impulsive element, the element of thought or reason, and, between these two, an element capable of curbing impulses and cravings and capable also of taking orders from thought or reason. The name of the in-between element, *thumos,* is sometimes unsatisfactorily rendered by "anger," sometimes by "spirit" (in the sense in which a horse may be spirited). This tripartite structure of the individual soul matches, and not by accident, the tripartite structure of the Ideal State in which the auxiliaries—the soldier-police—keep the lowest class in order and are themselves subject to the direction of the educated governors or kings.

JUSTICE AND HAPPINESS. This political model gives Plato a sort of psychological schema for the conflicts and the controls which form the content of the moral life. Just as in his political thinking Plato sometimes treats the working class as a deplorable necessity, so in his ethical thinking he is inclined to treat our impulses and desires in similar fashion. "Desire" and "pleasure," like our term "passions," are often used as terms of abuse, as if the ideal life, if we could only attain it, would be purged of these anti-rational forces. His theory, however, does not require this hyper-puritanism. That a man should not be a mere weathercock to his fears, likings and hankerings does not entail that ideally he should be screened from them. Though gales may sink the ill-rigged or ill-steered sailing ship, no ship can sail without winds. Winds can be too weak as well as too strong.

Still applying his model of the Ideal State, Plato is now able to reach the ethical conclusion that as political well-being requires the regulated cooperation of its three classes, so personal well-being requires the rationally coordinated functioning of the soul's three parts or elements. This coordination of different functions, that is, justice, is not merely a means to a good life, which might, with luck, be had without it. The functionings of these parts or elements, in their proper coordination, are what constitute well-being—somewhat as harmony is not something that just happens to be necessary for music; it is the relation between the notes without which there would be no music.

PLEASURE. Of great psychological as well as ethical interest are Plato's frequent discussions of the worth and nature of pleasure. In the *Protagoras* Socrates champions, with apparent seriousness, a hedonistic calculus according to which the goodness of anything reduces to the long-term excess of the pleasures over the pains that it causes. In this view, no pleasure could itself be bad; it could only be inferior to a greater or a more enduring pleasure. Yet in the *Gorgias* Socrates argues that some pleasures are not merely relatively inferior but are absolutely bad. In the *Republic, Timaeus* and *Philebus* Plato gives an account of what pleasure is. With his eye on the pleasantness of various kinds of replenishment and recuperation, like eating when hungry and resting when tired, Plato argues that, with certain reservations, pleasure *is* the process of being restored to a "natural" condition. Aristotle frequently criticizes this definition.

Partly, though not entirely, on the basis of this definition Plato, in his *Philebus,* argues that the place of pleasure in the best life, far from being paramount, is inferior and subordinate to the place of thought and knowledge. Neither is all-sufficient, but the contribution of pleasure is a lot lower on the scale than that of thought and knowledge. One reason for its relatively lowly placing is derived from the doctrine of the limit and the unlimited, the *peras* and the *apeiron.* Some things, like temperature and weight, admit of continuous quantitative variation, in the sense that for a thing of any particular weight there are or might be things of greater and lesser weights. On the other hand, there are no degrees of such notions as one ton or seven pounds. The precise "How heavy?" of a thing fixes it at a determinate point on the scale of heavier—lighter. There is no more-or-less of this determinate weight. Impulses, desires, feelings, pleasure and pain are like weight or temperature. Things can give us more or less pleasure or pain, and we can be very or slightly scared or angry. If for a person in a particular situation there is a proper determinate degree of an impulse or a feeling, this determinate degree has to be fixed by some standard out-side that variably intense impulse or feeling itself. Nor can the scale of temperature by itself determine which point on that scale is the right temperature for this or that end, for example, for baking bread or for bodily health or comfort. It is from this application of the general theory of the limit and the unlimited that Aristotle's doctrine of the mean is developed. Of course, the general theory of the limit and the unlimited has applications in fields quite remote from the special field of ethics. It is, for example, largely in terms of the two polar notions of the limit and the unlimited that Aristotle tries to refute Zeno's seeming proofs of the impossibility of motion.

However, for what concerns us here, Plato tries to show that the place of pleasure is lower than that of thought and knowledge, since the right "How much?" is fixed by thought and knowledge for, *inter alia,* pleasure. At the end of the *Philebus* Plato attempts to describe the Good, or what constitutes the best life, in terms of such notions as truth, beauty, measure, harmony, proportion and order. The description remains somewhat nebulous, but it is interesting in suggesting that Plato, like ourselves, has found that his earlier parallel accounts of the Ideal State and of the individual soul in terms of a coordinated division of labor had been inadequate. Regulated departmentalization may be a necessary, but it is not a sufficient condition of the best life.

POLITICS. We can be reasonably sure that for some period during his younger days Plato had not only had political ambitions but had also tried to engage in active politics. The triumph of the popular party shut the door on Plato's hopes and plans, and henceforth his unabating and often vitriolic opposition to the democratic cause had to be literary and pedagogic. The dialogues of his first period are almost entirely unpolitical, save for the finale of his *Gorgias,* his *Crito,* and some incidental animadversions, for example in the *Meno,* on Pericles and Periclean democracy. It is in his two mammoth dialogues, the *Republic* and the *Laws,* together with his *Politicus,* that we find Plato's political diagnoses and prescriptions, ideals and antipathies.

THE IDEAL STATE: THE REPUBLIC. In the *Republic,* and especially in the political core of Books II–V, Plato delineates his famous Ideal State, or "Callipolis." Starting from the elementary but developing economy of a normal rustic community, Plato moves on to design a full-fledged city-state, the like of which has never yet existed and may never exist in the future, though some of its features are borrowed from the constitution of Sparta. Applying the economic principle of the division of labor, Plato sets up in his utopia three classes: the guardians, or ruling class; the auxiliary class;

and the laborers. Most of Plato's recommendations concern only the ruling class, i.e., the governors and their auxiliaries, the police-soldiers. Its members, women as well as men, possess complete political authority, in return for which they live a garrison life, with no private property and not even private families. Their posterity is arranged for on stud lines. The other members of the state have no say in its government and are not entitled to its higher education. Their whole mission is to be farmers and artisans, but, significantly, not sailors. The guardians are trained and employed for external warfare and internal police work, but not only for these functions. Unlike the rulers in Sparta, its rulers have to go through a grueling intellectual training, resulting, at least for the select few, in their becoming philosophers. The Ideal State depends both for its creation and for its preservation upon its kings' being philosophers or philosophers' being its kings. For they know and only they know wherein the public weal consists.

The avowed object of the Republic *as a whole*

is to exhibit the nature of justice,

both within the state and within the individual soul.

The Ideal State is therefore, constitutionally, a rigid aristocracy of power, intellect and breeding but not of estates or families. No provisions are made for any reforms being made to this constitution after its creation. It is of its *raison d'être* to be static and immutable. It is therefore disheartening to hear, in Books VIII and IX, that even this supposedly self-perpetuating aristocracy is doomed by some numerological mystery eventually to degenerate through plutocracy into democracy and tyranny. Apparently in these books Plato was thinking not so much of his dream constitution as of actual contemporary Greek states, although, as Aristotle proves in his *Politics,* it was not true in fact that democracies always declined into tyrannies or that tyrannies never emerged out of plutocracies or aristocracies. Presumably Plato's account of the single-track course of this inevitable degeneration was minatory in intent rather than diagnostic or prophetic. It was certainly not utopian.

Since Plato himself tells us in *Republic* VI that philosophers are generally held to be politically useless or even politically harmful, and since the Athenian aristocratic families had long since lost their powers, privileges, and very often their wealth, it is hard to suppose that Plato even hoped that his plan for his Ideal State would make any difference to the actual course of politics in Athens. So little is said in the *Republic* of the

lives to be led by *hoi polloi* in Callipolis that Plato could not have been trying to attract the Athenian demos to his elite-governed model state. It is a relevant fact that in the whole of the *Republic* nothing is said of fleets or sailors forming any part of the war strength of the Ideal State. The guardians have had soldiers' training. They include no admirals, and Callipolis has no Piraeus.

Was the *Republic* no more than the compensation dream of a politically thwarted aristocrat who happened to be in love with philosophy? Or did Plato write his *Republic* to interest and in some degree to influence some state in which the great families were still dominant? Certain clues suggest that the *Republic,* or rather the political gist of Books II–V, had originally been composed for delivery in Syracuse. In the conversational opening of the *Timaeus* Socrates gives his companions, of whom one is a Sicilian and another an Italian, a précis of a discourse that he had given on the previous day. This is a précis of the section of the *Republic* that has just been mentioned. Socrates' précis is then followed by the preamble to the unfinished *Critias,* which was to give the history of a war, "9,000 years ago," between Hellas, headed by Athens, and Atlantis. The description of Atlantis is an only slightly romanticized description of Carthage, against whose eastward expansion Syracuse, under Dionysius the Elder and his son, was the sole bulwark for the western Greeks.

Both Socrates' précis, and the preamble to the *Critias* are tacked, quite incongruously, on to the *Timaeus,* a cosmological and physiological address which we have independent reasons for thinking was composed by Plato in Syracuse in 367–366 and delivered before Dionysius the Younger near the end of Plato's sojourn in Syracuse. According to this interpretation the *Republic* would contain a positive political message—namely, that the Sicilian elite should preserve its dominance by giving up its possessions and eliminating its inter-family feuds and becoming instead an order or brotherhood of soldier-philosophers.

Plato vaults rather cavalierly from the economic principle that productive efficiency is maximized by coordinated specialization to the quite different principles (*a*) that each individual person is constituted by nature to perform just one social and economic role and not another; and (*b*) that people's souls are, in an analogous way, microcosms composed of parts or elements, each having its own natural function or role. Both political and individual well-being depend on the proper coordination of these constitutionally different roles. A society is healthy when each of its classes performs its peculiar function; and a soul or person is, so to speak, properly self-governed when each of its parts makes its peculiar contribution to its microcosmic commonwealth, without trespassing on the domains of the other parts. What his reason is to a man at his best, the guardians are to the Ideal State. Both individuals and states are organic wholes, and their parts stand to these wholes somewhat as the several organs of a creature stand to that creature—or rather as they stand if and only if all is internally well with it. This semi-biological view of the body politic is apt to appeal less to those who are told that they are constituted by nature to be only the body's thews or feet than to those who are assured that their role is that of the body's eyes or brain.

The avowed object of the *Republic* as a whole is to exhibit the nature of justice, both within the state and within the individual soul. Socrates undertakes the task of proving that justice is no mere means to well-being, as regular exercise is to health. It is, rather, an essential part of well-being. The man who thinks that if there were no risks of punishment or other ill consequences, he would choose to be unjust, shows that he does not realize that the idea of well-being without justice is like the idea, not of health without exercise, but of health without vigor. The elucidation of the concept of justice in terms of the coordination of specialized functions is meant both to give support to and to get support from the partly independent idea that in the Ideal State there would be three sharply demarcated classes of citizens, which in their disciplined coordination would render that state economically efficient, strong in war and safe from revolutions.

THE *LAWS*. Plato's Ideal State is a fairyland model rather than a plan. His *Laws,* on the contrary, is a would-be practicable plan. Under this "second-best" constitution the elite may possess modest estates, and private families are allowed. The lower ranks of society now have some political rights and powers, though careful regulations ensure that they will not attain political control. The rulers, though decently educated, are not required to be philosophers. The women are not warriors. Much of the *Laws* is a sort of Blue Book, in which detailed rules and regulations are laid down for the conduct of elections, legal proceedings, religious ceremonies, markets, schools and irrigation. Even the regimen of pregnant mothers and the games of infants are all but ordained. Comparatively few general issues of political theory are discussed. As a whole the *Laws* is a piece of detailed programmatic legislation. As its spokesman declares that the polity that he is to design is only second best to the Ideal State, scholars have naturally tended to concentrate their attention on the more utopian of the two schemes.

Early in the *Laws* the discussion leader had surprised his interlocutors and us by asserting, in the teeth of Books VIII and IX of the *Republic,* that for the realization of his planned polity there was required the conjunction of a great legislator and a good tyrant. This, with some corroborative clues, suggests that Plato wrote his *Laws* for practical adoption by Dionysius the Younger and that he may have been invited or encouraged by the young tyrant to do so. If so, the defeat of Dionysius by Dion in 356 made this legislative program a dead letter. Plato's uncompleted conversationalization of the *Laws* may have been intended to salvage as literature a work which had been composed as a realizable constitutional blueprint.

Greek prose reached its peak in the writing of Plato.

It is almost true to say that in

his philosophical writing Plato did not develop,

he created the art of incarnating

abstract argumentative thought in prose.

The *Laws,* outside Book X, is not even intended for philosophers. In its concrete legal, social and administrative prescriptions, however, students of Greek history and politics can find a good deal of interest. For inevitably Plato sometimes copies and often just improves on laws, regulations, codes, customs and expedients already obtaining in Athens or other Greek states. Political actualities can be read through Plato's political recommendations. Plato's limitations as a political theorist can be detected in his unquestioning retention, in principle if not in detail, of Greek ways which do not seem to us necessary conditions of social and political life. The state that Plato is designing is still a city-state. That the heyday of the city-state was already over was never dreamed by Plato, any more than it was by Aristotle. No modern statesman or political theorist would suggest remodeling Canada, say, or Russia or Ghana according to the prescriptions of the *Laws*—or even, retrospectively, Macedon or Rome.

Plato as a Writer

Greek prose reached its peak in the writing of Plato. His flexibility, his rich vocabulary, his easy colloquialism and his high rhetoric, his humor, irony, pathos, gravity, bluntness, delicacy and occasional ferocity, his mastery of metaphor, simile and myth, his swift delineation of character—his combination of these and other qualities puts him beyond rivalry.

Some of Plato's compositions, such as the *Menexenus, Apology, Symposium* and the first part of the *Phaedrus,* belong to rhetoric. In the *Critias* and much of the *Timaeus* the writing is descriptive. But it is Plato's philosophical writing that is historically of first importance. It is almost true to say that in this field Plato did not develop, he created the art of incarnating abstract argumentative thought in prose.

We should distinguish two steps in this creation.

(1) In his early, elenctic dialogues Plato gives dramatic form to dialectical debates. He does not, save often in the *Lysis* and occasionally elsewhere, just sandwich dialectic with drama; he so blends them that the tussle between persons is itself the pitting of counterarguments against arguments. The conversations are duels, and the duelists' weapons are arguments. We hear the *pros* and the *contras* of the debate in the challenges and the resistances, the sarcasms and the sulks of the debaters. Their very tones of voice, petulant, scornful, complacent, worried, eager and flabbergasted, ring to us of the reactions of human disputants to the twists and turns of the argumentation. When a cogent argument is produced, a man has scored against a man; and when a man has lost a point to an opponent, a weak argument has been rebutted. The wits and tempers of the debaters and the logical merits and demerits of their arguments are depicted on one canvas and by the same brush strokes. In that moment when our hearts are for or against Socrates or Thrasymachus, our heads are for or against the conceptual points that they make against one another. We are in one breath partisans for or against persons and judges of their premises and conclusions. Our hero is also a dialectical tactician, and he is our hero partly because his dialectical tactics are good. He gets a dual allegiance from us; hence the wrench that we feel when we find Socrates occasionally scoring an invalid point against Protagoras or Thrasymachus. Our twin allegiances are here at variance. The young Athenians, for whom especially Plato wrote these dialogues, must, like us, have taken sides and must thereby effortlessly have made their hero's arguments their own. A dialogue did not have to be committed to memory. It could not be forgotten.

(2) In Plato's late dialogues the tussle between persons has nearly disappeared. Socrates in most of the *Philebus* and in much of the *Theaetetus,* and the Eleatic stranger in the *Sophist* and *Politicus* are not dueling, and their interlocutors are not being maneuvered into surrender. So little dramatic life is in these dialogues that we can wonder whether their recitals interested any of the auditors other than the philosophically sophisticated young men from the Academy. The Eleatic stranger and even the Socrates of the *Philebus* have almost no character. Much the same is true of the *Parmenides.* In the discussion in Part I old Parmenides is a powerful de-

structive philosopher, but one who strikes us as almost the pure professional philosopher. We do not like him or dislike him. In Part II, though the discussion reverts to the old pattern of question–answer disputation, it is completely formalized and depersonalized. Contradictory conclusions are deduced from theses, but there is no battling for these theses or against these conclusions. Here the questioner and answerer have no tones of voice. This part of the dialogue must be literally an Academic exercise.

The undramatic character of these late dialogues should not, however, be construed as evidence merely of the failing literary powers of the now aged Plato. He is no longer wholeheartedly composing dialogues for the benefit of lay audiences, but this is only partly because he is losing his exoteric touch. He is now composing for the colleagues and the partly trained students in the Academy. These dialogues are, consciously or unconsciously, adjusted to recipients like those to whom Aristotle's lecture courses are given. For such sophisticated recipients abstract issues generate their own intellectual excitements and their own impersonal partisanships. The impersonality of Plato's late dialogues, like that of Aristotle's lectures, reflects the emergence of philosophy as an inquiry with an impetus, with techniques and even with an academic curriculum of its own. Plato is now creating professional philosophical prose. As disputing for the sake of victory gives way to discussion for the sake of discovery, so the literature of the elenctic duel gives way to the literature of cooperative philosophical investigation. The university has come into being.

BIBLIOGRAPHY

Editions and Translations

A critical edition of the Greek text of Plato's works may be found in *Platonis Opera,* John Burnet, ed., 5 vols (Oxford, 1899–1907). There are improved Greek texts by various editors with French translations in the Budé series, 13 vols. in 25 parts (Paris, 1920–1956), and with English translations in the Loeb series, in 12 vols. (London and New York, 1921–1953). The dialogues in English may be found in *The Dialogues of Plato,* translated with analyses and introductions by Benjamin Jowett, 4th ed., rev., 4 vols. (Oxford, 1953), D. J. Allan and H. E. Dale, gen. eds.

Modern editions and translations of, and commentaries on, individual dialogues include the following: *Gorgias,* revised text with introduction, commentary, and appendix on Socrates, Callicles, and Nietzsche by E. R. Dodds (Oxford, 1959); *Plato's Phaedo,* translated with introduction, notes, and appendices by R. S. Bluck (London, 1955); *Plato's Phaedo,* translated, with introduction and commentary, by R. Hackforth (Cambridge, 1955); *Plato's Phaedrus,* translated, with commentary, by R. Hackforth (Cambridge, 1952); *Plato's Examination of Pleasure,* translation of the *Philebus,* with introduction and commentary, by R. Hackforth (Cambridge, 1945); *Philebus and Epinomis,* translated, with introduction, by A. E. Taylor, edited by

Raymond Klibansky with Guido Calogero and A. C. Lloyd (London and Edinburgh, 1956); *The Republic of Plato,* translated, with introduction and notes, by F. M. Cornford (Oxford, 1941); *Plato's Statesman,* translated by J. B. Skemp (New Haven, 1952); *Plato's Cosmology,* the *Timaeus* translated, with running commentary by F. M. Cornford (London, 1937); *Plato's Theory of Knowledge,* the *Theaetetus* and *Sophist* translated, with commentary by F. M. Cornford (London, 1935); *Plato and Parmenides,* the *Parmenides* translated, with running commentary, by F. M. Cornford (New York and London, 1939); *Plato's Cretan City: A Historical Interpretation of the Laws,* by G. R. Morrow (Princeton, 1960).

For the *Platonic Letters* see Ludwig Edelstein, *Plato's Seventh Letter* (Leiden, 1966), and G. R. Morrow, *Studies in the Platonic Epistles,* translation with commentary (Urbana, Ill., 1935).

General Accounts

Bluck, R. S., *Plato's Life and Thought.* London, 1949.
Field, G. C., *Plato and His Contemporaries.* London, 1930.
———, *The Philosophy of Plato.* Oxford, 1949.
Grube, G. M. A., *Plato's Thought.* London, 1935.
Koyré, Alexandre, *Introduction à la lecture de Platon,* translated by L. C. Rosenfield as *Discovering Plato.* New York, 1945.
Robin, Léon, *Platon.* Paris, 1935.
Shorey, Paul, *What Plato Said.* Chicago, 1933.
Taylor, A. E., *Plato: The Man and His Work.* London, 1926.
Wilamowitz-Moellendorf, Ulrich von, *Platon,* 2 vols. Berlin, 1919; 3d ed., Vol. I, Berlin, 1948.
Zeller, Eduard, *Die Philosophie der Griechen,* 6th ed. Hildesheim, 1963.

Particular Aspects of Plato's Work

Allen, R. E., ed., *Studies in Plato's Metaphysics.* London, 1965. Reprints articles by Cherniss, Ryle, Vlastos, Geach, Owen, et al.
Bambrough, Renford, ed., *New Essays on Plato and Aristotle.* London, 1965. Contains articles specially written for it by Vlastos, Hare, Ryle, Owen, MacKinnon, et al.
Cherniss, H. F., *Aristotle's Criticism of Plato and the Academy.* Baltimore, 1944.
———, *The Riddle of the Early Academy.* Berkeley, 1945.
Gould, John, *The Development of Plato's Ethics.* Cambridge, 1955.
Lasserre, François, *The Birth of Mathematics in the Age of Plato.* London, 1964.
Merlan, Philip, *From Platonism to Neoplatonism.* The Hague, 1953.
Murphy, N. R., *The Interpretation of Plato's Republic.* Oxford, 1951.
Robinson, Richard, *Plato's Earlier Dialectic,* 2d. ed. Oxford, 1953.
Ross, W. D., *Plato's Theory of Ideas.* Oxford, 1953.
Ryle, Gilbert, "Letters and Syllables in Plato." *Philosophical Review,* Vol. 59 (1960), 431–451.
Skemp, J. B., *The Theory of Motion in Plato's Later Dialogues.* Cambridge, 1942.
Solmsen, Friedrich, *Plato's Theology.* Ithaca, N.Y., 1942.
Stenzel, Julius, *Plato's Method of Dialectic,* translated from the 2d German ed. (1931) by D. J. Allan. Oxford, 1940.
Stenzel, Julius, *Zahl und Gestalt bei Platon und Aristoteles,* 2d ed. Leipzig, 1933. Translated by D. J. Allan as *Number and Form in Plato and Aristotle.* Oxford, 1940.
Tate, J., "Plato and 'Imitation.'" *Classical Quarterly,* Vol. 26 (1932), 161–169.
Vlastos, Gregory, Introduction to *Plato's Protagoras,* Benjamin Jowett's translation, extensively revised by Martin Ostwald, edited by Gregory Vlastos. New York, 1956, Pp. 7–58.
———, "Anamnesis in the Meno." *Dialogue,* Vol. 4 (1965), 143–167.

Wedberg, A. E. C., *Plato's Philosophy of Mathematics.* Stockholm, 1955.

Bibliographies

Cherniss, H. F., "Plato Studies, 1950–57." *Lustrum,* Vol. 4 (1959), 5–308; Vol. 5 (1960), 323–648.
Rosenmeyer, T. G., "Platonic Scholarship, 1945–1955." *Classical Weekly,* Vol. 50 (1957), 172–182, 185–196, 197–201, 209–211.

The following annotated bibliography prepared by Richard Kraut provides a review of some of the major scholarly works on Plato since the publication of the Encyclopedia of Philosophy. *For a review of recent scholarly work on Socrates, please note the entry on Socrates.*

For general overviews of Plato's thought, see G. Vlastos, ed., *Plato,* 2 vols., (Garden City, NY, 1971), J. Gosling, *Plato* (London, 1973), and R. Kraut, *The Cambridge Companion to Plato* (Cambridge, 1992).

For treatments of some of the central themes of Plato's metaphysics, see N. White, *Plato on Knowledge and Reality* (Indianapolis, 1976), R. Patterson, *Image and Reality in Plato's Metaphysics* (Indianapolis, 1985), T. Penner, *The Ascent From Nominalism* (Dordrecht, 1987), J. Moravesik, *Plato and Platonism* (Oxford, 1992), G. Fine, *On Ideas* (Oxford, 1993), and M. McCabe, *Plato's Individuals* (Princeton, NJ, 1994). His later metaphysical development is treated by K. Sayre, *Plato's Late Ontology* (Princeton, NJ, 1983) and K. Dorter, *Form and Good in Plato's Eleatic Dialogues* (Berkeley, 1994).

For general treatments of Plato's moral philosophy, see T. Irwin, *Plato's Moral Theory* (Oxford, 1977), M. Nussbaum, *The Fragility of Goodness* (Cambridge, 1986), T. Irwin, *Plato's Ethics* (Oxford, 1995). His political philosophy is surveyed in G. Klosko, *The Development of Plato's Political Theory* (New York, 1986). His attack on the artists is the subject of I. Murdoch, *The Fire and the Sun* (Oxford, 1977). His conception of love is discussed by G. Santas, *Plato and Freud* (Oxford, 1988) and A. Price, *Love and Friendship in Plato and Aristotle* (Oxford, 1989).

The two most influential scholars of recent decades who wrote in English about Plato were G. Vlastos and G. Owen. The former's essays about Plato can be found in *Platonic Studies* (Princeton, NJ, 1981) and *Studies in Greek Philosophy,* vol 2, edited by D. Graham (Princeton, NJ, 1995). The latter's essays on Plato are collected together in *Logic, Science and Dialectic,* edited by M. Nussbaum (Ithaca, NY, 1986).

For treatments of individual dialogues, see:
Laws: R. Stalley, *An Introduction to Plato's Laws* (Oxford, 1983), T. Saunders, *Plato's Penal Code* (Oxford, 1991);
Parmenides: R. Allen, *Plato's Parmenides* (Minneapolis, 1983), Mitchell Miller, *Plato's Parmenides* (Princeton, NJ, 1986), C. Meinwald, *Plato's Parmenides* (Oxford, 1991);
Phaedo: D. Gallop, *Plato, Phaedo* (Oxford, 1975), D. Bostock, *Plato's Phaedo* (Oxford, 1986);
Phaedrus: C. Griswold, *Self-Knowledge in Plato's Phaedrus* (New Haven, 1986), G. Ferrari, *Listening to the Cicadas* (Cambridge, 1987);
Philebus: G. Striker, *Peras und Apeiron* (Göttingen, 1970), G. Gosling, *Plato: Philebus* (Oxford, 1975);
Republic: N. White, *A Companion to Plato's Republic* (Indianapolis, 1979), J. Annas, *An Introduction to Plato's Republic* (Oxford, 1981), C. Reeve, *Philosopher-Kings* (Princeton, NJ, 1988);
Symposium: S. Rosen, *Plato's Symposium* (New Haven, 1987);
Timaeus: G. Vlastos, *Plato's Universe* (Seattle, 1975);

Theaetetus: J. McDowell, *Plato: Theaetetus* (Oxford, 1973), D. Bostock, *Plato's Theaetetus* (Oxford, 1988), M. Burnyeat, *The Theaetetus of Plato* (Indianapolis, 1990).

Chronological and stylometric issues are treated by L. Brandwood, *The Chronology of Plato's Dialogues* (Cambridge, 1990) and G. Ledger *Re-counting Plato* (Oxford, 1989).

Different methods of interpreting the dialogues are discussed in E. Tigerstedt, *Interpreting Plato* (Uppsala, 1977), C. Griswold, ed., *Platonic Writings, Platonic Readings* (London, 1988), and J. Klagge and N. Smith, eds., *Methods of Interpreting Plato and his Dialogues* (Oxford, 1992).

– GILBERT RYLE

PLATONISM, MATHEMATICAL

At least with reference to mathematics, "Platonism" in its most general meaning affirms the objective existence of abstract mathematical entities and the objectivity of truth about them. The terms can be specified in various ways. The most interesting is to understand objectivity in terms of philosophical realism. This gives rise to a contrast of Platonism and constructivism, where different degrees of the one and the other influence what mathematics is acceptable. Michael Dummett (1973) has given a new version of the intuitionist critique of Platonism, with its rejection of the logical law of excluded middle, using meaning-theoretic arguments. Dummett's arguments help to make clear that acceptance of nonconstructive classical mathematics, at least where impredicative set-theoretic devices are involved, is bound up with realistic conceptions.

We should distinguish between

Platonism with regard to mathematical objects,

and Platonism with regard to truth.

We should distinguish, however, between Platonism with regard to mathematical objects (Platonism$_1$), as opposed to regarding them as in some way constructions of our own, and Platonism with regard to truth (Platonism$_2$), which would hold that any properly formulated mathematical question has a true or false answer, whether or not it is possible to discover it. Intuitionism rejects both. Some classic Platonist arguments, such as those given in defense of impredicative concept formations by Ramsey, Bernays, and Gödel, are primarily defenses of Platonism$_1$. Dummett's primary target is Platonism$_2$. Many of Gödel's arguments, particularly in his discussion of the continuum problem (1964), are in defense of Platonism$_2$. Gödel's position has become much better understood in recent years, in particular as

more documentation has become available (cf. Gödel, 1995).

It is possible to hold Platonism$_1$ and embrace classical logic and set theory without accepting Platonism$_2$. W. V. O. Quine holds such a position in the context of a view of meaning that has much in common with Dummett's but includes a holism that Dummett rejects. Other recent writers (Tait, 1986, and Maddy, 1992) seem also to hold a view of this kind, for quite different reasons (Maddy, 1989 and 1990 defend Platonism$_2$).

Recent research in mathematical logic has some bearing on these issues. Platonism$_2$ hangs in the air if we have no hope of finding principles to decide questions in set theory that are undecidable by currently standard axioms. The continuum hypothesis (CH) was shown to be thus undecidable by Gödel and Paul Cohen; Gödel nonetheless hoped that new axioms would be found to decide it. Classical problems of descriptive set theory, also shown undecidable, are decided in a satisfying way by strong axioms of infinity. But these axioms leave CH undecided. It is still not known whether persuasive principles that decide CH will be found.

Other research has shown that much more of ordinary mathematics than had previously been thought can be developed in quite weak theories that can be understood in a non-Platonist way. Although mathematically straightforward statements that can be proved only by impredicative means can be given, they are not easy to come by without using such concepts in their formulation.

"Platonism" is also used in a weaker sense, to contrast with nominalism, that is (in this context) the rejection of abstract objects, at least abstract mathematical objects. Nominalism faces the difficulty that the language of mathematics speaks of objects, and it is hard to imagine how it could be so understood that these objects are not abstract. In this sense Platonism amounts to no more than accepting mathematical language at face value and accepting at least a substantial part of what is affirmed in mathematics as true. This would appear to make it a truism, as some writers (e.g., Tait, 1986) in fact say, but some nominalist strategies work by not accepting mathematical language at face value, and the most influential attempt of recent years (Field, 1980) denies that central parts of mathematics (arithmetic, analysis, set theory) are true and that truth is what the mathematician aims at.

Is there some difficulty with Platonism, even in this weak sense, that motivates the nominalist strategy? Two difficulties have had currency in recent years, both most dramatically presented by Benacerraf. The first (Benacerraf, 1965) is that mathematical objects do not have a well-defined identity, as is shown by the fact that, in foundational work, different constructions of number systems in terms of other objects (e.g., sets or numbers of other, perhaps more basic, systems) "identify" given numbers with different objects, and there seems to be no objective ground on which to choose between them. This fact is a reflection of the general fact that what matters in mathematics is structure, so that, for mathematical purposes, a system of numbers can be any system of objects with relations on them satisfying purely formal conditions. This observation has been used as the basis for programs to eliminate reference to mathematical objects, which are thus in the direction of nominalism even if not strictly nominalistic. But one can also reply that this is simply how mathematical objects are; they can at least metaphorically be described as positions in patterns (Resnik, 1981); the phenomenon pointed to is an instance of Quine's (1968) inscrutability of reference.

The second difficulty is that of giving an adequate epistemology for knowledge of abstract objects, particularly if what is demanded is a naturalistic theory (cf. Benacerraf, 1973). It is not obvious that reference to abstract objects is what is decisive for this difficulty; for example, one might discern it for logical truths that do not involve an abstract ontology or for statements involving some of the devices that have been proposed to eliminate reference to mathematical objects, such as modality. Moreover, it arises with more force (as Benacerraf admits) for stronger mathematical theories, embodying Platonism in the stronger sense considered above.

[See also Constructivism; Dummett, Michael; Gödel, Kurt; Intuitionism; Mathematical Logic; Metaphysics; Modality; Quine, Willard Van Orman; Realism; Set Theory.]

BIBLIOGRAPHY

Benacerraf, P. "What Numbers Could Not Be," *Philosophical Review*, Vol. 74 (1965), 47–73. Rept. in P. Benacerraf and H. Putnam, eds., *Philosophy of Mathematics: Selected Readings*, 2d ed. (Cambridge, 1983).

———. "Mathematical Truth," *Journal of Philosophy*, Vol. 70 (1973), 661–79. Rept. in P. Benacerraf and H. Putnam, eds., *Philosophy of Mathematics: Selected Readings*, 2d ed. (Cambridge, 1983).

———, and H. Putnam, eds. *Philosophy of Mathematics: Selected Readings*, 2d ed. Cambridge, 1983.

Bernays, P. "Sur le platonisme dans les mathématiques," *L'Enseignement mathématique*, Vol. 34 (1935), 52–69. Translated by C. Parsons in P. Benacerraf and H. Putnam, eds., *Philosophy of Mathematics: Selected Readings*, 2d ed. (Cambridge, 1983).

Dummett, M. "The Philosophical Basis of Intuitionistic Logic," in *Truth and Other Enigmas* (London, 1978).

Field, H. *Science without Numbers: A Defense of Nominalism*. Princeton, NJ, 1980.

Gödel, K. "Russell's Mathematical Logic," In P. A. Schilpp, ed., *The Philosophy of Bertrand Russell* (Evanston, IL, 1994). Rept. in *Collected Works*, Vol. 2.

———. "What Is Cantor's Continuum Problem?," rev. ed., in P. Benacerraf and H. Putnam, eds., *Philosophy of Mathematics: Selected Readings* (Englewood Cliffs, NJ, 1964; 2d ed., Cambridge, 1983). Rept. in *Collected Works*, Vol. 2.

———. *Collected Works*, S. Feferman et al., eds. Oxford, Vol. 1, 1986; Vol. 2, 1990; Vol. 3, 1995.

Maddy, P. "The Roots of Contemporary Platonism," *Journal of Symbolic Logic*, Vol. 54 (1989), 1, 121–44.

———. *Realism in Mathematics*. Oxford, 1990.

———. "Indispensability and Practice," *Journal of Philosophy*, Vol. 89 (1992), 275–89.

Quine, W. V. O. *Ontological Relativity and Other Essays*. New York, 1968.

Resnik, M. "Mathematics as a Science of Patterns: Ontology and Reference," *Noûs*, Vol. 15 (1981), 529–50.

Tait, W. W. "Truth and Proof: The Platonism of Mathematics," *Synthese*, Vol. 69 (1986), 341–70.

– CHARLES PARSONS

PLOTINUS

Plotinus (205–270), usually considered the founder of Neoplatonism. Plotinus was probably born in Lykopolis, Upper Egypt, and he may have been a Hellenized Egyptian rather than a Greek. He turned to the study of philosophy when he was 28. Disappointed by several teachers in Alexandria, he was directed by a friend to Ammonius Saccas, who made a profound impresson on

Because the content of Plotinus's writings seems to point to a complete absence of political interests, the problem of Plotinus's involvement in affairs of state is controversial. (Corbis/Araldo de Luca)

him. Of Ammonius's teachings we know extremely little, but a promising line of investigation has been opened up in a comparison of Plotinus's doctrines with those of Origen the Christian, also a student of Ammonius. Of other students of Ammonius, Origen the Pagan and Longinus deserve special mention. Plotinus was Ammonius's pupil for 11 years. He left Ammonius to join the expeditionary army of Emperor Gordianus III that was to march against Persia, hoping to acquire firsthand knowledge of Persian and Indian wisdom, in which he had become interested through Ammonius. When Gordianus was slain in Persia in 244, probably at the instigation of his successor, Philip the Arabian, Plotinus had to flee from the army camp—which could mean that he was politically involved in some way. Plotinus reached Antioch in his flight and from there proceeded to Rome, where he arrived in the same year. In Rome he conducted a school of philosophy and after ten years started writing. At about this time he gained influence over, or the confidence of, the new emperor, Gallienus, and it is possible that his philosophy was meant to aid the emperor in some way in his attempted rejuvenation of paganism. In any case, Plotinus asked the emperor to grant him land in order to found some kind of community, the members of which would live according to the laws (or *Laws*) of Plato.

Despite the emperor's favorable attitude, a cabal of courtiers brought the plan to nothing, indicating that they may have seen in it some political implications. However, because the contents of Plotinus's writings and some facts of his life seem to point to a complete absence of political interests, the problem of Plotinus's involvement in affairs of state is controversial. Nevertheless it is strangely coincidental that his literary activity began in the first year of Gallienus's rule. Moreover, when Plotinus died (probably from leprosy, about two years after the assassination of Gallienus), he was not in Rome but on the estate of one of his friends (of Arabic origin), and only one of his pupils, a physician, was present. These circumstances make it difficult to rule out the possibility that Plotinus had left Rome and that his pupils had all dispersed at the death of Gallienus (between March and August of 268) because he and they were afraid they would be affected by the anti-Gallienus reaction; this would again contradict a completely apolitical interpretation of Plotinus.

Plotinus's works, which were all written in the 16 years after 253, have come down to us only in the edition by his pupil Porphyry. Porphyry arranged the works according to content into six sections called enneads because each contains nine treatises; he arbitrarily created some treatises by dissecting or combining the originals. Independent of this arrangement, he indicated when each treatise was written by assigning it to one of three periods in the life of Plotinus: before Porphyry became Plotinus' student, 253–263; while Porphyry was his student, 263–268; after Porphyry left him, 268–270. Whether Porphyry numbered the treatises within each period in strictly chronological order is open to some doubt. The presentation of Plotinus given here follows the three periods of Porphyry with only a few forward or backward references. The standard citation to Plotinus's work designates the number of the ennead first, by Roman numeral; the treatise second, by arabic numeral; and the place of the treatise in Porphyry's chronological enumeration third, in brackets. The chapter number and, where relevant, the line number are also given in addition to the standard citation.

Contrary to the frequent attempts to present Plotinus's philosophy as a consistent whole, this presentation will stress all tensions by which the philosophy is permeated and leave it an open question whether Plotinus succeeded in reconciling them.

INFLUENCES. To understand the philosophy of Plotinus, a knowledge of some of the doctrines of Plato, Aristotle, the Neo-Pythagoreans, and the Stoics is very important.

In his dialogues Plato divided all reality into the realm of ideas (intelligibles) and the realm of sensibles, treating intelligibles alone as that which truly is (*ousia*), which implied that they are eternal and changeless (but see below). One of these ideas, the idea of the Good, he elevated above others, calling it beyond being (*epekeina ousias*). Comparable to the sun, it is the source of being and cognizability of all existents. In a lecture (or a lecture course) he seems to have identified the Good with the One.

Plato discussed the concept of the One in his dialogue *Parmenides*, ostensibly without any conclusion. In one passage he asserts hypothetically that if the One existed, it would be ineffable and unknowable. Whether this assertion was supposed to reveal the self-contradictory and, therefore, unacceptable character of the One, or on the contrary to express Plato's positive assertion as to the character of the One, is controversial.

In another dialogue, *The Sophist*, Plato seems to contradict his standard doctrine concerning the unchangeable character of the ideas by ascribing life, change, and knowledge to the realm of ideas.

As to the realm of the sensible, Plato in his *Timaeus* explains the origin of the cosmos in the form of a myth—as the work of a divine artisan (demiurge) who uses an ideal cosmos as model and fashions it out of something Plato calls "receptacle" and describes as void of any qualities, after ideas have in some way "entered" this void and by so doing created rudiments of the four elements. In addition to the physical universe the demiurge also fashions a cosmic soul and the immortal part of individual souls. The cosmic soul and the individual souls consist of a mixture of the same ingredients, on which mixture the demiurge imposes a numerical and a geometrical structure.

The immaterial and substantial character of the individual souls (or at least part of them) guarantees their pre-existence and post-existence (immortality). They are all subject to the law of reincarnation.

In the *Second Letter* (the authenticity of which was never doubted in antiquity, though today it finds virtually no defender), Plato, in a brief, and entirely obscure passage, seems to compress his whole philosophy into a formula reading: There are three realms, the first related to "the king," the second to the second, the third to the third. Plotinus was convinced that Plato is here describing the three realms of the One, Intelligence, and the Soul (whereas many Christian writers were convinced that Plato must have darkly anticipated the doctrine of the Trinity).

From Aristotle, Plotinus drew an important presentation of Plato's philosophy, ostensibly different from the one professed by Plato in his dialogues. According to Aristotle, Plato had assumed a realm of mathematicals mediating between ideas and sensibles (other sources identified this realm with that of the soul). Aristotle also attributed to Plato the view that two opposite principles, the One and the Indeterminate Dyad, are the supreme principles constitutive of everything, particularly of ideas and mathematicals—a doctrine Aristotle related to a similar, equally dualistic doctrine of the Pythagoreans. Aristotle represented Plato as having identified the Indeterminate Dyad with the receptacle and as having seen in it the principle of evil.

Plotinus also adopted Aristotle's doctrine of Intelligence (nous) as superior to the rest of the soul. Aristotle implied that it alone is immortal, the rest being merely the "form" of the body, hence incapable of separate existence. Aristotle designated the supreme deity as Intelligence contemplating (that is, intelligizing) itself; the cognitive activity of the Intelligence differed from sensation in that its objects (immaterial intelligibles) are identical with the acts by which Intelligence grasps them.

Plotinus was also aware of Academic and Neo-Pythagorean attempts to take over and modify the two-opposite-principles doctrine by elevating the One above the Indeterminate Dyad (sometimes above another One, coordinated with the Dyad), which thus changed

Plato's dualism into monism culminating in a transcendent One. Plotinus also knew of the syntheses of Plato's and Aristotle's philosophy attempted by some Platonists, especially of the second century A.D., most prominently Albinus and Apuleius. Another influence was the strictly materialistic and immanentistic Stoic doctrine of the omnipresence of the divine in the cosmos. Finally, two Neo-Pythagorean teachers are particularly relevant as sources for Plotinus: Moderatus, who seems to have taken his cue from Plato's *Parmenides,* distinguishing a first One above being from a second and a third; and Numenius, who distinguished the supreme god from the divine artisan, creator of the cosmos.

Plotinus's Philosophy First Period, 253–263

Plotinus subdivided Plato's realm of intelligibles into three: the One, Intelligence, and the Soul (presupposed in IV 8 [6], Ch. 6; V 4 [7], Ch. 1; VI 9 [9], Chs. 1 f.; V 1 [10], Ch. 10; V 2 [11]).

THE ONE. Following what are at best hints in Plato, Plotinus developed a full-fledged theory of the One as the highest principle, or cause. Precisely because it is the principle of everything that is—and is therefore omnipresent—it is itself above being (absolutely transcendental: VI 9 [9], Ch. 4, ll. 24 f., Ch. 7, ll. 28 f.; V 4 [7], Ch. 1, ll. 4–8; V 2 [11], Ch. 1). Since it is above being, it is fully indetermined (qualityless), although it may be called the Good as the object of universal desire. Because it is one, it is entirely undifferentiated (without multiplicity: V 4 [7]; VI 9 [9], Ch. 3, ll. 39–45). As every act of cognition, even of self-cognition, presupposes the duality of object and subject, Plotinus repeatedly and strongly states that the One is void of any cognition and is ignorant even of itself (VI 9 [9], Ch. 6, l. 42; III 9 [13], Chs. 7, 9). He tries to mitigate this statement in some places, hesitatingly attributing to the One some kind of self-awareness (V 4 [7], Ch. 2, l. 16) or quasi awareness of its "power" to engender being (V 1 [10], Ch. 7, l. 13). In other places he distinguishes the ordinary kind of ignorance from the ignorance of the One and says that there is nothing of which the One is cognizant but that there is also nothing of which it is ignorant (VI 9 [9], Ch. 6, ll. 46–50).

INTELLIGENCE. The realm of the One is "followed" by that of Intelligence (intellect, spirit, mind—all somewhat inadequate translations of the Greek word *nous*). Here, for the first time, multiplicity appears. Roughly, this realm (hypostasis) corresponds to Plato's realm of ideas and, therefore, to that of true being. But whereas Plato's ideas are self-sufficient entities outside the Intelligence that contemplates them, Plotinus develops a doctrine of the later Platonists (perhaps originating with Antiochus of Ascalon) which interpreted ideas as thoughts of God and insists that intelligibles do not exist outside the Intelligence (V 9 [5], Chs. 7 f.; III 9 [13], Ch. 1). The structure of the second hypostasis also differs from that of Plato's ideal realm in that Plotinus assumes the existence of ideas of individuals; the resulting difficulty that the infinity of individuals would demand an infinity of ideas Plotinus meets by assuming that the sensible world is, as the Stoa had it, subject to cyclical destruction and regeneration and that in each of these worlds the same indistinguishable individuals, for which one idea would suffice, would exist (V 7 [18], Ch. 1).

To understand the philosophy of Plotinus,

a knowledge of some of the doctrines of Plato,

Aristotle, the Neo-Pythagoreans,

and the Stoics is very important.

Another difference between Plato's and Plotinus's realm of ideas is that Plotinus assumed the existence of souls in this realm (IV 8 [6], Ch. 3). This doctrine creates a special problem. The ideal Socrates, unlike the soul of Socrates, must be composed of soul and body. It should follow that the soul of the empirical Socrates should be only a copy of that of the ideal Socrates, a consequence which, however, Plotinus rejects in places (V 9 [5], Ch. 13; VI 4 [22] Ch. 14) and approaches in others (III 9 [13], Ch. 3; V 2 [II], Ch. 1, 1.19).

Finally, Plotinus's realm of Intelligence contains even archetypal matter.

Despite all this multiplicity Intelligence remains one. In it everything is contained in everything without losing its identity, just as in mathematics every theorem contains all the others and, thus, the totality of mathematics (V 9 [5], Chs. 6, 9; IV 3 [27], Ch. 2).

Plotinus found it necessary to relate his doctrine of the One and Intelligence to the doctrine of the two opposite principles that figures in Aristotle's obscure presentation of Plato's philosophy in the *Metaphysics* (A6, 987a29 ff.). In that difficult passage (the text of which may be faulty), Plato is said to have identified ideas with numbers. Plotinus also found it necessary to relate his philosophy to the doctrine identifying the soul with number, the best-known example of which was Xenocrates' definition of the soul as self-changing number. Thus, Plotinus calls the realm of Intelligence the realm of number and calls the soul number (V 1 [10], Ch. 5). But as he conceives number to be derived from the interaction of One with plurality and yet elevates

the One above the realm of Intelligence (being), he seems to assign to his One a double role, a doctrine very close to the Neo-Pythagorean assumption of a double One, one superior and transcendental and another inferior, present in the realm of Intelligence, or number (V 1 [10], Ch. 5).

SOUL. Below the hypostasis of Intelligence Plotinus locates that of the Soul. Some souls remain unembodied; others "descend" into bodies. These bodies are either celestial or terrestrial. Celestial bodies offer no resistance to the soul's dwelling in them and thus these souls do not suffer from their incarnation (IV 8 [6], Ch. 2); terrestrial bodies, however, do offer resistance, and governing them may involve the soul to such an extent that it becomes alienated from Intelligence, its true home, and thus "sinks." In addition to these souls of individual bodies, Plotinus also assumes the existence of a cosmic soul (IV 8 [6], Ch. 7; III 9 [13], Ch. 3; II 2 [14], Ch. 2; I 2 [19], Ch. 1); thus, the world at large is one living organism. Probably the realm of the Soul does not consist of these individual souls alone; rather, they are all only individualizations of something we could call Soul in general (compare IV 3 [27], Ch. 4). In any case, all souls form only one Soul, and this unity implies that all souls intercommunicate by extrasensory means (IV 9 [8]).

Plotinus sometimes proves, sometimes merely assumes, not only the incorporeality, substantiality, and immortality of all the individual souls of men, animals, and even plants (IV 7 [2], Chs. 2–8[iii], 14), but also proves or assumes reincarnation, in the course of which the same soul may pass from the body of a man into that of a beast or a plant (III 4 [15], Ch. 2). Plato's best-known proof of immortality is based on the absolute simplicity and, therefore, indissolubility of the human soul. But Plato also taught that the soul is tripartite, and perhaps in an effort to reconcile these two doctrines, Plotinus assumes that the simple and, therefore, immortal soul on its "way" to the body receives additional, lower parts as accretions. This seems to be similar to a doctrine usually associated with Gnosticism—a downward journey of the soul, during which it passes the several planetary spheres, each of which adds something to it.

EMANATION. The explanation of the relation of the three hypostases to one another leads to one of the most characteristic doctrines of Plotinus, but it is a strangely ambiguous one. This relation is described as "emanation," or "effulguration," of Intelligence from the One and of Soul from Intelligence—an emanation which, however, leaves the emanating entity undiminished (VI 9 [9], Ch. 9; V 1 [10], Chs. 3, 5–7; compare III 8 [30], Ch. 8, 1. 11). The emanating entity thus remains outside of its product and yet is also present in it (VI 4 [7], Ch. 3; VI 9 [9], Ch. 7), a position sometimes described as dynamic pantheism to distinguish it from immanentist pantheism. This emanation Plotinus describes as entirely involuntary: what is full must overflow, what is mature must beget (V 4 [7], Ch. 1, ll. 26–41; V 1 [10], Ch. 6, l. 37; V 2 [11], Ch. 1, l. 8; compare IV 3 [27], Ch. 13). Seen in this way, there is no fault, no guilt involved in emanation, nor is any justification of why the One had to become multiple necessary. On the contrary, the process deserves praise; without it the One would have remained mere potentiality, and its hidden riches would not have appeared (IV 8 [6], Ch. 5 f.). But sometimes, particularly when discussing the Soul's descent, Plotinus speaks of emanation in an entirely different manner. Even the emanation of Intelligence from the One, let alone that of Soul from Intelligence, he describes in such terms as "apostasy" and "falling away." It is recklessness and the desire to belong to nobody but oneself that cause Intelligence to break away from the One (VI 9 [9], Ch. 5, l. 29). The Soul is motivated to break away from Intelligence by the desire to govern, which causes the Soul to become too immersed in bodies; by a craving for that which is worse; by a will to isolation (V 2 [11], Ch. 1; IV 8 [6], Ch. 4, l. 10; V 1 [10], Ch. 1). Matter emanates from Soul as the result of the Soul's wish to belong to itself (III 9 [13], Ch. 3). The "lowest" kind of Soul (the vegetative) is called the most foolhardy (V 2 [11], Ch. 2, l. 6). Thus, instead of an outflow, we should speak, rather, of a fall—with all its implications of will, guilt, necessity of punishment, and so on. These two interpretations—we shall call the former optimistic and the latter pessimistic—are difficult to reconcile.

INTELLIGENCE AND SOUL. Let us now consider the constitution of the second and third hypostases in additional detail. On the whole, Plotinus teaches that the One is in no way engaged in producing Intelligence. But sometimes he speaks as if Intelligence were the result of some kind of self-reflection of the One: The One turns to itself; this turning is vision; and this vision is Intelligence (V 1 [10], 7, l. 6—but the text is uncertain). Once more, we see that it is not easy for Plotinus to deprive the One of all self-awareness (consciousness). In any case, Intelligence is already multiple and, thus, less perfect than the One. However, the outflow from the One would not be sufficient to produce Intelligence. Rather, this flow must come to a stop—congeal, as it were. Incipient Intelligence must turn back to its source to contemplate it, and only by this act does Intelligence become fully constituted (V 2 [11], Ch. 1, l. 10). The emanation continues, and Soul emerges, again constituted by its turning toward the source, which is Intel-

ligence (V 1 [10], Ch. 6, l. 47; V 2 [11], Ch. 1, l. 18; III 9 [13], Ch. 5). In Soul, multiplicity prevails over unity, and perfection has therefore decreased.

From Soul emanates matter, the totally indetermined (III 9 [13], Ch. 3; III 4 [15], Ch. 1). Because Plotinus tends to split the Soul into a higher, lower, and lowest kind, it is only the lowest which is the source of matter. Matter, when illuminated by the Soul, becomes the physical world, the model of which is in the realm of Intelligence (Soul thus corresponds to Plato's divine artisan, the demiurge). Thus, Plotinus's system would seem to be entirely monistic. But sometimes Plotinus speaks as if matter existed by and in itself, "waiting" to be ensouled (IV 8 [6], Ch. 6, ll. 18–20; V 2 [11], Ch. 1).

Plotinus teaches that the One is in no way engaged in producing Intelligence, yet sometimes he speaks as if Intelligence were the result of some kind of self-reflection of the One.

Emanation must be described in temporal terms. But, of course, it is in fact an entirely timeless event (VI [10], Ch. 6, l. 19). Once the sensible world, particularly the human body, has been constituted, the Soul in the acts of incarnation becomes submerged in the realm of the temporal. The clash between a pessimistic and an optimistic evaluation of the emanative process can now be repeated in Plotinus's evaluation of incarnation.

INCARNATION. The Platonist cannot easily ignore either the myth of the *Phaedrus,* implying that souls "fall" by some kind of failing, or the otherworldly mood of the *Phaedo,* implying that the soul should try to flee the body and be polluted as little as possible by it. But just as it is difficult for a Platonist to forget that according to the *Timaeus,* the first incarnation of the soul is the work of the divine artisan himself and, thus, a blameless event, so it is equally difficult for him to forget the myth of the *Republic,* according to which embodiment seems to be the result of some universal necessity. As a result, Plotinus had to resolve a contradiction. Sometimes he did so by trying to prove that there is no true contradiction (IV 8 [6], Ch. 5). But recognizing that such an assertion is in the last resort unsatisfactory, even when it is assumed that only part of the Soul descends (IV 7 [2], Ch. 13, l. 12; IV 8 [6], Ch. 7, l. 7), he adopted a theory which he explicitly claims as his innovation (he otherwise presents himself as an orthodox Platonist). According to this theory, a true fall has never taken place. Actually, even when in a body, the soul still lives its original "celestial" life and remains unseparated from Intelligence. Only we are not aware of this "hidden" life of the soul; in other words, we are partly unconscious of what happens in our minds (IV 8 [6], Ch. 8). What is true of the Soul in relation to Intelligence is even truer of the relation between our embodied selves and Intelligence. Not even when present in us does Intelligence discontinue its activity (V 1 [10], Ch. 12).

Plotinus also makes an optimistic and a pessimistic evaluation of the deterioration which has taken place in the soul as a result of its incarnation. On the whole, he tries to prove that no real deterioration has taken place, but he often feels that he must find reasons why the soul should try to escape the body and return home. One of these reasons is that the body prevents the soul from exercising the activity peculiar to it (IV 8 [6], Ch. 2, l. 43), which means, of course, that some deterioration does take place.

DUALISM. There are some dualistic traits in the philosophy of Plotinus, particularly the recognition of the Indeterminate Dyad (as opposed to the One), to which he also refers simply as the Indeterminate (II 4 [12], Ch. 11, l. 37). Aristotle presented Plato's philosophy as a dualistic system, identifying the Indeterminate Dyad with Plato's receptacle and also with matter, in his own sense of the word; in other words according to him, Plato's ideas, being the product of the interaction of the two opposite principles, contain matter. Aristotle furthermore asserted that the Indeterminate Dyad is also the principle of evil. Plotinus is willing to recognize the Indeterminate as a second principle and to see in matter the principle of evil, but he refuses to recognize the existence of evil in the realm of Intelligence (ideas). He is thus forced to recognize the existence of two kinds of matter, one in the realm of the sensible and the result of the last emanative step, the other in the realm of Intelligence ("intelligible matter"), which does not have some of the properties usually associated with matter—specifically, it is not evil. He justifies this by the assumption that everything, including matter in the physical world, must have its archetype in the realm of Intelligence (II 4 [12], Chs. 2 f., 11, 14). Whether the assumption of intelligible matter can be reconciled with monism appears dubious; its "origin" is never made clear by Plotinus.

As to matter in the realm of the sensible, it is sheer indeterminacy, incorporeal, and, thus, different from the Stoic conception of matter (II 4 [12], Chs. 1, 4, 9, 10). It remains as unaffected by the ideas (or "ratios,"

logoi, by which Stoic term Plotinus often designates ideas as present in the soul qua formative powers) as the mirror is unaffected by what it reflects. Precisely because this matter is indeterminate, it is evil (II 4 [12], Ch. 16, l. 19), which means that evil is not something positive, but sheer privation.

There is a strange parallelism between matter and the One, because both are entirely indeterminate. Therefore, they both elude ordinary concepts, and Plotinus faces the question of what it means to know them. As far as matter is concerned, Plotinus likens it sometimes to darkness, and the mental act by which we grasp it to "unthinking thinking," or the soul's reduction to indefiniteness (II 4 [12], Chs. 6, 11)—concepts reminding us of Plato's pseudo thinking (nothos logismos), declared by him to be the appropriate way to think the receptacle.

KNOWLEDGE OF THE ONE. But much more important for Plotinus is the problem how the One, in spite of its being ineffable, can be known. In the pseudo(?)-Platonic Epinomis (992B), the author insists that in order to know the One (whatever "knowledge" means here), the soul must itself become one; the Platonic Letters also seem to teach some kind of suprarational insight. Perhaps starting from passages such as these and also from passages in Aristotle and Theophrastus in which some kind of infallible knowledge of certain objects is described as a kind of touching (thinganein), Plotinus asserts that to "know" the One means to become one with it, which the soul can accomplish only by becoming as simple or as "alone" as the One. In the moment of such a union the soul has become God or, rather, is God; the soul has reascended to its original source (VI 9 [9], Ch. 9 f.). Among the terms Plotinus uses to describe this condition are "ecstasy," "simplicity," "self-surrender," "touching," and "flight of the alone to the alone" (VI 9 [9], Chs. 3, 11). This ecstasy—repeatedly experienced by Plotinus himself—is undoubtedly the climactic moment of man's life. It is not expressible in words (compare Plato, Epistle VII, 341D); only he who has experienced it knows what it means to be ravished away and full of God.

For this reascent man prepares himself by the acquisition of all the perfections (virtues, aretai). However, each of these perfections acquires different meanings according to the level on which man's spiritual life takes place—thus, there is a social fairness, above it another kind of fairness, and so on. Man also prepares himself by the exercise of dialectics (I 2 [19]; I 3 [20]). The preliminary stages of achievement Plotinus calls "becoming Godlike" (I 6 [1], Ch. 8), a condition often described by Platonists preceding Plotinus as the ultimate goal of Plato's philosophy.

FREE WILL AND DEMONOLOGY. Among the other topics treated in this period, Plotinus' defense of the freedom of the will—only "reasonable" souls are free; others are subject to fate, εἱμαρμένη (III 1 [3])—and his demonology deserve special mention. In regard to demonology Plotinus tries to steer a middle course between two theories, one identifying demons with the supreme parts of our soul, and the other assuming the existence of demons as extra-psychical beings (III 4 [15]).

Second Period, 263–268

POLEMICS. More than two-fifths of Plotinus's total literary output was produced during the brief period between 263 and 268, when Porphyry was studying with Plotinus. Perhaps Porphyry's presence worked as a powerful stimulus. A considerable part of the output of this period is devoted to polemics with other schools, notably on the doctrine of categories and against Gnosticism.

Categories. Plotinus rejects both the Aristotelian and the Stoic versions of this doctrine, adhering to the principle that there can be no categories common to the realms of the sensible and the intelligible. In application to the realm of the sensible he corrects and modifies Aristotle's categories; to the realm of Intelligence he tries to apply Plato's five genera—being, identity, diversity, rest, and change (VI 1–3 [42–44]).

Ideal Numbers. Aristotle presented Plato as professing the existence of ideal numbers (twoness, threeness, and so on, as distinguished from ordinary numbers—two, three, and so on). And he devoted much effort to the criticism of the theory of ideal numbers. Plotinus defends the theory of ideal numbers—which differ from nonideal numbers in that they do not consist of addible unities and are therefore not addible themselves (V 5 [32], Ch. 4)—and, objecting to any nominalist or abstractionist theory of numbers, attributes to them subsistence. Specifically, after having divided the realm of Intelligence into three layers—Being, Intelligence (in a restricted sense of the word), and the original Living Being—he assigns ideal numbers to the uppermost layer and explains that only because of their existence can Being divide itself into beings (VI 6 [34]), Chs. 8, 16). In this context he also introduces a peculiar concept of infinity: The truly infinite is a thing which has no limits imposed on it from without but only from within (VI 6 [34], Chs. 17 f., but compare V 5 [32], Ch. 4).

Polemic against Gnosticism. Of all the polemics of Plotinus, the most significant is the one against Gnosticism. One could say that when facing Gnostic pessimism pointblank, Plotinus overcompensates for the pessimistic and Gnostic strand present in himself and

responds with an almost unlimited optimism. The fundamental mood underlying Gnosticism is alienation from a hostile world, and Gnosticism undertakes to explain this mood and to open the road to escape from the world. The explanation is in the form of a history of the origin of the visible cosmos; according to Gnosticism, this cosmos is the result of the activity of an evil god sometimes identified with the Creator-God of the Old Testament or with Plato's divine artisan. This evil god is only the last in a succession of beings. The manner in which this succession takes place consists in a number of voluntary acts by which divinities of an ever lower order originate. The relation between these deities is often personal, based on such traits as curiosity, oblivion, daring, ambition. Man, as he exists in this evil world, contains in himself a spark of what was his original, divine substance, now imprisoned in his body owing to the scheming of the evil god. At a certain moment a messenger-savior in some way breaks the power of the evil god and makes it possible for those who hear the whole story (acquire gnosis) to regain their original standing and free themselves from the tyranny of the evil god.

Plotinus treats Gnosticism as a strictly philosophic system. He simply compares its doctrines with his own and with those of Plato; its salvationary aspects are of little interest to him (compare III 2 [47], Ch. 9). In the succession of divine beings he sees only a superfluous multiplication of the three hypostases of his own system (compare V 5 [32], Chs. 1 f.). To the cosmic drama which results in the creation of the visible cosmos he opposes his view of a totally undramatic, unconscious emanation, a product of necessity without arbitrariness and, contradicting even Plato's *Timaeus* (40B–45A), without planning (V 8 [31], Ch. 7) and, therefore, entirely blameless. The cosmos, product of the activities of the Soul (or Intelligence or both), he considers to be beautiful. Whereas Gnosticism sees the visible universe filled with spirits inimical to man, most outstanding among them being the rulers of the celestial bodies (planets), Plotinus sees in these spirits powers related to man in brotherly fashion. What is true in Gnosticism can, according to him, be found in Plato. The Gnostic objection that Plato did not penetrate the mysteries of the intelligible world Plotinus considers ridiculously presumptuous (II 9 [33]; compare V 8 [31], Ch. 8).

PROBLEMS. In the second period Plotinus was also concerned with the problems inherent in his own system, especially with the relation between the intelligible world and the sensible world and with the structure of the intelligible world.

The One. First, Plotinus tries to elucidate the nature of the One still further. He does this particularly in the context of a discussion concerning the nature of human freedom, in which he also asks whether the One should be considered as a necessary being or as a free one (*ens necessarium* or *ens liberum*)—in theistic terms, whether God must exist or has freely chosen to exist. In what is perhaps his most profound theological discussion, Plotinus tries to establish the concept of the One as Lord of itself and thus not having to serve even itself, so that in the One freedom and necessity coincide (VI 8 [39], Chs. 7–21). And without any vacillation he excludes any kind of consciousness from the One (V 6 [24], Chs. 2, 4 f.).

The insistence that memory and sensation,

in their ordinary senses,

are absent from the realm of Intelligence

and even from that of the celestial sphere

Plotinus explains with his theory

that the universe is one animated organism.

Intelligence and Soul. As far as Intelligence is concerned, Plotinus reiterates his doctrine that it contains ideas within itself (V 5 [32], Chs. 1 f.), and he again tries to explain how, in spite of being one, it still contains multiplicity (VI 4 [22], Ch. 4; VI 5 [23], Ch. 6). With regard to souls Plotinus tries to explain how they can remain distinct from one another although they all are only one soul (VI 4 [22], Ch. 6; IV 3 [27], Chs. 1–8; compare IV 9 [8], Ch. 5).

Both Intelligence and Soul are supposed to be present in the sensible world and, therefore, present in what is extended, although they themselves are not extended. Starting from the famous discussion in Plato's *Parmenides* (131b), in which the attempt is made to explain how one idea can be present in many particulars, Plotinus tries to show that just because Intelligence and Soul are not extended, they can be omnipresent and ubiquitous in what is extended (VI 4 [22], especially VI 5 [23], Ch. 11). And also in this context he tries to establish the concept of differentiated unity (VI 4 [22], Ch. 4), that is, the noncontradictory character of "one" and "many."

Intelligence, Soul, Change. Probably the most formidable difficulty facing Plotinus is the result of his theory treating Intelligence and Soul as metaphysical principles on the one hand and as present in man on the other (that is, as both transcendent and immanent) and, therefore, in some way engaged in mental life, particularly in sensing and remembering. As metaphysical principles—that is, members of the realm of the intelligible—Intelligence and Soul should be unchangeable, whereas in man they seem to be involved in change. From this difficulty Plotinus tries to extricate himself in many ways, of which two will be presented.

On the one hand he keeps even the human soul away as much as possible from the processes of sensing, remembering, desiring, experiencing pleasure and pain, and so on (III 6 [26], Ch. 1–5). Sometimes he insists that the soul simply notices all these processes without being affected by what it perceives (IV 6 [41]; IV 4 [28], Ch. 19). Sometimes he insists that it is not the soul itself but only some trace of it which is engaged in these activities (IV 4 [28], Chs. 18 f.; compare VI 4 [22], Ch. 15, l. 15), and this ties in with the theory that the soul did not really—or not in its entirety—descend (VI 4 [22], Ch. 16). Sometimes he introduces the concept of a double soul, a higher and a lower, with only the lower being changeable. This doubling of the soul Plotinus carries to such extremes that he assumes two imaginative faculties and two faculties of memory, each belonging to its respective soul and each remembering in a different manner and different events. This is particularly the case after man's death; the higher soul no longer remembers anything it experienced while in the body, whereas the lower soul still remembers (IV 3 [27], Chs. 25–32; IV 4 [28], Ch. 1, l. 5). Sometimes he suggests that all the mental activities involving change happen not to the soul but to the composite of soul and body (IV 4 [28], Ch. 17), leaving undecided how anything can affect a whole without affecting the part which belongs to it.

On the other hand, when it comes to Intelligence and Soul as metaphysical principles (and even to the world soul and astral souls), Plotinus disallows them memory entirely (IV 4 [28], Chs. 6–17). As to sensing, he distinguishes two kinds, one serving such practical purposes as self-preservation, the other purely theoretical; it is only the theoretical kind which he ascribes to metaphysical entities, the implication obviously being that this kind of sensation does not cause any change in the perceiver (IV 4 [28], Ch. 24). Why they should still be called Intelligence and Soul remains somewhat unclear.

Perhaps the most striking example of the real effects of the Soul's falling away from Intelligence (despite everything said by Plotinus to minimize these effects) is that the cosmic soul, as it falls away, engenders time because of an inability to contemplate the totality of Intelligence simultaneously (III 7 [45], Ch. 11).

Ethics. The difficulties created for the explanation of the cognitive aspects of man's mental life without the assumption of a real change (passibility) of the soul return with even greater significance in the field of ethics.

If there is no actual fall of the soul and if no deterioration of its nature has taken place as the result of incarnation (III 6 [26], Ch. 5), why is purifying the soul necessary? Yet the concept of purification plays a central role in the ethics of Plotinus (compare I 6 [1]; I 2 [19]); he even describes the perfections—wisdom, self-control, justice, courage—as purifications. Plotinus tries to help himself by a metaphor: The soul is merely covered with mud, which, however, has never penetrated it. According to another explanation, what the soul has acquired because of its fall is nothingness, and all it has to do, therefore, is to get rid of nothing (VI 5 [23], Ch. 12, ll. 16–23).

Cosmic Sympathy. The insistence that memory and sensation, in their ordinary senses, are absent from the realm of Intelligence and even from that of the celestial sphere Plotinus explains with his theory that the universe is one animated organism. The sympathy existing among parts of one organism make memory and sensation superfluous, since the mutual affection need not be perceived. This leads to characteristic explanations of the efficacy of magic, prayers, and astrology. All these activities (and prophecies) are made possible by the fact that each part of the universe affects the others and is affected by them, not by mechanical causation nor by influencing the will of deities—particularly stars—but exclusively by mutual sympathy (IV 3 [27], Ch. 11; IV 4 [28], Chs. 40 f.). In this doctrine of sympathy many scholars see the influence of the Stoa, particularly Posidonius, on Plotinus.

Matter. As to matter, Plotinus in the writings of this period—with less ambiguity than in other periods—characterizes it as the result of the last step of the emanative process, thus fully preserving the monistic character of his system (II 5 [25], Ch. 5; compare I 8 [51], Ch. 7).

Some other problems discussed by Plotinus are distinctly occasional pieces and somewhat peripheral with regard to the system. Thus, we find a theory of vision, explained by sympathy (IV 5 [29]; II 8 [35]); a discussion of the Stoic concept of the complete interpenetration of bodies (II 7 [37]); a cosmology without the assumption of ether (II 1 [40]).

Third Period, 268–270

As is to be expected, some earlier themes recur in the third period. In fact, one of the essays of the third period (V 3 [49]) contains what is perhaps the most comprehensive presentation of the basic tenets of Plotinus's philosophy. Plotinus proves that there must be a One preceding all multiplicity and that this One must be ineffable (V 3 [49], Chs. 12 f., 17). To explain its presence in us and the fact that we know about it although we do not know it, he says that those full of and pos-

sessed by the divine also feel that something greater than themselves is present in them, although they cannot say what it is (V 3 [49], Ch. 14). Once more facing the problem of how the One, which is absolutely simple, can be the source of multiplicity, Plotinus is on the verge of admitting that the One is at least potentially (though it is a potentiality *sui generis*) many (V 3 [49], Chs. 15 f.; compare VI 5 [23], Ch. 9). The same essay contains what is probably the most detailed and the most impressive description of the upward journey of the soul to reach the goal of ecstatic union, described by the formula "through light light" (V 3 [49], Ch. 17, ll. 28–37; compare V 5 [32], Chs. 4–9). As advice on how to achieve this union, Plotinus says "strip yourself of everything" (V 3 [49], 17, l. 38). Furthermore, Plotinus still feels he must prove that ideas are not external to Intelligence (V 3 [49], Chs. 5–13).

Plotinus insists on the all-pervasive character of providence, thus rejecting Aristotle's dichotomy of the universe into a sublunar sphere dominated by necessity and a supralunar world to which providence is restricted.

On the whole, the writings of Plotinus's last period are dominated by two themes. The first concerns theodicy, the origin and justification of evil, and the second asks what man's true self is.

THEODICY. To explain the origin of evil, Plotinus tries to reconcile the view that matter, though void of any quality and actually only deficiency, is still evil in some sense of the word and is the source of all evil (I 8 [51], Chs. 8, 10). In so doing, he sometimes comes dangerously close to the Gnostic theory that matter imprisons the soul (I 8 [51], Ch. 14, ll. 48–50) and to a completely dualistic system (I 8 [51], Ch. 6, l. 33). Nevertheless, his optimism is particularly strong in this period; he has high praise for the beauty of the visible cosmos (III 2 [47], Ch. 12, l. 4), and rejects the idea of an evil creator of the cosmos (III 2 [47], Ch. 1). His theodicy is a blend of Platonic arguments, drawn especially from Book X of the *Laws,* and Stoic arguments. Perfection of the whole demands imperfection of the parts (III 2 [47], Chs. 11, 17; III 3 [48]) and the existence of evil (I 8 [51], Chs. 8–15). At the same time he minimizes the importance of evil by insisting that it exists only for the wicked one (III 2 [47], Ch. 6). Furthermore, he points out that the cosmic order rewards and punishes everybody according to his merits and assigns each one an appropriate place, thus making for a completely harmonious whole (III 2 [47], Ch. 4). Ultimately, his theodicy is based on convictions characteristic of most theodicies—that to designate a particular as evil is to lose sight of the whole, that everything participates in the good as far as it can, and that evil is only absence of the good (III 2 [47], Chs. 3, 5; I 8 [51], Chs. 1–5).

Providence. Closely connected with the problem of theodicy is the problem of providence. Plotinus insists on the all-pervasive character of providence, thus rejecting Aristotle's dichotomy of the universe into a sublunar sphere dominated by necessity and a supralunar world to which providence is restricted. He replaces Aristotle's distinction by the dichotomy of good and wicked men; only the wicked are subject to necessity (III 2 [47], Ch. 9; compare III 1 [3], Chs. 8–10). But this providence is entirely impersonal (compare VI 7 [38], Ch. 1) and actually coincides with the order of the universe.

TRUE SELF AND HAPPINESS. The second major theme of Plotinus's last period is that of ascertaining what man's true self is—that is, of ultimately obeying the divine command "Know thyself." Attendant subproblems are the explanations of wherein man's true happiness consists and of the concept of self-knowledge. It is extremely difficult for Plotinus to give a consistent account of what constitutes man's true self. He cannot simply identify it with Intelligence or Soul (as he did in IV 7 [1], Ch. 1, l. 24 or in I 4 [46], Chs. 8–16, where it is identified with the "higher" soul), precisely because both, in their character of metaphysical entities, remain transcendent; however, he rejects the idea that man is truly the composite of soul and body (I 4 [46], Ch. 14, l. 1) because this would grant the body too much importance. One of the solutions favored by Plotinus is that Intelligence is man's true self, but only if and when he succeeds in identifying himself with it. On the other hand, no such identification is actually necessary, because Intelligence is always in and with us even though we are not aware of it. (*Mutatis mutandis* this can also be applied to the relation of man and whatever is to be conceived the highest divinity: compare VI 5 [23], Ch. 12). Once more the concept of the unconscious plays a decisive role in the system of Plotinus (I 4 [46], Chs. 9 f.; V 3 [49], Chs. 3 f.). All this ties in with the idea that self-knowledge occurs only when the subject, the act, and the object of knowledge coincide— which takes place only on the level of Intelligence— whereas neither man as a whole nor Soul can possess full self-knowledge (V 3 [49], Chs. 3, 6). The One is,

of course, above any kind of self-knowledge (V 3 [49], Chs. 10–13).

The thesis that only Intelligence is man's true self (if and when he makes full use of it) serves also as a basis for a discussion of the problem of man's happiness. If by "man" we mean the composite of body and soul, man cannot experience happiness, nor can he if he is body alone. However, if by "man" we mean the true self, it is obvious that happiness consists in the exercise of Intelligence—that is, in contemplation. But as the activity of Intelligence is uninterrupted (here in the argument Plotinus switches from Intelligence as immanent to transcendent Intelligence; see I 1 [53], Ch. 13, l. 7) man is actually always happy, although he may remain unconscious of it (I 4 [46], Chs. 4, 9, 13–16). Why this should apply only to the sage remains unclear.

The formidable problem of how the soul, the essence of which is unchangeability, can ever become evil also vexed Plotinus to the end (compare I 8 [51], Ch. 4, 12, 15). In the work of his last period he explains that as the soul at its descent acquires additional parts, evil resides only in them. Thus, the ethical task of man is not so much to separate the soul from the body as it is to separate it from these adventitious parts (I 1 [53], Ch. 12, l. 18). In this context the problem of who is the subject of punishments in after-life also emerges; Plotinus answers that it is that "composite" soul (I 1 [53], Ch. 12). Why we should call soul an entity which is or can become evil, "suffer" punishment, and so on, after Soul has been presented as belonging to the realm of the unchangeable, remains unanswered; so do virtually all questions resulting from the dual character of Intelligence and Soul as metaphysical (transcendental) entities on the one hand and human (immanent) entities on the other.

There is almost something providential in the fact that the very last of Plotinus' essays, written at a time when death was approaching him, reasserts that all things participate in the One (the Good) and discusses the question of how to reconcile the two theses that life is good and yet death no evil, though it deprives us of something good (I 7 [54], Ch. 3). The battle between the pessimistic and the optimistic strands in Plotinus continued to the very end of his activity. Optimism ultimately won: Life is good—though not for the wicked one; death is good, because it will permit the soul to live an unhampered life.

BIBLIOGRAPHY

Works by Plotinus

When completed, the edition of Plotinus's *Enneads* by P. Henry and H. R. Schwyzer will replace the others. Of the *editio maior* (with full critical apparatus), two volumes, containing Enneads I–III and

IV–V, have appeared (Paris, 1951, 1959); of the *editio minor* (with abbreviated apparatus), one volume (Oxford, 1964). For Ennead VI, in addition to older editions, see the one by Bréhier cited below.

Translations accompanied by Greek texts, with notes, are available in French by Émile Bréhier, in 6 vols. (Paris, 1924–1938), and in German by R. Harder, W. Theiler, and R. Beutler (Hamburg, 1956—), in progress. For translations without Greek texts, see the English by Stephen MacKenna and B. S. Page, 3d ed. (London, 1962), and the Italian (with commentary) by Vincento Cilento, 3 vols. (Bari, Italy, 1947–1949).

Works on Plotinus

For an introduction to all problems of Plotinian scholarship, the best is H. R. Schwyzer's article "Plotinus" in A. Pauly and G. Wissowa, eds., *Realencyklopädie der classischen Altertumswissenschaft*, Vol. XXI (1951), pp. 471–592. See also appropriate sections in Eduard Zeller, *Die Philosophie der Griechen*, Vol. III, Pt. 2, 4th or 5th ed. (Leipzig, 1903; 1923), and Friedrich Ueberweg and Karl Praechter, *Die Philosophie des Altertums*, 12th ed. (Berlin, 1926). Two works on Plotinus are William Inge, *The Philosophy of Plotinus*, 2 vols. (London, 1929), and Émile Bréhier, *La Philosophie de Plotin* (Paris, 1952; new ed. in prep.), translated into English by J. Thomas as *Philosophy of Plotinus* (Chicago, 1958). There is a bibliography by B. Mariën in Vol. III of the Cilento translation cited above; see also Wilhelm Totok, *Handbuch der Geschichte der Philosophie*, Vol. I (Frankfurt, 1964—).

— PHILIP MERLAN

PLURALISM

Pragmatism and Continental hermeneutics have combined to produce a decided turn toward forms of pluralism in twentieth-century philosophy (Geyer; B. Singer). This has led to the rejection of any one favored epistemological method (e.g., the scientific method, scriptural exegesis, introspection) and any one favored basis for the reconstruction of reality (e.g., mind, matter). Neopragmatists propose to replace the notion of truth with notions such as 'fitting', 'useful', and 'warranted'. Given that what is 'fitting' is relative to the problem being faced and the means at one's disposal, we are left with the possibility of a plurality of ways of conceiving the world and of achieving our aims within it.

Moral pluralism opposes the monistic view that there is any one method of determining what is morally right (e.g., the utilitarian calculus or Kantian universalizability), and it also opposes the relativistic view that all things have value only with respect to a particular cultural context. Pluralists insist that a good life typically involves the desire, not for one, but for many kinds of 'goods', often of incommensurable value; moreover, the realization of certain 'goods' may conflict with and even preclude the realization of others. As such, pluralists believe that moral conflicts are inevitable and that there are not one but many alternative ways of resolving such conflicts (Kekes). The trend toward pluralism has also been influenced by our growing awareness of different cultures with nonequivalent conceptions of reality and 'the good life'.

Moral pluralism opposes the monistic view that there is any one method of determining what is morally right, and it also opposes the relativistic view that all things have value only with respect to a particular cultural context.

The modern nation-state has evolved beyond the belief that it manifests the cultural orientation of a single 'race', usually its majority. The reality is that every nation is composed of numerous groups with different cultural orientations. And the state is considered the primary guarantor that minority views will be presented, respected, and given a voice in determining policy (Guttman). The rejection of the view that a Eurocentric male-dominated culture is the norm to be achieved universally has led to the demand that the cultures of non-Europeans, women, and minorities be recognized and granted equal voice (Taylor). In this way pluralism is considered by many to be an essential part of the liberal democratic state, and this has manifested itself in terms of educational policy as the rejection of monoculturalism and the demand for a multicultural orientation.

One form of multiculturalism has focused on the need of suppressed groups to have their cultures recognized. Such a demand for recognition may motivate certain proposals—for example, to replace a Eurocentric focus with an Afrocentric focus or a male-centered orientation with a feminist-centered orientation. Some argue that because of the past harms inflicted upon such groups, ostensibly because they were different, they are justified in embracing those differences in order to cleanse them of the negative valuations imposed by the hegemonic culture. It is right for such groups to adopt a separatist posture if this is the best means of achieving a redefinition of themselves that is positive and self-affirming (Young). Where members of the hegemonic culture have inflicted unjust harms on members of an oppressed group, some argue that the oppressed group has the right to cultural restitution. The domination of culture A by culture B may not be the result of culture

A's not offering viable options; rather, it may be the result of unjust injuries and harms visited on culture A by culture B. In such cases groups sharing culture A have a right to 'moral deference', affirmative action, and the preservation of their culture (Mosley, Nickel, Thomas).

Many have been concerned that multiculturalism might degenerate into a bedlam of different groups, each espousing its own brand of cultural authenticity. Critics argue that this would amount to merely replacing one culture's hegemony with another culture's hegemony. Multiculturalism in this sense would fail to reflect the pluralist maxim that no orientation is 'fitting' for every situation and that for a given end there may be several equally 'fitting' means (West, Yates).

An alternative form of multiculturalism, closer to pluralism, emphasizes the importance of diversity and cross-cultural communication. On this view the more cultural orientations there are for consideration, the better the likelihood of finding or constructing a 'fitting' adaptation to some current problem (Rorty). For this reason every culture should be allowed the opportunity of articulating itself to the public at large and of thereby influencing the manner in which individuals construct their character.

Pluralism does not end with the insistence on an equal voice for every culture but extends itself to the view that different biological species often have interests that may conflict with the interests of human beings. Some have argued that, just as racism and sexism accord special preference to white males and victimize women and non-Europeans, so speciesism accords special preference to the interests of human beings and unjustly victimizes nonhuman species (P. Singer). The insistence on a plurality of interests and capacities has been extended to include the interests of other animal species, as well as trees, rivers, and ecological systems (Wenz).

[See also Affirmative Action; Animal Rights and Welfare; Pragmatism; Racism; Social and Political Philosophy; Speciesism.]

BIBLIOGRAPHY

Geyer, M. "Multiculturalism and the Politics of General Education," *Critical Inquiry*, Vol. 19 (1993), 499–533.

Guttman, A. "The Challenge of Multiculturalism in Political Ethics," *Philosophy and Public Affairs*, Vol. 22, No. 3 (Summer 1993), 171–206.

Kekes, J. *The Morality of Pluralism*. Princeton, NJ, 1993.

Mosley, A. "Preferential Treatment and Social Justice," in C. Peden and Y. Hudson, eds., *Terrorism, Justice, and Social Values* (Lewiston, NY, 1990).

Nickel, J. W. "Ethnocide and Indigenous Peoples," *Journal of Social Philosophy*, Vol. 25 (1994), 84–98.

Rorty, A. "The Advantages of Moral Diversity," *Social Philosophy and Policy*, Vol. 9, No. 2 (Summer 1992), 38–62.

Singer, B. "Pragmatism and Pluralism." *The Monist*, Vol. 75, No. 4 (October 1992), 477–91.

Singer, P. *Animal Liberation*. New York, 1990.

Taylor, C. *Multiculturalism and the Politics of Recognition*. Princeton, NJ, 1992.

Thomas, L. "Moral Deference," *Philosophical Forum*, Vol. 24, Nos. 1–3 (Spring 1992–93), 233–50.

Wenz, P. "Minimal, Moderate, and Extreme Moral Pluralism." *Environmental Ethics*, Vol. 15 (1993), 61–74.

West, C. *Beyond Eurocentricism and Multiculturalism*. Monroe, MA, 1993.

Yates, S. A. "Multiculturalism and Epistemology," *Public Affairs Quarterly*, Vol. 6 (1992), 435–56.

Young, M. Y. *Justice and the Politics of Difference*. Princeton, NJ, 1990.

— ALBERT MOSLEY

POSTSTRUCTURALISM

Poststructuralism is the name bestowed in the English-speaking philosophical and literary communities upon the ideas of several French philosophers whose work arose as a distinctly philosophical response to the privileging of the human sciences that characterized the structuralism of, among others, Claude Lévi-Strauss (anthropology), Louis Althusser (Marxism), Jacques Lacan (psychoanalysis), and Roland Barthes (literature). One can locate the emergence of poststructuralism in Paris in the late 1960s: Michel Foucault published *Les Mots et les choses* in 1966; Jacques Derrida published *De la grammatologie, L'écriture et la différence,* and *La voix et le phénomène* in 1967; Gilles Deleuze published *Différence et répétition* in 1968 and *Logique du sens* in 1969.

Like their structuralist predecessors, the poststructuralists draw heavily from the ideas of Karl Marx and Sigmund Freud. But unlike the structuralists, they draw at least as much from the third so-called master of suspicion—Friedrich Nietzsche. Nietzsche's critique of truth, his emphasis upon interpretation and differential relations of power, and his attention to questions of style in philosophical discourse became central motifs for the poststructuralists as they turned away from the human sciences and toward philosophical-critical analyses of: writing and textuality (Derrida); relations of power, discourse, and the construction of the subject (Foucault); desire and language (Deleuze); questions of aesthetic and political judgment (Jean-François Lyotard); and questions of sexual difference and gender construction (Luce Irigaray, Julia Kristeva, Hélène Cixous).

Most of the poststructuralist philosophers began working in an intellectual environment dominated by Jean-Paul Sartre's existentialism, and they all studied and were profoundly influenced by Maurice Merleau-Ponty's thinking on language and corporeality, Martin Heidegger's critique of the history of metaphysics, and Lacanian psychoanalysis. Like existentialism, a philosophical "movement" with which poststructuralism has a complicated relationship, it is impossible to locate any set of themes that unite all poststructuralist philosophers. That said, one can note certain motifs appearing frequently in their works: an attention to questions of language, power, and desire that emphasizes the context in which meaning is produced and makes problematic all universal truth and meaning claims; a suspicion of binary, oppositional thinking, often opting to affirm that which occupies a position of subordination within a differential network; a suspicion of the figure of the humanistic human subject, challenging the assumptions of autonomy and transparent self-consciousness while situating the subject as a complex intersection of discursive, libidinal, and social forces and practices; a resistance to claims of universality and unity, preferring instead to acknowledge difference and fragmentation.

The impact of poststructuralism upon philosophy, literary studies, and social theory has been extensive.

The impact of poststructuralism upon philosophy, literary studies, and social theory has been extensive. Twenty-five years ago, Continental philosophy was dominated by issues related to phenomenology, existentialism, and the works of Edmund Husserl, Heidegger, and Sartre; today the scope of Continental philosophy is focused increasingly on issues that originate in the works of post-1960 French thinkers. Derrida and deconstruction have been major forces in literary theory and criticism since the early 1970s. Since then Derrida has become a major influence in philosophical studies, and, together with Foucault, they have had the widest influence on English-language theorists.

Since 1980 other significant poststructuralist texts have begun attracting philosophical readers: Deleuze's important and innovative readings of major philosophical figures (Hume, Spinoza, Leibniz, Kant, Nietzsche, Bergson) and his analyses, alone and in collaboration with Félix Guattari, of psychoanalysis, cinema, art, literature, and contemporary culture; Lyotard's essays on postmodernism, politics, aesthetics, and art history, plus his important reflections on Kant's *Critique of Judgment;* Luce Irigaray's critical rereadings of Freud, the philosophical canon, and her reflections on language and sexual difference; Hélène Cixous's engendering writing and thinking its relations to the body, particularly the feminine body; Julia Kristeva's thinking on semiotics, abjection, and desire in language. Less influential but nevertheless significant poststructuralist work also is found in Pierre Bourdieu's reflexive sociology; Jean-Luc Nancy and Philippe Lacoue-Labarthe's work on aesthetics,

politics, and questions of community; and Jean Baudrillard's sociological reflections on contemporary cultural practices.

[See also Deconstruction; Derrida, Jacques; Existentialism; Foucault, Michel; Freud, Sigmund; Heidegger, Martin; Hume, David; Husserl, Edmund; Kant, Immanuel; Leibniz, Gottfried Wilhelm; Marx, Karl; Merleau-Ponty, Maurice; Nietzsche, Friedrich Wilhelm; Phenomenology; Sartre, Jean-Paul; Spinoza, Benedict (Baruch).]

BIBLIOGRAPHY

Gilles Deleuze's most important works include *Différence et répétition,* Paris, 1968 (translated by P. Patton as *Difference and Repetition,* New York, 1994); *Logique du sens,* Paris, 1968 (translated by M. Lester as *The Logic of Sense,* New York, 1990); and, with Félix Guattari, *L'Anti-Oedipe,* Paris, 1972 (translated by R. Hurley, M. Seem, and H. R. Lane as *Anti-Oedipus,* Minneapolis, 1983); *Mille plateaux,* Paris, 1980 (translated by B. Massumi as *A Thousand Plateaus,* Minneapolis, 1987); and *Qu'est-ce que la philosophie?* Paris, 1991 (translated by H. Tomlinson and G. Burchell as *What Is Philosophy?* New York, 1994). Jean-François Lyotard's best-known works include *La condition postmoderne,* Paris, 1979 (translated by G. Bennington and B. Massumi as *The Postmodern Condition,* Minneapolis, 1983) and *Le différend,* Paris, 1983 (translated by G. Van Den Abbeele as *The Differend: Phrases in Dispute,* Minneapolis, 1988).

Among the better secondary works are G. Bennington, *Lyotard: Writing the Event,* Manchester, 1988; R. Bogue, *Deleuze and Guattari,* New York, 1989; V. Descombes, *Le Même et l'autre: Quarante-cinq ans de philosophie française (1933–1978),* Paris, 1979 (translated by L. Scott-Fox and J. M. Harding as *Modern French Philosophy,* Cambridge, 1980); P. Dews, *Logics of Disintegration: Post-Structuralist Thought and the Claims of Critical Theory,* London, 1987; M. Frank, *Was ist Neostrukturalismus?* Frankfurt, 1983 (translated by S. Wilke and R. Gray as *What Is Neostructuralism?* Minneapolis, 1989); and A. Schrift, *Nietzsche's French Legacy: A Genealogy of Poststructuralism,* New York, 1995.

— ALAN D. SCHRIFT

PRACTICAL REASON APPROACHES

Practical-reasoning theory is a kind of metaethical view—alongside noncognitivism and other cognitivisms such as naturalism and rational intuitionism—that aims to understand ethics as rooted in practical reason.

Tradition divides the faculty of reason into two parts: theoretical and practical. Theoretical reason concerns what we should believe, practical reason what we should do. Beliefs aim to represent reality and are mistaken or in error when they do not. Theoretical reason's task, therefore, is to discover what is true of the independent order of fact to which belief is answerable. But what about practical reason? What could make it the case that an action is something a person ought to do?

Plainly, ethical convictions also aim at a kind of objectivity. If Jones thinks he should devote all his resources to conspicuous consumption but Smith thinks that he (Jones) should donate some to help the poor, their convictions conflict. Only one, at most, can be true.

Practical-reasoning theories aim to explain the objective purport of ethical conviction, but in a way that respects a fundamental distinction between theoretical and practical reason. Like noncognitivism, these theories sharply distinguish between ethics and those theoretical disciplines that aim to represent some independent reality, whether the order of nature or some supersensible metaphysical realm. They therefore reject both naturalism and rational intuitionism. But they also deny noncognitivism, since they hold that ethical propositions can be true or false.

According to practical-reasoning theories, objectivity consists not in accurate representation of an independent order, but in demands that are universally imposed within an agent's own practical reasoning. What marks ethics off from science is its intrinsically practical character, its hold on us as agents. It is because there is such a thing as practical reason, a form rational agents' deliberations must take, that there is such a thing as ethics.

But what form does rational deliberation take? Uncontroversially, practical reasoning includes reasoning from ends to means. The interesting debates concern what else it involves, if anything, and how instrumental reasoning is itself to be understood. Humeans maintain that means–end reasoning exhausts practical reason and that instrumental reason can be reduced to the use of theoretical reason in discovering means to ends. They tend not to be practical-reasoning theorists, however, since they argue that ethics fundamentally concerns what engages human sympathy or moral sentiment rather than what it is rational for a person to do. By contrast, practical-reasoning theorists deny that practical reason can be reduced to theoretical reason. As Christine Korsgaard has argued, even instrumental practical reason directs an agent who has already used theoretical reason in determining that B is the only means to his end A to undertake B (or to give up A as an end). In this way instrumental practical reasoning parallels the structure of *modus ponens* in theoretical reasoning (the move from "p" and "if p, then q" to "q").

Pursuing the analogy with theoretical reasoning (while insisting on irreducibility) further suggests that instrumental reasoning cannot exhaust practical reason. When we reason from our beliefs—for example, with *modus ponens*—we reason from their contents, not from the fact of our believing them. We reason from p and if p, then q, not from the facts that we believe that p and that we believe that if p, then q. Similarly, when we adopt an end, we do not simply select it by sheer fiat. Rather, we choose it as something (we think) there is some reason to do. Thus, when we reason from our ends, we do not reason from the fact that they are our

ends but from our commitments to them as things it makes sense to do. That is why instrumental rationality is so uncontroversial. As R. M. Hare argued, it is questionable at best that it follows from the facts that a person's end is to kill someone in the most grisly possible way and that using a cleaver is such a way that the person ought, or has some normative reason, to use a cleaver. What is uncontroversial is simply that the support of reasons transfers from end to means, other things being equal, and from not taking the (only available) means to renouncing the end, other things being equal. It follows only that a person ought to use a cleaver or give up my end.

According to practical-reasoning theories,

objectivity consists not in

accurate representation of an independent order,

but in demands that are universally imposed

within an agent's own practical reasoning.

On grounds such as these, practical-reasoning theorists tend to hold that instrumental rationality cannot exhaust practical reason. But how are we to deliberate about ends? What makes something a reason for adopting an end? Since they hold that reasons for action are necessarily connected to the agent's deliberative perspective, practical-reasoning theorists generally adopt what Korsgaard has called the internalism requirement, according to which a reason must be something the agent could, in principle, be moved by in deliberation and act on. This makes it a necessary condition of something's being a reason for an agent that she would be moved by it insofar as she deliberated rationally.

But what then is rational deliberation? Practical-reason theorists are loath to derive a deliberative ideal by independently specifying paradigm reasons for acting and holding that deliberation is rational when it responds appropriately to them. That would theorize practical reason too much on the model of theoretical reason. Rather, they maintain that rational deliberation must be understood formally, so that reason for acting is a status consideration inherit when it is such that it would move an agent who formed her will in accordance with that deliberative ideal.

The aspects that have been considered so far are relatively common among practical-reasoning theories, although not, perhaps, universal. Within these theories, however, there is a major division between neo-Hobbesians and neo-Kantians. Although nothing on the surface of practical-reasoning theory might suggest this result, it is notable that both camps attempt to vindicate the commonsense idea that moral obligations are supremely authoritative. Both argue that (at least some central) moral demands are demands of practical reason.

Neo-Hobbesianism

Recent versions of this view have their roots in ideas advanced by Kurt Baier in the late 1950s and attempt to address a significant problem faced by Baier's early view. Baier argued that reasons for acting must ultimately connect with the agent's interests. This does not reduce all practical reasoning to prudential reasoning, since other forms may advance agents' interests also. Specifically, Baier argued that morality may be viewed as a system of practical reasoning that is in the interest of everyone alike. Since it is mutually advantageous for everyone to regard moral obligations as supremely authoritative, Baier concluded that they actually do create overriding reasons for acting.

David Gauthier objected to Baier's theory that, while it is in the interest of each that all regard interest-trumping moral reasons as supreme, it is unclear how this can show that an individual agent should so regard them, since it will still most advance her interest to act prudentially when morality conflicts with self-interest. Why, then, might it not be true that instrumental and prudential reasoning exhaust practical reason, even if a person should hope to live in a world in which other people view things differently and (mistakenly) treat moral reasons as authoritative?

Gauthier is himself responsible for the major recent neo-Hobbesian practical-reasoning theory. Like Baier, Gauthier begins from the premise that practical reasoning must work to advance the agent's interests, although here his account is more nearly "internalist," since he understands a person's interests to consist in what she would herself prefer were she to be fully informed. Also like Baier, Gauthier argues that the fact that mutual advantage may require individuals to constrain their pursuit of self-interest can be used to show that practical reason counsels this constraint. However, it is not enough that it be true that everyone would do better if everyone so constrained their prudential reasoning. The crucial point for Gauthier is that individuals can do better if they constrain self-interest by a willingness to abide by mutually advantageous agreements.

Two agents who appear to each other to be unconstrained pursuers of self-interest simply cannot make agreements, however mutually advantageous the agreements might be, if these agreements would require the agents to act contrary to their own interests. In what have come to be known as prisoner's dilemma situa-

tions, therefore, mutually advantageous rational agreement between such persons is impossible. If each believes the other will rationally defect from the agreement on the condition that doing so is in her interest, then neither can rationally make the agreement.

Practical-reasoning theorists

tend to hold that instrumental rationality

cannot exhaust practical reason.

Personal advantage therefore counsels presenting oneself to others as someone who is not an unconstrained maximizer of self-interest. Of course, it is possible, theoretically, for someone to do this while still deliberating as an unconstrained prudential reasoner. But it may not be practically possible, Gauthier argues, at least not for normal human beings. Human motivation may be sufficiently translucent—through involuntary response, for example—so that the least costly way of appearing to others as someone who can be relied upon to keep mutually advantageous, interest-constraining agreements is actually to be such a person. If that is so, then instrumental and prudential reason will not support themselves as principles to guide rational deliberation. On the contrary, they will recommend that agents deliberate in terms of an alternative conception of practical reason that counsels keeping mutually advantageous agreements, even when this is contrary to self-interest.

As a practical-reasoning theorist, Gauthier believes that reasons for acting cannot be understood except in relation to what should guide a rational agent in deliberation. And he believes that a rational agent is someone whose dispositions of choice and deliberation serve her best and most advance her interest. But just as indirect forms of ethical consequentialism, such as character- and rule-consequentialism, face the objection that they are unstable and threaten to collapse either into act-consequentialism or deontology, Gauthier's indirect consequentialist theory of rationality may face the same objection. What motivates the move away from unconstrained prudence, on the grounds that it cannot support itself in the agent's practical thinking, is a view about the role a principle of rational conduct must be able to play in the deliberations of an autonomous rational agent that may be more Kantian than Hobbesian in inspiration.

Neo-Kantianism

This contemporary tradition may be held to date from Thomas Nagel's *The Possibility of Altruism* (1970) and

John Rawls's reinvigoration of Kantian moral and political philosophy in *A Theory of Justice* (1971) and "Kantian Constructivism in Moral Theory" (1980). Nagel's book was read as having both a modest and a more ambitious agenda. His more modest goal, suggested by his title, was to show how such "objective" (or, as he later termed them, "agent-neutral") considerations as "that acting would be relative *someone's* pain" can be genuine reasons for acting. A consideration can be rationally motivating, he argued, even if the agent lacks any relevant desire for acting on it other than one that is motivated by the awareness of that very consideration. A person may be moved, for instance, by considering long-term interests. And if motivation at a distance is possible with prudence, it can happen with altruism as well. Altruistic and other agent-neutral considerations can be rationally motivating.

Nagel's more ambitious agenda was to argue that practical reasoning is subject to a formal constraint that effectively requires that any genuine reason for acting be agent neutral. Stressing the "motivational content" of genuine practical judgments, Nagel argued that avoiding a kind of solipsism is possible only if an agent is able to make the same practical judgment of himself from an impersonal standpoint as he does from an egocentric point of view. Since accepting practical judgments from one's own point of view normally motivates, Nagel maintained, making the same judgment of oneself from an impersonal standpoint should normally motivate also. But this will be so only if the reasons for acting that ground practical judgments are agent neutral. So it is a necessary condition for avoiding practical solipsism that agents take considerations such as that something will advance their own ends or interests as reasons only if they regard them as instantiating more general, agent-neutral reasons, such as that acting will advance someone's ends or interests. Nagel later retreated from this strong claim in a direction that is arguably even more Kantian. Autonomous agency, he later argued, involves an agent's acting on reasons she can endorse from an objective standpoint, and such a set of reasons will include both agent-relative and agent-neutral ones.

Neo-Kantian practical-reasoning theories have been put forward by a number of philosophers, including Alan Gewirth, Stephen Darwall, and Christine Korsgaard. Korsgaard's sympathetic reconstruction of Kant's own arguments in a series of papers has been especially influential. Common to all these neo-Kantian approaches has been the idea that the practical reasoning of an autonomous agent has a formal structure, with its own internal standards and constraints, and that these provide the fundamental truth and objectivity conditions for ethical thought and discourse. Thus, Gewirth maintains that fundamental moral principles are derivable from propositions to which a rational agent is committed from within the deliberative standpoint in acting. And Korsgaard argues that even instrumental theorists are committed to the "hypothetical imperative" as a practical norm. Since, however, we regard ourselves to be free as agents to adopt and renounce ends, practical reason cannot possibly be exhausted by any mere consistency constraint, such as the hypothetical imperative. It follows, the neo-Kantians argue, that practical reason requires norms to regulate the choice of ends no less than to guide the choice of means. In choosing ends for reasons we commit ourselves implicitly to principles of choice as valid for all. But such a commitment is not, they claim, a hypothesis about some independently existing order of normative fact to which we might have cognitive access. That, after all, is precisely the difference between theoretical and practical reason. So the standards to which deliberation is subject must ultimately be based on some formal principle of impartial endorsement that is internal to free practical reasoning itself. And this will be so, they conclude, only if practical reasoning is regulated by some such principle as the categorical imperative, which requires that one act only on principles that one can will to regulate the deliberation and choices of all. If moral demands are ultimately grounded in the categorical imperative also, it will follow that moral demands are demands of practical reason.

[See also Consequentialism; Ethical Theory; Hare, Richard M.; Kant, Immanuel; Naturalism; Rationality; Rawls, John.]

BIBLIOGRAPHY

Baier, K. *The Moral Point of View.* Ithaca, NY, 1958.
Darwall, S. *Impartial Reason.* Ithaca, NY, 1983.
Falk, W. D. *Ought, Reasons, and Morality.* Ithaca, NY, 1986.
Gauthier, D. "Morality and Advantage," *Philosophical Review,* Vol. 76 (1967), 460–75.
———. *Morals by Agreement.* Oxford, 1986.
Gewirth, A. *Reasons and Morality.* Chicago, 1978.
Korsgaard, C. "The Source of Normativity," in G. Peterson, ed., *The Tanner Lectures on Human Values.* Salt Lake City, 1994.
Nagel, T. *The Possibility of Altruism.* Oxford, 1970.
———. *The View from Nowhere.* New York, 1986.
Rawls, J. *A Theory of Justice.* Cambridge, MA, 1971.
———. "Kantian Constructivism in Moral Theory," *Journal of Philosophy,* Vol. 77 (1980), 515–72.

— STEPHEN DARWALL

PRAGMATICS

Pragmatics was defined by Morris (1938) as the branch of semiotics which studies the relation of signs to interpreters, in contrast with semantics, which studies the relation of signs to designata. In practice, it has often been treated as a repository for any aspect of utterance meaning beyond the scope of existing semantic machinery, as in the slogan 'Pragmatics = meaning minus truth conditions' (Gazdar, 1979). There has been some doubt about whether it is a homogeneous domain (Searle, Kiefer, & Bierwisch, 1980).

A more positive view emerges from the work of Grice, whose *William James Lectures* (1967) are fundamental. Grice showed that many aspects of utterance meaning traditionally regarded as conventional, or semantic, could be more explanatorily treated as conversational, or pragmatic. For Gricean pragmatists, the crucial feature of pragmatic interpretation is its inferential nature: the hearer is seen as constructing and evaluating a hypothesis about the communicator's intentions, based, on the one hand, on the meaning of the sentence uttered, and on the other, on contextual information and general communicative principles that speakers are normally expected to observe. (For definition and surveys see Levinson, 1983.)

The Semantics–Pragmatics Distinction

In early work, the semantics–pragmatics distinction was often seen as coextensive with the distinction between truth-conditional and non-truth-conditional meaning (Gazdar, 1979). On this approach, pragmatics would deal with a range of disparate phenomena, including (a) Gricean conversational inference, (b) the inferential recognition of illocutionary-force, and (c) the conventional meanings of illocutionary-force indicators and other non-truth-conditional expressions such as 'but', 'please', 'unfortunately' (Recanati, 1987). From the cognitive point of view, these phenomena have little in common.

Within the cognitive science literature in particular, the semantics–pragmatics distinction is now more generally seen as coextensive with the distinction between decoding and inference (or conventional and conversational meaning). On this approach, all conventional meaning, both truth-conditional and non-truth-conditional, is left to linguistic semantics, and the aim of pragmatic theory is to explain how the gap between sentence meaning and utterance interpretation is inferentially bridged. A pragmatic theory of this type is developed in Sperber and Wilson (1986).

Implicature

Grice's distinction between saying and implicating cross-cuts the semantics–pragmatics distinction as defined above. For Grice, 'what is said' corresponds to the truth-conditional content of an utterance, and 'what is implicated' is everything communicated that is not part of what is said. Grice saw the truth-conditional content of an utterance as determined partly by the conventional (semantic) meaning of the sentence uttered, and partly by contextual (pragmatic) factors governing disambiguation and reference assignment. He saw conventional (semantic) implicatures as determined by the meaning of discourse connectives such as 'but', 'moreover' and 'so', and analyzed them as signaling the performance of higher-order speech acts such as contrasting, adding and explaining (Grice, 1989). An alternative analysis is developed in Blakemore (1987).

In practice, pragmatics has often been treated as a repository for any aspect of utterance meaning beyond the scope of existing semantic machinery, as in the slogan

"Pragmatics = meaning minus truth conditions."

Among nonconventional (pragmatic) implicatures, the best known are the conversational ones: these are beliefs that have to be attributed to the speaker in order to preserve the assumption that she was obeying the 'cooperative principle' (with associated maxims of truthfulness, informativeness, relevance, and clarity), in saying what she said. In Grice's framework, generalized conversational implicatures are 'normally' carried by use of a certain expression, and are easily confused with conventional lexical meaning (Grice, 1989). In Grice's view, many earlier philosophical analyses were guilty of such confusion.

Grice's account of conversational implicatures has been questioned on several grounds:

(1) The status and content of the cooperative principle and maxims have been debated, and attempts to reduce the maxims or provide alternative sources for implicatures have been undertaken (Davis, 1991; Horn, 1984; Levinson, 1987; Sperber & Wilson, 1986).

(2) Grice claimed that deliberate, blatant maxim-violation could result in implicatures, in the case of metaphor and irony in particular. This claim has been challenged, and alternative accounts of metaphor and irony developed, in which no maxim-violation takes place (Blakemore, 1992; Hugly & Sayward, 1979; Sperber & Wilson, 1986).

(3) Pragmatic principles have been found to make a substantial contribution to explicit communication, not only in disambiguation and reference assignment, but in enriching the linguistically encoded meaning in various ways. This raises the question of where the borderline between explicit and implicit communication

should be drawn (Sperber & Wilson, 1986, 1995). It has even been argued that many of Grice's best-known cases of generalized conversational implicature might be better analyzed as pragmatically determined aspects of what is said (Carston, 1988; Recanati, 1989).

(4) The idea that the context for utterance interpretation is determined in advance of the utterance has been questioned, and the identification of an appropriate set of contextual assumptions is now seen as an integral part of the utterance-interpretation process (Blakemore, 1992; Sperber & Wilson, 1986).

Prospects

Within the cognitive science literature, several approaches to pragmatics are currently being pursued. There are computational attempts to implement the Gricean program via rules for the recognition of coherence relations among discourse segments (Asher & Lascarides, 1995; Hobbs, 1985). Relations between the Gricean program and speech-act theory are being reassessed (Tsohatzidis, 1994). The cognitive foundations of pragmatics and the relations of pragmatics to neighboring disciplines are still being explored (Sperber & Wilson, 1995; Sperber, 1994). Despite this diversity of approaches, pragmatics now seems to be established as a relatively homogenous domain.

[See also Cognitive Science; Grice, Herbert Paul; Metaphor; Philosophy of Language; Reference; Semantics.]

BIBLIOGRAPHY

Asher, N., and A. Lascarides. "Lexical Disambiguation in a Discourse Context," *Journal of Semantics*, Vol. 12 (1995), 69–108.

Blakemore, D. *Semantic Constraints on Relevance.* Oxford, 1987.

———. *Understanding Utterances.* Oxford, 1992.

Carston, R. "Explicature, Implicature and Truth-Theoretic Semantics," in R. Kempson, ed., *Mental Representation: The Interface Between Language and Reality* (Cambridge, 1988).

Davis, S., ed. *Pragmatics: A Reader.* Oxford, 1991.

Gazdar, G. *Pragmatics: Implicature, Presupposition and Logical Form.* New York, 1979.

Grice, H. P. "Logic and Conversation," *William James Lectures* (Cambridge, MA, 1967).

———. *Studies in the Way of Words.* Cambridge, MA, 1989.

Hobbs, J. "On the Coherence and Structure of Discourse," Center for the Study of Language and Information (October, 1985).

Horn, L. "A New Taxonomy for Pragmatic Inference: Q-based and R-based Implicature," in D. Schiffrin, ed., *Meaning, Form and Use in Context* (Washington, DC, 1984).

Hugly, P., and C. Sayward. "A Problem About Conversational Implicature," *Linguistics and Philosophy*, Vol. 3 (1979), 19–25.

Levinson, S. *Pragmatics.* Cambridge, 1983.

———. "Minimization and Conversational Inference," in J. Verschueren and M. Bertuccelli-Papi, eds., *The Pragmatic Perspective* (Amsterdam, 1987).

Morris, C. "Foundations of the Theory of Signs," in O. Neurath, R. Carnap, and C. Morris, eds., *International Encyclopedia of Unified Science* (Chicago, 1938).

Recanati, F. *Meaning and Force.* Cambridge, 1987.

———. "The Pragmatics of What Is Said," *Mind and Language*, Vol. 4 (1989), 295–329.

Searle, J., F. Kiefer, and M. Bierwisch, eds. *Speech-Act Theory and Pragmatics.* Dordrecht, 1980.

Sperber, D. "Understanding Verbal Understanding," in J. Khalfa, ed., *What Is Intelligence?* (Cambridge, 1994).

Sperber, D., and D. Wilson. *Relevance: Communication and Cognition.* Oxford, 1986.

———. "Postface" to the second edition of *Relevance.* Oxford, 1995.

Tsohatzidis, S., ed. *Foundations of Speech-Act Theory: Philosophical and Linguistic Perspectives.* London, 1994.

– DEIRDRE WILSON

PRAGMATISM

Not unexpectedly, given that pragmatism is not a doctrine but a method (as Charles Peirce put it), the tradition of classical pragmatism is formidably diverse. Even the method—the pragmatic maxim—is differently interpreted by different pragmatists; and this diversity is compounded by the different doctrines and interests of the various pragmatists. But there is a pattern discernible within the diversity: a shift from Peirce's reformist, scientific philosophy, anchored by his realism about natural kinds and laws and about the objects of perception, through William James's more nominalist pragmatism, his insistence that "the trail of the human serpent is over everything" (1907, p. 37), through John Dewey's proposal that the concept of warranted assertibility replace the concept of truth, to the radicalism of F. C. S. Schiller's avowedly Protagorean relativization of truth to human interests.

Contemporary pragmatisms are no less diverse, but the spectrum has shifted to the left. The more conservative neopragmatists are as akin to James as to Peirce, and the most radical go beyond Schiller's relativism to an anti-philosophical, sometimes anti-scientific, even anti-intellectual, stance—a stance so much at odds with the aspirations of the founders of pragmatism as to put one in mind of Peirce's complaints about writers who persisted in "twisting [the pragmatists'] purpose and purport all awry" (*Collected Papers*, 5.464).

Nicholas Rescher describes his philosophy as pragmatic idealism: idealism, because it holds that "reality . . . as humans deal with it is *our* reality—our thought-world as we conceive and model it" (1994, p. 377); pragmatic, because it holds that, though our picture of reality is a mental construction, it is not a free construction but is objectively constrained by success or failure in practice, in prediction and attainment of purpose.

In some ways—not least in philosophizing unapologetically in the grand systematic manner—Rescher is much like Peirce; indeed, his conception of the interlocking cognitive, evaluative, and practical aspects of rationality takes him further than Peirce into some of the territory of value theory. In other ways Rescher's pragmatism is more reminiscent of James: *inter alia,* for its stress on practical consequences and on a pluralism of perspectival truth-claims. So, too, is his idealism. *Qua* pragmatist Peirce denies the intelligibility of the in-principle-incognizable; *qua* "objective idealist" he maintains that "matter is just effete mind" (*Collected Papers,* 6.25). Rescher's idealism sounds more like the Jamesian serpent—or Deweyan interactionism.

The more radical neopragmatists go beyond Schiller's relativism to an anti-philosophical, sometimes even anti-intellectual stance at odds with the aspirations of the founders of pragmatism.

In repudiating metaphysical realism and endorsing internal realism, Hilary Putnam evinced some sympathy with Peircean conceptions of truth and reality. But his conceptual relativism—"Our language cannot be divided into two parts, a part that describes the world 'as it is anyway' and a part that describes our conceptual contribution" (1992, p. 123)—sounded more like James. However, his argument against the irrealism of Nelson Goodman (himself classifiable as a left-wing Jamesian of the boldest nominalist stripe) stressed the distinction between wholly conventional names such as "Sirius" and only partially conventional general terms such as "star." Putnam thus recalled Peirce's realism of natural kinds, and perhaps divided our language after all. It is not surprising, then, to find that most recently, in his Dewey lectures, he tends to a more realist stance.

Sympathetic in the 1950s and 1960s to the positivists' aspiration to "a scientific single theory that explains everything" (Putnam, 1992, p. 2), Putnam is since then inclined to a pluralistic, problem-centered approach to philosophy. Here, as in his defense of democracy as a precondition for the application of intelligence to the solution of social problems, he acknowledges Dewey.

A year before the publication of W. V. O. Quine's "Two Dogmas," Morton G. White had invoked Dewey in describing the analytic-synthetic distinction as "an untenable dualism." Rejecting that distinction, adopting a holism of verification, insisting on the underdetermination of theory by data, Quine describes himself as going beyond C. I. Lewis's pragmatic a priori to a

"more thorough pragmatism" that emphasizes pragmatic considerations in theory-choice generally. "Pragmatic" here suggests the relatively unconstrained rather than, as in Rescher, a kind of constraint. Quine refers approvingly to Schiller's view of truth as man-made as one of pragmatism's main contributions to empiricism. But he hopes to avoid Schiller's relativism by means of a naturalism that views philosophy as internal to science. This differs significantly from Peirce's and Dewey's aspiration to make philosophy scientific by applying the method of science to philosophical questions.

As another of pragmatism's main contributions Quine mentions Peirce's and Dewey's connecting belief and meaning to behavior. But Quine's behaviorism is more stringent, in part because of the influence of B. F. Skinner, and in part because Quine's extensionalism leaves him uneasy, as Peirce was not, with any irreducibly dispositional talk.

As Putnam's allusions to the existentialist character of James's ethics indicate, some hope a neopragmatism might heal the analytic-Continental rift. One example is Karl-Otto Apel's grafting of pragmatic elements from Peirce and Jürgen Habermas onto Alfred Tarski's semantic conception of truth. Another is Joseph Margolis's attempt, emphasizing both the biological roots and the "deep historicity" of human injury, and proposing a reconciliation of a modest realism with a weak relativism, to marry themes from Peirce with themes from Martin Heidegger.

Richard Rorty describes himself as accommodating themes from Dewey with themes from Heidegger. Maintaining that "revolutionary movements within an intellectual discipline require a revisionist history of that discipline" (1983, p. xvii), Rorty dismisses Peirce as having merely given pragmatism its name. And he urges in the name of pragmatism that the project of a philosophical theory of knowledge should be abandoned; that science is exemplary only as a model of human solidarity; that philosophy is more akin to literature than to science; that it should be in the service of democratic politics; that truth is "not the kind of thing one should expect to have a philosophically interesting theory about" (1983, p. xiv) and that to call a statement true is just to give it "a rhetorical pat on the back" (1983, p. xvii); that pragmatism is antirepresentationalism.

There is some affinity between Rorty and Schiller. But Peirce, who was a pioneer of the theory of signs, of representation, and who desired "to rescue the good ship Philosophy for the service of Science from the hands of the lawless rovers of the sea of literature" (*Collected Papers,* 5.449), would disagree with Rorty's pragmatism in every particular. So too, except perhaps for his description of the best ethical writing as akin to "novels and dramas of the deeper sort" (1891, p. 316), would James. And so, most to the point, would Dewey, who hoped to renew the philosophical theory of knowledge by making it more scientific, and whose political philosophy is infused by the hope that the application of scientific methods would enable intelligent social reform, and by the conviction that a free society is a prerequisite of a flourishing science.

[See also Democracy; Dewey, John; Goodman, Nelson; Habermas, Jürgen; Heidegger, Martin; James, William; Naturalism; Peirce, Charles Sanders; Pragmatism; Putnam, Hilary; Quine, Willard Van Orman; Rationality; Realism.]

BIBLIOGRAPHY

Apel, K.-O. "C. S. Peirce and the Post-Tarskian Problem of an Adequate Explication of the Meaning of Truth: Towards a Transcendental-Pragmatic Theory of Truth," in E. Freeman, ed., *The Relevance of Charles Peirce* (La Salle, IL, 1983).

Bernstein, R. "The Resurgence of Pragmatism," *Social Research*, Vol. 59 (1992), 813–40.

Goodman, N. *Ways of Worldmaking*. Hassocks, Sussex, 1978.

James, W. *Pragmatism*, edited by F. Burkhardt and F. Bowers. Cambridge, MA, and London, 1975.

———. "The Moral Philosopher and the Moral Life," *International Journal of Ethics*, Vol. 1 (1891); in G. Bird, ed., *William James: Selected Writings* (1994).

Margolis, J. *Pragmatism without Foundations*. Oxford, 1986.

Peirce, C. S. *Collected Papers*, edited by C. Hawthorne, P. Weiss, and A. Burks. Cambridge, MA, 1931–1958.

Putnam, H. *Renewing Philosophy*. Cambridge, MA, 1992.

———. *Words and Life*. Cambridge, MA, 1994. Sec 3, "The Inheritance of Pragmatism."

———. "Sense, Nonsense and the Senses: An Inquiry into the Powers of the Human Mind," *Journal of Philosophy*, Vol. XC1.9 (1994), 447–517.

Quine, W. V. O. "Two Dogmas of Empiricism," *Philosophical Review*, Vol. 60 (1951), 20–43.

———. "The Pragmatists' Place in Empiricism," in R. J. Mulvaney and P. M. Zeltner, eds., *Pragmatism: Its Sources and Prospects* (Columbia, SC, 1981).

Rescher, N. *A System of Pragmatic Idealism*, 3 vols. Princeton, NJ, 1992–94.

———, et al. *Philosophy and Phenomenological Research*, Vol. 54 (1994), 377–457.

Rorty, R. *The Consequences of Pragmatism*. Hassocks, Sussex, 1983.

Thayer, H. S. *Meaning and Action: A Critical History of Pragmatism*. Indianapolis, 1968.

White, M. G. "The Analytic and the Synthetic: An Untenable Dualism," in Sidney Hook, ed., *John Dewey, Philosopher of Science and Freedom* (New York, 1950).

— SUSAN HAACK

PRAGMATIST EPISTEMOLOGY

William James's observation that "when . . . we give up the doctrine of objective certitude, we do not thereby give up the quest or hope of truth itself" (1956, p. 17) succinctly expresses one important epistemological theme of traditional pragmatism: accommodation of a thoroughgoing fallibilism with a modest optimism about the possibility of successful truth seeking. Also characteristic of that tradition is its naturalism, its acknowledgment of the biological, and the social as well as the logical elements in the theory of knowledge, and its respect for science as, in Charles Peirce's words, "the epitome of man's intellectual development" (*Collected Papers*, 7.49). Since 1968 these ideas have been variously worked out by some who are fully aware of their roots in pragmatism and have also entered the thinking of many who are not. More surprising, some self-styled neopragmatists defend epistemological positions (or anti-epistemological positions) quite unlike these classically pragmatist themes.

An important epistemological theme of traditional pragmatism accommodates a thoroughgoing fallibilism with a modest optimism about the possibility of successful truth seeking.

Both fallibilism and naturalism are prominent themes in W. V. O. Quine's epistemology, themes of which he acknowledges the pragmatist ancestry; his fallibilism, furthermore, like Peirce's, extends to mathematics and logic, and his naturalism, like Peirce's, has an evolutionary character. And he shares the pragmatists' regard for science. However, he seems drawn beyond a view of epistemology as resting in part on empirical assumptions about human cognitive capacities to conceiving of it as internal to the sciences of cognition; and thence, under pressure of the implausibility of supposing that psychology or biology could answer the questions about evidence, justification, and so forth, with which epistemology has traditionally been concerned, he seems drawn to a revolutionary scientism that would abandon the traditional questions in favor of questions the sciences can be expected to answer. Unlike his fallibilism and his modest, reformist naturalism, neither his scientism nor his revolutionary displacement of epistemology falls within the tradition of pragmatism.

Nicholas Rescher's approach, from its insistence that we humans "cannot function, let alone thrive, without knowledge of what goes on around us" (1994, p. 380) to its stress on the provisional, tentative character of all our estimates of truth, is unambivalently within the pragmatist tradition. But Rescher takes issue with

Peirce's definition of truth, and therefore conceives of progress in terms of improvement over earlier stages rather than closeness to a supposed final stage.

Focusing on criteria of evidence and justification rather than on guidelines for the conduct of inquiry, Susan Haack adapts from the pragmatist tradition: her fallibilism, expressed in the thesis that justification comes in degrees; her weak, reformist naturalism, expressed in the thesis that our criteria of evidence have built into them empirical presuppositions about human cognitive capacities; her account of perception; and her strategy for the metajustification of criteria of justification.

In stark contrast to Rescher or Haack, Richard Rorty urges in the name of pragmatism that the philosophical theory of knowledge is misconceived; and, in contrast to Quine, that epistemology should be, not replaced by the psychology of cognition, but simply abandoned. Rorty likens his repudiation of epistemology to Dewey's critique of the "spectator theory." What Dewey intended, however, was to reform epistemology, to replace the quest for certain knowledge of eternal, unchanging objects with a realistic account of fallible, experimental, empirical inquiry. Rorty's revolutionary attitude derives from his conception of justification as a matter exclusively of our practices of defending and criticizing beliefs, not grounded in any connection of evidence and truth. This "conversationalist" conception of justification is motivated by his rejection of any conception of truth as meaning more than "what you can defend against all comers."

Often accused of relativism, Rorty denies the charge. He escapes it, however, only by shifting from contextualism ("A is justified in believing that p iff (if and only if) he can defend p by the standards of his community") to tribalism (". . . iff he can defend p by the standards of our community" [1979, p. 308]). But tribalism is arbitrary if our practices of criticizing and defending beliefs are, as Rorty holds, not grounded in any connection of evidence and truth.

In not-so-stark contrast to Rorty, Stephen Stich urges in the name of pragmatism that it is mere epistemic chauvinism to care whether one's beliefs are true, and that justified beliefs are those that conduce to whatever the subject values. True, Stich cheerfully embraces relativism (and rejects tribalism since he thinks our epistemic practices too preoccupied with truth); and he looks to the sciences of cognition to help us "improve" our cognitive processing so as better to achieve what we really value. But, as more overtly in Rorty, the effect is profoundly anti-epistemological and "pragmatist" in quite another sense than the traditional one.

[See also Dewey, John; Epistemology; James, William; Naturalism; Peirce, Charles Sanders; Quine, Willard Van Orman.]

BIBLIOGRAPHY

Haack, S. *Evidence and Inquiry.* Oxford, 1993.
James, W. *The Will to Believe* [1897]. New York, 1956.
Peirce, C. S. *Collected Papers,* edited by C. Hawthorne, P. Weiss, and A. Burks. Cambridge, MA, 1931–1958.
Quine, W. V. O. "Epistemology Naturalized," in *Ontological Relativity and Other Essays* (New York, 1967).
———. "Natural Kinds," in *Ontological Relativity and Other Essays* (New York, 1969).
———. "The Pragmatists' Place in Empiricism," in R. J. Mulvaney and P. M. Zeltner, eds., *Pragmatism: Its Sources and Prospects* (Columbia, SC, 1981), 21–40.
Rescher, N. *A System of Pragmatic Idealism,* Vol. 1, *Human Knowledge in Idealistic Perspective* (Princeton, NJ, 1992).
———. "Précis of *A System of Pragmatic Idealism,*" *Philosophy and Phenomenological Research,* Vol. 54, (1994) 377–90.
Rorty, R. *Philosophy and the Mirror of Nature.* Princeton, NJ, 1979.
Stich, S. P. *The Fragmentation of Reason.* Cambridge, MA, 1990.

– SUSAN HAACK

PRESUPPOSITION

Consider the following famous example from Bertrand Russell.

(1) The present king of France is bald.

According to Russell, (1) is false because it asserts the existence of the present king of France. However, following Strawson (1952), a number of philosophers and linguists have maintained that, if there is no present king of France, an utterance of (1) fails to have a determinate truth value—in Strawson's words, the question of whether (1) is true or false "does not arise." On this view, (1) therefore does not assert or even entail the existence of the present king of France but rather "presupposes" his existence.

The Range of Phenomena

Sentences like (1) are argued to presuppose the existence of a particular individual, but there are many other presupposition effects. It has been argued, for example, that factive verbs such as "know" and "regret" presuppose the truth of their complement clauses and that "certain aspectuals"—a class of verbs such as "quit" and "continue"—also presuppose certain actions having taken place (this class covers the example "Have you stopped beating your dog?"). It also appears that a number of modifiers introduce presupposition effects, for example "again," "too," "even," and so forth. Karttunen (1973) argued that in propositional-attitude environments such as "Fred wants to sell his unicorn" it is presupposed that Fred believes he has a unicorn. A number of additional constructions that invoke presupposition effects have been explored, including those triggered by phonological stress. So, for example, if I say "I didn't go to the BASEBALL game," it arguably presupposes that I went to some other kind of game.

Presupposition Versus Entailment

The philosophical controversy surrounding presupposition comes in at the very beginning—determining whether these are genuine cases of presupposition or are merely cases of entailment. To illustrate, consider (2)–(4):

(2) Fred stopped washing the dishes.
(3) Fred didn't stop washing the dishes.
(4) Fred had been washing the dishes.

According to the presupposition thesis, both (2) and (3) presuppose (4). Hence, if (4) is false, then (2) and (3) must lack determinate truth values. Alternatively, according to the entailment analysis, (2) entails (4).

The doctrine of presupposition remains somewhat controversial, but at the same time it has found interesting applications.

Should (4) be false, then according to the entailment analysis (2) will be false and (3) will be true. This dispute has all the makings of a stalemate, since it turns on speakers' intuitions about whether sentences lack genuine truth values under the relevant conditions or are merely false. Indeed, Strawson (1964) came to doubt whether the matter could in fact be settled by "brisk little formal argument[s]" and offered that each view could be reasonable, depending on one's interests. Others have put more stock in brisk little formal arguments, notably Wilson (1975), who offered an extensive critique of the presuppositional analysis.

The Projection Problem

One of the most interesting questions to surface is the so-called projection problem for presupposition, first observed by Langendoen and Savin (1971). This problem involves the question of what happens when a construction with a presupposition is embedded in more complex constructions (e.g., in propositional-attitude constructions or in the scope of negation). To illustrate, when (2) is negated, yielding (3), it continues to presuppose (4)—the presupposition is said to be projected. Other constructions, such as "doubts that," do not always project presuppositions, and still others (such as the "wants" case from Karttunen, discussed above) project something weaker than the original presupposition. The question is therefore whether projection presup-

position is arbitrary or whether it obeys certain specific rules. Much subsequent work has attempted to articulate those "projection rules" (see Gazdar, 1979; Heim, 1991; Karttunen, 1973; and Soames, 1979, 1982, for important examples).

Semantic Versus Pragmatic Presupposition

If one accepts that there are genuine instances of presupposition, there remains the question of whether presupposition is a reflex of semantics or pragmatics—that is, whether the presupposition follows from the meaning of the sentence or is merely part of the conversational background. Stalnaker (1974) gave several arguments in favor of the pragmatic alternative, including the interesting observation that, in a case like (5),

(5) If Eagleton hadn't been dropped from the Democratic ticket, Nixon would have won the election

there seems to be a presupposition that Nixon lost, although the effect is weak, and, in the right context or given appropriate information, that presupposition can be overruled. This graded effect suggests that pragmatic phenomena are in play. Stalnaker also observed that the pragmatic alternative is useful in separating the question of entailment relations from the question of presupposition and in working out solutions to the projection problem. (But see Wilson, 1975, for criticism of pragmatic accounts of presupposition.)

Applications

The doctrine of presupposition remains somewhat controversial, but at the same time it has found interesting applications. For example, van Fraassen (1968, 1970) argued that presupposition might be employed in the treatment of the "liar paradox" and proposed that liar sentences are neither true nor false owing to a presupposition failure. Presupposition has also played an important role in work on the semantics of propositional attitudes, much of it extending from the work of Karttunen (1973). Heim (1992), for example, has updated the initial Karttunen analysis with features of Stalnaker's presuppositional analysis. Still other research (including unpublished work by Saul Kripke) has investigated the interplay of presupposition and the analysis of discourse anaphora.

[See also Anaphora; Kripke, Saul Aaron; Liar Paradox; Philosophy of Language; Russell, Bertrand Arthur William; Strawson, Peter F.]

BIBLIOGRAPHY

Gazdar, G. *Pragmatics*. New York, 1979.
Grice, P. "Presupposition and Conversational Implicature," in P. Cole, ed., *Radical Pragmatics* (New York, 1981).

Heim, I. "On the Projection Problem for Presuppositions," in S. Davis, ed., *Pragmatics* (Oxford, 1991).

——. "Presupposition Projection and the Semantics of Attitude Verbs," *Journal of Semantics*, Vol. 9 (1992), 183–221.

Karttunen, L. "Presuppositions of Compound Sentences," *Linguistic Inquiry*, Vol. 4 (1973), 169–93.

Langendoen, D. T., and H. Savin. "The Projection Problem for Presupposition," in C. Filmore and D. T. Langendoen, eds., *Studies in Linguistic Semantics* (New York, 1971).

Soames, S. "A Projection Problem for Speaker Presuppositions," *Linguistic Inquiry*, Vol. 10 (1979), 623–66.

——. "How Presuppositions Are Inherited: A Solution to the Projection Problem," *Linguistic Inquiry*, Vol. 13 (1982), 483–545.

Stalnaker, R. "Pragmatic Presuppositions," in M. Munitz and D. Unger, eds., *Semantics and Philosophy* (New York, 1974).

Strawson, P. *Introduction to Logical Theory*. New York, 1952.

——. "Identifying Reference and Truth-Values," *Theoria*, Vol. 3 (1964), 96–118.

van Fraassen, B. "Presupposition, Implication, and Self-Reference," *Journal of Philosophy*, Vol. 65 (1968), 136–52.

——. "Truth and Paradoxical Consequences," in R. L. Martin, ed., *The Paradox of the Liar* (New Haven, 1970).

Wilson, D. *Presuppositions and Non-Truth-Conditional Semantics*. London, 1975.

— PETER LUDLOW

PRIOR, ARTHUR NORMAN

Arthur Norman Prior was born on December 4, 1914, at Masterton, near Wellington, New Zealand. He acknowledged an early philosophical debt to John Findlay. But his first academic post was at Canterbury University College, where he succeeded Karl Popper. He was the visiting John Locke Lecturer at Oxford in 1956, and in 1958 he was appointed a professor of philosophy at the University of Manchester. After short periods as a visiting professor at the University of Chicago and at the University of California at Los Angeles, he moved in 1966 to a tutorial fellowship at Balliol College, Oxford, and Oxford University appointed him to a concurrent readership. He died in 1969.

Prior's early intellectual interests were very much religious in character. He was influenced for several years by the theologian Arthur Miller, who combined a strict adherence to Presbyterian doctrine with an equally strong support for socialism and opposition to nationalism. But Prior's pacifism weakened, and he served from 1942 to 1945 in the New Zealand air force. And the central focus of his interests gradually shifted—helped by an occasional bout of atheism—from theology to ethics and logic. He exchanged ideas with a wide circle of friends and acquaintances, and his hospitality to students was legendary.

Prior's first book, *Logic and the Basis of Ethics* (1946) traced seventeenth-, eighteenth-, and nineteenth-century anticipations of G. E. Moore's criticism of the so-called naturalistic fallacy. But his main claim to fame lies in his pioneering work on the formal logic of temporal relationships. His most important investigations in this field were published in *Time and Modality* (1957), *Past, Present, and Future* (1967), and *Papers on Time and Tense* (1968). But he also wrote on several logical topics in this Encyclopedia; he published a substantial survey of the current state of logical inquiry under the title of *Formal Logic* (1955; 2d ed., 1962); and a posthumous volume of papers, *Objects of Thought* (1971), was edited by P. T. Geach and A. J. P. Kenny.

Prior almost always used the Polish style of notation in the discussion of logical proofs and principles and was a convinced, though largely unsuccessful, champion of its virtues. The major inadequacy in his tense logic, however, was a failure to discuss or accommodate aspectual differences—roughly, differences between the meanings expressed by verbs in a perfect tense and those expressed by verbs in an imperfect tense (see Galton, 1984). Other criticisms may be found in L. J. Cohen's (1958) review of *Time and Modality* and in his subsequent controversy with Prior (*Philosophy*, Vol. 34 [1959]). In his *Formal Logic* Prior displayed an impressively wide acquaintance with logical systems outside the field of tense logic, and this book remains a useful text for anyone interested in comparisons between different axiomatizations of the propositional calculus, between different kinds of logical quantification, between different modal logics, or between different three-valued or institutionist logics. But the treatment of metalogical issues in the book is occasionally rather selective: for example, in its discussion of completeness proofs for the predicate calculus as against its treatment of completeness proofs for the propositional calculus.

Outside the brilliant originality of his work on tense logic, perhaps Prior's most striking idea was expressed in "The Runabout Inference-Ticket" (1960), where he argued that, if the meaning of a logical connective consisted just in the logical uses to which it can be put (as many seemed to hold), then it would be easy to invent a connective with a meaning that would enable one to infer any conclusion from any premises.

[See also Modal Logic; Nationalism; Pacifism.]

BIBLIOGRAPHY

Works by Prior

Formal Logic. Oxford, 1955; 2d ed., 1962.

Logic and the Basis of Ethics; Oxford, 1946.

Objects of Thought, ed. P. T. Geach and A. J. P. Kenny. Oxford, 1971.

Papers on Time and Tense. Oxford, 1968.

Past, Present, and Future. Oxford, 1967.

"The Runabout Inference-Ticket." *Analysis,* Vol. 21 (1960), 38–9.
Time and Modality. Oxford, 1957.

Works on Prior

Cohen, L. J. Review of *Time and Modality, Philosophical Quarterly,*
    Vol. 8 (1958), 266–71.
Galton, A. *The Logic of Aspect.* Oxford, 1984.

    – L. J. COHEN

PROBABILITY

The word probability is used in a wide variety of contexts in science, ordinary language, and philosophy. We say that the evidence for a scientific hypothesis or law cannot render it certain but can only confer a certain probability on it. We agree that the probability of heads on the toss of an ordinary coin is a half. Probability is fundamental to quantum mechanics; does that mean that the universe is fundamentally probabilistic? A moral agent is not responsible for predicting the future, but he is responsible for taking into account the probable consequences of his actions. The ideas of probability and uncertainty thus enter into philosophy in a number of areas: epistemology, metaphysics, philosophy of science, ethics, and others.

Keynes construed probability as measuring the logical force as an inconclusive argument based on all the available evidence. (UPI/Corbis-Bettmann)

But what is probability? Philosophers and mathematicians have offered a number of ways of understanding the term. None has been accepted universally, and thus a review of the current diversity of interpretations of probability is offered here, with the understanding that more than one interpretation may be useful to our understanding. This entry emphasizes the (few) changes that have occurred since the early 1970s.

There are three main kinds of interpretation of probability. The first construes probability as objective and empirical; these interpretations include but are not limited to the interpretation of probability as a relative frequency. The second construes probability as objective and logical: as measuring the force of an inconclusive argument. The third construes probability as subjective: as reflecting the propensity of an agent to act or to gamble on alternatives.

Objective empirical interpretations of probability construe it as an empirical property of the world: whether a statement of probability is true or false is a matter for empirical investigation. The view is inspired by the use of probability in connection with ideal gambling apparatus, the study of stochastic processes found in nature (for example, statistical mechanics), the theory of errors of measurement, and such special studies as meteorology and epidemiology.

Richard von Mises (1957) was perhaps the staunchest defender of this view. The details of his view are controversial, but it is a controversy that has not aroused much heat in recent years. Some writers (Cramér, 1951) found the conditions of randomness and the existence of limits unnecessary, given that we are dealing with models of natural phenomena. These writers (they include many philosophers and the majority of statisticians) adopt the view that all we have to know about probability is that it has the mathematical properties it is generally assumed to have and that for all practical purposes it can be measured by empirical relative frequencies.

Probability, on these interpretations, is essentially a property of infinite (or 'long') sequences. Yet we often talk of the probabilities of unique events, for example, the probability of heads on the next toss of this coin, or the probability of error in the measurement just made. A somewhat different empirical interpretation of probability was offered by Popper (1959) to accommodate these uses. This is the propensity interpretation of probability. On this view probability is relativized not to a sequence of trials but to a chance setup (Hacking, 1965), for example, tossing a U.S. quarter in a certain apparatus. This setup has a certain propensity to produce heads. Probability is an abstract (objective, empirical) property of the setup that is reflected in frequencies.

On any of these objective interpretations of probability, probability is relative. Thus, an event ('heads') has a probability relative only to a sequence of tosses, a chance setup, a model of tossed coin behavior. The same event may, therefore, have different probabilities relative to different sequences or setups. This is no embarrassment for the theory but presents a difficulty, recognized and discussed by Reichenbach (1949): the practical problem of which sequence or setup to take into account when using probabilities as a guide to action and choice. This has come to be known as the problem of the reference class. Relatively little has been written on this problem in recent years from the point of view under discussion.

A moral agent is not responsible

for predicting the future,

but he is responsible for taking into account

the probable consequences of his actions.

Objective logical interpretations such as that put forward by John Maynard Keynes (1921) construe probability as measuring the logical force of an inconclusive argument based on all the available evidence. This approach focuses on another usage for emphasis: given what we know, there is little probability of rain tomorrow; the evidence indicates with high probability that the vector of this disease is a flying insect; the evidence renders this scientific hypothesis more probable than not.

Keynes did not offer a definition of probability. Rudolf Carnap (1950) launched a program to define probability by means of a measure on the sentences of a formal first-order language. Carnap hoped to find a unique additive, normalized measure m for the 'language of science' that would embody all rational constraints on probabilities. For m to be additive is for $m(s \lor t) = m(s) + m(t)$, when $s \land t$ is logically false, and for it to be normalized is for $0 \leq m(s) \leq 1$, for all s in the language.

Among the problems facing this view are those of finding an appropriate first-order language of science, showing that it is possible to define a function m on such a rich language, finding rational criteria that will dictate the choice of a single function. Considerable thought has been devoted to the second problem, though mainly in computer science (see Bacchus, 1992). The first and third proved daunting, and even Carnap became doubtful that the project was feasible, turning instead toward a partly subjective interpretation

of probability. Little effort has been devoted since the 1960s to finding answers to the first and third problems.

An alternative objective logical approach, pursued by Kyburg (1961), took for granted (as Carnap did) the existence of objective knowledge of relative frequencies and focused on applying that knowledge in particular cases. Probabilities are construed as intervals, reflecting the logical force of argument, and are based on the knowledge of relevant statistics. The interpretation depends on a solution to Reichenbach's problem of the reference class (see Kyburg, 1983).

In response to Keynes, Frank Ramsey (1931) argued for a subjective approach to probability: while logic can determine relations among the agent's degrees of belief, it is no part of logic to measure the force of an inconclusive argument. Ramsey offered a dutch book argument in support of this position: if my degrees of belief represent the odds at which I am willing to bet on either side of a proposition, then a clever bettor can make a set of bets that I will be willing to take under which I am bound to lose no matter what happens, unless my degrees of belief conform to the probability calculus.

Probability, on this view, becomes a subjective matter: an agent may assign any probability he likes to a proposition. It is required only that the set of probabilities the agent assigns to a set of related propositions be coherent—satisfy the probability calculus.

The subjective view became important in statistics and philosophy when de Finetti (1937) showed that under certain conditions the probabilities that two agents assign to a proposition will converge as they get more evidence. This appears to mitigate the subjective aspect of this interpretation of probability, though it does require that the agents stick to their original probability assessments and update their degrees of belief in accord with Bayes's theorem, as discussed below. A modern exposition of the subjective point of view can be found in Howson and Urbach (1989).

Bayes's theorem is an uncontroversial theorem of the probability calculus. It says that the probability of a hypothesis h, given evidence e, is the initial or prior probability of the hypothesis h, multiplied by the probability of e given h, divided by the prior probability of the evidence e. Bayesianism is ambiguous. The term is used to characterize at least those who take Bayes's theorem to be the most important way of updating probabilities in the light of new evidence. For this to make sense, it is not required that probabilities be assigned to sentences or propositions rather than to sequences or chance setups. The problem of assigning a probability to having urn A on the basis of a sample drawn from the urn, given that you know the composition of balls in both urn A and urn B, and that you know the chance of having been given urn A is a perfectly classical problem to which the frequency interpretation can give a perfectly classical answer. What excludes those who adopt an objective empirical view of probability from being called Bayesians is the fact that they reject the idea of assigning probabilities to sentences or to particular determinate facts.

An interesting (partial) defense of the subjective Bayesian position is provided by Earman (1992). Earman believes that subjective Bayesianism is the only game in town; but half the time he believes it will not work. He offers careful arguments on both sides.

The subjective Bayesian position is defended—as much as any position is—by philosophers who write on these subjects. This includes many philosophers who have given up hope of finding objective standards for inductive or scientific inference and who have embraced a general relativistic view of inference. For some such thinkers even the standards of subjective probability are too rigid; but for many others subjective probability represents the right mix between subjectivity and objectivity. Yet others find the arguments purporting to support the probability axioms as rational standards for belief (the dutch book arguments) lacking in cogency.

Little new work is being done in philosophy on probability. What is written tends to concern the subjective interpretation, pro or con, and for the most part to sound familiar. The empirical interpretation attracts little attention, in part, perhaps, because it is in reasonably coherent shape. Philosophers seem to have abandoned the goal of providing a compelling logical measure for all first-order languages. Kyburg's logical view has not caught on (see Kyburg, 1994).

The ideas of probability and uncertainty

enter into philosophy in a number of areas,

including epistemology, metaphysics,

philosophy of science, and ethics.

The most active research in this area is being pursued by computer scientists interested in artificial intelligence (AI; see Bacchus, 1992; Cheeseman, 1988; Fagin & Halpern, 1989; Nilsson, 1986; Paris, 1995). Some of what is done there simply recapitulates the history of philosophical research in the area, but there is one new slant that may appear to help the subjectivist view to appear plausible. The focus of work in AI is largely practical, and that motivates a concentration on the relations among probabilities: If X's degrees of belief are probabilities, and we know that they are subject to such and such constraints, then what might (or should) his

belief in proposition S be? We can consider this problem quite independently, according to this view, from the problem of the source of the original degrees of belief.

This is not philosophically satisfying without some view as to the source of these original degrees of belief. A weak account takes them simply to be assumptions (Cheeseman) and so not to need justification. A more common approach is simply to leave their source unspecified. It is indeed perfectly proper to separate the two problems of accounting for the original beliefs of the agent and of providing an account of the relations among degrees of belief in related statements.

[See also Artificial Intelligence; Bayesianism; Carnap, Rudolph; Philosophy of Science.]

BIBLIOGRAPHY

Bacchus, F. *Representing and Reasoning with Probabilistic Knowledge.* Cambridge, MA, 1992.

Carnap, R. *The Logical Foundations of Probability.* Chicago, 1950.

Cheeseman, P. "Inquiry into Computer Understanding," *Computational Intelligence,* Vol. 4 (1988), 58–66.

Cramér, H. *Mathematical Methods of Statistics.* Princeton, NJ, 1951.

Earman, J. *Bayes or Bust.* Cambridge, MA, 1992.

Fagin, R., and J. Y. Halpern. "Uncertainty, Belief, and Probability," in *Proceedings of IJCAI 1989* (Detroit, 1989).

Finetti, B. de. "Foresight: Its Logical Laws, Its Subjective Sources," in H. E. Kyburg and H. Smokler, eds., *Studies in Subjective Probability,* 2d ed. (New York, 1980). First appeared in French as "La Prévision: Ses lois logiques, ses sources subjectives," *Annales de l'Institut Henri Poincaré,* Vol. 7 (1937), 1–68.

Hacking, I. *Logic of Statistical Inference.* Cambridge, 1965.

Halpern, J. Y. "An Analysis of First Order Probability," *Artificial Intelligence,* Vol. 46 (1990), 311–50.

Howson, C., and P. Urbach. *Scientific Reasoning.* LaSalle, IL, 1989.

Keynes, J. M. *A Treatise on Probability.* London, 1921.

Kyburg, H. E. *Probability and the Logic of Rational Belief.* Middletown, CT, 1961.

———. "The Reference Class," *Philosophy of Science,* Vol. 50 (1983), 374–97.

———. "Believing on the Basis of Evidence," *Computational Intelligence,* Vol. 10 (1994), 3–20.

Mises, R. von. *Probability, Statistics, and Truth.* London, 1957.

Nilsson, N. "Probabilistic Logic," *Artificial Intelligence,* Vol. 28 (1986), 71–88.

Paris, J. B. *The Uncertain Reasoner's Companion: A Mathematical Perspective.* Cambridge, 1995.

Popper, K. "The Propensity Interpretation of Probability," *British Journal for the Philosophy of Science,* Vol. 10 (1959), 25–42.

Ramsey, F. P. *The Foundations of Mathematics and Other Essays.* New York, 1931.

Reichenbach, H. *Theory of Probability.* Berkeley, 1949.

– HENRY E. KYBURG

PROJECTIVISM

Projectivism has its roots in David Hume's remark in the *Treatise* about the mind's "propensity to spread itself over external objects." We sometimes speak of properties of objects where in fact the features we notice are "projections" of our internal sentiments (or other qualities of our experience). The family of metaethical views claiming that value is a projection of our conative and affective physiological states is called projectivism by Simon Blackburn (1984), and the name has stuck. Blackburn proposes that "we say that [we] *project* an attitude or habit or other commitment which is not descriptive onto the world, when we speak and think as though there were a property of things which our sayings describe, which we can reason about, know about, be wrong about, and so on" (1984, pp. 170–71). In ethics projectivism is popular because it provides an explanation of how it is that moral judgment can have the logical role that it seems to have in deciding what to do. Believing that something has some property typically provides me with a reason to act only in conjunction with the desire to promote (or oppose) the realization of that property. But believing that something is good is (or has been taken historically to be) sufficient by itself to provide a person with a reason to act. Nor is this a coincidence; it is not that we humans happen to like good things, as we happen to like to eat sugary things. Rather, it is part of the logic of judgments of goodness that they provide reasons. How can this be? Projectivists explain: the judgment that something is good is the projection of our affinity toward it, our "appetite," as Hobbes puts it.

There are three varieties of projectivism to distinguish. The most straightforward is the error theory, advanced by J. L. Mackie (1977; see also Robinson, 1948), according to which our projection of value into the world is an illusion. Ordinary moral judgments presuppose an objectivity or independence of moral properties that is simply not to be had, and so they are in error. Mackie sees moral thought and language much as an atheist sees religious talk and language. The believers are not conceptually confused, but they are ontologically mistaken. The second sort of projectivism regards moral properties as Lockean "secondary qualities," not illusions, but real properties that consist in dispositions to affect human perceivers in certain ways. According to John MacDowell (1987), a leading exponent, just as we do not understand what the blueness of an object is except as the disposition to look blue to us, so we do not understand what goodness is except as the disposition to seem good to us. The projection involved in attribution of secondary qualities, including values, involves no error at all.

A third sort of projectivism is noncognitivism, or as it is more commonly called in discussions of projectivism, expressivism. The expressivist holds that moral judgments do not state propositions at all but rather serve to express some noncognitive mental state of the judge. Like secondary-quality theorists, expressivists deny that there is any mistake involved in moral judgment; true, there are no moral properties, and we speak as though there are, but this "speaking as though" is just a misleading feature of the surface grammar. In fact, according to expressivists, moral judgments do not serve the same semantic function as most declarative sentences, even though they look the same.

> *In ethics projectivism is popular*
>
> *because it provides an explanation*
>
> *of how it is that moral judgment*
>
> *can have the logical role*
>
> *that it seems to have in deciding what to do.*

Blackburn's projectivist position (the most influential one of the 1980s) develops an expressivist analysis of moral language with enough logical richness and complexity to model real moral deliberation and argument. His idea is easier to make out against the background of common criticisms of expressivism. Richard Brandt (1959), among others, noted that people's ordinary thinking about moral judgments runs contrary to expressivism. We have generally believed that normative judgments are used to state facts, that they are true or false, and when we change our moral views we come to regard our earlier views as mistaken, not merely as different. (By contrast, when one's taste in dessert changes, one generally regards the old preference as merely different or, at worst, childish.) Brandt complained that expressivists had given no explanation of why we are so confused. Blackburn's theory is designed to meet such objections. While maintaining an underlying expressivist semantics, he tries to show why we speak and think as though moral judgments state facts, can be true or false, and so on.

Imagine that people initially spoke about ethics in a language like English but having a quite explicitly expressivist structure. Rather than saying, "Voting for this health-care bill is morally wrong," they said, "Boo, voting for this health care bill!" Now imagine that these speakers valued a kind of consistency of sentiment, so that it was regarded as a confusion if someone said, "Boo, eating mammals, and hooray, eating cows!" And suppose they also believed that some moral sensibilities could never survive reflection by a rational person, so that expressing one of those sensibilities would be conclusive evidence that the speaker simply had not thought carefully about the subject. The expressivist community might "invent a predicate answering to that attitude, and treat commitments as if they were judgments, and then use all the natural devices for debating truth" (Blackburn 1984, p. 195). Since Blackburn's theory seeks to defend realist-style reasoning without realist metaphysics, he calls it 'quasi-realism'.

An important objection to Blackburn's quasi-realism is made by Crispin Wright (1988) and Bob Hale (1990). Our moral language has a realist surface structure, and quasi-realism seeks to vindicate this structure without giving in to realist metaphysics. But if quasi-realism is successful—if every realist-sounding thing we say can be endorsed in good faith by the quasi-realist—then how will a quasi-realist be distinguishable from a full-blooded realist? As Wright puts it, Blackburn's program confronts a dilemma: either it does not account for all the realist logical features of moral language, in which case it fails, or it succeeds in accounting for all of them, "in which case it makes good all the things which the projectivist started out wanting to deny: that the discourse in question is genuinely assertoric, aimed at truth, and so on" (1988, p. 35).

Despite these difficulties, projectivism deserves to be taken seriously, not just in the metaphysics of value, but in other metaphysical domains as well. For example, there have been projectivists about mental states (Dennett, 1987—judging that someone has intentional states is taking "the intentional stance" toward the person), causes (saying that one event caused another is projecting one's psychological propensity to associate events of the first kind with events of the second in temporal sequence), probability (Finetti, 1972—judgments of probability project one's degree of credence into the world), and logical impossibility (Blackburn, 1984—projecting a certain kind of inconceivability). With the exception of the first, all of these sorts of projectivism are plausibly attributed to Hume, who should be regarded as the prototype projectivist.

[See also Error Theory; Ethical Theory; Hobbes, Thomas; Hume, David; Mackie, John Leslie; Realism.]

BIBLIOGRAPHY

Ayer, A. J. *Language, Truth, and Logic.* Harmondsworth, Middlesex, 1971.
Blackburn, S. *Spreading the Word.* Oxford, 1984.
———. *Essays in Quasi-Realism.* New York, 1993.
Brandt, R. *Ethical Theory.* Englewood Cliffs, NJ, 1959.
de Finetti, B. *Probability, Induction, and Statistics.* London, 1972.
Dennett, D. *The Intentional Stance.* Cambridge, MA, 1987.
Geach, P. T. "Ascriptivism," *Philosophical Review,* Vol. 69 (1960), 221–25.
Gibbard, A. *Wise Choices, Apt Feelings.* Cambridge, MA, 1990.
Hale, B. "Can There Be a Logic of Attitudes?" in J. Haldane, ed., *Reality, Representation, and Projection* (London, 1990).
Harman, G. *The Nature of Morality.* New York, 1977.
MacDowell, J. *Projection and Truth in Ethics.* Lawrence, KS, 1987.
Mackie, J. L. *Ethics: Inventing Right and Wrong.* Harmondsworth, 1977.
Robinson, R. "The Emotivist Theory of Ethics," *Proceedings of the Aristotelian Society,* Vol. 22 (1948), supplement, 79–106.
Smart, J. J. C. *Ethics, Persuasion, and Truth.* London, 1984.
Stevenson, C. L. *Facts and Values.* New Haven, 1963.
Wright, C. "Realism, Anti-Realism, Irrealism, Quasi-Realism," in P. French, T. Uehling, and H. Wettstein, eds., *Realism and Antirealism,* Midwest Studies in Philosophy. Vol. 12 (Minneapolis, 1988).

– JAMES DREIER

PROOF THEORY

Briefly, Hilbert's program (HP), inaugurated in the 1920s, aimed to secure the foundations of mathematics by giving finitary consistency proofs of formal systems such as for number theory, analysis, and set theory, in which informal mathematics can be represented directly. These systems are based on classical logic and implicitly or explicitly depend on the assumption of "completed infinite" totalities. Consistency of a system S (containing a modicum of elementary number theory) is sufficient to ensure that any finitarily meaningful statement about the natural numbers that is provable in S is correct under the intended interpretation. Thus, in Hilbert's view, consistency of S would serve to eliminate the "completed infinite" in favor of the "potential infinite" and thus secure the body of mathematics represented in S. Hilbert established the subject of proof theory as a technical part of mathematical logic by means of which his program was to be carried out; its methods are described below.

In 1931 Gödel's second incompleteness theorem raised a prima facie obstacle to HP for the system Z of elementary number theory (also called Peano arithmetic—PA) since all previously recognized forms of finitary reasoning could be formalized within it. In any case Hilbert's program could not possibly succeed for any system such as set theory in which *all* finitary notions and reasoning could unquestionably be formalized. These obstacles led workers in proof theory to modify HP in two ways. The first was to seek reductions of various formal systems S to more constructive systems S'. The second was to shift the aims from foundational ones to more mathematical ones. Examples of the first modification are the reductions of PA to intuitionistic arithmetic HA and Gentzen's consistency proof of PA by finitary reasoning coupled with quantifier-free transfinite induction up to the ordinal ε_0, $TI(\varepsilon_0)$, both obtained in the 1930s. The second modification of proof theory was promoted especially by Georg Kreisel starting in the early 1950s; he showed how constructive mathematical information could be extracted from nonconstructive proofs in number theory. The pursuit of proof theory along the first of these lines has come to be called relativized Hilbert program or reductive proof theory, while that along the second line is sometimes called the program of unwinding proofs or, perhaps better, extractive proof theory. In recent years there have been a number of applications of the latter both in mathematics and in theoretical computer science. Keeping the philosophical relevance and limitations of space in mind, the following account is devoted entirely to developments in reductive proof theory, though the two sides of the subject often go hand in hand.

Methods of Finitary Proof Theory

Hilbert introduced a special formalism called the epsilon calculus to carry out his program (the nomenclature is related neither to the ordinal ε_0 nor to the membership symbol in set theory), and he proposed a particular substitution method for that calculus. Following Hilbert's suggestions, Wilhelm Ackermann and John von Neumann obtained the first significant results in finitary proof theory in the 1920s. Then, in 1930, another result of the same character for more usual logical formalisms was obtained by Jacques Herbrand, but there were troublesome aspects of his work. In 1934 Gerhard Gentzen introduced new systems, the so-called sequent calculi, to provide a very clear and technically manageable vehicle for proof theory, and reobtained Herbrand's fundamental theorem via his cut-elimination theorem. Roughly speaking, the latter tells us that every proof of a statement in quantificational logic can be normalized to a direct proof in which there are no detours ("cuts") at any stage via formulas of a complexity higher than what appears at later stages. Sequents have the form $\Gamma \rightarrow \Delta$, where Γ and Δ are finite sequences of formulas (possibly empty). $\Gamma \rightarrow \Delta$ is derivable in Gentzen's calculus LK just in case the formula $A \supset B$ is derivable in one of the usual calculi for classical predicate logic, where A is the conjunction of formulas in Γ and B is the disjunction of those in Δ.

Introduction of Infinitary Methods to Proof Theory

Gentzen's theorem as it stood could not be used to establish the consistency of PA, where the scheme of induction resists a purely logical treatment, and for this reason he was forced to employ a partial cut-elimination argument whose termination was guaranteed by the principle $TI(\varepsilon_0)$. Beginning in the 1950s, Paul Lorenzen and then, much more extensively, Kurt Schütte began to employ certain infinitary extensions of Gentzen's calculi (cf. Schütte, 1960, 1977). This was done first of all for elementary number theory by replacing the usual rule of universal generalization by the so-called ω-rule, in the form: from $\Gamma \rightarrow \Delta, A(\mathbf{n})$ for each $n = 0,1,2, \ldots$, infer $\Gamma \rightarrow \Delta,(x)A(x)$. Now derivations are well-founded trees (whose tips are the axioms $A \rightarrow A$), and each such is assigned an ordinal as length in a natural way. For this calculus LK_ω, one has a full cut-elimination theorem, and every derivation of a statement in PA can be transformed into a cut-free derivation of the same in LK_ω whose length is less than ε_0. Though infinite, the derivation trees involved are recursive and can be described finitarily, to yield another consistency proof of PA by $TI(\varepsilon_0)$. Schütte extended these methods to systems RA_α of ramified analysis (α an ordinal) in which existence of sets is posited at finite and transfinite levels up to α, referring at each stage only to sets introduced at lower levels. Using a suitable extension of LK_ω to RA_α, Schütte obtained cut-elimination theorems giving natural ordinal bounds for cut-free derivations in terms of the so-called Veblen hierarchy of ordinal functions. In 1963 he and Feferman independently used this to characterize (in that hierarchy) the ordinal of predicative analysis, defined as the first α for which $TI(\alpha)$ cannot be justified in a system RA_β for $\beta < \alpha$. William Tait (1968) obtained a uniform treatment of arithmetic, ramified analysis, and related unramified systems by means of the cut-elimination theorem for LK extended to a language with formulas built by countably infinite conjunctions (with the other connectives as usual). Here the appropriate new rule of inference is: from $\Gamma \rightarrow \Delta, A_n$, for each $n = 0,1,2, \ldots$, infer $\Gamma \rightarrow \Delta, A$, where A is the conjunction of all the A_n's.

Brief mention should also be made of the extensions of the other methods of proof theory mentioned above, concentrating on elimination of quantifiers rather than cut elimination. In the 1960s Burton Dreben and his students corrected and extended the Herbrand approach (cf. Dreben & Denton, 1970). Tait (1965) made useful conceptual reformulations of Hilbert's substitution method; a number of applications of this method to subsystems of analysis have been obtained in the 1990s by Grigori Mints (1994). Another approach stems from Gödel's functional interpretation, first presented in a lecture in 1941 but not published until 1958 in the journal *Dialectica*; besides the advances with this made by Clifford Spector in 1962, more recently there have been a number of further applications both to subsystems of arithmetic and to subsystems of analysis (cf. Feferman 1993). Finally, mention should be made of the work of Prawitz (1965) on systems of natural deduction, which had also been introduced by Gentzen in 1934 but not further pursued by him; for these a process of normalization takes the place of cut elimination. While each of these other methods has its distinctive merits and advantages, it is the methods of sequent calculi in various finitary and infinitary forms that have received the most widespread use.

Proof Theory of Impredicative Systems

The proof theory of impredicative systems of analysis was initiated by Gaisi Takeuti in the 1960s. He used partial cut-elimination results and established termination by reference to certain well-founded systems of ordinal diagrams (cf. Takeuti, 1987). In 1972 William Howard determined the ordinal of a system ID_1 of one arithmetical inductive definition, in the so-called Bachmann hierarchy of ordinal functions; the novel aspect of this was that it makes use of a name for the first uncountable ordinal in order to produce the countable (and in fact recursive) ordinal of ID_1. In a series of contributions by Harvey Friedman, Tait, Feferman, Wolfram Pohlers, Wilfried Buchholz, and Wilfried Sieg stretching from 1967 into the 1980s, the proof theory of systems of iterated inductive definitions ID_α and related impredicative subsystems of analysis was advanced substantially. The proof-theoretic ordinals of the ID_α were established by Pohlers in terms of higher Bachmann ordinal function systems (cf. Buchholz et al., 1981). The methods here use cut-elimination arguments for extensions of LK involving formulas built by countably and uncountably long conjunctions. In addition, novel "collapsing" arguments are employed to show how to collapse suitable uncountably long derivations to countable ones in order to obtain the countable (again recursive) ordinal bounds for these systems. An alternative functorial approach to the treatment of iterated inductive definitions was pioneered by Jean-Yves Girard (1985).

Hilbert's program aimed to secure

the foundations of mathematics

by giving finitary consistency proofs

of formal systems such as for

number theory, analysis, and set theory.

In 1982 Gerhard Jäger initiated the use of the so-called admissible fragments of Zermelo-Fraenkel set theory as an illuminating tool in the proof theory of predicatively reducible systems (cf. Jäger, 1986). This was extended by Jäger and Pohlers (1982) to yield the proof-theoretical ordinal of a strong impredicative system of analysis; that makes prima facie use of the name of the first (recursively) inaccessible ordinal. Michael Rathjen (1994) has gone beyond this to measure the ordinals of much stronger systems of analysis and set theory in terms of systems of recursive ordinal notations involving the names of very large (recursively) inaccessible ordinals, analogous to the so-called large cardinals in set theory.

Significance of the Work for HP and Reductive Proof Theory

Ironically for the starting point with Hilbert's aims to eliminate the "completed infinite" from the foundations of mathematics, these developments have required the use of highly infinitary concepts and objects to explain the proof-theoretical transformations involved in an understandable way. It is true that in the end these can be explained away in terms of transfinite induction applied to suitable recursive ordinal notation systems. Even so, one finds few who believe that one's confidence in the consistency of the systems of analysis and set theory that have been dealt with so far has been increased as a result of this body of work. However, while the intrinsic significance of the determination of the proof-theoretic ordinals of such systems has not been established, that work can still serve behind the scenes as a tool in reductive proof theory. It is argued in Feferman (1988) that one has obtained thereby foundationally significant reductions, for example of various (prima facie) infinitary systems to finitary ones, impredicative to predicative ones, and nonconstructive to constructive ones. With a field that is still evolving at the time of writing, it is premature to try to arrive at more lasting judgments of its permanent value.

[See also Gödel, Kurt; Mathematical Logic; Set Theory.]

BIBLIOGRAPHY

Buchholz, W., S. Feferman, W. Pohlers, and W. Sieg. *Iterated Inductive Definitions and Subsystems of Analysis: Recent Proof-theoretical Studies.* Lecture Notes in Mathematics 897. New York, 1981.
——, and K. Schütte. *Proof Theory of Impredicative Systems.* Naples, 1988.
Dreben, B., and J. Denton. "Herbrand-style Consistency Proofs," in J. Myhill, A. Kino, and R. E. Vesley, eds., *Intuitionism and Proof Theory* (Amsterdam, 1970), 419–33.
Feferman, S. "Hilbert's Program Relativized: Proof-theoretical and Foundational Reductions," *Journal of Symbolic Logic*, Vol. 53 (1988), 364–84.
——. "Gödel's *Dialectica* Interpretation and Its Two-way Stretch," in G. Gottlob et al., eds., *Computational Logic and Proof Theory*, Lecture Notes in Computer Science 713 (New York, 1993).

Gentzen, G. *The Collected Papers of Gerhard Gentzen*, ed. M. Szabo. Amsterdam, 1969.

Girard, J.-Y. "Introduction to Π^1_2 Logic," *Synthese*, Vol. 62 (1985).

———. *Proof Theory and Logical Complexity*. Naples, 1987.

Hilbert, D., and P. Bernays. *Grundlagen der Mathematik*. Vols. 1–2, 2d ed. Berlin, 1968–70.

Howard, W. "A System of Abstract Constructive Ordinals," *Journal of Symbolic Logic*, Vol. 37 (1972), 355–74.

Jäger, G. *Theories for Admissible Sets: A Unifying Approach to Proof Theory*. Naples, 1986.

———, and W. Pohlers. "Eine beweistheoretische Untersuchung von $(\Delta^1_2\text{-CA}) + (BI)$ und verwandter Systeme," *Sitzungsber. Bayerische Akad. Wissenschaft Math. Nat. Klasse* (1982), 1–28.

Kreisel, G. "A Survey of Proof Theory," *Journal of Symbolic Logic*, Vol. 33 (1965), 321–88.

Mints, G. E. *Selected Papers in Proof Theory*. Naples, 1992.

———. "Gentzen-type Systems and Hilbert's Epsilon Substitution Method. I," in D. Prawitz et al., eds., *Logic, Methodology, and Philosophy of Science IX* (1994).

Myhill, J., A. Kino, and R. E. Vesley, eds., *Intuitionism and Proof Theory*. Amsterdam, 1970.

Pohlers, W. "Contributions of the Schütte School in Munich to Proof Theory," in G. Takeuti, *Proof Theory* (Amsterdam, 1987).

———. *Proof Theory: An Introduction*. Lecture Notes in Mathematics 1407. [New York], 1989.

Prawitz, D. *Natural Deduction*. Stockholm, 1965.

Rathjen, M. "Admissible Proof Theory and Beyond," in D. Prawitz et al., eds., *Logic, Methodology and Philosophy of Science IX* (1994).

Schütte, K. *Beweistheorie*. Berlin, 1960.

———. *Proof Theory*. Berlin, 1977.

Sieg, W. "Hilbert's Program Sixty Years Later," *Journal of Symbolic Logic*, Vol. 53 (1988), 338–48.

Simpson, S. G. "Partial Realizations of Hilbert's Program," *Journal of Symbolic Logic*, Vol. 53 (1988), 349–63.

Tait, W. "The Substitution Method," *Journal of Symbolic Logic*, Vol. 30 (1965), 175–92.

———. "Normal Derivability in Classical Logic," in J. Barwise, ed., *The Syntax and Semantics of Infinitary Languages*, Lecture Notes in Mathematics 72 (New York, 1968).

Takeuti, G. *Proof Theory*, 2d ed. Amsterdam, 1987.

— SOLOMON FEFERMAN

PROPERTIES

Our every assertion or thought involves properties or relations. Most simply, we predicate some property of some thing: the earth is round. Sometimes we refer to properties by name or by description: red is the color of blood. Sometimes our quantifiers range over properties: galaxies come in many shapes and sizes.

This familiarity with properties, however, does not reveal what properties are. Indeed, the question is equivocal, both in ordinary and in philosophical discourse. There are different conceptions of properties, equally legitimate, corresponding to the different roles that properties have been called upon to play (Bealer, 1982; Lewis, 1983, 1986). And for each conception there are different theories as to what sort of entity, if any, is best suited to play the role. The most funda-mental division is between abundant and sparse conceptions of properties. On an abundant conception every meaningful predicate expresses some property or relation, including 'is blue or round', 'is on top of a turtle', 'is identical with the planet Mars'; a property's instances need not resemble one another in any intrinsic respect. Abundant properties are needed to serve as "meanings," or components of "meanings," in a compositional semantics for language. On a sparse conception of properties a predicate expresses a property only if the objects satisfying the predicate resemble one another in some specific intrinsic respect; perhaps 'has unit positive charge' and 'is ten kilograms in mass' are examples. Sparse properties are needed to provide an objective basis for the scientist's project of discovering the fundamental classifications of things and the laws that govern them. Properties, whether abundantly or sparsely conceived, are neither language- nor mind-dependent: they existed before there were beings to talk and think about them; they would have existed even had there never been such beings.

There are different conceptions of properties,

equally legitimate,

corresponding to the different roles

that properties have been called upon to play.

In this article only conceptions of properties are explicitly distinguished and discussed, although much of what is said applies also to relations and to propositions. Other philosophers' terms for 'property' in the abundant sense include 'attribute' (Quine, 1970), 'propositional function' (Russell, 1919), and 'concept' (Bealer, 1982; Frege, 1884); 'universal' and 'quality' have for the most part been interpreted sparsely. Ordinary language allows abundant or sparse readings of 'characteristic', 'feature', 'trait', and more.

Abundant Conceptions of Properties

How abundant are the properties on the abundant conception? Whenever there are some things, no matter how scattered or dissimilar from one another, there is the abundant property of being one of those things. Thus, for any class of things, there is at least one abundant property had by all and only the members of that class. It follows that there are at least as many abundant properties as classes of things and that the abundant properties outrun the predicates of any ordinary language. (There are nondenumerably many classes of things—assuming an infinity of things—but at most denumerably many predicates in any ordinary language.) Abundant properties, owing to their very abundance, must be transcendent, rather than immanent: they are not present in their instances as constituents or parts. It is not plausible to suppose that an object has a distinct constituent for each and every class to which it belongs.

If we say that whenever there are some things, there is exactly one property had by all and only those things, then a property may be identified with the class of its instances. For example, the property of being human may be identified with the class of human beings. But there is a well-known objection to this identification (Quine, 1970). Consider the property expressed by 'is a creature with a heart' and the property expressed by 'is a creature with kidneys'. If properties are "meanings," or semantic values, of predicates, then the properties expressed by these two predicates are distinct. Yet, these predicates, we may suppose, are coextensive: as a matter of fact, any creature with a heart has kidneys, and vice versa; the class of creatures with a heart is identical with the class of creatures with kidneys. Thus, distinct properties correspond to the same class and cannot be identified with that class.

Different responses to the objection invoke different criteria of individuation for properties, that is, different criteria for deciding when properties, introduced, say, via predicates that express them, are one and the same. One response simply denies that 'is a creature with a heart' and 'is a creature with kidneys' express distinct properties. More generally, properties expressed by coextensive predicates are identical. Call this an extensional conception of properties. A property so conceived may be identified with the class of its instances. Extensional conceptions of properties are adequate to the semantic analysis of mathematical language and extensional languages generally (Tarski, 1946).

A second response holds that 'is a creature with a heart' and 'is a creature with kidneys' express distinct properties, because it is logically possible for something to satisfy one predicate without satisfying the other. On this response properties expressed by necessarily coextensive predicates are identical; properties expressed by accidentally coextensive predicates are distinct. Call this an intensional conception of properties. If one accepts the standard analyses of logical possibility and necessity in terms of possibilia, then a property, on the intensional conception, may be identified with the function that assigns to each possible world the set of possible objects that has the property at the world. If one holds that each object exists at, and has properties at, only one world, then a property may more simply be iden-

tified with the class of (actual and) possible objects that has the property (Lewis, 1986). Properties, on the intensional conception, are appropriate semantic values for predicates of (standard) modal languages and intensional languages generally (Carnap, 1947; Kripke, 1963).

A third response holds that the properties expressed by 'is a creature with a heart' and 'is a creature with kidneys' are distinct because they are structured entities with different constituents: the property expressed by 'is a creature with a heart' has the property expressed by 'is a heart' as a constituent; the property expressed by 'is a creature with kidneys' does not. On this response properties have a quasi-syntactic structure that parallels the structure of predicates that express them. Call two predicates isomorphic if they have the same syntactic structure and corresponding syntactic components are assigned the same semantic values. On a structured conception of properties, properties expressed by isomorphic predicates are identical; properties expressed by nonisomorphic predicates are distinct. (Structured conceptions are sometimes called hyperintensional because they allow necessarily coextensive predicates to express distinct properties.) Structured conceptions subdivide according to whether the unstructured semantic values are intensional or extensional and according to whether the relevant structure is surface grammatical structure, or some hypothetical deep structure, or structure after analysis in terms of some chosen primitive vocabulary. Structured properties may be identified with sequences of unstructured properties and other unstructured semantic values. Structured properties, on one version or another, have a role to play in the semantic analysis of propositional attitudes and of hyperintensional languages generally (Carnap, 1947; Cresswell, 1985).

Thus far, this article has assumed that predicates of ordinary language are satisfied by objects once and for all. In fact, most ordinary language predicates are tensed; they may be satisfied by objects at some times but not at others. For example, 'is sitting' is true of me now, but was false of me ten minutes ago. On a tensed conception of properties, whether or not a property holds of an object may also be relative to times. Most simply, tensed properties may be identified with functions from times to untensed properties. Tensed properties may be taken as semantic values for tensed predicates.

We have, then, a plurality of abundant conceptions of properties. Which is correct? One need not and should not choose. A plurality of conceptions is needed to account for the multiple ambiguity in our ordinary talk of properties. And it seems that both structured and intensional conceptions are needed for compositional semantics: structured properties are needed to provide distinct semantic values for predicates, such as 'is a polygon with three sides' and 'is a polygon with three angles', that are necessarily coextensive without being synonymous; intensional properties are needed to provide distinct semantic values for unstructured predicates that are accidentally coextensive. To accept a plurality of conceptions, it suffices to find, for each conception, entities that satisfy that conception's criteria of individuation.

Realists with respect to some conception of properties hold that entities satisfying the individuation criteria for the conception exist. Realists divide into reductionists and antireductionists. Reductionists identify properties, under the various conceptions, with various set-theoretic constructions (in ways already noted): class, functions, or sequences of actual or possible objects (Lewis, 1986). Antireductionists reject some or all of these identifications. For some antireductionists, classes are suspect or esoteric entities; classes are to be explained, if at all, in terms of properties, not vice versa (Bealer, 1982; Russell, 1919). For other antireductionists the problem is not with classes, but with the possibilia that comprise them (on intensional conceptions). Possible but nonactual entities are to be explained, if at all, in terms of uninstantiated properties, not vice versa (Plantinga, 1976). According to the antireductionist, properties are basic or primitive; it is merely posited that there are entities satisfying the appropriate individuation criteria. Some entities, after all, must be taken as basic; according to the antireductionist, properties are an acceptable choice.

Eliminativists hold that, strictly speaking, there are no properties. They take aim, typically, at intensional conceptions, at conceptions with modal criteria of individuation. They claim that modal notions, such as logical possibility and necessity (whether taken as primitive or analyzed in terms of possibilia), incorrigibly lack the clarity and precision required of a rigorous scientific semantics or philosophy (Quine, 1970). Eliminativists have the burden of showing how ordinary and philosophical discourse ostensibly referring to properties can be paraphrased so as to avoid such reference; or, failing that, of showing that such discourse is dispensable, merely a *façon de parler*.

Sparse Conceptions of Properties

On an abundant conception any two objects share infinitely many properties and fail to share infinitely many others, whether the objects are utterly dissimilar or exact duplicates. On a sparse conception the sharing of properties always makes for genuine similarity; exact duplicates have all of their properties in common. Whatever

the sparse properties turn out to be, there must be enough of them (together with sparse relations) to provide the basis for a complete qualitative description of the world, including its laws and causal features. The sparse properties correspond one-to-one with a select minority of the abundant properties, on some intensional conception. ('Intensional', because distinct sparse properties may accidentally be instantiated by the same objects.) Those abundant properties that correspond to sparse properties are called natural (or perfectly natural, since naturalness presumably comes in degrees; Lewis, 1983, 1986). The naturalness of properties is determined not by our psychological makeup, or our conventions, but by nature itself.

How sparse are the properties, on a sparse conception? First, there is the question of uninstantiated properties. If sparse properties are transcendent, there is no difficulty making room for uninstantiated sparse properties; perhaps uninstantiated sparse properties are needed to ground laws that come into play only if certain contingent conditions are satisfied (Tooley, 1987). If, on the other hand, sparse properties are immanent, are present in their instances, then uninstantiated sparse properties must be rejected, because they have nowhere to be (Armstrong, 1978, 1989). Of course, uninstantiated sparse properties may nonetheless possibly exist, where this is understood according to one's favored interpretation of modality.

Second, there is the question of the compounding of sparse properties (and relations). Disjunctions and negations of natural properties are not themselves natural: their instances need not resemble one another in any intrinsic respect. For example, instances of the property having-unit-positive-charge-or-being-ten-kilograms-in-mass need not resemble one another in either their charge or their mass. It follows that there are no disjunctive or negative sparse properties (Armstrong, 1978).

The case of conjunctive sparse properties is less clear. There are two views. According to the first, since instances of a conjunction of natural properties, such as having-unit-positive-charge-and-being-ten-kilograms-in-mass, resemble one another in some—indeed, at least two—intrinsic respects, there exists a sparse property corresponding to the conjunction. According to the second view, the sparse properties must be nonredundant; they must be not only sufficient for describing the world but minimally sufficient. On this view conjunctive sparse properties are excluded on grounds of redundancy: a putative conjunctive sparse property would hold of an object just in case both conjuncts hold.

Similarly, structural sparse properties, such as being-a-molecule-of-H_2O, may be admitted on the grounds that they make for similarity among their instances. Or they may be excluded on grounds of redundancy: a putative structural sparse property would hold of an object just in case certain other sparse properties and relations hold among the object and its parts. But the exclusion of structural (and conjunctive) sparse properties faces a problem. It rules out a priori the possibility that some properties are irresolvably infinitely complex: they are structures of structures of structures, and so on, without ever reaching simple, fundamental properties or relations (Armstrong, 1978). A sparse conception that allowed for this possibility would have to allow some redundancy; and if some redundancy, why not more? This suggests that conjunctive and structural sparse properties should generally be admitted. (An alternative treatment makes use of degrees of naturalness and has it that conjunctive and structural properties are natural to some lesser degree than the properties in terms of which they are defined; a world with endless structure has no perfectly natural properties.)

If structural sparse properties are admitted, the sparse properties will not be confined to fundamental physical properties; there will be sparse properties of macroscopic, as well as microscopic, objects. For example, the sparse properties will include specific shape-and-size properties, such as being-a-sphere-ten-meters-in-diameter (which are arguably structural properties definable in terms of sparse distance relations). However, the vast majority of ordinary-language predicates—'is red', 'is human', 'is a chair', to name a few—fail to express natural properties to which sparse properties correspond; rather, these predicates express properties that, when analyzed in fundamental physical terms, are disjunctive (perhaps infinitely so) and probably extrinsic. (This judgment could be overturned, however, if there are irreducible natural properties applying to macroscopic objects—most notably, irreducible phenomenological properties of color, sound, and such.)

What are the properties on a sparse conception? There are three principal theories (or clusters of theories, since they each subdivide). According to the first, the properties sparsely conceived are just some of the properties abundantly conceived: the properties that are perfectly natural. What makes some properties natural and others unnatural? One version of the theory simply takes naturalness to be a primitive, unanalyzable distinction among abundant properties (Quinton, 1957; see also Armstrong, 1989; Lewis, 1986). But since a property is natural in virtue of the resemblances among its instances, it might seem more appropriate to take instead some relation of partial resemblance as primitive and to define naturalness in terms of resemblance. The resulting version, called resemblance nominalism, can be worked out in different ways with different primitive resemblance relation (Price, 1953; see also Armstrong,

1989; Goodman, 1951; Lewis, 1983). The chief objection to the view is that partial resemblance between ordinary objects, no less than naturalness of properties, cries out for analysis. When two objects partially resemble one another, the objection goes, they must have constituents that exactly resemble one another, perhaps constituents that are literally identical. More generally, it is argued, properties must be constituents of objects if properties are to play a role in the explanation of the natures and causal powers of objects; one cannot explain an object's nature or causal powers by invoking a class to which it belongs. Sparse properties, then, must be immanent, not transcendent, entities.

A plurality of conceptions is needed

to account for the multiple ambiguity

in our ordinary talk of properties.

What are these constituents of ordinary things? Not ordinary spatial or temporal constituents—or, at least, not always. For even an object with no spatial or temporal extension might have a complex nature and stand in relations of partial resemblance. If sparse properties are immanent, then they must be nonspatiotemporal constituents of things. There are two prominent theories as to the nature of these constituents. The first theory takes them to be universals (Armstrong, 1978, 1989). They are repeatable: each of them is, or could be, multiply instantiated. And they are wholly present in their instances: an immanent universal is located—all of it—wherever each of its instances is located. When objects resemble one another by having a sparse property in common, there is something literally identical between the objects. It follows that universals fail to obey commonsense principles of location, such as that nothing can be (wholly) in two places at the same time. But that is no objection. Such principles were framed with particulars in mind; it would beg the question against universals to require them to meet standards set for particulars.

On the other theory of sparse properties as immanent, the nonspatiotemporal constituents of ordinary particulars are themselves particulars, called tropes (Armstrong, 1989; Lewis, 1986; Williams, 1966) or abstract particulars (Campbell, 1981). When ordinary particulars partially resemble one another by having some sparse property—say, their mass—in common, then there are distinct, exactly resembling, mass tropes as constituents of each. On a trope theory sparse properties can be identified with maximal classes of exactly resembling tropes (perhaps including merely possible tropes). Exact resemblance between tropes is taken as primitive by trope theory; but it is a simple and natural primitive compared to the partial resemblance relation taken as primitive by an adequate resemblance nominalism.

A possible disadvantage of a universals theory is that it requires two fundamentally distinct kinds of entities: universal and particulars. An ordinary particular cannot simply be identified with a bundle of coinstantiated universals, lest numerically distinct but qualitatively identical particulars be identified with one another. On a universals theory there must be some nonqualitative, nonrepeatable constituent of ordinary particulars to ground their numerical identity. A trope theory, on the other hand, needs only tropes to make a world. Ordinary particulars can be identified with bundles of coinstantiated tropes; numerically distinct but qualitatively identical particulars are then bundles of numerically distinct but exactly resembling tropes.

The great advantage of a universals theory is that it promises to analyze all resemblance in terms of identity: exact resemblance is identity of all qualitative constituents; partial resemblance is partial identity, identity of at least one qualitative constituent. But it is unclear whether the promise can be kept. Objects instantiating different determinates of a determinable—such as unit-positive and unit-negative charge—seem to partially resemble one another by both being charged without there being any analysis of this resemblance in terms of the identity of constituent universals or, for that matter, the exact resemblance of constituent tropes. A universals theory and a trope theory would then have to fall back upon primitive partial resemblance between universals, or tropes. Some of the advantages of these theories over resemblance nominalism would be forfeited.

Of the three basic theories of sparse properties—resemblance nominalism, a theory of immanent universals, and a theory of tropes—only one can be true; the theories posit incompatible constituent structure to the world. However, assuming each theory is internally coherent, and adequate to the needs of science, the question arises, What sort of evidence could decide between them? It seems that a choice between the theories will have to be made, if at all, on the basis of pragmatic criteria such as simplicity, economy, and explanatory power. There is as yet no philosophical consensus as to what that choice should be.

[See also Armstrong, David M.; Carnap, Rudolph; Eliminative Materialism, Eliminativism; Frege, Gottlob; Goodman, Nelson; Kripke, Saul Aaron; Metaphysics; Quine, Willard Van Orman; Realism; Reduction, Reductionism; Russell, Bertrand Arthur William.]

BIBLIOGRAPHY

Armstrong, D. M. *Universals and Scientific Realism.* 2 vols. Cambridge, 1978.
———. *Universals: An Opinionated Introduction.* Boulder, CO, 1989.
Bealer, G. *Quality and Concept.* Oxford, 1982.
Campbell, K. "The Metaphysic of Abstract Particulars," in *Midwest Studies in Philosophy,* Vol. 6 (Minneapolis, 1981).
Carnap, R. *Meaning and Necessity.* Chicago, 1947.
Cresswell, M. *Structured Meanings.* Cambridge, MA, 1985.
Frege, G. *Die Grundlagen der Arithmetik* [1884]. Translated by J. L. Austin as *The Foundations of Arithmetic.* Oxford, 1950.
Goodman, N. *The Structure of Appearance.* Cambridge, MA, 1951.
Kripke, S. "Semantical Considerations on Modal Logic," *Acta Philosophica Fennica,* Vol. 16 (1963), 83–94.
Lewis, D. "New Work for a Theory of Universals," *Australasian Journal of Philosophy,* Vol. 61 (1983), 343–77.
———. *On the Plurality of Worlds.* Oxford, 1986.
Plantinga, A. "Actualism and Possible Worlds," *Theoria,* Vol. 42 (1976), 139–60.
Price, H. H. *Thinking and Experience.* London, 1953.
Quine, W. V. O. *Philosophy of Logic.* Englewood Cliffs, NJ, 1970.
Quinton, A. "Properties and Classes," *Proceedings of the Aristotelian Society,* Vol. 58 (1957), 33–58.
Russell, B. *Introduction to Mathematical Philosophy.* London, 1919.
Tarski, A. *Introduction to Logic.* 2d ed. Oxford, 1946.
Tooley, M. *Causation.* Oxford, 1987.
Williams, D. C. "The Elements of Being," in *The Principles of Empirical Realism* (Springfield, IL, 1966).

— PHILLIP BRICKER

PROPOSITIONAL KNOWLEDGE, DEFINITION OF

The traditional definition of propositional knowledge, emerging from Plato's *Meno* and *Theaetetus,* proposes that such knowledge—knowledge that something is the case—has three essential components. These components are identified by the view that knowledge is justified true belief. Knowledge, according to the traditional definition, is belief of a special kind, belief that satisfies two necessary conditions: (1) the truth of what is believed and (2) the justification of what is believed. While offering various accounts of the belief condition, the truth condition, and the justification condition for knowledge, many philosophers have held that those three conditions are individually necessary and jointly sufficient for propositional knowledge.

The belief condition requires that one accept, in some manner, any proposition one genuinely knows. This condition thus relates one psychologically to what one knows. It precludes that one knows a proposition while failing to accept that proposition. Some contemporary philosophers reject the belief condition for knowledge, contending that it requires a kind of mentalistic representation absent from many cases of genuine knowledge. Some other contemporary philosophers endorse the belief condition but deny that it requires actual assent to a proposition. They propose that, given the belief condition, a knower need only be disposed to assent to a proposition. Still other philosophers hold that the kind of belief essential to propositional knowledge requires assent to a known proposition, even if the assent need not be current or ongoing. The traditional belief condition is neutral on the exact conditions for belief and for the objects of belief.

Knowledge, according to the traditional definition,

is belief that satisfies two necessary conditions:

the truth of what is believed,

and the justification of what is believed.

The truth condition requires that genuine propositional knowledge be factual, that it represent what is actually the case. This condition precludes, for example, that astronomers before Copernicus knew that the Earth is flat. Those astronomers may have believed—even justifiably believed—that the Earth is flat, as neither belief nor justifiable belief requires truth. Given the truth condition, however, propositional knowledge without truth is impossible. Some contemporary philosophers reject the truth condition for knowledge, but they are a small minority. Proponents of the truth condition fail to agree on the exact conditions for the kind of truth essential to knowledge. Competing approaches to truth include correspondence, coherence, semantic, and redundancy theories, where the latter theories individually admit of variations. The truth condition for knowledge, generally formulated, does not aim to offer an exact account of truth.

The justification condition for propositional knowledge guarantees that such knowledge is not simply true belief. A true belief may stem just from lucky guesswork; in that case it will not qualify as knowledge. Propositional knowledge requires that the satisfaction of its belief condition be suitably related to the satisfaction of its truth condition. In other words, a knower must have adequate indication that a belief qualifying as knowledge is actually true. This adequate indication, on a traditional view of justification suggested by Plato and Kant, is suitable evidence indicating that a proposition is true. True beliefs qualifying as knowledge, on this traditional view, must be based on justifying evidence.

Contemporary philosophers acknowledge that justified contingent beliefs can be false; this is fallibilism about epistemic justification, the kind of justification appropriate to propositional knowledge. Given fallibilism, the truth condition for knowledge is not supplied by the justification condition; justification does not entail truth. Similarly, truth does not entail justification; one can lack evidence for a proposition that is true.

Proponents of the justification condition for knowledge do not share an account of the exact conditions for epistemic justification. Competing accounts include epistemic coherentism, which implies that the justification of any belief depends on that beliefs coherence relations to other beliefs, and epistemic foundationalism, which implies that some beliefs are justified independently of any other beliefs. Recently, some philosophers have proposed that knowledge requires not evidence but reliable (or truth-conducive) belief formation and belief sustenance. This is reliabilism about the justification condition for knowledge. Whatever the exact conditions for epistemic justification are, proponents of the justification condition maintain that knowledge is not merely true belief.

Although philosophers have not agreed widely on what specifically the defining components of propositional knowledge are, there has been considerable agreement that knowledge requires, in general, justified true belief. Traditionally, many philosophers have assumed that justified true belief is sufficient as well as necessary for knowledge. This is a minority position now, owing mainly to Gettier counterexamples to this view. In 1963 Edmund Gettier challenged the view that if one has a justified true belief that p, then one knows that p. Gettier's counterexamples are:

(I) Smith and Jones have applied for the same job. Smith is justified in believing that (i) Jones will get the job, and that (ii) Jones has ten coins in his pocket. On the basis of (i) and (ii), Smith infers, and thus is justified in believing, that (iii) the person who will get the job has ten coins in his pocket. As it turns out, Smith himself will actually get the job, and he also happens to have ten coins in his pocket. So, although Smith is justified in believing the true proposition (iii), Smith does not know (iii).

(II) Smith is justified in believing the false proposition that (i) Jones owns a Ford. On the basis of (i), Smith infers, and thus is justified in believing, that (ii) either Jones owns a Ford or Brown is in Barcelona. As it turns out, Brown is in Barcelona, and so (ii) is true. So although Smith is justified in believing the true proposition (ii), Smith does not know (ii).

Gettier counterexamples are cases where one has a justified true belief that p but lacks knowledge that p. The Gettier problem is the difficulty of finding a modification of, or an alternative to, the traditional justified-true-belief analysis that avoids difficulties from Gettier counterexamples.

Contemporary philosophers have not reached a widely accepted solution to the Gettier problem. Many philosophers take the main lesson of Gettier counterexamples to be that propositional knowledge requires a fourth condition, beyond the justification, belief, and truth conditions. Some philosophers have claimed, in opposition, that Gettier counterexamples are defective because they rely on the false principle that false evidence can justify one's beliefs. There are, however, examples similar to Gettier's that do not rely on any such principle. Here is one such example inspired by Keith Lehrer and Richard Feldman:

(III) Suppose that Smith knows the following proposition, *m*: Jones, whom Smith has always found to be reliable and whom Smith has no reason to distrust now, has told Smith, his officemate, that *p*: He, Jones, owns a Ford. Suppose also that Jones has told Smith that *p* only because of a state of hypnosis Jones is in and that *p* is true only because, unknown to himself, Jones has won a Ford in a lottery since entering the state of hypnosis. Suppose further that Smith deduces from *m* its existential generalization, *o*: There is someone, whom Smith has always found to be reliable and whom Smith has no reason to distrust now, who has told Smith, his officemate, that he owns a Ford. Smith, then, knows that *o*, since he has correctly deduced *o* from *m*, which he also knows. Suppose, however, that on the basis of his knowledge that *o*, Smith believes that *r*: Someone in the office owns a Ford. Under these conditions, Smith has justified true belief that *r*, knows his evidence for *r*, but does not know that *r*.

Gettier counterexamples of this sort are especially difficult for attempts to analyze the concept of propositional knowledge.

One noteworthy fourth condition consists of a "defeasibility condition" requiring that the justification appropriate to knowledge be "undefeated" in that an appropriate subjunctive conditional concerning defeaters of justification be true of that justification. A simple defeasibility condition requires of our knowing that *p* that there be no true proposition, *o*, such that if *q* became justified for us, *p* would no longer be justified for us. If Smith genuinely knows that Laura removed books from the office, then Smith's coming to believe with justification that Laura's identical twin removed books from the office would not defeat the justification for Smith's belief regarding Laura herself. A different approach claims that propositional knowledge requires

justified true belief sustained by the collective totality of actual truths. This approach requires a precise, rather complex account of when justification is defeated and restored.

The importance of the Gettier problem arises from the importance of a precise understanding of the nature, or the essential components, of propositional knowledge. A precise understanding of the nature of propositional knowledge, according to many philosophers, requires a Gettier-resistant account of knowledge.

[See also Coherentism; Epistemology; Kant, Immanuel; Plato; Reliabilism; Truth.]

BIBLIOGRAPHY

BonJour, L. *The Structure of Empirical Knowledge.* Cambridge, MA, 1985.

Carruthers, P. *Human Knowledge and Human Nature.* New York, 1992.

Chisholm, R. *Theory of Knowledge,* 3d ed. Englewood Cliffs, NJ, 1989.

Goldman, A. *Epistemology and Cognition.* Cambridge, MA, 1986.

Lehrer, K. *Theory of Knowledge.* Boulder, CO, 1990.

Lewis, C. I. *An Analysis of Knowledge and Valuation,* La-Salle, IL, 1946.

Moser, P. *Knowledge and Evidence.* New York, 1989.

———, and A. vander Nat, eds. *Human Knowledge: Classical and Contemporary Approaches,* 2d ed. New York, 1995.

Pollock, J. *Contemporary Theories of Knowledge.* Lanham, MD, 1986.

Shope, R. *The Analysis of Knowing.* Princeton, NJ, 1983.

Sosa, E. *Knowledge in Perspective.* New York, 1991.

— PAUL K. MOSER

PROPOSITIONS

On one use of the term, propositions are objects of assertion, what successful uses of declarative sentences say. As such, they determine truth values and truth conditions. On a second, they are the objects of certain psychological states (such as belief and wonder) ascribed with verbs that take sentential complements (such as 'believe' and 'wonder'). On a third use, they are what are (or could be) named by the complements of such verbs. Many assume that propositions in one sense are propositions in the others.

After some decades of skepticism about the worth of positing propositions, the last quarter of the twentieth century saw renewed interest in and vigorous debate over their nature. This can be traced in good part to three factors: the development in intensional logic of formal models of propositions; (not altogether unrelated) attacks on broadly Fregean accounts of propositions; and a spate of work on the nature of belief and its ascription.

"Possible-worlds semantics" is a collection of methods for describing the semantical and logical properties of expressions such as 'necessarily'; these methods developed out of work done by Saul Kripke, Richard Montague, and others in the 1960s. It illuminated the logic and semantics of modal terms such as 'necessarily', of conditionals and tenses, and other constructions as well. In such semantics one assigns a sentence a rule that determines a truth value relative to various "circumstances of evaluation" (possible worlds, times, whatever); a sentence like *it is necessary that S* has its truth value determined by the rule so associated with S. The success of such accounts made it natural to hypothesize that propositions, *qua* what's named by expressions of the form *that S,* could be identified with such rules—equivalently, with sets of circumstances such rules pick out.

After some decades of skepticism

about the worth of positing propositions,

the last quarter of the twentieth century

saw renewed interest in and vigorous debate

over their nature.

Such a conception of proposition provides too crude an account of objects of belief or assertion: it implausibly makes all logically equivalent sentences express the same belief and say the same thing. A partial solution to this problem supposes that propositional identity is partially reflected in sentential structure, taking propositions themselves to be structured. Given the working hypothesis that a proposition's structure is that of sentences expressing it, critical to determining the proposition a sentence (use) expresses are the contributions made by sentence parts (on that use).

Frege suggested that associated with names and other meaningful expressions are "ways of thinking" or *senses* of what the expressions pick out; one might suppose that sense and sentence structure jointly determine proposition expressed. Sense, in the case of names and other singular terms, has standardly been taken to be given by describing how one thinks of the referent. For example, the sense of 'Aristotle' for me might be given by 'the author of the *Metaphysics*'; if so, my uses of 'Aristotle taught Alexander' and 'the author of the *Metaphysics* taught Alexander' would, on a Fregean view, express the same proposition.

During the 1970s Kripke, David Kaplan, and others argued convincingly that this view is untenable: it is obvious, on reflection, that the truth conditions of the assertion or belief that Aristotle was *F* depend on Aristotle in a way in which the truth conditions of the assertion or belief that the author of the *Metaphysics* was *F* do not. So either ways of thinking are somehow tied to the objects they present (so that the way I think of Aristotle could not present anything but Aristotle), or the contributions of expressions to propositions must be something other than senses.

The success of accounts of intensional language that ignored sense in favor of constructions from references, along with the apparent failure of Fregean accounts, led in the 1980s to debate over the merits of what is variously called direct-reference theory, Millianism, and (neo-) Russellianism, espoused at various times by a wide variety of theorists including Kaplan, Mark Richard, Nathan Salmon, and Scott Soames. On such views sense is irrelevant to individuating a proposition; indeed, it is irrelevant to semantics. In particular, what a name contributes to a proposition is its referent: the proposition that Twain is dead is the same singular proposition as the proposition that Clemens is.

Neo-Russellians identify the object of assertion and the referent of a 'that' clause with a Russellian proposition. They allow that there is such a thing as a "way of grasping" a proposition and that belief in a singular proposition is mediated by such. Against the intuition that, for example, A: Mo believes that Twain is dead, and B: Mo believes that Clemens is dead, might differ in truth value, direct-reference accounts typically suggest that a pragmatic explanation is appropriate. Just as an ironic use of a sentence can convey a claim without literally expressing it, so a sentence about Mo's beliefs might convey information about Mo's way of grasping a singular proposition, without that information being part of what the sentence literally says. If this is so, intuitions about A and B are explained pragmatically.

Those unhappy with this account of propositions have looked elsewhere. Many accounts of propositions identify the proposition determined by S with some construction from linguistic items associated with S and the semantic values of S's parts. James Higginbotham has identified the referents of 'that' clauses with phrase markers that may be annotated with referents; Richard has suggested that the referent of a 'that' clause be identified with something like the singular proposition it determines paired off with the sentence itself. In making linguistic items constitutive of propositions, these views run counter to ones, like Frege's and Russell's, that closely tie meaning and synonymity to propositional determination. On linguistic views of propositions the synonymity of 'groundhog' and 'woodchuck' does not assure the identity of the proposition that groundhogs are pests with the proposition that woodchucks are.

Other theorists (Gareth Evans, for example) have attempted to revive a version of Frege's views of propositions.

Many philosophers continue to doubt the utility of positing propositions. Quineans argue that meaning and reference must be determined by behaviorally manifest facts but that such facts woefully underdetermine assignments of meaning and reference; they conclude that there is nothing about language that need or could be explained by positing propositions. Stephen Schiffer has argued that propositions are a sort of "linguistic posit": that we accept nominalizations of the form *that S* as referring to singular terms and have coherent criteria for using sentences in which those terms occur is itself sufficient for its being true that there are propositions. Such a deflationist view implies neither the possibility of a substantive account of propositions (on which, for example, the proposition expressed by a sentence is compositionally determined), nor that propositions play a substantive role in explaining semantic phenomena.

[See also Frege, Gottlob; Intensional Logic; Kripke, Saul Aaron; Meaning; Philosophy of Language; Quine, Willard Van Orman; Reference; Russell, Bertrand Arthur William.]

BIBLIOGRAPHY

Evans, G. *The Varieties of Reference*. Oxford, 1982.

Frege, G. "Uber Sinn und Bedeutung," *Zeitschrift für Philosophie and Philosophische Kritik,* Vol. 100 (1892), 25–50. Translated by P. Geach and M. Black as "On Sense and Reference," in P. Geach and M. Black, eds., *Translations from the Philosophical Writings of Gottlob Frege* (Cambridge, 1952).

Horwich, P. *Truth*. Cambridge, MA, 1990.

Kaplan, D. "Demonstratives," in J. Perry et al., eds., *Themes from Kaplan* (Oxford, 1989).

Kripke, S. *Naming and Necessity*. Cambridge, MA, 1980.

Lewis, D. "Attitudes *de dicto* and *de se*," *Philosophical Review*, Vol. 88 (1979), 513–43.

Montague, R. *Formal Philosophy*, edited by R. Thomason. New Haven, 1974.

Quine, W. V. O. *Word and Object*. Cambridge, MA, 1960.

Richard, M. *Propositional Attitudes*. Cambridge, 1990.

Salmon, N., and S. Soames, eds. *Propositions and Attitudes*. Oxford, 1988.

Schiffer, S. "A Paradox of Meaning," *Noûs*, Vol. 28, 279–324.

Stalnaker, R. *Inquiry*. Cambridge, MA, 1984.

— MARK E. RICHARD

PROVABILITY

Even though provability logic did not come into its own until the early seventies, it has its roots in two older fields: metamathematics and modal logic. In metamathematics, we study what theories can say about themselves. The first—and most outstanding—results are Gödel's two incompleteness theorems.

If we take a sufficiently strong formal theory T—say, Peano arithmetic—we can use Gödel numbering to construct in a natural way a predicate $Prov(x)$ in the language of T that expresses "x is the Gödel number of a sentence which is provable in T." About T we already know that it satisfies modus ponens:

If it is provable that A implies B, then, if A is provable, B is provable as well.

Now it turns out that, using Gödel numbering and the predicate *Prov*, we can express modus ponens in the language of T, and show that in T we can actually prove this formalized version of modus ponens:

$$Prov(\ulcorner A \to B \urcorner) \to (Prov(\ulcorner A \urcorner) \to Prov(\ulcorner B \urcorner)).$$

When we rephrase both the normal and the formalized version of modus ponens using the modal operator $\Box$, reading $\Box A$ as "A is provable in T," we get the modal rule

$$(1) \qquad \frac{A \to B \quad A}{B}$$

and the modal axiom

$$(2) \qquad \Box(A \to B) \to (\Box A \to \Box B).$$

Indeed both the rule and the axiom are well known from the basic modal logic K.

Similarly, we can show that if there is a proof of the sentence A in T, then T itself can check this proof, so T proves $Prov(\ulcorner A \urcorner)$—we shall call this principle *Prov*-completeness. Again, though in a less straightforward way than in the case of modus ponens, we can formalize the principle itself and see that T actually proves:

$$Prov(\ulcorner A \urcorner) \to Prov(\ulcorner Prov(\ulcorner A \urcorner) \urcorner).$$

When we rephrase the principle of *Prov*-completeness and its formalization in modal logical terms, we get the modal rule that is usually called necessitation:

$$(3) \qquad \frac{A}{\Box A},$$

and the modal axiom

(4) $$\Box A \rightarrow \Box\Box A,$$

which is the transitivity axiom 4 well known from modal systems such as K4 and S4.

Finally, one might wonder whether T proves the intuitively valid principle that "all provable sentences are true," i.e., whether T proves $Prov(\ulcorner A \urcorner) \rightarrow A$. Unexpectedly, this turns out not to be the case at all. Löb proved in 1953, using Gödel's technique of diagonalization, that T proves $Prov(\ulcorner A \urcorner) \rightarrow A$ only in the trivial case that T already proves A itself!

Löb's Theorem has a formalization that can also be proved in T. Writing both the theorem and its formalization in modal terms, we get the modal rule

(5) $$\frac{\Box A \rightarrow A}{A},$$

and the modal axiom

(6) $$\Box(\Box A \rightarrow A) \rightarrow \Box A,$$

usually called W (for well-founded) by modal logicians.

Now we can define provability logic, which goes by various names in the literature—PRL, GL (for Gödel/ Löb), L (for Löb), and, in modal logic texts, $KW4$. It is generated by all the modal formulas that have the form of a tautology of propositional logic, plus the rules (1),(3),(5) and axioms (2),(4),(6) given above. One can prove that rule (5) and axiom (4) already follow from the rest, so that PRL is equivalently given by the well-known system K plus the axiom $\Box(\Box A \rightarrow A) \rightarrow \Box A$.

The main "modal" theorem about PRL—but one with great arithmetical significance—is the "fixed point theorem," which D. de Jongh and G. Sambin independently proved in 1975. The theorem says essentially that "self-reference is not really necessary." Suppose that all occurrences of the propositional variable p in a given formula A are under the scope of $\Box$-es, for example, $A(p) = \neg\Box p$ or $A(p) = \Box(p \rightarrow q)$. Then there is a formula B in which p does not appear, such that all propositional variables that occur in B already appear in $A(p)$, and such that $PRL \vdash B \leftrightarrow A(B)$. This B is called a fixed point of $A(p)$. Moreover, the fixed point is unique, or more accurately, if there is another formula B' such that $PRL \vdash B' \leftrightarrow A(B')$, then we must have $PRL \vdash B \leftrightarrow B'$. Most proofs of the fixed point theorem in the literature give an algorithm by which one can compute the fixed point.

For example, suppose that $A(p) = \neg\Box p$. Then the fixed point produced by the algorithm is $\neg\Box\bot$, and indeed we have $PRL \vdash -\Box\bot \leftrightarrow -\Box(-\Box\bot)$. If we read this arithmetically, the direction from left to right is just the formalized version of Gödel's second incompleteness theorem. Thus, if T does not prove a contradiction, then it is *not* provable in T that T does not prove a contradiction.

Provability logic has its roots in two older fields,

metamathematics and modal logic.

The landmark result in provability logic is Solovay's "arithmetical completeness theorem" of 1976. This theorem says essentially that the modal logic PRL captures *everything* that Peano arithmetic can say in modal terms about its own provability predicate. Before formulating Solovay's theorem more precisely, we turn to the semantics of PRL.

Provability logic has a suitable Kripke semantics, just like many other modal logics. Unaware of the arithmetical relevance of PRL, Krister Segerberg proved in 1971 that it is sound and complete with respect to finite irreflexive transitive frames, and even with respect to finite trees. This completeness theorem immediately gives a decision procedure to decide for any modal formula A whether A follows from PRL or not. Looking at the procedure a bit more precisely, it can be shown that PRL is "very decidable": like the well-known modal logics K, T, and $S4$, it is decidable in PSPACE. This means that there is a Turing machine that, given a formula A as input, answers whether A follows from PRL; the size of the memory that the Turing machine needs for its computations is only polynomial in the length of A.

The modal completeness theorem was an important first step in Solovay's proof of the arithmetical completeness of PRL. Suppose that PRL does not prove the modal formula A. Then there is a finite tree such that A is false at the root of that tree. Now Solovay devised an ingenious way to describe the tree in the language of Peano arithmetic. Thus he found a translation f from modal formulas to sentences of arithmetic, such that Peano arithmetic does not prove $f(A)$. Such a *translation* f respects the logical connectives (so, e.g., $f(B \wedge C) = f(B) \wedge f(C)$), and $\Box$ is translated as $Prov$ (so $f(\Box B) = Prov(\ulcorner f(B) \urcorner)$). Thus Solovay's arithmetical completeness theorem gives an alternative way to construct many nonprovable sentences. For example, we know that PRL does not prove $\Box p \vee \Box\neg p$, so by the theorem, there is an arithmetical sentence $f(p)$ such that Peano arithmetic does not prove $Prov(\ulcorner f(p) \urcorner) \vee Prov(\ulcorner \neg f(p) \urcorner)$. In particular, if we suppose that Peano arithmetic does not prove any false sentences, this implies that neither $f(p)$ nor $\neg f(p)$ is provable in Peano arithmetic.

In recent years, logicians have investigated many other systems of arithmetic that are weaker than Peano arithmetic. They have given a partial answer to the question: "For which theories of arithmetic does Solovay's arithmetical completeness theorem still hold?" It certainly holds for theories T that satisfy the following two conditions:

1. T proves induction for formulas in which all quantifiers are bounded (like the quantifier $\forall x \leq y + z$) and T proves that for all x, its power 2^x exists. In more technical terms: T extends $I\Delta_0 + EXP$.
2. T does not prove any false Σ_1 sentences.

For such theories, it is also clear that PRL is sound if we read $\square$ as $Prov_T$ (where $Prov_T$ is a natural provability predicate with respect to a sufficiently simple axiomatization of T). To sum up, we have the following theorem: If T satisfies 1 and 2, and A is a modal sentence, then

$$PRL \vdash A \Leftrightarrow \text{for all translations } f,\ T \vdash f(A).$$

This result shows a strength of provability logic: for many different theories, PRL captures exactly what those theories say about their own provability predicates. At the same time this is of course a weakness: for example, provability logic does not point to any differences between those theories that are finitely axiomatizable and those that are not.

In order to be able to speak in a modal language about such distinctions between theories, researchers have extended provability logic in many different ways, only a few of which are mentioned here. One way is to add a binary modality, $\triangleright$, where for a given theory T, the modal sentence $A \triangleright B$ stands for "$T + B$ is interpretable in $T + A$." It appears that the interpretability logic of $I\Delta_0 + superexp$ is different from the interpretability logic of Peano arithmetic.

Another way to extend the framework of PRL is to add propositional quantifiers, so that one can express principles like Goldfarb's:

$$\forall p \forall q \exists r \square((\square p \vee \square q) \leftrightarrow \square r).$$

Finally, one can of course study predicate provability logic. Vardanyan proved that the set of always provable sentences of predicate provability logic is not even recursively enumerable, so it has no reasonable axiomatization.

[See also Gödel, Kurt; Kripke, Saul Aaron; Mathematical Logic; Modal Logic; Philosophical Logic.]

BIBLIOGRAPHY

Artemov, S. N., and L. D. Beklemishev. "On Propositional Quantifiers in Provability Logic," *Notre Dame Journal of Formal Logic*, Vol. 34 (1993), 401–19.

Boolos, G. *The Logic of Provability.* New York, 1993.

de Jongh, D. H. J., M. Jumelet, and F. Montagna. "On the Proof of Solovay's Theorem," *Studia Logica*, Vol. 50 (1991), 51–70.

Smoryński, C. *Self-reference and Modal Logic.* New York, 1985.

Solovay, R. M. "Provability Interpretations of Modal Logic," *Israel Journal of Mathematics*, Vol. 25 (1976), 287–304.

Visser, A. "Interpretability Logic," in P. P. Petkov, ed., *Mathematical Logic (Proceedings, Chaika, Bulgaria, 1988)* (New York, 1990).

– RINEKE VERBRUGGE

PUTNAM, HILARY

Hilary Putnam (b. 1926), after receiving a B.A. from Pennsylvania (1948) and a year spent at Harvard (1948–1949), studied at UCLA, taking his doctorate in 1951 with a dissertation titled "The Concept of Probability: An Application to Finite Sequences." He taught at Northwestern (1952–1953), Princeton (1953–1961) and MIT (1961–1965), becoming Walter Beverly Pearson professor at Harvard in 1965. Since 1995 he has been Cogan University Professor there. He has been influential in most areas of philosophy, particularly in the philosophy of language, of logic, of mathematics, and of science.

Putnam has been influential in most areas of philosophy, particularly in the philosophy of language, of logic, of mathematics, and of science.

Putnam is sometimes thought of as often changing his mind. (See, for example, the *Dictionary of Philosophers' Names*.) Sometimes he has. But in central respects he has held a single, though developing, position since the mid-1950s, a position that in some aspects resembles the later Wittgenstein's. This article sets out some constant central themes.

Putnam was among those American philosophers to benefit directly from the intellectual exodus from Europe caused by Nazism. He was a student of Rudolf Carnap and of Hans Reichenbach. Though his approach to issues is quite different from theirs, Reichenbach in particular had a lasting and often acknowledged influence on Putnam's thought. Putnam's innovations stand out when it is noted. In *Realism with a Human Face* (1990; p. 289), Putnam remarks,

> In *Theory of Relativity and A Priori Knowledge* (1922) Reichenbach listed a number of statements . . . each of which Kant would have regarded as synthetic *a priori,* and each of which can be held immune from revision . . . , but which *collectively imply statements that are empirically testable,* and that Kant would, therefore, have to regard as *a posteriori.*

Certain principles had, in Kant's time, as good a claim as any to fix how particular spatial, temporal, and other concepts are to be applied, and thereby which concepts those were; to be intrinsic to the concepts involved, thus 'conceptual truths', thus a priori. Relativity theory allows us to see how they are at least jointly testable, so that some may turn out false. Such, it seems, is a fate to which a priori truths are liable.

Putnam reports Reichenbach as making a related point to his classes. Considering questions such as 'How can we show that that blackboard is wider than this ashtray?', he argued that any system of measurement, or of observation, treats some propositions that seem empirical (such as 'mere translation does not make things grow or shrink') as axiomatic. One cannot sensibly apply the system while doubting these propositions; they are not subject to confirmation or refutation within the system. But it could prove reasonable to replace the system with another in which these propositions are testable, so possibly false. In that sense they are empirical.

There are two contrasting reactions to these points. One is: what this shows is that every concept commits itself to a particular empirical theory. If the theory proves false, then the concept is incoherent, so without application and to be discarded. This was Paul Feyerabend's reaction, and it is also Paul Churchland's.

The other reaction is: if we are confronted with situations that force giving up what seemed conceptual truths, it may appear that the concepts whose applications seemed to be governed by those principles are, in fact, otherwise governed. Perhaps the application of the concept 'straight line' to items in the world is not governed by the Euclidean parallel postulate, but rather in such and such other way. That reaction grants face value to Reichenbach's point that the same proposition that is axiomatic in one system may be testable and false in another. This was Putnam's reaction. He developed the position and drew its implications in a powerful series of papers in the 1950s and 1960s (see Putnam, 1962a–d). Part of the idea is that what principles govern the application of a concept depends in part on how the world in fact is. Putnam defined that role for the world in "The Meaning of 'Meaning' " (1975). This last article, though not published until 1975, was completed by 1968.

By the early seventies, Putnam had begun to emphasize some new themes. For one thing, he became increasingly impressed with what he calls the 'interest relativity' of such notions as explanation and cause. The general point is: what a concept counts as applying to—the correct way of applying it—varies with the circumstances in which it is to be applied. A concept may count, on one occasion, as fitting what it does not count as fitting on another. That is continuous with Putnam's earlier reaction to Reichenbach. The point then was: what it is reasonable to judge as to how a concept operates depends on the conditions in which such judgments are made. The point now is: what those conditions are depends not just on how the world is, but may vary from occasion to occasion, given the world as it is. Not coincidentally, this point went along with other developments in Putnam's thought.

The first of these developments is what he calls 'internal realism', first presented in 1976, and amplified in his writings of 1981, 1983, 1987a, 1987b, and elsewhere. The position includes four points. First, there are mundane, true things to say about what our words and thoughts are about: "the word 'gold' means (refers to) gold; this is gold"; "This is a chair; this is what 'chair' refers to," and so forth. Second, there are philosophical dicta that sound much like such mundanities, or their denials, or generalizations of these, but that say, or try to say, something quite different. They are bad answers to the following pseudo-problem. On the one hand, there are thoughts and words—items that purport to represent the world as being thus and so; on the other hand, the items the world in fact contains, which are what and how they are independent of what we think, or do not think, about them. How are our words and thoughts related to these items? How, if at all, does their truth depend on how those items are? And how could they be so related? Internal realism holds that the problem rests on a mistake; hence so do any 'solutions', which take it at face value.

Third, the mundane remarks (point one) are correct because they are a feature of how these words are (or are to be) used. But that formulation depersonalizes things misleadingly. The standard for the correctness of a statement cannot be fixed independently of what users of the relevant words and concepts—that is, human beings—are prepared to recognize as correct: what Putnam identifies as our (human) perceptions of rationality and reasonableness. What it is for a statement to be correct depends on the sorts of beings we are, and is not reducible to some set of principles that would have to hold anyway. Fourth, it is part of what we are prepared to recognize as rational that any concept might be applied correctly in different ways in different circumstances. What sometimes counts as the cause of the explosion may not at other times. It is because human rationality is occasion-sensitive that the problem mentioned in point two is a pseudo-problem. We cannot sensibly take a 'God's-eye view' of how we relate to the world, trying to say how our concepts would apply without us.

The occasion-sensitivity of rationality does not mean that truth is relative, or that there are no objective facts—given a framework, or setting, in which concepts are to be applied. Nor does giving up on a God's-eye view mean a deflationist account of truth. Putnam insists that we cannot comprehend what truth is without understanding the role of truth in our lives, notably in our activities of asserting, and of treating assertions in the ways we do; and that deflationism does not help us understand the role of truth in human life.

In arguing against the possibility

of a God's-eye view,

Putnam has produced what are probably

his most discussed arguments.

In arguing against the possibility of a God's-eye view, Putnam has produced what are probably his most discussed arguments. In one he identifies the God's-eye view (what John McDowell has called 'the view of the cosmic alien') as one from which we may consider our own language as an uninterpreted calculus with a range of possible interpretations, and then ask which interpretation is the right one. In what he first saw as a generalization of the Skolem paradox, he argues that, in that case, *nothing* could make one interpretation the right one, so we could not ever be talking about anything (or about one thing rather than others). But we cannot pose serious problems without talking about definite things. This is a reductio of the idea of a God's-eye view (see "Models and Reality," Philosophical Papers, Volume 3).

In another argument Putnam considers the (apparent) question whether we might be brains in a vat: that we are, and always have been, nothing but brains, kept alive by a bath of nutrients, fed computer-generated stimuli through electrodes. He argues that if the God's-

eye view is possible, then that we are, and that we are not such brains should both be possibilities. But for the words of the question to mean what a God's-eye view requires them to means we must be using them in ways that entail that we are not brains in vats. For, as argued in "The Meaning of 'Meaning'," what our words mean depends, *inter alia,* on how we are in fact connected to the world, and not just on what we may anyway be aware of. For our 'brain' to mean *brain,* and our 'vat' to mean *vat,* we must be connected to the world as brains in ways vats could not be. So we cannot formulate what, from a God's-eye view, ought to be a possibility, in a way that makes it possible. That is another reductio of the idea of a God's-eye view (see Putnam, 1981).

Equally important to internal realism are Putnam's arguments against a causal theory of reference: arguments, based on the interest-relativity of causation, that our being causally linked to the world as we, in fact, are is not enough in itself to make some one interpretation of our language correct—once it is granted that the language we speak may coherently be viewed by us as less than fully interpreted, so open to interpretation. These arguments appear in many replies to critics, and notably in "Realism with a Human Face" (1990).

At about the time Putnam began to develop internal realism, he also began to change his way of thinking about human psychology, rejecting a picture of it, and with that, a view he once espoused—functionalism. Viewed one way, a human being is an organism constructed in a particular way, a particular battery of mechanisms arranged to interact with each other and the environment in given ways. If, while taking that view, we ask what it is for someone to believe that Mars is a planet, or to have *any* propositional or other attitude—to be in a mood, experience an emotion, and so on—it is tempting to look for an answer by trying to identify some state(s) of some mechanism(s) such that for someone to believe that is for him to be structured like that. In that frame of mind, for example, one might speak seriously of someone having a "token of a mentalese sentence" in his "belief box." This is the picture Putnam rejects.

Against it Putnam notes that to ascribe belief to someone is to relate that person to the world as we view it, and to ourselves, as on the same side as ours, or a different one, with respect to such and such question as to how the world is, and so on. Given internal realism, this means that there will be different truths to tell on different occasions as to what a given person, as he is at a given time, then believes. So for someone to be as said to be when we say him to believe thus and so, cannot be for him to have some particular mechanism, otherwise identifiable, in some particular state. And so on for other mental states (see Putnam, 1989).

Putnam has been refining the ideas discussed above, notably the idea of a distinction between ordinary and philosophic statements, and applying them in new areas, such as philosophy of mathematics. The above indicates a few main themes, omitting Putnam's striking arguments for them.

[See also Carnap, Rudolph; Functionalism; Kant, Immanuel; Rationality; Realism; Reference; Wittgenstein, Ludwig Josef Johann.]

BIBLIOGRAPHY

Works by Putnam

"The Analytic and the Synthetic" [1962a], reprinted in *Mind, Language and Reality, Philosophical Papers, Volume 2* (Cambridge, 1975).

"It Ain't Necessarily So" [1962b], reprinted in *Mathematics, Matter and Method, Philosophical Papers, Volume 1* (Cambridge, 1975).

"Dreaming and 'Depth Grammar'" [1962c], in *Philosophical Papers, Volume 2* (Cambridge, 1975).

"What Theories Are Not" [1962d], in *Philosophical Papers, Volume 1* (Cambridge, 1975).

"The Meaning of 'Meaning,'" in *Philosophical Papers, Volume 2* (Cambridge, 1975).

"Realism and Reason" [1976], reprinted in *Meaning and the Moral Sciences* (London, 1978).

Reason, Truth and History. Cambridge, 1981.

"Models and Reality," reprinted in *Realism and Reason, Philosophical Papers, Volume 3* (Cambridge, 1983).

The Many Faces of Realism. LaSalle, IL, 1987.

"Realism with a Human Face," in *Realism with a Human Face, Philosophical Papers, Volume 4* (Cambridge, MA, 1990).

Renewing Philosophy. Cambridge, MA, 1992.

Words and Life. Cambridge, MA, 1994.

Works on Putnam

Clark, P., and B. Hale, eds. *Reading Putnam.* Oxford, 1994.
Ebbs, G. *Rule-Following and Realism.* Cambridge, MA, 1996.
Rorty, R. "Solidarity or Objectivity," in J. Rajchman and C. West, eds., *Post-analytical Philosophy* (New York, 1985).

— CHARLES TRAVIS

PYTHAGORAS AND PYTHAGOREANISM

Pythagoras was an Ionian Greek born on the island of Samos, probably about 570 B.C. His dislike of the policies of the Samian tyrant Polycrates caused him to immigrate to Crotona in southern Italy. There he founded a society with religious and political, as well as philosophical, aims which gained power in the city and considerably extended its influence over the surrounding area. A certain Cylon, however, stirred up a revolt against the society in which a number of its leading members were killed, and Pythagoras retired to Metapontum. The community recovered its influence until

The influence of Pythagorean thought on the history of philosophy and religion has been exercised largely through the medium of Plato. (Corbis/Gianni Dagli Orti)

a more serious persecution took place in the middle of the fifth century, from which the survivors scattered to various parts of the Greek world—notably Thebes, Phleius, and Tarentum. In these places "they preserved their original ways and their science, although the sect was dwindling, until, not ignobly, they died out" (in the late fourth century), to quote the epitaph written by a contemporary.

NATURE OF THE EVIDENCE. The obstacles to an appraisal of classical Pythagoreanism are formidable. There exists no Pythagorean literature before Plato, and it was said that little had been written, owing to a rule of secrecy. Information from the Christian era is abundant but highly suspect. Pythagoras himself, though a fully historical figure, underwent a kind of canonization. His life was quickly obscured by legend, and piety attributed all the school's teaching to him personally. Moreover, the dispersion of the school inevitably led to divergences of doctrine in the various groups. Aristotle makes it clear that by the late fifth century some Pythagoreans were teaching one thing and some another. A further reason for division was that the universal genius of Pythagoras, for whom religion and science were two aspects of the same integrated world view, was beyond the scope of lesser men. Some naturally inclined more to the religious and superstitious; others, to the intellectual and scientific side, as is confirmed by later references to the division between *acusmatici* and *mathematici*.

As early evidence there are several references to Pythagoras in works of his contemporaries or near contemporaries (for instance, Xenophanes satirized his belief in the transmigration of souls), a valuable reference in Plato to the relationship between astronomy and harmonics in the Pythagorean system, a quantity of information from Aristotle (who at least would not confuse the Pythagoreans with Plato, as later writers excusably did), and some quotations from pupils of Aristotle who were personally acquainted with the last generation of the school.

Given the nature of the sources, the following is a fairly conservative summary of Pythagoreanism before Plato.

MAN AND THE COSMOS. In contrast with the Milesians, the Pythagoreans were not motivated by disinterested scientific curiosity. For Pythagoras, philosophy was the basis of a way of life, leading to salvation of the soul. "Their whole life," said a fourth-century writer, "is ordered with a view to following God, and it is the governing principle of their philosophy." At philosophy's center, therefore, were man and his relation to other forms of life and to the cosmos. Purity was to be sought by silence, self-examination, abstention from flesh and beans, and the observance of other primitive taboos which the Pythagoreans interpreted symbolically. Of the recognized gods they worshiped Apollo, guardian of the typically Greek ideal of moderation ("nothing too much"), of whom Pythagoras was believed to be an incarnation.

Behind both the superstition and the science was the notion of kinship or sympathy. The kinship and essential unity of all life made possible the belief in the transmigration of souls and accounted for the prohibition of meat: a sheep might house the soul of an ancestor. Not only animate nature in our sense but the whole world was akin, for the cosmos itself was a living, breathing creature. The cosmos was one, eternal, and divine; men were divided and mortal. But the essential part of man, his soul, was not mortal; it was a fragment of the divine, universal soul that was cut off and imprisoned in a mortal body. Men should therefore cultivate and purify the soul, preparing it for a return to the universal soul of which it was a part. Until then, since it was still con-

taminated by the body, it must tread the wheel of reincarnation, entering a new body of man or animal after the death of its previous tenement.

There exists no Pythagorean literature before Plato, and it was said that little had been written, owing to a rule of secrecy.

These tenets were also taught by the religious movement known as Orphism, from which the religious side of Pythagoreanism can hardly be separated. (Pythagoras himself was said in the fifth century to have written books under the name of Orpheus.) But whereas the Orphics sought salvation by purely religious means— sacramental ceremonies and the observance of ritual prohibitions—Pythagoras added a new way, the way of philosophy.

Philosophy, for Pythagoras as for others, meant the use of reason and observation to gain understanding of the universe. The link between this procedure and his overriding aim of salvation seems to have been the principle that like is known by like, a widespread tenet of pre-Socratic thought, common to such diverse systems as the philosophicoreligious synthesis of Empedocles and the scientific atomism of Democritus. Hence, an understanding of the divine universe would bring man's nature closer to its own. In this conception we meet the typically Pythagorean conception of *kosmos*, a word which combines in an untranslatable way the notion of orderly arrangement or structural perfection with that of beauty. Closely linked with it is *peras*, meaning limit. An organic whole, particularly one that, like the universe, lives forever, must of necessity exhibit limit and order in the highest degree. What is unlimited has no *telos* (end) and is *a-teles*, which means both "endless" and "incomplete." But the world is a perfect whole, a model of order and regularity, supremely exemplified in Greek eyes by the ceaseless wheeling of the heavenly bodies in (as they believed) perfect circles, bringing about the unvarying succession of day and night and seasons. It was said of Pythagoras that he was the first to call the world *kosmos*, "from its inherent order." By studying this order, we reproduce it in our own souls, and philosophy becomes an assimilation to the divine, as far as that is possible within the limitations imposed by our mortal bodies.

THE DOCTRINE THAT THINGS ARE NUMBERS. The Pythagoreans studied mathematics in a cosmic context, and for them numbers always retained a mystical significance as the key to the divine cosmos. "They supposed the whole heaven to be a *harmonia* and a number," said Aristotle. *Harmonia,* though specially applied to music, could signify any well-organized structure of parts fitted together in due proportion. Its effect in music seems to have burst on Pythagoras as a revelation of the whole cosmic system. We may accept the many later statements that he discovered the numerical ratios underlying the intervals which the Greeks called consonant and used as the basis of their scale. They involve only the numbers 1 to 4—1:2, octave; 3:2, fifth; 4:3, fourth. These numbers add up to 10, a sacred number for the Pythagoreans, which was symbolized by the dotted triangle (*tetractys*), "source and root of everlasting nature." From the discovery that the sounds they recognized as beautiful depended on inherent, objective, mathematical order, they leaped to the conclusion that number was the key to the element of order in nature as a whole.

With this innovation the Pythagoreans would seem to have taken the momentous step from explanation in terms of matter (as the Milesians had sought it) to explanation in terms of form. Yet philosophy was not quite ready for that step, nor could the distinction between matter and form be clearly grasped. They saw simply the ultimate, single nature (*physis*) of things in their mathematical structure. There seems little doubt that probably until well on in the fifth century they thought it possible to speak of things as actually made up of "numbers" that were regarded simultaneously as units, geometrical points, and physical atoms. Lines are made of points; surfaces, of lines; solids, of surfaces; and physical bodies, of solids. In this scheme two points made a line; three, the minimum surface (triangle); four, the minimum solid (tetrahedron). A later theory spoke of the "fluxion" of point into line, line into surface, and so on, which gave a geometrical progression (1, 2, 4, 8) instead of the arithmetical (1, 2, 3, 4), and the sequence of point, line, square, cube. Based on continuity, it seems designed to avoid the problem of incommensurable magnitudes or irrational numbers.

Whenever they were discovered (probably not much later than 450), incommensurables had dealt a blow to the original "things are numbers" doctrine, the idea that geometrical figures—and thus ultimately the physical world—are based on a series of integers. No ratio between integers can either describe the relation between the diagonal of a square and its side or serve as the basis of construction of a right triangle. If, however, magnitudes are regarded as continuous and hence infinitely divisible, the existence of incommensurable or irrational magnitudes (those which cannot be expressed as a ratio of natural numbers) could be explained and the difficulty overcome.

THE ULTIMATE PRINCIPLES. The analysis went further than that outlined above, for numbers themselves have their elements. The ultimate principles were limit and the unlimited, which were equated with good and bad respectively; moral concepts went side by side with physical concepts in this extraordinary system. Abstractions as well as physical phenomena were equated with numbers; for instance, justice was 4, the first square number, symbolizing equality or requital. After limit and the unlimited came odd and even, instances respectively of these two. They generated the unit (considered to be outside the number series, and both odd and even), from the unit sprang numbers, and from numbers came the world. There seems no doubt that the scheme goes back to an ultimate duality that corresponds to the moral dualism of Pythagoreanism, but one can also see how monistically minded Neoplatonic commentators could speak of the cosmos as originating from the One. In general terms, *kosmos* was achieved by the imposition of limit on the unlimited in order to make the limited, just as the imposition of definite ratios on the indefinite range of musical pitch produced the *harmonia* of the scale.

COSMOGONY AND COSMOLOGY. Cosmogony starts with the planting of a unit in the infinite. Aristotle called it, among other things, a seed; and since limit was associated with male and unlimited with female, the Pythagoreans probably thought of the generation of the living cosmos as taking place as did that of other animals. It grows by drawing in and assimilating the unlimited outside, that is, by conforming it to limit and giving it numerical structure. Physically the process resembles inspiration, and the unlimited is also called breath.

The unit seed had the nature of fire and in the completed cosmos (which evidently grew from the center outward) became a fire at its center. There are traces of two different cosmological schemes, a geocentric one which spoke of a fire at the center of the earth, and a more remarkable one attributed, in later sources at least, to the fifth-century Pythagorean Philolaus, which made the earth a planet. (Copernicus in *De Revolutionibus* says that reading of this Pythagorean doctrine gave him courage to consider explaining the heavenly motions on the basis of a moving earth.) According to this latter scheme, earth, planets, sun, and moon—and an extra body called the counterearth—all revolved about the center of the universe, which was occupied by a fire invisible to man because he lived on the opposite side of the earth. It was known that the moon's light is borrowed, and the idea was extended to the sun, whose heat and light were said to be reflected from the central fire. The moon was eclipsed by the interposition of both the earth and the counterearth and, according to some, of further, otherwise unknown, planetary bodies. These caused the comparatively frequent lunar eclipses.

In this system, the mixture of religion and science in Pythagoreanism is well brought out. Fire was given the central position, not for any scientific reason but because it was regarded with religious awe—and the center is the most "honorable" place. It was lauded with such titles as Hearth of the Universe, Tower of Zeus, and Throne of Zeus. Yet the same thinkers were aware that with the earth in orbit "the phenomena would not be the same" as in a geocentric scheme (presumably they were thinking of the lack of stellar parallax and variations in the apparent size of the sun and moon). They pointed out that even with a central earth, an observer would be separated from the center by the distance of its radius, and they argued that the visible effect would be as negligible in one case as in the other. This assumes that the heavenly bodies are at vast distances from the earth; and it is not known how, if at all, this system was related to the theory later known as the harmony of the spheres.

The Pythagoreans studied mathematics

in a cosmic context,

and for them numbers always retained

a mystical significance

as the key to the divine cosmos.

In any case, there are many divergent versions of this doctrine. In outline, the idea was that large bodies in motion must inevitably produce a sound; that the speeds of the heavenly bodies, judged by their distances, are in the ratios of the musical consonances; and that therefore the sound made by their simultaneous revolution is concordant. We do not hear it because it has been with us from birth, and sound is perceptible only by contrast with silence. It has been plausibly argued that in the original version Pythagoras, like Anaximander, took only three orbits into account (sun, moon, and all the stars); this would relate it to his original musical discovery about the fourth, fifth, and octave. Later versions speak of seven, eight (Plato), and ten orbits. In any form, the doctrine emphasizes the universal importance, in Pythagorean eyes, of mathematical and musical laws and their intimate relation to astronomy.

NEO-PYTHAGOREANISM. The influence of Pythagorean thought on the history of philosophy and religion has been exercised largely through the medium of Plato, who enthusiastically adopted its main doctrines of the immortality of the soul, philosophy as an assimilation to the divine, and the mathematical basis of the cosmos. Later antiquity regarded him as a Pythagorean source, so that post-Platonic writings are of little help in distinguishing Pythagorean from original Platonic material in the dialogues. The Neo-Pythagorean movement, which started in the first century B.C., was an amalgam of early Pythagorean material with the teachings of Plato, the Peripatetics, and the Stoics. All of this material was credited to Pythagoras, who was revered as the revealer of esoteric religious truths. The interests of Neo-Pythagoreanism were religious and, in accordance with the prevailing tendencies of the time, it emphasized the mystical and superstitious sides of the earlier doctrine, its astral theology and number-mysticism, to the detriment of philosophical thinking. It cannot be called a system, but rather is a trend which in different forms continued until the rise of Neoplatonism in the third century A.D., when it lost its identity in that broader and more powerful current. Besides contributing to Neoplatonism, it influenced Jewish thought through Philo of Alexandria and Christian thought through Clement of Alexandria. Prominent Neo-Pythagoreans were Cicero's acquaintance, Nigidius Figulus, and Apollonius of Tyana, a wandering mystic and ascetic of the first century A.D., credited with miraculous and prophetic powers. Numenius of Apamea in the late second century was called both Pythagorean and Platonist, and was the immediate precursor of Neoplatonism.

BIBLIOGRAPHY

Delatte, A., *Études sur la littérature pythagoricienne*. Paris, 1915. For specialists.

Fritz, K. von, *Pythagorean Politics in South Italy: An Analysis of the Sources*. New York, 1940.

Guthrie, W. K. C., "Pythagoras and the Pythagoreans," in his *History of Greek Philosophy*, Vol. I. Cambridge, 1962. Pp. 146–340. References to much of the literature of the subject will be found in this general account.

Minar, E. L., Jr., *Early Pythagorean Politics*. Baltimore, 1942.

Morrison, J. S., "Pythagoras of Samos." *Classical Quarterly*, N. S. Vol. 6 (1956), 135–156.

Thesleff, H., *An Introduction to the Pythagorean Writings of the Hellenistic Period*. Turku, Finland, 1961. For specialists.

Timpanaro-Cardini, Maria, *Pitagorici: testimonianze e frammenti*, 2 vols. Florence, 1958 and 1962. Texts from H. Diels and W. Kranz, eds., *Fragmente der Vorsokratiker*, translated into Italian, with introduction and commentary.

Van der Waerden, B. L., "Die Arithmetik der Pythagoreer." *Mathematische Annalen*, Vol. 120 (1948), 127–153 and 676–700. For specialists.

———, *Die Astronomie der Pythagoreer*. Amsterdam, 1951. For specialists. Both this and the other van der Waerden work do not require a knowledge of Greek; texts are given in German.

— W. K. C. GUTHRIE

Q

QUALIA

The word quale (or qualia) derives from the Latin for "quality." As used by Clarence Irving Lewis and those following him, it refers to qualities such as color patches, tastes, and sounds of phenomenal individuals. In this sense the term means what Berkeley meant by sensible qualities or later philosophers meant by 'sensa', or 'sense data'. Since the demise of sense-data theories, the term qualia has come to refer to the qualitative, or phenomenal, character of conscious, sensory states, so mental states, not phenomenal individuals, are the subjects of predication. Another expression for this aspect of mental life is the "raw feel" of experience, or "what it's like" to have certain sensory experiences. Qualia are part of the phenomenon of the subjectivity of consciousness, and they pose one of the most difficult problems for a materialist solution to the mind–body problem.

In contemporary philosophy of mind, the problem of qualia has confronted both of the principal versions of materialism: the central-state identity theory and functionalism. Regarding the former, J. J. C. Smart (1959) posed the problem this way: even if one admits that sensations are identical to brain states, the qualitative character of a sensation seems itself to be a nonphysical property of the sensation and therefore an obstacle to a materialist reduction. In response Smart developed a "topic-neutral" analysis of qualia—the idea that our very notion of a quale is of a property of sensation that has a tendency to be caused by certain stimuli and cause certain judgments of similarity on our part. Functionalism is largely an outgrowth of this sort of analysis.

Another sort of argument against materialist reductions of qualia has its roots in René Descartes and was revived by Saul Kripke (1980). If we consider any proposed reduction of the sort "Pain is the firing of C-fibers," it seems quite conceivable that it is false: there could be pain without C-fibers and C-fibers without pain. Yet since it is widely accepted that true identity statements are necessarily true, what seems conceivable with respect to pain and C-fibers shouldn't be. Hence, they must not be identical. Again, one sort of response has been to argue that a proper analysis of our notion of pain (or any other quale) would reveal that it was a functional notion, and this explains the conceivability

of pain without C-fibers since pains could be realized in a variety of physical structures. With the right functional identity statement the felt contingency wouldn't arise.

In contemporary philosophy of mind,

the problem of qualia has confronted

both of the principal versions of materialism:

the central-state identity theory and functionalism.

For these reasons, among others, functionalism replaced the central-state identity theory as the dominant materialist doctrine in the philosophy of mind. With respect to qualia functionalism is the thesis that what it's like to have a certain sensory experience is analyzable in terms of the causal relations that hold among that experience, other mental states (e.g., beliefs, desires, and other sensory experiences), and stimuli and behavior. However, both the inverted qualia and absent qualia hypotheses pose serious problems for a functionalist theory of qualia.

The inverted qualia hypothesis is the idea that two creatures could be functionally identical and yet differ in their qualia. The most popular version of this hypothesis is the possibility of an inverted spectrum. Suppose Jack and Jill react exactly the same ways, both behaviorally and functionally, to light of every wavelength. However, it turns out that the way red looks to Jack is qualitatively similar to the way green looks to Jill, and similarly for yellow and blue. All the similarity relations among color experiences would be the same for the two, so there is no reason to think there need be a functional difference between them. Yet their qualia would differ. Hence, qualia can't be identified with functional states or properties.

The absent qualia hypothesis goes a step further. On this scenario, there is a creature that is functionally identical to a normal human being, and yet it has no conscious, qualitative experience at all; there is nothing it is like to be it. Ned Block (1980) proposed one way of making this possibility compelling. He has us imagine the entire nation of China organized—say by telephone connections—so as to realize the functional description of a human being. It seems ludicrous, he argues, to suppose the nation as a whole is experiencing anything.

Finally, another sort of argument (due to Jackson, 1982) against a materialist reduction of qualia is the knowledge argument: if any version of physicalism is true, then someone in possession of all the physical facts should be able to determine what the qualitative character of a state is like. Yet it seems obvious that someone who knew all the neurophysiology and psychology there was to know, but who had never seen red, wouldn't know what it was like to see red. Hence, the qualitative character of sensations of red must not be a physical property.

Some philosophers have taken these and similar arguments to show that qualia are not physical properties (where functional counts as a form of physical for these purposes). One of the biggest problems with adopting this position is that it seems to lead to epiphenomenalism, the position that qualia do not causally interact with physical events. Yet it seems clear that when we cry out from pain it's the pain, the phenomenal experience, that is causing the crying. Though some are willing to abide epiphenomenalism. (e.g., Jackson, 1982), most philosophers have sought other solutions.

Another sort of response in the spirit of nonmaterialism is to maintain that what these qualia-related arguments show is that we don't understand how physical processes give rise to qualitative experience. The mind–body problem is essentially an epistemological problem, and what we need are new conceptual tools to establish an explanatory connection between physical descriptions of what's going on in our brains and phenomenal descriptions. Philosophers taking this line (e.g., Levine, 1983, McGinn, 1991, and Nagel, 1974) differ as to how much of a problem it is that we seem unable to explain qualia in physical terms.

There are a number of materialist responses to the problem of qualia. Some philosophers argue that absent and inverted qualia are not possible, after all, and that functionalism provides the best theory of the nature of qualitative character (e.g., Lycan, 1987). Other philosophers, impressed by the inverted and absent qualia hypotheses, argue that a return to the central-state identity theory for sensory qualia is warranted. Sydney Shoemaker (1984), arguing that inverted qualia, but not absent qualia, are possible, adopts an in-between position: having qualia at all is a matter of functional organization, but which qualia one has is determined by how the functional states are physically realized.

Finally, some philosophers argue for eliminativism with respect to qualia (e.g., Dennett, 1991, Rey, 1983). That is, they argue that our intuitive conception of qualitative character is so primitive, contradictory, or incoherent that it is unlikely that any real property of our mental states satisfies it.

[See also Berkeley, George; Descartes, René; Eliminative Materialism, Eliminativism; Functionalism; Kripke, Saul Aaron; Philosophy of Mind; Physicalism; Reduction; Smart, John Jamieson Carswell.]

BIBLIOGRAPHY

Block, N. "Are Absent Qualia Impossible?" *Philosophical Review*, Vol. 89 (1980), 257–74.

———. "Troubles with Functionalism," in N. Block, ed., *Readings in Philosophy of Psychology*, Vol. 1 (Cambridge, MA, 1980).

Block, N., and J. A. Fodor. "What Psychological States Are Not," *Philosophical Review*, Vol. 81 (1972), 159–81.

Churchland, P. "Reduction, Qualia, and the Direct Introspection of Brain States," *Journal of Philosophy*, Vol. 82 (1985), 8–28.

Clark, A. *Sensory Qualities*. Oxford, 1993.

Davies, M., and G. W. Humphreys, eds. *Consciousness: Psychological and Philosophical Essays*. Oxford, 1993.

Dennett, D. C. "Quining Qualia," in A. J. Marcel and E. Bisiach, eds., *Consciousness in Contemporary Science* (Oxford, 1988).

———. *Consciousness Explained*. Boston, 1991.

Flanagan, O. *Consciousness Reconsidered*. Cambridge, MA, 1992.

Hardin, C. L. *Color for Philosophers: Unweaving the Rainbow*. Indianapolis, 1988.

Jackson, F. "Epiphenomenal Qualia," *Philosophical Quarterly*, Vol. 32, (1982), 127–36.

Kripke, S. *Naming and Necessity*. Cambridge, MA, 1980.

Levine, J. "Materialism and Qualia: The Explanatory Gap," *Pacific Philosophical Quarterly*, Vol. 64 (1983), 354–61.

Lycan, W. G. *Consciousness*. Cambridge, MA, 1987.

McGinn, C. *The Problem of Consciousness*. Oxford, 1991.

Nagel, T. "What Is It Like to Be a Bat?" *Philosophical Review*, Vol. 82 (1974), 435–50.

———. *The View from Nowhere*. New York, 1986.

Rey, G. "A Reason for Doubting the Existence of Consciousness," in R. Davidson, G. E. Schwartz, and D. Shapiro, eds., *Consciousness and Self-Regulation*, Vol. 3 (New York, 1983).

Smart, J. J. C. "Sensations and Brain Processes." *Philosophical Review*, Vol. 68 (1959), 109–30.

Shoemaker, S. *Identity, Cause, and Mind*. Cambridge, 1984. Specifically, chapters 9, 14, and 15.

– JOSEPH LEVINE

QUINE, WILLARD VAN ORMAN

Willard Van Orman Quine, Edgar Pierce Professor of Philosophy Emeritus, at Harvard, author of twenty-one books and scores of journal articles and reviews, has made many significant contributions to metaphysics, epistemology, philosophy of language, philosophy of science, philosophy of mind, logic, philosophy of logic, and set theory, and ethics (and ethical theory). These contributions are of a stature that firmly places Quine among the titans of twentieth-century Anglo-American philosophy.

In most of his publications following *Word and Object* (1960), Quine has sought to sum up, clarify, and expand on various themes found in that book. Quine can occasionally be seen changing his mind regarding some detail of his prior thought, but by and large he remains remarkably consistent.

Naturalism

The keystone of Quine's systematic philosophy is naturalism. Roughly, naturalism is the view that there is no suprascientific justification for science *and* that it is up to science to determine both what there is (ontology) and how we know what there is (epistemology). Moreover, Quine maintains that the best current science tentatively and fallibly plumps for a physicalist ontology and an empiricist epistemology.

Quine can occasionally be seen changing his mind

regarding some detail of his prior thought,

but by and large he remains remarkably consistent.

ONTOLOGY: PHYSICALISM. Since he maintains that what a (formalized) theory says there is is determined by the range of values of the bound variables of that theory, and since the bound variables of the best current scientific theory of the world (viz., physics) range over both physical objects and numbers, then, given his naturalism, Quine's physicalism embraces both concrete objects and abstract objects. He is a scientific realist regarding (observable and unobservable) physical objects and a Platonic realist regarding numbers (or sets). However, in *Pursuit of Truth* (1980) Quine downgrades the philosophical importance of ontology, including physicalism. He does so because of ontological relativity (i.e., indeterminacy of reference). The thesis is that a theory's ontology can be supplanted *salva veritate* by any one-to-one mapping of it. Ontological relativity thus engenders an attitude of indifference toward various equally apt ontologies for a given theory, including physical theory so called. At the same time it highlights the importance of a theory's ideology, that is, its lexicon of predicates. The philosophical point of Quine's thesis is, then, that what a theory says there is is less important to our understanding of the world than what a theory says about what there is.

There are two further senses in which Quine may be said to be a physicalist. First, as expected, he rejects Cartesian dualism of mind and body in favor of materialism. In this regard, he endorses Donald Davidson's anomalous monism: token identity, type diversity. Second, he is a physicalist in the sense in which physicalism is opposed to phenomenalism in epistemology (see below).

EPISTEMOLOGY: EMPIRICISM. If the best current scientific theory (tentatively and fallibly) proffers a physicalist answer to the question of what there is, then what does it proffer in response to the question of how we know what there is? The answer is, in a word, empiricism. Quine maintains that it is a finding of science that all that we come to know about the world begins with the activation of our nerve endings.

So, Quine endorses the naturalization of both ontology and epistemology. And although he downgrades the philosophical importance of ontology, he maintains the philosophical importance of epistemology. The central question of epistemology, according to Quine, is How do we acquire our theory of the world and why does it work so well? Any answer to this question must explain the relation between one's empirical data (the "meager input") and one's theory of the world (the "torrential output"). Much of what Quine wrote after *Word and Object* is, ultimately, devoted to answering this question. His own distinctive answer may be called externalized empiricism in order to differentiate it from approaches of other naturalized epistemologists (e.g., Donald Davidson). Quine's empiricism is externalized in the sense that he takes sets of activated nerve endings as his data and sets of sentences as his theory of the world (as opposed, say, to impressions and ideas, respectively).

In Quine's hands, the general relation, R_1, holding between sets of activated nerve endings and sets of sentences gets analyzed into two relations. There is the causal relation, R_2, holding between holophrastically construed observation sentences and their respective patterns of activated nerve endings, and there is the logical relation, R_3, holding between those same observation sentences, now analytically construed, and standing sentences. Quine schematizes how the child or the race, beginning with verbal responses conditioned to their respective patterns of nerve endings (R_2), could have gone on to achieve verbal reference to bodies, substances, unobservables, and abstract objects (R_3). Moreover, his account of R_3 explains how observation sentences are logically related to theoretical sentences in such a way that no bridge principles are needed for linking observation and theoretic sentences. His account also highlights the hypothetico-deductive method of prediction and falsification and the moderately holistic character of theory revision.

RECIPROCAL CONTAINMENT. Externalized empiricism is Quine's contribution to answering the central epistemological question of how we acquire our theory of the world and why it works so well. As such, his epistemology (empiricism) "contains" his ontology (physicalism): *nihil in mente quod non prius in sensu.* However, Quine's epistemologizing always takes place within some accepted theory of the world (the best one he can muster at the time), so his epistemology (empiricism) is itself contained within his ontology (physicalism). This latter containment is the central lesson of naturalism: there is no first philosophy. It is this latter containment that also makes Quine's epistemology such a radical departure from the tradition.

Changes of Mind

Even though Quine's thought has been remarkably consistent since his first works appeared in the 1930s, he changed his mind on a few important matters. First, he downgraded the importance of ontology, discussed above. Second, in the context of radical translation, Quine dropped the idea that the linguist can translate the native's "Gavagai" as her own "Lo, a rabbit" just in case the native's stimulus meaning for "Gavagai" is approximately the same as the linguist's for "Lo, a rabbit." The problem is with making scientific sense of this "implicit homology assumption" regarding different people's nerve endings. Quine changed to the position that the linguist can translate the native's "Gavagai" as her own "Lo, a rabbit" just in case the linguist can empathize with the native to the extent that she can confidently conjecture that, were she in the native's position when he uttered (or assented to) "Gavagai," then she would have done likewise for "Lo, a rabbit." In this way the linguist is (tentatively) equating the native's "Gavagai" with her own "Lo, a rabbit" without relying on an implicit homology assumption. Third, since, according to Quine's externalized empiricism, the meager input underdetermines the torrential output, then it is conceivable that there could be two (or more) global theories of the world that are empirically equivalent,

logically compatible, equally simple, and so forth. Would both be true? Quine's empiricism encourages an ecumenical response: both would be true. His naturalism encourages a sectarian response: only one would be true. Quine himself vacillated on the issue but eventually endorsed the sectarian response. This suggests that his commitment to naturalism runs deeper than his commitment to empiricism.

[See also Anomalous Monism; Davidson, Donald; Epistemology; Ethical Theory; Ethics; Metaphysics; Naturalism; Naturalized Epistemology; Ontology; Philosophy of Language; Philosophy of Mind; Philosophy of Science; Physicalism; Reference; Set Theory.]

BIBLIOGRAPHY

Among Quine's post–*Word and Object* books that bear directly on the topics discussed here are:

The Ways of Paradox and Other Essays. New York, 1966; enlarged ed., Cambridge, MA, 1976.

Ontological Relativity and Other Essays. New York, 1969.

Roots of Reference. La Salle, IL, 1974.

Theories and Things. Cambridge, MA, 1981.

Other of Quine's later books of interest are:

Set Theory and Its Logic. Cambridge, MA, 1963; rev. ed., 1969.

Philosophy of Logic. Englewood Cliffs, NJ, 1970; Cambridge, MA, 1986.

With J. S. Ullian, *The Web of Belief.* New York, 1970; rev. ed., 1978.

The Time of My Life. Cambridge, MA, 1985.

Quiddities. Cambridge, MA, 1987.

The secondary literature on Quine is immense and still growing. It includes:

Barrett, R., and R. Gibson, eds. *Perspectives on Quine.* Oxford, 1990.

Davidson, D., and J. Hintikka, eds. *Words and Objections.* Dordrecht, 1969.

Gibson, R. F., Jr. *The Philosophy of W. V. Quine: An Expository Essay.* Tampa, FL, 1982.

Hahn, L. E., and P. A. Schilpp, eds. *The Philosophy of W. V. Quine.* La Salle, IL, 1986.

Hookway, C. *Quine: Language, Experience, and Reality.* Stanford, CA, 1988.

Romanos, G. D. *Quine and Analytic Philosophy.* Cambridge, MA, 1983.

— R. F. GIBSON

R

RACISM

Racism is the view that the human species is composed of different racial groups that can be arranged hierarchically from least to most superior. Before Charles Darwin racist theories were typically formulated in terms of lineage and type: current groups were claimed to be the progeny of certain original types, each of which exemplified a distinctive form of behavior. The current achievements of any existing group or nation were then explained by reference to the admixture of racial types from which it had descended. Darwin introduced the notion of race as a subspecies—a group within a particular species that has been isolated genetically from other members of that species and has as a result developed distinct morphological and/or behavioral attributes (Banton). Social Darwinism made the survival of a particular race the mark of its fitness. Eugenicists went further to argue that we should use our knowledge to create a superior class of human beings for the future. Recent attempts to provide justification for racist orientations include a resuscitation of the claim that Africans and African Americans have lower IQs than do Europeans and European Americans (Levin). In response some argue that research that could produce

Demonstrators march on Washington, D.C., in protest of racism. (Corbis/Bettmann)

harm by furthering racist views should not be carried out; others argue that we have a moral obligation to pursue the truth no matter how uncomfortable it might be (Block & Dworkin). Clearly, however, the results of such research could be used equally to harm or help. If, for instance, it were found that people with high melanin content in their skin responded to a particular chemical compound that affected mental functioning, then it might be possible to manipulate that compound to either boost or retard intellectual performance.

Darwin introduced the notion of race

as a subspecies—a group within a particular species

that has been isolated genetically from

other members of that species

and has as a result developed

distinct morphological or behavioral attributes.

Some philosophers have argued that the very concept of a race is an artifact of European expansionism, that races exist only as a grouping convenient to the classifier. Rejecting Europe's cultural imperialism thus requires that we reject classification by races (Appiah). In a similar vein certain biologists have argued that the concept of race has no biological validity (Alland). Other biologists insist there is compelling evidence for the existence of races (Dobzansky, Nei & Roychoudhury). However, even if races were sociohistorical creations, that would be no argument against their current existence (Goldberg).

Marxists argue that racism—belief in the superiority of one race over other races—is an ideological ploy to divide the lower classes so that the European and non-European proletariat fight one another instead of fighting capitalism. Others argue that racial differences are often independent of class differences and cannot be reduced to them. Many of the latter link race to nationalist sentiments and to the demand of reparation for past harms perpetuated into the present (Outlaw).

Racism may be independent of individual intent, as is often the case with institutional racism, where implementation of certain procedures causes unnecessary harm to groups historically considered inferior, without the implementer's intentionally willing such harm. Practices such as requiring training and experience that is irrelevant for a particular employment or educational opportunity, or recruiting through personal networks,

often serve to perpetuate the effects of overt racist acts of the past and so are examples of institutional racism (Ezorsky, West).

[See also Social and Political Philosophy.]

BIBLIOGRAPHY

Alland, A., Jr. *Human Diversity.* New York, 1973.
Appiah, K. A. *In My Father's House: Africa in the Philosophy of Culture.* New York, 1992.
Banton, M. *Racial Theories.* New York, 1987.
Block, N. J., and G. Dworkin. *The IQ Controversy.* New York, 1976.
Dobzansky, T. *Mankind Evolving.* New York, 1962.
Ezorsky, G. *Racism and Justice: The Case for Affirmative Action.* Ithaca, NY, 1991.
Goldberg, D. T. "Racist Discourse and the Language of Class," in A. Zegeye, L. Harris, and J. Maxted, eds., *Exploitation and Exclusion: Race and Class in Contemporary US Society* (New York, 1991).
———. *Racist Culture-Philosophy and the Politics of Meaning.* Cambridge, 1993.
Levin, M. "Race, Biology, and Justice," *Public Affairs Quarterly,* Vol. 8 (1994), 267–85.
Mayr, E. *The Growth of Biological Thought: Diversity, Evolution, and Inheritance.* Cambridge, MA, 1982.
Nei, M., and A. K. Roychoudhury. "Genetic Relationship and Evolution of Human Races," *Evolutionary Biology,* Vol. 14 (1983), 1–59.
Outlaw, L. "Race and Class in the Theory and Practice of Emancipatory Social Transformation," in L. Harris, ed., *Philosophy Born of Struggle* (Dubuque, IA, 1983).
West, C. *Race Matters.* Boston, 1993.

— ALBERT MOSLEY

RATIONALITY

Philosophers have, at least characteristically, aspired to possess rationality but have not thereby sought exactly the same thing. Portrayed vaguely, rationality is reasonableness, but not all philosophers take rationality as dependent on reasons; nor do all philosophers have a common understanding of reasons or of reasonableness. Some theorists consider rationality to obtain in cases that lack countervailing reasons against what has rationality; they thus countenance rationality as, in effect, a default status. In ordinary parlance, persons can have rationality; so, too, can beliefs, desires, intentions, and actions, among other things. The rationality appropriate to action is practical, whereas that characteristic of beliefs is, in the language of some philosophers, theoretical.

Many philosophers deem rationality as instrumental, as goal oriented. You have rationality, according to some of these philosophers, in virtue of doing your best, or at least doing what you appropriately think adequate, to achieve your goals. If ultimate goals are not themselves subject to assessments of rationality, then rationality is purely instrumental, in a manner associated with

David Hume's position. Rationality, according to this view, is a minister without portfolio; it does not require any particular substantive goals of its own but consists rather in the proper pursuit of one's ultimate goals, whatever those goals happen to be. Many decision-theoretic and economic approaches to rationality are purely instrumentalist. If, however, ultimate goals are susceptible to rational assessment, as an Aristotelian tradition and a Kantian tradition maintain, then rationality is not purely instrumental. The latter two traditions regard certain rather specific (kinds of) goals, such as human well-being, as essential to rationality. Their substantialist approach to rationality lost considerable influence, however, with the rise of modern decision theory.

When relevant goals concern the acquisition of truth and the avoidance of falsehood, so-called epistemic rationality is at issue. Otherwise, some species of nonepistemic rationality is under consideration. One might individuate species of nonepistemic rationality by the kind of goal at hand: moral, prudential, political, economic, aesthetic, or some other. Some philosophers have invoked rationality "all things considered" to resolve conflicts arising from competing desires or species of rationality; even so, there are various approaches to rationality "all things considered" in circulation. The standards of rationality are not uniformly epistemic, then, but epistemic rationality can play a role even in what some call nonepistemic rationality. Regarding economic rationality, for instance, a person seeking such rationality will, at least under ordinary conditions, aspire to epistemically rational beliefs concerning what will achieve the relevant economic goals. Similar points apply to other species of nonepistemic rationality. A comprehensive account of rationality will characterize epistemic and nonepistemic rationality, as well as corresponding kinds of irrationality (e.g., weakness of will).

Taking rationality as deontological, some philosophers characterize rationality in terms of what is rationally obligatory and what is merely rationally permissible. If an action, for instance, is rationally obligatory, then one's failing to perform it will be irrational. Other philosophers opt for a nondeontological evaluative conception of rationality that concerns what is good (but not necessarily obligatory) from a certain evaluative standpoint. Some of the latter philosophers worry that, if beliefs and intentions are not voluntary, then they cannot be obligatory. Still other philosophers understand rationality in terms of what is praiseworthy, rather than blameworthy, from a certain evaluative standpoint. The familiar distinction between obligation, goodness and praiseworthiness thus underlies three very general approaches to rationality.

Following Henry Sidgwick, William Frankena has distinguished four conceptions of rationality: (1) an egoistic conception implying that it is rational for one to be or do something if and only if this is conducive to one's own greatest happiness (e.g., one's own greatest pleasure or desire satisfaction); (2) a perfectionist conception entailing that it is rational for one to be or do something if and only if this is a means to or a part of one's moral or nonmoral perfection; (3) a utilitarian conception implying that it is rational for one to be or do something if and only if this is conducive to the greatest general good or welfare; and (4) an intuitionist conception implying that it is rational for one to be or do something if and only if this conforms to self-evident truths, intuited by reason, concerning what is appropriate. The history of philosophy represents, not only these conceptions of rationality, but also modified conceptions adding further necessary or sufficient conditions to one of (1)–(4).

The rationality appropriate to action is practical,

whereas that characteristic of beliefs is,

in the language of some philosophers, theoretical.

Given an egoistic conception of rationality, one's being rational will allow for one's being immoral, if morality requires that one not give primacy to oneself over other people. Rationality and morality can then conflict. Such conflict is less obvious on a utilitarian conception of rationality. In fact, if morality is itself utilitarian in the way specified (as many philosophers hold), a utilitarian conception of rationality will disallow rational immorality. A perfectionist conception of rationality will preclude rational immorality only if the relevant perfection must be moral rather than nonmoral; achieving nonmoral perfection will, of course, not guarantee morality. As for an intuitionist conception of rationality, if the relevant self-evident truths do not concern what is morally appropriate, then rational immorality will be possible. An intuitionist conception will bar conflict between rationality and morality only if it requires conformity to all the self-evident truths about what is morally appropriate that are relevant to a situation or person. So, whether rationality and morality can conflict will depend, naturally enough, on the exact requirements of the conception of rationality at issue.

Richard Brandt has suggested that talk of what it would be rational to do functions to guide action by both recommending action and by making a normative claim that evaluates the available action relative to a standard. An important issue concerns what kind of strategy of using information to choose actions will enable one to achieve relevant goals as effectively as any other available strategy. Brandt has offered a distinctive constraint on such a strategy: a rational decision maker's preferences must be able to survive their being subjected to repeated vivid reflection on all relevant facts, including facts of logic. This constraint suggests what may be called (5) a relevant-information conception of rationality: rationality is a matter of what would survive scrutiny by all relevant information.

A relevant-information conception of rationality depends, first, on a clear account of precisely when information is relevant and, second, on an account of why obviously irrational desires cannot survive scrutiny by all relevant information. Evidently, one could have a desire caused by obviously false beliefs arising just from wishful thinking, and this desire could survive a process of scrutiny by all relevant information where the underlying false beliefs are corrected. In any case, a relevant-information conception of rationality will preclude rational immorality only if it demands conformity to all relevant moral information.

The egoistic, perfectionist, utilitarian, and relevant-information conceptions of rationality are nonevidential in that they do not require one's having evidence that something is conducive to self-satisfaction, perfection, general welfare, or support from all relevant information. Many philosophers would thus fault those conceptions as insufficiently sensitive to the role of relevant evidence in rationality. If relevant evidence concerns epistemic rationality, we again see the apparent bearing of epistemic rationality on rationality in general. The latter bearing deserves more attention in contemporary work on nonepistemic rationality.

Philosophers currently divide over internalism and externalism about rationality. If rationality demands reasons of some sort or other, the dispute concerns two senses of talk of a person's having a reason to perform an action. An internalist construal of this talk implies that the person has some motive that will be advanced by the action. An externalist construal, in contrast, does not require that the person have a motive to be advanced by the action. Bernard Williams, among others, has suggested that any genuine reason for one's action must contribute to an explanation of one's action and that such a contribution to explanation must be a motivation for the action. He concludes that externalism about rationality is false, on the ground that external reasons do not contribute to explanation of action in the required manner. Externalism about rationality does allow that reasons fail to motivate, but this, according to externalists, is no defect whatever. Externalists distinguish between merely motivating reasons and justifying reasons, contending that only the latter are appropriate to rationality understood normatively; what is merely motivating in one's psychological set, in any case, need not be justifying. Perhaps, then, disputes between internalists and externalists will benefit from attention to the distinction between justifying and merely motivating reasons.

Modern decision theory assumes that, in satisfying certain consistency and completeness requirements, a person's preferences toward the possible outcomes of available actions will determine, at least in part, what actions are rational for that person by determining the personal utility of outcomes of those actions. In rational decision making under certainty one definitely knows the outcomes of available actions. In decision making under risk one can assign only various definite probabilities less than 1 to the outcomes of available actions. (Bayesians assume that the relevant probabilities are subjective in that they are determined by a decision maker's beliefs.) In decision making under uncertainty one lacks information about relevant states of the world and hence cannot assign even definite probabilities to the outcomes of available actions. Acknowledging that rationality is purely instrumental (and thus that even Hitler's Nazi objectives are not necessarily rationally flawed), Herbert Simon has faulted modern decision theory on the ground that humans rarely have available the facts, consistent preferences, and reasoning power required by standard decision theory. He contends that human rationality is "bounded" in that it does not require utility maximization or even consistency. Rather, it requires the application of a certain range of personal values (or preferences) to resolve fairly specific problems one faces, in a way that is satisfactory, rather than optimal, for one. Simon thus relies on actual human limitations to constrain his account of rationality.

Contemporary theorists divide over the significance of human psychological limitations for an account of rationality. The controversy turns on how idealized principles for rationality should be. This raises the important issue of what exactly makes some principles of rationality true and others false. If principles of rationality are not just stipulative definitions, this issue merits more attention from philosophers than it has received. Neglect of this metaphilosophical issue leaves the theory of rationality as a subject of ongoing philosophical controversy.

[See also Aristotle; Bayesianism; Decision Theory; Hume, David; Kant, Immanuel; Sidgwick, Henry.]

BIBLIOGRAPHY

Audi, R. *Intention and Reason.* Ithaca, NY, 1993.

Benn, S. I., and G. W. Mortimore, eds. *Rationality and the Social Sciences.* London, 1976.

Brandt, R. *A Theory of the Good and the Right.* Oxford, 1979.

Elster, J., ed. *Rational Choice.* New York, 1986.

Frankena, W. "Concepts of Rational Action in the History of Ethics," *Social Theory and Practice,* Vol. 9 (1983), 165–97.

Gauthier, D. *Morals by Agreement.* Oxford, 1986.

Hollis, M., and S. Lukes, eds. *Rationality and Relativism.* Oxford, 1982.

Mele, A. *Irrationality.* New York, 1987.

Moser, P., ed. *Rationality in Action.* Cambridge, 1990.

Nozick, R. *The Nature of Rationality.* Princeton, NJ, 1993.

Rescher, N. *Rationality.* Oxford, 1988.

Sidgwick, H. *The Methods of Ethics,* 7th ed. London, 1907.

Simon, H. *Reason in Human Affairs.* Stanford, CA, 1983.

Slote, M. *Beyond Optimizing: A Study of Rational Choice.* Cambridge, MA, 1988.

Williams, B. "Internal and External Reasons," in R. Harrison, ed., *Rational Action* (Cambridge, 1979).

— PAUL K. MOSER

RAWLS, JOHN

John Rawls is widely regarded as one of the most significant political philosophers of the twentieth century. He was born in Baltimore, Maryland, in 1921. Educated at Princeton, he taught at Cornell and the Massachusetts Institute of Technology before joining the faculty of Harvard University in 1962. Rawls's *A Theory of Justice,* published in 1971, revitalized political theory as an academic discipline and rejuvenated interest in the substantive social issues that had long been neglected by academic philosophers. Rawls continued to refine and defend his theory in a series of articles and lectures, the most important of which he revised and collected in his 1993 work, *Political Liberalism.*

Justice as Fairness

The primary objective of Rawls's political theory is to articulate and defend a conception of justice for a modern democratic regime. The theory begins with the idea of society as a "fair system of cooperation between free and equal persons." The principles of justice for such a society characterize its fair terms of cooperation by specifying its citizens' basic rights and duties and by regulating the distribution of its economic benefits. To formulate his particular conception of justice, Rawls invokes the familiar theory of the social contract, according to which the legitimate rules for a society are arrived at by the autonomous agreement of its members. Rawls's version of the contract theory is distinctive, however, in its insistence upon the essential fairness of the point of view from which the agreement itself is conceived. This enables Rawls to appeal to the justificatory force of "pure procedural justice," the idea that the fundamental fairness of a procedure can ensure the justice of its outcome, provided that there is no independent criterion for the justice of that result. Fairness thus characterizes both the terms of the contractual agreement and the conditions in which that agreement is made. Rawls appropriately names the resulting theory "justice as fairness."

Rawls's A Theory of Justice *(1971) revitalized political theory as an academic discipline and rejuvenated interest in the substantive social issues that had long been neglected by academic philosophers.*

Rawls's contractarian or "constructivist" theory represents this fundamental ideal of fairness by situating the contracting parties in a hypothetical "original position." The most important feature of this theoretical model is the "veil of ignorance," which denies to the parties any knowledge of their actual natural endowments, their social position, or even their conception of what makes for a good life. The parties consequently cannot determine how proposed principles would affect their interests personally. The veil of ignorance thereby reflects our conviction that it would be patently unreasonable to allow principles that favored any individuals or groups merely in virtue of their possession of morally arbitrary attributes such as their race or sex or because they happened to affirm a particular religious or philosophical doctrine.

The Principles of Justice

Though deprived of knowledge of their particular ends, attachments, and aspirations, the parties in the original position are still rationally motivated to further their conception of the good, whatever it is. They also have "higher-order interests" in developing and exercising the two "moral powers" that they share as free and equal beings: (1) the capacity to understand and act from a sense of justice and (2) the capacity to form, revise, and rationally pursue a conception of the good. The parties will therefore seek for themselves the best possible package of "primary goods," those all-purpose, socially regulable opportunities and resources needed to advance those interests. Rawls's enumeration of these primary goods includes basic rights and liberties, the powers and prerogatives of offices and positions, income and wealth, and the social bases of self-respect. Assuming that a society has reached a minimal level of economic development, Rawls argues that the following two principles for allocating the primary goods would be selected:

a- Each person has an equal right to a fully adequate scheme of equal basic liberties which is compatible with a similar scheme of liberties for all.

b- Social and economic inequalities are to satisfy two conditions. First, they must be attached to offices and positions open to all under conditions of fair equality of opportunity; and second, they must be to the greatest benefit of the least advantaged members of society. (Rawls, 1993, p. 291)

Since the first principle is given absolute priority over the second, Rawls argues that the basic liberties guaranteed by it, such as freedom of religion or the right to run for political office, cannot be sacrificed for any amount of personal or collective economic benefit. Such liberties can be limited only to protect the central range of application of other conflicting liberties, as when the right to a fair trial necessitates some restrictions on the freedom of the press. Specific rights are included in the protection of the first principle if agents in the original position would rationally require them. Freedom of religion, for example, would be insisted upon by the parties, for they could not risk the possibility that their religion, should they have one, would be a minority faith subject to repression by a dogmatic majority.

Rawls maintains that political theory

should formulate a coherent set of principles

that account for the considered convictions

that we actually hold.

The second principle deals with economic and social primary goods such as income and wealth. Its second condition, the so-called "difference principle," stipulates that any departures from equality of resources can be justified only if the resulting inequality benefits the least advantaged members of society. Thus, positions that require the development of talents and the expenditure of extraordinary effort might deserve greater eco-

nomic rewards, but only if the increased productivity generated by such a differential would improve the condition of the least well off. Rawls argues that this requirement would be the reasonable and rational choice of individuals who, owing to the fairness conditions imposed in the original position, did not know their natural and social endowments and therefore could not determine their actual position in the social order.

The first part (of the second principle) stipulates that even the limited inequalities that would satisfy the difference principle are permissible only if the positions that give rise to them are open to all under conditions of "fair equality of opportunity." This strong requirement goes beyond mere prohibition of discrimination based on arbitrary features such as gender or race. It demands that all individuals of like natural ability and similar motivation should have the same opportunities throughout their entire lives, a requirement that obviously necessitates equal access to education, health care, and other social resources.

Stability

A viable political theory, Rawls insists, must be practical. The well-ordered society that it mandates must be feasible and stable given realistic economic, cultural, and psychological assumptions. In *A Theory of Justice* Rawls argued that a society regulated by justice as fairness would be stable, since the laws of moral psychology show that its members would tend to acquire and maintain a common comprehensive moral doctrine that would sustain it. In *Political Liberalism,* however, he admits that a liberal, nonauthoritarian regime will be characterized by a plurality of reasonable though incompatible comprehensive religious and moral doctrines. Nonetheless, he believes that the requirement of stability can be met by justice as fairness if we understand it as a political theory. As such, it regulates only the "basic structure" of society: the background institutions that specify political and civil rights and determine entitlements to other socially regulated goods. Members of a well-ordered society may therefore hold deeply conflicting comprehensive religious and moral views yet still endorse a common *political* conception of justice as the focus of an "overlapping consensus." Rawls stresses, moreover, that this consensus can be more than a mere modus vivendi, a practical compromise based on a tenuous balance of power. Rather, it can express a genuine moral commitment that reflects ideas and values implicit in the society's political culture, such as its conception of the citizen as a free and equal person and its willingness to rely on reasonable standards of public discourse in the conduct of its political affairs.

Reflective Equilibrium

Rawls's methodology has been as influential and as controversial as his substantive views. Declining to ground his views on any deep metaphysical or other philosophical truths, Rawls maintains that political theory should formulate a coherent set of principles that account for the considered convictions that we actually hold. The process goes beyond mere summarization of particular considered judgments, however, for it also postulates theoretical models, mediating ideas, and principles at all levels of generality. All judgments and principles are held open to revision in light of other aspects of the theory, until no further changes are needed to develop a compelling and coherent view. The resulting theory is then said to be in "reflective equilibrium." It is also "objective," Rawls contends, because it would gain the assent of all reasonable individuals on due reflection.

[See also Justice; Moral Psychology; Rights.]

BIBLIOGRAPHY

Works by Rawls

"Outline of a Decision Procedure for Ethics," *Philosophical Review*, Vol. 60 (1951), 177–97.

"Two Concepts of Rules," *Philosophical Review*, Vol. 64 (1955), 3–32.

A Theory of Justice. Cambridge, MA, 1971. A somewhat revised 1975 version has been translated into several languages.

"Kantian Constructivism in Moral Theory: The Dewey Lectures 1980," *Journal of Philosophy*, Vol. 77 (1980), 515–72.

"Themes in Kant's Moral Philosophy," in E. Förster, ed., *Kant's Transcendental Deductions* (Stanford, CA, 1989).

Political Liberalism. New York, 1993. Contains revised versions of several important papers published between 1974 and 1993.

"The Law of Peoples," in S. Shute and S. Hurley, eds., *On Human Rights: The Oxford Amnesty Lectures 1993* (New York, 1993).

Works on Rawls

Arneson, R., et al. "Symposium on Rawlsian Theory of Justice: Recent Developments," *Ethics*, Vol. 99 (1989).

Barry, B. *The Liberal Theory of Justice: A Critical Examination of the Principal Doctrines in "A Theory of Justice," by John Rawls.* Oxford, 1973.

Blocker, H. G., and E. Smith, eds. *John Rawls' Theory of Social Justice: An Introduction.* Athens, OH, 1980.

Daniels, N., ed. *Reading Rawls: Critical Studies of "A Theory of Justice."* New York, 1975.

Kukathas, C., and P. Pettit. *Rawls: "A Theory of Justice" and Its Critics.* Stanford, CA, 1990.

Martin, R. *Rawls and Rights.* Lawrence, KA, 1985.

Nozick, R. *Anarchy, State, and Utopia.* New York, 1974. Chap. 7.

Pogge, T. W. *Realizing Rawls.* Ithaca, NY, 1989.

Sandel, M. *Liberalism and the Limits of Justice.* Cambridge, 1982.

Wellbank, J. H., D. Snook, and D. T. Mason. *John Rawls and His Critics: An Annotated Bibliography.* New York, 1982.

— ALAN E. FUCHS

REALISM

Contemporary philosophical realism is not a single thesis but rather a diverse family of positions, unified chiefly by their invocation of certain characteristic images and metaphors. The realist about a region of discourse typically holds, for example, that our central commitments in the area describe a world that exists anyway, independently of us; that cognition in the area is a matter of detection rather than projection or constitution; and that the objects of the discourse are real things and not just linguistic or social constructions. Debates over realism defined in terms such as these persist in nearly every philosophical subdiscipline: from ethics and the philosophy of mind to the philosophy of science and the philosophy of mathematics. (Although it is common to describe a philosopher as a realist or nonrealist *tout court*, realism in one area is generally independent of realism in another, and advocates of global realism and its opposite number, global nonrealism, are comparatively rare.) Contemporary discussion is concerned in part with the evaluation of these discipline-specific realist theses. But it is also concerned (and increasingly so) with the more basic question of how exactly the realist's distinctive imagery is to be understood.

We may epitomize the realist's stance by saying that to be a realist about a region of discourse is to regard it as describing a genuine domain of objective fact. But what is it for a discourse to describe a "domain of fact"? And what is it for a domain of fact to be "objective"? These questions are usefully approached by attempting a taxonomy of the alternatives to realism. The nonrealist rejects the realist's rhetoric of objectivity. But this rejection can take a number of more determinate forms, and their variety sheds considerable light on what realism requires.

The realist's most basic commitment is to the view that statements in the target area purport to describe a world—to say how things stand with some distinctive range of objects or facts. This claim is often glossed as the minimal requirement that statements in the area be capable of truth or falsity. Realism is thus opposed at this most basic level to nonfactualism (also called irrealism or noncognitivism): the view that declarative statements in the target area cannot be evaluated as true or false and so cannot serve a descriptive function. Nonfactualist theses have been advanced mainly in moral philosophy, where it has been suggested that moral utterances serve to express emotional attitudes (emotivism; Blackburn, 1984; Gibbard, 1990) or to endorse or proscribe certain courses of action (prescriptivism;

Hare, 1963; cf. Geach, 1963). But they have occasionally been proposed in other areas. Formalism in the philosophy of mathematics (the view that mathematics is a game with meaningless marks, manipulated according to formal rules) and instrumentalism in the philosophy of science (according to which theoretical statements function as uninterpreted tools for deriving predictions about future experience) are further examples of this kind of nonrealism.

To say that a region of discourse purports to describe a world is to say more than that its central commitments are apt for truth. It is to say, in addition, that they are aimed at truth—that they are typically put forward as genuine assertions about how things stand with their ostensible subject matter. Realism is thus opposed at this second level to fictionalism, the view that seeming assertions in the target area, though capable of truth, are in fact designed only to provide representations that are somehow "good" or "interesting" or "useful" for certain purposes. Fictionalist approaches have been developed mainly in the philosophy of science, where Bas van Fraassen's constructive empiricism provides a useful example (van Fraassen, 1980; cf. Churchland & Hooker, 1985). Van Fraassen agrees with the scientific realist, against the instrumentalist, that theoretical statements possess definite truth conditions and so constitute genuine representations of unobservable structures. However, he further maintains, this time against the realist, that the truth value of a theory is irrelevant to its acceptability from the standpoint of science. The aim of science on van Fraassen's view is empirical adequacy: the correct description of the observable world. Theories may posit unobservable things. But a good scientific theory—one that satisfies to some high degree all of the aspirations implicit in the scientific enterprise—may be largely false in its account of such matters, so long as it is a reliable guide to the observable world. In advancing a theory in what seems to be the assertoric mode, the scientist shows only that he accepts it as empirically adequate. Van Fraassen's fictionalism thus consists centrally in his contention that the endorsement of a scientific theory does not involve the belief that it is true or that the unobservables it posits exist. Generalizing, we may say that realism involves, in addition to the semantic thesis of truth aptitude, the pragmatic thesis of truth directedness, according to which the target discourse aims at truth, and the endorsement of a claim is normally an expression of one's belief that it is true. (See Field, 1980, for a fictionalist approach to the philosophy of mathematics.)

Before we have a position that is recognizable as realist we must add one further ingredient. It is not enough that our central commitments aspire to truth.

They must also be true, or at least not wildly mistaken. Realism is thus opposed at this third level to a conception of the target area as involving a fundamental mistake about what the world contains. This "error-theoretic" alternative to realism is typified by J. L. Mackie's view of morality (Mackie, 1977). According to Mackie, ethical discourse purports to describe a range of objective prescriptions: constraints on action that are somehow built into the fabric of nature. But since it can be shown (Mackie held) that there are no such items, it follows that morality is based on a mistake— the entities it purports to describe do not exist; the properties it trades in are not instantiated—and hence that moral discourse demands reconstrual, if not outright rejection. A more familiar instance of the error-theoretic approach is atheism, the view that theological discourse is vitiated by the mistaken supposition that God exists. Agnostic versions are also possible, though in fact they have played no significant role outside the philosophy of religion.

A philosopher who holds that our core commitments in an area succeed in providing a true account of their intended subject matter may be called a minimal realist about that area. It is sometimes suggested that there is nothing more to realism than this minimal view and hence that once the questions of truth aptitude, truth directedness, and truth have been settled, there is no further space for debate about whether the discourse is to be understood "in a realistic fashion." There are, however, at least two reasons to resist this claim.

The first concerns the classification of reductionist positions. The behaviorist thesis that psychological statements can be reduced without remainder to claims about overt bodily movements and the like is clearly compatible with minimal realism about the mind. And yet the view that there is nothing more to being in pain than exhibiting "pain behavior" has generally been regarded as a clear alternative to a robust realism about mental states. It has thus become customary to insist that the realist's commitment to the truth of our views in the target area be a commitment to their truth on a literal or face-value construal. (Blackburn, 1984, chap. 5; cf. Wright, 1983.) The behaviorist translation of a simple psychological statement such as "Nadja is dreaming of Paris" will typically be a long conjunction of conditional claims describing the outward behavior Nadja would exhibit if prompted by various stimuli. But this paraphrase has a very different "surface form" from the psychological claim whose meaning it is meant to capture. And this suggests that on the behaviorist's account, the correct interpretation of psychological statements is not a face-value interpretation and hence that while he may endorse a version of minimal realism about the mental, the behaviorist should not be classed as a realist without qualification.

The second and more serious reason to resist the identification of realism with minimal realism is that minimal realism by itself involves no commitment to the mind independence or objectivity of the disputed subject matter. Kant's transcendental idealism has generally been regarded as a paradigmatic alternative to full-blown realism about the external world; and yet it is fully compatible with minimal realism as defined above. Objects in space and time are real, for Kant, in the sense that much of what common sense and science have to say about them is literally true. And yet there is another sense in which they are not fully real. The structure of the spatiotemporal world is "conditioned" for Kant by the structure of the mind that experiences it. Empirical investigation is therefore not addressed to a domain of fact that is altogether "independent of us." Clearly, Kant's position should not be described as a species of realism without qualification, its consistency with minimal realism notwithstanding.

The realist's most basic commitment

is to the view that statements in the target area

purport to describe a world—

to say how things stand

with some distinctive range of objects or facts.

Much of the most important work on realism has been devoted to explicating the commitment to objectivity that seems a necessary component of any fully realist position. The most natural thought is to identify objectivity directly with a straightforward sort of mind independence. A state of affairs will then count as objective if it would have obtained (or could have obtained) even if there were no minds or mental activity. But this precludes realism about the mind itself and also about any discourse in the social sciences that concerns itself with the products of human thought and action. And this is implausible. It should be possible to be a realist about psychology, for example, while conceding that the facts it describes are obviously mind dependent in the sense that they would not have obtained if there were no minds.

One influential approach to this problem is due to Michael Dummett, whose work is largely responsible for the current prominence of realism as a theme in Anglophone philosophy (Dummett, 1978; cf. Wright,

1992). On Dummett's view the dispute over realism, though ultimately an issue in metaphysics, is best approached by recasting it as a dispute within the philosophy of language about how to construct a theory of meaning for the target discourse. A theory of meaning in Dummett's sense is a representation in propositional form of what a competent speaker knows in virtue of which he understands his language. Dummett identifies realism with the view that a meaning theory must take the form of a classical two-valued semantic theory: an assignment of truth conditions to sentences that respects the principle of bivalence, according to which every sentence is determinately either true or false. Realism's slogan is: to understand a sentence is to know its truth condition. The leading alternative—sometimes called semantic antirealism—holds instead that to understand a sentence is to know the conditions under which it is correctly asserted. A view of this sort assigns each declarative sentence a class of "verification conditions," each of which must be the sort of condition a competent human being can in principle recognize as obtaining. A semantic theory constructed upon such a basis will generally fail to respect bivalence. The only notion of truth it makes available will be epistemically constrained: truth will be identified with knowable truth, and falsity with knowable falsity. On a view of this sort we shall not be entitled to say in advance that every well-formed question must have an answer, or that every statement of the form "*p* or not-*p*" must be true. This rejection of bivalence (and the closely related law of excluded middle) is the hallmark of semantic antirealism. To suppose that the only notion of truth we possess for a region of discourse is an epistemically constrained one is to suppose that the facts in the area are (as it were) cut to fit our intellectual capacities. Conversely, to insist that bivalence must hold regardless of our cognitive limitations is to conceive of the facts at which our thought is directed as obtaining (in one sense) independently of us.

A closely related proposal has been advanced by Hilary Putnam (1978, 1987). Putnam identifies full-blown "metaphysical" realism directly with the view that truth is epistemically unconstrained. As Putnam frames the issue, the metaphysical realist's characteristic thought is that an ideal theory might be false, where an ideal theory is one that satisfies perfectly every criterion we normally employ in deciding what to believe in the target area. In the scientific case, for example, an ideal theory would be one that supplies accurate predictions of experimental outcomes while simultaneously displaying every internal theoretical virtue that scientists consider in the context of theory choice: simplicity, elegance, explanatory power, "intrinsic plausibility," and the like. It is natural to suppose that such a theory could be false. After all, the theoretical virtues that provide our only grounds for choice among empirically equivalent hypotheses seem importantly subjective. A theory that strikes us as particularly powerful because it provides informative answers to interesting questions might strike creatures with different interests as unacceptably silent on important matters; a theory that strikes us as "intrinsically plausible" might strike creatures with different histories or cultures as strange and unlikely. The thought that an ideal theory can be false thus seems a natural expression of an appropriate human modesty, according to which we can have no guarantee in advance that our contingent, biologically, and historically conditioned sense of theoretical virtue must be a reliable guide to the facts about the physical world.

Much of the most important work on realism

has been devoted to explicating

the commitment to objectivity

that seems a necessary component

of any fully realist position.

Putnam rejects this natural thought. Metaphysical realism presupposes a concept of truth that is radically divorced from our notion of correct assertion. But according to Putnam such a concept is unattainable. Putnam's case for his view, like Dummett's, defies simple summary; but in rough outline it proceeds as follows. The only serious effort to explain an epistemically unconstrained notion of truth is a version of the correspondence theory of truth. This approach proceeds in two stages. First, subsentential expressions such as names and predicates are associated with objects and properties as their referents. Then truth as a feature of sentences is defined recursively according to a scheme well known to logicians. Putnam's central contention is that there is no credible account of the first stage. Every attempt to explain in realist terms how a word manages to refer to one object rather than another—that is, every attempt to explain how language "hooks on" to the world—is either plainly unsatisfactory or implies a radical indeterminacy of reference.

Putnam's alternative is to identify truth directly with "ideal acceptability," a position he calls internal realism. The position is realist, not simply because it is compatible with what has here been called minimal realism, but also because it eschews reductionism while remaining compatible with all of the ordinary denials of mind dependence that are part of our scientifically informed world view. Since it is plainly correct by ordinary standards to assert that mountains exist even when no one is aware of them, the internal realist will agree that mountains do not depend in this literal sense on our thought and are therefore in that sense objective. Still, the view does imply an internal connection at the global level between the way the world is and the way we are disposed to conceive of the world in what Peirce called "the ideal limit of inquiry." According to the internal realist, we should not say (as the idealist would) that the mind somehow constructs the world but rather that "the mind and the world together make up the mind and the world" (Putnam, 1978).

It remains uncertain whether the efforts of Dummett, Putnam, and others to describe a plausible alternative to realism on the matter of objectivity can succeed. It is to be noted that the arguments they provide indict any epistemically unconstrained notion of truth whatsoever, and hence that if they succeed at all they imply a global antirealism according to which every region of human thought that satisfies the condition of minimal realism is directed at a region of fact that is somehow constituted in part by our thought about it. But this can be rather hard to believe. The difficulty emerges most dramatically when we consider discourse about the past. Most of us are inclined to believe that every (nonvague) question about the past must have an answer. There is a fact of the matter, we suppose, as to whether Genghis Khan was right-handed, even if we cannot in principle obtain any pertinent evidence. But it is likely that neither "Genghis Khan was right-handed" nor its denial is assertible. Any view according to which this implies that the statement is neither true nor false is therefore bound to strike us as initially incredible. Perhaps more important, there is reason to doubt whether a commitment to an epistemically constrained notion of truth always implies a rejection of the realist's rhetoric of objectivity and independence. It is conceivable, for example, that a moral realist for whom the demands of morality are entirely independent of our passions and interests might nonetheless insist that the moral facts—because they represent rationally compelling demands on human action—must be accessible in principle to human beings. Moral truth would then be epistemically constrained; and yet the realist's rhetoric of objectivity and independence would not be undermined.

To be a realist about a region of discourse is to hold at a minimum that our core commitments in the area are largely true when interpreted "at face value." However, this minimal characterization fails to capture the realist's commitment to the objectivity or mind independence of his subject matter. In some cases this further commitment can be understood as the requirement that the concept of truth appropriate to the target area be epistemically unconstrained. It remains unclear, however, whether this characterization is adequate to every case. The search for a fully general account of the realist's commitment to objectivity is perhaps the central open question in this part of philosophy.

[See also Dummett, Michael; Kant, Immanuel; Mackie, John Leslie; Meaning; Metaphysics; Peirce, Charles Sanders; Philosophy of Language; Philosophy of Mind; Philosophy of Science; Putnam, Hilary; Reference; Truth.]

BIBLIOGRAPHY

Blackburn, S. *Spreading the Word.* Oxford, 1984.
———. "How to Be an Ethical Anti-Realist," in *Essays in Quasi-Realism* (New York, 1993).
Churchland, P., and C. Hooker, eds. *Images of Science.* Chicago, 1985.
Devitt, M. *Realism and Truth.* Cambridge, MA, 1991.
Dummett, M. *Truth and Other Enigmas.* Cambridge, MA, 1978. Especially the essays "Realism," "Truth," and "The Philosophical Basis of Intuitionistic Logic."
———. *The Seas of Language.* Oxford, 1994. Especially the essays "What Is a Theory of Meaning II" and "Realism."
Field, H. *Science without Numbers.* Princeton, NJ, 1980.
Geach, P. "Ascriptivism," *Philosophical Review,* Vol. 69 (1960), 221–25.
Gibbard, A. *Wise Choices, Apt Feelings.* Cambridge, MA, 1990.
Hare, R. M. *Freedom and Reason.* Oxford, 1963.
Honderich, T., ed. *Morality and Objectivity: A Tribute to J. L. Mackie.* London, 1985.
Mackie, J. L. *Ethics: Inventing Right and Wrong.* New York, 1977.
Putnam, H. *Meaning and the Moral Sciences.* Boston, 1978.
———. *The Many Faces of Realism.* La Salle, IL, 1987.
van Fraassen, B. *The Scientific Image.* Oxford, 1980.
Wright, C. *Frege's Conception of Numbers as Objects.* Aberdeen, 1983.
———. *Truth and Objectivity.* Cambridge, MA, 1992.

— GIDEON ROSEN

RECURSION THEORY

Since 1960 recursive function theory (or recursion theory, as it is often called) has seen both new results on existing problems, particularly on degrees of unsolvability, and growth into new areas, particularly—under the influence of computer science—studies of the complexity of computations.

Recall that a set R of natural numbers is said to be Turing reducible to another set S if membership in R can be effectively decided by using an oracle for S. We further say that R and S are Turing equivalent if each is Turing reducible to the other. This equivalence relation partitions the collection of sets into so-called degrees of unsolvability. And Turing reducibility induces a partial ordering of these degrees.

The 1983 book by Manuel Lerman surveys known results on the structure of the degrees of unsolvability. Since publication of that book, Barry Cooper has shown that the jump operation, which is the operation of forming the recursively enumerable nonrecursive set K but relative to an oracle S, is definable from the partial ordering. Questions about automorphisms of the degrees continue to be worked on.

Classically, recursion theory dealt with functions defined on the set N of natural numbers, or—equivalently—on the set of words over some finite alphabet. This can be generalized in two directions. First, the theory extends very naturally to functions taking as arguments both members of N and total functions from N into N. This extended theory is included in the book by Hartley Rogers (1987). Beginning with work by Stephen Kleene in 1959, this sort of extension has been iterated to produce "higher type" recursion theory. We get a type hierarchy by taking the objects of type 0 to be the natural numbers, and the objects of type $k + 1$ to be the functions mapping objects of type k to the natural numbers. And the theory of recursive partial functions extends to functions taking as arguments these objects of higher type.

And there is a second direction in which recursion theory has been generalized. Identifying N with the first infinite ordinal ω, one might ask what other ordinals can usefully serve as the base set for a recursion theory. The answer turns out to be the so-called admissible ordinals. For example, the next admissible ordinal after ω is the "Church-Kleene" ordinal ω_1^{CK}, the least ordinal that is not the order type of a recursive well-ordering of N. The 1957 work of Friedberg and Muenik answering Post's problem was carried over, in the 1970s, to the context of an arbitrary admissible ordinal.

The growing field of computer science has greatly influenced work in recursion theory, with each field contributing to the other. At the heart of recursion theory is the concept of an "effective procedure": a mechanical procedure specified by explicit instructions for calculating the values of a function. In the context of computer science, those explicit instructions are a "program." And an effective procedure is one for which, in principle, a computer program could be written.

In another direction, Yiannis Moschovakis, in his 1993 paper, attempts to see how the concept of "an algorithm" might be made into a mathematically precise notion. He further relates this concept to Frege's notion of sense.

The concept of an effective procedure bears on the philosophy of mathematics, in particular on the notion of a "proof." A proof of a sentence σ (in some formal system) must be something that whose correctness we can verify. A proof of σ is not the same thing as σ itself; a proof must convincingly establish that σ is indeed a theorem of the system. But to accomplish that, it must be possible to go over the proof, line by line, and mechanically verify its correctness. That is, there must be an effective procedure that, given σ and a putative proof of σ (as its input), will eventually halt and announce (as its output) the acceptability of the proof if and only if the proof is indeed correct.

Church's thesis identifies the informal notion of a function computable by an effective procedure with the mathematically precise notion of a recursive function. Alan Turing's original paper on what we now call Turing machines was guided by a desire to capture formally the notion of an effective procedure. Emil Post's work was similarly motivated. The equivalence of the Turing computability and Post computability to Alonzo Church's notion of λ-calculability has in no small measure contributed to the universal acceptance of Church's thesis as the correct formalization of an informal notion.

Classically, recursion theory dealt with

functions defined on the set N of natural numbers,

or—equivalently—

on the set of words over some finite alphabet.

In particular, under Church's thesis we can conclude that what is provable in a given formal system must be *recursively enumerable*. A sentence σ is provable if and only if there exists a string π of symbols that is its proof. And the predicate "π is a proof of σ" must be recursive, or at least recursively enumerable. (It matters not at all whether we encode here strings of symbols by means of a Gödel numbering or whether we develop directly the theory of recursive functions that operate on strings of symbols.) It follows from this fact that the set of provable sentences must be recursively enumerable.

Gödel's incompleteness theorem stems from the fact that what is provable in a formal system, be it first-order Peano arithmetic or the system in Whitehead and Russell's *Principia Mathematica* (1910–1913), is recursively enumerable, while what is true, say, in arithmetic, is not recursively enumerable. And hence a gap must remain.

But the recursive functions are the functions that are effectively computable in an ideal sense: no restrictions are imposed on the length of time the mechanical procedure might consume before producing its output, only that its output—if any—must appear in some finite length of time. Similarly, no restrictions are imposed on the amount of scratch paper that might be consumed while executing the procedure. And this idealized concept is exactly what is required for theoretical analysis of what, in principle, can be calculated.

If, however, one seeks to apply recursion theory to computer science, one finds the theory to be if anything too ideal. Even a simple computer can do everything a Turing machine can do in terms of reading a symbol, replacing it by a different symbol, and turning to the next (or to the preceding) symbol. But the Turing machine, an idealized device, never runs out of tape, and never breaks down, regardless of how long a time it runs. To an actual computer, memory space and running time are vitally important.

There are recursive functions f such that for large integers n, the number of steps required to calculate $f(n)$ is astronomically large. To be more precise, Michael Rabin proved that for any total recursive function g, we can find another total recursive function f taking only the values 0 and 1, such that for any choice of instructions I to compute f, the number of steps I uses to find $f(n)$ exceeds $g(n)$ for all but finitely many values of n. Taking $g(m) = 2^m$ and observing that 2^{100} microseconds is many times the age of the universe, one sees that some recursive functions, although computable in an idealized sense, are not "feasible" to compute in practice, at least for large inputs.

But this raises the question whether this informal notion of a computation that is feasible to execute in some practical sense admits any useful formalization at all. In recent years, as computers have become faster and their memory space has become larger, any quantitative estimates of what is feasible might seem foolhardy, to say the least.

In the early 1970s, through work of Stephen Cook, Richard Karp, and others, the proposal emerged that "polynomial time computability" might to be a useful formal notion to approximate the idea of feasible computability. Suppose that f is a recursive function defined on words (strings of symbols) over a finite alphabet. (For numerical computations, that finite alphabet might be the digits for base-10 notation.) One says that f is polynomial time computable if there are instructions I for f and a polynomial p such that for each input w, we obtain $f(w)$, following I, in no more than $p(|w|)$ steps, where $|w|$ is the length of the word w. And, as with recursive sets, one says that a set of words is polynomial time decidable (or belongs to P, for short) if its characteristic function is polynomial time computable.

While this description leaves many details open, such as the choice of formalization of recursiveness, it turns out that those details do not matter: they may affect the degree of the polynomial, but they do not affect the issue of whether or not such a bounding polynomial exists. And thus we obtain a stable notion.

The polynomial time computable functions form a subclass of the primitive recursive functions. And decidable problems can be examined anew. Take for example the satisfiability problem for propositional logic: given a formula φ of propositional logic, is there a truth assignment under which φ comes out true? This problem is well known to be decidable, that is, the set of satisfiable formulas is recursive. But is it in P? It is strongly conjectured by workers in the field that the answer is negative.

In fact, the satisfiability problem is typical of a broader class of decision problems that go under the name of "NP" (for nondeterministic polynomial time). That is, when the formula φ is indeed satisfiable, then a Turing machine, operating nondeterministically (when more than one instruction is applicable, the machine can "guess" which to use) can verify satisfiability in polynomial time. There is a rough (and imperfect) analogy here; the relation of NP to P is like the relation of recursive enumerability to recursiveness. But at least we can prove that some recursively enumerable sets are not recursive. The question whether $P = NP$ remains the most important open problem in theoretical computer science.

[See also Frege, Gottlob; Gödel, Kurt; Mathematical Logic; Philosophical Logic; Proof Theory; Russell, Bertrand Arthur William; Sense.]

BIBLIOGRAPHY

Barwise, J., ed. *Handbook of Mathematical Logic.* Amsterdam, 1978.
Cooper, S. B. "The Jump is Definable in the Structure of the Degrees of Unsolvability," *Bulletin of the American Mathematical Society,* Vol. 23 (1990), 151–58.
Lerman, M. *Degrees of Unsolvability.* Berlin, 1983.
Moschovakis, Y. N. "Sense and Denotation as Algorithm and Value," in J. Oikkonen and J. Väänänen, eds., *Logic Colloquium '90* (1993), 210–49.
Rogers, H. *Theory of Recursive Functions and Effective Computability.* New York, 1967.
Odifreddi, P. *Classical Recursion Theory.* Amsterdam, 1989.
Shoenfield, J. R. *Recursion Theory.* Berlin, 1993.

— HERBERT B. ENDERTON

REDUCTION, REDUCTIONISM

Reduction is the absorption or subsumption of one theory, conceptual scheme, or mode of discourse by another. The notion of reduction is employed in a number of family-resemblance related ways relevant to metaphysics, and it involves three interrelated dimensions or axes: ontological, semantic, and scientific. Ontologically reductionist positions typically assert that there are systematic identities between entities, kinds, properties, and facts posited respectively in a "higher-level" discourse and in a "lower-level," reducing, discourse. Semantically reductionist positions typically assert that there are systematic semantic equivalences between statements in a higher-level and in a lower-level discourse. Scientific reductionist positions typically assert that the laws and phenomena described in some scientific theory or theories are systematically explainable by those described in some other scientific theory, explainable in a way that absorbs the reduced theory into the reducing one.

Semantically reductionist projects

have often been viewed as a major means

of implementing ontological reductions.

Semantically reductionist projects have often been viewed as a major means of implementing ontological reductions. An example is logicism in philosophy of mathematics. Semantically, the logicist maintains that all the key concepts and terms of classical mathematics are definable via the terms and concepts of logic and set theory, in such a way that all of pure mathematics is derivable (under these definitions) from logic plus fundamental assumptions about classes. (Logicists such as Frege and Russell considered set theory part of logic.) This definitional reduction, says the logicist, effects an ontological reduction of all the entities posited in pure mathematics to classes.

Another semantically reductionist position often linked to ontological reductionism is phenomenalism. Semantically, the phenomenalist maintains that every meaningful statement about empirical fact is equivalent to some statement about immediate experience, actual or possible. Ontologically, this position sometimes has been regarded as undergirding metaphysical idealism—as effecting an ontological reduction of everything real to something mental.

Scientifically reductionist projects, too, often have been viewed as a way to implement ontological reductions—although normally not by means of semantic-equivalence relations. In philosophy of science the received view is that reduction involves empirical, a posteriori, hypotheses asserting systematic identities between items in the ontologies of the reduced theory and the reducing theory: the reduced theory gets explained by being shown derivable from the reducing theory together with these identity hypotheses. Thus, scientific reduction is standardly regarded as a species of ontological reduction.

Paradigm examples of scientific reduction have a part/whole aspect: laws and phenomena involving complex wholes are explained in terms of laws and phenomena involving the parts of which those wholes are composed. (This is called microreduction.) A frequently cited example is the microreduction of classical thermodynamics to statistical molecular mechanics. The key empirical hypothesis is that a gas's temperature is identical to its mean molecular kinetic energy. From this identity statement, together with the principles of molecular mechanics, the principles of thermodynamics can be derived—for example, the Boyle/Charles law, asserting that a gas's temperature is directly proportional to its pressure and inversely proportional to its volume.

Some philosophers, however, deny that scientific reduction requires intertheoretic identity hypotheses. They maintain that genuine microreduction can be underwritten by universally quantified biconditional "bridge laws," even if these bridge laws express nomic correlations between distinct properties. On this alternative view the key empirical hypothesis in the reduction just mentioned is that temperature in gases is nomically coextensive with mean molecular kinetic energy—not that the two properties are identical.

A variety of reductionist positions have been advocated in recent metaphysics. Often these are regarded as articulating a materialist metaphysical stance toward their subject matter. In philosophy of mind, for instance, it has been claimed that human psychology is microreducible to neurobiology—and that this reductionist thesis articulates a materialist conception of the mental. More generally, it has been claimed that each of the "special sciences" is microreducible to some other science, and hence (since microreduction is transitive) that all the special sciences are ultimately microreducible to fundamental microphysics. (This unity of science hypothesis is often regarded as articulating a general materialist metaphysics.) And in metaethics, it has been claimed (1) that there are genuine, objective, moral properties and facts (so-called moral realism) and (2) that these are reducible to properties and facts describable in the nonmoral language of science.

Reductionism is often contrasted with the "emergentism" of philosophical thinkers such as Samuel Alexander, Lloyd Morgan, and C. D. Broad. These emergentists were not substance-dualists; they held that all concrete particulars are, or are wholly composed out of, physical entities. But they were not full-fledged physicalists either, because they denied that physics is a causally complete science. They maintained that at various junctures in the course of evolution, complex physical entities came into existence (living beings, for example, and conscious beings) that had certain nonphysical, "emergent," properties. These properties, they claimed, are fundamental force-generating properties, over and above the force-generating properties of physics; when

such a property is instantiated by an individual, the total causal forces operative within the individual are a combination of physical and nonphysical forces, and the resulting behavior of the individual is different from what it would have been had the emergent force(s) not been operative alongside the lower-level forces. Furthermore, although emergent properties are supervenient upon lower-level properties, there is no explanation for why any given emergent property always gets instantiated when certain specific lower-order properties are instantiated; nor is there any explanation for why emergent properties generate the specific nonphysical forces they do. These facts are metaphysically and scientifically basic, in much the same way that the fundamental laws of physics are basic. They are unexplained explainers.

Although emergentism is not widely espoused

in metaphysics or the philosophy of mind,

reduction is a widely debated issue.

Although emergentism is not widely espoused in metaphysics or the philosophy of mind, reduction is a widely debated issue. In philosophy of mind three broad camps can be distinguished among philosophers who espouse some version of materialism. First are the reductive materialists, who typically maintain both (1) that scientific reduction of psychology is a prerequisite for the reality of human mentality and (2) that psychology is indeed reducible to natural science, and ultimately to physics. Second are the eliminative materialists, who typically embrace thesis (1) of reductive materialism but then argue that thesis (2) is probably false. On their view humans do not really have beliefs, desires, hopes, fears, or the other mental states of commonsense psychology at all; these are posits of a radically false, prescientific, theory. Third are the nonreductive materialists, who deny thesis (1) of reductive materialism and who typically agree, with eliminative materialists that thesis (2) of reductive materialism is probably false.

Although there are various versions of nonreductive materialism in philosophy of mind, four core tenets are commonly embraced. First, mental properties and facts are determined by, or supervenient upon, physical properties and facts. Second (and contrary to emergentism), physics is a causally complete science; the only fundamental force-generating properties are physical properties. More specifically, the human body does not instantiate any fundamental force-generating properties other than physical ones. Third, mental properties nonetheless have genuine causal/explanatory efficacy, via the physical properties that "realize" mental properties on particular occasions of instantiation. Thus, even though physics is a causally complete science, human behavior and human mental occurrences are causally explainable at both mental and physical levels of description; these different explanatory levels do not exclude one another but instead are compatible and complementary. Fourth (and again contrary to emergentism), psychophysical supervenience relations are in principle explainable rather than being fundamental and *sui generis;* so the laws and causal generalizations of psychology are explainable too. These four tenets of nonreductive materialism can be generalized beyond philosophy of mind, for instance by extending them to the whole hierarchy of intertheoretic relations among the various sciences.

One influential nonreductive materialist position is the anomalous monism of Donald Davidson. He holds that although concrete, spatiotemporally located, mental events and states are identical to concrete physical events and states (a form of ontological monism), nevertheless mental types—that is, kinds and/or properties—are neither identical to, nor lawfully coextensive with, physical types. (The monism is "anomalous" because it rejects bridge laws expressing either nomological coextensions or identities between mental and physical kinds or properties.) His argument for this position relies largely on the contention that the correct assignment of mental and actional properties to a person is always a holistic matter, involving a global, diachronic, "intentional interpretation" of the person.

Nonreductive materialists frequently argue that psychophysical reductionism runs afoul of the evident physical possibility that mental properties might be multiply realizable physicochemically, either across creatures with radically different physical constitutions or even within single creatures: realizable in humans by certain physicochemical properties instantiable only in organic matter and in silicon-based Martians by quite different physicochemical properties instantiable only in silicon; or realizable in humans, say, by a variety of distinct physicochemical properties. Multiple realizability would block the coextensiveness of mental and physical predicates (in certain physically possible worlds, at least, if not in the actual world) and hence would block reduction via bridge laws or property identities. Likewise, in philosophy of science it is sometimes argued that the properties posited in higher-level sciences are in general multiply realizable by various distinct lower-level properties—and thus that physics and the various special sciences are interrelated, not via a

hierarchy of microreduction (as the unity of science hypothesis asserts), but rather in accordance with the core tenets of nonreductive materialism.

[See also Anomalous Monism; Davidson, Donald; Eliminative Materialism, Eliminativism; Frege, Gottlob; Metaphysics; Moral Realism; Multiple Realizability; Philosophy of Mind; Philosophy of Science; Properties; Russell, Bertrand Arthur William; Set Theory; Supervenience.]

BIBLIOGRAPHY

Alexander, S. *Space, Time and Diety.* London, 1920.
Beckermann, A., H. Flohr, and J. Kim, eds. *Emergence or Reduction? Essays on the Prospects of Nonreductive Physicalism.* Berlin, 1992.
Broad, C. D. *The Mind and Its Place in Nature.* London, 1925.
Causey, R. "Attribute-identities in Microreductions," *Journal of Philosophy,* Vol. 69 (1972), 407–22.
Churchland, P. M. "Eliminative Materialism and Propositional Attitudes," *Journal of Philosophy,* Vol. 78 (1981), 67–90.
Davidson, D. "Mental Events," in L. Foster and J. W. Swanson, eds., *Experience and Theory* (Amherst, 1970).
Fodor, J. "Special Sciences (Or: The Disunity of Science as a Working Hypothesis)," *Synthese,* Vol. 28 (1974), 97–115.
Hellman, G., and F. Thompson. "Physicalism: Ontology, Determination, and Reduction," *Journal of Philosophy,* Vol. 72 (1975), 551–64.
Horgan, T. "Nonreductive Materialism and the Explanatory Autonomy of Psychology," in S. J. Wagner and R. Warner, eds., *Naturalism: A Critical Appraisal* (Notre Dame, IN, 1993).
Kemeny, J. G., and P. Oppenheim. "On Reduction," *Philosophical Studies,* Vol. 7 (1956), 6–19.
Kim, J. "The Myth of Nonreductive Materialism," *Proceedings and Addresses of the American Philosophical Association,* Vol. 63 (1989), 31–47.
McLaughlin, B. "The Rise and Fall of British Emergentism," in A. Beckermann, H. Flohr, and J. Kim, eds., *Emergence or Reduction? Essays on the Prospects of Nonreductive Physicalism* (Berlin, 1992).
Morgan, C. L. *Emergent Evolution.* London, 1923.
Nagel, E. *The Structure of Science.* New York, 1961.
Oppenheim, P., and H. Putnam. "Unity of Science as a Working Hypothesis," in H. Feigl, M. Scriven, and G. Maxwell, eds., *Minnesota Studies in the Philosophy of Science,* Vol. 2 (Minneapolis, 1958).
Putnam, H. "On Properties," in N. Rescher, ed., *Essays in Honor of Carl G. Hempel* (Dordrecht, 1969).
Quine, W. V. O. "Ontological Reduction and the World of Numbers," *Journal of Philosophy,* Vol. 61 (1964), 209–16.
Shaffner, K. "Approaches to Reduction," *Philosophy of Science,* Vol. 34 (1967), 137–47.
Sklar, L. "Types of Inter-theoretic Reduction," *British Journal for the Philosophy of Science,* Vol. 17 (1967), 109–24.

– TERENCE E. HORGAN

REFERENCE

Reference is usually conceived as the central relation between language or thought and the world. To talk or think about something is to refer to it. Twentieth-century philosophy has found such relations particularly problematic. One paradigm of reference is the relation between a proper name and its bearer. On a more theoretical conception all the constituents of an utterance or thought that contribute to determining whether it is true refer to their contributions (e.g., a predicate refers to a property). In analytic philosophy discussion of reference was dominated until the 1960s by the views of Frege and Russell and modifications of them (e.g., by Strawson). Criticisms of assumptions common to those views then provoked a revolution in the theory of reference. The alternatives include causal and minimalist theories.

Objections to Descriptivism

One model of reference is that of descriptive fit. The paradigm is a definite description (e.g., "the tallest tree") that refers to whatever it accurately describes. Frege and Russell assimilated the reference of ordinary proper names to this case by supposing that speakers associate them with descriptions. Similar accounts were later given of mass terms (e.g., "blood"), natural-kind terms (e.g., "gorilla"), and theoretical terms in science (e.g., "inertia"). It was conceded that most terms are associated with vague and context-dependent clusters of descriptions and that reference might be to whatever they least inaccurately described, but such liberalizations did not challenge the underlying idea that descriptive fit determines reference. However, Keith Donnellan, Saul Kripke, and Hilary Putnam proposed counterexamples to that idea. Suppose, for instance, that speakers associate the name "Jonah" with the Bible story. Traditional descriptivism concludes that the sentence "Although Jonah existed, those things happened only to someone else" is untrue. For if one person satisfied the relevant descriptions, "Jonah" would refer to him. But then descriptivism proves too much, for philosophical reflection cannot show that the Bible story is not a mere legend that grew up about a real person; if those things really happened to someone else, of whom no word reached the biblical writer, the name "Jonah" would still refer to the former, not the latter. Similarly, traditional descriptivism permits someone who thinks of gorillas primarily as ferocious monkeys to conclude falsely that the sentence "Gorillas exist, but they are not ferocious monkeys" is untrue.

A second criticism was this. Say that a term t rigidly designates an object x if and only if t designates (refers to) x with respect to all possible circumstances (except perhaps for circumstances in which x does not exist). Most descriptions designate nonrigidly: "the tallest tree" designates one tree with respect to present circumstances, another with respect to possible circumstances in which the former is outgrown. The descriptions that traditional descriptivists associated with names were

nonrigid. However, names designate rigidly: although we can envisage circumstances in which the Danube would have been called something else instead, we are still using our name "Danube" to hypothesize circumstances involving the very same river. Thus, most descriptions do not behave like names.

The second criticism was met by a modification of descriptivism. The descriptions associated with a name were rigidified by a qualifying phrase such as "in present circumstances". "The tallest tree in present circumstances" rigidly designates what "the tallest tree" nonrigidly designates. The first criticism is less easily met. Some descriptivists used deferential descriptions such as "the person referred to in the Bible as 'Jonah'". A more general strategy is to exploit the success of any rival theory of reference by building that theory into the associated descriptions. However, such moves jeopardize the connection between reference and speakers' understanding (a connection that descriptivism was intended to secure) as the descriptions that speakers supposedly associate with names become less and less accessible to the speakers themselves.

It is in any case clear that, as Russell recognized, not all reference is purely descriptive. If the sentence "It is hot now" is uttered at different times in exactly similar circumstances, associated with exactly the same descriptions, those descriptions are not what determines that it changes its reference from one time to the other. The reference of a token of "now" is determined by the time of its production and the invariant linguistic meaning of "now", the rule that any such token refers to the time of its production. Similarly, the presence of an object to the speaker or thinker plays an ineliminably nondescriptive role in the reference of demonstratives such as "this".

Nondescriptivism

THE KRIPKE—PUTNAM PICTURE. Kripke and Putnam proposed an alternative picture. Something x is singled out, usually demonstratively ("this river," "this kind of animal"). A name n, proper or common, is conferred on x ("Danube," "gorilla"). The name is passed on from one speaker to another, the latter intending to preserve the former's reference. Such intentions are self-fulfilling: n continues to refer to x. The beliefs that speakers would express in sentences containing n play no role in making n refer to x, so it can turn out that most of them are false. The picture involves two kinds of deference. Synchronically, there is division of linguistic labor: ordinary speakers defer to experts (e.g., in deciding which animals "gorilla" refers to). Diachronically, later speakers defer to earlier ones in a historical chain. Thus, reference typically depends on both the natural environment of the initial baptism (to fix the demonstrative reference) and the social environment of the later use. An individual speaker's understanding plays only a minor role. The account may be generalized (e.g., to many adjectives and verbs).

To talk about something is to refer to it.

Twentieth-century philosophy

has found such relations problematic.

The picture needs qualification. Gareth Evans pointed out that a name can change its reference as a result of misidentification, even if each speaker intends to preserve reference. What matters is not just the initial baptism but subsequent interaction between word and object. Such concessions do not constitute a return to descriptivism.

CAUSAL THEORIES. The Kripke–Putnam picture is often developed into a causal theory of reference, on which for n to refer to x is for a causal chain of a special kind to connect n to x. Such a theory goes beyond the original picture in at least two ways. First, although that picture required later uses of n to depend causally on the initial baptism, it did not require the initial baptism to depend causally on x. Kripke allowed reference to be fixed descriptively (not just demonstratively), as in "I name the tallest tree 'Albie' "; he merely insisted that the description did not give the meaning of the name. There is no causal connection between the name "Albie" and the tree Albie. Second, Kripke and Putnam did not attempt to define the notions they used in causal terms; the notion of an intention to preserve reference is not obviously causal.

Causal theories are often motivated by a desire to naturalize linguistic and mentalistic phenomena by reducing them to the terms of physical science. Such theories are therefore not restricted to proper names. Causal theorists will postulate that our use of the words "tall" and "tree" is causally sensitive to tallness and trees respectively, hoping thereby to explain the reference of "Albie". One problem for causal theories is that any word is at the end of many intertwined causal chains with different beginnings. It is extremely difficult to specify in causal terms which causal chains carry reference. For this reason, causal theories of reference remain programmatic.

DIRECT REFERENCE. Consonant with the Kripke–Putnam picture, but independent of causal theories of reference, is the theory of direct reference developed by David Kaplan. A term t directly refers to an object x in a given context if and only if the use of t in that context contributes nothing to what is said but x itself. For Kap-

lan, proper names, demonstratives, and indexicals such as "now" refer directly. Ruth Barcan Marcus had earlier made the similar suggestion that proper names are mere tags. The reference of a directly referential term may be determined relative to context by its context-independent linguistic meaning, as for "now"; the claim is that what "now" contributes to the proposition expressed by an utterance of "It is hot now" is not its invariant linguistic meaning but the time itself.

Although all direct reference is rigid designation, not all rigid designation is direct reference: "the square of 7" rigidly designates 49, but the reference is not direct, for the structure of the description figures in the proposition expressed by "The square of 7 is 49". On one view all genuine reference is direct, sentences of the form "The F is G" being quantified on the pattern of "Every F is G" (as Russell held); "the F" is neither a constituent nor a referring term.

If "Constantinople" and "Istanbul" have the same direct reference, the proposition (C) expressed by "Constantinople is crowded" is the proposition (I) expressed by "Istanbul is crowded", so believing (C) is believing (I), even if one would not express it in those words. Similarly, when a term of a directly referential type fails to refer, sentences in which it is used express no proposition. The view is anti-Fregean. In suitable contexts Frege would attribute different senses but the same reference to "Constantinople" and "Istanbul" and a sense but no reference to an empty name; for him the sense, not the reference, is part of what is said or thought. Russell held that logically proper names are directly referential but concluded that ordinary names are not logically proper. The challenge to defenders of the direct-reference view is to explain away the appearance of sameness of reference without sameness of thought and absence of reference without absence of thought, perhaps by postulating senselike entities in the act rather than the content of thought. The theory of direct reference concerns content, not the mechanisms of reference.

MINIMALISM. Traditional theorizing about reference is ambitious; the possibility of a broad and deep theory such as it seeks has been questioned by Richard Rorty, Robert Brandom, Paul Horwich, and others. The following schema constitutes a minimal account of reference ("a" is replaceable by singular terms):

(R) For any x, "a" refers to x if and only if $x = a$.

"London" refers to London and nothing else. A minimalist account adds to (R) the claim that (R) exhausts the nature of reference.

Some qualifications are necessary. First, if anything but a singular term replaces "a" in (R), the result is ill formed, for only singular terms should flank the identity sign. If expressions of other syntactic categories refer, those categories will require their own schemas. The schema for predicates might be:

(R') For any x, "F" refers to x if and only if x = Fness.

Second, the notion of a singular term must be explained (can "my sake" replace "a"?). Third, (R) does not say which singular terms refer. When "a" does not refer, (R) may not express a proposition. Fourth, (R) cannot be generalized by the prefix "In all contexts": "today" used tomorrow does not refer to today. Rather, (R) should be understood as instantiated by sentences in different contexts (e.g., uttered tomorrow with "today" for "a"). Fifth, when one cannot understand the term "a", one cannot understand (R). Thus, one will find many instances of (R) unintelligible.

Causal theories are often motivated

by a desire to naturalize linguistic

and mentalistic phenomena by reducing them

to the terms of physical science.

One's grasp of the minimal theory is not a grasp of each of many propositions; it is more like one's grasp of a general pattern of inference. For (R) the pattern is in the sentences that express the propositions, not in the propositions themselves (it is not preserved when a synonym replaces the unquoted occurrence of "a"). This generality does not satisfy all philosophers. Many accept the minimal theory but reject minimalism, because they postulate a deeper (e.g., causal) theory of reference that explains (R) and (R'). Although the reductionist demand for strictly necessary and sufficient conditions for reference in more fundamental terms may be overambitious, a good picture of reference might still reveal more than (R) and (R') without meeting that demand.

[See also Frege, Gottlob; Indexicals; Kripke, Saul Aaron; Marcus, Ruth Barcan; Philosophy of Language; Putnam, Hilary; Russell, Bertrand Arthur William; Sense; Strawson, Peter F.]

BIBLIOGRAPHY

Almog, J., J. Perry, and H. Wettstein, eds. *Themes from Kaplan.* New York, 1989.

Brandom, R. "Reference Explained Away: Anaphoric Reference and Indirect Description," *Journal of Philosophy,* Vol. 81 (1984), 469–92.

Devitt, M. *Designation.* New York, 1981.

Evans, G. *The Varieties of Reference.* Oxford, 1982.

Fodor, J. *Psychosemantics: The Problem of Meaning in the Philosophy of Mind.* Cambridge, MA, 1987.

French, P., T. Uehling, and H. Wettstein, eds. *Contemporary Perspectives in the Philosophy of Language,* Midwest Studies in Philosophy, Vol. 5 (Minneapolis, 1979).

Horwich, P. *Truth.* Oxford, 1990.

Kripke, S. *Naming and Necessity.* Oxford, 1980.

Lewis, D. "Putnam's Paradox," *Australasian Journal of Philosophy,* Vol. 62 (1984), 221–36.

Neale, S., *Descriptions.* Cambridge, MA, 1990.

Putnam, H. *Philosophical Papers,* Vol. 2, *Mind, Language, and Reality* (Cambridge, 1975).

Récanati, F. *Direct Reference: From Language to Thought.* Oxford, 1993.

Rorty, R. *Philosophy and the Mirror of Nature.* Princeton, NJ, 1980.

Schwartz, S., ed. *Naming, Necessity, and Natural Kinds.* Ithaca, NY, 1977.

– TIMOTHY WILLIAMSON

REID, THOMAS

The significance of Thomas Reid (1710–1796) lies in his criticism of the empiricist doctrines of his day and in the great influence he had on subsequent English-language and European philosophy. He became a minister of the Church of Scotland in 1737 and a regent at King's College, Aberdeen, in 1751. He was appointed to the Chair of Moral Philosophy at Glasgow University in 1764, succeeding Adam Smith. He displayed his greatest originality in the debate with his fellow Scotsman and near contemporary David Hume. Reid's first published work, the *Inquiry* of 1764, dealt with sense perception, a central area of Hume's many-sided skepticism.

Sense Perception and Skepticism

In sense perception a perceiver sees or touches external objects and makes judgments about them. In considering Reid's dispute with Hume we need to distinguish psychological and epistemological aspects. According to Hume's psychological account the perceiver has an impression and, insofar as she makes a judgment and forms a belief, she has an idea that is copied from the impression. The judgment itself is an idea whose particular vividness is due to the fact that it is embedded in impressions. This psychological model raises epistemological issues such as the following: if the idea is simply copied from the impression, and the impression is the only connection we have with the external world, then the judgment that we build on the idea copied from the impression will be warranted only within narrow limits. Insofar as ordinary judgments drawn from sense perception involve claims concerning objects that are distinct from us and have a permanent existence, those claims must remain illegitimate.

Reid's Psychological Account

Reid holds that this skeptical model misrepresents the psychological facts. Sense perception, he argues, involves sensations, but that does not mean that judgments are copied from sensations. Instead, the sensation naturally suggests the presence of the external object by triggering in the perceiver a conception and a judgment. The latter, however, have no similitude to the sensation. In emphasizing that our conceptions and judgments are original acts related to objects, Reid offers an early statement of the intentionality of mental acts. When a conception or judgment is occasioned by the sensation, the corresponding perception is of the external object itself. Reid never deals extensively with thoughts about what does not exist, although at some points, especially in connection with universals, he is ready to embrace a view, akin to A. Meinong's, that there are acts with nonexistent objects. Now, if our conceptions are not copied from sensations, how do we get them? Reid adopts an innatist view: in the appropriate circumstances we get our conceptions "by our constitution."

Epistemological Aspects

Reid outlines his epistemological position at two levels. At the more superficial level he insists that judgments involved in sense perception are irresistible and that our assent is not left to us. But even if one takes Reid's theologically inspired naturalism into account, this approach seems unable to answer critical questions: are not many false judgments irresistible for those who make them? But Reid's epistemology also operates at a more sophisticated level. He notes that, according to the empiricist philosophers who follow Descartes, we have complete authority in judging what our own mental states are. But, Reid remarks, although consciousness may have been particularly favored by philosophers, it is only one of the various faculties that are given to us originally, in just the same way as consciousness is. He shows that it is inconsistent to rely on consciousness alone and to deny a similar authority to our other faculties. The very detection of errors of judgment stands or falls with our ability to make reliable use of our faculties most of the time. Here the epistemological and psychological aspects of Reid's work overlap. Because our psychological faculties are relevant for his epistemology, Reid draws up a list of the "first principles of common sense," a summary of what we can usually derive from our faculties.

Although his vocabulary is psychological, Reid is taking a line adopted by a number of contemporary philosophers critical of skepticism. These philosophers have argued that, if doubt is to be intelligible, it must be local. The skeptic who believes that she can generalize doubt must be reminded that a background of certainty is required if doubt is to be effective.

Reid, by making explicit the veracity

of our faculties among his first principles,

has provided the main element

of metamental evaluation.

The American philosopher Keith Lehrer has sought an anticipation of his own coherentist epistemology in Reid. Lehrer observes that knowledge requires not only sources of information, but also the metamental evaluation of those sources, including the elimination of claims undermining the value of our information. Reid, by making explicit the veracity of our faculties among his first principles, has provided the main element of metamental evaluation. This elegant approach goes beyond anything that Reid himself wrote, but it correctly captures one aspect of his epistemology: the shift from the evaluation of judgments, which may be considered singularly by way of clear-cut criteria, to a second-order evaluation of our faculties themselves.

[*See also* Coherentism; Descartes, René; Hume, David; Nativism, Innatism; Nonexistent Objects; Perception; Skepticism.]

BIBLIOGRAPHY

Works by Reid

Inquiry into the Human Mind. 1764.
Essays on the Intellectual Powers of Man. 1785.
Essays on the Active Powers of Man. 1788.
Philosophical Works, 8th ed. Edinburgh, 1895.
Philosophical Orations, trans. S. D. Sullivan, ed. D. D. Todd. Carbondale, IL, 1989. Includes bibliography.
Practical Ethics, ed. K. Haakonssen. Princeton, NJ, 1990. Includes a substantial introduction.

Works on Reid

Alston, W. P. "Thomas Reid on Epistemic Principles," *History of Philosophy Quarterly,* Vol. 2 (1985), 435–52.
Barker, S. F., and T. L. Beauchamp, eds. *Thomas Reid: Critical Interpretations.* Philadelphia, 1976.
Brentano, F. "Was an Reid zu loben," *Grazer philosophische Studien,* Vol. 1 (1975), 1–18.
Dalgarno, M., and E. Matthews, eds. *The Philosophy of Thomas Reid.* Dordrecht, 1989.
Daniels, N. *Thomas Reid's "Inquiry": The Geometry of Visibles and the Case for Realism,* 2d ed. Stanford, CA, 1989.
Ferreira, M. J. *Scepticism and Reasonable Doubt.* Oxford, 1986.

Gallie, R. D. *Thomas Reid and the "Way of Ideas."* Dordrecht, 1989.

Lacoste, L. M. *Claude Buffier and Thomas Reid.* Kingston, 1982.

Rowe, W. L. *Thomas Reid on Freedom and Morality.* Ithaca, NY, 1991.

Schulthess, D. "Reid and Lehrer: Metamind in History," *Grazer philosophische Studien,* Vol. 40 (1991), 135–47.

Wood, P. B. "Thomas Reid, Natural Philosopher." Ph.D. diss., University of Leeds, 1984.

– DANIEL SCHULTHESS

RELEVANT ALTERNATIVES

On the relevant alternatives theory the main ingredient that must be added to true belief to make knowledge is that one be in a position to rule out all the relevant alternatives to what one believes. The important implication here is that some alternatives to what one believes are not relevant, so one can know in the face of some uneliminated possibilities of error.

This approach is largely motivated by its ability to handle cases similar to the following (adapted from Dretske, 1970). In all of our cases Wilma is now describing the epistemic state Fred was in earlier today when he had a good, clear look at what he confidently took to be—and what, in fact, were—some zebras at the local zoo. In ordinary case O nothing unusual was going on during Fred's trip to the zoo, and nothing funny is transpiring in Wilma's conversational setting as she says, "Fred knew that the animals he was seeing were zebras." By contrast, in case F the zoo was displaying convincing fake zebras—cleverly painted mules—in nine of its ten zebra exhibits. We may suppose that Fred was fooled by all nine sets of fakes before he finally encountered the real zebras. But it is that final episode that Wilma is currently talking about (and thus she is discussing a true belief of Fred's) when, unaware that there were any fakes at the zoo, she says, "Fred knew that the animals he was seeing were zebras." It seems that, since Fred did in fact know that the animals were zebras in case O, but did not know it in case F, Wilma is speaking the truth in O but is saying something false in F.

What accounts for this difference? In each case Fred believed—we may suppose with equal confidence—that the animals he was seeing were zebras. In each case this belief of Fred's was true. And we may suppose that Fred was equally justified in holding this belief in the two cases. What seems to block Fred from having knowledge in case F is that he could not rule out the possibility that he was seeing fake zebras. But Fred seems equally incapable of ruling out that alternative to what he believes in case O.

On the relevant alternatives approach the alternative that Fred was seeing fakes is, like other remote, fanciful alternatives, an irrelevant alternative in case O. But, because of the abundance of fake zebras that inhabited his surroundings in case F, that he was seeing fakes is a relevant alternative in that example. Thus, while Fred was incapable of ruling out that alternative in either case, this inability prevents him from knowing only in case F, where that alternative is relevant.

Some alternatives to what one believes are not relevant, so one can know in the face of some uneliminated possibilities of error.

That believers need not be in a position to rule out all the alternatives to what they believe in order to be knowers seems to promise some relief from skepticism. For many of the most powerful skeptical arguments reach the conclusion that we do not know what we ordinarily take ourselves to know by means of intuitively plausible claims to the effect that we are in no position to rule out various skeptical hypotheses (e.g., that one is a bodiless brain in a vat, that one is the victim of a powerful deceiving demon, etc.). But if these skeptical hypotheses are not relevant alternatives to what we believe, then our inability to rule them out does not preclude our having knowledge.

Several problems plague this antiskeptical strategy. One is that, absent some fairly clear criteria for when an alternative is relevant together with a non-question-begging argument to the effect that skeptical hypotheses do not meet these criteria, the bald claim that these hypotheses are irrelevant packs little punch against the skeptic. Another is that this strategy does not explain the persuasiveness of the skeptical arguments in question. If our concept of knowledge were such that alternatives such as the skeptical hypotheses are just irrelevant, then it seems the skeptic's inference (from our inability to rule out her hypothesis to our not knowing we think we know) would not have the intuitive pull it has for many of us. This second problem can perhaps be avoided by a different relevant alternatives strategy that allows the speaker's conversational context to affect which alternatives are relevant and does not simply declare the skeptic's hypotheses irrelevant.

In case F the presence and proximity of fakes in Fred's surroundings account for why the alternative that he is seeing fakes is relevant there. But consider another case exactly like case O with respect to the features pertaining to Fred and his surroundings. In this new case S, however, something funny *is* going on in Wilma's conversational context: she is discussing philosophical skepticism with her friend Betty, and, because Fred was in no position to rule out various skeptical hypotheses they have been discussing, she agrees with the skeptically inclined Betty that "Fred didn't know that the animals he was seeing were zebras." Here it can be maintained that because various skeptical alternatives have been brought up and taken seriously, those alternatives are relevant in case S, though they are irrelevant in O, and Wilma is therefore speaking a truth when in S she says that Fred did not know.

This approach seems to explain the power of the skeptical arguments: we find the skeptic's attack persuasive because she *makes* her alternatives relevant and thereby creates a context in which her skeptical assertions are true. That the skeptic speaks the truth here is a significant concession to the skeptic. But this approach protects the truth values of the claims to knowledge that we make in more ordinary contexts, where no skeptics are muddying the conversational waters with ordinarily irrelevant alternatives to what we believe. And it does so while, at the same time, explaining the persuasiveness of the skeptic's attack.

[See also Skepticism.]

BIBLIOGRAPHY

DeRose, K. "Contextualism and Knowledge Attributions," *Philosophy and Phenomenological Research*, Vol. 52 (1992), 913–29.
Dretske, F. "Epistemic Operators," *Journal of Philosophy*, Vol. 67 (1970), 1007–23.
Goldman, A. I. "Discrimination and Perceptual Knowledge," *Journal of Philosophy*, Vol. 73 (1976), 771–91.
Stine, G. "Skepticism, Relevant Alternatives, and Deductive Closure," *Philosophical Studies*, Vol. 29 (1976), 249–61.
Yourgrau, P. "Knowledge and Relevant Alternatives," *Synthese*, Vol. 55 (1983), 175–90.

— KEITH DEROSE

RELIABILISM

Reliabilism is a type of externalist theory concerning the nature of epistemically justified belief. According to theories of the reliabilist type, a belief held by an individual is epistemically justified just in case that belief is reliably connected to the truth. According to "process reliabilism," developed and defended in detail by Alvin Goldman (1979, 1986, 1988, 1991), an individual's belief is justified provided the process that produces the belief is a reliable one. A belief-producing process is reliable just in case it is of a type that results in true beliefs more often than false ones. According to the "reliable indicator theory," a belief is justified just in case the individual's having that belief is a reliable indication that the belief is true, where reliable indication is defined in terms of objective probability. Versions of

this kind of theory have been defended by Armstrong (1973), Alston (1989), Plantinga (1993a, 1993b), and Swain (1979), among others. In what follows, Goldman's reliable process theory will be the primary example of reliabilism under discussion.

In an early presentation of the process reliability theory, Goldman says: "The justificational status of a belief is a function of the reliability of the process or processes that cause it, where (as a first approximation) reliability consists in the tendency of a process to produce beliefs that are true rather than false" (1979, p. 9). It is not enough, however, to define justification merely in terms of having been caused by a reliable process. Suppose Mary has excellent memory but has been led to believe otherwise by a normally reliable authority. On a given occasion, she seems to remember a childhood event and comes to believe that this event occurred, despite contrary evidence. Then, even though the belief is produced by a reliable process (memory), justification is lacking. The contrary evidence should have led Mary to be suspicious of the deliverances of her memory, and to resist believing. To cover this kind of scenario, Goldman adds to the quoted suggestion a further stipulation to rule out defeaters:

(PR) S's belief in p at t is justified = def. S's belief in p at t results from a reliable cognitive process, and there is no reliable or conditionally reliable process available to S which, had it been used by S in addition to the process actually used, would have resulted in S's not believing p at t. (Goldman, 1979, p. 13)

For purposes of illustration, we may take the definition (PR) to represent the core idea behind process reliabilism.

There are three primary kinds of problems that face process reliabilism as exemplified in (PR). First, there are possible scenarios involving systematic deception by a Cartesian evil demon which suggest that an individual's belief can be epistemically justified but not produced by a reliable process. Imagine two kinds of worlds, one in which things are as we believe them to be in our world, and another in which we have the same phenomenal experiences but are systematically deceived by an evil demon. If our beliefs are epistemically justified in the "normal" world, then they should also be justified in the "demon" world, according to this line of objection. But, in demon worlds, our beliefs would not be produced by reliable processes. This kind of objection is inspired, in part, by the internalist conviction that only those properties of a person's beliefs that are internally accessible to that person are relevant to justification. In a demon world, beliefs may fully satisfy such internal conditions, just as they do in "normal" worlds, while being mostly false.

The reliabilist can respond to this first problem in several ways. The most direct response is simply to deny the legitimacy of the examples. Since the environment, in a demon world, conspires against reliable belief production, individuals in such a world have few, if any, justified beliefs. While bold, such a response will seem highly counterintuitive to many. A related reply grants that there is a legitimate, internalistic, subjective notion of justification that holds even in demon worlds. There is, however, a stronger, objective notion of justification, captured by the reliabilist approach, which correctly distinguishes between demon worlds and more hospitable epistemic environments (see Goldman, 1988). It might be argued that this stronger notion is more suitable for larger theoretical purposes, such as the provision of a definition of knowledge and the provision of an account of the social influences on individual knowledge. Yet a third possible reply is to grant the examples, continue to maintain that there is only one significant kind of epistemic justification, and modify the reliabilist account so that subjects in demon worlds have epistemically justified beliefs after all (Goldman, 1986).

According to theories of the reliabilist type,

a belief held by an individual

is epistemically justified just in case that belief

is reliably connected to the truth.

A second problem for reliabilism is illustrated by examples in which individuals arrive at true beliefs in a highly reliable manner, but are not aware that the process is a reliable one. Such examples cast doubt on the sufficiency of process reliabilism. Laurence Bonjour (1985) suggests an example in which an individual, Norman, has a rare but highly reliable clairvoyant ability. Norman is unaware that he has this ability. On certain occasions, Norman's clairvoyant ability causes him to have beliefs, for no apparent reason, concerning the whereabouts of the President of the United States. When this happens, the beliefs are invariably correct, and are irresistibly held by Norman, even when he has evidence suggesting that the President is elsewhere. Such beliefs, although reliably produced in Norman, are not epistemically justified, so it is argued.

There are, again, several responses that the reliabilist can make. The boldest, and perhaps most counterintuitive, is simply to deny the example. Although a subject like Norman violates internalist requirements that

one must be aware of one's evidence, or at least of one's reliability, the reliabilist might argue that such requirements are unacceptable on independent grounds and should not determine the results in this kind of example. A less counterintuitive reply takes note of the fact that Goldman's initial insight into the reliabilist nature of epistemic justification requires that a subject has not forsaken available processes that might have resulted in a different belief, even when coupled with the original, reliable process. Norman, for example, has failed to take into account the fact that he has no evidence for the whereabouts of the President or, even worse, has failed to take into account some contrary evidence. Taking such things into account, it might be argued, is a process that Norman could and should have used. Had he done so, he would not have believed what he does, despite his clairvoyant promptings.

The third, and perhaps most troubling problem facing the process reliabilist's program is a technical one having to do with the exact specification, in a given case, of the process that will be taken to have produced a subject's belief. This is known as the "generality problem." It was noted by Goldman himself (1979) and developed in detail by Richard Feldman (1985). Suppose that Laura sees a sheep in the field, but the sheep is at some distance and could fairly easily be confused with a large dog. Although not quite sure what she is seeing, Laura comes to believe that there is a sheep in the field. Is her belief justified? For the reliable process theory, the answer depends on the type of process that led to the belief, for it is only types of processes that can have the statistical features required for reliability. It seems, however, that Laura's coming to believe that there is a sheep in the field is the "result" of a variety of types of processes, including: perceiving something, perceiving something at a distance of two hundred yards, perceiving something that is a sheep in broad daylight on Saturday, March 9, 1996, and so forth. Some of these process types are highly reliable (the last one, for example, is perfectly reliable, since it can only be exemplified once, and it results on that occasion in a true belief), while some are considerably less reliable. Laura's belief is either justified or not, depending upon which of these process types is chosen to instantiate the definition (PR). And, so the objection goes, there is no nonarbitrary way to make such a choice. Hence, process reliabilism is hopelessly indeterminant and arbitrary.

The reliabilist might respond to the generality problem by trying to find a way of specifying the belief-forming processes whose reliability will determine epistemic justification (see, for example, Goldman, 1986). It has also been suggested, by Goldman himself (1986), that justification might be construed as permissibility in accordance with rules, where the rules specify those basic reliable processes that one may follow in forming beliefs. Goldman has also proposed that specific kinds of reliable processes might be identified as "epistemically virtuous," with beliefs being justified provided they are formed in accordance with virtuous processes (1991).

Other versions of reliabilism may be able to avoid the generality problem by defining justification in terms of reliability related features of an individual's epistemic situation other than the process that results in the belief. One example is Plantinga's theory, which says that a belief is warranted provided that it has been reliably produced by a properly functioning faculty in an environment of the type for which it was designed (1993b). On a view of this kind, reliability becomes a feature of faculties, rather than processes.

[See also Armstrong, David M.; Epistemology; Truth.]

BIBLIOGRAPHY

Alston, W. "An Internalistic Externalism," in *Epistemic Justification: Essays in the Theory of Knowledge* (Ithaca, NY, 1989). Presents and defends a reliable indication version of reliabilism.

Armstrong, D. *Belief, Truth, and Knowledge.* Cambridge, 1973. An early presentation of a reliable indication theory.

Bonjour, L. *The Structure of Empirical Knowledge.* Cambridge, MA, 1985. See particularly Chapter 3, where important criticisms of externalist theories are developed.

Feldman, R. "Reliability and Justification," *Monist*, Vol. 68 (1985), 159–74. Presentation of the generality problem.

Goldman, A. "What is Justified Belief?" in George S. Pappas, *Justification and Knowledge* (Dordrecht, 1979). Early statement of the reliable process theory.

———. *Epistemology and Cognition.* Cambridge, MA, 1986. See particularly Part 1, in which the reliable process theory is defended, and in which the "rules" version is introduced.

———. "Strong and Weak Justification." *Philosophical Perspectives*, Vol. 2 (1988), 51–69. Suggestion that there are two forms of justification.

———. "Epistemic Folkways and Scientific Epistemology," in *Liaisons: Philosophy Meets the Cognitive and Social Sciences* (Cambridge, MA, 1991). Suggestion that reliability and epistemic virtue are connected.

Plantinga, A. *Warrant: The Current Debate.* Oxford, 1993a. See especially Chapter 9, in which detailed criticisms of process and other forms of reliabilism are presented.

———. *Warrant and Proper Function.* Oxford, 1993b. Presentation of the properly functioning faculties view.

Swain, M. *Reasons and Knowledge.* Ithaca, NY, 1979. See especially Chapter 4, which develops the reliable indication theory.

— MARSHALL SWAIN

RELIGIOUS EXPERIENCE

Most of the philosophical work on religious experience that has appeared since 1960 has been devoted to its phenomenology and epistemic status. Two widely shared assumptions help account for this—that religious beliefs and practices are rooted in religious feelings and that whatever justification they have largely derives from them.

The majority of the discussions of the nature of religious experience are a reaction to Walter Stace, who believed that mysticism appears in two forms. Extrovertive mysticism is an experience of nature's unity and of one's identity with it. Introvertive mysticism is an experience of undifferentiated unity that is devoid of concepts and images; it appears to be identical with what others have called "pure consciousness"—a state in which one is conscious but conscious of nothing.

R. C. Zaehner argued that Stace's typology ignores love mysticism in India and the West. There are two types of introvertive mysticism—monistic (pure consciousness) and theistic. The latter is a form of mutual love that unites God and the mystic in an experience without images and with very little, if any, conceptual content. The most effective defense of a position of this sort is Nelson Pike's. Pike argues that the principal forms of mystical prayer in Christianity (quiet, rapture, and full union) are phenomenologically theistic. He defends his analysis against William Forgie, who denies that the identification of the experience's object with God can be part of its phenomenological content.

Phenomenological analyses of religious consciousness presuppose that we can distinguish descriptions of religious experience from interpretations.

Phenomenological analyses of religious consciousness presuppose that we can distinguish descriptions of religious experience from interpretations. Ninian Smart proposed two tests for distinguishing descriptions—that the accounts be autobiographical and that they be relatively free from doctrinal concepts. The question of criteria remains vexed, however (see Wainwright, 1981, chap. 1).

Others have argued that, because religious experience is significantly constituted by the concepts, beliefs, expectations, and attitudes that the mystic brings to it, attempts to distinguish interpretation from description are misguided. For example, an influential article by Steven Katz contends that a mystic's experiences are largely shaped by his or her tradition. This has two consequences. First, there are no "pure" or "unmediated" mystical experiences and, second, there are as many types of mystical experiences as there are traditions.

Katz's "constructivism" has been attacked by Robert Forman and Anthony Perovitch among others. Since pure consciousness is devoid of content, it is difficult to

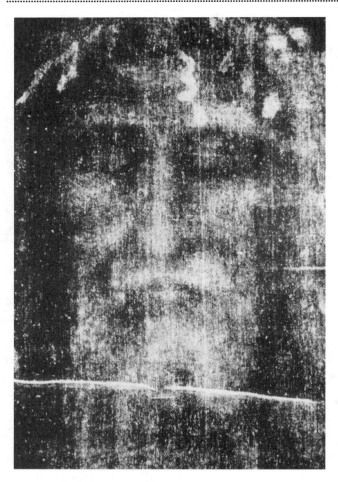

The Holy Shroud of Turin is believed to show the facial impression of Jesus Christ. (Corbis/Donald Lees)

see how it could be constituted by contents that the mystic brings to it. To argue that it must be mediated because all experience is mediated begs the question; on the face of it, pure consciousness is a counterexample to the thesis in question. Forman also argues that constructivism cannot adequately account for novelty—the fact that the mystic's experiences are often unlike what he or she expected.

Defenses of religious experience's cognitive validity have taken several forms. William Wainwright argues that mystical experiences are presumptively valid because they are significantly similar to sense experiences. Both experiences have what George Berkeley called "outness"—the subject has the impression of being immediately presented with something transcending his or her own consciousness. Corrigible and independently checkable claims about objective reality are spontaneously made on the basis of both types of experience.

There are tests in each case both for determining the reality of the experience's apparent object and for determining the genuineness of apparent perceptions of it. The nature of the tests, however, is determined by the nature of the experiences' alleged objects. Since the apparent objects of religious experience and ordinary perceptual experience differ, so too will the tests for veridical experiences of those objects.

Richard Swinburne's defense of religious experience's cognitive validity is based on the principle of credulity, which roughly states that apparent cognitions are innocent until proven guilty. This is a basic principle of rationality; without it we would be unable to justify our reliance on memory, sense perception, and rational intuition. The principle implies that there is an initial presumption in favor of how things seem to us, although this presumption can be overriden. What is true of apparent cognitions in general is true of religious experiences. They too should be accepted in the absence of good reasons for thinking them deceptive. Swinburne argues that there are none.

The most sustained defense of religious experience's epistemic credentials is William Alston's. Whereas Wainwright and Swinburne concentrate on perceptual (or perception-like) experiences, Alston focuses on perceptual practices. Doxastic (belief-forming) practices are basic when they provide our primary access to their subject matter. The reliability of a basic doxastic practice like memory cannot be established without circularity; any attempt to justify it relies on its own outputs. Alston argues that sense-perceptual practice and "Christian mystical practice" are epistemically on a par. Since both doxastic practices are basic, neither's reliability can be established without circularity. Both practices are socially established, internally consistent, and consistent with the outputs of other well-established practices. They are also self-supporting in the sense that they have the outputs we would expect them to have if they were reliable (successful predictions in the first case, for example, and moral and spiritual improvement in the second). Alston concludes that it is unreasonable to engage in sense-perceptual practice while rejecting the rationality of engaging in Christian mystical practice. The rationality at issue, however, is not epistemic. Neither practice can be shown to be epistemically rational, since it is impossible to establish their reliability without circularity. Alston intends to show only that it is practically or pragmatically rational to engage in them, although it should be noted that engaging in them involves accepting their outputs as true and therefore *believing* that they are reliable. Alston concedes that the existence of competing mystical practices weakens his case but denies that it destroys it. Critiques of Alston's work have tended to focus on this point (see, for example, Hasker, 1986).

The most significant attacks on religious experience's cognitive validity to have appeared since 1960 are Wayne Proudfoot's and Richard Gale's. Proudfoot argues that an experience's noetic quality should be identified with its embedded causal judgment (that the experience is caused by a tree, for example, or by God) and this judgment's affective resonance. The incorporated causal judgment has no intrinsic authority; it is merely one hypothesis among others and should be accepted only if it provides a better overall explanation of the experience than its competitors'. While the causal hypotheses embedded in religious experiences could be correct, they are in fact suspect; they appear to be artifacts of the subject's religious or cultural tradition and not products of nonnatural causes.

Proudfoot's identification of an experience's noetic quality with an incorporated causal judgment and its affective resonance is more plausible in some cases than others. Given my background knowledge, I believe that a certain sort of pain in one's tooth is caused by cavities. Believing this, and having a pain of that sort, I spontaneously form the belief that my pain is caused by a cavity. While my pain is not noetic, the experience as a whole is, since it incorporates a causal judgment. But the experience lacks "outness." It thus differs from sense perception, which (because of this quality) seems to have an intrinsic authority that noetic experiences like my toothache lack. Religious experiences are also diverse. Some, like my toothache, involve spontaneous causal attributions and nothing more. Others, however, are perception-like and have the same claim to intrinsic authority that sense perceptions do.

Richard Gale, on the other hand, argues that religious experience lacks the authority of sense experience. The only way of establishing religious experience's cognitivity is by showing that the tests for it are similar to those for sense experience. Arguments for religious experience's cognitive validity fail because the dissimilarities are too great. Alston and Wainwright contend that these dissimilarities can be explained by differences in the experiences' apparent objects. Gale objects that explaining the disanalogies does not explain them away and that there is a "tension" or "inconsistency" in claiming that the tests are similar (as they must be if the defense of religious experience's cognitivity is to be successful) and yet different in nature. The first point is dubious. Only relevant disanalogies count. The point of Wainwright's and Alston's explanations is to show that the disanalogies are not relevant—that is, that the features that tests for sense experiences have and tests for religious experiences lack are not ones we would expect the latter to

have if religious experiences were veridical perceptions of their apparent objects.

Gale's most original (and controversial) contribution is his contention that veridical experiences of God are conceptually impossible. The argument is roughly this. Talk of veridical experiences is in place only where it makes sense to speak of their objects as existing "when not actually perceived" and as being "the common object of different" experiences of that type. Sense experiences exhibit this feature because their objects are "housed in a space and time that includes both the object and the perceiver." Religious experiences do not exhibit this feature because there are no "analogous dimensions to space and time" that house both God and the perceiver. Gale attempts to establish this by refuting P. F. Strawson's claim that a "no space world . . . of objective sounds" is conceptually possible. We could neither reidentify sounds in such a world nor distinguish between numerically distinct but qualitatively identical ones. It would make no sense, therefore, to speak of sounds as the common objects of distinct auditory experiences or as existing when unperceived. Talk of veridical experiences of objective sounds would thus be out of place. A fortiori, talk of veridical experiences would be out of place in a nonspatial and nontemporal world. Therefore, since no common space (and, on some accounts, no common time) houses God and the mystic, talk of veridical perceptions of God is inappropriate.

A few general observations about discussions of religious experience since 1960 are in order. First, most defenses of religious experience's cognitive validity have been offered by theists. Stace is one of the few who has attempted to establish the veridicality of pure consciousness and other nontheistic experiences that lack intentional structure. Second, philosophical discussions of religious experiences tend to abstract them from the way of life in which they occur and thereby impoverish our understanding of them. Whether this penchant for abstraction adversely affects the discussion of phenomenological and epistemological issues, however, is more doubtful. Finally, a philosopher's assessment of the cognitive value of religious experience is affected by his or her metaphysical predilections. For example, those who assign a low antecedent probability to theism will demand stronger arguments for theistic experiences' cognitive validity than those who do not. One's assessment of religious experience cannot be separated from one's general assessment of the relevant religious hypotheses.

[See also Berkeley, George; Constructivism, Conventionalism; Constructivism, Moral; Intuition; Memory; Perception; Philosophy of Religion; Rationality; Strawson, Peter F.; Theism.]

BIBLIOGRAPHY

Alston, W. P. *Perceiving God.* Ithaca, NY, 1991.

Davis, C. F. *The Evidential Force of Religious Experience.* Oxford, 1989.

Forgie, W. J. "Theistic Experience and the Doctrine of Unanimity," *International Journal for Philosophy of Religion,* Vol. 15 (1984), 13–30.

———. "Pike's Mystic Union and the Possibility of Theistic Experience," *Religious Studies,* Vol. 30 (1994), 231–42.

Forman, R. K. C. "Introduction: Mysticism, Constructivism, and Forgetting," in R. K. C. Forman, ed., *The Problem of Pure Consciousness* (New York, 1990).

Gale, R. *On the Nature and Existence of God.* Cambridge, 1991. Chap. 8.

Gutting, G. *Religious Belief and Religious Skepticism.* Notre Dame, IN, 1982. Chap. 5.

Hasker, W. "On Justifying the Christian Practice," *New Scholasticism,* Vol. 60 (1986), 144–49.

Katz, S. T. "Language, Epistemology, and Mysticism," in S. T. Katz, ed., *Mysticism and Philosophical Analysis* (London, 1978).

Perovitch, A. N., Jr. "Does the Philosophy of Mysticism Rest on a Mistake?" in R. K. C. Forman, ed., *The Problem of Pure Consciousness* (New York, 1990).

Pike, N. *Mystic Union: An Essay in the Phenomenology of Mysticism.* Ithaca, NY, 1992.

Proudfoot, W. *Religious Experience.* Berkeley, 1985.

Smart, N. "Interpretation and Mystical Experience," *Religious Studies,* Vol. 1 (1965), 75–87.

Stace, W. T. *Mysticism and Philosophy.* Philadelphia, 1960.

Swinburne, R. *The Existence of God.* Oxford, 1979. Chap. 13.

Wainwright, W. J. *Mysticism: A Study of Its Nature, Cognitive Value, and Moral Implications.* Brighton, England, 1981.

Yandell, K. E. *The Epistemology of Religious Experience.* Cambridge, 1992.

Zaehner, R. C. *Concordant Discord.* Oxford, 1970.

— WILLIAM J. WAINWRIGHT

RELIGIOUS PLURALISM

The fact that there is a plurality of religions is significant in different ways from different points of view. From a skeptical point of view their different and often incompatible beliefs confirm the understanding of religion as delusion. Thus, Bertrand Russell wrote that "It is evident as a matter of logic that, since [the great religions of the world] disagree, not more than one of them can be true" (1957, xi). From the point of view of an exclusive and unqualified commitment to any one religion the fact of religious plurality is readily coped with by holding that all religions other than one's own are false, or false insofar as their belief systems differ from one's own. But from a point of view that sees religion as a worldwide phenomenon that is not to be dismissed in toto as delusion but as the human response to a divine/transcendent/ultimate reality, the fact of plurality poses a major philosophical problem. On the one hand, the "great world religions" seem—to many impartial observers, at any rate—to affect human life for both good and ill to more or less the same extent. But on the other hand their respective belief systems, although having important similarities, also include starkly incompatible elements. According to some the Real (a term at home in the Judeo-Christian tradition and corresponding to the Sanskrit *sat* and the Arabic *al-Haqq*) is personal but according to others not personal. And within each group of religions there are wide differences. Is the ultimate Person the Christian Trinity or the Qur'anic Allah, or the Adonai of Judaism, or Vishnu, or Shiva? Is the nonpersonal Ultimate the Brahman of advaitic Hinduism, or the Tao, or the Dharmakaya or Void or Nirvana of the Buddhist traditions? And how could the Real be all of these at once? The logic of religious difference here is in fact very complex, as is shown by William Christian's analysis (1987).

From a point of view that sees religion as a worldwide phenomenon that is not to be dismissed in toto as delusion but as the human response to a divine/transcendent/ultimate reality, the fact of plurality poses a major philosophical problem.

The problem is particularly acute for a major form of religious apologetic that has become prominent in the 1980s and 1990s. This holds that the basic empiricist principle that it is rational, in the absence of specific overriding considerations, to base beliefs on experience should be applied impartially to all forms of putatively cognitive experience, including religious experience—unless, again, there are specific overriding considerations to the contrary. This has been argued directly by William Alston (1991) and others and indirectly by Alvin Plantinga (in Plantinga & Wolterstorff, 1983), whose defense of the rationality of holding "properly basic" religious beliefs presupposes religious experience as their ground.

Most of the philosophers who employ this kind of apologetic have applied it only to specifically Christian beliefs. But it is evident that precisely the same argument is available for the belief systems of other religions. If Christian religious experience renders it epistemically justifiable (subject to the possibility of specific reasons to the contrary) to hold Christian beliefs, then Buddhist religious experience renders it epistemically justifiable, with the same qualification, to hold Buddhist beliefs, Muslim religious experience to hold Muslim beliefs, and so on. Thus, anyone who maintains that the Christian belief system is true, but that the belief systems of Buddhists, Muslims, and so on are false insofar as they differ from it, has implicitly reversed the original apologetic and is presenting Christian religious experience as the sole exception to the general rule that religious experience gives rise to false beliefs!

Alston, recognizing the challenge posed by the fact of religious diversity to the experiential apologetic, has responded by saying that in this situation it is proper for the Christian to continue within her own belief system, despite the existence of other equally well-justified alternatives, while, however, she seeks "a way to show in a non-circular way which of the contenders is correct" (1991, p. 278).

An alternative use of the experiential apologetic rejects the assumption that only one of the different religious belief systems can be true. This approach (Hick, 1989) distinguishes between, on the one hand, the ultimate religious reality, the Real, beyond the scope of our (other than purely formal) human conceptualities, and, on the other hand, the range of ways in which that reality is humanly conceived, and therefore humanly experienced, and therefore humanly responded to within the different religiocultural ways of being human. The epistemology operating here is one that, in the Kantian tradition, recognizes an important contribution by the perceiver to the form a reality is perceived to have. As Thomas Aquinas wrote, "Things known are in the knower according to the mode of the knower" (*Summa Theologica*, II/II, 1, 2). And in religious knowing the mode of the knower differs from religion to religion. From this point of view the fact of religious diversity does not constitute a challenge to the experiential apologetic but rather a series of examples of its valid application.

Other philosophical responses to the fact of religious plurality, not specifically related to the experiential apologetic, include the "perennial philosophy" (e.g., Schuon, 1975; Smith, 1976), which distinguishes between the essence (or esoteric core) of religion and its accidental (or exoteric) historical forms. In their esoteric essence all the great traditions converge in a transcendental unity, the Absolute Unity that is called God. Experientially, this sees the mystics of the different religions as participating in an identical experience, although they articulate it in the different ways provided by their traditions. This view is opposed by those (e.g., Katz, 1978) who hold that all experience is concept laden and that mystical experience accordingly takes different forms within the different traditions.

There is also the view of John Cobb (in Kellenberger, 1993) that the religions are directed toward different ultimates, particularly the personal reality worshiped in

the theistic religions and the nonpersonal process of the universe experienced in Buddhism. Yet other constructive suggestions include those of Joseph Runzo (1986), James Kellenberger (1989), and the authors included in the symposium *Inter-Religious Models and Criteria* (Kellenberger, 1993).

[See also *Philosophy of Religion; Religious Experience; Russell, Bertrand Arthur William; Thomas Aquinas, St.*]

BIBLIOGRAPHY

Alston, W. P. *Perceiving God*. Ithaca, NY, 1991.
Christian, W. A. *Doctrines of Religious Communities*. New Haven, 1987.
Godlove, T. F. *Religion, Interpretation, and Diversity of Belief*. Cambridge, 1989.
Hick, J. *An Interpretation of Religion*. London, 1989.
Katz, S. T., ed. *Mysticism and Philosophical Analysis*. Oxford, 1978.
Kellenberger, J. *God: Relationships with and without God*. London, 1989.
————, ed. *Inter-Religious Models and Criteria*. London, 1993.
Krieger, D. J. *The New Universalism*. Maryknoll, NY, 1991.
Plantinga, A., and N. Wolterstorff, eds. *Faith and Rationality*. Notre Dame, IN, 1983.
Runzo, J. *Reason, Relativism, and God*. London, 1986.
Russell, B. *Why I Am Not a Christian*. London, 1957.
Schuon, F. *The Transcendent Unity of Religions*. Rev. ed. New York, 1975.
Smith, H. *Forgotten Truth*. Philadelphia, 1976.
Vroom, H. M. *Religions and the Truth*. Amsterdam, 1988.

— JOHN HICK

RICOEUR, PAUL

[*This entry consists of five articles written by Don Ihde. In the first, Ihde presents an overview of the French philosopher's contributions to the field. In the second, he discusses Ricoeur's ethical theory. The third presents the philosopher's views on evil. In the fourth article, Ihde discusses Paul Ricoeur's contribution to the study of metaphor. The last article describes Ricoeur's "philosophy of the will."*]

RICOEUR, PAUL

Paul Ricoeur is one of France's most prominent and prolific contemporary philosophers. As of 1995 his bibliography ran to 120 pages of entries, including twenty-one books (in French). Ricoeur's earliest original works reflect the influence of phenomenology, in particular the phenomenology of Edmund Husserl. The earliest systematic project was a massive "philosophy of the will" that was to deal with the concepts of freedom, will, evil, finitude, and the notion of humanity. Three books, *Freedom and Nature: The Voluntary and the Involuntary* (1950), *Fallible Man* (1960), and *The Symbolism of Evil* (1960) formed the core of this early work. The first of these was the most thoroughly phenome-

nological, dealing with the experience of human freedom. Its tone is existential in its focus on the human
subject acting within an experiential field of decision.
This work is contemporaneous with works of Jean-Paul
Sartre and Maurice Merleau-Ponty and structurally
similar to the existential phenomenology of both in that
they interpret human action within situations or contexts. But already in this work the dialectical notion of
a "diagnostics" was employed; this dialectic sought to
deal with and integrate other methodologies into a
much broadened notion of Husserlian phenomenology.
Nonphenomenological sciences could provide clues or
"indices" for hard-to-detect experiential phenomena.
Fallible Man began the more religious turn often taken
by Ricoeur's work, and in this work the notions of limit-
concepts, largely Kantian in style, situate the notion of
humanity as dialectically finite and infinite: humanity
is "between" the finite and the infinite. Humanity, however, is marked by a fault line between these dimensions,
and this occasions the experience of evil. *The Symbolism
of Evil* explores this "fault" and introduces a much more
hermeneutic approach and explores the concepts and
experience of evil through the hermeneutic analysis of
a cycle of religio-cultural myths.

Ricoeur's earliest original works

reflect the influence of phenomenology,

in particular the phenomenology of Husserl.

The incorporation of these increasingly hermeneutic
concerns also marks *Freud and Philosophy* (1965) and
The Conflict of Interpretations (1969), which immediately follow the first project. Increasingly dialectical,
with a careful interrogation of some other bodies of
theory, these works attempt to enrich hermeneutic theory by carefully undertaking critical studies of structuralism, psychoanalysis, and the "hermeneutics of suspicion" that may be found in Freud, Marx, and Nietzsche.
These thinkers are suspicious of simple rationalities and
find various self-deceptive forces at work. Ricoeur terms
this attitude the hermeneutics of doubt, which contrasts
with the hermeneutics of belief arising both from classical hermeneutics (such as those associated with biblical hermeneutics), which implicitly holds to a belief that
interpretation may uncover some original meaning-
state, as well as hermeneutic phenomenology (including
the work of both Hans-Georg Gadamer and Martin
Heidegger). A hermeneutics of belief must be chastened
by a hermeneutics of suspicion.

Hermeneutics necessarily entails concerns with language. Ricoeur's habits of work are irenic and eclectic,

and for much of his mid-period of work he also finds
the notions of symbol, metaphor, and narrative to be
central to hermeneutic techniques. Ricoeur often enters
into dialogues and debates with ordinary-language philosophies, and he develops a major theory of metaphor
in *The Rule of Metaphor* (1975).

Ricoeur also has extended his hermeneutic concerns
to more historical topics, and another trilogy, the three-
volume *Time and Narrative,* marks yet another extension of his philosophy. Here concerns with both literary
and historical concepts come into play. Narrative, the
largest of the meaning units analyzed by Ricoeur, follows the progression from the symbol, his smallest unit,
through myth and metaphorical structure, to the culmination in grander narrative. Not only is this a movement from smaller to larger units, but it is also a movement to the fields of literature and history, beyond the
earlier fields of myth and religion.

There is also to be found a continuity of thematic
concerns throughout Ricoeur's career. If the earlier concentration upon a philosophy of the will necessarily
must deal with the individual, that concern marks his
very recent work as well. This can be seen in *Oneself as
Another* (1992), in which Ricoeur traces out the internal
dialectic of a complex notion of self, one in which one's
self is also developed in relation to other selves, within
oneself. In each thematic area one can find the examination of some region that is other, external, or exterior,
balanced and reflected back upon that which is the
same, internal or experienceable.

Ricoeur is a philosopher of complexity. He reads
carefully in a field, deals respectfully with alternative
approaches, and relates these dialectically to the core
continuities of his own work, which retains a
hermeneutic-phenomenological perspective. His work
contains balanced, pluralistic, and nonsimplistic theories of a wide range of phenomena. He is deeply informed in a wide range of religious, cultural, historical,
and social sciences, and his work is marked by ongoing
discussion and argumentation.

[*See also* Existentialism; Freud, Sigmund; Gadamer, Hans-
Georg; Heidegger, Martin; Hermeneutic Phenomenology; Her-
meneutic Philosophy; Husserl, Edmund; Marx, Karl; Merleau-
Ponty, Maurice; Metaphor; Nietzsche, Friedrich Wilhelm;
Sartre, Jean-Paul.]

BIBLIOGRAPHY

Works by Ricoeur

Fallible Man, translated by C. A. Kelbley. Chicago, 1965.
History and Truth, translated by C. A. Kelbley. Evanston, IL, 1966.
Freedom and Nature: The Voluntary and the Involuntary, translated by
   E. V. Kohak. Evanston, IL, 1966.
Husserl: An Analysis of His Phenomenology, translated by E. G. Ballard
   and L. E. Embree. Evanston, IL, 1967.

The Symbolism of Evil, translated by E. Buchanan. New York, 1967.

Freud and Philosophy: An Essay on Interpretation, translated by D. Savage. New Haven, 1970.

The Conflict of Interpretations: Essays in Hermeneutics, edited by D. Ihde. Evanston, IL, 1974.

The Rule of Metaphor: Multidisciplinary Studies of the Creation of Meaning in Language, translated by R. Czerny and K. Mc-Laughlin. Toronto, 1978.

Hermeneutics and the Human Sciences: Essays on Language, Action, and Interpretation, edited and translated by J. B. Thompson. Cambridge, MA, 1980.

Time and Narrative, Vols. I, II, and III, translated by K. McLaughlin and D. Pellauer. Chicago, 1984, 1985, 1988.

From Text to Action: Essays in Hermeneutics, translated by K. Blamey and J. B. Thompson. London, 1991.

Oneself as Another, translated by K. Blamey. Chicago, 1992.

– DON IHDE

RICOEUR, PAUL: ETHICAL THEORY

Paul Ricoeur does not develop a systematic or traditional ethical system, yet his works are rich in ethical insights. The three-volume *Time and Narrative* series is probably the richest in ethical suggestivity. Ricoeur argues that humans learn and locate ethical sensibilities through imagination, not simply the open imagination of sheer possibility, but a narrative-structured imagination that prefigures ethical possibilities. This he locates in fictive strategies developed primarily in literary types of narratives. Here possibility becomes concretely projective, but as fictive it is not yet historical.

Historical narrative, however, is relevant in that histories show consequences and provide a basis for ethical learning as well. Here the field of human actions is concretely traced out. Literary narrative prefigures, but historical narrative reconfigures. In Ricoeur's thought ethics is always developmental and is based upon a philosophical anthropology of human action. But human action takes its place within a meaning structure that is elucidated in narrative form. One can detect, even in this later development, links to the very earliest concerns of Ricoeur. The phenomenology of deciding within the context of the voluntary is Ricoeur's earliest examination of human structured possibility. The later development, both actional and hermeneutic, sees the mediation of ethical development in terms of the concrete, productive imagination that results in poetic, fictive, and historical narratives.

BIBLIOGRAPHY

Works by Ricoeur

Fallible Man, translated by C. A. Kelbley. Chicago, 1965.

"Guilt, Ethics, and Religion," in *Talk of God* (New York, 1969).

"The Antinomy of Human Reality and the Problem of Philosophical Anthropology," in *Readings in Existential Phenomenology* (Englewood Cliffs, NJ, 1976).

"The Problem of the Foundations of Moral Philosophy," *Philosophy Today*, Vol. 22, no. 3/4 (1978), 175–92.

– DON IHDE

RICOEUR, PAUL: EVIL, PROBLEM OF

Paul Ricoeur's theory of evil is complex and intercultural. It appears primarily in his *The Symbolism of Evil* (1960). Beginning with a phenomenology of symbolism, Ricoeur locates the foundational level of the experience of evil within symbolic "confessions" or expressions of evil experienced in defilement, sin, and guilt. All experience is open to primitive expressions. But expressions also always take place within already given contexts. These contexts are mythical and take a narrative shape. Primitive expressions thus reverberate with the higher-level myths.

> *Ricoeur locates the foundational level of the experience of evil within symbolic "confessions" or expressions of evil experienced in defilement, sin, and guilt.*

Defilement presumes evil as exterior, coming upon one through some kind of quasi-physical touch or stain. This is the most primitive stage. Here, notions of "touch not" found in many cultures predominate. Next, the notion of sin is taken up in contexts of relationships such as the contractual relationship between God and his people. Sin is a breach of relationships and thus occurs between a self and an other. Finally, guilt, the most developed notion, interiorizes evil and makes it a phenomenon of one's action and responsibility. Here some type of willing initiates evil. Ricoeur suggests these are three stages in the experience of evil, but they are stages that never totally exclude the earlier and more primitive aspects.

At the level of religio-cultural myths the experience of evil is placed in mythic narratives that give shape to the phenomenon. In this larger field Ricoeur locates—primarily out of the ancient sources of the Western traditions—four strands of mythic narrative. The first is the cycle of creation stories that describe the original disorder and chaos of the cosmos, which, through often violent acts of the deities, gradually attains order and authority. Here, evil is identified with the disorderly and chaotic, and the repetition of founding acts both founds and preserves the good as order. A second strand is the tragic group of myths in which the gods, implicitly amoral or even evil, often act against the needs of humans. The gods set boundaries and conditions in which to become fully humane often leads to tragic results. These limits often preclude moral action. This strand is associated with ancient Greek culture. To act heroically, humanely, or nobly often entails doom; the catharsis found through tragedy is its redemption. The "Adamic" cycle (the third strand) is biblical in origin and presumes a good God and his creation, but then it is by human action that evil enters the world. Evil is moral or ethical in that it results from acts of will and freedom. But its instigation is also associated with human action. The fourth strand is that of an evolution of a captured soul that gradually becomes enlightened and "returns" to a previously unified state with the divine. Here, the human is "fallen" into a material body, from which the soul must be liberated through a return to a presumed original unity with the divine. Ricoeur associates this strand with the origins of Greek philosophical thought.

While each of these myths of evil is unique, the elements of each interact in a "cycle of myths," with no one myth ever attaining clear ascendancy. The higher experience of evil, then, is a dialectical one in which the extreme poles of evil brought on by free will interact with and find an evil "already there." The cycle of myths keeps the experience of evil from any simple, rationalistic solution, but it also retains the sense of complexity and mystery through the multiple strands of this experience.

[See also Evil, Problem of.]

BIBLIOGRAPHY

Ricoeur, P. *The Symbolism of Evil*, translated by E. Buchanan. New York, 1967.
———. "Structure, Word, Event," *Philosophy Today*, Vol. 12. no. 2/4 (1968), 114–29.
———. "The Problem of the Double Sense as Hermeneutic Problem and as Semantic Problem," in *Myths and Symbols* (New York, 1969).

— DON IHDE

RICOEUR, PAUL: METAPHOR

Paul Ricoeur's contribution to the study of metaphor occurs most obviously in *The Rule of Metaphor* (1975), but the subject is a concern that runs through many of his works.

Ricoeur's theory of language is one that sees at its foundation a juncture of the experiential and the expressive, of experience and language. Symbols, the smallest meaning units in Ricoeur's repertoire, are expressions that describe primary experiences. Word and experience form a unity at this level. But even such primitives take their place in larger units, the largest being a narrative structure. But metaphors—and Ricoeur always stresses "living" or new metaphors as opposed to sedimented or "dead" metaphors—are medium-sized units that relate the various linguistic fields and roles in figurable ways. Although there can be "word metaphors," metaphor occurs primarily within a sentential context. Creative metaphor is a *deviance* from nonmetaphorical language that produces certain creative tensions. Arising from a primitive presemantic feature (such as found in symbols), metaphor may become predicative of new gestalts. Living, predicative metaphors are productive of possible creative imaginations. Ultimately, metaphors allow or stimulate redescriptions, which open new trajectories for human understanding. Rhetoric and hermeneutics are also skilled interpretive actions, and metaphor plays roles within them.

Ricoeur's theory of language is one that sees at its foundation a juncture of the experiential and the expressive, of experience and language.

Metaphors are, in this sense, the poetic inventions that simultaneously celebrate the sheer possibility of language and prefigure imaginative trajectories; they may eventuate in redescriptions, including those by which humans conceive of themselves. Metaphors have complex structures that include iconographic, imagistic, and referential capacities. They are projectively imaginative and provide the material for much of human self-interpretation and for the reconfiguration of human possibilities. Ricoeur rejects the traditional analysis of metaphor as analogy but also rejects the Heideggerian "direct" meaning of metaphor. He argues that metaphors have a linguistic structure that is complex and suggestive, thus placing metaphor in a central role for productive imagination.

[See also Metaphor.]

BIBLIOGRAPHY

Ricoeur, P. "Creativity in Language: Word, Polysemy, Metaphor," *Philosophy Today*, Vol. 17 (1973), 97–111.
———. "Metaphor and the Central Problem of Hermeneutics," *Graduate Faculty Philosophy Journal* (New York), Vol. 3 (1973–1974), 42–58.
———. *The Rule of Metaphor: Multidisciplinary Studies of the Creation of Meaning in Language,* translated by R. Czerny and K. McLaughlin, Toronto, 1978.

— DON IHDE

RICOEUR, PAUL: VOLUNTARY

Paul Ricoeur's "philosophy of the will" begins with *Freedom and Nature: The Voluntary and the Involuntary* (1950). Centrally influenced by a phenomenological method, Ricoeur locates the voluntary in the phenomenon of "deciding." Not distant from similar concepts of existentialist philosophers of the time, particularly Jean-Paul Sartre and Maurice Merleau-Ponty, decision is related to a *project* that is intended and must be decided. In the process one "decides oneself." Ricoeur undertakes a phenomenology of such decision making and attempts analyses of intentionality, motivation, need, and other related issues.

Whatever is voluntary, Ricoeur contends, always finds itself located within a context or field, which is involuntary. Moreover, even within human action there are limits that are associated with one's embodiment. In a careful depiction of the history of decision Ricoeur takes account of the moments of hesitation, the process of attention, and the interaction of determination and indetermination. Beginning from the most clearly voluntary experiences, the analysis moves outward to more and more difficult to enact decisional processes. These entail skills, habits, and other forms of patterned bodily activities.

Eventually, however, there are also limits to what can be voluntary, and at the horizons of decidability lie the phenomena of necessity, limits, and consent to inevitability. Growth and genesis, and a particularly interesting discussion of *birth*—which in Ricoeur's sense is not experienced directly but is indirectly mediated through the narratives of others—responds to the other authors of the era (in having an existential-phenomenological base) who also address these issues, such as Heidegger, Sartre, and others. It locates human freedom as a contextual freedom within, and in relation to, the involuntary. Ricoeur concludes that ours is an only or limited human freedom.

[See also Heidegger, Martin; Merleau-Ponty, Maurice; Phenomenology; Sartre, Jean-Paul.]

BIBLIOGRAPHY

Ricoeur, P. *Freedom and Nature: The Voluntary and the Involuntary,* translated by E. V. Kohak. Evanston, IL, 1966.
———. "Phenomenology of Freedom," in *Phenomenology and Philosophical Understanding* (London, 1975).

— DON IHDE

RIGHTS

The philosophical discussion of rights has tended to focus on foundational issues, such as whether talk about rights can be dispensed with entirely, and on the resolution of conflicts, for example between rights and the general welfare.

Rights and Duties

If a statement about one person's rights tells us no more than that some other person has certain duties or obligations, then in theory rights would simply be duties from another point of view. A number of reasons have been suggested for believing that this elimination is not possible. For one thing, it would require a mutual entailment between rights statements and duty statements. But (it is argued) the entailment does not hold in either direction. It is true that a claim right (i.e., a claim on someone else) might entail a duty; but, as Hohfeld long ago made us aware, since rights other than claim rights—liberty rights, powers, immunities—need not entail duties, not all rights have a corresponding and correlative duty. (Hohfeld was concerned only with legal relations, but Carl Wellman has argued that these distinctions pertain to moral rights as well as to legal rights.) Furthermore, it would seem that not every duty has a correlative right: It is sometimes said that though I may have a duty to give alms to the poor, no poor person has a right to receive alms from me.

It may be that all rights are duties, permissions,

or prohibitions without all duties, permissions,

and prohibitions being rights.

We might overcome the first objection by arbitrarily limiting the use of "rights" to talk about claim rights. But it may also be that even if liberties, powers, and immunities do not have duties as simple correlatives, there is nevertheless some other more complex relationship between statements about these kinds of rights and statements about duties; Wellman has defended such a view. A liberty, for example, might be the *absence* of a duty to do otherwise.

The other side of the argument—there are duties to which no rights correspond—is, strictly speaking, irrelevant to the question whether rights are superfluous. It may be that all rights are duties, permissions, or prohibitions without all duties, permissions, and prohibitions being rights. Nevertheless, the attempt to determine which duties, permissions, or prohibitions correlate with rights raises another objection to the attempt to dispense with rights. For if, as some suppose, having a duty toward Y will translate into Y's having a right only if it is up to Y to decide whether the duty must be fulfilled, then it can be argued that rights, even claim rights, do not simply reduce to duties—an essentially normative element would seem to be left over. That is, Y's authority over the duty cannot itself be translated into some claim about the duties of others.

This distinction between rights holders as mere beneficiaries of duties and rights holders as authorities over duties has consequences for the issue of the distribution of rights. Who is capable of holding a right? If holding a right carries with it the authority to determine whether the corresponding duty must be fulfilled, then certain entities cannot have rights: animals cannot and fetuses cannot have rights, to mention two hotly debated issues. Of course, to say that a certain sort of animal cannot have rights is not to say that there is no duty to treat the animal in certain ways.

A second sort of objection to the elimination of rights is based on a different sort of asymmetry. Rights, it is said, are grounds for duties and therefore cannot simply be duties under another name. Thus, Joseph Raz has argued that an individual capable of having rights will have a right if the fact that something is in her interest is a sufficient reason for holding some other person to be under a duty toward her. There will therefore be a duty when there is a right, but they are not just different names for the same thing. This position does not seem to be necessitated by Raz's desire to make well-being the basis for duty; it may be that well-being is the basis for both the right and the duty and that the two are nevertheless the same thing under different names.

Rights and Utility

Rights function to protect the individual against depredations on behalf of the general welfare. Each person has a right, for example, not to be killed, even if her killing would lead to a marginal gain in utility. While some writers see this need for rights as a refutation of straightforward utilitarianism, others have argued that there are versions of utilitarianism that can account for the existence of rights as limits to the public good. For example, L. W. Sumner argues that in the present state of our knowledge we simply cannot trust ourselves to make the right calculation of utility in certain types of circumstances, so that respect for rights in such circumstances may serve the function of keeping us headed for our consequentialist goal, in spite of ourselves.

Others have argued, however, that the ability to withstand utilitarian concerns is the very mark of a right. The interests protected by a right cannot simply be traded off either for greater future protection for those interests (Robert Nozick) or for any other collective goal whatever (Ronald Dworkin). This is the notion of rights as "trumps," and there are several different things it could mean. It could mean that rights are absolute, in the sense that the infringement of a right is never per-

missible, or it could mean that rights may be infringed only in the most extreme circumstances. The obvious possibility that rights themselves may come into conflict, so that one or the other must give way, makes both these interpretations implausible. Finally, it could mean that, while rights may vary as to the weight that they carry against other sorts of considerations, no right will yield to mere marginal improvements in utility. While this last reading is plausible, no one has yet been able to make clear precisely how rights are to be weighed against collective goals.

[See also Abortion; Animal Rights and Welfare; Biomedical Ethics; Rights; Social and Political Philosophy.]

BIBLIOGRAPHY

Dworkin, R. *Taking Rights Seriously.* Cambridge, MA, 1977.
Feinberg, J. *Social Philosophy.* Englewood Cliffs, NJ, 1973.
———. *Rights, Justice, and the Bounds of Liberty.* Princeton, NJ, 1980.
Gewirth, A. "Why Rights Are Indispensable." *Mind,* Vol. 95 (1986), 329–44.
Golding, M. "The Concept of Rights: A Historical Sketch," in E. Bandman and B. Bandman, eds., *Bioethics and Human Rights* (Boston, 1978).
Martin, R. *A System of Rights.* Oxford, 1993.
Martin, R., and J. Nickel. "Recent Work on the Concept of Rights," *American Philosophical Quarterly,* Vol. 17 (1980), 165–80.
Nozick, R. *Anarchy, State, and Utopia.* New York, 1974.
Raz, J. *The Morality of Freedom.* Oxford, 1986.
Sumner, L. W. *The Moral Foundation of Rights.* Oxford, 1987.
Thompson, J. J. *The Realm of Rights.* Cambridge, 1990.
Wellman, C. *A Theory of Rights.* Totowa, NJ, 1985.

— MICHAEL CORRADO

ROSS, WILLIAM DAVID

William David Ross, British Aristotelian scholar and moral philosopher, was born in 1877 in Scotland and was educated at the Royal High School in Edinburgh, Edinburgh University, and Balliol College, Oxford, where he took firsts in classical moderations and "greats." He was a fellow of Merton College from 1900 to 1902, when he was elected a fellow and tutor of Oriel. He was provost of Oriel from 1929 until his resignation in 1947.

Ross has been prominent in academic and public life. He was vice-chancellor of Oxford University (1941–1944), pro-vice-chancellor (1944–1947), president of the Classical Association (1932), and president of the British Academy (1936–1940). He has been chairman of Council of the Royal Institute of Philosophy continuously since 1940. In 1947 he served as president of the Union Académique Internationale.

Ross was awarded the Order of the British Empire for his work in the ministry of munitions and as a major on the special list during World War I. He was knighted in 1938. During World War II he was a member of the appellate tribunal for conscientious objectors and after the war was honored by the governments of Norway and Poland. Among his many public services were the chairmanships of three government departmental committees (1936–1937) and of the civil service arbitration tribunal (1942–1952). From 1947 to 1949 he was chairman of the important Royal Commission on the Press.

Ross's main contribution to philosophy,

as distinct from philosophical scholarship,

is in the field of ethics.

The qualities that made Ross successful in public life are those to which he owes his distinction as a philosopher. He is not only an Aristotelian scholar, but he also has an Aristotelian frame of mind—moderate, critical, balanced, thorough, and, above all, judicious. He values and possesses what Aristotle called "practical wisdom" no less than speculative ability.

Ross edited the Oxford translations of Aristotle, published between 1908 and 1931. He translated the *Metaphysics* and the *Ethics* himself, and he published definitive editions of a number of Aristotle's works. His *Aristotle* (London, 1923) is mainly expository, each chapter being concerned with a major aspect of Aristotle's work; this is still the best all-round exposition in English.

Ross was the leading opponent of the view of John Burnet and A. E. Taylor that the Socrates of Plato's dialogues is never a mouthpiece for Plato's own doctrines. In *Plato's Theory of Ideas* (Oxford, 1951), Ross rejected their contention that the theory of Ideas was originally the work of Socrates and not of Plato. This book traces the development of the theory of Ideas through Plato's thought. It includes a detailed discussion of Plato's cryptic doctrine of "ideal numbers," using Aristotle's account in the *Metaphysics* as a guide to the interpretation of the doctrine.

Ross's main contribution to philosophy, as distinct from philosophical scholarship, is in the field of ethics. In *The Right and the Good* (Oxford, 1930), he argued the case for intuitionism with a lucidity and thoroughness that made the book a classic. For some ten years it was the center of ethical controversy. In his *Foundations of Ethics* (Oxford, 1939) Ross restated his case and replied to his critics.

Ross's approach to ethics is Aristotelian. "The moral convictions of thoughtful and well-educated people are the data of ethics, just as sense-perceptions are the data

of a natural science" (*The Right and the Good,* p. 41). He appeals to what we mean by rightness and goodness and assumes that this guarantees the existence of what is meant and is a sure guide to its nature.

The germ of Ross's position is to be found in an article by H. A. Prichard, "Does Moral Philosophy Rest on a Mistake?" (*Mind,* Vol. 21, 1912, 21–152; reprinted in *Moral Obligation,* Oxford, 1949, pp. 1–17). Prichard was a pupil of John Cook Wilson, who also influenced Ross directly, an influence that appears in Ross's opposition to reductionism and in his view that knowledge and opinion are distinct in kind. The other main debt acknowledged by Ross is to G. E. Moore, whose arguments against ethical subjectivism he endorses, although he rejects Moore's "ideal utilitarianism."

Right and good are for Ross distinct, indefinable, and irreducible objective qualities. Rightness belongs to acts, independently of motives; moral goodness belongs to motives. Ross uses "act" for what is done and "action" for the doing of it. Thus, the doing of a right act may be a morally bad action—that is, a right act can be done from a morally bad motive; the inverse also holds. Nor can it ever be morally obligatory to act from a good motive. There are four kinds of good things—virtue, knowledge, pleasure, and the allocation of pleasure and pain according to desert. No amount of pleasure equals the smallest amount of virtue. In *Foundations of Ethics* Ross argued that virtue and pleasure are not good in the same sense—virtue is "admirable," pleasure only "a worthy object of satisfaction." What alone is common to the two senses is that they express a favorable attitude.

Ross's two main targets are ethical subjectivism and "ideal utilitarianism," which "ignores, or at least does not do full justice to, the highly personal character of duty" (*The Right and the Good,* p. 22). Specific duties are of three kinds—reparation, gratitude, and keeping faith. The "plain man" (to whom Ross, as a good Aristotelian, frequently appeals), in deciding what he ought to do, thinks as often of the past (a promise made, a debt incurred) as of future consequences. Ross does, however, admit among duties the utilitarian general duty of beneficence when it does not conflict with a specific duty. And "even when we are under a special obligation the tendency of acts to promote general good is one of the main factors in determining whether they are right" (*ibid.,* p. 3a).

Conflict of duties is one of the main problems facing an intuitionist, who cannot accept the utilitarian's "Do what will produce the most good." Ross says: "Do whichever act is more of a duty." To make sense of "more of a duty," he draws a distinction between prima-facie and actual duties and holds that conflict can only arise between prima-facie duties. An act is a prima-facie or "conditional" duty by virtue of being of a certain kind (for instance, the repaying of a debt) and would be an actual duty if it were not also of some other morally important kind or did not conflict with another more important prima-facie duty. Thus, if I have promised to lend money to a friend in need, I have a prima-facie duty to hand over the money. But suppose that before I have done so, I find that I need it for the legal defense of my son, charged with a crime of which I believe him innocent. I recognize a conflicting prima-facie duty to help him. Ross maintains that (*a*) one, and only one, of these two prima-facie duties is my actual duty; (*b*) I know each of them to be a prima-facie duty—this is self-evident; (*c*) I can have only an opinion about which is "more of a duty" and therefore my actual duty.

BIBLIOGRAPHY

A work by Ross not mentioned in the text is *Kant's Ethical Theory* (Oxford, 1954).

Some works on Ross are J. H. Muirhead, *Rule and End in Morals* (London, 1932); H. J. McCloskey, "Ross and the Concept of Prima Facie Duty," in *Australasian Journal of Philosophy,* Vol. 41 (1964), 336–345; G. E. Hughes, "Motive and Duty," in *Mind,* Vol. 53 (1944), 314–331, W. A. Pickard-Cambridge, "Two Problems About Duty," in *Mind,* Vol. 41 (1932), 72–96, 145–172, 311–340; P. F. Strawson, "Ethical Intuitionism," in *Philosophy,* Vol. 24 (1949), 23–33.

— A. K. STOUT

ROUSSEAU, JEAN-JACQUES

The writings of Jean-Jacques Rousseau continue to attract a wide range of readers throughout the world. Persistent questions concerning nationalism, political legitimacy, and the social costs of technological progress sustain an ongoing interest in Rousseau's major political writings (*The Social Contract, Considerations on the Government of Poland,* the first and second discourses). Controversies over childrearing, the nature of language, and the role of the media in public life keep alive his educational and cultural writings (*Emile, Essay on the Origin of Languages, Letter to d'Alembert on the Theater*). Speculations about psychology and the arts of autobiography draw readers to Rousseau's personal writings (*The Confessions, Reveries of a Solitary Walker, Rousseau Judge of Jean-Jacques*). And new attitudes regarding love, marriage, and eroticism provoke reconsideration of his romantic novel (*La Nouvelle Héloïse*). As the editors of a 1978 issue of *Daedalus* commemorating the bicentennial of Rousseau's death observed, Rousseau anticipated many of the moral, political, social, and aesthetic concerns that continue to preoccupy us today.

Three intellectual currents have contributed significantly to a growing body of scholarship on Rousseau.

Rousseau's writings on such subjects as childbearing, the status of women, and technological progress have continued to attract readers throughout the world. (Corbis/Leonard de Selva)

Feminist studies have offered fresh interpretations of his notoriously controversial writings about the nature, education, and status of women (see esp. *Emile,* book 5). Some feminist theorists (e.g., Okin, 1979) argue that Rousseau's advocacy of sexually differentiated social and political roles contradicts his egalitarian principles and undermines the logic and validity of his political theory. Others (e.g., Weiss, 1994) maintain that sexual differentiation constitutes a necessary social construct undergirding the unity of his entire system. At issue in many of these debates are fundamental questions about the usefulness for modern feminism of any theory that posits a close connection between a woman's essential "nature" and her moral role in society.

Deconstruction has also affected the content and direction of Rousseau criticism, especially among scholars in language and literature departments. The French philosophers and literary critics who originated this movement in the 1960s and 1970s gave prime place to Rousseau in the development of their ideas (see, e.g., Derrida, 1976). In seeking to expose the indeterminacy of the meaning of Rousseau's texts by examining details that are commonly overlooked (e.g., footnotes, metaphors, his choice of particular terms), deconstructionist critiques illuminate the multilayered quality of his prose and show that even an author committed to the truth may produce writings fraught with artifice.

A third important source of Rousseau criticism has been the legacy of Leo Strauss—a mid-twentieth-century political philosopher who is as well known for the habits of close textual analysis he passed on to his students as for the ideas put forth in his own writings (see, e.g., Strauss, 1953). Straussian interpretations take seriously Rousseau's claims that his political thought forms a single coherent system; they also emphasize his debt to classical sources. Most important, perhaps, the Straussian legacy includes a substantial number of English translations of Rousseau's work (e.g., by Allan Bloom, Victor Gourevitch, Christopher Kelly, Judith R. Bush, and Roger D. Masters)—thus making him more accessible to the general reader in North America.

Rousseau anticipated many of the moral,

political, social, and aesthetic concerns

that continue to preoccupy us today.

Rousseau specialists have benefited from the publication of Rousseau's *Oeuvres complètes* and *Correspondance complète*, from the appearance of scholarly journals and associations devoted to Rousseau studies (*Annales de la Société Jean-Jacques Rousseau*, *Études Jean-Jacques Rousseau*, and the *Proceedings* of the North American Association for the Study of Rousseau), and from the publication of papers delivered at various conferences held in 1978 to commemorate his death and in 1989 to mark his relationship to the French Revolution.

[See also Deconstruction; Derrida, Jacques; Nationalism.]

BIBLIOGRAPHY

Works by Rousseau

Oeuvres complètes. Ed. B. Gagnebin and M. Raymond. 5 vols. Paris, 1959–.
Correspondance complète de Jean-Jacques Rousseau. Ed. R. A. Leigh. 43 vols. Geneva, 1965–89.
Emile or On Education. Trans. A. Bloom. New York, 1979.
The Collected Writings of Jean-Jacques Rousseau. Ed. R. D. Masters and C. Kelly; trans. J. R. Bush, C. Kelly, and R. D. Masters. Hanover, NH, 1990–.

Works on Rousseau

Cranston, M. *Jean-Jacques: The Early Life and Work of Jean-Jacques Rousseau, 1712–1754.* New York, 1983.

———. *The Noble Savage: Jean-Jacques Rousseau, 1954–62.* Chicago, 1991.
Daedalus, "Rousseau for Our Time," special issue (Summer 1978).
de Man, P. *Allegories of Reading: Figural Language in Rousseau, Nietzsche, Rilke, and Proust.* New Haven, 1979.
Derrida, J. *Of Grammatology,* trans. G. Chakravorty Spivak. Baltimore, 1976.
Kelly, C. *Rousseau's Exemplary Life: The "Confessions" as Political Philosophy.* Ithaca, NY, 1987.
Launay, M. *Jean-Jacques Rousseau: Écrivain politique (1712–1762),* 2d ed. Geneva, 1989.
Masters, R. D. *The Political Philosophy of Rousseau.* Princeton, NJ, 1968.
Melzer, A. M. *The Natural Goodness of Man: On the System of Rousseau's Thought.* Chicago, 1990.
Miller, J. *Rousseau, Dreamer of Democracy.* New Haven, 1984.
Okin, S. M. *Women in Western Political Thought.* Princeton, NJ, 1979.
Roosevelt, G. G. *Reading Rousseau in the Nuclear Age.* Philadelphia, 1990.
Schwartz, J. *The Sexual Politics of Jean-Jacques Rousseau.* Chicago, 1984.
Shklar, J. N. *Men and Citizens: A Study of Rousseau's Social Theory.* Cambridge, 1969.
Starobinski, J. *J.-J. Rousseau: La transparence et l'obstacle.* Paris, 1971. Translated by A. Goldhammer as *Jean-Jacques Rousseau: Transparency and Obstruction.* Chicago, 1988.
Strauss, L. *Natural Right and History.* Chicago, 1953.
Weiss, P. A. *Gendered Community: Rousseau, Sex, and Politics.* New York, 1993.

— GRACE G. ROOSEVELT

RULE FOLLOWING

In 1982 Saul Kripke published *Wittgenstein on Rules and Private Language* and ushered in a new era of Wittgenstein interpretation. Although elements of Kripke's view of Wittgenstein could be found in the preceding literature (notably in Robert Fogelin's *Wittgenstein*), nothing had captured attention like his presentation of the 'rule-following considerations'.

Kripke presented his essay as a reconstruction of the problems Wittgenstein is addressing between around §140 and §203 of the *Philosophical Investigations*. These issue in the form of a paradox—that there can be no such thing as the meaning of a word: no fact of the matter that entails that a word is used according to a rule, whereby some applications of it are determined to be correct and other applications incorrect. In §201 Wittgenstein wrote "This [is] our paradox: no course of action could be determined by a rule, because every course of action can be made out to accord with the rule. The answer [is] if everything can be made out to accord with the rule, then it can also be made out to conflict with it. And so there would be neither accord nor conflict here."

The paradox is developed by Kripke through the figure of a "bizarre skeptic." The defender of common sense, here the view that words do indeed have meanings and obey rules, is challenged to show what this meaning consists in. The facts he or she can adduce typically include past applications and present dispositions to apply words in new cases. They may also include flashes of consciousness—for instance, if we associate a particular image with a term. But, Kripke's skeptic argues, these are not the kinds of facts that can determine the actual rule that governs the meaning of a word. The skeptic adduces three kinds of problems. First, our dispositions are finite, whereas a rule can cover a potential infinity of new cases. Second, our dispositions sometimes fail to match the relevant rules: this is precisely what happens when we mistakenly apply words to things to which they do not in fact apply.

There can be no such thing as the meaning of

a word; no fact of the matter that entails that

a word is used according to a rule, whereby some

applications of it are determined to be correct

and other applications incorrect.

Third, the existence of a rule has normative implications. It determines correctness and incorrectness of application of the term it governs. Our dispositions, by contrast, have no such implication. There is nothing intrinsically wrong about bending our dispositions from moment to moment, in the way that there is about applying a term in a way that fails to accord with its meaning. Finally, the addition of flashes of consciousness is unlikely to help, for, as Wittgenstein himself said, any such fact itself stands in need of interpretation. A flash of consciousness cannot comprehend all the possible applications of a term and sort them into those that are correct and those that are not.

Kripke illustrates these points with the case of a strange arithmetical operator, 'quus'. For two numbers n and m, n quus m is identical with n plus m for sufficiently small or common numbers, but the two results (or calculations) diverge when n and m are greater than a certain value (the function is therefore reminiscent of Goodman's predicate 'grue'). We do not mean n quus m when we talk of n plus m. But our dispositions with 'plus' might match those of people who in fact use the term to mean quus; we might give the answer n quus m when we attempt to add n and m, since we make mistakes; and finally there is nothing right or wrong about having one disposition or another.

The conclusion is paradoxical, since nothing seems more certain than that we do succeed in attaching reasonably determinate meanings to terms. It may be true that the 'open texture' of terms suggests that meanings are never fully precise, capable of determining their application in any circumstances, however outlandish. Nevertheless, over an indefinite normal range of cases, there is no doubt that some applications are correct and others not, and any interpretation of us according to which we mean something along the lines of the 'quus' function is incorrect. Yet so long as the skeptic wins, we have no conception of our right to say such things. Kripke's own solution to the paradox is that the skeptic wins on his chosen ground. There is indeed no fact of the matter whether one rule rather than another governs the use of a term. But we can advance a 'skeptical solution' (Hume's phrase from a different context) to the doubts. What there is instead is a practice of regarding ourselves and others in certain lights. We dignify each other as meaning one thing or another by our terms, and this ongoing practice is all that there is.

Kripke's work generated enormous interest and a variety of responses in the literature. Some outraged students of Wittgenstein argued that it was not at all his intention to produce a paradox but to lay bare the oversimplifications, or desire for a simple theory, that trap people into finding rule following problematic (Baker & Hacker, 1984). Many writers queried whether Wittgenstein could consistently have been content with a 'non-truth-conditional' account of rule following, which is what Kripke offers him, since Wittgenstein's abhorrence of theory and his belief that philosophy leaves everything as it is would make it impossible for him to say that it is not strictly speaking true that the application of words is correct or incorrect. Some (McDowell, 1981) detected a mischievous dislike of soft, humanly oriented facts in the setting up of the paradox and argued that a proper appreciation of the human constitution of rule following had wide implications for the notion of objectivity, as it occurs in domains such as aesthetics or ethics. Some (McGinn, 1984) found that Kripke had not looked hard enough for natural facts with which to identify the obtaining of a rule; others (Blackburn, 1985) embraced the thought that since the loss of a normative element in meaning was the main problem underlying the paradox, and since naturalistic theories of normativity have been proposed in many guises, a more generous sense of how to talk about facts solves the paradox. Paul Boghossian (1989) provided a summary of the state of the debate and a controversial contribution to it.

[See also Goodman, Nelson; Hume, David; Kripke, Saul Aaron; Philosophy of Language; Wittgenstein, Ludwig Josef Johann.]

BIBLIOGRAPHY

Baker, G. P., and P. M. S. Hacker. *Scepticism, Rules, and Language.* Oxford, 1984.

Blackburn, S. "The Individual Strikes Back," *Synthese,* Vol. XX (1985).

Boghossian, P. "The Rule-Following Considerations," *Mind,* Vol. 98 (1989).

McDowell, J. "Non-Cognitivism and Rule-Following," in S. Holtzman and C. Leich, *Wittgenstein: To Follow a Rule* (London, 1981).

McGinn, C. *Wittgenstein on Meaning.* Oxford, 1984.

Wittgenstein, L. *Philosophical Investigations.* Oxford, 1953.

— SIMON BLACKBURN

RUSSELL, BERTRAND ARTHUR WILLIAM

Bertrand Arthur William Russell (1872–1970), British philosopher, mathematician, and social reformer, was born in Trelleck, Wales. Russell was the grandson of Lord John Russell, who introduced the Reform Bill of 1832 and later twice served as prime minister under Queen Victoria. John Stuart Mill, a close friend of Russell's parents, was his godfather in an informal sense. Russell's parents died when he was a little child. Both of them had been freethinkers, and his father's will had provided that he and his brother were to have as their guardians friends of his father's who shared the latter's unorthodox opinions. As the result of litigation the will was set aside by the Court of Chancery and the two boys were placed in the care of their paternal grandparents. Lord John Russell died two years later, and it was the boys' grandmother who determined the manner of their upbringing. Russell was not sent to school but received his early education from a number of Swiss and German governesses and, finally, English tutors. He entered Cambridge University in October 1890 and studied mathematics and philosophy at Trinity College from 1890 to 1894. He was a fellow of Trinity College from 1895 to 1901 and lecturer in philosophy there from 1910 to 1916. In 1916 Russell was dismissed by Trinity College because of his pacifist activities. He was reinstated in 1919 but resigned before taking up his duties.

What is generally considered Russell's most important work in philosophy was done between 1900 and the outbreak of the first world war. From 1916 until the late 1930s Russell did not hold any academic position and supported himself by writing and public lecturing. During this period he wrote some of his most influential books on social questions, including *Marriage and Morals* (London, 1929) and his two books on education— *On Education, Especially in Early Childhood* (London, 1926) and *Education and the Social Order* (London, 1932). These views were put into practice in Russell's experimental school, the Beacon Hill

In awarding Russell the Nobel Prize for Literature, the committee described him as "one of our time's most brilliant spokesmen of rationality." (Corbis/Bettmann)

School, which he started with his second wife, Dora, in 1927. Russell left the school in 1934 after he and Dora were divorced (the school itself continued until 1943). Russell returned to more concentrated work in philosophy around 1936. He moved to the United States in 1938, teaching first at the University of Chicago and then at the University of California at Los Angeles. In 1940 he accepted an invitation from the Board of Higher Education of New York City to join the department of philosophy at City College. However, he never had an opportunity to take up this appointment, having been found unfit for this position in a remarkable opinion by a judge who felt he had to protect "public health, safety and morals." From 1941 until 1943 Russell lectured at the Barnes Foundation in Philadelphia (these lectures were later expanded into *A History of Western Philosophy*). Dr. Albert Barnes, the head of this foundation, dismissed Russell in January 1943, on three days' notice. In this instance Russell successfully brought action for wrongful dismissal. In 1944 he returned to Cambridge where he had been reelected to a fellowship at Trinity College.

Russell was a candidate for Parliament on three occasions and was defeated each time: In 1907 he ran at

Wimbledon as a candidate of the National Union of Women's Suffrage Societies, in 1922 and 1923 he stood as the Labour party candidate for Chelsea. Russell was jailed twice—in 1918 for six months on a count of an allegedly libelous article in a pacifist journal and in 1961, at the age of 89, for one week, in connection with his campaign for nuclear disarmament.

In 1908 Russell was elected a fellow of the Royal Society. He became an honorary fellow of the British Academy in 1949, and in the same year he was awarded the Order of Merit. Russell twice served as president of the Aristotelian Society and for many years was president of the Rationalist Press Association. In 1950 he received the Nobel Prize for Literature. In making the award, the committee described him as "one of our time's most brilliant spokesmen of rationality and humanity, and a fearless champion of free speech and free thought in the West."

Russell had three children and was married four times. In 1931, upon the death of his brother, he became the third earl Russell.

Writing in 1935 the German historian Rudolf Metz referred to Russell as "the only British thinker of the age who enjoys world-wide repute." At that time his works could not circulate in Germany, Italy, or Russia. Now they are available in every major and a great number of minor languages. It is safe to say that not since Voltaire was there a philosopher with such an enormous audience. Russell also shared with Voltaire a glittering and graceful prose style and a delicious sense of humor. It was perhaps Russell's gay irreverence as much as the substance of his heretical opinions that so deeply offended several generations of moralists and religious conservatives.

In the following section we shall briefly recount some of the highlights and formative influences in Russell's eventful life and sketch his views on political and social issues. Although these views are certainly logically independent of his more technical work as a philosopher, they deal with questions that have traditionally been discussed by philosophers, and they also help one to understand the basic motives inspiring Russell's thought.

Life and Social Theories

Russell's childhood and adolescence were unhappy. The atmosphere in his grandmother's house was one of puritan piety and austerity, and his loneliness, he recalled, was almost unbearable. Only virtue was prized—"virtue at the expense of intellect, health, happiness, and every mundane good." At the age of five Russell reflected that if he lived to be seventy, he would have endured only a fourteenth part of his life, and he felt

the long-spread-out boredom ahead of him to be unendurable. In adolescence, he remarked, he was continually on the verge of suicide, from which, however, he was "restrained by the desire to know more mathematics." His grandmother had gradually moved from Scottish Presbyterianism to Unitarianism. As a child Russell was taken on alternate Sundays to the parish church and to the Presbyterian church, while at home he was taught the tenets of Unitarianism. When he was fourteen he began to question theological doctrines and in the course of four years abandoned successively belief in free will, immortality, and God, the last as the result of reading John Stuart Mill's *Autobiography*. For some time, however, Russell had metaphysical attachments that served as substitutes for religion, and it was not until the end of the first world war that he became a militant opponent of all forms of supernaturalism.

At the age of five Russell reflected

that if he lived to be seventy,

he would have endured

only a fourteenth part of his life,

and he felt the long-spread-out boredom

ahead of him to be unendurable.

EARLY PLATONISM AND HEGELIANISM. Under the influence of J. M. E. McTaggart and F. H. Bradley, Russell came, in his early years at Cambridge, to believe "more or less" in the Absolute and the rest of the apparatus of British Hegelianism. "There was a curious pleasure," Russell wrote in retrospect, "in making oneself believe that time and space are unreal, that matter is an illusion, and that the world really consists of nothing but mind." In a "rash moment," however, he turned "from the disciples to the Master." Hegel's remarks in the philosophy of mathematics he found "both ignorant and stupid," and in other ways Hegel's work appeared a "farrago of confusions." After that Russell was converted by G. E. Moore to a "watered down" version of Plato's theory of Ideas, regarding the subject matter of mathematics as eternal and unchanging entities whose exactness and perfection is not duplicated anywhere in the world of material objects. Eventually Russell abandoned this "mathematical mysticism" as "nonsense." Following Ludwig Wittgenstein he came to believe "very reluctantly" that mathematics consists of tautologies. As to the timelessness of mathematics, Russell now regarded this as resulting from nothing more than that the pure mathematician is not talking about time. Aside from this, it became emotionally difficult for him to remain attached to "a world of abstraction" in the midst of the slaughter of the Great War. "All the high-flown thoughts that I had had about the abstract world of ideas," he wrote later, "seemed to me thin and rather trivial in view of the vast suffering that surrounded me." The nonhuman world, he added, "remained as an occasional refuge, but not as a country in which to build one's permanent habitation." Since his abandonment of Platonism, Russell wrote, he was not been able to find religious satisfaction in any philosophical doctrine that he could accept.

PACIFISM. Russell was interested in social questions throughout his life. He was an early member of the Fabian Society and for some time in the 1890s, under the influence of Sidney and Beatrice Webb, championed imperialism and supported the Boer War. In 1901 he had a quasi-religious experience. He became "suddenly and vividly aware of the loneliness in which most people live" and felt the need to find ways of "diminishing this tragic isolation." In the course of a few minutes he changed his mind about the Boer War, about harshness in the education of children and in the administration of the criminal law, as well as about fierceness in personal relations. This experience led him to write his famous essay "A Free Man's Worship" (1903). Although Russell became a pacifist right then, for another ten years or more he was preoccupied with work in mathematical logic and theory of knowledge. It was not until the war that he became passionately concerned about social issues. It is probable, he observed later, that "I should have remained mainly academic and abstract but for the War." The war, however, "shook him" out of many prejudices and made him reexamine a number of fundamental questions. He recalled:

> I had watched with growing anxiety the policies of all the European Great Powers in the years before 1914, and was quite unable to accept the superficial melodramatic explanations of the catastrophe which were promulgated by all the belligerent governments. The attitude of ordinary men and women during the first months amazed me, particularly the fact that they found a kind of pleasure in the excitement. (*Selected Papers of Bertrand Russell*, p. xi)

He decided that he had been quite mistaken in believing the claims of pacifists that wars were the work of devious tyrants who forced them on reluctant populations. Although he was not then familiar with the theories of psychoanalysis, Russell concluded that the majority of human beings in our culture were filled with destructive and perverse impulses and that no scheme for reform would achieve any substantial improvement in human affairs unless the psychological structure of the average person was suitably transformed.

Russell recalled that his decision to oppose the war was made particularly difficult by his passionate love of England. Nevertheless, he had no doubt as to what he had to do. "When the war came I felt as if I heard the voice of God. I knew that it was my business to protest, however futile protest might be. My whole nature was involved. As a lover of truth, the national propaganda of all the belligerent nations sickened me. As a lover of civilisation, the return to barbarism appalled me" (*Portraits From Memory*, p. 27). Russell remarked that he never believed much tangible good would come from opposition to the war, but he felt that "for the honor of human nature," those who "were not swept off their feet" should stand their ground. He patiently argued in lectures and books that the slaughter of millions of men was not justified by any of the possible gains of a defeat of the Central Powers. Russell's pacifism was not mystical. It was not then and was not his contention at any time that the use of force is always wrong, that war can never possibly be justified. He maintained that *this* war in *these* circumstances was not worth all the pain and misery, and the lying of all the parties. Consistently with his general position, Russell favored the Allies during the Second World War on the ground that the defeat of the Nazis was essential if human life was to remain tolerable. The Kaiser's Germany by contrast was "only swashbuckling and a little absurd," allowing a good deal of freedom and democracy.

Prior to the war there had been strong pacifist sentiment in all the major Western countries, especially among the intellectuals and the powerful socialist and liberal parties. When war came only a tiny minority of these pacifists remained true to its convictions. Overwhelmed by their need to conform and in many cases by what Russell would have regarded as their own primitive impulses, many of them became the most violent jingoists. Russell was bitterly attacked for his pacifist activities not only, as one might have expected, by conservatives and professional patriots but also by many of his erstwhile friends. H. G. Wells, for example, publicly heaped abuse on Russell when he was already in trouble with the authorities. Russell's political philosophy, according to Wells, amounted to a "tepid voluntaryism," and he (unlike Wells) had no right to speak for British socialism. Wells even abused Russell's work as a mathematical philosopher. Russell, he wrote, is that "awe-inspiring" man who "objected to Euclid upon grounds no one could possibly understand, in books no one could possibly read" (Preface to P. H. Loyson, *The Gods in the Battle,* London, 1917).

Russell remarked that he never believed

much tangible good would come

from opposition to the war, but he felt that

"for the honor of human nature,"

those who "were not swept off their feet"

should stand their ground.

At Cambridge, Russell's teacher and friend Mc-Taggart led a move for his ouster. Meetings addressed by Russell were broken up by violent mobs without any police interference. Eventually he was prosecuted by the government. For writing a pamphlet on the case of a conscientious objector he was fined £100. When he would not pay the fine the government sold parts of his library, including rare books on mathematics, which Russell was never able to recover. In 1918 he was sentenced to six months' imprisonment for an article in *The Tribunal,* a pacifist weekly, in which he had written that "unless peace comes soon . . . the American garrison, which will by that time be occupying England and France, . . . will no doubt be capable of intimidating strikers, an occupation to which the American army is accustomed when at home." In a fierce denunciation that accompanied the sentence, the magistrate, Sir John Dickinson, referred to Russell's offense as "a very despicable one" and added that Russell "seems to have lost all sense of decency." It should be added that as the result of the intervention of Arthur Balfour, Russell was treated with consideration while in prison—he finished there his *Introduction to Mathematical Philosophy* and began work on *The Analysis of Mind.*

Attitude toward the Soviet Union. Russell's isolation was not ended with the return of peace. This was due to his failure to support the Bolshevist regime in Russia. Like many Western socialists he at first welcomed the news of the revolution, but, wanting to see things for himself, he visited Russia in 1920 and came back totally disillusioned. Some of Russell's friends argued that any criticism of the revolution would only play into the hands of the reactionaries who wanted to reestablish the old order. After some hesitation Russell decided to publish the truth as he saw it. Russia, he later wrote, "seemed to me one vast prison in which the jailors were cruel bigots. When I found my friends applauding these men as liberators and regarding the regime that they were creating as a paradise, I wondered in a bewildered manner whether it was my friends or I that were mad."

The little book in which he recorded his views of the Soviet Union, *The Theory and Practise of Bolshevism* (1920), was remarkable for, among other things, its prescience. Long before most Westerners had heard of Stalin, Russell predicted, point by point, the reactionary features that came to characterize the Soviet system under Stalin—its militarism and nationalism, the hostility to free art and science, its puritanism, and the gradual ascendancy of bureaucrats and sycophants over the early idealists. Russell was able to reprint the book in 1947 without a single alteration. His isolation after his return from Russia was even greater than during the war. The patriots had not yet forgiven him his opposition to the war, while the majority of his former political friends denounced him for his opposition to the Soviet regime. But Russell never played to the galleries. As on many other occasions he acted in accordance with his favorite Biblical text—"Thou shalt not follow a multitude to do evil."

Education and Sexual Morality. Probably the most controversial of Russell's opinions are those relating to education and sexual morality. These were closely connected with his observations of the joy people took in the fighting and killing during the war. Russell wrote that he thought he saw the inward and outward defeats that led to cruelty and admiration of violence and that these defeats were, in turn, largely the outcome of what had happened to people when they were very young. A peaceful and happy world could not be achieved without drastic changes in education. In sexual matters, although not only in these, irrational prohibitions and dishonesty were exceedingly harmful. "I believe," he wrote in *Marriage and Morals,* "that nine out of ten who have had a conventional upbringing in their early years have become in some degree incapable of a decent and sane attitude towards marriage and sex generally" (p. 249). Conventional education was judged to be at fault in a great many other ways as well. Its general tendency was to cramp creative impulses and to discourage a spirit of critical inquiry. While a certain amount of discipline is necessary, very much of the coercion traditionally employed cannot be justified. The child who is coerced "tends to respond with hatred, and if, as is usual, he is not able to give free vent to his hatred, it festers inwardly, and may sink into the unconscious with all sorts of strange consequences throughout the rest of life."

Although puritanical moralists were or professed to be violently shocked by Russell's views on sex and education, it is worth emphasizing that his recommendations are not extreme and that unlike his opponents he stated his position temperately and without recourse to personal abuse. Russell may be characterized as a "libertarian" in education, but he was strongly opposed to the view of other educational pioneers who played down the importance of intellectual training and encouraged originality without insisting on the acquisition of technical skill. Similarly, although he may quite fairly be called a champion of free love, it is grossly misleading to describe Russell as an advocate of "wild living." On the contrary, he disavowed any such intentions. He wrote:

> The morality which I should advocate does not consist simply in saying to grown-up people or adolescents: "follow your impulses and do as you like." There has to be consistency in life; there has to be continuous effort directed to ends that are not immediately beneficial and not at every moment attractive; there has to be consideration for others; and there should be certain standards of rectitude. (*Marriage and Morals*, p. 243)

But this does not mean that we should be "dominated by fears which modern discoveries have made irrational." Russell could see nothing wrong in sexual relations before marriage, and he advocated temporary, childless marriages for most university students. This, he wrote, "would afford a solution to the sexual urge neither restless nor surreptitious, neither mercenary nor casual, and of such a nature that it need not take up time which ought to be given to work" (*Education in the Modern World*, pp. 119–120). It would be wrong to regard Russell as an enemy of the institution of marriage. He did indeed object to keeping a marriage going when no love is left, and, what shocked people a great deal, he remarked that a "permanent marriage" need not exclude "temporary episodes," but he also emphatically affirmed that "marriage is the best and most important relation that can exist between two human beings . . . something more serious than the pleasure of two people in each other's company" (*Marriage and Morals*, p. 115).

Russell's views on sexual morality featured prominently in the New York City case of 1940. When his appointment was announced, Bishop Manning of the Episcopal church wrote an inflammatory letter to all New York City newspapers in which he denounced Russell's subjectivism in ethics and his position on religion and morality. It was unthinkable that "a man who is a recognized propagandist against both religion and morality, and who specifically defends adultery" should be held up "before our youth as a responsible teacher of philosophy." The bishop's letter was the beginning of a campaign of vilification and intimidation. The ecclesiastical journals, the Hearst press, and numerous Democratic politicians joined in the chorus of abuse. Russell was described as "the Devil's minister to men," as an advocate of "the nationalization of women," as "the mastermind of free love and of hatred for parents," and also, needless to say, as an exponent of communism.

The climax of the campaign was a taxpayer's suit by a Mrs. Jean Kay of Brooklyn demanding that Russell's appointment be annulled. The case was heard before Justice McGeehan, who had previously shown his notions of tolerance by trying to have a portrait of Martin Luther removed from a courthouse mural illustrating legal history. In a startling decision, which was bitterly criticized by legal experts as in many respects grossly improper, McGeehan voided Russell's appointment on three grounds: First, Russell had not been given a competitive examination; second, he was an alien and there was no reason to suppose that the post in question could not be competently filled by an American citizen; and, finally, the appointment would establish "a chair of indecency." Elaborate arguments were adduced in behalf of this last claim. Among other things it was maintained that Russell's doctrines would tend to bring his students "and in some cases their parents and guardians in conflict with the Penal Law." In some fashion not explained by the judge, Russell's appointment would lead to "abduction" and rape. Russell's opposition to the laws that make homosexuality a crime was misread as advocacy of a "damnable felony . . . which warrants imprisonment for not more than 20 years in New York State." Evasive actions of the mayor of New York, Fiorello La Guardia, prevented any effective appeal against this monstrous decision, and Russell was never able to take up his position at City College. In 1950, shortly after receiving the Nobel prize, he returned to New York to deliver the Machette lectures at Columbia University. He received a rousing reception that was compared with the acclaim given Voltaire in 1784 on his return to Paris, the place where he had been imprisoned and from which he had later been banished. As for McGeehan, it is safe to say that he will go down in history as a minor inquisitor who used his one brief moment in the limelight to besmirch and injure a great and honest man.

McGeehan did not pass judgment on Russell's competence as a philosopher, but other opponents of the appointment were not so restrained. Thus, Joseph Goldstein, attorney for Mrs. Kay, described Russell as "lecherous, libidinous, lustful, venerous, erotomaniac, aphrodisiac, irreverent, narrow-minded, untruthful, and bereft of moral fiber." After a few gratuitous lies about Russell's private life, he concluded:

> He is not a philosopher in the accepted meaning of the word; not a lover of wisdom; not a searcher after wisdom; not an explorer of that universal science which aims at the explanation of all phenomena of the universe by ultimate causes . . . all his alleged doctrines which he calls philosophy are just cheap, tawdry, worn-out, patched-up fetishes and propositions, devised for the purpose of misleading the people.

In the present encyclopedia a somewhat different view is taken of the value of Russell's philosophy. Some of his most important theories in epistemology and metaphysics will be discussed in the next section, his contributions to logic and the foundations of mathematics will be covered in the following section, and his views on ethics and religion will be dealt with in the last section. However, a number of Russell's most interesting ideas are not at all or only briefly discussed in the present article. Many of these are treated elsewhere in the encyclopedia.

Epistemology and Metaphysics

Russell exercised an influence on the course of Anglo-American philosophy in the twentieth century second to that of no other individual. Yet, unlike many influential thinkers, he neither founded nor attached himself to any definite movement. Although he wanted above all to be empirical, he always had reservations of one sort or another to the proposition that all acceptable beliefs can be derived from purely empirical premises, and although his stress on analysis as the proper philosophical method is one of the chief sources of the analytical bent that philosophy currently has in English-speaking countries, he never accepted the view that philosophy is nothing but analysis.

EARLY REALISM. Russell's first distinctive philosophical work was colored by a violent reaction against the absolute idealism then dominant in England, which was ultimately based on the thought of G. W. F. Hegel and whose outstanding British exponent was F. H. Bradley. According to Bradley if we try to think through the implications of any fact whatever, we will inevitably be forced to conclude that everything that there is constitutes a single, immediate unity of consciousness. In Russell's view the main weapon used to bludgeon people into submission to this result was the "doctrine of internal relations," according to which any relational fact—for example, that x is above y—is really a fact about the natures of the terms involved. This doctrine in effect refuses to take relations as ultimate.

It follows from this position that whenever x and y are related, each "enters into the nature of the other." For when x is above y, then being above y is part of the nature of x and being below x is part of the nature of y. Hence, y is part of the nature of x and x is part of the nature of y. Since everything is related to everything else in one way or another, it follows that everything else enters into the nature of any given thing, which is just another way of saying that there is no "other thing" relative to a given thing. In other words, the only thing that exists is one all-comprehensive entity. From the related principle that when we are aware of something, that something enters into the nature of the awareness or of the mind that has the awareness, it follows that it is impossible to conceive of anything that is not included within consciousness. Thus, the one all-comprehensive entity is a unity of consciousness.

Although in his youth Russell, with most of his philosophical contemporaries, was caught up in this philosophy, he and G. E. Moore became disenchanted with it shortly before the turn of the century. Russell came to hold that in sense perception we are as immediately aware of the relations between things as of the things themselves and therefore that any philosophy which denied ultimate reality to relations must be mistaken. Moreover, he came to think that mathematics would be impossible if we held that every relation enters into the nature of its terms; for in mathematics we must understand what our units *are* before we can know anything about their relations to other units. Russell therefore argued for a "doctrine of external relations," according to which relations have a reality over and above the terms they relate and do not enter into the definition of the terms they relate. This led him to a kind of philosophical atomism that thenceforth was characteristic of his philosophy. We may think of the basic core of atomism, which runs through all the shifts in Russell's later philosophizing, as being constituted by the following principles:

(1) There are nonmental facts that are what they are whether or not any mind ever becomes aware of them. This does not follow from the doctrine of external relations, but that doctrine enabled Russell to reject the idealistic argument based on the doctrine of internal relations and thus left him free to hold his native realist convictions with a good conscience.

(2) A particular proposition (for example, that my car is in the garage) can be unqualifiedly true "in isolation." This follows from the thesis that facts are "atomic" in the sense that any given fact could hold, whatever is the case with the rest of the world, together

with the correspondence theory of truth—that what makes a true proposition true is its correspondence with an objective fact. Hegelians, on the other hand, had argued that since one could not adequately think about any particular fact without inflating it into the absolute totality of being, whenever one is saying something short of everything, what he is saying is not quite true in any absolute sense.

Russell's first distinctive philosophical work

was colored by a violent reaction against the

absolute idealism then dominant in England,

which was ultimately based on the thought of Hegel

and whose outstanding British exponent

was F. H. Bradley.

---

(3) An important corollary of (2) is the usefulness of analysis as a method in philosophy. If it is possible to get an adequate grasp of the parts of a totality without considering their place in the whole, then it is possible to give an illuminating account of something complex by showing how its simple parts are related to form the whole. Hegelians had argued that analysis cannot get started because we cannot understand what any part is without already seeing how it fits into the whole, which means already knowing everything about the whole. The conviction that analysis is the proper method of philosophy has remained the most prominent strand in Russell's thought.

Intoxicated by his release from idealism, Russell, as he later put it, tended to accept as objectively real anything that the absolute idealists had not succeeded in showing to be unreal. Numbers, points of space, general properties like roundness, physical objects as they appear to sense perception, were all regarded as having an independent existence. Under the influence of Alexius Meinong this extreme realism was reinforced by an extreme form of the referential theory of meaning, the view that in order for a linguistic expression to have a meaning there must be something that it means, something to which it refers. In this stage of Russell's thought, represented most fully by *The Principles of Mathematics* and to a lesser extent by *The Problems of Philosophy,* Russell was inclined to think that the meaningfulness of the sentence "The car is in the garage" required that there be objectively existing referents not only for the words "car," "garage," and "in" but even

for the words "the" and "is." An objectively existing "isness" soon proved to be too much for Russell's self-proclaimed "robust sense of reality." He came to think that terms belonging to the logical framework of sentences, such as "the," "is," "or," could perform their function without each being correlated with extralinguistic referents. Nevertheless, a modified form of the referential theory of meaning continued to dominate Russell's thinking.

LOGICAL CONSTRUCTIONISM. Russell's decisive shift away from the full-blooded realism of *The Principles of Mathematics* came with the development of logical constructionism. The theory can be generally stated as follows. We start with a body of knowledge or supposed knowledge which we feel strongly inclined to accept but which has the following drawbacks: (1) the knowledge claims do not seem to be adequately justified, (2) there are unresolved problems about the natures of the entities involved, and (3) we feel uncomfortable about committing ourselves to the existence of such entities. If we can show that this body of knowledge could be formulated in terms of relations between simpler, more intelligible, more undeniable entities and that when so formulated there is a decisive justification for it, we will have made a philosophical advance. We will have converted the problematic to the unproblematic, the obscure to the clear, the uncertain to the certain. Russell called this technique logical constructionism because the problematic entities were said, in a possibly misleading metaphor, to be "constructed" out of the simpler ones.

Reduction of Mathematics to Logic. The technique of logical constructionism was first employed in the theory of mathematics worked out by Russell and A. N. Whitehead and published in *Principia Mathematica* (3 vols., 1910–1913). In the *Principia* the authors set out to show that all of pure mathematics can be stated in terms of logic, using no undefined terms other than those required for logic in general—for example, implication, disjunction, class membership, and class inclusion. In the course of carrying out this reduction, various more or less problematic mathematical entities were "constructed" out of what were thought to be less problematic entities. Thus, numbers were defined as classes of classes: Zero is the class of all empty classes. The number 1 is the class of all classes each of which is such that any member is identical with any other member. The number 2 is the class of all classes each of which is such that it includes a member not identical with another member and such that any member is identical with one or the other of these. If one is puzzled about what sort of entity a number is (it does not seem to be in space or time and is not perceivable by the senses) or is uncomfortable about assuming that such queer entities exist, he will presumably be reassured by the discovery that he can think of numbers as classes of classes of familiar, unproblematic entities. Of course analogous problems may arise with respect to the entities made use of in this first reduction—for example, classes. And in fact various difficulties in doing mathematics in terms of classes led Russell to try to "construct" classes out of "propositional functions." (See the section on logic and mathematics, below.) Starting from a given point we may well have to perform a series of reductions before we get down to maximally intelligible, indubitable entities.

Construction of Physical Objects. After *Principia Mathematica,* Russell applied the technique of logical constructionism to our knowledge of physical objects, both in physical science and in common sense. Physical theories are formulated in terms of a variety of unperceivable entities—electromagnetic fields, protons, energy quanta, forces exerted at a point, etc. There are serious problems in the philosophy of science both about the content of our concepts of such entities and about the basis for our accepting their existence. We can try to show that such entities can be inferred from what we know about perceivable entities, but how could we get an empirical basis for a principle correlating observed and unobserved entities? Or we can try to show that unobserved entities have to be *postulated* in order to give an adequate explanation of observed happenings, but it seems impossible to show conclusively that no adequate explanation could be given purely in terms of observables. If we apply the constructionist principle, "Whenever possible, substitute constructions out of known entities for inferences to unknown entities," to this problem, we shall try to show that electromagnetic fields can be construed as complexes of less problematic entities related in various ways. Russell devoted a large proportion of his philosophical energy to trying to show that scientific entities can be constructed out of undeniable data of perception. But it will be easier to illustrate this kind of analysis by taking ordinary physical objects like trees and buildings, for Russell thought that they raise analogous problems, although in less obvious ways.

There is a long tradition, dominant since the time of Descartes, according to which common sense is mistaken in supposing that we directly perceive physical objects. According to this tradition what we are directly and indubitably aware of in sense perception is something private to the individual observer. There are several sources of this view, the most important of which are, first, the fact that the content of one's perception can change with, for example, changes in perspective, lighting, and physiological condition of the observer, without there being any change in the physical object which, according to common sense, one is perceiving, and, second, the fact that in dreams and hallucinations one can have experiences which are intrinsically indistinguishable from those one has when one is "really" seeing a tree, but in these cases no tree is present. In dreams and hallucinations one is really aware of *something* which is not a physical object and is not perceivable by anyone else. And since these experiences are intrinsically just like those in which a physical object is present, one must be perceiving these private objects in the latter cases as well. This consideration is reinforced by the first, which is designed to show that even where a physical object admittedly is involved, I am often aware of different things without the physical object's undergoing any change.

The conclusion of these arguments is that the colors, shapes, sounds, etc., of which we are directly aware in sense perception (sense data) are private objects which must be distinguished from the entities in the physical world (if any) which we suppose ourselves to be perceiving. This conclusion inevitably gives rise to the question how, if at all, I can start from the private objects of whose existence I can be certain and show that public, physical objects like trees exist. No generally accepted solution to this problem has emerged in several centuries of discussion. Here again Russell tried to avoid the necessity for an inference by showing that the public physical objects can be construed as a complex structure of data of immediate experience. At first Russell aimed at a solipsistic reduction in which a given physical object would be constructed out of the actually experienced data of a single observer, but he soon came to lower his aspiration and to admit into the construction data experienced by others, as well as data that *would* have been experienced by others if they had been in a certain place. The view, then, is that a tree can be regarded as a system of all the actual and possible sense experiences that would be regarded as figuring in perceptions of that tree. This is a form of the position known as phenomenalism, and it is subject to the difficulties to which that position is notoriously subject, particularly the apparent impossibility of specifying which experiences go into defining a particular physical object without referring to that physical object or others in the specification.

Construction of Mind. Until about 1920 Russell was a mind–matter dualist. As we have just seen, physical objects were regarded as complex structures of data of the sort given in sense perception. Now, although the mind might be partly constituted by data that are given to "inner sense"—that is, things which are the objects of *introspective* awareness, such as images and feelings—

it seemed to Russell, as it had to most philosophers, that in any act of awareness, be it directed to the external or to the internal world, there is in addition to the data of which one is aware a subject or self which has the experience or which performs the act of awareness. But as the spirit of logical constructionism took increasing hold of Russell, he came to feel that there was no real warrant for believing in a subject of awareness which performs acts. He became convinced that one cannot really find any such constituent of the experience; its apparent obviousness is a reflection of the grammar of the sentences in which we speak about such matters—we say "*I* saw a flash of light" rather than "A flash of light occurred." As it presents itself, a minimal piece of consciousness does not involve a relation between two components. It is a unitary whole. Only the flash of light is given. The "I" and the "saw" are added interpretations. If we have no real basis for accepting a subject or mind as an ultimate entity, then the logical constructionist will try to show that it can be exhibited as a complex of entities of which we are directly assured by our experience. Here Russell followed the lead of William James, who had earlier formulated a view known as neutral monism, according to which both mind and matter consisted of the data of immediate experience, the difference between them lying in the grouping of the constituents. Thus, if I am looking at a tree the visual datum (an irregularly shaped green splotch) of which I am directly aware is both part of my mind and part of the tree. When grouped together with other experiences from this and other perspectives that would be said to be experiences of that tree, it goes to make up a tree; when grouped with other data bound together in a single conscious field, along with other data related to these by memory, it goes to make up a mind. If this theory is acceptable, traditional puzzles about the mind–body relation are dissolved. We are faced not with two radically distinct kinds of stuff but with two different kinds of arrangement of the same elementary components. (That is, some of the components are the same. Russell considered images to be peculiar to mind.) It is in the light of this theory that one should consider Russell's notorious view that what one perceives is always his own brain. Whenever I have any sense perception whatever, I do so because a certain kind of physical activity is going on in my brain. This activity, as a physical process, is to be regarded, like all physical processes, as a construction out of the sort of data given in immediate experience. And since whatever may be the case otherwise, my brain is always active when I perceive, the data of which I am aware enter into the constitution of my brain, whatever other entities they may enter into. Hence the paradoxical view

that whenever one is conscious he is aware of his own brain.

When Russell abandoned the subject of experience as an ultimate constituent of the world he rejected sense data and thenceforth spoke simply of sense experiences.

After Principia Mathematica, *Russell applied*

the technique of logical constructionism

to our knowledge of physical objects,

both in physical science and in common sense.

But he would have represented his view more clearly by saying that he had given up belief in anything other than sense data. For in the old paradigm of *subject aware of sense data,* it was the subject exercising awareness that was abandoned. In *The Analysis of Mind* Russell set out to construct the conscious mind out of sensations and images. (Insofar as facts regarded as mental do not consist of consciousness, Russell's strategy was to give a behavioristic analysis. Thus, desire, belief, and emotions can be regarded as made up, at least in part, of dispositions to behave in one way rather than another in certain circumstances.) The results are admittedly equivocal. Russell was always too honest to overlook glaring deficiencies in his analyses. One that particularly bothered Russell was this: On a common-sense basis it seems clear that one must distinguish between simply having a sensation and taking that sensation as an indication of a tree, and there seems to be an important difference between simply having an image and employing that image in, for example, thinking about a forthcoming election. If this analysis of mind is to be made to work, one must give an account of the reference of perception and thought in terms of the interrelations of data. Thus, we might hold that to take a sensation as an indication of a tree is to be disposed to have the sensation of surprise if certain other sensations were to follow. But apart from difficulties about the nature of these dispositions, which are themselves neither images nor sensations, this is all extremely difficult to work out in detail, and it is equally difficult to make sure that one has shown that it can be done.

It is clear that logical constructionism is based on a tendency opposite to that of the realism briefly espoused by Russell in his youth. Logical constructionism wields Ockham's razor with a heavy hand. We begin with those entities whose existence is indubitable because they are given in immediate experience, and we then try to show that anything we might wish to say about anything else can be stated in terms of relations between these indubitable entities. In other words, anything we want to say about something else is not really about something else. Thus, we try to represent all our knowledge as having to do with as few kinds of entities as possible, thereby reducing the possibility of error.

LOGICAL ATOMISM. Thus far we have concentrated on the epistemological side of logical constructionism, its concern with reducing the number of assumptions we make and with exhibiting clearly the basis for what we claim to know. But it also has a metaphysical side, although Russell wavered about this. Sometimes he talked as if his constructionism was metaphysically neutral. At such times he said that in showing that minds can be constructed out of sensations and images we do not show that there is no ultimate, irreducible subject of awareness; we show merely that everything we *know* about minds can be expressed without assuming the existence of such an entity. At other times, however, he claimed that by showing that minds can be constructed out of sensations and images we have shown what minds really are—we have revealed their metaphysical status. And by carrying through constructions of everything that can be constructed out of simpler entities we will have developed a complete metaphysical scheme.

Ideal Language. The most systematic presentation of this metaphysical side of logical constructionism is found in the set of lectures *The Philosophy of Logical Atomism,* which Russell gave in 1918. Here Russell made explicit the principle on which a metaphysical interpretation of logical constructionism depends—namely, isomorphism of the structure of an ideal language and of the structure of reality. If we can determine in outline how the world would be described in an ideal language, we will have, in outline, an account of what the world is like. The restriction to an "ideal" language is essential. Since there are alternative ways of stating the same body of facts, it could not be the case that all these ways reflect the real structure of the world. In this approach to metaphysics the basic metaphysical commitment is to the identity of structure between reality and an ideal language, and one shows one's hand metaphysically by choosing one rather than another set of criteria for an ideal language.

For Russell the most important requirement for an ideal language was an empiricist one, formulated in the "principle of acquaintance": "Every proposition which we can understand must be composed wholly of constituents with which we are acquainted." In other words, we can understand a linguistic expression only if it either refers to something we have experienced or is defined by other expressions which are so used. This principle plays a part in the constructions we have been surveying, as do the considerations we have already made explicit. That is, Russell held not only that if physical objects were not defined in terms of sense experiences we would have no way of *knowing* anything about them but also—and even more important—we would not be able to *understand* talk about them. In logical atomism this principle is reflected in the requirement that the expressions which figure in the "atomic" sentences in terms of which everything is to be expressed must get their meaning through direct correlation with experience. They will, therefore, be names of particular sense data and terms for properties of sense data and relations between sense data. Russell was forced to exclude the logical framework of sentences from this requirement ("is," "the," etc.), but he was recurrently uneasy about this exclusion and recurrently disturbed by the question how, in that case, we can understand them.

In addition to the need for its undefined terms getting their meaning through correlation with immediately experienced items, the ideal language will have to satisfy some more strictly logical requirements. These will include the absence of vagueness and having one and only one expression for each meaning. But the most important restriction concerns the form of the basic sentences. An atomic sentence will be one that contains a single predicate or relational term and one or more than one name, the whole sentence asserting that the entity named has the indicated property ("This is white") or that the entities named stand in the indicated relation ("This is above that"). If a sentence (1) has this form, (2) contains only terms that get their meaning through correlation with experienced items, and (3) has to do with entities that cannot be analyzed into anything simpler, then it is an atomic sentence. It is clear that for Russell the sentences which satisfy these requirements will all state a minimal fact about a momentary content of sense experience.

Logical atomism can then be presented as the thesis that all knowledge can be stated in terms of atomic sentences and their truth-functional compounds. A truth-functional compound of two sentences is one whose truth or falsity is a determinate function of the truth or falsity of the components. Thus, "I am leaving and you are staying" is a truth-functional compound of "I am leaving" and "You are staying." For the compound is true if and only if both its components are true. There is an empiricist motivation for maintaining this thesis. Atomic sentences, in the sense specified above, can be conclusively verified or falsified by a single experience, and as long as we are dealing only with truth-functional compounds of these no further problem can arise concerning their truth or falsity. Consider a "contrary-to-fact conditional," such as "If I had offered him more money, he would have accepted the job." As it stands this sentence is not a truth-functional compound of its constituents. For in saying it we are presupposing that both its constituents are false, yet this does not settle the question whether the whole statement is true or false. There is a corresponding puzzle about what empirical evidence would settle the question. Obviously I cannot go back in time and offer him more money and see what he will do. If we could find some way to restate this as a (very complicated) truth-functional compound of atomic sentences, it would become clear which experiences would verify or falsify it.

Pluralism and Knowledge by Acquaintance. The metaphysical correlate of this sketch of the ideal language brings together two of Russell's deepest convictions, the logical independence of particular facts (pluralism) and the dependence of knowledge on the data of immediate experience. In this view reality consists of a plurality of facts, each of which is the sort of fact which could be infallibly discerned in a single moment of experience and each of which could conceivably be what it is even if nothing else were in existence. All the familiar and seemingly relatively simple objects in the world of common sense are really extremely complicated complexes of atomic facts of these sorts.

For Russell the most important requirement

for an ideal language was an empiricist one:

"Every proposition which we can understand

must be composed wholly of constituents

with which we are acquainted."

Russell was well aware that logical atomism in this extreme form was untenable. For example, he insisted that generalizations could not be truth-functional compounds of atomic sentences. The most promising way of so construing them would be to take, for example, "All lemons are yellow" as a conjunction of a large number of atomic sentences of the form "This lemon is yellow," "That lemon is yellow," .... But as Russell points out, even if it were possible to list *all* the lemons, the conjunction would say the same thing as the original universal generalization only if we added the conjunct "and that is all the lemons there are." And this last addition is not an atomic sentence. Moreover, Russell had doubts about so-called intensional contexts, such as "Smith believes that the White Sox will win," where

the truth or falsity of the compound is clearly independent of the truth or falsity of the components. Whether Smith has this belief does not in any way depend on whether the White Sox win. Russell always hoped that neutral monism would help him to get out of this difficulty. If we could construct beliefs out of sensations and images we might be able to restate this fact as some truth-functional derivative of atomic sentences.

Later Doubts. Russell came to have more fundamental doubts about logical atomism, including doubts concerning the very notion of a logical atom. How can we ever be sure that we are dealing with something which cannot be further analyzed into parts? How can one be sure that yellowness is an absolutely simple property? More basically, what makes a property *logically* simple? Does the fact that one can explain the word "yellow" to someone by saying "Something is yellow if it has the same color as the walls of your room" show that being the same color as the walls of your room is logically a *part* of yellowness? If so, then yellowness is not absolutely simple. If not, what does count against logical simplicity? Moreover, if there are alternative minimum vocabularies, then a simple, undefined term in one mode of formulation may turn out to be definable in another. Thus, on one systematization "pleasure" might be defined as the satisfaction of desire, whereas on a different systematization "desire" would be defined as the belief that something is pleasant. Russell gave up the belief that we can know that we have gotten down to ultimate simples and even the belief that there must be absolute simples. He came to think, in more relativistic terms, of a class of things that can be taken as simple at a given stage of analysis. In those terms he tended to fall back on sense experiences that are as apparently simple as anything we can find. Such experiences, even if not absolutely simple, can be regarded as being independent of anything except their possible components.

LATER DEVELOPMENTS. Despite Russell's frank admissions that logical atomism does not work as a depiction of the structure of an ideally adequate language, he did not develop an alternative metaphysics. On the principle of isomorphism, if one cannot represent general statements as functions of atomic statements, then one must admit general facts as ultimate constituents of the world. Later this metaphysical implication did not seem to bother Russell as it once did. This is partly because he was less preoccupied with metaphysics and partly because the principle of isomorphism had been so heavily qualified as to remove most of the cutting edge. In his major philosophical works of the 1940s, *An Inquiry Into Meaning and Truth and Human Knowledge,* he was more concerned with the nature of atomic facts thought of as the ultimate pieces of empirical data and the kinds of inferences required to get from these to the rest of what one wants to count as knowledge than he was with inferring a metaphysical structure from the logical form which an adequate statement of our knowledge would assume.

In these works there is a major shift in his view of the structure of atomic facts. Russell had earlier interpreted the word "this" in "This is red" as referring to a particular, something that has qualities and stands in relations but is not itself a quality or relation or set of qualities or relations. This is the traditional concept of substance as the substratum of properties, which was still alive in the realm of sense data even after physical objects and minds were no longer taken to be substances. But eventually the sense datum as substratum of properties went the way of physical objects, minds, and numbers. Here, too, Russell became convinced that there is no empirical warrant for assuming the existence of any such thing. In sense experience I am aware of a variety of qualities and their interrelations, but I am not also aware of something that *has* qualities. The bearer of qualities turns out to be the shadow of the usual grammatical form of the sentences used to report atomic facts. (There is a subject of the sentence—for example, "this"—which does not refer to any quality.) Russell's latest position was that the subject of qualities is simply a construction out of a set of compresent qualities. Thus, in the ideal language "This is red" would be restated as "Red is compresent with . . . ," where in place of the dots we have a specification of the other properties involved in that experience, for example, being round, being in the middle of the visual field, having ragged edges. It might be thought that this necessarily involves giving up the idea of absolute simples, for what takes the place of things in this view is bundles of qualities. But in this theory qualities themselves are regarded as the ultimate particulars (possibly simple) of which the world consists. Thus, in "Red is compresent with . . . ," "red" does not refer to a particular exemplification of redness. If we took that line we would have to suppose that there is something which distinguishes *this* exemplification from other exemplifications of just the same color, and that would have to be something as unempirical as a substratum. Instead, it is taken to refer to the color conceived as a "scattered particular," something which can exist in a number of different places at the same time. And such a particular might well be simple.

Russell continued to think of common-sense physical objects and the entities of physics as constructions out of entities of the sort which are given in sense experience. But he came to require less similarity to sense data in the elements of these constructions. His view was that although all ultimate entities have basic structural similarities to sense experiences, they need not involve only qualities which are given in sense experience. They may have qualities that it is impossible for us to be aware of. This uncertainty does not carry with it any serious gap in our knowledge, since for physical science it is the structure of external events which is important. In the 1940s Russell became increasingly concerned with the principles that are required to justify inferences from sense experience to unexperienced events and complexes of unexperienced events. The simplest form this takes is, for example, the inference that my desk has continued to exist in my office throughout the night, when no one was observing it. In Russell's view this is an inference from certain sense experiences to structurally similar events spatiotemporally connected with them in certain ways. He felt that the principle of induction by simple enumeration (the more often one has observed *A* and *B* to be associated, the more it is likely that they are invariably correlated) is insufficient to justify such inferences. What is needed, he believed, was a set of assumptions having to do with spatiotemporal connections of events of like structures. In *Human Knowledge* he presented a set of such assumptions. He did not claim that they can be *known* to be true. His point was a Kantian one: we must accept these assumptions if we are to accept the inferences to unobserved events that we all do accept in the course of our daily life.

Russell's entire philosophical career was dominated by the quest for certainty. In recent years he was driven to admit that it was less attainable than he had hoped, but nevertheless the desire to approximate it as much as possible continued to shape his thinking about knowledge and the nature of the world. Because of this desire he was continually preoccupied with the problem of how to formulate those pieces of knowledge that are rendered indubitable by experience. And because of it he consistently attempted to analyze anything that appears dubitable into constituents about which there can be no doubt. Even where he was forced to admit that inferences beyond the immediately given are inevitable, he strived to reduce the principles of such inferences to the minimum. Russell is distinguished from other seekers after absolute certainty chiefly by the ingenuity of his constructions and by the candor with which he admitted the failures of the quest.

Logic and Mathematics

REDUCTION OF MATHEMATICS TO LOGIC. Russell's main work in logic and mathematics was concerned with the problem of bringing the two together and with the interpretation of mathematics—arithmetic in particular—as a simple extension of logic, involving no undefined ideas and no unproved propositions except purely logical ones. Russell achieved this synthesis at the beginning of the twentieth century, a little later than Gottlob Frege, but independently of him; in working it out in detail he had the collaboration of A. N. Whitehead. By current standards Russell's work lacks rigor, and in this respect it compares unfavorably with that of Frege; at an early stage, however, Russell did notice a difficulty that had escaped Frege's attention, the paradox about the self-membership of classes, which will be examined later. Because of its complexity it will be best to treat Russell's picture of the logical foundations of mathematics systematically rather than historically, with occasional comments about the actual development of his thought. We shall also separate from the outset two elements of Russell's treatment of his and other paradoxes, the theory of "types" and the theory of "orders," which Russell himself ran together, and thereby give a slightly clearer picture of his intention than his own writings immediately furnish.

Definition of "Similarity." Russell took over from Giuseppe Peano the reduction of all other arithmetical notions to complications of the three arithmetically undefined ideas of "zero," "number," and "successor" and defined these in terms of the theory of logical relations between classes or sets. In particular, he defined a number as a class of classes with the same number of members; for example, he defined the number 2 as the class of pairs. This procedure may seem unnatural (do we really mean by "2" the class of two-membered classes?) and circular. To the charge of unnaturalness Russell's answer was that his definition (together with the definitions of addition, etc.) gives all the ordinary results (2 + 2 = 4, for example) and that for a pure mathematician this is enough; another answer can be given only after it has been made clearer what Russell meant by a class. With regard to the charge of circularity, Russell defined the complex "having the same number of members," or "similarity," as he called it, not in terms of "number" (or of his definition of "number") but in other terms altogether.

At this point some notions from the logic of relations have to be introduced. A relation is said to be one to one if whatever has that relation to anything has it to one thing only and if whatever has anything standing in that relation to it has one thing only standing in that relation to it. (In strictly monogamous countries, "husband of" is a one-to-one relation in this sense.) Here the phrase "one only" does not presuppose the notion of the number 1. The sentence "*x* stands in the relation *R* to one thing only" means "For some *y*, whatever *x*

stands in the relation *R* to is identical with *y*." The domain of a relation is the set of objects that stand in that relation to anything (the domain of "husband of" is the class of all husbands); the relation's converse domain is the set of all objects to which anything stands in that relation (the converse domain of "husband of" is the class of individuals that have husbands—that is, the class of wives). A class *A* is similar to (that is, has the same number of members as) another class if there is some one-to-one relation of which the first class is the domain and the second the converse domain.

Russell consistently attempted to analyze anything that appears dubitable into constituents about which there can be no doubt.

One can see that in a monogamous country the class of husbands will be similar in this sense to the class of wives, but one might think that two sets of objects could have the same number of members without there being any relation at all that pairs them off in the way that "husband of" does in our example. This, however, is a mistake when the term "relation" is understood as widely as it was by Russell. A relation in Russell's sense is, roughly, anything that can be expressed by a sentence with two gaps in it where names might go, and this covers not only obvious relating expressions like "_____ shaves ( )" or "_____ is the husband of ( )" but also ones like "Either _____ is identical with *A*, or *B* is identical with ( )." Take any set of two objects *C* and *D*. The relation "Either _____ is identical with *A* and ( ) with *C*, or _____ is identical with *B* and ( ) with *D*" (where all dashes must be replaced by the same name, and similarly with the bracketed blanks) will be a one-to-one relation in which *A* stands to *C* alone and *B* to *D* alone and in which *C* has *A* alone standing to it and *D* has *B* alone—that is, it will be a one-to-one relation of which the class with *A* and *B* as sole members is the domain and the class with *C* and *D* as sole members the converse domain; there are analogous relations in the case of larger classes. (Where the classes are infinitely large these relations will not be expressible in a language with only finite expressions, and perhaps that means that they will not be expressible in any language. Some philosophers would regard this as a serious difficulty; others would not.)

Axiom of Infinity. Similarity, then, or having-the-same-number-of-members, is defined in terms of notions from the logic of relations: one to one, domain, and converse domain. The number-of-members of a given class is the class of classes similar to it, and a class of classes is a number (strictly, a cardinal number) if there is some class of which it is the number-of-members. This last step gives rise to another difficulty: Suppose there are (as there might well be) no more than a certain number n of objects in the universe. Then there will be no classes with more than n members and so, by the above definition, no cardinal numbers greater than n. This makes a great part of arithmetic (for example, the principle that every number has a successor different from itself) subject to the hypothesis (sometimes called the axiom of infinity) that there are an infinite number of objects.

Formal implication is not

(to use Russell's "realistic" language)

a relation between propositions but one between

what he called "propositional functions."

Russell came to accept this last consequence of his definitions, but at an earlier stage he had thought that the axiom of infinity was provable, as follows: If we assume that every property demarcates a class, we must admit that some classes are empty (have no members), for example, there are no objects not identical with themselves. (The number 0 is precisely the class of classes with no members.) Thus, even if the universe contains no ordinary objects at all, there will still be at least one object of a more abstract sort, the universe itself considered as an empty class. And if there is this object there will also be two further objects of a still more abstract sort: the class of classes which has the first empty class as its one member and the empty class of classes. That makes three objects, call them A, B, and C. In addition to these there will be four classes of classes of classes—the class with B as its sole member, that with C as its sole member, that containing both B and C as members, and the empty class of classes of classes. And so on ad infinitum.

Russell Paradox and the Theory of Types. Russell was led to abandon the above demonstration (which, as he said, has anyway "an air of hocus-pocus about it") by his discovery of the paradox of self-membership, mentioned earlier. If we can concoct classes with some members that are themselves classes, some that are classes of classes, and so on as we please (if, in other words, we can treat classes, classes of classes, etc., as so many sorts of classifiable "objects"), we can, it seems, argue as follows: The most obvious classes do not contain themselves as members—for example, the class of men is not itself a man and so is not itself a member of the class of men (that is, of itself). On the other hand, the class of non-men *is* a non-man (is one of the things that are not men) and thus *is* a member of itself. We can therefore divide classes into two broad classes of classes—the class of classes that are members of themselves and the class of classes that are not. Now take the class of classes that are not members of themselves: Is it a member of itself or not? If it is, it must possess the defining property of this class to which *ex hypothesi* it belongs—that is, it must be not-a-member-of-itself. (Thus, if it is a member of itself, it is not a member of itself.) And if it is not a member of itself, *ipso facto* it possesses its own defining property and so *is* a member of itself. (If it is not, it is.) Let p be the proposition that our class *is* a member of itself; it follows even from the attempt to deny it, so it *must* be true—but it entails its own denial, so it *must* be false. There is clearly something wrong here.

Russell thought the error lay in treating a class seriously as an object. Perhaps it is an object in a sense, but not in the same sense in which genuine individuals are objects—and classes of classes are different again. They are, as he put it, of different "logical type." In particular, in an intelligible sentence you cannot replace an individual name by a class name or a class name by the name of a class of classes, or vice versa, and still have the sentence make sense. If "Russell is dead" makes sense, "The class of men is dead" does not, and if "The class of men is three-membered" makes sense (even if false), "Russell is three-membered" does not. And where a sentence makes no sense (as opposed to being merely false), its denial makes no sense either. Since "The individual I is a member of the class-of-individuals C" makes sense, "The class-of-individuals C is a member of the class-of-individuals C" does not and neither does "The class-of-individuals C is not a member of the class-of-individuals C"—and so on at higher points in the hierarchy. This being granted, the paradox with which we began simply cannot be intelligibly formulated and thus disappears from the system.

At this point it would be wise to remove a possible source of confusion. The relation of class membership is different from the relation of class inclusion. One class is included in another if all the members of the former are members of the latter; for example, the class of men is included in the class of animals—all men are animals. But the class of men is not a member of the class of animals; that is, the class of men is not an animal (or, more strictly, "The class of men is an animal" is nonsense). The class of men is a member, rather, of the class of classes-of-animals—it is a class of animals. And the class of classes of animals is included in (but is not a member of) the class of classes of living things—any class of animals, in other words, is a class of living things. Inclusion thus relates classes of the same logical type; membership, on the other hand, relates an entity with another entity of the logical type one above its own. The membership of an individual in a class of individuals is membership in a sense different from the membership of a class of individuals in a class of classes, and similarly for inclusion—there is a hierarchy not only of classes but also of membership and inclusion relations.

All this, besides solving a technical problem, is not without some attraction for philosophical common sense. Even apart from paradoxes it seems an artificial "multiplication of entities" to suppose that in addition to the individual objects which form the members of the lowest type of classes there are classes, classes of classes, and so on, and Russell devoted some attention to the problem of showing how what appears to be talk about these rather strange objects is in reality just more and more oblique talk about quite ordinary ones. To see just how he shows this it is necessary to look more closely at what might be called his "straight" language, into which this talk of classes, etc., does not enter and into which, once this talk *has* been introduced, it can always be "translated back."

LOGIC. From what has been said so far, it is clear that the "logic" to which Russell reduced arithmetic covered, implicitly or explicitly, such subjects as class membership and class inclusion, identity, and some sort of theory of relations. This is that part of logic that we first encounter when we work back to logic from arithmetic. We must now try and work forward to the same point from the fundamentals of logic.

Russell thought of logic as being at bottom "the theory of implication" (to quote the title of one of his early papers). And from the first he considered it important to distinguish implication from inference. He objected to the view that logic is primarily about thinking—conception, judgment, and inference, as some of the traditional logic texts put it. The connection of logic with inference is rather that logic is concerned with that in the real world which makes inference justified, and this is implication. "Where we validly infer one proposition from another," he wrote in 1903, "we do so in virtue of a relation which holds between the two propositions whether we perceive it or not: the mind, in fact, is as purely receptive in inference as common sense supposes it to be in perception of sensible objects" (*Principles of Mathematics*, p. 33).

Material Implication. Even in Russell's purely objective, nonpsychological sense "implication" is ambiguous. Implication may be a relation between complete propositions, in which case it is called "material" im-

plication and holds whenever it is not the case that the implying proposition is true and the implied proposition false. Before enlarging and commenting upon this account, certain grammatical and metaphysical clarifications are in order. Russell originally believed that sentences symbolized abstract objects called "propositions" and that material implication was a relation between these objects in exactly the same sense that marriage might be a relation between two people. He later dropped this view and regarded propositions, like classes, as mere "logical constructions," but he still used the old forms of words (as being, no doubt, accurate enough for practical purposes). In particular, the partly symbolic form "p implies q" (or "p materially implies q") freely occurs in all his writings, and we ought to be clear about what he means by it. Generally it is simply a variant of "If p then q," or completely symbolically "$p \supset q$" ("p hook q"), where the phrase "If ___ then ( )"—or the hook—is not a transitive verb expressing a relation between objects but a conjunction, or, as we now say, a "sentential connective." "If p then q" is thus not a statement about two objects symbolized by "p" and "q" but rather a complex statement about whatever the statements represented by "p" and "q" are about. For example, "If James is going to come, John will stay away" is not about two objects symbolized by "James is going to come" and "John will stay away," nor is it about these subordinate sentences themselves; rather, it links these two sentences to make a more complex statement about James and John. And if we say "That James is going to come implies that John will stay away," this is just a verbal variant of "If James is going to come then John will stay away"; that is, the linking expression "That ___ implies that ( )" has the same meaning as the conjunction "If ___ then ( )." The general form "That p implies that q" thus has the same sense as the form "If p then q" or "$p \supset q$," and Russell's "p implies q" is thus just a loose way of saying "That p implies that q." In a similar way Russell often uses "p is true" and "p is false" as variants of "It is the case (is true) that p" and "It is not the case (is false) that p"; although sometimes he may really be talking about sentences in such a way that the sentence "John will stay away" may be described as true if and only if John will stay away and as false if and only if he will not, and the sentence "James is going to come" may be said to "imply" the sentence "John will stay away" if and only if the sentence "If James is going to come then John will stay away" is true.

The assertion that an implication is true if and only if it is not the case that the implying statement (antecedent) is true and the implied statement (consequent) false is not intended as a definition of the form "If p then q." It is simply an informal attempt to fix our attention on the relation (or quasi relation) that Russell intended. In his earliest works, like Frege and C. S. Peirce before him, Russell took this relation to be indefinable, and "the discussion of indefinables—which forms the chief part of philosophical logic—is the endeavour to see clearly, and to make others see clearly, the entities concerned, in order that the mind may have that kind of acquaintance with them which it has with redness or the taste of a pineapple" (*Principles of Mathematics*, 1st ed., Preface; 2d ed., p. xv). Later he preferred to take as undefined the conjunction "or" and the negative prefix "it is not the case that" (or just "not") and to define "If *p* then *q*" as an abbreviation of "Either not *p* or *q*"; later still he followed H. M. Sheffer and Jean Nicod in using the stroke form "*p* | *q*" (which is true if and only if the component statements are not both true) and defined "if," "not," and "or" in terms of it. But for Russell the central part of logic has always been the study of implication, whether taken as undefined or not.

Since the form "If *p* then *q*" as understood by Russell is true as long as it is not the case that the antecedent is true and the consequent false, it is automatically true if the antecedent is false (for then it is not the case that the antecedent is true and thus not the case that the antecedent-is-true-and-the-consequent-false) or the consequent true (for then it is not the case that the consequent is false and thus not the case that the-antecedent-is-true-and-the-consequent-false). In other words, a false proposition materially implies, and a true one is materially implied by, any proposition whatever. But implication is supposed by Russell to justify inference, and the mere fact that "Grass is pink" is false would not seem to justify us in inferring the 25th proposition of Euclid from it, and the mere fact that Euclid's proposition is true would not seem to justify us in inferring it from "Grass is green"—geometry would be much easier if we could do this. Russell's explanation is that the first of these inferences cannot be performed because we cannot get it started (the premise not being true) and that the second inference is justified but we cannot know it to be so unless we already know the conclusion, so that we will not need it. In other words, "Infer a true proposition from anything at all" is a rule with no practical use, but this does not make it logically wrong.

Formal Implication and Propositional Functions. Implications are of practical use when we know their truth without knowing either the falsehood of their antecedents or the truth of their consequents, and this happens most often when a material implication is an instance or particularization of an implication in the second of Russell's senses, a "formal" implication.

Formal implication is not (to use Russell's "realistic" language) a relation between propositions but one between what he calls "propositional functions." One might say roughly that formal implication is a relation between properties and that one property formally implies another if it is never present without the other; for example, being human formally implies being mortal (nothing is human without being mortal). Formal implication is clearly involved in the notion of class inclusion—*A* is included in *B* if being a member of *A* formally implies being a member of *B*. But the notion of a propositional function is wider than that of a property. It is what is meant by an "open sentence," a sentence in which some expression—say, a name—has been replaced by a variable. "Socrates is a man" expresses a proposition; "*x* is a man" expresses a propositional function. Sometimes, more simply, Russell uses the term "propositional function" for the open sentence itself.

Classes of classes

are related to functions of functions

as classes are related to functions.

And the proposition that Socrates is a man may be said to be the *value* of the propositional function "*x* is a man" for the value "Socrates" of the argument *x*. The propositional function "*x* is a man" formally implies "*x* is mortal" if *x*'s being a man materially implies that *x* is mortal whatever *x* may be—that is, if we have "For any *x*, if *x* is a man then *x* is mortal." Russell writes this sort of implication as "$\varphi x \supset_x \psi x$." At one stage he treated this notion, for systematic purposes, as undefined, but even then he regarded it as complex in meaning, being built up from material implication together with the prefix "for any *x*," called a quantifier. Writing this last as "(*x*)," we may spell out the sense of a formal implication by writing it as "$(x) : \varphi x \supset \psi x$." It should be noted that whereas a propositional function is not a proposition, a formal implication between such functions *is* a proposition. The propositional function "*x* is a man" is neither true nor false; only its various values are true or false. But "For any *x*, if *x* is human then *x* is mortal" is as it were complete and is as it happens true. The quantifier is said here to "bind" the variable *x*, or, in the terminology Russell took over from Peano, *x* is in this context not a "real" but an "apparent" variable.

A propositional function may also have more than one expression in a proposition replaced by a variable, as in "*x* shaves *y*," "*x* gives *y* to *z*," and "If *x* shaves *y* then *x* does not shave *z*." In such cases the function corresponds to a relation (two-termed or many-termed) rather than to a property, and such functions may again be linked by formal implication, as in "For any x and y, if x is a child of y then x detests y"—that is, "All children detest their parents." Symbolically, we have here the form "$\varphi xy \supset_{x,y} \psi xy$," or "$(x,y) : \varphi xy \supset \psi xy$." Again, formal implication may link a propositional function and a complete proposition, as in "If anything is in that box I'm very much mistaken," which is of the form "For any x, if φx then p" or "$\varphi x \supset_x p$." Moreover, the expression whose place is taken in a propositional function by a variable need not be a name. It might, for example, be a sentence—"If p then q" is a propositional function of which "If James is going to be there then John will not come" is the value when "James is going to be there" is the value of the argument p and "John will not come" the value of the argument q. If we prefix quantifiers to forms of this sort we obtain further formal implications, including the laws of propositional logic themselves—for example, "For any p, q, and r, if p implies q then if q implies r, p implies r," which may be written "$(p,q,r) : (p \supset q) \supset ((q \supset r) \supset (p \supset r))$" or "$(p \supset q) \supset_{p,q,r} ((q \supset r) \supset (p \supset r))$."

A further case of special interest is that in which a variable replaces a verb or equivalent expression, as in "$\varphi(\text{Socrates})$," where φ stands indifferently for "is a man," "smokes," "is running," etc. With appropriate quantifiers this function will yield such formal implications as "$(\varphi) : \varphi a \supset \varphi b$," "$\varphi a \supset_\varphi \varphi b$" (roughly, "Whatever a does, b does," or "Whatever goes for a goes for b"). However, Russell says not that "$\varphi(\text{Socrates})$" and "If $\varphi(\text{Socrates})$ then $\varphi(\text{Plato})$" are functions of the verb or predicate φ but that they are functions of the *function* φx or, as he writes it in this type of context, the function $\varphi \hat{x}$ (the significance of this accenting or "capping" will be indicated later). His aim here is in part to bring out what Peirce and Frege called the "unsaturatedness" of verbs: The function of verbs can be understood only in relation to names and sentences; we use verbs to *make statements* about objects, not to name a special sort of object. The additional associated variables also enable one to represent unambiguously such complexes as "shaving oneself"—if φ is "shaves," shaving oneself is $\varphi \hat{x} \hat{x}$, as opposed to simply shaving ($\varphi \hat{x} \hat{y}$). But Russell was hampered by not having the word "functor" to designate what makes a function out of its argument; it is more natural to speak of "Socrates is a man" as a propositional function of "Socrates," of "x is a man" as the same propositional function of "x," and of "is a man" as the functor which forms this function in both cases than to speak of "$\hat{x}$ is a man" as a propositional function and to treat it in practice as a functor (Frege and W. E. Johnson were

more accurate here, although they, too, lacked the term "functor").

This part of Russell's "philosophical grammar" can now be set out fairly straightforwardly: Sentences may be built out of other units in various ways—out of other sentences by connectives, as in "$p \supset q$," and out of names by verbs, as in "φx," "φxy," and "$\varphi x \supset \psi x$" (which may be conceived of as constructed out of the subsentences "φx" and "ψx" by the connective "$\supset$" or out of the name "x" by the complex verb "$\varphi \hat{x} \supset \psi \hat{x}$," "$\psi$'s-if-it-$\psi$'s"). The rest of the hierarchy goes on from here—there are, for example, functors that form sentences out of verbs (that is, out of functors that form sentences out of names) and functors that form sentences out of these again, and so on ad infinitum. Functors may require one or more than one argument to make a sentence (the difference between "is a man" and "shaves," in the transitive sense), and when more arguments than one are required they may or may not be of the same type (for example, "If $\hat{x}$ is a man then $\hat{p}$" requires a name and sentence).

Quantification. Of functors that form sentences from verbs, the most important are quantifications, such as "$(x)\hat{\varphi}x$" (which makes a sentence out of the verb whose place in the sentence is kept by "φ"), represented in English by such words as "everything." "Everything" is, or is constructed out of, the universal quantifier; there are many other quantifiers. Russell distinguished one other basic quantifier, "something." "Something is a man" expands in his language to "For some x, x is a man," or symbolically "$(\exists x)(x \text{ is a man})$."

Given the quantifier "something" and negation we can construct the complex "It is not the case that (for some x (x is a man))" or "For no x is x a man." Here we have the philosophical beginnings of the number series. The number 0 makes its appearance as part of a quantification, for we could write the preceding form as "$(0x)(x \text{ is a man})$." And the series can be continued. "Some" means "*At least* one," and "*At most* one thing is a man" is "For some x, if anything is human it is identical with x"—that is, "For some x: for any y, if y is human y is identical with x." The combination of "At least one thing is a man" with "At most one thing is a man" gives us "Exactly one thing is a man"; that is, "$(1x)(x \text{ is a man})$." "$(2x)(x \text{ is a man})$" is, similarly, "At least two things are men, and at most two things are men"—that is, "(For some x and for some y, x is a man, y is a man, and y is not identical with x) and (for some x and for some y: for any z, if z is a man z is either identical with x or identical with y)." Apparent occurrences of numbers as objects can be analyzed away in terms of this primary sense; "1 and 1 is 2" for instance, becomes "For any φ and for any ψ, if exactly one thing φ's, exactly one thing ψ's, and nothing does both, then exactly two things either-φ-or-ψ." Numbers are inseparable components of functors of functors of names, or, as Russell would say, functions of functions, but the naturalness of this analysis is disguised in his own work by the fact that before he brings arithmetic into the picture he introduces the language of classes and defines numbers in terms of classes. (The notation "$(0x)φx$," etc., is not Russell's.)

DESCRIPTIONS. Before going on to Russell's discussion of classes, we should note that "$(x)\hat{φ}x$," "$(\exists x)\hat{φ}x$," and also "$(0x)\hat{φ}x$," "$(2x)\hat{φ}x$," and so on, are *functions* of functions of names, not *arguments* of such functions—that is, they are not names. "Something," "nothing," "exactly one thing," etc., are not names, although, like names, they go with verbs to make sentences. They go, so to speak, on the other side of verbs: they "govern" the verbs; the verbs do not govern them. And although Russell's hierarchy of types of functors or "functions" provides innumerable ways of constructing sentences (and so of constructing functions), it provides no way of constructing genuine names. It is of the essence of the expressions represented by Russell's variables of lowest type (x, y, z, etc.)—that is, individual names—that they are logically structureless; they pick out individuals, and that is all. But in common speech and in mathematics we do seem to construct names, or at least ways of designating objects, out of expressions of other types: For example, "the man who broke the bank at Monte Carlo" seems to function as a name, yet it seems to be constructed from the verb "broke the bank at Monte Carlo." On Russell's view this appearance is illusory, and sentences in which such apparent names occur can always be replaced by paraphrases expressed entirely in Russell's language of structureless names, functions of functions, etc. However, he regarded it as useful for logical symbolism to reproduce at this point, although with greater precision, some of the devices of common speech and to have, as it were, a secondary language imposed on the primary one.

"The φ-er," or "The thing that φ's," when it occurs as the apparent subject of a further verb—that is, in a context of the form "The φ-er ψ's"—is in reality a functor, in some ways like a quantifying expression, of which the verbs "φ's" and "ψ's" are arguments; in fact "The thing that φ's ψ's" amounts precisely to "Exactly one thing φ's, and whatever φ's ψ's," whose first component has been analyzed above and whose second component is a simple formal implication. Expressions of this kind are especially important in mathematics when the contained functor φ is relational in form, as in "The φ-er of y"—that is, "The thing that φ's y." "The square root of y" (the number which yields y when multiplied by

itself) is such an expression. Russell called expressions of this kind "descriptive functions." They include most "functions" in the ordinary mathematical sense. It is a little inaccurate, of course, to use name symbols like "y" for numbers, which on Russell's view are not genuine individuals, but once the devices which yield class language and number language have been worked out, Russell's analysis of descriptive functions can be reproduced at the new level in a transposed form. This language of classes and numbers, to which we shall now turn, is itself a case of a secondary language containing apparent names (like "The class of persons that shave themselves") that disappear from the primary-language paraphrase.

CLASSES, FUNCTIONS, AND PROPERTIES. Russell represented the form "The class of things that φ" as "$\hat{x}(φx)$"—usually read as "the x's such that φx"—and represented "y is a member of the class of φ-ers" as "$y \in \hat{x}(φx)$." Alternatively we may read "$\hat{x}(φx)$" simply as "φ-er" and "$y \in \hat{x}(φx)$" as "y is a φ-er." The expression "y is a φ-er" is true if and only if y φ's. One can in fact simply define "$y \in \hat{x}(φx)$" as "φy." Given this definition, other concepts associated with class theory are easily introduced. For example, as noted earlier, "The class of φ-ers is included in the class of ψ-ers" amounts to the formal implication "For any x, if x is a φ-er then x is a ψ-er."

Classes of classes are related to functions of functions as classes are related to functions. To say that a given class—$\hat{x}(φx)$, for example—is a member of the class of two-membered classes (or, as Russell would write it, "$\hat{x}(φx) \in 2$") is just to say that exactly two things φ—i.e., the class of classes that Russell identifies with the number 2 is just the correlate in the class hierarchy of the function of functions $(2x)\hat{φ}x$.

Counting Classes. There are two difficulties in Russell's views concerning classes. One is that classes, and, for that matter, numbers, can themselves be counted, as can individuals, but a number of classes would have to be not a class of classes but a class of classes of classes, and a number of numbers would similarly have to be a class of classes of classes of classes. This means that when we say "The number of numbers between 2 and 5 is 2," the first "2" has a sense quite different (belongs to a place quite different in the type hierarchy) from the second; and this seems a little implausible. Russell at this point is content to speak of the "systematic ambiguity" of the key expressions of his symbolic language. Given the proof of "$1 + 1 = 2$," for instance, considered as a statement about numbers of individuals, an analogous proof can always be constructed for the analogous statements about numbers of classes, numbers of numbers, etc., so that in practice it does not matter at which place in the type hierarchy we are working, provided we keep the types going up in order.

Ludwik Borkowski has suggested what may be a better solution: Suppose we always express quantification by a sign followed by a variable; for Russell's "(x)" we might put "$(\forall x)$," by analogy with "$(\exists x)$." We might then use the term "quantifier" not for this expression as a whole but for the initial sign, which can then be described as a functor which constructs a sentence out of a variable followed by a sentence, usually an "open" sentence in which the variable just mentioned occurs. We might then say that the initial sign "$\forall$" or "$\exists$"— or in the case of numerical quantifiers "0" or "1" or "2," etc.—is of the same logical type whatever the type of the variable that comes between it and the sentence following it. For counting properties (and, therefore, classes), we would have prefixes like "(2φ)"—for example, "$(2\varphi)\varphi(\text{Socrates})$" would mean "Socrates has exactly two properties" or, better, "Exactly two things are true of Socrates"; and "(2φ)" is different from "$(2x)$," but the "2" is exactly the same in both contexts.

Counting Functions. The other difficulty in Russell's theory is that classes dissolve into functions, but we do not count classes and functions in quite the same way. We would say, for example, that any two-membered class has four sub-classes, in the sense that there are four ways of selecting members from such a class (both members, the first only, the second only, and neither). The corresponding theorem about functions would seem to be this: If exactly two things φ, then for exactly four ψ's, whatever ψ's φ's. But in fact there will always be vastly more than four ψ's meeting this condition. Suppose, for example, that there are just two men in a room—i.e., $(2x)(x$ is a man in the room)—and that one of them wears spectacles, spats, spotted socks, a red tie, and striped trousers; this much alone gives us five ψ's (namely, "_____ is a man in the room wearing spectacles," "_____ is a man in the room wearing spats," etc.), such that whatever ψ's is a man in the room. The key point here is simply that we count classes as being the same when they have the same members, but we do not count propositional functions as being the same merely because they are satisfied by the same arguments, and all the numerical concepts that are built up from the concept of identity must be similarly adjusted. For instance: "At most one class is a sub-class of $\hat{x}(\varphi x)$" does not mean "For some ψ: for any χ, if $\hat{x}(\chi x)$ is a subclass of $\hat{x}(\varphi x)$, then χ-ing is the same as ψ-ing," but rather it means "For some ψ: for any χ, if $\hat{x}(\chi x)$ is a sub-class of $\hat{x}(\varphi x)$, then whatever χ's ψ's and whatever ψ's χ's." It is the same when we move up a type and count numbers themselves. If we write "$(0x)(\varphi x)$" for "It is not the case that (for some x, φx)" and "$(0'x)(\varphi x)$" for "For any

x, if x φ's then x is not identical with itself," we may say that these are different functions of functions—but whatever function either of them applies to the other applies to also; thus, they determine a single class of classes and a single "number," 0. The class and number language which Russell superimposed on his basic one is such that this is the way these quasi entities are counted.

Russell lumped together all his

type and order restrictions

under the general head of avoiding "vicious circles,"

and the theory of types with the theory of orders

worked into it is called the "ramified" theory of types.

Extensionality. One very radical way of simplifying this whole problem (one which Russell considered from time to time) is to say that functions (properties, relations, etc.) are to be counted in just the same way that classes are; i.e., that if $\varphi\hat{x}$ and $\psi\hat{x}$ characterize precisely the same objects (are formally equivalent), they are the same function. This is called the principle or law of extensionality; it in effect simply identifies a function with its "extension"—that is, with the class which it determines. The objection to this principle is simply its extreme implausibility in particular cases. For example, it seems obvious that even when two individuals and these two only are the men in a certain room wearing spats and the men in that room wearing spectacles, being a man in the room with spats is something different from being a man in it with spectacles.

Quine's Criticism. Logicians such as W. V. Quine, following Ernst Zermelo and John von Neumann, have developed systems in which classes, classes of classes, etc., are treated not as logical constructions but as genuine objects, and Russell's paradox is dealt with not by saying that "x is (is not) a member of x" is meaningless but by denying that "$x\varphi$'s" always implies that x is a member of the class of φ-ers. This account runs into difficulty when we try to handle certain nonmathematical properties of these supposed objects. Russell's view seems to have the advantage of not unnecessarily "multiplying entities," but Quine argues that Russell succeeds in dispensing with classes only by making genuine objects of properties or functions. This is said on the ground that in the course of his treatment of classes and numbers Russell is compelled to quantify over predicate variables—that is, to employ quantifiers like "$(\exists\varphi)$" (for example, in defining "Exactly as many things ψ as χ" as "*For some relation* φ, whatever φ's anything ψ's and vice versa, whatever is φ'd by anything χ's and vice versa, and whatever φ's or is φ'd by anything φ's or is φ'd by that thing only"). This, Quine says, is to make properties and relations (like φ-ing) the "values of bound variables," and to do this is to treat them as existing.

This amounts to saying that to generalize an expression by quantifying over it is *ipso facto* to make it a name of an object; but this claim may be contested. We do not elucidate "He must have killed him somehow" by translating it "There must be some way in which he killed him" (which, taken literally, suggests that there are objects called "ways") but rather vice versa: we understand "somehow" directly as a generalization of qualifications like "with a knife," and the "way" line of talk is merely a variant of this. Even "something" is often to be understood as a generalized adjective rather than as a generalized individual name—for example, when I say "I am something that Jones is not—logical." It seems more plausible to interpret "I *have* something that Jones has not—logicality" as a verbal variant of the preceding sentence than to say that the latter alone brings out what I am really doing. And the logical rules for such higher-order quantifications are simple—we proceed from the specific case to the generalization, from "I am logical and Jones is not" to "For some A, I am A and Jones is not A," exactly as we do from "I am logical but not intelligent" to "For some individual x, x is logical but not intelligent."

Elimination of Abstract Terms. Russell might more plausibly be said to "hypostatize" or "reify" abstractions on the ground that there are some contexts from which it seems impossible to eliminate from his basic language his symbols for "abstracts," that is, φx, etc. This part of his system is developed more tidily in Alonzo Church's calculus of λ-conversion, in which the property of φ-ing is represented not by "$\varphi \hat{x}$" but by "$\lambda x \varphi x$," and of "ψ-ing if one φ's" by "$\lambda x \,.\, \varphi x \supset \psi x$." The basic rule of this calculus is that the *application* of $\lambda x \varphi x$ to an object a, symbolized by $(\lambda x \varphi x)a$, is equivalent to the plain φa, and similarly $(\lambda x \,.\, \varphi x \supset \psi x)a$ is equivalent to $\varphi a \supset \psi a$. And where we have a function of functions f, we can in general similarly replace $f(\lambda x \varphi x)$ by $f(\varphi)$—but not always. For instance, it is an obvious law that any such function f which holds for any φ whatever will hold for χ-ing-if-one-ψ's, as in formula F:

$$(f) : (\varphi) \, f(\varphi) \,.\, \supset \,.\, f(\lambda x \,.\, \psi x \supset \chi x).$$

Here the expression with λ seems uneliminable. We cannot replace it with "$\psi \supset \chi$," for this is meaningless—the hook joins sentence forms, not predicate forms. Where we have a specific f the elimination is again possible; for example, if f is the function "applying to exactly two objects," then $f(\lambda x \,.\, \psi x \supset \chi x)$ will amount to $(2y) : (\lambda x \,.\, \psi x \supset \chi x)y$ and thus to $(2y)(\psi y \supset \chi y)$. But where the f itself is a variable, as it is in formula F, nothing of this sort is done. We could indeed (following Stanisław Leśniewski) introduce a symbol for the predicate "χ-ing-if-one-φ's" by a special definition; for example

$$[\supset \psi \chi]x =_{Df} \varphi x \supset \psi x$$

and so replace F with G:

$$(f) : (\varphi)f(\varphi) \,.\, \supset \,.\, f([\supset \psi \chi]),$$

but then it would be impossible to eliminate the defined symbol from G in favor of the symbols by which it is defined, and it seems an odd sort of definition that would be thus limited. (Church's use of λ can in fact be regarded as simply a generalization of Leśniewski's procedure.)

The uneliminability of "abstracts" from these contexts is an odd and perhaps awkward fact, but it need not be taken to imply that there are abstract objects, for "abstracts" need not be regarded as a kind of name. In expositions of the λ-calculus it is often said that the form $\lambda x \varphi x$ corresponds to the ordinary-language quasi noun "φ-ing," but this is not strictly correct, as may be seen from the fundamental equation "$(\lambda x \varphi x)a = \varphi a$." If "$\varphi$" here represents not a name but a verb ("φa" means "a φ's"), then so must "$\lambda x \varphi x$" ("$(\lambda x \varphi x)a$" also means "a φ's"), so that if f in $f(\varphi)$ is a function with not names but predicates as arguments, so it must be in "$f(\lambda x \varphi x)$."

RAMIFIED THEORY OF TYPES. We may now describe the added feature which makes Russell's own presentation of his theory of types more complex than the presentation so far given here. Russell divides functions into types not only according to the types of argument which they take but also according to whether they do or do not involve an internal reference to all functions of (what appear to be) their own type. For example, the function "$\hat{x}$ has all the qualities of a great general" has individual-name arguments, just as "$\hat{x}$ is brave" does, but unlike "$\hat{x}$ is brave" it has a "for all φ" within itself—it amounts to "For all φ, if whoever is a great general φ's, then $\hat{x}$ φ's." Russell therefore regarded it as of a different type, or, as he often said, of a different order, from "$\hat{x}$ is brave." Functions that do not thus involve a reference to all functions of (what appear to be) their own type he calls "predicative" functions and symbolizes them by putting an exclamation mark or "shriek" after the symbol, as in "φ!x." Functions cannot in fact (on Russell's view) strictly contain references to all functions of *their own* type or order but references only to ones of orders below their own. A function of individuals, which contains a reference to all predicative functions of individuals, is not itself predicative and cannot be regarded as being among the functions to which it implicitly refers. Having all the properties of a great general, for example, is not itself a property of a great general, at least not in the same sense of "property"— it is a second-order property.

What this means in practice might be illustrated as follows: It seems that if there were no facts about *x*— that is, if for no φ, φ*x*—then there would be at least one fact about *x*, namely the fact that there are no facts about it, and hence it cannot be that there are no facts about *x*. In symbols, from

$$(1) \qquad \psi x \supset (\exists\varphi)(\varphi x)$$

it seems possible to obtain

$$(2) \qquad \sim(\exists\varphi)(\varphi x) \, . \supset (\exists\varphi)(\varphi x)$$

by letting ψ*x̂* in (1) be, in particular, ∼(∃φ)(φ*x̂*); and from (2) it follows by a kind of *reductio ad absurdum* that for any given *x* we have (∃φ)(φ*x*). But on Russell's view this proof will not do, for (1) ought to have been written

$$(3) \qquad \psi!x \supset (\exists\varphi)(\varphi!x)$$

and here ∼(∃φ)(φ!*x̂*), not being itself predicative, is not a permissible substitution for ψ!*x̂*. It is worth noting, however, that our final conclusion, (∃φ)(φ!*x*), *can* be proved from (3) in a different way—by letting our ψ!*x̂* be χ!*x̂* ⊃ χ!*x̂* ("*x̂* χ's-if-it-χ's"), which *is* predicative and is true of any *x*, so that what it implies must be true of any *x* also. (The new argument is as follows: There is always some fact about *x*, since at least it is a fact that *x* is red-if-it-is-red, square-if-it-is-square, etc.)

Axiom of Reducibility. Russell lumped together all his type and order restrictions under the general head of avoiding "vicious circles," and the theory of types with the theory of orders worked into it is called the "ramified" theory of types. One trouble with it is that it vitiates certain essential arguments in the higher reaches of mathematics, and to save these Russell introduced an "axiom of reducibility," that to every function of any order there corresponds a predicative function which is formally equivalent to it—that is, which holds for exactly the same arguments as the given function. This means that any argument like our allegedly invalid

proof of (∃φ)(φ*x*) above, where it is worth saving, can in principle be replaced by one like our second and valid one; the axiom of reducibility does not itself enable us to find this valid argument but entitles us to proceed as if we had it. It is, however, an intuitively dubious principle and can be dispensed with if we can content ourselves with the theory of types in the "simple" form in which it has been stated in earlier sections.

Semantic Paradoxes. It was pointed out by F. P. Ramsey that those paradoxes which Russell listed and which cannot be eliminated (as can, for example, the paradox of the class of all classes not members of themselves) by the "simple" theory of types always contain some implicitly or explicitly "semantic" feature; that is, they all have to do with the relation of language to what it is about and all involve conceptions like truth and meaning. A typical example is the paradox of the liar, of the man who says "What I am now saying is false" and says nothing else but this, so that what he says is true if it is false and false if it is true. Such paradoxes are now generally dealt with by assuming not only a hierarchy of "parts of speech" in one's basic language (this is what the simple theory of types amounts to) but also a hierarchy of languages—a basic language, a "metalanguage" in which we discuss the meaning and truth of expressions in the basic language, a "metametalanguage" in which we deal similarly with the metalanguage, and so on.

It is both easy and necessary to criticize Russell's theories concerning the logical and semantic paradoxes, and his work in logic and the foundations of mathematics generally, but he remains, more than any other one person, the founder of modern logic.

Ethics and the Critique of Religion

ETHICS. Much of Russell's life, as we saw in an earlier section, was devoted to the advocacy of certain moral and political ideals. In this sense of the word "moralist," in which it has no derogatory implications, Russell was certainly a moralist and frequently a very passionate one at that. Unlike many other moralists he was also concerned with what are now referred to as "metamoral" or "metaethical" issues. He repeatedly addressed himself to questions about the status of moral principles— what, if anything, they mean, what kind of disagreement there is between people who support opposite moral positions, and whether inferences from nonmoral premises to a moral conclusion can ever be valid. In discussing Russell's ethics, we will be concerned only with his metamoral theories.

Early Views. In his first important essay on this subject, "The Elements of Ethics" (1910), Russell defended a position closely akin to that of G. E. Moore in *Prin-*

cipia Ethica. "*Good* and *bad,*" he wrote, "are qualities which belong to objects independently of our opinions, just as much as *round* and *square* do; and when two people differ as to whether a thing is good, only one of them can be right, though it may be very hard to know which is right." The goodness or badness of a thing cannot be inferred from *any* of its other properties. "Knowledge as to what things exist, have existed, or will exist, can throw absolutely no light upon the question as to what things are good." Russell was by no means unaware at this time of the wide appeal of the familiar arguments for subjectivism—the "divergence of opinion" on moral questions and the difficulty of "finding arguments to persuade people who differ from us in such a question" ("The Elements of Ethics," in Wilfrid Sellars and John Hospers, eds., *Readings in Ethical Theory,* New York, 1952, pp. 6–7). But he did not then regard these arguments as having any logical force. "Difficulty in discovering the truth," he wrote, "does not prove that there is no truth to be discovered" (*ibid.,* p. 6). Like Moore, he argued that if subjectivism were true it would follow that in a moral dispute there is never really any "difference of opinion" between the disputing parties. If when *A* says *x* is good and *B* says *x* is bad, *A* and *B* were really talking about their respective feelings or desires, they might well both be right at the same time and "there would be no subject of debate between them." At that time Russell regarded this as plainly false. "As a matter of fact," he observed, "we consider some tastes better than others: we do not hold merely that some tastes are ours and other tastes are other people's" (*ibid.*). When "The Elements of Ethics" was reprinted in 1952 in *Readings in Ethical Theory,* the anthology mentioned above, Russell added a footnote in which he explained that "not long after publishing this paper [he] came to disagree with the theory that it advocates." He explained that the change in his views was originally due to Santayana's criticisms in his *Winds of Doctrine,* but he added that he "found confirmation" for his later position "in many other directions." Russell's later position was first mentioned very briefly in a 1921 preface to a paperback reprint of "A Free Man's Worship"; it was explained in some detail in *What I Believe* (1925) and in *The Outline of Philosophy* (1927), and it received its fullest formulations in *Religion and Science* (1935), *Power* (1938), "Reply to My Critics" (in P. A. Schilpp, ed., *The Philosophy of Bertrand Russell,* 1944), and *Human Society in Ethics and Politics* (1955).

The Subjectivity of Values. Except on one basic issue, Russell's later position is a point-by-point denial of the earlier theory. "Good" and "bad" are no longer regarded as qualities belonging to objects, and in this respect they are now explicitly contrasted with "square" and "sweet":

"If two men differ about values, there is not a disagreement as to any kind of truth, but a difference of taste" (*Religion and Science,* pp. 237–238); "There are no facts of ethics" (*Power,* p. 257); "I see no property analogous to truth that belongs or does not belong to an ethical judgment" ("Reply to My Critics," p. 723). "Taste" in the first of these passages is used in a very broad sense to cover all kinds of psychological states and attitudes, including desires. Russell did not, of course, deny the plain fact that people regard some tastes as better than others and some desires as higher than other desires, but now he was willing to maintain that this merely means that the tastes or desires are their own. "What we 'ought' to desire is merely what someone else wishes us to desire" (*What I Believe,* p. 29).

Russell was quite ready to have his later theory classified as a form of "the doctrine of the subjectivity of values" (*Religion and Science,* p. 237), but it differs in some significant respects from the older theories that have gone by that name. If somebody maintains that pleasure, for example, or the love of God, is intrinsically good, or good "on its own account," this must not be taken to be equivalent to the statement that he approves of it or in some way desires it. Like the advocates of the so-called emotive theory of ethics, Russell maintained that intrinsic moral judgments, grammatical appearances notwithstanding, are not statements or assertions at all but *expressions* of desire. "A judgment of intrinsic value," he wrote in *Power,* "is to be interpreted, not as an assertion, but as an expression of desire concerning the desires of mankind. When I say 'hatred is bad,' I am really saying: 'would that no one felt hatred.' I make no assertion; I merely express a certain type of wish" (*Power,* p. 257).

Both here and in his capacity as a reformer Russell placed much emphasis on the distinction between purely personal and what he called "impersonal" desires. A hungry man's desire for food or an ambitious man's desire for fame are examples of the former; a desire for the abolition of the death penalty or the end of racial discrimination, independently of whether the person in question stands to gain from these changes, are examples of the latter. In moral judgments we express certain of our impersonal desires. A king who says, "Monarchy is better than republican forms of government," is using the word "better" in its properly moral sense if he is expressing not just his desire to remain king but a desire that nations have monarchical systems regardless of his own personal position. Russell occasionally wrote as if the desire expressed by moral judgments must be a second-order desire—that is, a desire that everybody have a certain first-order desire—but as several of his own examples make clear, this was not part of his position. What is essential is that the desire be impersonal. In this connection he also observed that the philosophers who stressed the "universality" of moral principles were in a sense quite right. This universality, however, does not consist in any a priori character or logical necessity. What is universal is the *object of the desire* expressed by a moral judgment. "The wish, as an occurrence, is personal, but what it desires is universal. . . . It is this curious interlocking of the particular and the universal which has caused so much confusion in ethics" (*Religion and Science*, p. 236).

It has been argued that a subjectivist

cannot consistently make moral judgments.

All he can say is that some people

have one kind of feeling or attitude

while other people feel differently.

As we shall see, Russell had a tendency to overestimate the scope of application of his subjectivism, but in a number of places he pointed out quite explicitly that large classes of everyday moral judgments and disputes do not come within the purview of the theory. "Ethical controversies are very often as to means, not ends" (*Power*, p. 259). "The framing of moral rules, so long as the ultimate Good is supposed known, is matter for science" (*Religion and Science*, p. 228). It follows from this that if human beings could agree about ultimate ends, all moral disputes would in principle be decidable by an appeal to facts even though the intrinsic judgments would still be not bona fide propositions but expressions of wishes. In fact, however, Russell insisted, there is no such agreement about ends. In "The Elements of Ethics" he had conceded that there were *some* ultimate ethical differences but had maintained that people in fact "differ very little in their judgments of intrinsic value." Many of the commonly observed differences are wrongly regarded as ultimate because what are really disagreements about means are mistaken for disagreements about ends. In his subjectivist phase Russell seemed to think that differences about ends are not at all uncommon. Behind such disputes as, for example, the subjection of women or the persecution of religious minorities, which do involve questions of means, he wrote, "there is generally a difference as to ends," and this sometimes becomes "nakedly apparent," as in Nietzsche's criticisms of Christian ethics. In Christianity, all men are valued equally, but for Nietzsche the

majority exists only as means to the superman. This, Russell maintained, is an example of a dispute about ends, and "it cannot be conducted, like scientific controversies, by appeals to facts" (*Power*, p. 259).

In "The Elements of Ethics" Russell quite properly observed that the mere existence of widespread ethical disagreement (if it is indeed widespread) does not establish any form of subjectivism. Although he evidently came to believe that ethical disagreement is more widespread than he had thought earlier, he did not offer this as evidence for his new theory. What he does offer as evidence is the undecid*ability* of ethical disputes. He wrote:

[The chief ground for adopting this view] is the complete impossibility of finding any arguments to prove that this or that has intrinsic value. . . . We cannot *prove*, to a color-blind man, that grass is green and not red. But there are various ways of proving to him that he lacks a power of discrimination which most men possess, whereas in the case of values there are no such ways . . . since no way can be even imagined for deciding a difference as to values, the conclusion is forced upon us that the difference is one of taste, not one as to any objective truth. (*Religion and Science*, p. 238)

If three men argue, one saying "The good is pleasure," the second "The good is pleasure for Aryans and pain for Jews," and the third "The good is to praise God and glorify him forever," they cannot, as people engaged in a scientific dispute, "appeal to facts," for facts, it seems obvious, "are not relevant to the dispute" (*Power*, p. 257).

Russell's later view agreed with the earlier position on only one significant point, its opposition to naturalism. By "naturalism" is here meant the theory that there *is* a logical connection between some moral judgments and factual premises where the latter are not necessarily confined to empirical statements but may also include metaphysical doctrines. We saw how in "The Elements of Ethics" Russell had insisted that from statements concerning what exists nothing can be inferred about "the goodness of anything." "It is logically impossible," he repeated in the course of expounding his later position, "that there should be evidence for or against" a moral judgment, but now this is maintained because a moral judgment "makes no assertion" and hence possesses neither truth nor falsehood (*Religion and Science*, pp. 236–237).

"Incredibility" of Russell's Subjectivism. Rather than attempt a detailed critical evaluation of Russell's subjectivism, we will discuss one objection that has been urged by a number of his critics and that, in one form or

another, has been leveled against nearly all forms of subjectivism. It has been argued that a subjectivist cannot consistently make moral judgments. All he can say is that some people have one kind of feeling or attitude while other people feel differently. More specifically, how can Russell's subjectivism be reconciled with his judgments as a moral critic and reformer?

It may be replied that as a matter of pure logic there is no inconsistency between holding that moral judgments are expressions of taste and using moral language to express one's own tastes. Russell, it might be said, would be inconsistent only if he claimed that *his* moral judgments, unlike those of his opponents, are more than expressions of taste. Then he would indeed be like the man who, in the course of an argument about the value of a piece of music, remarked to his opponent "It is all a matter of taste, except that my taste is better than yours." However, while this answer is valid as far as it goes, it does not meet the heart of the objection. For Russell seems to be saying—or at least he would like to be able to say—that his moral judgments (for example, his judgment that democracy is a better system than totalitarianism or that the sexual code advocated in *Marriage and Morals* is superior to that associated with orthodox religion) are in some sense rational or right or well-grounded while the judgments of his opponents are irrational, wrong, or unsupported by the evidence.

Russell apparently did not, when he first advanced his subjectivism, see any serious problem here, but in the 1940s and 1950s he repeatedly expressed dissatisfaction with his own theory on this ground. Thus, in "Reply to My Critics" he wrote:

> What are "good" desires? Are they anything more than desires that you share? Certainly there *seems* to be something more. Suppose, for example, that some one were to advocate the introduction of bull-fighting in this country. In opposing the proposal, I should *feel,* not only that I was expressing my desires, but that my desires in the matter are *right,* whatever that may mean. As a matter of argument, I can, I think, show that I am not guilty of logical inconsistency in holding to the above interpretation of ethics and at the same time expressing strong ethical preferences. But in feeling I am not satisfied. (*The Philosophy of Bertrand Russell,* p. 724)

To this he added: "I can only say that, while my own opinions as to ethics do not satisfy me, other people's satisfy me still less." More than a decade later Russell expressed himself even more strongly. In a letter to the *Observer* (October 6, 1957) he comments on Philip

Toynbee's review of *Why I Am Not a Christian:* "What Mr. Toynbee says in criticism of my views on ethics has my entire sympathy. I find my own views argumentatively irrefutable, but nevertheless incredible. I do not know the solution."

Some unbelievers have gone out of their way to praise the greatness of Jesus and to admit that religious belief is at least of great value to individual believers and to society. Russell makes no such concessions.

It is doubtful whether in such comments Russell is really fair to his own subjectivism. Let us recall that the theory was never meant to apply to anything other than what are variously called intrinsic or fundamental value judgments and differences. The questions whether happiness is better than unhappiness and love better than hate are frequently cited as such ultimate moral issues, but it would be hard to find anybody who seriously maintains that suffering is good on its own account or that hate is better than love, although of course people have often maintained that in certain situations and for certain reasons suffering and hate are preferable to enjoyment and love. However, on occasions there do appear to be real value differences of an ultimate kind. Thus, some people would maintain that dignity is "more important" or "nobler" than happiness. Many who do not despise happiness at all would maintain without hesitation that a man who chose to suffer a great deal rather than compromise his integrity (where it is assumed that he would in fact have suffered much less if he had not stood his ground) lived a better life than he would have if he had made the opposite choice. Or, again, there is sometimes disagreement as to whether a person suffering from a fatal illness should be told the truth, although there may be full agreement about the consequences of both telling and not telling him the truth. Russell's subjectivism does apply to this kind of intrinsic moral disagreement, and in such situations he could not, consistently with his theory, claim that the moral judgment he endorses is "more rational" or better supported than that of his opponents.

However, the examples Russell offered when expressing dissatisfaction with his subjectivism were not at all of this ultimate kind, and this applies to all or nearly all the positions he advocated in his social and political writings. The man who says that the good is pleasure for Aryans and pain for Jews, if he is willing to engage in moral argument at all—if he is not, the problem does not arise—presumably does not *just* say this but proceeds to make all kinds of factual claims about the psychological and physical qualities of Aryans and Jews, respectively, about the laws of heredity, and about various other matters which he regards as justifying his moral position. Similarly, the man who maintains that "the good is to praise God and glorify him forever" presupposes that there is a God, and a God of a certain kind, probably also that he has revealed himself in certain ways, and, if challenged (or perhaps even without being challenged), he will make claims about the hollowness of all earthly satisfactions and the greater reliability, intensity, and duration of the satisfactions derived from glorifying God. Again, a man, who advocates the introduction of bullfighting into the United States would not *just* advance this proposal but would give reasons having to do, perhaps, with the benefits to be derived from engaging in dangerous sports and the special thrills experienced by the spectators. All these supporting factual claims are discussable, and it may be possible to show that they are mistaken or highly implausible. If so, it might well be possible to regard the case of one side in such a dispute as well supported and the other as unsupported by the evidence. In all cases in which the person is willing to support his moral judgment by factual premises, it is perfectly consistent for Russell to assert that one position is "more rational" than the other, where "more rational" does not merely mean that Russell shares the attitude of the person taking this position.

What seems to be amiss here is not Russell's subjectivism but his view (which is not logically implied by it) that the theory applies to cases like the dispute about bullfighting. In his later period Russell seems to be guilty of a gross overestimate of the prevalence of ultimate moral disagreements. It is true, as he observes in *Power,* that behind disagreements about means there is frequently disagreement about ends, but it is very doubtful that the ends in question are in most cases *ultimate* ends. To give a simple illustration of a very common type: two people may offer conflicting moral judgments about a bill to legalize abortion. The man who opposes the legislation may give as his reason (or as one of his reasons) that it would remove one of the conditions restraining unmarried people from engaging in sexual intercourse, whereas the other man might offer this as his reason (or one of his reasons) for supporting the legislation. Although the disagreement may in the immediate context be properly described as one about an end, it is clearly not about an ultimate end. In all likelihood the parties to the dispute would differ about

the effects of a freer sex life on personal happiness, on society at large, on the future of religious institutions, and many other things. It is doubtful that either of them would maintain that suffering as such is better than happiness or that hate is better than love.

Even people who advocate what by most contemporary standards would be regarded as "outlandish" moral positions can usually be seen to share many of the intrinsic value judgments of the rest of mankind. Thus, Schopenhauer and other champions of asceticism recommend the suppression of desires, including those that to most human beings seem the most natural and the most innocent, but they do so *not* because in their opinion suppression of these desires would make people unhappy but, on the contrary, because it would enable them to achieve greater happiness or at least because it would reduce suffering to a minimum. In Norman Mailer's bizarre novel *An American Dream* the main character offers a defense of murder, but this unusual position is justified by the argument that "murder offers the promise of vast relief. It is never unsexual." It is accompanied by "exhilaration" which must come "from possessing such strength." It should be noted that murder is here justified not because it causes suffering but because, according to the character, it leads to "exhilaration." In other writings Mailer tells us that the "modern soul marooned in . . . emptiness, boredom and a flat, dull terror of death" would be well advised to pass through "violence, cannibalism, insanity, perversion" and other states and activities that are usually considered highly undesirable, but these recommendations are offered not for their own sake but because they will lead the person "back to life."

As for the really intrinsic clashes of the kind mentioned earlier, to which Russell's subjectivism would apply, one wonders if the consequences of the theory are there really so paradoxical. No doubt people do in such disputes regard their position as superior to that of their opponents—the man who admires integrity will feel contempt for the "cowardly" compromiser, and the compromiser will think the man who chooses to suffer a fool. Here, however, unless there are some *hidden* differences concerning matters of fact, it seems not at all incredible to maintain that calling one position superior simply amounts to expressing one's own preference for it.

None of the above is meant to prove that Russell's subjectivism is a correct account of the logical status of moral judgments, but it would indicate that the favorite objection of his critics can be disposed of without much difficulty.

CRITIQUE OF RELIGION. No such doubts as Russell expressed about his subjectivism in ethics mark his views on religion. Unlike many academic philosophers whose position is very similar to his, Russell did not hesitate to express his convictions publicly and without equivocation or compromise. After he abandoned the Platonic theory of ideas, Russell was a forthright opponent of religion in more senses than one: he regarded the basic doctrines of (supernaturalistic) religions as intellectually indefensible, he argued that religious belief was not on balance a force for good but quite the opposite, and he hoped and believed that religion would eventually die out. "I am myself," he wrote in 1922, "a dissenter from all known religions, and I hope that every kind of religious belief will die out. . . . I regard religion as belonging to the infancy of human reason and to a stage of development which we are now outgrowing" (*Sceptical Essays,* p. 101). In a television interview 37 years later he slightly qualified this prediction. If great wars and great oppressions continue so that many people will be leading very unhappy lives, religion will probably go on, but "if people solve their social problems religion will die out" (*Bertrand Russell Speaks His Mind,* p. 31).

God. Russell wavered between calling himself an agnostic and describing himself as an atheist. He evidently did not attach too much importance to this distinction, but he made it clear that if he was to be classified as an agnostic, it would have to be in a sense in which an agnostic and an atheist are "for practical purposes, at one." In the television interview mentioned earlier the interviewer asked Russell, "Do you think it is certain that there is no such thing as God, or simply that it is just not proved?" "No," Russell answered, "I don't think it is certain that there is no such thing—I think that it is on exactly the same level as the Olympic gods, or the Norwegian gods; they also may exist, the gods of Olympus and Valhalla. I can't prove they don't, but I think the Christian God has no more likelihood than they had. I think they are a bare possibility" (*ibid.,* pp. 24–25). He explained his views more fully in an interview published in *Look* magazine in 1953. An agnostic, in any sense in which he can be regarded as one, Russell said, "may hold that the existence of God, though not impossible, is very improbable; he may even hold it so improbable that it is not worth considering in practice" (Leo Rosten, ed., *A Guide to the Religions of America,* New York, 1955, p. 150).

Immortality. On survival, Russell's position was similarly negative. All the evidence indicates that what we regard as our mental life is "bound up with brain structure and organized bodily energy." There is every reason to believe that mental life ceases when the body decays. Russell admitted that this argument was "only one of probability" but added that "it is as strong as those upon which most scientific conclusions are based" (*Why I Am*

Not a Christian, p. 51). It is conceivable that evidence from psychical research might change the balance of probability some day, but, writing in 1925, Russell considered such evidence far weaker "than the physiological evidence on the other side." He never saw any reason to modify this judgment.

Russell's views on the body–mind problem are known as "neutral monism," and it would be inaccurate to call him a materialist. However, he always emphasized that as a theory about man's place in the universe his philosophy was closely akin to materialism. "Emotionally," he wrote in 1928, "the world is pretty much the same as it would be if the materialists were in the right" (*In Praise of Idleness,* p. 143). The opponents of materialism, he added, have been actuated by the desire to prove that the mind is immortal and that the "ultimate power" in the universe is mental and not physical. On both these points, Russell made clear, he agreed with materialism. When he returned to the subject in 1959 he had not changed his opinion at all. "I still think," he wrote then, "that man is cosmically unimportant, and that a Being, if there were one, who could view the universe impartially, without the bias of *here* and *now,* would hardly mention man, except perhaps in a footnote at the end of the volume" (*My Philosophical Development,* p. 213).

Objections to Fideism. Although, needless to say, Russell rejected the traditional arguments for the existence of God and immortality, he greatly preferred the rationalistic theology of such philosophers as Aquinas and Descartes to the fideism of Pascal, Rousseau, Kierkegaard, and their numerous modern followers. "The rejection of reason in favor of the heart," he wrote, "was not, to my mind, an advance." He remarked that "no one thought of this device so long as reason appeared to be on the side of religious belief" (*A History of Western Philosophy,* p. 720). There are two fatal objections to the practice of justifying religious belief by an appeal to the emotions of the heart. To begin with, the heart says different things to different men and to the same man at different times, but even if the heart said the same thing to all men this would still not be evidence for the existence of anything outside our emotions, and the fideists, no less than the rationalistic believers, mean to make claims about objective fact, not merely about their own emotions. At bottom, Russell concluded, the only reason offered for the acceptance of the new theology was "that it allows us to indulge in pleasant dreams. This is an unworthy reason, and if I had to choose between Thomas Aquinas and Rousseau, I should unhesitatingly choose the Saint" (*ibid.,* p. 721).

Some unbelievers have gone out of their way to praise the greatness of Jesus and to admit that religious belief, although perhaps not true, is at least of great value to individual believers and to society. Russell made no such concessions. Although he granted that some of Christ's maxims were indeed admirable (especially those consistently disregarded by Christian dignitaries) he found much in the teachings of Jesus to be defective, in particular his doctrine of eternal damnation. "Either in the matter of virtue or in the matter of wisdom," Russell concludes, Christ does not "stand as high as some other people known to history"—for example, Buddha and Socrates (*Why I Am Not a Christian,* p. 19).

Harmfulness of Religious Belief. Russell's views about the nature of the emotions which inspire religious belief ("it is based, primarily and mainly, upon fear") and also about the harmful influence of religious organizations are very similar to those of Hume, Holbach, and other eighteenth-century freethinkers. He, however, devoted rather more attention to the bad effects of the habit of accepting propositions on faith—in the absence of or even in opposition to the evidence. It is an error, Russell contends, to suppose that a person who does not form his beliefs on the basis of evidence in one domain can remain open-minded and scientific in another. Furthermore, somebody holding comfortable beliefs on faith dimly realizes that they are myths and "becomes furious when they are disputed." Such a person will therefore do his best to suppress all critics who might remind him of the feeble backing of his beliefs. Russell makes it clear that in this context he is not criticizing Christianity only. "The important thing," he writes, "is not what you believe, but how you believe it." The objections to "faith" do not depend on what the faith in question may be. "You may believe in the verbal inspiration of the Bible or of the Koran or of Marx's *Capital.* Whichever of these beliefs you entertain, you have to close your mind against evidence; and if you close your mind against evidence in one respect, you will also do so in another, if the temptation is strong." The person who bases his belief on reason will support it by argument rather than by persecution and will abandon his position if the argument goes against him. If, however, his belief is based on faith, he will conclude that argument is useless and will "therefore resort to force either in the form of persecution or by stunting and distorting the minds of the young whenever he has the power to control their education" (*Human Society in Ethics and Politics,* pp. 207–208).

"The World is Horrible." Russell never denied that in some respects a "godless" philosophy like his had to be gloomy. The beginning of wisdom, he teaches, is acceptance of the fact that the universe does not care about our aspirations and that happiness and unhappiness are not meted out in accordance with what people deserve. "The secret of happiness," he observed during a television program commemorating his 92d

birthday, "is to face the fact that the world is horrible." What Russell meant by this becomes clear from a story related by his biographer, Alan Wood. Wood's wife had expressed her opinion that it seemed horribly unjust that the young men who had been killed in the war should not somehow or somewhere have a second chance to achieve happiness. "But the universe *is* unjust," Russell replied, "the secret of happiness is to face the fact that the world is horrible, horrible, *horrible* . . . you must feel it deeply and not brush it aside . . . you must feel it right here"—hitting his breast—"and then you can start being happy again" (*Bertrand Russell: The Passionate Sceptic,* p. 237). Once a person has stopped looking at the universe in terms of anthropomorphic demands, he can concentrate on what is attainable and not waste his time in self-pity and cosmic complaints. For those whose philosophy is shaped not by a respect for facts but by their wishes Russell was always been scathing in his contempt. He expressed his amazement that courage is praised in all types of situations but not when it comes to forming a view about the world. "Where traditional beliefs about the universe are concerned," he wrote, "craven fears . . . are considered praiseworthy, while intellectual courage, unlike courage in battle, is regarded as unfeeling and materialistic." Writing in 1957, he noted that this attitude was perhaps less widespread than it was in his youth, but he added that it "still inspires vast systems of thought which have their root in unworthy fears." "I cannot believe," he concluded, "that there can ever be any good excuse for refusing to face the evidence in favor of something unwelcome. It is not by delusion, however exalted, that mankind can prosper, but only by unswerving courage in the pursuit of truth" (*Fact and Fiction,* p. 46).

[*See also Modal Logic.*]

BIBLIOGRAPHY

Biography

There is a good deal of autobiographical material in Russell's *Portraits From Memory and Other Essays* (London and New York, 1956); in *Fact and Fiction* (London and New York, 1962); in his introduction to *Selected Papers of Bertrand Russell* (New York, 1927); in "My Religious Reminiscences," in *The Rationalist Annual,* Vol. 55 (1938), 3–8; in "My Mental Development," in P. A. Schilpp, ed., *The Philosophy of Bertrand Russell* (Evanston and Chicago, Ill., 1944); and in *My Philosophical Development* (London and New York, 1959). Alan Wood, *Bertrand Russell: The Passionate Sceptic* (London and New York, 1956), is the only full-length biographical study of Russell. H. W. Leggett, *Bertrand Russell* (New York, 1950), is a short pictorial biography.

G. H. Hardy, *Bertrand Russell and Trinity* (Cambridge, 1942), traces the controversy between Russell and the fellows of Trinity College over his pacifist activities during World War I. *Rex Versus Bertrand Russell, Report of the Proceedings Before the Lord Mayor* (London, 1916), gives the text of the first of Russell's trials.

D. H. Lawrence, *Letters to Bertrand Russell* (New York, 1948), reproduces Lawrence's letters to Russell during World War I; Russell's letters to Lawrence have not been preserved.

Russell's part in the Beacon Hill School is most fully described in Joe Park, *Bertrand Russell on Education* (Columbus, Ohio, 1963). The Park volume also contains a complete list of Russell's writings on educational topics. Details about the City College case of 1940 can be found in John Dewey and Horace M. Kallen, eds., *The Bertrand Russell Case* (New York, 1941); in a publication by the American Civil Liberties Union entitled *The Story of the Bertrand Russell Case—The Enlightening Record of the Obstruction by Courts and Officials of the Appointment of Bertrand Russell to a Professorship at the College of the City of New York* (New York, 1941); and in Paul Edwards, "How Bertrand Russell Was Prevented From Teaching at City College," which is an appendix to Russell's *Why I Am Not a Christian and Other Essays on Religion and Related Subjects* (London and New York, 1957).

Epistemology and Metaphysics

Principles of Mathematics (Cambridge, 1903) was Russell's first major philosophical work. Its position is one of Platonic realism. In the preface to the second edition (1937) Russell sets forth his later disenchantment with this position. For a nonmathematical exposition of Russell's early realism, see "Meinong's Theory of Complexes and Assumptions," in *Mind*, Vol. 13 (1904), 204–219; 336–354; 509–524. Russell's criticisms of the idealist theory of truth are to be found in "The Monistic Theory of Truth," in *Philosophical Essays* (New York, 1910), a revised version of "The Nature of Truth," in *Mind*, Vol. 15 (1906), 528–533. *Philosophical Essays* also contains two influential essays by Russell attacking the pragmatist theory of truth.

The shift from realism to logical constructionism can be followed in a number of articles, the most important of which is "On Denoting," in *Mind*, Vol. 14 (1905), 479–493. This, together with other important but otherwise largely unavailable essays, is reprinted in Russell's *Logic and Knowledge*, R. C. Marsh, ed. (London, 1956). Russell's "On the Relations of Universals and Particulars," in *PAS*, Vol. 12 (1911–1912), 1–24, reprinted in *Logic and Knowledge,* is a classic presentation of the largely Platonic theory of universals Russell still held at that time. *Problems of Philosophy* (New York, 1912) gives an excellent semipopular account of the general state of Russell's thinking then. Russell's early attempts to represent physical objects as logical constructions can be seen in *Our Knowledge of the External World* (Chicago, 1914) and in two essays, "The Ultimate Constituents of Matter," in *The Monist*, Vol. 25 (1915), 399–417, and "The Relations of Sense-data to Physics," in *Scientia*, No. 4 (1914), both reprinted in *Mysticism and Logic* (London, 1918). Other important essays in this collection are "On Scientific Method in Philosophy" (1914); "On the Notion of Cause," originally published in *PAS*, Vol. 13 (1912–1913), 1–26; and "Knowledge by Acquaintance and Knowledge by Description," originally published in *PAS*, Vol. 11 (1910–1911), 108–128. See also "The Philosophy of Logical Atomism," in *The Monist*, Vol. 28 (1918), 495–527; Vol. 29 (1919), 32–63, 190–222, and 345–380; reprinted in *Logic and Knowledge* (see above). The analysis of basic concepts and principles of physical science is pushed further in *The Analysis of Matter* (New York, 1927). Logical constructionism is applied to mental phenomena in *The Analysis of Mind* (New York, 1921). Russell's increasing concern with psychological aspects of meaning can be traced in "On Propositions, What They Are and How They Mean," in *PAS*, Supp. Vol. 2 (1919), 1–43, reprinted in *Logic and Knowledge;* in Ch. 10 of *The Analysis of Mind;* and in Russell's most extensive work on meaning and empirical data, the rich but chaotic *An Inquiry Into Meaning and Truth* (New York, 1940). Russell's latest thoughts on meaning and various other problems concerning empirical knowledge, particularly in the physical sciences, are given a relatively systematic presentation in *Human Knowledge, Its Scope and Limits* (New York, 1948).

In several works Russell has summarized his philosophy and/or its development. The most important of these are "Logical Atomism," in J. H. Muirhead, ed., *Contemporary British Philosophy*, First Series (London, 1924), reprinted in *Logic and Knowledge* (see above); "My Mental Development," in P. A. Schilpp, ed., *The Philosophy of Bertrand Russell* (see above); and the very interesting recent work *My Philosophical Development* (London and New York, 1959). The last-named work also contains some of Russell's polemics against recent Oxford philosophers and their criticisms of his views. Russell's *A History of Western Philosophy* (London and New York, 1946) and *The Wisdom of the West* (London and New York, 1959), aside from their intrinsic interest, are of great value to students of Russell's thought in showing us his mature evaluations of the great philosophers of past ages.

The critical literature on different aspects of Russell's epistemology and metaphysics is vast. *The Philosophy of Bertrand Russell* (see above) contains a number of excellent discussions, together with Russell's replies. Special mention should also be made of C. A. Fritz, *Bertrand Russell's Construction of the External World* (London, 1952); Erik Götlind, *Bertrand Russell's Theories of Causation* (Uppsala, 1952); J. O. Urmson, *Philosophical Analysis—Its Development Between Two World Wars* (Oxford, 1956); and G. J. Warnock, *English Philosophy Since 1900* (London, 1958). The books by Urmson and Warnock contain detailed appraisals of Russell's logical atomism. Russell's logical atomism as well as his neutral monism and his theories about truth and induction are sympathetically discussed by D. J. O'Connor in Ch. 26 of his *Critical History of Western Philosophy* (New York, 1964). *Rivista critica di storia della filosofia*, Vol. 8, No. 2 (1953), 101–335, and several articles in *Philosophy*, Vol. 35 (January 1960), 1–50, are devoted to Russell's philosophy, including Anthony Quinton's useful sketch of the development of Russell's ideas in epistemology and metaphysics, "Russell's Philosophical Development," 1–13.

Logic and Mathematics

Of Russell's own works on logic and mathematics, see *Principles of Mathematics* (Cambridge, 1903; 2d ed., London, 1937); *Principia Mathematica*, 3 vols., written with A. N. Whitehead (Cambridge, 1910–1913; 2d ed., 1927; paperback ed. up to *56, 1962); *Introduction to Mathematical Philosophy* (London, 1919); and the papers "On Denoting" (1905), "Mathematical Logic as Based on the Theory of Types" (1908), "The Philosophy of Logical Atomism" (1918), and "Logical Atomism" (1924), all of which are reprinted in R. C. Marsh, ed. *Logic and Knowledge* (London, 1956).

On Frege's parallel work, see his *Grundlagen der Arithmetik* (Breslau, 1884), translated by J. L. Austin as *The Foundations of Arithmetic* (Oxford, 1950); and P. T. Geach and Max Black, eds., *Translations From the Philosophical Writings of Gottlob Frege* (Oxford, 1952).

Important critical discussions of Russell's work occur in W. E. Johnson, *Logic*, Pt. II (Cambridge, 1922), Chs. 3 and 6; F. P. Ramsey, *The Foundations of Mathematics* (London, 1931), papers I and II; W. V. Quine, *From a Logical Point of View* (Cambridge, Mass., 1953), essays I, V, and VI; and G. E. Moore, *The Commonplace Book of G. E. Moore, 1919–1953*, Casimir Lewy, ed. (London and New York, 1963), Notebook II, item 4, and Notebook V, item 13.

On formal implication, see A. N. Prior, "The Theory of Implication," in *Zeitschrift für mathematische Logik und Grundlagen der*

Mathematik, Vol. 9 (1963), 1–6. On simplifications of type theory, see Alonzo Church, "A Formulation of the Simple Theory of Types," in *Journal of Symbolic Logic,* Vol. 5 (1940), 56–68, and Ludwik Borkowski, "Reduction of Arithmetic to Logic Based on the Theory of Types," in *Studio Logica,* Vol. 8 (1958), 283–295.

Ethics and Religion

Russell's early views on ethics are in "The Elements of Ethics," Ch. 1 of *Philosophical Essays* (New York, 1910); it has been reprinted in Wilfrid Sellars and John Hospers, eds., *Readings in Ethical Theory* (New York, 1952), pp. 1–34. The fullest statements of his later position are in Ch. 9 of *Religion and Science* (London and New York, 1935) and in *Human Society in Ethics and Politics* (London and New York, 1955). There are critical discussions of Russell's views in Lillian W. Aiken, *Bertrand Russell's Philosophy of Morals* (New York, 1963); in Justus Buchler, "Russell and the Principles of Ethics," in P. A. Schilpp, ed., *The Philosophy of Bertrand Russell* (see above); and in D. H. Monro, "Russell's Moral Theories," in *Philosophy,* Vol. 35 (1960), 30–50.

Russell's earlier views on religion are in "The Essence of Religion," in *The Hibbert Journal,* Vol. 11 (1912), 46–62. His first published discussion of the arguments for the existence of God is contained in Ch. 15 of *A Critical Exposition of the Philosophy of Leibniz* (Cambridge, 1900; 2d ed., London and New York, 1937). His later views are expounded in several of the essays in *Why I Am Not a Christian* (London and New York, 1957) and in Pt. II, Ch. 7, of *Human Society in Ethics and Politics* (see above). The BBC debate with Father F. C. Copleston (1948), "The Existence of God," is available in the British edition, but not in the American edition, of *Why I Am Not a Christian,* but it has been reprinted in Paul Edwards and Arthur Pap, eds., *A Modern Introduction to Philosophy,* 2d ed. (New York, 1965), and in John Hick, ed., *The Existence of God* (New York, 1964). Several chapters in *The Scientific Outlook* (London and New York, 1931) and in *Religion and Science* (see above) contain criticisms of the attempts of certain scientists to derive theological conclusions from physics and biology. Russell's objections to the fideistic position are found in Ch. 12, Bk. 3, of *A History of Western Philosophy* (London and New York, 1946). His objections to William James' defense of religion are contained in Ch. 29, Bk. 3, of the same work and in Ch. 5 of *Philosophical Essays* (see above). Russell's views on religion are criticized in H. G. Wood, *Why Mr. Bertrand Russell Is Not a Christian* (London, 1928); C. H. D. Clark,

Christianity and Bertrand Russell (London, 1958); G. S. Montgomery, *Why Bertrand Russell Is Not a Christian* (New York, 1959); and E. S. Brightman's contribution to the Schilpp volume, "Russell's Philosophy of Religion," pp. 537–556.

Social and Political Theory

In addition to the works mentioned in the first section of the present article, the following among Russell's books dealing with social and political questions have been influential: *Principles of Social Reconstruction* (London, 1916); *Roads to Freedom: Socialism, Anarchism and Syndicalism* (London, 1918); *The Problems of China* (New York, 1922); *Power: A New Social Analysis* (London and New York, 1938); *Authority and the Individual* (London, 1949); and *New Hopes for a Changing World* (London and New York, 1951). Ch. 17 of *New Hopes* contains a moving discussion of the problems of growing old and facing death. Russell's fullest discussion of Marxism can be found in *Freedom and Organization 1814–1914* (London and New York, 1934; New York edition entitled *Freedom versus Organization*), which is in effect a history of the main social and intellectual forces of the nineteenth century.

Other Writings

Philosophical discussions sooner or later crop up in most of Russell's writings. Some of his most delightful occasional pieces have been collected in *Sceptical Essays* (London and New York, 1927); in *In Praise of Idleness* (London and New York, 1935); and in *Unpopular Essays* (London and New York, 1950). The last of these contains his "Auto-obituary," which was first published in 1936. *Bertrand Russell Speaks His Mind* (London, 1960) is a most interesting volume containing the unedited text of a series of television interviews, dealing with a great variety of topics, which took place in the spring of 1959.

The Basic Writings of Bertrand Russell, 1903–1959, R. E. Egner and L. E. Dennon, eds. (New York, 1961), is a very useful anthology of writings by Russell. The Schilpp volume contains an extremely comprehensive bibliography up to 1944.

(Life and Social Theories, Ethics and Critique of Religion)
— PAUL EDWARDS
(Epistemology and Metaphysics)
— WILLIAM P. ALSTON
(Logic and Mathematics)
— A. N. PRIOR

S

SARTRE, JEAN-PAUL

Jean-Paul Sartre, French existentialist, was born in Paris in 1905 and studied at the École Normale Supérieure from 1924 to 1928. After passing his agrégation in 1929 he taught philosophy in a number of *lycées,* both in Paris and elsewhere. From 1933 to 1935, he was a research student at the Institut Français in Berlin and at the University of Freiburg. From 1936 on he published a philosophical novel, *La Nausée* (1938), and a collection of stories, *Le Mur* (1939; *The Wall*), as well as a number of philosophical studies. At the outbreak of war in 1939, he was called up by the French Army and in 1940 was captured by the Germans. Released after the armistice, he returned to Paris, where he continued to teach philosophy until 1944. During these years he completed *L'Être et le néant* (1943; *Being and Nothingness*), his major philosophical work. He was also active in the resistance, and at the end of the war he emerged as the dominant figure in the existentialist movement. During the early postwar years he wrote a number of novels and plays which made him world-famous. As one of the founders (with Simone de Beauvoir and Maurice Merleau-Ponty) of *Les Temps modernes,* a review devoted to the discussion of political and literary questions from a generally existentialist point of view, he took an active part in the ideological controversies of the time. In 1951 he unsuccessfully attempted to found a new political movement that was to be radically to the left but noncommunist. Sartre's political activities, which provided the occasion for acrimonious disputes with his friends Albert Camus and Maurice Merleau-Ponty, have led him into periods of cooperation with the French Communist party, of which, however, he has often been highly critical. His most recent philosophical work, *Critique de la raison dialectique* ("Critique of Dialectical Reason"; 1960) of which only Volume I has appeared, is a restatement of Marxism that is intended to show its underlying harmony with existentialism.

PHILOSOPHICAL ORIENTATION. Sartre's philosophical culture appears to have been formed almost entirely within the tradition of Continental rationalism and idealism—that is, the line of thinkers that leads from Descartes to Kant and then from Hegel to the twentieth-century phenomenology of Husserl and Heidegger. Allusions to philosophers outside this tradition are rare in Sartre's writings, and generally he seems not to regard empiricism or positivism—and certainly not materialism—as serious philosophical alternatives. Although a great deal of Sartre's work has been criticism, often extremely violent, of the various forms of dualism and

---

The central theme

that runs through all Sartre's work

is his passionate interest in human beings.

---

idealism that are peculiar to the Cartesian tradition, it has been, in a profound sense, internal criticism, and his leading ideas, almost without exception, bear the mark of their derivation from one or another of the philosophers he has attacked. At different stages in his career, his thought has seemed to be most strongly influenced first by Husserl, then by Heidegger and Hegel, and finally, during the past decade, by a rather highly alembicated Marx. This is not to deny that Sartre is in many respects an original thinker but, rather, to define the tradition within which his innovations find their place. He has also, of course, drawn extensively on extraphilosophical disciplines like psychology and, to some extent, sociology, but his way of using their results mainly as supporting evidence for conclusions already reached by independent dialectical analysis strongly suggests that in his view the fundamental truths about man and his relation to the world are still the province of a kind of philosophical inquiry that owes very little to the special sciences. As for the physical sciences and mathematics, these find only passing and perfunctory mention in his writings and have clearly had no influence on his thought. By contrast, his very wide literary culture has exerted a constant and powerful influence on his philosophy, and in a sense it can be said that his whole philosophy is an energetic reaffirmation of the primacy of the world of human experience to which literature and art are also addressed.

CENTRAL THEME. Despite the great diversity of his writings, which range from abstruse ontological dialectic to political journalism and film scenarios, the central theme that runs through all Sartre's work is his passionate interest in human beings. Sometimes he has expressed his sense of the primacy of human existence (conceived as a consciously sustained relationship to oneself, to other human beings, and to the world at large) in a rather exaggerated way—as, for example, when he has a character in the play *Le Diable et le bon Dieu* declare that "only human beings really exist." Yet there can be no doubt of the profoundly moral and, in an authentic sense, humanistic character of his philosophy. While Sartre's deepest interest is in individual human beings, his effort to understand them, to form a general concept of human being, has nevertheless been heavily dependent on a number of other such conceptions, among them the Christian, the Cartesian, and the Hegelian theories of man. All of these Sartre for one reason or another rejects, but he does not regard them as just unfortunate philosophical mistakes. Instead, they express in his view an aspiration of human beings that runs so deep as to be virtually definitive of what it is to be a human being: the aspiration to found one's own individual being in a rational necessity of some sort. Sartre's whole philosophy can be seen as an attempt to describe a mode of being—human being—whose essence is just this aspiration, which he thinks is necessarily doomed to failure. This combination of a rejection of all forms of rationalism, theistic and otherwise, with a recognition of the permanent validity of the demand they express may fairly be regarded as the most characteristic feature of Sartre's thought. It is also the key to his moral philosophy, the fundamental imperative of which is to recognize and accept this unresolvable contradiction that defines human nature.

STAGES OF DEVELOPMENT. Although Sartre has attempted, often with great success, to communicate this conception of man through his novels and plays and his political and literary criticism, it is in his philosophical writings that the most detailed exposition and defense of it are to be found. These writings can be conveniently divided into three main groups that roughly coincide with successive periods in Sartre's intellectual development. The first group comprises his contributions to phenomenological psychology, beginning with "La Transcendance de l'égo" (1936) and including *L'Imaginaire* (1940) and *Esquisse d'une théorie des émotions* (1939). The principal work of the second period, in which Sartre emerges as a full-fledged ontologist of human existence, is *L'Être et le néant* (1943); however, with it should be associated *L'Existentialisme est un humanisme* (1946), his somewhat unsuccessful attempt at a simplified statement of the central doctrines of *L'Être et le néant*, as well as a number of critical studies, such as *Baudelaire* (1947), *Réflexions sur la question juive* (1946), and *Saint Genet: comédien et martyre* (1952), in which Sartre's ontological categories are applied to the analysis of human personality. It should be emphasized

that there is no sharp break between this period and the earlier one and that many of the ideas that Sartre develops fully in *L'Être et le néant* had begun to emerge in his phenomenological studies. By contrast, the work of his most recent period, in which he has been attempting an extensive restatement of Marxism that would do justice to the essential insights of his own form of existentialism, seems to involve a much more radical recasting of his whole mode of thought. How extensive this revision will prove to be is hard to judge until the *Critique de la raison dialectique* has been completed.

Psychology

In the three essays that belong to his first period, Sartre is concerned to describe a particular structure of consciousness, very much in the Husserlian manner, without the aid of any master concept of human existence. It is clear, however, that these descriptions are intended as contributions to the working out of such a concept and that Sartre already has a rather clear idea of what its general contours will be. It is obvious, too, that although Sartre is using a descriptive phenomenological method that he learned from Husserl, the results it produces in his hands take him steadily away from Husserl toward a position that has a greater affinity with that of Heidegger.

THE SELF. In "La Transcendance de l'égo," Sartre's first philosophical publication, the divergence from Husserl's views was already abundantly clear. Sartre here argued that Husserl had failed to push his phenomenological reduction far enough; that he had not really succeeded in his aim of "bracketing-off" the world from the sphere of pure consciousness; and that by identifying pure transcendental consciousness with the self, he had produced an inconsistent amalgam of radically disparate elements. According to Sartre, the self, unlike pure consciousness, does not disclose itself exhaustively to immediate intuition and for precisely this reason belongs among the objects that transcend consciousness—that is, in the world. Since the world is constituted by the intentional acts of pure consciousness, the self must also be treated as the result of a synthetic act of organization of this kind and not as itself the agency by which these syntheses are made.

What is not altogether clear in this essay is how radical a revision of Husserl's whole position Sartre felt himself committed to by his own conclusions. It is significant that even at this early, prepolitical stage in his philosophical career, Sartre felt it necessary to answer the Marxist charge that phenomenology is a kind of crypto-idealism that makes man a spectator instead of a deeply committed agent in the historical process. If the self forms part of the world, as Sartre claims to have shown, then it cannot be isolated from history either, and the Marxist charge falls to the ground. But whether the "bracketing-off" operation, even when it is carried out as rigorously as Sartre would wish, is still doomed to break down before the stubbornly unconceptualizable fact of existence Sartre did not make clear.

THE EMOTIONS. In his essay on the emotions, Sartre presents both Husserl and Heidegger, without any emphasis on their divergencies, as providing the necessary conceptual framework within which psychological phenomena can be adequately understood. Experience, according to the phenomenological view, is not just an aggregate of heterogeneous items of mental content but a structured whole whose two poles are pure consciousness, as a constitutive, meaning-conferring activity, and the world, conceived as the transcendent correlate of these intentional acts of consciousness. Sartre argues that emotion can be understood only if it is set in the context of this total "human reality." It must, accordingly, be treated as a spontaneous activity of consciousness and not as something that is passively suffered or undergone. Emotion is in fact not a physiological phenomenon but a certain total mode of relating oneself to the world; its peculiar strategy is that of a "magical transformation" of given situations that bypasses the necessity for dealing with them by rational, step-by-step methods. Thus, sadness makes the world appear sad so that it offers no opening to our efforts to change it, and in this way it justifies our passivity by making purposeful effort seem pointless. This self-imposed passivity Sartre calls a "degradation of consciousness," a concept which is a clear forerunner of the "bad faith" that figures so largely in his later work.

L'Imaginaire is by far the most ambitious

of Sartre's studies in phenomenological psychology.

This analysis also poses a problem to which, in one form or another, Sartre has felt obliged to return again and again: How can emotion (or any other mental function) be interpreted as a spontaneous and purposive activity without attributing an intolerably sophisticated kind of self-consciousness to those who have the emotion? Sartre's way of meeting this difficulty is to set up an intermediate kind of self-awareness between explicit or reflective consciousness of self (as when I am writing and think to myself, "I am writing") and events of which we are completely unconscious (for example, the circulation of the blood). This intermediary is exemplified by the awareness that I have of what I am doing—my intention—while I am doing it but not thinking about what I am doing. Sartre calls it a "non-positional" consciousness and argues that strategies of action, such as those which he takes to be characteristic of the emotions, can be attributed to it without any of the incongruities that would result if explicit or verbal self-awareness were required.

THE IMAGINATION. *L'Imaginaire* is by far the most ambitious of Sartre's studies in phenomenological psychology, and it also makes a much more direct approach to his later ontological themes than the others do. Once again, the point of departure is an alleged misconception of a psychological phenomenon—in this instance, the imagination—that is due to a positivistic refusal to appreciate the importance of the structural organization of our experience. As a result, perception and imagination are confused with one another, and both are conceived as the having of picturelike simulacra of objects before the mind, the only difference between them being caused by superior vivacity, immediacy, and so forth of our perceptions. Against this view, Sartre insists that imagination is an activity of consciousness—an "imaging consciousness"—and that the object of this intentional activity is not some discrete item of psychic content but the very person or thing itself of which we are said to "have an image." Imagination is, in short, an alternative mode of consciousness, addressed to the same objects as perceptual consciousness but—and this is the crucial point in Sartre's theory—to these objects *as they are not,* at least at the time of imagining them. Counterposed to the world, human consciousness sets up, through imagination, alternative "unreal" states of affairs, and the measure of their unreality and of the reality of perceptual objects is the fact that although the latter are never exhaustively given to intuition, imaginal objects are exhausted by our awareness of them. Again, Sartre argues that the self-awareness involved is of the nonpositional kind, and once again, he insists that even when the appearance of passivity in relation to our imaginal experiences seems most undeniable (as, for example, in the case of hallucinations and psychosis), this can be shown to be the work of a spontaneous activity of consciousness that, as it were, imprisons itself. Finally, in answering the question whether imagination is merely a mental function that contingently characterizes human beings but which they might well be without, Sartre explicitly identifies imagination with the reality-negating function which he says is essential to human consciousness. Consciousness through imagination "constitutes, isolates, and negates" the world; it can do this only because it is itself nonbeing. Here Sartre initiates his characterization of the ontological status of consciousness that is, he thinks, presupposed by all the descriptions he has given of its distinct functions and that was to be fully worked out in the second main period in his philosophical career.

Ontology

There can be no doubt that *L'Être et le néant* owes more to the thought of Martin Heidegger than to any other single philosopher. In many respects Sartre's account of "the human reality" is no more than an amplified restatement of the doctrines in Heidegger's *Sein und Zeit*. There are, however, major differences. Heidegger, unlike Sartre, has never been interested in the detailed analysis of the structures of consciousness. Instead, he has described the ontic counterparts of these intentional structures, and in this way he has tried to convey the special character of human being by showing what its "world" is like. In Sartre's view, such a description of the human world must be supplemented by an account of the structure of the consciousness that "founds" this world; he repeatedly criticizes Heidegger for having, in effect, suppressed consciousness. Again, Heidegger has professed himself to be uninterested in any "humanistic" interpretation of his doctrines that would seek to draw ethical consequences from them. By contrast, Sartre is unequivocally committed to the use of his ontological apparatus for the purpose of a general clarification of the human predicament. Finally, Sartre's conclusions with respect to the possibility of a general ontology that would set forth a concept of being as such from which the concepts of conscious and nonconscious being could then be derived seem to be entirely negative. Heidegger, on the other hand, has never declared such a project to be impossible, and in his later writings he has, if anything, given even greater weight to the general concept of being.

The subtitle of *L'Être et le néant* is "Essai d'ontologie phénoménologique." A long tradition of usage that contrasts being—the subject of ontology—with appearance—the subject of phenomenology—might seem to make this collocation of terms highly incongruous. Sartre explains that his kind of ontology, like phenomenology, is purely descriptive in character and does not undertake to explain human experience by reference to extraphenomenal realities in the manner of Descartes or Kant. Such explanations are, he says, the work of metaphysics, not of ontology; ontology, as conceived by Sartre, seems to differ from the more familiar kind of phenomenology only by virtue of the superior generality of the concepts it employs—that is, the concepts of being and nonbeing.

BEING AND APPEARING. In the introduction to *L'Être et le néant*, entitled "A la Recherche de l'être," Sartre first takes up the claim of contemporary phenomenalism to have overcome the traditional duality of appearance and reality by contructing both the "physical" and the "mental" out of series of "appearances" that are themselves neutral with respect to this distinction. He concludes that such a treatment of the being of objects is entirely justified insofar as it denies that there is any screen of sensations or mental contents behind which reality lurks. Being itself appears. On the other hand, Sartre insists, against the idealists, that being is completely independent of the fact of its appearing and is "transcendent" in the sense that it can never be exhausted by any finite set of its appearances. A question thus arises as to the nature—as Sartre says, the "being"—of this appearing that supervenes upon being and of the relationship between the being of things and the being of their appearing. This is the general problem of the book as a whole.

Imagination is an alternative mode of consciousness, addressed to the same objects as perceptual consciousness, but addressed to these objects as they are not, at least at the time of imagining them.

In order to set up his inquiry in this way, Sartre has to break sharply with Husserl on several points. Most important, in order to establish the transphenomenality of objects, by which is meant their irreducibility to appearances, he drastically reinterprets the Husserlian notion of intentionality. For Husserl intentionality was an internal structure of mental states by virtue of which they were directed toward objects, but it was by no means necessary that these objects should be independent of consciousness. Sartre adds the stipulation that they must be so independent. Otherwise, he argues, objects would owe their being to consciousness, and this he declares to be impossible. His proof is that since objects, whatever their status, are never exhaustively given to an instantaneous intuition, a "constitutive consciousness," as conceived by Husserl, could reproduce this central feature of our consciousness of objects only by intending the infinite series of appearances that compose the object and at the same time not intending all those that are not presently given. This it manifestly cannot do, and thus, Sartre concludes, the transcendence of objects is established.

BEING-FOR-ITSELF AND BEING-IN-ITSELF. Just as Sartre presents the transphenomenality of objects as the background against which they appear, he also argues that the being of consciousness is similarly transphenomenal in the sense of not being dependent on its appearing to itself in explicit, reflective self-awareness. Instead, this reflective self-consciousness is said to presuppose the antecedent existence of a prereflective consciousness in much the same way as consciousness of objects is held by Sartre to presuppose their transphenomenal status. The chief characteristic of this being of consciousness—or "being-for-itself," as Sartre calls it—is its activity. It is incapable of being acted on from without, and it consists in and is exhausted by its own intentional, meaning-conferring acts. By contrast, the being of things—"being-in-itself"—is characterized in terms of a complete incapacity for any relationship to itself; it is, in Sartre's highly metaphorical language, "opaque," and it "coincides exactly with itself." All that can strictly be said of it is that it is. In this way, by establishing these two radically distinct types of being and by rejecting both the idealistic and the realistic accounts of their rapport, Sartre has put himself under an obligation to provide a more satisfactory account of the relationship between being-in-itself and being-for-itself and of the relationship of both to the generic concept of being. The last question is not answered until the structures of conscious being have been examined in very great detail, which takes up the major portion of the book.

Conscious Being. Sartre's principal clue in his attempt to describe conscious being is the human ability to ask questions and receive negative answers. For him negation is not, of course, just a logical function of judgment. Negative judgments themselves are said to require, as a condition of their being possible at all, an extralogical or ontic counterpart which is nonbeing, and Sartre, accordingly, has to ask what the origin of this nonbeing is. He rejects the Hegelian view that being and nonbeing are logically interdependent in favor of the Heideggerian notion of nonbeing as a kind of circumambient medium in which being is contingently suspended. At the same time, however, he criticizes Heidegger for having failed to show how nonbeing can appear in particularized or local form within the world, and he argues that this is possible only if there is a being that is, or generates its own, nothingness. This being turns out to be human consciousness, whose distinguishing feature is thus to constitute itself by contrast with or as other than its physical milieu, its body, its past, and, indeed, everything whatsoever. By its self-detaching activity, it creates, as it were, a hole in being-in-itself, and the latter, as the horizon that surrounds this focus of negation, becomes a "world." Because consciousness projects being-in-itself against a backdrop of nonbeing, it inescapably apprehends actuality in the context of possibility—that is, of the alternative possibilities of development of which the actual is suscepti-

ble. It also apprehends itself as a bridge between the actual and the possible and as having to determine which of these possibilities is to be realized. Finally, human consciousness is free because it is forced to think of itself as—and thus is—other than the world and unincorporable into any causal sequences it may discern within the world. The feeling of anguish, Sartre says, is our experience of this freedom.

The Problem of Freedom. In the face of this freedom, human beings can adopt either of two fundamentally different attitudes. They can attempt to conceal their freedom from themselves by a variety of devices, the most typical of which is belief in some form of psychological determinism. All of these efforts are doomed to failure, Sartre argues, because human beings can try to conceal their freedom only to the extent that they recognize it. The attempt succeeds only in producing a paradoxical internal duality of consciousness in which consciousness thinks of itself as a thing at the same time that it gives covert recognition to its freedom. This state, which has to be carefully distinguished both from lying to others and from the Freudian conception of a manipulation of consciousness by subconscious forces, is called "bad faith." Its antithesis is an acceptance of one's own freedom and a recognition that human beings are the absolute origin of, and are solely responsible for, their own acts. On the contrast between these two life-attitudes is based the whole of Sartre's ethic. But while Sartre severely condemns all attempts by human consciousness to objectify itself and put itself on a level with things, he basically defines human being as precisely this self-contradictory effort to achieve the status of a thing while remaining a consciousness that contemplates itself as a thing. Indeed, he goes so far as to define value as this impossible combination of being-for-itself and being-in-itself, and in this impossibility he sees the ultimate reason for the hopeless character of the human enterprise (which he also describes as the attempt to make oneself God). This effort must fail, for while human beings are absolutely responsible for their choices, their existence is not the result of a choice. It is simply a fact, and its uneliminable contingency makes it impossible for human beings to be ontologically self-sufficient in the way that a God must be.

Time. Large sections of *L'Être et le néant* are devoted to discussions of temporality as a structure of conscious being and to analysis of the relationship of one consciousness to another. In his treatment of time, Sartre relies heavily on Heidegger's works and adopts his view of past, present, and future as internal structures of conscious being and thus as so many different ways in which consciousness is what it is not and is not what it is. We are what we were in the past but in the mode of not being it any longer, and we are our future in the mode of not yet being it. Similarly, in the present, consciousness is inescapably tied to the world and to its situation within the world, but once again, it is tied in such a way as to reinforce the distinction between it and the world. For Sartre, temporality in all its dimensions is an activity of consciousness by which the latter negates and transcends itself. There is no place in Sartre's philosophy for time conceived as one dimension of a spatio-temporal continuum which itself exists tenselessly.

Sartre rejects the Hegelian view that being

and nonbeing are logically interdependent

in favor of the Heideggerian notion

of nonbeing as a kind of circumambient medium

in which being is contingently suspended.

Other Minds. In his analyses of the reciprocal relationships of consciousnesses, Sartre very clearly goes beyond Heidegger. He argues, first, that it cannot be proved by analogical arguments or otherwise that there are other minds (and to this extent, he thinks, solipsism expresses a truth); rather, it is the case that my own apprehension of my existence is so structured that it presupposes the existence of other conscious beings. This is particularly clear in the case of feelings of shame, which presuppose that my body is accessible to another observer. In general, my experience of myself is inseparable from this public dimension of my existence. In Husserl, Sartre finds this fact recognized only in the form of a logical requirement that has to be met if there is to be an intersubjectively shareable world, not in a way that accounts for our actual encounters with others. Only Heidegger is said to have grasped the relationship of consciousnesses in a way that makes it not just an internal requirement of our conceptual system but a feature of our being that is presupposed by that system. Sartre, however, feels that Heidegger's very general account of *Mitsein* ("being-together") has to be supplemented by an analysis of the experience in which I apprehend myself as I am perceived by another consciousness—that is, as an object, reified and deprived of the transcendence that is central to my own sense of my being. This is the experience of being looked at by someone else. In relation to this intrusive "other," I can adopt either of two courses of action. I can try to dominate it and suppress its transcendence

by which my own is threatened, or I can try to make myself into an object to be dominated by the liberty of the other person. In either case, I am destined to fail because I must recognize my liberty (or that of the other) in order to suppress it. What is impossible in either option is a moral consensus that is more than an accidental convergence of independent individual projects.

ACTION, LIBERTY, AND CHOICE. The last section of *L'Être et le néant* deals with human action and human liberty, and it takes the form of an analysis of the relationship between human consciousness and the milieu or situation in which consciousness finds itself. The principal thesis is that this situation, conceived as the intentional object of conscious activity, cannot determine the direction that will be taken or the direction that ought to be taken by the human activity of which it is the premise. Moral autonomy is thus presented as equally inconsistent both with causal determinism and with any kind of natural moral law. It is conscious human being that first isolates particular situations so that they are experienced as incomplete and as calling for complementation through human action; it is only by that same conscious existence that these situations can be assigned the goals toward which they are to develop. It follows that not only the means used to reach a given goal but the goal itself and any general moral principles that may have dictated its selection must be thought of as choices that are subject to no causal influences and no rational controls at all. Such choices are, in the last analysis, "unjustifiable" because the reasoning that is commonly thought of as providing independent guidance for choice is itself an expression of that choice. Such a choice is not, however, to be conceived as a single mental episode; rather, it is human action itself considered as doing one thing rather than another from among the multiple possibilities with which human consciousness endows each actual situation. Taken together, these choices form a system within which particular choices are derivative specifications of what Sartre calls a "total choice of oneself" although they are not deducible from the latter, and even the most extreme passivity or acquiescence is, at bottom, an autonomous choice of this total kind. What I do not choose is the necessity for choosing itself or the situation in which I am obliged to choose. In another sense, however, Sartre argues that by acting in that situation and by conferring on it the meaning it is to have for me, I may be said to accept it and to make myself responsible for it. The individual human person is in fact a choice, and by himself he defines a complete moral universe.

Our choices or "projects" are not necessarily the objects of a reflective self-awareness. Normally, our understanding of our own actions will be in the mode of the nonpositional consciousness previously described. A properly conceived psychoanalytic method would therefore address itself to the task of interpreting the system of choices that our actions express and would reject all reductions of these choices to occult non-choicelike states of the unconscious. Existential psychoanalysis, as conceived by Sartre, must treat empirical needs and desires as simply symbolizations of the total choices by which our relation to being is defined; the meanings it disengages from human behavior must always be treated as internal to the consciousness of the person whose behavior it is, even if only in the mode of "bad faith." In these interpretations, the analyst would be guided, Sartre thinks, by the expressive values of certain qualities in our experience through which the nature of our relationship to being is conveyed. The main example that is offered of this expressive function of qualities is that of "sliminess," whose "metaphysical coefficient" Sartre rather extravagantly declares to be a fear that being-in-itself will absorb being-for-itself.

The general conclusion that Sartre reaches with respect to the relationship between these two kinds of being is that a synthesis of the two that would compose a total being *causa sui* is impossible and that the general concept of being is therefore in a permanent state of disintegration. What is lacking is the kind of mutual entailment by which being-in-itself would presuppose being-for-itself and vice versa, rather in the way that one consciousness, according to Sartre, presupposes the existence of others. But while being-for-itself does presuppose being-in-itself, the latter remains radically independent. The project of constituting an ontologically self-sufficient being is in fact peculiar to being-for-itself, which is thus one of the terms in this relationship between the two kinds of being and the relation itself. It is also a hopeless undertaking because a genuine logical synthesis is precluded by the negating action of human consciousness which perpetually creates anew the distinctions such a synthesis is intended to overcome.

Social Philosophy

At the end of *L'Être et le néant*, Sartre promised that it would be followed by a full-scale treatment of the ethical implications of the doctrine of human reality expounded in it. This book has never appeared, and in the light of Sartre's current preoccupations it seems unlikely that it ever will. In later years, he turned more and more toward a kind of dialectical sociology that seems very remote from the individualism that was characteristic of his earlier moral theory. He now criticizes severely his own lack of understanding of the way the moral autonomy of the individual is qualified by

the fact that he lives in an exploitative society. True moral freedom is now projected into a future that will not be realized until the dialectic of human antagonism has run its course, and of this future Sartre says we can know nothing. Nevertheless, while Sartre is clearly dissatisfied with the virtually total neglect, in his earlier work, of the social aspect of morality, his present description of existentialism as an "enclave within Marxism" substantially exaggerates the degree to which his fundamental position has changed. He is still not a materialist or a determinist in the orthodox Marxist manner, and he is still strongly critical of the refusal by contemporary Marxists to deal with individual personality except in the most crudely schematic way. It is true that he now holds that a material fact—scarcity—is the motor that sets the dialectic of human social relationships going, but he would presumably still want to say that this "natural" fact assumes its human significance only within the context of a conscious project of some sort. Furthermore, Sartre has always recognized that human beings in some sense stand in a passive relation to the products of their own spontaneity, and what he has done in his recent work is simply to give a new emphasis to this kind of passivity which he now conceives in relation to the dual fact of natural scarcity and the resulting dialectic of human antagonism. He still argues that human beings have to be understood by methods that are entirely different from those used in the study of nature, and he still regards scientific inquiry as assuming its full significance only within the context of a dialectical comprehension of man. A final judgment on the degree to which Sartre has really modified his views in the direction of Marxism and not just expanded them to take account of aspects of human life to which Marxist criticism had forcibly drawn his attention must, of course, await the completion of *Critique de la raison dialectique*.

Again and again, when Sartre seems most

deeply involved in some hopelessly sterile logomachy,

he will offer an insight that makes

the tortuous complications of his terminology

seem a small price to pay in return.

Any appraisal of Sartre's achievement as a philosopher must reckon with the fact that even in his most technical philosophical works he is never really a pure philosopher in the sense of one who is primarily concerned to secure the theoretical underpinnings of some system of ideas. His argumentation is often both skimpy and lacking in rigor; he seems to be unaware of, or unconcerned by, the grossly metaphorical character of many of his leading ideas; and he has allowed free rein to the special bias of his sensibility in a way that is indefensible in abstruse theoretical work. At the same time, his work shows many of the defects that are typical of the grand tradition of philosophical system builders—in particular, an almost total lack of any capacity for critical detachment in relation to his own philosophical theses. His ideas may quite literally be said to define reality for him in a way and to a degree that makes it impossible for him to submit them to any kind of empirical or pragmatic test by which their merits might be compared with those of other philosophical points of view. This is the more unfortunate since it often seems that what Sartre is trying to do, while continuing to use for his own purposes the philosophical vocabulary of rationalism and idealism, is to work out ideas that at many points have clear affinities with tendencies in contemporary pragmatism and sometimes even in analytical philosophy. In any case, after all these criticisms have been registered, the extraordinary fecundity and energy of Sartre's mind must be recognized. Again and again, when he seems most deeply involved in some hopelessly sterile logomachy, he will offer an insight that makes the tortuous complications of his terminology seem a small price to pay in return. In this respect he is like Hegel, whom, among the great philosophers, he may most resemble. Sartre himself will probably not be ranked as a "great philosopher" in the histories of the future, but he is without doubt an immensely stimulating and acute critical mind.

BIBLIOGRAPHY

Works by Sartre

Philosophical

"La Transcendance de l'égo." *Recherches philosophiques*, Vol. 6 (1936), 65–123. Translated by Forrest Williams and Robert Kirkpatrick as *The Transcendence of the Ego*. New York, 1937.

Esquisse d'une théorie des émotions. Paris, 1939. Translated by Bernard Frechtman as *The Emotions: Outline of a Theory*. New York, 1948. Translated by Philip Mairet as *Sketch for a Theory of the Emotions*. London, 1962.

L'Imaginaire: Psychologie phénoménologique de l'imagination. Paris, 1940. Translated by Bernard Frechtman as *The Psychology of Imagination*. New York, 1948.

L'Être et le néant: Essai d'ontologie phénoménologique. Paris, 1943. Translated by Hazel E. Barnes as *Being and Nothingness*. New York, 1956.

L'Existentialisme est un humanisme. Paris, 1946. Translated by Philip Mairet as *Existentialism and Humanism*. London, 1948.

Situations I & III. Paris, 1947, 1949. Two volumes of philosophical and literary essays. The two most important pieces are "La Liberté cartésienne" and "Matérialisme et révolution," both of which have been translated by Annette Michelson in *Literary and Philosophical Essays*. New York, 1955.

Questions de méthode and *Critique de la raison dialectique*, Vol. I. Paris, 1960. Translated by Hazel E. Barnes as *The Problem of Method*. London, 1964.

Literary Works

La Nausée. Paris, 1938. Translated by Lloyd Alexander as *Nausea*. New York, 1949.

Réflexions sur la question juive. Paris, 1946. Translated by George J. Becker as *Anti-Semite and Jew*. New York, 1948.

Baudelaire. Paris, 1947. Translated by Martin Turnell under the same title. Norfolk, Conn., 1950.

Huis clos and *Les Mouches*, in *Théâtre*, Vol. I. Paris, 1947. Translated by Stuart Gilbert as *No Exit* and *The Flies*, in *Two Plays*. New York, 1947.

Le Diable et le Bon Dieu. Paris, 1952. Translated by Kitty Black as *Lucifer and the Lord*. London, 1952.

Saint Genet: Comédien et martyre. Paris, 1952. Translated by Bernard Frechtman as *Saint Genet: Actor and Martyr*. New York, 1963.

Works on Sartre

Ayer, A. J., "Novelist-Philosophers: J. P. Sartre." *Horizon*, Vol. 12 (1945), 12–26, 101–110. Highly critical estimate by contemporary analytical philosopher.

Desan, Wilfred, *The Tragic Finale*. Cambridge, Mass., 1954. Careful explication of some central themes of Sartre's ontology.

Jeanson, Francis, *Le Problème morale et la pensée de Sartre*. Paris, 1947. Preface by Sartre. Probably the best treatment of the ethical aspect of Sartre's philosophy.

Murdoch, Iris, *Sartre: Romantic Rationalist*. New Haven, 1953. Balanced appreciation of Sartre as a philosopher and a man of letters.

Spiegelberg, Herbert, "The Phenomenology of Jean Paul Sartre," in *The Phenomenological Movement*, 2 vols. The Hague, 1960. Vol. II, Ch. 10. A detailed bibliography.

Warnock, Mary, *The Philosophy of Sartre*. London, 1965. An analytical philosopher's view of Sartre.

— FREDERICK A. OLAFSON

SARTRE, JEAN-PAUL (UPDATE)

Jean-Paul Sartre (1905–80), wrote several major works after this Encyclopedia's first edition appeared, most notably the second volume of his *Critique of Dialectical Reason* and his multivolume study of Flaubert, *The Family Idiot*. A large amount of material has been published posthumously, including diaries and letters, essays, the scenario for a biographical film on Freud, and the very important *Notebooks for an Ethics,* which he had promised at the end of *Being and Nothingness*. This subsequent work expands and modifies, but does not essentially change, his previous philosophical achievements, especially in philosophical psychology, social ontology, the philosophy of history, and ethics.

Philosophical Psychology

Sartre's concept of freedom expanded beyond the meaning-giving noetic freedom of *Being and Nothingness*. Not only did it come to include the "positive" freedom that overcomes socioeconomic scarcity, but it recognized the limits placed on an agent by class, peers, and especially early childhood experience. This last is particularly evident in his study of Flaubert's life and work. The family emerges as the major vehicle mediating social norms and values. So Sartrean freedom became less individualistic or omnipotent than his earlier work seemed to imply. Still, the maxim of Sartrean humanism remained the conviction that "you can always make something out of what you have been made into." If his vintage existentialist writings stressed the first part of this claim, his later work underscored the second.

His relation to Freud, accordingly, became more nuanced. Though he continued to reject the Freudian unconscious, the concept of comprehension (the translucency of praxis to itself) began to serve as a functional equivalent, especially in *The Family Idiot*. Thus, Flaubert is supposed to have comprehended more than he knew, and the reader of *The Family Idiot* is enabled to know Flaubert better than he knew, but not better than he comprehended, himself. Sartre's quarrel with the unconscious continued to be its supposed denial of human freedom and responsibility, features that comprehension preserves.

Social Ontology

If the vintage existentialist Sartre is a philosopher of consciousness, the later Sartre is a philosopher of praxis, defined as purposive human action in its material environment and sociohistorical context. The shift to praxis breaks the logjam in social ontology created by Sartre's looking/looked-at paradigm of interpersonal relations. Collective action (group praxis) and positive reciprocity are now possible in a way that was unthinkable in *Being and Nothingness*. Free organic praxis, the model of which is the Marxist notion of labor, is dialectical, totalizing, and translucent (it comprehends what it is about). In his later work Sartre accords a threefold primacy—namely, epistemic, ontological, and moral—to individual praxis.

Sartre speaks of the "translucency of individual praxis" as opposed to the opacity of the practico-inert, which he implies is the "intelligible limit of intelligibility." He distinguishes two forms of reason: the analytic, roughly Aristotelian logic, which is structural, abstract, and proper to the practico-inert, and the dialectical, which incorporates temporality in its comprehension and thus is processive and concrete. He re-

spects the explanatory power of each but finds that dialectical reason, as totalizing, is closer to the lived reality of individual praxis. The intelligibility of social and historical causes is an enrichment of constitutive individual praxis.

The ontological primacy of praxis stems from Sartre's claim that "there are only individuals and real relations among them." Individual praxis alone is constitutive of whatever concrete reality obtains. So, abstract and impersonal processes such as colonialism or ideas such as racism, for example, are sustained by innumerable organic praxes that the practico-inert absorbs and transforms. The basic motive for forming groups is to liberate serialized (socially impotent) praxes from the alienating mediation of the practico-inert, supplanting the latter by the practical mediation of the praxes themselves.

If the vintage existentialist Sartre

is a philosopher of consciousness,

the later Sartre is a philosopher of praxis.

Such "dialectical nominalism" avoids methodological and ontological holism and individualism. Its vehicle is the "mediating third," the organic individual acting *as* group member, wherein each organic praxis makes itself "the same" "here" as the other member's praxes "there" in terms of action and practical concern. The model is the combat group or team where each participant becomes a member by acting with the others-as-same in a common project against the others-as-other. There is no collective subject, except organic praxes-in-practical relation. Yet group praxis is a qualitative enrichment of individual praxes, supporting new predicates such as "power" and "right/duty," and not a mere psychological attitude.

Sartre is fundamentally a moralist. His project of "existentializing" Marxist philosophy is an attempt to underscore those factors, abstract but especially concrete, that mediate historical change and individual action, since "it is men whom we judge and not physical forces" (*Search for a Method,* p. 47). The epistemic and ontological primacy culminates in the ethical primacy of individual praxis. Even the most impersonal and "necessary" social processes such as the rise of industrial capitalism or the spread of racist ideologies find their originating and sustaining power in free organic praxis to which moral judgments can be ascribed.

Philosophy of History

Though historicity has been a basic existentialist concept since Martin Heidegger, Sartre gave history short shrift in *Being and Nothingness*. But his *War Diaries* reveal him to have been occupied with the theory of history in response to the successes in that field of his erstwhile friend Raymond Aron, as well as in reaction to the events of the Phony War in which he was then engaged. Only after the war did he resume these reflections, first in the posthumously published *Notebooks for an Ethics* under the rubric of morality and history, and then *ex professo* in the two volumes of his *Critique of Dialectical Reason*. In the latter the challenge is to discover whether history has only one meaning/direction *(sens)* and, if so, what the ontological and socioeconomic conditions for such might be. His hypothesis, and the claims it is only that (though frequent reference to "dialectical necessity" suggests otherwise), is that the fact of material *scarcity* (there are not enough of the world's goods to go around) has turned practico-inert mediation into the vehicle of violence and rendered history as we know it an unrelenting war of all against all.

What one might call his principle of totalization ("a man totalizes his era to the precise extent that he is totalized by it," *The Family Idiot*, 5:394)—a notion anticipated in C. Wright Mills's *The Sociological Imagination*—guides Sartre's approach to History with a Hegelian "H." Thus, Stalin's dialectical, totalizing relation to the Soviet Union in the 1930s (the subject of volume 2 of the *Critique*), or Flaubert's relation to the bourgeois literary world of Second Empire France (especially as analyzed in volume 5 of *The Family Idiot*), enables us to comprehend the agent and the age in spiraling interaction. Facts of individual biography illuminate historical phenomena, and vice versa, by a synthesis of historical materialism and existential psychoanalysis that Sartre calls the "progressive-regressive" method. By this method the investigator uncovers the social conditions—for example, the nature of provincial bourgeois families and of Flaubert's intrafamilial relationships in French society at the time—by a regressive movement in order to chart progressively the agent's interiorization and exteriorization of these conditions in the project of living in this world historically. Rather than merely appealing to examples of historical movements or ideal types, this method aims to comprehend the concrete reality that is the organic individual as a "singular universal" interiorizing and exteriorizing these conditions.

Ethics

With the availability of several manuscripts from the 1960s as well as the *Notebooks for an Ethics* and interviews given by Sartre toward the end of his life it is common to speak of Sartre's three attempts to formulate an ethics. The first is his well-known ethics of authenticity, elaborated during the 1940s. The *Notebooks* corrects many misunderstandings of this ethics and of Sartre's image as a moral relativist and nihilist. A series of unpublished notes for lectures in the 1960s, the second, "dialectical" ethics uses the language of the *Critique* to promote the value of "integral humanity." His so-called ethics of the "We" is a tape dialogue with Benny Lévy cut short by Sartre's death. Still unpublished in its entirety, this third attempt appears to be of mainly biographical interest.

[See also Authenticity; Consciousness in Phenomenology, Sartre; Existentialism; Freud, Sigmund; Heidegger, Martin; Violence.]

BIBLIOGRAPHY

For a complete annotated bibliography of Sartre's works see M. Contat and M. Rybalka, eds., *The Writings of Jean-Paul Sartre* (Evanston, IL, 1973), updated in *Magazine littéraire* 103–4 (1975), 9–49, and by Michel Sicard in *Obliques* 18–19 (May 1979), 331–47. Rybalka and Contat have compiled an additional bibliography of primary and secondary sources published since Sartre's death in *Sartre: Bibliography, 1980–1992* (Bowling Green, OH: CNRS Editions, 1993).

Works by Sartre

Critique de la Raison Dialectique, précédée de questions de méthode, Vol. 1, *Théorie des ensembles pratiques*. Paris, 1960. Reprinted in new annotated edition, 1985. Prefatory essay translated by H. E. Barnes as *Problem of Method* (London, 1964) and *Search for a Method* (New York, 1963). Vol. 1 translated by A. Sheridan-Smith as *Critique of Dialectical Reason*, Vol. 1, *Theory of Practical Ensembles*. London, 1976.

L'Idiot de la famille, 3 vols. Paris, 1971–72. Vol. 3 rev. ed., 1988. Translated by C. Cosman as *The Family Idiot*, 5 vols. Chicago, 1981–93.

Between Existentialism and Marxism, translated by J. Mathews. London, 1974.

Oeuvres Romanesques. Paris, 1981.

Cahiers pour une morale, composed 1947–48. Paris, 1983. Translated by D. Pellauer as *Notebooks for an Ethics*. Chicago, 1992.

Le Scénario Freud. Paris, 1984. Translated by Q. Hoare as *The Freud Scenario*. Chicago, 1985.

Critique de la raison dialectique, Vol. 2 (*inachevé*), *L'Intelligibilité de l'histoire*, edited by A. Elkhaim-Sartre. Paris, 1985. Translated by Q. Hoare as *Critique of Dialectical Reason*, Vol. 2 (unfinished), *The Intelligibility of History*. London, 1991.

Ecrits de jeunesse, edited by M. Contat and M. Rybalka. Paris, 1990.

Works on Sartre

Anderson, T. C. *Sartre's Two Ethics. From Authenticity to Integral Humanity*. Chicago, 1993.

Aronson, R. *Sartre's Second Critique*. Chicago, 1987.

Barnes, H. E. *Sartre and Flaubert*. Chicago, 1981.

Busch, T. *The Power of Consciousness and the Force of Circumstances in Sartre's Philosophy*. Bloomington, IN, 1990.

Catalano, J. *A Commentary on Sartre's Critique of Dialectical Reason*, Vol. 1. Chicago, 1986.

Cumming, R. *Phenomenology and Deconstruction*, Vol. 2, *Method and Imagination*. Chicago, 1992.

Detmer, D. *Freedom as Value. A Critique of the Ethical Theory of Jean-Paul Sartre.* La Salle, IL, 1988.

Flynn, T. R. *Sartre and Marxist Existentialism: The Test Case of Collective Responsibility.* Chicago, 1984.

Hollier, D. *Politique de la prose: Jean-Paul Sartre et l'an quarante.* Paris, 1982. Translated by J. Mehlman as *The Politics of Prose: Essay on Sartre.* Minneapolis, 1986.

Howells, C., ed. *The Cambridge Companion to Sartre.* Cambridge, 1992.

Lévy, B. *Le Nom de l'homme: Dialogue avec Sartre.* Lagrasse, 1984.

McBride, W. *Sartre's Political Theory.* Bloomington, IN, 1991.

Schilpp, P. *The Philosophy of Jean-Paul Sartre.* LaSalle, IL, 1981.

— THOMAS R. FLYNN

SCHOPENHAUER, ARTHUR

Arthur Schopenhauer (1788–1860), was a German philosopher of pessimism who gave the will a leading place in his metaphysics. He was born in Danzig. His father, a successful businessman of partly Dutch ancestry, was an admirer of Voltaire and was imbued with a keen dislike of absolutist governments. When Danzig surrendered to the Prussians in 1793, the family moved to Hamburg and remained there until the father's death (apparently by suicide) in 1805. Schopenhauer's mother was a novelist who in later years established a salon in Weimar, which brought him into contact with a number of literary figures, including Goethe. His relations with his mother, however, were bitter and antagonistic and eventually led to a more or less complete estrangement.

EDUCATION. Schopenhauer's early education was somewhat unconventional. He spent two years in France in the charge of a friend of his father, and for another period he accompanied his parents on a prolonged tour of France, England (where he attended school in London for several months), Switzerland, and Austria. After his father's death he was tutored privately in the classics for a time and then entered the University of Göttingen as a medical student, studying, among other subjects, physics, chemistry, and botany. At Göttingen he first read Plato and Kant, and the powerful and lasting impression their writings made upon him directed his interests decisively toward philosophy. In consequence he left Göttingen in 1811 for Berlin, which was at that time the chief philosophical center in Germany, and worked there for two years, attending the lectures of Fichte and Schleiermacher (both of whom he found profoundly disappointing) and making preparatory notes for a doctoral thesis. When the uprising against Napoleon led to the closing of the university, Schopenhauer, for whom nationalistic sentiment held little appeal, retired to Rudolstadt to write his thesis, subsequently published there in 1813 under the title of *Über die vierfache Wurzel des Satzes vom zureichenden*

Schopenhauer lived a solitary life, profoundly resentful at the lack of recognition he felt was his due. (Corbis/Bettmann)

Grunde (On the Fourfold Root of the Principle of Sufficient Reason).

EARLY CAREER. Apart from producing a short book on the perception of color, *Über das Sehn und die Farben* (Leipzig, 1816), which was inspired by a previous essay on the same subject by Goethe, Schopenhauer employed the next four years writing his principal work, *Die Welt als Wille und Vorstellung (The World as Will and Idea).* From the very first stages of the composition of this work, Schopenhauer believed that the ideas he was striving to express were of major importance, and when it was published at Leipzig in 1818 (dated 1819), he was confident that its significance would immediately be recognized. In this expectation he was to be quickly disappointed; the scanty reviews his book received were generally tepid in tone, and the number of copies sold was small. Nevertheless, its publication helped him to obtain the post of lecturer at the University of Berlin, where he chose to give lectures at the same hours as Hegel, who was then at the height of his reputation and popularity. From the start, Schopenhauer advertised his opposition to Hegelian conceptions. He spoke of sophists who, having arisen after Kant, "first exhausted the thinking power of their time with barbarous and mysterious speech, then scared it away from philosophy and brought the study into discredit," and he made it clear that he regarded his own mission as one of repairing the damage that had been done. Schopenhauer's lectures, however, were a failure; Hegel's authority was too firmly established to be undermined in this manner, and Schopenhauer's audience dwindled away.

LATER CAREER. Schopenhauer made no further attempt to establish himself academically. From then on he lived a solitary life, profoundly resentful at the lack of the recognition he felt to be his due and confirmed in his opinion that the dominant Hegelian philosophy was the product of a charlatan who, by an artful combination of sophistry and rhetoric, had succeeded in corrupting the intellects of an entire generation. Despite his disappointment, however, Schopenhauer continued to write, producing books that were in effect elaborations and developments of themes already adumbrated in his main work. He published an essay entitled *Über den Willen in der Natur* (Frankfurt, 1836); and a volume on ethics and the problem of free will, *Die beiden Grundprobleme der Ethik* (Frankfurt, 1841), which contained the two essays "Über die Freiheit des Willens" (1839) and "Über die Grundlage der Moral" (1840). In 1844 he brought out a second edition of *Die Welt als Wille und Vorstellung*, greatly expanded by the addition of fifty supplementary chapters. He also contemplated translating Kant's *Critique of Pure Reason* into English and Hume's *Dialogues Concerning Natural Religion* (a work he greatly admired) into German. There can be little doubt that he would have performed both of these tasks well, for his knowledge of English was excellent; but unfortunately nothing came of either project. Finally, Schopenhauer published a collection of essays and aphorisms called *Parerga und Paralipomena* (2 vols., Berlin, 1851), and with this work he began to be widely known. Discussions of his ideas appeared in foreign as well as in German periodicals, and his system was made the subject of lectures in a number of major European universities. By the time of his death in Frankfurt, he had a growing circle of admirers in England, Russia, and the United States, while nearer home the influence of his writings was soon to show itself in the work of such thinkers as Nietzsche and Jakob Burckhardt.

CHARACTER. Schopenhauer's personality, which is reflected in much of his writing, was complex and compounded of curiously diverse elements. Although intellectually self-assured to the point of arrogance, he had a brooding, introspective disposition, and he betrayed an extreme susceptibility to irrational fears and anxieties. Thus, he always slept with a loaded pistol near him, and he took compulsive precautions against disease; he once remarked that if nothing alarmed him, he grew alarmed at this very condition—"as if there must still be something of which I am only ignorant for a time." His manner could be truculent and overbearing; as many of his aphorisms make clear, his view of others was colored by a deep suspiciousness and cynicism, and his general outlook on life and existence was unrelievedly pessimistic. Yet this did not prevent him from taking pleasure in many things—art and music, good food and wine, travel, and, despite his notorious essay on the subject, women. And while he detested bores, in company that he found sympathetic he appears to have been a lively and entertaining talker, displaying a sharp, satirical wit.

The Nature of Philosophical Thinking

Schopenhauer's philosophy is best approached from a position that clearly recognizes his indebtedness to Kant, whom he believed to have been indisputably the greatest thinker of modern times. Schopenhauer's chief charge against his own philosophical contemporaries in Germany (Schelling, Fichte, and Hegel)—was that under the pretense of carrying forward and developing Kantian ideas, they had in fact attempted to philosophize in a fashion that Kant himself had ruled out as wholly inadmissible. For if Kant had shown anything, it was that metaphysical speculation in the old "transcendent" sense was useless as a means of achieving knowledge of what lay beyond all human experience. Such knowledge is in principle unattainable, and it followed that any philosopher, whatever his procedure might be, who tried to establish such things as the existence of God and the immortality of the soul was engaged in a hopeless quest. Rationalist metaphysicians like Descartes had employed deductive a priori arguments in an endeavor to prove certain fundamental propositions of theology, and Kant had sufficiently exposed the inadequacy of these arguments by a series of devastating refutations. Yet according to Schopenhauer, Kant's strictures had not prevented some of his self-appointed successors from speaking as if they had mysterious access to truths necessarily outside the range of human cognition—a "little window opening on to the supernatural world," as it were. He suggested, too, that writing in this way appeared more expedient to many academic teachers of philosophy than the honest alternative of expounding truthfully and directly the anti-dogmatic theses contained in the *Critique of Pure Reason.*

While he accepted Kant's reasons for rejecting metaphysical theorizing in the sense described above, Schopenhauer was nevertheless far from wishing to claim that all philosophical speculation concerning the ultimate nature of the world must be deemed illicit and misconceived. The impulse to seek some general interpretation of reality and of the place of human existence within it was too deeply embedded in the human mind to be totally ignored or set aside. Man, Schopenhauer held, is an *animal metaphysicum,* a creature who cannot avoid wondering at the existence of the world and raising questions concerning its fundamental character and significance—questions which empirical science is unable adequately to resolve, for they lie beyond its sphere.

Schopenhauer believed

that the ideas he was striving to express in

The World as Will and Idea *(1818)*

were of major importance,

and he was confident that its significance

would immediately be recognized.

Religion, it is true, attempts in its own way to meet this pervasive need, although not in a manner susceptible to rational justification or certification. For the tenets and concepts of religious faiths, whatever those who subscribe to them may believe to the contrary, can never be more than "allegories" or imaginative figures, and treating them as if they represented literal truths about a higher order of things leads straightway to manifest absurdities and contradictions. By contrast, the concern of philosophical thinking is not with the metaphorical intimation of ideas which are beyond the grasp of the human intellect; rather, such thinking aims at truth *sensu proprio.* It follows, therefore, that any solution of "the riddle of the world" that philosophy purports to provide must not be one that involves overstepping the boundaries within which all human knowledge is set and confined. The determination of exactly where these boundaries lie is accordingly of primary importance as a preliminary to all philosophical inquiry.

Perception and Thought

Schopenhauer's theory of knowledge may be said to start with Kant's distinction between *phenomena* (what appears to a perceiving mind) and *noumena* (things as they are in themselves). In our perceptual consciousness of the world, we are in fact aware of it only as mediated through our sense organs and intellect—a point Schopenhauer expressed by saying that, so conceived, the world is "idea" or "representation" *(Vorstellung).* Moreover, everything that presents itself to us in perception necessarily conforms to a certain formal and categorial framework that underlies and finds expression in all departments of our common-sense and scientific knowledge. Thus Schopenhauer was at one with Kant in holding that the human mind cannot (as the British empiricists had suggested) be envisaged as a mere passive recipient of sense impressions, but on the contrary plays an essentially active part in shaping and organizing the sensory material. It is the structure of the intellect, comprising "sensibility" and "understanding," which ensures that this sensory material apprises us of a realm of external objective phenomena, spatially and temporally ordered and standing in determinate causal relations both with one another and with ourselves as percipients. Space and time as forms of sensibility, together with causality considered as the sole category of the understanding (here Schopenhauer diverged from Kant), are therefore "subjective in origin," while at the same time they are necessary conditions of our knowledge of the world as idea. According to Schopenhauer, it is also the case that their valid employment is restricted to this sphere; they have no application to anything not given, or that could not be given, in sense experience.

Schopenhauer distinguished a further class of ideas, namely, what he termed "ideas of Reflection," or sometimes "ideas of ideas" *(Vorstellungen von Vorstellungen).* It is in terms of these that we think about and communicate the contents of our phenomenal experience. In other words, they are the general concepts by virtue of which we can classify phenomena according to common features that are of interest or importance to us, forming thereby a conceptual structure or system which may be said to mirror or copy the empirical world. The function of this system is essentially a practical one; it provides a means of memorizing, and generalizing from, our observations of how things behave under varying conditions, and hence of putting to use what we learn from experience. Schopenhauer insisted, moreover, that this system cannot legitimately be separated from the foundation of empirical reality upon which it is based, and he claimed that concepts and abstract notions that cannot be traced back to experience are comparable to bank notes "issued by a firm which has nothing but other paper obligations to back it with." Consequently, metaphysical theories that pretend to offer an account of the world purely a priori, and that in doing so employ terms or propositions not susceptible to empirical interpretation, are empty of cognitive content; they "move in the air without support." Indeed, such theories often represent no more than the development, by laborious deductive steps, of the implications of a small group of initial axioms or definitions, yielding systems of empty tautologies.

Thus far, Schopenhauer would appear to have placed fairly stringent limits upon the scope of human inquiry. Attempts to transcend these limits by appealing to the resources of deductive reasoning alone are necessarily impossible, since they involve fundamentally wrong ideas concerning the nature of logical inference. These ideas can never provide us with information of which we were not previously cognizant, for such inference merely makes explicit what is already implicitly asserted in the premises from which it proceeds. Equally, there can be no justification for trying to extend the use of nonlogical, formative principles like the principle of causality in order to establish matters of nonempirical fact, after the manner of some earlier metaphysicians. Schopenhauer even accused Kant of inconsistency in this matter, on the ground that he wrote as though the existence of things-in-themselves, which for Kant are by definition incapable of being experienced, could be validly inferred from the phenomenal data, thereby disregarding his own prohibition. Nonetheless, Schopenhauer considered that the Kantian notion of the thing-in-itself remained a fertile one. Properly conceived, it offered the needed clue to the discovery of a legitimate and correct philosophical interpretation of existence.

The Will

According to Schopenhauer, it is not true that the thing-in-itself, the noumenal reality that underlies the world of phenomenal appearances, is beyond the range of all possible human experience. To realize this, it is necessary to take account of the facts of self-consciousness, that is, our own intimate knowledge of ourselves. Self-awareness has two distinct aspects. From one point of view, namely, the standpoint of ordinary perception, I cannot avoid regarding myself as an "object," as much a physical entity as a building or a tree is. In this sense, I necessarily conform to the conditions that constitute the "world as idea" in general; I am a body that occupies space, endures through time, and causally responds to stimuli.

INDIVIDUAL WILL. My inner experience also assures me that I am nevertheless more than "an object among objects," for I do not appear to myself under this aspect alone. I am also aware of myself from within as a self-

moving, active being whose overt perceptible behavior directly expresses my will. This inner consciousness that each one of us has of himself as will is primitive and irreducible. Thus, Schopenhauer claimed that the will reveals itself immediately to everyone as the "in-itself" of his own phenomenal being and that the awareness we have of ourselves as will is quite different from the awareness we have of ourselves as body. At the same time, however, he emphatically denied that the operations of a man's will and the movements he makes with his body are two distinct series of events—events of the first kind being thought of as causally productive of events of the second kind. Schopenhauer believed that dualistic conceptions of the relation of will and body, deriving largely from Descartes, had wrought havoc in philosophy, and he argued instead that a man's body is simply the "objectification" of his will as it appears under the conditions of external perception; what I will and what in physical terms I do are one and the same thing, but viewed from different standpoints.

THE WILL IN NATURE. What has just been discussed represents the cornerstone of Schopenhauer's metaphysic. For it was his contention that we should not assume the above distinction between the phenomenal appearance and the thing as it is in itself to apply only insofar as we ourselves are concerned. On the contrary, just as my own phenomenal being and activity is ultimately intelligible as the expression of my inner will, so may the rest of the phenomenal world be understood to share the same fundamental character that we recognize to be ours. Here was the "great extension" of the concept of will whereby Schopenhauer claimed that all phenomena—human and nonhuman, animate and inanimate—might be interpreted in a way that gave the world as a whole a new dimension of significance and that at the same time was not open to the insuperable objections vitiating traditional metaphysical doctrines. The latter claim may reasonably be doubted. Schopenhauer often displayed considerable perspicacity in detecting errors and inconsistencies in the theories of other philosophers, but he did not always show a comparable critical acumen with regard to his own ideas. Even so, the picture he drew of the world, in accordance with his conception of its inner essence, is not without a certain novelty and horrific fascination, standing as it does at the opposite pole from all those metaphysical systems which have, in one way or another, endeavored to present ultimate reality as if it were the incarnation of rational or moral order. For Schopenhauer, the real was not the rational (as Hegel, for instance, implied that it was); on the contrary, "will" was for him the name of a nonrational force, a blind, striving power whose operations are without ultimate purpose or design. So portrayed, nature in all its aspects, ranging from the simplest physical structures to the most complex and highly developed organisms, takes on the character of an endless, and in the last analysis meaningless, struggle for existence, in which all is stress, conflict, and tension. The mechanistic models, the rationalistic schemes and constructions, in terms of which we find it useful to try to systematize the phenomenal data for scientific and practical purposes, merely serve to disguise from view the true nature of the underlying reality; the proper task of philosophy lies, not in seeking (as so many previous thinkers had sought) to reinforce these misconceptions by consoling and sophistical arguments, but rather in removing the veil of deception and setting the truth in a clear light.

HUMAN NATURE. As indicated above, Schopenhauer took as the starting point of his theory of the world the nature of man himself, regarded as the embodiment of will. Man is the microcosm in which all that is fundamental to reality as a whole (the macrocosm) may be plainly discerned. And it is in connection with what he wrote about human nature that Schopenhauer's doctrine of the will can perhaps be most profitably considered. For this doctrine, far from being merely an extravagant philosophical fantasy, foreshadows much that was central to the later development of psychological theory; it represents a highly significant contribution with genuinely revolutionary implications.

Schopenhauer's theory of knowledge may be said

to start with Kant's distinction between

phenomena *(what appears to a perceiving mind)*

and noumena *(things as they are in themselves).*

Will and Intellect. What Schopenhauer had to say on the subject of human nature revolved about his conception of the role of the intellect in human behavior. We like to suppose that in principle, everything we do lies within the province of our reason and is subject to our control; only if this is so can we deem ourselves to be truly our own masters. Traditionally, philosophers have given their support to such beliefs; according to Schopenhauer, however, the situation is quite the reverse. For the will is not, as Descartes and others have taught, a sort of instrument or component of the intellectual faculty, mysteriously controlling our actions from on high by means of independent acts of rational choice. As has already been seen, Schopenhauer argued that will and body are simply the same thing viewed under different

aspects, and he further claimed that the intellect, far from being the original source and spring of the will and the master of the body, is in fact no more than the will's servant and appendage. From an epistemological point of view, this governance of the intellect by the will manifests itself in the forms of knowledge under which the world appears to us—for example, as a causally governed system. To see things as causes or effects is to see them in terms of their potential uses, that is, as possible means to the gratification of the will.

Motivation. According to Schopenhauer, however, the primacy of will exhibits itself in a number of other important ways. Thus he gave various illustrations, drawn from everyday experience, of the manner in which we are often quite unaware of the true import and significance of our responses to circumstances and situations. Believing ourselves to be activated by some consideration that we find acceptable on moral or other grounds, we miss the real motive and might well be shocked or embarrassed if we knew it. Although we are inwardly and immediately aware of ourselves *as* will, our own consciously formulated conceptions of what we desire or what we are intending are, in fact, a highly unreliable guide when the question under consideration is *what* we will. Sometimes, indeed, Schopenhauer seems to have been making the extreme claim that conscious acts of choice never really determine behavior at all. He suggested in a number of instances that our conduct is not ultimately decided by resolves intellectually arrived at after weighing the pros and cons of alternative courses of action; the real decision is made by the will below the level of rationally reflective consciousness, the sole role of the intellect being to put before the will the various possibilities that lie open to the agent and to estimate the consequences that would ensue upon their actualization. In this sense, we never really form more than a "conjecture" of what we shall do in the future, although we often take such conjectures for resolves; what we have decided to do becomes finally clear to us only a posteriori, through the deed we perform. As it stands, this doctrine gives rise to obvious difficulties. *Some* cases doubtless occur that we should be inclined to describe in some such manner as Schopenhauer recommends, but it does not follow that every case of deliberate action can be so characterized. Indeed, it may be claimed against all positions of this sort that it is only in virtue of our knowledge of what it is to act in accordance with consciously formed choices that the explanation of certain actions in terms of secret or concealed determinations of the will becomes intelligible.

Unconscious Mental Activity. The above-mentioned difficulties do not invalidate Schopenhauer's exceptionally perceptive and shrewd observations regarding much human motivation. These observations retain their importance even if the more bizarre speculations he based upon them are rejected; and Schopenhauer in fact connected them with a wider theory of human nature that, considering the time in which he wrote, manifested an astonishing prescience. According to this theory, the entire perspective in terms of which we are disposed to view our characters and doings is distorted. We customarily think of ourselves as being essentially free and rational agents, whereas in fact the principal sources and springs of our conduct consist in deep-lying tendencies and drives of whose character we are often wholly unaware. "Consciousness," Schopenhauer wrote, "is the mere surface of our mind, of which, as of the earth, we do not know the inside but only the crust," and in consequence we often put entirely false constructions upon the behavior in which these basic impulses are expressed. He suggested, moreover, that the ignorance we display, the rationalizations which in all innocence we provide, may themselves have a motive, although not one we are aware of. Thus, he frequently wrote of the will as preventing the rise to consciousness of thoughts and desires that, if known, would arouse feelings of humiliation, embarrassment, or shame. Another example of the same process is to be found in instances of memory failure. It is not a mere accident that we do not remember certain things, since there may be powerful inducements for us not to do so; events and experiences can be "completely suppressed," becoming for us as if they had never taken place, simply because unconsciously we feel them to be unendurable. And in extreme cases this can lead to a form of insanity, with fantasies and delusions replacing what has thus been extruded from consciousness.

Schopenhauer referred to sexuality

as a "demon"

that strives to pervert, confuse,

and overthrow everything.

Sexuality. Freud himself recognized the similarity between ideas like those above and some of the leading conceptions of psychoanalytical theory. Certainly there are striking parallels, and perhaps most obviously between what Schopenhauer had to say about the sexual instinct and the Freudian account of libido. For instance, Schopenhauer claimed that the sexual urge represents the "focus of the will." Apart from the instinct to survive, it is the most powerful motive of all and exercises a pervasive influence in every area of human

life. Yet despite this, the amount of attention sexuality had received from most philosophers and psychologists had been remarkably small; it is as though a veil had been thrown over it, through which, however, the subject kept showing through. Nevertheless, Schopenhauer was far from extolling the operations of the sexual drive. Although he thought it necessary to expose honestly the stark reality that human beings seek to hide by falsely romanticizing and idealizing their primitive passions, he also made it clear that he considered sexuality to be a source of great mischief and suffering. Thus he referred to it as a "demon" that "strives to pervert, confuse and overthrow everything," and spoke of sexual desires as being inherently incapable of achieving lasting satisfaction; according to Schopenhauer, the end of love is always disillusion. In other words, here, as elsewhere, conformity to the dictates of the will ultimately results in unhappiness, which is the universal condition of human existence.

PESSIMISM AND ANTIRATIONALISM. In sum, Schopenhauer's doctrine of the will constituted, in a variety of ways, a reaction against the then dominant eighteenth-century, or "Enlightenment," conceptions of human nature. He not only rejected the Cartesian belief in the primacy of intellect or reason in man, but also, by implication, repudiated the "mechanistic" model according to which writers like Hume sought to explain human personality and motivation in terms of the combination and association of atomistically conceived impressions and ideas. In place of this model, he substituted one of dynamic drive and function that was oriented toward the biological rather than the physical sciences and that stressed the importance of unconscious rather than conscious mental processes. Furthermore, Schopenhauer's writings represent a complete departure from the strain of optimism that underlay so much eighteenth-century thinking about history and society. Schopenhauer utterly rejected such ideas as the inevitability of human progress and the perfectibility of man and replaced them with a picture of mankind in general as doomed to an eternal round of torment and misery. Radical changes in the social structure, however "scientifically" applied, would solve nothing, for the evil condition of life as we find it is merely the reflection of the aggressive and libidinous urges rooted in our own natures. All that can usefully be employed are certain palliatives in the form of social and legal controls which give the individual minimal protection against the incursions of his neighbors; and with such measures men have long been familiar.

Art and Aesthetic Experience

The pre-eminent position that Schopenhauer assigned to art (certainly no other major philosopher has elevated it to a higher status) is not difficult to understand in the light of his general theory. In this theory, our modes of knowledge and understanding, as well as the activities in which we normally engage, are regarded as being determined by the will. Scientific inquiry was the supreme instance of this, since (Schopenhauer believed) its essential function was one of providing, through the discovery of empirical uniformities, practical techniques for satisfying our wants and desires.

THE AESTHETIC ATTITUDE. The artist's concern, however, is not with action, or the possibility of action, at all, but with what Schopenhauer termed "contemplation" or "will-less perception." This type of perception must not be confused with perception of the ordinary everyday kind, wherein things are looked at from the standpoint of practical interest and appear under the aspect of particular phenomenal objects. For it is the mark of aesthetic contemplation that in the enjoyment of artistic experience "we keep the sabbath of the penal servitude of willing"; the world is seen in abstraction from the various aims, desires, and anxieties that accompany our normal apprehension of it, with the result that it presents itself to us in a completely different light.

It is a further consequence of such detachment (and on this point Schopenhauer followed Kant) that all judgments of taste or aesthetic value are disinterested: they cannot have as their basis some titillation of sensual appetite, for instance; nor can they be grounded upon considerations of social utility, or even of moral purpose. To speak of a natural scene or of a work of art or literature as "beautiful" is to judge it in and for itself, and quite outside the framework of cause and consequence within which our ordinary perceptual judgments have their natural place and from which they derive their significance.

THE AESTHETIC OBJECT. The claim that aesthetic awareness presupposes a distinctive attitude of mind and attention is clearly separable from the contention, also advanced by Schopenhauer, that in such awareness the content of our experience is of a radically different kind from that involved in ordinary sense perception. Surprising as it may seem in the light of some of his earlier pronouncements, Schopenhauer held that the subjective conditions which define and universally determine our perception at the everyday level are wholly in abeyance in the case of aesthetic apprehension, and that to this complete "change in the subject" there is a corresponding change in the object. As aesthetic observers, we are no longer confronted with a multiplicity of individual things and events that are spatiotemporally and causally interrelated, but instead are presented with the "permanent essential forms of the world and all its phenomena," which Schopenhauer termed the "Ideas"

(*Ideen*). This conception of fundamental Ideas, which Schopenhauer adapted from Plato to serve the purposes of his own, very different, theory of art, helps us to understand why he regarded art not merely as a kind of knowledge, but as a kind of knowledge vastly superior to any found in the sphere of the natural sciences. In his view, the natural sciences can never do more than discover regularities at the stage of phenomenal appearance, whereas works of genuine art exhibit to the beholder the nature of the archetypal forms of which the particular phenomena of sense perception are necessarily incomplete and inadequate expressions. Artistic productions may, in fact, be said to be the vehicles through which the artist communicates his profound discoveries and insights and thereby enables others to share his vision.

Schopenhauer's doctrine of the will constituted a reaction against the then dominant eighteenth-century, or "Enlightenment," conceptions of human nature.

The notion that the proper objects of artistic perception are Platonic Ideas in the sense described above gives rise to obvious objections. It certainly fits somewhat uneasily into Schopenhauer's system insofar as that originally seemed to be based upon the postulate that phenomenal representation and noumenal will between them exhaust the field of possible human knowledge. And quite apart from this, the theory of Ideas raises problems on its own account. It appears paradoxical, for instance, to suggest that a picture of, say, apples in a bowl is not a picture of things of the sort we can all see and touch in the ordinary way, but of something set mysteriously apart from these and situated in a realm beyond the range of normal vision. Even so, it is at least to Schopenhauer's credit that he recognized some of the difficulties presented by much that we are prone to think and say about artistic portrayals of experience. The concept of perception, for instance, seems to play a significantly different role in the context of aesthetic appraisal and criticism from the role it plays in other contexts. Again, the specific sense in which certain art forms (painting, for example) are concerned with "representing" reality is notoriously difficult to analyze. The claim that the artist sees something literally distinct from what we ordinarily see is, no doubt, hard to defend; on the other hand, the (different) claim that he sees and is able to portray ordinary things in unfamiliar ways, and under fresh and revealing aspects, appears to contain an obvious truth. Schopenhauer himself never clearly distinguished between these two claims. Theoretically he subscribed to the first, but much that he said in his discussion of concrete cases accords better with the second. Not only did he often stress the particularity of the artist's observation of phenomena; he also suggested that the artist's unique mode of presenting individual objects, scenes, or situations succeeds in illuminating for us whole ranges of our experience to which we have previously been blind. He argued, however, that it would be a mistake to suppose that we can ever convey by verbal description what we learn from our direct acquaintance with particular works of art. For what these works communicate will in the end always elude anything we try to say about them. "The transition from the Idea to the concept," he wrote, "is always a fall."

Schopenhauer thought that

all forms of artistic activity

—with one important exception—

could be explained in terms of his theory of Ideas.

The exception was music.

MUSIC. Schopenhauer thought that all forms of artistic activity—with one important exception—could be understood and explained in terms of his theory of Ideas. The exception was music. Music is not concerned with the representation of phenomena or the fundamental forms that underlie phenomena, but has as its subject the will itself, the nature of which it expresses directly and immediately. Thus, of all the arts, music stands closest to the ultimate reality of things which we all bear within ourselves and speaks "the universal imageless language of the heart." Schopenhauer's ideas, in this instance and in general, produced a deep impression upon Richard Wagner, who in his opera *Tristan und Isolde* tried to realize in musical form the leading conceptions of Schopenhauer's theory of the world. It is a curious irony that Schopenhauer, far from reciprocating Wagner's admiration, spoke of his music with actual distaste.

Ethics and Mysticism

Although the world, viewed from a purely contemplative standpoint, presents a spectacle that can be aesthetically enjoyed, it does not follow that the operations of the agency which underlies all that we perceive can afford us any kind of moral guidance or solace. On the contrary, the ethical significance of existence lies in its ultimate horror. Unlike many other metaphysicians, Schopenhauer concluded from his system, not that we should gratefully seek to make our lives conform to the pattern implicit in the nature of reality, but rather that true salvation consists in a total rejection of this pattern. The moral worth of individuals lies in their capacity to liberate themselves from the pressures and urges of the rapacious will.

INALTERABILITY OF CHARACTER. It is not altogether easy to see how liberation is possible. Schopenhauer had claimed that human beings, like everything else in nature, are in essence expressions of will. How, then, can they become otherwise? Furthermore, he insisted upon a strictly deterministic interpretation of human character and action, one that makes the type of freedom of choice postulated by traditional libertarian doctrines inconceivable. What a person does is always and necessarily a manifestation of his inner disposition, which remains fixed and is unalterable by any resolutions he may form to be different. The individual discovers what he is really like by observing his behavior over the course of his life. He will find that this behavior conforms to certain invariant patterns of reaction and response, so that if the same circumstances recur, his conduct in the face of them will be the same as it was before. Such consistent behavior patterns are the outward manifestation of the individual noumenal essence, or timeless character, which each man is in himself—a conception Schopenhauer claimed to have derived from Kant's discussion of the foundations of moral responsibility, though the consequences he drew from it were in fact far removed from any drawn by Kant. Nor can some of these consequences be said to have been logically very happy; for instance, Schopenhauer seems to have employed the notion of a man's character so elastically that it ruled out the possibility of any imaginable state of affairs falsifying his thesis concerning its innate and unchangeable nature.

ETHICAL VARIATION. Schopenhauer's claim that a man cannot change his character at will does not, however, commit him to the view that the dispositions of different individuals do not show significant ethical variations. For an explanation of the fact that there are good as well as evil persons in the world, he returned to the fundamental tenets of his metaphysic. It is a feature of the good, as contrasted with the self-centered or egotistical, individual that he comprehends himself and his relations with others from a "higher" standpoint, which enables him to recognize, however obscurely or inarticulately, the common unitary nature shared by all things. Egoism rests upon the assumption that the individual is a self-sufficient unit, to which all else is foreign. But the individual appears to be set apart from his fellows by an impassable gulf only when apprehended in accordance with the spatiotemporal scheme that informs our everyday "will-governed" way of looking at things. A profounder insight, such as is exhibited intuitively in the behavior of the just and compassionate man who "draws less distinction between himself and others than is usually done," involves awareness of the illusory character of the phenomenal world. Those who possess this awareness no longer see their fellow creatures as alien objects to be overcome or manipulated in pursuit of their own egocentric aims, but rather as "themselves once more," homogeneous with their own being and nature. Thus, in the last analysis, the distinction between virtue and vice has its source in radically different modes of viewing those around us; and this distinction could, Schopenhauer believed, be adequately explicated and justified in the terms provided by his own philosophical system.

Schopenhauer frequently quoted the

Brahman formula tat tvam asi *("that thou art")*

when discussing the metaphysical unity of things

that underlies the realm of appearance.

DENIAL OF THE WILL. Schopenhauer frequently quoted the Brahman formula, *tat tvam asi* ("that thou art"), when discussing the metaphysical unity of things that underlies the realm of appearance. Indeed, all his writings on ethical and related subjects show affinities with the doctrines advanced in the Upanishads and in Buddhist texts—affinities which he freely acknowledged. Like the Indian teachers, he considered all human life to be enmeshed in suffering, and following them, he often used the word *māyā* to refer to the illusory phenomenal world to which, as empirical individuals, we belong. Total release from the enslavement of the will, as compared with the identification of himself with others that is displayed in the conduct of the morally good man, in fact occurs only when a person finally ceases to feel any attachment to earthly things and when all desire to participate in the life of the world completely vanishes. Such an attitude of mind, which Schopenhauer attributed to ascetics and mystics of all times, becomes possible when a man's will "turns and denies itself," and when what in the eyes of ordinary men is the very essence and substance of reality appears to him as "nothing." But Schopenhauer was insistent

that this "turning of the will," which is a highly mysterious process, is not something a man can bring about through his own deliberate volition, since the process involves the complete "abolition" of his previous personality. This "turning of the will" comes to him, as it were, "from outside" and springs from an insight which wholly transcends the will and the world. Such mystical insight, moreover, is necessarily incommunicable and indescribable; all knowledge, including that attainable by philosophy, here reaches its limit, and we are left with only "myths and meaningless words" which express no positive content. "The nature of things before or beyond the world, and consequently beyond the will," Schopenhauer declared at the close of his main work, "is open to no investigation." The end of philosophy is silence.

Importance and Influence

Schopenhauer's critics have not failed to draw attention to discrepancies and inconsistencies in his system. These certainly exist, and his natural clarity of expression, which contrasts so sharply with the obscure and cloudy terminology favored by his philosophical contemporaries in Germany, makes them comparatively easy to detect. On the other hand, these discrepancies should not be allowed to stand in the way of a proper appreciation of what was important and influential in Schopenhauer's thought. The nineteenth century witnessed a decline in the fascination that achievements in physics and mathematics had previously exercised over philosophy, and there was a tendency in speculative thought to explore new ways of interpreting and conceptualizing human life and experience. In this development Schopenhauer played a central role. Both through his theory of will, with its psychological implications, and also through the new metaphysical status he gave to art, he helped to bring about a profound shift in the intellectual and imaginative climate. In this connection, the impression made by his ideas upon novelists like Tolstoy, Conrad, Proust, and Thomas Mann is particularly noteworthy. Among philosophers, the impact of Schopenhauer's thought was weaker and certainly never approached that produced by Hegel's writings; while in more recent times, when philosophical speculation in general has been at a discount, he has attracted little interest. Yet such neglect is undeserved, and the significance of his contribution should not be underestimated. He realized more fully than the majority of his contemporaries the implications of the Kantian critique of traditional metaphysics, and some of the things he himself had to say about the nature of a priori knowledge have a strikingly modern ring. Again, it is worth emphasizing his "instrumentalist" view of human thinking, which anticipated William James and the American pragmatist school, and also his highly perceptive attacks upon the Cartesian theory of personality and self-consciousness, which in important respects foreshadowed present-day approaches to problems in the philosophy of mind. (In particular, his theory of the double knowledge we have of ourselves as agents in the world has interesting contemporary analogues.) Finally, it should be remembered that possibly the greatest philosopher of modern times, Ludwig Wittgenstein, read Schopenhauer and was influenced by him. The extent of this influence appears most clearly in the notebooks Wittgenstein kept during World War I (*Notebooks 1914–1916*, translated by G. E. M. Anscombe, Oxford, 1961), but signs of it are also to be found in the *Tractatus Logico-philosophicus* (translated by D. F. Pears and B. F. McGuiness, London, 1961), particularly in the sections on ethics and the limits of language in the latter part of the work.

BIBLIOGRAPHY

Works by Schopenhauer

The most recent edition of Schopenhauer's collected works in German is *Sämtliche Werke*, A. Hübscher, ed., 2d ed., 7 vols. (Wiesbaden, 1946–1950).

There are two English translations of *Die Welt als Wille und Vorstellung: The World as Will and Idea*, translated by R. B. Haldane and J. Kemp, 3 vols. (London, 1883), and *The World as Will and Representation*, translated by E. F. J. Payne, 2 vols. (Indian Hills, Colo., 1958). Translations of other writings of Schopenhauer include *On the Fourfold Root of the Principle of Sufficient Reason and On the Will in Nature*, translated by K. Hillebrand (London, 1888); *The Basis of Morality*, translated by A. B. Bullock (London, 1903); *Selected Essays of Schopenhauer*, translated by T. B. Saunders (London, 1951); *Essay on the Freedom of the Will*, translated by K. Kolenda (New York, 1960); and *The Will to Live: Selected Writings of Arthur Schopenhauer*, Richard Taylor, ed. (New York, 1962).

Works on Schopenhauer

Modern commentaries on Schopenhauer are scarce, but F. C. Copleston, *Schopenhauer, Philosopher of Pessimism* (London, 1946), provides a careful and levelheaded survey from a critical and explicitly Roman Catholic point of view. There is also an interesting discussion of Schopenhauer's philosophy by Richard Taylor in D. J. O'Connor, ed., *A Critical History of Western Philosophy* (New York, 1964). The view of Schopenhauer presented in the present article is given at greater length in Patrick Gardiner, *Schopenhauer* (Harmondsworth, England, 1963).

Among earlier works, the following may be mentioned as dealing with particular aspects of Schopenhauer's thought and influence: G. Simmel, *Schopenhauer und Nietzsche* (Leipzig, 1907); R. A. Tsanoff, *Schopenhauer's Criticism of Kant's Theory of Experience* (New York, 1911); and A. Baillot, *Influence de la philosophie de Schopenhauer en France* (Paris, 1927). See also William Caldwell, *Schopenhauer's System in Its Philosophical Significance* (Edinburgh, 1896); and Israel Knox, *The Aesthetic Theories of Kant, Hegel, and Schopenhauer* (New York, 1936). For interpretations by writers deeply influenced by Schopenhauer's philosophy, see Friedrich Nietzsche, "Schopenhauer als Erzieher," in *Unzeitgemässe Betrachtungen* (Leipzig, 1873–1874); and Thomas Mann's introduction to *The Living Thoughts of Schopenhauer* (London, 1939). Schopenhauer's influence upon Wittgenstein is considered in G. E. M. Anscombe, *An Introduction to Wittgenstein's Tractatus* (London, 1959), Ch. 13, and Erik Stenius, *Wittgenstein's Tractatus* (Oxford, 1960), Ch. 11.

The most complete life of Schopenhauer is W. Schneider, *Schopenhauer, eine Biographie* (Vienna, 1937). In English, see William Wallace, *Life of Schopenhauer* (London, 1890); and Helen Zimmern, *Arthur Schopenhauer: His Life and Philosophy* (London, 1876; rev. ed., London, 1932).

— PATRICK GARDINER

SCIENCE, RESEARCH ETHICS OF

Sustained work on the ethics of scientific research by journalists, scholars, practitioners, and government officials began in the early 1980s, in the aftermath of scandals featuring researchers. One such researcher was Dr. John Long, a respected investigator of Hodgkin's disease at Massachusetts General Hospital. He had to resign and relinquish a large government grant after his collaborator discovered from a data logbook that Long had falsified results in response to a journal referee's

The notion of answerability may serve to identify specific ethical concerns regarding scientific research. (Corbis/Kevin Fleming)

criticism that their reported data were scanty (Kohn, 1986).

In an atmosphere of accountability the term that first gained currency was "fraud in science." This language clearly signaled that the self-correction processes of science were not protections against deception and cheating. In time the broader notion of misconduct took hold, especially in regulations of federal funding agencies. Eventually, emphasis on proper conduct came to the fore with the currency of the terms "research ethics," "responsible conduct in science," and especially "integrity" (Davis, 1990).

An important philosophical task is to delineate the subject matter of this part of ethics. The terms 'science', 'research', and 'ethics' require explication in light of their ultimate connection with institutions and of growing, but still partial, understanding of what scientists do (Galison, 1987; Latour and Woolgar, 1986).

The 1992 National Academy of Sciences report, *Responsible Science,* emphasizes "the research process," which includes "proposing, performing, evaluating, and reporting research activities" (p. 4). A broader view includes the social interactions of individuals and institutions; these interactions are governed by conventions and practices of research groups and peer communities (Zwolinek, 1992). Because the policies and procedures of universities, laboratories, funding agencies, scientific journals and societies, and peer review systems exert powerful influence on research processes, these components should, it seems, be encompassed as well. More external but also influential are pressures from journalists in the popular and scientific press.

What fields are included within the sciences? It seems that certain contextual features and research methods rather than the content or aims of investigation are determinative. Discussion concentrates on empirical research in fields that rely on substantial external funding (Davis, 1990).

The starting point for unpacking 'ethics' in the context of scientific research is the notion of misconduct. The definitions issued by U.S. government funding agencies in the late 1980s helped to clarify this notion, characterizing it as "serious deviation from accepted practices in proposing, carrying out, or reporting results from research" (NIH, 1988, p. 36347; NSF, 1991, p. 2228690). "Serious deviation" included fabrication, falsification, and plagiarism. Some scientists contest the "deviation from accepted practice" conception, holding that it is vague and threatens to curtail creativity because it leaves innovation indistinguishable from unethical conduct (Buzzelli, 1994).

This objection ignores context, especially the role of peer assessments, which serve to distinguish the innovative from the routine. If peers are expected to separate the innovative from the routine, they can also be expected to distinguish innovative research from conduct ethically unacceptable according to established standards for conducting research (Buzzelli, 1994; Zwolenik, 1992).

This response points to the central position of standards of practice and care in research communities. Many count on these standards as a guide to conduct and a basis for identifying misconduct (Buzzelli, 1994). This foundation of consensus places the burden for special ethical standards where it seems to belong and allows standards to be tailored to the character and circumstances of research and to evolve. The community-standards orientation, however, faces difficulties, notably from differences and conflicts between research programs about methodology. Rules of method carry normative force and are themselves subject to scientific debate (Schmaus, 1990). Furthermore, evidence indicates that research communities need to clarify their standards for conducting research (identifying underlying ethical considerations) and to delineate practices that serve the standards, while remaining ready to reassess as circumstances change (Swayze, 1993).

The starting point for unpacking "ethics"

in the context of scientific research

is the notion of misconduct.

In view of the considerable differences in standards and conventions across research communities, the question arises whether there are shared core principles or ethical commitments that underlie specific standards. Some scientists favor the notion of integrity, which at root is the idea of moral wholeness or freedom from corruption, especially in relation to truth and fair dealing. Ascribed to persons, the notion of integrity implies constancy in meeting demands of morality. "Integrity of the research process" is understood as "adherence by scientists and their institutions to honest and verifiable methods" in research (NAS, p. 4). For the broader view of the research process (see above), this notion is inadequate.

Avoidance of deception, a key ethical commitment in science, seems to some philosophers the undergirding principle (Gert, 1993). However, it does not encompass (apparently) uncontroversial instances of ethical concern, such as violations of confidentiality in peer review. This principle is not well suited to addressing structures of science (e.g., peer review) or the relations of scientists and scientific research to the wider society. These latter dimensions are too integral to the doing of science and too salient in public discussion to be excluded.

What may serve to identify specific ethical concerns is the notion of answerability. For what are scientists answerable? Bench level practices include treatment of human and animal research subjects, advising and mentoring graduate students and postdoctoral fellows, gathering, recording, storing, and sharing data, preparing research reports, authorial practices, and practices related to intellectual property (Weil, 1993a). With closer ties between scientists and commerce threatening reliable judgment, conflict of interest must be included. In the structures of science, peer review is salient. Debate about the primary obligation to society pits a narrow interpretation, the obligation to pursue knowledge, against a broader conception, including, for example, a duty to avoid harmful consequences of research. Whether the broader conception can be derived from inherent features of science or must derive from conventions scientists have reasons to adopt is also debated (Davis, 1993; Kaiser, 1993). Favoring the latter position is its consonance with the foundation of consensus.

[See also Applied Ethics.]

BIBLIOGRAPHY

Buzzelli, D. E. "NSF's Definition of Misconduct in Science," *Centennial Review*, Vol. 38 (1994), 1–19.
Davis, M. "The New World of Research Ethics: A Preliminary Map," *International Journal of Applied Philosophy*, Vol. 5 (1990), 1–10.
———. "Science: After Such Knowledge, What Responsibility?" Center for the Study of Ethics in the Professions, Illinois Institute of Technology, Chicago, 1992.
Galison, P. L. *How Experiments End*. Chicago, 1987.
Gert, B. "Morality and Scientific Research," in *Ethics, Values, and the Promise of Science* (Research Triangle Park, NC, 1993).
Hackett, E. J. "A Social Control Perspective on Scientific Misconduct," *Journal of Higher Education* (May/June 1994), 242–60.
Kaiser, M. "Some Thoughts on the Responsibility of Scientists in Relation to the Growth of Fish-farming in Norway," *Studies in Research Ethics* [Göteborg, Sweden], No. 2 (1993), 19–32.
Kohn, A. *False Prophets: Fraud and Error in Science and Medicine*. Oxford, 1986.
Latour, B. *Science in Action: How to Follow Scientists and Engineers through Society*. Philadelphia, 1987.
———, and S. Woolgar. *Laboratory Life: The Construction of Scientific Facts*. Princeton, NJ, 1986.
National Academy of Sciences (NAS). *Responsible Science: Ensuring the Integrity of the Research Process*, Vol. 1. Washington, DC, 1992.
National Institutes of Health (NIH). "Responsibilities of PHS Awardee and Applicant Institution for Dealing with and Reporting Possible Misconduct in Science," *Federal Register*, Vol. 53 (1988), p. 36347.
National Science Foundation (NSF). "Misconduct in Science and Engineering: Final Rule." *Federal Register*, Vol. 56 (1991), p. 2228690.
Schmaus, W. "Honesty and Methods," *Accountability in Research: Policies and Quality Assurance*, Vol. 1 (1990), 147–53.
Swayze, J., M. Anderson, and K. S. Louis. "Ethical Problems in Academic Research," *American Scientist*, Vol. 81 (Nov.–Dec., 1993), 542–53.
Weil, V. "Ethics in Scientific Research and Graduate Education," *Studies in Research Ethics* [Göteborg, Sweden]. No. 2 (1993a), 1–58.
———. "Teaching Ethics in Science," in *Ethics, Values, and the Promise of Science* (Research Triangle Park, NC, 1993b).
Zwolenik, J. J. "New Definitions of Misconduct: Priorities for the 1990s," *Knowledge*, Vol. 14, No. 2 (December 1992), 168–173.

— VIVIAN WEIL

SCIENTIFIC THEORIES

Theories and models are two main artifacts produced by science. Divergent analyses of their functions, structures, and interpretations have been advanced that constrain interpreting other aspects of science.

Functions of Theories

Theories use theoretical laws to provide generalized descriptions that go beyond what is directly observable unaided by apparatus or contrived experimental circumstances. Theoretical realism maintains that the function of theories is systematic description and explanation and that, to be adequate, all aspects of a theory's descriptions must be correct. Reductionism further requires that nonobservable content be reduced to the observable or some other empirical basis. Instrumentalism construes the function of theories to be prediction of directly observable phenomena and requires only adequate description of directly observable aspects.

Structure of Theories

Theories utilize specialized concepts, are expressed in technical language, and often invoke mathematical structures. Different philosophical analyses give each feature priority.

OPERATIONALISM. For Percy W. Bridgman theories link concepts that are operationally defined via mixes of basic measurement procedures constituting the concepts' entire meaning. The subject matter of science is operations, not absolute physical matter. Behaviorist S. S. Stevens operationally defined concepts as referring to mixes of objective gross physical behaviors. E. C. Tolman extended the notion to include stimulus-response overt behaviors mediated by intervening variables.

SYNTACTIC ANALYSES. Logical positivism sought a theoretically adequate language for science where every sentence was true or false and contingent ones were empirically testable, hence meaningful. The syntax was symbolic logic. Descriptive vocabulary was trifurcated into mathematical and logical expressions, terms V_O de-

Ancient scientists produced two main artifacts: theories and models. (Corbis/Historical Picture Archive)

scriptive of directly observable conditions, and the remainder V_T. Empirical testability was problematic only for "theoretical" expressions containing V_T terms. Restricting admissible V_T terms to those defined by correspondence rules C guaranteeing reference to something real ensured testability and meaningfulness.

Initially, V_T terms were shorthand abbreviations for complex directly observable conditions, hence eliminable explicit definitions. Technical difficulties handling dispositional concepts and the inadvisability of identifying theoretical entities with specific measurement procedures led Rudolf Carnap to introduce reduction sentences providing separate partial definitions of V_T terms for different experimental circumstances. Later, Carl G. Hempel allowed interpretative systems that enabled testing observable consequences of entire theories without requiring each V_T term be tied contextually to specific directly observable consequences.

Embedded into this reformed language is the received view on theories (RV): a theory TC is set T of theoretical laws containing V_T terms conjoined with correspondence rules C as the axioms for a symbolic logic theory, where V_O terms refer to directly observables and referents of V_T terms are determined by C and V_O. Meaningfulness of terms and semantic reference are thus identified with ontological commitment, which means that positivistic-insistence theoretical terms referring to fictitious theoretical entities such as the luminiferous ether should be disallowed. The RV embodies theoretical realism, but the describable range of phenomena varies with allowed C. If only explicit definitions are allowed, the descriptive scope and range of ontological commitment are that of instrumentalism and many reductionisms. However, only instrumentalism would allow V_T terms not made referential by C.

Critics branded the RV untenable: Peter Achinstein, Hilary Putnam, and Frederick Suppe argued its V_T/V_O-term distinction could not coherently be drawn in any epistemologically significant manner. Norwood Russell Hanson argued that all observation is theory laden. Kenneth Schaffner and Wilfrid Sellars argued that correspondence rules were a heterogeneous confusion of meaning relationships, experimental design, measurement, and causal relationships. Patrick Suppes and Suppe argued that they did not accurately reflect how theories are connected to observational data. Achinstein and Putnam mistakenly charged that partial interpretation notions associated with more liberal C were incoherent. Suppes, Stephen Toulmin, and others questioned the appropriateness of first-order predicate logic formalism. Alternative views rooted in history of science by Thomas Kuhn, Paul Feyerabend, Hanson, and Toulmin offered portraits conflicting with the RV. By the early 1970s few philosophers of science subscribed to the RV.

Another fundamental defect was that the RV improperly individuated theories. Linguistic entities contain language forms as constitutive parts, so changes in linguistic form create new entities. Since symbolic logic axiomatizations are proper parts of theories on the RV, theories are linguistic entities. Real scientific theories admit of alternative linguistic formulations (e.g., difference equation, partial differential equation, and Hamiltonian formulations of classical mechanics) and so are not linguistic entities. Furthermore, correspondence rules C are individuating parts, so development of new observational techniques yields replacement C'. Contrary to actual scientific practice, on the RV such formulation changes are changes in theory.

SEMANTIC CONCEPTIONS (SC). Evert Beth, Suppe, Suppes, and Bas C. van Fraassen developed analyses construing theories as mathematical structures describing state-transition behavior mapped onto real-world systems. These theory structures were identified with configured state spaces (van Fraassen), relational systems (Suppe), or set-theoretic predicates (Suppes) that represent states of systems as simultaneous values of variables and behaviors as state sequences allowed by theoretical laws. Linguistic formulations referred variously to theory structures or real-world systems and are not proper individuating theory parts. Alternative linguistic formulations are allowed. That no particular logic is imposed enables the SC to incorporate quantum logics.

Theoretical realism maintains

that the function of theories

is systematic description and explanation and that,

to be adequate, all aspects of a theory's descriptions

must be correct.

The SC does not embrace any particular epistemology. Suppes, Suppe, and van Fraassen incorporate it into quite different views about testing, confirmation, and scientific knowledge. An observational–theoretical distinction is not essential to the SC, and only van Fraassen imposes one.

Since theories are not linguistic entities, empirical-content issues are not conflated with questions of meaningfulness of terms or linguistic ontological commitment. One propounds a theory with a theory hypothesis: theory structure T stands in mapping relationship M to class P of actual or possible real-world systems wherein T represents state-change behaviors in P. The M are unlike correspondence rules, concerning just representation of P by T, not meaning relations, experimental design, or causal interactions. Observational or experimental testing practices are included in neither T nor M and so are not individuating theory parts. However, Suppes and Suppe used the SC to analyze how date and experiment mediate connections between theory and world. Van Fraassen and Suppe analyzed linguistic relations between formulations, theory structures, and real-world systems.

STRUCTURALIST APPROACH. Closely related to SCs is the structuralist approach of Joseph Sneed, Wolfgang Stegmüller, and C. U. Moulines, which began with Sneed's application of Suppes's version of the SC to the problem of theoretical terms. Sneed argued that theoretical terms are those that in some contexts can be measured only by utilizing the theory. Sneed claims that circular testing is avoided, since a theory's empirical content varies with application and theory portions used to measure a theoretical term are not parts of the theory's empirical content in that application. A theory structure's inner core and a set of intended core-augmenting applications individuate theories. Theoretical cores and their extensions were exploited to investigate dynamics of theorizing—displaying how theories can develop and be extended while remaining the same theory and explicating Kuhn's normal science where paradigm theories undergo progressive development via puzzle solving.

OTHER APPROACHES. Despite lingering disputes over the relative superiority of syntactical versus semantic approaches, there has been no prominent development of syntactical theory analyses since the RV's demise. Maria Dalla Chiara, Giuliano Toraldo di Francia, M. Prezełecki and Ryzard Wójcicki produced neopositivistic semantic structural analyses reminiscent of the RV but using set theory, not symbolic logic.

Theories and Models

The term model encompasses metamathematical models (mathematical structures satisfying formulae under some referential interpretation), scientific theories, and scientific models including iconic scale models. Suppes proposed analyzing models in science via metamathematical models. Under SC and structuralist approaches theory structures and physical systems are metamathematical models of theory formulations. Since V_O terms refer to directly observable conditions, and correspondence rules impose meaning relations between V_O and V_T terms, the RV interpretation of TC can be represented using metamathematical models.

Scientific models can be metamathematical models for equations or sentences. Some scientific models are simplified, often physical, analogues or icons of more complex structures or systems. Philosophers typically construe such models as having only heuristic or explanatory roles and incapable of providing new knowledge. Nevertheless, Norman Campbell claimed they were essential components of RV theories, claiming the choice of C would be irrational unless the V_T laws were given meaning by reference to familiar iconic models. Mary Hesse and Rom Harré argued that such models are essential for RV theories to be explanatory and indispensable for hypothesis discovery.

Experimental scientific results often are presented as models of data that are structural enhancements of embedded observational data. Science increasingly regards simulation models as just another form of experiment.

Such models are not mere heuristics or explanatory analogues but yield new knowledge. Work by Suppes and Suppe shows that both sorts of models can be analyzed as mathematical structures similar to SC theory structures but where mapping relations to the world differ from the *M* of adequate theories.

Realism, Quasi-realism, and Antirealism

Philosophers worry about ontological commitments of scientific theories. Theoretical realism, instrumentalism, and reductionism were the classic responses, asserting respectively that recourse to theoretical terms did or did not carry ontological commitments to hypothesized entities or that such commitments were reducible to observational or prior ontological commitments. As Dudley Shapere noted, such polarized philosophical options are artificial, since scientists often selectively make ontological commitments to some but not all theoretical terms.

Modern instrumentalism-realism-reductionism debates are closely tied to the RV. Defense of instrumentalism by Ramsey sentences (which eliminate theoretical terms by existentially quantifying them so as to enable the same V_O predictions) or Craig's theorem (for a theory *TC* with V_T there is theory *T'* without any of the V_T having the same V_O consequences) makes sense only in the context of RV construal of theories as axiomatic symbolic logic systems, assumption of an observational-theoretical term division, and conflation of meaning and reference issues with ontological commitment. Post-RV ontological commitment debates tend to ignore instrumentalism. David Lewis used modified Ramsey sentences to give a realist reductionistic account in terms of old or prior terms rather than observables.

On semantic approaches meaning and ontology issues get separated. When linguistic theory formulations *L* refer to theory structures, the only ontological commitments are mathematical. When propounding a theory as adequate, one asserts that a theory structure *T* stands in mapping *M* to possible real-world systems *P*. Choice of *M* determines ontological commitments.

Requirements on *M* for adequate theories are controversial. Realism asserts that scientific theories must be literally true to be adequate: each state variable in *T* is characteristic of *P* systems and the state transitions of *P* systems are exactly those allowed by *T*. Citing potentially unlimited factors not reflected in *T* affecting state variables, Suppe claims that literal truth is unattainable. Rather, the epistemologically attainable adequacy standard is a quasi-realism where *M* counterfactually asserts that the systems in *P* would behave in accordance with *T* were they isolated from outside influences. Ian Hacking and Nancy Cartwright advance entity realisms

where theoretical terms refer but theories do not provide literally true descriptions of phenomena.

Antirealisms deny that adequate theories must be literally true, because not all state variables or other features of *T* need correspond to features in *P*. *M* determines which do. Let *T** be the *T* portion corresponding to *P* under *M*. *T* is empirically adequate when *T** provides a literally true characterization of *P*. Antirealism thus is realism with restricted scope. Van Fraassen's antirealism identifies *T** with actual observable portions of *P*. Empirical adequacy notions are applications of his theory of semi-interpreted languages where full semantic interpretations are given to theoretical assertions, including probabilistic and modal ones, using abstract semantic spaces. Freely chosen *loc* functions map world features into these semantic spaces, but not all features correspond to anything in the world. *Loc* functions specify range of ontological commitment. For scientific theories the *T* are embedded into semantic spaces, and empirical adequacy consists in *P* corresponding to the *T** portion.

Philosophers worry about

ontological commitments of scientific theories.

Since empirical adequacy is literal-truth realism restricted to *T**, antirealism seems liable to the objections raised above against realisms. However, semi-interpreted languages are compatible with quasi-realism. Quasi-realisms with quite restricted ontological commitments are possible, but empirical adequacy would be replaced by counterfactual truth conditions.

Arthur Fine proposed the natural ontological attitude (NOA) as neutral common ground between realism and antirealisms: scientific statements are referential and true in some unanalyzed sense of truth; commitment to entities is only as strong as our belief assertions about them are true. Semantic and structuralist approaches augment NOA with metamathematical or semi-interpreted-language truth analyses.

[See also Carnap, Rudolph; Kuhn, Thomas; Philosophy of Science; Putnam, Hilary; Realism; Reduction, Reductionism; Sellars, Wilfrid; Set Theory.]

BIBLIOGRAPHY

Beth, E. "Towards an Up-to-Date Philosophy of the Natural Sciences," *Methodos*, Vol. 1 (1949), 178–85.

Bridgman, P. W. *The Nature of Physical Theory*. Princeton, NJ, 1936.

Carnap, R. "Testability and Meaning," Parts 1 and 2, *Philosophy of Science*, Vol. 3 (1936), 420–66, Vol. 4 (1937), 1–40.

Cartwright, N. *How the Laws of Physics Lie*. New York, 1983.

Fine, A. *The Shaky Game: Einstein, Realism, and the Quantum Theory*. Chicago, 1986.

Hacking, I. *Representing and Intervening*. Cambridge, 1983.

Hempel, C. G. *Fundamentals of Concept Formation in Empirical Science*. Chicago, 1952.

Hesse, M. *Models and Analogies in Science*. Notre Dame, IN, 1966.

Lewis, D. "How to Define Theoretical Terms," in *Philosophical Papers*, Vol. 1. New York, 1983.

Przełecki, M., K. Szaniawski, and R. Wójcicki, eds. *Formal Methods in the Methodology of Science*. Wrocław, Poland, 1976. Contains a number of semantic approaches, most of them resembling the received view.

Sneed, J. *The Logical Structure of Mathematical Physics*. Dordrecht, 1971.

Stegmüller, W. *The Structure and Dynamics of Theories*. New York, 1976.

Stevens, S. S. "The Operational Definition of Psychological Concepts," *Psychological Review*, Vol. 42 (1935), 517–26.

Suppe, F. *The Structure of Scientific Theories*, 2d ed. Urbana, IL, 1977. Introduction and afterword provide a comprehensive account of the development of the positivistic received view, criticisms of it that led to its eventual demise, and postpositivistic attempts to understand scientific theorizing, including the semantic conception. Comprehensive bibliography.

———. *The Semantic Conception of Theories and Scientific Realism*. Urbana, IL, 1989. Extensive bibliography.

———. Facts, *Theories, and Scientific Observation*. Urbana, IL, 1996. Extensive bibliography.

Suppes, P. "A Comparison of the Meaning and Use of Models in Mathematics and the Empirical Sciences," in H. Freudenthal, ed., *The Concept and the Role of the Model in Mathematics and Natural and Social Sciences* (Dordrecht, 1961).

———. "Models of Data," in E. Nagel, P. Suppes, and A. Tarski, eds., *Logic, Methodology, and Philosophy of Science: Proceedings of the 1960 International Congress* (Stanford, CA, 1962).

———. "What Is a Scientific Theory?" in S. Morgenbesser, ed., *Philosophy of Science Today* (New York, 1967).

Tolman, E. C. *Purposive Behavior in Animals and Men*. New York, 1932.

van Fraassen, B. C. "Meaning Relations and Modalities," *Noûs*, Vol. 3 (1969), 155–68. Extends theory of semi-interpreted languages to include modal operators.

———. "On the Extension of Beth's Semantics of Physical Theories," *Philosophy of Science*, Vol. 37 (1970), 325–39. Develops a semantic conception of theories based upon his theory of semi-interpreted languages.

———. *The Scientific Image*. New York, 1980.

— FREDERICK SUPPE

SELF

In its normal use the English expression "self" is not even quite a word, but something that makes an ordinary object pronoun into a reflexive one (e.g., "her" into "herself"). The reflexive pronoun is used when the object of an action or attitude is the same as the subject of that action or attitude. If I say Mark Twain shot *himself* in the foot, I describe Mark Twain not only as the shooter but as the person shot. In this sense "the self" is just the person doing the action or holding the attitude that is somehow in question. "Self" is also used as a prefix for names of activities and attitudes, identifying the special case where the object is the same as the agent: self-love, self-hatred, self-abuse, self-promotion, self-knowledge.

"The self" often means more than this, however. In psychology it is often used for that set of attributes that a person attaches to himself or herself most firmly, the attributes that the person finds it difficult or impossible to imagine himself or herself without. The term identity is also used in this sense. Typically, one's sex is a part of one's self or one's identity; one's profession or nationality may or may not be.

In philosophy the self is the agent, the knower

and the ultimate locus of personal identity.

In philosophy the self is the agent, the knower and the ultimate locus of personal identity. If the thought of future reward or punishment is to encourage or deter me from some course of action, I must be thinking of the person rewarded as me, as myself, as the same person who is now going to endure the hardship of righteousness or pass up the enjoyments of sin in favor of this ultimate reward. But this same self comes up in much more mundane transactions. If I pick up the cake and shove it in this mouth rather than that one, is it not because I think it will be me, the very same person who picks up the cake, that will have the pleasure of tasting it?

A straightforward view of the self would be that the self is just the person and that a person is a physical system. This view has been challenged on two fronts. First, the nature of freedom and consciousness has convinced many philosophers that there is a fundamentally nonphysical aspect of persons. The second challenge stems from puzzling aspects of self-knowledge. The knowledge we have of ourselves seems very unlike the knowledge we have of other objects in several ways, and this has led some philosophers to rather startling conclusions about the self. In his *Tractatus*, Ludwig Wittgenstein tells us that "I am my world" and that " 'the world is my world' " (1961, 5.63, 5.641). This should lead us to the rather surprising conclusion that I am the world, or that at least Wittgenstein was. He draws at least one conclusion that would follow from this: "at death the world does not alter, but comes to an end."

The contemporary philosopher Thomas Nagel has been led to a possibly less radical but still quite dramatic view. According to Nagel, when he says "I am Tom Nagel," at least in certain philosophical moods, the "I" refers to the "objective self," which is not identical with but merely contingently related to the person Tom Nagel. This self could just as well view the world from the perspective of someone other than him (Nagel, 1983). We need to discuss the puzzling features of self-knowledge that give rise to such views.

Self-Knowledge

"Self-knowledge" seems to have a straightforward meaning: cases of knowledge in which the knower and the known are identical. But this does not seem sufficient. The philosopher Mach once got on the end of a bus and saw a scruffy, unkempt, bookish-looking sort of person at the other end. He thought to himself.

(1) That man is a shabby pedagogue.

In fact, Mach was seeing himself in a large mirror at the far end of the bus. He eventually realized this and thought to himself:

(2) I am that man.
(3) I am a shabby pedagogue.

Now consider Mach at the earlier time. Did Mach have self-knowledge? In our straightforward sense it seems that he did. He knew that a certain person was a shabby pedagogue and, furthermore, that person was him. The knower and the known were the same. But this is not what we mean by self-knowledge. Self-knowledge is something Mach really had only when he got to step (3), when he would have used the word "I" to express what he knew.

Self-knowledge seems peculiar. First, it seems "essentially indexical." Statement (3) expresses self-knowledge because of the word "I"; it is hard to see how Mach could have expressed self-knowledge without using the first person. If he said "Mach is a shabby pedagogue," he would be claiming to know only what everyone else may have known. It does not seem that there is any objective characterization D of Mach, such that knowing that *he* is a shabby pedagogue amounts to knowing that D is a shabby pedagogue (Castañeda, 1966, 1968; Perry, 1990, 1993).

Secondly, we seem immune to certain sorts of misidentification with respect to self-knowledge. If we learn, in certain ways, that someone is in pain, then we cannot miss the fact that it is we who are in pain. That is, if Mach discovers that he has a headache in the ordinary way that a person discovers she has a headache, he can scarcely be wrong about *who* has the headache, if the range of choices is "I/you/that man," and so forth. Of course he can be wrong if the range of choices is "Mach/

Freud/Wittgenstein," and so on, for he might not realize which of those people he is (Shoemaker, 1984).

Third, self-knowledge seems to play a unique cognitive role. If Mach desires that *he* do so and so, and believes that *he* can do so and so by executing such and such a movement, then he will execute that movement without further ado (Perry, 1990).

Agent-Relative Knowledge

At least some of these peculiarities of self-knowledge can be explained by taking self-knowledge to be a species of agent-relative knowledge. There are two quite different ways of cognizing objects (people, things, places, and times). We can think of them via their relationship to us, the role they are playing in our lives at the moment of thought: the object I see; the present moment; the place I'm at; the person I'm talking to. We need to think about things in the first way, when we are picking up information about them perceptually or interacting with them, since ways of knowing and acting are tied to these agent-relative roles. I can learn about the here and now by looking; I can learn about the person I am talking to by asking questions, and so forth.

But these agent-relative roles cannot be our only ways of thinking about objects of more than passing interest to us. Different objects play the same agent-relative roles at different times, and at any given time many of the objects we wish to retain information about will not be playing any agent-relative role for us. And we cannot accumulate information along such roles. Suppose I am in Tokyo on Tuesday but return to Palo Alto on Friday. From the facts that on Tuesday I truly thought "Japanese is the official language *here*" and on Friday I truly thought "Senator Stanford used to live near *here*" it does not follow that there is some place where Japanese is the official language and near which Senator Stanford used to live.

In order to retain and accumulate information about objects, to construct and maintain a coherent picture of the world, we need to have a way of conceiving of objects as existing independently of us, as occupying and then ceasing to occupy various agent-relative roles. That is, we need objective ways of thinking about objects. We keep track of them by names or descriptions that do not depend on their relationship to us: Cordura Hall, 4 P.M., June 23, 1995, the southernmost town in Santa Clara County, Aurora Fischer. These serve as our fundamental ways of thinking about those objects. Recognition consists in connecting our objective ways of thinking of objects with the roles those objects play at a given moment. Consider the knowledge I might express with "Today is July 4." This is knowledge that a certain day, objectively conceived ("July 4"), is playing a certain role in my life; it is the present day, the day on which the thinking and speaking take place. This kind of knowledge, "knowing what day it is," is quite crucial to successful application of other, more objective knowledge. If I know that the party is on July 4 and know that today is July 4, then I will form the right expectations about what the day will be like.

Similarly, I may be in Kansas City and know that Kansas City is a good place for a steak dinner. But if I do not know that I am in Kansas City, if I do not realize that Kansas City is playing the "here" or "this city" role in my life at this moment, I will not be able to apply the knowledge that Kansas City is a good place for a steak dinner.

And again, I may know that Aurora Fischer has important information about my schedule, but unless I realize that the person I am talking to is Aurora Fischer, I will not apply this information and say, "Can *you* tell me where this afternoon's meeting is?"

Self-knowledge is knowledge

about a person by that very person,

with the additional requirement

that the person be cognized

via the agent-relative role of identity.

These kinds of knowledge are, like self-knowledge, "essentially indexical." We use "now" and "today" to express our knowledge of what time it is and "here" to express our knowledge of where we are. These locutions are not reducible to names or objective descriptions, just as "I" was not. I cannot express what I say when I say, "The meeting starts right now" by saying "the meeting starts at D" for any description D of the present moment.

We are also immune to certain sorts of misidentification when we use certain methods of knowing. There is a way of finding out what is going on around one, namely opening one's eyes and looking (Evans, 1985). Now when one learns what is going on in this way, one can hardly fail to identify the time at which this is happening as now and the place as here. And finally, the forms of thought we express with "now" and "here" seem to have a unique motivational role. If I want to do something here and now, I will simply do it.

Self-Knowledge as Agent-Relative Knowledge

"Self" is really the name of such an agent-relative role, that of identity. As with other agent-relative roles, there are special ways of knowing and acting that are associated with identity. If Mach had wished to know, during the interval while he was confused, if the shabby pedagogue he was seeing had lint on his vest, he would have had to walk over to him and look. If Mach had wanted to know if he himself had lint on his vest, he could have simply lowered his head and looked. Had he done this, he would have had no doubt about whom the lint was on. If Mach found lint and wanted to brush it off, he would engage in self-brushing, a quick movement of the hand across one's front that each of us can use to remove lint from our own vest and no one else's.

Unlike the other agent-relative roles, identity is permanent. I will talk to many people, be in many places, live through many times in the course of my life. But there is only one person I will ever be identical with, myself. Hence, accumulation along "I" is valid, unlike accumulation along "here" or "now" or "that man."

Earlier we rejected the straightforward account of self-knowledge, as knowledge about a person by that very person. Now we can put forward an alternative. Self-knowledge is knowledge about a person by that very person, with the additional requirement that the person be cognized via the agent-relative role of identity. This agent-relative role is tied to normally self-informative methods of knowing and normally self-effecting ways of acting. When these methods are employed, there will be immunity of misidentification as to who is known about, or who is acted upon.

This role can serve as a person's fundamental concept of himself or herself. In this way our self-conceptions have structures that are different from our conceptions of other individuals of importance to us. If we understand the special way in which a person's self-knowledge is structured, we do not need to postulate anything but the person himself or herself for the knowledge to be about.

[See also Identity; Indexicals; Personal Identity; Philosophy of Mind; Reduction, Reductionism; Wittgenstein, Ludwig Josef Johann.]

BIBLIOGRAPHY

Castañeda, H.-N. " 'He': A Study in the Logic of Self-Consciousness," *Ration*, Vol. 8 (1966), 130–57.
———. "On the Logic of Attributions of Self-Knowledge to Others," *Journal of Philosophy*, Vol. 65 (1968), 439–56.
Evans, G. "Understanding Demonstratives," in *Collected Papers* (Oxford, 1985).
———. *The Varieties of Reference.* Oxford, 1982.
Nagel, T. "The Objective Self," in C. Ginet and S. Shoemaker, eds., *Knowledge and Mind* (Oxford, 1983).
Perry, J. *The Problem of the Essential Indexical.* New York, 1993.
———. "Self-Notions," *Logos*, Vol. 11 (1990), 17–31.
Shoemaker, S. *Identity, Cause, and Mind.* Cambridge, 1984.

Wittgenstein, L. *Tractatus Logico-Philosophicus,* translated by D. F. Pears and B. F. McGuinness. London, 1961.

– JOHN PERRY

SELLARS, WILFRID STALKER

Wilfrid Stalker Sellars (1912–1989), American philosopher and teacher, was born in Ann Arbor, Michigan, the son of Roy Wood Sellars, the American critical realist, who taught at the University of Michigan. His early education took place in the United States and in France, where he attended the lycées Montaigne and Louis le Grand; it was continued at the University of Michigan (B.A., 1933), the University of Buffalo (M.A., 1934), and Oxford University, where he was a Rhodes scholar and received a B.A. with first-class honors in philosophy, politics, and economics. He received an M.A. from Oxford in 1940. After a year at Harvard University he began his career as a teacher of philosophy in 1938 at the University of Iowa. During the war he spent several years as an officer in the Naval Reserve, and in 1946 he went to the University of Minnesota, where he eventually became professor of philosophy, chairman of the philosophy department, founding coeditor of the journal *Philosophical Studies,* and a member of Herbert Feigl's Minnesota Center for the Philosophy of Science. In 1959 he joined the faculty of Yale University, and in 1963 he moved to the University of Pittsburgh, where he became University Professor of Philosophy and Research Professor of the Philosophy of Science. Apart from numerous interludes as visiting professor at other institutions, he remained at Pittsburgh until his death.

Although Sellars became an extremely prolific writer, in the early years of his career he had great difficulty putting his ideas on paper. His first scholarly essay, third in his list of publications, was "Realism and the New Way of Words"; it underwent seventeen major revisions, Sellars said in his "Autobiographical Reflections," before it finally appeared in print. In spite of its striking originality, his early work was strongly influenced by the logical empiricist movement, particularly by the work of Rudolf Carnap; in one essay, "Epistemology and the New Way of Words," he declared that philosophy "is properly conceived as the pure theory of empirically meaningful languages." From today's vantage point the most significant of his early essays would appear to be "Concepts as Involving Laws and Inconceivable without Them" (1948) and "A Semantical Solution of the Mind–Body Problem" (1953). Both show him to have been well ahead of his time in analytic philosophy. In the former he offered a clarification of necessity and natural law that anticipated the treatment of these no-

tions in recent possible-world semantics, and in the latter he developed a distinctly functionalist view of intentional states.

Sellars's best-known philosophical work

is the lengthy essay

"Empiricism and the Philosophy of Mind,"

which originated in lectures he gave in 1956

attacking what he called "the myth of the given."

Sellars's best-known philosophical work is the lengthy essay "Empiricism and the Philosophy of Mind." This essay originated in lectures that Sellars gave in 1956 attacking what he called "the myth of the given." The cluster of ideas making up this doctrine was, he thought, the source of important errors in both the theory of knowledge and the philosophy of mind; and by exposing it for what it is, he hoped to lay the groundwork for an acceptable form of empiricism and for a proper understanding of mental and sensory phenomena. The basic epistemic error prompted by the myth was the idea that empirical knowledge rests on a foundation of certain truth which is "given"—that is, knowable without inference—and provides the ultimate evidence for anything knowable by inference. The root error in the philosophy of mind prompted by the myth was the claim that, merely by having sensory experiences and conscious thoughts, we gain theoretically satisfactory conceptions of those experiences and thoughts. These corresponding errors are related by the belief, commonly held by those who accept the myth, that foundational empirical knowledge concerns the sensory and psychological items, the mere having of which supposedly results in their being adequately conceived of or understood.

In attacking the errors he saw in the myth Sellars defended the view that empirical knowledge cannot have a foundation—that the supposedly basic knowledge of psychological fact presumed by the myth cannot exist independently of general knowledge relating psychological experience to linguistic and other behavior—and that theoretically adequate conceptions of anything can be obtained only by a process of learning and can be known to be adequate only by reference to scientific theorizing about the sensory and cognitive capabilities of human beings. He argued that "empirical knowledge . . . is rational not because it has a *foundation* but because it is a self-correcting enterprise which can put *any* claim in jeopardy, though not *all* at once" (1991, pp. 127–196). As for commonsense sensory and psychological concepts, he argued that it is illuminating to think of them as resulting from an attempt to explain intelligent, nonhabitual human behavior by postulating appropriate "inner episodes" in substantially the way that theoretical scientists explain facts about observable objects by postulating unobservable micro-causes. In arguing this point he added that, when concepts of such inner episodes are developed, people can learn to use them in making first-person reports of what they are experiencing. Seen this way, psychological concepts are fundamentally intersubjective rather than private, and they are as subject to revision as any concept of theoretical science.

In "Philosophy and the Scientific Image of Man" (1960), Sellars developed the thesis that, although theoretical science is a natural development of commonsense thought about the world, it is not evidentially dependent upon it. Like David Hume, Sellars thought that scientific thinking yields a theoretical picture of humans in the world that is incompatible with the commonsense, or, as he called it, the "manifest," image of the same reality. These clashing images are not on a par, he thought; in purely descriptive respects, the scientific image is an improvement upon the manifest image, containing "successor concepts" to commonsense counterparts. (Water, on this view, is not identical with H_2O; the technical concept of H_2O applies to a common ingredient in most puddles, wells, clouds, and seas—one that is not accurately singled out by any commonsense concept.) A philosophically adequate picture of humans in the world is not fully descriptive, however; it is partly normative. Working out such a picture is an important philosophical task that has yet to be accomplished: the scientific image is not yet complete, and serious problems exist about how some normative matters can be incorporated into a significantly different image.

In later writings Sellars worked out highly original ideas on most central fields of philosophy. He produced, as Johanna Seibt observed, a unique scheme of "full scope nominalism," which purports to demonstrate the expendability of abstract entities for all their supposed explanatory functions; he worked out (he was the first to do so) a sophisticated "conceptual role" semantics; he developed a neo-Kantian view of moral obligation and the moral point of view; and he had original things to say about central figures and issues in the history of philosophy. At a time when systematic philosophy was decidedly out of fashion, he pursued the synoptic vision of humans in the world that Plato spoke of in the *Republic*. In parody of Kant he liked to tell his students that, in philosophy, analysis without synthesis must be blind.

[See also Carnap, Rudolph; Functionalism; Hume, David; Kant, Immanuel; Philosophy of Mind; Plato.]

BIBLIOGRAPHY

Works by Sellars

"Autobiographical Reflections," in H.-N. Castañeda, ed., *Action, Knowledge, and Reality: Critical Studies in Honor of Wilfrid Sellars* (Indianapolis, 1975).
Philosophical Perspectives: History of Philosophy. Atascadero, CA, 1977.
Philosophical Perspectives: Metaphysics and Epistemology. Atascadero, CA, 1977.
Pure Pragmatics and Possible Worlds: The Early Essays of Wilfrid Sellars, edited by J. F. Sicha. Atascadero, CA, 1980. Sellars's most significant early writings.
Science, Perception, and Reality. Atascadero, CA, 1991.
Naturalism and Ontology. Atascadero, CA, 1992.
Science and Metaphysics. Atascadero, CA, 1992.

Work on Sellars

Seibt, J. *Properties as Processes: A Synoptic Study of Sellars' Nominalism.* Atascadero, CA, 1990.

– BRUCE AUNE

SEMANTICS

The entry semantics by Donald Kalish in the 1967 edition of the *Encyclopedia of Philosophy* remains an excellent overview of the approach to the field that developed out of philosophical logic. Since the mid-1960s major advances in the application of the kinds of logical and philosophical techniques described there as pure semantics to the (descriptive) semantic analysis of natural languages have given rise to the formal semantics of natural language, which in turn has stimulated the development of new formal tools and techniques. Here we review the rapid growth of formal semantics, influenced especially by the work of Richard Montague. We outline central theoretical issues and note that formal semantics has become increasingly "naturalized" as a branch of linguistics. We will mention some controversies and critiques as well as some recent developments, and briefly describe some of the alternative stances concerning central issues.

By the 1960s the rigorous study of the syntax of natural language by Noam Chomsky and his followers (Chomsky, 1957, 1965; Newmeyer, 1980) had made it more plausible that natural languages might be describable as complex but not "unruly" formal languages. Montague claimed further that natural languages could be treated as interpreted formal languages using the same techniques of formal semantics and pragmatics that he and others were successfully developing and applying to the description of artificial languages of logic. The title of his 1970 paper, "English as a Formal Language," embodied his claim, and in a relatively small number of papers written before his untimely death in

1971 (especially Montague, 1970a, 1970b, 1973, reprinted in the collection Montague, 1974), he set forth an explicit theoretical framework for formal semantics and pragmatics applicable to both artificial and natural languages, and illustrated its workings with explicit syntactic and semantic rules for "fragments" of both English and intensional logic. (See also Lewis, 1970; Cresswell, 1973; Dowty et al [eds.], 1981; Gamut, 1991.)

By the 1960s the rigorous study

of the syntax of natural language

by Noam Chomsky and his followers

had made it more plausible that natural languages

might be describable as complex

but not "unruly" formal languages.

Central to Montague's theory of "universal grammar" (Montague, 1970b) is an algebraic interpretation of the "compositionality principle," the principle that the meaning of an expression is a function of the meanings of its parts and of their mode of syntactic combination. According to Montague, both the syntax and the semantics of a language should be expressed as algebras, and the compositionality principle becomes the requirement of a homomorphism from the syntactic algebra to the semantic algebra.

In Montague's conception of syntax, following the logical tradition, syntactic rules recursively form well-formed expressions from other well-formed expressions, starting from basic ("lexical") expressions, and semantic rules then specify how the interpretation of the resulting expression is obtained from the interpretation of the (syntactic) parts. Syntactic and semantic rules thus come in pairs of the following sort, where A, B, and C are syntactic categories, F_i is a syntactic operation on expressions, and G_j is some semantic operation on interpretations, yielding an interpretation as result.

Syntactic rule n: if $\alpha \in$ A and $\beta \in$ B, then $F_i (\alpha, \beta) \in$ C.

Semantic rule n: If α is interpreted as α' and β is interpreted as β', then $F_i(\alpha, \beta)$ is interpreted as $G_j(\alpha', \beta')$.

For an artificial language, the elements of the syntactic algebra might be the well-formed expressions of various categories; but for a natural language, the ambiguity of surface strings conflicts with the homomorphism requirement. Montague's fragments illustrate two different means for the required "disambiguation": by adding elements such as brackets to the generated strings, or by taking the "derivation tree" or "analysis tree" of the expression as the relevant syntactic structure. Some linguists (such as Chomsky, 1975) have expressed skepticism about whether a disambiguated syntactic structure can be independently motivated for natural languages, suspecting that compositionality is a requirement that is not met for natural languages. Some linguists working at the interface between Chomskyan syntax and formal semantics use a level of logical form, a disambiguated syntactic representation that serves as the input to semantic interpretation.

It is still customary to distinguish theory of reference from theory of meaning, a distinction often analyzed in terms of *extensions* and *intensions,* whose history traces from Frege (1892), through Carnap (1956), to Montague. Montague's general framework makes only structural constraints on the nature of the semantic algebras, but typically the extensions are set-theoretic constructs built from two truth-values and a domain of entities. Montague analyzed intensions as functions from possible worlds to extensions: propositions as functions from possible worlds to truth values, properties as functions from possible worlds to sets of individuals, and so forth, using a typed intensional logic.

Many critics of possible-worlds semantics argue that the possible-world reconstruction of intensions is "not intensional enough." When propositions are analyzed as sets of possible worlds, all necessarily equivalent sentences are treated as expressing the same proposition, and necessary equivalence is predicted to license substitution *salva veritate* in intensional contexts such as "Jones believes that _____". One response is to treat the problematic contexts as "hyperintensional" (a term coined by M. J. Cresswell, 1985), and construct semantic values more fine-grained than Montagovian intensions, for example, "structured meanings" (Lewis, 1970; Cresswell, 1985). Another response is to argue about the nature of the problematic data and defend the adequacy of possible worlds semantics (as in Stalnaker, 1984.) A third approach is to blame the set-theoretic metatheory, in which possible-worlds semantics is formulated, and replace it with a (much more intensional) property theory (Turner, 1986, 1987; Chierchia & Turner, 1987). Some semanticists advocate working with possible situations, where situations are taken as parts of worlds (Kratzer, 1989; see also Barwise, 1981), as a means of achieving more fine-grained semantic values and simultaneously making possible a more straightforward account of other phenomena such as tense, aspect, nominalizations, and the semantics of event sentences. The semantics of propositional attitudes remains one of the most difficult problems in semantics.

What is more basic than the use of possible worlds is the principle that truth conditions and entailment relations are among the crucial data for a semantic theory, and the working hypothesis that a semantics that is model-theoretic is better able to capture such data than an axiomatic or proof-theoretic approach.

An algebraic approach to semantic structure is implicit in Montague's work and explicit in Link (1983, 1987). On the algebraic perspective, the actual semantic values are not directly significant; what is important for the explanation of semantic properties of expressions is the algebraic structures on the space of semantic values. Link's analysis of the semantics of mass and count expressions employs a nonatomic semilattice structure underlying the semantics of the mass nouns, and an atomic-semilattice for the semantics of the count nouns (Link, 1983).

Other areas of formal semantics in which there has been productive work by philosophers and linguists (with linguists increasingly playing the major role in the United States) include the treatment of indefinite and definite articles, the semantics of quantification and anaphora, the semantics of nominalizations, of event sentences, and of tense and aspect. Linguists commonly devote greater attention to the syntax-semantics interface and to issues of universals and typology across natural languages, and philosophers and logicians commonly devote greater attention to the logical, metaphysical, and epistemological underpinnings of semantic theories; but the division of labor is not sharp.

Important extensions and revisions of Montague's theory include the development of approaches that more closely integrate formal pragmatics, the study of the interaction of language and aspects of the context in which language is used, with formal semantics. Such approaches include 'file change semantics' (Heim, 1982), 'discourse representation theory' (Kamp, 1981; Kamp & Reyle, 1993), and 'dynamic semantics' (Groenendijk & Stokhof, 1990, 1991; Chierchia, 1995). The dynamic perspective, viewing the semantic values of sentences not as ("static") truth conditions but as "context-change potentials" (Heim's term), appears to offer a better and more integrated account of anaphora, quantification, presupposition, and the semantics of a variety of context-dependent expressions.

The development of formal semantics opens up new tools for investigating questions concerning the universality vs. language-particularity of semantics (see Bach, 1986, on "natural language metaphysics").

There continue to be a wide range of approaches to semantics within philosophy, linguistics, psychology,

anthropology, and other fields. Given the nonpsychologism of most formal semantics, inherited from its Fregean roots, its principal competitors are theories with a greater emphasis on mental representations or on the cognitive role of natural language expressions. Some, like Fodor (1975, 1987), posit a universal language of thought and see semantics as translation into the language of thought. Others, who can have versions compatible with formal semantics, seek to anchor the semantic interpretation of expressions to their conceptual role, emphasizing the logical space of distinctions we are able and disposed to draw. Continuing philosophical problems include the classic problems of intentionality and knowledge raised by Brentano and Wittgenstein and the integration of the philosophy of mind with semantics and the philosophy of language.

[See also Anaphora; Carnap, Rudolph; Chomsky, Noam; Frege, Gottlob; Intensional Logic; Language of Thought; Logical Form; Meaning; Philosophical Logic; Philosophy of Language; Philosophy of Mind; Pragmatics; Properties; Propositions; Reference; Syntax; Wittgenstein, Ludwig Josef Johann.]

BIBLIOGRAPHY

Bach, E. "Natural Language Metaphysics." in R. Barcan Marcus, G. J. W. Dorn, P. Weingartner, eds., *Logic, Methodology and Philosophy of Science*, Vol. 7 (1986), 573–95.

Barwise, J. "Scenes and Other Situations," *Journal of Philosophy*, Vol. 78 (1981), 369–97.

Carnap, R. *Meaning and Necessity*, 2d ed. with supplements. Chicago, 1956.

Chierchia, G. *Dynamics of Meaning: Anaphora, Presupposition and the Theory of Grammar*. Chicago, 1995.

———, and R. Turner. "Semantics and Property Theory," *Linguistics and Philosophy*, Vol. 11 (1987).

Chomsky, N. *Syntactic Structures*. The Hague, 1957.

———. *Aspects of the Theory of Syntax*. Cambridge, MA, 1965.

———. "Questions of Form and Interpretation," *Linguistic Analysis*, Vol. 1 (1975), 75–109; also in R. Austerlitz, ed., *The Scope of American Linguistics* (Philadelphia, 1975).

Cresswell, M. J. *Logics and Languages*. London, 1973.

———. *Structured Meanings*. Cambridge, MA, 1985.

Dowty, D., R. Wall, and S. Peters, eds. *Introduction to Montague Semantics*. Dordrecht, 1981.

Fodor, J. A. *The Language of Thought*. New York, 1975.

———. *Psychosemantics: The Problem of Meaning in the Philosophy of Mind*. Cambridge, MA, 1987.

Frege, G. "Über Sinn und Bedeutung." *Zeitschrift für Philosophie und philosophische Kritik*, Vol. 100 (1892), 25–50. Translated as "On Sense and Reference," in P. T. Geach and M. Black, eds., *Translations from the Philosophical Writings of Gottlob Frege* (Oxford, 1952).

Gamut, L. T. F. *Logic, Language, and Meaning, Vol. II: Intensional Logic and Logical Grammar*. Chicago, 1991.

Groenendijk, J., and M. Stokhof. "Dynamic Montague Grammar," in L. Kalman and L. Polos, eds., *Papers from the Second Symposium on Logic and Language* (Budapest, 1990).

———. "Dynamic Predicate Logic," *Linguistics and Philosophy*, Vol. 14 (1991).

Heim, I. *The Semantics of Definite and Indefinite NP's*, Ph.D. dissertation, Amherst, MA, 1982.

Kamp, H. "A Theory of Truth and Semantic Representation," in J. Groenendijk, T. Janssen, and M. Stokhof, eds., *Formal Methods in the Study of Language; Proceedings of the Third Amsterdam Colloquium* (Amsterdam, 1981). Reprinted in J. Groenendijk, T. M. V. Janssen, and M. Stokhof, eds., *Truth, Interpretation and Information* (Dordrecht, 1984).

Kamp, H., and U. Reyle. *From Discourse to Logic*. Dordrecht, 1993.

Kratzer, A. "An Investigation of the Lumps of Thought," *Linguistics and Philosophy*, Vol. 12 (1989), 607–53.

Lewis, D. "General Semantics," *Synthese*, Vol. 22 (1970), 18–67; reprinted in D. Davidson and G. Harman, eds., *Semantics of Natural Language* (Dordrecht, 1972).

Link, G. "The Logical Analysis of Plurals and Mass Terms: A Lattice-Theoretic Approach," in R. Bauerle et al., eds., *Meaning, Use and Interpretation of Language* (Berlin, 1983).

———. "Algebraic Semantics of Event Structures," in J. Groenendijk, M. Stokhof, and C. Veltman, eds., *Proceedings of the Sixth Amsterdam Colloquium* (Amsterdam, 1987).

Montague, R. "English as a Formal Language," in B. Visentini et al., eds., *Linguaggi nella Societa e nella Tecnica* (Milan, 1970a).

———. "Universal Grammar." *Theoria*, Vol. 36 (1970b), 373–98; reprinted in Montague (1974).

———. "The Proper Treatment of Quantification in Ordinary English," in K. J. J. Hintikka, J. M. E. Moravcsik, and P. Suppes, eds., *Approaches to Natural Language* (Dordrecht, 1973).

———. *Formal Philosophy: Selected Papers of Richard Montague*, edited and with an introduction by R. Thomason (New Haven, 1974).

Newmeyer, F. J. *Linguistic Theory in America*. New York, 1980.

Stalnaker, R. C. *Inquiry*. Cambridge, MA, 1984.

Turner, R. "Formal Semantics and Type-Free Theories," in J. Groenendijk, D. de Jongh, and M. Stokhof, eds., *Studies in Discourse Representation Theory and the Theory of Generalized Quantifiers* (Dordrecht, 1986).

———. "A Theory of Properties." *Journal of Symbolic Logic*, Vol. 52 (1987), 455–72.

– BARBARA H. PARTEE

SENSE

Sense is the distinctive central notion in theories of thought and language inspired by the later work of Gottlob Frege ("sense" translates Frege's *Sinn*). For Frege what we think (not the act of thinking it) is a thought, an abstract object. Thoughts have quasi-syntactic structure. Any simple or complex constituent of a thought, even the thought itself, is a sense; thus, senses are abstract. Frege assumes that it is irrational to assent to a thought and simultaneously dissent from it. Since someone misled about astronomy may rationally combine assent to the thought that Hesperus is Hesperus with dissent from the thought that Hesperus is Phosphorus, the thoughts are distinct. Although the names "Hesperus" and "Phosphorus" have the same reference, they express different sense, two modes of presentation of one planet. The role of a sense is to present the thinker with a reference—that is, something on which

the truth value (truth or falsity) of the thought depends; if the sense fails to present a reference, the thought lacks a truth value. For Frege the truth value of a thought is independent of where, when, and by whom it is thought. Thus, what reference a constituent sense presents is independent of when, where, and by whom it is thought. Sense determines reference, not vice versa.

Any simple or complex constituent of a thought,

even the thought itself, is a sense;

thus, senses are abstract.

Frege used his notion of sense to analyze the semantics of thought attributions in natural language, as in the sentence "Someone doubts that Hesperus is Phosphorus". On Frege's account expression within such "that" clauses refer to their customary senses. This explains the presumed failure of the inference from that sentence and "Hesperus is Phosphorus" to "Someone doubts that Hesperus is Hesperus": the two names have different references within "that" clauses, for their customary senses are different. If sense determines reference, then the sense of "Hesperus" in "Someone doubts that Hesperus is Phosphorus" defers from its sense in "Hesperus is Phosphorus", since the reference differs. By appeal to iterated attributions such as "He doubts that she doubts that Hesperus is Phosphorus", it can be argued that Frege is committed to an infinite hierarchy of senses. His account involves the assignment of senses to natural-language expressions. However, in order to understand many words (e.g., proper names and natural kind terms), there is arguably no particular way in which one must think of their reference; they do not express senses common to all competent speakers. Fregeans therefore distinguish sense from linguistic meaning but in doing so sacrifice Frege's original account of thought attributions.

Sense must also be distinguished from linguistic meaning for context-dependent expressions such as "I". Two people may think "I am falling" and each refer to themselves, not the other. Since the references are distinct and sense determines reference, the senses are distinct, even though the mode of presentation is the same. Others cannot think the sense that one expresses with "I"; they can only think about it. Communication here does not amount to the sharing of thoughts, and "You think that I am falling" does not attribute to the hearer the thought that the speaker expresses with "I am falling". In contrast, the linguistic meaning of "I" is the same for everyone; it consists in the rule that each token of "I" refers to its producer. Unlike a sense, the rule determines reference only relative to context. Such cases reveal tensions within Frege's conception of sense. Sense cannot be both what determines reference and how it is determined. Since senses can be qualitatively identical but numerically distinct, they are not purely abstract objects, if qualitatively identical purely abstract objects must be numerically identical.

Although Fregeans distinguish sense from linguistic meaning, they still treat a given speaker on a given occasion as expressing senses in words. Frege gave the impression that the sense expressed by a word was a bundle of descriptions that the speaker associated with it: the word refers to whatever best fits the descriptions. However, this descriptive model of reference has fared badly for proper names and natural-kind terms. Nondescriptive models may also allow different routes to the same reference, but that is a difference in sense only if it is a difference in presentation to the thinker.

In spite of these problems a role for something like sense remains. An account is needed of the deductions that thinkers are in a position to make. When, for example, is one in a position to deduce "Something is black and noisy" from "That is black" and "That is noisy"? It is necessary but not sufficient that the two tokens of "that" refer to the same thing, for, even if they do, the thinker may lack evidence to that effect: perhaps one refers through sight, the other through hearing. What is needed is more like identity of sense than identity of reference. Thus, the theory of rational inference may still require a notion of sense. It does not follow that thinkers are always in a position to know whether given senses are identical, for it is not obvious that they are always in a position to know what deductions they are in a position to make.

[See also Frege, Gottlob; Reference; Semantics.]

BIBLIOGRAPHY

Burge, T. "Sinning against Frege," *Philosophical Review*, Vol. 88 (1979), 398–432.

Campbell, J. "Is Sense Transparent?" *Aristotelian Society Proceedings*, Vol. 88 (1987–88), 273–92.

Dummett, M. *Frege: Philosophy of Language*, 2d ed. London, 1981.

Forbes, G. "The Indispensability of *Sinn*," *Philosophical Review*, Vol. 99 (1990), 535–63.

Kripke, S. *Naming and Necessity*. Oxford, 1980.

McDowell, J. "On the Sense and Reference of a Proper Name," *Mind*, Vol. 86 (1977), 159–85.

Peacocke, C. "Sense and Justification," *Mind*, Vol. 101 (1992), 793–816.

Perry, J. *The Problem of the Essential Indexical and Other Essays*. Oxford, 1993.

Salmon, N. *Frege's Puzzle*. Atascadero, CA, 1986.

— TIMOTHY WILLIAMSON

SENSIBILITY THEORIES

Sensibility theories concern moral realism and its rivals moral relativism and noncognitivism. Misunderstandings have tended to prevent any consensus here (e.g., Sturgeon, 1986, p. 139 n.34, in analyzing Hare and Blackburn unintentionally but seriously misquotes Hare). Realism claims there are moral truths and properties to discover and know, and these truths and properties are objective in that they exist independently of beliefs and practices per se. Relativism claims moral truths are subjective in that they are relative to and dependent on endorsement by a relevant group's or individual's beliefs or practices. Noncognitivism claims there are no moral truths to know. This entry discusses the views of Blackburn (combining elements of realism and relativism into a view called projectivism); Harman (relativism); McDowell (realism); and so-called Cornell realists, Boyd, Brink, and Sturgeon. Our abilities to perceive moral properties and be motivated by them constitute our moral sensibility, which is the focus of this debate on whether objective moral knowledge exists.

Our abilities to perceive moral properties and be motivated by them constitute our moral sensibility, which is the focus of the debate on whether objective moral knowledge exists.

On motivation the key issue concerns the prescriptive nature of morality. How can morality objectively and universally prescribe grounds for action that constrain and motivate us if, as David Hume suggests, belief alone is inert and motivation always depends on the contingent presence of desire in the subject? Must there be a mysterious moral sense that detects queer moral properties? McDowell rejects Hume's belief/desire model and accepts internalism, which claims that knowledge that an act is moral implies some motivation to do that act. Externalism denies this. Harman and some noncognitivists such as Mackie are also internalists. But, though some standard accounts of moral realism omit Brink, his externalist moral realism seems the most defensible version of realism. Completely apathetic people who know they should give to famine relief are counterexamples to internalism. Dancy's alleged counterexample to externalism is looking before crossing the street without any desire to look. But this seems a habitual reflex rather than voluntary action relevant for morality. Externalism dodges Mackie's noncognitivist arguments by avoiding the necessity of postulating a mysterious moral sense or queer moral properties to sense, since externalism denies that morality has a strange and necessary motivational power over us. Rather, externalists think morality gives us intellectual grounds to be moral, which we might not care to be. But the desire to be moral is so common it is taken for granted and too often forgotten by the internalists.

Far from thinking morality is threatened by its dependence on our desires to move us, Blackburn claims, "We cannot become corrupt overnight" (1985, p. 14). But this seems somewhat naive, since we can easily imagine a corrupting evening.

The issue of perception concerns whether moral properties are like secondary qualities such as color and what explanatory role morality can play analogous to explanation in empirical science. Sturgeon (relying on Boyd) argues against Harman on moral explanations. McDowell would agree with Sturgeon that values can have causal relations, suggesting values can form moral explanations. The force of the abolitionists' moral arguments, for example, can help explain the end of slavery. Harman thinks no moral explanations can avoid reduction to nonmoral explanations. But this seems irrelevant, since biological explanations, for example, would still be significant even if one can reduce them to chemical explanations. Harman is led to relativism because he thinks morality, unlike science, is closed to discovery by observation. But we seem to observe moral values, or their absence, when we see, for example, courage, cowardice, honesty, and so forth.

Harris summarizes three serious flaws in Harman's relativism, which states that inner judgments (judgments of people rather than outer judgments, judgments of acts) are relative to culture. First, consider "Hitler showed himself to be evil by ordering the extermination of Jews." Harris claims, "if Harman is right, this should sound odd because it is an inner judgment and Hitler and the Nazi[s] . . . did not share our moral sensibilities. But surely there is a perfectly straightforward sense in which it is not odd" (1992, p. 31). Second, sometimes the impropriety of blaming people when they could not have been expected to act differently seems to be based on moral considerations rather than Harman's distinction between inner and outer judgments (e.g., Hitler was exposed to more moral views than some cannibals were and so it is more reasonable to criticize Hitler). Third, outer judgments may be more important for morality than the inner judgments Harman emphasizes.

Returning to science and morality, Blackburn claims, "that moral properties supervene upon natural ones is not a scientific fact, and it *is* criterial of incompetence in moralizing to fail to realize that they must do so" (1985, p. 14). But Brink denies this, since he insists "ethical supernaturalism can be defended" (1989, p. 211). Cornell realists, however, try to reduce moral properties to natural ones (e.g., utility). Brink's realism has other problems concerning self-evidence as perception. First, Brink seems to argue invalidly that there are no "self-evidently true" beliefs because no belief is "self-justifying" (1988, p. 117); for he admits: "Truth and justification appear to be distinct properties of beliefs" (p. 31). Second, Brink goes too far to conclude that "justification . . . should not guarantee truth" merely from his premise that justification need not guarantee truth (p. 31). A second argument is a justification that guarantees the truth of its conclusion. Third, Brink claims, "no belief about the world can also be the reason for thinking that that belief is true" (p. 117). Brink claims "neither moral nor non-moral beliefs can be self-evident" (p. 211). But what of counterexamples such as "Some belief exists," "Something exists," and "The world exists"? Further, any denial of a clear contradiction (e.g., "Ra did not create everything in the world including Ra") is self-justifying and self-evident.

Blackburn's view also has problems concerning perception. Blackburn thinks we project values onto the world rather than have causal relations with them. But McDowell thinks values are secondary qualities in the world. Blackburn claims, "Colours really exist, although the reality which contains them is not independent of the fact that there also exist human modes of perception" (1985, p. 13). But many nonhuman animals perceive color, and the wavelengths making up the spectrum of white light would still exist after human extinction. McDowell claims, "No doubt it is true that a given thing is red in virtue of some microscopic textural property of its surface; but a predication understood only in such terms—not in terms of how the object would look—would not be an ascription of the secondary quality of redness" (1985, p. 112). But he gives no argument for this key claim. Further, to say a thing reflects the red part of the spectrum is to say something about how it would look to an observer of that wavelength.

McDowell thinks pain, which is observable, gives us moral reason to avoid a painful act. Cornell realists would agree. But a masochist or extreme skeptic can still deny that we directly observe the evil in all pain. Further, Blackburn (1985, pp. 13–15) and Sinnott-Armstrong (1980, pp. 90 and 95) present several differences between values and secondary qualities that collectively help undermine McDowell's view.

In conclusion, Cornell realists rebut many of the attacks on realism, but they fail to provide any affirmative case for realism. They seem content to defend moral realism as no more objectionable than scientific realism, which has many controversies of its own.

[See also Ethical Theory; Hare, Richard M.; Hume, David; Mackie, John Leslie; Moral Realism; Moral Relativism; Perception; Projectivism.]

BIBLIOGRAPHY

Blackburn, S. "Errors and the Phenomenology of Value," in T. Honderich, ed., *Morality and Objectivity* (London, 1985).

Boyd, R. N. "How to Be a Moral Realist," in G. Sayre-McCord, ed., *Essay on Moral Realism* (Ithaca, NY, 1988).

Brink, D. O. *Moral Realism and the Foundations of Ethics*. Cambridge, 1989.

Dancy, J. "Intuitionism," in P. Singer, ed., *A Companion to Ethics* (Oxford, 1991).

Harman, G. *The Nature of Morality: An Introduction to Ethics.* Oxford, 1977.

Harris, C. E., Jr. *Applying Moral Theories*, 2d ed. Belmont, CA, 1992.

McDowell, J. "Values and Secondary Qualities," in T. Honderich, ed., *Morality and Objectivity* (London, 1985).

Mackie, J. L. *Ethics: Inventing Right and Wrong.* Harmondsworth, Middlesex, 1977.

Sinnott-Armstrong, W. "Moral Experience and Justification," *Southern Journal of Philosophy*, Vol. 29, Supplement (1990), 89–96.

Sturgeon, N. L. "Moral Explanations," in D. Copp and D. Zimmerman, eds., *Morality, Reason, and Truth: New Essays on the Foundations of Ethics* (Totowa, NJ, 1984).

———. "What Difference Does it Make Whether Moral Realism Is True?" *Southern Journal of Philosophy*, Vol. 24, Supplement (1986), 115–41.

— STERLING HARWOOD

SET THEORY

Modern set theory began with a single discovery in 1963—the proof by Paul Cohen of Stanford University that Cantor's continuum problem is undecidable on the basis of the accepted axioms of set theory.

The continuum problem asks for the cardinality of the real number continuum in terms of Cantor's system of infinite cardinal numbers, $\aleph_0, \aleph_1, \aleph_2, \ldots$ The 'continuum hypothesis', proposed by Cantor, is that the continuum has cardinality equal to the first uncountable cardinal, $\aleph_1$. In a classic monograph published in 1940, Gödel had proved that the continuum hypothesis could not be disproved—it is consistent with the Zermelo-Fraenkel axioms of set theory. Cohen's 1963 result showed that the continuum hypothesis could not be proved in Zermelo-Fraenkel set theory, and hence is undecidable.

Important though the resolution of the continuum problem was in its own right—the problem was the first of the twenty-three "most significant open problems of mathematics" listed by David Hilbert in his famous address of 1900—by far the greatest significance of Cohen's result lay in the method he used. Cohen invented a new technique, known as 'forcing', that can be used to construct models of set theory having particular properties. Using this method, one starts with a countable transitive model M of (Zermelo-Fraenkel) set theory and constructs a second transitive model N of set theory called a 'generic extension' of M, such that (1) $M \subseteq N$, and (2) M and N have the same set of ordinals. The method of forcing enables this to be done in such a way that certain properties of N can be controlled within M. In particular, Cohen was able to control within the initial model M certain aspects of the cardinal arithmetic of N—specifically that M and N have the same set of cardinals and, in N, the continuum has cardinality unequal to $\aleph_1$.

Following Cohen's breakthrough, Robert Solovay showed that the method of forcing had wide applicability. In particular, he developed a general theory of forcing and applied it to establish the undecidability of a number of open problems of set theory. Soon afterward, Dana Scott and Robert Solovay independently developed an alternative treatment of the method of forcing, the method of 'Boolean-valued models'. In this approach, one starts with a given universe of set theory—the universe one is working in—and constructs a class of 'Boolean-valued sets' in which the characteristic function of each 'set' has values ranging over a given (complete) Boolean algebra B. In the Boolean-valued universe, any set-theoretic proposition has a Boolean truth-value in the Boolean algebra B. The axioms of set theory and all the axioms of predicate logic have Boolean value 1. The value of other propositions can depend on the choice of B. By choosing the algebra B appropriately, a Boolean universe can be obtained in which the truth value of a particular proposition Φ can be made to be less than 1, which demonstrates that Φ cannot be a theorem of set theory.

Many undecidability results were obtained by constructing a particular Boolean algebra using a technique called 'iterated forcing', developed initially by Solovay and Tony Martin. Iterated forcing enables the construction of a generic extension N of a model M that has the properties one could obtain in principle by an increasing transfinite sequence $N_1, N_2, N_3, \ldots N_\alpha, \ldots$ of generic extensions. In the 1980s, Saharon Shelah developed a refinement of iterated forcing known as 'proper forcing'.

The method of forcing led to several developments in the theory of large cardinals. A 'large cardinal axiom' arises from the postulation of a certain set-theoretic property P when it is demonstrated that any set X for which P(X) holds must have 'large' cardinality. One of the criteria for an uncountable cardinal κ being called a 'large cardinal' is that κ is regular (i.e., equal to its own cofinality) and such that $2^\lambda < \kappa$ for all cardinals $\lambda < \kappa$. Such cardinals are said to be 'inaccessible' and are fixed points in the sequence of alephs, i.e., $\aleph_\kappa = \kappa$. Moreover, if κ is an inaccessible cardinal, then V_κ, the set of all sets of rank less than κ, is a model of set theory. By virtue of Gödel's incompleteness theorem, it follows that the existence of a cardinal having any particular 'large cardinal property' cannot be proved.

Important though the resolution

of the continuum problem was in its own right,

by far the greatest significance of Cohen's result

lay in the method he used.

An example of a large cardinal property is the property P that says a set X of uncountable cardinality κ supports a κ-additive, two-valued measure defined on all subsets of X that vanishes on all singletons and is unity on X. The cardinality of such a set is said to be a 'measurable cardinal'. Measurable cardinals are fixed points for the function that enumerates the inaccessible cardinals. Despite a number of attempts to prove that measurable cardinals do not exist, it remains a possibility that the existence of such a cardinal is consistent with the Zermelo-Fraenkel axioms, and their present status is thus controversial.

The technique used by Gödel to prove that the continuum hypothesis is consistent with Zermelo-Fraenkel set theory involved his notion of 'constructibility'. The class of all constructible sets, L, is obtained by mimicking the recursive construction of the set-theoretic hierarchy by iteration of the power set operation, but instead of taking $V_{\alpha+1}$ to be the set of all subsets of V_α, one takes $L_{\alpha+1}$ to be the set of all subsets of L_α that are definable by means of a first-order formula interpreted over L_α (with constant symbols referring to fixed elements of L_α). In the case of limit ordinals γ, L_γ is defined to be the union of all L_α for $\alpha < \gamma$, just as the V_α-hierarchy. Gödel proved that L is a model of the Zermelo-Fraenkel axioms in which the continuum hypothesis is true. Scott proved that in the universe L there can be no measurable cardinals. In the early 1970s, Ronald Jensen developed a powerful analysis of the constructible hierarchy called the 'fine structure theory', which led to a number of major results both in set the-

ory and in other areas of mathematics. In the 1980s generalizations of Jensen's techniques to structures other than the constructible hierarchy led to further advances in the theory of large cardinals.

[See also Gödel, Kurt; Mathematical Logic.]

BIBLIOGRAPHY

Barwise, J. ed. *Handbook of Mathematical Logic.* Amsterdam, 1977. Provides considerable coverage of the various advances made in the 1960s and the 1970s.

Devlin, K. *Constructibility.* New York, 1983. This is the standard reference for work on constructibility.

Jech, T. *Set Theory.* San Diego, CA, 1978. This is a comprehensive information source for the earlier work on forcing and large cardinals.

Shelah, S. "Around Classification Theory of Models," in *Lectures Notes on Mathematics Series,* Vol. 1182 (New York, 1986).

———. "Classification Theory and the Number of Non-Isomorphic Models," 2d rev. ed., *Studies in Logic and the Foundations of Mathematics,* Vol. 92 (1991).

– KEITH DEVLIN

SIDGWICK, HENRY

Henry Sidgwick (1838–1900) is renowned for giving classical utilitarianism its most sophisticated dress and greatly advancing substantive moral theory. Celebrated for his clarity and cool impartiality, Sidgwick was actually haunted by the specter of skepticism in religion and morality. If he turned utilitarianism into a respectable academic philosophy, patiently distinguishing total from average utility, utilitarian from egoistic reasons, he also reluctantly brought it into the crisis of the Enlightenment.

Educated in classics and mathematics at Trinity College, Cambridge, Sidgwick spent his entire adult life at Cambridge, becoming Knightbridge Professor in 1883. His extensive interests also covered theology, biblical criticism, poetry, ethics, political economy, jurisprudence, political theory, sociology, epistemology, metaphysics, and parapsychology (he was a founder and president of the Society for Psychical Research). He vastly influenced the Cambridge moral sciences curriculum and was a guiding force in the cause of women's higher education and the founding of Newnham College. In 1876 he married Eleanor Mildred Balfour, a force in her own right in psychical research and educational reform.

Sidgwick's masterpiece, *The Methods of Ethics* (1874), was a sustained effort at independent, secular moral theory resulting from his decade of "storm and stress" over the defense and reform of Christianity. It also reveals that, however indebted Sidgwick was to his chief mentor, J. S. Mill, his hedonism was more consistently Benthamite, while his overall position was more eclectic, reconciling utilitarianism with arguments from Aristotle, Kant, Joseph Butler, Clarke, Whewell, John Grote, and T. H. Green. It rejects the empiricism and reductionism of earlier utilitarianism, and adheres to a sophisticated fallibilist intuitionism involving various tests for reducing the risk of error with respect to basic noninferentially known propositions: (1) clarity and precision, (2) ability to withstand careful reflection, (3) mutual consistency, and (4) consensus of experts.

Sidgwick vastly influenced

the Cambridge moral sciences curriculum

and was a guiding force in

the cause of women's higher education

and the founding of Newnham College.

The Methods is largely a systematic critical comparison of the 'methods' of ethical egoism, commonsense or intuitional morality, and utilitarianism—for Sidgwick, the going procedures for determining, on principle, what one ought to do (though he would later devote as much attention to idealism and evolutionism). He takes the notion of 'ought' or 'right' as fundamental and irreducible and gives an internalist account of moral approbation. But he also holds that it is a plausible and significant (not tautological) proposition that ultimate good is pleasure or desirable consciousness; egoism and utilitarianism hence reduce to egoistic and universalistic hedonism. He then shows that earlier utilitarians exaggerated the conflict with common sense, confused the utilitarian and egoist positions, and failed to give their view rational foundations. His exhaustive examination of commonsense morality, after the manner of Aristotle, reveals time and again that such principles as veracity, fidelity, justice, and benevolence are either too vague and indeterminate or too conflicting and variably interpreted to form a system of rational intuitions. Indeed, common sense is even unconsciously utilitarian, since it is apt to resort to that view to complete its own system—for example, to settle conflicts between the duty to speak the truth and the duty to keep one's promises.

Thus, commonsense morality thought through ends in utilitarianism, though utilitarianism grounded on 'philosophical intuitionism', and utilitarianism can in turn rationalize much of commonsense morality as the (indirect) means to the greatest happiness. But no such reconciliation of utilitarianism and egoism is forthcoming, each being, on reflection, equally defensible. Kan-

tian universalizability, the essence of justice, comports with either egoism or utilitarianism and cannot decide between them, though it is another self-evident principle. Sidgwick dismally concludes that there is a dualism of practical reason rendering it incoherent. Without help from epistemology or theology, he has no rational way to settle conflicts between individual self-interest and universal good.

Sidgwick's other intellectual and reformist interests often radiated from his fears about the implications of the dualism of practical reason. Although *The Principles of Political Economy* (1883) and *The Elements of Politics* (1891) tend rather to assume the utilitarian standpoint, they bespeak his concern that human emotions be shaped in a more deeply utilitarian direction, encouraging sympathetic, benevolent sentiments and reigning in egoistic ones. Both his reformism and his philosophical and scientific pursuits were brought to bear on the potential for such societal evolution and the perhaps limited place of reason and religion within it. Never as sanguine as Comte, Mill, or Spencer, his concern for reform was tempered by fear that skepticism and egoism would lead to social deterioration. If Sidgwick was as good at defending an agent-relative egoism as an agent-neutral utilitarianism, this was scarcely the result he sought.

Only by reading *The Methods* in the context of Sidgwick's other work and activities is there some hope of determining whether he was a true government house utilitarian, advocating that the publicity of moral principles be subject to felicific calculations congenial to paternalistic governments, or a defender of the plain person's capacity for genuine moral self-direction, as his focus on 'method' might suggest. At least, a sense of his view as a truly comprehensive moral and political one deeply informed by Kantianism and idealism makes it harder to view him as a naive 'encyclopedist' with no grasp of social theory or the historicity of his own philosophy. But whether he began, in his last decades, to doubt the quest for certainty enough to approximate the pragmatist *via media* is a very difficult question that has put Sidgwick back in the middle of debates over the shape and origins of contemporary liberalism.

[*See also Aristotle; Butler, Joseph; Ethical Egoism; Justice; Kant, Immanuel; Liberalism; Mill, John Stuart; Skepticism.*]

BIBLIOGRAPHY

Works by Sidgwick

The Ethics of Conformity and Subscription. London, 1870.
The Methods of Ethics. London, 1874, 1877, 1884, 1890, 1893, 1901, 1907.
The Principles of Political Economy. London, 1883, 1887, 1901.

The Scope and Method of Economic Science. London, 1885.

Outlines of the History of Ethics for English Readers. London, 1886, 1888, 1892, 1896, 1902.

The Elements of Politics. London, 1891, 1897, 1908, 1919.

Practical Ethics: A Collection of Addresses and Essays. London, 1898, 1909.

Philosophy, Its Scope and Relations. Edited by J. Ward. London, 1902.

Lectures on the Ethics of T. H. Green, H. Spencer, and J. Martineau. Edited by E. E. Constance Jones. London, 1902.

The Development of European Polity. Edited by E. M. Sidgwick. London, 1903.

Miscellaneous Essays and Addresses. Edited by E. M. Sidgwick and A. Sidgwick. London, 1904.

Lectures on the Philosophy of Kant and Other Philosophical Lectures and Essays. Edited by J. Ward. London, 1905.

The Complete Works of Henry Sidgwick. Edited by B. Schultz. Charlottesville, VA, 1995. Contains, as a data base, all of Sidgwick's published works and a selection of his correspondence. Includes a comprehensive Sidgwick bibliography.

Works on Sidgwick

Kloppenberg, J. *Uncertain Victory: Social Democracy and Progressivism in European and American Thought, 1870–1920.* Oxford, 1986. The most extensive effort to link Sidgwick to pragmatism and progressivism in general.

MacIntyre, A. *Three Rival Versions of Moral Enquiry.* Notre Dame, IN, 1990. Presents Sidgwick as the arch-representative of the encyclopedist version, as opposed to genealogy and tradition.

Schneewind, J. B. *Sidgwick's Ethics and Victorian Moral Philosophy.* Oxford, 1977. The single most significant philosophical treatment of Sidgwick's ethics, providing the basis for the interpretation of him as a defender of the ordinary person's capacity for moral self-direction.

Schultz, B., ed. *Essays on Henry Sidgwick.* New York, 1992. Covers both Sidgwick's work in its historical context and the current philosophical interest in Sidgwick.

Williams, B. "The Point of View of the Universe: Sidgwick and the Ambitions of Ethics," *Cambridge Review,* 7 May 1982, pp. 183–91. Nicely surveys Sidgwick's ethics and points up why he could be considered a government house utilitarian.

– BART SCHULTZ

SKEPTICISM

Skepticism regarding a subject matter is the view that knowledge about the subject matter is not possible. Many subject matters have come under skeptical attack. It has been argued, for example, that it is not possible to obtain knowledge about the external world, about as-yet-unobserved states of affairs, and about minds other than one's own. This entry will focus upon skepticism about knowledge of the external world.

The Cartesian Skeptical Argument

The following skeptical argument is suggested by Descartes's first meditation. Consider the skeptical hypothesis SK: There are no physical objects; all that exists is my mind and that of an evil genius, who causes me to have sense experience just like that which I actually have (sense experience representing a world of physical ob-

jects). This hypothesis, says the skeptic, is logically possible and incompatible with propositions implying the existence of the external world, such as that I have hands. The skeptic then claims that (1) if I know that I have hands, then I know that not-SK. To justify premise (1), the skeptic points out that the proposition that I have hands entails not-SK, and he asserts this closure principle: if S knows that φ and S knows that φ entails ψ, then S knows that ψ. The skeptical argument's other premise is that (2) I do not know that not-SK. To justify this premise, the skeptic points out that, if SK were true, then I would have sense experience exactly similar to that which I actually have. Since my sensory evidence does not discriminate between the hypothesis that SK and the hypothesis that not-SK, this evidence does not justify me in believing not-SK rather than SK. Lacking justification for my belief that not-SK, I do not know that not-SK. From (1) and (2) it follows that I do not know that I have hands. A similar argument can be given for each external-world proposition that I claim to know.

Those who think that minds

are physical in nature might well balk

at the skeptic's claim that

the evil-genius hypothesis is logically possible.

Those who think that minds are physical in nature might well balk at the skeptic's claim that the evil-genius hypothesis is logically possible. Accordingly, the skeptic will replace that hypothesis with this updated version of SK: I am a brain in a vat connected to a computer which is the ultimate cause of my (thoroughly unveridical) sense experience.

To see how the foregoing pattern of skeptical reasoning can be extended to other subject matters, let the target knowledge claim be that there are minds other than my own, and let the skeptical hypothesis be that the complex patterns of bodily behavior that I observe are not accompanied by any states of consciousness. The analogue to premise (2) will in this case be supported by the claim that, if the skeptical hypothesis were true, then I would have behavioral evidence exactly similar to that which I actually have.

Denying the Logical Possibility of SK

Let us consider two radical responses to the Cartesian skeptical argument. The evil-genius and vat hypotheses both depend on the assumption that the external world is mind-independent in such a way that it is logically possible for sense experience to represent there to be a physical world of a certain character even though there is no physical world, or at least no physical world of that character. An idealist will deny this assumption of independence. He will maintain that facts about physical objects hold simply in virtue of the holding of the right facts about sense experience. The idealist will then deny that the skeptical hypotheses are logically possible: any world in which the facts of sense experience are as they actually are is a world in which there is an external reality of roughly the sort we take there to be. Thus premise (2) is false: I know that not-SK in virtue of knowing the necessary falsity of SK.

The second radical response to the skeptical argument rests on a verificationist constraint on the meaningfulness of sentences. Like the idealist, the verificationist holds that the sentence "I am a victim of thoroughgoing sensory deception" fails to express a logically possible hypothesis. Given that the sentence fails to express a proposition for which sense experience could in principle provide confirming or disconfirming evidence, the verificationist counts the sentence as meaningless. Since the sentence expresses no proposition at all, it does not express a proposition that is possibly true.

The antirealist puts forward a similar view. He maintains that one's understanding of a sentence's meaning consists in a recognitional capacity that is manifestable in one's use of the sentence. Suppose that the conditions under which a sentence X is true transcend our powers of recognition. Then one's understanding of X's meaning could not be identified with one's grasping of X's recognition-transcendent truth conditions (since such a grasping could not, in turn, be identified with a manifestable recognitional capacity). This conception can be applied to sentences that allegedly express skeptical hypotheses. If we cannot detect the obtaining of their truth conditions, then what we understand when we understand skeptical sentences' meanings must be something other than their truth conditions. Grasping such sentences' meanings instead consists in grasping the detectable conditions under which they are warrantedly assertible. Thus, it would turn out that an allegedly problematic "skeptical" hypothesis fails to make any coherent claims about putative conditions in the world that outstrip our capacity for knowledge.

Attacking Premise (1)

Premise (1) has come under attack by those who think that the skeptic has succeeded in stating a hypothesis that is genuinely logically possible and not known to be false. On this strategy the closure principle is denied. This opens up the possibility that I know that I have hands even though I do not know that not-SK. For example, one might deny closure by maintaining that knowing that φ requires knowing only that the *relevant* alternative hypotheses to φ do not obtain. Skeptical hypotheses, it is then said, are not relevant alternatives to the propositions involved in ordinary knowledge claims.

Attacking Premise (2)

Let us turn to antiskeptical strategies that do not challenge premise (1) and that accept that SK is indeed logically possible. On these strategies premise (2) is attacked. For example, Kant tried to show via a transcendental argument that, in allowing knowledge of certain key features of one's own mind, the Cartesian is already committed to the possibility of knowledge of the external world. Kant argued (in "Refutation of Idealism" in *Critique of Pure Reason*) that, in order to have knowledge of one's own temporally ordered inner states, one must also have knowledge of spatial objects outside one's mind, whose temporal ordering is related to that of one's inner states. A prima facie difficulty for the Kantian strategy is that arguing for a connection between knowledge of one's mind and knowledge of the external world seems to require the assumption of verificationism or idealism, which would render superfluous the rest of the transcendental argument.

The inference to the best explanation strategy relies on the idea that, even if two incompatible explanatory hypotheses are equally supported by the available evidence, I am still justified in rejecting one hypothesis if the other offers a better explanation of the evidence. It might be maintained that the ordinary hypothesis that the world is roughly as I take it to be offers a better explanation of my sensory evidence than does SK, in virtue of its greater simplicity. Thus, I can justifiably reject SK. The proponent of this strategy needs to specify the respect in which SK is more complex than the ordinary hypothesis and to make it plausible that hypotheses that are complex in the specified way are less likely to be true than simpler ones.

Another way to attack premise (2) is to deny that knowledge that not-SK requires possession of sensory evidence that figures in the justification of a belief that not-SK. This denial could be based on a reliabilist theory of knowledge, according to which knowing that φ is a matter of having a reliably produced true belief that φ. If reliabilism is correct, then in arguing that I do not know that not-SK the skeptic would have the difficult burden of showing that there is in fact some flaw in the belief-producing mechanism that yields my belief that not-SK (thereby rendering that belief unjustified).

Finally, one can use considerations from the philosophy of language and the philosophy of mind to argue that SK is in fact false. According to semantic externalism, the Cartesian commits an error in attempting to construct thought experiments involving massive deception. He naively assumes that, starting with a subject S of thought and experience who is ensconced in a normal external environment, we can hold fixed the contents of S's thoughts and the meanings of his sentences while varying (in thought) S's external environment in such a way that S's thoughts come out predominantly false of his environment. According to the semantic externalist, the Cartesian fails to realize that the contents of one's thoughts and the meanings of one's sentences depend in certain ways on one's external environment.

According to semantic externalism,

the Cartesian commits an error

in attempting to construct thought experiments

involving massive deception.

For example, Donald Davidson argues that, when we interpret a speaker's sentences as expressing various beliefs that he holds, we are constrained to attribute beliefs to him that are by and large true of the causal environment with which he interacts. This is because there is no rational basis for preferring one interpretation that finds him to be massively mistaken in his beliefs over another such interpretation. It is constitutive of beliefs and of sentential meanings that they are what are correctly attributed in correct interpretation, on Davidson's view. Thus, it follows from the very nature of belief and meaning that, contrary to what SK states, one is not massively mistaken.

To see another manifestation of this anti-Cartesian line of thought, consider Hilary Putnam's Twin Earth, a planet just like Earth but for the circumstances that the clear, thirst-quenching liquid that the Twin Earthians call "water" is composed of XYZ molecules rather than H_2O molecules. The Twin Earthians' term "water" does not refer to water but rather to the liquid on Twin Earth with which they interact. Hence, my Twin Earth counterpart's word "water" does not have the same meaning as my word, and when he says "water is wet" he does not thereby express the thought that water is wet. Similarly, the semantic externalist maintains that, when my envatted twin in a treeless world uses the word "tree" in thought he does not refer to trees. Instead, he refers to the entities in his external environment that play a causal role with respect to his uses of "tree," a causal role that is analogous to that played by trees with respect to normal uses of "tree" in a tree-filled world. These entities might be states of the computer that sys-

tematically cause the brain in a vat to have "tree-like" sense experience. When he thinks the sentence "A tree has fallen," he does not thereby express the mistaken thought that a tree has fallen. Instead, he expresses a thought about computer states, which thought may well be true of his environment. In general, the brain in a vat is not massively mistaken about his world, contrary to what the Cartesian maintains.

We can use these considerations, together with the assumption that I have knowledge of the contents of my own thoughts, against premise (2) in the following way: I am now thinking that a tree has fallen; if SK is true, then I am not now thinking that a tree has fallen; thus, SK is false. This argument, however, is powerless against versions of the skeptical hypothesis on which the brain in a vat is indirectly causally linked to ordinary objects. If, for example, there are programmers of the computer who refer to trees, then it becomes plausible to suppose that the brain does so as well. Further, there is a prima facie problem as to whether I can claim knowledge of the contents of my own thoughts, given semantic externalism. Such knowledge seems to require independent knowledge of the content-determining causal environment in which I am located, knowledge the antiskeptical argument was meant to provide.

[See also Davidson, Donald; Descartes, René; Epistemology; Inference to the Best Explanation; Kant, Immanuel; Philosophy of Language; Philosophy of Mind; Putnam, Hilary; Reliabilism; Verifiability Principle.]

BIBLIOGRAPHY

Ayer, A. J. *Language, Truth, and Logic.* New York, 1952. Verificationism.

Berkeley, G. *Three Dialogues between Hylas and Philonous.* Indianapolis, 1984. Idealism.

Brueckner, A. "Semantic Answers to Skepticism," *Pacific Philosophical Quarterly*, Vol. 72 (1992), 200–1. Semantic externalism.

Davidson, D. "A Coherence Theory of Truth and Knowledge," in E. LePore, ed., *Truth and Interpretation* (Oxford, 1986). Semantic externalism.

Descartes, R. *Meditations on First Philosophy*, in *The Philosophical Works of Descartes*, vol. 1, translated by Haldane and Ross. New York, 1955. The Cartesian skeptical argument.

Dretske, F. "Epistemic Operators," *Journal of Philosophy*, Vol. 67 (1970), 1007–1023. Denying the closure principle.

Dummett, M. "What Is a Theory of Meaning? (II)," in G. Evans and J. McDowell, eds., *Truth and Meaning* (Oxford, 1976). Antirealism.

Goldman, A. "What Is Justified Belief?" in G. Pappas, ed., *Justification and Knowledge* (Dordrecht, 1979). Reliabilism.

Kant, I. *Critique of Pure Reason*, translated by N. K. Smith. New York, 1965. Transcendental arguments.

Nozick, R. *Philosophical Explanations*, Chap. 3. Cambridge, MA, 1981. Denying the closure principle.

Putnam, H. "Meaning and Reference," *Journal of Philosophy*, Vol. 70 (1973), 699–711. Semantic externalism.

———. *Reason, Truth, and History*, Chap. 1. Cambridge, 1981. Semantic externalism.

Stroud, B., "Transcendental Arguments," *Journal of Philosophy*, Vol. 65 (1968), 241–56. Transcendental arguments.

Vogel, J. "Cartesian Skepticism and Inference to the Best Explanation," *Journal of Philosophy*, Vol. 87 (1990), 658–66.

– ANTHONY BRUECKNER

SMART, JOHN JAMIESON CARSWELL

John Jamieson Carswell Smart was born in Scotland in 1920. Working for almost all his career in Australia, he has been a leading figure in the development of the naturalistic and science-oriented approach to philosophy characteristic of the period following the mid-century dominance of conceptual analysis.

Educated at Glasgow (M.A. 1946, with honors in philosophy, mathematics, and natural philosophy) and Oxford, he came under the influence of Gilbert Ryle and the linguistic analytic movement of that time. After a short period as a junior research fellow at Corpus Christi College, he accepted, at the age of twenty-nine, the chair of philosophy at the University of Adelaide. Smart moved to a readership at La Trobe University in Melbourne in 1972 and filled a chair in the Research School of Social Sciences of the Australian National University from 1976 until his retirement in 1985, following which he continued to be active in philosophy.

Smart came to see philosophy

as best pursued through reflection on

the methods and successes of natural science.

Soon after his arrival in Australia, Smart came to see philosophy as best pursued through reflection on the methods and successes of natural science. Showing the influence of David Hume and of the contemporary American philosopher Willard Van Orman Quine, Smart's metaphysics and epistemology have been consistently empiricist. He is extensionalist in logic, is nominalist in metaphysics, holds a regularity view of natural law, and is realist in the interpretation of scientific theories. In ethics he has defended an act utilitarian consequentialism, not flinching from some of its more controversial implications.

Most of Smart's mature work has centered on three major themes—physical realism, materialism, and utilitarianism.

In a series of papers beginning with "The River of Time" (1949) and continuing through to *Our Place in the Universe* (1989), Smart argues for the four-dimensional space–time conception of the cosmos, which implies the equal reality of past, present, and future and the unreality of any flow of time. *Philosophy and Scientific Realism* (1963) saw the first appearance of another continuing theme: a realist stance toward unobservable theoretical entities in the natural sciences that appeals to inference to the best explanation. The complex, interlocking set of experimental results that we have now obtained and validated about electrons, for instance, would constitute an incredible set of coincidences, for which there could be no intelligible accounting, unless the electron theory were close to the literal truth concerning those levels that transcend our direct observation.

Smart is a materialist: there are no spiritual or nonphysical mental realities. Our minds are our brains; our states of mind are states or processes occurring in the nervous system. Smart's "Sensations and Brain Processes" (1959) was an early expression of this central-state materialism. He expanded and defended its claims in subsequent discussions, both of the general issue and of its implications for secondary qualities, particularly color.

From *An Outline of a System of Utilitarian Ethics* (1961) on, Smart has presented the utilitarian view that the actual consequences of our behavior determine its moral value. The consequences to consider concern the happiness of all sentient beings, judged from a natural, secular point of view. He recognizes the difficulties that questions of justice generate for an unbending utilitarian theory and has not been able to reach a definitive resolution of this conflict in his ethical thought. In *Ethics, Persuasion, and Truth* (1984) Smart presents a sophisticated subjectivist theory of the meaning and logical status of moral judgments.

Our Place in the Universe is his philosophic testament. Recapitulating many of the central themes of his writings, it draws them together in a naturalistic vision—of spatio-temporal physical reality and of the living, conscious systems to be found on earth—that is suffused with an attractive natural piety.

[See also Consequentialism; Hume, David; Inference to the Best Explanation; Philosophy of Mind; Physicalism, Materialism; Quine, Willard Van Orman.]

BIBLIOGRAPHY

Works by Smart

An Outline of a System of Utilitarian Ethics. Melbourne, 1961. Rev. ed., J. J. C. Smart and B. Williams, *Utilitarianism, For and Against.* London, 1973.

Philosophy and Scientific Realism. London, 1963.

Between Science and Philosophy: An Introduction to the Philosophy of Science. New York, 1968.

Ethics, Persuasion, and Truth. London, 1984.

Essays, Metaphysical and Moral. Oxford, 1987. This collects the more important of over 120 journal articles and book chapters.
Our Place in the Universe. Oxford, 1989.

Work on Smart

Pettit, P., R. Sylvan, and J. Norman, eds. *Metaphysics and Morality: Essays in Honour of J. J. C. Smart.* Oxford, 1987.

– KEITH CAMPBELL

SOCIAL AND POLITICAL PHILOSOPHY

It is generally agreed that the central task of social and political philosophy is to provide a justification for coercive institutions. Coercive institutions range in size from the family to the nation-state and world organizations, such as the United Nations, with their narrower and broader agendas for action. Yet essentially they are institutions that at least sometimes employ force or the threat of force to control the behavior of their members to achieve either minimal or wide-ranging goals. To justify such coercive institutions, we need to show that the authorities within these institutions have a right to be obeyed and that their members have a corresponding duty to obey them. In other words, we need to show that these institutions have legitimate authority over their members.

In philosophical debate at the end of the twentieth century, a number of competing justifications for coercive institutions have been defended: (1) a libertarian justification, which appeals to an ideal of liberty; (2) a socialist justification, which appeals to an ideal of equality; (3) a welfare liberal justification, which appeals to an ideal of contractual fairness; (4) a communitarian justification, which appeals to an ideal of the common good; and (5) a feminist justification, which appeals to an ideal of a gender-free society. Each of these justifications must be examined so as to determine which, if any, are morally defensible.

Libertarianism

Libertarians frequently cite the work of F. A. Hayek, particularly his *Constitution of Liberty* (1960), as an intellectual source of their view. Hayek argues that the libertarian ideal of liberty requires "equality before the law" and "reward according to market value," but not "substantial equality" or "reward according to merit." Hayek further argues that the inequalities due to upbringing, inheritance, and education that are permitted by an ideal of liberty actually tend to benefit society as a whole.

In basic accord with Hayek, contemporary libertarians such as John Hospers, Robert Nozick, and Jan Narveson define liberty negatively as "the state of being unconstrained by other persons from doing what one wants" rather than positively as "the state of being assisted by other persons in doing what one wants." Libertarians go on to characterize their social and political ideal as requiring that each person have the greatest amount of liberty commensurate with the same liberty for all. From this ideal libertarians claim that a number of more specific requirements, in particular a right to life, a right to freedom of speech, press, and assembly, and a right to property, can be derived.

The libertarian's right to life is not a right to receive from others the goods and resources necessary for preserving one's life; it is simply a right not to be killed. So understood, the right to life is not a right to receive welfare. In fact, there are no welfare rights in the libertarian view. Accordingly, the libertarian's understanding of the right to property is not a right to receive from others the goods and resources necessary for one's welfare, but rather a right to acquire goods and resources either by initial acquisition or by voluntary agreement.

By defending rights such as these, libertarians can support only a limited role for coercive institutions. That role is simply to prevent and punish initial acts of coercion—the only wrongful actions for libertarians. Thus, libertarians are opposed to all forms of censorship and paternalism, unless they can be supported by their ideal of liberty.

Libertarians do not deny that it is a good thing for people to have sufficient goods and resources to meet their basic nutritional needs, but they do deny that coercive institutions can be used to provide for such needs. Such good things as the provision of welfare to the needy are requirements of charity rather than justice, libertarians claim. Accordingly, failure to make such provisions is neither blameworthy nor punishable.

Socialism

In contrast with libertarians, socialists take equality to be the ultimate social and political ideal. In the *Communist Manifesto,* Karl Marx and Friedrich Engels maintain that the abolition of bourgeois property and bourgeois family structure is a necessary first requirement for building a society that accords with the political ideal of equality. In the *Critique of the Gotha Program,* Marx provides a much more positive account of what is required to build such a society: the distribution of social goods must conform, at least initially, to the principle from each according to his ability, to each according to his contribution. But when the highest stage of communist society has been reached, Marx adds, distribution will conform to the principle "from each according to his ability, to each according to his need." Contemporary socialists such as Kai Nielsen and Carol Gould continue to endorse these tenets of Marxism.

At first hearing, these tenets of Marxism might sound ridiculous to someone brought up in a capitalist society. The obvious objection is, How can you get persons to contribute according to their ability if income is distributed on the basis of their needs and not on the basis of their contributions?

The answer, according to socialists, is to make the work that must be done in a society as enjoyable in itself as possible. As a result, people will want to do the work they are capable of doing because they find it intrinsically rewarding. For a start socialists might try to get people to accept presently existing, intrinsically rewarding jobs at lower salaries—top executives, for example, would work for $300,000, rather than $900,000, a year. Yet ultimately, socialists hope to make all jobs as intrinsically rewarding as possible, so that once people are no longer working primarily for external rewards and are making their best contributions to society, distribution can proceed on the basis of need.

Socialists propose to implement their egalitarian ideal by giving workers democratic control over the workplace. They believe that if workers have more to say about how they do their work, they will find their work intrinsically more rewarding. As a consequence, they will be more motivated to work, because their work itself will be meeting their needs. Socialists believe that extending democracy to the workplace will necessarily lead to socialization of the means of production and the end of private property. By making jobs intrinsically as rewarding as possible, in part through democratic control of the workplace and an equitable assignment of unrewarding tasks, socialists believe people will contribute according to their ability even when distribution proceeds according to need. Liberation theology has also provided an interpretation of Christianity that is sympathetic to this socialist ideal.

Nor are contemporary socialists disillusioned by the collapse of the Soviet Union and the transformation of the countries in Eastern Europe. Judging the acceptability of the socialist ideal of equality by what took place in these countries would be as unfair as judging the acceptability of the libertarian ideal of liberty by what takes place in countries such as Guatemala or South Korea, where citizens are arrested and imprisoned without cause. Actually, a fairer comparison would be to judge the socialist ideal of equality by what takes place in countries such as Sweden and to judge the libertarian ideal of liberty by what takes place in the United States. Even these comparisons, however, are not wholly appropriate, because none of these countries fully conforms to those ideals.

Welfare Liberalism

Finding merit in both the libertarian's ideal of liberty and the socialist's ideal of equality, welfare liberals attempt to combine both liberty and equality into one political ideal that can be characterized by contractual fairness.

A classic example of this contractual approach is found in the political works of Immanuel Kant. Kant claims that a civil state ought to be founded on an original contract satisfying the requirements of freedom, equality, and independence. According to Kant, it suffices that the laws of a civil state are such that people would agree to them under conditions in which the requirements of freedom, equality, and independence obtain.

How can you get persons

to contribute according to their ability

if income is distributed on the basis of their needs

and not on the basis of their contributions?

The Kantian ideal of a hypothetical contract as the moral foundation for coercive institutions has been further developed by John Rawls in *A Theory of Justice* (1971). Rawls, like Kant, argues that principles of justice are those principles that free and rational persons who are concerned to advance their own interests would accept in an initial position of equality. Yet Rawls goes beyond Kant by interpreting the conditions of his "original position" to explicitly require a "veil of ignorance." This veil of ignorance, Rawls claims, has the effect of depriving persons in the original position of the knowledge they would need to advance their own interests in ways that are morally arbitrary.

According to Rawls, the principles of justice that would be derived in the original position are (1) a principle of equal political liberty; (2) a principle of equal opportunity; (3) a principle requiring that the distribution of economic goods work to the greatest advantage of the least advantaged. Rawls holds that these principles would be chosen in the original position because persons so situated would find it reasonable to follow the conservative dictates of the "maximin strategy" and maximize the minimum, thereby securing for themselves the highest minimum payoff. In *Political Liberalism* (1993) Rawls explains how these principles could be supported by an overlapping consensus and thus would be compatible with a pluralistic society whose members endorse diverse comprehensive conceptions of the good.

Communitarianism

Another prominent social and political ideal defended by contemporary philosophers is the communitarian ideal of the common good. As one might expect, many contemporary defenders of a communitarian social and political ideal regard their conception as rooted in Aristotelian moral theory. Alasdair MacIntyre in *After Virtue* (1981) sees his social and political theory as rooted in Aristotelian moral theory, but one that has been refurbished in certain respects. Specifically, MacIntyre claims that Aristotelian moral theory must, first of all, reject any reliance on a metaphysical biology. Instead, MacIntyre proposes to ground Aristotelian moral theory on a conception of a practice. A practice, for MacIntyre, is "any coherent and complex form of socially established cooperative human activity through which goods internal to that form of activity are realized in the course of trying to achieve those standards of excellence which are appropriate to and partially definitive of that form of activity, with the result that human powers to achieve excellence, and human conceptions of the ends and goods involved are systematically extended." As examples of practices, MacIntyre cites arts, sciences, games, and the making and sustaining of family life.

MacIntyre then partially defines the virtues in terms of practices. A virtue, such as courage, justice, or honesty is "an acquired human quality the possession and exercise of which tends to enable us to achieve those goods which are internal to practices and the lack of which prevents us from achieving any such goods." However, MacIntyre admits that the virtues that sustain practices can conflict (e.g., courage can conflict with justice), and that practices so defined are not themselves above moral criticism.

Accordingly, to further ground his account, MacIntyre introduces the conception of a telos or good of a whole human life conceived as a unity. It is by means of this conception that MacIntyre proposes morally to evaluate practices and resolve conflicts between virtues. For MacIntyre, the telos of a whole human life is a life spent in seeking that telos; it is a quest for the good human life, and it proceeds with only partial knowledge of what is sought. Nevertheless, this quest is never undertaken in isolation but always within some shared tradition. Moreover, such a tradition provides additional resources for evaluating practices and for resolving conflicts while remaining open to moral criticism itself.

MacIntyre's characterization of the human telos in terms of a quest undertaken within a tradition marks a second respect in which he wants to depart from Aristotle's view. This historical dimension to the human telos, which MacIntyre contends is essential for a rationally acceptable communitarian account, is absent from Aristotle's view.

A third respect in which MacIntyre's account departs from Aristotle's concerns the possibility of tragic moral conflicts. As MacIntyre points out, Aristotle recognized only those moral conflicts that are the outcome of wrongful or mistaken action. Yet MacIntyre, following Sophocles, wants to recognize the possibility of additional conflicts between rival moral goods that are rooted in the very nature of things.

Rather than draw out the particular requirements of his own social and political theory, MacIntyre usually defends his theory by attacking rival theories; by and large, he has focused his attacks on liberal social and political theories and in this respect shares common ground with contemporary deconstructionists. Thus, MacIntyre argues in his *Privatization of the Good* that virtually all forms of liberalism attempt to separate rules defining right action from conceptions of the human good. MacIntyre contends that these forms of liberalism not only fail but have to fail because the rules defining right action cannot be adequately grounded apart from a conception of the good. For this reason, MacIntyre claims, only some refurbished Aristotelian theory that grounds rules supporting right action in a complete conception of the good can ever hope to be adequate.

Feminism

Defenders of a feminist social and political ideal present a distinctive challenging critique to defenders of other social and political ideals. In his *The Subjection of Women,* John Stuart Mill, one of the earliest male defenders of women's liberation, argues that the subjection of women was never justified but was imposed upon women because they were physically weaker than men; later this subjection was confirmed by law. Mill argues that society must remove the legal restrictions that deny women the same opportunities enjoyed by men. However, Mill does not consider whether because of past discrimination against women it may be necessary to do more than simply removing legal restrictions: he does not consider whether positive assistance may also be required.

Usually it is not enough simply to remove unequal restrictions to make a competition fair among those who have been participating. Positive assistance to those who have been disadvantaged in the past may also be required, as would be the case in a race where some were unfairly impeded by having to carry ten-pound weights for part of the race. To render the outcome of such a race fair, we might want to transfer the ten-pound weights to the other runners in the race and thereby advantage the previously disadvantaged runners for an equal period of time. Similarly, positive assistance, such as affirmative action or preferential treatment programs, may be necessary if women who have been disadvantaged in the past by sexism are now going to be able to compete fairly with men. According to feminists, the argument for using affirmative action or preferential treatment to overcome sexism in society is perfectly analogous to the argument for using affirmative action or preferential treatment to overcome racism in society.

Would the most morally defensible

social and political ideal

apply only within a nation-state,

or would it apply more broadly

to distant peoples and future generations as well?

In *Justice, Gender, and the Family* (1989), Susan Okin argues for the feminist ideal of a gender-free society, in which basic rights and duties are not assigned on the basis of a person's biological sex. Since a conception of justice is usually thought to provide the ultimate grounds for the assignment of rights and duties, we can refer to this ideal of a gender-free society as "feminist justice."

Okin goes on to consider whether John Rawls's welfare liberal conception of justice can support the ideal of a gender-free society. Noting Rawls's failure to apply his original position-type thinking to family structures, Okin is skeptical about the possibility of using a welfare liberal ideal to support feminist justice. She contends that in a gender-structured society like our own, male philosophers cannot achieve the sympathetic imagination required to see things from the standpoint of women; nor can they do the original position-type thinking required by the welfare liberal ideal, because they lack the ability to put themselves in the position of women. According to Okin, original position-type thinking can really be achieved only in a gender-free society.

Yet at the same time that Okin despairs of doing original position-type thinking in a gender-structured

society like our own, she herself purportedly does a considerable amount of just that type of thinking. For example, she claims that Rawls's principles of justice "would seem to require a radical rethinking not only of the division of labor within families but also of all the nonfamily institutions that assume it." She also claims that "the abolition of gender seems essential for the fulfillment of Rawls's criterion of political justice."

Applications

Assuming that either libertarianism, socialism, welfare liberalism, communitarianism, feminism, or some combination of these ideals can be shown to be the most morally defensible, questions of application will still arise. For example, would the most morally defensible social and political ideal apply only within a nation-state, or would it apply more broadly to distant peoples and future generations as well? Would it justify war or violence, or would it require some form of pacifism in international relations? Would it apply only to human beings or would it apply more broadly to animals and other living beings? These are important questions of application that must be answered.

Until recently, there was very little discussion of this last question. It was just widely assumed, without much argument, that social and political ideals apply only to humans. However, this lack of argument has recently been challenged by defenders of animal rights on grounds of speciesism. Speciesism, they claim, is the prejudicial favoring of the interests of members of one's own species over the interests of other species. Determining whether this charge of speciesism can be sustained is vital to providing a justification of coercive institutions, particularly those of animal experimentation and factory farming, and thus is vital to fulfilling the central task of social and political philosophy as well.

[See also *Affirmative Action; Animal Rights and Welfare; Aristotle; Censorship; Communitarianism; Deconstruction; Democracy; Distant Peoples and Future Generations; Feminist Social and Political Philosophy; Justice; Kant, Immanuel; Liberalism; Liberation Theology; Liberty; Marx, Karl; Marxism; Mill, John Stuart; Nationalism and International Relations; Pacifism; Paternalism; Pluralism; Racism; Rawls, John; Rights; Speciesism; Violence.*]

BIBLIOGRAPHY

Gould, C. *Rethinking Democracy.* Cambridge, 1988.
Hayek, F. A. *The Constitution of Liberty.* Chicago, 1960.
Hospers, J. *Libertarianism.* Los Angeles, 1971.
MacIntyre, A. *After Virtue.* Notre Dame, IN, 1981.
———. *Three Rival Versions of Moral Enquiry.* Notre Dame, IN, 1990.

———. "The Privatization of the Good," *Review of Politics,* Vol. 52 (1990), 1–20.

Marx, K., and F. Engels. *The Communist Manifesto.* 1888.

Mill, J. S. *The Subjection of Women* [1869]. Indianapolis, 1988.

Narveson, J. *The Libertarian Idea.* Philadelphia, 1988.

Nielson, K. *Liberty and Equality.* Totowa, NJ, 1985.

Nozick, R. *Anarchy, State, and Utopia.* New York, 1974.

Okin, S. *Justice, Gender, and the Family.* New York, 1988.

Rawls, J. *A Theory of Justice.* Cambridge, MA, 1971.

———. *Political Liberalism.* New York, 1993.

Sterba, J. P. *How to Make People Just.* Totowa, NJ, 1988.

— JAMES P. STERBA

SOCIAL EPISTEMOLOGY

Social epistemology has been an important field in philosophy since the early 1980s. It encompasses a wide variety of approaches that regard investigation of social aspects of inquiry to be relevant to discussions of justification and knowledge. The approaches range from the acknowledgment that individual thinkers can be aided by others in their pursuits of truth to the view that both the goals of inquiry and the manner in which those goals are attained are profoundly social.

Individualistic, rather than social, epistemologies have dominated philosophy since at least the time of Descartes and throughout the history of analytic philosophy. The writings of Peirce and Wittgenstein, which present social epistemologies, are among the few exceptions, and they had little effect on epistemological work when they were published. Even the move to naturalized epistemology, taken by many epistemologists after Quine's polemics in its favor, retained individualistic assumptions about knowledge and justification. Quine argued that epistemologists should attend to actual, rather than ideal, conditions of production of knowledge, but he concluded that "epistemology . . . falls into place as a chapter of psychology" (1969, p. 82), ignoring sociology of knowledge altogether.

Movements outside of epistemology motivated and cleared the way for social epistemology. First, and most important, the proliferation of interdisciplinary research on social aspects of scientific change following the publication of Kuhn's *The Structure of Scientific Revolutions* pressured naturalistic epistemologists to take sociology of knowledge seriously. In particular the skeptical and relativistic conclusions of sociologists and anthropologists of science such as Barry Barnes, David Bloor, Steven Shapin, Simon Schaffer, Bruno Latour, Steve Woolgar, Harry Collins, Karin Knorr-Cetina, and Andy Pickering moved naturalistic epistemologists of science to take social accounts of scientific change seriously yet draw their own epistemic conclusions. Second, influential work during the late 1970s in philosophy of language and philosophy of mind—core fields of philosophy—by Putnam, Burge, and others eschewed individualism and began producing social accounts. A more general openness to social approaches in philosophy followed.

Social epistemologies vary along two dimensions. First, there is a range of views about goals of inquiry. This range is the result of a more general, and older, debate in epistemology: goals range from correspondence truth to pragmatic success to socially constituted truths. Second, attempts to attain epistemic goals are evaluated for different subjects of inquiry. Some social epistemologists evaluate the attempts of individual human beings, assessing the influence of social processes on individual reasoning and decision making. Others evaluate the aggregate efforts of groups of people, who may work together or separately. Such disagreements about the unit of inquiring subject for epistemic assessments are the defining debate for social epistemology. Therefore, examples are given of the twofold range of views with more attention on the second.

Goldman, Kitcher, and Kornblith take truth (or significant truth) to be a central goal of all kinds of inquiry. They assess various social processes and practices, such as communication control (Goldman, 1992), intellectual rivalry and credit seeking (Goldman, 1992; Kitcher, 1993), and reliance on experts (Kornblith, 1994) for their conduciveness to attaining truths. Some hold that, although truth is the ultimate epistemic goal, it is mediated by coherence of belief; they examine social processes for their conduciveness to coherence. For example, Lehrer (1990) argues that individual reasoning yields more coherent belief if it makes use of all the information residing in a community, and Thagard (1993) argues that delays in the transmission of information across a community can be conducive to finding a theory with maximal explanatory coherence.

Although the majority of social epistemologists regard truth as the most important epistemic goal, there are a range of other, less traditional, positions. Giere (1988), for example, claims that the goal of scientific inquiry is the attainment of theories that model the world through similarity relations rather than state truths about it and that social practices such as credit seeking should be assessed for their conduciveness to producing good models. More radically, Longino (1990) claims that the goal of scientific inquiry is to produce theories that are "empirically adequate" within a scientific community that satisfies particular criteria of objectivity; differences in values between members of the scientific community increase objectivity. Solomon (1994) claims that scientific goals are composed of empirical and pragmatic goals. Fuller (1993) writes of a range of epistemic goals espoused by scientific communities.

The most radical position is one that claims that our social epistemic practices construct truths rather than discover them and, furthermore, negotiate the goals of inquiry rather than set them in some nonarbitrary manner. Work in the "strong program" in sociology of science—notably by Latour, Shapin, and Woolgar—is frequently guided by such social constructivism. Rorty (1979) has similar views. Most contemporary epistemologists and philosophers of science are motivated by their disagreement with social constructivism, and they argue for the less radical positions described above.

The second dimension along which social epistemologies vary is the unit of inquiry that they assess. The most conservative social epistemology looks only at the effects of social processes on individual reasoning: Goldman's work on the effects of communication control (1992) and rhetoric (1994), Kornblith's work on suggestibility (1987) and reliance on experts (1994), and Coady's work on the role of trust in knowledge (1992) fall into this category. The claim is that individual human beings reason better when placed in a social situation where there is, for example, control of information that could mislead, criticism that employs rhetorical strategies, influence of others' beliefs, consultation with experts, and acceptance on trust of others' beliefs. Epistemic terms such as 'knows' and 'is justified' are, in practice, applied to individual human beings.

Many social epistemologists go further and regard division of cognitive labor as the most important component of the social nature of inquiry. It is wasteful to duplicate the efforts of others, beyond the minimum required to check robustness of results. Different individuals or research groups should, for the sake of efficiency, pursue different avenues of inquiry, especially when there is more than one promising direction to follow. Here it is the distribution of cognitive labor across a community, rather than the decisions of any particular individual, that is epistemically valuable. Kitcher (1993), Goldman (1992), and Shaked have argued that the desire for credit leads to effective division of cognitive labor; Thagard (1993) has argued that the same result is achieved by delays in dissemination of information; Giere (1988) thinks that interests and variation in cognitive resources distribute research effort; Solomon (1992) has argued that cognitive biases such as salience, availability, and representativeness can result in effective distribution of belief and thereby research effort.

Cognitive labor can be divided, not only for discovery and development of new ideas, but also for storage of facts, theories, and techniques that are widely accepted. Just as books contain information that no individual could retain, information is also stored in communities in ways that are accessible to most or all members of those communities, but not duplicated within each head. This is achieved when experts on different subjects, or with different experiences or techniques, comprise a useful variety of resources within a community. Campbell (1979), Kitcher (1993), and Lehrer (1990), among many others, hold that knowledge is social in this way.

Social epistemology encompasses a wide variety of approaches that regard investigation of social aspects of inquiry to be relevant to discussions of justification and knowledge.

Cognitive labor can also be divided for epistemic work in the process of coming to consensus. In traditional philosophies of science, consensus is presented as the outcome of the *same* decision of each member of a scientific community: a good consensus is the result of each scientist's choosing the best theory. Sarkar (1983) and Solomon (1994) each offer normative accounts of coming to consensus in which the epistemic work of selecting the best theory is distributed across the scientific community and no individual scientist need make a fair overall assessment of the merits of each theory.

More radically, social groups can be understood as having emergent epistemic qualities that are due to something other than the sum of the activities, memories, and abilities of their members. Gilbert (1987) argues that group knowledge need have no coincidences with the knowledge ascribed to members of a group. Hacking (1990) identifies conceptual change with linguistic change in a social group. Longino (1990) presents four conditions for objective knowledge: these are social conditions of openness, responsiveness to criticism, standards of inquiry, and equality of intellectual authority in a community of inquirers. Fuller (1993) argues that the goals of a science become apparent only through examining the activities and products of the relevant scientific community. Schmitt (1994) argues that group justificatory processes can achieve, through interactions, more than the sum of individual justifications. Solomon (1994) has argued that good distribution of biasing factors across a community is conducive to scientific progress.

It is not surprising to find that this variety of social epistemologies goes together with many different connections to other disciplines. Economics, artificial intelligence (especially distributed computation), cognitive science, race and gender studies, sociology of science, anthropology, and European philosophers (e.g., Foucault, Habermas) get frequent mention, either for the data or for the methodologies that they supply. It is likely that epistemological theories are not completely general (applying to all disciplines) but that they are at least in part relative to particular domains of application.

When epistemologies are deeply social, recommendations for inquiry will often be applicable to communities, or institutions, rather than to individuals. A future task for social epistemologists is to spell out the details of such recommendations. The traditional focus on individual epistemic responsibility may disappear or be transformed by the addition of new, socially relevant, recommendations.

[See also Artificial Intelligence; Cognitive Science; Constructivism, Conventionalism; Descartes, René; Epistemology; Foucault, Michel; Habermas, Jürgen; Kuhn, Thomas; Naturalized Epistemology; Peirce, Charles Sanders; Philosophy of Language; Philosophy of Mind; Putnam, Hilary; Quine, Willard Van Orman; Truth; Wittgenstein, Ludwig Josef Johann.]

BIBLIOGRAPHY

Barnes, B., and D. Bloor. "Relativism, Rationalism, and the Sociology of Knowledge," in M. Hollis and S. Lukes, eds., *Rationality and Relativism* (Cambridge, MA, 1982).

Campbell, D. "A Tribal Model of the Social System Vehicle Carrying Scientific Knowledge," *Knowledge: Creation, Diffusion, Utilization*, Vol. 1. No. 2 (1979), 181–200.

Coady, C. A. J. *Testimony: A Philosophical Study.* Oxford, 1992.

Fuller, S. *Philosophy of Science and Its Discontents*, 2d ed. New York, 1993.

Giere, R. *Explaining Science: A Cognitive Approach.* Chicago, 1988.

Gilbert, M. "Modelling Collective Belief," in F. Schmitt, ed., *Synthese*, Vol. 73, No. 1 (1987), 185–204.

Goldman, A. *Liaisons: Philosophy Meets the Cognitive and Social Sciences.* Cambridge, MA, 1992.

Hacking, I. *The Taming of Chance.* Cambridge, 1990.

Kitcher, P. *The Advancement of Science.* Oxford, 1993.

Kornblith, H. "Some Social Features of Cognition," in F. Schmitt, ed., *Synthese*, Vol. 73, No. 1 (1987), 27–41.

———. "A Conservative Approach to Social Epistemology," in F. Schmitt, ed., *Socializing Epistemology* (Lanham, MD, 1994).

Kuhn, T. *The Structure of Scientific Revolutions*, 2d ed. Chicago, 1970.

Latour, E., and S. Woolgar, *Laboratory Life: The Construction of Scientific Facts*, 2d ed. Princeton, NJ, 1986.

Lehrer, K. *Theory of Knowledge.* Boulder, CO, 1990.

Longino, H. *Science as Social Knowledge.* Princeton, NJ, 1990.

McMullin, E., ed. *The Social Dimensions of Science.* Notre Dame, IN, 1992.

Quine, W. V. O. "Epistemology Naturalized," in *Ontological Relativity and Other Essays.* New York, 1969.

Rorty, R. *Philosophy and the Mirror of Nature.* Princeton, NJ, 1979.

Sarkar, H. *A Theory of Method.* Berkeley, 1983.

Schmitt, F., ed. *Synthese*, Vol. 73, No. 1 (1987). Special issue on social epistemology.

———, ed. *Socializing Epistemology.* Lanham, MD, 1994.

Shapin, S., and S. Schaffer. *Leviathan and the Air Pump: Hobbes, Boyle, and the Experimental Life.* Princeton, NJ, 1985.

Solomon, M. "Scientific Rationality and Human Reasoning," *Philosophy of Science*, Vol. 59 (1992), 439–55.

———. "A More Social Epistemology," in F. Schmitt, ed., *Socializing Epistemology* (Lanham, MD, 1994).

Thagard, P. "Societies of Minds: Science as Distributed Computing," *Studies in the History and Philosophy of Science*, Vol. 24 (1993), 49–67.

– MIRIAM SOLOMON

SOCRATES

Socrates (c. 470–399 B.C.), of Athens, was perhaps the most original, influential, and controversial figure in the history of Greek thought. Very little is known about his life. He died by drinking hemlock after having been condemned to death for "not believing in the gods the state believes in, and introducing different new divine powers; and also for corrupting the young," according to the indictments recorded in Plato's *Apology* and Xenophon's *Apology*. Philosophy before him was "pre-Socratic"; he was the "hinge," or the orientation point, for most subsequent thinkers and the direct inspiration of Plato. There is no agreement, however, on the exact nature of Socrates' philosophical contribution or on whether anything certain can be said of the historical Socrates. This controversy is known as the Socratic problem, which arises because Socrates wrote nothing on philosophy, unless, perhaps, jottings of self-examination not for publication (cf. Epictetus, *Discourses* II, 1, 32). Not only a historical problem is involved in the nature of the evidence, but also a philosophical puzzle in the character of Socrates embedded in Plato's dialogues.

Two extreme answers which would put an end to further controversy have been put forth in this century. Professors John Burnet and A. E. Taylor have argued that the Socrates of Plato's dialogues, and only he, is the historical Socrates, and agnostics suggest that we know nothing of Socrates, the earliest reports being versions of a literary myth of no greater historical validity than stage Agamemnons.

There are two arguments for the latter view. (1) None of the primary evidence is historical in purpose or character. Aristophanes' comedy *The Clouds* (423 B.C.) is a satire on intellectuals, and Socrates, the chief character, is a mere type. The Socratic dialogues of Socrates' friends and admirers (Plato and the fragmentary minor Socratics—for example, Antisthenes and Aeschines) were not intended as biography but as live philosophy, mostly written well after Socrates' death, where "Socrates" illustrates the writers' arguments, which differ from one another. Xenophon also knew Socrates, but much in his memoirs is probably secondhand and

Socrates was perhaps the most original, influential, and controversial figure in the history of Greek thought. (Corbis/Gianni Dagli Orti)

tainted with the suspect fancies of Greek apologetics. It is demonstrable that the first two chapters of Xenophon's *Memorabilia* are a reply to a literary pamphlet written some time after 394 by the Sophist Polycrates. This pamphlet put a fictitious prosecuting speech into the mouth of Anytus, one of Socrates' accusers. Aristotle, who was not born until 15 years after Socrates' death, probably derived his historical assessment from the earlier suspect literature; anyway, his "historical" comments are often protreptic interpretations for his own philosophy. The frequent references in later antiquity must derive from these suspect sources or from an oral tradition hardening into collected "Sayings of Socrates" (see Hibeh Papyrus 182), an equally untrustworthy source. (2) All the evidence is riddled with contradiction, and not only of details. The whole presentation of one reporter is scarcely consistent with that of another; indeed, the Socratics were bitterly critical of one another. There are no objective facts against which to resolve these inconsistencies.

It should, however, be protested against extreme agnosticism that contradiction among the reports cannot by itself prove them all wholly mythical. Doubt thrown on part of a historical anecdote does not necessarily in-

validate the whole. It does not follow from two contradictory pieces of evidence that neither of them can be true or be explained. We are looking for a common stimulus to divergent interpretations where cancellation by naive abstraction proves nothing. Contradiction should lead to a critical examination of the value of a piece of evidence against the background and context of the individual reporter. Second, literary genres are never mutually exclusive. None of the evidence can be thus dismissed. Who can say that Plato's Socrates is a figment of his literary imagination or that Aristophanes did not reflect current opinions of Socrates? *The Clouds* itself helped to create a historical prejudice about Socrates which was later used against him at his trial; Plato's *Apology* is geared to this historical atmosphere. Polycrates' fictional speech probably embodied another part of the historical prejudice, and Xenophon's account is not invalidated because it is a reply to a fictional speech although its value for us is limited by our knowledge of Xenophon. Aristotle can be shown to have distinguished (*Metaphysics* 987a29 ff. and 1078b9 ff.) between the Platonic and the historical Socrates in the history of a subject, the theory of Forms, on which twenty years in the Platonic Academy must have made him expert. There is no reason to suspect misrepresentation.

It seems to follow that while the skeptics are right in not accepting any evidence per se as having firsthand historical certainty, all the evidence has a right to be regarded as historical interpretations of varying value, from which it may be difficult but not impossible to separate historical plausibility. It is clear this could not be done by simple corroboration but by an estimate of the peculiarities of each reporter's view of Socrates. Only by an intensive study of Plato and the others may we hope to gauge the "lenses" through which they saw Socrates and thus interpret their evidence. Then and only then may corroboration play a significant part.

The question arises whether one reporter should take precedence over the rest. The likeliest candidate is Plato, but he should not be taken as absolutely as Burnet and Taylor take him. For although they argued that it was unlikely that Plato would misrepresent his revered master, it is still more improbable that a man of Plato's ability could postpone his own philosophical progression and, contrary to his Socrates' methods, preach another's philosophy until after he was sixty, when the character of Socrates retired into the background of Plato's dialogues. Nor is it easy to see why a historical criterion should work for Plato's Socrates and not for other writers of the same genre. But it is impossible to believe that the development of "Socrates' " doctrine in the course of the dialogues, which were written after his death, can be other than Plato's; Aristotle was right to make his distinction. Plato's Socrates, too, is an interpretation. Weight should be given, however, to Plato's sincere attachment to Socrates and to his insight into Socrates' thought. Also, although Socratic doctrine must still be disentangled from a study of the development of Plato's thought (and probably never will be to everybody's satisfaction), Plato does give by far the most coherent and convincing picture of Socrates' personality. That Plato thought this personality of prime philosophical importance is the most fruitful thing we know of the historical Socrates. From such principles a plausible account of Socrates may be attempted.

EARLY LIFE AND PERSONAL CIRCUMSTANCES. Our sources insist that Socrates was remarkable for living the life he preached. But information is sparse. He was the son of Sophroniscus (only in later sources described as a stone-mason), of the deme Alopeke, and Phaenarete, a midwife, an occupation translated by Socrates into philosophical activity. The father was a close friend of the son of Aristides the Just, and the young Socrates was familiar with members of the Periclean circle. Later, he was obviously at home in the best society, but he had no respect for social status. His financial resources were adequate to entitle him to serve as a hoplite in the Peloponnesian War, where his courage in the campaigns of Potidaea, Delium, and Amphipolis is offered as evidence that there was a complete concord between his words and character. His later absorption in philosophy and his mission made him neglect his private affairs, and he fell to a level of comparative poverty, which was in tune with his arguments on the unimportance of material goods and his own simple needs. He was probably more in love with philosophy than with his family, but that his wife Xanthippe was a shrew is a late tale and that he was not without interest in parental and filial duties is obvious in his thought for his sons' future in Plato's *Crito*. But all personal considerations, including his own life, were subordinated to "the supreme art of philosophy"; tradition holds that by refusing to compromise his principles, he deliberately antagonized the court which was trying him for impiety and forced an avoidable death penalty. Plato's *Crito* and *Phaedo*, set during Socrates' last days, give a moving and convincing picture of a man at one with himself.

CONTEMPORARY PHILOSOPHY. In Plato's *Phaedo* (96A) Socrates describes his youthful enthusiasm for philosophies that concentrated on physical descriptions of the universe, which were then in vogue, and his subsequent disillusionment with all material explanations of causation. Although the tone and context of Plato's theory of Forms forbid literal acceptance of the whole passage, the general outline is probably correct. The contemporary Ion of Chios recorded that as a young man Socrates was a pupil of Archelaus. Archelaus's

teacher, Anaxagoras, was linked with Socrates' name to stir a prejudice which persisted from Aristophanes' *Clouds* to the trial. But by the time we have any descriptive picture of Socrates, he had abandoned any interest in physics and was immersed in ethical and logical inquiries. It is more helpful to see Socrates against the background of the Sophists. Almost the only information to be derived with any certainty from *The Clouds* is that Socrates (then about 47) was regarded as a Sophist. Polycrates was still attacking him as such after his death, and Plato and Xenophon go to great pains to

---

Philosophy before him was "pre-Socratic";

he was the "hinge," or the orientation point,

for most subsequent thinkers

and the direct inspiration of Plato.

---

distinguish him from other Sophists. The Sophists were itinerant professors teaching for a fee the skill (*sophia*) of *arete* (excellence, in the sense of how to make the best of yourself and get on). Socrates was the Athenian Sophist inasmuch as his life was dedicated to the same new intellectual inquiry into education—the science of effecting *arete*. He might claim that he took no fees and gave no formal instruction, but he would start and dominate an argument wherever the young and intelligent would listen, and people asked his advice on matters of practical conduct and educational problems. Sophists frequently studied language and rhetoric as an obvious key to private and political success; Socrates' interest in words and arguments was notorious. Plato lightheartedly compared him with Prodicus, the specialist in subtle discriminations of the meanings of apparently synonymous words. The terrorist government of Thirty banned any public utterance by him. His very method of argument, dialectic, characterized by destructive cross-examination, could be confused with, and sometimes in Plato falls to the level of, the combative eristic technically practiced by Sophists, who concentrated almost exclusively on technique. The similarities are real. The distortion arises from seeing Socrates simply as the Athenian counterpart of the Sophistic phenomenon. Plato suggests that he differed fundamentally in moral purpose and intellectual standards and so should be contrasted to them.

POLITICAL AND SOCIAL INFLUENCE. Like all generalizations, the classification of Socrates as a Sophist carries such half-truths as the charge, reflected in Polycrates' pamphlet, that Socrates was politically dangerous, the enemy of democracy, and the inspiration of the notorious politicians Alcibiades and Critias. The politician Anytus could not formally bring this charge at the trial since the effective deployment of political attack in the courts was barred by the amnesty decree of 403. But the anti-Sophistic prejudice was real enough in the sensitive restored democracy, which remembered its earlier animosity against supposed political interference by freethinking, unscrupulous Sophists in Pericles' circle.

Nevertheless, in the strict sense the political influence of Socrates is a mirage. The only two public acts recorded by his apologists (see Plato's *Apology* 32Bf.) were refusals to involve himself in state actions he thought wrong; both were courageous personal protests of no political significance. In the *Apology* (31D; cf. *Gorgias* 521C–E, 473E) Socrates explicitly denies political participation. Nor was he a power behind the scenes, for his friends Critias and Charmides when in power tried ineffectively to muzzle his caustic comments (Xenophon, *Memorabilia* I, 2, 32 f.). The association with Alcibiades is testified to by the rash of "Alcibiades dialogues" by the Socratics, and Socrates could not fairly disown his influence by simply denying that he was responsible because he had no financial contract or profession as a teacher. But his influence was always personal, not political. No characteristic political philosophy emerged from the Socratics; even Plato may have conceived his doctrine of philosopher-kings through pondering the injustice of Socrates' conviction and death rather than from what Socrates had said (*Epistle* VII 324C–326B).

However, in the wider Greek sense of "political" there was reason for fearing Socrates as a social force. Where *arete,* education, and state were fused in one image (see Plato, *Protagoras* 325C–326E), an educator critical of received assumptions was a revolutionary. Socrates not only publicly raised such fundamental questions as "What is *arete?*" and "Who are its teachers?," but also by discrediting through their own representatives the accepted educational channels and by creating a climate of questioning and doubt, he was suspected by conservative minds of the dangerous game of discomfiting all authority before a circle of impressionable youths and subtracting from the state the stability of tradition (see the encounter with Anytus in *Meno* 90A–95A). It was also apparent that the values by which Socrates lived, his indifference to material wealth and prosperity, and his freedom from desire and ambition were themselves a living criticism of the actual social and economic structures of Athens. In fact, Socrates claimed the right of independent criticism of all institutions and of politicians who did not seem to know what they were doing or compromised their prin-

ciples; the Athenian democracy was distinguished merely by relying on a majority of ignoramuses. But he did not oppose the authority of law, and in Plato's *Crito* he rejected his friends' plan to smuggle him out of the country by putting forward a theory of social contract imbued with the true Athenian's emotional regard for his country as for a parent. He claimed that he had ruined himself financially in service to the state; yet his unsettling effect on the young and his persistent criticism were intolerable to any establishment. A gadfly, however patriotic (*Apology* 30E), will, if it does not go away by itself, eventually be removed as a poisonous nuisance. That Socrates was not attacked until he was seventy argues that his influence was not so wide as has been suspected (that is, that many did not take him seriously), unless he was saved by the power of his friends or by the charm and sincerity of his own personality.

These discussions, or "dialectics,"

whereby Socrates engaged in his

question-and-answer investigations,

were, for Plato at least,

the very marrow of the Socratic legacy.

RELIGION. The charge made against Socrates of disbelief in the state's gods implied un-Athenian activities which would corrupt the young and the state if publicly preached. Meletus, who brought the indictment, counted on an anti-intellectualist smear that had precedents in the impiety trials of Pericles' friends. The prejudice against Socrates, who was neither a heretic nor agnostic as some Sophists undoubtedly were, had persisted from *The Clouds* and was perhaps fostered by the conduct of Alcibiades in the scandalous parody of the Mysteries in 415 B.C. But Socrates provoked hostility. Two outbursts of feeling are recorded in court. One was at the mention of Socrates' daimonion (hinted at in the charge as a notorious religious innovation), a divine sign apprehended by him alone as a voice from god forbidding a contemplated action. Plato and Xenophon played this feature down, but it was regarded as unique in Socrates (Plato, *Republic* 496C) and was quite distinct from other accepted forms of religious communion. The claim set him dangerously apart from his fellows. The second instance involved the pronouncement of the Delphic oracle to his friend Chaerephon. The oracle said that no man was wiser than Socrates, and Socrates had the audacity to use this as justification of his mission as examiner-extraordinary of the views and conduct of every notable in Athens, claiming that in exposing their false conceit, he proved the god right—he at least knew that he knew nothing. Although this was characteristic Socratic irony—the expression of only half-serious suggestions with a curious mixture of humility and presumption—Socrates clearly thought his mission was divinely inspired, and this involved criticism of the received mythology enshrined in the work of the poets and religious experts. In Plato's *Euthyphro* Socrates challenged both popular conceptions of piety and that of the fanatic who preaches strict interpretation of "scriptural authority." His logical and moral objections to the confused and scandalous standards of anthropopathic deities were aimed at a truer redefinition of piety. He was no mystic. Religion appears to have been a branch of ethics for him, and conscious right conduct in religious matters he held to be dependent on a rational inquiry into what piety was. Yet, the accounts portray, besides the restless searcher for understanding, a man of sincere practice in traditional cult forms, with a simple faith in the providence of a divinity that was good and without contradiction. It was apparently possible for Socrates to contain his religious purification within the terms of the Olympian pantheon.

THE PHILOSOPHICAL PERSONALITY. The political and religious attack on Socrates by his enemies, although understandable, conveys an unsatisfactory picture of the intellectual dynamite which released Plato. Socrates' friends and followers placed his contributions in the fields of morals and logic, but they present a philosophical personality, not a philosophical system. The most striking feature of the evidence is that it required the invention of a new literary and philosophical genre, the Socratic dialogue, to convey his influence. The difference between Xenophon and Plato is as much one of form as of content. The shrewd moral confidant of Xenophon's anecdotal account could have been only of local interest; the character of Socrates in the organic dialogues of Plato has stimulated all Western philosophy. In the dialogues the common Socratic element is not quotation of doctrine, which varies, not the philosophy of Socrates, but Socrates philosophizing.

Socrates philosophized by joining in a discussion with another person who thought he knew what justice, courage, or the like is. Under Socrates' questioning it became clear that neither knew, and they cooperated in a new effort, Socrates making interrogatory suggestions that were accepted or rejected by his friend. They failed to solve the problem but, now conscious of their lack of knowledge, agreed to continue the search whenever possible. These discussions, or "dialectics," whereby

Socrates engaged in his question-and-answer investigations, were, for Plato at least, the very marrow of the Socratic legacy. For those who had not heard Socrates at it, the "Socratic dialogue" was invented.

Plato revealed the advantages of dialectic by contrasting the method with contemporary Sophistic education typified by the set lecture of dictated information or expounded thesis and the eristic technical exercise of outsmarting opponents. For Socrates knowledge was not acceptance of secondhand opinion which could be handed over for a sum of money like a phonograph record (or encyclopedia) but a personal achievement gained through continual self-criticism. Philosophy involved not learning the answers but searching for them—a search more hopeful if jointly undertaken by two friends, one perhaps more experienced than the other but both in love with the goal of truth and reality and willing to subject themselves honestly to the critical test of reason alone.

Socrates was the first openly to canvass this conception of the operation of philosophy and is still the best illustration of it. He thought himself uniquely gifted to stimulate the operation in others. He disclaimed authority on his own part, pleading the ignorance of the searcher; this did not prevent him from directing the argument, which is a different matter from feeding information. An intellectual midwife (Plato, *Theaetetus* 149; already in *The Clouds*), he tested the wind eggs of others and assisted fertile production. Wind eggs predominated, and the *elenchos* (cross-examination) exposing them followed a set pattern: the subject claims knowledge of some matter evidenced in a proposition defining what is usually an ethical term; a series of questions from Socrates elicits a number of other propositions which, when put together, prove the contrary of the original definition. But obstetrics is essentially a personal affair; what is really tested is the person and his false conceit. The premises and argumentation of the *elenchus* are tailored to each individual, even to the extent, in the case of a hostile witness, of fallacious argument. At this point the establishment of truth is not at stake; the question of whether the person will destroy for himself the main blockage of his thought, his false confidence, is the issue. Socrates' zeal for this demolition work produced such aporia (the perplexity of no way out) that he was accused of simply numbing his victims like a sting ray. Plato had to point out, in the illustration with commentary of Socratic *elenchus* which forms the first half of *Meno*, that false conceit was paralysis, and that Socratic disillusionment was the stimulus, of philosophy. "The life not tested by criticism is not worth living" (*Apology* 38A).

Even so, the destructive logic could have stifled, sterilized, and offended more than it did had it not been for an element Plato termed *eros*, denoting not only the passionate attachments Socrates inspired but also that quality of passion in the enthusiasm of a great teacher who fires his associates with his own madness. The young especially felt a personal attraction which was not, despite some ribald stories, physical—Socrates was a popeyed man with a flattened snub nose and could be compared to a Silenus (Plato, *Symposium* 215)—but for his character and his conversations.

Plato's picture is vivid: of a genial but disturbing personality, a social grace and disreputable appearance; a placidity radiating a calm like that found at the center of a storm; the puckish humor and wit offsetting the sharpness of mind and clarity of thought and tireless concentration; the freshness and unexpectedness of his arguments, his power of not exhausting a subject but of opening it up; the warmth of his attachments, his eccentricities, mischievousness, simplicity, deviousness, modesty, and presumption; the knack of bringing a gathering or person to life and leaving it exhausted; the practical example of his life and the uncompromising idealism of his death; a man whose talk foreigners came to Athens to hear; whose homely, not to say vulgar, instances could suddenly uncover penetrating and embarrassing truths; talk with which the best brains in Athens literally fell in love, a talk and beauty of inner man, which they took to be the touchstone of truth and right; above all, the affection in Plato's writing—this picture astonishingly still conveys the magnetism of the personality. And Plato would have us believe that Socrates, as the human embodiment of a philosophical attitude directed by a passionate love of truth and knowledge, finally inspired in his associates the love of *sophia* itself. This claim, of course, may still be tested by the reader of Plato's dialogues.

PHILOSOPHICAL DOCTRINES. Our knowledge of Socratic doctrine is severely limited by his own refusal to formulate his inquiries into a system and by the personal variations of his interpreters. There are indications, however, that the expert skill (*sophia*) for which he so "lovingly" searched in the operation of "philosophy" gained a new meaning through him. His version of *sophia*, unlike that in most pre-Socratic thought, was concerned almost exclusively with the ethics of human conduct (this is the evidence of both Aristotle and the Socratics). "Socrates was the first to call philosophy down from the heavens" (Cicero, *Tusculan Disputations* V, 4, 10). His opposition to the contemporary cult of successful living was based on a new concept of the psyche, to which he assigned for the first time moral and intellectual status, making it the dominant factor in human conduct. This conception was quite different both from popular ideas on the soul and from the psychology of philosophers like Heraclitus (Fr. 119) and the Pythagoreans (see Empedocles, Fr. 115). Socrates advocated the Delphic motto "Know thyself" and suggested that introspection showed how man achieves his real personality—the perfectly efficient realization of his being (*arete*)—when the psyche is in control of the physical and the intellectual and moral part of the psyche is in control of the rest of it (see *Meno* 88E). Happiness (*eudaimonia*), then, depends not on external or physical goods but on knowingly acting rightly. The proper condition of the psyche is thus of prime importance, and the task of philosophy is its care, training, or doctoring (Plato, *Apology* 29Df.). As there is only one proper condition, being good implies the capacity for any virtue; although different virtues are distinguishable, virtue is a unity and a form of knowledge.

Socrates was a man of essentially practical aims who dismissed physics and theoretical mathematics as useless (Xenophon, *Memorabilia* IV, 7). Through his new interpretation of human fulfillment, he was seeking a way by which *arete* and right action could be guaranteed. His own character probably suggested the importance of self-control. Only a man in control of himself is in control of his actions; the self-discipline of moral reason frees a man from the slavery of distracting appetites so that he can do what he wishes—that is, pursue true happiness. Above all, only rationally controlled action is not self-defeating. No one voluntarily makes a mistake. By "voluntarily" he meant consistently with one's true will—that is, to be really happy. Socrates was, of course, familiar with the experience of yielding to temptation, but he explained that in such cases one does not really believe that what one does is bad and does not really know that what is rejected is good. For Socrates "good" was a term of utility signifying advantage for the doer. Thus, he argued that no one would deliberately choose what will harm him or knowingly reject what will benefit him most. If a wrong choice is made, it must be an intellectual mistake, an error which the man who knows could not make. *Arete,* according to another Socratic epigram, is (that is, depends on) knowledge. Socrates was thus hunting for a practical science of right conduct which through its rational organization was infallible, predictable, and teachable. It is this search which the earliest Socratic dialogues of Plato are probably testing.

Clearly, the key to such a science is the interpretation of knowledge, and the evidence here displays a confusion over different types of knowing. Socrates is sometimes represented as comparing his moral expert with other experts of practical skills, suggesting the slogan

"Efficiency (*arete*) is know-how," but he seems to have recognized the moral inadequacy of mere technical expertise. Most frequently, Socrates wanted to know what a thing is (*arete,* justice, or the like) on the assumption that it is impossible to be good (just, or the like) on purpose unless one first knows what it is. If one knows what it is, one can say what it is (unlike the Sophists, who professed to teach *arete* but could not coherently state what *arete* was). Now, since he held that a correct rational account (logos) of what good is was not only a necessary, but even a sufficient, condition of being good, the prime practical business of the philosopher involved the examination of moral terms and the attempt to define them. This is the evidence of Aristotle (*Metaphysics* 1078b17 ff.) and the main activity of the Socrates in the early Platonic dialogues. ("What is courage, piety, beauty, justice, *arete?*" he asked in the *Laches, Euthyphro, Hippias Major, Republic* I, *Protagoras,* and *Meno.*)

Socrates' championship of reason

took deep root in Greek thought,

possibly all the more so

because he did not expound a system.

The failure of the attempt is of much interest. The Platonic Socrates rejected as inadequate definition by instance or enumeration and answers which were too narrow or too wide. The equivalence sought appears to be more than mere verbal identification. Above all, Socrates was not seeking the conventional meaning of the word but what the thing really is—the essence of what is denoted by the word. He seems to have been groping for an analytical formula of the type "Clay is earth mixed with water," which explicates the essential nature or structure of the thing in question. The hope was that if one could recognize for certain with one's mind what was the essential ingredient which made all just acts just, one could recognize any instance and also reproduce an example at will and so act justly. The success of this attempt at real definition was precluded by certain assumptions about the kind of answer and confusion over the type of question involved (see R. Robinson, *Plato's Earlier Dialectic,* 2d ed., Ch. 5); yet even if Socrates had been able to explicate "justice" to his own satisfaction, the question of how knowledge of its description could prescribe our conduct would have remained. The analogies to which Socrates was addicted tended to obscure the idiosyncrasies of moral terms. Nevertheless, a dia-

logue like *Euthyphro* is still an excellent introduction to the problem of definition.

In the *Metaphysics* (1078b17 ff.) Aristotle qualified Socratic definitions as universal. If Socrates did search (as he did in the early dialogues) for a single ingredient which was the same in all instances and for an explanation of them, he was at least logically committed to a theory of universals, which, however, was probably not systematically investigated until Plato constructed, partly from Socratic "definitions," his theory of Forms. Aristotle should be believed when he stated that Socrates did not himself make the universals or definitions exist apart, as the Platonic Socrates did later in the middle dialogues.

Aristotle also said that induction (epagoge) and syllogizing are characteristic of Socrates (*loc. cit.*). Induction probably does not mean the full inductive procedure of the scientist, but merely argument from analogy—by all accounts, one of Socrates' notorious habits, which he most dangerously employed. Syllogizing is "adding together" premises to discover deductively a conclusion; in the aporetic dialogues it is the method by which Socrates elicited conclusions which destroy as contradictories the originally proposed definitions. But if he did hope to construct a science of living, the syllogisms would have been the necessary arguments developing the premises of the real definitions of "what-a-thing-is" into a rational system or science.

Socrates' championship of reason took deep root in Greek thought, possibly all the more so because he did not expound a system. He himself was probably concerned simply with continually testing in public the possibility in action of his rationally dominated ethic, but he never really doubted that it was possible. If he overstressed the power of reason in psychology, this may be partly attributed to his own unique strength of character, which conformed his actions to his thinking. It is also attributable to the paradoxical fusion of *eros*-passion with the rational in him. His reason was infused with desire for the end of good and truth, which attracted his mind by its beauty so that he was in love with it. Plato, too, was infected; with rational detachment he demonstrated the Socratic willingness to "follow the argument (logos) wherever it might lead" in the dialogues. We are also shown how the logos led Socrates to a martyrdom which Plato used to canonize him in emotionally moving prose. It must have been the fusion of logos and *eros* that was so highly infectious; the Socratic evidence is inexplicable unless it was the gift of the historical Socrates. However, what really matters now is not such a historical supposition, but that the Platonic Socrates' love of *sophia* (philosophy) is still contagious. Yet, the incarnation of philosophy in Plato could not have come so convincingly alive had there not been a man who was regarded by Plato as "the finest, most intelligent, and moral man of his generation" (Plato, *Phaedo* 118) and who was also the greatest of mental midwives.

THE SOCRATICS. Socrates established no school. The logos led his associates in different directions, and each was critical of the others. Plato cultivated the seeds in ethics, logic, and epistemology that flowered into a rational system. Of the minor Socratics our evidence is sparse. Antisthenes, stressing the self-sufficiency of virtue and its dependence on knowledge, developed the aspect of self-discipline and freedom from convention. His ascetic tendencies were sneered at by the hedonist Aristippus of Cyrene. Socrates' views on pleasure are hard to discover (see, for example, the hedonistic calculus in Plato, *Protagoras* 351B ff.), but Aristippus's insistence on the intelligent control of pleasure as distinct from slavish adherence or abstinence does not clash with what we hear of Socrates in Plato's *Symposium*, for example. Euclides of Megara may have fused Socratic and Eleatic elements; his school was notorious for an interest, possibly stimulated by Socrates, in the methodology of argument. Phaedo, who wrote at least one Socratic dialogue (Diogenes Laërtius, II, 105, and Cicero, *Tusculan Disputations* IV, 37, 80), founded a school in Elis; Simmias and Cebes were active in Thebes; their doctrines are not known. Aeschines of Sphettus (an Athenian deme), probably a contemporary of Plato, wrote dialogues admired by the ancients for their style and for the fidelity of the portrait of Socrates; indeed, a malicious tale accused him of passing off material of Socrates obtained from Xanthippe as his own. The Stoic Panaetius classed his dialogues as "genuine," together with those of Plato, Xenophon, and Antisthenes. Aeschines' portrait possibly had the smallest ingredient of orginality; it would still be limited by his own capacities and insight. Enough survives of Aeschines' *Alcibiades* and *Aspasia* to give a tantalizing glimpse of these works. Socratic themes briefly appear, but the fragments are too truncated to allow Socrates' personality to emerge, and they are of more historical than philosophical interest. Like Xenophon, Aeschines had no subsequent philosophical influence.

Socrates' influence spread far beyond his contemporaries. The ancients regarded him as the root of most subsequent philosophy. The main stem rose through the Platonic Academy (not least Socratic in its skeptical Middle and New periods), from which Aristotle himself came. From Antisthenes a link (possibly tenuous) was traced through Diogenes to Cynicism. Through So-cratic elements in Cynicism and the Platonic Academy, Stoicism tried to graft itself onto the Socratic tradition, although it was later Stoics like Panaetius and Epictetus who expressly admired the influence of Socrates. Even the hedonistic Cyrenaic school stems from Aristippus. It is possible that Socrates' philosophy may still be growing. "Even now although Socrates is dead the memory of what he did or said while still alive is just as helpful or even more so to men" (Epictetus, *Discourses* IV, 1, 169).

BIBLIOGRAPHY

Primary Sources

In this section and the next sections works are listed to follow the development of themes in the text.

Aristophanes, *The Clouds,* V. Coulon, ed., translated by H. van Daele, Vol. I, 6th ed. Les Belles Lettres. Paris, 1958. Greek text with English translation by B. B. Rogers. Loeb Classical Library. Cambridge, Mass., and London, 1924.

Plato, *Dialogues,* John Burnet, ed. Oxford Classical Texts, 1902–1906. Translated by B. Jowett, 4th ed., rev., 4 vols. Oxford, 1953.

Xenophon, *Memorabilia,* translated by E. C. Marchant. Loeb Classical Library.

Xenophon, *Apology* and *Symposium,* translated by O. J. Todd. Loeb Classical Library, 1922.

Aeschines, *Fragmenta,* H. Krauss, ed. Leipzig, 1911.

Aischines von Sphettos, H. Dittmar, ed. Berlin, 1912.

Antisthenes, *Fragmenta,* A. Winkelmann, ed. Zurich, 1842.

Aristippus, *Fragmenta,* E. Mannebach, ed. Leiden and Cologne, 1961.

Aristotle. See T. Deman, *Le Témoignage d'Aristote sur Socrate.* Paris, 1942.

Diogenes Laërtius, *Lives of Eminent Philosophers,* 2 vols. Loeb Classical Library. See Book 2, 18 ff.

Socratic Problem

Magalhães-Vilhena, V. de, *Le Problème de Socrate.* Paris, 1952. This book and the following work give a good conspectus of the literature.

Magalhães-Vilhena, V. de, *Socrate et la légende platonicienne.* Paris, 1952.

Vogel, C. J. de, "The Present State of the Socratic Problem." *Phronesis,* Vol. 1 (1955), 26 ff.

Historicity of Platonic Socrates

Burnet, John, *Greek Philosophy, Thales to Plato.* London, 1914.

Burnet, John, "The Socratic Doctrine of the Soul." *Proceedings of the British Academy,* Vol. 7 (1915–1916).

Taylor, A. E., *Varia Socratica.* Oxford, 1911.

Taylor, A. E., *Socrates.* London, 1935.

Skeptics

Dupréel, E., *La Légende socratique.* Brussels, 1922.

Gigon, O., *Sokrates.* Bern, 1947.

Gigon, O., *Kommentar zu Xenophons Memorabilien.* Basel, 1953—. Vol. I (1953) and Vol. II (1956) have been published thus far.

Joel, K., *Der echte und der Xenophontische Sokrates.* Berlin, 1893–1901. For Xenophon.

Chroust, A.-H., *Socrates, Man and Myth*. London, 1957. For Polycrates.

Other General Constructions

Zeller, Eduard, *Die Philosophie der Griechen*. Leipzig, 1875, 1922. Translated by O. Reichel as *Socrates and the Socratic Schools*. London, 1885. See Part 2, Section 1.

Maier, Heinrich, *Sokrates*. Tübingen, 1913.

Stenzel, Julius, "Sokrates," in August Pauly and Georg Wissowa, eds., *Realencyclopädie der classischen Altertumswissenschaft*, second series, Vol. III, Part 1 (1927), Cols. 811 ff.

Ritter, C., *Sokrates*. Tübingen, 1931.

Festugière, A.-J., *Socrate*. Paris, 1934.

Jaeger, Werner, *Paideia*, 3 vols. Berlin, 1936–1947. Translated under the same title by Gilbert Highet. Oxford, 1939–1944. See Vol. II.

Versényi, Laszlo, *Socratic Humanism*. New Haven, 1963.

With Special Reference to Platonic Socrates

Diès, A., *Autour de Platon*. Paris, 1927.

Field, G. C., *Plato and His Contemporaries*. London, 1930.

Hackforth, Reginald, *Composition of Plato's Apology*. Cambridge, 1933.

Robinson, Richard, *Plato's Earlier Dialectic*, 2d ed. Oxford, 1953.

Gould, John, *The Development of Plato's Ethics*. Oxford, 1955.

— I. G. KIDD

SOCRATES (UPDATE)

Scholars continue to find themselves unable to agree about the historicity of any of the extant portraits of Socrates. One recent discussion, however, stands out for its painstaking review of the evidence: Gregory Vlastos's three chapters (2–4) on the historical Socrates in *Socrates: Ironist and Moral Philosopher*. Vlastos lists two groups of dialogues as falling within the early period: (1) what he calls the "elenctic dialogues" (*Apology, Charmides, Crito, Euthyphro, Gorgias, Hippias Minor, Ion, Laches, Protagoras,* and *Republic* I) and (2) what Vlastos calls "transitional dialogues" (*Euthydemus, Hippias Major, Lysis, Menexenus,* and *Meno*). From careful study of characterizations of Socrates and his philosophical views Vlastos identifies ten theses by which the Socrates of the early dialogues can be distinguished from the Socrates of the middle period and later dialogues. Vlastos concludes that the Socrates of the early dialogues is the historical Socrates; the Socrates of the later dialogues is only a character who speaks for Plato himself. Vlastos goes on to contrast the Socrates of Plato's early period with the Xenophontic Socrates and then to speculate about what it was that led Plato to modify his philosophical views, in the middle period, away from those of Socrates.

Most work on Socrates since the late 1970s shares Vlastos's view that a coherent picture of Socrates and Socratic philosophy can be found in the early dialogues of Plato. Whether this coherence is indicative of an authentically historical Socratic philosophy—as opposed to a coherent philosophy attributable only to a character named Socrates in Plato's early works—will no doubt remain the focus of intense scholarly controversy.

The Trial

Until the early 1980s scholars had assumed that the motivation for the trial of Socrates was essentially some political prejudice against him. A prima facie problem for this view has always been that Socrates was charged with a religious crime, impiety. This problem was typically overcome by an appeal to the amnesty decree of 403 B.C., which forbade prosecution for crimes committed prior to the amnesty itself. Thomas C. Brickhouse and Nicholas D. Smith have disputed this account, arguing that the amnesty would not have made

Because Socrates appears to equate virtue with the sort of knowledge he claims to lack, it would appear to follow that Socrates cannot be wholly virtuous.

a political charge impossible and would not have prevented Socrates' prosecutors from appealing to the evidence traditionally supposed to have provided the real motives for the prosecution. Other studies have also questioned whether Socrates' political views would have merited a legal attack. Given no legal impediment to an explicitly political charge, and only ambiguous evidence of serious political motives for the trial, Brickhouse and Smith conclude that the religious charge accurately reflects the ground for the prosecution. This new interpretation allows a more straightforward understanding of Plato's account of the trial: we need not assume that Socrates is evading the "real" issues or making a defense that is largely irrelevant to the jurors' most serious concerns simply because he does not plainly address the political concerns scholars have cited.

Philosophical Method and Epistemology

One major dispute among scholars has been about whether or not the *elenchos*, Socrates' method of asking questions and generating contradictions from his interlocutors' answers, can be used to construct and justify positive philosophical doctrines. One reason for doubting the "constructivist" understanding of Socrates' philosophizing is Socrates' own notorious profession of ignorance. If Socrates thought his elenchos could be used to generate and secure positive philosophical doctrine, why was he so persistent in his own disclaimers of knowledge?

Constructivists have attempted to answer this question by noting that Socrates does not always proclaim his own or others' ignorance; in fact, he occasionally makes and grants to others a variety of knowledge claims. Those inclined to the "constructivist" position have seen one sort of knowledge in Socrates' disclaimers of knowledge and at least another sort in the knowledge claims he makes and grants to others. The sort of knowledge he disclaims is constitutive of wisdom of the "greatest things" (see *Ap.* 22d7), and the reason Socrates is the "wisest of men" is that he alone recognizes just how deficient he is in *this* sort of knowledge (see *Ap.* 23b2–4). When Socrates claims to have knowledge or grants it to others, it is not this sort of knowledge, but some other sort.

Ethics

Other interesting work has been done on Socratic ethics, in particular the relationships between goodness, virtue, and happiness (*eudaimonia*). No one doubts that Socrates is a eudaimonist—one who believes that eudaimonia is the final end or goal. But a number of different views have been published about exactly how Socrates saw the way the goodness of something was linked to its value in the pursuit of happiness, especially in the role virtue or excellence (*arete*) played in this pursuit. Is virtue merely instrumental to the pursuit of happiness, or is it in some way constitutive of the happy life? Also, is the possession of virtue necessary or even sufficient for happiness, or can one be virtuous, but not happy, or happy, but not virtuous? Scholars have offered different answers to these questions. No one has doubted, however, that Plato depicts Socrates himself as an exemplar of whatever goodness or virtue—and happiness—a human being can achieve. But because Socrates appears to equate virtue with the sort of knowledge he claims to lack, it would appear to follow that Socrates cannot be wholly virtuous. And yet he will regard himself as enjoying "inconceivable happiness," he claims, if only he will be allowed to pursue his elenctic mission in the afterlife unmolested (see *Ap.* 41c3–4). This can be true only if Socrates supposes either that virtue is not necessary for happiness or that he will be given in death the knowledge that he lacked in life.

Socrates' account of the "unity of the virtues," one of the salient features of Socratic ethics, has been the topic of a number of important studies. Many commentators now accept the view that the "unity thesis"

defended in the *Protagoras* asserts that the different virtue names refer to one and the same cognitive state. Nevertheless, commentators remain divided over whether Socrates' belief that the virtues are really identical is consistent with all of his statements, made elsewhere in the early dialogues, that some virtues are proper parts of other virtues or of virtue as a whole. Commentators who seek to show how Socrates' various remarks form a coherent theory of virtue have generally tried to show how each of the virtues other than wisdom are all in some way parts of wisdom. No consensus has emerged, however, regarding exactly how these relationships must be understood.

[See also Plato.]

BIBLIOGRAPHY

Benson, H. H. "The Problem of the Elenchus Reconsidered," *Ancient Philosophy,* Vol. 7 (1987), 67–85.
———. "The Priority of Definition and the Socratic *Elenchos,*" *Oxford Studies in Ancient Philosophy,* Vol. 8 (1990), 19–65.
———. ed. *Essays on the Philosophy of Socrates.* New York, 1992.
Brickhouse, T. C., and N. D. Smith. *Socrates on Trial.* Princeton, NJ, 1989.
———. *Plato's Socrates.* New York, 1994.
Irwin, T. H. *Plato's Moral Theory.* Oxford, 1977.
Kraut, R. *Socrates and the State.* Princeton, NJ, 1983.
Stokes, M. *Plato's Socrates Conversations: Drama and Dialectic in Three Dialogues.* Baltimore, 1986.
Vlastos, G. *Socrates: Ironist and Moral Philosopher.* Ithaca, NY, 1991.
———. *Socratic Studies,* edited by M. Burnyeat. Cambridge, 1994.
Woodruff, P. "Plato's Early Theory of Knowledge," in S. Everson, ed., *Companions to Ancient Thought,* Vol. 1, *Epistemology* (Cambridge, 1990).

– NICHOLAS D. SMITH
THOMAS C. BRICKHOUSE

SPECIESISM

This is the name of a form of bias or discrimination that is much discussed in the contemporary debates over the moral status of animals. It amounts to discriminating on the basis of species; that is, it takes the fact that, say, baboons and humans belong to different species as a reason in itself to draw moral differences between them and on several counts.

First, speciesism sometimes manifests itself in consideration of who or what may be members of the moral community, of who or what is morally considerable (see Clark, Frey, Regan, Singer). For example, it is sometimes said that creatures who have experiences or are sentient count morally; to go on to affirm that (some) animals have experiences and are sentient but to deny that they count morally solely because they are not of the right species is a form of speciesism. If it really is the fact that creatures have experiences and are sentient that matters, then animals count; what has to be shown is why the fact that it is a baboon and not a human who has these characteristics matters morally.

Second, speciesism sometimes manifests itself in claims about pain and suffering. For instance, we usually take pain and suffering to be evils, to be things that blight a life and lower its quality, and animals can feel pain and suffer. Thus, suppose one pours scalding water on a child and on a cat: it seems odd to say that it would be wrong to scald the child but not wrong to scald the cat, since both feel pain and suffer, both have the quality of their lives diminished, and both instinctively reveal pain-avoidance behavior. To claim that scalding the child is wrong, but that scalding the cat is not wrong solely on the basis of the species to which each belongs is not in itself to give a reason why or how species-membership is morally relevant, let alone morally decisive (see Rachels, Sapontzis).

Is the life of a human being

in a permanent vegetative state

more valuable than the life

of a perfectly healthy baboon?

Third, speciesism sometimes manifests itself in claims about the value of life. Most of us think human life is more valuable than animal life; yet to think this solely on the basis of species exposes one to an obvious problem. If it is true that normal adult human life is more valuable than animal life, it by no means follows that all human life is more valuable than animal life, since it is by no means the case that all human lives are even remotely approximate in their quality. Thus, some human lives have a quality so low that those who are presently living those lives seek to end them; this, of course, is what the contemporary concern with euthanasia and physician-assisted suicide is all about. Indeed, some humans live in permanently vegetative states, where, as best we can judge, all talk of the quality of life seems beside the point. Are even these human lives more valuable than the lives of perfectly healthy baboons? To say that they are solely because they are human lives, lives lived by members of the species *homo sapiens,* even though it is true that healthy baboons can do all manner of things, can have all manner of experiences, is in effect to say that species-membership makes the crucial difference in value. It is not apparent exactly how it does this (see Frey). Of course, certain religions and cultural traditions may hold that humans have greater value than do animals, no matter what the quality or kind of lives lived; but these very same religions have put forward moral views that many today do not endorse, and these very same cultural traditions have held that, for example, whites are superior to blacks.

[See also Animal Rights and Welfare; Euthanasia.]

BIBLIOGRAPHY

Clark, S. R. L. *The Moral Status of Animals.* Oxford, 1977.
———. *The Nature of the Beast.* Oxford, 1982.
Frey, R. G. *Interests and Rights: The Case Against Animals.* Oxford, 1980.
———. *Rights, Killing, and Suffering: Moral Vegetarianism and Applied Ethics.* Oxford, 1984.
———. "Moral Standing, The Value of Lives, and Speciesism," *Between the Species.* Vol. 4 (1988): 191–201.
Rachels, J. *Created from Animals: The Moral Implications of Darwinism.* New York, 1990.
Regan, T. *The Case for Animal Rights.* Berkeley, 1983.
Regan, T., and P. Singer, eds. *Animal Rights and Human Obligations,* 2nd ed. Englewood Cliffs, NJ, 1989.
Sapontzis, S. F. *Morals, Reason, and Animals.* Philadelphia, 1987.
Singer, P. *Animal Liberation,* 2nd ed. New York, 1990.
———. *Practical Ethics,* 2nd ed. Cambridge, 1993.

– R. G. FREY

SPINOZA, BENEDICT (BARUCH)

Benedict (Baruch) Spinoza (1632–1677), rationalist metaphysician, is of all philosophers the one whose life has least apparent connection with his work. The objectivity and impersonality of his philosophical style betray a rare concern for truth and clarity, and for nothing else. As a Jew, Spinoza had relatively few ties with his Dutch neighbors; as a Jew expelled from the synagogue for his unorthodoxy (1656), he had few ties with his Jewish neighbors. He had a rabbinical education and then went to a German tutor, Van Den Ende. He lived in Amsterdam, his birthplace, until 1660 and then in Rijnsburg and Voorburg, earning his living by grinding and polishing lenses and discussing philosophical problems with his friends, both in conversation and in correspondence. He published an account of Descartes's philosophy (*Renati Descartes Principiorum Philosophiae, Pars I et II,* Amsterdam, 1663) and the *Tractatus Theologico-politicus* (Amsterdam, 1670), the latter anonymously. He refused the chair of philosophy at Heidelberg in 1673 because he thought it would have cost him his independence and tranquillity. He died of consumption, aggravated by the dust from lens grinding.

Spinoza's manifest determination to think through his own thoughts, in relative isolation from others, accounts both for his independence from external influences apart from purely philosophical ones and for his

The objectivity and impersonality of Spinoza's philosophical style betray a rare concern for truth and clarity. (Corbis/Bettmann)

almost total lack of influence for long after his death. The *Ethics* appeared in a collection of works published immediately after his death, and the *Tractatus de Intellectus Emendatione* was not discovered for publication until the late eighteenth century. Spinoza tried to protest the political assassination of Jan De Witt in 1672, but a friend prevented him—and probably thereby saved his life—by locking him up. Spinoza corresponded with and met Leibniz, who had read the *Tractatus Theologico-politicus*. He also corresponded with Henry Oldenburg and Christian Huygens. If every fact that we now possess about Spinoza's life were lost to us, his writings would be no more difficult to interpret than they are now, for the difficulties are considerable.

Fortunately, on at least one point Spinoza enlightened us: his motives. Like Hobbes, he was aware of the uncertainty that accompanies all worldly pursuits; like Hobbes he saw in such pursuits an endless and unsatisfying search, a perpetual transition from one object of desire to the next; but unlike Hobbes, he did not take it for granted that such a continuous restlessness constitutes the core of the human condition. He tells us in the *Tractatus de Intellectus Emendatione* that he resolved to search for a good that would so fill the mind that all dependence on contingent circumstance and uncertainty would end. He follows Plato and Aristotle in rejecting wealth, reputation, and pleasure as candidates for the role of such a good. He concludes that the supreme good consists in the enjoyment of a human nature which, because it is perfectly aware of its place in and its unity with the whole natural scheme of things, accepts the inevitability and necessity of that natural order. The knowledge requisite to attain such an awareness includes natural science, an understanding of politics, morals, education, and the material and technological bases of social life. "We must in no way despise technology. . . ."

Spinoza's philosophy is itself a part of this practical knowledge to be acquired with a view to attaining the supreme good. But since the supreme good is ultimately defined in terms of the philosophical conclusions reached within Spinoza's system, this is of little interpretative value. It is thus brought home at the outset that the self-enclosed character of Spinoza's thought constitutes the central difficulty in interpreting it. Not that Spinoza was uninfluenced by or was not reacting to either his immediate or his more distant predecessors. Spinoza may be partially expounded as the critic of Descartes, the critic of Hobbes, and even as a dissident follower of Maimonides; but what his criticisms amount to is clear only from within his own system. Some commentators have evaded this difficulty by separating strands in Spinoza's thought and treating them in isolated fashion, and to some extent a procedure of this kind is inevitable. But insofar as the commentator abstracts, he tends to falsify. How, then, can one think himself inside the system without surrendering the possibility of judging it in terms other than its own? Interestingly and surprisingly, an answer to this question is also contained within Spinoza's system, for his system contains an account of the nature of the "outsider."

Suppose, he said in a letter, that a parasitic worm living in the bloodstream tried to make sense of its surroundings: from the point of view of the worm, each drop of blood would appear as an independent whole and not as a part of a total system. The worm would not recognize that each drop behaves as it does in virtue of the nature of the bloodstream as a whole. But in fact the nature of the blood can be understood only in the context of a larger system in which blood, lymph, and other fluids interact; and this system in turn is a part of a still larger whole. If we men begin with the bodies that surround us in nature and treat them as independent wholes, the relation between which is contingent and given, then we shall be in error precisely as the worm is in error. We must grasp the system as a whole before we can hope to grasp the nature of the part, since the nature of the part is determined by its role in the total system. This epistemological point is found elsewhere in seventeenth-century writers, notably in Pascal. It marks a decisive break with Cartesian mechanistic rationalism (the machine which is the body in the Cartesian system can be thought of as an independent whole and not as a part of a larger system of nature) and with Hobbesian empiricism (the worm is essentially an empiricist). Thus, the image formed by the person who does not grasp the system of nature is like that of the parasitic worm; to have grasped the system of nature is to move not from part to whole but from whole to part. The whole is a single system which has two names, "God" and "Nature." But the point of the two names cannot be grasped until the unity of Spinoza's exposition of the system is understood, and this unity resides in the system's deductive and quasi-geometrical character.

Ideal of Rational Understanding

Spinoza's use of a deductive geometrical method of exposition is easily misunderstood. It is not just that he shares with Descartes, Hobbes, and Leibniz an interest in geometrical problems and a high regard for the power of geometrical methods, nor is it only a preference for deductive methods in the interests of clarity which leads him to write as he does. Rather, it is that the content of Spinoza's philosophy requires a deductive mode of exposition in the strictest sense of "requires." That is, the criterion of truth and certitude set out in the philosophy is such that unless Spinoza's philosophy were expounded deductively, it could not possess the truth and certitude which he wishes to claim for it. If, in Spinoza's view, a proposition is to be true and certain, its truth and certainty can be exhibited only when that proposition is shown to be part of a total deductive system of such propositions, the truth of each of which depends upon its connection with all the others. Spinoza's deductive system is presented as geometrical because Euclidean geometry provided for him, as for his contemporaries, the paradigm case of an axiomatized system. As with all such systems, the axioms and the primitive terms can be understood only in terms of the propositions which are consequently derived, just as the consequent propositions must be referred back to the axioms and primitive terms. Furthermore, when such a system is an attempt to set forth the total character of the universe, the system takes on a specially self-enclosed character.

Any criticism of any part of such a system is inevitably a criticism of the whole. Spinoza's confidence in his manner of exposition was probably reinforced not only by mathematical parallels but also by the fact that he wrote in the academic Latin of the day, a language whose vocabulary had been purged of ambiguity to an unusually high degree. Those characteristics of academic Latin which ensured that by the seventeenth century no genuine poet could use it lent to those who wrote in it an illusion of quasi-mathematical precision. There is, of course, more than one way to approach Spinoza's philosophy; but the unusually close links between its form and its content suggest that if one begins by setting out the form which, in Spinoza's view, all rational understanding must take, then the way in which form determines content (as well as vice versa) will become clear.

Spinoza refused the chair of philosophy at Heidelberg in 1673 because he thought it would cost him his independence and tranquillity.

To explain anything is to know its cause. The cause of any being is that which not only brings that being into existence but also makes that being what it is and not another thing. Not only does the cause of a being make that being what it is, it also necessarily produces the effect that it does. There is, therefore, in Spinoza an intimate relationship between essence (what something is) and cause (what makes it what it is). This concept of cause is a scholastic one put to new purposes. The relationship between cause and essence was anticipated in medieval scholastic philosophy in discussions of the divine causality of the real essence of created beings; but since for the Scholastics the causality which mattered was that of finite *contingent* existence, that causality which brings into being one actual, existent world out of all the possibilities open to God, there was not for the Scholastics the intimate and necessary connection between the concept of cause and that of essence which there was for Spinoza.

The properties of any being are divided into those which that being possesses essentially and necessarily and those which it possesses accidentally and contingently. To understand any being, to have genuine knowledge of it, is to know its essential properties. (This is also a radically revised scholastic concept. For the Scholastics the world is a collection of finite, created substances; and according to them, the explanation of the existence of those substances which happen to exist is to be found in the creating will of God. For Spinoza, however, a plurality of substances is ruled out by his concept of rational understanding.) According to Spinoza's ideal of rational understanding, to explain is to show the necessary connection of essential properties with the substance of which they are properties, that is, to show that they *are* essential properties. If a property is contingent and accidental, then it can only be due to the action of some second substance on the first, and we explain the existence of the property by exhibiting it as necessarily connected with the essence of that substance. Thus, an explanation terminates in showing how a substance is the cause of its own essential properties, solely by being the substance that it is. To explain is to exhibit as *causa sui*. But from this it follows that there is and can be only one ultimate explanation, only one cause, only one substance. Suppose there were two substances. The properties which constitute their relationship or lack of it could not be necessary and essential properties of either. Thus, the relationship would be unintelligible; and for Spinoza it is unintelligible that there could be such a relationship. It follows that all rational understanding consists in showing how some feature of the universe necessarily has the role it has as some kind of essential property of the one substance which is *causa omnium rerum* and *causa sui* at one and the same time. Thus, the necessity for the existence of only one total explanation dictates that a true philosophy will consist of one set of necessarily connected propositions, any one of which or any subset of which is justified by exhibiting its place in the deductive order. The same necessity dictates that there can be only one substance in the universe, and that all relations are internal and necessary, none external and contingent. Thus, Spinoza's method of exposition and the content of his metaphysics are inexorably linked.

In his Cartesian preoccupation with necessary truth

Spinoza neglects the kind of logical investigation

that Aristotle undertook in the De Interpretatione.

Spinoza's originality here lies in the way in which he uses Aristotelian and Cartesian notions in combination, criticizing each in the light of the other. From Descartes he accepts the deductive ideal; from Aristotle, the concept of substance and the concept of an essential property. He assumes with Aristotle that all propositions are of subject–predicate form, but, contrary to Aristotle, he believes that in every case to attach a predicate to a subject is to assign a property to a substance. In his Cartesian preoccupation with necessary truth Spinoza neglects the kind of logical investigation that Aristotle undertook in the *De Interpretatione,* in which the anal-

ysis of sentences led him to accept contingent statements; and in failing to distinguish the identifying from the describing functions of expressions (also investigated in *De Interpretatione*), he cannot distinguish between a substance incorrectly identified and a substance incorrectly described. Hence, description and identification are totally assimilated; and if anything is really a property, then to ascribe it to its subject will be to utter a necessary truth. But to say—as this might suggest— that Spinoza's monism springs from conceptual confusion is not to say that he made a simple mistake; it is, rather, to point out the consequences of failing to make certain conceptual distinctions, consequences which can be appreciated only when they are developed as fully as Spinoza developed them.

Spinoza's program is a priori in the sense that it sets an ideal of understanding before the intellect; it does not start from any one particular puzzlement or inadequacy. It is this a priori program which impresses upon the intellect a single pattern of understanding and explanation. For Spinoza there are not sciences, there is science; and there are not alternative deductive forms in which understanding can usefully be expressed. There is *one* deductive form in which all understanding *must* be expressed. To interpret Spinoza, therefore, as the ancestor of modern conceptions of science can be dangerously misleading.

"Deus Sive Natura"

The unity of Spinoza's system is not only the product of his deductive ideals; it is also in part the outcome of his theological preoccupations. These preoccupations have been grotesquely underestimated both by those who have wanted to see in Spinoza an anticipation of their own atheism and materialism, and by those who have wanted to condemn Spinozism as atheistic, as did Moses Mendelssohn in the eighteenth century, when he defended his dead friend Lessing against the charge of Spinozism. But such writers as Novalis, Goethe, Coleridge, and Edward Caird, who have stressed the theological content of Spinoza's thought, have been almost as misleading.

It is true that Spinoza follows his native Judaism in affirming the existence and the unity of God. It is true that in a letter to Oldenburg he affirms the identity of his doctrine with that of St. Paul and "I might dare to say with that of all the ancient Hebrews. . . ." It is true that the first book of the *Ethics* is entitled "De Deo." But since "God" is the name of the one substance whose other name is "Nature," the contrast between God and the world, a contrast which is at the heart of both Judaism and Christianity, is obliterated. The one substance can have nothing outside itself to limit it. It is and therefore must be undetermined from outside itself and unbounded; hence, Spinoza calls it infinite. Thus, not only the unity and existence but also the infinity of God are preserved in Spinozism, although all three, it is clear, are given a new sense.

Spinoza has, of course, no need of a proof of the existence of God apart from his proof of the existence of the one substance. But in his demonstration that to perceive the essence of the one substance is to perceive the necessity of its existence, he reproduces a form of the Ontological Argument which Descartes used to prove the existence of God—that the essence of God (or of substance) entails its existence. Moreover, he does not rest his case for the identity of God and nature solely upon the deduction of the necessity of there being only one substance. He produces detailed arguments to show that an infinite and necessary divine being could not exist alongside a finite and contingent nature external to the divine being. If it did, it would then be the case that God was limited and therefore determined by something other than himself. And if God were so limited, he would be finite and unfree. Equally, if God were limited by a purely contingent being, his relationship to that being could only be contingent, and therefore not all the properties of God would be necessary ones. But all these conclusions are absurd, for a God who is finite or unfree, or of whom any contingent truths are true, *ex hypothesi* could not be God. Thus, there can be nothing which falls outside the divine being and which is not necessitated by it.

It will, perhaps, clarify Spinoza's conception of God if we consider first what he rejects of traditional theology and then that in which he purports to agree with it. On a traditional Jewish view—in a scholastic work such as Moses Maimonides' *Guide of the Perplexed*—the only ground of creation lies in the free and mysterious will of God, and there is no necessity that what has actually been created should have been created; there is simply the divine fiat. On this view, explanation terminates with a brute fact, the fact that God created thus and not otherwise; and for Spinoza there are no ultimate brute facts, let alone this one. Both his ideal of understanding generally and his conception of the divine lead straight to a rejection of the orthodox doctrine of creation. Nonetheless, Spinoza is prepared to conceive of God as the creator of the world—in a sense which the orthodox Jew or Christian might well take to be Pickwickian—provided God is understood to be the immanent and continuing cause of the world and not its transient first cause. He thus rejects the view, found among many of his contemporaries and notably in Newton's *Scholium*, that God is the first, efficient, external cause of the world's being and motion but that

thereafter the world continues according to divinely ordained mechanical laws. The scientist looks and need look only as far as those laws; the theologian looks beyond, to the lawmaker. This deistic compromise allows science and theology their own territories; Spinoza's doctrine of the one substance insists upon a unitary doctrine in which every issue between them must be resolved. At least two questions arise for Spinoza which cannot arise for deism. How is the origin of motion to be accounted for, if not along Newtonian lines? And what attitude is to be taken toward the biblical accounts of divine creation? Answers to these questions are indeed furnished in Spinoza's writings.

How is the origin of motion to be accounted for,

if not along Newtonian lines?

And what attitude is to be taken

toward the biblical accounts of divine creation?

The second orthodox theological doctrine which Spinoza rejects is belief in divine teleology. It is not just that he rejects all forms of the Argument from Design; he rejects the very conception of God's having purposes, designs, or desires for the world. To suppose this is to suppose that God wishes to bring about some state of affairs which does not yet exist; and to suppose this is to suppose that there is something which God at present lacks but which he needs or desires. This is absurd. God *ex hypothesi* can lack nothing. The rejection of this doctrine has further consequences. If God has no purposes, a fortiori he can have no moral purpose for mankind. At once traditional Jewish morality is brought in question, and with it the status of the Scriptures. Spinoza provides answers to these questions in his analysis of religion.

What of orthodoxy does Spinoza accept? He is, as has already been shown, prepared to say of God much of what orthodoxy says—that God is free, infinite, and a necessary being; he is also prepared to say, like some orthodox theologians, that when we ascribe predicates to God, we must do so in quite a different sense from that in which we would ascribe them to anything else. This is partly because "God" is the name of the whole intelligible system of which all finite beings are mere parts; but for Spinoza this also rests partly upon a view that the divine essence can be considered apart from its relation to its attributes: in the *Tractatus Theologico-politicus* he says of the divine names that Jehovah is a name which points to "the absolute essence of God without reference to created things," and *El Shaddai* and the other divine names point to attributes.

Anticipations of Spinoza's type of pantheism can be found in the Jewish mystical traditions. When both Jewish and Christian Scholastics spoke of God's knowledge of his creatures, they found it difficult to hold that his creatures were external objects to God, about whom God could know contingent truths. In answer to this problem a sixteenth-century cabalist, Moses Cordovero, wrote in words which are almost reproduced by Spinoza (*Ethics* II, Prop. VII, *Scholium*): "But the creator is Himself knowledge, the knower and the object known. His knowledge does not arise from His directing His thoughts to things outside of Him, since in comprehending and knowing Himself, He comprehends and knows everything that exists" (*A Garden of Pomegranates*). Thus, Spinoza could and did legitimately claim to be developing one strain in the Jewish theological tradition.

Opposition to Dualism

"The mind and the body are one and the same thing. . . ." The unity of the one substance is incompatible with any dualism, and Spinoza's theology therefore attacks the dualism of God and the created world. The second great dualism under attack from Spinoza is that of body and mind. Spinoza has sometimes been presented as primarily continuing and correcting Descartes, but here he is explicitly detaching himself from the Cartesian tradition. It is certainly true that the study of Descartes was seminal for Spinoza, and there are obvious debts both of doctrine and of terminology. Nonetheless, Spinoza's philosophy is in one crucial respect at the opposite pole from that of Descartes. Descartes presents an epistemology from which he derives a metaphysics; Spinoza presents a metaphysics without which his epistemology could scarcely be intelligible. This difference is in the end what determines their difference on the body–mind problem. For Descartes the question "What certain truths can I grasp?" leads to a differentiation between the clear and distinct apprehension which I have of my own existence as a conscious thinking thing and the guarantees which I possess of the existence of extended material substance, guarantees which I possess only because a perfect being—God—would not allow me to be deceived in my sense experience. The status of mind is necessarily quite different from that of body; I am a mind but only have a body. This leads to a deep inability to connect mind and body in the Cartesian tradition. When Malebranche sees mental events and bodily events as two independent series of events which God providentially synchronizes so that my decision to move my hand and the hand's

subsequent movement follow from each other just *as if* the one caused the other, he is truer to Descartes's original position than Descartes is in his resort to the pineal gland. The role of God in Descartes's system of thought is essentially that of filling epistemological gaps. (Thus Descartes, the nominally orthodox Catholic, treats God with a great deal less respect than does Spinoza, the explicitly heretical Jew.)

Both the nature of the role assigned to God's mysterious action and the purely contingent character of the explanation involved rule out any such solution for Spinoza. But he does not need a solution of this or any other kind, since according to his premises the problem cannot, so he believes, arise. Spinoza is neither an occasionalist like Malebranche, nor an epiphenomenalist who sees mental events as the effect of bodily causes, nor an interactionist envisaging reciprocal causality between body and mind. Body and mind are not causally related at all; they are identical, because thought and extension are two attributes under which the one substance is conceived. Spinoza's doctrine of substance and attributes is not merely an assertion of the unity of the single substance but an attempt to explain the relationship between that unity and the multiplicity of finite beings.

SUBSTANCE AND ATTRIBUTES. Substance is that which is in itself and is conceived through itself; it can be conceived independently of the conception of anything else. To be conceivable is not to be imaginable, for imagination is very low and unreliable in the grades of experience and knowledge. To be conceivable is to be capable of being thought without contradiction. And since for Spinoza what can exist in itself and what can be conceived by itself are one and the same, to know what can and must be thought is also to know what can and must exist. But substance is not characterless; to grasp its essence is to perceive its attributes. Spinoza defines an attribute as "that which intellect perceives in substance as constituting its essence" (*Ethics* I, Def. IV). Each of the attributes of the one substance is infinite, expresses the eternal and infinite essence of the one substance, and is conceived through itself. Although there can be no plurality of substances, there must be an infinity of attributes, each distinctly conceivable from all the others.

The argument which carries us from the one substance to a plurality of attributes seems little better than a linguistic conjuring trick. Sometimes the attributes are spoken of merely as aspects under which we conceive the one substance; sometimes they are spoken of almost as if they possess an independent reality. The argument here appears to be of the form that because we can think of X as Y and of X as Z, we can therefore think of Y

and Z as identical in some sense (but also as different). Clearly, where X is the name of a substance and Y and Z are names of properties, this is false. The fact that two properties are properties of the same thing in no sense makes them identical.

Why is Spinoza deceived by so obvious a fallacy? The answer surely lies in the fact that the premises from which he starts never permit him to formulate clear criteria of identity and difference. Two distinct reasons for this failure to formulate the needed criteria can be detected. One is the metaphysical desire to exhibit everything as the same in respect of its being a manifestation of the one substance. The other is the assimilation of causal and logical relations. To say of one thing that it is the cause of another is, for Spinoza, to point to a relation of entailment. But Spinoza has no clear theory of entailment, of logical necessity, or of analytic truth. These are notions upon which he habitually relies without ever passing beyond formulations which blend Cartesian references to clarity of conception with scholastic phrases of the "in itself" and "through itself" variety. Yet unless a clear meaning can be assigned to the notion of a relation which is both causal and logical, Spinoza cannot hope to identify clearly the terms of this relation. His use of the word "idea" helps him to avoid clarity at this point. Sometimes an "idea" appears to be a proposition, sometimes a concept, and sometimes a concept or proposition as it is entertained in thought.

Anticipations of Spinoza's type of pantheism

can be found in the Jewish mystical traditions.

When we pass from the one substance to its attributes, therefore, there is no way of making the transition intelligible. Indeed, grave difficulties occur. Since the one substance cannot be bounded in any way, it follows that the number of its attributes cannot be bounded. "The more reality or being anything has, the more attributes it possesses" (*Ethics* I, 9). But of the infinite number of infinite attributes, each of which is a necessary expression of the one substance, there are only two which we grasp, thought and extension. Why only two? If everything is a necessary consequence of the nature of the whole, there ought to be available a demonstration of how it is necessarily true that, as Spinoza says (*Ethics* II, Axiom 5), "We feel and perceive no particular things save bodies and modes of thought." It is worth noting that Spinoza originally avoids the need for proof on this point by introducing this proposition as an axiom. But one of his correspondents, Ehrenfried von Tschirnhaus, asked him if it can be proved "that

we cannot know any attributes of God other than thought and extension." Spinoza's answer is that in thinking we can grasp no more than the essence of mind and "that the essence of mind is the idea of the body, which idea does not involve or express any of God's attributes except for extension and thought." But this is merely repeating the assertion for which proof has been requested.

EXTENSION. The twin attributes under which we conceive the one substance are, then, to be thought of as different ways of envisaging one and the same reality. All reality can be thought of as a series of *res extensae,* physical bodies ordered in causal series, or equally as a series of ideas ordered in intelligible logical sequences. The two sequences will correspond exactly, not because of any external contingent correspondence between them but because they are the same causal sequence viewed in two different ways. The manner in which we think of extended substance is due to our modes of thinking or, rather, to our modes of imagining, rather than to the nature of extension as it is in itself. For we think of extended substance as divided into separate bodies which occupy a limited area in space and endure for a limited amount of time, but extension itself cannot be thought of as other than enduring always and existing everywhere. We may in our imagining conceive of extended substance as made up of separate bodies. "It is mere folly or insanity to suppose that extended substance is made up of parts or bodies really distinct from each other" (Ep. 29). And the manner in which we think of thought will depend upon the grade of thinking to which our particular finite mind has attained.

Immediately below the infinite attributes in the metaphysical hierarchy come infinite modes, which are eternal, just as the attributes of which they are the modes of existence are eternal. The infinite and eternal mode of extension Spinoza calls motion-and-rest. And finally on the Spinozistic scale there are modes of extension which are finite. The finite modes, which constitute individual bodies, of the kind of which the universe of ordinary physical objects is made up, are configurations of fundamental particles (*corpora simplicissima*) moving together in different ways.

It is at this point, rather than in his conception of total explanation, that Spinoza anticipates in the most striking way the development of theoretical physics. For Spinoza, motion-and-rest is an eternal mode; he treats movement as ultimate, rest as a special case of movement, and the system of moving bodies as one in which each state of the system must be explained in terms of prior states of the system rather than in terms of the initial activity of a Prime Mover outside the system. Moreover, the explanation of change is in terms of different distributions of motion-and-rest among the ultimate particles, which thus come to resemble points at which energy is concentrated in the system. Thus, they are more like the quanta of modern physics than the atoms of classical physics. The configurations which compose individual physical objects as we know them are part of a hierarchy of such systems in which there is an ascent from the ultimate particles at one end of the scale to that total configuration which is the entire physical universe and which Spinoza presents as a single individual in which all the other entities are parts, under the title "the face of the whole universe" (*facies totius universi*).

It is worth emphasizing not only the kinship of this physical theory to theories which date from the close of the nineteenth century but also the extent to which this part of Spinoza's doctrine is independent of the rest. Some sense can perhaps be made of the metaphysical monism as an ideal of total explanation; and some sense can certainly be made of the physical theory. But how the precise content of the physics derives from the metaphysics not only cannot be understood, but also is unintelligible even in Spinoza's own terms. He says explicitly that finite things cannot follow from any infinite attribute of God but only from such an attribute as it is affected by some finite mode (*Ethics* I, 28), and this line of argument seems to involve him in both asserting and denying that the finite can follow from the infinite. Since, according to Spinoza, everything that is must follow from God and his infinite attributes, if there are finite modes, they also must follow from an infinite cause. If not, how do they come into being? How could there ever be any finite modes to affect the infinite attributes?

Individuals, then, are configurations which maintain themselves in being and possess a drive toward self-preservation (*conatus in suo esse perseverandi*). The hierarchy of individuals is a hierarchy of power; the higher an individual is on the scale, the less it is acted on by external forces and the more its changes come from within itself. No physical event is external to the *facies totius universi,* so that it is necessarily highest on the scale. Moreover, in the hierarchy of individuals, the more an individual is acted upon by others without its *conatus in suo esse perseverandi* being defeated, the higher it is on the scale. In Spinoza there is an equation between being more or less active as a causal agent upon others, being more or less in interaction with others, and being more or less real. The basis of this hierarchy is the more fundamental equation of ultimate reality with ultimate causality. The hierarchy that emerges in the end is the Aristotelian one: the inorganic, the vegetative, the animal, and the human. The human body is more real than animal bodies because it maintains itself in being more effectively and also interacts more with its environment.

THOUGHT. Corresponding to the infinite mode of extension, motion-and-rest, is the infinite and eternal mode of thought, intellect. Just as the infinite mode of extension covers all that is physical, so the infinite mode of intellect covers all that can be thought. There is a hierarchy of ideas, just as there is a hierarchy of bodies, and just as there is a highest-order body, the *facies totius universi,* so there is a highest-order idea, the infinite idea of God. Neither ideas nor bodies belong to the one substance, conceived as the cause of all (*natura naturans*), but to the finite modes of the infinite attributes, which come into existence through the mediation of the infinite modes. The relationship between ideas and bodies can be envisaged from the standpoint of either. Every body has an idea corresponding to it, which is its soul (*anima*). The human body's idea alone is worthy of being called a mind (*mens*). Or, from the standpoint of the idea, every idea has that of which it is an idea (*ideatum*), its body. The human mind is the idea of the human body.

Sometimes an "idea" appears to be a proposition, sometimes a concept, and sometimes a concept or proposition as it is entertained in thought.

What can this mean? In any ordinary sense of "idea," even in a Cartesian sense, this saying appears largely enigmatic. Surely, we are inclined to say, my mind contains the ideas of many things other than my body. Spinoza's answer is that if I have an adequate idea of something other than my own body, then this idea is not just something in *my* mind, but insofar as my mind apprehends it, my mind becomes more than merely *mine.* It is, rather, the infinite and eternal mode of intellect which is at work.

The whole paradox would not have arisen had Spinoza distinguished logical from psychological statements as we customarily distinguish them. The word "idea" bedevils everything. For Descartes and for Locke in their very different ways an idea is at least something belonging to an individual mind. And this use of "idea" creates for them an epistemological problem: how can we know that there are independent external realities that correspond to our ideas? This is certainly a misleading question which drives Descartes to the Ontological Argument and Locke to something he knows not what; but for Spinoza the question cannot even arise.

Ideas and that of which they are ideas do not have to be brought together because they have never been separated. An idea and its *ideatum* are the same thing viewed in two ways. But because Spinoza uses the misleading vocabulary of Descartes and Locke, his avoidance of their question does not save him from unintelligibility. Instead, this unintelligibility is pushed a stage further back, onto the word "idea" itself. But in order to understand Spinoza's use of this term, we must look to his systematic theory of knowledge.

Theory of Knowledge

In the *Ethics* Spinoza distinguishes three levels at which the mind operates. He gives a Hobbesian or empiricist account of the first, a corrected Cartesian account of the second, and blends his own metaphysics with traditional theology for the third. Thus, for Spinoza the empiricist versus rationalist controversy does not arise, for the two parties to it are describing different phenomena.

CONFUSED IDEAS. The first level is that of vague or confused experience, where notions are formed by whatever causal associations our bodies enter into. There is a physiological explanation for the formation of such notions. Whatever ideas we form at this level are essentially images (*imaginationes*) rather than thoughts (although Spinoza uses the word *cogitatio* to cover all the contents of the mind) and are essentially passive rather than active. The connections between one image and another are those of mechanical association rather than of any logical connection.

Out of the modification of the body which results from recurrent interaction with other bodies, general ideas are formed. The repetition of similar experiences when similar interactions occur results in the abstraction of a composite image, and this is what constitutes a general idea. Likewise, it is by physiological processes of association that ordinary language is built up, the recurrent association of one image with others resulting in the one coming to be taken as a sign for the others. How far we share general ideas and the meanings of ordinary language depends, therefore, upon how far we share experiences, upon how far our bodies have undergone similar modifications. Ordinary language, reflecting as it does the changes and chances of causal interaction, cannot furnish us with a precise instrument of thought. Moreover, what is founded on sense experience and expressed in ordinary language cannot be genuine knowledge. In so arguing, Spinoza makes use of Hobbes's nominalist account of language and knowledge, but for purposes quite other than those for which Hobbes used it. Spinoza takes this account to be an account not of the rational man's use of language but

of ordinary, prerational, confused discourse. In criticizing Hobbes, Spinoza is mainly in the right. Indeed, he is insufficiently radical. A merely naturalistic, causal account of language and belief omits the rule-governed character of language, for a rule of language is not just a record of regular sequences which a majority of language users happen to follow but at once an expression of standards of meaningfulness and a means of generating a wide range of significant utterances for the person who knows how to utter and to follow them. An empiricist, nominalist, Hobbesian account of language can give no account of the logical connections in language and makes meaning dependent on reference, while in fact it is necessary to understand reference in the light of a more general doctrine of meaning; and on a Hobbesian account we cannot explain how we can both understand and utter meaningful assertions about what we have never experienced and perhaps never will experience. But this last consideration, although important for the refutation of Hobbes, is quite alien to Spinoza, whose account of the second level of the mind leaves experience behind altogether.

ADEQUATE IDEAS. As bodies interact with each other, similarities between the experiences of interaction of different bodies result in the building up of certain universal notions. These notions are the general ideas referred to above and are the work of imagination out of intellect. Nonetheless, such are the interactions of bodies that quite inescapably we build up certain "common notions" which have two characteristics: *all* men share them, and they are adequate ideas of characteristics possessed by *all* bodies. What is universally the case in the mode of extension will universally have its counterpart in the mode of thought. Thus, what is true of all bodies will be impressed upon every mind. What are these ideas, and what does it mean to call them adequate?

Common notions are ideas of characteristics that every individual thing that participates in the mode of extension must necessarily possess. The most elementary spatial and physical properties of bodies are the subject matter of common notions, and upon them is built the whole scheme of scientific knowledge. Euclidean geometry, with its elementary concepts of line and point, is one example of a science which makes use of common notions. To call an idea adequate is to say that it stands in a certain logical relation to other ideas and that we can see the necessity that it should be thus and not otherwise. Moreover, we cannot have an adequate idea without being conscious that the idea is adequate. If we know, we necessarily know that we know. I can never be puzzled as to whether I know; but I can, because I possess not only adequate ideas but also ideas of those ideas, realize that in the light of the criteria which adequate ideas provide, many of my other ideas are found wanting. They lack clarity, they are confused; I cannot perceive any necessary relationship between them and my other ideas. Thus, I can study what I already know and hence derive a method for knowing more, for replacing confusion with clarity and the perception of necessity. The task of correcting the understanding depends, then, upon my original possession of at least one adequate idea to furnish me with a criterion of adequacy, necessity, and truth. But how do I know that this original idea is adequate? For Spinoza this question simply cannot arise because "Truth is the criterion of itself and of the false, as light manifests itself and the dark" and "Truth is its own norm." A true idea is always and necessarily self-evident; to call an idea true is to say that it exhibits the logical necessity of the relationship between the characteristics of that of which it is an idea. Our idea of extension is true insofar as it states what properties any extended thing necessarily possesses.

It follows both from Spinoza's physiological account of the origin of our ideas and from his logical elucidation of the concept of truth that no idea can be wholly false. For if our ideas originate in and reflect the interactions of our bodies, every idea must have to some extent, no matter how confused it may be, its *ideatum.* By *ideatum* Spinoza means that in the mode of extension to which the given idea is the counterpart in the mode of thought. Equally, if the truth of an idea resides in its logical relationships with other ideas, every idea by virtue of being an idea must stand in some such relationships with other ideas, no matter how confusedly. It follows that although ideas may be wholly true, to be false is to be less than true, not to be wholly other than true. Our ideas are in a hierarchy, with the physiologically produced images at the bottom and those ideas which form part of a logically interlocking system in which the necessity of the relationship of every item to every other item is manifest at the top. There can be only one such system, for any system which covered less than everything would leave its relationship to what was outside it unintelligible and unexplained, and therefore it would not be a system of ideas whose every feature was manifestly logically necessary. In other words, the necessity of the single total system of ideas is the same as the necessity for there being one, and only one, substance. Rational inquiry (for Spinoza there can be no ultimate distinction between the natural scientist, the philosopher, and the theologian) will always attempt to approach this ideal, as indeed Spinoza attempts to approach it in the *Ethics,* but there is a very good reason why one can never hope to attain it with any completeness. My ideas can only be the counterparts of those interactions in which my body participates. If I could extend my ideas so that they embraced the entire universe in the mode of thought, it could only be because my body was coextensive with the physical universe. In other words, "I" would be God and "my" body would be nature.

INTUITIVE IDEAS. The total system of ideas is the *infinita idea Dei* (infinite idea of God), and only God possesses a totally adequate idea of himself. Insofar as I approach the possession of such an idea, I necessarily approach the condition of God and I necessarily become God to some extent. Hence the aptness of Novalis's tag about Spinoza as "the God-intoxicated man." This third and highest grade of knowledge, which is that of the divine mind, Spinoza calls *scientia intuitiva* (intuitive knowledge).

SPINOZA AND DESCARTES. Spinoza's originality is nowhere more apparent than in the difference from Descartes which is apparent in his theory of knowledge. Descartes is a deeply inconsistent thinker in that he declares clarity and distinctness to be the criteria of truth but still seeks a guarantee that his clear and distinct ideas do in fact correspond to what is the case in the realm of physical bodies. The inconsistency resides in the attempt *both* to find a guarantee for the truth of an idea in the idea itself and its relationship with other ideas *and* yet to mean by "truth" roughly a sort of correspondence to an external reality. This inconsistency could be avoided either by abandoning the criteria of clarity and distinctness or by rejecting the dualism of thought and extension. Most empiricist thinkers have chosen to abandon the criteria of clarity and distinctness; Spinoza chose to reject the dualism of thought and extension.

The price which empiricism paid for its choice was to divorce the realm of necessity from that of knowledge and thus to render unintelligible the way in which advances in knowledge could alter our views as to what statements express necessary truths. ("A straight line is the shortest distance between two points" was until recently taken to be a necessary truth; the physics of relativity have shown it to be empirically false.) The price which Spinoza had to pay for his rejection of Cartesian dualism was the assimilation of all truth to necessary truth. By accepting this in the way he does, Spinoza avoids the characteristic difficulties of Cartesianism. As has already been noted, he does not have to build an epistemological bridge between ideas and the physical world and he does not have to invoke God, as Descartes does, in the role of metaphysical bridge builder. Second, he is not involved in the circularity of the *Cogito.* Descartes accepts the *Cogito* because it is clear and distinct, and he accepts the criterion of clarity and distinctness because he finds that these properties appertain to his grasp of the *Cogito*. Third, Descartes's demonstration of how we can come to grasp the truth involves him in the desperate task of explaining how, according to his account, error can be possible. His explanation is that intellectual error is a consequence of the will's mistakenly accepting or rejecting what the intellect presents to it. But this suggests that we can either choose to believe or choose not to believe a given proposition. Spinoza avoids any suggestion of this by an account of truth which allows for error and falsity from the outset. Since error and falsity are a privation of truth, in recognizing what is true, we also gradually come to recognize what is false. Moreover, since the sequence of ideas in my mind is a counterpart of the causal sequence of modifications of my body as it undergoes and initiates changes, there can be no question of real alternative possibilities of acceptance or rejection of an idea that is arising, and therefore no question of choice.

The way in which Spinoza makes this last point has led to a charge of inconsistency, formulated by Stuart Hampshire, as follows. Spinoza's theory of knowledge entails that all mental life is determined. Yet the announced aim of his philosophy is practical, to correct the understanding, and by attaining the crown of the intellectual life, to attain to beatitude. But if it is determined, as a physical sequence is determined, that we should think what and as we do, then how can we hope to change and improve our intellectual life? The inconsistency here is apparent rather than real. Certainly, unless certain conditions are satisfied, I cannot possibly change intellectually—and in the case of most men these conditions are not satisfied. Spinoza is clear on this. But if my mind is determined in a certain way, then it will be determined in such a way that I not only can and do, but also must, improve and correct it. This determination of the mind will accompany a certain determined sequence of modifications of the body. What appears under the aspect of thought as my decision to improve my understanding will appear under the aspect of extension as a set of physiological changes. But in order to elucidate the relationship between the mental and the physiological any further, Spinoza's psychology must be set out more systematically.

Psychology

Spinoza's psychology is parallel to his theory of knowledge, and for a very good reason. Both the ordinary concept of an emotion and the ordinary concept of the will are, according to Spinoza, confused notions. In reality they are only ideas, functioning in various ways and viewed under various aspects. Thus, both Spinoza's

theory of knowledge and his psychology are accounts of those elusive entities, ideas. Corresponding to the three stages of confused experience and images, scientific understanding, and *scientia intuitiva* are the stages which constitute human bondage, human freedom, and the intellectual love of God. These are psychological stages in that they are distinguished as different conditions of the mind. Spinoza's basic psychological concept is equally physiological: the human being, like any other being, is a unity inspired by a *conatus in suo esse perseverandi* (a drive toward self-preservation). Modifications of the body impinge upon the mind in the form of confused ideas which we experience differently, depending upon whether or not the individual's power of preserving itself is increased or diminished. If it is maintained or increased, what we experience is pleasure (*laetitia*); if it is decreased, what we experience is pain (*tristitia*). Pleasure is distinguished from mere pleasurable sensation (*titillatio*); and pain is sadness rather than physical pain. Pleasure and pain are thus outcomes of external causes impinging upon the individual *conatus*. Desire is *conatus* consciously directed toward some specific object. Spinoza then explains the individual emotions as involving different combinations of desire, pleasure, and pain, further differentiated by their association with other ideas. But, before discussing Spinoza's view of the emotions further, one precaution must be taken.

In Spinoza there is an equation between being more or less active as a causal agent upon others, being more or less in interaction with others, and being more or less real.

There is no single word in Spinoza which means what we mean by "emotion." The words which are liable to be translated by "emotion" are *affectus* and *passio*, but both of these words have a meaning defined by their place in the Spinozan system. An *affectus* is a modification, initially one of the body. A *passio* is something undergone, a modification effected by an external cause, as contrasted with one initiated from within the individual. "Affect, which is called a passion of the soul, is a confused idea by which the mind affirms of its body a power of endurance greater or lesser than before, and by which the mind is determined to think one thing rather than another" (*Ethics* III). The idea is said to be confused because from it we gain no insight into the genuine cause of the affect. Just as our general ideas at the level of confused experience are formed by mechanical association, so also are our desires. By association that which has been customarily linked with pleasure becomes an object of desire, and that which has been customarily linked with pain becomes an object of aversion. When the ordinary, and not philosophically enlightened, man explains his preferences, he gives reasons which have nothing to do with the true causes of his

---

There is no single word in Spinoza

which means what we mean by "emotion."

---

desire or aversion; this is what Spinoza means when he calls the ideas of such a man confused. In regard to the association of one idea with another or with feelings of pleasure, such an agent is completely passive; he regards himself as an agent, but he is merely reflecting the causal interchange between his own *conatus* and external powers. It would be wrong to think of Spinoza as asserting that feelings are merely associated with ideas; for Spinoza feelings *are* ideas. What does he mean? An affect is a modification of the body; every modification of a body has an idea as its counterpart. An inadequate idea and an adequate idea are alike in being counterparts of such a modification, and they do not differ in their relation to action. An idea, although it may be passive in respect of the agent's initiation, is never just a passive image. To have an idea is always to move or to be moved in a certain way. All thinking is action; all movement has its accompaniment in idea. Hence, it is less odd than it would be outside the context of Spinoza's system to assert that an affect is an idea. As it is with feeling and emotion, so it is more obviously with will. "There is in the mind no act of will save that which an idea as idea involves" (*Ethics* II, 49), and, in the same passage, "A particular act of will and a particular idea are one and the same." Spinoza believes that the popular conception of the will as active is a product of the mistake of supposing the intellect to be passive. Men argue mistakenly that since thought cannot move us to action, and we *are* moved to action, something else—the will—must so move us. Spinoza's assertion that ideas are active and move us to act places him against all those who have wanted to mark an ultimate dichotomy between fact-stating and action-guiding discourse.

Spinoza's treatment of particular emotions is often detailed and subtle. He is aware of the possible complexity of the emotions due to a multiplicity of associations and of that intertwining of pleasure and pain which results in such phenomena as ambivalence. Just as Spinoza is a nominalist in his treatment of *experientia saga* in the theory of knowledge, so he is also a nomi-

nalist in his treatment of the emotions. These only are particular emotions. "There is in the mind no faculty of understanding as such, or desiring as such, or loving as such." Moreover, one man's experience of emotion need not resemble another's; what constitutes the two emotions as the same emotion is their common relationship to pleasure and pain as defined in terms of *conatus*. All emotion, reflecting as it does the striving of the individual to maintain itself in being, as this is reflected in the seeking of pleasure and the avoidance of pain, has reference to the individual self. We are pleased at the happiness of others because we, by having regard to and for the happiness of others, increase our own powers. We wish other men to be rational because there is a general advantage in men's being rational. This at first sight resembles a Hobbesian egoism, but Spinoza's account of motivation at the level of the passions differs from a Hobbesian egoism in two striking ways. To maintain myself in being is to maintain in being what is part of the eternal order of things. "The power whereby each individual thing and therefore man maintains his being is the power of God or nature" (*Ethics* IV, 4). Moreover, the necessity of the self-maintaining character of the individual follows from the axioms of the system; it is not just contingently true that men regard their own self-interest. This is in a way true also of Hobbes, but the detail of the Hobbesian theory of human nature is independent of Hobbes's physical theorizing in a way which is not true of Spinoza's system.

SIMILARITY TO FREUD. The derivation of the psychology from the metaphysical axioms makes it as dangerous to compare Spinoza with Freud as it is to compare him with modern theoretical physicists. But the resemblance is nonetheless not an illusory one. The Spinozan *conatus* is one ancestor of the Freudian *libido;* and the Spinozan thesis of confused ideas which men cite as reasons for what they seek and avoid, items which in fact are not the causes which move them, is the ancestor of the Freudian thesis of rationalization. Spinoza and Freud were both interested in the plasticity of the emotions. Spinoza also anticipated Freud in the view that to become aware of the causes which move us is no longer to fall victim to them; but whereas Freud regarded his assertions as empirical and contingent, derived from and confirmed by observation, for Spinoza the parallel assertions are a priori truths. Nonetheless, the comparison of Freud and Spinoza suggests that one way of regarding rationalist metaphysical systems may be as deductive frameworks from which possible scientific theories can be derived. The vindication of a given metaphysical system would then lie in its providing us with concepts by means of which we may frame theories and explanations. A system such as that of Spinoza, with implications for both psychology and physics, compatible with empirical findings in these fields, and suggestive of possible new observations and inquiries, would rank higher than a system which was either barren of such consequences or whose consequences were incompatible with the empirical findings.

HUMAN BONDAGE AND FREEDOM. If human bondage consists in being moved by causes of which we are unaware because our ideas are confused, the transition to freedom is made solely by our ideas becoming adequate. When our ideas are adequate, we are no longer moved by something external to us; what initiates our movement is within us, and by definition we are free. The view that we become free by understanding the causes of our actions requires elucidation in two ways. First, Spinoza is not involved in denying the occurrence of the familiar experience of being able to identify the emotions which move one but of still being subject to them. To understand the cause of our actions is not to identify an emotion in common-sense fashion, for such an emotion is a confused idea. It is to replace the confused idea with an adequate idea. Hence, we no longer have the same emotion. To have adequate ideas is, moreover, to grasp and to be guided by "the law of one's own nature." "An emotion which is a passion ceases to be a passion as soon as we form a clear and distinct idea of it" (*Ethics* V, 3).

We are delivered from the bondage of passion by understanding because "the mind has greater power over the passions, and is less subject to them, in so far as it understands all things as necessary." We see the true causes of things being as they are and cannot then want them otherwise. It is not that we cease to have the desires which we formerly had. "For all desires by which we are determined to any action may arise as well from adequate as from inadequate ideas" (*Ethics* V, 4, *Scholium*). But these desires now are aimed at a goal which is common to all men and which is constant for each man. Consequently, one is rescued both from struggle with others and from the condition in which "we are in many ways driven about by external causes, and like the waves of the sea driven by contending winds, we are swayed hither and thither, unconscious of the issue and our destiny."

It is crucial for Spinoza that rational understanding is not merely a means to something else. It is at once means and end. The goals which understanding reveals are the goals of freedom and rationality, and these are one and the same. This freedom, which consists in knowing the causes which move one, and thus making the causes internal and not external to the agent, is of course not only compatible with but also requires complete determinism. Belief in free decision is among the illusions, the confused ideas, which the free man has discarded. From this there follow large consequences for the understanding of moral predicates.

Morality, Religion, Political Philosophy

According to Spinoza, the elements of the ordinary man's conventional moral code are a belief in free will, a use of praise and blame depending on this belief, and a use of such predicates as "good" and "evil" in the belief that they denote characteristics of that to which they are ascribed. In fact, Spinoza thinks, men call good whatever gives them pleasure, and evil whatever gives them pain, and these predicates express characteristics of those who use them and not of the objects about which they are used. But in fact all conventional use of moral predicates is out of place, for such a use presupposes that things could be other than they are, that men could have failed where they have succeeded and succeeded where they have failed, and that the world could be improved. To suppose this is to fail to see that everything occurs necessarily; it is to imply a contingency in the universe which the free man knows to be an inadequate idea. The *conatus suo esse perseverandi* is the foundation of virtue, in the true sense of that word, for "by virtue and power I understand the same thing" (*Ethics* IV, Def. 8). There is a link between the ordinary conventional use of moral predicates and what the free man knows, for the ordinary use of "good" and "evil" which refers to pleasure and pain refers to the effects of the *conatus*, before we are conscious of the true nature of pleasure, pain, and desire. After we become conscious of it, we equally seek to maintain the power of our being; but we now know what that power truly consists in, namely, knowledge. The virtuous life, the life of knowledge, can be described in terms both of attitudes and emotions and of goals.

We are delivered from the bondage of passion

by understanding because

"the mind has greater power over the passions,

and is less subject to them,

in so far as it understands all things as necessary."

There is no pain in the life of the free man, a fact which follows logically from the definitions of pain and of freedom. For when we are free, we are moved only by causes internal to our being; and pain is caused by the impinging upon us of external causes which decrease our power and vitality. Consequently, freedom and pain are incompatible. As we free ourselves from the impact of the external, as our ideas become adequate, so our ideas become part of the infinite idea of God; and even then, although they cease to be only the ideas of a particular body, the fundamental relationship between thought and extension is still preserved. For the essence of body is also imperishable and eternal (*Ethics* V, 22 and 23). In becoming God, the mind loses all distinction of subject and object: "the love of God to man and the intellectual love of man to God are one and the same."

In reaching this point, Spinoza's philosophy reaches its final goal. It has specified a good, the intellectual love of God, with which the mind can be filled and thus be impervious to change and circumstance. The distinction between true and illusory goods has been finally made.

VIEWS ON RELIGION. It is clear that Spinoza's conception of the religious life is at odds with that of all traditional religion, particularly with the Judaism which excommunicated him. In Spinoza's own view, however, there can be no clash between philosophy and revelation. The Old Testament is to be interpreted in two ways: as allegories of intellectual truth, and as fitted for the social, moral, and intellectual needs of a primitive people. The Hebrew prophets could not have spoken other than as they did; the philosophically enlightened man cannot accept what they said, if he is asked to treat it as a literal truth. But the unenlightened modern man needs allegory, anthropomorphism, threat, bribes, and promises to keep him law-abiding and to support him emotionally, just as much as the audience of the prophets did. It would be wrong, therefore, to try to deprive him of it. Spinoza's great emphasis is not upon skepticism about popular religion but upon the need to preserve freedom of inquiry for those who wish it.

POLITICAL PHILOSOPHY. In Spinoza's political philosophy too the necessity of freedom is central. As in every other part of his philosophy he uses Hobbes in an attempt to go beyond him. He accepts as completely as Hobbes does the fact that politics is entirely a matter of power. He also accepts a Hobbesian version of the social contract in which we hand over power to a sovereign in return for a restraint upon the anarchy which threatens all possibility of peace and survival. It is not surprising that he accepts the Hobbesian equation of "have a right to" with "have the power to," for this is consistent with his own critique of conventional morality. But we can see the beginnings of the breach with Hobbes when we consider that, although both held that when a contract is no longer to our advantage, we are

therefore under no obligation to keep it ("to be under obligation" means "to find advantages in"), the Spinozan and Hobbesian conceptions of advantage are at opposite extremes. For Hobbes, advantage lies in satisfying as many of one's desires as possible without being preyed upon by others. For Spinoza, advantage lies in escaping from the bondage of just those desires which Hobbesian man aspires to satisfy. Consequently, Spinoza wishes to see a state in which civil peace secures above all freedom for diverse opinions, provided only that these do not lead to seditious acts. The imposition of irrational beliefs upon unwilling subjects, so he argues, produces precisely the civil strife which men wish to avoid. This is quite unlike Hobbes, who sees opinion as a source of contention and who thinks that we hand over to the sovereign and to his magistrates the right to set standards for the expression of opinions and even for the meaning of words.

It is clear that Spinoza's conception of the religious life is at odds with that of all traditional religion, particularly with the Judaism which excommunicated him.

This difference is rooted in the contrast between Hobbes's view that reason is merely a means to the ends set by the desires and Spinoza's that the desires must be transformed by the ends which rational inquiry sets for rational men. It is, therefore, not surprising that while Hobbes sees security in monarchy, Spinoza, after comparing different types of constitutions, concludes that the best type is a democracy in which the owners of property rule. Here there is an interesting coincidence between systems and environment. For if Hobbes's system points toward monarchy, so did his social experience of the English Civil War. Spinoza's ideal is clearly not merely a product of abstract reasoning but also of the tolerance of Amsterdam and its mercantile bourgeois democracy.

For a century after his death Spinoza's thought was substantially ignored. From the time of Goethe, and as a result of the influence of Goethe and of Schelling, he has been continually reinterpreted. The two most prevalent interpretations of Spinoza are equally enthusiastic and equally incorrect. For Goethe and Coleridge, Spinoza was a pantheist and mystic; for G. V. Plekhanov,

Spinoza was a monistic materialist. The one tradition underlines *Deus,* the other *Natura;* both miss the essential Spinozan point which lies in the *sive* (the equation). Equally, idealist commentators, such as Edward Caird and H. H. Joachim, or an analytical philosopher like Stuart Hampshire, are apt to import into Spinoza interests which were not his. The corrective to these interpretations lies in stressing Spinoza's attempt to achieve complete deductive unity in the metaphysics. From the axioms and definitions to the final consequences, the system stands or falls as a whole. If this is not the right way to do philosophy, we can understand why this is so only by a study of the system as a whole. What Spinoza has left us is, because it is the most complete and hard-headed exposition of rationalist metaphysics, the best evidence we have of its impossibility.

BIBLIOGRAPHY

Works by Spinoza

Spinoza Opera, C. Gebhardt, ed., 4 vols. Heidelberg, 1924.

Translations

The Chief Works of Spinoza, translated by R. H. M. Elwes, 2 vols. London, 1883; New York, 1955 and 1956.
The Principles of Descartes' Philosophy, translated by H. H. Briton. Chicago, 1905.
Short Treatise on God, Man and His Well-being, translated by A. Wolf. London, 1910.
Ethics, translated by W. H. White and A. H. Stirling. Oxford, 1927.
Correspondence of Spinoza, translated by A. Wolf. London, 1928.
The Political Works, edited and translated by A. G. Wernham. Oxford, 1958.

Works on Spinoza

Caird, Edward, *Spinoza.* Edinburgh and London, 1902.
Hallett, H. F., *Benedict de Spinoza, The Elements of His Philosophy.* London, 1957.
Hampshire, Stuart, *Spinoza.* Harmondsworth, 1951; London, 1956.
Joachim, H. H., *A Study of Spinoza's Ethics.* Oxford, 1901.
Joachim, H. H., *Commentary on Spinoza's Tractatus de Intellectus Emendatione.* Oxford, 1940.
Oko, Adolph S., *The Spinoza Bibliography.* Boston, 1964.
Parkinson, G. H. R., *Spinoza's Theory of Knowledge.* Oxford, 1954.
Pollock, F., *Spinoza: His Life and Philosophy.* London, 1880.
Roth, Leon, *Spinoza, Descartes and Maimonides.* Oxford, 1924.
Roth, Leon, *Spinoza.* London, 1954.
Saw, R. L., *The Vindication of Metaphysics: A Study in the Philosophy of Spinoza.* New York, 1951.
Strauss, L., *Die Religionskritik Spinoza als Grundlage seiner Bibelwissenschaft.* Berlin, 1930.
Wolfson, H. A., *The Philosophy of Spinoza,* 2 vols. Cambridge, Mass., 1954; New York, 1958.

– ALASDAIR MACINTYRE

SPINOZA, BENEDICT (BARUCH) (UPDATE)

The years following 1967 witnessed a major renewal of interest in Spinoza's philosophy. One factor facilitating this renewal was the decline—or at least moderation—of a linguistically oriented mode of philosophizing that had typically regarded Spinoza's metaphysical aims with deep suspicion and had frequently sought to locate the grounds of his doctrines in alleged linguistic or logical confusions. More positively, interest was stimulated by the publication, within a two-year period, of three groundbreaking interpretive studies (Curley, 1969; Gueroult, 1968; and Matheron, 1969). Increasingly, philosophers have interpreted Spinoza's metaphysical, ethical, political, and religious thought in ways that emphasize its relations to a modern scientific and naturalistic understanding of the universe.

Metaphysics

One important example of this trend concerns the interpretation of the relations holding among substance, attributes, and modes. Spinoza asserts that nothing exists except substance and modes and that all modes (including all individual things) are "in" and "conceived through" a single substance (God or Nature). Traditionally, this assertion has been understood to mean that all things inhere in God as qualities in a subject or substratum, so that the ontological status of ordinary individual things is reduced to that of mere qualities. Curley (1969), however, denied that the relation of inherence was central to Spinoza's conception of being "in and conceived through," emphasizing instead the causal character of these relations. Since attributes constitute (by definition, *Ethics,* pt. 1, def. 4) the essence of substance, this causal conception of the substance/mode relation led Curley to an interpretation of the divine attributes as fundamental pervasive facts about the universe, corresponding to the most basic laws of nature. He then interpreted the infinite modes (which, according to Spinoza [*Ethics,* pt. 1, prop. 21], follow from the "absolute nature" of the attributes) as facts corresponding to less basic nomological generalizations, which are logically entailed by the most basic laws of nature. Finally, he construed finite modes as particular facts about the universe, following from other particular facts in concert with the laws of nature associated with the attributes and infinite modes, though not from the laws of nature alone. Spinoza's doctrine that all modes are in and conceived through a single substance becomes, on this interpretation, not a doctrine about the relation of qualities to a single substratum, but rather a version of determinism about the relation of individual things to a naturalized conception of "God" as the single basic nomic structure of the universe.

While not denying the significance of the causal aspect of the substance/mode relation, and without ascribing to Spinoza acceptance of a Lockean substratum,

Bennett (1984) nevertheless sought to reinstate an aspect of subject/quality inherence as part of the meaning of "in and conceived through." His way of doing so, while contrasting with Curley's interpretation, provides another example of the trend toward reading Spinoza in ways congenial to modern scientific naturalism. On Bennett's reading Spinoza's substance monism primarily expresses "the field metaphysic," according to which (1) the ultimate substantial independent reality (at least insofar as that reality is considered as extended) is space itself and (2) individual extended things are, at the deepest level, simply strings of spatiotemporally continuous place-times, strings whose elements are associated with one another by the changing distributions, through spatial regions, of physical qualities of space itself. This interpretation, if correct, provides a sense in which individual extended things would be "adjectival" upon the one extended substance. (It would then be necessary to apply a similar account to the attribute of thought.)

Spinoza asserts that nothing exists

except substance and modes and that

all modes (including all individual things)

are "in" and "conceived through"

a single substance (God or Nature).

One well-known problem facing any interpretation of the substance/mode relation is the question of how merely temporary and local finite modes can "follow from" the nature of the eternal and infinite substance. One solution would begin by interpreting the attributes as essential natures of substance that are expressible (as Curley suggested) in the most basic laws of nature. These laws, when taken in connection with the plausibly Spinozistic requirement that the one substance (because infinite and unlimited) must manifest or express itself with the greatest amount of reality/perfection possible, would then logically and causally determine the entire infinite series of finite modes as the uniquely most perfect set of temporary and local self-manifestations or self-expressions (considered as distributions of qualities, in something like the way Bennett described) of the one substance. This infinite series would itself be an infinite mode, composed of finite, spatiotemporally limited parts. Such an interpretation could hope to explain how a substance both causes and is qualified by its modes and to do so in a way that is compatible with the absolute necessitarianism that Spinoza seems to enunciate in *Ethics*, pt. 1, props. 29, 33, and elsewhere. Absolute necessitarianism also seems to be required by what Gueroult (1968) identifies as Spinoza's most fundamental assumption: the doctrine that all things are intelligible or conceivable. For, when combined with Spinoza's doctrines that things must be understood or conceived through their causes (*Ethics*, pt. 1, ax. 4) and that causes necessitate (*Ethics*, pt. 1, ax. 3), this assumption of universal conceivability (arguably embodied in *Ethics*, pt. 1, ax. 2) requires that everything be necessary.

It is worth emphasizing that Spinoza would not distinguish between "logical" and "causal" necessitarianism, since for him logical consequence is not primarily a formal matter (as it was for Leibniz), but rather an expression of the laws of thought, a causal power both isomorphic to and identical with the dynamic causal power manifested in extension. Spinoza is often criticized for conflating the logical and the psychological, but his apparent failure to distinguish them sharply is intentional: logical consequence is best understood, on his view, as an aspect of divine psychology (i.e., the psychology of Nature itself).

Ethics, Politics, and Religion

Since 1967 there has also been increased interest in the naturalistic aspects of Spinoza's ethics, politics, and religion. Spinoza uses four fundamental terms of positive moral evaluation: 'good', 'virtue', 'free man', and 'in accordance with reason'. Each of these terms is definable naturalistically: 'good' as "what we certainly know to be useful to us" (*Ethics*, pt. 4, def. 1), where 'useful' is itself defined in terms of self-preservation; 'virtue' as "power" (*Ethics*, pt. 4, def. 8); 'free man' in terms of causal self-sufficiency (*Ethics*, pt. 1, def. 8) or of action in accordance with reason (*Ethics*, pt. 4, prop. 67); and 'in accordance with reason' itself in terms of self-preserving action produced by a specific natural, adequate cognitive faculty (*Ethics*, pt. 4, prop. 18 scholium). (Because every individual necessarily endeavors to preserve itself, certain cognitions of the world are also desires; when these cognitions are adequate, they are rational desires. Hence, reason is intrinsically practical.) His moral theory is also a species of virtue ethics, inasmuch as the ultimate aim is neither the production of an end nor the performance of actions in accordance with duty or law, but rather the achievement and maintenance of a virtuous ("free," "blessed") state of being. Spinoza (seeking to avoid what he regards as the subjectivity of the common usage of 'good') defines a "good" action as one that certainly enables us to come closer to this state rather than as what someone who has already achieved this state would do; hence, there may be circumstances for Spinozistic ethics in which it would be "good" to do something other than what a "free" or "virtuous" person would do.

Like his ethical theory, Spinoza's political theory is naturalistic, treating "right" as coextensive with power and identifying the permissible with the actual, just as his metaphysics identifies the possible with the actual. There is, for Spinoza, a particularly close relationship between personal freedom and political freedom. Just as the human being is an individual whose freedom lies in his or her ability to achieve self-preservation through his or her own power and activity, so a political state is an individual whose freedom lies in its ability to preserve itself through its own power and activity (Matheron, 1969). One underlying purpose of Spinoza's political theorizing is to show that a political state that is free in the sense of allowing free thought and expression and thereby fostering the existence of citizens who are personally free is also the most free in the sense of being best able to maintain and enhance its own existence. In Spinoza's view one central political problem for a free state is the role of religion. While retaining scripture for the nonphilosophical masses, he seeks to derive from its own text the inessentiality to true religion of any particular dogmas or practices beyond the practice of justice and charity toward others (*Theological-Political Treatise*, chap. 13). Whereas the vulgar perceive God as a personal and supernatural lawgiver, the more philosophical understand God as Nature and His laws as the immutable laws of nature. Thus, natural science itself proves to be the best expression of the religious impulse—that is, the impulse to love God and to find one's blessedness in doing so.

[See also Virtue Ethics.]

BIBLIOGRAPHY

Works by Spinoza

The Collected Works of Spinoza. Vol. 1, trans. E. Curley. Princeton, NJ, 1985. Upon its publication this became the standard English translation of the works it contains: *Ethics; Treatise on the Emendation of the Intellect; Short Treatise on God, Man, and His Well-Being; Principles of Descartes' Philosophy;* and the *Correspondence* (through 1665). The remainder of his philosophical works will appear in Vol. 2. (The 1967 article on Spinoza erroneously describes Spinoza's *Treatise of the Emendation of the Intellect [Tractatus de Intellectus Emendatione]* as having been discovered only in the nineteenth century. In fact, it was included [along with the *Ethics, Political Treatise, Correspondence,* and a *Hebrew Grammar*] in the *Opera posthuma* published shortly after Spinoza's death; it is the *Short Treatise on God, Man, and His Well-Being* that was discovered [in a Dutch transcription] in the nineteenth century.)
Ethics; Treatise on the Emendation of the Intellect; Selected Letters, trans. S. Shirley. 2d ed. Indianapolis, 1992.

Tractatus Theologico-politicus, trans. S. Shirley. Leiden, 1989.

Works on Spinoza

Bennett, J. *A Study of Spinoza's "Ethics."* Indianapolis, 1984.
Curley, E. *Spinoza's Metaphysics: An Essay in Interpretation.* Cambridge, MA, 1969.
———. *Behind the Geometrical Method: A Reading of Spinoza's "Ethics."* Princeton, NJ, 1988.
———, and P.-F. Moreau. *Spinoza: Issues and Directions.* Leiden, 1990.
Donagan, A. *Spinoza.* Chicago, 1988.
Garrett, D., ed. *The Cambridge Companion to Spinoza.* Cambridge, 1996.
Gueroult, M. *Spinoza.* 2 vols. Paris, 1968–74.
Matheron, A. *Individu et communauté chez Spinoza.* Paris, 1969.
Yovel, Y., ed. *God and Nature: Spinoza's Metaphysics.* Leiden, 1991.

– DON GARRETT

STEVENSON, CHARLES L.

Charles L. Stevenson (1908–1979) constructed the first thorough account of the emotivist or expressivist theory of moral language. His position is called noncognitivism because it emphasizes the conative side of ethical practice rather than the search for ethical knowledge and truth. In a series of articles and in his widely discussed 1944 book *Ethics and Language,* Stevenson argued that, since evaluative utterances are not, or not primarily, fact stating, they are not subject to assessment in terms of truth and falsity. Ethical disagreements, he said, often involve disagreement in belief, but they always involve disagreement in attitude. Disagreement in attitude can be resolved by argument if it is rooted in disagreement in belief; but we recognize that some disagreement in attitude may be fundamental, in which case we will be unable to reach agreement by rational methods.

Ethical disagreements, said Stevenson,

often involve disagreement in belief,

but they always involve disagreement in attitude.

By the time *Ethics and Language* appeared, emotivism had been sketched by A. J. Ayer, who claimed that ethical utterances are disguised commands and exclamations. Others had introduced behavioral accounts of meaning, emphasized attention to the use of moral language, and questioned the rationality of morality. Stevenson's contribution was to integrate these new ideas into a coherent theory, to distinguish the "theoretical" nature of his approach from normative ethics, or moralizing, and to emphasize the distinction between descriptive meaning and emotive meaning.

Stevenson argued that we can explain the meaning of an utterance such as "X is good" only if we can find a similar expression that is free from ambiguity and confusion and allows us to do and say everything we can do and say with the original expression. A "subjectivist" definition such as "This is good = I approve of this" at best accounts for the descriptive meaning of "This is good," but it completely neglects the emotive meaning. Stevenson characterized the emotive meaning of a word as its tendency, "arising through the history of its usage, to produce (result from) *affective* responses in people" (1963, p. 21). By leaving out any mention of emotive meaning the subjectivist definition makes it impossible to understand the nature of ethical disagreement, which is fundamentally a clash of attitudes. Stevenson's suggestion is that a proper analysis of "This is good" will satisfy the following pattern: "This is good = I approve of this; do so as well." The first element of the *definiens* (I approve of this) gives a subjectivist "descriptive meaning," and the second element of the *definiens* (Do so as well) gives the emotive meaning.

In a "second pattern of analysis," Stevenson dealt with cases in which the descriptive and emotive meanings are more closely related. In this connection he introduced the idea of a "persuasive definition." When we give such a definition we are trying to attach a new descriptive meaning to terms such as 'courage' or 'justice' while keeping the emotive meaning unchanged. The point of doing this is to change the direction of interests and attitudes, which is also the point of making a straightforward ethical judgment.

Stevenson earned degrees at Yale and Cambridge before receiving his Ph.D. from Harvard in 1935. He then taught at Harvard and at Yale, where his views about ethics were not popular. In 1946 he joined the philosophy department at the University of Michigan and remained there until his retirement. In addition to his landmark writings on ethical theory, he wrote about aesthetics and the arts, especially music and poetry. He was a talented amateur musician and frequently performed on the piano or the cello with his friends and family.

[See also Ethical Theory; Rationality.]

BIBLIOGRAPHY

Ayer, A. J. *Language, Truth and Logic.* New York, 1952.
Goldman, A. I., and J. Kim, eds. *Values and Morals: Essays in Honor of William Frankena, Charles Stevenson, and Richard Brandt.* London, 1978.
Stevenson, C. L. *Ethics and Language.* New Haven, 1944.
———. *Facts and Values.* New Haven, 1963.
Urmson, J. O. *The Emotive Theory of Ethics.* New York, 1969.

— RICHARD GARNER

STRAWSON, P. F.

P. F. Strawson succeeded Gilbert Ryle as Waynflete Professor of Metaphysical Philosophy at the University of Oxford in 1968, retiring in 1987. He was knighted in 1977. Since 1966 he has published seven books, including *The Bounds of Sense* (1966) and *Skepticism and Naturalism* (1985). In these and other writings he has continued to explore a wide-ranging set of problems in metaphysics, epistemology, the philosophy of language, and the history of philosophy, including their interrelations, displaying the same profundity and abstractness of argument as in his earlier works, notably *Individuals.*

The Bounds of Sense, a book with links to part 1 of *Individuals,* is a critical and constructive study of Kant's *Critique of Pure Reason,* in which Strawson attempts to determine what insights can be extracted from Kant's arguments when certain Kantian errors are eliminated. The chief error is transcendental idealism, which Strawson argues is both hard to interpret and incoherent, especially when applied to the self. Another error is Kant's conception of the necessities for which he argues, as corresponding to features we impose on experience and as classifiable as synthetic a prioris. Rather, Strawson suggests, the "necessities represent limits to what we can conceive of . . . as possible general structures of experience" (1966, p. 15).

Strawson, drawing on the transcendental deduction,

claims that a self-conscious subject

must acknowledge that some of his experiences

are of an objective realm.

Strawson, drawing on the transcendental deduction, claims that a self-conscious subject must acknowledge that some of his experiences are of an objective realm. The argument is that there can be a concept of oneself, the possessor of the experiences, only if there is the complexity of thought that is brought by regarding some experiences as being of objects independent of oneself. Further, drawing on the analogies, Strawson suggests that thinking of such objects itself requires that there be a "background of persistences and alterations" that are regular and that objects must fall under causal concepts. It follows that there is no genuine problem corresponding to the traditional one associated with empiricism: of how to construct, and defend, a conception of the external world starting from self-consciously ascribed inner (sense-datum) experiences. Strawson also analyzes and adds to Kant's more critical arguments, for example, the attack on rational psychology in the paralogisms.

Strawson's study of Kant has inspired a debate as to whether Strawson himself has adequately defended the necessities. It has also inspired attempts to interpret transcendental idealism in a more sympathetic way.

In *Subject and Predicate in Logic and Grammar,* a book with clear links to part 2 of *Individuals,* Strawson returned to what distinguishes subject terms from predicate terms. Strawson's main thesis is that a variety of semanticological marks of the distinction can be viewed as consequences of a more fundamental contrast. In certain basic sentences the role of subject terms is to pick out spatiotemporal particulars, and the fundamental (though not only) role of predicate terms is to pick out a principle of classification (or a concept), according to which such particulars can be grouped. The subject–predicate distinction applies to sentences outside this basic class because of analogies with the basic case. In the second part of the book Strawson specifies a progressively rich range of functions a language must perform and speculates about different ways, in relation to the grammar of languages, they might be performed. Although displaying a brilliant sense of the role of elements in natural language, this style of speculative grammar has not attracted many other philosophers.

Skepticism and Naturalism: Some Varieties considers various traditional philosophical debates, which take the form of a choice between endorsing or being skeptical of certain natural beliefs or attitudes. In the case of skepticism about the external world, Strawson argues—inspired by Hume and Wittgenstein—that our nature makes it impossible to entertain skepticism seriously, and so the skeptic's arguments lapse. Strawson thereby recommends us not to rely on the type of transcendental argument he himself extracted from Kant. It has been extensively debated whether the psychological claims yield a proper reply. Strawson proposes different strategies to avoid revision of other fundamental beliefs, concerning, for example, secondary qualities, mentality, and meaning. In this book Strawson displays an interest in the abstract dynamics of philosophical disputes, a theme developed in *Analysis and Metaphysics: An Introduction to Philosophy.* In it Strawson outlines his conception of philosophy as analytical, rather than revisionary, and as displaying connections between our fundamental categories rather than reducing concepts to a limited range of simple categories. A theme of this book, as well as many of Strawson's articles—for example, those dealing with perception and the theory of language—is that philosophy should offer realistic descriptions of its subject matter, not oversimplifying in

the interests of neatness of theory, nor springing from a mistaken desire to make philosophy like science. Given this stance, Strawson has criticized the programs of other leading philosophers such as Quine, Davidson, and Dummett.

Strawson's writings, with their goal of providing a realistically rich description—innocent of the pretensions of reduction and revision—of our basic thought about and contact with the world, have inspired many other recent philosophers, notably Gareth Evans and John McDowell.

[See also Davidson, Donald; Dummett, Michael; Epistemology; Hume, David; Kant, Immanuel; Meaning; Metaphysics; Perception; Philosophy of Language; Quine, Willard Van Orman; Self; Skepticism; Wittgenstein, Ludwig Josef Johann.]

BIBLIOGRAPHY

Works by Strawson

The Bounds of Sense. London, 1966.
Logico Linguistic Papers. London, 1971. Includes "Meaning and Truth," in which Strawson discusses Davidson.
Freedom and Resentment. London, 1974. Includes the very famous title paper, which attempts, along characteristically Strawsonian lines, to dissolve the conflict between responsibility and determinism, and other influential papers on perception.
Subject and Predicate in Logic and Grammar. London, 1974.
Skepticism and Naturalism: Some Varieties. New York, 1985.
Analysis and Metaphysics: An Introduction to Philosophy. Oxford, 1992.

Works on Strawson

Philosophia, Vol. 10 (1981), 141–328. A collection of articles about many aspects of Strawson's work and a reply by Strawson.
Philosophical Subjects. van Straaten, Z., ed. Oxford, 1980. Contains discussions of Strawson by Evans, McDowell, and Ishiguro and replies by Strawson.
Sen, P. B., and R. R. Verma. *The Philosophy of P. F. Strawson.* New Delhi, 1995. Contains important discussions by Putnam, Dummett, and Cassam and replies by Strawson.

– PAUL F. SNOWDON

SUBJECTIVIST EPISTEMOLOGY

A subjectivist epistemology is one that implies the standards of rational belief are those of the individual believer or those of the believer's community. Thus, subjectivism can come in either an individualistic form or a social form. A key negative test of subjectivism is whether an account implies that by being rational one is assured of having beliefs that are more reliable than they would be otherwise—that is, more reliable than they would be if one were not rational. Thus, reliabilist accounts of rational beliefs are paradigmatically objective. So are traditional foundationalist accounts. By contrast, if an account implies that the standards one must meet if one's beliefs are to be rational are those that one would regard as intellectually defensible were one to be ideally reflective (Foley, 1987, 1993), then the account is subjective. Similarly, an account is subjective if it implies that one's beliefs are rational if they meet the standards of one's community (Rorty, 1979) or the standards of the recognized experts in one's community (Stich, 1985). Likewise, an account is subjective if it implies that one's beliefs are rational if they meet the standards of the human community at large, provided nothing else in the account implies that adhering to such standards will reliably produce true beliefs.

One of the considerations favoring a subjectivist

epistemology is that it provides an attractive way

of describing what is going on in skeptical scenarios.

One of the considerations favoring a subjectivist epistemology is that it provides an attractive way of describing what is going on in skeptical scenarios—for example, one in which everything appears normal from my subjective point of view even though my brain has been removed from my body and placed in a vat, where it is being fed sensory experiences by a deceiving scientist. In such a scenario, almost everything I believe about my immediate surroundings would be false. Hence, I would have little knowledge about these surroundings, but what I believe about them might nonetheless be rational. Indeed, my beliefs would be as rational as my current beliefs about my surroundings. The most plausible explanation as to why this is so is that there is at least one important sense of rational belief according to which having rational beliefs is essentially a matter of meeting subjectively generated standards. Thus, by being envatted I may be deprived of the opportunity of having knowledge about my surroundings, but I am not necessarily also deprived of an opportunity of having rational beliefs.

[See also Classical Foundationalism; Epistemology; Reliabilism; Social Epistemology.]

BIBLIOGRAPHY

Foley, R. *The Theory of Epistemic Rationality.* Cambridge, MA, 1987.
———. *Working without a Net.* New York, 1993.
Rorty, R. *Philosophy and the Mirror of Nature.* Princeton, NJ, 1979.
Stich, S. "Could Man Be an Irrational Animal?" *Synthese,* Vol. 64 (1985), 115–35.

— RICHARD FOLEY

SUBJECTIVITY

Subjectivity is, primarily, an aspect of consciousness. In a sense, conscious experience can be described as the way the world appears from a particular mental subject's point of view. The very idea that there is a distinction between appearance and reality seems to presuppose the distinction between subjective and objective points of view.

There are two principal controversies surrounding subjectivity: first, whether subjectivity, as it is manifested in consciousness, is an essential component of mentality; and, second, whether subjectivity presents an obstacle to naturalistic theories of the mind.

Most philosophers agree that intentionality—the ability to represent—is characteristic of mentality. However, there is strong disagreement over whether subjectivity is also necessary. Those philosophers who think it is (e.g., Searle, 1992) argue that true (or what they call "original") intentionality can be attributed only to a conscious subject. On this view representational properties can be ascribed only to unconscious states, or to states of unconscious machines, in a derivative, or metaphorical, sense. The basic argument for this position is that, without a conscious subject interpreting a representation, there is nothing to determine its content, and therefore there is no representation at all.

Other philosophers reject this assimilation of intentionality and subjectivity, arguing that a theory of intentionality—one that applies equally to conscious and unconscious states—can be developed independently of a theory of subjectivity (e.g., Dretske, 1981, and Fodor, 1987). In particular they argue that conditions for the determination of representational content can be given in objective, even physicalistic, terms.

With respect to the second question—whether or not subjectivity presents a problem—one might argue as follows. A complete inventory of the world should, if it is truly complete, capture everything there is and everything going on. It seems natural to suppose that such a complete description is in principle possible and is in fact the ideal aim of natural science. But how could facts that are essentially accessible only from a particular subject's point of view be included; and, if they can't, doesn't this undermine the idea that the natural world constitutes a coherent, lawful, and objective whole?

For example, take the very fact of one's own existence. You could read through this hypothetical exhaustive description of the world, and it would include a description of a body at a particular spatiotemporal location, with particular physiological (or even nonphysical) processes going on inside it. However, what would be missing is the fact that this is your body—

this is you. No collection of facts stable in objective terms seem to add up to the fact that this body is yours.

Or take the problem of personal identity. From a point of view outside the subject, what it is that makes one the same person across time, whether it be a matter of bodily or psychological continuity, seems to admit of borderline cases, or matters of degree, or other sorts of indeterminacy. Yet from the point of view of the subject, what it is to be oneself seems to be a clear-cut, all-or-nothing matter. Either one continues to exist or one doesn't. It is hard to reconcile the objective and subjective perspectives on this question.

Two principal controversies surrounding subjectivity

are whether subjectivity as it is manifested in

consciousness is an essential component of mentality;

and whether subjectivity presents an obstacle

to naturalistic theories of the mind.

One particularly difficult manifestation of the problem of subjectivity is how to account for the fact that there is "something it is like" to be certain objects (say a human being), or occupy certain states (say, visual experiences), but not others (say, a rock, and its states). This is also known as the problem of qualia. From an objective point of view there would seem to be nothing special about the neurological activity responsible for conscious experience that would explain what it's like for the subject.

Many philosophers argue that subjectivity does not present a special puzzle. For some (e.g., Searle, 1992) it is just a fact that the world contains both objective facts and irreducibly subjective facts; their relation requires no explanation and produces no mystery. For most, though, the demystification of the subjective is accomplished by some sort of reductionist strategy (e.g., Lycan, 1987, 1990, and Rosenthal, 1986). One influential model of subjectivity is the internal monitoring, or higher-order thought model. On this view, which fits well with a functionalist approach to the mind–body problem in general, subjectivity is principally a matter of some mental states representing other mental states. If this is what subjectivity amounts to, then any model of the mind that builds in the requisite architectural features will explain subjectivity. We already have a model of this sort of internal scanning with computers.

Advocates for the view that subjectivity presents no special mystery sometimes point to the perspectival character of indexical expressions such as "I" and "here" for support. The idea is that it is generally acknowledged that the meaning of such expressions cannot be captured in nonindexical terms (see Perry, 1979), yet this doesn't give rise to any special philosophical problem or mystery. There are theories that take into account the special behavior of such terms consistent with a general theory that applies to nonindexical terms as well. Similarly, goes the argument, subjective phenomena can be incorporated into a more general theory of the world that applies to nonsubjective phenomena as well.

Yet another approach to the problem of subjectivity is eliminativism (e.g., Churchland, 1985, and Dennett, 1991). Proponents of this view will grant that none of the models proposed to account for subjectivity really explains it, but, they argue, that is due to the fact that our intuitive conception of subjectivity—indeed of consciousness in general—is too confused or incoherent to be susceptible of scientific explanation. Subjectivity just isn't a real phenomenon, so there's nothing in the end to explain.

[See also Eliminative Materialism, Eliminativism; Indexicals; Personal Identity; Philosophy of Mind; Qualia; Self.]

BIBLIOGRAPHY

Churchland, P. "Reduction, Qualia, and the Direct Introspection of Brain States," *Journal of Philosophy*, Vol. 82 (1985).
Dennett, D. C. *Consciousness Explained*. Boston, 1991.
Dretske, F. *Knowledge and the Flow of Information*. Cambridge, MA, 1981.
Fodor, J. A. *Psychosemantics: The Problem of Meaning in the Philosophy of Mind*. Cambridge, MA, 1987.
Levine, J. "Could Love Be Like a Heatwave?: Physicalism and the Subjective Character of Experience," *Philosophical Studies*, Vol. 49 (1986).
Lycan, W. G. *Consciousness*. Cambridge, MA, 1987.
———. "What Is the 'Subjectivity' of the Mental?" *Philosophical Perspectives*, Vol. 4 (1990), 109–30.
McGinn, C., *The Subjective View*. New York, 1983.
———. *The Problem of Consciousness*. Oxford, 1991.
Nagel, T. "What Is It Like to Be a Bat?" *Philosophical Review*, Vol. 83 (1974), 435–50.
———. *The View from Nowhere*. New York, 1986.
Perry, J. "The Problem of the Essential Indexical," *Noûs*, Vol. 13 (1979), 3–21.
Rosenthal, D. "Two Concepts of Consciousness," *Philosophical Studies*, Vol. 49 (1986), 329–59.
Searle, J. *The Rediscovery of the Mind*. Cambridge, MA, 1992.
van Gulick, R. "Physicalism and the Subjectivity of the Mental," *Philosophical Topics*, Vol. 16 (1985), 51–70.

– JOSEPH LEVINE

SUPERVENIENCE

The core idea of the leading notion of supervenience is that there is an instance of supervenience when, but only when there cannot be a difference of some one sort without a difference of another sort (Lewis, 1986). According to this idea, if there can be no *A*-difference without a *B*-difference, then, and only then *A*-respects supervene on *B*-respects. Thus, for example, mental respects supervene on physical respects if and only if (iff) there can be no mental difference without a physical difference; and moral respects supervene on nonmoral respects iff there can be no moral difference without a nonmoral difference. This notion of supervenience is the notion of dependent-variation: variations in supervenient *A*-respects depend on variations in subvenient *B*-respects in that the former require the latter. Exact similarity in subvenient respects thus excludes the possibility of variation in supervenient respects. So, if mental respects supervene on physical respects, then exact similarity in physical respects excludes the possibility of difference in mental respects. Let us say that any *x* and *y* are *A*-duplicates just in case they are exactly alike in every *A*-respect; and likewise for *B*-duplicates. Then, *A*-respects supervene on *B*-respects, when, but only when *B*-duplicates cannot fail to be *A*-duplicates.

World-strong supervenience implies global,

but there has been controversy

over whether global implies world-strong,

and even over whether it implies world-weak.

Various technical definitions have been proposed that formulate different types of dependent-variation (Kim, 1993). Quantifying over possible worlds (i.e., ways the world might be or counterfactual situations), the following characterize two types:

World-Weak Supervenience. In any world *w*, *B*-duplicates in *w* are *A*-duplicates in *w*.
World-Strong Supervenience. For any worlds *w* and *w**, and any individuals *x* and *y*, if *x* in *w* is a *B*-duplicate of *y* in *w**, then *x* in *w* is an *A*-duplicate of *y* in *w**.

Thus, according to world-weak supervenience, intraworld *B*-duplicates are invariably intraworld *A*-duplicates; while according to world-strong supervenience, both intraworld and cross-world *B*-duplicates are invariably *A*-duplicates. Strong implies weak, but not conversely; hence the names "strong" and "weak." Subversions of each can be formulated by restricting the range of worlds, for example, to the nomologically possible worlds.

There is another intuitive notion of supervenience that is related to the notion of dependent-variation. It

is the notion of a purely modal dependence-determination relationship. The dependence idea is that possessing a supervenient property requires possessing some subvenient property; the determination idea is that possession of that subvenient property will suffice for possession of the supervenient property. Thus, on this conception of supervenience, possessing a supervenient property requires possessing some subvenient property whose possession suffices for the possession of that supervenient property. A pair of technical definitions of property-supervenience have been proposed that distinguish strong and weak versions (Kim, 1993):

Operator-Weak Supervenience. Necessarily, for any *A*-property *F*, if something has *F*, then there is at least one *B*-property *G* such that it has *G*, and whatever has *G* has *F*.
Operator-Strong Supervenience. Necessarily, for any *A*-property *F*, if something has *F*, then there is at least one *B*-property *G* such that it has *G*, and necessarily whatever has *G* has *F*.

Of course, strong implies weak, but not conversely. Subversions of each can be formulated by restricting the kind of necessity in question.

On trivial assumptions, if necessity can be understood as universal quantification over possible worlds, then operator-weak implies world-weak supervenience, and operator-strong implies world-strong. However, the converse implications fail. The reason is that both operator-weak and operator-strong imply that if something has an *A*-property, then it has some *B*-property (Haugeland, 1982; McLaughlin, 1995). But neither world-weak nor world-strong has that implication. The operator definitions are, however, arguably equivalent to the corresponding world-definitions in a special case of property-supervenience—understood as a relationship between nonempty sets of properties—namely, when the sets of properties in question are closed under Boolean operations of complementation and either conjunction or disjunction.

A third determinate of the relation of dependent-variation has been formulated (Haugeland, 1982; Hellman & Thomson, 1975; Horgan, 1982; Kim, 1993; Paull & Sider, 1992; Post, 1987):

Global Supervenience (1). Worlds that are *B*-duplicates (i.e., that are exactly alike in respect of the pattern of distribution of *B*-respects over individuals within them) are *A*-duplicates (i.e., exactly alike in respect of the pattern of distribution of *A*-respects over individuals within them).

Consider global property-supervenience. We are typically interested in the pattern of distribution of properties irrespective of the particular individuals they are distributed over. Thus, sameness of distributional pattern is typically understood not to require that the properties be distributed over numerically the same individuals. (On some theories of possible worlds, individuals are world-bound, and so properties could not possibly be distributed over numerically the same individuals in different worlds.) Nor is it typically required that properties be distributed over individuals that share some other sort of property. For, then, that other sort of property, whatever it is, will trivially globally supervene on any property whatsoever. To see this, suppose it was required for worlds to have the same distribution of B-properties, that B-properties in the worlds be distributed over individuals with the same spatial-temporal locations (or with counterpart spatial-temporal locations, if locations are world-bound). Then, properties such has having such-and-such a spatial-temporal location will trivially global-supervene on any property whatsoever. For, then, to be property duplicates of any sort, worlds would have to be spatial-temporal property duplicates (McLaughlin, 1995). Given such considerations, the notion of global supervenience is arguably best formulated as follows:

Global Supervenience (2). For any isomorphism, I, worlds that are B-duplicates under I are A-duplicates under I.

Thus, for example, mental respects globally supervene on physical respects just in case for any isomorphism, I, worlds that are physical-duplicates under I are mental-duplicates under I.

World-strong supervenience implies global, but there has been controversy over whether global implies world-strong, and even over whether it implies world-weak. Global implies neither in virtue of logical form; but the question is whether a global supervenience thesis will metaphysically necessitate the truth of corresponding world-strong and world-weak supervenience theses (Paull & Sider, 1992). It can be seen, however, that global fails to metaphysically necessitate world-weak, and thus that it fails also to so necessitate world-strong. It is incompatible with the world-weak supervenience of A-properties on B-properties for two individuals within a world to be B-duplicates yet fail to be A-duplicates. But that is compatible with the global supervenience of A-respects on B-respects. To see this, suppose, for the sake of argument, that states have unique constitutive properties, that mental properties are constitutive of mental states, physical properties of physical

states, and that no such constitutive mental property is a physical property. Then, since such states will have distinct unique constitutive properties, no mental state is a physical state. Consider, then, properties such as having such-and-such a mental property as a constitutive property; call these mental-event-constituting properties; and call properties such as having such-and-such a physical property as a constitutive property, physical-event-constituting properties. Any two mental events will be exactly alike in respect of physical-event-constituting properties since they will lack any such property. However, since two mental events can differ in respect of their mental-event-constituting properties, world-weak supervenience fails. Nevertheless, global supervenience may very well hold in this case. If the assumptions are coherent, then global supervenience fails to imply world-weak, and thus fails as well to imply world-strong (McLaughlin, 1995).

Definitions of "multiple domain supervenience" have been formulated, which characterize notions of world-weak and world-strong supervenience that do not require that B-duplicates be A-duplicates, but only that there be some appropriate relationship (e.g., constitution) between the bearers of B-properties and the bearers of A-properties relative to which if two individuals are B-duplicates, individuals to which they bear the appropriate relationship, respectively, are A-duplicates. We lack sufficient space to formulate those definitions here. Suffice it to note that global supervenience is arguably equivalent to multiple domain world-strong supervenience (Kim, 1993).

Supervenience has been employed for a wide variety of philosophical purposes: to help characterize the relationship of mereological determination, the relationship of realization, the notion of emergence, the relationship between macrocausal relationships and the microcausal mechanisms that implement them, the relationship between special science laws and initial physical conditions and physical laws, and the notion of reduction, just to name some purposes (see Horgan, 1984; Kim, 1993; Post, 1987; Savellos & Yalcin, 1995).

Every variety of supervenience considered here seems required for reducibility. One source of interest in supervenience, however, is that it seems compatible with irreducibility. Neither world-weak, world-strong, nor global supervenience implies reducibility. Notice, for example, that if complementation is a property-forming operator, then the property not-P, world-weakly, world-strongly, and globally supervenes on property P. Moreover, operator-strong supervenience with merely nomological necessity fails to imply reducibility as well. If reducibility does not require an explanatory connection, however, then it is an open question whether the operator-strong supervenience with metaphysical necessity—and even whether the world-strong and the global supervenience across metaphysically possible worlds of one natural family of properties (e.g., mental properties) on another (e.g., physical properties)—suffices for reduction. Indeed, this is a topic of dispute. In any event, nonreductionists have in many cases conceded various varieties of supervenience, but denied reducibility is possible. Thus, it has been claimed, for instance, that while mental respects supervene on physical respects, mental respects fail to reduce to physical respects (Davidson, 1980).

Since supervenience of every variety is required for reducibility, supervenience theses serve another purpose: they yield tests for whether reductive programs can succeed. Any would-be program of reduction according to which *A*-respects reduce to *B*-respects will imply some world-strong (indeed, some operator-strong) supervenience thesis to the effect that *A*-respects supervene on *B*-respects. A single counterexample can show that a strong supervenience thesis is false, and thus show that the program cannot succeed. Thus, suppose, for instance, that there is a program of attempting to reduce thinking that *P* to a kind of neurophysiological process. For the program to succeed, it will have to be that there can be no difference between individuals in respect to thinking that *P* without a difference in respect to their neurophysiological processes. If there is a single counterexample to this, then the reductive program is doomed to failure. (Twin-Earth thought-experiments might be invoked to try to provide such a counterexample.) Arguments that appeal to such counterexamples to reject reductive programs are arguments by appeal to false implied supervenience theses (FISTs) (McLaughlin, 1995).

[See also Davidson, Donald; Logical Form; Metaphysics; Philosophy of Mind; Properties.]

BIBLIOGRAPHY

Davidson, D. *Actions and Events.* Oxford, 1980.
Haugeland, J. "Weak Supervenience," *American Philosophical Quarterly,* Vol. 19 (1982), 93–103.
Hellman, G., and F. Thomson. "Physicalism: Ontology, Determination, and Reduction," *Journal of Philosophy,* Vol. 72 (1975), 551–64.
Horgan, T. "Supervenience and Microphysics," *Pacific Philosophical Quarterly,* Vol. 63 (1982), 29–43.
———. ed. *Southern Journal of Philosophy 22: The Spindel Conference on Supervenience Supplement.* Memphis, TN, 1984.
Kim, J. *Supervenience and Mind.* Cambridge, 1993.
Lewis, D. *On the Plurality of Worlds.* Oxford, 1986.
McLaughlin, B. P. "Varieties of Supervenience," in E. Savellos and U. Yalcin, eds., *Supervenience: New Essays* (Cambridge, 1995).
Paull, R. C., and T. R. Sider. "In Defense of Global Supervenience," *Philosophy and Phenomenological Research,* Vol. 52 (1992), 833–54.
Post, J. *The Faces of Existence.* Ithaca, NY, 1987.
Savellos, E., and U. Yalcin. *Supervenience: New Essays.* Cambridge, 1995.

– BRIAN P. MCLAUGHLIN

SYNTAX

Syntax is the theory of the construction of sentences out of words. In linguistics, syntax is distinguished from morphology, or the theory of the construction of words

The dawn of syntax is marked by the realization that the structure of sentences is hierarchical— that behind the linear order of words and morphemes there is another organization of larger or smaller constituents nested one within another.

out of minimal units of significance, only some of which are words. According to this division, it is a matter of morphology that the word "solubility" decomposes into "dissolve" + "able" + "ity"; but it is a matter of syntax to analyze the construction of the sentence, "That substance is able to dissolve."

Although syntax is a traditional grammatical topic, it was only with the rise of formal methods growing out of the study of mathematical logic that the subject attained sufficient explicitness to be studied in depth, in works by Harris (1957) and Chomsky (1957). Since then a flourishing field has been created; for it was rapidly discovered that the syntax of human languages was far more complex than at first appeared. In this respect, the development of syntax is comparable to other fields of cognitive science such as human vision, problem-solving capacities, and the organization of common-sense knowledge, all of which gave rise to difficult problems once the goal of fully explicit representation was put in place.

The dawn of syntax is marked by the realization that the structure of sentences is hierarchical; that is, that behind the linear order of words and morphemes that is visible in natural languages there is another organization in terms of larger or smaller constituents nested one within another. Description of sentences at this level is said to give their phrase structure. Moreover, phrases of a given kind can occur within others of the same kind: it is this recursive feature of language that enables sentences of arbitrary complexity to be constructed. The realization that phrase structure is recursive is very old. Assuming the categories of a complete noun phrase (NP) and sentence (S), Arnauld (1662) gives the examples (rendered here in English):

(1) ($_S$The divine law commands that [$_S$kings are to be honored])

(2) ($_S$[$_{NP}$Men [$_S$who are pious]] are charitable)

remarking that in (1) the embedded element "kings are to be honored" is a sentence occurring within a sentence, and that in (2) the relative clause has all the structure of a sentence, except that the relative pronoun "who" has replaced the subject.

In linguistic theory the recursive structure of syntax is expressed by principles of combination modeled after the clauses of an inductive definition. However, far more complex devices seem to be required for a compact description that helps to reveal the basis of the native speaker's ability. Chomsky's introduction of grammatical transformations opened the way to a variety of formalisms and developments (see Atkinson, Kilby, & Roca, 1988, for a useful overview). Chomsky also initiated the conception of linguistic theory as a study of the acquisition of a system of linguistic knowledge, or competence. Any human language is acquirable under ordinary experiential conditions by any normal child. The space between empirical evidence and the resulting linguistic competence is sufficiently great that a kind of readiness for language, universal grammar in Chomsky's terminology, is presupposed. Contemporary theory seeks to probe the basis for this readiness in terms of innate rules and principles of grammar. For a recent statement, see Chomsky and Lasnik (in Jacobs et al., 1993).

Within philosophy too the theory of syntax came to play an important role in the systematization of mathematics, and assumed central importance in Carnap (1934). Carnap distinguished between grammatical syntax, of the sort that a linguist might give in a description of a language, and logical syntax, whose aim was not only to specify the class of sentences (or wellformed formulae of a calculus) but also to use formal methods in constructing a theory of logical consequence and logical truth. Carnap employed the distinction between grammatical form and logical form, which plays a crucial part in Wittgenstein's views both in the *Tractatus* and in the *Philosophical Investigations,* and has become part of the lore of analytic philosophy. The scope of logical syntax in Carnap's terms took on much of the role of semantics in later philosophical discussion. Even with the later distinction between syntax and model-theoretic semantics, syntactic properties of formalized languages are still crucial for properties of systems of logic (soundness and completeness), and proof theory is established as a part of the syntax of mathematics.

In linguistic theory syntax and semantics have become increasingly intertwined disciplines, as it was realized that there are explanatory issues in relating linguistic forms to the specific meanings, or range of meanings, associated with them. Lappin (ed., 1995) contains a number of useful expositions on this theme; see also Larson and Segal (1995). The current research climate is in practice very different from conceptions associated with "ordinary language" philosophy: the contemporary view is not that ordinary speech lacks an exact logic, but rather that a diligent, collaborative effort is required to find out what the logic is. The concentration on logic implies that syntactic investigations have a metaphysical dimension. The patterns of inference of ordinary language call for formalization as part of a general account of the structure of individual human languages, or human language in general, and this formalization may in turn lead to proposals for reification, as in Davidson's (1967) hypothesis that references to events are pervasive in ordinary action sentences.

In linguistic theory syntax and semantics

have become increasingly intertwined disciplines.

On the side of linguistics proper, the problems of morphology have been treated in a progressively more syntactic manner as, for instance, our example "solubility" can be seen as built up by rules of a sort familiar from syntax. The result is the area now called morphosyntax, where the question whether morphology is a distinct level of linguistic organization is under active debate; see Hendrick (1995) for recent discussion.

[See also Carnap, Rudolph; Chomsky, Noam; Davidson, Donald; Language; Logical Consequence; Logical Form; Mathematical Logic; Philosophy; Philosophy of Language; Proof Theory; Semantics; Wittgenstein, Ludwig Josef Johann.]

BIBLIOGRAPHY

Arnauld, A. *La Logique, ou l'art de penser* [1662]. Translated by J. Dickoff and P. James as *The Art of Thinking* (Indianapolis, 1964).

Atkinson, M., D. Kilby, and I. Roca. *Foundations of General Linguistics,* 2d ed. London, 1988.

Carnap, R. *The Logical Syntax of Language.* London, 1937.

Chomsky, N. *Syntactic Structures.* The Hague, 1957.

———, and H. Lasnik. "The Theory of Principles and Parameters," in J. Jacobs, A. von Stechow, W. Sternfeld, and T. Vennemann, eds., *Syntax: An International Handbook of Contemporary Research* (Berlin and New York, 1993).

Davidson, D. "The Logical Form of Action Sentences," in N. Rescher, ed., *The Logic of Decision and Action* (Pittsburgh, 1967).

Harris, Z. "Co-Occurrence and Transformations in Linguistic Structure," *Language 33,* Vol. 3 (1957).

Hendrick, R. "Morphosyntax," in G. Webelhuth, ed., *Government and Binding Theory and the Minimalist Program* (Oxford, 1995).

Lappin, S., ed. *The Handbook of Contemporary Semantic Theory.* Oxford, 1995.

Larson, R., and G. Segal. *Knowledge of Meaning.* Cambridge, MA, 1995.

— JAMES HIGGINBOTHAM

T

TESTIMONY

An important, and relatively neglected, topic within epistemology is that of how the users of a common language may come to know things at second hand, by learning from what others tell them—either in person, or through the written word. Knowledge gained in this way is, within analytic philosophy, said to be gained through 'testimony'. Tellings of all kinds—serious assertoric utterances intended to inform their audiences—are instances of testimony. The information (or misinformation) recorded in train timetables, birth registers, minutes of meetings, official records, diaries, letters, historical works, textbooks, and all kinds of purported factual published and unpublished writings is also 'testimony' in an extended sense.

How exactly does testimony effect the spreading

of knowledge from one person to another

within a linguistic community?

Philosophical concern with testimony is about whether (and if so, how) knowledge, or justified belief, may be acquired by means of it. Plato (in the *Theaetetus*) and Augustine (in *De Magistro*), despising its second-hand character, denied that knowledge, as opposed to mere belief, can ever be acquired through it. Supporting their claim, one might argue that knowledge requires true understanding, which comes only with thinking through for oneself, not from relying on another's report. But while this may hold for some very special subject matters such as religious or moral belief, it is absurd to deny that I can understand the proposition that the sun is an enormous and very distant ball of burning gases when I read this in a book, or that this afternoon's meeting is postponed when I am so told by a colleague. And it seems undeniable that we learn things, come to know them, in this way.

But how exactly does testimony effect the spreading of knowledge from one person to another within a linguistic community? The testifier asserts something to be so, and her audience, trusting her, comes to believe it. But what a person asserts is true, flukes apart, only if she is sincere and her belief about her subject matter

is correct. Thus, one central issue in the epistemology of testimony is whether a hearer is epistemically entitled to take the sincerity and competence of her informant on trust, or if she should believe what she is told only when she has evidence of this. David Hume famously took a reductionist position on this question, while Thomas Reid opposed this, asserting the naturalness and justifiedness of the complementary human dispositions to truthfulness and trustfulness.

The place of testimony within our system of empirical knowledge as a whole may also be investigated. Do we have a core of empirically based knowledge, gained through perception and retained in memory, which is independent of any reliance on testimony; or is all of our knowledge infected by dependence on testimony? Since any social creature's learning of language depends on teaching of word meanings by initiates, and all she knows is expressed by her in that language, it will require difficult argument to establish that we have any testimony-free knowledge.

[See also Augustine, St.; Epistemology; Hume, David; Plato; Reid, Thomas.]

BIBLIOGRAPHY

Chakrabarti, A., and B. K. Matilal, eds. *Knowing from Words*. Synthese Library, Vol. 230. Dordrecht, 1994.

Coady, C. A. J. *Testimony: A Philosophical Study*. Oxford, 1992.

Fricker, E. "Telling and Trusting: Reductionism and Anti-reductionism in the Epistemology of Testimony," *Mind*, Vol. 104 (1995), 393–411.

Hume, D. *An Enquiry Concerning Human Understanding*, in P. H. Nidditch, ed., *Hume's Enquiries* (Oxford, 1975). Sec. 10, "Of Miracles."

Reid, T. *An Enquiry into the Human Mind*, ed. T. Duggan. Chicago, 1970. Chap. 6, sec. 24.

— ELIZABETH FRICKER

THALES OF MILETUS

Thales of Miletus has since early antiquity been regarded as the founder of the Ionian school of natural philosophy. Evidence suggests that he was a Milesian of Greek origin who flourished around 580 B.C. and that his field of distinguished activities included practical and political matters. There are indications that he visited Mesopotamia and Egypt, that he predicted the possibility of an eclipse in 585 B.C., and that he proposed a simple doctrine on the origin and nature of the world.

Thales of Miletus is regarded as the founder of the Ionian school of natural philosophy. (Corbis/Bettmann)

The most ancient references to Thales depict him as a man of exceptional wisdom. Later commentators associate him with specific discoveries in physics, metaphysics, astronomy, geometry, and engineering. Modern studies have hailed him as a proponent of the rational approach. However, recent conservative reconstructions of Thales' ideas have called for the abandonment or modification of earlier estimates. In the absence of primary sources, several scholars have argued that the earliest testimony of Herodotus, Plato, and Aristotle must be preferred to later reports stemming from the doxographic tradition. Such a preference is necessary, they maintain, since Thales left no written documents, and most of the post-Aristotelian compilers depended for their comments on Aristotle's reports. When the ancient evidence is carefully examined, these commentators hold, a believable picture of Thales' thought

emerges. The following is an outline of his thought, based on the early sources.

Thales was very much concerned with the political conditions and developments in Asia Minor during his time: as an advisor he showed foresight in urging the Ionians to form a confederation against the Persians. As a "learned person" (*sophos*) he showed remarkable vision, correctly anticipating a solar eclipse during a battle between the Lydeans and the Persians. As an engineer he made the Halys River passable for King Croesus by diverting its waters.

In his speculations Thales asserted with unprecedented boldness that the world originated in water and was sustained by water and that the earth floated on water. Inasmuch as there is natural change everywhere, he went on to claim, the world is animated, and even apparently inanimate objects possess *psyche,* the principle of self-motion.

A fuller interpretation of the above necessarily takes one outside the area of the historically confirmable; yet one must propose some interpretation beyond the hard evidence if later fabrications are to be discarded. On the basis of Aristotle's cautious remarks it can be inferred that Thales thought of the world as perfectly understandable through the idea of water—an element essential to life (and thus to self-motion), versatile, common, and powerful enough to account for every physical phenomenon.

While there is very little else that may be safely associated with Thales' life and thought, post-Aristotelian commentators persist in crediting him with many specific discoveries. They suggest that he discovered the solstices and measured their cycles, that he discovered the five celestial zones (arctic, antarctic, equator, and the tropics), the inclination of the zodiac, the sources of the moon's light, and more. He is said to have explained the rise of the Nile as due to the etesian winds, and in geometry, to have discovered proofs for the propositions that the circle is bisected by its diameter, that

> *Thales asserted with unprecedented boldness*
>
> *that the world originated in water*
>
> *and was sustained by water*
>
> *and that the earth floated on water.*

the angles at the base of an isosceles triangle are equal, that two triangles are identical when they have one side and the angles formed by it with the other sides equal, and that in two intersecting straight lines the opposite angles at the intersection are equal. He was supposedly responsible for the axiomatization of the field of geometry, and he was further credited with measuring the height of the pyramids and the distance of ships at sea.

Most of these unsubstantiated ascriptions must be judged as unhistorical and inconsistent with the temper of the Milesian's thought. Thales was the last representative of a tradition that respected myth, was fond of intuitions, and did not concern itself with proofs. To be sure, he was also the founder of a new approach, that of attempting to comprehend the world through reason alone.

BIBLIOGRAPHY

Burnet, John, *Early Greek Philosophy*, 4th ed. London, 1930. Pp. 40–50.

Dicks, D. R., "Thales." *Classical Quarterly*, Vol. 9 (1959). 294–309.

Diels, H., and Kranz, W., *Die Fragmente der Vorsokratiker*, 7th ed. Berlin, 1954. Vol. I, pp. 67–81.

Guthrie, W. K. C., *A History of Greek Philosophy*, 4th ed. Cambridge, 1962. Vol. I, pp. 45–72.

Hölscher, V., "Anaximander und die Anfänge der Philosophie." *Hermes*, Vol. 81 (1953), 252–277, 385–417.

Kirk, G. S., and Raven, J. E., *The Presocratic Philosophers*. Cambridge, 1957. Pp. 74–88.

Snell, Bruno, "Die Nachrichten über die Lehre des Thales und die Anfänge der griechischen Philosophie und Literaturgeschichte." *Philologus*, Vol. 96 (1944), 170–182.

— P. DIAMANDOPOULOS

THEISM, ARGUMENTS FOR/AGAINST

Philosophy of religion enjoyed a renaissance in the final third of the twentieth century. Its fruits include important contributions to both natural theology, the enterprise of arguing for theism, and natural atheology, the enterprise of arguing against it. In natural theology philosophers produced new versions of ontological, cosmological, and teleological arguments for the existence of God. In natural atheology problems of evil, which have always been the chief arguments against theism, were much discussed, and philosophers debated proposed solutions to both the logical problem of evil and the evidential problem of evil.

Natural Theology

Building on work by Charles Hartshorne and Norman Malcolm, Alvin Plantinga (1974) formulated a model ontological argument for the existence of God that employs the metaphysics of possible worlds. Let it be stipulated that being unsurpassably great is logically equivalent to being maximally excellent in every possible world and that being maximally excellent entails being omnipotent, omniscient, and morally perfect. The main premise of Plantinga's argument is that there is a possible world in which unsurpassable greatness is exemplified. From these stipulations and this premise he concludes, first, that unsurpassable greatness is exemplified in every possible world and hence in the actual world and, second, that there actually exists a being who is omnipotent, omniscient, and morally perfect and who exists and has these properties in every possible world. The argument is valid in a system of modal logic that can plausibly be claimed to apply correctly to possible worlds. Plantinga reports that he thinks its main premise is true and so considers it a sound argument.

In natural atheology problems of evil,

which have always been

the chief arguments against theism,

were much discussed in the

final third

of the twentieth century.

However, he acknowledges that it is not a successful proof of the existence of God. A successful proof would have to draw all its premises from the stock of propositions accepted by almost all sane or rational persons. The main premise of this argument is not of that sort; a rational person could understand it and yet not accept it. In other words, not accepting the argument's main premise is rationally permissible. But Plantinga maintains that accepting that premise is also rationally permissible. Since he regards it as rational to accept the argument's main premise, he holds that the argument shows it to be rational to accept its conclusion. As he sees it, even though his ontological argument does not establish the truth of theism, it does establish the rational permissibility of theistic belief.

According to William L. Rowe (1975), Samuel Clarke has given us the most cogent presentation of the cosmological argument we possess. It has two parts. The first argues for the existence of a necessary being, and the second argues that this being has other divine attributes such as omniscience, omnipotence, and infinite goodness. As Rowe reconstructs it in contemporary terms, the first part of the argument has as its main premise a version of the principle of sufficient reason, according to which every existing thing has a reason for its existence either in the necessity of its own nature or in the causal efficacy of some other beings. It is then argued that not every existing thing has a reason for its existence in the causal efficacy of some other beings. It follows that there exists a being that has a reason for its existence in the necessity of its own nature. Next it is argued that a being that has a reason for its existence in the necessity of its own nature is a logically necessary being. It may then be concluded that there exists a necessary being.

Rowe takes care to ensure that his version of Clarke's argument is deductively valid. What is more, he maintains that the principle of sufficient reason that is its main premise is not known to be false because no one has set forth any convincing argument for its falsity. However, he claims that the argument is not a proof of the existence of a necessary being. As Rowe sees it, an argument is a proof of its conclusion only if its premises are known to be true, and no human knows that the principle of sufficient reason is true. Hence, even if the argument is sound, it is not a proof of its conclusion. Rowe leaves open the possibility that it is reasonable for some people to believe that the argument's premises are true, in which case the argument would show the reasonableness of believing that a necessary being exists. If the second part of the argument made it reasonable to believe that such a necessary being has other divine attributes, then the theist might be entitled to claim that the argument shows the reasonableness of theistic belief. So Rowe invites the theist to explore the possibility that his cosmological argument shows that it is reasonable to believe in God, even though it perhaps fails to show that theism is true.

Richard Swinburne's teleological argument is part of a cumulative case he builds for theism (Swinburne, 1979). Other parts of the case involve arguments from consciousness and morality, from providence, from history and miracles, and from religious experience. Each part of the case is supposed to increase the probability of theism; the case as a whole is supposed to yield the conclusion that, on our total evidence, theism is more probable than not. The existence of order in the universe is supposed to increase significantly the probability of theism, even if it does not by itself render theism more probable than not.

In constructing his teleological argument, Swinburne appeals to general physical considerations rather than specifically biological order. There is a vast uniformity in the powers and liabilities of material objects that underlies the regularities of temporal succession described by the laws of nature. In addition, material objects are made of components of very few fundamental kinds. Either this order is an inexplicable brute fact or it has

some explanation. Explanatory alternatives to theism such as the committee of minor deities suggested by Hume seem to Swinburne less probable than theism, because theism leads us to expect one pattern of order throughout nature, while we would expect different patterns in different parts of the universe if its order were the product of a committee. So the alternatives are that the temporal order of the world has no explanation and that it is produced by God.

It is a consequence of Bayes theorem that this order increases the probability of theism if and only if it is more probable if God exists than if God does not exist. Swinburne offers two reasons for thinking that the order of the universe is more probable on theism than on its negation. The first is that the order seems improbable in the absence of an explanation and so cries out for explanation in terms of a common source. The second is that there are reasons for God to make an orderly universe: one is that order is a necessary condition of beauty, and there is good reason for God to prefer beauty to ugliness in creating; another is that order is a necessary condition of finite rational agents growing in knowledge and power, and there is some reason for God to make finite creatures with the opportunity to grow in knowledge and power.

The teleological argument plays a limited role in Swinburne's natural theology. Since it is an inductive argument, it does not prove the existence of God. Swinburne does not claim that by itself it shows that theism is more probable than not; nor does he claim that by itself it establishes the rational permissibility of belief in God.

Hence, only modest claims should be made on behalf of these three arguments for theism. Their authors are well aware that they do not prove the existence of God. However, they may show that belief in God is reasonable or contributes to a cumulative case for the rationality of theistic belief.

Problems of Evil

According to J. L. Mackie (1955), the existence of a God who is omniscient, omnipotent, and perfectly good is inconsistent with the existence of evil. If this is correct, we may infer that God does not exist from our knowledge that evil does exist. A solution to this logical problem of evil would be a proof that the existence of God is, after all, consistent with the existence of evil. One way to prove consistency would be to find a proposition that is consistent with the proposition that God exists and that, when conjoined with the proposition that God exists, entails that evil exists. This is the strategy employed in Alvin Plantinga's free-will defense against the logical problem of evil (Plantinga, 1974).

The intuitive idea on which the free-will defense rests is simple. Only genuinely free creatures are capable of producing moral good and moral evil. Of course, God could create a world without free creatures in it, but such a world would lack both moral good and moral evil. If God does create a world with free creatures in it, then it is partly up to them and not wholly up to God what balance of moral good and evil the world contains. The gift of creaturely freedom limits the power of an omnipotent God. According to Plantinga, it is possible that every free creature God could have created would produce at least some moral evil. Hence, it is possible that God could not have created a world containing moral good but no moral evil.

According to J. L. Mackie,

the existence of a God who is omniscient,

omnipotent, and perfectly good

is inconsistent with the existence of evil.

Consider the proposition that God could not have created a world containing moral good but no moral evil and yet creates a world containing moral good. The free-will defense claims that this proposition is consistent with the proposition that God is omniscient, omnipotent, and perfectly good. But these two propositions entail that moral evil exists and thus that evil exists. Hence, if the defense's consistency claim is true, the existence of a God who is omniscient, omnipotent, and perfectly good is consistent with the existence of evil. Therefore, the free-will defense is a successful solution of the logical problem of evil if its consistency claim is true. That claim certainly appears to be plausible.

Most philosophers who have studied the matter are prepared to grant that the existence of God is consistent with the existence of evil. The focus of discussion has shifted from the logical to the evidential problem of evil. The evils within our ken are evidence against the existence of God. The question is whether they make theism improbable or render theistic belief unwarranted or irrational.

William L. Rowe (1988) presents the evidential problem of evil in terms of two vivid examples of evil. Bambi is a fawn who is trapped in a forest fire and horribly burned; she dies after several days of intense agony. Sue is a young girl who is raped and beaten by her mother's boyfriend; he then strangles her to death. According to Rowe, no good state of affairs we know of is such that an omnipotent, omniscient being's obtaining it would morally justify that being's permitting the suffering and death of Bambi or Sue. From this premise he infers that no good state of affairs is such that an omnipotent, omniscient being's obtaining it would morally justify that being in permitting the suffering and death of Bambi or Sue. If there were an omnipotent, omniscient, and morally perfect being, there would be some good state of affairs such that the being's obtaining it would morally justify the being's permitting the suffering and death of Bambi or Sue. Hence, it may be concluded that no omnipotent, omniscient, and morally perfect being exists.

The first step in this argument is an inductive inference from a sample, good states of affairs known to us, to a larger population, good states of affairs without qualification. So it is possible that no good state of affairs known to us morally justifies such evils but some good state of affairs unknown to us morally justifies them. But Rowe argues that the inference's premise gives him a reason to accept its conclusion. We are often justified in inferring from the known to the unknown. If I have encountered many pit bulls and all of them are vicious, I have a reason to believe all pit bulls are vicious.

William P. Alston (1991) challenges Rowe's inference. As he sees it, when we justifiably infer from the known to the unknown, we typically have background knowledge to assure us that the known sample is likely to be representative of the wider population. We know, for example, that character traits are often breed-specific in dogs. According to Alston, we have no such knowledge of the population of good states of affairs because we have no way of anticipating what is in the class of good states of affairs unknown to us. He likens Rowe's reasoning to inferring, in 1850, from the fact that no one has yet voyaged to the moon that no one will ever do so.

The disagreement between Rowe and Alston illustrates the lack of a philosophical consensus on a solution to the evidential problem of evil. It is safe to predict continued debate about whether horrible evils such as the suffering and death of Bambi or Sue provide sufficient evidence to show that theistic belief is unjustified or unreasonable.

[See also Bayesianism; Evil, Problem of; Hume, David; Mackie, John Leslie; Modal Logic; Philosophy of Religion; Religious Experience.]

BIBLIOGRAPHY

Alston, W. P. "The Inductive Argument from Evil and the Human Cognitive Condition," in James E. Tomberlin, ed., *Philosophical Perspectives*. Vol. 5, *Philosophy of Religion* (Atascadero, CA, 1991).

Mackie, J. L. "Evil and Omnipotence," *Mind,* Vol. 64 (1955), 200–12.

Plantinga, A. *The Nature of Necessity.* Oxford, 1974.

Rowe, W. L. *The Cosmological Argument.* Princeton, NJ, 1975.

———. "Evil and Theodicy," *Philosophical Topics,* Vol. 16, no. 2 (1988), 119–32.

Swinburne, R. *The Existence of God.* Oxford, 1979.

— PHILLIP L. QUINN

THOMAS AQUINAS, ST.

St. Thomas Aquinas (c. 1224–1274), Catholic theologian and philosopher, was born at Roccasecca, Italy, the youngest son of Landolfo and Teodora of Aquino. At about the age of five he began his elementary studies under the Benedictine monks at nearby Montecassino. He went on to study liberal arts at the University of Naples. It is probable that Aquinas became a master in arts at Naples before entering the Order of Preachers (Dominicans) in 1244. He studied in the Dominican courses in philosophy and theology, first at Paris and, from 1248 on, under Albert the Great at Cologne. In 1252 he was sent to the University of Paris for advanced study in theology; he lectured there as a bachelor in theology until 1256, when he was awarded the magistrate (doctorate) in theology. Accepted after some opposition from other professors as a fully accredited member of the theology faculty in 1257, Aquinas continued to teach at Paris until 1259.

Aquinas's philosophy is mainly

a rethinking of Aristotelianism,

with significant influences from Stoicism,

Neoplatonism, Augustinism, and Boethianism.

Aquinas then spent almost ten years at various Dominican monasteries in the vicinity of Rome, lecturing on theology and philosophy (including an extensive study of the major works of Aristotle) and performing various consultative and administrative functions in his order. In the fall of 1268 Aquinas returned for his second professorate in theology at the University of Paris. He engaged in three distinct controversies: against a group of conservative theologians who were critical of his philosophic innovations; against certain radical advocates of Aristotelianism or Latin Averroism; and against some critics of the Dominicans and Franciscans and their right to teach at the university. Many of Aquinas's literary works were in process or completed at this time. It is thought that he was provided with secretarial

help in this task, partly in view of the fact that his own handwriting was practically illegible. Called back to Italy in 1272, Aquinas taught for a little more than a year at the University of Naples and preached a notable series of vernacular sermons there. Illness forced him to discontinue his teaching and writing toward the end of 1273. Early in 1274 he set out for Lyons, France, to attend a church council. His failing health interrupted the trip at a point not far from his birthplace, and he died at Fossanova in March of that year.

The writings of Thomas Aquinas were produced during his twenty years (1252–1273) as an active teacher. All in Latin, they consist of several large theological treatises, plus recorded disputations on theological and philosophical problems (the "Disputed Questions" and "Quodlibetal Questions"), commentaries on several books of the Bible, commentaries on 12 treatises of Aristotle, and commentaries on Boethius, the pseudo-Dionysius, and the anonymous *Liber de Causis.* There are also about forty miscellaneous notes, letters, sermons, and short treatises on philosophical and religious subjects. Although Aquinas's philosophic views may be found in almost all his writings (thus the "Exposition of the Book of Job" reads like a discussion among philosophers), certain treatises are of more obvious interest to philosophers. These are listed in detail at the end of this article.

GENERAL PHILOSOPHICAL POSITION. In the main, Aquinas's philosophy is a rethinking of Aristotelianism, with significant influences from Stoicism, Neoplatonism, Augustinism, and Boethianism. It also reflects some of the thinking of the Greek commentators on Aristotle and of Cicero, Avicenna, Averroës, ibn-Gabirol, and Maimonides. This may suggest that we are dealing with an eclectic philosophy, but actually Aquinas reworked the speculative and practical philosophies of his predecessors into a coherent view of the subject which shows the stamp of his own intelligence and, of course, the influence of his religious commitment.

One of the broad characteristics of Aquinas's work in philosophy is a temperamental tendency to seek a middle way on questions that have been given a wide range of answers. This spirit of moderation is nowhere better illustrated than in his solution to the problem of universals. For centuries philosophers had debated whether genera and species are realities in themselves (Plato, Boethius, William of Champeaux) or mere mental constructs (Roscelin, Peter Abelard). What made this odd discussion important was the conviction (certainly shared by Aquinas) that these universals (such as humanity, justice, whiteness, dogness) are the primary objects of human understanding. Most thinkers in the

Middle Ages felt that if something is to be explained, it must be treated in universal terms. Therefore, the problem of universals was not simply an academic question.

Aquinas's position on this problem is now called moderate realism. He denied that universals are existing realities (and frequently criticized Plato for having suggested that there is a world of intelligible Forms), but he also insisted that men's universal concepts and judgments have some sort of foundation in extramental things. This basis for the universality, say of humanity, would consist in the real similarity found among all individual men. It was not that Aquinas attributed an actual, existent universal nature to all individual men: that would be an extreme realism. Rather, only individuals exist; but the individuals of a given species or class resemble each other, and that is the basis for thinking of them as universally representative of a common nature.

Aquinas's spirit of compromise as a philosopher was balanced by another tendency, that toward innovation. His original Latin biographers all stress this feature of his work. Aquinas introduced new ways of reasoning about problems and new sources of information, and he handled his teaching in a new way. In this sense Thomas Aquinas was not typical of the thirteenth century and was perhaps in advance of his contemporaries.

FAITH AND RATIONAL KNOWLEDGE. As Aquinas saw it, faith (*fides*) falls midway between opinion and scientific knowledge (*scientia*); it is more than opinion because it involves a firm assent to its object; and it is less than knowledge because it lacks vision. Both are intellectual acts and habits of assent: in the case of faith a person is not sufficiently moved by the object to accept it as true, so, by an act of will, he inclines himself to believe. Knowledge implies assent motivated by a personal seeing of the object without any direct influence from will. Where objects of belief have to do with divine matters which exceed man's natural cognitive capacity, the disposition to believe such articles of religious faith is regarded as a special gift from God. Reason (*ratio*) is another type of intellectual activity: simple understanding and reasoning differ only in the manner in which the intellect works. Through intellection (understanding) one knows simply by seeing what something means, while through reason one moves discursively from one item of knowledge to another. (These functions of believing and knowing are treated in many places by Aquinas: *Summa Contra Gentiles* III, 147; *In Boethii de Trinitate,* Ques. II and III; *Summa Theologiae* I, Ques. 79–84.)

Aquinas thought that philosophy entailed reasoning from prior knowledge, or present experience, to new

Aquinas's philosophic views may be found in almost all his writings. (Corbis)

knowledge (the way of discovery) and the rational verification of judgments by tracing them back to more simply known principles (the way of reduction). Where the basic principles are grasped by man's natural understanding of his sensory experiences, the reasoning processes are those of natural science and philosophy. If one starts to reason from judgments accepted on religious faith, then one is thinking as a theologian. Questions V and VI of *In Boethii de Trinitate* develop Aquinas's methodology of the philosophical sciences: philosophy of nature, mathematics, and metaphysics. He distinguished speculative or theoretical reasoning from the practical: the purpose of speculation is simply to know; the end of practical reasoning is to know how to act. He described two kinds of theology: the philosophical "theology," metaphysics, which treats divine matters as principles for the explanation of all things, and the theology taught in Scripture, which "studies divine things for their own sakes" (*In Boethii de Trinitate* V, 4 c).

Thus philosophy, for Aquinas, was a natural type of knowledge open to all men who wish to understand the meaning of their ordinary experiences. The "philosophers" whom he habitually cited were the classic Greek, Latin, Islamic, and Jewish sages. Christian teachers mentioned by Aquinas were the "saints" (Augustine, John of Damascus, Gregory, Ambrose, Dionysius, Isidore, and Benedict); they were never called Christian philosophers. The word "theology" was rarely used by Aquinas. In the first question of his *Summa Theologiae* he formally calls his subject sacred doctrine (*sacra doctrina*) and says that its principles, unlike those of philosophy, are various items of religious faith. Thus, Thomas Aquinas was by profession a theologian, or better, a teacher of sacred doctrine who also studied and wrote about philosophy. He obviously used a good deal of pagan and non-Christian philosophy in all his writings. His own understanding of these philosophies was influenced by his personal faith—as almost any man's judgment is influenced by his stand for or against the claim of religious faith—in this sense Thomism is a "Christian philosophy." Aquinas did not ground his philosophical thinking on principles of religious belief, however, for this would have destroyed his distinction between philosophy and sacred doctrine, as presented in the opening chapters of the first book of *Summa Contra Gentiles*. One of the clearest efforts to maintain the autonomy of philosophy is found in Aquinas's *De Aeternitate Mundi* (about 1270), in which he insists that, as far as philosophical considerations go, the universe might be eternal. As a Christian, he believed that it is not eternal.

Among interpreters of Aquinas there has been much debate whether his commentaries on Aristotle deal with his personal thinking. It is generally agreed even by non-Thomists (W. D. Ross, A. E. Taylor) that these expositions are helpful to the reader who wishes to understand Aristotle. It is not so clear whether the mind of Aquinas is easily discernible in them. One group of Thomists (Étienne Gilson, Joseph Owens, A. C. Pegis) stresses the more obviously personal writings (such as the two *Summa*s) as bases for the interpretation of his thought; another school of interpretation (J. M. Ramírez, Charles De Koninck, J. A. Oesterle) uses the Aristotelian commentaries as the main sources for Aquinas's philosophic thought.

Theory of Knowledge. The Thomistic theory of knowledge is realistic. (This theory is presented in *Summa Theologiae* I, 79–85; *Quaestiones Disputatae de Veritate* I, 11; *In Libros Posteriorum Analyticorum* I, 5;

II, 20.) Men obtain their knowledge of reality from the initial data of sense experience. Apart from supernatural experiences which some mystics may have, Aquinas limited human cognition to sense perception and the intellectual understanding of it. Sense organs are stimulated by the colored, audible, odorous, gustatory, and tactile qualities of extramental bodies; and sensation is the vital response through man's five external sense powers to such stimulation. Aquinas assumed that one is cognitively aware of red flowers, noisy animals, cold air, and so on. Internal sensation (common, imaginative, memorative, and cogitative functions) works to perceive, retain, associate, and judge the various impressions (phantasms) through which things are directly known. Man's higher cognitive functions, those of understanding, judging, and reasoning, have as their objects the universal meanings that arise out of sense experience. Thus, one sees and remembers an individual apple on the level of sensation—but he judges it to be healthful because it contains vitamins, or for any other general reason, on the level of intellectual knowledge. Universals (health, humanity, redness) are not taken as existing realities but are viewed as intelligibilities (*rationes*) with a basis in what is common to existents. As a moderate realist, Aquinas would resent being classified as a Platonist; yet he would defend the importance of our knowledge of the general and common characteristics of things.

Although human cognition begins with the knowing of bodily things, man can form some intellectual notions and judgments concerning immaterial beings: souls, angels, and God. Aquinas taught that man does this by negating certain aspects of bodies (for instance, a spirit does not occupy space) and by using analogy. When the notion of power is attributed to God, its meaning is transferred from an initially physical concept to the analogous perfection of that which can accomplish results in the immaterial order. Aquinas did not think that men, during earthly life, can know the nature of God in any adequate, positive way.

Discursive reasoning was taken as an intellectual process moving from or toward first principles in logical processes of demonstration (the ways of discovery and reduction, described above). In one way, sense experience is the first principle (starting point) for all of man's natural knowledge. This is one aspect of Aquinas's empiricism. Following Aristotle's *Posterior Analytics*, Aquinas taught that many sensations combine to form a unified memory, and many memories constitute sense experience. From this manifold of experience, by a sort of sensory induction, there arises within human awareness a beginning (*principium*) of understanding. Such first principles are not demonstrated (they naturally emerge from sense cognition), but they become the roots for consequent intellectual reasoning. A doctor who tries a variety of remedies to treat headaches eventually notices that one drug works well in almost all cases—at some point he grasps the universal "Drug *A* is a general remedy for headache." From this principle he proceeds rationally to order his practice. If he becomes a teacher of medicine, he uses such a theoretical principle to instruct others. This is the basis of the life of reason.

PHILOSOPHY AND THE PHYSICAL WORLD. In his exposition of the *Liber de Causis* (Lect. 1), Aquinas described a sequence of philosophic studies: logic, mathematics, natural philosophy (physics), moral philosophy, and, finally, metaphysics. The first kind of reality examined in this course would be that of the physical world. (At the start of the next century, Duns Scotus criticized Aquinas for attempting to base his metaphysics and his approaches to God on physics.) Interpreters still debate whether Aquinas himself felt that this was the order to be followed in learning philosophy, or whether he was merely reporting one way that the "philosophers" had taught it. In any case, the philosophical study of bodies, of mobile being in the Aristotelian sense, was important to Aquinas. One group of his writings (*De Principiis Naturae*, parts of Book II of the *Summa Contra Gentiles*, the treatise *De Aeternitate Mundi*) offers a quite personal treatment of this world of bodies. Another set of writings (the commentaries on Aristotle's *Physics* and *De Generatione et Corruptione*) shows how indebted Aquinas was to Aristotle in his theory of physical reality.

Matter and Form. The philosophy of nature (*phusis*) was understood as the study of a special kind of beings, those subject to several kinds of change. Physical beings have primary matter as one component and, depending on their species or kind, substantial form as their other integral principle. Neither matter nor form is a thing by itself; matter and form are simply the determinable and determining factors within any existing physical substance. Like Aristotle, Aquinas took it that there are many species of bodily substances: all the different kinds of inanimate material (wood, gold, water, etc.) and all the species of plants and animals. Within each such species there is one specifying principle (the substantial form of wood, potato plant, or dog), and the many individual members of each species are differentiated by the fact that the matter constituting dog *A* could not also constitute dog *B* (so viewed, matter is said to be quantified, or marked by quantity).

Change. Being mobile, physical beings are subject to four kinds of change (*motus*): of place (locomotion), of size (quantitative change), of color, shape, and so on

(qualitative change), and of species of substance (generation and corruption, substantial change). Basically, prime matter is that which remains constant and provides continuity during a change from one substance to another. When a pig eats an apple, that part of the apple really assimilated by the pig becomes the very substance of the pig; some factor in the apple, the prime matter, must continue on into the pig. All four types of change are explained in terms of the classic theory of four causes. The final cause is the answer to the question "why" something exists or occurs; the agent or efficient cause is the maker or producer of the change; the material cause is that out of which the change comes; and the formal cause is the specifying factor in any event or existent. So used, "cause" has the broad meaning of *raison d'être*.

One of the broad characteristics of Aquinas's work in philosophy is a temperamental tendency to seek a middle way on questions that have been given a wide range of answers.

Space and Time. Certain other points in Aquinas's philosophy of nature further illustrate the influence of Aristotle. Place, for instance, is defined as the "immobile limit of the containing body" (*In IV Physicorum* 6). Moreover, each primary type of body (the four elements still are earth, air, fire, and water) is thought to have its own "proper" place. Thus, the place for fire is "up" and that for earth is "down." Some sort of absolute, or box, theory of space may be presupposed; yet in the same passage Aquinas's discussion of the place of a boat in a flowing river indicates a more sophisticated understanding of spatial relativity. Time is defined, as in Aristotle, as the measure of motion in regard to "before" and "after." Eternity is a type of duration differing from time in two ways: the eternal has neither beginning nor termination, and the eternal has no succession of instants but exists entirely at once (*tota simul*).

Encouragement of Science. Doubtless Aquinas's philosophy of the physical world was limited and even distorted by certain views and factual errors derived from Aristotle and from thirteenth-century science. Apart from the mistaken hypothesis that each element has its proper place in the universe, Aquinas also used the Eudoxian astronomy, which placed the earth at the center of a system of from 49 to 53 concentric spheres. (Besides the Commentary on *De Caelo* II, 10, and the Commentary on *Meteorologia* II, 10; see *Summa Contra Gentiles* I, 20, and *Summa Theologiae* I, 68, 4 c.) At times Aquinas showed an open mind on such questions and an ability to rise above the limitations of his period. His Commentary on Aristotle's *Metaphysics* (Lect. 1 on Book III and Lect. 9 on Book XII) provides a key instance. Pointing out that astronomers differ widely on the number and motions of the planets, Aquinas recommended that one study all the reports and theories of such scientists, even though these scientific explanations are not the last word on the matter and are obviously open to future revision. He further compared the study of physical science to the work of a judge in a court of law. One should listen to, and try to evaluate, all important testimony before attempting to formulate one's own judgment on the problems of contemporary science. This is Aquinas at his best, hardly a philosophical dogmatist.

HUMAN FUNCTIONS AND MAN'S NATURE. Anthropology, or psychology, in the classical sense of the study of man's psyche, forms an important part of Aquinas's philosophy. His view of man owed much to the Aristotelian treatise *On the Soul,* to the Christian Platonism of Augustine and John of Damascus, and to the Bible. This part of Aquinas's thought will be found in *Scriptum in IV Libros Sententiarum* ("Commentary on the *Sentences*") I, Dists. 16–27; *Summa Contra Gentiles* II, 58–90; *Quaestio Disputata de Anima;* the *Libros de Anima;* and *Summa Theologiae* I, 75–90.

Aquinas's usual way of working out his theory of human nature was first to examine certain activities in which man engages, then to reason to the kinds of operative powers needed to explain such actions, and finally to conclude to the sort of substantial nature that could be the subject of such powers. He described the biological activities of man as those of growth, assimilation of food, and sexual reproduction. A higher set of activities included sensory perception, emotive responses to what is perceived, and locomotion: these activities man shares with brute animals. A third group of activities comprises the cognitive functions of understanding, judging, and reasoning, as well as the corresponding appetitive functions of affective inclination toward or away from the objects of understanding. To these various functions Aquinas assigned generic powers (operative potencies) of growth, reproduction, sensory cognition and appetition, physical locomotion, and intellectual cognition and appetition (will).

Re-examining these functional powers in detail, Aquinas distinguished five special sense powers for the cognition of physical individuals: sight, hearing, smell, taste, and touch. These functions and powers are called

external because their proper objects are outside the mental awareness of the perceiver: this is essential to epistemological realism. Following these are four kinds of internal sensory activities: the perceptual grasping of a whole object (*sensus communis*), the simple retention of sensed images (imagination), the association of retained images with past time (sense memory), and concrete discrimination or judgment concerning individual things (cogitative sense, particular reason). Still on the level of sensory experience, Aquinas (here influenced by John of Damascus) described two kinds of appetition (emotion): a simple tendency toward or away from what is sensed as good or evil (this affective power is called the concupiscible appetite), and a more complicated sensory inclination to meet bodily threats, obstacles, and dangers by attacking or avoiding them or by putting up with them (this affective power is called irascible appetite). Eleven distinct kinds of sensory passions (emotions) are attributed to these two sensory appetites: love, desire, delight, hate, aversion, and sorrow to the concupiscible; fear, daring, hope, despair, and anger to the irascible. Much of this psychological analysis is quite sophisticated, employing data from Greek, Roman, and early Christian thought and also using the physiological and psychological treatises of Islamic and Jewish scholars. It also forms the basis of the analysis of human conduct in Thomistic ethics.

Aquinas thought that philosophy entailed reasoning from prior Knowledge, or present experience, to new Knowledge (the way of discovery) and the rational verification of judgments by tracing them back to more simply known principles (the way of reduction).

On the higher level of distinctively human experience, Aquinas found various other activities and powers. These are described in his commentary on Book III of Aristotle's *De Anima*, in the *Summa Contra Gentiles* (II, 59–78), and in Questions 84–85 of the *Summa Theologiae*. The general capacity to understand (*intellectus*) covers simple apprehension, judging, and reasoning. The objects of intellection are universal aspects (*rationes*) of reality. Since universal objects do not exist in nature, Aquinas described one intellectual action as the abstraction of universal meanings (*intentiones*) from the individual presentations of sense experience. This abstractive power is called agent intellect (*intellectus agens*). A second cognitive function on this level is the grasping (*comprehensio*) of these abstracted meanings in the very act of cognition; this activity is assigned to a different power, the possible intellect (*intellectus possibilis*). Thus, there are two quite different "intellects" in Thomistic psychology: one abstracts, the other knows. No special power is required for intellectual memory; the retention of understandings is explained by habit formation in the possible intellect.

Will. Affective responses to the universal objects of understanding are functions of intellectual appetition. Considered quite different from sensory appetition, this is the area of volition, and the special power involved is the will (*voluntas*). Aquinas distinguished two kinds of volitional functions. First, there are those basic and natural tendencies of approval and affective approach to an object that is judged good or desirable without qualification. In regard to justice, peace, or a perfectly good being, for instance, Aquinas felt that a person's will would be naturally and necessarily attracted to such objects. This natural movement of the will is not free. Second, there are volitional movements toward or away from intellectually known objects that are judged as partly desirable or as partly undesirable. Such movements of will are directed by intellectual judgments evaluating the objects. In this case volition is said to be "deliberated" (specified by intellectual considerations) and free. It is in the act of decision (*arbitrium*) that man is free. Aquinas did not talk about "free will"; the term *libera voluntas* is found only twice in all his works, and then in a nontechnical usage; rather, he spoke of free choice or decision (*liberum arbitrium*). Man, by virtue of his intellectual powers, is free in some of his actions.

Soul. Although Aquinas sometimes spoke as if these various "powers" of man were agents, he formally stressed the view that it is the whole man who is the human agent. A human being is an animated body in which the psychic principle (*anima*) is distinctive of the species and determines that the material is human. In other words, man's soul is his substantial form. Some of man's activities are obviously very like those of brutes, but the intellectual and volitional functions transcend materiality by virtue of their universal and abstracted character. Aquinas took as an indication of the immateriality of the human soul the fact that it can understand universal meanings and make free decisions. The soul is a real part of man and, being both immaterial and real, it is spiritual. From certain other features of man's higher activities, especially from the unity of conscious experience, Aquinas concluded to the simplicity and integration of man's soul: it is not divisible into parts. This, in turn, led him to the conclusion that the soul is incapable of corruption (disintegration into parts) and thus is immortal.

Since Aquinas thought the soul incapable of being partitioned, he could not explain the coming into being of new human souls by biological process. He was thus forced to the view that each rational soul is originated by divine creation from nothing. Human parents are not the total cause of their offspring; they share the work of procreation with God. This view explains why Aquinas put so much stress on the dignity and sanctity of human reproduction, which he regarded as more than a biological function. When he claimed, in his ethics, that the begetting and raising of children is the primary purpose of married life, he was not thinking of simple sexual activity but of a human participation in God's creative function. This does not mean that man is the highest of God's creatures; Aquinas speculated that there are other kinds of purely intellectual beings with activities, powers, and natures superior to those of men. These are angels. Thomas Aquinas is called the Angelic Doctor in Catholic tradition because of his great interest in these purely spiritual but finite beings. They would constitute the highest realm of the universe.

METAPHYSICS AND REAL BEING. Aquinas devoted much thought to the question "What does it mean to be?" Many Thomists think that his greatest philosophical ability was shown in the area of metaphysics. His general theory of reality incorporates much of the metaphysics of Aristotle, and some interpreters have seen Thomistic metaphysics as but a baptized Aristotelianism. Recent Thomistic scholarship has selected two non-Aristotelian metaphysical teachings for new emphasis: the theory of participation and the general influence of Platonic metaphysics (L. B. Geiger, Cornelio Fabro, R. J. Henle), and the primacy of *esse*, the fundamental act of being (Gilson, Jacques Maritain, G. P. Klubertanz). Because *esse*, which simply means "to be," is sometimes translated as "existence," this second point of emphasis is called by some writers the existentialism of Thomistic metaphysics. It has little, however, to do with present-day existentialism. A major treatment of metaphysical problems is to be found in Aquinas's long Commentary on Aristotle's *Metaphysics,* but here again the problem is to decide how much is Thomistic. Some very competent scholars (Pegis, Gilson) regard this work as a restatement of Aristotelianism; others (De Koninck, Herman Reith) consider the Commentary to be a key exposition of Aquinas's own metaphysics. It is admitted by all that there are some explanations in it that are not found in Aristotle.

Metaphysics, for Aquinas, was the effort to understand reality in general, to find an ultimate explanation of the manifold of experience in terms of the highest causes. His predecessors had variously described the subject matter of this study as existing immaterial substances, as the most universal and common aspects of being, as the first causes of all things, and as the divine being in itself. Commenting on these opinions in the Prologue to his Commentary on the *Metaphysics,* Aquinas remarked: "Although this science considers these items, it does not think of each of them as its subject; its subject is simply being in general." In this sense, he called the study of being "first philosophy."

Analogy. It is distinctive of Aquinas's thought to maintain that all existing realities, from God down to the least perfect thing, are beings—and that "being" has in this usage an analogical and not a univocal meaning. In a famous passage (*In I Sententiarum* 19, 5, 2, ad 1) Aquinas describes three sorts of analogy: one in which a given perfection is present in one item but only attributed to another; one in which one perfection exists in a somewhat different way in two or more items; and one in which some sort of remote resemblance or community is implied between two items which have no identity either in existence or in signification. "In this last way," Aquinas adds "truth and goodness, and all things of this kind, are predicated analogously of God and creatures." In later works the notion of proportionality is introduced to develop the concept of the analogy of being. Vision in the eye is a good of the body in somewhat the same way that vision in the intellect is a good of the soul. Similarly, the act of being in a stone is proportional to the act of being in a man, as the nature of a stone is proportional to the nature of man. Whereas some interpreters feel that the analogy of proportionality is the central type of analogy of being, others insist that Aquinas used several kinds of analogy in his metaphysics.

Being and Essence. One early but certainly personal presentation of the metaphysics of Aquinas is to be found in the brief treatise *De Ente et Essentia,* which was strongly influenced by Avicenna. His usage of basic terms of analysis, such as being (*ens*), essence (*essentia*), nature, quiddity, substance, accident, form, matter, genus, species, difference, immaterial substance (*substantia separata*), potency, and act, is clearly but rather statically defined in this *opusculum*. Additional precisions, particularly on the meaning of element, principle, cause, and *esse,* are to be found in the companion treatise, *De Principiis Naturae*. A more dynamic approach to being and its operations is offered in the *Quaestiones Disputatae de Potentia Dei* and in Part I of the *Summa Theologiae.*

Fundamental in the metaphysical thinking of Aquinas is the difference between *what* a being is and the fact *that* it is. The first is a question of essence; the second is the act of being, *esse*. Essences are many (various kinds of things—stones, cows, air, men) and are known through simple understanding, without any necessity of adverting to their existence or nonexistence. For a thing *to be* is entirely another matter; the fact that something exists is noted in human experience by an act of judgment. Many essences of things are material, but there is nothing about *esse* that requires it to be limited to materiality. This proposition (to be is not necessarily to be material) is the "judgment of separation" (*In Boethii de Trinitate* V, 3). Many Thomists now regard it as a fundamental point of departure for Aquinas's metaphysical thinking.

There are also certain most general features of real beings which transcend all division into genera and species; these are convertible with metaphysical being. In other words, they are coextensive and really identical with being. Such transcendentals are thing (*res*), something (*aliquid*), one, true, good, and (according to some interpreters) beautiful. The more important of these transcendentals suggest that every being is internally undivided but externally distinct from all else (*unum*), that every being has some intelligible meaning (*verum*), and that every being is in some way desirable (*bonum*). The theory of transcendentals is much more expanded and stressed in later scholasticism than in Aquinas's own writings. He barely touches upon it in Questions I and XXI of *De Veritate* and in the discussion of God's attributes in *Summa Theologiae* (I, Ques. 6, 11, 16).

Potency and Act. Potency and act are important principles in Aquinas's metaphysical explanation of the existence and operation of things. In *De Potentia Dei* (I, 1) Aquinas pointed out that the name "act" first designated any activity or operation that occurs. Corresponding to this sort of operational act is a dual meaning of potency (or power). Consider the activity of sawing wood: the passive potency of wood to be cut is required (water, for instance, cannot be sawed); also required is the active potency of the sawyer to do the cutting. In addition, in the same text, Aquinas says that the notion of "act" is transferred to cover the existence of a being. Essential potency, the metaphysical capacity to exist, would correspond to this act of being (*esse*). In this way the theory of act and potency was applied to all levels of being. At the highest level, God was described as Pure Act in the existential order, but this did not prevent Aquinas from attributing to God an active potency for operating.

Finality. Still another dimension of metaphysical reality, for Aquinas, was that of finality. He thought of all activities as directed toward some end or purpose, a basic assumption in Aristotle. But Aquinas developed this tendential, vector characteristic of being and applied it to the inclination of possible beings to become actual. The finality of being, in Thomism, is that dynamic and ongoing inclination to be realized in their appropriate perfections that is characteristic of all realities and capacities for action. In this sense the finality of being is an intrinsic perfectionism in the development of all beings. Aquinas also held that all finite beings and events are tending toward God as Final Cause. This is metaphysical finality in the sense of order to an external end. This theme runs through Book III of *Summa Contra Gentiles.*

Since Aquinas thought the soul

incapable of being partitioned,

he could not explain the coming into being

of new human souls by biological process.

PHILOSOPHY AND GOD. The consideration of the existence and nature of God was approached by Aquinas both from the starting point of supernatural revelation (the Scriptures), which is the way of the theologian, and from the starting point of man's ordinary experience of finite beings and their operations, which is the way of the philosopher: "The philosophers, who follow the order of natural cognition, place the knowledge of creatures before the divine science; that is, the philosophy of nature comes before metaphysics. On the other hand, the contrary procedure is followed among the theologians, so that the consideration of the Creator precedes the consideration of creatures" (*In Boethii de Trinitate,* Prologue). In the same work (II, 3 c) we are told that the first use of philosophy in sacred doctrine is "to demonstrate items that are preambles to faith, such as those things that are proved about God by natural processes of reasoning: that God exists, that God is one," and so on.

Aquinas recognized two types of demonstration, one moving from cause to effects and the other from effects back to their cause. The arguments that he selected to establish that God exists use the second procedure and are technically called *quia* arguments. In other words, these proofs start with some observed facts of experience (all Aquinas's arguments to God's existence are a posteriori) and conclude to the ultimate cause of these facts. Well aware of his debt to his predecessors, Aquinas outlined three arguments for the existence of God in *De Potentia Dei* (III, 5 c). The first shows that, since the act of being is common to many existents, there must

be one universal cause of all (Plato's argument, Aquinas noted); the second argument starts from the fact that all beings in our experience are imperfect, not self-moved, and not the source of their actual being, and the reasoning concludes to the existence of a "mover completely immobile and most perfect" (Aristotle's argument); the third argument simply reasons from the composite nature of finite beings to the necessary existence of a primary being in which essence and the act of existing are identical (Avicenna's proof). Aquinas felt that these two pagan philosophers and an Islamic thinker had successfully established the conclusion "that there is a universal cause of real beings by which all other things are brought forth into actual being."

The "Five Ways." The most famous of the arguments are the "Five Ways" (*Quinque Viae*) of reasoning to the conclusion that God exists (*Summa Theologiae* I, 2, 3, c). All these ways employ the principle of causality and start from empirical knowledge of the physical world. They are not entirely original with Aquinas, depending not only on Plato, Aristotle, and Avicenna but also on Augustine and especially on Moses Maimonides. The First Way begins with the point that things in the world are always changing or moving and concludes to the existence of one, first, moving Cause. The Second Way argues from the observation of efficient production of things in the universe to the need of an existing, first, efficient Cause. The Third Way reasons from the contingent character of things in the world (none of them has to be) to the existence of a totally different kind of being, a necessary one (which has to be). The Fourth Way argues from the gradations of goodness, truth, and nobility in the things of man's experience to the existence of a being that is most true, most good, and most noble. The Fifth Way starts from the orderly character of mundane events, argues that all things are directed toward one end (the principle of finality), and concludes that this universal order points to the existence of an intelligent Orderer of all things. At the end of his statement of each "way," Thomas simply said, "and this is what all men call God," or words to that effect. Obviously, he presupposed a common meaning of the word "God" in the dictionary or nominal sense. There is disagreement among interpreters as to whether the "ways" are five distinct proofs or merely five formulations of one basic argument. Most Thomists now favor the second view.

Aquinas favored the argument from physical motion (*prima autem et manifestior via est*). The *Summa Contra Gentiles* (I, 13) offers an extended version of this first argument and frankly indicates its relation to the ideas in the last books of Aristotle's *Physics*. The other four ways are but briefly suggested in the *Summa Contra*

Gentiles. In another, much neglected, work (*Compendium Theologiae* I, 3) the first way is stated clearly and concisely. Before attempting to establish in detail the various attributes of God, such as divine unity, one should consider whether he exists. Now, all things that are moved must be moved by other things; furthermore, things of an inferior nature are moved by superior beings. (Aquinas's examples are chosen from thirteenth-century physics and astronomy, in which the four basic elements were thought to be under dynamic influence of the stars, and lower celestial bodies were considered to be moved about by those at a greater distance from the earth. How much of the force of this argument may depend on outmoded science is a matter of debate in present-day Thomism.

Aquinas next argues that the process in which *A* moves *B*, *B* moves *C*, and so on cannot be self-explanatory. His way of saying this is "This process cannot go on to infinity." He concludes that the only possible explanation of the series of physical motions observed in the universe requires the acceptance of the existence of a different sort of "mover"—a being that is not moved by another, in other words, a first mover. This would have to be a real being, of course, and of a quite different nature from bodily things. He eventually suggests that this "first mover existing above all else" is what Christians call God.

In the same passage from the *Compendium*, two other facets of the argument from motion are introduced. First, Aquinas claims that all causes observed as acting in the physical universe are instrumental in character and must be used, as it were, by a primary agent. This primary agent is again another name for God. To suppose that the universe is self-explanatory is, to Aquinas, like thinking that a bed could be constructed by putting the tools and material together, "without any carpenter to use them." This is an important case of the conception of God as a divine craftsman. In the second place, this text suggests briefly that an infinite series of moved movers is an impossibility; the length of the series has nothing to do with its explanatory function, if all its members be finite. Finally, any such series requires a first mover (primary in the sense of causality, not necessarily of chronological priority). This first mover would be a Supreme Being. It is obvious that many of the attributes of God are aleady implied in the argument for divine existence.

Knowledge of God. Regarding the nature and attributes of God, Aquinas's greatest emphasis fell on how little we really know about the Supreme Being. In a series of articles (*Summa Theologiae* I, 86–88) on the objects of human knowledge, he reiterated his position that man is naturally equipped to understand directly the natures of material things; further, that man is aware of his own psychic functions as they occur but that all man's understanding of the nature of his own soul, of immaterial substances such as angels, and of infinite immaterial being (God) is achieved by dint of discursive and indirect reasoning. There is, of course, a wide gap between material and immaterial substances. Yet both these types of finite beings fall within the same logical genus, as substances, and thus bodies and created spirits have some aspects in common. On the other hand, God is an immaterial being of an entirely different nature from that of bodies or even of created spirits. Between God and creatures there is no univocal community: that is to say, God does not fall within the same genus, either real or logical, as any other being. Hence, God's nature transcends all species and genera. Man's natural knowledge of God's nature is therefore very imperfect, achieved by negating various imperfections found in finite beings: thus, God is not in time, not in place, not subject to change, and so on. Furthermore, man may reach some semipositive knowledge of God by way of analogy: thus, God is powerful but not in the finite manner of other beings; he is knowing, willing, and so on.

Regarding the nature and attributes of God, Aquinas's greatest emphasis fell on how little we really know about the Supreme Being.

Providence. Divine providence is that attribute of God whereby he intelligently orders all things and events in the universe. As Aquinas explained it in the *Summa Contra Gentiles* (III), God both establishes the plan (*ratio*) in accord with which all creatures are kept in order and executes this plan through continued governance of the world. Literally, providence means "foresight," and this required Aquinas to face certain problems traditionally associated with any theory of divine foreknowledge. First of all, he insisted that such a view of divine providence does not exclude chance events from the universe. In one sense, a chance event occurs apart from the intention of the agent. However, what is intended by one agent may involve another agent who is unaware of the intention of the first. Hence, a plurality of real but imperfect agents sets the stage for chance: God knows this and permits it to occur.

Evil. In the *Quaestiones Disputatae de Malo* and elsewhere Aquinas agreed with Augustine that evil (both physical and moral) is a privation of goodness, of perfection, in being or in action. This does not deny the fact that evil really occurs but asserts that it is like a wound in being (the phrase is Maritain's); and, like any defect, evil is important by virtue of what is lacking. As to why a perfectly good God will allow evil to occur, Aquinas argued that the possibility of evil is necessary so that many goods may be possible. "If there were no death of other animals, there would not be life for the lion; if there were no persecution from tyrants, there would be no occasion for the heroic suffering of the martyrs" (*Summa Theologiae* I, 22, 2, ad 2).

Freedom. Aquinas also did not admit that divine fore-knowledge is opposed to the exercise of human freedom. His explanation of this point (in *Summa Theologiae* I, 103, 7 and 8) is complicated and not easy to state briefly. In effect, human freedom does not imply absolute indeterminism (action that is uncaused). What a man does freely is caused by himself, as a knowing and willing agent. God makes man capable of choosing well or ill, permits man to do so freely, and knows what man will accomplish. What appears to be necessitated from one point of view may be quite contingent and free from another viewpoint. From God's vantage point in eternity, human actions are not affairs of past or future but are events within the all-inclusive present of a divine observer who witnesses these events but does not determine them.

ETHICS AND POLITICAL PHILOSOPHY. The fore-going problems and considerations fall within Aquinas's speculative philosophy. His practical philosophy, aimed at the intelligent performance of actions, is divided into ethics, economics (treating problems of domestic life), and politics. In all three areas the thinking is teleological; finality, purposiveness, and the means–end relation all are aspects of Thomistic teleology. Rationally controlled activities must be directed to some goal; they are judged good or bad in terms of their attainment of that goal and in terms of the means by which they attain (or fail to attain) that end.

Aquinas dealt with the theoretical analysis of ethical activities in a long series of works: the *Scriptum in IV Libros Sententiarum*, Book III; *Summa Contra Gentiles* III, 114–138; the *In X Libros Ethicorum; Quaestiones Disputatae de Malo;* and the *Summa Theologiae,* Part II. Most of these works take the approach of moral theology, viewing moral good and evil in terms of accord or discord with divine law, which is revealed in Scripture and developed and interpreted in Christian tradition. Aquinas himself did not consider moral theology to be a part of philosophy, and it will not be further considered here, except as throwing incidental light on his ethical position.

Voluntary Action. Aquinas's ethics consists of a study of good and evil in human conduct, from the point of view of man's achievement of ultimate happiness. Not all the actions in which man is involved are truly human but only those accomplished under control of man's intellect and will. The primary characteristic of human conduct, according to Aquinas, is not so much freedom as voluntariness. His description of voluntary activity is a development of the teaching of Aristotle. Several factors are required for a voluntary action. There must be sufficient knowledge on the part of a moral agent that a given action is within his power; he cannot be entirely ignorant of the kind of action that he is performing or of the means, circumstances, and end of his action. Violence, under certain conditions, modifies the voluntariness of one's actions—as do certain kinds of uncontrollable feelings. Furthermore, as Aquinas saw it there are two opposites to what is voluntary. The "involuntary" is a contrary: it represents a diminution of voluntariness. Thus, an action that is partly involuntary is also partly voluntary and is, to a greater or lesser extent, imputable to the agent. On the other hand, the "not-voluntary" is the contradictory of what is voluntary, and an agent who is not voluntary is not morally responsible for his action.

Natural Law. Most surveys of ethical theories classify Aquinas's ethics as a natural law theory. He described natural law as a rational participation in the eternal law of God and suggested that all men have a sufficient knowledge of what is morally right (the *justum*) to be able to regulate their own actions. In a famous passage (*Summa Theologiae* I–II, 94, 2) Aquinas explained the way in which he thought that rules of natural law are known. The judgment of *synderesis* (an intellectual quality enabling any man to intuit the first principle of practical reasoning) is simply the proposition "Good should be done and sought after; evil is to be avoided." (Most modern Thomists take this rule as a formal principle in the Kantian sense, requiring further knowledge to fill in the content of specific moral rules.) Aquinas then proceeded to describe three kinds of inclinations natural to man: that of man's substantial nature toward the conservation of its own existence and physical well-being, that of man's animal nature to seek such biological goods as sexual reproduction and the care of offspring, and that of man's reason whereby he tends toward universal goods, such as consideration of the interests of other persons and the avoidance of ignorance. All three kinds of inclinations are presented as natural and good, provided they are reasonably pursued. They form the bases from which one may conclude to a number of rules of natural moral law. Aquinas never attempted to make an exhaustive listing of the precepts of such a law; nor did he consider such a codification advisable.

In point of fact, the natural law approach to moral theory is not the only, and not the best, classification of Aquinas's ethics. Particularly in view of various shifts in the meaning of "law" since the time of Aquinas (notably a growing stress on law as a fiat of legislative will), it can be positively misleading to limit Aquinas's ethics to a natural law position. He defines law in general as "any ordinance of reason that is promulgated for the common good by one who has charge of a community" (*Summa Theologiae* I–II, 90, 4 c). "Reason" is the key word in this definition. Right reason (*recta ratio*) is the justification of ethical judgment in Aquinas's thought. "In the case of volitional activities, the proximate standard is human reason (*regula proxima est ratio humana*) but the supreme standard is eternal law. Therefore, whenever a man's action proceeds to its end in accord with the order of reason and of eternal law, then the act is right; but when it is twisted away from this rightness, then it is called a sin" (*ibid.*, 21, 1 c).

Reason, Goodness, and Justice. Thomistic ethics requires a person to govern his actions as reasonably as he can, keeping in mind the kind of agent that he is and the position that he occupies in the total scheme of reality. Man's own good is achieved by the governance of his actions and feelings under rational reflection—and God does not require anything else. "For we do not offend God, except by doing something contrary to our own good" (*Summa Contra Gentiles* III, 121–122). It is a part of being reasonable to respect the good of others. The moral good, then, is not so much what men are obligated to do by an all-powerful legislator; rather, it is that which is in accord with the reasonable perfecting of man. In becoming a better agent within himself, man is making himself more fit for ultimate happiness and for the vision of God. This kind of ethics resembles a self-perfectionist theory, without idealist overtones.

Aquinas based much of his teaching on ethical rules on the theory of natural justice found in Book V of the *Nicomachean Ethics*. All things have specific natures which do not change: dogs are dogs and stones are stones. Certain functions are taken as natural and appropriate to given natures: eating is an act expected of a dog but not of a stone. Human nature shares certain functions with the higher brutes but is distinguished by the performance of rational activities. Some of these typical functions are always the same in relation to man's nature and ethical rules pertaining to these do not change. Aquinas's example of such an immutable rule of justice is simply "Theft is unjust." Other ethical judgments, however, are not essential to justice (for example, detailed ordinances which contain many variable factors); these secondary rules are by no means absolute and immutable. Examples would be rules concerned with taxation, buying and selling, and other such circumstantially variable regulations. Moral law is composed of both types of rules and is neither absolute nor immutable in all its requirements.

Conscience. In *De Veritate* (XVII) Aquinas referred to moral conscience as a concrete intellectual judgment whereby the individual agent decides for himself that a given action or feeling is good or bad, right or wrong, to be done or not to be done. Conscience was not considered a special power or moral sense, nor was it viewed as the source of universal moral convictions. For Aquinas it was simply a man's best practical judgment concerning a concrete moral problem. As such, moral conscience is a person's internal guide to good action; one acts immorally in going against his conscience, for it is his best judgment on a matter. If it is not his best judgment, then the person is clearly required to make a better effort to reach a conscientious decision. Reasonable consideration of a proposed action includes thinking of the kind of action that it is (the formal object), the purpose to which it is directed (the end), and the pertinent circumstances under which it is to be performed. These three moral determinants were used by Aquinas to complete the theory of right reasoning in *De Malo* (II, 4 c, ad 2, ad 5).

Family. Aquinas also considered man in his social relations. In the *Summa Contra Gentiles* (III, cc. 122–126) the family is regarded as a natural and reasonable type of small society, designed to provide for the procreation and raising of children and for the mutual good of husband and wife. (The material on matrimony in the so-called *Supplement* to the *Summa Theologiae* was excerpted from Book IV of the *Scriptum in IV Libros Sententiarum* and does not represent Aquinas's mature thought.) The main reason why people get married, Aquinas thought, is to raise children, so his approach to the family was child-oriented. There should be but one husband and wife in a family; they should stay together until the children are fully grown and educated; they should deal honestly and charitably with each other as marriage partners. Many of Aquinas's arguments for monogamy and the indissolubility of the marriage bond are but restatements of similar reasonings in Aristotle's *Politics*.

Political Theory. Aquinas's family, living in southern Italy, had been closely allied with the imperial government: his father and at least two of his brothers were in the service of Emperor Frederick II. Aquinas thus grew up with monarchic loyalties. On the other hand, early in life he joined the Dominicans, a religious community remarkable for its democratic and liberal practices. As a result Aquinas's political philosophy (in *De Regno*, in *In Libros Politicorum*, and in *Summa Theologiae*, I–II, *passim*) stressed the ideal of the limited monarchy, or that kind of state which Aristotle had called the *politeia*. The purpose of the state is described as to provide for temporal peace and welfare. Political society is quite different from ecclesiastical society (the church), whose end is otherworldly. Here again Aquinas always stressed the central role of reason: "Divine justice (*ius divinum*) which stems from grace does not cancel human justice which comes from natural reason." There is no detailed theory of government in Aquinas's writings.

ART AND AESTHETICS. In his theory of art Aquinas was quite abstract and intellectualistic, taking Aristotle's *Rhetoric, Poetics,* and *Nicomachean Ethics* (Book VI) as his major sources. He used a new awareness of the spiritual and moral dimensions of the beautiful, found seminally in the mystical Neoplatonism of Dionysius the Pseudo-Areopagite, to develop the fragmentary aesthetics of Aristotelianism. Most of these precisions are found in Aquinas's commentary on the fourth chapter of Dionysius's *De Divinis Nominibus.*

Art is understood to be a special habit, or acquired skill, of the practical intellect, which is simply man's possible intellect applied to problems of action. Prudence, the key practical habit in moral discourse, is defined as right reason in doing things (*recta ratio agibilium*). Similarly, art is defined as right reason in making things (*recta ratio factibilium*). These two practical habits are not confused. Elsewhere it is explained: "The principle of artifacts is the human intellect which is derived by some sort of similitude from the divine intellect, and the latter is the principle of all things in nature. Hence, not only must artistic operations imitate nature but even art products must imitate the things that exist in nature" (*In I Politicorum* 1). Some artifacts are merely useful; others may be beautiful; and still others may exist only in the order of thought (Aquinas took seriously the dictum that logic is an art).

He regarded the beautiful and the good as really identical but insisted that they differ in their formal meanings (*rationes*). Where the good is simply that which all desire, the beautiful is that which gives pleasure when perceived (*quod visum placet*). Three aspects of the beautiful are distinguished: integrity (*integritas sive perfectio*), due proportion (*debita proportio sive consonantia*), and brilliance (*claritas*). Each of these aesthetic factors is taken as capable of variation in degree and appeal.

These notions on the general meaning of beauty were used not to describe the attraction of a life of sacrifice but of spiritual perfection as a member of a religious community, such as the Dominicans. "In fact," Aquinas wrote, "there are two kinds of beauty. One is spiritual and it consists in a due ordering and overflowing of spiritual goods. Hence, everything that proceeds from a lack of spiritual good, or that manifests intrinsic disorder, is ugly. Another kind is external beauty which consists in a due ordering of the body" (*Contra Impugnantes Dei Cultum et Religionem* 7, ad 9). He was ac-

tually defending the practice of begging, as used in the mendicant orders. Aquinas agreed that there is something distasteful about begging but argued that it is an admirable exercise of humility, when religiously motivated. Here again the concept of purpose, teleological order, is central.

Man's own good is achieved by the governance

of his actions and feelings under rational reflection—

and God does not require anything else.

Metaphysical participation recurs as a key theme in Aquinas's discussion of the manner in which the manifold of creation shares in the transcendent beauty of God. All lower beauties are but imperfect manifestations of one highest *pulchritudo.* This is Dionysian mystical aesthetics and is presented in *In Dionysii de Divinis Nominibus* (IV, 5–6).

AUTHORITY AND INFLUENCE. Aquinas has been given a special position of respect in the field of Catholic scholarship, but this does not mean that all Catholic thinkers agree with him on all points. Within three years of his death a number of propositions closely resembling his philosophic views were condemned as errors by Bishop Tempier of Paris. This episcopal condemnation was formally revoked in 1325. Thomistic thought met much criticism in the later Middle Ages. Since the Renaissance nearly all the popes have praised Aquinas's teaching; the one who provided for the first collected edition of his works (St. Pius V) also did the same for St. Bonaventure, a Franciscan, and proclaimed both Doctors of the Church. In the ecclesiastical law of the Catholic church, revised in 1918, canon 589:1 states that students for the priesthood are required to study at least two years of philosophy and four of theology, "following the teaching of St. Thomas." Further, canon 1366:2 directs professors in seminaries to organize their teaching "according to the method, teaching and principles of the Angelic Doctor."

Actually, Thomism has never been the only kind of philosophy cultivated by Catholics, and from the fourteenth century to the Enlightenment, Thomism was rivaled and sometimes obscured by Scotism and Ockhamism.

In 1879, with the publication of the Encyclical *Aeterni Patris* by Pope Leo XIII, the modern revival of Thomism started. While this document praised Thomism throughout, Pope Leo added this noteworthy qualification: "If there be anything that ill agrees with the discoveries of a later age, or, in a word, improbable in whatever way—it does not enter Our mind to propose that for imitation to our age" (Étienne Gilson, ed., *The Church Speaks to the Modern World,* New York, 1954, p. 50).

In 1914 a group of Catholic teachers drew up a set of 24 propositions which, they felt, embodied the essential points in the philosophy of Aquinas. The Sacred Congregation of Studies, with the approval of Pope Pius X, published these "Twenty-four Theses" as clear expressions of the thought of the holy Doctor. (Original Latin text in *Acta Apostolicae Sedis,* Vol. 6, 1914, 384–386; partial English version in Charles Hart, *Thomistic Metaphysics,* Englewood Cliffs, N.J., 1959, *passim.*)

God's being and that of created things

do not belong within the same genus,

but there is some remote resemblance

between divine and nondivine beings.

The first six theses attempt a formulation of the general metaphysical position of Aquinas. All beings are composed of potential and actual principles, with the exception of God, who is pure act. The divine *esse* (act of being) is utterly simple (that is, without parts or constituents) and infinite in every way. Other beings are composite; their acts of existing are limited in character and merely participated. In general, metaphysical being may be understood in terms of analogy: God's being and that of created things do not belong within the same genus, but there is some remote resemblance between divine and nondivine beings. To satisfy competing theories of analogy which developed in Renaissance Thomism, the theses describe this metaphysical analogy in terms of both attribution (following Suárez) and proportionality (following Cajetan). The real distinction between essence and *esse* is stressed in the fifth thesis, while the difference between substance and accidents is stated in the sixth (accidents *exist in* some substance but never, in the natural course of things, exist by themselves). Marking a transition to special metaphysics (cosmology and philosophical psychology), the seventh proposition treats a spiritual creature as composed of essence and *esse,* and also of substance and accidents, but denies that there is any composition of matter and form in spirits.

A series of theses (VIII to XIII) describe bodily beings as constituted of prime matter and substantial form, neither of which may exist by itself. As material, bodies are extended in space and subject to quantification. Matter as quantified is proposed as the principle which individuates bodies. The location of a body in place is also attributed to quantity. Thesis XIII distinguishes nonliving from living bodies and makes the transition to a group of propositions concerned with human nature and its activities. The life principle in any plant or animal is called a soul, but, in the case of the human animal, the soul is found to be a principle of a very special kind. Theses XIV to XXI focus on the vital nature and functions of man. His soul is capable of existing apart from the human body; it is brought into existence directly by God's creative action; it is without constituent parts and so cannot be disintegrated, that is to say, the human soul is immortal. Moreover, man's soul is the immediate source of life, existence, and all perfection in the human body. Subsequent propositions emphasize the higher human functions of cognition and volition, and they distinguish sensitive knowledge of individual bodies and their qualities from intellectual understanding of the universal features of reality. Willing is subsequent to intellectual cognition, and the free character of volitional acts of choice is strongly asserted.

The last three theses offer a summary of Aquinas's philosophic approach to God. The divine existence is neither directly intuited by the ordinary man nor demonstrable on an a priori basis. It is capable of a posteriori demonstration using any of the famous arguments of the Five Ways; these arguments are briefly summarized. Thesis XXIII reaffirms the simplicity of God's being and maintains the complete identity between the divine essence and *esse.* The final thesis asserts the creation by God of all things in the universe and stresses the point that the coming into existence and the motion of all creatures are to be attributed ultimately to God as First Cause.

These 24 theses represent a rigid and conservative type of Thomism. Many modern Catholic philosophers, while recognizing that these propositions do express some of the basic themes in the speculative thought of Aquinas, doubt that it is possible to put the wisdom of any great philosopher into a few propositions and prefer to emphasize the open-minded spirit with which Aquinas searched for information among his predecessors and approached the problems of his own day. After all, it was Aquinas who remarked that arguments from authority are appropriate in sacred teaching but are the weakest sort of evidence in philosophic reasoning.

BIBLIOGRAPHY

Works by Thomas Aquinas

Collected Editions

Opera Omnia, 25 vols. Parma, 1852–1873. Reprinted New York, 1948–1950. A noncritical but almost complete edition.

Opera Omnia, 34 vols. Paris, 1871–1882. A noncritical but almost complete edition.

S. Thomae Aquinatis, Opera Omnia. Rome, 1882—. This is the incomplete Leonine edition of the Latin works (many Latin works are published separately in Turin). Vols. I–III contain some of the commentaries on Aristotle, notably that on the *Physics;* Vols. IV–XII contain the *Summa Theologiae,* with Cajetan's *Commentary;* Vols. XIII–XV contain the *Summa Contra Gentiles,* with the *Commentary* by Sylvester of Ferrara; Vol. XVI is the Index. Announced for publication next are the *Quaestiones Disputatae,* the *Commentary on Job,* and the *Commentary on the Nicomachean Ethics.*

Individual Works

Scriptum in IV Libros Sententiarum (1252–1257), Pierre Mandonnet and M. F. Moos, eds., 4 vols. Paris, 1929–1947. No English version.

De Ente et Essentia (1253), Ludwig Baur, ed. Münster, 1933. Translated by Armand Maurer as *On Being and Essence.* Toronto, 1949.

De Principiis Naturae (1253), J. J. Pauson, ed. Fribourg, 1950. Translated by V. J. Bourke in V. J. Bourke, ed., *The Pocket Aquinas.* New York, 1960. Pp. 61–77.

Contra Impugnantes Dei Cultum et Religionem (1256), R. M. Spiazzi, ed., in *Opuscula Theologica,* Vol. I. Turin, 1954. Translated by J. Proctor as *An Apology for the Religious Orders.* Westminster, Md., 1950.

Quaestiones Disputatae de Veritate (1256–1259), R. M. Spiazzi, ed. Turin, 1949. Translated by R. W. Mulligan and others as *Truth,* 3 vols. Chicago, 1952–1954.

Quaestiones Quodlibetales (1256–1272), R. M. Spiazzi, ed. Turin, 1949. No English version.

In Librum Boethii de Trinitate Expositio (1257–1258), Bruno Decker, ed. Leiden, 1959. Partially translated by Armand Maurer as *Division and Methods of the Sciences.* Toronto, 1953.

In Librum Dionysii de Divinis Nominibus (1258–1265), Ceslas Pera, ed. Turin, 1950. Partially translated by V. J. Bourke in *The Pocket Aquinas.* New York, 1960. Pp. 269–278.

Summa de Veritate Catholicae Fidei Contra Gentiles (1259–1264), Vols. XIII–XV of the Leonine edition. Rome, 1918–1930. Also published in a one-volume "manual" edition. Turin and Rome, 1934. Translated by A. C. Pegis, J. F. Anderson, V. J. Bourke, and C. J. O'Neil as *On the Truth of the Catholic Faith,* 5 vols. New York, 1955–1957.

De Emptione et Venditione (1263), translated and edited by Alfred O'Rahilly as "Notes on St. Thomas on Credit." *Irish Ecclesiastical Record,* Vol. 31 (1928), 164–165. Translation reprinted in *The Pocket Aquinas.* New York, 1960. Pp. 223–225.

Quaestiones Disputatae de Potentia Dei (1265), R. M. Spiazzi, ed. Turin, 1949. Translated by Lawrence Shapcote as *On the Power of God.* Westminster, Md., 1952.

Commentaries on Aristotle (1265–1273), listed in next section.

De Regno (1265–1266), Jean Perrier, ed. Paris, 1949. Translated by G. B. Phelan and I. T. Eschmann as *On Kingship.* Toronto, 1949.

Compendium Theologiae (1265–1269), R. A. Verardo, ed. Turin, 1954. Translated by Cyril Vollert as *Compendium of Theology.* St. Louis, 1957.

Summa Theologiae (1265–1273), Vols. IV–XII of the Leonine edition. Rome, 1918–1930. Reprinted Turin, 1934. Translated by the English Dominican Fathers as *The Summa Theologica,* 22 vols. London, 1912–1936. Revision of part of the English Dominican Fathers' translation appears in *Basic Writings of Saint Thomas Aquinas,* A. C. Pegis, ed. New York, 1945.

Quaestiones, Disputatae de Spiritualibus Creaturis (1267), L. W. Keeler, ed. Rome, 1938. Translated by John Wellmuth and Mary Fitzpatrick as *On Spiritual Creatures.* Milwaukee, 1949.

Quaestio Disputata de Anima (1269), R. M. Spiazzi, ed. Turin, 1949. Translated by J. P. Rowan as *The Soul.* St. Louis, 1949.

Quaestiones Disputatae de Malo (1269–1272), R. M. Spiazzi, ed. Turin, 1949. Partially translated by A. C. Pegis as *On Free Choice.* New York, c. 1945.

Quaestiones Disputatae de Virtutibus (1269–1272), R. M. Spiazzi, ed. Turin, 1949. Partially translated by J. P. Reid as *The Virtues in General.* Providence, R.I., 1951.

In Job Expositio (1269–1272), in Vol. XVII of Leonine edition. Rome, 1962. No English version.

In Evangelium Joannis Expositio (1269–1272), Raphael Cai, ed. Turin, 1952. No English version.

De Unitate Intellectus (1270), L. W. Keeler, ed. Rome, 1936. Translated by Sister Rose E. Brennan as *The Unicity of the Intellect.* St. Louis, 1946.

De Substantiis Separatis (1271), F. J. Lescoe, ed. West Hartford, Conn., 1962. Translated by F. J. Lescoe as *Treatise on Separate Substances.* West Hartford, Conn., 1960.

De Aeternitate Mundi (1271), R. M. Spiazzi, ed. Turin, 1954. Translated by Cyril Vollert as *On the Eternity of the World.* Milwaukee, 1965.

In Librum de Causis (1271), H. D. Saffrey, ed. Fribourg, 1954. No English version.

Commentaries on Aristotle

In Libros Peri Hermeneias, in Vol. I of the Leonine edition. Rome, 1882. Also edited by R. M. Spiazzi. Turin, 1955. Translated by Jean Oesterle as *Aristotle on Interpretation—Commentary by St. Thomas and Cajetan.* Milwaukee, 1962.

In Libros Posteriorum Analyticorum, in Vol. I of the Leonine edition. Rome, 1882. Translated by Pierre Conway. Quebec, 1956.

In VIII Libros Physicorum, in Vol. II of the Leonine edition. Rome, 1884. Also edited by P. M. Maggiolo. Turin, 1954. Translated by R. J. Blackwell and others as *Commentary on Aristotle's Physics.* London and New Haven, 1963.

In Libros de Caelo et Mundo, in Vol. III of the Leonine edition. Rome, 1886. Also edited by R. M. Spiazzi. Turin, 1952. No English version.

In Libros de Generatione et Corruptione, in Vol. III of the Leonine edition. Rome, 1886. Also edited by R. M. Spiazzi. Turin, 1952. No English version.

In Libros Meteorologicorum, in Vol. III of the Leonine edition. Rome, 1886. Also edited by R. M. Spiazzi. Turin, 1952. No English version.

In Libros de Memoria et Reminiscentia, et de Sensu et Sensato, R. M. Spiazzi, ed. Turin, 1949. No English version.

In XII Libros Metaphysicorum, R. M. Spiazzi, ed. Turin, 1950. Translated by J. P. Rowan as *Commentary on the Metaphysics of Aristotle,* 2 vols. Chicago, 1961.

In Libros de Anima, R. M. Spiazzi, ed. Turin, 1955. Translated by Kenelm Foster and Silvester Humphries as *Aristotle's De Anima With the Commentary of St. Thomas.* London and New Haven, 1951.

In Libros Politicorum, R. M. Spiazzi, ed. Turin, 1951. Translation of Book III, Lectures 1–6 by E. L. Fortin and Peter D. O'Neill in Ralph Lerner and Muhsin Mahdi, eds., *Medieval Political Philosophy.* New York, 1963. Pp. 297–334.

In X Libros Ethicorum, R. M. Spiazzi, ed. Turin, 1949. Translated. by C. I. Litzinger as *Commentary on the Nicomachean Ethics,* 2 vols. Chicago, 1964.

Works on Thomas Aquinas

Guides

Bergomo, Petri de, *Tabula Aurea in Omnia Opera S. Thomae Aquinatis.* Bologna, 1485. Reprinted in Vol. XXV of *S. Thomae, Opera Omnia.* Parma, 1873.

Deferrari, Roy J.; Barry, Sister M. Inviolata; and McGuiness, Ignatius, *A Lexicon of St. Thomas Aquinas, Based on the Summa Theologica and Selected Passages of His Other Works.* Washington, 1949.

Indices . . . in Summam Theologiae et Summam Contra Gentiles, in Vol. XVI of the Leonine edition. Reprinted with some omissions in *Editio Leonina Manualis.* Rome, 1948.

Schütz, Ludwig, *Thomas-Lexikon.* Paderborn, 1895. Reprinted New York, 1949. The most useful concordance.

Studies

Anderson, J. F., *An Introduction to the Metaphysics of St. Thomas Aquinas.* Chicago, 1953. Collection of basic texts with clear explanations; useful for the theory of analogy.

Bourke, V. J., *Aquinas' Search for Wisdom.* Milwaukee, 1965. A factual biography excluding pious legends and situating Aquinas's thought in the context of his life.

Callahan, Leonard, *A Theory of Esthetic According to St. Thomas.* Washington, 1927. Rethinks the original theory but also interprets the fragmentary maxims of Aquinas on beauty and art.

Chenu, M. D., *Towards Understanding Saint Thomas.* Chicago, 1964. Masterful introduction to the advanced study of the works of Thomas Aquinas.

Copleston, F. C., *Aquinas.* London, 1955. This is a well-written exposition of the philosophy of Aquinas, with some effort to meet the criticisms of British analysts.

De Koninck, Charles, "Introduction à l'étude de l'âme." *Laval théologique et philosophique,* Vol. 3 (1947), 9–65. Reprinted in Stanislas Cantin, *Précis de psychologie thomiste.* Quebec, 1948. LXXXIII, 173.

Descoqs, Pedro, *Thomisme et scolastique.* Paris, 1927. Representative Suarezian criticism of the metaphysics of Aquinas; insists that there are other valid positions in philosophy.

Duns Scotus, John, *De Primo Principio,* translated and edited by Evan Roche. St. Bonaventure, N.Y., 1948. Important for fourteenth-century criticism by Duns Scotus of the general metaphysics and natural theology of Aquinas.

Fabro, Cornelio, *La nozione metafisica di partecipazione secondo S. Tommaso.* Milan, 1939; 2d ed., Turin, 1950. Outstanding study of the metaphysics of Thomism, stressing the Platonic elements.

Garrigou-Lagrange, Réginald, *Reality: A Synthesis of Thomistic Thought.* St. Louis, 1950. Adapted from a long article in the *Dictionnaire de théologie catholique,* this work represents a most conservative type of Thomism.

Geiger, L. B., *La Participation dans la philosophie de saint Thomas.* Paris, 1942. Excellent discussion of the Platonic themes in Aquinas's metaphysics; with Fabro and Geiger it has become clear that Thomism is not a "baptized" Aristotelianism.

Gilby, Thomas, *The Political Thought of Thomas Aquinas.* Chicago, 1958. Work of popularization which offers, however, a rather balanced view of the monarchic and democratic elements in Aquinas's ideas on government.

Gilson, Étienne, *The Christian Philosophy of St. Thomas Aquinas.* New York, 1956. With "Catalogue of St. Thomas's Works" by I. T. Eschmann. A highly esteemed exposition: the French original followed the order of the *Summa Contra Gentiles;* this English revision stresses the idea that Thomism is a Christian philosophy.

Grabmann, Martin, *Die Werke des hl. Thomas von Aquin,* 3d ed. Münster, 1949. The most complete study of the chronology and authenticity of the writings of Aquinas.

Henle, R. J., *Saint Thomas and Platonism.* The Hague, 1956. Good example of a careful textual study using the method of parallel passages taken in chronological sequence.

Jaffa, H. V., *Thomism and Aristotelianism. A Study of the Commentary by Thomas Aquinas on the Nicomachean Ethics.* Chicago, 1952. A sharp criticism of Aquinas as an interpreter of Aristotle's practical philosophy.

Klubertanz, G. P., *St. Thomas Aquinas on Analogy.* Chicago, 1960. Advanced and difficult study of all that Aquinas has written on metaphysical analogy; stresses the pluralism inherent in the theory; several types of analogy are at work.

Kluxen, Wolfgang, *Philosophische Ethik bei Thomas von Aquin.* Mainz, 1964. Important discussion of the relation between moral theology and ethics.

Maritain, Jacques, *Art and Scholasticism.* New York, 1930. An almost classic account of the aesthetic theory of Aquinas, with some adaptation to artistic problems in the twentieth century.

Maritain, Jacques, *The Angelic Doctor: The Life and Thought of St. Thomas Aquinas,* rev. ed. New York, 1958. Popular work stressing papal approval of Thomistic philosophy and the special status of Aquinas in Catholic educational programs.

Meyer, Hans, *The Philosophy of St. Thomas Aquinas.* St. Louis, 1944. In the guise of an exposition of Aquinas's thought, this is actually a trenchant critique of Thomism.

Oesterle, John A., *Ethics: Introduction to Moral Science.* Englewood Cliffs, N.J., 1957. Representative textbook emphasizing the autonomy and strictly philosophical character of Thomistic ethics.

Owens, Joseph, *An Elementary Christian Metaphysics.* Milwaukee, 1963. Advanced textbook in the tradition of the Christian philosophy interpretation of Aquinas.

Pieper, Josef, *Guide to Thomas Aquinas,* translated by Richard and Clara Winston. New York, 1962. A readable and elementary introduction by a noted German Thomist.

Rahner, Karl, *Geist im Welt. Zur Metaphysik der endliche Erkenntnis bei Thomas von Aquin.* Innsbruck and Leipzig, 1939. Outstanding German study of the theory of knowledge.

Ramírez, J. M., *De Auctoritate Doctrinae Sancti Thomae Aquinatis.* Salamanca, 1952. Representative of the well-informed and broadminded views of some Spanish Dominicans on the status of Thomism in Catholic philosophy.

Rommen, Heinrich, *The State in Catholic Thought.* St. Louis, 1945. Situates Thomistic political philosophy in the broader context of Catholic thinking as a whole.

Reith, Herman, *The Metaphysics of St. Thomas Aquinas.* Milwaukee, 1958. Standard exposition, not difficult to read. Includes 200 pages of quotations from many works of Aquinas.

Ryan, J. K., "St. Thomas and English Protestant Thinkers." *New Scholasticism,* Vol. 22, No. 1 (1948), 1–33; No. 2 (1948), 126–208. Excellent survey of the reactions to, and criticisms of, Aquinas in post-Reformation British thought.

Smith, Gerard, *Natural Theology: Metaphysics II.* New York, 1951. On Aquinas's philosophical approach to God; Ch. 16 discusses divine foreknowledge and human freedom.

Ude, Johannes, *Die Autorität des hl. Thomas von Aquin als Kirchenlehrer.* Salzburg, 1932. Basic study of the question "Must Catholics agree in philosophy and theology with Thomas Aquinas?" The answer is "No."

Walz, Angelus, *Saint Thomas d'Aquin,* French adaption by Paul Novarina. Louvain and Paris, 1962. One of the best biographies; this French printing has much more information than the English version, *Saint Thomas Aquinas,* translated by S. T. Bullough. Westminster, Md., 1951.

Wittmann, Michael, *Die Ethik des hl. Thomas von Aquin.* Munich, 1933. Good historical study of Thomistic ethics in relation to Aristotle, the Stoics, and the Fathers of the Church.

Works on Thomism

Bourke, V. J., *Thomistic Bibliography, 1920–1940.* St. Louis, 1945.

Bulletin thomiste (since 1921). Le Saulchoir, Belgium. (This Dominican study center moved after World War II to Étiolles, Soisy-sur-Seine, France.) Offers very complete listings and evaluations of works on all aspects of the life, writings, thought, and historical relations of Aquinas. The bulletin is numbered in three-year cycles but appears periodically in smaller fascicles. (For American readers there is a Canadian suboffice: Centre annexe du Bulletin thomiste, Institut d'Études Médiévales, 831 avenue Rockland, Montreal.)

Mandonnet, Pierre, and Destrez, Jean, *Bibliographie thomiste.* Le Saulchoir, Belgium, 1921; rev. ed., M. D. Chenu, ed., Paris, 1960.

Répertoire bibliographique. Annual supplement to *Revue philosophique de Louvain* (Belgium).

Wyser, Paul, *Thomas von Aquin* and *Der Thomismus,* fascicles 13–14 and 15–16 of *Bibliographische Einführungen in das Studium der Philosophie.* Fribourg, Switzerland, 1948 ff.

— VERNON J. BOURKE

TIME, BEING, AND BECOMING

The major debate in the philosophy of time, being, and becoming is between defenders of the tenseless theory of time and defenders of the tensed theory of time. The tenseless theory implies that temporal features of events consist only of relations of simultaneity, earlier, and later and that all events are ontologically equal, regardless of when they occur. The tensed theory implies that the basic temporal concepts are of the future, present, and past and that present events have a superior ontological status to past or future events; present events exist, but past events no longer exist, and future events do not yet exist. For most of the twentieth century the debate between tenseless theorists and tensed theorists concerned whether tensed sentences (types or tokens) can be translated by tenseless sentences. If a noon, July 1, 1994, utterance of "the event E is no longer present" is translated by "the event E is earlier than noon, July 1, 1994," this would show that the tensed utterance conveys the same temporal information as the tenseless sentence—namely, that the event E is earlier than noon, July 1, 1994, and is equally as real as the events on noon, July 1, 1994. If the tensed utterance cannot be translated, then it arguably conveys a different sort of temporal information—namely, that event E no longer has presentness or no longer "exists" in the present tensed sense.

The major development in the 1980s and 1990s is the development of the so-called new tenseless theory of time and responses to this theory by defenders of the

tensed theory. The new tenseless theory is that tensed sentences cannot be translated by tenseless sentences but that it is nonetheless true that tensed sentences convey only the temporal information conveyed by tenseless sentences. The new theory implies that tensed sentences have only tenseless truth conditions. For example, it may be argued that a noon, July 1, 1994, utterance of "the event E is no longer present" is true if and only if the event E occurs earlier than noon, July 1, 1994. Since facts involving the relations of earlier, later, and simultaneous are both necessary and sufficient to make tensed sentences true, there is no need to suppose that tensed sentences commit us to facts about what is present, past, or future.

The major development in the 1980s and 1990s was the development of the so-called new tenseless theory of time and responses to this theory by defenders of the tensed theory.

The new tenseless theory of time appears to be correct insofar as it implies that tensed sentences cannot be translated by tenseless ones; however, its further implication that tensed sentences have only tenseless truth conditions may be challenged. It appears to be false, for example, that "Jane is running" as uttered at noon, July 1, 1994, is true if and only if Jane runs at noon, July 1, 1994. There are possible worlds in which the mentioned sentence-utterance, call it U, is true and yet it is false that Jane is running at noon, July 1, 1994. Suppose that times are sets of simultaneous events and that "noon, July 1, 1994" refers to the set of simultaneous events that is actually 1,993 years, six months and twelve hours after the conventionally assigned birthdate of Jesus. There is a possible world exactly similar to the actual world except for the fact that the utterance U belongs to a different set of simultaneous events, a set that includes every event included in noon, July 1, 1994 (which means it includes Jane's running), except for some minor difference; say, the set does not include the decision actually made by David to have lunch. Since U occurs simultaneously with Jane's running in this world, U is true; nonetheless, it does not occur at noon, July 1, 1994. Thus, a necessary condition of the truth of the utterance of "Jane is running" is not that it occur at noon, July 1, 1994.

How might a defender of the new tenseless theory respond to this argument? The defender might modify the tenseless theory so that it implies that the tenseless truth conditions are world indexed. It would imply that "Jane is running" as uttered at noon, July 1, 1994, in world W is true if and only if Jane runs at noon, July 1, 1994, in world W. Since the possible world is mentioned in the truth-condition sentence, the objection based on what occurs in a different possible world is avoided. However, this response does not seem satisfactory, since by mentioning the world the truth-condition sentence is no longer relevant to the meaning or semantic content of the utterance U. The reason for this is that the criterion for the truth of a world-indexed truth-condition sentence implies that any sentence with the same truth value as U in world W may be placed after the biconditional and we will have a true truth-condition sentence. For example, if Jane runs at the mentioned time and snow is white in world W, then "Jane is running" as uttered at noon, July 1, 1994, in world W is true if and only if snow is white in world W. But this sentence fails to give us any idea about the meaning of "Jane is running" and thus cannot be said to capture the temporal ontology implied by the sentence-utterance. In order for a truth-condition sentence to explain the meaning of a sentence-utterance, it must state the necessary and sufficient conditions of the utterance's truth in each world in which the utterance occurs, not simply in one world.

The above-mentioned problems with the new tenseless theory of time may be avoided by tenseless theorists if they reject the idea that the truth conditions of tensed sentence-utterances involve dates; they may argue instead that the truth conditions are facts about the temporal relation of the event described by the utterance to the utterance itself. But this version of the new theory faces a distinct set of problems. Suppose there are two simultaneous utterances U and S of the sentence type "Jane is running." These two utterances, or what is stated by these two utterances, are logically equivalent. But they are not logically equivalent if their truth conditions are facts about the temporal relation of the event reported by U and S. The tenseless truth condition of U would be "U occurs simultaneously with Jane's running," and the truth condition of S would be "S occurs simultaneously with Jane's running," but "U occurs simultaneously with Jane's running" neither entails nor is entailed by "S occurs simultaneously with Jane's running." The utterance U could have occurred even if S did not occur, and vice versa. Thus, this version of the new tenseless theory also does not appear to succeed.

If the new tenseless theory of time cannot succeed in supplying the requisite truth conditions, then it is reasonable to conclude that tensed utterances have tensed truth conditions. But different proponents of the tensed theory offer different accounts of the nature of these

truth conditions. Some argue the conditions require that events possess transient properties of futurity, presentness, or pastness, but other defenders of the tensed theory argue that there are logical difficulties in the way of admitting such properties and claim that tenses do not commit us to any sort of properties, relations, or individuals. One problem with the latter version of the tensed theory is that its proponents have not explained what sort of item the tenses refer to or ascribe. If the "is" in "Jane is running" does not ascribe a property or relation and does not refer to an individual, then what is the ontological category of the item to which the "is" has a semantic relation?

The version of the tensed theory that implies that tenses ascribe properties of futurity, presentness, or pastness has an answer to this question, but it implies an infinite regress of property ascriptions. For example, if "Jane is running" is true just in case Jane's running exemplifies presentness, then the "exemplifies" must be present tensed, implying that the exemplification of presentness by Jane's running itself exemplifies presentness. But since the last occurrence of "exemplifies" is also present tensed, it implies a further exemplification of presentness, and so on infinitely. This regress is benign, but the fact nonetheless remains that this version of the tensed theory commits us to a complicated ontology. It is safe to say that no consensus has been reached as to the correct version of the tensed theory or whether it is better justified than the tenseless theory.

BIBLIOGRAPHY

Le Poidevin, R. *Change, Cause, and Contradiction: A Defense of the Tenseless Theory of Time.* Cambridge, 1992.

Mellor, D. H. *Real Time.* Cambridge, 1981.

Oaklander, L. N. *Temporal Relations and Temporal Becoming.* Lanham, MD, 1984.

Oaklander, L. N., and Q. Smith, eds. *The New Theory of Time.* New Haven, 1994. This book contains essays by M. Beer, B. Garrett, H. S. Hestevold, D. Kaplan, D. Kiernan-Lewis, M. MacBeath, D. H. Mellor, L. N. Oaklander, G. Schlesinger, Q. Smith, C. Williams, and D. Zeilicovici.

Priest, G. "Tense, *Tense,* and TENSE," *Analysis,* Vol. 46 (1987), 184–87.

Smart, J. J. C. "Time and Becoming," in P. van Inwagen, ed., *Time and Cause* (Boston, 1981).

Smith, Q. *Language and Time.* New York, 1993.

Smith, Q., and L. N. Oaklander. *Time, Change, and Freedom.* New York, 1995.

Sosa, E. "The Status of Becoming: What Is Happening Now," *Journal of Philosophy,* Vol. 77 (1979), 26–42.

– QUENTIN SMITH

TIME, DIRECTION OF

Our experience of the temporality of things seems to be an experience of a radically asymmetric structure of the world. We have an access to knowledge of past events that is not given us to events in the future. That is, we have records and memories of past events but not of future events. Our concerns with the past (regret, for example) are radically unlike our concerns for the future (anxious anticipation, for example). Intuitively we take it that the direction of causation or determination among events is always from past to future. Some also have metaphysical intuitions about the asymmetry. The past, they say, is "fixed" and has "determinate reality," whereas the future remains ontologically merely a realm of open possibilities.

One might take these asymmetric features of time as irreducible primitives and our awareness of them as also immune to further analysis or understanding. Or one might argue for some basic asymmetric metaphysical structure of time as grounding all of the asymmetries noted above. The idea of "branching" models, familiar from tense logics, is sometimes proposed as our clue to this fundamental structure of time.

Alternatively, one could seek some naturalistic account of the asymmetries, holding them to be founded on a pervasive asymmetry in time of physical processes as characterized by fundamental physics. Such an account, if successful, would go some way to resolving the mystery of the direction of time. But carrying out this reductivist program is not a simple task.

Several fundamental asymmetries occur in the world described by physics. Alleged lawlike time asymmetries present in weak interactions do not seem suitable for grounding the intuitive time asymmetries. More promising are the asymmetries of entropy increase in thermodynamics and that asymmetry of radiation in which we encounter outbound but not inbound spherically coherent patterns of wave radiation. No agreed-upon explanatory account for these asymmetries yet exists, although the mainstream of physical thought seeks an origin for them in deep facts about the cosmological structure of the universe.

How are these physical asymmetries of systems in time supposed to ground our intuitive temporal asymmetries? One can easily be misled by the familiar example, that of our using entropic facts to determine if the film of an entropy-changing process is being run in the correct time order, into thinking that the proposal is that we somehow determine the order in time of events in our experience by consulting entropic facts about the events, a claim that is surely false. But it is not such an epistemically motivated claim that the naturalist is making.

Rather, the claim is that the facts about the physical asymmetries fully account, in an explanatory way, for all of our intuitive asymmetries, such as having mem-

The idea of "branching" models, familiar from tense logics, is sometimes proposed as our clue to this fundamental structure of time. (Corbis/Bettmann)

ories or records of the past and not the future or taking causation to be future directed. The analogy is often drawn to our use of the facts about gravity as a force to explain everything there is to explain about our intuitions about up and down spatial directions. Just as we now realize that "down" is just the local direction of the gravitational force, as it is said, we should also realize that "future" is just the local direction of time in which entropy is increasing for isolated systems.

It should be noted that it is not enough for such an account that there be a lawlike or quasi-lawlike correlation of the physical process with the intuitive temporal direction. The fact that some weak interaction processes are lawlike asymmetric with regard to left–right asymmetry does not mean that our intuitive distinction between left- and right-handed objects is somehow explanatorily grounded on the asymmetry of the weak interaction processes. For the naturalistic program to be plausible one would need a set of explanations that invoked the physical asymmetry and that accounted for the asymmetries of records, memories, and causation and that even explained the origin of our direct awareness of the time order of events in our experience, much as gravity's workings on the inner ear accounts for our ability to determine noninferentially which direction is downward at our location.

Our concerns with the past (regret, for example)

are radically unlike our concerns for the future

(anxious anticipation, for example).

One important proposal for carrying out the naturalistic program has its origin with H. Reichenbach. The basic structure of the program is to argue that records of the past are systems in the world with surprisingly low "macroentropy" given their environments (such as the famous footprint on the beach whose sand grains have an order not possessed by the surrounding randomly distributed grains). The presence of this low macroentropy must, it is argued, be accounted for by means of a past interaction of the system with some outside system (such as the foot that pressed the footprint into the otherwise smooth beach). Such systems then serve as records of their past interactions. The fact that the explaining interactions are all in the same time direction, the direction we call the past, is accounted for by the physical asymmetry of entropic processes. Other asymmetries are then grounded on the asymmetries of records. This imaginative proposal has been subjected to skeptical criticism that notes, for example, high macroentropy records (surprisingly disordered states) and the difficulties encountered in deriving the macroentropy asymmetry from the underlying physics of microentropy asymmetry.

Another imaginative proposal is that of D. Lewis. He analyzes causation in terms of counterfactual conditionals and outlines our intuitive grounds for stipulating when such conditionals are true. Considerations of the multiply correlated but physically spread-out consequences of a single local cause (such as occurs in wave spreading) leads, he claims, to a temporal asymmetry of our evaluation of the truth of counterfactual conditionals in cases such as this and hence to a temporal asymmetry in our notion of the causal relation.

Even were the naturalistic program successfully carried out, the issue of how to deal with our immediately sensed time of direct experience in a world of physically asymmetric time remains, as A. Eddington emphasized, problematic.

[See also Causation; Conditionals; Philosophy of Physics; Philosophy of Science.]

BIBLIOGRAPHY

Boltzmann, L. "On Zermelo's Paper 'On the Mechanical Explanation of Irreversible Processes,' " in S. Brush, ed., *Kinetic Theory*, Vol. 2, *Irreversible Processes* (Oxford, 1966).
Davies, P. *The Physics of Time Asymmetry.* Berkeley, 1974.
Earman, J. "An Attempt to Add a Little Direction to 'The Problem of the Direction of Time,' " *Philosophy of Science,* Vol. 41 (1974), 15–47.
Eddington, A. *The Nature of the Physical World.* Cambridge, 1929.
Grünbaum, A. "The Anisotropy of Time," in *Philosophical Problems of Space and Time,* 2d ed. (Dordrecht, 1973).
Horwich, P. *Asymmetries in Time.* Cambridge, MA, 1987.
Lewis, D. "Counterfactual Dependence and Time's Arrow," in *Philosophical Papers,* Vol. 2 (Oxford, 1986).
Mehlberg, H. *Time, Causality, and Quantum Theory.* Dordrecht, 1980.
Reichenbach, H. *The Direction of Time.* Berkeley, 1956.
Sklar, L. "The Direction of Time," in *Physics and Chance* (Cambridge, 1993).
———. "Up and Down, Left and Right, Past and Future," in *Philosophy and Spacetime Physics* (Berkeley, 1985).

– LAWRENCE SKLAR

TRUTH

All mainstream theories of truth—correspondence, coherence, pragmatist—presuppose that 'truth' is the name of a substantive, explanatorily significant property. The nature of truth may be difficult to explain, but that truth has a nature is taken for granted. The thought seems to be that, just as a scientist might want to explain what it is that makes some substances acidic, so a philosopher will want to explain what makes true sentences (propositions, beliefs, etc.) true. However, there are alternative theories, now generally called deflationary, that challenge this preconception. For proponents of such views, there is no analogy between 'true' and terms such as 'acidic'. The predicate 'true' is an expressive convenience, not the name of a property requiring deep analysis.

Two factors incline philosophers toward deflationism: the existence of what seem to be insuperable objections to all traditional theories of truth and the thought that the behavior and significance of 'true' can be quite satisfactorily accounted for on a rather minimal basis. Indeed, because deflationary theories are so minimalist, it might be better to speak of deflationary views or approaches rather than theories.

An early version of such an approach to truth is Ramsey's redundancy theory, according to which "It is true that Caesar was murdered" means no more than that Caesar was murdered. Any difference is entirely "stylistic": for example, we may use "It is true that" to speak more emphatically. Because it stresses the use of 'true' in performing such special speech acts, this approach is sometimes also called the performative theory.

More recent views, such as Quine's disquotational theory, do not claim "that p" and "It is true that p" are synonymous. Rather, what matters about 'true' is given by certain logical equivalences. Thus, "All that glisters is not gold" is true if and only if all that glisters is not gold; "France is hexagonal" is true if and only if France is hexagonal; and so on. Appending "is true" to a quoted sentence is just like canceling the quotation marks ("disquotation"). Thus, 'true' offers a way of replacing talk about the world with logically equivalent talk about words. However, a move to the level of talk about words ("semantic ascent") gives us new things to generalize over (i.e., linguistic objects, sentences), thereby enabling us to express agreement and disagreement with sentences that we cannot specify—for example, because we do not know exactly what they are ("What the President said is true") or because there are too many of them ("Every sentence of the form 'P or not P' is true"). Accordingly, 'true' is an indispensable logical device.

The disquotational theory treats 'true' as a predicate of sentences. A similar account of the meaning and utility of the truth predicate can be given, mutatis mutandis, if we prefer to think of 'true' as predicated of propositions. The axioms of such a theory will be: the proposition "All that glisters is not gold" is true if and only if all that glisters is not gold, and so forth. Horwich's minimal theory takes this form.

Notice that while, on the redundancy/performative theory, to think of truth as any sort of property is, in Ramsey's words, just "linguistic muddle," on the disquotational and minimal theories we can see truth as a property, a complete theory of which is given by the appropriate equivalences. Of course, we cannot write this "theory" down, since it will have infinitely many axioms. But since these axioms share a common structure, we can indicate more or less what they are. (Only more or less because, without some restrictions on admissible substitutions, a schema like " 'p' is true if and only if p" will generate semantic paradoxes.)

Tarski's semantic theory, in its original form, can also be considered deflationary. For although Tarski defines "true-in-L" (where L is a particular formalized language) in terms of a generalized notion of reference (again for L), which he calls "satisfaction," he defines the relation of "satisfies" in a highly deflationary manner. However, though strongly influenced by Tarski's work, Davidson's view of truth is *not* deflationary. Davidson can sound like a deflationist, in that he denies the need for an analysis of truth and so rejects all traditional theories. But he insists that truth plays an indispensable explanatory role in the theory of meaning. He therefore concludes that we must accept the concept of truth as a primitive.

There are many objections to deflationism. Some, mostly rather technical, concern whether a deflationary account can even be given an adequate formulation. For example, disquotational truth, as described above, does not immediately apply to sentences involving indexical expressions ("I," "here," etc.) or to sentences of foreign languages. This latter problem is particularly significant, since the natural response is to expand the disquotation schema, allowing us to substitute on the right-hand side proper translations of foreign sentences quoted on the left: thus, "La France a huit côtés" is true if and only if France is octagonal. The question then arises as to whether we can explain "proper translation" without invoking a prior understanding of truth. A related problem arises for the minimal theory in connection with explaining the identity conditions for propositions.

" 'What is truth?' said jesting Pilate

and would not stay for an answer."

If deflationists are to be believed,

he did not miss much.

However, perhaps the deepest source of skepticism with respect to deflationism is sheer incredulity in the face of its claim that truth is not a theoretically significant concept. Many (perhaps most) philosophers see truth as playing a crucial explanatory role in metaphysics, epistemology, philosophy of language, or even psychology. Deflationists have no master argument to prove them wrong. All they can do is to examine each purported explanatory use of truth and try to argue either that the explanation in question does not require a substantive notion of truth, that there is really nothing to explain, or that there is an alternative explanation that does not invoke truth at all.

" 'What is truth?' said jesting Pilate and would not stay for an answer." If deflationists are to be believed, he did not miss much.

[See also Davidson, Donald; Epistemology; Metaphysics; Philosophy of Language; Propositions; Quine, Willard Van Orman.]

BIBLIOGRAPHY

Davidson, D. "The Structure and Content of Truth," *Journal of Philosophy,* Vol. 87 (1990), 280–328.
Field, H. "The Deflationary Conception of Truth," in C. Wright and G. McDonald, eds., *Fact, Science, and Morality* (New York, 1987).
Horwich, P. *Truth.* Oxford, 1990.
Leeds, S. "Theories of Reference and Truth," *Erkenntnis,* Vol. 13 (1978), 111–29.

Putnam, H. "On Truth," in L. Cauman et al., eds., *How Many Questions?* (Indianapolis, 1983).

Quine, W. V. O. *Pursuit of Truth.* Cambridge, MA, 1990.

Ramsey, F. "Facts and Propositions," *Proceedings of the Aristotelian Society,* supp. vol. 7 (1927), 153–70; repr. in D. H. Mellor, ed., *F. P. Ramsey, Philosophical Papers* (Cambridge, 1990).

Soames, S. "What Is a Theory of Truth?" *Journal of Philosophy,* Vol. 81 (1984), 411–29.

Strawson, P. F. "Truth," *Proceedings of the Aristotelian Society,* supp. vol. 24 (1950), 125–26.

Tarski, A. "The Semantic Conception of Truth," *Philosophy and Phenomenological Research,* Vol. 4 (1944), 341–75.

Williams, M. "Do We (Epistemologists) Need a Theory of Truth?" *Philosophical Topics,* Vol. 14 (1986), 223–42.

Wright, C. *Truth and Objectivity.* Cambridge, MA, 1992.

– MICHAEL WILLIAMS

TRUTHLIKENESS

Truth is the aim of inquiry. Despite this, progress in an inquiry does not always consist in supplanting falsehoods with truths. The history of science is replete with cases of falsehoods supplanting other falsehoods. If such transitions are to constitute epistemic progress, then it must be possible for one falsehood better to realize the aim of inquiry—be more truthlike, be closer to the truth, or have more verisimilitude—than another. The notion of truthlikeness is thus fundamental for any theory of knowledge that endeavors to take our epistemic limitations seriously without embracing epistemic pessimism.

Given that truthlikeness is not only a much-needed notion but rich and interesting, it is surprising that it has attracted less attention than the simpler notion of truth. The explanation is twofold. First, if knowledge requires truth, then falsehoods cannot constitute knowledge. The high value of knowledge has obscured other epistemic values such as the comparative value of acquiring more truthlike theories. Second, if knowledge requires justification, then the notion of probability often takes center stage. There has been a long and deep confusion between the notions of subjective probability (seemingly true) and the notion of truthlikeness (similarity to the truth; Popper, 1972). This, together with the high degree of development of the theory of probability, obscured the necessity for a theory of truthlikeness.

Sir Karl Popper was the first to notice the importance of the notion (1972, chap. 10 and Addenda). Popper was long a lonely advocate of both scientific realism and fallibilism: that, although science aims at the truth, most theories have turned out to be false and current theories are also likely to be false. This seems a bleak vision indeed and fails to do justice to the evident progress in science. Popper realized that the picture would be less bleak if a succession of false (and falsified) theories could nevertheless constitute steady progress toward the truth. Further, even if actually refuted by some of the data, the general observational accuracy of a false theory might be good evidence for the theory's approximate truth, or high degree of truthlikeness. That our theories, even if not true, are close to the truth, may be the best explanation available for the accuracy of their observable consequences (Boyd, 1983; Putnam, 1978, chap. 2).

Note that truthlikeness is no more an epistemic notion than is truth. How truthlike a theory is depends only on the theory's content and the world, not on our knowledge. The problem of our epistemic access to the truthlikeness of theories is quite different from the logically prior problem of what truthlikeness consists in.

Popper proposed a bold and simple account of truthlikeness: that theory B is more truthlike than theory A if B entails all the truths that A entails, A entails all the falsehoods that B entails, and either B entails at least one more truth than A or A entails at least one more falsehood than B (Popper, 1972).

This simple idea undoubtedly has virtues. Let the *Truth* be that theory that entails all and only truths (relative to some subject matter). On Popper's account the Truth is more truthlike than any other theory, and that is as it should be. The aim of an inquiry is not just some truth or other. Rather, it is the truth, the whole truth, and nothing but the truth about some matter— in short, the Truth—and the Truth realizes that aim better than any other theory. The account also clearly separates truthlikeness and probability. The Truth generally has a very low degree of (subjective) probability, but it definitely has maximal truthlikeness. Furthermore, the account yields an interesting ranking of truths—the more a truth entails, the closer it is to the Truth.

Popper's account also has some defects. For example, it does not permit any falsehood to be closer to the Truth than any truth. (Compare Newton's theory of motion with denial of Aristotle's theory.) But its most serious defect is that it precludes any false theory being more truthlike than any other (Miller, 1974; Tichý, 1974). The flaw is simply demonstrated. Suppose theory A entails a falsehood, say f, and we attempt to improve on A by adding a new truth, say t. Then the extended theory entails both t and f and hence entails their conjunction: $t \& f$. But $t \& f$ is a falsehood not entailed by A. Similarly, suppose A is false and we attempt to improve it by removing one of its falsehoods, say f. Let g be any falsehood entailed by the reduced theory B. Then $g \supset f$ is a truth entailed by A but not B. (If B entailed both g and $g \supset f$, it would entail f.) So truths cannot be added without adding falsehoods, nor falsehoods subtracted without subtracting truths.

Maybe this lack of commensurability could be overcome by switching to quantitative measures of true and false logical content. Indeed, Popper proposed such accounts, but the problem they face is characteristic of the content approach, the central idea of which is that truthlikeness is a simple function of two factors—truth value and logical content/strength (Kuipers, 1982; Miller, 1978). If truthlikeness were such a function, then among false theories truthlikeness would vary with logical strength alone. There are only two well-behaved options here: truthlikeness either increases monotonically with logical strength, or else it decreases. But strengthening a false theory does not itself guarantee either an increase or a decrease in truthlikeness. If it is hot, rainy, and windy (h&r&w), then both of the following are logical strengthenings of the false claim that it is cold (~h): it is cold, rainy, and windy (~h&r&w); it is cold, dry, and still (~h&~r&~w). The former involves an increase, and the latter a decrease, in truthlikeness.

The history of science is replete with cases of falsehoods supplanting other falsehoods.

A quite different approach takes the likeness in truthlikeness seriously (Hilpinen, 1976: Niiniluoto, 1987; Oddie, 1981; Tichý, 1974, 1976). An inquiry involves a collection of possibilities, or possible worlds, one of which is actual. Each theory selects a range of possibilities from this collection—that theory's candidates for actuality. A proposition is true if it includes the actual world in its range. Each complete proposition includes just one such candidate. The Truth, the target of the inquiry, is the complete true proposition—that proposition that selects the actual world alone. If worlds vary in their degree of likeness to each other, then a complete proposition is the more truthlike the more like actuality is the world it selects. This is a promising start, but we need to extend it to incomplete propositions. The worlds in the range of an incomplete proposition typically vary in their degree of likeness to actuality, and the degree of truthlikeness of the proposition should be some kind of function thereof: average likeness is a simple suggestion that yields intuitively pleasing results. (For a survey, see Niiniluoto, 1987, chap. 6.) The framework can also be utilized in the analysis of related notions such as approximate truth or closeness to being true (Hilpinen, 1976; Weston, 1992).

There are two related problems with this program. The first concerns the measure of likeness between worlds. It would be a pity if this simply had to be postulated. The second concerns the size and complexity of worlds and the number of worlds that propositions typically select. Fortunately, there is available a handy logical tool for cutting the complexity down to a finite, manageable size (Niiniluoto, 1977; Tichý, 1974, 1976). We can work with kinds of worlds rather than whole words. The kinds at issue are specified by the constituents of first-order logic (Hintikka, 1965), a special case of which are the maximal conjunctions of propositional logic (like h&r&w, ~h&r&w, ~h&~r&~w). Constituents have two nice features. First, each depicts in its surface structure the underlying structure of a kind of world. And, second, like the propositional constituents, they are highly regular in their surface structure, enabling degree of likeness between constituents to be extracted. (The world in which it is cold, rainy, and windy [~h&r&w] is more like the world in which it is hot, rainy, and windy [h&r&w] than it is like the world in which it is cold, dry, and still [~h&~r&~w]. In the propositional case, just add up the surface differences.) Since every statement is logically equivalent to a disjunction of constituents, we have here the elements of a quite general account of truthlikeness, one that can be extended well beyond standard first-order logic (Oddie, 1986, chap. 5).

Not just any features count in a judgment of overall likeness. Such judgments clearly presuppose a class of respects of comparison. The possibilities specified by h&r&w and ~h&r&w differ in one weather respect and agree on two, whereas those specified by h&r&w and ~h&~r&~w differ in all three. But now consider the following two states (where ≡ is the material biconditional): hot≡rainy, and hot≡windy. The possibility specified by h&r&w can equally be specified by h&(h≡r)&(h≡w); ~h&r&w by ~h&~(h≡r)&~(h≡w); and ~h&~r&~w by ~h&(h≡r)&(h≡w). Counting differences in terms of these new features does not line up with our intuitive judgments of likeness. Unless there is some objective reason for counting the hot-rainy-windy respects rather than the hot-(hot≡rainy)-(hot≡windy) respects, truthlikeness (unlike truth) seems robbed of objectivity.

This is the main objection to the likeness program (Miller, 1974). If sound, however, it would reach far indeed, for perfectly analogous arguments would establish a similar shortcoming in a host of important notions—similarity in general, structure, confirmation, disconfirmation, fit of theory to data, accuracy, and change (Oddie, 1986, chap. 6). The advocate of the objectivity of such notions simply has to grasp the nettle and maintain that some properties, relations, and magnitudes are more basic or fundamental than others. Realists, of course, should not find the sting too sharp to bear.

[See also Aristotle; Confirmation Theory; Philosophy of Science; Propositions; Putnam, Hilary; Realism; Truth.]

BIBLIOGRAPHY

Boyd, R. "On the Current Status of the Issue of Scientific Realism," *Erkenntniss,* Vol. 19 (1983), 45–90.

Hilpinen, R. "Approximate Truth and Truthlikeness," in M. Przelecki, K. Szaniawski, and R. Wojcicki, eds., *Formal Methods in the Methodology of the Empirical Sciences* (Dordrecht, 1976).

Hintikka, J. "Distributive Normal Forms in the Calculus of Predicates," in J. N. Crossley and M. A. Dummett, eds., *Formal Systems and Recursive Functions* (Amsterdam, 1965).

Kuipers, T. A. F. "Approaching Descriptive and Theoretical Truth," *Erkenntnis,* Vol. 18 (1982), 343–87.

———, ed. *What Is Closer-to-the-Truth?* Amsterdam, 1987.

Miller, D. "Popper's Qualitative Theory of Verisimilitude," *British Journal for the Philosophy of Science,* Vol. 25 (1974), 166–77.

———. "Distance from the Truth as a True Distance," in J. Hintikka, I. Niiniluoto, and E. Saarinen, eds., *Essays in Mathematical and Philosophical Logic* (Dordrecht, 1978).

Niiniluoto, I. "On the Truthlikeness of Generalizations," in R. E. Butts and J. Hintikka, eds., *Basic Problems in Methodology and Linguistics* (Dordrecht, 1977).

———. *Truthlikeness.* Dordrecht, 1987.

Oddie, G. "Verisimilitude Reviewed," *British Journal for the Philosophy of Science,* Vol. 32 (1981), 237–65.

———. *Likeness to Truth.* Dordrecht, 1986.

Popper, K. R. *Conjectures and Refutations,* 4th ed. London, 1972.

Putnam, H. *Meaning and the Moral Sciences.* London, 1978.

Tichý, P. "On Popper's Definitions of Verisimilitude," *British Journal for the Philosophy of Science,* Vol. 25 (1974), 155–60.

———. "Verisimilitude Redefined," *British Journal for the Philosophy of Science,* Vol. 27 (1976), 25–42.

Weston, T. "Approximate Truth and Scientific Realism," *Philosophy of Science,* Vol. 59 (1992), 53–74.

– GRAHAM ODDIE

V

VAGUENESS

A term is vague if, and only if, capable of having borderline cases. All borderline cases are inquiry resistant. Bill Clinton is a borderline case of 'chubby' because no amount of conceptual or empirical investigation can settle the question of whether Clinton is chubby. This is not vagueness in the sense of being underspecific. If the president's spokesman states that Clinton weighs between 100 and 400 pounds, reporters will complain that the assertion is too *obvious* to be informative—not that the matter is indeterminate.

Typically, borderline cases lie between clear negative cases and clear positives. Moreover, the transition from clear to borderline cases will itself be unclear. If a thousand men queue in order of weight, there is no definite point at which the definitely non-chubby end and the borderline chubby begin. This higher order vagueness ascends to higher levels: there is no definite point at which the definitely definite cases end and the indefinitely definite ones begin, and so on for unlimited iterations of 'definite'.

Vagueness is responsible for Eubulides' 2,400-year-old sorites paradox. This conceptual slippery-slope argument can be compactly formulated with the help of mathematical induction:

> Base step: A collection of one million grains of sand is a heap.
> Induction step: If a collection of n grains of sand is a heap, then so is a collection of $n - 1$ grains.
> Conclusion: One grain of sand is a heap.

Long dismissed as a sophism, the sorites gained respect in the twentieth century. Within the last twenty years, it has acquired a stature comparable to Eubulides' other underestimated paradox, the liar.

Eubulides may have intended the sorites to support Parmenides' conclusion that all is one. For one solution is to deny the base step on the grounds that there really are no heaps. Since a sorites paradox can be formulated for any vague predicate for ordinary things ('cloud', 'chair', 'person'), the solution only generalizes by a rejection of common sense. In any case, this radical position has been championed by a few contemporary metaphysicians. A less strident group hopes that the sorites will be rendered obsolete by science's tendency to replace vague predicates by precise ones.

C. S. Peirce was the first to propose that logic be revised to fit vagueness. Peirce developed a form of many-valued logic. 'Clinton is chubby' is assigned a degree of truth between 1 (full truth) and 0 (full falsehood), say 0.5. Truth values of compound statements are then calculated on the basis of rules. Disjunctions are assigned the same truth value as their highest disjunct. Conditionals count as fully true only when the antecedent has a truth value at least as high as the consequent. This undermines the induction step of the sorites. As the progression heads into the borderline zone, the consequent has a value a bit lower than the antecedent. Although a small departure from full truth is normally insignificant, the sorites accumulates marginal differences into a significant difference.

Typically, borderline cases lie between

clear negative cases and clear positives.

If a thousand men queue in order of weight,

there is no definite point at which

the definitely non-chubby end

and the borderline chubby begin.

Supervaluationists deny that borderline statements have any truth value at all. Words mean what we decide them to mean. Since there has been no practical need to decide every case, our words are only partially meaningful. We are free to fill in the gaps as we go along. If a statement would come out true regardless of how the gaps were filled, then we are entitled to deem the statement as true. This modest departure from truth-functionality lets the supervaluationists count 'Clinton is chubby or Clinton is not chubby' as true even though neither disjunct has a truth value. Indeed, all the tautologies of classical logic will be endorsed by this principle. All the contradictions will be likewise rejected. This suggests a solution to the sorites paradox. For every precisification of 'heap' makes the induction step come out false.

Other forms of deviant logic, such as intuitionism and relevance logic, have been applied to the sorites.

However, deviant logics have been criticized as an over-reaction by the epistemic theorists. Instead of changing the center of our web of belief, they urge revision of our more peripheral beliefs about language. In particular, the epistemicists say that the data can be accommodated by the conservative hypothesis that vagueness is just a special form of ignorance—'Clinton is chubby' has an *unknown* truth value. The induction step of the sorites is plain false; there is an n such that n grains of sand makes a heap but $n - 1$ does not. Although the epistemic view is committed to hidden thresholds for any finite sequence, it is compatible with the absence of thresholds for infinite sequences. 'Shortest tall man' could be as empty as 'smallest fraction'. Since the meaning of a term covers infinitely many possible instances, the epistemic view is not committed to *semantic* thresholds. Nevertheless, it is committed to the principle that an F can be arbitrarily close to a non-F.

Epistemicism is frequently characterized as the view that the world is precise. However, epistemicists side with those who believe that vagueness and precision are solely features of *representations*. Those who believe that there are vague objects view the vagueness of language as reflective of a deeper, metaphysical phenomenon.

[See also Intuitionism; Liar Paradox; Peirce, Charles Sanders; Philosophy of Language.]

BIBLIOGRAPHY

Evans, G. "Can There Be Vague Objects?" *Analysis*, Vol. 38 (1978), 208.

Fine, K. "Vagueness, Truth, and Logic," *Synthese*, Vol. 30 (1975), 265–30.

Sorensen, R. *Blindspots*. Oxford, 1988.

Wheeler, S. "Megarian Paradoxes as Eleactic Arguments," *American Philosophical Quarterly*, Vol. 20 (1983), 287–95.

Williamson, T. *Vagueness*. London, 1994.

— ROY A. SORENSON

VERIFIABILITY PRINCIPLE

The doctrines associated with the slogan that meaning is the mode of verification continued to develop in the last four decades of the twentieth century. While the exact formulation of the principle was itself controversial, the essential idea was to link semantic and epistemic concerns by letting the meaning of an expression be its role within an empirical epistemology. At the same time the fortunes of logical empiricism, the movement associated with verificationism, changed substantially as well. First, as philosophers who conspicuously did not identify themselves with logical empiricism moved to center stage, the movement as a separately identifiable phenomenon virtually ceased to exist. This did not dispose of verificationism, however, for often the later philosophers' views were strikingly similar to the logical empiricism that they supposedly replaced, just as the criticisms of logical empiricism were often pioneered by the logical empiricists themselves. The second major change in the fortunes of this view was the renewal of interest in the history of philosophy of science, especially in the histories of the logical empiricists themselves. Now freed from the myopia that comes from being part of the fray, philosophers were able to explore the roots of logical empiricism, what held it together as a movement, which of its doctrines were central or peripheral, and even which views look more plausible in hindsight than they did before their systematic interconnection could be appreciated.

One root of verificationism

lies in the increasing professionalization

of both the sciences and philosophy

around the turn of the century.

One root of verificationism lies in the increasing professionalization of both the sciences and philosophy around the turn of the century. The sciences tended to emphasize the importance of empirical investigation, to explore its scope and limits, and to deplore as metaphysical any claims not based on evidence. Correspondingly, many philosophers claimed for themselves a non-empirical source of knowledge concerning things higher or deeper than mere observation could reveal, that is, concerning metaphysics. Logical empiricism grew out of methodological discussions within science rather than philosophy, and many of its central proponents were trained in the sciences. True, logical empiricism made special accommodation for the a priori domains of mathematics and logic. But these were technical subjects of use within the sciences and for which there were increasingly well-developed modes of conflict resolution. Moreover, the way in which the accommodation was reached, namely through the logical analysis of language, especially the language of science, comported well with a basic empiricism and provided no comfort to traditional philosophy. A second root of verificationism lies in Russell's reaction to the paradox that bears his name (viz. a contradiction that arises when sets can contain themselves) and in Wittgenstein's further elaboration of a related idea. In order to avoid the paradox, Russell had restricted the grammar so that apparent assertions of sets containing themselves were no longer well formed. Similarly, Wittgenstein emphasized that some combinations of words were neither true nor false but just nonsensical; they were, he said, metaphysical.

This seemed to offer the ideal diagnosis of the sought-after distinction: scientifically respectable claims were either empirically meaningful in virtue of having some appropriate relation to the observations that would be the source of their justification, or else they were true in virtue of the language itself; traditional metaphysics, by contrast, was simply unintelligible. Phrased in this way, the verifiability principle leaves as a separate question the issue of what the appropriate relation to observation would be.

It has also become clearer what the logical status of the principle itself is. Initially, these philosophers could imagine that they were saying something about language in general or about the language of science. But as it became apparent that there were alternative languages to be considered, it became obvious that the principle could be put as a proposal for a language or as an analytic or empirical claim either about a particular language or about a range of languages. Perhaps the dominant form of the principle is as a proposal for a language to explicate the linguistic practices that are already largely in place in the sciences. As a proposal, it is not a claim, and hence neither true nor false, but not thereby unintelligible. If the proposal is adopted, the corresponding claim about the language that has those rules would be analytic. There would also be the empirical claim that we had adopted such a language and even empirical claims about that language if it were specified as, say, the language that is now used in contemporary physics.

So construed, many of the objections that were first made to the principle (and which continued to be made through the period in question) can be seen to be wrong-headed. The most persistent of these criticisms is that the principle renders itself an unintelligible claim. Whether construed as a proposal, as an analytic claim, or as an empirical one, this is just a (willful) misunderstanding. The same can be said for the criticism that it renders all philosophy meaningless. Equally misguided is the repeated objection that the principle cannot be right because we can understand a sentence without knowing whether it is true. Obviously, the principle in no way denies this truism.

Potentially more serious is the idea that all attempts to specify the principle have failed and are thus likely to continue to do so. Reinforcing this idea are papers by Hempel which, while they are not really histories, strike many readers as signed confessions of complicity in a series of disasters. In defense of the principle it must be said that, except for those immediately around Wittgenstein, complete verifiability was virtually never at issue. Even in the *Aufbau*, where the general question is raised many times, all but one formulation are much more liberal. Similarly, strict falsifiability was never pro-posed as a criterion of meaningfulness. Concerning the more fertile ground of confirmation and disconfirmation, the difficulties seem to have arisen because the formulations tried both to link semantic and epistemic concerns *and* to specify a complete theory of confirmation. This latter task is so difficult that we should not expect early success nor conclude from failure that the enterprise is misguided—any more than we give up physics simply because we still lack the final theory.

There were, of course, other sources of difficulty. Many attempts, such as Ayer's, tried to apply a criterion of meaningfulness at the level of whole sentences even though those sentences could contain meaningless parts. More successful in this regard was Carnap's "Methodological Character of Theoretical Concepts" (1956), which applied the criterion at the level of primitive terms. In a paper that was famous despite being unpublished for many years, David Kaplan provided two counterexamples to Carnap's criterion. These examples were widely regarded as decisive, but Creath showed that one of the examples missed its mark and the criterion could be patched in a natural way so as to avoid the other. Less easily dismissed is Rozeboom's criticism that Carnap's criterion ties meaningfulness to a particular theory when it should apply only to the language. Finally, Carnap's criterion, like many others, seems to presuppose that the theory/observation distinction can be drawn at the level of vocabulary. There came to be general agreement that this presupposition is mistaken and distorts any criterion based on it. In fairness, it must be admitted that some theory/observation distinction is essential to a healthy empiricism and that Carnap was from the very beginning fully aware of the limitations of formulating the distinction in this way. Finding a satisfactory way is still an unsolved problem.

W. V. O. Quine is often associated with the demise of logical empiricism, and his "Two Dogmas of Empiricism" is often thought to have rejected verificationism decisively. It would be more accurate to say that he rejected the idea that individual sentences could be separately confirmed, but he did not resist linking meaningfulness with confirmation holistically construed. Indeed, his demand that behavioral criteria be provided for analyticity to render it intelligible is exactly parallel to Carnap's demand for correspondence rules to render theoretical terms meaningful. Moreover, Quine's argument from the indeterminacy of translation to the unintelligibility of interlinguistic synonymy makes sense only if meaning and confirmation are somehow linked as in the verifiability principle.

So what then of this link between semantic and epistemic issues? At least there is much to be said for it. A theory of meaning should give accounts of meaningfulness (having a meaning), of synonymy (having the same meaning), and of understanding (knowing the meaning). The verifiability principle provides *a* way of doing these things not provided by simply identifying various entities as "the meanings" of expressions. Moreover, it provides *a* defense against wholesale skepticism by tying what we know to how we know. And finally, it provides *a* way of dealing with the so-called a priori by making those claims knowable in virtue of knowing the meanings of the expressions involved. No doubt there are others ways, perhaps even equally systematic ways, of accomplishing these ends, and no doubt these other paths should be investigated as well. But the basic idea behind the verifiability principle, namely that semantical and epistemic questions should be linked, is far from refuted, and its promise is far from exhausted.

[See also *Analyticity; Carnap, Rudolph; Epistemology; Language; Meaning; Philosophy; Philosophy of Science; Quine, Willard Van Orman; Russell, Bertrand Arthur William; Semantics; Skepticism; Wittgenstein, Ludwig Josef Johann.*]

BIBLIOGRAPHY

Ayer, A. J. *Language, Truth and Logic.* London, 1936.
———. "The Principle of Verifiability," *Mind,* Vol. 45 (1936), 199–203.
Carnap, R. "On the Character of Philosophic Problems," trans. W. M. Malisoff, *Philosophy of Science,* Vol. 1 (1934), 5–19.
———. "The Methodological Character of Philosophic Problems," in H. Feigl and M. Scriven, eds., *The Foundations of Science and the Concepts of Psychology and Psychoanalysis* (Minneapolis, 1956).
———. "On the Use of Hilbert's ∈-Operator in Scientific Theories," in Y. Bar-Hillel et al., eds., *Essays on the Foundations of Mathematics* (Jerusalem, 1961).
Creath, R. "On Kaplan on Carnap on Significance," *Philosophical Studies,* Vol. 30 (1976), 393–400.
———. "Was Carnap a Complete Verificationist in the *Aufbau?*" *PSA 1982,* Vol. 1, 384–93.
Glymour, C. *Theory and Evidence.* Princeton, NJ, 1980.
Hempel, C. G. "Problems and Changes in the Empiricist Criterion of Meaning," *Revue internationale de philosophie,* Vol. 4 (1950), 41–63.
Kaplan, D. "Significance and Analyticity: A Comment on Some Recent Proposals of Carnap," in J. Hintikka, ed., *Rudolf Carnap, Logical Empiricist: Materials and Perspectives* (Dordrecht, 1975).
Quine, W. V. O. "Two Dogmas of Empiricism," *Philosophical Review,* Vol. 60 (1951), 20–43.
———. *Word and Object.* Cambridge, MA, 1960.
Rozeboom, W. "A Note on Carnap's Meaning Criterion," *Philosophical Studies,* Vol. 11 (1960), 33–38.

– RICHARD CREATH

VIOLENCE

"Violence" is derived from the Latin *violentia,* "vehemence," which itself comes from *vis* ("force") + *latus* ("to carry") and means, literally, intense force. Violence shares its etymology with violate, "injure." "Violence" is used to refer to swift, extreme force (e.g., a violent storm) and to forceful injurious violation (e.g., rape, terrorism, war).

Violence has received some philosophical consideration since ancient times, but only in the twentieth century has the concept of violence itself been of particular concern to philosophers. Perhaps this is due to the exponential growth in the efficiency of and access to the means of violence in the modern era, to the unprecedented carnage the twentieth century has seen, or to the emergence of champions of nonviolence such as Mohandas Gandhi and Martin Luther King, Jr. Beyond clarifying the concept of violence, philosophical argument has turned to the moral and cultural justifiability of violence to achieve personal, social, or political ends.

Beyond clarifying the concept of violence, philosophical argument has turned to the moral and cultural justifiability of violence to achieve personal, social, or political ends.

Philosophers do not achieve consensus about the concept. Often, violence is taken to consist in overt physical manifestations of force. These may be on the scale of individuals (e.g., mugging) or of nations (e.g., war). In its primary use "violence" refers to swift, extreme physical force typically involving injury and violation to persons or property. There is increasing philosophical interest in a wider use of the term extending beyond the overtly physical to covert, psychological, and institutional violence. In this broader sense racism, sexism, economic exploitation, and ethnic and religious persecution all are possible examples of violence; that is, all involve constraints that injure and violate persons, even if not always physically.

Concerning the moral and political justifiability of using violence to achieve personal or social ends, again philosophers disagree. Some have taken violence to be inherently wrong (e.g., murder), while most have taken it to be an open question whether violence is normatively justifiable. Terrorism presents a special case. It is aimed at randomly selected innocent victims in an effort to create general fear, thus sharpening focus on the terrorists' cause or demands. This random targeting of innocents accounts for the near universal moral condemnation of terrorism, despite the dominant view that violence in general is not inherently wrong.

Arguments purporting to justify violence do not value it in itself but as a means to an end sufficiently good to outweigh the evils of the injury or violation involved. Often, such justifiable violence is seen as a necessary means to important ends; that is, the good achieved by justifiable violence could not be achieved without it. Arguments challenging the justifiability of violence tend to reject the claim to necessity, arguing for nonviolent means, or to deny the claim that violation and injury are outweighed by the ends achieved. Such arguments may be against violence per se or merely against particular violent acts.

Georges Sorel's *Reflections on Violence* (1908) is the earliest extensive philosophical work devoted to the subject. While Marx saw a role for violence in history, it was secondary to the contradictions inherent in collapsing systems. Sorel synthesizes Marx's proletarianism, Proudon's anarchism and Bergson's voluntarism, defending revolutionary trade unionism in its efforts to destroy the existing institutional order. Sorel advocates the violent general strike as the means of class warfare against the state and owners of industry.

In *On Violence* (1969) Hannah Arendt reviews the twentieth-century apologists for violence in an effort to explain the increasing advocacy of violence, especially by the new left. She questions Mao Zedong's "Power grows out of the barrel of a gun" and articulates the position that power and violence are opposites. For Arendt the extreme of violence is one against all while the extreme of power is all against one. Power is acting in concert with others while violence is acting with implements against others. Loss of power leads some to try to replace it with violence. But violence is the opposite of power and cannot stand in its stead. Arendt concedes that violence can be justified but insists that it is only in defense against clear, present, immediate threats to life where the violence does not exceed necessity and its good ends are likely and near.

Despite civil rights leader Martin Luther King Jr.'s message of nonviolence, riots broke out after followers learned of his assassination in 1968. (Corbis/Bettmann)

1067

Newton Garver's "What Violence Is" (1968) extends the discussion to covert, psychological, and institutional violence. According to Garver, "Any institution which systematically robs certain people of rightful options generally available to others does violence to those people" (p. 420). Despite his sympathy with nonviolence, Garver claims that it is not a viable social goal. Violence between nations may be reduced but not eliminated.

[See also Arendt, Hannah; Marx, Karl; Pacifism; Racism; Social and Political Philosophy.]

BIBLIOGRAPHY

Arendt, H. *On Violence.* New York, 1969.
Cotta, S. *Why Violence? A Philosophical Interpretation.* Gainesville, FL, 1985.
Garver, N. "What Violence Is," in R. Wasserstrom, ed., *Today's Moral Problems* (New York, 1975).
Gray, G. *On Understanding Violence Philosophically.* New York, 1970.
Holmes, R. L. "Violence and the Perspective of Morality," in *On War and Morality* (Princeton, NJ, 1989).
Schaffer, J. A., ed. *Violence: Award Winning Essays in the Council for Philosophical Studies Competition.* New York, 1971.
Sorel, G. *Reflections on Violence* [1908], translated by T. E. Hulme and J. Roth. Glencoe, IL, 1950.
Wolff, R. P. "On Violence," *Journal of Philosophy,* Vol. 66 (1969), 601–16.

— DUANE L. CADY

VIRTUE EPISTEMOLOGY

Virtue epistemology has a broad and a narrow sense. In the narrow sense the central claim of virtue epistemology is that, minor qualifications aside, knowledge is true belief resulting from an intellectual virtue. On this view the intellectual virtues are stable dispositions for arriving at true beliefs and avoiding false beliefs in a particular field. Put another way, the intellectual virtues are abilities of persons to reliably determine the truth. Plausible examples of such abilities are cognitive faculties such as vision and introspection, and cognitive habits such as careful evidence gathering. On this view knowledge is understood to be true belief arising from a reliable cognitive character.

In the broad sense virtue epistemology is the position that the intellectual virtues are the appropriate focus of epistemological inquiry, whether or not knowledge can be defined in terms of the virtues and whether or not the virtues can be understood as dispositions toward true belief. In this broader sense the intellectual virtues continue to be understood as character traits of cognitive agents, but it is left open whether such traits make the agent reliable or whether agent reliability is even

relevant for the most important kinds of epistemic evaluation.

Virtue and Knowledge

A major motivation for applying virtue epistemology to the analysis of knowledge is that the position explains a wide range of our pretheoretical intuitions about who knows and who does not. Thus suppose we think of a virtue as a faculty for believing the truth in a specific area and we think that knowledge derives from such abilities. This would explain why beliefs caused by clear vision, mathematical intuition, and reliable inductive reasoning typically have positive epistemic value and why beliefs caused by wishful thinking, superstition, and hasty generalization do not. The former beliefs are grounded in what are plausibly intellectual virtues, whereas the latter beliefs derive from intellectual vices.

Virtue epistemology also seems to provide the theoretical resources for answering important kinds of skepticism. By making important kinds of epistemic evaluation depend on instancing the intellectual virtues, the approach potentially explains how justification and knowledge are possible for beings like us, even if we cannot rule out skeptical possibilities involving evil demons or brains in vats. The main idea is that actually instancing the virtues is what gives rise to knowledge, even if we would not have the virtues, or they would not have their reliability, in certain nonactual situations.

Perhaps most important, virtue epistemology promises a way of understanding the kind of normativity that is involved in justified belief and knowledge. As in ethics, a virtue theory in epistemology competes with purely consequentialist and purely deontological approaches. Virtue epistemology seems to provide a better account of epistemic normativity than either of these alternatives. Thus, until the early 1960s almost all of contemporary epistemology took a deontological approach, making justified belief depend on doing one's epistemic duty or perhaps following the right epistemic norms. But this kind of normativity will not turn true belief into knowledge. Consider the case of a meticulously dutiful believer who is also the victim of a Cartesian deceiver. Suppose that as a result of her predicament her beliefs about the world are massively false but that she occasionally forms a true belief purely by accident. Such a person has true belief that is justified in the deontological sense and yet still does not have knowledge. Virtue theory typically requires more than deontological justification and therefore can avoid this particular kind of problem.

An example of a purely consequentialist theory is process reliabilism, or the theory that a belief is justified just in case it is formed by a reliable process. But process theories are hampered by counter examples involving strange and fleeting reliable processes. Consider a person who has been given a clean bill of health but who suffers from a brain tumor, one effect of which is to reliably cause the belief that he has a brain tumor. This example shows that a belief can be formed by a reliable process and yet fail to be justified in any sense relevant for having knowledge. The problem, according to virtue theory, is that not all reliable processes are epistemically significant. But if we stipulate that knowledge must arise from the stable faculties (or virtues) of the believer, then this kind of counter example is avoided.

Broadly, virtue epistemology

is the position that the intellectual virtues

are the appropriate focus of epistemological inquiry.

But even if virtue epistemology seems promising along these lines, the perceived intractability of traditional problems has led others to advocate a shift in the focus of epistemological inquiry. These theorists agree that the intellectual virtues should play a central role in epistemology, but they prefer to ask different questions and engage in different projects. Jonathan Kvanvig, for example, argues that the individual synchronic focus of traditional epistemology should be replaced by a social genetic approach and that such a shift is best achieved by focusing on the intellectual virtues. On such an approach questions such as whether S knows p at t are replaced by questions about cognitive development, the corporate nature of knowledge acquisition, and the cognitive impact of social structures on persons and communities.

Lorraine Code's topic is epistemic responsibility, or the responsibility to know well. Code thinks that such responsibility is related but not reducible to our moral responsibility to live well. James Montmarquet investigates the topic of doxastic responsibility, or the kind of responsibility for beliefs that can ground moral responsibility for actions. Both theorists emphasize the social and moral dimensions of epistemology, and both argue that a focus on the intellectual characters of persons is the most fruitful approach for investigating the relevant questions of responsibility.

Accordingly, virtue epistemology can be divided into two main camps. The first camp comprises philosophers who are interested in the traditional topics of epistemology such as the analysis of knowledge and the nature of epistemic justification. These philosophers argue that virtue epistemology provides new insights into old problems. (See Goldman, 1992; Greco, 1993; Plantinga, 1993; Sosa, 1991; and Zagzebski, 1993.) The second camp explicitly advocates a shift away from the traditional problems of epistemology and argues that virtue epistemology is the best vehicle for achieving the new focus. (See Code, 1987; Kvanvig, 1992; and Montmarquet, 1993.)

The Nature of the Virtues

As is the case with the moral virtues, the intellectual virtues may be given a consequentialist, a deontological. or a "pure virtue theory" account. Depending on the account that is adopted, one will get a different understanding of the nature of the virtues and a different sense of the importance of the virtues for an analysis of knowledge.

On a consequentialist account an intellectual virtue is a stable disposition to achieve some cognitive end, where that end is not to be defined in terms of the virtues themselves. For example, a common move is to define intellectual virtue in terms of truth, so that an intellectual virtue is a reliable (i.e., truth-conducive) cognitive faculty or habit of the believer. Alternatively, one might give a deontological account of the virtues. Here an intellectual virtue is understood as a stable disposition to do one's duty, or perhaps to be guided by the right norms, where again duty and right norm are not to be understood in terms of the virtues themselves. Finally, on a pure virtue theory the virtues continue to be understood as stable dispositions of the cognitive agent, but such dispositions are not defined in terms of the good or the right. Rather, such notions are defined in terms of the virtues. For example, a pure virtue account might understand the epistemic good in terms of what the virtuous person would believe.

Other disputes concerning the nature of the intellectual virtues also have their analogs in virtue ethics. For example, virtue epistemologists differ over whether and how intellectual virtues involve the will, whether the virtues are subject to our control, and whether they are appropriate sources of praise and blame. (See especially Montmarquet, 1993; Plantinga, 1993; and Zagzebski, 1993.) There is also disagreement over the degree to which the intellectual virtues are social in nature and over the extent to which the intellectual virtues are analogous to the moral virtues. (See especially Code, 1987; Montmarquet, 1993; and Zagzebski, 1993.)

What all virtue epistemologies have in common is a focus on the stable dispositions (i.e., faculties, abilities, or habits) of epistemic agents and the attempt to understand important epistemic notions in terms of these dispositions. For example, a consequentialist like Ernest Sosa understands an intellectual virtue as a faculty for arriving at true belief and then defines both knowledge and justification in terms of belief caused by an intellectual virtue. Alternatively, a nonconsequentialist like Montmarquet understands virtues as qualities a truth-desiring person would want to have and then defines epistemic justification in terms of virtuous belief. In each case the more basic kind of epistemic evaluation concerns the character (or virtue) of the cognitive agent, and then further kinds of epistemic evaluation are understood in terms of these.

[See also Epistemology; Skepticism; Truth.]

BIBLIOGRAPHY

Code, L. Epistemic Responsibility. Hanover, NH, 1987.

Goldman, A. "Epistemic Folkways and Scientific Epistemology," in Liaisons: Philosophy Meets the Cognitive and Social Sciences (Cambridge, 1992).

Greco, J. "Virtues and Vices of Virtue Epistemology," Canadian Journal of Philosophy, Vol. 23 (1993), 413–32.

Kvanvig, J. L. The Intellectual Virtues and the Life of the Mind. Savage, MD, 1992.

Montmarquet, J. A. Epistemic Virtue and Doxastic Responsibility. Lanham, MD, 1993.

Plantinga, A. Warrant and Proper Function. Oxford, 1993.

Sosa, E. Knowledge in Perspective. Cambridge, 1991.

Zagzebski, L. "Intellectual Virtue in Religious Epistemology," in E. Radcliffe and C. White, eds., Faith in Theory and Practice (Chicago, 1993).

– JOHN GRECO

VIRTUE ETHICS

In 1930 C. D. Broad first proposed to divide ethical theories into two classes, teleological and deontological, thereby introducing a dichotomy that quickly became standard in ethics. Teleological theories were defined as ones that hold that the moral rightness of an action is always determined by its tendency to promote certain consequences deemed intrinsicially good; deontological theories, as ones that deny this claim. Broad's dichotomy was widely accepted as being exhaustive, but in fact there are two fundamental classes of normative moral judgments that do not fit easily into it. First, it focuses on rightness or obligation, excluding moral judgments concerning what is admirable, good, excellent, or ideal. Second, it concerns only actions and their consequences, saying nothing about moral judgments concerning persons, character, and character traits.

The contemporary movement known as virtue ethics is usually said to have begun in 1958 with Elizabeth Anscombe's advice to do ethics without the notion of a 'moral ought'. Although her own critique of moral-

obligation concepts (viz., that they have meaning only within religious frameworks that include the notion of a divine lawgiver) did not gain widespread acceptance among secular ethicists, her constructive proposal to look for moral norms not in duty concepts but within the virtues or traits of character that one needs to flourish as a human being quickly caught on. Soon thereafter philosophers such as Alasdair MacIntyre, Philippa Foot, Edmund Pincoffs, and many others began to articulate and defend a third option in normative ethics: one whose chief concern was not a theory of morally right action but rather those traits of character that define the morally good or admirable person.

The contemporary movement known as virtue ethics is usually said to have begun in 1958 with Elizabeth Anscombe's advice to do ethics without the notion of a "moral ought."

Phrases such as "revival of" or "return to" often precede mention of virtue ethics in contemporary discussions, and it is generally true that questions about the virtues occupy a much more prominent place in ancient and medieval moral philosophy than in moral theories developed since the Enlightenment. But it is important to note that the conscious awareness of virtue ethics as a distinct way of theorizing about ethics arose from within contemporary Anglo-American ethical theory. Virtue ethics took root as a reaction against the underlying common assumptions of both teleological and deontological ethical theories and has achieved its greatest critical success as a protest against these accepted ways of doing normative ethics. Accordingly, one can view virtue ethics as having two complementary aspects: a critical program that presents a critique of the prevailing assumptions, methods, and aspirations of normative teleological and deontological moral theories; and a constructive program, in which an alternative virtue-oriented normative moral conception is developed and defended.

The Critical Program

At this first level virtue theorists are not necessarily committed to defending a full-scale alternative to existing ethical theory programs but rather to showing why such approaches are systematically unable to account satisfactorily for moral experience. Major criticisms made by virtue theorists against their opponents include the following.

OVERRELIANCE ON RULE MODELS OF MORAL CHOICE. Utilitarians and Kantians, it is held, both mistakenly view universal and invariable principles and laws as being exhaustive of ethics. But real-life moral exemplars do not simply deduce what to do from a hierarchy of timeless, universal principles and rules. They possess sound judgment skills that enable them to respond appropriately to the nuances of each particular situation in ways that go beyond mere mechanical application of rules.

OVERLY RATIONALISTIC ACCOUNTS OF MORAL AGENCY. Traditional moral theorists, it is held, too often assign a merely negative role in the moral life for desires and emotions. However, morally admirable people are not simply people who do their duty, but people who do so with the right kinds of emotions. Additionally, though many teleologists and deontologists do acknowledge the importance of motives in ethics, they typically mislocate them in abstractions such as "the greatest happiness principle" or "the moral law" rather than in particular persons and our relationships to them.

FORMALISM. Mainstream teleological and deontological theorists tend to focus exclusively on conceptual analyses of their favored duty-concepts and then on logical arguments based on such analyses. Additionally, they tend to view moral questions as arising only when an individual agent is trying to decide what to do in certain problematic situations. These methodological commitments result in a view of morality that is impoverished and overly restrictive. Virtue theorists, on the other hand, are much more open to drawing connections between morality and other areas of life such as psychology, anthropology, history, art, and culture. Their long-term agent-perspective also enables them correctly to view moral deliberation and choice as involving much more than snapshot decisions.

The Constructive Program

In offering their alternative, virtue theorists face the fundamental task of showing how and why a virtue-oriented conception of ethics is superior to its act- and duty-based competitors. In what ways is moral experience better understood once virtue-concepts become the primary tools of analysis? Here one may distinguish two general tendencies: radical virtue ethics attempts to interpret moral experience and judgment without employing duty-concepts at all (or at least by claiming that such concepts are always derivable from more fundamental ones concerning good people—e.g., 'morally right' acts might be defined simply as those acts performed by moral exemplars); moderate virtue ethics seeks to supplement standard act approaches with an account of the virtues. The former approach tends to view teleological and deontological ethical theories as totally misguided; the latter sees them merely as incomplete. Major issues confronting constructive virtue ethics programs include the following.

DEFINING MORAL VIRTUE. What counts as a moral virtue and why? Is there any plausible way to distinguish between moral and nonmoral virtues? How exactly do virtues relate to actions, reasons, principles, rules, desires, emotions? Are virtues beneficial to their possessors, and, if so, are they too self-centered to count as moral traits?

JUSTIFYING THE VIRTUES. How can we establish the validity of those character traits defined as moral virtues, once the option of appealing to the value of the acts that the virtues tend to encourage is ruled out? Traditionally, moral virtues have been defined as traits that human beings need in order to live well or flourish. But does the idea of flourishing provide solid enough ground on which to base the moral virtues? Is it still possible to speak accurately of *a* single human function, or is human life more variously textured that the classical picture allows? How and why is evidence of flourishing necessarily evidence of moral virtuousness? On the other hand, if one declines to issue pronouncements about "the human *telos*" and instead opts for a softer, more pluralistic functionalism that seeks to define virtues in terms of different kinds of human purposes or practices, can one still arrive at a substantive notion of the virtues that holds that they are more than local cultural products?

APPLYING THE VIRTUES. How do the virtues relate to one another in real life? Is there anything to the ancient "unity of virtues" thesis (which, on the Aristotelian model, views *phronesis* or practical wisdom as generating and uniting all of the moral virtues), or does it make sense to hold that a person might possess one moral virtue such as courage and nevertheless lack others? How many different moral virtues are there? Are some more fundamental than others? Can they be ranked in order of importance? Do virtues ever conflict with one another? What kinds of specific practical guidance do we get from the virtues, especially in cases where they appear to conflict with one another (e.g., honesty vs. kindness, love vs. fidelity)?

It should come as no surprise that radical virtue-ethics approaches have attracted far fewer followers than more moderate versions and that the critical program has had a much stronger influence on contemporary ethical theory than has the constructive program. Those who turn to late twentieth-century work in virtue ethics in hopes of finding greater consensus on either theoretical or normative issues than exists among ethical theorists elsewhere are bound to be disappointed. Still, it is no small sign of virtue ethics' success that contemporary ethical theorists of all persuasions are addressing questions of character, agency, and motivation as never before—and that there now exist greater realism and humility among contemporary philosophers concerning how ethical theory should proceed and what it might reasonably accomplish.

[See also Anscombe, Elizabeth; Consequentialism; Deontological Ethics; Ethical Theory; Kant, Immanuel.]

BIBLIOGRAPHY

Ansombe, G. E. M. "Modern Moral Philosophy," *Philosophy,* Vol. 33 (1958), 1–19; reprt. in her *Collected Philosophical Papers,* Vol. 3 (Minneapolis, 1981). The *locus classicus* of the contemporary genre.

Aristotle. *Ethica Nicomachea* [approx. 330 B.C.E.]. Translated by Terence Irwin as *Nichomachean Ethics.* Indianapolis, 1985. The most important classical source. See esp. bk. 2 for his definition of moral virtue; 1 and 10.6–9 on human flourishing; 6.5–13 on practical wisdom.

Broad, C. D. *Five Types of Ethical Theory.* London, 1930. See pp. 206–7 for Broad's division of ethical theories into deontological and teleological.

Foot, P. *Virtues and Vices.* Berkeley, 1978.

Flanagan, O., and A. O. Rorty, eds. *Identity, Character, and Morality: Essays in Moral Psychology.* Cambridge, 1990. Nineteen commissioned essays; see esp. part 5.

French, P. A., T. E. Uehling, and H. K. Wettstein, eds. *Ethical Theory: Character and Virtue.* Midwest Studies in Philosophy, Vol. 13. Notre Dame, IN, 1988. Twenty-nine commissioned essays.

Kruschwitz, R. B., and R. C. Roberts, eds. *The Virtues: Contemporary Essays in Moral Character.* Belmont, CA, 1987. Seventeen essays. The first anthology on the topic. Includes an extensive bibliography of relevant works published up to 1985.

MacIntyre, A. *After Virtue,* 2d ed. Notre Dame, IN, 1984. The most influential single book on the topic.

Philosophia, Vol. 20 (1990). Double issue on virtue, with special reference to Philippa Foot's work. Thirteen commissioned essays.

Pincoffs, E. L. *Quandaries and Virtues.* Lawrence, KS, 1986.

Slote, M. *From Morality to Virtue.* New York, 1992.

Statman, D., ed., *Virtue Ethics.* Edinburgh, 1996.

Wallace, J. *Virtues and Vices.* Ithaca, NY, 1978.

— ROBERT B. LOUDEN

WITTGENSTEIN, LUDWIG JOSEF JOHANN

Ludwig Josef Johann Wittgenstein (1889–1951), philosopher, was born in Vienna, the youngest of eight children. Ludwig's paternal grandfather, a convert from Judaism to Protestantism, had been a wool merchant in Saxony before moving to Vienna. Ludwig's father, Karl Wittgenstein, had, as a strong-willed boy, rebelled against a classical education, running away to America when he was 17. After two years he returned to Vienna and underwent a brief training in engineering. He went to work as a draftsman, designed and largely directed the construction of a steel-rolling mill, became its manager, in ten years' time was the head of a large steel company, and subsequently organized the first cartel of the Austrian steel industry. Ludwig's mother was the daughter of a Viennese banker. She was a Roman Catholic, and Ludwig was baptized in the Catholic church. Ludwig had four brothers and three sisters; all the children were generously endowed with artistic and intellectual talent. Their mother was devoted to music, and their home became a center of musical life. Johannes Brahms was a frequent visitor and a close friend of the family. One of Ludwig's brothers, Paul, became a distinguished pianist.

Ludwig was educated at home until he was 14. He was an indifferent student, and apparently his greatest interest was in machinery; a sewing machine that he constructed was much admired. His parents decided to send him to a school at Linz, in Upper Austria, that provided preparation in mathematics and the physical sciences rather than a classical education. After three years at Linz, Wittgenstein studied mechanical engineering for two years at the Technische Hochschule at Charlottenburg, in Berlin. He left this school in the spring of 1908 and went to England. In the summer of 1908 he experimented with kites at a kiteflying station in Derbyshire. That fall he registered as a research student of engineering at the University of Manchester. He engaged in aeronautical research for three years and designed a jet-reaction engine and a propeller.

Wittgenstein's interest began to shift to pure mathematics and then to the philosophical foundations of mathematics. He chanced upon Bertrand Russell's *Principles of Mathematics* and was greatly excited by it. He decided to give up engineering and to study with Russell at Cambridge. At the beginning of 1912 he was ad-

mitted to Trinity College, where he remained for the three terms of 1912 and the first two terms of 1913. Under Russell's supervision he applied himself intensively to logical studies and made astonishing progress. Soon he was engaged in the research that culminated in the logical ideas of the *Tractatus*.

In the spring of 1913 he submitted to hypnosis

with the hope that in the hypnotic trance

he could give clear answers

to questions about difficulties in logic.

Wittgenstein's most intimate friend during those early years at Cambridge was David Pinsent, a fellow student, to whom he later dedicated the *Tractatus*. When they met in the spring of 1912, Wittgenstein, in addition to studying logic, was doing experiments in the psychological laboratory on rhythm in music. He and Pinsent were united by strong musical interests. They had a repertoire of forty of Schubert's songs, whose melodies Wittgenstein would whistle while Pinsent accompanied him on the piano. Wittgenstein could play the clarinet and had an excellent memory for music and an unusual gift for sight-reading. He retained a deep interest in music throughout his life; in his philosophical writings there are many allusions to the nature of musical understanding.

In 1912, Wittgenstein was doing his first extensive reading in philosophy, and according to Pinsent he expressed "naive surprise" that the philosophers whom he had "worshipped in ignorance" were after all "stupid and dishonest and make disgusting mistakes!" He and Pinsent made holiday junkets to Iceland and Norway, Wittgenstein paying all expenses. Pinsent found Wittgenstein a difficult companion: irritable, nervously sensitive, often depressed. But when he was cheerful he was extremely charming. Sometimes he was depressed by the conviction that his death was near at hand and that he would not have time to perfect his new ideas in logic, sometimes by the thought that perhaps his logical work was of no real value. Even so, his general frame of mind was less morbid than before he had come to Cambridge. For a number of years previously there had hardly been a day, he told Pinsent, in which he had not thought of suicide "as a possibility." Coming to study philosophy with Russell had been his "salvation."

Wittgenstein worked with fierce energy at his logical ideas. In the spring of 1913 he submitted to hypnosis with the hope that in the hypnotic trance he could give clear answers to questions about difficulties in logic. He entertained a plan of going to live in seclusion in Norway for some years, devoting himself to logical problems. The reasons he gave to Pinsent were that he could do better work in the absence of all distractions, but he also said that "he had no right to live in a world" where he constantly felt contempt for other people and irritated them by his nervous temperament. Wittgenstein acted on his plan and lived in Norway from the latter part of 1913 until the outbreak of World War I. He stayed on a farm at Skjolden and later built a hut, where he lived in complete seclusion.

Wittgenstein was dismayed by the insincerity,

vanity, and coldness of the human heart.

Human kindness and human concern were

for him more important attributes in a person

than intellectual power or cultivated taste.

During this period Wittgenstein corresponded with Russell. His letters were warmly affectionate and were full of the excitement of his logical discoveries. However, he expressed the conviction that he and Russell had such different "ideals" that they were not suited for true friendship. Two people can be friends, he said, only if both of them are "pure," so that they can be completely open with one another without causing offense. A relationship founded on "hypocrisy" is intolerable. He and Russell should break off entirely or else limit their communications to their logical work. Both of them have weaknesses, but especially himself: "My life is *full* of the most hateful and petty thoughts and acts (this is *no* exaggeration)." "Perhaps you think it is a waste of time for me to think about myself; but how can I be a logician if I am not yet a man! *Before everything else* I must become pure."

When war broke out Wittgenstein entered the Austrian Army as a volunteer. He served in an artillery group on a vessel on the Vistula and later in an artillery workshop at Cracow. He was ordered to an officers' training school and subsequently served on the eastern front and later with mountain artillery in the southern

Tyrol. During these years he continued to work at his book, writing down his philosophical thoughts in notebooks that he carried in his rucksack. He completed the book in August 1918; when he was taken prisoner by the Italians in November, he had the manuscript with him. From his prison camp near Monte Cassino he wrote to Russell, to whom the manuscript was subsequently delivered by diplomatic courier through the offices of a mutual friend, J. M. Keynes.

While serving on the eastern front Wittgenstein bought at a bookshop in Galicia a copy of one of Tolstoy's works on the Gospels, which apparently made a deep impression on him. In the prison camp in Italy he read a standard version of the Gospels, possibly for the first time, and is reported to have been disturbed by much that he found in it and to have questioned its authenticity, perhaps because of the differences from Tolstoy's version.

Wittgenstein was anxious to have his book, *Logisch-philosophische Abhandlung,* published immediately. Shortly after his release from imprisonment and his return to Vienna, in August 1919, he offered it to a publisher. He believed that his book finally solved the problems with which he and Russell had struggled. From Russell's letters, however, he concluded that Russell had not understood his main ideas, and he feared that no one would. He and Russell met in Holland in December 1919 to discuss the book. Russell undertook to write an introduction for it, but the following May, Wittgenstein wrote to Russell that the introduction contained much misunderstanding and he could not let it be printed with his book. Subsequently the publisher with whom he had been negotiating rejected the book. Wittgenstein wrote to Russell, in July 1920, that he would take no further steps to have it published and that Russell could do with it as he wished. The German text was published in 1921 in Wilhelm Ostwald's *Annalen der Naturphilosophie.* The following year it was published in London with a parallel English translation, under the title *Tractatus Logico-philosophicus.* A new and improved English translation was published in 1961.

Most of the notebooks used in the preparation of the *Tractatus* were destroyed on Wittgenstein's order. Three of them, however, from the years 1914–1916, were accidentally preserved and were published in 1961 with a parallel English translation. The notebooks present a vivid picture of the intensity of Wittgenstein's struggles with the problems of the *Tractatus,* and they sometimes help to show what the problems were.

Soon after his return to civilian life Wittgenstein decided to become a schoolteacher. He attended a teacher-training course in order to receive a certificate, and in the fall of 1920 he began teaching classes of children aged nine and ten in the village of Trattenbach in Lower Austria. He was an exacting teacher. He did not get on with his colleagues and was often depressed. When he was transferred to another village he was somewhat happier, for one of the teachers, Rudolf Koder, was a talented pianist. The two of them devoted many afternoons to music, Wittgenstein playing the clarinet or whistling. He remained a schoolteacher until 1926. In 1924 he prepared a dictionary of six to seven thousand words for the use of pupils in the elementary schools of the Austrian villages; this small book was published in 1926.

When his father died, in 1913, Wittgenstein inherited a large fortune. In the summer of the following year he wrote to Ludwig von Ficker, editor of the literary review *Der Brenner,* proposing to send a large sum of money to be distributed among needy Austrian poets and artists. The poets Rainer Maria Rilke and Georg Trakl received sizable gifts of money from this anonymous source. Upon his return to civilian life after the war, Wittgenstein gave his fortune to two of his sisters. Part of the reason for this action was that he did not want to have friends for the sake of his money, but undoubtedly it was largely due to his inclination toward a simple and frugal life.

During his years as a teacher, until Frank Ramsey visited him in 1923, Wittgenstein probably gave no thought to philosophy. Ramsey, a brilliant young mathematician and philosopher at Cambridge, had just completed a review of the *Tractatus* and was eager to discuss the book with its author. He found Wittgenstein living in extreme simplicity in a small village. In explaining his book, to which he was willing to devote several hours a day for a fortnight or more, Wittgenstein would become very excited. He told Ramsey, however, that he would do no further work in philosophy because his mind was "no longer flexible." He believed that no one would understand the *Tractatus* merely by reading it but that some day some person would, independently, think those same thoughts and would derive pleasure from finding their exact expression in Wittgenstein's book.

After his resignation as a schoolteacher in 1926, Wittgenstein inquired at a monastery about the possibility of entering upon monastic life, but he was discouraged by the father superior. In the summer of that year he worked as a gardener's assistant with the monks at Hütteldorf, near Vienna. Meanwhile, one of his sisters had commissioned the architect Paul Engelmann to build a mansion for her in Vienna. Engelmann, a friend of Wittgenstein's, proposed to him that they undertake it jointly. Wittgenstein agreed and actually became the directing mind in the project, which occupied him for two years. The building has been described by

G. H. von Wright as "characteristic of its creator. It is free from all decoration and marked by a severe exactitude in measure and proportion. Its beauty is of the same simple and static kind that belongs to the sentences of the *Tractatus.*" During the same period Wittgenstein did some work in sculpture.

Moritz Schlick, a professor in Vienna, had been deeply impressed by the *Tractatus.* He managed to establish contact with Wittgenstein and apparently prevailed upon him to attend one or two meetings of the group founded by Schlick, known as the Vienna circle. Subsequently Schlick and Friedrich Waismann paid visits to Wittgenstein, in which he expounded some ideas that were passed on to other members of the circle.

In January 1929 he returned to Cambridge to devote himself again to philosophy. What produced this renewal of interest is unknown, but it is said that it was provoked by a lecture he heard L. E. J. Brouwer give in Vienna in 1928 on the foundations of mathematics. Wittgenstein found he would be eligible to receive the Ph.D. degree from Cambridge if he submitted a dissertation, whereupon he submitted the *Tractatus*. Russell and G. E. Moore were appointed to give him an oral examination, which they did in June 1929. Moore found the occasion "both pleasant and amusing." Trinity College granted Wittgenstein a research fellowship. At this time he published a short paper, "Some Remarks on Logical Form," which he soon came to think was weak and confused. This paper and the *Tractatus* were the sole philosophical writings of his that were published in his lifetime.

Wittgenstein began to give lectures in January 1930. He remained at Cambridge until the summer of 1936, when he went to live for a year in his hut in Norway and to begin writing the *Philosophical Investigations*. In 1937 he returned to Cambridge and two years later succeeded Moore to the chair of philosophy.

Wittgenstein's lectures made a powerful impression on his auditors. They were given without notes or preparation. Each lecture was new philosophical work. Wittgenstein's ideas did not come easily. He carried on a visible struggle with his thoughts. At times there were long silences, during which his gaze was concentrated, his face intensely alive, and his expression stern, and his hands made arresting movements. His hearers knew that they were in the presence of extreme seriousness, absorption, and force of intellect. When he spoke his words did not come fluently, but they came with force and conviction. His face was remarkably mobile and expressive when he talked. His eyes were often fierce, and his whole personality was commanding. His lectures moved over a wide range of topics and were marked by great richness of illustration and comparison.

Wittgenstein attacked philosophical problems energetically, even passionately. Unlike many other philosophers, who really want to retain the problems rather than to solve them, Wittgenstein's desire was to clear them up, to get rid of them. He exclaimed to a friend: "My father was a business man and I am a business man too!" He wanted his philosophical work to be businesslike, to settle things.

When he was not working at philosophy Wittgenstein could sometimes, with a friend, put on a charming mood of mock seriousness in which he said nonsensical things with utmost gravity. These lighthearted moments were, however, comparatively infrequent. Most commonly his thoughts were somber. He was dismayed by the insincerity, vanity, and coldness of the human heart. He was always troubled about his own life and was often close to despair. Human kindness and human concern were for him more important attributes in a person than intellectual power or cultivated taste. He had an acute need for friendship, and his generosity as a friend was striking. At the same time it was not easy to maintain a friendly relationship with him, for he was easily angered and inclined to be censorious, suspicious, and demanding.

In World War II Wittgenstein found it impossible to remain a spectator. He obtained a porter's job at Guy's Hospital in London and worked there from November 1941 to April 1943. He was then transferred to the Royal Victoria Infirmary in Newcastle, where he served as a "lab boy" in the Clinical Research Laboratory until the spring of 1944. He impressed the doctors for whom he worked by the prolonged and concentrated thought he gave to their medical problems. This hard thinking would often result in a new way of looking at the problems. At Newcastle, Wittgenstein devised a simple technique for estimating the area of war wounds that proved of value in determining their treatment.

In 1944 he resumed his lectures at Cambridge. But he became increasingly dissatisfied with his role as a teacher. He feared that his influence was positively harmful. He was disgusted by what he observed of the half understanding of his ideas. "The only seed I am likely to sow is a jargon," he said. He strongly disliked universities and academic life. He felt an increasing need to live alone, perhaps occasionally seeing a friend, and to devote his remaining energies (for several years he had been repeatedly unwell) to finishing the *Investigations*.

In the fall of 1947 he finally resigned his chair. He sought a secluded life, first in the Irish countryside near Dublin, then in an isolated cottage on the west coast of Ireland. He worked hard when his health permitted it. In the summer of 1949 he went to spend three months with a friend in the United States. Upon his return to England, in the fall, he was discovered to have cancer. He wrote that he was not shocked by this news because he had no wish to continue living. During part of 1950 he visited his family in Vienna, then went to Oxford to live with a friend, and afterward made a trip to Norway. In 1951 he moved to the home of his physician in Cambridge. Wittgenstein had expressed an aversion to spending his last days in a hospital, and his doctor had invited him to come to his own home to die. Wittgenstein was deeply grateful for this offer. Knowing that death was imminent, he continued hard at work. The philosophical thoughts that he wrote in his notebooks at this time are of the highest quality.

On April 27 he was taken violently ill. When his doctor informed him that the end had come he said, "Good!" His last words, before he lost consciousness, were "Tell them I've had a wonderful life!" He died on April 29, 1951.

The *Tractatus*

The *Tractatus* is a comprehensive work of extreme originality, yet it is less than eighty pages long. It is arranged as a series of remarks numbered in decimal notation. The following propositions are distinguished by their numbering as the primary theses of the book:

(1) The world is everything that is the case.
(2) What is the case, the fact, is the existence of states of affairs.
(3) A logical picture of facts is a thought.
(4) A thought is a sentence with a sense.
(5) A sentence is a truth-function of elementary sentences.
(6) The general form of a truth-function is $[\bar{p},\bar{\xi},N(\bar{\xi})]$.
(7) Whereof one cannot speak, thereof one must be silent.

Erik Stenius has perceptively remarked that the book has a "musical" structure and that the numbering brings out a "rhythm of emphasis": these seven main propositions are "forte" places in the rhythm.

THE PICTURE THEORY. In a notebook Wittgenstein wrote (*Notebooks,* p. 39): "My *whole* task consists in explaining the nature of sentences." (The German *Satz* will be translated sometimes as "sentence," sometimes as "proposition.") What makes it possible for a combination of words to represent a fact in the world? How is it that by producing a sentence I can *say* something—can *tell* someone that so-and-so is the case?

Wittgenstein's explanation consists in the striking idea that a sentence is a *picture*. He meant that it is *literally* a picture, not merely *like* a picture in certain respects. Apparently this thought first occurred to him during the war, when he saw in a magazine an account of how a motorcar accident was represented in a law court by means of small models (see *Notebooks,* p. 7). So he said: "A proposition is a picture of reality. A proposition is a model of reality as we think it to be" (*Tractatus,* 4.01). The dolls and toy cars could be manipulated so as to depict different ways in which the accident might have taken place. They could be used to construct different propositions about the accident—to put forward different accounts, different models of what took place. Wittgenstein's general conception was that when we put a sentence together we construct a model of reality. "In a proposition a situation is, as it were, put together experimentally" (4.031).

One would not normally think that a sentence printed on a page is a picture. According to the *Tractatus* it really is a picture, in the ordinary sense, of what it represents. Wittgenstein conceived the proof of this to be that although words we have not previously encountered have to be explained to us, when we meet for the first time a sentence that is composed of familiar words, we understand the sentence without *further* explanation. "I understand a sentence without having had its sense explained to me" (4.021). This can appear to one as a remarkable fact. If it is a fact, the only possible explanation would be that a sentence *shows* its sense. It shows how things are if it is true (4.022). This is exactly what a picture does. A sentence composed of old words is able to communicate a new state of affairs by virtue of being a picture of it.

In any picture, according to the *Tractatus,* there has to be a one-to-one correspondence between the elements of a picture and the things in the state of affairs its represents. If one element of a picture stands for a man and another for a cow, then the relationship between the picture elements might show that the man is milking the cow. A picture is a *fact,* namely the fact that the picture elements are related to one another in a definite way. A picture fact shows that the things the picture elements stand for are related in the *same* way as are the picture elements.

Since a sentence is held to be a picture, there must be as many elements to be distinguished in it as in the state of affairs it portrays. The two must have the same logical or mathematical multiplicity. Again, this does not *seem* to be true of our ordinary sentences. For Wittgenstein this meant not that it is not true but that our sentences possess a concealed complexity that can be exhibited by analysis.

According to the *Tractatus* a picture must have something *in common* with what it pictures. This common thing is the picture's "form of representation." There are different kinds of pictures, different pictorial notations, different methods of projection. But all pictures must have in common with reality the same logical form

in order to be able to picture reality at all, either truly or falsely. This logical form, also called "the form of reality," is defined as the possibility that things in the world are related as are the elements of the picture (2.18, 2.151). Sentences, since they are pictures, have the same form as the reality they depict.

WHAT CANNOT BE SAID. A picture can depict reality, but it cannot depict its own form of representation. It depicts (represents) its subject from "outside," but it cannot get outside itself to depict its own form of representation. A picture of another form might depict the representational form of a given picture; for instance, a picture in sound might depict the representational form of a picture in color. But in order for the one to represent the form of the other, there must be something that is the same in both. "There must be something identical in a picture and what it depicts, to enable the one to be a picture of the other at all" (2.161). Therefore, *logical* form, the form of reality, which *all* pictures must possess, cannot be depicted by any picture.

A thought consists not of words

"but of psychical constituents that have

the same sort of relation to reality as words.

What those constituents are I don't know."

This consideration must apply to sentences, too. We make assertions by means of sentences. With a sentence we say something. We say how things are. Things in the world are related in a certain way, and we try to describe that. But we cannot describe how our sentences succeed in representing reality, truly or falsely. We cannot say what the form of representation is that is common to all sentences and that makes them pictures of reality. We cannot say how language represents the world. We cannot state in any sentence the pictorial form of all sentences. "What can be said can only be said by means of a sentence, and so nothing that is necessary for the understanding of *all* sentences can be said" (*Notebooks,* p. 25).

This doctrine implies that in a sense one cannot say what the meaning of a sentence is. With regard to the sentence "*a* is larger than *b,*" one can explain to a person what "*a*" and "*b*" each refer to and what "larger" means, but there is not a further explanation to give him, namely what "*a* is larger than *b*" means. We understand the elements of a sentence, and we see how they are combined. But we cannot say what this combination means. Yet we *grasp* its meaning. In some sense we know what it means, because the sentence *shows* its meaning. Anything that can be said can be said clearly, but not everything that is understood can be said. In a letter to Russell, Wittgenstein remarked that his "main contention" was this distinction between what can be said in propositions—i.e., in language—and what cannot be said but can only be shown. This, he said, was "the cardinal problem of philosophy."

THE NATURE OF THOUGHT. The picture theory of propositions is at the same time an account of the nature of thought. Wittgenstein said: "A thought is a sentence with a sense" (*Tractatus*, 4). This implies that thinking is impossible without language. Since a thought is a sentence and a sentence is a picture, a thought is a picture. The totality of true thoughts would be a true picture of the world.

The view that a thought is a sentence seems to imply that the words of a sentence could be the constituents of a thought. But in a letter written to Russell shortly after the *Tractatus* was completed, Wittgenstein explicitly denied this. A thought consists not of words "but of psychical constituents that have the same sort of relation to reality as words. What those constituents are I don't know." "I don't know *what* the constituents of a thought are but I know *that* it must have such constituents which correspond to the words of Language" (*Notebooks*, pp. 130, 129). It would appear from these remarks that Wittgenstein's view was not that a thought and a sentence with a sense are one and the same thing but that they are two things with corresponding constituents of different natures. Each of these two things is a picture. "Thinking is a kind of language. For a thought too is, of course, a logical picture of a sentence, and therefore it just is a kind of sentence" (*Notebooks*, p. 82).

To say that a state of affairs is conceivable (thinkable) means that we can make a picture of it (*Tractatus*, 3.001). A thought "contains" the possibility of a state of affairs, for the logical form of the thought is the possibility that things in the world are combined in the way the constituents of the thought are combined. Whatever is conceivable is possible. In a spoken or written sentence a thought is "made perceptible to the senses." All thoughts can be stated in sentences; what cannot be stated cannot be thought.

A consequence of these views is that the form of representation of propositions (the form of reality, logical form), which cannot be stated, also cannot be thought. Language *shows* us something we cannot *think*. A function of philosophy is to indicate (*bedeuten*) what cannot be said (or thought) by presenting clearly what can be said. According to the *Tractatus,* therefore, there is a

realm of the unthinkable which, far from being a mere wind egg, is the foundation of all language and all thought. In some way we *grasp* this foundation of thought (what we do here cannot really be said); it is mirrored *in* our thoughts, but it cannot be an object of thought.

Obviously the *Tractatus* is a thoroughly metaphysical work; this is not a minor tendency of the book. Yet it was once widely regarded as being antimetaphysical in its outlook. There is some excuse for this interpretation, since at the end of the book Wittgenstein said that the correct philosophical method would be to prove to anyone who wants to say something metaphysical that he has failed to give a meaning to certain signs in his sentences (6.53). But Wittgenstein did not reject the metaphysical; rather, he rejected the possibility of *stating* the metaphysical.

NAMES AND OBJECTS. The conception of propositions, and therefore of language, in the *Tractatus* rests on the notion of a *name*. This is defined as a "simple sign" employed in a sentence. A simple sign is not composed of other signs, as, for example, the phrase "the king of Sweden" is. The word "John" would satisfy this requirement of a simple sign. But a further requirement of a *name* is that it should stand for a simple thing, which is called an "object." According to the *Tractatus* the object for which a name stands *is the meaning* of the name (3.203). It is easy to determine whether a sign is composed of other signs but not whether it stands for something *simple.*

Wittgenstein conceived of objects as *absolutely* simple and not merely as simple relative to some system of notation. "Objects make up the substance of the world. That is why they cannot be composite. . . . Substance is what exists independently of what is the case. . . . Objects are identical with the fixed, the existent. . . . The configuration of objects is the changing, the mutable" (2.021, 2.024, 2.027, 2.0271).

A name is not a picture of the object it stands for, and therefore a name does not *say* anything. A picture in language—i.e., the sentence—can be formed only by a combination of names. This combination pictures a configuration of objects. The combination of names is like a *tableau vivant* (4.0311). (One might think here, for example, of a group of people posed to represent *The Last Supper.*) A name is a *substitute* for an object, and a combination of names portrays a configuration of objects—i.e., a state of affairs (*Sachverhalt*).

A reader of the *Tractatus* will be perplexed to know what examples of *names* and of *objects* would be. No examples are given. It is said that names occur only in "elementary" propositions, but there are no examples of the latter notion. Wittgenstein was not able to come to any conclusion about examples. The *Notebooks* show that he was very vexed by this problem. He struggled with the question of whether "points of the visual field" might be simples (see, for example, p. 45). Sometimes he wondered whether any *ordinary* name whatsoever might not be a "genuine" name. And he wondered whether his *watch* might not be a "simple object" (*Notebooks*, pp. 60–61). His final conviction that there are absolutely simple objects was purely a priori. He wrote in his notes:

> It seems that the idea of the *simple* is already to be found contained in that of the complex and in the idea of analysis, and in such a way that we come to this idea quite apart from any examples of simple objects, or of propositions which mention them, and we realize the existence of the simple object—*a priori*—as a logical necessity. (*Notebooks*, p. 60)

The "logical necessity" arises from the requirement that propositions have a *definite sense*. "The demand for simple things *is* the demand for definiteness of sense" (*Notebooks*, p. 63). As it is put in the *Tractatus*, "The requirement that simple signs be possible is the requirement that sense be definite" (3.23). An indefinite sense would be no sense at all. A proposition might be ambiguous, but the ambiguity would be between definite alternatives: either *this* or *that*.

The sentences of everyday language are in perfect logical order. This order rests on the simples—that which is fixed, unchangeable, *hard* (*das Harte: Notebooks*, p. 63). The simples and their configurations—that is what order *is*. Wittgenstein said: "Our problems are not abstract, but perhaps the most concrete that there are" (*Tractatus*, 5.5563).

ELEMENTARY PROPOSITIONS. A combination of genuine names is an elementary proposition. It is not analyzable into other propositions. "It is obvious that the analysis of propositions must bring us to elementary propositions which consist of names in immediate combination" (4.221). An elementary proposition shows (represents) a certain configuration of simple objects.

The picture theory is meant to hold for *all* genuine propositions, not merely for elementary propositions. Wittgenstein said without qualification: "A proposition is a picture of reality" (4.01, 4.021). Elementary and nonelementary propositions are equally pictures: the difference is that in an elementary proposition the pictorial nature is manifest. "It is *evident* that we perceive (*empfinden*) an elementary proposition as the picture of a state of affairs" (*Notebooks*, p. 25). But Wittgenstein admitted that most sentences do not *seem* to be pictures.

At first sight a sentence—one set out on the printed page, for example—does not seem to be a picture of the reality with which it is concerned. But no more does musical notation at first sight seem to be a picture of music, nor our phonetic notation (letters) to be a picture of our speech. And yet these sign-languages prove to be pictures, even in the ordinary sense, of what they represent. (*Tractatus*, 4.011)

All genuine propositions, according to the *Tractatus*, are analyzable into elementary propositions. This analysis of our ordinary propositions, with their complicated modes of symbolizing—their various "methods of projection"—will make manifest their concealed pictorial nature. In his introduction to the *Tractatus*, written for the first English edition, Russell said:

> Mr. Wittgenstein is concerned with the conditions for a logically perfect language—not that any language is logically perfect, or that we believe ourselves capable, here and now, of constructing a logically perfect language, but that the whole function of language is to have meaning, and it only fulfils this function in proportion as it approaches to the ideal language which we postulate.

That this is an incorrect account of the *Tractatus* is sufficiently shown by Wittgenstein's remark "All the propositions of our everyday language are actually in perfect logical order, just as they are" (5.5563). The analysis achieved by the philosophical logician will not create order where previously there was no order; instead, it will make evident what is already there.

Every genuine proposition has one and only one complete analysis into elementary propositions (3.25). This is so even if every fact consists of infinitely many states of affairs and every state of affairs is composed of infinitely many simple objects (4.2211). The completely analyzed proposition will consist of simple names; the meaning of each simple name will be a simple object; the particular way in which the names are combined in the proposition will *say* that the simple objects in the world are related in the same way. To understand the completely analyzed proposition one need only understand the names—i.e., know what objects they stand for. What their combination means will be immediately evident. Understanding a proposition requires *merely* understanding its constituents (4.024).

As Rush Rhees has remarked, the idea that there are elementary propositions is not an arbitrary assumption. Wittgenstein was trying to solve the question of how language and thought can be related to reality. His basic intuition was that language pictures reality. If this is so, then among the sentences of language there must be some that *show their sense immediately,* which, of course, does not mean that their truth is self-evident. Wittgenstein had no criteria for identifying elementary propositions and could give no general account of their subject matter. But if his intuition was right, then there must be elementary propositions—that is, propositions which show their sense immediately and of which all other propositions are "truth-functions." If this were not so, no sentence could say anything or be understood (Rush Rhees, "The *Tractatus:* Seeds of Some Misunderstandings," pp. 218–219).

THEORY OF TRUTH-FUNCTIONS. A truth-function of a single proposition *p* is a proposition whose truth or falsity is uniquely determined by the truth or falsity of *p*; for example, *not-p* (*p* is false) is a truth-function of *p*. A truth-function of two propositions *p, q* is a proposition whose truth or falsity is uniquely determined by the truth or falsity of *p, q*; for instance, "*p, q* are both true" is a truth-function of *p, q*. According to the *Tractatus* (5) every genuine proposition is a truth-function of elementary propositions. (It is an interesting and difficult question whether this doctrine follows from the picture theory or, on the other hand, is even compatible with it.) If two nonelementary propositions *r* and *s* are truth-functions of some of the same elementary propositions, then *r* and *s* will be internally related: for instance, one of them may logically follow from the other, or they may be contradictories or contraries of each other. If we see the internal structure of two propositions, we know what logical relations hold between them. We do not need, in addition, a knowledge of logical principles. We can actually do without the formal principles of logic, "for in a suitable notation we can recognize the formal properties of propositions by mere inspection of the propositions themselves" (6.122).

Wittgenstein employed a technique (known as the method of truth tables) for making manifest the truth conditions of a proposition that is a truth-function of other propositions—that is, for exhibiting the relation between the truth or falsity of the latter and the truth or falsity of the former.

There are two limiting cases among the possible groupings of truth conditions of propositions. One case would be when a proposition was true for all truth possibilities of the elementary propositions; this proposition is called a *tautology.* The other would be when a proposition was false for all the truth possibilities; this proposition is called a *contradiction.* Although it is convenient to refer to tautologies and contradictions as "propositions," they are actually degenerate cases, not genuine propositions. They are not pictures of reality.

They do not determine reality in any way. They have no truth conditions, since a tautology is *un*conditionally true and a contradiction *un*conditionally false. Wittgenstein compared a genuine proposition, a picture, to "a solid body that restricts the freedom of movement of others." In contrast a tautology (for example, "He is here, or he is not here") "leaves open to reality the whole of logical space." No restriction is imposed on anything. A contradiction (for example, "He is here, and he is not here") "fills the whole of logical space and leaves no point of it for reality" (4.461, 4.462, 4.463).

Wittgenstein's picture theory

and his explanation of logical truth

lead to an interesting doctrine of necessity and

also to a denial of any knowledge of the future.

According to the *Tractatus* the so-called propositions of logic, logical truths, principles of logic are all tautologies. They express no thoughts. They say nothing. We could do without them. But they are not nonsense, for the fact that a certain combination of propositions yields a tautology reveals something about the structures of the constituent propositions. "That the propositions of logic are tautologies *shows* the formal—logical—properties of language, of the world" (6.12).

NECESSITY. Wittgenstein's picture theory and his explanation of logical truth lead to an interesting doctrine of necessity and also to a denial of any knowledge of the future. Genuine propositions say only how things are, not how things must be. The only necessity there can be is embodied in tautologies (and the equations of mathematics). Neither tautologies nor equations say anything about the world. Therefore, there is no necessity in the world. "Outside of logic everything is accidental" (6.3). One proposition can be inferred from another proposition only if there is an internal, structural connection between them. The existence of one state of affairs cannot be inferred from the existence of another, entirely different, state of affairs (5.135). But that is what an inference to a *future* state of affairs would have to be. Thus Wittgenstein declared that we do not *know* whether the sun will rise tomorrow (6.36311).

WILL AND ACTION. If we conceive of an act of will (a volition) as one occurrence and the transpiring of what is willed as an entirely different occurrence, it follows from the foregoing doctrines that there can be, at most, a merely accidental correlation between one's will and what happens in the world. I cannot *make* anything happen—not even a movement of my body. "The world is independent of my will" (6.373). In his notes Wittgenstein gave this idea dramatic expression: "I cannot bend the happenings of the world to my will: I am completely powerless" (*Notebooks,* p. 73).

ETHICS. According to the picture theory a proposition and its negation are both possible; which one is true is accidental. Wittgenstein drew the conclusion that there can be no propositions of ethics. His thought here was that if anything has value, this fact cannot be accidental: the thing *must* have that value. But everything in the world is accidental. Therefore there is no value in the world. "In the world everything is as it is, and everything happens as it does happen: *in* it no value exists—and if it did, it would have no value" (*Tractatus,* 6.41).

This view is an absolute denial not of the existence of value but of its existence *in the world.* Propositions can state only what is in the world. What belongs to ethics cannot be stated; it is "transcendental" (6.421). The world, and what is in the world, is neither good nor evil. Good and evil exist only in relation to the subject (the ego). But this "subject" to which Wittgenstein referred is also "transcendental." It is not in the world but is a "limit" of the world (5.5632).

THE MYSTICAL. In the view of the *Tractatus* there are a variety of things that cannot be stated: the form of representation of propositions, the existence of the simple objects that constitute the substance of the world, the existence of a metaphysical subject, of good and evil—these things are all unsayable. Wittgenstein seems to have believed that we have thoughts on these matters only when we view the world as a *limited whole.* This latter experience is what he called "the mystical" (6.45).

Although one cannot *say* anything on these metaphysical topics included in the mystical, this is not because they are absurd but because they lie beyond the reach of language. "Unsayable things do indeed exist" (*Es gibt allerdings Unaussprechliches:* 6.522). This itself is something unsayable. It is one of those sentences of his own of which Wittgenstein declared that although they can produce philosophical insight, they are actually nonsensical and eventually must be "thrown away" (6.54). The final proposition of the book ("Whereof one cannot speak, thereof one must be silent") is not the truism one might take it to be, for it means that there *is* a realm about which one can say nothing.

THE *TRACTATUS* AND LOGICAL POSITIVISM. The *Tractatus* exerted a considerable influence on the so-called Vienna circle of logical positivism. Moritz Schlick, the leader of this movement, declared that the *Tractatus* had brought modern philosophy to a "decisive turning point." It is true that there is some agreement between the predominant views of the Vienna circle and the positions of the *Tractatus*—for example, that all genuine propositions are truth-functions of elementary propositions, that logical truths are tautologies and say nothing, and that philosophy can contain no body of doctrine but is an activity of clarifying thoughts.

But there are fundamental differences. The Vienna circle did not adopt the picture theory of propositions, which is the central idea of the *Tractatus.* A conspicuous doctrine of the circle was that all genuine propositions are reducible to propositions that report "direct perception" or what is "immediately given in experience." This doctrine is not found in the *Tractatus.* A corollary to it is the famous positivist thesis "The meaning of a statement is its method of verification." But the topic of verification is not even brought into the *Tractatus.* The only proposition there that seems to resemble this thesis is the following: "To understand a proposition means to know what is the case if it is true" (4.024). Even here nothing is explicitly said about verification, and a comment immediately following this remark shows that Wittgenstein was not thinking about verification. A proposition, he said, "is understood by anyone who understands its constituents." That is to say, if you understand the words in a sentence, you thereby understand the sentence. There is no mention of a requirement that you must know how to verify what it says.

As previously noted, Wittgenstein was tempted by the suggestion that "points in the visual field" are examples of the simples out of which all meaning is composed. But the final view of the *Tractatus* is that the simples are fixed, immutable things, which exist "independently of what is the case." If so, they cannot be described by propositions and cannot be *given in experience.* The *Tractatus* does not contain, therefore, an empiricist theory of meaning. What it holds is that to understand any sentence one must know the references of the names that compose it; that is all. When you understand a sentence you know how reality is constituted if the sentence is true, regardless of whether you know how to verify what it says. The picture theory is not a verification theory of meaning. It is ironical that the role of *verification* in meaning and understanding receives much attention in Wittgenstein's later philosophy, which obviously is not positivistic, but none at all in the reputedly positivistic *Tractatus.*

Logical positivism and the author of the *Tractatus* were both opposed to metaphysics, but in different ways. For positivism there is nothing at all behind metaphysical propositions except possibly their authors' emotions. "Metaphysicians are musicians without musical ability," said Rudolf Carnap. In the view of the *Tractatus* one may gain insights into the presuppositions and limits of language, thought, and reality. These metaphysical insights cannot be stated in language, but *if* they could be, they would be true insights and not mere muddles or expressions of feeling.

The foregoing sketch of the *Tractatus* has omitted many of its important topics. Wittgenstein wrote in his notes, "My work has extended from the foundations of logic to the nature of the world." In his preface to the *Tractatus* he expressed the opinion that he had obtained the final solution of the problems treated in the book, but he added that one value of his work is that "it shows how little is achieved when these problems are solved."

The "New" Philosophy

In 1929, Wittgenstein returned to Cambridge, after an absence of more than fifteen years, to resume philosophical research and to lecture. From then until his death he did a huge amount of writing. Among the first works of this period were two large typescript volumes. One, which was composed in the period 1929–1930, has been published under the title *Philosophische Bemerkungen.* The other is a systematic work of nearly 800 typewritten pages written between 1930 and 1932. In both of these volumes Wittgenstein re-examined the problems of the *Tractatus* and revised what he had written there. This led him to questions he had not previously considered. Perhaps it can be said that he found that the logical investigations of the *Tractatus* and its supreme problem of the relation of language to reality had drawn him more and more into questions in the philosophy of psychology. These volumes seem to show that the change from the *Tractatus* to the *Philosophical Investigations* was an intensive but continuous development rather than a sudden revolution.

In 1933–1934, Wittgenstein dictated to his students a set of notes that came to be called the *Blue Book,* and in 1934–1935 he dictated another set, later known as the *Brown Book.* (Although Wittgenstein always wrote in German, the *Blue Book* and the *Brown Book* were dictated in English.) Both circulated widely in typescript, and Wittgenstein's new ideas began to create a stir. The *Blue Book* is clear and lively and is perhaps the beginner's best introduction to Wittgenstein. Nevertheless, it is a comparatively superficial work; Wittgenstein never regarded it as more than a set of class notes. The *Brown Book,* on the other hand, he regarded for a short time as a draft of something that might be published. He worked at a revision but gave it up in 1936, when he began to write the *Philosophical Investigations.* Wittgenstein refrained from publishing the *Investigations* during his lifetime, but his explicit wish was that it be published posthumously, a wish that he probably did not have with respect to any of the rest of the voluminous work he produced between 1929 and 1951.

The *Philosophical Investigations* was published in 1953 in two parts. Part I was written in the period 1936–1945 and Part II between 1947 and 1949. Concurrently with the *Investigations,* Wittgenstein did other writing, which was closely related to the topics of the *Investigations* or even overlapped it. From the years 1937–1944 there are extensive manuscripts on the philosophy of logic and mathematics. *Remarks on the Foundations of Mathematics,* published in 1956, consists of selections, made by the editors, from this material. A quantity of writing in the form of loose notes, probably from the years 1947–1949, is of the same subject matter and quality as the latter part of Part I of the *Investigations.* Wittgenstein's last manuscript notebooks, from the years 1949–1951, treating questions about belief, doubt, knowledge, and certainty, also contain much material that should eventually be published.

Philosophical Investigations

Wittgenstein believed that the *Investigations* could be better understood if one saw it against the background of the *Tractatus.* A considerable part of the *Investigations* is an attack, either explicit or implicit, on the earlier work. This development is probably unique in the history of philosophy—a thinker producing, at different periods of his life, two highly original systems of thought, each system the result of many years of intensive labors, each expressed in an elegant and powerful style, each greatly influencing contemporary philosophy, and the second being a criticism and rejection of the first.

Apparently it is possible for a serious student of Wittgenstein to form the impression that "the *Investigations* basically contains an application of the main ideas of the *Tractatus* to several concrete problems, the only difference being the use of language-games instead of the language of the natural sciences which formed the theoretical background of the *Tractatus.*" This view is thoroughly mistaken, as will be seen.

THE WHOLE OF LANGUAGE. It is held in the *Tractatus* that any proposition presupposes the whole of language. "If objects are given, then at the same time we are given *all* objects. If elementary propositions are given, then at the same time *all* elementary propositions are given" (5.524). "If all objects are given, then at the same time all *possible* states of affairs are also given" (2.0124). An elementary proposition is a combination of names, and in order to understand the proposition one must in some sense "know" the objects for which the names stand. In understanding any proposition at all one must know some objects, and therefore, as stated, one must know all objects and all possibilities. Any proposition whatsoever carries with it the whole of "logical space." This view is connected with the idea that there is an *essence* of propositions. The essence of propositions is "the essence of all description, and thus the essence of the world" (5.4711). The essence of propositions is the same as "the universal form of proposition" (*Die allgemeine Satzform*). That there is a universal form of proposition is proved by the fact that all possibilities—i.e., all forms of proposition—"must be *foreseeable*" (*Notebooks,* p. 89; Tractatus, 4.5).

The Tractatus *assumes that there is a universal form of language, just as it assumes that there is a universal form of number— that which is common to all numbers. The* Investigations *rejects this assumption.*

The *Investigations* emphatically rejects the idea that each proposition carries with it the whole of language. A sentence does presuppose a "language game," but a language game will be only a small segment of the whole of language. An example of a language game is the following, which appears at the beginning of the *Investigations* (Sec. 2): There are a builder and his helper. The building materials are blocks, pillars, slabs, and beams. The two men have a language consisting of the words "block," "pillar," "slab," "beam." The builder calls out one of the words and the helper brings the building material that he has learned to bring at that call. Wittgenstein called the words and the actions with which they are joined a language game (*Sprachspiel*). He said that it is *complete in itself* and could even be conceived to be the entire language of a tribe. If we think it is incomplete we are only comparing it with our more complex language. In the *Brown Book* there is the analogy of someone's describing chess without mentioning pawns. As a description of chess it is incomplete, yet we can also say that it is a complete description of a simpler game (*Blue and Brown Books,* p. 77). This simpler game does not presuppose chess, nor does the part played, for example, by the word "block" in the game of Sec. 2 imply its use in descriptions or questions.

According to the *Tractatus* every form of proposition can be anticipated because a new form of proposition would represent a new combination of simple objects in logical space. It would be like grouping the pieces on a chessboard in a new way. It would be a different arrangement of what you already have. But in Wittgenstein's later philosophy a new language game would embody a new "form of life," and this would not merely be a rearrangement of what was there before. Suppose the people of a certain tribe use language to describe events that are occurring or have occurred (such as men walking, running, or fighting, or the weather), or that they believe have occurred, but they do not have any *imaginative* use of language. They do not lie, pretend, make supposals, or engage in any imaginative play. Nor does any behavior of pretending occur: the children do not ever, for example, walk on all fours and growl as if they were lions. These people would not understand kidding. If one of us said to them something obviously false and then laughed, they would not know how to take it. (We should remember that among ourselves we differ greatly in our responsiveness to joking and pretense.) What these people lack is not words but the behavior and reactions that enter into the language games of imagination. Are they capable of *foreseeing* a use of language to convey a play of imagination? They do not even understand it when they encounter it. A new use of language embedded in a new form of life could not be anticipated, any more than could the rise of nonobjective painting.

THE ESSENCE OF LANGUAGE. The *Tractatus* assumes that there is a universal form of language, just as it assumes (6.022) that there is a universal form of number—that which is common to all numbers. The *Investigations* rejects this assumption. There is nothing common to the various forms of language that makes them language. There is not something common to all language games, just as there is not something common to all *games.* We are asked to consider the various kinds of games there are (for example, board games, card games, ball games) and the variety within each kind. If we pick out a feature common to two games we shall find that it is absent from some other place in the spectrum of games. Not all games are amusing, not all involve winning or losing, not all require competition between players, and so on. What makes all of them games, what gives unity to those activities, is not some feature present in all games but a multitude of relationships "overlapping and criss-crossing." Wittgenstein employed the analogy of a family resemblance. One can often see a striking resemblance between several generations of the same family. Studying them at close hand one may find that there is no feature common to all of the family. The eyes or the build or the temperament are not always the same. The family resemblance is due to many features that "overlap and criss-cross." The unity of games is like a family resemblance. This is also the case with sentences, descriptions, and numbers.

> Why do we call something a "number": Well, perhaps because it has, a—direct—relationship with several things that have hitherto been called number; and this can be said to give it an indirect relationship to other things we call the same name. And we extend our concept of number as in spinning a thread we twist fibre on fibre. And the strength of the thread does not reside in the fact that some one fibre runs through its whole length, but in the overlapping of the fibres. (Sec. 67)

One of the remarkable features of the *Investigations* is the detail and ingenuity of Wittgenstein's examination of some sample concepts (*reading, deriving, being guided:* Secs. 156–178) in order to bring out the variety of cases that fall under them and to prove that they are not united by an essence. If these concepts do not have an essential nature, then neither do the concepts of *description, proposition,* and *language.* The *Tractatus* was wrong in a most fundamental assumption.

ABSOLUTE SIMPLES. The *Tractatus* held that the ultimate elements of language are names that designate simple objects. In the *Investigations* it is argued that the words "simple" and "complex" have no *absolute* meaning. It has to be *laid down,* within a particular language game, what is to be taken as simple and what composite. For example, is one's visual image of a tree simple or composite? The question makes no sense until we make some such stipulation as that if one sees merely the trunk, it is simple, but if one sees trunk and branches, it is composite.

> But isn't a chess board, for instance, obviously, and absolutely composite?—You are probably thinking of the composition out of thirty-two white and thirty-two black squares. But could we not also say, for instance, that it was composed of the colours black and white and the schema of squares? And if there are quite different ways of looking at it, do you still want to say that the chessboard is absolutely "composite"? . . . Is the colour of a square on a chessboard simple, or does it consist of pure white and pure yellow? And is white simple, or does it consist of the colours of the rainbow?—Is this length of 2 cm. simple, or does it consist of two parts, each 1 cm. long? But why not of one bit 3 cm. long, and one bit 1 cm. long measured in the opposite direction? (Sec. 47)

By such examples Wittgenstein tried to show that the ideas of "simple" and "complex" are necessarily relative

to a language game. The notion of a simplicity that is not relative but absolute, because all of language is based on it, is a philosophical "super-concept." We have an image but we do not know how to apply it: we do not know what would be an example of an absolute simple.

The more closely we examine actual language,

the sharper becomes the conflict between it

and our philosophical ideal.

In the *Tractatus* the existence of simple objects was conceived as following from the requirement that the sense of sentences be *definite.* In the *Investigations* this requirement is regarded as another philosophical illusion. We have imagined an "ideal" of language that will not satisfy actual needs. A sharp boundary has not been drawn between, for example, games and activities that are not games. But why *should* there be one *in general?* Precision and exactness are relative to some particular purpose. The guests are to arrive exactly at one o'clock, but *this* notion of exactness would not employ the instruments and measurements of an observatory. "No *single* ideal of exactness has been laid down; we do not know what we should be supposed to imagine under this head" (Sec. 88). Losing sight of the fact that there are different standards of exactness for different purposes, we have supposed that there is a certain state of complete exactness underneath the surface of our everyday speech and that logical analysis can bring it to light. We have supposed, therefore, that a proposition would have one and only one complete analysis.

In searching for the ideal of perfect exactness we become dissatisfied with ordinary words and sentences. We do not find in actual language the pure and clear-cut structure that we desire. The more closely we examine actual language, the sharper becomes the conflict between it and our philosophical ideal. The latter now begins to seem empty. We do not even understand how it could be realized in actual language. We have been bewitched by a *picture.* Instead of trying to perceive in our language a design too fine to grasp, we need to see more clearly what is really there. We should abandon preconceived ideas and hypotheses and turn to *description,* the purpose of which will be to remove our philosophical perplexities. The substitution of description for analysis, and the new conception that nothing is hidden, is a major change from the *Tractatus.*

MEANING AS USE. If the picture theory is the central feature of the *Tractatus,* it is important to see how Wittgenstein's new thinking judged that theory. Surprisingly, there is not much explicit discussion of it, and the remarks that do occur are usually enigmatic. But if we take a long view of the new philosophy, there can be no question that it rejects the picture theory. In the later work as well as the earlier, Wittgenstein was concerned with the question, How can a sentence say something; how can language represent reality? The first sentence of the *Blue Book* is "What is the meaning of a word?" and it might equally well have been "What is the meaning of a sentence?" Both philosophical systems are centered on the same question, but the answer given in the second is entirely different. Instead of holding that a sentence has meaning or sense because it is a picture, the *Investigations* says that the meaning of a sentence is its "use" (*Gebrauch*) or "employment" (*Verwendung*) or "application" (*Anwendung*).

Some readers of Wittgenstein have doubted that he spoke of the use of a *sentence,* and others have thought that in any case it is wrong to speak this way. There is no question on the first point. Wittgenstein spoke of the "use" of a sentence in many passages. For example: "But doesn't the fact that sentences have the same sense consist in their having the same *use?*" (*Investigations,* Sec. 20); there are "countless different kinds of use of what we call 'symbols,' 'words,' 'sentences'" (Sec. 23).

The other objection may be important. Some philosophers want to say that a *sentence* cannot have a use. Words have a use; we learn the use of words, not of sentences. We understand sentences without having their sense explained to us, because we understand the use of the words that compose them.

What is espoused here is really the ground of the picture theory of the *Tractatus* (cf. *Tractatus,* 4.021, 4.026, 4.027). In the *Investigations* there is more than one objection to the above argument. Wittgenstein denied that we always understand a sentence, even if it is a grammatically correct sentence whose words we do understand. If someone says, for example, that the sentence "This is here" (saying which, he points to an object in front of him) makes sense to him, "then he should ask himself in what special circumstances this sentence is actually used. There it does make sense" (Sec. 117). "A philosopher says that he understands the sentence 'I am here,' that he means something by it, thinks something—even when he doesn't think at all how, on what occasions, this sentence is used" (Sec. 514). Wittgenstein was saying that these sentences have sense only in special circumstances; in other circumstances we do not understand them—that is, we do not know what to *do* with them.

The view of the *Tractatus* is entirely different. An elementary sentence is a combination of names, and if we know what the names refer to, then we understand the sentence, for it *shows* its sense. "Circumstances" have nothing to do with it. The *Investigations* regards this view as absurd. What does the sentence "I am here" *show?* Certainly it does not show its *use.* What can it mean to say that it shows its sense? A significant sentence is a tool with which a certain job is done. By looking at a sentence you cannot always tell whether it is a tool and, if it is, what job it is used for. The *Investigations* denies the claim that was the basis of the picture theory, namely that "we understand the sense of a propositional sign without its having been explained to us" (*Tractatus,* 4.02).

In holding that (in many cases) the meaning of an expression is its use, Wittgenstein was not declaring that the words "meaning" and "use" are general synonyms. By the "use" of an expression he meant the special circumstances, the "surroundings," in which it is spoken or written. The use of an expression is the *language game* in which it plays a part. Some readers have arrived at the mistaken idea that by the "use" of an expression Wittgenstein meant its *ordinary* or its *correct* use: they have thought that he was an "ordinary-language philosopher." But Wittgenstein studied any use of language, real or imaginary, that may illuminate a philosophical problem. Often he *invented* language games that corresponded to no actual use of language (see, for example, *Blue and Brown Books,* pp. 103–104, 110). The language games are "*objects of comparison* which are meant to throw light on the facts of our language by way not only of similarities, but also of dissimilarities" (*Investigations,* Sec. 130).

The *Tractatus* holds that language is ultimately composed of names, that the meaning of a name is a simple object, and that the sense of a sentence arises from the names that compose it. One name stands for one thing, another for another thing, and the combination pictures a state of affairs (4.0311). Thus, naming is prior to the sense of sentences (although it is also said that a name has meaning only in a sentence: 3.3). A sentence says something because it is composed of names that stand for things. In the *Investigations* two objections are made against this notion of the priority of names. First, the meaning of a word is never the thing, if there is one, that corresponds to the word (Sec. 40). Second, before one can find out what a name stands for one must already have mastered the language game to which the name belongs. In order to learn the name of a color, a direction, a sensation, one must have some grasp of the activities of placing colors in an order, of reading a map, of responding to the words, gestures, and behavior that are expressions of sensation. Merely pointing at something and saying a word achieves nothing. The kind of use the word will have, the special circumstances in which it will be said, must be understood before it can even *be* a name.

One could say that the *Tractatus* conceives of a significant sentence as having the nature of a mechanism. If the parts fit, then the whole thing works: you have a picture of reality. If the parts do not fit, they are like cog-wheels that do not mesh. There is, as it were, a clash of meanings. But in the *Investigations* we read: "When a sentence is called senseless, it is not as it were its sense that is senseless" (Sec. 500). If someone said to us, for example, "My head is asleep," we should be perplexed. It would be no help if he said: "You know what it is for an arm or a leg to be asleep. I have the same thing, except that it is my head." Here we do not know what the "same" *is*. It is not that we see that the meaning of "head" is incompatible with the meaning of "asleep." We do not perceive a clash of meanings. But we do not know what behavior and circumstances go with this sentence. It is not that we see that it *cannot* have a use (because the words do not fit together). The fact is that it does not have a use: we do not know in what circumstances one should say it. "Look at the sentence as an instrument, and at its sense as its employment!" (Sec. 421). Instead of the fundamental notion being the right combination of words and the sense of the sentence being explained in terms of it, it is the other way round: whether the sentence has an "employment" (*Verwendung*) is what is fundamental. This would be our only criterion for whether there is a sense-making combination of parts.

One additional criticism of the picture theory will be noted. Suppose that a sentence were a picture. There would still be a question of how we should apply the picture. If someone showed you a drawing of a cube and told you to bring him one of those things, you might in good faith bring him a triangular prism instead of a cube. More than one way of taking the drawing was possible. It suggests a cube, but it is possible to interpret the drawing differently. A picture represents an old man walking up a steep path leaning on a stick. But could it not also represent him as sliding down the hill in that position? For us it is more natural to take it in the first way, but the explanation of this does not lie in anything intrinsic to the picture. A picture of a green leaf might be understood to be a representation of the color green, or of a specific shade of green, or of leaf shape in general, or of a particular shape of leaf, or of foliage in general, and so on. How a picture is used will determine what it is a picture of. It cannot, therefore, be a fundamental explanation of the sense of sentences to say that they are pictures. Wittgenstein hinted that the picture theory is plausible because we tend to think of portraits that hang on our walls and are, as it were, "idle." If we consider instead an engineer's machine

drawing or an elevation with measurements, then the *activity* of using the picture will be seen to be the important thing (Sec. 291).

LOGICAL COMPULSION. Our discussion may suggest the following view: How a word, sentence, or picture is *interpreted* determines what use is made of it. How a man responds to an order, for example, depends on how he *understands* it, and whether the one who gave the order will be satisfied with that response will depend on what he *meant* by it. If someone understands the algebraic formula determining a numerical series, then he will know what numbers should occur at various places in the expansion of the series. What a person deduces from a proposition will depend entirely on his understanding of the proposition. Wittgenstein once wrote (in a pre-*Tractatus* notebook): "What propositions follow from a proposition must be completely settled before that proposition can have a sense" (*Notebooks*, p. 64). By virtue of grasping the meaning or sense of an expression we know how to employ it: we know when to say it and what action it calls for. Instead of meaning being identical with use, it comes before use, and use is based on it. When you hear a sentence and understand it or give an order and mean it, the action required in responding to the sentence or obeying the order is already, in a queer sense, taken in your mind. In your act of meaning or understanding, "your mind as it were flew ahead and took all the steps" before they were taken physically (*Investigations*, Sec. 188). In taking, or accepting, those physical steps, you would be ratifying what has already transpired in your mind. To do differently would be inconsistent with the previous mental act. Consistency, rationality, requires you to take these steps or draw these conclusions. Understanding carries compulsion with it.

This idea of "logical compulsion" is vigorously attacked in the *Investigations* and in Wittgenstein's writings on the foundations of mathematics. Was Wittgenstein rejecting deductive reasoning and logical necessity? No. He was rejecting this *picture* of logical necessity, namely that when I have understood a proposition and there is a question of what follows from it, I *have* to deduce such-and-such consequences because it was already settled in my understanding of the proposition that it would have those consequences. Wittgenstein's criticism of this imagery creates a continuity between his philosophy of psychology and his philosophy of logic. A part of his criticism could be put as follows: Suppose that two people, *A* and *B*, have received the same instruction in elementary arithmetic. They have been given the same rules and illustrations and have worked through the same examples. Later, when they are required to perform some arithmetical operation, *A* does it right and *B* wrong, although *B* thinks he has done it correctly. We shall say that *A understood* the problem and *B* did not. What does this come to? It could have been that the *sole* difference between them was that *A wrote down* correct numbers and *B* incorrect ones. If this fact is our *criterion* of a difference of understanding, then it is wrong-headed to postulate a difference of understanding to *explain* the fact that *A* and *B* wrote down different answers.

The inclination to insert an act or state of understanding as an intermediary between, for example, hearing an order and executing it is an example of what is called in the *Brown Book (Blue and Brown Books,* p. 143) "a general disease of thinking." It consists in always looking for (and "finding") mental states and acts as the sources of our actions. Other examples of this inclination are thinking that one must know where one's pain is before one can point to the place, thinking that we call various shades of red by the name "red" because we see something in common in all of them, thinking that we speak of "looking in our memory for a word" and of "looking in the park for a friend" because we have noticed a similarity between the two cases.

The assumption of mental states to explain our actions comes from a "one-sided diet." If we let our view range over the family of cases of "differences of understanding," we shall discover some in which the only difference between two people who understood a certain proposition differently consists in their having drawn different conclusions from it.

Must we believe, then, that our understanding does not reach beyond the particular training we received and the examples we studied? No. There is a good sense in which it reaches beyond, for we do go on to apply rules in new cases in what we agree is the same way we were taught. Does this agreement have to be explained by the fact that our understanding has penetrated to the essence of the examples? No. This agreement is one of the "extremely general facts of nature" (*Investigations,* pp. 56, 230) that underlie our concepts. We do handle new cases in the same way. If this strikes us as mysterious, it is a symptom of our confusion. We are trying to imagine that the future steps are taken in the mind, "in a queer sense," before they are taken in reality—as if the mind were a machine that already contained its future movements (*Investigations,* Secs. 193–195).

Wittgenstein was saying that our understanding of a rule is not a state that forces us to apply the rule in a particular way. Someone who has received the ordinary instruction in arithmetic or chess and has applied it normally in the past could go on in the future in a different way but *still be a rational person.* Perhaps he could even give a reasonable defense of his divergence.

If this is true, it makes it seem that there are no *rules,* for a rule forbids some things and requires others. It appears that anything goes, anything can be justified. But then understanding, meaning, language itself all crumble away because they imply rules.

The idea that the content of a rule can be fixed only by a practice provides a transition to one of the most subtle topics of the Investigations, *namely the treatment of "private language."*

Wittgenstein was not denying, however, that there are rules and that we follow them. He held that the way a rule is applied in particular cases *determines its meaning.* A rule, as it is formulated in a sentence, "hangs in the air" (*Investigations,* Sec. 198). What puts it on the ground, gives it content, is what we say and do in actual cases. And on this there is overwhelming agreement: we nearly always say and do the same. It is this agreement that determines whether a particular action is in accordance with a rule. Rather than to say that we agree *because* we follow rules, it is more perceptive to say that our agreement fixes the meaning of the rules, defines their content. In a sense the content of the rules grows as our practice grows. Instead of thinking of mankind as coerced by the rules of logic and mathematics, we should consider that human practice establishes what the rules are.

PRIVATE RULES. The idea that the content of a rule can be fixed only by a practice provides a transition to one of the most subtle topics of the *Investigations,* namely the treatment of "private language." The conception that a significant sentence is a picture was replaced in Wittgenstein's thought by the conception that the sense of a sentence is determined by the circumstances in which it is uttered. Swinging a stick is a *strike* and pushing a piece of wood is a *move*—in the circumstances of games. Likewise, saying some words is *making a decision*—in certain circumstances. In one set of circumstances saying a particular sentence would be *asserting* something; in other circumstances saying those same words would be *asking* a question; in still others it would be *repeating* what someone had said.

This is a difficult conception to grasp. We feel a strong inclination to say that the only thing that determines the sense of what someone says is what goes on in his mind as he says it. As Locke put it, "Words, in their primary or immediate signification, stand for nothing but *the ideas in the mind of him that uses them.*" Whether some words you uttered expressed a question or an assertion is solely a matter of whether there was a question or an assertion *in your mind.* What the occasion was, what happened before and after, what persons were present—those circumstances are irrelevant to the sense of your words. The only "circumstance" that matters is the mental occurrence at the time of utterance.

Wittgenstein fought hard and resourcefully against this objection. One technique he used was to describe different cases of deciding, asserting, intending, expecting, and so on. The purpose of this was to show that when one utters some words that express, for instance, a decision, one cannot pick out anything that occurred (for example, a thought, an image, some spoken words, a feeling) such that one wants to call *that* the act of deciding.

This technique, although powerful, may provoke the response that the only thing proved is the *intangibility,* the *indescribability,* of the mental phenomenon in question. William James remarked about the *intention of saying a thing* before one has said it: "It is an entirely definite intention, distinct from all other intentions, an absolutely distinct state of consciousness, therefore; and yet how much of it consists of definite sensorial images, either of words or of things? Hardly anything!" This intention has "a nature of its own of the most positive sort, and yet what can we say about it without using words that belong to the later mental facts that replace it? The intention *to-say-so-and-so* is the only name it can receive" (*Principles of Psychology,* New York, 1890, Vol. I, p. 253). Likewise, the decision *to stay an hour longer* cannot be expressed in any other words than those, yet it is a quite definite mental occurrence; one knows it is there!

Wittgenstein opposed this conception not with further description but with an argument. It is the following: If a decision or expectation or sensation were a state or event that was logically independent of circumstances, then no one, not even the subject of the supposed event, could ever determine that it had occurred. First, how would one learn what, for example, deciding is? Since circumstances are supposed to be irrelevant, one could not learn it by observing other people. Apparently one would have to learn what deciding is *from one's own case.* But as Wittgenstein remarked: "If I know it only from my own case, then I know only what *I* call that, not what anyone else does" (*Investigations,* Sec. 347). Thus it would be unverifiable whether two people refer to the same phenomenon by the word "deciding." But worse is to come. One could not even take comfort in the thought "At least I know what *I* call 'deciding.'" You might believe that you have always called the same thing by that name. Yet nothing could determine that

this belief was right or wrong. Perhaps the private object constantly changes but you do not notice the change because your memory constantly deceives you (*Investigations,* p. 207)! The idea that you might have a language with logically private rules—i.e., rules that only you could understand because only you could know to what the words refer—is a self-contradictory idea. Following a rule implies *doing the same,* and what "the same" *is* can only be defined by a practice in which more than one person participates.

Wittgenstein's rejection of the intrinsically private, inner object is a consequence of his new conception of meaning. Language requires rules, and following a rule implies a customary way of doing something. It could not be that only once in the history of mankind was a rule followed (Sec. 199). An expression has a meaning only if there is a regular, a uniform, connection between saying the expression and certain circumstances. When we call something *measuring,* for example, a part of the uniformity we require is a constancy in the results of measurement (Sec. 242). A person can be *guided by a signpost* only if there is a regular way of responding to signposts. The meaning of an expression is its *use*—that is to say, the *language game* in which it occurs—that is to say, the uniform relation of the expression to certain *circumstances.* Wittgenstein made explicit the connection between this view of the nature of meaning and his attack on "private" mental contents when he said that following a rule is a *practice* and *therefore* one cannot follow a rule "privately" (Sec. 202).

BIBLIOGRAPHY

Works by Wittgenstein

Tractatus Logico-philosophicus. London, 1922. Contains the German text of *Logisch-philosophische Abhandlung,* with English translation on facing pages, and an introduction by Bertrand Russell. Republished with a new translation by D. F. Pears and B. F. McGuinness. London, 1961.

"Some Remarks on Logical Form." *PAS,* Supp. Vol. 9 (1929), 162–171.

Philosophical Investigations, G. E. M. Anscombe, Rush Rhees, and G. H. von Wright, eds., translated by G. E. M. Anscombe. Oxford, 1953. Contains German text of *Philosophische Untersuchungen,* with English translation on facing pages.

Remarks on the Foundations of Mathematics, G. E. M. Anscombe, Rush Rhees, and G. H. von Wright, eds., translated by G. E. M. Anscombe. Oxford, 1956. Parallel German and English texts.

The Blue and Brown Books: Preliminary Studies for the Philosophical Investigations. Oxford, 1958. With a preface by Rush Rhees.

Notebooks 1914–1916, G. E. M. Anscombe and G. H. von Wright, eds., translated by G. E. M. Anscombe. Oxford, 1961. Parallel German and English texts.

Philosophische Bemerkungen. Frankfurt, 1964.

"A Lecture on Ethics." *Philosophical Review,* Vol. 74 (1965). A paper delivered at Cambridge in 1929 or 1930.

Works on Wittgenstein

Biography

Gasking, D. A. T., and Jackson, A. C., "Ludwig Wittgenstein," memorial notice. *Australasian Journal of Philosophy*, Vol. 29 (1951).

Malcolm, Norman, *Ludwig Wittgenstein: A Memoir*. London, 1958.

Russell, Bertrand, "Ludwig Wittgenstein," memorial notice. *Mind*, Vol. 60 (1951).

Ryle, Gilbert, "Ludwig Wittgenstein," memorial notice. *Analysis*, Vol. 12 (1951).

Von Wright, G. H., "Ludwig Wittgenstein: A Biographical Sketch," Malcolm, *op. cit.*

Wisdom, John, "Ludwig Wittgenstein, 1934–1937." *Mind*, Vol. 61 (1952).

"Tractatus"

Anscombe, G. E. M., *An Introduction to Wittgenstein's Tractatus*. London, 1959.

Black, Max, *A Companion to Wittgenstein's Tractatus*. Cambridge, 1964.

Colombo, G. C. M., critical introduction and notes to the Italian translation of the *Tractatus*. Milan and Rome, 1954.

Daitz, E., "The Picture Theory of Meaning," in Antony Flew, ed., *Essays in Conceptual Analysis*. London, 1956.

Griffin, James, *Wittgenstein's Logical Atomism*. Oxford, 1964.

Hartnack, Justus, *Wittgenstein og den moderne Filosofi*. Copenhagen, 1960. Translated into German as *Wittgenstein und die moderne Philosophie*. Stuttgart, 1962.

Hintikka, Jaakko, "On Wittgenstein's Solipsism." *Mind*, Vol. 67 (1958).

Keyt, David, "Wittgenstein's Notion of an Object." *Philosophical Quarterly*, Vol. 13 (1963).

Keyt, David, "A New Interpretation of the *Tractatus* Examined." *Philosophical Review*, Vol. 74 (1965).

Maslow, Alexander, *A Study in Wittgenstein's Tractatus*. Berkeley and Los Angeles, 1961.

Pitcher, George, *The Philosophy of Wittgenstein*. Englewood Cliffs, N.J., 1964.

Ramsey, F. P., critical notice of the *Tractatus*, in R. F. Braithwaite, ed., *The Foundations of Mathematics*. London, 1931.

Rhees, Rush, "Miss Anscombe on the *Tractatus*." *Philosophical Quarterly*, Vol. 10 (1960).

Rhees, Rush, "The *Tractatus*: Seeds of Some Misunderstandings." *Philosophical Review*, Vol. 72 (1963).

Russell, Bertrand, "The Philosophy of Logical Atomism," in *Logic and Knowledge*, R. C. Marsh, ed. London, 1956.

Schlick, Moritz, "The Turning Point in Philosophy," in A. J. Ayer, ed., *Logical Positivism*. Glencoe, Ill., 1959.

Stenius, Eric, *Wittgenstein's Tractatus*. Oxford, 1960.

Wienpahl, Paul D., "Wittgenstein and the Naming Relation." *Inquiry*, Vol. 7 (1964).

"Blue and Brown Books," "Investigations," "Remarks on the Foundations of Mathematics"

Albritton, Rogers, "On Wittgenstein's Use of the Term 'Criterion.'" *Journal of Philosophy*, Vol. 56, No. 22 (1959).

Ayer, A. J., and Rhees, Rush, "Can There Be a Private Language?" *PAS*, Supp. Vol. 28 (1954). Symposium.

Ayer, A. J., "Privacy." *Proceedings of the British Academy*, Vol. 45 (1959).

Bambrough, Renford, "Universals and Family Resemblances." *PAS*, Vol. 61 (1960–1961).

Bouwsma, O. K., "The Blue Book." *Journal of Philosophy*, Vol. 58, No. 6 (1961).

Buck, R. C., "Non-other Minds," in R. J. Butler, ed., *Analytical Philosophy*. Oxford, 1962.

Carney, J. D., "Private Language: The Logic of Wittgenstein's Argument." *Mind*, Vol. 69 (1960).

Cavell, Stanley, "The Availability of Wittgenstein's Later Philosophy." *Philosophical Review*, Vol. 71 (1962).

Chihara, C. S., "Wittgenstein and Logical Compulsion." *Analysis*, Vol. 21 (1961).

Chihara, C. S., "Mathematical Discovery and Concept Formation." *Philosophical Review*, Vol. 72 (1963).

Cook, J. W., "Wittgenstein on Privacy." *Philosophical Review*, Vol. 74 (1965).

Cowan, J. L., "Wittgenstein's Philosophy of Logic." *Philosophical Review*, Vol. 70 (1961).

Dummett, Michael, "Wittgenstein's Philosophy of Mathematics." *Philosophical Review*, Vol. 68 (1959).

Feyerabend, Paul K., "Wittgenstein's *Philosophical Investigations*." *Philosophical Review*, Vol. 64 (1955).

Fodor, J. A., and Katz, J. J., "The Availability of What We Say." *Philosophical Review*, Vol. 72 (1963).

Gasking, D. A. T., "Avowals," in R. J. Butler, ed., *Analytical Philosophy*, Oxford, 1962.

Hardin, C. L., "Wittgenstein on Private Languages." *Journal of Philosophy*, Vol. 56 (1959).

Hartnack, Justus, *Wittgenstein og den moderne Filosofi*, above.

Kreisel, Georg, "Wittgenstein's *Remarks on the Foundations of Mathematics*." *British Journal for the Philosophy of Science*, Vol. 9 (1958).

Kreisel, Georg, "Wittgenstein's Theory and Practice of Philosophy." *British Journal for the Philosophy of Science*, Vol. 11 (1960).

Malcolm, Norman, *Dreaming*. New York, 1959.

Malcolm, Norman, *Knowledge and Certainty*. Englewood Cliffs, N.J., 1963. See "Wittgenstein's *Philosophical Investigations*" and "Knowledge of Other Minds."

Malcolm, Norman, "Behaviorism as a Philosophy of Psychology," in T. W. Wann, ed., *Behaviorism and Phenomenology*, Chicago, 1964.

Moore, G. E., "Wittgenstein's Lectures in 1930–1933," in *Philosophical Papers*. New York, 1959.

Nell, E. J., "The Hardness of the Logical 'Must.'" *Analysis*, Vol. 21 (1961).

Pitcher, George, *The Philosophy of Wittgenstein*. Englewood Cliffs, N.J., 1964.

Rhees, Rush, Preface to *The Blue and Brown Books*. Oxford, 1958.

Rhees, Rush, "Wittgenstein's Builders." *PAS*, Vol. 60 (1959–1960).

Rhees, Rush, "Some Developments in Wittgenstein's View of Ethics." *Philosophical Review*, Vol. 74 (1965).

Strawson, P. F., critical notice of *Philosophical Investigations*. *Mind*, Vol. 63 (1954).

Thomson, Judith J., "Private Languages." *American Philosophical Quarterly*, Vol. 1 (1964).

Waismann, Friedrich, "Notes on Talks With Wittgenstein." *Philosophical Review*, Vol. 74 (1965).

Wellman, Carl, "Wittgenstein and the Egocentric Predicament." *Mind*, Vol. 68 (1959).

Wellman, Carl, "Our Criteria for Third-person Psychological Sentences." *Journal of Philosophy*, Vol. 58 (1961).

Wellman, Carl, "Wittgenstein's Conception of a Criterion." *Philosophical Review*, Vol. 71 (1962).

Wisdom, John, *Philosophy and Psychoanalysis*. Oxford, 1953.

Wisdom, John, "A Feature of Wittgenstein's Technique." *PAS*, Supp. Vol. 35 (1961).

— NORMAN MALCOLM

WITTGENSTEIN, LUDWIG JOSEF JOHANN (UPDATE)

Of Ludwig Josef Johann Wittgenstein's philosophical writings available in print, by far the greater part was published after the 1967 *Encyclopedia of Philosophy.* The year 1967 also saw the publication on microfilm of Wittgenstein's *Nachlass.* In addition to the *Nachlass* itself and the posthumously published material from it, there has become available since 1967 a considerable body of Wittgenstein's letters, records of conversations with him, and notes taken by students at his lectures. Altogether, vastly more material is available to the student of Wittgenstein than there was in the mid-1960s. The *Tractatus* and the *Philosophical Investigations* remain, however, the central works for anyone trying to understand Wittgenstein's philosophy. The other writings do give a far fuller understanding of how Wittgenstein's later thought developed; they make clear important continuities between earlier and later work that had been difficult to see earlier. The recognition of these continuities can, for example, be seen in several of the essays in Peter Winch (1969), including Winch's own introductory essay on the unity of Wittgenstein's philosophy. Hidé Ishiguro (1969), in that volume, established that Wittgenstein's connection between meaning and use was not new in his later philosophy. He had always tied meaning to use; what was new in the later work, Ishiguro argued, was the willingness to consider a great variety of different kinds of use besides stating of facts; and Winch notes also the importance in Wittgenstein's later work of the idea that what we call "stating a fact" can itself be many different sorts of thing. A very important continuity noted by Anthony Kenny (1973) lies in Wittgenstein's conception of philosophy itself, including the contrast he made between philosophy and natural science, and the central role he gave to descriptions (rather than proofs) within philosophy.

The material written in the late 1940s and just before Wittgenstein's death shows how Wittgenstein's thought developed after the completion of what was published as Part I of *Philosophical Investigations.* He mentioned to friends his intention (never carried out) of replacing much of what is in the last thirty pages or so of Part I with what is in Part II, along with related material (subsequently published as *Remarks on Philosophical Psychology* and *Last Writings on Philosophical Psychology,* Vol. 1). His comment helps make clear how he saw the investigations of psychological concepts that occupy so much of Part II of the *Investigations* and of the related manuscripts. He is not turning away from the central questions about language in the *Investigations* to new and unrelated topics. Those questions themselves led him repeatedly into detailed examination of such matters as how what is going on in our minds bears on whether we speak with understanding or rather only as parrots might. The late writings show also his concern with the question, important to him from the 1930s onward, how what is given in experience is relevant to the concepts we grasp. These issues are closely related also to the investigations in *Remarks on Colour* (1977), drawn from manuscripts from the last eighteen months of Wittgenstein's life.

The Tractatus *and the* Philosophical Investigations *remain the central works for anyone trying to understand Wittgenstein's philosophy.*

Wittgenstein was greatly stimulated by G. E. Moore's attempts to reply to skeptical arguments by asserting things he took it to be plain that he knew (for example, that the earth had existed for a long time) and by Moore's discussion of the paradoxical character of saying "I believe he has gone out, but he has not." Moore's paradox about belief provides a focus for some of Wittgenstein's discussions of psychological concepts in Part II of the *Investigations* and the related manuscripts. Moore's commonsense response to skepticism provided the impetus for Wittgenstein's treatment of skepticism and knowledge in *On Certainty.* He criticized Moore for having misunderstood the concept of knowledge on the model of that of belief and doubt; and indeed *On Certainty* is to some degree continuous with Wittgenstein's other discussions of psychological concepts. But it also stands on its own as an investigation of how certainty forms a part of our various language games and of the role played in those language games by empirical propositions that are not questioned. Wittgenstein's methods in *On Certainty* have been applied by other philosophers in discussions of religious and ethical claims, but he himself does not attempt to apply general principles about doubt, certainty, or knowledge to ethics or religion. (Some of his views about ethics and religion, as well as about art and other topics, have been gathered from various manuscripts and published in *Culture and Value.*)

There is a group of questions about how Wittgenstein saw the relation between facts and the language games in which we are engaged and about how far his approach, in his later philosophy, involves some kind of idealism or relativism. Do facts exercise any sort of control on the character of our concepts? If there were people who engaged in language games very different from ours—if there were, for example, people who thought one could travel to the moon while in a dream—would we be in a position to criticize such people as fundamentally in error? Several of Wittgenstein's works published after 1967 are particularly relevant to these questions, including *On Certainty, Zettel* (a collection of remarks Wittgenstein had cut from various manuscripts, mostly from the late 1940s), and Wittgenstein's "Remarks on Frazer's *Golden Bough*" (included in Wittgenstein, 1993). Wittgenstein's discussions of mathematics also bear directly on the question how free we are in our development of concepts: what would we be getting wrong if our mathematics, or our logic, were very different? In these discussions Wittgenstein is frequently responding to Gottlob Frege's conception of objectivity in logic and mathematics.

Reception of Wittgenstein's Philosophy

Philosophers are far from agreement on how Wittgenstein's philosophical achievements can be assimilated or indeed whether they should be. There are many philosophers who regard Wittgenstein's influence as pernicious and who think that the best response to his philosophy is to ignore it. This view rests sometimes on the idea that his philosophy developed to meet his personal needs and is irrelevant to the genuine interests of contemporary philosophy. A second kind of response to Wittgenstein involves making a sharp distinction between, on the one hand, the important philosophical claims and arguments that are thought to be in his work or implied by it and, on the other, his own understanding of his philosophy as not involving disputable theses or explanations and as aiming to dissolve philosophical problems rather than to find the correct answers. If that distinction is made, it may then be held that we should simply ignore his views about philosophy (which it may also be held are inconsistent with his own practice) and should instead pay attention to the theses and arguments (on which, on this view, his reputation must properly rest). Philosophers who read Wittgenstein in this way do not agree among themselves whether the theses in question are true, the arguments sound; nor do they agree about what the extractible theses are supposed to be. Thus, for example, those who ascribe to him theses about the necessary conditions for a language disagree about whether these conditions include the necessity that a speaker of any language have been at least at some time a member of a community of speakers. A third distinct kind of response to Wittgenstein takes seriously his conception of philosophical problems as dependent upon our misunderstandings of the work-

ings of our language; they arise when language is allowed to go "on holiday." And so any adequate approach to these problems depends on coming to see how we are led into them; it will not issue in solutions that leave unchanged our idea of the problems themselves. Finally, some elements of Wittgenstein's approach to philosophical problems, and his criticisms of standard philosophical moves in response to them, have also been treated as important and interesting by those who, like Richard Rorty, wish to see analytical philosophy replaced by some other kind of intellectual activity.

The philosophical disputes about Wittgenstein's work have been focused to a considerable degree on the issues discussed by Norman Malcolm in the original *Encyclopedia* piece, including the relation between meaning and use, the possibility of a private language, and the objectivity of rules. Much recent controversy has been inspired by the writings of Michael Dummett and Saul Kripke. Dummett reads Wittgenstein as putting forward an anti-realist theory of meaning; Kripke has argued that Wittgenstein in the *Investigations* presents a new skeptical problem and a skeptical solution to it. Responses to Dummett and Kripke have made clear the importance of understanding Wittgenstein's aims, his desire to show how our misconceptions can make something perfectly ordinary appear problematic; thus, it is the step in our arguments at which the ordinary first appears problematic which we fail to note, and to which we need to attend.

[See also Dummett, Michael; Frege, Gottlob; Kripke, Saul Aaron; Philosophy; Skepticism.]

BIBLIOGRAPHY

Works by Wittgenstein

Philosophical Remarks, ed. R. Rhees, trans. R. Hargreaves and R. White. Oxford, 1964; 2d ed., 1975.

Zettel, ed. G. E. M. Anscombe and G. H. von Wright, trans. G. E. M. Anscombe. Oxford, 1967; 2d ed., 1981.

On Certainty, ed. G. E. M. Anscombe and G. H. von Wright, trans. G. E. M. Anscombe and D. Paul. Oxford, 1969.

Proto-tractatus, ed. B. F. McGuinness, T. Nyberg, and G. H. von Wright, trans. D. F. Pears and B. F. McGuinness. Ithaca, NY, 1971.

Philosophical Grammar, ed. R. Rhees, trans. A. Kenny. Oxford, 1974.

Remarks on Colour, ed. G. E. M. Anscombe, trans. L. McAlister and M. Schättle. Oxford, 1977.

Remarks on the Foundations of Mathematics, ed. G. H. von Wright, R. Rhees, and G. E. M. Anscombe, trans. G. E. M. Anscombe, 3d ed. Cambridge, MA, 1978.

Culture and Value, ed. G. H. von Wright, trans. P. Winch. Oxford, 1980.

Remarks on the Philosophy of Psychology. Vol. 1, ed. G. E. M. Anscombe and G. H. von Wright, trans. G. E. M. Anscombe. Chicago, 1980. Vol. 2, ed. G. H. von Wright and H. Nyman, trans. C. G. Luckhardt and M. A. E. Aue. Chicago, 1980.

Last Writings on the Philosophy of Psychology, ed. G. H. von Wright and H. Nyman, trans. C. G. Luckhardt and M. A. E. Aue. 2 vols. Chicago, 1982–92.

Werkausgabe. 8 vols. Frankfurt, 1989.

Philosophical Occasions, 1912–1951, ed. J. Klagge and A. Nordmann. Indianapolis, 1993. Contains all Wittgenstein's shorter published writings; some letters and records of lectures; also a full account of the Wittgenstein *Nachlass.*

Wienerausgabe, ed. M. Nedo. 22 vols. Vienna, 1993–.

The Published Works of Ludwig Wittgenstein, ed. H. Kaal and A. McKinnon. Electronic text database.

Lectures and Conversations

Wittgenstein's Lectures, Cambridge, 1930–32, ed. D. Lee. Oxford, 1980.

Wittgenstein's Lectures, Cambridge, 1932–1935, ed. A. Ambrose. Totowa, NJ, 1979.

Wittgenstein's Lectures on the Foundations of Mathematics, Cambridge, 1939, ed. C. Diamond. Ithaca, NY, 1976; Chicago, 1989.

Wittgenstein's Lectures on Philosophical Psychology 1946–47, ed. P. T. Geach. Chicago, 1988.

Ludwig Wittgenstein and the Vienna Circle: Conversations Recorded by Friedrich Waismann, ed. B. F. McGuinness, trans. J. Schulte and B. F. McGuinness. Oxford, 1979.

Works on Wittgenstein

Anscombe, G. E. M. "The Question of Linguistic Idealism," in *From Parmenides to Wittgenstein* (Oxford, 1981).

Canfield, J. V., ed. *The Philosophy of Wittgenstein.* 15 vols. New York, 1986. Comprehensive collection of over 250 articles.

Cavell, S. *The Claim of Reason.* Oxford, 1979.

Conant, J. "Kierkegaard, Wittgenstein, and Nonsense," in T. Cohen et al., eds., *Pursuits of Reason* (Lubbock, TX, 1993).

Diamond, C. *The Realistic Spirit: Wittgenstein, Philosophy, and the Mind.* Cambridge, MA, 1991.

Dummett, M. *Truth and Other Enigmas.* London, 1978.

Goldfarb, W. "I Want You to Bring Me a Slab: Remarks on the Opening Sections of the *Philosophical Investigations,*" *Synthese,* Vol. 56 (1983).

———. "Kripke on Wittgenstein on Rules," *Journal of Philosophy,* Vol. 82 (1985).

Holtzman, S. H., and Leich, C. M., eds. *Wittgenstein: To Follow a Rule.* London, 1981.

Hacker, P. M. S. *Insight and Illusion: Themes in the Philosophy of Wittgenstein.* Oxford, 1972; rev. 2d ed., 1986.

Ishiguro, H. "Use and Reference of Names," in P. Winch, ed., *Studies in the Philosophy of Wittgenstein* (London, 1969).

Kenny, A. *Wittgenstein.* Harmondsworth, Middlesex, 1973.

Kripke, S. *Wittgenstein on Rules and Private Language.* Cambridge, MA, 1982.

Malcolm, N. *Nothing Is Hidden: Wittgenstein's Criticism of His Early Thought.* Oxford, 1986.

McDowell, J. *Selected Papers,* Vol. 1. Cambridge, MA, 1996.

McGuinness, B. F. *Wittgenstein—A Life: Young Ludwig: 1889–1921.* London, 1988.

Monk, R. *Ludwig Wittgenstein: The Duty of Genius.* New York, 1990.

Pears, D. F. *The False Prison.* 2 vols. Oxford, 1987–88.

Rhees, R. *Discussions of Wittgenstein.* London, 1970.

Shanker, S. G., ed. *Ludwig Wittgenstein: Critical Assessments.* 4 vols. Beckenham, Kent, 1986. Comprehensive collection of 104 articles.

Shanker, V. A., and S. G. Shanker. *A Wittgenstein Bibliography.* Beckenham, Kent, 1986. Covers primary sources and over 5,400 items on Wittgenstein.

Sluga, H., and D. Stern, eds. *Cambridge Companion to Wittgenstein.* Cambridge, 1996. Includes a full bibliography of Wittgenstein's writings and good selective bibliography of secondary literature.

Winch, P., ed. *Studies in the Philosophy of Wittgenstein.* London, 1969.

Wright, C. *Wittgenstein on the Foundations of Mathematics.* London, 1980.

– CORA DIAMOND

WOLLSTONECRAFT, MARY

Mary Wollstonecraft (1757–97) has long been recognized as one of the most influential feminist theorists in history, largely through her *Vindication of the Rights of Woman* (1792). Late twentieth-century scholarship also began to explore her other texts and their significance.

Wollstonecraft's work is a product of the late Enlightenment, emphasizing the need to achieve virtue and progress through development of reason and sensibility. It also reflects ideas of the Dissenters and political radicals who stood among the relatively few English supporters of the French Revolution. Wollstonecraft's early mentors were Richard Price and Joseph Priestley. The

Mary Wollstonecraft demanded an end to unnatural distinctions based on sex and family relations. (John Opie, R.A., National Portrait Gallery, London)

circle with whom she continued to associate included writers and artists such as William Blake, Thomas Paine, Henry Fuseli, and William Godwin. Like them, she opposed slavery, standing armies, and many elements of political patriarchy such as primogeniture, aristocracy, and probably monarchy. She shared their critique of the corrupting influence of political and social institutions structured around "unnatural distinctions" based on rank, property, religion, or profession.

As she wrote in the Rights of Woman,

if observation could not prove that men

had more natural capability for reason than women,

they could claim no superiority over women

and certainly no right to rule them.

Wollstonecraft's most distinctive and well-known contribution was to extend this analysis to demand an end to unnatural distinctions based on sex and family relations. As she wrote in the *Rights of Woman,* if observation could not prove that men had more natural capability for reason than women, they could claim no superiority over women and certainly no right to rule them. In analysis shaped by Locke and Rousseau (but one that attacked Rousseau for his views on women), she concluded that education, experience, and the "present constitution of society," and not nature, created most observed character differences between men and women.

She argued that unnatural distinctions between women and men tended toward the same effects as other unjust power relations: they corrupt the character of all parties to the relationship, rendering the dominant party dependent on its power and making the subordinate party resort to cunning and unvirtuous strategies of self-preservation. In the case of women she pointed to the use of beauty as what might now be called a "weapon of the weak." Unlike more well-known democratic theorists of her era, she applied an antipatriarchal analysis commonly used on institutions such as government to the family itself.

She advocated altering the social practices such as dress, courtship, employment, and family relations that had given men power over women and kept both from virtue. She sought expanded work opportunities for women. She proposed development of a public school system educating girls and boys and children of different classes similarly and together, at least for the early years of their schooling, and wanted girls to study sub-

jects that had been forbidden to them. Her final, unfinished novel, *Maria, or the Wrongs of Woman,* underscored the necessity of women's ability to support themselves, divorce, and have rights over their children.

Although most famous for her arguments on women's rights, other contributions are worth noting. Her *Vindication of the Rights of Men* (1790) was one of the first attacks on Edmund Burke's *Reflections on the Revolution in France,* and it engaged his work on the sublime and the beautiful, thus integrating aesthetics and politics in a critique of Burke's defense of monarchy, aristocracy, and pomp. Her further exploration of the French Revolution in the *Historical and Moral View of the Origin and Progress of the French Revolution* (1794) contains an underrated inquiry into the nature of political history and the relationship between ideals and human action. Wollstonecraft's *Letters Written during a Short Residence in Sweden, Norway, and Denmark* influenced the early generation of English Romantics, including Coleridge, Southey, Wordsworth, and Percy Bysshe Shelley and his wife, Wollstonecraft's daughter, Mary Shelley.

[See also Beauty; Locke, John; Rousseau, Jean-Jacques.]

BIBLIOGRAPHY

Works by Wollstonecraft

The Works of Mary Wollstonecraft, ed. J. Todd and M. Butler. New York, 1989. Includes all of Wollstonecraft's works (other than letters). Among the most important are:

Mary: A Fiction (1788).

A Vindication of the Rights of Men, in a Letter to the Right Honorable Edmund Burke (1790).

A Vindication of the Rights of Woman with Strictures on Moral and Political Subjects (1792).

An Historical and Moral View of the Origin and Progress of the French Revolution; and the Effect It Has Produced in Europe (1794).

Letters Written during a Short Residence in Sweden, Norway, and Denmark (1796).

Maria, or the Wrongs of Woman (post.).

Works on Wollstonecraft

Poovey, M. *The Proper Lady and the Woman Writer: Ideology as Style in the Works of Mary Wollstonecraft, Mary Shelley, and Jane Austen.* Chicago, 1982.

Sapiro, V. *A Vindication of Political Virtue: The Political Theory of Mary Wollstonecraft.* Chicago, 1992.

Tomalin, C. *The Life and Death of Mary Wollstonecraft.* New York, 1974.

– VIRGINIA SAPIRO

WOMEN IN THE HISTORY OF PHILOSOPHY

The standard twentieth-century histories of European philosophy do not include women as important, original contributors to the discipline's past. Some relegate a few to footnotes; most omit women entirely. Recent research, inspired by the influence of feminist theory, and by a renewed interest in the historiography of philosophy, has uncovered numerous women who contributed to philosophy over the centuries.

Women's representation in philosophy's history was not always as marginal as it came to be by the opening of the twentieth century. For example, in the seventeenth century, Thomas Stanley's history mentioned twenty-four women philosophers of the ancient world, while Gilles Ménage discussed some seventy, including women Platonists, Academicians, Dialecticians, Cyrenaics, Megarians, Cynics, Peripatetics, Epicureans, Stoics, and Pythagoreans. With respect to the moderns, the seventeenth-century treatises of Jean de La Forge and Marguerite Buffet provided doxographies of women philosophers. Even in the nineteenth century, when women were virtually being erased from the standard histories, Lescure, Joël, Foucher de Careil, and Cousin wrote special studies on female philosophers.

Women's representation in philosophy's history

was not always as marginal as it came to be

by the opening of the twentieth century.

In recent years *A History of Women Philosophers*, volume 1, *600 BC–500 AD*, edited by Mary Ellen Waithe, has provided a detailed discussion of the following figures: Themistoclea, Theano I and II, Arignote, Myia, Damo, Aesara of Lucania, Phintys of Sparta, Perictione I and II, Aspasia of Miletus, Julia Domna, Makrina, Hypatia of Alexandria, Arete of Cyrene, Asclepigenia of Athens, Axiothea of Philesia, Cleobulina of Rhodes, Hipparchia the Cynic, and Lasthenia of Mantinea. In addition to the medieval and Renaissance philosophers discussed in the second volume of Waithe's *History* (Hildegard of Bingen, Heloise, Herrad of Hohenbourg, Beatrice of Nazareth, Mechtild of Magdeburg, Hadewych of Antwerp, Birgitta of Sweden, Julian of Norwich, Catherine of Siena, Oliva Sabuco de Nantes Barrera, Roswitha of Gandersheim, Christine de Pisan, Margaret More Roper, and Teresa of Avila), scholars have recently begun to focus attention on such humanist and Reformation figures as Isotta Nogarola, Laura Cereta, Cassandra Fidele, Olimpia Morata, and Caritas Pickheimer.

The Seventeenth Century

In the early modern period women's initial published philosophical endeavors inserted argumentation into the largely literary genre of the *querelle des femmes,* or woman question. Thus, Marie de Gournay, adopted daughter of Montaigne, in *The Equality of Men and Women* (1622) replaced persuasive force based on example with skeptical and fideistic arguments; Anna Maria van Schurman's *Whether a Maid May Be a Scholar?* (1659) and Sor Juana Inés de la Cruz's "Response to Sor Filotea" (1700) utilized scholastic models of argumentation to discuss woman's nature and her relation to learning. By 1673, when Bathsua Makin published *An Essay to Revive the Ancient Education of Gentlewomen,* an unbroken, explicitly acknowledged line of influence ran from Gournay through van Schurman to Makin. In the second half of the century, partly in response to the writings of Erasmus, Vives, and Fénelon, a number of treatises on the education of girls appeared, stressing its importance for religion and society. Authors included the Port Royal educator Sister Jacqueline Pascal and Madame de Maintenon.

In the second half of the Age of Reason women also produced numerous works on morals and the passions, including the maxims of Marguerite de La Sablière, Marquise de Sablé, and Queen Christina of Sweden. Perhaps the most well-known seventeenth-century woman writer of moral psychology is Madeline de Scudéry, of whom Leibniz said that she had "clarified so well the temperaments and the passions in her . . . conversations on morals."

Another type of philosophical writing by women, the treatment of natural philosophy, begins to appear after 1660. In Paris Jeanne Dumée and, in England, Aphra Behn argued in defense of Copernicus. But by far the most prolific female philosopher then was Margaret Cavendish, who published over a half dozen books on natural philosophy in which she advanced a unique combination of hard-nosed materialism together with an organic model of natural change and a denial of mechanism.

Of Anne Conway Leibniz said, "My philosophical views approach somewhat closely those of the late Countess of Conway." Her metaphysical treatise argued against Descartes, Spinoza, and Hobbes in favor of a monistic vitalism. On the Continent Princess Elisabeth of Bohemia, whose letters to Descartes had exposed the weakness of the latter's published views on mind–body interaction and free will, discussed Conway's philosophy with a Quaker correspondent. Seventeenth-century England also produced Mary Astell, who in the appendix to the *Letters Concerning the Love of God* (1695) argued against occasionalism. In *A Serious Proposal to the Ladies, Part II* (1697), Astell offered women a manual for improving their powers of reasoning, a work that was influenced by Descartes and the Port Royal logicians. Damaris Cudworth Masham also argued against occasionalism in *Discourse Concerning the Love of God* (1696). In *Occasional Thoughts* (1705) she defended a number of Lockean views on knowledge, education, and the relative merits of reason and revelation. Masham also corresponded with Leibniz on metaphysical issues, especially his views on substance; yet despite this scholarly career, she stood in need of defense against the charge that the arguments addressed to Leibniz could not have been written by a woman. It was Catherine Trotter Cockburn who came to her defense. Cockburn wrote a number of philosophical works, including *A Defence of Mr. Locke's Essay of Human Understanding* (1702) and a vindication of the views of Samuel Clarke.

In France in the final years of the seventeenth century, Gabrielle Suchon published, arguably, the most ambitious philosophical text that had yet been written by a woman on the Continent: *Treatise of Morals and of Politics* (1693), which included book-length treatments of liberty, science, and authority. Excerpts of her work were published in the scholarly journals of the time, but since the *Treatise* was published under a pseudonym, Suchon fell into oblivion by the late eighteenth century. (Anonymous authorship similarly led to Conway's erasure.)

The Eighteenth Century

In England Catherine Macaulay published a critical treatment of Hobbes's political philosophy and her magnum opus, *Letters on Education* (1790), to which Mary Wollstonecraft explicitly acknowledges her debt in her own *Vindication of the Rights of Woman* (1792). By the end of the century Mary Hays's *Female Biography* (1803) demonstrated that English women were beginning to trace a history of feminist social and political philosophy that reached back about one hundred years to Mary Astell. At the turn of the century, with the growing professionalization of philosophy and placement of it against the *belles lettres* and religion, women were producing philosophy stripped of its moorings within discussions of the woman question and theology, and written in journalistic style, as evidenced in Mary Shepherd's book-length treatments of causation, skepticism, and knowledge of the external world, with their attendant criticisms of such figures as Hume and Berkeley.

In Enlightenment France Anne Dacier published a translation and commentary for the writings of Marcus Aurelius and entered the debate about the ancients versus the moderns in her *The Causes of the Corruption of Taste* (1714). Dacier's salonist friend, the Marquise de Lambert, published a number of works on morals, the passions, education, and woman's status, which contin-

Catherine the Great's correspondence with Voltaire was published posthumously in Russia. (Corbis/Bettmann)

ued to be published a century later. Sophie de Grouchy, Marquise de Condorcet, added to her translation of Adam Smith's *Theory of the Moral Sentiments* her own blend of rationalist ethics and moral sentiment theory in her eight letters on sympathy.

Prior to the French Revolution philosophy of education, in particular, critical responses to Rousseau's *Émile*, occupied a prominent place in women's philosophical writings, as exemplified in Louise d'Epinay's *The Conversations of Emilie* (1774) and the works of Mme de Genlis. In addition to her work on education Louise-Marie Dupin also left an extensive manuscript. *Observations on the Equality of the Sexes and of Their Difference*, which she dictated to her secretary, Rousseau. The French Revolution moved the issue of woman's education into the arena of the rights of a woman as a citizen. Perhaps the most famous of these treatises is Olympe de Gouge's *Declaration of the Rights of Woman* (1791).

In the area of natural philosophy there is no question but that Emilie Du Châtelet deserves recognition as an important figure of the eighteenth century. Her *Principles of Physics* (1740) and her letters on the "active force" controversy (1742) attempt to reconcile what she takes to be most useful in Newtonian mechanics and Leibnizian philosophy. Du Châtelet also published a *Discourse on Happiness* (1779) and essays on the existence of God, the formation of color, and grammatical structure.

By the end of the century French women were producing broad critiques of culture and the arts, as evidenced in the mathematician Sophie Germain's *General Considerations on the State of the Sciences and Letters* (1833) and Madame de Staël's *On the Influence of the Passions on the Happiness of Individuals and Nations* (1796).

Germany spawned two critical treatments of Kant's views on women: the first by an unidentified "Henriette" and the second by Amalia Holst. In Switzerland Marie Huber's publications included three Enlightenment texts on the principles of natural religion: *The World Unmask'd* (English translation, 1736), *The State of Souls Separated from their Bodies* (English translation, 1736), and *Letters on the Religion Essential to Man* (English translation, 1738).

In Russia Catherine the Great's correspondence with Voltaire was published posthumously. Finally, in Italy Laura Bassi publicly disputed philosophical theses and published five lectures on natural philosophy; Maria Agnesi discussed logic, metaphysics, and Cartesian physics in *Philosophical Propositions* (1738): and Giuseppa Barbapiccola translated and wrote a critical introduction for Descartes's *Principles of Philosophy* (1731).

The information now available about women philosophers and ongoing research on this topic will provide us with a richer picture of philosophy's significant figures, topics, and styles of argumentation. It is to be hoped that future histories of philosophy will reflect this richer panorama of the past.

[*See also* Berkeley, George; Descartes, René; Feminist Philosophy; Hobbes, Thomas; Hume, David; Hypatia; Kant, Immanuel; Leibniz, Gottfried Wilhelm; Locke, John; Rousseau, Jean-Jacques; Spinoza, Benedict (Baruch); Wollstonecraft, Mary.]

BIBLIOGRAPHY

The Seventeenth Century

Astell, M. *Letters Concerning the Love of God between the Author of the Proposal to the Ladies and Mr. John Norris* (London, 1695); *A Serious Proposal to the Ladies Part II: Wherein a Method is offer'd for the Improvement of their Minds* (London, 1697); *Some Reflections Upon Marriage* (London, 1700); *The Christian Religion as Profess'd by a Daughter of the Church of England* (London, 1705).

Behn, A. "The Translator's Preface," in B. le Bovier de Fontenelle, *A Discovery of New Worlds*, trans. A. Behn (London, 1688).

Cavendish, M. L., Duchess of Newcastle. *Philosophical and Physical Opinions* (London, 1655); *Orations of Divers Sorts* (London, 1662); *Philosophical Letters: or, Modest Reflections upon some Opinions in Natural Philosophy Maintained By Several Famous and Learned Authors of this Age* (London, 1664); *Observations upon Experimental Philosophy* (London, 1666); *Grounds of Natural Philosophy* (London, 1668).

Conway, A., Viscountess. *The Principles of the Most Ancient and Modern Philosophy* (Latin translation: Amsterdam, 1690; English retranslation: London, 1692: both reprinted: The Hague, 1982); *The Conway Letters*, ed. M. H. Nicholson and S. Hutton (Oxford, 1992).

Christina, Queen of Sweden. *L'Ouvrage de loisir* [ca. 1670–80] and *Les Sentiments héroïques* [ca. 1670–80], with *Réflexions diverses sur la Vie et sur les Actions du Grand Alexandre, Les Vertues et vices de Caesar*, and correspondence, in J. Arckenholtz, *Mémoires concernant Christine, reine de Suède*, 4 vols. (Leipzig, 1751–60).

Dumée, J. *Entretien sur l'opinion de Copernic touchant la mobilité de la terre* (Paris, n.d.); ms. ca. 1680, Bibliothèque Nationale Fonds français 1941.

Elisabeth, Princess of Bohemia. Her letters in: *Oeuvres de Descartes*, ed. C. Adam and P. Tannery (Paris, 1897–1913; rev. ed. 1964–74): N. Malebranche. *Correspondance, actes et documents 1638–1689*, ed. A. Robinet, Vol. 18 (Paris, 1961); *Papers of William Penn*, Vol. 1, ed. M. Dunn and R. Dunn (Philadelphia, 1981).

Gournay, M. le Jars de. *L'Egalité des hommes et des femmes* (Paris, 1622); *L'Ombre de la Damoiselle de Gournay* (Paris, 1626); *Les Advis ou Les Presens de la Demoiselle de Gournay* (Paris, 1634).

Juana Inés de la Cruz, Sor, *Carta athenagórica de la madre Juana Inés de la Cruz* (Puebla de los Angeles, 1690); *Fama, y obras póstumas del fenix de Mexico, Decima Musa, Poetisa Americana* (Madrid, 1700); *Obras completas*, ed. A. Méndez Plancarte [A. Salceda], 4 vols. (Mexico City, 1951–57).

Lettres, Opuscules et Mémoires de Mme. Périer et de Jacqueline, Soeurs de Pascal, ed. P. Faugère (Paris, 1845).

Maintenon, F. d'Aubigné. *Lettres sur l'éducation des filles*, ed. Th. Lavallée (Paris, 1854); *Entretiens sur l'éducation des filles*, ed. Th. Lavallée (Paris, 1854); *Lettres historiques et édifiantes adressées aux dames de St.-Louis*, ed. Th. Lavallée, 2 vols. (Paris, 1856); *Conseils et instructions aux demoiselles pour leur conduite dans le monde*, 2 vols. (Paris, 1857).

Makin, B. *An Essay to Revive the Antient Education of Gentlewomen* (London, 1673).

Masham, D. C. *A Discourse Concerning the Love of God* (London, 1696; French translation, 1705); *Occasional Thoughts in Reference to a Vertuous or Christian Life* (London, 1705); letters to Locke in *The Correspondence of John Locke*, ed. E. S. de Beer, 8 vols. (Oxford, 1976–85); letters to Leibniz in *Die Philosophischen Schriften von Leibniz*, ed. C. I. Gerhardt, 7 vols. (Berlin, 1875–90).

Réflexions ou Sentences et Maximes morales de Monsieur de la Rochefoucauld, Maximes de Madame la marquise de Sablé. Pensées diverses de M. L. D. et les Maximes chrétiennes de M**** [Mme. de La Sablière] (Amsterdam, 1705).

Schurman, A. M. van. *Amica dissertatio inter Annam Mariam Schurmanniam et Andr. Rivetum de capacitate ingenii muliebris ad scientias* (Paris, 1638); *Opuscula, hebraea, graeca, latina, gallica, prosaica et metrica* (Leiden, 1648).

Scudéry, M. de. *Discours sur la gloire* (Paris, 1671); *Conversations sur divers sujets*, 2 vols. (Paris, 1680); *Conversations nouvelles sur divers sujets*, 2 vols. (Paris, 1684); *Conversations morales*, 2 vols. (Paris, 1686); *Nouvelles Conversations de morale*, 2 vols. (Paris, 1688); *Entretiens de morale*, 2 vols. (Paris, 1692).

Suchon, G. *Traité de la morale et de la Politique* (Lyon, 1693); *[Traité] Du célibat Volontaire, ou la Vie sans engagement, par Demoiselle Suchon* (Paris, 1700).

The Eighteenth Century

Agnesi, M. G. *Propositiones Philosophicae* (Milan, 1738).

Barbapiccola, G. E. *I Principii della Filosopfia* (Turin, 1722).

Bassi, L. M. C. *Philosophica Studia* [forty-nine theses disputed for the doctorate] (Bologna, 1732); *De acqua corpore naturali elemento aliorum corporum parte universi* [theses for a disputation] (Bologna, 1732); the following appear in *De Bononiensi Scientiarum et Artium Instituto atque Academia Commentarii: De aeris compressione* (1745); *De problemate quodam hydrometrico* (1757); *De problemate quodam mechanico* (1757); *De immixto fluidis aere* (1792).

Cockburn, C. Trotter. *The Works of Mrs. Catherine Cockburn, Theological, Moral, Dramatic, and Poetical,* ed. T. Birch (London, 1751).

Dacier, A. L. *Réflexions morales de l'empereur Marc Antonin* (Paris, 1690–91; English translation: London, 1692); *Des Causes de la corruption du goût* (Paris, 1714).

D'Épinay, L. *Les Conversations d'Émilie* (Leipzig, 1774; Paris, 1781).

Documents of Catherine the Great: The Correspondence with Voltaire and the Instruction of 1767 in the English text of 1768, ed. W. F. Reddaway (Cambridge, 1931).

Du Châtelet, G. E. Le Tonnelier De Breteuil, Marquise. *Institutions de Physique* (Paris, 1740); *Réponse de Madame**** [du Châtelet] *à la lettre que M. de Mairan . . . lui a écrite le 18 février sur la question des forces vives* (Brussels, 1741); *Dissertation sur la Nature et la Propagation du Feu* (Paris, 1744); *Principes Mathématiques de la Philosophie Naturelle,* 2 vols. (Paris, 1756); *Réflexions sur le Bonheur* in *Opuscules philosophiques et littéraires, la plupart posthumes ou inédits* (Paris, 1796); essays in Ira O. Wade, *Studies on Voltaire with Some Unpublished Papers of Mme du Châtelet* (Princeton, NJ, 1947).

Dupin, L. *Portefeuille de Mme Dupin* (Paris, 1884).

Genlis, S. F. du Crest de Saint-Aubin, Comtesse de. *Adèle et Théodore ou lettres sur l'éducation* (Paris, 1782; English translation: London, 1783); *Discours sur la suppression des couvents de religieuses et l'éducation publique des femmes* (Paris, 1790).

Germain, S. *Oeuvres philosophiques de Sophie Germain, suivies de pensées et de lettres inédites* (Paris, 1879; 1896).

Gouges, O. de. *Les Droits de la Femme* (Paris, [1791]); *Oeuvres,* ed. Groult (Paris, 1986).

Grouchy, S. de, Marquise de Condorcet. *Lettres sur la Sympathie,* in *Théorie des Sentimens Moraux,* Vol. 2 (Paris, 1798).

Holst, A., *Über die Bestimmung des Weibes zur öhern Geistesbildung* (Berlin, 1802).

Huber, M., *Le monde fou préféré au monde sage* (Amsterdam, 1731); *Le système des anciens et des modernes, . . . sur l'état des âmes séparées des corps* (London, 1731), both in English translation as *The World Unmask'd, or the Philosopher the greatest Cheat in Twenty Four Dialogues . . . To which is added, The State of Souls Separated from their Bodies . . . In Answer to a Treatise entitled, An Enquiry into Origenism* (London, 1736); *Lettres sur la religion essentielle à l'homme, distinguée de ce qui n'en est que l'accessoire* (Amsterdam, 1738; English translation, 1738).

Lambert, A. de. *Réflexions Nouvelles Sur Les Femmes par une Dame de la Cour de France* (Paris, 1727); *Lettres sur la véritable éducation* (Paris/Amsterdam, 1729); *Traité de l'Amitié, Traité de la Vieillesse, Réflexions sur les Femmes, sur le Goût, sur les Richesses* (Amsterdam, 1732); *Oeuvres complètes . . .* (Paris, 1808).

Macaulay, C. S. *Loose Remarks on Certain Positions to be found in Mr. Hobbes's Philosophical Rudiments of Government and Society* (London, 1767); *Letters on Education* (London, 1790).

Shepherd, M. *An Essay Upon the Relation of Cause and Effect, controverting the Doctrine of Mr. Hume . . .* (London, 1824); *Essays on the Perception of an External Universe* (London, 1827); "Lady Mary Shepherd's Metaphysics," *Fraser's Magazine for Town and Country,* Vol. 5, no. 30 (July 1832).

Staël, G. de. *De l'influence des passions sur le bonheur des individus et de nations* (Paris, 1796).

Wollstonecraft, M. *Thoughts on the Education of Daughters* (London, 1787); *A Vindication of the Rights of Men* (London, 1790); *A Vindication of the Rights of Woman* (London, 1792).

Works on Women Philosophers

Albistur, M., and D. Armogathe. *Histoire du féminisme français,* Vol. 1. Paris, 1977.

Buffet, M. *Nouvelles observations sur la langue française . . . Avec les éloges d'illustres sçavantes tant anciennes que modernes* (Paris, 1668).

Cousin, V. *Jacqueline Pascal: Premières études sur les femmes illustres et la société du XVIIe siècle.* Paris, 1844. *Madame de Sablé: Nouvelles Études sur la société et les femmes illustres du dix-septième siècle.* Paris, 1854. *La Société Française au XVIIe Siècle d'après Le Grand Cyrus de Mlle de Scudéry.* 2 vols. Paris, 1858.

Dronke, P. *Women Writers of the Middle Ages.* Cambridge, 1984.

Foucher de Careil, L. *Descartes et la Princesse Palatine, ou de l'influence du cartésianisme sur les femmes au XVIIe siècle.* Paris, 1862.

———. *Descartes, la princesse Elisabeth et la reine Christine.* Paris, 1909.

Harth, E. *Cartesian Women.* Ithaca, NY, 1992.

Joël, K. *Die Frauen in der Philosophie.* Hamburg, 1896.

King, M. L. *Women of the Renaissance.* Chicago, 1991.

Kristeller, P. O. "Learned Women of Early Modern Italy: Humanists and University Scholars," in P. Labalme, ed., *Beyond Their Sex: Learned Women of the European Past* (New York, 1980).

La Forge, J. de. *Le Cercle des femmes sçavantes.* Paris, 1663.

Le Doeuff, M. "Long Hair, Short Ideas," in *The Philosophical Imaginary* (Stanford, CA, 1989).

Lescure, M. de. *Les femmes philosophes.* Paris, 1881.

Ménage, G. *Historia mulierum philosopharum.* Lyon, 1690; English translation, 1702; new English edition by B. Zedler, Lanham, MD, 1984.

Merchant, C. *The Death of Nature: Women, Ecology, and the Scientific Revolution.* New York, 1980.

O'Neill, E. "Disappearing Ink: Early Modern Women Philosophers and Their Fate in History," in J. Kourany, ed., *Philosophy in a Different Voice* (Princeton, NJ, 1996).

Schiebinger, L. *The Mind Has No Sex? Women in the Origins of Modern Science.* Cambridge, MA, 1989.

Stanley, T. *A History of Philosophy.* 3 vols. London, 1687.

Waithe, M. E., ed. *A History of Women Philosophers.* 3 vols. Dordrecht, 1987–91.

Wilson, K., and F. Warnke, eds. *Women Writers of the Seventeenth Century.* Athens, GA, 1989.

– EILEEN O'NEILL

WRIGHT, GEORG HENRIK VON

Georg Henrik von Wright, Finnish philosopher belonging to the Swedish-speaking minority, was born in

1916. He was a professor at the University of Helsinki from 1946 to 1948 and from 1952 to 1961, and, in between, at the University of Cambridge (1948–1951). Since 1961 he has been a research professor at the Academy of Finland.

Von Wright himself describes the main influence on his philosophy as coming from Eino Kaila, his teacher in Finland, as well as from Ludwig Wittgenstein and G. E. Moore. From Kaila stems his interest in formal matters and his use of logical methods. From Moore he may have gotten his unpretentiousness and unrelenting search for clarity. That Wittgenstein had a profound personal influence on von Wright is not in doubt—he was first Wittgenstein's student, then his successor as professor in Cambridge, and finally, with G. E. M. Anscombe and Rush Rhees, one of his literary executors—yet it is not obvious just how his philosophy has been influenced by Wittgenstein.

Wright has combined to an unusual extent

the passionate commitment of the humanist

and the detached objectiveness

of the academic philosopher.

Throughout life von Wright has combined, to an extent that is not usual, two rather different approaches to philosophy, one the passionate commitment of the humanist, the other the detached objectiveness of the academic philosopher. The former approach has been exemplified by a number of books in Swedish such as *Thought and Prophecy* (1955), *Humanism as a Way of Life and Other Essays* (1978), and *Science and Reason* (1986). As a thinker of predominantly pessimistic views regarding the future of humankind, von Wright has won wide public acclaim in the Nordic countries, particularly in Sweden.

Internationally, however, it is for his academic work that von Wright is known. He has written on induction and probability (*The Logical Problem of Induction* [1941], *A Treatise on Induction and Probability* [1951]), and on ethics (*The Varieties of Goodness* [1963]). But his main reputation lies in modal logic and theory of action.

In *An Essay in Modal Logic* (1951), von Wright developed his method of distributive normal forms and analyzed a number of modal systems, one of which is nowadays often referred to as the Gödel/Feys/von Wright system. In this work von Wright explicitly recognized the possibility of epistemic and doxastic logic (that is, logics in which the modal box operator is interpreted as "the agent knows that" and "the agent believes that"); these themes were later developed by von Wright's former student Jaakko Hintikka.

His paper "Deontic Logic" (1951) opened up the field of deontic logic and was the first in a long series of papers and books in which von Wright elaborated and deepened his analysis. One of his most important insights is that the study of deontic logic requires a logic of action as a basis (*Norm and Action*, 1963). He is unusual among early action theorists in letting his logic of action inform his philosophy of action and vice versa.

According to von Wright, to act is to interfere with the course of nature: to bring about a change, to bring about an event. This view has led him to question the relationship between action and causality; an explanation of human action in purely causal terms will always omit something important. In *Explanation and Understanding* (1973) this view drives him to an examination of practical syllogisms; they do not possess logical validity in the ordinary sense of the word, nevertheless they may be valid as explanations *ex post actu*.

[See also Anscombe, Elizabeth; Modal Logic; Probability; Wittgenstein, Ludwig Josef Johann.]

BIBLIOGRAPHY

Schilpp, P. A., and L. E. Hahn. *The Philosophy of Georg Henrik von Wright.* The Library of Living Philosophers, Vol. 19. La Salle, IL, 1989.

– KRISTER SEGERBERG

Index